Small Business Sourcebook

ISSN 0883-3397

Small Business Sourcebook

The Entrepreneur's Resource

TWENTY-NINTH EDITION

Volume 3

Specific Small Business Profiles
General Small Business Topics

(Entries 17565-28812)

Sonya D. Hill
Project Editor

Detroit • New York • San Francisco • New Haven, Conn • Waterville, Maine • London

Small Business Sourcebook, 29th edition

Project Editor: Sonya D. Hill

Editorial Support Services: Charles Beaumont

Composition and Electronic Prepress: Gary Leach

Manufacturing: Rita Wimberley

Gale
27500 Drake Rd.
Farmington Hills, MI, 48331-3535

ISBN-13: 978-1-4144-6919-5 (set)
ISBN-10: 1-4144-6919-5 (set)
ISBN-13: 978-1-4144-6920-1 (vol. 1)
ISBN-10: 1-4144-6920-9 (vol. 1)
ISBN-13: 978-1-4144-6921-8 (vol. 2)
ISBN-10: 1-4144-6921-7 (vol. 2)
ISBN-13: 978-1-4144-6986-7 (vol. 3)
ISBN-10: 1-4144-6986-1 (vol . 3)
ISBN-13: 978-1-4144-6987-4 (vol . 4)
ISBN-10: 1-4144-6987-X (vol . 4)
ISBN-13: 978-1-4144-6988-1 (vol . 5)
ISBN-10: 1-4144-6988-8 (vol . 5)
ISBN-13: 978-1-4144-7694-0 (vol . 6)
ISBN-10: 1-4144-7694-9 (vol . 6)

ISSN 0883-3397

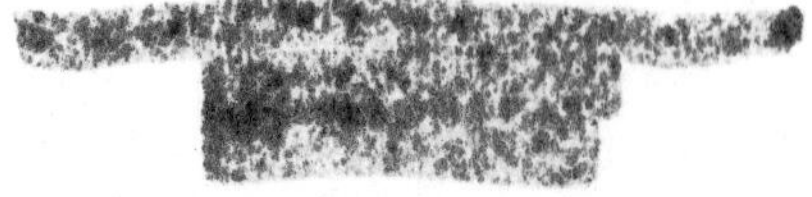

Printed in the United States of America
1 2 3 4 5   16 15 14 13 12

FD109

Contents

Introduction

The appeal of small business ownership remains perpetually entrenched in American culture as one of the most viable avenues for achieving the American Dream. To many entrepreneurs going into business for themselves represents financial independence, an increased sense of identity and self-worth, and the fulfillment of personal goals. Small business owners strive to make their mark in today's competitive marketplace by establishing healthy businesses that can, over time, become legacies handed down from one generation to the next. Entrepreneurs from each generation tackle the obstacles and adversities of the current business and economic climate to test their business savvy and generate opportunities. Today's entrepreneurs face many of the problems of their predecessors, as well as some distinctly new challenges.

With the rightsizing, downsizing, and reorganization of-corporate America, many individuals have decided to confront the risks of developing and operating their own businesses. Small business ownership is rapidly becoming a viable alternative to what is perceived as an equally unstable corporate environment. These entrepreneurs, many of whom have firsthand experience with the problems and inefficiencies inherent in today's large corporations, seek to improve upon an archaic business model and to capitalize on their own ingenuity and strengths. Led by their zeal, many would-be entrepreneurs let their desire, drive, and determination overshadow the need for business knowledge and skill. Ironically, aids in obtaining these components of entrepreneurial success are widely available, easily accessible, and often free of charge.

Small Business Sourcebook (*SBS*) is a six-volume annotated guide to more than 21,199 listings of live and print sources of information designed to facilitate the start-up, development, and growth of specific small businesses, as well as over 26,073 similar listings on general small business topics. An additional 8,679 state-specific listings and over 1,997 U.S. federal government agencies and offices specializing in small business issues, programs, and assistance are also included. *SBS* covers 340 specific small business profiles and 99 general small business topics.

Features of This Edition

This edition of *Small Business Sourcebook* has been revised and updated, incorporating thousand of changes to names, addresses, contacts, and descriptions of listings from the previous edition.

Contents and Arrangement

The geographical scope of *SBS* encompasses the United States and Canada, with expanded coverage for resources pertaining to international trade and for resources that have a U.S. or Canadian distributor or contact. Internet sites that are maintained outside of the U.S. and Canada are also included if they contain relevant information for North American small businesses. Resources that do not relate specifically to small businesses are generally not included.

The information presented in *SBS* is grouped within four sections: Specific Small Business Profiles, General Small Business Topics, State Listings, and Federal Government Assistance. Detailed outlines of these sections may be found in the Users' Guide following this Introduction. Also included is a Master Index to Volumes 1 through 6.

Specific Small Business Profiles This section includes the following types of resources: start-up information, associations and other organizations, educational programs, directories of educational programs, reference works, sources of supply, statistical sources, trade periodicals, videocassettes/audiocassettes, trade shows and conventions, consultants, franchises and business opportunities, computerized databases, computer systems/software, Internet databases, libraries, and research centers-all arranged by business type. Entries range from Accounting Service to Word Processing Service, and include such businesses as Airbag Replacement Service Centers, Computer Consulting, Damage Restoration Service, and Web Site Design.

General Small Business Topics This section offers such resources as associations, books, periodicals, articles, pamphlets, educational programs, directories of educational programs,videocassettes/audiocassettes, trade shows and conventions, consultants, computerized databases, Internet databases, software,libraries, and research centers, arranged alphabetically by business topic.

State Listings Entries include government, academic, and commercial agencies and organizations, as well as select coverage of relevant state-specific publications; listings are arranged alphabetically by state, territory, and Canadian province. Some examples include small business development consultants, educational programs, financing and loan programs, better business bureaus, and chambers of commerce.

Federal Government Assistance Listings specializing in small business issues, programs, assistance, and policyare arranged alphabetically by U.S. government agency or office; regional or branch offices are listed alphabetically by state.

Master Index All entries in Volumes 1 through 6 are arranged in one alphabetic index for convenience.

Entries in *SBS* include (as appropriate andavailable):

- Organization, institution, or product name
- Contact information, including contact name, address and phone, toll-free, and fax numbers
- Author/editor, date(s), and frequency
- Availability, including price
- Brief description of purpose, services, or content
- Company and/or personal E-mail addresses
- Web site addresses

SBS also features the following:

Guide to Publishers—An alphabetic listing of 2,425 companies, associations, institutions, and individuals that publish the periodicals, directories, guidebooks, and other publications noted in the Small Business Profiles and General Topics sections. Users are provided with full contact information, including address, phone, fax,and e-mail and URL when available. The Guide to Publishers facilitates contact with publishers and provides a one- stop resource for valuable information.

Method of Compilation

SBS was compiled by consulting small business experts and entrepreneurs, as well as a variety of resources, including direct contact with the associations, organizations, and agencies through telephone surveys, Internet research, or through materials provided by those listees; government resources; and data obtained from other relevant Gale directories. *SBS* was reviewed by a team of small business advisors, all of whom have numerous years of expertise in small business counseling and identification of small business information resources. The last and perhaps most important resource we utilize is direct contact with our readers, who provide valuable comments and suggestions to improve our publication. *SBS* relies on these comprehensive market contacts to provide today's entrepreneurs with relevant, current, and accurate informationon all aspects of small business.

Available in Electronic Formats

Licensing. *Small Business Sourcebook* is available for licensing. The complete database is provided in a fielded format and is deliverable on such media as disk or CD-ROM. For more information, contact Gale's Business Development Group at1-800-877-GALE, or visit our website at www.gale.com/bizdev.

Comments and Suggestions Welcome

Associations, agencies, business firms, publishers, and other organizations that provide assistance and information to the small business community are encouraged to submit material about their programs, activities, services, or products. Comments and suggestions from users of this directory are also welcomed and appreciated. Please contact:

Project Editor
Small Business Sourcebook
Gale, Cengage Learning
27500 Drake Rd.
Farmington Hills, MI 48331-3535
Phone: (248) 699-4253
Fax: (248) 699-8070
E-mail: BusinessProductsgale.com
URL: www.gale.com

User's Guide

Small Business Sourcebook (*SBS*) provides information in a variety of forms and presentations for comprehensive coverage and ease of use. The directory contains four parts within two volumes:

- Specific Small Business Profiles
- General Small Business Topics
- State Listings
- Federal Government Assistance

Information on specific businesses is arranged by type of business; the many general topics that are of interest to the owners, operators, or managers of all small businesses are grouped in a separate section for added convenience. Users should consult the various sections to benefit fully from the information *SBS* offers. For example, an entrepreneur with a talent or interest in the culinary arts could peruse a number of specific small business profiles, such as Restaurant, Catering, Cooking School, Specialty Food/Wine Shop, Bakery/Doughnut Shop, Healthy Restaurant, or Candy/Chocolate Store. Secondly, the General Small Business Topics section could be consulted for any applicable subjects, such as Service Industry, Retailing, Franchising, and other relevant topics. Then, the appropriate state within the State Listings section would offer area programs and offices providing information and support to small businesses, including venture capital firms and small business development consultants. Finally, the Federal Government Assistance section could supply relevant government offices, such as procurement contacts.

Features Included in Volumes 1 through 3

List of Small Business Profiles. This list provides an alphabetic outline of the small businesses profiled, with cross-references for related profiles and for alternate names by which businesses may be identified. The page number for each profile is indicated.

Standard Industrial Classification (SIC) Codes for Profiled Small Businesses. This section lists four-digit SIC codes and corresponding classification descriptions for the small businesses profiled in this edition. The SIC system, which organizes businesses by type, is a product of the Statistical Policy Division of the U.S. Office of Management and Budget. Statistical data produced by government, public, and private organizations is usually categorized according to SIC codes, thereby facilitating the collection, comparison, and analysis of data as well as providing a uniform method for presenting statistical information. Hence, knowing the SIC code for a particular small business increases access and the use of a variety of statistical data from many sources.

Guide to Publishers. This resource lists alphabetically the companies, associations, institutions, and individuals that publish the periodicals, directories, guidebooks, and other publications noted in the "Small Business Profiles" and "General Topics" sections. Users are provided with full contact information, including address, phone, fax, and e-mail and URL when available. The "Guide" facilitates contact with publishers and provides a one-stop resource for valuable information.

Glossary of Small Business Terms. This glossary defines nearly 400 small business terms, including financial, governmental, insurance, procurement, technical, and general business definitions. Cross-references and acronyms are also provided.

Small Business Profiles A-Z. A total of 340 small businesses is represented in volumes 1 through 3. Profiles are listed alphabetically by business name. Entries within each profile are arranged alphabetically by resource type, within up to 17 subheadings.These subheadings are detailed below:

- ***Start-up Information***—Includes periodical articles, books, manuals, book excerpts, kits, and other sources of information. Entries offer title; publisher; address; phone, fax, toll-free numbers; company e-mail and URL addresses; and a description. Bibliographic data is provided for cited periodical articles whenever possible.
- ***Associations and Other Oganizations***—Includes trade and professional associations whose members gather and disseminate information of interest to small business owners. Entries offer the association's

name; address; phone, toll-free and fax numbers; company e-mail address; contact name; purpose and objective; a description of membership; telecommunication services; and a listing of its publications, including publishing frequency.

- ***Educational Programs***—Includes university and college programs, schools, training opportunities, association seminars, correspondence courses, and other educational programs.Entries offer name of program or institution, sponsor name, address, phone, toll-free and fax numbers, e-mail and URL addresses; and description of program.
- ***Directories of Educational Programs***—Includes directories and other publications that list educational programs. Entries offer name of publication; publisher name, address, and phone, toll-free and fax numbers; editor; frequency or date of publication; price; and description of contents, including directory arrangement and indexes.
- ***Reference Works***—Includes handbooks, manuals, textbooks, guides, directories, dictionaries, encyclopedias, and other published reference materials. Entries offer name of publication; publisher name, address, and phone, toll-free and fax numbers; e-mail and URL addresses; and, when available, name of author or editor, publication year or frequency, and price. A brief description is often featured.
- ***Sources of Supply***—Includes buyer's guides,directories, special issues of periodicals, and other publications that list sources of equipment, supplies, and services related to the operation of the profiled small business. Entries offer publication name; publisher name, address, and phone, toll-free and fax numbers; e-mail and URL addresses; and, when available, editor's name, frequency or publication year, and price. A brief description of the publication, including directory arrangement and indexes, is often provided.
- ***Statistical Sources***—Includes books, reports, pamphlets, and other sources of statistical data of interest to an owner, operator or manager of the profiled small business, such as wage, salary, and compensation data; financial and operating ratios; prices and costs; demographics; and other statistical information. Entries offer publication/data source name; publisher (if applicable); address; phone, toll-free and fax numbers of data source; publication date or frequency; and price. A brief description of the publication/data source is often provided.
- ***Trade Periodicals***—Includes trade journals, newsletters, magazines, and other serials that offer information about the management and operation of the profiled small business. Such periodicals often contain industry news; trends and developments; reviews; articles about new equipment and supplies; and other information related to business operations. Entries offer publication name; publisher name, address, phone, toll-free and fax numbers, and e-mail and URL addresses; editor name; publication frequency; andprice. A brief description of the publication's content is also included, when known.
- ***Videocassettes/Audiocassettes***—Includes videocassettes, audiocassettes, and other audiovisual media offering information on the profiled small business. Entries offer program title; distributor name, address, phone, toll-free and fax numbers, and e-mail and URL addresses; description of program; release date; price; and format(s).
- ***Trade Shows and Conventions***—Includes tradeshows, exhibitions, expositions, conventions, and other industry meetings that provide prospective and existing business owners with the opportunity to meet and exchange information with their peers, review commercial exhibits, establish business or sales contacts, and attend educational programs. Entries offer event name; sponsor or management company name, address, phone, toll-free and fax numbers, and e-mail and URL addresses; a description of the event, including audience, frequency, principal exhibits, and dates and locations of event for as many years ahead as provided by the event's sponsor.
- ***Consultants***—Includes consultants and consulting organizations that provide services specifically related to the profiled small business. Entries offer individual consultant or consulting organization name, address, and phone, toll-free and fax numbers; company and individual e-mail addresses; and a brief description of consulting services. (For e-mail and URL addresses, see the Small Business Development Consultants subheadings in the State Listings section in Volume 2.)
- ***Franchises and Business Opportunities***—Includes companies granting franchise licenses for enterprises falling within the scope of the profiled small business, as well as other non-franchised business opportunities that operate within a given network or system. Entries offer franchise name, address, phone, toll-free and fax numbers, and e-mail and URL addresses, as well as a description of the franchise or business opportunity, which has been expanded whenever possible to include the number of existing franchises, the founding date of the franchise, franchise fees, equity capital requirements, royalty fees, any managerial assistance offered, and available training.
- ***Computerized Databases***—Includes diskettes, magnetic tapes, CD-ROMs, online systems, and other computer-readable databases. Entries offer database name; producer name, address, phone, toll-free and fax numbers, e-mail and URL addresses; description; and available format(s), including vendor name.

(Many university and public libraries offer online information retrieval services that provide searches of databases, including those listed in this category.)

- ***Computer Systems/Software***—Includes softwar-eand computerized business systems designed to assist in the operation of the profiled small business. Entries offer name of the software or system; publisher name, address, phone, toll-free and fax-numbers; price; and description.
- ***Libraries***—Includes libraries and special collections that contain material especially applicable to the profiled small business. Entries offer library or collection name; parent organization (where applicable); address; phone, toll-free and fax numbers; e-mail and URL addresses; contact name and title; scope of collection; and description of holdings, subscriptions, and services.
- ***Research Centers***—Includes university-related and independently operated research institutes and information centers that generate, through their research programs, data related to the operation of the profiled small business. Also listed are associations and other business-related organizations that conduct research programs. Entries offer name of organization; address; phone, toll-free and fax numbers; company web site address; contact name and personale-mail; a description of principal fields of research or services; publications, including title and frequency; and related conferences.

Features Included in Volumes 2 through 6

General Small Business Topics. This section offers chapters on different topics in the operation of any small business, for example, venture capital and other funding, or compensation. Chapters are listed alphabetically by small business topic; entries within each chapter are arranged alphabetically, within up to 14 subheadings, by resource type:

- ***Associations and OtherOrganizations***—Includes trade and professional associations that gather and disseminate information of interest to small business owners. Entries offer the association's name; address; phone, toll-free and fax numbers; organization e-mail and URL addresses; contact name;purpose and objectives; a description of membership; telecommunication services; and a listing of its publications, including publishing frequency.
- ***Educational Programs***—Includes university and college programs, schools, training opportunities, association seminars, correspondence courses, and other educational programs. Entries offer name of program or institution, sponsor name, address, phone, toll-free and fax numbers, e-mail and URL addresses, and description of program.
- ***Directories of Educational Programs***—Includes directories and other publications that list educational programs. Entries offer name of publication; publisher name, address, phone, toll-free and fax numbers, and e-mail and URL addresses; editor; frequency or date of publication; price; and description of contents, including arrangement and indexes.
- ***Reference Works***—Includes articles, handbooks, manuals, textbooks, guides, directories, dictionaries, encyclopedias, and other published reference materials. Entries offertitle of article, including bibliographic information; name of publication; publisher name, address, phone, toll-free and fax numbers, and e-mail and URL addresses; and, when available, name of author oreditor, publication year or frequency, and price. A brief descriptionis often featured.
- ***Sources of Supply***—Includes buyer's guides,directories, special issues of periodicals, and other publications that list sources of equipment, supplies, and services. Entries offer publication name; publisher name, address, phone, toll-free and fax numbers, and e-mail and URL addresses; editor's name, frequency or publication year, price, and a brief description of the publication, when available.
- ***Statistical Sources***—Includes books, reports, pamphlets, and other sources of statistical data of interest to an owner, operator, or manager of a small business, such as wage, salary, and compensation data; financial and operating ratios; prices and costs; demographics; and other statistical information. Entries offer publication/data source name; publisher (if applicable); address; phone, toll-free and fax numbers of data source; publication date or frequency; and price. A brief description is often provided.
- ***Trade Periodicals***—Includes journals, newsletters, magazines, and other serials. Entries offer name of publication; publisher name, address, phone, toll-free and fax numbers, and e-mail and URL addresses; and name of editor, frequency, and price.A brief description of the periodical's content is included when known.
- ***Videocassettes/Audiocassettes***—Includes videocassettes, audiocassettes, and other audiovisual media. Entries offer program title; distributor name, address, phone, toll-free and fax numbers, and e-mail and URL addresses; price; description of program; release date; and format(s).
- ***Trade Shows and Conventions***—Includes tradeshows, exhibitions, expositions, seminars, and conventions. Entries offer event name; sponsor or management company name, address, phone, toll-free and fax numbers, and e-mail and URL ad-

dresses; frequency of event; and dates and locations of the event for as many years ahead as known.

- ***Consultants***—Includes consultants and consulting organizations. Entries offer individual consultant or-consulting organization name, address, and phone, toll-free and fax numbers; company and individual e-mail addresses; and a brief description of consulting services. (See also Consultants in the State Listings section.)
- ***Computerized Databases***—Includes diskettes, CD-ROMs, magnetic tape, online systems and other computer-readable databases. Entries offer database name; producer, address, phone, toll-free and fax numbers, and e-mail and URL addresses; description; and available format(s), including vendor name. (Many university and public libraries offer online information retrieval services that provide searches of databases, including those listed in this category.)
- ***Computer Systems/Software***—Includes software and computerized business systems. Entries offer name of the software or system; publisher name, address, phone, toll-free and fax numbers, and e-mail and URL addresses; price; and description.
- ***Libraries***—Includes libraries and special collections that contain material applicable to the small business topic. Entries offer library or collection name, parent organization (where applicable), address, phone and fax numbers, e-mail and URL addresses, scope of collection, and description of holdings and services.
- ***Research Centers***— Includes university-related and independently operated research institutes and information centers that generate, through their research programs, data related to specific small business topics. Entries offer name of organization, address, phone, toll-free and fax numbers, e-mail and URL addresses, a description of principal fields of research or services, and related conferences.

State Listings. This section lists various sources of information and assistance available within given states, territories, and Canadian provinces; entries include governmental, academic, and commercial agencies, and are arranged alphabetically within up to 15 subheadings by resource type:

- ***Small Business Development Center Lead Office***— Includes the lead small business development center (SBDC) for each state.
- ***Small Business Development Centers***—Includes any additional small business development centers (SBDC) in the state, territory, or province. SBDCs provide support services to small businesses, including individual counseling, seminars, conferences, and learning center activities.
- ***Small Business Assistance Programs***—Includes state small business development offices and other programs offering assistance to small businesses.
- ***SCORE Offices***—Includes SCORE office(s) for each state. The Service Corps of Retired Executives Association (SCORE), a volunteer program sponsored by the Small Business Administration, offers counseling, workshops, and seminars across the U.S. for small business entrepreneurs.
- ***Better Business Bureaus***—Includes various better business bureaus within each state. By becoming a member of the local Better Business Bureau, a small business owner can increase the prestige and credibility of his or her business within the community, as well as make valuable business contacts.
- ***Chambers of Commerce***—Includes various chambers of commerce within each state. Chambers of Commerce are valuable sources of small business advice and information; often, local chambers sponsor SCORE counseling several times per month for a small fee, seminars, conferences, and other workshops to its members. Also, by becoming a member of the local Chamber of Commerce, a small business owner can increase the prestige and credibility of his or herbusiness within the community, as well as make valuable business contacts.
- ***Minority Business Assistance Programs***—Includes minority business development centers and other sources of assistance for minority-owned business.
- ***Financing and Loan Programs***—Includes venture capital firms, small business investment companies (SBIC), minority enterprise small business investment companies (MESBIC), and other programs that provide funding to qualified small businesses.
- ***Procurement Assistance Programs***—Includes state services such as counseling, set-asides, and sheltered-market bidding, which are designed to aid small businesses in bidding on government contracts.
- ***Incubators/Research and Technology Parks***—Includes small business incubators, which provide newly established small business owners with work sites, business services, training, and consultation; also includes research and technology parks, which sponsor research and facilitate commercialization of new technologies.
- ***Educational Programs***—Includes university and college programs, as well as those sponsored by other organizations that offer degree, nondegree, certificate, and correspondence programs in entrepreneurship and in small business development.
- ***Legislative Assistance***—Includes committees, subcommittees, and joint committees of each state's

senate and house of representatives that are concerned with small business issues and regulations.

- ***Consultants***—Includes consultants and consulting firms offering expertise in small business development.
- ***Publications***—Includes publications related to small business operations within the profiled state.
- ***Publishers***—Includes publishers operating in or for the small business arena within the profiled state.

Federal Government Assistance. This section lists federal government agencies and offices, many with additional listings for specific offices, as well as regional or district branches. Main agencies or offices are listed alphabetically; regional, branch, ordistrict offices are listed after each main office or agency.

Master Index. This index provides an alphabetic listing of all entries contained in Volumes 1 throgh 6. Citations are referenced by their entry numbers. Publication titles are rendered in italics.

Acknowledgements

The editors would like to extend sincere thanks to the following members of the Small Business Sourcebook advisory board for their expert guidance, recommendations, and suggestions for the ongoing development of this title:

Susan C. Awe
Assistant Director,
William J. Parish Memorial Business Library

Jill Clever
Business Technology Specialist,
Toledo-Lucas County Public Library

Jules Matsoff
District Manager,
Service Corps of Retired Executives (SCORE) Milwaukee Chapter

Ken MacKenzie
President,
Southeast Business Appraisal

The editors would also like to thank the individuals from associations and other organizations who provided information for the compilation of this directory.

List of Small Business Profiles

This list is an outline of the 341 small businesses profiled in this edition of Small Business Sourcebook. The beginning page number of each profile is provided. For convenience, this index also provides cross-references to small businesses known by alternate names, businesses contained within other small business profiles, and synonymous or related businesses.

Standard Industrial Classification (SIC) Codes for Profiled Small Businesses

Included here are the four-digit SIC codes and corresponding classification descriptions for the businesses profiled in this edition. The SIC system, which organizes businesses by type, is a product of the Statistical Policy Division of the U.S. Office of Management and Budget. Statistical data produced by government, public, and private organizations usually are categorized according to SIC codes, thereby facilitating the collection, comparison, and analysis of data as well as providing a uniform method for presenting statistical information. Hence, knowing the SIC code for a particular small business increases the access to, and the use of, a variety of statistical data from many sources. The following SIC codes were obtained from the 1987 edition of the Standard Industrial Classification Manual, the most recent version available. (The term "nec" stands for "not elsewhere classified.")

Accounting Service

7291 Tax return preparation services

8721 Accounting, auditing, and bookkeeping services

Adult Day Care Center

8322 Individual and family social services (includes adult day carecenters)

Advertising Service

7311 Advertising agencies (includes advertising consultants)

7312 Outdoor advertising agencies

7313 Radio, television, and publishers' advertising representatives

7319 Advertising, nec

7331 Direct mail advertising services

8999 Services, nec (includes advertising copywriters)

Airbag Replacement Service Centers

7538 General automotive repair shops

7539 Automotive repair shops, nec

Air Charter Service

4512 Air transportation, scheduled (includes air cargo and passenger carriers)

4513 Air courier services

4522 Air transportation, nonscheduled (includes charter service)

Air-conditioning/Heating and Cooling Contractor

1711 Plumbing, heating, and air-conditioning contractors

Air Purification/Cleaning Service

7699 Repair shops and related services, nec (includes furnace cleaning service)

Ambulance Service

4119 Local passenger transportation, nec (includes ambulance service, road)

4522 Air transportation, nonscheduled (includes ambulance service, air)

Amusement Arcade

7993 Coin-operated amusement devices

Amusement/Water Park

7996 Amusement parks

7999 Amusement and recreation services, nec (includes waterslides and wave pools)

Animal Breeder

0279 Animal specialties, nec (includes kennels, breeding and raising own stock)

0752 Animal specialty services, except veterinary (includes breeding of animals other than farm animals)

Animal Clinic

0742 Veterinary service for animal specialties (includes animal hospitals for pets and other animals)

Antique Shop

5932 Used merchandise stores (includes retail antique stores)

7641 Reupholstery and furniture repair (includes antique furniture repair and restoration)

7699 Repair shops and related services, nec (includes antique repair and restoration, except furniture)

Apartment Locating Service

6531 Real Estate Agents and Managers

Appliance Store

5722 Household appliance stores

Appraisal Service

7389 Business services, nec (includes appraisers, except real estate)

6531 Real estate agents and managers (includes appraisers, realestate)

Aquarium Maintenance/Leasing Service

7359 Equipment rental and leasing, nec

8999 Services, nec

Archery/Target/Shooting Range

7999 Amusement and recreation services, nec (includes archery ranges, shooting galleries, shooting ranges, and trap-shooting facilities, except membership)

Architectural Restoration/Conservation

8712 Architectural Services

Art Gallery

5932 Used merchandise stores (includes retailers of art objects)

5999 Miscellaneous retail stores, nec (includes art dealers)

8412 Museums and art galleries (includes noncommercial art galleries)

Art Supplies Store

5999 Miscellaneous retail stores, nec (includes retail artists' supplies and materials stores)

Assisted Living Facilities

8051 Skilled nursing care facilities (includes extended care facilities and skilled nursing homes)

8052 Intermediate care facilities (includes intermediate care nursing homes)

8059 Nursing and personal care facilities, nec (includes rest homeswith health care)

Association Management Service

8611 Business associations

8621 Professional membership organizations

8631 Labor unions and similar labor organizations

8641 Civic, social, and fraternal associations

8699 Membership organizations, nec

8741 Management services (does not include operating staff)

Auctioneer

5154 Livestock (includes wholesale livestock auctioning)

5999 Miscellaneous retail stores, nec (includes retail general merchandise auction rooms)

7389 Business services, nec (includes auctioneering services)

Auto Supply Store

5531 Auto and home supply stores

Automobile Detailing/Painting Service

7532 Automotive paint shops

7542 Carwashes (includes detailing, cleaning and polishing, new autos on a contract or fee basis; washing and polishing, automotive; waxing and polishing, automotive)

Automobile/Truck Leasing Service

7513 Truck rental and leasing, without drivers

7514 Passenger car rental, without drivers

7515 Passenger car leasing, without drivers

Baby Store

5999 Miscellaneous retail stores, nec (includes retail baby)

Bagel Shop

2051 Bread and other bakery products, except cookies and crackers (includes bagels)

5461 Retail bakeries (includes retail bagel stores)

Bait and Tackle Shop

5941 Sporting goods stores and bicycle shops (includes bait and tackle shops and fishing equipment, retail)

Bakery/Doughnut Shop

5461 Retail bakeries

Bar/Cocktail Lounge

5813 Drinking places alcoholic beverages (includes bars, cocktail lounges, saloons, tap rooms, taverns, and like establishments)

Beauty Supply Center

5087 Service establishment equipment and supplies (includes wholesale barber shop and beauty parlor equipment and supplies)

Bed and Breakfast Operation

7011 Hotels and motels (includes bed and breakfast inns)

Beekeeping

0279 Animal specialties, nec (includes apiaries and bee farms)

Beeper/Paging Service

4812 Radiotelephone communications (includes beeper and paging services)

Bicycle Shop

5941 Sporting goods stores and bicycle shops

7699 Repair shops and related services, nec (includes bicycle repair shops)

Billiards Hall

7999 Amusement and recreation services, nec (includes billiard parlors)

Blacktop Surfacing Business

1771 Concrete work (includes blacktop work: private driveways and private parking areas contractors)

Blind Cleaning/Installation

2431 Millwork (includes wood blinds and shutters)

2591 Drapery hardware and window blinds and shades

Body Care Shop

5999 Miscellaneous retail stores, nec (includes cosmetics stores)

Book Publishing

2731 Books; publishing or publishing and printing

Bookbinder

2789 Bookbinding and related work

Bookkeeping

8721 Accounting, auditing, and bookkeeping services

Bookstore

5932 Used merchandise stores (includes used book retailers)

5942 Bookstores

Bottled Water Service

5149 Groceries and related products, nec (includes natural spring and mineral water bottling and distribution services)

5499 Miscellaneous food stores (includes mineral water, retail)

Bowling Alley

7933 Bowling centers

Brewery Operation

2082 Malt beverages

Bridal Shop/Bridal Consultant

5621 Women's clothing stores (includes retail bridal shops, exceptcustom designers)

Building/Home Inspection

7389 Business services, nec (includes safety inspection, except automotive)

Building Maintenance/Custodial Service

7349 Building cleaning and maintenance services, nec (includes interior building cleaning services, contract janitorial services, and like enterprises)

Bulletin Board Service

4822 Telegraph and other message communications (includes electronic mail services)

7379 Computer related services, nec

Business Broker Service

7389 Business services, nec (includes business brokers buying andselling business enterprises)

Business Consulting Service

8748 Business consulting services, nec

Business Services Operation

8744 Facilities support management services (includesbasemaintenance, providing personnel on continuing basis)

Butcher Shop

5423 Meat and fish (seafood) markets, including freezer provisioners

5499 Miscellaneous food stores (includes retail poultry dealers)

Cable Network

1623 Water, Sewer, Pipeline, and Communications and Power Line Construction (includes cable television line construction-contractors)

1731 Electrical Work (includes cable television hookup-contractors)

4841 Cable and Other Pay Television Services

Calligraphy Service

7389 Business services, nec (includes lettering services)

Camera Shop

5946 Camera and photographic supply stores

7699 Repair shops and related services, nec (includes camera repair shops)

Campground Management

7033 Recreational vehicle parks and campsites

Candy/Chocolate Shop

5441 Candy, nut, and confectionery stores

Car Alarm and Stereo Store

5531 Auto and home supply stores (includes automobile accessorydealers, retail)

5731 Radio, television, and consumer electronics stores (includesautomotive stereo equipment, retail)

Car Inspection Service

7549 Automotive services, except repair services and car washes(includes inspection service, automotive)

Car Towing Service

7549 Automotive services, except repair services and car washes(includes automotive towing and wrecker services)

Car Wash

7542 Car washes

Career Counseling

7389 Business services, nec (includes career counseling service)

Carpentry Service

1751 Carpentry work

Catering Service

5812 Eating places (includes caterers)

CD-ROM Developer/Producer

7372 Prepackaged software (includes pre-packaged computer software publishers)

7379 Computer related services, nec (includes database developers)

Cellular Phone/Telephone Business

4812 Radiotelephone communications

5999 Miscellaneous retail stores, nec (includes telephone stores, retail)

Charter Boat Service

4499 Water transportation service, nec (includes boat rental, commercial)

Check Cashing Service

6099 Functions related to depository banking, nec (includes check cashing agencies)

Children's Apparel Shop

5611 Men's and boys' clothing stores

5641 Children's and infants' wear stores

5651 Family clothing stores

5699 Miscellaneous apparel and accessory stores (includes children's wear)

5932 Used merchandise stores (includes retail second hand clothing stores)

Children's Day Care Center

8351 Child day care services

Chimney Sweeping Business

7349 Building cleaning and maintenance services, nec (includeschimney cleaning service)

Christmas Decoration Store

5999 Miscellaneous retail stores, nec

Christmas Tree Farm

0811 Timber tracts (includes Christmas tree growing)

Clipping Service

7389 Business services, nec (includes press clipping service)

Clothing Designer

2311 Men's and boys' suits, coats, and overcoats

2325 Men's and boys' separate trousers and slacks

2329 Men's and boys' clothing, nec

2331 Women's, misses', and juniors' blouses and shirts

2335 Women's, misses', and juniors' dresses

2337 Women's, misses', and juniors' suits, skirts, and coats

2361 Girls', children's, and infants' dresses, blouses, and shirts

Clothing Store

5611 Men's and boys' clothing and accessory stores

5621 Women's clothing stores

5632 Women's accessory and specialty stores

5641 Children's and infants' wear stores

5651 Family clothing stores

5699 Miscellaneous apparel and accessory stores

5932 Used merchandise stores (includes retail secondhand clothing stores)

Coffee Service

5149 Groceries and related products, nec (includes coffee, wholesale)

Coin/Stamp Dealer

5961 Catalog and mail order houses (includes retail mail order coinand stamp businesses)

5999 Miscellaneous retail stores, nec

Comedy Club

5813 Drinking placesMalcoholic beverages (includes nightclubs)

Comic Book/Collectibles Store

5999 Miscellaneous retail stores, nec

Commercial/Graphic Art Business

7336 Commercial art and graphic design

Commercial Mail Receiving Agency

7389 Business services, nec (includes post office contract stations)

Compact Disc/Record Store

5735 Recorded and prerecorded tape stores

Computer Consulting

7379 Computer related services, nec (includes computer consultants

Computer Data Storage Company

3572 Computer storage devices

Computer Learning/Training Center

8243 Data processing schools

Computer Maintenance and Repair Service

7378 Computer maintenance and repair

Computer Programming and Data Processing Service

7374 Computer processing and data preparation services

Computer Store

5734 Computer and computer software stores

Computer System Integrators

7371 Computer programming services

7373 Computer integrated systems design

7379 Computer related services, nec (includes computer consultants and database developers)

Computerized Billing Service

7374 Computer processing and data preparation and processing services

Computerized Matching Service

7299 Miscellaneous personal services, nec (includes dating services)

7375 Information retrieval services

Concession Stand Business

5812 Eating places (includes concession stands in airports and sports arenas, and refreshment stands)

7999 Amusement and recreation services, nec (concession operators andamusement concessions)

Consignment Shop

5932 Used merchandise stores (includes clothing stores, secondhand retail; furniture stores, secondhand retail; home furnishing stores, secondhand retail)

Construction Company

1521 General contractors—single family houses

1522 General contractors—residential buildings other than single-family

Consumer Electronics Store

5731 Radio, television, and consumer electronics stores

Convenience Store

5411 Grocery stores (includes retail convenience food stores)

Cooking School

8299 Schools and educational services, nec (includes cooking schools)

Copy Shop

7334 Photocopying and duplicating services

Cosmetics Business

2844 Perfumes, cosmetics, and other toilet preparations

5122 Drugs, drug proprietaries, and druggists' sundries (includes cosmetics—wholesale)

5963 Direct selling establishments (includes canvassers , headquarters for retail sale of merchandise, and direct selling organizations—retail)

5999 Miscellaneous retail stores, nec (includes cosmeticss-tores—retail)

Costume Shop

7299 Miscellaneous personal services, nec (includes costume rental)

7922 Theatrical producers and miscellaneous theatrical services(includes theatrical costume design)

Craft Artisan

3269 Pottery products, nec (includes art and ornamental ware; pottery; ceramic articles for craft shops; cookware; crockery; china, earthenware and stoneware figures; kitchen articles; coarse earthenware; lamp bases; and vases)

Craft/Hobby Shop

5945 Hobby, toy, and game shops (includes retail hobby stores and craft kit and supply retailers)

5947 Gift, novelty, and souvenir shops pottery; ceramic articles for craft shops; cookware; crockery; china, earthenware and stoneware figures; kitchen articles; coarse earthenware; lamp bases; and vases)

Create Your Own...Store

3269 Pottery Products, nec

5947 Gift, Novelty, and Souvenir Shops

5999 Micellaneous Retail Stores, nec

Credit Card Issuing Service

6153 Short-Term Business Credit Institutions, Except Agricultural (includes credit card service, collection by central agency)

7389 Business Services, nec (includes credit card service collection by individual firms)

Credit Repair Service

7299 Miscellaneous personal services, nec (includes debt counseling and adjustment services)

Credit Reporting and Collection Service

7322 Adjustment and collection services

7323 Credit reporting services

Damage Restoration Service

1790 Special trade contractors, nec (includes cleaning building exteriors, dampproofing buildings, dewatering, fireproofing buildings, steam cleaning of building exteriors, and waterproofing)

Dance School

7911 Dance studios, schools, and halls

Delicatessen/Sandwich Shop

5812 Eating places (includes sandwich bars or shops and submarine sandwich shops)

Desktop Publishing Company

2711 Publishing, or publishing and printing newspapers

2721 Publishing, or publishing and printing periodicals

2731 Publishing, or publishing and printing books

2741 Miscellaneous publishing

Dial-it Services

4813 Telephone communications, except radio-telephone

Diaper Service

7219 Laundry and garment services, nec

Disc Jockey Service

8999 Services, nec

Domestic Help/Maid Service

7349 Building cleaning and maintenance services, nec (includes housekeeping and office cleaning services)

8811 Private households (includes private households employing cooks, maids, and other domestic help)

Driving School

8249 Vocational schools, nec (includes truck driving schools)

8299 Schools and educational services, nec (includes automobile driving instruction)

Drug Store/Pharmacy

5912 Drug stores and proprietary stores

Dry Cleaning Service/Coin-Operated Laundry

7215 Coin-operated laundries and dry cleaning services

7216 Dry cleaning plants, except rug cleaning

Editorial/Freelance Writing Business

8999 Services, nec (includes writing and ghostwriting services)

Electrical Contractor

1731 Electrical work (includes trade contractors engaged in on-site electrical work)

Electrical Lighting Supply Store

5719 Miscellaneous home furnishings stores (includes retail lamp and shade shops)

Employee Leasing Service

7363 Help supply services

Employment Agency

361 Employment agencies

Engraving/Monogramming Service

3479 Coating, engraving, and allied services, nec (includes jewelryand silverware engraving)

7389 Business services, nec (includes advertising embroidery services, embossing services, and identification engraving services)

Environmental Consultant

8748 Business consulting services, nec

Environmental Store

5999 Miscellaneous retail stores, nec

Estate Planning

8811 Private Households

Estate Sales Business

6530 Real estate agents and managers

Executive Recruiting Agency

7361 Employment agencies (includes executive placement)

Fashion Accessories Business

3961 Costume jewelry and costume novelties, except precious metal

5137 Women's, children's, and infants' clothing and accessories

5632 Women's accessory and specialty stores

Fax Service

4822 Telegraph and other message communications (includes facsimile transmission services)

Film and Video Production Operation

7812 Motion picture and videotape production services

Financial Planning Service

282 Investment Advice

Fish and Seafood Store

5421 Meat and fish (seafood) markets, including freezer provisioners

Fish Farm

0273 Animal aquaculture (includes fish farms except hatcheries)

Floor Covering/Restoration Business

5713 Floor covering stores—retail

Florist

5992 Florists

Food Delivery Service

5812 Eating places

5963 Direct selling establishments (includes door-to-door selling organizations and mobile lunch wagons)

5999 Miscellaneous retail stores, nec

Formalwear Rental Business

7299 Miscellaneous personal services, nec (includes tuxedo rental)

Freight Forwarding Service

4731 Arrangement of transportation of freight and cargo (includes freight forwarding services)

Fund Raising Consultant

7389 Business services, nec (includes fund raising on a contract or fee basis)

Funeral Service

7261 Funeral services and crematories

Fur Farm

0271 Fur-bearing animals and rabbits

Fur Store

5632 Women's accessory and specialty stores (includes fur shops and furriers)

Furniture Restoration Service

7641 Reupholstery and furniture repair

Gambling Organizations/Service

7011 Hotels and Motels (includes casino hotels)

7993 Coin-Operated Amusement Devices

7999 Amusement and Recreation Services, nec (includes gambling establishments not primarily operating coin-operated machines and lotteries, operation of)

9311 Public Finance Taxation, and Monetary Policy (includes gambling control boards-government and lottery control boards-government)

Genealogy Service

7299 Miscellaneous personal services, nec (includes genealogical investigation service)

Gift Basket Service

5961 Catalog and mail-order houses

Gift/Card Shop

5943 Stationery stores

5947 Gift, novelty, and souvenir shops (includes card shops)

Glass Repair and Replacement Service

1751 Carpentry work (includes prefabricated window and door installation)

7536 Automotive glass replacement shops

Golf Shop

5941 Sporting goods stores and bicycle shops (includes retail golf goods and equipment stores)

Gourmet Coffee/Tea House

5499 Miscellaneous food stores (includes coffee stores, retail)

5812 Eating places (includes coffee shops)

Greenhouse/Garden Center/Nursery Business

0181 Ornamental floricultural and nursery products (includes greenhouses for floral products, growing of nursery stock, growing of potted plants)

5261 Retail nurseries, lawn and garden supply stores (includes nursery stock, seeds, and bulbs, retail)

Greeting Card Publishing

2771 Greeting card publishing and printing

8999 Services, nec (includes hand painting of greeting cards)

Grocery Store

5411 Grocery stores

Gunsmith/Gun Shop

5941 Sporting good stores and bicycle shops (includes firearms,retail)

7699 Repair shops and related services, nec (includes gunsmith shops)

Hair Replacement/Electrolysis Clinic

7299 Miscellaneous personal services, nec (includes depilatory salons, electrolysis, and hair weaving or replacement services)

Hair Salon/Barber Shop

7231 Beauty shops (includes beauty and barber shops combined)

7241 Barber shops

Handwriting Analysis Consultant

7389 Business services, nec (includes handwriting analysis)

Hardware Store

5251 Hardware stores

Hat Store

5611 Men's and boys' clothing and accessory stores (includes retail hat stores)

5621 Women's accessory and specialty stores (includes retail millinery stores)

Hazardous Waste Disposal Business

4953 Refuse systems (includes hazardous waste material disposal sites)

Healthy Restaurants

5812 Eating Places

Health Food Store

5499 Miscellaneous food stores (includes health food stores)

Hearing Aid Testing and Fitting Service

5999 Miscellaneous retail stores, nec (includes hearing aids, retail)

8099 Health and allied services, nec (includes hearing testing service)

Herb Farm

0191 General farms, primarily crop

2833 Medical chemicals and botanical products (includes herb grinding, grading, and milling)

5499 Miscellaneous food stores (includes spice and herb stores)

Home Accessory Store

5714 Drapery, curtain, and upholstery stores

5719 Miscellaneous home furnishings stores

Home Furnishings Store

5712 Furniture stores

5719 Miscellaneous home furnishings stores

5932 Used merchandise stores (including antique and secondhand retail furniture stores)

Home Health Care Service

8082 Home health care services

Horse Riding Academy

752 Animal specialty services, except veterinary (includes boarding and training horses)

Hotel/Motel/Resort Operation

7011 Hotels and motels (includes resort hotels)

Housesitting Service

8999 Services, nec

Ice Cream/Frozen Yogurt Shop

5451 Dairy products stores (includes retail packaged ice cream stores)

5812 Eating places (includes retail dairy bars)

563 Direct selling establishments (includes ice cream wagons)

Image Consultant

8299 Schools and educational services, nec (includes personal development schools)

8743 Public relations services

Import/Export Service

4731 Arrangement of the transportation of freight and cargo

Incubator

7389 Business services, nec

8748 Business consulting services, nec

Information Broker

7375 Information retrieval services

Insulation Contractor

1742 Plastering, dry wall, acoustical, and insulation work (includes insulation installation contractors)

Insurance Agency

6411 Insurance agents, brokers, and services

Interior Design Service

7389 Business services, nec (includes interior decoration consulting services and interior design services)

Internet/Online Service Provider

4822 Telegraph and other message communications (includes electronicmail services)

7379 Computer related services, nec

Investment/Securities Broker

6211 Security brokers, dealers, and flotation companies

Jewelry Store

5632 Women's accessory and specialty stores (includes costume jewelry stores)

5944 Jewelry stores

7631 Watch, clock, and jewelry repair

Job Training/Retraining

8331 Job training and vocational rehabilitation services (includesjob training)

Kiosk/Pushcart/Vendor Business

5812 Eating places (includes box lunch stands, concession stands,food bars, hamburger and hot dog stands, ice cream stands, refreshment stands, and soft drink stands)

Landscaping Service

0781 Landscape counseling and planning services

0782 Lawn and garden services

0783 Ornamental shrub and tree services

Lawn Maintenance Service

0782 Lawn and garden services

0783 Ornamental shrub and tree services

Limousine Service

4119 Local passenger transportation, nec (includes hearse and limousine rental, with drivers)

7514 Passenger car rental (includes limo rental, w/o drivers)

Lingerie Shop

5632 Lingerie storesMretail

Liquor Store

5921 Liquor stores

Literary Agency

7389 Business services, nec (includes agents and brokers for authors and non-performing artists)

Locksmith

7699 Repair shops and related services, nec (includes locksmith shops and made-to order lock parts)

Luggage and Leather Goods Business

5948 Luggage and leather goods stores

Lumberyard

5211 Lumber and other building materials dealers

Machine Shop/Metalorking Shop

3541 Machine tools, metal cutting types

3542 Machine tools, metal forming types

3544 Special dies and tools, die sets, jigs and fixtures, and industrial molds

3545 Cutting tools, machine tool accessories, and machinists' precision measuring devices

3549 Metalworking machinery, nec

Mail Order Business

5961 Catalog and mail order houses

Management Consulting Service

8742 Management consulting services

Manufacturer's Representative

7389 Business services, nec

Marine Shop

5551 Boat dealers (includes retail marine supply dealers)

Market Research and Analysis

8732 Commercial, economic, sociological, and educational research

8742 Management consulting services

Martial Arts Studio

7999 Amusement and recreation services, nec (includes Judo and Karate instruction)

Masonry, Stonework, and Plastering Contractors

1741 Masonry, stone setting, and other stonework

1742 Plastering, dry wall, acoustical, and insulation work

Massage Therapist

7299 Massage parlor 8049 Offices and clinics of health practitioners,nec

Mediation Service

7389 Business services, nec (includes arbitration and conciliationservices)

Medical and Dental Instrument Manufacturing

3841 Surgical and medical instruments and apparatus

3843 Dental equipment and supplies

Medical Claims Service

6411 Insurance agents, brokers, and service (includes processing ofmedical claims on a contract or fee basis)

Medical Laboratory Service

8071 Medical laboratories

Medical Supplies Store

5047 Medical, dental, and hospital equipment and supplies

Medical Transcription Service

7374 Computer processing and data preparation and processing services

Messenger/Delivery/Subpoena Service

4215 Courier services, except by air (includes letter, mail, package,and parcel delivery services)

4822 Telegraph and other message communication (includes cablegrams, mailgrams, electronic mail, and other message services)

7389 Business services, nec (includes process serving services)

Miniature Golf Course Operation

7999 Amusement and recreation services, nec (includes miniature golf course operations)

Modeling School/Agency

7363 Help supply services (includes modeling services)

8299 Schools and educational services, nec (includes modeling schools)

Mortgage Broker

6162 Mortgage bankers and loan correspondents (includes mortgage brokers using own money)

6163 Loan brokers (includes mortgage brokers arranging for loans but using money of others)

6211 Security brokers, dealers, and flotation companies (includes buying and selling mortgages)

Motorcycle/Moped Store

5571 Motorcycle dealers

Movie Theatre Operation

7832 Motion picture theatres, except drive-ins

7833 Drive-in motion picture theatres

Moving Service

4212 Local trucking, without storage (includes furniture and other moving services)

4214 Local trucking, with storage (includes furniture and household goods moving services)

Music School

8299 Schools and educational services, nec (includes music schools)

Music Shop

5736 Musical instrument stores

5932 Used merchandise stores (includes retailers of secondhand musical instruments)

7699 Repair shops and related services, nec (includes musical instrument repair shops)

Musical Instrument Repair/Piano Tuning Service

7699 Repair shops and related services, nec (includes musical instrument repair shops and piano tuning and repair)

Nail Salon

7231 Beauty shops (includes manicure and pedicure salons)

Nanny Service

7299 Miscellaneous personal services, nec (includes babysitting bureaus)

New Age Services and Supplies

5999 Miscellaneous retail stores, nec

8999 Services, nec

New and Used Car Dealer

5511 Motor vehicle dealers (new and used)

5521 Motor vehicle dealers (used only)

Newsletter Publishing

2721 Periodicals; publishing or publishing and printing

2741 Miscellaneous publishing (includes business service newsletterspublishing and/or printing)

Novelty Items Business

2499 Wood products, nec (includes wood and wood fiber novelties)

2514 Metal household furniture (includes metal novelty furniture)

2679 Converted paper and paperboard products, nec (includes papernovelties)

3199 Leather goods, nec (includes leather novelties)

3229 Pressed and blown glass and glassware, nec (includes novelty glassware made in glassmaking plants)

3231 Glass products, made of purchased glass (includes glassnovelties)

3499 Fabricated metal products, nec (includes metal novelties and specialties, except advertising novelties)

3961 Costume jewelry and costume novelties, except precious metal andgems

3999 Manufacturing industries, nec (includes bone, beaded and shell novelties)

Nursing Home/Long-Term Care Center

8051 Skilled nursing care facilities

8052 Intermediate care facilities (includes intermediate care nursing homes)

8059 Nursing and personal care facilities, nec (includes convalescent homes, rest homes, and like facilities)

Nutritional Consultant/Diet Planner

7299 Miscellaneous personal services, nec (includes diet workshops)

8049 Offices and clinics of health practitioners, nec (includes offices of nutritionists and offices of dietitians)

Office Design Service

7389 Business services, nec (includes interior decorating and design services)

Office Supply/Equipment Store

5943 Stationery stores (includes retail office forms and supplies stores)

Online Store

5734 Computer and computer software stores

7375 Information retrieval services

Paint/Wall Covering Center

5231 Paint, glass, and wallpaper stores

Painting Contractors

1721 Painting and paperhanging contractors

Party Entertainment Services

7929 Bands, orchestras, actors, and other entertainers and entertainment groups

Party/Reunion Planning Service

7359 Equipment rental and leasing, nec (includes party supplies rental and leasing)

8999 Services, nec

Pawnbroker

5932 Used merchandise stores (includes pawnshops)

Payroll Preparation Service

8721 Accounting, auditing, and bookkeeping services (includes payrollaccounting service)

Periodical/Newspaper Publishing

2721 Periodicals; publishing or publishing and printing

Personal Shopping Service

7299 Miscellaneous personal services, nec (includes shopping servicesfor individuals)

Pest Control Service

0851 Forestry services (includes forest pest control)

7342 Disinfecting and pest control services

Pet Boarding/Grooming Service

0279 Animal specialties, nec (includes breeding kennels)

0752 Animal specialty services (includes boarding kennels, doggrooming services, and related services)

Pet Cemetery

0782 Lawn and garden services (includes independent cemetery upkeep services)

6531 Real estate agents and managers (includes cemetery management services)

6553 Cemetery subdividers and developers (includes animal cemetery operations)

Pet Obedience School

0752 Animal specialty services, except veterinary (includes training of pets and other animal specialties)

Pet Shop

5999 Miscellaneous retail stores, nec (includes pet shops)

Pet Sitting Service

0752 Animal specialty services, except veterinary

Photo Finishing Center

7384 Photo finishing laboratories

7819 Services allied to motion picture production (includes motion picture film processing)

Photographer, Commercial

7335 Commercial photography

Photographic Studio

7221 Photographic studios, portrait

Physical Fitness Center

7991 Physical fitness facilities

Physical Therapy Clinic/Practice

8049 Offices and clinics of health practitioners, nec (includes offices of physical therapists)

Pizzeria

5812 Eating places (includes pizza parlors and pizzerias)

Plant Leasing Service

7359 Equipment rental and leasing, nec (includes plants)

Plumbing Service

1711 Plumbing, heating, and air-conditioning contractors

Porcelain Refinishing Service

1799 Special trade contractors, nec

Power Washing Service

1799 Special trade contractors, nec (includes cleaning of building exteriors)

7349 Building cleaning and maintenance services, nec (includes cleaning of building interiors)

7542 Car washes (includes automotive washing and polishing)

Prepaid Phone Card Business

4812 Radiotelephone communications

4813 Telephone communications, except radiotelephone

Print/Frame Shop

7699 Repair shops and related services, nec (includes custom picture framing services)

Printing Business

2752 Commercial printing, lithographic

2754 Commercial printing, gravure

2759 Commercial printing, nec

2761 Manifold business form printers

Private Investigation/Personal Security Service

7381 Detective, guard, and armored car services

Private Label Product Manufacturer/Retailer

3999 Manufacturing industries, nec

5399 Miscellaneous general mer chandise stores

5499 Miscellaneous food stores 5699 Miscellaneous apparel and accessory stores

5999 Miscellaneous retail stores, nec

Professional Organizer

7299 Miscellaneous personal services, nec

7389 Business services, nec

Property Management

6531 Real estate agents and managers

Public Relations Consultant

8743 Public relations services

Public Warehousing/Ministorage Operation

4221 Farm product warehousing and storage

4222 Refrigerated warehousing and storage

4225 General warehousing and storage

4226 Special warehousing and storage, nec (includes fur storage, household goods warehousing and storage, whiskey warehousing, and like enterprises)

Quick Oil Change Service

5541 Gasoline service stations (includes automobile servicestations—retail)

7538 General automotive repair shops

Radio Station

4832 Radio broadcasting stations

Radon Testing Service

1799 Special trade contractors, nec

8734 Testing laboratories

Real Estate Agency

6531 Real estate agents and managers

Real Estate Investment Service

6798 Real estate investment trusts

Recording Studio

7399 Business services, nec (includes recording studios operating on a contract or fee basis)

Recreational Vehicle Dealer

5561 Recreational vehicle dealers

Recycling Business

5093 Scrap and waste materials

Rental Service

7299 Miscellaneous personal services, nec (includes clothing rental)

7352 Medical equipment rental and leasing

7353 Heavy construction equipment and leasing

7359 Equipment rental and leasing, nec

7377 Computer rental and leasing

7999 Amusement and recreation services, nec (includes pleasure boat rental, canoe and rowboat rental, bicycle, motorcycle and moped rental, and sporting goods rental)

Restaurant

5812 Eating places (includes sit-down, carry-out, and fast food)

Resume Service

7338 Secretarial anc court reporting services (includes resumewriting services)

Roofing Contractor

1761 Roofing, siding, and sheet metal work

Satellite Dish Service

4841 Cable and other pay television services (includes directbroadcast satellite services and satellite master antenna systems services)

Screen Printing Business

2261 Finishers of broadwoven fabrics of cotton (includes printing andfinishing of cotton broadwoven fabrics)

2262 Finishers of broadwoven fabrics of manmade fiber and silk(includes printing manmade fiber and silk broadwoven fabrics)

2759 Commercial printing, nec (includes screen printing on glass, plastics, paper, and metal, including highway signs)

Security Systems Service

7382 Security systems services

Seminar Planner/Lecturer

8999 Services, nec (including lecturers)

Service Station/Auto Repair and Service Shop

5541 Gasoline service stations

7532 Top, body, and upholstery repair shops and paint shops

7533 Automotive exhaust system repair shops

7534 Tire retreading and repair shops

7536 Automotive glass replacement shops

7537 Automotive transmission repair shops

7538 General automotive repair shops

7539 Automotive repair shops, nec

Sewer and Drain Cleaning Business

7699 Repair shops and related services, nec (includes sewer cleaning and rodding and septic tank cleaning) Sewing Center 5722 Household appliance stores (includes retail sewing machine stores)

5949 Sewing, needlework, and piece goods stores

7699 Repair shops and related services, nec (includes sewing machine repair shops)

Shoe Repair Shop

7251 Shoe repair shops and shoeshine parlors

Shoe Store

5661 Shoe stores

Sign Shop

3993 Signs and advertising specialties

7389 Business services, nec (includes sign painting shops)

Silk Plant Shop

5999 Miscellaneous retail stores, nec (includes artificial flowers—retail)

Skating Rink Operation

7999 Amusement and recreation services, nec (includes ice and rollerskating rink operations)

Ski Shop

5941 Sporting goods stores and bicycle shops

Software Publishing

7372 Packaged software

Solar Energy Design/Contracting Business

1711 Plumbing, heating, and air-conditioning contractors (includes solar heating apparatus contractors)

1742 Plastering, dry wall, acoustical, and insulation work (includes solar reflecting insulation film contractors)

Specialized Staffing

7361 Employment Agencies

7363 Help Supply Services

Specialty Foods/Wine Shop

5499 Miscellaneous food stores

5921 Liquor stores (includes packaged wine—retail)

Sports Promotional Services

7941 Professional Sports Clubs and Promoters

Sporting Goods Store

5941 Sporting goods stores and bicycle shops

Surveying Service

8713 Surveying services (includes surveying: land, water, and aerial)

Swimming Pool/Hot Tub Business

1799 Special trade contractors, nec (includes swimming pool construction contractors)

5999 Miscellaneous retail stores, nec (includes hot tubs, retail)

7389 Business services, nec (includes swimming pool cleaning and maintenance services)

7999 Amusement and recreation services, nec (includes swimming pooloperations)

Tailor Shop

5699 Miscellaneous apparel and accessory stores (includes customtailor shops) 7219 Laundry and garment services, nec (includes tailorshops, except custom or merchant tailors)

Talent Agency

7922 Theatrical producers and miscellaneous theatrical services (includes agents)

Tanning Parlor/Sauna

7299 Miscellaneous personal services (includes steam baths and tanning salons)

Tattoo Parlor

7299 Miscellaneous personal services, nec (includes tattoo parlors)

Tax Preparation Business

7291 Tax return preparation services

8721 Accounting, auditing, and bookkeeping services

Taxicab/Van Shuttle Service

4121 Taxicabs

Taxidermy Service

7699 Repair shops and related services, nec (includes taxidermy)

Teacher Supply Store

5999 Miscellaneous retail stores, nec

Telemarketing Service

7389 Business services, nec (includes telemarketing services operating on a contract or fee basis)

Telephone Answering Service

7389 Business services, nec (includes answering services)

Television/Radio Repair Service

7622 Radio and television repair shops

Television Station

4833 Television broadcasting stations

Temporary Employment Agency

7363 Help supply services (includes temporary help services

Tennis Court/Racquet Club Operation

7997 Membership sports and recreation clubs (includes racquetball and tennis clubs)

7999 Amusement and recreation services, nec (includes nonmembership racquetball and tennis court operations)

Tire Dealer

5531 Auto and home supply stores (includes retail tire dealers) 7534 Tire retreading and repair shops

Tobacco Shop

5993 Tobacco stores and stands

Tour Guide Operation/Adventure Service

4725 Tour operations

7999 Amusement and recreation services, nec (includes tour guides)

Toy Business

5945 Hobby, toy, and game shops

Trade Show/Conference Management Service

7389 Business services, nec (includes trade show arrangement)

Translating/Interpreting Service

7389 Business services, nec (includes translation service)

Travel Agency

4724 Travel agencies

Trucking Business

4212 Local trucking, without storage services

4213 Trucking, except local

4214 Local trucking, with storage services

Tutoring Service

8299 Schools and educational services, nec (includes tutoring services)

Typesetting Business

2791 Typesetting

Typing/Stenographic Service

7338 Secretarial and court reporting services (includes stenographic and typing services)

Upholstery/Carpet Services

1752 Floor laying and other floor work, nec (includes carpet laying and removing services)

5714 Drapery, curtain, and upholstery stores (includes upholstery materials stores)

7217 Carpet and upholstery cleaning

Vending Machine Merchandising and Service Business

5962 Automatic merchandising machine operators (includes retail sale of products through vending machines)

7359 Equipment rental and leasing services, nec (includes vending machine rental businesses)

Videocassette Rental Store

5735 Recorded and prerecorded tape stores (includes retail videotape stores)

7841 Videotape rental establishments

Vision Center

5995 Optical goods stores

Voice Mail Service

4813 Telephone communications, except radiotelephone (includes voice telephone communications)

Water Conditioning Service

7389 Business services, nec (includes water softener services)

Web Site Design

7371 Computer programming services (includes custom computer programsor systems software development and computer software systems analysis and design)

Weight Reduction/Control Center

7991 Physical fitness facilities (includes reducing facilities and slenderizing salons)

Welcome Service

7389 Business service, nec (includes welcoming service)

Window Dressing Business

3993 Signs and advertising specialties (includes advertising displays, except printed, and window and lobby cutouts and displays)

7319 Advertising, nec (includes display advertising services, exceptoutdoor)

Word Processing Service

7338 Secretarial and court reporting services (includes wordprocessing services)

List of General Small Business Topics

This section covers sources of assistance applicable to a variety of small businesses. Resources are arranged by topic and include associations, educational programs, directories of educational programs, reference works, sources of supply, statistical sources, periodicals, videocassettes/audiocassettes, trade shows and conventions, consultants, computerized databases, computer systems/software, Internet databases, libraries, and research centers.

ASSOCIATIONS AND OTHER ORGANIZATIONS

17565 ■ Audio Engineering Society
60 E 42nd St., Rm. 2520
New York, NY 10165-2520
Ph:(212)661-8528
Fax:(212)682-0477
Co. E-mail: hq@aes.org
URL: http://www.aes.org
Contact: Roger Furness, Exec. Dir.
Description: Engineers, administrators, and technicians who design or operate recording and reproducing equipment for radio, television, motion picture, and recording studios, or who produce, install, and operate disc, magnetic tape, and sound amplifying equipment; educators who use recording in teaching, or who teach acoustics, electronics, and other sciences basic to the recording and reproducing of sound; administrators, sales engineers, and technicians in the sound industry and related fields. Operates educational and research foundation. **Publications:** *Journal of the Audio Engineering Society: Audio/Acoustics/Applications* (10/year).

17566 ■ Canadian Academy of Recording Arts and Sciences
345 Adelaide St. W, 2nd Fl.
Toronto, ON, Canada M5V 1R5
Ph:(416)485-3135
Free: 888-440-5866
Fax:(416)485-4978
Co. E-mail: membership@carasonline.ca
URL: http://www.carasonline.ca
Contact: Melanie Berry, Pres./CEO
Description: Individuals actively working within the Canadian music industry. Promotes advancement in the field of recording and related disciplines. Conducts educational and charitable programs; maintains hall of fame.

17567 ■ Canadian Independent Music Association
30 St. Patrick St., 2nd Fl.
Toronto, ON, Canada M5T 3A3
Ph:(416)485-3152
Fax:(416)485-4373
Co. E-mail: cima@cimamusic.ca
URL: http://www.cirpa.ca
Contact: Duncan McKie, Pres./CEO
Description: Works to secure a strong and economically stable Canadian independent music and sound recording industry.

17568 ■ Canadian Recording Industry Association–L'association de l'industrie canadienne de L'enregistrement
85 Mowat Ave.
Toronto, ON, Canada M6K 3E3
Ph:(416)967-7272
Fax:(416)967-9415
Co. E-mail: info@cria.ca
URL: http://www.cria.ca
Contact: Graham Henderson, Pres.
Description: Record companies and manufacturers. Promotes high standards of ethics and practice in the recording industry. Represents members' interests.

17569 ■ Content Delivery and Storage Association
39 N Bayles Ave.
Port Washington, NY 11050
Ph:(516)767-6720
Fax:(516)883-5793
Co. E-mail: mporter@contentdeliveryandstorage.org
URL: http://www.cdsaonline.org
Contact: Martin Porter, Exec. Dir.
Description: Serves as the advocate for the growth and development of all recording media and as a forum for the exchange of information regarding global trends and innovations. Provides members an opportunity to join forces and be a strong industry voice allowing them to grow and expand their business. Encompasses all facets of the recording media. **Publications:** *Mediaware* (9/year).

17570 ■ National Academy of Recording Arts and Sciences
3402 Pico Blvd.
Santa Monica, CA 90405
Ph:(310)392-3777
Fax:(310)399-3090
Co. E-mail: memservices@grammy.com
URL: http://www.grammy.com
Contact: Jimmy Jam, Chm.
Description: Musicians, producers and other recording professionals. Dedicated to improving the cultural environment and quality of life for music and its makers. The Recording Academy is internationally known for the Grammy Awards and is responsible for numerous groundbreaking outreach, professional development, cultural enrichment, education and human service programs. **Publications:** *Grammy Magazine* (periodic); *The Grammy Winners Book* (annual); *Program Book* (annual);Journal (semiannual).

17571 ■ National Association of Recording Merchandisers
9 Eves Dr., Ste. 120
Marlton, NJ 08053
Ph:(856)596-2221
Fax:(856)596-3268
Co. E-mail: donio@narm.com
URL: http://www.narm.com
Contact: Jim Donio, Pres.
Description: Serves the music and other prerecorded entertainment software industry as a forum for insight and dialogue; members include retailers, wholesalers, distributors, entertainment software suppliers, and suppliers of related products and services. **Publications:** *NARM Convention Official Guide* (annual); *NARM Membership Directory and Buyer's Guide* (annual); *NARM News Bits* (monthly); *NARM Research Briefs* (monthly).

17572 ■ Society of Professional Audio Recording Services
441 W 53rd St.
New York, NY 10019
Ph:(212)765-7500
Fax:(212)765-7450
Co. E-mail: info@spars.com
URL: http://www.spars.com
Contact: Kirk Imamura, Pres./Dir.
Description: Recording and video studio owners; suppliers, manufacturers, producers, engineers, and recording service users involved with audio commercial facilities. Works to improve every phase of business operations and to provide members with the opportunity to play an effective role in shaping the future of their industry. Acts as a forum for the industry; maintains a high technical cultural standard; addresses interested parties on issues confronting the industry's present and future equipment needs. Analyzes, evaluates, and comments upon the use of professional audio equipment; fosters the dissemination of information concerning techniques of studio management and technical innovation; conducts educational activities. Assists in the development of projects, undertakings, and studies related to the industry; considers and deals with intratrade problems; attempts to reform abuses and inculcate principles of justice and equity in the audio recording industry. .

DIRECTORIES OF EDUCATIONAL PROGRAMS

17573 ■ *Directory of Private Accredited Career Schools and Colleges of Technology*
Pub: Accrediting Commission of Career Schools and Colleges of Technology
Contact: Michale S. McComis, Exec. Dir.
Released: On web page. **Price:** Free. **Description:** Covers 3900 accredited post-secondary programs that provide training programs in business, trade, and technical fields, including various small business endeavors. Entries offer school name, address, phone, description of courses, job placement assistance, and requirements for admission. Arrangement is alphabetical.

REFERENCE WORKS

17574 ■ *The Big Payback: The History of the Business of Hip-Hop*
Pub: New American Library/Penguin Group
Ed: Dan Charnas. **Price:** $24.95. **Description:** The complete history of hip-hop music is presented, by following the money and the relationship between artist and merchant. In its promise of economic security and creative control for black artist-entrepreneurs, it is the culmination of dreams of black nationalists and civil rights leaders.

17575 ■ *Here Come the Regulars: How to Run a Record Label on a Shoestring Budget*
Pub: Faber & Faber, Inc.
Ed: Ian Anderson. **Released:** October 1, 2009. **Price:** $15.00. **Description:** Author, Ian Anderson launched

his own successful record label, Afternoon Records when he was 18 years old. Anderson shares insight into starting a record label, focusing on label image, budget, blogging, potential artists, as well as legal aspects.

17576 ■ *The Rhythm of Success: How an Immigrant Produced His Own American Dream*
Pub: Penguin Group (USA) Inc.
Ed: Emilio Estefan. **Released:** January 10, 2010. **Price:** $24.95. **Description:** Emilio Estafan, husband to singer Gloria Estefan and founder of the Latin pop legend Miami Sound Machine, is the classic example of the American dream. He shares his guiding principles that entrepreneurs need to start and grow a business.

17577 ■ "Scoring Music" in *Canadian Business* (Vol. 81, December 8, 2008, No. 21, pp. S3)
Pub: Rogers Media Ltd.
Ed: Jay Somerset. **Description:** Boyd Devereaux, who plays with the Toronto Maple Leafs, collaborates with musicians through his record label Elevation Records. Devereaux won a Stanley Cup with the Detroit Red Wings in 2002 and has released five limited edition discs through Elevation records.

17578 ■ "Sound Fundamentals" in *Hispanic Business* (September 2007, pp. 12, 14, 16)
Pub: Hispanic Business
Ed: Michael T. Mena. **Description:** Profile of Ozomatli, a Los Angeles-based multicultural, multi-ethnic musical group that has topped Billboard's Latin Pop chart without relying on record sales. Members explain how they run the group like a small business.

17579 ■ "Welcome to Babesland" in *Women In Business* (Vol. 62, June 2010, No. 2, pp. 33)
Pub: American Business Women's Association
Ed: Leigh Elmore. **Description:** Music group, Four Bitchin' Babes will be performing at the 2010 American Business Women's Association's National Women's Leadership Conference. The group has been in the industry for 20 years and has released nine albums. The Four Bitchin' Babes consist of Sally Fingerett, Nancy Moran, Deirdre Flint, and Debi Smith.

17580 ■ "When the Longtime Star Fades" in *Harvard Business Review* (Vol. 88, September 2010, No. 9, pp. 117)
Pub: Harvard Business School Publishing
Ed: Jimmy Guterman. **Description:** A fictitious aging employee scenario is presented, with contributors offering advice. The scenarios focuses on an older employee's match with a rapidly changing industry; suggestions include consolidating a niche business around the employee, and also engaging the older employee in solving the productivity issue.

SOURCES OF SUPPLY

17581 ■ *Broadcast Engineering—Equipment Reference Manual*
Pub: Penton Media Inc.
Contact: Brad Dick, Editorial Dir.
E-mail: bdick@primediabusiness.com
Released: Annual, fall. **Publication Includes:** List of more than 1,400 manufacturers and distributors of communications equipment for radio, television, and recording applications. **Entries Include:** For manufacturers—Company name, address. For distributors and dealers—Company name, address, phone, product or service provided, geographic area covered. **Arrangement:** Manufacturers are alphabetical; dealers and distributors are geographical. **Indexes:** Product/service.

TRADE PERIODICALS

17582 ■ *etracks Newsletter*
Pub: Society of Professional Audio Recording Services
Contact: Shirley P. Kaye
Released: Periodic. **Price:** Included in membership. **Description:** Examines technical developments in audio equipment and techniques of audio studio management. Discusses industry issues and trends. Recurring features include reports on Society programs, services, and activities. Remarks: Available only via e-mail, or on website.

17583 ■ *Journal of the Audio Engineering Society*
Pub: Audio Engineering Society Inc.
Contact: Christine Carleo
Ed: John Vanderkooy, Editor. **Released:** Monthly, except Jan., Feb. and July, Aug. when it is published Bimonthly. **Price:** $50 members; $280 nonmembers print; $525 nonmembers online; $695 nonmembers print and online. **Description:** Newsletter reporting engineering developments and scientific progress in audio engineering for audio professionals, educators, executives, consumers, and students.

17584 ■ *Pro Sound News*
Pub: New Bay Media, LLC
Contact: Allison Smith, Specialty Sales
E-mail: asmith@nbmedia.com
Released: Monthly. **Description:** Audio industry magazine covering recording and sound production.

17585 ■ *Sound & Video Contractor*
Pub: Penton Media Inc.
Contact: Shahla Hebets, Publisher
E-mail: shahla.hebets@penton.com
Released: Monthly. **Description:** Magazine covering management and technical topics for the systems contracting industry.

TRADE SHOWS AND CONVENTIONS

17586 ■ The NAMM Show
NAMM I International Music Products Association
5790 Armada Dr.
Carlsbad, CA 92008
Ph:(760)438-8001
Free: 800-767-6266
Fax:(760)438-7327
Co. E-mail: info@namm.com
URL: http://www.namm.com
Released: Annual. **Audience:** Retail music merchants; manufacturers of musical instruments and accessories; manufacturers of acoustical equipment; sheet music publishers. **Principal Exhibits:** Musical instruments and accessories, acoustical equipment, and sheet music publications. **Dates and Locations:** 2012 Jan 19-22, Nashville, TN; 2013 Jan 17-20, Nashville, TN.

17587 ■ NAMM - Summer Session
NAMM I International Music Products Association
5790 Armada Dr.
Carlsbad, CA 92008
Ph:(760)438-8001
Free: 800-767-6266
Fax:(760)438-7327
Co. E-mail: info@namm.com
URL: http://www.namm.com
Released: Annual. **Audience:** All attendees must be owners or employees of companies in the music-products industry, either retailers or suppliers-closed trade show. **Principal Exhibits:** Musical instruments and accessories, acoustical equipment, and sheet music publications. **Dates and Locations:** 2011 Jul 21-23, Nashville, TN; 2012 Jul 12-14, Nashville, TN; 2013 Jul 11-13, Nashville, TN.

CONSULTANTS

17588 ■ Engineering Harmonics Inc.
29A Leslie St.
Toronto, ON, Canada M4M 3C3
Ph:(416)465-3378
Fax:(416)465-9037
Co. E-mail: 2009-info@engineeringharmonics.com
URL: http://www.engineeringharmonics.com
Contact: Paul Alegado, Principle
E-mail: pgiddings@atsengineeringharmonies.com
Scope: Specializing in audio, audio and video, control, and communication based systems. **Publications:** "Designing Sound for Frank Gehry's Vision"; "Precis of WDCH PSVC System"; "PSVC Design Challenges at WDCH"; "Power and Ground Update"; "Noise Reduction Systems"; "Mandating the House Audio System," Overture Hall; "Betting on Legends," Nov, 2008; "Examining our Roots, Defining our Future," Dec, 2008; "Walking The Hall: A Guide to Tuning a Loudspeaker System," Nov, 2007; "National Ballet School," Nov, 2007; "The Puzzle of PA for a Hall-in-the-Round," Aug, 2007; "A House for All Seasons," Aug, 2006; "Hooray for LA," Jan, 2004; "A Kodak Moment," Apr, 2002.

17589 ■ Jacek Figwer Associates Inc.
85 The Valley Rd.
Concord, MA 01742
Ph:(508)369-0155
Fax:(508)369-6073
Contact: Jozef Jacek Figwer, President
Scope: Offers consulting services in acoustics and related fields, including: Architectural acoustics, noise and vibration control, office acoustics, sound system design, noise masking systems, sound recording and broadcast studio design and audio-visual systems. Serves private industries as well as government agencies. Active worldwide. **Publications:** "Sound Reinforcement Systems".

17590 ■ Jess Barker, Document Research/ Retrieval L.L.C.
209A S Macoupin St.
Gillespie, IL 62033-1605
Ph:(217)839-3219
Free: 888-316-3773
Fax:877-522-7537
Co. E-mail: documentretrieval@frontiernet.net
URL: http://www.documentresearch.biz
Contact: James Barker, Principle
Scope: A full service title search company that provides Title Reports to investors who are interested in making offers on properties.

17591 ■ Lougheed Resource Group Inc.
17608 Deer Isle Cir.
Winter Garden, FL 34787
Ph:(407)654-1212
Fax:(407)654-5419
Co. E-mail: info@lrgconstruction.com
URL: http://www.lrgconstruction.com
Contact: Karen Lougheed, Owner
E-mail: karen@lrgmanagement.com
Scope: Construction consultants specializing in project strategies, scope preparation, contract negotiation, project management, document and code evaluation, peer reviews, scheduling/estimates, dispute resolution, and forensic analysis expert testimony.

17592 ■ Triad Studios
4572 150th Ave. NE
Redmond, WA 98052
Ph:(425)881-9322
Fax:(425)881-3645
Co. E-mail: info@triadstudios.com
Contact: Eric Janko, Principle
E-mail: ejanko@atstriadstudios.com
Scope: Firm has expertise in recording studio design, acoustics, and sound issues. The firm serves the music industry in the Northwest.

LIBRARIES

17593 ■ Bowling Green State University–Music Library and Sound Recordings Archives
Wm. T. Jerome Library, 3rd Fl.
Bowling Green, OH 43403
Ph:(419)372-2307
Fax:(419)372-2499
Co. E-mail: mlsra@bgsu.edu
URL: http://www.bgsu.edu/colleges/library/music
Contact: Susannah Cleveland, Hd.Libn. of MLSRA
Scope: Popular music, recording industry, classical music. **Services:** Library open to the public with restrictions; researchers should contact Library prior to making extended visit. **Holdings:** 60,000 books and scores; 1700 bound periodical volumes; 16,000 pieces of popular sheet music; 6 drawers of popular music posters. **Subscriptions:** 200 journals and other serials.

17594 ■ Delaware State Museums Division of Historical and Cultural Affairs–Johnson Victrola Museum
Museum Sq.
375 S. New St.
Dover, DE 19901
Ph:(302)744-5055
Co. E-mail: stacey.johnson@state.de.us
URL: http://history.delaware.gov/museums/jvm/jvm_main.shtml
Contact: Stacey Johnson, Site Supv.
Scope: Sound recording industry, Victor Talking Machine Company. **Services:** Library open to the public for reference and by appointment only. **Holdings:** Books; reference materials; advertisement; manuscripts; patents.

17595 ■ Recording Industry Association of America Reference Library
1025 F St. NW, 10th Fl.
Washington, DC 20004
Ph:(202)775-0101
Fax:(202)775-7253
URL: http://www.riaa.com
Contact: Mitch Bainwol, Chm./CEO
Scope: Audio and video recording industry, trade association that represents the U.S. recording industry. **Services:** Library not open to the public. **Holdings:** Books; magazines; clippings; other reference materials. **Subscriptions:** 50 journals and other serials; 6 newspapers.

Recreational Vehicle Dealer

ASSOCIATIONS AND OTHER ORGANIZATIONS

17596 ■ BlueRibbon Coalition
4555 Burley Dr., Ste. A
Pocatello, ID 83202-1945
Ph:(208)237-1008
Free: 800-BLUE-RIB
Fax:(208)237-9424
Co. E-mail: brmem@sharetrails.org
URL: http://www.sharetrails.org
Contact: Mr. Greg Mumm, Exec. Dir.
Description: Represents individuals, organizations and businesses involved in off highway recreation such as snowmobiling, motorcycle trail riding, mountain biking, ATVing, hiking, horseback riding, 4x4ing, rock hounding and boating. Seeks to preserve access for off highway recreation; promotes conservation of natural resources; encourages cooperation among members and government land managers. .

17597 ■ Canadian Recreational Vehicle Association–Association Canadienne du Vehicule Recreatif
2175 Sheppard Ave., Ste. 310
Toronto, ON, Canada M2J 1W8
Fax:(416)491-1670
URL: http://www.crva.ca/index.html
Description: Suppliers (122) and manufacturers (49) of recreational vehicles. Represents the interests of the industry before consumers and government agencies; provides for information exchange. Collects statistics; sponsors educational programs; presents awards. Ensures a continuity of professional standards beneficial to the RV industry and ultimately to the interest of the consumer.

17598 ■ Recreation Vehicle Dealers Association of America
3930 University Dr.
Fairfax, VA 22030-2515
Ph:(703)591-7130
Free: 888-687-7832
Fax:(703)359-0152
Co. E-mail: info@rvda.org
URL: http://www.rvda.org
Contact: Michael A. Molino CAE, Pres.
Description: Firms that have as their principal business the retail sale of recreation vehicles (commonly known as travel trailers, camping trailers, truck campers, and motor homes) and who maintain a permanent business establishment oPEN for business and service on what they sell year-round. Provides information and liaison on government regulation of safety, trade, warranty, and franchising; fosters improved dealer-manufacturer relations; encourages communications among dealers and state and local RV associations. Offers education programs and training, advertising, sales, and service information. Provides public relations and publicity among the RV dealers and the rest of the industry, the public, and the government; works to improve standards of service to the consumer; sponsors local retail RV shows and dealer seminars. Supports improved availability and quality of campgrounds. Maintains speakers' bureau; compiles statistics; sponsors educational programs. Maintains the Recreation Vehicle Rental Association and Recreation Vehicle Aftermarket Division to help improve the professional quality of rental and service businesses. **Publications:** *RV Executive Today* (monthly); *RV Technician Magazine* (quarterly).

17599 ■ Recreation Vehicle Industry Association
1896 Preston White Dr.
Reston, VA 20191
Ph:(703)620-6003
Fax:(703)620-5071
Co. E-mail: dstuebing@rvia.org
URL: http://www.rvia.org
Contact: Ms. Diane Stuebing, Member Services Coor.
Description: Recreation vehicle manufacturers, manufacturers' representatives, and suppliers of accessories and equipment used by manufacturers. Seeks to provide a unified recreation vehicle organization for manufacturers and component parts suppliers of motor homes, travel trailers, fifth wheel trailers, horse trailer conversions, sport-utility trailers, truck campers and folding camping trailers. Promotes and represents the growth and concerns of the industry to federal and state government departments, the media, and the public. Collects shipment statistics, technical data, and consumer and media information. Monitors industry compliance with safety standards and the activities of federal and state governments that affect the RV industry. Provides legal and public relations services. Sponsors market research. **Publications:** *Recreation Vehicle Industry Association—Industry Profile Report* (annual); *Recreation Vehicle Market Report* (monthly); *Survey of RV Financing* (annual).

17600 ■ Recreation Vehicle Rental Association
3930 University Dr.
Fairfax, VA 22030-2515
Ph:(703)591-7130
Fax:(703)359-0152
Co. E-mail: info@rvda.org
URL: http://www.rvra.org
Description: Dealers involved in the rental of recreation vehicles such as folding trailers, travel trailers, and motor homes. Works to improve the professionalism of the RV rental dealer through educational programs and promote the use of rentals by disseminating information. Compiles statistics; conducts seminars. .

REFERENCE WORKS

17601 ■ "Business For Sale: Your Cold Calling?" in *Inc.* (December 2007, pp. 34)
Pub: Gruner & Jahr USA Publishing
Ed: Elaine Appleton Grant. **Description:** Profile of a recreational outfitting company in northern New England with an asking price of $6.185 million, with gross revenue of $9.4 million in 2007.

17602 ■ Recreation Vehicle Industry Association—Membership Directory and Industry Buyer's Guide
Pub: Recreation Vehicle Industry Association
Ed: Karen Mason, Editor. **Released:** Annual, February; latest edition 2009. **Covers:** Approximately 500 member recreation vehicle manufacturers, component parts suppliers, and associate firms; RV-related state and regional associations. **Entries Include:** For businesses—Company name, address, phone, fax, name of contact, subsidiary and branch names and locations, product provided. For associations—Association name, address, phone. **Arrangement:** Separate sections for manufacturers, suppliers, finance firms, associate firms, manufacturers reps, and related associations. **Indexes:** Product/service, geographical, company name and brand names.

17603 ■ RV Business—RV Industry Directory Issue
Pub: TL Enterprises Inc.
Released: Annual, Latest edition 2010. **Price:** $19. 95, individuals 1-4 copies; $14.95, individuals 5 or more copies. **Publication Includes:** About 250 recreational vehicle manufacturers, 700 suppliers, and 600 distributors, wholesalers, manufacturers' representatives, and others in the industry; limited international coverage. **Entries Include:** For manufacturers—Company name, address, phone, fax, names of key personnel, location of branch plants, types of vehicles made, brand names. For suppliers, and distributors—Company name, address, phone, fax, names of key personnel, products. For representatives—Company name, address, phone, fax, names and titles of key personnel, companies represented. **Arrangement:** Classified by line of business or type of service. **Indexes:** Company name, brand names for manufacturers, supplier products.

17604 ■ The RVDA Membership Directory and Resource Guide
Pub: Recreation Vehicle Dealers Association of North America
Released: Annual, Latest edition 2008. **Covers:** Over 900 retail sales firms handling travel trailers, camping trailers, truck campers, and motor homes in the United States and Canada that are open for business twelve months of the year. **Entries Include:** Company name, address, phone, and owner's or manager's name. **Arrangement:** Alphabetical. **Indexes:** Geographical, membership status.

STATISTICAL SOURCES

17605 ■ The Market Outlook for Leisure and Recreational Vehicles
Pub: Business Trend Analysts, Inc.
Released: 2005 -2006. **Price:** $1295.00. **Description:** Since the last decline in the value of manufacturers' sales of recreational vehicles (RVs) in 2001, this market has exhibited positive-sometimes almost overwhelming-growth.

17606 ■ RMA Annual Statement Studies
Pub: Robert Morris Associates (RMA)
Released: Annual. **Price:** $175.00 2006-07 edition, $105.00. **Description:** Contains composite balance

sheets and income statements for more than 360 industries, including the accounting, auditing, and bookkeeping industries. Also contains five years of comparative historical data for discerning trends. Includes 16 commonly used ratios, computed for most of the size groupings for nearly every industry.

TRADE PERIODICALS

17607 ■ *Escapees Magazine*
Pub: Escapees, Inc.
Contact: Janice Lasko, Managing Editor
Released: Bimonthly. **Description:** Provides members with the opportunity to exchange ideas and information on traveling in recreational vehicles. Carries hints for modifying vehicles for full-time living, saving and earning money, and keeping in touch with others. Recurring features include technical advice, travel in Mexico and abroad, housekeeping hints, where to find free and inexpensive parking, book reviews, announcements of rallies and other events, and information about the Escapee support network and RV Park system.

17608 ■ *ISTVS Newsletter*
Pub: International Society for Terrain-Vehicle Systems
Ed: Dvoralai Wulfsohn, Editor, dw@kvl.dk. **Released:** 2-3/year. **Description:** Concerned with off-road vehicle research. Recurring features include news of the Society and a calendar of events.

17609 ■ *RV Business*
Pub: TL Enterprises Inc.
Contact: Sherman Goldenberg, Publisher
E-mail: sgoldenberg@affinitygroup.com
Ed: Bruce Hampson, Editor, bhampson@affinitygroup.com. **Released:** Monthly. **Description:** Magazine about the business of manufacturing, distributing, and selling travel trailers, conversion vehicles, and motorhomes and related parts, accessories, and services.

17610 ■ *Trailer Life*
Pub: TL Enterprises Inc.
Contact: Terry Thompson, VP, Sales
Released: Monthly. **Price:** $15.97; $27.97 two years. **Description:** Magazine for recreational vehicle (RV) enthusiasts.

17611 ■ *Woodall's Northeast Outdoors*
Pub: Woodall Publications Corp.
Released: Bimonthly. **Price:** $20. **Description:** Magazine serving campers and RVers in the Northeast.

17612 ■ *Woodall's Southern RV*
Pub: Woodall Publications Corp.
Ed: Brent Peterson, Editor. **Released:** Bimonthly. **Price:** $20 retail price. **Description:** Magazine on recreational vehicles and campgrounds.

TRADE SHOWS AND CONVENTIONS

17613 ■ Annual Rockford RV, Camping and Travel Show
Showtime Productions Inc.
PO Box 4372
Rockford, IL 61110
Fax:(815)877-9037
Co. E-mail: brenda@showtimeproduction.net
URL: http://www.showtimeproduction.net
Released: Annual. **Principal Exhibits:** RVs, camping and travel.

17614 ■ Eastern Sports & Outdoor Show
Reed Exhibitions North American Headquarters
383 Main Ave.
Norwalk, CT 06851
Ph:(203)840-4800
Fax:(203)840-5805
Co. E-mail: export@reedexpo.com
URL: http://www.reedexpo.com
Released: Annual. **Audience:** General public. **Principal Exhibits:** Recreational vehicles, boats, hunting and fishing equipment, clothing, and related outdoor products, resorts, SUVs, retailers and manufacturers, motorcycles, ATVs, travel and tourism.

17615 ■ Fort Wayne Sports, Vacation, and Boat Show
Trio Enterprises, Inc.
3624 Maxim Dr.
Fort Wayne, IN 46815
Ph:(219)483-2638
Free: 800-446-2638
Fax:(219)484-0876
Released: Annual. **Audience:** General public. **Principal Exhibits:** Recreational vehicles, boats, and travel and vacation information.

17616 ■ Idaho Sportsmen's Show
Spectra Productions, Inc.
PO Box 333
Eagle, ID 83616
Ph:(208)939-6426
Free: 800-635-2274
Fax:(208)939-6437
Co. E-mail: david@spectraproductions.com
URL: http://www.spectraproductions.com
Released: Annual. **Audience:** General public. **Principal Exhibits:** Recreational vehicles and sporting goods, including fishing, hunting, and camping equipment and supplies. **Dates and Locations:** 2011 Mar 03-06.

17617 ■ Kansas Sports, Boat, & Travel Show
Industrial Expositions, Inc.
1675 Larimer St., No.700
PO Box 480084
Denver, CO 80248-0084
Ph:(303)892-6800
Free: 800-457-2434
Fax:(303)892-6322
Co. E-mail: info@iei-expos.com
URL: http://www.iei-expos.com/
Released: Annual. **Audience:** General public. **Principal Exhibits:** Recreational vehicles, boats, sports equipment, and travel destination information; fishing and hunting equipment, supplies, and services.

17618 ■ Maryland RV Show
Maryland Recreational Vehicle Dealers Association, Inc.
729 MD Rt. 3 N.
Gambrills, MD 21054
Ph:(410)987-6300
Fax:(410)987-6300
Co. E-mail: info@mdrv.com
URL: http://www.mdrv.com
Released: Semiannual. **Audience:** General public. **Principal Exhibits:** Recreational vehicles and accessories; campground displays.

17619 ■ The National RV Trade Show
Recreation Vehicle Industry Association
1896 Preston White Dr.
Reston, VA 20195-0999
Ph:(703)620-6003
Fax:(703)620-5071
URL: http://www.rvia.org
Released: Annual. **Audience:** RV dealers, warehouse distributors, accessory/part store personnel, and campground representatives. **Principal Exhibits:** Recreational vehicles, component parts, services, and accessories.

17620 ■ Tacoma RV Show
O'Loughlin Trade Shows (Tacoma, Washington)
PO Box 110849
Tacoma, WA 98411-0849
Ph:(253)756-2121
Fax:(253)756-6898
URL: http://www.otsusa.com
Released: Annual. **Audience:** General public. **Principal Exhibits:** Recreational vehicles, motor homes, and related accessories. **Dates and Locations:** 2011 Mar 17-20, Tacoma, WA.

Recycling Business

ASSOCIATIONS AND OTHER ORGANIZATIONS

17621 ■ Canadian Association of Recycling Industries–Association Canadienne des Industries du Recyclage
682 Monarch Ave., Unit 1
Ajax, ON, Canada L1S 4S2
Ph:(905)426-9313
Fax:(905)426-9314
Co. E-mail: donna.turner-cari@on.aibn.com
URL: http://www.cari-acir.org
Contact: Donna Turner
Description: Companies engaged in the recycling of used materials and products. Seeks to advance the recycling industries; promotes reuse of products containing nonrenewable resources. Represents members' interests; conducts promotional and advocacy activities. **Publications:** *The Pulse* (monthly).

17622 ■ Canadian Environmental Network–Reseau canadien de l'environment
39 McArthur Ave., Level 1-1
Ottawa, ON, Canada K1L 8L7
Ph:(613)728-9810
Fax:(613)728-2963
Co. E-mail: info@cen-rce.org
URL: http://www.cen-rce.org
Contact: Ms. Olivier Kolmel, Chm.
Description: Environmental organizations. Seeks to advance the projects and activities of members. Promotes ecologically sustainable development. Serves as a clearinghouse on environmental issues; provides support and assistance to members. **Publications:** *Canadian Environmental Network News* (annual).

17623 ■ EarthSave Canada
SPEC Bldg.
2150 Maple St.
Vancouver, BC, Canada V6J 3T3
Ph:(604)731-5885
Fax:(604)731-5805
URL: http://www.earthsave.ca
Contact: Dave Steele, Pres.
Description: Seeks to increase the awareness of the health, ethical, and environmental impacts of food choices. Promotes transition to a plant-based diet for optimum health, environmental sustainability, and compassion. **Publications:** *Canada EarthSaver* (bimonthly).

17624 ■ Institute of Scrap Recycling Industries
1615 L St. NW, Ste. 600
Washington, DC 20036-5610
Ph:(202)662-8500
Fax:(202)626-0900
Co. E-mail: robinwiener@isri.org
URL: http://www.isri.org
Contact: Robin Wiener, Pres.
Description: Represents processors, brokers, and consumers engaged in the recycling of ferrous, nonferrous, paper, plastics, glass, textiles, rubber and electronics scrap. Conducts specialized education and research programs. **Publications:** *Institute of Scrap Recycling Industries Directory of Members* (annual); *ISRI Focus*; *Scrap Magazine* (bimonthly).

17625 ■ Municipal Waste Association
127 Wyndham St. N, Ste. 100
Guelph, ON, Canada N1H 4E9
Ph:(519)823-1990
Fax:(519)823-0084
Co. E-mail: mwa@municipalwaste.ca
URL: http://www.municipalwaste.ca
Contact: Vivian De Giovanni, Exec. Dir.
Description: Municipal waste management professionals. Promotes more effective and environmentally sustainable removal of solid wastes. Facilitates sharing of municipal waste management, reduction, recycling, and reuse information and facilities. Conducts continuing professional education courses for members; operates job hotline; represents members' interests before government agencies and the public. Sponsors research; compiles statistics. **Publications:** *For R Information* (quarterly).

17626 ■ Recycling Council of Alberta
PO Box 23
Bluffton, AB, Canada T0C 0M0
Ph:(403)843-6563
Fax:(403)843-4156
Co. E-mail: info@recycle.ab.ca
URL: http://www.recycle.ab.ca
Contact: Jason London, Pres.
Description: Promotes and facilitates waste reduction, recycling and resource conservation in the province of Alberta. **Publications:** *Connector* (quarterly); *Enviro Business Guide* .

17627 ■ Saskatchewan Environmental Society
Box 1372
Saskatoon, SK, Canada S7K 3N9
Ph:(306)665-1915
Fax:(306)665-2128
Co. E-mail: info@environmentalsociety.ca
URL: http://www.environmentalsociety.ca
Contact: Allyson Brady, Exec. Dir.
Description: Seeks to support and encourage the creation of a global community in which all needs are met in sustainable ways. **Publications:** *SES Newsletter* (bimonthly).

17628 ■ Society Promoting Environmental Conservation
2060-B Pine St.
Vancouver, BC, Canada V6J 4P8
Ph:(604)736-7732
Fax:(604)736-7115
Co. E-mail: admin@spec.bc.ca
URL: http://www.spec.bc.ca
Contact: Joanna Robinson, Pres.
Description: Promotes environmental research, advocacy, and education. **Publications:** *SPECTRUM* (quarterly).

17629 ■ Steel Recycling Institute
680 Andersen Dr.
Pittsburgh, PA 15220-2700
Ph:(412)922-2772
Free: 800-876-7274
Co. E-mail: gcrawford@steel.org
URL: http://www.recycle-steel.org
Contact: Mr. Gregory L. Crawford, Exec. Dir.
Description: Educates the solid waste management industry, government, business and the consumer about the economic and environmental benefits of recycling steel. .

17630 ■ U.S. Composting Council
One Comac Loop 14B1
Ronkonkoma, NY 11779
Ph:(631)737-4931
Fax:(631)737-4939
Co. E-mail: uscc@compostingcouncil.org
URL: http://www.compostingcouncil.org
Contact: Dr. Stuart Buckner, Exec. Dir.
Description: Supports the recycling of all organic materials in the waste stream, including compostable materials from solid waste, wastewater, and agriculture that are not otherwise recycled. (Composting is a way of naturally recycling organic wastes and converting them into beneficial products that are safe to the public and the environment.) Works to improve public and market acceptance of composting processes and products; defines compost product standards; ensures that composting products are defined as "recycled" in federal, state, and local regulations and legislation; removes procedural and regulatory barriers; provides product classification and quality control for product liability and controlled use issues; and serves as an information clearinghouse. Maintains speakers' bureau; compiles statistics; and conducts research and educational programs. **Publications:** *Compost Facility Operating Guide*; *Composting Council Cap*; *Farmer's Field Guide to Compost Production and Use*; *Field Guide to Compost Use*; *Landscape Architecture Specifications for Compost Utilization* .

17631 ■ Yukon Conservation Society
302 Hawkins St.
Whitehorse, YT, Canada Y1A 1X6
Ph:(867)668-5678
Fax:(867)668-6637
Co. E-mail: ycs@ycs.yk.ca
URL: http://www.yukonconservation.org
Contact: Karen Baltgailis, Exec. Dir.
Description: Seeks to protect Canada's natural environment; particularly that of the Yukon region. Encourages the conservation of Yukon wilderness, wildlife and natural resources. **Publications:** *Walk Softly* (quarterly).

REFERENCE WORKS

17632 ■ "Austin Energy May Build $2.3B Biomass Plant" in *Austin Business JournalInc.* (Vol. 28, July 25, 2008, No. 19, pp. A1)
Pub: American City Business Journals
Ed: Kate Harrington. **Description:** An approval from the Austin City Council is being sought by Austin

Energy for a 20-year supply contract with Nacogdoches Power LLC to build a $2.3 billion biomass plant in East Texas. The 100-megawatt biomass plant, which is to run on waste wood, will have Austin Energy as its sole buyer.

17633 ■ "Battling Back from Betrayal" in *Harvard Business Review* (Vol. 88, December 2010, No. 12, pp. 130)
Pub: Harvard Business School Publishing
Ed: Daniel McGinn. **Description:** Stephen Greer's scrap metal firm, Hartwell Pacific, lost several million dollars due to a lack of efficient and appropriate inventory audits, accounting procedures, and new-hire reference checks for his foreign operations. Greer believes that balancing growth with control is a key component of success.

17634 ■ "Boyd's Pawn Shop Looks More Like a Mini-Mall With Plenty For Sale" in *The Hawk Eye* (January 2, 2011)
Pub: McClatchy-Tribune Information Services
Ed: Rex L. Troute. **Description:** Profile of Brian Boyd, aka 'the king of pawn' and his shop located in West Burlington, Iowa. Boyd also operates a redemption center at the rear of his shop and collects nearly 42 million cans and bottles annually.

17635 ■ *The Complete Idiot's Guide to Starting and Running a Thrift Store*
Pub: Alpha Publishing House
Ed: Ravel Buckley, Carol Costa. **Released:** January 5, 2010. **Price:** $18.95. **Description:** Thrift stores saw a 35 percent increase in sales during the falling economy in 2008. Despite the low startup costs, launching and running a thrift store is complicated. Two experts cover the entire process, including setting up a store on a nonprofit basis, choosing a location, funding, donations for saleable items, recruiting and managing staff, sorting items, pricing, and recycling donations.

17636 ■ "Developer Tries to Bring Homes to Buda" in *Austin Business JournalInc.* (Vol. 28, December 26, 2008, No. 41, pp. 1)
Pub: American City Business Journals
Ed: Kate Harrington. **Description:** Real estate developer Jeremiah Venture LP is planning a residential, single-family development on about 600 acres near Buda, Texas. The company also plans to construct a membrane waste treatment plant, and has applied to do land application. However, several groups have come forward to ask for more information on the application due to concerns about soil density.

17637 ■ "Electronics Recycler Poised to Grow" in *Austin Business Journal* (Vol. 31, July 22, 2011, No. 20, pp. A1)
Pub: American City Business Journals Inc.
Ed: Cody Lyon. **Description:** Electronic Recycling and Trading Inc. has leased 138,000 square feet of space in North Austin, Texas. The company requires more space for bigger equipment.

17638 ■ *The Green Guide for Business: The Ultimate Environment for Businesses of All Sizes*
Pub: Profile Books Limited
Ed: Roger East, Hannah Bullock, Chris Goodall. **Released:** May 10, 2010. **Description:** Everyone wants to go green these days, but for small businesses that's easier said than done. How do you measure a company's carbon footprint? Are dryers or hand towels more eco-friendly? Recycled paper or FSC-certified? All these questions and more are explored.

17639 ■ "Greening the Auto Industry" in *Business Journal-Serving Phoenix & the Valley of the Sun* (Vol. 30, July 23, 2010, No. 46, pp. 1)
Pub: Phoenix Business Journal
Ed: Patrick O'Grady. **Description:** Thermo Fluids Inc. has been recycling used oil products since 1993 and could become Arizona's first home for oil filter recycling after retrofitting its Phoenix facility to include a compaction machine. The new service could help establish Thermo Fluids as a recycling hub for nearby states.

17640 ■ *Greening Your Small Business: How to Improve Your Bottom Line, Grow Your Brand, Satisfy Your Customers and Save the Planet*
Pub: Prentice Hall Press
Ed: Jennifer Kaplan. **Released:** November 3, 2009. **Price:** $19.95. **Description:** A definitive resource for anyone who wants their small business to be cutting-edge, competitive, profitable, and eco-conscious. Stories from small business owners address every aspect of going green, from basics such as recycling waste, energy efficiency, and reducing information technology footprint, to more in-depth concerns such as green marketing and communications, green business travel, and green employee benefits.

17641 ■ *Institute of Scrap Recycling Industries—Membership Directory*
Pub: Institute of Scrap Recycling Industries Inc.
Contact: Robin Wiener, President
E-mail: robinwiener@isri.org
Released: Annual, August. **Covers:** Member processors, brokers, and consumers of scrap ferrous and nonferrous metals, paper, glass, plastics, rubber, and textiles; suppliers to the industry. **Entries Include:** Company name, address, phone, contact name, product or service provided. **Arrangement:** Information is arranged geographically, by firm name and by individual name in separate sections.

17642 ■ "Kiosk Outfit ecoATM Now Recycling Video Games" in *San Diego Union-Tribune* (October 7, 2010)
Pub: San Diego Union-Tribune
Ed: Mike Freeman. **Description:** ecoATM makes automated kiosks to buy back cell phones will now include video games as part of their recycling business.

17643 ■ "Recycling 202: How to Take Your Recycling Practices to the Next Level" in *Black Enterprise* (Vol. 41, September 2010, No. 2, pp. 38)
Pub: Earl G. Graves Publishing Co. Inc.
Ed: Tamara E. Holmes. **Description:** Consumer Electronics Association and other organizations, manufacturers and retailers list ways to recycle all household items.

17644 ■ *Recycling and Waste Management Guide to the Internet*
Pub: Government Institutes
Contact: Roger M. Guttentag, Author
Price: $72, individuals. **Covers:** More than 350 web sites, discussion lists, and news groups on the internet covering waste management and recycling issues. **Entries Include:** Site name, address, subject, site summary, contact name and e-mail. **Arrangement:** Alphabetical. **Indexes:** Subject.

17645 ■ "Shifting Gears" in *Business Journal-Serving Phoenix & the Valley of the Sun* (Vol. 31, November 12, 2010, No. 10, pp. 1)
Pub: Phoenix Business Journal
Ed: Patrick O'Grady. **Description:** Automotive parts recyclers in Arizona are benefiting from the challenging national economic conditions as well as from the green movement. Recyclers revealed that customers prefer recycled parts more because they are cheaper and are more environmentally friendly. Other information about the automotive parts recycling industry is presented.

17646 ■ "Survey: Most Approve of Donating Used Pacemakers to Medically Underserved" in *Crain's Detroit Business* (Vol. 25, June 1, 2009)
Pub: Crain Communications Inc. - Detroit
Description: According to a survey conducted by University of Michigan Cardiovascular Center, 87 percent of those with pacemakers and 71 percent of the general population would donate the device to patients in underserved nations.

17647 ■ "Unilever to Sustainably Source All Paper and Board Packaging" in *Ice Cream Reporter* (Vol. 23, July 20, 2010, No. 8, pp. 1)
Pub: Ice Cream Reporter
Description: Unilever, a leader in the frozen dessert market, has developed a new sustainable paper and board packaging sourcing policy that will reduce environmental impact by working with suppliers to source 75 percent of paper and board packaging from sustainably managed forests or from recycled material. Unilever is parent company to Breyers, Haagen-Dazs, Klondike, Popsicle and other ice cream brands.

17648 ■ "A Whiff of TV Reality" in *Houston Business Journal* (Vol. 40, January 22, 2010, No. 37, pp. A1)
Pub: American City Business Journals
Ed: Christine Hall. **Description:** Houston, Texas-based Waste Management Inc.'s president and chief operation officer, Larry O'Donnell shares some of his experience as CBS Television Network reality show 'Undercover Boss' participant. O'Donnell believes the show was a great way to show the customers how tough their jobs are and reveals that the most difficult job was being a sorter at the recycling center.

17649 ■ "Xerox Diverts Waste from Landfills" in *Canadian Electronics* (Vol. 23, February 2008, No. 1, pp. 1)
Pub: CLB Media Inc.
Description: Xerox Corporation revealed that it was able to divert more than two billion pounds of electronic waste from landfills through waste-free initiatives. The company's program, which was launched in 1991, covers waste avoidance in imaging supplies and parts reuse. Environmental priorities are also integrated into manufacturing operations.

STATISTICAL SOURCES

17650 ■ *Standard & Poor's Industry Surveys*
Pub: Standard & Poor's Corp.
Released: Annual. **Price:** $3633.00. **Description:** Two-volume book that examines the prospects for specific industries, including trucking. Also provides analyses of trends and problems, statistical tables and charts, and comparative company analyses.

TRADE PERIODICALS

17651 ■ *Composting News*
Pub: McEntee Media Corp.
Ed: Ken McEntee, Editor, ken@recycle.cc. **Released:** Monthly. **Price:** $83, individuals; $93, Canada and Mexico; $105, other countries. **Description:** Covers news and trends in the composting industry. Also reports on compost product prices. Recurring features include letters to the editor, interviews, news of research, a calendar of events, reports of meetings, and notices of publications available.

17652 ■ *Environmental Quality Management*
Pub: John Wiley & Sons Inc.
Contact: Isabelle Cohen-DeAngelis, Exec. Ed.
E-mail: icohen@wiley.com
Ed: Ginger Griffin, Editor, gjgriffin@earthlink.net. **Released:** Quarterly. **Price:** $775 print only; $1,005 U.S., Canada, and Mexico institutional, print only; $1,029 institutions, other countries print only. **Description:** Journal featuring articles on and case studies of successful environmental quality improvement efforts. Covers current thinking in benchmarking, total quality management, information technology, environmental auditing, and waste reduction and recycling.

17653 ■ *Plastic Recycling Update*
Pub: Resource Recycling
Contact: Judy Roumpf
Ed: Jerry Powell, Editor, editor@resource-recycling.com. **Released:** Monthly. **Price:** $58, individuals. **Description:** Markets newsletter that covers all aspects of plastic waste recovery.

17654 ■ *Re-News*
Pub: Recycling Council of Ontario
Ed: John Hanson, Editor, john@rco.on.ca. **Released:** Monthly. **Price:** Included in membership. **Description:** Promotes recycling and waste reduction through an examination of social, economic, and environmental trends in current and developing markets, technologies, and government initiatives. Covers local, regional, federal, and international programs. Recurring features include a calendar of events.

17655 ■ *Recycling Today*
Pub: G.I.E. Media, MC
Contact: DeAnne Toto, Managing Editor
E-mail: dtoto@gie.net
Released: Monthly. **Description:** Magazine covering recycling of secondary raw materials and solid-waste management.

17656 ■ *Remgro Recycling Equipment Marketing News*
Pub: Bruce Mooney Associates Inc.
Ed: Bruce C. Mooney, Editor. **Released:** Annual. **Price:** Free. **Description:** Promotes the sale of equipment and systems for processing household recyclables and solicits inquiries for the company's processing products. Lists prices.

17657 ■ *Resource Recycling*
Pub: Resource Recycling
Contact: Rick Downing, Advertising Dir
E-mail: rick@resource-recycling.com
Released: Monthly. **Price:** $52. **Description:** Journal reporting on all aspects of recycling and composting of solid waste, from collection and materials processing to markets and governmental policies.

17658 ■ *Scrap*
Pub: Institute of Scrap Recycling Industries Inc.
Contact: Ellen Ross, Dir of Production
E-mail: ellenross@scrap.org
Released: Bimonthly. **Price:** $44 companies; $40 libraries government & non-profit organizations; $52 Canada and Mexico first class; $139 other countries; $73 two years companies; $66 libraries govt. & non profit organizations, 2 years; $86 Canada and Mexico 2 years; $230 other countries airmail 2 years. **Description:** Magazine for the scrap processing and recycling industry.

17659 ■ *Waste Recovery Report*
Pub: ICON Inc.
Ed: Released: Monthly. **Price:** $60, U.S. and Canada; $75, elsewhere. **Description:** Contains news of the recycling, waste-to-energy, and other resource recovery fields. Supplies news on legislative and regulatory changes, new facilities and technologies, and environmental concerns. Recurring features include news of research, reports of meetings, notices of publications available, and a calendar of events.

TRADE SHOWS AND CONVENTIONS

17660 ■ GLOBE - International Environmental Industry Trade Fair and Conference
GLOBE Foundation of Canada
World Trade Centre
578 999 Canada Pl.
Vancouver, BC, Canada V6C 3E1
Ph:(604)775-7300
Free: 800-274-6097
Fax:(604)666-8123
Co. E-mail: info@globe.ca
URL: http://www.globe.ca
Released: Biennial. **Audience:** Trade professionals. **Principal Exhibits:** Environmental equipment, supplies, and services.

FRANCHISES AND BUSINESS OPPORTUNITIES

17661 ■ Expense Reduction Consulting
Expense Reduction Consulting, Inc.
27902 Meadow Dr., No. 130
Evergreen, CO 80439
Free: 877-255-2511
Fax:(954)255-7786
Co. E-mail: vic@ercinc.com
URL: http://www.ercfranchise.com
No. of Franchise Units: 25. **Founded:** 1993. **Franchised:** 2005. **Description:** ERC Franchises employ a finely tuned methodology that has helped companies minimize indirect costs. This methodology along with proprietary web based tools and Knowledge Base, assist franchisees in increasing their client's bottom lines by decreasing their indirect costs. **Equity Capital Needed:** $73,360-$82,210. **Franchise Fee:** $45,000. **Financial Assistance:** Assistance with franchise fee. **Training:** 5 days at ERC University coupled with a 1 year long sales training program and ongoing support is provided as long as you are an ERC franchisee.

17662 ■ Ink Solution & Postal
9524 Hebron Commerce Dr.
Charlotte, NC 28273
Free: (866)482-4657
Fax:(704)523-8720
No. of Franchise Units: 19. **Founded:** 2001. **Franchised:** 2007. **Description:** Inkjet & toner cartridge recycling/postal services. **Equity Capital Needed:** $118,000. **Franchise Fee:** $29,000. **Royalty Fee:** 4%. **Financial Assistance:** No. **Training:** Provides 1 week training at headquarters, 1 week at franchisee's location, 1 week at corporate store and ongoing support.

17663 ■ Shred-It
Shred-it
2794 S Sheridan Way
Oakville, ON, Canada L6J 7T4
Ph:(905)829-2794
No. of Franchise Units: 53. **No. of Company-Owned Units:** 65. **Founded:** 1988. **Franchised:** 1992. **Description:** Mobile paper shredding and recycling operation, serving medical, financial, government and large and small business. Offers on-site shredding and recycling of shredded material. **Equity Capital Needed:** $300,000-$500,000 net worth required. **Franchise Fee:** $75,000. **Financial Assistance:** No. **Training:** 1 week in the field at time of opening. Provides 8 manuals on all aspects of the business.

LIBRARIES

17664 ■ California Department of Conservation–Division of Recycling–Resource Center (801 K)
801 K St.
MS-18-58
Sacramento, CA 95814-3530
Ph:(916)323-3836
Free: 800-REC-YCLE
Fax:(916)327-2144
Co. E-mail: doriis@calrecycle.ca.gov
URL: http://www.consrv.ca.gov
Contact: Patti Holmes, Lib.Coord.
Scope: Recycling, waste reduction, resource conservation. **Services:** Library open to the public with restrictions. **Holdings:** 300 books; 400 reports; 277 videocassettes. **Subscriptions:** 93 journals and other serials.

17665 ■ California Integrated Waste Management Board Library
1001 I St.
PO Box 4025
Sacramento, CA 95812-4025
Ph:(916)341-6198
Fax:(916)319-7239
Co. E-mail: mvanbaaren@ciwmb.ca.gov
URL: http://www.ciwmb.ca.gov/
Contact: Michael VanBaaren, Staff Svcs.Anl.
Scope: Waste management, recycling, source reduction, landfill technology. **Services:** Interlibrary loan; copying; Library open to the public for reference use only. **Holdings:** 8000 books; reports; manuscripts; patents; archives; microfiche. **Subscriptions:** 117 journals and other serials; 2 newspapers.

17666 ■ Institute for Local Self-Reliance
2001 S. St., NW, Ste. 570
Washington, DC 20009
Ph:(202)898-1610
Fax:(202)332-0463
Co. E-mail: info@ilsr.org
URL: http://www.ilsr.org
Contact: Neil Seldman, Pres.
Scope: Recycling and waste utilization, energy, alternative energy sources, cities and neighborhoods, ecology and environment, local economic development, materials policy, economic development, sustainable communities.

17667 ■ Long Island Lighting Company Resource Center
131 Hoffman Ln.
Central Islip, NY 11722
Ph:(516)436-4003
Fax:(516)436-4036
Contact: Carolyn Jaskot, Curric.Rsrc.Spec.
Scope: Energy, electricity, public utilities, business management. **Services:** Library not open to the public. **Holdings:** 1570 books; 100 periodical titles; videocassettes; audiocassettes. **Subscriptions:** 30 journals and other serials; 2 newspapers.

17668 ■ Pennsylvania Environmental Council Library
1315 Walnut St., Ste. 532
Philadelphia, PA 19107
Ph:(215)545-4570
Fax:(215)545-4594
URL: http://www.pecpa.org
Contact: Don Welsh, Pres./CEO
Scope: Solid waste and energy issues, water issues, air pollution, transportation, growth management, land use, industrial sites reuse, mediation, population. **Services:** Copying; faxing; Library open to the public by appointment. **Holdings:** 400 books; 100 reports; 40 videotapes; 10 slide shows. **Subscriptions:** 200 journals and other serials.

RESEARCH CENTERS

17669 ■ Brown University–Center for Environmental Studies
135 Angell St., Box 1943
Providence, RI 02912
Ph:(401)863-3449
Fax:(401)863-3503
Co. E-mail: j_timmons_roberts@brown.edu
URL: http://envstudies.brown.edu
Contact: Prof. J. Timmons Roberts PhD, Dir.
E-mail: j_timmons_roberts@brown.edu
Scope: Environmental studies, with special focus on Narragansett Bay, solid waste management in Rhode Island, social research, forest ecology, climate change, hazardous waste reduction, energy conservation, environmental health, environmental justice, and recycling at the University. **Educational Activities:** The Brown is Green Campus Environmental Stewardship Initiative; Farm Fresh Rhode Island (weekly), develops local food system that values the environment, health and quality of life of Rhode Island farmers and eaters, links local farmers and buyers; Lectures and seminars; Project 20/20 (weekly), promotes the use of high-efficiency lighting in low-income households in Providence; Science and policy-related courses; Sustainability Consulting Partnership (SCP) (weekly), creates professional development opportunities for Brown University students to apply their interdisciplinary backgrounds to business sustainability topics; Tours, by appointment.

17670 ■ Community Environmental Council
26 W Anapamu St., 2nd Fl.
Santa Barbara, CA 93101
Ph:(805)963-0583
Fax:(805)962-9080
Co. E-mail: ddavis@cecmail.org
URL: http://www.cecsb.org/index.php
Contact: David D. Davis, CEO/Exec.Dir.
E-mail: ddavis@cecmail.org
Scope: Environmental problem-solving through design and implementation of innovative environmental management systems, focusing on increasing the use of secondary, recycled materials in the manufacturing process, finding ways to reduce the amount of waste generated, and expanding markets for recycled materials. Specific areas of research include recycling, hazardous waste, and composting systems. **Services:** Community gardens; Integrated pest management; Testimony, in legal and political matters at the national, state, and local levels; Videos and other multi-media presentations; Watershed restoration. **Publications:** Newsletter, proceedings and white papers. **Educational Activities:** Land use education; Public Policy Seminars.

17671 ■ Cornell University–Cornell Waste Management Institute
Bradfield Hall
Department of Crop & Soil Sciences
Ithaca, NY 14853
Ph:(607)255-1187
Fax:(607)255-2644
Co. E-mail: cwmi@cornell.edu
URL: http://cwmi.css.cornell.edu
Contact: Prof. Murray B. McBride, Dir.
E-mail: cwmi@cornell.edu
Scope: Solid waste management, including composting, collaborative decision making, risk communication, assessing benefits and impacts of land application of sewage sludges, waste prevention, managing agricultural solid wastes. **Services:** Technical assistance, to communities, including a series of audio-visual and print resources addressing waste disposal, land use, and water contamination problems. **Publications:** Fact sheets; Training manuals; Videos.

17672 ■ Earthworm, Inc.
35 Medford St.
Somerville, MA 02143
Ph:(617)628-1844
Fax:(617)628-2773
Co. E-mail: info@earthwormrecycling.org
URL: http://www.earthwormrecycling.org
E-mail: info@earthwormrecycling.org
Scope: Recycling, resource recovery, solid waste management, environmental quality, hazardous waste, and earthworms. **Publications:** Earthworm Recycling Guide.

17673 ■ Ecology Action Centre–Centre d'Action Écologique
2705 Fern Ln.
Halifax, NS, Canada B3K 4L3
Ph:(902)429-2202
Fax:(902)405-3716
Co. E-mail: info@ecologyaction.ca
URL: http://www.ecologyaction.ca
Contact: Mark Butler
E-mail: info@ecologyaction.ca
Scope: Environmental issues, including acid rain, deforestation, hazardous wastes, recycling, nuclear power, ecosystem stability, species extinction, global warming, pesticides, and waste management. **Services:** Briefs preparation and research, on ocean habitat and biodiversity. **Publications:** Between the Issues Newsletter (bimonthly). **Educational Activities:** Diverse volunteer opportunities; Educational workshops, on environmental and science topics.

Rental Service

START-UP INFORMATION

17674 ■ *Legal Guide for Starting and Running a Small Business*
Pub: NOLO
Ed: Fred Steingold. **Released:** April 2008. **Price:** $34.99. **Description:** Information for starting a new business focusing on choosing a business structure, taxes, employees and independent contractors, trademark and service marks, licensing and permits, leasing and improvement of commercial space, buying and selling a business, and more.

ASSOCIATIONS AND OTHER ORGANIZATIONS

17675 ■ American Rental Association
1900 19th St.
Moline, IL 61265-4179
Ph:(309)764-2475
Free: 800-334-2177
Fax:(309)764-1533
URL: http://www.ararental.org
Contact: Chris Wehrman, CEO
Description: Firms engaged in the rental of event and party equipment, tools, machinery, and other products; includes independent, franchised, and chain store operators. Associates are suppliers of equipment, merchandise, and other items. Seeks to foster better business methods; promote study of economic trends in the rental industry. **Publications:** *Cost of Doing Business Report*; *Rental Management* (monthly).

17676 ■ Association of Progressive Rental Organizations
1504 Robin Hood Trail
Austin, TX 78703
Ph:(512)794-0095
Free: 800-204-2776
Fax:(512)794-0097
Co. E-mail: robert.briley@aaronrents.com
URL: http://www.rtohq.org
Contact: Robert Briley, Pres.
Description: Represents dealer and industry suppliers. Serves rental dealers in the home appliance, furniture, and consumer electronics industry who market their products with a rental-purchase plan. Purposes are to: foster trade and commerce; collect and disseminate information; represent members before legislative committees, government bureaus, and other bodies in matters affecting the industry. Encourages competition among members and increased use of industry services; establishes advertising standards to prevent misleading and false advertising; considers and deals with common problems of management, including those involving production, distribution, employment, and financial functions within the rental industry. Sponsors workshops and seminars in accounting, sales, customer satisfaction and relations, personnel, inventory management, management development, and legal issues; makes available training materials. Conducts government relations program; compiles statistics. **Publications:** *Progressive Rentals Magazine* (bimonthly); *Rental-To-Own Almanac* (annual); *Rental Viewpoint Online* (biweekly); *RTO Today* (weekly).

17677 ■ Equipment Leasing and Finance Association
1825 K St. NW, Ste. 900
Washington, DC 20006
Ph:(202)238-3400
Fax:(202)238-3401
Co. E-mail: wsutton@elfaonline.org
URL: http://www.elfaonline.org
Contact: William G. Sutton, Pres./CEO
Description: Individuals, companies, divisions, or subsidiaries whose principal activity is the leasing of equipment to other commercial users. Includes companies that function or operate in the capacity of brokers and that do not write leases on their own forms, as well as bank-related lessors. Promotes understanding of problems involved in equipment leasing; works to advance the interests of members so they may better serve the public. Compiles statistics. .

17678 ■ International Furniture Rental Association
5229 College Hill Rd.
Woodstock, VT 05091
Co. E-mail: info@ifra.org
URL: http://www.ifra.org
Description: Companies whose major business is the leasing and rental of home furnishings and accessories; suppliers of products and services to these companies are associate members. Dedicated in upholding ethical standards of the furniture rental industry and providing quality products and service. Conducts industry exposition and statistical surveys. Promotes industry through nationwide consumer education program. Works to safeguard against adverse legislation and regulation. **Publications:** *Furniture Rental Association of America—Newsletter* (bimonthly).

REFERENCE WORKS

17679 ■ "$550 Cash Rent on 330 Acres in Iowa" in *Farm Industry News* (November 30, 2011)
Pub: Penton Business Media Inc.
Ed: Karen McMahon. **Description:** A farmer in Iowa accepted a bid for $550/acre for his 330-acre farm for one year. The next closest bid was $350/acre. This rent will amount to more than the farmer paid for all of his land in the 1960s and 1970s. High rents are not alarming because of the high profitability farmers are currently receiving from crops.

17680 ■ "The 2011 Rental Readers' Choice Award Winners" in *Rental Product News* (Vol. 33, October 2011)
Pub: Cygnus Business Media
Ed: Jenny Lescohier. **Description:** Rental Product News conducted a survey asking readers what they considered to be the best product in their rental industry. A listing of winners is provided.

17681 ■ "AF Expands in New Green Building in Gothenburg" in *Ecology,Environment & Conservation Business* (September 24, 2011, pp. 2)
Pub: HighBeam Research
Description: AF signed a ten-year tenancy contract with Skanska for the premises of its new green building in Gothenburg, Sweden. AF offers qualified services and solutions for industrial processes, infrastructure projects and the development of products and IT systems.

17682 ■ "Antwerpen Takes on Chrysler Financial Over Foreclosure Sales" in *Baltimore Business Journal* (Vol. 28, July 30, 2010, No. 12, pp. 1)
Pub: Baltimore Business Journal
Ed: Gary Haber. **Description:** Antwerpen Motorcars Ltd. aims to fight the scheduled foreclosure sale of real estate it leases in Baltimore County, including the showroom for its Hyundai dealership on Baltimore National Pike in Catonsville, Maryland. The company is planning to file papers in court to stop the scheduled August 11, 2010 auction sought by Chrysler Financial Services Americas LLC.

17683 ■ "Apartment Tower in River North Fetches More Than $90 Million" in *Crain's Chicago Business* (Vol. 34, October 24, 2011, No. 42, pp. 17)
Pub: Crain Communications Inc.
Ed: Alby Gallun. **Description:** Apartment tower in River North was sold for over $90 million to a Texas pension fund adviser. Details are included.

17684 ■ "Asterand Eyes Jump to Ann Arbor; TechTown Tenant" in *Crain's Detroit Business* (Vol. 25, June 22, 2009)
Pub: Crain Communications Inc. - Detroit
Ed: Tom Henderson. **Description:** Asterand PLC is considering a move to Ann Arbor from its current location as anchor tenant at TechTown, an incubator and technology park associated with Wayne State University. The university believes the Ann Arbor location's rent is too expensive for the tissue bank company.

17685 ■ "BancVue to Expand" in *Austin Business JournalInc.* (Vol. 29, November 27, 2009, No. 38, pp. 1)
Pub: American City Business Journals
Ed: Kate Harrington. **Description:** Significant growth of BancVue in the past six years has prompted the company to look for a site that could increase its office space from 25,000 square feet to 65,000 square feet. BancVue offers bank and credit union software solutions and is planning to lease or buy a property in Austin, Texas.

17686 ■ "Banks Could Greet Tenants in One Year" in *Business Courier* (Vol. 26, October 16, 2009, No. 25, pp. 1)
Pub: American City Business Journals, Inc.
Ed: Lucy May. **Description:** The Banks project's initial phase is expected to start in 60 days, which may mean that the project's first tenant could move in by the end of 2010 or beginning of 2011. Carter,

an Atlanta-based firm has partnered with Dawson Company in this riverfront development. The first phase will include 80,000 square feet of retail and 300 apartments.

17687 ■ "Before Signing a Lease" in *Business Owner* (Vol. 35, September-October 2011, No. 5, pp. 14)
Pub: DL Perkins Company
Description: The following terms are essential to investigate before renewing or negotiating a lease for a small business: Term, Neighbors, Actual Usable Space, Gross or Net, Tenant Improvements, Renewal Option, Purchase Option, Cancelation Option, Sublease or Assignment, Security Deposit, Code Restrictions and Zoning, Parking, Relief and Lease Agreement.

17688 ■ "Beware of Bad Blade Rentals" in *Rental Product News* (Vol. 33, June 2011)
Pub: Cygnus Business Media
Ed: Jenny Lescohier. **Description:** Blade rentals, despite their return on investment, can result in lost revenue because if handled incorrectly customers can injure themselves.

17689 ■ "Beware of E15" in *Rental Product News* (Vol. 33, October 2011)
Pub: Cygnus Business Media
Ed: Curt Bennink. **Description:** Environmental Protection Agency (EPA) set a new regulation that grants partial waivers to allow gasoline containing up to 15 percent ethanol (E15) to be introduced into commerce for use in model year 2001 and newer light-duty motor vehicles, subject to certain conditions.

17690 ■ "Biggest UM Landlords" in *Crain's Detroit Business* (Vol. 25, June 15, 2009, No. 24, pp. 1)
Pub: Crain Communications Inc. - Detroit
Description: University of Michigan will purchase the two million-square-foot Pfizer campus in June 2009. The university is the largest occupier of commercial real estate off campus in and around Ann Arbor, Michigan.

17691 ■ "BRIEF: Montana Street Pawn Shop Closing Doors" in *Montana Standard* (November 6, 2010)
Pub: Montana Standard
Ed: John Grant Emeigh. **Description:** First National Pawn located in Butte, Montana will close its doors after losing its lease. Co-owner Pat Evenson reported the lease situation coupled with the economy prompted the decision to close.

17692 ■ "Buyers' Market" in *Baltimore Business Journal* (Vol. 27, November 20, 2009, No. 28, pp. 1)
Pub: American City Business Journals
Ed: Daniel J. Sernovitz. **Description:** Some business owners in Maryland are removing their leases and purchasing buildings due to the lower costs of real estate. This trend has enabled small business owners to avoid rent hikes, while setting equity into their companies. The pros and cons of owning buildings and how business owners assess their return on investment are examined.

17693 ■ "Cash Rents Reach Sky-High Levels" in *Farm Industry News* (November 23, 2011)
Pub: Penton Business Media Inc.
Ed: Karen McMahon. **Description:** Strong commodity prices are driving land values creating a hot rental market for farm land. Highest rents occur when farmers compete head-to-head for land.

17694 ■ "Cold-Storage Cargo Facility a Late Bloomer" in *Houston Business Journal* (Vol. 40, August 28, 2009, No. 16, pp. 1A)
Pub: American City Business Journals
Ed: Jennifer Dawson. **Description:** Trammell Crow Company leased half of the 61,000 square foot IAH International Air Cargo Centre II to Tradewinds Cargo Handling. The facility, located at George Bush Intercontinental Airport, is intended to be a destination of fresh flowers and food from Latin America.

17695 ■ *The Commonsense Way to Build Wealth: One Entrepreneur Shares His Secrets*
Pub: Griffin Publishing Group
Ed: Jack Chou. **Released:** September 2004. **Price:** $19.95. **Description:** Entrepreneurial tips to accumulate wealth, select the proper business or franchise, choose and manage rental property, and how to negotiate a good lease.

17696 ■ "Cupcake Maker Grabs Outpost" in *Crain's New York Business* (Vol. 27, August 15, 2011, No. 33, pp. 16)
Pub: Crain Communications Inc.
Ed: Jermaine Taylor. **Description:** Family-owned miniature cupcake maker, Baked by Melissa, singed a ten-year lease, expanding their stores to five. The business was started three years ago by advertising executive Melissa Bushell.

17697 ■ "Customer Preferences Control Skid Steer Choices" in *Rental Product News* (Vol. 33, June 2011)
Pub: Cygnus Business Media
Ed: Jenny Lescohier. **Description:** Understanding the types of controls available on skid steer equipment is essential. The article provides a comprehensive guide to using and maintaining skid steers for rental agencies.

17698 ■ "Delta Looks at Downtown Departure" in *Business Courier* (Vol. 27, October 1, 2010, No. 22, pp. 1)
Pub: Business Courier
Ed: Dan Monk. **Description:** Delta Air Lines Inc. has been looking for a smaller office for its reservations center in downtown Cincinnati, Ohio. Delta has informed the city of its plan to seek proposals on office space alternatives in advance of the 2011 lease expiration. Insights on the current employment status at the reservations center are also given.

17699 ■ "Developers Poised to Pull Trigers" in *Boston Business Journal* (Vol. 30, November 12, 2010, No. 42, pp. 1)
Pub: Boston Business Journal
Ed: Craig M. Douglas. **Description:** Large residential projects are expected to break ground in Boston, Massachusetts in 2011, as real estate developers expect growth for the industry. Real estate experts expect more than 2,000 rental units to be available by 2011. Information on key real estate projects in Boston is presented.

17700 ■ *Dictionary of Real Estate Terms*
Pub: Barron's Educational Series, Incorporated
Ed: Jack P. Friedman, Jack C. Harris, J. Bruce Lindeman. **Released:** October 2008. **Price:** $13.99. **Description:** More than 2,500 real estate terms relating to mortgages and financing, brokerage law, architecture, rentals and leases, property insurance, and more.

17701 ■ "The Display Group Is Super-Sized" in *Michigan Vue* (Vol. 13, July-August 2008, No. 4, pp. 34)
Pub: Entrepreneur Media Inc.
Description: Profile of the Display Group, located in downtown Detroit, this company provides custom designed mobile marketing displays as well as special event production services for trade show displays. The rental house and design service is also beginning to see more business due to the film initiative, which provides incentives for films that are shooting in Michigan.

17702 ■ "Do You Need to Reinvent Your Managers?" in *Rental Product News* (Vol. 33, June 2011)
Pub: Cygnus Business Media
Ed: Dick Detmer. **Description:** Rental business owners need to assess their management and be sure they perform as true leaders of the organization.

17703 ■ "Docs Might Hold Cure for Real Estate, Banks" in *Baltimore Business Journal* (Vol. 28, November 5, 2010, No. 26, pp. 1)
Pub: Baltimore Business Journal
Ed: Gary Haber. **Description:** Health care providers, including physicians are purchasing their office space instead of renting it as banks lower interest rates to 6 percent on mortgages for medical offices. The rise in demand offers relief to the commercial real estate market. It has also resulted in a boom in building new medical offices.

17704 ■ "Doctors Buy In to Medical Timeshares" in *Houston Business Journal* (Vol. 40, December 11, 2009, No. 31, pp. 1)
Pub: American City Business Journals
Ed: Mary Ann Azevedo. **Description:** Memorial Hermann Hospital System has leased to doctors three examination rooms and medical office space in the Memorial Hermann Medical Plaza in line with its new timeshare concept. The concept was designed to bring primary care physicians to its Texas Medical Center campus.

17705 ■ "easyhome Ltd. Discovers Employee Fraud at an Easyfinancial Kiosk Company" in *Internet Wire* (October 14, 2010)
Pub: Comtex
Description: Canada's leading merchandise leasing company and provider of financial services, easyhome Ltd., reported employee fraud totaling $3.4 million that was perpetrated against the firm's easyfinancial services business.

17706 ■ "Empty Office Blues" in *Business Journal Portland* (Vol. 26, December 4, 2009, No. 39, pp. 1)
Pub: American City Business Journals Inc.
Ed: Wendy Culverwell. **Description:** Portland's office vacancy rates could reach almost 15 percent by the end of 2010 due to job reductions and mergers.

17707 ■ "Ethnic Businesses Ending Vacancies" in *Business First-Columbus* (Vol. 26, August 20, 2010, No. 51, pp. 1)
Pub: Business First
Ed: Carrie Ghose. **Description:** The Morse Road commercial corridor in Columbus, Ohio has several immigrant-owned businesses that were recognized as instrumental in preventing widespread vacancies when the Northland Mall closed in 2002. The ethnic stores have created a diverse destination that attracted traffic and more businesses.

17708 ■ "Extra Rehab Time Boosts M-B's Off-Lease Profits" in *Automotive News* (Vol. 86, October 31, 2011, No. 6488, pp. 22)
Pub: Crain Communications Inc.
Ed: Arlena Sawyers. **Description:** Mercedes-Benz Financial Services USA is holding on to off-lease vehicles in order to recondition them and the move is boosting profits for the company.

17709 ■ "Firms Sue Doracon to Recoup More Than $1M in Unpaid Bills" in *Baltimore Business Journal* (Vol. 28, July 9, 2010, No. 9, pp. 1)
Pub: Baltimore Business Journal
Ed: Scott Dance. **Description:** Concrete supplier Paul J. Rach Inc., Selective Insurance Company, and equipment leasing firm Colonial Pacific Leasing Corporation intend to sue Baltimore, Maryland-based Doracon Contracting Inc. for $1 million in unpaid bills. Doracon owed Colonial Pacific $794,000 and the equipment is still in Doracon's possession. Selective Insurance and Paul J. Rach respectively seek $132,000 and $88,000.

17710 ■ "Formaspace Finds a Bigger Home" in *Austin Business JournalInc.* (Vol. 29, December 4, 2009, No. 39, pp. 1)
Pub: American City Business Journals
Ed: Kate Harrington. **Description:** Formaspace Technical Furniture has signed a lease for 56,700 square feet in Harris Ridge Business Center at Northeast Austin, Texas, which represents one of the area's largest leases for 2009. The new lease enables Formaspace to hire new employees, invest in new equipment, and take advantage of a taxing designation created for manufacturers.

17711 ■ "Furniture Chain Moving to Harford" in *Baltimore Business Journal* (Vol. 27, January 22, 2010, No. 38, pp. 1)
Pub: American City Business Journals
Ed: David J. Sernovitz. **Description:** Manchester, Connecticut-based Bob's Discount Furniture signed a lease for 672,000 square feet of space in Harford

County, Maryland. The site will become the discount furniture retailer's distribution center in mid-Atlantic US. As many as 200 jobs could be generated when the center opens.

17712 ■ "Generation Y Driving Portland Multifamily Market" in *Daily Journal of Commerce, Portland* (October 29, 2010)
Pub: Dolan Media Newswires
Ed: Nick Bjork. **Description:** Generation Y, young adults between the ages of 18-30, are interested in multifamily residents in the Portland, Oregon area. Developers in the area, particularly North Portland, have recognized this trend and are looking into multifamily investments.

17713 ■ "Go Back to Basics to Maximize Skid Steer ROI" in *Rental Product News* (Vol. 33, October 2011)
Pub: Cygnus Business Media
Ed: Jenny Lescohier. **Description:** There are two types of rental customers in the market for skid steers: the small contractor or weekend warrior who rents for a day or a week and the longer-term rental going to large contractor firms.

17714 ■ "Groundbreaking 2.0" in *Philadelphia Business Journal* (Vol. 30, September 23, 2011, No. 32, pp. 1)
Pub: American City Business Journals Inc.
Ed: Natalie Kostelni. **Description:** University Place Associates, the developer of 2.0 University Place in West Philadelphia, Pennsylvania, will break ground on a five-story, 97,000-square-foot office building in December 2011. The decision follows the Citizenship and Immigration Services signing of a 15-year lease as anchor tenant.

17715 ■ "Higher Thread Count for Metropole" in *Business Courier* (Vol. 26, September 25, 2009, No. 22, pp. 1)
Pub: American City Business Journals, Inc.
Ed: Lisa Biank Fasig, Lucy May. **Description:** Cincinnati Center City Development Corporation is under contract to buy the 225-unit apartment building called Metropole Apartments and 21c Museum Hotel is the lead candidate for the space. Advocates of some residents of the low-income rental complex complain that this move could leave them homeless.

17716 ■ "How Fast Can This Thing Go Anyway?" in *Inc.* (March 2008, pp. 94-101)
Pub: Gruner & Jahr USA Publishing
Ed: Stephanie Clifford. **Description:** Founder of Zipcar, an auto rental company, tell how he brought a new CEO into the company to boost revenue. The new CEO instituted a seven-step strategy to increase business.

17717 ■ "Independence's Day Keeps on Getting Brighter" in *Business Courier* (Vol. 27, June 11, 2010, No. 6, pp. 1)
Pub: Business Courier
Ed: Lucy May. **Description:** Reports show that residential and commercial development continues in Independence, Kentucky despite the recession, with a 144-unit apartment complex under construction. The city recorded 152 new-home closings in 2009, or 25 percent of all new homes closed in Boone, Campbell, and Kenton counties.

17718 ■ "Industrial RE Market Shows Signs of Health" in *Business Courier* (Vol. 27, August 20, 2010, No. 16, pp. 1)
Pub: Business Courier
Ed: Jon Newberry. **Description:** Cincinnati, Ohio's industrial real estate sector has experienced growth during the first half of 2010. The industry has seen a large net loss of occupied space in 2009.

17719 ■ "Investors Eye Old Buildings" in *Business Journal-Portland* (Vol. 24, October 19, 2007, No. 34, pp. 1)
Pub: American City Business Journals, Inc.
Ed: Wendy Culverwell. **Description:** Office vacancy rates in downtown Portland has dipped to around five percent, causing brokers and investors to search for older buildings in the Class B and Class C categories where the rent is also cheaper. Some notable older and cheaper buildings will be renovated for use.

17720 ■ "Is this a Buying Opportunity?" in *Canadian Business* (Vol. 82, April 27, 2009, No. 7, pp. 46)
Pub: Rogers Media
Ed: Andy Holloway. **Description:** Home prices in Canada are down by as much as 14.2 percent in 2009 compared to prices in 2008, making homes more affordable now. Some housing experts believe that homes are still good investments as prices of rent and properties always recover. Meanwhile, a survey found that Canadians under 35 plan to buy a home within two years.

17721 ■ "Is It Time for a Change?" in *Rental Product News* (Vol. 33, October 2011)
Pub: Cygnus Business Media
Ed: Jenny Lescohier. **Description:** Management software for running a rental business is examined.

17722 ■ "Joint Venture Plans Bronzeville Project" in *Business Journal-Milwaukee* (Vol. 25, October 5, 2007, No. 1, pp. A1)
Pub: American City Business Journals, Inc.
Ed: Rich Kirchen. **Description:** Proposal for construction of an apartment building and possible expansion of Northtown Mall in Milwaukee, Wisconsin is being planned by developers in the city's Bronzeville area. The project for rehabilitating the existing mall and building of a 50-unit apartment would amount to about $12.5 million.

17723 ■ "Leaning Tower" in *Business Courier* (Vol. 27, June 4, 2010, No. 5, pp. 1)
Pub: Business Courier
Ed: Jon Newberry. **Description:** New York-based developer Armand Lasky, owner of Tower Place Mall in downtown Cincinnati, Ohio has sued Birmingham, Alabama-based Regions Bank to prevent the bank's foreclosure on the property. Regions Bank claims Lasky was in default on an $18 million loan agreement. Details on the mall's leasing plan is also discussed.

17724 ■ "Lytle Place Listing Seen as Bellweather" in *Business Courier* (Vol. 27, December 3, 2010, No. 31, pp. 1)
Pub: Business Courier
Ed: Dan Monk. **Description:** Denver, Colorado-based Apartment Investment and Management Company (AIMCO) has offered the 25-story One Lytle Place Apartments for sale through CB Richard Ellis for the third time in three years. The potential sale could define the recovery for Cincinnati, Ohio's struggling apartment industry.

17725 ■ "Market for Retail Space Flat, but Recovery Still Uncertain" in *Sacramento Business Journal* (Vol. 28, August 26, 2011, No. 26, pp. 1)
Pub: Sacramento Business Journal
Ed: Kelly Johnson. **Description:** The retail market in the Sacramento, California region remains challenged with the stock market volatility being the latest of its hurdles. The overall vacancy was 13.1 percent as of mid-2011, but retail real estate professionals express hopes that the worst is behind. A list and description of the region's winners and losers in retail vacancies is provided.

17726 ■ "A New Way to Arrive in Style" in *Inc.* (Vol. 33, September 2011, No. 7, pp. 54)
Pub: Inc. Magazine
Ed: Matthew Rist. **Description:** EagleRider is a franchise offering various two-wheeled rentals, including BMWs and Harley-Davidsons at more than 100 locations worldwide.

17727 ■ "Nothing But Green Skies" in *Inc.* (November 2007, pp. 115-120)
Pub: Gruner & Jahr USA Publishing
Ed: Alison Stein Wellner. **Description:** Profile of Enterprise Rent-A-Car, one of the largest family-owned businesses in the U.S. Andy Taylor, CEO, discusses the company's talks about the idea of offering carbon off-sets for a few years.

17728 ■ "Old Ford Plant to Sign New Tenants" in *Business Courier* (Vol. 27, August 13, 2010, No. 15, pp. 1)
Pub: Business Courier
Ed: Dan Monk. **Description:** Ohio Realty Advisors LLC, a company handling the marketing of the 1.9 million-square-foot former Ford Batavia plant is on the brink of landing one distribution and three manufacturing firms as tenants. These tenants are slated to occupy about 20 percent of the facility and generate as many as 250 jobs in Ohio.

17729 ■ "The Perks of Going Public" in *Austin Business Journal* (Vol. 31, July 15, 2011, No. 19, pp. A17)
Pub: American City Business Journals Inc.
Ed: Christopher Calnan. **Description:** HomeAway Inc. launched a $216 million initial public offering. Austin Ventures has generated more than $32 million from the IPO.

17730 ■ "Plans for $160M Condo Resort in Wisconsin Dells Moves Forward" in *Commercial Property News* (March 18, 2008)
Pub: Nielsen Company
Description: Plans for the Grand Cambrian Resort in the Wisconsin Dells is discussed. The luxury condominium resort will include condos, townhomes, and condo-hotel style residences, two water parts, meeting space and indoor entertainment space, as well as a spa, four restaurants and retail offerings.

17731 ■ "Priced-Out Tenants Flocking to Class B" in *Boston Business Journal* (Vol. 27, October 19, 2007, No. 38, pp. 1)
Pub: American City Business Journals Inc.
Ed: Michelle Hillman. **Description:** Tenants who usually rent top-tier office buildings are migrating to building that are not as expensive. The shift from Class A to Class B buildings is influenced by the high rental cost of the flashy office towers.

17732 ■ "Proposed Accounting Changes Could Complicate Tenant's Leases" in *Baltimore Business Journal* (Vol. 28, July 2, 2010, No. 8, pp. 1)
Pub: Baltimore Business Journal
Ed: Daniel J. Sernovitz. **Description:** The Financial Accounting Standards Board has proposed that companies must indicate the value of real estate leases as assets and liabilities on balance sheets instead of expenses. The proposals could cause some companies to document millions of dollars in charges on their books or find difficulty in getting loans.

17733 ■ "Protect Your Assets" in *Black Enterprise* (Vol. 38, January 2008, No. 6, pp. 38)
Pub: Earl G. Graves Publishing Co. Inc.
Ed: Trevor Delaney. **Description:** Owner of rental properties seeks advice for incorporating versus getting an LLC for the business.

17734 ■ "Questions to Ask Your Customers Before They Rent a Generator" in *Rental Product News* (Vol. 33, October 2011)
Pub: Cygnus Business Media
Ed: Jenny Lescohier. **Description:** According to a national strategic account manager at Kohler Rental Power, the most important factors when choosing a generator include volts, amps and phase. Understanding the relationship between these three electrical values will help rent the power equipment to customers.

17735 ■ "Rent Check" in *Boston Business Journal* (Vol. 31, July 29, 2011, No. 27, pp. 1)
Pub: Boston Business Journal
Ed: Lisa van der Pool. **Description:** Merchants at Newbury Street in Boston, Massachusetts are concerned with the annual increase of already inflated rents that prevent many small businesses from expanding.

17736 ■ *Rental Management—Who's Who in the Rental Industry Issue*
Pub: American Rental Association
Ed: Brian Alm, Editor, brian.alm@ararental.org. **Released:** Annual, July. **Price:** $25, individuals member price; $75, individuals non-member price. **Publica-**

tion Includes: Lists of about 8,500 member rental companies, branch locations, services, and suppliers to the rental industry in the United States, limited international coverage; also lists association officers, other associations in the industry, and ARA state and local groups. **Entries Include:** For rental firms—Company name, address, phone, key personnel and kind of rental service provided (construction, general tool, health, party). For suppliers—Company name, address, phone, products or service. For associations—Organization name, contact name, address, phone. For officers—Name, company, address, phone; listings for present officers include first name of spouse; listings for past presidents show the year(s) of tenure. **Arrangement:** Rental firms are listed geographically; associations are by country or state; current officers are hierarchical, past officers are listed alphabetically, past presidents are chronological; suppliers are alphabetical. **Indexes:** Personal name.

17737 ■ "Renters' Review – Secret Shoppers Strike Again" in *Rental Product News* (Vol. 33, June 2011)
Pub: Cygnus Business Media
Description: Staff of Rental Product News set out to rent various items from three different rental sources in order to evaluate the rental experience from the eyes of the average customer.

17738 ■ "Restaurateurs Follow High-End Apartments Into Kendall Square" in *Boston Business Journal* (Vol. 31, July 22, 2011, No. 26, pp. 3)
Pub: Boston Business Journal
Ed: Lisa van der Pool. **Description:** Kendall Square in Cambridge, Massachusetts is attracting restaurants, 16 of which have opened since 2009. The influx of restaurants is being driven by lower commercial rents.

17739 ■ "Restoring Grandeur" in *Business Courier* (Vol. 26, December 4, 2009, No. 32, pp. 1)
Pub: American City Business Journals, Inc.
Ed: Dan Monk. **Description:** Eagle Realty Group intends to spend more than $10 to restore the historic 12-story Phelps apartment building in Lytle Park in Cincinnati. Its president, Mario San Marco, expressed the need to invest in the building in order to maintain operations. The building could be restored into a hotel catering to executives and consultants.

17740 ■ "A Rise in Rental Units" in *Philadelphia Business Journal* (Vol. 30, October 7, 2011, No. 34, pp. 1)
Pub: American City Business Journals Inc.
Ed: Natalie Kostelni. **Description:** Housing developers have been stepping up the construction of new apartment complexes throughout the suburbs of Pennsylvania in order to capture growing demand for rental properties. BPG Properties Ltd. has nearly 1,000 new apartments under construction.

17741 ■ "Sales Tax Proposed to Revive KRM" in *Business Journal-Milwaukee* (Vol. 25, October 26, 2007, No. 4, pp. A1)
Pub: American City Business Journals, Inc.
Ed: Rich Kirchen. **Description:** City and county officials are proposing a $13 increase in rental car fees to finance the Kenosha-Racine-Milwaukee line. The Alliance of Cities proposed sales tax are backed by Milwaukee-area business groups, however it failed to generate support from the public.

17742 ■ "Shedding Light on Innovation" in *Rental Product News* (Vol. 33, June 2011)
Pub: Cygnus Business Media
Ed: Rod Dickens. **Description:** Light tower manufacturers have introduced numerous new products that feature alternative power sources, LED lighting and a second generation of performance and value.

17743 ■ "State Center Lease Deal High for Md." in *Baltimore Business Journal* (Vol. 28, August 6, 2010, No. 13, pp. 1)
Pub: Baltimore Business Journal
Ed: Daniel J. Sernovitz. **Description:** The proposed $1.5 billion State Center development project in Midtown Baltimore might cause the State of Maryland to pay the most expensive rental rates in the city. The state will have to pay an effective rental rate of $34 per square foot, including expenses, on the leasing. Other details of the redevelopment project are discussed.

17744 ■ "State Wants to Add Escape Clause to Leases" in *Sacramento Business Journal* (Vol. 28, October 14, 2011, No. 33, pp. 1)
Pub: Sacramento Business Journal
Ed: Michael Shaw. **Description:** California Governor Jerry Brown's administration has decided to add escape clauses to new lease agreements, which created new worry for building owners and brokers in Sacramento, California. Real estate brokers believe the appropriation of funds clauses have been making the lenders nervous and would result in less competition.

17745 ■ "Survey: Apartment Rents Continue to Climb as Home Market Slows" in *Business Review, Albany New York* (November 23, 2007)
Pub: American City Business Journals, Inc.
Ed: Michael DeMasi. **Description:** Survey by Sunrise Management and Consulting shows that asking rents for apartments in the Capital Region increased for the thirteenth consecutive time. The survey, which was conducted between August and October 2007, also showed that Albany County, New York had the highest average asking rent, followed by Rensselaer County, Saratoga County, and Schenectady County.

17746 ■ "Survey Says Commercial Real Estate Headed for Turbulence" in *Commercial Property News* (March 17, 2008)
Pub: Nielsen Company
Description: Commercial real estate sector is declining due to the sluggish U.S. economy. According to a recent survey, national office, retail and hospitality markets are also on the decline.

17747 ■ "Take the Right Approach to Concrete Polishing Rentals" in *Rental Product News* (Vol. 33, June 2011)
Pub: Cygnus Business Media
Ed: Jenny Lescohier. **Description:** A recent trend in flooring is concrete polishing for a practical, beautiful and sustainable way to decorate homes and businesses. Things to keep in mind when assessing the value of adding concrete polishing equipment to an existing rental store are evaluated.

17748 ■ "Tulsa-Based Dollar Thrifty Adds Franchises" in *Journal Record* (December 7, 2010)
Pub: Dolan Media Newswires
Ed: D. Ray Tuttle. **Description:** Dollar Thrifty Automotive Group Inc. opened 31 franchise locations in 2010 as part of its expansion plan in the U.S.

17749 ■ "UC May Expand into Old Ford Plant" in *Business Courier* (Vol. 26, December 25, 2009, No. 35, pp. 1)
Pub: American City Business Journals, Inc.
Ed: Dan Monk. **Description:** Developer Stuart Lichter is planning to acquire University of Cincinnati (UC) as a tenant at a two-story office building on a 132-acre site where a vacant Ford transmission plant is located. Details of the transaction are outlined.

17750 ■ "Welcome Back" in *Canadian Business* (Vol. 82, April 27, 2009, No. 7, pp. 25)
Pub: Rogers Media
Ed: Sarka Halas. **Description:** Some Canadian companies such as Gennum Corporation have taken advantage of corporate sale-leasebacks to raise money at a time when credit is hard to acquire. Corporate sale-leasebacks allow companies to sell their property assets while remaining as tenants of the building. Sale-leasebacks allow firms to increase capital while avoiding the disruptions that may result with moving.

17751 ■ "Where the Loans Are" in *Boston Business Journal* (Vol. 30, October 22, 2010, No. 39, pp. 1)
Pub: Boston Business Journal
Ed: Craig M. Douglas. **Description:** Massachusetts-based community banks have been investing in multi-family apartment projects. Lending has decline during the first half of 2010. A $264 million increase in multifamily loans has also been observed.

STATISTICAL SOURCES

17752 ■ *RMA Annual Statement Studies*
Pub: Robert Morris Associates (RMA)
Released: Annual. **Price:** $175.00 2006-07 edition, $105.00. **Description:** Contains composite balance sheets and income statements for more than 360 industries, including the accounting, auditing, and bookkeeping industries. Also contains five years of comparative historical data for discerning trends. Includes 16 commonly used ratios, computed for most of the size groupings for nearly every industry.

TRADE PERIODICALS

17753 ■ *Heavy Equipment Guide*
Pub: Baum Publications Ltd.
Contact: Robin McCabe
E-mail: circulation@baumpub.com
Released: 10/yr. **Description:** Trade publication for the construction, mining, truck, and municipal industries.

17754 ■ *Rental Management*
Pub: American Rental Association
Contact: April Peterson, Circulation Mgr
E-mail: april.peterson@ararental.org
Released: Monthly. **Price:** $85. **Description:** Magazine for business owners who rent equipment to consumers, industries, institutions and commercial firms.

17755 ■ *Rental Product News*
Pub: Cygnus Business Media
Released: 10/yr. **Price:** Free to qualified subscribers. **Description:** Product rental management trade magazine.

TRADE SHOWS AND CONVENTIONS

17756 ■ American Rental Association Annual Convention and Rental Trade Show
American Rental Association
1900 19th St.
Moline, IL 61265
Ph:800-334-2177
Fax:(309)764-1533
URL: http://www.ararental.org
Released: Annual. **Audience:** Owners and managers of rental equipment stores. **Principal Exhibits:** Equipment for rental, including party, construction, industrial, and do-it-yourself equipment.

17757 ■ Association of Progressive Rental Organizations Annual Convention and Trade Show
Association of Progressive Rental Organizations
1504 Robin Hood Trail
Austin, TX 78703
Free: 800-204-2776
Fax:(512)794-0097
URL: http://www.rtohq.org/
Released: Annual. **Audience:** Rental-purchase store owners, managers, and suppliers. **Principal Exhibits:** Products of interest to rent-to-own dealers, such as audio products, computers, home appliances, home furniture, video products, jewelry, advertising, electronics, fabric protection, marketing, promotional services, and related equipment, supplies, and services. **Dates and Locations:** 2011 Jul 11-14, Little Rock, AR.

FRANCHISES AND BUSINESS OPPORTUNITIES

17758 ■ Abrakadoodle Remarkable Art Education
Abrakadoodle, Inc.
1800 Robert Fulton Dr., Ste. 205
Reston, VA 20191

Ph:(703)860-6570
Fax:(703)860-6574
Co. E-mail: info@abrakadoodle.com
URL: http://www.abrakadoodle.com
No. of Franchise Units: 70. **No. of Company-Owned Units:** 2. **Founded:** 2002. **Franchised:** 2004. **Description:** Arts education program. **Equity Capital Needed:** $100,000 net worth. **Franchise Fee:** $22,400-$35,900. **Financial Assistance:** No. **Managerial Assistance:** Monthly teleconferences, annual meetings and an interactive web-based forum and Intranet. **Training:** Provides 5 days at headquarters with ongoing support.

17759 ■ Affiliated Car Rental LC
105 Hwy. 36
Eatontown, NJ 07724
Free: 800-367-5159
Fax:(732)290-8305
No. of Franchise Units: 254. **Founded:** 1987. **Franchised:** 1987. **Description:** Vehicle rentals. **Equity Capital Needed:** $44,980-$71,800. **Franchise Fee:** $5,000-$11,600. **Royalty Fee:** Varies. **Financial Assistance:** Limited third party financing available. **Training:** Provides 2 days at headquarters, 2 days onsite with ongoing support.

17760 ■ Colortyme
Colortyme, Inc.
5501 Headquarters Dr.
Plano, TX 75024
Ph:(972)403-4905
Free: 800-411-8963
Fax:(972)403-4923
No. of Franchise Units: 191. **Founded:** 1979. **Franchised:** 1982. **Description:** Provides a specialized inventory of rental products, such as televisions, audio-video equipment, appliances, furniture, jewelry, papers and computers. **Equity Capital Needed:** $412,075-$627,000. **Franchise Fee:** $25,000. **Royalty Fee:** 5%. **Financial Assistance:** Limited third party financing available. **Training:** Provides 2 weeks at headquarters, 2-4 weeks at franchisee's location, and ongoing support.

17761 ■ Cool Daddy's
4188 Roswell Rd.
Atlanta, GA 30342
Ph:(404)352-9996
Fax:(404)352-9106
No. of Franchise Units: 1. **No. of Company-Owned Units:** 1. **Founded:** 2000. **Franchised:** 2005. **Description:** Frozen drink party rentals & entertainment. **Equity Capital Needed:** $105,000-$187,500. **Franchise Fee:** $25,000. **Royalty Fee:** 6%. **Financial Assistance:** Limited third party financing available. **Training:** Provides 2 weeks at headquarters. 1 week at franchisee's location, with ongoing support.

17762 ■ Dollar Thrifty Automotive Group Canada Inc.
6050 Indian Line
Mississauga, ON, Canada L4V 1G5
Ph:(905)671-7858
Free: 800-667-5925
Fax:(905)612-1893
Co. E-mail: lynn.jordan@dtag.com
URL: http://www.thrifty.com
No. of Franchise Units: 66. **No. of Company-Owned Units:** 54. **Founded:** 1985. **Franchised:** 1985. **Description:** Daily, weekly, monthly rental of all passenger vehicles and light trucks. **Equity Capital Needed:** $50,000-$300,000. **Franchise Fee:** $5,000-$50,000. **Training:** Yes.

17763 ■ Grand Rental Station
True Value Specialty Co., LLC
203 Jandus Rd.
Cary, IL 60013-2861
Free: 800-833-3004
Co. E-mail: pagee@truserv.com
URL: http://www.grandrental.com
No. of Franchise Units: 475. **Founded:** 1910. **Franchised:** 1985. **Description:** Industry leading store design, cooperative supply of rental and sale products. General rental store. Grand Rental Station/Taylor Rental Centers is the largest general rental store in the USA. **Equity Capital Needed:** $250,000-$325,000. **Franchise Fee:** $1,500. **Royalty Fee:** 1.2%. **Financial Assistance:** Third party financing available. **Managerial Assistance:** Store sign, inventory space, inventory supply, advertising, computerization and operational guidance are provided. **Training:** Offers 1 week of training program at company headquarters.

17764 ■ Joe Loue Tout Rent All Inc.
28 Vanier
Chateauguay, QC, Canada J6J 3W8
Ph:(450)692-6268
Free: 800-361-2020
Fax:(450)692-2848
Co. E-mail: mrjoe@videotron.ca
URL: http://www.joelouetout.ca
No. of Franchise Units: 80. **Founded:** 1982. **Franchised:** 1982. **Description:** Tool and equipment rental centre, offering full line of services from procurement of specific legalized stationary, rental inventory of tools, equipment and recreational vehicles. **Equity Capital Needed:** $40,000-$400,000. **Franchise Fee:** $20,000. **Training:** Yes.

17765 ■ Nation-Wide General Rental Centers, Inc.
5510 Hwy. 9 N
Alpharetta, GA 30004
Ph:(770)664-7765
Free: 800-227-1643
Fax:(770)664-0052
Co. E-mail: office@nation-widerental.com
URL: http://www.nation-widerental.com
No. of Franchise Units: 412. **Founded:** 1976. **Description:** Complete line for contractor, home owner & party. **Equity Capital Needed:** $45,000 cash plus $10,000 working capital; package $120,000-$250,000. **Franchise Fee:** None. **Financial Assistance:** Yes. **Training:** Offers 1 week training program with ongoing support.

17766 ■ Party Central
True Value Specialty Company, LLC
203 Jandus Rd.
Cary, IL 60013-2861
Free: 800-833-3004
No. of Franchise Units: 475. **Founded:** 1910. **Franchised:** 1985. **Description:** Rental store. **Equity Capital Needed:** $250,000-$325,000. **Franchise Fee:** $1,500. **Training:** Yes.

17767 ■ Priceless Rent-A-Car
Bundy American Corp.
105 Main St.
Laurel, MD 20707
Ph:(240)581-1359
Fax:(240)581-1385
No. of Franchise Units: 50. **Founded:** 1996. **Franchised:** 1996. **Description:** Automobiles is the main area of interest and offers rentals. **Equity Capital Needed:** $134,600-$636,500. **Franchise Fee:** $8,000. **Financial Assistance:** None. **Training:** Yes.
.

17768 ■ Rent-A-Tire Canada, Inc.
16 Victoria St. N
Kitchener, ON, Canada N2H 6S2
Ph:(519)578-3800
Fax:(519)578-2822
Co. E-mail: info@rentatirecanada.com
URL: http://www.rentatirecanada.com
No. of Company-Owned Units: 1. **Founded:** 2000. **Franchised:** 2002. **Description:** Specialists in tire, custom wheel and automotive accessories. Offering the "affordable alternative" of rent-to-own purchases.

17769 ■ Rent A Wreck
7710 5th St. SE, Ste. 204
Calgary, AB, Canada T2H 2L9
Ph:(403)259-6666
Free: 800-668-8591
Fax:(403)259-6776
Co. E-mail: info@rent-a-wreck.ca
URL: http://www.rent-a-wreck.ca
No. of Franchise Units: 62. **Founded:** 1976. **Franchised:** 1977. **Description:** The franchise specializes in renting high-quality, clean and dependable used vehicles at reasonable price. Strong brand awareness, international name recognition, national reservation network, national and regional marketing initiative, training, ongoing support and used car sales program are provided. **Equity Capital Needed:** $80,000-$200,000. **Franchise Fee:** $20,000-$35,000. **Training:** Yes.

17770 ■ Rent 'N Drive
Rent 'n Drive Franchising LLC
1440 Plumridge Rd.
Lincoln, NE 68527
Ph:(402)467-4994
Fax:(402)466-3819
No. of Franchise Units: 1. **No. of Company-Owned Units:** 1. **Founded:** 1990. **Franchised:** 1996. **Description:** Used car, van, and truck rentals. **Equity Capital Needed:** $83,000-$189,000, depending on fleet size. **Franchise Fee:** $7,500. **Financial Assistance:** No. **Training:** Yes. Yes.

17771 ■ Scooter Planet
2620 Regatta Dr., Ste. 102
Las Vegas, NV 89128
Ph:(702)869-0099
Fax:(702)446-6071
No. of Franchise Units: 1. **Founded:** 2004. **Franchised:** 2004. **Description:** Recreational equipment rental franchise. **Equity Capital Needed:** $75,000 estimated. **Franchise Fee:** $29,500. **Financial Assistance:** No. **Training:** Yes.

17772 ■ Taylor Rental
TruServ Specialty Co., LLC
203 Jandus Rd.
Cary, IL 60013-2861
Free: 800-833-3004
Co. E-mail: pagee@truserv.com
URL: http://www.taylorrental.com
No. of Franchise Units: 475. **Founded:** 1910. **Franchised:** 1985. **Description:** A 100% member-owned Co-Operative, offering the Rental Industry's most complete Rental Franchise. Full line general rental stores offering tools, party & event & contractor equipment to the homeowner & professional contractor. Grand Rental Station/Taylor Rental/Party Central offer the benefits of national name recognition, strong purchasing power, modern store design & effective advertising programs. New & existing business opportunities available. **Equity Capital Needed:** $250,000-$325,000. **Franchise Fee:** $1,500. **Training:** Yes.

17773 ■ U-Save Car & Truck Rental
Franchise Services of North America, Inc.
4780 I-55 N, Ste. 300
Jackson, MS 39211
Ph:(601)713-4333
Free: 800-438-2300
Fax:(601)982-9850
Co. E-mail: info@usave.net
URL: http://www.usave.net
No. of Franchise Units: 169. **Founded:** 1979. **Franchised:** 1979. **Description:** Auto rental. **Equity Capital Needed:** $300,000 net worth; $60,000 liquid. **Franchise Fee:** $20,000. **Financial Assistance:** Up to $150,000 fleet financing. **Training:** Initial training program focuses on management, marketing, and operational techniques.

17774 ■ Wheel Fun Rentals
Freetime Inc.
4526 Telephone Rd., Ste. 202
Ventura, CA 93004
Ph:(805)650-7770
Fax:(805)650-7771
No. of Franchise Units: 93. **No. of Company-Owned Units:** 13. **Founded:** 1987. **Franchised:** 2000. **Description:** Bicycle and specialty products rental. **Equity Capital Needed:** $85,000-$259,000. **Franchise Fee:** $29,000. **Royalty Fee:** 6%. **Financial Assistance:** Limited third party financing available. **Training:** Offers 7 days training headquarters, at franchisee's location and ongoing as needed.

START-UP INFORMATION

17775 ■ *55 Surefire Food-Related Businesses: You Can Start for Under $5000*
Pub: Entrepreneur Press
Ed: Cheryl Kimball. **Released:** March 1, 2009. **Price:** $17.95. **Description:** Advice is given to start 55 various food-related companies and goes beyond restaurant or catering services. Home-based, retail and mail order ventures are covered, as well as food safety and standards.

17776 ■ "Ahead of the Pack" in *Small Business Opportunities* (Fall 2010)
Pub: Harris Publications Inc.
Description: Profile of an organic fast-food business that is carving out a niche that is gaining favor. Elevation Burger is a unique concept offering healthier burgers in sustainable buildings.

17777 ■ "'Crazy' Or Not, Restaurateurs Are Finding Ways to Open New Eateries" in *Baltimore Business Journal* (Vol. 28, October 8, 2010)
Pub: Baltimore Business Journal
Ed: Joanna Sullivan. **Description:** New restaurants have been opening in Maryland. However, 515 restaurants have closed down due to the economic crisis. Comments from restaurateurs are also provided.

17778 ■ *Culinary Careers: How to Get Your Dream Job in Food with Advice from Top Culinary Professionals*
Pub: Crown Business Books
Ed: Rick Smilow, Anne E. McBride. **Released:** May 4, 2010. **Price:** $16.99. **Description:** Top culinary experts offer advice for working in or owning a food service firm.

17779 ■ "Franchises with an Eye on Chicago" in *Crain's Chicago Business* (Vol. 34, March 14, 2011, No. 11, pp. 20)
Pub: Crain Communications Inc.
Description: Profiles of franchise companies seeking franchisees for the Chicago area include: Extreme Pita, a sandwich shop; Hand and Stone, offering massage, facial and waxing services; Molly Maid, home-cleaning service; Primrose Schools, private accredited schools for children 6 months to 6 hears and after-school programs; Protect Painters, residential and light-commercial painting contractor; and Wingstop, a restaurant offering chicken wings in nine flavors, fries and side dishes.

17780 ■ "Jean-Rober's 'oui'" in *Business Courier* (Vol. 27, August 6, 2010, No. 14, pp. 1)
Pub: Business Courier
Ed: Dan Monk. **Description:** Jean-Robert de Cavel will open his new restaurant in Cincinnati, Ohio. The culinary arts program at Cincinnati State Technical and Community College offered him $100,000 to be its 'chef in residence'. He was able to energize students, boost enrollment, and increase the stature of the culinary program.

17781 ■ "Proven Success Pays Off" in *Small Business Opportunities* (January 2011)
Pub: Harris Publications Inc.
Ed: Description: Industry pioneers of the fast-casual restaurant launch new venture with sales of $43 million. Profile of Newk's Express Cafe and its founders is included.

17782 ■ *Small Business Desk Reference*
Pub: Penguin Books (USA) Incorporated
Ed: Gene Marks. **Released:** December 2004. **Description:** Comprehensive guide for starting or running a successful small business, focusing on buying a business or franchise, writing a business plan, financial management, accounting, legal issues, human resources management, operations, marketing, sales, customer service, taxes, insurance, and ethics. Information for launching a restaurant, property management firm, retail outlet, consulting firm, and service business is included.

17783 ■ *Start and Run a Delicatessen: Small Business Starters Series*
Pub: How To Books
Ed: Deborah Penrith. **Released:** November 9, 2010. **Price:** $30.00. **Description:** Information for starting and running a successful delicatessen is provided. Insight is offered into selecting a location, researching the market, writing a business plan and more.

17784 ■ *Start Small, Finish Big*
Pub: Business Plus/Warner Business Books
Ed: Fred DeLuca with John P. Hayes. **Released:** April 2009. **Price:** $16.95. **Description:** Fred DeLuca is profiled; after founding the multi-billion dollar chain of Subway sandwich restaurants, DeLuca is committed to helping microentrepreneurs, people who start successful small businesses with less than $1,000.

17785 ■ "Thirsty Lion on the Prowl" in *Business Journal Portland* (Vol. 27, November 5, 2010, No. 36, pp. 1)
Pub: Portland Business Journal
Ed: Wendy Culverwell. **Description:** Concept Entertainment Inc.'s impending launch of the Thirsty Lion Pub and Grill at the Washington Square in downtown Portland, Oregon is part of its West Coast expansion plan. A discussion of the planning involved in realizing Thirsty Lion is discussed, along with pub offerings that are expected to be enjoyed by customers.

ASSOCIATIONS AND OTHER ORGANIZATIONS

17786 ■ Association of Food Industries
3301 Rte. 66, Ste. 205, Bldg. C
Neptune, NJ 07753
Ph:(732)922-3008
Fax:(732)922-3590
Co. E-mail: info@afius.org
URL: http://afi.mytradeassociation.org
Contact: Tom White, Chm.
Description: Food processors, importers, and import agents nationally; food brokers in the New York metropolitan market and overseas food exporters. Maintains arbitration tribunal, government relations, and information services. **Publications:** *Standard Import Contract* .

17787 ■ Beverage Network
44 Pleasant St., Ste. 110
Watertown, MA 02472
Ph:(617)715-9670
Fax:(617)812-7740
Co. E-mail: jcraven@bevnet.com
URL: http://www.bevnet.com
Contact: John Craven, Ed.
Description: Beverage distributors dealing primarily in "new wave specialty non-alcoholic" products and some specialty food items. Serves as a forum for the exchange of information among members. Assists members in identifying new products. .

17788 ■ Broker Management Council
PO Box 150229
Arlington, TX 76015
Ph:(682)518-6008
Fax:(682)518-6476
Co. E-mail: assnhqtrs@aol.com
URL: http://www.bmcsales.com
Contact: Pamela L. Bess, Exec. Dir.
Description: Foodservice sales and marketing companies specializing in institutional and restaurant food and allied products. Aims to: facilitate communication and exchange of management information; increase efficiency and reduce the cost of doing business; promote a favorable image of brokers in order to enhance their acceptance. Compiles statistics; conducts specialized education program. .

17789 ■ Canadian Restaurant and Foodservices Association–Association Canadienne des Restaurateurs et des Services Alimentaires
316 Bloor St. W
Toronto, ON, Canada M5S 1W5
Ph:(416)923-8416
Free: 800-387-5649
Fax:(416)923-1450
Co. E-mail: info@crfa.ca
URL: http://www.crfa.ca
Contact: Garth Whyte, Pres./CEO
Description: Restaurant and food service corporations, hotels, caterers, and food service suppliers and educators. Seeks to create a favorable business environment for members. Represents members' interests before government; conducts trade research. Makes available group buying programs and other services to members; owns and operates three industry trade shows. **Publications:** *Canadian Foodservice Industry Operations Report* (biennial); *Foodservice Facts* (annual); *Legislation Guide* (quarterly).

17790 ■ Commercial Food Equipment Service Association
2216 W Meadowview Rd., Ste. 100
Greensboro, NC 27407
Ph:(336)346-4700

Fax:(336)346-4745
Co. E-mail: cstrickland@cfesa.com
URL: http://www.cfesa.com
Contact: Carla Strickland, Exec. Dir.
Description: Represents firms that repair food preparation equipment used by restaurants, hotels, and institutions. Provides training and education for members and their employees. **Publications:** *Commercial Food Equipment Service Association—Directory* (annual); *On Target* (bimonthly);Membership Directory (annual).

17791 ■ Foodservice Equipment Distributors Association
2250 Point Blvd., Ste. 200
Elgin, IL 60123-7887
Ph:(224)293-6500
Free: 800-677-9605
Fax:(224)293-6505
Co. E-mail: feda@feda.com
URL: http://www.feda.com
Contact: Raymond W. Herrick CAE, Exec. VP
Description: Distributors of foodservice equipment, such as ovens, ranges, dishwashing machines, china, utensils, and cutlery for hotels, restaurants, and institutions. Conducts specialized education programs. **Publications:** *FEDA News and Views* (bimonthly);Membership Directory (periodic).

17792 ■ International Foodservice Manufacturers Association
2 Prudential Plz.
180 N Stetson Ave., Ste. 4400
Chicago, IL 60601
Ph:(312)540-4400
Fax:(312)540-4401
Co. E-mail: ifma@ifmaworld.com
URL: http://www.ifmaworld.com
Contact: Larry Oberkfell, Pres./CEO
Description: National and international manufacturers and processors of food, food equipment, and related products for the away-from-home food market. Associate and allied members provide support services to the industry through marketing, publishing, distribution, consulting, promotion, research, advertising, public relations, and brokering. Activities are aimed at marketing, merchandising, sales training, and market research. Compiles statistics. **Publications:** *IFMA World* (9/year);Membership Directory (annual).

17793 ■ National Barbecue Association
455 S Fourth St., Ste. 650
Louisville, KY 40202
Free: 888-909-2121
Fax:(502)589-3602
Co. E-mail: nbbqa@hqtrs.com
URL: http://www.nbbqa.org
Contact: Kell Phelps, Pres.
Description: Industry professionals and barbecue enthusiasts including restaurants, caterers, specialty equipment retailers, grill manufacturers and distributors, smoker manufacturers and distributors, food product suppliers and distributors, sauces and spice distributors, backyard hobbyists. **Publications:** *National Barbecue News* (monthly); *NBBQA Barbecue Buyers' Guide* (annual).

17794 ■ National Black McDonald's Operators Association
PO Box 820668
South Florida, FL 33082-0668
Ph:(954)389-4487
Fax:(954)349-5408
Co. E-mail: nbmoa1@aol.com
URL: http://www.nbmoa.org
Contact: Roland G. Parrish, Chm./CEO
Description: Black owners of McDonald's restaurants. Provides a forum for the exchange of ideas on the improvement of community relations and on the operation and management of restaurants. Seeks to build and improve the McDonald's restaurant image throughout the community. Sponsors training seminars on marketing, better sales practices, labor relations and profit sharing. Conducts charitable programs. .

17795 ■ National Council of Chain Restaurants
325 7th St. NW, Ste. 1100
Washington, DC 20004
Ph:(202)783-7971
Free: 800-673-4692
Fax:(202)737-2849
Co. E-mail: info@nrf.com
URL: http://www.nccr.net
Contact: Rob Green, Exec. Dir.
Description: Represents major multi-unit, multi-state foodservice, restaurant and lodging companies in the U.S. Activities are directed to legislative and regulatory matters affecting members. .

17796 ■ National Restaurant Association Educational Foundation
175 W Jackson Blvd., Ste. 1500
Chicago, IL 60604-2702
Ph:(312)715-1010
Free: 800-765-2122
Co. E-mail: info@restaurant.org
URL: http://www.nraef.org
Contact: Linda Bacin, Interim Exec. Dir.
Description: Serves as an educational foundation supported by the National Restaurant Association and all segments of the foodservice industry including restaurateurs, foodservice companies, food and equipment manufacturers, distributors and trade associations. Advances the professional standards of the industry through education and research. Offers video training programs, management courses and careers information. Conducts research and maintains hall of fame. .

17797 ■ National Restaurant Association I Multi-Unit Architects, Engineers and Construction Officers Executive Study Group
1200 17th St. NW
Washington, DC 20036
Ph:(202)973-3678
Free: 800-424-5156
Fax:(202)331-2429
URL: http://www.restaurant.org/education/study-groups/maeco
Contact: Dawn Sweeney, Pres./CEO
Description: Professional architects, engineers, and construction officers from member companies of the National Restaurant Association who are involved in the construction and equipping of food service and hospitality facilities. Provides a forum for the sharing of common goals, concerns, ideas, and problems. .

17798 ■ North American Association of Food Equipment Manufacturers
161 N Clark St., Ste. 2020
Chicago, IL 60601
Ph:(312)821-0201
Fax:(312)821-0202
Co. E-mail: info@nafem.org
URL: http://www.nafem.org
Contact: Deirdre T. Flynn, Exec. VP
Description: Represents manufacturers of commercial food service equipment and supplies for restaurant, hotel, and institutional use. Conducts certification program. **Publications:** *NAFEM for Operators* (quarterly); *NAFEM in Print* (quarterly).

17799 ■ Society for Foodservice Management
15000 Commerce Pkwy., Ste. C
Mount Laurel, NJ 08054
Ph:(856)380-6829
Fax:(856)439-0525
Co. E-mail: sfm@ahint.com
URL: http://www.sfm-online.org
Contact: Carol Bracken-Tilley, Pres.
Description: Operates or maintains food service and vending facilities in businesses and industrial plants, or supply food products, equipment, or other essential industry services. Serves the needs and interests of onsite employee food service executives and management. Provides an opportunity for the exchange of experiences and opinions through study, discussion, and publications; develops greater efficiency and more economical methods of providing high-quality food and service at a reasonable cost; assists members in solving specific operating and management problems; keeps pace with the rapidly changing conditions of the employee food service segment of the industry. Develops and encourages the practice of high standards and professional conduct among management and executive personnel; provides job placement and management personnel recruiting service; sends representative to the U.S. Air Force Hennessey Award Team, which selects the Air Force base having the most superior food service. **Publications:** *Journal of Foodservice Systems* (quarterly).

DIRECTORIES OF EDUCATIONAL PROGRAMS

17800 ■ *Directory of Private Accredited Career Schools and Colleges of Technology*
Pub: Accrediting Commission of Career Schools and Colleges of Technology
Contact: Michale S. McComis, Exec. Dir.
Released: On web page. **Price:** Free. **Description:** Covers 3900 accredited post-secondary programs that provide training programs in business, trade, and technical fields, including various small business endeavors. Entries offer school name, address, phone, description of courses, job placement assistance, and requirements for admission. Arrangement is alphabetical.

REFERENCE WORKS

17801 ■ "$50 Million Project for West Chester" in *Business Courier* (Vol. 24, December 14, 2008, No. 35, pp. 1)
Pub: American City Business Journals, Inc.
Ed: Laura Baverman. **Description:** Commercial developer Scott Street Partners is planning to invest $50 million for the development of a site south of the Streets of West Chester retail center. The 31-acre project will generate 1,200 jobs, and will bring in offices, restaurants and a hotel. The development plans and the features of the site are discussed as well.

17802 ■ "$100 Million Complex To Be Built...On a Bridge" in *Business Courier* (Vol. 27, November 12, 2010, No. 28, pp. 1)
Pub: Business Courier
Ed: Lucy May. **Description:** A development firm closed a deal with the Newport Southbank Bridge Company for a $100M entertainment complex that will be built on tope of the Purple People Bridge. The proposed project will cover 150,000 square feet with attractions such as restaurants, a boutique hotel, and pubs.

17803 ■ "2010 Book of Lists" in *Austin Business JournalInc.* (Vol. 29, December 25, 2009, No. 42, pp. 1)
Pub: American City Business Journals
Description: Rankings of companies and organizations within the business services, finance, healthcare, hospitality and travel, insurance, marketing and media, professional services, real estate, education and technology industries in Austin, Texas are presented. Rankings are based on sales, business size, and other statistics.

17804 ■ "2010 Book of Lists" in *Tampa Bay Business Journal* (Vol. 30, December 22, 2009, No. 53, pp. 1)
Pub: American City Business Journals
Description: Rankings of companies and organizations within the human resources, banking and finance, business services, healthcare, real estate, technology, hospitality and travel, and education industries in the Greater Tampa Bay area are presented. Rankings are based on sales, business size, and more.

17805 ■ "Airmall Mulls I-95 Travel Plazas Bid" in *Boston Business Journal* (Vol. 29, September 2, 2011, No. 17, pp. 3)
Pub: American City Business Journals Inc.
Ed: Alexander Jackson. **Description:** Airmall USA is planning to move its food courts from the Baltimore/Washington International Thurgood Marshall Airport to the new travel plazas on Interstate 95. The plazas are up for bid.

17806 ■ "All Fired Up!" in *Small Business Opportunities* (November 2008)
Pub: Entrepreneur Media Inc.
Ed: Stan Roberts. **Description:** Profile of Brixx Wood Fired Pizza, which has launched a franchising program due to the amount of interest the company's founders received over the years; franchisees do not need experience in the food industry or pizza restaurant service business in order to open a franchise of their own because all franchisees receive comprehensive training in which they are educated on all of the necessary tools to effectively run the business.

17807 ■ "Anja Carroll; Media Director-McDonald's USA" in *Advertising Age* (Vol. 79, November 17, 2008, No. 34, pp. 6)
Pub: Crain Communications, Inc.
Ed: Emily Bryson York. **Description:** Profile of Anja Carroll who is the media director for McDonald's USA and has the challenge of choosing the right mix of media for the corporation.

17808 ■ "Aramark Rolls Out Ballpark Food Truck" in *Nation's Restaurant News* (Vol. 45, August 8, 2011, No. 16, pp. 4)
Pub: Penton Media Inc.
Ed: Ron Ruggless. **Description:** Aramark installed its first ballpark food truck serving Asian-inspired noodle bowls at the outfield concourse at Coors Field in Colorado.

17809 ■ "Are You Looking for an Environmentally Friendly Dry Cleaner?" in *Inc.* (Vol. 30, December 2008, No. 12, pp. 34)
Pub: Mansueto Ventures LLC
Ed: Shivani Vora. **Description:** Greenopia rates the greenness of 52 various kinds of businesses, including restaurants, nail salons, dry cleaners, and clothing stores. The guidebooks are sold through various retailers including Barnes & Noble and Amazon.com.

17810 ■ "Bars, Restaurants to Offer Prix Fixe Menus, Space to Race Patrons" in *Boston Business Journal* (Vol. 29, July 22, 2011, No. 11, pp. 1)
Pub: American City Business Journals Inc.
Ed: Alexander Jackson. **Description:** Restaurants and bar owners in Baltimore, Maryland have changed the way they do business as the Baltimore Grand Prix approaches. Owners have gone so far as to offering new services or renting out their entire restaurants to companies for the three-day event in September.

17811 ■ "Baskin-Robbins Tests New Upscale Concept" in *Ice Cream Reporter* (Vol. 21, September 20, 2008, No. 10, pp. 1)
Pub: Ice Cream Reporter
Description: Baskin-Robbins is opening its new upscale store, Cafe 31 in an effort to invigorate its brand. The shop will serve fondues, cakes and other treats prepared by an in-store chef.

17812 ■ "Beyond Grits: The Many Varieties of Southern Cuisine" in *Women In Business* (Vol. 62, June 2010, No. 2, pp. 14)
Pub: American Business Women's Association
Ed: Debbie Gold. **Description:** Southern cuisine is believed to be associated with grits, but the cuisine is not always with grits and offers varieties from Europe, Native American and African cooking. Southern cuisine varieties include soul food, Creole food, Cajun food and Low Country food. Examples are provided.

17813 ■ "A Bigger Slice; Buscemi's Adds Licensees, Profits" in *Crain's Detroit Business* (Vol. 23, October 15, 2007, No. 42, pp. 3)
Pub: Crain Communications Inc. - Detroit
Ed: Brent Snavely. **Description:** Six new licensees have opened under the Original Buscemi's Inc. The firm was founded in 1958 and expects to open nine more restaurants by the end of 2008.

17814 ■ "BK Franchisees Lose Sleep Over Late-Night Rule" in *Advertising Age* (Vol. 79, August 11, 2008, No. 31, pp. 1)
Pub: Crain Communications, Inc.
Ed: Emily Bryson York. **Description:** Burger King's corporate headquarters mandates that franchisees remain open until at least 2 a.m. Three Miami operators have filed a lawsuit that alleges the extended hours can be dangerous, do not make money and overtax the workforce.

17815 ■ "BK Menu Gives Casual Dining Reason to Worry" in *Advertising Age* (Vol. 79, November 17, 2008, No. 43, pp. 12)
Pub: Crain Communications, Inc.
Ed: Emily Bryson York. **Description:** Burger King is beginning to compete with such casual dining restaurants as Applebees and the Cheesecake Factory with new premium menu items, including thicker burgers and ribs; statistical data regarding the casual dining segment which continues to fall and Burger King, whose sales continue to rise is included.

17816 ■ "Blue Tractor Barbeque and Brewery, Cafe Havana" in *Crain's Detroit Business* (Vol. 23, October 1, 2007, No. 40, pp. 15)
Pub: Crain Communications Inc. - Detroit
Ed: Daniel Duggan. **Description:** Two restaurants are converted from a Buddhist Temple to become the most unique spaces in Ann Arbor, Michigan.

17817 ■ "Book of Lists 2010" in *Philadelphia Business Journal* (Vol. 28, December 25, 2009, No. 45, pp. 1)
Pub: American City Business Journals
Description: Rankings of companies and organizations within the banking, biotechnology, economic development, healthcare, hospitality, law and accounting, marketing and media, real estate, and technology industries in the Philadelphia, Pennsylvania area are presented. Rankings are based on sales, business size, and more.

17818 ■ "Burger Heirs' Long-Bottled Fight Plays Out" in *Business Courier* (Vol. 24, January 11, 2008, No. 40, pp. 1)
Pub: American City Business Journals, Inc.
Ed: Dan Monk. **Description:** Discussion of an heir to the Burger Brewing Co. Michael Cundall who has filed for permission to pursue efforts to question the legality of a 1984 transaction in which the Cundall family sold its share of the Central Investment Corp. (CIC). The court ruled that Cundall may continue fighting for his claim that his uncle, John Koons, breached fiduciary duties by pressuring the family to sell its CIC stake. Details of the court rulings are given.

17819 ■ "Burger Market Sizzling with Newcomers" in *Boston Business Journal* (Vol. 29, June 10, 2011, No. 5, pp. 1)
Pub: American City Business Journals Inc.
Ed: Ryan Sharrow. **Description:** The burger trend in Maryland is on the rise with burger joints either opening up or expanding into several branches. Startup costs for this kind of business range between $250,000 to $400,000. With a growth rate of roughly 17 percent in 2009, this so-called better burger segment of the burger categories is expected to dominate the market for quite some time.

17820 ■ "Burritos New Bag for Shopping Developer" in *Houston Business Journal* (Vol. 40, December 4, 2009, No. 30, pp. 4A)
Pub: American City Business Journals
Ed: Allison Wollam. **Description:** Houston, Texas-based Rob Johnson is the newest franchisee for Bullritos and plans to open eight area locations to market the quick-casual burrito concept. The former shopping center developer was looking for a new business sector after selling off his shopping center holdings.

17821 ■ "Choice Bits" in *Crain's Cleveland Business* (Vol. 30, June 29, 2009, No. 25, pp. 19)
Pub: Crain Communications, Inc.
Description: Ross Farro, Cleveland area restaurateur who was featured in the New York Times story about casual dining chains competing over lunch traffic through pricing.

17822 ■ "Chuy's Gears Up to Serve Atlants, Other Untapped Cities" in *Austin Business Journal* (Vol. 31, June 17, 2011, No. 15, pp. 1)
Pub: American City Business Journals Inc.
Ed: Cody Lyon. **Description:** Chuy's Holdings Inc. plans to expand into the Southeastern United States, particularly in Atlanta, Georgia. The restaurant, which secured $67.5 million in debt financing in May 2011, added 20 stores in five years and plans to open eight locations in 2011.

17823 ■ "City Board Tweaks Internet Cafe Ordinance" in *Ocala Star-Banner* (July 19, 2011)
Pub: Ocala Star-Banner
Ed: Susan Latham Carr. **Description:** Ocala Planning and Zoning Commission revised the proposed draft of the Internet Café ordinance by eliminating the cap on the number of locations allowed, but keeping fees and number of devices the same.

17824 ■ "City Hopes Casino Will Be $333M Jackpot" in *Business First Buffalo* (October 5, 2007, pp. 1)
Pub: American City Business Journals, Inc.
Ed: James Fink. **Description:** Construction of the $333 million Seneca Buffalo Creek Casino, which includes a hotel, spa and restaurants, is schedule to begin in October 2007. The 5,000 square-foot casino is expected to generate revenue and provide 1,000 jobs for the City of Buffalo, New York.

17825 ■ "Cluster Truck Events Updates on Curbside Dining Sweeps in Las Vegas" in *Food & Beverage Close-Up* (November 4, 2011)
Pub: Close-Up Media
Description: Gourmet food trucks will provide mobile dining for attendees of the South Point Gourmet Food Truck Fest held in Las Vegas, Nevada November 5, 2011.

17826 ■ "Come One, Come All" in *Black Enterprise* (Vol. 38, October 2007, No. 3, pp. 58)
Pub: Earl G. Graves Publishing Co. Inc.
Ed: Tennille M. Robinson. **Description:** Ways to market a restaurant are cited.

17827 ■ "Competitive Restaurant Scene Lures Buyers to Saratoga Springs" in *Business Review, Albany New York* (Vol. 34, October 26, 2007)
Pub: American City Business Journals, Inc.
Ed: Robin K. Cooper. **Description:** Restaurant industry in Saratoga Springs, New York, a competitive market, with the city having 102 licensed restaurants and 28,499 residents in 2006. Buyers tend to acquire restaurants in Saratoga Springs, New York due to its good market condition. Examples of restaurant acquisitions in Saratoga Springs are given.

17828 ■ *Council on Hotel, Restaurant and Institutional Education—Member Directory and Resource Guide*
Pub: International Council on Hotel, Restaurant & Institutional Education
Contact: Kathy McCarthy, CEO
E-mail: kmccarty@chrie.org
Released: Biennial, March of even years. **Covers:** Over 2,000 educational programs and institutions in the hotel, restaurant, and tourism industries. **Entries Include:** Name, address, phone, fax. **Arrangement:** Alphabetical. **Indexes:** Geographical, membership category.

17829 ■ "Counter Service" in *Nation's Restaurant News* (Vol. 45, September 26, 2011, No. 20, pp. 8)
Pub: Penton Media Inc.
Description: As food trucks continue their momentum, a study was conducted showing how many consumer would visit a food truck. Nearly two thirds of 18-44 year olds would likely visit a food truck, while individuals over the age of 65 only 38 percent would eat from a food truck.

17830 ■ "Counting Crabs: Supply Dips, Putting Crimp on Memorial Day Feast" in *Boston Business Journal* (Vol. 29, June 3, 2011, No. 4, pp. 1)
Pub: American City Business Journals Inc.
Ed: Scott Dance. **Description:** Restaurateurs in Baltimore City experienced low supply of crabs this Memorial Day 2011 owing to the early season and

the fact that many small crabbers took time off during the weekend. Sales were cut in half compared with previous Memorial Day weekends and prices rose to as much as $185 to $200 per box of crabs. Normal supply is expected, though, as summer pushes on.

17831 ■ "Credit Crunch Takes Bite Out Of McDonald's" in *Advertising Age* (Vol. 79, September 29, 2008, No. 36, pp. 1)
Pub: Crain Communications, Inc.

Ed: Emily Bryson York. **Description:** McDonald's will delay its launch of coffee bars inside its restaurants due to the banking crisis which has prompted Bank of America to halt loans to the franchise chains.

17832 ■ "Culture, Community and Chicken Fingers" in *Entrepreneur* (Vol. 37, July 2009, No. 7, pp. 96)
Pub: Entrepreneur Media, Inc.

Ed: Jason Daley. **Description:** Raising Cane's Chicken Fingers founder Todd Graves shares his experiences in running the company - from getting funding to plans for company. Graves believes that the company wants franchisees to live and breathe the brand, and that the key to its success is doing one thing and doing it right. Cane's Pillar Program, a financial support program for franchisees, is also discussed.

17833 ■ "Deals Still Get Done at Drake's Coq d'Or" in *Crain's Chicago Business* (Vol. 31, November 17, 2008, No. 46, pp. 35)
Pub: Crain Communications, Inc.

Ed: Shia Kapos. **Description:** Chicago's infamous Coq d'Or, a restaurant and lounge located at the Drake Hotel, is still a favorite establishment for noted executives but the eatery is now trying to cater to younger professionals through marketing and offering new beverages that appeal to that demographic. Many find it the perfect environment in which to close deals, relax or network.

17834 ■ *Directory of Chain Restaurant Operators*
Pub: Chain Store Guide

Released: Annual, Latest edition 2010. **Price:** $425, individuals Directory; $495, individuals online lite; $1,175, individuals online pro; $695, individuals online lite plus. **Covers:** 7,100 chain restaurant and chain hotel operators, nontraditional foodservice operators and food service management operators who operate 2 or more food service locations. **Entries Include:** 32,500 chain restaurant buyers, chefs, executives—company name, address, phone and fax numbers; 15,000 personal e-mail and web addresses; type of business; listing type; total annual sales; food service sales; system wide sales; percent of sales of alcohol; percent of sales from Internet; alcohol types served; total units; company owned units; units franchised to and from; trade names; co-branded names and numbers; food service management location types; trading areas; foreign trading areas; units by primary menu types and type of foodservice; self distributing and catering services indicators; franchise affiliations names and locations; primary distributors names and locations; parent and subsidiary company names and locations; regional; divisional; and branch office locations; distribution centers locations; year founded; public company indicator; key personnel with titles. For chain hotel operators—includes number of restaurants in hotels. For food service management operators—includes number of food service management accounts and total number of locations served. **Arrangement:** Geographical. **Indexes:** Alphabetical, type of food service, menu type, franchisee, food service management, state, exclusions.

17835 ■ "Don's Pomeroy House a Strongsville Staple" in *Crain's Cleveland Business* (Vol. 30, June 1, 2009, No. 21, pp. 12)
Pub: Crain Communications, Inc.

Ed: Kathy Ames Carr. **Description:** Profile of Don's Pomeroy House, an upscale restaurant inside a 162-year-old brick mansion. The building is listed on the National Register of Historic Places and features a main restaurant, pub and outdoor patio.

17836 ■ "Drought Takes Toll on Farmers, Restaurants" in *Saint Louis Business Journal* (Vol. 31, August 12, 2011, No. 51, pp. 1)
Pub: Saint Louis Business Journal

Ed: E.B. Solomont. **Description:** The drought in St. Louis, Missouri has adversely impacted farmers and restaurants in the areas. Diners can expect to lose some ingredients from their menus.

17837 ■ "Dunnellon Welcomes Internet Cafe Jobs" in *Ocala Star-Banner* (August 18, 2011)
Pub: Ocala Star-Banner

Ed: Fred Hiers. **Description:** Despite the fact that a few Internet cafes offering patrons to win cash and are facing legal challenges, the city's planning commission would welcome the cafes in order to provide more jobs for its residents.

17838 ■ "Eat, Drink and Be a Success" in *Entrepreneur* (Vol. 37, August 2009, No. 8, pp. 70)
Pub: Entrepreneur Media, Inc.

Ed: Joel Holland. **Description:** Profile of Fritz Brogan, who is a full time student but also runs a successful bar and restaurant named Gin & Tonic and Kitchen. The bar was built with their target audience in mind which happens to be Brogan's college friends.

17839 ■ "Eat Up!" in *Entrepreneur* (Vol. 36, April 2008, No. 4, pp. 104)
Pub: Entrepreneur Media, Inc.

Ed: Tracy Stapp. **Description:** Provides a list of the top restaurant franchises. The restaurant franchises presented are picked out from the 2008 Franchise 500 ranking and are listed according to category.

17840 ■ "Entrepreneurship: As Cool As It Gets" in *Canadian Business* (Vol. 80, January 29, 2007, No. 3, pp. 10)
Pub: Rogers Media

Ed: Norman de Bono. **Description:** The proposed construction of a restaurant with ice in Dubai by the Canadian firm Iceculture Inc. for the Sharaf Group is discussed. The growth of the clientele of Iceculture Inc. is described.

17841 ■ *Everything I Know About Business I Learned at McDonald's: The 7 Leadership Principles that Drive Break Out Success*
Pub: The McGraw-Hill Companies

Ed: Paul Facella. **Released:** 2009. **Price:** $24.95. **Description:** McDonald's management philosophy is as simple as its menu, but don't underestimate the effectiveness of founder Ray Kroc's business plan.

17842 ■ "Explosive Growth: Wings Over To Triple In Size By 2010" in *Small Business Opportunities* (Fall 2007)
Pub: Harris Publications Inc.

Ed: Michael L. Corne. **Description:** Profile of Wings Over, a franchised chain of restaurants offering chicken wings in 22 flavors; all items are cooked to order.

17843 ■ "A Failed Promise: A Dream Job Gone...or Just Delayed?" in *Restaurant Business* (Vol. 107, September 2008, No. 9, pp. 34)
Pub: Ideal Media

Ed: Patricia Cobe, Joan M. Lang, Dana Tanyeri. **Description:** Profile of Jeremy Lycanwas, executive chef who taught at the California Culinary Academy. Lycanwas tells of accepting a position as executive chef from his mentor, and later started his own restaurant.

17844 ■ "Fair Exchange" in *Food and Drink* (Winter 2010, pp. 84)
Pub: Schofield Media Group

Ed: Don Mardak. **Description:** Bartering can assist firms in the food and beverage industry to attract new customers, maximize resources, and reduce cash expenses.

17845 ■ "The Final Piece; Lowe's to Fill Last Big Parcel Near Great Lakes Crossing" in *Crain's Detroit Business* (March 10, 2008)
Pub: Crain Communications, Inc.

Ed: Daniel Duggan. **Description:** Silverman Development Co. is developing a Lowe's home-improvement store on the last major retail parcel near the intersection of I-75 and Joslyn Road, an area which was once desolate but is now home to several restaurants and other retail facilities.

17846 ■ "Food-Truck Learnings Travel Indoors" in *Nation's Restaurant News* (Vol. 45, June 27, 2011, No. 13, pp. 3)
Pub: Penton Media Inc.

Ed: Lisa Jennings. **Description:** Challenges faced by owners of food truck businesses are discussed. Ways a food truck can be used to promote a restaurant's menu are covered.

17847 ■ "For Staying True: Bobby Flam: Jumbo's Restaurant, Miami" in *Inc.* (Volume 32, December 2010, No. 10, pp. 102)
Pub: Inc. Magazine

Ed: Leigh Buchanan. **Description:** Profile of Bobby Flam, owner of Jumbo's Restaurant in Miami, Florida.

17848 ■ "Former NFL Player Tackles a New Restaurant Concept" in *Inc.* (Vol. 33, September 2011, No. 7, pp. 32)
Pub: Inc. Magazine

Ed: Nadine Heintz. **Description:** Matt Chatham, former NFL player, launched SkyCrepers, a chain of fast-serve crepe shops with his wife Erin. Chatham entered Babson College's MBA program after retiring from football.

17849 ■ "Franchisees Lose Battle Against BK" in *Advertising Age* (Vol. 79, June 2, 2008, No. 22, pp. 46)
Pub: Crain Communications, Inc.

Ed: Emily Bryson York. **Description:** Burger King has had continuing litigation with former franchisees from New York, Luan and Elizabeth Sadik, who claim that Burger King's double cheeseburger, along with additional problems, created the environment for their eventual insolvency. Burger King has since terminated its test of selling the double cheeseburger for $1, although the company declined to comment on the reason for this decision.

17850 ■ "Fries With That?" in *Canadian Business* (Vol. 81, September 29, 2008, No. 16, pp. 33)
Pub: Rogers Media Ltd.

Ed: Calvin Leung. **Description:** Profile of Toronto-based New York Fries, which has four stores in South Korea, is planning to expand further as well as into Hong Kong and Macau; the company also has a licensee in the United Arab Emirates whom is also planning to expand.

17851 ■ "Game On at Jordan's New Spot" in *Crain's Chicago Business* (Vol. 34, October 24, 2011, No. 42, pp. 34)
Pub: Crain Communications Inc.

Ed: Laura Bianchi. **Description:** Michael Jordan partnered with Cornerstone Restaurant Group to launch Michael Jordan's Steakhouse in Chicago. Details are included.

17852 ■ "Hard Rock on Pike" in *Puget Sound Business Journal* (Vol. 29, September 5, 2008, No. 20, pp. 1)
Pub: American City Business Journals

Ed: Jeanne Lang Jones. **Description:** A branch of the Hard Rock Cafe is opening in 2009 in the Liberty Building on Pike Street in downtown Seattle, Washington. The location is being renovated as a green building; the restaurant and concert venue will seat 300 patrons and has a rooftop deck and memorabilia shop.

17853 ■ "Health Care Leads Sectors Attracting Capital" in *Hispanic Business* (Vol. 30, March 2008, No. 3, pp. 14)
Pub: Hispanic Business

Ed: Scott Williams. **Description:** Discusses the capital gains of Hispanic-owned companies and other Hispanic leaders in the investment and retail fields in the year 2007. Sectors like health care, media, food and technology saw a healthy flow of capital due to successful mergers, acquisitions and increased private equity investments.

17854 ■ "Here's the Deal" in *Crain's Cleveland Business* (Vol. 30, June 15, 2009, No. 23, pp. 14)
Pub: Crain Communications, Inc.
Description: Incentives being offered by hotels, restaurants, golf courses and major chains in order to promote bookings for meetings or conferences in the Cleveland area are listed.

17855 ■ "Holy Wasabi! Sushi Not Just For Parents Anymore" in *Chicago Tribune* (March 13, 2008)
Pub: McClatchy-Tribune Information Services
Ed: Christopher Borrelli. **Description:** Wicker Park cooking school, The Kid's Table, specializes in cooking classes for pre-teens; Elena Marre who owns the school was surprised when she was asked to plan a children's party in which she would teach a course in sushi making. More and more adolescents and small children are eating sushi.

17856 ■ "Homes, Not Bars, Stay Well Tended" in *Advertising Age* (Vol. 79, January 28, 2008, No. 4, pp. 8)
Pub: Crain Communications, Inc.
Ed: Jeremy Mullman. **Description:** Due to the downturn in the economy, consumers are drinking less at bars and restaurants; however, according to the Distilled Spirits Council of the United States, they are still purchasing expensive liquor to keep in their homes.

17857 ■ "How I Did It: George Naddaff: From Spit 'n' Shine Boy To Boston Chicken and Beyond" in *Inc.* (February 2008, pp. 98-101)
Pub: Gruner & Jahr USA Publishing
Ed: Leigh Buchanan. **Description:** Profile of George Naddaff, founder of Boston Chicken as well as numerous other business ventures.

17858 ■ "Hyde Park Hungry for Expansion at Cap" in *Business First-Columbus* (October 12, 2007, pp. A1)
Pub: American City Business Journals, Inc.
Ed: Dan Eaton. **Description:** The Cap, an area developed for the retail and restaurant industry, is experiencing major changes such as Hyde Park Restaurant System's planned expansion, and the expected departure of other tenants. The expansion of Hyde Park will lead to the relocation of Schakolad Chocolate Factory.

17859 ■ *In-N-Out Burger: A Behind-the-Counter Look at the Fast-Food Chain That Breaks All the Rules*
Pub: HarperCollins Publishers
Ed: Stacy Perman. **Released:** April 2009. **Price:** $24. 99. **Description:** Business analysis of the factors that helped In-N-Out Burgers, a family owned burger chain in California, along with a history of its founding family, the Synders.

17860 ■ "In the Raw: Karyn Calabrese Brings Healthy Dining to a New Sophisticated Level" in *Black Enterprise* (Vol. 41, September 2010)
Pub: Earl G. Graves Publishing Co. Inc.
Ed: Sonia Alleyne. **Description:** Profile of Karyn Calabrese whose businesses are based in Chicago, Illinois. Calabrese has launched a complete line of products (vitamins and beauty items), services (spa, chiropractic, and acupuncture treatments), and restaurants to bring health dining and lifestyles to a better level.

17861 ■ "Inn at Saratoga Owners Buy Caribbean Hotel" in *Business Review, Albany New York* (Vol. 34, November 2, 2007, No. 31, pp. 3)
Pub: American City Business Journals, Inc.
Ed: Robin K. Cooper. **Description:** Bob Israel, owner of the Inn at Saratoga in Saratoga Springs, New York, made a $3 million to $4 million acquisition of the 22-room Mafolie Hotel and Restaurant in the Island of St. Thomas in the Caribbean. This is Israel's first real estate venture out of Saratoga Springs.

17862 ■ "Internet Cafe Logging in to Chardon Plaza?" in *News-Herald* (July 16, 2011)
Pub: Journal Register Ohio
Ed: Betsy Scott. **Description:** Pearl's High Rollers Inc. applied for an Internet sweepstakes café license that would reside in a vacant space in Chardon Plaza. City officials have created regulations for such businesses and Pearl's applied for a license and is awaiting approval.

17863 ■ "Internet Café 'Sweepstakes' Expanding in Arkansas" in *Arkansas Business* (Vol. 28, September 5, 2011, No. 36, pp. 1)
Pub: Arkansas Business Publishing Group
Ed: Mark Friedman. **Description:** Despite the fact that video games resembling casino games in Lucky's Business Center in Little Rock, representatives of the Internet café insist they are not offering gambling but a type of sweepstakes promotion and that business model is thriving. Lucky's, Cancun Cyber Café & Business Center Inc., and Wild Rides Business Center & Internet Café has opened in the area in the last few weeks.

17864 ■ "Invasion of the New York Pizza" in *Charlotte Observer* (February 5, 2007)
Pub: Knight-Ridder/Tribune Business News
Ed: Leigh Dyer. **Description:** Dozens of new pizza restaurants are cropping up in the Charlotte, North Carolina area, a result of New Yorker transplants.

17865 ■ "It Sure Beats Pizza: San Francisco Company Delivers Gourmet Lunches to Businesses" in *Inc.* (Vol. 33, November 2011, No. 9, pp. 30)
Pub: Inc. Magazine
Ed: Bobbie Gossage. **Description:** Gastronaut caters daily meals to local companies. The firm was started by two former chefs at Google and employs 24 people to deliver buffet-style meals to eight businesses, with lunches costing $16 to $18 per serving.

17866 ■ "It's all Kosher at Downtown Eatery/Bakery" in *AZ Daily Star* (July 10, 2008)
Pub: Arizona Daily Star
Ed: Valerie Vinyard. **Description:** Rabbi James Botwright and partner Wayne Anderson are profiled. Details of how the partners opened their bakery and eatery in Tucson, Arizona. Botwright, who attended culinary school in San Francisco, learned much from his grandfather who was a pastry chef.

17867 ■ "The Kitchen is Closed; Eateries Forced Out by Soaring Rents, Declining Revenues" in *Crain's New York Business* (January 21, 2008)
Pub: Crain Communications, Inc.
Ed: Lisa Fickenscher. **Description:** Many restaurants have already closed in the area and experts expect many more will follow due to skyrocketing rents and declining revenues.

17868 ■ "Learn New Ideas from Experienced Menu Makers" in *Nation's Restaurant News* (Vol. 45, June 27, 2011, No. 13, pp. 82)
Pub: Penton Media Inc.
Ed: Nancy Kruse. **Description:** National Restaurant Association Restaurant, Hotel-Motel Show featured the Food Truck Spot, a firm committed to all aspects of mobile catering, foodtruck manufacturers, leasers of fully equipped truck and a food-truck franchising group.

17869 ■ *Lessons in Service From Charlie Trotter*
Pub: Ten Speed Press
Ed: Edmund Lawler. **Released:** March 2004. **Price:** $24.95. **Description:** Chef Charlie Trotter, owner of a restaurant, shares insight into managing any business successfully.

17870 ■ "Looking To Hire Young? Be Careful" in *Boston Business Journal* (Vol. 30, November 19, 2010, No. 43, pp. 1)
Pub: Boston Business Journal
Ed: Lisa van der Pool. **Description:** The Massachusetts Commission Against Discrimination (MCAD) has been using undercover job applicants to expose discrimination. Cabot's Ice Cream and Restaurant has been accused of denying older workers equal employment opportunities. MCAD has discovered unfair hiring practices such as hiring high school and college students.

17871 ■ "Losing the Top Job - And Winning It Back" in *Harvard Business Review* (Vol. 88, October 2010, No. 10, pp. 136)
Pub: Harvard Business School Publishing
Ed: Alison Beard. **Description:** Michael Mack chronicles the changes in perspectives that occurred when he was fired from Garden Fresh, a restaurant firm he co-owned. Once again at the company helm, he is now more receptive to outside input and acknowledges the importance of work-life balance.

17872 ■ "Lux Coffees, Breads Push Chains to React" in *Advertising Age* (Vol. 77, June 26, 2006, No. 26, pp. S14)
Pub: Crain Communications, Inc.
Ed: Kate MacArthur. **Description:** Fast-food giants such as McDonald's, Burger King, Dunkin' Donuts and Subway have adjusted their menus in order to become more competitive with gourmet coffee shops and bakeries like Panera Bread and Starbucks which have taken a large share in the market. Statistical data included.

17873 ■ "MBA Project Turns on Tastebuds" in *The Business Journal - Serving Phoenix and the Valley of the Sun* (Vol. 28, August 15, 2008, No. 50)
Pub: American City Business Journals, Inc.
Ed: Angela Gonzales. **Description:** Amol Khade, Venkat Nallapati and Govind Arora, master of business administration graduates from Thunderbird School of Global Management, have opened an Indian restaurant, called The Daba, in Tempe, Arizona. The Indian name of the restaurant means 'a place for travelers to stop for rest and food'. Franchise plans for the restaurant are discussed.

17874 ■ "McD's Dollar-Menu Fixation Sparks Revolt" in *Advertising Age* (Vol. 79, June 2, 2008, No. 22, pp. 1)
Pub: Crain Communications, Inc.
Ed: Emily Bryson York. **Description:** McDonald's franchisees say that low-cost dollar-menu offerings are impacting their bottom line and many have discontinued the dollar-menu altogether due to rising commodity costs, an increase in minimum wage and consumers trading down to the lower-price items.

17875 ■ "McD's Picks a Soda Fight; Takes on 7-Eleven With $1 Pop as Economy Softens" in *Crain's Chicago Business* (April 14, 2008)
Pub: Crain Communications, Inc.
Ed: David Sterrett. **Description:** McDonald's Corp. is urging franchise owners to slash prices on large soft drinks to one dollar this summer to win customers from convenience store chains like 7-Eleven.

17876 ■ "McD's Tries to Slake Consumer Thirst for Wider Choice of Drinks" in *Advertising Age* (Vol. 79, June 9, 2008, No. 23, pp. 1)
Pub: Crain Communications, Inc.
Ed: Natalie Zmuda; Emily Bryson York. **Description:** McDonald's is testing the sale of canned and bottled drinks in about 150 locations in an attempt to offer more options to consumers who are going elsewhere for their beverage choices.

17877 ■ "McD's Warms Up For Olympics Performance" in *Advertising Age* (Vol. 79, July 7, 2008, No. 26, pp. 8)
Pub: Crain Communications, Inc.
Ed: Description: Overview of McDonald's marketing plans for the company's sponsorship of the Olympics which includes a website, an alternate-reality game, names featured on U.S. athletes and on-the-ground activities.

17878 ■ "Menchie's Tops Restaurant Business' Future 50 List" in *Ice Cream Reporter* (Vol. 23, August 20, 2010, No. 9, pp. 4)
Pub: Ice Cream Reporter
Description: Menchie's, frozen yogurt shop, announced it placed first in the Restaurant Business

Magazine's Future 50, ranking the franchise the fastest-growing in the food industry.

17879 ■ "More SouthPark Shopping" in *Charlotte Business Journal* (Vol. 25, July 16, 2010, No. 17, pp. 1)
Pub: Charlotte Business Journal
Ed: Will Boye. **Description:** Charlotte, North Carolina-based Bissel Companies has announced plans to expand its retail presence at the Siskey and Sharon properties in SouthPark. Bissel Companies has requested a rezoning to a mixed-use development classification so that it can utilize the entire ground floor of the Siskey building for restaurant and retail uses.

17880 ■ *My Life From Scratch: A Sweet Journey of Starting Over, One Cake at a Time*
Pub: Broadway Books
Released: June 8, 2010. **Price:** $14.00. **Description:** Lively account of Old World recipes, Bullock-Prado, a former Hollywood film developer and sister to actress Sandra Bullock, recounts the joys and heartbreak of running her own patisserie in Montpelier, Vermont. Having fled Los Angeles with her husband, Ray for the simpler pleasures of a small town near the Green Mountains, she opened her own bake shop, Gesine Confectionary in 2004, mostly on the fame of the macaroons she refashioned from her German mother's favorite almond treat, mandelhoernchen (and the casual mention of her sister in an interview). Her memoir follows one day in a busy baker's life, from waking at 3 a.m. to prepare the batter and bake her croissants, scones, and sticky buns, before opening her shop at 7 a.m., through the hectic lunch, and 3 p.m. tea time.

17881 ■ "New CEO For Friendly's" in *Ice Cream Reporter* (Vol. 23, September 20, 2010, No. 10, pp. 1)
Pub: Ice Cream Reporter
Description: Friendly Ice Cream Corporation named Harsha V. Agadi as new chief executive officer. Agadi has 24 years experience in food service, most recently serving as CEO of Church's Chicken.

17882 ■ "A New Flavor for Second Street: Lamberts Chef Backs New Restaurant" in *Austin Business JournalInc.* (Vol. 28, January 2, 2009)
Pub: American City Business Journals
Ed: Sandra Zaragoza. **Description:** Chef Larry McGuire has teamed up with the Icon Group to develop the La Condesa restaurant and the Malverde lounge in the Second Street district. The La Condesa restaurant will be a Mexico City-inspired restaurant, while the Malverde lounge atop the La Condesa will host DJs and live music.

17883 ■ "A New Mix of Tenants Settles In" in *Crain's New York Business* (Vol. 24, January 14, 2008, No. 2, pp. 26)
Pub: Crain Communications, Inc.
Ed: Andrew Marks. **Description:** More and more nonfinancial firms are relocating downtown due to the new retailers and restaurants that are reshaping the look and feel of lower Manhattan.

17884 ■ "New Technology, Growing Fan Base Fuel Truck Trend" in *Nation's Restaurant News* (Vol. 45, June 13, 2001, No. 12, pp. 16)
Pub: Penton Media Inc.
Ed: Ron Ruggless. **Description:** Food trucks drove more interest at this year's National Restaurant Association Restaurant Hotel-Motel Show in Chicago. The trend continues to show long-term growth.

17885 ■ "Nighttime Shuttle to Connect Detroit, Ferndale, Royal Oak" in *Crain's Detroit Business* (Vol. 24, October 6, 2008, No. 40, pp. 24)
Pub: Crain Communications, Inc.
Ed: Nancy Kaffer. **Description:** With hopes of bridging the social gap between the cities and suburbs, Chris Ramos has launched The Night Move, a new shuttle service that will ferry passengers between Royal Oak, Ferndale and downtown Detroit. The cost for a round trip ticket is $12.

17886 ■ "Nurturing Talent for Tomorrow" in *Restaurants and Institutions* (Vol. 118, September 15, 2008, No. 14, pp. 90)
Pub: Reed Business Information
Description: Hormel Foods Corporation and The Culinary Institute of America (CIA) have teamed to develop The Culinary Enrichment and Innovation Program that supports future culinary leaders by providing creative and competitive staff development. Sixteen students attend four three-day sessions at the CIA's campus in Hyde Park, New York; sessions include classroom teaching, one-on-one interaction with leading culinarians, and hands-on kitchen time.

17887 ■ "Ohio Franchise Buys 21 Jacksonville Area Papa John's" in *Florida Times-Union* (December 20, 2010)
Pub: Florida Times-Union
Ed: Mark Basch. **Description:** Ohio-based Papa John's pizza franchise acquired 21 of the restaurants in Duval, Clay and St. Johns counties in Jacksonville, Florida.

17888 ■ "Old Friends Make Old Buildings Successful Restaurants" in *Crain's Detroit Business* (Vol. 24, February 4, 2008, No. 5, pp. 14)
Pub: Crain Communications Inc. - Detroit
Ed: Brent Snavely. **Description:** Profiles of Jon Carlson and Gregory Lobdell, founders of ten new restaurants in Ann Arbor, Royal Oak, and Traverse City, Michigan, and their plans to add four more in the near future.

17889 ■ "On the Green: Sheila Johnson Adds $35 Million Golf Resort To Her Expanding Portfolio" in *Black Enterprise* (January 2008)
Pub: Earl G. Graves Publishing Co. Inc.
Ed: Donna M. Owens. **Description:** Profile of Sheila Johnson, CEO of Salamander Hospitality LLC, made history when she purchased the Innisbrook Resort and Golf Club, making her the first African American woman to own this type of property. The resort includes four championship golf courses, six swimming pools, four restaurants, eleven tennis courts, three conference halls, and a nature preserve.

17890 ■ "Ordering Pizza Hut From Your Facebook Page?" in *Advertising Age* (Vol. 79, November 10, 2008, No. 42, pp. 50)
Pub: Crain Communications, Inc.
Ed: Emily Bryson York. **Description:** Fast-food chains are experimenting with delivery/takeout services via social networks such as Facebook and iPhone applications. This also allows the chains to build valuable databases of their customers.

17891 ■ *The Pampered Chef*
Pub: Doubleday Broadway Publishing Group
Ed: Doris Christopher. **Price:** $24.95.

17892 ■ "Paying the Price" in *Baltimore Business Journal* (Vol. 28, July 9, 2010, No. 9, pp. 1)
Pub: Baltimore Business Journal
Ed: Emily Mullin. **Description:** Crab prices have never been higher in Baltimore, Maryland and businesses have been led to count on strengthening demand for seafood. For instance, the average price for a dozen large crabs has increased by 5 percent to $58.90. How restaurants have responded to the increase in prices is discussed, along with factors that might have caused the harvest of smaller crabs.

17893 ■ "Pepsi Co. Breaches the Walls of Coke Fortress McDonald's" in *Globe & Mail* (March 13, 2007, pp. B1)
Pub: CTVglobemedia Publishing Inc.
Ed: Keith McArthur. **Description:** Soft drinks giant Pepsi Co. has entered an agreement with fast food chain McDonald's for offering its products in outlets across Canada. Earlier Coca-Cola Co. used to offer its exclusive products in these outlets.

17894 ■ "Personal Pizza Goes Franchise Route" in *Atlanta Journal-Constitution* (December 22, 2010)
Pub: Atlanta Journal-Constitution
Ed: Bob Townsend. **Description:** Your Pie, developer of the personal-size pizza franchise concept is profiled.

17895 ■ "A Piece of the Action" in *Black Enterprise* (Vol. 38, January 2008, No. 6, pp. 42)
Pub: Earl G. Graves Publishing Co. Inc.
Ed: Alan Hughes. **Description:** Andre Williams, owner of Kaze Sushi restaurant, offered generous incentive plan-equity in the business in order to acquire Chef Kaze Chan and Chef Hari Chan. Williams' entrepreneurial pursuits are discussed.

17896 ■ "Plan B Saloon Opened New Year's Eve" in *Bellingham Business Journal* (Vol. February 2010, pp. 7)
Pub: Sound Publishing Inc.
Description: Plan B Saloon, located in Bellingham, Washington, opened New Year's Eve 2010. The bar/restaurant will feature classic American food consisting of sandwiches and burgers and will host local musicians on Friday and Saturday nights.

17897 ■ "Plans for $160M Condo Resort in Wisconsin Dells Moves Forward" in *Commercial Property News* (March 18, 2008)
Pub: Nielsen Company
Description: Plans for the Grand Cambrian Resort in the Wisconsin Dells is discussed. The luxury condominium resort will include condos, townhomes, and condo-hotel style residences, two water parts, meeting space and indoor entertainment space, as well as a spa, four restaurants and retail offerings.

17898 ■ "Proposed Triangle Redo in Motion" in *Crain's Cleveland Business* (Vol. 28, October 15, 2007, No. 41, pp. 1)
Pub: Crain Communications, Inc.
Ed: Stan Bullard. **Description:** Zaremba Homes and MRN Ltd. are partnering to redevelop the so-called Triangle section of University Circle. The proposed project will include a total of 434 new rental and for-sale residential suites and as much as 227,000 square feet of retail and restaurant space.

17899 ■ "Quiznos Franchisees Walloped by Recession" in *Advertising Age* (Vol. 79, October 20, 2008, No. 39, pp. 3)
Pub: Crain Communications, Inc.
Ed: Emily Bryson York. **Description:** While the recession has taken a toll on the entire restaurant industry, a number of Quiznos franchisees claim to have been disproportionately affected due to lackluster marketing, higher-than-average commodity costs, competition with Subway and a premium-pricing structure that is incompatible with a tight economy.

17900 ■ "Ready, Aim, (Cool) Fire" in *Saint Louis Business Journal* (Vol. 32, September 2, 2011, No. 1, pp. 1)
Pub: Saint Louis Business Journal
Ed: E.B. Solomont. **Description:** Coolfire Originals' CEO Jeff Keane is co-producing 'Welcome Sweetie Pie's' with Los Angeles, California-based Pilgrims Films and Television Films for the Oprah Winfrey Network. The reality show focuses on restaurant owner Robbie Montgomery of Sweetie Pie's in St. Louis, Missouri.

17901 ■ "Ready for the Back Burner" in *Barron's* (Vol. 88, March 17, 2008, No. 11, pp. 47)
Pub: Dow Jones & Company, Inc.
Ed: Vito J. Racanelli. **Description:** McDonald's has promised to return $15 billion to $17 billion to shareholders in 2007-2009 but headwinds are rising for the company. December, 2007 same-store sales were flat and the company's traffic growth in the U.S. is slowing. Its shares are likely to trade in tandem with the market until recession fears recede.

17902 ■ "A Recipe for Change" in *Canadian Business* (Vol. 80, October 22, 2007, No. 21, pp. 25)
Pub: Rogers Media
Ed: Erin Pooley. **Description:** Market conditions have changed and customers around the world are demanding low-fat alternatives. Labor costs have risen and so did the price of foodstuffs. The impacts of this on fast food restaurants as well as the measures they have taken to cope with the new demands are discussed.

17903 ■ "Recipe for Disaster?" in *Sacramento Business Journal* (Vol. 25, July 4, 2008, No. 18, pp. 1)
Pub: American City Business Journals, Inc.
Ed: Mark Anderson. **Description:** Restaurateurs are challenged with balancing rising operating costs and what customers are willing to pay for their services. Flour prices in 2008 have increased by 46 percent from April 2007. Other views on the situation, as well as trends, forecasts and statistics on sales, outlook on economic conditions, consumer price index, and the typical split of restaurant revenue, are presented.

17904 ■ "Recovery on Tap for 2010?" in *Orlando Business Journal* (Vol. 26, January 1, 2010, No. 31, pp. 1)
Pub: American City Business Journals
Ed: Melanie Stawicki Azam, Richard Bilbao, Christopher Boyd, Anjali Fluker. **Description:** Economic forecasts for Central Florida's leading business sectors in 2010 are presented. These sectors include housing, film and TV, sports business, law, restaurants, aviation, tourism and hospitality, banking and finance, commercial real estate, retail, health care, insurance, higher education, and manufacturing. According to some local executives, Central Florida's economy will slowly recover in 2010.

17905 ■ "Reinventing the Cheeseburger" in *Inc.* (November 2007, pp. 124-125)
Pub: Gruner & Jahr USA Publishing
Ed: Chris Lydgate. **Description:** Profile of Burgerville's Tom Mears, who turned his drive-through burger restaurant green.

17906 ■ "Report: McD's Pepsi Score Best With Young Hispanics" in *Brandweek* (Vol. 49, April 21, 2008, No. 16, pp. 8)
Pub: VNU Business Media, Inc.
Ed: Della de Lafuente. **Description:** According to a new report, in order to reach Hispanic Gen Yers, marketing strategists need to understand this demographic's "bi-dentity," something which has proved an elusive task to many marketers. Another trend is the emergence of Latinas who have careers, as opposed to just jobs. There is an opportunity to tap this new, young and empowered female market with innovative messaging. Statistical data included.

17907 ■ *The Restaurant Manager's Handbook: How to Set Up, Operate, and Manage a Financially Successful Food Service Operation*
Pub: Atlantic Publishing Company
Released: September 25, 2007. **Price:** $79.95. **Description:** Insight is offered on running a successful food service business. Nine new chapters detail restaurant layout, new equipment, principles for creating a safer work environment, and new effective techniques to interview, hire, train, and manage employees.

17908 ■ *Restaurant Marketing for Owners and Managers*
Pub: John Wiley & Sons, Incorporated
Ed: Patti J. Shock, John T. Bowen, John M. Stefanelli. **Released:** October 2003. **Price:** $30.00. **Description:** Tools for combining marketing theory to practice in a restaurant business are covered.

17909 ■ "Restaurants Dish Up Meal Deals To Attract Customers" in *Crain's Detroit Business* (Vol. 24, October 6, 2008, No. 40, pp. 1)
Pub: Crain Communications, Inc.
Ed: Nathan Skid. **Description:** Restaurateurs are devising many creative and rewarding incentives to get customers to frequent their establishments during this economic crisis. Innovative ways in which even higher-end establishments are drawing in business are discussed.

17910 ■ "Restaurants Rewrite Menu to Get Financing" in *Saint Louis Business Journal* (Vol. 31, August 19, 2011, No. 52, pp. 1)
Pub: Saint Louis Business Journal
Ed: Peter Solomont. **Description:** St. Louis, Missouri-based restaurants are finding new ways to secure financing. The weak economy has made it difficult for restaurants to secure bank financing.

17911 ■ "Restaurants Slammed by Economy" in *Business Courier* (Vol. 24, April 4, 2008, No. 52, pp. 1)
Pub: American City Business Journals, Inc.
Ed: Lisa Biank Fasig. **Description:** Restaurants in Cincinnati are closing some of their stores due to growing costs of fuel, eggs and meat. The establishments are also affected by lower consumer spending that was brought on by unemployment, higher grocery prices and foreclosures. The economic problems in Cincinnati are also compared to those in other cities.

17912 ■ "Restaurants Stewing Over Food Prices" in *The Business Journal-Milwaukee* (Vol. 25, August 22, 2008, No. 48, pp. A1)
Pub: American City Business Journals, Inc.
Ed: David Doege. **Description:** Many restaurant operators in the Milwaukee area are changing their menus, increasing prices and decreasing workers' hours amid the soaring prices of commodities. The prices of some staples have risen by over 50 percent since 2006. The impacts of the continued rise in food prices are examined further.

17913 ■ "Restaurateurs Follow High-End Apartments Into Kendall Square" in *Boston Business Journal* (Vol. 31, July 22, 2011, No. 26, pp. 3)
Pub: Boston Business Journal
Ed: Lisa van der Pool. **Description:** Kendall Square in Cambridge, Massachusetts is attracting restaurants, 16 of which have opened since 2009. The influx of restaurants is being driven by lower commercial rents.

17914 ■ "Ritz Kapalua Sells 93 Suites for $176M to Fund Renovation" in *Commercial Property News* (March 17, 2008)
Pub: Nielsen Company
Description: Ritz-Carlton, Kapalua in Lahaina, Hawaii sold ninety-three of its units in order to fund renovations of 463 rooms and suites along with construction of a new spa and fitness center, new and expanded restaurants and pools and an environmental education center for children.

17915 ■ "Salad Creations To Open 2nd Location" in *Crain's Detroit Business* (Vol. 24, March 3, 2008, No. 9, pp. 26)
Pub: Crain Communications Inc. - Detroit
Ed: Brent Snavely. **Description:** Salad Creations, a franchise restaurant that allows customers to create their own salads and also offers soups and sandwiches; Salad Creations plans to open a total of five locations by the end of 2008.

17916 ■ "Seasonal Franchises" in *Franchising World* (Vol. 42, August 2010, No. 8, pp. 50)
Pub: International Franchise Association
Ed: Jennifer Lemcke. **Description:** Seasonal franchises, such as tax businesses can be slow during the summer months. Restaurants are slow during the months of January and February. The various challenges faced by seasonal franchises are examined.

17917 ■ *Setting the Table*
Pub: HarperCollins Publishers Inc.
Ed: Danny Meyer. **Price:** $29.95. **Description:** Renowned restauranteur profiles his success in the hospitality business.

17918 ■ "Seward Restaurant Garners Accolades" in *Alaska Business Monthly* (Vol. 27, October 2011, No. 10, pp. 9)
Pub: Alaska Business Publishing Company
Ed: Nancy Pounds. **Description:** Resurrection Road House of Seward, Alaska won the Wine Spectator's Aware of Excellence in 2011. The award honors restaurants that handle at least 100 gourmet wines that are skillfully paired with the cuisine.

17919 ■ "Social Networkers for Hire" in *Black Enterprise* (Vol. 40, December 2009, No. 5, pp. 56)
Pub: Earl G. Graves Publishing Co., Inc.
Ed: Brittany Hutson. **Description:** Companies are utilizing social networking sites in order to market their brand and personally connect with consumers and are increasingly looking to social media specialists to help with this task. Aliya S. King is one such web strategist, working for ICED Media by managing their Twitter, Facebook, YouTube and Flickr accounts for one of their publicly traded restaurant clients.

17920 ■ "Soured Relationship Plays Out in Courts" in *The Business Journal-Serving Greater Tampa Bay* (Vol. 28, September 19, 2008, No. 39)
Pub: American City Business Journals, Inc.
Ed: Janet Leiser. **Description:** Heirs of developer Julian Hawthorne Lifset won a court battle to end a 50-year lease with Specialty Restaurants Corp. in Rocky Point. The decision opens the Tampa Bay prime waterfront property for new development.

17921 ■ "Speakers Address Authenticity, R&D Evolution" in *Nation's Restaurant News* (Vol. 45, October 24, 2011, No. 32, pp. 32)
Pub: Penton Media Inc.
Ed: Bret Thorn. **Description:** Culinary trends are discussed, along with an examination of the food truck trend and how this small sector is creating a great influence on food and communication with customers and delivery expectations.

17922 ■ "Startup to Serve Bar Scene" in *Austin Business JournalInc.* (Vol. 29, December 18, 2009, No. 41, pp. 1)
Pub: American City Business Journals
Ed: Christopher Calnan. **Description:** Startup ATX Innovation Inc. of Austin, Texas has developed a test version of TabbedOut, a Web-based tool that would facilitate mobile phone-based restaurant and bar bill payment. TabbedOut has been tested by six businesses in Austin and will be available to restaurant and bar owners for free. Income would be generated by ATX through a 99-cent convenience charge per transaction.

17923 ■ "Sweet Tea; Neil Golden" in *Advertising Age* (Vol. 79, November 17, 2008, No. 43, pp. 4)
Pub: Crain Communications, Inc.
Ed: Emily Bryson York. **Description:** McDonald's launch of iced coffee and sweat tea, which were promoted via price cuts over the summer, helped to boost sales at the fast-food chain.

17924 ■ "Taco Bell; David Ovens" in *Advertising Age* (Vol. 79, November 17, 2008, No. 43, pp. S2)
Pub: Crain Communications, Inc.
Ed: Emily Bryson York. **Description:** Due to the addition of new products such as a low-calorie, low-fat Fresco menu; a fruity iced beverage; and a value initiative, Taco Bell now accounts for half of Yum Brands' profits. The chain has also benefited from a new chief marketing officer, David Ovens, who oversees ad support.

17925 ■ "Taking a Pounding; Recession Fears Weigh Down Steakhouse Operator Morton's" in *Crain's Chicago Business* (March 31, 2008)
Pub: Crain Communications, Inc.
Ed: Monee Fields-White. **Description:** Morton's Restaurant Group Inc. has seen a 50 percent drop in shares in the past six months due to the economy and cutbacks in corporate expense accounts; business customers provide the restaurant about 80 percent of its revenue.

17926 ■ "Tap Into Food Truck Trend to Rev Up Sales, Build Buzz" in *Nation's Restaurant News* (Vol. 45, February 7, 2011, No. 3, pp. 18)
Pub: Penton Media Inc.
Ed: Brian Sacks. **Description:** Food truck trend is growing, particularly in New York City, Philadelphia, Washington DC, and Los Angeles, California. Man entrepreneurs are using a mobile food component to market their food before opening a restaurant.

17927 ■ "This Week: McD's Eyes Ad Plan, Shifts Breakfast Biz" in *Crain's Chicago Business* (Vol. 30, February 2007, No. 6, pp. 1)
Pub: Crain Communications, Inc.
Ed: Kate MacArthur. **Description:** McDonald's is moving its national breakfast ad account from DDB Chicago to Arnold Worldwide of Boston and Moroch

of Dallas in an attempt to change its marketing strategy. It is also doing a study to keep abreast of consumer trends.

17928 ■ "Tim Hortons Aims for Breakfast Breakout" in *Globe & Mail* (February 13, 2006, pp. B3)
Pub: CTVglobemedia Publishing Inc.
Ed: Andy Hoffman. **Description:** Fast food chain Tim Hortons will be launching its new breakfast menu with more combinations that include bacons, eggs and coffee. Tim Horton is subsidiary of Wendy's International Inc and has 290 outlets in America.

17929 ■ "TiVo, Domino's Team to Offer Pizza Ordering by DVR" in *Advertising Age* (Vol. 79, November 17, 2008, No. 43, pp. 48)
Pub: Crain Communications, Inc.
Ed: Brian Steinberg. **Description:** Domino's Pizza and TiVo are teaming up to make it possible for customers to order from the restaurant straight from their DVR. The companies see that this kind of interactive television and consumer experience will only serve to generate more sales as the customer can be exposed to a fuller range of menu selections and will not have to interrupt their viewing, while workers can spend more time making the product.

17930 ■ "To Live and Thrive in L.A." in *Canadian Business* (Vol. 81, October 13, 2008, No. 17, pp. 78)
Pub: Rogers Media Ltd.
Ed: Rachel Pulfer. **Description:** Toronto entrepreneur Shereen Arazm thrived in Los Angeles, California as the queen of nightlife. Arazm holds or has held ownership stakes in bars, nightspots and restaurants that include the Geisha House, Concorde, Shag, Parc and Central, and Terroni L.A.

17931 ■ "Top Coffee Has Concord Ties" in *Charlotte Observer* (February 7, 2007)
Pub: Knight-Ridder/Tribune Business News
Ed: Adam Bell. **Description:** McDonald's highly rated premium coffee is supplied by Concord's S&D Coffee, one of three McDonald's coffee suppliers. The blend outranked Starbucks and Dunkin' Donuts coffee by Consumer Reports.

17932 ■ "Travel Tears" in *Crain's Chicago Business* (Vol. 31, November 17, 2008, No. 46, pp. 3)
Pub: Crain Communications, Inc.
Ed: Bob Tita. **Description:** Hotels, restaurants and conventions are seeing a decline in profits due to corporate travel cutbacks and the sagging economy. City and state revenues derived from taxes on tourism-related industries are also suffering.

17933 ■ "Truffled Ahead: Farms for Rare Delicacy Gain Ground In State" in *Puget Sound Business Journal* (Vol. 29, December 26, 2008, No. 36)
Pub: American City Business Journals
Ed: Steve Wilhelm. **Description:** Twenty farmers in Washington started small plots for truffles, which are irregular fungi growing around tree roots and are considered restaurant delicacies. These truffles could generate $35,000 per acre, although they need a decade to mature.

17934 ■ "Union, Uneven But Imaginative, Works" in *Crain's Chicago Business* (Vol. 34, September 12, 2011, No. 37, pp. 30)
Pub: Crain Communications Inc.
Ed: Alison Neumer Lara. **Description:** Japanese restaurant, Union Sushi & Barbecue Bar opened in Chicago this year. Union is a hip and urban place for business and leisure diners.

17935 ■ "'Unknown' Muted Grand Prix Impact" in *Boston Business Journal* (Vol. 29, September 9, 2011, No. 18, pp. 3)
Pub: American City Business Journals Inc.
Ed: Alexander Jackson. **Description:** Baltimore Grand Prix caught restaurateurs, hoteliers and street vendors in Baltimore, Maryland unprepared for the thousands of race fans who attended the inaugural event over Labor Day weekend. The race popularity is relatively unknown to them and some felt they were not able to make as much money as they had hoped.

17936 ■ "Velvet Ice Cream" in *Ice Cream Reporter* (Vol. 23, November 20, 2010, No. 12, pp. 7)
Pub: Ice Cream Reporter
Description: Velvet Ice Cream will open its Ye Olde Mill for private corporate parties around the holidays. Their facility can accommodate groups ranging from 30 to 125 individuals. The historic site houses the company headquarters, an ice cream museum, and a restaurant.

17937 ■ "Waite, Cancer Survivor, Readies Sch'dy 'Big House' after Long Delay" in *Business Review, Albany New York* (October 26, 2007)
Pub: American City Business Journals, Inc.
Ed: Michael DeMasi. **Description:** Stephen Waite, owner of Big House Brewing Company, will be opening its new nightclub called Big House Underground. The nightclub is part of a $3.25 million project Waite started in 2005, which was delayed due to his battle with tonsil cancer. Details of turning the building into a restaurant, bar and nightclub are provided.

17938 ■ "Want a Facial With That Steak?" in *Charlotte Observer* (February 5, 2007)
Pub: Knight-Ridder/Tribune Business News
Ed: Jen Aronoff. **Description:** Profile of Burke Myotherapy Massage & Spa and Schell's Bistro. Lynn Shell moved her massage therapy business into a 106-year old home that had been used as a restaurant. She opened her own eatery on the first floor and offers massage therapy upstairs.

17939 ■ "What'll You Have Tonight?" in *Barron's* (Vol. 88, July 4, 2008, No. 28, pp. 22)
Pub: Dow Jones & Co., Inc.
Ed: Neil A. Martin. **Description:** Shares of Diageo could rise by 30 percent a year from June 2008 after it slipped due to U.S. sales worries. The company also benefits from the trend toward more premium alcoholic beverage brands worldwide especially in emerging markets.

17940 ■ "What's Cooking?" in *Entrepreneur* (Vol. 36, April 2008, No. 4, pp. 98)
Pub: Entrepreneur Media, Inc.
Ed: Eileen Figure Sandlin. **Description:** Unique and unusual restaurants have the potential to attract customers and provide them with fresh menu options. Outlining goals, strategies and details on proposed concept and target market can also help in restaurant planning. Other tips on how to plan launching your own restaurant are provided.

17941 ■ "While Competitors Shut Doors, Subway Is Still Growing" in *Advertising Age* (Vol. 79, July 21, 2008, No. 28, pp. 4)
Pub: Crain Communications, Inc.
Ed: Emily Bryson York. **Description:** Subway, the largest fast-food chain, with 22,000 U.S. locations, is adding 800 this year, despite the economic downturn that has caused competitors such as Starbucks to close stores and McDonald's to focus its expansion abroad.

17942 ■ "Whopper; Russ Klein" in *Advertising Age* (Vol. 79, November 17, 2008, No. 43, pp. S10)
Pub: Crain Communications, Inc.
Ed: Emily Bryson York. **Description:** Burger King has seen a double digit increase in the sales of its Whopper hamburger despite the economic recession that has hit many in the restaurant industry particularly hard. For most of the spring, U.S. same-store-sales gains beat McDonald's.

SOURCES OF SUPPLY

17943 ■ *Directory of Foodservice Distributors*
Pub: Chain Store Guide
Released: Annual, Latest edition 2011. **Price:** $425, individuals Directory; $495, individuals online lite; $1,175, individuals online pro. **Covers:** About 4,700 companies in the United States and Canada with at least $500,000 in sales to foodservice companies. Included companies must distribute more than one product line and obtain no more than 95% of its total sales volume from self-manufactured merchandise. **Entries Include:** Company name, address, phone and fax numbers, e-mail and web addresses; Internet order processing indicator and sales percentage; total sales; foodservice and wholesale sales; product lines; total units served; foodservice accounts served; trading areas; distribution center locations; markets served; buying/marketing group name and location; subsidiaries names and locations; divisional, regional and branch office locations; year founded; public company indicator; key personnel with titles; 20,500 foodservice distribution contacts; 9,642 Name, address, phone, fax. **Arrangement:** Geographical. **Indexes:** Product lines, alphabetical, exclusions.

STATISTICAL SOURCES

17944 ■ *Fast Food and Multi-Unit Restaurant Business*
Pub: Business Trend Analysts, Inc.
Released: 2006-2007. **Price:** $3795.00. **Description:** Profiles the fast food industry, covering hamburger, hot dog, roast beef, chicken, and pizza outlets; seafood restaurant chains; and Mexican restaurant chains. Provides information on demographics, sales, promotional spending, and new products and menu expansion. Also contains profiles of leading marketers.

17945 ■ *RMA Annual Statement Studies*
Pub: Robert Morris Associates (RMA)
Released: Annual. **Price:** $175.00 2006-07 edition, $105.00. **Description:** Contains composite balance sheets and income statements for more than 360 industries, including the accounting, auditing, and bookkeeping industries. Also contains five years of comparative historical data for discerning trends. Includes 16 commonly used ratios, computed for most of the size groupings for nearly every industry.

17946 ■ *Standard & Poor's Industry Surveys*
Pub: Standard & Poor's Corp.
Released: Annual. **Price:** $3633.00. **Description:** Two-volume book that examines the prospects for specific industries, including trucking. Also provides analyses of trends and problems, statistical tables and charts, and comparative company analyses.

TRADE PERIODICALS

17947 ■ *ConcepTrac*
Pub: Technomic Information Services
Ed: Eric Giandelone, Editor, egiandelone@technomic.com. **Released:** Monthly. **Price:** $395, individuals. **Description:** Provides news on chain restaurant development. Includes information on decor, atmosphere, service styles, cooking preparation methods, and unit economics.

17948 ■ *Cooking for Profit*
Pub: CP Publishing, Inc.
Released: Monthly. **Price:** $30; $55 two years; $52 Canada; $98 Canada 2 years; $85 other countries; $160 other countries 2 years. **Description:** Food service trade publication for owners/operators of food service businesses. Profiles successful operations, offers management tips, recipes with photos and step-by-step instructions, new and improved uses and maintenance of gas equipment.

17949 ■ *Cornell Hoospitality Quarterly*
Pub: Cornell University School of Hotel Administration
Ed: J. Bruce Tracey, Editor. **Released:** Quarterly. **Price:** $296 institutions combined print and electronic access; $290 institutions print only; $95 print & online; $31 single issue. **Description:** Magazine of applied research and ideas for hotel and restaurant managers.

17950 ■ *CRFA National Hospitality News*
Pub: Canadian Restaurant and Foodservices Association (CRFA)
Ed: David Harris, Editor. **Released:** 5/year. **Price:** Included in membership. **Description:** Informs members of association activities and industry

concerns, including labor shortages, sales tax reform, and government issues. Recurring features include news of research, reports of meetings, notices of publications available, statistics, and the columns titled National Infostats, The Personnel File, and Focus on Ottawa. Remarks: Reprints articles in French.

17951 ■ *Fancy Food & Culinary Products*
Pub: Talcott Communication Corp.
Contact: Erika Flynn, Contributing Ed.
Released: Monthly. **Price:** $26; $37 two years; $47 Canada 3 years; $32 Canada; $60 other countries. **Description:** Trade magazine for specialty food retailers.

17952 ■ *The Food & Beverage Journal*
Pub: Journal Publications Inc.
Contact: Michael Walsh, Publisher
Ed: Ellen Walsh, Editor, ewalsh@fbworld.com. **Released:** Bimonthly. **Price:** $30; $40 two years. **Description:** Trade magazine for the food and beverage industry in the western U.S.

17953 ■ *Hospitality Design*
Pub: Nielsen Business Media
Contact: Tara Mastrelli, Managing Editor
E-mail: tmastrelli@hdmag.com
Released: 10/yr. **Price:** $79; $94 Canada; $139 other countries by airmail. **Description:** Magazine covering design of restaurants, hotels, facilities, clubs, cruise ships, etc.

17954 ■ *HOTELS*
Pub: Marketing & Technology Group
Released: Monthly. **Description:** Magazine covering management and operations as well as foodservice and design in the hospitality industry.

17955 ■ *Journal of Foodservice Business Research*
Pub: Routledge Journals
Ed: David A. Cranage, Editor. **Released:** Quarterly. **Price:** $90 online; $95 print & online. **Description:** Journal on restaurant and foodservice management.

17956 ■ *The National Culinary Review*
Pub: American Culinary Federation Inc.
Ed: Kay Orde, Editor, korde@acfchefs.net. **Released:** Monthly. **Price:** $60; $200 other countries. **Description:** Trade magazine covering food and cooking.

17957 ■ *Pastry Art & Design*
Pub: Haymarket Group Ltd.
Contact: Jeff Dryfoos, Publisher
E-mail: jdryfoos@chocolatiermagazine.com
Ed: Tish Boyle, Editor. **Released:** Bimonthly. **Price:** $50; $100 two years; $60 Canada; $120 Canada for two years; $60 other countries; $120 other countries for two years. **Description:** Trade magazine for professional chefs.

17958 ■ *Restaurant Business*
Pub: VNU Business Publications
Contact: Scott Allmendinger, Gp. Publisher
E-mail: sallmendinger@idealmediallc.com
Released: Monthly. **Price:** $119; $212 Canada; $468 other countries rest of the world. **Description:** Trade magazine for restaurants and commercial food service.

17959 ■ *Restaurant Hospitality*
Pub: Penton Media Inc.
Contact: Michael Sanson, Editor-in-Chief
E-mail: msanson@penton.com
Released: Monthly. **Description:** Dedicated to the success of full service restaurants and edited for chefs and other commercial foodservice professionals. Includes new food and equipment products and trends, menu and recipe ideas, industry news, new technology, food safety, emerging new concepts, consumer attitudes and trends, labor and training, and profiles of successful operations.

17960 ■ *TECHNOMIC Foodservice Digest*
Pub: Technomic Information Services
Contact: Jan Sneesby
Ed: Jan Sneesby, Editor, jsneesby@technomic.com. **Released:** Monthly. **Price:** $295, individuals. **Description:** Contains abstracted citations from 100 publications on business developments in the foodservice industry. Recurring features include a column titled As I See It on forces and factors shaping the industry.

VIDEOCASSETTES/ AUDIOCASSETTES

17961 ■ *Food Services*
RMI Media
1365 N. Winchester St.
Olathe, KS 66061-5880
Ph:(913)768-1696
Free: 800-745-5480
Fax:800-755-6910
Co. E-mail: actmedia@act.org
URL: http://www.actmedia.com
Released: 1987. **Description:** Methods of food preparation and equipment maintenance used in the food industry are discussed. **Availability:** VHS; 3/4U.

17962 ■ *Inside Business Today*
GPN Educational Media
1550 Executive Drive
Elgin, IL 60123
Ph:(402)472-2007
Free: 800-228-4630
Fax:800-306-2330
Co. E-mail: askgpn@smarterville.com
URL: http://www.shopgpn.com
Released: 1989. **Description:** Leaders in business and industry tell their success stories in this extensive series. **Availability:** VHS; 3/4U.

17963 ■ *The Key to Cleanliness*
Film Library/National Safety Council California Chapter
4553 Glencoe Ave., Ste. 150
Marina Del Rey, CA 90292
Ph:(310)827-9781
Free: 800-421-9585
Fax:(310)827-9861
Co. E-mail: California@nsc.org
URL: http://www.nsc.org/nsc_near_you/FindYourLocalChapter/Pages/California.aspx
Released: 198?. **Description:** This is an explanation of what food poisoning is and how to avoid it through sanitary work habits like taking that extra moment. **Availability:** VHS; 3/4U.

TRADE SHOWS AND CONVENTIONS

17964 ■ Annual Hotel, Motel, and Restaurant Supply Show of the Southeast
Leisure Time Unlimited, Inc.
708 Main St.
PO Box 332
Myrtle Beach, SC 29577
Ph:(843)448-9483
Free: 800-261-5591
Fax:(843)626-1513
Co. E-mail: dickensshow@sc.rr.com
Released: Annual. **Audience:** Hospitality industry, managers, and buyers. **Principal Exhibits:** Carpeting, furniture, coffee makers, produce companies, wine and beer and food companies, and services to motels, hotels, and restaurants.

17965 ■ ApEx
Canadian Restaurant and Food Services Association
316 Bloor St. W.
Toronto, ON, Canada M5S 1W5
Ph:(416)923-8416
Free: 800-387-5649
Fax:(416)923-1450
Co. E-mail: info@crfa.ca
URL: http://www.crfa.ca
Audience: Trade. **Principal Exhibits:** Products and services for the restaurant and hospitality industry, as well as institutions, convenience stores, delis and bakeries. **Dates and Locations:** 2011 Apr 03-04, Moncton, NB.

17966 ■ IH/M & RS - International Hotel/Motel & Restaurant Show
George Little Management, LLC (New York, New York)
1133 Westchester Ave., Ste. N136
White Plains, NY 10606
Ph:(914)421-3200
Free: 800-272-SHOW
Co. E-mail: cathy_steel@glmshows.com
URL: http://www.glmshows.com
Released: Annual. **Audience:** Representatives from mass feeding, lodging, and healthcare industries. **Principal Exhibits:** Products and services for lodging and food serving properties, including: technology, uniforms, linens and bedding, tabletop accessories, guest amenities and services, food and beverages, cleaning maintenance, food service equipment and supplies, franchising information, finance and management furnishings and fixtures, fitness equipment, and leisure and entertainment services. **Dates and Locations:** 2011 Dec 12-15, New York, NY.

17967 ■ International Restaurant & Foodservice Show of New York
Reed Exhibitions North American Headquarters
383 Main Ave.
Norwalk, CT 06851
Ph:(203)840-4800
Fax:(203)840-5805
Co. E-mail: export@reedexpo.com
URL: http://www.reedexpo.com
Released: Annual. **Principal Exhibits:** Equipment, supplies, and services for the food products, foodservice, restaurant, and institutional food service industries.

17968 ■ Michigan Restaurant Show
Michigan Restaurant Association
225 W. Washtenaw St.
Lansing, MI 48933
Ph:(517)482-5244
Free: 800-968-9668
Fax:(517)482-7663
URL: http://www.michiganrestaurant.org
Released: Annual. **Audience:** Food service industry professionals. **Principal Exhibits:** Equipment, supplies, and services for the food service industry.

17969 ■ Mid-America Restaurant Softserve and Pizza Show
Ohio Restaurant Association
1525 Bethel Rd. Ste. 301
Columbus, OH 43220
Ph:(614)442-3535
Free: 800-282-9049
Fax:(614)442-3550
Co. E-mail: info@ohiorestaurant.org
URL: http://www.ohiorestaurant.org
Released: Annual. **Audience:** Restaurant owner, managers, institutions, country clubs. **Principal Exhibits:** Food distributors, manufacturers, equipment, beverages.

17970 ■ National Prepared Food Festival
Star Consulting
24 Foley St.
Dublin 1, Ireland
Ph:353 1 8881160
Fax:353 1 8881161
URL: http://www.starconsultinggroup.com/
Released: Annual. **Audience:** Foodservice professionals, chefs, and restaurant owners. **Principal Exhibits:** Manufacturers of frozen, prepared, and refrigerated foods.

17971 ■ Nightclub & Bar/Beverage Retailer/ Food and Beverage Convention & Tradeshow
Oxford Publishing Inc.
307 W Jackson Ave.
Oxford, MS 38655
Ph:(662)236-5510
Free: 800-247-3881

Fax:(662)236-5541
Co. E-mail: oxfordpublishing@oxpub.com
URL: http://www.oxfordpublishinginc.com
Released: Semiannual. **Audience:** Owners and managers of bars, clubs, and restaurants; corporate executives and food/beverage managers of hotels, resorts, state buyers, retailers. **Principal Exhibits:** Equipment, supplies, and services for nightclubs, restaurants, bars, hotels, casinos, and retailers of alcoholic beverages. **Dates and Locations:** 2011 Mar 08-09, Las Vegas, NV.

17972 ■ Ottawa Wine and Food Show
Player Expositions International
255 Clemow Ave.
Ottawa, ON, Canada K1S 2B5
Ph:(613)567-6408
Fax:(613)567-2718
URL: http://www.playerexpo.com
Released: Annual. **Audience:** Restaurant, hotels, clubs, catering-fine food stores, specialty food stores, wine clubs, and the general public. **Principal Exhibits:** Fine wines and foods, and beer from around the world.

17973 ■ West Ex: The Rocky Mountain Regional Hospitality Exposition
Colorado Restaurant Association
430 E. 7th Ave.
Denver, CO 80203
Ph:(303)830-2972
Free: 800-522-2972
Fax:(303)830-2973
Co. E-mail: info@coloradorestaurant.com
URL: http://www.coloradorestaurant.com
Released: Annual. **Audience:** Food service and restaurant industry personnel. **Principal Exhibits:** Food service and lodging products, equipment, and services.

CONSULTANTS

17974 ■ Beer Associates
96 Atlantic Ave.
PO Box 356
Lynbrook, NY 11563
Ph:(516)593-2270
Fax:(516)593-8735
Co. E-mail: beerconsul@aol.com
URL: http://www.beerassociates.com
Contact: Ira B. Beer, President and General Manager
Scope: Management and planning consultants to the food service industry, providing clients with advice and counsel on subjects of project programming, feasibility, space allocation, arrangement of kitchen equipment and dining areas, selection and specification of equipment. Devises energy conservation systems and specifies such equipment as it relates to food service facilities. Assists with bidding and procurement of equipment, an important service to domestic and overseas clients. Project management and concept development services: Also offered. Prepares energy consumption projections for food service equipment, as well as scope of support system requirements. Full range of management consulting in the food service and hospitality fields. Industries served: Fortune 500 companies, banking and financial organizations, general business and industry groups, municipal and government agencies, and education and health providers and organizations, publishing companies, professional services organizations. **Seminars:** Integrating Food Service Facilities Plans into Engineering Documents; Specifications: Key to a Successful Project.

17975 ■ Cini-Little International Inc.
20251 Century Blvd., Ste. 375
Germantown, MD 20874-1114
Ph:(301)528-9700
Fax:(301)528-9711
Co. E-mail: info@cinilittle.com
URL: http://www.cinilittle.com
Contact: William V. Eaton, Principle
E-mail: weaton@atscinilittle.com
Scope: Offers a full range of independent management and design consulting services in all aspects of food service to industries such as hospitality, business, and health care. Services include feasibility studies and or operations analyses, food service programs and concepts, operational training programs and manuals, food service contractor selection, contract documents, review of contractor submittal and site inspections. Offers consulting in materials management, materials handling, vertical horizontal transport elevator escalator moving sidewalks to all segments of the construction, hospitality, health-care and related industries.

17976 ■ Clevenger Associates
11803 101st Avenue Ct. E, Ste. 203
Puyallup, WA 98373-3473
Ph:(253)841-7811
Fax:(253)841-7435
Co. E-mail: info@clevengerassoc.com
URL: http://www.clevengerassoc.com
Contact: Trine Loepfe, Mgr
E-mail: trine@atsclevengerassoc.com
Scope: Offers food service and laundry/valet design and consulting. Will design new and remodeled space; specify equipment, and follow-up to ensure quality and likeness to specifications. Industries served: hotels, restaurants, clubhouses, health care, educational, institutional corrections, convention centers, business and industry.

17977 ■ Erin Services Inc.
111 Travelers Way
PO Box 1048
Saint Simons Island, GA 31522-5632
Ph:(912)638-9916
Free: 800-862-5361
Fax:(912)638-5701
Co. E-mail: dennisd@ns.technonet.com
Contact: Dennis J. Donnelly III, President
E-mail: dennis179@yahoo.com
Scope: Offers assistance in technical proposal production, marketing, and research. Industries served: Food service, janitorial, landscaping, hospitality and lodging, parks, and recreational.

17978 ■ GEC Consultants Inc.
4604 Birchwood Ave.
Skokie, IL 60076-3835
Ph:(847)674-6310
Fax:(847)674-3946
Co. E-mail: experts@gecconsultants.com
URL: http://www.gecconsultants.com
Contact: Lloyd M. Gordon, CEO
E-mail: legal@gecconsultants.com
Scope: Consulting in all areas of bar and restaurant operations. Restaurant manager development appraises existing locations or sites. Studies the feasibility of projects. Develop new concepts. Assist in expanding, existing food operations, marketing, expert witness (legal) for hospitality/restaurant industry. **Publications:** "How You Can Fight Back to Minimize This Recession!"; "New Thoughts On Leases"; "The Use of Job Analysis to Actually Reduce Payroll Costs"; "Do You Need a Feasibility Study?"; "Combat Negative Hospitality"; "How To Run A Successful Night club"; "Are Capitalists In Your Cabinet?"; "Marketing For The 21st Century"; "Profitability In The Banquet Industry"; "Starting a Restaurant, Bar or Catering Business"; "How To Find And Retain Suitable Employees"; "26 Things To Do To Plan A Restaurant"; "Wall Fabric or Paint: Decor Magic It's Your Call"; "The Art of Cafe Ambiance"; "Why You Need A Consultant". **Seminars:** How to increase restaurant profit, Member MSPC Speakers Bureau; Raising Capital for New Development and Expansion.

17979 ■ George Hawkins & Associates
3849 Amber Way Cir. SW
Roanoke, VA 24018
Ph:(540)774-8547
Fax:(540)774-2192
Co. E-mail: ghawkins@infi.net
Contact: George K. Hawkins, President
E-mail: ghawkins@infi.net
Scope: Offers food service facilities and management consulting expertise. Industries served: Food service.

17980 ■ Hostline
School of Hotel Administration Library
Cornell University
G80 Statler Hall
Ithaca, NY 14853-6902
Ph:(607)254-4503
Fax:(607)255-0021
Co. E-mail: hostline@cornell.edu
URL: http://www.nestlelib.cornell.edu/hostline
Contact: Mihoko Hosoi, Mgr
E-mail: hostline@cornell.edu
Scope: Provides reference service for the hospitality industry in the following areas hotel management, franchising and management contracts, tourism and travel, food and beverage management, hospitality marketing and branding, real estate, technology updates, hospitality law, architecture and interior design, hospitality financial structures, cookery/food science/sanitation, hotel and restaurant accounting, human resource management and company background. Provides information on particular issues, trends, and theories specific facts in statistics; references for quick updates and background review and referrals to other information sources. Access to the Hospitality Database, which indexes more than 80hospitality journals and newsletters; the Hotel School Library's collection of 26, 000 volumes and 1000 periodicals and newsletters; the Cornell University Library's holdings of seven million books and serial volumes and seven million microforms; multiple databases designed for the hospitality and general business and industry and academic experts. Expertise in gathering key information, providing published information, bibliographic citations and photocopied documents suited to the requested research topic.

17981 ■ The Hysen Group
41740 6 Mile Rd., Ste. 103
Northville, MI 48168
Ph:(248)347-0700
Free: 800-347-0687
Fax:(248)347-0660
Co. E-mail: consult@hysengroup.com
URL: http://www.hysengroup.com
Contact: P. Paul Hysen, Principle
E-mail: paul@atshysengroup.com
Scope: Provides design, engineering and management consulting activities relating to all types of food service facilities.

17982 ■ Isaksen Foodservice Consultants Inc.
11228 Georgia Ave.
Silver Spring, MD 20902-2712
Ph:(301)933-2100
Fax:(301)933-2101
Co. E-mail: isaksen@erols.com
Contact: Rosemarie Kellinger, Vice President
Scope: Consultants to architects, developers, and owners regarding layout and design of food service equipment for health care, elder care, country clubs, bakeries, hotels, hospitals, restaurants, nursing homes, schools, prisons and other institutions, as well as government agencies. Also space planning, lighting and acoustic design, laundry layout and design and food service area construction and installation supervision services. **Publications:** "Contemporary Long Term Care," Oct, 1997; "Pantries Take on Non-Institutional Look"; "Hospitality Profiles," Nov, 1994; "Interview: Ron Isak sen of Isak sen Food services Strategies"; "Food service Equipment and Supplies Specialist," Sep, 1991; "Winning Kitchens Show Their Metal"; "Food service Equipment and Supplies Specialist," Jun, 1991; "Isak sen, Others Devote Time to Charity," Restaurants and Institutions, Feb, 1991; "Nothing Fishy About Proper Seafood Refrigeration," Food service Equipment and Supplies Specialist, Oct, 1990; "Seven Great Kitchen Design Ideas". **Seminars:** Recipe for Success: New Concepts in Nutrition for the Aging; Integration of Food Delivery Systems with Decentralized Cluster Concepts.

17983 ■ James S. Taffae Associates Inc.
3909 Welker Ave.
Des Moines, IA 50312-3057
Ph:(515)274-0723

Fax:(515)279-7736
Co. E-mail: jstassoc@aol.com
Contact: James S. Taffae, President
E-mail: jstassoc@aol.com
Scope: Firm works primarily with architects and owners offering food facility design consulting services for various types of buildings. Work includes layout and design of food service facilities, including equipment selection, specification writing, detail drawings and budget estimating. Industries served: Food service industry (schools K thru 12, colleges and universities, clubs, health care facilities, correctional facilities, hospitals and restaurants). **Special Services:** AutoCAD Drafting Services.

17984 ■ Jeff Fetter Associates
181 Hitchcock Rd.
Salinas, CA 93908-9451
Ph:(831)455-0410
Contact: Jeff Fetter, Owner
Scope: Food service facilities engineering and design consultant. Industries served: Food service and hospitality.

17985 ■ JKM Associates
3545 S Ocean Blvd., Apt. 406
Palm Beach, FL 33480
Ph:(561)586-8859
Fax:(561)588-1219
Contact: James K. Maragos, Principle
Scope: Firm provides and conducts food service management advisory services including operating procedures and systems. Also offers services in food service design and litigation support. Industries served: restaurants, schools and colleges, industrial food service, and hospitals.

17986 ■ Market Discoveries Inc.
82-50 217th St.
Queens Village, NY 11427
Ph:(718)464-0690
Fax:(718)468-6089
Contact: Arlene Spiegel, President
Scope: Provides operational, management and marketing services for all aspects of food service and food retail business facilities. Also offers expertise in strategic planning, business and development. Industries served: restaurants, hotels, specialty food, supermarkets, franchise, fast food, entertainment and contract management companies. **Seminars:** How to Develop a Healthy Deli; Supermarkets - The New Competition; How to Upscale in a Downscale Market; How to Identify Profit Opportunities in90s; How to Develop an Effective Sales Force; How to Get Free Publicity; What Makes You So Special; Taste of Tuscany Food Program; Full Service Nutrition Analysis.

17987 ■ Neumeier Consulting Inc.
601 Academy Ave.
PO Box 928
Owings Mills, MD 21117-1301
Ph:(410)902-0464
Free: 800-827-5715
Fax:(410)902-5890
Co. E-mail: miken@comcast.net
Contact: Michael A. Neumeier, President
E-mail: miken@atscomcast.net
Scope: Specializes in the design and management of retirement accounts. Offers retirement planning courses for adults of any age. **Seminars:** Retirement Planning Today[R].

17988 ■ Nisonger Associates Inc.
202 Elm St.
Milford, OH 45150-1185
Ph:(513)248-1441
Fax:(513)248-1445
Co. E-mail: info@nisongerassoc.com
URL: http://www.nisongerassoc.com
Contact: Harry T. Nisonger, President
E-mail: nisongerai@aol.com
Scope: Food service consultants offering management and design services to the food service, lodging, health care, and leisure time industries, as well as to schools, private clubs and other institutions, and government agencies. Not only will the firm evaluate and prescribe, but it will take the project through the implementation process. Services include financial planning, menu development, facilities design, operations assessment, programming, systems studies, corporate valuations, contract and lease negotiations, consumer surveys, market and feasibility studies, prototype planning, and expert witness services. Construction division formed to provide clients with design or build services for fast track projects with cost efficiencies.

17989 ■ Peter Cooke Associates
1480 Endicott Ter.
Teaneck, NJ 07666
Ph:(201)837-1686
Fax:(201)837-8301
Contact: Peter Cooke, Owner
Scope: Provides food service facility design.

17990 ■ Progressive Sales
Roosevelt Ave., Ste. 1163, Puerto Nueva
PO Box 10876
San Juan, PR 00920
Ph:(787)782-7474
Fax:(787)793-6479
Co. E-mail: account@@progressivesales.net
URL: http://www.progressivesales.net
Contact: Vicente Berdeguer, Principle
E-mail: berdeguer@atsprogressivesales.net
Scope: Provides a full range of consulting services to all types of food service facilities including design and specifications. Industries served: restaurants, hospitals, cafeterias, and government agencies. **Seminars:** Designing Food Service Facilities.

17991 ■ R.D. Network Inc.
PO Box 375
Lafayette Hill, PA 19444
Ph:(215)482-4461
Free: 877-482-4991
Fax:(215)836-0378
Co. E-mail: info@rdnetwork.com
URL: http://www.rdnetwork.com
Contact: Melissa Altman, Principle
E-mail: info@rdnetwork.com
Scope: Dietitians, diet technicians, and certified dietary managers available nationwide and worldwide through an international registry for consulting positions to wellness and employee education programs, drug or alcohol rehabilitation, hospital, LTC, nutrition and labeling communications, nutrition consultation, weight control classes, healthcare staff supplementation, media and program development, and all nutrition and food-related needs. Expert witness and speakers bureau also available. Industries served: healthcare, food industry, food service, restaurateurs, supermarkets, pharmaceutical companies, home health agencies, insurance companies, HMOs, and government agencies. **Seminars:** Healthy Dining Etiquette for Executives and Sales Staff Diet and Wellness; Cardiovascular Nutrition; Starting a Nutrition Consulting Practice; AIDS and Diet Therapy; Nutrition Care for Your Parents in Their Elder Years; Increase Your Energy-Increase Your Sales.

17992 ■ Riedel Marketing Group
5327 E Pinchot Ave.
Phoenix, AZ 85018-2963
Ph:(602)840-4948
Fax:(602)840-4928
Co. E-mail: ajr@4rmg.com
URL: http://www.4rmg.com
Contact: A. J. Riedel, Senior Partner
E-mail: ajr@4rmg.com
Scope: The house wares and food service industry strategic marketing planning experts. Help manufacturers of house wares and food products solve marketing problems and identify and exploit marketing opportunities. Provides a full-range of strategic marketing planning services including development of marketing strategy, development of fact-based sales presentations, category management, definition of market opportunities and new product development exclusively to the house wares and food service industries. **Publications:** "Your Key Consumer: Her Take on the International Home & Housewares Show," Mar, 2008; "What's Hot, What's Not: The Consumer Speaks," Mar, 2006; "HIPsters SPEAK: What We Love to Buy and Why," Apr, 2005; "Influentials: Who They Are and Why You Should Care," Jun, 2004; "The Seven Secrets to Selling More Housewares," Jan, 2003. **Seminars:** Consumers Speak: What We Love to Buy and Why, What Do Those Consumers Think; The Seven Secrets to Selling More House wares. **Special Services:** Home Trend Influentials Panel.

FRANCHISES AND BUSINESS OPPORTUNITIES

17993 ■ 5 & Diner
5 & Diner Of North America, LLC
24 Main St.
Maynard, MA 01754
Ph:(480)962-7104
Fax:(480)962-0159
No. of Franchise Units: 16. **No. of Company-Owned Units:** 2. **Founded:** 1989. **Franchised:** 1989. **Description:** 1950's diner. **Equity Capital Needed:** Stand alone /in-line-net worth $500,000, food court net-worth $100,000. **Franchise Fee:** $25,000$35,000. **Financial Assistance:** No. **Training:** Yes.

17994 ■ A&W Food Services of Canada Inc.
171 W Esplanade, Ste. 300
North Vancouver, BC, Canada V7M 3K9
Ph:(604)988-2141
Fax:(604)988-5531
Co. E-mail: awfranchise@aw.ca
URL: http://www.awfranchise.com
No. of Franchise Units: 738. **No. of Company-Owned Units:** 10. **Founded:** 1956. **Franchised:** 1957. **Description:** A quick service hamburger chain in Canada with 600 restaurants. The annual sales in 2007 were $658 million. The main products include Burger Family, A&W Root Beer, fresh Onion Rings and Chubby Chicken. **Equity Capital Needed:** Approximately $300,000. **Franchise Fee:** $55,000 for 20 year term. **Training:** Provides 4-6 weeks of in-store training and ongoing support.

17995 ■ ABC Country Restaurants Inc.
15373 Fraser Hwy., Ste. 202
Surrey, BC, Canada V3R 3P3
Ph:(604)583-2919
Fax:(604)583-8488
Co. E-mail: info@abcCountry.ca
URL: http://www.abcCountry.ca
No. of Franchise Units: 27. **No. of Company-Owned Units:** 3. **Founded:** 1972. **Franchised:** 1976. **Description:** The restaurants offer fresh food, such as Smokehouse Barbeque, roast beef dinners, focaccia Stacker sandwiches, fresh pies and desserts. Complimentary liquor, wine and beer are also served. **Equity Capital Needed:** $600,000. **Franchise Fee:** $50,000. **Training:** Provides 4-6 weeks before and ongoing support.

17996 ■ Amato's
312 St. John St.
Portland, ME 04102
Ph:(207)828-5981
Fax:(207)761-0977
No. of Franchise Units: 30. **No. of Company-Owned Units:** 12. **Founded:** 1902. **Franchised:** 2002. **Description:** Italian take out pizza, pasta, and sandwiches. **Equity Capital Needed:** $75,000 liquid, investment range $380,000-$500,000. **Franchise Fee:** $25,000 full scale, $15,000 xpress. **Financial Assistance:** No. **Training:** Yes.

17997 ■ Andrew Smash
Smash International, Inc.
PO Box 12233
Eugene, OR 97440
Ph:(541)465-9088
Fax:(541)465-9088
No. of Company-Owned Units: 1. **Founded:** 1995. **Franchised:** 1998. **Description:** Meatless burger and smoothie restaurant. **Equity Capital Needed:** $100,000-$175,000. **Franchise Fee:** $10,000-$20,000. **Financial Assistance:** No. **Training:** Yes.

17998 ■ Applebee's Neighborhood Grill & Bar
Applebee's International, Inc.
11201 Renner Blvd.
Lenexa, KS 66207

Ph:(913)967-4000
No. of Franchise Units: 1,014. **No. of Company-Owned Units:** 234. **Founded:** 1980. **Franchised:** 1983. **Description:** Restaurant. **Equity Capital Needed:** Net worth in excess of $3,000,000; $300,000-$500,000 in liquidity. **Franchise Fee:** $35,000 U.S.; $40,000 International. **Financial Assistance:** No. **Training:** Yes.

17999 ■ Arby's
Triarc Restaurant Group
1155 Perimeter Ctr. W, Ste. 700
Atlanta, GA 30338
Ph:(678)514-4100
Free: 800-487-2729
No. of Franchise Units: 2,411. **No. of Company-Owned Units:** 1,150. **Founded:** 1964. **Franchised:** 1965. **Description:** Fast-food restaurant, specializing in roast beef sandwiches, chicken, and subs. **Equity Capital Needed:** $336,500-$2,404,500. **Franchise Fee:** $37,500. **Royalty Fee:** 4%. **Financial Assistance:** Limited third party. **Training:** Yes.

18000 ■ Asian Chao/Maki of Japan/Chao Cajun
385 Commerce Way
Longwood, FL 32750
Ph:(407)830-5338
Fax:(407)830-7258
No. of Franchise Units: 20. **No. of Company-Owned Units:** 45. **Founded:** 1991. **Franchised:** 2001. **Description:** Asian fast food. **Equity Capital Needed:** $330,000-$475,000. **Franchise Fee:** $30,000. **Royalty Fee:** 6%. **Financial Assistance:** Third party financing available. **Training:** Provides 2 weeks training at headquarters, 2 weeks onsite and ongoing support.

18001 ■ Austin Grill
505 Huntmar Park Dr., Ste. 350
Herndon, VA 20170
Ph:(703)230-5560
Fax:(703)964-0505
No. of Company-Owned Units: 7. **Founded:** 1988. **Franchised:** 2007. **Description:** Tex-Mex restaurant. **Equity Capital Needed:** $882,000-$2,800,000. **Franchise Fee:** $50,000. **Royalty Fee:** 5%. **Financial Assistance:** No.

18002 ■ Back Yard Burgers Inc.
500 Church St., Ste. 200
Nashville, TN 37219
Ph:(901)367-0888
Fax:(901)367-0999
No. of Franchise Units: 138. **No. of Company-Owned Units:** 43. **Founded:** 1986. **Franchised:** 1988. **Description:** Quick-service restaurant offering hamburgers, chicken and desserts. **Equity Capital Needed:** $1,000,000-$2,000,000 total investment; $750,000 net worth, $500,000 cash liquidity. **Franchise Fee:** $25,000. **Royalty Fee:** 4%. **Financial Assistance:** No. **Training:** Provides 6 weeks at headquarters, 2 weeks at franchisee's location with ongoing support.

18003 ■ Baja Sol Tortilla Grill
2922 Upper 55th St.
Inver Grove Heights, MN 55076
Ph:(612)280-1467
Fax:(952)944-2001
No. of Franchise Units: 10. **No. of Company-Owned Units:** 4. **Founded:** 1995. **Franchised:** 1995. **Description:** Fresh Mexican food. **Equity Capital Needed:** $186,000-$400,000 total investment; $500,000 net worth, $100,000 cash liquidity. **Franchise Fee:** $30,000. **Royalty Fee:** 5%. **Financial Assistance:** No. **Training:** Provides 4 weeks at headquarters with ongoing support.

18004 ■ Bandana's Bar-B-Q
15450 S Outer Forty, Ste. 100
St. Louis, MO 63017
Ph:(636)537-8200
Fax:(636)537-8444
No. of Franchise Units: 6. **No. of Company-Owned Units:** 25. **Founded:** 1996. **Franchised:** 2004. **Description:** Barbecue restaurant. **Equity Capital Needed:** $417,700-$1,390,000 total investment; $250,000 cash liquidity. **Franchise Fee:** $40,000. **Royalty Fee:** 5%. **Financial Assistance:** Third party financing available. **Training:** Provides 5 weeks at headquarters, 10 days onsite with ongoing support.

18005 ■ Bar-B-Cutie
5120 Virginia Way, Ste. B-23
Brentwood, TN 37027
Ph:(615)372-0707
Fax:(615)372-0705
No. of Franchise Units: 13. **No. of Company-Owned Units:** 2. **Founded:** 1950. **Franchised:** 2003. **Description:** Barbecue restaurant. **Equity Capital Needed:** $329,500-$450,000 total investment; $500,000 net worth, $200,000 cash liquidity. **Franchise Fee:** $25,000. **Royalty Fee:** 5%. **Financial Assistance:** Third party financing available. **Training:** Provides 3 weeks at headquarters, 1 week onsite with ongoing support.

18006 ■ Beef O'Bradys Family Sports Pubs
Family Sports Concepts Inc.
5510 LaSalle St., Ste. 200
Tampa, FL 33607
Ph:(813)226-2333
Fax:(813)200-3305
No. of Franchise Units: 213. **No. of Company-Owned Units:** 4. **Founded:** 1985. **Franchised:** 1988. **Description:** Family sports restaurant. **Equity Capital Needed:** $160,000-$662,500 total investment. **Franchise Fee:** $35,000-$40,000. **Royalty Fee:** 4%. **Financial Assistance:** Yes. **Training:** 8 week training at headquarters included with 2 weeks onsite and ongoing support.

18007 ■ Benihana
Benihana Inc.
8685 NW 53rd Ter.
Miami, FL 33166
Ph:(305)593-0770
Fax:(305)592-6371
No. of Franchise Units: 30. **No. of Company-Owned Units:** 60. **Founded:** 1964. **Franchised:** 1970. **Description:** Food and service. a restaurant for a period of 12-16 weeks until properly trained in general restaurant management and food preparation. **Equity Capital Needed:** Minimum $2,000,000. **Franchise Fee:** &40,000-$50,000. **Financial Assistance:** No. **Training:** Yes.

18008 ■ Big Apple Bagels
BAB, Inc.
500 Lake Cook Rd., Ste. 475
Deerfield, IL 60015
Ph:(847)948-7520
Fax:(847)405-8140
Co. E-mail: tcervini@babcorp.com
URL: http://www.babcorp.com
No. of Franchise Units: 147. **No. of Company-Owned Units:** 1. **Founded:** 1992. **Franchised:** 1993. **Description:** A bakery style cafe featuring our three brands, made from scratch daily Big Apple Bagels and My Favorite Muffin, and freshly roasted Brewster's Coffee. Product offering includes made to order gourmet sandwiches, salads, soups, and espresso beverages. **Equity Capital Needed:** $174,800-$349,500. **Franchise Fee:** $25,000. **Financial Assistance:** No. **Managerial Assistance:** Ongoing support in operations, marketing, and menu development provided by field reps and in-house staff. **Training:** Extensive training covers all aspects of operations and management, combines hands-on experience at our corporate store training facility with classroom presentations by management and key note vendors.

18009 ■ Big Boy Family Restaurant
Big Boy Restaurants International L.L.C.
4199 Marcy St.
Warren, MI 48091
Ph:(586)755-8113
Free: 800-244-2694
Fax:(586)757-4737
No. of Franchise Units: 118. **No. of Company-Owned Units:** 20. **Founded:** 1936. **Franchised:** 1952. **Description:** Full-service family restaurant, featuring in-store bakery, breakfast, dinner, soup, salad and fruit bar. **Equity Capital Needed:** $750,000. **Franchise Fee:** $40,000. **Financial Assistance:** No. **Training:** Yes.

18010 ■ Blenz Coffee
535 Thurlow St., Ste. 300
Vancouver, BC, Canada V6E 3L2
Ph:(604)682-2995
Fax:(604)684-2542
No. of Franchise Units: 25. **No. of Company-Owned Units:** 2. **Founded:** 1990. **Franchised:** 1992. **Description:** Coffee beverages and coffee beans. **Equity Capital Needed:** $30,000-$70,000+ equity. **Financial Assistance:** No. **Training:** Yes.

18011 ■ Blimpie Subs & Salads
Blimpie International, Inc.
9311 E Via De Ventura
Scottsdale, AZ 85258
Ph:(480)362-4800
Fax:(480)505-0910
Co. E-mail: info@blimpie.com
URL: http://www.blimpie.com
No. of Franchise Units: 847. **No. of Company-Owned Units:** 1. **Founded:** 1964. **Franchised:** 1970. **Description:** National quick-service restaurant, serving fresh-sliced submarine sandwiches and salads. **Equity Capital Needed:** $145,900-$397,800. **Franchise Fee:** $18,000. **Royalty Fee:** 6%. **Financial Assistance:** Available through third party sources. **Training:** Training includes 1 week at headquarters, 2 weeks onsite and ongoing support.

18012 ■ Boardwalk Fresh Burgers & Fries
Branded Concepts, Inc.
9220 Rumsey Rd., Ste. 101
Columbia, MD 21045
Ph:(410)715-0500
Fax:(410)715-0711
No. of Franchise Units: 10. **Founded:** 1981. **Franchised:** 1983. **Description:** Fast Food. **Equity Capital Needed:** $152,000-$594,500. **Franchise Fee:** $30,000. **Royalty Fee:** 6%. **Financial Assistance:** Third party financing available. **Training:** Yes.

18013 ■ Bojangles' Chicken 'n Biscuits
Bojangles' Restaurants, Inc.
9432 Southern Pine Blvd.
Charlotte, NC 28273
Ph:(704)527-2675
Free: 800-366-9921
Fax:(704)523-6803
Co. E-mail: bojbizopp@crs-services.com
URL: http://www.bojangles.com
No. of Franchise Units: 309. **No. of Company-Owned Units:** 194. **Founded:** 1977. **Franchised:** 1979. **Description:** Fast-service chicken and biscuits restaurant. **Equity Capital Needed:** $500,000 liquid assets; $1,000,000 minimum net worth. **Franchise Fee:** $25,000. **Financial Assistance:** Franchise secures own financing. Different sources are available. **Managerial Assistance:** Ongoing training, marketing, and Operations is part of the franchise support. **Training:** Offers an 5 week training program at as well as a one week training program at Bojangles' University.

18014 ■ Boneheads Grilled Fish & Piri Piri Chicken
Raving Brands
2349 Peachtree Rd.
Atlanta, GA 30305
Ph:(404)351-3500
Co. E-mail: salesleads@ravingbrands.com
URL: http://www.eatboneheads.com
No. of Franchise Units: 35. **No. of Company-Owned Units:** 1. **Founded:** 2005. **Franchised:** 2005. **Description:** A culinary experience where people seeking fresh, flavorful food in a relaxed environment can indulge in fire-grilled fish seasoned with Boneheads signature spices and chicken dishes marinated with Piri Piri sauces. From the sumptuous Mahi Mahi to the fiery-skewered shrimp, Boneheads pays homage to the Piri Piri pepper, a South African spice with serious sauce-making capabilities. **Equity Capital Needed:** $500,000 net worth; $150,000

liquid. **Franchise Fee:** $25,000. **Financial Assistance:** Provides assistance. **Training:** Raving Brands University classroom and onsite training provided.

18015 ■ Boston Pizza International Inc.
610-5600 Parkwood Way
Richmond, BC, Canada V6V 2M4
Ph:(604)270-1108
Fax:(604)270-4553
Co. E-mail: Franchising@bostonpizza.com
URL: http://www.bostonpizza.com
No. of Franchise Units: 340. **No. of Company-Owned Units:** 3. **Founded:** 1964. **Franchised:** 1968. **Description:** The franchise promotes casual dining, restaurant, and sports bar concept. **Equity Capital Needed:** $600,000-$800,000. **Franchise Fee:** $60,000. **Training:** Offers 7 weeks training.

18016 ■ The Boston's Gourmet Pizza
Boston Pizza International
1501 LBJ Fwy., Ste. 450
Dallas, TX 75234
Ph:(972)484-9022
Free: 800-277-8721
Fax:(972)484-7630
No. of Franchise Units: 154. **No. of Company-Owned Units:** 4. **Founded:** 1963. **Franchised:** 1968. **Description:** Casual restaurant specializing in pizza. **Equity Capital Needed:** $300,000-$350,000 equity, $900,000-$1,000,000 total. **Franchise Fee:** $35,000 U.S. **Financial Assistance:** No. **Training:** Yes.

18017 ■ Buffalo Philly's - Wings, Cheesesteaks N' More
Buffalo Philly's Franchising, LLC
1812 Efty Ct.
Woodbridge, VA 22191
Ph:(703)490-3428
Fax:(703)490-3427
No. of Franchise Units: 5. **No. of Company-Owned Units:** 1. **Founded:** 2000. **Franchised:** 2004. **Description:** A fast casual concept wings and cheesesteaks. **Equity Capital Needed:** $200,000-$300,000. **Franchise Fee:** $18,000. **Financial Assistance:** No. **Training:** Yes.

18018 ■ Buffalo Wild Wings Grill & Bar
Buffalo Wild Wings International, Inc.
5500 Wayzata Blvd., Ste. 1600
Minneapolis, MN 55416
Free: 800-499-9586
Fax:(952)593-9787
No. of Franchise Units: 495. **No. of Company-Owned Units:** 278. **Founded:** 1982. **Franchised:** 1991. **Description:** Sports theme, family, wings and 12 sauces. **Equity Capital Needed:** $1,389,200-$3,148,200 total investment. **Franchise Fee:** $42,500. **Royalty Fee:** 5%. **Financial Assistance:** No. **Training:** Includes 4 week training at headquarters, 2-3 weeks onsite and ongoing support.

18019 ■ Buffalo Wings & Rings
Buffalo Wings & Rings, LLC
564 Old State Rte. 74
Cincinnati, OH 45244
Ph:(513)831-9464
Fax:(954)783-5177
No. of Franchise Units: 51. **No. of Company-Owned Units:** 2. **Founded:** 1986. **Franchised:** 1988. **Description:** Casual dining featuring wings. **Equity Capital Needed:** $1,113,000-$1,410,500. **Franchise Fee:** $35,000. **Royalty Fee:** 5%. **Financial Assistance:** Limited third party financing available. **Training:** Yes.

18020 ■ Burger King Corp.
5505 Blue Lagoon Dr.
Miami, FL 33126
Ph:(305)378-7579
Fax:(305)378-7721
No. of Franchise Units: 10,144. **No. of Company-Owned Units:** 1,079. **Founded:** 1954. **Franchised:** 1961. **Description:** Highly-recognized fast food hamburger restaurant. Worldwide brand with over 6,800 points of distribution. New, lower cost facility design and flexible ownership guidelines continue to make an attractive franchise investment. **Equity Capital Needed:** $1,500,000 net worth, plus $500,000 in liquid assets. **Franchise Fee:** $40,000. **Financial Assistance:** No. **Training:** Yes.

18021 ■ Cafe Fondue Franchise Systems Inc.
281 W 80th Pl.
Merrillville, IN 46410
Ph:(219)793-1511
Fax:(219)793-1511
No. of Company-Owned Units: 1. **Founded:** 1998. **Franchised:** 2003. **Description:** Fondue - specialty restaurant. **Equity Capital Needed:** $136,000-$307,000. **Franchise Fee:** $35,000. **Royalty Fee:** 4%. **Financial Assistance:** Equipment and franchise fee assistance. **Training:** Provides 2 weeks training at headquarters and 2 weeks onsite.

18022 ■ Carl's Jr.
CKE Restaurants, Inc.
6307 Carpinteria Ave., Ste. A
Carpinteria, CA 93013
Ph:(805)745-7842
Free: (866)253-7655
Fax:(714)780-6320
No. of Franchise Units: 712. **No. of Company-Owned Units:** 399. **Founded:** 1945. **Franchised:** **Description:** 1984. **Equity Capital Needed:** Minimum $300,000 liquid; $1,000,000 net worth; $300,000 liquid per restaurant, 3 restaurant minimum **Franchise Fee:** $35,000. **Financial Assistance:** No. **Training:** Yes.

18023 ■ Casey's Grill & Bar
10 Kingsbridge Garden Cir., Ste. 600
Mississauga, ON, Canada L5R 3K6
Ph:(905)568-0000
Free: 800-361-3111
Fax:(905)568-0080
Co. E-mail: Franchising@primerestaurants.com
URL: http://www.caseysbarandgrill.com
No. of Franchise Units: 33. **No. of Company-Owned Units:** 1. **Founded:** 1979. **Description:** Casual dining restaurant that offers "grilled" food such as AAA steak house burgers and AAA steaks, and fresh cut fries. **Equity Capital Needed:** $630,000-$720,000 startup capital; $1,400,000-$1,600,000 investment required. **Franchise Fee:** $50,000. **Training:** Yes.

18024 ■ Casino Tony Goes Restaurant
15 Anderson St.
Trenton, NJ 08611
Ph:(609)213-2984
No. of Franchise Units: 2. **No. of Company-Owned Units:** 1. **Founded:** 1935. **Franchised:** 2005. **Description:** Quick-service Italian restaurant specializing in Italian hot dogs. **Equity Capital Needed:** $386,100-$591,800. **Franchise Fee:** $30,000. **Royalty Fee:** 6%. **Financial Assistance:** Limited third party financing available. **Training:** Offers 2 weeks at headquarters with ongoing support.

18025 ■ Central Park Restaurants
Central Park of America, Inc.
5751 Uptain Rd., Ste. 210
Chattanooga, TN 37411-5672
Ph:(423)855-0991
Fax:(423)899-5923
No. of Franchise Units: 25. **Founded:** 1982. **Franchised:** 1988. **Description:** Drive-thru hamburger restaurant. **Equity Capital Needed:** $300,000-$550,000. **Franchise Fee:** $20,000. **Financial Assistance:** No. **Training:** Yes.

18026 ■ The Cereal Bowl
13941 SW 112th St.
Miami, FL 33128
Ph:(305)428-2695
Fax:(305)662-2695
No. of Franchise Units: 23. **No. of Company-Owned Units:** 1. **Founded:** 2005. **Franchised:** 2007. **Description:** Cereal cafe. **Equity Capital Needed:** $186,000-$341,000. **Franchise Fee:** $25,000. **Financial Assistance:** No. **Training:** Yes.

18027 ■ Charley's Grilled Subs
Gosh Enterprises, Inc.
2500 Farmers Dr., Ste. 140
Columbus, OH 43235-5706
Ph:(614)923-4700
Free: 877-278-2798
Fax:(614)923-4701
Co. E-mail: dmoore@charleys.com
URL: http://www.charleys.com
No. of Franchise Units: 353. **No. of Company-Owned Units:** 30. **Founded:** 1986. **Franchised:** 1991. **Description:** Features freshly grilled steak and chicken subs, fresh-cut fries and old-fashioned fresh squeezed lemonade. **Equity Capital Needed:** $103,027-$445,300 total investment; $100,000 liquid. **Franchise Fee:** $24,500. **Royalty Fee:** 6%. **Financial Assistance:** Assists in working with preferred lenders. **Training:** Requires 4 week training program at various corporate locations in Columbus, OH.

18028 ■ Charo Chicken Systems, Inc.
1077 Pacific Coast Hwy.
Seal Beach, CA 90740
Ph:(714)960-2348
No. of Franchise Units: 20. **No. of Company-Owned Units:** 4. **Founded:** 1985. **Franchised:** 1998. **Description:** Flame-broiled chicken, salads, and sides. **Equity Capital Needed:** $400,000. **Franchise Fee:** $25,000. **Financial Assistance:** Yes. **Training:** Yes.

18029 ■ Checkers / Ralley's
Checkers Drive-In Restaurants, Inc.
4300 W Cypress St., Ste. 600
Tampa, FL 33607
Ph:(813)283-7000
Free: 888-913-9135
Fax:(813)283-7208
Co. E-mail: fumiat@checkers.com
URL: http://www.checkers.com
No. of Franchise Units: 507. **No. of Company-Owned Units:** 323. **Founded:** 1985. **Franchised:** 1985. **Description:** Restaurants offering burgers, fish and chicken sandwiches, hot dogs, fries, and soft drinks. **Equity Capital Needed:** $750,000 net worth, $250,000 liquid. **Franchise Fee:** $40,000. **Financial Assistance:** No. **Training:** 4-6 weeks initial training and ongoing support.

18030 ■ Cheeburger Cheeburger Restaurants, Inc.
15951 McGregor Blvd.
Ft. Myers, FL 33908
Free: 800-487-6211
Fax:(941)437-1512
No. of Franchise Units: 53. **No. of Company-Owned Units:** 1. **Founded:** 1986. **Franchised:** 1990. **Description:** Family restaurant. **Equity Capital Needed:** $355,500-$495,000. **Franchise Fee:** $29,500. **Financial Assistance:** Limited third party financing available. **Training:** Yes.

18031 ■ Chester's International, LLC
3500 Colonnade Pky., Ste. 325
Birmingham, AL 35243
Free: 800-288-1555
Fax:(205)298-0332
Co. E-mail: franchising@chestersinternational.com
URL: http://www.chestersinternational.com
No. of Franchise Units: 22. **No. of Company-Owned Units:** 1. **Founded:** 1952. **Franchised:** 2004. **Description:** Offers consumers a high-quality chicken product, cooked with a unique taste and style. The company's secret is a breading recipe and process that has been successful for more than 30 years. Chester's uses only real chicken that is specially marinated and offers double breaded bone-in, tenders and potato wedges, as well as sandwiches, wraps, salads and breakfast. **Equity Capital Needed:** $105,857-$407,000 total investment; $50,000-$100,000 liquid. **Franchise Fee:** $15,000-$20,000. **Financial Assistance:** Third party assistance offered. **Training:** Offers turn-key supply, marketing support and ongoing operations support. Franchisees benefit from Chester's University, where employees participate in a hands-on, 5 day training program in a high-tech classroom and in-store settings, plus onsite training and grand opening support.

18032 ■ Chicken Connection Franchise Corp.
International Restaurant Management Group
4104 Aurora St.
Coral Gables, FL 33146-1416
Ph:(305)476-1611
Fax:(305)476-9622
No. of Company-Owned Units: 7. **Founded:** 1997. **Franchised:** 1998. **Description:** Variety of chicken items. **Equity Capital Needed:** $240,500-$424,500. **Franchise Fee:** $30,000. **Financial Assistance:** Yes. **Training:** Yes.

18033 ■ Chicken Delight
395 Berry St.
Winnipeg, MB, Canada R3J 1N6
Ph:(204)885-7570
Fax:(204)831-6176
No. of Franchise Units: 26. **No. of Company-Owned Units:** 11. **Founded:** 1952. **Franchised:** 1952. **Description:** Pressure-fried chicken and fresh-dough pizza, plus other tasty selections. **Equity Capital Needed:** $150,000-$350,000. **Franchise Fee:** $20,000. **Royalty Fee:** 5%. **Financial Assistance:** No. **Managerial Assistance:** Provides on-site operational training, manuals and marketing ideas. Also monitors the progress of all franchisees on a monthly basis. **Training:** Offers an intensive 4 week, in-field training program at our corporate stores.

18034 ■ Church's Chicken
AFC Enterprises, Inc.
980 Hammond Dr., Bldg. 2, Ste. 1100
Atlanta, GA 30328
Free: 800-639-3495
Fax:(770)512-3290
No. of Franchise Units: 1,414. **No. of Company-Owned Units:** 269. **Founded:** 1952. **Franchised:** 1972. **Description:** Fast-food chicken restaurant specializing in Southern-style dishes. **Equity Capital Needed:** Minimum investment $1,500,000; minimum liquid equity $650,000 (per unit); must develop 3+. **Franchise Fee:** $15,000. **Financial Assistance:** No. **Training:** Offers 4 weeks Management in Training conducted in operating restaurants. Ongoing operational support, advice, and new product training.

18035 ■ CiCi's Pizza
CiCi Enterprises, Inc.
1080 W Bethel Rd.
Coppell, TX 75019
Ph:(972)745-4200
Fax:(469)675-6405
No. of Franchise Units: 578. **No. of Company-Owned Units:** 13. **Founded:** 1985. **Franchised:** 1988. **Description:** Pizza, pasta, salad bar and dessert on an all-you-can-eat lunch and dinner buffet. Also offers a value-priced take-out menu. **Equity Capital Needed:** $461,343-$714,912 total investment range. **Franchise Fee:** $30,000. **Financial Assistance:** No. **Training:** Yes.

18036 ■ City Wok
City Wok, LLC
73744 Hwy. 11, No. 3
Palm Beach, CA 92260
Ph:(760)346-7764
Free: 800-563-8592
No. of Franchise Units: 1. **No. of Company-Owned Units:** 4. **Founded:** 1990. **Franchised:** 2004. **Description:** Authentic Chinese cuisine. **Equity Capital Needed:** $243,400-$568,500. **Franchise Fee:** $30,000. **Royalty Fee:** 5%. **Financial Assistance:** No. **Training:** Yes.

18037 ■ Cora Breakfast and Lunch
2798 Thamesgate Dr., Unit 9
Mississauga, ON, Canada 4LT 4E8
Ph:(905)673-2672
Fax:(905)673-8271
Co. E-mail: franchising@chezcora.com
URL: http://www.chezora.com
No. of Franchise Units: 120. **No. of Company-Owned Units:** 3. **Founded:** 1987. **Franchised:** 1994. **Description:** Cora offers original breakfast platters in Canada. **Equity Capital Needed:** $600,000-$850,000. **Franchise Fee:** $45,000. **Training:** Provides 4-6 week training program consisting of theoretical and practical training.

18038 ■ Corn Dog Factory
Corn Dog Factory Intl.
442 N Main St., Ste. 100
Bountiful, UT 84010
Ph:(801)298-1900
No. of Franchise Units: 15. **Founded:** 1974. **Franchised:** 2001. **Description:** The franchise offers restaurant, drive-in, carryout and delivery facilities. **Equity Capital Needed:** $90,000 and up. **Franchise Fee:** $10,000/cobrand opt. **Financial Assistance:** No. **Training:** Yes.

18039 ■ The Counter
8571 Higuera St.
Culver City, CA 90232
Ph:(310)559-3355
Fax:(310)559-3356
No. of Franchise Units: 21. **No. of Company-Owned Units:** 2. **Founded:** 2003. **Franchised:** 2005. **Description:** Build-your-own-burger restaurant. **Equity Capital Needed:** $591,100-$2,500,000. **Franchise Fee:** $50,000. **Royalty Fee:** 6%. **Financial Assistance:** Third party financing available. **Training:** Offers 2 weeks at headquarters, 2 weeks at franchisees location and ongoing support.

18040 ■ Country Kitchen International
Kitchens Investment Group, Inc.
1289 Deming Way, Ste. 212
Madison, WI 53717
Ph:(608)833-9633
Fax:(608)826-9080
No. of Franchise Units: 127. **No. of Company-Owned Units:** 21. **Founded:** 1939. **Franchised:** 1939. **Description:** Family restaurant. **Equity Capital Needed:** $350,000. **Franchise Fee:** $40,000. **Financial Assistance:** No. **Training:** Yes.

18041 ■ Cousins Subs
Cousins Subs Systems, Inc.
N83 W13400 Leon Rd.
Menomonee Falls, WI 53051
Ph:(262)253-7700
Free: 800-238-9736
Fax:(262)253-7710
Co. E-mail: betterfranchise@counsinssubs.com
URL: http://www.cousinssubs.com
No. of Franchise Units: 145. **No. of Company-Owned Units:** 16. **Founded:** 1972. **Franchised:** 1985. **Description:** Submarine sandwich operation, with over 20 years of expertise. Volume-oriented, fast-service concept in an upscale, in-line, strip or free-standing location, some with drive-up windows. Franchising opportunities available for single, multi-unit and area developer franchisees, seminars and training classes. A corporate area representative meets with each franchise location management 3 times per month to maintain communications and assist in problem solving. **Equity Capital Needed:** $80,000 cash, $106,700-$288,300 total investment. **Franchise Fee:** $17,500 ltd. time. **Financial Assistance:** No. **Training:** Includes a store building seminar for site selection, lease negotiation and construction 30 days of hands-on training, plus 10 days of opening assistance and training. National and local store marketing support.

18042 ■ Crepemaker
Oui Du Crepes, Inc.
14365 SW 142nd St.
Miami, FL 33186
Ph:(305)233-1113
No. of Franchise Units: 16. **No. of Company-Owned Units:** 3. **Founded:** 1992. **Franchised:** 2001. **Description:** Casual fast food. **Equity Capital Needed:** $110,000-$315,000. **Franchise Fee:** 25,000. **Financial Assistance:** No. **Training:** Yes.

18043 ■ D'Angelo Grilled Sandwiches
Papa Gino's Inc.
600 Providence Hwy.
Dedham, MA 02026
Ph:(781)467-1668
Fax:(781)329-8796
No. of Franchise Units: 51. **No. of Company-Owned Units:** 139. **Founded:** 1967. **Franchised:** 1988. **Description:** Fast casual restaurant. **Equity Capital Needed:** $127,000 liquid capital; $400,000 net worth. **Franchise Fee:** $20,000. **Financial Assistance:** No. **Training:** Yes.

18044 ■ De Dutch Pannekoek House Restaurants
8484 162 St., Unit 108
Surrey, BC, Canada V4N 1B4
Ph:(604)543-3101
Fax:(604)543-3107
Co. E-mail: moliver@dedutch.com
URL: http://www.dedutch.com
No. of Franchise Units: 20. **No. of Company-Owned Units:** 1. **Founded:** 1975. **Franchised:** 1995. **Description:** De Dutch Pannekoek is a casual dining restaurant specializing in breakfast, lunch and brunch. The restaurant offers a unique menu with equally attractive timings. **Equity Capital Needed:** $350,000-$750,000. **Franchise Fee:** $42,500, includes training fee. **Training:** Provides 7 weeks at corporate training unit in Vancouver and an additional 2-3 weeks at new location.

18045 ■ Denny's, Inc.
Franchise Development
203 E Main St.
Spartanburg, SC 29319
Free: 800-304-0222
Fax:(864)597-7708
Co. E-mail: franchisedevelopment@dennys.com
URL: http://www.dennys.com
No. of Franchise Units: 1,452. **No. of Company-Owned Units:** 226. **Founded:** 1953. **Franchised:** 1963. **Description:** Full-service family restaurant - 24-hour operation. **Equity Capital Needed:** $1,000,000 net worth; $350,000 liquid assets. **Franchise Fee:** $40,000. **Financial Assistance:** No. **Training:** Yes.

18046 ■ Dickey's Barbecue Pit
Dickey's Barbecue Restaurants, Inc.
4514 Cole Ave., Ste. 1100
Dallas, TX 75205
Ph:(972)248-9899
Fax:(972)248-8667
Co. E-mail: rdickeyjr@dickeys.com
URL: http://www.rickeys.com
No. of Franchise Units: 146. **No. of Company-Owned Units:** 6. **Founded:** 1941. **Franchised:** 1994. **Description:** Dickey's uses the latest in barbeque technology along with several proprietary concepts and recipes. Tasty, fresh food served in a fast casual dining approach featuring slowly smoked tender meat, a hot variety of veggies, cold crisp salads, desserts and soft-serve ice cream. **Equity Capital Needed:** $150,000-$180,000, 3,000 sq. ft.; $500,000 for 3,000 sq, ft. end capital; renovate average $350,000. **Franchise Fee:** $25,000. **Financial Assistance:** No. **Training:** Official training site where new franchisees and managers spend 2 weeks learning about operations, marketing and accounting.

18047 ■ The Dogout
PO Box 4567
Oceanside, CA 92052
Free: 800-794-0117
Co. E-mail: info@thedogout.com
URL: http://www.thedogout.com
No. of Franchise Units: 7. **No. of Company-Owned Units:** 1. **Founded:** 2002. **Franchised:** 2002. **Description:** Restaurants and food delivery services. **Equity Capital Needed:** $200,000-$400,000. **Franchise Fee:** $25,000. **Financial Assistance:** No. **Training:** Training includes information system & financial management; market analysis and location selection; image development; opening assistance and operational assistance.

18048 ■ East Side Mario's
Prime Restaurant Group Inc.
10 Kingsbridge Garden Cir., Ste. 600
Mississauga, ON, Canada L5R 3K6
Ph:(905)568-0000
Free: 800-361-3111

Fax:(905)568-0080
Co. E-mail: franchising@primerestaurants.com
URL: http://www.eastsidemarios.com
No. of Franchise Units: 99. **No. of Company-Owned Units:** 5. **Founded:** 1979. **Description:** Offers good food in an exuberant atmosphere with an American Italian setting. Serves foods like Linguine Chicken Tettrazini and Peppercorn Steak Sandwich. **Equity Capital Needed:** $500,000-$840,000 start-up capital; $1,300,000-$2,100,000 investment required. **Franchise Fee:** $50,000. **Royalty Fee:** 5%. **Financial Assistance:** No. **Training:** Yes.

18049 ■ Edo Japan
4838 32nd St. SE
Calgary, AB, Canada T2B 2S6
Ph:(403)215-8800
Fax:(403)215-8801
No. of Franchise Units: 21. **No. of Company-Owned Units:** 2. **Founded:** 1977. **Franchised:** 1981. **Description:** The original teppan/ teriyaki-style, fast-food outlet that places emphasis on nutrition, high-quality food and the availability of vegetarian-style dishes. All menu items are prepared fresh, in full view of the customers. The teppan-style menu brings customers back again and again. Has a highly successful, very profitable, fast-food concept. There are 90+ restaurants in US and Canada. **Equity Capital Needed:** $200,000-$350,000. FFE $25,000. **Royalty Fee:** 6%. **Financial Assistance:** No. **Training:** Provides 21 days at headquarters, followed by 14 days at franchisee's location and ongoing support.

18050 ■ El Pollo Loco
El Pollo Loco, Inc.
3535 Harbor Blvd., Ste. 110
Costa Mesa, CA 92656
Ph:(714)599-5202
Free: 800-99P-OLLO
Fax:(714)599-5802
No. of Franchise Units: 250. **No. of Company-Owned Units:** 163. **Founded:** 1975. **Franchised:** 1980. **Description:** Restaurants specializing in Mexican-style broiled chicken. **Equity Capital Needed:** $417,000-$740,000. **Franchise Fee:** $40,000. **Financial Assistance:** No. **Training:** Yes.

18051 ■ Empress Chili
10592 Taconic Terr.
Cincinnati, OH 45215
Ph:(513)771-1441
No. of Franchise Units: 18. **Founded:** 1992. **Description:** Fast food restaurant. **Equity Capital Needed:** $65,000. **Franchise Fee:** $6,000. **Financial Assistance:** No. **Training:** Yes.

18052 ■ The Extreme Pita
2187 Dunwin Dr.
Mississauga, ON, Canada L5L 1X2
Ph:(905)820-7887
Free: 888-729-7482
Fax:(905)820-8448
Co. E-mail: seanb@extremepita.com
URL: http://www.extremepita.com
No. of Franchise Units: 227. **No. of Company-Owned Units:** 2. **Founded:** 1997. **Franchised:** 1999. **Description:** Food industry, providing fast, healthy food with exceptional quality and service. **Equity Capital Needed:** $181,500-$308,000 (+/-). **Franchise Fee:** $20,000. **Training:** At least 6 weeks of training.

18053 ■ Famous Sam's, Inc.
16012 Metcalf Ave., Ste. 1
Overland Park, KS 66085
Ph:(913)239-0266
Free: 888-866-8808
Fax:(913)239-9768
No. of Franchise Units: 29. **Founded:** 1979. **Franchised:** 1989. **Description:** Entertainment restaurant and sports bar. **Equity Capital Needed:** $586,000-$1,200,000. **Franchise Fee:** $30,000. **Royalty Fee:** 5%. **Financial Assistance:** No. **Training:** Offers 2 weeks at headquarters and ongoing support.

18054 ■ Farmer Boys
Farmer Boys Food, Inc.
3452 University Ave.
Riverside, CA 92501
Ph:(909)275-9900
Fax:(909)275-9930
No. of Franchise Units: 48. **No. of Company-Owned Units:** 17. **Founded:** 1981. **Franchised:** 1997. **Description:** Restaurants and food delivery services. **Equity Capital Needed:** $515,375-$795,505. **Franchise Fee:** $40,000. **Royalty Fee:** 5%. **Financial Assistance:** Third party financing available. **Training:** Yes.

18055 ■ Fazoli's Restaurants
Fazoli's Franchising Systems, LLC
2470 Palumbo Dr.
Lexington, KY 40509
Ph:(859)825-6259
Fax:(859)268-2263
No. of Franchise Units: 96. **No. of Company-Owned Units:** 126. **Founded:** 1990. **Franchised:** 1991. **Description:** Italian food - fast. Walk-up, take-out and drive-thru operation with approximately 100 seats. **Equity Capital Needed:** $250,000 liquid; $750,000 total investment capability. **Franchise Fee:** $30,000. **Financial Assistance:** No. **Training:** Yes.

18056 ■ The Firkin Group of Pubs
Firkin Pub International, Inc.
20 Steelcase Rd. W, No. 1C
Markham, ON, Canada L3R 1B2
Ph:(905)305-9792
Fax:(905)305-9719
Co. E-mail: larry@firkinpubs.com
URL: http://www.firkinpubs.com
No. of Franchise Units: 15. **No. of Company-Owned Units:** 15. **Founded:** 1987. **Franchised:** 1987. **Description:** Restaurants and food delivery services. **Equity Capital Needed:** $350,000. **Franchise Fee:** $30,000. **Royalty Fee:** 5%. **Financial Assistance:** Third party financing available. **Training:** Training provided at headquarters and ongoing support.

18057 ■ Five Guys
10440 Furnace Rd., Ste. 205
Lorton, VA 22079
Ph:(703)339-9500
No. of Franchise Units: 415. **No. of Company-Owned Units:** 62. **Founded:** 1997. **Franchised:** 2002. **Description:** Fresh made burgers and fries. **Equity Capital Needed:** $300,000-$550,000; $30,000 dev. Fee/store. **Franchise Fee:** $25,000. **Training:** Yes.

18058 ■ The Flame Broiler, Inc.
3525 Hyland Ave., Ste. 270
Costa Mesa, CA 92626
Ph:(714)424-0223
Fax:(714)424-0225
No. of Franchise Units: 92. **No. of Company-Owned Units:** 3. **Founded:** 1995. **Franchised:** 1999. **Description:** Chicken bowl specialist. **Equity Capital Needed:** $232,400-$317,400. **Franchise Fee:** $25,000. **Financial Assistance:** No. **Training:** Yes.

18059 ■ Flamers Charbroiled
F.C.I. Food Group
500 S 3rd St.
Jacksonville Beach, FL 32250
Ph:(904)241-3737
Fax:(904)241-1301
No. of Franchise Units: 78. **No. of Company-Owned Units:** 6. **Founded:** 1987 **Franchised:** 1987. **Description:** Gourmet hamburgers and chicken. **Equity Capital Needed:** $164,000-$263,500. **Franchise Fee:** $30,000. **Financial Assistance:** No. **Training:** Yes.

18060 ■ Flying Biscuit
Raving Brands
1718 Peachtree St. NW, Ste. 1070
Atlanta, GA 30309
Ph:(404)351-3500
URL: http://www.flyingbiscuit.com
No. of Franchise Units: 3. **No. of Company-Owned Units:** 2. **Founded:** 1993. **Franchised:** 2005. **Description:** Open for breakfast, lunch and dinner. Menu features a variety of healthy and hearty dishes. **Equity Capital Needed:** $750,000 net worth; $200,000 liquid. **Franchise Fee:** $25,000. **Financial Assistance:** No. **Training:** Raving Brands University classroom and onsite training provided.

18061 ■ Fox and Fiddle Corporation
44 Upjohn Rd.
North York, ON, Canada M3B 2W1
Ph:(416)385-7705
Fax:(416)385-1718
Co. E-mail: alanna@pegasusgroup.ca
URL: http://www.foxandfiddle.com
No. of Franchise Units: 17. **No. of Company-Owned Units:** 2. **Founded:** 1981. **Franchised:** 1999. **Description:** The franchise offers a perfect mix of high quality food and meal preparation, great entertainment, bar genius and friendly fun atmosphere. **Equity Capital Needed:** $500,000-$1,000,000. **Franchise Fee:** $40,000. **Training:** Yes.

18062 ■ Fresh City
Fresh City Franchising, LLC
145 Rosemary St., Ste. F
Needham, MA 02494
Ph:(781)453-0200
Fax:(781)453-8686
No. of Franchise Units: 4. **No. of Company-Owned Units:** 9. **Founded:** 1997. **Franchised:** 2002. **Description:** Fresh, fast, and casual. **Equity Capital Needed:** $1,750,000. **Franchise Fee:** $30,000. **Financial Assistance:** No. **Training:** Yes.

18063 ■ Friendly's Restaurants Franchise LLC
Friendly Ice Cream Corp.
1855 Boston Rd.
Wilbraham, MA 01095
Ph:(413)543-2400
Free: 800-576-8088
Fax:(413)543-2820
No. of Franchise Units: 239. **No. of Company-Owned Units:** 253. **Founded:** 1935. **Franchised:** 1997. **Description:** Full service restaurant with ice cream treats. **Equity Capital Needed:** $147,600-$1,979,350. **Franchise Fee:** $15,000-$35,000. **Royalty Fee:** 4%. **Financial Assistance:** Limited third party financing available. **Training:** provides 12 weeks training and ongoing support.

18064 ■ Frisch's Restaurants, Inc.
Elias Brothers
2800 Gilbert Ave.
Cincinnati, OH 45206
Ph:(513)559-5304
No. of Franchise Units: 39. **No. of Company-Owned Units:** 103. **Founded:** 1947. **Franchised:** 1953. **Description:** Family restaurant with drive-thru. **Equity Capital Needed:** $1,000,000-$150,000 liquid. **Franchise Fee:** $30,000. **Financial Assistance:** No. **Training:** Yes.

18065 ■ Fuddruckers, Inc.
Magic Restaurants
5700 Mopac Expy. S, Ste. C300
Austin, TX 78749
Ph:(512)275-0421
Fax:(512)275-0670
No. of Franchise Units: 99. **No. of Company-Owned Units:** 113. **Founded:** 1980. **Franchised:** 1983. **Description:** Upscale restaurant that serves fresh ground beef patties from on-premises butcher shop and freshly baked buns from on-premises bakery. Breast of chicken, fish fillet, hot dogs, salads, fries, onion rings, fresh cookies, brownies, pies, milk shakes and beverages with unlimited refills are also available. **Equity Capital Needed:** $740,000-$1,500,000 total investment; $1,500,000 net worth, $550,000 cash liquidity. **Franchise Fee:** $50,000. **Royalty Fee:** 5%. **Financial Assistance:** Third party financing available. **Training:** Provides 6 week training program with ongoing support.

18066 ■ Genghis Grill - The Mongolian Stir Fry
Genghis Grill Franchise Concepts, LP
The Centre Bldg. 7
4099 McEwen, Ste. 305
Dallas, TX 75244
Ph:(214)774-4240
Free: 888-GEN-GHIS
Fax:(214)774-4243
No. of Franchise Units: 43. **No. of Company-Owned Units:** 28. **Description:** Full service restaurant and bar. **Equity Capital Needed:** $320,000-$643,000. **Franchise Fee:** $30,000. **Royalty Fee:** 5%. **Financial Assistance:** Third party financing available. **Training:** Yes.

18067 ■ Golden Chick
Golden Franchising Corp.
1131 Rockingham Dr., Ste. 250
Richardson, TX 75080
Ph:(972)831-0911
Fax:(972)831-0401
No. of Franchise Units: 84. **No. of Company-Owned Units:** 6. **Founded:** 1967. **Franchised:** 1972. **Description:** Quick service chicken restaurant. **Equity Capital Needed:** $150,000. **Franchise Fee:** $20,000. **Financial Assistance:** No. **Training:** Yes.

18068 ■ Golden Corral Buffet & Grill
Investors Management Corp.
5151 Glenwood Ave.
Raleigh, NC 27612
Ph:(919)881-4479
Free: 800-284-5673
Fax:(919)881-5252
Co. E-mail: abagwell@goldencorral.net
URL: http://www.goldencorralfranchise.com
No. of Franchise Units: 376. **No. of Company-Owned Units:** 103. **Founded:** 1973. **Description:** Family Style restaurant specializing in steaks, chicken, and seafood. **Equity Capital Needed:** $2,500,000 net worth; $500,000 liquid. **Franchise Fee:** $50,000. **Financial Assistance:** Yes. **Training:** Offers 3-phase/12 week training program, including classroom, lab, and in-store practical experience.

18069 ■ Golden Griddle Family Restaurants
Golden Griddle Corporation
305 Milner Ave., Ste. 900
Toronto, ON, Canada M1B 3V4
Ph:(416)609-2200
Fax:(416)609-2207
Co. E-mail: jmoyer@goldengriddlecorp.com
URL: http://www.goldengriddlecorp.com
No. of Franchise Units: 27. **No. of Company-Owned Units:** 3. **Founded:** 1964. **Franchised:** 1976. **Description:** A family food franchise serving breakfast, dining and meals for all occasions. **Equity Capital Needed:** $100,000-$500,000. **Franchise Fee:** $25,000. **Training:** 4-6 weeks training and ongoing support included.

18070 ■ Grampa's Catfish House
100 Shadow Oaks
Sherwood Oaks, AR 72120
Ph:(501)834-5400
Fax:(501)834-3611
No. of Franchise Units: 2. **No. of Company-Owned Units:** 2. **Founded:** 1970. **Franchised:** 2005. **Description:** Catfish, seafood & Southern foods. **Equity Capital Needed:** $121,000-$234,000. **Franchise Fee:** $25,000. **Royalty Fee:** $300/week. **Training:** Includes 2 weeks training at headquarters, 2 weeks at franchisee's location and ongoing support. .

18071 ■ Grandy's,
Souper Brands, Inc.
401 Corporate Dr., Ste. 244
Lewisville, TX 75057
Ph:(972)434-9225
Fax:(972)434-9244
No. of Franchise Units: 65. **No. of Company-Owned Units:** 5. **Founded:** 1973. **Franchised:** 1977. **Description:** Quick service restaurant. **Equity Capital Needed:** $150,000 capital; $350,000 net worth. **Franchise Fee:** $29,500. **Financial Assistance:** No. **Training:** Yes.

18072 ■ The Great Canadian Bagel
1270 Central Pky. W, Ste. 303
Mississauga, ON, Canada L5C 4P4
Ph:(905)566-1903
Fax:(905)566-1402
Co. E-mail: edk@greatcanadianbagel.com
URL: http://www.greatcanadianbagel.com
No. of Franchise Units: 47. **No. of Company-Owned Units:** 3. **Founded:** 1993. **Franchised:** 1994. **Description:** Alternative to fast foods. The Great Canadian Bagel (TGCB) is a healthy way to enjoy a sandwich, snack or meals. TGCB is aggressively pursuing non-production/nontraditional locations: office buildings, malls, hospitals, etc. **Equity Capital Needed:** $120,000. **Franchise Fee:** $20,000. **Training:** 3 weeks and ongoing support provided.

18073 ■ The Great Steak & Potato Co.
Nicar Franchising Inc.
9311 E Via De Ventura
Scottsdale, AZ 85258
Ph:(480)362-4800
Fax:(480)505-0910
Co. E-mail: franchiseinfo@thegreatsteak.com
URL: http://www.kahalacorp.com
No. of Franchise Units: 133. **No. of Company-Owned Units:** 1. **Founded:** 1985. **Franchised:** 1986. **Description:** Specializing in cheese steaks, grilled sandwiches, fries, and fresh squeezed lemonade offers the flexibility of operating as inline mall units, in mall food courts, airports, strip centers and freestanding units. **Equity Capital Needed:** $160,900-$511,800. **Franchise Fee:** $30,000. **Royalty Fee:** 6%. **Financial Assistance:** Limited third party financing available. **Training:** Offers 2 week training program at headquarters, onsite training the first 2 weeks, and ongoing support at existing locations as needed.

18074 ■ Great Wraps!
4 Executive Park E, Ste. 315
Atlanta, GA 30329
Ph:(404)248-9900
Fax:(404)248-0180
No. of Franchise Units: 98. **No. of Company-Owned Units:** 1. **Founded:** 1978. **Franchised:** 1983. **Description:** Fast-food franchisor operating in major regional mall food courts. Serves hot, grilled, pita-wrapped sandwiches with beef and lamb, steak and cheese, fresh vegetables and strips of chicken breast, plus fresh salads, such as Greek and Caesar, fries and soft drinks. **Equity Capital Needed:** $225,000-$350,000 total investment; $70,000 liquid. **Franchise Fee:** $22,500. **Financial Assistance:** No. **Training:** Yes.

18075 ■ Hamburger Mary's Bar & Grille
Hamburger Mary's International, LLC
8288 Santa Monica Blvd.
West Hollywood, CA 90046
Ph:(949)729-8000
Free: 888-834-6279
Fax:(949)675-9979
No. of Franchise Units: 14. **No. of Company-Owned Units:** 1. **Founded:** 1972. **Franchised:** 1998. **Description:** Full service bar and restaurants. **Equity Capital Needed:** Purchase price, liquor license and improvements; approximately $225,000-$1,250,000. **Franchise Fee:** $50,000. **Royalty Fee:** 5%/month. **Financial Assistance:** No. **Training:** Yes.

18076 ■ Hardee's
CKE Restaurants, Inc.
100 N Broadway, Ste. 1200
St. Louis, MO 63102
Free: (866)253-7655
No. of Franchise Units: 1,226. **No. of Company-Owned Units:** 469. **Founded:** 1961. **Franchised:** 1962. **Description:** Fast-food restaurants featuring hamburgers and related products. Hands-on and classroom training are provided. Managerial assistance is offered. **Equity Capital Needed:** $1,085,000-$1,583,500. **Franchise Fee:** $35,000. **Royalty Fee:** 4%. **Financial Assistance:** Limited third party financing available. **Managerial Assistance:** Offers 8 weeks management training. **Training:** Provides training at franchisee's location, at grand opening and ongoing support.

18077 ■ Harvey's
Cara Operations Limited
199 Four Valley Dr.
Vaughan, ON, Canada L4K 0B8
Ph:(905)760-2244
Free: 888-854-4402
Fax:(866)230-9355
Co. E-mail: Franchising@cara.com
URL: http://www.harveys.ca
No. of Franchise Units: 217. **No. of Company-Owned Units:** 30. **Founded:** 1959. **Franchised:** 1962. **Description:** New traditional, free standing restaurants serving excellent charbroiled hamburger. **Equity Capital Needed:** $150,000-$200,000 unencumbered. **Franchise Fee:** $25,000. **Training:** Offers 8 weeks of training.

18078 ■ Hero Certified Burgers
78 Signet Dr., Ste. 201
Toronto, ON, Canada M9L 1T2
Ph:(416)740-2304
Free: (866)216-4376
Fax:(416)740-5398
Co. E-mail: franchise@heroburgers.com
URL: http://www.heroburgers.com
No. of Franchise Units: 14. **Founded:** 2003. **Franchised:** 2003. **Description:** Our goal is to deliver the best tasting food and the highest quality service in a clean environment for a fair price. Our commitment to quality ensures that all our burgers are from natural free-range beef and hormone-free and antibiotic-free, cooked medium-well. **Equity Capital Needed:** $60,000-$80,000. **Franchise Fee:** $25,000. **Training:** Provides training and ongoing support.

18079 ■ The Honeybaked Ham Co. and Cafe
The HBH Franchise Co. LLC
3875 Mansell Rd.
Alpharetta, GA 30022
Ph:(678)966-3254
Free: (866)968-7424
Fax:(678)966-3134
URL: http://www.honeybakedonline.com
No. of Franchise Units: 183. **No. of Company-Owned Units:** 280. **Founded:** 1957. **Franchised:** 1998. **Description:** Specialty retailer of high quality spiral-sliced hams and turkeys. **Equity Capital Needed:** $350,000 net worth with $100,000 available as equity contribution. **Franchise Fee:** $30,000. **Financial Assistance:** No. **Training:** Comprehensive 14 day program at corporate training store.

18080 ■ Hooters of America, Inc.
1815 The Exchange
Atlanta, GA 30339
Ph:(770)951-2040
Fax:(770)933-9464
No. of Franchise Units: 210. **No. of Company-Owned Units:** 90. **Founded:** 1985. **Franchised:** 1988. **Description:** Business of restaurant and food delivery services. **Equity Capital Needed:** $800,000. **Franchise Fee:** $75,000. **Financial Assistance:** No. **Training:** Yes.

18081 ■ Howard Johnson
Wyndham Hotel Group
22 Sylvan Way
Parsippany, NJ 07054
Free: 888-222-7484
No. of Franchise Units: 500+. **Founded:** 1954. **Franchised:** 1954. **Description:** Licensor of Howard Johnson guest lodging facilities. **Equity Capital Needed:** Varies depending upon project. **Franchise Fee:** $10,000 minimum; $100/room. **Financial Assistance:** Yes. **Training:** Yes.

18082 ■ Huddle House
Huddle House, Inc.
5901-B Peachtree Dunwoody Rd., Ste. 450
Atlanta, GA 30328
Ph:(770)325-1300
Free: 800-868-5700
Fax:(770)394-1970
Co. E-mail: franchiseinfo@huddlehouse.com
URL: http://www.huddlehouse.com
No. of Franchise Units: 430. **No. of Company-Owned Units:** 20. **Founded:** 1964. **Franchised:** 1966. **Description:** Twenty-four hour fastfood restaurants featuring breakfast items, steaks, sandwiches,

and seafood. **Equity Capital Needed:** $100,000 cash; $200,000-$750,000 total investment; $25,000 franchising fee. **Franchise Fee:** $25,000. **Financial Assistance:** No. **Training:** 7 week performance-based program covering all aspects of operations. Ongoing support in operations and field support.

18083 ■ Hudson's Grill of America, Inc.
16970 Dallas Pky., Ste. 402
Dallas, TX 75248
Ph:(972)931-9237
Fax:(972)931-1326
No. of Franchise Units: 17. **No. of Company-Owned Units:** 2. **Founded:** 1985. **Franchised:** 1985. **Description:** Offers a limited bar-and-grill type menu in a casual family dining atmosphere. Lunch and dinner are featured with a full-service bar available. **Equity Capital Needed:** $125,000 start-up cash; $500,000 total investment required. **Franchise Fee:** $25,000. **Financial Assistance:** Yes. **Training:** Yes.

18084 ■ HuHot Mongolian Grill
223 E Main St.
Missoula, MT 59802
Ph:(406)251-4303
Fax:(406)327-1232
No. of Franchise Units: 32. **No. of Company-Owned Units:** 6. **Founded:** 1999. **Franchised:** 2002. **Description:** Mongolian grill restaurant. **Equity Capital Needed:** $782,000-$982,000. **Franchise Fee:** $35,000. **Royalty Fee:** 5%. **Financial Assistance:** Third party financing available. **Training:** Provides 3 weeks training at headquarters and ongoing support.

18085 ■ Humpty's Restaurants International Inc.
2505 Macleod Trl. S
Calgary, AB, Canada T2G 5J4
Ph:(403)269-4675
Fax:(403)266-1973
Co. E-mail: info@humptys.com
URL: http://www.humptys.com
No. of Franchise Units: 46. **No. of Company-Owned Units:** 4. **Founded:** 1977. **Franchised:** 1986. **Description:** Full-service family restaurant open 24 hours a day. Stir fry's to gourmet burgers available along with award-winning breakfast menu. **Equity Capital Needed:** $495,000-$625,000. **Franchise Fee:** $25,000. **Training:** Provides 7 weeks of training.

18086 ■ IHOP
DineEquity, Inc.
450 N Brand Blvd., 4th Fl.
Glendale, CA 91203
Ph:(818)240-6055
Free: 888-774-4467
Fax:(818)246-6096
No. of Franchise Units: 1,502. **No. of Company-Owned Units:** 11. **Founded:** 1958. **Franchised:** 1958. **Description:** Full-service family restaurant, serving breakfast, lunch, dinner, snacks and desserts, including a variety of pancake specialties and featuring the cook's Daily Special. Wine and beer are served in some locations. **Equity Capital Needed:** $500,000 liquid; $1,500,000 net worth. **Franchise Fee:** $50,000 single/$40,000 multi. **Financial Assistance:** No. **Training:** Yes.

18087 ■ Indigo Joe's Sports Pub & Restaurant
Neighborhood Sports Pub Concepts, Inc.
23412 Moulton Pky., Ste. 131
Laguna Hills, CA 92653
Free: 888-303-5637
Fax:(949)457-3541
No. of Franchise Units: 36. **No. of Company-Owned Units:** 1. **Founded:** 1994. **Franchised:** 2003. **Description:** Neighborhood sports pub and restaurant. **Equity Capital Needed:** $300,000 liquid. **Franchise Fee:** $30,000. **Financial Assistance:** No. **Training:** Yes.

18088 ■ Izzo's Illegal Burrito
422 Pinewold Dr.
Houston, TX 77056
Ph:(713)965-8108
Fax:(225)706-7001
No. of Franchise Units: 2. **No. of Company-Owned Units:** 4. **Founded:** 2001. **Franchised:** 2006. **Description:** Fast-casual Mexican food. **Equity Capital Needed:** $544,500-$859,100. **Franchise Fee:** $40,000. **Royalty Fee:** 5%. **Financial Assistance:** No. **Training:** Includes 12 days training at headquarters, 7 days onsite and ongoing support.

18089 ■ Jerry's Subs and Pizza
Jerry's Systems, Inc.
15942 Shady Grove Rd.
Gaithersburg, MD 20877
Free: 800-990-9176
Fax:(301)948-3508
No. of Franchise Units: 135. **No. of Company-Owned Units:** 3. **Founded:** 1954. **Franchised:** 1981. **Description:** Fresh-dough pizza and stuffed submarine sandwiches, served in upscale retail outlets, featuring take-out service and self-service dining. **Equity Capital Needed:** $250,000-$350,000. **Franchise Fee:** $25,000. **Royalty Fee:** 6%. **Financial Assistance:** Limited third party financing available. **Training:** Yes.

18090 ■ Joey's Only Seafood Restaurant
514-42 Ave., SE
Calgary, AB, Canada T2G 1Y6
Ph:(403)243-4584
Free: 800-661-2123
Fax:(403)243-8989
Co. E-mail: rob@joeysonly.ca
URL: http://www.joeysonly.ca
No. of Franchise Units: 100. **No. of Company-Owned Units:** 3. **Founded:** 1985. **Franchised:** 1992. **Description:** Full-service mid-casual family style seafood restaurant. **Equity Capital Needed:** $80,000 minimum Streetside; $180,000 minimum Full Service. **Franchise Fee:** $25,000. **Training:** Yes.

18091 ■ Johnny Rockets Group Inc.
25550 Commercentre Dr., Ste. 200
Lake Forest, CA 92630
Ph:(949)643-6100
Fax:(949)643-6200
URL: http://www.johnnyrockets.com
No. of Franchise Units: 140. **No. of Company-Owned Units:** 56. **Founded:** 1986. **Franchised:** 1987. **Description:** Hamburger malt shop. **Equity Capital Needed:** $641,000-$920,000. **Franchise Fee:** $49,000. **Royalty Fee:** 5-7%. **Financial Assistance:** No. **Training:** Available at headquarters with ongoing support.

18092 ■ Jugo Juice
416 Meridian Rd. SE, Ste. A8
Calgary, AB, Canada T2A 1X2
Ph:(403)207-5850
Free: 877-377-5846
Fax:(403)207-5875
Co. E-mail: contact@jugojuice.com
URL: http://www.jugojuice.com
No. of Franchise Units: 140. **Founded:** 1998. **Franchised:** 2002. **Description:** Offers premiere made to order smoothies and juices supplemented with signature food items such as wraps and salads. **Equity Capital Needed:** $80,000-$350,000. **Franchise Fee:** $25,000. **Training:** 5 day training and opening support with ongoing field and operational support.

18093 ■ Just Fresh Franchise Systems Inc.
Just Fresh Enterprises, Inc.
8040 Arrowridge Rd.
Charlotte, NC 28273
Ph:(704)992-1818
Fax:(704)992-5699
Co. E-mail: info@justfresh.com
URL: http://www.justfresh.com
No. of Franchise Units: 7. **No. of Company-Owned Units:** 7. **Founded:** 1993. **Franchised:** 2004. **Description:** Fast-casual restaurant franchise. Just Fresh capitalizes on the multiple trends of juice, gourmet coffee, bagels and premium quality, made-to-order sandwiches, salads, pizza and soup. **Equity Capital Needed:** $500,000-$675,000. **Franchise Fee:** $25,000. **Royalty Fee:** 5%. **Financial Assistance:** No. **Training:** Provides 3 weeks training at headquarters and ongoing support.

18094 ■ Keg Restaurants Ltd.
10100 Shellbridge Way
Richmond, BC, Canada V6X 2W7
Ph:(604)276-0242
Fax:(604)276-2681
Co. E-mail: thekeg@kegrestaurants.com
URL: http://www.kegsteakhouse.com
No. of Franchise Units: 54. **No. of Company-Owned Units:** 33. **No. of Operating Units:** 100. **Founded:** 1971. **Franchised:** 1974. **Description:** Steakhouse restaurant leader. **Equity Capital Needed:** 3,000,000-$4,500,000. **Franchise Fee:** $50,000. **Financial Assistance:** available upon qualifying. **Training:** Provides 2 weeks training.

18095 ■ Kelly's Cajun Grill Franchise Corp.
4104 Aurora St.
Coral Gables, FL 33146-1416
Ph:(305)476-1611
Fax:(305)476-9622
No. of Franchise Units: 74. **No. of Company-Owned Units:** 40. **Founded:** 1991. **Franchised:** 1996. **Description:** Cajun restaurant. **Equity Capital Needed:** $250,000-$500,000. **Franchise Fee:** $30,000. **Financial Assistance:** No. **Training:** Yes.

18096 ■ KFC - Canada
YUM! RESTAURANTS INTERNATIONAL (CANADA) COMPANY
101 Exchange Ave.
Vaughan, ON, Canada L4K 5R6
Ph:(416)664-5200
Free: 800-268-5435
Fax:(416)739-0118
Co. E-mail: franchisecanada@yum.com
URL: http://www.yumfranchises.ca
No. of Franchise Units: 728. **Founded:** 1954. **Description:** Chicken restaurants selling both on and off-thebone chicken products with fries and salads. **Equity Capital Needed:** $350,000-$1,200,000. **Franchise Fee:** $45,500 U.S. funds. **Financial Assistance:** No. **Training:** Yes.

18097 ■ The Krystal Co.
One Union Sq.
Chattanooga, TN 37402
Free: 800-458-5912
Fax:(423)757-1588
Co. E-mail: jschmidt@krystalco.com
URL: http://www.krystal.com
No. of Franchise Units: 185. **No. of Company-Owned Units:** 246. **Founded:** 1932. **Franchised:** 1990. **Description:** Fast food hamburger concept, offering proven, destination-oriented products. Restaurants are open 24 hours. **Equity Capital Needed:** $525,000-$625,000 per restaurant. **Franchise Fee:** $32,500. **Financial Assistance:** No. **Training:** Provide in the restaurant training, computer training at home office. Also, provides area directors in the field to assist with business.

18098 ■ La Salsa
CKE Restaurants, Inc.
6307 Carpinteria Ave., Ste. A
Carpinteria, CA 93103
Ph:(805)745-7842
Free: (866)253-7655
Fax:(714)780-6320
No. of Franchise Units: 41. **No. of Company-Owned Units:** 54. **Founded:** 1979. **Franchised:** 1989. **Description:** Fast and casual dining. **Equity Capital Needed:** Minimum of $200,000 liquid and $800,000 net worth per store w/3 store commitment. **Franchise Fee:** First-third $20,000. **Financial Assistance:** No. **Training:** Yes.

18099 ■ Le Muffin Plus
2464 Jean-Talon East
Montreal, QC, Canada H2E 1W2
Ph:(514)281-2067
Fax:(514)281-6405
Co. E-mail: info@cafedepot.ca
No. of Franchise Units: 21. **No. of Company-Owned Units:** 2. **Founded:** 1984. **Description:** Specializing in healthy sandwiches, salads, muffins, and hot meals. **Equity Capital Needed:** $100,000. **Franchise Fee:** $20,000. **Training:** Yes.

18100 ■ The Lion And Rose Pub
The Lion and Rose Franchise, Ltd.
PO Box 27313
San Antonio, TX 78227
Ph:(210)798-5301
Co. E-mail: franchise@thelionandrose.com
URL: http://www.thelionandrose.com
No. of Company-Owned Units: 2. **Founded:** 2004. **Franchised:** 2006. **Description:** Offers an opportunity to own and operate your own business. Currently looking for qualified franchise owner/operators in Texas and the near southwest U.S. **Equity Capital Needed:** $285,500-$875,500. **Franchise Fee:** $25,000. **Financial Assistance:** No. **Training:** Access to operations manuals, unique recipes, operational systems, vendor relations and training materials with ongoing support from team of managers and staff.

18101 ■ The Little Dooey Barbeque & Blues
16930 W Catawba Ave., Ste. 102
Cornelius, NC 28031
Ph:(704)895-2512
Fax:(704)895-2432
No. of Franchise Units: 1. **No. of Company-Owned Units:** 3. **Founded:** 1985. **Franchised:** 2004. **Description:** Barbecue restaurant. **Equity Capital Needed:** $928,000-$1,600,000. **Franchise Fee:** $35,000. **Royalty Fee:** 5%. **Financial Assistance:** No.

18102 ■ Long John Silver's
Yum! Brands
1900 Colonel Sanders Ln.
Louisville, KY 40213-1914
Free: 800-544-5774
No. of Franchise Units: 542. **No. of Company-Owned Units:** 760. **Founded:** 1969. **Franchised:** 1970. **Description:** Seafood chain in the fish and seafood segment. Offers a menu of fish, seafood and chicken. Eat-in, take-out and drive-thru. **Equity Capital Needed:** Minimum net worth $400,000; Minimum liquidity $200,000. **Franchise Fee:** $20,000 domestic. **Financial Assistance:** No. **Training:** Yes.

18103 ■ Mama Fu's Asian House
Mama Fu's Franchise Group, Inc.
512 E. Riverside Dr., Ste. 250
Austin, TX 78704
Ph:(515)949-3211
Fax:800-905-2147
No. of Franchise Units: 6. **No. of Company-Owned Units:** 6. **Founded:** 2002. **Franchised:** 2003. **Description:** Pan-Asian food. **Equity Capital Needed:** $150,000 liquid; $1,000,000 net worth. **Franchise Fee:** $28,000/Multi unit. **Royalty Fee:** 5%. **Financial Assistance:** No.

18104 ■ Manchu Wok (Canada) Inc.
85 Citizen Ct., Unit 9
Markham, ON, Canada L6G 1A8
Ph:(954)427-2163
Free: 800-361-8864
Fax:(905)946-7201
Co. E-mail: mariellen_clark@manchuwok.com
URL: http://www.manchuwok.com
No. of Franchise Units: 60. **No. of Company-Owned Units:** 18. **Founded:** 1980. **Franchised:** 1990. **Description:** Oriental quick-service restaurant chains in Canada. Operates in food courts of large regional malls. **Equity Capital Needed:** $248,000-$512,000. **Franchise Fee:** $30,000. **Training:** 3 weeks real estate, marketing, field support, and product development included.

18105 ■ Mandarin Restaurant Franchise Corp.
8 Clipper Ct.
Brampton, ON, Canada L6W 4T9
Ph:(905)451-4100
Fax:(905)456-3411
Co. E-mail: info@mandarinbuffet.com
URL: http://www.mandarinbuffet.com
No. of Franchise Units: 20. **No. of Company-Owned Units:** 1. **Founded:** 1979. **Franchised:** 1993. **Description:** Mandarin is known for fresh and quality food, buffet restaurant serving Chinese and Canadian food and a-lacarte and take-out. **Equity Capital Needed:** $3,000,000. **Franchise Fee:** 10% of total construction cost. **Training:** 1-3 years and ongoing support provided.

18106 ■ Mary Browns Inc.
250 Shield's Ct., Ste. 7
Markham, ON, Canada L3R 9W7
Ph:(905)513-0044
Fax:(905)513-0050
Co. E-mail: sean@marybrowns.com
URL: http://www.marybrowns.com
No. of Franchise Units: 80. **No. of Company-Owned Units:** 4. **Founded:** 1969. **Franchised:** 1969. **Description:** Committed in serving high quality and innovative food items. Serves white meat chicken filet sandwiches, mini nuggets unique to Mary Brown's, chicken fingers, salads and our famous hand-cut taters, all cooked in 100% canola oil. **Equity Capital Needed:** $100,000+. **Franchise Fee:** $25,000. **Training:** Offers 3 weeks initial training and ongoing support.

18107 ■ McDonald's Corp.
Kroc Dr.
Oak Brook, IL 60521
Ph:(630)623-6196
No. of Franchise Units: 22,591. **No. of Company-Owned Units:** 8,180. **Founded:** 1955. **Franchised:** 1955. **Description:** Food-service retailer, with restaurants in 70 countries. 85% of franchises in the U.S. are locally-owned and operated support. **Equity Capital Needed:** Minimum $175,000 non-borrowed personal resources. **Franchise Fee:** $45,000. **Financial Assistance:** No. **Training:** Franchisees required to participate in a training and evaluation program which may, on a part-time basis, take 2 years or longer to complete.

18108 ■ McDonald's Restaurants of Canada Ltd.
McDonald's Pl.
Toronto, ON, Canada M3C 3L4
Ph:(416)443-1000
Fax:(416)446-3420
Co. E-mail: mcdfranon@ca.mcd.com
URL: http://www.mcdonalds.ca/franchising
No. of Franchise Units: 1,136. **No. of Company-Owned Units:** 297. **Founded:** 1967. **Franchised:** 1968. **Description:** McDonald's, the quick service restaurant provides quality service, cleanliness and value. **Equity Capital Needed:** $500,000, unencumbered funds. **Franchise Fee:** $45,000. **Training:** Offers 1-2 years training.

18109 ■ McGhin's Southern Pit Bar-B-Que
2964 N Expy.
Griffin, GA 30223
Ph:(770)412-8222
Fax:(770)229-5838
No. of Franchise Units: 1. **No. of Company-Owned Units:** 1. **Founded:** 1984. **Franchised:** 2006. **Description:** Barbecue restaurant. **Equity Capital Needed:** $288,000-$800,000. **Franchise Fee:** $30,000. **Royalty Fee:** $500/week. **Financial Assistance:** Yes. **Training:** Provides 3 weeks training at headquarters, 1 week at franchisee's location, and ongoing support.

18110 ■ The Melting Pot Restaurants, Inc.
8810 Twin Lakes Rd.
Tampa, FL 33614
Ph:(813)425-6208
Free: 800-783-0867
Fax:(813)367-0076
No. of Franchise Units: 138. **No. of Company-Owned Units:** 4. **Founded:** 1975. **Franchised:** 1984. **Description:** Offers a unique opportunity to stand apart from the competition. Select the franchise system that offers a unique concept, coupled with training, education and outstanding support. **Equity Capital Needed:** $325,000-$400,000 liquid, $886,695-$1,544,695 or more total investment. **Franchise Fee:** $45,000. **Financial Assistance:** No. **Training:** Franchisees and their managers pay their own costs of lodging, meals and transportation during training.

18111 ■ Mexicali Rosa's
3232 Carp Rd.
Perth, ON, Canada K0A 1L0
Ph:(613)839-0324
Free: 877-477-3950
Fax:(613)839-0591
Co. E-mail: info@mexicalrosas.com
URL: http://www.mexicalirosas.com
No. of Franchise Units: 16. **Founded:** 1977. **Franchised:** 1986. **Description:** Authentic, California-style Mexican Restaurants with a large emphasis on Fun, Flavour and Integrity. Our menu features Canada's best nachos, hand-rolled enchiladas and tamales, sizzling fajitas, chimichangas and Award-winning Chilis and Margaritias. **Equity Capital Needed:** $250,000-$800,000. **Franchise Fee:** $25,000 **Training:** Assistance with site selection, restaurant design and construction with ongoing operational, advertising, and central purchasing support.

18112 ■ Mister Bar-B-Que
Smokey P., Inc.
1134 Grove Dr.
Rockledge, FL 32955
Ph:(321)639-0038
Free: 888-766-5399
Fax:(321)639-4318
No. of Franchise Units: 1. **Founded:** 1988. **Franchised:** 1997. **Description:** Freshly prepared barbecued meats, fish, and burgers. **Equity Capital Needed:** $160,000. **Franchise Fee:** $15,000. **Financial Assistance:** No. **Training:** Yes.

18113 ■ Moe's Southwest Grill
200 Glenridge Point Pky., Ste. 200
Atlanta, GA 30342
Ph:(404)255-3250
Fax:(404)255-4978
URL: http://www.moes.com
No. of Franchise Units: 421. **No. of Company-Owned Units:** 4. **Founded:** 2000. **Franchised:** 2001. **Description:** Fresh-Mex quick-service restaurant. **Equity Capital Needed:** $450,615-$768,843. **Franchise Fee:** $30,000. **Royalty Fee:** 5%. **Financial Assistance:** Third party assistance available. **Training:** 2 weeks at corporate headquarters, 1 week onsite, and ongoing support included.

18114 ■ Montana Mike's Steakhouse
Stockade Franchising, LP
2908 N Plum St.
Hutchinson, KS 67502-8400
Ph:(620)669-9372
Fax:(620)669-0531
No. of Franchise Units: 21. **Founded:** 1998. **Franchised:** 1998. **Description:** Casual dining full service steakhouse. **Equity Capital Needed:** $1,000,000 net worth; $250,000 liquid assets. **Franchise Fee:** $20,000. **Financial Assistance:** No. **Training:** Yes. Yes.

18115 ■ Mr. Goodcents Subs & Pastas
Mr. Goodcents Franchise Systems, Inc.
8997 Commerce Dr.
DeSoto, KS 66018
Ph:(913)583-8400
Free: 800-648-2368
Fax:(913)583-3500
Co. E-mail: frandev@mrgoodcents.com
URL: http://www.mrgoodcents.com
No. of Franchise Units: 100. **No. of Company-Owned Units:** 1. **Founded:** 1989. **Franchised:** 1990. **Description:** Quick service restaurant serving lunch and dinner featuring submarine sandwiches with fresh meat and cheese on bread. **Equity Capital Needed:** $75,000. **Franchise Fee:** $20,000. **Financial Assistance:** No. **Training:** 30 days of comprehensive in-house training.

18116 ■ Mr. Greek Mediterranean Grill
44 Upjohn Rd
Toronto, ON, Canada M3B 2W1
Ph:(416)444-3266
Free: 888-674-7335

Fax:(416)444-3484
Co. E-mail: Vicki.raios@mrgreek.com
URL: http://www.mrgreek.com
No. of Franchise Units: 20. **No. of Company-Owned Units:** 4. **Founded:** 1988. **Franchised:** 1994. **Description:** Full service restaurant, take out, food court. **Equity Capital Needed:** $350,000-$500,000. **Franchise Fee:** $35,000. **Financial Assistance:** No. **Training:** Offers 12 weeks training with ongoing support.

18117 ■ Mr. Greek Rxpress
Mr. Greek Mediterranean Grill
44 Upjohn Rd
Toronto, ON, Canada M3B 2W1
Ph:(416)444-3266
Free: 888-674-7335
Fax:(416)444-3484
Co. E-mail: Vicki.raios@mrgreek.com
URL: http://www.mrgreek.com
No. of Franchise Units: 20. **No. of Company-Owned Units:** 4. **Founded:** 1988. **Franchised:** 2003. **Description:** Mr. Greek Express is a quick-service restaurant concept with a limited menu of the most popular specialty dishes of the Mr. Greek Mediterranean Grill franchise, as well as some dishes available only at the Mr. Greek Express locations. The Express units are counter-service restaurants offering seating and take-out and, where possible, drive-through facilities. Great Food, Served Fast. The Mr. Greek Express is an outstanding business opportunity for highly motivated, customer-oriented individuals who have the desire to succeed. **Equity Capital Needed:** $350,000-$500,000. **Franchise Fee:** $35,000. **Training:** Offers 10 weeks training and ongoing support.

18118 ■ Mr. Hero Restaurants
Restaurant Developers Corp.
7010 Engle Rd., Ste. 100
Middleburg Heights, OH 44130
Free: 888-860-5082
No. of Franchise Units: 103. **No. of Company-Owned Units:** 7. **Founded:** 1965. **Franchised:** 1970. **Description:** Specialty sandwiches & fast food. **Equity Capital Needed:** $113,000-$305,000. **Franchise Fee:** $18,000. **Royalty Fee:** 5.5%. **Financial Assistance:** Third party financing available. **Training:** Offers 4 weeks at headquarters, 1 week at franchisees location with ongoing support.

18119 ■ Mr. SUB
4576 Yonge St., Ste. 600
Toronto, ON, Canada M2N 6N4
Ph:(416)225-5545
Free: 800-668-SUBS
Fax:(416)225-5536
Co. E-mail: info@mrsub.ca
URL: http://www.mrsub.ca
No. of Franchise Units: 300. **No. of Company-Owned Units:** 2. **Founded:** 1968. **Franchised:** 1971. **Description:** Submarine restaurants serving fresh food like subs, wraps, soups, salads and a variety of beverages. **Equity Capital Needed:** Varies. **Franchise Fee:** $15,000. **Training:** Provides 3 weeks training and ongoing support.

18120 ■ Mucho Burrito
2187 Dunwin Dr.
Mississauga, ON, Canada L5L 1X2
Ph:(905)820-7887
Free: 888-729-7482
Fax:(905)820-8448
Co. E-mail: seanb@extremepita.com
URL: http://www.muchoburrito.com
No. of Franchise Units: 50. **Founded:** 2006. **Franchised:** 2006. **Description:** Restaurant. **Equity Capital Needed:** $212,800$547,100+/-. **Franchise Fee:** $25,000. **Training:** At least 4 (four) to 5 1/2 weeks training.

18121 ■ Nando's Flame Grilled Chicken
13931 Sparwood Pl., Unit 130
Richmond, BC, Canada V6V 1X2
Ph:(604)303-0881
Fax:(604)303-0882
Co. E-mail: askus@nandoscanada.com
URL: http://www.nandoscanada.com
No. of Franchise Units: 29. **No. of Company-Owned Units:** 1. **Founded:** 1994. **Franchised:** 1999. **Description:** Dining restaurant specialist in flame grilled chicken, expanded across the world. **Equity Capital Needed:** $700,000+. **Franchise Fee:** $35,000. **Training:** Provides full training.

18122 ■ Nathan's
Nathan's Famous Systems, Inc.
1 Jericho Plz.
Jericho, NY 11753
Ph:(516)338-8500
Fax:(516)338-7220
No. of Franchise Units: 204. **No. of Company-Owned Units:** 6. **Founded:** 1916. **Franchised:** 1989. **Description:** Offers a large variety of menu items, all-beef frankfurters and fresh-cut French fries in a contemporary atmosphere. Offers 8 different prototypes, ranging from countertop modular to free-standing restaurants. **Equity Capital Needed:** $50,000-$200,000 liquid. **Franchise Fee:** $30,000-$37,500. **Financial Assistance:** No. **Training:** Yes.

18123 ■ New England Hot Dog Company, LLC
100 Commings Ctr., Ste. 231G
Beverly, MA 01907
Ph:(978)922-5105
Fax:(978)922-0750
No. of Company-Owned Units: 1. **Founded:** 2004. **Franchised:** 2005. **Description:** Gourmet hot dog and ice cream restaurant. **Equity Capital Needed:** $135,000-$250,000. **Franchise Fee:** $30,000. **Training:** Yes.

18124 ■ Nothing But Noodles
9383 E. Bahia Suite 100
Scottsdale, AZ 85260
Ph:(480)513-7008
Fax:(480)513-7989
No. of Franchise Units: 33. **No. of Company-Owned Units:** 1. **Founded:** 2001. **Franchised:** 2002. **Description:** Noodles, pasta, and salads. **Equity Capital Needed:** $352,400-$441,800. **Franchise Fee:** $25,000. **Royalty Fee:** 6%. **Financial Assistance:** No.

18125 ■ O'Charley's Restaurants
O'Charley's Inc.
3038 Sidco Dr.
Nashville, TN 37204
Ph:(615)782-8980
Free: 877-772-0001
Fax:(615)782-5043
No. of Franchise Units: 7. **No. of Company-Owned Units:** 230. **Founded:** 1973. **Franchised:** 2002. **Description:** Casual dining, with emphasis on cuisine and service. **Equity Capital Needed:** $3,000,000 net worth. **Franchise Fee:** $50,000. **Financial Assistance:** No. **Training:** Yes.

18126 ■ Off the Grill Franchising, LLC
1728 General George Patton Dr., Ste. 200
Brentwood, TN 37027
Ph:(615)370-0700
Free: 877-OTG-2100
Fax:(615)371-1405
No. of Franchise Units: 13. **No. of Company-Owned Units:** 2. **Founded:** 1999. **Franchised:** 1999. **Description:** Carry out and delivery; steaks, burgers, and chicken. **Equity Capital Needed:** $250,000. **Franchise Fee:** $25,000. **Financial Assistance:** No. **Training:** Yes.

18127 ■ Orange Julius Canada Limited
5045 S Service Rd., Ste. 3000
PO Box 430
Burlington, ON, Canada L7R 3Y3
Ph:(905)639-1492
Fax:(905)681-3623
Co. E-mail: tammie.verna@idq.com
URL: http://www.orangejulius.com
No. of Franchise Units: 56. **Founded:** 1930. **Franchised:** 1940. **Description:** Snack and drink franchise of North America easily accessible for pedestrians. **Equity Capital Needed:** $100,000+. **Franchise Fee:** $30,000. **Training:** Yes. s.

18128 ■ Otter's Chicken Tenders
1110 Gilmore Ave.
Nashville, TN 37204
Ph:(615)832-7501
Fax:(615)523-1489
No. of Company-Owned Units: 2. **Founded:** 2003. **Franchised:** 2006. **Description:** Chicken tenders. **Equity Capital Needed:** $291,500-$429,000. **Franchise Fee:** $30,000. **Royalty Fee:** 5%. **Financial Assistance:** No. **Training:** Includes 4-6 weeks training at headquarters, 1 week onsite and ongoing support.

18129 ■ Panchero's Mexican Grill
Panchero's Franchise Corp.
2475 Coral Ct., Ste. B
Coralville, IA 52241
Ph:(319)545-6565
Free: 888-MEX-BEST
Fax:(319)545-6570
No. of Franchise Units: 56. **No. of Company-Owned Units:** 15. **Founded:** 1992. **Franchised:** 1996. **Description:** Mexican food. **Equity Capital Needed:** Net worth $750,000; liquid $250,000. **Franchise Fee:** $30,000. **Financial Assistance:** No. **Training:** Yes.

18130 ■ The Pantry Restaurants
1812 152 St., Ste. 203
Surrey, BC, Canada V4A 4N5
Ph:(604)536-4111
Fax:(604)536-4103
Co. E-mail: rvillalpando@rammp.net
URL: http://www.thepantry.ca/restaurant_franchise_canada.html
No. of Franchise Units: 16. **No. of Company-Owned Units:** 1. **Founded:** 1975. **Franchised:** 1977. **Description:** Pantry Hospitality Corp. is a restaurant, which focuses mainly on prime rib, certified angus beef steaks, with an assortment of seafood and pasta dishes. **Equity Capital Needed:** $500,000-$700,000. **Franchise Fee:** $50,000. **Training:** 6 weeks and ongoing support provided.

18131 ■ Pepe's Mexican Restaurants
Pepe's, Inc.
1325 W 15th St.
Chicago, IL 60608
Ph:(312)733-2500
No. of Franchise Units: 50. **Founded:** 1967. **Franchised:** 1967. **Description:** Full-service Mexican restaurant franchise, featuring a full range of Mexican items, including beer, wine and liquor. **Equity Capital Needed:** $75,000-$200,000. **Franchise Fee:** $15,000. **Financial Assistance:** No. **Training:** Yes.

18132 ■ The Perfect Pita
The Perfect Pita, LLC
3193 S Stafford St.
Arlington, VA 22206
Free: (866)856-PITA
Fax:(703)549-0740
No. of Company-Owned Units: 3. **Founded:** 1994. **Franchised:** 2004. **Description:** Homemade Mediterranean carryout restaurant. **Equity Capital Needed:** $162,000-$423,000. **Franchise Fee:** $15,000. **Financial Assistance:** Yes. **Training:** Yes.

18133 ■ Perkins Restaurant & Bakery
The Restaurant Co.
6075 Poplar Ave., Ste. 800
Memphis, TN 38119
Ph:(901)766-6400
Free: 800-877-7375
Fax:(901)766-6482
No. of Franchise Units: 300. **No. of Company-Owned Units:** 163. **Founded:** 1958. **Franchised:** 1958. **Description:** Full-service, family-style restaurants offering breakfast, lunch and dinner entrees. More than half of the restaurants feature signature bakery. **Equity Capital Needed:** $500,000 liquid; $1,500,000 net. **Franchise Fee:** $20,000. **Financial Assistance:** No. **Training:** Yes.

18134 ■ The Philly Connection
The Philly Franchising Co.
120 Insterstate N Pky. E, Ste. 112
Atlanta, GA 30339-2103
Ph:(770)952-6152

Free: 800-886-8826
Fax:(770)952-3168
No. of Franchise Units: 130. **No. of Company-Owned Units:** 1. **Founded:** 1984. **Franchised:** 1987. **Description:** Fast-food franchise, specializing in Philly cheese steaks, hoagies and salads. **Equity Capital Needed:** $154,000-$261,500. **Franchise Fee:** $20,000. **Royalty Fee:** 6%. **Financial Assistance:** Limited third party financing available. **Training:** Provides 80 hours at training facility.

18135 ■ Pizza Delight
774 Main St., Ste. 400
Moncton, NB, Canada E1C 9Y3
Ph:(506)853-0990
Free: 877-853-0990
Fax:(506)853-4131
Co. E-mail: ktoner@pizzadelight.ca
URL: http://www.pizzadelight.com
No. of Franchise Units: 96. **Founded:** 1968. **Franchised:** 1969. **Description:** Family restaurants, specialists in pizza, pasta, salads and rotisserie chicken with delivery services too. **Equity Capital Needed:** $100,000-$150,000 unencumbered equity. **Franchise Fee:** $15,000-$30,000. **Training:** Offers 3-4 weeks of training.

18136 ■ Pizza Hut Canada
Yum! Restaurants International (Canada) Company
101 Exchange Ave.
Vaughan, ON, Canada L4K 5R6
Ph:(416)664-5200
Free: 800-268-5435
Fax:(416)739-0118
Co. E-mail: franchisecanada@yum.com
URL: http://www.yumfranchises.ca
No. of Franchise Units: 304. **Founded:** 1958. **Description:** Restaurant specialized in pan pizza, thin crust pizza, pastas, garlic bread and salads. **Equity Capital Needed:** $350,000-$1,200,000. **Franchise Fee:** $45,500 U.S. Funds. **Royalty Fee:** 6%. **Training:** Yes.

18137 ■ Pizza Ranch, Inc.
204 19th St. SE
PO Box 465
Orange City, IA 51041
Ph:(712)707-8800
Free: 800-321-3401
Fax:(712)707-8825
No. of Franchise Units: 156. **No. of Company-Owned Units:** 1. **Founded:** 1981. **Franchised:** 1984. **Description:** Pizza and chicken restaurant. **Equity Capital Needed:** $660,000-$1,691,000. **Franchise Fee:** $30,000. **Financial Assistance:** No. **Training:** Yes.

18138 ■ Pluckers Wing Bar
MD Pluckers Franchising L.P.
811 Barton Springs Rd., Ste. 520
Austin, TX 78704
Ph:(512)236-9110
Fax:(512)236-9113
No. of Franchise Units: 2. **No. of Company-Owned Units:** 1. **Founded:** 1995. **Franchised:** 2000. **Description:** Chicken wings, hamburgers, cheesesteakes and more. **Equity Capital Needed:** $70,000-$225,000. **Franchise Fee:** $18,000. **Financial Assistance:** No. **Training:** Yes.

18139 ■ Popeyes Chicken & Biscuits
AFC Enterprises, Inc.
5555 Glenridge Connector NE, Ste. 300
Atlanta, GA 30342
Ph:(404)459-4450
Free: 800-639-3780
Fax:(404)459-4523
Co. E-mail: popeyesfranchising@afce.com
URL: http://www.popeyesfranchising.com
No. of Franchise Units: 1,533. **No. of Company-Owned Units:** 37. **Founded:** 1972. **Franchised:** 1976. **Description:** Fast-food chicken restaurant specializing in cajun-style dishes. Serves authentic red beans and rice, spicy chicken, mashed potatoes and gravy and many other cajun-style side dishes. **Equity Capital Needed:** $750,000-$1,500,000 total investment; $900,000 required cash liquidity. **Franchise Fee:** $30,000. **Financial Assistance:** No. **Training:** Popeyes Operations Management Training (OMT) Program must be attended by up to four management employees prior to the opening of a restaurant. The OMT Program covers an extensive range of subjects related to the operation of a restaurant. This 6 week program indoctrinates employee of job station areas and restaurant administration management, application of job skills and techniques, and classroom materials needed in the management of a restaurant.

18140 ■ Port of Subs
Port of Subs, Inc.
5365 Mae Anne Ave., No. A-29
Reno, NV 89523
Ph:(775)747-0555
Free: 800-245-0245
Fax:(775)747-1510
No. of Franchise Units: 115. **No. of Company-Owned Units:** 25. **Founded:** 1972. **Franchised:** 1985. **Description:** Submarine sandwich franchise, featuring unique front-line method of preparing specialty sandwiches, soups, salads and party platters. Bread is baked fresh daily on premises. **Equity Capital Needed:** $80,000 liquid assets, $250,000 net worth. **Franchise Fee:** $20,000. **Financial Assistance:** No. **Managerial Assistance:** operations assistance. **Training:** Offers 2+ weeks of training, plus 2 weeks in the franchisees unit during initial opening.

18141 ■ Prime Restaurants of Canada Inc.
Prime Restaurant Group Inc.
10 Kingsbridge Garden Cir., Ste. 600
Mississauga, ON, Canada L5R 3K6
Ph:(905)568-0000
Free: 800-361-3111
Fax:(905)568-0080
Co. E-mail: franchising@primerestaurants.com
URL: http://www.primerestaurants.com
No. of Franchise Units: 139. **No. of Company-Owned Units:** 11. **Founded:** 1980. **Franchised:** 1982. **Description:** The pub has achieved "total value" by "raising the bar" in terms of food quality, service entertainment and decor. **Equity Capital Needed:** $288,000-$840,000 start-up; $500,000-$2,100,000 total investment. **Franchise Fee:** $40,000-$50,000.

18142 ■ Qdoba Mexican Grill
Qdoba Restaurant Corp.
4865 Ward Rd., Ste. 500
Wheat Ridge, CO 80033
Ph:(720)898-2300
Fax:(720)898-2396
No. of Franchise Units: 490. **No. of Company-Owned Units:** 147. **Founded:** 1995. **Franchised:** 1997. **Description:** Specialist in Mexican food. **Equity Capital Needed:** $2,000,000 net worth; $500,000 liquid. **Franchise Fee:** $30,000. **Financial Assistance:** No. **Training:** Yes.

18143 ■ Quizno's Subs
The Quizno's Corp.
1001 17th St., Ste. 175
Denver, CO 80202-2212
Ph:(720)359-3300
Free: 800-335-4782
No. of Franchise Units: 2,772. **No. of Company-Owned Units:** 62. **Founded:** 1981. **Franchised:** 1983. **Description:** Italian deli theme, specializing in subs, soups, salads and pasta. **Equity Capital Needed:** $157,547-$217,527, estimated initial investment for new store. **Franchise Fee:** $5,000-$12,500. **Financial Assistance:** Assistance with third party financing. **Training:** Twenty two day training program includes classroom and in-store training. Grand opening and initial onsite assistance.

18144 ■ Rally's Hamburgers
Checkers Drive-In Restaurants, Inc.
4300 West Cypress St., Ste. 600
Tampa, FL 33607
Ph:(813)283-7000
Fax:(813)283-7317
No. of Franchise Units: 378. **No. of Company-Owned Units:** 98. **Founded:** 1985. **Franchised:** 1986. **Description:** Double drive-thru burgers, fries, and cola. **Equity Capital Needed:** $472,100-$644,100 (excludes land). **Franchise Fee:** $30,000. **Financial Assistance:** Yes. **Training:** Yes.

18145 ■ Ranch 1 Grilled Chicken
9311 E Via De Ventura
Scottsdale, AZ 85258
Ph:(480)362-4800
Free: 800-438-2590
No. of Franchise Units: 15. **Founded:** 1991. **Franchised:** 1993. **Description:** Grilled & fried chicken quick service restaurant. **Equity Capital Needed:** $148,400-$518,300. **Franchise Fee:** $30,000. **Royalty Fee:** 6%. **Financial Assistance:** Limited third party financing available. **Training:** Provides 1 week training at headquarters, 2 weeks at franchisee's location, and ongoing support.

18146 ■ Rice King
Rice King Foods, Inc.
8396 Vickers St., Ste. 205
San Diego, CA 92111
Ph:(858)505-8677
Free: 800-418-4421
Fax:(858)505-8668
No. of Franchise Units: 35. **No. of Company-Owned Units:** 3. **Founded:** 1982. **Franchised:** 1996. **Description:** Asian fast food restaurant. **Equity Capital Needed:** $174,000-$382,000. **Franchise Fee:** $13,000. **Financial Assistance:** Yes. **Training:** Yes.

18147 ■ Ricky's All Day Grill
1901 Rosser Ave., Ste. 401
Burnaby, BC, Canada V5C 6S3
Ph:(604)637-7272
Free: 888-597-7272
Fax:(604)637-8874
Co. E-mail: franchising@rickysr.com
URL: http://www.rickys-restaurants.com
No. of Franchise Units: 55. **No. of Company-Owned Units:** 2. **Founded:** 1960. **Franchised:** 1978. **Description:** Offers awesome, affordable meals for breakfast, lunch and dinner. **Equity Capital Needed:** $650,000-$950,000 investment required; $350,000 start-up capital required. **Franchise Fee:** $45,000. **Training:** Comprehensive pre-opening and post-opening training, and ongoing training programs.

18148 ■ Rockin'Baja Lobster
Rockin'Baja Lobster, LLC
19712 MacArthurs Blvd., Ste. 210
Irvine, CA 92612
Ph:(949)719-3800
Free: 877-762-2252
Fax:(949)721-4053
No. of Company-Owned Units: 40. **Founded:** 1992. **Franchised:** 2003. **Description:** Baja cantina and grill. **Equity Capital Needed:** $240,400-$1,200,000. **Franchise Fee:** $30,000. **Royalty Fee:** 5%. **Financial Assistance:** Third party financing available. **Training:** Provides 2 weeks training at headquarters and ongoing support.

18149 ■ Rockwell's Bar & Grill
1812 152nd St., Unit 203
Surrey, BC, Canada V4A 4N5
Ph:(604)536-4111
Fax:(604)536-4103
Co. E-mail: franchise@rockwell.ca
URL: http://www.rockwells.ca
No. of Franchise Units: 3. **No. of Company-Owned Units:** 1. **Founded:** 2001. **Franchised:** 2001. **Description:** Casual full service dining. **Equity Capital Needed:** $800,000-$1,000,000. **Franchise Fee:** $50,000. **Training:** Provides 6 weeks training and ongoing support.

18150 ■ Rollerz
Kahala Corp.
9311 E Via De Ventura
Scottsdale, AZ 85258
Ph:(480)362-4800
Free: 800-438-2590

Fax:(480)443-1972
No. of Franchise Units: 7. **Founded:** 1999. **Franchised:** 1999. **Description:** Fast foods restaurant that offers delivery service too. **Equity Capital Needed:** $143,400-$441,300. **Franchise Fee:** $30,000. **Royalty Fee:** 6%. **Financial Assistance:** Limited third party financing available. **Training:** Provides 1 week at headquarters, 2 weeks at franchisee's location and ongoing support.

18151 ■ Ronzio Pizza
Ronzio Management, Inc.
111 John St.
Lincoln, RI 02865
Ph:(401)334-9750
Fax:(401)312-0378
No. of Franchise Units: 21. **Founded:** 1986. **Franchised:** 1992. **Description:** Pizza & sub shops. **Equity Capital Needed:** $250,000 net worth; $136,500-$207,500 total investment. **Franchise Fee:** $15,000. **Financial Assistance:** No. **Training:** Yes.

18152 ■ Roy Rogers Restaurants
Roy Rogers Franchise Company, LLC
321 Ballenger Center Dr., Ste. 201
Fredrick, MD 21703
Ph:(301)695-8563
Fax:(301)695-5066
No. of Franchise Units: 36. **No. of Company-Owned Units:** 17. **Founded:** 1968. **Franchised:** 2003. **Description:** Quick service restaurant. **Equity Capital Needed:** $915,250-$1,472,250. **Franchise Fee:** $30,000. **Financial Assistance:** No. **Training:** Yes.

18153 ■ St. Louis Bar and Grill
St. Louis Franchise Limited
2040 Yonge St., Ste. 200B
Toronto, ON, Canada M4S 1Z9
Ph:(416)485-1094
Free: (866)674-0606
Fax:(416)480-1512
Co. E-mail: kathy@stlouisfranchise.com
URL: http://www.stlouiswings.com
No. of Franchise Units: 28. **No. of Company-Owned Units:** 2. **Founded:** 1992. **Franchised:** 2002. **Description:** 20 year history in the bar and restaurant industry in owner-operated locations. **Equity Capital Needed:** 400,000-$600,000 investment required; $200,000 minimum. **Franchise Fee:** $40,000. **Training:** Yes.

18154 ■ Salad Creations
Lett-Us Franchise, LLC
4171 W Hillsboro Blvd., Ste. 4
Coconut Creek, FL 33073
Ph:(954)590-2467
Fax:(954)590-2484
URL: http://www.saladcreations.net
No. of Franchise Units: 81. **No. of Company-Owned Units:** 1. **Founded:** 2002. **Franchised:** 2003. **Description:** "Fresh is fabulous!" at Salad Creations, a growing franchise offering selections that fit the needs & wants of educated consumers in an exciting, welcoming environment. Consumers are always seeking healthful alternatives to traditional fast food. Along with our menu of healthful & tasty choices, we invite our guests to create meals with the assistance of enthusiastic & service focused "salad chefs." **Equity Capital Needed:** $75,000-$225,000. **Franchise Fee:** $25,000. **Financial Assistance:** No. **Training:** Provides 12 days training at the Salad University, consists of operational and psychological training.

18155 ■ Saladworks LLC
Eight Tower Bridge
161 Washington St., Ste. 300
Conshohocken, PA 19428
Ph:(610)825-3080
Free: 800-230-8447
Fax:(610)825-3280
No. of Franchise Units: 100+. **No. of Company-Owned Units:** 4. **Founded:** 1986. **Franchised:** 1991. **Description:** Restaurant franchise, meeting the drive-in, carryout and delivery requirements of the customers. **Equity Capital Needed:** $381,150-$698,400. **Franchise Fee:** $35,000. **Financial Assistance:** Yes. **Training:** Yes.

18156 ■ Salsarita's Fresh Cantina
Salsarita's Inc.
2908 Oak Lake Blvd., Ste. 205
Charlotte, NC 28208
Ph:(704)540-9447
Fax:(704)540-9448
No. of Franchise Units: 16. **Founded:** 2000. **Franchised:** 2000. **Description:** Fresh Mexican in a cantina atmosphere. **Equity Capital Needed:** $125,000 liquid; $350,000 net worth. **Franchise Fee:** $20,000. **Financial Assistance:** Yes. **Training:** Yes.

18157 ■ Sammy J. Peppers Restaurant & Lounge
1075 Lougheed Hwy.
Coquitlam, BC, Canada V3K 6N5
Ph:(604)524-1422
Fax:(604)525-0745
Co. E-mail: sjpcoquitlam@sjpeppers.com
URL: http://www.sammyjpeppers.com
No. of Company-Owned Units: 5. **Founded:** 1996. **Franchised:** 2004. **Description:** We offer an extensive, unique and bold menu with an upbeat and energetic atmosphere in our restaurants. Peppers and spices are very dominant in our menu offerings. We are a casual family restaurant with an entertainment lounge area. We currently have 5 locations in BC. Franchise opportunities are available throughout BC and Alberta. We are also seeking sites in the USA. **Equity Capital Needed:** $750,000-$1,500,000. **Franchise Fee:** $50,000. **Training:** Offers 4-6 weeks training in Vancouver, BC.

18158 ■ Sawmill Prime Rib & Steak House
4810 Calgary Trl. South, 2nd Fl.
Edmonton, AB, Canada T6H 5H5
Ph:(780)463-4499
Fax:(780)463-3183
Co. E-mail: lmccullough@sawmillrestaurant.com
URL: http://www.sawmillrestaurant.com
No. of Franchise Units: 4. **No. of Company-Owned Units:** 2. **Founded:** 1976. **Franchised:** 2004. **Description:** Offers fine dining and formal service in a comfortable atmosphere. Serving only "AAA" Alberta Beef, an extensive salad shrimp & oyster bar, as well as an array of seafood, chicken, bison and lamb. Adjoining pub/patio has lighter menu. **Equity Capital Needed:** $1,500,000. **Franchise Fee:** $50,000. **Training:** Yes.

18159 ■ Sbarro The Italian Eatery
401 Broadhollow Rd.
Melville, NY 11747
Ph:(631)715-4150
Fax:(516)715-4183
No. of Company-Owned Units: 280. **Founded:** 1959. **Franchised:** 1977. **Description:** Italian eateries. **Equity Capital Needed:** $250,000-$850,000 liquid capital over $150,000, additional in high cost areas. **Franchise Fee:** $15,000-45,000. **Royalty Fee:** 7%. **Financial Assistance:** No. **Training:** Yes.

18160 ■ Scores Rotisserie & Ribs
8250 Decarie Blvd., Ste. 310
Montreal, QC, Canada H7P 2P5
Ph:(905)361-6701
Free: (866)341-9782
Fax:(514)341-5635
Co. E-mail: jrussel@scores.ca
URL: http://www.scores.ca
No. of Franchise Units: 42. **Founded:** 1995. **Franchised:** 1996. **Description:** Casual dining concept featuring Rotisserie Chicken, BBQ Ribs and an "ALL YOU CAN EAT" salad and soup bar. **Equity Capital Needed:** $700,000-$950,000 investment required; $280,000-$450,000 start-up capital required. **Franchise Fee:** $60,000, includes training. **Training:** Provides 8 weeks training.

18161 ■ Seattle Sutton's Franchise Corp.
611 E Stevenson Rd.
Ottawa, IL 61350
Ph:888-795-6135
Fax:(815)795-3493
No. of Franchise Units: 5. **No. of Company-Owned Units:** 1. **Founded:** 1985. **Franchised:** 1996. **Description:** Manufacturing freshly prepared healthy meals. **Equity Capital Needed:** $5,000,000 franchise kitchen; $500,000 distributorship. **Franchise Fee:** $35,000. **Financial Assistance:** No. **Training:** Yes.

18162 ■ Select Sandwich
Select Food Services, Ltd.
155 Gordon Baker Rd., Ste. 214
Toronto, ON, Canada M2H 3N5
Ph:(416)391-1244
Free: (866)567-5648
Fax:(416)391-5244
Co. E-mail: crkahn@selectsandwich.com
URL: http://www.selectsandwich.com
No. of Franchise Units: 30. **Founded:** 1979. **Franchised:** 1980. **Description:** An established brand leader operating quick-service gourmet sandwich restaurants. Now expanding nationally. **Equity Capital Needed:** $250,000. **Franchise Fee:** $25,000. **Training:** Offers 6 weeks training.

18163 ■ Shakey's Pizza & Buffet
Shakey's USA, Inc.
2200 W Valley Blvd.
Alhambra, CA 91803
Ph:(626)576-0616
Free: 888-444-6686
Fax:(626)284-6870
URL: http://www.shakeys.com
No. of Franchise Units: 35. **No. of Company-Owned Units:** 25. **Description:** The franchise offers food service, well-known for a variety of pizza. **Equity Capital Needed:** $500,000 liquid per unit. **Franchise Fee:** $35,000. **Financial Assistance:** No. **Training:** Yes.

18164 ■ Shane's Rib Shack
Petrus Brands
1425 Ellsworth Industrial Blvd. NW, Ste. 38
Atlanta, GA 30318
Ph:(404)856-4320
Fax:(404)856-4334
URL: http://www.shanesribshack.com
No. of Franchise Units: 64. **No. of Company-Owned Units:** 2. **Founded:** 2002. **Franchised:** 2005. **Description:** Fast casual concept specializes in choice cut pork BBQ, baby back ribs, crispy chicken tenders, homemade side items and made from scratch peach cobbler. **Equity Capital Needed:** $500,000 net worth; $150,000 liquid. **Franchise Fee:** $30,000. **Financial Assistance:** No. **Training:** Raving Brands University classroom and onsite training provided. From register operation to food preparation, from hiring staff to accounting procedures, you'll improve your management skills, setup your back office and develop airtight sales and marketing plan.

18165 ■ Shoeless Joe's Limited
8555 Jane St, Unit 201
Vaughan, ON, Canada L4K 5N9
Ph:(905)760-1295
Fax:(905)760-1296
Co. E-mail: franchising@shoelessjoes.ca
URL: http://www.shoelessjoes.ca/our_teamfranchises.htm
No. of Franchise Units: 34. **No. of Company-Owned Units:** 2. **Founded:** 1985. **Franchised:** 1987. **Description:** The franchise offers restaurant and bar service with a North American sports theme. **Equity Capital Needed:** $350,000-$450,000 start-up capital required; $650,000-$950,000 total investment. **Franchise Fee:** $45,000. **Training:** Provides 8 weeks training and ongoing support.

18166 ■ Silver Mine Subs
8010 S County Rd. 5, Unit 203
Fort Collins, CO 80528
Ph:(970)266-2600
Fax:(970)267-3538
No. of Franchise Units: 20. **No. of Company-Owned Units:** 1. **Founded:** 1996. **Franchised:** 2002. **Description:** Is a food franchise with restaurant, drive-in, carryout and delivery facilities. **Equity Capital Needed:** $212,850-$321,350. **Franchise Fee:** $12,500-$20,000. **Financial Assistance:** No. **Training:** Yes.

18167 ■ Sizzler USA Franchise, Inc.
Sizzler USA Inc.
6101 W Centinga Ave., Ste. 300
Culver City, CA 90230
Ph:(310)846-8750
Fax:(310)848-8794
No. of Franchise Units: 239. **No. of Company-Owned Units:** 74. **Founded:** 1958. **Franchised:** 1963. **Description:** Casual restaurant dining. **Franchise Fee:** $30,000. **Financial Assistance:** No. **Training:** Yes.

18168 ■ Skyline Chili, Inc.
4180 Thunderbird Ln.
Fairfield, OH 45014
Ph:(513)874-1188
Fax:(513)874-3591
No. of Franchise Units: 98. **No. of Company-Owned Units:** 37. **Founded:** 1949. **Franchised:** 1957. **Description:** Maker of chili and franchisor of restaurants offering chili and related products. **Equity Capital Needed:** $200,000-$400,000 start-up cash minimum; total investment varies. **Franchise Fee:** $20,000. **Financial Assistance:** No. **Training:** Yes.

18169 ■ Smitty's
Smitty's Canada Ltd.
501 18th Ave. SW, Ste. 600
Calgary, AB, Canada T2S 0C7
Ph:(403)229-3838
Fax:(403)229-3899
Co. E-mail: franchiseinquiry@smittys.ca
No. of Franchise Units: 115. **No. of Company-Owned Units:** 8. **Founded:** 1960. **Franchised:** 1960. **Description:** Restaurants providing a full menu, which comprises breakfast, lunch, and dinner items. Even though experts in pancakes, waffles, and eggs, Smitty's franchises offers sandwiches and burgers and include liquor service during hours. **Equity Capital Needed:** $150,000 cash. **Franchise Fee:** $35,000 + GST. **Training:** Yes.

18170 ■ Sonic Drive In Restaurants
Sonic Corp.
300 Johnny Bench Dr.
Oklahoma City, OK 73104
Ph:(405)225-5000
Free: 800-569-6656
Fax:(405)225-5963
No. of Franchise Units: 3,079. **No. of Company-Owned Units:** 446. **Founded:** 1954. **Franchised:** 1959. **Description:** Drive-in fast-food restaurant offering hamburgers, hot dogs, French fries and onion rings. **Equity Capital Needed:** $1,102,300-$3,046,700. **Franchise Fee:** $45,000. **Royalty Fee:** 2-5%. **Financial Assistance:** Third party financing available. **Training:** Provides 1 week training at headquarters, 11 weeks onsite, 1 day to 1 week additional training with ongoing support.

18171 ■ Soul Fixins' Restaurant
Soul Fixins Franchise Corp. LLC
225 W 28th St.
New York, NY 10001
Ph:(212)736-1345
No. of Franchise Units: 1. **Founded:** 1993. **Franchised:** 2004. **Description:** Soul food restaurant. **Equity Capital Needed:** $274,000-$524,000. **Franchise Fee:** $30,000. **Royalty Fee:** 5%. **Financial Assistance:** Third party financing available. **Training:** Includes training at headquarters, franchisee's location and ongoing.

18172 ■ The Steak Escape
Escape Enterprises, Ltd.
222 Neilston St.
Columbus, OH 43215
Ph:(614)224-0300
Fax:(614)224-6460
No. of Franchise Units: 101. **No. of Company-Owned Units:** 8. **Founded:** 1982. **Franchised:** 1983. **Description:** Specialty restaurant for grilled sandwiches, salads, freshly cut French fries. **Equity Capital Needed:** Grill: $350,000 net worth, $100,000 cash; Express: $175,000 net worth $50,000 cash. **Franchise Fee:** $15,000-$25,000. **Financial Assistance:** No. **Training:** Provides 3 weeks training at headquarters, 1 week at franchisee's location and ongoing support.

18173 ■ Steak N Shake
The Steak N Shake Co.
36 S Pennsylvania, Ste. 500
Indianapolis, IN 46204
Ph:(317)633-4100
Fax:(317)655-7317
No. of Franchise Units: 51. **No. of Company-Owned Units:** 437. **Founded:** 1934. **Franchised:** 1939. **Description:** A restaurant offering quick-seared steak burgers, thin French fries, genuine chili and hand dipped milk shakes. Offers drive-thru and take-out service, in an environment reminiscent of the 50's. **Equity Capital Needed:** $1,500,000 net worth; $500,000 liquid. **Franchise Fee:** $40,000. **Financial Assistance:** No. **Training:** Provides on-the-job training program, utilizing personal instructions, training videos and workbooks.

18174 ■ Steak-Out Charbroiled Delivery
Steak-Out Franchising, Inc.
3091 Governors Lake Dr., Ste. 500
Norcross, GA 30071
Ph:(678)533-6000
Free: 877-878-3257
Fax:(678)291-0222
Co. E-mail: jmccord@steakout.com
URL: http://www.steakout.com
No. of Franchise Units: 42. **No. of Company-Owned Units:** 2. **Founded:** 1986. **Franchised:** 1987. **Description:** Full meal delivery chain featuring charbroiled steaks, chicken, seafood, burgers, chef salads & deserts. Steak-Out serves the busy office worker that doesn't have time to go for lunch & the on-the-go family that needs a wholesome meal when there is no time to cook. Steak-Out features delivery, carry-out & catering. **Equity Capital Needed:** $100,000 liquid; $400,000 net worth. **Franchise Fee:** $30,000. **Financial Assistance:** Third party and SBA approved. **Training:** Training is 4 weeks in the store and at headquarters for 3 to 4 management employees. Complete support in site finding, store opening, marketing and ongoing.

18175 ■ Strings Italian Cafe/Strings Italian Express
Strings Franchises Inc.
11344 Coloma Rd., Ste. 545
Gold River, CA 95670
Ph:(916)635-3990
Fax:(916)631-9775
No. of Franchise Units: 15. **No. of Company-Owned Units:** 3. **Founded:** 1987. **Franchised:** 1989. **Description:** It is a franchise of Italian restaurants. **Equity Capital Needed:** $159,500-$385,700. **Franchise Fee:** $37,500. **Financial Assistance:** No. **Training:** Yes.

18176 ■ Suki Hana & Chicken Connection
International Restaurant Management Group
4104 Aurora St.
Coral Gables, FL 33146-1416
Ph:(305)476-1611
Fax:(305)476-9622
No. of Franchise Units: 6. **No. of Company-Owned Units:** 16. **Founded:** 1989. **Franchised:** 1998. **Description:** A restaurant providing Japanese-style food. **Equity Capital Needed:** $240,500-$507,000. **Franchise Fee:** $30,000. **Financial Assistance:** No. **Training:** Yes.

18177 ■ Sunset Grill
5100 Erin Mills Town Centre
PO Box 53036
Mississauga, ON, Canada L5M 5A7
Ph:(905)286-5833
Fax:(905)829-1142
Co. E-mail: info@sunsetgrill.ca
URL: http://www.sunsetgrill.ca
No. of Franchise Units: 64. **No. of Company-Owned Units:** 5. **Founded:** 1985. **Franchised:** 2003. **Description:** Sunset Grill, Famous all-day Breakfast. Toronto's favorite breakfast restaurant franchising a one-shift breakfast concept. **Equity Capital Needed:** $150,000-$200,000. **Franchise Fee:** $45,000. **Training:** Yes.

18178 ■ Supper Thyme USA
Supper Thyme USA Franchise Services
7102 S 141st St.
Omaha, NE 68137
Ph:(402)933-4521
Fax:(402)614-5900
No. of Franchise Units: 31. **Founded:** 2003. **Franchised:** 2004. **Description:** Homemade meal preparation service. **Equity Capital Needed:** $130,900-$238,500. **Franchise Fee:** $35,000. **Financial Assistance:** No. **Training:** Yes.

18179 ■ Sweet Peppers Deli
Sweet peppers Franchise Systems, LLC
PO Box 1368
Columbus, OH 39703
Ph:(662)327-6982
Free: 888-222-9550
Fax:(662)327-1672
No. of Franchise Units: 14. **No. of Company-Owned Units:** 5. **Founded:** 1984. **Franchised:** 2002. **Description:** Fast casual, deli-style restaurant. **Equity Capital Needed:** $200,000. **Franchise Fee:** $25,000. **Financial Assistance:** No. **Training:** Yes.

18180 ■ Taco Bell of Canada
A Division of Tricon Global Restaurants (Canada) Inc.
101 Exchange Ave.
Vaughan, ON, Canada L4K 5R6
Ph:(416)664-5200
Free: 800-268-5435
Fax:(416)739-0118
Co. E-mail: franchisecanada@yum.com
URL: http://www.yumfranchises.com
No. of Franchise Units: 56. **Founded:** 1962. **Description:** Offers quick-service Mexican-style food specializing in tacos, burritos, nachos and fries. **Equity Capital Needed:** $350,000-$1,200,000. **Franchise Fee:** $45,500 U.S. **Training:** Offers 12 weeks minimum.

18181 ■ Taco Del Mar
Taco Del Mar franchising Corp.
6830 NE Bothell Way Ste. C-492
Kenmore, WA 98028
Ph:(206)624-7060
Fax:(206)624-7065
No. of Franchise Units: 276. **No. of Company-Owned Units:** 1. **Founded:** 1992. **Franchised:** 1995. **Description:** Fast casual Mexican restaurant. **Equity Capital Needed:** $148,000-$294,000. **Franchise Fee:** $23,000. **Financial Assistance:** No. **Training:** Yes.

18182 ■ Taco John's International, Inc.
808 West 20th St.
Cheyenne, WY 82001
Ph:(307)635-0101
Fax:(307)772-0369
No. of Franchise Units: 419. **No. of Company-Owned Units:** 9. **Founded:** 1969. **Franchised:** 1969. **Description:** A fast-food chain offering Mexican food. **Equity Capital Needed:** $150,000 liquid; $400,000 net worth. **Franchise Fee:** $22,500. **Financial Assistance:** No. **Training:** Yes.

18183 ■ The Taco Maker
PO Box 362888
San Juan, PR 00936-2888
Ph:(787)273-3160
No. of Franchise Units: 134. **No. of Company-Owned Units:** 4. **Founded:** 1978. **Franchised:** 1978. **Description:** Fresh made Mexican fast food. **Equity Capital Needed:** Capability of financing $70,000-$255,000. **Franchise Fee:** $30,000-$35,000. **Royalty Fee:** 5%. **Financial Assistance:** Third party financing available. **Training:** Yes.

18184 ■ Taco Mayo
Taco Mayo Franchise Systems, Inc.
10405 Greenbriar Pl.
Oklahoma City, OK 73159
Ph:(405)691-8226
No. of Franchise Units: 76. **No. of Company-Owned Units:** 16. **Founded:** 1978. **Franchised:** 1980. **Description:** Quick service Tex-Mex restau-

rant. **Equity Capital Needed:** $100,000-$120,000, includes franchise fee. **Franchise Fee:** $15,000. **Financial Assistance:** No. **Training:** Yes.

18185 ■ Taco Palace
814 E Hwy. 60
PO Box 87
Monett, MO 65708
Ph:(573)216-1739

No. of Franchise Units: 8. **No. of Company-Owned Units:** 2. **Founded:** 1985. **Franchised:** 1997. **Description:** Mexican fast food. **Equity Capital Needed:** $99,000-$139,000. **Franchise Fee:** $33,950. **Royalty Fee:** 0-4%. **Financial Assistance:** No. **Training:** Provides unlimited training at headquarters, 10 days at franchisee's location, and ongoing support.

18186 ■ Taco Time Canada Inc.
MTY TIKI Ming Enterprises
7156 Fisher St., SE
Calgary, AB, Canada T2H 0W5
Ph:(403)543-3490
Free: 800-471-5722
Fax:(403)543-3499
Co. E-mail: snickerson@tacotimecanada.com
URL: http://www.tacotimecanada.com

No. of Franchise Units: 119. **Founded:** 1978. **Franchised:** 1978. **Description:** Offers fast food in a friendly environment. **Equity Capital Needed:** $200,000-$350,000. **Franchise Fee:** $25,000. **Training:** Offers 2 weeks at corporate plus onsite at opening.

18187 ■ TacoTime
Taco Time International, Inc.
9311 E Via De Ventura
Scottsdale, AZ 85258
Ph:(480)362-4800
Free: 800-547-8907
URL: http://www.tacotime.com

No. of Franchise Units: 170. **Founded:** 1959. **Franchised:** 1960. **Description:** A restaurant specializing in Mexican food. **Equity Capital Needed:** $144,900-$721,800. **Franchise Fee:** $30,000 **Royalty Fee:** 6%. **Financial Assistance:** Limited third party financing available. **Training:** Provides 2-4 weeks training at headquarters and ongoing support.

18188 ■ Teriyaki Experience
Made in Japan Japanese Restaurants
7420 E Mary Sharon Dr.
Scottsdale, AZ 85266
Ph:(905)337-7777
Fax:(905)337-0331
Co. E-mail: info@teriyakiexperience.com
URL: http://www.teriyakieexperience.com

No. of Franchise Units: 135. **Founded:** 1986. **Franchised:** 1986. **Description:** A fast food franchise serving in food courts of shopping centres and airports. **Equity Capital Needed:** $180,000-$329,000 single store. **Franchise Fee:** $25,000. **Financial Assistance:** No. **Training:** Provides 12 day training pre-opening; onsite prior to opening and assistance during opening.

18189 ■ Teriyaki Stix
4833 N Edgewood Dr.
Provo, UT 84604
Ph:(801)224-6502
Free: 800-653-4581
Co. E-mail: franchise@hogiyogi.com
URL: http://www.hogiyogi.com

No. of Franchise Units: 54. **No. of Company-Owned Units:** 1. **Founded:** 1995. **Franchised:** 1998. **Description:** Japanese fast food restaurant. **Equity Capital Needed:** $135,200-$452,500. **Franchise Fee:** $25,000-$30,000. **Royalty Fee:** 6%. **Financial Assistance:** No. **Training:** Provides 8 days of training at headquarters.

18190 ■ Tony Roma's, Famous for Ribs
Roma Corp. USA
1700 Alma Dr., Ste. 400
Plano, TX 75075
Ph:(214)343-7800
Free: (214)343-7840

No. of Franchise Units: 141. **No. of Company-Owned Units:** 36. **Founded:** 1972. **Franchised:** 1974. **Description:** Casual restaurant, specializing in ribs. **Equity Capital Needed:** $350,000 liquid, per unit; $750,000 total. **Franchise Fee:** $50,000. **Financial Assistance:** No. **Training:** Yes.

18191 ■ Topper's Pizza
551 Bryne Drive, Unit N
Barrie, ON, Canada L4N 9Y3
Ph:(705)735-2127
Free: 877-558-5581
Fax:(705)735-4821
Co. E-mail: franchiseinfo@toppers.ca
URL: http://www.toppers.ca

No. of Franchise Units: 30. **No. of Company-Owned Units:** 6. **Founded:** 1982. **Franchised:** 1998. **Description:** Delivers great tasting pizzas at a competitive price. **Equity Capital Needed:** $200,000-$250,000. **Franchise Fee:** $25,000. **Training:** Offers 4-6 of training weeks.

18192 ■ Triple O's
1126 SE Marine Dr.
Vancouver, BC, Canada V5X 2V7
Ph:(604)321-6631
Fax:(604)325-1499
Co. E-mail: franchise-info@whitespot.ca
URL: http://www.tripleos.com

No. of Franchise Units: 44. **No. of Company-Owned Units:** 4. **Founded:** 1928. **Description:** White Spot Limited has developed a unique and proven "fast casual" concept. The Triple O's concept offers what many other quick service restaurant don't - high quality, unique tasting food made fresh, just for you. No one can beat Triple O's taste - award winning Triple "O" burger, fresh-cut fries and classic shakes. **Equity Capital Needed:** $500,000-$1,500,000 total investment. **Franchise Fee:** $40,000.

18193 ■ Tropik Sun Fruit & Nut
Diversifoods Inc.
899 Lakewood Dr.
Lakeforest, IL 60045
Ph:(847)968-4415

No. of Franchise Units: 90. **No. of Company-Owned Units:** 4. **Founded:** 1980. **Franchised:** 1980. **Description:** "Fun Munchies," gifts, drinks and popcorn. **Equity Capital Needed:** $35,000-$50,000 liquid. **Franchise Fee:** $20,000. **Financial Assistance:** No. **Training:** Yes.

18194 ■ Tubby's Sub Shops, Inc.
18357 E 14 Mile Rd.
Fraser, MI 48026
Ph:(586)293-5099
Free: 800-752-0644
Fax:(586)293-5088

No. of Franchise Units: 70. **No. of Company-Owned Units:** 2. **Founded:** 1968. **Franchised:** 1978. **Description:** Specialty submarine sandwich shop, featuring grilled sandwiches, soups, salads and ice cream. **Equity Capital Needed:** $500,000 net worth; $75,000 cash/assets convertible to cash. **Franchise Fee:** $5,000-$13,000 (varies by type of store). **Financial Assistance:** No. **Training:** Classroom sessions where very facet of your business is covered. Additional onsite assistance is given just prior to opening and during your first few weeks of operation.

18195 ■ Turtle Jack's Grillhouse Restaurant Inc.
Tortoise Restaurant Group Inc.
3370 S Service Rd., Ste. 201
Burlington, ON, Canada L7N 3M6
Ph:(905)332-6833
Fax:(905)332-0456
Co. E-mail: info@tortoise.ca
URL: http://www.tortoise.ca

No. of Franchise Units: 7. **No. of Company-Owned Units:** 5. **Founded:** 1992. **Description:** Tortoise Restaurant Group Inc., is a Management group that owns and operates concepts under the name of Turtle Jack's. Offers consistent execution of a simple philosophy including high quality food, enthusiastic service in a clean and comfortable environment has been key to the company's success. **Equity Capital Needed:** $600,000. **Franchise Fee:** $50,000. **Training:** Offers 12 weeks of training.

18196 ■ Tuscano's Italian Style Subs
Noble Roman's Inc.
1 Virginia Ave., Ste. 800
Indianapolis, IN 46204
Ph:(317)634-3377
Free: 800-585-0669

No. of Franchise Units: 60. **No. of Company-Owned Units:** 6. **Founded:** 2003. **Franchised:** 2003. **Description:** Subs - cold or grilled. **Equity Capital Needed:** $20,000-$175,000. **Franchise Fee:** $6,000-$15,000. **Financial Assistance:** No. **Training:** Yes.

18197 ■ Urban Kitchen
155 Gordon Baker Rd., Ste. 214
Toronto, ON, Canada M2H 3NP
Ph:(416)391-1244
Free: (866)567-5648
Fax:(416)391-5244
Co. E-mail: crkahn@selectsandwich.com

No. of Franchise Units: 3. **Founded:** 2007. **Franchised:** 2007. **Description:** Restaurant. **Equity Capital Needed:** $400,000-$500,000. **Franchise Fee:** $30,000. **Training:** Provides 6 weeks training.

18198 ■ Villa Enterprises
25 Washington St.
Morristown, NJ 07960
Ph:(973)285-4800
Fax:(973)401-0121

No. of Franchise Units: 88. **No. of Company-Owned Units:** 144. **Founded:** 1964. **Franchised:** 1999. **Description:** Quick service pizza & Italian restaurant. **Equity Capital Needed:** $296,950-$584,000. **Franchise Fee:** $25,000-$35,000. **Royalty Fee:** 6%. **Financial Assistance:** Limited third party financing available. **Training:** Training provided 3 weeks at corporate headquarters, 3 weeks at franchisee's location and ongoing support.

18199 ■ Virginia Barbeque
Virginia Barbeque Franchise Co.
1814 Country Rd.
Beaverdam, VA 23105
Free: 800-429-9965

No. of Franchise Units: 14. **No. of Company-Owned Units:** 2. **Founded:** 2000. **Franchised:** 2004. **Description:** Quick service "Genuine Southern" barbeque. **Equity Capital Needed:** $81,500-$221,500. **Franchise Fee:** $25,000. **Royalty Fee:** 6%. **Financial Assistance:** Limited third party financing available. **Training:** Provides 2 weeks at headquarters and 1 week at franchisee's location.

18200 ■ A & W Restaurant
YUM! Brands
1900 Colonel Sanders Ln.
Louisville, KY 40213-1914
Free: (866)298-6986

No. of Franchise Units: 322. **Founded:** 1919. **Franchised:** 1925. **Description:** Restaurants, serving hamburgers, hot dogs and root beer. **Equity Capital Needed:** $912,000-$1,623,500. **Franchise Fee:** $20,000. **Royalty Fee:** 5%. **Financial Assistance:** No. **Training:** Provides 2 weeks training and ongoing support.

18201 ■ We Toss'em, They're Awesome Pizza Factory
Pizza Factory Inc.
49430 Rd. 426
PO Box 989
Oakhurst, CA 93644
Ph:(559)683-3377
Free: 800-654-4840
Fax:(559)683-6879

No. of Franchise Units: 121. **Founded:** 1979. **Franchised:** 1985. **Description:** Pizzeria. **Equity Capital Needed:** $137,000-$426,000. **Franchise Fee:** Full, Mid, Express $20,000. **Financial Assistance:** No. **Training:** Yes.

18202 ■ Wendy's Restaurants of Canada Inc.
240 Wyecroft Rd.
Oakville, ON, Canada L6K 2G7
Ph:(905)849-7685
Fax:(905)849-5545
Co. E-mail: jane_dann@wendys.com
URL: http://www.wendys.com
No. of Franchise Units: 230. **No. of Company-Owned Units:** 137. **Founded:** 1969. **Description:** Wendy's Restaurant supplies quality hamburgers, including, chicken sandwiches and nuggets, garden sensations salads, French fries, soft drinks, baked potatoes, chili, kids' meals and a fresh dairy dessert. **Equity Capital Needed:** $1,300,000+/-. **Franchise Fee:** $40,000. **Training:** Initial 16-26 weeks of training provided.

18203 ■ Western Sizzlin
PO Box 12167
Roanoke, VA 24023-2167
Ph:(540)345-3195
Free: 800-247-8325
No. of Franchise Units: 142. **No. of Company-Owned Units:** 6. **Founded:** 1962. **Franchised:** 1966. **Description:** Family style steak house, buffet and bakery. **Equity Capital Needed:** $861,000-$2,660,000. **Franchise Fee:** $30,000. **Financial Assistance:** No. **Training:** Yes.

18204 ■ Wetzel's Pretzels
Wetzel's Pretzels, LLC
35 Hugus Alley, Ste. 300
Pasadena, CA 91103
Ph:(626)432-6900
Fax:(626)432-6904
No. of Franchise Units: 236. **No. of Company-Owned Units:** 11. **Founded:** 1994. **Franchised:** 1996. **Description:** Pretzels. **Equity Capital Needed:** $156,300-$369,950. **Franchise Fee:** $35,000. **Royalty Fee:** 7%. **Financial Assistance:** Limited third party financing available. **Training:** Offers 2 weeks at headquarters, 4 days at franchisees location and ongoing support.

18205 ■ Whata Lotta Pizza
7011 Warner Ave., Unit M
Huntington Beach, CA 92647
Ph:(714)848-6148
Free: 888-425-6882
Fax:(714)849-2029
Co. E-mail: info@whatalottapizza.com
URL: http://www.4alotta.com
No. of Franchise Units: 50. **No. of Company-Owned Units:** 8. **Founded:** 1992. **Franchised:** 2005. **Description:** Restaurant franchise. **Equity Capital Needed:** $90,000-$208,500. **Franchise Fee:** $25,000. **Financial Assistance:** Yes. **Training:** Yes.

18206 ■ White Spot Restaurants
1126 SE Marine Dr.
Vancouver, BC, Canada V5X 2V7
Ph:(604)321-6631
Fax:(604)325-1499
Co. E-mail: franchise-info@whitespot.ca
URL: http://www.whitespot.com
No. of Franchise Units: 40. **No. of Company-Owned Units:** 24. **Founded:** 1928. **Description:** The franchise is a family restaurant and offers site and design assistance, extensive training and ongoing support and marketing expertise. **Equity Capital Needed:** $750,000-$2,500,000. **Franchise Fee:** $75,000. **Training:** Offers 3-10 weeks of training, and assistance with staff and management.

18207 ■ Wienerschnitzel/Tastee-Freez
Galardi Group, Inc.
7700 Irvine Center Dr., Ste. 550
Irvine, CA 92618
Ph:(949)892-2619
Free: 800-764-9353
Fax:(949)892-2615
Co. E-mail: KPeters@GalardiGroup.com
URL: http://www.tastee-freez.com
No. of Franchise Units: 370. **Founded:** 1950. **Franchised:** 1950. **Description:** Fast food, including soft-serve ice cream and desserts. Plans available for free-standing building/food court/seasonal stores considered. **Equity Capital Needed:** $150,000-$250,000 liquid; $1,200,000 total investment. **Franchise Fee:** $32,000. **Royalty Fee:** 4%. **Financial Assistance:** Yes. **Managerial Assistance:** Provides ongoing field support, marketing support, product development, area meetings, equipment advisor and store lay-out assistance. **Training:** Consists of 2 weeks at the corporate office - total operation and business training given.

18208 ■ Wimpy's Diner Inc.
3559 St. Clair Ave., E
Scarborough, ON, Canada M1K 1L6
Ph:(416)269-4679
Free: 888-594-6797
Fax:(416)269-8484
Co. E-mail: info@wimpysdiner.ca
URL: http://www.whimpysdiner.net
No. of Franchise Units: 43. **Founded:** 1988. **Franchised:** 1992. **Description:** Full menu Diner Style Restaurant chain with a nostalgic 50's and 60's atmosphere, serving Famous burgers, Home style breakfast, Lunch, Dinner specials and other entrees. **Equity Capital Needed:** $150,000. **Franchise Fee:** $20,000. **Training:** Provides 4-8 weeks training.

18209 ■ Wing Zone
WZ Franchise Corp.
900 Circle 75 Pkwy., Ste. 930
Atlanta, GA 30339
Ph:(404)875-5045
Free: 877-333-WING
Fax:(404)875-6631
No. of Franchise Units: 90. **No. of Company-Owned Units:** 2. **Founded:** 1991. **Franchised:** 1999. **Description:** Take-Out and delivery buffalo wings. **Equity Capital Needed:** $247,500-$312,500. **Franchise Fee:** $25,000. **Royalty Fee:** 5%. **Financial Assistance:** Third party financing available. **Training:** Offers 12 days training at headquarters, 10 days at franchisee's location and ongoing support.

18210 ■ Winger's Grill & Bar
Winger's Franchising, Inc.
404 East 4500 S, Ste. A12
Salt Lake City, UT 84107
Ph:(801)261-3700
Fax:(801)261-1615
No. of Franchise Units: 30. **No. of Company-Owned Units:** 9. **Founded:** 1993. **Franchised:** 1997. **Description:** Casual dining for smaller markets. **Equity Capital Needed:** $250,000 per unit. **Franchise Fee:** $30,000. **Financial Assistance:** No. **Training:** Yes.

18211 ■ Wings to Go
Wings to Go, Inc.
846 Ritchie Hwy., Ste. 1B
Severna Park, MD 21146
Free: 800-552-9464
Fax:(870)932-1795
No. of Franchise Units: 87. **No. of Company-Owned Units:** 1. **Founded:** 1985. **Franchised:** 1989. **Description:** Retail restaurants, specializing in authentic buffalo-style chicken wings. **Equity Capital Needed:** $219,500-$354,500. **Franchise Fee:** $20,000. **Financial Assistance:** No. **Training:** Yes.

18212 ■ Wingstop
Wingstop Restaurants, Inc.
1101 E Arapaho Rd., Ste. 150
Richardson, TX 75081
Ph:(972)686-6500
Fax:(972)686-6502
Co. E-mail: info@wingstop.com
URL: http://www.wingstop.com
No. of Franchise Units: 94. **No. of Company-Owned Units:** 2. **Founded:** 1994. **Franchised:** 1998. **Description:** Non-vegetarian restaurant famous for buffalo-style chicken wings throughout southern United States. **Equity Capital Needed:** $55,000-$70,000 available; $181,800-$250,000 total investment. **Franchise Fee:** $20,000. **Financial Assistance:** Yes. **Training:** Yes.

18213 ■ Woody's Bar-B-Q
4745 Sutton Park Ct.
Jacksonville, FL 32224
Ph:(904)992-0556
Fax:(904)992-0551
No. of Franchise Units: 40. **No. of Company-Owned Units:** 1. **Founded:** 1980. **Franchised:** 1989. **Description:** Restaurant featuring smoked pork, beef, turkey, chicken, and barbecued ribs. **Equity Capital Needed:** $200,000-$300,000. **Franchise Fee:** $35,000. **Financial Assistance:** Third party financing available. **Training:** Includes 6 week training class in a company store for 2 people. Provides an in-store training and grand opening team along with ongoing field support and management, as well as advertising and promotion.

18214 ■ WOW Cafe & Wingery
WOW Cafe & Wingery Franchise Account L.L.C.
109 New Camellia Blvd., Ste. 200
Covington, LA 70433
Ph:(985)792-5776
No. of Franchise Units: 56. **Founded:** 2001. **Franchised:** 2002. **Description:** All American Cafe. **Equity Capital Needed:** $224,400-$752,500. **Franchise Fee:** $5,000-$35,000. **Royalty Fee:** 5%. **Financial Assistance:** Third party financing available. **Training:** Provides 15 days training at headquarters, 14 days at franchisee's location and ongoing support.

18215 ■ Yaya's Flame Broiled Chicken
CSC, Inc.
521 S Dort Hwy.
Flint, MI 48503
Ph:(810)235-6550
Free: 800-754-1242
Fax:(810)235-5210
No. of Franchise Units: 10. **No. of Company-Owned Units:** 7. **Founded:** 1986. **Franchised:** 1988. **Description:** Flame-broiled chicken, marinated with Yaya's special blend of herbs and spices. Side dishes include baked beans, mashed potatoes, rice pilaf, coleslaw and potato salad. No fried or frozen products. We specialize in flavor and nutrition. **Equity Capital Needed:** $300,000-$400,000. **Franchise Fee:** $15,000. **Financial Assistance:** No. **Training:** Yes.

18216 ■ Yeung's Lotus Express Franchise Corp.
4104 Aurora St.
Coral Gables, FL 33146-1416
Ph:(305)476-1611
Fax:(305)476-9622
No. of Franchise Units: 22. **No. of Company-Owned Units:** 19. **Founded:** 1987. **Franchised:** 1998. **Description:** Chinese food restaurant. **Equity Capital Needed:** $250,000-$500,000. **Franchise Fee:** $30,000. **Financial Assistance:** No. **Training:** Yes.

18217 ■ Yogurt & Such Cafe
Yogurt & Such Franchise Systems, Inc.
438 Woodbury Rd.
Plainview, NY 11803
Ph:(516)783-2655
No. of Franchise Units: 6. **No. of Company-Owned Units:** 3. **Founded:** 1982. **Franchised:** 1989. **Description:** A foods - restaurant franchise offering drive-in, carryout and delivery services. **Equity Capital Needed:** $95,000-$150,000 cash required. **Franchise Fee:** $25,000. **Financial Assistance:** No. **Training:** Yes.

18218 ■ Yum! Restaurants International (Canada) Company
101 Exchange Ave.
Vaughan, ON, Canada L4K 5R6
Ph:(416)664-5200
Free: 800-268-5435
Fax:(416)739-0118
Co. E-mail: franchisecanada@yum.com
URL: http://www.yumfranchises.ca
No. of Franchise Units: 1,050. FND 1954. **Description:** One of the world's largest restaurant chain with 30,000 units and $30 billion annual sales. Our franchises include Pizza Hut Canada, KFC-Canada,

and Taco Bell of Canada. **Equity Capital Needed:** $350,000-$1,200,000. **Franchise Fee:** $45,500 U.S. **Financial Assistance:** No. **Training:** Yes.

18219 ■ Zoo Pizza
3273 N Shepard
Milwaukee, WI 53211
No. of Company-Owned Units: 1. **Founded:** 1994. **Description:** Pizzeria. **Equity Capital Needed:** $300,000-$400,000. **Franchise Fee:** $89,000. **Training:** No.

18220 ■ ZOUP!
Zoup! Systems LLC
28290 Franklin Rd.
Southfield, MI 48034
Ph:(248)663-1111
Free: 800-940-9687
Fax:(248)663-9880
Co. E-mail: franchise@zoup.com
URL: http://www.zoupfranchise.com
No. of Franchise Units: 31. **No. of Company-Owned Units:** 3. **Founded:** 1997. **Franchised:** 2003. **Description:** Quick, casual soup restaurant. **Equity Capital Needed:** $235,400-$437,600. **Franchise Fee:** $39,000 for single. **Royalty Fee:** 6%. **Financial Assistance:** Third party financing available. **Training:** Offers 3 weeks at headquarters, 1 week onsite and ongoing support.

18221 ■ Zyng Asian Grill
PO Box 72108, RPO Atwater
Montreal, QC, Canada H3J 2Z6
Ph:(514)288-8808
Free: 888-EAT-ZYNG
Fax:(514)227-5302
Co. E-mail: ckassab@zyng.com
URL: http://www.zyng.com
No. of Franchise Units: 4. **Founded:** 1998. **Description:** Offers new full-service restaurant concept with noodle-based soups and grilled meals-in-bowls. Menu includes beer and wine, with table service and jazz music. **Equity Capital Needed:** $300,000-$500,000. **Franchise Fee:** $25,000. **Managerial Assistance:** Individual and area development agreements available. **Training:** Provides 4 weeks and ongoing support.

COMPUTER SYSTEMS/ SOFTWARE

18222 ■ Bottom Line Service System
Bottom Line Software
6528 E 101st St., Ste. 430
PMB 145
Tulsa, OK 74133
Ph:(530)573-0777
Fax:(530)573-0772
Co. E-mail: sales@blss.com
URL: http://www.bottom-line-software.com
Price: $495 single user version; $2595 network version. **Description:** The Bottom Line Service System is a Windows based service management system designed specifically to meet the needs of customer service businesses. HVAC, Refrigeration, Plumbing, Electrical and Mechanical service and installation companies use our system with great deal of success.

18223 ■ PayMaster Hospitality
Computer Aid Corp.
501 Church St., NE, Ste. 306
Vienna, VA 22180
Ph:(703)281-7486
Fax:(703)281-3461
URL: http://www.paymaster-pro.com/
Price: Computer Aid for pricing.

18224 ■ Restaurant Financial Management System
Rapp Industries, Inc.
233 Rock Rd., No. 113
Glen Rock, NJ 07452
Ph:(201)670-9084
Free: 800-999-1159
Fax:(201)444-4595
Co. E-mail: bobrapp@compuserve.com
URL: http://www.rappind.com
Price: $495.00. **Description:** Available for IBM computers and MS-DOS compatibles. Restaurant accounting system including payroll, accounts payable, general ledger and menu costing, tip allocation, and sales entry by category.

LIBRARIES

18225 ■ American Beverage Association Information Center
1101 16th St., NW
Washington, DC 20036
Ph:(202)463-6732
Fax:(202)659-5349
Co. E-mail: info@ameribev.org
URL: http://www.ameribev.org/
Contact: Susan K. Neely, Pres./CEO
Scope: Beverage industry. **Services:** Library open to the public for reference use only. **Holdings:** 500 books, articles, papers, and historical materials. **Subscriptions:** 115 journals and other serials.

18226 ■ American Institute of Food Distribution, Inc.–Information and Research Center
1 Broadway Plaza, 2nd Fl.
Elmwood Park, NJ 07407
Ph:(201)791-5570
Fax:(201)791-5222
Co. E-mail: jkastrinsky@foodinstitute.com
URL: http://www.foodinstitute.com/
Contact: Brian Todd, Pres./CEO
Scope: Food industry. **Services:** Center open to the public on fee basis. **Subscriptions:** 400 journals and other serials.

18227 ■ California Culinary Academy Library
625 Polk St.
San Francisco, CA 94102
Ph:800-229-2433
Free: 888-897-3222
Co. E-mail: bgk@baychef.com
URL: http://www.baychef.com
Contact: Beth Klein, Dean, Lib.Svcs.
Scope: Culinary arts, nutrition, restaurant and hospitality industry. **Services:** Library open to the public by special appointment only. **Holdings:** 3500 books. **Subscriptions:** 90 journals and other serials.

18228 ■ Canadian Restaurant & Foodservices Association Resource Centre
316 Bloor St., W.
Toronto, ON, Canada M5S 1W5
Ph:(416)923-8416
Free: 800-387-5649
Fax:(416)923-1450
Co. E-mail: info@crfa.ca
URL: http://www.crfa.ca/research/
Contact: Mimy Taylor, Info.Coord.
Scope: Food service, quantity cooking, legislation, administration, management, statistics, training, customer attitude surveys. **Services:** Copying; Center open to the public on fee basis. **Holdings:** 1000 books. **Subscriptions:** 100 journals and other serials.

18229 ■ City College of San Francisco Culinary Arts and Hospitality Studies Department–Alice Statler Library
50 Phelan Ave.
Statler Wing, Rm. 10
San Francisco, CA 94112
Ph:(415)239-3460
Fax:(415)239-3026
Co. E-mail: aniosi@ccsf.edu
URL: http://www.ccsf.edu/library/alice/statler.html
Contact: Andrea Niosi, Libn.
Scope: Public hospitality industries - hotels, motels, restaurants, catering services, cookery and nutrition; tourism; beverages. **Services:** Copying; Library open to the public for reference use only. **Holdings:** 10,000 books; 3500 pamphlets; 900 menus; videotapes; archives. **Subscriptions:** 80 journals and other serials.

18230 ■ Cornell University–The Nestle Library
G80 Statler Hall
School of Hotel Administration
Ithaca, NY 14853-6901
Ph:(607)255-3673
Fax:(607)255-0021
Co. E-mail: hotelref@cornell.edu
URL: http://www.hotelschool.cornell.edu/research/library
Contact: Donald Schnedeker, Dir.
Scope: Hotel, motel, and restaurant management, administration, accounting, quantity cookery, food facilities engineering, sanitation, advertising, sales promotion, public relations, marketing, hospitality law, franchising, real estate, tourist industry, resort development. **Services:** Interlibrary loan; Library open to the public by appointment on a fee basis. **Holdings:** 37,000 volumes; 17,000 microforms; 500 computer files; 1000 reels of microfilm; 16,500 microfiche; 1500 videos. **Subscriptions:** 500 serials; 12 newspapers.

18231 ■ Culinary Institute of America–Conrad N. Hilton Library
1946 Campus Dr.
Hyde Park, NY 12538-1499
Ph:(845)451-1322
Co. E-mail: c_crawfo@culinary.edu
URL: http://library.culinary.edu/
Contact: Christine Crawford-Oppenheimer, Info.Svcs. Libn.
Scope: Cookery, food service, restaurant management, hospitality. **Services:** Interlibrary loan; copying; Library open to the public by appointment. **Holdings:** 84,000 volumes; 30,000 menus; 3800 DVDs and videos. **Subscriptions:** 280 journals and other serials.

18232 ■ National Restaurant Association–Information Services and Library
1200 17th St., NW
Washington, DC 20036
Ph:(202)331-5900
Free: 800-424-5156
Fax:(202)331-2429
URL: http://www.restaurant.org
Contact: Mr. B. Hudson Riehle, Sr. VP
Scope: Foodservice industry, restaurants, cookery. **Services:** Library open to non-members and students for a fee (fee-based services available to non-members). **Holdings:** 5000 books; 2000 subject clipping files. **Subscriptions:** 150 journals and other serials.

18233 ■ Noble and Associates Library
2155 W. Chesterfield Blvd.
Springfield, MO 65807
Ph:(417)875-5000
Co. E-mail: julie.tumy@noble.net
URL: http://www.noble.net
Contact: Julie Tumy, Pres.
Scope: Food, food service, advertising, construction, agriculture. **Services:** Interlibrary loan; copying; SDI; Library not open to the public. **Holdings:** 500 books; 1000 reports. **Subscriptions:** 300 journals and other serials; 5 newspapers.

18234 ■ Prince Edward Island Food Technology Centre–Information Services
PO Box 2000
Charlottetown, PE, Canada C1A 7N8
Ph:(902)368-5548
Fax:(902)368-5549
Co. E-mail: peiftc@gov.pe.ca
URL: http://www.gov.pe.ca/ftc/
Contact: Kathy MacEwen, Lib.Techn.
Scope: Agriculture, food, technology, food research. **Services:** Interlibrary loan; Library open to the public by permission only. **Holdings:** 200 books; 9 bound periodical volumes. **Subscriptions:** 38 journals and other serials.

Resume Service

START-UP INFORMATION

18235 ■ "Home Work" in *Black Enterprise* (Vol. 37, October 2006, No. 3, pp. 78)
Pub: Earl G. Graves Publishing Co. Inc.

Ed: James C. Johnson. **Description:** Information on starting a resume-writing service is profiled.

ASSOCIATIONS AND OTHER ORGANIZATIONS

18236 ■ Professional Association of Resume Writers and Career Coaches
1388 Brightwaters Blvd. NE
St. Petersburg, FL 33704-1336
Ph:(727)821-2274
Free: 800-822-7279
Fax:(727)894-1277
Co. E-mail: parwhq@aol.com
URL: http://www.parw.com
Contact: Frank Fox, Exec. Dir.
Description: Represents the interests of professional resume writers, employment interview trainers, and career coaches. Acts as a clearinghouse for information on career topics. Provides educational programs. Offers certification for Certified Professional Resume Writers (CPRW) and for Certified Employment Interview Professionals (CEIP). **Publications:** *The Spotlight* (monthly).

REFERENCE WORKS

18237 ■ "'Resume Mining' Services Can Save Time, Money" in *HR Specialist* (Vol. 8, September 2010, No. 9, pp. 7)
Pub: Capitol Information Group Inc.
Description: Low-cost resume mining services can help human resource departments save time and money by searching online resume databases for candidates matching specific job qualifications.

18238 ■ "Tracking Your Fleet Can Increase Bottom Line" in *Contractor* (Vol. 56, November 2009, No. 11, pp. 26)
Pub: Penton Media, Inc.

Ed: Candace Roulo. **Description:** GPS fleet management system can help boost a contractor's profits, employee productivity, and efficiency. These are available as a handheld device or a cell phone that employees carry around or as a piece of hardware installed in a vehicle. These lets managers track assets and communicate with employees about jobs.

ASSOCIATIONS AND OTHER ORGANIZATIONS

18239 ■ American Subcontractors Association
1004 Duke St.
Alexandria, VA 22314-3588
Ph:(703)684-3450
Free: 888-374-3133
Fax:(703)836-3482
Co. E-mail: asaoffice@asa-hq.com
URL: http://www.asaonline.com
Contact: Timmy McLaughlin, Pres.

Description: Construction subcontractors of trades and specialties such as foundations, concrete, masonry, steel, mechanical, drywall, electrical, painting, plastering, roofing and acoustical. Formed to deal with issues common to subcontractors. Works with other segments of the construction industry in promoting ethical practices, beneficial legislation and education of construction subcontractors and suppliers. Manages the Foundation of the American Subcontractors Association (FASA). **Publications:** *Action ASA* (monthly); *The Contractor's Compass* (quarterly).

18240 ■ Asphalt Roofing Manufacturers Association
Public Information Department
750 National Press Bldg.
529 14th St. NW
Washington, DC 20045
Ph:(202)207-0917
Fax:(202)223-9741
URL: http://asphaltroofing.org
Contact: Reed Hitchcock, Exec. VP

Description: Manufacturers of asphalt shingles, roll-goods, built-up roofing systems (BUR) and modified bitumen roofing systems. Compiles statistics. **Publications:** *ARMA eNewsletter* (quarterly); *ARMA Government Issues Newsletter* (quarterly); *Publication and Audio-Visual Directory* (biennial);Membership Directory (annual).

18241 ■ Canadian Roofing Contractors Association–Association Canadienne des Entrepreneurs en Couverture
2430 Don Reid Dr., Ste. 100
Ottawa, ON, Canada K1H 1E1
Ph:(613)232-6724
Free: 800-461-2722
Fax:(613)232-2893
Co. E-mail: crca@on.aibn.com
URL: http://www.roofingcanada.com
Contact: John E. Hill, Exec. Dir.

Description: Roofing contractors. Seeks to advance the building industries. Facilitates communication and cooperation among members; represents members' interests before labor and industrial organizations, government agencies, and the public. **Publications:** *Roofing Canada* (semiannual).

18242 ■ National Roofing Contractors Association
10255 W Higgins Rd., Ste. 600
Rosemont, IL 60018-5607
Ph:(847)299-9070
Free: 800-323-9545
Fax:(847)299-1183
URL: http://www.nrca.net
Contact: Bill Good, Exec. VP

Description: Roofing, roof deck, and waterproofing contractors and industry-related associate members. Assists members to successfully satisfy their customers through technical support, testing and research, education, marketing, government relations, and consultation. **Publications:** *Professional Roofing* (monthly).

18243 ■ National Roofing Foundation
10255 W Higgins Rd., Ste. 600
Rosemont, IL 60018-5607
Ph:(847)299-9070
Fax:(847)493-7959
Co. E-mail: bjudson@roofingindustryalliance.net
URL: http://www.nrca.net/rp/related/nrf
Contact: Geoff Craft, Pres.

Description: Sponsors programs and projects that support the highest-quality programs for roofing contractors, ensures timely and forward-thinking industry responses to major economic and technological issues, and enhances the long-term viability and attractiveness of the roofing industry. .

18244 ■ Roof Coatings Manufacturers Association
750 National Press Bldg.
529 14th St. NW
Washington, DC 20045
Ph:(202)207-0919
Fax:(202)223-9741
Co. E-mail: questions@roofcoatings.org
URL: http://www.roofcoatings.org
Contact: Russ Snyder, Exec. VP

Description: Corporations involved in the manufacture and distribution of cold-process protective roof coatings. Represents manufacturers and suppliers; conducts market research on the size, volume, and number of roof coating companies in the U.S.; provides financial management surveys, business studies, industry statistics, and technical information. Sponsors educational and training seminars. **Publications:** *RCMA Report* (bimonthly); *Roof Coatings Manufacturers Association Membership Directory* (annual).

18245 ■ Roof Consultants Institute
1500 Sunday Dr., Ste. 204
Raleigh, NC 27607
Ph:(919)859-0742
Free: 800-828-1902
Fax:(919)859-1328
Co. E-mail: jbirdsong@rci-online.org
URL: http://www.rci-online.org
Contact: James R. Birdsong, Exec. VP/CEO

Description: Individuals organized to promote the field of roof consultation. (Roof consultants are individuals that provide advice to architects, engineers, and building owners on the latest and most appropriate technology in the roofing industry.) Maintains certification program; conducts research in roofing technology. **Publications:** *International Directory of Roofing Professionals*; *RCItems* (monthly).

18246 ■ Tile Roofing Institute
230 E Ohio St., Ste. 400
Chicago, IL 60611
Ph:(312)670-4177
Fax:(312)644-8557
Co. E-mail: info@tileroofing.org
URL: http://www.tileroofing.org
Contact: Richard K. Olson, Technical Dir.

Description: Manufacturers and suppliers of clay and concrete roofing tiles; cement companies; mineral pigment producers; and others furnishing equipment and materials for manufacturing roof tiles. Promotes the use of "firesafe" roof construction, especially clay and concrete tile roofs; educates the architectural, design, and construction industries regarding the advantages of tile roofs; presents to the home-owning public the advantages and economies of tile roofs. Conducts international programs for architects, builders, building inspectors, and roofing contractors; provides sound/slide presentations, speakers, mailers, and specifications relating to tile roof construction. .

REFERENCE WORKS

18247 ■ *ENR—Top 600 Specialty Contractors Issue*
Pub: McGraw-Hill Inc.

Released: Annual, latest edition 2010. **Price:** $82, individuals yearly subscription. **Publication Includes:** Lists of the 600 largest U.S. Specialty subcontractors with sub-lists of top firms in mechanical contracting (50 firms), electrical (50), excavation-foundation (20), steel erection (20), roofing (20), sheet metal (20), demolition-wrecking (20), glazing curtain wall (20), masonry (20), concrete (20), utilities (20), painting (20), wall/ceiling (20), and asbestos abatement (20). **Entries Include:** Company name, headquarters location, total value of contracts received in preceding year and of foreign contracts, construction specialties, rank. **Arrangement:** By revenue.

18248 ■ "For Putting Down Roots in Business: Amy Norquist: Greensulate, New York City" in *Inc.* (Volume 32, December 2010, No. 10, pp. 106)
Pub: Inc. Magazine

Ed: Christine Lagorio. **Description:** Profile of Amy Norquist who left her position at an environmental nonprofit organization to found Greensulate. Her firm insulates rooftops with lavender, native grasses and succulents called sedum in order to eliminate carbon from the atmosphere.

18249 ■ "Housing Slide Picks Up Speed" in *Crain's Chicago Business* (Vol. 31, April 21, 2008, No. 16, pp. 2)
Pub: Crain Communications, Inc.

Ed: Eddie Baeb. **Description:** According to Tracy Cross & Associates Inc., a real estate consultancy, sales of new homes in the Chicago area dropped 61 percent from the year-earlier period which is more bad news for homebuilders, contractors and real estate agents who are eager for an indication that market conditions are improving.

18250 ■ *Low-Slope Roofing Materials Guide*
Pub: National Roofing Contractors Association
Contact: Alison Lavalley CAE
Released: Biennial, January. **Price:** $95, members; $175, individuals retail price. **Covers:** Approximately 250 manufacturers and suppliers of low-slope roof membrane, metal roof panels, cements and coatings, insulation board, and roof fastener products for commercial, industrial, and institutional purposes. **Entries Include:** Company name, location, phone, name and title of contact, description of products, warranty information. **Arrangement:** Alphabetical. **Indexes:** Company name, trade name, product.

18251 ■ *National Roofing Contractors Association—Membership Directory*
Pub: National Roofing Contractors Association
Contact: Lori Ogles, Dir. of Membership
E-mail: logles@nrca.net
Released: Annual, July. **Covers:** 5,000 contractors applying all types of commercial and residential roofing; 600 associate member manufacturers, suppliers, and distributors; 300 foreign members; and 100 institutions and related industries. **Entries Include:** Company name, address, phone, and names of voting representatives. **Arrangement:** Alphabetical. **Indexes:** Geographical, voting representative, Alphabetical, member product guide.

18252 ■ *Roofing Contractor—Single Ply Systems Index Issue*
Pub: BNP Media
Contact: Jill Nash, Publisher
E-mail: nashj@bnpmedia.com
Ed: Chris King, Editor, kingc@bnpmedia.com. **Released:** Annual, February, 2005. **Publication Includes:** List of manufacturers of single ply roofing products. **Entries Include:** Company name, address, phone, products. **Arrangement:** Classified by product.

18253 ■ *Steep-Slope Roofing Materials Guide*
Pub: National Roofing Contractors Association
Contact: Alison Lavalley CAE
Released: Biennial, January; Latest edition 2007-2008. **Price:** $95, members; $175, nonmembers. **Covers:** Over 75 manufacturers of approximately 500 products used for steep residential roofs; coverage includes Canada. **Entries Include:** Product name, description, specifications and applications, manufacturer name, address, phone, fax, telex, name and title of contact, geographical area served. **Arrangement:** Classified by product type. **Indexes:** Product/service, company name.

STATISTICAL SOURCES

18254 ■ *Market for Roofing and Siding*
Pub: Business Trend Analysts, Inc.
Released: 2001-2002. **Price:** $2495.00. **Description:** Examines national and regional markets for roofing and siding, for both new installations and replacements/additions. Current and projected demand is also quantified by material type.

18255 ■ *RMA Annual Statement Studies*
Pub: Robert Morris Associates (RMA)
Released: Annual. **Price:** $175.00 2006-07 edition, $105.00. **Description:** Contains composite balance sheets and income statements for more than 360 industries, including the accounting, auditing, and bookkeeping industries. Also contains five years of comparative historical data for discerning trends. Includes 16 commonly used ratios, computed for most of the size groupings for nearly every industry.

TRADE PERIODICALS

18256 ■ *Professional Roofing*
Pub: National Roofing Contractors Association
Contact: Carl Good, Publisher
E-mail: cgood@nrca.net
Released: Monthly. **Description:** Roofing industry magazine.

TRADE SHOWS AND CONVENTIONS

18257 ■ Southeast Roofing and Sheet Metal Spectacular Trade Exposition
Florida Roofing, Sheet Metal, and Air Conditioning Contractors Association FRSA
4111, Metric Dr., Ste. 6
Winter Park, FL 32792
Ph:(407)671-3772
Fax:(407)679-0010
Co. E-mail: frsa@floridaroof.com
URL: http://www.floridaroof.com
Released: Annual. **Audience:** Roofing, and sheet metal, contractors, architects, specifiers, and building officials. **Principal Exhibits:** Roofing and sheet metal supplies, products and services. **Dates and Locations:** 2011 Jun 23-25, Orlando, FL.

CONSULTANTS

18258 ■ A/R/C Associates Inc.
601 N Fern Creek Ave., Ste. 100
Orlando, FL 32803-4899
Ph:(407)896-7875
Fax:(407)898-6043
Co. E-mail: info@arc-arc.com
URL: http://www.arc-arc.com
Contact: Donald G. Dorner, President
E-mail: jjw@atsarc-arc.com
Scope: Architectural firm with specialized capacities in roof consulting and construction technology. Services include: Facility evaluation reports, construction document preparation, bidding and negotiation, construction contract observation and contract administration; roof consulting-roof investigation and analysis, roof inspection and maintenance scheduling, roof litigation and expert testimony, and historical roof preservation and restoration.

18259 ■ Roofing Materials Science & Technology
9037 Monte Mar Dr.
Los Angeles, CA 90035-4235
Ph:(310)559-6090
Fax:(310)559-6090
Co. E-mail: rmstlaaly@aol.com
URL: http://www.roofsandroofing.com
Contact: Dr. Heshmat O. Laaly, President
E-mail: rmstlaaly@aol.com
Scope: Offers roofing and waterproofing inspection and diagnostics. Presents seminars and consultation on state of the art roofing and waterproofing technology, tailored to individual needs and held on premises. Provides litigation expert testimony and maintains comprehensive roofing library, documentation center, and materials showroom. Developed and patented photovoltaic single ply roofing membrane which provides free electricity for household. Industries served: Commercial and institutional roofing, residential roofing and waterproofing, information dissemination on construction materials. **Publications:** "The Science and Technology of Traditional and Modern Roofing Systems," 1992. **Seminars:** State of the Art in Roofing Technology.

FRANCHISES AND BUSINESS OPPORTUNITIES

18260 ■ Jet-Black World's Most Beautiful Driveway's & Parking Lots
Jet-Black International
990 Lone Oak Rd., Ste. 142
Eagan, MN 55121
Ph:(651)686-6200
Free: 888-538-2525
Fax:(651)379-9559
No. of Franchise Units: 102. **No. of Company-Owned Units:** 3. **Founded:** 1987. **Franchised:** 1993. **Description:** Asphalt and concrete maintenance. **Equity Capital Needed:** $65,000-$105,000. **Franchise Fee:** $20,000. **Financial Assistance:** No. **Training:** Yes.

LIBRARIES

18261 ■ Construction Consultants Library
4600 College Blvd., Ste. 104
Overland Park, KS 66211-1606
Ph:(913)491-8626
Free: 800-533-8626
Fax:(913)491-9469
Co. E-mail: callahanmt@cclcc.com
URL: http://www.cclcc.com
Contact: Michael T. Callahan, Pres.
Scope: Construction, waterproofing, facility asset management, roofing, concrete. **Services:** Library open to the public with restrictions. **Holdings:** 500 books. **Subscriptions:** 6 journals and other serials.

ASSOCIATIONS AND OTHER ORGANIZATIONS

18262 ■ Canadian Broadcast Distribution Association–Association Canadienne de Distribution de Radiodiffusion
2233 Argentina Rd., Ste. 100
Mississauga, ON, Canada L5N 2X7
Ph:(905)826-3451
Fax:(905)826-4873
Co. E-mail: info@cbda.ca
URL: http://cbda.ca
Contact: Don Braden, Exec. Dir.
Description: Users of satellite telecommunications services. Seeks to advance the satellite communications industries. Serves as a forum for the exchange of information among members; represents members' commercial and regulatory interests.

18263 ■ Electronics Technicians Association International
5 Depot St.
Greencastle, IN 46135
Ph:(765)653-8262
Free: 800-288-3824
Fax:(765)653-4287
Co. E-mail: eta@eta-i.org
URL: http://www.eta-i.org
Contact: Teresa Maher CSS, Pres.
Description: Skilled electronics technicians. Provides placement service; offers certification examinations for electronics technicians and satellite, fiber optics, and data cabling installers. Compiles wage and manpower statistics. Administers FCC Commercial License examinations and certification of computer network systems technicians and web and internet specialists. **Publications:** *The High-Tech News* (bimonthly).

REFERENCE WORKS

18264 ■ *Broadcasting & Cable Yearbook*
Pub: R.R. Bowker L.L.C.
Released: Annual, latest edition 2010. **Price:** $395, individuals softbound. **Covers:** Over 17,000 television and radio stations in the United States, its territories, and Canada; cable MSOs and their individual systems; television and radio networks, broadcast and cable group owners, station representatives, satellite networks and services, film companies, advertising agencies, government agencies, trade associations, schools, and suppliers of professional and technical services, including books, serials, and videos; communications lawyers. **Entries Include:** Company name, address, phone, fax, names of executives. Station listings include broadcast power, other operating details. **Arrangement:** Stations and systems are geographical, others are alphabetical. **Indexes:** Alphabetical.

18265 ■ *Directory of Computer & Consumer Electronics Retailers*
Pub: Chain Store Guide
Released: Annual, Published June, 2008. **Covers:** 4,500 U.S. and Canadian companies operating almost 61,000 stores with at least $500,000 in computer sales, $1 million in consumer electronics, or other included product line sales. Almost 800 distributors, each also with $500,000 in sales of these product lines, are also included. **Entries Include:** Company name, address, phone and fax numbers, web and e-mail addresses; Internet order processing indicator; type of business; product lines; computer brands; network software; operating systems; total sales; consumer electronic sales; computer product sales; sales percentage by product group; sales percentage by customer type; services provided; total stores; units by trade name; trading areas; distribution center locations; projected openings and remodelings; private label credit care indicator; number of agents/resellers; wireless reseller name and location; franchise group headquarters name and location; buying group name; mail order catalog indicator; export indicator; average number of checkouts; year founded; public company indicator; parent company name and location; subsidiaries names and locations; divisional office locations; key personnel with titles. **Arrangement:** Geographical, separate sections for retailers and distributors. **Indexes:** Product lines, alphabetical, computer brand, exclusions.

18266 ■ "Give Me Liberty With DirecTV" in *Barron's* (Vol. 89, July 13, 2009, No. 28, pp. M5)
Pub: Dow Jones & Co., Inc.
Ed: Fleming Meeks. **Description:** Shares of Liberty Entertainment look cheap at $25.14 and the same goes for DirecTV at $23.19. A merger between the two companies was announced and the deal will likely close by September 2009. Barclays Capital has a target of $30 for Liberty Media and $32 for DirecTV.

18267 ■ *Telecommunications Directory*
Pub: Gale
Released: Annual, Latest edition 23rd; April, 2012. **Price:** $993, individuals. **Covers:** Two volumes-North America and International, Cover approximately 6,000 national and international voice and data communications networks, electronic mail services, teleconferencing facilities and services, facsimile services, Internet access providers, videotex and teletext operations, transactional services, local area networks, audiotex services, microwave systems/networkers, satellite facilities, and others involved in telecommunications, including related consultants, advertisers/marketers; associations, regulatory bodies, and publishers. **Entries Include:** Company or organization name, address, phone, fax, year established, name and title of contact, executive officers and board of directors, function or type of service; geographical area served; NAICS and SIC codes; number of employees; general description, including telecommunications-related activities; product/service; specific applications; means of access and equipment required; publications; intended market and availability; pricing; stock exchanges traded and ticker symbols; financial figures. **Arrangement:** Alphabetical by company name; within geographic region. **Indexes:** Name of firm/acronym, personal name, geographical (with name, address, phone, and director), and function/type of service (with name, address, phone). Indexes are cumulative.

TRADE PERIODICALS

18268 ■ *The Orbiter*
Pub: Society of Satellite Professionals International
Contact: Celia Hartmann, Associate Editor
Ed: Linda Thornberg, Editor. **Released:** 6/year. **Price:** Included in membership. **Description:** Covers member and chapter activities, developments in commercial satellite communications technology and applications, and activities of corporate sponsors. Recurring features include a calendar of events, reports of meetings, and columns titled Letter from the President and Corporate Corner.

18269 ■ *Ottawa Letter*
Pub: CCH Canadian Ltd.
Contact: Anna Wong
E-mail: awong@cch.ca
Released: Biweekly. **Price:** $920. **Description:** Reports on current events and topics of Canada, such as free trade, human rights, employment, and defense. Also provides statistics, lending, and foreign exchange rates.

18270 ■ *Satellite News*
Pub: Access Intelligence L.L.C.
Ed: Paul Dykewicz, Editor, pdykewicz@pbimedia.com. **Released:** 50/year. **Price:** $1,197. **Description:** Provides business insights and analysis into the commercial satellite industry including new satellite applications, developing technologies, and unfolding partnerships. Recurring features include columns titled Satellite Spotlight, DBS News, Satellite News, Newsmaker Interiews, Satellite Circuit, and Satellite News Financial Ticker.

18271 ■ *Wireless Satellite & Broadcasting*
Pub: Information Gatekeepers Inc.
Ed: Tony Carmona, Editor. **Released:** Monthly. **Price:** $695, U.S. and Canada; $745, elsewhere. **Description:** Covers developments in technology, business activity, and regulation for the statellite and broadcasting telecommunications industry.

18272 ■ *Worldwide Videotex Update*
Pub: Worldwide Videotex
Contact: Mark Wright
Released: Monthly. **Price:** $165, U.S. and Canada; $180, elsewhere outside North America; $25, single issue U.S. and Canada; $30, single issue outside North America. **Description:** Reports on electronic mail, online services, satellite communication, videotex, teleconferencing, teletext, and other television related technologies. Focuses on information of interest to marketers.

VIDEOCASSETTES/ AUDIOCASSETTES

18273 ■ *Financial Aspects*
SatNews Publishers
800 Siesta Way
Sonoma, CA 95476
Ph:(707)939-9306

Fax:(707)939-9235
Co. E-mail: design@satnews.com
URL: http://www.satnews.com
Released: 1992. **Price:** $495.00. **Description:** Covers various financial aspects of satellite communications services, including typical fees, risk management, and future supply and demand. Part of the "Satellite Training Series." **Availability:** VHS.

18274 ■ *Satellite & Antenna Technology Basics*
SatNews Publishers
800 Siesta Way
Sonoma, CA 95476
Ph:(707)939-9306
Fax:(707)939-9235
Co. E-mail: design@satnews.com
URL: http://www.satnews.com
Released: 1992. **Price:** $595.00. **Description:** The technological aspects of satellites and antennas are covered, including information on frequency bands, scrambling, television standards, and channel capacity. Part of the "Satellite Training Series." **Availability:** VHS.

18275 ■ *Satellite Fundamentals*
SatNews Publishers
800 Siesta Way
Sonoma, CA 95476
Ph:(707)939-9306
Fax:(707)939-9235
Co. E-mail: design@satnews.com
URL: http://www.satnews.com
Released: 1992. **Price:** $595.00. **Description:** Pelton and Baylin discuss various aspects of satellites, including launching, satellite orbits, the environment of space, and how satellites function. Part of the "Satellite Training Series." **Availability:** VHS.

18276 ■ *Satellite Training Series*
SatNews Publishers
800 Siesta Way
Sonoma, CA 95476
Ph:(707)939-9306
Fax:(707)939-9235
Co. E-mail: design@satnews.com
URL: http://www.satnews.com
Released: 1992. **Description:** A series of instructional tapes that gives a complete training program on every aspect of the satellite industry. Appropriate for non-technical persons in the satellite communications industry. Tapes are available individually. **Availability:** VHS.

18277 ■ *The World Satellite Marketplace*
SatNews Publishers
800 Siesta Way
Sonoma, CA 95476
Ph:(707)939-9306
Fax:(707)939-9235
Co. E-mail: design@satnews.com
URL: http://www.satnews.com
Released: 1992. **Price:** $595.00. **Description:** Discusses the world marketplace for various satellite services, including fixed satellite services, mobile satellite services, and radio determining services. Part of the "Satellite Training Series." **Availability:** VHS.

CONSULTANTS

18278 ■ Rainbow Network Communications
620 Hicksville Rd.
Bethpage, NY 11714
Ph:(516)803-0300
Fax:(516)918-6940
Co. E-mail: mcsupport@rainbow-media.com
URL: http://www.rncnetwork.com
Contact: John Barbieri, Vice President
E-mail: tagreco@rainbow-media.com
Scope: Telecommunications consultants. Offers services in network operations facilities; satellite services, including teleport, down-linking, local channel, microwave and transponder services and production services.

18279 ■ W & J Partnership
18876 Edwin Markham Dr.
PO Box 2499
Castro Valley, CA 94546-0499
Ph:(510)583-7751
Fax:(510)583-7645
Co. E-mail: jemorgan@wjpartnership.com
URL: http://www.wjpartnership.com
Contact: Judith E. Morgan, Partner
E-mail: jemorgan@atswjpartnership.com
Scope: Management and technical consulting in complex network design, operations, administration, maintenance and products for large enterprises, carriers and service providers (wire-line and wireless) and governments, especially VoIP, security; R and D for vendors. Review product plans and investment opportunities. Software and hardware: Architectures, design, development and testing for manufacturers. No work for vendors and business at the same time. **Seminars:** Fiber Optics Communications; Networks & Networks Management; Structured Cabling; Public Safety Radio; Computer and Communications Security Systems; Hands-On Fiber Optic Communications; Cabling & Wiring for Local Communications. **Special Services:** Systems Software; Networking Software; Communications Embedded Systems; SAP; Siebel; Software and Firmware Quality Assurance.

LIBRARIES

18280 ■ Intelsat Library
3400 International Dr., NW
Box 40
Washington, DC 20008
Ph:(202)944-6800
Fax:(202)944-7898
Co. E-mail: library@intelsat.com
URL: http://www.intelsat.com/home.asp
Contact: Rosa Liu, Mgr., Lib./Rec.
Scope: Satellite communication, network infrastructure, telecommunication services. **Services:** Interlibrary loan; Library not open to the public. **Holdings:** 9000 books; 750 bound periodical volumes; technical reports; e-books. **Subscriptions:** 325 journals and other serials.

ASSOCIATIONS AND OTHER ORGANIZATIONS

18281 ■ Screen Printing Technical Foundation
10015 Main St.
Fairfax, VA 22031
Ph:(703)385-1335
Free: 888-385-3588
Fax:(703)273-0456
Co. E-mail: sptf@sgia.org
URL: http://www.sgia.org/sptf
Contact: Dawn Hohl, Technical Training Mgr.
Description: Participants include corporations, institutions, and individuals interested in screen-printing. Advances the screen-printing industry. Conducts technical research and hands-on training programs to address production problems and processes. Sponsors educational programs and prepares educational materials. **Publications:** *SPTF Update* (quarterly).

18282 ■ Specialty Graphic Imaging Association
10015 Main St.
Fairfax, VA 22031-3489
Ph:(703)385-1335
Free: 888-385-3588
Fax:(703)273-0456
Co. E-mail: sgia@sgia.org
URL: http://www.sgia.org
Contact: Michael E. Robertson, Pres./CEO
Description: Printers who use screen printing and/or digital printing; associate members are suppliers and manufacturers; educational institutions. Provides training and information on technical, managerial, governmental, safety, and research issues. Conducts safety, environmental, and print quality recognition programs. Compiles statistics; conducts research programs. **Publications:** *Guide to Digital Garment Decoration*; *Operating Rate Survey* (biennial); *SGIA Journal* (quarterly); *SGIA News* (monthly); *Who's Who in SGIA* (annual).

REFERENCE WORKS

18283 ■ "A Life of Spice" in *Entrepreneur* (Vol. 37, September 2009, No. 9, pp. 46)
Pub: Entrepreneur Media, Inc.
Ed: Jason Daley. **Description:** Matt and Bryan Walls have successfully grown their Atlanta, Georgia-based Snorg Tees T-shirt company. The company has expanded its product offering and redesigned its Website to be more user-friendly. The company has registered between $5 and 10 million in 2008.

18284 ■ *Screen Printing—Buyer's Guide Issue*
Pub: ST Media Group International Inc.
Ed: Gail Flower, Editor, gail.flower@stmediagroup.com. **Released:** Annual, July. **Publication Includes:** List of about 500 manufacturers and distributors of products and equipment used in the screen printing industry. **Entries Include:** Company name, address, phone; branch office locations, phone number, name of sales contact, product lines, geographic area served. **Arrangement:** Alphabetical. **Indexes:** Product, trade name, fax number, editorial reference.

18285 ■ *Who's Who in SGIA*
Pub: Screenprinting and Graphic Imaging Association International
Contact: Michael Robertson, President
E-mail: miker@sgia.org
Released: Annual, August. **Covers:** About 3,800 screen printers and graphic imaging companies, suppliers of screen printing equipment and graphic imaging materials, and investors in the Screen Printing Technical Foundation; international coverage. **Entries Include:** Company name, address, phone, fax, e-mail, name of contact, products or services. **Arrangement:** Classified by type of business, then geographical. **Indexes:** Alphabetical by company, within state or country.

SOURCES OF SUPPLY

18286 ■ *Screen Printing—Distributor/Dealer Directory Section*
Pub: ST Media Group International Inc.
Ed: Tom Frecska, Editor. **Released:** Monthly. **Price:** $5 per issue; $42 per year. **Publication Includes:** Listings of over 135 dealers and distributors of screen printing equipment, materials, and services. **Entries Include:** Company name, address, phone, fax, name and title of contact, geographical area served, and product/service. **Arrangement:** Geographical.

TRADE PERIODICALS

18287 ■ *Screen Printing*
Pub: ST Media Group International Inc.
Contact: Steve Duccilli, Gp. Publisher
E-mail: steve.duccilli@stmediagroup.com
Released: Monthly. **Price:** $42 U.S.; $66 U.S., 2 years; $86 U.S., 3 years; $62 Canada surface; $100 Canada surface, 2 years; $30 Canada surface, 3 years; $97 Canada, international air; $170 Canada, international air, 2 years; $235 Canada, international air, 3 years; $65 Mexico/foreign-surface. **Description:** Trade magazine covering screen printing with ground-breaking industry reports and management information.

VIDEOCASSETTES/ AUDIOCASSETTES

18288 ■ *Basic Screen Printing*
Crystal Productions
1812 Johns Dr.
Box 2159
Glenview, IL 60025-6519
Ph:(847)657-8144
Free: 800-255-8629
Fax:(847)657-8149
Co. E-mail: custserv@crystalproductions.com
URL: http://www.crystalproductions.com
Price: $39.95. **Description:** Teaching aid for art education introduces screen printing on paper and fabric. **Availability:** VHS.

18289 ■ *Photo Screen Printing*
Crystal Productions
1812 Johns Dr.
Box 2159
Glenview, IL 60025-6519
Ph:(847)657-8144
Free: 800-255-8629
Fax:(847)657-8149
Co. E-mail: custserv@crystalproductions.com
URL: http://www.crystalproductions.com
Price: $39.95. **Description:** Artist Alex Wood presents the photo emulsion process, including color separation, registration, and exposure, in this teaching aid for art education. **Availability:** VHS.

18290 ■ *Printing*
Morris Video
12881 Knott St.
Garden Grove, CA 92841
Ph:(310)533-4800
Fax:(310)320-3171
Released: 1978. **Price:** $24.95. **Description:** Many aspects of the printing industry are featured. **Availability:** VHS.

18291 ■ *Printing Basics for Non-Printers 1: An Abridged Guide to Printing Fundamentals*
Cambridge Educational
c/o Films Media Group
132 West 31st Street, 17th Floor
Ste. 124
New York, NY 10001
Free: 800-257-5126
Fax:(609)671-0266
Co. E-mail: custserve@films.com
URL: http://www.cambridgeol.com
Price: $39.95. **Description:** Explains how to save money and get your ideas across when dealing with designers and production artists. **Availability:** VHS.

TRADE SHOWS AND CONVENTIONS

18292 ■ The Imprinted Sportswear Show, Atlantic City
Nielsen Business Media
770 Broadway
New York, NY 10003-9595
Ph:(646)654-4500
Co. E-mail: bmcomm@nielsen.com
URL: http://www.nielsenbusinessmedia.com/
Released: Annual. **Audience:** Trade only. **Principal Exhibits:** Trade show source for the imprinted sportswear/textile screen printing/embroidery industry; t-shirts, pre-prints, and other apparel; design software; screen printing supplies and equipment; transfers, lettering embroidery equipment and supplies. **Dates and Locations:** 2011 Mar 11-13, Atlantic City, NJ.

FRANCHISES AND BUSINESS OPPORTUNITIES

18293 ■ Bad Ass Coffee Co.
166 W 2700 South
Salt Lake City, UT 84115
Ph:(801)463-1966
Free: 888-422-3277
Fax:(801)463-2606
No. of Franchise Units: 41. **Founded:** 1991. **Franchised:** 1998. **Description:** Coffee and logo wear. **Equity Capital Needed:** $207,000-$326,000 total investment; $100,000 cash liquidity. **Franchise Fee:** $35,000. **Royalty Fee:** 6%. **Financial Assistance:** Third party financing available. **Training:** Provides 2 weeks at headquarters, onsite if requested with ongoing support.

18294 ■ Printwear Xpress
Printwear Xpress Franchise Corp.
1819 Wazee St.
Denver, CO 80202
Ph:(303)771-7100
Free: 888-241-0337
Fax:(303)771-7133
Co. E-mail: info@printwearxpress.com
URL: http://www.printwearxpress.com
No. of Company-Owned Units: 1. **Founded:** 2007. **Franchised:** 2007. **Description:** Printwear Xpress (PWX)combines shopping experience, technology & customer service to deliver a highly competitive business model. PWX stores are modern, attractive & well merchandised to help customers select the right product for their needs. Production is showcased to illustrate the capabilities of the business & customer service is second to none. PWX stores are located in neighborhood strip centers & don't require an anchor tenant. **Equity Capital Needed:** $148,200-$169,600. **Franchise Fee:** $29,900. **Royalty Fee:** 5%. **Financial Assistance:** Third party financing available. **Training:** Offers 1 week classroom in Denver and 1 week onsite during opening, as well as vendor training.

RESEARCH CENTERS

18295 ■ Western Michigan University–Paper and Imaging
Department of Paper Engineering, Chemical Engineering, & Ima
A-217 Parkview Campus
Kalamazoo, MI 49008
Ph:(269)276-3500
Fax:(269)276-3501
Co. E-mail: said.abubakr@wmich.edu
Contact: Said Abubakr, Chm.
E-mail: said.abubakr@wmich.edu
Scope: Pulping, papermaking, coating, recycling, and printing. **Educational Activities:** Barrier coating symposium; Flexo Day; Gravure Day; Industrial seminars include courses on coated paper manufacture, paper coating advances, fundamentals of papermaking, paper recycling, de-inking, specialty coatings and laminations, and printing; Litho Day; Paper coating course.

START-UP INFORMATION

18296 ■ "Macomb County, OU Eye Business Incubator" in *Crain's Detroit Business* (Vol. 24, February 11, 2008, No. 6, pp. 1)
Pub: Crain Communications Inc. - Detroit

Ed: Chad Halcom. **Description:** Officials in Macomb County, Michigan are discussing plans to create a defense-themed business incubator in the county. Macomb County was awarded $282,000 in federal budget appropriation for the project.

18297 ■ "Secure Fortune: New Twist In Security: The Marketplace Is Going Digital" in *Small Business Opportunities* (November 2007)
Pub: Harris Publications Inc.

Description: Profile of EYESthere, providing digital video security franchise opportunities.

18298 ■ "Secure Future" in *Small Business Opportunities* (November 2010)
Pub: Harris Publications Inc.

Ed: Stan Roberts. **Description:** Fed up with the corporate world, this first-time business owner sells security equipment over the phone. Last year, sales hit $4 million. Profile of the founder of SmartWatch Security & Sound, Madelaine Lock is included.

18299 ■ "Securing a Fortune" in *Small Business Opportunities* (Fall 2010)
Pub: Harris Publications Inc.

Description: Profile of Whelan Security based in Saint Louis and is a private security company operating in 17 states. The family owned business started as a safety patrol unit.

ASSOCIATIONS AND OTHER ORGANIZATIONS

18300 ■ ASIS International
1625 Prince St.
Alexandria, VA 22314-2818
Ph:(703)519-6200
Fax:(703)519-6299
Co. E-mail: asis@asisonline.org
URL: http://www.asisonline.org
Contact: Michael J. Stack, CEO

Purpose: Security professionals responsible for loss prevention, asset protection and security for businesses, government, or public organizations and institutions. Sponsors educational programs on security principles (basic through advanced levels) and current security issues. Administers professional certification programs (CPP, PCI, PSP). Offers networking opportunities to professionals; provides an online service for employment and resumes, publishes books, directories, and other resources. **Publications:** *ASIS Security Industry Buyers Guide* (annual); *Dynamics* (bimonthly); *Security Journal* (quarterly); *Security Management* (monthly).

18301 ■ Canadian Fire Alarm Association–Association Canadienne D'Alarme Incendie
85 Citizen Ct., Unit 5
Markham, ON, Canada L6G 1A8
Ph:(905)944-0030
Free: 800-529-0552
Fax:(905)479-3639
Co. E-mail: admin@cfaa.ca
URL: http://www.cfaa.ca
Contact: Gerry Landmesser, Pres.

Description: Promotes improved fire safety through use of fire alarms. Facilitates communication and cooperation among members; represents members' commercial and regulatory interests; sponsors research and educational programs.

18302 ■ Canadian Security Association–L'Association Canadienne de la Securite
50 Acadia Ave., Ste. 201
Markham, ON, Canada L3R 0B3
Ph:(905)513-0622
Free: 800-538-9919
Fax:(905)513-0624
Co. E-mail: staff@canasa.org
URL: http://www.canasa.org
Contact: Karen McGee, Pres.

Description: Alarm and security equipment manufacturers, installers, monitors, and private security guard services. Seeks to advance the industry and enhance the professionalism of members. Serves as a clearinghouse on security systems and services; acts a unified voice representing the national electronic security industry. Conducts lobbying activities; sponsors continuing professional development programs for members; sets standards of practice and ethics for the security systems and services industries. **Publications:** *English/French EFlash* (monthly).

18303 ■ Electronic Privacy Information Center
1718 Connecticut Ave. NW, Ste. 200
Washington, DC 20009
Ph:(202)483-1140
Fax:(202)483-1248
Co. E-mail: epic-info@epic.org
URL: http://www.epic.org
Contact: Marc Rotenberg, Pres.

Description: Interested individuals. Advocates for electronic privacy, free expression, public voice. Sponsors educational and research programs; compiles statistics; conducts litigation. **Publications:** *EPIC Alert* (biweekly).

18304 ■ Electronic Security Association
2300 Valley View Ln., Ste. 230
Irving, TX 75062
Ph:(214)260-5970
Free: 888-447-1689
Fax:(214)260-5979
Co. E-mail: webmaster@alarm.org
URL: http://www.alarm.org
Contact: Merlin Guilbeau, Exec. Dir.

Description: Represents electronic safety, security and systems professionals. **Publications:** *National Burglar and Fire Alarm Association—Membership Directory* (annual).

18305 ■ International Association of Professional Security Consultants
575 Market St., Ste. 2125
San Francisco, CA 94105
Ph:(415)536-0288
Fax:(415)764-4915
Co. E-mail: iapsc@iapsc.org
URL: http://www.iapsc.org
Contact: Richard Grassie CPP, Pres.

Description: Security management, technical, training and forensic consultants. Promotes understanding and cooperation among members and industries or individuals requiring such services. Seeks to enhance members' knowledge through seminars, training programs and educational materials. Works to foster public awareness of the security consulting industry; serves as a clearinghouse for consultants' requirements. Maintains code of conduct, ethics and professional standards. Offers consultant referral service; operates speakers' bureau. **Publications:** *Consultants Directory* (annual); *News* (quarterly).

18306 ■ International Security Management Association
PO Box 623
Buffalo, IA 52728
Ph:(563)381-4008
Fax:(563)381-4283
Co. E-mail: isma3@aol.com
URL: http://www.isma.com
Contact: Susan W. Pohlmann, Consulting Business Mgr.

Description: Senior security executives of multinational business firms and chief executive officers of full service security services companies. Aims to assist senior security executives in coordinating and exchanging information about security management and to establish high business and professional standards. .

18307 ■ Jewelers' Security Alliance
6 E 45th St.
New York, NY 10017
Free: 800-537-0067
Fax:(212)808-9168
Co. E-mail: jsa2@jewelerssecurity.org
URL: http://www.jewelerssecurity.org
Contact: John J. Kennedy, Pres.

Description: Advocates for crime prevention in the jewelry industry. Provides crime information and assistance to the jewelry industry and law enforcement. **Publications:** *Annual Report on Crime Against the Jewelry Industry in U.S.* (annual); *JSA Manual of Jewelry Security* (biennial); *JSA Newsletter* (quarterly);Bulletins (periodic).

18308 ■ National Association of Security Companies
444 N Capitol St. NW, Ste. 345
Washington, DC 20001
Ph:(202)347-3257

Fax:(202)393-7006
Co. E-mail: information@nasco.org
URL: http://www.nasco.org
Contact: Jim McNulty, Chm.
Description: Major security guard companies. Monitors legislation affecting the industry. .

18309 ■ National Council of Investigation and Security Services
7501 Sparrows Point Blvd.
Baltimore, MD 21219-1927
Free: 800-445-8408
Fax:(410)388-9746
Co. E-mail: nciss@comcast.net
URL: http://www.nciss.org
Contact: Carolyn Ward, Exec. Dir.
Purpose: Monitors national and state legislative and regulatory activities. Develops and encourages the practice of high standards of personal and professional conduct. Acquires, preserves, and disseminates data and valuable information; promotes the purpose of investigation and guard companies. Provides information about state legislation and regulatory activities that could have an impact on a particular firm or on the industry in general; acts as spokesman for the industry before legislative and regulatory bodies at both federal and state levels. **Publications:** *NCISS Report* (quarterly).

18310 ■ Nine Lives Associates
Executive Protection Institute
16 Penn Pl., Ste. 1570
New York, NY 10001
Ph:(212)268-4555
Free: 800-947-5827
Fax:(212)563-4783
Co. E-mail: info@personalprotection.com
URL: http://www.personalprotection.com/nla.cfm
Contact: Dr. Jerry Heying, Pres./CEO
Description: Law enforcement, correctional, military, and security professionals who have been granted Personal Protection Specialist Certification through completion of the protective services program offered by the Executive Protection Institute; conducts research; EPI programs emphasize personal survival skills and techniques for the protection of others. Provides professional recognition for qualified individuals engaged in executive protection assignments. Maintains placement service. Operates speakers' bureau; compiles statistics. .

18311 ■ Security Industry Association
635 Slaters Ln., Ste. 110
Alexandria, VA 22314
Ph:(703)683-2075
Free: (866)817-8888
Fax:(703)683-2469
Co. E-mail: info@siaonline.org
URL: http://www.siaonline.org
Contact: Gordon Hope, Chm.
Description: Security equipment manufacturers and distributors. Seeks for the advancement of companies in the security products industry. Promotes the export of American security products. Conducts research programs, educational programs, technical seminars, communications with related industries and other activities. Maintains speakers' bureau; compiles statistics. .

DIRECTORIES OF EDUCATIONAL PROGRAMS

18312 ■ *Directory of Private Accredited Career Schools and Colleges of Technology*
Pub: Accrediting Commission of Career Schools and Colleges of Technology
Contact: Michale S. McComis, Exec. Dir.
Released: On web page. **Price:** Free. **Description:** Covers 3900 accredited post-secondary programs that provide training programs in business, trade, and technical fields, including various small business endeavors. Entries offer school name, address, phone, description of courses, job placement assistance, and requirements for admission. Arrangement is alphabetical.

REFERENCE WORKS

18313 ■ "Actiontec and Verizon Team Up for a Smarter Home" in *Ecology,Environment & Conservation Business* (November 5, 2011, pp. 3)
Pub: HighBeam Research
Description: Verizon is implementing Actiontec Electronics' SG200 Service Gateway as a basic component of its Home Monitoring and Control service. This new smart home service allows customers to remotely check their homes, control locks and appliances, view home-energy use and more using a smartphone, PC, or FiOS TV.

18314 ■ "Altegrity Acquires John D. Cohen, Inc." in (November 19, 2009, pp. 14)
Pub: Investment Weekly News
Description: John D. Cohen, Inc., a contract provider of national security policy guidance and counsel to the federal government, was acquired by Altegrity, Inc., a global screening and security solutions provider; the company will become part of US Investigations Services, LLC and operate under the auspices of Altegrity's new business, Altegrity Security Consulting.

18315 ■ "American Chemistry Council Launches Flagship Blog" in *Ecology,Environment & Conservation Business* (October 29, 2011, pp. 5)
Pub: HighBeam Research
Description: American Chemistry Council (ACC) launched its blog, American Chemistry Matters, where interactive space allows bloggers to respond to news coverage and to discuss policy issues and their impact on innovation, competitiveness, job creation and safety.

18316 ■ *American Society for Industrial Security—Annual Membership Directory*
Pub: ASIS International
Contact: Ann Longmore-Etheridge
Released: Annual, May/June. **Covers:** 37,000 member management specialists in the private and public sectors who formulate security policy and direct security programs to prevent terrorism, document piracy, industrial espionage, counterfeiting, insurance fraud, arson, employee theft, white-collar crime, computer crime, organized crime, etc. **Entries Include:** Member name, title, address, phone, company affiliation. **Arrangement:** Alphabetical. **Indexes:** Geographical, affiliated organization/company, personal name.

18317 ■ "AMT's Partner Program Enables New Security Business Models" in *Internet Wire* (August 12, 2010)
Pub: Comtex
Description: AMT, technical provider of physical access control Software as a Service (Saas) solutions, has developed a new Partner Program that allows partners to outsource any technical abilities lacking to AMT with no upfront fees.

18318 ■ "And The Winner Is..." in *Canadian Business* (Vol. 81, March 3, 2008, No. 3, pp. 21)
Pub: Rogers Media
Ed: Joe Castaldo. **Description:** Thirty out of 141 Canadian chief executive officers think that Hilary Clinton would be best for U.S.-Canada relations if elected as U.S. president. Findings also revealed that 60 respondents believe that presidential candidate John McCain would be best on handling issues of international military-security. Views on the candidates' performance and their ability to deal with the declining U.S. economy as well as international trade issues are also given.

18319 ■ "At Wine Kiosk, Show ID, Face Camera, Swipe Card and Blow" in *Pittsburgh Post-Gazette* (November 28, 2010)
Pub: Pittsburgh-Post Gazette
Ed: Dennis B. Roddy. **Description:** New technology installed on wine kiosks enables sellers to abide by the law. This technology tests blood alcohol levels and warns people if they have recently used a mouthwash before testing.

18320 ■ "Auto Bankruptcies Could Weaken Defense" in *Crain's Detroit Business* (Vol. 25, June 8, 2009, No. 23, pp. 1)
Pub: Crain Communications Inc. - Detroit
Ed: Chad Halcom. **Description:** Bankruptcy and supplier consolidation of General Motors Corporation and Chrysler LLC could interfere with the supply chains of some defense contractors, particularly makers of trucks and smaller vehicles.

18321 ■ "AVG Introduces Security Software Suite for SMBs 551179" in *eWeek* (October 12, 2010)
Pub: Ziff Davis Enterprise
Description: AVG Technologies is offering its AVG Internet Security 2011 Business Edition and AVG Anti-Virus Business Edition designed to give Internet-active SMB owners protection. The system protects online transactions and email communications as well as sensitive customer data and AVG Anti-Virus 2011 Business edition offers real-time protection against the latest online threats.

18322 ■ "Behind the Scenes: Companies At the Heart of Everyday Life" in *Inc.* (February 2008, pp. 26-27)
Pub: Gruner & Jahr USA Publishing
Ed: Athena Schindelheim. **Description:** Profiles of companies providing services to airports, making the environment safer and more efficient, as well as more comfortable for passengers and workers. Centerpoint Manufacturing provides garbage bins that can safely contain explosions producing thousands of pounds of pressure; Infax, whose software displays arrival and departure information on 19-foot-wide screens; Lavi Industries, whose products include security barricades, hostess stands, and salad-bar sneeze guards; and SATech maker of rubber flooring that helps ease discomfort for workers having to stand for long periods of time.

18323 ■ "Blues at the Toy Fair: Industry Reeling From Recalls, Lower Sales Volumes" in *Crain's New York Business* (February 18, 2008)
Pub: Crain Communications Inc.
Ed: Elisabeth Cordova. **Description:** Over 1,500 toy developers and vendors will attend the American International Toy Fair, expected to be low-key due to recent recalls of toys not meeting American safety standards. Toy retailers and manufacturers, as well as the Chinese government, are promoting product testing to prevent toxic metals in toys.

18324 ■ "Border Boletin: UA to Take Lie-Detector Kiosk to Poland" in *Arizona Daily Star* (September 14, 2010)
Pub: Arizona Daily Star
Ed: Brady McCombs. **Description:** University of Arizona's National Center for Border Security and Immigration Research will send a team to Warsaw, Poland to show border guards from 27 European Union countries the center's Avatar Kiosk. The Avatar technology is designed for use at border ports and airports to assist Customs officers detect individuals who are lying.

18325 ■ "Bracing for Impact" in *Playthings* (Vol. 106, September 1, 2008, No. 8, pp. 15)
Pub: Reed Business Information
Ed: J. Tol Broome Jr. **Description:** A good risk management plan for any company consists of making correct decisions in the following six key areas: operational, reputation, regulatory, legal, liquidity, and disaster.

18326 ■ "Building Targeted for Marriott in Violation" in *Business Journal-Milwaukee* (Vol. 28, December 24, 2010, No. 12, pp. A1)
Pub: Milwaukee Business Journal
Ed: Sean Ryan. **Description:** Milwaukee, Wisconsin's Department of Neighborhood Services has ordered structural improvements and safeguards for the Pioneer Building after three violations from structural failures were found. Pioneer was among the five buildings wanted by Jackson Street Management LLC to demolish for the new Marriott Hotel.

18327 ■ "Businesses Still on the Mend" in *Boston Business Journal* (Vol. 29, September 9, 2011, No. 18, pp. 1)
Pub: American City Business Journals Inc.

Ed: Scott Dance. **Description:** The 9/11 terrorist attacks have caused many companies in the US to dramatically shift course in response to changes in the economy. The concern that the cost of being unprepared for future disasters could be larger has remained among many companies.

18328 ■ "Buyer's Guide: Room for Improvement" in *Entrepreneur* (Vol. 35, October 2007, No. 10, pp. 62)
Pub: Entrepreneur Media Inc.

Ed: Amanda C. Kooser. **Description:** Buyers guide for wireless routers is presented. Price, features and availability of the Belkin N1 Vision, Buffalo Wireless-N Nfinit Router, D-Link Xtreme Gigabit Router DIR 655, Linksys Wireless-N Gigabit Security Router, Netgear RangeMax Next Wireless-N Router and Zyxel NBG-460N are provided.

18329 ■ "Cents and Sensibility" in *Playthings* (Vol. 107, January 1, 2009, No. 1, pp. 19)
Pub: Reed Business Information

Ed: Pamela Brill. **Description:** Recent concerns over safety, phthalate and lead paint and other toxic materials, as well as consumers going green, are issues discussed by toy manufacturers. Doll manufacturers also face increase labor and material costs and are working to design dolls that girls will love.

18330 ■ "CMS Products and Avecto Team for Business Security Product Solutions" in *Wireless News* (November 11, 2009)
Pub: Close-Up Media

Description: CMS Products, a provider of data security, backup, content management and disaster recovery, has agreed on a strategic partnership with Avect, a provider in least privilege management. The partnership will allow the companies to bundle their products.

18331 ■ "Comcast Launches New Home Security Service, Developed in Portland" in *The Oregonian* (June 7, 2011)
Pub: McClatchy-Tribune Regional News

Ed: Mike Rogoway. **Description:** Comcast introduced its new high-end home security system that provides 24-hour monitoring and control of homes and utilities, along with Web and mobile access.

18332 ■ "Consumer Trust in E-Commerce Web Sites: a Meta-Study" in *ACM Computing Surveys* (Vol. 43, Fall 2011, No. 3, pp. 14)
Pub: Association for Computing Machinery

Ed: Patricia Beatty, Ian Reay, Scott Dick, James Miller. **Description:** Trust is at once an elusive, imprecise concept, and a critical attribute that must be engineered into e-commerce systems. Engineering trust is examined.

18333 ■ *Contingency Planning and Disaster Recovery: A Small Business Guide*
Pub: John Wiley & Sons, Incorporated

Ed: Donna R. Childs, Stefan Dietrich. **Released:** October 2002. **Description:** Four keys issues to help a business plan for disasters include: preparation, response, recovery, and sample IT solutions in order to secure property and confidential data files and covers the six types of disasters: human errors, equipment failures, third-party failures, environmental hazards, fires and other structural catastrophes, and terrorism and sabotage.

18334 ■ "Contractors Scramble for Jobs" in *Business Journal Portland* (Vol. 26, December 18, 2009, No. 41, pp. 1)
Pub: American City Business Journals Inc.

Ed: Andy Giegerich. **Description:** Contractors in Portland area are expected to bid for capital construction projects that will be funded by municipalities in the said area. Contracts for companies that work on materials handling, road improvement, and public safety structure projects will be issued.

18335 ■ *Corporate Radar: Tracking the Forces That Are Shaping Your Business*
Pub: Amacom

Ed: Karl Albrecht. **Released:** December 2008. **Price:** $24.95. **Description:** Ways for a business to assess the forces operating in the external environment that can affect the business and solutions to protect from outside threats.

18336 ■ "Council Power Shift Could Benefit Business" in *Business Courier* (Vol. 26, November 6, 2009, No. 28, pp. 1)
Pub: American City Business Journals, Inc.

Ed: Lucy May. **Description:** A majority in the Cincinnati City Council, which is comprised of reelected members, might be created by Charlie Winburn's impending return to the council. It would be empowered to decide on public safety, stock options taxes, and environmental justice. How the presumed majority would affect the city's economic progress is discussed.

18337 ■ "Credit Card Crackdown" in *Business Journal-Portland* (Vol. 24, November 23, 2007, No. 38, pp. 1)
Pub: American City Business Journals, Inc.

Ed: Andy Giegerich. **Description:** Oregon's U.S. Senator Ron Wyden is sponsoring Credit Card Safety Act of 2007, a bill that requires credit card companies to reduce the jargon of credit card agreements and require the Federal Reserve Board to launch a public education campaign among credit card users. The legislation will also impose a rating system for credit card contracts with five being the safest for consumers to use.

18338 ■ "Data Security is No. 1 Compliance Concern" in *HRMagazine* (Vol. 53, October 2008, No. 10, pp. 32)
Pub: Society for Human Resource Management

Ed: Aliah D. Wright. **Description:** Electronic data protection and data privacy are the leading ethics and compliance issues faced by companies today.

18339 ■ "Dealing With Dangers Abroad" in *Financial Executive* (Vol. 23, December 2007, No. 10, pp. 32)
Pub: Financial Executives International

Ed: Jeffrey Marshall. **Description:** Clear processes and responsibilities for risk management for all companies going global are essential. U.S. toy manufacturer, Matel was put into crisis mode after its Chinese-made toys were recalled due to the use of lead-based paint or tiny magnets in its products.

18340 ■ "Defense Budge Ax May Not Come Down So Hard On the Region" in *Baltimore Business Journal* (Vol. 28, August 20, 2010, No. 15, pp. 1)
Pub: Baltimore Business Journal

Ed: Daniel J. Sernovitz. **Description:** U.S. Defense Secretary Robert M. Gates' planned budget cuts are having little effect on Maryland's defense industry. Gates will reduce spending on intelligence service contracts by 10 percent.

18341 ■ "Despite Hot Toys, Holiday Sales Predicted To Be Ho-Ho-Hum" in *Drug Store News* (Vol. 29, November 12, 2007, No. 14, pp. 78)
Pub: Drug Store News

Ed: Doug Desjardins. **Description:** Summer toy recalls have retailers worried about holiday sales in 2007. Mattel was heavily impacted from the recall of millions of toys manufactured in China.

18342 ■ *Doing Business Anywhere: The Essential Guide to Going Global*
Pub: John Wiley and Sons, Inc.

Ed: Tom Travis. **Released:** 2007. **Price:** $24.95. **Description:** Plans are given for new or existing businesses to organize, plan, operate and execute a business on a global basis. Trade agreements, brand protection and patents, ethics, security as well as cultural issues are among the issues addressed.

18343 ■ "Eagle's Wine Kiosk Is Area's 1st" in *Pittsburgh Post-Gazette* (October 28, 2010)
Pub: Pittsburgh-Post Gazette

Ed: Bob Batz Jr. **Description:** Giant Eagle Market District store at Settlers Ridge opened the first self-serve wine kiosk in Western Pennsylvania. The kiosk will have a built-in breathalyzer panel to ensure safety.

18344 ■ *Electronic Commerce*
Pub: Course Technology

Ed: Gary Schneider, Bryant Chrzan, Charles McCormick. **Released:** May 1, 2010. **Price:** $117.95. **Description:** E-commerce can open the door to more opportunities than ever before for small business. Packed with real-world examples and cases, the book delivers comprehensive coverage of emerging online technologies and trends and their influence on the electronic marketplace. It details how the landscape of online commerce is evolving, reflecting changes in the economy and how business and society are responding to those changes. Balancing technological issues with the strategic business aspects of successful e-commerce, the new edition includes expanded coverage of international issues, social networking, mobile commerce, Web 2.0 technologies, and updates on spam, phishing, and identity theft.

18345 ■ *Electronic Commerce: Technical, Business, and Legal Issues*
Pub: Prentice Hall PTR

Ed: Oktay Dogramaci; Aryya Gangopadhyay; Yelena Yesha; Nabil R. Adam. **Released:** August 1998. **Description:** Provides insight into the goals of using the Internet to grow a business in the areas of networking and telecommunication, security, and storage and retrieval; business areas such as marketing, procurement and purchasing, billing and payment, and supply chain management; and legal aspects such as privacy, intellectual property, taxation, contractual and legal settlements.

18346 ■ "Encouraging Study in Critical Languages" in *Occupational Outlook Quarterly* (Vol. 55, Summer 2011, No. 2, pp. 23)
Pub: U.S. Bureau of Labor Statistics

Description: Proficiency in particular foreign languages is vital to the defense, diplomacy, and security of the United States. Several federal programs provide scholarships and other funding to encourage high school and college students to learn languages of the Middle East, China, and Russia.

18347 ■ "Enforcer In Fantasyland" in *Crain's New York Business* (Vol. 24, February 25, 2008, No. 8, pp. 10)
Pub: Crain Communications Inc.

Ed: Hilary Potkewitz. **Description:** Patent law, particularly in the toy and game industry, is recession-proof according to Barry Negrin, partner at Pryor Cashman. Negrin co-founded his patent practice group. Despite massive recalls of toys and the concern over toxic toys, legal measures are in place in this industry.

18348 ■ "EOTech Product Improves Holographic Gun Sights" in *Crain's Detroit Business* (Vol. 24, February 4, 2008, No. 5, pp. 9)
Pub: Crain Communications Inc. - Detroit

Description: L-3 Communications EOTech Inc. procured new business contracts to fulfill military and law enforcement's demand for improved holographic sites used on handheld weapons.

18349 ■ "Eve in the Sky: A Look at Security Tech from All Angles" in *Bellingtham Business Journal* (October 2008, pp. 23)
Pub: Sun News Inc.

Ed: Lance Henderson. **Description:** High tech solutions to security issues in any company are not the only things to be considered; a low-tech evaluation of a building and its security fixtures, such as door knobs, locks, doors and windows as well as lighting are important aspects to security any office.

18350 ■ "Familiar Fun" in *Crain's Cleveland Business* (Vol. 28, October 22, 2007, No. 42, pp. 3)
Pub: Crain Communications Inc.
Ed: John Booth. **Description:** Marketing for the 2007 holiday season has toy retailers focusing on American-made products because of recent recalls of toys produced in China that do not meet U.S. safety standards.

18351 ■ "Finalist: Private Company, Less Than $100M" in *Crain's Detroit Business* (Vol. 25, June 22, 2009, No. 25)
Pub: Crain Communications Inc. - Detroit
Ed: Sherri Begin Welch. **Description:** Profile of family-owned Guardian Alarm Company is presented. The firm has expanded to include medical monitoring and video equipment of doors and windows.

18352 ■ "Fly Phishing" in *Canadian Business* (Vol. 80, October 22, 2007, No. 21, pp. 42)
Pub: Rogers Media
Ed: Andy Holloway. **Description:** Symantec Corporation's report shows consumers and companies have effectively installed network defenses that prevent unwanted access. Phishing packages are readily available and are widely used. Other details of the Internet Security Threat Report are presented.

18353 ■ "The Fort" in *Hawaii Business* (Vol. 53, November 2007, No. 5, pp. 19)
Pub: Hawaii Business Publishing
Ed: Jason Ubay. **Description:** DRFortress' flagship data center The Fort located at Honolulu's Airport Industrial Park provides companies a place to store their servers in an ultra-secure environment. Anything stored in here that requires power has a back up and in case of an outage generators can supply power up to 80 hrs. The Fort caters to major carriers and Internet service providers.

18354 ■ "Freeing the Wheels of Commerce" in *Hispanic Business* (July-August 2007, pp. 50, 52, 54)
Pub: Hispanic Business
Ed: Keith Rosenblum. **Description:** SecureOrigins, a border-based partnership with high-tech innovators is working to move goods faster, more efficiently, and securely.

18355 ■ "Frost and Sullivan" in *Investment Weekly News* (December 19, 2009, pp. 150)
Pub: Investment Weekly News
Description: Demand for video analytics solutions concerning security and business intelligence is growing, especially in such regions as the Middle East, Europe and Africa. Significant advancements in the field of intelligent analysis of video hold promising opportunities in security applications.

18356 ■ "General Clark Stresses Ethanols Role In National Security At Ag Connect" in *Farm Industry News* (January 11, 2011)
Pub: Penton Business Media Inc.
Description: General Clark stressed the role of ethanols in national security at the AgConnect.

18357 ■ "GM's Volt Woes Cast Shadow on E-Cars" in *Wall Street Journal Eastern Edition* (November 28, 2011, pp. B1)
Pub: Dow Jones & Company Inc.
Ed: Sharon Terlep. **Description:** The future of electric cars is darkened with the government investigation by the National Highway Traffic Safety Administration into General Motor Company's Chevy Volt after two instances of the car's battery packs catching fire during crash tests conducted by the Agency.

18358 ■ "Government Says Self-Regulation of Online Privacy is Coming Up Short" in *Advertising Age* (Vol. 81, December 6, 2010, No. 43, pp. 1)
Pub: Crain Communications, Inc.
Ed: Edmund Lee. **Description:** U.S. Federal Trade Commission and the Department of Commerce are concerned about the current state of digital privacy and stated that self-regulation has not been sufficient to date.

18359 ■ "A Hacker in India Hijacked His Website Design and Was Making Good Money Selling It" in *Inc.* (December 2007, pp. 77-78, 80)
Pub: Gruner & Jahr USA Publishing
Ed: Darren Dahl. **Description:** John Anton, owner of an online custom T-shirt business and how a company in India was selling software Website templates identical to his firm's Website.

18360 ■ "Homing In On the Future" in *Black Enterprise* (Vol. 38, October 2007, No. 3, pp. 61)
Pub: Earl G. Graves Publishing Co. Inc.
Ed: Sean Drakes. **Description:** More and more people are wanting new homes wired automated systems that integrate multiple home devices such as computers, audio/visual entertainment, security, communications, utilities, and lighting and environmental controls.

18361 ■ "Hopkins' Security, Reputation Face Challenges in Wake of Slaying" in *Baltimore Business Journal* (Vol. 28, August 6, 2010, No. 13)
Pub: Baltimore Business Journal
Ed: Gary Haber. **Description:** The slaying of Johns Hopkins University researcher Stephen Pitcairn has not tarnished the reputation of the elite school in Baltimore, Maryland among students. Maintaining Hopkins' reputation is important since it is Baltimore's largest employer with nearly 32,000 workers. Insights on the impact of the slaying among the Hopkins' community are also given.

18362 ■ "How Business Intelligence Can Affect Bottomline" in *Canadian Electronics* (Vol. 23, February 2008, No. 1, pp. 6)
Pub: CLB Media Inc.
Ed: Mark Borkowski. **Description:** Business intelligence has an important role in delivering the right information in a secured manner. However, coping with data volume, cost, workload, time, availability and compliance have been a problem for business intelligence projects. Ways to avoid problems in business intelligence projects and examples of business intelligence applications are provided.

18363 ■ "How Foreigners Could Disrupt U.S. Markets" in *Barron's* (Vol. 90, September 13, 2010, No. 37, pp. 30)
Pub: Barron's Editorial & Corporate Headquarters
Ed: Jim McTague. **Description:** An informal meeting by the House Homeland Security Panel concluded that U.S. stock exchanges and related trading routes can be the subject of attacks from rogue overseas traders. A drop in funding for the U.S. Department of Defense is discussed.

18364 ■ "iControl Networks Powers Comcast's XFINITY (Reg) Home Security Service" in *Benzinga.com* (June 9, 2011)
Pub: Benzinga.com
Ed: Benzinga Staff. **Description:** Comcast's XFINITY Home Security Service is powered by iControl Networks' OpenHome (TM) software platform. The service provides intrusion and fire protection along with interactive features such as home monitoring, home management, and energy management services with Web and mobile access.

18365 ■ "Identity Crisis: The Battle For Your Data" in *Canadian Business* (Vol. 81, March 17, 2008, No. 4, pp. 12)
Pub: Rogers Media
Description: Nigel Brown explains that businesses must protect their data through encryption and tightening up access to data. Brown also points out that banks and merchants bear most of the costs for identity fraud and leaves individuals with a lot of pain and heartache in clearing their name.

18366 ■ "Identity Thieves Hit a New Low" in *Information Today* (Vol. 26, February 2009, No. 2, pp. 1)
Pub: Information Today, Inc.
Ed: Phillip Britt. **Description:** Identity thieves are opening credit lines after reading obituaries. Actual identity theft cases are examined.

18367 ■ "Importers Share Safety Liability" in *Feedstuffs* (Vol. 80, January 21, 2008, No. 3, pp. 19)
Pub: Miller Publishing Company, Inc.
Description: Pet food and toys containing lead paint are among products from China being recalled due to safety concerns. American Society for Quality's list of measures that outsourcing companies can take to help ensure safer products being imported to the U.S.

18368 ■ "In the Mobikey of Life" in *Canadian Business* (Vol. 81, July 21, 2008, No. 11, pp. 42)
Pub: Rogers Media Ltd.
Ed: John Gray. **Description:** Toronto-based Route1 has created a data security software system that allows employees to access files and programs stored in the head office without permanently transferring data to the actual computer being used. Mobikey technology is useful in protecting laptops of chief executive officers, which contain confidential financial and customer data.

18369 ■ "Intel to Buy McAfee Security Business for 768B" in *eWeek* (August 19, 2010)
Pub: Ziff Davis Enterprise
Description: Intel will acquire security giant McAfee for approximately $7.68 billion, whereby McAfee would become a wholly owned subsidiary of Intel and would report to Intel's Software and Services Group.

18370 ■ "Kids, Computers and the Social Networking Evolution" in *Canadian Business* (Vol. 81, October 27, 2008, No. 18, pp. 93)
Pub: Rogers Media Ltd.
Ed: Penny Milton. **Description:** Social networking was found to help educate students in countries like the U.S., Canada and Mexico. Schools that embrace social networking teach students how to use computers safely and responsibility in order to counter threats to children on the Internet.

18371 ■ "Local Company Seeks Patent For Armored Trucks" in *Crain's Detroit Business* (Vol. 24, February 4, 2008, No. 5, pp. 10)
Pub: Crain Communications Inc. - Detroit
Description: Profile of James LeBlanc Sr., mechanical engineer and defense contractor, discusses his eleven utility patents pending for a set of vehicles and subsystems that would work as countermeasures to explosively formed projectiles.

18372 ■ "Macho Men" in *Canadian Business* (Vol. 81, November 10, 2008, No. 19, pp. 23)
Pub: Rogers Media Ltd.
Ed: Sharda Prashad. **Description:** Professors Robin Ely and Debra Meyerson found that oil rigs decreased accidents and increased productivity when they focused on improving safety and admitting errors rather than on a worker's individual strength. Professor Jennifer Berdahl shows there is pressure for men to be seen as masculine at work, which makes them avoid doing 'feminine' things such as parental leaves.

18373 ■ "Making Factory Tours Count" in *Playthings* (Vol. 107, January 1, 2009, No. 1, pp. 14)
Pub: Reed Business Information
Ed: Malcolm Denniss. **Description:** The importance of touring an overseas toy supplier's manufacturing facility is stressed. Strategies for general factory visits are outlined in order to determine safety-related quality assurance issues in production.

18374 ■ "Melamine Analytical Methods Released" in *Feedstuffs* (Vol. 80, October 6, 2008, No. 41, pp. 2)
Pub: Miller Publishing Company
Description: Romer Labs has released new validations for its AgraQuant Melamine enzyme-linked immunosorbent assay. The test kit screens for melamine in feed and diary products, including pet foods, milk and milk powder. Melamine by itself is nontoxic in low doses, but when combined with cyanuric acid it can cause fatal kidney stones. The Chinese dairy industry is in the midst of a huge melamine crisis; melamine-contaminated dairy and food products from China have been found in more than 20 countries.

18375 ■ "Microsoft Releases Office Security Updates" in *Mac World* (Vol. 27, November 2010, No. 11, pp. 66)
Pub: Mac Publishing
Ed: David Dahlquist. **Description:** Office for Mac and Mac Business Unit are Microsoft's pair of security- and stability-enhancing updates for Office 2008 and Office 2004. The software will improve the stability and compatibility and fixes vulnerabilities that would allow attackers to overwrite Mac's memory with malicious code.

18376 ■ "Mimosa Systems Gains 150,000 New NearPoint Users" in *Information Today* (Vol. 26, February 2009, No. 2, pp. 31)
Pub: Information Today, Inc.
Description: Mimosa System's NearPoint archive solution features email and file archiving, e-discovery, archive virtualization, and disaster recovery capabilities.

18377 ■ "Mobile Security for Business V5" in *SC Magazine* (Vol. 20, August 2009, No. 8, pp. 55)
Pub: Haymarket Media, Inc.
Description: Review of F-Secure's Mobile Security for Business v5 which offers protection for business smartphones that can be centralized for protection monitoring by IT administrators.

18378 ■ "Nampa Police Department: Electronic Systems Just One Tool in Business Security Toolbox" in *Idaho Business Review* (October 29, 2010)
Pub: Dolan Media Newswires
Ed: Brad Carlson. **Description:** Police departments and private security firms can help small businesses with hard security and business consultants can assist with internal audit security and fraud prevention.

18379 ■ "New Wave of Business Security Products Ushers in the Kaspersky Anti-Malware Protection System" in *Internet Wire* (October 26, 2010)
Pub: Comtex
Description: Kaspersky Anti-Malware System provides anti-malware protection that requires minimal in-house resources for small businesses. The system offers a full range of tightly integrated end-to-end protection solutions, ensuring unified protection across an entire network, from endpoint and mobile device protection to file server, mail server, network storage and gateway protection. It provides flexible centralized management, immediate threat visibility and a level of responsiveness not seen in other anti-malware approaches.

18380 ■ "New Ways To Think About Data Loss: Data Loss Is Costly and Painful" in *Franchising World* (Vol. 42, August 2010, No. 8, pp. 21)
Pub: International Franchise Association
Ed: Ken Colburn. **Description:** Information for maintaining data securely for franchised organizations, including smart phones, tablets, copiers, computers and more is given.

18381 ■ *Nine Lives Associates—Membership Directory*
Pub: Executive Protection Institute
Ed: Dr. Richard W. Kobetz, Editor, rwk@crosslink.com. **Released:** Annual, March. **Covers:** 2,000 individuals certified as personal protection specialists through completion of a training program. **Entries Include:** Specialist name and title, address, phone, company name. **Arrangement:** Classified by class completed.

18382 ■ "No Lines, No Waiting" in *The Business Journal-Serving Greater Tampa Bay* (Vol. 28, August 15, 2008, No. 34, pp. 1)
Pub: American City Business Journals, Inc.
Ed: Jane Meinhardt. **Description:** Voda LLC, which was founded to commercialize developments by David Fries, develops outdoor sensor networks used for environmental monitoring by markets like research, the security industry, and the government. Fries already licensed 12 technologies for clients for about $130,000 per technology. Other information on Voda LLC is presented.

18383 ■ "Not In Our Backyard" in *Canadian Business* (Vol. 80, October 22, 2007, No. 21, pp. 76)
Pub: Rogers Media
Ed: Anrew Nikiforuk. **Description:** Alberta Energy and Utilities Board's proposed construction of electric transmission line has let to protests by landowners. The electric utility was also accused of spying on ordinary citizens and violating impartiality rules. Details of the case between Lavesta Area Group and the Board are discussed.

18384 ■ "Now Entering A Secure Area" in *Women Entrepreneur* (January 14, 2009)
Pub: Entrepreneur Media Inc.
Ed: Aliza Sherman. **Description:** Despite the fact that the field of government intelligence and security is dominated by males, many women entrepreneurs are finding opportunities for their products and services in homeland security. Profiles of several women who have found such opportunities are included.

18385 ■ "Obama Plan May Boost Maryland Cyber Security" in *Boston Business Journal* (Vol. 29, May 20, 2011, No. 2, pp. 1)
Pub: American City Business Journals Inc.
Ed: Scott Dance. **Description:** May 12, 2011 outline of the cyber security policies of President Obama may improve the cyber security industry in Maryland as the state is home to large defense and intelligence activities. Details of the proposed policies are discusses as well as their advantages to companies that deal in developing cyber security plans for other companies.

18386 ■ "Online Security Crackdown: Scanning Service Oversees Site Security at David's Bridal" in (Vol. 84, July 2008, No. 7, pp. 46)
Pub: Chain Store Age
Ed: Samantha Murphy. **Description:** Online retailers are beefing up security on their Websites. Cyber thieves use retail systems in order to gain entry to consumer data. David's Bridal operates over 275 bridal showrooms in the U.S. and has a one-stop wedding resource for new brides planning weddings.

18387 ■ "Oracle and Tauri Group Honored by Homeland Security and Defense Business Council" in *Wireless News* (December 15, 2009)
Pub: Close-Up Media
Description: Selected as members of the year by the Homeland Security and Defense Business Council were Oracle, a software company that has provided thought leadership and strategic insights as well as The Tauri Group, an analytical consultancy, that has demonstrated a unique understanding of the role of small business and its vital contribution to the success of the country's security.

18388 ■ "Out Front and Strong" in *WorkingUSA* (Vol. 11, December 2008, No. 4, pp. 477)
Pub: Blackwell Publishers Ltd.
Ed: Jessica Wilkerson. **Description:** History of the Tennessee Committee on Occupational Safety and Health that formed in East Tennessee in 1979 is explored. The article addresses how local women contributed to the organization at the grassroots.

18389 ■ "Panda Security for Business 4.05" in *SC Magazine* (Vol. 21, July 2010, No. 7, pp. 50)
Pub: Haymarket Media Inc.
Description: Profile of Panda Security for Business, software offering endpoint security protection for computer desktops and servers is presented.

18390 ■ "PC Connection Acquires Cloud Software Provider" in *New Hampshire Business Review* (Vol. 33, March 25, 2011, No. 6, pp. 8)
Pub: Business Publications Inc.
Description: Merrimack-based PC Connection Inc. acquired ValCom Technology, a provider of cloud-based IT service management software. Details of the deal are included.

18391 ■ "Prevent Identity Theft: Simple Steps To Protect Yourself Against Identity Theft" in *Small Business Opportunities* (January 2008)
Pub: Harris Publications Inc.
Ed: Frank W. Abagnale. **Description:** Expert shares tips to help individuals and businesses protect themselves from identity theft.

18392 ■ "Protection One Introduces Home and Business Security iPhone App" in *Wireless News* (November 13, 2009)
Pub: Close-Up Media
Description: Protection One, Inc., a provider of security systems to business and residential customers, has developed an application that allows users to access their security panels and receive real-time updates from their iPhone or iPod touch devices.

18393 ■ "The Quality Revolution" in *Canadian Business* (Vol. 81, November 10, 2008, No. 19, pp. 128)
Pub: Rogers Media Ltd.
Ed: Andrew Nikiforuk. **Description:** John Volpe believes that the pursuit of quantity of food choices leads to tasteless meals, expanding waistlines, and food poisoning and stresses emphasis on food quality and food security.

18394 ■ "Ready for the Worst? How to Disaster-Proof Your Business" in *Inc.* (Vol. 33, September 2011, No. 7, pp. 38)
Pub: Inc. Magazine
Ed: J.J. McCorvey, Dave Smith. **Description:** Twelve products to and services designed to help small businesses run smoothly in the event of a disaster are outlined.

18395 ■ "Remote Control: Working From Wherever" in *Inc.* (February 2008, pp. 46-47)
Pub: Gruner & Jahr USA Publishing
Ed: Ryan Underwood. **Description:** New technology allows workers to perform tasks from anywhere via the Internet. Profiles of products to help connect to your office from afar include, LogMein Pro, a Web-based service that allowsaccess to a computer from anywhere; Xdrive, an online service that allows users to store and swap files; Basecamp, a Web-based tools that works like a secure version of MySpace; MojoPac Freedom, is software that allows users to copy their computer's desktop to a removable hard drive and plug into any PC; WatchGuard Firebox X Core e-Series UTM Bundle, hardware that blocks hackers and viruses while allowing employees to work remotely; TightVNC, a free open-source software that lets you control another computer via the Internet.

18396 ■ "Rep. Loretta Sanchez Holds a Hearing on Small Business Cyber Security" in *Political/Congressional Transcript Wire* (July 29, 2010)
Pub: CQ Roll Call
Description: U.S. House Committee on Armed Services, Subcommittee on Terrorism, Unconventional Threats and Capabilities held a hearing on small business cyber security innovation.

18397 ■ "Research and Market Adds Report: Endpoint Security for Business" in *Wireless News* (October 26, 2009)
Pub: Close-Up Media
Description: Summarizes Research and Markets Adds Report: Endpoint Security for Business: Desktops, Laptops & Mobile Devices 2009-2014; highlights include a detailed analysis of where the industry is at present and forecasts regarding how it will develop over the next five years.

18398 ■ "Retailers Report 'Shrinkage' of Inventory on the Rise" in *Arkansas Business* (Vol. 26, September 28, 2009, No. 39, pp. 17)
Pub: Journal Publishing Inc.
Ed: Mark Friedman. **Description:** According to a National Retail Security Survey report released last June, retailers across the country have lost about $36.5 billion in shrinkage, most of it at the hands of employees and shoplifters alike. Statistical data included.

18399 ■ "Safety Managers Need to Be Safety Experts" in *Indoor Comfort Marketing* (Vol. 70, May 2011, No. 5, pp. 10)
Pub: Industry Publications Inc.

Ed: Mike Hodge. **Description:** It is imperative to have a good safety manager in place for all heating and cooling firms.

18400 ■ "Sales Communications in a Mobile World" in *Business Communication Quarterly* (December 2007, pp. 492)
Pub: Sage Publications USA

Ed: Daniel T. Norris. **Description:** Salespeople can take advantage of the latest mobile technologies while maintaining a personal touch with clients and customers through innovation, formality in interactions, client interactions, and protection and security of mobile data.

18401 ■ "Scanning the Field" in *Business Courier* (Vol. 26, January 8, 2010, No. 38, pp. 1)
Pub: American City Business Journals, Inc.

Ed: Jon Newberry. **Description:** Anti-terror detection systems developer Valley Force Composite Technologies Inc. of Kentucky plans to enter the market with its high-resolution ODIN and Thor-LVX screening systems. These systems are expected to meet the increasing demand for airport security equipment.

18402 ■ "SECO Manufacturing" in *Point of Beginning* (Vol. , 2008, No. , pp.)
Pub: BNP Media

Description: Seco Manufacturing's 3015-Series lock features an all-metal tilting holder with an improved brass front locking lever for improved security for any building.

18403 ■ "Security Alert: Data Server" in *Entrepreneur* (Vol. 36, February 2008, No. 2, pp. 28)
Pub: Entrepreneur Media Inc.

Ed: Amanda C. Kooser. **Description:** Michael Kogon is the founder of Definition 6, a technology consulting and interactive marking firm. He believes in the philosophy that the best way to keep sensitive data safe is not to store it. Details on the security policies of his firm are discussed.

18404 ■ "A Security Risk?" in *Canadian Business* (Vol. 80, October 22, 2007, No. 21, pp. 36)
Pub: Rogers Media

Ed: Joe Castaldo. **Description:** Garda World Security Corporation declared a C$1.5 million loss in the second quarter of 2007. The company's securities have been falling since June and hit a 52-week low of $15.90 in September. Details of the physical and cash-handling firm's strategy to integrate its acquisitions are discussed.

18405 ■ *Selling Online: Canada's Bestselling Guide to Becoming a Successful E-Commerce Merchant*
Pub: John Wiley and Sons Canada Ltd.

Ed: Jim Carroll; Rick Broadhead. **Released:** September 6, 2002. **Description:** Helps individuals build online retail enterprises; this updated version includes current tools, information and success strategies, how to launch an online storefront, security, marketing strategies, and mistakes to avoid.

18406 ■ "Selling Your Company" in *Inc.* (March 2008, pp. 78)
Pub: Gruner & Jahr USA Publishing

Ed: Myra Goodman. **Description:** Owner of a safety consulting company seeks advice for selling the firm.

18407 ■ "Sign of Progress" in *Playthings* (Vol. 106, October 1, 2008, No. 9, pp. 4)
Pub: Reed Business Information

Ed: Cliff Annicelli. **Description:** The ramifications of the toy recalls in 2007 are discussed. Mandates for lead-free toys and other safety issues are having an impact on the American toy industry.

18408 ■ "Some Atlantic Beach Leaders Leery About Convenience Store Safety Measure" in *Florida Times-Union* (November 3, 2010)
Pub: Florida Times-Union

Ed: Drew Dixon. **Description:** Jacksonville, Florida authorities are proposing a new ordinance that would require convenience stores to upgrade safety measures to protect store workers and customers from robbery and other crimes.

18409 ■ "STAR TEC Incubator's Latest Resident Shows Promise" in *The Business Journal-Serving Greater Tampa Bay* (August 8, 2008)
Pub: American City Business Journals, Inc.

Ed: Jane Meinhardt. **Description:** Field Forensics Inc., a resident of the STAR Technology Enterprise Center, has grown after being admitted into the business accelerator. The producer of defense and security devices and equipment has doubled 2007 sales as of 2008.

18410 ■ "State Democrats Push for Changes to Plant Security Law" in *Chemical Week* (Vol. 172, July 19, 2010, No. 17, pp. 8)
Pub: Access Intelligence

Ed: Kara Sissell. **Description:** Legislation has been introduced to revise the existing U.S. Chemical Facility Anti-Terrorism Standards (CFATS) that would include a requirement for facilities to use inherently safer technology (IST). The bill would eliminate the current law's exemption of water treatment plants and certain port facilities and preserve the states' authority to establish stronger security standards.

18411 ■ "A Survey of DHT Security Techniques" in *ACM Computing Surveys* (Vol. 43, Summer 2011, No. 2, pp. 8)
Pub: Association for Computing Machinery

Ed: Guido Urdaneta, Guillaume Pierre, Maarten Van Steen. **Description:** Peer-to-peer networks based on distributed hash tables (DHTs) have received considerable attention since their introduction in 2001. Unfortunately, DHT-based systems have been shown to be difficult to protect against security attacks. An overview of techniques reported in literature for making DHT-based systems resistant to the three most important attacks that can be launched by malicious nodes participating in the DHT is given: the Sybil attack, the Eclipse attack, and routing and storage attacks.

18412 ■ *Surviving in the Security Alarm Business*
Pub: Butterworth-Heinemann

Ed: Lou Sepulveda. **Released:** 1998. **Price:** $19.95.

18413 ■ "Symantic Completes Acquisition of VeriSign's Security Business" in *Internet Wire* (August 9, 2010)
Pub: Comtex

Description: Symantec Corporation acquired VeriSign's identity and authentication business, which includes Secure Sockets Layer (SSL) and Code Signing Certificate Services, the Managed Public Key Infrastructure (MPKI) Services, the VeriSign Trust Seal, the VeriSign Identity Protection (VIP) Authentication Service and the VIP Fraud Protection Service (FDS). The agreement also included a majority stake in VeriSign Japan.

18414 ■ "Taking a Chance" in *Baltimore Business Journal* (Vol. 28, July 16, 2010, No. 10, pp. 1)
Pub: Baltimore Business Journal

Ed: Scott Dance. **Description:** North Avenue in Baltimore, Maryland is considered a rough neighborhood due to the dangers of prostitution and drug dealing. However, some entrepreneurs have taken the risk of building their businesses on North Avenue as revitalization efforts grow. One of the challenges for businesses in rough neighborhoods is bringing customers to their stores or offices.

18415 ■ "Taking the Steps Into the Clouds" in *New Hampshire Business Review* (Vol. 33, March 25, 2011, No. 6, pp. 19)
Pub: Business Publications Inc.

Ed: Tim Wessels. **Description:** Cloud services include Internet and Web security, spam filtering, message archiving, work group collaboration, IT asset management, help desk and disaster recovery backup.

18416 ■ "Tauri Group Partner Joining Homeland Security and Defense" in *Wireless News* (December 15, 2009)
Pub: Close-Up Media

Description: Managing partner Cosmo DiMaggio III of the Tauri Group, a provider of analytic consulting for homeland security, defense and space clients, has been elected to the Board of Directors at Homeland Security and Defense Business Council.

18417 ■ "Tech Data Launches Unified Communications and Network Security Specialized Business Units" in *Wireless News* (October 22,2009)
Pub: Close-Up Media

Description: Responding to the growing demand for unified communications and network security, Tech Data announced the formation of two new Specialized Business Units.

18418 ■ "Tech Investing: March's Long Road" in *Canadian Business* (Vol. 80, January 29, 2007, No. 3, pp. 67)
Pub: Rogers Media

Ed: Calvin Leung. **Description:** The efforts of March Networks, a manufacturer of digital surveillance equipment, from the decline in the price of its shares at the beginning of the year 2007 are described.

18419 ■ "Technology Protects Lottery" in *Arkansas Business* (Vol. 26, September 28, 2009, No. 39, pp. 1)
Pub: Journal Publishing Inc.

Ed: George Waldon. **Description:** Arkansas Lottery Commission was initially criticized for what was seen as a major breach in security protocol by revealing the exact location of 26 million lottery tickets during a publicity stunt in which the media was invited to the main distribution center; however, due to the high-tech security that has been implemented the tickets are worthless until their status is changed after passing through multiple security scans.

18420 ■ "Tektronix Buys Arbor Networks for Security Business" in *eWeek* (August 9, 2010)
Pub: Ziff Davis Enterprise

Description: Tektronix Communications, provider of communications test and network intelligence solutions will acquire Arbor Networks. The deal will help Tektronix build a brand in security. Details of the transaction are included.

18421 ■ "This Year's Model" in *Playthings* (Vol. 107, January 1, 2009, No. 1, pp. 23)
Pub: Reed Business Information

Ed: Karyn M. Peterson. **Description:** Toy manufacturers, as well as retailers, address the need to exceed safety and quality demands by consumers when developing new toys and games for children.

18422 ■ "Thomas and His Washington Friends" in *CFO* (Vol. 23, October 2007, No. 10, pp. 18)
Pub: CFO Publishing Corporation

Ed: Alix Stuart. **Description:** Reliance on Chinese suppliers to America's toymakers may become quite costly as Congress considers legislation that would increase fines to as high as $50 million for companies selling tainted products. The legislation would also require independent mandatory testing for makers of products for children.

18423 ■ "The Total Cost of Ignorance: Avoiding Top Tech Mistakes" in *Black Enterprise* (Vol. 38, October 2007, No. 3, pp. 64)
Pub: Earl G. Graves Publishing Co. Inc.

Ed: Alwin A.D. Jones. **Description:** Cost of data loss for any small business can be devastating; lack of security is another mistake companies make when it comes to technology.

18424 ■ "Tougher Securities Rules on the Way" in *Globe & Mail* (February 21, 2007, pp. B1)
Pub: CTVglobemedia Publishing Inc.
Ed: Janet McFarland. **Description:** The Canadian Securities Administration will implement new regulation for the securities industry by early next year. Securities companies will now have to register its employee details and earnings according to this new rule.

18425 ■ "Toy Scares Drive Business" in *Boston Business Journal* (Vol. 27, November 23, 2007, No. 43, pp. 1)
Pub: American City Business Journals, Inc.
Ed: Joan Goodchild. **Description:** Several Boston businesses have tapped into the lead content scare in toys and other products manufactured in China. ConRoy Corporation LLC launched Toy Recall Alert!, an online tool to alert consumers about new recalls while Hybrivet Systems introduced screening test kit, LeadCheck. Other new products pertaining to toy safety are discussed.

18426 ■ "Toy Story" in *Forbes* (Vol. 180, October 15, 2007, No. 8, pp. 102)
Pub: Forbes Inc.
Description: Three voluntary recalls of Chinese-made toys were announced by American toymakers, sending Mattel stocks plummeting.

18427 ■ "Toy Story: U.S.-Made a Hot Seller" in *Crain's Detroit Business* (Vol. 23, December 17, 2007, No. 51, pp. 3)
Pub: Crain Communications Inc. - Detroit
Ed: Chad Halcom. **Description:** American Plastic Toys, located in Walled Lake, Michigan reports all its toys are made in the U.S. and have passed all U.S. safety standards. Revenue for American Plastic Toys reached nearly $33 million in 2005, and the company expects to exceed that because of recent toy safety recalls of products produced in China.

18428 ■ "Tragedies Add Demand for Inspiron's Alert System" in *Crain's Cleveland Business* (Vol. 28, October 29, 2007, No. 43, pp. 5)
Pub: Crain Communications, Inc.
Ed: Chuck Soder. **Description:** Inspiron Logistics Corp. has seen huge growth over the past months for its Wireless Emergency Notification System which colleges and universities have rushed to buy since the April 16 shootings at Virginia Tech. The company now makes more than half of its revenue by selling the systems to colleges whereas previous to the shootings the academic market accounted for just 20 percent of the company's sales.

18429 ■ "Twitter Hack: Made in Japan? User Says Attack Showed Security Flaw" in *Houston Chronicle* (September 24, 2010, pp. 3)
Pub: Houston Chronicle
Ed: Tomoko A. Hosaka. **Description:** Details of the attack on Twitter caused by a Japanese computer hacker are revealed.

18430 ■ "Unbound ID Raises $2 Million" in *Austin Business JournalInc.* (Vol. 28, December 12, 2008, No. 39, pp. 1)
Pub: American City Business Journals
Ed: Christopher Calnan. **Description:** Austin, Texas-based Unbound ID Corporation has secured $2 million in funding from venture capital firm Silverton Partners. The company has developed identity management software for network directories. The market for identity management technology is expected to grow to more than $12.3 billion by 2014.

18431 ■ "U.S. Enters BlackBerry Dispute Compromise Sought Over Security Issues" in *Houston Chronicle* (August 6, 2010)
Pub: Houston Chronicle
Ed: Matthew Lee. **Description:** U.S. State Department is working for a compromise with Research in Motion, manufacturer of the BlackBerry, over security issues. The Canadian company makes the smartphones and foreign governments believe they pose a security risk.

18432 ■ "Vandal-Resistant Mortise Locks" in *Building Design and Construction* (Vol. 49, September 1, 2008, No. 12, pp. 78)
Pub: Reed Business Information
Description: Stanley Security Solutions offers mortise locks with a vandal-resistant feature that includes a clutch mechanism designed to break away when excessive force is applied either by kicking or standing on the lever. Once the mortise lock breaks away it can be easily reset to its original position without sustaining damage.

18433 ■ "VeriFone Announces Global Security Solutions Business" in *Marketing Weekly News* (October 3, 2009)
Pub: Investment Weekly News
Description: Focused on delivering innovative security solutions, VeriFone Holdings, Inc. announced the formation of its Global Security Solutions Business Unit, including VeriShield Protect, an end-to-end encryption to protect cardholder data throughout the merchant and processor systems. The business will focus on consulting, sales and implementation of these new products in order to help retailers and processors protect customer data.

18434 ■ "Video Surveillance Enters Digital Era, Makes Giant Strides" in *Arkansas Business* (Vol. 26, September 28, 2009, No. 39, pp. 1)
Pub: Journal Publishing Inc.
Ed: Jamie Walden. **Description:** Arkansas business owners are finding that the newest technology in video surveillance is leading to swift apprehension of thieves due to the high-quality digital imagery now being captured on surveillance equipment. Motion detection software for these systems is enhancing the capabilities of these systems and providing opportunities for businesses that would normally have problems integrating these systems.

18435 ■ "Watchful Eye: Entrepreneur Protects Clients and His Bottom Line" in *Black Enterprise* (Vol. 38, March 2008, No. 8, pp. 46)
Pub: Earl G. Graves Publishing Co. Inc.
Ed: Tennille M. Robinson. **Description:** Profile of Elijah Shaw, founder of Icon Services Corporation, a full service security and investigative service; Shaw shares his plans to protect clients while growing his business.

18436 ■ "Wegmans Uses Database for Recall" in *Supermarket News* (Vol. 56, September 22, 2008, No. 38)
Pub: Penton Business Media, Inc.
Ed: Carol Angrisani. **Description:** Wegmans used data obtained through its loyalty card that, in turn, sent automated telephone calls to every customer who had purchased tainted pet food when Mars Petcare recalled dog food products.

18437 ■ "What the Future Holds for Consumers" in *Black Enterprise* (Vol. 41, August 2010, No. 1, pp. 47)
Pub: Earl G. Graves Publishing Co. Inc.
Ed: Sheiresa Ngo. **Description:** The way people purchase goods and service has changed with technology. With an increased focus on security (as well as privacy and fairness) the U.S. Congress began regulating the credit card industry with the Fair Credit Reporting Act of 1970 and the Credit Card Accountability, Responsibility, and Disclosure (CARD) Act of 2009.

18438 ■ "Who Gets the Last Laugh?" in *Barron's* (Vol. 88, March 31, 2008, No. 13, pp. 17)
Pub: Dow Jones & Company, Inc.
Ed: Leslie P. Norton. **Description:** Nord/LB will take a charge of 82.5 million euros to cover potential losses apparently related to Vatas' refusal to take the shares of Remote MDx Inc. after buying the shares. Remote MDx's main product is an ankle bracelet to monitor criminals; the firm has lost over half of its market cap due to the Nord/LB troubles and questions about its revenues.

18439 ■ "Windstream Expands Business Service Into Monroe" in *Marketing Weekly News* (January 23, 2010, pp. 77)
Pub: Investment Weekly News
Description: Windstream Corp. announces the expansion of its data and voice services into Monroe, N.C., which will give local businesses a new choice for advanced communication services and network security.

STATISTICAL SOURCES

18440 ■ *RMA Annual Statement Studies*
Pub: Robert Morris Associates (RMA)
Released: Annual. **Price:** $175.00 2006-07 edition, $105.00. **Description:** Contains composite balance sheets and income statements for more than 360 industries, including the accounting, auditing, and bookkeeping industries. Also contains five years of comparative historical data for discerning trends. Includes 16 commonly used ratios, computed for most of the size groupings for nearly every industry.

TRADE PERIODICALS

18441 ■ *Newsline*
Pub: National Burglar and Fire Alarm Association
Ed: Amanda Johnston, Editor. **Released:** 6/year. **Price:** Included in membership. **Description:** Provides news on the security industry, including marketing tips for small businesses and false alarm prevention ideas. Recurring features include interviews, a calendar of events, reports of meetings, news of educational opportunities, book reviews, and notices of publications available.

18442 ■ *Police & Security News*
Pub: Days Communications
Contact: Cindie Bonsall, Gen Mgr
E-mail: cbonsall@policeandsecuritynews.com
Released: Bimonthly. **Price:** $18 by mail; $75 other countries mail. **Description:** Tabloid for the law enforcement and private security industries. Includes articles on training, new products, and new technology.

18443 ■ *Security*
Pub: BNP Media
Contact: Bill Zalud, Ed. Emeritus
E-mail: zaludb@bnpmedia.com
Released: Monthly. **Description:** Magazine presenting news and technology for loss prevention and asset protection.

18444 ■ *Security Management*
Pub: ASIS International
Contact: Sherry Harowitz, Editor-in-Chief
E-mail: sharowitz@asisonline.org
Released: Monthly. **Price:** $48 Free to members; $115 nonmembers; $115 out of country. **Description:** Loss prevention and security magazine.

18445 ■ *Security Sales & Integration*
Pub: Bobit Business Media
Released: Monthly. **Description:** Magazine covering the security industry.

VIDEOCASSETTES/ AUDIOCASSETTES

18446 ■ *Executive Protection Video Catalog*
Gun Video
4585 Murphy Canyon Rd.
San Diego, CA 92123
Ph:(858)569-4000
Free: 800-942-8273
Fax:(858)569-0505
Co. E-mail: info2@gunvideo.com
URL: http://www.gunvideo.com
Price: $29.95. **Description:** A discussion of various high-tech security devices, including instructions on their use. Includes information on where they can be bought. **Availability:** VHS.

TRADE SHOWS AND CONVENTIONS

18447 ■ ISC Chicago
Reed Exhibitions North American Headquarters
383 Main Ave.
Norwalk, CT 06851
Ph:(203)840-4800
Fax:(203)840-5805
Co. E-mail: export@reedexpo.com
URL: http://www.reedexpo.com
Released: Biennial. **Audience:** Security equipment dealers and installers, corporate, industrial and institutional security managers and directors. **Principal Exhibits:** Residential, commercial, industrial and institutional security equipment, systems and services.

CONSULTANTS

18448 ■ Lenow International Inc.
1503 Union Ave., Ste. 210
PO Box 3092
Memphis, TN 38173-0092
Ph:(901)726-0735
Fax:(901)725-4079
Co. E-mail: nlenow@compuserve.com
URL: http://www.lenowinternational.com
Contact: Nate Lenow, President
E-mail: nate@lenowinternational.com
Scope: Acts as a consultant for investigative strategies to resolve civil or criminal investigations. Conducts surveys or evaluations to prevent crime directed toward business, in particular crime involving fraudulent activity. Recommends security procedures or equipment to aid loss prevention by business. Available to serve as expert witness in forensic security and fraud examination. Referral source for investigative agencies. Industries served: Corporate security departments, private investigative agencies, small business, and government agencies. **Publications:** "Competitive Intelligence," Law Enforcement Quarterly. **Seminars:** Automate your reports with software, Tennessee Association of Investigators, May, 2000; Use of Computer as an Investigative Tool; Criminal Investigation.

18449 ■ Protection Management Associates Inc.
8632 E Sells Dr., Ste. 302
Scottsdale, AZ 85251-2927
Ph:(480)949-5637
Fax:(602)994-0493
Contact: Loren E. Newland, President
Scope: Provides litigation support and expert witness services to corporations and facilities, designed to limit claims of negligence with respect to security adequacy. Performs security management assessments and audits designed to evaluate effectiveness of security design and administration. Industries served: hotels, hospitals, apartment houses, nursing homes, casinos and resorts, and government agencies. **Publications:** "Hotel Protection Management: the Inn keepers Guide to Guest Protection and Reasonable Care".

FRANCHISES AND BUSINESS OPPORTUNITIES

18450 ■ Direct Link
10700 Montgomery Rd., Ste. 300
Cincinnati, OH 45242
Free: 800-216-4196
Fax:(513)563-2691
Co. E-mail: inquiry@homehelpers.cc
URL: http://www.HomeHelpers.cc
No. of Franchise Units: 440. **Founded:** 1997. **Franchised:** 1997. **Description:** In-home emergency monitoring system for seniors. **Equity Capital Needed:** $21,100-$30,800. **Franchise Fee:** $18,900. **Financial Assistance:** Financing available. **Training:** Extensive training includes operations, payroll, recruitment, accounting, scheduling and client relations.

18451 ■ EYESthere
EYESthere Franchise Inc.
10725 SW Barbur Blvd.
Portland, OR 97219
Ph:(503)726-3937
Co. E-mail: info@eyesthere.com
URL: http://www.eyesthere.com
No. of Company-Owned Units: 5. **Founded:** 2006. **Franchised:** 2007. **Description:** Custom designs solutions that protect and empower businesses with live and recorded video. Franchises help protect our customer's premises, property, people and transactions and empower the owners, employees and customers with EYESthere unique Digital Video solutions **Equity Capital Needed:** $190,000-$310,000. **Franchise Fee:** $45,000. **Royalty Fee:** 6-10%. **Financial Assistance:** Limited third party financing available. **Managerial Assistance:** Customized P2C Operating Systems to track sales leads through the site survey, sales proposals, contract & installation cycle. **Training:** Provides 2 weeks at headquarters, 2 weeks at franchisee's location and ongoing support.

18452 ■ MonitorClosely.com
Monitor Closely.com, LLC
901 King St., Ste. 101
Alexandria, VA 45242
Free: 800-797-7505
No. of Franchise Units: 117. **Founded:** 2006. **Franchised:** 2006. **Description:** Digital surveillance systems. **Equity Capital Needed:** $45,000-$60,000. **Franchise Fee:** $39,500. **Royalty Fee:** 8%. **Financial Assistance:** Limited third party financing available. **Training:** Provides 4 days training at headquarters and ongoing support.

18453 ■ SHIELD Security Systems
Shield Development, Ltd.
5170 Genesee St.
Bowmansville, NY 14026
Ph:(716)681-6677
Fax:(716)636-8819
Co. E-mail: franchise@SHIELDsecurity.net
URL: http://www.SHIELDsecurity.net
No. of Franchise Units: 7. **No. of Company-Owned Units:** 2. **Founded:** 1976. **Franchised:** 2000. **Description:** Sales and installation of burglar and fire alarm systems. **Equity Capital Needed:** $74,275-$125,550. **Franchise Fee:** $40,000. **Royalty Fee:** 5%. **Financial Assistance:** Third party financing available. **Training:** 3-5 days of pre-training at corporate office, 3 days at franchisee location, and online for 8 weeks and ongoing support.

18454 ■ Signature Alert Security
746 E Winchester St., Ste. 110
Salt Lake City, UT 84107
Ph:(801)743-0101
Free: 800-957-1030
Fax:(801)743-0808
No. of Franchise Units: 36. **No. of Company-Owned Units:** 3. **Founded:** 1999. **Franchised:** 2003. **Description:** Sales, installation, and monitoring of security systems. **Equity Capital Needed:** $42,950-$50,500. **Franchise Fee:** $21,000. **Royalty Fee:** $2/customer/month. **Financial Assistance:** Assistance with franchisee fee. **Training:** Includes 5 days training at corporate headquarters, 2 days at franchisee's location and ongoing support.

18455 ■ Sonitrol Corp.
Automated Security Holdings
1000 Westlakes Dr., Ste. 150
Berwyn, PA 19312
Ph:(610)725-9706
Fax:(610)725-9707
No. of Franchise Units: 178. **No. of Company-Owned Units:** 57. **Founded:** 1964. **Franchised:** 1965. **Description:** Franchises auto intrusion alarm systems. **Equity Capital Needed:** $245,000-$500,000. **Franchise Fee:** $25,000-$55,000. **Royalty Fee:** 4.5%. **Financial Assistance:** No. **Training:** Includes training at headquarters, franchisee's location and ongoing.

RESEARCH CENTERS

18456 ■ University of Louisville–National Crime Prevention Institute
206 Mccandless Hall
Louisville, KY 40292
Ph:(502)852-8577
Free: 800—334-8635
Fax:(502)852-0335
Co. E-mail: marianna.perry@louisville.edu
URL: http://louisville.edu/ncpi/
Contact: Marianna Perry, Dir.
E-mail: marianna.perry@louisville.edu
Scope: Crime prevention, including research on physical and electronic security and review of loss reduction techniques employed in communities across the United States. **Services:** Crime Prevention Information Center.

START-UP INFORMATION

18457 ■ *How to Start a Home-Based Event Planning Business*
Pub: Globe Pequot Press

Ed: Jill Moran. **Released:** July 2007. **Price:** $18.95. **Description:** Guide to starting and growing a business planning events from a home-based firm.

ASSOCIATIONS AND OTHER ORGANIZATIONS

18458 ■ Canadian Society of Professional Event Planners
312 Oakwood Ct.
Newmarket, ON, Canada L3Y 3C8
Ph:(905)868-8008
Free: (866)467-2299
Fax:(905)895-1630
Co. E-mail: info@canspep.ca
URL: http://canspep.ca
Contact: Rose Timmerman-Gitzi, Pres.

Description: Provides a forum for entrepreneurs in the meetings, conferences and event planning profession to meet, share ideas, gain new and valuable information about the industry and work together to form a strong presence in the marketplace. Promotes professionalism and builds awareness of independent meeting planning industry to the target markets. **Publications:** *The Independent* (quarterly); Directory (annual). **Telecommunication Services:** electronic mail, rtgevents@rogers.com.

18459 ■ Connected International Meeting Professionals Association
9200 Bayard Pl.
Fairfax, VA 22032
Ph:(512)684-0889
Fax:(267)390-5193
Co. E-mail: susan@cimpa.org
URL: http://www.cimpa.org
Contact: Andrea Sigler PhD, Pres./CEO

Description: Meeting planners, incentive organizers, travel agents, tour operators, and seminar organizers in 42 countries. Works to improve the skills of professional conference and convention planners. Serves as a clearinghouse of information on new travel destinations and planning technologies, techniques, and strategies. Facilitates exchange of information among Internet professionals. Produces a television program on travel and meetings. Conducts educational courses and awards Certified Internet Meeting Professional designation. Conducts research programs and placement service. Sponsors training courses on the Internet. **Publications:** *Course Catalog* (quarterly); *How to Comply with the American Disability Act*; *How To Plan Meetings on the Internet*; *Job Leads* (monthly); *Journal of Technology, Meetings and Incentives*; *Marketing to Meeting Planners*; *Meeting Checklists*; *Organizing Meetings on the Internet*; *Tech-Savvy Meeting Professional* (bimonthly).

18460 ■ International Association of Speakers Bureaus
3933 S McClintock Dr., Ste. 505
Tempe, AZ 85282
Ph:(480)839-1423
Fax:(480)603-4141
Co. E-mail: info@iasbweb.org
URL: http://www.iasbweb.org
Contact: Gail Davis, Pres.

Description: Maintains speakers' bureau representing 15 countries. Focuses on continuing education for its members, promotes awareness among meeting planners and raises the bar on accepted practices in the speakers' bureau industry. .

18461 ■ National Speakers Association
1500 S Priest Dr.
Tempe, AZ 85281
Ph:(480)968-2552
Fax:(480)968-0911
Co. E-mail: information@nsaspeaker.org
URL: http://www.nsaspeaker.org
Contact: Kristin Arnold MBA, Pres.-Elect

Description: Professional speakers. Works to increase public awareness of the speaking profession, advance the integrity and visibility of professional speakers, and provide a learning and communication vehicle to professional speakers. Sponsors workshops, conventions, and labs. **Publications:** *Voices of Experience* (10/year); *Who's Who in Professional Speaking: The Meeting Planner's Guide* (annual).

EDUCATIONAL PROGRAMS

18462 ■ Design for Presentations
EEI Communications
66 Canal Center Plz., Ste. 200
Alexandria, VA 22314
Ph:(703)683-7453
Free: 888-253-2762
Fax:(703)683-7310
Co. E-mail: train@eeicom.com
URL: http://www.eeicom.com/training

Price: $745.00. **Description:** Seminar for professionals with experience using Microsoft PowerPoint, but minimal formal design training. Covers enhancing presentation design; creating more effective grids and graphs; using color and typeface effectively, and how to avoid ten design disasters. **Locations:** Silver Spring, MD; Alexandria, VA; Hunt Valley, MD; and Columbia, MD.

REFERENCE WORKS

18463 ■ "The Art and Business of Motivation Speaking: Your Guide" in *Inc.* (Volume 32, December 2010, No. 10, pp. 124)
Pub: Inc. Magazine

Ed: Leigh Buchanan. **Description:** Profile of Josh Shipp that discusses his career as a motivational speaker.

18464 ■ "BBB Hires Marketing Firm to Attract More Businesses" in *Baltimore Business Journal* (Vol. 27, January 1, 2010, No. 35, pp. 1)
Pub: American City Business Journals

Ed: Julekha Dash. **Description:** Better Business Bureau (BBB) of Greater Maryland hired Bystry Carson & Associates Ltd. to assist in its rebranding efforts in order to entice more businesses. Bystry Carson will promote BBB's new mission at lectures, seminars, and networking events, as well as educate businesses about the agency through blogs and Twitter. BBB's services are also outlined.

18465 ■ "Calendar" in *Crain's Detroit Business* (Vol. 24, October 6, 2008, No. 40, pp. 22)
Pub: Crain Communications, Inc.

Description: Listing of events in the Detroit area include conferences addressing entrepreneurialism, economic development, manufacturing, marketing, the housing crisis and women business ownership.

18466 ■ "The Center of Success: Author Explores How Confidence Can Take You Further" in *Black Enterprise* (Vol. 38, March 2008, No. 8)
Pub: Earl G. Graves Publishing Co. Inc.

Ed: Ayana Dixon. **Description:** Motivational speaker and author, Valorie Burton, provides a 50-question confidence quotient assessment to help business owners and managers develop confidence in order to obtain goals.

18467 ■ "Chamber Offers Seminar on Web Design" in *Charlotte Observer* (February 6, 2007)
Pub: Knight-Ridder/Tribune Business News

Ed: Joe DePriest. **Description:** Belmont Chamber of Commerce and Gaston College Small Business Center will offer seminars on online Web design.

18468 ■ "Conference Calendar" in *Marketing to Women* (Vol. 21, March 2008, No. 3, pp. 7)
Pub: EPM Communications, Inc.

Description: Listing of current conferences and events aimed at women entrepreneurs and leaders.

18469 ■ "Convention Calendar" in *Black Enterprise* (Vol. 37, February 2007, No. 7, pp. 68)
Pub: Earl G. Graves Publishing Co. Inc.

Description: Listing of conventions and trade show of interest to minority and women business leaders.

18470 ■ "Datebook" in *Crain's Chicago Business* (Vol. 31, April 28, 2008, No. 17, pp. 18)
Pub: Crain Communications, Inc.

Description: Listing of events in the Detroit area include conferences addressing entrepreneurialism, economic development, and women business ownership.

18471 ■ "Economy Forcing Meeting Planners to Think Fast" in *Crain's Cleveland Business* (Vol. 30, June 15, 2009, No. 23, pp. 15)
Pub: Crain Communications, Inc.
Ed: Amy Ann Stoessel. **Description:** Meeting planners are working hard to meet lower corporate budgets when planning events.

18472 ■ *From Entrepreneur to Infopreneur: Make Money with Books, E-Books, and Other Information Products*
Pub: John Wiley & Sons, Incorporated
Ed: Stephanie Chandler. **Released:** November 2006. **Price:** $19.95. **Description:** Infopreneurs sell information online in the forms of books, e-books, special reports, audio and video products, seminars, and more.

18473 ■ "Here's the Deal" in *Crain's Cleveland Business* (Vol. 30, June 15, 2009, No. 23, pp. 14)
Pub: Crain Communications, Inc.
Description: Incentives being offered by hotels, restaurants, golf courses and major chains in order to promote bookings for meetings or conferences in the Cleveland area are listed.

18474 ■ "The Jobs Man" in *Business Courier* (Vol. 26, December 25, 2009, No. 35, pp. 1)
Pub: American City Business Journals, Inc.
Ed: Lucy May. **Description:** Entrepreneur Bob Messer, a volunteer for Jobs Plus Employment Network in Cincinnati's Over-the-Rhine neighborhood, regularly conducts a seminar that aims to help attendees prepare for employment. Jobs Plus founder Burr Robinson asked Messer to create the seminar in order to help unemployed jobseekers. So far, the program has helped 144 individuals with full time jobs in 2009.

18475 ■ "Not Enough Room" in *Austin Business JournalInc.* (Vol. 29, November 13, 2009, No. 36, pp. A1)
Pub: American City Business Journals
Ed: Jacob Dirr. **Description:** Hotel and convention business in downtown Austin, Texas lost nearly $5.3 million when Dell Inc. relocated its annual convention to Las Vegas. However, lack of capital caused the postponement of various hotel projects which need to be finished in order to attract well-attended conventions. Makeover projects on Austin's Waller Creek and Sixth Street are discussed.

18476 ■ "Not Your Father's Whiteboard" in *Inc.* (Vol. 33, November 2011, No. 9, pp. 50)
Pub: Inc. Magazine
Ed: Adam Baer. **Description:** Sharp's new interactive whiteboard is really a 70-inch touch screen monitor with software for importing presentations from any Windows 7 computer.

18477 ■ "On Beyond Powerpoint: Presentations Get a Wake-Up Call" in *Inc.* (November 2007, pp. 58-59)
Pub: Gruner & Jahr USA Publishing
Ed: Michael Fitzgerald. **Description:** New software that allows business presentations to be shared online are profiled, including ProfCast, audio podcasts for sales, marketing, and training; SmartDraw2008, software that creates professional graphics; Dimdim, an open-Web conferencing tool; Empressr, a hosted Web service for creating, managing, and sharing multimedia presentations; Zentation, a free tool that allows users to watch slides and a videos of presenter; Spresent, a Web-based presentation tool for remote offices or conference calls.

18478 ■ "People/Calendar" in *Brandweek* (Vol. 49, April 21, 2008, No. 16, pp. 30)
Pub: VNU Business Media, Inc.
Description: Listing of current conferences, tradeshows and events concerning the marketing industry.

18479 ■ "Polite Conversation" in *Mergers & Acquisitions: The Dealmaker's Journal* (March 1, 2008)
Pub: SourceMedia, Inc.
Description: In January, industry leaders and dealmakers met at Davos to discuss topics ranging from the possibility of a recession to what lies ahead in the deal market.

18480 ■ "Prepping for the Unpredictable" in *Crain's Cleveland Business* (Vol. 30, June 15, 2009, No. 23, pp. 16)
Pub: Crain Communications, Inc.
Ed: Joel Hammond. **Description:** Michael Ferrara, event planner and designer for Executive Caterers discusses the many events he has planned.

18481 ■ "Save the Date" in *Mergers & Acquisitions: The Dealmaker's Journal* (March 1, 2008)
Pub: SourceMedia, Inc.
Description: Listing of conferences and forums that deal with business and investing, particularly with mergers and acquisitions. Includes dates, locations and Internet addresses.

18482 ■ "Speak Better: Five Tips for Polished Presentations" in *Women Entrepreneur* (September 19, 2008)
Pub: Entrepreneur Media Inc.
Ed: Suzannah Baum. **Description:** Successful entrepreneurs agree that exemplary public speaking skills are among the core techniques needed to propel their business forward. A well-delivered presentation can result in securing a new distribution channel, gaining new customers, locking into a new referral stream or receiving extra funding.

18483 ■ "Tic-Tac-Show" in *American Printer* (Vol. 128, August 1, 2011, No. 8)
Pub: Penton Media Inc.
Description: Graph Expo has become the US print industry's main event. There will be as many as 500 exhibitors at this year's event and the Graphic Arts Show Company lists over 30 co-located events as well as 53 new sessions in the seminar program's 28 education categories.

18484 ■ "Tired of PowerPoint? Try This Instead" in *Harvard Business Review* (Vol. 88, September 2010, No. 9, pp. 30)
Pub: Harvard Business School Publishing
Ed: Daniel McGinn, Stephanie Crowley. **Description:** Usefulness of graphic recording, also known as storyboarding or visual facilitation, during client meetings is illustrated.

18485 ■ "Tourism Bureau Seeks Hotel Tax Hike" in *Baltimore Business Journal* (Vol. 27, December 18, 2009, No. 32, pp. 1)
Pub: American City Business Journals
Ed: Rachel Bernstein. **Description:** Baltimore, Maryland's tourism agency, Visit Baltimore, has proposed a new hotel tax that could produce $2 million annually for its marketing budget, fund improvements to the city's 30-year-old convention center and help it compete for World Cup soccer games. Baltimore hotel leaders discuss the new tax.

18486 ■ "The Weeks Ahead" in *Crain's New York Business* (Vol. 24, January 14, 2008, No. 2, pp. 20)
Pub: Crain Communications, Inc.
Description: Listing of events in the Detroit area include conferences addressing entrepreneurialism, economic development, and women business ownership.

TRADE PERIODICALS

18487 ■ *Sharing Ideas News Magazine*
Pub: Royal Publishing Inc.
Contact: Michael MacFarlane, President
E-mail: michael@speakandgrowrich.com
Released: Quarterly. **Price:** $100 U.S.; $124 Canada and Mexico; $175 out of country other foreign. **Description:** Magazine for professional speakers, meeting planners, and bureaus.

18488 ■ *Tips*
Pub: Toastmasters International Inc.
Contact: Beth Curtis, Assoc. Editor
Ed: Suzanne Frey, Editor. **Released:** Bimonthly. **Price:** Included in membership. **Description:** Contains leadership tips, organization, and club programming suggestions. Recurring features include a calendar of events and news of speech competitions and awards.

18489 ■ *The Toastmaster*
Pub: Toastmasters International Inc.
Contact: Suzanne Frey
Released: Monthly. **Description:** Magazine covering leadership, communication and public speaking.

VIDEOCASSETTES/ AUDIOCASSETTES

18490 ■ *Delivering Successful Presentations*
American Management Association
1601 Broadway
New York, NY 10087-7327
Ph:877-566-9441
Free: 800-262-9699
Fax:(518)891-0368
Co. E-mail: customerservice@amanet.org
URL: http://www.amanet.org
Price: $215.00. **Description:** Presents techniques on how to become a successful presenter. **Availability:** VHS.

18491 ■ *Making Effective Presentations*
AJN Video Library/Lippincott Williams & Wilkins
American Journal of Nursing
345 Hudson St., 16th Fl.
New York, NY 10014
Ph:(212)886-1200
Free: 800-256-4045
Fax:(212)886-1276
Co. E-mail: info@nursingcenter.com
URL: http://www.nursingcenter.com
Price: $285.00. **Description:** Offers vignettes that demonstrate do's and don'ts in making stronger, more compelling presentations. Furnishes step-by-step instruction on how to prepare, deliver, and wrap up an effective presentation. Also provides helpful hints on planning and rehearsing, speaking from an outline, using audiovisuals, and fine-tuning. Includes study guide. **Availability:** VHS.

CONSULTANTS

18492 ■ National Speakers Association
1500 S Priest Dr.
Tempe, AZ 85281
Ph:(480)968-2552
Fax:(480)968-0911
Co. E-mail: information@nsaspeaker.org
URL: http://www.nsaspeaker.org
Contact: Mark Sanborn, Accounting Manager
E-mail: mark@atsnsaspeaker.org
Scope: An association for experts who speak professionally. Members include experts in a variety of industries and disciplines, who reach audiences as trainers, educators, humorists, motivators, consultants and authors. Provides resources and education designed to enhance the business skills and platform performance of professional speakers. **Publications:** "Speaker Magazine"; "Voices of Experience".

START-UP INFORMATION

18493 ■ "Pump Up the Profits: Teaching Small Biz How to Handle Fuel and Reduce Costs!" in *Small Business Opportunities* (March 2008)
Pub: Harris Publications Inc.

Description: Profile of 4Refuel, a company that delivers diesel and biodiesel fuel to customers individual fuelings.

18494 ■ "Rev Up Your Engine" in *Small Business Opportunities* (Fall 2010)
Pub: Harris Publications Inc.

Description: Industry giant Meineke is adding franchisees whose average sales top $500,000 annually. Profile of Meineke is also included.

ASSOCIATIONS AND OTHER ORGANIZATIONS

18495 ■ Automotive Service Association
PO Box 929
Bedford, TX 76095-0929
Ph:(817)283-6205
Free: 800-272-7467
Fax:(817)685-0225
Co. E-mail: asainfo@asashop.org
URL: http://www.asashop.org
Contact: Ron Pyle, Pres./Chief Staff Exec.

Description: Automotive service businesses including body, paint, and trim shops, engine rebuilders, radiator shops, brake and wheel alignment services, transmission shops, tune-up services, and air conditioning services; associate members are manufacturers and wholesalers of automotive parts, and the trade press. Represents independent business owners and managers before private agencies and national and state legislative bodies. Promotes confidence between consumer and the automotive service industry, safety inspection of motor vehicles, and better highways. **Publications:** *AutoInc* (monthly).

18496 ■ Canadian Automotive Repair and Service Council–Service d'Entretien et de Reparation Automobiles du Canada
57 Auriga Dr., Ste. 203
Ottawa, ON, Canada K2E 8B2
Ph:(613)798-0500
Free: 888-224-3834
Fax:(613)798-9963
Co. E-mail: askus@cars-council.ca
URL: http://www.cars-council.ca
Contact: Jennifer Steeves, Exec. Dir.

Description: Seeks to advance the automotive service industry. Facilitates communication and cooperation among members; represents members' interests before industrial organizations, government agencies, organizations, and the public.

18497 ■ Gasoline and Automotive Service Dealers Association
372 Doughty Blvd., Ste. 2C
Inwood, NY 11096
Ph:(516)371-6201
Fax:(516)371-1579
Co. E-mail: gasda@nysassrs.com
URL: http://www.nysassrs.com/gasda/gasdamainpage.htm
Contact: Ralph Bombardiere, Exec. Dir.

Description: Owners/operators or dealers of service stations or automotive repair facilities; interested individuals. Aims to educate, inform and help increase professionalism of members and of the industry. Offers periodic technical training clinics and other educational programs including advanced automotive technical training, prepaid group legal services plan and group health insurance and liaison with government agencies. Informs members of political and legislative action or changes affecting their industry. .

18498 ■ Inter-Industry Conference on Auto Collision Repair
5125 Trillium Blvd.
Hoffman Estates, IL 60192-3600
Ph:(847)590-1198
Free: 800-422-7872
Fax:800-590-1215
Co. E-mail: john.edelen@i-car.com
URL: http://www.i-car.com
Contact: Elise Quadrozzi, Chair

Description: Automobile manufacturers, collision repair shops, insurance companies, tool, equipment and supply manufacturers, vocational institutions and related industrial organizations such as auto dismantlers and recyclers, appraisers and technical publishers. Works to improve the quality, safety and efficiency of collision repair, especially on newly manufactured fuel-efficient automobiles, through education in the collision repair and insurance industries. Serves as a forum providing for communication among insurance claims representatives, body shop owners and managers and interested individuals. Conducts classes to improve skills of repair technicians, insurance claims personnel and other interested individuals. Offers courses on unibody repair, refinishing, plastic repair, electronics, steering and suspension and advanced vehicle systems; also conducts collision repair research. Offers welding qualification test through its Welding Qualification Program. **Publications:** *Communications*; *I-CAR E-newsletter* (biweekly).

18499 ■ International Midas Dealers Association
4831 Las Virgenes Rd., Ste. 159
Calabasas, CA 91302
Free: 888-916-4111
Fax:800-443-2143
Co. E-mail: david@franchiselegalsupport.com
URL: http://www.imdaonline.org
Contact: David Scott Levaton Esq., Exec. Dir./Legal Counsel

Description: Midas auto service shop franchisees. **Publications:** *IMDA Today* .

18500 ■ National Auto Body Council
191 Clarksville Rd.
Princeton Junction, NJ 08550
Free: 888-667-7433
Fax:(609)799-7032
Co. E-mail: info@autobodycouncil.org
URL: http://www.autobodycouncil.org
Contact: Cynthia Prisco, Mgr.

Description: Members from the collision repair industry. Seeks to promote pride in professionalism and increase consumer confidence. .

18501 ■ National Automotive Radiator Service Association
3000 Village Run Rd., Ste. 103, No. 221
Wexford, PA 15090-6315
Ph:(412)847-5747
Free: 800-551-3232
Fax:(724)934-1036
Co. E-mail: info@narsa.org
URL: http://www.narsa.org
Contact: Wayne Juchno, Exec. Dir.

Description: Represents operators of automotive radiator and air conditioning repair shops and cooling system service businesses as well as manufacturers and suppliers for the trade. Maintains hall of fame. **Publications:** *Automotive Cooling Journal* (monthly); *NARSA Service Reports* (bimonthly);Membership Directory (annual).

18502 ■ National Institute for Automotive Service Excellence
101 Blue Seal Dr. SE, Ste. 101
Leesburg, VA 20175
Ph:(703)669-6600
Free: 888-273-8378
Fax:(703)669-6123
Co. E-mail: tmolla@ase.com
URL: http://www.ase.com
Contact: Tim Zilke, Pres./CEO

Description: Governed by a 40-member board of directors selected from all sectors of the automotive service industry and from education, government, and consumer groups. Encourages and promotes the highest standards of automotive service in the public interest. Conducts continuing research to determine the best methods for training automotive technicians; encourages the development of effective training programs. Tests and certifies the competence of automobile, medium/heavy truck, collision repair, school bus and engine machinist technicians as well as parts specialists. **Publications:** *ASE Catalogs of Tests* (annual); *ASE Certification Test Registration Booklet* (semiannual).

18503 ■ New York State Association of Service Stations and Repair Shops
6 Walker Way
Albany, NY 12205
Ph:(518)452-4367
Fax:(518)452-1955
Co. E-mail: state@nysassrs.com
URL: http://www.nysassrs.com
Contact: Ralph Bombardiere

Description: Service station dealers united for: passage of national, state, and local legislation supportive of the service station dealer; promotion of fraternity and unity among dealers in New York State and throughout the country; achievement of the highest standards of service and safety for the motoring public. Conducts trade exhibits and seminars in automotive mechanics. .

18504 ■ SAE International
400 Commonwealth Dr.
Warrendale, PA 15096-0001
Ph:(724)776-4841
Free: 877-606-7323
Fax:(724)776-0790
Co. E-mail: customerservice@sae.org
URL: http://www.sae.org
Contact: Richard E. Kleine EdD, Pres.
Description: Collects and disseminates information on mobility technology. Fosters information exchange among the worldwide automotive and aerospace communities. Conducts educational programs. **Publications:** *Aerospace Engineering* (monthly); *Automotive Engineering* (monthly); *Bosch Handbook* (annual).

18505 ■ Service Station Dealers of America/ National Coalition of Petroleum Retailers and Allied Trades
1532 Pointer Ridge Pl., Ste. E
Bowie, MD 20716
Ph:(301)390-4405
Fax:(301)390-3161
Co. E-mail: pfiore@wmda.net
URL: http://www.ssda-at.org
Contact: Mr. Paul Fiore, Exec. VP
Description: Service station operators and affiliated state and local associations. Works for the betterment of its members as a voice on Capitol Hill, with federal regulators, with the media, in the courts and with suppliers. .

18506 ■ Society of Collision Repair Specialists
PO Box 909
Prosser, WA 99350
Ph:(302)423-3537
Free: 877-841-0660
Fax:877-851-0660
Co. E-mail: info@scrs.com
URL: http://www.scrs.com
Contact: Aaron Schulenburg, Exec. Dir.
Description: Businesses; associations; individual owners and managers of auto collision repair shops, suppliers, insurance and educational associates. Distributes management and technical information; maintains industry standards; works to promote professionalism within the industry. .

18507 ■ Society of Independent Gasoline Marketers of America
3930 Pender Dr., Ste. 340
Fairfax, VA 22030
Ph:(703)709-7000
Fax:(703)709-7007
Co. E-mail: sigma@sigma.org
URL: http://www.sigma.org
Contact: Kenneth A. Doyle CAE, Exec. VP
Description: Represents chain gasoline marketers, wholesale and retail. Works to inform members of current governmental and legislative activities; represents the marketers' interests before government and legislative and regulatory agencies; and provides statistical data on industry. **Publications:** *Society of Independent Gasoline Marketers Membership Directory* (annual); *Society of Independent Gasoline Marketers of America—Weekly Report* (weekly); *Statistical Report* (annual).

18508 ■ Truck-Frame and Axle Repair Association
364 W 12th St.
Erie, PA 16501
Free: 877-735-1687
Fax:877-735-1688
Co. E-mail: leafspg@aol.com
URL: http://www.taraassociation.com
Contact: Bill Hinchcliffe, Pres.
Description: Owners and operators of heavy-duty truck repair facilities and their mechanics; allied and associate members are manufacturers of heavy-duty trucks and repair equipment, engineers, trade press and insurance firms. Seeks to help members share skills and technical knowledge and keep abreast of new developments and technology to better serve customers in areas of minimum downtime, cost and maximum efficiency. Conducts studies and surveys regarding safety, fuel conservation and heavy-duty truck maintenance and repairs. Has formed TARA's Young Executives to help make young people at members' repair facilities more proficient in normal business functions and to ensure the future of the Association. **Publications:** *Truck-Frame and Axle Repair Association—Membership Directory* (annual).

DIRECTORIES OF EDUCATIONAL PROGRAMS

18509 ■ *Directory of Private Accredited Career Schools and Colleges of Technology*
Pub: Accrediting Commission of Career Schools and Colleges of Technology
Contact: Michale S. McComis, Exec. Dir.
Released: On web page. **Price:** Free. **Description:** Covers 3900 accredited post-secondary programs that provide training programs in business, trade, and technical fields, including various small business endeavors. Entries offer school name, address, phone, description of courses, job placement assistance, and requirements for admission. Arrangement is alphabetical.

REFERENCE WORKS

18510 ■ "21st Century Filling Station" in *Austin Business JournalInc.* (Vol. 29, December 11, 2009, No. 40, pp. 1)
Pub: American City Business Journals
Ed: Jacob Dirr. **Description:** Clean Energy Fuels Corporation announced plans for the construction of a $1 million, 17,000 square foot compressed natural gas fueling station at or near the Austin-Bergstrom International Airport (ABIA). Clean Energy Fuels hopes to encourage cab and shuttle companies in the ABIA to switch from gasoline to natural gas.

18511 ■ "Auto Repair Business Owner Sentenced" in *Ventura County Star* (November 20, 2010)
Pub: Ventura County Star
Ed: Raul Hernandez. **Description:** Oxnard, California auto repair business owner was sentenced to jail for grand theft and falsification of smog certificate information.

18512 ■ "Bill Lee's Auto Repair Business Chugs Along Despite Life's Obstacles" in *Bradenton Herald* (August 22, 2010)
Pub: Bradenton Herald
Ed: Grace Gagliano. **Description:** Profile of Bill Lee's Professional Automotive Services located in Bradenton, Florida. The auto repair business was opened 26 years ago and provides repair for an assortment of fleet vehicles, including truck repair.

18513 ■ "Casey's Buys Second Marion Convenience Store" in *Gazette* (December 14, 2010)
Pub: Gazette
Ed: Dave DeWitte. **Description:** Casey's General Stores Inc. has acquired a Short Stop convenience store on Marion's west side in Iowa. The new store includes a car and truck wash.

18514 ■ "Convenience Store Owners Will Request New Zoning Once More" in *Daily Republic* (November 1, 2010)
Pub: McClatchy Tribune Information Services
Ed: Tom Lawrence. **Description:** Zoning change has been requested for a proposed convenience store in Mitchell, South Dakota. Details are included.

18515 ■ "Fees Fueling Frustration for Region's Gas Retailers" in *Business First Buffalo* (December 7, 2007, pp. 1)
Pub: American City Business Journals, Inc.
Ed: David Bertola. **Description:** Credit card fees are a major cause of concern to gas retailers along with higher gasoline prices. Statistical details included.

18516 ■ "Fix-It Career: Jobs in Repair" in *Occupational Outlook Quarterly* (Vol. 54, Fall 2010, No. 3, pp. 26)
Pub: U.S. Bureau of Labor Statistics
Ed: Elka Maria Torpey. **Description:** Auto mechanics and HVAC technician occupations require repair skills. Advantages for individuals with proper skills are outlined.

18517 ■ "Hy-Vee Plans Expansion, Convenience Store in Cedar Rapids" in *Gazette* (November 26, 2010)
Pub: Gazette
Ed: George Ford. **Description:** Hy-Vee Inc. is awaiting approval to expand its supermarket in Cedar Rapids, Iowa. Hy-Vee is a food and drug store chain will construct a convenience store and gas station on the site.

18518 ■ "Kroger Forges Ahead with Fuel Centers" in *Business Courier* (Vol. 26, December 25, 2009, No. 35, pp. 1)
Pub: American City Business Journals, Inc.
Ed: Jon Newberry. **Description:** Cincinnati-based grocery chain Kroger Company plans to construct more fuel centers near supermarkets and food stores despite declining profit margins in gasoline sales. Statistical data included.

18519 ■ "Merchants Association Working on Deal for Large Wholesale Warehouse" in *Austin Business JournalInc.* (September 19, 2008)
Pub: American City Business Journals
Ed: Jean Kwon. **Description:** Greater Austin Merchants Association planning to buy a former Dell Outlet Factory in Austin, Texas and convert it into a warehouse for convenience stores and gas stations.

18520 ■ "OSHA Proposes Historic Safety Penalty on BP" in *Workforce Management* (Vol. 88, November 16, 2009, No. 12, pp. 8)
Pub: Crain Communications, Inc.
Ed: Mark Schoeff Jr. **Description:** Labor Secretary Hilda Solis has warned that she aims to toughen the enforcement of workplace laws; OSHA, the Occupational Safety and Health Administration, an agency within the Department of Labor, is penalizing BP Products North America Inc. for their failure to improve workplace safety.

18521 ■ "Sellers Shift Gears" in *Crain's Detroit Business* (Vol. 25, June 22, 2009, No. 25, pp. 3)
Pub: Crain Communications Inc. - Detroit
Description: Of the 14 new car Chrysler dealerships in the Detroit area who had franchises terminated, Joe Ricci of Dearborn will sell used cars at his new business called All American Buyer's Service; Lochmoor Automotive Group in Detroit will focus on Mahindra & Mahindra trucks; Mt. Clemens Dodge, Clinton Township is also selling Mahindra & Mahindra trucks; and Monicatti Chrysler Jeep, Sterling Heights, will offer service along with selling used cars.

18522 ■ "Service With a Smile...And Comfy Chairs" in *Crain's Chicago Business* (Vol. 31, April 28, 2008, No. 17, pp. 46)
Pub: Crain Communications, Inc.
Ed: Phuong Ly. **Description:** O'Hare Auto Group has improved the experience of waiting for service on one's vehicle by offering wireless Internet, comfortable chairs and plasma TVs. The company also has long service hours, running from 6 a.m. to midnight Monday through Thursday so customers don't have to take time off work.

18523 ■ "Some Atlantic Beach Leaders Leery About Convenience Store Safety Measure" in *Florida Times-Union* (November 3, 2010)
Pub: Florida Times-Union
Ed: Drew Dixon. **Description:** Jacksonville, Florida authorities are proposing a new ordinance that would require convenience stores to upgrade safety measures to protect store workers and customers from robbery and other crimes.

18524 ■ "Thomas Morley; President, The Lube Stop Inc., 37" in *Crain's Cleveland Business* (Vol. 28, November 19, 2007, No. 46, pp. F-12)
Pub: Crain Communications, Inc.

Ed: David Bennett. **Description:** Profile of Thomas Morley, president of The Lube Stop Inc., who is dedicated to promoting the company's strong environmental record as an effective way to differentiate Lube Stop from its competition. Since Mr. Morley came to the company in 2004, Lube Stop has increased sales by 10 percent and has boosted its operating profits by 30 percent.

18525 ■ *Undercar Digest—Buyer's Guide Issue*
Pub: MD Publications Inc.

Ed: James R. Wilder, Editor, jwilder@mdpublications.com. **Released:** Annual, Latest edition 2011. **Price:** $10, individuals. **Publication Includes:** List of automotive aftermarket manufacturers and suppliers of mufflers, exhaust pipes, brakes, chassis, steering, suspension, driveline, shop equipment and tools, and other products. **Entries Include:** Company name, address, phone, fax, name and title of contact, products. **Arrangement:** Alphabetical. **Indexes:** Product, warehouse distributors, franchise headquarters.

STATISTICAL SOURCES

18526 ■ *RMA Annual Statement Studies*
Pub: Robert Morris Associates (RMA)

Released: Annual. **Price:** $175.00 2006-07 edition, $105.00. **Description:** Contains composite balance sheets and income statements for more than 360 industries, including the accounting, auditing, and bookkeeping industries. Also contains five years of comparative historical data for discerning trends. Includes 16 commonly used ratios, computed for most of the size groupings for nearly every industry.

TRADE PERIODICALS

18527 ■ *AutoGlass*
Pub: National Glass Association

Released: 6/yr. **Price:** $24.95; $34.95 other countries. **Description:** Trade publication for auto glass manufacturers, distributors, and installers.

18528 ■ *The Blue Seal*
Pub: National Institute for Automotive Service Excellence

Ed: Martin Lawson, Editor. **Released:** Quarterly. **Description:** Covers news of the Institute's efforts to certify auto, medium/heavy truck, engine machinists, collision repair technicians, and parts specialists. Discusses industry trends, vehicle repair tips, and training information, and highlights activities of ASE-certified technicians.

18529 ■ *BodyShop Business*
Pub: Babcox

Ed: Jason Stahl, Editor, jstahl@babcox.com. **Released:** Monthly. **Price:** Free to qualified subscribers. **Description:** Magazine providing management and technical information that can be applied to running an efficient and profitable collision repair shop.

18530 ■ *Cooling Journal*
Pub: NARSA
Contact: Mike Dwyer, Exec. Dir.
E-mail: mdwyer@ahint.com

Released: Monthly. **Price:** $60; $110 two years; $97 Canada; $184 Canada 2 years. **Description:** Automotive trade magazine.

18531 ■ *Engine Builder*
Pub: Babcox

Ed: Doug Kaufman, Editor, dkaufman@babcox.com. **Released:** Monthly. **Price:** Free to qualified subscribers. **Description:** Magazine covering management topics, technical information, and new product news for owners and managers of leading volume rebuilding businesses.

18532 ■ *Franchise Focus*
Pub: International Midas Dealers Association
Contact: Jennifer Gentry
Ed: Jennifer Gentry, Editor, jennifer@robstan.com. **Released:** Bimonthly. **Price:** Included in membership. **Description:** Informs member Midas franchisees of activities performed on their behalf by the Association. Reports on all negotiations between the Association and Midas International, including updates on Association committees, which meet with Midas officials on a regular basis. Recurring features include reports of meetings and conventions and a calendar of events.

18533 ■ *Gasoline and Automotive Service Dealers Association—Bulletin*
Pub: Gasoline and Automotive Service Dealers Association (GASDA)
Ed: Released: Monthly. **Price:** Included in membership. **Description:** Reports on industry news, laws, and regulations affecting service station operators in New York. Updates Association news and provides general tips on operation. Recurring features include news of research, news of educational opportunities and Association programs, reports of meetings, and a calendar of events.

18534 ■ *Motor Age*
Pub: Adams Business Media
Released: Monthly. **Price:** $49; $75 two years; $90 other countries. **Description:** Magazine for auto repair shops.

18535 ■ *Motor Magazine*
Pub: Motor Information Systems
Contact: Dave Marlowe, Assoc. Publisher
E-mail: dmarlowe@motor.com
Released: Monthly. **Price:** $60 other countries surface mail; $120 other countries airmail; $96 two years and other countries; surface mail; $216 two years and other countries; airmail. **Description:** Magazine for the automotive aftermarket trade, professional technicians, and shop owners.

18536 ■ *NARSA National Newsletter*
Pub: National Automotive Radiator Service Association (NARSA)
Ed: Mike Dwyer, Editor, mdwyer@narsa.org. **Released:** 24/year. **Price:** Included in membership. **Description:** Covers issues of interest to radiator service station operators and others in the auto repair industry. Recurring features include news of conferences and a calendar of events.

18537 ■ *Professional Tool & Equipment News*
Pub: Cygnus Business Media
Contact: Larry Greenberger, Publisher
E-mail: larry.greenberger@cygnusb2b.com
Released: 9/yr. **Price:** $35; $65 two years; $50 Canada and Mexico; $95 Canada and Mexico two years; $75 out of country; $145 out of country two years; $10 single issue. **Description:** Magazine for automotive shop owners and technicians. Reports on new tools and equipment.

18538 ■ *Restoration*
Pub: International Society for Vehicle Preservation
Released: Semiannual. **Price:** $20 members; $3 single issue. **Description:** Technical magazine covering the how-to of vehicle restoration.

18539 ■ *SHOPtalk–Engine Professional*
Pub: Automotive Engine Rebuilders Association
Contact: Maria Hoeppner
Ed: Maria Hoeppner, Editor, mariahoeppner@charter.net. **Released:** Monthly. **Price:** Free. **Description:** Recurring features include interviews, news of research, a calendar of events, reports of meetings, news of educational opportunities, and notices of publications available.

18540 ■ *Skinned Knuckles*
Pub: SK Publications
Released: Monthly. **Price:** $26; $49 two years; $3.25 single issue; $40 Canada; $77 Canada 2 years; $43 in Australia; $83 two years in Australia; $45 in Europe; $87 two years in Europe; $47 other countries. **Description:** Consumer magazine covering automobile restoration.

18541 ■ *Truck Parts & Service*
Pub: Kona Communications Inc.
Released: Monthly. **Price:** $50. **Description:** Trade magazine for truck parts and service market.

18542 ■ *Undercar Digest*
Pub: MD Publications Inc.
Ed: Jim Wilder, Editor, jwilder@undercardigest.com. **Released:** Monthly. **Price:** $49. **Description:** Magazine for the undercar service and supply industry.

18543 ■ *Underhood Service*
Pub: Babcox
Released: Monthly. **Description:** Magazine covering service and repair shops doing 50%or more of service underhood.

VIDEOCASSETTES/ AUDIOCASSETTES

18544 ■ *Anti-Lock Brake Systems Explained*
Bergwall Productions, Inc.
1 DIckinson Drive, Brandywine BUilding 5, Ste. 105
PO Box 1481
Chadds Ford, PA 19317
Ph:(610)361-0334
Free: 800-934-8696
Fax:(610)361-0092
URL: http://www.bergwall.com
Released: 1989. **Price:** $369.00. **Description:** The operation and repair of anti-lock brake systems are examined for the benefit of auto mechanics. This series is also available as a single tape for the same cost. **Availability:** VHS.

18545 ■ *Basic Electricity for Auto Mechanics*
Bergwall Productions, Inc.
1 DIckinson Drive, Brandywine BUilding 5, Ste. 105
PO Box 1481
Chadds Ford, PA 19317
Ph:(610)361-0334
Free: 800-934-8696
Fax:(610)361-0092
URL: http://www.bergwall.com
Released: 1989. **Price:** $359.00. **Description:** Electrical basics are explained, with special emphasis on their importance to the auto mechanic. The series is also available on one tape for the same cost. **Availability:** VHS.

18546 ■ *Distributorless Ignition*
Bergwall Productions, Inc.
1 DIckinson Drive, Brandywine BUilding 5, Ste. 105
PO Box 1481
Chadds Ford, PA 19317
Ph:(610)361-0334
Free: 800-934-8696
Fax:(610)361-0092
URL: http://www.bergwall.com
Released: 1988. **Price:** $369.00. **Description:** Various types of electronic ignition systems are examined from a mechanic's point of view. This series is also available as a single tape at the same cost. **Availability:** VHS.

18547 ■ *Saab*
Direct Cinema Ltd.
PO Box 10003
Santa Monica, CA 90410-1003
Ph:(310)636-8200
Free: 800-525-0000
Fax:(310)636-8228
Co. E-mail: orders@directcinemalimited.com
URL: http://www.directcinema.com
Released: 1986. **Description:** How to tune-up and maintain the Saab engine. **Availability:** VHS; 3/4U.

18548 ■ *Safety in the Auto Shop*
Bergwall Productions, Inc.
1 DIckinson Drive, Brandywine BUilding 5, Ste. 105
PO Box 1481
Chadds Ford, PA 19317
Ph:(610)361-0334
Free: 800-934-8696

Fax:(610)361-0092
URL: http://www.bergwall.com
Released: 1985. **Price:** $299.00. **Description:** This safety program shows how to be accident free in a body shop. **Availability:** VHS.

18549 ■ *Small Engines*
Bergwall Productions, Inc.
1 DIckinson Drive, Brandywine BUilding 5, Ste. 105
PO Box 1481
Chadds Ford, PA 19317
Ph:(610)361-0334
Free: 800-934-8696
Fax:(610)361-0092
URL: http://www.bergwall.com
Released: 1989. **Price:** $399.00. **Description:** Small engine construction and repair are explained for the benefit of auto mechanics. Also available as one tape at the same cost. **Availability:** VHS.

18550 ■ *Vehicle Maintenance*
RMI Media
1365 N. Winchester St.
Olathe, KS 66061-5880
Ph:(913)768-1696
Free: 800-745-5480
Fax:800-755-6910
Co. E-mail: actmedia@act.org
URL: http://www.actmedia.com
Released: 1989. **Price:** $89.00. **Description:** Another series on the subject of fixing car engines is offered. **Availability:** VHS; 3/4U.

TRADE SHOWS AND CONVENTIONS

18551 ■ National Automotive Radiator Service Association Annual Trade Show and Convention
National Automotive Radiator Service Association
PO Box 97
East Greenville, PA 18041
Ph:(215)541-4500
Fax:(215)679-4977
Released: Annual. **Audience:** Trade professionals. **Principal Exhibits:** Manufacturers in the automotive cooling industry.

FRANCHISES AND BUSINESS OPPORTUNITIES

18552 ■ AAMCO Transmissions, Inc.
American Driveline, Inc.
201 Gibraltar Rd.
Horsham, PA 19044
Ph:(267)464-1690
Free: 800-523-0402
Fax:(215)956-0340
Co. E-mail: franchise@aamco.com
URL: http://www.aamco.com
No. of Franchise Units: 895. **Founded:** 1963. **Franchised:** 1963. **Description:** Chain of transmission service centers, specializing in all types of automobile transmission and related repairs. The company philosophy is to continue to increase its competitive advantage and market share through technical expertise and customer satisfaction. AAMCO provides a complete A to Z training course at its corporate headquarters. No automotive experience is needed. Operational, technical and sales support is provided on an ongoing basis. **Equity Capital Needed:** Total investment $232,500-$299,700, cash required $65,000. **Franchise Fee:** $39,500. **Financial Assistance:** Third party financing assistance. **Training:** Offers 3 weeks training at home office, plus in field support.

18553 ■ All Night Auto
3872 Rochester Rd.
Troy, MI 48083
Ph:(248)619-9020
Free: 877-877-6444
Fax:(248)619-0596
No. of Franchise Units: 4. **No. of Company-Owned Units:** 1. **Founded:** 1994. **Franchised:** 1999. **Description:** Full service automotive repair shop. **Equity Capital Needed:** $100,000 minimum. **Franchise Fee:** $25,000. **Financial Assistance:** Yes. **Training:** Provides 3-4 weeks of training.

18554 ■ All Tune and Lube
ATL International, Inc.
8334 Veterans Hwy.
Millersville, MD 21108
Ph:(410)987-1011
Free: 800-935-8863
Fax:(410)987-4827
Co. E-mail: alltune@erols.com
URL: http://www.alltuneandlube.com
No. of Franchise Units: 300. **Founded:** 1986. **Franchised:** 1986. **Description:** Automotive servicing. "One stop" total car care, including tune-ups, brakes, exhaust, engine replacement and more. **Equity Capital Needed:** $35,000+. **Franchise Fee:** $32,000. **Financial Assistance:** Financing available. **Managerial Assistance:** Provides operation staff visits, toll-free telephone assistance, and newsletters. **Training:** All Tune and Lube provides extensive training at headquarters and in the individual center locations. Provides 1 week of center management training and operational support.

18555 ■ Automotive Maintenance Solutions
Sheldrick Inc.
1404 7th Ave.
Hendersonville, NC 28792
Ph:(828)696-9611
Fax:(828)693-0823
No. of Franchise Units: 1. **No. of Company-Owned Units:** 1. **Founded:** 1962. **Franchised:** 2002. **Description:** Auto service and repair shop. **Franchise Fee:** $25,000. **Financial Assistance:** No. **Training:** Yes.

18556 ■ Big O Tires
823 Donald Ross Rd.
Juno Beach, FL 33408
Ph:(561)803-7015
Free: 800-622-2446
Fax:(858)672-6201
Co. E-mail: franchise@big0tires.com
URL: http://www.bigotires.com
No. of Franchise Units: 458. **No. of Company-Owned Units:** 31. **Founded:** 1962. **Franchised:** 1982. **Description:** Retail tire and under-car service centers. **Equity Capital Needed:** Varies. **Franchise Fee:** $30,000. **Financial Assistance:** Yes. **Training:** 7-week training program, including classroom and hands-on application in a fully operational retail training store and ongoing support through regional schools, seminars, and clinics.

18557 ■ Brake Masters
Brake Masters Systems, Inc.
6179 E Broadway Blvd.
Tucson, AZ 85711
Ph:(520)631-7200
Free: 877-524-7541
Fax:(866)459-8731
No. of Franchise Units: 42. **No. of Company-Owned Units:** 52. **Founded:** 1983. **Franchised:** 1994. **Description:** Brake repair and lubrication services. **Equity Capital Needed:** Cash $75,000-$150,000; Total investment $175,000-$650,000. **Franchise Fee:** $22,950. **Financial Assistance:** Banks, SBA, third party, assist with loan application. **Training:** Training includes classroom instruction, as well as several weeks of on the job training in stores.

18558 ■ Car-X Associates Corp.
7150 Granite Cir.
Toledo, OH 43617
Ph:(419)865-6900
Free: 800-359-2359
Co. E-mail: dmaltzman@carx.com
URL: http://www.carx.com
No. of Franchise Units: 159. **No. of Company-Owned Units:** 7. **Founded:** 1971. **Franchised:** 1973. **Description:** Automobile maintenance and repair, including exhaust systems, brakes and suspension systems. **Equity Capital Needed:** $100,000 minimum cash required. **Franchise Fee:** $25,000. **Financial Assistance:** Third party financing. **Training:** Initial training for 3 weeks, plus 2 weeks at new shop at opening. Ongoing support and training programs.

18559 ■ ColorAll Technologies
ColorAll Technologies Intl., Inc.
1520 N Powerline Rd.
Pompano Beach, FL 33069
Ph:(954)969-1599
Free: 877-412-6567
Fax:(954)969-1679
No. of Franchise Units: 75. **Founded:** 1990. **Franchised:** 1998. **Description:** Onsite auto appearance & repair management. **Equity Capital Needed:** $100,000. **Franchise Fee:** $75,000, includes equipment. **Financial Assistance:** No. **Training:** Yes.

18560 ■ Dent Clinic Canada 2000, Inc.
5551 45th St., Ste. 2
Red Deer, AB, Canada T4N 1L2
Ph:(403)250-3386
Free: 888-722-3368
Fax:(403)340-3191
Co. E-mail: franchising@dentclinic.com
URL: http://www.dentclinic.com
No. of Franchise Units: 10. **Founded:** 1993. **Franchised:** 1996. **Description:** Dent clinic deals with paint less dent repair and other auto body services. **Equity Capital Needed:** $80,000. **Franchise Fee:** $20,000. **Training:** Yes.

18561 ■ Dent Doctor
11301 W Markham St.
Little Rock, AR 72211
Ph:(501)224-0500
Fax:(501)224-0507
No. of Franchise Units: 20. **No. of Company-Owned Units:** 2. **Founded:** 1986. **Franchised:** 1990. **Description:** Paint less dent removal services for both wholesale and retail vehicle owners. Dent Doctor franchisees operate from both mobile and fixed locations. Dent Doctor franchisees remove minor dents, door dings and nail damage from vehicles with a special process that requires no painting for a fraction of the costs and time to repair it in the body shop. **Equity Capital Needed:** $80,000. **Franchise Fee:** $13,900-$23,900. **Financial Assistance:** Yes. **Managerial Assistance:** Toll-free management hotline is available for management issues, as well as an annual meeting to keep all franchisees up to date on the latest technology. **Training:** An intensive 8 week training program is required to learn the Dent Doctor painless dent removal system. Dent Doctor also offers ongoing refresher training.

18562 ■ Dr. Vinyl & Associates, Ltd.
201 NW Victoria Dr.
Lee's Summit, MO 64086
Ph:(816)525-6060
Free: 800-531-6600
Fax:(816)525-6333
No. of Franchise Units: 253. **No. of Company-Owned Units:** 2. **Founded:** 1972. **Franchised:** 1981. **Description:** Mobile repair, reconditioning and after-market sales and services to auto dealers and other commercial accounts, such as vinyl, leather, velour, fabric, bumper, windshield, plastic and paint less dent repair, application of striping, body moldings, deck racks, graphics, gold plating, etc. **Equity Capital Needed:** $55,000-$85,000. **Franchise Fee:** $38,950. **Financial Assistance:** Yes. **Managerial Assistance:** Ongoing technical assistance via newsletter, conventions and telephone. **Training:** (Missouri for combined classroom and field training and 4-5 days in franchisees territory). Training also available for franchisees employees or sub-contractors.

18563 ■ The Doctor's Touch
PO Box 770
Lee's Summit, MO 64064
Ph:(801)525-6060
Free: 800-531-6600

Fax:(816)525-6333
Founded: 2005. **Franchised:** 2007. **Description:** Automotive exterior repair services. **Equity Capital Needed:** $56,300-$85,950. **Franchise Fee:** $38,950. **Royalty Fee:** 7%. **Financial Assistance:** Limited in-house financing available. **Training:** Provides 3 weeks training at headquarters and ongoing support.

18564 ■ Econo Lube N' Tune
128 S Tryon St., Ste. 900
Charlotte, NC 28202
Free: 800-275-5200
No. of Franchise Units: 173. **No. of Company-Owned Units:** 95. **Founded:** 1973. **Franchised:** 1978. **Description:** Auto service, lube, tune and brakes. **Franchise Fee:** $39,500. **Financial Assistance:** Yes. **Training:** Yes.

18565 ■ Honest-1 Auto Care, Inc.
7430 E Butherus Dr., Ste. B
Scottsdale, AZ 85260
Ph:(480)223-1300
Free: 877-466-3781
Fax:(480)223-1301
No. of Franchise Units: 23. **Founded:** 2003. **Franchised:** 2003. **Description:** Automotive maintenance and repair. **Equity Capital Needed:** $90,000 liquid; $350,000 net worth; total investment $174,200$292,200. **Franchise Fee:** $30,000. **Financial Assistance:** Yes. **Training:** Yes.

18566 ■ Lee Myles Transmissions
Lee Myles Associates Corp.
847 Fern Avenue
Reading, PA 19607
Ph:(610)370-6900
Free: 800-533-6953
No. of Franchise Units: 70. **Founded:** 1947. **Franchised:** 1964. **Description:** Automotive transmission service and repair. **Equity Capital Needed:** $75,000 cash on total investment of $135,000-$210,000. **Franchise Fee:** $30,000. **Financial Assistance:** Third party financing. **Training:** Offers 2 week training program in the classroom and onsite followed up with continuous support.

18567 ■ Lentz USA Service Centers
Lentz USA Franchise Corp.
1001 Riverview Dr.
Kalamazoo, MI 49001
Ph:(269)342-2200
Free: 800-354-2131
Fax:(269)342-9461
No. of Franchise Units: 23. **No. of Company-Owned Units:** 11. **Founded:** 1983. **Franchised:** 1989. **Description:** Automotive under car repair facility. Lentz USA is a specialty shop, concentrating on exhaust, brakes and suspension services. It is a middle-end to high-end service store with 10,000 associated warranty locations nationwide. **Equity Capital Needed:** $50,000 liquid assets. **Franchise Fee:** $20,000. **Financial Assistance:** Yes. **Training:** Yes.

18568 ■ Maaco Franchising, Inc.
Maaco Enterprises, Inc.
381 Brooks Rd.
King of Prussia, PA 19406
Ph:(610)265-6606
Free: 800-296-2226
Fax:(610)337-6176
Co. E-mail: Fslprv@maaco.com
URL: http://www.maaco.com
No. of Franchise Units: 500. **Founded:** 1972. **Franchised:** 1972. **Description:** Maaco Auto Painting & Bodyworks Centers are complete production auto paint and body repair centers. No prior automotive experience necessary. **Equity Capital Needed:** $90,000 minimum cash required. **Franchise Fee:** $40,000. **Financial Assistance:** Third party financing available to qualified applicants. **Training:** 4 weeks formal training at corporate headquarters, continuing operational support thereafter. Assistance in financing, site selection and installation of equipment.

18569 ■ The Master Mechanic
3250 Ridgeway Dr., Unit 1
Mississauga, ON, Canada L5L 5Y6
Ph:(905)820-2552
Fax:(905)820-2558
Co. E-mail: hugh@mastermechanic.ca
URL: http://www.mastermechanic.ca
No. of Franchise Units: 39. **Founded:** 1985. **Franchised:** 1985. **Description:** Full-service automotive repair garages to the retail market. Professional service for imported and domestic cars and vans. Specializing in general repairs, tune-ups, alignments, engine performance and drive ability. franchisees. Onsite assistance by franchisor. **Equity Capital Needed:** $175,000-$225,000. **Franchise Fee:** $25,000. **Financial Assistance:** Financing possible for 50%. **Training:** Procedures and technical training are conducted onsite and at existing locations and head office. Management training courses provided by specialists in management and automotive servicing. Business training by franchisor accountants.

18570 ■ Meineke Car Care Centers, Inc.
Meineke Discount Muffler Shops, Inc.
128 S Tyron St., Ste. 900
Charlotte, NC 28202
Free: 800-275-5200
Fax:(704)372-4826
Co. E-mail: franchise.info@meineke.com
URL: http://www.ownameineke.com
No. of Franchise Units: 863. **No. of Company-Owned Units:** 15. **Founded:** 1972. **Franchised:** 1972. **Description:** Meineke Discount Muffler Shops, Inc. offers fast, courteous service in the merchandising of automotive exhaust systems, brakes, shock absorbers, struts, C.V. joints and oil changes. Unique inventory control and group purchasing power enables Meineke to adhere to a 'Discount Concept' and deliver quality service. No mechanical skills required. **Equity Capital Needed:** $187,589-$336,877 personal investment. **Franchise Fee:** 15,000-$30,000. **Financial Assistance:** Third party financing or leasing option is available to qualified individuals. **Training:** 4 weeks training at the Meineke University Campus in Charlotte, NC. In addition, Meineke provides Continuous field supervision and group operational meetings. is open, franchisees receive ongoing sales analysis and operational analysis, including personnel, facility, service and sales review. Dealers also receive customer service assistance in the form of counseling and mediation assistance.

18571 ■ Merlin 200,000 Mile Shops
Merlin's Franchising, Inc.
3815 E Main St., Ste. D
St. Charles, IL 60174
Ph:(630)513-8207
Free: 800-652-9900
Fax:(630)513-1388
Co. E-mail: twilliams@merlins.com
URL: http://www.merlins.com
No. of Franchise Units: 48. **No. of Company-Owned Units:** 11. **Founded:** 1975. **Franchised:** 1975. **Description:** Merlin is an upscale 'under-car' service chain with one of the highest average sales per shop statistics in its industry. Its marketing strategies are rooted in building long-term customer relationships. Merlin offers a special equity assistance program to 'proven' industry veterans. Industry experience is not always necessary. Candidates must have significant experience in managing employees & serving customers. Merlin is expanding in IL, IN, MI, GA, TX & WI. **Equity Capital Needed:** $20,000 required; $100,000-$250,000 total investment. **Franchise Fee:** $$30,000. **Financial Assistance:** Third parties - banks, SBA, leasing companies. Equity assistance is available to qualified Special candidates with significant industry experience. **Training:** 6 week management training program at training center and selected company-operated shops. Each franchisee receives a minimum of four visits/year by field personnel as well as manuals, ongoing electronic and printed communications, ongoing training, employee recruitment programs, etc.

18572 ■ Midas
Midas International Corp.
1300 Arlington Heights Rd.
Itasca, IL 60143
Ph:(630)438-3000
Free: 800-365-0007
Fax:(630)438-3700
Co. E-mail: midasfranchise@midas.com
URL: http://www.midasfran.com
No. of Franchise Units: 2,300+. **No. of Company-Owned Units:** 110. **Founded:** 1956. **Franchised:** 1956. **Description:** Provider of automotive service, including brakes, exhaust, steering/suspension services, as well as batteries, climate control and maintenance services. Midas gives you the name people know, the product people want, and the warranty people trust. If you have business management experience, a dedication to customer service and the desire to take on the challenge of single or multiple unit ownership, contact us now. **Equity Capital Needed:** $50,000 cash; $200,000 net worth, $150,000-$400,000 total investment range. **Franchise Fee:** $30,000. **Financial Assistance:** Third parties. **Training:** Several weeks onsite participation with certified technicians, shop managers and owners. 3 week training program at Midas Institute of Technology in Palatine, IL. We want to share with you the best of what we've learned before you even open your bays for business.

18573 ■ Mighty Distributing System of America
MDSA, LLC
650 Engineering Dr.
Norcross, GA 30092
Ph:(770)448-3900
Free: 800-829-3900
Fax:(770)446-8627
No. of Franchise Units: 105. **No. of Company-Owned Units:** 4. **Founded:** 1963. **Franchised:** 1970. **Description:** Wholesale suppliers of automotive parts for the automotive industry. **Equity Capital Needed:** $138,100-$266,900. **Franchise Fee:** $15,500. **Royalty Fee:** 5%. **Financial Assistance:** No. **Training:** Offers 4-5 days at headquarters, 5-10 days at franchisees location with ongoing support.

18574 ■ Milex Complete Auto Care
Moran Industries, Inc.
4444 W 147th St.
Midlothian, IL 60445
Ph:(708)389-5922
Free: 800-581-8468
Fax:(708)389-5948
No. of Franchise Units: 30. **Founded:** 1967. **Franchised:** 1967. **Description:** Auto service center. **Equity Capital Needed:** $60,000 cash; $144,150-$189,225 total investment. **Franchise Fee:** $30,000. **Financial Assistance:** Yes. **Training:** Yes.

18575 ■ Mister Transmission (International) Limited
9675 Yonge St., 2nd Fl.
Richmond Hill, ON, Canada L4C 1V7
Ph:(905)884-1511
Free: 800-373-8432
Fax:(905)884-4727
Co. E-mail: info@mistertransmission.com
URL: http://www.mistertransmission.com
No. of Franchise Units: 85. **Founded:** 1963. **Franchised:** 1969. **Description:** Mister Transmission offers transmission repair services in Canada. **Equity Capital Needed:** $120,000-$150,000. **Franchise Fee:** $25,000. **Training:** Yes.

18576 ■ Mr. Lube (Canada)
725 Eaton Way, Ste. 110
Delta, BC, Canada V3M 6S5
Ph:(905)828-0909
Free: 877-258-0858
Fax:(905)568-4242
Co. E-mail: franchising@mrlube.com
URL: http://www.mrlube.com
No. of Franchise Units: 103. **Founded:** 1976. **Description:** Service station that provides maintenance services and automotive lubrication. **Equity Capital Needed:** $800,000-$1,500,000. **Franchise Fee:** $50,000. **Training:** 3 months training.

18577 ■ Mr. Transmission/Transmission USA
Moran Industries, Inc.
4444 W 147th St.
St. Midlothian, IL 60445
Ph:(708)389-5922
Free: 800-581-8468
Fax:(708)389-9882
No. of Franchise Units: 104. **Founded:** 1956. **Franchised:** 1976. **Description:** Transmission repair and services. **Equity Capital Needed:** $147,544-$178,840. **Franchise Fee:** $30,000. **Royalty Fee:** 7%. **Financial Assistance:** Limited third party and in-house financing available. **Training:** Offers 2 weeks at headquarters, 3 weeks at franchisees location, 1 week operations visit at location when open with ongoing support.

18578 ■ Precision Tune Auto Care, Inc.
Precision Auto Care, Inc.
748 Miller Dr. SE
PO Box 5000
Leesburg, VA 20175
Ph:(703)777-9095
Free: 800-438-8863
Fax:(703)669-1539
URL: http://www.precision-tune.com
No. of Franchise Units: 400. **No. of Company-Owned Units:** 5. **Founded:** 1975. **Franchised:** 1978. **Description:** Auto care, quick lube. **Equity Capital Needed:** $100,000 or more. **Franchise Fee:** $25,000. **Financial Assistance:** Yes. **Training:** Yes.

18579 ■ Speedy Transmission Centers
Autotech Franchise Systems Inc.
235 NE 6th Ave., Ste. H
Delray Beach, FL 33483
Ph:(561)274-0445
Free: 800-336-0310
Fax:(561)274-6456
Co. E-mail: speedytrans@mindspring.com
URL: http://www.speedytransmission.com
No. of Franchise Units: 20. **Founded:** 1983. **Franchised:** 1983. **Description:** Provides repair, replacement and servicing of components to the automotive drive train, including transmission repair, both automatic and standard. **Equity Capital Needed:** Cash investment $40,000; approximate total investment $100,000. **Franchise Fee:** $19,500. **Financial Assistance:** Financing available from equipment supplier to qualified applicants. **Managerial Assistance:** Provide management manuals, as well as continuous consultation. Newsletters and local meetings are used to update management skills. A toll-free number is available for use by franchisees requiring assistance. The franchisor assists in the selection of real estate, the obtaining of necessary licenses and in obtaining skilled labor for the center. **Training:** Franchisee attends a 3 week training course in either Atlanta, GA or Boca Raton, FL. Included in this period is 1 week of classroom operational training. Training can vary depending on the background and experience of the franchisee. Ongoing management training classes are provided by the franchisor in local areas.

18580 ■ Sprayglo Auto Refinishing & Body Repair
Sprayglo USA Inc.
340 Smith Street
Clayton, GA 30525
Ph:877-677-7294
Fax:877-677-7294
Co. E-mail: info@sprayglo.com
URL: http://www.sprayglo.com
No. of Franchise Units: 8. **No. of Company-Owned Units:** 13. **Founded:** 1986. **Franchised:** 1995. **Description:** Automotive painting and body repair. **Equity Capital Needed:** $216,800-$296,000. **Franchise Fee:** $20,000. **Royalty Fee:** 6%. **Financial Assistance:** Equipment leasing can reduce start-up costs along with available financing of initial inventory requirements. **Training:** 30 days at training facilities, and 2 weeks at site location. All paint, materials, and equipment available from franchisor.

18581 ■ Tilden Your Total Car Care Centers
Tilden Associates
300 Hempstead Tpke., Ste. 110
West Hempstead, NY 11552
Ph:(516)746-7911
Free: 800-845-3367
Fax:(516)746-1288
No. of Franchise Units: 41. **Founded:** 1923. **Franchised:** 1996. **Description:** Offers maintenance and repair services for automobiles. **Equity Capital Needed:** $155,433-$200,133. **Franchise Fee:** $29,900. **Royalty Fee:** 6%. **Financial Assistance:** Limited third party financing available. **Training:** Offers 2 weeks at headquarters, 1 week at franchisee's location and ongoing as needed.

18582 ■ Transmission Depot
2006 Hwy 7, Unit 3
Concord, ON, Canada L4K 1W6
Ph:(416)800-3191
Free: (866)785-7118
Fax:(416)783-4902
Co. E-mail: rkeene@transmissiondepot.ca
URL: http://www.transmissiondepot.ca
No. of Franchise Units: 8. **No. of Company-Owned Units:** 1. **Founded:** 1995. **Franchised:** 2000. **Description:** Offers transmission repair to both wholesale and retail clients. **Equity Capital Needed:** $65,000. **Franchise Fee:** $25,000. **Training:** Yes.

18583 ■ Tuffy Auto Service Centers
Tuffy Associates Corp.
7150 Granite Cir.
Toledo, OH 43617
Ph:(419)865-6900
Free: 800-228-8339
Fax:(419)865-7343
Co. E-mail: jacobs@tuffy.com
URL: http://www.tuffy.com
No. of Franchise Units: 200. **No. of Company-Owned Units:** 23. **Founded:** 1970. **Franchised:** 1971. **Description:** complete automotive repair franchise. **Equity Capital Needed:** $100,000 of liquid capital. **Franchise Fee:** $25,000. **Financial Assistance:** Third party financing available. **Training:** 3 weeks initial training and ongoing support.

18584 ■ Tunex Automotive Specialists
Franchise Sales Dept.
12608 S 125 W, Ste. C
Draper, UT 84020
Ph:(801)676-8882
Free: 800-448-8639
Fax:(801)676-8887
Co. E-mail: info@tunex.com
URL: http://www.tunex.com
No. of Franchise Units: 30. **No. of Company-Owned Units:** 1. **Founded:** 1974. **Franchised:** 1995. **Description:** Offers diagnostic services and repairs of engine related systems. **Equity Capital Needed:** $150,000-$235,000 total investment required, 30%liquid. **Franchise Fee:** $25,000. **Financial Assistance:** Provides third party sources. **Training:** 2 weeks initial training and 1 week during start-up of franchisees business.

18585 ■ Valvoline Instant Oil Change
Ashland Inc.
3499 Blazer Pky.
Lexington, KY 40509
Ph:(859)357-7303
Free: 800-622-6846
Fax:(859)357-6919
Co. E-mail: jjtaylor@ashland.com
URL: http://www.viocfranchise.com
No. of Franchise Units: 612. **No. of Company-Owned Units:** 300. **Founded:** 1986. **Franchised:** 1988. **Description:** Automobile oil change service. **Equity Capital Needed:** $800,000-$1,000,000 liquid assets/$1,000,000 net worth. **Franchise Fee:** $30,000. **Financial Assistance:** Yes. **Training:** Yes.

18586 ■ Ziebart
Ziebart International Corp.
1290 E. Maple Rd.
Troy, MI 48007-1290
Ph:(248)588-4100
Free: 800-877-1312
Fax:(248)588-0718
No. of Franchise Units: 400. **No. of Company-Owned Units:** 16. **Founded:** 1954. **Franchised:** 1963. **Description:** Automotive application of detailing-accessories and protection services. **Equity Capital Needed:** $145,000-$250,000. **Franchise Fee:** $25,000. **Financial Assistance:** Yes. **Training:** Yes.

COMPUTERIZED DATABASES

18587 ■ *Audatex Collision Estimating Database*
Solera Holdings Inc.
15030 Avenue of Science, Ste. 100
San Diego, CA 92128
Ph:(858)946-1900
Free: 800-366-4237
Fax:(858)946-1073
Co. E-mail: SRCusomerService@audatex.com
URL: http://www.audatex.com
Description: A cost estimating system that contains component data on automobile collision repairs by specific make and model for U.S., Canadian, and imported automobiles. Data are taken from repair estimates prepared by insurance company adjustors, independent appraisers, and automobile body repair shops. Provides labor and replacement cost estimates for specific parts (e.g., bumper, fender, hood) and such accident information as point of impact and insurance coverage (i.e., collision and/or liability). **Availability:** Online: Solera Holdings Inc. **Type:** Software.

18588 ■ *International Petroleum Encyclopedia*
PennWell Corp.
1421 S Sheridan Rd.
Tulsa, OK 74112
Ph:(918)835-3161
Free: 800-331-4463
Fax:(918)831-9497
Co. E-mail: headquarters@pennwell.com
URL: http://www.pennwell.com
Description: Provides articles and Information on the energy Industry. Offers country reports; maps of North America, Middle East, Asia-Pacific, China, Latin America, Africa, Former Soviet Union, and Europe; industry statistics; stratigraphic charts; a directory of state-owned oil companies; articles covering subsalt seismic imaging and a survey of enhanced oil recovery projects. Offers the option of selecting from major articles or from a select group included in *Oil and Gas Journal*. Corresponds to the print version *International Petroleum Encyclopedia*. **Availability:** CD-ROM: PennWell Corp. **Type:** Full text; Statistical.

LIBRARIES

18589 ■ Automotive Service Association Library
1901 Airport Fwy.
PO Box 929
Bedford, TX 76095-0929
Ph:(817)283-6205
Free: 800-272-7467
Fax:(817)685-0225
Co. E-mail: asainfo@asashop.org
URL: http://www.asashop.org
Contact: Denise Caspersen, Res.Mgt.Spec.
Scope: Automotive repair. **Services:** Library open to the public for reference use only. **Holdings:** 130 video recordings; 8000 reports and industry related articles. **Subscriptions:** 50 journals and other serials.

18590 ■ Western Maryland Public Libraries–Regional Library
100 S. Potomac St.
Hagerstown, MD 21740
Ph:(301)739-3250
Fax:(301)739-5839
Co. E-mail: jthompson@washcolibrary.org
URL: http://www.westmdlib.info
Contact: Joe Thompson, Assoc.Dir.
Scope: Small business; antiques and collectibles; Civil Service and vocational tests; small scale farm-

ing. **Services:** Interlibrary loan; copying; Library open to the public with restrictions. **Holdings:** 62,000 books; 2500 audiovisuals. **Subscriptions:** 3 newspapers.

Sewer and Drain Cleaning Business

ASSOCIATIONS AND OTHER ORGANIZATIONS

18591 ■ NASSCO
11521 Cronridge Dr., Ste. J
Owings Mills, MD 21117
Ph:(410)486-3500
Fax:(410)486-6838
Co. E-mail: kathy.romans@trelleborg.com
URL: http://www.nassco.org
Contact: Kathy Romans, Pres.
Description: Companies providing services including sewer evaluation, cleaning, inspection, and rehabilitation; manufacturers and suppliers of sewer service equipment; consulting engineers and municipal government officials. Serves as a forum for discussion of needs, ideas and information among members. Works to: improve standards and procedures for sewer evaluation, maintenance, rehabilitation and worker safety; promote members' services and assist in marketing sewer service of equipment, materials and supplies; educate owners, engineers and inspectors about sewer rehabilitation methods and procedures. Conducts training seminars in maintenance and rehabilitation, inspection and safety. Provides referral services. **Publications:** *Manual of Practices* .

18592 ■ Sump and Sewage Pump Manufacturers Association
PO Box 647
Northbrook, IL 60065-0647
Ph:(847)559-9233
Fax:(847)559-9235
Co. E-mail: hdqtrs@sspma.org
URL: http://www.sspma.org
Description: Manufacturers of residential sump pumps (cellar drainers) and sewage pumps. Seeks to: develop and promulgate quality standards; implement a certification and labeling program for all products conforming to these standards; investigate market size and activity; promote improved provisions in building codes on the use of sump and sewage pumps. .

REFERENCE WORKS

18593 ■ "Acing the Test" in *Contractor* (Vol. 57, January 2010, No. 1, pp. 32)
Pub: Penton Media, Inc.
Ed: Robert P. Mader. **Description:** A ward winning mechanical system retrofitting of a middle school in Ohio is discussed. The school now operates at 37,800 Btu/sq. ft and reduced a significant amount of pollutants from being emitted into the environment.

18594 ■ "Are EO Programs Right for Your Business?" in *Contractor* (Vol. 56, October 2009, No. 10, pp. 49)
Pub: Penton Media, Inc.
Ed: Susan Linden McGreevy. **Description:** Some of the laws regarding equal opportunity programs are discussed. Suggestions for mechanical contractors who are considering certification to qualify for these programs are presented.

18595 ■ "Be Proactive - Closely Review Contracts" in *Contractor* (Vol. 56, July 2009, No. 7, pp. 19)
Pub: Penton Media, Inc.
Ed: Al Schwartz. **Description:** Contract disputes can make subcontractors suffer big financial losses or even cause a new subcontractor to fail. Subcontractors should scour the plans and specifications for any references to work that might remotely come under their scope and to cross out any line in the contract that does not accurately reflect the work that they agreed to.

18596 ■ "Be Wary of Dual-Flush Conversion Kits" in *Contractor* (Vol. 56, September 2009, No. 9, pp. 66)
Pub: Penton Media, Inc.
Ed: John Koeller; Bill Gauley. **Description:** Recommendation of untested dual-flush conversion devices for tank-type toilets in the United States have been questioned. The products are being advertised as having the ability to convert single-flush to a dual-flush toilet. No evidence of water conservation from using such devices has been recorded.

18597 ■ "BIM and You: Know Its Benefits and Risks" in *Contractor* (Vol. 57, January 2010, No. 1, pp. 46)
Pub: Penton Media, Inc.
Ed: Susan Linden McGreevy. **Description:** Building Information Modeling is intended to be "collaborative" and this could raise legal issues if a contractor sends an electronic bid and it is filtered out. Other legal issues that mechanical contractors need to consider before using this technology are discussed.

18598 ■ "Climate Right Systems Provides Pre-Assembled Equipment Packages" in *Contractor* (Vol. 56, July 2009, No. 7, pp. 1)
Pub: Penton Media, Inc.
Description: Climate Right Systems offers completely engineered, assembled, and tested equipment packages for hydronic heating and cooling. This package does away with the need to custom fabricate on-site and lets mechanical and plumbing contractors expand their offerings without added overhead and risk.

18599 ■ "Commercial Water Efficiency Initiatives Announced" in *Contractor* (Vol. 56, November 2009, No. 11, pp. 5)
Pub: Penton Media, Inc.
Ed: Robert P. Mader. **Description:** Plumbing engineers John Koeller and Bill Gauley are developing a testing protocol for commercial toilets. The team said commercial toilets should have a higher level of flush performance than residential toilets for certification. The Environmental Protection Agency's WaterSense program wants to expand the program into the commercial/institutional sector.

18600 ■ "Contractors Fret Over Credit, People, Government" in *Contractor* (Vol. 57, February 2010, No. 2, pp. 7)
Pub: Penton Media, Inc.
Ed: Robert P. Mader. **Description:** Telephone interviews with 22 plumbing and HVAC contractors reveal that only two had sales increases for 2009 and that overall, contractors were down anywhere from seven to 25 percent. In the repair/service market, the residential sector was holding its own but the commercial portion was lagging behind.

18601 ■ "Corporate Park Retrofits for Water Savings" in *Contractor* (Vol. 56, October 2009, No. 10, pp. 5)
Pub: Penton Media, Inc.
Description: Merrit Corporate Park in Norwalk, Connecticut has been interested in improving building efficiency and one of their buildings has been retrofitted with water-efficient plumbing systems which will allow them to save as much as two million gallons of water. ADP Service Corp. helped the park upgrade their plumbing system.

18602 ■ "The Customer Is Right Even If He's Wrong" in *Contractor* (Vol. 57, February 2010, No. 2, pp. 12)
Pub: Penton Media, Inc.
Ed: Al Schwarz. **Description:** Mechanical contractors should note that customers will make a judgment based upon the impression that they form on their first meeting. Contractors can maintain a professional image by washing their trucks and having the personnel dress uniformly. Contractors have every right to demand that employees clean up and make a better impression on customers.

18603 ■ "Got to be Smarter than the Average Bear" in *Contractor* (Vol. 56, September 2009, No. 9, pp. 82)
Pub: Penton Media, Inc.
Ed: Bob Mader. **Description:** International Association of Plumbing and Mechanical Officials Green Technical Committee has debated the need for contractors to have certifications in installing green plumbing. Some have argued that qualifications would discourage homeowners from improving their properties. Comments from executives are also included.

18604 ■ "Grainger Show Highlights Building Green, Economy" in *Contractor* (Vol. 57, February 2010, No. 2, pp. 3)
Pub: Penton Media, Inc.
Ed: Candace Roulo. **Description:** chief U.S. economist told attendees of the Grainger's 2010 Total MRO Solutions National Customer Show that the economic recovery would be subdued. Mechanical contractors who attended the event also learned about building sustainable, green products, and technologies, and economic and business challenges.

18605 ■ "Green Pipe Helps Miners Remove the Black" in *Contractor* (Vol. 57, January 2010, No. 1, pp. 1)
Pub: Penton Media, Inc.
Description: Lyons Co. Mechanical Contractors and Engineers installed a piping system for the River View Coal Mine facility's shower rooms. Lyons used Aquatherm's polypropylene piping system which creates seamless connections in the piping.

18606 ■ "Hansen Mechanical Performs Boiler Upgrade at Brookfield Zoo" in *Contractor* (Vol. 57, February 2010, No. 2, pp. 7)
Pub: Penton Media, Inc.
Description: Hansen Mechanical installed a donated boiler in the Brookfield Zoo from Weil-McLain. The boilers were installed in the zoo's 'The Swamp' and 'The Living Coast' exhibits.

18607 ■ "Homebuilders Continue to be Our Nemesis" in *Contractor* (Vol. 56, July 2009, No. 7, pp. 50)
Pub: Penton Media, Inc.
Ed: Bob Mader. **Description:** Homebuilders rank high on the greed scale along with Wall Street brokers. There is this one instance when a builder gave copies of another contractor's quotes that have just been blackened out and another instance when one builder let other bidders visit a site while the current mechanical contractor is working.

18608 ■ "How to Detect and Prevent Employee Fraud" in *Contractor* (Vol. 56, October 2009, No. 10, pp. 57)
Pub: Penton Media, Inc.
Ed: James R. Leichter. **Description:** Mechanical contractors can prevent employee fraud by handing out a detailed employment policy manual to their employees and making sure that their invoices are numbered. It is also highly advised to have bank statements reconciled by a third party.

18609 ■ "IAPMO GTC Debates Supplement" in *Contractor* (Vol. 56, September 2009, No. 9, pp. 3)
Pub: Penton Media, Inc.
Ed: Robert P. Mader. **Description:** Green Technical Committee of the International Association of Plumbing and Mechanical Officials is developing a Green Plumbing and Mechanical Supplement. The supplement provides for installation of systems by licensed contractors and installers. Comments from officials are also presented.

18610 ■ "IAPMO GTC Finalizes Green Supplement" in *Contractor* (Vol. 57, January 2010, No. 1, pp. 1)
Pub: Penton Media, Inc.
Description: International Association of Plumbing and Mechanical Officials' Green Technical Committee finalized the Green Plumbing & Mechanical Code Supplement. The supplement was created to provide a set of provisions that encourage sustainable practices and work towards the design and construction of plumbing and mechanical systems.

18611 ■ "IAPMO GTC Votes to Limit Showers to 2.0-GPM" in *Contractor* (Vol. 56, September 2009, No. 9, pp. 1)
Pub: Penton Media, Inc.
Ed: Robert P. Mader. **Description:** Green Technical Committee of the International Association of Plumbing and Mechanical Officials has voted to limit showers to 2.0 GPM. It is also developing a Green Plumbing and Mechanical Supplement. Comments from executives are also supplied.

18612 ■ "IAPMO Seeks Group Participants" in *Contractor* (Vol. 56, September 2009, No. 9, pp. 37)
Pub: Penton Media, Inc.
Description: International Association of Plumbing and Mechanical Officials is accepting applications for task groups that will develop its Uniform Plumbing Code and Uniform Mechanical Code. The codes are developed using American National Standards Institute accredited consensus process. Task groups are assigned to address a specific topic or problem.

18613 ■ "Keep Customers Out of the Yellow Pages" in *Contractor* (Vol. 56, November 2009, No. 11, pp. 47)
Pub: Penton Media, Inc.
Ed: Matt Michel. **Description:** Mechanical contractors should keep customers away from the Yellow Pages where they could find their competition by putting stickers on the water heater or the front of the directory. Giving out magnets to customers and putting the company name on sink rings and invoices are other suggestions.

18614 ■ "LA Passes HET Ordinance, California Greens Code" in *Contractor* (Vol. 56, September 2009, No. 9, pp. 1)
Pub: Penton Media, Inc.
Ed: Candace Ruolo. **Description:** Los Angeles City Council has passed a Water Efficiency Requirements ordinance. The law mandates lower low-flow plumbing requirements for plumbing fixtures installed in new buildings and retrofits. Under the ordinance, a toilet's maximum flush volume may not exceed 1.28-gpf.

18615 ■ "The Latest on E-Verify" in *Contractor* (Vol. 56, September 2009, No. 9, pp. 58)
Pub: Penton Media, Inc.
Ed: Susan McGreevy. **Description:** United States government has required federal contractors to use its E-Verify program to verify the eligibility of incoming and existent employees. The use of the program is seen to eliminate Social Security mismatches.

18616 ■ "Major Advances in Heat Pump Technology" in *Contractor* (Vol. 57, January 2010, No. 1, pp. 42)
Pub: Penton Media, Inc.
Ed: Mark Eatherton. **Description:** Tax credits make ground-source heat pump technology more economically feasible. Suggestions on how to choose the right ground-source heat pump technology to install in a house are discussed.

18617 ■ "Most Popular Tools? The Survey Says" in *Contractor* (Vol. 57, February 2010, No. 2, pp. 1)
Pub: Penton Media, Inc.
Ed: Robert P. Mader. **Description:** According to a survey of individuals in the field, mechanical contractors are purchasing more of their tools at home centers and they are also increasingly working in the service, repair, and retrofit markets. The survey also found that the reciprocating saw is the most used corded power tool. Additional purchasing habits of mechanical contractors are listed.

18618 ■ "A Necessary Balancing Act: Bookkeeping" in *Contractor* (Vol. 56, November 2009, No. 11, pp. 22)
Pub: Penton Media, Inc.
Ed: Al Schwartz. **Description:** Pros and cons of getting a bookkeeper or a certified public accountant for the subcontractor are discussed. A bookkeeper can help a subcontractor get new accounting software up and running while an accountant will more than likely keep after the books at regular intervals throughout the year.

18619 ■ "Niche Markets, Green Will Be Okay in 2010" in *Contractor* (Vol. 57, January 2010, No. 1, pp. 1)
Pub: Penton Media, Inc.
Ed: Robert P. Mader . **Description:** Mechanical contractors will see most of their work stemming from niche markets, such as green work, as well as service work in 2010. It is said that things will turn around for the industry in 2012 and 2013 and one forecast believes that anything outside of the institutional or more public sector work could be down 15 to 30 percent.

18620 ■ "Papal Permit Trumps the Plumbing Codes" in *Contractor* (Vol. 57, February 2010, No. 2, pp. 20)
Pub: Penton Media, Inc.
Ed: Dave Yates. **Description:** Despite the plumbing code, a plumbing contractor was able to convince the inspector to approve his application to install a sacristy sink which drains into the ground instead of the sewer system. Details of the church's system are presented.

18621 ■ "PMA Launches Online Education Program" in *Contractor* (Vol. 56, October 2009, No. 10, pp. 8)
Pub: Penton Media, Inc.
Description: Plumbing & Mechanical Association of Georgia launched an online program that covers technical and business management that will help contractors run their businesses. Future courses will include math for plumbers, graywater systems, and recession-proofing your business.

18622 ■ "Pre-Certified LEED Hotel Prototype Reduces Energy Use, Conserves Water" in *Contractor* (Vol. 57, January 2010, No. 1, pp. 3)
Pub: Penton Media, Inc.
Ed: Candace Roulo. **Description:** Marriott International Inc.'s LEED pre-certified prototype hotel will reduce a hotel's energy and water consumption by 25 percent and save owners approximately $100,000. Their Courtyard Settler's Ridge in Pittsburgh will be the first hotel built based on the prototype.

18623 ■ "Public Bathroom Pressure Woes Resolved" in *Contractor* (Vol. 56, September 2009, No. 9, pp. 44)
Pub: Penton Media, Inc.
Ed: Dave Yates. **Description:** Design and construction of a public bathroom's plumbing system in the United States are discussed. Installed plumbing fixtures with flush valves would not function properly. The installation of Grundfos SQE variable-speed pumps has resolved problems with the bathroom's water pressure.

18624 ■ "Selling a Job When There's Buyer's Remorse" in *Contractor* (Vol. 56, December 2009, No. 12, pp. 37)
Pub: Penton Media, Inc.
Ed: H. Kent Craig. **Description:** Advice on how contractors should manage low-profit jobs in the United States are presented. Efforts should be made to try and find at least one quality field foreman or superintendent. Contractors should also try to respectfully renegotiate the terms of the job.

18625 ■ "Software Solutions Increase Productivity" in *Contractor* (Vol. 57, February 2010, No. 2, pp. 26)
Pub: Penton Media, Inc.
Ed: William Feldman; Patti Feldman. **Description:** Singletouch is a real-time data capture solution for mechanical and other contractors that work in jobs that require materials and workload tracking. Contractors get information on extreme weather and sudden changes in the cost of materials. The OptimumHVAC optimization software by Optimum Energy is designed to optimize energy savings in commercial buildings.

18626 ■ "Technology to the Rescue" in *Contractor* (Vol. 56, July 2009, No. 7, pp. 22)
Pub: Penton Media, Inc.
Ed: Candace Ruolo. **Description:** Features of several products that will make the job of a mechanical contractor easier are discussed. These include Ridgid's line of drain and sewer inspection cameras and monitors, Motion Computing's Motion F5 tablet rugged tablet PC, the JobClock from Exaktime, and the TeleNav Track tool for mobile workforce management.

18627 ■ "Tracking Your Fleet Can Increase Bottom Line" in *Contractor* (Vol. 56, November 2009, No. 11, pp. 26)
Pub: Penton Media, Inc.
Ed: Candace Roulo. **Description:** GPS fleet management system can help boost a contractor's profits, employee productivity, and efficiency. These are available as a handheld device or a cell phone that employees carry around or as a piece of hardware installed in a vehicle. These lets managers track assets and communicate with employees about jobs.

18628 ■ "Trade Craft: Take Pride in Your Trade, Demand Excellence" in *Contractor* (Vol. 56, October 2009, No. 10, pp. 24)
Pub: Penton Media, Inc.
Ed: Al Schwartz. **Description:** There is a need for teaching, developing, and encouraging trade craft. An apprentice plumber is not only versed in the mechanical aspects of the trade but he also has a working knowledge of algebra, trigonometry, chemistry, and thermal dynamics. Contractors should be demanding on their personnel regarding their trade craft and should only keep and train the very best people they can hire.

18629 ■ "Train Now to Get the Competitive Edge" in *Contractor* (Vol. 56, October 2009, No. 10, pp. 58)
Pub: Penton Media, Inc.
Ed: Merry Beth Hall. **Description:** Due to the harsh economic climate, mechanical contractors would be well-served to train their employees while they have time to take them out of the field. This will help ensure that they are not behind when the economic recovery happens. Suggestions on how to choose the best type of training are presented.

18630 ■ "Use Social Media to Enhance Brand, Business" in *Contractor* (Vol. 56, December 2009, No. 12, pp. 14)
Pub: Penton Media, Inc.
Ed: Elton Rivas. **Description:** Advice on how plumbing contractors should use online social networks to increase sales is presented including such issues as clearly defining goals and target audience. An additional advantage to this medium is that advertisements can easily be shared with other users.

18631 ■ "Water Efficiency Bill Move Through Congress" in *Contractor* (Vol. 56, July 2009, No. 7, pp. 20)
Pub: Penton Media, Inc.
Ed: Kevin Schwalb. **Description:** National Association, a plumbing-heating-cooling contractor, was instrumental in drafting the Water Advanced Technologies for Efficient Resource Use Act of 2009 and they are also backing the Water Accountability Tax Efficiency Reinvestment Act. The first bill promotes WaterSense-labeled products while the other promotes water conservation through tax credits.

SOURCES OF SUPPLY

18632 ■ *Plumbing Engineer—Product Directory Issue*
Pub: TMB Publishing Inc.
Contact: John Mesenbrink, Editor-in-Chief
Released: Monthly, 12 times a year. **Price:** $50, individuals one year. **Covers:** Over 400 plumbing products from approximately 250 manufacturers. **Entries Include:** Company name, phone, fax, website, and e-mail; name of engineering contact with the firm.

TRADE PERIODICALS

18633 ■ *Indiana Contractor*
Pub: Indiana Association of Plumbing Heating Cooling Contractors Inc.
Contact: Brenda A. Dant
E-mail: brenda@iaphcc.com
Released: Quarterly. **Description:** Official publication of the Indiana Association of Plumbing, Heating, Cooling Contractors, Inc.

FRANCHISES AND BUSINESS OPPORTUNITIES

18634 ■ Rooter-Man
A-Corp
268 Rangeway Rd.
N Billerica, MA 01862
Ph:(978)667-1144
Free: 800-700-8062
Fax:(978)663-0061
Co. E-mail: info@rooterman.com
URL: http://www.rooterman.com
No. of Franchise Units: 445. **Founded:** 1970. **Franchised:** 1981. **Description:** A successful and proven system built around the exclusive use of the Rooter-Man Trademark territory. With your license you will have access to the management skills and know how of professionals who have had years of experience in the plumbing, and drain clearing industries. **Equity Capital Needed:** $25,000. **Franchise Fee:** $7,950. **Financial Assistance:** Financing available for initial franchise up to 50% for a period of 5 years. **Training:** A complete 2 day training program devoted to advanced techniques in both practical and management training. Training will consist of 2 days at various locations across the country. Provides unlimited ongoing support by personal coach.

ASSOCIATIONS AND OTHER ORGANIZATIONS

18635 ■ American Needlepoint Guild
2424 American Ln.
Madison, WI 53704-3102
Ph:(608)443-2476
Fax:(608)443-2474
Co. E-mail: membership@needlepoint.org
URL: http://www.needlepoint.org
Contact: Sue Haines, VP, Chapters and Areas
Description: Males and females of all ages who enjoy needlepoint. Seeks to provide educational and cultural development through participation in and encouragement of interest in the art and history of needlepoint. Sponsors amateur and professional needlework exhibits; offers correspondence courses and teacher and judging certification programs; sponsors annual seminar. **Publications:** *Needle Pointers* (bimonthly);Newsletter (bimonthly).

18636 ■ American Sewing Guild
9660 Hillcroft, Ste. 510
Houston, TX 77096
Ph:(713)729-3000
Fax:(713)721-9230
Co. E-mail: ddias@asg.org
URL: http://www.asg.org
Contact: Denise Dias, Chair
Description: Home sewers and people interested in sewing. Provides current sewing information and advice through lectures, demonstrations, classes, seminars, and fashion shows. Seeks to improve communication between home sewers and sewing industry. Encourages the development of neighborhood workshop groups. .

18637 ■ The National Needle Arts Association
1100-H Brandywine Blvd.
Zanesville, OH 43701-7303
Ph:(740)455-6773
Free: 800-889-8662
Fax:(740)452-2552
Co. E-mail: tnna.info@offinger.com
URL: http://www.tnna.org
Contact: Matt Bryant, Pres.
Description: Manufacturers, retailers and distributors of upscale needle art products (needlepoint, embroidery, cross stitch, crochet, knitting, books and accessories). Advances its community of professional businesses by encouraging the passion for needle arts though education, industry knowledge exchange and a strong marketplace. **Publications:** *Directory of Exhibitors* (semiannual).

REFERENCE WORKS

18638 ■ "35-Year-Old Downtown Fabric Store Closes Doors" in *The Times and Democrat* (September 29, 2009)
Pub: The Times and Democrat
Description: Warren's Fashion Fabrics Inc., a 35-year-old retail fabric, decor and sewing store, officially closed its doors due, in part, to the changing tide of the industry in which fewer women sew and products from countries such as China are so cheap.

18639 ■ *Enterprising Women in Urban Zimbabwe: Gender, Microbusiness, and Globalization*
Pub: Indiana University Press
Ed: Mary Johnson Osirim. **Released:** April 1, 2009. **Price:** $39.95. **Description:** An investigation into the business and personal experiences of women entrepreneurs in the microenterprise sector in Zimbabwe. Many of these women work as market traders, crocheters, seamstresses, and hairdressers.

18640 ■ "Fabric, Craft Store Opens in North Bibb" in *Macon Telegraph* (July 17, 2010)
Pub: Macon Telegraph
Ed: Linda S. Morris. **Description:** Ohio-based Jo-Ann Fabrics and Craft Stores opened a new shop in Macon, Georgia. The store will feature items for crafters, hobbyists, needle artists and seamstresses.

18641 ■ "Group Sewing for Area Charities" in *Messenger-Inquirer* (July 7, 2010)
Pub: Messenger-Inquirer
Ed: Beth Wilberding. **Description:** Hobby Lobby in Owensboro, Kentucky features a weekly sewing group that made 656 pillowcases for area agencies.

18642 ■ "How-To Workshops Teach Sewing, Styles" in *St. Louis Post-Dispatch* (September 14, 2010)
Pub: St. Louis Post-Dispatch
Ed: Kalen Ponche. **Description:** Profile of DIY Style Workshop in St. Charles, Missouri, where sewing, designing and teaching is offered. The shop is home base for DIY Style, a Website created by mother and daughter to teach younger people how to sew.

18643 ■ "Jo-Ann Fabric and Craft Stores Joins ArtFire.com to Offer Free Online Craft Marketplace" in *Internet Wire* (January 26, 2010)
Pub: Comtex News Network, Inc.
Description: Jo-Ann Fabric and Craft Stores has entered into a partnership with ArtFire.com which will provide sewers and crafters all the tools they need in order to make and sell their products from an online venue.

18644 ■ "Jo-Ann Launches Quilt Your Colors Contest to Celebrate National Sewing Month" in *Internet Wire* (September 10, 2010)
Pub: Comtex
Description: Jo-Ann Fabric and Craft Stores featured a contest to create a quilt in order to promote National Sewing Month.

18645 ■ "Liora Manne to Debut Fabric Line" in *Home Textiles Today* (Vol. 31, May 24, 2011, No. 13, pp. 4)
Pub: Reed Business Information
Description: Textile and product designer Liora Manne will debut her new decorative fabric collection at the Showtime in High Point, North Carolina in June 2011. More than 22 fabric patterns and solid colors using Manne's patented Lamontage textile design process will be featured and can be used for indoor/outdoor decorative fabrics, furniture, decorative pillows, upholstery and more.

18646 ■ "Make It Yourself: Home Sewing, Gender, and Culture, 1890-1930" in *Business History Review* (Vol. 84, Autumn 2010, No. 3, pp. 602)
Pub: Harvard Business School
Ed: Alexis McCrossen. **Description:** Review of the publication, 'Make It Yourself: Home Sewing, Gender, and Culture, 1890-1930, a nonfiction work.

18647 ■ "Readers Share How Sewing Shaped the Fabric of Their Lives" in *Virginian-Pilot* (September 14, 2010)
Pub: Virginian-Pilot
Ed: Jamesetta Walker. **Description:** People discuss the ways sewing has help enrich their lives, from public service projects and conventions centered on sewing.

18648 ■ "Remodeled Stores Help Fabric Retailer Stitch Up Profit Growth" in *Investor's Business Daily* (January 7, 2010, pp. A06)
Pub: Investor's Business Daily
Ed: Marilyn Much. **Description:** Overview of the successful plan implemented by Darrell Webb for Jo-Ann Fabric and Craft stores to stimulate growth and generate revenue; changes include better inventory controls and remodeling; statistical data included.

18649 ■ "Sewing Is a Life Skill; Teaching To Sew Is An Art" in *Virginia-Pilot* (August 31, 2010)
Pub: Virginian-Pilot
Ed: Jamesetta Walker. **Description:** In conjunction with National Sewing Month, the American Sewing Guild is sponsoring a two-day workshop featuring Stephanie Kimura.

18650 ■ "Sewing Resurgence" in *Northeast Mississippi Daily Journal* (June 11, 2010)
Pub: Northeast Mississippi Daily Journal
Ed: Ginna Parsons. **Description:** Information about the growing trend in sewing is discussed.

18651 ■ "Sewing Shoppe Is All His" in *News & Observer* (October 8, 2010)
Pub: News & Observer
Ed: Sue Stock. **Description:** Profile of My Sewing Shoppe, authorized sales and service dealers for Pfaff and Singer sewing machines, and also sells items for sewing, embroider and quilting. The store is located in Raleigh, North Carolina area.

18652 ■ "S.M. Whitney Co. (1868-2010)" in *Canadian Business* (Vol. 83, October 12, 2010, No. 17, pp. 27)
Pub: Rogers Media Ltd.
Ed: Angelina Chapin. **Description:** A history of S.M. Whitney Company is presented. The cotton company was opened in 1868. The cotton is sold to textile manufacturers after crops have been picked, ginned

and baled. The company closed down in 2010 after chief executive officer Barry Whitney decided to sell his last bale of cotton.

18653 ■ "Suddenly, Sewing Is Hip Again for Kids, Moms and Crafters" in *Atlanta Journal-Constitution* (August 29, 2010)
Pub: Atlanta Journal-Constitution
Ed: Rosalind Bentley. **Description:** Across Atlanta, Georgia, along with the entire nation, sewing classes are increasing in popularity.

18654 ■ "Sunbrella Engages Consumers Via Social Media" in *Home Textiles Today* (Vol. 31, May 24, 2011, No. 13, pp. 4)
Pub: Reed Business Information
Description: Performance fabric brand Sunbrella is marketing to social media, such as Facebook and Twitter, in order to boost consumer interest and retailer support.

18655 ■ "Ultimate Business of the Week: McDougals Sewing Center" in *Houston Chronicle* (December 2, 2010)
Pub: Houston Chronicle
Description: Profile of family owned, McDouglas Sewing Center located in Houston, Texas. The shop offers computerized sewing machines, supplies, classes and repairs.

TRADE PERIODICALS

18656 ■ *Sew News*
Pub: Primedia Consumer Media and Magazine Group
Contact: Beth Bradley, Assoc. Ed.
Released: 6/yr. **Price:** $21.98; $38.98 two years; $27.98 Canada; $33.98 other countries; $50.98 two years; $62.98 institutions 2 years. **Description:** Magazine on fashion sewing home decor, products, and patterns. Includes interviews with designers.

VIDEOCASSETTES/ AUDIOCASSETTES

18657 ■ *Cotton Production*
CEV Multimedia
1020 SE Loop 289
Lubbock, TX 79404
Ph:(806)745-8820
Free: 877-610-5017
Fax:800-243-6398
Co. E-mail: cev@cevmultimedia.com
URL: http://www.cevmultimedia.com
Price: $59.95. **Description:** Outlines all areas of the cotton industry from planting to clothing production. **Availability:** VHS.

18658 ■ *How to Make Money in a Home-Based Sewing Business*
Nancy's Notions Ltd.
333 Beichl Ave.
P.O. Box 683
Beaver Dam, WI 53916-0683
Ph:(920)887-7321
Free: 800-725-0361
Fax:800-255-8119
Co. E-mail: customerservice@nancysnotions.com
URL: http://www.nancysnotions.com
Released: 1989. **Description:** Turn your hobby into a money-making operation with these sew-for-profit tips. **Availability:** VHS.

TRADE SHOWS AND CONVENTIONS

18659 ■ Industrial Fabrics Association International Expo
Industrial Fabrics Association International
1801 County Rd. B W
Roseville, MN 55113-4061
Ph:(651)222-2508
Free: 800-225-4324
Fax:(651)631-9334
Co. E-mail: generalinfo@ifai.com
URL: http://www.ifai.com
Released: Annual. **Principal Exhibits:** Industrial and commercial fabric equipment, supplies, and services.

FRANCHISES AND BUSINESS OPPORTUNITIES

18660 ■ Color-Glo International
CGI International Inc.
7111-7115 Ohms Ln.
Minneapolis, MN 55439
Ph:(952)835-1338
Free: 800-333-8523
Fax:(952)835-1395
Co. E-mail: cgiinc@aol.com
URL: http://www.colorglo.com
No. of Franchise Units: 120. **No. of Company-Owned Units:** 1. **Founded:** 1978. **Franchised:** 1984. **Description:** Fabric re-dyeing and restoration service franchises. **Equity Capital Needed:** $18,000-$27,500. **Franchise Fee:** $16,750-$25,000. **Financial Assistance:** Yes. **Managerial Assistance:** Company offers continuous training and seminars; and supports location with accounts, payroll, inventory, and news updates. **Training:** Corporate and on-site training provided in marketing, operations, applications, and technique. Company trainers spend 1 week with new location.

18661 ■ Hometown Threads
209 Hudson Trace
Augusta, GA 30907
Ph:(706)737-7687
Fax:(706)737-7690
URL: http://www.hometownthreads.com
No. of Franchise Units: 44. **No. of Company-Owned Units:** 4. **Founded:** 1998. **Franchised:** 2001. **Description:** Retail embroidery store located within Wal-Mart encourage shoppers to create and buy custom designed gifts and products. **Equity Capital Needed:** Total investment $165,000. **Franchise Fee:** $29,000. **Royalty Fee:** 6%. **Financial Assistance:** Third party financing options available. **Training:** Offers 3 weeks training at headquarters, 2 weeks at franchisees location with ongoing support.

LIBRARIES

18662 ■ Center for the History of American Needlework Library
1445 E. Cruikshank Rd.
Valencia, PA 16059-3709
Ph:(724)586-5325
Co. E-mail: charlottearn@hotmail.com
Contact: Lisa Johnson, Hd.Libn.
Scope: Needlework, embroidery, lacemaking, textile fabrics, weaving, spinning, costume. **Services:** Library open to the public for reference use only. **Holdings:** 2000 books; 7000 leaflets/magazines; 3500 slides; textile collection.

ASSOCIATIONS AND OTHER ORGANIZATIONS

18663 ■ Shoe Service Institute of America
305 Huntsman Ct.
Bel Air, MD 21015
Ph:(410)569-3425
Fax:(410)569-8333
Co. E-mail: don@shoeglue.com
URL: http://www.ssia.info
Contact: Donald Rinaldi, Pres.
Description: Finders (wholesalers) of shoe repair supplies and equipment. Supplier members are manufacturers, tanners and distributors. **Publications:** *Shoe Service Institute of America—Membership Directory* (annual).

FRANCHISES AND BUSINESS OPPORTUNITIES

18664 ■ Heel Quik! & Heel/Sew Quik!
Heel Quik!, Inc.
2359 Windy Hill Rd., Ste. 400
Marietta, GA 30067
Ph:(770)951-9440
Fax:(770)933-8268
No. of Franchise Units: 730. **No. of Company-Owned Units:** 2. **Founded:** 1984. **Franchised:** 1985. **Description:** Instant shoe repair, clothing alterations and monogramming. **Equity Capital Needed:** $20,000-$85,000. **Franchise Fee:** $17,500. **Financial Assistance:** No. **Training:** Yes.

Shoe Store

START-UP INFORMATION

18665 ■ "Stepping Out" in *Small Business Opportunities* (Get Rich At Home 2010)
Pub: Harris Publications Inc.
Ed: Description: Earn $1 million a year selling flip flops? A Flip Flop Shop franchise will help individuals start their own business.

18666 ■ "Well-Heeled Startup" in *Business Journal Portland* (Vol. 27, November 12, 2010, No. 37, pp. 1)
Pub: Portland Business Journal
Ed: Erik Siemers. **Description:** Oh! Shoes LLC expects to receive about $1.5 million in funding from angel investors, while marketing a new line of high heel shoes that are comfortable, healthy, and attractive. The new line of shoes will use the technology of athletic footwear while having the look of an Italian designer. Oh! Shoes hopes to generate $35 million in sales by 2014.

ASSOCIATIONS AND OTHER ORGANIZATIONS

18667 ■ Footwear Distributors and Retailers of America
1319 F St. NW, Ste. 700
Washington, DC 20004-1121
Ph:(202)737-5660
Fax:(202)645-0789
Co. E-mail: info@fdra.org
URL: http://www.fdra.org
Contact: Matt Rubel, Chm.
Description: Volume shoe store chains. Conducts traffic, foreign sourcing, customs, leadership and employment relations' seminars. .

18668 ■ National Shoe Retailers Association
3037 W Ina Rd.
Tucson, AZ 85741
Free: 800-673-8446
Co. E-mail: info@nsra.org
URL: http://www.nsra.org
Contact: Alan Miklofsky, Chm.
Description: Proprietors of independent shoe stores and stores with major shoe departments. Provides business services and professional development programs including bankcard processing, shipping, freight discounts, free website listing, employee training; conducts research; monitors legislation. **Publications:** *Business Performance Report* (biennial).

18669 ■ Pedorthic Footwear Association
2025 M St. NW, Ste. 800
Washington, DC 20036
Ph:(202)367-1145
Free: 800-673-8447
Fax:(202)367-2145
Co. E-mail: info@pedorthics.org
URL: http://www.pedorthics.org
Contact: Kristi Hayes, Pres.
Description: Professionals involved in the field of pedorthics. (Pedorthics is the design, manufacture, fit and modification of shoes and foot orthoses to alleviate foot problems caused by disease, overuse, or injury). **Publications:** *When the Shoe Fits* .

REFERENCE WORKS

18670 ■ "Adidas' Brand Ambitions" in *Business Journal Portland* (Vol. 27, December 10, 2010, No. 41, pp. 1)
Pub: Portland Business Journal
Ed: Erik Siemers. **Description:** Adidas AG, the second-largest sporting goods brand in the world, hopes to increase global revenue by 50 percent by 2015. The German company, which reported $14.5 billion sales, plans to improve its U.S. market. The U.S. is Adidas' largest, but also the most underperforming market for the firm.

18671 ■ *American Shoemaking Directory*
Pub: Shoe Trades Publishing Co.
Released: Annual. **Price:** $60, individuals. **Covers:** Shoe manufacturers in the United States, Puerto Rico, and Canada. **Entries Include:** Company name, address, phone, fax, names of executives, product information brand names. Also key personnel; Plant output, trade sold, and sales offices included. **Arrangement:** Geographical. **Indexes:** Brands, company.

18672 ■ "Apparel" in *Retail Merchandiser* (Vol. 51, July-August 2011, No. 4, pp. 14)
Pub: Phoenix Media Corporation
Description: NPD Group Inc. released current sales statistics for the women's apparel market along with men's apparel. It also reported annual shoes sales for 2010. Statistical data included.

18673 ■ "Design program in Athletic Footwear" in *Occupational Outlook Quarterly* (Vol. 55, Fall 2011, No. 3, pp. 21)
Pub: U.S. Bureau of Labor Statistics
Description: The Fashion Institute of Technology offers the only certificate program in performance athletic footwear design in the U.S. The program focuses on conceptualizing and sketching shoe designs and covers ergonomic, anatomical, and material considerations for athletic footwear design.

18674 ■ "EEOC Sues Charlotte-Based Lebo's" in *Charlotte Observer* (February 7, 2007)
Pub: Knight-Ridder/Tribune Business News
Ed: Mike Drummond. **Description:** The U.S. Equal Employment Opportunity Commission filed a pregnancy discrimination lawsuit against Lebo's Shoe Stores, located in Charlotte, North Carolina. The suit alleges the store withdrew an offer to hire a woman after finding out she was pregnant.

18675 ■ "Energy Outfitter Wings Into Houston" in *Houston Business Journal* (Vol. 40, December 4, 2009, No. 30, pp. 2A)
Pub: American City Business Journals
Ed: Ford Gunter. **Description:** Red Wing Shoe Company Inc. has launched its personal protective equipment (PPE) line for oil and gas industry crewmen in North America by opening a 13,000 square foot distribution hub in Houston, Texas. The Houston facility was created to supply directly the oil and gas industry and to carry inventory for select distributors.

18676 ■ "Hot Kicks, Cool Price" in *Black Enterprise* (Vol. 37, December 2006, No. 5, pp. 34)
Pub: Earl G. Graves Publishing Co. Inc.
Ed: Topher Sanders. **Description:** Stephon Marbury of the New York Nicks introduced a new basketball shoe, the Starbury One, costing $14.98. The shoes are an addition to the Starbury clothing line and although the privately owned company would not disclose figures; stores sold out of a month's worth of inventory in merely three days.

18677 ■ "How to Keep Your Cool and Your Friends in a Heat Wave" in *Canadian Business* (Vol. 83, August 17, 2010, No. 13-14, pp. 79)
Pub: Rogers Media Ltd.
Ed: Angelina Chapin. **Description:** A buyer's guide of menswear clothing for businessmen is presented. The products include an antiperspirant and deodorant, men's dress shorts, shoes and bamboo fabric undershirt.

18678 ■ "Laced Up and Ready to Run" in *Barron's* (Vol. 89, July 6, 2009, No. 27, pp. 12)
Pub: Dow Jones & Co., Inc.
Ed: Christopher C. Williams. **Description:** Shares of Foot Locker could raise from $10 to about $15 a share with the improvement of the economy. The company has benefited from prudent management and merchandising as well as better cost cutting, allowing it to better survive in a recession.

18679 ■ "Life's Work: Manolo Blahnik" in *Harvard Business Review* (Vol. 88, December 2010, No. 12, pp. 144)
Pub: Harvard Business School Publishing
Ed: Alison Beard. **Description:** Shoe designer Manolo Blahnik recounts his beginnings in the shoe industry and the influence art has had on his work, as well as balancing art and commerce. He also discusses the importance of quality materials and craftsmanship and the benefits of managing an independent, family-owned business.

18680 ■ "Portland Wooing Under Armour to West Coast Facility" in *Baltimore Business Journal* (Vol. 27, January 29, 2010, No. 39, pp. 1)
Pub: American City Business Journals
Ed: Andy Giegerich. **Description:** Baltimore, Maryland sports apparel maker, Under Armour, is planning a west coast expansion with Portland, Oregon among the sites considered to house its apparel and footwear design center. Portland officials counting on the concentration of nearly 10,000 activewear workers in the city will help lure the company to the city.

18681 ■ "Research Reports: How Analysts Size Up Companies" in *Barron's* (Vol. 88, July 14, 2008, No. 28, pp. M13)
Pub: Dow Jones & Co., Inc.
Ed: Anita Peltonen. **Description:** Shares of Bankrate and AutoZone both get a "Buy" rating from analysts

while Zions Bancorporation's shares are downgraded from "Outperform" to "Neutral". The shares of Jet Blue Airline and Deckers Outdoor, a manufacturer of innovative footwear, are also rated and discussed. Statistical data included.

18682 ■ "Retail News: Children's Boutique Relocates to Conway" in *Sun News* (June 4, 2010)
Pub: The Sun News
Description: Little Angel's Children's Boutique and Big Oak Frame Shop have moved to downtown locations in Conway, South Carolina. Little Angel's will sell children's clothing and accessories, shoes and gifts, while the frame shop will offer custom framing along with the sale of stationary, invitations and local prints.

18683 ■ "Retail Woes: The Shoe Doesn't Fit for Gerald Loftin's Stock Picks" in *Black Enterprise* (Vol. 38, July 2008, No. 12, pp. 40)
Pub: Earl G. Graves Publishing Co. Inc.
Ed: Steve Garmhausen. **Description:** Each of the three stocks that Gerald Loftin picked in May 2007 have lost money; DSW, the designer shoe retailer, fell by 63.7 percent; paint and coatings retailer Sherwin-Williams Co. fell by 7.2 percent; and Verizon Communications Inc. fell by 1.4 percent. Statistical data included.

18684 ■ "Rough Q1 Begs Question: Is the Crocs Craze Over?" in *Brandweek* (Vol. 49, April 21, 2008, No. 16, pp. 16)
Pub: VNU Business Media, Inc.
Ed: Eric Newman. **Description:** Crocs, a rubber shoemaker, announced last week that it missed its expected first quarter revenues by 15 percent. The popular rubber sandals are suffering in sales due to a number of factors including a tougher economic environment, less expensive, knock-off brands, the cold weather delay of the spring season and fading consumer interest in plastic shoes.

18685 ■ *Shoe Factory Buyer's Guide*
Pub: Shoe Trades Publishing Co.
Released: Annual, Latest edition 2008. **Price:** $59, individuals. **Covers:** Over 600 suppliers and their representatives to the shoe manufacturing industries in the United States and Canada. **Entries Include:** Company name, address, phone, fax, trade and brand names, list of products or services. **Arrangement:** Classified by type of product or service. **Indexes:** Product, trademark.

18686 ■ "Shop Around" in *Houston Chronicle* (December 7, 2010, pp. 3)
Pub: Houston Chronicle
Ed: Tara Dooley. **Description:** Profile of Diana Candida and Maria Martinez who partnered to open Beatniks, a shop carrying vintage clothing, art from various artists, dance shoes, and jewelry.

18687 ■ *Sneaker Wars: The Enemy Brothers Who Founded Adidas and Puma and the Family Feud that Forever Changed the Business of Sport*
Pub: Ecco
Ed: Barbara Smit. **Released:** 2009. **Price:** $26.95. **Description:** A history of Puma and Adidas shoes and the two German brothers who built the empires.

18688 ■ "Stepping Up" in *Baltimore Business Journal* (Vol. 28, October 22, 2010, No. 24, pp. 1)
Pub: Baltimore Business Journal
Ed: Erik Siemers. **Description:** Uner Armour Inc. will release its Micro G line of four basketball sneakers on October 23, 2010. The company's executives mentioned that Under Armour's goal is to appeal to customers, and not to chip away at Nike Inc.'s supremacy in basketball shoes. The new sneakers will range from $80 to $110.

18689 ■ *The Towering World of Jimmy Choo: A Story of Power, Profits, and the Pursuit of the Perfect Shoe*
Pub: Bloomsbury USA
Ed: Lauren Goldstein Crowe, Sagra Maceira de Rosen. **Released:** 2009. **Description:** Profile of Jimmy Choo and his pursuit to manufacture the perfect shoe.

18690 ■ "Unpleasant Surprise" in *Barron's* (Vol. 88, March 24, 2008, No. 12, pp. 60)
Pub: Dow Jones & Company, Inc.
Ed: Shirley A. Lazo. **Description:** Discusses the $175 million that footwear company Genesco received in a settlement with Finish Line and UBS is considered as a stock distribution and is taxable as dividend income. Railroad company CSX raised its quarterly common payout from 15 cents to 18 cents.

18691 ■ "Walk This Way" in *Barron's* (Vol. 90, August 23, 2010, No. 34, pp. 13)
Pub: Barron's Editorial & Corporate Headquarters
Ed: Christopher C. Williams. **Description:** Crocs and Skechers are selling very popular shoes and sales show no signs of winding down. The shares of both companies are attractively prices.

18692 ■ "Zappo's CEO On Going to Extremes for Customers" in *Harvard Business Review* (Vol. 88, July-August 2010, No. 7-8, pp. 41)
Pub: Harvard Business School Publishing
Ed: Tony Hsieh. **Description:** Footwear firm Zappos. com Inc. improved corporate performance through enhanced customer service. Enhancements include highly visible phone numbers, avoidance of scripts, and viewing call centers as marketing departments.

STATISTICAL SOURCES

18693 ■ *The Athletic Footwear Market*
Pub: Rector Press, Ltd.
Contact: Lewis Sckolnick, Pres
Released: 2009. **Price:** Contact Rector Press.

18694 ■ *Market Outlook for Footwear*
Pub: Business Trend Analysts, Inc.
Released: 2005-2006. **Price:** $2995.00. **Description:** An in-depth investigation of the size and growth of the U.S. market for men's, women's, and children's footwear, including all types of dress shoes, casual footwear, boots, slippers, athletic shoes, work shoes, and more.

18695 ■ *RMA Annual Statement Studies*
Pub: Robert Morris Associates (RMA)
Released: Annual. **Price:** $175.00 2006-07 edition, $105.00. **Description:** Contains composite balance sheets and income statements for more than 360 industries, including the accounting, auditing, and bookkeeping industries. Also contains five years of comparative historical data for discerning trends. Includes 16 commonly used ratios, computed for most of the size groupings for nearly every industry.

TRADE PERIODICALS

18696 ■ *Shoe Retailing Today*
Pub: National Shoe Retailers Association
Contact: Nancy Hultquist
Ed: Nancy Hultquist, Editor. **Released:** Quarterly. **Price:** Included in membership; $35, individuals; $55, elsewhere. **Description:** Provides news of activities and developments in independent shoe retailing. Recurring features include member news, calendar of events, product reference guide and vendor profiles.

TRADE SHOWS AND CONVENTIONS

18697 ■ China International Footwear Fair
Neway International Trade Fairs Ltd.
9/F, Fortis Tower
77 Gloucester Rd.
Wan Chai, People's Republic of China
Ph:852 2561 5566
Fax:852 2811 9156
Co. E-mail: info@newayfairs.com
URL: http://www.newayfairs.com
Principal Exhibits: Footwear and accessories, manufacturing, and manufacturing materials.

FRANCHISES AND BUSINESS OPPORTUNITIES

18698 ■ The Athlete's Foot
1346 Oakbrook Dr., Ste. 170
Norcross, GA 30093
Ph:(770)514-4500
Free: 800-524-6444
Fax:(770)514-4903
Co. E-mail: franchiseinfo@theathletesfoot.com
URL: http://www.theathletesfoot.com
No. of Franchise Units: 151. **Founded:** 1972. **Franchised:** 1973. **Description:** Retailer specializing in athletic footwear. **Equity Capital Needed:** $209,950-$495,250; $250,000 net worth, $100,000-$150,000 cash liquidity. **Franchise Fee:** $10,000-$25,000. **Royalty Fee:** 5%. FAS Third party financing available. **Training:** Provides 5 days at headquarters, 5 days at opening with ongoing support.

18699 ■ Kiddie Kobbler Ltd.
PO Box 27038
Kingston, ON, Canada K7M 8W5
Ph:(613)592-5515
Fax:(613)592-5314
Co. E-mail: kiddiekobblerltd@rogers.com
URL: http://www.kiddiekobbler.com
No. of Franchise Units: 15. **Founded:** 1946. **Franchised:** 1968. **Description:** Children's shoe stores with brand name footwear for all seasons plus dance and athletic footwear, accessories, and apparel too. **Equity Capital Needed:** $175,000-$300,000. **Franchise Fee:** $30,000. **Training:** 3 weeks in an existing location.

18700 ■ Les Franchises Panda Ltee/Panda Franchises Ltd.
259 Labelle Blvd. Suite 201
Rosemere, QC, Canada J7A 2H3
Ph:(450)818-9741
Free: 888-357-2632
Fax:(450)622-2939
Co. E-mail: linda@pandashoes.com
URL: http://www.pandashoes.com
No. of Franchise Units: 31. **No. of Company-Owned Units:** 1. **Founded:** 1972. **Franchised:** 1999. **Description:** Children's shoe specialist. **Equity Capital Needed:** $125,000 start-up; $200,00-$350,000 total investment. **Franchise Fee:** $25,000. **Training:** Yes. .

18701 ■ Shoes-n-Feet
The Toe Box
15015 Main St., Ste. 211
Bellevue, WA 98007
Ph:(425)830-1605
Free: 888-994-FEET
Fax:(425)562-5005
Co. E-mail: jb.smith@shoesnfeet.com
URL: http://www.shoesnfeet.com
No. of Franchise Units: 8. **No. of Company-Owned Units:** 1. **Founded:** 1998. **Franchised:** 2003. **Description:** Education based healthy shoe store servicing the baby-boomer generation. **Equity Capital Needed:** $185,000-$226,500. **Franchise Fee:** $25,000. **Royalty Fee:** 5%. **Financial Assistance:** No. **Training:** Provides up to 160 hours training at headquarters and at franchisee's location as needed with ongoing support.

18702 ■ Z-Coil Pain Relief Footwear
Z-Tech, Inc.
6932 4th St. N.W.
Albuquerque, NM 87107
Ph:(505)345-2222
Free: 800-268-6239
Fax:(505)938-5770
Co. E-mail: franchise@zcoil.com
URL: http://www.zcoil.com
No. of Franchise Units: 66. **No. of Company-Owned Units:** 1. **Founded:** 1995. **Franchised:** 2005. **Description:** Retailing of revolutionary line of footwear specifically designed for foot, leg and back pain relief. **Equity Capital Needed:** $88,150-$160,800. **Franchise Fee:** $15,000. **Financial Assistance:** Limited third party financing available. **Training:** Offers 5 day training program and ongoing support.

LIBRARIES

18703 ■ National Shoe Retailers Association Library
7150 Columbia Gateway Dr., Ste. G
Columbia, MD 21046
Ph:(410)381-8282
Free: 800-673-8446
Fax:(410)381-1167
Co. E-mail: info@nsra.org
URL: http://www.nsra.org
Contact: Chuck Schuyler, Pres.

Scope: Footwear, business start-up, employee relations, marketing. **Services:** Library not open to the public. **Holdings:** 500 periodicals, clippings, business records, and archival materials.

ASSOCIATIONS AND OTHER ORGANIZATIONS

18704 ■ International Sign Association
1001 N Fairfax St., Ste. 301
Alexandria, VA 22314
Ph:(703)836-4012
Fax:(703)836-8353
Co. E-mail: info@signs.org
URL: http://www.signs.org
Contact: Lori Anderson, Pres./CEO
Description: Manufacturers, users, and suppliers of on-premise signs and sign products produced by more than 400,000 employees in all 50 states and 69 countries. Exists to support, promote and improve the $30 billion-a-year sign industry, which sustains the nation's nearly $3 trillion-a-year retail industry. .

REFERENCE WORKS

18705 ■ "Bright Lights, Big Impact: Why Digital Billboards are Growing in Popularity" in *Inc.* (March 2008, pp. 61-62)
Pub: Gruner & Jahr USA Publishing
Ed: Sarah Goldstein. **Description:** Clear Channel provides high tech digital billboards which allow companies to change advertising as often as necessary during a contract period. The Outdoor Advertising Association of America predicts the growth of digital billboards at several hundred per year over the next few years. CEO of Magic Media believes all billboards will eventually go digital.

18706 ■ "First the Merger: Then, The Culture Clash. How To Fix the Little Things That Can Tear a Company Apart" in *Inc.* (January 2008)
Pub: Gruner & Jahr USA Publishing
Ed: Elaine Appleton Grant. **Description:** Ways three CEOs handled the culture classes that followed after company mergers; companies profiled include Fuel Outdoor, an outdoor advertising company; Nelson, an interior design and architecture firm; and Beber Silverstein, an ad agency.

18707 ■ "Sign, Sign, Everywhere a Sign: How I Did It: Richard Schaps" in *Inc.* (October 2007, pp. 128)
Pub: Gruner & Jahr USA Publishing
Ed: Stephanie Clifford. **Description:** Richard Schaps shares the story of selling his outdoor-advertising firm, Van Wagner for $170 million and sharing the wealth with his employees. Schaps then started another outdoor-sign company.

18708 ■ *Signs of the Times Magazine—Buyers' Guide Issue*
Pub: ST Media Group International Inc.
Contact: Wade Swormstedt, Editor & Publisher
E-mail: wade.swormstedt@stmediagroup.com
Released: Annual, December. **Publication Includes:** List of more than 600 manufacturers and distributors of equipment and supplies for the sign industry; trade associations, consultants, trade shows, and other related organizations. **Entries Include:** For manufacturers and distributors—Company name, address, phone, name of sales contact; manufacturer listings also include product lines. For others—Organization name, address, phone; trade show listings include dates. **Arrangement:** Alphabetical. **Indexes:** Product, fax number, trade name.

18709 ■ *Signs of the Times Magazine—Sign Erection and Maintenance Directory Section*
Pub: ST Media Group International Inc.
Released: Monthly. **Publication Includes:** List of over 750 companies that erect or maintain electrical signs. **Entries Include:** Company name, address, phone, services. **Arrangement:** Geographical. **Indexes:** Product.

18710 ■ *Signs of the Times Magazine—Sign Supply Distributors Directory Section*
Pub: ST Media Group International Inc.
Contact: Nancy Bottoms, Assoc. Publisher
E-mail: nancy.bottoms@stmediagroup.com
Released: Monthly. **Price:** $39 per year -13 issues; $59, Canada Surface mail; $94, Canada 1st Class mail; $62, other countries Surface mail. **Publication Includes:** List of more than 80 suppliers of products and services used by sign companies; all listings are paid. **Entries Include:** Name of firm, address, phone, code indicating type of product. **Arrangement:** Geographical.

STATISTICAL SOURCES

18711 ■ *RMA Annual Statement Studies*
Pub: Robert Morris Associates (RMA)
Released: Annual. **Price:** $175.00 2006-07 edition, $105.00. **Description:** Contains composite balance sheets and income statements for more than 360 industries, including the accounting, auditing, and bookkeeping industries. Also contains five years of comparative historical data for discerning trends. Includes 16 commonly used ratios, computed for most of the size groupings for nearly every industry.

TRADE PERIODICALS

18712 ■ *Sign Business*
Pub: National Business Media Inc.
Contact: Rich Adams, Advisory Board
Released: Monthly. **Price:** $88 3 years; $64 two years; $85 other countries print & digital edition; $38. **Description:** Trade magazine for signage and graphics.

18713 ■ *SignCraft*
Pub: Signcraft Publishing Company Inc.
Contact: Bill McIltrot
E-mail: bill@signcraft.com
Released: 7/yr. **Price:** $39; $69 two years; $49 other countries; $91 other countries 2 years. **Description:** Trade magazine.

18714 ■ *Signs of the Times*
Pub: ST Media Group International Inc.
Contact: Tedd Swormstedt, Pres./CEO
E-mail: tedd.swormstedt@stmediagroup.com
Released: 13/yr. **Price:** $39 U.S.; $60 two years U.S.; $86 3 years; $59 Canada; $101 two years Canada; $141 Canada 3 years; $62 other countries; $112 two years international; $156 other countries 3 years; $5 single copy. **Description:** Signs of the Times covers the latest technological information and product news for the sign industry and also provides in-depth analyses and regular columns by top industry experts.

FRANCHISES AND BUSINESS OPPORTUNITIES

18715 ■ FASTSIGNS International Inc.
2542 Highlander Way
Carrollton, TX 75006
Ph:(214)346-5600
Free: 800-827-7446
Fax:(972)248-8201
Co. E-mail: mark.jameson@fastsigns.com
URL: http://www.fastsigns.com
No. of Franchise Units: 22. **Founded:** 1985. **Franchised:** 1986. **Description:** FASTSIGNS centers produce sign and graphic solutions for businesses worldwide. Unparalleled training and support have resulted in exceptional per store average unit volumes, and franchisee satisfaction. FASTSIGNS continues to receive accolades as a premier business to business franchise system. **Equity Capital Needed:** $240,000 investment required (Canadian); start-up capital required $85,000 (Canadian). **Franchise Fee:** $34,500 (Canadian). **Training:** Provides 3 weeks training.

18716 ■ Signal Graphics Business Centers
848 Broadway
Denver, CO 80203
Ph:(303)779-6789
Free: 800-852-6336
Fax:(303)779-8445
Co. E-mail: info@signalgraphics.com
URL: http://www.signalgraphics.com
No. of Franchise Units: 34. **No. of Company-Owned Units:** 3. **Founded:** 1974. **Franchised:** 1982. **Description:** A high volume business without the heavy investment & the complexity associated with traditional printing shops. Expanded portfolio of products & services well beyond the scope of our competition, including printing, copying, packaging and shipping. A unique approach and a low franchise fee & royalty. **Equity Capital Needed:** $50,000 minimum cash. **Franchise Fee:** $25,000. **Financial Assistance:** We have relationships for financing. We work with you to create a loan package to present to these institutions, or you can present your loan independently. **Training:** A easy-to-learn system that empowers franchise owners with many advantages. Provides initial training, grand opening assistance, and ongoing support.

18717 ■ SIGNARAMA, Inc.
2121 Vista Pky.
West Palm Beach, FL 33411
Ph:(561)640-5570
Free: 800-286-8671

Fax:(561)478-4340
Co. E-mail: franchise@signarama.com
URL: http://www.signarama.com
No. of Franchise Units: 36. **Founded:** 1986. **Franchised:** 1987. **Description:** One of the largest Sign Franchise with over 650 stores in 25+ countries. Rated 1 in industry past 5 years running by Entrepreneur Magazine's Franchise 500 issues. Our Full-Service Sign Centres utilize the latest in computerized sign making technology. Sign-ARama maintains support personnel in Toronto to handle growth in Canada. **Equity Capital Needed:** $40,000-$42,000, total includes franchise fee, equipment and furnishings. **Franchise Fee:** $42,500. **Financial Assistance:** Yes. **Training:** Offers 5 weeks training and ongoing support.

18718 ■ Signs First
Monotag Corp.
PO Box 11569
Memphis, TN 38111
Free: 800-852-2163
No. of Franchise Units: 33. **Founded:** 1966. **Franchised:** 1987. **Description:** Computer aided design sign stores. **Equity Capital Needed:** $30,000-$118,000. **Franchise Fee:** $7,500-$17,500. **Royalty Fee:** 6%. **Financial Assistance:** Third party financing available. **Training:** Offers 2 weeks training at headquarters, at franchisee's location, regional locations and ongoing support.

18719 ■ Signs Now
Allegra Network, LLC
47585 Galleon Dr.
Plymouth, MI 48170
Free: 800-726-9050
Fax:(248)596-8601
Co. E-mail: phill@signsnow.com
URL: http://www.signsnowfranchise.com
No. of Franchise Units: 184. **Founded:** 1983. **Franchised:** 1986. **Description:** Computerized 24-hour sign shop, offering signs and graphics for business and retail. **Equity Capital Needed:** Total investment range $169,832-$333,322; $100,000 liquid. **Franchise Fee:** $45,000 MatchMaker, $35,000 startup & 20,000 resale. **Financial Assistance:** Third party financing to qualified individuals. **Training:** Provides 3 week program at headquarters followed by onsite training.

18720 ■ Signs by Tomorrow
8681 Robert Fulton Dr.
Columbia, MD 21046
Ph:(410)312-3600
Free: 800-765-7446
Co. E-mail: sales@signsbytomorrow.com
URL: http://www.signsbytomorrow.com
No. of Franchise Units: 190. **No. of Company-Owned Units:** 1. **Founded:** 1986. **Franchised:** 1987. **Description:** Computerized sign shops offering signs and graphics for virtually all sizes of businesses. Franchisees responsibility is to manage the sales and administrative areas in servicing a business-to-business clientele during regular working hours. **Equity Capital Needed:** $160,000-$284,000; $250,000 net worth, $50,000 liquidity. **Franchise Fee:** $34,500. **Financial Assistance:** Assist in the location of lenders and the preparation of documents for loan applications. A success rate of 100%. Minimum cash $50,000. **Managerial Assistance:** Quick start marketing program, direst mail lists and materials, discount on yellow page add, periodic visits, and advanced training. **Training:** Training includes 2 weeks at headquarters, 2 weeks of onsite, and assistance with the grand opening.

REFERENCE WORKS

18721 ■ "Austin's GMP Growth Top in Nation" in *Austin Business JournalInc.* (Vol. 29, January 8, 2010, No. 44, pp. 1)
Pub: American City Business Journals
Ed: Jacob Dirr. **Description:** Austin's gross metropolitan product (GMP) has grown by 2 percent, putting it in the top 5 for GMP growth among the largest 100 American metropolitan areas. Insights into the area's business and technology services are examined.

TRADE PERIODICALS

18722 ■ *Interior Design*
Pub: Reed Business Information
Contact: Helene Oberman, Managing Editor
E-mail: hoberman@interiordesign.net
Released: 15/yr. **Price:** $59.95; $87 Canada; $187 other countries. **Description:** Interior designing and furnishings magazine.

18723 ■ *Paint & Decorating Retailer Magazine*
Pub: Paint and Decorating Retailers Association
Released: Monthly. **Price:** Free to qualified subscribers. **Description:** Magazine serving retailers of paint and decorating products.

VIDEOCASSETTES/ AUDIOCASSETTES

18724 ■ *Dried Flower Arranging and Silk Flower Making*
Aspen Publishers
7201 McKinney Circ.
Frederick, MD 21704
Ph:(301)698-7100
Free: 800-234-1660
Fax:800-901-9075
URL: http://www.aspenpublishers.com
Released: 1980. **Description:** How to make decorative arrangements such as centerpieces and wall pieces from dried flowers is demonstrated. Making realistic silk flowers is also shown. **Availability:** VHS; 3/4U.

TRADE SHOWS AND CONVENTIONS

18725 ■ Charlotte Gift and Jewelry Show
Charlotte Gift and Jewelry Show
3710 Latrobe Dr., Ste. 110
Charlotte, NC 28211
Ph:(704)365-4150
Fax:(704)365-4154
Co. E-mail: michael@charlottegiftshow.com
URL: http://www.charlottegiftshow.com
Released: Quarterly. **Audience:** Trade buyers. **Principal Exhibits:** Gifts, housewares, jewelry, crafts, silk plants and flowers, tabletop, glassware, collectibles, accessories, home decorating accessories, basketry, and other related products.

LIBRARIES

18726 ■ American Floral Art School–Floral Library
634 S. Wabash Ave., Ste. 210
Chicago, IL 60605
Ph:(312)922-9328
Co. E-mail: americanfl@americanfloralartschool.com
URL: http://www.americanfloralartschool.com
Contact: James Moretz, Owner/Dir.
Scope: Flower arrangement and symbolism, floral design, language of flowers. **Services:** Library is accessible on a restricted basis. **Holdings:** 6000 books; 500 uncataloged items; periodicals; photographs; video tapes. **Subscriptions:** 60 journals and other serials; 2 newspapers.

Skating Rink Operation

ASSOCIATIONS AND OTHER ORGANIZATIONS

18727 ■ Ice Skating Institute
6000 Custer Rd., Bldg. 9
Plano, TX 75023
Ph:(972)735-8800
Fax:(972)735-8815
Co. E-mail: pmartell@skateisi.org
URL: http://www.skateisi.org
Contact: Peter Martell, Exec. Dir.

Description: Represents ice rink owners and managers; builders and suppliers for the industry; skaters; ice skating instructors. Seeks to educate ice arena owners, operators, and instructors and to increase public interest in ice skating. Provides information on building ice facilities. Provides recreational ice skater class programs, and a national test registration program to identify and record skating skill development in free-style, couple and pair skating, ice dancing, figures, hockey, and speed skating. Sponsors Ice Skating Hall of Fame, annual conference and trade show and annual recreational ice skating competitions. Offers professional certification courses through ISI's Ice Arena Institute of Management. **Publications:** *ISI EDGE* (bimonthly); *Recreational Ice Skater Team Competition Standards*; *Recreational Ice Skating* (quarterly); *Skaters and Coaches Handbook*-;Membership Directory (annual).

18728 ■ Professional Skaters Association
3006 Allegro Park SW
Rochester, MN 55902
Ph:(507)281-5122
Fax:(507)281-5491
Co. E-mail: office@skatepsa.com
URL: http://skatepsa.com
Contact: Jimmie Santee, Exec. Dir.

Description: Professional ice skaters engaged in the teaching, coaching and performing of ice skating. Strives to form a cohesive body of all professional ice skaters for the benefit of the profession, to protect the interests of members' pupils, to advance all aspects of both ice figure skating and recreational skating, and to promote high ethical and professional standards in the field. Grades teachers on the basis of on-ice proficiency and oral examination. Operates placement service. **Publications:** *Coaches Manual*; *Professional Skater* (bimonthly); *Professional Skaters Association—Membership Directory* (annual); *Professional Skaters Association—Rating Systems Manual* (periodic); *Skaters Handbook* .

18729 ■ Roller Skating Association International
6905 Corporate Dr.
Indianapolis, IN 46278
Ph:(317)347-2626
Fax:(317)347-2636
Co. E-mail: rsa@rollerskating.com
URL: http://www.rollerskating.org
Contact: Susan Melenchuk, Exec. Dir.

Description: Independent roller skating rink operators; associate members are rink managers, teachers, and suppliers and manufacturers. Promotes the business and recreational sport of roller skating. Provides business and marketing information to skating center owners. **Publications:** *Roller Skating Business* (bimonthly); *Roller Skating Manufacturer's Newsletter* .

STATISTICAL SOURCES

18730 ■ *RMA Annual Statement Studies*
Pub: Robert Morris Associates (RMA)
Released: Annual. **Price:** $175.00 2006-07 edition, $105.00. **Description:** Contains composite balance sheets and income statements for more than 360 industries, including the accounting, auditing, and bookkeeping industries. Also contains five years of comparative historical data for discerning trends. Includes 16 commonly used ratios, computed for most of the size groupings for nearly every industry.

TRADE PERIODICALS

18731 ■ *American Hockey Magazine*
Pub: Touchpoint Publishing
Contact: Jim McEwen, President
E-mail: jim@tpgsports.com
Released: 10/yr. **Price:** $35; $44 Canada Canadian first class; $48 other countries other foreign. **Description:** U.S.A. Hockey (sports association) magazine.

18732 ■ *The ISI EDGE*
Pub: Ice Skating Institute
Contact: Carol Jackson
Ed: Carol Jackson Editor, cjackson@skateisi.org. **Released:** Bimonthly. **Description:** Provides information of interest to member ice rinks: promotional ideas, management tips, energy saving suggestions, and instructional information.

18733 ■ *Rinksider*
Pub: Target Publishing Company Inc.
Released: Bimonthly. **Price:** $20; $35 two years; $45 3 years. **Description:** Trade newspaper for roller rink operators.

TRADE SHOWS AND CONVENTIONS

18734 ■ FUN Expo
Reed Exhibitions North American Headquarters
383 Main Ave.
Norwalk, CT 06851
Ph:(203)840-4800
Fax:(203)840-5805
Co. E-mail: export@reedexpo.com
URL: http://www.reedexpo.com
Released: Annual. **Principal Exhibits:** Amusement and recreation products for family and location based entertainment centers, small amusement parks and family oriented businesses such as bowling centers, skating rinks, sports parks, miniature golf courses, golf driving ranges, family restaurants, resorts and other entertainment/recreation businesses. **Dates and Locations:** 2011 Mar 01-03, Las Vegas, NV.

18735 ■ Roller Skating Association Convention and Trade Show
Roller Skating Association International
6905 Corporate Dr.
Indianapolis, IN 46278
Ph:(317)347-2626
Fax:(317)347-2636
Co. E-mail: rsa@rollerskating.com
URL: http://www.rollerskating.org
Released: Annual. **Audience:** Roller skating rink operators and managers; skating teachers. **Principal Exhibits:** Skate manufacturers, suppliers; novelty companies; snack bar items; sound and lighting; flooring; and arcade games. **Dates and Locations:** 2011 Mar 01-04, Orlando, FL.

LIBRARIES

18736 ■ National Museum of Roller Skating Archives
4730 South St.
Lincoln, NE 68506
Ph:(402)483-7551
Fax:(402)483-1465
Co. E-mail: directorcurator@rollerskatingmuseum.com
URL: http://www.rollerskatingmuseum.com
Contact: James Vannurden, Dir. & Cur.
Scope: Roller skating, skating rules, roller skating history. **Services:** Library open to the public by appointment. **Holdings:** 1500 books; 8000 photographs; 125 periodical titles; papers of individuals prominent in roller skating; patents; prints; medals; trophies; films; costumes; archival materials; memorabilia. **Subscriptions:** 18 journals and other serials.

ASSOCIATIONS AND OTHER ORGANIZATIONS

18737 ■ Cross Country Ski Areas Association
259 Bolton Rd.
Winchester, NH 03470
Ph:(603)239-4341
Free: 877-779-2754
Fax:(603)239-6387
Co. E-mail: ccsaa@xcski.org
URL: http://www.xcski.org
Contact: Ms. Chris Frado, Pres./Exec. Dir.

Description: Owners and operators of cross country ski facilities; suppliers to the industry; individuals engaged in businesses related to cross-country skiing. Seeks to foster, stimulate, and promote cross country skiing in North America; to protect the legitimate interests of the cross-country ski area. Serves as a clearinghouse for cross-country ski areas of all sizes. Compiles and distributes information concerning ongoing developments in the cross country ski industry. Provides trail signs for ski areas to adequately inform or instruct the skier. Works with national groups such as the SnowSports Industries America, National Ski Patrol System, Professional Ski Instructors of America, and Canadian Ski Council. Compiles statistics on the ski industry. **Publications:** *Cross Country Close to Home: A Ski Area Development Manual*; *Nordic Network* (quarterly).

18738 ■ Eastern Winter Sports Representatives Association
PO Box 88
White Haven, PA 18661
Ph:(570)443-7180
Fax:(570)443-0388
Co. E-mail: ewsra@uplink.net
URL: http://www.ewsra.org
Contact: Chris Bremer, Board Member

Description: Independent company sales representatives for firms associated with the snow-ski industry. Conducts preview showings of hard and soft goods for retailers. .

18739 ■ Midwest Winter Sports Representatives Association
PO Box 76
Hazelhurst, WI 54531
Ph:(715)358-6262
Fax:(866)623-6155
Co. E-mail: mwsragayle@aol.com
URL: http://www.midwestwinterreps.com
Contact: Bruce Marsh, Pres.

Description: Manufacturers' representatives serving the Midwest ski industry. Coordinates buying shows. **Publications:** *Buyers Guide* (annual).

18740 ■ National Brotherhood of Skiers
1525 E 53rd St., Ste. 418
Chicago, IL 60615
Ph:(773)955-4100
URL: http://www.nbs.org
Contact: Haymon T. Jahi, Pres.

Description: Minority ski clubs. Promotes winter sports among minorities, with emphasis on youth. Seeks to locate and develop talented ski racers through local, regional, and national competitions. Promotes the development of Olympic-quality minority skiers. Offers two-year athletic scholarships for qualified youth to attend Ski Academies. Encourages participation in United States Ski Association competitions. Supports Building Skills and Talents programs and community-based youth motivational improvement programs. **Publications:** *NBS Directory* (annual); *Skiers Edge* (quarterly).

18741 ■ National Ski Patrol System
133 S Van Gordon St., Ste. 100
Lakewood, CO 80228
Ph:(303)988-1111
Free: 800-222-4754
Fax:(303)988-3005
Co. E-mail: nsp@nsp.org
URL: http://www.nsp.org
Contact: Tim White, Exec. Dir.

Description: Promotes ski safety and handling of injuries at ski areas. Assists municipal and federal agencies in cold weather disasters and in rescue attempts involving air crashes, mountain accidents, and blizzards; all members are trained in winter emergency care, receive special training in cold weather survival and rescue, must pass Ski Patrol proficiency and toboggan handling tests, and are trained in avalanche recognition and rescue. Maintains inventory of winter rescue equipment and patrol supplies. **Publications:** *Ski Patrol Magazine* (quarterly); *Winter Catalog* .

18742 ■ National Ski and Snowboard Retailers Association
1601 Feehanville Dr., Ste. 300
Mount Prospect, IL 60056-6035
Ph:(847)391-9825
Fax:(847)391-9827
Co. E-mail: info@nssra.com
URL: http://www.nssra.com
Contact: Brad Nelson, Chm.

Description: Ski & snowboard stores. Represents the interests of members and provides services beneficial to their businesses. Compiles statistics. **Publications:** *NSSRA Newsletter* (quarterly).

18743 ■ National Snow Industries Association–Association Nationale des Industries de la Neige
245 Victoria Ave., Ste. 810
Westmount, QC, Canada H3Z 2M6
Ph:(514)939-7370
Free: 800-263-6742
Fax:(514)939-7371
Co. E-mail: central.station@nsia.ca
URL: http://www.nsia.ca/P1/home.asp
Contact: Anna Di Meglio, Pres.

Description: Manufacturers and distributors of snow sports equipment including skis, snowboards, and winter outdoor products. Promotes participation in winter sports; works to insure a healthy business climate for members. Sponsors research programs; compiles industry statistics and marketing. **Publications:** *Scoop* (quarterly); *Show Directory* (annual).

18744 ■ National Sporting Goods Association
1601 Feehanville Dr., Ste. 300
Mount Prospect, IL 60056
Free: 800-815-5422
Fax:(847)391-9827
Co. E-mail: info@nsga.org
URL: http://www.nsga.org/i4a/pages/index.cfm?pageid=1
Contact: Matt Carlson, Pres./CEO

Description: Provides services, education and information to assist member to profit in a competitive marketplace. **Publications:** *NSGA Buying Guide* (annual); *NSGA Retail Focus* (bimonthly); *Sports Participation-Series I & II* (annual).

18745 ■ Professional Ski Instructors of America
133 S Van Gordon St., Ste. 200
Lakewood, CO 80228
Ph:(303)987-9390
Fax:(303)988-9489
Co. E-mail: mist@thesnowpros.org
URL: http://www.psia.org
Contact: Eric Sheckleton, Chm.

Description: Professional-certified Alpine and Nordic ski teachers. Promotes ski instruction by professional teachers. Developed American Teaching Method (ATM), which has received international recognition. Sponsors and publishes results of educational research through the Professional Ski Instructors of America Educational Foundation; develops clinics and management seminars. Establishes a library of books and publications on ski technique, teaching, and ski history. **Publications:** *Convention Proceedings* (annual); *PSIA Accessories Catalog*; *Ski School Management* (3/year).

18746 ■ SnowSports Industries America
8377-B Greensboro Dr.
McLean, VA 22102
Ph:(703)556-9020
Fax:(703)821-8276
Co. E-mail: siamail@snowsports.org
URL: http://www.snowsports.org
Contact: David Ingemie, Pres.

Description: Manufacturers, distributors, and suppliers of ski, snowboard, on-snow, and outdoor action sports apparel, equipment, footwear, and accessories. Monitors activities at the federal level to protect the interest of on-snow product manufacturers and distributors. Provides information on the on-snow industry to the media. Promotes snow sports through market development programs. Conducts research programs. Operates 14 committees. **Publications:** *Retailer/Rep Advisor* (biennial); *SIA Member Update* (semimonthly); *SIA Trade Show Directory* (annual).

18747 ■ Western Winter Sports Representatives Association
726 Tenacity Dr., Unit B
Longmont, CO 80504
Ph:(303)532-4002
Free: (866)929-4572
Co. E-mail: info@wwsra.com
URL: http://www.wwsra.com
Contact: Cami Garrison, Dir.

Description: Representatives in the ski industry. Sponsors buyers' shows in the Eastern U.S. Membership and activities are focused in the western part of the U.S. **Publications:** *Ski Show Directory-Sporting Goods Directory* (semiannual).

REFERENCE WORKS

18748 ■ *QuickBooks for the New Bean Counter: Business Owner's Guide 2006*
Pub: Wheatmark

Ed: Joseph L. Catallini. **Released:** July 2006. **Price:** $21.95. **Description:** Profile of QuickBooks software, offering insight into using the software's accounting and bookkeeping functions.

18749 ■ *SIA Snow Sports Book*
Pub: SnowSports Industries America

Released: Annual, August. **Covers:** 1,000 manufacturers, distributors, and suppliers of ski, snowboard, on-snow, and in-line skate apparel, equipment, and accessories who are members of SIA and who exhibit at the SIA show. **Entries Include:** Company name, address, phone, names of management, sales representatives, and products (including trade or brand names). **Arrangement:** Alphabetical. **Indexes:** Product by brand name, personnel.

18750 ■ "VC Boosts WorkForce; Livonia Software Company to Add Sales, Marketing Staff" in *Crain's Detroit Business* (March 24, 2008)
Pub: Crain Communications, Inc.

Ed: Tom Henderson. **Description:** WorkForce Software Inc., a company that provides software to manage payroll processes and oversee compliance with state and federal regulations and with union rules, plans to use an investment of $5.5 million in venture capital to hire more sales and marketing staff.

TRADE PERIODICALS

18751 ■ *Cross Country Skier*
Pub: Country Skier L.L.C.
Contact: Ron Bergin, Editor & Publisher

Released: Quarterly. **Price:** $12.75; $24.95 two years. **Description:** Magazine emphasizing touring, destinations, and technique in cross-country skiing.

18752 ■ *Ski*
Pub: Time4 Media Inc.

Released: 8/yr, from September to May. **Price:** $10. **Description:** Magazine of the ski life.

18753 ■ *Skiing*
Pub: Time4 Media Inc.
Contact: Rick Kahl, Editor-in-Chief

Released: 7/yr (issued monthly Sept. thru April). **Price:** $10. **Description:** Skiing magazine.

18754 ■ *Sporting Goods Dealer*
Pub: Bill Communications Inc.
Contact: Mark Sullivan, Publisher
E-mail: msullivan@sgdealer.com
Ed: Mike Jacobsen, Editor, mjacobsen@sgdealer.com. **Released:** Bimonthly. **Description:** Magazine which offers expert reporting on trends affecting team dealers and retailers who service schools, colleges, pro and local teams.

VIDEOCASSETTES/ AUDIOCASSETTES

18755 ■ *Old School*
Tapeworm Video Distributors
25876 The Old Road 141
Stevenson Ranch, CA 91381
Ph:(661)257-4904
Fax:(661)257-4820
Co. E-mail: sales@tapeworm.com
URL: http://www.tapeworm.com
Price: $14.95. **Description:** Presents the first snowboarding competition at Ski Cooper Colorado 1980. **Availability:** VHS.

18756 ■ *Ski Tips 5: Skiing with Shaped Skis Made Easy*
TMW Media Group
2321 Abbot Kinney Blvd., Ste. 101
Venice, CA 90291
Ph:(310)577-8581
Free: 800-262-8862
Fax:(310)574-0886
Co. E-mail: general@tmwmedia.com
URL: http://www.tmwmedia.com
Released: 1997. **Price:** $29.95. **Description:** Shows skiers how to properly use shaped skis for the best performance. **Availability:** VHS.

18757 ■ *Space Cowboys: Dysfunctional Superheroes II*
Tapeworm Video Distributors
25876 The Old Road 141
Stevenson Ranch, CA 91381
Ph:(661)257-4904
Fax:(661)257-4820
Co. E-mail: sales@tapeworm.com
URL: http://www.tapeworm.com
Released: 1997. **Price:** $14.95. **Description:** Presents footage of snowboarders, skateboarders, and freestyle BMX riders. **Availability:** VHS.

18758 ■ *Steep Snow*
Keen Media
857 Pulpit Rock Circle N.
Colorado Springs, CO 80918
Ph:(719)593-2155
Free: 800-363-5336
Fax:(719)593-2888
Co. E-mail: jim@keenmedia.com
URL: http://www.keenmedia.com
Price: $34.95. **Description:** Provides instruction on techniques, equipment, and weather and terrain for hunters, hikers, skiers, and others finding it necessary to cross steep snow. **Availability:** VHS.

TRADE SHOWS AND CONVENTIONS

18759 ■ The SIA Snow Show
SnowSports Industries America
8377-B Greensboro Dr.
McLean, VA 22102-3587
Ph:(703)556-9020
Fax:(703)821-8276
Co. E-mail: SIAmail@snowsports.org
URL: http://www.thesnowtrade.org
Released: Annual. **Audience:** Members of SIA to exhibit or attend as a raw material or service providers, attendees are retail or corporate buyers only. **Principal Exhibits:** Ski, snowboard, outdoor sports, snowshoe companies with equipment, clothing, and accessories.

18760 ■ Ski Dazzle - Los Angeles Ski Show and Snowboard Expo
Ski Dazzle, LLC.
1550 S. Coast Hwy.
Laguna Beach, CA 92651
Ph:(949)497-4977
Fax:(949)497-4123
Co. E-mail: support@skidazzle.com
URL: http://www.skidazzle.com
Released: Annual. **Audience:** Snow skiing, snow boarding and winter sports enthusiasts/consumers. **Principal Exhibits:** Ski equipment and snow boarding, clothing, and accessories; travel-related products and services.

18761 ■ Toronto Ski, Snowboard and Travel Show
Canadian National Sportsmen's Shows (Toronto, Ontario)
703 Evans Ave., Ste. 202
Toronto, ON, Canada M9C 5E9
Ph:(416)695-0311
Free: 888-69-52677
Fax:(416)695-0381
URL: http://www.sportsmensshows.com
Released: Annual. **Audience:** General public. **Principal Exhibits:** Ski and snowboard manufacturers, retailers; ski resorts, tourist bureaus, travel agencies, hotels, ski clinics and demonstrations, associations, clubs, ski swap and sale.

LIBRARIES

18762 ■ Canadian Ski Museum Archives
301-1960 Scott St.
Ottawa, ON, Canada K1Z 8L8
Ph:(613)722-3584
Fax:(613)722-2914
Co. E-mail: info@skimuseum.ca
URL: http://www.skimuseum.ca
Contact: Ryan Scranton
Scope: Skiing, snowboarding, ski history, Canadian winter sport. **Services:** Library open to the public with restrictions. **Holdings:** 2000 books; archival materials, photographs.

18763 ■ U.S. National Ski Hall of Fame and Museum–Roland Palmedo National Ski Library
PO Box 191
Ishpeming, MI 49849
Ph:(906)485-6323
Fax:(906)486-4570
Co. E-mail: skihall@uplogon.com
URL: http://www.skihall.com
Scope: Skiing. **Services:** Copying; Library open to the public for reference use only. **Holdings:** 1300 volumes; 20 VF drawers of reports, pamphlets, clippings; 180 films. **Subscriptions:** 7 journals and other serials.

START-UP INFORMATION

18764 ■ *The 100 Best Businesses to Start When You Don't Want To Work Hard Anymore*
Pub: Career Press Inc.
Ed: Lisa Rogak. **Price:** $16.99. **Description:** Author helps burned-out workers envision a new future as a small business owner. Systems analysis, adventure travel outfitting, bookkeeping, food delivery, furniture making, and software development are among the industries examined.

18765 ■ "Local Startup Hits Big Leagues" in *Austin Business JournalInc.* (Vol. 28, December 19, 2008, No. 40, pp. 1)
Pub: American City Business Journals
Ed: Christopher Calnan. **Description:** Qcue LLC, an Austin, Texas-based company founded in 2007 is developing a software system that can be used by Major League Baseball teams to change the prices of their single-game tickets based on variables affecting demand. The company recently completed a trial with the San Francisco Giants in 2008.

18766 ■ "OtherInbox Ready for Revenue: Software Startup Expects Profits in '09" in *Austin Business JournalInc.* (Vol. 28, January 2, 2009)
Pub: American City Business Journals
Ed: Christopher Calnan. **Description:** Founder of Austin, Texas-based OtherBox Inc. expects the company to generate revenue through subscriptions and advertising and also reach profitability in 2009. The company's email management tool sends secondary mail to an alternate location thereby freeing up the work inbox for more urgent messages.

ASSOCIATIONS AND OTHER ORGANIZATIONS

18767 ■ Business Software Alliance
1150 18th St. NW, Ste. 700
Washington, DC 20036
Ph:(202)872-5500
Fax:(202)872-5501
Co. E-mail: info@bsa.org
URL: http://www.bsa.org
Contact: Robert Holleyman II, Pres./CEO
Description: Computer software publishers. Promotes the free world trade of business software by combating international software piracy, advancing intellectual property protection, and increasing market access. **Publications:** *Guide to Software Management* (annual); *Software Review* (quarterly).

18768 ■ Entertainment Software Association
575 7th St. NW, Ste. 300
Washington, DC 20004
Co. E-mail: esa@theesa.com
URL: http://www.theesa.com
Contact: Michael D. Gallagher, Pres.
Description: Represents the interactive entertainment software publishing industry. Established an autonomous rating board to rate interactive entertainment software. Established a program to combat piracy in the United States and around the world. Represents members on industry issues at the federal and state level. Provides market research and information. .

18769 ■ Free Software Foundation
51 Franklin St., Ste. 500
Boston, MA 02110-1301
Ph:(617)542-5942
Fax:(617)542-2652
Co. E-mail: info@fsf.org
URL: http://www.fsf.org
Contact: Richard M. Stallman, Pres./Founder
Description: Promotes computer users' right to use, study, copy, modify, and redistribute computer programs; development and use of free (as in freedom) software, particularly the GNU operating system and free (as in freedom) documentation; promotes ethical and political issues of freedom in the use of software. **Publications:** *GNU's Bulletin* (annual).

18770 ■ International Computer Music Association
1819 Polk St., Ste. 330
San Francisco, CA 94109
Fax:(734)878-3031
Co. E-mail: icma@umich.edu
URL: http://www.computermusic.org
Contact: Tae Hong Park, Pres.
Description: Composers, computer software and hardware developers, researchers and musicians. Works to advance individuals and institutions involved in the technical, creative and performance aspects of computer music. Provides networking opportunities; sponsors research and projects; holds competitions. .

18771 ■ Society for Software Quality
PO Box 27634
San Diego, CA 92198
Co. E-mail: info@ssq.org
URL: http://www.ssq.org
Contact: Merle Kemble, Pres.
Description: Software professionals. Seeks to advance the art, science, and technology of software quality assurance. Promotes professional development of members and encourages high standards in the field. Fosters communication between the public and the industry. Assists colleges and universities in developing and implementing curricula in quality evaluation and methodologies. Operates speakers' bureau. .

18772 ■ Software and Information Industry Association
1090 Vermont Ave. NW, 6th Fl.
Washington, DC 20005-4095
Ph:(202)289-7442
Free: 800-388-7478
Fax:(202)289-7097
URL: http://www.siia.net
Contact: Kenneth Wasch, Pres.
Description: Seeks to promote the interest of the software and information industries. Protects intellectual property and advocate a legal and regulatory environment that benefits the industry. Serves as a resource to members. .

REFERENCE WORKS

18773 ■ "A Dog-Day Pooch" in *Canadian Business* (Vol. 79, September 11, 2006, No. 18, pp. 19)
Pub: Rogers Media
Ed: Andrew Wahl. **Description:** Acquisition deal of Hummingbird Ltd by Canadian software maker Open Text Corp., is discussed.

18774 ■ "Abacast, Citadel Strike Radio Ad Deal" in *Business Journal Portland* (Vol. 27, December 31, 2010, No. 44, pp. 3)
Pub: Portland Business Journal
Ed: Erik Siemers. **Description:** Software firm Abacast Inc. has partnered with Citadel Media to aid the latter's advertising sales. Citadel provides radio networks and syndicated programs to 4,200 affiliate stations.

18775 ■ "ACC Game Development Program Opens" in *Austin Business JournalInc.* (Vol. 28, October 31, 2008, No. 33, pp. 1)
Pub: American City Business Journals
Ed: Sandra Zaragoza. **Description:** Austin, Texas-based Austin Community College has launched its Game Development Institute. The institute was created to meet the gaming industry's demand for skilled workers. One hundred students have enrolled with the institute.

18776 ■ "All Those Applications, and Phone Users Just Want to Talk" in *Advertising Age* (Vol. 79, August 11, 2008, No. 31, pp. 18)
Pub: Crain Communications, Inc.
Ed: Mike Vorhaus. **Description:** Although consumers are slowly coming to text messaging and other data applications, a majority of those Americans surveyed stated that they simply want to use their cell phones to talk and do not care about other activities. Statistical data included.

18777 ■ "AMT's Partner Program Enables New Security Business Models" in *Internet Wire* (August 12, 2010)
Pub: Comtex
Description: AMT, technical provider of physical access control Software as a Service (Saas) solutions, has developed a new Partner Program that allows partners to outsource any technical abilities lacking to AMT with no upfront fees.

18778 ■ "Angel Investments Tripled in 2009" in *Austin Business JournalInc.* (Vol. 29, January 8, 2010, No. 44, pp. 1)
Pub: American City Business Journals
Ed: Christopher Calnan. **Description:** Central Texas Angel Network (CTAN) has invested $3.5 million in 12 ventures, which include 10 in Austin, Texas in 2009 to triple the amount it invested during 2008. The largest recipient of CTAN's investments is life sciences, which attracted 20 percent of the capital,

while software investments fell to 18 percent. The new screening process that helps startups secure CTAN capital is explored.

18779 ■ "Apps For Anybody With an Idea" in *Advertising Age* (Vol. 79, October 20, 2008, No. 39, pp. 29)
Pub: Crain Communications, Inc.
Ed: Beth Snyder Bulik. **Description:** Apple's new online App Store is open to anyone with an idea and the ability to write code and many of these developers are not only finding a sense of community through this venue but are also making money since the sales are split with Apple, 30/70 in the developer's favor.

18780 ■ "Arctic IT Honored" in *Alaska Business Monthly* (Vol. 27, October 2011, No. 10, pp. 10)
Pub: Alaska Business Publishing Company
Ed: Nancy Pounds. **Description:** Arctic Information Technology Inc. was named to Everything Channel's 2011 Computer Reseller News (CRN) Next-Generation 250 list. The firm provides business software and network infrastructure solutions.

18781 ■ "Arizona Firms In Chicago Go For Gold With '08 Games" in *The Business Journal - Serving Phoenix and the Valley of the Sun* (Vol. 28, August 8, 2008, No. 49, pp. 1)
Pub: American City Business Journals, Inc.
Ed: Patrick O'Grady. **Description:** More than 20 U.S. athletes will wear Arizona-based eSoles LLC's custom-made insoles to increase their performance at the 2008 Beijing Olympics making eSoles one of the beneficiaries of the commercialization of the games. Translation software maker Auralog Inc saw a 60 percent jump in sales from its Mandarin Chinese language applications.

18782 ■ "Attivio Brings Order to Data" in *Information Today* (Vol. 26, February 2009, No. 2, pp. 14)
Pub: Information Today, Inc.
Ed: Marji McClure. **Description:** Profile of Attivio, the high tech firm offering next-generation software that helps businesses to consolidate data and eliminate enterprise silos.

18783 ■ "AVG Introduces Security Software Suite for SMBs 551179" in *eWeek* (October 12, 2010)
Pub: Ziff Davis Enterprise
Description: AVG Technologies is offering its AVG Internet Security 2011 Business Edition and AVG Anti-Virus Business Edition designed to give Internet-active SMB owners protection. The system protects online transactions and email communications as well as sensitive customer data and AVG Anti-Virus 2011 Business edition offers real-time protection against the latest online threats.

18784 ■ "BancVue to Expand" in *Austin Business JournalInc.* (Vol. 29, November 27, 2009, No. 38, pp. 1)
Pub: American City Business Journals
Ed: Kate Harrington. **Description:** Significant growth of BancVue in the past six years has prompted the company to look for a site that could increase its office space from 25,000 square feet to 65,000 square feet. BancVue offers bank and credit union software solutions and is planning to lease or buy a property in Austin, Texas.

18785 ■ "Bar Hopping: Your Numbers At a Glance" in *Inc.* (January 2008, pp. 44-45)
Pub: Gruner & Jahr USA Publishing
Ed: Michael Fitzgerald. **Description:** Software that helps any company analyze data include Crystal Xcelsius, a program that takes data from Excel documents and turns them into animated gauges, charts and graphs; CashView, a Web-based application that tracks receivables and payables; iDashboards, a Web-based programs that produces animated gauges, maps, pie charts and graphs; Corda Human Capital Management, that transforms stats like head count, productivity, and attrition into graphs and dials; NetSuite, a Web-based application that tracks key indicators; and Cognos Now, that gauges, dials, and graphs data.

18786 ■ "BayTSP, NTT Data Corp. Enter Into Reseller Pact to Market Online IP Monitoring" in *Professional Services Close-Up* (Sept. 11, 2009)
Pub: Close-Up Media
Description: Due to incredible interest from distributors and content owners across Asia, NTT Data Corp. will resell BayTSP's online intellectual property monitoring, enforcement, business intelligence and monetization services in Japan.

18787 ■ "Behind the Scenes: Companies At the Heart of Everyday Life" in *Inc.* (February 2008, pp. 26-27)
Pub: Gruner & Jahr USA Publishing
Ed: Athena Schindelheim. **Description:** Profiles of companies providing services to airports, making the environment safer and more efficient, as well as more comfortable for passengers and workers. Centerpoint Manufacturing provides garbage bins that can safely contain explosions producing thousands of pounds of pressure; Infax, whose software displays arrival and departure information on 19-foot-wide screens; Lavi Industries, whose products include security barricades, hostess stands, and salad-bar sneeze guards; and SATech maker of rubber flooring that helps ease discomfort for workers having to stand for long periods of time.

18788 ■ "Being all a-Twitter" in *Canadian Business* (Vol. 81, December 8, 2008, No. 21, pp. 22)
Pub: Rogers Media Ltd.
Ed: Andrew Wahl. **Description:** Marketing experts suggest that advertising strategies have to change along with new online social media. Companies are advised to find ways to incorporate social software because workers and customers are expected to continue its use.

18789 ■ "Best Managed Companies (Canada)" in *Canadian Business* (Vol. 82, Summer 2009, No. 8, pp. 38)
Pub: Rogers Media
Ed: Calvin Leung. **Description:** Agrium Inc. and Barrick Gold Corporation are among those that are found to be the best managed companies in Canada. Best managed companies also include software firm Open Text Corporation, which has grown annual sales by 75 percent and annual profits by 160 percent since 1995. Open Text markets software that allow firms to manage word-based data, and has 46,000 customers in 114 countries.

18790 ■ "Beyond Microsoft and Yahoo!: Some M&A Prospects" in *Barron's* (Vol. 88, March 17, 2008, No. 11, pp. 39)
Pub: Dow Jones & Company, Inc.
Ed: Eric J. Savitz. **Description:** Weak quarterly earnings report for Yahoo! could pressure the company's board to cut a deal with Microsoft. Electronic Arts is expected to win its hostile $26-a-share bid for Take-Two Interactive Software. Potential targets and buyers for mergers and acquisitions are mentioned.

18791 ■ "Beyond YouTube: New Uses for Video, Online and Off" in *Inc.* (October 2007, pp. 53-54)
Pub: Gruner & Jahr USA Publishing
Ed: Leah Hoffmann. **Description:** Small companies are using video technology for embedding messages into email, broadcasting live interactive sales and training seminars, as well as marketing campaigns. Experts offer insight into producing and broadcasting business videos.

18792 ■ *The Big Switch*
Pub: W. W. Norton & Company, Inc.
Ed: Nicholas Carr. **Released:** January 19, 2009. **Price:** $16.95 paperback. **Description:** Today companies are dismantling private computer systems and tapping into services provided via the Internet. This shift is remaking the computer industry, bringing competitors such as Google to the forefront ant threatening traditional companies like Microsoft and Dell. The book weaves together history, economics, and technology to explain why computing is changing and what it means for the future.

18793 ■ "Blog Buzz Heralds Arrival of IPhone 2.0" in *Advertising Age* (Vol. 79, June 9, 2008, No. 40, pp. 8)
Pub: Crain Communications, Inc.
Ed: Abbey Klaasen. **Description:** Predictions concerning the next version of the iPhone include a global-positioning-system technology as well as a configuration to run on a faster, 3G network.

18794 ■ *Business Feasibility Analysis Pro*
Pub: Prentice Hall PTR
Ed: Palo Alto Software. **Released:** August 2006. **Price:** $28.40. **Description:** Profile of software developed to support small business management and/or entrepreneurship text. Step-by-step instructions are provided.

18795 ■ "BusinessOnLine Launches a New Web-Based Search Engine Optimization Tool" in *Internet Wire* (October 19, 2009)
Pub: Comtex News Network, Inc.
Description: First Link Checker, a complimentary new search engine optimization tool that helps site owners optimize their on-page links by understanding which of those links are actually being counted in Google's relevancy algorithm, was developed by BusinessOnLine, a rapidly growing Internet marketing agency. This tool will make it easy for the average web master to ensure that their internal link structure is optimized.

18796 ■ "CarBiz Inc. Speaking At NABD" in *Canadian Corporate News* (May 14, 2007)
Pub: Comtex News Network Inc.
Description: CarBiz Inc., a leading provider of software, consulting, and training solutions to the United States' automotive industry, had two of its executive officers speak at the National Alliance of Buy Here - Pay Here Dealers (NABD), a conference that draws over 2,000 dealers, service providers, and experts from across the United States.

18797 ■ "A Case Study: Real-Life Business Planning" in *Entrepreneur* (February 3, 2009)
Pub: Entrepreneur Media Inc.
Ed: Tim Berry. **Description:** Provides a case study of a two-day planning meeting for Palo Alto Software in which the executives of the company met for their annual planning cycle and discussed ways in which the company needed to change in order to stay viable in today's tough economic climate.

18798 ■ "Cerner Works the Business Circuit" in *Business Journal-Serving Metropolitan Kansas City* (Vol. 26, October 5, 2007, No. 4, pp. 1)
Pub: American City Business Journals, Inc.
Ed: Rob Roberts. **Description:** Cerner Corporation is embracing the coming of the electronic medical record exchange by creating a regional health information organization (RHIO) called the CareEntrust. The RHIO convinced health insurers to share claims data with patients and clinicians. At the Center Health Conference, held October 7 to 10, Cerner will demonstrate the software it developed for CareEntrust to the 40,000 healthcare and information technology professionals.

18799 ■ "ChemSW Software Development Services Available for Outsourcing" in *Information Today* (Vol. 26, February 2009, No. 2, pp. 30)
Pub: Information Today, Inc.
Description: ChemSW software development services include requirements analysis, specification development, design, development, testing, and system documentation as an IT outsourcing solution. The company can also develop software tracking systems for satellite stockrooms, provide asset management integration solutions and more.

18800 ■ "ClickFuel Launches New Products to Help Small and Mid-Sized Businesses Bolster Their Brand Online" in *Internet Wire* (Dec. 3,2009)
Pub: Comtex News Network, Inc.
Description: Boostability, a provider of Enterprise Search Engine Optimization (SEO) software technol-

ogy, has partnered with ClickFuel, a firm that designs, tracks and manages Internet marketing campaigns in order to leverage Boostability's technology in order to deliver comprehensive SEO solutions to small and mid-size businesses; three new products will also become available for these business clients to help them manage all facets of their online presence.

18801 ■ "ClickFuel Unveils Internet Marketing Tools for Small Businesses" in *Internet Wire* (October 19, 2009)
Pub: Comtex News Network, Inc.
Description: ClickFuel, a firm that manages, designs and tracks marketing campaigns has unveiled a full software suite of affordable services and technology solutions designed to empower small business owners and help them promote and grow their businesses through targeted Internet marketing campaigns.

18802 ■ "Clouds in the Forecast" in *Information Today* (Vol. 28, September 2011, No. 8, pp. 10)
Pub: Information Today, Inc.
Ed: Paula J. Hane. **Description:** Cloud computing is software, applications, and data stored remotely and accessed via the Internet with output displayed on a client device. Recent developments in cloud computing are explored.

18803 ■ *Computer Accounting Essentials with Microsoft Office Accounting 2010*
Pub: McGraw-Hill Higher Education
Ed: Carol Yacht, Susan Crosson. **Released:** March 10, 2010. **Description:** Step-by-step guide to using Microsoft's Office Professional 2007 Accounting program.

18804 ■ "Contec Innovations Inc.: MovieSet.com First to Mobilize Content Using BUZmob" in *Canadian Corporate News* (May 16, 2007)
Pub: Comtex News Network Inc.
Description: Contec Innovations Inc., a provider of mobile infrastructure software, announced that MovieSet.com is the first Internet portal to mobilize their content using BUZmob, the company's new mobile publishing service that allows content publishers to enable mobile access to their feed-based content on any mobile device or network in real-time.

18805 ■ "Cut Energy Waste" in *Inc.* (Vol. 31, January-February 2009, No. 1, pp. 42)
Pub: Mansueto Ventures LLC
Description: Carbon Control, Edison, and Saver software programs help companies cut carbon emissions by reducing the amount of energy consumed by computers while they are idle.

18806 ■ "Dear Customer: Managing E-Mail Campaigns" in *Inc.* (March 2008, pp. 58-59)
Pub: Gruner & Jahr USA Publishing
Ed: Ryan Underwood. **Description:** Internet services that help firms manage their online business including email marketing, to manage subscriber lists, comply with spam regulations, monitor bouncebacks, and track potential customers are profiled. Constant Contact, MobileStorm Stun, Campaign Monitor, Pop Commerce, Emma, and StrongMail E-mail Server are among software and services highlighted.

18807 ■ "Descartes Launches Ocean Shipment Management Suite" in *Canadian Corporate News* (May 16, 2007)
Pub: Comtex News Network Inc.
Description: Descartes Systems Group, a global on-demand software-as-a-service (SaaS) logistics solutions provider, launched the latest release of its Descartes Ocean Shipment Management Suite. The release integrates customs compliance services with Descartes' Rate Builder solution, a central database for global shipment and rate information, and Descartes Global Logistics Network (GLN) messaging capabilities.

18808 ■ "Design Programs for HVAC Sizing Solutions" in *Contractor* (Vol. 57, January 2010, No. 1, pp. 44)
Pub: Penton Media, Inc.
Ed: William Feldman; Patti Feldman. **Description:** Rhvac 8 is an HVAC design program that lets users calculate peak heating and cooling load requirements for rooms, zones, systems, and entire buildings. The HVAC Pipe Sizer software for the iPhone enables quick sizing of a simple piping system.

18809 ■ "Don't Touch My Laptop, If You Please Mr. Customs Man" in *Canadian Electronics* (Vol. 23, June-July 2008, No. 4, pp. 6)
Pub: Action Communication Inc.
Ed: Mark Borkowski. **Description:** Canadian businessmen bringing electronic devices to the US can protect the contents of their laptops by hiding their data from US border agents. They can also choose to clean up the contents of their laptop using file erasure programs.

18810 ■ "DST Turns to Banks for Credit" in *The Business Journal-Serving Metropolitan Kansas City* (Vol. 27, October 3, 2008, No. 3, pp. 1)
Pub: American City Business Journals, Inc.
Ed: Rob Roberts. **Description:** Kansas City, Missouri-based DST Systems Inc., a company that provides sophisticated information processing, computer software services and business solutions, has secured a new five-year, $120 million credit facility from Enterprise Bank and Bank of the West. The deal is seen to reflect that the region and community-banking model remain stable. Comments from executives are also provided.

18811 ■ "Eagles Measure Suite Success" in *Philadelphia Business Journal* (Vol. 30, September 9, 2011, No. 30, pp. 1)
Pub: American City Business Journals Inc.
Ed: John George. **Description:** Philadelphia Eagles have a new software program that helps suite holders keep track of how their suite is being used and whether they are getting a return on their investment. The software allows suite holders to better utilize and distribute their tickets.

18812 ■ "EBSCO Adds New Features to EBSCOhost Content Viewer" in *Information Today* (Vol. 26, February 2009, No. 2, pp. 31)
Pub: Information Today, Inc.
Description: EBSCOhost Content Viewer historical digital archive collection provides a visual overview of a displayed document, highlighting search keywords on the page as well as providing a document map that shows the number of times a given keyword is mentioned in a periodical, monograph, article, or other document. For periodical content, the viewer lets users browse multiple issues in a volume without leaving the interface; features include zoom and pan technology similar to online maps.

18813 ■ "Elastic Path Software Joins Canada in G20 Young Entrepreneur Summit" in *Internet Wire* (June 14, 2010)
Pub: Comtex
Description: The Canadian Youth Business Foundation hosted the G20 Young Entrepreneur Summit and announced that Harry Chemko of British Columbia's Elastic Path Software will be a member of the Canadian delegation at the G20 Young Entrepreneur Summit. Details are included.

18814 ■ "Elemental Nabs $5.5 Million" in *The Business Journal-Portland* (Vol. 25, July 18, 2008, No. 19, pp. 1)
Pub: American City Business Journals, Inc.
Ed: Aliza Earnshaw. **Description:** Elemental Technologies Inc., a Portland, Oregon-based software company got $5.5 million in new funding, bringing its total invested capital to $7.1 million in nine months since October 2008. The company plans to launch Badaboom, software for converting video into various formats, later in 2008.

18815 ■ "The Emergence of Governance In an Open Source Community" in *Academy of Management Journal* (Vol. 50, No. 5, October 2007, pp. 1079)
Pub: Academy of Management
Ed: Siiobhan O'Mahony, Fabrizio Ferraro. **Description:** Study examined the method of self-governance among small communities producing collective goods, focusing on an open source software community. Results revealed that a combination of bureaucratic and democratic practices helped its governance system.

18816 ■ "Empire of Pixels" in *Entrepreneur* (Vol. 37, September 2009, No. 9, pp. 50)
Pub: Entrepreneur Media, Inc.
Ed: Jason Daley. **Description:** Entrepreneur Jack Levin has successfully grown Imageshack, an image-hosting Web service. The Website currently gets 50 million unique visitors a month. Levin has launched Y-Frog, an application that uses Imageshack to allow Twitter users to add images to their posts.

18817 ■ *The Entrepreneurial Culture Network Advantage Within Chinese and Irish Software Firms*
Pub: Edward Elgar Publishing, Incorporated
Ed: Tsang. **Released:** October 2006. **Price:** $95.00. **Description:** Ways national cultural heritage influences entrepreneurial ventures are discussed.

18818 ■ "Ex Libris Rosetta Hits the Market" in *Information Today* (Vol. 26, February 2009, No. 2, pp. 30)
Pub: Information Today, Inc.
Description: Ex Libris Rosetta, the latest version of the Ex Libris Group's Digital Preservation System supports the acquisition, validation, ingest, storage, management, preservation, and dissemination of digital objects, allowing libraries the infrastructure and technology to preserve and facilitate access to digital collections. The firm's Ex Libris Rosseta Charter Program helps users develop strategic collaboration between Ex Libris and its customers to improve the product.

18819 ■ "Fly Phishing" in *Canadian Business* (Vol. 80, October 22, 2007, No. 21, pp. 42)
Pub: Rogers Media
Ed: Andy Holloway. **Description:** Symantec Corporation's report shows consumers and companies have effectively installed network defenses that prevent unwanted access. Phishing packages are readily available and are widely used. Other details of the Internet Security Threat Report are presented.

18820 ■ "The Folly of Google's Latest Gambit" in *Barron's* (Vol. 89, July 13, 2009, No. 28, pp. 23)
Pub: Dow Jones & Co., Inc.
Ed: Eric J. Savitz. **Description:** Google will enter the operating systems business with the introduction of the Google Chrome OS but its success is dubious because the project is still a year or so away while Microsoft will release an updated version of Windows by then; another problem is that Google already has another OS called Android which will overlap with the Chrome OS's market.

18821 ■ "Forsys Metals Corporation Goes "Live" With Q4's On-Demand Disclosure Management Software" in *Canadian Corporate News* (May 16, 2007)
Pub: Comtex News Network Inc.
Description: Forsys Metals Corp. selected Q4 Web Systems to automate its corporate website disclosure with Q4's software platform which also automates and simplifies many of the administrative tasks that Forsys was doing manually, allowing them to focus their internal resources on the business.

18822 ■ "Game On! African Americans Get a Shot at $17.9 Billion Video Game Industry" in *Black Enterprise* (Vol. 38, July 2008, No. 12, pp. 56)
Pub: Earl G. Graves Publishing Co. Inc.
Ed: Carolyn M. Brown. **Description:** Despite the economic crisis, consumers are still purchasing the hottest video games and hardware. Tips for African American developers who want to become a part of this industry that lacks content targeting this demographic are offered.

18823 ■ "Game On" in *Canadian Business* (Vol. 80, February 12, 2007, No. 4, pp. 15)
Pub: Rogers Media
Ed: Calvin Leung. **Description:** The plan of president of TransGaming Vikas Gupta to create innovative software programs for games that can be played in different operating systems is discussed.

18824 ■ "Game Plan" in *Canadian Business* (Vol. 79, September 11, 2006, No. 18, pp. 50)
Pub: Rogers Media
Ed: Joe Castaldo. **Description:** Strategies adopted by gaming companies to revitalize their business and give a stimulus to their falling resources are presented.

18825 ■ "German Win Through Sharing" in *Canadian Business* (Vol. 83, September 14, 2010, No. 15, pp. 16)
Pub: Rogers Media Ltd.
Ed: Jordan Timm. **Description:** German economic historian Eckhard Hoffner has a two-volume work showing how German's relaxed attitude toward copyright and intellectual property helped it catch up to industrialized United Kingdom. Hoffner's research was in response to his interest in the usefulness of software patents. Information on the debate regarding Canada's copyright laws is given.

18826 ■ "Getting Rid of Global Glitches: Choosing Software For Trade Compliance" in *Black Enterprise* (Vol. 41, September 2010, No. 2, pp. 48)
Pub: Earl G. Graves Publishing Co. Inc.
Ed: Marcia Wade Talbert. **Description:** Compliance software for trading with foreign companies must be compatible with the U.S. Census Bureau's Automated Export System (www.aesdirect.gov). It has to be current with regulatory requirements for any country in the world. Whether owners handle their own compliance or hire a logistics company, they need to be familiar with this software in order to access reports and improve transparency and efficiency of theft supply chain.

18827 ■ "Global: Put It on Autopilot" in *Entrepreneur* (Vol. 35, October 2007, No. 10, pp. 110)
Pub: Entrepreneur Media Inc.
Ed: Laurel Delaney. **Description:** A business that aims to enter the global market must first streamline its global supply chain (GSC). A streamlined GSC can be achieved by laying out the company's processes and by automating it with supply chain management software. Advantages of GSC automation such as credibility are provided.

18828 ■ "Google Edges into Wireless E-Mail" in *Globe & Mail* (February 19, 2007, pp. B5)
Pub: CTVglobemedia Publishing Inc.
Ed: Simon Avery. **Description:** Google Inc. has introduced a free mobile e-mail service in Canada. The mobile users can read, send, and search messages using the new software.

18829 ■ "Google Places a Call to Bargain Hunters" in *Advertising Age* (Vol. 79, September 29, 2008, No. 36, pp. 13)
Pub: Crain Communications, Inc.
Ed: Abbey Klaassen. **Description:** Google highlighted application developers who have created tools for its Android mobile phone in the device's unveiling; applications such as ShopSavvy and CompareEverywhere help shoppers to find bargains by allowing them to compare prices in their local areas and across the web.

18830 ■ *Graduate Assistantship Directory in Computing*
Pub: Association for Computing Machinery
Contact: Mark Mandelbaum
Entries Include: Institution name, address, name and title of contact, degrees offered, area of expertise, financial aid offered, stipend amount, department facilities (hardware and software), school enrollment, required exams, admission deadlines. **Database Covers:** Fellowships and assistantships in the computer sciences offered at U.S. and Canadian educational institutions. **Arrangement:** Geographical.

18831 ■ "A Hacker in India Hijacked His Website Design and Was Making Good Money Selling It" in *Inc.* (December 2007, pp. 77-78, 80)
Pub: Gruner & Jahr USA Publishing
Ed: Darren Dahl. **Description:** John Anton, owner of an online custom T-shirt business and how a company in India was selling software Website templates identical to his firm's Website.

18832 ■ "His Banking Industry Software Never Caught On, so Bill Randle is Now Targeting the Health Care Market" in *Inc.* (March 2008)
Pub: Gruner & Jahr USA Publishing
Ed: Alex Salkever. **Description:** Profile of Bill Randle, bank executive turned entrepreneur; Randle tells how he changed his focus for his company from banking software to healthcare software. The firm employs ten people who secure online billing and recordkeeping systems for hospitals and insurers. Randle discusses critical decisions that will impact his firm in the coming year. Three experts offer advice.

18833 ■ "Holiday Sales Look Uncertain for Microsoft and PC Sellers" in *Puget Sound Business Journal* (Vol. 29, November 28, 2008, No. 32)
Pub: American City Business Journals
Ed: Todd Bishop. **Description:** Personal computer makers face uncertain holiday sales for 2008 as a result of the weak U.S. economy and a shift toward low-cost computers. Personal computer shipments for the fourth quarter 2008 are forecast to drop 1 percent compared to the same quarter 2007.

18834 ■ "How Hard Could It Be? Adventures In Software Demol'ling" in *Inc.* (December 2007, pp. 99-100)
Pub: Gruner & Jahr USA Publishing
Ed: Joel Spolsky. **Description:** Founder and CEO of Fog Creek Software, a New York City software developer shares insight into his software demo tour used to promote his firm's products.

18835 ■ "HR Tech on the Go" in *Workforce Management* (Vol. 88, November 16, 2009, No. 12, pp. 1)
Pub: Crain Communications, Inc.
Ed: Ed Frauenheim. **Description:** Examination of the necessity of mobile access of human resources software applications that allow managers to recruit, schedule and train employees via their mobile devices; some industry leaders believe that mobile HR applications are vital while others see this new technology as hype.

18836 ■ "iControl Networks Powers Comcast's XFINITY (Reg) Home Security Service" in *Benzinga.com* (June 9, 2011)
Pub: Benzinga.com
Ed: Benzinga Staff. **Description:** Comcast's XFINITY Home Security Service is powered by iControl Networks' OpenHome (TM) software platform. The service provides intrusion and fire protection along with interactive features such as home monitoring, home management, and energy management services with Web and mobile access.

18837 ■ "Image Conscious" in *Canadian Business* (Vol. 81, March 17, 2008, No. 4, pp. 36)
Pub: Rogers Media
Ed: Andrew Wahl. **Description:** Idee Inc. is testing an Internet search engine for images that does not rely on tags but compares its visual data to a database of other images. The company was founded and managed by Leila Boujnane as an off-shoot of their risk-management software firm. Their software has already been used by image companies to track copyrighted images and to find images within their own archives.

18838 ■ "Ingrian and Channel Management International Sign Distribution Agreement" in *Canadian Corporate News* (May 16, 2007)
Pub: Comtex News Network Inc.
Description: Channel Management International (CMI), a Canadian channel management and distribution company, and Ingrian Networks, Inc., the leading provider of data privacy solutions, announced a Canadian distribution agreement to resell Ingrian encryption solutions to the Canadian market.

18839 ■ "Inside Intel's Effectiveness System for Web Marketing" in *Advertising Age* (Vol. 81, January 25, 2010, No. 4, pp. 4)
Pub: Crain's Communications
Ed: Beth Snyder Bulik. **Description:** Overview of Intel's internally developed program called Value Point System in which the company is using in order to evaluate and measure online marketing effectiveness.

18840 ■ "Intel to Buy McAfee Security Business for 768B" in *eWeek* (August 19, 2010)
Pub: Ziff Davis Enterprise
Description: Intel will acquire security giant McAfee for approximately $7.68 billion, whereby McAfee would become a wholly owned subsidiary of Intel and would report to Intel's Software and Services Group.

18841 ■ "iPhone Apps Big Business" in *Austin Business JournalInc.* (Vol. 28, November 14, 2008, No. 35, pp. 1)
Pub: American City Business Journals
Ed: Christopher Calnan. **Description:** Members of the computer software industry in Austin, Texas have benefited from developing applications for Apple Inc.'s iPhone. Pangea Software Inc.'s revenues have grown by developing iPhone applications. Lexcycle LLC, on the other hand, has created an application that enables users to read books on the iPhone.

18842 ■ "iPhone Apps In a Flash" in *Entrepreneur* (Vol. 37, October 2009, No. 10, pp. 38)
Pub: Entrepreneur Media, Inc.
Description: Ansca is developing Corona, a software development kit for the Apple iPhone. The kit reduces development time and allows individuals with knowledge of software to develop iPhone applications.

18843 ■ "Is It Time to Ban Swearing at Work?" in *HR Specialist* (Vol. 8, September 2010, No. 9, pp. 2)
Pub: Capitol Information Group Inc.
Description: Screening software has been developed to identify profanity used in business correspondence.

18844 ■ "iSymmetry's Technological Makeover Or, How a Tech Company Finally Grew Up and Discovered the World Wide Web" in *Inc.* (October 2007)
Pub: Gruner & Jahr USA Publishing
Description: Profile of iSymmetry, an Atlanta, Georgia-based IT recruiting firm, covering the issues the company faces keeping its technology equipment up-to-date. The firm has devised a program that will replace its old server-based software systems with on-demand software delivered via the Internet, known as software-as-a-service. Statistical information included.

18845 ■ "Johnny Royal of Luthier Society Unveils Archimedes 1.0 Trailer" in *Internet Wire* (October 22, 2009)
Pub: Comtex News Network, Inc.
Description: Luthier Society, a social media and viral branding agency, has released the first viral video for the company's ROI weighted-value software platform named Archimedes 1.0; users of the software will be able to determine the depth of their outreach efforts, saturation rate, value of their Internet presence and the geo-spatial location of their audience; this will give a true, monetized value for ROI (Return on Investment) in social media marketing.

18846 ■ "Keeping Up With the Joneses: Outfitting Your Company With Up-To-Date Technology is Vital" in *Black Enterprise* (November 2007)
Pub: Earl G. Graves Publishing Co. Inc.
Ed: Sonya A. Donaldson. **Description:** Small businesses, whether home-based or not, need to keep up with new technological developments including hardware, software, and the Internet.

18847 ■ "Lights, Camera, Action: Tools for Creating Video Blogs" in *Inc.* (Volume 32, December 2010, No. 10, pp. 57)
Pub: Inc. Magazine
Ed: John Brandon. **Description:** A video blog is a good way to spread company news, talk about products, and stand out among traditional company blogs. New editing software can create two- to four-

minute blogs using a webcam and either Windows Live Essentials, Apple iLife 2011, Powerdirector 9 Ultra, or Adobe Visual Communicator 3.

18848 ■ "Make Relationships Count: CRM Software That Works" in *Black Enterprise* (Vol. 38, February 2008, No. 7, pp. 60)
Pub: Earl G. Graves Publishing Co. Inc.
Ed: Fiona Haley. **Description:** Customer relationship management (CRM) software can help any small business keep track of clients. Descriptions of the latest CRM software offered are profiled, including Salesforce.com, Microsoft Dynamics, and Saga Software.

18849 ■ "Media Software and Data Services" in *MarketingMagazine* (Vol. 115, September 27, 2010, No. 13, pp. 78)
Pub: Rogers Publishing Ltd.
Description: Media software and data services information in Canada is presented.

18850 ■ "Meetings Go Virtual" in *HRMagazine* (Vol. 54, January 2009, No. 1, pp. 74)
Pub: Society for Human Resource Management
Ed: Elizabeth Agnvall. **Description:** Microsoft Office Live Meeting conferencing software allows companies to schedule meetings from various company locations, thus saving travel costs.

18851 ■ "Microsoft Clicks Into High Speed" in *Hispanic Business* (Vol. 30, July-August 2008, No. 7-8, pp. 54)
Pub: Hispanic Business, Inc.
Ed: Derek Reveron. **Description:** Microsoft's diversity hiring and vendor diversity program to capture more Hispanic consumer and business-to-business market is described. One of the main goals of these programs is to hire more Hispanic executives and managers who will help the company develop and market products and services that will appeal and benefit Hispanic consumers.

18852 ■ "Microsoft Goes Macrosoft" in *Barron's* (Vol. 89, July 27, 2009, No. 30, pp. 25)
Pub: Dow Jones & Co., Inc.
Ed: Mark Veverka. **Description:** Microsoft reported a weak quarter on the heels of a tech rally which suggests the economy has not turned around. Marc Andreesen describes his new venture-capital fund as focused on "classic tech" and that historical reference places him in the annals of the last millennium.

18853 ■ "Microsoft Releases Office Security Updates" in *Mac World* (Vol. 27, November 2010, No. 11, pp. 66)
Pub: Mac Publishing
Ed: David Dahlquist. **Description:** Office for Mac and Mac Business Unit are Microsoft's pair of security- and stability-enhancing updates for Office 2008 and Office 2004. The software will improve the stability and compatibility and fixes vulnerabilities that would allow attackers to overwrite Mac's memory with malicious code.

18854 ■ "Mimosa Systems Gains 150,000 New NearPoint Users" in *Information Today* (Vol. 26, February 2009, No. 2, pp. 31)
Pub: Information Today, Inc.
Description: Mimosa System's NearPoint archive solution features email and file archiving, e-discovery, archive virtualization, and disaster recovery capabilities.

18855 ■ "More Leading Retailers Using Omniture Conversion Solutions to Boost Sales and Ecommerce Performance" in *Internet Wire* (Sept. 22,2009)
Pub: Comtex News Network, Inc.
Description: Many retailers are utilizing Omniture conversion solutions to improve the performance of their ecommerce businesses; recent enhancements to Omniture Merchandising and Omniture Recommendations help clients drive increased conversion to their Internet ventures.

18856 ■ "My Favorite Tool for Organizing Data" in *Inc.* (Vol. 33, November 2011, No. 9, pp. 46)
Pub: Inc. Magazine
Ed: Abram Brown. **Description:** Intelligence software firm uses Roambi, a Web-based service that turns spreadsheet data into interactive files for iPhones and iPads.

18857 ■ "New Database Brings Doctors Out of the Dark" in *Business Courier* (Vol. 26, October 23, 2009, No. 26, pp. 1)
Pub: American City Business Journals, Inc.
Ed: James Ritchie. **Description:** A database created by managed care consulting firm Praesentia allows doctors in Cincinnati to compare average reimbursements from health insurance companies to doctors in different areas. Specialist doctors in the city are paid an average of $172.25 for every office consultation.

18858 ■ "New IPhone Also Brings New Way of Mobile Marketing" in *Advertising Age* (Vol. 79, June 16, 2008, No. 24, pp. 23)
Pub: Crain Communications, Inc.
Ed: Abbey Klaassen. **Description:** Currently there are two kinds of applications for the iPhone and other mobile devices: native applications that allow for richer experiences and take advantage of features that are built into a phone and web applications, those that allow access to the web through specific platforms. Marketers are interested in creating useful experiences for customers and opening up the platforms which will allow them to do this.

18859 ■ "New Sprint Phone Whets Appetite for Applications" in *The Business Journal-Serving Metropolitan Kansas City* (Vol. 26, July 25, 2008)
Pub: American City Business Journals, Inc.
Ed: Suzanna Stagemeyer. **Description:** Firms supporting the applications of the new Samsung Instinct, which was introduced by Sprint Nextel Corp. in June 2008, have reported usage rates increase for their products. Handmark, whose mobile services Pocket Express comes loaded with Instinct, has redirected employees to meet the rising demand for the services. Other views and information on Instinct, are presented.

18860 ■ "New Wave of Business Security Products Ushers in the Kaspersky Anti-Malware Protection System" in *Internet Wire* (October 26, 2010)
Pub: Comtex
Description: Kaspersky Anti-Malware System provides anti-malware protection that requires minimal in-house resources for small businesses. The system offers a full range of tightly integrated end-to-end protection solutions, ensuring unified protection across an entire network, from endpoint and mobile device protection to file server, mail server, network storage and gateway protection. It provides flexible centralized management, immediate threat visibility and a level of responsiveness not seen in other anti-malware approaches.

18861 ■ "Nonprofit NAIC Acquires Software Developer as For-Profit Arm" in *Crain's Detroit Business* (Vol. 25, June 22, 2009, No. 25, pp. 10)
Pub: Crain Communications Inc. - Detroit
Ed: Sherri Begin Welch. **Description:** Details of National Association of Investors Corporation's acquisition of a Massachusetts investment software developer in order to offer more products to investment clubs and individual investors nationwide.

18862 ■ "Not Your Father's Whiteboard" in *Inc.* (Vol. 33, November 2011, No. 9, pp. 50)
Pub: Inc. Magazine
Ed: Adam Baer. **Description:** Sharp's new interactive whiteboard is really a 70-inch touch screen monitor with software for importing presentations from any Windows 7 computer.

18863 ■ "Nothing Like a Weak Team Or An Unrealistic Schedule To Start a Project Off Right" in *Inc.* (November 2007, pp. 85-87)
Pub: Gruner & Jahr USA Publishing
Ed: Joel Spolsky. **Description:** Five easy ways to fail meeting a project deadline are discussed by the owner of a software development company: start with second-rate team of developers, set weekly milestones, negotiate a deadline, divide tasks equitably, and work until midnight.

18864 ■ "OCE Boosts JetStream Productivity" in *American Printer* (Vol. 128, August 1, 2011, No. 8)
Pub: Penton Media Inc.
Description: New Oce JetStream 1400 and 3000 digital full-color inkjet presses are profiled. The new models promise higher speed to grow print volume.

18865 ■ "Oce Business Services: Discovery Made Easy" in *Information Today* (Vol. 26, February 2009, No. 2, pp. 31)
Pub: Information Today, Inc.
Ed: Barbara Brynko. **Description:** Oce Business Services provides document process management and electronic discovery through its CaseData repertoire of legal management solutions.

18866 ■ "Off the RIM" in *Canadian Business* (Vol. 80, January 15, 2007, No. 2, pp. 7)
Pub: Rogers Media
Ed: John Gray. **Description:** The reasons for the rise and fall in stock prices of the software company, Research In Motion Ltd., from September 2006 to January 2007, are analyzed.

18867 ■ "Office Retooled" in *Canadian Business* (Vol. 80, March 26, 2007, No. 7, pp. 67)
Pub: Rogers Media
Ed: Andrew Wahl. **Description:** The merits and demerits of using new Google Apps Premier Edition are presented.

18868 ■ "Office Tech: A Pretty Little Vista" in *Canadian Business* (Vol. 80, January 29, 2007, No. 3, pp. 61)
Pub: Rogers Media
Ed: Andrew Wahl. **Description:** The features of the new version of Microsoft Windows Vista OS and Microsoft Office 2007 are described.

18869 ■ "Omniture's Next Version of SearchCenter Delivers Landing Page Optimization" in *Internet Wire* (September 24, 2009)
Pub: Comtex News Network, Inc.
Description: Omniture, Inc., a leading provider of online business optimization software, has announced a new release of Omniture SearchCenter; this latest version will allow search engine marketers to test landing pages across campaigns and ad groups.

18870 ■ "On Beyond Powerpoint: Presentations Get a Wake-Up Call" in *Inc.* (November 2007, pp. 58-59)
Pub: Gruner & Jahr USA Publishing
Ed: Michael Fitzgerald. **Description:** New software that allows business presentations to be shared online are profiled, including ProfCast, audio podcasts for sales, marketing, and training; SmartDraw2008, software that creates professional graphics; Dimdim, an open-Web conferencing tool; Empressr, a hosted Web service for creating, managing, and sharing multimedia presentations; Zentation, a free tool that allows users to watch slides and a videos of presenter; Spresent, a Web-based presentation tool for remote offices or conference calls.

18871 ■ *Open Source Solutions for Small Business Problems*
Pub: Charles River Media
Ed: John Locke. **Released:** May 2004. **Price:** $35. 95. **Description:** Open source software provides solutions to many small business problems such as tracking electronic documents, scheduling, accounting functions, managing contact lists, and reducing spam.

18872 ■ "Oracle and Tauri Group Honored by Homeland Security and Defense Business Council" in *Wireless News* (December 15, 2009)
Pub: Close-Up Media
Description: Selected as members of the year by the Homeland Security and Defense Business Council were Oracle, a software company that has

provided thought leadership and strategic insights as well as The Tauri Group, an analytical consultancy, that has demonstrated a unique understanding of the role of small business and its vital contribution to the success of the country's security.

18873 ■ "Our Gadget of the Week" in *Barron's* (Vol. 88, March 24, 2008, No. 12, pp. 47)
Pub: Dow Jones & Company, Inc.
Ed: Tiernan Ray. **Description:** Review of the $299 Apple Time Capsule, which is a 500-megabyte hard disk drive and a Wi-Fi router, rolled into one device. The device allows users to create backup files without the need for sophisticated file management software.

18874 ■ "Owner of IT Firm MK2 Tying Future to Software" in *Crain's Cleveland Business* (Vol. 30, June 15, 2009, No. 23, pp. 3)
Pub: Crain Communications, Inc.
Ed: Chuck Soder. **Description:** Donald Kasper, owner of MK2 Technologies LLC of Cleveland, Ohio discusses his recent acquisition of a portion of ProSource Solution. The move will help expand the two companies' custom software development plans.

18875 ■ "Paging Dr. Phil" in *Canadian Business* (Vol. 79, September 25, 2006, No. 19, pp. 21)
Pub: Rogers Media
Ed: John Gray. **Description:** Increasing corporate crimes in software industry is discussed by focusing on recent case of Hewlett and Packard.

18876 ■ "Panda Security for Business 4.05" in *SC Magazine* (Vol. 21, July 2010, No. 7, pp. 50)
Pub: Haymarket Media Inc.
Description: Profile of Panda Security for Business, software offering endpoint security protection for computer desktops and servers is presented.

18877 ■ "The Paper Shredder" in *Business Courier* (Vol. 26, September 11, 2009, No. 20, pp. 1)
Pub: American City Business Journals, Inc.
Ed: Dan Monk. **Description:** DotLoop Company, owned by entrepreneur Austin Allison, is developing the DotLoop software, which eliminates paperwork in the processing of real estate contracts. The software allows realtors to take control of the negotiation process and is adaptable to the rules of different US states.

18878 ■ "Paperless Bookkeeping Program" in *Fleet Owner Online* (February 15, 2011)
Pub: Penton Business Media Inc.
Description: TruckTax launched its new paperless bookkeeping system to help manage bookkeeping tasks, accounting and business tax information and filings for truckers.

18879 ■ "PC Connection Acquires Cloud Software Provider" in *New Hampshire Business Review* (Vol. 33, March 25, 2011, No. 6, pp. 8)
Pub: Business Publications Inc.
Description: Merrimack-based PC Connection Inc. acquired ValCom Technology, a provider of cloud-based IT service management software. Details of the deal are included.

18880 ■ "PC Running Slowly? How to Rev Up Your Machine" in *Inc.* (Vol. 33, November 2011, No. 9, pp. 46)
Pub: Inc. Magazine
Ed: John Brandon. **Description:** Software that keeps PCs tuned up and running smoothing are profiled: AUSLO6ICS BOOSTSPEED 5, $50; Tuneup Utilities 2011, $40; Slimware Slimcleaner 1.9, free; and IOBIT Advanced Systemcare Pro 4, $20 a year.

18881 ■ "PopCap Games Achieves Significant Increase in Return on Ad Spend With Omniture SearchCenter" in *Internet Wire* (September 15, 2009)
Pub: Comtex News Network, Inc.
Description: PopCap Games, a leading computer games provider, is using Omniture SearchCenter together with Omniture SiteCatalyst to increase revenue from its search engine marketing campaign. Omniture, Inc. is a leading provider of Internet business optimization software.

18882 ■ "The Power of Negative Thinking" in *Inc.* (Volume 32, December 2010, No. 10, pp. 43)
Pub: Inc. Magazine
Ed: Jason Fried. **Description:** A Website is software and most businesses have and need a good Website to generate business. Understanding for building a powerful Website is presented.

18883 ■ "Power Ranger" in *Inc.* (November 2007, pp. 131)
Pub: Gruner & Jahr USA Publishing
Ed: Nitasha Tiku. **Description:** Surveyor software is designed to power down computers when not in use, in order to save energy.

18884 ■ *Practical Tech for Your Business*
Pub: Kiplinger Books and Tapes
Ed: Michael J. Martinez. **Released:** 2002. **Description:** Advice is offered to help small business owners choose the right technology for their company. The guide tells how to get started, network via the Internet, create an office network, use database software, and conduct business using mobile technology.

18885 ■ "Precision Crop Control with Valley Irrigation/CropMetrics Partnership" in *Farm Industry News* (January 6, 2011)
Pub: Penton Business Media Inc.
Description: Irrigation systems have become a precision farming tool since partnering with agronomic software systems to apply products across the field by prescription. Valley Irrigation and CropMetrics have partnered in order to variably control water, fertilizer and other crop management products through a center pivot irrigation system.

18886 ■ "Press Release: Trimble Introduces CFX-750 Display" in *Farm Industry News* (January 4, 2011)
Pub: Penton Business Media Inc.
Description: Trimble is offering a touch screen display called the CFX-750. The new 8-inch full-color display allows farmers to choose the specific guidance, steering and precision agriculture capabilities that best fit their farm's particular needs. The display can be upgraded as business needs change, including the addition of GLONASS capabilities, or the addition of section and rate control for crop inputs such as seed, chemicals and fertilizer.

18887 ■ "Programs Provide Education and Training" in *Contractor* (Vol. 56, September 2009, No. 9, pp. 56)
Pub: Penton Media, Inc.
Ed: William Feldman; Patti Feldman. **Description:** Opportunity Interactive's Showroom v2 software provides uses computer graphics to provide education and training on HVAC equipment and systems. It can draw heat pump balance points for a specific home. Meanwhile, Simutech's HVAC Training Simulators provide trainees with 'hands-on' HVACR training.

18888 ■ "Protection One Introduces Home and Business Security iPhone App" in *Wireless News* (November 13, 2009)
Pub: Close-Up Media
Description: Protection One, Inc., a provider of security systems to business and residential customers, has developed an application that allows users to access their security panels and receive real-time updates from their iPhone or iPod touch devices.

18889 ■ "Providers Ride First Wave of eHealth Dollars" in *Boston Business Journal* (Vol. 31, June 10, 2011, No. 20, pp. 1)
Pub: Boston Business Journal
Ed: Julie M. Donnelly. **Description:** Health care providers in Massachusetts implementing electronic medical records technology started receiving federal stimulus funds. Beth Israel Deaconess Medical Center was the first hospital to qualify for the funds.

18890 ■ *Publishers, Distributors, and Wholesalers of the United States*
Pub: R.R. Bowker L.L.C.
Released: Annual, latest edition 2010. **Price:** $500, individuals in 2 volumes; hard cover. **Covers:** Over 196,066 publishers, distributors, and wholesalers; includes associations, museums, software producers and manufacturers, and others not included in 'Books in Print'. **Entries Include:** Publisher name, editorial and ordering addresses, e-mail, websites, phone, Standard Address Numbers (SANs), International Standard Book Number prefix. **Arrangement:** Alphabetical; distributors and wholesalers are listed separately. **Indexes:** ISBN prefix, abbreviation, type of business, imprint name, geographical, inactive and out of business company name, toll-free phone and fax, wholesaler and distributor.

18891 ■ "Publishing Technology Introduces IngentaConnect Mobile" in *Information Today* (Vol. 26, February 2009, No. 2, pp. 33)
Pub: Information Today, Inc.
Description: College undergraduates will find Publishing Technology's newest publisher product, IngentaConnect Mobile helpful. The product allows users to read articles and abstracts on mobile devices. According to a recent study, 73 percent of young adults with wireless hand-held devices use them to access non-voice data on any given day.

18892 ■ "Putting the App in Apple" in *Inc.* (Vol. 30, November 2008, No. 11, pp.)
Pub: Mansueto Ventures LLC
Ed: Nitasha Tiku. **Description:** Aftermarket companies are scrambling to develop games and widgets for Apple's iPhone. Apple launched a kit for developers interested in creating iPhone-specific software along with the App Store, and an iTunes spinoff. Profiles of various software programs that may be used on the iPhone are given.

18893 ■ *QuickBooks All-in-One Desk Reference for Dummies*
Pub: John Wiley & Sons, Incorporated
Ed: Stephen L. Nelson. **Released:** January 2007. **Price:** $29.99 (US), $42.99 (Canadian). **Description:** Compilation of nine self-contained minibooks to get the most from QuickBooks accounting software. Companion Web site with sample business plan workbook and downloadable profit-volume cost analysis workbook included.

18894 ■ *QuickBooks Simple Start for Dummies*
Pub: John Wiley & Sons, Incorporated
Ed: Stephen L. Nelson. **Released:** October 2004. **Price:** $21.99. **Description:** Profile of Intuits new accounting software geared to micro businesses. Advice is offered on daily, monthly, and yearly accounting activities covering records, sales tax, and reports.

18895 ■ *QuickBooks X on Demand*
Pub: Que
Ed: Gail Perry. **Released:** December 2006. **Price:** $34.99. **Description:** Step-by-step training for using various small business financial software programs; includes illustrated, full color explanations.

18896 ■ *QuickBooks X for Dummies*
Pub: John Wiley & Sons, Incorporated
Ed: Stephen L. Nelson. **Released:** November 2006. **Price:** $21.99. **Description:** Key features of QuickBooks software for small business are introduced. Invoicing and credit memos, recoding sales receipts, accounting, budgeting, taxes, payroll, financial reports, job estimating, billing, tracking, data backup, are among the features.

18897 ■ "Quickoffice's MobileFiles Pro App Enables Excel Editing On-the-Go" in *Information Today* (Vol. 26, February 2009, No. 2, pp. 31)
Pub: Information Today, Inc.
Description: Quickoffice Inc. introduced MobileFiles Pro, which features editable Microsoft Office functionality for the iPone and iPod touch. The application allows users to edit and save Microsoft Excel files in .xls format, transfer files to and from PC and Mac desktops via Wi-Fi, and access and synchronize with Apple MobileMe accounts.

18898 ■ "Remote Control: Working From Wherever" in *Inc.* (February 2008, pp. 46-47)
Pub: Gruner & Jahr USA Publishing

Ed: Ryan Underwood. **Description:** New technology allows workers to perform tasks from anywhere via the Internet. Profiles of products to help connect to your office from afar include, LogMein Pro, a Web-based service that allowsaccess to a computer from anywhere; Xdrive, an online service that allows users to store and swap files; Basecamp, a Web-based tools that works like a secure version of MySpace; MojoPac Freedom, is software that allows users to copy their computer's desktop to a removable hard drive and plug into any PC; WatchGuard Firebox X Core e-Series UTM Bundle, hardware that blocks hackers and viruses while allowing employees to work remotely; TightVNC, a free open-source software that lets you control another computer via the Internet.

18899 ■ "RES Stakes Its Claim in Area" in *Philadelphia Business Journal* (Vol. 28, January 29, 2010, No. 50, pp. 1)
Pub: American City Business Journals

Ed: Peter Key. **Description:** RES Software Company Inc. of Amsterdam, Netherlands appointed Jim Kirby as president for the Americas and Klaus Besier as chairman in an effort to boost the firm's presence in the US. Brief career profiles of Kirby and Besier are included. RES develops software that allows management of information flow between an organization and its employees regardless of location.

18900 ■ "Route Optimization Impacts the Bottom Line" in *Contractor* (Vol. 56, November 2009, No. 11, pp. 48)
Pub: Penton Media, Inc.

Ed: Dave Beaudry. **Description:** Plumbing and HVAC businesses can save a significant amount of money from route optimization. The process begins with gathering information on a fleet and a routing software tool can determine the effectiveness of current route configurations and identify preferable route plans.

18901 ■ *Salesforce.com Secrets of Success: Best Practices for Growth and Profitability*
Pub: Prentice Hall Business Publishing

Ed: David Taber. **Released:** May 15, 2009. **Price:** $34.99. **Description:** Guide for using Salesforce.com; it provides insight into navigating through user groups, management, sales, marketing and IT departments in order to achieve the best results.

18902 ■ "Save the Date" in *Barron's* (Vol. 90, September 13, 2010, No. 37, pp. 35)
Pub: Barron's Editorial & Corporate Headquarters

Ed: Mark Veverka. **Description:** Mark Hurd is the new Co-President of Oracle after being forced out at Hewlett-Packard where he faced a harassment complaint. HP fired Hurd due to expense account malfeasance. Hurd is also set to speak at an Oracle trade show in San Francisco on September 20, 2010.

18903 ■ "Scitable Puts Nature Education on the Map" in *Information Today* (Vol. 26, February 2009, No. 2, pp. 29)
Pub: Information Today, Inc.

Description: Nature Education, a division of the Nature Publishing Group, released its first product, Scitable, a free online resource for undergraduate biology students and educators. The service includes over 180 overviews of key genetics concepts as well as social networking features, including groups and functionality, that lets students work with classmates and others. Teachers can use the service to set up public or private groups for students.

18904 ■ "Second Cup?" in *Canadian Business* (Vol. 81, July 21, 2008, No. 11, pp. 50)
Pub: Rogers Media Ltd.

Ed: Calvin Leung. **Description:** Profile of James Gosling who is credited as the inventor of the Java programming language; however, the 53-year-old software developer feels ambivalent for being credited as inventor since many people contributed to the language. Netscape and Sun Microsystems incorporation of the programming language into Java is presented.

18905 ■ "Sense of Discovery" in *Business Journal Portland* (Vol. 27, November 19, 2010, No. 38, pp. 1)
Pub: Portland Business Journal

Ed: Erik Siemers. **Description:** Tigard, Oregon-based Exterro Inc. CEO Bobby Balachandran announced plans to go public without the help of an institutional investor. Balachandran believes Exterro could grow to a $100 million legal compliance software company in the span of three years. Insights on Exterro's growth as market leader in the $1 billion legal governance software market are also given.

18906 ■ "Serials Solutions Launches 360 Resource Manager Consortium Edition" in *Information Today* (Vol. 26, February 2009, No. 2, pp. 32)
Pub: Information Today, Inc.

Description: Serials Solutions new Serials Solutions 360 Resource Manager Consortium Edition helps consortia, groups and member libraries with their e-resource management services. The products allows users to consolidate e-resource metadata and acquisition information into one place, which enables groups to manage holdings, subscriptions, licensing, contacts, and cost information and to streamline delivery of information to members.

18907 ■ "A Side Project Threatens To Get Totally Out of Control and I Think, 'How Fun'" in *Inc.* (October 2007, pp. 81-82)
Pub: Gruner & Jahr USA Publishing

Ed: Joel Spolsky. **Description:** Profile of Fog Creek Software, makers of project-management software for other software developers. Fog Creek's owner discusses his idea to create a new product for his firm.

18908 ■ "Skype on Steroids" in *Inc.* (Vol. 31, January-February 2009, No. 1, pp. 46)
Pub: Mansueto Ventures LLC

Ed: Nitasha Tiku. **Description:** Free software called VoxOx allows users to make calls over the Internet and connects all email and IM accounts.

18909 ■ "Slow but Steady into the Future" in *Barron's* (Vol. 88, July 7, 2008, No. 27, pp. M)
Pub: Dow Jones & Co., Inc.

Ed: Mark Veverka. **Description:** Investors are advised to maintain their watch on the shares of business software company NetSuite. The company's chief executive officer, Zach Nelson, claims that the company has a 10-year lead on its competitors with the development of software-as-a service.

18910 ■ "Small is Bountiful for Intuit" in *Barron's* (Vol. 90, September 13, 2010, No. 37, pp. 22)
Pub: Barron's Editorial & Corporate Headquarters

Ed: Mark Veverka. **Description:** Finance software maker Intuit wants to tap the underserved small business market. One analyst sees Intuit's shares rising 25 percent to 55 percent in the next 12 months from September 2010.

18911 ■ "A Software Company's Whimsical Widgets Were an Instant Hit. But Its Core Product Was Getting Overshadowed" in *Inc.* (Jan. 2008)
Pub: Gruner & Jahr USA Publishing

Ed: Alex Salkever. **Description:** A widget designed as a marketing tool tuned into a hit on Facebook. Should ChipIn shift its focus?

18912 ■ *The Software Encyclopedia*
Pub: R.R. Bowker L.L.C.
Contact: Charlie Friscia, Director
E-mail: charlie.friscia@bowker.com

Released: Annual, latest edition May, 2008. **Price:** $460, individuals for set of 2 volumes; soft cover. **Description:** Contains listings of over 44,600 software programs from 4,646 publishers and distributors. **Arrangement:** Two alphabetical sections for software, one by title, the other by system/application; also, one alphabetical section for publishers. **Indexes:** Title, system/application.

18913 ■ "Software Solutions Increase Productivity" in *Contractor* (Vol. 57, February 2010, No. 2, pp. 26)
Pub: Penton Media, Inc.

Ed: William Feldman; Patti Feldman. **Description:** Singletouch is a real-time data capture solution for mechanical and other contractors that work in jobs that require materials and workload tracking. Contractors get information on extreme weather and sudden changes in the cost of materials. The OptimumHVAC optimization software by Optimum Energy is designed to optimize energy savings in commercial buildings.

18914 ■ "Software Solutions from Trane and Carrier" in *Contractor* (Vol. 56, July 2009, No. 7, pp. 38)
Pub: Penton Media, Inc.

Ed: William Feldman; Patti Feldman. **Description:** Trane Trace 700 software helps HVAC contractors optimize the design of a building's HVAC system and aids in the evaluation of various key energy-saving concepts, including daylighting, high-performance glazing, and other optimization strategies. Carrier's E20-II family of software programs lets contractors increase the accuracy of an HVAC system estimate.

18915 ■ "Software's Last Hurrah" in *Canadian Business* (Vol. 81, December 24, 2007, No. 1, pp. 27)
Pub: Rogers Media

Ed: Andrew Wahl. **Description:** Canada's software industry could be facing a challenge with IBM's acquisition of Cognos, which was the country's last major independent business intelligence company and was also IBM's largest acquisition ever. Next in line to Cognos in terms of prominence is Open Text Corporation, which could also be a possible candidate for acquisition, as analysts predict.

18916 ■ "Startup on Cusp of Trend" in *Austin Business JournalInc.* (Vol. 29, January 8, 2010, No. 44, pp. 1)
Pub: American City Business Journals

Ed: Christopher Calnan. **Description:** Austin-based Socialware Inc. introduced a new business called social middleware, which is a software that is layered between the company network and social networking Website used by workers. The software was designed to give employers a measure of control over content while allowing workers to continue using online social networks.

18917 ■ "The State of the Art in End-User Software Engineering" in *ACM Computing Surveys* (Vol. 43, Fall 2011, No. 3, pp. 21)
Pub: Association for Computing Machinery

Description: Most programs today are not written by professional software developers but by people with expertise in other domains working towards goals for which they need computational support. A discussion of empirical research about end-user software engineering activities and the technologies designed to support them is presented. Several crosscutting issues in the design of EUSE tools, including the roles of risk, reward, and domain complexity, and self-efficacy in the design of EUSE tools and the potential of educating users about software engineering principles are also examined.

18918 ■ "The Story Of Diane Greene" in *Barron's* (Vol. 88, July 14, 2008, No. 28, pp. 31)
Pub: Dow Jones & Co., Inc.

Ed: Mark Veverka. **Description:** Discusses the ousting of Diane Greene as a chief executive of VMWare, a developer of virtualization software, after the firm went public; in this case Greene, a brilliant engineer, should not be negatively impacted by the decision because it is common for companies to bring in new executive leadership that is more operations oriented after the company goes public.

18919 ■ "A Survey of Combinatorial Testing" in *ACM Computing Surveys* (Vol. 43, Summer 2011, No. 2, pp. 11)
Pub: Association for Computing Machinery

Ed: Changhai Nie, Hareton Leung. **Description:** Combinatorial Testing (CT) can detect failures triggered by interactions of parameters in the Software Under Test (SUT) with a covering array test suite generated by some sampling mechanisms. Basic concepts and notations of CT are covered.

18920 ■ "A Survey of Comparison-Based System-Level Diagnosis" in *ACM Computing Surveys* (Vol. 43, Fall 2011, No. 3, pp. 22)
Pub: Association for Computing Machinery
Ed: Elias P. Duarte Jr., Roverli P. Ziwich, Luiz C.P. Albini. **Description:** The growing complexity and dependability requirements of hardware, software, and networks demand efficient techniques for discovering disruptive behavior in those systems. Comparison-based diagnosis is a realistic approach to detect faulty units based on the outputs of tasks executed by system units. This survey integrates the vast amount of research efforts that have been produced in this field.

18921 ■ "Taking the Steps Into the Clouds" in *New Hampshire Business Review* (Vol. 33, March 25, 2011, No. 6, pp. 19)
Pub: Business Publications Inc.
Ed: Tim Wessels. **Description:** Cloud services include Internet and Web security, spam filtering, message archiving, work group collaboration, IT asset management, help desk and disaster recovery backup.

18922 ■ "Tech Deal Couples Homegrown Firms" in *The Business Journal-Serving Greater Tampa Bay* (Vol. 28, July 4, 2008, No. 28, pp. 1)
Pub: American City Business Journals, Inc.
Ed: Michael Hinman. **Description:** Tampa Bay, Florida-based Administrative Partners Inc. was acquired by Tribridge Inc. resulting in the strengthening of the delivery of Microsoft products to clients. Other details of the merger of the management consulting services companies are presented.

18923 ■ "Technology to the Rescue" in *Contractor* (Vol. 56, July 2009, No. 7, pp. 22)
Pub: Penton Media, Inc.
Ed: Candace Ruolo. **Description:** Features of several products that will make the job of a mechanical contractor easier are discussed. These include Ridgid's line of drain and sewer inspection cameras and monitors, Motion Computing's Motion F5 tablet rugged tablet PC, the JobClock from Exaktime, and the TeleNav Track tool for mobile workforce management.

18924 ■ "Technology: What Seems To Be the Problem? Self Service Gets a Tune-Up" in *Inc.* (February 2008, pp. 43-44)
Pub: Gruner & Jahr USA Publishing
Ed: Darren Dahl. **Description:** Self-service software can save companies money when responding to customer service phone calls, text or email messages. More companies are relying on alternatives such as automated Web-based self-service systems.

18925 ■ "Ted Stahl: Executive Chairman" in *Inside Business* (Vol. 13, September-October 2011, No. 5, pp. NC6)
Pub: Great Lakes Publishing Company
Ed: Miranda S. Miller. **Description:** Profile of Ted Stahl, who started working in his family's business when he was ten years old is presented. The firm makes dies for numbers and letters used on team uniforms. Another of the family firms manufactures stock and custom heat-printing products, equipment and supplies. It also educates customers on ways to decorate garments with heat printing products and offers graphics and software for customers to create their own artwork.

18926 ■ "Thinking Strategically About Technology" in *Franchising World* (Vol. 42, August 2010, No. 8, pp. 9)
Pub: International Franchise Association
Ed: Bruce Franson. **Description:** Nearly 25 percent of companies waste money from their technology budget. Most of the budget is spent on non-strategic software. Ways to spend money on technology for any franchise are examined.

18927 ■ "A Timely Boon for Small Investors" in *Barron's* (Vol. 88, March 24, 2008, No. 12, pp. 48)
Pub: Dow Jones & Company, Inc.
Ed: Theresa W. Carey. **Description:** Nasdaq Data Store's new program called Market Replay allows investors to accurately track stock price movements. The replay can be as long as a day of market time and allows investors to determine whether they executed stock trades at the best possible price.

18928 ■ "Touching the Future" in *Canadian Business* (Vol. 81, July 21, 2008, No. 11, pp. 41)
Pub: Rogers Media Ltd.
Ed: Matt McClearn. **Description:** Microsoft Corp. has launched a multi-touch product which is both a software and hardware technology called Microsoft Surface. The innovative product allows people to use it at the same time, however touch-based computers are reported to be around $100,000. Other features and benefits of the product are presented.

18929 ■ "Trust But Verify: FMLA Software Isn't Foolproof, So Apply a Human Touch" in *HR Specialist* (Vol. 8, September 2010, No. 9, pp. 3)
Pub: Capitol Information Group Inc.
Description: Employers are using software to track FMLA information, however, it is important for employers to review reasons for eligibility requirements, particularly when an employee is reportedly overstepping the bounds within leave regulations due to software error.

18930 ■ "Two Field Service Management Solutions" in *Contractor* (Vol. 56, November 2009, No. 11, pp. 37)
Pub: Penton Media, Inc.
Ed: William Feldman; Patti Feldman. **Description:** Bella Solutions Field Service Software v. 4.2 is a web based solution for HVAC service contractors that enables scheduling of emergency, one-time, multi-visit or periodically recurring jobs with drag and drop appointments. VaZing is another web based solution that costs $99 per month for contractors. It can handle line-item discounting and invoices aside from scheduling.

18931 ■ "Two Ways to Find New Customers" in *Inc.* (Vol. 31, January-February 2009, No. 1, pp. 41)
Pub: Mansueto Ventures LLC
Description: Latest software programs that help sales staff connect to new leads are profiled. Salesconx provides online leads while Demandbase reports users on a particular Website.

18932 ■ "Unbound ID Raises $2 Million" in *Austin Business JournalInc.* (Vol. 28, December 12, 2008, No. 39, pp. 1)
Pub: American City Business Journals
Ed: Christopher Calnan. **Description:** Austin, Texas-based Unbound ID Corporation has secured $2 million in funding from venture capital firm Silverton Partners. The company has developed identity management software for network directories. The market for identity management technology is expected to grow to more than $12.3 billion by 2014.

18933 ■ "Unbreakable" in *Canadian Business* (Vol. 79, October 9, 2006, No. 20, pp. 111)
Pub: Rogers Media
Ed: Robert Hercz. **Description:** The features and functions of Neutrino, an embedded operating system developed by QNX Software Systems are discussed.

18934 ■ "uTest Discusses the Evolution of Crowdsourcing Models at CrowdConf 2010" in *Internet Wire* (October 1, 2010)
Pub: Comtex
Description: World's largest software testing marketplace, uTest, announces its first conference dedicated to the emerging field of crowdsourcing along with the future of distributed work. A panel of experts will discuss common misconceptions about crowdsourcing using real-world examples.

18935 ■ "Video Surveillance Enters Digital Era, Makes Giant Strides" in *Arkansas Business* (Vol. 26, September 28, 2009, No. 39, pp. 1)
Pub: Journal Publishing Inc.
Ed: Jamie Walden. **Description:** Arkansas business owners are finding that the newest technology in video surveillance is leading to swift apprehension of thieves due to the high-quality digital imagery now being captured on surveillance equipment. Motion detection software for these systems is enhancing the capabilities of these systems and providing opportunities for businesses that would normally have problems integrating these systems.

18936 ■ "A Virtual Jog Mode for CAM" in *Modern Machine Shop* (Vol. 84, November 2011, No. 6, pp. 22)
Pub: Gardner Publications
Ed: Edwin Gasparraj. **Description:** In many cases, CAM programming required a specific, user-defined path. Siemens PLMs Generic Motion Controller is an alternative that defines the tool path within CAM. The program is a virtual 'teach' mode that enables the user to capture cutter locations by jogging machines axes within CAM.

18937 ■ "The Virtual Office" in *Canadian Business* (Vol. 80, April 9, 2007, No. 8, pp. 64)
Pub: Rogers Media
Ed: Andrew Wahl. **Description:** The business operation of Eloqua which runs all its IT systems using its own online software is discussed.

18938 ■ "What Has Sergey Wrought?" in *Barron's* (Vol. 89, July 13, 2009, No. 28, pp. 8)
Pub: Dow Jones & Co., Inc.
Ed: Alan Abelson. **Description:** Sergey Aleynikov is a computer expert that once worked for Goldman Sachs but he was arrested after he left the company and charged with theft for bringing with him the code for the company's proprietary software for high-frequency trading. The stock market has been down for four straight weeks as of July 13, 2009 which reflects the reality of how the economy is still struggling.

18939 ■ "Will the Force Be With Salesforce?" in *Barron's* (Vol. 88, March 24, 2008, No. 12, pp. 20)
Pub: Dow Jones & Company, Inc.
Ed: Mark Veverka. **Description:** Shares of Salesforce.com are likely to drop from the $44.83-a-share level in the face of a deteriorating economy and financial sector and thus lower demand for business software. The company is unlikely to deliver on its ambitious earnings forecasts for 2008 especially with strengthening competition from Oracle.

18940 ■ "Women Losing IT Ground" in *Marketing to Women* (Vol. 21, February 2008, No. 2, pp. 6)
Pub: EPM Communications, Inc.
Description: According to a study conducted by The National Center for Women & Information Technology, women in technology are losing ground. Statistical data included.

18941 ■ "Yammer Gets Serious" in *Inc.* (Volume 32, December 2010, No. 10, pp. 58)
Pub: Inc. Magazine
Ed: Eric Markowitz. **Description:** Yammer, an internal social network for companies, allows coworkers to share ideas and documents in real-time. Details of this service are included.

18942 ■ "Yes, No, and Somewhat Likely: Survey the World with Web Polls" in *Inc.* (October 2007, pp. 58-59)
Pub: Gruner & Jahr USA Publishing
Ed: Don Steinberg. **Description:** Online tools for surveying customers, employees and the general public include Zoomergan zPro and Zoomerang Sample, software designed to send surveys and allows viewing results; SurveyMonkey software creates, administers and allows viewing online surveys and results; Vizu software places a one-question poll

on a particular Website; and Vovici EFM Feedback, a subscription service providing ongoing surveys to customers or employees.

18943 ■ "Zeon Solutions Teams with Endeca for SaaS Version of Endeca InFront" in *Entertainment Close-Up* (October 25, 2011)
Pub: Close-Up Media
Description: Zeon Solutions, an enterprise e-commerce and Website development firm announced a special licensing partnership with Endecca Technologies. Endeca is an information management software company that provides small and mid-size retailers with high-performance Customer Experience Management technology.

STATISTICAL SOURCES

18944 ■ *RMA Annual Statement Studies*
Pub: Robert Morris Associates (RMA)
Released: Annual. **Price:** $175.00 2006-07 edition, $105.00. **Description:** Contains composite balance sheets and income statements for more than 360 industries, including the accounting, auditing, and bookkeeping industries. Also contains five years of comparative historical data for discerning trends. Includes 16 commonly used ratios, computed for most of the size groupings for nearly every industry.

18945 ■ *Standard & Poor's Industry Surveys*
Pub: Standard & Poor's Corp.
Released: Annual. **Price:** $3633.00. **Description:** Two-volume book that examines the prospects for specific industries, including trucking. Also provides analyses of trends and problems, statistical tables and charts, and comparative company analyses.

TRADE PERIODICALS

18946 ■ *Cutter IT Journal*
Pub: Cutter Information Corp.
Ed: Ed Yourdon, Editor. **Released:** Monthly. **Price:** Free. **Description:** Provides IT managers with practical and objective views on the latest technology and management trends.

18947 ■ *Datamation*
Pub: Reed Business Information
Contact: Renee Munshi, Sen. Ed.
Released: Semimonthly. **Description:** Magazine on computers and information processing.

18948 ■ *DCLNews*
Pub: Data Conversion Laboratory
Contact: Mark Gross
Ed: Released: Monthly. **Price:** Included in membership;. **Description:** E-journal providing you insider information on XML and SGML, along with the latest technology and e-publishing news.

18949 ■ *Dr. Dobb's Journal*
Pub: United Business Media
Released: Monthly. **Price:** $25; $99.95 CD-ROM library. **Description:** Magazine covering computer programming.

18950 ■ *ENT*
Pub: 1105 Media Inc.
Contact: Scott Bekker, Editor-in-Chief
E-mail: sbekker@entmag.com
Released: 18/yr. **Price:** $54.95 Canada and Mexico; $64.95 other countries. **Description:** Publication providing news and analysis for Windows NT enterprise users.

18951 ■ *Maximum PC*
Pub: Future Network USA
Contact: Michael Brown, Review Ed.
E-mail: michael@maximumpc.com
Released: Monthly. **Price:** $14.95; $24.95 12 CDs; $29.95 other countries; $49.95 other countries two years; $1.95 single issue. **Description:** Consumer magazine covering computing, hardware and software reviews, games and work programs for personal computer users.

18952 ■ *Media Computing*
Pub: Dreamscape Productions
Ed: Sheridan Tatsuno, Editor, statsuno@aol.com. **Released:** Monthly. **Price:** $495, institutions in the U.S. and Canada; $550, institutions elsewhere. **Description:** Supplies analysis of multimedia, internet, intranet, and web computing issues. Recurring features include interviews and reports of meetings.

18953 ■ *Productivity Software*
Pub: Worldwide Videotex
Released: Monthly. **Price:** $150. **Description:** Provides information on computer software.

18954 ■ *Softletter*
Pub: Rick Chapman
Ed: Rick Chapman, Editor, jtarter@softletter.com. **Released:** Semimonthly. **Price:** $399, individuals. **Description:** Analyzes market trends and company strategies in microcomputer software publishing and development. Recurring features include industry statistics and case studies.

18955 ■ *Software*
Pub: John Wiley & Sons Inc.
Ed: Prof. Andy J. Wellings, Editor. **Released:** 12/yr. **Price:** $3,410 other countries print; $4,612 institutions, other countries print; $2,976 institutions, other countries print; $2,353 institutions print. **Description:** Journal for those who design, implement, or maintain computer software.

18956 ■ *Software Process*
Pub: John Wiley & Sons Inc.
Contact: Prof. Darren Dalcher, Editor-in-Chief
E-mail: d.dalcher@mdx.ac.uk
Released: 7/yr. **Price:** $209 print; $363 other countries print; $727 institutions, other countries print; $469 institutions, other countries print; $370 institutions print. **Description:** Journal for those involved in the software development process. Features experience reports, research papers, and critical discussion.

18957 ■ *Software Tech News*
Pub: Data & Analysis Center for Software
Ed: Released: Quarterly. **Price:** Free. **Description:** Disseminates information and news about software technology and engineering, especially as required by the U.S. Department of Defense.

VIDEOCASSETTES/ AUDIOCASSETTES

18958 ■ *How to Keep Score in Baseball*
Tapeworm Video Distributors
25876 The Old Road 141
Stevenson Ranch, CA 91381
Ph:(661)257-4904
Fax:(661)257-4820
Co. E-mail: sales@tapeworm.com
URL: http://www.tapeworm.com
Released: 1995. **Description:** Explains how to use charts and formulas to record statistics and scores. **Availability:** VHS.

TRADE SHOWS AND CONVENTIONS

18959 ■ COMDEX
Ziff-Davis, Inc.
28 E. 28th St.
New York, NY 10016-7930
Ph:(212)503-3500
Co. E-mail: info@ziffdavis.com
URL: http://www.ziffdavis.com
Released: Annual. **Audience:** Volume resellers and value-adders of small computers and related items; only a virtual trade show since 2003. **Principal Exhibits:** Small computer systems, related peripherals, software, accessories, services, and supplies.

18960 ■ Computer Game Developers' Conference
CMP Media LLC (San Mateo, California)
2800 Campus Dr.
San Mateo, CA 94403
Ph:(650)513-4300
Co. E-mail: cmp@cmp.com
URL: http://www.cmp.com
Released: Annual. **Principal Exhibits:** Equipment, supplies, and services for developers and producers of computer games.

CONSULTANTS

18961 ■ Century Small Business Solutions
152 N El Camino Real
Encinitas, CA 92024-2849
Ph:(760)633-4725
Contact: John R. Todd, Principle
Scope: Focuses on improving the profitability of growth-oriented small businesses through business planning, controlling expenses, marketing to find new customers and tax planning to minimize taxes. **Seminars:** QuickBooks training and Budgeting for your Small Business.

18962 ■ CheckMark Software Inc.
724 Whalers Way, Bldg. H, Ste. 101
Fort Collins, CO 80525-7578
Ph:(970)225-0522
Free: 800-444-9922
Fax:(970)225-0611
Co. E-mail: info@checkmark.com
URL: http://www.checkmark.com
Contact: Terry Stone, Dir of Sales
E-mail: rgilmore@checkmark.com
Scope: Developer of accounting software tools for small businesses and provides fast, easy to use, affordable accounting and payroll solutions to small and medium sized businesses. Provides payroll software and multiledger integrated accounting software. **Special Services:** MultiLedger™; Payroll.

18963 ■ Creative Computer Resources Inc.
5001 Horizons Dr., Ste. 200
Columbus, OH 43220-5291
Ph:(614)384-7557
Free: (866)720-0209
Fax:(614)573-6331
Co. E-mail: team@planet-ccr.com
URL: http://www.planet-ccr.com
Contact: M. Erik Mueller, President
E-mail: merikm@atsplanet-ccr.com
Scope: Firm offers information systems support, custom software development, website design, development and implementation. Provides information technology support and management services to small and mid-size businesses.

18964 ■ DacEasy Inc.
1715 N Brown Rd.
Lawrenceville, GA 30043
Ph:(770)492-6414
Free: 800-322-3279
Fax:(770)724-2874
Co. E-mail: sales@daceasy.com
URL: http://www.daceasy.com
Contact: Marchell Gillis
E-mail: marchell.gillis@sage.com
Scope: Develops an accounting system for small businesses that integrates accounting, invoicing, payroll, communications, and management software into a single package. **Seminars:** DacEasy Training. **Special Services:** DacEasy.

18965 ■ David Collison
2328 NE Smokey Hill Dr.
Lees Summit, MO 64086-7018
Ph:(816)524-6099
Co. E-mail: dcollison@kc.rr.com
Contact: David E. Collison, Principle
E-mail: dcollison@kc.rr.com
Scope: Consultant in software development, robot integration, and user interfaces.

18966 ■ On-Q Software Inc.
13764 SW 11th St.
Miami, FL 33184
Ph:(305)553-2400
Free: 800-553-2862

Fax:(305)220-2666
Co. E-mail: info@on-qsoftware.com
URL: http://www.on-qsoftware.com
Contact: Terry Cajigas, Principle
E-mail: hcajigas@on-qsoftware.com
Scope: Provides the small business community with simple to use, feature rich software. Provides software solutions including time and fixed fee billing, due date tracking and practice manager.

18967 ■ Profit Associates Inc.
26 Hunters Forest Dr.
PO Box 81018
Charleston, SC 29414
Ph:(843)763-5718
Free: 800-688-6304
Fax:(843)763-5719
Co. E-mail: bobrog@profit-associates.com
URL: http://www.profit-associates.com
Contact: Bob Rogers, Managing Director
E-mail: bobrog@profit-associates.com
Scope: A team of management and turnaround specialists providing consulting services. Focuses on the problems of small to medium-sized businesses in the manufacturing, distribution, construction, software. Specializes in employee productivity and incentives, management reengineering, profit and expense controls, production planning, strategic business planning, marketing and public relations, or ISO 9000 support. **Seminars:** Essential Elements of a Good Incentive Program; Why Look at Management Reengineering; The Profit & Expense Control Process; The Executive Coaching Alternative.

18968 ■ Rothman Consulting Group Inc.
38 Bonad Rd.
Arlington, MA 02476
Ph:(781)641-4046
Fax:(781)641-2764
Co. E-mail: jr@jrothman.com
URL: http://www.jrothman.com
Contact: Johanna Rothman, President
E-mail: jr@jrothman.com
Scope: Works with software organizations to improve product development practices. Works with clients to find the leverage points that will increase their effectiveness as organizations and as managers, helping ship the night product at the right time, and recruit and retain the best people.

18969 ■ RSA - The Security Division of EMC
174 Middlesex Tpke.
Bedford, MA 01730
Ph:(781)515-5000
Free: 877-772-4900
Fax:(781)515-5010
Co. E-mail: conferenceinfo@rsa.com
URL: http://www.rsa.com
Contact: Dennis Hoffman, Vice President
Scope: Firm develops and markets platform independent software developer's kits, end user products, and provides comprehensive consulting services in the cryptographic sciences. **Publications:** "Proofs for Two-Server Password Authentication," 2005; "On the security of RSA encryption in TLS," 2002; "Efficient finite field basis conversion involving dual bases," 1999; "Broadband Network and Device Security"; "Wireless Security"; "XmlSecurity". **Special Services:** BSAFE; TIPEM; RSA SecurID[R]; RSA[R]; RSA ClearTrust[R].

18970 ■ SiteShapers
4070 Goldfinch St., Ste. D
San Diego, CA 92103
Ph:(619)231-6907
Fax:(619)231-7061
Co. E-mail: inquiry@siteshapers.com
URL: http://www.siteshapers.com
Contact: Irene Jernigan, Principal
E-mail: jaime@atssiteshapers.com
Scope: Conducts needs assessment and marketing productivity workshops for high-technology manufacturers and service firms. Specializes in web site strategies and design, marketing strategies, planning, research and promotion. Serves electronics and software, instruments and health care industries.

18971 ■ S.V. Writing Services
4471 Park Bristol Pl.
San Jose, CA 95136-2510
Ph:(408)972-2476
Fax:(408)224-8496
Co. E-mail: nahal@ix.netcom.com
Contact: Tarlochan S. Nahal, President
Scope: Firm specializes in computer hardware and software documentation; online documentation; wafer processing equipment manuals; desktop publishing and illustration. Uses in-house Macintosh Quadra and Pentium-based computers running Inter leaf, Frame Maker, Word Perfect, Microsoft Word, and Ventura. Serves the semiconductor, electronics, and computer hardware or software industries.

18972 ■ Users First Inc.
2162 Pine Knoll Ave.
PO Box 26385
Columbus, OH 43229
Ph:(614)523-2177
Fax:(614)899-7886
Co. E-mail: mjlmail@aol.com
Contact: Dr. Martha Lindeman, President
E-mail: lindemam@franklin.edu
Scope: Design and/or test user interfaces for any type of computer or telephony systems or for the computer-telephony integration. Participates in any phase of the design and development process. Provide off-site prototyping and usability evaluation services. Customize training materials for combined training/consulting workshops for specific projects. Serves all industries. **Publications:** "A New Design Framework for Computer-Telephony Integration"; "Human Factors and Voice Interactive Systems"; "Automatic Speech Recognition".

LIBRARIES

18973 ■ Boston University–Corporate Education Center Library
1 Exec. Dr., Ste. 301
Chelmsford, MA 01824-2558
Ph:(978)649-8200
Free: 800-288-7246
Fax:(978)649-2145
URL: http://butrain.bu.edu
Scope: Software engineering, business administration and management, computer programming languages, program methodology, project management, computer science, social work. **Services:** Interlibrary loan; copying; SDI; Library open to the public by appointment. **Holdings:** 5000 books. **Subscriptions:** 150 journals and other serials; 10 newspapers.

18974 ■ Follett Software Company Resource Center
1391 Corporate Dr.
McHenry, IL 60050-7041
Ph:(815)344-8700
Free: 800-323-3397
Fax:(815)344-8774
Co. E-mail: rmaihofer@fsc.follett.com
URL: http://www.fsc.follett.com
Contact: Robert Maihofer
Scope: Computers. **Services:** SDI; Library not open to the public. **Holdings:** 100 books; 50 reports. **Subscriptions:** 34 journals and other serials; 3 newspapers.

18975 ■ IBM Corporation–Burlington Technical Library
967-B, 1000 River St.
Essex Junction, VT 05452-4299
Ph:(802)769-6519
Fax:(802)769-6501
Co. E-mail: karenlyn@us.ibm.com
URL: http://www.ibm.com/us/en/
Contact: Karen Kromer Lynch, Tech.Lib.Mgr.
Scope: Semiconductor manufacturing, chemistry, computing, solid-state electronics, physics, business and professional, project management, programming, management science, mathematics. **Services:** Interlibrary loan; Center not open to the public. **Holdings:** 10,000 books; 100 reels of microfilm. **Subscriptions:** 160 journals and other serials.

18976 ■ IBM Corporation–Library/Information Resource Center
Dept. LVUS, B/908 Z/9819
11400 Burnet Rd.
Austin, TX 78758
Ph:(512)823-0404
Co. E-mail: gillen@us.ibm.com
URL: http://www.ibm.com/us/en/
Contact: Bev Gerzcvske, Mgr.
Scope: Computer architecture, RISC, personal computing, telecommunications, management, human factors, communications. **Services:** Interlibrary loan; Library not open to the public. **Holdings:** 11,000 books; 500 bound periodical volumes; 400 videotapes; 200 audiocassettes; 2000 reels of microfilm. **Subscriptions:** 300 journals, newsletters, and other serials; 15 newspapers.

18977 ■ Mentor Graphics Corporation Library
8005 SW Boeckman Rd.
Wilsonville, OR 97070
Ph:(503)685-7000
Free: 800-592-2210
URL: http://www.mentor.com/
Contact: Rachel Berrington, Corp.Libn.
Scope: Software engineering, electronics manufacturing, EDA industry. **Services:** Interlibrary loan; copying; SDI; Library not open to the public. **Holdings:** Figures not available.

18978 ■ UNISYS Corporation–Technical Information Center
41100 Plymouth Rd.
Plymouth, MI 48170
Ph:(313)451-4512
Contact: Mark Stuart Berna, Libn.
Scope: Computer technology, banking, imaging, business. **Services:** Library not open to the public. **Holdings:** 1800 books. **Subscriptions:** 72 journals and other serials; 5 newspapers.

18979 ■ UNISYS Corporation–West Coast Information Center
25725 Jeronimo Rd., MS-260
Mission Viejo, CA 92691
Ph:(714)380-5061
Fax:(714)380-5138
Contact: M. Patricia Feeney, Mgr., Tech.Info.Ctr.
Scope: Computer architecture, computer programming, software design, hardware engineering design, data communications, management. **Services:** Interlibrary loan; center open to the public at librarian's discretion. **Holdings:** 5000 books; 3500 technical reports; 3000 other cataloged items. **Subscriptions:** 225 journals and other serials.

RESEARCH CENTERS

18980 ■ Carnegie Mellon University–Software Engineering Institute
4500 5th Ave.
Pittsburgh, PA 15213-2612
Ph:(412)268-5800
Free: 888—201-4479
Fax:(412)268-6257
Co. E-mail: info@sei.cmu.edu
URL: http://www.sei.cmu.edu
Contact: Paul D. Nielsen, Dir./CEO
E-mail: info@sei.cmu.edu
Scope: Software engineering, including software process, software risk management, disciplined engineering of software-intensive systems, product lines, cyber security, survivable systems, COTS-based systems, software components, trustworthy networks, software engineering education, and technology transition. **Services:** CERT Coordination Center. **Publications:** news@sei; SEI Annual Report. **Educational Activities:** Conferences; Software Engineering Process Group Conference; Workshops, continuing education, and special training courses. **Awards:** IEEE Process Improvement Award, cosponsored with IEEE.

18981 ■ Massachusetts Institute of Technology–CADLAB
MIT Rm. 3-458
77 Massachusetts Ave.
Cambridge, MA 02139

Ph:(617)258-6016
Fax:(617)452-2461
Co. E-mail: drwallac@mit.edu
URL: http://cadlab.mit.edu
Contact: Prof. David Wallace, Co-Dir.
E-mail: drwallac@mit.edu
Scope: Computer-aided engineering software, including graphics and geometric design. Develops software with applications in a wide range of industrial and manufacturing areas, including aerospace, automotive, and discrete parts manufacturing.

18982 ■ Montana State University, Bozeman–Information Technology Center
Renne Library Basement
PO Box 173240
Bozeman, MT 59717-3240
Ph:(406)994-1010
Fax:(406)994-4600
Co. E-mail: gwen@cns.montana.edu
URL: http://www.montana.edu/itcenter/index.html
Contact: Dr. Gwen Jacobs
E-mail: gwen@cns.montana.edu
Scope: Computer systems (especially software development), computer and information networks, and administrative information systems. **Services:** Computer software consultation. **Educational Activities:** Computer seminar courses.

18983 ■ University of Illinois at Chicago–Electronic Visualization Laboratory
SEO Rm. 1120, MC 152
Department of Computer Science
851 S Morgan St.
Chicago, IL 60607-7053
Ph:(312)996-3002
Fax:(312)413-7585
Co. E-mail: spiff@uic.edu
URL: http://www.evl.uic.edu
Contact: Jason Leigh, Dir.
E-mail: spiff@uic.edu
Scope: Computer graphics and interactive techniques, including virtual reality, multimedia, scientific visualization, new methodologies for informal science and engineering education, paradigms for information display, televisualization (distributed graphics over networks), algorithm optimization for scalable and parallel computing, sonification, and abstract mathematical visualization.

18984 ■ University of North Florida–Institute of Police Technology and Management
12000 Alumni Dr.
Jacksonville, FL 32224-2678
Ph:(904)620-4786
Fax:(904)620-2453
Co. E-mail: info@iptm.org
URL: http://www.iptm.org
Contact: Leonard R. Jacob, Dir.
E-mail: info@iptm.org
Scope: Develops software products for police agencies, including a computer management system that collects and tracks records for a drug investigative unit or task force. This system, Drug-Trak for Windows, provides reports based on people, vehicles, businesses, aircraft, watercraft, and telephone numbers. **Services:** Offers management and supervisory training, drug investigation and enforcement, and specialty courses; Trains in-service law enforcement officers in traffic safety, criminal investigation, and microcomputer training. **Publications:** Traffic Accident Investigations and Traffic Accident Reconstruction.

Solar Energy Design/Contracting Business

ASSOCIATIONS AND OTHER ORGANIZATIONS

18985 ■ Air-Conditioning Heating and Refrigeration Institute
2111 Wilson Blvd., Ste. 500
Arlington, VA 22201
Ph:(703)524-8800
Fax:(703)562-1942
Co. E-mail: ahri@ahrinet.org
URL: http://www.ahrinet.org
Contact: Ray Hoglund, Chm.
Description: Manufacturers of air conditioning, refrigeration and heating products and components. Develops and establishes equipment and application standards and certifies performance of certain industry products; provides credit and statistical services to members. Provides representation and technical assistance to government entities in federal, state and local legislative matters; provides public relations, consumer education and promotional programs for the industry. **Publications:** *ARI Curriculum Guide*; *Minuteman* (monthly).

18986 ■ Alternative Energy Resources Organization
432 N Last Chance Gulch
Helena, MT 59601-5014
Ph:(406)443-7272
Fax:(406)442-9120
Co. E-mail: aero@aeromt.org
URL: http://www.aeromt.org
Contact: Jonda Crosby, Exec. Dir.
Description: Promotes sustainable agriculture, resource conservation and transportation choices through community education and citizen representation. Provides current programs that focus on sustainable agriculture, farm improvement clubs, beginning and retiring farmers, smart growth, and a more localized food system for greater community self-reliance. **Publications:** *Abundant Montana* (annual); *AERO Sun-Times* (quarterly); *Big Sky or Big Sprawl Montana at the Crossroads*; *Montana's Sustainable Agriculture Farming with Foresight*; *Sustainable Agriculture Curriculum-Grades 4-6* .

18987 ■ American Solar Energy Society
4760 Walnut St., Ste. 106
Boulder, CO 80301
Ph:(303)443-3130
Fax:(303)443-3212
Co. E-mail: ases@ases.org
URL: http://www.ases.org
Contact: Shaun McGrath, Exec. Dir.
Description: Professional energy society organized to promote a wide utilization of solar energy through the application of science and technology. Encourages basic and applied research and development. Conducts workshops; organizes forums inviting researchers, policymakers, practitioners and consumers for discussion, analysis, and debate. Promotes education by compiling and disseminating information to schools, universities, and the community. **Publications:** *Advances in Solar Energy* (annual); *Solar Today* (bimonthly).

18988 ■ Renew the Earth
1850 Centennial Park Dr., Ste. 105
Reston, VA 20191
Ph:(703)689-4670
Co. E-mail: steve@renew-the-earth.org
URL: http://www.renew-the-earth.org
Contact: Ms. Debbie Reed, Exec. Dir.
Description: Individuals and groups working toward a sustainable future by promoting a safe and healthy environment. Coordinates National Awards for Environmental Sustainability program to recognize positive environmental programs. Operates the Environmental Success Index, a clearinghouse of more than 1600 working environmental projects available to community groups, the media, businesses, policy makers, and individuals dedicated to implementing and promoting positive environmental change. Moving toward developing an international program. **Publications:** *Environmental Success Index* (annual).

18989 ■ Solar Energy Industries Association
575 7th St. NW, Ste. 400
Washington, DC 20004
Ph:(202)682-0556
Fax:(202)682-0559
Co. E-mail: info@seia.org
URL: http://www.seia.org
Contact: Rhone Resch, Pres./CEO
Description: Manufacturers, installers, distributors, contractors, and engineers of solar energy systems and components. Aims to accelerate and foster commercialization of solar energy conversion for economic purposes. Maintains Solar Energy Research and Education Foundation. Compiles statistics; offers computerized services. .

18990 ■ Solar Rating and Certification Corporation
400 High Point Dr., Ste. 400
Cocoa, FL 32926
Ph:(321)213-6037
Fax:(321)821-0910
Co. E-mail: srcc@solar-rating.org
URL: http://www.solar-rating.org
Contact: Eileen Prado, Exec. Dir.
Purpose: Serves as a rating and certification board for domestic solar hot water and pool heating panels and systems. .

REFERENCE WORKS

18991 ■ "$40M Fund Created for Big Energy Project" in *Austin Business JournalInc.* (Vol. 29, November 27, 2009, No. 38, pp. 1)
Pub: American City Business Journals
Ed: Christopher Calnan. **Description:** A group of Texas businessmen, called Republic Power Partners LP, is planning to raise $40 million in order to launch an alternative energy project. The 6,000-megawatt initiative would generate solar, biomass and wind power in West Texas and could cost as much as $10 billion.

18992 ■ "Acing the Test" in *Contractor* (Vol. 57, January 2010, No. 1, pp. 32)
Pub: Penton Media, Inc.
Ed: Robert P. Mader. **Description:** A ward winning mechanical system retrofitting of a middle school in Ohio is discussed. The school now operates at 37,800 Btu/sq. ft and reduced a significant amount of pollutants from being emitted into the environment.

18993 ■ "Adventures at Hydronicahh" in *Contractor* (Vol. 56, October 2009, No. 10, pp. 42)
Pub: Penton Media, Inc.
Ed: Mark Eatherton. **Description:** Design and installation of a solar thermal system for a hydronic heating project is described. This portion has two 32-square feet of flat plate glazed solar collectors that are tied to a 120-gallon reverse indirect DHW heater.

18994 ■ "Alternative Energy Calls for Alternative Marketing" in *Indoor Comfort Marketing* (Vol. 70, June 2011, No. 6, pp. 8)
Pub: Industry Publications Inc.
Ed: Richard Rutigliano. **Description:** Advice for marketing solar energy products and services is given.

18995 ■ "Aquarium's Solar Demonstration Project Exceeds Expectations" in *Contractor* (Vol. 57, February 2010, No. 2, pp. 1)
Pub: Penton Media, Inc.
Ed: Candace Roulo. **Description:** Seattle Aquarium cafe installed flat-plate solar collectors to preheat water and data has shown that the system has allowed them to off-set almost double their expected consumption of natural gas. It is estimated that rthe solar panels will shrink the aquarium's carbon footprint by 2.5 tons of carbon dioxide each year.

18996 ■ "Big Energy Deals Power OptiSolar's Local Growth" in *Sacramento Business Journal* (Vol. 25, August 22, 2008, No. 25, pp. 1)
Pub: American City Business Journals, Inc.
Ed: Celia Lamb. **Description:** Solar energy projects are driving Sacramento, California-based OptiSolar's growth. The company is set to begin construction of its first photovoltaic project in Ontario. It also plans to build the world largest photovoltaic project in San Luis Obispo County.

18997 ■ "Bold Goals Will Require Time" in *Contractor* (Vol. 56, October 2009, No. 10, pp. S2)
Pub: Penton Media, Inc.
Ed: Ted Lower. **Description:** Offering a broad range of courses is the Radiant Panel Association (RPA), an organization that holds education as its top priority. The RPA must lead the industry by raising the educational bar for future installers.

18998 ■ "The Business of Activism" in *Entrepreneur* (Vol. 37, September 2009, No. 9, pp. 43)
Pub: Entrepreneur Media, Inc.
Ed: Mary Catherine O'Connor. **Description:** San Francisco, California-based business incubator Virgance has been promoting sustainable projects by

partnering with businesses. The company has launched campaigns which include organizing homeowners in negotiating with solar installers. The company is also planning to expand its workforce.

18999 ■ "Can HOAs Stop You From Going Green?" in *Contractor* (Vol. 56, July 2009, No. 7, pp. 39)
Pub: Penton Media, Inc.
Ed: Susan Linden McGreevy. **Description:** There have been cases concerning homeowners' associations objections to the installation of wind turbines and solar panels. Precedence with the courts show that they will look at several factors when deciding to uphold restrictions on property use including whether the item encroaches on the rights of others, is likely to adversely affect property values, and also the state of enforcement.

19000 ■ "Chicago Botanic Garden Builds Green Research Facility" in *Contractor* (Vol. 56, December 2009, No. 12, pp. 5)
Pub: Penton Media, Inc.
Ed: Candace Roulo. **Description:** Chicago Botanic Garden has built a laboratory and research facility in Illinois. The facility is set to receive a United States Green Building Council LEED Gold certification. The building features a solar photovoltaic array, radiant flooring and water-conserving plumbing products.

19001 ■ "China's Transition to Green Energy Systems" in *Energy Policy* (Vol. 39, October 2011, No. 10, pp. 5909-5919)
Pub: Reed Elsevier Reference Publishing
Ed: Wei Li, Guojun Song, Melanie Beresford, Ben Ma. **Description:** The economics of home solar water heaters and their growing popularity in Dezhous City, China is discussed.

19002 ■ "Chinese Solar Panel Manufacturer Scopes Out Austin" in *Austin Business JournalInc.* (Vol. 29, October 30, 2009, No. 34, pp. 1)
Pub: American City Business Journals
Ed: Jacob Dirr. **Description:** China's Yingli Green Energy Holding Company Ltd. is looking for a site in order to construct a $20 million photovoltaic panel plant. Both Austin and San Antonio are vying to house the manufacturing hub. The project could create about 300 jobs and give Austin a chance to become a player in the solar energy market. Other solar companies are also considering Central Texas as an option to set up shop.

19003 ■ *Directory of SRCC Certified Collectors and Solar Water Heating Systems Ratings*
Pub: Solar Rating & Certification Corp.
Contact: Jim Huggins
Released: Irregular, Latest edition 2010. **Price:** Free. **Covers:** Nearly 20 manufacturers of solar collectors and water heaters certified by the organization. **Entries Include:** Company name, address, system model and description, including technical specifications, thermal performance ratings, etc. , for one or more systems. **Arrangement:** Classified by type of system. **Indexes:** Company name.

19004 ■ "Doing the Right Thing" in *Black Enterprise* (Vol. 38, July 2008, No. 12, pp. 50)
Pub: Earl G. Graves Publishing Co. Inc.
Ed: Tamara E. Holmes. **Description:** More business owners are trying to become more environmentally friendly, either due to their belief in social responsibility or for financial incentives or for both reasons. Tips for making one's business more environmentally responsible are included as well as a listing of resources that may be available to help owners in their efforts.

19005 ■ "East Coast Solar" in *Contractor* (Vol. 57, February 2010, No. 2, pp. 17)
Pub: Penton Media, Inc.
Ed: Dave Yates. **Description:** U.S. Department of Energy's Solar Decathlon lets 20 college student-led teams from around the world compete to design and build a solar-powered home. A mechanical contractor discusses his work as an advisor during the competition.

19006 ■ "Eco Smart Home Will Showcase Green Technology" in *Contractor* (Vol. 56, September 2009, No. 9, pp. 3)
Pub: Penton Media, Inc.
Ed: Steve Spaulding. **Description:** Eco Smart World Wide is building the Eco Smart Demonstration House to promote the latest in sustainable, renewable and high-efficiency practices and products. The company will use insulated concrete forms in the construction of the building. Features and dimensions of the structure are also presented.

19007 ■ "Election Could Undo Renewable Energy Quotas" in *The Business Journal - Serving Phoenix and the Valley of the Sun* (Vol. 28, July 11, 2008, No. 45, pp. 1)
Pub: American City Business Journals, Inc.
Ed: Patrick O'Grady. **Description:** Competition for the three open seats in the Arizona Corporation Commission is intense, with 12 candidates contesting for the three slots. The commission's mandates for renewable energy and infrastructure investment will also be at stake.

19008 ■ "ESolar Partners With Penglai on Landmark Solar Thermal Agreement for China" in *Business of Global Warming* (January 25, 2010, pp. 8)
Pub: Investment Weekly News
Description: Penglai Electric, a privately-owned Chinese electrical power equipment manufacturer, and eSolar, a global provider of cost-effective and reliable solar power plants, announced a master licensing agreement in which eSolar will build at least 2 gigawatts of solar thermal power plants in China over the next 10 years.

19009 ■ "Everett Dowling" in *Hawaii Business* (Vol. 54, August 2008, No. 2, pp. 32)
Pub: Hawaii Business Publishing
Ed: Jason Ubay. **Description:** Real estate developer Everett Dowling, president of Dowling Company Inc., talks about the company's sustainable management and services. The company's office has been retrofitted to earn a Leadership in Energy and Environmental Design (LEED) certification. Dowling believes that real estate development can be part of the sustainable solution.

19010 ■ "Final State Budget Is a Mixed Bag of Key Industries" in *The Business Journal - Serving Phoenix and the Valley of the Sun* (Vol. 28, July 4, 2008, No. 44, pp. 3)
Pub: American City Business Journals, Inc.
Ed: Mike Sunnucks; Patrick O'Grady. **Description:** Approved by Governor Janet Napolitano and passed by the Arizona Legislature, the $9.9 billion state budget is beneficial to some industries in the business community. The tax cap for on Arizona Lottery has been removed which is beneficial to the industry, while the solar energy industry and real estate developers stand to lose from the spending bill. Other details of the finance budget are presented.

19011 ■ "Florida's Bright Upside" in *Tampa Bay Business Journal* (Vol. 29, November 6, 2009, No. 46, pp. 1)
Pub: American City Business Journals
Ed: Michael Hinman. **Description:** Florida's Public Service Commission (PSC) decision on a power purchase agreement that could add 25 megawatts of solar energy on Tampa Electric Company's offerings is presented. The decision could support the growing market for suppliers and marketers of renewable energy such as Jabil Circuit Inc., which manufactures photovoltaic modules. Details of the agreement are discussed.

19012 ■ "For Giving Us a Way To Say Yes To Solar: Lynn Jurich and Edward Fenster" in *Inc.* (Volume 32, December 2010, No. 10, pp. 110)
Pub: Inc. Magazine
Description: Profile of entrepreneurs Lynn Jurich and Edward Fenster, cofounders of SunRun. The firm installs solar panels at little or no cost and homeowners sign 20-year contracts to buy power at a fixed price.

19013 ■ "FSU's OGZEB Is Test Bed for Sustainable Technology" in *Contractor* (Vol. 56, October 2009, No. 10, pp. 1)
Pub: Penton Media, Inc.
Ed: Candace Roulo. **Description:** Florida State University has one of 14 off-grid zero emissions buildings (OGZEB) in the U.S. ; it was built to research sustainable and alternative energy systems. The building produces electricity from 30 photovoltaic panels and it also has three AET water heating solar panels on the roof.

19014 ■ "Fuel for Thought; Canadian Business Leaders on Energy Policy" in *Canadian Business* (Vol. 81, September 15, 2008, No. 14-15, pp. 12)
Pub: Rogers Media Ltd.
Ed: Joe Castaldo. **Description:** Most Canadian business leaders worry about the unreliability of the oil supply but feel that Canada is in a better position to benefit from the energy supply crisis than other countries. Many respondents also highlighted the need to invest in renewable energy sources.

19015 ■ "Germans Win Solar Decathlon - Again" in *Contractor* (Vol. 56, November 2009, No. 11, pp. 1)
Pub: Penton Media, Inc.
Ed: Robert P. Mader. **Description:** Students from Technische Universtat Darmstadt won the U.S. Department of Energy's Solar Decathlon by designing and building the most attractive and efficient solar-powered home. The winner's design produced a surplus of power even during three days of rain and photovoltaic panels covered nearly every exterior surface.

19016 ■ "Got to be Smarter than the Average Bear" in *Contractor* (Vol. 56, September 2009, No. 9, pp. 82)
Pub: Penton Media, Inc.
Ed: Bob Mader. **Description:** International Association of Plumbing and Mechanical Officials Green Technical Committee has debated the need for contractors to have certifications in installing green plumbing. Some have argued that qualifications would discourage homeowners from improving their properties. Comments from executives are also included.

19017 ■ "Green Light" in *The Business Journal-Portland* (Vol. 25, July 11, 2008, No. 18, pp. 1)
Pub: American City Business Journals, Inc.
Ed: Erik Siemers. **Description:** Ecos Consulting, a sustainability consulting company based in Portland, Oregon, is seeing a boost in revenue as more businesses turn to sustainable practices. The company's revenue rose by 50 percent in 2007 and employees increased from 57 to 150. Other details about Ecos' growth are discussed.

19018 ■ "Greenhouse Announces Merger With Custom Q, Inc." in *Investment Weekly* (January 30, 2010, pp. 338)
Pub: Investment Weekly News
Description: In accordance with an Agreement and Plan of Share Exchange, GreenHouse Holdings, Inc., an innovative green solutions provider, has gone public via a reverse merger with Custom Q, Inc.

19019 ■ "How Green Is The Valley?" in *Barron's* (Vol. 88, July 4, 2008, No. 28, pp. 13)
Pub: Dow Jones & Co., Inc.
Description: San Jose, California has made a good start towards becoming a leader in alternative energy technology through the establishment of United Laboratories' own lab in the city. The certification process for photovoltaic cells will be dramatically shortened with this endeavor.

19020 ■ "Hydronicahh - Everything in Modulation" in *Contractor* (Vol. 56, December 2009, No. 12, pp. 24)
Pub: Penton Media, Inc.
Ed: Mark Eatherton. **Description:** Management and the environmental impact of a home hydronic system are discussed. Radiant windows have the potential to reduce energy consumption. A variable speed delta T pump is required for the construction of a hydronic wood pit.

19021 ■ "It's Always 55 Degrees F" in *Contractor* (Vol. 56, September 2009, No. 9, pp. 38)
Pub: Penton Media, Inc.
Ed: Carol Fey. **Description:** Geothermal-exchange heating and cooling systems can save businesses up to 60 percent on energy costs for heating and cooling. Geothermal systems get heat from the earth during winter. Design, features and installation of geothermal systems are also discussed.

19022 ■ "Letting the Sunshine In" in *Barron's* (Vol. 89, July 6, 2009, No. 27, pp. 11)
Pub: Dow Jones & Co., Inc.
Ed: Katherine Cheng. **Description:** Solar energy industry leaders believe the industry needs aid from the US government regarding the funding of its research efforts and lowering solar energy costs. The climate change bill passed by the US House of Representatives signifies the US government's desire to significantly reduce carbon dioxide emissions.

19023 ■ "Magpower May Build Solar Panels Here" in *Austin Business Journal* (Vol. 31, May 13, 2011, No. 10, pp. A1)
Pub: American City Business Journals Inc.
Ed: Christopher Calnan. **Description:** RRE Austin Solar LLC CEO Doven Mehta has revealed plans to partner with Portugal-based Magpower SA, only if Austin energy buys electricity from planned solar energy farm in Pflugerville. Austin Energy has received 100 bids from 35 companies to supply 200 megawatts of solar- and wind-generated electricity.

19024 ■ "N.E.'s Largest Solar Site Set for Scituate Landfill" in *Boston Business Journal* (Vol. 30, December 17, 2010, No. 47, pp. 1)
Pub: Boston Business Journal
Ed: Kyle Alspach. **Description:** A closed 12-acre landfill in Scituate, Massachusetts is the proposed site for a 2.4-megawatt solar power plant. The town government will buy the power at a discounted rate, saving it $200,000 annually.

19025 ■ "On Growth Path of Rising Star" in *Boston Business Journal* (Vol. 31, June 24, 2011, No. 22, pp. 3)
Pub: Boston Business Journal
Ed: Kyle Alspach. **Description:** 1366 Technologies Inc. of Lexington, Massachusetts is considered a rising solar power technology company. The firm secured $150 million loan guarantee from the US Department of Energy that could go to the construction of a 1,000 megawatt solar power plant.

19026 ■ "One on One With SEIA's President, CEO" in *Contractor* (Vol. 57, January 2010, No. 1, pp. 40)
Pub: Penton Media, Inc.
Ed: Dave Yates. **Description:** Solar Energy Industries Association President and CEO Rhone Resch says that the deployment of solar systems in the U.S. has exploded since 2005 and that there is a need to make inroads for shaping the U.S. energy policy. Resch says one of the hurdles they face is that there are no universal standards.

19027 ■ "Proposal Ruffles Builders" in *Austin Business Journallnc.* (Vol. 29, November 20, 2009, No. 37, pp. 1)
Pub: American City Business Journals
Ed: Jacob Dirr. **Description:** A proposal that requires heating, ventilation and cooling equipment checking for a new commercial building having an area of at least 10,000 square feet might cost 25 cents to 50 cents per square foot for the owners. This may lead to higher housing costs. Both the Building and Fire Code Board of Appeals and the Mechanical Plumbing and Solar Board have recommended the plan.

19028 ■ "PSC Approves $130M TECO Solar Project" in *Tampa Bay Business Journal* (Vol. 30, December 18, 2009, No. 52, pp. 1)
Pub: American City Business Journals
Ed: Michael Hinman. **Description:** Florida's Public Service Commission has endorsed Tampa Electric Company's plan to add 25 megawatts of solar energy to its portfolio. TECO's plan needed the approval by PSC to defray additional costs for the project through ratepayers.

19029 ■ "San Diego Museum Receives LEED Certification" in *Contractor* (Vol. 57, January 2010, No. 1, pp. 14)
Pub: Penton Media, Inc.
Description: San Diego Natural History Museum received an LEED certification for existing buildings. The certification process began when they committed to displaying the Dead Sea Scrolls in 2007 and they had to upgrade their buildings' air quality and to control for air moisture, temperature, and volume. They reduced their energy consumption by upwards of 20 percent.

19030 ■ "Saudi Overtures" in *The Business Journal-Portland* (Vol. 25, August 15, 2008, No. 23, pp. 1)
Pub: American City Business Journals, Inc.
Ed: Aliza Earnshaw. **Description:** Saudi Arabia's huge revenue from oil is creating opportunities for Oregon companies as the country develops new cities, industrial zones, and tourism centers. Oregon exported only $46.8 million worth of goods to Saudi Arabia in 2007 but the kingdom is interested in green building materials and methods, renewable energy and water quality control, and nanotechnology all of which Oregon has expertise in.

19031 ■ "Seeing Green in Going Green" in *The Business Journal-Serving Greater Tampa Bay* (Vol. 28, July 4, 2008, No. 28, pp. 1)
Pub: American City Business Journals, Inc.
Ed: Janet Leiser. **Description:** Atlanta, Georgia-based developer IDI Corp. is pushing for Leadership in Energy and Environmental Design certification for the warehouse that is currently under construction at Madison Business Center along Port Sutton and U.S. 41. The industrial building is the first in Tampa Bay to seek certification for LEED as set by the U.S. Green Building Council.

19032 ■ "Silicon Success: Solar Energy Shines for Dawn Alston Paige" in *Black Enterprise* (Vol. 38, October 2007, No. 3, pp. 46)
Pub: Earl G. Graves Publishing Co. Inc.
Ed: Evan Mynatt. **Description:** Dawn Alson Paige, senior vice president and co-founder of Piedmont Investment Advisors predicted MBMC Electronic Materials to climb to $50 in 12 to 18 months, however the stock rose higher hitting $61 in early August, due to the international push for alternative energy.

19033 ■ "Solar Choices" in *Contractor* (Vol. 56, October 2009, No. 10, pp. 32)
Pub: Penton Media, Inc.
Ed: Tom Scheel. **Description:** Price, performance, and ease of installation of a flat plate versus an evacuated tube collector for a plumbing and heating job are compared. The better choice with regards to weight, aesthetics, efficiency in warm or cool climates, year round load, and space heating is discussed.

19034 ■ "Solar Credit Lapse Spur Late Demand" in *The Business Journal - Serving Phoenix and the Valley of the Sun* (Vol. 28, July 18, 2008)
Pub: American City Business Journals, Inc.
Ed: Patrick O'Grady. **Description:** Businesses looking to engage in the solar energy industry are facing the problems of taxation and limited solar panel supply. Solar panels manufacturers are focusing more on the European market. Political issues surrounding the federal tax credit policy on solar energy users are also discussed.

19035 ■ "Solar Hot Water Sales Are Hot, Hot, Hot" in *Contractor* (Vol. 56, December 2009, No. 12, pp. 22)
Pub: Penton Media, Inc.
Ed: Dave Yates. **Description:** Plumbing contractors in the United States can benefit from the increased sales of solar thermal water systems. Licensed plumbers have the base knowledge on the risks associated from heating and storing water. Safety issues associated with solar water heaters are also included.

19036 ■ "Sustainability Is Top Priority for GreenTown Chicago" in *Contractor* (Vol. 56, November 2009, No. 11, pp. 1)
Pub: Penton Media, Inc.
Ed: Candace Roulo. **Description:** GreenTown Chicago 2009 conference tackled energy-efficient practices and technologies, green design and building, and sustainable policies. Water conservation was also a topic at the conference and one mayor who made a presentation said that reducing the water loss in the system is a priority in the city's endeavor.

19037 ■ "Top 50 Exporters" in *Hispanic Business* (Vol. 30, July-August 2008, No. 7-8, pp. 42)
Pub: Hispanic Business, Inc.
Ed: Hildy Medina. **Description:** Increases in exports revenues reported by food exporters and green companies in a time of economic slowdown in the U.S are described. Food exporters have benefited from the growth of high-volume grocery stores in underdeveloped countries and the German governments' promotion of solar energy has benefited the U.S. solar heating equipment and solar panel manufactures.

19038 ■ "UA Turns Ann Arbor Green" in *Contractor* (Vol. 56, September 2009, No. 9, pp. 5)
Pub: Penton Media, Inc.
Ed: Robert P. Mader. **Description:** Instructors at the United Association of Plumbers and Steamfitters have studied the latest in green and sustainable construction and service at the Washtenaw Community College in Michigan. Classes included building information modeling, hydronic heating and cooling and advanced HVACR troubleshooting. The UA is currently focusing on green training.

19039 ■ "University Data Center Goes Off-Grid, Is Test Bed" in *Contractor* (Vol. 57, February 2010, No. 2, pp. 1)
Pub: Penton Media, Inc.
Ed: Candace Roulo. **Description:** Syracuse University's Green Data Center has gone off-grid through the use of natural gas fired turbines. It is expected to use 50 percent less energy than a typical computer center. The center's heating and cooling system setup is also discussed.

19040 ■ "Warm Floors Make Warm Homes" in *Contractor* (Vol. 56, October 2009, No. 10, pp. S18)
Pub: Penton Media, Inc.
Ed: Lisa Murton Beets. **Description:** Three award winning radiant floor-heating installations are presented. The design and the equipment used for these systems are discussed.

19041 ■ "Was Mandating Solar Power Water Heaters For New Homes Good Policy?" in *Hawaii Business* (Vol. 54, August 2008, No. 2, pp. 28)
Pub: Hawaii Business Publishing
Description: Senator Gary L. Kooser of District 7 Kauai-Niihau believes that the mandating of energy-efficient water heaters for new single-family homes starting in 2010 will help cut Hawaii's oil consumption. Ron Richmond of the Hawaii Solar Energy Association says that the content of SB 644 has negative consequences as it allows for choice of energy and not just solar, and it also eliminates tax credits for new homebuyers.

19042 ■ "Water Conservation Helps GC's Building Attain LEED Gold Status" in *Contractor* (Vol. 56, September 2009, No. 9, pp. 5)
Pub: Penton Media, Inc.
Description: Green contractor Marshall Erdman has built a new office building using green design. The facility is seen to become a prime Leadership in Energy and Environmental Design (LEED) building model. Details of the building's design and features are also provided.

19043 ■ "Water Distiller" in *Canadian Business* (Vol. 81, September 29, 2008, No. 16, pp. 52)
Pub: Rogers Media Ltd.
Ed: Matthew McClearn. **Description:** Les Fairn's invention of a water distiller called a Solarsphere was

recognized in the Great Canadian Invention Competition. Fairn's invention resembles a buoy that uses the sun's energy to vaporize dirty water then leaves the impurities behind in a sump. The invention has an application for producing potable water in impoverished countries.

19044 ■ "Yates Helps Turn Log Home Green" in *Contractor* (Vol. 56, December 2009, No. 12, pp. 40)
Pub: Penton Media, Inc.
Description: Upgrading and greening of a log home's HVAC system in Pennsylvania is discussed. F. W. Behler Inc. president Dave Yates was chosen to manage the project. A large coil of R-flex was used to connect the buffer tank to the garage's radiant heat system.

19045 ■ "Yates Turns Log Home Green - Part Three" in *Contractor* (Vol. 57, January 2010, No. 1, pp. 5)
Pub: Penton Media, Inc.
Description: Dave Yates of F.W. Behler Inc. discusses remodeling a log home's HVAC system with geo-to-radiant heat and thermal-solar systems. The solar heater's installation is discussed.

19046 ■ "Yudelson Challenges San Antonio Groups" in *Contractor* (Vol. 56, October 2009, No. 10, pp. 6)
Pub: Penton Media, Inc.
Description: Green building consultant and author Jerry Yudelson made a presentation for the Central Texas Green Building Council and Leadership San Antonio where he discussed the European approach to sustainability and how it can be used for designing green buildings. Yudelson also discussed how to use sustainable practices for planning 25 years into the future.

TRADE PERIODICALS

19047 ■ *Wind Energy Weekly*
Pub: American Wind Energy Association
Ed: Thomas O. Gray, Editor, tom_gray@igc.org. **Released:** Weekly. **Price:** Included in membership; $595, nonmembers. **Description:** Provides wind energy trade news, plus covers energy and environmental policy. Recurring features include news of research, reports of meetings, job listings, and notices of publications available. Remarks: Available only via E-mail account.

TRADE SHOWS AND CONVENTIONS

19048 ■ World Energy Engineering Congress
Association of Energy Engineers
4025 Pleasantdale Rd., Ste. 420
Atlanta, GA 30340
Ph:(770)447-5083
Fax:(770)446-3969
Co. E-mail: info@aeecenter.org
URL: http://www.aeecenter.org
Released: Annual, Fall. **Audience:** Energy engineers, managers, facility managers, and VPs of operations. **Principal Exhibits:** Energy equipment, supplies, and services. **Dates and Locations:** 2011 Oct 12-14, Chicago, IL.

CONSULTANTS

19049 ■ CPIX Risk Services
1500 727 - 7th Ave. SW
Calgary, AB, Canada T2P 0Z5
Ph:(403)261-6061
Fax:(403)261-6068
Co. E-mail: insurance@cpix.com
URL: http://www.cpix.com
Contact: Sam Jackson, President
E-mail: sam@atscpix.com
Scope: Provider of Energy Insurance Reciprocal (EIR)-based insurance solutions to the energy industry. Offers risk services to reduce, manage and control the cost of risk in four specialized areas: safety and loss control, risk surveys, loss control program audits, facility inspections, hazard analysis, job observations, task analysis, impact forecasting; support, training, loss investigation, claims management, loss information sharing, on going audits and inspections; alternative risk financing; and mentoring offers periodic workshops, guest lectures, program structure evaluation and a forum for idea development and evaluation.

COMPUTERIZED DATABASES

19050 ■ *Energy Design Update*
Wolters Kluwer Law & Business
76 9th Ave., 7th Fl.
New York, NY 10011
Ph:(212)771-0600
Free: 800-234-1660
Fax:(212)771-0885
URL: http://www.aspenpublishers.com
Description: Contains the complete text of *Energy Design Update*, a monthly newsletter providing information on energy-efficient building design and construction. Covers regulatory trends, standards, and legal decisions. Features profiles of energy-conserving homes in North America, a calendar of national and international events, an annual special report on superinsulation, news of research, reviews of related computer software, new product and materials reviews, and construction tips. **Availability:** Online: Wolters Kluwer Law & Business. **Type:** Full text.

LIBRARIES

19051 ■ Alternative Energy Resources Organization AERO Library
432 N. Last Chance Gulch
Helena, MT 59601-5014
Ph:(406)443-7272
Fax:(406)442-9120
Co. E-mail: aero@aeromt.org
URL: http://www.aeromt.org
Contact: Jonda Crosby, Exec.Dir.
Scope: Sustainable agriculture, renewable energy, community self-reliance. **Services:** Full Library access to members; open to the public for reference use only. **Holdings:** 550 books; 120 bound periodical volumes; 3 VF drawers of topical resource material. **Subscriptions:** 15 journals and other serials.

19052 ■ Arizona State University–Architectural and Environmental Design Library
College of Architecture
PO Box 871705
Tempe, AZ 85287-1705
Ph:(480)965-6400
Fax:(480)727-6965
Co. E-mail: deborah.koshinsky@asu.edu
URL: http://www.asu.edu
Contact: Deborah Koshinsky, Hd.Archv./Libn.
Scope: Architecture, city planning, landscape architecture, industrial design, interior design, graphic design. **Services:** Interlibrary loan; copying; Library open to the public; special collections open to the public by appointment. **Holdings:** 50,000 volumes; 150 cassette and tape recordings; 563 titles on microfilm; 125 films and videocassettes; archives; microfiche. **Subscriptions:** 140 journals and other serials.

19053 ■ Arizona State University–Architectural and Environmental Design Library–Solar Energy Collection (PO Box)
PO Box 871705
Tempe, AZ 85287-1705
Ph:(480)965-6370
Co. E-mail: deborah.koshinsky@asu.edu
URL: http://lib.asu.edu/architecture/collections/solar-energy
Contact: Deborah Koshinsky, Hd.Arch./Env. Design Libn.
Scope: Photovoltaics, solar thermal, architectural design, wind power, energy conservation, other renewable energy. **Services:** Interlibrary loan; copying; Library open to the public. **Holdings:** 18,000 archival items; technical papers and reports; pamphlets; brochures; clippings; reprints; product information.

19054 ■ Ball State University–Center for Energy Research/Education/Service (CERES)
Architecture Bldg., AB 018
2000 W. University Ave.
Muncie, IN 47306
Ph:(765)285-1135
Fax:(765)285-5622
Co. E-mail: ceres@bsu.edu
URL: http://cms.bsu.edu/Academics/CentersandInstitutes/CERES.aspx
Contact: Robert J. Koester, Dir.
Scope: Energy, solar energy, community planning, design, building performance analysis, computer simulation. **Services:** Copying; Center open to the public with restrictions. **Holdings:** 200 books; 200 technical reports. **Subscriptions:** 20 journals and other serials.

19055 ■ Boston Architectural Center–Alfred Shaw and Edward Durell Stone Library
320 Newbury St., 6th Fl.
Boston, MA 02115
Ph:(617)585-0155
Free: (87)
Fax:(617)585-0151
Co. E-mail: library@the-bac.edu
URL: http://www.the-bac.edu/x459.xml
Contact: Susan Lewis, Lib.Dir.
Scope: Architectural design and history, building technology, urban planning, urban design, landscape architecture, photography, interior design, energy conservation, solar energy. **Services:** Copying; Library open to the public for reference only. **Holdings:** 25,000 books; 800 bound periodical volumes; 800 student theses; 40,000 slides; 500 other cataloged items; archives. **Subscriptions:** 120 journals and other serials.

19056 ■ Burt Hill Kosar Rittelmann Associates Library
400 Morgan Ctr.
101 E. Diamond St.
Butler, PA 16001-5977
Ph:(724)285-4761
Fax:(724)285-6815
Co. E-mail: dianne.sinz@burthill.com
URL: http://www.burthill.com
Contact: John Brock, Dir.
Scope: Energy use in buildings, solar energy, building products and design, architecture, engineering, interior design. **Services:** Library not open to the public. **Holdings:** 12,000 volumes. **Subscriptions:** 176 journals and other serials.

19057 ■ Florida Solar Energy Center Research Library
1679 Clearlake Rd.
Cocoa, FL 32922-5703
Ph:(321)638-1000
Fax:(321)638-1010
Co. E-mail: rickling@fsec.ucf.edu
URL: http://www.fsec.ucf.edu/en/about/facilities/library.htm
Contact: Iraida B. Rickling, Univ.Libn.
Scope: Solar and other alternative sources of energy, science, technology. **Services:** Interlibrary loan; copying; Library open to the public with restrictions. **Holdings:** 13,000 books; 2364 bound periodical volumes; 12,477 technical documents; 7715 vertical files; 7572 slides; 56,522 microfiche; 10 films; 213 videotapes. **Subscriptions:** 212 journals and other serials.

19058 ■ Northeast Sustainable Energy Association Library
50 Miles St.
Greenfield, MA 01301-3212
Ph:(413)774-6051

Fax:(413)774-6053
Co. E-mail: nesea@nesea.org
URL: http://www.nesea.org
Scope: Solar energy, alternative energy sources, sustainable transportation and building practices, solar electric vehicles, renewable energy, the environment. **Services:** Copying (5 cents per copy); Library open to the public for reference use only. **Holdings:** 200 books. **Subscriptions:** 30 journals and other serials.

19059 ■ Sustainable Buildings Industries Council Library
1112 16th St. NW, Ste. 240
Washington, DC 20036
Ph:(202)628-7400
Fax:(202)393-5043
URL: http://www.sbicouncil.org
Scope: Passive solar energy - design, construction, technology, industry. **Services:** Library open to the public by appointment. **Holdings:** Documents from national laboratories, government contractors and agencies, and private programs.

19060 ■ U.S. Dept. of Energy–Energy Library
1000 Independent Ave., SW
Forrestal Bldg. Rm. GA-138
Washington, DC 20585
Ph:(202)586-9535
Fax:(202)586-1661
Co. E-mail: forrestal.library@hq.doe.gov
URL: http://management.energy.gov/program_support/library.htm
Contact: Denise B. Diggin, Libn.
Scope: Energy resources and technologies; economic, environmental, and social aspects of energy; energy regulation; energy statistics; management. **Services:** Interlibrary loan; SDI; Library open to DOE Headquarters staff and authorized contractors. **Holdings:** 500,000 million volumes of books, journals, technical reports, government documents. **Subscriptions:** 1600 journals and other serials.

RESEARCH CENTERS

19061 ■ Ball State University–Center for Energy Research/Education/Service
Architecture Bldg., Rm. 018
Muncie, IN 47306
Ph:(765)285-1135
Fax:(765)285-5622
Co. E-mail: ceres@bsu.edu
URL: http://www.bsu.edu/ceres
Contact: Prof. Robert J. Koester, Dir.
E-mail: ceres@bsu.edu
Scope: Interrelation of disciplines in energy related methods of analysis, performance evaluation, and decision making, including studies of community planning, urban design, building design, materials technology, computer application, solar and other alternative energy sources, energy education methodologies, and economic analysis. **Publications:** Annual Report. **Educational Activities:** Workshops, energy awareness programs, periodic public lectures, and guest lecture program.

19062 ■ California State Polytechnic University, Pomona–John T. Lyle Center for Regenerative Studies
4105 W University Dr.
Pomona, CA 91768
Ph:(909)869-5155
Fax:(909)869-5188
Co. E-mail: crs@csupomona.edu
URL: http://www.csupomona.edu/lAtcrs
Contact: Kyle D. Brown PhD, Dir.
E-mail: crs@csupomona.edu
Scope: Regenerative technologies, including integrated agriculture/aquaculture systems, agroforestry, passive solar heating and cooling, waste water recycling, and small scale intensive agriculture.

19063 ■ Department of Energy–National Renewable Energy Laboratory
1617 Cole Blvd.
Golden, CO 80401-3393
Ph:(303)275-3000
Fax:(303)275-3097
Co. E-mail: dan_arvizu@nrel.gov
URL: http://www.nrel.gov
Contact: Dr. Dan E. Arvizu, Dir.
E-mail: dan_arvizu@nrel.gov
Scope: Renewable energy technologies, including the fundamental nature of light and its interaction with matter, focusing on the development of cost-effective solar technologies capable of producing significant amounts of energy. Studies encompass the areas of photovoltaics, alternative fuels, wind energy, transportation technologies, and energy efficiency technologies (active and passive solar). Specific areas include production of biomass fuel, photon conversion for the production of hydrogen from water, and the development of high-efficiency semiconductor solar cells. **Services:** Technology transfer. **Educational Activities:** Regional and national renewable energy conferences.

19064 ■ University of Central Florida–Florida Solar Energy Center
1679 Clearlake Rd.
Cocoa, FL 32922-5703
Ph:(321)638-1000
Fax:(321)638-1010
Co. E-mail: solarinfo@fsec.ucf.edu
URL: http://www.fsec.ucf.edu/en
Contact: Prof. James Fenton PhD, Dir.
E-mail: solarinfo@fsec.ucf.edu
Scope: Photovoltaics, energy-efficient building design, solar water heating, energy-efficient, industrialized housing, innovative air conditioning systems, electrical end-uses, photoelectrochemical processes, solar waste detoxification, production, storage and utilization of hydrogen, and other energy efficiency, and solar energy activities for the state of Florida. Program objectives include research and development, testing, certification, establishment of standards, educational services, and information dissemination. Responsible for mandatory certification of all solar energy systems manufactured and/or sold in Florida. **Services:** Self-guided tours, open to the public. **Publications:** Annual Report; Photocatalyst Report; Solar Collector Newsletter. **Educational Activities:** Distance learning program; Short courses, on solar and energy efficiency.

19065 ■ University of Oregon–Solar Energy Center
Department of Physics
1274 University of Oregon
Eugene, OR 97403-1274
Ph:(541)346-4745
Fax:(541)346-5861
Co. E-mail: fev@uoregon.edu
URL: http://solardata.uoregon.edu
Contact: Frank Vignola PhD, Dir.
E-mail: fev@uoregon.edu
Scope: Solar resource monitoring and assessment, and analysis of climate in terms of architectural response. **Services:** Monitoring the solar resource, in the region; Monitoring performance of photovoltaic systems, in the field; Solar Energy exhibits, films, lectures, and demonstrations (occasionally). **Publications:** Solar Newsletter (semiannually). **Educational Activities:** Workshops and Solar Seminars (occasionally), on a wide range of topics associated with energy resources and architectural applications.

19066 ■ University of Tennessee, Knoxville–Energy, Environment and Resources Center
311 Conference Center Bldg.
Knoxville, TN 37996-4134
Ph:(865)974-4251
Fax:(865)974-1838
Co. E-mail: barkenbu@utk.edu
URL: http://eerc.ra.utk.edu/
Contact: Jack N. Barkenbus PhD, Exec.Dir.
E-mail: barkenbu@utk.edu
Scope: Critical issues in energy, environment, natural resources, science and technology policy, and economic development. Of particular interest are waste management, clean technologies, sustainable development, water, and environmental education. **Services:** Speakers' bureau. **Publications:** The Review of Policy Research (quarterly); Working paper series. **Educational Activities:** Energy, Environment, and Resource Fields Seminars.

19067 ■ University of Wisconsin—Madison–Solar Energy Laboratory
1343 Engineering Research Bldg.
1500 Engineering Dr.
Madison, WI 53706-1687
Ph:(608)263-5626
Fax:(608)262-8464
Co. E-mail: klein@engr.wisc.edu
URL: http://sel.me.wisc.edu
Contact: Prof. Sanford A. Klein PhD, Dir.
E-mail: klein@engr.wisc.edu
Scope: Computer programs used in solar energy research, development, and design; solar and non-solar air conditioning and heating systems.

ASSOCIATIONS AND OTHER ORGANIZATIONS

19068 ■ National Staff Development Council
504 S Locust St.
Oxford, OH 45056
Ph:(513)523-6029
Free: 800-727-7288
Fax:(513)523-0638
Co. E-mail: nsdcoffice@nsdc.org
URL: http://www.learningforward.org
Contact: Stephanie Hirsh, Exec. Dir.
Description: Provides assistance and support to local school district personnel whose primary responsibility is the administration, supervision, and coordination of staff development programs. Promotes public policy favorable to the development of comprehensive district-based staff development programs. Provides information on effective staff development programs, new models of staff development, theories of adult learning, planning and funding of district-based staff development programs, and relevant research. Sponsors regional workshops on topics such as conducting effective staff development programs. **Publications:** *Journal of Staff Development* (quarterly); *The Learning Principal* (8/year); *Teachers Teaching Teachers* (8/year).

19069 ■ OAS Staff Association
1889 F St. NW, Ste. 691
Washington, DC 20006
Ph:(202)458-6230
Fax:(202)458-3466
Co. E-mail: staffadmin@oas.org
URL: http://staff.oas.org/english/default.asp
Contact: Carla Sorani, Pres.
Description: Staff members of the Organization of American States General Secretariat. Serves as a union to negotiate employment conditions and labor rights with the OAS administration. **Publications:** *Staff News* .

REFERENCE WORKS

19070 ■ *Alternative Travel Directory*
Pub: Transitions Abroad Publishing
Contact: Bill Nolting, Author
Ed: Ron Mader, Editor. **Released:** Annual, January; latest edition 7th. **Price:** $19.95, individuals. **Covers:** Over 2,000 sources of information on international employment, education, and specialty travel opportunities. **Entries Include:** Source name, address, phone, description, cost dates. **Arrangement:** Classified by subject and country. **Indexes:** Geographical.

19071 ■ "Area Hurt By Doctor Deficiency" in *The Business Journal-Serving Metropolitan Kansas City* (Vol. 27, October 17, 2008, No. 5, pp. 1)
Pub: American City Business Journals, Inc.
Ed: Rob Roberts. **Description:** Kansas City, Missouri may face a shortage of doctors, according to the Metropolitan Medical Society of Greater Kansas City. Over the next ten years the city needs to recruit more doctors in order to address the problem. Practicing physicians are having difficulties recruiting.

19072 ■ "Bankruptcies" in *Crain's Detroit Business* (Vol. 24, September 29, 2008, No. 39, pp. 4)
Pub: Crain Communications, Inc.
Description: Current list of business that filed for Chapter 7 or 11 protection in U.S. Bankruptcy Court in Detroit include manufacturers, real estate companies, a printing company and a specialized staffing company.

19073 ■ *Complete Guide to Public Employment*
Pub: Impact Publications
Ed: Ron Krannich, PhD, Editor. **Released:** Triennial, Latest edition 3rd. **Price:** $19.95, individuals paper. **Publication Includes:** List of federal, state, and local government agencies and departments, trade and professional associations, contracting and consulting firms, nonprofit organizations, foundations, research organizations, political support groups, and other organizations offering public service career opportunities. **Entries Include:** Organization name, address, phone, name and title of contact. Complete title is "Complete Guide to Public Employment: Opportunities and Strategies with Federal, State, and Local Government;" Trade and Professional Associations; Contracting and Consulting Firms; Foundations; Research Organizations; and Political Support Groups. **Arrangement:** Classified by type of service. **Indexes:** Subject.

19074 ■ *Directory of Contract Staffing Firms*
Pub: C.E. Publications Inc.
Contact: Jerry A. Erickson, Publisher
Released: Annual. **Covers:** Nearly 1,300 contract firms actively engaged in the employment of engineering, IT/IS, and technical personnel for 'temporary' contract assignments throughout the world. **Entries Include:** Company name, address, phone, name of contact, email, web address. **Arrangement:** Alphabetical. **Indexes:** Geographical.

19075 ■ *Federal Jobs Digest*
Pub: Federal Jobs Digest
Contact: Peter E. Ognibene
Released: 25x/yr. **Price:** $125, U.S.; $152.75, Canada; $183.75, individuals Europe; $112.50, libraries. **Covers:** Over 10,000 specific job openings in the federal government in each issue. Vacancies from over 300 Federal Agencies are covered. **Entries Include:** Position name, title, General Schedule (GS) grade, and Wage Grade (WG), closing date for applications, announcement number, application address, phone, and name of contact. **Arrangement:** By federal department or agency, then geographical.

19076 ■ *INSIGHT Into Diversity*
Pub: INSIGHT Into Diversity
Ed: Lucy Knapp-Yanni, Editor. **Released:** Monthly. **Price:** $15, individuals subscription per/year; $8, individuals subscription for 1/2 year. **Covers:** In each issue, about 300 positions at a professional level (most requiring advanced study) available to women, minorities, veterans, and the handicapped; listings are advertisements placed by employers with affirmative action programs. **Entries Include:** Company or organization name, address, contact name; description of position including title, requirements, duties, application procedure, salary, etc. **Arrangement:** Classified by profession.

19077 ■ *Journal of the American Medical Association—Physician Service Opportunities Overseas Section*
Pub: American Medical Association
Contact: Gwenn Gregg
E-mail: gwenn_gwegg@ama-assn.org
Released: Irregular, latest edition August 2002. **Publication Includes:** List of more than 60 organizations that provide assignments overseas for physicians from the United States. **Entries Include:** Organization name, address, phone, contact person, countries served, and medical specialties sought. **Arrangement:** Alphabetical.

19078 ■ "King of the Crib: How Good Samaritan Became Ohio's Baby HQ" in *Business Courier* (Vol. 27, June 18, 2010, No. 7, pp. 1)
Pub: Business Courier
Ed: James Ritchie. **Description:** Cincinnati's Good Samaritan hospital had 6,875 live births in 2009, which is more than any other hospital in Ohio. They specialize in the highest-risk pregnancies and deliveries and other hospitals are trying to grab Good Samaritan's share in this niche.

19079 ■ *National Directory for Employment in Education*
Pub: American Association for Employment in Education
Contact: B.J. Bryant, Exec. Dir.
Released: Annual, winter; latest edition 2008-2009. **Price:** $20, nonmembers Processing fee $2; $10, members processing fee $2. **Covers:** about 600 placement offices maintained by teacher-training institutions and 300 school district personnel officers and/or superintendents responsible for hiring profesional staff. **Entries Include:** Institution name, address, phone, contact name, email address, and website. **Arrangement:** Geographical. **Indexes:** Personal name, subject-field of teacher training, institutions which provide vacancy bulletins and placement services to non-enrolled students.

19080 ■ "The People Puzzle; Re-Training America's Workers" in *The Economist* (Vol. 390, January 3, 2009, No. 8612, pp. 32)
Pub: The Economist Newspaper Inc.
Description: With thousands of workers losing their jobs, America is now facing the task of getting them back to work. With an overall unemployment rate of 6.7 percent, the federal government has three main ways for leading workers back to employment: training them for new jobs, providing unemployment insurance in order to replace lost wages during the period of job-hunting; and matching employers who desire a skill with workers who have that skill. Specialized

staffing agencies provide employers and potential employees with the help necessary to find a job in some of the more niche markets.

19081 ■ "Q&A With Devin Ringling: Franchise's Services Go Beyond Elder Care" in *Gazette* (October 2, 2010)
Pub: The Gazette
Ed: Bill Radford. **Description:** Profile of franchise, Interim HealthCare, in Colorado Springs, Colorado; the company offers home care services that include wound care and specialized feedings to shopping and light housekeeping. It also runs a medical staffing company that provides nurses, therapists and other health care workers to hospitals, prisons, schools and other facilities.

19082 ■ *SER Network Directory*
Pub: SER-Jobs for Progress National Inc.
Contact: Alex Martinez, Exec. Dir.
Released: Annual, Latest edition 2009. **Covers:** Approximately 130 affiliated agencies in 90 U.S. cities of SER ("Service, Employment, Redevelopment")-Jobs for Progress National, Inc., an organization of Hispanics that provides employment and training, services to disadvantaged youth and adults, especially Hispanics. **Entries Include:** Organization name, address, phone, name of president, services provided, satellite offices, if any. **Arrangement:** Geographical.

19083 ■ "Sign of the Times: Temp-To-Perm Attorneys" in *HRMagazine* (Vol. 54, January 2009, No. 1, pp. 24)
Pub: Society for Human Resource Management
Ed: Bill Leonard. **Description:** A growing number of law firms are hiring professional staff on a temp-to-perm basis according to the president of Professional Placement Services in Florida. Firms can save money while testing potential employees on a temporary basis.

19084 ■ "Staffing Firm Grows by Following Own Advice-Hire a Headhunter" in *Crain's Detroit Business* (Vol. 24, October 6, 2008, No. 40, pp. 1)
Pub: Crain Communications, Inc.
Ed: Sherri Begin. **Description:** Profile of Venator Holdings L.L.C., a staffing firm that provides searches for companies in need of financial-accounting and technical employees; the firm's revenue has increased from $1.1 million in 2003 to a projected $11.5 million this year due to a climate in which more people are exiting the workforce than are coming in with those particular specialized skills and the need for a temporary, flexible workforce for contract placements at companies that do not want to take on the legacy costs associated with permanent employees. The hiring of an external headhunter to find the right out-of-state manager for Venator is also discussed.

19085 ■ "Work To Do" in *Canadian Business* (Vol. 81, July 22, 2008, No. 12-13, pp. 22)
Pub: Rogers Media Ltd.
Ed: Jane Bao. **Description:** Recruiting firm Manpower revealed that 36 percent of Canadian employers had trouble filling positions in 2007, highlighting the labor shortage and the need to bring in more workers. Underemployment of immigrants costs up to $6 billion to Canada's economy every year. Other views regarding Canada's labor shortage and on its economic impact are presented.

SOURCES OF SUPPLY

19086 ■ *Atlanta JobBank*
Pub: Adams Media Corp.
Contact: Michael Kelly
E-mail: michael.kelly@adamsmedia.com
Released: latest edition 15th. **Price:** $17.95, individuals Paperback. **Covers:** 3,900 employers in the state of Georgia, including Albany, Columbus, Macon, and Savannah. **Entries Include:** Firm or organization name, address, local phone, toll-free phone, fax, description of organization, subsidiaries, other locations, recorded jobline, name and title of contact, typical titles for common positions, educational backgrounds desired, number of employees, benefits offered, training programs, internships, parent company, revenues, e-mail and URL address, projected number of hires. **Arrangement:** Classified by industry. **Indexes:** Alphabetical.

19087 ■ *Boston JobBank*
Pub: Adams Media Corp.
Released: Annual, latest edition 20th. **Price:** $17.95, individuals Paperback. **Covers:** Over 7,000 employers in Massachusetts. **Entries Include:** Firm or organization name, address, local phone, toll-free phone, fax, e-mail, URL, recorded jobline, hours, names of management, name and title of contact, titles of common positions, entry-level positions, fringe benefits offered, stock exchange listing, description of organization, subsidiaries, location of headquarters, educational background desired, projected number of hires, training programs, internships, parent company, number of employees, revenues, other U.S. Locations, and international locations. **Arrangement:** Classified by industry. **Indexes:** Alphabetical.

19088 ■ *California Job Journal*
Pub: California Job Journal
Contact: Kathy Masera, Publisher
Ed: Clayton Babcock, Editor. **Released:** Weekly, Latest edition 2011. **Price:** Free. **Covers:** Employment issues and job openings in California from entry-level to executive positions. **Entries Include:** Company name, address, phone, type of business, name and title of contact; comprehensive description of position and required skills/background, salary and/or benefits offered. **Arrangement:** Classified by field of employment.

19089 ■ *Carolina JobBank*
Pub: Adams Media Corp.
Released: latest edition 7th. **Price:** $12.21, individuals Paperback. **Covers:** 4,600 employers in North Carolina and South Carolina. **Entries Include:** Firm or organization name, address, local phone, toll-free phone, fax, e-mail, URL, recorded jobline, description of organization, subsidiaries, other locations, hours, names of management, name and title of contact, location of headquarters, typical titles for common positions, educational backgrounds desired, projected number of hires, company benefits, stock exchange listing, training programs and internships, parent company, number of employees, revenues. **Arrangement:** Classified by industry. **Indexes:** Alphabetical.

19090 ■ *Chicago JobBank*
Pub: Adams Media Corp.
Released: Annual, Latest edition 19th. **Price:** $17.95, individuals Paperback; $9, individuals sale price. **Covers:** About 5,500 major employers in northern and central Illinois including Aurora, Peoria, Rockford, and Springfield. **Entries Include:** Firm or organization name, address, local phone, toll-free phone, fax, e-mail, URL, description of organization, hours, recorded jobline, subsidiaries, names of management, name and title of contact, names of management, headquarters locations, typical titles for entry-level and middle-level positions, educational backgrounds desired, company benefits, stock exchange listing, training programs, internships, parent company, number of employees, revenues, other U.S. Locations, international locations. **Arrangement:** Classified by industry. **Indexes:** Alphabetical.

19091 ■ *Dallas/Ft. Worth JobBank*
Pub: Adams Media Corp.
Released: Annual, latest edition 14th. **Price:** $9, individuals Paperback. **Covers:** 4,000 employers in the Dallas/Ft. Worth, Texas, area including Abilene, Amarillo, Arlington, Garland, Irving, Lubbock, Plano. **Entries Include:** Firm or organization name, address, local phone, toll-free phone, fax, e-mail, URL, recorded jobline, hours, description of organization, subsidiaries, names of management, name and title of contact, location of headquarters, typical titles for common positions, educational backgrounds desired, company benefits, stock exchange listing, training programs, internships, parent company, number of employees, revenues, projected number of hires. **Arrangement:** Classified by industry. **Indexes:** Alphabetical.

19092 ■ *Denver JobBank*
Pub: Adams Media Corp.
Ed: Steven Graber, Editor. **Released:** latest edition 14th. **Price:** $17.95, individuals 4 used & new. **Covers:** 3,500 employers in Denver and the rest of Colorado including Aurora, Boulder, Colorado Springs, Lakewood. **Entries Include:** Firm or organization name, address, local phone, toll-free phone, fax, e-mail, URL, description of organization, subsidiaries, other locations, hours, recorded jobline, names of management, name and title of contact, headquarters location, projected number of hires; listings may also include typical titles for common positions, educational backgrounds desired, company benefits, stock exchange listing, training programs, internships, parent company, number of employees, revenues. **Arrangement:** Classified by industry. **Indexes:** Alphabetical.

19093 ■ *Federal Career Opportunities*
Pub: Federal Research Service Inc.
Released: Biweekly, Latest edition 2010. **Price:** $19.97, members per copy; $59.95, members 6 issues; $99.95, members 12 issues; $39.95, members 26 issues. **Covers:** more than 3,000 current federal job vacancies in the United States and overseas; includes permanent, part-time, and temporary positions. **Entries Include:** Position title, location, series and grade, job requirements, special forms, announcement number, closing date, application address. **Arrangement:** Classified by occupation.

19094 ■ *Florida JobBank*
Pub: Adams Media Corp.
Released: latest edition 16th. **Price:** $17.95, individuals payment with order; $9, individuals sale price. **Covers:** 5,500 employers in Florida including Fort Lauderdale, Jacksonville, Miami, Orlando, Tampa. **Entries Include:** Firm or organization name, address, local phone, toll-free phone, fax, e-mail addresses, web addresses, description of organization, subsidiaries, hours, recorded jobline, name and title of contact, headquarters location, typical titles for common positions, educational backgrounds desired, number of projected hires, company benefits, stock exchange listing, training programs, internships, parent company, number of employees, revenues, other U.S. Locations, international locations. **Arrangement:** Classified by industry. **Indexes:** Alphabetical.

19095 ■ *Houston JobBank*
Pub: Adams Media Corp.
Released: Annual, latest edition 12th. **Price:** $17.95, individuals 3 used & new. **Covers:** Over 4,000 employers in Houston, Texas and the surrounding areas including Bayton, Beaumont, Galveston, Pasadena. **Entries Include:** Firm or organization name, address, local phone, toll-free phone, fax, recorded jobline, e-mail, URL, hours, name and title of contact; description of organization; headquarters location, subsidiaries, operations at the facility, names of management, typical titles for common positions, educational backgrounds desired, number of projected hires, fringe benefits offered, stock exchange listing, training programs, internships, parent company, number of employees, revenues, other U.S. locations, international locations. **Arrangement:** Classified by industry. **Indexes:** Alphabetical.

19096 ■ *International Employment Hotline*
Pub: International Employment Hotline
Contact: Lisa Law, Publisher
E-mail: lisa@internationaljobs.org
Released: Monthly. **Price:** $69, individuals per 1 year; $21, individuals per 3 months; $39, individuals per 6 months; $129, individuals per 2 years. **Covers:** Temporary and career job openings overseas and advice for international job hunters. **Entries Include:** Company name, address, job title, description of job, requirements, geographic location of job. **Arrangement:** Geographical.

19097 ■ *Los Angeles JobBank*
Pub: Adams Media Corp.
Released: Annual, latest edition 17th. **Price:** $16.95, individuals Paperback. **Covers:** Over 7,900 southern California employers including Orange, Riverside, San Bernardino, San Diego, Santa Barbara and Ventura counties. **Entries Include:** Firm or organization name, address, local phone, toll-free phone, fax,

e-mail, URL, recorded jobline, hours, subsidiaries, other locations, names of management, name and title of contact, description of organization, number of employees, headquarters location, typical titles for common positions, educational backgrounds desired, fringe benefits offered, stock exchange listing, training programs, internships, parent company, number of employees, revenues, corporate headquarters, and number of projected hires. Projected hires. **Arrangement:** Classified by industry. **Indexes:** Alphabetical.

19098 ■ *Metropolitan Washington DC JobBank*
Pub: Adams Media Corp.
Contact: Michael Kelly
E-mail: michael.kelly@adamsmedia.com
Released: Latest edition 17th. **Price:** $17.95, individuals Paperback. **Covers:** 6,900 employers in Washington, D.C. , Greater Baltimore, and Northern Virginia. **Entries Include:** Firm or organization name, address, local phone, toll-free phone, fax, recorded jobline, name and title of contact, description of organization, subsidiaries, other locations, names of management, hours, titles for common positions, educational backgrounds desired, company benefits, stock exchange listing, location of headquarters, training programs, internships, parent company, number of employees, revenues, email and URL address, projected number of hires. **Arrangement:** Classified by industry. **Indexes:** Alphabetical.

19099 ■ *National JobBank*
Pub: Adams Media Corp.
Released: Annual, Latest edition 2010. **Price:** $475, individuals payment with order. **Covers:** Over 20,000 employers nationwide. **Entries Include:** Firm or organization name, address, local phone, toll-free phone, fax, contact name and title, description of organization, headquarters location, names of management, number of employees, other locations, subsidiaries, parent company, projected number of hires, training offered, internships, hours, recorded jobline, typical titles for common positions, educational backgrounds desired, stock exchange (if listed), fringe benefits offered. Several state and regional volumes are available and described separately. **Arrangement:** Geographical. **Indexes:** Geographical and classified by industry.

19100 ■ *San Francisco Bay Area JobBank*
Pub: Adams Media Corp.
Contact: Michael Kelly
E-mail: michael.kelly@adamsmedia.com
Released: Latest edition 18th. **Price:** $17.95, individuals Paperback. **Covers:** About 5,600 employers in the San Francisco Bay area and the Northern half of California including Oakland, Sacramento, San Jose, and Silicon Valley. **Entries Include:** Firm or organization name, address, local phone, toll-free phone, fax, e-mail, URL, recorded jobline, hours, description of organization, subsidiaries, other locations, number of employees, name and title of contact, headquarters location, typical titles for common positions, educational backgrounds desired, company benefits, stock exchange listing, training programs, internships, parent company, and number of employees, revenues, corporate headquarters, and number of projected hires. **Arrangement:** Classified by industry. **Indexes:** Alphabetical.

19101 ■ *Seattle JobBank*
Pub: Adams Media Corp.
Contact: Michael Kelly
Released: latest edition 13th. **Price:** $17.95, individuals Paperback. **Covers:** About 4,800 employers in Washington state, including Spokane, Tacoma, and Bellevue. **Entries Include:** Firm or organization name, address, local phone, toll-free phone, fax, e-mail, URL, description of organization, subsidiaries, name and title of contact, headquarters location, recorded jobline, typical titles for common positions, educational backgrounds desired, projected number of hires, company benefits, stock exchange listing, training programs, internships, parent company, number of employees, revenues. **Arrangement:** Classified by industry. **Indexes:** Alphabetical.

TRADE PERIODICALS

19102 ■ *Graduating Engineer & Computer Careers*
Pub: Career Recruitment Media
Contact: Matt Summer, VP, Sales and Mktg.
E-mail: msummer@alloyeducation.com
Released: Quarterly. **Price:** $16.95. **Description:** Magazine focusing on employment, education, and career development for entry-level engineers and computer scientists.

19103 ■ *Insight into Diversity*
Pub: INSIGHT Into Diversity
Contact: Sarah Zeveski, Advertising Dir
Ed: Michael Rainey, Editor. **Released:** Monthly. **Description:** Journal for business, academia, non-profit organizations and the government to use in recruiting females, Native Americans, minorities, veterans, and persons with disabilities.

19104 ■ *Mobility*
Pub: Employee Relocation Council
Contact: Jerry Holloman, VP/Publisher
E-mail: jholloman@worldwideerc.org
Released: Monthly. **Price:** $48. **Description:** Magazine for professionals in the relocation industry.

19105 ■ *NSBE Magazine*
Pub: NSBE Publications
Contact: Pamela Sharif, Publisher
Released: 3/yr. **Price:** $20; $35 other countries; $15 students. **Description:** Journal providing information on engineering careers, self-development, and cultural issues for recent graduates with technical majors.

19106 ■ *Public Personnel Management*
Pub: International Personnel Management Association
Contact: Neil Reichenberg, Exec. Ed.
Released: Quarterly. **Price:** $130 print & online; $175 other countries print & online; $100 online only. **Description:** Journal for human resource executives and managers in the public sector. Contains articles on trends, case studies, legislation, and industry research.

19107 ■ *Staffing Industry Analysts*
Pub: Staffing Industry Analysts Inc.
Contact: Craig Johnson, Analyst and Assoc. Ed.
E-mail: basin@staffingindustry.com
Released: Bimonthly, 22/year. **Description:** Focuses on the temporary help and employment services industry. Provides information on economic forecasts, employment indicators, finance, labor and market trends, stocks, and statistics.

VIDEOCASSETTES/ AUDIOCASSETTES

19108 ■ *Specialty Nursing*
Moonbeam Publications, Inc.
PO Box 5150
Traverse City, MI 49696
Ph:(616)922-0533
Free: 800-445-2391
Fax:800-334-9789
Co. E-mail: custserv@moonbeampublications.com
URL: http://www.moonbeampublications.com
Released: 1988. **Price:** $250.00. **Description:** Features highlights from a meeting of the National Federation of Specialty Nursing Organizations. **Availability:** VHS; 3/4U.

CONSULTANTS

19109 ■ Columbia Consultants
8950 Old Annapolis Rd., Rte. 108, Ste. 226
Columbia, MD 21045
Ph:(410)992-4700
Free: 800-783-7574
Fax:(410)992-4518
Contact: Anela Brooks, Principle
E-mail: abrooks@columbiaconsultants.net
Scope: A complete personnel service offering placement of both permanent and temporary employees. Provides professional services and integrated solutions.

19110 ■ The Purchasing Department
34 Claremont Ave.
Maplewood, NJ 07040-2118
Fax:(973)275-0749
Co. E-mail: eostpd@aol.com
Contact: James Thomas Milway, Principle
E-mail: jtmtpd@aol.com
Scope: Provides state of the art procurement arrangements, process re-engineering and outsourcing assistance to any business wishing to achieve purchasing savings and efficiencies to improve bottom line results. Available to provide contract services to businesses requiring specialized supplemental assistance to back up own personnel on special projects. **Seminars:** Green Purchasing: Buying Recycled Products; Ethics; Measuring Purchasing Performance; Supplier Teaming and Quality; Preparing for ISO 9000 in the Purchasing Department.

19111 ■ SBR International
3 - 14 College St.
The Graeme Bldg.
Toronto, ON, Canada M5G 1K2
Ph:(416)962-7500
Fax:(416)962-7505
Co. E-mail: bizdev@sbr-global.com
URL: http://www.sbr-global.com
Contact: Chris Anstead, Managering Director
Scope: Specializes in the leasing of multi-disciplinary, high-performance work teams at customer in-house cost, under a mixed military/general contracting model. Engagements include BPR, IE, SA, market and competitor intelligence, logistics, strategy, audit, workouts/turnarounds, M and A support/targeting, statistics and micro-economic modeling, PMO support. **Seminars:** Electronic counter measures; Strategic planning; Project management.

FRANCHISES AND BUSINESS OPPORTUNITIES

19112 ■ AtWork Personnel Services
3215 John Sevier Hwy.
Knoxville, TN 37920
Free: 800-383-0804
Fax:(865)573-1171
No. of Franchise Units: 36. **Founded:** 1990. **Franchised:** 1992. **Description:** Staffing service. **Equity Capital Needed:** $143,600-$226,800. **Franchise Fee:** $0-$25,000. **Royalty Fee:** 6.1-1.6%. **Financial Assistance:** Limited in-house financing available. **Training:** Training includes 5 days minimum at headquarters, 3-5 days onsite, 2 days of meeting and ongoing support.

19113 ■ Lloyd Staffing
445 Broadhollow Rd., Ste. 119
Melville, NY 11747
Ph:(631)777-7600
Free: 888-292-6678
Fax:(631)777-7626
Co. E-mail: info@lloydstaffing.com
URL: http://www.lloydstaffing.com
No. of Franchise Units: 5. **No. of Company-Owned Units:** 6. **Founded:** 1971. **Franchised:** 1988. **Description:** Specialized staffing services. **Equity Capital Needed:** $93,500-$158,300. **Franchise Fee:** $20,000. **Financial Assistance:** Yes. **Training:** Yes.

19114 ■ Party Personnel Franchise Systems
11720 Hadley
Overland Park, KS 66210
Ph:(913)451-0218
Fax:(913)451-8941
No. of Franchise Units: 1. **No. of Company-Owned Units:** 1. **Founded:** 1993. **Franchised:** 2003. **Description:** Hospitality & entertainment staffing. **Equity Capital Needed:** $22,500-$40,000. **Franchise Fee:** $15,000. **Royalty Fee:** 3%. **Financial Assistance:** No. **Training:** Training includes 2 weeks at headquarters, 1 week/year at franchisee's location and ongoing support.

COMPUTERIZED DATABASES

19115 ■ *HireDiversity.com*
Hispanic Business Inc.
425 Pine Ave.
Santa Barbara, CA 93117-3709
Ph:(805)964-4554

Fax:(805)964-5539
URL: http://www.hispanicbusiness.com
Price: Free. **Entries Include:** Name, address, phone, employment history, salary requirements, level of management experience, education, geographical preference, and language. **Database Covers:** Over 95,000 resumes of multicultural professionals and recent college graduates who are seeking employment with Fortune 500 companies; job listings with a large variety of companies.

19116 ■ *Library Literature & Information Science Full Text*
EBSCO Publishing
10 Estes St.
Ipswich, MA 01938
Ph:(978)356-6500
Free: 800-653-2726
Fax:(978)356-6565
Co. E-mail: information@ebscohost.com
URL: http://www.ebscohost.com/wilson
Description: Contains more than 240,000 citations and indexing to more than 400 English and foreign language periodicals and journals, monographs, conference proceedings, pamphlets, and library school theses, as well as full text of articles from January 1994. Includes reviews of books, periodicals, and audiovisual materials in the library and information science area. Features periodical indexing from 1984. Provides hotlinks to websites featured in the articles. **Availability:** Online: EBSCO Publishing, Wolters Kluwer Health, Wolters Kluwer Health. **Type:** Bibliographic; Full text.

LIBRARIES

19117 ■ Brandeis University–Center for Youth and Communities Library
415 South St.
Waltham, MA 02453
Ph:(781)736-3770
Fax:(781)736-3773
Co. E-mail: melchior@brandeis.edu
URL: http://cyc.brandeis.edu
Contact: Alan Melchior, Sr.Res.Assoc.
Scope: Employment and income research, youth employment and education, employee benefits, welfare reform, public/private partnership, networking in social programs. **Services:** Library open to the public by appointment. **Holdings:** 3000 volumes.

19118 ■ Colorado Department of Labor & Employment–Labor Market Information Library
633 17th St., Ste. 400
Denver, CO 80202-3660
Ph:(303)318-8700
Free: 800-685-0891;
Fax:(303)318-8710
Co. E-mail: workers.comp@state.co.us
URL: http://lmigateway.coworkforce.com/lmigateway/
Scope: Labor market information. **Services:** Library open to the public for reference use only. **Holdings:** 100 books; 1000 unbound reports; 500 unbound periodicals; all official Colorado labor force estimates. **Subscriptions:** 20 journals and other serials.

19119 ■ District of Columbia Public Library–Business, Economics and Vocations Division
Martin Luther King Memorial Library
901 G St. NW, Rm. 107
Washington, DC 20001
Ph:(202)727-1171
Fax:(202)727-1129
Co. E-mail: commentssuggestions.dcpl@dc.gov
URL: http://dclibrary.org
Contact: David Robinson, Div.Mgr.
Scope: Business; statistics, economics, vocations, investment, real estate, import, export, accounting, taxation, business report writing, organizational behavior, commerce, management, marketing, labor, transportation. **Services:** Interlibrary loan; copying; division open to the public. **Holdings:** 55,639 books; 1150 bound periodical volumes; 471 business directories; 6000 pamphlets; 508 telephone directories; 5521 reels of microfilm; 88 microcards; 7268 microfiche. **Subscriptions:** 428 journals and other serials; 35 newspapers and financial services.

19120 ■ New York Department of Labor–Labor Research Library
Averill Harriman State Office Campus, Bldg. 12, Rm. 480
Albany, NY 12240-0013
Ph:(518)457-1292
Fax:(518)457-6199
Co. E-mail: ashley.hibbard@labor.state.ny.us
Contact: R. Ashley Hibbard, Sr.Libn.
Scope: Employment, statistics, economic and business conditions, personnel management, unions, unemployment insurance, wages and hours, labor legislation, vocational education and guidance. **Services:** Interlibrary loan; copying; Library open to the public with restrictions. **Holdings:** 3000 titles (books and documents); 20 VF drawers. **Subscriptions:** 175 journals and other serials.

RESEARCH CENTERS

19121 ■ University of Texas at Arlington–Center for Research on Organizational and Managerial Excellence
Management Department, Box 19467
Arlington, TX 76019
Ph:(817)272-3866
Fax:(817)272-3122
Co. E-mail: wheeler@uta.edu
URL: http://www.uta.edu/ra/real/editprofile.php?onlyview=1&pid=512
Contact: Kenneth G. Wheeler PhD, Dir.
E-mail: wheeler@uta.edu
Scope: Corporate restructuring and the effect on human resource function and the workforce; employee absenteeism and turnover; corporate strategic decision making; organizational stress; employee job satisfaction; work group effectiveness; employee selection; and work schedule effects on employee attitudes and health; work adjustment of employees with impairments and disabilities. **Publications:** Working papers.

START-UP INFORMATION

19122 ■ "Local Flavor" in *Entrepreneur* (Vol. 35, November 2007, No. 11, pp. 110)
Pub: Entrepreneur Media Inc.
Ed: Nichole L. Torres. **Description:** Local food products are growing in the market today as consumers are becoming interested in where their food comes; you can start a business by investigating the kinds of foods popular in your region.

ASSOCIATIONS AND OTHER ORGANIZATIONS

19123 ■ American Cheese Society
2696 S Colorado Blvd., Ste. 570
Denver, CO 80222-5954
Ph:(720)328-2788
Fax:(720)328-2786
Co. E-mail: info@cheesesociety.org
URL: http://www.cheesesociety.org
Contact: Nora Weiser, Exec. Dir.
Description: Represents producers, manufacturers, retailers, distributors and others interested in the specialty and farmstead cheese industry. Aims to promote cheese appreciation and to provide useful information on cheese making in a farm, house, or a manufacturing plant environment. Includes activities such as annual conferences, cheese tasting and workshops on cheese making. Conducts discussions on the technical and economical aspects of cheese making. Sponsors competitions; maintains speakers' bureau. .

19124 ■ Greek Food and Wine Institute
34-80 48th St.
Long Island City, NY 11101
Ph:(718)729-5277
Co. E-mail: info@gfwi.org
URL: http://www.gfwi.org
Description: Food, wine and spirits producers, importers, and distributors from Greece and the U.S. Educates food and wine trade and consumers about the quality, variety, uses, and healthfulness of Greek foods, wines, and spirits. Conducts educational programs. **Publications:** *Gastronomia* (semiannual); *Greek Wine Manual: Guide Sommeliers & Wine Professionals* .

19125 ■ International Dairy-Deli-Bakery Association
PO Box 5528
Madison, WI 53705-0528
Ph:(608)310-5000
Fax:(608)238-6330
Co. E-mail: iddba@iddba.org
URL: http://www.iddba.org
Contact: Carol Christison, Exec. Dir.
Description: Companies and organizations engaged in the production, processing, packaging, marketing, promotion, and/or selling of cheese and cheese products, bakery, or delicatessen and delicatessen-related items. Aims to further the relationship between manufacturing, production, marketing and distribution channels utilized in the delivery of deli, dairy, and bakery foods to the marketplace. Develops and disseminates information concerning deli, dairy, and bakery foods. **Publications:** *Dairy-Deli-Bake Digest* (monthly); *IDDBA and You* (monthly); *Trainer's Tool Kit*; *Who's Who in Dairy-Deli-Bakery* (periodic).

19126 ■ National Association for the Specialty Food Trade
136 Madison Ave., 12th Fl.
New York, NY 10016
Ph:(212)482-6440
Free: 800-627-3869
Fax:(212)482-6459
Co. E-mail: info@nasft.org
URL: http://www.specialtyfood.com
Contact: Ann Daw, Pres.
Description: Represents manufacturers, distributors, processors, importers, retailers, and brokers of specialty and gourmet foods. **Publications:** *Specialty Food Magazine* (10/year).

19127 ■ Opimian, the Wine Society of Canada–La Societe Opimian
5165 Sherbrooke St. W, Ste. 420
Montreal, QC, Canada H4A 1T6
Ph:(514)483-5551
Free: 800-361-9421
Fax:(514)481-9699
Co. E-mail: opim@opim.ca
URL: http://www.opim.ca
Contact: Pierre Chanzonkov, Gen. Mgr.
Description: Individuals interested in wine. Promotes increased public appreciation of wine. Conducts educational programs.

DIRECTORIES OF EDUCATIONAL PROGRAMS

19128 ■ *Major Food & Drink Companies of the World*
Pub: Graham & Whiteside
Ed: Heather Brewin, Editor. **Released:** Annual, Latest edition 16th; Published May, 2012. **Price:** $1,460, individuals. **Covers:** Over 9,200 worldwide companies involved in the food and drink industry. **Entries Include:** Company name, address, phone and names and titles of key personnel.

REFERENCE WORKS

19129 ■ "At Wine Kiosk, Show ID, Face Camera, Swipe Card and Blow" in *Pittsburgh Post-Gazette* (November 28, 2010)
Pub: Pittsburgh-Post Gazette
Ed: Dennis B. Roddy. **Description:** New technology installed on wine kiosks enables sellers to abide by the law. This technology tests blood alcohol levels and warns people if they have recently used a mouthwash before testing.

19130 ■ "Bagging Profits; High-End Grocers Expand Despite Stale Economy" in *Crain's Detroit Business* (Vol. 24, March 24, 2008, No. 12, pp. 1)
Pub: Crain Communications, Inc.
Ed: Nancy Kaffer. **Description:** Discusses the expansion plans of several high-end grocery stores in the Detroit area and the reasons why, despite the poor economy, these gourmet grocers are doing well. Statistical data included.

19131 ■ "The Bear Arrives - With Bargain Hunters" in *Barron's* (Vol. 88, July 7, 2008, No. 27, pp. M3)
Pub: Dow Jones & Co., Inc.
Ed: Kopin Tan. **Description:** US stock markets have dropped 20 percent below their highs, entering the bear market at the end of June 2008. It was also the worst performance of the stock markets during June. Wine maker Constellation Brands, however, reported a 50 percent rise in net income for the first quarter of 2008.

19132 ■ "The Believer" in *Inc.* (December 2007, pp. 130-138)
Pub: Gruner & Jahr USA Publishing
Ed: Leigh Buchanan. **Description:** Profile of Selena Cuffe, wine importer and socially conscious woman entrepreneur, who is focusing her talents on helping South Africa get wine products to America.

19133 ■ *Beverage Marketing Directory*
Pub: Beverage Marketing Corp.
Contact: Brian Sudano, Mng. Dir.
Released: Annual, Latest edition 33rd; 2011. **Price:** $1,435, individuals softcover or in PDF format; $5,495, individuals database on CD-ROM; $5,495, Canada database on CD-ROM. **Covers:** Over 25,500 beer wholesalers, wine and spirits wholesalers, soft drink bottlers and franchisors, breweries, wineries, distilleries, alcoholic beverage importers, bottled water companies; and trade associations, government agencies, micro breweries, juice, coffee, tea, milk companies, and others concerned with the beverage and bottling industries; coverage includes Canada. **Entries Include:** Beverage and bottling company listings contain company name, address, phone, names of key executives, number of employees, brand names, and other information, including number of franchisees, number of delivery trucks, sales volume. Suppliers and related companies and organizations listings include similar but less detailed information. **Arrangement:** Geographical. **Indexes:** Personnel, supplier's product, company name.

19134 ■ "Booze Makers Battle Over Turkey Day" in *Advertising Age* (Vol. 78, October 29, 2007, No. 43, pp. 4)
Pub: Crain Communications, Inc.
Ed: Jeremy Mullman. **Description:** Beer and wine marketers are jockeying for position in regards to the Thanksgiving holiday.

19135 ■ "Cheap Thrills: Where to Look When You're Craving a Low-Price Wine" in *Chicago Tribune* (January 12, 2009)
Pub: McClatchy-Tribune Information Services
Ed: Bill Daley. **Description:** Wines priced $15 and above are being hit the hardest by the economic

downturn while cheaper wines, specifically those priced between $3 and $6, are seeing a growth in sales.

19136 ■ "Closures Pop Cork on Wine Bar Sector Consolidation" in *Houston Business Journal* (Vol. 40, January 22, 2010, No. 37, pp. A2)
Pub: American City Business Journals
Ed: Allison Wollam. **Description:** Wine bar market in Houston, Texas is in the midst of a major shift and heads toward further consolidation due to the closure of pioneering wine bars that opened in the past decade. The Corkscrew owner, Andrew Adams, has blamed the creation of competitive establishments to the closure which helped wear out his concept.

19137 ■ "Construction Firms Support NAACP Plan" in *Business Courier* (Vol. 27, September 24, 2010, No. 21, pp. 1)
Pub: Business Courier
Ed: Lucy May. **Description:** Executives of Turner Construction Company and Messer Construction Company expressed their support for the Cincinnati National Association for the Advancement of Colored People Construction Partnership Agreement. The agreement involves the setting of rules for the involvement of firms owned by African Americans in major projects in Cincinnati.

19138 ■ "Dancing With Giants: Acquisition and Survival of the Family Firm" in *Family Business Review* (Vol. 19, December 2006, No. 4, pp. 289)
Pub: Family Firm Institute Inc.
Ed: Adam Steen, Lawrence S. Welch. **Description:** Responses of family firms to mergers and acquisitions are analyzed taking the example of the takeover of an Australian wine producer and family firm.

19139 ■ "Eagle's Wine Kiosk Is Area's 1st" in *Pittsburgh Post-Gazette* (October 28, 2010)
Pub: Pittsburgh-Post Gazette
Ed: Bob Batz Jr. **Description:** Giant Eagle Market District store at Settlers Ridge opened the first self-serve wine kiosk in Western Pennsylvania. The kiosk will have a built-in breathalyzer panel to ensure safety.

19140 ■ "Food & Wine Publisher Tries His Hand at Saber Rattling" in *Advertising Age* (Vol. 77, December 4, 2006, No. 49, pp. 16)
Pub: Crain Communications, Inc.
Description: French vineyards are facing a massive overproduction crisis due to a falling number in the amount of wine the French are drinking per week.

19141 ■ "Fromm Family Foods Converts Old Feed Mill Into Factory for Gourmet Pet Food" in *Wisconsin State Journal* (August 3, 2011)
Pub: Capital Newspapers
Ed: Barry Adams. **Description:** Fromm Family Foods, a gourmet cat and dog food company spent $10 million to convert an old feed mill into a pet food manufacturing facility. The owner forecasts doubling or tripling its production of 600 tons of feed per week in about five years.

19142 ■ "Gallo Family Vineyards to Raise Funds for Meals On Wheels" in *Food & Beverage Close-Up* (November 4, 2011)
Pub: Close-Up Media
Description: Gallo family is committed to raising funds for Meals On Wheels Association of America and hosts a fundraiser annually.

19143 ■ "Grape Expectations" in *Canadian Business* (Vol. 80, Winter 2007, No. 24, pp. 57)
Pub: Rogers Media
Ed: Joe Castaldo. **Description:** Laura McCain-Jensen bought a 15-acre vineyard in the Niagara wine country after a trip to Ontario for her husband's hair transplant. The vineyard has since been renamed Creekside Estate Winery and now produces two celebrity-branded wines under the name of golfer Mike Weir and hockey player Wayne Gretsky.

19144 ■ "Growing Pains" in *Canadian Business* (Vol. 81, July 22, 2008, No. 12-13, pp. 35)
Pub: Rogers Media Ltd.
Ed: Alex Mylnek. **Description:** Laughing Stock Vineyards' Cynthia Enns and David Enns plan to target young buyers by using social media. The Enns however, are concerned that targeting younger buyers may affect Laughing Stock's image as a premium brand. Additional information regarding the company's future plans is presented.

19145 ■ "Heat Brings Out Flavor, Not Visitors to Wineries" in *Saint Louis Business Journal* (Vol. 31, August 12, 2011, No. 51, pp. 1)
Pub: Saint Louis Business Journal
Ed: Rick Desloge. **Description:** St. Louis, Missouri's wine industry seems to benefit from the heat wave. The hot weather is expected to give grapes more flavor.

19146 ■ "Homes, Not Bars, Stay Well Tended" in *Advertising Age* (Vol. 79, January 28, 2008, No. 4, pp. 8)
Pub: Crain Communications, Inc.
Ed: Jeremy Mullman. **Description:** Due to the downturn in the economy, consumers are drinking less at bars and restaurants; however, according to the Distilled Spirits Council of the United States, they are still purchasing expensive liquor to keep in their homes.

19147 ■ "J&J Snack Rakes in Sales" in *Philadelphia Business Journal* (Vol. 28, September 25, 2009, No. 32, pp. 1)
Pub: American City Business Journals
Ed: Peter van Allen. **Description:** Analysts expect J&J Snack Foods Corporation to boost earnings by 48 percent for fiscal year ending September 2009. Stable commodity prices have benefited the company.

19148 ■ "Lawyers Cash In On Alcohol" in *Business Journal Portland* (Vol. 27, November 19, 2010, No. 38, pp. 1)
Pub: Portland Business Journal
Ed: Andy Giegerich. **Description:** Oregon-based law firms have continued to corner big business on the state's growing alcohol industry as demand for their services increased. Lawyers, who represent wine, beer and liquor distillery interests, have seen their workload increased by 20 to 30 percent in 2009.

19149 ■ "LCB Puts a Cork in Kiosk Wine Sales" in *Times Leader* (December 22, 2010)
Pub: Wilkes-Barre Publishing Company
Ed: Andrew M. Seder. **Description:** The Pennsylvania Liquor Control Board closed down thirty Pronto Wine Kiosks located in supermarkets throughout the state. The Board cited mechanical and technological issues such as products not dispensing.

19150 ■ "LCB Turning Off Wine Vending Machines" in *Pittsburgh Post-Gazette* (September 20, 2011)
Pub: PG Publishing Company
Ed: Tracie Mauriello. **Description:** Grocery store shoppers will no longer be able to purchase a bottle of wine from wine kiosks in Pennsylvania.

19151 ■ "Leinie's Charts National Craft Beer Rollout" in *The Business Journal-Milwaukee* (Vol. 25, August 29, 2008, No. 49, pp. A1)
Pub: American City Business Journals, Inc.
Ed: Rich Rovito. **Description:** Jacob Leinenkugel Brewing Co. is expected to complete the national rollout of its craft beer brands, while the launch of a new beer is prepared for this fall. The rollout is will likely benefit MillerCoors LLC, and will leave Alaska as the only state without Leinenkugel beer. Other views and information on Leinenkugel's national rollout are presented.

19152 ■ "Little Cheer in Holiday Forecast for Champagne" in *Advertising Age* (Vol. 88, November 17, 2008, No. 43, pp. 6)
Pub: Crain Communications, Inc.
Ed: Jeremy Mullman. **Description:** Due to a weak economy that has forced consumers to trade down from the most expensive alcoholic beverages as well as a weak U.S. dollar that has driven already lofty Champagne prices higher, makers of the French sparkling wine are anticipating a brutally slow holiday season.

19153 ■ "Millennials: The Great White Hope for Wine Industry" in *Advertising Age* (Vol. 81, December 6, 2010, No. 43, pp. 2)
Pub: Crain Communications, Inc.
Ed: E.J. Shultz. **Description:** Generation offers category of most growth potential in 30 years and 7-Eleven and vintner are taking notice.

19154 ■ "Moet, Rivals Pour More Ad Bucks Into Bubbly" in *Advertising Age* (Vol. 88, September 3, 2007, No. 35, pp. 4)
Pub: Crain Communications, Inc.
Ed: Jeremy Mullman. **Description:** In an attempt to revive sluggish sales, champagne companies are raising their advertising budgets, transforming themselves from light-spending seasonal players to year-round heavyweights in the advertising world.

19155 ■ "New Recipes Added to IAMS Naturals Pet Food Line" in *MMR* (Vol. 28, August 1, 2011, No. 11, pp. 17)
Pub: Racher Press Inc.
Description: Procter & Gamble Company's IAMS brand has created a new pet food line called IAMS Naturals for pet owners wishing to feed their pets natural, wholesome food. IAMS Sensitive Naturals has ocean fish and its first ingredient for dogs with sensitivities. IAMS Simple & Natural features chicken with no fillers.

19156 ■ "The Price Is Right: What You Can Learn From the Wine Industry" in *Advertising Age* (Vol. 88, February 11, 2008, No. 6, pp. 14)
Pub: Crain Communications, Inc.
Ed: Lenore Skenazy. **Description:** In California a wine study was conducted in which participants' brains were hooked up to an MRI so researchers could watch what was happening in both the taste centers as well as the pleasure centers; the participants were given three different wines but were told that the samples were from a variety of wines that differed radically in price; surprisingly, the differences did not affect the taste centers of the brain, however, when the participants were told that a sample was more expensive, the pleasure centers were greatly affected.

19157 ■ "Russian Renaissance" in *Chicago Tribune* (September 22, 2008)
Pub: McClatchy-Tribune Information Services
Ed: Alex Rodriguez. **Description:** Winemakers from Russia are returning to the craft and quality of winemaking now that they are free from Soviet restraints.

19158 ■ "Secaucus-Based Freshpet is Barking Up the Right Tree" in *Record* (September 8, 2011)
Pub: North Jersey Media Group
Ed: Rebecca Olles. **Description:** Freshpet produces a variety of nutritious, refrigerated pet foods and treats for cats and dogs. The firm introduced five new recipes and treats to its grain-free line called Vital line. The Vital line mimics the ancestral diets of dogs and cats.

19159 ■ "Seward Restaurant Garners Accolades" in *Alaska Business Monthly* (Vol. 27, October 2011, No. 10, pp. 9)
Pub: Alaska Business Publishing Company
Ed: Nancy Pounds. **Description:** Resurrection Road House of Seward, Alaska won the Wine Spectator's Aware of Excellence in 2011. The award honors restaurants that handle at least 100 gourmet wines that are skillfully paired with the cuisine.

19160 ■ "Silver Springs Creamery Opens Retail" in *Bellingham Business Journal* (Vol. March 2010, pp. 3)
Pub: Sound Publishing Inc.
Description: Eric Sundstrom, owner of Silver Springs Creamery, announced the opening of its on-site retail store that will sell the farm's goat and cow cheese, yogurt, ice cream and flesh milk.

19161 ■ "A Soggy Harvest" in *Business Journal-Portland* (Vol. 24, October 5, 2007, No. 32, pp. 1)
Pub: American City Business Journals, Inc.
Ed: Robin J. Moody. **Description:** Vintners in Willamette Valley are facing a tough challenge with a rainy wine harvest season and a delay in the ripening of grapes due to a cool spring and August. Rain decreased the sugar content of grapes and poses a danger with molds. The economic impact of the rainy harvest season in wine making is discussed.

19162 ■ "The Spirit of a Man: Kedar Massenburg's Intoxicating Style of Conducting Business" in *Black Enterprise* (Vol. 38, March 2008)
Pub: Earl G. Graves Publishing Co. Inc.
Ed: Sonia Alleyne. **Description:** Profile of Kedar Massenburg, personal trainer at The Gym in Montvale, New Jersey. Massenburg also operates an independent record label and management company as well as Kedar Beverages LLC founded in 2005. His latest venture is winemaking.

19163 ■ "The Trouble With $150,000 Wine" in *Barron's* (Vol. 88, July 7, 2008, No. 27, pp. 33)
Pub: Dow Jones & Co., Inc.
Ed: Orley Ashenfelter. **Description:** Review of the book, "The Billionaire's Vinegar: The Mystery of the World's Most Expensive Bottle of Wine," which discusses vintners along with the marketing and distribution of wine as well as the winemaking industry as a whole.

19164 ■ "Top 50 Exporters" in *Hispanic Business* (Vol. 30, July-August 2008, No. 7-8, pp. 42)
Pub: Hispanic Business, Inc.
Ed: Hildy Medina. **Description:** Increases in exports revenues reported by food exporters and green companies in a time of economic slowdown in the U.S are described. Food exporters have benefited from the growth of high-volume grocery stores in underdeveloped countries and the German governments' promotion of solar energy has benefited the U.S. solar heating equipment and solar panel manufactures.

19165 ■ "What'll You Have Tonight?" in *Barron's* (Vol. 88, July 4, 2008, No. 28, pp. 22)
Pub: Dow Jones & Co., Inc.
Ed: Neil A. Martin. **Description:** Shares of Diageo could rise by 30 percent a year from June 2008 after it slipped due to U.S. sales worries. The company also benefits from the trend toward more premium alcoholic beverage brands worldwide especially in emerging markets.

19166 ■ *Wine Investment for Portfolio Diversification: How Investing in Wine Can Yield Greater Returns than Stocks and Bonds*
Pub: Wine Appreciation Guild, Ltd.
Ed: Mahesh Kumar. **Released:** October 2005. **Price:** $45.00. **Description:** Analysis of the performance of investments in fine wines, particularly Bordeaux, is presented. History verifies that wine has traditionally been a sound investment offering a higher expected return over the market relative to its overall contribution of risk. Wine can be used as an effective means of diversifying one's portfolio.

19167 ■ "The Wine Spectator" in *Business Courier* (Vol. 27, November 26, 2010, No. 30, pp. 1)
Pub: Business Courier
Ed: Dan Monk. **Description:** Vintner Select, a wine distributor, will introduce an internationally known portfolio of more than 50 German and Austrian wines. The company now distributes about 900 different wine labels from 220 producers in 10 countries to smaller, independent retailers in Indiana, Kentucky and Ohio.

19168 ■ "Wirtz Partners With California Liquor Wholesaler To Expand Reach" in *Chicago Tribune* (December 17, 2008)
Pub: McClatchy-Tribune Information Services
Ed: Mike Hughlett. **Description:** Young's Market Co. and Wirtz Beverage Group have tentatively agreed to a joint venture that will give both companies a larger reach in the wine and liquor distribution business.

19169 ■ "Yao Ming Courts China's Wine Boom" in *Wall Street Journal Eastern Edition* (November 28, 2011, pp. B4)
Pub: Dow Jones & Company Inc.
Ed: Jason Chow. **Description:** Yao Ming, the former NBA 7-foot 6-inch Chinese basketball star, is set to cash in on the market potential for wine in China. He has created his own winery in California, Yao Family Wines, which will produce wines solely for the Chinese market.

19170 ■ "Your Turn in the Spotlight" in *Inc.* (Volume 32, December 2010, No. 10, pp. 57)
Pub: Inc. Magazine
Ed: John Brandon. **Description:** Examples of three video blogs created by entrepreneurs to promote their businesses and products are used to show successful strategies. Wine Library TV promotes a family's wine business; SHAMA.TV offers marketing tips and company news; and Will It Blend? promotes sales of a household blender.

SOURCES OF SUPPLY

19171 ■ *Beverage Industry—Annual Manual Issue*
Pub: BNP Media
Released: Annual, Latest edition 2010. **Publication Includes:** List of over 1,700 companies supplying equipment and materials to the soft drink, beer, wine, bottled water, and juice industries; industry associations; bottling and supply franchise companies; beer importers distributors; manufacturers' representatives; soft drink distributors. **Entries Include:** For suppliers—Company name, address, phone, code to indicate products. For associations—Name, address, phone, name of president; some association listings also include meeting date and location and names of other executives. For franchise companies—Name, address, phone, names and titles of executives, number of plants, number of franchised plants, products, foreign involvement. For beer importers and distributors—Name, address, phone, names and titles of key executives, brands handled. For manufacturers' representatives—Name, address, phone, names of contacts, market areas, products represented. **Arrangement:** State associations and supplier associations are geographical; other listings are alphabetical. **Indexes:** Trade name, product/service.

STATISTICAL SOURCES

19172 ■ *The Cheese Market*
Pub: Rector Press, Ltd.
Contact: Lewis Sckolnick, Pres
Released: 2009. **Price:** Contact Rector Press. **Description:** Examines the growth areas within Analyzes consumer attitudes and buying habits and identifies trends that will affect market growth. Focuses on the specialty cheese segment as well as on low-fat, low-sodium, and low-cholesterol varieties. Also covers distribution and marketing strategies, and provides profiles of major cheese marketers.

19173 ■ *The U.S. Pasta Market*
Pub: Business Trend Analysts, Inc.
Released: 2002. **Price:** $1,695.00. **Description:** Provides in-depth coverage of the markets for all types of pasta products, including dry pasta, shelf-stable pasta mixes and dinners, fresh pasta, frozen pasta, and canned pasta products.

TRADE PERIODICALS

19174 ■ *The Art of Eating*
Pub: The Art of Eating
Contact: Edward Behr, Publisher
Released: Quarterly. **Price:** $88 two years; $48; $58 other countries; $12.50 single issue. **Description:** Consumer publication featuring essays on food and wine.

19175 ■ *Bread Pudding Recipe Exchange*
Pub: Prosperity & Profits Unlimited, Distribution Services
Contact: A. Doyle
Ed: A. Doyle, Editor. **Released:** Annual. **Price:** $2, U.S.; $3, Canada; $4, elsewhere. **Description:** Presents recipe possibilities for bread pudding, sample greetings, and more.

19176 ■ *The Cheese Reporter*
Pub: The Cheese Reporter Publishing Company Inc.
Contact: Moira Crowley, Asst. Ed.
E-mail: editorial@cheesereporter.com
Released: Weekly. **Price:** $130 yearly mailed subscription periodical mail; $185 yearly mailed subscription first class mail; $250 Canada and Mexico yearly mailed subscription periodical mail; $355 other countries 2 years foreign airmail; $195 two years yearly mailed subscription periodical mail; $35 weekly mailed subscription periodical mail; $35 4 weeks mailed subscription periodical mail; $60 12 weeks mailed subscription periodical mail. **Description:** Newspaper (tabloid) serving the cheese and dairy industry.

19177 ■ *The Food & Beverage International*
Pub: Journal Publications Inc.
Contact: Rodney Ruppert, Web Asst.
Released: Bimonthly. **Description:** Trade magazine covering the food and beverage industry.

19178 ■ *Gourmet News*
Pub: United Publications Inc.
Released: Monthly. **Description:** Business newspaper for the specialty food industry.

19179 ■ *The National Culinary Review*
Pub: American Culinary Federation Inc.
Ed: Kay Orde, Editor, korde@acfchefs.net. **Released:** Monthly. **Price:** $60; $200 other countries. **Description:** Trade magazine covering food and cooking.

19180 ■ *Uncorked*
Pub: The California Wine Club
Ed: Bruce Boring, Editor. **Released:** Monthly. **Price:** Included in membership. **Description:** Profiles wineries and the wine industry. Recurring features include interviews, news of research, reports of meetings, book reviews, and columns titled Up Close & Personal, Fun Facts, To Your Health, Recipes, What They Say, Tasting Notes, Alumni Notes, and Questions & Answers.

19181 ■ *The Wine Advocate*
Pub: Robert M. Parker, Jr.
Contact: Robert M. Parker Jr., Publisher
Released: Bimonthly, 6/year. **Price:** $75, individuals; $90, Canada; $100, other countries. **Description:** Serves as an independent guide to fine wines.

19182 ■ *Wine Enthusiast Magazine*
Pub: Wine Enthusiast Co.
Contact: Susan Kostrzewa, Exec. Ed.
E-mail: skostrze@wineenthusiast.net
Price: $29.95; $49.95 two years; $69.95 3 years; $49.95 Canada; $79.95 other countries. **Description:** Magazine reporting news on wines and spirits; includes profiles of industry leaders from around the world as well as a consumer wine report.

19183 ■ *Wine News*
Pub: T.E. Smith Inc.
Contact: Todd M. Wernstrom, Exec. Ed.
Released: Bimonthly. **Price:** $25; $60 out of country. **Description:** Consumer magazine covering wine, food, and related travel.

19184 ■ *Wine & Spirits Magazine*
Pub: Wine & Spirits Magazine Inc.
Contact: Joshua Greene, Editor & Publisher
Released: Monthly, 8/yr. **Price:** $29.95; $51.95 two years; $15 first class mail; $10 Canada and Mexico. **Description:** Magazine containing consumer buying information on wine and spirits with in-depth articles on regions and trends in food and wine.

19185 ■ *Wines & Vines*
Pub: Hiaring Co.
Contact: Tina Caputo, Managing Editor
Ed: Jim Gordon, Editor. **Released:** Monthly. **Price:** $38; $48 Canada and Mexico; $85 other countries; $59 two years USA. **Description:** Periodical on wine industry.

VIDEOCASSETTES/ AUDIOCASSETTES

19186 ■ *Cheese 101*
International Dairy-Deli-Bakery Association (IDDBA)
636 Science Dr.
PO Box 5528
Madison, WI 53705-0528
Ph:(608)310-5000
Fax:(608)238-6330
Co. E-mail: iddba@iddba.org
URL: http://www.iddba.org
Price: $50.00. **Description:** Discusses the high margin, high profit product, cheese and explains how they differ in taste and the qualities of 16 varieties. **Availability:** VHS.

19187 ■ *Cheese Classics of America*
International Dairy-Deli-Bakery Association (IDDBA)
636 Science Dr.
PO Box 5528
Madison, WI 53705-0528
Ph:(608)310-5000
Fax:(608)238-6330
Co. E-mail: iddba@iddba.org
URL: http://www.iddba.org
Price: $100.00. **Description:** Merchandising and training video. **Availability:** VHS.

19188 ■ *International Cheese Classics*
International Dairy-Deli-Bakery Association (IDDBA)
636 Science Dr.
PO Box 5528
Madison, WI 53705-0528
Ph:(608)310-5000
Fax:(608)238-6330
Co. E-mail: iddba@iddba.org
URL: http://www.iddba.org
Price: $100.00. **Description:** Merchandising and training video. **Availability:** VHS.

19189 ■ *Jancis Robinson's Wine Course*
PBS Home Video
Catalog Fulfillment Center
PO Box 751089
Charlotte, NC 28275-1089
Ph:800-531-4727
Free: 800-645-4PBS
Co. E-mail: info@pbs.org
URL: http://www.pbs.org
Released: 1998. **Price:** $99.95. **Description:** Hosted by expert Jancis Robinson, editor of the Oxford Companion to Wine, this series gives the viewer a lighthearted introduction to the world of wine. Covers how wine is made, how to taste it and how to store it. Five hours on five videocassettes. **Availability:** VHS; DVD.

TRADE SHOWS AND CONVENTIONS

19190 ■ Dairy-Deli-Bake Seminar and Expo
International Dairy-Deli-Bakery Association
PO Box 5528
Madison, WI 53705-0528
Ph:(608)310-5000
Fax:(608)238-6330
Co. E-mail: iddba@iddba.org
URL: http://www.iddba.org
Released: Annual. **Audience:** Retailers, wholesalers, distributors, brokers, and manufacturers of the dairy, deli, and bakery industry. **Principal Exhibits:** Dairy, deli, and bakery products, packaging, and equipment. **Dates and Locations:** 2011 Jun 05-07, Anaheim, CA.

19191 ■ International Fancy Food and Confection Show/Winter
National Association for the Specialty Food Trade, Inc.
120 Wall St., 27th Fl.
New York, NY 10005
Ph:(212)482-6440
Fax:(212)482-6459
URL: http://www.fancyfoodshows.com
Released: Annual. **Audience:** Retailers, brokers, importers, buyers, chefs, caterers and related personnel. **Principal Exhibits:** Pates, cheeses, specialty meats and seafood, condiments, sauces, mustards, vinegars, chocolates, fine candies, biscuits, cookies, cakes, jams, jellies, preserves, coffees, teas, fruits, nuts, special beverages, beer, wine, ice creams, desserts, and cooking accessories.

19192 ■ Ottawa Wine and Food Show
Player Expositions International
255 Clemow Ave.
Ottawa, ON, Canada K1S 2B5
Ph:(613)567-6408
Fax:(613)567-2718
URL: http://www.playerexpo.com
Released: Annual. **Audience:** Restaurant, hotels, clubs, catering-fine food stores, specialty food stores, wine clubs, and the general public. **Principal Exhibits:** Fine wines and foods, and beer from around the world.

FRANCHISES AND BUSINESS OPPORTUNITIES

19193 ■ Auntie Anne's Inc.
48-50 W Chestnut St., Ste. 200
Lancaster, PA 17603
Ph:(717)435-1479
Fax:(717)435-1471
Co. E-mail: LindaE@auntieannesinc.com
URL: http://www.auntieannesfranchising.com
No. of Franchise Units: 1,100. **No. of Company-Owned Units:** 14. **Founded:** 1988. **Franchised:** 1990. **Description:** Serves fresh, hot hand-rolled soft pretzels. **Equity Capital Needed:** $197,875-$439,100. **Franchise Fee:** $30,000. **Financial Assistance:** No. **Training:** 2 week training program is provided for owners, including onsite training at time of store opening.

19194 ■ Blenz Coffee
535 Thurlow St., Ste. 300
Vancouver, BC, Canada V6E 3L2
Ph:(604)682-2995
Fax:(604)684-2542
No. of Franchise Units: 25. **No. of Company-Owned Units:** 2. **Founded:** 1990. **Franchised:** 1992. **Description:** Coffee beverages and coffee beans. **Equity Capital Needed:** $30,000-$70,000+ equity. **Financial Assistance:** No. **Training:** Yes.

19195 ■ Borvin Beverage
Borvin Beverage Franchise Corp.
1022 King St.
PO Box 1417-All
Alexandria, VA 22314
Fax:(703)836-6654
No. of Franchise Units: 1. **No. of Company-Owned Units:** 1. **Founded:** 1992. **Franchised:** 1994. **Description:** Wine distribution and wholesale. **Equity Capital Needed:** $250,000 liquid assets; $50,000 net worth. **Franchise Fee:** $25,000-$75,000. **Financial Assistance:** Yes. **Training:** Yes.

19196 ■ Bulk Barn Foods Limited
55 Leek Crescent
Richmond Hill, ON, Canada L4B 3Y2
Ph:(905)886-6756
Fax:(905)886-3717
Co. E-mail: francesspatafora@bulkbarn.ca
URL: http://www.bulkbarn.ca
No. of Franchise Units: 170. **Founded:** 1982. **Franchised:** 1982. **Description:** Specialized bulk retailer in Canada, offering bulk and packaged products, including a range of candy making, cake making and decorating, snacks, health foods, vitamins and supplements. **Equity Capital Needed:** $500,000 minimum investment required; $150,000 start-up and onsite. **Franchise Fee:** $35,000. **Financial Assistance:** No. **Managerial Assistance:** Site selection, lease negotiations, advisory council provided. **Training:** Ongoing support provided.

19197 ■ Cafe Fondue Franchise Systems Inc.
281 W 80th Pl.
Merrillville, IN 46410
Ph:(219)793-1511
Fax:(219)793-1511
No. of Company-Owned Units: 1. **Founded:** 1998. **Franchised:** 2003. **Description:** Fondue - specialty restaurant. **Equity Capital Needed:** $136,000-$307,000. **Franchise Fee:** $35,000. **Royalty Fee:** 4%. **Financial Assistance:** Equipment and franchise fee assistance. **Training:** Provides 2 weeks training at headquarters and 2 weeks onsite.

19198 ■ Cena
12501 N Hwy. 395, Ste. 3
Spokane, WA 99218
Ph:(509)448-1725
Free: 888-667-2362
Fax:(509)448-9380
No. of Franchise Units: 10. **No. of Company-Owned Units:** 1. **Founded:** 2004. **Franchised:** 2005. **Description:** Meal preparation/assembly center and wine shop. **Equity Capital Needed:** $148,400-$205,500; express/kiosk option available. **Franchise Fee:** $30,000. **Royalty Fee:** 5%. **Financial Assistance:** No. **Training:** Provides 4 days training at headquarters, 3 days onsite and ongoing support.

19199 ■ Crescent Wines
2255 King George Hwy., Ste. 108
Surrey, BC, Canada V4A 5A4
Ph:(604)542-0211
Co. E-mail: whiterock@crescentwines.com
URL: http://www.crescentwines.com
No. of Franchise Units: 2. **No. of Company-Owned Units:** 1. **Founded:** 1996. **Description:** Wine making. **Equity Capital Needed:** $50,000-$100,000. **Franchise Fee:** $20,000. **Training:** Offers full-training and ongoing support.

19200 ■ Desert Moon Fresh Mexican Grill
Desert Moon Holdings Corp., Inc.
521 Berlin Cross Keys Rd., PMB 13
Sicklerville, NJ 08081
Ph:(845)267-3300
Free: 877-564-6362
Fax:(845)267-2548
No. of Franchise Units: 15. **No. of Company-Owned Units:** 3. **Founded:** 1992. **Franchised:** 1999. **Description:** Specializes in Mexican food delicacies. **Equity Capital Needed:** $350,000. **Franchise Fee:** $25,000. **Financial Assistance:** Yes. **Training:** Yes.

19201 ■ Entrees Made Easy
4858 E Baseline Rd., Ste. 104
Mesa, AZ 85206
Ph:(480)985-7900
Fax:(480)985-7909
No. of Franchise Units: 21. **No. of Company-Owned Units:** 2. **Founded:** 2004. **Franchised:** 2006. **Description:** Meal preparation service. **Equity Capital Needed:** $172,800-$296,500. **Franchise Fee:** $30,000. **Royalty Fee:** 5%. **Financial Assistance:** No. **Training:** 1 week training at headquarters, 1 week onsite and ongoing support.

19202 ■ The Honeybaked Ham Co. and Cafe
The HBH Franchise Co. LLC
3875 Mansell Rd.
Alpharetta, GA 30022
Ph:(678)966-3254
Free: (866)968-7424
Fax:(678)966-3134
URL: http://www.honeybakedonline.com
No. of Franchise Units: 183. **No. of Company-Owned Units:** 280. **Founded:** 1957. **Franchised:** 1998. **Description:** Specialty retailer of high quality spiral-sliced hams and turkeys. **Equity Capital Needed:** $350,000 net worth with $100,000 available as equity contribution. **Franchise Fee:** $30,000. **Financial Assistance:** No. **Training:** Comprehensive 14 day program at corporate training store.

19203 ■ Pretzels Plus
639 Frederick St.
Hanover, PA 17331
Ph:(717)633-7927
Free: 800-559-7927
Fax:(717)633-5078
No. of Franchise Units: 24. **Founded:** 1991. **Franchised:** 1992. **Description:** Soft pretzels. **Equity Capital Needed:** $80,000. **Franchise Fee:** $12,000. **Financial Assistance:** No. **Training:** Yes.

19204 ■ Rosevine Winery
2424 N. Federal Hwy., Ste. 455
Boynton Beach, FL 33426
Ph:(561)416-9096
Fax:(561)416-9098
No. of Company-Owned Units: 2. **Founded:** 2003. **Franchised:** 2004. **Description:** Make-your-own-wine retail shops. **Equity Capital Needed:** $246,000-$425,000. **Franchise Fee:** $35,000. **Royalty Fee:** 6%. **Financial Assistance:** No. **Training:** Offers 3-5 days training at franchisees location, 10 days at 1810 Winery and ongoing support.

19205 ■ Sushi Shop
MTY Group
3465 Thimens Blvd.
Montreal, QC, Canada H4R 1V5
Ph:(514)336-8885
Free: (866)891-6633
Fax:(514)336-9222
Co. E-mail: info@sushishop.com
URL: http://www.sushishop.com
No. of Franchise Units: 111. **No. of Company-Owned Units:** 3. **Founded:** 2000. **Franchised:** 2001. **Description:** The franchise offers retail selling of products and by-products of Sushi. **Equity Capital Needed:** $175,000-$250,000 investment required; $75,000-$150,000 start-up capital required. **Franchise Fee:** $30,000. **Training:** Yes.

19206 ■ A Taste Above
120 Carlton St., Ste. 207
Toronto, ON, Canada M5A 4K2
Ph:(416)935-0050
Fax:(416)935-0463
Co. E-mail: info@atasteabove.com
URL: http://www.atasteabove.com
No. of Company-Owned Units: 1. **Founded:** 2004. **Franchised:** 2004. **Description:** Chef prepared gourmet cuisine prepared in our own kitchens vacuumed packed, cooler fresh in measured quantities of serving per pack for home and commercial use. **Franchise Fee:** From $30,000. **Training:** Yes.

19207 ■ Vitner's Cellar Franchising International, Inc.
4020 Somers Dr.
Burton, MI 48529
Ph:(810)742-9463
Free: 800-480-7417
Fax:(810)743-9466
Co. E-mail: info@vintnerscellar.com
No. of Franchise Units: 46. **No. of Company-Owned Units:** 1. **Founded:** 1993. **Franchised:** 1994. **Description:** Produce and sell wine onsite year round. **Equity Capital Needed:** $119,500-$191,000. **Franchise Fee:** $45,000. **Financial Assistance:** Yes. **Training:** Yes.

19208 ■ We're Rolling Pretzel Co.
WRPC Inc.
2500 W State St.
PO Box 6160
Alliance, OH 44601
Ph:(330)823-0575
Free: 888-549-7655
Fax:(330)821-9808
URL: http://www.wererolling.com
No. of Franchise Units: 31. **No. of Company-Owned Units:** 14. **Founded:** 1996. **Franchised:** 2000. **Description:** Soft pretzel company. **Equity Capital Needed:** $65,000-$154,000. **Franchise Fee:** $15,000. **Royalty Fee:** 5%. **Financial Assistance:** Third party financing available. **Training:** Offers 7 days at headquarters and 7 days onsite.

19209 ■ Wetzel's Pretzels
Wetzel's Pretzels, LLC
35 Hugus Alley, Ste. 300
Pasadena, CA 91103
Ph:(626)432-6900
Fax:(626)432-6904
No. of Franchise Units: 236. **No. of Company-Owned Units:** 11. **Founded:** 1994. **Franchised:** 1996. **Description:** Pretzels. **Equity Capital Needed:** $156,300-$369,950. **Franchise Fee:** $35,000. **Royalty Fee:** 7%. **Financial Assistance:** Limited third party financing available. **Training:** Offers 2 weeks at headquarters, 4 days at franchisees location and ongoing support.

19210 ■ Wine Lovers, Inc.
387 Wellington Street
P.O. Box 25028
London, ON, Canada N6H 4V6
Ph:(519)913-2423
Fax:(519)471-1442
Co. E-mail: info@wineloversonline.com
URL: http://www.wineloversonline.com
Description: Wine Lovers has established a business model that allows potential franchise owners a 'Turn Key' operation that allows minimal investments with minimal risk. We have established suppliers, equipment and management training.

19211 ■ Wine Not Custom Wineries
380 Spring Gate Blvd.
Box 80
Thornhill, ON, Canada L4J 4K6
Free: 888-946-3668
Fax:888-946-3668
Co. E-mail: sales@wineryfranchise.com
URL: http://www.winenotinternational.com
No. of Franchise Units: 9. **Founded:** 2002. **Description:** Our wineries are full service, federally bonded wineries equipped with state of the art fermentation equipment, professional tasting bar & lounge areas. We also provide direct retail & wholesale sales, customized labeling & a unique customer participation experience. **Equity Capital Needed:** $125,000-$438,500; $200,000-$600,000 with bistro. **Franchise Fee:** $50,000. **Financial Assistance:** No. **Training:** training begins at Head Office covering all aspects of wine making, tasting, customer service, marketing, purchasing, inventory and operations. Part two is on location at your winery utilizing your winery systems and equipment and ongoing support.

19212 ■ WineStyles Inc.
5100 Copans Rd., Ste. 310
Margate, FL 33063
Ph:(954)984-0070
Fax:(954)984-0074
No. of Franchise Units: 71. **Founded:** 2002. **Franchised:** 2002. **Description:** Wine store. **Equity Capital Needed:** $229,500-$380,500. **Franchise Fee:** $25,000. **Royalty Fee:** 6%. **Financial Assistance:** Third party financing available. **Training:** Offers 5 days at headquarters, 3 days onsite and ongoing support.

19213 ■ ZamLows Sugarfree Low-Carb
ZamLows Franchising Company
222 Pitts Rd.
Friendship, TN 38034
Ph:(731)660-3045
Free: 877-660-3045
Fax:(731)660-5612
No. of Company-Owned Units: 1. **Founded:** 2001. **Franchised:** 2004. **Description:** Low-carb grocery for diabetics and dieters. **Equity Capital Needed:** $122,000-$247,000. **Franchise Fee:** $20,000. **Financial Assistance:** No. **Training:** Yes.

COMPUTERIZED DATABASES

19214 ■ *Wine On Line*
Wine On Line International
400 E 59th St., Ste. 9F
New York, NY 10022
Ph:(212)755-4363
Co. E-mail: info@punchin.com
URL: http://www.wineonline.net
Description: Contains information about wines. Includes descriptions, ratings, production methods, serving advice, pricing, and a shopping service for domestic and foreign wines, tasting kits, wine racks, books, and videocassettes. Provides information on restaurant wine lists, wine tastings, sales of wines and wine products, and wine tours and events. Also provides information on award-winning wines; related organizations; a calendar of events; media reprints of features, columns, and articles; and question and answer forum. **Availability:** Online: Punch In International Syndicate, Wine On Line International. **Type:** Directory; Transactional.

LIBRARIES

19215 ■ American Institute of Food Distribution, Inc.–Information and Research Center
1 Broadway Plaza, 2nd Fl.
Elmwood Park, NJ 07407
Ph:(201)791-5570
Fax:(201)791-5222
Co. E-mail: jkastrinsky@foodinstitute.com
URL: http://www.foodinstitute.com/
Contact: Brian Todd, Pres./CEO
Scope: Food industry. **Services:** Center open to the public on fee basis. **Subscriptions:** 400 journals and other serials.

19216 ■ Napa Valley Wine Library Association Library
1492 Library Ln.
St. Helena, CA 94574-1143
Ph:(707)963-5244
Fax:(707)963-5264
Co. E-mail: director@shpl.org
URL: http://www.shpl.org
Contact: Jennifer Baker, Lib.Dir.
Scope: Grapes, viticulture, wine and winemaking. **Services:** Interlibrary loan; copying; Library open to the public. **Holdings:** 6000 books; 200 bound periodical volumes; 12 VF drawers; 99 reels of microfilm. **Subscriptions:** 55 journals and other serials.

19217 ■ St. Joseph's University–Academy of Food Marketing–Campbell Library (157 M)
157 Mandeville Hall
5600 City Ave.
Philadelphia, PA 19131
Ph:(610)660-1196
Fax:(610)660-1604
Co. E-mail: pat.weaver@sju.edu
URL: http://www.sju.edu/resources/libraries/campbell/index.html
Contact: Pat Weaver, Dir.
Scope: Food marketing. **Services:** Interlibrary loan; copying; Library open to the public for reference use only, reciprocal privileges extended to food industry libraries and organizations. **Holdings:** 1500 books; 1650 bound periodical volumes; 200 items in corporation files; 256 reels of microfilm; journals and doctoral dissertations; 753 microfiche; 500 subject information files. **Subscriptions:** 320 journals and other serials.

19218 ■ University of California, Davis–University Libraries I Special Collections
100 NW Quad
Shields Library, 1st Fl.
Davis, CA 95616-5292
Ph:(530)752-1621
Fax:(916)754-5758
Co. E-mail: dmorrison@ucdavis.edu
URL: http://www.lib.ucdavis.edu/dept/specol/
Contact: Ms. Daryl Morrison, Dept.Hd.
Scope: Reference. **Services:** Copying; collections open to the public for reference use only. **Holdings:** 129,500 books; 17,200 lin.ft. of archives and manuscripts. **Subscriptions:** 40 journals and other serials; 2 newspapers.

RESEARCH CENTERS

19219 ■ Texas Tech University–Texas Wine Marketing Research Institute
PO Box 41162
Lubbock, TX 79409-1240
Ph:(806)742-3077
Fax:(806)742-3042
Co. E-mail: tim.dodd@ttu.edu
URL: http://www.depts.ttu.edu/hs/texaswine
Contact: Dr. Tim H. Dodd
E-mail: tim.dodd@ttu.edu
Scope: Wine marketing, including supermarkets, wine tourism, restaurants and winery sales. Also studies the Texas wine and wine grape industry. **Publications:** Profile of the Texas Wine Industry (annually); Research articles; Research reports.

19220 ■ University of British Columbia–Wine Research Centre
2205 East Mall
Faculty of Land & Food Systems
Vancouver, BC, Canada V6T 1Z4
Ph:(604)822-0005
Fax:(604)822-5143
Co. E-mail: hjjvv@interchange.ubc.ca
URL: http://www.landfood.ubc.ca/wine
Contact: Dr. Hennie J.J. van Vuuren, Dir.
E-mail: hjjvv@interchange.ubc.ca
Scope: Enology and viticulture.

START-UP INFORMATION

19221 ■ *The 100 Best Businesses to Start When You Don't Want To Work Hard Anymore*
Pub: Career Press Inc.
Ed: Lisa Rogak. **Price:** $16.99. **Description:** Author helps burned-out workers envision a new future as a small business owner. Systems analysis, adventure travel outfitting, bookkeeping, food delivery, furniture making, and software development are among the industries examined.

ASSOCIATIONS AND OTHER ORGANIZATIONS

19222 ■ Association of Golf Merchandisers
PO Box 7247
Phoenix, AZ 85011-7247
Ph:(602)604-8250
Fax:(602)604-8251
Co. E-mail: info@agmgolf.org
URL: http://www.agmgolf.org
Contact: Desane Blaney, Exec. Dir.
Description: Golf buyers and vendors. Dedicated to maximizing members' learning and earning capabilities. Conducts continuing educational programs; provides networking opportunities, scholarships and a forum for communication; compiles statistics. **Publications:** *AGM Merchandise Manual* .

19223 ■ Athletic Equipment Managers Association
460 Hunt Hill Rd.
Freeville, NY 13068
Ph:(607)539-6300
Fax:(607)539-6340
Co. E-mail: aema@frontiernet.net
URL: http://www.equipmentmanagers.org
Contact: Dorothy Cutting, Office Mgr.
Description: Athletic equipment managers and others who handle sports equipment for junior high and high schools, colleges, recreation centers, and professional sports; individuals involved in athletic management and coaching or the handling or purchasing of athletic, physical education, or recreational equipment. Aims to improve the profession of equipment management and promote a better working relationship among those interested in problems of management. Works collectively to facilitate equipment improvement for greater safety among participants in all sports. Conducts workshops and clinics. Maintains job placement service. **Publications:** *The Scoreboard* (3/year).

19224 ■ Canadian Sporting Goods Association–Association Canadienne d'Articles de Sport
300 rue du Saint-Sacrement St., Ste. 420
Montreal, QC, Canada H2Y 1X4
Ph:(514)393-1132
Free: 888-393-3002
Fax:(514)393-9513
Co. E-mail: csga@csga.ca
URL: http://csga.ca
Contact: Mr. Gord Cundell, Pres.
Description: Sporting goods sales representatives, manufacturers, suppliers, distributors, retailers, and importers. Represents members' interests in international trade matters; functions as liaison between members and government agencies involved in the manufacture and trade of sporting goods. Conducts industry surveys; makes available discount programs and services to members. **Publications:** *CSGA Info-Bulletin Newsletter* (weekly); *CSGA Sport-Trade Directory* .

19225 ■ National Ski and Snowboard Retailers Association
1601 Feehanville Dr., Ste. 300
Mount Prospect, IL 60056-6035
Ph:(847)391-9825
Fax:(847)391-9827
Co. E-mail: info@nssra.com
URL: http://www.nssra.com
Contact: Brad Nelson, Chm.
Description: Ski & snowboard stores. Represents the interests of members and provides services beneficial to their businesses. Compiles statistics. **Publications:** *NSSRA Newsletter* (quarterly).

19226 ■ National Sporting Goods Association
1601 Feehanville Dr., Ste. 300
Mount Prospect, IL 60056
Free: 800-815-5422
Fax:(847)391-9827
Co. E-mail: info@nsga.org
URL: http://www.nsga.org/i4a/pages/index.cfm?pageid=1
Contact: Matt Carlson, Pres./CEO
Description: Provides services, education and information to assist member to profit in a competitive marketplace. **Publications:** *NSGA Buying Guide* (annual); *NSGA Retail Focus* (bimonthly); *Sports Participation-Series I & II* (annual).

19227 ■ Paddlesports Industry Association
PO Box 5204
Frankfort, KY 40602
Ph:(502)395-1513
Fax:(502)227-8086
Co. E-mail: canoeky@aol.com
URL: http://www.paddlesportsindustry.org
Contact: Ed Councill, Pres.
Description: Renters and outfitters of canoes, kayaks, and rafts; manufacturers and distributors of equipment and products. Promotes safety in non-power watercraft; seeks to protect the nation's waterways and the rights of the public to use them. Provides members with legislative representation; on-water liability insurance; member service programs; certification courses; and professional development. .

19228 ■ Soccer Industry Council of America
8505 Fenton St., Ste. 211
Silver Spring, MD 20910
Ph:(301)495-6321
Fax:(301)495-6322
Co. E-mail: info@sgma.com
URL: http://www.sgma.com
Contact: Tom Cove, Pres./CEO
Description: Subsidiary organization of the Sporting Goods Manufacturers Association. Manufacturers, suppliers, and retailers of soccer apparel, footwear and equipment; others involved in the soccer industry. Promotes the growth of soccer in the U.S. Supports grassroots programs that offer playing opportunities to economically-disadvantaged youth, as well as the physically and mentally handicapped. Publishes statistical abstract and overview of the American soccer marketplace. **Publications:** *National Soccer Participation Survey* (annual); *Retail Soccer USA*; *Soccer in the USA* .

19229 ■ Sporting Goods Manufacturers Association
8505 Fenton St., Ste. 211
Silver Spring, MD 20910
Ph:(301)495-6321
Fax:(301)495-6322
Co. E-mail: info@sgma.com
URL: http://www.sgma.com
Contact: Tom Cove, Pres./CEO
Description: Manufacturers of athletic clothing, footwear, and sporting goods. Seeks to increase sports participation and create growth in the sporting goods industry. Owns and operates the largest sports products trade show in the world. **Publications:** *American Sports Data Analysis Participation Summary Report* (periodic); *SGMA Recreation Market Report* (periodic); *Sports Edge NewsWire* (semi-weekly).

19230 ■ Trade Association of Paddlesports
11781 A. Watertank Rd.
Burlington, WA 98233
Ph:(559)340-8277
Co. E-mail: info@gopaddle.org
URL: http://www.gopaddle.org
Contact: Mr. Tim Rosenhan, Pres.
Description: Manufacturers, retailers, outfitters, importers and liveries of paddlesports equipment. Seeks to support, encourage and promote the paddlesports trade in North America. Provides information and referrals on sources of insurance for paddlesports businesses; undertakes research projects; develops and maintains safety, warning and product performance standards; conducts statistical surveys; co-organized the National River Cleanup Week; conducts educational programs; lobbies on behalf of the industry. .

19231 ■ Water Sports Industry Association
PO Box 568512
Orlando, FL 32856-8512
Ph:(407)251-9039

Fax:(407)251-9039
Co. E-mail: info@wsia.net
URL: http://www.wsia.net
Contact: Larry Meddock, Exec. Dir.
Description: Manufacturers and distributors of water sports equipment including skis, boats, wet suits, and towlines. Regular members are manufacturers and importers whose revenues are primarily derived from the water sports industry; associate members are firms with sales and manufacturing interests not primarily directed towards watersports. Monitors legislation affecting the water sports industry and keeps manufacturers and distributors informed of such action. Promotes the sports of water skiing, wakeboarding, kneeboarding, tubing and riding personal watercraft. .

REFERENCE WORKS

19232 ■ "Adidas' Brand Ambitions" in *Business Journal Portland* (Vol. 27, December 10, 2010, No. 41, pp. 1)
Pub: Portland Business Journal
Ed: Erik Siemers. **Description:** Adidas AG, the second-largest sporting goods brand in the world, hopes to increase global revenue by 50 percent by 2015. The German company, which reported $14.5 billion sales, plans to improve its U.S. market. The U.S. is Adidas' largest, but also the most underperforming market for the firm.

19233 ■ "Always Striving" in *Women In Business* (Vol. 61, December 2009, No. 6, pp. 28)
Pub: American Business Women's Association
Ed: Kathleen Leighton. **Description:** Jennifer Mull discusses her responsibilities and how she attained success as CEO of Backwoods, a gear and clothing store founded by her father in 1973. She places importance on being true to one's words and beliefs, while emphasizing the capacity to tolerate risks in business. Mull defines success as an evolving concept and believes there must always be something to strive for.

19234 ■ "Arizona Firms In Chicago Go For Gold With '08 Games" in *The Business Journal - Serving Phoenix and the Valley of the Sun* (Vol. 28, August 8, 2008, No. 49, pp. 1)
Pub: American City Business Journals, Inc.
Ed: Patrick O'Grady. **Description:** More than 20 U.S. athletes will wear Arizona-based eSoles LLC's custom-made insoles to increase their performance at the 2008 Beijing Olympics making eSoles one of the beneficiaries of the commercialization of the games. Translation software maker Auralog Inc saw a 60 percent jump in sales from its Mandarin Chinese language applications.

19235 ■ "Athletes' Performance Building $10 Million Facility In ASU Park" in *The Business Journal - Serving Phoenix and the Valley of the Sun* (Vol. 28, August 8, 2008, No. 49, pp. 1)
Pub: American City Business Journals, Inc.
Ed: Jan Buchholz. **Description:** Athletes' Performance's planned facility at Arizona State University is scheduled to begin in November 2008 and expected to be completed by September 2009. The new building will almost double the company's training space as it will expand from around 19,000 square feet to 35,000 square feet.

19236 ■ "Buck-ing the Trend?" in *Baltimore Business Journal* (Vol. 28, August 13, 2010, No. 14, pp. 1)
Pub: Baltimore Business Journal
Ed: Gary Haber. **Description:** Baltimore Orioles' new manager Buck Showalter has managed to win games for fans. However, not all businesses around Camden Yards were boosted by the Orioles' surge as street vendors complained of worsening business.

19237 ■ "Cabela's Repays Incentives as Sales Lag" in *Business Journal-Milwaukee* (Vol. 28, November 19, 2010, No. 7, pp. A1)
Pub: Milwaukee Business Journal
Ed: Stacy Vogel Davis. **Description:** Cabela's has given back $266,000 to the government of Wisconsin owing to its failure to meet projected revenue goals for its Richfield, Wisconsin store. It has also failed to meet sales tax and hiring projection. The company received $4 million in incentives from Washington County.

19238 ■ "Can the State Afford a Big Time College Football Program?" in *Hawaii Business* (Vol. 53, March 2008, No. 9, pp. 26)
Pub: Hawaii Business Publishing
Description: Jill Nunokawa, civil rights at University of Hawaii, believes that athletics are extra-curricular and that the state needs to focus on priorities. State representative K. Mark Takai says that a football program brings pride and inspiration and can generate revenue and provide economic opportunities.

19239 ■ "Chiefs Hope Renovations Score Big With Sponsors" in *The Business Journal-Serving Metropolitan Kansas City* (Vol. 26, July 11, 2008)
Pub: American City Business Journals, Inc.
Ed: James Dornbrook. **Description:** Kansas City Chiefs officials expect to obtain 12 to 14 new major sponsors with the completion of the Arrowhead Stadium renovations. The new sponsorship opportunities will include naming rights for the stadium and practice facility. The team's marketing strategies are discussed.

19240 ■ "Design program in Athletic Footwear" in *Occupational Outlook Quarterly* (Vol. 55, Fall 2011, No. 3, pp. 21)
Pub: U.S. Bureau of Labor Statistics
Description: The Fashion Institute of Technology offers the only certificate program in performance athletic footwear design in the U.S. The program focuses on conceptualizing and sketching shoe designs and covers ergonomic, anatomical, and material considerations for athletic footwear design.

19241 ■ "Fight Against Fake" in *The Business Journal-Portland* (Vol. 25, July 18, 2008, No. 19, pp. 1)
Pub: American City Business Journals, Inc.
Ed: Erik Siemers. **Description:** Companies, such as Columbia Sportswear Co. and Nike Inc., are fighting the counterfeiting of their sportswear and footwear products through the legal process of coordinating with law enforcement agencies to raid factories. Most of the counterfeiting factories are in China and India. Other details on the issue are discussed.

19242 ■ "Fledgling Brands May Take the Fall With Steve & Barry's" in *Advertising Age* (Vol. 79, July 7, 2008, No. 26, pp. 6)
Pub: Crain Communications, Inc.
Ed: Natalie Zmuda. **Description:** Steve & Barry's, a retailer that holds licensing deals with a number of designers and celebrities, may have to declare bankruptcy; this leaves the fate of the retailer's hundreds of licensing deals and exclusive celebrity lines in question.

19243 ■ "Great Expectations" in *Canadian Business* (Vol. 81, April 14, 2008, No. 6, pp. 34)
Pub: Rogers Media
Ed: Andy Holloway. **Description:** Therma Blades Inc. says that the reports that say their Therma Blade ice skates were not working properly were inaccurate. The major mistake of the company was to fail to manage the public's expectation when they touted the blades as revolutionary. Therma Blades Inc. has since tested the product with the help of 120 players and physiological testing done on elite level players show that there was a 10 percent improvement in energy efficiency.

19244 ■ "Hitting the Green" in *Canadian Business* (Vol. 81, July 22, 2008, No. 12-13, pp. 34)
Pub: Rogers Media Ltd.
Ed: Andy Holloway. **Description:** RBC is sponsoring the Canadian Open golf tournament, which is the second-oldest event in the PGA Tour. RBC is expected to receive television exposure on CBS and the Golf Channel. Additional information relating to the sponsorship is presented.

19245 ■ "HOK Sport May Build Own Practice" in *The Business Journal-Serving Metropolitan Kansas City* (Vol. 26, August 29, 2008, No. 51, pp. 1)
Pub: American City Business Journals, Inc.
Ed: Rob Roberts. **Description:** HOK Sport Venue Event is considering a spin-off from its parent company, HOK Group Inc. HOK Sport spokeswoman Gina Leo confirms that the firm is exploring structures, including a management buyout. Some of HOK Sport Venue Event's Minnesota projects are discussed.

19246 ■ "An Ice Boost in Revenue; Wings Score With Expanded Corporate Sales" in *Crain's Detroit Business* (Vol. 25, June 1, 2009, No. 22)
Pub: Crain Communications Inc. - Detroit
Ed: Bill Shea. **Description:** Stanley Cup finals always boost business for the Detroit area, even during a recession. The Red Wings corporate office reported corporate sponsorship revenue luxury suite rentals, Legends Club seats and advertising were up 40 percent this year over 2008.

19247 ■ "Insider" in *Canadian Business* (Vol. 80, Winter 2007, No. 24, pp.)
Pub: Rogers Media
Ed: Zena Olijnyk. **Description:** Luluemon Athletica started in 1998 after Dennis Wilson takes a yoga class and notices a demand from women for breathable clothes. The company opened their first outlet in Vancouver in November 2000 then opened their first U.S. store in 2003 until finally going public July 27, 2007 where its stocks doubled in value within days of trading.

19248 ■ "It's a New Game: Killerspin Pushes Table Tennis to Extreme Heights" in *Black Enterprise* (Vol. 37, October 2006, No. 3, pp. 73)
Pub: Earl G. Graves Publishing Co. Inc.
Ed: Bridget McCrea. **Description:** Profile of Robert Blackwell and his company Killerspin L.L.C., which is popularizing the sport of table tennis. Killerspin has hit $1 million in revenues due to product sales primarily generated through the company's website, magazines, DVDs, and event ticket sales.

19249 ■ "Lawyers Sued Over Lapsed Lacrosse Patent" in *Crain's Detroit Business* (Vol. 25, June 8, 2009, No. 23, pp. 5)
Pub: Crain Communications Inc. - Detroit
Ed: Chad Halcom. **Description:** Warrior Sports Inc., a manufacturer of lacrosse equipment located in Warren, Michigan is suing the law firm Dickinson Wright PLLC and two of its intellectual property lawyers over patent rights to lacrosse equipment.

19250 ■ "Marathon Money" in *Hawaii Business* (Vol. 53, December 2007, No. 6, pp. 127)
Pub: Hawaii Business Publishing
Ed: Jolyn Okimoto Rosa. **Description:** Discusses the effects of the Honolulu Marathon on small businesses' sales. The Running Room, for instance, experience growth in sales starting from the training season up to the end of the race, as a surge of Hawaiian residents and tourists come into the store for items such as running shoes and blister kits. The marathon's impact on Hawaii's tourism is examined as well.

19251 ■ "NFL Labor, Legal Issues Hang Over Detroit Lions' Rebuilding Efforts" in *Crain's Detroit Business* (Vol. 26, January 11, 2010, No. 2)
Pub: Crain Communications, Inc.
Ed: Bill Shea. **Description:** Overview of the possible outcomes regarding labor talks with Detroit Lion's players as well as the outcome of a U.S. Supreme Court decision that could boost franchise values but at the expense of fans and corporate sponsors.

19252 ■ "Nike's Next Splash" in *The Business Journal-Portland* (Vol. 25, August 22, 2008, No. 24, pp. 1)
Pub: American City Business Journals, Inc.
Ed: Erik Siemers. **Description:** Business analysts expect Nike to bid for the endorsement services of swimmer Michael Phelps after the swimmer's contract

with Speedo expires. The company, however, is a lightweight in the swimming apparel market and is not focusing on swimming as a growth sector.

19253 ■ "One Paddle, Two Paddle" in *Hawaii Business* (Vol. 53, October 2007, No. 4, pp. 65)
Pub: Hawaii Business Publishing
Ed: Kyle Galdeira. **Description:** Oiwi Ocean Gear's strategy may not give instant profits, but it works well for the company's goal of providing high-quality apparel for paddlers. The apparel company produces and markets swimwear, paddling jerseys and active wear. The company's strategy is compared with the selling of mass-produced clothes lower prices.

19254 ■ "Packers Still Want Marketing Deal With Favre" in *The Business Journal-Milwaukee* (Vol. 25, August 15, 2008, No. 47, pp. A1)
Pub: American City Business Journals, Inc.
Ed: Mark Kass. **Description:** The Green Bay Packers plan to offer a $20 million marketing agreement to quarterback Brett Favre, including a clothing, merchandise, and collectibles line. The team is pursuing the agreement despite trading Favre to the New York Jets on 6 August 2008.

19255 ■ "Portland Wooing Under Armour to West Coast Facility" in *Baltimore Business Journal* (Vol. 27, January 29, 2010, No. 39, pp. 1)
Pub: American City Business Journals
Ed: Andy Giegerich. **Description:** Baltimore, Maryland sports apparel maker, Under Armour, is planning a west coast expansion with Portland, Oregon among the sites considered to house its apparel and footwear design center. Portland officials counting on the concentration of nearly 10,000 activewear workers in the city will help lure the company to the city.

19256 ■ "Recovery on Tap for 2010?" in *Orlando Business Journal* (Vol. 26, January 1, 2010, No. 31, pp. 1)
Pub: American City Business Journals
Ed: Melanie Stawicki Azam, Richard Bilbao, Christopher Boyd, Anjali Fluker. **Description:** Economic forecasts for Central Florida's leading business sectors in 2010 are presented. These sectors include housing, film and TV, sports business, law, restaurants, aviation, tourism and hospitality, banking and finance, commercial real estate, retail, health care, insurance, higher education, and manufacturing. According to some local executives, Central Florida's economy will slowly recover in 2010.

19257 ■ "Retail Center Pitched" in *Business Courier* (Vol. 27, June 18, 2010, No. 7, pp. 1)
Pub: Business Courier
Ed: Dan Monk. **Description:** Jeffrey R. Anderson Real Estate Inc.'s plan for a retail center in Butler County, Ohio could have three department stores in the 1.1 million-square-foot property. An outdoor sports retailer is also part of the plans.

19258 ■ "Sabathia Deal Makes Dollars and Sense" in *The Business Journal-Milwaukee* (Vol. 25, July 11, 2008, No. 42, pp. A1)
Pub: American City Business Journals, Inc.
Ed: Mark Kass. **Description:** It was reported that the Milwaukee Brewers' acquisition of CC Sabathia will mean that the team will pick up an estimated $5 million in salary that Sabathia is owed for the remainder of the season. Because of this, the team will not make a profit in 2008. The acquisition of Sabathia is expected to cause an increase in attendance and merchandise revenue over the remainder of the season.

19259 ■ "Sheets Energy Strips Unveils New Vending Machines" in *Food and Beverage Close-Up* (August 12, 2011)
Pub: Close-Up Media
Description: Sheets Energy Strips is installing vending machines in malls, office buildings, stadiums and arenas in New York, New Jersey, Connecticut and Florida. These machines will offer 4 packs, 10 packs and Sheets branded hats and T-shirts.

19260 ■ *Sporting Goods and Activewear Buyers*
Pub: Briefings Media Group
Ed: Patrick Snyder, Editor, psnyder@douglaspublications.com. **Released:** Annual, Latest edition 2004-2005 edition. **Price:** $1,299, individuals CD-ROM. **Covers:** 18,400 buyers and 10,700 stores in the sporting goods and activewear industry, covering the United States, Puerto Rico, the Virgin Islands, and Canada. **Entries Include:** Store name, address, phone, fax; e-mail; URL; names and titles of key personnel; financial data; branch/subsidiary name and address; products and/or services provided; sales volume; type of store; number of stores; buying groups. **Arrangement:** Geographical. **Indexes:** Store name, new listings, mail order, buying group, online retailer.

19261 ■ "Surfing's Next Safari" in *Entrepreneur* (Vol. 37, July 2009, No. 7, pp. 24)
Pub: Entrepreneur Media, Inc.
Ed: Dennis Romero. **Description:** Profile of Firewire Surfboards, a San Diego-based maker of lightweight surfboards, aims to capture surfing enthusiasts' attention with its use of unusual and high-tech materials. Firewire's biggest challenge is the preference for old-school surfboards, but the company is determined to revolutionize how surfboards should be made. The company's various innovations and experiences are also discussed.

19262 ■ "Tigers Put to Test; Can Team Win Back Fans, Advertisers?" in *Crain's Detroit Business* (Vol. 24, October 6, 2008, No. 40, pp. 1)
Pub: Crain Communications, Inc.
Ed: Bill Shea. **Description:** Despite the enormous amount of money the Detroit Tigers' owner Mike Ilitch spent on player salaries, a record $137.6 million this season, the team finished in last-place; ticket sales and advertising dollars for next season are expected to fall dramatically. Additional speculation regarding the future of the ball team is included.

19263 ■ "To the Extreme" in *Entrepreneur* (Vol. 36, February 2008, No. 2, pp. 21)
Pub: Entrepreneur Media Inc.
Ed: Lindsay Holloway. **Description:** Extreme sports are increasing in number, with companies seeing the market potential of these sports for the 10- to 30-year-old age group. Entrepreneurs are launching innovated products catering to extreme sports-related markets. Details on the opportunities provided by the growth of extreme sports are discussed.

19264 ■ "Under Armour Wants to Equip Athletes, Too" in *Boston Business Journal* (Vol. 29, July 8, 2011, No. 9, pp. 1)
Pub: American City Business Journals Inc.
Ed: Ryan Sharrow. **Description:** Baltimore sportswear maker Under Armour advances plans to enter into the equipment field, aiming to strengthen its hold on football, basketball and lacrosse markets where it already has a strong market share. The company is now cooking up licensing deals to bolster the firm's presence among athletes.

19265 ■ "Viewing Ironman As Gold, R.I. Firm Buys Its Parent" in *The Business Journal-Serving Greater Tampa Bay* (Vol. 28, September 19, 2008)
Pub: American City Business Journals, Inc.
Ed: Pete Williams. **Description:** Providence Equity Partners purchased World Triathlon Corp., parent company of the Ironman Triathlon, for an undisclosed sum. The acquisition means that the World Triathlon Headquarters will move to Tampa, Florida, and allows Providence Equity Partners to stage or license rights to Ironman and half-Ironman distance events.

19266 ■ "What Players in the Midmarket Are Talking About" in *Mergers & Acquisitions: The Dealmaker's Journal* (March 1, 2008)
Pub: SourceMedia, Inc.
Description: Sports Properties Acquisition Corp. went public at the end of January; according to the company's prospectus, it is not limiting its focus to just teams, it is also considering deals for stadium construction companies, sports leagues, facilities, sports-related advertising and licensing of products, in addition to other related segments.

STATISTICAL SOURCES

19267 ■ *RMA Annual Statement Studies*
Pub: Robert Morris Associates (RMA)
Released: Annual. **Price:** $175.00 2006-07 edition, $105.00. **Description:** Contains composite balance sheets and income statements for more than 360 industries, including the accounting, auditing, and bookkeeping industries. Also contains five years of comparative historical data for discerning trends. Includes 16 commonly used ratios, computed for most of the size groupings for nearly every industry.

TRADE PERIODICALS

19268 ■ *Mountainwest Golf*
Pub: Harris Publishing Inc.
Contact: Magdalene Mercado, Gp. Sec.
Released: Quarterly. **Price:** $8.95; $15.95 two years; $21.95 3 years; $28.95 other countries; $55.95 other countries 2 years; $81.95 other countries 3 years; $23.95 Canada; $45.95 Canada 2 years; $66.95 Canada 3 years. **Description:** Magazine covering local golfing.

19269 ■ *NSSRA Newsletter*
Pub: National Ski & Snowboard Retailers Association
Contact: Thomas B. Doyle, President
E-mail: tdoyle@nssra.com
Released: Quarterly. **Price:** Included in membership. **Description:** Informs ski and snowboard retail stores on critical industry issues such as guidelines and litigation exposure and marketing.

19270 ■ *Out Your Backdoor*
Pub: Out Your Backdoor
Contact: Jeff Potter, Editor & Publisher
E-mail: jeff@outyourbackdoor.com
Released: Monthly. **Description:** Magazine focusing on bicycling, adventure, culture, the outdoors, hobbies, and sports.

19271 ■ *Sporting Goods Dealer*
Pub: Bill Communications Inc.
Contact: Mark Sullivan, Publisher
E-mail: msullivan@sgdealer.com
Ed: Mike Jacobsen, Editor, mjacobsen@sgdealer.com. **Released:** Bimonthly. **Description:** Magazine which offers expert reporting on trends affecting team dealers and retailers who service schools, colleges, pro and local teams.

19272 ■ *The Team Line-Up*
Pub: National Sporting Goods Association
Contact: T. Doyle
E-mail: tdoyle@nsga.org
Ed: Thomas B. Doyle, Editor, tdoyle@nsga.org. **Released:** Quarterly. **Price:** Included in membership. **Description:** Intended for member athletic team distributors who specialize in supplying equipment to high schools, colleges, and organized teams. Monitors athletic rule-making bodies and carries articles on such topics as safety and sports equipment and the liability of sports equipment manufacturers in lawsuits concerning sports injuries. Recurring features include notices of rules changes and rules committee meetings.

19273 ■ *USA Table Tennis Magazine*
Pub: USA Table Tennis
Contact: Larry Hodges, Exec. Dir.
E-mail: larry@larrytt.com
Released: Bimonthly. **Price:** $20, Included in membership. **Description:** Covers the sport of table tennis.

VIDEOCASSETTES/ AUDIOCASSETTES

19274 ■ *Air Raid*
Tapeworm Video Distributors
25876 The Old Road 141
Stevenson Ranch, CA 91381

Ph:(661)257-4904
Fax:(661)257-4820
Co. E-mail: sales@tapeworm.com
URL: http://www.tapeworm.com
Price: $19.95. **Description:** Exciting aerial feats in motorcross, snowboarding, surfing, skateboarding, wakeboarding, and BMX racing. **Availability:** VHS.

19275 ■ *The Best of Golf in Paradise*
Tapeworm Video Distributors
25876 The Old Road 141
Stevenson Ranch, CA 91381
Ph:(661)257-4904
Fax:(661)257-4820
Co. E-mail: sales@tapeworm.com
URL: http://www.tapeworm.com
Released: 1996. **Price:** $19.95. **Description:** Johnny Bench presents resort destinations, celebrity bloopers, instruction, tips, and golf gadgets. **Availability:** VHS.

19276 ■ *Coach Curry's Quarterback Clinic: Developing the Quarterback*
Karol Media
Hanover Industrial Estates
375 Stewart Rd.
PO Box 7600
Wilkes Barre, PA 18773-7600
Ph:(570)822-8899
Free: 800-526-4773
Co. E-mail: sales@karolmedia.com
URL: http://www.karolmedia.com
Released: 1997. **Price:** $19.95. **Description:** Provides football drills and instruction. **Availability:** VHS.

19277 ■ *The Coach's 10 Commandments of Positive Athletic Parenting*
Karol Media
Hanover Industrial Estates
375 Stewart Rd.
PO Box 7600
Wilkes Barre, PA 18773-7600
Ph:(570)822-8899
Free: 800-526-4773
Co. E-mail: sales@karolmedia.com
URL: http://www.karolmedia.com
Released: 1997. **Price:** $12.95. **Description:** Coach George Curry explains to parents how to give positive support to their kids, the team, and to coaches, and how to avoid negative behavior. **Availability:** VHS.

19278 ■ *How to Be the Kid with the Perfect Swing*
Tapeworm Video Distributors
25876 The Old Road 141
Stevenson Ranch, CA 91381
Ph:(661)257-4904
Fax:(661)257-4820
Co. E-mail: sales@tapeworm.com
URL: http://www.tapeworm.com
Price: $19.95. **Description:** Dave Griffin's Baseball School presents basic techniques to "hit like a pro." **Availability:** VHS.

19279 ■ *Playing and Coaching Winning Baseball and Softball*
Karol Media
Hanover Industrial Estates
375 Stewart Rd.
PO Box 7600
Wilkes Barre, PA 18773-7600
Ph:(570)822-8899
Free: 800-526-4773
Co. E-mail: sales@karolmedia.com
URL: http://www.karolmedia.com
Released: 1997. **Price:** $19.95. **Description:** Instruction and guidance for little league coaches. **Availability:** VHS.

19280 ■ *Ski Tips 5: Skiing with Shaped Skis Made Easy*
TMW Media Group
2321 Abbot Kinney Blvd., Ste. 101
Venice, CA 90291
Ph:(310)577-8581
Free: 800-262-8862
Fax:(310)574-0886
Co. E-mail: general@tmwmedia.com
URL: http://www.tmwmedia.com
Released: 1997. **Price:** $29.95. **Description:** Shows skiers how to properly use shaped skis for the best performance. **Availability:** VHS.

19281 ■ *Soccer Strategies and Fitness Techniques*
Service Quality Institute
9201 E. Bloomington Fwy.
Minneapolis, MN 55420-3437
Ph:(952)884-3311
Free: 800-548-0538
Fax:(952)884-8901
URL: http://www.customer-service.com
Price: $14.95. **Description:** Coach Tom Fitzgerald teaches offensive and defensive strategies and gives advice on Soccer fitness. **Availability:** VHS.

19282 ■ *Space Cowboys: Dysfunctional Superheroes II*
Tapeworm Video Distributors
25876 The Old Road 141
Stevenson Ranch, CA 91381
Ph:(661)257-4904
Fax:(661)257-4820
Co. E-mail: sales@tapeworm.com
URL: http://www.tapeworm.com
Released: 1997. **Price:** $14.95. **Description:** Presents footage of snowboarders, skateboarders, and freestyle BMX riders. **Availability:** VHS.

19283 ■ *Steep Snow*
Keen Media
857 Pulpit Rock Circle N.
Colorado Springs, CO 80918
Ph:(719)593-2155
Free: 800-363-5336
Fax:(719)593-2888
Co. E-mail: jim@keenmedia.com
URL: http://www.keenmedia.com
Price: $34.95. **Description:** Provides instruction on techniques, equipment, and weather and terrain for hunters, hikers, skiers, and others finding it necessary to cross steep snow. **Availability:** VHS.

19284 ■ *"Winning Soccer" Soccer Skills*
Service Quality Institute
9201 E. Bloomington Fwy.
Minneapolis, MN 55420-3437
Ph:(952)884-3311
Free: 800-548-0538
Fax:(952)884-8901
URL: http://www.customer-service.com
Price: $14.95. **Description:** Coach Tom Fitzgerald discusses four components of soccer, fitness, technique, tactics and psychological dimensions. **Availability:** VHS.

TRADE SHOWS AND CONVENTIONS

19285 ■ American Alliance for Health, Physical Education, Recreation, and Dance - National Conference and Exposition
American Alliance for Health, Physical Education, Recreation, and Dance
1900 Association Dr.
Reston, VA 20191-1598
Ph:(703)476-3400
Free: 800-213-7193
Fax:(703)476-9527
Co. E-mail: info@aahperd.org
URL: http://www.aahperd.org
Released: Annual. **Audience:** Health and physical education teachers, coaches, athletic directors, trainers, officials, dance teachers, and related professionals and students. **Principal Exhibits:** Physical educational sporting goods, supplies, equipment, publishers, and service organization representatives.

19286 ■ Annual Allegheny Sport, Travel and Outdoor Show
Expositions Inc.
PO Box 550, Edgewater Br.
Cleveland, OH 44107-0550
Ph:(216)529-1300
Fax:(216)529-0311
Co. E-mail: expoinc@oinc.com
URL: http://www.expoinc.com
Released: Annual. **Principal Exhibits:** Sports, travel and outdoor show.

19287 ■ Annual Reading Sport, Travel and Outdoor Show
Eastern Fishing and Outdoor Exposition Inc.
PO Box 4720
Portsmouth, NH 03801
Ph:(603)431-4315
Fax:(603)431-1971
Co. E-mail: info@sportshows.com
URL: http://www.sportshows.com
Released: Annual. **Audience:** Greater Washington DC area. **Principal Exhibits:** Sports, travel and outdoor show.

19288 ■ Annual Rockford RV, Camping and Travel Show
Showtime Productions Inc.
PO Box 4372
Rockford, IL 61110
Fax:(815)877-9037
Co. E-mail: brenda@showtimeproduction.net
URL: http://www.showtimeproduction.net
Released: Annual. **Principal Exhibits:** RVs, camping and travel.

19289 ■ Asiafit
Neway International Trade Fairs Ltd.
9/F, Fortis Tower
77 Gloucester Rd.
Wan Chai, People's Republic of China
Ph:852 2561 5566
Fax:852 2811 9156
Co. E-mail: info@newayfairs.com
URL: http://www.newayfairs.com
Released: Annual. **Principal Exhibits:** Asia fitness equipment, sporting goods & facilities.

19290 ■ Cincinnati Travel, Sports, and Boat Show
Hart Productions, Inc.
2234 Bauer Rd., Ste. B
Batavia, OH 45103
Ph:(513)797-7900
Free: 877-704-8190
Fax:(513)797-1013
URL: http://www.hartproductions.com
Released: Annual. **Audience:** General public. **Principal Exhibits:** Showcasing a world of travel and recreation featuring vacation travel exhibits, boats, sporting goods, fishing and hunting equipment and seminars. **Dates and Locations:** 2011 Jan 14-23, Cincinnati, OH.

19291 ■ Detroit Boat Show
Michigan Boating Industries Association
32398 5 Mile Rd.
Livonia, MI 48154-6109
Ph:(734)261-0123
Free: 800-932-2628
Fax:(734)261-0880
Co. E-mail: boatmichigan@mbia.org
URL: http://www.mbia.org
Released: Annual. **Audience:** Trade professionals and general public. **Principal Exhibits:** Boats, fishing equipment, boat-related accessories, charter rentals, nautical attire, trailer and outboard motors, and personal watercraft.

19292 ■ Eastern Fishing and Outdoor Exposition
Eastern Fishing and Outdoor Exposition Inc.
PO Box 4720
Portsmouth, NH 03801
Ph:(603)431-4315
Fax:(603)431-1971
Co. E-mail: info@sportshows.com
URL: http://www.sportshows.com
Released: Annual. **Audience:** Metro Boston/ Worcester Market. **Principal Exhibits:** Fishing and outdoor sports.

19293 ■ Eastern Sports & Outdoor Show
Reed Exhibitions North American Headquarters
383 Main Ave.
Norwalk, CT 06851
Ph:(203)840-4800
Fax:(203)840-5805
Co. E-mail: export@reedexpo.com
URL: http://www.reedexpo.com
Released: Annual. **Audience:** General public. **Principal Exhibits:** Recreational vehicles, boats, hunting and fishing equipment, clothing, and related outdoor products, resorts, SUVs, retailers and manufacturers, motorcycles, ATVs, travel and tourism.

19294 ■ Fort Wayne Sports, Vacation, and Boat Show
Trio Enterprises, Inc.
3624 Maxim Dr.
Fort Wayne, IN 46815
Ph:(219)483-2638
Free: 800-446-2638
Fax:(219)484-0876
Released: Annual. **Audience:** General public. **Principal Exhibits:** Recreational vehicles, boats, and travel and vacation information.

19295 ■ FUN Expo
Reed Exhibitions North American Headquarters
383 Main Ave.
Norwalk, CT 06851
Ph:(203)840-4800
Fax:(203)840-5805
Co. E-mail: export@reedexpo.com
URL: http://www.reedexpo.com
Released: Annual. **Principal Exhibits:** Amusement and recreation products for family and location based entertainment centers, small amusement parks and family oriented businesses such as bowling centers, skating rinks, sports parks, miniature golf courses, golf driving ranges, family restaurants, resorts and other entertainment/recreation businesses. **Dates and Locations:** 2011 Mar 01-03, Las Vegas, NV.

19296 ■ H2X Canada Hardware & Home Improvement Expo & Conference
Messe Frankfurt Inc. (Atlanta, Georgia)
1600 Parkwood Cir., Ste. 515
Atlanta, GA 30339
Ph:(770)984-8016
Fax:(770)984-8023
Co. E-mail: info@usa.messefrankfurt.com
URL: http://www.usa.messefrankfurt.com
Released: Annual. **Audience:** Volume buyers, including retailers and manufacturers' representatives. **Principal Exhibits:** Hardware, housewares, giftware, paint, wallcovering, and products for leisure living, and home improvement.

19297 ■ The Imprinted Sportswear Show, Long Beach
Nielsen Business Media
770 Broadway
New York, NY 10003-9595
Ph:(646)654-4500
Co. E-mail: bmcomm@nielsen.com
URL: http://www.nielsenbusinessmedia.com/
Released: Annual. **Audience:** Buyers of imprinted sportswear, screen printing/embroidery equipment, supplies and apparel. **Principal Exhibits:** T-shirts, pre-prints, and other apparel; design software; screen-printing supplies and equipment; transfers, lettering, embroidery equipment and supplies.

19298 ■ The Imprinted Sportswear Show, Orlando
Nielsen Business Media
770 Broadway
New York, NY 10003-9595
Ph:(646)654-4500
Co. E-mail: bmcomm@nielsen.com
URL: http://www.nielsenbusinessmedia.com/
Released: Annual. **Audience:** Buyers of imprinted sportswear, screen printing/embroidery equipment, supplies, and apparel. **Principal Exhibits:** T-shirts, pre-prints, apparel, design software, screen-printing supplies and equipment, transfers, lettering, and embroidery equipment and supplies.

19299 ■ JAGEN UND FISCHEN - International Exhibition for Hunters, Fishermen and Marksmen
Kallman Worldwide, Inc.
4 North St., Ste. 800
Waldwick, NJ 07463-1842
Ph:(201)251-2600
Fax:(201)251-2760
Co. E-mail: info@kallman.com
URL: http://www.kallman.com
Principal Exhibits: Equipment, supplies, and services for hunters, fishermen, and marksmen.

19300 ■ Kansas City Sportshow
General Sports Shows Inc.
1301 2nd Ave. S.
Minneapolis, MN 55403
Ph:(612)827-5833
Free: 800-777-4766
Fax:(612)827-1242
Co. E-mail: info@generalsportshows.com
URL: http://www.generalsportshows.com
Released: Annual. **Principal Exhibits:** Sports.

19301 ■ Kansas Sports, Boat, & Travel Show
Industrial Expositions, Inc.
1675 Larimer St., No.700
PO Box 480084
Denver, CO 80248-0084
Ph:(303)892-6800
Free: 800-457-2434
Fax:(303)892-6322
Co. E-mail: info@iei-expos.com
URL: http://www.iei-expos.com/
Released: Annual. **Audience:** General public. **Principal Exhibits:** Recreational vehicles, boats, sports equipment, and travel destination information; fishing and hunting equipment, supplies, and services.

19302 ■ Louisville Boat, RV & Sportshow
Douglas Expositions Inc.
10000 Shelbyville Rd., No. 111
Anchorage, KY 40223-2950
Ph:(502)244-5660
Fax:(502)244-5160
Released: Annual. **Principal Exhibits:** Sports, boating and vacations, hunting and fishing, recreational vehicles.

19303 ■ Milwaukee Journal Sentinel Sports Show
Milwaukee Journal Sentinel
PO Box 661
Milwaukee, WI 53201
Ph:(414)224-2000
Fax:(414)225-5000
URL: http://www.journalsentinel.com
Released: Annual. **Principal Exhibits:** Sports equipment, supplies, and services.

19304 ■ Northwest Sportshow
General Sports Shows Inc.
1301 2nd Ave. S.
Minneapolis, MN 55403
Ph:(612)827-5833
Free: 800-777-4766
Fax:(612)827-1242
Co. E-mail: info@generalsportshows.com
URL: http://www.generalsportshows.com
Released: Annual. **Audience:** Sporting enthusiasts, sporting goods professionals. **Principal Exhibits:** Boating, fishing, hunting, camping, RVing. **Dates and Locations:** 2011 Mar 30 - Apr 03, Minneapolis, MN.

19305 ■ Outdoor Retailer Summer Market
VNU Expo (Laguna Beach, California)
310 Broadway
Laguna Beach, CA 92651
Ph:(946)376-6200
Free: 800-486-2701
Fax:(949)497-5290
Co. E-mail: interbike@wyoming.com
URL: http://www.vnuexpo.com
Released: Annual. **Audience:** Owners and managers of the specialty sports retail stores. **Principal Exhibits:** Human-powered outdoor sports goods. **Dates and Locations:** 2011 Aug 04-07, Salt Lake City, UT.

19306 ■ Outdoor Retailer Winter Market
VNU Expo (Laguna Beach, California)
310 Broadway
Laguna Beach, CA 92651
Ph:(946)376-6200
Free: 800-486-2701
Fax:(949)497-5290
Co. E-mail: interbike@wyoming.com
URL: http://www.vnuexpo.com
Released: Annual. **Audience:** Owners and managers of specialty sports retail stores. **Principal Exhibits:** Human-powered outdoor sports goods. **Dates and Locations:** 2011 Jan 19-23, Salt Lake City, UT.

19307 ■ Rocky Mountain Snowmobile & Icefishing Expo
Industrial Expositions, Inc.
1675 Larimer St., No.700
PO Box 480084
Denver, CO 80248-0084
Ph:(303)892-6800
Free: 800-457-2434
Fax:(303)892-6322
Co. E-mail: info@iei-expos.com
URL: http://www.iei-expos.com/
Released: Annual. **Audience:** Snowmobilers. **Principal Exhibits:** Snowmobiles, clothing and accessories, recreational vehicles, travel and accommodations.

19308 ■ Scuba ExtaSea Expo
Industrial Expositions, Inc.
1675 Larimer St., No.700
PO Box 480084
Denver, CO 80248-0084
Ph:(303)892-6800
Free: 800-457-2434
Fax:(303)892-6322
Co. E-mail: info@iei-expos.com
URL: http://www.iei-expos.com/
Released: Annual. **Audience:** General public. **Principal Exhibits:** Scuba diving, snorkeling, travel and accessories.

19309 ■ The Shooting, Hunting, and Outdoor Trade Show
Reed Exhibitions Contemporary Forums
11900 Silvergate Dr.
Dublin, CA 94568
Ph:(925)828-7100
Fax:800-329-9923
Co. E-mail: info@cforums.com
URL: http://www.contemporaryforums.com
Audience: Federally licensed firearms dealers and legitimate sporting goods dealers. **Principal Exhibits:** Shooting and hunting equipment and products; sports accessories, clothing, and supplies.

19310 ■ United States Professional Tennis Association Convention
United States Professional Tennis Association
3535 Briarpark Dr., Ste. One
Houston, TX 77042
Ph:(713)978-7782
Free: 800-USPTA-4U
Fax:(713)978-7780
Co. E-mail: uspta@uspta.org
URL: http://www.uspta.org
Released: Annual. **Audience:** Tennis-teaching professionals, industry delegates, and general public. **Principal Exhibits:** Tennis equipment, supplies, and services.

19311 ■ Washington Sportmen's Show
O'Loughlin Trade Shows (Portland, Oregon)
PO Box 80750
Portland, OR 97280
Ph:(503)246-8291
Free: 800-343-6973
Fax:(503)246-1066
URL: http://www.oloughlintradeshows.com
Released: Annual. **Principal Exhibits:** Sportsmen's show.

19312 ■ World Fishing and Outdoor Exposition
Eastern Fishing and Outdoor Exposition Inc.
PO Box 4720
Portsmouth, NH 03801
Ph:(603)431-4315
Fax:(603)431-1971
Co. E-mail: info@sportshows.com
URL: http://www.sportshows.com
Released: Annual. **Audience:** Metro New York City Market. **Principal Exhibits:** Fishing and outdoor sports. **Dates and Locations:** 2011 Mar 03-06, Suffern, NY.

FRANCHISES AND BUSINESS OPPORTUNITIES

19313 ■ Golf Etc.
Golf Etc. of America Inc.
2201 Commercial Ln.
Granbury, TX 76048-5698
Free: 800-806-8633
Co. E-mail: sales@golfetc.com
URL: http://www.GolfEtc.com
No. of Franchise Units: 65. **Founded:** 1992. **Description:** Sales of golf clubs and golf accessories. **Equity Capital Needed:** $179,500. **Franchise Fee:** $15,000. **Financial Assistance:** No. **Training:** Provides training at corporate office in Granbury, TX. Follow-up with regards to merchandising, ordering, club fitting, pro line selections, hottest accessories, advertising, trends and strategic planning. Internet linked owner info and monthly newsletter.

19314 ■ Play it Again Sports
Winmark Corp.
605 Highway 169 N, Ste. 400
Minneapolis, MN 55441
Free: 800-592-8049
URL: http://www.playitagainsports.com
NFU 328. **Founded:** 1983. **Franchised:** 1988. **Description:** Sells new and used sports equipment and clothing. Franchisees purchase discount inventory through closeouts and overruns and accept used equipment in trade from customers, reducing retail prices by 40-60%. **Equity Capital Needed:** $236,400-$374,500; Approximately 30% cash requirement. **Franchise Fee:** $25,000. **Financial Assistance:** No in-house financing available. Support given in developing 3 year business plan and cash flow analysis to use in securing loans. **Managerial Assistance:** Owner only website provides resources and operational support tools to franchisee. **Training:** Training includes product acquisition, inventory management, staff hiring and training, customer service, advertising and marketing, and merchandising. Ongoing regional meetings and national training conferences held annually.

ASSOCIATIONS AND OTHER ORGANIZATIONS

19315 ■ International Gay Rodeo Association
PO Box 460504
Aurora, CO 80046-0504
Co. E-mail: admin.assistant@igra.com
URL: http://www.igra.com
Contact: Tommy Channel, Admin. Asst.
Description: Gay rodeo associations in the United States and Canada. Promotes public interest in rodeo events and seeks to increase participation in rodeo by gay people. Facilitates communication and cooperation among members; sponsors competitions. **Publications:** *Safety Video*; *2005 Rodeo Resource Guidebook* .

DIRECTORIES OF EDUCATIONAL PROGRAMS

19316 ■ *Encyclopedia of Sports Business Contacts*
Pub: Global Sports Productions Ltd.
Ed: Edward T. Kobak, Jr., Editor. **Released:** Biennial, latest edition 1st. **Price:** $79.95, individuals perfect bound; plus shipping charges $13.50. **Covers:** Sports organizations, associations, clubs, leagues, teams, corporate sponsors, sports media, facilities, sports agents and lawyers, organizations for the physically challenged, and manufacturers and retailers of sporting goods. **Entries Include:** Company name, address, phone, fax, email and web addresses, names and titles of key personnel.

19317 ■ *International Sports Directory*
Pub: Global Sports Productions Ltd.
Ed: Edward T. Kobak, Jr., Editor. **Released:** Latest edition 3rd. **Price:** $45, individuals perfect bound; plus shipping charges $5.25. **Covers:** International men's and women's professional club sports, Olympic and multi-sport international games, sports federations, publications, Olympic committees, sports information centers, and IOC recognized sports federations. **Entries Include:** Company name, address, phone, fax, e-mail and web addresses, names and titles of key personnel.

REFERENCE WORKS

19318 ■ "10 Trends That Are Shaping Global Media Consumption" in *Advertising Age* (Vol. 81, December 6, 2010, No. 43, pp. 3)
Pub: Crain Communications, Inc.
Ed: Ann Marie Kerwin. **Description:** Ad Age offers the statistics from the TV penetration rate in Kenya to the number of World Cup watchers and more.

19319 ■ "Advertisers Hooked on Horns, their Playground" in *Austin Business JournalInc.* (Vol. 28, July 25, 2008, No. 19, pp. A1)
Pub: American City Business Journals
Ed: Sandra Zaragoza. **Description:** Renovation of the D.K. Royal-Texas Memorial Stadium has increased its advertising revenue from $570,000 in 1993 to $10 in 2008. Sponsorship has grown in the past years due to the revenue-sharing agreement, a ten-year contract through 2015 between the University of Texas and IMG College Sports.

19320 ■ "Arizona Firms In Chicago Go For Gold With '08 Games" in *The Business Journal - Serving Phoenix and the Valley of the Sun* (Vol. 28, August 8, 2008, No. 49, pp. 1)
Pub: American City Business Journals, Inc.
Ed: Patrick O'Grady. **Description:** More than 20 U.S. athletes will wear Arizona-based eSoles LLC's custom-made insoles to increase their performance at the 2008 Beijing Olympics making eSoles one of the beneficiaries of the commercialization of the games. Translation software maker Auralog Inc saw a 60 percent jump in sales from its Mandarin Chinese language applications.

19321 ■ "Athletes' Performance Building $10 Million Facility In ASU Park" in *The Business Journal - Serving Phoenix and the Valley of the Sun* (Vol. 28, August 8, 2008, No. 49, pp. 1)
Pub: American City Business Journals, Inc.
Ed: Jan Buchholz. **Description:** Athletes' Performance's planned facility at Arizona State University is scheduled to begin in November 2008 and expected to be completed by September 2009. The new building will almost double the company's training space as it will expand from around 19,000 square feet to 35,000 square feet.

19322 ■ *Athletic Business—Professional Directory Section*
Pub: Athletic Business Publications Inc.
Ed: Andrew Cohen, Editor. **Released:** Monthly, Latest edition 2010. **Price:** $8 per issue. **Publication Includes:** List of architects, engineers, contractors, and consultants in athletic facility planning and construction; all listings are paid. **Entries Include:** Company name, address, phone, fax and short description of company. **Arrangement:** Alphabetical.

19323 ■ "Back to Business" in *Retail Merchandiser* (Vol. 51, September-October 2011, No. 5, pp. 18)
Pub: Phoenix Media Corporation
Ed: Eric Slack. **Description:** National Football League owners and players have reached a labor agreement for the next ten years. America's football league can once again focus on providing fans with a great product both on and off the field.

19324 ■ "Bars, Restaurants to Offer Prix Fixe Menus, Space to Race Patrons" in *Boston Business Journal* (Vol. 29, July 22, 2011, No. 11, pp. 1)
Pub: American City Business Journals Inc.
Ed: Alexander Jackson. **Description:** Restaurants and bar owners in Baltimore, Maryland have changed the way they do business as the Baltimore Grand Prix approaches. Owners have gone so far as to offering new services or renting out their entire restaurants to companies for the three-day event in September.

19325 ■ *The Blind Side*
Pub: W. W. Norton & Company, Inc.
Ed: Michael Lewis. **Released:** 2007. **Price:** $13.95. **Description:** The evolving business of football, viewed through the rise of the left tackle, Michael Oher.

19326 ■ "Blues Asking Price Out of Their League" in *Saint Louis Business Journal* (Vol. 32, September 23, 2011, No. 4, pp. 1)
Pub: Saint Louis Business Journal
Ed: Amy Kurtovic. **Description:** St. Louis Blues owner Dave Checketts wanted the hockey team sold before the start of the season and he believed the team could fetch $200 million or more. However, Hockey insiders believe the price was too high when considering the team's high debt ratio and several other National Hockey League teams on the market.

19327 ■ "The Board Shorts Executive" in *Hawaii Business* (Vol. 53, January 2008, No. 7, pp. 33)
Pub: Hawaii Business Publishing
Ed: Mike Markrich. **Description:** Vans Triple Crown of Surfing executive director Randy Rarick believes that the surfing business requires knowledge of the sport and integity to the game's lifestyle and spirit. His organization manages surfing events, and has generated jobs for the locals. Plans for Vans Triple Crown are supplied.

19328 ■ "Buck-ing the Trend?" in *Baltimore Business Journal* (Vol. 28, August 13, 2010, No. 14, pp. 1)
Pub: Baltimore Business Journal
Ed: Gary Haber. **Description:** Baltimore Orioles' new manager Buck Showalter has managed to win games for fans. However, not all businesses around Camden Yards were boosted by the Orioles' surge as street vendors complained of worsening business.

19329 ■ "Calling An Audible" in *The Business Journal-Milwaukee* (Vol. 25, August 1, 2008, No. 45, pp. A1)
Pub: American City Business Journals, Inc.
Ed: David Dedge. **Description:** Tough economic conditions are forcing entertainment businesses in Milwaukee, Wisconsin, to try new business strategies to keep attracting customers. These strategies include keeping prices steady despite increasing costs and new sales promotions.

19330 ■ "Can the State Afford a Big Time College Football Program?" in *Hawaii Business* (Vol. 53, March 2008, No. 9, pp. 26)
Pub: Hawaii Business Publishing
Description: Jill Nunokawa, civil rights at University of Hawaii, believes that athletics are extra-curricular and that the state needs to focus on priorities. State representative K. Mark Takai says that a football program brings pride and inspiration and can generate revenue and provide economic opportunities.

19331 ■ "Chew On This: Soul Fans to 'Chew' Games' First Play" in *Philadelphia Business Journal* (Vol. 30, September 30, 2011, No. 33, pp. 3)
Pub: American City Business Journals Inc.
Ed: John George. **Description:** Arena football team Philadelphia Soul extended its marketing partnership

with Just Born Inc. The team's fans will enter a contest where the winner will be allowed to select the team's first play during a home game.

19332 ■ "Chiefs Hope Renovations Score Big With Sponsors" in *The Business Journal-Serving Metropolitan Kansas City* (Vol. 26, July 11, 2008)
Pub: American City Business Journals, Inc.
Ed: James Dornbrook. **Description:** Kansas City Chiefs officials expect to obtain 12 to 14 new major sponsors with the completion of the Arrowhead Stadium renovations. The new sponsorship opportunities will include naming rights for the stadium and practice facility. The team's marketing strategies are discussed.

19333 ■ "City Eyeing Tax Breaks for Arena" in *Boston Business Journal* (Vol. 29, June 3, 2011, No. 4, pp. 1)
Pub: American City Business Journals Inc.
Ed: Daniel J. Sernovitz. **Description:** Baltimore City is opting to give millions of dollars in tax breaks and construction loans to a group of private investors led by William Hackerman who is proposing to build a new arena and hotel at the Baltimore Convention Center. The project will cost $500 million with the state putting up another $400 million for the center's expansion.

19334 ■ "The Colt Effect" in *Hawaii Business* (Vol. 53, January 2008, No. 7, pp. 30)
Pub: Hawaii Business Publishing
Ed: David K. Choo. **Description:** Participation at the Bowl Championship Games can help the University of Hawaii financially. Playing at a prominent sports event could provoke donations from alumni and increase enrollment at the university. Examples of universities that earned generous income by becoming a part of prestigious sporting events are presented.

19335 ■ "Contracting Firm Sees Timing Right for Expansion" in *Tampa Bay Business Journal* (Vol. 29, November 13, 2009, No. 47, pp. 1)
Pub: American City Business Journals
Ed: Janet Leiser. **Description:** Construction management company Moss & Associates LLC of Fort Lauderdale, Florida has launched its expansion to Tampa Bay. Moss & Associates has started the construction of the Marlins stadium in Miami, Florida's Little Havana section. It also plans to diversify by embarking on other government development, such as health care facilities and airports.

19336 ■ "Detroit Scores When Tigers Play; Studies Predict Winning Economy" in *Crain's Detroit Business* (Vol. 24, March 31, 2008, No. 13)
Pub: Crain Communications, Inc.
Ed: Bill Shea. **Description:** East Lansing-based Anderson Economic Group and the Detroit Regional Chamber predict that the economic impact of the Detroit Tigers will be very positive for the region due to an unexpected World Series trip two years ago followed by another strong season in 2007, player acquisitions and the popular Jim Leyland again managing the team. Statistical data included.

19337 ■ "DHR Hires Carr for Sports Group" in *Crain's Detroit Business* (Vol. 25, June 8, 2009, No. 23, pp. 5)
Pub: Crain Communications Inc. - Detroit
Ed: Sherri Begin Welch. **Description:** Lloyd Carr, former head football coach for University of Michigan, has taken a position with DHR International in order to expand its searches for collegiate and professional sports organizations, recruit athletic directors, head coaches and other executives.

19338 ■ "Eagles Measure Suite Success" in *Philadelphia Business Journal* (Vol. 30, September 9, 2011, No. 30, pp. 1)
Pub: American City Business Journals Inc.
Ed: John George. **Description:** Philadelphia Eagles have a new software program that helps suite holders keep track of how their suite is being used and whether they are getting a return on their investment. The software allows suite holders to better utilize and distribute their tickets.

19339 ■ "Easy Answers? Hall No" in *Charlotte Business Journal* (Vol. 25, December 17, 2010, No. 39, pp. 1)
Pub: Charlotte Business Journal
Ed: Erik Spanberg. **Description:** Charlotte, North Carolina-based NASCAR Hall of Fame has been trying to recover from its shaky start, but still bullish on the future as officials intensify promotions. Sports museums and halls of fame are mainly dependent on families and always search for new exhibits and great appearances to boost attendance.

19340 ■ "Economics at Play When Allocating Seats to Series" in *Boston Business Journal* (Vol. 27, October 26, 2007, No. 39, pp. 1)
Pub: American City Business Journals Inc.
Ed: Jesse Noyes, Naomi R. Kooker. **Description:** Business executives are trying to obtain as many baseball tickets to the World Series as possible. Allocating corporate seats to the Series is about maintaining tight relationships and influence clients. It is a key to business relationships.

19341 ■ "Five-Ring Circus" in *Entrepreneur* (Vol. 35, November 2007, No. 11, pp. 76)
Pub: Entrepreneur Media Inc.
Ed: Scott Bernard Nelson. **Description:** China's economy is growing and is expected to do well even after the 2008 Olympics, but growth could slow from eleven percent to eight or nine percent. Chinese portfolio concerns with regard to health and environmental records and bureaucratic fraud are discussed.

19342 ■ "For DVD Company, No Extra Innings: Capturing a Season Takes Fast Work" in *Boston Business Journal* (Vol. 27, December 7, 2007)
Pub: American City Business Journals Inc.
Ed: Terry Lefton. **Description:** Details of the development of MLB's annual World Series film by MLB Productions are discussed. The company is compelled to produce the film in a short period of time due to a promised November 27, 2007 delivery date. According to Elizabeth Scott, MLB vice president of programming and business affairs, she was concerned about the things that could directly affect sales.

19343 ■ "Game On at Jordan's New Spot" in *Crain's Chicago Business* (Vol. 34, October 24, 2011, No. 42, pp. 34)
Pub: Crain Communications Inc.
Ed: Laura Bianchi. **Description:** Michael Jordan partnered with Cornerstone Restaurant Group to launch Michael Jordan's Steakhouse in Chicago. Details are included.

19344 ■ "Getting in the Game" in *Baltimore Business Journal* (Vol. 27, October 16, 2009, No. 23, pp. 1)
Pub: American City Business Journals
Ed: Ryan Sharrow. **Description:** Crystal Palace FC USA is finalizing a deal with a North Carolina development team to build a 7,000 seat stadium by early 2012 in spite of efforts by Baltimore Mayor Sheila Dixon to bring in professional soccer's DC United. The planned stadium is in the Carroll Camden Industrial area near M&T Bank Stadium. Plans for the new stadium are included.

19345 ■ "Goodbye, Locker Room: Hello, Boardroom" in *Inc.* (Vol. 33, October 2011, No. 8, pp. 30)
Pub: Inc. Magazine
Ed: Issie Lapowsky, Kasey Wehrum. **Description:** In 2005, the National Football League started the NFL Business Management and Entrepreneurial Program. Since the onset of the program, 700 players have participated in the program which takes place at the business schools of Harvard, the University of Pennsylvania, Northwestern and Stanford.

19346 ■ "Goodyear Extends Exclusive Deal to Supply NASCAR's Tires" in *Charlotte Observer* (February 4, 2007)
Pub: Knight-Ridder/Tribune Business News
Ed: David Poole. **Description:** Goodyear tires will continue to be the exclusive tire provider at NASCAR's Nextel Cup, Busch and Truck series through the year 2012.

19347 ■ "Grand Prix Didn't Fill Up City's Hotels" in *Boston Business Journal* (Vol. 29, September 16, 2011, No. 19, pp. 1)
Pub: American City Business Journals Inc.
Ed: Alexander Jackson. **Description:** Baltimore Grand Prix inaugural race failed to fill the hotels in Baltimore, Maryland as hoteliers reported rooms to spare during the three-day event. City officials expected downtown hotels to nearly sell out Labor Day weekend.

19348 ■ "Great Expectations" in *Canadian Business* (Vol. 81, April 14, 2008, No. 6, pp. 34)
Pub: Rogers Media
Ed: Andy Holloway. **Description:** Therma Blades Inc. says that the reports that say their Therma Blade ice skates were not working properly were inaccurate. The major mistake of the company was to fail to manage the public's expectation when they touted the blades as revolutionary. Therma Blades Inc. has since tested the product with the help of 120 players and physiological testing done on elite level players show that there was a 10 percent improvement in energy efficiency.

19349 ■ "Hedge-Fund Titan Cohen Plans Bid for Dodgers" in *Wall Street Journal Eastern Edition* (November 25 , 2011, pp. C3)
Pub: Dow Jones & Company Inc.
Ed: Matthew Futterman, Gregory Zuckerman. **Description:** Steven A. Cohen, the founder and head of hedge-fund SAC Capital Advisors LLC is looking to make an offer at the bankruptcy auction for the financially-troubled Los Angeles Dodgers baseball team.

19350 ■ "High-Tech, Niche Options Change Sports Marketing" in *Crain's Detroit Business* (Vol. 24, March 17, 2008, No. 11, pp. 14)
Pub: Crain Communications, Inc.
Ed: Leah Boyd. **Description:** Sports advertisers have an ever-increasing menu of high-tech or niche marketing options such as interactive campaigns through cell phones and electronic banners which can span arenas.

19351 ■ "Hitting the Green" in *Canadian Business* (Vol. 81, July 22, 2008, No. 12-13, pp. 34)
Pub: Rogers Media Ltd.
Ed: Andy Holloway. **Description:** RBC is sponsoring the Canadian Open golf tournament, which is the second-oldest event in the PGA Tour. RBC is expected to receive television exposure on CBS and the Golf Channel. Additional information relating to the sponsorship is presented.

19352 ■ "HOK Sport May Build Own Practice" in *The Business Journal-Serving Metropolitan Kansas City* (Vol. 26, August 29, 2008, No. 51, pp. 1)
Pub: American City Business Journals, Inc.
Ed: Rob Roberts. **Description:** HOK Sport Venue Event is considering a spin-off from its parent company, HOK Group Inc. HOK Sport spokeswoman Gina Leo confirms that the firm is exploring structures, including a management buyout. Some of HOK Sport Venue Event's Minnesota projects are discussed.

19353 ■ "An Ice Boost in Revenue; Wings Score With Expanded Corporate Sales" in *Crain's Detroit Business* (Vol. 25, June 1, 2009, No. 22)
Pub: Crain Communications Inc. - Detroit
Ed: Bill Shea. **Description:** Stanley Cup finals always boost business for the Detroit area, even during a recession. The Red Wings corporate office reported corporate sponsorship revenue luxury suite rentals, Legends Club seats and advertising were up 40 percent this year over 2008.

19354 ■ "It's Back to Business for the Ravens" in *Boston Business Journal* (Vol. 29, July 29, 2011, No. 12, pp. 1)
Pub: American City Business Journals Inc.
Ed: Scott Dance. **Description:** The Baltimore Ravens football team has been marketing open sponsorship packages following the end of the National Football

League lockout. Team officials are working to get corporate logos and slogans on radio and television commercials and online advertisements.

19355 ■ "LED Screen Technology Takes Centre Stage" in *Canadian Electronics* (Vol. 23, June-July 2008, No. 4, pp. 17)
Pub: Action Communication Inc.
Ed: Ed Whitaker. **Description:** Display technologies based on light emitting diodes are becoming more popular due to their flexibility, versatility and reproducibility of displays. These are being increasingly used in different applications, such as advertising and concerts.

19356 ■ "Local Startup Hits Big Leagues" in *Austin Business Journalinc.* (Vol. 28, December 19, 2008, No. 40, pp. 1)
Pub: American City Business Journals
Ed: Christopher Calnan. **Description:** Qcue LLC, an Austin, Texas-based company founded in 2007 is developing a software system that can be used by Major League Baseball teams to change the prices of their single-game tickets based on variables affecting demand. The company recently completed a trial with the San Francisco Giants in 2008.

19357 ■ "Looking for a Sales Tax Extension" in *Milwaukee Business Journal* (Vol. 27, January 29, 2010, No. 18, pp. A1)
Pub: American City Business Journals
Ed: Mark Kass. **Description:** Milwaukee, Wisconsin-area business executives believe the extension of the Miller Park 0.1 percent sales tax could help fund a new basketball arena to replace the 21-year-old Bradley Center in downtown Milwaukee. However, any sales tax expansion that includes the new basketball arena would need approval by Wisconsin's legislature.

19358 ■ "The Major Leagues: Have Front-Office Positions Opened Up for Blacks?" in *Black Enterprise* (Vol. 37, February 2007, No. 7, pp.)
Pub: Earl G. Graves Publishing Co. Inc.
Ed: Alexis McCombs. **Description:** Major leave sports teams are hiring more African Americans to manage and coach teams. Statistical data included.

19359 ■ *Marketing Outrageously: How to Increase Your Revenue by Staggering Amounts*
Pub: Bard Press
Ed: Jon Spoelstra. **Released:** July 25, 2001. **Price:** $24.95. **Description:** Creative marketing strategies are defined. The book shows how considering marketing problems as outrageously but consistently can benefit any small business. The author talks about his own experience when there were not adequate funds for marketing and advertising and the outrageous approach he created to promote sports teams.

19360 ■ "Minor-League Baseball's Sliders Plan Stock Offering" in *Crain's Detroit Business* (Vol. 25, June 15, 2009, No. 24, pp. 3)
Pub: Crain Communications Inc. - Detroit
Ed: Bill Shea. **Description:** New minor-league baseball team is raising funds to build a new stadium in Waterford Township, Michigan because banks are unwilling to provide loans for the project. Owners of the Midwest Sliders in Ypsilanti, Michigan are waiting for the federal Securities and Exchange Commission to approve a Regulation A public offering.

19361 ■ "Moms Dis Super Bowl Ads" in *Marketing to Women* (Vol. 21, March 2008, No. 3, pp. 6)
Pub: EPM Communications, Inc.
Description: According to a survey by the Marketing to Moms Coalition, although 80 percent of moms tune into the Super Bowl most complain that the advertisements are not appropriate for a family sports viewing experience.

19362 ■ "Money Ball" in *Canadian Business* (Vol. 80, October 22, 2007, No. 21, pp. 40)
Pub: Rogers Media
Ed: Andy Holloway. **Description:** Rising Canadian dollar has a positive impact on the sports industry. Canadian team executives earn revenues in Canadian dollar, but pay expensive American dollar. Athletes who play in the Canadian Football Leagues benefit most from the increasing rate.

19363 ■ "Money and the Mayhem" in *Canadian Business* (Vol. 83, September 14, 2010, No. 15, pp. 52)
Pub: Rogers Media Ltd.
Ed: Greg Hudson. **Description:** Ultimate Fighting Championship (UFC) has hired Tom Wright as director of operations for Canada, who finally managed to get mixed martial arts sanctioned in Ontario. Canada is UFC's largest market after the US and accounting for about 15-20 percent in annual revenue.

19364 ■ "Nation of Islam Businessman Who Became Manager for Muhamnmad Ali Dies" in *Chicago Tribune* (August 28, 2008)
Pub: McClatchy-Tribune Information Services
Ed: Trevor Jensen. **Description:** Profile of Jabir Herbert Muhammad who died on August 25, after heart surgery; Muhammad lived nearly all his life on Chicago's South Side and ran a number of small businesses including a bakery and a dry cleaners before becoming the manager to famed boxer Mohammad Ali.

19365 ■ "Newcomers Join Roster of Indoor Sports Venues" in *Business Review, Albany New York* (Vol. 34, October 12, 2007, No. 28, pp. 1)
Pub: American City Business Journals, Inc.
Ed: Adam Sichko. **Description:** Indoor sports scene in Albany, New York is growing, with several indoor training facilities with a special attention to baseball and softball being built. These facilities include the $2.2 million Extra Innings facility in Ballston Corporate Technology Park and the Warning Track facility on Route 9 in Malta. The market for indoor sports, which is seen as saturated, is analyzed.

19366 ■ "NFL Labor, Legal Issues Hang Over Detroit Lions' Rebuilding Efforts" in *Crain's Detroit Business* (Vol. 26, January 11, 2010, No. 2)
Pub: Crain Communications, Inc.
Ed: Bill Shea. **Description:** Overview of the possible outcomes regarding labor talks with Detroit Lion's players as well as the outcome of a U.S. Supreme Court decision that could boost franchise values but at the expense of fans and corporate sponsors.

19367 ■ "Nike's Next Splash" in *The Business Journal-Portland* (Vol. 25, August 22, 2008, No. 24, pp. 1)
Pub: American City Business Journals, Inc.
Ed: Erik Siemers. **Description:** Business analysts expect Nike to bid for the endorsement services of swimmer Michael Phelps after the swimmer's contract with Speedo expires. The company, however, is a lightweight in the swimming apparel market and is not focusing on swimming as a growth sector.

19368 ■ "Packers Still Want Marketing Deal With Favre" in *The Business Journal-Milwaukee* (Vol. 25, August 15, 2008, No. 47, pp. A1)
Pub: American City Business Journals, Inc.
Ed: Mark Kass. **Description:** The Green Bay Packers plan to offer a $20 million marketing agreement to quarterback Brett Favre, including a clothing, merchandise, and collectibles line. The team is pursuing the agreement despite trading Favre to the New York Jets on 6 August 2008.

19369 ■ "Palace Adds Marketing Arm; College Sponsorships First Step In New Effort" in *Crain's Detroit Business* (October 1, 2007)
Pub: Crain Communications Inc. - Detroit
Ed: Bill Shea. **Description:** Palace Sports and Entertainment is restructuring itself from operating the Detroit Piston's basketball team and concert venues into a marketing company that also runs sports teams and venues. The firm signed a deal to handle sponsorship sales for colleges and universities.

19370 ■ "Peter Bynoe Trades Up" in *Black Enterprise* (Vol. 38, July 2008, No. 12, pp. 30)
Pub: Earl G. Graves Publishing Co. Inc.
Ed: Alexis McCombs. **Description:** Chicago-based Loop Capital Markets L.L.C. has named Peter Bynoe managing director of corporate finance. Bynoe was previously a senior partner at the law firm DLA Piper U.S. L.L.P., where he worked on stadium deals.

19371 ■ "Pro Teams Shift Ad Budgets; Naming Rights Deals Near $1 Billion" in *Brandweek* (Vol. 49, April 21, 2008, No. 16, pp. 18)
Pub: VNU Business Media, Inc.
Ed: Barry Janoff. **Description:** More and more professional sports marketers are spending less of their advertising budgets on traditional media outlets such as television, print and radio; the growing trend in sports marketing is in utilizing new media venues such as the Internet in which innovative means are used to encourage interaction with fans.

19372 ■ "Race Benefits: Changes Afoot for Ironman" in *Business Journal Serving Greater Tampa Bay* (Vol. 30, October 29, 2010, No. 45, pp. 1)
Pub: Tampa Bay Business Journal
Ed: Margaret Cashill. **Description:** World Triatholon Corporation, organizer of the Ironman World Championship 70.3, will move the sports event from Florida to Nevada in 2011. A replacement event, the 5150 Triathlon Series, will be held in 2011 and the series finale will be staged in Florida's Clearwater Beach. How hotels and motels in the area will benefit from the 5150 Triathlon Series is discussed.

19373 ■ "Race-Week Schedule Filling Up With Galas, Nonprofit Fundraisers" in *Boston Business Journal* (Vol. 29, July 22, 2011, No. 11, pp. 1)
Pub: American City Business Journals Inc.
Ed: Alexander Jackson. **Description:** Baltimore, Maryland-based businesses and nonprofit groups have been planning their own events to coincide with the Baltimore Grand Prix during the Labor Day weekend. They also plan to partner with others in hopes of drumming up new business, raising money or to peddle their brands.

19374 ■ "Raptor Opens Consultancy" in *Austin Business Journal* (Vol. 31, July 8, 2011, No. 18, pp. 1)
Pub: American City Business Journals Inc.
Ed: Christopher Calnan. **Description:** Boston hedge fund operator Raptor Group launched Raptor Accelerator, a consulting business providing sales and advisory services to early-stage companies in Central Texas. Aside from getting involved with the startups in which the Raptor Group invests, Raptor Accelerator will target firms operating in the sports, media, entertainment, and content technology sectors.

19375 ■ "The Reality of Fantasy Sports" in *Entrepreneur* (Vol. 37, September 2009, No. 9, pp. 52)
Pub: Entrepreneur Media, Inc.
Ed: Jason Ankeny. **Description:** United States fantasy sports business has grown into a $1 billion industry. Fantasy gaming in the country remains affordable and accessible despite the increase in the prices of tickets to sports games. Comments from analysts are also presented.

19376 ■ "Recovery on Tap for 2010?" in *Orlando Business Journal* (Vol. 26, January 1, 2010, No. 31, pp. 1)
Pub: American City Business Journals
Ed: Melanie Stawicki Azam, Richard Bilbao, Christopher Boyd, Anjali Fluker. **Description:** Economic forecasts for Central Florida's leading business sectors in 2010 are presented. These sectors include housing, film and TV, sports business, law, restaurants, aviation, tourism and hospitality, banking and finance, commercial real estate, retail, health care, insurance, higher education, and manufacturing. According to some local executives, Central Florida's economy will slowly recover in 2010.

19377 ■ "Reds Hit Ratings Homer" in *Business Courier* (Vol. 27, July 30, 2010, No. 13, pp. 1)
Pub: Business Courier

Ed: Steve Watkins, James Ourand. **Description:** Cincinnati Reds fans have tuned in to their TVs and radios as their team made a hottest start to a season. The Reds TV ratings have increased 49 percent during the first six months of 2010 and continued to rise while the Reds' games broadcast on WLW-AM reported the highest average audience share per game of any Major League Baseball team.

19378 ■ "Rooting for Hispanic Dollars" in *Hispanic Business* (October 2007, pp. 76, 80)
Pub: Hispanic Business

Description: Sports franchises are working to gain and retain the Hispanic market.

19379 ■ "Sabathia Deal Makes Dollars and Sense" in *The Business Journal-Milwaukee* (Vol. 25, July 11, 2008, No. 42, pp. A1)
Pub: American City Business Journals, Inc.

Ed: Mark Kass. **Description:** It was reported that the Milwaukee Brewers' acquisition of CC Sabathia will mean that the team will pick up an estimated $5 million in salary that Sabathia is owed for the remainder of the season. Because of this, the team will not make a profit in 2008. The acquisition of Sabathia is expected to cause an increase in attendance and merchandise revenue over the remainder of the season.

19380 ■ *Scorecasting*
Pub: Crown Business Books

Ed: Tobias Moskowitz, L. Jon Wertheim. **Released:** January 25, 2011. **Price:** $26.00. **Description:** Behavioral economist and veteran writer partner to write about research and studies revealing the hidden forces that shape how basketball, baseball, football and hockey games are played, won and lost.

19381 ■ "Sheets Energy Strips Unveils New Vending Machines" in *Food and Beverage Close-Up* (August 12, 2011)
Pub: Close-Up Media

Description: Sheets Energy Strips is installing vending machines in malls, office buildings, stadiums and arenas in New York, New Jersey, Connecticut and Florida. These machines will offer 4 packs, 10 packs and Sheets branded hats and T-shirts.

19382 ■ "Sounders Kicking Ball to Fans" in *Puget Sound Business Journal* (Vol. 29, November 28, 2008, No. 32, pp. 1)
Pub: American City Business Journals

Ed: Greg Lamm. **Description:** Major League Soccer expansion team, Seattle Sounders FC, hopes to build fan support leading to its inaugural season 2009-2010 by tapping online social networks. The club launched fan clubs with actual powers over its decision making and Websites similar to Facebook.

19383 ■ "Spillover Effects" in *Crain's Detroit Business* (Vol. 24, October 6, 2008, No. 40, pp. 29)
Pub: Crain Communications, Inc.

Description: Earlier this year, the Detroit Regional Chamber estimated that the Detroit Tiger's baseball team's 81 home games would have a $277 million positive economic impact on the region. Due to the poor performance of the team, fewer fans are spending money on tickets, which translates into fewer dollars coming into the region. Lower viewership on television has also been a result of the Tiger's losing season.

19384 ■ "Squeeze Play" in *Baltimore Business Journal* (Vol. 28, September 3, 2010, No. 17, pp. 1)
Pub: Baltimore Business Journal

Ed: Daniel J. Sernovitz. **Description:** The Baltimore Grand Prix is seen to benefit businesses in Baltimore, Maryland's Inner Harbor. It is also seen to create a rift between the city government and some office workers.

19385 ■ "Stadium Developers Seek a Win With the State" in *The Business Journal-Serving Metropolitan Kansas City* (Vol. 26, August 22, 2008)
Pub: American City Business Journals, Inc.

Ed: Rob Roberts. **Description:** Three Trails Redevelopment LLC is hoping to win $30 million in state tax credits from the Missouri Development Finance Board for the construction of an 18,500-seat Wizards stadium. The project is contingent on state tax incentives and the company remains optimistic about their goal.

19386 ■ "Still No Arena Financing Plan" in *Sacramento Business Journal* (Vol. 28, May 27, 2011, No. 13, pp. 1)
Pub: Sacramento Business Journal

Ed: Kelly Johnson. **Description:** The government of Sacramento, California has yet to devise a plan to finance the construction of a proposed stadium. The arena is estimated to cost $387 million. A brief description of the facility is also included.

19387 ■ "Study: Austin is Ready for a Pro Sports Team" in *Austin Business JournalInc.* (Vol. 29, December 25, 2009, No. 42, pp. 1)
Pub: American City Business Journals

Ed: Kate Harrington. **Description:** A study shows that Austin, Texas, with a total income of about $62 billion annually, is capable of hosting teams in the NBA, NHL, NFL and Major League Soccer. The capacity of 82 markets in the US and Canada was verified to assess their financial ability to support professional sports teams. Factors affecting Austin's ability to host a professional team are also presented.

19388 ■ "Super Bowl Events Get Tax Breaks" in *Business Journal-Serving Phoenix and the Valley of the Sun* (Vol. 7, October 12, 2007, No. 28)
Pub: American City Business Journals, Inc.

Ed: Mike Sunnucks. **Description:** Cities of Glendale and Phoenix, Arizona increased sales taxes in September 2007 and have issued tax exemptions for professional sporting events like the Super Bowl. Phoenix is planning to exempt events included in the 2009 NBA All-Star Game. National Football League's tax abatement requirement to cities hosting the Super Bowl is discussed.

19389 ■ "Teams Buy Into Screen Scene" in *Business First Buffalo* (October 5, 2007, pp. 1)
Pub: American City Business Journals, Inc.

Ed: James Fink. **Description:** Buffalo Bills, Buffalo Sabres, University of Buffalo, and Buffalo Bisons have all purchased new ribbon informational boards and video scoreboards to enhance their marketing strategies and improve the experience of sports fans. Vision boards of University of Buffalo and Sabres were installed by Daktronics, while Bills bought a Mitsubishi Diamond Vision board. The features that make the new scoreboards good promotional tools are described.

19390 ■ "Ted Stahl: Executive Chairman" in *Inside Business* (Vol. 13, September-October 2011, No. 5, pp. NC6)
Pub: Great Lakes Publishing Company

Ed: Miranda S. Miller. **Description:** Profile of Ted Stahl, who started working in his family's business when he was ten years old is presented. The firm makes dies for numbers and letters used on team uniforms. Another of the family firms manufactures stock and custom heat-printing products, equipment and supplies. It also educates customers on ways to decorate garments with heat printing products and offers graphics and software for customers to create their own artwork.

19391 ■ "Tigers Put to Test; Can Team Win Back Fans, Advertisers?" in *Crain's Detroit Business* (Vol. 24, October 6, 2008, No. 40, pp. 1)
Pub: Crain Communications, Inc.

Ed: Bill Shea. **Description:** Despite the enormous amount of money the Detroit Tigers' owner Mike Ilitch spent on player salaries, a record $137.6 million this season, the team finished in last-place; ticket sales and advertising dollars for next season are expected to fall dramatically. Additional speculation regarding the future of the ball team is included.

19392 ■ "Tim Tebow Foundation to Hold Pink 'Cleats for a Cure' Auction" in *Travel & Leisure Close-Up* (October 20, 2011)
Pub: Close-Up Media

Description: Tim Tebow Foundation partnered with XV Enterprises to hold the 'Cleats for a Cure' auction on eBay. Tebow is auctioning off a pair of pink cleans he wore during the Denver Broncos vs. Tennessee Titans game October 3, 2010. All funds will go toward finding a cure for breast cancer.

19393 ■ "To the Extreme" in *Entrepreneur* (Vol. 36, February 2008, No. 2, pp. 21)
Pub: Entrepreneur Media Inc.

Ed: Lindsay Holloway. **Description:** Extreme sports are increasing in number, with companies seeing the market potential of these sports for the 10- to 30-year-old age group. Entrepreneurs are launching innovated products catering to extreme sports-related markets. Details on the opportunities provided by the growth of extreme sports are discussed.

19394 ■ "Under Armour Wants to Equip Athletes, Too" in *Boston Business Journal* (Vol. 29, July 8, 2011, No. 9, pp. 1)
Pub: American City Business Journals Inc.

Ed: Ryan Sharrow. **Description:** Baltimore sportswear maker Under Armour advances plans to enter into the equipment field, aiming to strengthen its hold on football, basketball and lacrosse markets where it already has a strong market share. The company is now cooking up licensing deals to bolster the firm's presence among athletes.

19395 ■ "'Unknown' Muted Grand Prix Impact" in *Boston Business Journal* (Vol. 29, September 9, 2011, No. 18, pp. 3)
Pub: American City Business Journals Inc.

Ed: Alexander Jackson. **Description:** Baltimore Grand Prix caught restaurateurs, hoteliers and street vendors in Baltimore, Maryland unprepared for the thousands of race fans who attended the inaugural event over Labor Day weekend. The race popularity is relatively unknown to them and some felt they were not able to make as much money as they had hoped.

19396 ■ "Used to Being Courted" in *Business Courier* (Vol. 24, March 14, 2008, No. 49, pp. 1)
Pub: American City Business Journals, Inc.

Ed: Dan Monk. **Description:** College basketball coach Sean Miller is reported to be earning up to $900,000 a year. A look into the contract at regional universities show Thad Matta makes over $2 million in a year and that UK's Billy Gillispie makes over $2.7 million.

19397 ■ "USF Plans $30M Sports Complex" in *Tampa Bay Business Journal* (Vol. 29, October 23, 2009, No. 44, pp. 1)
Pub: American City Business Journals

Ed: Jane Meinhardt. **Description:** University of South Florida (USF) is going to build a new sports complex with the aid of a $30 million loan from BB&T. The project, which is also comprised of new and renovated athletic facilities on USF's Tampa campus, is projected to create more than $37 million in revenue in its first year. Revenues from the said facilities are expected to achieve an annual growth of at least four percent.

19398 ■ "Vanity Plates" in *Canadian Business* (Vol. 82, April 27, 2009, No. 7, pp. 26)
Pub: Rogers Media

Ed: Andy Holloway. **Description:** Politicians in the U.S. called for the review of firms that availed of the bailout money but are under deals for naming rights of sports stadiums. Angus Reid's Corporate Reputation and Sponsorship Index found for example, that there is little correlation between sponsoring arenas on having a better brand image. It is suggested that firms who enter these deals build closer to people's homes.

19399 ■ "Viewing Ironman As Gold, R.I. Firm Buys Its Parent" in *The Business Journal-Serving Greater Tampa Bay* (Vol. 28, September 19, 2008)
Pub: American City Business Journals, Inc.
Ed: Pete Williams. **Description:** Providence Equity Partners purchased World Triathlon Corp., parent company of the Ironman Triathlon, for an undisclosed sum. The acquisition means that the World Triathlon Headquarters will move to Tampa, Florida, and allows Providence Equity Partners to stage or license rights to Ironman and half-Ironman distance events.

19400 ■ "Wells' Is Title Sponsor for Volleyball Championship" in *Ice Cream Reporter* (Vol. 22, August 20, 2008, No. 9, pp. 4)
Pub: Ice Cream Reporter
Description: Wells' Dairy was chosen to sponsor the 29th Annual National Association of Intercollegiate Athletics (NAIA) Volleyball National Championship to be held in Sioux City, Iowa. Blue Bunny will sponsor the 2008 NAIA Women's Volleyball National Championship, also a Wells' brand.

19401 ■ "What Players in the Midmarket Are Talking About" in *Mergers & Acquisitions: The Dealmaker's Journal* (March 1, 2008)
Pub: SourceMedia, Inc.
Description: Sports Properties Acquisition Corp. went public at the end of January; according to the company's prospectus, it is not limiting its focus to just teams, it is also considering deals for stadium construction companies, sports leagues, facilities, sports-related advertising and licensing of products, in addition to other related segments.

19402 ■ "What Women Watch on TV" in *Marketing to Women* (Vol. 21, February 2008, No. 2, pp. 6)
Pub: EPM Communications, Inc.
Description: According to BIGresearch, women are more likely to watch sports than they are soap operas. Statistical data included.

19403 ■ "Winning Gold" in *The Business Journal-Milwaukee* (Vol. 25, August 8, 2008, No. 46, pp. A1)
Pub: American City Business Journals, Inc.
Ed: Rich Rovito. **Description:** Johnson Controls Inc. of Milwaukee, Wisconsin is taking part in the 2008 Beijing Olympics with the installation of its sustainable control equipment and technology that monitor over 58,000 points in 18 Olympic venues. Details of Johnson Controls' green products and sustainable operations in China are discussed.

19404 ■ "With Traffic Jam in Super Bowl, Can Any Auto Brand Really Win?" in *Advertising Age* (Vol. 81, December 6, 2010, No. 43, pp. 1)
Pub: Crain Communications, Inc.
Ed: Rupal Parekh, Brian Steinberg. **Description:** Car marketers are doubling down for Super Bowl XLV in Arlington, Texas and asking their ad agencies to craft commercials unique enough to break through the clutter and to capture viewers' attention.

TRADE PERIODICALS

19405 ■ *The American Quarter Horse Journal*
Pub: American Quarter Horse Association
Contact: Doug Hayes, Advertising Dir
E-mail: dhayes@aqha.org
Released: 10/yr. **Price:** $25; $50 Canada; $80 other countries. **Description:** Magazine promoting advancement and improvement of the breeding and performance of the American Quarter Horse.

19406 ■ *Cutting Horse Chatter*
Pub: National Cutting Horse Association
Contact: Alan Gold, Publisher
E-mail: alan@chatteronline.com
Released: Monthly. **Description:** Magazine promoting the cutting horse industry.

19407 ■ *Deer and Turkey Show Previews*
Pub: Target Communications Corp.
Contact: Glenn Helgeland, Editor & Publisher
Released: 1/yr, 5 different states, 1 issue/state. **Description:** Five magazines on 5 deer and turkey hunting shows.

19408 ■ *The Quarter Racing Journal*
Pub: American Quarter Horse Association
Contact: Doug Hayes, Dir. of Business Dev.
E-mail: dhayes@aqha.org
Released: Monthly. **Price:** $25; $80 other countries; $50 Canada; $60 3 years; $135 Canada 3 years; $225 other countries 3 years. **Description:** Magazine promoting breeding and performance of the racing Quarter Horse.

19409 ■ *South Carolina Wildlife*
Pub: South Carolina Department of Natural Resources
Contact: Tricia Way, Editorial Asst.
E-mail: wayt@dnr.sc.gov
Ed: David Lucas, Editor, lucasd@dnr.sc.gov. **Released:** Bimonthly. **Price:** $18; $30 two years. **Description:** Magazine promoting resource management, wildlife, and better understanding of South Carolina's environment. Official publication of the state department of natural resources.

TRADE SHOWS AND CONVENTIONS

19410 ■ International Sport Summit
E.J. Krause & Associates, Inc.
6550 Rock Spring Dr., Ste. 500
Bethesda, MD 20817
Ph:(301)493-5500
Fax:(301)493-5705
Co. E-mail: ejkinfo@ejkrause.com
URL: http://www.ejkrause.com
Released: Annual. **Audience:** Trade professionals. **Principal Exhibits:** Equipment, supplies, and services for sports facilities and events.

19411 ■ Michigan Interscholastic Athletic Administrators Mid-Winter Conference
Michigan Interscholastic Athletic Administrator Association
35445 Hathaway
Livonia, MI 48150-2513
Ph:(734)422-3569
Fax:(734)762-9957
URL: http://www.miaaa.com
Released: Annual. **Audience:** Educators in the field of secondary interscholastic athletic administration. **Principal Exhibits:** Sports supplies, athletic equipment, clothing, publications, fund raisers, and athletic training supplies, and awards companies.

CONSULTANTS

19412 ■ Jim Castello Marketing Communications Consultants
711 Red Wing Dr.
Lake Mary, FL 32746
Ph:(407)321-6322
Contact: James E. Castello Jr., President
Scope: Consultant develops creative ideas and marketing strategies, including collateral programs, public relations, advertising, and brochures. Industries served: All golf related industry/business, golf manufacturers, golf resorts, golf residential developments, golf professionals, golf clothing, golf accessories, golf associations, and golf travel. **Seminars:** How To Seminar for Family Fun Center Entrepreneurs; How To Seminar for Creativity in Golf Marketing; The Golf Business on the Internet.

FRANCHISES AND BUSINESS OPPORTUNITIES

19413 ■ Awards Express
United Trophy Company
2400 First Ave. North
Birmingham, AL 35203
Ph:(205)322-4999
Free: 800-874-5008
Fax:(205)322-4941
No. of Franchise Units: 1. **Founded:** 1965. **Franchised:** 2006. **Description:** Trophies, awards, and recognition and promotional products. **Equity Capital Needed:** $25,000-$50,000. **Franchise Fee:** $12,500. **Financial Assistance:** Yes. **Training:** Yes.

19414 ■ i9 Sports
1723 S Kings Ave.
Brandon, FL 33511
Free: 800-975-2937
Fax:(813)662-9114
Co. E-mail: franchisesales@i9sports.com
URL: http://www.i9sports.com
No. of Franchise Units: 134. **No. of Company-Owned Units:** 2. **Founded:** 2002. **Franchised:** 2003. **Description:** They provide Amateur sports leagues, tournaments & events. **Equity Capital Needed:** $44,900-$72,900. **Franchise Fee:** $19,900. **Royalty Fee:** 7.5%. **Financial Assistance:** Third party financing available. **Training:** 1 week provided at headquarters, 2 days of onsite, and optional refresher training available.

19415 ■ Puckmasters International
2300-2850 Shaughnessy St.
Port Coquitlam, BC, Canada V3C 6K5
Ph:(604)552-4373
Free: 888-775-7825
Fax:(604)552-7709
Co. E-mail: info@puckmasters.com
URL: http://www.puckmasters.com
No. of Franchise Units: 20. **No. of Company-Owned Units:** 1. **Founded:** 1993. **Franchised:** 1996. **Description:** Hockey training centers. **Equity Capital Needed:** $130,000-$695,000. **Franchise Fee:** $30,000. **Royalty Fee:** 6%. **Training:** 14 days at headquarters, 9 days at franchisees location and ongoing support.

19416 ■ Skyhawks
Skyhawks Sports Camps
6311 E Mt. Spokane Park Dr.
Mead, WA 99021
Free: 800-376-9142
Fax:888-466-2318
No. of Franchise Units: 68. **Founded:** 1979. **Franchised:** 2007. **Description:** Youth sports programs. **Equity Capital Needed:** Standard: $40,000-$68,000, including franchise fee. **Franchise Fee:** $15,000. **Financial Assistance:** No. **Training:** Yes.

19417 ■ Velocity Sports Performance
151 Kalmus Drive, Bldg. C, Suite-200
Costa Mesa, CA 92626
Ph:(714)640-3360
Fax:(866)269-7024
URL: http://www.velocitysp.com
No. of Franchise Units: 65. **No. of Company-Owned Units:** 5. **Founded:** 1999. **Franchised:** 2002. **Description:** Training for Sports. **Equity Capital Needed:** $554,800-$1,500,000. **Franchise Fee:** $54,000. **Royalty Fee:** 6%. **Financial Assistance:** Limited third party financing available. **Training:** Includes 2 weeks training at corporate headquarters, 1 week at franchisee's location, and periodic conferences and quarterly sales training.

COMPUTERIZED DATABASES

19418 ■ *CSW Stats*
Computer Sports World
c/o VegasInsider.com Inc.
5300 NW 33rd Ave., Ste. 119
Fort Lauderdale, FL 33309
Ph:(702)233-5738
Free: 800-321-5562
Fax:(702)294-1322
Co. E-mail: dandros@vegasinsider.com
URL: http://www.cswstats.com
Description: Contains information on professional and collegiate sports. Covers football, including the National Football League (NFL), Canadian Football League (CFL), and National Collegiate Athletic Association (NCAA); basketball, including the National

Basketball Association (NBA) and National Collegiate Athletic Association; major league baseball; golf, including the Professional Golfer's Association (PGA) and Ladies Professional Golfer's Association (LPGA); boxing; tennis; skiing; auto racing; and indoor soccer. Includes schedules, past and current standings, statistics, injury reports, weather conditions affecting sports events, betting information, and game summaries and results. Provides continuous changes in scores and line movements for games in progress. For horseracing, covers entries (including late scratches) for each race at more than 40 racetracks, as well as post performances, charts, morning programs, and results. **Availability:** Online: Computer Sports World, Computer Sports World. **Type:** Directory; Full text.

19419 ■ *Sports CustomWire*
Comtex News Network Inc.
625 N Washington St., Ste. 301
Alexandria, VA 22314
Ph:(703)820-2000
Free: 800-266-8399
Fax:(703)820-2005
Co. E-mail: cs@comtex.com
URL: http://www.comtex.com
Description: Features breaking news on professional and amateur sporting events in the United States, International games, and world competitions. Delivers such news items as final scores and commentary, team transactions and standings, player achievements and injury reports, franchise development news, and feature stories on industry personalities. **Availability:** Online: Comtex News Network Inc., Comtex News Network Inc. **Type:** Full text.

ASSOCIATIONS AND OTHER ORGANIZATIONS

19420 ■ American Congress on Surveying and Mapping
6 Montgomery Village Ave., Ste. 403
Gaithersburg, MD 20879
Ph:(240)632-9716
Fax:(240)632-1321
Co. E-mail: curtis.sumner@acsm.net
URL: http://www.acsm.net
Contact: Curtis W. Sumner, Exec. Dir.
Description: Professionals, technicians, and students in the field of surveying and mapping including surveying of all disciplines, land and geographic information systems, cartography, geodesy, photogrammetry, engineering, geophysics, geography, and computer graphics; American Association for Geodetic Surveying, American Cartographic Association, and National Society of Professional Surveyors. Objectives are to: advance the sciences of surveying and mapping; promote public understanding and use of surveying and mapping; speak on the national level as the collective voice of the profession; provide publications to serve the surveying and mapping community. Member organizations encourage improvement of university and college curricula for surveying and mapping. **Publications:** *Cartography and Geographic Information Science* (quarterly); *Surveying and Land Information Science* (quarterly).

19421 ■ National Society of Professional Surveyors
6 Montgomery Village Ave., Ste. 403
Gaithersburg, MD 20879-3557
Ph:(240)632-9716
Fax:(240)632-1321
Co. E-mail: curtis.sumner@acsm.net
URL: http://www.nspsmo.org
Contact: Curtis W. Sumner, Exec. Dir.
Description: Consists of professional surveyors, preprofessionals, technicians, and students. Encourages members to adopt and adhere to standards of ethical and professional behavior and to provide a professional service to the public. Maintains liaison with other professional societies; promotes public confidence in services rendered by members; monitors laws and regulations affecting the profession; helps to develop curricula for teaching surveying. **Publications:** Membership Directory (periodic).

19422 ■ Professional Surveyors Canada–Geometres professionnels du Canada
3 - 11 Bellerose Dr., Ste. 367
St. Albert, AB, Canada T8N 5C9
Ph:(780)470-5110
Free: 800-241-7200
Co. E-mail: info@psc-gpc.ca
URL: http://www.psc-gpc.ca
Contact: Sarah J. Cornett BSc, Exec. Dir.
Description: Represents the interests of professional surveyor in Canada. Aims to build and enable a strong multi-faced community of surveying professionals. Works on behalf of its members to encourage and enable an environment where their work is valued as underpinning the fabric of society for the safety and economic well being of Canadians.

19423 ■ Surveyors Historical Society
628 Ridge Ave.
Lawrenceburg, IN 47025-1912
Ph:(812)537-2000
Fax:(812)537-2000
Co. E-mail: shs9@embarqmail.com
URL: http://www.surveyhistory.org/surveyor's_historical_society.htm
Contact: Roger Woodfill, Admin.
Description: Persons interested in the history of surveying. Dedicated to the preservation of surveying instruments, records, memorabilia, and relics. Seeks to educate the public about the history of surveying. Organizes displays of surveying memorabilia and instruments. Conducts research projects. Operates speakers' bureau and museum; compiles statistics. **Publications:** *Backsights* (semiannual);Membership Directory (annual).

DIRECTORIES OF EDUCATIONAL PROGRAMS

19424 ■ *Directory of Private Accredited Career Schools and Colleges of Technology*
Pub: Accrediting Commission of Career Schools and Colleges of Technology
Contact: Michale S. McComis, Exec. Dir.
Released: On web page. **Price:** Free. **Description:** Covers 3900 accredited post-secondary programs that provide training programs in business, trade, and technical fields, including various small business endeavors. Entries offer school name, address, phone, description of courses, job placement assistance, and requirements for admission. Arrangement is alphabetical.

REFERENCE WORKS

19425 ■ "Ask Inc." in *Inc.* (October 2007, pp. 73-74)
Pub: Gruner & Jahr USA Publishing
Description: An online marketing research firm investigates the use of online communities such as MySpace and Second life in order to recruit individuals to answer surveys.

19426 ■ "Blacks Go Broadband: High Speed Internet Adoption Grows Among African Americans" in *Black Enterprise* (Vol. 38, February 2008)
Pub: Earl G. Graves Publishing Co. Inc.
Ed: Cliff Hocker. **Description:** Number of black households using broadband Internet services tripled since 2005 according to a survey conducted by Pew Internet and American Life Project.

19427 ■ "Broadband Reaches Access Limits in Europe" in *Information Today* (Vol. 26, February 2009, No. 2, pp. 22)
Pub: Information Today, Inc.
Ed: Jim Ashling. **Description:** Eurostat (the Statistical Office of the European communities) reports results from is survey regarding Internet use by businesses throughout its 27-member states. Iceland, Finland and the Netherlands provide the most access at broadband speeds, followed by Belgium, Spain and France.

19428 ■ "Crime and Punishment" in *Canadian Business* (Vol. 81, December 24, 2007, No. 1, pp. 21)
Pub: Rogers Media
Ed: Joe Castaldo. **Description:** Cmpass Inc.'s survey of 137 Canadian chief executive officers showed that they want tougher imposition of sentences on white-collar criminals, as they believe that the weak enforcement of securities laws gives an impression that Canada is a country where it is easy to get away with fraud.

19429 ■ "Currency: I'm Otta Here" in *Entrepreneur* (Vol. 35, October 2007, No. 10, pp. 72)
Pub: Entrepreneur Media Inc.
Ed: C.J. Prince. **Description:** Liberum Research revealed that 193 chief financial officers (CFOs) at small companies have either resigned or retired during the first half of 2007. A survey conducted by Tatum found that unreasonable expectations from the management and compliance to regulations are the main reasons why CFOs are leaving small firms. The chief executive officer's role in making CFOs stay is also discussed.

19430 ■ "The Duty of Wealth: Canadian Business Leaders on Nepotism and Philanthropy" in *Canadian Business* (Vol. 80, Winter 2007, No. 24)
Pub: Rogers Media
Ed: Joe Castaldo. **Description:** Fifty-one percent of the respondents in a survey of business leaders say that the decision to allow adult children to join a family firm should be based on the circumstances at the time. He CEOs that were surveyed also believed that billionaires should donate an average of forty percent of their estates and keep the rest for their family.

19431 ■ "ForeSee Finds Satisfaction On Web Sites, Bottom Line" in *Crain's Detroit Business* (Vol. 24, February 25, 2008, No. 8, pp. 3)
Pub: Crain Communications Inc. - Detroit
Ed: Tom Henderson. **Description:** Ann Arbor-based ForeSee Results Inc. evaluates user satisfaction on Web sites. The company expects to see an increase of 40 percent in revenue for 2008 with plans to expand to London, Germany, Italy and France by the end of 2009.

19432 ■ "Hot Air: On Global Warming and Carbon Tax" in *Canadian Business* (Vol. 81, October 13, 2008, No. 17, pp. 12)
Pub: Rogers Media Ltd.
Ed: Joe Castaldo. **Description:** Survey of Canadian business leaders revealed that the environment is a key issue in Canada's federal elections. Respondents

believe that Prime Minister Stephen Harper's views on global warming and climate change are closer to their own views. Other key information on the survey is presented.

19433 ■ "Keep Them Posted" in *Entrepreneur* (Vol. 35, October 2007, No. 10, pp. 39)
Pub: Entrepreneur Media Inc.
Ed: Gwen Moran. **Description:** Survey by the Pew Internet and American Life Project found that 12 million American adults maintain blogs, which are created for personal and business reasons. Blogs are effective in giving a business a personal touch while informing the public about its operations and products. Tips on how to create an effective business blog are presented.

19434 ■ "May I Handle That For You?" in *Inc.* (March 2008, pp. 40, 42)
Pub: Gruner & Jahr USA Publishing
Ed: Taylor Mallory. **Description:** According to a recent survey, 53 percent of all companies outsource a portion of their human resources responsibilities. Ceridian, Administaff, Taleo, KnowledgeBank, and CheckPoint HR are among the companies profiled.

19435 ■ "Merger Brings New Force to Hispanic Marketing Industry" in *Hispanic Business* (July-August 2007, pp. 60)
Pub: Hispanic Business
Description: Merger between Latin Force LLC, a marketing strategy firm and Geoscape International Inc., a consumer intelligence and data analytics company is discussed.

19436 ■ "More Businesses Will Shift Health Costs to Workers" in *Business Review, Albany New York* (Vol. 34, November 16, 2007, No. 33, pp. 1)
Pub: American City Business Journals, Inc.
Ed: Barbara Pinckney. **Description:** Survey conducted by consulting firm Benetech Inc. showed that sixty percent of employers are planning to increase payroll deductions to pay for health insurance premiums. More than ninety percent of the employers prefer HMO plans, followed by Preferred Provider Organizations. Other details of the survey are discussed.

19437 ■ "Nanotech Impact is Smaller Than Hoped For" in *Boston Business Journal* (Vol. 27, October 26, 2007, No. 39, pp. 1)
Pub: American City Business Journals Inc.
Ed: Jackie Noblett. **Description:** Survey by the Massachusetts Technology Collaborative showed that nanotechnology firms are within the early stages of operations and need funding to make them profitable. Details on some nanotech companies and their operations and difficulties in developing or mass producing their products are discussed.

19438 ■ "The Next Generation: African Americans Are Successfully Launching Businesses Earlier In Life" in *Black Enterprise* (January 2008)
Pub: Earl G. Graves Publishing Co. Inc.
Ed: Tennille M. Robinson. **Description:** According to a survey conducted by OPEN, a team dedicated small business at American Express, Generation Y individuals are three times more likely to start their own company. Three African American individuals who did just that are profiled.

19439 ■ "Praise for Tax Cuts" in *Canadian Business* (Vol. 80, November 19, 2007, No. 23, pp. 16)
Pub: Rogers Media
Ed: Joe Castaldo. **Description:** A Compas Inc. survey found that most of the 158 business leaders polled are in favor of federal tax cuts. The findings revealed that the respondents gave an average of 74 percent to the mini-budget, an unusual score for a government initiative. Other opinions on the government's tax relief are presented.

19440 ■ "Reading the Public Mind" in *Harvard Business Review* (Vol. 88, October 2010, No. 10, pp. 27)
Pub: Harvard Business School Publishing
Ed: Andrew O'Connell. **Description:** Examination of the various methods for obtaining public opinion and consumer preferences is provided; an outline of the disadvantages and benefits of both are also given.

19441 ■ "Survey: Apartment Rents Continue to Climb as Home Market Slows" in *Business Review, Albany New York* (November 23, 2007)
Pub: American City Business Journals, Inc.
Ed: Michael DeMasi. **Description:** Survey by Sunrise Management and Consulting shows that asking rents for apartments in the Capital Region increased for the thirteenth consecutive time. The survey, which was conducted between August and October 2007, also showed that Albany County, New York had the highest average asking rent, followed by Rensselaer County, Saratoga County, and Schenectady County.

19442 ■ "Survey Profile" in *Small Business Economic Trends* (April 2008, pp. 19)
Pub: National Federation of Independent Business
Ed: William C. Dunkelberg, Holly Wade. **Description:** Two graphs and a table presenting the profile of small businesses that participated in the National Federation of Independent Business (NFIB) survey are provided. The actual number of firms, their industry types, and the number of full and part-time employees are also given.

19443 ■ "Survey Says Commercial Real Estate Headed for Turbulence" in *Commercial Property News* (March 17, 2008)
Pub: Nielsen Company
Description: Commercial real estate sector is declining due to the sluggish U.S. economy. According to a recent survey, national office, retail and hospitality markets are also on the decline.

19444 ■ "Tell Us What You Really Think Collecting Customer Feedback" in *Inc.* (Vol. 30, December 2008, No. 12, pp. 52)
Pub: Mansueto Ventures LLC
Ed: Ryan Underwood. **Description:** According to a recent survey, nearly 77 percent of online shoppers review consumer-generated reviews of products before making a purchase.

19445 ■ "To Offshore Or Not To Offshore?" in *Converting* (Vol. 25, October 1, 2007, No. 10, pp. 10)
Pub: Reed Business Information Inc.
Ed: Mark Spaulding. **Description:** Offshore manufacturing and the issue of buying raw materials from foreign suppliers by American companies is discussed. Results of a study conducted by Cap Gemini and Pro Logis regarding offshore manufacturing, especially to China, are presented.

19446 ■ "Yes, No, and Somewhat Likely: Survey the World with Web Polls" in *Inc.* (October 2007, pp. 58-59)
Pub: Gruner & Jahr USA Publishing
Ed: Don Steinberg. **Description:** Online tools for surveying customers, employees and the general public include Zoomergan zPro and Zoomerang Sample, software designed to send surveys and allows viewing results; SurveyMonkey software creates, administers and allows viewing online surveys and results; Vizu software places a one-question poll on a particular Website; and Vovici EFM Feedback, a subscription service providing ongoing surveys to customers or employees.

TRADE PERIODICALS

19447 ■ *CE News*
Pub: Mercor Media
Contact: Shanon M. Fauerbach, Editorial Inquiries
Released: Monthly. **Description:** Trade magazine serving civil engineers and land surveyors engaged in land development, highways, bridges, structural, environmental, geotechnical, water resources, and industrial engineering projects including surveying.

19448 ■ *Geomatica*
Pub: Canadian Institute of Geomatics
Contact: Carol Railer, Advertising Mgr
E-mail: editgeo@magma.ca
Ed: Mike Pinch, Editor. **Released:** Quarterly. **Price:** $275 Canada. **Description:** Surveying and mapping journal.

19449 ■ *NAMS News Online*
Pub: National Association of Marine Surveyors Inc.
Ed: Chris LaBure, Editor. **Released:** Semiannual. **Description:** Provides news of interest to marine surveyors, underwriters, and adjusters. Covers developments at the International Maritime Bureau, government regulations affecting the field, the national marine conference, and regional meetings. Recurring features include news of research, news of members, information on publications available, and columns titled Cargo and Yachts.

19450 ■ *The Ontario Land Surveyor*
Pub: Association of Ontario Land Surveyors
Contact: Maureen V. Mountjoy, Dep. Registrar
E-mail: maureen@aols.org
Released: Quarterly. **Description:** Surveying magazine.

19451 ■ *Professional Surveyor*
Pub: Reed Business Geo, Inc.
Contact: Neil Sandler, Publisher
E-mail: neil@profsurv.com
Released: Monthly. **Price:** $20 Canada; $72 other countries; Free to qualified subscribers. **Description:** Magazine for land surveyors, mappers, and civil engineers.

TRADE SHOWS AND CONVENTIONS

19452 ■ California Land Surveyors Association Conference
California Land Surveyors Association
795 Farmers Ln., No. 11
PO Box 9098
Santa Rose, CA 95405-9990
Ph:(707)578-6016
Fax:(707)578-4406
Co. E-mail: clsa@californiasurveyors.org
URL: http://www.californiasurveyors.org
Released: Annual. **Audience:** Land surveyors and civil engineers. **Principal Exhibits:** Land surveying equipment, computers, vehicles, software, and two-way communication systems.

COMPUTER SYSTEMS/ SOFTWARE

19453 ■ Land Survey Calculator
Dynacomp, Inc.
4768 Rte. 89
Romulus, NY 14487
Ph:(315)257-9303
Free: 800-828-6772
Fax:(315)549-7118
Co. E-mail: info@dynacompsoftware.com
Price: $19.95. **Description:** Available for PC computers. Program for performing land survey calculations.

19454 ■ Sight Survey Professional 2009
Simplicity Systems, Inc.
PO Box 9646
PO Box 556
Asheville, NC 28815
Ph:(828)338-2516
Free: 800-777-7978
Co. E-mail: support@carlsonsw.com
URL: http://www.carlsonsw.com/PL_Simplicity.html
Price: Description: Available for Windows 95/98/NT/2000/XP compatibles. Coordinate geometry program for land surveyors. Integrates COGO and CAD.

LIBRARIES

19455 ■ Alberta Land Surveyor's Association Library
10020 - 101A Ave., Ste. 1000
Edmonton, AB, Canada T5J 3G2
Ph:(403)429-8805
Free: 800-665-2572

Fax:(403)429-3374
Co. E-mail: info@alsa.ab.ca
URL: http://www.ccls-ccag.ca/educ-resources-Library.html
Contact: Brian E. Munday, Exec.Dir.
Scope: Surveying. **Services:** Copying; Library open to the public at librarian's discretion. **Holdings:** books and videos.

19456 ■ British Columbia Land Surveyors Foundation–Anna Papove Memorial Library
2400 Bevan Ave., Ste. 301
Sidney, BC, Canada V8L 1W1
Ph:(250)655-7222
Fax:(250)655-7223
Co. E-mail: janice.henshaw@telus.net
URL: http://www.bclandsurveyors.bc.ca
Contact: Janice Henshaw, Exec.Dir.
Scope: Surveying - land, water, air; boundaries. **Services:** Library open to the public. **Holdings:** 900 books; 100 serials; 100 reports; 100 VF drawers; 5 videotapes; 50 other cataloged items; archival records. **Subscriptions:** 10 journals and other serials from land surveying associations.

19457 ■ Washington State Department of Natural Resources–Public Land Survey Office
Natural Resources Bldg., 3rd Fl.
1111 Washington St., SE
PO Box 47000
Olympia, WA 980504-700
Ph:(360)902-1190
Fax:(360)902-1191
Co. E-mail: plso@dnr.wa.gov
URL: http://www.dnr.wa.gov/htdocs/plso/
Contact: Mick Sprouffske, Unit Supv./Surveyor
Scope: Cadastral and geodetic survey information. **Services:** Copying; office open to the public for a fee. **Holdings:** 300,000 aperture cards of survey maps; 300 reels of microfilm of original government survey notes; 3500 field books from private surveyors; 500,000 scanned images of survey maps and historic survey documents.

RESEARCH CENTERS

19458 ■ Hope College–Carl Frost Center for Social Science Research
100 E 8th St., Ste. 220
Holland, MI 49422-9000
Ph:(616)395-7556
Fax:(616)395-7410
Co. E-mail: hill@hope.edu
URL: http://www.hope.edu/frostcenter
Contact: Dr. Martin Hill, Dir.
E-mail: hill@hope.edu
Scope: Social science research in conjunction with corporate, educational, governmental, and nonprofit organizations. Research includes mail, telephone and web surveys, questionnaire design, data management and analysis, focus group discussions, etc. **Publications:** Reports.

Swimming Pool/Hot Tub Business

ASSOCIATIONS AND OTHER ORGANIZATIONS

19459 ■ Association of Pool and Spa Professionals
2111 Eisenhower Ave., Ste. 500
Alexandria, VA 22314
Ph:(703)838-0083
Fax:(703)549-0493
Co. E-mail: memberservices@apsp.org
URL: http://www.apsp.org
Contact: Mr. Bill Weber, Pres./CEO
Description: Builders, dealers, designers, service companies, retail stores, engineers, manufacturers, distributors, public officials, suppliers, and service persons concerned with public and residential swimming pools, spas, and hot tubs. Aims to raise spa and pool industry standards; expand interest and use of swimming pools, spas, and hot tubs; seeks to achieve uniformity in federal, state, and local regulations affecting swimming pool, spa, and hot tub operations. Promotes the industry to the consumer; protects interests of the industry through government relations and technical programs. Establishes voluntary standards for the design and construction of swimming pools and spas. Compiles cost of doing business data and other statistics. **Publications:** *AQ* (quarterly).

19460 ■ Diving Equipment and Marketing Association
3750 Convoy St., Ste. 310
San Diego, CA 92111-3741
Ph:(858)616-6408
Free: 800-862-3483
Fax:(858)616-6495
Co. E-mail: info@dema.org
URL: http://www.dema.org
Contact: Tom Ingram, Exec. Dir.
Description: International recreational scuba diving and snorkeling organizations and associations promoting or reporting diving activities, individuals or organizations providing educational, retail, travel, media or other services in the field. Aims to promote advancement within the diving equipment industry, encourage the growth of diving activities, and enhance public enjoyment of recreational diving. Cooperates with domestic governmental and private agencies that develop standards or are involved in regulating activities affecting the diving industry and related products. Seeks to establish continuing education programs to instruct and assist industry members in business, quality control and the marketing of diving products. Organizes conferences dealing with topics such as governmental regulations, product standards, quality control, and standardized bookkeeping methods. **Publications:** *DEMA News & Industry Report* (monthly).

19461 ■ International Association of Plumbing and Mechanical Officials
4755 E Philadelphia St.
Ontario, CA 91761
Ph:(909)472-4100
Free: 800-854-2766
Fax:(909)472-4150
Co. E-mail: iapmo@iapmo.org
URL: http://www.iapmo.org
Contact: Mr. Dwight Perkins, Sr. Dir. of Field Services
Description: Government agencies, administrative officials, plumbing officials, mechanical officials, plumbing and mechanical product manufacturers, trade associations, and members of associations related to the plumbing field. Sponsors and writes uniform plumbing codes, uniform mechanical code, uniform solar energy code and uniform swimming pool, spa and hot tub code. Sponsors speakers' bureau. **Publications:** *Directory of Listed Plumbing Products* (weekly); *Directory of Listed Plumbing Products for Mobile Homes and Recreational Vehicles* (bimonthly); *Official* (bimonthly); *Uniform Mechanical Illustrated Training Manual* (periodic); *Uniform Plumbing Code Illustrated Training Manual* .

19462 ■ National Swimming Pool Foundation
4775 Granby Cir.
Colorado Springs, CO 80919-3131
Ph:(719)540-9119
Fax:(719)540-2787
Co. E-mail: info@nspf.org
URL: http://www.nspf.org
Contact: Mr. Tom Lachocki, CEO
Description: Aims to improve public health by creating a safer aquatic environment through education and research and to attract more people to aquatic exercise. Works toward its mission with educational products like the Aquatic Safety Compendium, Certified Pool/Spa Operator training, Certified Pool/Spa Inspector training and the World Aquatic Health Conference. Provides program for pool and spa operators and health officials, certifying over 200,000 from 45 countries. **Publications:** *Aquatic Risk Management* (periodic); *Emergency Response Planning Book* (periodic); *Pool Math Workbook* (periodic).

REFERENCE WORKS

19463 ■ "Everyone Out of the Pool" in *Barron's* (Vol. 89, July 20, 2009, No. 29, pp. 18)
Pub: Dow Jones & Co., Inc.
Ed: Sandra Ward. **Description:** Shares of Pool Corp. could drop as continued weakness in the housing market weakens the market for swimming pool equipment. The company's shares are trading at $18.29, about 20 times projected 2009 earnings of $0.91 a share.

SOURCES OF SUPPLY

19464 ■ *AQUA—Buyers' Guide Issue*
Pub: Athletic Business Publications Inc.
Ed: Scott Webb, Editor, scottw@aquamagazine.com. **Released:** Annual, Latest edition 2009. **Covers:** Swimming pool and spa product manufacturers, distributors, representatives, and trade shows. **Entries Include:** Company name, address, phone, fax, E-mail, toll-free phone, website, name and title of contact, number of employees, geographical area served for distributors and representatives only, year established, products manufactured (or sold in the case of the distributors & representatives). **Arrangement:** Alphabetical; distributors and representatives also listed geographical by state. **Indexes:** Brand name; product manufactured; state covered (distributors & representatives).

STATISTICAL SOURCES

19465 ■ *RMA Annual Statement Studies*
Pub: Robert Morris Associates (RMA)
Released: Annual. **Price:** $175.00 2006-07 edition, $105.00. **Description:** Contains composite balance sheets and income statements for more than 360 industries, including the accounting, auditing, and bookkeeping industries. Also contains five years of comparative historical data for discerning trends. Includes 16 commonly used ratios, computed for most of the size groupings for nearly every industry.

TRADE PERIODICALS

19466 ■ *AQUA Magazine*
Pub: Athletic Business Publications Inc.
Contact: Jenna Danninger, Assoc. Ed.
Released: Monthly. **Description:** Trade magazine for spa and pool professionals.

19467 ■ *Pool & Spa Marketing*
Pub: Hubbard Marketing & Publishing Ltd.
Contact: Jason Cramp, Asst. Ed. and Magazine Designer
Ed: David Barnsley, Editor. **Price:** $98 other countries; $77. **Description:** Magazine covering the pool and spa industry.

VIDEOCASSETTES/ AUDIOCASSETTES

19468 ■ *Pool Maintenance: Complete Guide to Spa & Hot Tub*
Nightingale-Conant Corp.
6245 W. Howard St.
Niles, IL 60714
Ph:(847)647-0300
Free: 800-560-6081
URL: http://www.nightingale.com
Description: How to care and maintain your spa or hot tub. **Availability:** VHS.

TRADE SHOWS AND CONVENTIONS

19469 ■ Atlantic City Pool and Spa Show
Northeast Spa & Pool Association
6B South Gold Dr.
Hamilton, NJ 08691
Ph:(732)972-9111

Fax:(609)689-9110
Co. E-mail: info@nespapool.org
URL: http://www.nespapool.org

Released: Annual. **Audience:** Swimming pool and spa industry retailers, builders, installers, service companies, and pool operators. **Principal Exhibits:** Pools, spas, pumps, filters, heaters, chemicals, toys/games, outdoor furniture, enclosures, covers (pool, spa), parts, accessories, decks, pool tables, wood-burning stoves, Christmas products, saunas, tanning beds, computer software. **Dates and Locations:** 2011 Jan 25-27.

19470 ■ IHS Adana
Tuyap Fairs and Exhibitions Organization Inc.
Gazeteciler Mahallesi
Saglam Fikir Sokak No. 19
80300 Istanbul, Turkey
Ph:90 212 21 23 100
Fax:90 212 21 23 098
Co. E-mail: artlink@tuyap.com
URL: http://www.tuyap.com.tr

Released: Biennial. **Audience:** Builders, architects, and other industry professionals. **Principal Exhibits:** Heating, cooling, air conditioning, natural gas, installation, insulation, latest technologies.

CONSULTANTS

19471 ■ Bucher, Willis & Ratliff Corp.
1828 E Southwest Loop 323, Ste. 202
Tyler, TX 75701-1657
Ph:(816)363-2696
Free: 800-748-8276
Fax:(816)363-0027
Co. E-mail: ddreiling@bwrcorp.com
URL: http://www.bwrcorp.com
Contact: Steven Hileman, Exec VP
E-mail: shileman@bwrcorp.com

Scope: Professional consulting engineers, planners and architects offering engineering services in studying the feasibility, planning, design, specification writing and inspection of construction for bridges, highways, streets, dams, airports, industrial and domestic water and waste treatment facilities, environmental compliance, water and sewerage systems and cross country utilities. Also offers planning services in comprehensive planning, recreational planning, urban renewal planning, airport planning, transportation planning, off-street parking and zoning for statewide, regional and local governmental agencies, as well as architectural services in the design of governmental centers, group housing, schools, swimming pools and commercial and industrial buildings. **Seminars:** The New Normal: Development Trends in a Changing Economy, 2010; Quality of life, Oct, 2008; Transportation Workshop, Sep, 2008; Infrastructure workshop, Jun, 2008; Housing Workshop, May, 2008; Community development, Apr, 2008; Focus session, Mar, 2008.

19472 ■ Milton Costello, Consulting Engineer
4 Sandstone Ln.
Stony Brook, NY 11790-3102
Ph:(631)751-3030
Fax:(516)691-6550
Co. E-mail: poolengr@prodigy.net
Contact: Sydell Costello, Mgr
E-mail: poolengr07@gmail.com

Scope: Consulting engineer specializing in aquatic facilities, swimming pool projects, auditoriums, park complexes and open water recreation facilities and soil mechanics structures and related construction failures. Expert witness in swimming pool and related aquatic safety injury cases.

19473 ■ Short Elliott Hendrickson Inc.
3535 Vadnais Center Dr.
Saint Paul, MN 55110
Ph:(651)490-2000
Free: 800-325-2055
Fax:(651)490-2150
Co. E-mail: info@sehinc.com
URL: http://www.sehinc.com
Contact: Mark Benson, Mgr
E-mail: dhagen@sehinc.com

Scope: Expertise in airport planning and design, architectural design, electrical or mechanical engineering, environmental engineering, heavy civil, municipal engineering, transportation, urban design, waste water engineering, water engineering. **Publications:** "Sending the Right Signals: Project Management for Telecommunication Sites on Water Tanks," Journal of Protective Coatings & Linings, May, 2008; "The Transportation Aspect of Disaster Planning," 2008; "Performance Or Preference? a Look at Selected Systems for Water Tank Interiors," Journal of Protective Coatings & Linings, May, 2007; "Old Tanks, Tight Budgets: How Does the Job Get Done," Journal of Protective Coatings & Linings, May, 2005; "Painting for Antenna Installations on Water Storage Facilities," Today Magazine, Feb, 2003; "Bioterrorism, Cyberterrorism and Water Supplies," Wisconsin Water Well Association Journal, Jan, 2003; "They're Water Storage Tanks," Today Magazine, Jul, 2002. **Special Services:** SEH[R].

19474 ■ Veenstra & Kimm Inc.
860 22nd Ave., Ste. 4
Coralville, IA 52241-1565
Ph:(515)225-8000
Free: 800-241-8000
Fax:(515)225-7848
Co. E-mail: vk@v-k.net
URL: http://www.v-k.net
Contact: Timothy A. Moreau, Office Mgr
E-mail: tmoreau@v-k.net

Scope: The practice includes a wide range of consulting services involving sewer systems and wastewater treatment plants, water supply, distribution, storage and treatment, streets and highways, airports, bridges, land surveys and site planning, swimming pools, solid waste disposal systems, and expert testimony on engineering matters in litigations.

FRANCHISES AND BUSINESS OPPORTUNITIES

19475 ■ ASP-America's Swimming Pool Co.
3986 Lake St.
Macon, GA 31204
Ph:(478)254-4495

No. of Franchise Units: 72. **Founded:** 2001. **Franchised:** 2005. **Description:** Swimming pool maintenance & repairs. **Equity Capital Needed:** $49,200-$89,500. **Franchise Fee:** $22,000-$37,000. **Royalty Fee:** 8-5%. **Financial Assistance:** No. **Training:** Provides 12 days training at headquarters, 2 days onsite and ongoing support.

LIBRARIES

19476 ■ Chemtura Corporation Library
1801 U.S. Hwy. 52, W.
West Lafayette, IN 47906
Ph:(765)497-6275
Fax:(765)497-6680
Co. E-mail: annharmon@chemtura.com
URL: http://www.e1.greatlakes.com/corp/common/jsp/index.jsp
Contact: Ann Harmon, Corp.Libn.

Scope: Chemistry - bromine, organic, polymer; flame retardants; pool chemicals; business resources. **Services:** Copying; SDI; Library not open to the public. **Holdings:** 4000 books; 2000 bound periodical volumes; 10,000 reports; 5000 archival materials; 100 microfiche; 600 reels of microfilm. **Subscriptions:** 250 journals and other serials; 5 newspapers.

19477 ■ International Swimming Hall of Fame–Henning Library
One Hall of Fame Dr.
Fort Lauderdale, FL 33316
Ph:(954)462-6536
Fax:(954)525-4031
Co. E-mail: ischmid@ishof.org
URL: http://www.ishof.org/
Contact: Bob Duenkel, Exec.Dir./Cur.

Scope: Swimming history and instruction, sports medicine and psychology, pool care and management, diving and water polo, swim officiating, synchronized swimming. **Services:** Copying; research services; photo duplication; Library open to the public by appointment. **Holdings:** 7601 books; 130 bound periodical volumes; 307 scrapbooks; 110 theses and dissertations; 92 archives; guidebooks; swimmers' biographies; games, charts, tables for swimming officiating. **Subscriptions:** 20 journals and other serials.

Tailor Shop

DIRECTORIES OF EDUCATIONAL PROGRAMS

19478 ■ *Directory of Private Accredited Career Schools and Colleges of Technology*
Pub: Accrediting Commission of Career Schools and Colleges of Technology
Contact: Michale S. McComis, Exec. Dir.
Released: On web page. **Price:** Free. **Description:** Covers 3900 accredited post-secondary programs that provide training programs in business, trade, and technical fields, including various small business endeavors. Entries offer school name, address, phone, description of courses, job placement assistance, and requirements for admission. Arrangement is alphabetical.

REFERENCE WORKS

19479 ■ "A Family's Fortune" in *Canadian Business* (Vol. 80, Winter 2007, No. 24, pp. 103)
Pub: Rogers Media
Ed: Graham F. Scott. **Description:** James Richardson started as a tailor before moving into the grain business because his clients paid him in sacks of wheat and barley. The James Richardson and Sons Ltd. entered the radio business in 1927 but later sold it off in 1951.

TRADE PERIODICALS

19480 ■ *The Custom Tailor*
Pub: Custom Tailors and Designers Association of America Inc.
Ed: Suzanne Kilgore, Editor. **Released:** 3/yr. **Price:** $50. **Description:** Custom tailoring magazine.

VIDEOCASSETTES/ AUDIOCASSETTES

19481 ■ *How to Make Money in a Home-Based Sewing Business*
Nancy's Notions Ltd.
333 Beichl Ave.
P.O. Box 683
Beaver Dam, WI 53916-0683
Ph:(920)887-7321
Free: 800-725-0361
Fax:800-255-8119
Co. E-mail: customerservice@nancysnotions.com
URL: http://www.nancysnotions.com
Released: 1989. **Description:** Turn your hobby into a money-making operation with these sew-for-profit tips. **Availability:** VHS.

FRANCHISES AND BUSINESS OPPORTUNITIES

19482 ■ Heel Quik! & Heel/Sew Quik!
Heel Quik!, Inc.
2359 Windy Hill Rd., Ste. 400
Marietta, GA 30067
Ph:(770)951-9440
Fax:(770)933-8268
No. of Franchise Units: 730. **No. of Company-Owned Units:** 2. **Founded:** 1984. **Franchised:** 1985. **Description:** Instant shoe repair, clothing alterations and monogramming. **Equity Capital Needed:** $20,000-$85,000. **Franchise Fee:** $17,500. **Financial Assistance:** No. **Training:** Yes.

ASSOCIATIONS AND OTHER ORGANIZATIONS

19483 ■ Association of Talent Agents
9255 Sunset Blvd., Ste. 930
Los Angeles, CA 90069
Ph:(310)274-0628
Fax:(310)274-5063
Co. E-mail: shellie@agentassociation.com
URL: http://www.agentassociation.com
Contact: Sandy Bresler, Pres.
Description: Talent agencies that have clients in the Screen Actors Guild, American Federation of Television and Radio Artists, Directors Guild of America, Writers Guild of America, East, and Writers Guild of America, West. Negotiates terms of franchise agreements with these guilds and maintains liaison with their representatives. Assists members with contract problems, interpretations, rulings, residual matters, and arbitrations. Employs legal counsel to prepare opinions upon request and to file briefs in arbitrations and labor commission hearings. Maintains liaison with labor commission representatives in San Francisco and Los Angeles, CA, and intervenes on behalf of individual members having special problems. Conducts seminars and symposia. **Publications:** *Employment Law* .

19484 ■ International Entertainment Buyers Association
9 Music Sq. W
Nashville, TN 37203
Ph:(615)251-9000
Fax:(615)866-0116
Co. E-mail: info@ieba.org
URL: http://www.ieba.org
Contact: Tiffany Davis, Exec. Dir.
Description: Talent buyers and sellers, artists, managers, agents, venue operators and managers, and entertainment organizations; others with an interest in the entertainment industry, including advertisers, promoters, lighting, sound, and film technicians, and staging, production, and music businesses. Promotes professional advancement of members; seeks to ensure provision of high-quality entertainment purchasing services to customers. Serves as a clearinghouse on talent agencies and upcoming performances; facilitates exchange among members; represents members' commercial and professional interests. .

REFERENCE WORKS

19485 ■ *Billboard's International Talent and Touring Guide*
Pub: Crown Publishing Group
Released: Annual, Latest edition 2010. **Price:** $149, individuals. **Covers:** Over 30,000 artists, managers and agents from 69 countries worldwide, including the USA. and Canada; tour facilities and services; venues; entertainers, booking agents, hotels, and others in the entertainment industry; international coverage. **Entries Include:** Company name, address, phone, fax, names and titles of key personnel. **Arrangement:** Classified by line of business; venues are then geographical. **Indexes:** Product/service.

19486 ■ "A Digital Makeover for the Modeling Business" in *Inc.* (February 2008, pp. 82-86, 88-89)
Pub: Gruner & Jahr USA Publishing
Ed: David H. Freedman. **Description:** Ways the Ford Modeling Agency is using the online You Tube to realign its business are presented. Products to help a firm grow its presence on the Internet are included.

19487 ■ *Hollywood Representation Directory*
Pub: Nielsen Business Media
Released: Latest edition 38th. **Price:** $64.95, individuals. **Covers:** Over 2,000 agencies and management companies, and over 10,000 agents and personal managers within those companies. Majority of listings are located in Los Angeles and New York. **Entries Include:** company name, staff names and titles, address, phone, fax, e-mail address, web site address, company type, types of clients, and guild and organization affiliations. **Arrangement:** Alphabetical by company. **Indexes:** Client category, affiliation, individual names.

19488 ■ *International Television and Video Almanac*
Pub: Quigley Publishing Company Inc.
Ed: Eileen Quigley, Editor. **Released:** Annual, January; latest edition 2011. **Price:** $235, individuals. **Covers:** "Who's Who in Motion Pictures and Television and Home Video," television networks, major program producers, major group station owners, cable television companies, distributors, firms serving the television and home video industry, equipment manufacturers, casting agencies, literary agencies, advertising and publicity representatives, television stations, associations, list of feature films produced for television; statistics, industry's year in review, award winners, satellite and wireless cable provider, primetime programming, video producers, distributors, wholesalers. **Entries Include:** Generally, company name, address, phone; manufacturer and service listings may include description of products and services and name of contact; producing, distributing, and station listings include additional detail, and contacts for cable and broadcast networks. **Arrangement:** Classified by service or activity. **Indexes:** Full.

19489 ■ *Talk Show Yearbook*
Pub: Broadcast Interview Source Inc.
Ed: Mitchell P. Davis, Editor. **Released:** Annual, winter. **Price:** $185, individuals. **Covers:** more than 700 contacts at radio and television talk shows. **Entries Include:** Name of contact, format, market, address, phone, fax, name of talk show, station call letters, ADI information. **Arrangement:** Geographical. **Indexes:** Station call letters or network name.

TRADE PERIODICALS

19490 ■ *Variety*
Pub: Reed Business Information
Ed: Dana Harris, Editor, dana.harris@variety.com. **Released:** Weekly, 50/yr. **Price:** $259; $25 monthly. **Description:** Newspaper (tabloid) reporting on theatre, television, radio, music, records, and movies.

TRADE SHOWS AND CONVENTIONS

19491 ■ International Association of Fairs and Expositions Trade Show
International Association of Fairs and Expositions
3043 E. Cairo
Springfield, MO 65802
Ph:(417)862-5771
Free: 800-516-0313
Fax:(417)862-0156
Co. E-mail: iafe@fairsandexpos.com
URL: http://www.fairsandexpos.com
Released: Annual. **Audience:** Fair managers, staffs, and board members; carnival owners and staffs; concessionaires; talent and other agencies related to the fair industry. **Principal Exhibits:** Talent agencies, concessionaires, novelties, amusement devices, insurance, ribbons, plaques, attractions, and equipment. Products and services for the fair industry.

Tanning Parlor/Sauna

ASSOCIATIONS AND OTHER ORGANIZATIONS

19492 ■ Suntanning Association for Education
PO Box 1181
Gulf Breeze, FL 32562
Free: 800-536-8255
Fax:(850)384-7325
Co. E-mail: suntanningedu@gmail.com
URL: http://www.suntanningedu.com
Contact: Joe Schuster
Description: Companies and individuals involved in the indoor tanning industry. Educates members and the public about indoor tanning. Conducts educational and training program for salon operators; sponsors research. .

REFERENCE WORKS

19493 ■ "Looking Like a Million Bucks" in *Entrepreneur* (Vol. 37, August 2009, No. 8, pp. 102)
Pub: Entrepreneur Media, Inc.
Ed: Jason Daley. **Description:** Sunset Tan's Jeff Bozz says he and Devin Haman are executive producers of the show and that they want to stretch the truth a bit and make fun of it. Haman says the business is all about VIP service for everyone and that they want all their clients to feel like celebrities.

FRANCHISES AND BUSINESS OPPORTUNITIES

19494 ■ Aruba Tanning Franchise
Aruba Franchising Group, LLC
3456 Emmorton Rd.
Abingdon, MD 21009
Ph:(813)935-5087
Fax:(813)425-5799
No. of Company-Owned Units: 2. **Founded:** 2005. **Franchised:** 2007. **Description:** Tanning salon. **Equity Capital Needed:** $242,000-$630,000. **Franchise Fee:** $29,500. **Financial Assistance:** No. **Training:** Yes.

19495 ■ Executive Tans
CSE International LLC
603 Park Point Dr., No. 224
Golden, CO 80401
Ph:(303)988-9999
Free: 877-393-2826
Fax:(303)988-5390
No. of Franchise Units: 35. **Founded:** 1991. **Franchised:** 1995. **Description:** Tanning salon. **Equity Capital Needed:** $258,000-$448,000. **Franchise Fee:** $25,000. **Royalty Fee:** $795/month. **Financial Assistance:** Third party financing available. **Training:** Includes 1 week training at headquarters, 1 week at franchisee's location and ongoing support.

19496 ■ Image Sun Tanning Centers
TC Franchising Inc.
5514 Metro Pky.
Sterling Heights, MI 48310
Free: (866)313-8266
Fax:(586)314-0516
Co. E-mail: franchise@ateimagesun.com
URL: http://www.imagesun.com
No. of Franchise Units: 31. **No. of Company-Owned Units:** 5. **Founded:** 1996. **Franchised:** 2000. **Description:** Tanning salon. **Equity Capital Needed:** $187,000-$440,000. **Franchise Fee:** $25,000. **Financial Assistance:** Third party financing available. **Training:** Up to 1 week and 5 days onsite with ongoing support.

19497 ■ Mama Mio Pregnancy Spa & Imaging Centre
Becoming Mom
5685 Deerfield Blvd.
Mason, OH 45040
Ph:(813)935-5087
Fax:(813)425-5799
No. of Company-Owned Units: 1. **Founded:** 2006. **Franchised:** 2007. **Description:** Maternity spa. **Equity Capital Needed:** $250,000-$460,000. **Franchise Fee:** $37,500. **Financial Assistance:** No. **Training:** Yes.

19498 ■ Palm Beach Mega Tan
Palm Beach Franchise Corp.
1411 King St., E
Courtice, ON, Canada L1E 2J6
Ph:(905)434-8168
Free: 888-878-7882
Fax:(905)434-2579
Co. E-mail: info@palmbeachmegatan.com
URL: http://www.palmbeachmegatan.com
No. of Franchise Units: 25. **No. of Company-Owned Units:** 3. **Founded:** 1992. **Franchised:** 2001. **Description:** Upscale and professional tanning salon franchise. Extensive in-house training with ongoing support. State of the art equipment, looks better and gets fast effective tanning results. Secure and successful operating system comes with extensive manuals. President nominated for Canadian Woman Entrepreneur of the Year 2003, Business Excellence Award 2002, Canadian Salon of the Year Award 1995 and 1997. **Equity Capital Needed:** $50,000 start-up capital; $270,000 total investment. **Franchise Fee:** $20,000. **Training:** Classroom and in-salon training provided, ongoing annual training and ongoing support.

19499 ■ The Palms Tanning Resort
8577 E Arapahoe Rd., Ste. A
Greenwood Village, CO 80112
Free: (866)725-6748
Fax:(303)688-3789
No. of Franchise Units: 2. **No. of Company-Owned Units:** 3. **Founded:** 2003. **Franchised:** 2003. **Description:** Tanning salon. **Equity Capital Needed:** $489,750-$517,000. **Franchise Fee:** $35,000. **Royalty Fee:** 6%. **Financial Assistance:** Third party financing available. **Training:** Offers 1 week+ training at headquarters, 1 week+ onsite and ongoing support.

19500 ■ Planet Beach Franchising Corporation
5161 Taravella rd.
Marrero, LA 70072
Ph:(504)361-5550
Free: 888-290-8266
Fax:(504)361-5540
No. of Franchise Units: 340. **No. of Company-Owned Units:** 1. **Founded:** 1995. **Franchised:** 1996. **Description:** Tanning spa franchise. **Equity Capital Needed:** Liquid capital $50,000 (market specific). **Franchise Fee:** $10,000 non-uv; $30,000 with uv. **Financial Assistance:** Yes. **Training:** Yes.

19501 ■ Sol'exotica Tanning Spa
Sol'exotica Franchising Inc.
27 Legend Ct.
Box 10067
Ancaster, ON, Canada L8K 1P2
Ph:(905)529-3826
Free: (866)432-1826
Fax:(905)529-8070
Co. E-mail: franchising@solexotica.com
URL: http://www.solexotica.com
No. of Franchise Units: 25. **Founded:** 1994. **Franchised:** 2007. **Description:** Tanning salon. **Equity Capital Needed:** $45,000-$200,000. **Franchise Fee:** $35,000. **Training:** Yes.

19502 ■ SunBanque Island Tanning
Sunbanque Corp.
2384 Yonge St., Ste. 1400
Toronto, ON, Canada M4P 3J4
Ph:(416)488-5838
No. of Franchise Units: 10. **No. of Company-Owned Units:** 5. **Founded:** 1983. **Franchised:** 1983. **Description:** Offers sun tanning services. **Equity Capital Needed:** $30,000-$40,000. **Franchise Fee:** $5,000. **Financial Assistance:** Yes. **Training:** Yes.

19503 ■ Tropi Tan
5152 Commerce Rd.
Flint, MI 48507
Ph:(810)230-6789
Free: (866)818-1826
Fax:(810)230-1115
No. of Franchise Units: 14. **No. of Company-Owned Units:** 5. **Founded:** 1979. **Description:** Tanning services. **Franchise Fee:** $25,000. **Financial Assistance:** No. **Training:** Yes.

ASSOCIATIONS AND OTHER ORGANIZATIONS

19504 ■ National Tattoo Association
485 Business Park Ln.
Allentown, PA 18109-9120
Ph:(610)433-7261
Fax:(610)433-7294
Co. E-mail: curt@nationaltattoo.com
URL: http://www.nationaltattooassociation.com
Contact: Florence Makofske, Treas.
Description: Tattoo artists and enthusiasts. Promotes tattooing as a viable contemporary art form; seeks to upgrade standards and practices of tattooing. Offers advice on selecting a tattoo artist and studio. Holds seminars for tattoo artists to improve skills and learn better hygienic practices. Operates museum and biographical archives. .

REFERENCE WORKS

19505 ■ "King Ink" in *Inc.* (November 2007, pp. 98-102, 104, 106, 108)
Pub: Gruner & Jahr USA Publishing
Ed: Max Chafkin. **Description:** Profile of Mario Barth, whose goal is to build the Starbucks of tattoo parlors; the tattoo industry is worth $2.3 billion in the U.S.

19506 ■ "Verizon Small Business Awards Give Companies a Technology Edge" in *Hispanic Business* (July-August 2009, pp. 32)
Pub: Hispanic Business
Ed: Patricia Marroquin. **Description:** Verizon Wireless awards grants to twenty-four companies in California. The winning businesses ranged from barbershop to coffee shop, tattoo parlor to florist.

TRADE PERIODICALS

19507 ■ *Tattoo*
Pub: Paisano Publications L.L.C.
Released: Monthly. **Price:** $37.95; $67.95 two years. **Description:** Magazine for tattoo enthusiasts.

TRADE SHOWS AND CONVENTIONS

19508 ■ National Tattoo Association Convention
National Tattoo Association
485 Business Park Ln.
Allentown, PA 18109-9120
Ph:(610)433-7261
Co. E-mail: nattat2@fast.net
URL: http://www.nationaltattooassociation.com
Released: Annual. **Audience:** Trade professionals and general public. **Principal Exhibits:** Tattooing, jewelry, books, t-shirts, and other tattoo related items. **Dates and Locations:** 2011 Apr 12-17, Reno, NV.

LIBRARIES

19509 ■ Lyle Tuttle Tattooing–Tattoo Art Museum Library
837 Columbus Ave.
San Francisco, CA 94133
Ph:(707)462-4406
Fax:(707)462-4433
Co. E-mail: lyletutt@pacific.net
Contact: Lyle Tuttle, Dir.
Scope: Tattooing and related arts. **Services:** Copying; Library open to the public. **Holdings:** 200 books; drawings; tattoo equipment; memorabilia; art reproductions.

Tax Preparation Business

START-UP INFORMATION

19510 ■ *The 100 Best Businesses to Start When You Don't Want To Work Hard Anymore*
Pub: Career Press Inc.
Ed: Lisa Rogak. **Price:** $16.99. **Description:** Author helps burned-out workers envision a new future as a small business owner. Systems analysis, adventure travel outfitting, bookkeeping, food delivery, furniture making, and software development are among the industries examined.

ASSOCIATIONS AND OTHER ORGANIZATIONS

19511 ■ American Taxation Association
9201 University City Blvd.
Charlotte, NC 28223
Ph:(704)687-7696
Co. E-mail: americantaxationassociation@aaahq.org
URL: http://aaahq.org/ata/index.htm
Contact: Hughlene Burton, Pres.
Description: Membership comprises primarily university professors teaching federal income tax, federal estate, and/or gift tax courses; other members are practitioners, including certified public accountants. Seeks to further taxation education. Researches the impact of the tax process, particularly tax code sections, on the social and economic structure of the U.S. Maintains speakers' bureau. .

19512 ■ Canadian Institute of Chartered Accountants–Institut Canadien des Comptables Agrees
277 Wellington St. W
Toronto, ON, Canada M5V 3H2
Ph:(416)977-3222
Fax:(416)977-8585
Co. E-mail: jan.burns@cica.ca
URL: http://www.cica.ca
Contact: Nigel Byars, Exec. VP
Description: Sets national accounting, auditing, and financial reporting standards. Maintains an active professional development program for its members. Represents the profession's viewpoint on federal legislation issues and matters of national concern. Confers with other national organizations to achieve worldwide harmonization of accounting and auditing standards. **Publications:** *Directory of Canadian Chartered Accountants* (periodic).

19513 ■ Canadian Tax Foundation–Association Canadienne d'Etudes Fiscales
595 Bay St., Ste. 1200
Toronto, ON, Canada M5G 2N5
Ph:(416)599-0283
Free: 877-733-0283
Fax:(416)599-9283
Co. E-mail: lchapman@ctf.ca
URL: http://www.ctf.ca
Contact: FCA Larry Chapman, Exec. Dir./CEO
Description: Individuals and organizations with an interest in taxation. Promotes increased awareness of the Canadian Tax Code and the social ramifications of taxation. Serves as a clearinghouse on taxation; sponsors research and educational programs. **Publications:** *Canadian Tax Journal* (quarterly).

19514 ■ Institute of Tax Consultants
7500 212th SW, Ste. 205
Edmonds, WA 98026-7617
Ph:(425)774-3521
Co. E-mail: kraemerc@juno.com
URL: http://www.taxprofessionals.homestead.com/welcome.html
Contact: Carol Kraemer CCCE, Registrar
Description: Aims to provide tax practitioners with the opportunity to upgrade their professionalism through certification. Conducts educational programs and certification examinations. .

19515 ■ National Association of Tax Professionals
PO Box 8002
Appleton, WI 54914-8002
Free: 800-558-3402
Co. E-mail: natp@natptax.com
URL: http://www.natptax.com
Contact: Michael D. Whittle EA, Pres.
Description: Serves professionals who work in all areas of tax practice, including individual practitioners, enrolled agents, certified public accountants, accountants, attorneys and certified financial planners. **Publications:** *TAXPRO Quarterly Journal* (quarterly); *TAXPRO Weekly E-Mail* (weekly).

19516 ■ National Society of Accountants
1010 N Fairfax St.
Alexandria, VA 22314
Ph:(703)549-6400
Free: 800-966-6679
Fax:(703)549-2984
Co. E-mail: members@nsacct.org
URL: http://www.nsacct.org
Contact: John G. Ams, Exec. VP
Description: Professional organization and its affiliates represent 30,000 members who provide auditing, accounting, tax preparation, financial and estate planning, and management services to approximately 19 million individuals and business clients. Most members are sole practitioners or partners in small to mid-size accounting firms. **Publications:** *National Society of Accountants Technology Advisor* (8/year); *NSAlert* (biweekly).

19517 ■ National Tax Association
725 15th St. NW, No. 600
Washington, DC 20005-2109
Ph:(202)737-3325
Fax:(202)737-7308
Co. E-mail: natltax@aol.com
URL: http://www.ntanet.org
Contact: Ms. Charmaine J. Wright, Sec.
Description: Government and corporate tax officials, accountants, consultants, economists, attorneys, and others interested in the field of taxation. Promotes nonpartisan academics, study of taxation; encourages better understanding of the common interests of national, state, and local governments in matters of taxation and public finance; and disseminates higher quality research through publications and conferences. **Publications:** *National Tax Journal* (quarterly); *Proceedings of the Annual Conference on Taxation* (annual).

19518 ■ Society of Professional Accountants of Canada–La societe des comptables professionnels du Canada
250 Consumers Rd., Ste. 1007
Toronto, ON, Canada M2J 4V6
Ph:(416)350-8145
Free: 877-515-4447
Fax:(416)350-8146
Co. E-mail: president@professionalaccountant.org
URL: http://www.professionalaccountant.org
Contact: Mr. John Singer RPA, VP
Description: Professional accountants and individuals working to pass qualifying accountancy examinations. Promotes ongoing professional education among accountants; encourages students to enter the accounting field; works to advance the profession of accounting. Gathers and disseminates information on accounting; sponsors educational programs; conducts professional accountancy qualifying examinations. **Publications:** *Professional Accountant* (quarterly).

19519 ■ Tax Executives Institute
1200 G St. NW, Ste. 300
Washington, DC 20005-3814
Ph:(202)638-5601
Fax:(202)638-5607
Co. E-mail: asktei@tei.org
URL: http://www.tei.org
Contact: Timothy J. McCormally, Exec. Dir.
Description: Professional society of executives administering and directing tax affairs for corporations and businesses. Maintains TEI Education Fund. **Publications:** *The Tax Executive* (bimonthly); *Value-Added Taxes - A Comparative Analysis* .

REFERENCE WORKS

19520 ■ "2011 Tax Information of Interest" in *Business Owner* (Vol. 35, November-December 2011, No. 6, pp. 10)
Pub: DL Perkins Company
Description: Compilation of 2011 tax information to help small business take advantage of all tax incentives.

19521 ■ "Accrual vs. Cash Accounting, Explained" in *Business Owner* (Vol. 35, July-August 2011, No. 4, pp. 13)
Pub: DL Perkins Company
Description: Cash method versus accrual accounting methods are examined, using hypothetical situations.

19522 ■ "Adler Blanchard & Freeman Reports New SmartKeeper Bookkeeping Service" in *Professional Services Close-Up* (March 24, 2011)
Pub: Close-Up Media
Description: Profile of Adler Blanchard & Freeman (AB&F) accountants and business advisors. The firm

has expanded its client offerings to include their new SmartKeeper Business and Personal Bookkeeping Service for small to mid-sized companies and individuals.

19523 ■ *Beat the Taxman 2006: Easy Ways to Save Tax in Your Small Business*
Pub: John Wiley & Sons, Incorporated
Ed: Stephen Thompson. **Released:** May 2006. **Price:** $21.95. **Description:** Tax advice is given to help small businesses maximize returns for 2006.

19524 ■ *Beat the Taxman 2007: Easy Ways to Save Tax in Your Small Business, 2007 Edition For the 2006 Tax Year*
Pub: John Wiley & Sons, Incorporated
Ed: Stephen Thompson. **Released:** December 2006. **Price:** $26.99. **Description:** Year-round tax planner for entrepreneurs; the book is written in a question and answer format to help small business owners save money on annual taxes.

19525 ■ *Beat the Taxman: Easy Ways to Tax Save in Your Small Business*
Pub: John Wiley & Sons, Incorporated
Ed: Stephen Thompson. **Released:** May 2008. **Price:** $26.95. **Description:** Concise tax planner to help entrepreneurs take advantage of current tax laws.

19526 ■ "A Bigger Deal" in *Crain's Cleveland Business* (Vol. 28, November 12, 2007, No. 45, pp. 1)
Pub: Crain Communications, Inc.
Ed: Shawn A. Turner. **Description:** In an attempt to boost its revenue CBiz Inc., a provider of accounting and business services, is looking to balance its acquisitions of smaller companies with larger ones as part of its overall growth strategy.

19527 ■ "Bookkeeping Service Opens First Sacramento Franchise" in *Sacramento Bee* (April 13, 2011)
Pub: Sacramento Bee
Ed: Mark Glover. **Description:** Franchise bookkeeping service called BookKeeping Express opened its new office in Roseville, California; its first shop in the area.

19528 ■ "Businesses Balk at 1099 Provision in Health Reform Law" in *Baltimore Business Journal* (Vol. 28, August 13, 2010, No. 14, pp. 1)
Pub: Baltimore Business Journal
Ed: Scott Dance. **Description:** Small business advocates and accountants have criticized the Internal Revenue Service Form 1099 provision in the health care reform law as not worth the cost of time and money. Critics believe the policy would create a deluge of the documents that is too much for the companies or the IRS to handle. Details of the provision are also discussed.

19529 ■ "Changing the Rules of the Accounting Game" in *Canadian Business* (Vol. 81, December 8, 2008, No. 21, pp. 19)
Pub: Rogers Media Ltd.
Ed: Al Rosen. **Description:** Interference from world politicians in developing accounting standards is believed to have resulted in untested rules that are inferior to current standards. European lawmakers have recently asked to change International Financial Reporting Standards.

19530 ■ "Channeling for Growth" in *The Business Journal-Serving Greater Tampa Bay* (Vol. 28, July 11, 2008, No. 29, pp. 1)
Pub: American City Business Journals, Inc.
Ed: Margie Manning. **Description:** HSN Inc., one of the largest employers in Tampa Bay, Florida, is expected to spend an additional $9.7 million annually as it plans to hire more accounting, internal audit, legal, treasury and tax personnel after its spin-off to a public company. Details on the company's sales growth are provided.

19531 ■ "Convergence Collaboration: Revising Revenue Recognition" in *Management Accounting Quarterly* (Vol. 12, Spring 2011, No. 3, pp. 18)
Pub: Management Accounting Quarterly
Ed: Jack T. Ciesielski, Thomas R. Weirich. **Description:** While revenue recognition is critical, regulations have been developed on an ad hoc basis until now. The joint FASB/IASB proposed accounting standard on revenue recognition is a meaningful convergence of standards that will require a major adjustment for financial statement preparers. The proposal is a radical departure from the way revenue has been recognized by the U.S. GAAP. For industries such as consulting, engineering, construction, and technology, it could dramatically change revenue recognition, impacting the top line. The new proposed standard, its potential impact, and the critical role that contracts play is examined thoroughly.

19532 ■ "Crash Pads" in *Business Courier* (Vol. 24, November 2, 2008, No. 29, pp. 1)
Pub: American City Business Journals, Inc.
Ed: Jon Newberry. **Description:** Francisca Webster accumulated $4 million in mortgage debt in about 2 months. She filed a lawsuit against her tax preparer and her mortgage broker contending that the defendants had breached their fiduciary duties to her and made fraudulent misrepresentations to her. The other details of the case are supplied.

19533 ■ *Deduct It!: Lower Your Small Business Taxes*
Pub: NOLO
Ed: Stephen Fishman. **Released:** November 2009. **Price:** $34.99. **Description:** Ways to maximize business tax deductions for any type of small business owner (sole proprietor, partnership, LLC, corporation).

19534 ■ "Defer Tax with Installment Sale Election" in *Business Owner* (Vol. 35, September-October 2011, No. 5, pp. 12)
Pub: DL Perkins Company
Description: It is critical to consult with a tax professional before selling any high-value asset in order to minimize taxes.

19535 ■ "DHS Finalizes Rules Allowing Electronic I-9s" in *HR Specialist* (Vol. 8, September 2010, No. 9, pp. 5)
Pub: Capitol Information Group Inc.
Description: U.S. Department of Homeland Security issued regulations that give employers more flexibility to electronically sing and store I-9 employee verification forms.

19536 ■ *Directory of Global Professional Accounting and Business Certifications*
Pub: John Wiley & Sons, Incorporated
Ed: Lal Balkaran. **Released:** February 9, 2007. **Price:** $35.00. **Description:** Resource for international accounting, auditing, and business professions.

19537 ■ "Do Fair Value Adjustments Influence Dividend Policy?" in *Accounting and Business Research* (Vol. 41, Spring 2011, No. 2, pp. 51)
Pub: American Institute of CPAs
Ed: Igor Goncharov, Sander van Triest. **Description:** The impact of positive fair value adjustments on corporate distributions is examined using a Russian setting that requires disclosure of unrealized fair value adjustments in income. It was found that there is no rise in dividends due to positive fair value adjustments and that on the contrary, a negative relationship exists between adjustments and dividend changes.

19538 ■ "Down to the Wire for Your Taxes" in *Women In Business* (Vol. 63, Spring 2011, No. 1, pp. 22)
Pub: American Business Women's Association
Ed: Maureen Sullivan. **Description:** A look at a last-minute checklist to consult before filing annual corporate tax returns for a small business owner is presented. Enlisting professional help for small business taxes is always a good investment. However, small business owners have to make sure their records back up their filing when planning to go it alone.

19539 ■ *EBay Income: How ANYONE of Any Age, Location, and/or Background Can Build a Highly Profitable Online Business with eBay (Revised 2nd Edition)*
Pub: Atlantic Publishing Company
Released: December 1, 2010. **Price:** $24.95. **Description:** A complete overview of eBay is given and guides any small company through the entire process of creating the auction and auction strategies, photography, writing copy, text and formatting, multiple sales, programming tricks, PayPal, accounting, creating marketing, merchandising, managing email lists, advertising plans, taxes and sales tax, best time to list items and for how long, sniping programs, international customers, opening a storefront, electronic commerce, buy-it now pricing, keywords, Google marketing and eBay secrets.

19540 ■ "Economic Crisis and Accounting Evolution" in *Accounting and Business Research* (Vol. 41, Summer 2011, No. 3, pp. 2159)
Pub: American Institute of CPAs
Ed: Gregory Waymire, Sudipta Basu. **Description:** Financial reporting changes at the face of economic crises are studied using a punctuated equilibrium evolution. Findings show that financial reporting has a minor impact but may amplify economic crises. Attempts to enhance accounting amid economic crises may not be as beneficial as planned.

19541 ■ *Electronic Commerce: Technical, Business, and Legal Issues*
Pub: Prentice Hall PTR
Ed: Oktay Dogramaci; Aryya Gangopadhyay; Yelena Yesha; Nabil R. Adam. **Released:** August 1998. **Description:** Provides insight into the goals of using the Internet to grow a business in the areas of networking and telecommunication, security, and storage and retrieval; business areas such as marketing, procurement and purchasing, billing and payment, and supply chain management; and legal aspects such as privacy, intellectual property, taxation, contractual and legal settlements.

19542 ■ *Employer Legal Forms Simplified*
Pub: Nova Publishing Company
Ed: Daniel Sitarz. **Released:** August 2007. **Price:** $24.95. **Description:** Business reference containing the following forms needed to handle employees in any small business environment: application, notice, confidentiality, absence, federal employer forms and notices, and many payroll forms. All forms are included on a CD that comes in both PDF and text formats. Adobe Acrobat Reader software is also included on the CD. The forms are valid in all fifty states and Washington, DC.

19543 ■ "Finally, Justice" in *Canadian Business* (Vol. 82, April 27, 2009, No. 7, pp. 12)
Pub: Rogers Media
Ed: John Gray. **Description:** Former investment adviser Alex Winch feels that he was vindicated with the Canadian Court's ruling that Livent Inc. founders Garth Drabinsky and Myron Gottlieb were guilty of fraud. Drabinsky filed a libel case on Winch over Winch's letter that complained over Livent's accounting procedures. Winch also criticized the inconsistent accounting during Drabinsky's term as chief executive of another firm.

19544 ■ "Foreign (In)Direct Investment and Corporate Taxation" in *Canadian Journal of Economics* (Vol. 44, November 2011, No. 4, pp. 1497)
Pub: Blackwell Publishers Ltd.
Ed: Georg Wamser. **Description:** Foreign investments of multinational firms are often complex in that they involve conduit entities. In particular, a multinational can pursue either a direct or an indirect investment strategy, where the latter involves an intermediate corporate entity and is associated with enhanced opportunities for international tax planning. As a consequence, in the case of indirect investments, the role of corporate taxation in destination countries may change. An investigation into the effects of corporation taxation on foreign investment decisions of German multinationals, taking explicitly into account that firms choose in a first stage the investment regime, (direct vs. indirect) is provided.

19545 ■ "Getting More Out of Retirement" in *Agency Sales Magazine* (Vol. 39, November 2009, No. 10, pp. 48)
Pub: MANA
Ed: Joshua D. Mosshart. **Description:** Overview of the Tax Increase Prevention and Reconciliation Act, which lets employees convert to a Roth IRA in 2010.

The benefits of conversion depend on age and wealth and it is best to consult a tax advisor to determine the best strategy for retirement planners.

19546 ■ "Give Until It Works" in *Hispanic Business* (Vol. 30, March 2008, No. 3, pp. 26)
Pub: Hispanic Business
Ed: Rick Munarriz. **Description:** Donating to qualified charities and non-profit organizations for maximizing tax advantage to be availed on the income tax bill is examined. The amount that can be deducted from the total taxable amount is usually less then the actual amount donated and must be made during that calendar year.

19547 ■ *Home Business Tax Deductions: Keep What You Earn*
Pub: NOLO
Ed: Stephen Fishman. **Released:** November 2006. **Price:** $34.99. **Description:** Home business tax deductions are outlined. Basic information on the ways various business structures are taxed and how deductions work is included.

19548 ■ "How To: Manage Your Cash Better" in *Inc.* (Volume 32, December 2010, No. 10, pp. 69)
Pub: Inc. Magazine
Description: A monthly guide to policies, procedures and practices for managing cash for a small business.

19549 ■ "IFRS Monopoly: the Pied Piper of Financial Reporting" in *Accounting and Business Research* (Vol. 41, Summer 2011, No. 3, pp. 291)
Pub: American Institute of CPAs
Ed: Shyam Sunder. **Description:** The disadvantages of granting monopoly to the international financial reporting standards (IFRS) are examined. Results indicate that an IFRS monopoly removes the chances for comparing alternative practices and learning from them. An IFRS monopoly also eliminates customization of financial reporting to fit local differences in governance, business, economic, and legal conditions.

19550 ■ "Internal Auditor Wants Ethics Review of City's Casper Golf Contract" in *Business Courier* (Vol. 27, September 10, 2010, No. 19, pp. 1)
Pub: Business Courier
Ed: Dan Monk. **Description:** Mark Ashworth, an internal auditor for Cincinnati, Ohio is pushing for an ethics review of management contract for seven city-owned golf courses. Ashworth wants the Ohio Ethics Commission to investigate family ties between a superintendent for the Cincinnati Recreation Commission and Billy Casper Golf.

19551 ■ "IRS Announces New Standards for Tax Preparers" in *Bellingham Business Journal* (Vol. February 2010, pp. 9)
Pub: Sound Publishing Inc.
Ed: Isaac Bonnell. **Description:** A new oversight plan was announced by the Internal Revenue Services (IRS) that will require tax professionals to pass a competency test and register with the government in order to ensure greater accountability in the industry.

19552 ■ "It's Time to Take Full Responsibility" in *Harvard Business Review* (Vol. 88, October 2010, No. 10, pp. 42)
Pub: Harvard Business School Publishing
Ed: Rosabeth Moss Kanter. **Description:** A case for corporate responsibility is cited, focusing on long-term impact and the effects of public accountability.

19553 ■ *JK Lasser's Small Business Taxes 2077: Your Complete Guide to a Better Bottom Line*
Pub: John Wiley & Sons, Incorporated
Ed: Barbara Weltman. **Released:** November 2006. **Price:** $17.95. **Description:** J.K. Lasser's guide that offers tax facts and strategies for small businesses. The book helps to maximize deductions while learning tax planning strategies.

19554 ■ "Kaboom!" in *Canadian Business* (Vol. 81, November 10, 2008, No. 19, pp. 18)
Pub: Rogers Media Ltd.
Ed: Al Rosen, Mark Rosen. **Description:** International Financial Reporting Standards (IFRS) is a good idea in theory but was implemented in a hurry and had poor quality standards from the beginning.

19555 ■ "Know Your Numbers" in *Inc.* (Volume 32, December 2010, No. 10, pp. 39)
Pub: Inc. Magazine
Ed: Norm Brodsky. **Description:** Ways to maximize profit and minimize tax burden are presented.

19556 ■ "Lifesavers" in *Black Enterprise* (Vol. 41, December 2010, No. 5, pp. 38)
Pub: Earl G. Graves Publishing Co. Inc.
Ed: Tamara E. Holmes. **Description:** Profile of Interventional Nephrology Specialists Access Center and founders Dr. Omar Davis and Dr. Natarsha Grant; the center generated $5.5 million in revenue for 2009. Details on how they run their successful center are included.

19557 ■ "Living in a 'Goldfish Bowl'" in *WorkingUSA* (Vol. 11, June 2008, No. 2, pp. 277)
Pub: Blackwell Publishers Ltd.
Ed: John Lund. **Description:** Recent changes in laws, regulations and even the reporting format of labor organization annual financial reports in both the U.S. and Australia have received surprisingly little attention, yet they have significantly increased the amount of information available both to union members and the public in general, as reports in both countries are available via government Websites. While such financial reporting laws are extremely rare in European countries, with the exception of the UK and Ireland, the U.S. and Australian reporting systems have become among the most detailed in the world. After reviewing these changes in financial reporting and the availability of these reports, as well as comparing and contrasting the specific reporting requirements of each country, this paper then examines the cost-benefit impact of more detailed financial reporting.

19558 ■ *Make Sure It's Deductible*
Pub: McGraw-Hill Inc.
Ed: Evelyn Jacks. **Released:** November 2006. **Price:** $22.95. **Description:** Tax planning, strategies are provided to help small businesses maximize deductions.

19559 ■ *Make Your Life Tax Deductible: Easy Techniques to Reduce Your Taxes and Start Building Wealth Immediately*
Pub: McGraw-Hill Companies
Ed: David Meier. **Released:** December 2005. **Price:** $16.95 (US), $22.95 (Canadian). **Description:** Over 150 tax deductions are listed to help small business owners lower taxes and boost profits.

19560 ■ "May I Handle That For You?" in *Inc.* (March 2008, pp. 40, 42)
Pub: Gruner & Jahr USA Publishing
Ed: Taylor Mallory. **Description:** According to a recent survey, 53 percent of all companies outsource a portion of their human resources responsibilities. Ceridian, Administaff, Taleo, KnowledgeBank, and CheckPoint HR are among the companies profiled.

19561 ■ *MBA In a Day*
Pub: John Wiley and Sons, Inc.
Ed: Steven Stralser, PhD. **Released:** 2004. **Price:** $34.95. **Description:** Management professor presents important concepts, business topics and strategies that can be used by anyone to manage a small business or professional practice. Topics covered include: human resources and personal interaction, ethics and leadership skills, fair negotiation tactics, basic business accounting practices, project management, and the fundamentals of economics and marketing.

19562 ■ "Merger Mania: Regional Snaps Up HVS" in *The Business Journal-Serving Greater Tampa Bay* (Vol. 28, September 26, 2008, No. 40, pp. 1)
Pub: American City Business Journals, Inc.
Ed: Alexis Muellner. **Description:** It was reported that Harper Van Scoik & Co. LLP has finalized a merger with Carr Riggs & Ingram LLC. The agreement, effective October 1, 2008, is a merger of HVS assets into CRI. Bill Carr, a managing partner, revealed that HVS' $5 million in revenue will take CRI from $78 million to $82 million in revenue.

19563 ■ "My Favorite Tool for Managing Expenses" in *Inc.* (Volume 32, December 2010, No. 10, pp. 60)
Pub: Inc. Magazine
Ed: J.J. McCorvey. **Description:** Web-based service called Expensify is outlined. The service allows companies to log expenses while away from the office using the service's iPhone application.

19564 ■ "New Century's Fall Has a New Culprit" in *Barron's* (Vol. 88, March 31, 2008, No. 13, pp. 20)
Pub: Dow Jones & Company, Inc.
Ed: Jonathan R. Laing. **Description:** Court examiner Michael Missal reports that New Century Financial's auditor contributed to New Century's demise by its negligence in permitting improper and imprudent practices related to New Century's accounting processes. New Century's bankruptcy filing is considered the start of the subprime-mortgage crisis.

19565 ■ "New Institutional Accounting and IFRS" in *Accounting and Business Research* (Vol. 41, Summer 2011, No. 3, pp. 309)
Pub: American Institute of CPAs
Ed: Peter Wysocki. **Description:** A new framework for institutional accounting research is presented. It has five fundamental components – efficient versus inefficient results, interdependencies, causation, level of analysis, and institutional structure. The use of the framework for evaluation accounting institutions such as the international financial reporting standards is discussed.

19566 ■ "Olympus is Urged to Revise Board" in *Wall Street Journal Eastern Edition* (November 28, 2011, pp. B3)
Pub: Dow Jones & Company Inc.
Ed: Phred Dvorak. **Description:** Koji Miyata, once a director on the board of troubled Japanese photographic equipment company, is urging the company to reorganize its board, saying the present group should resign their board seats but keep their management positions. The company has come under scrutiny for its accounting practices and costly acquisitions.

19567 ■ "Paperless Bookkeeping Program" in *Fleet Owner Online* (February 15, 2011)
Pub: Penton Business Media Inc.
Description: TruckTax launched its new paperless bookkeeping system to help manage bookkeeping tasks, accounting and business tax information and filings for truckers.

19568 ■ "Pick and Save" in *Entrepreneur* (Vol. 36, April 2008, No. 4, pp. 66)
Pub: Entrepreneur Media, Inc.
Ed: C.J. Prince. **Description:** Business owners can purchase the needed big equipment to offset this year's expected profit. They can also switch to annualized computing of quarterly income and estimated tax payments to pay less estimated taxes for the first half of the year. Other tips on tax planning are provided.

19569 ■ "Privacy Concern: Are 'Group' Time Sheets Legal?" in *HR Specialist* (Vol. 8, September 2010, No. 9, pp. 4)
Pub: Capitol Information Group Inc.
Description: Under the Fair Labor Standards Act (FLSA) employers are required to maintain and preserve payroll or other records, including the number of hours worked, but it does not prescribe a particular order or form in which these records must be kept.

19570 ■ "Proposed Accounting Changes Could Complicate Tenant's Leases" in *Baltimore Business Journal* (Vol. 28, July 2, 2010, No. 8, pp. 1)
Pub: Baltimore Business Journal
Ed: Daniel J. Sernovitz. **Description:** The Financial Accounting Standards Board has proposed that companies must indicate the value of real estate

leases as assets and liabilities on balance sheets instead of expenses. The proposals could cause some companies to document millions of dollars in charges on their books or find difficulty in getting loans.

19571 ■ *QuickBooks All-in-One Desk Reference for Dummies*
Pub: John Wiley & Sons, Incorporated
Ed: Stephen L. Nelson. **Released:** January 2007. **Price:** $29.99 (US), $42.99 (Canadian). **Description:** Compilation of nine self-contained minibooks to get the most from QuickBooks accounting software. Companion Web site with sample business plan workbook and downloadable profit-volume cost analysis workbook included.

19572 ■ *QuickBooks Simple Start for Dummies*
Pub: John Wiley & Sons, Incorporated
Ed: Stephen L. Nelson. **Released:** October 2004. **Price:** $21.99. **Description:** Profile of Intuits new accounting software geared to micro businesses. Advice is offered on daily, monthly, and yearly accounting activities covering records, sales tax, and reports.

19573 ■ "Quicken Starter Edition 2008" in *Black Enterprise* (Vol. 38, March 2008, No. 8, pp. 54)
Pub: Earl G. Graves Publishing Co. Inc.
Ed: Sonya A. Donaldson. **Description:** Profile of Quicken Starter Edition 2008 offering programs that track spending; it will also categorize tax deductible expenses.

19574 ■ *Reading Financial Reports for Dummies*
Pub: John Wiley and Sons, Inc.
Ed: Lita Epstein. **Released:** January 2009. **Price:** $21.99. **Description:** This second edition contains more new and updated information, including new information on the separate accounting and financial reporting standards for private/small businesses versus public/large businesses; updated information reflecting 2007 laws on international financial reporting standards; new content to match SEC and other governmental regulatory changes over the last three years; new information about how the analyst-corporate connection has changed the playing field; the impact of corporate communications and new technologies; new examples that reflect the current trends; and updated Websites and resources.

19575 ■ "Reform or Perish" in *Canadian Business* (Vol. 82, April 27, 2009, No. 7, pp. 20)
Pub: Rogers Media
Ed: Al Rosen. **Description:** It is believed that Canada needs to fix its financial regulatory framework in order to provide more oversight on accounting procedures that is often left up to auditors. While the U.S. has constantly rebuilt its regulatory framework, Canada has not instituted reforms on its regulations. Canada entered the recession with a strong system but needs to build more substance into it.

19576 ■ *Sarbanes-Oxley for Dummies, 2nd Ed.*
Pub: John Wiley and Sons, Inc.
Ed: Jill Gilbert Welytok. **Released:** February 2008. **Price:** $21.99. **Description:** Provides the latest Sarbanes-Oxley (SOX) legislation with procedures to safely and effectively reduce compliance costs. Topics include way to: establish SOX standards for IT professionals, minimize compliances costs for every aspect of a business, survive a Section 404 audit, avoid litigation under SOX, anticipate future rules and trends, create a post-SOX paper trail, increase a company's standing and reputation, work with SOX in a small business, meet new SOX standards, build a board that can't be bought, and to comply with all SOX management mandates.

19577 ■ *Sarbanes-Oxley for Small Businesses: Leveraging Compliance for Maximum Advantage*
Pub: John Wiley & Sons, Incorporated
Ed: Peggy M. Jackson. **Released:** November 2006. **Price:** $39.95. **Description:** Book lists five ways the Sarbane Oxley Act helps small businesses.

19578 ■ *Schaum's Outline Financial Management, Third Edition*
Pub: McGraw-Hill
Ed: Jae K. Shim; Joel G. Siegel. **Released:** May 2007. **Price:** $22.95 (CND). **Description:** Rules and regulations governing corporate finance, including the Sarbanes-Oxley Act are discussed.

19579 ■ "SEC Extends Small Business Deadline for SOX Audit Requirement" in *HRMagazine* (Vol. 53, August 2008, No. 8, pp. 20)
Pub: Society for Human Resource Management
Description: Securities and Exchange Commission has approved a one-year extension of the compliance date for smaller public companies to meet the Section 404(b) auditor attestation requirement of the Sarbanes-Oxley Act.

19580 ■ *Self-Employed Tax Solutions: Quick, Simple, Money-Saving, Audit-Proof Tax and Recordkeeping Basics*
Pub: The Globe Pequot Press
Ed: June Walker. **Released:** January 1, 2009. **Price:** $17.95. **Description:** A simple system for maintaining tax records and filing tax forms for any small business is explored.

19581 ■ *Small Business Tax Deductions 2006*
Pub: Continuing Education of the Bar-California
Ed: Stephen Fishman. **Released:** June 2006. **Price:** $99.00. **Description:** Allowable tax deductions for small business in 2006 are explained.

19582 ■ *Smart Tax Write-Offs, 5th Ed.*
Pub: Rayve Productions, Inc.
Ed: Norm Ray. **Released:** February 2008. **Price:** $15.95. **Description:** Guidebook to help small business owners take advantage of legitimate tax deductions for home-based and other entrepreneurial businesses.

19583 ■ "Smart Year-End Tax Moves" in *Business Owner* (Vol. 35, November-December 2011, No. 6, pp. 8)
Pub: DL Perkins Company
Description: Managing small business and individual taxes is more important in a bad economy. It is imperative to seek all tax incentives that apply to your business.

19584 ■ "Spotlight on Principles-based Financial Reporting" in *Business Horizons* (September-October 2007, pp. 359)
Pub: Elsevier Technology Publications
Ed: Laureen A. Maines. **Description:** Employment of principles-based standards in order to generate reliable financial reporting and to reduce misrepresentations is discussed. Rules-based standards are distinguished from principles-based standards.

19585 ■ "Statistical Data of Interest" in *Business Owner* (Vol. 35, July-August 2011, No. 4, pp. 7)
Pub: DL Perkins Company
Description: Sources of federal tax revenue are presented; payroll taxes, 36 percent; corporate income tax, 12 percent, other 4 percent, excise taxes, 3 percent, individual income tax, 45 percent.

19586 ■ "Surviving an IRS Audit: Tips for Small Businesses" in *Agency Sales Magazine* (Vol. 39, July 2009, No. 7, pp. 52)
Pub: MANA
Ed: Joshua D. Mosshart. **Description:** It is a good idea to enlist the services of a tax professional even if an audit is expected to go smoothly since the IRS is likely to scrutinize the unreported income and personal as well as business expenses of a small business during an audit.

19587 ■ *Tax Savvy for Small Business*
Pub: NOLO
Ed: Frederick W. Daily. **Released:** November 2006. **Price:** $36.99. **Description:** Strategies to help small business owners claim all legitimate deductions and keep accurate records.

19588 ■ *Tax Smarts for Small Business*
Pub: Sourcebooks, Incorporated
Ed: James O. Parker. **Released:** December 2006. **Price:** $27.95. **Description:** Tax guide for small businesses.

19589 ■ "Test Your Structural Integrity" in *Entrepreneur* (Vol. 37, August 2009, No. 8, pp. 60)
Pub: Entrepreneur Media, Inc.
Ed: Jennifer Lawler. **Description:** Tax considerations can be important when choosing a business structure. For example, profits are taxed to the corporation in a C corp while profits are taxed only once at an S corp or a limited liability company. Meeting a tax professional should be done prior to switching to a different structure.

19590 ■ "Throughput Metrics Meet Six Sigma" in *Management Accounting Quarterly* (Vol. 12, Spring 2011, No. 3, pp. 12)
Pub: Management Accounting Quarterly
Ed: Shaun Aghili. **Description:** Throughput accounting (TA) metrics can be combined with six sigma's DMAIC methodology and various time-tested analysis and measurement tools for added effectiveness in resolving resource constraint issues. The goal is to optimize not only the output of a specific department but that of the entire system, by implementing a cost accounting system that is conducive to system optimization while increasing product quality, process integrity, or ideally, both.

19591 ■ *Top Tax Savings Ideas: How to Survive in Today's Tough Tax Environment*
Pub: Entrepreneur Press
Ed: Thomas J. Stemmy. **Released:** March 2004. **Price:** $18.95 (US), $26.95 (Canadian). **Description:** Tax deductions, fringe benefits, and tax deferrals for small businesses.

19592 ■ "ValienteHernandez Acquired" in *The Business Journal-Serving Greater Tampa Bay* (Vol. 28, September 12, 2008, No. 38, pp. 1)
Pub: American City Business Journals, Inc.
Ed: Alexis Muellner. **Description:** Minnesota accounting firm LarsonAllen LLP has acquired Florida-based ValienteHernandez PA, creating a company with 35 employees to be based in ValienteHernandez's newly built office in Tampa Bay Area. Other details about the merger are provided.

19593 ■ "Welcome Back" in *Canadian Business* (Vol. 82, April 27, 2009, No. 7, pp. 25)
Pub: Rogers Media
Ed: Sarka Halas. **Description:** Some Canadian companies such as Gennum Corporation have taken advantage of corporate sale-leasebacks to raise money at a time when credit is hard to acquire. Corporate sale-leasebacks allow companies to sell their property assets while remaining as tenants of the building. Sale-leasebacks allow firms to increase capital while avoiding the disruptions that may result with moving.

19594 ■ "Where Women Work" in *Marketing to Women* (Vol. 21, April 2008, No. 4, pp. 8)
Pub: EPM Communications, Inc.
Description: According to the U.S. Census Bureau, 60 percent of America's professional tax preparers are women. Also features additional trends concerning women in the workplace. Statistical data included.

19595 ■ *Working Papers, Chapters 1-14 for Needles/Powers/Crosson's Financial and Managerial Accounting*
Pub: Cengage South-Western
Ed: Belverd E. Needles, Marian Powers, Susan V. Crosson. **Released:** May 10, 2010. **Price:** $62.95. **Description:** Appropriate accounting forms for completing all exercises, problems and cases in the text are provided for financial management of a small company.

19596 ■ "Year-End Tax Tips" in *Hawaii Business* (Vol. 53, December 2007, No. 6, pp. 136)
Pub: Hawaii Business Publishing

Ed: Kathleen Bryan. **Description:** Tax planning tips for the end of 2007, in relation to the tax breaks that are scheduled to expire, are presented. Among the tax breaks that will be expiring at the 2007 year-end are sales tax deduction in the state and local level, premiums on mortgage insurance, and deduction on tuition. The impacts of these changes are discussed.

TRADE PERIODICALS

19597 ■ *Canadian MoneySaver*
Pub: Dale Ennis
Contact: Dale Ennis

Ed: Dale Ennis, Editor. **Released:** 11/year. **Price:** $19.95, Canada U.S. $36 elsewhere. **Description:** Examines taxes, investment, and financial planning in Canada. Recurring features include interviews, book reviews, and notices of publications available.

19598 ■ *CPA Client Tax Letter*
Pub: The American Institute of Certified Public Accountants

Ed: Maria Luzarraga Albanese, Editor. **Released:** Quarterly. **Price:** $119, members; $148.75, nonmembers. **Description:** Covers tax planning, including laws and legislation.

19599 ■ *The Exempt Organization Tax Review*
Pub: Tax Analysts

Released: Monthly. **Description:** Journal covering tax exemption laws and policies, including summaries of court opinions, IRS rulings, related regulations and administrative pronouncements, and analysis of current issues.

19600 ■ *Farm Tax Saver*
Pub: Sara Wyant

Ed: Released: Monthly. **Description:** Monitors changes in tax laws and analyzes how they affect farm families. Covers areas such as social security tax, tax shelters, tax on investments, and tax records required on transportation costs. Recurring features include editorials and news of research.

19601 ■ *Financial and Estate Planning*
Pub: CCH Inc.

Released: Monthly. **Price:** $1,479 CD-ROM; $1,465 print. **Description:** Monthly plus the monthly Estate Planning Review; financial planning to build and preserve wealth; forms and planning aids; will and trust forms and clauses; investment plans; insurance and annuity forms; tax planning and administration for estates and trusts; in-depth articles offering new planning ideas; analysis of court decisions; new rulings and legislative developments; year begins first of any month.

19602 ■ *The Insurance Tax Review*
Pub: Tax Analysts

Released: Monthly. **Price:** $699. **Description:** Trade magazine covering tax issues for the insurance industry.

19603 ■ *International Tax and Public Finance*
Pub: Springer Netherlands
Contact: John D. Wilson, Editor-in-Chief

Released: Bimonthly. **Price:** $1,013 institutions print or online; $1,215.60 institutions print & enchanced access. **Description:** Journal covering tax and public finance worldwide.

19604 ■ *Intertax*
Pub: Kluwer Academic/Plenum Publishing Corp.
Contact: Michael A. Olesnicky, Assoc. Ed.

Released: Monthly. **Price:** $901 print or online; $1,201 print or online; $662 print or online; $1,171 print & online; $1,562 print & online; $861 print & online. **Description:** Journal covering tax information worldwide.

19605 ■ *Journal of the American Taxation Association*
Pub: American Accounting Association
Contact: Jay Soled, Assoc. Ed.
E-mail: jaysoled@andromeda.rutgers.edu

Ed: Richard C. Sansing, Editor. **Released:** Semiannual, with a third conference supplement. **Price:** $120 print; $160 online from volume 21 to current issue; $175 online and print. **Description:** Academic journal covering accounting and taxation.

19606 ■ *The Journal of Taxation*
Pub: RIA Group
Contact: Carol Conjura, Department Ed.

Released: Monthly. **Price:** $370 print; $535 online/print bundle; $415 online. **Description:** Journal for sophisticated tax practitioners.

19607 ■ *Partnership Tax Planning & Practice*
Pub: CCH Inc.

Ed: James Rooney, Editor. **Released:** Monthly. **Price:** $439. **Description:** Explanatory comments on partnership, taxation, full text of pertinent code and acquisition provisions, post 1954 revenue rulings, revenue procedures.

19608 ■ *The Practical Tax Lawyer*
Pub: American Law Institute-American Bar Association
Contact: Mark T. Carroll, Director
E-mail: mcarroll@ali-aba.org

Released: Quarterly. **Price:** $75; $59 members special for ABA tax section members; $40 online; $99 print and online; $169 two years print and online; $139 two years special for ABA tax section; $89 two years online only. **Description:** Professional legal magazine covering advice to tax practitioners.

19609 ■ *Practical Tax Strategies*
Pub: RIA Group
Contact: Irving Evall, Editorial Advisory Board

Released: Monthly. **Price:** $250 print; $385 online/print; $280 online. **Description:** Magazine covering taxes and accounting.

19610 ■ *The Tax Executive*
Pub: Tax Executives Institute Inc.
Contact: Timothy McCormally, Exec. Dir.
E-mail: tmccormally@tei.org

Released: Bimonthly. **Price:** $22 single issue; $120 regular; $110 institutions; $145 other countries; $135 institutions, other countries; $110 government. **Description:** Professional journal covering business tax issues.

19611 ■ *Tax Notes Today*
Pub: Tax Analysts
Contact: Christopher Bergin, Pres./Publisher

Released: Weekly. **Price:** $1,999. **Description:** Trade magazine covering Federal tax news and reports.

19612 ■ *Tax Practice Bulletin*
Pub: Tax Management Inc.

Ed: Glenn B. Davis, Editor. **Released:** Biweekly. **Price:** $735 includes Tax Practice Series CD-ROM; $930 with state forms; $102 bulletin only. **Description:** Answers most of the common questions tax professionals face in daily practice. Provides analyses by expert practitioners.

19613 ■ *Tax Savings Report*
Pub: National Taxpayers Union

Ed: Peter Sepp, Editor. **Released:** 10/year. **Price:** $39, individuals. **Description:** Imparts tax savings tips and ideas on how to best use IRS regulations to the taxpayer's advantage. Discusses such topics as expense deductions, tax planning for senior citizens, job hunting expense deductions, and child care tax credit. Recurring features include columns titled Answers to Your Tax Questions and Tax Briefs.

19614 ■ *Taxes—The Tax Magazine*
Pub: CCH Inc.

Released: Monthly. **Price:** $349. **Description:** Magazine on tax laws and regulations.

19615 ■ *The TaxLetter*
Pub: MPL Communications Inc.

Released: Monthly. **Price:** $89. **Description:** Acts as a consumer newsletter that specializes in personal tax-planning, offering timely advice, information, and recommendations on personal and business tax-planning strategies. Features columns titled ShelterWatch, RRSP Watch, Looking Out for No. 1, Managing Your Money, and Tax-Wise Investor.

19616 ■ *TAXPRO Monthly*
Pub: National Association of Tax Professionals
Contact: Susan Lucius

Ed: Char DeCoster, Editor, cdecosteratsnatptax.com. **Released:** Monthly. **Price:** Included in membership. **Description:** Helps to communicate the purposes of the Association, which are to foster high standards in the tax preparation profession and to promote and protect the interests of tax practitioners. Includes tax law and regulations, statistics, and news of members.

19617 ■ *Valuation Researcher*
Pub: Valuation Research Corp.
Contact: Theresa Miller

Ed: Theresa Miller, Editor, tmiller@valuationresearch.com. **Released:** 6/year. **Price:** Free. **Description:** Publishes valuation news and information for use in asset management, finance, and tax planning.

19618 ■ *Worldwide Tax Daily*
Pub: Tax Analysts
Contact: Robert Goulder, Editor-in-Chief

Released: Weekly. **Price:** $999. **Description:** Professional magazine covering international tax news.

VIDEOCASSETTES/ AUDIOCASSETTES

19619 ■ *CPE Network: Tax & Accounting Report*
Bisk Education
9417 Princess Palm Ave.
Tampa, FL 33619
Free: 800-874-7877
Co. E-mail: info@bisk.com
URL: http://www.bisk.com

Price: $1200.00. **Description:** Provides information on current tax regulations and current accounting and auditing changes. Video newsletter published 11 times per year. **Availability:** VHS.

TRADE SHOWS AND CONVENTIONS

19620 ■ Institute of Internal Auditors - USA International Conference
Institute of Internal Auditors (Altamonte Springs, Florida)
247 Maitland Ave.
Altamonte Springs, FL 32701-4201
Ph:(407)937-1100
Fax:(407)937-1101
URL: http://www.theiia.org

Released: Annual. **Audience:** All levels of internal auditors from every industry. **Principal Exhibits:** Internal auditing equipment, supplies, and services, software, computer related equipment.

19621 ■ New Jersey Accounting, Business & Technology Show & Conference
Flagg Management, Inc.
353 Lexington Ave.
New York, NY 10016
Ph:(212)286-0333
Fax:(212)286-0086
Co. E-mail: flaggmgmt@msn.com
URL: http://www.flaggmgmt.com

Released: Annual. **Audience:** CPAs, accounting professionals, business and financial executives of New Jersey, Fortune 1000 corporations, business owners and managers, IT managers. **Principal Exhibits:** Information and technology, financial and business services, computer accounting systems, software, tax preparation, accounting, audit, practice management software - windows, and computer and business systems. Banking, insurance, financial and business software. Internet, online systems and middle market software and investment services. **Dates and Locations:** 2011 May 18-19, Secaucus, NJ.

CONSULTANTS

19622 ■ The Business Advisor
6 Main st.
Hamilton, ON, Canada L9S 1M8
Ph:(705)431-0511
Fax:(705)431-0522
Contact: Jacob M. Hoeppner, President
Scope: Assists in the preparation and implementation of efficient systems and procedures. Advises on business and management methods and procedures. Provides temporary interim management solutions for businesses requiring leadership to re-evaluate business direction and operations. Offers accounting and tax advice. Prepares for business succession.

19623 ■ Hollingsworth & Associates
395 Wellington Rd. S, Ste. 101
London, ON, Canada N6C 4P9
Ph:(519)649-2001
Fax:(519)649-7880
Co. E-mail: jack@hollingsworth.net
Contact: Jill Rogers, Principle
E-mail: jack@hollingsworth.net
Scope: Acts as management accountants, tax and management consultants, and offsite controllers. Consulting services include software selection, and financial information systems. Accounting and tax preparation.

19624 ■ John Alan Cohan
433 N Camden Dr., Ste. 100
Beverly Hills, CA 90210
Ph:(310)278-0203
Free: 800-255-1529
Fax:(310)859-8656
Co. E-mail: johnalancohan@aol.com
URL: http://www.johnalancohan.com
Contact: Cohan John Alan, Principle
Scope: Consultant assists in the development of business plans for startups in the fields of livestock, horses, farming, or aviation. Also provides tax consultations and tax opinion letters to support deductions.

19625 ■ Mitchell & Titus L.L.P.
1101 New York Ave. NW
Washington, DC 20005
Ph:(212)709-4500
Fax:(212)709-4680
Co. E-mail: newyork.office@mitchelltitus.com
URL: http://www.mitchelltitus.com
Contact: Ronald Benjamin, Partner
E-mail: ronald.benjamin@mitchelltitus.com
Scope: Firm provides assurance, advisory business services, transaction support and tax services. Specializes in auditing and accounting services, tax planning and preparation services management and business advisory services. **Publications:** "ITEM Club Budget preview report," 2010; "Year end personal planning," 2010; "Steering towards the future using the Pre Budget Report to help the UK rebound," 2009; "Be careful what you wish for," 2009; "Year end personal planning," 2009. **Seminars:** Budget Seminar 2010, Mar, 2010.

FRANCHISES AND BUSINESS OPPORTUNITIES

19626 ■ Accountants, Inc.
Select Appointments
111 Anza Blvd., No. 400
Burlingame, CA 94010
Ph:(650)579-1111
Free: 800-491-9411
No. of Franchise Units: 16. **No. of Company-Owned Units:** 22. **Founded:** 1986. **Franchised:** 1994. **Description:** Placement for accounting & finance candidates. **Equity Capital Needed:** $144,400-$193,700 + franchise fee. **Franchise Fee:** $30,000. **Financial Assistance:** Yes. **Training:** Yes.

19627 ■ Cash Plus
Cash Plus, Inc.
3002 Dow Ave., Ste, 120
Tustin, CA 92780
Ph:(714)731-2274
Free: 888-707-2274
Fax:(714)731-2099
No. of Franchise Units: 91. **No. of Company-Owned Units:** 2. **Founded:** 1984. **Franchised:** 1988. **Description:** Check cashing service and related services, including money orders, wire transfers, cash advances, mailboxes, notary, UPS, fax, snacks, tax filing and other items. **Equity Capital Needed:** $190,200-$269,700. **Franchise Fee:** $35,000. **Financial Assistance:** Provides guidance on credit applications and business plans used by franchisees seeking third party financing. **Training:** Provides training including easy-to-run computerized operating system, promotions and check verification and payday advance process.

19628 ■ CFO Today Inc.
545 E Tennessee St.
Tallahassee, FL 32308
Ph:(850)681-1941
Free: 888-643-1348
Fax:(850)561-1374
URL: http://www.cfotoday.com
No. of Franchise Units: 103. **No. of Company-Owned Units:** 1. **Founded:** 1989. **Franchised:** 1990. **Description:** Offers regional franchise program through which a regional owner solicits local franchisees. Local franchisees operate an accounting and tax practice, utilizing special marketing techniques, in addition to operational and computer systems, to provide tax, record keeping and other services to clients. **Equity Capital Needed:** $24,400-$40,000. **Franchise Fee:** $24,000. **Royalty Fee:** Varies. **Financial Assistance:** No. **Training:** Provides 5 days training at corporate headquarters and 1 day onsite, with ongoing support.

19629 ■ Colbert/Ball Tax Service
2616 S Loop West, Ste. 110
Houston, TX 77076
Ph:(713)592-5555
Free: 888-288-8675
Fax:(713)395-1606
No. of Franchise Units: 140. **No. of Company-Owned Units:** 5. **Founded:** 1995. **Franchised:** 2000. **Description:** Full service tax preparation. **Equity Capital Needed:** $24,378-$37,406. **Franchise Fee:** $10,000. **Financial Assistance:** Yes. **Training:** Yes.

19630 ■ Electronic Tax Filers (ETF)
The St. Simons Corporation
PO Box 2077
Cary, NC 27512-2077
Ph:(919)469-0651
Free: 800-945-9277
Fax:(919)460-5935
No. of Franchise Units: 44. **No. of Company-Owned Units:** 2. **Founded:** 1990. **Franchised:** 1990. **Description:** E-filing and refund loans. **Equity Capital Needed:** $25,000. **Franchise Fee:** $10,500. **Financial Assistance:** Yes. **Training:** Yes.

19631 ■ ExpressTax Service Inc.
Express Tax Service, Inc.
3030 Hartley Rd., Ste. 320
Jacksonville, FL 32257
Free: 888-417-4461
Fax:(904)262-0031
URL: http://www.expresstaxservice.com
No. of Franchise Units: 404. **Founded:** 1997. **Franchised:** 2002. **Description:** Tax preparation and electronic filing services. **Equity Capital Needed:** $15,375-$40,100/Co-located $3,500-$8,000. **Franchise Fee:** $1,500$2,500. **Financial Assistance:** No. **Training:** Yes.

19632 ■ Instant Tax Service
ITS Financial, LLC
1 S Main St., Ste. 1400
Dayton, OH 45402
Ph:888-870-1040
Fax:888-297-2199
Co. E-mail: franchise@instanttaxservice.com
No. of Franchise Units: 1,197. **No. of Company-Owned Units:** 16. **Founded:** 2000. **Franchised:** 2004. **Description:** Provides tax return preparation, electronic filing, refund options and financial services. **Equity Capital Needed:** $39,000-$89,000, total investment required. **Franchise Fee:** $34,000. **Financial Assistance:** Yes. **Managerial Assistance:** Provides 24/7 team support, software instructions, complete marketing solutions and state of the industry overviews, including current tax laws. **Training:** Yes.

19633 ■ Jackson Hewitt Tax Service
Cendant Corp.
3 Sylvan Way, 2nd Fl.
Parsippany, NJ 07054
Ph:(973)496-1040
Free: 800-475-2904
Fax:(973)496-2760
No. of Franchise Units: 4,200. **Founded:** 1960. **Franchised:** 1986. **Description:** Awards franchise territories to individuals who are dedicated to producing the highest-quality tax return possible. The Company utilizes a proprietary computerized tax interview system, designed to maximize deductions, reduce math errors and produce an accurate tax return for every customer. The Super fast Refund is the trademark for a refund anticipation loan, which allows customers their refund minus fees in 24 hours or less. cannot receive financing from banks. **Equity Capital Needed:** $47,430-$75,205. **Franchise Fee:** $25,000. **Financial Assistance:** Yes. **Managerial Assistance:** Over 40 field support members in place to help franchisees develop their skills in getting and retaining customers. Trainers will thoroughly teach how to train staff so your preparers will be up-to-date on the latest tax laws. Provides franchisees with a toll-free number to help with any questions that may arise. Provides franchisees with a strong advertising support team. **Training:** 5 day training program designed to teach business partners the skills necessary to launch a new franchise operation. This also includes workshops, seminars and group discussions. Extensive 2 days of training for electronic filing system.

19634 ■ Ledgerplus
259 E 7th Ave.
Tallahassee, FL 32303
Ph:(850)561-1374
Free: 888-643-1348
No. of Franchise Units: 156. **No. of Company-Owned Units:** 5. **Founded:** 1989. **Franchised:** 1991. **Description:** Accounting, tax & consultation. **Equity Capital Needed:** $29,000. **Franchise Fee:** $16,000. **Financial Assistance:** Yes. **Training:** Yes.

19635 ■ Ledgers Professional Services
4-17705 Leslie St.
Newmarket, ON, Canada L3Y 3E3
Ph:(905)898-6320
Free: (866)836-6620
Co. E-mail: sales@ledgers.com
URL: http://www.ledgers.com
No. of Franchise Units: 50. **No. of Company-Owned Units:** 1. **Founded:** 1994. **Franchised:** 1996. **Description:** Provides a comprehensive suite of services to small businesses, including bookkeeping, payroll and personal income taxes to corporate financial statement preparation and tax returns. **Equity Capital Needed:** $10,000. **Franchise Fee:** $20,000. **Royalty Fee: Financial Assistance: Training:** Provides 5 days training.

19636 ■ Liberty Tax Service
800 Denison St., Unit 18
Markham, ON, Canada L3R 5M9
Ph:(905)943-2640
Free: 800-790-3863
Fax:(866)902-1245
Co. E-mail: kstrongoli@libtax.com
URL: http://www.libertytaxcanada.ca
No. of Franchise Units: 233. **No. of Company-Owned Units:** 19. **Founded:** 1972. **Franchised:** 1982. **Description:** Tax preparation service. **Equity Capital Needed:** $33,350-$54,900. **Franchise Fee:** $25,000. **Training:** Provides 5 days training.

19637 ■ Padgett Business Services
400 Blue Hill Dr., Ste. 201
Westwood, MA 02090
Free: 877-729-8725
Co. E-mail: padgett@smallbizpros.com
URL: http://www.smallbizpros.com
No. of Franchise Units: 400. **Founded:** 1966. **Franchised:** 1975. **Description:** Padgett provides an array of services to small businesses, such as consulting, financial reporting, government compliance, payroll and tax preparation services. Padgett also offers credit card processing, pension and 125 plan administration, equipment financing and workers' compensation payment service. **Equity Capital Needed:** Total investment and net worth &105,955; liquid or cash $78,750. **Franchise Fee:** $56,000. **Financial Assistance:** Third party financing up to $75,000. Also enrolled in the SBA registry. **Training:** Initial training 12 days + field visits, covering marketing, operations, and software. Ongoing training and support is provided through regular seminars in marketing, operations, tax, etc. Support is delivered through toll-free telephone and a wide range of information and material is provided via the company's web site.

19638 ■ Tax Centers of America
1611 E Main St.
Russellville, AR 72802
Ph:(479)968-4796
Free: 800-364-2012
Fax:(479)968-8012
Co. E-mail: moreinfo@tcoa.net
URL: http://www.tcoa.net
No. of Franchise Units: 193. **No. of Company-Owned Units:** 1. **Founded:** 1992. **Franchised:** 1995. **Description:** Tax centers. **Equity Capital Needed:** $20,100$63,749. **Franchise Fee:** $10,000-$36,000. **Royalty Fee:** $30-55/return. **Financial Assistance:** Assistance available with franchise fee. **Training:** Offers 4 days of training and ongoing support.

COMPUTERIZED DATABASES

19639 ■ *Daily Tax Report*
The Bureau of National Affairs Inc.
1801 S Bell St.
Arlington, VA 22202
Free: 800-372-1033
Co. E-mail: customercare@bna.com
URL: http://www.bna.com
Description: Contains the complete text of the *Daily Tax Report.* Covers U.S. tax and pension legislation; pertinent court and agency rulings; accounting standards; pension rules; agency personnel charges; federal budget activity; International Revenue Service (IRS) and treasury policy; Congressional deliberations; and executive policy-making. Includes such sections as the following: Today's Summaries—contains a brief overview and summary of the day's most important news and developments in tax law and policy. Congressional and Presidential Calendars—contains the Summary of Congressional actions and a schedule of Presidential activities including bills introduced, scheduled for hearings, and enacted. Taxation, Budget, and Accounting—contains news reports of legislative and regulatory developments affecting tax policy including reports of federal budget developments, coverage of policy, personnel, and administrative changes in the IRS and Treasury Department, and developments in pension rules, policies, and legislation. Court Decisions—provides reports of federal court decisions including summaries of facts and holdings and partial text of options. rulings, revenue procedures, notices, and other announcements arranged by Internal Revenue Code Section. Court Decisions—provides reports of federal court decisions including summaries of facts and holdings and partial text of options. **Availability:** Online: Thomson Reuters, The Bureau of National Affairs Inc. **Type:** Full text.

19640 ■ *e-JEP*
American Economic Association
2014 Broadway, Ste. 305
Nashville, TN 37203
Ph:(615)322-2595
Fax:(615)343-7590
Co. E-mail: aeainfo@vanderbilt.edu
URL: http://www.vanderbilt.edu/AEA
Description: Contains the full text of the *Journal of Economic Perspectives.* Includes articles, reports, and other material for economists and economics professionals. Features analysis and critiques of recent research findings and developments in public policy. Includes coverage of global economics issues and developments. Features articles on education in economics, employment issues for economists, and other issues of concern to professional economists. **Availability:** Online: American Economic Association, Thomson Reuters; CD-ROM: American Economic Association. **Type:** Full text.

19641 ■ *Federal Income Taxation of Corporations and Shareholders*
Thomson Reuters
395 Hudson St., 4th Fl.
New York, NY 10014
Ph:(212)367-6300
Free: 800-431-9025
Co. E-mail: ria@thomson.com
URL: http://ria.thomsonreuters.com
Description: Contains the full text of the seventh edition of *Federal Income Taxation of Corporations and Shareholders*, a treatise on the subject of corporate taxation. Covers all areas of corporate income taxation. Focuses on tax issues in the lifecycle of corporations. Includes details and analysis of how shareholders and corporations are affected by the Internal Revenue Code, the IRS, and by tax-related court decisions. **Availability:** Online: Thomson Reuters, Thomson Reuters. **Type:** Full text.

19642 ■ *Federal Taxes Weekly Alert*
Thomson Reuters
395 Hudson St., 4th Fl.
New York, NY 10014
Ph:(212)367-6300
Free: 800-431-9025
Co. E-mail: ria@thomson.com
URL: http://ria.thomsonreuters.com
Description: Contains weekly updates, news, and time-critical information on U.S. federal taxes and taxation. Includes details on the latest actions and developments in Congress, as well as decisions and opinions from the courts, the federal treasury, the IRS, and other agencies. Includes updates on pending and current legislation. Includes comprehensive and authoritative analysis of federal tax laws, regulations, and issues, with specific attention given to their application and impact. **Availability:** Online: Thomson Reuters, Thomson Reuters. **Type:** Full text.

19643 ■ *IRS Practice and Procedure*
Thomson Reuters
395 Hudson St., 4th Fl.
New York, NY 10014
Ph:(212)367-6300
Free: 800-431-9025
Co. E-mail: ria@thomson.com
URL: http://ria.thomsonreuters.com
Description: Contains the full text of the second edition of IRS Practice and Procedure, a treatise on the subject of IRS procedures. Clarifies IRS procedures and policies. Includes detailed procedural information on such activities as drafting a ruling request, preparing for an appeals conference, and dealing with an IRS revenue officer. Covers recent changes in tax laws, civil and criminal penalties, and IRS access to foreign-based records. **Availability:** Online: Thomson Reuters, Thomson Reuters. **Type:** Full text.

19644 ■ *IRS Publication 334: Tax Guide for Small Business*
U.S. Department of the Treasury
1111 Constitution Ave. NW
Washington, DC 20224
Ph:(202)622-2000
Free: 800-829-3676
Fax:(202)622-6642
URL: http://www.irs.ustreas.gov
Description: Contains the complete text of the 2009 edition of *IRS Publication 334 (Tax Guide for Small Business)*, covering information on U.S. federal tax law and tax return preparation for small businesses. Enables the user to search by topic and to retrieve IRS listings of technical authorities. **Availability:** Online: U.S. Department of the Treasury. **Type:** Full text; Directory.

19645 ■ *ProQuest Accounting & Tax*
ProQuest LLC
789 E Eisenhower Pky.
PO Box 1346
Ann Arbor, MI 48106-1346
Ph:(734)761-4700
Free: 800-521-0600
Fax:(734)761-6450
Co. E-mail: info@proquest.com
URL: http://www.proquest.com
Description: Contains citations and abstracts to more than 2300 key publications in accounting, financial management, taxation, and auditing worldwide. Also provides citations to articles in more than 800 newspapers, business journals, dissertations and news magazines. Titles include *The Internal Auditor, Inside Public Accounting, Journal of Accounting and Finance Research, Journal of the American Taxation Association*, and the *National Tax Journal.* **Availability:** Online: ProQuest LLC, ProQuest LLC, ProQuest LLC. **Type:** Bibliographic.

19646 ■ *State Tax Notes*
Tax Analysts
400 S Maple Ave., Ste. 400
Falls Church, VA 22046
Ph:(703)533-4400
Free: 800-955-2444
Co. E-mail: cservice@tax.org
URL: http://www.taxanalysts.com
Description: Follows tax developments in every state, and keeps track of interstate trends. Covers multi-state Organizations, state tax conferences, tax decisions from courts nationwide, rulings and regulations from revenue departments, and legislation from all 50 states each week. **Availability:** Online: LexisNexis Group. **Type:** Full text.

19647 ■ *State Tax Today*
Tax Analysts
400 S Maple Ave., Ste. 400
Falls Church, VA 22046
Ph:(703)533-4400
Free: 800-955-2444
Co. E-mail: cservice@tax.org
URL: http://www.taxanalysts.com
Description: Covers tax news and documents from every state, the District of Columbia, and all U.S. possessions, complete with summaries and full text of legislation. Includes proposed and finalized regulations, *Revenue Rulings & Procedures*, supreme, appellate, and tax court opinions, and private letter rulings. **Availability:** Online: Tax Analysts. **Type:** Full text.

19648 ■ *The Tax Directory*
Tax Analysts
400 S Maple Ave., Ste. 400
Falls Church, VA 22046
Ph:(703)533-4400
Free: 800-955-2444
Co. E-mail: cservice@tax.org
URL: http://www.taxanalysts.com
Description: Contains information on more than 20,000 tax professionals. Vol. One Government Officials Worldwide including state and federal officials, including taxwriting committees U.S. Department of Treasury and IRS, Tax Court Judges, International Financial Specialists, Tax and Business Journalists, Professional Associations, and Tax Groups and Coalitions. Vol. Two Corporate Tax Managers including names and contact information for tax managers in largest U.S corporations. Entries including industry description derived from the Securities and Exchange Commission's four-digit Standard Industry Classification code used by the listed companies for filing purposes. **Availability:** Online: LexisNexis Group; CD-ROM: Tax Analysts. **Type:** Directory.

19649 ■ *Tax Management Memorandum*
The Bureau of National Affairs Inc.
1801 S Bell St.
Arlington, VA 22202

Free: 800-372-1033
Co. E-mail: customercare@bna.com
URL: http://www.bna.com/tax-accounting-t5000
Description: Reviews current news and developments in business tax planning. Includes professional practitioners' commentary on new issues, developments, trends, and strategies. **Availability:** Online: The Bureau of National Affairs Inc. **Type:** Full text.

19650 ■ *Tax Notes Today*
Tax Analysts
400 S Maple Ave., Ste. 400
Falls Church, VA 22046
Ph:(703)533-4400
Free: 800-955-2444
Co. E-mail: cservice@tax.org
URL: http://www.taxanalysts.com
Description: Provides daily tax news coverage, including the complete text of items to be published in *Tax Notes*. Includes news items and feature articles on tax developments, tax policy issues, and congressional developments. Also provides the complete text of all Internal Revenue Service (IRS) regulations and selected relevant court opinions, summaries of tax-related correspondence between the U.S. Treasury and the tax bar, IRS letter rulings and Technical Advice Memoranda, *Congressional Record* items, IRS manual changes, and public comments on IRS regulations. Also provides the complete text of such documents as the IRS General Counsel Memoranda, Technical Memoranda, and Actions on Decisions; IRS revenue rulings and revenue procedures; the House-Senate Conference Committee Report on the Tax Reform Act of 1986; and tax-related news releases and reports from the IRS, U.S. Treasury, General Accounting Office, Congressional Budget Office, and other sources. Also contains the complete text of IRS publications for taxpayers' use in preparing tax returns, and references to individuals and organizations involved in tax-related issues from *The Federal Tax Directory*. Beginning with September 1985, the complete text of federal court decisions affecting taxation is available. **Availability:** Online: ProQuest LLC, LexisNexis Group, PricewaterhouseCoopers LLP. **Type:** Full text.

19651 ■ *Weekly Report*
The Bureau of National Affairs Inc.
1801 S Bell St.
Arlington, VA 22202
Free: 800-372-1033
Co. E-mail: customercare@bna.com
URL: http://www.bna.com/tax-accounting-t5000
Description: Contains the complete text of *Tax Management Weekly Report*, a newsletter covering legislative, regulatory, judicial, and policy actions related to taxation and accounting. Provides summaries of selected cases, Internal Revenue Service (IRS) rulings and procedures, private letter rulings by code section, and general counsel and technical memoranda. **Availability:** Online: The Bureau of National Affairs Inc., Thomson Reuters. **Type:** Full text.

COMPUTER SYSTEMS/ SOFTWARE

19652 ■ Accountant's Relief
AccountantsWorld
140 Fell Ct.
Hauppauge, NY 11788
Ph:888-999-1366
Free: 800-829-7354
Fax:800-927-1283
Co. E-mail: contactus@accountantsworld.com
URL: http://www.accountantsworld.com
Description: Available for IBM computers and compatibles. System prepares 53 tax forms and schedules and calculates various personal and business taxes.

19653 ■ BNA Estate and Gift Tax Planner
BNA Software Inc.
1801 S Bell St.
Arlington, VA 22202
Ph:800-424-2938
Free: 800-424-2938
Fax:(703)341-2938
Co. E-mail: software@bna.com
URL: http://www.bnasoftware.com
Price: Contact BNA. **Description:** Available for IBM computers. System calculates federal and state taxes for the estates of spouses.

19654 ■ BNA Income Tax Planner
BNA Software Inc.
1801 S Bell St.
Arlington, VA 20037
Ph:800-424-2938
Free: 800-424-2938
Fax:(703)341-2938
Co. E-mail: software@bna.com
URL: http://www.bnasoftware.com
Price: Contact BNA. **Description:** Available for IBM computers and compatibles. Calculates federal and state individual income taxes.

19655 ■ FAS Fixed Asset Programs–Sage Software SB, Inc.
Best Software, Inc.
2325 Dulles Corner Blvd., Ste. 800
Herndon, VA 20171
Ph:(703)793-2700
Free: 800-368-2405
Fax:(703)793-2770
URL: http://www.sagenorthamerica.com
Price: Description: Windows based. System calculates taxes and provides comparisons of tax liability over a certain number of years.

19656 ■ TAX/PACK: Professional 1040
Alpine Data, Inc.
Division of Analytical Processes Corp.
737 S Townsend Ave.
Montrose, CO 81401
Ph:(805)525-1040
Free: 800-525-1040
Fax:(970)249-8511
Co. E-mail: info@taxpack.com
URL: http://www.alpinedata.com
Price: $410 (with laser), $245 (without laser). **Description:** Available for IBM computers and compatibles. Provides tax form preparation.

19657 ■ Tax Preparer
HowardSoft
7852 Ivanhoe Ave.
La Jolla, CA 92037
Ph:(858)454-0121
Fax:(858)454-7559
Co. E-mail: support@howardsoft.com
URL: http://www.howardsoft.com
Price: $229.00. **Description:** Available for IBM and Apple II computers and compatibles. System automating the preparation of tax returns. Handles IRS worksheets, recordkeeping, stocks, bonds, rental, accounts, and depreciated assets.

19658 ■ Tax Preparer: California Supplement
HowardSoft
7852 Ivanhoe Ave.
La Jolla, CA 92037
Ph:(858)454-0121
Fax:(858)454-7559
Co. E-mail: support@howardsoft.com
URL: http://www.howardsoft.com
Price: $149.00. **Description:** Available for IBM and Apple II computers and compatibles. System providing automated tax preparation for California state income taxes.

19659 ■ Tax$imple
AJV Computerized Data Management, Inc.
8 Emery Ave.
Randolph, NJ 07869
Ph:(973)989-8955
Free: 800-989-8955
Fax:(973)366-5877
Co. E-mail: support@taxsimple.com
URL: http://www.taxsimple.com/
Price: Contact TaxSimple for Pricing. **Description:** Available for IBM computers and compatibles. System for tax professionals offering tax form input, calculations, tables, schedules, and printing options.

LIBRARIES

19660 ■ Baker & McKenzie Library
BCE Pl.
181 Bay St., Ste. 2100
PO Box 874
Toronto, ON, Canada M5J 2T3
Ph:(416)863-1221
Fax:(416)863-6275
URL: http://www.bakernet.com/BakerNet/default.htm
Contact: Irene Batna, Libn.
Scope: Law - corporate, commercial, labor, tax. **Services:** Interlibrary loan; Library not open to the public. **Holdings:** Figures not available.

19661 ■ Bensfield & Associates Library
6912 W. Cermak Rd.
Berwyn, IL 60402
Ph:(708)795-7600
Fax:(708)795-7614
Co. E-mail: jbensfield@compuserve.com
Contact: John P. Bensfield
Scope: Taxation. **Holdings:** 100 bound periodical volumes.

19662 ■ Brooklyn Public Library Business Library
280 Cadman Plaza, W.
Tillary St.
Brooklyn, NY 11201
Ph:(718)623-7000
Co. E-mail: busref@brooklynpubliclibrary.org
URL: http://www.brooklynpubliclibrary.org/business
Contact: Dionne Mack-Harvin, Exec.Dir.
Scope: Accounting, advertising, business management, business procedure, career development and employment, finance, insurance, investment, public relations, small business, real estate. **Services:** Copying; Library open to the public. **Holdings:** 133,000 books; 730,000 microfiche; 22,000 reels of microfilm; 1000 directories; 120 videocassettes and DVDs; selective U.S. government documents depository. **Subscriptions:** 700 journals and other serials; 5 newspapers.

19663 ■ Caixa Geral do Depositos SA CGD Mediateca e Centro de Informacao Europeia
Edificio-Sede da CGD, Av Joao XXI, 63
P-1000 Lisbon, Portugal
Co. E-mail: ana.monteiro@cgd.pt
URL: http://www.cgd.pt
Scope: Finance. **Services:** Centre open to the public. **Holdings:** 40,000 volumes. **Subscriptions:** 1000 journals and other serials.

19664 ■ CMA Ontario–Member Services Centre
70 University Ave., Ste. 101
Toronto, ON, Canada M5J 2M4
Ph:(416)204-3142
Fax:(416)977-1365
Co. E-mail: msc@cma-ontario.org
Contact: Patricia Black, Mgr., Member Svcs.Ctr.
Scope: Accounting, management, finance, strategy, taxation, investments. **Services:** Copying; SDI; Library not open to the public. **Holdings:** 2069 books; 267 videocassettes; 184 audiocassettes; 6 videodiscs. **Subscriptions:** 53 journals and other serials; 2 newspapers.

19665 ■ Deloitte & Touche–Toronto North Library
5140 Yonge St., Ste. 1700
Toronto, ON, Canada M2N 6L7
Ph:(416)229-2100
Fax:(416)601-5700
URL: http://www.deloitte.com
Contact: Lynn Idnurm
Scope: Tax. **Services:** Library not open to the public. **Holdings:** Books; bound periodical volumes.

19666 ■ Deloitte & Touche LLP Library
350 S. Grand Ave., Ste. 200
Two California Plaza
Los Angeles, CA 90071-3462
Ph:(213)688-0800

Fax:(213)688-0100
URL: http://www.deloitte.com
Contact: Elizabeth Carranza, Hd.Libn.
Scope: Auditing, taxation, management consultation, actuarial services, employee benefits, valuation consultation. **Services:** Library not open to the public. **Holdings:** Figures not available.

19667 ■ Epstein, Becker, & Green, PC Law Library
250 Park Ave., 12th Fl.
New York, NY 10177-0077
Ph:(212)351-4571
Fax:(212)661-0989
Co. E-mail: eegan@ebglaw.com
URL: http://www.ebglaw.com
Contact: Elaine M. Egan, Dir., Lib.Svcs.
Scope: Law - labor and employment, litigation, health, corporate, elder law, taxation. **Services:** Interlibrary loan; Library not open to the public. **Holdings:** 1500 books. **Subscriptions:** 250 journals and other serials; 10 newspapers.

19668 ■ Ernst & Young Center for Business Knowledge
1 Victory Pk., Ste. 2000
2323 Victory Ave.
Dallas, TX 75219
Ph:(214)969-8000
Fax:(214)969-8587
URL: http://www.ey.com
Contact: Tommy M. Yardley, Reg.Res.Mgr.
Scope: Consulting, accounting, tax accounting, auditing. **Services:** Center open to the public at librarian's discretion.

19669 ■ Ernst & Young Library
875 E. Wisconsin Ave.
Milwaukee, WI 53202
Ph:(414)273-5900
URL: http://www.ey.com
Contact: Julie Porter, Sr.Mgr.
Scope: Taxation, tax law, accounting, auditing. **Services:** Performs searches on fee basis for clients only. **Holdings:** 1200 books. **Subscriptions:** 35 journals and other serials.

19670 ■ Ernst & Young LLP Center for Business Knowledge
5 Times Sq.
New York, NY 10019
Ph:(212)773-3000
Fax:(212)773-6350
Co. E-mail: center_for_business_knowledge@ey.com
URL: http://www.ey.com/cbk
Scope: Accounting and auditing, taxation, finance. **Services:** Interlibrary loan; Library open to clients and SLA members. **Holdings:** 3500 books. **Subscriptions:** 500 journals and other serials.

19671 ■ Fenwick & West LLP Law Library
Silicon Valley Center
801 California St.
Mountain View, CA 94041-2008
Ph:(650)988-8500
Fax:(650)938-5200
Co. E-mail: library@fenwick.com
URL: http://www.fenwick.com
Contact: Sharon McNally Lahey, Lib.Mgr.
Scope: Securities, corporate, employment, International taxation, intellectual property. **Services:** Interlibrary loan; copying; Library not open to the public. **Holdings:** 10,000 books. **Subscriptions:** 350 journals and other serials; 8 newspapers.

19672 ■ Greene Radovsky Maloney Share Library
4 Embarcadero Ctr., Ste. 4000
San Francisco, CA 94111
Ph:(415)981-1400
Fax:(415)777-4961
Co. E-mail: info@grmslaw.com
URL: http://www.greeneradovsky.com
Scope: Taxation. **Services:** Interlibrary loan; copying; Library not open to the public. **Holdings:** 1200 books; 75 bound periodical volumes. **Subscriptions:** 150 journals and other serials; 10 newspapers.

19673 ■ Huddleston, Bolen LLP Law Library
611 3rd Ave.
PO Box 2185
Huntington, WV 25701
Ph:(304)529-6181
Fax:(304)522-4312
Co. E-mail: laldridge@huddlestonbolen.com
URL: http://www.huddlestonbolen.com/
Contact: Lauren Aldridge, Law Libn.
Scope: Taxation/estate, corporate/securities/banking, federal litigation, labor. **Services:** Library not open to the public. **Holdings:** 35,000 books.

19674 ■ Illinois CPA Society–Information & Research Center
550 W. Jackson, Ste. 900
Chicago, IL 60661-5716
Ph:(312)601-4613
Free: 800-993-0407 (Illinois
Fax:(312)906-8045
Co. E-mail: research@icpas.org
URL: http://www.icpas.org
Contact: Michele Courtney, Asst.Dir.
Scope: Accounting; auditing; taxation; business. **Services:** Library open to the public with restrictions. **Holdings:** 5500 books; 50 bound periodical volumes; 225 microfilms. **Subscriptions:** 120 journals and other serials.

19675 ■ KPMG–Research Centre
777 Dunsmuir St.
PO Box 10426
Vancouver, BC, Canada V7Y 1K3
Ph:(604)691-3000
Fax:(604)691-3031
URL: http://www.kpmg.ca
Contact: Julian Richards, Libn.
Scope: Accounting, tax, general business, stocks. **Services:** SDI; Library not open to the public. **Holdings:** 1000 books; 70 bound periodical volumes. **Subscriptions:** 50 journals and other serials; 6 newspapers.

19676 ■ Polsinelli Shalton Welte Suelthaus PC Law Library
700 W. 47th St., Ste. 1000
Kansas City, MO 64112
Ph:(816)753-1000
Fax:(816)753-1536
Co. E-mail: bfullerton@pswlaw.com
URL: http://www.pswlaw.com/
Contact: Karin L. Weaver
Scope: Law - tax, bankruptcy, real estate; litigation; product liability. **Services:** Interlibrary loan; copying; SDI; Library open to clients only. **Holdings:** 15,000 books. **Subscriptions:** 1500 journals and other serials; 10 newspapers.

19677 ■ Power Budd LLP Law Library
First Canadian Place, Ste. 7210
Toronto, ON, Canada M5X 1C7
Ph:(416)642-8580
Fax:(416)640-2777
Co. E-mail: lrhodes@powerbudd.com
Contact: Lesley Rhodes, Libn.
Scope: Energy, environmental and corporate law. **Services:** Library not open to the public. **Holdings:** Figures not available.

19678 ■ PricewaterhouseCoopers–Research Centre
1250 Boul Rene-Levesque O
Bureau 2800
Montreal, QC, Canada H3B 2G4
Ph:(514)205-5105
Fax:(514)876-1502
Co. E-mail: dany.lessard@ca.pwc.com
URL: http://www.pwc.com/ca
Contact: Dany Lessard, Mgr.
Scope: Accounting, tax, management, business, finance. **Subscriptions:** 200 journals and other serials.

19679 ■ Protape, Inc. Library
1540 Broadway
New York, NY 10036
Contact: Richard Sobelsohn
Scope: Accounting, law, real estate, English, math, insurance, travel, taxation, stock broker, medical billing, claims adjusting, private investigation, paralegal. **Services:** Library not open to the public. **Holdings:** 25,000 books; 250 bound periodical volumes. **Subscriptions:** 65 journals and other serials; 20 newspapers.

19680 ■ Reid and Riege, PC Library
1 Financial Plaza
Hartford, CT 06103
Ph:(860)278-1150
Fax:(860)240-1002
Co. E-mail: info@reidandriege.com
URL: http://www.reidandriege.com/
Contact: Mary Ann Veenstra, Libn.
Scope: Law - tax, corporate. **Services:** Interlibrary loan; copying; Library not open to the public. **Holdings:** 10,000 books; 100 bound periodical volumes. **Subscriptions:** 30 journals and other serials.

19681 ■ Tax Executives Institute, Inc. Library
1200 G. St. NW, Ste. 300
Washington, DC 20005-3814
Ph:(202)638-5601
Fax:(202)638-5607
Co. E-mail: asktei@tei.org
URL: http://www.tei.org
Contact: Timothy J. McCormally, Exec.Dir.
Scope: Taxation; tax - legislation, administration, management. **Services:** Library open to TEI members upon written request. **Holdings:** 500 books; 500 professional memoranda. **Subscriptions:** 20 journals and other serials.

19682 ■ Trumbull County Law Library Association Library
120 High St., NW
Warren, OH 44481
Ph:(330)675-2525
Fax:(330)675-2527
URL: http://www.tclla.org
Contact: George W. Baker, J.D., Dir.
Scope: Law - Ohio, labor, tax. **Services:** Copying; Library open to the public with restrictions. **Holdings:** 32,000 books; 67,000 microfiche. **Subscriptions:** 7 newspapers.

19683 ■ U.S. Dept. of the Treasury–Treasury Library
1500 Pennsylvania Ave. NW, Rm. 1428
Washington, DC 20220
Ph:(202)622-0990
Co. E-mail: library.reference@do.treas.gov
URL: http://www.ustreas.gov/offices/management/privacy-records
Contact: Judy Lim-Sharpe, Chf.Libn.
Scope: Taxation, public finance, law, domestic and International economics, economic conditions and management. **Services:** Interlibrary loan within D.C.; copying; Library open to the public by appointment for reference use only. **Holdings:** 70,000 books and bound periodical volumes; 500,000 microforms. **Subscriptions:** 300 journals and other serials; 6 newspapers.

19684 ■ U.S. Tax Court Library
400 2nd St., NW
Washington, DC 20217
Ph:(202)521-4585
Fax:(202)521-4574
Co. E-mail: tclib@ustaxcourt.gov
Contact: Elsa B. Silverman, Libn.
Scope: Federal tax law - income, estate, and gift. **Services:** Interlibrary loan; Library not open to the public. **Holdings:** 60,000 books; 9000 bound periodical volumes; Congressional Record, Federal Register, and federal tax legislation. **Subscriptions:** 200 journals and other serials.

19685 ■ Willamette Management Associates Library
8600 W. Bryn Mawr Ave., Ste. 950
Chicago, IL 60631
Ph:(773)399-4300

Fax:(773)399-4310
Co. E-mail: vaplatt@willamette.com
URL: http://www.willamette.com
Contact: Victoria A. Platt, Info.Spec.
Scope: Business valuation, tax, gift and estate, finance. **Services:** Interlibrary loan; copying. Library not open to the public.

19686 ■ Zuckerman Spaeder LLP Library
1800 M. St., NW, Ste. 1000
Washington, DC 20036
Ph:(202)778-1878
Fax:(202)822-8106
Co. E-mail: jfaubell@zuckerman.com
URL: http://www.zuckerman.com
Contact: Jeanne Trahan Faubell, Lib.Dir.
Scope: Law - bankruptcy, business and corporate law, securities litigation, political law, real estate; civil and criminal litigation, American Indian law. **Services:** Interlibrary loan; copying; Library open to the public with restrictions. **Holdings:** 4500 volumes. **Subscriptions:** 35 journals and other serials; 10 newspapers.

RESEARCH CENTERS

19687 ■ American Institute for Economic Research
250 Division St.
PO Box 1000
Great Barrington, MA 01230
Ph:(413)528-1216
Free: 888—528-1216
Fax:(413)528-0103
Co. E-mail: info@aier.org
URL: http://www.aier.org
Contact: Charles Murray, Pres./CEO
E-mail: info@aier.org
Scope: Economic and financial problems as applicable to individuals as well as private and public organizations, including all aspects of personal, community, and governmental economic and financial problems, money and banking, governmental fiscal policies, industrial development and production, domestic and foreign aid, taxation, life insurance, retirement, and investments. **Publications:** Economic Education Bulletin (monthly); Research reports (semimonthly). **Educational Activities:** Conferences and consultations with educators and economists; Summer program for graduate students, two available for 4-weeks.

19688 ■ American Law Institute
4025 Chestnut St.
Philadelphia, PA 19104
Ph:(215)243-1600
Fax:(215)243-1636
Co. E-mail: lliebman@law.columbia.edu
URL: http://www.ali.org
Contact: Prof. Lance Liebman, Dir.
E-mail: lliebman@law.columbia.edu
Scope: Tax law, property law, commercial law, tort law, international law, family law, and law of trusts. **Publications:** ALI Reporter; Annual meeting proceeding; Annual report; Model Penal Code and the Uniform Commercial Code (occasionally); Principles of the Law (occasionally); Restatements of the Law (periodically).

19689 ■ Auburn University–Center for Governmental Services
2236 Haley Ctr.
Auburn University, AL 36849-5268
Ph:(334)844-4781
Free: 800—446-0376
Fax:(334)844-1919
Co. E-mail: vealdon@auburn.edu
URL: http://www.auburn.edu/outreach/cgs
Contact: Dr. Don-Terry Veal, Dir.
E-mail: vealdon@auburn.edu
Scope: Special topics and issues to broaden understanding of public policy and to promote informed decision making. Conducts research in the public sector, including government in Alabama, local government finance, election administration, taxation, and public management. Conducts program evaluations and designs municipal and county personnel and finance systems. Also conducts telephone and mail survey research services for state and local government and university researchers of attitudes and opinions, citizen satisfaction, public policy assessment, and demographic analysis. **Services:** Technical assistance, to municipalities, counties, and state agencies in solving specific problems. **Educational Activities:** Annual County Government Officials Conference, on management; Annual Public Personnel Administrators Conference.

19690 ■ Canadian Tax Foundation–L'Association Canadienne d'Études Fiscales
595 Bay St., Ste. 1200
Toronto, ON, Canada M5G 2N5
Ph:(416)599-0283
Free: 877—733-0283
Fax:(416)599-9283
Co. E-mail: lchapman@ctf.ca
URL: http://www.ctf.ca
Contact: Larry Chapman, Exec.Dir./CEO
E-mail: lchapman@ctf.ca
Scope: Taxation and public finance, including both staff and sponsored studies on federal, provincial, and municipal taxes and expenditures, and intergovernmental fiscal trends. **Services:** Information service, for members. **Publications:** Annual Conference Report; Annual Report (monthly); Canadian Tax Highlights (monthly); Canadian Tax Journal (bimonthly); Canadian Tax Papers Series (occasionally); Finances of the Nation (annually); Tax Memos; Tax for the Owner Manager (quarterly); Taxation of Private Corporations and Their Shareholders (occasionally). **Educational Activities:** National tax and corporate management tax conferences (annually); Regional conferences (annually).

19691 ■ Cascade Policy Institute
4850 SW Scholls Ferry Rd., Ste. 103
Portland, OR 97225
Ph:(503)242-0900
Fax:(503)242-3822
Co. E-mail: info@cascadepolicy.org
URL: http://www.cascadepolicy.org
Contact: John A. Charles Jr., Pres./CEO
E-mail: info@cascadepolicy.org
Scope: Explores voluntary market-oriented answers to national, regional, and state public policy issues. Areas of research include environment, education, transportation, healthcare and taxation. **Publications:** Cascade Commentaries (weekly); Cascade Quickpoints (weekly); Cascade Update (semiannually). **Educational Activities:** Intern program, summer program for graduate students; Lecture series (annually), features national experts.

19692 ■ Citizens for Tax Justice
1616 P St. NW, Ste. 200
Washington, DC 20036
Ph:(202)299-1066
Fax:(202)299-1065
Co. E-mail: ctj@tasctj.org
URL: http://www.ctj.org
Contact: Robert S. McIntyre, Dir.
E-mail: ctj@tasctj.org
Scope: Federal, state and local tax systems. **Publications:** CTJ Update (quarterly); Studies and analyses.

19693 ■ Competitive Enterprise Institute
1899 L St. NW, 12th Fl.
Washington, DC 20036
Ph:(202)331-1010
Fax:(202)331-0640
Co. E-mail: info@cei.org
URL: http://cei.org
Contact: Fred L. Smith Jr., Founder/Pres.
E-mail: info@cei.org
Scope: Domestic economic policy issues, including deregulation of industry, deficit reduction, privatization, antitrust, free trade, free-market environmentalism, intellectual property, technology and innovation, transportation deregulation, global warming, entrepreneurship and risk and insurance. **Publications:** CEI Planet (bimonthly). **Awards:** Julian Simon Award (annually); Warren Brookes Journalism Fellowship.

19694 ■ Employee Benefit Research Institute
1100 13 St. NW, Ste. 878
Washington, DC 20005
Ph:(202)659-0670
Fax:(202)775-6312
Co. E-mail: salisbury@ebri.org
URL: http://www.ebri.org
Contact: Dallas L. Salisbury, Pres./CEO
E-mail: salisbury@ebri.org
Scope: Employee benefits in the public and private sectors, including studies on individual retirement accounts, retirement income, flexible benefits, financing health care for the elderly, health care costs, long-term care, employee benefits and federal tax policy, social security, changing benefits, and government regulation of employee benefit plans. **Services:** Congressional briefings. **Publications:** EBRI Issue Brief (monthly); EBRI Notes (monthly); Pension Investment Report (quarterly). **Educational Activities:** American Savings Education Council; Choose to Save Education Program; Fellows program, for academics, media, retirees; Policy forums (biennially). **Awards:** EBRI Lillywhite Award (annually).

19695 ■ Florida TaxWatch
PO Box 10209
Tallahassee, FL 32302
Ph:(850)222-5052
Fax:(850)222-7476
Co. E-mail: dcalabro@floridataxwatch.org
URL: http://www.floridataxwatch.org
Contact: Dominic M. Calabro, Pres./CEO
E-mail: dcalabro@floridataxwatch.org
Scope: State government productivity and cost savings, state budgeting and taxation, internal auditing, program analysis, and taxpayer education. **Publications:** Budget Watch Series; Report and Recommendations of the Government Cost Savings Task Force (annually); Research reports (occasionally). **Educational Activities:** Ideas in Action Forum. **Awards:** Prudential Financial-Davis Productivity Awards, providing cash awards and recognition to Florida's highly productive government workers.

19696 ■ The Fraser Institute
1770 Burrard St., 4th Fl.
Vancouver, BC, Canada V6J 3G7
Ph:(604)688-0221
Free: 800—665-3558
Fax:(604)688-8539
Co. E-mail: brett.skinner@fraserinstitute.org
URL: http://www.fraserinstitute.org
Contact: Brett J. Skinner PhD, Pres.
E-mail: brett.skinner@fraserinstitute.org
Scope: Studies industrial organization, economics of discrimination, housing, marketing boards, taxation, labor markets, energy markets, the environment and other general economic issues through economic analysis. The Institute's objective is to provide a base of well-supported information about the functions of the competitive market system. **Publications:** Annual Report; Fraser Forum (monthly); Public Policy Sources and Economic Freedom of the World (10/year). **Educational Activities:** Roundtables (monthly); Seminars (periodically).

19697 ■ Free Market Foundation
2001 Plano Pky., Ste. 1600
Plano, TX 75075
Ph:(972)941-4444
Fax:(972)423-6162
Co. E-mail: info@libertyinstitute.org
URL: http://www.libertylegal.org
Contact: Kelly J. Shackelford, Pres./CEO
E-mail: info@libertyinstitute.org
Scope: Public policy, focusing on limited government, free enterprise, limited taxation, and traditional family values. **Services:** Provides public service announcements for radio stations. **Publications:** Legislative Bulletins; Lone Star Report; Voter's Guide. **Educational Activities:** Sponsors briefings on issues affecting Texas.

19698 ■ Hoover Institution on War, Revolution and Peace
434 Galvez Mall
Stanford University
Stanford, CA 94305-6010

Ph:(650)723-1754
Free: 877—466-8374
Fax:(650)723-1687
URL: http://www.hoover.org
Contact: John Raisian PhD, Dir.
Scope: Political, economic, and social change in modern times, including the study of foreign areas, economic-structural transition, U.S. foreign policy, national security affairs, geopolitical questions, international political and economic thought, U.S. government spending and taxation, federal budget deficits, welfare and income redistribution, and regulation and deregulation of industry. Analyzing social, political, and economic change and formulating a diverse range of ideas and proposals on public policy and central aspects of the research mission of the Hoover Institution. **Publications:** Essays in Public Policy; Hoover Digest; Hoover Institution Annual Report; Quarterly Newsletter; Syndicated newspaper column; Viewpoints. **Educational Activities:** National Fellows Program; Seminars and individual lectures.

19699 ■ Institute for Research on the Economics of Taxation
1710 Rhode Island Ave. NW, 11th Fl.
Washington, DC 20036
Ph:(202)463-1400
Fax:(202)463-6199
Co. E-mail: sentin@iret.org
URL: http://www.iret.org
Contact: Stephen J. Entin, Pres./Exec.Dir.
E-mail: sentin@iret.org
Scope: Examination of effects of federal, state, and local tax, spending, regulatory, and monetary policies on economic output and incomes. Advises and educates policymakers, businesses, media and individuals about progrowth, free market policy options for optimal functioning of the domestic and international economy. Also provides constructive and objective analysis of proposals for tax reform and reform of social security, medicare, and other health care programs. **Publications:** Congressional Advisory; Economic Policy Bulletin; Papers, Bylines, and testimony. **Educational Activities:** Congressional Staff Seminar Series (annually), attended by congressional staff, academic and other lecturers; Policy meetings (monthly), periodic congressional, business and media briefings on public policy issues and events.

19700 ■ International Association of Assessing Officers–Research and Technical Services Department
314 W 10th St.
Kansas City, MO 64105
Ph:(816)701-8100
Free: 800—616-4226
Fax:(816)701-8149
Co. E-mail: library@iaao.org
URL: http://www.iaao.org
Contact: Lisa Daniels, Exec.Dir.
E-mail: library@iaao.org
Scope: Conducts research and surveys for U.S., state, and local government agencies and organizations in areas of assessment administration, computer-assisted appraisal techniques, mapping in assessment, property taxation, economic development, salaries, assessment office resources, and assessment practices. **Publications:** Fair and Equitable (monthly); Journal of Property Tax Assessment and Administration (quarterly). **Educational Activities:** Conference (annually), September or October; Workshops, one-day courses.

19701 ■ League of California Cities
1400 K St., Ste. 400
Sacramento, CA 95814
Ph:(916)658-8200
Fax:(916)658-8240
Co. E-mail: okabel@cacities.org
URL: http://www.cacities.org
Contact: Chris McKenzie, Exec.Dir.
E-mail: okabel@cacities.org
Scope: Local, regional, and statewide issues in California, including administrative services, community services, employee relations, environmental quality, housing, community and economic development, public safety, revenue and taxation, and transportation and public works. **Services:** Legal Service Program, provides legal inquiry, educational, and litigation-oriented service to city attorneys. **Publications:** Priority Focus (weekly); Special interest newsletters; Special reports; Western City Magazine (monthly). **Educational Activities:** Professional development and training for elected and appointed city officials and city staff.

19702 ■ National Bureau of Economic Research
1050 Massachusetts Ave.
Cambridge, MA 02138-5398
Ph:(617)868-3900
Fax:(617)868-2742
Co. E-mail: op@nber.org
URL: http://www.nber.org
Contact: Dr. James Poterba, Pres./CEO
E-mail: op@nber.org
Scope: Quantitative analysis of American economy, including productivity, capital formation, taxation, pensions and social insurance, business cycles, financial institutions and processes, labor economics, international economic relations, health economics, and the economics of aging. **Publications:** Macroeconomics Annual; NBER Digest; NBER Reporter; Tax Policy and the Economy (annually). **Educational Activities:** Six-week summer institute for economists.

19703 ■ National Center for Policy Analysis
12770 Coit Rd., Ste. 800
Dallas, TX 75251-1339
Ph:(972)386-6272
Fax:(972)386-0924
Co. E-mail: media@ncpa.org
URL: http://www.ncpa.org
Contact: John C. Goodman PhD, Pres./CEO
E-mail: media@ncpa.org
Scope: Public policy issues, including but not limited to, taxation, health care, social security and Medicare, pensions and retirement, security, energy and the environment. **Publications:** Daily Policy Digest (daily); Health Policy Digest (weekly); NCPA Alert (bimonthly); Today at the NCPA (daily); What's New at the NCPA (weekly). **Educational Activities:** Hatton Sumners Distinguished Lecture Series; Public policy forums.

19704 ■ New York Public Interest Research Group
9 Murray St., 3rd Fl.
New York, NY 10007-2223
Ph:(212)349-6460
Fax:(212)349-1366
Co. E-mail: nyc@nypirg.org
URL: http://www.nypirg.org
Contact: Rebecca Weber, Exec.Dir.
E-mail: nyc@nypirg.org
Scope: Advocates the rights of consumers and conducts studies to protect consumer interests in such areas as toxic waste, tax policies, environmental resources, drinking water, incineration, recycling, utility rate reform, nuclear power, government and political reform, standardized testing, higher education, and mass transit. **Publications:** Council Watch; NYPIRG AGENDA (quarterly). **Educational Activities:** Conferences (3/year), throughout the state.

19705 ■ Peter G. Peterson Institute for International Economics
1750 Massachusetts Ave. NW
Washington, DC 20036-1903
Ph:(202)328-9000
Fax:(202)659-3225
Co. E-mail: kstewart@piie.com
URL: http://www.iie.com
Contact: Dr. C. Fred Bergsten, Dir.
E-mail: kstewart@piie.com
Scope: Principal research areas are finance, trade and investment, globalization, and regional and country studies. Understand the international economic issues confronting policymakers and to devise practical policy responses. Consult with government officials and nongovernment observers of international economic affairs. **Publications:** Books; Policy briefs; Policy analyses; Working papers. **Educational Activities:** Briefings on leading international economic policy issues; Policy conferences; Press conferences; Seminars.

19706 ■ Taxpayers' Federation of Illinois
430 E Vine St., Ste. A
Springfield, IL 62703
Ph:(217)522-6818
Fax:(217)522-6823
Co. E-mail: tom@iltaxwatch.org
URL: http://www.taxpayfedil.org
Contact: J. Thomas Johnson, Pres.
E-mail: tom@iltaxwatch.org
Scope: Illinois tax issues, including income, property, and sales taxes; general public policy issues, especially spending and performance analysis in areas such as education, health care, and government administration. **Services:** Lobbying. **Publications:** Annual report; Illinois Tax Facts Newsletter (monthly). **Educational Activities:** Seminars and addresses, for civic groups and legislators.

19707 ■ Texas Public Policy Foundation
900 Congress Ave., Ste. 400
Austin, TX 78701
Ph:(512)472-2700
Fax:(512)472-2728
Co. E-mail: brollins@texaspolicy.com
URL: http://www.texaspolicy.com
Contact: Brooke L. Rollins, Pres./CEO
E-mail: brollins@texaspolicy.com
Scope: State public policy issues, focusing on free enterprise, limited government, individual responsibility and freedom, tax policy, honesty in government, private initiative, economic growth, and open and responsive government. Specific areas of research include Texas fiscal policy, education, health care, transportation, insurance, telecommunications, water and natural resources, tort reform, and the role of government. **Services:** Offers information to the media, government officials, leaders in business, and the community. **Publications:** Newsletters; Policy Issue Papers; Reports; Videos. **Educational Activities:** Conferences, seminars, and policy forums; Policy Orientation for the Texas Legislature; Policy Primer Series.

19708 ■ University of Arkansas at Little Rock–Institute for Economic Advancement
2801 S University Ave.
Little Rock, AR 72204-1099
Ph:(501)569-8519
Fax:(501)569-8538
Co. E-mail: jlyoungquist@ualr.edu
URL: http://www.aiea.ualr.edu/
Contact: Jim Youngquist, Exec.Dir.
E-mail: jlyoungquist@ualr.edu
Scope: Business and economics, industrial development, labor statistics, demographics, government and taxes, economic development and U.S. census.

19709 ■ University of Michigan–Office of Tax Policy Research
Stephen M. Ross School of Business
701 Tappan St., Rm. W7715
Ann Arbor, MI 48109-1234
Ph:(734)763-3068
Fax:(734)763-4032
Co. E-mail: jslemrod@umich.edu
URL: http://www.bus.umich.edu/OTPR/
Contact: Prof. Joel Slemrod PhD, Dir.
E-mail: jslemrod@umich.edu
Scope: Tax policy, including compliance, capital gains, reform, international taxation, and income dynamics. **Publications:** Tax Research News (semiannually). **Educational Activities:** Conference on relevant tax issues (annually).

19710 ■ University of Toronto–Institute for Policy Analysis
Joseph L. Rotman School of Management
105 St. George St.
Toronto, ON, Canada M5S 3E6
Ph:(416)978-1888
Fax:(416)978-4629
Co. E-mail: ihorstmann@rotman.utoronto.ca
URL: http://www.rotman.utoronto.ca/riib/
Contact: Prof. Ig Horstmann, Co-Dir.
E-mail: ihorstmann@rotman.utoronto.ca
Scope: Analyses of social and economic policy, including studies on fiscal policy and taxation, applied econometrics, urban and regional economics,

public expenditures, non-market decision making, economics of higher education, industry studies, and macro-econometric models. **Services:** Advisory services, to decision makers within government and industry; Research training, both in quantitative analysis in social sciences. **Publications:** Annual Report; Working Papers. **Educational Activities:** Graduate instruction; Seminars; Special conferences, all for participants in its policy and economic analysis program; Workshops.

19711 ■ Utah Foundation
10 W Broadway, Ste. 307
Salt Lake City, UT 84101
Ph:(801)355-1400
Fax:(801)355-1470
Co. E-mail: steve@utahfoundation.org
URL: http://www.utahfoundation.org
Contact: Stephen J. Kroes, Pres.
E-mail: steve@utahfoundation.org
Scope: Public education, higher education, tax and fiscal policy, state economy, environment, health and welfare, etc. in Utah. **Publications:** Research Reports (5/year); Special reports (occasionally); Statistical Review of Government in Utah (biennially).

19712 ■ Washington Research Council
16300 Christensen Rd., Ste. 207
Tukwila, WA 98188
Ph:(206)467-7088
Free: 800—294-7088
Fax:(206)467-6957
Co. E-mail: rsdavis@researchcouncil.org
URL: http://www.researchcouncil.org/mx/hm.asp?id=home
Contact: Richard S. Davis, Pres.
E-mail: rsdavis@researchcouncil.org
Scope: Review and analysis of state and local government policies regarding taxation and expenditures. **Services:** Specialty research, as requested by Council members or local organizations with interests in state governmental policies. **Publications:** How Washington Compares; Special Reports; State Budget Trends; WRC Notebook (monthly). **Educational Activities:** Annual meeting, in the spring for members and guests. **Awards:** Pathfinder.

Taxicab/Van Shuttle Service

ASSOCIATIONS AND OTHER ORGANIZATIONS

19713 ■ American Public Transportation Association
1666 K St. NW, Ste. 1100
Washington, DC 20006
Ph:(202)496-4800
Fax:(202)496-4324
Co. E-mail: info@apta.com
URL: http://www.apta.com
Contact: Michael J. Scanlon, Chm.
Description: Motor bus and rapid transit systems; organizations responsible for planning, designing, constructing, financing and operating transit systems; business organizations which supply products and services to transit, academic institutions and state associations and departments of transportation. Represents the public interest in improving transit. Encourages cooperation among its members, their employees, the general public and compliance with the letter and spirit of equal opportunity principles. Seeks to: collect information relative to public transit; assist in the training, education and professional development of all persons involved in public transit; and engage in activities which promote public transit. Provides a medium for exchange of experiences, discussion, and a comparative study of public transit affairs; Promotes research. **Publications:** *Passenger Transport* (biweekly).

19714 ■ Chartered Institute of Logistics and Transport in North America–Institut agree de la logistique et des transports Amerique du Nord
275 Slater St., Ste. 900
Ottawa, ON, Canada K1P 5H9
Ph:(613)688-1438
Fax:(613)688-0966
Co. E-mail: cuylits@ciltna.com
URL: http://www.ciltna.com
Contact: Hazem Ghonima, CEO
Description: Professionals in the transportation industries. Promotes high standards of ethics and practice among members; encourages study and interest in transportation and related fields. Makes available continuing professional education opportunities to members. **Publications:** *Pegasus* (quarterly).

19715 ■ National Bus Traffic Association
111 K St. NE, 9th Fl.
Washington, DC 20002
Ph:(202)898-2700
Fax:(202)842-0850
URL: http://www.bustraffic.org
Description: Establishes by the intercity regular route bus carriers. Serves as tariff publisher for its industry. .

19716 ■ Taxicab, Limousine and Paratransit Association
3200 Tower Oaks Blvd., Ste. 220
Rockville, MD 20852
Ph:(301)984-5700
Fax:(301)984-5703
Co. E-mail: info@tlpa.org
URL: http://www.tlpa.org
Contact: Alfred LaGasse, CEO
Description: Ground transportation fleet owners operating 108,000 passenger vehicles including taxicabs, limousines, sedans, airport shuttles, paratransit, and non-emergency medical. **Publications:** *Transportation Leader* (quarterly).

19717 ■ Transportation Association of Canada–Association des Transports du Canada
2323 St. Laurent Blvd.
Ottawa, ON, Canada K1G 4J8
Ph:(613)736-1350
Fax:(613)736-1395
Co. E-mail: secretariat@tac-atc.ca
URL: http://www.tac-atc.ca
Contact: Raymond Mantha, Pres.
Description: Government agencies and private organizations involved in transportation. Maintains technical information service; compiles statistics.

19718 ■ United Motorcoach Association
113 S West St., 4th Fl.
Alexandria, VA 22314-2824
Ph:(703)838-2929
Free: 800-424-8262
Fax:(703)838-2950
Co. E-mail: info@uma.org
URL: http://www.uma.org
Contact: Victor S. Parra, Pres./CEO
Description: Represents bus and motorcoach companies. Concerns itself with issues related to buses such as safety standards and regulations. **Publications:** *Operating Ratio Study*; *Safety and Courtesy Video*;Membership Directory (annual).

REFERENCE WORKS

19719 ■ "21st Century Filling Station" in *Austin Business JournalInc.* (Vol. 29, December 11, 2009, No. 40, pp. 1)
Pub: American City Business Journals
Ed: Jacob Dirr. **Description:** Clean Energy Fuels Corporation announced plans for the construction of a $1 million, 17,000 square foot compressed natural gas fueling station at or near the Austin-Bergstrom International Airport (ABIA). Clean Energy Fuels hopes to encourage cab and shuttle companies in the ABIA to switch from gasoline to natural gas.

19720 ■ "Business Start-Up a Learning Experience for Young Bellingham Entrepreneur" in *Bellingham Herald* (July 18, 2010)
Pub: Bellingham Herald
Ed: Dave Gallagher. **Description:** Profile of 21-year-old entrepreneur, Chase Larabee, who developed an online program that helps airport fixed-based operators handle refueling, hotel and transportation reservations and other requests from private airplane pilots.

19721 ■ "City's Streetcar Utility Estimate Way Off Mark" in *Business Courier* (Vol27, November 19, 2010, No. 29. , pp. 1)
Pub: Business Courier
Ed: Dan Monk, Lucy May. **Description:** Duke Energy Corporation has released new estimates that show moving electric and gas lines alone for Cincinnati, Ohio's proposed streetcar project could cost more than $20 million. However, the city has only estimated the relocation to cost $5 million in federal grant applications.

19722 ■ "Funkhouser Wants Region to Get On Board Light Rail" in *Business Journal-Serving Metropolitan Kansas City* (November 30, 2007)
Pub: American City Business Journals, Inc.
Ed: Suzanna Stagemeyer. **Description:** Mark Funhouser, Mayor of Kansas City, is planning to construct a regional multimodal public transit system. A previous light rail plan was rescinded due to logistical, financial and legal problems. Details of the light transit plans are discussed.

19723 ■ *How to Start a Home-Based Senior Care Business: Check-in-Care, Transportation Services, Shopping and Cooking*
Pub: The Globe Pequot Press
Ed: James L. Ferry. **Released:** January 1, 2010. **Price:** $18.95. **Description:** Information is provided to start a home-based senior care business.

19724 ■ "MV Transportation Winds $133M Contract" in *Black Enterprise* (Vol. 38, November 2007, No. 4, pp. 30)
Pub: Earl G. Graves Publishing Co. Inc.
Ed: Marcia A. Wade. **Description:** MV Transportation won a $133 million contract to operate 139 fixed-route buses in the San Gabriel and Pomona valley areas of California.

19725 ■ "People; E-Commerce, Online Games, Mobile Apps" in *Advertising Age* (Vol. 80, October 19, 2009, No. 35, pp. 14)
Pub: Crain's Communications
Ed: Nat Ives. **Description:** Profile of People Magazine and the ways in which the publisher is moving its magazine forward by exploring new concepts in a time of declining newsstand sales and advertising pages; among the strategies are e-commerce such as the brand People Style Watch in which consumers are able highlight clothing and jewelry and then connect to retailers' sites and a channel on Taxi TV, the network of video-touch screens in New Your City taxis.

19726 ■ "People; E-Commerce, Online Games, Mobile Apps: This Isn't Your Mom's People" in *Advertising Age* (Vol. 80, October 19, 2009, No. 35)
Pub: Crain's Communications
Ed: Nat Ives. **Description:** Profile of People Magazine and the ways in which the publisher is moving its magazine forward by exploring new concepts in a time of declining newsstand sales and advertising

pages; among the strategies are e-commerce such as the brand People Style Watch in which consumers are able highlight clothing and jewelry and then connect to retailers' sites and a channel on Taxi TV, the network of video-touch screens in New Your City taxis.

19727 ■ "Taxis Are Set to Go Hybrid" in *Philadelphia Business Journal* (Vol. 30, September 16, 2011, No. 31, pp. 1)
Pub: American City Business Journals Inc.
Ed: Natalie Kostelni. **Description:** Taxis are going hybrid in several major states such as New York, California and Maryland where it is mandated, but it is yet to happen in Philadelphia, Pennsylvania with the exception of one taxi company. Freedom Taxi is awaiting Philadelphia Parking Authority's sign off.

19728 ■ *The Transportation Leader—Buyer's Guide Issue*
Pub: Taxicab, Limousine & Paratransit Association
Released: Annual, Latest edition 2009. **Publication Includes:** List of manufacturers of taxicabs, minibuses, vans, limousines, parts, service equipment, wheelchair lifts, communications systems; also includes consultants, insurance agencies, advertising services, propane or natural gas systems; dealers in used vehicles, two-way radios, and meters; and other companies servicing the for-hire vehicle fleet industry (taxicabs, limousines, vans, and minibuses). **Entries Include:** Company name, address, phone, contact person, and brief description of product or service. **Arrangement:** Alphabetical. **Indexes:** Product or service, provided by vendor.

STATISTICAL SOURCES

19729 ■ *RMA Annual Statement Studies*
Pub: Robert Morris Associates (RMA)
Released: Annual. **Price:** $175.00 2006-07 edition, $105.00. **Description:** Contains composite balance sheets and income statements for more than 360 industries, including the accounting, auditing, and bookkeeping industries. Also contains five years of comparative historical data for discerning trends. Includes 16 commonly used ratios, computed for most of the size groupings for nearly every industry.

TRADE PERIODICALS

19730 ■ *Bus Ride*
Pub: Power Trade Media L.L.C.
Contact: Maria Galioto, Marketplace Advertising
E-mail: mgalioto@busride.com
Ed: David Hubbard, Editor, david@busride.com. **Released:** Monthly. **Price:** $39; $64; $42 Canada; $69 two years Canada; $98 Canada 3 years; $75 other countries; $125 two years and other countries; $175 two years 3 years. **Description:** Magazine for managers of bus, motorcoach and transit operations.

19731 ■ *Commercial Carrier Journal*
Pub: Randall-Reilly Publishing Co.
Contact: Stacy McCants, Publisher
E-mail: smccants@rrpub.com
Released: Monthly. **Description:** Magazine containing management, maintenance, and operations information for truck and bus fleets.

19732 ■ *In the Driver's Seat*
Pub: Ontario Safety League
Ed: Terry Thompson, Editor. **Released:** Monthly. **Price:** Included in membership. **Description:** Commercial driver safety newsletter.

19733 ■ *Transportation Leader*
Pub: Taxicab, Limousine & Paratransit Association
Released: Quarterly. **Price:** $16; $26 U.S. via airmail. **Description:** Magazine for owners and operators of taxicab, limousine, livery, van, and minibus fleets. Includes information on vehicles, marketing, public relations, legal issues, industry meetings and conventions, industry products and more.

LIBRARIES

19734 ■ Alabama Department of Transportation–Research & Development Bureau–Research Library (1409)
1409 Coliseum Blvd.
Montgomery, AL 36110
Ph:(334)206-2210
Fax:(334)264-2042
Co. E-mail: harrisi@dot.state.al.us
URL: http://www.dot.state.al.us/docs
Contact: Jeffrey W. Brown, Res. & Dev.Engr.
Scope: Transportation. **Services:** Interlibrary loan; Library not open to the public. **Holdings:** 1000 books; 5000 reports. **Subscriptions:** 8 journals and other serials.

19735 ■ California State Department of Motor Vehicles–Licensing Operations Division - Research and Development Branch–Traffic Safety Research Library (2415)
2415 1st Ave., MS F-126
Sacramento, CA 95818
Ph:(916)657-3079
Fax:(916)657-8589
Co. E-mail: dluong@dvm.ca.gov
Contact: Douglas Luong, Staff Svcs.Anl.
Scope: Automobile transportation. **Services:** Copying; Library not open to the public. **Holdings:** 500 books; 10,000 bound periodical volumes; reports; manuscripts. **Subscriptions:** 20 journals and other serials.

19736 ■ Connecticut Department of Transportation–ConnDOT Library and Information Center
2800 Berlin Tpke.
Newington, CT 06111-4116
Ph:(860)594-3035
Fax:(860)594-3039
Co. E-mail: betty.ambler@po.state.ct.us
URL: http://www.ct.gov/dot/site/default.asp
Contact: Betty Ambler, Libn.
Scope: Transportation. **Services:** Interlibrary loan; copying; Library open to the public by appointment. **Holdings:** 10,000 books; 10,000 reports.

19737 ■ Kansas Department of Transportation Library
700 S.W. Harrison St.
Eisenhower State Office Bldg., 4th Fl., W.
Topeka, KS 66603-3745
Ph:(785)291-3854
Fax:(785)291-3717
Co. E-mail: library@ksdot.org
Contact: Marie Manthe, Libn.
Scope: Transportation. **Services:** Interlibrary loan; Library open to the public. **Holdings:** 3000 books; 20,000 reports; 175 CD-ROMs; 100 videos **Subscriptions:** 100 journals and other serials.

19738 ■ Kentucky Transportation Center Library
University of Kentucky
176 Raymond Bldg.
Lexington, KY 40506-0281
Ph:(859)257-2155
Free: 800-432-0719
Fax:(859)257-1815
Co. E-mail: lwhayne@engr.uky.edu
URL: http://www.kyt2.com/
Contact: Laura Whayne, Libn.
Scope: Transportation. **Services:** Interlibrary loan; copying; Library open to the public. **Holdings:** 6000 books; 9000 reports; 800 videotapes. **Subscriptions:** 300 journals and other serials.

19739 ■ K.T. Analytics, Inc. Library
885 Rosemount Rd.
Oakland, CA 94610
Ph:(510)839-7702
Fax:(510)839-9887
Scope: Parking management, transportation systems management, demand management, transit planning, congestion pricing, road tolling, fleet management, intelligent transportation systems, air quality. **Services:** Library not open to the public; **Holdings:** 500 reports; 200 manuscripts. **Subscriptions:** 10 journals and other serials.

19740 ■ Missouri Highway and Transportation Department–Division of Materials Library
PO Box 270
Jefferson City, MO 65102-0270
Ph:(573)751-6735
Fax:(573)526-5636
Co. E-mail: michael.meyerhoff@mail.modot.state.mo.us
URL: http://www.modot.org/
Contact: Mona Scott
Scope: Transportation. **Services:** Library not open to the public. **Holdings:** Figures not available.

19741 ■ Montana Department of Transportation Library
2701 Prospect Ave.
PO Box 201001
Helena, MT 59620-1001
Ph:(406)444-6338
Fax:(406)444-7204
Co. E-mail: ssillick@mt.gov
URL: http://www.mdt.mt.gov/research/unique/services.shtml
Contact: Susan Sillick
Scope: Transportation. **Services:** Interlibrary loan; copying. **Holdings:** 10,000 items; reports; CD-ROMs; video. **Subscriptions:** 10 journals and other serials.

19742 ■ New Jersey Department of Transportation–Research Library
1035 Parkway Ave.
PO Box 600
Trenton, NJ 08625-0600
Ph:(609)530-5289
Fax:(609)530-2052
Co. E-mail: library@dot.state.nj.us
URL: http://www.state.nj.us/transportation/refdata/library/
Contact: Carol Paszamant, Libn.
Scope: Transportation. **Services:** Interlibrary loan; Library open to the public by appointment. **Holdings:** 300 books; 11,000 reports. **Subscriptions:** 50 journals and other serials.

19743 ■ North Carolina Department of Transportation–Research and Development Library
PO Box 25201
Raleigh, NC 27611
Ph:(919)715-2463
Fax:(919)715-0137
Co. E-mail: rhhall@dot.state.nc.us
URL: http://www.ncdot.org/
Contact: Bob Hall
Scope: Transportation. **Services:** Interlibrary loan; copying; Library open to the public for reference use only. **Holdings:** 11,209 books; 20,021 reports; 132 videos. **Subscriptions:** 57 journals and other serials.

19744 ■ North Dakota Department of Transportation–Materials and Research Division Library
300 Airport Rd.
Bismarck, ND 58504-6005
Ph:(701)328-6901
Fax:(701)328-0310
Co. E-mail: gweisger@nd.gov
Contact: Gerri Weisgerber, Adm. Staff Off.
Scope: Transportation. **Services:** Library not open to the public. **Holdings:** 6600 reports. **Subscriptions:** 5 journals and other serials.

19745 ■ South Carolina Department of Transportation Library
955 Park St., Rm. 110
Columbia, SC 29202
Ph:(803)737-9897
Fax:(803)737-0824
Co. E-mail: adcockda@dot.state.sc.us
URL: http://www.dot.state.sc.us
Contact: Ann Adcock, Mgr.
Scope: Transportation, engineering, mass transit. **Services:** Interlibrary loan; transportation related research; Library open to the public. **Holdings:** 5500 books; 90 bound periodical volumes; 1900 reports; 250 videos. **Subscriptions:** 41 journals and other serials; 10 newspapers.

19746 ■ Vermont Agency of Transportation–Policy and Planning Division Library
133 State St.
Montpelier, VT 05633
Ph:(802)828-2544
Fax:(802)828-3983
Contact: Sandy Aja
Scope: Transportation. **Holdings:** Figures not available.

RESEARCH CENTERS

19747 ■ Southwest Region University Transportation Center
Texas Transportation Institute
Texas A&M University System
3135 TAMU
College Station, TX 77843-3135
Ph:(979)845-5815
Fax:(979)845-9761
Co. E-mail: d-burke@tamu.edu
URL: http://swutc.tamu.edu
Contact: Dock Burke, Dir.
E-mail: d-burke@tamu.edu
Scope: Transportation of passengers and property. **Educational Activities:** Graduate instruction.

DIRECTORIES OF EDUCATIONAL PROGRAMS

19748 ■ *Directory of Private Accredited Career Schools and Colleges of Technology*
Pub: Accrediting Commission of Career Schools and Colleges of Technology
Contact: Michale S. McComis, Exec. Dir.
Released: On web page. **Price:** Free. **Description:** Covers 3900 accredited post-secondary programs that provide training programs in business, trade, and technical fields, including various small business endeavors. Entries offer school name, address, phone, description of courses, job placement assistance, and requirements for admission. Arrangement is alphabetical.

VIDEOCASSETTES/ AUDIOCASSETTES

19749 ■ *Taxidermy by Video*
Allied Video Corp.
810 S. Cincinnati Ave.
PO Box 702618
Tulsa, OK 74119
Ph:(918)587-6477
Free: 800-926-5892
Fax:(918)587-1550
Co. E-mail: info@alliedvd.com
URL: http://www.alliedvd.com
Released: 1987. **Description:** This series reveals the secret techniques of professional taxidermy, covering all its aspects, including mounting and finishing. Such popular animals as the Mallard Duck, White Tail Deer and Large Mouth Bass are fully examined. **Availability:** VHS.

Teacher Supply Store

REFERENCE WORKS

19750 ■ "Commentary. On Federal Reserve's Cut of Interest Rates" in *Small Business Economic Trends* (January 2008, pp. 3)
Pub: National Federation of Independent Business
Description: Federal Reserve cut interest rates and announced its economic outlook on September 18, 2007 to stimulate spending. The cut in interest rates, however, may not help in supporting consumer spending because savers may lose interest income. The expected economic impact of the interest rate cuts and the U.S. economic outlook are also discussed.

19751 ■ "Commentary. Small Business Economic Trends" in *Small Business Economic Trends* (February 2008, pp. 3)
Pub: National Federation of Independent Business
Ed: William C. Dunkelberg, Holly Wade. **Description:** Commentary on the economic trends for small businesses in the U.S. is presented. Analysis of the U.S. Federal Reserve Board's efforts to prevent a recession is given. Reduction in business inventories is also discussed.

19752 ■ *Educational Dealer—Buyers' Guide Issue*
Pub: Fahy-Williams Publishing Inc.
Contact: J. Kevin Fahy, Publisher
E-mail: kfahy@fwpi.com
Released: Annual, August. **Publication Includes:** List of approximately 2,000 suppliers of educational materials and equipment. **Entries Include:** Company name, address, phone, products or services. **Arrangement:** Classified by product or service.

19753 ■ "Going Dutch" in *Canadian Business* (Vol. 81, October 27, 2008, No. 18, pp. 40)
Pub: Rogers Media Ltd.
Description: Experts like Philippe Bergevin suggest that current economic conditions in Canada are similar to those of the Netherlands in the 1970s. The Organisation for Economic Co-operation suggested that Canada should instead invest in sovereign wealth funds similar to Norway's policy.

19754 ■ "Risk and Reward" in *Canadian Business* (Vol. 81, October 13, 2008, No. 17, pp. 21)
Pub: Rogers Media Ltd.
Ed: Calvin Leung. **Description:** Macro-economist and currency analyst Mark Venezia believes that stable financial institutions, free-market reforms, and the role of central banks in keeping inflation and exchange rates stable could make emerging-market bonds strong performers for better future returns. Venezia's other views on emerging-market bonds are discussed.

19755 ■ "Sense and Consensus" in *Canadian Business* (Vol. 81, October 13, 2008, No. 17, pp. 22)
Pub: Rogers Media Ltd.
Ed: David Wolf. **Description:** Stock analysts' agree that earning estimates are seen to be optimistic in relation to their global economic outlook. Analysts are expected to cut earnings projections by fall because it may negatively affect the Canadian stock market. Other view on market analysis are presented.

TRADE PERIODICALS

19756 ■ *Educational Dealer*
Pub: Fahy-Williams Publishing Inc.
Contact: Kevin J. Fahy, Publisher
E-mail: kfahy@fwpi.com
Released: 5/yr. **Description:** Trade magazine for school supply dealers, distributors, and retailers. Includes articles on retailing, cataloging, marketing, management, product lines, trends, and industry news.

19757 ■ *Teacher Magazine*
Pub: Editorial Projects in Education Inc.
Ed: Virginia B. Edwards, Editor. **Released:** 9/yr. **Price:** $81. **Description:** Professional magazine for elementary and secondary school teachers.

TRADE SHOWS AND CONVENTIONS

19758 ■ Ed Expo
National School Supply and Equipment Association
NSSEA
8300 Colesville Rd., Ste. 250
Silver Spring, MD 20910
Ph:(301)495-0240
Free: 800-395-5550
Fax:(301)495-3330
Co. E-mail: NSSEA@nssea.org
URL: http://www.nssea.org
Released: Annual. **Audience:** Dealers and distributors of educational supplies. **Principal Exhibits:** Educational supplies and instructional materials. **Dates and Locations:** 2011 Apr 07-09, San Antonio, TX.

19759 ■ The School Equipment Show
National School Supply and Equipment Association
NSSEA
8300 Colesville Rd., Ste. 250
Silver Spring, MD 20910
Ph:(301)495-0240
Free: 800-395-5550
Fax:(301)495-3330
Co. E-mail: NSSEA@nssea.org
URL: http://www.nssea.org
Released: Annual. **Audience:** School supply and equipment dealers. **Principal Exhibits:** Manufacturers of school products and school equipment (excluding textbooks). **Dates and Locations:** 2011 Nov 30 - Dec 02, San Antonio, TX.

REFERENCE WORKS

19760 ■ *Customer Inter@ctions Buyer's Guide & Directory Issue*
Pub: Technology Marketing Corp.
Contact: Ray Tompkins
E-mail: rtompkins@tmcnet.com
Ed: Linda Driscoll, Editor. **Released:** Annual, December. **Price:** $25. **Publication Includes:** Over 1100 domestic and foreign suppliers of equipment, products, and services to the telecommunications/telemarketing industry. **Entries Include:** Company name, address, phone, names of key sales personnel; type of firm, sales, products and services. **Arrangement:** Alphabetical and by product. **Indexes:** Service, product.

STATISTICAL SOURCES

19761 ■ *Successful Telemarketing*
Pub: McGraw-Hill
Ed: Bob Stone and John Wyman. **Released:** 1991. **Price:** 1992 - Hardcover $19.95. **Description:** Provides information on various uses of telemarketing, including advertising, sales promotions, and fundraising.

VIDEOCASSETTES/ AUDIOCASSETTES

19762 ■ *Hot Line to Sales*
Downtown Community TV Center (DCTV)
87 Lafayette St.
New York, NY 10013
Ph:(212)966-4510
Fax:(212)226-3053
URL: http://www.dctvny.org
Released: 1985. **Price:** $395.00. **Description:** Sales should increase if the salespeople make proper use of the telephone. **Availability:** VHS; 3/4U.

19763 ■ *90 Telemarketing Selling Skills for the '90s*
American Media, Inc.
4621 121st St.
Urbandale, IA 50323-2311
Ph:(515)224-0919
Free: 888-776-8268
Fax:(515)327-2555
Co. E-mail: custsvc@ammedia.com
URL: http://www.ammedia.com
Released: 1990. **Price:** $1595.00. **Description:** Segments from various Billue seminars have been put together to provide this up-to-date course on telemarketing skills. **Availability:** VHS.

19764 ■ *90 Telemarketing Skills in 90 Minutes*
Downtown Community TV Center (DCTV)
87 Lafayette St.
New York, NY 10013
Ph:(212)966-4510
Fax:(212)226-3053
URL: http://www.dctvny.org
Released: 1985. **Price:** $495.00. **Description:** Learn how to sell by the phone from a man who doubled his income for five years straight in that line of work. **Availability:** VHS.

19765 ■ *Phoning for Profits*
1st Financial Training Services
1515 E. Woodfield Rd., Ste. 345
Schaumburg, IL 60173
Ph:(847)969-0900
Free: 800-442-8662
Fax:(847)969-0521
URL: http://www.1stfinancialtraining.com
Released: 1987. **Price:** $250.00. **Description:** Using the phone as a communication tool is a good way to increase sales. **Availability:** VHS; 3/4U.

19766 ■ *Secrets of Telemarketing Scripts*
Instructional Video
2219 C St.
Lincoln, NE 68502
Ph:(402)475-6570
Free: 800-228-0164
Fax:(402)475-6500
Co. E-mail: feedback@insvideo.com
URL: http://www.insvideo.com
Price: $75.00. **Description:** Consultant Judy Lanier demonstrates how to develop a workable telemarketing script. Shows a team of people developing a script and reveals the result. **Availability:** VHS.

19767 ■ *Selling on the Phone*
American Media, Inc.
4621 121st St.
Urbandale, IA 50323-2311
Ph:(515)224-0919
Free: 888-776-8268
Fax:(515)327-2555
Co. E-mail: custsvc@ammedia.com
URL: http://www.ammedia.com
Released: 1987. **Price:** $475.00. **Description:** A quick training film for telephone salespeople, from call planning to close. **Availability:** VHS; 3/4U.

19768 ■ *Setting Up a Telemarketing Program*
Instructional Video
2219 C St.
Lincoln, NE 68502
Ph:(402)475-6570
Free: 800-228-0164
Fax:(402)475-6500
Co. E-mail: feedback@insvideo.com
URL: http://www.insvideo.com
Price: $75.00. **Description:** Consultant Judy Lanier explains how to set up a business to business telemarketing operation, covering sales, marketing, operations, and customer base. **Availability:** VHS.

19769 ■ *Telemarketing Skills in Minutes*
American Media, Inc.
4621 121st St.
Urbandale, IA 50323-2311
Ph:(515)224-0919
Free: 888-776-8268
Fax:(515)327-2555
Co. E-mail: custsvc@ammedia.com
URL: http://www.ammedia.com
Released: 1987. **Description:** On four tapes, a thorough training program for telephone salespeople. **Availability:** VHS; 3/4U.

19770 ■ *Telephone Manners*
Encyclopedia Britannica
331 N. LaSalle St.
Chicago, IL 60654
Ph:(312)347-7159
Free: 800-323-1229
Fax:(312)294-2104
URL: http://www.britannica.com
Released: 1989. **Description:** This valuable new program demonstrates every important step in telephone usage including identifying yourself and your organization, personalizing your calls, repeating all instructions given, taking notes of important messages, remembering calls on hold, listening to the caller's mood as well as the message, using common courtesey word and conveying warmth. **Availability:** VHS; 3/4U.

19771 ■ *Telephone Selling: A New Approach*
Video Arts, Inc.
c/o Aim Learning Group
8238-40 Lehigh
Morton Grove, IL 60053-2615
Free: 877-444-2230
Fax:(416)252-2155
Co. E-mail: service@aimlearninggroup.com
URL: http://www.aimlearninggroup.com
Released: 1991. **Price:** $790.00. **Description:** Keith Einstein shares his three-point approach to telephone sales. **Availability:** VHS; 8mm; 3/4U; Special order formats.

19772 ■ *What Is Telemarketing and How Do I Get Started?*
1st Financial Training Services
1515 E. Woodfield Rd., Ste. 345
Schaumburg, IL 60173
Ph:(847)969-0900
Free: 800-442-8662
Fax:(847)969-0521
URL: http://www.1stfinancialtraining.com
Released: 1987. **Price:** $425.00. **Description:** Starting a career in telemarketing is explained in this tape. **Availability:** VHS; 3/4U.

TRADE SHOWS AND CONVENTIONS

19773 ■ Call Center Conference & Exposition
Advanstar Communications
641 Lexington Ave., 8th Fl.
New York, NY 10022
Ph:(212)951-6600

Fax:(212)951-6793
Co. E-mail: info@advanstar.com
URL: http://www.advanstar.com
Released: Annual. **Audience:** Managers of call centers, customer service and telemarketing operations, help desks, direct-marketing agencies, telcos, and other call intensive organizations. **Principal Exhibits:** Companies offering stand-alone and/or integrated products and services that improve call center productivity and profitability.

19774 ■ Incoming Call Center Management
Advanstar Communications
641 Lexington Ave., 8th Fl.
New York, NY 10022
Ph:(212)951-6600
Fax:(212)951-6793
Co. E-mail: info@advanstar.com
URL: http://www.advanstar.com
Released: Annual. **Audience:** Call Center Managers. **Principal Exhibits:** Call center industry management.

COMPUTERIZED DATABASES

19775 ■ *Big Yellow: Yellow Pages on the Web*
SuperMedia LLC
2200 W Airfield Dr.
DFW Airport, TX 75261
Free: 800-555-4833
URL: http://www.supermedia.com
Description: Provides all Business listings for the U.S., including current advertising information. Ability to search by Business name, location, heading, zip code, person, email and more. Also provides categories and hierarchies of listings for browsing. Allows creation of customized directory for personal usage. **Availability:** Online: SuperMedia LLC. **Type:** Directory.

19776 ■ *FONE*Data*
Melissa DATA Corp.
22382 Avenida Empresa
Rancho Santa Margarita, CA 92688-2112
Ph:(949)858-3000
Free: 800-MEL-ISSA
Fax:(949)589-5211
URL: http://www.melissadata.com
Description: Contains 99,000 telephone numbers with location information for areas in the United States and Canada. Enables the user to calculate the distance between two coordinates. Offers more than 10 megabytes of current phone number information. Comprises the following 4 files: Telephone Database File—provides information on area codes, city, state, county FIPS code, longitude and latitude coordinates, and ZIP Code. County Database File—contains data on 3300 counties in the United States, including FIPS code, county name, state, time zone, Area of Dominant Influence (ADI) code, Metropolitan Statistical Area (MSA) code, and county type by alphabetical rank. MSA Database File—provides MSA code, MSA name, and MSA population. Contains 350 records. DMA Database File—contains DMA code, DMA name, percent of U.S. population, DMA rank, and number of households with televisions. Contains 215 records. **Availability:** Online: Melissa DATA Corp; CD-ROM: Melissa DATA Corp. **Type:** Directory; Statistical.

RESEARCH CENTERS

19777 ■ Columbia University–Columbia Institute for Tele-Information
Uris Hall, Ste. 1A
Columbia Business School
3022 Broadway
New York, NY 10027
Ph:(212)854-4222
Fax:(212)854-1471
Co. E-mail: sr2132@columbia.edu
URL: http://www4.gsb.columbia.edu/citi/
Contact: Prof. Eli M. Noam, Dir.
E-mail: sr2132@columbia.edu
Scope: Economic, management, and policy issues of telecommunications, electronic mass-media, and computer systems. Research has focused on the continuing transformation of the information industry, specifically relating to integration and decentralization. Other areas of research include private and public networking, the economics of networks, studies of telecommunications in the U.S., Europe, the Pacific Basin, Latin America, Africa, and Western Asia, visions of the communications future, globalization of communications media, the future of local communication, video software, free speech and new electronic media, pricing of access in network industries, economics of technology adoption in the public network, American competitiveness in global information markets, specialization and performance in the personal computer industry, economics of electronic stock exchanges, marketing in the motion picture industry, quality choices in network industries, and cryptology. **Publications:** CITI Working Paper Series; Information Exchange Newsletter (semiannually). **Educational Activities:** Seminars.

ASSOCIATIONS AND OTHER ORGANIZATIONS

19778 ■ Association of Teleservices International
12 Academy Ave.
Atkinson, NH 03811
Ph:(603)362-9489
Free: (866)896-ATSI
Fax:(603)362-9486
Co. E-mail: admin@atsi.org
URL: http://www.atsi.org
Contact: Mike Fultz, Pres.

Description: Telephone answering and voice message service providers. Seeks to foster growth and development in the industry. Represents the industry before Congress and regulatory agencies; negotiates with telephone companies. Holds seminars and workshops on the latest telecommunications technology; compiles statistics. Maintains hall of fame. **Publications:** *Connections* (bimonthly); *TeleCommunicator* (biweekly).

19779 ■ Canadian Call Management Association
24 Olive St., Unit 10
Grimsby, ON, Canada L3M 2B6
Ph:(905)309-0224
Free: 800-896-1054
Fax:(905)309-0225
Co. E-mail: info@camx.ca
URL: http://www.camx.ca/call-center/index_ang.cfm
Contact: Linda Osip, Exec. Dir.

Description: Call centers and message exchanges. Promotes excellence in the handling of voice and electronic messages. Represents members' interests; facilitates technical advancement in the field of telecommunications. **Publications:** *Advisor* (bimonthly).

VIDEOCASSETTES/ AUDIOCASSETTES

19780 ■ *Telephone Manners*
Encyclopedia Britannica
331 N. LaSalle St.
Chicago, IL 60654
Ph:(312)347-7159
Free: 800-323-1229
Fax:(312)294-2104
URL: http://www.britannica.com
Released: 1989. **Description:** This valuable new program demonstrates every important step in telephone usage including identifying yourself and your organization, personalizing your calls, repeating all instructions given, taking notes of important messages, remembering calls on hold, listening to the caller's mood as well as the message, using common courtesey word and conveying warmth. **Availability:** VHS; 3/4U.

TRADE SHOWS AND CONVENTIONS

19781 ■ Incoming Call Center Management
Advanstar Communications
641 Lexington Ave., 8th Fl.
New York, NY 10022
Ph:(212)951-6600
Fax:(212)951-6793
Co. E-mail: info@advanstar.com
URL: http://www.advanstar.com
Released: Annual. **Audience:** Call Center Managers. **Principal Exhibits:** Call center industry management.

CONSULTANTS

19782 ■ Telecommunications Consultants of America
117 N Prospect Ave.
Bergenfield, NJ 07621
Ph:(201)384-0660
Free: 800-282-3411
Fax:(201)384-6751
Contact: John C. Fuhrman, President
Scope: Produces telecommunications economies through increased efficiencies and/or alternate methods. Analyzes and audits phone services, files claims and negotiates orders with the communications carrier, and designs networks and station software. Active throughout the U.S., Canada, Puerto Rico, and Mexico. Clients from all types of organizations and industries, including government. **Publications:** "Telemanagement," Prentice Hall. **Seminars:** Introduction to Telecommunications Management, a 5-day seminar.

LIBRARIES

19783 ■ Museum of Independent Telephony–Archives Collection
412 S. Campbell
Abilene, KS 67410
Ph:(785)263-2681
Fax:(785)263-0380
Co. E-mail: heritagecenterdk@sbcglobal.net
URL: http://www.heritagecenterdk.com/museum_of_independent_telephony.html
Contact: Jeff Sheets
Scope: Telephone history and technology. **Services:** Copying; collection open to the public. **Holdings:** 1000 books; 1000 bound periodical volumes; 1000 other cataloged items; 500 manuscripts; 120 boxes of loose periodicals; 150 tapes. **Subscriptions:** 10 journals and other serials.

19784 ■ Ohio Bell–Corporate Information Resource Center
45 Erieview Plaza, Rm. 820
Cleveland, OH 44114-1813
Ph:(216)822-2740
Contact: John Jakovcic, Asst.Mgr.
Scope: Business, management, telecommunications, personnel, computers, marketing, Ohio Bell and Bell System history. **Services:** Interlibrary loan; copying; Library open to the public at librarian's discretion. **Holdings:** 5000 books. **Subscriptions:** 150 journals and other serials; 10 newspapers.

Television/Radio Repair Service

ASSOCIATIONS AND OTHER ORGANIZATIONS

19785 ■ Electronics Technicians Association International
5 Depot St.
Greencastle, IN 46135
Ph:(765)653-8262
Free: 800-288-3824
Fax:(765)653-4287
Co. E-mail: eta@eta-i.org
URL: http://www.eta-i.org
Contact: Teresa Maher CSS, Pres.

Description: Skilled electronics technicians. Provides placement service; offers certification examinations for electronics technicians and satellite, fiber optics, and data cabling installers. Compiles wage and manpower statistics. Administers FCC Commercial License examinations and certification of computer network systems technicians and web and internet specialists. **Publications:** *The High-Tech News* (bimonthly).

19786 ■ International Society of Certified Electronics Technicians
3608 Pershing Ave.
Fort Worth, TX 76107-4527
Ph:(817)921-9101
Free: 800-946-0201
Fax:(817)921-3741
Co. E-mail: info@iscet.org
URL: http://www.iscet.org
Contact: Mack Blakely, Exec. Dir.

Description: Technicians in 50 countries who have been certified by the society. Seeks to provide a fraternal bond among certified electronics technicians, raise their public image and improve the effectiveness of industry education programs for technicians. Offers training programs in new electronics information. Maintains library of service literature for consumer electronic equipment, including manuals and schematics for out-of-date equipment. Offers all FCC licenses. Sponsors testing program for certification of electronics technicians in the fields of audio, communications, computer, consumer, industrial, medical electronics, radar, radio-television and video. **Publications:** *ISCET Update* (quarterly).

DIRECTORIES OF EDUCATIONAL PROGRAMS

19787 ■ *Directory of Private Accredited Career Schools and Colleges of Technology*
Pub: Accrediting Commission of Career Schools and Colleges of Technology
Contact: Michale S. McComis, Exec. Dir.

Released: On web page. **Price:** Free. **Description:** Covers 3900 accredited post-secondary programs that provide training programs in business, trade, and technical fields, including various small business endeavors. Entries offer school name, address, phone, description of courses, job placement assistance, and requirements for admission. Arrangement is alphabetical.

REFERENCE WORKS

19788 ■ "Don't' Hate the Cable Guy" in *Saint Louis Business Journal* (Vol. 31, August 5, 2011, No. 50, pp. 1)
Pub: Saint Louis Business Journal

Ed: Angela Mueller. **Description:** Charter Communications named John Birrer as senior vice president of customer experience. The company experienced problems with its customer services.

19789 ■ "For Apple, It's Showtime Again" in *Barron's* (Vol. 90, August 30, 2010, No. 35, pp. 29)
Pub: Barron's Editorial & Corporate Headquarters
Ed: Eric J. Savitz. **Description:** Speculations on what Apple Inc. will unveil at its product launch event are presented. These products include a possible new iPhone Nano, a new update to its Apple TV, and possibly a deal with the Beatles to distribute their songs over iTunes.

TRADE PERIODICALS

19790 ■ *The High-Tech News*
Pub: ETA International
Ed: Bryan Allen, Editor, bryan@eta-i.org. **Released:** Monthly. **Price:** Included in membership. **Description:** Serves member technicians with news of the Association and the electronics industry, including items on service, education, employment, management, and events. Contains information on membership, management, telecommunications, and business and technical training programs. Recurring features include editorials, news of research, letters to the editor, book reviews, and a calendar of events.

LIBRARIES

19791 ■ Antique Wireless Association Library/Museum
PO Box 421
Bloomfield, NY 14469
Co. E-mail: tpflab@aol.com
URL: http://www.antiquewireless.org
Contact: Thomas Peterson, Jr., Musm.Dir.
Scope: History of radio, television, telegraph; electricity; communication. **Services:** Library open to the public by appointment. **Holdings:** 2000 books; 5000 radio/electronic magazines. **Subscriptions:** 40 journals and other serials.

ASSOCIATIONS AND OTHER ORGANIZATIONS

19792 ■ Alliance of Canadian Cinema, Television and Radio Artists
625 Church St., 3rd Fl.
Toronto, ON, Canada M4Y 2G1
Ph:(416)489-1311
Free: 800-387-3516
Fax:(416)489-8076
Co. E-mail: national@actra.ca
URL: http://www.actra.ca
Contact: Ferne Downey, Natl. Pres.
Description: Performing artists in the television, radio, film, and other recorded media. Seeks to obtain equitable compensation and safe working conditions for members. Represents members in negotiations with employers; monitors workplace conditions in the film and broadcasting industries. **Publications:** *Inter-ACTRA News* (quarterly).

19793 ■ Associated Press Broadcast
AP Broadcast News Center
1100 13th St., Ste. 700
Washington, DC 20005
Ph:(202)641-9921
Free: 800-342-5127
Co. E-mail: lperryman@ap.org
URL: http://www.apbroadcast.com
Contact: Lee Perryman, Deputy Dir. of Broadcast Services
Description: Broadcast stations in the United States that are members of the Associated Press. Advances journalism through radio and television. Cooperates with the AP in order to make available accurate and impartial news. Serves as a liaison between radio and television stations that are members of the AP and representatives of those stations. .

19794 ■ Association for Interactive Marketing
1430 Broadway, 8th Fl.
New York, NY 10018
Free: 888-337-0008
Fax:(212)391-9233
URL: http://www.interactivehq.org/
Contact: Kevin M. Nooman, Exec. Dir.
Description: Organizations, corporations, and individuals interested in the interactive television industry. Promotes the interests and image of the interactive television industry through political action and press releases. Provides reporters with research assistance, expert opinions, and contact information. Works to keep members updated on issues affecting the industry. Maintains speakers' bureau; conducts research and educational programs; offers placement service. Hosts networking events around the country, seminars, and conferences. .

19795 ■ Association of Public Television Stations
2100 Crystal Dr., Ste. 700
Arlington, VA 22202
Ph:(202)654-4200
Fax:(202)654-4236
Co. E-mail: pbutler@apts.org
URL: http://www.apts.org
Contact: Patrick Butler, Pres./CEO
Description: Public television licensees whose goal is to organize efforts of public television stations in areas of planning and research and in representation before the government. Maintains current information on the public television system including such areas as licensee characteristics, financing and industry trends; makes projections on system growth and income. Monitors social, economic and demographic trends that have an impact on public television services. Prepares and disseminates general information about public television to policymaking agencies, the press, and the public. **Publications:** *Communique* (quarterly); *Transitions* (quarterly); *Update* (quarterly).

19796 ■ Broadcast Cable Credit Association
550 W Frontage Rd., Ste. 3600
Northfield, IL 60093
Ph:(847)881-8757
Fax:(847)784-8059
Co. E-mail: info@bccacredit.com
URL: http://www.bccacredit.com
Contact: Mary M. Collins, Pres./CEO
Description: A subsidiary of the Broadcast Cable Financial Management Association. Television and radio stations; cable television networks; national sales representatives. Provides industry specific credit reports on individual agencies, advertisers, or buying services (local or national). **Publications:** *BCCA Credit Handbook* (annual); *Credit and Collection Survey*; *The Financial Manager for the Media Professional/Credit Topics* (bimonthly); *Update* (monthly).

19797 ■ Broadcast Education Association
1771 N St. NW
Washington, DC 20036-2800
Ph:(202)429-3935
Fax:(202)775-2981
Co. E-mail: 20hbirks@nab.org
URL: http://www.beaweb.org
Contact: Heather Birks, Exec. Dir.
Description: Universities and colleges; faculty and students; promotes improvement of curriculum and teaching methods, broadcasting research, television and radio production, and programming teaching on the college level. **Publications:** *Journal of Broadcasting and Electronic Media* (quarterly).

19798 ■ Cabletelevision Advertising Bureau
830 Third Ave., 2nd Fl.
New York, NY 10022
Ph:(212)508-1200
Fax:(212)832-3268
Co. E-mail: joleenm@cabletvadbureau.com
URL: http://www.thecab.tv
Contact: Mr. Sean Cunningham, Pres./CEO
Description: Ad-supported cable networks. Provides marketing and advertising support to members and promotes the use of cable by advertisers and ad agencies locally, regionally, and nationally. **Publications:** *Cable Network Profiles* (annual); *TV Facts* (annual).

19799 ■ Canadian Association of Broadcasters–Association Canadienne des Radiodiffuseurs
PO Box 627, Sta. B
Ottawa, ON, Canada K1P 5S2
Ph:(613)233-4035
Fax:(613)233-6961
Co. E-mail: cab@cab-acr.ca
URL: http://www.cab-acr.ca
Contact: Mr. Elmer Hildebrand, Chm.
Description: Collective voice of the majority of Canada's private radio and television stations, networks, and specialty services. Develops industry-wide strategic plans, works to improve the financial health of the industry, and promotes private broadcasting's role as Canada's leading programmer and local service provider.

19800 ■ CTAM - Cable and Telecommunications Association for Marketing
201 N Union St., Ste. 440
Alexandria, VA 22314
Ph:(703)549-4200
Fax:(703)684-1167
Co. E-mail: info@ctam.com
URL: http://www.ctam.com
Contact: Char Beales, Pres./CEO
Description: Network of cable and telecommunications professionals dedicated to the pursuit of marketing excellence. Provides its members with competitive marketing resources including education, research, networking and leadership opportunities. **Publications:** *CTAM Quarterly Journal* (quarterly).

19801 ■ International Radio and Television Society Foundation
420 Lexington Ave., Ste. 1601
New York, NY 10170
Ph:(212)867-6650
Fax:(212)867-6653
Co. E-mail: membership@irts.org
URL: http://www.irts.org
Contact: Joyce M. Tudryn, Pres.
Description: Individuals interested in management, sales, or executive production in the radio, television, and cable industries and their allied fields. Seeks to educate members through seminars. Conducts summer internships for college students majoring in communications. **Publications:** *International Radio and Television Society Foundation—Roster Yearbook* (annual).

19802 ■ Jones/NCTI
9697 E Mineral Ave.
Centennial, CO 80112
Ph:(303)797-9393
Free: (866)575-7206
Fax:(303)797-9394
Co. E-mail: info@jonesncti.com
URL: http://www.jonesncti.com
Contact: Glenn R. Jones, Chm./CEO
Description: Provides comprehensive broadband training for the cable television industry. Offers career training resources and courses in areas ranging from

customer service procedures to optical fiber system design, installation, and maintenance. **Publications:** *Spanish/English CATV Dictionary* .

19803 ■ National Association of Broadcasters
1771 N St. NW
Washington, DC 20036
Ph:(202)429-5300
Fax:(202)429-4199
Co. E-mail: nab@nab.org
URL: http://www.nab.org
Contact: Gordon H. Smith, Pres./CEO
Description: Serves as the voice for the nation's radio and television broadcasters. Advances the interests of members in federal government, industry and public affairs; improves the quality and profitability of broadcasting; encourages content and technology innovation; and spotlights the important and unique ways stations serve their communities. Delivers value to its members through advocacy, education and innovation. Relies on the grassroots strength of its television and radio members and state broadcast associations. Helps broadcasters seize opportunities in the digital age. Offers broadcasters a variety of programs to help them grow in their careers, promote diversity in the workplace and strengthen their businesses. .

19804 ■ National Association of Television Program Executives
5757 Wilshire Blvd., Penthouse 10
Los Angeles, CA 90036-3681
Ph:(310)453-4440
Fax:(310)453-5258
Co. E-mail: info@natpe.org
URL: http://www.natpe.org
Contact: Rick Feldman, Pres./CEO
Description: Program directors of television stations, networks, and multiple station groups; persons engaged in television programming (including cable, DBS and multimedia) or production; representatives of related businesses, such as station representatives, advertising agencies, film and package show producers and distributors and research organizations. Seeks to contribute to the improvement of television programming by providing a forum for discussion of ideas and exchange of information concerning programming, production and related fields. Maintains NATPE Educational Foundation. Sponsors faculty development program, seminars and international exchange program. Sponsors six faculty internships. .

19805 ■ National Cable and Telecommunications Association
25 Massachusetts Ave. NW, Ste. 100
Washington, DC 20001-1413
Ph:(202)222-2300
Fax:(202)222-2514
Co. E-mail: webmaster@ncta.com
URL: http://www.ncta.com
Contact: Michael Powell, Pres./CEO
Description: Franchised cable operators, programmers, and cable networks; associate members are cable hardware suppliers and distributors; affiliate members are brokerage and law firms and financial institutions; state and regional cable television associations cooperate, but are not affiliated, with the organization. Serves as national medium for exchange of experiences and opinions through research, study, discussion, and publications. Represents the cable industry before Congress, the Federal Communications Commission and various courts on issues of primary importance. Conducts research program in conjunction with National Academy of Cable Programming. Sponsors, in conjunction with Motion Picture Association of America, the Coalition Opposing Signal Theft, an organization designed to deter cable signal theft and to develop anti-piracy materials. Provides promotional aids and information on legal, legislative and regulatory matters. Compiles statistics. **Publications:** *Cable Industry Overview* (semiannual).

19806 ■ North American Broadcasters Association
PO Box 500, Sta. A
Toronto, ON, Canada M5W 1E6
Ph:(416)598-9877
Fax:(416)598-9774
Co. E-mail: contact@nabanet.com
URL: http://www.nabanet.com/nabaweb
Contact: Leonardo Ramos Mateos, Pres.
Description: Network broadcasters in North America concerned with international matters that affect broadcasting. Seeks to identify, study and provide solutions to international questions concerning broadcasting. Creates opportunities for North American broadcasters to share information, identify common interests and reach on issues of an international nature. Works with other international broadcasters' associations and unions toward gaining an effective voice in international circles on matters that affect broadcasting. Organizes international conferences in conjunction with other broadcasting associations.

19807 ■ Public Broadcasting Management Association
939 S Stadium Rd.
Columbia, SC 29201-4724
Ph:(803)799-5517
Fax:(803)771-4831
Co. E-mail: rick@pbma.org
URL: http://www.pbma.org
Contact: Rick Lehner, Exec. Dir.
Description: Represents finance, human resources, information systems, and administrative managers in public broadcasting. .

19808 ■ Radio-Television News Directors' Association
2175 Sheppard Ave. E, Ste. 310
Toronto, ON, Canada M2J 1W8
Ph:(416)756-2213
Free: 877-25R-TNDA
Fax:(416)491-1670
Co. E-mail: info@rtndacanada.com
URL: http://www.rtndacanada.com
Contact: Andy LeBlanc, Pres.
Description: Radio and television news executives and personnel. Promotes the professional development of broadcast journalists in Canada. Sponsors national scholarship program.

19809 ■ Television Bureau of Advertising
3 E 54th St., 10th Fl.
New York, NY 10022-3108
Ph:(212)486-1111
Fax:(212)935-5631
Co. E-mail: info@tvb.org
URL: http://www.tvb.org
Contact: Steve Lanzano, Pres./CEO
Description: Television stations, station sales representatives, and program producers/syndicates. Strives to increase advertiser dollars to U.S. spot television. Represents television stations to the advertising community. .

DIRECTORIES OF EDUCATIONAL PROGRAMS

19810 ■ *Directory of Private Accredited Career Schools and Colleges of Technology*
Pub: Accrediting Commission of Career Schools and Colleges of Technology
Contact: Michale S. McComis, Exec. Dir.
Released: On web page. **Price:** Free. **Description:** Covers 3900 accredited post-secondary programs that provide training programs in business, trade, and technical fields, including various small business endeavors. Entries offer school name, address, phone, description of courses, job placement assistance, and requirements for admission. Arrangement is alphabetical.

REFERENCE WORKS

19811 ■ "10 Trends That Are Shaping Global Media Consumption" in *Advertising Age* (Vol. 81, December 6, 2010, No. 43, pp. 3)
Pub: Crain Communications, Inc.
Ed: Ann Marie Kerwin. **Description:** Ad Age offers the statistics from the TV penetration rate in Kenya to the number of World Cup watchers and more.

19812 ■ "A&E Networks" in *Brandweek* (Vol. 49, April 21, 2008, No. 16, pp. SR9)
Pub: VNU Business Media, Inc.
Ed: Anthony Crupi. **Description:** Provides contact information for sales and marketing personnel for the A&E Networks as well as a listing of the station's top programming and an analysis of the current season and the target audience for those programs running in the current season. A&E has reinvented itself as a premium entertainment brand over the last five years and with its $2.5 million per episode acquisition of The Sopranos, the station signaled that it was serious about getting back into the scripted programming business. The acquisition also helped the network compete against other cable networks and led to a 20 percent increase in prime-time viewers.

19813 ■ "ABC" in *Brandweek* (Vol. 49, April 21, 2008, No. 16, pp. SR6)
Pub: VNU Business Media, Inc.
Ed: John Consoli. **Description:** Provides contact information for sales and marketing personnel for the ABC network as well as a listing of the station's top programming and an analysis of the current season and the target audience for those programs running in the current season.

19814 ■ "ACTRA Phones It In" in *Canadian Business* (Vol. 80, January 15, 2007, No. 2, pp. 8)
Pub: Rogers Media
Ed: Denis Seguin. **Description:** The strike held by the members of the ACTRA or Canadian Cinema, Television and Radio Artists from January 8 2007, due to the contract dispute with the trade association representing Canadian producers, is discussed.

19815 ■ "Advertisers Don't Party With CBS's Swingers" in *Advertising Age* (Vol. 79, July 7, 2008, No. 26, pp. 1)
Pub: Crain Communications, Inc.
Ed: Brian Steinberg. **Description:** Broadcast networks that are trying to air edgier programming such as CBS's "Swingtown" but are running into problems with advertisers who are fearful of consumer complaints and backlash when running commercials during such fare.

19816 ■ "Advertising May Take a Big Hit in Southwest/AirTran Merger" in *Baltimore Business Journal* (Vol. 28, October 1, 2010, No. 21, pp. 1)
Pub: Baltimore Business Journal
Ed: Gary Haber. **Description:** Advertising on television stations and the publishing industry in Baltimore could drop as a result of the merger between rival discount airlines Southwest Airlines and AirTran Airways. Southwest is among the top advertisers in the U.S., spending $126 million in 2009. No local jobs are expected to be affected because neither airline uses a local advertising firm.

19817 ■ "Alliance Atlantis Takes a Cheekier Attitude to Life" in *Globe & Mail* (March 5, 2007, pp. B5)
Pub: CTVglobemedia Publishing Inc.
Ed: Keith McArthur. **Description:** Alliance Atlantis Communications Inc. is re-branding its human life ministry Life Network specialty channel as Slice. The new channel is being promoted with an advertising campaign.

19818 ■ "As Seen On TV" in *Canadian Business* (Vol. 80, November 5, 2007, No. 22, pp. 93)
Pub: Rogers Media
Ed: Zena Olijnyk. **Description:** StarBrand Media Inc. is one of the companies providing fans with information on how and where to purchase the items that television characters are using. StarBrand created the style section found on different television shows' Websites, such as that of the Gossip Girl and Smallville. The benefits of using sites like StarBrand are evaluated.

19819 ■ "Astral Media Set to Broadcast Coast to Coast" in *Globe & Mail* (February 24, 2007, pp. B5)
Pub: CTVglobemedia Publishing Inc.
Ed: Grant Robertson. **Description:** The decision of Astral Media Inc. to acquire Standard Broadcasting

Corp. Ltd. for $1.2 billion, with a view to increase its broadcast coverage, is discussed.

19820 ■ "At 5-Year Mark, News 9 Makes Presence Felt in Competition for Ad Dollars" in *Business Review, Albany New York* (October 5, 2007)
Pub: American City Business Journals, Inc.
Ed: Barbara Pinckney. **Description:** The 24-hour news channel Capital News 9 can be watched live by viewers on their cell phones beginning late 2007 or early 2008 as part of a deal between Time Warner Cable and Sprint Nextel Corporation to bring Sprint's Pivot technology. News 9 marked its fifth year and plans to continue expanding coverage and provide better services to viewers.

19821 ■ "Autoline Goes West" in *Michigan Vue* (Vol. 13, July-August 2008, No. 4, pp. 6)
Pub: Entrepreneur Media Inc.
Ed: Dave Gibbons. **Description:** Profile of Blue Sky Productions, a Detroit-based production company that produces the nationally syndicated television series "Autoline", which traditionally probes inside the Detroit auto industry; the company recently decided to shoot in Southern California, an area that now has an immense auto industry but has been virtually ignored by the media. Blue Sky originally slated four shows but ended up producing eleven due to the immense amount of material they discovered concerning the state of California's auto market.

19822 ■ *Bacon's Radio/TV/Cable Directory, Volume 1*
Pub: Cision US Inc.
Contact: Stephen Newman, CEO
Released: Annual, Latest edition 2012. **Price:** $650, individuals. **Covers:** over 13,500 radio and television stations, including college radio and public television stations, and cable companies. **Entries Include:** For radio and television stations—Call letters, address, phone, names and titles of key personnel, programs, times broadcast, name of contact, network affiliation, frequency or channel number, target audience data. For cable companies—Name, address, phone, description of activities. **Arrangement:** Geographical.

19823 ■ "The Best Five-Month Run Since 1938" in *Barron's* (Vol. 89, August 3, 2009, No. 31, pp. M3)
Pub: Dow Jones & Co., Inc.
Ed: Kopin Tan. **Description:** US stock markets ended July 2009 registering the highest five-month rise since 1938. The shares of Cablevision could rise as the company simplifies its structure and spins off its Madison Square Garden unit. The shares of Potash Corp. could fall as the company faces lower earnings due to falling potash purchases.

19824 ■ "Betting on a Happy Ending" in *Barron's* (Vol. 88, July 7, 2008, No. 27, pp. 14)
Pub: Dow Jones & Co., Inc.
Ed: Dimitra DeFotis. **Description:** Shares of Time Warner, priced at $14.69 each, appear under-priced as financial analysts discount the value of the company. The company should be worth more than $20 a share as the company is spinning off Time Warner Cable.

19825 ■ "'Biggest Loser' Adds Bit of Muscle to Local Economy" in *Crain's Detroit Business* (Vol. 26, January 4, 2010, No. 1, pp. 1)
Pub: Crain Communications, Inc.
Ed: Chad Halcom. **Description:** NBC's weight-loss reality show, "The Biggest Loser" has helped the local economy and generated a new crop of local startup businesses due to past contestants that were from the Detroit area.

19826 ■ "Black Network Shifts Gears: Struggling Channel To Focus On Broadband TV" in *Black Enterprise* (Vol. 38, November 2007, No. 4, pp. 34)
Pub: Earl G. Graves Publishing Co. Inc.
Ed: Wendy Isom. **Description:** Rick Newberger, president and CEO of Black Family Channel's television platform discusses its plans to switch to broadband format programming offering various channels simultaneously with fewer costs.

19827 ■ "Branding Specialist" in *Black Enterprise* (Vol. 38, July 2008, No. 12, pp. 1)
Pub: Earl G. Graves Publishing Co. Inc.
Ed: Faith Chukwudi. **Description:** Interview with Wonya Lucas who is the chief marketing officer for Discovery Communications and is known for building strong brands by understanding her audience and generating buy-in throughout the organization; Lucas discusses her role in the corporation, guerilla marketing techniques, and what companies tend to overlook in marketing their products or services.

19828 ■ *Broadcast Engineering—Equipment Reference Manual*
Pub: Penton Media Inc.
Contact: Brad Dick, Editorial Dir.
E-mail: bdick@primediabusiness.com
Released: Annual, fall. **Publication Includes:** List of more than 1,400 manufacturers and distributors of communications equipment for radio, television, and recording applications. **Entries Include:** For manufacturers—Company name, address. For distributors and dealers—Company name, address, phone, product or service provided, geographic area covered. **Arrangement:** Manufacturers are alphabetical; dealers and distributors are geographical. **Indexes:** Product/service.

19829 ■ *Broadcasting & Cable Yearbook*
Pub: R.R. Bowker L.L.C.
Released: Annual, latest edition 2010. **Price:** $395, individuals softbound. **Covers:** Over 17,000 television and radio stations in the United States, its territories, and Canada; cable MSOs and their individual systems; television and radio networks, broadcast and cable group owners, station representatives, satellite networks and services, film companies, advertising agencies, government agencies, trade associations, schools, and suppliers of professional and technical services, including books, serials, and videos; communications lawyers. **Entries Include:** Company name, address, phone, fax, names of executives. Station listings include broadcast power, other operating details. **Arrangement:** Stations and systems are geographical, others are alphabetical. **Indexes:** Alphabetical.

19830 ■ "CBC Eyes Partners for TV Downloads" in *Globe & Mail* (February 9, 2006, pp. B1)
Pub: CTVglobemedia Publishing Inc.
Ed: Grant Robertson. **Description:** The details on Canadian Broadcasting Corp.'s distribution agreement with Google Inc. and Apple Computer Inc. are presented.

19831 ■ "CBS" in *Brandweek* (Vol. 49, April 21, 2008, No. 16, pp. SR6)
Pub: VNU Business Media, Inc.
Ed: John Consoli. **Description:** Provides contact information for sales and marketing personnel for the CBS network as well as a listing of the station's top programming and an analysis of the current season and the target audience for those programs running in the current season.

19832 ■ "CBS Television Distribution" in *Brandweek* (Vol. 49, April 21, 2008, No. 16, pp. SR13)
Pub: VNU Business Media, Inc.
Ed: Marc Berman. **Description:** Provides contact information for sales and marketing personnel for CBS Television Distribution as well as a listing of the station's top programming and an analysis of the current season and the target audience for those programs running in the current season. Due to the unprecedented, decade-plus advantage of first-run leaders such as Wheel of Fortune, Oprah, Judge Judy and Entertainment Tonight, CBS is poised to remain a leader among the syndicates.

19833 ■ "Comcast Networks" in *Brandweek* (Vol. 49, April 21, 2008, No. 16, pp. SR9)
Pub: VNU Business Media, Inc.
Ed: Anthony Crupi. **Description:** Provides contact information for sales and marketing personnel for the Comcast networks as well as a listing of the station's top programming and an analysis of the current season and the target audience for those programs running in the current season. Experts believe Comcast will continue to acquire more stations into their portfolio.

19834 ■ "Commercials Make Us Like TV More" in *Harvard Business Review* (Vol. 88, October 2010, No. 10, pp. 36)
Pub: Harvard Business School Publishing
Ed: Leif Nelson. **Description:** Research indicates that people prefer commercial interruption over uninterrupted shows due to the break creating a reactivation of the initial pleasure when beginning a desirable activity.

19835 ■ *CPB Public Broadcasting Directory*
Pub: Corporation for Public Broadcasting
Released: Annual. **Covers:** Public television and radio stations, national and regional public broadcasting organizations and networks, state government agencies and commissions, and other related organizations. **Entries Include:** For radio and television stations—Station call letters, frequency or channel, address, phone, licensee name, licensee type, date on air, antenna height, area covered, names and titles of key personnel. For organizations—Name, address, phone, name and title of key personnel. **Arrangement:** National and regional listings are alphabetical; state groups and the public radio and television stations are each geographical; other organizations and agencies are alphabetical. **Indexes:** Geographical, personnel, call letter, licensee type (all in separate indexes for radio and television).

19836 ■ "CRTC Signals CHUM Deal Will Get Nod" in *Globe & Mail* (May 2, 2007, pp. B3)
Pub: CTVglobemedia Publishing Inc.
Ed: Grant Robertson. **Description:** The likely approval of Canadian Radio-Television and Telecommunications Commission to the proposed acquisition of CHUM Ltd. by CTVglobemedia Inc. is discussed.

19837 ■ "CTV's CHUM Proposal Gets Chilly Reception" in *Globe & Mail* (May 1, 2007, pp. B1)
Pub: CTVglobemedia Publishing Inc.
Ed: Grant Robertson. **Description:** The possible violation of broadcast regulations in case of acquisition of CHUM Ltd. by CTV Inc. for $1.4 billion is discussed.

19838 ■ "The CW" in *Brandweek* (Vol. 49, April 21, 2008, No. 16, pp. SR8)
Pub: VNU Business Media, Inc.
Ed: John Consoli. **Description:** Provides contact information for sales and marketing personnel for the CW network as well as a listing of the station's top programming and an analysis of the current season and the target audience for those programs running in the current season. Purchases of advertising feel that Warner Bros. and CBS made a mistake merging The WB and UPN into the new CW rather than folding UPN into the more-established WB; compared to last season ratings are down more than 20 percent across the board.

19839 ■ "Detroit Pawn Shop to be Reality TV Venue" in *UPI NewsTrack* (July 10, 2010)
Pub: United Press International-USA
Description: TruTV will present a new series called 'Hardcore Pawn' to compete with the History Channel's successful show 'Pawn Stars'. The show will feature American Jewelry and Loan in Detroit, Michigan and its owner Les Gold, who runs the store with his wife and children.

19840 ■ "Discovery Networks" in *Brandweek* (Vol. 49, April 21, 2008, No. 16, pp. SR9)
Pub: VNU Business Media, Inc.
Ed: Anthony Crupi. **Description:** Provides contact information for sales and marketing personnel for the Discovery networks as well as a listing of the station's top programming and an analysis of the current season and the target audience for those programs running in the current season. The networks flagship station returned to the top 10 in 2007, averaging 1.28 million viewers.

19841 ■ "Disney-ABC Domestic Television Distribution" in *Brandweek* (Vol. 49, April 21, 2008, No. 16, pp. SR13)
Pub: VNU Business Media, Inc.

Ed: Marc Berman. **Description:** Provides contact information for sales and marketing personnel for Disney-ABC Domestic Television Distribution as well as a listing of the station's top programming and an analysis of the current season and the target audience for those programs running in the current season.

19842 ■ "Don't' Hate the Cable Guy" in *Saint Louis Business Journal* (Vol. 31, August 5, 2011, No. 50, pp. 1)
Pub: Saint Louis Business Journal

Ed: Angela Mueller. **Description:** Charter Communications named John Birrer as senior vice president of customer experience. The company experienced problems with its customer services.

19843 ■ "The Endless Flow of Russell Simmons" in *Entrepreneur* (Vol. 37, September 2009, No. 9, pp. 24)
Pub: Entrepreneur Media, Inc.

Ed: Josh Dean. **Description:** Entrepreneur Russell Simmons has successfully grown his businesses by focusing on underserved markets. Simons has never given up on any business strategy. He has also entered the music, clothing and television industries.

19844 ■ "Exiting Stage Left" in *Baltimore Business Journal* (Vol. 28, June 18, 2010, No. 6, pp. 1)
Pub: Baltimore Business Journal

Ed: Scott Dance. **Description:** Film professionals including crew members and actors have been leaving Maryland to find work in other states such as Michigan, Louisiana, and Georgia where bigger budgets and film production incentives are given. Other consequences of this trend in local TV and film production are discussed.

19845 ■ "Fox" in *Brandweek* (Vol. 49, April 21, 2008, No. 16, pp. SR3)
Pub: VNU Business Media, Inc.

Ed: John Consoli. **Description:** Provides contact information for sales and marketing personnel for the Fox network as well as a listing of the station's top programming and an analysis of the current season and the target audience for those programs running in the current season. In terms of upfront advertising dollars, it looks as if Fox will be competing against NBC for third place due to its success at courting the 18-49-year-old male demographic.

19846 ■ "Fox Cable Entertainment Networks" in *Brandweek* (Vol. 49, April 21, 2008, No. 16, pp. SR10)
Pub: VNU Business Media, Inc.

Ed: Anthony Crupi. **Description:** Provides contact information for sales and marketing personnel for the Fox Cable Entertainment networks as well as a listing of the station's top programming and an analysis of the current season and the target audience for those programs running in the current season.

19847 ■ *Freelancing for Journalists*
Pub: Routledge

Ed: Diana Harris. **Released:** January 1, 2010. **Price:** $110.00. **Description:** Comprehensive guide showing the specific skills required for those wishing to freelance in newspapers, magazines, radio, television, and as online journalists.

19848 ■ "Hitting the Green" in *Canadian Business* (Vol. 81, July 22, 2008, No. 12-13, pp. 34)
Pub: Rogers Media Ltd.

Ed: Andy Holloway. **Description:** RBC is sponsoring the Canadian Open golf tournament, which is the second-oldest event in the PGA Tour. RBC is expected to receive television exposure on CBS and the Golf Channel. Additional information relating to the sponsorship is presented.

19849 ■ "How to Boost Your Super Bowl ROI" in *Advertising Age* (Vol. 80, December 7, 2009, No. 41, pp. 3)
Pub: Crain's Communications

Ed: Abbey Klaassen. **Description:** Internet marketing is essential, even for the corporations that can afford to spend $3 million on a 30-second Super Bowl spot; last year, Super Bowl advertising reached an online viewership of 99.5 million while 98.7 million people watched the game on television validating the idea that public relations must go farther than a mere television ad campaign. Social media provides businesses with a longer shelf life for their ad campaigns. Advice is also given regarding ways in which to strategize a smart and well-thought plan for utilizing the online marketing options currently available.

19850 ■ "It Could Be Worse" in *Barron's* (Vol. 89, July 27, 2009, No. 30, pp. 5)
Pub: Dow Jones & Co., Inc.

Ed: Alan Abelson. **Description:** Media sources are being fooled by corporate America who is peddling an economic recovery rather than reality as shown by the report of a rise in existing home sales which boosted the stock market even if it was a seasonal phenomenon. The phrase "things could be worse" sums up the reigning investment philosophy in the U.S. and this has been stirring up the market.

19851 ■ "Johnson Publishing Expands: Moving Into Television and Internet To Extend Brand" in *Black Enterprise* (October 2007)
Pub: Earl G. Graves Publishing Co. Inc.

Ed: Tamara E. Holmes. **Description:** Johnson Publishing Company has followed the lives of black families in both Ebony and Jet magazines. The media firm has expanded its coverage by developing entertainment content for television, the Internet and other digital arenas.

19852 ■ "KXAN Seeks Larger Studio, Office Space" in *Austin Business Journal* (Vol. 31, May 27, 2011, No. 12, pp. A1)
Pub: American City Business Journals Inc.

Ed: Cody Lyon. **Description:** Austin NBC affiliate KXAN Television is opting to sell its property north of downtown and relocate to another site. The station is now inspecting possible sites to house its broadcasting facility and employees totaling as many as 200 people. Estimated cost of the construction of the studios and offices is $13 million plus another million in moving the equipment.

19853 ■ "Lifetime Networks" in *Brandweek* (Vol. 49, April 21, 2008, No. 16, pp. SR10)
Pub: VNU Business Media, Inc.

Ed: Anthony Crupi. **Description:** Provides contact information for sales and marketing personnel for the ABC network as well as a listing of the station's top programming and an analysis of the current season and the target audience for those programs running in the current season. Lifetime will still produce its original signature movies but will now focus its emphasis more clearly on series development in order to appeal to a younger, hipper female demographic.

19854 ■ "Local TV Hits Media Radar Screen" in *Business Courier* (Vol. 27, July 2, 2010, No. 9, pp. 1)
Pub: Business Courier

Ed: Dan Monk. **Description:** Fort Wright, Kentucky-based broadcasting company Local TV LLC has acquired 18 television stations since its founding in 2007, potentially boosting its chances of becoming a media empire. In the last twelve months that ended in March 2010, Local TV LLC has posted total revenues of $415 million. How Local TV LLC has entered into cost-sharing deals with other stations is also discussed.

19855 ■ "Looking Like a Million Bucks" in *Entrepreneur* (Vol. 37, August 2009, No. 8, pp. 102)
Pub: Entrepreneur Media, Inc.

Ed: Jason Daley. **Description:** Sunset Tan's Jeff Bozz says he and Devin Haman are executive producers of the show and that they want to stretch the truth a bit and make fun of it. Haman says the business is all about VIP service for everyone and that they want all their clients to feel like celebrities.

19856 ■ "Marketing: You Are On the Air: Radio and TV Producers Are Looking For Shows Starring Smart CEOs" in *Inc.* (December 2007, pp. 67-69)
Pub: Gruner & Jahr USA Publishing

Ed: Sarah Goldstein. **Description:** Many successful entrepreneurs are being hired to host television and radio shows in order to share business expertise.

19857 ■ *Matthews Media Directory*
Pub: Marketwire
Contact: Lisa Davis

Released: Semiannual, Latest edition 50th. **Covers:** Daily newspapers, radio and television stations, trade magazines, networks and newswires and press galleries in Canada.

19858 ■ "MEC, Churchill Downs Saddle Up in Racing Deal" in *Globe & Mail* (March 6, 2007, pp. B1)
Pub: CTVglobemedia Publishing Inc.

Ed: Greg Keenan. **Description:** The formation of a company called TrackNet Media Group LLC by Magna Entertainment Corp. and Churchill Downs Inc. for the broadcast of horse races on television is discussed. The efforts of the two companies to revive public interest in horse racing are described.

19859 ■ *Media, Organizations and Identity*
Pub: Palgrave Macmillan

Ed: Lilie Chouliaraki, Mette Morsing. **Released:** January 19, 2010. **Price:** $90.00. **Description:** The mass media, press and television are a essential in the formation of corporate identity and the promotion of business image and reputation. This book offers a new perspective into the interrelationships between media and organizations over three dimensions: media as business, media in business and business in the media.

19860 ■ "Mentoring Support" in *Black Enterprise* (Vol. 38, July 2008, No. 12, pp. 64)
Pub: Earl G. Graves Publishing Co. Inc.

Description: With his relocation from his multicultural team in New York to the less diverse Scripps Networks' headquarters in Knoxville, Earl Cokley has made it a top priority to push for more diversity and mentoring opportunities within the management of the media and marketing company.

19861 ■ *Mississippi News Media Directory*
Pub: News Media Directories

Released: Annual, Latest edition 2010. **Price:** $45, individuals; $65, individuals CD; $85, individuals Combo-Directory and CD. **Covers:** Newspapers, periodicals, radio and television broadcasting stations, and press services operating in Mississippi. **Entries Include:** Publisher or company name, address, phone, names and titles of key personnel, publication title, call letters, hours of operation, and frequency. **Arrangement:** Classified by type of media. **Indexes:** Title, call letters, county index.

19862 ■ "Moms Dis Super Bowl Ads" in *Marketing to Women* (Vol. 21, March 2008, No. 3, pp. 6)
Pub: EPM Communications, Inc.

Description: According to a survey by the Marketing to Moms Coalition, although 80 percent of moms tune into the Super Bowl most complain that the advertisements are not appropriate for a family sports viewing experience.

19863 ■ "Moving Into the Digital Space: How New Media Create Opportunities for Minorities" in *Black Enterprise* (February 2008)
Pub: Earl G. Graves Publishing Co. Inc.

Ed: Sonia Alleyne. **Description:** The Internet is becoming an alternative to traditional sources of entertainment; nearly 16 percent of American households who use the Internet watch television online. One such Internet show features a variety of African American lifestyles.

19864 ■ "MTV Networks" in *Brandweek* (Vol. 49, April 21, 2008, No. 16, pp. SR10)
Pub: VNU Business Media, Inc.
Ed: Anthony Crupi. **Description:** Provides contact information for sales and marketing personnel for the MTV networks as well as a listing of the station's top programming and an analysis of the current season and the target audience for those programs running in the current season. MTV networks include MTV, VH1, Nickelodeon and Comedy Central.

19865 ■ "NBC" in *Brandweek* (Vol. 49, April 21, 2008, No. 16, pp. SR6)
Pub: VNU Business Media, Inc.
Ed: John Consoli. **Description:** Provides contact information for sales and marketing personnel for the NBC network as well as a listing of the station's top programming and an analysis of the current season and the target audience for those programs running in the current season. NBC also devised a new strategy of announcing its prime-time schedule 52 weeks in advance which was a hit for advertisers who felt this gave them a better opportunity to plan for product placement. Even with the station's creative sales programs, they could face a challenge from Fox in terms of upfront advertisement purchases.

19866 ■ "NBC Universal Cable" in *Brandweek* (Vol. 49, April 21, 2008, No. 16, pp. SR11)
Pub: VNU Business Media, Inc.
Ed: Anthony Crupi. **Description:** Provides contact information for sales and marketing personnel for the NBC Universal Cable networks as well as a listing of the station's top programming and an analysis of the current season and the target audience for those programs running in the current season. The network's stations include USA, Sci Fi and Bravo. Ad revenue for the network grew 30 percent in the first quarter.

19867 ■ "NBC Universal Domestic Television Distribution" in *Brandweek* (Vol. 49, April 21, 2008, No. 16, pp. SR13)
Pub: VNU Business Media, Inc.
Ed: Marc Berman. **Description:** Provides contact information for sales and marketing personnel for NBC Universal Domestic Television Distribution as well as a listing of the station's top programming and an analysis of the current season and the target audience for those programs running in the current season.

19868 ■ "Network TV" in *Canadian Business* (Vol. 79, September 11, 2006, No. 18, pp. 136)
Pub: Rogers Media
Ed: Gerry Blackwell. **Description:** The functions and features of the new Mediasmart LCD TV offered by Hewlett-Packard are discussed.

19869 ■ "New Sony HD Ads Tout Digital" in *Brandweek* (Vol. 49, April 21, 2008, No. 16, pp. 5)
Pub: VNU Business Media, Inc.
Description: Looking to promote Sony Electronics' digital imaging products, the company has launched another campaign effort known as HDNA, a play on the words high-definition and DNA; originally Sony focused the HDNA campaign on their televisions, the new ads will include still and video cameras as well and marketing efforts will consist of advertising in print, Online, television spots and publicity at various venues across the country.

19870 ■ "Nortel Makes Customers Stars in New Campaign" in *Brandweek* (Vol. 49, April 21, 2008, No. 16, pp. 8)
Pub: VNU Business Media, Inc.
Ed: Mike Beirne. **Description:** Nortel has launched a new television advertising campaign in which the business-to-business communications technology provider cast senior executives in 30-second TV case studies that show how Nortel's technology helped their businesses innovate.

19871 ■ "Not the Six O'Clock News" in *Canadian Business* (Vol. 80, January 15, 2007, No. 2, pp. 10)
Pub: Rogers Media
Ed: Marlene Rego. **Description:** The proposal by Paul Jay, the chief executive officer of Independent World Television, to launch The Real News Project, is discussed. The objective of the project is to establish an independent news and current affairs network solely through viewers.

19872 ■ "Our World with Black Enterprise" in *Black Enterprise* (Vol. 37, February 2007, No. 7, pp. 145)
Pub: Earl G. Graves Publishing Co. Inc.
Description: Our World with Black Enterprise is a television broadcast that features roundtable discussions and interviews with important African American figures.

19873 ■ "Political Ads Big Boost to Local Media" in *Baltimore Business Journal* (Vol. 28, October 22, 2010, No. 24, pp. 1)
Pub: Baltimore Business Journal
Ed: Scott Dance. **Description:** Information about the intense demand for advertising time from political campaigns in Baltimore, Maryland is provided. The surge in political advertisement spending would mean big money for local broadcasters, because they see a surging demand for local advertising time for virtually any time of day.

19874 ■ "Prime-Time Exposure" in *Inc.* (March 2008, pp. 66, 68)
Pub: Gruner & Jahr USA Publishing
Ed: Adam Bluestein. **Description:** Product placement in television shows has increase sales for many companies. Tips for placing products or services into TV shows are explained: consider hiring an agency, target efforts, dream up a plot point, be ready to go on short notice, and work the niches.

19875 ■ "Private TV Industry's Profit Climbs Four Percent" in *Globe & Mail* (March 29, 2006, pp. B6)
Pub: CTVglobemedia Publishing Inc.
Ed: Simon Tuck. **Description:** The private television industry in Canada is experiencing 4 percent increase in its profits, i.e. $242.2 millions. The revenues of CTV contributed more to this increase in profits.

19876 ■ "Pro Teams Shift Ad Budgets; Naming Rights Deals Near $1 Billion" in *Brandweek* (Vol. 49, April 21, 2008, No. 16, pp. 18)
Pub: VNU Business Media, Inc.
Ed: Barry Janoff. **Description:** More and more professional sports marketers are spending less of their advertising budgets on traditional media outlets such as television, print and radio; the growing trend in sports marketing is in utilizing new media venues such as the Internet in which innovative means are used to encourage interaction with fans.

19877 ■ "Recovery on Tap for 2010?" in *Orlando Business Journal* (Vol. 26, January 1, 2010, No. 31, pp. 1)
Pub: American City Business Journals
Ed: Melanie Stawicki Azam, Richard Bilbao, Christopher Boyd, Anjali Fluker. **Description:** Economic forecasts for Central Florida's leading business sectors in 2010 are presented. These sectors include housing, film and TV, sports business, law, restaurants, aviation, tourism and hospitality, banking and finance, commercial real estate, retail, health care, insurance, higher education, and manufacturing. According to some local executives, Central Florida's economy will slowly recover in 2010.

19878 ■ "Reds Hit Ratings Homer" in *Business Courier* (Vol. 27, July 30, 2010, No. 13, pp. 1)
Pub: Business Courier
Ed: Steve Watkins, James Ourand. **Description:** Cincinnati Reds fans have tuned in to their TVs and radios as their team made a hottest start to a season. The Reds TV ratings have increased 49 percent during the first six months of 2010 and continued to rise while the Reds' games broadcast on WLW-AM reported the highest average audience share per game of any Major League Baseball team.

19879 ■ "Scripps' Dinner Bell" in *Business Courier* (Vol. 24, October 19, 2008, No. 27, pp. 1)
Pub: American City Business Journals, Inc.
Ed: Dan Monk. **Description:** Discusses the split of E.W. Scripps Co.'s Food Network into a separate publicly traded company Scripps Networks Interactive could produce expansion into Asia and Europe.

19880 ■ "Scripps Networks" in *Brandweek* (Vol. 49, April 21, 2008, No. 16, pp. SR12)
Pub: VNU Business Media, Inc.
Ed: Anthony Crupi. **Description:** Provides contact information for sales and marketing personnel for the Scripps networks as well as a listing of the station's top programming and an analysis of the current season and the target audience for those programs running in the current season. Scripps networks include HGTV and the Food Network. HGTV boasts on of the industry's best commercial-retention averages, keeping nearly 97 percent of its viewers during advertising breaks.

19881 ■ "Sony Pictures Television" in *Brandweek* (Vol. 49, April 21, 2008, No. 16, pp. SR13)
Pub: VNU Business Media, Inc.
Ed: Marc Berman. **Description:** Provides contact information for sales and marketing personnel for Sony Pictures Television Distribution as well as a listing of the station's top programming and an analysis of the current season and the target audience for those programs running in the current season.

19882 ■ "Spillover Effects" in *Crain's Detroit Business* (Vol. 24, October 6, 2008, No. 40, pp. 29)
Pub: Crain Communications, Inc.
Description: Earlier this year, the Detroit Regional Chamber estimated that the Detroit Tiger's baseball team's 81 home games would have a $277 million positive economic impact on the region. Due to the poor performance of the team, fewer fans are spending money on tickets, which translates into fewer dollars coming into the region. Lower viewership on television has also been a result of the Tiger's losing season.

19883 ■ "A Sports Extravaganza - To Go" in *Canadian Business* (Vol. 79, June 19, 2006, No. 13, pp. 21)
Pub: Rogers Media
Ed: Andy Holloway. **Description:** Television broadcasting industry in Canada utilizing advanced technologies like mobile television and internet protocol television in broadcasting major sports events. Large number of new technologies are being invented to support increasing demand.

19884 ■ "State Expects Increase of $50 Million from Film Bills; Come Back, Al Roker" in *Crain's Detroit Business* (March 24, 2008)
Pub: Crain Communications, Inc.
Ed: Bill Shea. **Description:** Overview of the new film initiative and its incentives designed to entice more film work to Michigan; the measures could bring $50 million to $100 million in movie production work for the rest of this year compared to the $4 million total the state saw last year. Also discusses the show "DEA" which was filmed in Detroit and stars Al Roker.

19885 ■ "Storytelling Star of Show for Scripps" in *Business Courier* (Vol. 26, November 13, 2009, No. 29, pp. 1)
Pub: American City Business Journals, Inc.
Ed: Dan Monk. **Description:** Rich Boehne, CEO Of the EW Scripps Company in Cincinnati has authorized a new training program in storytelling for employees at Scripps' 10 television stations. He believes that the training will improve the quality of broadcasting content. His plans to improve quality of newspaper content are also discussed.

19886 ■ "Study: New Moms Build A Lot of Brand Buzz" in *Brandweek* (Vol. 49, April 21, 2008, No. 16, pp. 7)
Pub: VNU Business Media, Inc.
Description: According to a new survey which sampled 1,721 pregnant women and new moms, this demographic is having 109 word-of-mouth conversations per week concerning products, services and brands. Two-thirds of these conversations directly involve brand recommendations. The Internet is driving these word-of-mouth, or W-O-M, conversations among this segment, beating out magazines, television and other forms of media.

19887 ■ "Summit, Lions Gate are in Talks to Merge Studios" in *Wall Street Journal Eastern Edition* (November 29, 2011, pp. B2)
Pub: Dow Jones & Company Inc.
Ed: Erica Orden, Michelle Kung. **Description:** Movie studio Summit Entertainment LLC is in talks with television producer Lions Gate Entertainment Corporation about a possible merger. Previous talks have taken place, but no deal was ever reached. Such a deal would create a large, independent studio able to compete in the market with the big Hollywood giants.

19888 ■ "Survey: More Buyers Expect to Spend Less in Most Media" in *Advertising Age* (Vol. 79, July 7, 2008, No. 26, pp. 3)
Pub: Crain Communications, Inc.
Ed: Megan McIlroy. **Description:** Marketers are decreasing their budgets for advertising in television, radio, newspaper and outdoor due to the economic downturn. Statistical data concerning advertising agencies and marketers included.

19889 ■ "Telemundo" in *Brandweek* (Vol. 49, April 21, 2008, No. 16, pp. SR8)
Pub: VNU Business Media, Inc.
Ed: John Consoli. **Description:** Provides contact information for sales and marketing personnel for the Telemundo network as well as a listing of the station's top programming and an analysis of the current season and the target audience for those programs running in the current season.

19890 ■ "Television Broadcasting" in *MarketingMagazine* (Vol. 115, September 27, 2010, No. 13, pp. 16)
Pub: Rogers Publishing Ltd.
Description: Market statistics covering the Canadian television broadcasting industry are covered.

19891 ■ *Television & Cable Factbook*
Pub: Warren Communications News
Contact: Michael C. Taliaferro, Managing Editor
E-mail: info@warren-news.com
Released: Annual, Latest edition 2012. **Price:** $945, individuals first copy, print or online; $295, individuals second copy, print or online; $195, individuals third copy, print or online & subsequent seats; $995, individuals full online data, additional per seat. **Covers:** Commercial and noncommercial television stations and networks, including educational, low-power and instructional TV stations, and translators; United States cable television systems; cable and television group owners; program and service suppliers; and brokerage and financing companies. **Entries Include:** For stations—Call letters, licensee name and address, studio address and phone; identification of owners, sales and legal representatives and chief station personnel; rates, technical data, map of service area, and Nielsen circulation data. For cable systems—Name, address, basic and pay subscribers, programming and fees, physical plant; names of personnel and ownership. Ownership. **Arrangement:** Geographical by state, province, city, county, or country. **Indexes:** Call letters, product/service, name, general subject.

19892 ■ "Telus Tunes in to the TV Revolution" in *Globe & Mail* (February 18, 2006, pp. B4)
Pub: CTVglobemedia Publishing Inc.
Ed: Eric Reguly. **Description:** The business growth plans of chief executive officer Darren Entwistle of Telus Corp. are presented.

19893 ■ "Top of the Food Chain" in *Entrepreneur* (Vol. 37, October 2009, No. 10, pp. 19)
Pub: Entrepreneur Media, Inc.
Ed: Jennifer Wang. **Description:** Television producer Mark Burnett discusses his latest reality television production, Shark Tank. The show pits venture capitalists against entrepreneurs in a contest to obtain business funding.

19894 ■ "Transform Your Life" in *Black Enterprise* (Vol. 37, January 2007, No. 6, pp. 14)
Pub: Earl G. Graves Publishing Co. Inc.
Description: Through the magazine, television and radio programs, events, and the website, the various platforms of Black Enterprise will provide the tools necessary to achieve success in business ventures, career aspirations, and personal goals.

19895 ■ "Trib TV Station Switching to Fox" in *Crain's Chicago Business* (Vol. 31, March 31, 2008, No. 13, pp. 14)
Pub: Crain Communications, Inc.
Ed: Michelle Greppi. **Description:** Signaling the new Tribune owner Sam Zell's divergence from previous management is the company's shift of its KSWB-TV station in San Diego to News Corp.'s Fox from CW Television Network.

19896 ■ "Turner Broadcasting System" in *Brandweek* (Vol. 49, April 21, 2008, No. 16, pp. SR13)
Pub: VNU Business Media, Inc.
Ed: Anthony Crupi. **Description:** Provides contact information for sales and marketing personnel for the Turner Broadcasting System networks as well as a listing of the station's top programming and an analysis of the current season and the target audience for those programs running in the current season. Recent acquisitions are also discussed.

19897 ■ "TV Revenue Slide Hits CanWest Profit" in *Globe & Mail* (January 13, 2006, pp. B3)
Pub: CTVglobemedia Publishing Inc.
Ed: Grant Robertson. **Description:** CanWest Global Communications Corp. posted drop in profits by 14 percent for first quarter 2006. The downward trend in profits is attributed to low television revenues.

19898 ■ "Twentieth Television" in *Brandweek* (Vol. 49, April 21, 2008, No. 16, pp. SR16)
Pub: VNU Business Media, Inc.
Ed: Marc Berman. **Description:** Provides contact information for sales and marketing personnel for Twentieth Television as well as a listing of the station's top programming and an analysis of the current season and the target audience for those programs running in the current season.

19899 ■ "Univision" in *Brandweek* (Vol. 49, April 21, 2008, No. 16, pp. SR8)
Pub: VNU Business Media, Inc.
Ed: John Consoli. **Description:** Provides contact information for sales and marketing personnel for the Univision network as well as a listing of the station's top programming and an analysis of the current season and the target audience for those programs running in the current season. Univision is the No. 1 network on Friday nights in the 18-34 demographic, beating all English-language networks.

19900 ■ "Waco Pawn Shop Owners Say Reality Isn't Much Like 'Pawn Stars' TV Show" in *Waco Tribune-Herald* (August 15, 2010)
Pub: Waco Tribune-Herald
Ed: Mike Copeland. **Description:** Area pawn shop owners report that the television show on cable TV does not represent the true life operations of a pawn shop. The Las Vegas shop represented on TV boasts 30 employees and 21 on-call experts, which is not the case in reality.

19901 ■ "Warner Bros. Domestic Television Distribution" in *Brandweek* (Vol. 49, April 21, 2008, No. 16, pp. SR16)
Pub: VNU Business Media, Inc.
Ed: Marc Berman. **Description:** Provides contact information for sales and marketing personnel for Warner Bros. Domestic Television Distribution as well as a listing of the station's top programming and an analysis of the current season and the target audience for those programs running in the current season.

19902 ■ *The Weather Channel*
Pub: Harvard Business School Press
Ed: Frank Batten with Jeffrey L. Cruikshank. **Released:** 2002. **Price:** $29.95. **Description:** Frank Batten illustrates the power of a resourceful growth strategy along with details the journey he successfully took his small, private newspaper into the cable industry.

19903 ■ "What Women Watch on TV" in *Marketing to Women* (Vol. 21, February 2008, No. 2, pp. 6)
Pub: EPM Communications, Inc.
Description: According to BIGresearch, women are more likely to watch sports than they are soap operas. Statistical data included.

19904 ■ "A Whiff of TV Reality" in *Houston Business Journal* (Vol. 40, January 22, 2010, No. 37, pp. A1)
Pub: American City Business Journals
Ed: Christine Hall. **Description:** Houston, Texas-based Waste Management Inc.'s president and chief operation officer, Larry O'Donnell shares some of his experience as CBS Television Network reality show 'Undercover Boss' participant. O'Donnell believes the show was a great way to show the customers how tough their jobs are and reveals that the most difficult job was being a sorter at the recycling center.

SOURCES OF SUPPLY

19905 ■ *BIA's Television Yearbook*
Pub: BIA Financial Network Inc.
Released: Annual, Latest edition 2011. **Price:** $630, individuals. **Covers:** U.S. Television markets and their inclusive stations, television equipment manufacturers, and related service providers and trade associations. **Entries Include:** For stations—Call letters, address; name and phone of general manager, owner, and other key personnel; technical attributes, rep firm, network affiliation, last acquisition date and price and ratings for total day and prime time. For others—Company or organization name, address, phone, description. **Arrangement:** Classified by market. **Indexes:** Numerical by market rank; call letters.

TRADE PERIODICALS

19906 ■ *Broadcast Engineering*
Pub: Penton Media Inc.
Contact: Jonathan Chalon, VP/Entertainment Technology
E-mail: jonathon.chalon@penton.com
Ed: Brad Dick, Editor, brad.dick@penton.com. **Released:** Monthly, 24 regular issues US/CAN, 12 (World/Asia). **Description:** Magazine on television broadcast cable, telco, satellite equipment, products & technology.

19907 ■ *Broadcaster*
Pub: Business Information Group
Contact: James A. Cook, Sen. Publisher
E-mail: jcook@broadcastermagazine.com
Released: Monthly. **Price:** $45.95 Canada plus taxes; $45.95 in U.S.; $59.95 other countries. **Description:** Magazine covering communications industry.

19908 ■ *Cable Yellow Pages*
Pub: Teton Media Inc.
Contact: Glenn Schrader, Assoc. Pub.
Released: Annual. **Price:** $32.95. **Description:** Cable TV industry directory.

19909 ■ *TV Guide*
Pub: TV Guide Magazine
Contact: Gary Kleinman, VP, Assoc. Publisher
E-mail: gary.kleinman@tvguide.com
Released: Weekly. **Price:** $15.96 28 issues. **Description:** Special interest publication serving cable television customers and cable television system companies.

19910 ■ *TV International Daily*
Pub: Informa Publishing Group
Contact: Mr.
Released: Daily. **Price:** $1,995, U.S. via fax; $1,995, U.S. via e-mail; $2,495, U.S. via fax and e-mail. **Description:** Provides news on international television, cable, satellite, digital, and pay and pay-per-view. Remarks: Available via fax or e-mail.

VIDEOCASSETTES/ AUDIOCASSETTES

19911 ■ *Community TV: A Portrait of DCTV*
Downtown Community TV Center (DCTV)
87 Lafayette St.
New York, NY 10013
Ph:(212)966-4510
Fax:(212)226-3053
URL: http://www.dctvny.org

Released: 1989. **Description:** The relationship between this progressive independent station and network TV, as well as the history of porta-pak journalism is examined. **Availability:** VHS; 3/4U.

TRADE SHOWS AND CONVENTIONS

19912 ■ NAB Show
National Association of Broadcasters
1771 N. St. NW
Washington, DC 20036
Ph:(202)429-5300
Free: 800-342-2460
Fax:(202)429-4199
Co. E-mail: nab@nab.org
URL: http://www.nab.org

Released: Annual. **Audience:** Radio and television broadcasters and related broadcasting industry professionals. **Principal Exhibits:** Radio and television broadcasting equipment, supplies, and services; supplies and services for production, post-production, computing, multimedia, telecommunications and corporate communications. **Dates and Locations:** 2011 Apr 11-14, Las Vegas, NV.

19913 ■ Radio-Television News Directors Association International Conference & Exhibition
Radio-Television News Directors Association
1600 K St., NW, Ste. 700
Washington, DC 20006-2838
Ph:(202)659-6510
Free: 800-807-8632
Fax:(202)223-4007
Co. E-mail: rtnda@rtnda.org
URL: http://www.rtnda.org

Released: Annual. **Audience:** Professionals from the television, radio and cable industries, along with representatives from government, publications and special interest groups. **Principal Exhibits:** Equipment, supplies, and services for the radio and television news industries, including cameras, recorders, weather equipment, computers, and software.

CONSULTANTS

19914 ■ A & A Research
690 Sunset Blvd.
Kalispell, MT 59901-3641
Ph:(406)752-7857
Free: 800-735-1554
Fax:(406)752-0194
Contact: Judith Doonan, President

Scope: Offers marketing research services, specializing in newspaper readership and advertising studies. Also specializes in audience research and programming studies for radio and television stations, minority broadcasting, new business and retail marketing research, and advertising consulting and research. Also prepares public opinion polls. Serves private industries as well as government agencies. **Seminars:** Three R's of Advertising; Precision Advertising; Audience Research Workshop; Use of Research in Radio Programming.

19915 ■ Baker Scott & Co.
16 South Ave. W
Cranford, NJ 07016
Ph:(973)263-3355
Fax:(973)263-9255
Co. E-mail: exec.search@bakerscott.com
URL: http://www.bakerscott.com
E-mail: exec.search@bakerscott.com

Scope: Consulting services include executive recruiting, employment attitude surveys, and screening organization plans. Industries served: telecommunication, cable TV, broadcasting entertainment, and financial institutions. The firm is integrated horizontally across functional discipline such as accounting, administration, call center, data processing, engineering, finance, general operations, marketing and technical and plant operations. **Seminars:** Offers seminar programs on interview techniques, management skills, and customer service.

19916 ■ The Benchmark Co.
907 S Congress Ave., Ste. 7
Austin, TX 78704
Ph:(512)707-7500
Free: 800-688-7010
Fax:(512)707-7757
Co. E-mail: thebenc@earthlink.net
URL: http://www.thebenchmarkcompany.net
Contact: Bob McDonald, VP of Research
E-mail: rob@diningoutwithrobbalon.com

Scope: Full service consultants to the communications industry, specializing in radio and television. Also serves newspapers and ad agencies with extensive market research. **Publications:** "Radio in the 90S; Audience, Promotion and Marketing Strategies". **Seminars:** The Rules of the Ratings Game Seminar.

19917 ■ Bentley Miller Lights Inc.
96 Glenmore Rd.
Toronto, ON, Canada M4L 3M3
Ph:(416)699-4786
Co. E-mail: bentley@bentleymiller.com
URL: http://www.bentleymiller.com
Contact: Bentley Miller, President
E-mail: bentley@bentleymiller.com

Scope: A lighting design/consulting company which offers lighting design and photography services for both private and government television production groups. Also offers systems design for television studios. This includes, client consultation, equipment specifying, supervising installation through system debugging and commissioning. Firm also offers lighting design services ranging from large scale spectaculars to news, drama and children's programs. Industries served: television producers, both private and public, government agencies, communications media, film and digital based media, performing arts, and education. **Publications:** "Ace lightning and the carnival of the doom".

19918 ■ Bob Page Communications Inc.
111 Cloister Ct., Ste. 120
Chapel Hill, NC 27514-2294
Ph:(919)967-1134
Fax:(919)967-1134
Co. E-mail: rcpageiii@mindspring.com
Contact: Robert C. Page III, President
E-mail: rcpageiii@mindspring.com

Scope: Offers counsel, programs and implementation in public relations, marketing, and advertising. Industries served: financial institutions, manufacturers, developers, food service, retirement communities, resorts, newspapers, television stations, sports franchises, and trade associations.

19919 ■ Cable Ad Ventures Corp.
95 Mountainview Terr.
Hillsdale, NJ 07642-1023
Ph:(201)666-5131
Co. E-mail: j@cavcorp.com
Contact: Jay L. Campbell, President
E-mail: j@cavcorp.com

Scope: A firm specializing in the cable television field, working with programmers, advertisers and producers in developing original programming for cable television distribution. Company also produces television programming; works in representing companies in placing existing or new television programs in the cable marketplace.

19920 ■ Conly Productions
1563 Oneida St.
Denver, CO 80220-1750
Ph:(303)393-6240
Fax:(303)393-6240
Co. E-mail: conlymusic@aol.com
Contact: Paul F. Conly, Owner

Scope: Provides audiovisual production consulting including all phases of production for television, radio, or multi-image shows: pre-production, location scouting, scripting, casting, ideography or still photography, post-production services, editing, sound effects, audio sweetening, music scoring. Also consults on equipment purchasing audiovisual installations.

19921 ■ D.E.M. Allen & Associates Ltd.
130 Cree Crescent
Winnipeg, MB, Canada R3J 3W1
Ph:(204)889-9202
Fax:(204)831-6650
Co. E-mail: gneilson@dema.mb.ca
URL: http://www.dema.mb.ca
Contact: Gord Neilson, Principal
E-mail: wriesterer@atsdema.mb.ca

Scope: Telecommunications consultants, experienced in AM, FM and television broadcasting, CATV systems, LF/HF, VHF/UHF and microwave systems and satellite earth stations; RF measurements and evaluations related to SCADA; LMCS in the millimeters portion of the spectrum as well as the 2.5Ghz MDS/MMDS field; electromagnetic compatibility and electromagnetic immunity including non-ionizing radiation evaluation and measurement. Services include planning, design, supervision and adjustment of broadcast transmitting facilities, including specifications, tender evaluation, preparation of reports, technical briefs for Federal Regulatory bodies, evaluation and measurements associated with RF propagation and electromagnetic energy throughout the radio frequency spectrum. Industries served: Broadcast, communications and national defense agencies.

19922 ■ DeMers Programming Media Consultants
4503 Adelphi Ln.
Austin, TX 78750
Ph:(610)363-2636
Fax:(610)363-2198
Co. E-mail: info@demersprogramming.com
URL: http://www.demersprogramming.com
Contact: Sean Hoots, Mgr
E-mail: sean@demersprogramming.com

Scope: Programming and marketing consultants offering advice for broadcasters and broadcast related businesses. Services include: music and format controls, strategic planning, talent coaching and acquisition, research and promotional planning. Serves private and government sectors. **Publications:** "12 Steps To A One Share - Uncovering The Clutter," Feb, 2005; "Get Your Mind Out Of The Clutter - DeMers Dispatch Winter '05"; "See Spot Run... Over The Golden Goose"; "Radio's Attention Deficit Disorder"; "Program The Seller"; "At Issue: Staying Creative"; "Take A Hard Look At Your Special Programming"; "A Fresh Coat Of Paint"; "Guerrilla Radio". **Seminars:** Diary Keepers Plus Research; Marketing, Merchandising and Money.

19923 ■ Elder Engineering Inc.
35 Auckland Ln.
PO Box 10
King City, ON, Canada L7B 1C1
Ph:(905)833-5141
Fax:(905)833-2101
Co. E-mail: eldeng@sympatico.ca
Contact: Joan Elder, Office Mgr
E-mail: eldeng@sympatico.ca

Scope: Expertise regarding communications and broadcast transmitting systems encompasses feasibility study, frequency search, site selection, propagation tests, and protection analysis. Experienced with antenna design, contour predictions, equipment specification, technical brief, bid selection, tuning, testing, certification and proof of performance for newer improved transmitting facilities in LF to UHF bands; design studies for broadband multi station AM, FM, TV or DRB antenna and transmission systems at a common site, point-to-point STL, microwave distant learning, MDS, or teleconferencing systems. Industries served: radio, television, broadcasters and applicants, power utilities, government agencies, radio communications licensees, and manufacturers.

19924 ■ Financial Solutions Inc.
309 W Jefferson St.
La Grange, KY 40031
Ph:(502)225-9900
Free: 877-952-9766
Fax:(502)225-9997
Co. E-mail: robin@lawsonfinancial.net
URL: http://www.lawsonfinancial.net
Contact: Robin H. Lawson, Owner
E-mail: robin@lawsonfinancial.net
Scope: Offers financial brokerage services to the broadcasting industry in the Midwest United States. **Publications:** "Eighty percent of Americans agree they would benefit from having basic financial education and information," 2009; "Finra Investor Education Survey, 2007"; "How Are Mutual Funds Taxed". **Seminars:** Long Term Care, Estate Planning, Retirement, Financial Management.

19925 ■ Forsyth Consulting
9 Laurier Ave.
Toronto, ON, Canada M4X 1S2
Ph:(416)964-0812
Fax:(416)964-1304
Co. E-mail: ajforsyth9@rogers.com
Contact: Andrew J. Forsyth, President
E-mail: ajforsyth9@rogers.com
Scope: Specialized in regulatory affairs applicable to radio, television, cable, and satellite. Provides CRTC applications and interventions, compliance strategies and analysis, strategic planning and market positioning, creative programming, management sales, talent and formative development, acquisitions, benefit package strategies, and broadcast property sale representation. Industries served: Broadcasting.

19926 ■ SEMO Communications Corp.
107 Semo Ln.
PO Box C
Sikeston, MO 63801
Ph:(573)471-6599
Free: 800-635-8230
Fax:(573)471-6878
Co. E-mail: cableme@semocommunications.com
URL: http://www.semocommunications.com
Contact: Tyrone Garrett, President
E-mail: cableme@semocommunications.com
Scope: Consults on cable television systems and other communications services.

19927 ■ Stewart/Laurence Associates Inc.
PO Box 811146
PO Box 131
Boca Raton, FL 33496
Ph:(732)972-8000
Fax:(732)972-8003
Co. E-mail: info@stewartlaurence.com
URL: http://www.stewartlaurence.com
Contact: Shelley Miller, Vice President
Scope: An executive search firm assists corporations with the recruitment of top level management personnel. It recruits key executives (President, CEO, CFO, General Manager, VP Sales, VP Mktg, etc.) for startup, high tech and venture capital companies internationally. Fields of expertise include: medical device and bio medical technology, Internet/Intranet, digital and graphic imaging, software, networking, telecommunications, and wireless/WAP.

19928 ■ Technology Group Communications
8750 W Bryn Mawr Ave., Ste. 460
Chicago, IL 60631-3545
Ph:(773)695-9601
Fax:(773)675-2635
Contact: Alan G. Kraus, President
Scope: Established to provide in-depth engineering and integration services to the growing high performance enterprise network market. The firm has the ability to turnkey design, install, test and maintain large scale data communications networks of fiber, coax, twisted pair, and wireless media. Experience and expertise in all aspects of multi-product local area networking integration and installation. Projects have included the complete design, installation and certification of major facility networks for large manufacturing, educational and office facilities.

19929 ■ Victory Studios
2247 15th Ave. W
Seattle, WA 98119
Ph:(206)282-1776
Free: 888-282-1776
Fax:(206)282-3535
Co. E-mail: matt@victorystudios.com
URL: http://www.victorystudios.com
Contact: Doug Ramsey, Director
E-mail: dramsey@atsvictorystudios.com
Scope: Offers marketing, distribution, and syndication consultation regarding television programming for program producers. Also provides production services through an affiliate company, American Production Services. Work involves editing, audio narration, recording, computer graphics, NTSC-PAL, video and audio duplication, and camera equipment rental (stages and grip truck), and multimedia services. Industries served: Broadcast and industrial media, and government agencies.

19930 ■ Walter S. Wydro Consultants
57 Woodhill Rd.
Newtown, PA 18940-3013
Ph:(215)860-2288
Fax:(215)860-5502
Contact: Walter S. Wydro, President
Scope: Engineering consultants in telecommunications and cable television, offering research and development of new products, system growth analysis, financial and technical evaluation and planning for municipal services, and litigation testimony.

COMPUTERIZED DATABASES

19931 ■ *BaselineFT's In Production Database*
New York Times Media Group
3415 S Sepulveda Blvd., Ste. 200
Los Angeles, CA 90034
Ph:(310)482-3400
Free: 800-858-3669
Fax:(310)393-7799
URL: http://www.baselineresearch.com
Description: Lists more than 5000 film and television projects that are either announced, in preproduction, production, post-production, or awaiting release. Monitors activity in the entertainment industry through press releases, local film commissions, industry sources, and phone calls to producers. **Availability:** Online: New York Times Media Group. **Type:** Full text.

LIBRARIES

19932 ■ Alliance for Children and Television–Resource Library
1400 Rene-Levesque Blvd. E., Ste. 713
Montreal, QC, Canada H2L 2M2
Ph:(514)597-5417
Fax:(514)597-5205
Co. E-mail: cfortier@act-aet.tv
URL: http://www.act-aet.tv
Contact: Caroline Fortier, Exec.Dir.
Scope: Television and children, media, broadcasting. **Services:** Library open with permission only. **Holdings:** Figures not available.

19933 ■ CBC/Radio Canada Maritimes–Broadcast Materials, Halifax Centre
PO Box 3000
Halifax, NS, Canada B3J 3E9
Ph:(902)420-4160
Fax:(902)420-4281
Co. E-mail: doug.kirby@cbc.ca
URL: http://archives.cbc.ca
Contact: Doug Kirby, Media Lib./Archv.Coord.
Scope: Television news, children's television, television comedy, agriculture and resources television, performance and programming television. **Services:** Library open to the public by appointment. **Holdings:** 100,000 television archival items. **Subscriptions:** 13 newspapers.

19934 ■ National Press Club–Eric Friedheim Library & News Information Center
529 14th St. NW, 13th Fl.
Washington, DC 20045
Ph:(202)662-7523
Fax:(202)879-6725
Co. E-mail: info@press.org
URL: http://press.org/library
Contact: Julie Schoo, Dir./Libn.
Scope: Current events; journalism - craft, history; print and broadcast media. **Services:** Copying; audio cassette copying (fee); Library open to members. **Holdings:** 2500 books; NPC luncheon audiocassettes & videotapes; newsletters; microfilm; CDs. **Subscriptions:** 250 newspapers, magazines, journals, and newsletters.

19935 ■ Right Management Consultants–Corporate Research Center
1818 Market St., 33rd Fl.
Philadelphia, PA 19103
Ph:(215)988-1588
Free: 800-237-4448
Co. E-mail: contactus@right.com
URL: http://www.right.com
Scope: Career management, executives, change management, human resource issues. **Services:** Interlibrary loan; Center not open to the public. **Holdings:** 700 books. **Subscriptions:** 70 journals and other serials; 4 newspapers.

19936 ■ TV Ontario Library
PO Box 200, Sta. Q
Toronto, ON, Canada M4T 2T1
Ph:(416)484-2665
Fax:(416)484-2646
Co. E-mail: rvolpatti@tvo.org
URL: http://www.tvo.org
Contact: Ms. Rechilde Volpatti, Supv.
Scope: Educational television, television production, broadcasting, distance education, communications, multimedia, children and television. **Services:** Interlibrary loan; copying; Library open to the public for reference use only. **Holdings:** 10,000 books; TV Ontario documents, program guides, and newspaper clippings. **Subscriptions:** 200 journals and other serials.

19937 ■ University of California, Los Angeles–UCLA Film and Television Archive–Research and Study Center (46 Po)
46 Powell Library
PO Box 951517
Los Angeles, CA 90095-1517
Ph:(310)206-5388
Fax:(310)206-5392
Co. E-mail: arsc@ucla.edu
URL: http://www.cinema.ucla.edu
Contact: Mark Quigley, Mgr., Res. & Study Ctr.
Scope: U.S. theatrical films and broadcast television programs, theatrical newsreels, films of recognized importance in world film history, television news programs, animated films. **Services:** Archive open to the public for scholarly and project-oriented onsite research only. **Holdings:** 220,000 motion picture prints and negatives; 95,000 television films and tapes.

RESEARCH CENTERS

19938 ■ Massachusetts Institute of Technology–Media Lab
Bldg. E14 & E15
77 Massachusetts Ave.
Cambridge, MA 02139-4307
Ph:(617)253-5960
Co. E-mail: communications@media.mit.edu
URL: http://www.media.mit.edu
Contact: Ellen Hoffman, Dir. of Commun.
E-mail: communications@media.mit.edu
Scope: New information technologies in the areas of biomechatronics, neuroengineering, machines with common sense, viral communications, advanced sensor networks, innovative interface design, and sociable robots. Projects range from wearable sensors for monitoring health, to new programming tools for children.

19939 ■ Texas Tech University–Center for Communications Research
College of Mass Communications, Box 43082
Lubbock, TX 79409-3082
Ph:(806)742-3385
Fax:(806)742-1085
Co. E-mail: p.muhlberger@ttu.edu
URL: http://www.depts.ttu.edu/masscom/about/ccr.php
Contact: Prof. Peter Muhlberger PhD, Dir.
E-mail: p.muhlberger@ttu.edu

Scope: Public opinion and consumer surveys, communication experiments, economic and policy studies, and television/radio production and testing, including studies on communication immunization and functions, and television personality and viewers' preference. **Publications:** Journal of Broadcasting and Electronic Media; Journal of Media Economics; Journalism Educator; Journalism Quarterly; Public Opinion Quarterly.

Temporary Employment Agency

ASSOCIATIONS AND OTHER ORGANIZATIONS

19940 ■ American Staffing Association
277 S Washington St., Ste. 200
Alexandria, VA 22314-3675
Ph:(703)253-2020
Fax:(703)253-2053
Co. E-mail: asa@americanstaffing.net
URL: http://www.americanstaffing.net
Contact: Mr. Richard Wahlquist, Pres./CEO
Description: Promotes and represents the staffing industry through legal and legislative advocacy, public relations, education, and the establishment of high standards of ethical conduct. **Publications:** *ASA Managers Guide to Employment Law*; *Co-Employment Guide*; *Membership and Resource Directory*; *Staffing Success* (bimonthly).

19941 ■ Association of Manpower Franchise Owners
6737 W Washington St., Ste. 1300
Milwaukee, WI 53214
Ph:(414)276-2651
Fax:(414)276-7704
Co. E-mail: info@amfo.org
URL: http://www.amfo.org
Contact: Jane A. Svinicki CAE, Exec. Dir.
Description: Serves as a forum for exchange of ideas and information among members; acts as liaison between members and the parent company. Studies and critiques procedures and policies of Manpower International; solicits suggestions from members regarding smooth operation of a temporary employee service. Provides formalized procedure for resolution of grievances among members and between members and the parent company. .

19942 ■ National Association of Personnel Services
131 Prominence Ct., Ste. 130
Dawsonville, GA 30534
Ph:(706)531-0060
Fax:(866)739-4750
Co. E-mail: conrad.taylor@recruitinglife.com
URL: http://www.recruitinglife.com
Contact: Conrad Taylor, Pres.
Description: Private employment and temporary service firms. Compiles statistics on professional agency growth and development; conducts certification program and educational programs. Association is distinct from former name of National Association of Personnel Consultants. **Publications:** Membership Directory (annual).

19943 ■ National Association of Professional Employer Organizations
707 N St. Asaph St.
Alexandria, VA 22314
Ph:(703)836-0466
Fax:(703)836-0976
Co. E-mail: info@napeo.org
URL: http://www.napeo.org
Contact: Brian Fayak, Pres.
Description: Professional employer organizations. Seeks to enhance professionalism in the professional employer industry. Sponsors educational and public information programs. Maintains speakers' bureau; compiles statistics. .

REFERENCE WORKS

19944 ■ "AT&T To Acquire Black Telecom Firm" in *Black Enterprise* (Vol. 38, January 2008, No. 6, pp. 24)
Pub: Earl G. Graves Publishing Co. Inc.
Ed: Alan Hughes. **Description:** Details of AT&T's acquisition of ChaseCom LP, a telecommunications company based in Houston, Texas, are covered.

19945 ■ "Calling All Recruiters: Agent HR Puts Staffing Agents In Charge" in *Black Enterprise* (Vol. 38, December 2007, No. 5, pp. 72)
Pub: Earl G. Graves Publishing Co. Inc.
Ed: Chana Garcia. **Description:** Recruiting and staffing agencies are seeing a drop in services due to slow economic growth. AgentHR partners with full-service recruiters who have three to five year's experience-specialists soliciting their own clients, provide staffing services, and manage their own accounts, thus combining the roles of recruiter and salesperson.

19946 ■ *The Directory of Toronto Recruiters*
Pub: Continental Records Company Ltd.
Contact: Neil Patte
Released: Annual, latest edition 2008. **Price:** $49. 95, individuals plus express post shipping cost and GST. **Covers:** More than 1,200 recruiting firms in the Toronto, Canada area. **Entries Include:** Firm name, address, phone, fax, e-mail, URL, name and title of contact, and industry and professional specialties.

19947 ■ "Impressive Numbers: Companies Experience Substantial Increases in Dollars, Employment" in *Hispanic Business* (July-August 2007)
Pub: Hispanic Business
Ed: Derek Reveron. **Description:** Profiles of five fastest growing Hispanic companies reporting increases in revenue and employment include Brightstar, distributor of wireless products; Greenway Ford Inc., a car dealership; Fred Loya Insurance, auto insurance carrier; and Group O, packaging company; and Diverse Staffing, Inc., an employment and staffing firm.

19948 ■ "Matchmakers Anticipating Tech Valley Boom" in *Business Review, Albany New York* (Vol. 34, November 2, 2007, No. 31, pp. 1)
Pub: American City Business Journals, Inc.
Ed: Adam Sichko. **Description:** Qualified candidates are coming to permanent placement companies after being downsized elsewhere. The top five projected fastest-growing and top five projected fasted-decreasing jobs in the Capital Region are presented.

19949 ■ "Overseas Overtures" in *Business Journal-Portland* (Vol. 24, October 26, 2007, No. 35, pp. 1)
Pub: American City Business Journals, Inc.
Ed: Robin J. Moody. **Description:** Oregon has a workforce shortage, specifically for the health care industry. Recruiting agencies, such as the International Recruiting Network Inc., answers the high demand for workforce by recruiting foreign employees. The difficulties recruiting companies experience with regards to foreign labor laws are investigated.

19950 ■ "Priority: Business For Sale" in *Inc.* (January 2008, pp. 28)
Pub: Gruner & Jahr USA Publishing
Ed: Elaine Appleton Grant. **Description:** Profile of an employment agency providing registered nurses to hospitals and nursing homes. The company began as an temporary placement agency for IT professionals and is now for sale at the asking price of $4.2 million.

19951 ■ "Q&A With Devin Ringling: Franchise's Services Go Beyond Elder Care" in *Gazette* (October 2, 2010)
Pub: The Gazette
Ed: Bill Radford. **Description:** Profile of franchise, Interim HealthCare, in Colorado Springs, Colorado; the company offers home care services that include wound care and specialized feedings to shopping and light housekeeping. It also runs a medical staffing company that provides nurses, therapists and other health care workers to hospitals, prisons, schools and other facilities.

19952 ■ "Regional Talent Network Unveils Jobs Web Site" in *Crain's Cleveland Business* (Vol. 30, June 1, 2009, No. 21, pp. 11)
Pub: Crain Communications, Inc.
Description: Regional Talent Network launched WhereToFindHelp.org, a Website designed to act as a directory of all Northeast Ohio resources that can help employers recruit and job seekers look for positions. The site also lists organizations offering employment and training services.

19953 ■ "Sign of the Times: Temp-To-Perm Attorneys" in *HRMagazine* (Vol. 54, January 2009, No. 1, pp. 24)
Pub: Society for Human Resource Management
Ed: Bill Leonard. **Description:** A growing number of law firms are hiring professional staff on a temp-to-perm basis according to the president of Professional Placement Services in Florida. Firms can save money while testing potential employees on a temporary basis.

19954 ■ "Temporary Measures" in *Occupational Outlook Quarterly* (Vol. 54, Fall 2010, No. 3, pp. 36)
Pub: U.S. Bureau of Labor Statistics
Description: Data on temporary help services employment from the U.S. Bureau of Labor Statistics suggests good news for all nonfarm workers. The data had been rising steadily for most of 2009.

19955 ■ "Temporary Theory" in *Canadian Business* (Vol. 80, November 5, 2007, No. 22, pp. 33)
Pub: Rogers Media
Ed: Joe Castaldo. **Description:** Employing a temporary manager is ideal for companies working on a strict budget and limited time. The strategy will

provide the company with the skills of an expert manager for a cost that is less than that of hiring a full-time manager. The usage of interim managers, specifically in short-term projects, is discussed.

19956 ■ "Work To Do" in *Canadian Business* (Vol. 81, July 22, 2008, No. 12-13, pp. 22)
Pub: Rogers Media Ltd.
Ed: Jane Bao. **Description:** Recruiting firm Manpower revealed that 36 percent of Canadian employers had trouble filling positions in 2007, highlighting the labor shortage and the need to bring in more workers. Underemployment of immigrants costs up to $6 billion to Canada's economy every year. Other views regarding Canada's labor shortage and on its economic impact are presented.

STATISTICAL SOURCES

19957 ■ *RMA Annual Statement Studies*
Pub: Robert Morris Associates (RMA)
Released: Annual. **Price:** $175.00 2006-07 edition, $105.00. **Description:** Contains composite balance sheets and income statements for more than 360 industries, including the accounting, auditing, and bookkeeping industries. Also contains five years of comparative historical data for discerning trends. Includes 16 commonly used ratios, computed for most of the size groupings for nearly every industry.

FRANCHISES AND BUSINESS OPPORTUNITIES

19958 ■ AHEAD Human Resources, Inc.
AHEAD Human Resources, Inc.
2209 Heather Ln.
Louisville, KY 40218
Free: 877-485-5858
Fax:(502)485-0801
No. of Franchise Units: 7. **Founded:** 1995. **Franchised:** 2000. **Description:** Temporary staffing. **Equity Capital Needed:** Need working capital. **Franchise Fee:** $17,700-$23,700. **Financial Assistance:** No. **Training:** Yes.

19959 ■ AtWork Medical Services
3215 John Sevier Hwy.
Knoxville, TN 37290
Free: 800-383-0804
Fax:(865)573-1171
No. of Franchise Units: 14. **Founded:** 1990. **Franchised:** 2003. **Description:** Temporary & full-time medical staffing services. **Equity Capital Needed:** $143,600-$226,800. **Franchise Fee:** $0-$25,000. **Royalty Fee:** 6.1.-1.6%. **Financial Assistance:** Limited in-house financing available. **Training:** Provides 5+ days at headquarters, 2-5 days onsite and ongoing support.

19960 ■ CareersUSA Franchise
Careers Franchising Inc.
6501 Congress Ave., Ste. 200
Boca Raton, FL 33487
Ph:(561)995-7000
Free: 888-CAR-EERS
Fax:(561)995-7001
Co. E-mail: tfeldman@careerusa.com
URL: http://www.careerusa.com
No. of Franchise Units: 9. **No. of Company-Owned Units:** 17. **Founded:** 1981. **Franchised:** 1987. **Description:** A temporary, temp-to-hire and direct hire placement staffing service specializing in clerical, administrative, accounting and light service personnel in varied industries and organizations. **Equity Capital Needed:** $110,000-$154,500. **Franchise Fee:** $14,500. **Financial Assistance:** 100% payroll funding. **Managerial Assistance:** Proprietary computerized software provided. **Training:** Comprehensive business and sales training including site selection advice, advertising support and staff status.

19961 ■ Express Employment Professionals
8516 NW Expy.
Oklahoma City, OK 73162
Free: 877-652-6400
Co. E-mail: franchising@expresspersonnel.com
URL: http://www.franchising.expresspersonnel.com
No. of Franchise Units: 550. **Founded:** 1983. **Franchised:** 1985. **Description:** Is an international fullservice staffing corporation with three distinct divisions available in one franchise agreement. The franchised offices provide clients with temporary help, full-time placements, and executive recruitment. **Equity Capital Needed:** $153,750-$242,500 depending on the market. Can be a combo of cash and equity. **Franchise Fee:** $35,000. **Financial Assistance:** Express finances temporary associate payroll. **Managerial Assistance:** Continuous follow-up training in the field and in regular seminars and workshops. **Training:** 2 week initial training at headquarters, 1 week in certified training office and ongoing field training and support. Followed by additional time in new office with assigned field representative.

19962 ■ Link Staffing Services
Personnel Concepts
1800 Bering Dr., Ste. 800
Houston, TX 77057
Ph:(713)784-4400
Free: 800-848-5465
Fax:(713)784-4454
Co. E-mail: franchise@linkstaffing.com
URL: http://www.linkstaffing.com
No. of Franchise Units: 55. **No. of Company-Owned Units:** 10. **Founded:** 1980. **Franchised:** 1994. **Description:** Supplies light industrial and industrial personnel to a variety of retail, commercial and manufacturing businesses. **Equity Capital Needed:** $93,000-$171,000. **Franchise Fee:** $30,000. **Royalty Fee:** 32%-40% of gross margin. **Financial Assistance:** Finance the field staff payroll, burden and accounts receivable. **Managerial Assistance:** Intranet accessible training available. **Training:** Support center classes include operations, management, sales and computer applications and an ongoing program of advanced curriculum including field training.

19963 ■ Pridestaff
7535 N Palm Ave., Ste. 101
Fresno, CA 93711-1393
Ph:(559)449-5804
No. of Franchise Units: 35. **No. of Company-Owned Units:** 3. **Founded:** 1978. **Franchised:** 1995. **Description:** Recruiting Agency. **Equity Capital Needed:** $162,000-$237,000. **Franchise Fee:** $32,000. **Financial Assistance:** No. **Training:** Yes.

19964 ■ Protingent Staffing
16650 NE 79th St., Ste. 200
Redmond, WA 98052
Ph:(425)284-7777
Free: (866)244-4396
Fax:(425)642-8001
Co. E-mail: franchiseinfo@protingent.com
URL: http://www.protingent.com
No. of Franchise Units: 2. **No. of Company-Owned Units:** 2. **Founded:** 2001. **Franchised:** 2007. **Description:** Technical staffing firm. **Equity Capital Needed:** $90,000-$132,000. **Franchise Fee:** $25,000. **Financial Assistance:** No. **Training:** Offers 2 weeks training at Seattle headquarters covering account management, recruiting, back office and client/candidate tracking system training.

19965 ■ Remedy Intelligent Staffing
Koosharem Corp.
3820 State St.
Santa Barbara, CA 93105
Free: 800-753-0196
Fax:(805)617-1309
Co. E-mail: franchise@remedystaff.com
URL: http://www.remedystaff.com
No. of Franchise Units: 89. **No. of Company-Owned Units:** 255. **Founded:** 1974. **Franchised:** 1987. **Description:** Recruiting Services. **Equity Capital Needed:** $117,000-$200,000. **Franchise Fee:** $30,000. **Financial Assistance:** No. **Training:** Includes classroom training, field training and online web courses in the areas of strategic planning, sales support, operations and client retention.

19966 ■ Spherion
925 N Point Pky.
Alpharetta, GA 30005
Ph:(678)867-3702
Free: 800-903-0082
Fax:(678)867-3190
No. of Franchise Units: 89. **No. of Company-Owned Units:** 285. **Founded:** 1946. **Franchised:** 1956. **Description:** Flexible staffing solutions. **Equity Capital Needed:** License $57,500-$135,700; Franchise fee $121,800-$391,700. **Franchise Fee:** $15,000. **Financial Assistance:** No. **Training:** Yes.

19967 ■ TRC Staffing Services, Inc.
115 Perimeter Center Pl. NE, Ste. 850
Atlanta, GA 30346
Ph:(770)392-1411
Free: 800-488-8008
No. of Franchise Units: 30. **No. of Company-Owned Units:** 23. **Founded:** 1980. **Description:** Provides office support, clerical, word processing, data processing, marketing and light industrial personnel to businesses. **Equity Capital Needed:** $15,000. **Franchise Fee:** $75,000 minimum liquid. **Financial Assistance:** No. **Training:** Yes.

Tennis Court/Racquet Club Operation

ASSOCIATIONS AND OTHER ORGANIZATIONS

19968 ■ American Sports Builders Association
8480 Baltimore National Pike, No. 307
Ellicott City, MD 21043
Ph:(410)730-9595
Free: (866)501-2722
Fax:(410)730-8833
Co. E-mail: info@sportsbuilders.org
URL: http://sportsbuilders.org
Contact: Sam Fisher, Chm.
Description: Contractors who install running tracks, synthetic turf fields, tennis courts and indoor sports surfaces; manufacturers who supply basic materials for construction; accessory suppliers, designers, architects, and consultants of facilities. Provides guidelines for tennis court construction, running track construction, fencing, synthetic turf field construction and lighting. Offers certification and awards programs. **Publications:** *Buyers Guide for Tennis Court Construction* (periodic); *Running Tracks: A Construction and Maintenance Manual* (semiannual); *Tennis and Track Construction Guidelines* (periodic);Membership Directory (annual).

19969 ■ American Tennis Association
9701 Apollo Dr., Ste. 301
Largo, MD 20774
Ph:(240)487-5953
Co. E-mail: fscott@americantennisassociation.org
URL: http://www.americantennisassociation.org
Contact: Dr. Franklyn Scott Jr., Pres.
Description: Persons interested in tennis. Promotes and develops tennis regardless of race. Supports training programs to develop Teaching Professionals. Sponsors training programs for young players; conducts 60 state and local tournaments. **Publications:** *ATA News* (quarterly).

19970 ■ International Health, Racquet and Sportsclub Association
Seaport Ctr.
70 Fargo St.
Boston, MA 02210
Ph:(617)951-0055
Free: 800-228-4772
Fax:(617)951-0056
Co. E-mail: info@ihrsa.org
URL: http://www.ihrsa.org
Contact: Joe Moore, Pres./CEO
Description: Health, racquet, and sport clubs; racquet sports manufacturers and suppliers. Promotes the continued growth of the health, racquet, and sports club industry in 70 countries. Aids member clubs in making educated business decisions. Sets standards for club management; offers group purchasing program. Organizes management training seminars. Compiles statistics; disseminates information. Conducts market research and educational programs; conducts sponsored membership promotion programs. Provides government relations and public relations services. **Publications:** *Club Business International* (monthly).

19971 ■ International Tennis Hall of Fame
194 Bellevue Ave.
Newport, RI 02840
Ph:(401)849-3990
Free: 800-457-1144
Co. E-mail: newport@tennisfame.com
URL: http://www.tennisfame.com
Contact: Tony Trabert, Pres.
Description: Seeks to foster interest in tennis, its history, and its athletic heroes. Supports junior tennis training programs; conducts amateur and professional grass-court competitions; maintains a museum. Produces video programs. Inducts new Hall of Fame members annually, including administrators, coaches, players, and writers. **Publications:** *Hall of Fame News* (quarterly).

19972 ■ Professional Tennis Registry
PO Box 4739
Hilton Head Island, SC 29938
Ph:(843)785-7244
Free: 800-421-6289
Fax:(843)686-2033
Co. E-mail: ptr@ptrtennis.org
URL: http://www.ptrtennis.org
Contact: Daniel Santorum, CEO/Exec. Dir.
Description: Tests, certifies, and registers international tennis teaching professionals; Certification requires successful completion of a written and on-court examinations. Sponsors workshops, tennis clinics, and charitable program. Holds competitions; compiles statistics; maintains placement service. **Publications:** *TennisPro* (bimonthly); *USPTR Membership Directory* (annual).

19973 ■ Sony Ericsson WTA Tour
1 Progress Plz., Ste. 1500
St. Petersburg, FL 33701
Ph:(727)895-5000
Fax:(727)894-1982
Co. E-mail: webmaster@wtatour.com
URL: http://www.sonyericssonwtatour.com
Contact: Stacey Allaster, Chm./CEO
Purpose: Works to increase and strengthen the global popularity and stature of the women's professional tennis tour, and to further advance the game as the preeminent sport for women worldwide. .

19974 ■ United States Professional Tennis Association
3535 Briarpark Dr., Ste. 1
Houston, TX 77042
Ph:(713)978-7782
Free: 800-USPTA-4U
Fax:(713)978-7780
Co. E-mail: uspta@uspta.org
URL: http://www.uspta.com
Contact: Tim Heckler, CEO
Description: Professional tennis instructors, tennis-teaching professionals and college coaches. Seeks to improve tennis instruction in the United States; maintains placement bureau and library. Offers specialized education; sponsors competitions; administrates an adult tennis league and a nationwide program to introduce children ages 3-10 to tennis. Sponsors annual "Tennis Across America" program each spring. **Publications:** *ADDvantage* (monthly).

19975 ■ United States Racquet Stringers Association
330 Main St.
Vista, CA 92084
Ph:(760)536-1177
Fax:(760)536-1171
Co. E-mail: usrsa@racquettech.com
URL: http://www.racquettech.com
Contact: David Bone, Exec. Dir.
Description: Racquet stringers; individuals interested in learning about the stringing of racquets and new patterns on the market. Conducts experiments with new racquets and patterns. Provides free stringing business consulting service. Offers Certification Program. Offers instruction-workshops and video instruction. **Publications:** *Racquet Sports Industry*; *RacquetTECH.com*; *The Stringer's Digest* (semiannual); *Total Racquet Service* .

19976 ■ United States Racquetball Association
1685 W Uintah St.
Colorado Springs, CO 80904-2969
Ph:(719)635-5396
Fax:(719)635-0685
Co. E-mail: jhiser@usra.org
URL: http://www.usra.org
Contact: James Hiser, Exec. Dir.
Description: Represents racquetball players and enthusiasts. Promotes racquetball as a sport; organizes racquetball to be a self-governing sport of, by, and for the players; encourages building of facilities for the sport; conducts racquetball events including annual national and international tournaments. Maintains hall of fame, junior player programs, and charitable programs. **Publications:** *Official USRA Rules*; *Racquetball Magazine* (bimonthly).

19977 ■ United States Squash Racquets Association
555 8th Ave., Ste. 1102
New York, NY 10018-4311
Ph:(212)268-4090
Fax:(212)268-4091
Co. E-mail: office@ussquash.com
URL: http://www.ussquash.com
Contact: Mr. Kevin Klipstein, CEO
Description: Member of United States Olympic Committee. Aims to establish and enforce uniformity in the rules of the game, standardize court specifications and schedules, and conduct tournaments. **Publications:** *National Court Survey* (triennial); *Squash Magazine* (10/year); *U.S. Squash Racquets Association—Official Yearbook* .

19978 ■ United States Tennis Association
70 W Red Oak Ln.
White Plains, NY 10604
Ph:(914)696-7000

Free: 800-990-8782
Co. E-mail: memberservices@usta.com
URL: http://www.usta.com
Contact: Karen Martin-Eliezer, Exec. Dir.

Description: Federation of local tennis clubs, educational institutions, recreation departments, and other groups and individuals interested in the promotion of tennis. Works to develop tennis as a means of healthful recreation and physical fitness and maintain high standards of fair play and sportsmanship. Sanctions thousands of tennis tournaments for all age groups throughout the U.S. each year. Sponsors Junior Program for boys and girls under 18 years of age; U.S. national tennis team; national championships for various age groups; National Circuit tournament for pro and amateur players; Davis Cup, Fed Cup, Olympics international matches; and adult recreational leagues. Compiles statistics on leading professional and amateur players. **Publications:** *Tennis Championships Magazine* (periodic); *Tennis USTA* (annual).

19979 ■ WTA Tour Players Association
1 Progress Plz., Ste. 1500
St. Petersburg, FL 33701
Ph:(727)895-5000
Fax:(727)894-1982
Co. E-mail: kwulff@wtatour.com
URL: http://www.sonyericssonwtatour.com
Contact: Stacey Allaster, Chm./CEO

Description: Professional women tennis players. Purpose is to represent members with regard to professional tournaments. **Publications:** *Getting Started* (annual); *Inside Women's Tennis* (monthly); *Media Guide* (annual); *Players Handbook* (annual); *Tournament Guide* (annual).

REFERENCE WORKS

19980 ■ "Growing Strong" in *Entrepreneur* (Vol. 35, November 2007, No. 11, pp. 36)
Pub: Entrepreneur Media Inc.

Ed: Nichole L. Torres. **Description:** Amy Langer founded Salo LL with partner John Folkestad. The company is growing fast since its 2002 launch, with over $40 million in projections for 2007. The finance and accounting staffing company tops the list of the fastest-growing women-led companies in North America.

TRADE PERIODICALS

19981 ■ *Black Tennis Magazine*
Pub: Black Tennis Magazine
Contact: Marcus Freeman

Released: Quarterly. **Price:** $15; $28 two years; $40 3 years. **Description:** Sports magazine featuring black tennis players, clubs, and parks.

19982 ■ *Tennis Magazine*
Pub: Miller Publishing Group L.L.C.
Contact: James Martin, Editor-in-Chief

Released: Annual, September. **Price:** $20 two years; $15. **Description:** Tennis magazine.

19983 ■ *Tennis Week*
Pub: Tennis Week
Contact: Randy Master, Publisher

Released: Monthly, 11/yr. **Price:** $40 special tournament & other package rates available; $30 website. **Description:** Tennis news publication including features, business and politics of the game, rankings, results, schedules coverage of camps, resorts, and tournaments.

VIDEOCASSETTES/ AUDIOCASSETTES

19984 ■ *Consistent Tennis Wins*
Tapeworm Video Distributors
25876 The Old Road 141
Stevenson Ranch, CA 91381
Ph:(661)257-4904
Fax:(661)257-4820
Co. E-mail: sales@tapeworm.com
URL: http://www.tapeworm.com

Released: 1996. **Price:** $39.95. **Description:** Host Tom Avery discusses tennis techniques such as ground strokes, volleys, warm-up routines and breathing. **Availability:** VHS.

TRADE SHOWS AND CONVENTIONS

19985 ■ United States Professional Tennis Association Convention
United States Professional Tennis Association
3535 Briarpark Dr., Ste. One
Houston, TX 77042
Ph:(713)978-7782
Free: 800-USPTA-4U
Fax:(713)978-7780
Co. E-mail: uspta@uspta.org
URL: http://www.uspta.org
Released: Annual. **Audience:** Tennis-teaching professionals, industry delegates, and general public. **Principal Exhibits:** Tennis equipment, supplies, and services.

LIBRARIES

19986 ■ International Tennis Hall of Fame and Tennis Museum Library
Newport Casino
194 Bellevue Ave.
Newport, RI 02840
Ph:(401)849-3990
Free: 800-457-1144
Fax:(401)849-8780
Co. E-mail: research@tennisfame.com
URL: http://www.tennisfame.com
Contact: Joanie Agler, Info.Res.Ctr.Coord.
Scope: Lawn tennis, court tennis, other racquet games. **Services:** Copying. **Holdings:** 5000 books; 300,000 photographs; periodicals; catalogs; Newport RI Social History. **Subscriptions:** 5 journals and other serials.

19987 ■ Racquet and Tennis Club Library
370 Park Ave.
New York, NY 10022-5968
Ph:(212)753-9700
Fax:(212)980-7180
Contact: Gerard J. Belliveau, Jr., Libn.
Scope: Sports, court and lawn tennis, early American sport. **Services:** Mail queries answered; copying; Library open to researchers by appointment. **Holdings:** 20,000 books. **Subscriptions:** 45 journals and other serials.

Tire Dealer

ASSOCIATIONS AND OTHER ORGANIZATIONS

19988 ■ Tire Industry Association
1532 Pointer Ridge Pl., Ste. G
Bowie, MD 20716-1883
Ph:(301)430-7280
Free: 800-876-8372
Fax:(301)430-7283
Co. E-mail: info@tireindustry.org
URL: http://www.tireindustry.org
Contact: Gary Albright, Pres./CEO
Description: Corporations engaged in all sectors of the replacement tire industry. Seeks to advance members' interests. Serves as a clearinghouse on economic and regulatory issues affecting the replacement tire industry; conducts educational programs; sponsors lobbying activities. .

19989 ■ Tire Retread and Repair Information Bureau
1013 Birch St.
Falls Church, VA 22046
Ph:(703)533-7677
Free: 877-394-6811
Fax:(703)533-7678
Co. E-mail: info@retread.org
URL: http://www.retread.org
Contact: Mr. David Stevens, Managing Dir.
Description: Retreaders, tire repair information, suppliers to the retread industry. Serves as information resource for the retread industry. Receives logistical support from industry associations, suppliers and retreaders. Operates speakers' bureau. .

REFERENCE WORKS

19990 ■ "Goodyear Extends Exclusive Deal to Supply NASCAR's Tires" in *Charlotte Observer* (February 4, 2007)
Pub: Knight-Ridder/Tribune Business News
Ed: David Poole. **Description:** Goodyear tires will continue to be the exclusive tire provider at NASCAR's Nextel Cup, Busch and Truck series through the year 2012.

19991 ■ "Miami's 'Big Wheels' Keep Latin America Rolling" in *Hispanic Business* (July-August 2007, pp. 46-47)
Pub: Hispanic Business
Ed: Frank Nelson. **Description:** Four top Hispanic owned exporters of tires are discussed. All four companies are based in Miami, Florida.

19992 ■ *Modern Tire Dealer—Facts/Directory Issue*
Pub: Bobit Business Media
Ed: Bob Ulrich, Editor, bob.ulrich@bobit.com. **Released:** Annual. **Publication Includes:** Directories of tire and car service suppliers, tire shop jobbers, and national and state associations. **Entries Include:** Generally, listings show company or organization name, address, phone, names and titles of key personnel. Listings for manufacturers include products. **Arrangement:** Manufacturers and national associations are alphabetical; jobbers and state associations are geographical. **Indexes:** Product.

19993 ■ *Tire Review—Sourcebook & Directory Issue*
Pub: Babcox
Ed: Jim Smith, Editor, jsmith@babcox.com. **Released:** Annual, latest edition 2007. **Publication Includes:** About 850 suppliers of tires, repair equipment, and automotive service supplies and equipment to tire dealers and retreaders. **Entries Include:** Company name, address, phone, name and title of contact, products, brand names, email and website addresses. **Arrangement:** Alphabetical. **Indexes:** Product, brand name.

19994 ■ *Who Makes It and Where Directory*
Pub: Tire Guides Inc.
Contact: Nancy Garfield, Chychrun, Sr. Publisher
Released: Annual, Latest edition 2011. **Price:** $8, single issue up to 24 copies. **Covers:** Over 600 tire, wheel, and tube manufacturers; international, domestic, and worldwide coverage. **Entries Include:** Company name, address, phone, website addresses, and toll free numbers. **Arrangement:** Classified by Department of Transportation identification code numbers. **Indexes:** Brand name.

STATISTICAL SOURCES

19995 ■ *World Markets for Tires and Rubber*
Pub: Business Trend Analysts, Inc.
Released: 2001-2002. **Price:** $2495.00. **Description:** Analyzes worldwide supply and demand for tires and natural and synthetic rubber. Competitor profiles provide insight to marketing strategies, R & D activities, financial performance, and more.

TRADE PERIODICALS

19996 ■ *Tire Business*
Pub: Crain Communications Inc.
Contact: Keith E. Crain, Editorial Dir.
Released: Semimonthly. **Price:** $79; $148 two years; $107 Canada; $194 two years Canada; $119 other countries; $208 two years all and other countries; $99 web only. **Description:** Newspaper (tabloid) serving independent tire dealers, retreaders, tire wholesalers and others allied to the tire industry.

19997 ■ *Tire Retreading/Repair Journal*
Pub: Tire Industry Association
Contact: LaKisha Pindell, Advertising Dir
E-mail: lpindell@tireindustry.org
Released: Monthly. **Price:** $60 U.S. and Canada; $70 other countries. **Description:** Magazine containing technical information on tire retreading and repair.

19998 ■ *Tire Review*
Pub: Babcox
Contact: Steve LaFerre, Sen. Ed.
E-mail: writecomm@aol.com
Released: Monthly. **Price:** Free to qualified subscribers. **Description:** Magazine containing news and business information about the tire, custom wheel, automotive service, and retreading industries.

TRADE SHOWS AND CONVENTIONS

19999 ■ World Tire Conference and Exhibition
Tire Industry Association
1532 Pointer Ridge Pl., Ste. G.
Bowie, MD 20716-1883
Ph:(301)430-7280
Free: 800-876-8372
Fax:(301)430-7283
Co. E-mail: info@tireindustry.org
URL: http://www.tireindustry.org
Released: Annual. **Audience:** Tire dealers, retreaders and repairs; trucking industry personnel; government personnel; environmentalists; recyclers. **Principal Exhibits:** Tire re-treading and repairing equipment; tires; reduction and removal; computer systems; waste to energy systems; allied services, including: brake equipment, wheel alignment, tire balancers, tire drangers, and service trucks; rubber recycling technologies; recycled rubber products.

FRANCHISES AND BUSINESS OPPORTUNITIES

20000 ■ Big O Tires
823 Donald Ross Rd.
Juno Beach, FL 33408
Ph:(561)803-7015
Free: 800-622-2446
Fax:(858)672-6201
Co. E-mail: franchise@big0tires.com
URL: http://www.bigotires.com
No. of Franchise Units: 458. **No. of Company-Owned Units:** 31. **Founded:** 1962. **Franchised:** 1982. **Description:** Retail tire and under-car service centers. **Equity Capital Needed:** Varies. **Franchise Fee:** $30,000. **Financial Assistance:** Yes. **Training:** 7-week training program, including classroom and hands-on application in a fully operational retail training store and ongoing support through regional schools, seminars, and clinics.

20001 ■ Canadian Tire Corp., Ltd
2180 Yonge St.
PO Box 770, Station K
Toronto, ON, Canada M4P 2V8
Ph:(416)480-3647
Fax:(416)480-3480
Co. E-mail: dealers@canadiantire.com
URL: http://www.canadiantire.ca/dealers
No. of Franchise Units: 485. **Founded:** 1922. **Franchised:** 1934. **Description:** Retailers of automotive, sports, leisure and home products. **Equity Capital Needed:** $125,000+. **Training:** Yes.

20002 ■ Rent-n-Roll Custom Wheels and Tires
SPF Mgt. Co., LLC
14620 N Nebraska Ave., Bldg. B
Tampa, FL 33613
Ph:(813)977-9800
Fax:(813)978-0584
No. of Franchise Units: 57. **No. of Company-Owned Units:** 6. **Founded:** 1999. **Franchised:** 2003. **Description:** Custom wheels & tires. **Equity Capital Needed:** $350,000-$500,000. **Franchise Fee:** $25,000. **Royalty Fee:** 4%. **Financial Assistance:** No. **Training:** Yes.

Tobacco Shop

ASSOCIATIONS AND OTHER ORGANIZATIONS

20003 ■ American Wholesale Marketers Association
2750 Prosperity Ave., Ste. 530
Fairfax, VA 22031
Ph:(703)208-3358
Free: 800-482-2962
Fax:(703)573-5738
Co. E-mail: info@awmanet.org
URL: http://www.awmanet.org
Contact: Bill Marshall, Pres.
Description: Represents the interests of distributors of convenience-related products. Its members include wholesalers, retailers, manufacturers, brokers and allied organizations from across the U.S. and abroad. Programs include strong legislative representation in Washington and a broad spectrum of targeted education, business and information services. Sponsors the country's largest show for candy and convenience related products in conjunction with its semi-annual convention. **Publications:** *Buying Guide and Membership Directory* (annual).

20004 ■ International Premium Cigar and Pipe Retailers
4 Bradley Park Ct., Ste. 2-H
Columbus, GA 31904-3637
Ph:(706)494-1143
Fax:(706)494-1893
Co. E-mail: info@ipcpr.org
URL: http://www.rtda.org
Description: Retailers of legal tobacco products and related items. Conducts marketing and merchandising programs. **Publications:** *Tobacco Retailers' Almanac* (annual).

20005 ■ Tobacco Merchants Association
PO Box 8019
Princeton, NJ 08543-8019
Ph:(609)275-4900
Fax:(609)275-8379
Co. E-mail: tma@tma.org
URL: http://www.tma.org
Contact: Farrell Delman, Pres.
Description: Manufacturers of tobacco products, leaf dealers, suppliers, distributors, and others related to the tobacco industry. Maintains records of trademarks. **Publications:** *Executive Summary* (weekly); *Issues Monitor* (biennial); *Legislative Bulletin* (biweekly); *Tobacco Barometer* (monthly); *Tobacco Trade Barometer* (monthly); *Tobacco Weekly* (weekly); *World Alert* (weekly).

20006 ■ Tobacconists' Association of America
19 S Wabash Ave.
Chicago, IL 60603
Ph:(312)351-2444
Co. E-mail: t-a-a@t-a-a.us
URL: http://www.t-a-a.com
Description: Retail tobacco merchants, usually one firm to an area or city, selling quality pipes, lighters, cigars, smokers, requisites, and personally blended tobaccos. .

REFERENCE WORKS

20007 ■ "Roll Your Own" in *Business North Carolina* (Vol. 28, March 2008, No. 3, pp. 66)
Pub: Business North Carolina
Ed: Amanda Parry. **Description:** Profile of U.S. Flue-Cured Tobacco Growers who process tobacco and make cigarettes. Details of the program are outlined.

20008 ■ "San Marcos May Ban Smoking" in *Austin Business Journal* (Vol. 31, June 17, 2011, No. 15, pp. 1)
Pub: American City Business Journals Inc.
Ed: Vicky Garza. **Description:** The City Council of San Marcos, Texas will hold a public hearing regarding a proposed citywide smoking ban. The city is moving towards the smoking ban because it appears a statewide ban may be enacted.

20009 ■ "Smoke Signals: Johnny Drake On What To Expect In a Fine Cigar" in *Black Enterprise* (Vol. 38, December 2007, No. 5, pp. 195)
Pub: Earl G. Graves Publishing Co. Inc.
Ed: Alan Hughes. **Description:** Profile of Johnny Drake, co-owner of the retail tobacco company Renaissance Cigar Emporium. According to the Retail Tobacco Dealers of America, 320 million handmade cigars are sold in the U.S. annually.

20010 ■ "What's Working Now: In Providing Jobs for North Carolinians" in *Business North Carolina* (Vol. 28, February 2008, No. 2, pp. 16)
Pub: Business North Carolina
Ed: Edward Martin, Frank Maley. **Description:** Individuals previously employed in the furniture, tobacco, or textile manufacturing sectors have gone back to school to be trained in new sectors in the area such as life sciences, finances and other emerging sectors.

TRADE PERIODICALS

20011 ■ *Cigar Aficionado*
Pub: M. Shanken Communications Inc.
Contact: Barry Abrams, Assoc. Publisher
E-mail: babrams@mshanken.com
Released: Bimonthly. **Price:** $19.95; $35.95 two years; $38 Canada; $70 Canada two years; $56 other countries; $102 other countries 2 years. **Description:** Men's lifestyle magazine directed toward those who wish to expand their knowledge of premium cigars.

20012 ■ *Convenience Distribution*
Pub: American Wholesale Marketers Association
Contact: Traci Carneal, Editor-in-Chief
E-mail: tracic@awmanet.org
Released: 10/yr. **Price:** $36 domestic; $66 other countries. **Description:** For service based distributors marketing to the retail trade.

20013 ■ *TMA Issues Monitor*
Pub: Tobacco Merchants Association of the U.S. Inc.
Contact: R. Crosby
Ed: Darryl Jayson, Editor. **Released:** Semiannual. **Price:** Included in membership. **Description:** Tracks issues and trends affecting the tobacco industry worldwide. Covers import and export news, related legislation, production and marketing information, and statistics.

20014 ■ *TMA Legislative Bulletin*
Pub: Tobacco Merchants Association of the U.S. Inc.
Contact: R. Crosby
Ed: Kay Carmello, Editor. **Released:** Biweekly. **Price:** Included in membership. **Description:** Reports on federal and state legislation and regulations affecting the tobacco industry.

20015 ■ *TMA Tobacco Weekly*
Pub: Tobacco Merchants Association of the U.S. Inc.
Contact: R. Crosby
Ed: David Goldstein, Editor. **Released:** Weekly. **Price:** Included in membership. **Description:** Summarizes key domestic tobacco industry issues as they develop at the federal, state, and local levels. Covers excise taxes, marketing and distribution, corporate finance, leaf and trade, health campaigns, and product liability.

20016 ■ *TMA Trademark Report*
Pub: Tobacco Merchants Association of the U.S. Inc.
Contact: R. Crosby
Ed: Kathy McCormick, Editor. **Released:** Monthly. **Price:** Included in membership. **Description:** Tracks tobacco product and tobacco accessory trademarks and brand names from test markets through registration. Covers renewals and cancellations.

20017 ■ *TMA World Alert*
Pub: Tobacco Merchants Association of the U.S. Inc.
Contact: R. Crosby
Ed: Marketa Stoy, Editor. **Released:** Weekly. **Price:** Included in membership. **Description:** Covers tobacco industry and corporate issues worldwide, on a country-by-country basis, including corporate finance, excise taxes, marketing and distribution developments, leaf and trade, and health campaigns.

20018 ■ *Tobacco Barometer: Cigarettes, Cigars, Smoking Tobacco, Chewing Tobacco and Snuff*
Pub: Tobacco Merchants Association of the U.S. Inc.
Contact: R. Crosby
Ed: Mark Schoenfeld, Editor. **Released:** Quarterly. **Price:** Included in membership. **Description:** Lists statistics on quarterly and cumulative production and sales of smoking tobacco, chewing tobacco, and snuff. Makes comparisons with the same period of the previous year, and has an analysis of current developments and trends. Recurring features include legislative and labor activities which affect the prices of these products.

20019 ■ *Tobacco Industry Litigation Reporter*
Pub: Thomson West
Ed: Kenneth Bradley, Esq., Editor, tomh@andrews-pub.com. **Released:** Monthly. **Price:** $2088.96. **Description:** Monitors major litigation brought against

the tobacco industry. Reports on discovery, protective orders, and cross-claims in asbestos cases and on the preemption provision of the Federal Cigarette Labeling and Advertising Act.

20020 ■ *Tobacco International*
Pub: Lockwood Trade Publications Inc.
Ed: Edward E. Ted Hoyt, III, Editor. **Released:** Monthly. **Price:** $40 U.S., Canada, and Mexico; $60 U.S., Canada, and Mexico two years; $85 other countries air mail; $150 other countries air mail, 2 years. **Description:** Trade magazine for tobacco leaf, tobacco products and allied industries.

20021 ■ *Tobacco Trade Barometer: Imports*
Pub: Tobacco Merchants Association of the U.S. Inc.
Contact: R. Crosby
Ed: Mark Schoenfeld, Editor. **Released:** Monthly. **Price:** Included in membership. **Description:** Carries statistics on imports of tobacco leaf and tobacco products. Gives tables on type, by country of origin, with quantities being brought in and their values. Quantity is given by weight and in pieces; value in U.S. dollars.

20022 ■ *US Tobacco Trade Barometer: Exports*
Pub: Tobacco Merchants Association of the U.S. Inc.
Contact: R. Crosby
Ed: Mark Schoenfeld, Editor. **Released:** Monthly. **Price:** Included in membership. **Description:** Carries statistics on exports of tobacco and tobacco products. Gives listings by country of destination, with quantities and values exported in the current month, in the year to date, and in comparison with previous periods.

VIDEOCASSETTES/ AUDIOCASSETTES

20023 ■ *All You Need to Know About Cigars!*
Tapeworm Video Distributors
25876 The Old Road 141
Stevenson Ranch, CA 91381
Ph:(661)257-4904
Fax:(661)257-4820
Co. E-mail: sales@tapeworm.com
URL: http://www.tapeworm.com
Price: $19.95. **Description:** Covers the history of cigars, the cigar lifestyle, and advice for both novices and connoisseurs. **Availability:** VHS.

20024 ■ *But a Good Cigar Is a Smoke!*
Tapeworm Video Distributors
25876 The Old Road 141
Stevenson Ranch, CA 91381
Ph:(661)257-4904
Fax:(661)257-4820
Co. E-mail: sales@tapeworm.com
URL: http://www.tapeworm.com
Released: 1997. **Price:** $14.95. **Description:** Presents an in depth look at every aspect of cigars. **Availability:** VHS.

20025 ■ *Cigars 101*
ELN Communications
155 North 35th St.
Seattle, WA 98103
Ph:(206)256-0420
Fax:(206)256-0419
Co. E-mail: eln@eln.com
URL: http://www.eln.com
Price: $19.95. **Description:** Provides how-to instruction in cutting, selecting, storing, and smoking cigars. **Availability:** VHS.

20026 ■ *The Havana: Cigar of Connoisseurs*
Janson Media
88 Semmens Rd.
Harrington Park, NJ 07640
Ph:(201)784-8488
Fax:(201)784-3993
URL: http://www.janson.com
Price: $24.95. **Description:** Documents the history and tradition of Cuban Havana cigars. **Availability:** VHS; DVD.

20027 ■ *Smoke in Your Eyes*
Tapeworm Video Distributors
25876 The Old Road 141
Stevenson Ranch, CA 91381
Ph:(661)257-4904
Fax:(661)257-4820
Co. E-mail: sales@tapeworm.com
URL: http://www.tapeworm.com
Price: $24.95. **Description:** Presents Vuelto Abajo, a prosperous tobacco growing region, its cigar factories, and personal interviews with cigar rollers. **Availability:** VHS.

FRANCHISES AND BUSINESS OPPORTUNITIES

20028 ■ Shefield Gourmet
2265 W Railway St.
PO Box 490
Abbotsford, BC, Canada V2S 2E3
Ph:(604)859-1014
Fax:(604)859-1711
No. of Franchise Units: 13. **Founded:** 1996. **Franchised:** 1996. **Description:** Tobacco products, coffees, and gifts. **Equity Capital Needed:** $70,000-$180,000 + inventory. **Franchise Fee:** $25,000. **Financial Assistance:** No. **Training:** Yes.

LIBRARIES

20029 ■ Imperial Tobacco Ltd.–Corporate Information Center
3711 St. Antoine St.
Montreal, QC, Canada H4C 3P6
Ph:(514)932-6161
Fax:(514)932-0383
Co. E-mail: rdumais@itl.ca
Contact: Robin Dumais, Assoc.Bus.Info.
Scope: Tobacco, management, science. **Services:** Interlibrary loan. **Holdings:** 6000 books; 10,000 pamphlets; 20 VF drawers of photographs and patents. **Subscriptions:** 360 journals and other serials.

20030 ■ Lorillard Tobacco Company Library
Box 21688
Greensboro, NC 27420-1688
Ph:(336)335-6896
Fax:(336)335-6640
Co. E-mail: lsklandanowski@lortobco.com
Contact: Lawrence M. Skladanowski, Lib.Mgr.
Scope: Tobacco products and manufacturing, tobacco chemistry. **Services:** Interlibrary loan; copying; Library open to the public by appointment. **Holdings:** 4200 books; 5700 bound periodical volumes; 1000 boxes of unbound periodicals. **Subscriptions:** 140 journals and other serials.

20031 ■ New York Public Library–The Research Libraries - Humanities and Social Sciences Library–Arents Tobacco Collection (5th A)
5th Ave. & 42nd St., Rm. 328
New York, NY 10018-2788
Ph:(212)642-0110
Fax:(212)302-4815
Co. E-mail: arnref@nypl.org
URL: http://legacy.www.nypl.org/research/chss/spe/rbk/arents/tobacco.html
Contact: Sarah Augusta Dickson, Libn.
Scope: Tobacco, herbals, history, medicine, law, manufacture, marketing; smoking and health. **Services:** Open to qualified researchers by card of admission secured in Special Collections Office. **Holdings:** 13,000 books and manuscripts; 150,000 cards and pieces of ephemera. **Subscriptions:** 10 journals and other serials.

20032 ■ Philip Morris Corporate Library
100 Park Ave., 17th Fl.
New York, NY 10017
Ph:(917)663-3863
Fax:(917)663-5317
Co. E-mail: david.deschenes@us.pm.com
Contact: David Deschenes, Dir./Sr.Res.Libn.
Scope: Business, marketing, finance, tobacco. **Services:** Library not open to the public. **Holdings:** 2000 books; microfiche; tobacco trade literature. **Subscriptions:** 160 journals and other serials; 20 newspapers.

20033 ■ PM USA Library
PO Box 26603
Richmond, VA 23261
Ph:(804)484-8897
URL: http://www.philipmorrisusa.com
Contact: Cornita Winston, Mgr.
Scope: Tobacco, chemistry, biochemistry, botany, physics, plant physiology. **Services:** Interlibrary loan. **Holdings:** 30,000 books; 10,000 bound periodical volumes; 350 AV programs; 5000 microfiche; 40 VF drawers of clippings; 7500 reels of microfilm of periodicals. **Subscriptions:** 300 journals and other serials; 6 newspapers.

20034 ■ Tobacco Merchants Association of the U.S.–Howard S. Cullman Library
PO Box 8019
Princeton, NJ 08543-8019
Ph:(609)275-4900
Fax:(609)275-8379
Co. E-mail: judith@tma.org
URL: http://www.tma.org/tmalive/FrmMain
Contact: Judith Mathus, Mgr., Info.Svcs./Res.Libn.
Scope: Tobacco industry and products. **Services:** Copying; Library open to the public for reference use only by appointment only. **Holdings:** 2000 books; 296 bound periodical volumes; 150 VF drawers of pamphlets, archives, and clippings; 18 shelves of government reports; 135 drawers of trademark file cards; 25 drawers of brand file cards. **Subscriptions:** 99 journals and other serials; 10 newspapers.

20035 ■ U.S. Bureau of Alcohol, Tobacco and Firearms–National Laboratory Center Library
6000 Ammendale Rd.
Beltsville, MD 20705-1250
Ph:(240)264-3770
Fax:(240)264-1493
Co. E-mail: susan.barned@atf.gov
Contact: Sue Barned, MLS, Libn.
Scope: Alcohol, analytical techniques, forensic sciences, firearms, tobacco, explosives. **Services:** Library not open to the public. **Holdings:** 4700 books; 4000 bound periodical volumes; 200 total journal titles; government documents; archives. **Subscriptions:** 42 journals and other serials.

20036 ■ U.S. Bureau of Alcohol, Tobacco, Firearms and Explosives Reference Library
99 New York Ave., NE
Washington, DC 20226
Ph:(202)927-7890
Co. E-mail: atfmail@atf.gov
URL: http://www.atf.gov
Contact: Vicki R. Herrmann, Libn.
Scope: Alcohol, tobacco, firearms, explosives. **Services:** Interlibrary loan; copying; SDI; reading room open to the public by appointment; archives open to the public with written permission. **Holdings:** 750 books; 100 bound periodical volumes; 1000 lin.ft. of indexed hearings, projects, tasks, and correspondence; 25 drawers of microfiche of historical documents; CD-ROMs. **Subscriptions:** 50 journals and other serials.

Tour Guide Operation/Adventure Service

START-UP INFORMATION

20037 ■ *The 100 Best Businesses to Start When You Don't Want To Work Hard Anymore*
Pub: Career Press Inc.
Ed: Lisa Rogak. **Price:** $16.99. **Description:** Author helps burned-out workers envision a new future as a small business owner. Systems analysis, adventure travel outfitting, bookkeeping, food delivery, furniture making, and software development are among the industries examined.

20038 ■ "Business Start-Up a Learning Experience for Young Bellingham Entrepreneur" in *Bellingham Herald* (July 18, 2010)
Pub: Bellingham Herald
Ed: Dave Gallagher. **Description:** Profile of 21-year-old entrepreneur, Chase Larabee, who developed an online program that helps airport fixed-based operators handle refueling, hotel and transportation reservations and other requests from private airplane pilots.

20039 ■ *Design and Launch an Online Travel Business in a Week*
Pub: Entrepreneur Press
Ed: Charlene Davis. **Released:** May 1, 2009. **Price:** $17.95. **Description:** Guide providing techniques and professional advice for starting an online travel business. Tips are given to build a Website, find qualified providers and to set up a payment system.

20040 ■ *Home-Based Travel Agent, 5th Edition*
Pub: The Intrepid Traveler
Ed: Kelly Monaghan. **Released:** March 2006. **Price:** $59.95. **Description:** Advice for starting and running a home-based travel agency is given.

20041 ■ "Online Fortunes" in *Small Business Opportunities* (Fall 2008)
Pub: Entrepreneur Media Inc.
Description: Fifty hot, e-commerce enterprises for the aspiring entrepreneur to consider are featured; virtual assistants, marketing services, party planning, travel services, researching, web design and development, importing as well as creating an online store are among the businesses featured.

ASSOCIATIONS AND OTHER ORGANIZATIONS

20042 ■ Adventure Travel Trade Association
601 Union St., 42nd Fl.
Seattle, WA 98101
Ph:(360)805-3131
Fax:(360)805-0649
Co. E-mail: info@adventuretravel.biz
URL: http://www.adventuretravel.biz
Contact: Mr. Shannon Stowell, Pres.
Description: Serves the adventure travel industry. Aims to grow the adventure travel industry overall and to help build up its member organizations. Provides exposure, marketing expertise, education, research, and discount to its members. .

20043 ■ Association of Canadian Travel Agencies–Association Canadienne des Agences de Voyages
2560 Matheson Blvd. E, Ste. 328
Mississauga, ON, Canada L4W 4Y9
Ph:(905)282-9294
Free: 888-257-2282
Fax:(905)282-9826
Co. E-mail: actacan@acta.ca
URL: http://www.acta.ca
Contact: David McCaig, Pres./COO
Description: Travel agents, tour operators, airlines, hotels, destination marketing organizations, cruise and rail lines, and automobile rental companies in Canada. Ensures consumers have professional and meaningful travel counseling by providing effective leadership in advocacy, public relations, research and education on behalf of the retail travel industry in Canada. **Publications:** *ACTA Voyage* (quarterly).

20044 ■ Canadian Tourism Research Institute
255 Smyth Rd.
Ottawa, ON, Canada K1H 8M7
Ph:(613)526-3280
Free: (866)711-2262
Fax:(613)526-4857
Co. E-mail: ctri@conferenceboard.ca
URL: http://www.conferenceboard.ca/topics/economics/CTRI/default.aspx
Contact: Anne Golden, Pres./CEO
Description: Represents travel and tourism businesses. Seeks to increase understanding of the needs and interests of tourists. Serves as a clearinghouse on tourism in Canada. Sponsors commercial tourism research.

20045 ■ International Association of Tour Managers - North American Region
24 Blevins Rd.
Kerhonkson, NY 12446-1302
Ph:(212)208-6800
Fax:(212)208-6800
Co. E-mail: chairman@tourmanager.org
URL: http://www.tourmanager.org
Contact: Mr. Scott Mcgraw CTM, Chm.
Description: Works to maintain the highest possible standards of tour management; guarantee excellence of performance; educate the travel world on the role of the tour manager (also referred to as tour director, tour escort, or tour leader) in the successful completion of the tour itinerary and in bringing business to related industries. Represents members in influencing legislation and advising on travel policy. Trains tour managers to plan, research, and lead tours to specific domestic and foreign destinations; operates Advisory Board in Professional Tour Management; offers placement service; conducts Professional travel agents, travel wholesalers, airlines, hotel associations, shipping lines, tourist organizations, restaurants, shops, and entertainment organizations Tour Management International Certificate Program. **Publications:** *The Professional Tour Manager* (quarterly).

20046 ■ The International Ecotourism Society
PO Box 96503
Washington, DC 20090-6503
Ph:(202)506-5033
Fax:(202)789-7279
Co. E-mail: info@ecotourism.org
URL: http://www.ecotourism.org
Contact: Dr. Kelly S. Bricker, Chair
Description: Works to generate and disseminate information about ecotourism. Represents members from academics, consultants, conservation professionals and organizations, governments, architects, tour operators, lodge owners and managers, general development experts, and ecotourists in more than 80 countries. Provides guidelines and standards, training, technical assistance, research and publications to foster sound ecotourism development. **Publications:** *Ecotourism: A Guide for Planners and Managers*; *Ecotourism: An Annotated Bibliography for Planners and Managers*; *Ecotourism Guidelines for Nature Tour Operations*; *The Environmental Tourist: An Ecotourism Revolution*; *Tourism, Ecotourism, and Protected Areas*;Membership Directory (annual).

20047 ■ International Galapagos Tour Operators Association
PO Box 1713
Lolo, MT 59847
Co. E-mail: exd@igtoa.org
URL: http://www.igtoa.org
Contact: Matt Kareus, Exec. Dir.
Description: Individuals and corporations conducting tours to the Galapagos Islands; educational and scientific institutions with an interest in the Islands and their ecosystems. Promotes tourism with the lowest possible environmental impact; seeks to preserve the unique ecosystems and species indigenous to the Galapagos Islands. Raises funds to support environmental protection initiatives; serves as a clearinghouse on low-impact nature tourism; facilitates communication and cooperation among members. .

20048 ■ National Tour Association
101 Prosperous Pl., Ste. 350
Lexington, KY 40509
Ph:(859)226-4444
Free: 800-682-8886
Fax:(859)226-4414
Co. E-mail: questions@ntastaff.com
URL: http://www.ntaonline.com
Contact: Cathy Greteman, Chair/CEO
Description: Operators of group tours and packaged travel; travel industry-related companies providing services/facilities to tour operators (hotels, attractions, restaurants); and destination marketing organizations such as convention and visitor bureaus, and state tourism departments. Seeks to: maintain a code of ethical standards within the tour industry; develop and increase public interest in packaged travel. Represents members before governmental bodies and agencies. Conducts research and educational programs. **Publications:** *Tuesday* (monthly);Directory (annual).

20049 ■ Tourism Industry Association of Canada–Association de L'Industrie Touristique du Canada
116 Lisgar St., Ste. 600
Ottawa, ON, Canada K2P 0C2
Ph:(613)238-3883
Co. E-mail: info@tiac.travel
URL: http://www.tiac.travel
Contact: David F. Goldstein, Pres./CEO
Description: Promotes viability of Canada's tourism industries. Serves as a unified voice for the industry in communications with government agencies responsible for tourism and related matters; conducts lobbying activities. **Publications:** *RVC Directory* (annual); *TIAC Talk* (weekly); *TIAC Talk Issue Focus* (periodic).

20050 ■ United States Tour Operators Association
275 Madison Ave., Ste. 2014
New York, NY 10016-1101
Ph:(212)599-6599
Fax:(212)599-6744
Co. E-mail: information@ustoa.com
URL: http://www.ustoa.com
Contact: Linda Kundell
Description: Represents wholesale tour operators, common carriers, associations, government agencies, suppliers, purveyors of travel services, trade press, communications media, and public relations and advertising representatives. Encourages and supports professional and financial integrity in tourism. Protects the legitimate interests of the consumer and the retail agent from financial loss from business conducted with members. Provides tour operators with an opportunity to formulate and express an independent industry voice on matters of common interest and self-regulation. Strives to facilitate and develop travel on a worldwide basis. .

DIRECTORIES OF EDUCATIONAL PROGRAMS

20051 ■ *Directory of Private Accredited Career Schools and Colleges of Technology*
Pub: Accrediting Commission of Career Schools and Colleges of Technology
Contact: Michale S. McComis, Exec. Dir.
Released: On web page. **Price:** Free. **Description:** Covers 3900 accredited post-secondary programs that provide training programs in business, trade, and technical fields, including various small business endeavors. Entries offer school name, address, phone, description of courses, job placement assistance, and requirements for admission. Arrangement is alphabetical.

REFERENCE WORKS

20052 ■ "2010 Book of Lists" in *Business Courier* (Vol. 26, December 26, 2009, No. 36, pp. 1)
Pub: American City Business Journals, Inc.
Description: Rankings of companies and organizations within the business services, education, finance, health care, hospitality and tourism, real estate, and technology industries in the Cincinnati, Ohio-Northern Kentucky area are presented. Rankings are based on sales, business size, or other statistics.

20053 ■ "B&B Hopes to Appeal to Fiat Execs" in *Crain's Detroit Business* (Vol. 25, June 15, 2009, No. 24, pp. 21)
Pub: Crain Communications Inc. - Detroit
Ed: Daniel Duggan. **Description:** Cobblestone Manor, a ten-room bed and breakfast in Auburn Hills, Michigan is hoping to provide rooms for Fiat executives. The owners have been working with travel organizations to promote the castle-like bed and breakfast which appeals to European visitors.

20054 ■ "Bill Kaneko" in *Hawaii Business* (Vol. 53, December 2007, No. 6, pp. 32)
Pub: Hawaii Business Publishing
Ed: David K. Choo. **Description:** Hawaii Institute for Public Affairs chief executive officer and president Bill Kaneko believes that the Hawaiian economy is booming, however, he also asserts that the economy is too focused on tourism and real estate. Kaneko has also realized the that the will of the people is strong while he was helping with the Hawaiian 2050 Sustainability Plan. The difficulties of making a sustainable Hawaii are discussed.

20055 ■ "The British Aren't Coming" in *Crain's Chicago Business* (Vol. 34, October 24, 2011, No. 42, pp. 3)
Pub: Crain Communications Inc.
Ed: Brigid Sweeney. **Description:** In a move to attract tourists back to Chicago, its Convention and Tourism Bureau is marketing in London, England, Mexico, and Canada, but not Germany or France because of budget constraints.

20056 ■ *Cruise Travel—Cruise Calendar Section*
Pub: World Publishing Co.
Ed: Charles Doherty, Editor. **Released:** Bimonthly, Three times yearly; April, August, and December. **Price:** $19.97, individuals per year. **Publication Includes:** Listing of cruises by major cruise lines worldwide. **Entries Include:** Cruise line company name, name of cruise ship, length of cruise, departure dates, destinations and ports-of-call, price range. **Arrangement:** Classified by cruising area, then port of departure.

20057 ■ "Cruising In Choppy Water" in *The Business Journal-Portland* (Vol. 25, August 22, 2008, No. 24, pp. 1)
Pub: American City Business Journals, Inc.
Ed: Erik Siemers. **Description:** Yacht builder Christensen Shipyards Inc. is experiencing robust business despite the slowing US economy, building four yachts a year as of 2008. The company expects revenues to hit $90 million and is opening a 500,000-square-foot plant in Tennessee.

20058 ■ "DePaul To Train Hotel Leaders" in *Chicago Tribune* (September 22, 2008)
Pub: McClatchy-Tribune Information Services
Ed: Kathy Bergen. **Description:** With help from a $7.5 million grant from the Conrad N. Hilton Foundation, DePaul University will dramatically expand its role as a training ground for the tourism-industry with the opening of a School of Hospitality.

20059 ■ "Destination Africa: A Look at How Tourism Could Change the Face and Economics of Africa" in *Black Enterprise* (February 2008)
Pub: Earl G. Graves Publishing Co. Inc.
Ed: Sonia Alleyne. **Description:** Countries in Africa are experiencing high rates of growth in tourism than the worldwide average. Statistical data included.

20060 ■ *Double or Nothing: How Two Friends Risked It All to Buy One of Las Vegas' Legendary Casinos*
Pub: HarperBusiness
Ed: Tom Breitling, with Cal Fussman. **Released:** March 2008. **Price:** $24.95. **Description:** Founders of a successful Internet travel agency share their experience from startup to selling the company.

20061 ■ "Doubletree Finds a Niche for Giving Back" in *Hotel and Motel Management* (Vol. 225, July 2010, No. 8, pp. 6)
Pub: Questex Media Group Inc.
Ed: Paul J. Heney. **Description:** Profile of Doubletree Hotel's community outreach programs that help employee volunteers work to educate children and the public about issues important to the environment.

20062 ■ *Driving With No Brakes: How a Bunch of Hooligans Built the Best Travel Company in the World*
Pub: Grand Circle Corporation
Ed: Alan and Harriet Lewis. **Price:** $19.95. **Description:** Inspirational book about how two courageous leaders built a remarkable company that can thrive in change and succeed in an unpredictable world. Important lessons for any business leader trying to create value in the 21st Century are included.

20063 ■ "Eco-Preneuring" in *Small Business Opportunities* (Jan. 2008)
Pub: Harris Publications Inc.
Description: Iceland Naturally is a joint marketing effort among tourism and business interests hoping to increase demand for Icelandic products including frozen seafood, bottled water, agriculture, and tourism in North America.

20064 ■ "Get Wrecked" in *Canadian Business* (Vol. 80, November 19, 2007, No. 23, pp. S13)
Pub: Rogers Media
Ed: Thomas Watson. **Description:** Key West economy has benefited from wrecks as salvaging lost items became a lucrative business. The USAFS General Hoyt S. Vanderberg is expected to be sunk and will provide a good opportunity for wreck dives. The trends in Key West tourism are evaluated.

20065 ■ "Goldbelt Inc.: Targeting Shareholder Development" in *Alaska Business Monthly* (Vol. 27, October 2011, No. 10, pp. 108)
Pub: Alaska Business Publishing Company
Ed: Tracy Kalytiak. **Description:** Profile of Goldbelt Inc., the company that has changed its original focus of timber to real estate to tourism and then to government contracting opportunities.

20066 ■ "Gov. Kasich to Put DOD On Short Leash" in *Business Courier* (Vol. 27, November 26, 2010, No. 30, pp. 1)
Pub: Business Courier
Ed: Dan Monk. **Description:** Ohio Governor-elect John Kasich proposed the privatization of the Ohio Department of Development in favor of a nonprofit corporation called JobsOhio. Kasich believes that the department has lost its focus by adding to its mission issues such as energy efficiency and tourism.

20067 ■ *A Guide to College Programs in Hospitality, Tourism, & Culinary Arts*
Pub: International Council on Hotel, Restaurant & Institutional Education
Contact: Kathy McCarthy, CEO
E-mail: kmccarty@chrie.org
Released: Biennial, latest edition 9th. **Price:** $29.95, members CD-ROM; $59.95, nonmembers CD-ROM; $149.95, members hardbound; $199.95, nonmembers hardbound. **Covers:** About 500 secondary and technical institutes, colleges, and universities; international coverage. **Entries Include:** School name, address, areas of study, degrees offered, name and title of contact, program description, financial aid information, tuition and fees, admission and graduation requirements. **Arrangement:** Alphabetical, geographical, specialization.

20068 ■ "Happy Trails: RV Franchiser Gives Road Traveling Enthusiasts a Lift" in *Black Enterprise* (Vol. 38, July 2008, No. 12, pp. 47)
Pub: Earl G. Graves Publishing Co. Inc.
Ed: Tamara E. Holmes. **Description:** Overview of Bates International Motor Home Rental Systems Inc., a growing franchise that gives RV owners the chance to rent out their big-ticket purchases to others when they are not using them; Sandra Williams Bate launched the company as a franchise in July 1997 and now has a fleet of 30 franchises across the country. She expects the company to reach 2.2 million for 2008 due to a marketing initiative that will expand the company's presence.

20069 ■ *Heads in Beds*
Pub: Prentice Hall PTR
Ed: Ivo Raza. **Released:** May 28, 2004. **Description:** Advice is given to help build brands, generate sales and grow profits through marketing for any hospitality or tourism business.

20070 ■ "Hola and Aloha" in *Hawaii Business* (Vol. 53, December 2007, No. 6, pp. 131)
Pub: Hawaii Business Publishing
Ed: Jason Ubay. **Description:** Juan Carlos Bianchetti is the trilingual owner of Ole Tours Hawaii, a travel wholesaler that targets Portuguese and Spanish-speaking visitors. The competition for American and

Japanese tourists is already tight, which is why Bianchetti opted to target a different segment of the Hawaii tourism market. Plans for the company's expansion in Kauai, Brazil, and Argentina, are mentioned.

20071 ■ "Hotels Get a Fill-Up" in *Crain's Detroit Business* (Vol. 25, June 1, 2009, No. 22, pp. 1)
Pub: Crain Communications Inc. - Detroit
Ed: Daniel Duggan. **Description:** Hot Rod Power Tour will have a $1 million economic impact on the area when it arrives in June 2009; the tour will bring 3,500 out-of-state custom vehicles to the event, whose owners will be needing hotel rooms.

20072 ■ "Ill Winds; Cuba's Economy" in *The Economist* (Vol. 390, January 3, 2009, No. 8612, pp. 20)
Pub: The Economist Newspaper Inc.
Description: Cuba's long-term economic prospects remain poor with the economy forecasted to grow only 4.3 percent for the year, about half of the original forecast, due in part to Hurricane Gustav which caused $10 billion in damage and disrupted the food-supply network and devastated farms across the region; President Raul Castro made raising agricultural production a national priority and the rise in global commodity prices hit the country hard. The only bright spot has been the rise in tourism which is up 9.3 percent over 2007.

20073 ■ "Indigenous Tourism Operators" in *International Journal of Entrepreneurship and Small Business* (Vol. 10, July 6, 2010, No. 4)
Pub: Publishers Communication Group
Ed: Andrews Cardow, Peter Wiltshier. **Description:** Emergent enthusiasm for tourism as a savior for economic development in the Chatham Islands of New Zealand is highlighted.

20074 ■ *JAX FAX—Travel Marketing Magazine*
Pub: Jet Airtransport Exchange Inc.
Contact: Marjorie Vincent, Bus. Mgr.
E-mail: marjorie@jaxfax.com
Released: Monthly. **Price:** $5 per copy; $15 per year; $12 per year group rate (5 or more); $3 back issues. **Covers:** over 6,000 specific scheduled and charter flights and tours to more than 80 destinations worldwide. **Entries Include:** Date of flight or tour, city of departure, destination, minimum and maximum prices, operator or wholesaler identification; contact name, address, phone, telex, telefax, commission rates. **Arrangement:** Geographical by destination. **Indexes:** Destination.

20075 ■ "Making Visitors Out Of Listeners" in *Hawaii Business* (Vol. 54, July 2008, No. 1, pp. 18)
Pub: Hawaii Business Publishing
Ed: Casey Chin. **Description:** Japanese workers are subscribing to the Official Hawaii Podcast in iTunes, which offers a free 20-minute, Japanese-language audio content on different topics, such as dining reviews and music from local artists. The concept is a way to attract Japanese travelers to come to Hawaii.

20076 ■ "Marathon Money" in *Hawaii Business* (Vol. 53, December 2007, No. 6, pp. 127)
Pub: Hawaii Business Publishing
Ed: Jolyn Okimoto Rosa. **Description:** Discusses the effects of the Honolulu Marathon on small businesses' sales. The Running Room, for instance, experience growth in sales starting from the training season up to the end of the race, as a surge of Hawaiian residents and tourists come into the store for items such as running shoes and blister kits. The marathon's impact on Hawaii's tourism is examined as well.

20077 ■ "The Next Waive" in *Hawaii Business* (Vol. 53, January 2008, No. 7, pp. 27)
Pub: Hawaii Business Publishing
Ed: Cathy S. Cruz-George. **Description:** Only 40,000 Koreans took a visit to Hawaii in 2007, a decline from the pre-September averages of 123,000 visits. The number of Korean visitors in Hawaii could increase if the visa waiver proposal is passed. Efforts to improve Hawaiian tourism are presented.

20078 ■ *OAG Business Travel Planner*
Pub: Reed Travel Group
Contact: Les Higgins, CEO
Released: Quarterly. **Covers:** 14,500 destination cities, military installations (U.S. only), and colleges and universities in North America; over 78,000 hotels and motels; calendar of events; city, state or province, and national tourist offices; tour operators; car rental agencies; airlines and charter air taxi firms, and airport limousine services; consulates and missions of foreign countries in North America; United States foreign service offices; hotel and motel systems, and toll free reservations services; airport club locations, frequent flyer and frequent guest information. **Entries Include:** For destinations—Place name, airport name and code or note on nearest air service; entries for larger cities include convention facilities, hotel name, address, phone, rates, location, number of meeting rooms, fax; whether member of the American Hotel and Motel Association. For calendar of events—Date, name and location of event, and names, addresses, and phone numbers of state and local tourism agencies. Separate toll-free section for hotel/motel systems and travel-related firms. Other listings include company or office name, address, phone. **Arrangement:** Primarily geographical.

20079 ■ *OAG Travel Planner European Edition*
Pub: OAG Worldwide
Contact: Oak Brook
Released: Quarterly. **Price:** $632, individuals Online; $705, individuals CD. **Covers:** Over 14,000 destination cities in Europe; 16,923 hotels; hotel chains and reservations services; calendars of events; city, regional, and national tourist offices; airline reservation numbers; car rental agencies; ground transportation information; U.S. military installations; consulates and missions of foreign countries in the United States and Canada; airport, ground, and rail services. **Entries Include:** Section for a country begins with climate, currency, documentary requirements, consulate, and other information; holiday and public event calendar for following six months; list of the country's tourist offices at home and abroad. For individual destinations—Place name, name and mileage from nearest airport, dialing code for each city; hotel name, address, phone, fax, telex, postal number, room rates, number of rooms, and quality rating, where applicable. **Arrangement:** Geographical.

20080 ■ "Orbitz Adds Parent Panel" in *Marketing to Women* (Vol. 21, March 2008, No. 3, pp. 5)
Pub: EPM Communications, Inc.
Description: Orbitz introduces the Orbitz Parent Panel in an attempt to better connect with traveling families.

20081 ■ "The Personal Touch: Entrepreneur Turns Good Taste, Love of Luxury Into Lucrative Venture" in *Black Enterprise* (October 2007)
Pub: Earl G. Graves Publishing Co. Inc.
Ed: Tamara E. Holmes. **Description:** Profile of Chaka Fattah Jr. who turned his taste for luxurious things into a successful luxury travel and concierge service catering to business owners, corporate executives, athletes, and entertainers.

20082 ■ "Plans for $160M Condo Resort in Wisconsin Dells Moves Forward" in *Commercial Property News* (March 18, 2008)
Pub: Nielsen Company
Description: Plans for the Grand Cambrian Resort in the Wisconsin Dells is discussed. The luxury condominium resort will include condos, townhomes, and condo-hotel style residences, two water parts, meeting space and indoor entertainment space, as well as a spa, four restaurants and retail offerings.

20083 ■ "Rock Hall Shifts Advertising to 'Significant Markets' in Region" in *Crain's Cleveland Business* (Vol. 28, July 23, 2007, No. 29, pp. 6)
Pub: Crain Communications, Inc.
Ed: John Booth. **Description:** Cleveland's Rock and Roll Hall of Fame and Museum is attempting a different marketing strategy this year with aims of reaching a broader audience in the Midwest and Great Lakes regions.

20084 ■ "Saudi Overtures" in *The Business Journal-Portland* (Vol. 25, August 15, 2008, No. 23, pp. 1)
Pub: American City Business Journals, Inc.
Ed: Aliza Earnshaw. **Description:** Saudi Arabia's huge revenue from oil is creating opportunities for Oregon companies as the country develops new cities, industrial zones, and tourism centers. Oregon exported only $46.8 million worth of goods to Saudi Arabia in 2007 but the kingdom is interested in green building materials and methods, renewable energy and water quality control, and nanotechnology all of which Oregon has expertise in.

20085 ■ *Selling the Invisible: A Field Guide to Modern Marketing*
Pub: Business Plus
Ed: Harry Beckwith. **Price:** $22.95. **Description:** Tips for marketing and selling intangibles such as health care, entertainment, tourism, legal services, and more are provided.

20086 ■ "Senate OKs Funds for Promoting Tourism" in *Crain's Detroit Business* (Vol. 24, March 31, 2008, No. 13, pp. 6)
Pub: Crain Communications, Inc.
Ed: Amy Lane. **Description:** Discusses the Senate proposal which allocates funds for Michigan tourism and business promotion as well as Michigan's No Worker Left Behind initiative, a program that provides free tuition at community colleges and other venues to train displaced workers for high-demand occupations.

20087 ■ "Small Dutch Islands Saba, Statia Content With Low-Key Niche" in *Travel Weekly* (Vol. 69, August 16, 2010, No. 33, pp. 22)
Pub: NorthStar Travel Media LLC
Ed: Gay Nagle Myers. **Description:** Small Caribbean islands market and promote their region for tourism by never competing with the bigger destinations. Saba and Statia are the two smallest islands in the Caribbean and rely on repeat guests, word-of-mouth recommendations and travel agents willing to promote them.

20088 ■ "State Tourism Likely to Decline Two Percent this Year" in *Crain's Detroit Business* (Vol. 24, April 14, 2008, No. 15, pp. 6)
Pub: Crain Communications, Inc.
Ed: Amy Lane. **Description:** Due to such national and state economic conditions such as unemployment, the housing crisis and rising gasoline and food prices, Michigan's tourism industry is likely to decline about 2 percent this year.

20089 ■ "Sunriver Venture Hits Snag" in *The Business Journal-Portland* (Vol. 25, August 1, 2008, No. 21, pp. 1)
Pub: American City Business Journals, Inc.
Ed: Robin J. Moody. **Description:** Portland, Oregon based-Sunwest Management Inc. has divided its Sunriver resort community to make way for a redevelopment plan. Sunwest owner Jon Harder and three partners formed SilverStar Destinations LLC to broker the purchase and redevelopment of the property. Details and description of the redevelopment project are also presented.

20090 ■ "The Superfluous Position" in *Entrepreneur* (Vol. 37, July 2009, No. 7, pp. 62)
Pub: Entrepreneur Media, Inc.
Description: Profile of an anonymous editor at a multimedia company that publishes tourism guides who shares his experiences in dealing with an office-mate who was promoted as creative manager of content. Everyone was irritated by this person, who would constantly do something to justify his new title. The biggest problem was the fact that this person didn't have a clear job description.

20091 ■ "The Way I Work" in *Inc.* (March 2008, pp. 102-104, 106)
Pub: Gruner & Jahr USA Publishing
Ed: Hannah Clark Steiman. **Description:** Profile of Howard Lefkowitz, CEO of Vegas.com, a Website that allows visitors to book flights, reserve hotel rooms, buy show tickets, make spa appointments, and coordinate any and all aspects of a trip to Las Vegas. The firm also runs brick-and-mortar box offices and concierge desks at various cities.

20092 ■ "Tourism Bureau Seeks Hotel Tax Hike" in *Baltimore Business Journal* (Vol. 27, December 18, 2009, No. 32, pp. 1)
Pub: American City Business Journals
Ed: Rachel Bernstein. **Description:** Baltimore, Maryland's tourism agency, Visit Baltimore, has proposed a new hotel tax that could produce $2 million annually for its marketing budget, fund improvements to the city's 30-year-old convention center and help it compete for World Cup soccer games. Baltimore hotel leaders discuss the new tax.

20093 ■ *Tourism and Entrepreneurship: International Perspectives*
Pub: Elsevier Science & Technology Books
Ed: Stephen Page, Jovo Ateljevic. **Released:** June 1, 2009. **Price:** $69.95. **Description:** Trends in tourism development are explored, focusing on the impact of entrepreneurship in the context of regional and local tourism development.

20094 ■ "Tourism Push Rising in Fall" in *Philadelphia Business Journal* (Vol. 30, August 26, 2011, No. 28, pp. 1)
Pub: American City Business Journals Inc.
Ed: Peter Van Allen. **Description:** Philadelphia is offering events for tourists this fall despite massive cuts for tourism promotion. Governor Tim Corbet slashed $5.5 million in funding for the state's tourism-promotion agencies which received $32 million in 2009. The agencies were forced to cooperate and fend for themselves using the hotel taxes that sustain them.

20095 ■ *The Travel Agent's Complete Desk Reference, 5th Edition*
Pub: The Intrepid Traveler
Ed: Kelly Monaghan. **Released:** August 25, 2009. **Price:** $39.95. **Description:** Reference book that provides essential information to the home-based travel agent.

20096 ■ "Travel In Style, Or Not: Finding a Company Travel Service for Every Budget" in *Inc.* (January 2008, pp. 36-37)
Pub: Gruner & Jahr USA Publishing
Ed: Larry Olmsted. **Description:** Profiles of various travel services to help small businesses. Firms profiled include Cassis Travel Services, providing first class bookings; Open from American Express, specializing in business class travel; Travelocity business, providing travel agents with 24/7 services; Diners Club Corporate Card, with many features; and Expedia Corporate Travel, allowing users to compare prices for airline tickets, hotels, and car rentals.

20097 ■ "Travel Tears" in *Crain's Chicago Business* (Vol. 31, November 17, 2008, No. 46, pp. 3)
Pub: Crain Communications, Inc.
Ed: Bob Tita. **Description:** Hotels, restaurants and conventions are seeing a decline in profits due to corporate travel cutbacks and the sagging economy. City and state revenues derived from taxes on tourism-related industries are also suffering.

20098 ■ "Turbulent Times and Golden Opportunity" in *Business Strategy Review* (Vol. 21, Spring 2010, No. 1, pp. 34)
Pub: Wiley-Blackwell
Ed: Don Sull. **Description:** For those feeling storm-tossed by today's economy, the author believes there's much to learn from Carnival Cruise Lines, a company that discovered that turbulence often has an upside.

20099 ■ "TW Trade Shows to Offer Seminars On Niche Selling, Social Media" in *Travel Weekly* (Vol. 69, October 4, 2010, No. 40, pp. 9)
Pub: NorthStar Travel Media LLC
Description: Travel Weekly's Leisure World 2010 and Fall Home Based Travel Agent Show focused on niche selling, with emphasis on all-inclusives, young consumers, groups, incentives, culinary vacations, and honeymoon or romance travel.

20100 ■ "Tweaking On-Board Activities, Equipment Saves Fuel, Reduces CO2" in *Canadian Sailings* (June 30, 2008)
Pub: Commonwealth Business Media
Description: Optimizing ship activities and equipment uses less fuel and therefore reduces greenhouse gas emissions. Ways in which companies are implementing research and development techniques in order to monitor ship performance and analyze data in an attempt to become more efficient are examined.

20101 ■ "Up In the Air" in *The Business Journal-Serving Greater Tampa Bay* (Vol. 28, July 18, 2008, No. 30, pp. 1)
Pub: American City Business Journals, Inc.
Ed: Margie Manning. **Description:** Views and information on Busch Gardens and on its future, are presented. The park's 3,769 employees worry for their future, after tourism industry experts have expressed concerns on possible tax cuts and other cost reductions. The future of the park, which ranks number 19 as the most visited park in the world, is expected to have a major impact on the tourism industry.

20102 ■ "The Visitor Rebound" in *Canadian Business* (Vol. 80, November 5, 2007, No. 22, pp. 23)
Pub: Rogers Media
Ed: Graham Silnicki. **Description:** Overnight visits to Canada are expected to fall by 5.3 percent in 2008, however spending is expected to drop by only 2 percent. Senior economist Alex Fritsche thinks that tourism from the U.S. will improve in 2009; the reasons for the expected growth in 2009 are examined.

20103 ■ "What's the Black Travel Market Worth?" in *Black Enterprise* (Vol. 38, January 2008, No. 6, pp. 54)
Pub: Earl G. Graves Publishing Co. Inc.
Ed: Aisha Sylvester. **Description:** African American travel market, both business and pleasure, is one of the top three fastest growing markets in the industry. Hugh Riley, director of marketing for the Caribbean Tourism Organization shares his ideas on the relationship between African American travelers and the Caribbean tourism industry.

20104 ■ "Where's the Lava" in *Hawaii Business* (Vol. 53, November 2007, No. 5, pp. 18)
Pub: Hawaii Business Publishing
Ed: Jason Ubay. **Description:** Hawaii Volcanoes National Park used to allow visitors to drive to the end of the paved coastal park road and view flowing lava that came from Kilauea until it reached the sea. On Father's Day morning in June 2007, Kilauea began erupting outside the park and the lava flows inland to Kahaualea and Wao Kele O Puna natural area reserves. In July 2007 321,217 visitors came to the park, a 14 percent increase compared to the same month in 2006.

20105 ■ "The World Is Your Hospital" in *Canadian Business* (Vol. 81, July 22, 2008, No. 12-13, pp. 62)
Pub: Rogers Media Ltd.
Ed: Sharda Prashad. **Description:** Medical tourism is seen as a booming industry around the world and is expected to grow to around $40 billion in 2010. Key information regarding medical tourism and services are presented. Views on the possible impact of medical tourism on Canada's health care industry, as well as medical tourism opportunities in Canada, are also given.

STATISTICAL SOURCES

20106 ■ *Travel Agencies and Tour Operators Market*
Pub: Rector Press, Ltd.
Contact: Lewis Sckolnick, Pres
Released: 2009. **Price:** Contact Rector Press.

TRADE PERIODICALS

20107 ■ *Bermuda Now*
Pub: Bermuda Department of Tourism
Ed: Melanie Astwood, Editor. **Released:** 4/year. **Price:** Free. **Description:** Offers promotional articles on Bermuda to encourage growth of the tourist industry and to keep the U.S. travel industry abreast of news about the island's visitors.

20108 ■ *Cruise Travel Magazine*
Pub: World Publishing Co.
Contact: Dale Jacobs, Production Mgr
E-mail: djacobs@centurysports.net
Ed: Charles Doherty, Editor. **Released:** Bimonthly. **Price:** $24.94; $50 Canada; $60 other countries. **Description:** Magazine covering consumer-oriented cruise-ship vacations.

20109 ■ *Cruise and Vacation Views*
Pub: Orban Communications Inc.
Contact: Jessica A. Agate, Assoc. Ed.
Released: Bimonthly. **Description:** Trade magazine for leisure travel professionals.

20110 ■ *Dude, Guest & Vacation Ranches*
Pub: Bibliotheca Press
Contact: A. Doyle
Ed: A. Doyle, Editor. **Released:** Irregular. **Price:** $7. 95, U.S.. **Description:** Lists dude, guest, and vacation ranches for tourists.

20111 ■ *Hideaways Newsletter*
Pub: Hideaways International
Contact: Michael F. Thiel, President/Founder
E-mail: mthiel@hideaways.com
Ed: Peg Aaronian, Editor, paaronian@hideaways.com. **Released:** Quarterly. **Price:** $129, Included in membership. **Description:** Features articles on issues of interest to villa vacationers and those seeking high quality, high service vacation options. Includes extensive reports on vacation accommodations; destination descriptions; members' ratings of villas, hotels, cruise ships, and yacht charters; travel tips; and news from recommended properties/cruise lines. Recurring features include compilations of quarterly travel surveys, and columns titled Members News, Members Forum, and Trade Winds. Occasional supplements focusing on one destination, i.e., the Caribbean, Paris, etc. Remarks: Subscription includes semiannual, full-color "Hideaways Guide."

20112 ■ *Hot Springs, Mineral Waters*
Pub: Bibliotheca Press
Contact: A. Doyle
Ed: A. Doyle, Editor. **Released:** Irregular. **Price:** $7. 95, U.S.. **Description:** Lists hot springs and mineral water locations for tourists.

20113 ■ *Hotel & Travel Index—International Edition*
Pub: Hotel & Travel Index International Edition
Contact: Bob Sullivan, VP/Publisher
E-mail: rsullivan@travelweekly.com
Released: Quarterly. **Price:** $125 U.S. and other countries one year. **Description:** International hotel directory.

20114 ■ *Journeywoman Online Magazine*
Pub: Journeywoman
Contact: Evelyn Hannon, Editor & Publisher
E-mail: editor@journeywoman.com
Released: Irregular. **Description:** Online publication offering female-centered travel tips and stories for single and married women.

20115 ■ *National Bus Trader*
Pub: National Bus Trader Inc.
Ed: Larry Plachno, Editor. **Released:** Monthly. **Price:** $25; $30 other countries. **Description:** Magazine for bus tour planners.

20116 ■ *OAG Flight-Finder Asia Pacific Plus*
Pub: OAG Worldwide
Released: Monthly. **Description:** Guide containing quick reference airline schedules within and between all countries of the Pacific geographic area; plus all schedules between the area and North America, Europe, the Middle East, Africa, and Central/South America.

20117 ■ *Southern Festivals*
Pub: Southern Festivals
Contact: Jim Taylor
Released: Bimonthly. **Description:** A statewide newspaper covering travel and tourism.

20118 ■ *Spa Magazine*
Pub: Islands Publishing Co.
Contact: Michelle Gamble, Publisher
Released: 7/yr. **Price:** $11.97 U.S.; $20.97 Canada; $36.97 other countries. **Description:** Magazine containing articles on travel, well-being, and 'renewal'.

20119 ■ *Travelweek*
Pub: Concepts Travel Media Ltd.
Contact: Michael Butler, Gp. Publisher
E-mail: mbutler@travelweek.ca
Released: Weekly (Thurs.). **Description:** Trade publication covering the travel industry.

20120 ■ *Tuesday*
Pub: National Tour Association
Ed: Julie Lawson, Editor. **Released:** Monthly. **Price:** Included in membership. **Description:** Promotes high standards in the tour industry and public interest in North American escorted tours. Provides information for group tour operators and suppliers in the U.S. and Canada. Carries legislative updates. Recurring features include Association and member news.

20121 ■ *Woodall's Northeast Outdoors*
Pub: Woodall Publications Corp.
Released: Bimonthly. **Price:** $20. **Description:** Magazine serving campers and RVers in the Northeast.

TRADE SHOWS AND CONVENTIONS

20122 ■ Annual Allegheny Sport, Travel and Outdoor Show
Expositions Inc.
PO Box 550, Edgewater Br.
Cleveland, OH 44107-0550
Ph:(216)529-1300
Fax:(216)529-0311
Co. E-mail: expoinc@oinc.com
URL: http://www.expoinc.com
Released: Annual. **Principal Exhibits:** Sports, travel and outdoor show.

20123 ■ Colorado RV Adventure Travel Show
Industrial Expositions, Inc.
1675 Larimer St., No.700
PO Box 480084
Denver, CO 80248-0084
Ph:(303)892-6800
Free: 800-457-2434
Fax:(303)892-6322
Co. E-mail: info@iei-expos.com
URL: http://www.iei-expos.com/
Released: Annual. **Audience:** General Public. **Principal Exhibits:** Recreational vehicles, accessories and travel.

20124 ■ Eastern Sports & Outdoor Show
Reed Exhibitions North American Headquarters
383 Main Ave.
Norwalk, CT 06851
Ph:(203)840-4800
Fax:(203)840-5805
Co. E-mail: export@reedexpo.com
URL: http://www.reedexpo.com
Released: Annual. **Audience:** General public. **Principal Exhibits:** Recreational vehicles, boats, hunting and fishing equipment, clothing, and related outdoor products, resorts, SUVs, retailers and manufacturers, motorcycles, ATVs, travel and tourism.

20125 ■ Fort Wayne Sports, Vacation, and Boat Show
Trio Enterprises, Inc.
3624 Maxim Dr.
Fort Wayne, IN 46815
Ph:(219)483-2638
Free: 800-446-2638
Fax:(219)484-0876
Released: Annual. **Audience:** General public. **Principal Exhibits:** Recreational vehicles, boats, and travel and vacation information.

20126 ■ Louisville Boat, RV & Sportshow
Douglas Expositions Inc.
10000 Shelbyville Rd., No. 111
Anchorage, KY 40223-2950
Ph:(502)244-5660
Fax:(502)244-5160
Released: Annual. **Principal Exhibits:** Sports, boating and vacations, hunting and fishing, recreational vehicles.

20127 ■ Travel Media Showcase
Atlantic City Convention & Visitors Authority
2314 Pacific Ave.
Atlantic City, NJ 08401
Ph:(609)449-7162
Fax:(609)345-2200
URL: http://www.atlanticcitynj.com/
Released: Annual. **Audience:** Trade. **Principal Exhibits:** Tourism industry and travel media convention.

FRANCHISES AND BUSINESS OPPORTUNITIES

20128 ■ GolfAhoy Golf & Cruise Travel Bureau
GolfAhoy (BVI) Ltd.
5328 Calgary Tr., Ste. 1165
Edmonton, AB, Canada T6H 4J8
Free: 877-415-5442
Fax:(780)669-5667
No. of Franchise Units: 46. **No. of Company-Owned Units:** 1. **Founded:** 1988. **Franchised:** 2001. **Description:** Golf tourism and cruise travel bureau. **Equity Capital Needed:** $16,040-$18,260 start-up. **Franchise Fee:** $14,960. **Financial Assistance:** No. **Training:** Yes.

20129 ■ Lantis Fireworks & Lasers
Lantis Franchising
PO Box 491
Draper, UT 84020
Free: 800-443-3040
No. of Franchise Units: 1. **No. of Company-Owned Units:** 2. **Founded:** 1988. **Franchised:** 1990. **Description:** Provide pyrotechnical and laser displays. **Equity Capital Needed:** $172,400-$274,000. **Franchise Fee:** $50,000. **Royalty Fee:** 6%. **Financial Assistance:** No. **Training:** Available at headquarters 4-6 weeks.

20130 ■ Outdoor Connection
424 Neosho
Burlington, KS 66839
Ph:(620)364-5500
Fax:(620)364-5563
No. of Franchise Units: 61. **No. of Company-Owned Units:** 2. **Founded:** 1988. **Franchised:** 1990. **Description:** Hunting and fishing travel service. **Equity Capital Needed:** $7,550-$12,250. **Franchise Fee:** $6,500. **Royalty Fee:** 4%. **Financial Assistance:** Assistance with franchise fee. **Training:** 2 days at headquarters, 2-3 days annual convention and ongoing support. ort.

LIBRARIES

20131 ■ Davenport University–Thomas F. Reed, Jr. Memorial Library
4123 W. Main St.
Kalamazoo, MI 49006
Ph:(616)382-2835
Free: 800-632-8928
Fax:(269)382-2657
Co. E-mail: kz_linc@davenport.edu
URL: http://www.davenport.edu/
Contact: Judith J. Bosshart, Dir.
Scope: Business, data processing, administrative services, accounting, humanities, paralegal, medical records, healthcare administration, computer and information processing. **Services:** Interlibrary loan; copying; faxing; Library open to the public for reference use only. **Holdings:** 14,200 books; 995 videotapes. **Subscriptions:** 12,000 journals and other serials; 6 newspapers.

20132 ■ Johnson and Wales University Charleston Campus–Barry L. Gleim Library
701 E. Bay St.
Charleston, SC 29403
Ph:(843)727-3045
Fax:(843)727-3078
Co. E-mail: Joanne.Letendre@jwu.edu
Contact: Joanne N. Letendre
Scope: Culinary arts, food service, hospitality management, travel and tourism. **Services:** Library open to the public with restrictions. **Holdings:** 10,681 books; 1230 videos; 6 CD-ROMs. **Subscriptions:** 174 journals and other serials; 5 newspapers.

20133 ■ Pannell Kerr Forster Library
29 Broadway
New York, NY 10006-3201
Ph:(212)867-8000
Fax:(212)687-4346
Co. E-mail: dsu@pkfny.com
URL: http://www.pkfnewyork.com
Contact: Di Su, Libn.
Scope: Research on hospitality, tourism, accounting, auditing, real estate. **Services:** Library not open to the public. **Holdings:** 2000 volumes; pamphlets; clippings. **Subscriptions:** 50 journals and other serials.

20134 ■ Simat, Helliesen & Eichner, Inc. Library
90 Park Ave., 27th Fl.
New York, NY 10016
Ph:(212)656-9200
Fax:(212)471-6000
Co. E-mail: newyork@h-e.com
URL: http://www.sh-e.com
Scope: Aviation, aircraft, aviation finance and safety, airport planning, tourism, travel, economics, business. **Services:** Interlibrary loan (within company only); copying; Library not open to the public. **Holdings:** 2500 titles; periodicals. **Subscriptions:** 550 journals and other serials.

20135 ■ Travel Industry Association of America Library
1100 New York Ave. NW, Ste. 450
Washington, DC 20005-3934
Ph:(202)408-8422
Fax:(202)408-1255
URL: http://www.tia.org
Contact: Suzanne D. Cook, Sr. VP, Res.
Scope: Travel and tourism. **Services:** Library not open to the public. **Holdings:** 3000 research documents; 3800 government documents; 250 unpublished travel research reports; 15,000 clippings; 20 tapes. **Subscriptions:** 27 journals and other serials.

20136 ■ University of Wisconsin—Stout–Library Learning Center
315 10th Ave.
Menomonie, WI 54751
Ph:(715)232-1215
Free: (80)
Fax:(715)232-1783
Co. E-mail: library@uwstout.edu
URL: http://www.uwstout.edu/lib/
Contact: Paul Roberts, Dir.
Scope: Industrial technology; hospitality and tourism; human development and family life education; home economics; business; vocational rehabilitation; early childhood education; manufacturing engineering; technology education. **Services:** Interlibrary loan; copying; document delivery; SDI; Center open to the public. **Holdings:** 226,551 books; 19,694 AV titles; 1,243,068 microforms; 1705 archives. **Subscriptions:** 1057 journals; 19 newspapers.

RESEARCH CENTERS

20137 ■ College of Forestry and Conservation–Institute for Tourism and Recreation Research
University of Montana
32 Campus Dr., No. 1234
Missoula, MT 59812-1234
Ph:(406)243-5686
Fax:(406)243-4845
Co. E-mail: request@forestry.umt.edu
URL: http://www.forestry.umt.edu/
Contact: Kate Cenis, Dir.
Description: Provides research data needed to support the state's tourism industry.

20138 ■ State University of New York at Buffalo–Center for Executive Development
108 Jacobs Management Center
Buffalo, NY 14260
Ph:(716)645-3200
Fax:(716)645-3501
Co. E-mail: mgt-ced@buffalo.edu
URL: http://www.mgt.buffalo.edu/executive
Contact: Courtney Walsh, Exec.Dir.
E-mail: mgt-ced@buffalo.edu
Scope: Administrates and coordinates market, tourism, and public policy research conducted by School of Management faculty, bringing faculty and student research expertise to bear upon specific business and economic issues. As a State Data Center Affiliate designate, the Center collects, analyzes, and distributes data for business and community planning purposes. **Educational Activities:** Seminars and training programs for industry, including a continuing education program in accounting.

20139 ■ University of Calgary–World Tourism Education and Research Centre
Scurfield Hall
Haskayne School of Business
2500 University Dr. NW
Calgary, AB, Canada T2N 1N4
Ph:(403)220-3800
Fax:(403)282-0266
Co. E-mail: brent.ritchie@haskayne.ucalgary.ca
URL: http://haskayne.ucalgary.ca/haskaynefaculty/research/centres/wterc
Contact: Dr. J.R. Brent Ritchie, Ch.
E-mail: brent.ritchie@haskayne.ucalgary.ca
Scope: Tourism, especially its role in global, social, and cultural development, management of tourism organizations and regions, and environmental and social considerations.

20140 ■ University of Central Florida–Dick Pope, Sr. Institute for Tourism Studies
Rosen College of Hospitality Management
9907 Universal Blvd.
Orlando, FL 32819
Ph:(407)903-8028
Fax:(407)903-8105
Co. E-mail: apizam@mail.ucf.edu
URL: http://www.hospitality.ucf.edu/dick_pope.html
Contact: Dr. Abraham Pizam, Dir.
E-mail: apizam@mail.ucf.edu
Scope: Tourism and travel industry in Florida, U.S., and other countries, including development of tourism forecasts and investigations of characteristics and motivations of travelers. Identifies and analyzes problems in the tourism industry. Provides primary data sources to aid in management decision making. **Publications:** Proprietary Research Reports. **Educational Activities:** Conferences; Faculty workshops; Industry seminars; Public and private research consultation opportunities; Research colloquiums (monthly); Sponsorship opportunities.

20141 ■ University of Colorado at Boulder–Business Research Division
420 UCB
Leeds School of Business
Boulder, CO 80309-0420
Ph:(303)492-8227
Fax:(303)492-3620
Co. E-mail: richard.wobbekind@colorado.edu
URL: http://leeds.colorado.edu/brd
Contact: Dr. Richard Wobbekind, Dir.
E-mail: richard.wobbekind@colorado.edu
Scope: Regional and local economic impact studies, and forecasting. **Services:** Provides businesspersons, city managers, planners, association executives, and others with information useful in the operation of their organizations. **Educational Activities:** Annual Colorado Business Economic Outlook Forum, in December.

Toy Business

START-UP INFORMATION

20142 ■ "Fun And Easy Gold Mines" in *Small Business Opportunities* (Fall 2008)
Pub: Entrepreneur Media Inc.
Description: Twenty-five businesses that cater to the booming children's market are profiled; day care services, party planning, special events video-making, tutoring, personalized children's toys and products and other services geared toward the kids market are included.

20143 ■ "Honoring Creativity" in *Playthings* (Vol. 107, January 1, 2009, No. 1, pp. 28)
Pub: Reed Business Information
Ed: Cliff Annicelli. **Description:** Toy & Game Inventors Expo is held annually in conjunction with the Chicago Toy & Game Fair. The event honors toy inventors in the categories of Game Design, Toy Design and Rising Stars, plus a lifetime achievement award. Profile of the company, Toying With Games, founded by Joyce Johnson and Colleen McCarthy-Evans are included in the article.

20144 ■ *The Specialty Shop: How to Create Your Own Unique and Profitable Retail Business*
Pub: AMACOM
Ed: Dorothy Finell. **Released:** February 27, 2007. **Price:** $21.95. **Description:** Advise to start retail businesses, including bakeries, gift shops, toy stores, book shops, tea houses, clothing boutiques, and other unique stores.

ASSOCIATIONS AND OTHER ORGANIZATIONS

20145 ■ Strawberry Shortcake Chat Group
138 E Main Cross St.
Greenville, KY 42345
Ph:(270)338-4318
Fax:(270)338-6856
Co. E-mail: jenniferbowles@bellsouth.net
URL: http://www.strawberrybonkers.com
Contact: Jennifer Bowles, Ed.
Description: Owners and admirers of Strawberry Shortcake dolls. Promotes collection and preservation of Strawberry Shortcake dolls. Facilitates communication among members; serves as a clearinghouse on Strawberry Shortcake dolls. .

20146 ■ Toy Industry Association
1115 Broadway, Ste. 400
New York, NY 10010
Ph:(212)675-1141
Co. E-mail: info@toyassociation.org
URL: http://www.toyassociation.org
Contact: Bryan Stockton, Chm.
Description: Provides business services to U.S. manufacturers and importers of toys. Manages American International Toy Fair; represents the industry before Federal, State and Local government on issues of importance; provides legal and legislative counsel; conducts educational programs; compiles industry statistics. **Publications:** *American International Toy Fair Official Directory* (annual); *Toy Challenges and Opportunities* (annual).

20147 ■ U.S.A. Toy Library Association
2719 Broadway Ave.
Evanston, IL 60201
Ph:(847)612-6966
Fax:(847)864-8473
Co. E-mail: jqi@comcast.net
URL: http://usatla.org/Welcome.html
Contact: Judith Q. Iacuzzi, Exec. Dir.
Description: Child care professionals, parents, and others interested in the role of toys and play in child development. Promotes the importance of play and the development of toy libraries in public and school libraries, hospitals, day care centers, and mobile collections. Seeks to broaden understanding of how toys can educate, increase parent-child interaction, and aid in development and therapy of disabled children.
.

REFERENCE WORKS

20148 ■ "The ABCs of a Good Show" in *Playthings* (Vol. 106, October 1, 2008, No. 9, pp. 18)
Pub: Reed Business Information
Ed: Karyn M. Peterson. **Description:** ABC Kids Expo 2008 made a strong showing with products for babies, kids and new/expecting parents. The new Naturally Kids section promoting eco-friendly products was the highlight of the show.

20149 ■ "ACC Game Development Program Opens" in *Austin Business JournalInc.* (Vol. 28, October 31, 2008, No. 33, pp. 1)
Pub: American City Business Journals
Ed: Sandra Zaragoza. **Description:** Austin, Texas-based Austin Community College has launched its Game Development Institute. The institute was created to meet the gaming industry's demand for skilled workers. One hundred students have enrolled with the institute.

20150 ■ "Bakugan Battle Brawlers" in *Advertising Age* (Vol. 79, November 17, 2008, No. 43, pp. S2)
Pub: Crain Communications, Inc.
Ed: Kate Fitzgerald. **Description:** Spin Master toys has a new hit, Bakugan Battle Brawlers, an interactive game board with 106 characters that battle with one another in tournaments. Bakugan tournaments are being held at Toys "R" Us stores.

20151 ■ "Blues at the Toy Fair: Industry Reeling From Recalls, Lower Sales Volumes" in *Crain's New York Business* (February 18, 2008)
Pub: Crain Communications Inc.
Ed: Elisabeth Cordova. **Description:** Over 1,500 toy developers and vendors will attend the American International Toy Fair, expected to be low-key due to recent recalls of toys not meeting American safety standards. Toy retailers and manufacturers, as well as the Chinese government, are promoting product testing to prevent toxic metals in toys.

20152 ■ "Cents and Sensibility" in *Playthings* (Vol. 107, January 1, 2009, No. 1, pp. 19)
Pub: Reed Business Information
Ed: Pamela Brill. **Description:** Recent concerns over safety, phthalate and lead paint and other toxic materials, as well as consumers going green, are issues discussed by toy manufacturers. Doll manufacturers also face increase labor and material costs and are working to design dolls that girls will love.

20153 ■ "The China Tax" in *Forbes* (Vol. 180, October 1, 2007, No. 6, pp. 35)
Pub: Forbes Inc.
Ed: Robyn Meredith. **Description:** U.S. consumers can see a rise in prices for goods made in China due to growing pressure from Congress to ensure safe products from that country. Taxing products imported from China could be levied in five different forms listed.

20154 ■ "Consignment Shop Offers Children's Clothes, Products" in *Frederick News-Post* (August 19, 2010)
Pub: Federick News-Post
Ed: Ed Waters Jr. **Description:** Sweet Pea Consignments for Children offers used items for newborns to pre-teens. The shop carries name brand clothing as well as toys, books and baby products.

20155 ■ "Counting on Cornhole: Popular Bean Bag Game Brings Crowds to Bars" in *Boston Business Journal* (Vol. 29, July 15, 2011, No. 10, pp. 1)
Pub: American City Business Journals Inc.
Ed: Alexander Jackson. **Description:** Cornhole game is being used by bars to spur business as the games hikes beer and food sales on slow weekdays. The game is played with two cornhole boards facing each other and is played with one or two people on one team who try to place a bag on the board.

20156 ■ "A Curious Appeal (Market for Scientific Toys)" in *Playthings* (Vol. 106, October 1, 2008, No. 9, pp. 26)
Pub: Reed Business Information
Ed: Pamela Brill. **Description:** Science and nature toys are still popular with children. Kits allow kids to make candy, soap, grow miniature gardens, catch bugs and more. These hands-on kits have manufacturers watching trends to create more toys in this category.

20157 ■ "Dealing With Dangers Abroad" in *Financial Executive* (Vol. 23, December 2007, No. 10, pp. 32)
Pub: Financial Executives International
Ed: Jeffrey Marshall. **Description:** Clear processes and responsibilities for risk management for all companies going global are essential. U.S. toy

manufacturer, Matel was put into crisis mode after its Chinese-made toys were recalled due to the use of lead-based paint or tiny magnets in its products.

20158 ■ "Despite Hot Toys, Holiday Sales Predicted To Be Ho-Ho-Hum" in *Drug Store News* (Vol. 29, November 12, 2007, No. 14, pp. 78)
Pub: Drug Store News
Ed: Doug Desjardins. **Description:** Summer toy recalls have retailers worried about holiday sales in 2007. Mattel was heavily impacted from the recall of millions of toys manufactured in China.

20159 ■ "Disney Has High Hopes for Duffy" in *Canadian Business* (Vol. 83, October 12, 2010, No. 17, pp. 14)
Pub: Rogers Media Ltd.
Ed: James Cowan. **Description:** The reintroduction of Duffy is expected to create a new, exclusive product line that distinguishes Disney's parks and stores from competitors. Duffy, a teddy bear, was first introduced at a Disney World store in Florida in 2002. The character was incorporated into the Disney mythology when its popularity grew in Japan.

20160 ■ "A Doll That Looks Like You: Will Custom Toys Take Off?" in *Inc.* (Volume 32, December 2010, No. 10, pp. 144)
Pub: Inc. Magazine
Ed: Shivani Vora. **Description:** Profiles of various companies that provide custom items that look like people.

20161 ■ "Down on the Boardwalk" in *Retail Merchandiser* (Vol. 51, September-October 2011, No. 5, pp. 56)
Pub: Phoenix Media Corporation
Ed: Eric Slack. **Description:** Classic board game, Monopoly, continues to be the most recognized game brand while staying fresh by entering new markets and gaming platforms for all walks of life. Monopoly is available in over 100 countries, translated into 43 languages and played by more than 1 billion people since its introduction, and the game is tailored to each geographic market it enters.

20162 ■ "Earth Angels" in *Playthings* (Vol. 106, September 1, 2008, No. 8, pp. 10)
Pub: Reed Business Information
Ed: Karyn M. Peterson. **Description:** ImagiPlay toy company has partnered with Whole Foods Market to distribute the company's wooden playthings across the country. The company's Earth-friendly business model is outlined.

20163 ■ "Enforcer In Fantasyland" in *Crain's New York Business* (Vol. 24, February 25, 2008, No. 8, pp. 10)
Pub: Crain Communications Inc.
Ed: Hilary Potkewitz. **Description:** Patent law, particularly in the toy and game industry, is recession-proof according to Barry Negrin, partner at Pryor Cashman. Negrin co-founded his patent practice group. Despite massive recalls of toys and the concern over toxic toys, legal measures are in place in this industry.

20164 ■ "Familiar Fun" in *Crain's Cleveland Business* (Vol. 28, October 22, 2007, No. 42, pp. 3)
Pub: Crain Communications Inc.
Ed: John Booth. **Description:** Marketing for the 2007 holiday season has toy retailers focusing on American-made products because of recent recalls of toys produced in China that do not meet U.S. safety standards.

20165 ■ "Fitness Made Fun" in *Playthings* (Vol. 106, September 1, 2008, No. 8, pp. 12)
Pub: Reed Business Information
Ed: Karyn M. Peterson. **Description:** Nintendo Wii has developed the Wii Fit game that allows gamers to engage in over forty physical activities through its Balance Board accessory, an engineered platform that senses weight and shifts in movement and balance. It also offers virtual trainers to talk participants through the activities and keeps track of the progress of multiple users.

20166 ■ "Game Changer" in *Canadian Business* (Vol. 83, June 15, 2010, No. 10, pp. 52)
Pub: Rogers Media Ltd.
Ed: Jordan Timm. **Description:** Ubisoft chose Ontario to be the site for its new development studio and it has appointed Jade Raymond as its managing director. Raymond was born in Montreal in 1975 and studied computer science at McGill. Raymond is said to possess the understanding of the game industry's technical, art, and business components.

20167 ■ *The Game Makers*
Pub: Harvard Business School Press
Ed: Philip E. Orbanes. **Released:** November 2003. **Price:** $29.95. **Description:** Profile of game expert and president of a specialty game company, author of books about games, Monopoly championship judge, senior vice president of research and development at Parker Brothers, and inventor of board and card games in highlighted.

20168 ■ "Going Green, Going Slowly" in *Playthings* (Vol. 106, September 1, 2008, No. 8, pp. 17)
Pub: Reed Business Information
Ed: Nancy Zwiers. **Description:** Sustainability and greener materials for both product and packaging in the toy industry has become important for protecting our environment. However, in a recent survey nearly 60 percent of responders stated environmental issues did not play a part in purchasing a toy or game for their children.

20169 ■ "Hobbies Hold Fast" in *Playthings* (Vol. 106, November 1, 2008, No. 1, pp. 6)
Pub: Reed Business Information
Ed: Karyn M. Peterson. **Description:** Profile of the 24th Annual iHobby Expo is presented. The event is a combined trade and consumer show offering a look at the latest releases in die-cast collectibles, model railroads and aircraft, slot cars, remote control vehicles, rocketry, robotics, military toys, wood/plastic model kits, games, etc.

20170 ■ "Importers Share Safety Liability" in *Feedstuffs* (Vol. 80, January 21, 2008, No. 3, pp. 19)
Pub: Miller Publishing Company, Inc.
Description: Pet food and toys containing lead paint are among products from China being recalled due to safety concerns. American Society for Quality's list of measures that outsourcing companies can take to help ensure safer products being imported to the U.S.

20171 ■ "Inside Out" in *Playthings* (Vol. 107, January 1, 2009, No. 1, pp. 3)
Pub: Reed Business Information
Description: Mattel signed on as the global master toy licensee for Cartoon Network's The Secret Saturdays while Toy Island signed a deal for wooden toys based on several leading Nick Jr. properties.

20172 ■ "The Last Ingredient?" in *Canadian Business* (Vol. 81, October 13, 2008, No. 17, pp. 88)
Pub: Rogers Media Ltd.
Ed: Rachel Pulfer. **Description:** Views and information on Cookie Jar Group's plan to acquire rights for Strawberry Shortcake and the Care Bears are discussed. The move would make Cookie Jar a major player in the global children's entertainment market. Cookie Jar chief executive, Michael Hirsh is believed to be securing funds for the planned $195 million acquisition.

20173 ■ "Look, Leap, and License" in *Retail Merchandiser* (Vol. 51, July-August 2011, No. 4, pp. 16)
Pub: Phoenix Media Corporation
Description: Toys highlighting the Licensing International Expo 2011 included a life-sized Cookie Monster, Papa Smurf, Power Rangers, Transformer, and margarita wrestlers. Taking licensed properties international was a common theme at this year's show.

20174 ■ "Look Out, Barbie, Bratz are Back" in *Canadian Business* (Vol. 83, August 17, 2010, No. 13-14, pp. 18)
Pub: Rogers Media Ltd.
Ed: Joe Castaldo. **Description:** California-based MGA Entertainment has wrestled back control over Bratz from Mattel after a six-year legal battle. However, MGA owner Isaac Larian could still face legal hurdles if Mattel pursues a retrial. He now has to revive the brand which virtually disappeared from stores when Mattel won the rights for Bratz.

20175 ■ "Making Factory Tours Count" in *Playthings* (Vol. 107, January 1, 2009, No. 1, pp. 14)
Pub: Reed Business Information
Ed: Malcolm Denniss. **Description:** The importance of touring an overseas toy supplier's manufacturing facility is stressed. Strategies for general factory visits are outlined in order to determine safety-related quality assurance issues in production.

20176 ■ "Mattel's Got a Monster Holiday Hit, But Will Franchise Have Staying Power?" in *Advertising Age* (Vol. 81, December 6, 2010, No. 43)
Pub: Crain Communications, Inc.
Ed: Beth Snyder Bulik. **Description:** Monster High transmedia play expands beyond dolls to merchandise, apparel and entertainment.

20177 ■ "Nat'l Instruments Connects with Lego" in *Austin Business JournalInc.* (Vol. 28, August 22, 2008, No. 23, pp. 1)
Pub: American City Business Journals
Ed: Laura Hipp. **Description:** Austin-based National Instruments Corporation has teamed with Lego Group from Denmark to create a robot that can be built by children and can be used to perform tasks. Lego WeDo, their latest product, uses computer connection to power its movements. The educational benefits of the new product are discussed.

20178 ■ *The Official American International Toy Fair Directory*
Pub: Toy Industry Association Inc.
Released: Annual, Latest edition 2009. **Covers:** About 1,500 toy, game, and holiday decoration manufacturers and their representatives. **Entries Include:** Company name, address, phone, e-mail, fax, website, booth number or location at Toy Fair, products, name of representative. **Arrangement:** Classified by show site and booth/room number. **Indexes:** Company name, product, exhibit location, member exhibitors and trade names.

20179 ■ "Paper Cache" in *Playthings* (Vol. 106, October 1, 2008, No. 9, pp. 9)
Pub: Reed Business Information
Ed: Karyn M. Peterson. **Description:** New toys in the paper play category are capturing children's imaginations with pirate ships and fairy houses and more they can build or design themselves. Hands-on paper and cardboard-based kits offer options for all ages.

20180 ■ "Play It Safe" in *Entrepreneur* (Vol. 35, November 2007, No. 11, pp. 26)
Pub: Entrepreneur Media Inc.
Ed: Gwen Moran. **Description:** U.S.-based toy manufacturers find opportunity from concerns regarding the recent recalls of toys that are made in China. The situation can provide better probability of parents buying toys made in the U.S. or Europe, where manufacturing standards are stricter.

20181 ■ *The Race for a New Game Machine: Creating the Chips Inside the Xbox 360 and the PlayStation 3*
Pub: Citadel Press
Ed: David Shippy, Mickie Phipps. **Released:** 2009. **Price:** $21.95. **Description:** The story of Microsoft and Sony's race to deliver the goods for the Xbox 360 and Playstation 3 is explored.

20182 ■ "Sign of Progress" in *Playthings* (Vol. 106, October 1, 2008, No. 9, pp. 4)
Pub: Reed Business Information
Ed: Cliff Annicelli. **Description:** The ramifications of the toy recalls in 2007 are discussed. Mandates for lead-free toys and other safety issues are having an impact on the American toy industry.

20183 ■ "The State of the Stores" in *Playthings* (Vol. 106, November 1, 2008, No. 10, pp. 8)
Pub: Reed Business Information
Ed: Dana French. **Description:** Investigation into the top twenty-five toy and game retailers shows that video games and related handheld and console systems as well as computer games were number one with America's children in 2007.

20184 ■ "This Year's Model" in *Playthings* (Vol. 107, January 1, 2009, No. 1, pp. 23)
Pub: Reed Business Information
Ed: Karyn M. Peterson. **Description:** Toy manufacturers, as well as retailers, address the need to exceed safety and quality demands by consumers when developing new toys and games for children.

20185 ■ "Thomas and His Washington Friends" in *CFO* (Vol. 23, October 2007, No. 10, pp. 18)
Pub: CFO Publishing Corporation
Ed: Alix Stuart. **Description:** Reliance on Chinese suppliers to America's toymakers may become quite costly as Congress considers legislation that would increase fines to as high as $50 million for companies selling tainted products. The legislation would also require independent mandatory testing for makers of products for children.

20186 ■ "A 'To Do' List" in *Playthings* (Vol. 107, January 1, 2009, No. 1, pp. 9)
Pub: Reed Business Information
Ed: Richard Gottlieb. **Description:** Profile of the Building Our Future Toy Conference held in October 2008. Participants discussed the industry's future and is seeking ways to understand the toys children want in today's society.

20187 ■ "Toy Scares Drive Business" in *Boston Business Journal* (Vol. 27, November 23, 2007, No. 43, pp. 1)
Pub: American City Business Journals, Inc.
Ed: Joan Goodchild. **Description:** Several Boston businesses have tapped into the lead content scare in toys and other products manufactured in China. ConRoy Corporation LLC launched Toy Recall Alert!, an online tool to alert consumers about new recalls while Hybrivet Systems introduced screening test kit, LeadCheck. Other new products pertaining to toy safety are discussed.

20188 ■ "Toy Story" in *Forbes* (Vol. 180, October 15, 2007, No. 8, pp. 102)
Pub: Forbes Inc.
Description: Three voluntary recalls of Chinese-made toys were announced by American toymakers, sending Mattel stocks plummeting.

20189 ■ "Toy Story: U.S.-Made a Hot Seller" in *Crain's Detroit Business* (Vol. 23, December 17, 2007, No. 51, pp. 3)
Pub: Crain Communications Inc. - Detroit
Ed: Chad Halcom. **Description:** American Plastic Toys, located in Walled Lake, Michigan reports all its toys are made in the U.S. and have passed all U.S. safety standards. Revenue for American Plastic Toys reached nearly $33 million in 2005, and the company expects to exceed that because of recent toy safety recalls of products produced in China.

20190 ■ "VTech Targets Tots With a Wee Wii" in *Advertising Age* (Vol. 79, September 8, 2008, No. 33, pp. 14)
Pub: Crain Communications, Inc.
Ed: Beth Snyder Bulik. **Description:** V-Motion is a video-game console targeting 3-to-7-year-olds and is manufactured by educational toy company VTech. The company is marketing the product as a kind of Wii for preschoolers and hopes to build a formidable brand presence in the kids' electronics market.

20191 ■ "Weathering the Economic Storm" in *Playthings* (Vol. 107, January 1, 2009, No. 1, pp. 10)
Pub: Reed Business Information
Ed: J. Tol Broome Jr. **Description:** Six steps for toy companies to survive the economic turndown are outlined: Outline your business model; seek professional input; meet with your banker; cut your costs; manage your inventory; and use your trade credit.

20192 ■ "Wham-O's Wisdom" in *Playthings* (Vol. 107, January 1, 2009, No. 1, pp. 13)
Pub: Reed Business Information
Ed: Tim Walsh. **Description:** Toy historian Tim Walsh discusses the history of the toy industry and shares secrets to his success. Walsh is the creator of toys and board games.

20193 ■ "Work for Play: Careers in Video Game Development" in *Occupational Outlook Quarterly* (Vol. 55, Fall 2011, No. 3, pp. 2)
Pub: U.S. Bureau of Labor Statistics
Ed: Drew Liming, Dennis Vilorio. **Description:** Game developers make a living creating the games the public enjoys playing. The video gaming industry reported sales over $10 billion in 2009 and employed 32,000 people in 34 states. Career options in video game development are featured.

20194 ■ "Xbox 360 Excels as a Media Hub" in *Hispanic Business* (October 2009, pp. 40)
Pub: Hispanic Business
Ed: Jeremy Nisen. **Description:** Xbox 360 video game console from Microsoft offers games, amazing graphics and state-of-the-art accessories. The trend towards purchase of the Xbox includes more than teenagers.

20195 ■ "Zakkamono Taps Growing Market for Collectibles" in *Hawaii Business* (Vol. 54, September 2008, No. 3, pp. 68)
Pub: Hawaii Business Publishing
Ed: Casey Chin. **Description:** Profile of Zakkamono, a business that designs and sells designer toys, shirts and other collectibles; the first toys being Mousubi and Miao figurines. Owners Zakka and Rae Huo say that one of the business' challenges is finding manufacturing resources. Other details about Zakkamono are discussed.

STATISTICAL SOURCES

20196 ■ *RMA Annual Statement Studies*
Pub: Robert Morris Associates (RMA)
Released: Annual. **Price:** $175.00 2006-07 edition, $105.00. **Description:** Contains composite balance sheets and income statements for more than 360 industries, including the accounting, auditing, and bookkeeping industries. Also contains five years of comparative historical data for discerning trends. Includes 16 commonly used ratios, computed for most of the size groupings for nearly every industry.

20197 ■ *Standard & Poor's Industry Surveys*
Pub: Standard & Poor's Corp.
Released: Annual. **Price:** $3633.00. **Description:** Two-volume book that examines the prospects for specific industries, including trucking. Also provides analyses of trends and problems, statistical tables and charts, and comparative company analyses.

TRADE PERIODICALS

20198 ■ *The Toy Book*
Pub: Adventure Publishing Group Inc.
Contact: Jonathan Samet, Group Publisher
E-mail: jsamet@adventurepub.com
Released: Monthly. **Price:** $48; $200 other countries airmail only; $80 two years; $56 Canada and Mexico; $100 3 years. **Description:** Tabloid for buyers in the toy and hobby industries.

20199 ■ *Toys & Games*
Pub: Chelsie Communications Inc.
Contact: Graham Kennedy, Publisher
Released: Bimonthly. **Price:** $21 Canada; $60 other countries. **Description:** Toys and games magazine.

TRADE SHOWS AND CONVENTIONS

20200 ■ Canadian Toy and Hobby Fair
Canadian Toy Association
7777 Keele St., Ste. 212
Concord, ON, Canada L4K 1Y7
Ph:(905)660-5690
Fax:(905)660-6103
Co. E-mail: info@cdntoyassn.com
URL: http://www.cdntoyassn.com
Released: Annual. **Audience:** Trade professionals. **Principal Exhibits:** Toys, games, books, and seasonal decorations and hobby products. **Dates and Locations:** 2011 Jan 30 - Feb 01, Toronto, ON.

20201 ■ CHA Winter Convention and Trade Show
Hobby Industry Association HIA
319 E. 54th St.
Elmwood Park, NJ 07407
Ph:(201)835-1200
Fax:(201)797-0657
Co. E-mail: info@craftandhobby.org
URL: http://www.hobby.org
Released: Annual. **Audience:** Owners, corporate officers and buyers from craft, hobby, DIY stores, general merchandise stores, wholesalers, and professional crafters. **Principal Exhibits:** Crafts, ceramics, floral accessories, dollhouse miniatures, aromatics, art materials and frames, jewelry findings, fabrics, needlework and quilting supplies, home decor, rubber stamps, stencils and scrapbooking supplies.

20202 ■ Just Kidstuff - A Division of the New York International Gift Fair
George Little Management, LLC (New York, New York)
1133 Westchester Ave., Ste. N136
White Plains, NY 10606
Ph:(914)421-3200
Free: 800-272-SHOW
Co. E-mail: cathy_steel@glmshows.com
URL: http://www.glmshows.com
Released: Semiannual. **Audience:** Buyers from specialty and department stores, giftshops, jewelry stores, interior designers, importers and distributors of home products, mail order catalogs. **Principal Exhibits:** Presents a wide variety of upscale products for children of all ages, including bedding, furniture, dolls, toys and games, gifts, clothes, books and educational products and accessories.

20203 ■ Supermarket Promotion Show
Association of Retail Marketing Services
10 Drs. James Parker Blvd., Ste. 103
Red Bank, NJ 07701-1500
Ph:(732)842-5070
Fax:(732)219-1938
Co. E-mail: info@goarms.com
URL: http://www.goarms.com
Released: Annual. **Audience:** Buyers of retail, consumer incentives. **Principal Exhibits:** Dinnerware, glassware, housewares, books, videos, games, sweepstakes, dolls, and plush toys suppliers.

FRANCHISES AND BUSINESS OPPORTUNITIES

20204 ■ Compuchild
Compuchild Services of America
1800 Halifax St.
Camel, IN 46032
Ph:(317)817-9817
Free: 800-619-5437
Fax:(317)818-8184
No. of Franchise Units: 69. **No. of Company-Owned Units:** 1. **Founded:** 1994. **Franchised:** 1995. **Description:** Computer education to children. **Equity Capital Needed:** $15,000. **Franchise Fee:** $12,500 or $17,500. **Financial Assistance:** No. **Training:** Yes.

20205 ■ Learning Express
29 Buena Vista St.
Ayer, MA 01434
Free: 800-436-8697
Fax:(978)889-1010
No. of Franchise Units: 160. **Founded:** 1987. **Franchised:** 1987. **Description:** Educational toy store. **Equity Capital Needed:** $100,000 capital requirement. **Franchise Fee:** $35,000. **Financial Assistance:** No. **Training:** Yes.

20206 ■ Once Upon a Child
Winmark Corp.
605 Highway 169 N., Ste. 400
Minneapolis, MN 55441
Ph:(763)520-8490
Free: 800-592-8049
Fax:(763)520-8501
URL: http://www.onceuponachild.com

No. of Franchise Units: 241. **Founded:** 1985. **Franchised:** 1993. **Description:** Franchises consignment shops featuring children's products including toys, books, furniture, and apparel. **Equity Capital Needed:** $204,200-$309,500; approximately 30% cash requirement. **Franchise Fee:** $25,000. **Financial Assistance:** No financing available from corporation; Support given in developing 3 year business plan and cash flow analysis to use in securing financing. **Training:** Program includes product acquisition, inventory management, retail store operations, advertising and marketing, proprietary point-of-sale computer system. Training conferences held annually. Owner only website provides tools, resources and a network of fellow franchisees.

COMPUTERIZED DATABASES

20207 ■ *Playthings*
Reed Business Information Ltd.
Quadrant House
The Quadrant
Surrey
Sutton SM2 5AS, United Kingdom
Ph:44 20 8652 3500
Fax:44 20 8652 8932
Co. E-mail: rbi.subscriptions@qss-uk.com
URL: http://www.rbi.co.uk

Description: Contains the full-text of *Playthings*, a monthly magazine providing coverage of the toy industry. Covers reporting on what toys are selling across the country along with in-depth analysis and statistics of toy trends. **Availability:** Online: Reed Business Information Ltd. **Type:** Full text; Directory.

Trade Show/Conference Management Service

START-UP INFORMATION

20208 ■ *How to Start a Home-Based Event Planning Business*
Pub: Globe Pequot Press

Ed: Jill Moran. **Released:** July 2007. **Price:** $18.95. **Description:** Guide to starting and growing a business planning events from a home-based firm.

20209 ■ *Mommy Millionaire: How I Turned My Kitchen Table Idea Into a Million Dollars and How You Can, Too!*
Pub: St. Martin's Press LLC

Ed: Kim Lavine. **Released:** February 19, 2008. **Price:** $14.95. **Description:** Advice, secrets and lessons for making a million dollars from a mom who turned her kitchen into a successful business; tools cover developing and patenting an idea, cold calling, trade shows, QVC, big retailers, manufacturing, and raising venture capital.

ASSOCIATIONS AND OTHER ORGANIZATIONS

20210 ■ Association for Convention Operations Management
191 Clarksville Rd.
Princeton Junction, NJ 08550
Ph:(609)799-3712
Fax:(609)799-7032
Co. E-mail: info@acomonline.org
URL: http://www.acomonline.org
Contact: Eric Blanc, Pres.

Description: Convention service directors and managers of hotels, convention centers, and convention bureaus. Works to increase the effectiveness, productivity and quality of meetings, conventions and exhibitions. Works to establish high ethical standards, improve professional management techniques and increase awareness of client, employer and provider needs. Maintains speakers' bureau, resource center, and placement services; compiles statistics. Conducts research and educational programs. .

20211 ■ Canadian National Exhibition–Exposition Nationale Canadienne
Press Bldg.
Exhibition Pl.
210 Princes Blvd.
Toronto, ON, Canada M6K 3C3
Ph:(416)263-3800
Fax:(416)263-3838
Co. E-mail: info@theex.com
URL: http://www.theex.com
Contact: Jim Melvin, Pres.

Description: Organizations sponsoring and participating in the Canadian National Exhibition. Promotes efficient and profitable operation of the exhibition. Facilitates cooperation among members; conducts promotional activities.

20212 ■ Center for Exhibition Industry Research
12700 Park Central Dr., Ste. 308
Dallas, TX 75251
Ph:(972)687-9242
Fax:(972)692-6020
Co. E-mail: info@ceir.org
URL: http://www.ceir.org
Contact: Carrie Freeman Parsons, Chair

Description: Promotes the growth, awareness and value of exhibitions and other face-to-face marketing events by producing and delivering research-based knowledge tools. Consists of exhibition organizers, service providers, exhibitors, CVBs and facilities. **Publications:** *Face-to-Face Marketing*; *Guru Reports*; *The Power of Exhibitions* .

20213 ■ Council of Protocol Executives
101 W 12th St., Ste. PH-H
New York, NY 10011
Ph:(212)633-6934
Fax:(212)633-6934
Co. E-mail: copeorg@aol.com
URL: http://www.councilofprotocolexecutives.org
Contact: Jim Cronin, Pres.

Description: Persons who coordinate executive level meetings and special events for governments, corporations, and professional and nonprofit organizations; dedicated to increasing the level of professionalism in the field. Works to develop new ideas in all areas of meeting planning and identify trends in the industry. Reviews and recommends new and existing facilities and suppliers; conducts educational programs covering topics such as invitations, sports marketing, wines, entertainment of foreign guests, and speakers and entertainers; facilitates networking among members. **Publications:** Newsletter (quarterly).

20214 ■ Exhibit Designers and Producers Association
10 Norden Pl.
Norwalk, CT 06855
Ph:(203)852-5698
Fax:(203)854-6735
Co. E-mail: jprovost@edpa.com
URL: http://www.edpa.com
Contact: Jeff Provost, Exec. Dir.

Description: Firms designing and building exhibits for trade shows and museums. Conducts educational and research programs. **Publications:** *EDP Action News* (bimonthly); *EDPA.COMmunications* (monthly); *EDPA Today* (quarterly).

20215 ■ Exposition Service Contractors Association
5068 W Plano Pkwy., Ste. 300
Plano, TX 75093
Ph:(972)447-8212
Free: 877-792-3722
Fax:(972)447-8209
Co. E-mail: info@esca.org
URL: http://www.esca.org
Contact: Larry Arnaudet, Exec. Dir.

Description: Engages in the provision of material and/or services normally furnished for trade shows, conventions, exhibitions and corporate meetings. Serves as a clearinghouse for the exchange of information among members and all other entities of the trade show and convention field. Seeks to promote and maintain progressive business and professional standards; advances better show techniques; improves the efficiency of material handling and on-site organization; enhances the use of manpower. **Publications:** *Guide to Exposition Service* (annual).

20216 ■ International Association of Conference Center Administrators
6832 Milan Dr.
Lincoln, NE 68526
Ph:(402)202-1973
Co. E-mail: mquinn@iacca.org
URL: http://www.iacca.org
Contact: Jimmy Huffman, Pres.

Description: Provides support to conference center administrators and furthers their professional development. Conducts educational programs; compiles statistics; offers information on legislative and legal trends. Offers professional certification. **Publications:** *IACCA Journal* (periodic).

20217 ■ International Association of Conference Centers
243 N Lindbergh Blvd.
St. Louis, MO 63141
Ph:(314)993-8575
Fax:(314)993-8919
Co. E-mail: info@iacconline.org
URL: http://www.iacconline.org
Contact: Tom Bolman CAE, Exec. VP

Description: Executive, resort, corporate, college/university, and nonresidential conference centers in 13 countries; firms providing products and services to conference centers; conference center personnel. Promotes members' interests and disseminates marketing information. Provides educational programs, speakers, and trainers within the industry; conducts public relations campaign. Maintains Internet site with searchable database of all members. **Publications:** *Conference Center Concept*;Membership Directory (annual).

20218 ■ International Association of Exhibitions and Events
12700 Park Central Dr., Ste. 308
Dallas, TX 75251
Ph:(972)458-8002
Fax:(972)458-8119
Co. E-mail: news@iaee.com
URL: http://www.iaee.com
Contact: Steven Hacker CAE, Pres.

Description: Managers and executives of shows, exhibits, and expositions; suppliers are associate members. Sponsors seminars to educate show managers. Conducts surveys, compiles statistics, and maintains placement service. Works to promote the exhibition industry throughout the world and to provide for the education and professional growth of its members. **Publications:** *E2: Exhibitions and*

Events (monthly); *Guidelines for Display Rules and Regulations*; *Hotel/Client Agreement Guidelines and Information*;Annual Report (annual).

20219 ■ Professional Convention Management Association
35 E Wacker Dr., Ste. 500
Chicago, IL 60601-2105
Ph:(312)423-7262
Free: 877-827-7262
Fax:(312)423-7222
Co. E-mail: president@pcma.org
URL: http://www.pcma.org
Contact: Deborah Sexton, Pres./CEO
Description: Represents the interests of meeting management executives from associations, non-profit organizations, corporations, independent meeting planning companies, and multi-management firms who recognize the importance of meetings to their organization. Provides education, research and advocacy to advance the meetings and hospitality industry. Empowers members with the tools they need to succeed as meeting professionals and to promote the value of the industry to their organizations and the general public. **Publications:** *Professional Convention Management Association—Membership Directory* (annual).

20220 ■ Trade Show Exhibitors Association
2301 S Lake Shore Dr., Ste. 1005
Chicago, IL 60616
Ph:(312)842-8732
Fax:(312)842-8744
Co. E-mail: membership@tsea.org
URL: http://www.tsea.org
Contact: Margit B. Weisgal CME, Pres./CEO
Description: Exhibitors working to improve the effectiveness of trade shows as a marketing tool. Purposes are to promote the progress and development of trade show exhibiting; to collect and disseminate trade show information; conduct studies, surveys, and stated projects designed to improve trade shows; to foster good relations and communications with organizations representing others in the industry; to undertake other activities necessary to promote the welfare of member companies. Sponsors Exhibit Industry Education Foundation and professional exhibiting seminars; the forum series of educational programs on key issues affecting the industry. Maintains placement services; compiles statistics. **Publications:** *Trade Show Ideas Magazine* (monthly);Membership Directory (annual).

DIRECTORIES OF EDUCATIONAL PROGRAMS

20221 ■ *Meeting Planners International—Oregon Chapter—Annual Membership Directory*
Pub: LLM Publications Inc.
Released: Annual, Latest edition 2007-2008. **Covers:** Members of the Meeting Planners International in Oregon. **Entries Include:** Name, contact information, product/service provided.

REFERENCE WORKS

20222 ■ "$3 Million in Repairs Prep Cobo for Auto Show" in *Crain's Detroit Business* (Vol. 26, January 4, 2010, No. 1, pp. 1)
Pub: Crain Communications, Inc.
Ed: Nancy Kaffer. **Description:** Overview of the six projects priced roughly at $3 million which were needed in order to host the North American International Auto Show; show organizers stated that the work was absolutely necessary to keep the show in the city of Detroit.

20223 ■ "2008 Woman of the Year Gala" in *Hispanic Business* (Vol. 30, July-August 2008, No. 7-8, pp. 58)
Pub: Hispanic Business, Inc.
Ed: Brynne Chappell. **Description:** Brief report on the sixth annual Women of the Year Awards gala which was held at JW Marriott Desert Ridge Resort and Spa is given; 20 women were honored with these awards for their professional contribution, commitment to the advancement of the Hispanic community and involvement with charitable organizations.

20224 ■ "ALA: Hot Topics for Librarianship" in *Information Today* (Vol. 28, September 2011, No. 8, pp. 17)
Pub: Information Today, Inc.
Ed: Barbara Brynko. **Description:** Highlights from the American Library Association Annual Conference and Exhibition are listed. Thousands of attendees sought out services, displays, demos, new product rollouts, and freebies. Emerging technology for librarians, staff development, gray literature, interlibrary loans, and next-generation interfaces were among the topics discussed.

20225 ■ "And In This Briefcase" in *Mergers & Acquisitions: The Dealmaker's Journal* (March 1, 2008)
Pub: SourceMedia, Inc.
Description: ACG San Diego decided to address the impact the changes in the economy will have on potential private equity transactions as well as what criteria private equity firms are looking for when assessing a company. At the opening of the chapter's 2008 breakfast meeting, real-world case studies were utilized with the audiences' participation in order to assess pre-deal risk scenarios.

20226 ■ *Annual Trade Show Directory*
Pub: Forum Publishing Co.
Released: Annual, Latest edition 2011. **Price:** $39. 95, individuals. **Covers:** over 2,400 merchandise trade shows throughout the United States and Canada. **Entries Include:** Company name, address, phone, estimated attendance and number of exhibitors, show description. **Arrangement:** Classified by product, then chronological. **Indexes:** Product, type of show.

20227 ■ "AREE Meets in Atlantic City" in *Indoor Comfort Marketing* (Vol. 70, June 2011, No. 6, pp. 28)
Pub: Industry Publications Inc.
Description: Highlights of the Atlantic Region Energy Expo are provided.

20228 ■ "Around the World in a Day" in *Agency Sales Magazine* (Vol. 39, August 2009, No. 8, pp. 36)
Pub: MANA
Ed: Jack Foster. **Description:** Highlights of Manufacturer's Agents National Association (MANA) member Les Rapchak one-day visit to Basra, Iraq are presented. Rapchak completed the trip via Frankfurt, Germany and Kuwait with a stop afterwards in Istanbul, Turkey. His purpose for the trip was to take part in a seminar at the State Company for Petrochemical Industries.

20229 ■ "Art Attack 2007 Comes to Minneapolis" in *Art Business News* (Vol. 34, November 2007, No. 11, pp. 11)
Pub: Pfingsten Publishing, LLC
Description: Overview of Art Attack 2007, an open studio and gallery crawl in the Northeast Minneapolis Arts District which featured artists working in glass, ceramics, jewelry, mosaics, mixed media, photography, painting, pottery, sculpture, textiles and wood.

20230 ■ "Art Miami Comes to Miami's Wynwood Art District" in *Art Business News* (Vol. 34, November 2007, No. 11, pp. 18)
Pub: Pfingsten Publishing, LLC
Description: In December, The Art Group will hold its Art Miami fair in the Wynwood Art District; the exhibitors range from painting, sculpture, video and works on paper.

20231 ■ "Artexpo Celebrates 30th Anniversary" in *Art Business News* (Vol. 34, November 2007, No. 11, pp. 18)
Pub: Pfingsten Publishing, LLC
Description: In honor of its 30th anniversary Artexpo New York 2008 will be an unforgettable show offering a collection of fine-art education courses for both trade and consumer attendees and featuring a variety of artists working in all mediums.

20232 ■ "An Artwork in Progress" in *Hawaii Business* (Vol. 53, March 2008, No. 9, pp. 45)
Pub: Hawaii Business Publishing
Ed: Jolyn Okimoto Rosa. **Description:** Art galleries in Honolulu, Hawaii holds the First Friday Gallery Walk and other special events, which draw crowd to and increase sales activities in the city's downtown. The district also advocates for the reintroduction of Honolulu's Chinatown to the people. Details regarding the art galleries' Chinatown revival and its local economic impact are discussed.

20233 ■ *Association Management—Convention Center & Convention Bureau Directory*
Pub: American Society of Association Executives
Contact: Keith C. Skillman
Ed: Debra Popovich, Editor. **Released:** Annual, February. **Price:** Free. **Publication Includes:** List of convention halls, centers, auditoriums, arenas, and convention and visitors bureaus in the United States, Canada, and abroad. **Entries Include:** Name of hall or CVB, phone, fax, and exhibit space available. **Arrangement:** Geographical.

20234 ■ "Attorney Panel Tackles Contract Questions" in *Agency Sales Magazine* (Vol. 39, September-October 2009, No. 9, pp. 8)
Pub: MANA
Ed: Jack Foster. **Description:** MANAfest conference tackled issues regarding a sales representative's contract. One attorney from the panel advised reps to go through proposed agreements with attorneys who are knowledgeable concerning rep laws. Another attorney advised reps to communicate with a company to ask about their responsibilities if that company is facing financial difficulty.

20235 ■ "Auto Show Aims to Electrify" in *Crain's Detroit Business* (Vol. 26, January 11, 2010, No. 2, pp. 1)
Pub: Crain Communications, Inc.
Ed: Ryan Beene. **Description:** Overview of the North American International Auto show include sixteen production and concept vehicles including eight from the Detroit 3. High-tech battery suppliers as well as hybrid and electric vehicles will highlight the show.

20236 ■ "Avanti Hosts Users Conference" in *American Printer* (Vol. 128, July 1, 2011, No. 7)
Pub: Penton Media Inc.
Description: Avanti Computer Systems Ltd. hosted its 19th annual users conference in Washington DC. In-plant and commercial printers were in attendance.

20237 ■ "BBB Hires Marketing Firm to Attract More Businesses" in *Baltimore Business Journal* (Vol. 27, January 1, 2010, No. 35, pp. 1)
Pub: American City Business Journals
Ed: Julekha Dash. **Description:** Better Business Bureau (BBB) of Greater Maryland hired Bystry Carson & Associates Ltd. to assist in its rebranding efforts in order to entice more businesses. Bystry Carson will promote BBB's new mission at lectures, seminars, and networking events, as well as educate businesses about the agency through blogs and Twitter. BBB's services are also outlined.

20238 ■ "Biz Assesses 'Textgate' Fallout; Conventions, Smaller Deals Affected" in *Crain's Detroit Business* (Vol. 24, March 31, 2008)
Pub: Crain Communications, Inc.
Ed: Tom Henderson. **Description:** Businesspeople who were trying to measure the amount of economic damage is likely to be caused due to Mayor Kwame Kilpatrick's indictment on eight charges and found that: automotive and other large global deals are less likely to be affected than location decisions by smaller companies and convention site decisions. Also being affected are negotiations in which Mexican startup companies were planning a partnership with the TechTown incubator to pursue opportunities in the auto sector; those plans are being put on hold while they look at other sites.

20239 ■ "Bottom-Fishing and Speed-Dating in India" in *Barron's* (Vol. 88, March 24, 2008, No. 12, pp. M12)
Pub: Dow Jones & Company, Inc.
Ed: Elliot Wilson. **Description:** Indian stocks have fallen hard in 2008, with Mumbai's Sensex 30 down 30 percent from its January 2008 peak of 21,000 to 14,995 in March. The India Private Equity Fair 2008 attracted 140 of the world's largest private equity firms and about 24 of India's fastest-growing corporations. Statistical data included.

20240 ■ "The British Aren't Coming" in *Crain's Chicago Business* (Vol. 34, October 24, 2011, No. 42, pp. 3)
Pub: Crain Communications Inc.
Ed: Brigid Sweeney. **Description:** In a move to attract tourists back to Chicago, its Convention and Tourism Bureau is marketing in London, England, Mexico, and Canada, but not Germany or France because of budget constraints.

20241 ■ "Calendar" in *Crain's Detroit Business* (Vol. 24, March 24, 2008, No. 12, pp. 25)
Pub: Crain Communications, Inc.
Description: Listing of events in the Detroit area include conferences addressing entrepreneurialism, economic development, and women business ownership.

20242 ■ "CarBiz Inc. Speaking At NABD" in *Canadian Corporate News* (May 14, 2007)
Pub: Comtex News Network Inc.
Description: CarBiz Inc., a leading provider of software, consulting, and training solutions to the United States' automotive industry, had two of its executive officers speak at the National Alliance of Buy Here - Pay Here Dealers (NABD), a conference that draws over 2,000 dealers, service providers, and experts from across the United States.

20243 ■ "Celebrate Success. Embrace Innovation" in *Black Enterprise* (Vol. 37, February 2007, No. 7, pp. 145)
Pub: Earl G. Graves Publishing Co. Inc.
Description: 2007 Women of Power Summit provides networking opportunities, empowerment sessions, and nightly entertainment. More than 500 executive women of color are expected to attend this inspiring summit in Phoenix, February 7-10.

20244 ■ "Change Is in the Air" in *Agency Sales Magazine* (Vol. 39, August 2009, No. 8, pp. 30)
Pub: MANA
Ed: Jack Foster. **Description:** Highlights of the Power-Motion Technology Representatives Association (PTRA) 37th Annual Conference, which projected an economic upturn, are presented. Allan Bealulieu of the Institute for Trend Research gave the positive news while Manufacturer's Agents National Association (MANA) president Brain Shirley emphasized the need to take advantage of a turnaround.

20245 ■ "Chattanooga at a Glance" in *Women In Business* (Vol. 62, June 2010, No. 2, pp. 29)
Pub: American Business Women's Association
Ed: Jill Yates Bagby. **Description:** City of Chattanooga, Tennessee is the location of the 2010 American Business Women's Association (ABWA) National Women's Leadership Conference. The city offers historical sites, parks and tourist attractions, as well as dining options.

20246 ■ "Clinic to Use Medical Summit to Pump Up Cardiology Center" in *Crain's Cleveland Business* (Vol. 28, October 1, 2007, No. 39, pp. 6)
Pub: Crain Communications, Inc.
Ed: Chuck Soder. **Description:** Overview of the Medical Innovation Summit, sponsored by the Cleveland Clinic and regional business recruitment group Team NEO, whose theme was cardiology. The goal for this year's summit went beyond finding companies for the cardiovascular center, it also looked to market the region to other industries with growth potential.

20247 ■ "Clusters Last Stand?" in *Canadian Electronics* (Vol. 23, February 2008, No. 1, pp. 6)
Pub: CLB Media Inc.
Description: Survival of technology clusters was the focus of Strategic Microelectronics Council's conference entitled, "The Power of Community: Building Technology Clusters in Canada". Clusters can help foster growth in the microelectronics sector, and it was recognized that government intervention is needed to maintain these clusters.

20248 ■ "Conference Calendar" in *Marketing to Women* (Vol. 21, February 2008, No. 2, pp. 1)
Pub: EPM Communications, Inc.
Description: Listing of current conferences and events concerning women, marketing and business.

20249 ■ "Convention Budgeting Best Practice" in *Franchising World* (Vol. 42, November 2010, No. 11, pp. 11)
Pub: International Franchise Association
Ed: Steve Friedman. **Description:** Franchise conventions can offer benefits to both franchisor and franchisee in terms of culture-building, professional education and networking. However, these conventions can be costly. Tips for planning a successful franchising convention on a budget are outlined.

20250 ■ "Convention Calendar" in *Black Enterprise* (Vol. 37, February 2007, No. 7, pp. 68)
Pub: Earl G. Graves Publishing Co. Inc.
Description: Listing of conventions and trade show of interest to minority and women business leaders.

20251 ■ "Datebook" in *Crain's Chicago Business* (Vol. 31, April 28, 2008, No. 17, pp. 18)
Pub: Crain Communications, Inc.
Description: Listing of events in the Detroit area include conferences addressing entrepreneurialism, economic development, and women business ownership.

20252 ■ "Datran Media Executives to Lead Industry Debates Across Q1 Conferences" in *Internet Wire* (January 22, 2010)
Pub: Comtex News Network, Inc.
Description: Datran Media, an industry-leading digital marketing technology company, will be sending members of its management team to several conferences in the early part of the first quarter of 2010; discussions will include Internet marketing innovations, e-commerce and media distribution.

20253 ■ "Designing Events Updates Online Suite" in *Wireless News* (October 25, 2009)
Pub: Close-Up Media
Description: Designing Events, an outsourcing and consulting firm for conferences and meetings, announced the release of an update to its Designing Events Online suite of web-based management and marketing tools; features include enhanced versions of online registration and collaboration, content management, session development, social media and conference websites.

20254 ■ "Detroit Hosts Conferences on Green Building, IT, Finance" in *Crain's Detroit Business* (Vol. 25, June 1, 2009, No. 22, pp. 9)
Pub: Crain Communications Inc. - Detroit
Ed: Tom Henderson. **Description:** Detroit will host three conferences in June 2009, one features green technology, one information technology and the third will gather black bankers and financial experts from across the nation.

20255 ■ "Developer Banks On East Submarket, Slowdown Not a Hinderance" in *The Business Journal-Serving Greater Tampa Bay* (August 1, 2008)
Pub: American City Business Journals, Inc.
Ed: Janet Leiser. **Description:** CLW Industrial Group and Cobalt Industrial REIT II have teamed up to develop a 14-acre area in northeast Hillsborough County, Florida. The $15 million industrial park project includes the 175,000-square-foot New Tampa Commerce Center, scheduled for completion in the first quarter of 2009.

20256 ■ "Developers Await Hotel" in *The Business Journal-Portland* (Vol. 25, July 11, 2008, No. 18, pp. 1)
Pub: American City Business Journals, Inc.
Ed: Wendy Culverwell. **Description:** Developers are eager to start the construction of a new hotel at the Oregon Convention Center in Portland, Oregon as hey say that the project will help boost the convention center neighborhood. The project, called The Westin Portland at the Convention Center, is partly handled by Ashforth Pacific Inc.

20257 ■ "The Display Group Is Super-Sized" in *Michigan Vue* (Vol. 13, July-August 2008, No. 4, pp. 34)
Pub: Entrepreneur Media Inc.
Description: Profile of the Display Group, located in downtown Detroit, this company provides custom designed mobile marketing displays as well as special event production services for trade show displays. The rental house and design service is also beginning to see more business due to the film initiative, which provides incentives for films that are shooting in Michigan.

20258 ■ "Dow Champions Innovative Energy Solutions for Auto Industry at NAIAS" in *Business of Global Warming* (January 25, 2010, pp. 7)
Pub: Investment Weekly News
Description: This year's North American International Auto Show in Detroit will host the "Electric Avenue" exhibit sponsored by the Dow Chemical Company. The display will showcase the latest in innovative energy solutions from Dow as well as electric vehicles and the technology supporting them. This marks the first time a non-automotive manufacturer is part of the main floor of the show.

20259 ■ "Downtowns Must Court Young, CEOs for Cities President Says" in *Crain's Detroit Business* (Vol. 24, October 6, 2008, No. 40, pp. 18)
Pub: Crain Communications, Inc.
Ed: Amy Lane. **Description:** It is important to produce more college graduates, and keep them in Michigan, according to CEOs for Cities President Carol Coletta when she spoke to a session at the West Michigan Regional Policy Conference which was held in September in Grand Rapids. Ways in which city leaders can connect students to communities, resulting in employees who have vested interest in the region, are also discussed.

20260 ■ "The Early Bird Gets the Worm" in *Black Enterprise* (Vol. 37, January 2007, No. 6, pp. 111)
Pub: Earl G. Graves Publishing Co. Inc.
Ed: Tykisha N. Lundy. **Description:** General Motors hosts the Black Enterprise Conference And Expo: Where Deals Are Made at Walt Disney World's Swan and Dolphin Resort, May 9-12. The conference will offer great information to entrepreneurs.

20261 ■ "East-Side Real Estate Forum Detours To Grand Rapids" in *Crain's Detroit Business* (Vol. 24, October 6, 2008, No. 40, pp. 17)
Pub: Crain Communications, Inc.
Ed: Daniel Duggan. **Description:** Tom Wackerman was elected chairman of the University of Michigan-Urban Land Institute Real Estate Forum and proposed that the annual conference be held in Grand Rapids due to the brisk economic activity he was finding there; although the idea was initially met with resistance, the plan to introduce East-siders to the West side began receiving more enthusiasm due to the revitalization of the area, which was once considered to have a bleak outlook. Many are hoping to learn the lessons of those who were able to change a negative economic climate into a positive one in which the cooperation of private business and government can work together to accomplish goals.

20262 ■ "Economy Forcing Meeting Planners to Think Fast" in *Crain's Cleveland Business* (Vol. 30, June 15, 2009, No. 23, pp. 15)
Pub: Crain Communications, Inc.

Ed: Amy Ann Stoessel. **Description:** Meeting planners are working hard to meet lower corporate budgets when planning events.

20263 ■ "Entrepreneurs Conference" in *Black Enterprise* (Vol. 38, February 2008, No. 7, pp. 163)
Pub: Earl G. Graves Publishing Co. Inc.

Description: Black Enterprise Entrepreneurs Conference and Expo will be held May 14-17, 2008 at the Charlotte Westin Hotel and Charlotte Convention Center in North Carolina. Entrepreneurs are given the opportunity to present their business ideas in the Bevator Pitch Competition for a chance to win products and services.

20264 ■ "Events Struggling with Fees" in *Philadelphia Business Journal* (Vol. 28, November 20, 2009, No. 40, pp. 1)
Pub: American City Business Journals

Ed: Peter van Allen. **Description:** Dad Vail Regatta organizers told Philadelphia officials their plans to move the rowing event out of Philadelphia into Rumson, New Jersey was due to rising fees from the city and the loss of corporate sponsorship. Smaller events have been left out of funding or transferred to other locations due, in part, to higher fees also.

20265 ■ "Finding Room for Financing" in *The Business Journal-Serving Metropolitan Kansas City* (Vol. 26, August 1, 2008, No. 47, pp. 1)
Pub: American City Business Journals, Inc.

Ed: Rob Roberts. **Description:** Kansas City officials are expecting to receive financing recommendations for a new 1,000-room convention headquarters hotel. The $300-million project could be financed either through private ownership with public subsidies, or through public ownership with tax-exempt bond financing. Other views and information on the project and its expected economic impact, are presented.

20266 ■ "Four Exhibition Considerations" in *American Printer* (Vol. 128, August 1, 2011, No. 8)
Pub: Penton Media Inc.

Description: Four questions to ask at the Graph Expo will help printers improve their own business.

20267 ■ "Grainger Show Highlights Building Green, Economy" in *Contractor* (Vol. 57, February 2010, No. 2, pp. 3)
Pub: Penton Media, Inc.

Ed: Candace Roulo. **Description:** chief U.S. economist told attendees of the Grainger's 2010 Total MRO Solutions National Customer Show that the economic recovery would be subdued. Mechanical contractors who attended the event also learned about building sustainable, green products, and technologies, and economic and business challenges.

20268 ■ "Grand Action Makes Grand Changes in Grand Rapids" in *Crain's Detroit Business* (Vol. 25, June 1, 2009, No. 22, pp. M012)
Pub: Crain Communications Inc. - Detroit

Ed: Amy Lane. **Description:** Businessman Dick DeVos believes that governments are not always the best to lead certain initiatives. That's why, in 1991, he gathered 50 west Michigan community leaders and volunteers to look consider the construction of an arena and expanding or renovating local convention operations. Grand Action has undertaken four major projects in the city.

20269 ■ "Half a World Away" in *Tampa Bay Business Journal* (Vol. 30, December 4, 2009, No. 50, pp. 1)
Pub: American City Business Journals

Ed: Jane Meinhardt. **Description:** Enterprise Florida has offered four trade grants for Florida's marine industry businesses to give them a chance to tap into the Middle East market at the Dubai International Boat Show on March 9 to 13, 2010. The grants pay for 50 percent of the exhibition costs for the qualifying business.

20270 ■ "Here's the Deal" in *Crain's Cleveland Business* (Vol. 30, June 15, 2009, No. 23, pp. 14)
Pub: Crain Communications, Inc.

Description: Incentives being offered by hotels, restaurants, golf courses and major chains in order to promote bookings for meetings or conferences in the Cleveland area are listed.

20271 ■ "Herrell's Launches New Corporate Identity at Fancy Food Show" in *Ice Cream Reporter* (Vol. 23, July 20, 2010, No. 8, pp. 3)
Pub: Ice Cream Reporter

Description: Herrell's ice cream introduced a new corporate branding at the Summer 2010 Fancy Food Show last summer. Slightly Mad Communications advertising agency developed the new brand to reflect the era of the early 1970s.

20272 ■ "Hotel Tax Eyed For Waukesha" in *The Business Journal-Milwaukee* (Vol. 25, August 29, 2008, No. 49, pp. A1)
Pub: American City Business Journals, Inc.

Ed: Rich Kirchen. **Description:** Midwest Airlines Center chairman Frank Gimbel wants Waukesha County to help in the funding of the $200-million expansion of the convention center through a hotel room tax. The Waukesha hotel industry is expected to oppose the new room tax. Other views and information on the planned new room tax in Waukesha are presented.

20273 ■ "How to Declutter Your Life Closet Cleanup: Putting a Lid on Clutter" in *Atlanta Journal-Constitution* (May 1, 2011)
Pub: Atlanta Journal-Constitution

Ed: Felicia Feaster. **Description:** The annual Closets and Home Organization Convention and Expo spotlights new products and services designed to help people get organized at home or the workplace. The organization sector is holding steady despite the recession and is expected to expand into garage organization.

20274 ■ *IAEM Membership Directory and Buyer's Guide*
Pub: International Association of Exhibitions and Events
Contact: Cathy Breden, COO
E-mail: cbrenden@iaee.com

Released: Annual, December. **Price:** Free. **Covers:** Over 1,600 show manager members and 1,700 associate members (including service suppliers, convention hall representatives, and others). **Entries Include:** Individual's name, title, firm name, address, phone and fax number. **Arrangement:** Member lists are alphabetical by personal name; classified by company name and product/service. **Indexes:** Association or company affiliation.

20275 ■ "IFA-AAG Professional Athlete Franchise Summit Scores" in *Franchising World* (Vol. 42, August 2010, No. 8, pp. 56)
Pub: International Franchise Association

Ed: Miriam L. Brewer. **Description:** The first International Franchise Association-Allied Athlete Group Franchise summit spotlighted athletes turned business owners addressing peers on franchising. The summit is expected to become an annual event.

20276 ■ "Industry/Events 2011" in *American Printer* (Vol. 128, July 1, 2011, No. 7)
Pub: Penton Media Inc.

Description: PMA, the Worldwide Community of Imaging Association launched its new CliQ with how-to tips, product reviews and monthly photo contests. PMA formed a partnership with the Consumer Electronics Association to make changes to this year's annual convention.

20277 ■ "IPEX Moves to London Venue" in *American Printer* (Vol. 128, July 1, 2011, No. 7)
Pub: Penton Media Inc.

Description: IPES 2014 is being relocated to London's ExCeL International Exhibition and Conference Centre from March 26 to April 2, 2014.

20278 ■ "Javo Beverage to Feature On-Demand Coffee System" in *GlobeNewswire* (October 20, 2009)
Pub: Comtex News Network, Inc.

Description: During the National Association of Convenience Store Show (NACS) at the Las Vegas Convention Center, Javo Beverage Company, Inc., a leading provider of premium dispensable coffee and tea-based beverages to the foodservice industry, will introduce its on-demand hot coffee system as well as a new line of products for the convenience store industry.

20279 ■ "Jay Berkowitz to Present Making Social Media Money Seminar at Affiliate Summit West" in *Entertainment Close-Up* (January 15, 2010)
Pub: Close-Up Media

Description: Highlights of Jay Berkowitz's conference, "Making Social Media Make Money" include ways in which to develop Internet marketing strategies that will maximize Website traffic and convert that traffic to sales.

20280 ■ "Kent Officials Seek Further KSU, City Unity" in *Crain's Cleveland Business* (Vol. 28, December 3, 2007, No. 48, pp. 3)
Pub: Crain Communications, Inc.

Ed: Jay Miller. **Description:** Kent State University and Portage County are searching for a developer who will use a three-acre parcel to bring new life to the city's sagging downtown and create an area that will better link the town and the Kent State campus. The project will include a hotel and conference center as well as retail and restaurant space.

20281 ■ "Kuno Creative to Present B2B Social Media Campaign Webinar" in *Entertainment Close-Up* (August 25, 2011)
Pub: Close-Up Media

Description: Kuno Creative, an inbound marketing agency, will host Three Steps of a Successful B2B Social Media Campaign. The firm is a provider of Website development, branding, marketing strategy, public relations, Internet marketing, and inbound marketing.

20282 ■ "Let's Put On a Show" in *Inc.* (November 2007, pp. 127)
Pub: Gruner & Jahr USA Publishing

Ed: Elaine Appleton Grant. **Description:** Profile of Jeff Baker, CEO of Image 4, designer of trade show exhibits. Baker shares details of the firm's commitment to being green.

20283 ■ "Local Green Technology on Display" in *Crain's Detroit Business* (Vol. 26, January 18, 2010, No. 3, pp. 1)
Pub: Crain Communications, Inc.

Ed: Ryan Beene. **Description:** Detroit's 2010 North American International Auto Show put the newest, most innovative green technologies on display showing that the Southeast Michigan automobile industry is gaining traction with its burgeoning e-vehicle infrastructure. Think, a Norwegian electric city-car manufacturer is eyeing sites in Southeast Michigan in which to locate its corporate headquarters and technical center for its North American branch.

20284 ■ "Look, Leap, and License" in *Retail Merchandiser* (Vol. 51, July-August 2011, No. 4, pp. 16)
Pub: Phoenix Media Corporation

Description: Toys highlighting the Licensing International Expo 2011 included a life-sized Cookie Monster, Papa Smurf, Power Rangers, Transformer, and margarita wrestlers. Taking licensed properties international was a common theme at this year's show.

20285 ■ *Mail Order in the Internet Age*
Pub: Morgan James Publishing, LLC

Ed: Ted Ciuba. **Released:** May 2004. **Price:** $19.95. **Description:** Direct response market, or mail order, for marketing and selling a product or service is discussed, with emphasis on how direct marketing compares favorably to other methods in terms of speed, ease, profitability, and affordability. Advice is given for writing ads; seminars to attend; and newsletters, mailing lists and magazines in which to subscribe.

20286 ■ "Major Golf Retail Show in the Rough for 2010" in *Orlando Business Journal* (Vol. 26, January 15, 2010, No. 33, pp. 1)
Pub: American City Business Journals
Ed: Anjali Fluker. **Description:** The 57th Annual PGA Merchandise Show in Orlando, Florida is projected to attract 39,000 attendees in 2010, compared with 41,000 in 2009. According to the Orange County Convention Center, economic benefits that could be obtained from the 2010 edition of the golf retail show might reach only $77 million, compared with $78 million generated last year.

20287 ■ "MANAfest Provides Reps with Tools for the Future" in *Agency Sales Magazine* (Vol. 39, September-October 2009, No. 9, pp. 36)
Pub: MANA
Ed: Jack Foster. **Description:** Former Harley Davidson director of communications Ken Schmidt was the keynote speaker at the MANAfest conference; he discussed how the company delivered itself from bankruptcy. Selling Power magazine publisher Gerhard Gschwandtner also made a presentation; he believes that there will be opportunities for sales people involved in relationship selling.

20288 ■ "Minnesota ABC Event Looks at Government Contracting" in *Finance and Commerce Daily Newspaper* (November 23, 2010)
Pub: Dolan Media Newswires
Ed: Brian Johnson. **Description:** Minnesota Associated Builders and Contractors hosted an event focusing on doing business with government agencies. Topics included bidding work, awarding jobs, paperwork, guidelines, certifications and upcoming projects.

20289 ■ "More Than 1,000 Attend Second WaterSmart" in *Contractor* (Vol. 56, November 2009, No. 11, pp. 3)
Pub: Penton Media, Inc.
Description: Over 1,000 plumbing and water conservation professionals attended the second WaterSmart Innovations Conference and Exposition in Las Vegas. Plumbing industry personalities made presentations during the conference and several innovative products were displayed at the trade show.

20290 ■ "Nobody Knows What To Do" in *Barron's* (Vol. 88, March 17, 2008, No. 11, pp. 40)
Pub: Dow Jones & Company, Inc.
Ed: Mark Veverka. **Description:** Attendees of the South by Southwest Interactive conference failed to get an insight on how to make money on the Web from former Walt Disney CEO Michael Eisner when Eisner said there's no proven business model for financing projects. Eisner said he finances his projects with the help of his connections to get product-placement deals.

20291 ■ "Norvax University Health Insurance Sales Training and Online Marketing Conference" in *Internet Wire* (January 27, 2010)
Pub: Comtex News Network, Inc.
Description: Overview of the Norvax University Marketing and Sales Success Conference Tour which includes insurance sales training seminars, proven and innovative online marketing techniques and a host of additional information and networking opportunities.

20292 ■ "Not Enough Room" in *Austin Business JournalInc.* (Vol. 29, November 13, 2009, No. 36, pp. A1)
Pub: American City Business Journals
Ed: Jacob Dirr. **Description:** Hotel and convention business in downtown Austin, Texas lost nearly $5.3 million when Dell Inc. relocated its annual convention to Las Vegas. However, lack of capital caused the postponement of various hotel projects which need to be finished in order to attract well-attended conventions. Makeover projects on Austin's Waller Creek and Sixth Street are discussed.

20293 ■ "Now See This" in *Entrepreneur* (Vol. 36, April 2008, No. 4, pp. 53)
Pub: Entrepreneur Media, Inc.
Ed: Mike Hogan. **Description:** New high definition (HD) products are to be introduced in 2008 at the Consumer Electronics Show and the Macworld Conference & Expo. HD lineup from companies such as Dell Inc. and Hewlett-Packard Co. are discussed.

20294 ■ "Nowspeed and OneSource to Conduct Webinar" in *Internet Wire* (December 14, 2009)
Pub: Comtex News Network, Inc.
Description: OneSource, a leading provider of global business information, and Nowspeed, an Internet marketing agency, will conduct a webinar titled "How to Develop Social Media Content That Gets Results" in order to provide marketers insight into how to develop and optimize effective social media content to get consumer results that translate into purchases and lead generation.

20295 ■ "Nowspeed's David Reske to Speak at SolidWorks World 2010 in Anaheim" in *Internet Wire* (January 7, 2010)
Pub: Comtex News Network, Inc.
Description: David Reske, managing director at Nowspeed, an Internet marketing agency based in the Boston area, will be presenting at SolidWorks World 2010; the convention's presentation will focus on proven methodologies, practical tips and real-world case studies in order to help attendees leverage the powerful Internet marketing innovations that are proving effective for businesses.

20296 ■ "O'Loughlin Cuts $6 Million for Chesterfield Doubletree" in *Saint Louis Business Journal* (Vol. 32, September 2, 2011, No. 1, pp. 1)
Pub: Saint Louis Business Journal
Ed: Angela Mueller. **Description:** Lodging Hospitality Management (LHM) acquired the Doubletree Hotel and Conference Center in Chesterfield, Missouri and added it as the 18th hotel in its portfolio. LHM chairman and CEO Bob O'Loughlin plans to invest nearly $15 million in the hotel, including $9 for renovation.

20297 ■ "One World" in *American Printer* (Vol. 128, August 1, 2011, No. 8)
Pub: Penton Media Inc.
Description: Graph Expo will highlight entrepreneurs focused on the connection between content, technology and business models.

20298 ■ "The Open Mobile Summit Opens in San Francisco Today: John Donahoe CEO eBay to Keynote" in *Benzinga.com* (November 2, 2011)
Pub: Benzinga.com
Ed: Benzinga Staff. **Description:** eBay's CEO, John Donahoe was keynote speaker at the 4th Annual Open Mobile Summit held in San Francisco, California. eBay is one of the 130 companies participating as speakers at the event.

20299 ■ "People/Calendar" in *Brandweek* (Vol. 49, April 21, 2008, No. 16, pp. 30)
Pub: VNU Business Media, Inc.
Description: Listing of current conferences, tradeshows and events concerning the marketing industry.

20300 ■ "People and Places" in *Entrepreneur* (Vol. 36, February 2008, No. 2, pp. 12)
Pub: Entrepreneur Media Inc.
Ed: Rieva Lesonsky. **Description:** Websites of different organizations that can provide entrepreneurs with business help are presented. Business-related events such as the Women in Charge conference and Xerox Smart Business Symposium are mentioned.

20301 ■ "PHCC Convention, Show Gets High Marks" in *Contractor* (Vol. 56, December 2009, No. 12, pp. 1)
Pub: Penton Media, Inc.
Ed: Robert P. Mader. **Description:** Plumbing-Heating-Cooling Contractors National Association has held its first convention and trade show in New Orleans, Louisiana. Attendees were treated to a variety of seminars and exhibitors during the event. Comments from event organizers are also given.

20302 ■ "Pipe Show Finds a Way for Smokers to Light Up" in *Crain's Chicago Business* (Vol. 31, April 28, 2008, No. 17, pp. 57)
Pub: Crain Communications, Inc.
Ed: H. Lee Murphy. **Description:** With the help of attorneys within its local membership of 150 pipe collectors, the Chicagoland Pipe Collectors Club will be allowed to smoke at its 13th International Pipe & Tobacciana Show at Pheasant Run Resort. The event is expected to draw 4,000 pipe enthusiasts from as far as China and Russia.

20303 ■ "Plan Your Next Event at Newport News Marriott at City Center" in *Benzinga.com* (July 29, 2011)
Pub: Benzinga.com
Ed: Benzinga Staff. **Description:** Newport News Marriott at City Center is promoting itself as the premier venue for business meetings, conventions and weddings.

20304 ■ "Plumbing, Heating Products Shine at Greenbuild" in *Contractor* (Vol. 57, January 2010, No. 1, pp. 3)
Pub: Penton Media, Inc.
Ed: Robert P. Mader. **Description:** Among the many exhibitors at Greenbuild 2009 was T&S Brass which showcased their low-flow pre-rinse spray valves and Watts Water Technologies which showed off their hot water recirculating system. Aquatherm and Acorn Engineering were also at the show.

20305 ■ "Plumbing, Heating Products Shine at Greenbuild Expo" in *Contractor* (Vol. 56, December 2009, No. 12, pp. 1)
Pub: Penton Media, Inc.
Ed: Robert P. Mader. **Description:** Greenbuild Show held in Phoenix, Arizona has showcased the latest in plumbing and heating products. Zurn displayed its EcoVantage line of fixtures and valves during the event. Meanwhile, Sloan Valve offered its washdown 1-pint/flush Alphine urinal.

20306 ■ "Polite Conversation" in *Mergers & Acquisitions: The Dealmaker's Journal* (March 1, 2008)
Pub: SourceMedia, Inc.
Description: In January, industry leaders and dealmakers met at Davos to discuss topics ranging from the possibility of a recession to what lies ahead in the deal market.

20307 ■ "Prepping for the Unpredictable" in *Crain's Cleveland Business* (Vol. 30, June 15, 2009, No. 23, pp. 16)
Pub: Crain Communications, Inc.
Ed: Joel Hammond. **Description:** Michael Ferrara, event planner and designer for Executive Caterers discusses the many events he has planned.

20308 ■ "Proposal for a Macomb County Visitors Bureau Draws Mixed Reaction" in *Crain's Detroit Business* (Vol. 24, March 31, 2008, No. 13)
Pub: Crain Communications, Inc.
Ed: Chad Halcom. **Description:** Discusses the newly formed M-59 Corridor Business Association and its proposal to create a convention and visitors bureau dedicated to the county's interests.

20309 ■ "Real-Life Coursework for Real-Life Business People" in *Women In Business* (Vol. 63, Summer 2011, No. 2, pp. 22)
Pub: American Business Women's Association
Ed: Leigh Elmore. **Description:** American Business Women's Association National Women's Leadership Conference provides members with academic business training courses. Members can take a variety of MBA-level courses that are taught by University of Kansas School of Business professors. Courses include marketing, management, leadership and communication and decision making.

20310 ■ "Renren Partners With Recruit to Launch Social Wedding Services" in *Benzinga.com* (June 7, 2011)
Pub: Benzinga.com

Ed: Benzinga Staff. **Description:** Renren Inc. and Recruit Company Ltd. partnered to build a wedding social media catering to engaged couples and newlyweds in China. The platform will integrate online wedding related social content and offline media such as magazine and wedding exhibitions.

20311 ■ "Rock Festival: High Spirited Conventioneers Celebrate Their Good Fortune" in *Canadian Business* (Vol. 81, March 31, 2008, No. 5)
Pub: Rogers Media

Ed: Jeff Sanford. **Description:** Soaring prices of commodities in the mining industry have been very good for the attendees of the 76th annual conference of the Prospectors & Developers Association of Canada. A speaker at the conference expects commodity prices to come off a bit but not fall dramatically as it did in the 1980's.

20312 ■ "RPA Preps for Building Radiant Conference, Show" in *Contractor* (Vol. 57, January 2010, No. 1, pp. 5)
Pub: Penton Media, Inc.

Description: Radiant Panel Association is accepting registrations for its Building Radiant 2010 Conference and Trade Show. The conference will discuss radiant heating as well as insurance and other legal matters for mechanical contractors.

20313 ■ "A Safe Bet" in *Entrepreneur* (Vol. 35, October 2007, No. 10, pp. 26)
Pub: Entrepreneur Media Inc.

Ed: Carol Tice. **Description:** U.S. Department of Defense has developed a program, called the Defense Venture Catalyst Initiative or DeVenCI, that will match defense officials to the products that they need. DeVenCI uses conferences to showcase the defense contractors and their technologies to defense managers. Details of how this program helps both contractors and defense officials are overviewed.

20314 ■ "Save the Date" in *Barron's* (Vol. 90, September 13, 2010, No. 37, pp. 35)
Pub: Barron's Editorial & Corporate Headquarters

Ed: Mark Veverka. **Description:** Mark Hurd is the new Co-President of Oracle after being forced out at Hewlett-Packard where he faced a harassment complaint. HP fired Hurd due to expense account malfeasance. Hurd is also set to speak at an Oracle trade show in San Francisco on September 20, 2010.

20315 ■ "Save the Date" in *Mergers & Acquisitions: The Dealmaker's Journal* (March 1, 2008)
Pub: SourceMedia, Inc.

Description: Listing of conferences and forums that deal with business and investing, particularly with mergers and acquisitions. Includes dates, locations and Internet addresses.

20316 ■ "Secrets To Trade Show Success" in *Women Entrepreneur* (September 12, 2008)
Pub: Entrepreneur Media Inc.

Ed: Lesley Spencer Pyle. **Description:** Trade shows require an enormous amount of work, but they are an investment that can pay off handsomely because they allow a business to get their product or service in front of their target market. Advice regarding trade shows is given including selecting the correct venue, researching the affair and following up on leads obtained at the event.

20317 ■ "Sherwin-Williams Workers Forgo Travel for Virtual Trade Show" in *Crain's Cleveland Business* (Vol. 28, October 15, 2007, No. 41)
Pub: Crain Communications, Inc.

Ed: John Booth. **Description:** Overview of CyberCoating 2007, a cutting-edge virtual three-dimensional trade show that exhibitors such as Sherwin-Williams Co.'s Chemical Coatings Division will take part in by chatting verbally or via text messages in order to exchange information and listen to pitches just like they would on an actual trade show floor.

20318 ■ "Show Dates" in *Art Business News* (Vol. 34, November 2007, No. 11, pp. 18)
Pub: Pfingsten Publishing, LLC

Description: Listing of conferences, trade shows and gallery openings for artists and those in the art industry.

20319 ■ "Silverdome Bidders Bring New Proposals" in *Crain's Detroit Business* (Vol. 24, March 17, 2008, No. 11, pp. 23)
Pub: Crain Communications, Inc.

Ed: Daniel Duggan. **Description:** Discusses the seven plans which have been proposed as part of the third round of bidding for the Pontiac Silverdome; proposals range from Global Baseball Inc., a baseball league that would pit a team from every country against one another, to an Indian casino, a musical "hall of fame", a convention center, a horse track, a hotel and an indoor water park.

20320 ■ "Six Tips To Maximize Networking Opportunities" in *Women Entrepreneur* (November 3, 2008)
Pub: Entrepreneur Media Inc.

Ed: Tamara Monosoff. **Description:** Networking events fall into the realm of business development as opposed to immediate sales opportunities. It is important to remember that these events provide a chance to build relationships that may someday help one's business. Tips to help make the most out of networking events are provided.

20321 ■ "Social Media Event Slated for March 25" in *Bellingham Business Journal* (Vol. February 2010, pp. 3)
Pub: Sound Publishing Inc.

Description: Center for Economic Vitality (CEV) and the Technology Alliance Group (TAG) will host the 2010 Social Media Conference at the McIntyre Hall Performing Arts & Conference Center in Mt. Vernon, Washington. The event will provide networking opportunities for attendees.

20322 ■ "Speak Better: Five Tips for Polished Presentations" in *Women Entrepreneur* (September 19, 2008)
Pub: Entrepreneur Media Inc.

Ed: Suzannah Baum. **Description:** Successful entrepreneurs agree that exemplary public speaking skills are among the core techniques needed to propel their business forward. A well-delivered presentation can result in securing a new distribution channel, gaining new customers, locking into a new referral stream or receiving extra funding.

20323 ■ "Sponsorship, Booths Available for Spring Business Showcase" in *Bellingham Business Journal* (Vol. February 2010, pp. 3)
Pub: Sound Publishing Inc.

Description: Third Annual Spring Business Showcase still have space available for vendors and sponsors. The event gives local businesses the opportunity to increase their visibility and provides a means to increase sales and build relationships.

20324 ■ "State of a Fair!" in *Small Business Opportunities* (March 2008)
Pub: Harris Publications Inc.

Ed: Shelly Buss. **Description:** State fairs are money-making venues; one company made $2 million in 12 days at the Minnesota State Fair.

20325 ■ "State Fairgrounds Adding Year-Round Attractions" in *Crain's Detroit Business* (Vol. 24, February 18, 2008, No. 7, pp. 17)
Pub: Crain Communications Inc. - Detroit

Ed: Robert Ankeny. **Description:** Michigan State Fairgrounds and Exposition Center shares its plans to become a year-round recreation, entertainment and education center.

20326 ■ "Success Products" in *Black Enterprise* (Vol. 37, February 2007, No. 7, pp. 135)
Pub: Earl G. Graves Publishing Co. Inc.

Ed: Tanisha A. Sykes. **Description:** Using innovative resources that are already at your fingertips instead of trying to reach out to companies first is a great way to discover whether you have a viable idea or product. Be motivated to start an e-newsletter letting people know about your products and attend conferences like The Motivation Show, the world's largest exhibition of motivational products and services related to performance in business.

20327 ■ "Tax-Free Zones Need Shows; Out-of-State Shoppers Are Key To Success" in *Crain's Detroit Business* (Vol. 24, January 28, 2008, No. 4)
Pub: Crain Communications Inc. - Detroit

Ed: Daniel Duggan. **Description:** Sales tax-free zones are being considered by Michigan's legislators in order to promote the state as a conference destination.

20328 ■ "Teachable Moments: Worth Every Penny" in *Pet Product News* (Vol. 64, December 2010, No. 12, pp. 34)
Pub: BowTie Inc.

Ed: Cheryl Reeves. **Description:** Pet bird retailers can attain both outreach to customers and enhanced profitability by staging educational events such as the annual Parrot Palooza event of Burlington, New Jersey-based Bird Paradise. Aside from attracting a global audience, Parrot Palooza features seminars, workshops, classes, and bird-related contests.

20329 ■ "Tic-Tac-Show" in *American Printer* (Vol. 128, August 1, 2011, No. 8)
Pub: Penton Media Inc.

Description: Graph Expo has become the US print industry's main event. There will be as many as 500 exhibitors at this year's event and the Graphic Arts Show Company lists over 30 co-located events as well as 53 new sessions in the seminar program's 28 education categories.

20330 ■ "Tool Time" in *Entrepreneur* (Vol. 36, March 2008, No. 3, pp. 90)
Pub: Entrepreneur Media Inc.

Ed: Nichole A. Torres. **Description:** DaVinci Institute holds an annual event in Colorado to display new products and inventions. Innovative Design Engineering Animation is a consulting company that helps inventors develop product through various stages. NineSigma Inc. has an online marketplace where inventors can post ideas for clients needing new products.

20331 ■ "Tourism Bureau Seeks Hotel Tax Hike" in *Baltimore Business Journal* (Vol. 27, December 18, 2009, No. 32, pp. 1)
Pub: American City Business Journals

Ed: Rachel Bernstein. **Description:** Baltimore, Maryland's tourism agency, Visit Baltimore, has proposed a new hotel tax that could produce $2 million annually for its marketing budget, fund improvements to the city's 30-year-old convention center and help it compete for World Cup soccer games. Baltimore hotel leaders discuss the new tax.

20332 ■ *Trade Show Exhibitors Association—Membership Directory and Industry Buyer's Guide*
Pub: Trade Show Exhibitors Association

Released: Continuous, Updated every month. **Covers:** About 2,300 members of the Trade Show Exhibitors Association. **Entries Include:** Name, address, phone, fax, e-mail, web site, name of contact. **Arrangement:** Classified by type of business or association. **Indexes:** Alphabetical by name.

20333 ■ "Tradeshow Attendance Incentives Add Up" in *Pet Product News* (Vol. 64, December 2010, No. 12, pp. 14)
Pub: BowTie Inc.

Ed: Mark E. Battersby. **Description:** Pointers on how pet specialty retailers can claim business travel tax and income tax deductions for expenses paid or incurred in participation at tradeshows, conventions, and meetings are presented. Incentives in form of these deductions could allow pet specialty retailers to gain business benefits, aside from the education and enjoyment involved with the travel.

20334 ■ *Tradeshow Week Data Book*
Pub: Tradeshow Week Inc.
Contact: Larry Dunn, Publisher
E-mail: ldunn@reedbusiness.com
Released: Annual, Latest edition 2010. **Price:** $305, individuals plus $25 shipping and handling. **Covers:** Nearly 5,300 trade and public shows with at least 5,000 net square feet of exhibit space scheduled in the United States and Canada up to five years from publication date. **Entries Include:** Show title, show management and sponsor, show description, location, dates, general contractor, estimated net square feet of exhibit space, number and profile of exhibitors and participants, fees, associated seminars, meetings and conferences, show history, future dates and sites. **Arrangement:** Classified by industry category. **Indexes:** Geographical, alphabetical, chronological, show management, show size, rotation pattern, new shows.

20335 ■ *Tradeshow Week Major Exhibit Hall Directory*
Pub: Tradeshow Week Inc.
Contact: Nancy Walker, Publisher
E-mail: nwalker@reedbusiness.com
Released: Annual, Latest edition 2009. **Price:** $250, individuals full web access (plus $25 shipping & handling). **Covers:** Exhibition facilities with at least 25,000 square feet of prime exhibit space, including convention centers, hotels, auditoriums, arenas, and other facilities in the United States, Canada, and Mexico. **Entries Include:** Hall name, address, facility manager name, title, and phone number, prime and total exhibit space size; utilities available; number of meeting rooms and capacity; parking sites; rates; new construction and expansions; recent openings. **Arrangement:** Geographical. **Indexes:** Hall size, floorplan.

20336 ■ "Travel Tears" in *Crain's Chicago Business* (Vol. 31, November 17, 2008, No. 46, pp. 3)
Pub: Crain Communications, Inc.
Ed: Bob Tita. **Description:** Hotels, restaurants and conventions are seeing a decline in profits due to corporate travel cutbacks and the sagging economy. City and state revenues derived from taxes on tourism-related industries are also suffering.

20337 ■ "A Vegas Sensation Inaugural Artexpo Las Vegas" in *Art Business News* (Vol. 34, November 2007, No. 11, pp. 1)
Pub: Pfingsten Publishing, LLC
Ed: Jennifer Dulin. **Description:** Overview of the first Artexpo Las Vegas which featured exhibitors, artists and buyers and was a wonderful place for networking.

20338 ■ "Wal-Mart Doesn't Sell Council" in *The Business Journal-Serving Metropolitan Kansas City* (Vol. 26, July 4, 2008, No. 43, pp. 1)
Pub: American City Business Journals, Inc.
Ed: Steve Vockrodt. **Description:** Wal-Mart Stores Inc. announced that it will move the location of its annual convention from Kansas City, Missouri to Orlando, Florida. The change of venue came after Rick Hughes, Kansas City Convention and Visitors Association president rejected Wal-Mart's proposal to subsidize a new hotel in the downtown area that is needed for the event.

20339 ■ "The Weeks Ahead" in *Crain's New York Business* (Vol. 24, January 14, 2008, No. 2, pp. 20)
Pub: Crain Communications, Inc.
Description: Listing of events in the Detroit area include conferences addressing entrepreneurialism, economic development, and women business ownership.

20340 ■ "Welcome to Babesland" in *Women In Business* (Vol. 62, June 2010, No. 2, pp. 33)
Pub: American Business Women's Association
Ed: Leigh Elmore. **Description:** Music group, Four Bitchin' Babes will be performing at the 2010 American Business Women's Association's National Women's Leadership Conference. The group has been in the industry for 20 years and has released nine albums. The Four Bitchin' Babes consist of Sally Fingerett, Nancy Moran, Deirdre Flint, and Debi Smith.

20341 ■ "Women of Power" in *Black Enterprise* (Vol. 41, November 2010, No. 4, pp. 94)
Pub: Earl G. Graves Publishing Co. Inc.
Description: Black Enterprise Women of Power Summit will be held February 23-26, 2011 at the Ritz Carlton in Orlando, Florida. Speakers will offer insight into career, household, and life in general.

20342 ■ "Women of Power Summit" in *Black Enterprise* (Vol. 38, February 2008, No. 7, pp. 163)
Pub: Earl G. Graves Publishing Co. Inc.
Description: Third annual Women of Power Summit, hosted by State Farm, will host over 700 executive women of color offering empowerment sessions, tips for networking, along with entertainment.

20343 ■ "Worry No. 1 at Auto Show" in *Crain's Detroit Business* (Vol. 24, January 21, 2008, No. 3, pp. 1)
Pub: Crain Communications Inc. - Detroit
Ed: Brent Snavely. **Description:** Recession fears clouded activity at the 2008 Annual North American International Auto Show. Automakers are expecting to see a drop in sales due to slow holiday retail spending as well as fallout from the subprime lending crisis.

20344 ■ "WQA's Leadership Conference Tackles Industry Issues" in *Contractor* (Vol. 56, October 2009, No. 10, pp. 3)
Pub: Penton Media, Inc.
Ed: Candace Roulo. **Description:** Water Quality Association's Mid-Year Leadership Conference held in Bloomingdale, Illinois in September 2009 tackled lead regulation, water softeners, and product efficiency. The possibility of a WQA green seal was discussed by the Water Sciences Committee and the Government Relations Committee meeting.

20345 ■ "Your Turn in the Spotlight" in *Inc.* (March 2008, pp. 30)
Pub: Gruner & Jahr USA Publishing
Ed: Elaine Appleton Grant. **Description:** Profile of a Tennessee business that produces events and concerts. The company offers a complete package of services handling staging, lighting, video, musical instrument rentals, and audio support. The founder has decided to sell the business and details of the asking price, price rationale, the pros and cons of buying the firm and its bottom line are examined.

TRADE PERIODICALS

20346 ■ *Association Meetings*
Pub: Primedia Business Magazines & Media
Contact: Melissa Fromento, Gp. Publisher
E-mail: mfromento@meetingsnet.com
Ed: Sue Pelletier, Editor, spelletier@meetingsnet.com. **Released:** Bimonthly. **Price:** $65 Canada; $98 other countries. **Description:** Magazine for association meeting planners.

20347 ■ *Corporate & Incentive Travel*
Pub: Coastal Communications Corp.
Contact: Harvey Grotsky, Publisher/Ed.-in-Ch.
E-mail: cccpublisher@att.net
Released: Monthly. **Description:** Magazine for corporate executives with the responsibility for site selection, staging and planning meetings, incentive travel programs, conferences, and conventions.

20348 ■ *Facility Manager*
Pub: International Association of Assembly Managers
Contact: Richard Church, Production Mgr
Ed: R.V. Baugus, Editor, rv.baugus@iaam.org. **Released:** Bimonthly. **Price:** $55 Free members; $85 two years North America; $110 out of state. **Description:** Magazine for managers of public assembly facilities.

20349 ■ *Healthcare Convention & Exhibitors Association—AIP Alert*
Pub: Healthcare Convention & Exhibitors Association
Ed: **Released:** 2/year. **Price:** Free. **Description:** Disseminates information to health care associations, exhibitors, and their Exhibitors Advisory Councils (EAC). Reports on innovative ideas and focuses on specific problems and solutions pertaining the effective display of health care products. Seeks to communicate the benefits of membership. Recurring features include news of research, reports of meetings and industry issues, news of educational opportunities, and notices of publications available.

20350 ■ *Meeting News*
Pub: Nielsen Business Media
Contact: Jay Boehmer, Sen. Ed.
E-mail: jboehmer@meetingnews.com
Released: 18/yr. **Price:** $89; $99 Canada; $205 other countries by airmail. **Description:** The newspaper for conventions, meetings, incentive travel and trade show professionals.

20351 ■ *Meetings & Conventions*
Pub: Northstar Travel Media
Contact: Lisa Grimaldi, Sen. Ed.
E-mail: lgrimaldi@mcmag.com
Released: Monthly. **Price:** Free to qualified subscribers. **Description:** Magazine focusing on meetings, conferences and trade show.

20352 ■ *Meetings & Incentive Travel*
Pub: Rogers Media Publishing
Contact: Stephen Dempsey, Editor & Publisher
E-mail: steve.dempsey@mtg.rogers.com
Released: 6/yr. **Price:** $98 two years CAN; $74 Canada; $95 U.S. **Description:** Magazine for corporate meeting planners and incentive travel executives.

20353 ■ *Sharing Ideas News Magazine*
Pub: Royal Publishing Inc.
Contact: Michael MacFarlane, President
E-mail: michael@speakandgrowrich.com
Released: Quarterly. **Price:** $100 U.S.; $124 Canada and Mexico; $175 out of country other foreign. **Description:** Magazine for professional speakers, meeting planners, and bureaus.

20354 ■ *Trade Show Ideas*
Pub: Trade Show Exhibitors Association
Contact: Amy Mandel CPS, DIR
Released: Monthly, combined (July/August). **Price:** Included in membership; $79 for subscription only. **Description:** Supplies news and information of interest to exhibit managers and their suppliers. Carries case studies, "how-to" items, checklists, and industry data. Recurring features include interviews, news of research and of educational opportunities, and reports of meetings. Also includes columns titled Destinations, Thoughts from the Corner Office, Market-Wise, Profiles and Member Network Exchange.

VIDEOCASSETTES/ AUDIOCASSETTES

20355 ■ *The Trade Show Advantage*
Creative Training Solutions
5 Timberline Dr.
Voorhees, NJ 08043
Ph:(856)784-3468
Free: 800-515-4114
Fax:(856)784-7087
Co. E-mail: mail@creativetraining.com
URL: http://www.creativetraining.com
Price: $395.00. **Description:** Shows how to set up a booth at a trade show. Includes everything from personal comportment to information on the typical trade show environment. Includes planning guide, handout, and audiocassette. **Availability:** VHS.

20356 ■ *Working the Booth: Trade Show Success*
American Media, Inc.
4621 121st St.
Urbandale, IA 50323-2311
Ph:(515)224-0919

Free: 888-776-8268
Fax:(515)327-2555
Co. E-mail: custsvc@ammedia.com
URL: http://www.ammedia.com
Released: 1992. **Price:** $395.00. **Description:** Details techniques on successfully setting up and maintaining a booth at a trade show. Stresses etiquette, professionalism, positivity, correct prospect handling, and salesmanship. **Availability:** VHS; 3/4U; 8mm.

TRADE SHOWS AND CONVENTIONS

20357 ■ Destinations Showcase
TBA
Ste. 400, 425 Carrall St.
Vancouver, BC, Canada V6B 6E3
Ph:(604)689-3448
Fax:(604)689-5054
Co. E-mail: canadainfo@pgi.com
URL: http://www.pgi.com
Released: Annual. **Audience:** Convention, meeting, trade show, and travel planners. **Principal Exhibits:** Convention center and convention bureau information. **Dates and Locations:** 2011 Jun 02-02, Rosemont, IL.

20358 ■ HSMAI Affordable Meetings Exposition and Conference
George Little Management, LLC (New York, New York)
1133 Westchester Ave., Ste. N136
White Plains, NY 10606
Ph:(914)421-3200
Free: 800-272-SHOW
Co. E-mail: cathy_steel@glmshows.com
URL: http://www.glmshows.com
Released: Annual. **Audience:** Planners, executives, and decision-makers from corporations and associations; religious, social, ethnic, sports, and educational groups. **Principal Exhibits:** Services for cost-conscious meeting planners. **Dates and Locations:** 2011 Sep 07-08, Washington, DC.

20359 ■ International Association of Fairs and Expositions Trade Show
International Association of Fairs and Expositions
3043 E. Cairo
Springfield, MO 65802
Ph:(417)862-5771
Free: 800-516-0313
Fax:(417)862-0156
Co. E-mail: iafe@fairsandexpos.com
URL: http://www.fairsandexpos.com
Released: Annual. **Audience:** Fair managers, staffs, and board members; carnival owners and staffs; concessionaires; talent and other agencies related to the fair industry. **Principal Exhibits:** Talent agencies, concessionaires, novelties, amusement devices, insurance, ribbons, plaques, attractions, and equipment. Products and services for the fair industry.

CONSULTANTS

20360 ■ Exhibit Center L.L.C.
3055 West 2100 South, Ste. A
Salt Lake City, UT 84119-1286
Ph:(801)908-6122
Fax:(801)908-0776
Contact: Chris Hatch, President
Scope: Graphics design consultants experienced in planning of exhibits and other industrial design projects. A specialty is the fabrication of portable displays and cusion displays for trade shows. Store interiors, high end lobbies, sets.

20361 ■ Intex Exhibit Systems L.L.C.
1846 Sequoia Ave.
Orange, CA 92868
Ph:(714)940-0369
Free: 800-331-6633
Fax:(714)935-0223
Co. E-mail: info@intexexhibits.com
URL: http://www.intexexhibits.com
Contact: Sue Bonas, Owner
E-mail: mdk@intexexhibits.com
Scope: Firm specializes in the design and production of exhibits, displays and pavilions for world fairs, tradeshows and similar events. Services include product design, industrial and engineering design for educational exhibits, museum exhibits and science and technology museology. Serves private industry as well as government agencies. **Publications:** "Trade Show Marketing," Sep, 2000; "Exhibitor Times," 1998. **Special Services:** Fastpack^{TM}; Panelflo^{TM}; affordable-1^{TM}; thegraphic arm^{TM}; Expression^{TM}; TigerMark^{TM}.

Translating/Interpreting Service

START-UP INFORMATION

20362 ■ "Can You Say $1 Million? A Language-Learning Start-Up Is Hoping That Investors Can" in *Inc.* (Vol. 33, November 2011, No. 9, pp. 116)
Pub: Inc. Magazine
Ed: April Joyner. **Description:** Startup, Verbling is a video platform that links language learners and native speakers around the world. The firm is working to raise money to hire engineers in order to build the product and redesign their Website.

ASSOCIATIONS AND OTHER ORGANIZATIONS

20363 ■ The American Association of Language Specialists
PO Box 27306
Washington, DC 20038-7306
Co. E-mail: admissions@taals.net
URL: http://www.taals.net
Description: Professional association of conference interpreters, translators, revisers and precis-writers. .

20364 ■ American Translators Association
225 Reinekers Ln., Ste. 590
Alexandria, VA 22314-2875
Ph:(703)683-6100
Fax:(703)683-6122
Co. E-mail: ata@atanet.org
URL: http://www.atanet.org
Contact: Dr. Nicholas Hartmann, Pres.
Description: Fosters the professional development of translators and interpreters and promotes the translation and interpretation professions. **Publications:** *ATA Chronicle* (monthly); *Translation and Interpretation Services Survey* (biennial); *Translator and Interpreter Programs in North America* .

20365 ■ Association of Legal Court Interpreters and Translators–Association des Traducteurs et Interpretes Judiciaires
438 St. Antoine E
Montreal, QC, Canada H2Y 1A5
Ph:(514)845-3113
Fax:(514)845-3006
Co. E-mail: admin@atij.ca
URL: http://www.atij.ca
Description: Interpreters and translators working in courts of law. Promotes professional advancement of members; seeks to insure high standards of practice in the field of court translation. Conducts continuing professional education programs; facilitates exchange of information among members.

20366 ■ Association of Visual Language Interpreters of Canada
110 - 39012 Discovery Way
Squamish, BC, Canada V8B 0E5
Ph:(604)617-8502
Fax:(604)567-8502
Co. E-mail: avlic@avlic.ca
URL: http://www.avlic.ca/index.php
Contact: Christie Reaume, Pres.
Description: Sign language interpreters. Promotes standardization of sign language; seeks to insure excellence in the practice of visual language interpretation. Conducts continuing professional development courses for members. **Publications:** *AVLIC News* (3/year). **Telecommunication Services:** electronic mail, president@avlic.ca.

20367 ■ Canadian Translators, Terminologists and Interpreters Council–Conseil des traducteurs, terminologues et interpretes du Canada
1 Nicholas St., Ste. 1202
Ottawa, ON, Canada K1N 7B7
Ph:(613)562-0379
Fax:(613)241-4098
Co. E-mail: info@cttic.org
URL: http://www.cttic.org
Contact: Kristel Blais, Admin. Dir.
Description: Provincial societies representing 3,000 translators and interpreters. Promotes advancement of the professions of translation and interpretation. Formulates standards of knowledge and practice for translators and interpreters; conducts certification examinations. Coordinates members' activities; represents members in international professional organizations; sponsors educational and research programs. **Publications:** *Action CTIC Action* (periodic); *Meta* (quarterly).

20368 ■ Literary Translators' Association of Canada–Association des Traducteurs et Traductrices Literariness du Canada
LB 601 Concordia University
1455 de Maisonneuve Blvd. W
Montreal, QC, Canada H3G 1M8
Ph:(514)848-2424
Co. E-mail: info@attlc-ltac.org
URL: http://www.attlc-ltac.org
Contact: Jo-Anne Elder, Pres.
Description: Literary translators. Promotes literary translation and the interests of literary translators in Canada. Networks with cultural associations and agencies worldwide; lobbies government and cultural agencies regarding funding and copyright. **Publications:** *Transmission* (quarterly); Membership Directory (annual).

20369 ■ National Council of Less Commonly Taught Languages
National African Language Resource Ctr.
4231 Humanities Bldg.
455 N Park St.
Madison, WI 53706
Ph:(608)265-7905
Fax:(608)265-7904
Co. E-mail: ncolctl@mailplus.wisc.edu
URL: http://www.ncolctl.org
Contact: Antonia Folarin Schleicher PhD, Exec. Dir.
Description: National organization that represents teachers of less commonly taught languages. Addresses the issue of national capacity in the LCTL by facilitating communications among member organizations and with the governmental, private, heritage, and overseas sectors of the language community. Increases the collective impact of LCTL constituencies on America's ability to communicate with peoples from all parts of the world.

REFERENCE WORKS

20370 ■ *American Translators Association—Membership Directory*
Pub: American Translators Association
Contact: Mr. Walter W. Bacak Jr., Exec. Dir.
E-mail: walter@atanet.org
Released: Annual, summer. **Description:** Includes more than 9,000 member translators, interpreters, and linguists in the United States and over 60 countries. **Entries Include:** Name, address, phone, languages in which member has ATA certification. **Arrangement:** Alphabetical.

20371 ■ "The Americans Are Coming" in *The Economist* (Vol. 390, January 3, 2009, No. 8612, pp. 44)
Pub: The Economist Newspaper Inc.
Description: Student recruitment consultancies, which help place international students at universities in other countries and offer services such as interpreting or translating guidelines, are discussed; American universities who have shunned these agencies in the past; the result has been that America underperforms in relation to its size with a mere 3.5 percent of students on its campuses that are from abroad.

20372 ■ "Arizona Firms In Chicago Go For Gold With '08 Games" in *The Business Journal - Serving Phoenix and the Valley of the Sun* (Vol. 28, August 8, 2008, No. 49, pp. 1)
Pub: American City Business Journals, Inc.
Ed: Patrick O'Grady. **Description:** More than 20 U.S. athletes will wear Arizona-based eSoles LLC's custom-made insoles to increase their performance at the 2008 Beijing Olympics making eSoles one of the beneficiaries of the commercialization of the games. Translation software maker Auralog Inc saw a 60 percent jump in sales from its Mandarin Chinese language applications.

20373 ■ *ATA Directory of Translators and Interpreters*
Pub: American Translators Association
Contact: Walter Bacak Jr., Exec. Dir.
E-mail: walter@atanet.org
Covers: over 5,800 member translators and interpreters. **Entries Include:** Name, address, languages in which proficient, subject competencies, professional background. **Arrangement:** Alphabetical, area of specialization, language. **Indexes:** Language-subject competency (with state).

20374 ■ "Encouraging Study in Critical Languages" in *Occupational Outlook Quarterly* (Vol. 55, Summer 2011, No. 2, pp. 23)
Pub: U.S. Bureau of Labor Statistics
Description: Proficiency in particular foreign languages is vital to the defense, diplomacy, and security

of the United States. Several federal programs provide scholarships and other funding to encourage high school and college students to learn languages of the Middle East, China, and Russia.

20375 ■ "The Future Is Another Country; Higher Education" in *The Economist* (Vol. 390, January 3, 2009, No. 8612, pp. 43)
Pub: The Economist Newspaper Inc.
Description: Due to the growth of the global corporation, more ambitious students are studying at universities abroad; the impact of this trend is discussed.

20376 ■ "Internet Translation Service Helps Burmese" in *News-Sentinel* (May 10, 2011)
Pub: New-Sentinel
Ed: Ellie Bogue. **Description:** Catherine Kasper Place, Parkview Health Community Outreach, Allen County-Fort Wayne Department of Health and Advantage Health have partnered to help the Burmese Community in the area by providing an online service that links doctors' offices with translators in order to provide better healthcare.

20377 ■ "Machine Transliteration Survey" in *ACM Computing Surveys* (Vol. 43, Fall 2011, No. 3, pp. 17)
Pub: Association for Computing Machinery
Ed: Sarvnaz Karimi, Falk Scholer, Andrew Turpin. **Description:** Machine transliteration is the process of automatically transforming the script of a word from a source language to a target language, while preserving pronunciation. The development of algorithms specifically for machine transliteration began over a decade ago based on the phonetics of source and target languages, followed by approaches using statistical and language-specific methods. In this survey, the key methodologies introduced in transliteration literature are reviewed. The approaches are categorized based on the resources and algorithms used, and the effectiveness is compared.

20378 ■ "Making Visitors Out Of Listeners" in *Hawaii Business* (Vol. 54, July 2008, No. 1, pp. 18)
Pub: Hawaii Business Publishing
Ed: Casey Chin. **Description:** Japanese workers are subscribing to the Official Hawaii Podcast in iTunes, which offers a free 20-minute, Japanese-language audio content on different topics, such as dining reviews and music from local artists. The concept is a way to attract Japanese travelers to come to Hawaii.

20379 ■ "Online Translation Service Aids Battlefield Troops" in *Product News Network* (August 30, 2011)
Pub: Thomas Publishing Company
Description: Linquist online service, LinGo Link provides real-time interpreter support to military troops overseas. Interpreters skilled in multiple languages and dialects are used in various areas and in multiple instances without requiring physical presence. The service is available through commercial cellular or WiFi services or tactical communications network. The system accommodates exchange of audio, video, photos, and text during conversations via smartphones and mobile peripheral devices.

20380 ■ "Speaking In Tongues: Rosetta Stone's TOTALE Adds 'Social' To Language Learning" in *Black Enterprise* (Vol. 41, September 2010, No. 2)
Pub: Earl G. Graves Publishing Co. Inc.
Ed: Sonya A. Donaldson. **Description:** As small businesses become more globalized, it is necessary to learn new languages in order to compete. Rosetta Stone's TOTALe is profiled.

20381 ■ "Web Translation Made Simple" in *Inc.* (Vol. 33, October 2011, No. 8, pp. 44)
Pub: Inc. Magazine
Ed: Adam Baer. **Description:** Smartling is a Web-based service that translates sites into more than 50 foreign languages. The software will begin translation right after setting up the account.

TRADE PERIODICALS

20382 ■ *Views*
Pub: R I D Publications
Contact: Stuart Nealy
Released: Monthly, except combined Aug./Setp. issue. **Price:** $36, U.S.; $36, elsewhere. **Description:** Newsletter for interpreters for the deaf.

TRADE SHOWS AND CONVENTIONS

20383 ■ American Translators Association Annual Conference
American Translators Association
225 Reinekers Ln., Ste. 590
Alexandria, VA 22314
Ph:(703)683-6100
Fax:(703)683-6122
Co. E-mail: ata@atanet.org
URL: http://www.atanet.org
Released: Annual. **Audience:** Translators and interpreters. **Principal Exhibits:** Publications, software and services. **Dates and Locations:** 2011 Oct 26-29, Boston, MA.

CONSULTANTS

20384 ■ DTS Language Services Inc.
7780 Brier Creek Pky., Ste. 325
Raleigh, NC 27617
Ph:(919)942-0666
Free: 800-524-0722
Fax:(919)942-0686
Co. E-mail: contact@dtstrans.com
URL: http://www.dtstrans.com
Contact: Henk Ypma, President
E-mail: dshaw@dtstrans.com
Scope: Offers a complete range of foreign language services, including translation of engineering and technical documentation, bids and proposals, instruction and training materials, correspondence, patents and legal documentation, advertising copy and brochures, and many other services. Maintains both English and foreign language word processing equipment to produce camera-ready copy of most materials in-house. Industries served: engineering, computer hardware, electronics industry, pharmaceuticals, telecommunications and software.

20385 ■ ENLASO Corp.
4888 Pearl East Cir., Ste. 300E
Boulder, CO 80301
Ph:(303)516-0857
Free: (866)415-6820
Fax:(303)516-1701
Co. E-mail: contact@translate.com
URL: http://www.translate.com
Contact: Yves Savourel, Mgr
E-mail: ysavourel@atstranslate.com
Scope: Services include translations from and into foreign languages. Specializes in technical and legal documents, patents, specifications and instruction manuals translation. Also active in advertising in foreign languages, including copy-writing, artwork, typesetting and video and audio. Serves private industries and government agencies. **Publications:** "Cross-Cultural Training and Localization," Feb, 2008; "Using Symbols and Icons in Localization"; "Marketing Communications, Culture, and Localization"; "Culture: Overlooked Web Globalization Ingredient"; "Documentation Localization Process Tune-Up"; "Multilingual Flash Production"; "How to Economize When Localizing Graphics"; "Xml Internationalization and Localization," Sams, Jun, 2001. **Seminars:** A growing market: Non-English speakers in the US. **Special Services:** Rainbow™; Album™; Horizon™; Lexikon™.

20386 ■ Languages Inc.
1010 Spring Mill Ave., Ste. 100
Conshohocken, PA 19428-2391
Ph:(215)763-7787
Free: 800-346-5071
Fax:(610)825-4430
Contact: Jeff Levin, Principle
Scope: Provides translations and narration services for corporate video and audiovisual products. In house capabilities include beta cam SP and AVID non linear editing, international video standards conversion, duplication and fulfillment. Also offers text translation in all fields and languages, as well as typesetting and mechanical production. Industries served: international corporations and production houses.

20387 ■ MiracleLink
53-36, 4th Fl., Changchun-dong
Seoul 11104, Republic of Korea
Ph:(718)937-8565
Fax:(718)937-8565
Co. E-mail: info@omnitr.com
URL: http://www.omnitr.com
E-mail: info@omnitr.com
Scope: Provides free Internet access to an international list of translators, interpreters, translation related consultation, software or website localization vendors, translation agencies, and other translation related resources books, associations, accreditations, business start up guide and vendors.

20388 ■ Rosetta Stone Associates
34 Franklin St., Ste. 200A
Nashua, NH 03064-2699
Ph:(603)883-9388
Free: 800-472-2896
Fax:(603)595-8673
Co. E-mail: info@mv.com
URL: http://www.mv.com/biz/rosetta/
Contact: Katrin Feldman, Principle
E-mail: jfurey@rosettastoneinc.net
Scope: Technical and scientific translation and localization services offered inmost major languages of the world. Subject matter is highly diverse, covering such areas as advertising, patents, user manuals, financial statements, contracts, technical and scientific journals, proposals, and correspondence. Typesetting services is available as needed. Provides qualified interpreters to handle foreign visits, conferences, seminars, and training programs. Additionally, provides language instruction for either individuals and groups tailored to client's specific needs. Industries served manufacturing, academia, finance, legal, computer, High technology, airlines, research, and government agencies. **Publications:** "Rosetta Stone Bought By Eurotext Translations," Oct, 2002. "Partnership with Eurotext," Ireland, Jun, 2000.

20389 ■ Suzuki, Myers & Associates Ltd.
46320 Ten Mile Rd.
PO Box 852
Novi, MI 48376-0852
Ph:(248)344-0909
Fax:(248)344-0092
Co. E-mail: office@suzukimyers.com
URL: http://www.suzukimyers.com
Contact: Amanda McClintock, Mgr
E-mail: amanda@atssuzukimyers.com
Scope: Offers marketing and sales assistance to firms approaching the Japan market, as well as cultural and communications training for staff who working in or with Japanese companies or subsidiaries, and public affairs assistance to firms approaching Japan. Assistance includes technical or promotional translating and interpreting. Industries served: Automotive OEM clients and their vendors, service firms, professionals, city and county development agencies, government agencies, and some retail operations. **Seminars:** Selling Goods and Services to the Japanese; Hosting Japanese; Education in Japan; Single in Japan; PR: The US/Japan Interface; Lawyers and the Japanese Client; A Japan Cultural Sampler.

20390 ■ Thomas J. Snow
27 Dennison Ave.
Binghamton, NY 13901-2106
Ph:(607)723-5702
Scope: Offers consulting in languages, information, and communication. Translation from and into any language of texts in any field of technology, including marketing literature and user documentation.

20391 ■ Transimpex Translations Inc.
602 Fairway
Belton, MO 64012
Ph:(816)561-3777
Free: 888-877-4679
Fax:(816)561-5515
Co. E-mail: translations@transimpex.com
URL: http://www.transimpex.com
Contact: Ingrid Pelger, Office Mgr

Scope: Offers industrial, legal, technical and scientific translation, interpreting, foreign language typesetting, advertising, audio and video presentation, localization/internationalization, translator/interpreter training, and expertise on translation and international trade worldwide. **Seminars:** Legal and Technical Translation Workshop; Starting and Operating a Translation Business; Translator Ethics; Language Identification; Translation and Localization for International Trade; Culture Training; T and I Training.

FRANCHISES AND BUSINESS OPPORTUNITIES

20392 ■ Language Leaders Franchising LLC
Foreign Language Network, L.L.C.
401 W. State St.
Geneva, IL 60134
Ph:(630)377-8794
No. of Company-Owned Units: 1. **Founded:** 1998. **Franchised:** 2004. **Description:** Foreign language education and interpreting. **Equity Capital Needed:** $18,700-$107,000. **Franchise Fee:** $10,000-$90,000. **Royalty Fee:** 15%. **Financial Assistance:** In-house assistance with franchise fee. **Training:** 2 days training at headquarters.

LIBRARIES

20393 ■ New Brunswick Translation Bureau Library
Marysville Pl., 1st Fl.
20 McGloin St.
Fredericton, NB, Canada E3A 5T8
Ph:(506)453-2920
Fax:(506)459-7911
Co. E-mail: chrystiane.mallaley@gnb.ca
URL: http://www.gnb.ca/0099/Translation/index-e.asp
Contact: Chrystiane Mallaley
Scope: Communications, terminology, lexicography, interpretation, language arts. **Services:** Interlibrary loan; copying. **Holdings:** 6500 books. **Subscriptions:** 250 journals and other serials; 6 newspapers.

20394 ■ University of Texas at Dallas–Center for Translation Studies–Translation Library (PO Box)
PO Box 830688
MS: JO51
Richardson, TX 75083-0688
Ph:(972)883-2092
Fax:(972)883-6303
Co. E-mail: schulte@utdallas.edu
URL: http://translation.utdallas.edu
Contact: Rainer Schulte, Dir.

Scope: Literary translations. **Services:** Library open to the public. **Holdings:** Literary works in translation; original source language texts.

RESEARCH CENTERS

20395 ■ University of Texas at Dallas–Center for Translation Studies
PO Box 830688-J051
PO Box 830688
Richardson, TX 75083-0688
Ph:(972)883-2092
Fax:(972)883-6303
Co. E-mail: schulte@utdallas.edu
URL: http://www.utdallas.edu/research/cts
Contact: Prof. Rainer Schulte, Dir.
E-mail: schulte@utdallas.edu

Scope: Literary translations, translation methodologies in the humanities, and cross-cultural communications. **Publications:** Translation Review (3/year). **Educational Activities:** Translation workshops.

START-UP INFORMATION

20396 ■ *The 100 Best Businesses to Start When You Don't Want To Work Hard Anymore*
Pub: Career Press Inc.
Ed: Lisa Rogak. **Price:** $16.99. **Description:** Author helps burned-out workers envision a new future as a small business owner. Systems analysis, adventure travel outfitting, bookkeeping, food delivery, furniture making, and software development are among the industries examined.

20397 ■ "Business Start-Up a Learning Experience for Young Bellingham Entrepreneur" in *Bellingham Herald* (July 18, 2010)
Pub: Bellingham Herald
Ed: Dave Gallagher. **Description:** Profile of 21-year-old entrepreneur, Chase Larabee, who developed an online program that helps airport fixed-based operators handle refueling, hotel and transportation reservations and other requests from private airplane pilots.

20398 ■ *Design and Launch an Online Travel Business in a Week*
Pub: Entrepreneur Press
Ed: Charlene Davis. **Released:** May 1, 2009. **Price:** $17.95. **Description:** Guide providing techniques and professional advice for starting an online travel business. Tips are given to build a Website, find qualified providers and to set up a payment system.

20399 ■ *Home-Based Travel Agent, 5th Edition*
Pub: The Intrepid Traveler
Ed: Kelly Monaghan. **Released:** March 2006. **Price:** $59.95. **Description:** Advice for starting and running a home-based travel agency is given.

20400 ■ "Online Fortunes" in *Small Business Opportunities* (Fall 2008)
Pub: Entrepreneur Media Inc.
Description: Fifty hot, e-commerce enterprises for the aspiring entrepreneur to consider are featured; virtual assistants, marketing services, party planning, travel services, researching, web design and development, importing as well as creating an online store are among the businesses featured.

ASSOCIATIONS AND OTHER ORGANIZATIONS

20401 ■ Adventure Travel Trade Association
601 Union St., 42nd Fl.
Seattle, WA 98101
Ph:(360)805-3131
Fax:(360)805-0649
Co. E-mail: info@adventuretravel.biz
URL: http://www.adventuretravel.biz
Contact: Mr. Shannon Stowell, Pres.
Description: Serves the adventure travel industry. Aims to grow the adventure travel industry overall and to help build up its member organizations. Provides exposure, marketing expertise, education, research, and discount to its members. .

20402 ■ American Society of Travel Agents
1101 King St., Ste. 200
Alexandria, VA 22314
Co. E-mail: askasta@asta.org
URL: http://www.astanet.com
Contact: William A. Maloney CTC, Exec. VP/COO
Description: Travel agents; allied members are representatives of carriers, hotels, resorts, sightseeing and car rental companies, official tourist organizations, and other travel interests. Aims to: promote and encourage travel among people of all nations and the use of professional travel agents worldwide; serve as an information resource for the travel industry worldwide; promote and represent the views and interests of travel agents to all levels of government and industry; promote professional and ethical conduct in the travel agency industry worldwide; facilitate consumer protection and safety for the traveling public. Maintains biographical archives and travel hall of fame. Conducts research and education programs. **Publications:** *ASTA Officials Directory* (annual); *Dateline ASTA* (weekly).

20403 ■ Association of Canadian Travel Agencies–Association Canadienne des Agences de Voyages
2560 Matheson Blvd. E, Ste. 328
Mississauga, ON, Canada L4W 4Y9
Ph:(905)282-9294
Free: 888-257-2282
Fax:(905)282-9826
Co. E-mail: actacan@acta.ca
URL: http://www.acta.ca
Contact: David McCaig, Pres./COO
Description: Travel agents, tour operators, airlines, hotels, destination marketing organizations, cruise and rail lines, and automobile rental companies in Canada. Ensures consumers have professional and meaningful travel counseling by providing effective leadership in advocacy, public relations, research and education on behalf of the retail travel industry in Canada. **Publications:** *ACTA Voyage* (quarterly).

20404 ■ Association of Destination Management Executives
PO Box 2307
Dayton, OH 45401-2307
Ph:(937)586-3727
Fax:(937)586-3699
Co. E-mail: info@adme.org
URL: http://www.adme.org
Contact: Fran Rickenbach CAE, Exec. VP
Description: Works to increase the professionalism of owners, CEOs and employees of destination management companies. Conducts educational conferences and meetings. **Publications:** *ADME Xpressions* (quarterly).

20405 ■ Association of Retail Travel Agents
4320 N Miller Rd.
Scottsdale, AZ 85251
Free: (866)369-8969
Co. E-mail: pat@artonline.com
URL: http://www.artaonline.com
Contact: Pat Funk, Exec. Dir.
Description: Represents retail travel agents and agencies in North America. Promotes the interests of retail travel agents through representation on industry councils, testimony before Congress and participation government proceedings. Conducts joint marketing and educational programs; sponsors work-study program. .

20406 ■ Association of Travel Marketing Executives
PO Box 3176
West Tisbury, MA 02575
Ph:(508)693-0550
Fax:(508)693-0115
Co. E-mail: admin@atme.org
URL: http://www.atme.org
Contact: Kristin Zern, Exec. Dir.
Description: Travel marketing executives working in an executive or managerial capacity related to marketing a travel product or service including airlines, cruise lines, hotels, and convention and visitors' bureaus. Prepares special reports; conducts Certified Travel Marketing Executive educational program; honors travel marketing executives. **Publications:** *ATMES Travel Marketing Newsletter - Market Flash*; *Directory of ATME Members* (annual); *Travel Marketing Decisions* (quarterly).

20407 ■ Canadian Institute of Travel Counsellors–Institut Canadiens des Conseillers en Voyages
505 Consumers Rd., Ste. 406
Toronto, ON, Canada M2J 4V8
Ph:(416)484-4450
Free: 800-589-5776
Fax:(416)484-4140
Co. E-mail: info@citc.ca
URL: http://www.citc.ca
Contact: Steve Gillick CTM, Pres./COO
Description: Represents individual travel professionals in Canada; promotes professional development through seminars, home study courses, conferences and workshops; offers professional certification programs leading to the Certified Travel Counsellor (CTC) and Certified Travel Manager (CTM) designations, and consumer awareness. **Publications:** *The Buzz* (monthly).

20408 ■ Canadian Tourism Research Institute
255 Smyth Rd.
Ottawa, ON, Canada K1H 8M7
Ph:(613)526-3280
Free: (866)711-2262
Fax:(613)526-4857
Co. E-mail: ctri@conferenceboard.ca
URL: http://www.conferenceboard.ca/topics/economics/CTRI/default.aspx
Contact: Anne Golden, Pres./CEO
Description: Represents travel and tourism businesses. Seeks to increase understanding of the needs and interests of tourists. Serves as a clearinghouse on tourism in Canada. Sponsors commercial tourism research.

20409 ■ European Travel Commission
50 W 23rd St., 11th Fl.
New York, NY 10010
Co. E-mail: etc@spring-obrien.com
URL: http://www.VisitEurope.com/us
Contact: Robert K. Franklin, Exec. Dir.
Purpose: Represents government tourism organizations cooperating to promote travel to Europe and

further international goodwill and economic prosperity. **Publications:** *VisitEurope* (monthly).

20410 ■ International Association of Tour Managers - North American Region
24 Blevins Rd.
Kerhonkson, NY 12446-1302
Ph:(212)208-6800
Fax:(212)208-6800
Co. E-mail: chairman@tourmanager.org
URL: http://www.tourmanager.org
Contact: Mr. Scott Mcgraw CTM, Chm.
Description: Works to maintain the highest possible standards of tour management; guarantee excellence of performance; educate the travel world on the role of the tour manager (also referred to as tour director, tour escort, or tour leader) in the successful completion of the tour itinerary and in bringing business to related industries. Represents members in influencing legislation and advising on travel policy. Trains tour managers to plan, research, and lead tours to specific domestic and foreign destinations; operates Advisory Board in Professional Tour Management; offers placement service; conducts Professional travel agents, travel wholesalers, airlines, hotel associations, shipping lines, tourist organizations, restaurants, shops, and entertainment organizations Tour Management International Certificate Program. **Publications:** *The Professional Tour Manager* (quarterly).

20411 ■ International Galapagos Tour Operators Association
PO Box 1713
Lolo, MT 59847
Co. E-mail: exd@igtoa.org
URL: http://www.igtoa.org
Contact: Matt Kareus, Exec. Dir.
Description: Individuals and corporations conducting tours to the Galapagos Islands; educational and scientific institutions with an interest in the Islands and their ecosystems. Promotes tourism with the lowest possible environmental impact; seeks to preserve the unique ecosystems and species indigenous to the Galapagos Islands. Raises funds to support environmental protection initiatives; serves as a clearinghouse on low-impact nature tourism; facilitates communication and cooperation among members. .

20412 ■ International Gay and Lesbian Travel Association
1201 NE 26th St., Ste. 103
Fort Lauderdale, FL 33305
Ph:(954)630-1637
Fax:(954)630-1652
Co. E-mail: iglta@iglta.org
URL: http://www.iglta.org
Contact: John Tanzella, Pres.
Description: Travel agents, tour operators, hoteliers, guesthouse and resort owners, travel clubs, and allied businesses interested in promoting travel services to the gay community. Works to: enhance member businesses; inform travel agents and consumers about properties, businesses, and destinations welcoming gay clientele; provide a networking opportunity for members. Offers familiarization trips to promote member businesses in locations of special appeal to gay travelers. Operates public awareness campaign. **Publications:** *IGLTA Connections* (annual).

20413 ■ National Association of Cruise-Oriented Agencies
7378 Atlantic Blvd., No. 115
Margate, FL 33063
Ph:(305)663-5626
Free: (866)816-7143
Co. E-mail: nacoafl@aol.com
URL: http://www.nacoaonline.com
Contact: Donna Kaye Esposito MCC, Pres.
Description: Professional association of travel agencies dedicated to the cruise vacation product. Provides educational and training programs, including Seminars-At-Sea, and Ship Inspection weekends. Offers Safe Sail insurances and Errors and Omissions insurance. **Publications:** *Now Sea This* .

20414 ■ National Tour Association
101 Prosperous Pl., Ste. 350
Lexington, KY 40509
Ph:(859)226-4444
Free: 800-682-8886
Fax:(859)226-4414
Co. E-mail: questions@ntastaff.com
URL: http://www.ntaonline.com
Contact: Cathy Greteman, Chair/CEO
Description: Operators of group tours and packaged travel; travel industry-related companies providing services/facilities to tour operators (hotels, attractions, restaurants); and destination marketing organizations such as convention and visitor bureaus, and state tourism departments. Seeks to: maintain a code of ethical standards within the tour industry; develop and increase public interest in packaged travel. Represents members before governmental bodies and agencies. Conducts research and educational programs. **Publications:** *Tuesday* (monthly);Directory (annual).

20415 ■ Opening Door
8049 Ormesby Ln.
Woodford, VA 22580-3211
Co. E-mail: contactus@accessiblevirginia.org
URL: http://www.travelguides.org
Description: Acts as clearinghouse and consultant to the travel and lodging industry for disabled travelers. Sponsors seminars on disability etiquette and the effect of the Americans with Disabilities Act on public accommodations. Maintains speakers' bureau. Conducts activities internationally. Publishes travel and access guides. **Publications:** *Virginia Travel Guide for Persons with Disabilities* (biennial).

20416 ■ Pacific Asia Travel Association
164 Loop Pl.
Trinidad, CA 95570
Ph:(707)232-2102
Fax:(707)540-6259
Co. E-mail: americas@pata.org
URL: http://www.pata.org
Contact: Bill Calderwood, CEO
Description: Represents Government tourist bureaus; cruise companies, airlines, railroads, commercial travel bureaus, hotels, tour operators and hotel associations throughout the world. Conducts marketing program to promote travel to the countries and islands of the Greater Pacific region; works to facilitate and unify entry and exit procedures in members' countries; provides travel information service to the industry disseminates travel news to the press and other media; coordinates market research to determine potential markets and the future impact of overseas travelers. Develops destination development task forces. Compiles statistics. **Publications:** *Pacific Asia Travel Association—Annual Report* (annual); *PATA Quarterly Statistical Report* (quarterly); *PATA Worldwide Chapter Directory* (annual).

20417 ■ Tourism Industry Association of Canada–Association de L'Industrie Touristique du Canada
116 Lisgar St., Ste. 600
Ottawa, ON, Canada K2P 0C2
Ph:(613)238-3883
Co. E-mail: info@tiac.travel
URL: http://www.tiac.travel
Contact: David F. Goldstein, Pres./CEO
Description: Promotes viability of Canada's tourism industries. Serves as a unified voice for the industry in communications with government agencies responsible for tourism and related matters; conducts lobbying activities. **Publications:** *RVC Directory* (annual); *TIAC Talk* (weekly); *TIAC Talk Issue Focus* (periodic).

20418 ■ The Travel Institute
148 Linden St., Ste. 305
Wellesley, MA 02482
Ph:(781)237-0280
Free: 800-542-4282
Fax:(781)237-3860
Co. E-mail: info@thetravelinstitute.com
URL: http://www.thetravelinstitute.com
Contact: Jack E. Mannix, Chm.
Description: Individuals who have been accredited as Certified Travel Counselors (CTC) or Certified Travel Associates (CTA) must meet the institute's testing and experience requirements. Seeks to increase the level of competence in the travel industry. Provides continuing education and examination and certification programs; conducts workshops and professional management seminars. Operates Travel Career Development Program to increase professional skills and Destination Specialist Programs to enhance the geographical knowledge of sales agents. Organizes study groups of instruction with enrolled student bodies in most major cities. **Publications:** *Travel Counselor* (bimonthly).

20419 ■ United States Tour Operators Association
275 Madison Ave., Ste. 2014
New York, NY 10016-1101
Ph:(212)599-6599
Fax:(212)599-6744
Co. E-mail: information@ustoa.com
URL: http://www.ustoa.com
Contact: Linda Kundell
Description: Represents wholesale tour operators, common carriers, associations, government agencies, suppliers, purveyors of travel services, trade press, communications media, and public relations and advertising representatives. Encourages and supports professional and financial integrity in tourism. Protects the legitimate interests of the consumer and the retail agent from financial loss from business conducted with members. Provides tour operators with an opportunity to formulate and express an independent industry voice on matters of common interest and self-regulation. Strives to facilitate and develop travel on a worldwide basis. .

20420 ■ U.S. Travel Association
1100 New York Ave. NW, Ste. 450
Washington, DC 20005-3934
Ph:(202)408-8422
Fax:(202)408-1255
Co. E-mail: feedback@ustravel.org
URL: http://www.tia.org
Contact: Roger J. Dow, Pres./CEO
Description: Corporations engaged in the hospitality and travel industries. Promotes increased profitability within the travel industries. Serves as a clearinghouse on the hospitality, travel, and related industries; represents members' interests on the national level; conducts industry research and surveys. Facilitates communication and cooperation among members. .

20421 ■ U.S. Travel Data Center
1100 New York Ave. NW, Ste. 450
Washington, DC 20005-3934
Ph:(202)408-8422
Fax:(202)408-1255
Co. E-mail: feedback@ustravel.org
URL: http://www.tia.org
Description: Conducts statistical, economic, and market research concerning travel; encourages standardized travel research terminology and techniques. Monitors trends in travel activity and the travel industry. Measures the economic impact of travel on geographic areas and the cost of travel in the U.S. Evaluates the effect of government programs on travel and the travel industry. Forecasts travel activity and expenditures. **Publications:** *Impact of Travel on State Economies* (annual); *National Travel Survey* (quarterly); *Survey of State Travel Offices* (annual).

DIRECTORIES OF EDUCATIONAL PROGRAMS

20422 ■ *Directory of Private Accredited Career Schools and Colleges of Technology*
Pub: Accrediting Commission of Career Schools and Colleges of Technology
Contact: Michale S. McComis, Exec. Dir.
Released: On web page. **Price:** Free. **Description:** Covers 3900 accredited post-secondary programs that provide training programs in business, trade, and technical fields, including various small business endeavors. Entries offer school name, address, phone, description of courses, job placement assistance, and requirements for admission. Arrangement is alphabetical.

REFERENCE WORKS

20423 ■ "2010 Book of Lists" in *Austin Business JournalInc.* (Vol. 29, December 25, 2009, No. 42, pp. 1)
Pub: American City Business Journals
Description: Rankings of companies and organizations within the business services, finance, healthcare, hospitality and travel, insurance, marketing and media, professional services, real estate, education and technology industries in Austin, Texas are presented. Rankings are based on sales, business size, and other statistics.

20424 ■ "2010 Book of Lists" in *Business Courier* (Vol. 26, December 26, 2009, No. 36, pp. 1)
Pub: American City Business Journals, Inc.
Description: Rankings of companies and organizations within the business services, education, finance, health care, hospitality and tourism, real estate, and technology industries in the Cincinnati, Ohio-Northern Kentucky area are presented. Rankings are based on sales, business size, or other statistics.

20425 ■ "2010 Book of Lists" in *Tampa Bay Business Journal* (Vol. 30, December 22, 2009, No. 53, pp. 1)
Pub: American City Business Journals
Description: Rankings of companies and organizations within the human resources, banking and finance, business services, healthcare, real estate, technology, hospitality and travel, and education industries in the Greater Tampa Bay area are presented. Rankings are based on sales, business size, and more.

20426 ■ "B&B Hopes to Appeal to Fiat Execs" in *Crain's Detroit Business* (Vol. 25, June 15, 2009, No. 24, pp. 21)
Pub: Crain Communications Inc. - Detroit
Ed: Daniel Duggan. **Description:** Cobblestone Manor, a ten-room bed and breakfast in Auburn Hills, Michigan is hoping to provide rooms for Fiat executives. The owners have been working with travel organizations to promote the castle-like bed and breakfast which appeals to European visitors.

20427 ■ "Bill Kaneko" in *Hawaii Business* (Vol. 53, December 2007, No. 6, pp. 32)
Pub: Hawaii Business Publishing
Ed: David K. Choo. **Description:** Hawaii Institute for Public Affairs chief executive officer and president Bill Kaneko believes that the Hawaiian economy is booming, however, he also asserts that the economy is too focused on tourism and real estate. Kaneko has also realized the that the will of the people is strong while he was helping with the Hawaiian 2050 Sustainability Plan. The difficulties of making a sustainable Hawaii are discussed.

20428 ■ *Bottin Touristique du Quebec*
Pub: Quebec Dans Le Monde
Released: Annual, Latest edition 15th; 2009-2010. **Price:** $51.95, individuals. **Covers:** Approximately 800 business, cultural and recreational travel agencies and agents in Quebec. **Entries Include:** Company name, address, phone, fax, agent name, address, phone, fax, activities. **Arrangement:** Alphabetical. **Indexes:** Subject, geographical.

20429 ■ "The British Aren't Coming" in *Crain's Chicago Business* (Vol. 34, October 24, 2011, No. 42, pp. 3)
Pub: Crain Communications Inc.
Ed: Brigid Sweeney. **Description:** In a move to attract tourists back to Chicago, its Convention and Tourism Bureau is marketing in London, England, Mexico, and Canada, but not Germany or France because of budget constraints.

20430 ■ "Cruising In Choppy Water" in *The Business Journal-Portland* (Vol. 25, August 22, 2008, No. 24, pp. 1)
Pub: American City Business Journals, Inc.
Ed: Erik Siemers. **Description:** Yacht builder Christensen Shipyards Inc. is experiencing robust business despite the slowing US economy, building four yachts a year as of 2008. The company expects revenues to hit $90 million and is opening a 500,000-square-foot plant in Tennessee.

20431 ■ "DePaul To Train Hotel Leaders" in *Chicago Tribune* (September 22, 2008)
Pub: McClatchy-Tribune Information Services
Ed: Kathy Bergen. **Description:** With help from a $7.5 million grant from the Conrad N. Hilton Foundation, DePaul University will dramatically expand its role as a training ground for the tourism-industry with the opening of a School of Hospitality.

20432 ■ "Destination Africa: A Look at How Tourism Could Change the Face and Economics of Africa" in *Black Enterprise* (February 2008)
Pub: Earl G. Graves Publishing Co. Inc.
Ed: Sonia Alleyne. **Description:** Countries in Africa are experiencing high rates of growth in tourism than the worldwide average. Statistical data included.

20433 ■ *Double or Nothing: How Two Friends Risked It All to Buy One of Las Vegas' Legendary Casinos*
Pub: HarperBusiness
Ed: Tom Breitling, with Cal Fussman. **Released:** March 2008. **Price:** $24.95. **Description:** Founders of a successful Internet travel agency share their experience from startup to selling the company.

20434 ■ "Doubletree Finds a Niche for Giving Back" in *Hotel and Motel Management* (Vol. 225, July 2010, No. 8, pp. 6)
Pub: Questex Media Group Inc.
Ed: Paul J. Heney. **Description:** Profile of Doubletree Hotel's community outreach programs that help employee volunteers work to educate children and the public about issues important to the environment.

20435 ■ *Driving With No Brakes: How a Bunch of Hooligans Built the Best Travel Company in the World*
Pub: Grand Circle Corporation
Ed: Alan and Harriet Lewis. **Price:** $19.95. **Description:** Inspirational book about how two courageous leaders built a remarkable company that can thrive in change and succeed in an unpredictable world. Important lessons for any business leader trying to create value in the 21st Century are included.

20436 ■ "Eco-Preneuring" in *Small Business Opportunities* (Jan. 2008)
Pub: Harris Publications Inc.
Description: Iceland Naturally is a joint marketing effort among tourism and business interests hoping to increase demand for Icelandic products including frozen seafood, bottled water, agriculture, and tourism in North America.

20437 ■ "F1 Makes Room(s) for Aspiring Entrepreneur" in *Austin Business Journal* (Vol. 31, July 1, 2011, No. 17, pp. 1)
Pub: American City Business Journals Inc.
Ed: Vicky Garza. **Description:** Formula One fan and graphic designer Danielle Crespo cashes in on the June 17, 2012 racing event in Austin, Texas via hosting a Website that allows users to book hotel rooms. She invested less than $100 and long hours on this enterprise which now has 74,000-plus visitors.

20438 ■ "Get Wrecked" in *Canadian Business* (Vol. 80, November 19, 2007, No. 23, pp. S13)
Pub: Rogers Media
Ed: Thomas Watson. **Description:** Key West economy has benefited from wrecks as salvaging lost items became a lucrative business. The USAFS General Hoyt S. Vanderberg is expected to be sunk and will provide a good opportunity for wreck dives. The trends in Key West tourism are evaluated.

20439 ■ "Goldbelt Inc.: Targeting Shareholder Development" in *Alaska Business Monthly* (Vol. 27, October 2011, No. 10, pp. 108)
Pub: Alaska Business Publishing Company
Ed: Tracy Kalytiak. **Description:** Profile of Goldbelt Inc., the company that has changed its original focus of timber to real estate to tourism and then to government contracting opportunities.

20440 ■ "Gov. Kasich to Put DOD On Short Leash" in *Business Courier* (Vol. 27, November 26, 2010, No. 30, pp. 1)
Pub: Business Courier
Ed: Dan Monk. **Description:** Ohio Governor-elect John Kasich proposed the privatization of the Ohio Department of Development in favor of a nonprofit corporation called JobsOhio. Kasich believes that the department has lost its focus by adding to its mission issues such as energy efficiency and tourism.

20441 ■ "Happy Trails: RV Franchiser Gives Road Traveling Enthusiasts a Lift" in *Black Enterprise* (Vol. 38, July 2008, No. 12, pp. 47)
Pub: Earl G. Graves Publishing Co. Inc.
Ed: Tamara E. Holmes. **Description:** Overview of Bates International Motor Home Rental Systems Inc., a growing franchise that gives RV owners the chance to rent out their big-ticket purchases to others when they are not using them; Sandra Williams Bate launched the company as a franchise in July 1997 and now has a fleet of 30 franchises across the country. She expects the company to reach 2.2 million for 2008 due to a marketing initiative that will expand the company's presence.

20442 ■ *Heads in Beds*
Pub: Prentice Hall PTR
Ed: Ivo Raza. **Released:** May 28, 2004. **Description:** Advice is given to help build brands, generate sales and grow profits through marketing for any hospitality or tourism business.

20443 ■ "Hola and Aloha" in *Hawaii Business* (Vol. 53, December 2007, No. 6, pp. 131)
Pub: Hawaii Business Publishing
Ed: Jason Ubay. **Description:** Juan Carlos Bianchetti is the trilingual owner of Ole Tours Hawaii, a travel wholesaler that targets Portuguese and Spanish-speaking visitors. The competition for American and Japanese tourists is already tight, which is why Bianchetti opted to target a different segment of the Hawaii tourism market. Plans for the company's expansion in Kauai, Brazil, and Argentina, are mentioned.

20444 ■ "An Ill Wind: Icelandic Bank Failures Chill Atlantic Canada" in *Canadian Business* (Vol. 81, November 10, 2008, No. 19, pp. 10)
Pub: Rogers Media Ltd.
Ed: Charles Mandel. **Description:** Bank failures in Iceland have put a stop to flights ferrying Icelanders to Newfoundland to purchase Christmas gifts, thereby threatening Newfoundland's tourism industry. The credit of Newfoundland's fisheries is also being squeezed since most of Atlantic Canadian seafood processors hold lines of credit from Icelandic banks.

20445 ■ "Ill Winds; Cuba's Economy" in *The Economist* (Vol. 390, January 3, 2009, No. 8612, pp. 20)
Pub: The Economist Newspaper Inc.
Description: Cuba's long-term economic prospects remain poor with the economy forecasted to grow only 4.3 percent for the year, about half of the original forecast, due in part to Hurricane Gustav which caused $10 billion in damage and disrupted the food-supply network and devastated farms across the region; President Raul Castro made raising agricultural production a national priority and the rise in global commodity prices hit the country hard. The only bright spot has been the rise in tourism which is up 9.3 percent over 2007.

20446 ■ "Indigenous Tourism Operators" in *International Journal of Entrepreneurship and Small Business* (Vol. 10, July 6, 2010, No. 4)
Pub: Publishers Communication Group
Ed: Andrews Cardow, Peter Wiltshier. **Description:** Emergent enthusiasm for tourism as a savior for economic development in the Chatham Islands of New Zealand is highlighted.

20447 ■ *The Itty Bitty Guide to Business Travel*
Pub: Chronicle Books LLC
Ed: Stacie Krajchir, Carrie Rosten. **Released:** April 2004. **Description:** Advice on all aspects of business travel, including low-price airfare, packing and coping with stress.

20448 ■ "Luxe Hotels on a Budget" in *Inc.* (Volume 32, December 2010, No. 10, pp. 60)
Pub: Inc. Magazine
Ed: Adam Baer. **Description:** Off & Away Website allows users to vie for discounted hotel rooms at more than 100 luxury properties. To compete, uses buy $1 bids and each time an individual bids the price of the room goes up by 10 cents.

20449 ■ "Making Visitors Out Of Listeners" in *Hawaii Business* (Vol. 54, July 2008, No. 1, pp. 18)
Pub: Hawaii Business Publishing
Ed: Casey Chin. **Description:** Japanese workers are subscribing to the Official Hawaii Podcast in iTunes, which offers a free 20-minute, Japanese-language audio content on different topics, such as dining reviews and music from local artists. The concept is a way to attract Japanese travelers to come to Hawaii.

20450 ■ "Marathon Money" in *Hawaii Business* (Vol. 53, December 2007, No. 6, pp. 127)
Pub: Hawaii Business Publishing
Ed: Jolyn Okimoto Rosa. **Description:** Discusses the effects of the Honolulu Marathon on small businesses' sales. The Running Room, for instance, experience growth in sales starting from the training season up to the end of the race, as a surge of Hawaiian residents and tourists come into the store for items such as running shoes and blister kits. The marathon's impact on Hawaii's tourism is examined as well.

20451 ■ "The Next Waive" in *Hawaii Business* (Vol. 53, January 2008, No. 7, pp. 27)
Pub: Hawaii Business Publishing
Ed: Cathy S. Cruz-George. **Description:** Only 40,000 Koreans took a visit to Hawaii in 2007, a decline from the pre-September averages of 123,000 visits. The number of Korean visitors in Hawaii could increase if the visa waiver proposal is passed. Efforts to improve Hawaiian tourism are presented.

20452 ■ "Not Enough Room" in *Austin Business JournalInc.* (Vol. 29, November 13, 2009, No. 36, pp. A1)
Pub: American City Business Journals
Ed: Jacob Dirr. **Description:** Hotel and convention business in downtown Austin, Texas lost nearly $5.3 million when Dell Inc. relocated its annual convention to Las Vegas. However, lack of capital caused the postponement of various hotel projects which need to be finished in order to attract well-attended conventions. Makeover projects on Austin's Waller Creek and Sixth Street are discussed.

20453 ■ *OAG Business Travel Planner*
Pub: Reed Travel Group
Contact: Les Higgins, CEO
Released: Quarterly. **Covers:** 14,500 destination cities, military installations (U.S. only), and colleges and universities in North America; over 78,000 hotels and motels; calendar of events; city, state or province, and national tourist offices; tour operators; car rental agencies; airlines and charter air taxi firms, and airport limousine services; consulates and missions of foreign countries in North America; United States foreign service offices; hotel and motel systems, and toll free reservations services; airport club locations, frequent flyer and frequent guest information. **Entries Include:** For destinations—Place name, airport name and code or note on nearest air service; entries for larger cities include convention facilities, hotel name, address, phone, rates, location, number of meeting rooms, fax; whether member of the American Hotel and Motel Association. For calendar of events—Date, name and location of event, and names, addresses, and phone numbers of state and local tourism agencies. Separate toll-free section for hotel/motel systems and travel-related firms. Other listings include company or office name, address, phone. **Arrangement:** Primarily geographical.

20454 ■ *OAG Travel Planner European Edition*
Pub: OAG Worldwide
Contact: Oak Brook
Released: Quarterly. **Price:** $632, individuals Online; $705, individuals CD. **Covers:** Over 14,000 destination cities in Europe; 16,923 hotels; hotel chains and reservations services; calendars of events; city, regional, and national tourist offices; airline reservation numbers; car rental agencies; ground transportation information; U.S. military installations; consulates and missions of foreign countries in the United States and Canada; airport, ground, and rail services. **Entries Include:** Section for a country begins with climate, currency, documentary requirements, consulate, and other information; holiday and public event calendar for following six months; list of the country's tourist offices at home and abroad. For individual destinations—Place name, name and mileage from nearest airport, dialing code for each city; hotel name, address, phone, fax, telex, postal number, room rates, number of rooms, and quality rating, where applicable. **Arrangement:** Geographical.

20455 ■ *Official Hotel Guide*
Pub: Northstar Travel Media L.L.C.
Released: Annual. **Covers:** in four volumes, 29,000 hotels, motels, and resorts worldwide. Volume 1 covers most of the U.S. ; Volume 2 covers the rest of the U.S. and the Western Hemisphere; Volume 3 covers Europe, the Middle East, Asia, and Africa. Volume 4 specialty travel guide includes listings of golf resorts and tennis resorts; health spas, dude ranches, bed and breakfasts, and casino & hotels in the United States; also includes lists of hotels in the Caribbean with golf, tennis, casinos, and all-inclusive. **Entries Include:** Hotel/motel/resort name, address, phone, fax, CRS's, number of rooms or units, rates, brief description of facilities, ratings, codes indicating credit cards accepted, email and website addresses, and travel agent's commission, if any. **Arrangement:** Geographical.

20456 ■ "Orbitz Adds Parent Panel" in *Marketing to Women* (Vol. 21, March 2008, No. 3, pp. 5)
Pub: EPM Communications, Inc.
Description: Orbitz introduces the Orbitz Parent Panel in an attempt to better connect with traveling families.

20457 ■ "The Personal Touch: Entrepreneur Turns Good Taste, Love of Luxury Into Lucrative Venture" in *Black Enterprise* (October 2007)
Pub: Earl G. Graves Publishing Co. Inc.
Ed: Tamara E. Holmes. **Description:** Profile of Chaka Fattah Jr. who turned his taste for luxurious things into a successful luxury travel and concierge service catering to business owners, corporate executives, athletes, and entertainers.

20458 ■ "Plans for $160M Condo Resort in Wisconsin Dells Moves Forward" in *Commercial Property News* (March 18, 2008)
Pub: Nielsen Company
Description: Plans for the Grand Cambrian Resort in the Wisconsin Dells is discussed. The luxury condominium resort will include condos, townhomes, and condo-hotel style residences, two water parts, meeting space and indoor entertainment space, as well as a spa, four restaurants and retail offerings.

20459 ■ "Recovery on Tap for 2010?" in *Orlando Business Journal* (Vol. 26, January 1, 2010, No. 31, pp. 1)
Pub: American City Business Journals
Ed: Melanie Stawicki Azam, Richard Bilbao, Christopher Boyd, Anjali Fluker. **Description:** Economic forecasts for Central Florida's leading business sectors in 2010 are presented. These sectors include housing, film and TV, sports business, law, restaurants, aviation, tourism and hospitality, banking and finance, commercial real estate, retail, health care, insurance, higher education, and manufacturing. According to some local executives, Central Florida's economy will slowly recover in 2010.

20460 ■ "Saudi Overtures" in *The Business Journal-Portland* (Vol. 25, August 15, 2008, No. 23, pp. 1)
Pub: American City Business Journals, Inc.
Ed: Aliza Earnshaw. **Description:** Saudi Arabia's huge revenue from oil is creating opportunities for Oregon companies as the country develops new cities, industrial zones, and tourism centers. Oregon exported only $46.8 million worth of goods to Saudi Arabia in 2007 but the kingdom is interested in green building materials and methods, renewable energy and water quality control, and nanotechnology all of which Oregon has expertise in.

20461 ■ "Save Money on Travel With These Websites for Frequent Fliers" in *Inc.* (Vol. 31, January-February 2009, No. 1, pp. 44)
Pub: Mansueto Ventures LLC
Description: Four Websites offering services to the business traveler are profiled: MissRefund.com will get the taxes and fuel surcharges back to any traveler canceling a flight; Vayama.com is a booking site focused on routes and destinations not generally available online; Airfarewatchdog.com searches for listing sites for best travel deals; and Yapta alerts users to good prices for particular flights.

20462 ■ *Selling the Invisible: A Field Guide to Modern Marketing*
Pub: Business Plus
Ed: Harry Beckwith. **Price:** $22.95. **Description:** Tips for marketing and selling intangibles such as health care, entertainment, tourism, legal services, and more are provided.

20463 ■ "Senate OKs Funds for Promoting Tourism" in *Crain's Detroit Business* (Vol. 24, March 31, 2008, No. 13, pp. 6)
Pub: Crain Communications, Inc.
Ed: Amy Lane. **Description:** Discusses the Senate proposal which allocates funds for Michigan tourism and business promotion as well as Michigan's No Worker Left Behind initiative, a program that provides free tuition at community colleges and other venues to train displaced workers for high-demand occupations.

20464 ■ "Small Dutch Islands Saba, Statia Content With Low-Key Niche" in *Travel Weekly* (Vol. 69, August 16, 2010, No. 33, pp. 22)
Pub: NorthStar Travel Media LLC
Ed: Gay Nagle Myers. **Description:** Small Caribbean islands market and promote their region for tourism by never competing with the bigger destinations. Saba and Statia are the two smallest islands in the Caribbean and rely on repeat guests, word-of-mouth recommendations and travel agents willing to promote them.

20465 ■ "State Tourism Likely to Decline Two Percent this Year" in *Crain's Detroit Business* (Vol. 24, April 14, 2008, No. 15, pp. 6)
Pub: Crain Communications, Inc.
Ed: Amy Lane. **Description:** Due to such national and state economic conditions such as unemployment, the housing crisis and rising gasoline and food prices, Michigan's tourism industry is likely to decline about 2 percent this year.

20466 ■ "The Way I Work" in *Inc.* (March 2008, pp. 102-104, 106)
Pub: Gruner & Jahr USA Publishing
Ed: Hannah Clark Steiman. **Description:** Profile of Howard Lefkowitz, CEO of Vegas.com, a Website that allows visitors to book flights, reserve hotel rooms, buy show tickets, make spa appointments, and coordinate any and all aspects of a trip to Las Vegas. The firm also runs brick-and-mortar box offices and concierge desks at various cities.

20467 ■ "Tourism Bureau Seeks Hotel Tax Hike" in *Baltimore Business Journal* (Vol. 27, December 18, 2009, No. 32, pp. 1)
Pub: American City Business Journals
Ed: Rachel Bernstein. **Description:** Baltimore, Maryland's tourism agency, Visit Baltimore, has proposed a new hotel tax that could produce $2 million annually for its marketing budget, fund improvements to the city's 30-year-old convention center and help it compete for World Cup soccer games. Baltimore hotel leaders discuss the new tax.

20468 ■ *Tourism and Entrepreneurship: International Perspectives*
Pub: Elsevier Science & Technology Books
Ed: Stephen Page, Jovo Ateljevic. **Released:** June 1, 2009. **Price:** $69.95. **Description:** Trends in tour-

ism development are explored, focusing on the impact of entrepreneurship in the context of regional and local tourism development.

20469 ■ "Tourism Push Rising in Fall" in *Philadelphia Business Journal* (Vol. 30, August 26, 2011, No. 28, pp. 1)
Pub: American City Business Journals Inc.
Ed: Peter Van Allen. **Description:** Philadelphia is offering events for tourists this fall despite massive cuts for tourism promotion. Governor Tim Corbet slashed $5.5 million in funding for the state's tourism-promotion agencies which received $32 million in 2009. The agencies were forced to cooperate and fend for themselves using the hotel taxes that sustain them.

20470 ■ *The Travel Agent's Complete Desk Reference, 5th Edition*
Pub: The Intrepid Traveler
Ed: Kelly Monaghan. **Released:** August 25, 2009. **Price:** $39.95. **Description:** Reference book that provides essential information to the home-based travel agent.

20471 ■ *The Travel Book*
Pub: Scarecrow Press Inc.
Contact: Jon O. Heise, Author
Released: Latest edition 2nd. **Covers:** Travel guides from throughout the world. **Arrangement:** Geographical by country. **Indexes:** Alphabetical.

20472 ■ "Travel In Style, Or Not: Finding a Company Travel Service for Every Budget" in *Inc.* (January 2008, pp. 36-37)
Pub: Gruner & Jahr USA Publishing
Ed: Larry Olmsted. **Description:** Profiles of various travel services to help small businesses. Firms profiled include Cassis Travel Services, providing first class bookings; Open from American Express, specializing in business class travel; Travelocity business, providing travel agents with 24/7 services; Diners Club Corporate Card, with many features; and Expedia Corporate Travel, allowing users to compare prices for airline tickets, hotels, and car rentals.

20473 ■ "Travel Tears" in *Crain's Chicago Business* (Vol. 31, November 17, 2008, No. 46, pp. 3)
Pub: Crain Communications, Inc.
Ed: Bob Tita. **Description:** Hotels, restaurants and conventions are seeing a decline in profits due to corporate travel cutbacks and the sagging economy. City and state revenues derived from taxes on tourism-related industries are also suffering.

20474 ■ "Turbulent Times and Golden Opportunity" in *Business Strategy Review* (Vol. 21, Spring 2010, No. 1, pp. 34)
Pub: Wiley-Blackwell
Ed: Don Sull. **Description:** For those feeling storm-tossed by today's economy, the author believes there's much to learn from Carnival Cruise Lines, a company that discovered that turbulence often has an upside.

20475 ■ "TW Trade Shows to Offer Seminars On Niche Selling, Social Media" in *Travel Weekly* (Vol. 69, October 4, 2010, No. 40, pp. 9)
Pub: NorthStar Travel Media LLC
Description: Travel Weekly's Leisure World 2010 and Fall Home Based Travel Agent Show focused on niche selling, with emphasis on all-inclusives, young consumers, groups, incentives, culinary vacations, and honeymoon or romance travel.

20476 ■ "Tweaking On-Board Activities, Equipment Saves Fuel, Reduces CO2" in *Canadian Sailings* (June 30, 2008)
Pub: Commonwealth Business Media
Description: Optimizing ship activities and equipment uses less fuel and therefore reduces greenhouse gas emissions. Ways in which companies are implementing research and development techniques in order to monitor ship performance and analyze data in an attempt to become more efficient are examined.

20477 ■ "Up In the Air" in *The Business Journal-Serving Greater Tampa Bay* (Vol. 28, July 18, 2008, No. 30, pp. 1)
Pub: American City Business Journals, Inc.
Ed: Margie Manning. **Description:** Views and information on Busch Gardens and on its future, are presented. The park's 3,769 employees worry for their future, after tourism industry experts have expressed concerns on possible tax cuts and other cost reductions. The future of the park, which ranks number 19 as the most visited park in the world, is expected to have a major impact on the tourism industry.

20478 ■ "The Visitor Rebound" in *Canadian Business* (Vol. 80, November 5, 2007, No. 22, pp. 23)
Pub: Rogers Media
Ed: Graham Silnicki. **Description:** Overnight visits to Canada are expected to fall by 5.3 percent in 2008, however spending is expected to drop by only 2 percent. Senior economist Alex Fritsche thinks that tourism from the U.S. will improve in 2009; the reasons for the expected growth in 2009 are examined.

20479 ■ "Website for Women 50+ Launches" in *Marketing to Women* (Vol. 21, April 2008, No. 4, pp. 5)
Pub: EPM Communications, Inc.
Description: Vibrantnation.com is an online community targeting women over age 50; members can share recommendations on a variety of topics such as vacation spots, retailers and financial issues.

20480 ■ "What Moms Want" in *Marketing to Women* (Vol. 21, February 2008, No. 2, pp. 6)
Pub: EPM Communications, Inc.
Description: According to a survey conducted by Eureka's Spa, moms would rather have an experience gift than flowers or chocolate. The top five dream gifts include a spa day, a weekend getaway, maid service, a bathroom makeover or a getaway weekend with girlfriends.

20481 ■ "What's the Black Travel Market Worth?" in *Black Enterprise* (Vol. 38, January 2008, No. 6, pp. 54)
Pub: Earl G. Graves Publishing Co. Inc.
Ed: Aisha Sylvester. **Description:** African American travel market, both business and pleasure, is one of the top three fastest growing markets in the industry. Hugh Riley, director of marketing for the Caribbean Tourism Organization shares his ideas on the relationship between African American travelers and the Caribbean tourism industry.

20482 ■ "Where's the Lava" in *Hawaii Business* (Vol. 53, November 2007, No. 5, pp. 18)
Pub: Hawaii Business Publishing
Ed: Jason Ubay. **Description:** Hawaii Volcanoes National Park used to allow visitors to drive to the end of the paved coastal park road and view flowing lava that came from Kilauea until it reached the sea. On Father's Day morning in June 2007, Kilauea began erupting outside the park and the lava flows inland to Kahaualea and Wao Kele O Puna natural area reserves. In July 2007 321,217 visitors came to the park, a 14 percent increase compared to the same month in 2006.

20483 ■ "The World Is Your Hospital" in *Canadian Business* (Vol. 81, July 22, 2008, No. 12-13, pp. 62)
Pub: Rogers Media Ltd.
Ed: Sharda Prashad. **Description:** Medical tourism is seen as a booming industry around the world and is expected to grow to around $40 billion in 2010. Key information regarding medical tourism and services are presented. Views on the possible impact of medical tourism on Canada's health care industry, as well as medical tourism opportunities in Canada, are also given.

STATISTICAL SOURCES

20484 ■ *RMA Annual Statement Studies*
Pub: Robert Morris Associates (RMA)
Released: Annual. **Price:** $175.00 2006-07 edition, $105.00. **Description:** Contains composite balance sheets and income statements for more than 360 industries, including the accounting, auditing, and bookkeeping industries. Also contains five years of comparative historical data for discerning trends. Includes 16 commonly used ratios, computed for most of the size groupings for nearly every industry.

20485 ■ *Travel Agencies and Tour Operators Market*
Pub: Rector Press, Ltd.
Contact: Lewis Sckolnick, Pres
Released: 2009. **Price:** Contact Rector Press.

TRADE PERIODICALS

20486 ■ *Andrew Harper's Hideaway Report*
Pub: Harper Associates Inc.
Contact: Andrew Harper, Editor & Publisher
Released: Monthly. **Price:** $135, U.S.; $165, elsewhere. **Description:** Reviews small and exclusive vacation resorts, executive retreats, and hotels for the sophisticated traveler.

20487 ■ *ARTAFAX*
Pub: Association of Retail Travel Agents
Ed: Nikole Williams, Editor, nikolew@grouptravelleader.com. **Released:** Daily. **Price:** Included in membership. **Description:** Reviews developments in the travel industry for retail travel agents. Covers topics such as ethics, tour operations, transportation services, educational opportunities, commissions, and political action in pertinent issues. Includes chapter and Association news.

20488 ■ *Austrian Information*
Pub: Austrian Press and Information Service
Contact: Ulf Pacher, Managing Editor
Released: Bimonthly. **Price:** Free. **Description:** Publishes about all aspects of Austria, including its history, government, society, arts, and culture.

20489 ■ *Corporate & Incentive Travel*
Pub: Coastal Communications Corp.
Contact: Harvey Grotsky, Publisher/Ed.-in-Ch.
E-mail: cccpublisher@att.net
Released: Monthly. **Description:** Magazine for corporate executives with the responsibility for site selection, staging and planning meetings, incentive travel programs, conferences, and conventions.

20490 ■ *Corporate Meetings & Incentives*
Pub: Primedia Business Magazines & Media
Contact: Melissa Fromento, Gp. Publisher
E-mail: mfromento@meetingsnet.com
Ed: Barbara Scofidio, Editor, bscofidio@meetingsnet.com. **Released:** Monthly. **Price:** $97 Canada; $123 Free to qualified subscribers in USA; $123 other countries. **Description:** Magazine for executives and travel professionals responsible for choosing sites and destinations for meeting and incentive travel programs.

20491 ■ *Cruise Connoisseur*
Pub: Traveling Times Inc.
Ed: Mirko A. Ilich, Editor. **Released:** 6/year. **Description:** Presents information on cruise destinations.

20492 ■ *Cruise and Vacation Views*
Pub: Orban Communications Inc.
Contact: Jessica A. Agate, Assoc. Ed.
Released: Bimonthly. **Description:** Trade magazine for leisure travel professionals.

20493 ■ *DogGone*
Pub: Doggone
Contact: Robyn Peters, Publisher
E-mail: roblipete@earthlink.net
Released: Bimonthly. **Price:** $25, U.S.; $38, Canada; $48, elsewhere. **Description:** Highlights destinations and travel tips for people who vacation with their dogs. Also covers creative activities for pets and their owners to enjoy together, travel advice, and personal stories. Recurring features include columns titled Products for Pooches, Travel Pointers, Road Trip, From the Groomer's Table, The Trainers Territory, A Dog's Haus, and Dining With Dogs.

20494 ■ *Dude, Guest & Vacation Ranches*
Pub: Bibliotheca Press
Contact: A. Doyle
Ed: A. Doyle, Editor. **Released:** Irregular. **Price:** $7.95, U.S.. **Description:** Lists dude, guest, and vacation ranches for tourists.

20495 ■ *El Planeta Platica*
Pub: Ron Mader
Contact: Ron Mader, Publisher
E-mail: ron@txinfinet.com; ronmader@aol.com
Released: Quarterly. **Price:** $25, U.S.. **Description:** Covers tourism in Latin America with an environmental slant. Features articles and a list of resources. Recurring features include book reviews.

20496 ■ *Entree*
Pub: Entree Travel
Contact: William Tomicki
Ed: William Tomicki, Editor, wtomicki@aol.com. **Released:** Monthly. **Price:** $75, individuals U.S.. **Description:** Features an insider's look at luxury hotels, cruises, tours, spas, restaurants, and travel around the world. Contains advice and tips on luxury travel, bargains, and services. Recurring features include book/wine reviews.

20497 ■ *Hideaways Newsletter*
Pub: Hideaways International
Contact: Michael F. Thiel, President/Founder
E-mail: mthiel@hideaways.com
Ed: Peg Aaronian, Editor, paaronian@hideaways.com. **Released:** Quarterly. **Price:** $129, Included in membership. **Description:** Features articles on issues of interest to villa vacationers and those seeking high quality, high service vacation options. Includes extensive reports on vacation accommodations; destination descriptions; members' ratings of villas, hotels, cruise ships, and yacht charters; travel tips; and news from recommended properties/cruise lines. Recurring features include compilations of quarterly travel surveys, and columns titled Members News, Members Forum, and Trade Winds. Occasional supplements focusing on one destination, i.e., the Caribbean, Paris, etc. Remarks: Subscription includes semiannual, full-color "Hideaways Guide."

20498 ■ *International Journal of Tourism Research*
Pub: John Wiley & Sons Inc.
Contact: Dimitrios Buhalis, Editorial Board
Ed: John Fletcher, Editor. **Released:** Bimonthly. **Price:** $500 other countries print only; $445 institutions print only; $561 institutions, other countries print only; $871 institutions, other countries print only; $617 institutions, other countries print with online; $489 institutions print with online; $959 institutions, other countries print with online. **Description:** Journal concerned with promoting the tourism and hospitality industries by keeping professionals abreast of current research and debate topics.

20499 ■ *Journeywoman Online Magazine*
Pub: Journeywoman
Contact: Evelyn Hannon, Editor & Publisher
E-mail: editor@journeywoman.com
Released: Irregular. **Description:** Online publication offering female-centered travel tips and stories for single and married women.

20500 ■ *Meetings & Incentive Travel*
Pub: Rogers Media Publishing
Contact: Stephen Dempsey, Editor & Publisher
E-mail: steve.dempsey@mtg.rogers.com
Released: 6/yr. **Price:** $98 two years CAN; $74 Canada; $95 U.S. **Description:** Magazine for corporate meeting planners and incentive travel executives.

20501 ■ *OAG Flight-Finder Asia Pacific Plus*
Pub: OAG Worldwide
Released: Monthly. **Description:** Guide containing quick reference airline schedules within and between all countries of the Pacific geographic area; plus all schedules between the area and North America, Europe, the Middle East, Africa, and Central/South America.

20502 ■ *Southern Festivals*
Pub: Southern Festivals
Contact: Jim Taylor
Released: Bimonthly. **Description:** A statewide newspaper covering travel and tourism.

20503 ■ *Spa Magazine*
Pub: Islands Publishing Co.
Contact: Michelle Gamble, Publisher
Released: 7/yr. **Price:** $11.97 U.S.; $20.97 Canada; $36.97 other countries. **Description:** Magazine containing articles on travel, well-being, and 'renewal'.

20504 ■ *Travel Trade*
Pub: Travel Trade
Contact: Seth Gittlitz, Mng. Dir.
E-mail: seth@traveltrade.com
Released: Weekly. **Price:** $20; $30 two years; $40 3 years. **Description:** Travel industry magazine.

20505 ■ *Travel Weekly*
Pub: Northstar Travel Media
Contact: Kimberly Scholz, Web Mng. Ed.
E-mail: kscholz@travelweekly.com
Released: Weekly (Mon.). **Price:** Free to qualified subscribers. **Description:** Travel industry magazine.

20506 ■ *Travel World News Magazine*
Pub: Travel Industry Network Inc.
Contact: Charles Gatt, Publisher
E-mail: charlie@travelworldnews.com
Ed: Carol A. Petro, Editor. **Released:** Monthly. **Price:** $25 by mail; $40 Canada; $60 other countries. **Description:** Magazine for the travel industry professional.

20507 ■ *TravelAge West*
Pub: Northstar Travel Media
Contact: Michelle Rosenberg, Publisher
E-mail: mrosenberg@travelagewest.com
Released: Biweekly. **Description:** Magazine for retail travel agents in western U.S. and western Canada.

20508 ■ *Traveling Times*
Pub: Traveling Times Inc.
Ed: Mirko A. Ilitch, Editor. **Released:** Quarterly. **Description:** Highlights popular vacation spots around the world.

20509 ■ *Travelweek*
Pub: Concepts Travel Media Ltd.
Contact: Michael Butler, Gp. Publisher
E-mail: mbutler@travelweek.ca
Released: Weekly (Thurs.). **Description:** Trade publication covering the travel industry.

20510 ■ *Woodall's Northeast Outdoors*
Pub: Woodall Publications Corp.
Released: Bimonthly. **Price:** $20. **Description:** Magazine serving campers and RVers in the Northeast.

VIDEOCASSETTES/ AUDIOCASSETTES

20511 ■ *Europe's Romantic Inns*
Cambridge Educational
c/o Films Media Group
132 West 31st Street, 17th Floor
Ste. 124
New York, NY 10001
Free: 800-257-5126
Fax:(609)671-0266
Co. E-mail: custserve@films.com
URL: http://www.cambridgeol.com
Description: Two-volume set tours the most exquisite inns in Europe. **Availability:** VHS.

20512 ■ *Going Places*
MPI Home Video
16101 S. 108th Ave.
Orland Park, IL 60467
Ph:(708)460-0555
Free: 800-323-0442
Fax:(708)873-3177
URL: http://www.mpihomevideo.com
Price: $79.98. **Description:** Eight-volume set features NBC's Al Roker exploring the world's most popular vacation spots. **Availability:** VHS.

20513 ■ *I Can Do It! Judi Wineland*
Direct Cinema Ltd.
PO Box 10003
Santa Monica, CA 90410-1003
Ph:(310)636-8200
Free: 800-525-0000
Fax:(310)636-8228
Co. E-mail: orders@directcinemalimited.com
URL: http://www.directcinema.com
Released: 1985. **Description:** Wineland describes the tribulations, maneuvers and backroom strategies that resulted in her multi-million dollar travel company. **Availability:** VHS; 3/4U; Special order formats.

20514 ■ *Inside Business Today*
GPN Educational Media
1550 Executive Drive
Elgin, IL 60123
Ph:(402)472-2007
Free: 800-228-4630
Fax:800-306-2330
Co. E-mail: askgpn@smarterville.com
URL: http://www.shopgpn.com
Released: 1989. **Description:** Leaders in business and industry tell their success stories in this extensive series. **Availability:** VHS; 3/4U.

TRADE SHOWS AND CONVENTIONS

20515 ■ Annual Reading Sport, Travel and Outdoor Show
Eastern Fishing and Outdoor Exposition Inc.
PO Box 4720
Portsmouth, NH 03801
Ph:(603)431-4315
Fax:(603)431-1971
Co. E-mail: info@sportshows.com
URL: http://www.sportshows.com
Released: Annual. **Audience:** Greater Washington DC area. **Principal Exhibits:** Sports, travel and outdoor show.

20516 ■ Annual Rockford RV, Camping and Travel Show
Showtime Productions Inc.
PO Box 4372
Rockford, IL 61110
Fax:(815)877-9037
Co. E-mail: brenda@showtimeproduction.net
URL: http://www.showtimeproduction.net
Released: Annual. **Principal Exhibits:** RVs, camping and travel.

20517 ■ Eastern Sports & Outdoor Show
Reed Exhibitions North American Headquarters
383 Main Ave.
Norwalk, CT 06851
Ph:(203)840-4800
Fax:(203)840-5805
Co. E-mail: export@reedexpo.com
URL: http://www.reedexpo.com
Released: Annual. **Audience:** General public. **Principal Exhibits:** Recreational vehicles, boats, hunting and fishing equipment, clothing, and related outdoor products, resorts, SUVs, retailers and manufacturers, motorcycles, ATVs, travel and tourism.

20518 ■ Fort Wayne Sports, Vacation, and Boat Show
Trio Enterprises, Inc.
3624 Maxim Dr.
Fort Wayne, IN 46815
Ph:(219)483-2638
Free: 800-446-2638
Fax:(219)484-0876
Released: Annual. **Audience:** General public. **Principal Exhibits:** Recreational vehicles, boats, and travel and vacation information.

20519 ■ Kansas Sports, Boat, & Travel Show
Industrial Expositions, Inc.
1675 Larimer St., No.700
PO Box 480084
Denver, CO 80248-0084
Ph:(303)892-6800
Free: 800-457-2434

Fax:(303)892-6322
Co. E-mail: info@iei-expos.com
URL: http://www.iei-expos.com/
Released: Annual. **Audience:** General public. **Principal Exhibits:** Recreational vehicles, boats, sports equipment, and travel destination information; fishing and hunting equipment, supplies, and services.

20520 ■ Louisville Boat, RV & Sportshow
Douglas Expositions Inc.
10000 Shelbyville Rd., No. 111
Anchorage, KY 40223-2950
Ph:(502)244-5660
Fax:(502)244-5160
Released: Annual. **Principal Exhibits:** Sports, boating and vacations, hunting and fishing, recreational vehicles.

20521 ■ Quad City Boat and Vacation Show
Iowa Show Productions Inc.
PO Box 2460
Waterloo, IA 50704-2460
Ph:(319)232-0218
Fax:(319)235-8932
Co. E-mail: info@iowashows.com
URL: http://www.iowashows.com/
Released: Annual. **Principal Exhibits:** Boats, fishing tackle, resorts, tourism associations, motorhomes.

20522 ■ Travel Media Showcase
Atlantic City Convention & Visitors Authority
2314 Pacific Ave.
Atlantic City, NJ 08401
Ph:(609)449-7162
Fax:(609)345-2200
URL: http://www.atlanticcitynj.com/
Released: Annual. **Audience:** Trade. **Principal Exhibits:** Tourism industry and travel media convention.

CONSULTANTS

20523 ■ The Tactix Group
1619 N 102 St.
Omaha, NE 68114
Ph:(402)393-3800
Fax:(402)393-5151
Co. E-mail: info@thetactixgroup.com
URL: http://www.thetactixgroup.com
Contact: Douglas R. Little, President
E-mail: dlittle@tactixinc.com
Scope: Offers integrated marketing system design and implementation, for customer relationship management. Serves manufacturing, distributing, high-tech, banking, and executive benefit industries. **Special Services:** Saleslogix (Client Server) Sales Automation Software.

FRANCHISES AND BUSINESS OPPORTUNITIES

20524 ■ All About Honeymoons
7887 E Bellview Ave., Ste. 540
Englewood, CO 80111
Free: 888-845-4488
No. of Franchise Units: 101. **No. of Company-Owned Units:** 1. **Founded:** 1994. **Franchised:** 2003. **Description:** Honeymoon resort, wedding and travel specialists. **Equity Capital Needed:** $32,900-$75,900. **Franchise Fee:** $9,500-$29,500. **Royalty Fee:** Varies. **Financial Assistance:** Limited third party financing available. **Training:** Yes.

20525 ■ Cruise Holidays
Carlson Travel Network
6442 City West Pkwy.
Minneapolis, MN 55344
Free: 800-824-1481
Co. E-mail: cruisefh@franchisehub.com
URL: http://www.cruiseholidays.com
No. of Franchise Units: 168. **No. of Company-Owned Units:** 4. **Founded:** 1984. **Franchised:** 1984. **Description:** Largest cruise-travel franchise in North America. Headquartered in Minneapolis & have over 200 locations throughout North America. **Equity Capital Needed:** $10,350-$160,350. **Franchise Fee:** $9,500$30,000. **Royalty Fee:** 3%. **Financial Assistance:** Limited third party financing available. **Training:** Provides 1 week at headquarters, at franchisee's location that varies and ongoing training and support.

20526 ■ Cruise Planners /American Express
CP Franchising, LLC
3300 University Dr., Ste. 602
Coral Springs, FL 33065
Ph:(954)344-8060
Free: 888-582-2150
Fax:(954)755-5898
Co. E-mail: franchising@cruiseplanners.com
URL: http://www.beacruiseagent.com
No. of Franchise Units: 740. **Founded:** 1994. **Franchised:** 1999. **Description:** Cruise agency. **Equity Capital Needed:** $9,995-$19,590, includes franchise fee, training, and airfare. **Franchise Fee:** 0-$9,995 depending on experience. **Financial Assistance:** Yes. **Managerial Assistance:** Business management software, toll-free support desk, free marketing Consultation. **Training:** Pre-training commencement materials, 5 day training seminar (includes airfare, hotel, ground transportation, all meals, ship inspections, classroom seminars, materials). Advanced training seminars available.

20527 ■ CruiseOne
WTH
1201 W Cypress Creek Rd., Ste. 100
Ft. Lauderdale, FL 33309
Ph:(954)958-3701
Free: 800-892-3928
Fax:(954)958-3697
Co. E-mail: franchise@cruiseone.com
URL: http://www.cruiseone.com
No. of Franchise Units: 685. **Founded:** 1992. **Franchised:** 1993. **Description:** Complete turnkey, low onetime investment. No monthly sales quota. No experience required. Complete training & support. Work from home or office. Full or part-time. Earn the highest commissions & bonuses. **Franchise Fee:** $9,800. **Financial Assistance:** Yes. **Managerial Assistance:** Six personalized websites & comprehensive marketing programs to help promote your business. Websites & reservation system have booking capability & online connectivity. **Training:** Comprehensive 8 day training program at corporate headquarters in Ft. Lauderdale. Included in franchise fee: R/T airfare, private hotel room, meals, classroom seminars, ship inspections, meet cruise line executives, additional ongoing training, toll-free support, sales & marketing, and seminars at sea.

20528 ■ Expedia CruiseShipCenters
1055 West Hastings, Ste. 400
Vancouver, BC, Canada V6E 2E9
Ph:(604)685-1221
Free: 888-783-0133
Fax:(604)685-1245
Co. E-mail: franchise@cruiseshipcenters.com
URL: http://www.cruiseshipcenters.ca
No. of Franchise Units: 117. **No. of Company-Owned Units:** 1. **Founded:** 1987. **Franchised:** 1987. **Description:** The center mainly deals with cruise sales in Canada. They have centers all across Canada and are a leading force worldwide. **Equity Capital Needed:** $60,000-$90,000 start up capital required; $125,000-$150,000 total investment. **Franchise Fee:** $43,000. **Training:** 3 weeks initially with lifetime of learning.

20529 ■ Outdoor Connection
424 Neosho
Burlington, KS 66839
Ph:(620)364-5500
Fax:(620)364-5563
No. of Franchise Units: 61. **No. of Company-Owned Units:** 2. **Founded:** 1988. **Franchised:** 1990. **Description:** Hunting and fishing travel service. **Equity Capital Needed:** $7,550-$12,250. **Franchise Fee:** $6,500. **Royalty Fee:** 4%. **Financial Assistance:** Assistance with franchise fee. **Training:** 2 days at headquarters, 2-3 days annual convention and ongoing support. ort.

20530 ■ Tix Travel and Ticket Agency Inc.
201 Main St.
Nyack-On-Hudson, NY 10960
Ph:(845)358-1007
Free: 800-20W-NTIX
Fax:(845)358-1266
URL: http://www.tixtravel.com
No. of Franchise Units: 400. **No. of Company-Owned Units:** 1. **Founded:** 1982. **Franchised:** 1989. **Description:** A travel agency and concert and sporting event tickets outlet. **Equity Capital Needed:** From $3,495. **Franchise Fee:** From $3,495. **Financial Assistance:** Yes. **Training:** Yes.

20531 ■ TPI Travel Services
Travel Pros Inc.
2901 W Busch Blvd., Ste. 408
Tampa, FL 33618-4566
Ph:(813)281-5670
Free: 800-393-7767
Co. E-mail: support@tpitravel.com
No. of Franchise Units: 460. **No. of Company-Owned Units:** 1. **Founded:** 1987. **Description:** Full service travel agency. **Equity Capital Needed:** $10,000. **Franchise Fee:** $4,995. **Financial Assistance:** Yes. **Training:** Yes.

20532 ■ Travel Lines Express Franchise Group
9858 Glades Rd.
Boca Raton, FL 33434
Ph:(561)482-9557
No. of Franchise Units: 50. **No. of Company-Owned Units:** 1. **Founded:** 1980. **Franchised:** 2003. **Description:** Full service home based travel agency. **Equity Capital Needed:** $1,000-$3,000. **Franchise Fee:** $300. **Financial Assistance:** No. **Training:** Yes.

20533 ■ Uniglobe Travel International Limited Partnership
1199 West Pender St., Ste. 900
Vancouver, BC, Canada V6E 2R1
Ph:(604)718-2614
Fax:(604)718-2678
Co. E-mail: jhenry@uniglobetravel.ca
URL: http://www.uniglobetravel.com
No. of Franchise Units: 122. **Founded:** 1981. **Franchised:** 1981. **Description:** International travel management system that specializes in providing travel services to the small to mid-size enterprise market. The travel organization has over 700 franchise and Global Partner locations in more than 30 countries in the Americas, Europe, Asia, and Africa. Operating under a well-recognized brand name, UNIGLOBE travel agencies specialize in providing travel services to corporate accounts and to leisure travelers. **Equity Capital Needed:** $10,000-$100,000. **Franchise Fee:** $5,000-$20,000.

20534 ■ Uniglobe Travel (USA), LLC
18662 MacArthur Blvd., Ste. 100
Irvine, CA 92612
Ph:(949)623-9000
Free: 800-863-1606
Fax:(949)623-9008
No. of Franchise Units: 1,100. **Founded:** 1980. **Franchised:** 1981. **Description:** Travel franchisor. A National TV advertising, consumer-recognized brand image, profitability software programs one-on-one travel agency business consultation, franchise operator and manager forums, preferred supplier override programs and unparalleled training in all facets of the travel industry. *Entrepreneur Magazine* awarded Uniglobe 1 in Travel Agency Franchising. **Equity Capital Needed:** $5,500-$20,200 conversion; $98,450-$134,950 start-up; $3,600-$13,500 home based. **Franchise Fee:** $3,000-$29,500. **Financial Assistance:** No. **Managerial Assistance:** Travel industry's most in-depth support program from front and back office to sales and marketing. Partial list of support programs includes software for agency management. Uniglobe's own back office system, management reports, productivity reports, corporate client reports, financial reports, commission tracking and billing reports. Budget and finance programs also. **Training:** Offers the industry's most in-depth training courses international management academy, advanced international management academy, Uni-

globe orientation, commercial sales, vacation sales, group and incentive sales, video-based training and financial management.

LIBRARIES

20535 ■ American Hotel & Lodging Association Information Center
1201 New York Ave. N.W., Ste. 600
Houston, TX 77204-3028
Ph:(202)289-3100
Free: 888-743-2515
Fax:(202)289-3199
Co. E-mail: informationcenter@ahla.com
URL: http://www.ahla.com
Contact: Lydia Westbrook, Res.Dir.
Scope: Hotels and restaurants; travel and tourism. **Services:** Library open to the public with restrictions by appointment only. **Holdings:** 2500 volumes; microfilms; archives. **Subscriptions:** 100 journals and other serials.

20536 ■ Davenport University–Thomas F. Reed, Jr. Memorial Library
4123 W. Main St.
Kalamazoo, MI 49006
Ph:(616)382-2835
Free: 800-632-8928
Fax:(269)382-2657
Co. E-mail: kz_linc@davenport.edu
URL: http://www.davenport.edu/
Contact: Judith J. Bosshart, Dir.
Scope: Business, data processing, administrative services, accounting, humanities, paralegal, medical records, healthcare administration, computer and information processing. **Services:** Interlibrary loan; copying; faxing; Library open to the public for reference use only. **Holdings:** 14,200 books; 995 videotapes. **Subscriptions:** 12,000 journals and other serials; 6 newspapers.

20537 ■ Johnson and Wales University Charleston Campus–Barry L. Gleim Library
701 E. Bay St.
Charleston, SC 29403
Ph:(843)727-3045
Fax:(843)727-3078
Co. E-mail: Joanne.Letendre@jwu.edu
Contact: Joanne N. Letendre
Scope: Culinary arts, food service, hospitality management, travel and tourism. **Services:** Library open to the public with restrictions. **Holdings:** 10,681 books; 1230 videos; 6 CD-ROMs. **Subscriptions:** 174 journals and other serials; 5 newspapers.

20538 ■ Midstate College–Barbara Fields Memorial Library I Special Collections
R. Dale Bunch Student Ctr., Rm. 403
411 W. Northmoor Rd.
Peoria, IL 61614-3542
Ph:(309)692-4092
Fax:(309)692-3893
Co. E-mail: zbrown@midstate.edu
URL: http://www.midstate.edu/
Contact: Zachary M. Brown, Lib.Dir.
Scope: Travel and tourism; court reporting, paralegal services; office assistant, office computer applications, business administration, business computer accounting; medical assistant, medical transcription, medical clinical office assistant; legal transcription, administrative assistant; computer information specialist; business administration. **Services:** Interlibrary loan; copying; faxing. **Holdings:** 8000 books; audiotapes; videotapes. **Subscriptions:** 100 journals and other serials; 4 newspapers.

20539 ■ Nadasdy Ferenc Museum Library
Varkerulet 1
H-9600 Sarvar, Hungary
Ph:(36)95 320158
Fax:(36)95 320158
Co. E-mail: nadasdy.sarvar@museum.hu
URL: http://www.museum.hu/museum/index_hu.php?ID=669
Contact: Takacs Zoltan, Dir.
Scope: Regional history. **Services:** Library open to the public with restrictions. **Holdings:** 4000 volumes.

20540 ■ Society for Accessible Travel and Hospitality Library
347 5th Ave., Ste. 605
New York, NY 10016
Ph:(212)447-7284
Fax:(212)447-1928
Co. E-mail: sathtravel@aol.com
URL: http://www.sath.org
Contact: Jani Nayar, Exec.Cood.
Scope: Travel advice on facilities for persons with disabilities. **Services:** Library opens to members only. **Holdings:** Travel guides for people with disabilities and literature provided by tourist offices, carriers, hotels, foreign organizations, destinations, and car rental agencies; statistics. **Subscriptions:** 5 journals and other serials; 3 newspapers.

20541 ■ Travel Industry Association of America Library
1100 New York Ave. NW, Ste. 450
Washington, DC 20005-3934
Ph:(202)408-8422
Fax:(202)408-1255
URL: http://www.tia.org
Contact: Suzanne D. Cook, Sr. VP, Res.
Scope: Travel and tourism. **Services:** Library not open to the public. **Holdings:** 3000 research documents; 3800 government documents; 250 unpublished travel research reports; 15,000 clippings; 20 tapes. **Subscriptions:** 27 journals and other serials.

RESEARCH CENTERS

20542 ■ College of Forestry and Conservation–Institute for Tourism and Recreation Research
University of Montana
32 Campus Dr., No. 1234
Missoula, MT 59812-1234
Ph:(406)243-5686
Fax:(406)243-4845
Co. E-mail: request@forestry.umt.edu
URL: http://www.forestry.umt.edu/
Contact: Kate Cenis, Dir.
Description: Provides research data needed to support the state's tourism industry.

20543 ■ Travel and Tourism Research Association
3048 W Clarkston Rd.
Lake Orion, MI 48362
Ph:(248)708-8872
Fax:(248)814-7150
Co. E-mail: cbrauer@ttra.com
URL: http://www.ttra.com
Contact: Connie Brauer, Admin.
E-mail: cbrauer@ttra.com
Scope: Travel and tourism, focusing on development and marketing within the travel industry. **Services:** Reference services, to assist the travel research and marketing industry in finding information sources and solving business problems. **Publications:** Annual conference proceedings; Journal of Travel Research (quarterly); Newsletter (quarterly). **Awards:** JTR Best Article Award; Slattery Marketing Award for Students, Professionals; Student Research Award; Travel Research Grant; Travel Research Student Contest.

START-UP INFORMATION

20544 ■ "Pump Up the Profits: Teaching Small Biz How to Handle Fuel and Reduce Costs!" in *Small Business Opportunities* (March 2008)
Pub: Harris Publications Inc.
Description: Profile of 4Refuel, a company that delivers diesel and biodiesel fuel to customers individual fuelings.

20545 ■ "Road Map To Riches" in *Small Business Opportunities* (September 2010)
Pub: Harris Publications Inc.
Description: Profile of Philip Nenadov who launched The Transportation Network Group during the recession. This franchise is low cost and can earn six figures while working from home by becoming a trucking agent.

ASSOCIATIONS AND OTHER ORGANIZATIONS

20546 ■ American Trucking Associations
950 N Glebe Rd., Ste. 210
Arlington, VA 22203-4181
Ph:(703)838-1700
Free: 888-333-1759
Co. E-mail: atamembership@trucking.org
URL: http://www.truckline.com
Contact: Bill Graves, Pres.
Description: Motor carriers, suppliers, state trucking associations, and national conferences of trucking companies. Works to influence the decisions of federal, state, and local government bodies; promotes increased efficiency, productivity, and competitiveness in the trucking industries; sponsors American Trucking Associations Foundation. Provides quarterly financial and operating statistics service. Offers comprehensive accounting service for all sizes of carriers. Promotes highway and driver safety; supports highway research projects; and studies technical and regulatory problems of the trucking industry. Sponsors competitions; compiles statistics. Maintains numerous programs and services including: Management Information Systems Directory; Compensation Survey; Electronic Data Interchange Standards. **Publications:** *North American Truck Fleet Directory* (annual).

20547 ■ Canadian Trucking Alliance–Alliance Canadienne du Camionnage
324 Somerset St. W
Ottawa, ON, Canada K2P 0J9
Ph:(613)236-9426
Free: (866)823-4076
URL: http://cantruck.ca/imispublic/cantruck
Description: Trucking companies. Seeks to advance the road transportation industries. Serves as a forum for the exchange of information among members; represents members' interests before labor and industrial organizations, government agencies, and the public. **Publications:** *Crossing International Borders: A Trucker's Guide* .

20548 ■ Distribution and LTL Carriers Association
950 N Glebe Rd., Ste. 210
Arlington, VA 22203
Ph:(703)838-7970
Fax:(703)838-7994
Co. E-mail: bfarrell@trucking.org
URL: http://www.dltl.org
Contact: Bob Farrell, Pres.
Description: Represents for-hire motor common carriers of general freight who specialize in less-than-truckload shipments throughout the U.S. Provides government relations, networking, business development programs, and publications. .

20549 ■ Freight Carriers Association of Canada
427 Garrison Rd., Unit 3 and 4
Fort Erie, ON, Canada L2A 6E6
Free: 800-559-7421
Fax:(905)994-0117
Co. E-mail: info@fca-natc.org
URL: http://www.fca-natc.org
Contact: Dave Sirgey, Pres.
Description: Canadian motor carriers involved in domestic transportation. Creates and provides statistical and operational information to all parties involved in motor carrier transportation. Offers statistical information. **Publications:** *Fuel Calculation Bulletin* (weekly); *News* (bimonthly).

20550 ■ International Truck Parts Association
1720-10 Ave. S, Ste. 4
PMB 199
Great Falls, MT 59405
Free: (866)346-5692
Fax:800-895-4654
Co. E-mail: info@itpa.com
URL: http://www.itpa.com
Contact: Venlo Wolfsohn, Exec. Dir.
Description: Represents companies specializing in the purchase and sale of used and rebuilt heavy-duty truck components. .

20551 ■ Mid-West Truckers Association
2727 N Dirksen Pkwy.
Springfield, IL 62702
Ph:(217)525-0310
Fax:(217)525-0342
Co. E-mail: info@mid-westtruckers.com
URL: http://www.mid-westtruckers.com
Description: Owners and operators of trucking companies. Serves as a unified voice for truckers nationwide; conducts lobbying. Sponsors services to members including: mass purchasing program, whereby members may purchase parts at wholesale rates; drug and alcohol testing program; assistance with international registration; license plate procurement; group insurance programs self-funded worker's Compensation Program. Conducts seminars and educational programs; maintains speakers' bureau. **Publications:** *Cost Summary Booklet*; *Keep on Truckin' News* (monthly).

20552 ■ National Private Truck Council
950 N Glebe Rd., Ste. 530
Arlington, VA 22203-4183
Ph:(703)683-1300
Fax:(703)683-1217
Co. E-mail: info@nptc.org
URL: http://www.nptc.org
Contact: Mr. George Mundell, Exec. VP/COO
Description: Represents private motor carrier truck fleets and their suppliers. **Publications:** *Fleet Owner* (bimonthly); *Membership Directory & Buyers' Guide* (annual); *Private Fleet Directory/FleetSeek*; *Weekly Update* (weekly).

20553 ■ National Tank Truck Carriers
950 N Glebe Rd., Ste. 520
Arlington, VA 22203
Ph:(703)838-1960
Fax:(703)838-8860
Co. E-mail: jconley@tanktruck.org
URL: http://www.tanktruck.org
Contact: John Conley, Pres.
Description: Common or contract "for-hire" tank truck carriers transporting liquid and dry bulk commodities, chemicals, food processing commodities, petroleum, and related products; allied industry suppliers. Promotes federal standards of construction, design, operation and use of tank trucks and equipment. Coordinates truck transportation system for shippers of bulk commodities. Secures improvements in tank specifications. Sponsors annual schools; conducts research. **Publications:** *Cargo Tank Hazardous Materials Regulations* (annual); *National Tank Truck Directory* (annual); *Washington Newsletter* (monthly).

20554 ■ National Truck Equipment Association
37400 Hills Tech Dr.
Farmington Hills, MI 48331-3414
Ph:(248)489-7090
Free: 800-441-NTEA
Fax:(248)489-8590
Co. E-mail: info@ntea.com
URL: http://www.ntea.com
Contact: Jim Carney, Exec. Dir.
Description: Serves as a trade group for commercial truck, truck body, truck equipment, trailer and accessory manufacturers and distributors. Advises members of current federal regulations affecting the manufacturing and installation of truck bodies and equipment; works to enhance the professionalism of management and improve profitability in the truck equipment business. **Publications:** *Excise Tax Bulletin* (periodic); *Membership Roster and Product Directory* (annual); *NTEA News* (monthly); *Truck Equipment Handbook* .

20555 ■ Owner-Operator Independent Drivers Association
1 NW OOIDA Dr.
Grain Valley, MO 64029-7903
Ph:(816)229-5791
Free: 800-444-5791

Fax:(816)229-0518
Co. E-mail: jjohnston@ooida.com
URL: http://www.ooida.com
Contact: Jim Johnston, Pres.
Description: Truck owner-operators, small fleet operators, and drivers. Lobbying association seeking to improve owner-operator working conditions. Provides national recognition and a channel for members to voice interests and concerns on changes that affect the trucking business. Addresses issues including: freight rates commensurate with costs; rules guaranteeing prompt payment for owner-operators; flexible hours of operation; taxes; safety initiatives. Offers medical, truck, dental, and accident programs. Sponsors research programs; compiles statistics; maintains speakers' bureau. **Publications:** *Land Line* (10/year); *Owner-Operator News* (quarterly).

20556 ■ Private Motor Truck Council of Canada–Association Canadienne du Camionnage d'Entreprise
1660 N Service Rd. E, Ste. 115
Oakville, ON, Canada L6H 7G3
Ph:(905)827-0587
Free: 877-501-PMTC
Fax:(905)827-8212
Co. E-mail: info@pmtc.ca
URL: http://www.pmtc.ca
Contact: Bruce J. Richards, Pres.
Description: Private truck fleet operators and others with an interest in the trucking industry. Represents members' interests before government and international regulatory bodies and the public. **Publications:** *The Counsellor* (quarterly); *Newsbriefs* (monthly).

20557 ■ Professional Truck Driver Institute
555 E Braddock Rd.
Alexandria, VA 22314-2182
Ph:(703)647-7015
Fax:(703)836-6610
Co. E-mail: ptdi@truckload.org
URL: http://www.ptdi.org
Contact: Chris Burruss, Pres.
Description: Stakeholders include carriers, schools, trade associations, manufacturers, insurance companies, regulatory bodies, funding organizations, and suppliers to the trucking industry. Develops skill and curriculum standards for truck driver training and standards for the certification of truck driver training courses; certifies commercial truck driver training courses and driver finishing programs. **Publications:** *Certification Standards and Requirements for Entry-Level Tractor-Trailer Driver Courses*; *Certification Standards and Requirements for Tractor-Trailer Driver Finishing Programs*; *Curriculum Standard Guidelines for Entry-Level Tractor-Trailer Driver Courses*; *Skill Standards for Entry-Level Tractor-Trailer Drivers*; *Skill Standards for Professional Solo Tractor-Trailer Drivers* .

20558 ■ Specialized Carriers and Rigging Association
2750 Prosperity Ave., Ste. 620
Fairfax, VA 22031-4312
Ph:(703)698-0291
Fax:(703)698-0297
Co. E-mail: info@scranet.org
URL: http://www.scranet.org
Contact: Joel M. Dandrea, Exec. VP
Description: Common carriers, crane and rigging companies, and millwright contractors engaged in the transportation of heavy and specialized articles, machinery, iron and steel, construction, and military traffic. Operates Heavy and Specialized Carriers Tariff Bureau. Conducts Fleet Safety and Outstanding Hauling, Rigging, and Millwright Job of the Year contests. Compiles statistics. **Publications:** *Lifting and Transportation International Magazine* (9/year); *Moving the World*; *Safety, Industrial Relations, and Government Affairs Special Reports* (periodic); *Specialized Carriers and Rigging Association-Newsletter* (weekly).

20559 ■ Trucking Management, Inc.
PO Box 860725
Shawnee, KS 66286
Ph:(913)568-5873
Co. E-mail: info@tmiweb.org
URL: http://www.tmiweb.org
Contact: David Smith, Pres./CEO
Description: Less-Than-Truckload (LTL) motor carriers. Promotes economic interests of unionized LTL motor carriers. Represents members' interests in public policy and economic issues. Works as the primary multi-employer bargaining arm of the unionized general freight trucking industry. .

20560 ■ Truckload Carriers Association
555 E Braddock Rd.
Alexandria, VA 22314-2182
Ph:(703)838-1950
Fax:(703)836-6610
Co. E-mail: tca@truckload.org
URL: http://www.truckload.org
Contact: Gary Salisbury, Chm.
Description: Engages in the truckload segment of the motor carrier industry. Represents dry van, refrigerated, flatbed and intermodel container carriers operating in the 48 contiguous states as well as Alaska, Mexico and Canada. Represents operators of over 200,000 trucks. .

DIRECTORIES OF EDUCATIONAL PROGRAMS

20561 ■ *Directory of Private Accredited Career Schools and Colleges of Technology*
Pub: Accrediting Commission of Career Schools and Colleges of Technology
Contact: Michale S. McComis, Exec. Dir.
Released: On web page. **Price:** Free. **Description:** Covers 3900 accredited post-secondary programs that provide training programs in business, trade, and technical fields, including various small business endeavors. Entries offer school name, address, phone, description of courses, job placement assistance, and requirements for admission. Arrangement is alphabetical.

REFERENCE WORKS

20562 ■ *American Motor Carrier Directory*
Pub: UBM Global Trade
Contact: Amy Middlebrook, Gp. Publisher
E-mail: amiddlebrook@cbizmedia.com
Released: Annual, December. **Publication Includes:** Lists of all licensed Less Than Truckload (LTL) general commodity carriers in the United States; includes specialized motor carriers and related services; includes refrigerated carriers, heavy haulers, bulk haulers, riggers, and specified commodity carriers; state and federal regulatory bodies governing the trucking industry; tariff publishing bureaus; freight claim councils; industry associations, etc. **Entries Include:** For carriers and services—Company name, address of headquarters and terminals, phones, tariffs followed, names of executives, insurance, and equipment information, services or commodities handled. Principal content of publication is listing of direct point-to-point services of LTL general commodity carriers throughout the United States and to Canada and Mexico. **Arrangement:** Alphabetical.

20563 ■ *Commercial Carrier Journal—Buyers' Guide Issue*
Pub: Reed Business Information (New York, New York)
Contact: Carol Hope Heavens
E-mail: cheavens@chilton.net
Released: Annual, October. **Price:** $10. **Publication Includes:** List of vehicles, components and accessories suppliers for the truck and bus fleet markets. **Entries Include:** Company name, address, phone, fax, e-mail, internet address, trade names. **Arrangement:** Classified by product and alphabetical.

20564 ■ "Compelling Opportunities" in *Barron's* (Vol. 88, March 10, 2008, No. 10, pp. 39)
Pub: Dow Jones & Company, Inc.
Ed: Neil A. Martin. **Description:** Michael L. Reynal, portfolio manager of Principal International Emerging Markets Fund, is bullish on the growth prospects of stocks in emerging markets. He is investing big on energy, steel, and transportation companies.

20565 ■ "Con-Way Project Back in High Gear" in *Business Journal Portland* (Vol. 27, November 5, 2010, No. 36, pp. 1)
Pub: Portland Business Journal
Ed: Wendy Culverwell. **Description:** Trucking firm Con-Way Inc. intends to sell parcels of land from a property comprising 16 blocks and 20 prime acres west of the Pearl District in Portland, Oregon. In 2009, Con-Way abandoned plans to sell the property. As Con-Way reclaims control over design and usage of the property, it also expressed willingness to cooperate with a master developer on a related real estate project.

20566 ■ "Credit Crunch Gives, Takes Away" in *The Business Journal-Serving Metropolitan Kansas City* (Vol. 27, October 17, 2008, No. 5, pp. 1)
Pub: American City Business Journals, Inc.
Ed: Suzanna Stagemeyer. **Description:** Although many Kansas City business enterprises have been adversely affected by the U.S. credit crunch, others have remained relatively unscathed. Examples of how local businesses are being impacted by the crisis are provided including: American Trailer & Storage Inc., which declared bankruptcy after failing to pay a long-term loan; and NetStandard, a technology firm who, on the other hand, is being pursued by prospective lenders.

20567 ■ "CSX Transportation: Supplier Diversity on the Right Track" in *Hispanic Business* (July-August 2009, pp. 34)
Pub: Hispanic Business
Description: CSX Transportation is a leader in delivering essential products, operating as many as 1,200 trains and a fleet of more than 100,000 freight cars. CSX attributes its success by valuing diversity in both hiring and supplier contracts.

20568 ■ "Dealer Gets a Lift with Acquisitions at Year's End" in *Crain's Detroit Business* (Vol. 26, January 11, 2010, No. 2, pp. 3)
Pub: Crain Communications, Inc.
Ed: Ryan Beene. **Description:** Alta Equipment Co., a forklift dealer, closed 2009 with a string of acquisitions expecting to double the firm's employee headcount and triple its annual revenue. Alta Lift Truck Services, Inc., as the company was known before the acquisitions, was founded in 1984 as Michigan's dealer for forklift manufacturer Yale Materials Handling Corp.

20569 ■ "Family Throne" in *Hawaii Business* (Vol. 53, March 2008, No. 9, pp. 51)
Pub: Hawaii Business Publishing
Ed: Cathy S. Cruz-George. **Description:** Jeanette and George Grace inherited Paradise Lua Inc., a portable toilet company founded by George's father. The toilets are rented by Aloha Stadium during football season and St. Patrick's Day block party among others. The company has 2,500 toilets and 20 pumping trucks and had earnings of $1.3 million in 2007.

20570 ■ "Freeing the Wheels of Commerce" in *Hispanic Business* (July-August 2007, pp. 50, 52, 54)
Pub: Hispanic Business
Ed: Keith Rosenblum. **Description:** SecureOrigins, a border-based partnership with high-tech innovators is working to move goods faster, more efficiently, and securely.

20571 ■ *Heavy Duty Representatives Profile Directory*
Pub: Heavy Duty Representatives Association
Ed: Cara R. Giebner, Editor. **Released:** Annual, January. **Covers:** About 75 independent sales agencies which sell heavy-duty components to the trucking and aftermarket industries. **Entries Include:** Name of company, address, phone, name and title of principal, experience in industry, sales territory, warehouse space, product lines, services. **Arrangement:** Alphabetical. **Indexes:** Geographical.

20572 ■ *Heavy Duty Trucking—Council of Fleet Specialists Equipment Buyer's Guide & Services Directory*
Pub: Newport Communications Div.
Contact: Jody Patterson
Ed: Doug Condra, Editor. **Released:** Annual, January. **Price:** $45 included in subscription; free to equip-

ment and maintenance managers. **Covers:** 500 Council of Fleet Specialists member manufacturers and wholesalers specializing in heavy-duty truck parts and repairs. **Entries Include:** Company name, address, phone, names of executives, parts or services manufactured or available; wholesaler listings also show area served. A special section of 'Heavy Duty Trucking' magazine prepared by the Council of Fleet Specialists, 315 Delaware, Kansas City, MO 64105 (816-421-2600). **Arrangement:** Wholesalers are geographical; manufacturers are alphabetical. **Indexes:** Wholesaler name.

20573 ■ "Is 'Tsunami' of Freight in our Future?" in *Business Courier* (Vol. 26, November 27, 2009, No. 31, pp. 1)
Pub: American City Business Journals, Inc.

Ed: Dan Monk. **Description:** Freight companies are planning for cargo-container shipping facilities on the riverfront of Cincinnati in light of the completion of the $5 billion Panama Canal expansion in 2015. The city's capability to utilize the growth in freight has been under investigation by authorities.

20574 ■ "iSymmetry's Technological Makeover Or, How a Tech Company Finally Grew Up and Discovered the World Wide Web" in *Inc.* (October 2007)
Pub: Gruner & Jahr USA Publishing

Description: Profile of iSymmetry, an Atlanta, Georgia-based IT recruiting firm, covering the issues the company faces keeping its technology equipment up-to-date. The firm has devised a program that will replace its old server-based software systems with on-demand software delivered via the Internet, known as software-as-a-service. Statistical information included.

20575 ■ "The Market's (Very) Tender Spring Shoots" in *Barron's* (Vol. 88, March 31, 2008, No. 13, pp. M3)
Pub: Dow Jones & Company, Inc.

Ed: Kopin Tan. **Description:** Expansion in price-earnings multiples and a lower credit-default risk index has encouraged fans of the spring-awakening theory. Shares of industrial truckers have gone up 32 percent in 2008 and some shares are pushing five-year highs brought on by higher efficiency and earnings from more load carried. The prospects of the shares of Foot Locker are also discussed.

20576 ■ *National Highway and Airway Carriers Directory*
Pub: National Highway Carriers Directory Inc.

Released: Semiannual, Latest edition 2010. **Price:** $295, individuals one issue only; $345, individuals for 2 issues per year, fall and spring, 1yr sub.; $395, individuals online. **Covers:** Over 2,500 motor and airway carriers. LTL, TL, intermodal, refrigerated freight forwarders, warehousing, Canadian Carriers, Brokers, North American Railroads and Ocean Carriers. **Entries Include:** Company name, address, phone, fax, names of key personnel, number of trucks, locations of terminals, terminal phone numbers, terminal fax numbers, kind of equipment insurance available, routes, tariffs, and points served direct in North America. **Arrangement:** Geographical, alphabetical.

20577 ■ *National Tank Truck Carrier Directory*
Pub: National Tank Truck Carriers Inc.

Released: Annual, Latest edition 57th; 2011. **Price:** $54, members; $80, nonmembers. **Covers:** For-hire tank truck carriers serving petroleum, chemical, and other industries in the United States, Canada, Australia, England, Europe, Japan, Mexico, and South Africa. Also lists major shippers who use tank trucks, intermodal bulk facilities, industry suppliers, and state related associations affiliated with the American Trucking Associations. **Entries Include:** Company name, address, phone, names of executives, list of products or services. **Arrangement:** Separate geographical sections for carriers and associations; shippers and industry suppliers are alphabetical. **Indexes:** Personal name, company name.

20578 ■ *National Truck Equipment Association—Market Resource Guide*
Pub: National Truck Equipment Association
Contact: Allison Kroll, Communications Dir.

Released: Annual, Latest edition 2011. **Price:** $50, nonmembers; $10, members. **Covers:** Over 1,500 distributors who install commercial truck bodies and related equipment on chassis-cabs, truck body and equipment manufacturers, and associates. **Entries Include:** Company name, address, phone, fax, e-mail, web site, name and title of contact; membership type and year began membership, products or services. **Arrangement:** Alphabetical. **Indexes:** Distributors are geographical; manufacturers and associates classified by product/service and geographical.

20579 ■ *NATSO—Membership Directory*
Pub: NATSO
Contact: Bobby Berkstresser, Chm.
E-mail: halfano@natso.com

Released: Annual. **Covers:** Over 1,300 North American travel plazas, truck stops, supplier firms, and corporate parent firms. **Entries Include:** Truck stop name, street and mailing addresses, phone, names of key personnel, corporate affiliations. Similar detail given for suppliers and corporate parent firms. **Arrangement:** Geographical. **Indexes:** Member truck stops by U.S. and interstate highway; supplier, product/service.

20580 ■ "Paperless Bookkeeping Program" in *Fleet Owner Online* (February 15, 2011)
Pub: Penton Business Media Inc.

Description: TruckTax launched its new paperless bookkeeping system to help manage bookkeeping tasks, accounting and business tax information and filings for truckers.

20581 ■ "Presidential Address: Innovation in Retrospect and Prospect" in *Canadian Journal of Electronics* (Vol. 43, November 2010, No. 4)
Pub: Journal of the Canadian Economics Association

Ed: James A. Brander. **Description:** Has innovation slowed in recent decades? While there has been progress in information and communications technology, the recent record of innovation in agriculture, energy, transportation and healthcare sectors is cause for concern.

20582 ■ "Ryder's Shock Absorbers Are In Place" in *Barron's* (Vol. 88, March 24, 2008, No. 12, pp. 19)
Pub: Dow Jones & Company, Inc.

Ed: Christopher C. Williams. **Description:** Shares of Ryder System Inc. are expected to continue rising on the back of rising earnings, forecast at $5.20 a share for 2009. The shares of the truck freight company hit a 52-week high of $62.27 each and may reach $70 a share.

20583 ■ "Sedo Keeps Trucking in Good Times and Bad" in *Crain's Chicago Business* (Vol. 31, April 28, 2008, No. 17, pp. 35)
Pub: Crain Communications, Inc.

Ed: Samantha Stainburn. **Description:** Discusses Seko Worldwide Inc., an Itasca-based freight forwarder, and its complicated road to growth and expansion on a global scale.

20584 ■ "Staffing Firms are Picking Up the Pieces, Seeing Signs of Life" in *Milwaukee Business Journal* (Vol. 27, February 5, 2010, No. 19)
Pub: American City Business Journals

Ed: Rich Rovito. **Description:** Milwaukee, Wisconsin-based staffing firms are seeing signs of economic rebound as many businesses turned to temporary employees to fill the demands for goods and services. Economic observers believe the growth in temporary staffing is one of the early indicators of economic recovery.

20585 ■ *Truck Frame & Axle Repair Association—Membership Directory*
Pub: Truck Frame and Axle Repair Association
Contact: Bob Razenberg, President
E-mail: razenberg@sbcglobal.net

Released: Biennial, August of odd years. **Price:** Free. **Covers:** About 150 regular and associate members that repair heavy-duty truck equipment or supply the industry. **Entries Include:** Firm name, address, phone, key personnel, coding to indicate specialties. **Arrangement:** Geographical.

20586 ■ "Truckers Walk Strike Line" in *Puget Sound Business Journal* (Vol. 29, October 24, 2008, No. 27, pp. 1)
Pub: American City Business Journals

Ed: Steve Wilhelm. **Description:** Teamsters Local 174 went on strike against Oak Harbor Freight Lines Inc. over alleged company violations of federal labor laws. The union also accuses the company of engaging directly with employees and holding mandatory meetings about contract negotiations.

STATISTICAL SOURCES

20587 ■ *RMA Annual Statement Studies*
Pub: Robert Morris Associates (RMA)

Released: Annual. **Price:** $175.00 2006-07 edition, $105.00. **Description:** Contains composite balance sheets and income statements for more than 360 industries, including the accounting, auditing, and bookkeeping industries. Also contains five years of comparative historical data for discerning trends. Includes 16 commonly used ratios, computed for most of the size groupings for nearly every industry.

20588 ■ *Standard & Poor's Industry Surveys*
Pub: Standard & Poor's Corp.

Released: Annual. **Price:** $3633.00. **Description:** Two-volume book that examines the prospects for specific industries, including trucking. Also provides analyses of trends and problems, statistical tables and charts, and comparative company analyses.

TRADE PERIODICALS

20589 ■ *American Trucker—Badger Edition*
Pub: Primedia Business

Released: Monthly. **Price:** $48. **Description:** Truck trader magazine.

20590 ■ *American Trucker—Buckeye Edition*
Pub: Primedia Business

Released: Monthly. **Price:** $48. **Description:** Truck trader magazine.

20591 ■ *American Trucker—Central States Edition*
Pub: Primedia Business

Released: Monthly. **Price:** $48; $60 other countries. **Description:** Truck trader magazine.

20592 ■ *American Trucker—Illinois Edition*
Pub: Primedia Business

Released: Monthly. **Price:** $48. **Description:** Truck Trader Magazine.

20593 ■ *American Trucker—South Central Edition*
Pub: Primedia Business

Released: Monthly. **Price:** $48. **Description:** Truck Trade magazine.

20594 ■ *Bulk Transporter*
Pub: Primedia Business Magazines
Contact: Mary Davis, Assoc. Ed.
E-mail: mary.davis@penton.com

Released: Monthly. **Description:** Magazine serving middle and upper management of private and for-hire tank fleets that carry liquid, dry, and gas bulk products.

20595 ■ *CALTRUX*
Pub: California Trucking Association
Contact: Michael Riley

Ed: Michael Riley, Editor, mriley@caltrux.org. **Released:** Monthly. **Price:** Included in membership. **Description:** Provides news, commentary, announcements, and advertising of interest to California truck fleet owners and managers. Carries legislative updates, news of developments in the state regulatory agencies, and a calendar of events.

20596 ■ *Commercial Carrier Journal*
Pub: Randall-Reilly Publishing Co.
Contact: Stacy McCants, Publisher
E-mail: smccants@rrpub.com

Released: Monthly. **Description:** Magazine containing management, maintenance, and operations information for truck and bus fleets.

20597 ■ *Fleet Equipment*
Pub: Babcox

Released: Monthly. **Description:** Magazine for equipment managers of truck, trailer, and bus fleets.

20598 ■ *Heavy Duty Trucking*
Pub: Newport Communications
Contact: Tom Berg, Equipment Ed.
E-mail: tberg@truckinginfo.com

Released: Monthly. **Price:** Free to qualified subscribers. **Description:** Magazine serving large, medium and small fleet managers whose firms operate class 6, 7 and 8 trucks in the U.S.

20599 ■ *In the Driver's Seat*
Pub: Ontario Safety League

Ed: Terry Thompson, Editor. **Released:** Monthly. **Price:** Included in membership. **Description:** Commercial driver safety newsletter.

20600 ■ *Keep on Truckin News*
Pub: Mid-West Truckers Association
Contact: Robert Jasmon

Ed: Don Schaefer, Editor, dhscubs@aol.com. **Released:** Monthly. **Price:** Included in membership. **Description:** Offers owners and operators of trucks information relating to the Association and the industry in general. Contains information on services available to members, including mass purchasing, international registration assistance, license plate procurement, drug testing, self-funded workers compensation, EPA Storm Water Permits, and group insurance plans. Reports on legislative and regulatory changes that affect the industry. Recurring features include news of members, news of research, and notices of Association activities.

20601 ■ *Land Line*
Pub: Owner-Operator Independent Drivers Association Inc.
Contact: Sandi Soendker, Managing Editor
E-mail: ooida@aol.com

Released: Monthly. **Price:** Free to qualified subscribers. **Description:** Business magazine for professional truckers.

20602 ■ *National Truck Rate Report*
Pub: U.S. Department of Agriculture
Contact: Elizabeth Longley

Ed: Alesia Swan, Editor, alesia.swan@usda.gov. **Released:** Weekly, always Wednesday. **Price:** $10, U.S. and Canada per month; $20, elsewhere per month mailed; $60, elsewhere per month faxed. **Description:** Lists truck rates per load to selected markets throughout the U.S. Also reports on trucks available in relation to shippers' needs. Recurring features include statistics on the total reported domestic and import truck shipments of fresh fruit and vegetables.

20603 ■ *SC & RA Newsletter*
Pub: Specialized Carriers & Rigging Association

Ed: Jennifer Callahan, Editor, jcallahan@scranet.org. **Released:** Weekly. **Price:** Included in membership. **Description:** Reports on current regulatory, safety, and industrial relations developments. Offers news of business opportunities. Recurring features include news of research, news of members, book reviews, and a calendar of events.

20604 ■ *Standard Trucking and Transportation Statistics*
Pub: American Trucking Associations Inc.

Ed: Bob Costello, Editor, bcostell@trucking.org. **Released:** Quarterly. **Price:** $78.75, members; $105, nonmembers. **Description:** Source for up-to-date statistics in the industry.

20605 ■ *Truck West*
Pub: Business Information Group
Contact: Lou Smrylis, Editorial Dir.
E-mail: lou@transportationmedia.ca

Released: Monthly. **Price:** $37.95 Canada taxes applicable; $66.95 U.S.; $66.95 out of country. **Description:** Magazine serving truck owners and operators in western Canada.

20606 ■ *Trucker's Connection*
Pub: Trucker's Connection Inc.
Contact: Mark Schiffmacher, CEO
E-mail: jerry@truckersconnection.com

Released: Monthly. **Price:** $26.95; $45 Canada; $90 other countries. **Description:** Trade magazine for over-the-road, long haul truck operators.

TRADE SHOWS AND CONVENTIONS

20607 ■ American Trucking Association Management Conference & Exhibition
American Trucking Association
950 N. Glebe Rd., Ste. 210
Arlington, VA 22203-4181
Ph:(703)838-1700
Co. E-mail: meetingsteam@trucking.org
URL: http://www.truckline.com

Released: Annual. **Audience:** Chief executive officers and upper level management of motor carrier companies, as well as executives from suppliers to the trucking industry. **Principal Exhibits:** Equipment, supplies, and services related to the trucking industry. **Dates and Locations:** 2011 Oct 15-18, Grapevine, TX.

20608 ■ Great American Trucking Show
Sellers Expositions
222 Pearl St., Ste. 300
New Albany, IN 47150
Ph:(812)949-9200
Free: 800-558-8767
Fax:(812)949-9600
URL: http://www.sellersexpo.com

Audience: Truck owners and operators, exempt haulers, company drivers and truck drivers for hire, aftermarket parts purchasers, purchasing agents, mechanics, fleet owner. **Principal Exhibits:** Trucks and related equipment, supplies, and services.

20609 ■ Mid-America Trucking Show
Exhibit Management Associates, Inc.
1404 Browns Ln., Ste. E
Louisville, KY 40207
Ph:(502)899-3892
Fax:(502)899-3952
Co. E-mail: clrockwell@truckingshow.com
URL: http://www.truckingshow.com

Released: Annual. **Audience:** Owner-operators, fleet operators, sales managers, and maintenance personnel. **Principal Exhibits:** Equipment, trucks, supplies, and services for the trucking industry.

20610 ■ Midwest Truck Show
Mid-West Truckers Association, Inc.
2727 N Dirksen Pkwy.
Springfield, IL 62702
Ph:(217)525-0310
Fax:(217)525-0342
Co. E-mail: info@mid-westtruckers.com
URL: http://www.mid-westtruckers.com

Released: Annual. **Audience:** Owners of trucking companies (for hire and private). **Principal Exhibits:** Trucks, trailers, financing information, computers, communication and satellite equipment insurance information, and related equipment, supplies, and services.

20611 ■ Service Specialists Association Annual Convention
Service Specialists Association
4015 Marks Rd., Ste. 2B
Medina, OH 44256
Ph:(330)725-7160
Free: 800-763-5717
Fax:(330)722-5638
Co. E-mail: trucksvc@aol.com
URL: http://www.truckservice.org

Released: Annual. **Audience:** Trade-Heavy Duty Aftermarket. **Principal Exhibits:** Exhibits related to truck repair operations, rebuilding departments, individuals who have maintained shop equipment such as hydraulic press or heat treating furnace.

20612 ■ Truckload Carriers Association
Truckload Carriers Association
555 E. Braddock Rd.
Alexandria, VA 22314
Ph:(703)838-1950
Fax:(703)836-6610
Co. E-mail: tca@truckload.org
URL: http://www.truckload.org

Released: Annual. **Principal Exhibits:** Trucking equipment, supplies, and services.

20613 ■ The Work Truck Show and Annual NTEA Convention
National Truck Equipment Association
37400 Hills Tech Dr.
Farmington Hills, MI 48331-3414
Ph:(248)489-7090
Free: 800-441-6832
Fax:(248)489-8590
Co. E-mail: info@ntea.com
URL: http://www.ntea.com

Released: Annual. **Audience:** Owners, commercial truck distributors, dealers, up fitters, manufacturers, buyers, users, sales, marketing, financial, administrative, engineers, and shop manag. **Principal Exhibits:** Chassis, commercial truck, bodies, mounted equipment, accessories, and supplies. **Dates and Locations:** 2011 Mar 08-10, Indianapolis, IN.

CONSULTANTS

20614 ■ Claude Travis & Associates
2550 Holtman Dr. NE
Grand Rapids, MI 49525-1815
Ph:(616)364-0869
Fax:(616)364-0869
Contact: Claude J. Travis Sr., Principal

Scope: Fleet consultant offering truck and fleet maintenance studies, fleet fuel economy testing and expert witness work relating to truck safety, trucks and truck products and accidents. Serves trucking companies, manufacturers of trucks and parts, government and lawyers.

LIBRARIES

20615 ■ American Truck Historical Society–Zoe James Memorial Library
PO Box 901611
Kansas City, MO 64190-1611
Ph:(816)891-9900
Fax:(816)891-9903
Co. E-mail: info@aths.org
URL: http://www.aths.org
Contact: Lee Young, Libn.

Scope: Trucks, truck companies, people in trucking. **Services:** Copying; Library open to the public. **Holdings:** 1100 books; 180 bound periodical volumes; 250 biographies; 700 company histories; 30,000 unbound periodicals; 500 slides; 100 videotapes; 100,000 photographs. **Subscriptions:** 45 journals and other serials.

20616 ■ Manitoba Trucking Association Library
25 Bunting St.
Winnipeg, MB, Canada R2X 2P5
Ph:(204)632-6600
Fax:(204)694-7134
Co. E-mail: info@trucking.mb.ca
URL: http://www.trucking.mb.ca
Contact: Bob Dolyniuk, Gen.Mgr.

Scope: Transportation. **Holdings:** Figures not available.

RESEARCH CENTERS

20617 ■ American Transportation Research Institute
950 N Glebe Rd., Ste. 210
Arlington, VA 22203
Ph:(703)838-1966
Fax:(770)432-0638
Co. E-mail: rbrewster@trucking.org
URL: http://www.atri-online.org
Contact: Rebecca Brewster, Pres./COO
E-mail: rbrewster@trucking.org
Scope: Truck-related research including driver fatigue, truck crashworthiness, and the commercial drivers license; productivity, including economics of highway transportation, regulation of weights on pavements and bridges, alternative fuels, and incident management; taxes, including measurement of pavement damage for cost allocation and rationalization of cost allocation procedures; and human resources, including the truck driver shortage, worker's compensation, and the factors affecting truck driver job satisfaction. **Publications:** Inventory of Truck Related Research (annually).

20618 ■ University of Michigan–Center for National Truck and Bus Statistics
Transportation Research Institute
2901 Baxter Rd.
Ann Arbor, MI 48109-2150
Ph:(734)764-0248
Fax:(734)764-2640
Co. E-mail: dfblower@umich.edu
URL: http://www.umtri.umich.edu/divisionPage.php?pageID=4
Contact: Dr. Daniel Blower, Dir.
E-mail: dfblower@umich.edu
Scope: Collection and analysis of statistical information on fatal accidents in the U.S. involving trucks and buses. Develops and applies multivariate statistical techniques to the identification of factors associated with accident risk. **Publications:** Truck and Bus Accident Factbook (annually). **Educational Activities:** Training opportunities, to graduate students.

20619 ■ University of New Brunswick–Transportation Group
Department of Civil Engineering
Fredericton, NB, Canada E3B 5A3
Ph:(506)453-5113
Fax:(506)453-3568
Co. E-mail: edh@unb.ca
URL: http://www.unb.ca/transpo
Contact: Dr. Eric D. Hildebrand, Coord.
E-mail: edh@unb.ca
Scope: Traffic and transportation systems planning and design, environmental impacts of transport facilities, economics of transport systems; aviation, highway and marine transport systems; policy and management of transport systems, road and motor vehicle safety. **Educational Activities:** Guest speakers from government and industry; Transportation Seminar.

Tutoring Service

START-UP INFORMATION

20620 ■ "Advantage Tutoring Center" in *Bellingham Business Journal* (Vol. February 2010, pp. 16)
Pub: Sound Publishing Inc.
Ed: Ashley Mitchell. **Description:** Profile of the newly opened Advantage Tutoring, owned by Mary and Peter Morrison. The center offers programs ranging from basic homework help to subject-specific enrichment.

20621 ■ "Fun And Easy Gold Mines" in *Small Business Opportunities* (Fall 2008)
Pub: Entrepreneur Media Inc.
Description: Twenty-five businesses that cater to the booming children's market are profiled; day care services, party planning, special events video-making, tutoring, personalized children's toys and products and other services geared toward the kids market are included.

20622 ■ *Start Your Own Tutoring and Test Prep Business: Your Step-by-Step Guide to Success*
Pub: Entrepreneur Press
Ed: Rich Mintzer. **Released:** September 9, 2010. **Price:** $17.95. **Description:** Are you an advocate of higher learning? Do you enjoy teaching others? Are you interested in starting a business that makes money and a positive impact? Keys for starting a successful tutoring and test preparation small business are presented.

ASSOCIATIONS AND OTHER ORGANIZATIONS

20623 ■ Independent Educational Consultants Association
3251 Old Lee Hwy., Ste. 510
Fairfax, VA 22030-1504
Ph:(703)591-4850
Free: 800-808-IECA
Fax:(703)591-4860
Co. E-mail: info@iecaonline.com
URL: http://www.iecaonline.com
Contact: Mark Sklarow, Exec. Dir.
Description: Represents the interests of established educational consultants. Brings family the knowledge and skills of an experienced professional. Gives advice to students with special circumstances such as learning or physical disabilities, emotional or behavioral issues. Helps members update knowledge and maintain skills through meetings, workshops, training programs, and information exchanges with colleges, schools, programs, and other consultants. Members are required to maintain the highest standards of ethical practice. **Publications:** Directory (annual).

REFERENCE WORKS

20624 ■ "An Educated Play on China" in *Barron's* (Vol. 88, June 30, 2008, No. 26, pp. M6)
Pub: Dow Jones & Co., Inc.
Ed: Mohammed Hadi. **Description:** New Oriental Education & Technology Group sells English-language courses to an increasingly competitive Chinese workforce that values education. The shares in this company have been weighed down by worries on the impact of the Beijing Olympics on enrollment and the Sichuan earthquake. These shares could be a great way to get exposure to the long-term growth in China.

20625 ■ "The Future Is Another Country; Higher Education" in *The Economist* (Vol. 390, January 3, 2009, No. 8612, pp. 43)
Pub: The Economist Newspaper Inc.
Description: Due to the growth of the global corporation, more ambitious students are studying at universities abroad; the impact of this trend is discussed.

20626 ■ "Pre-K Pressure" in *Hawaii Business* (Vol. 53, October 2007, No. 4, pp. 32)
Pub: Hawaii Business Publishing
Ed: David K. Choo. **Description:** Kindergarten admission in Hawaii is becoming more competitive. Parents, for example, prepare their children for the kindergarten admissions process by bringing them to the schools before the interview or by paying for tutorial services. The impacts of increased competition in school admissions on the life of Hawaiian children are discussed.

20627 ■ "Trend: Tutors to Help You Pump Up the Staff" in *Business Week* (September 22, 2008, No. 4100, pp. 45)
Pub: McGraw-Hill Companies, Inc.
Ed: Reena Janaj. **Description:** High-level managers are turning to innovation coaches in an attempt to obtain advice on how to better sell new concepts within their companies. Individuals as well as consulting firms are now offering this service.

TRADE PERIODICALS

20628 ■ *DETC News*
Pub: Distance Education & Training Council
Contact: Sally R. Welch
Ed: Sally R. Welch, Editor, sally@detc.org. **Released:** 2/year. **Description:** Discusses issues pertaining to distance study education and reports activities of the Council. Recurring features include news of research, book reviews, news of members, and a calendar of events.

20629 ■ *Exceptional Children*
Pub: Council for Exceptional Children
Ed: Margo Mastropieri, Editor. **Released:** Quarterly. **Price:** $75; $80 Canada; $110 other countries; $25 single issue; $155 institutions libraries; $160 institutions, Canada; $190 institutions, other countries; $130 two years; $135 Canada two years; $190 libraries two years. **Description:** Peer-reviewed journal about the education and development of infants, toddlers, children and youth with exceptionalities. disabled.

20630 ■ *Teaching Exceptional Children*
Pub: Council for Exceptional Children
Ed: Alec Peck, PhD, Editor, peck@bc.edu. **Released:** 6/yr. **Price:** $80; $135 two years; $90 two years Canada; $150 two years Canada; $210 out of country foreign-air printed matter; $355 out of country two years, foreign-air printed matter; $30 institutions single copy; $175 institutions; $295 two years institutional; $185 Canada. **Description:** Peer-reviewed journal exploring practical methods for teaching students who have exceptionalities and those who are gifted and talented.

FRANCHISES AND BUSINESS OPPORTUNITIES

20631 ■ ABC Tutors In Home Tutoring
7234 W 151st St.
Overland Park, KS 66223
Ph:(913)961-7800
Fax:(913)685-0533
No. of Franchise Units: 4. **No. of Company-Owned Units:** 1. **Founded:** 2004. **Franchised:** 2005. **Description:** Academic tutoring. **Equity Capital Needed:** $29,500-$52,500. **Franchise Fee:** $19,500. **Royalty Fee:** 4-6%. **Financial Assistance:** Limited in-house. **Training:** Provides 3 days of onsite training with ongoing support.

20632 ■ Academy for Mathematics & English
20 Wertheim Ct., Unit 12
Richmond Hill, ON, Canada L4B 3A8
Ph:(905)731-0404
Fax:(905)731-6178
Co. E-mail: balti@acadfor.com
URL: http://www.tutoringacademy.ca
No. of Franchise Units: 35. **No. of Company-Owned Units:** 2. **Founded:** 1993. **Franchised:** 1993. **Description:** Math tutoring system. Tutoring is also offered for English, Physics and Chemistry. **Equity Capital Needed:** $120,000-$150,000. **Franchise Fee:** $35,000. **Training:** 3 week initial training and ongoing support.

20633 ■ Chyten Educational Services
1723 Massachusetts Ave.
Lexington, MA 02420
Ph:(508)720-9827
No. of Franchise Units: 23. **No. of Company-Owned Units:** 4. **Founded:** 1999. **Franchised:** 2007. **Description:** Tutoring & test preparation. **Equity Capital Needed:** $113,900-$2340500. **Franchise Fee:** $37,500. **Royalty Fee:** 10%. **Financial Assistance:** Third party financing available. **Training:** Offers training up to 10 days at corporate headquarters, up to 3 days at franchisees location and ongoing support provided.

20634 ■ Club Z! In-Home Tutoring
Club Z! Inc.
15310 Aberly Dr., Ste. 185
Tampa, FL 33647
Ph:(813)931-5516
Free: 800-434-2582
Fax:(813)932-2485
Co. E-mail: leads@clubztutoring.com
URL: http://www.clubztutoring.com
No. of Franchise Units: 412. **No. of Company-Owned Units:** 1. **Founded:** 1995. **Franchised:**

1997. **Description:** In-home tutoring services. **Equity Capital Needed:** $32,500. **Franchise Fee:** $24,500. **Financial Assistance:** No. **Training:** Yes.

20635 ■ Huntington Center Services
Huntington Learning Centers, Inc.
496 Kinderkamack Rd.
Oradell, NJ 07649
Ph:(201)261-8400
Free: 800-653-8400
Co. E-mail: franchise@huntingtonlearningcenter.com
URL: http://www.huntingtonfranchise.com
No. of Franchise Units: 375. **No. of Company-Owned Units:** 33. **Founded:** 1977. **Franchised:** 1985. **Description:** Provides individualized instruction to school-aged children and adults in remedial and speed reading, study skills, spelling, phonics, mathematics, and Scholastic Aptitude Test (SAT) preparation. **Equity Capital Needed:** Total investment range $211,750-$377,450. **Franchise Fee:** $43,000. **Financial Assistance:** Third party financing. **Training:** Training program, provides detailed demographic data for desired location, site selection and start-up assistance.

20636 ■ Kumon Math and Reading Centres
640 Applewood Crescent
Vaughan, ON, Canada L4K 4B4
Ph:(416)490-1434
Free: 888-897-0789
Fax:(905)738-1765
Co. E-mail: franchisecanada@kumon.com
URL: http://www.kumon.com
No. of Franchise Units: 331. **No. of Company-Owned Units:** 4. **Founded:** 1988. **Franchised:** 1988. **Description:** Provides an individualized after school math and reading program for students. **Equity Capital Needed:** $50,000-$100,000. **Franchise Fee:** $1,000. **Training:** Yes.

20637 ■ The Learning Experience
4855 N. Technology Way, Ste. 700
Boca Raton, FL 33431
Ph:(561)886-6400
Fax:(561)886-6433
Co. E-mail: franchise@tlecorp.com
URL: http://www.thelearningexperience.com
No. of Franchise Units: 96. **No. of Company-Owned Units:** 19. **Founded:** 2001. **Franchised:** 2003. **Description:** The Learning Experience is one of the fastest growing childcare center operators in the Northeastern United States with current expansion in the Michigan and North Carolina markets. Through the development of detailed franchisee training, meticulous operational manuals and an unparalleled student curriculum, The Learning Experience remains on the cutting edge within the childcare industry. **Equity Capital Needed:** $150,000. **Franchise Fee:** $60,000. **Financial Assistance:** Helps identify third party lenders to provide financing, and assistance with developing loan packages. **Training:** Provides an in-depth orientation on every aspect of the business, including a sophisticated but user-friendly computer system. Offers reinforcement and support systems throughout tenure as a franchisee.

20638 ■ Mathnasium Learning Centers
5120 W Goldleaf Cir., Ste. 130
Los Angeles, CA 90056
Ph:(323)421-8000
Free: 877-531-MATH
Fax:(310)943-2111
Co. E-mail: franchise@mathnasium.com
URL: http://www.mathnasium.com
No. of Franchise Units: 313. **No. of Company-Owned Units:** 1. **Founded:** 2002. **Franchised:** 2003. **Description:** Mathnasium provides the most effective mathematics in education available to grade school children after school, in an attractive neighborhood learning center environment. The Mathnasium Method, developed over 30 years of hands-on experience, is engaging for students and builds confidence as it builds real understanding. Created to address a real need in the market by a team with unparalleled success in the industry, the business model is strong and the opportunity is now. **Equity Capital Needed:** $78,300-$107,500 initial investment range. **Franchise Fee:** $19,500. **Financial Assistance:** No. **Training:** Complete initial training at corporate headquarters and ongoing support.

20639 ■ Scholars Education Centre
Scholars Canada
101 N Syndicate
Thunder Bay, ON, Canada P7C 3V4
Ph:(807)345-2661
Fax:(807)768-5226
Co. E-mail: parry@scholarscanada.com
URL: http://www.scholarscanada.com
No. of Franchise Units: 9. **No. of Company-Owned Units:** 3. **Founded:** 1998. **Franchised:** 2000. **Description:** Offers Personalized Programs targeting the individual needs of students and their families. Credible, standardized Canadian assessments are used to obtain the information needed to personalize the student's program. **Equity Capital Needed:** $50,000-$80,000 + applicable taxes. **Franchise Fee:** $25,000 + applicable taxes. **Training:** 2 weeks training provided.

20640 ■ Sylvan Learning Center
Sylvan Learning, Inc.
1001 Fleet St.
Baltimore, MD 21202-4382
Ph:(410)843-6844
Free: 800-284-8214
Fax:(410)843-6265
Co. E-mail: sylvanfranchise@Educate.com
URL: http://www.sylvanfranchise.com
No. of Franchise Units: 890. **No. of Company-Owned Units:** 40. **Founded:** 1979. **Franchised:** 1980. **Description:** Offers services that supplements education programs in reading, mathematics, and other subjects for both children and adults. **Equity Capital Needed:** $188,000-$305,000. **Franchise Fee:** $42,000-$48,000. **Financial Assistance:** Third party financing available to qualified applicants. **Training:** Training at corporate headquarters and locally. Basic training, regional training, regional meetings, and annual conferences.

20641 ■ Tutoring Club
Tutoring Club, LLC
11241 Eastern Ave.
Henderson, NV 89052
Free: 888-674-6425
No. of Franchise Units: 126. **No. of Company-Owned Units:** 1. **Founded:** 1991. **Franchised:** 1999. **Description:** Center providing individualized after-school instruction. **Equity Capital Needed:** $83,400-$126,300. **Franchise Fee:** $34,500. **Royalty Fee:** 10%. **Financial Assistance:** Third party financing available. **Training:** Offers 2 weeks at headquarters, 1 day onsite with ongoing support.

LIBRARIES

20642 ■ American Federation of Teachers Library
555 New Jersey Ave., NW
Washington, DC 20001
Ph:(202)879-4400
Co. E-mail: online@aft.org
URL: http://www.aft.org
Contact: Bernadette Bailey
Scope: Labor, education. **Services:** Library open to members only. **Holdings:** 1400 books. **Subscriptions:** 300 journals and other serials; 11 newspapers.

20643 ■ Instructional Media Services, Inc.
PO Box 711
Merton, WI 53056
Ph:(262)369-9200
Fax:(262)538-1491
Co. E-mail: imsinfo@imseducates.com
URL: http://www.imseducates.com
Scope: Educational curriculum. **Services:** Center open to the public. **Holdings:** 20,000 16mm educational films; 10,000 video cassettes; 100 laser discs; 2500 museum specimens; miniature dioramas; Jonas miniature models; mounted plants and animals; museum artifacts. **Subscriptions:** 10 journals and other serials.

20644 ■ Oakland University–School of Education and Human Services–Educational Resources Laboratory (350 P)
350 Pawley Hall
Rochester Hills, MI 48309-4494
Ph:(248)370-4230
Fax:(248)370-4226
Co. E-mail: amphelps@oakland.edu
URL: http://www.oakland.edu/erl
Contact: Adelaide Phelps, Coord.
Scope: Education - general, pre-school-12th grade, multi-cultural diversity, career; children's literature. **Services:** Wireless computer lab; presentation equipment; laminator; book binder; poster maker; guest memberships with borrowing privileges available for purchase. **Holdings:** 30,000 books, journals, videotapes, DVDs, digital cameras and camcorders, and desktop and laptop computers. **Subscriptions:** 20 journals and other serials.

20645 ■ Traverse City Regional Educational Media Center–REMC 2 - Central
1101 Red Dr.
Traverse City, MI 49684-4465
Ph:(616)922-6217
Fax:(616)922-7870
Co. E-mail: swyckoff@tbaisd.k12.mi.us
URL: http://www.tbaisd.k12.mi.us
Contact: Mike Porter, Ctrl.Dir.
Scope: Educational curriculum; print and non-print media and materials. **Services:** Center open to the public with restrictions. **Holdings:** 15,000 videocassettes.

20646 ■ Wisconsin Literacy Resource Network
310 Price Pl.
PO Box 7874
Madison, WI 53707
Ph:(608)266-1272
Fax:(608)266-1690
Co. E-mail: muellej@board.tec.wi.us
URL: http://www.wtcsystem.edu/
Contact: Mark Johnson, Educ.Dir.
Scope: Literacy, basic education. **Holdings:** Figures not available.

Typesetting Business

ASSOCIATIONS AND OTHER ORGANIZATIONS

20647 ■ Printing Brokerage/Buyers Association
PO Box 744
Palm Beach, FL 33480
Ph:(215)821-6581
Free: 877-585-7141
Fax:(561)845-7130
URL: http://www.pbba.org
Description: Printing buyers/brokers/distributors, printers, typographers, binders, envelope and book manufacturers, packagers, color separation houses, pre-press service organizations, and related companies in the graphic arts industry. Promotes understanding, cooperation, and interaction among members while obtaining the highest standard of professionalism in the graphic arts industry. Gathers information on current technology in the graphic communications industry. Sponsors seminars for members to learn how to work with buyers, brokers and printers; also conducts technical and management seminars. Maintains referral service; compiles statistics. Conducts charitable programs. **Publications:** *BrokerRatings* (quarterly); *Corporate Print Buyer* (quarterly); *Hot Markets Annual Rankings of Buyers, Print Products and Geographies* (annual); *The Printer's Official Complete Guide to e-Everything-and How to Prevail!*; *Printing Brokerage Directory and Sourcebook* (annual).

20648 ■ Type Directors Club
347 W 36th St., Ste. 603
New York, NY 10018
Ph:(212)633-8943
Fax:(212)633-8944
Co. E-mail: director@tdc.org
URL: http://tdc.org
Contact: Carol Wahler, Exec. Dir.
Description: Serves as a professional society of typographic designers, type directors, and teachers of typography; sustaining members are individuals with interests in typographic education. Seeks to stimulate research and disseminate information. Provides speakers, classes and offers presentations on history and new developments in typography. **Publications:** *Typography 28* .

REFERENCE WORKS

20649 ■ "Agfa: M-Press Leopard Debuts" in *American Printer* (Vol. 128, June 1, 2011, No. 6)
Pub: Penton Media Inc.
Description: M-Press Leopard is a new version of the machine that offers advanced ink jet technology at a lower price point. Agfa Graphics introduced the new version that allows for new applications that require more manual handling.

20650 ■ "Avanti Hosts Users Conference" in *American Printer* (Vol. 128, July 1, 2011, No. 7)
Pub: Penton Media Inc.
Description: Avanti Computer Systems Ltd. hosted its 19th annual users conference in Washington DC. In-plant and commercial printers were in attendance.

20651 ■ "Avoid a Tablet Generation Gap" in *American Printer* (Vol. 128, July 1, 2011, No. 7)
Pub: Penton Media Inc.
Description: Individuals between the ages of 18-34 are the only generation that is more likely to own a laptop computer or netbook insead of a desktop computer. Statistical data included.

20652 ■ "Boston Printer Celebrates 60th Anniversary" in *American Printer* (Vol. 128, August 1, 2011, No. 8)
Pub: Penton Media Inc.
Description: Shawmut printing is celebrating its 60th anniversary. The family business plans to increase efficiency through automation, monitoring job progress online from start to finish.

20653 ■ "Business is Unbelievable" in *American Printer* (Vol. 128, August 1, 2011, No. 8)
Pub: Penton Media Inc.
Ed: Katherine O'Brien. **Description:** Most commercial printers have seen an increase in business over the last year.

20654 ■ "ContiTech Celebrates 100 Years" in *American Printer* (Vol. 128, July 1, 2011, No. 7)
Pub: Penton Media Inc.
Description: ContiTech celebrated 100 years in business. The firm started in 1911 after developing the first elastic printing blanket. Other milestones for the firm include its manufacturing process for compressible printing blankets, the Conti-Air brand and climate-neutral printing blankets.

20655 ■ "Crouser Offers UV Coating Price Report" in *American Printer* (Vol. 128, June 1, 2011, No. 6)
Pub: Penton Media Inc.
Description: Crouser and Associates will offer the 'Pricing Off-Line UV Coating' report that provides background information on all three types of protective printing coatings and price guidance. The report will also offer comparisons of four popular types of offline equipment.

20656 ■ "Customer OKs on Press" in *American Printer* (Vol. 128, August 1, 2011, No. 8)
Pub: Penton Media Inc.
Description: Printers discuss the value of having customers meet at the plant in order to okay print colors for projects.

20657 ■ "Design Center Shows Quality of Digital Paper" in *American Printer* (Vol. 128, June 1, 2011, No. 6)
Pub: Penton Media Inc.
Description: Digital Design Centers allows printers to customize marketing tools in order to promote their own digital printing capabilities.

20658 ■ "Digital Printing Walks the Plank" in *American Printer* (Vol. 128, August 1, 2011, No. 8)
Pub: Penton Media Inc.
Description: Digital print manufacturing is discussed.

20659 ■ "Feeding the Elephants While Searching for Greener Pastures" in *American Printer* (Vol. 128, July 1, 2011, No. 7)
Pub: Penton Media Inc.
Ed: Bob Rosen. **Description:** Three steps to help printers to build a new business while facing the challenges to the existing business are outlined.

20660 ■ "First U.S. :M-Press Tiger with Inline Screen Printing" in *American Printer* (Vol. 128, June 1, 2011, No. 6)
Pub: Penton Media Inc.
Description: Graphic Tech located in California bought :M-Press Tiger, the first in North America with an inline screen printing unit.

20661 ■ "Flint Group Raises Prices" in *American Printer* (Vol. 128, August 1, 2011, No. 8)
Pub: Penton Media Inc.
Description: Due to the rising cost for raw materials, Flint Group is raising their prices for inks and coatings in North American.

20662 ■ "Four Exhibition Considerations" in *American Printer* (Vol. 128, August 1, 2011, No. 8)
Pub: Penton Media Inc.
Description: Four questions to ask at the Graph Expo will help printers improve their own business.

20663 ■ "Fujifilm Invites Printers to Take the 'Onset Challenge'" in *American Printer* (Vol. 128, August 1, 2011, No. 8)
Pub: Penton Media Inc.
Description: Fujifilm North American Corporation's Graphic Systems Division offers a new five-step product selection and return-on-investment calculator for the Onset family of wide-format printers.

20664 ■ "Guide to Carbon Footprinting" in *American Printer* (Vol. 128, June 1, 2011, No. 6)
Pub: Penton Media Inc.
Description: PrintCity Alliance published its new report, 'Carbon Footprint & Energy Reduction for Graphic Industry Value Chain.' The report aims to help improve the environmental performance of printers, converters, publishers, brand owners and their suppliers.

20665 ■ "How to Save Money on Ink" in *American Printer* (Vol. 128, July 1, 2011, No. 7)
Pub: Penton Media Inc.
Description: Tips are shared to help graphic arts and printing companies save money on raw materials. Factors to consider once the type of ink is decided are also outlined.

20666 ■ "Improving the USPS" in *American Printer* (Vol. 128, July 1, 2011, No. 7)
Pub: Penton Media Inc.
Description: National Postal Forum held in San Diego, California May 1-4, 2011 hosted 4,000 attendees. Highlights of the event are provided.

20667 ■ "Industry/Events 2011" in *American Printer* (Vol. 128, July 1, 2011, No. 7)
Pub: Penton Media Inc.
Description: PMA, the Worldwide Community of Imaging Association launched its new CliQ with how-to tips, product reviews and monthly photo contests. PMA formed a partnership with the Consumer Electronics Association to make changes to this year's annual convention.

20668 ■ "Interchangeable or Irreplaceable?" in *American Printer* (Vol. 128, August 1, 2011, No. 8)
Pub: Penton Media Inc.
Description: Creating and maintaining customers is important for all graphic design and printing companies. Tips are shared to help maintain good customer satisfaction and repeat business.

20669 ■ "IPEX Moves to London Venue" in *American Printer* (Vol. 128, July 1, 2011, No. 7)
Pub: Penton Media Inc.
Description: IPES 2014 is being relocated to London's ExCeL International Exhibition and Conference Centre from March 26 to April 2, 2014.

20670 ■ "JDF Integration: 3 Key Tips" in *American Printer* (Vol. 128, August 1, 2011, No. 8)
Pub: Penton Media Inc.
Description: Three tips for implementing cross-vendor integrations are outlined.

20671 ■ "KBA, Graphic Art System Partner on Cold Foil" in *American Printer* (Vol. 128, June 1, 2011, No. 6)
Pub: Penton Media Inc.
Description: KBA North America has partnered with Graphic Art System to retrofit and equip presses with cold foil machines.

20672 ■ "Kodak Offers Cloud-Based Operating Option" in *American Printer* (Vol. 128, June 1, 2011, No. 6)
Pub: Penton Media Inc.
Description: Kodak partnered with VMware to offer its first Virtual Operating Environment option for Kodak Unified Workflow Solutions. The new feature enables cost savings, increased efficiency and failover protection.

20673 ■ *Literary Market Place*
Pub: Information Today Inc.
Contact: Thomas H. Hogan, Pres. & Publisher
Released: Annual, Latest edition 2012. **Price:** $339, individuals 2-volume set/softbound plus $25 shipping/handling; $305.10, individuals first time standing order. **Covers:** Over 12,500 firms or organizations offering services related to the publishing industry, including book publishers in the United States and Canada who issued three or more books during the preceding year, plus a small press section of publishers who publish less than three titles per year or those who are self-published. Also included: book printers and binders; book clubs; book trade and literary associations; selected syndicates, newspapers, periodicals, and radio and TV programs that use book reviews or book publishing news; translators and literary agents. **Entries Include:** For publishers—Company name, address, phone, address for orders, principal executives, editorial directors, and managers, date founded, number of titles in previous year, number of backlist titles in print, types of books published, ISBN prefixes, representatives, imprints, and affiliations. For suppliers, etc.—Listings usually show firm name, address, phone, executives, services, etc. **Arrangement:** Classified by line of business. **Indexes:** Principal index is 35,000-item combined index of publishers, publications, and personnel; several sections have geographical and/or subject indexes; translators are indexed by source and target language.

20674 ■ "Metallics Education" in *American Printer* (Vol. 128, June 1, 2011, No. 6)
Pub: Penton Media Inc.
Description: Guide 'Curious About Print: Your Guide to the World of Curious Metallics' provides hints and tips to help printers maximize selection and reproduction, advice on working with metallic and UV inks, and recommendations for gaining quantity without sacrificing quality.

20675 ■ "MFSA Officially Endorses Five-Day USPS Delivery" in *American Printer* (Vol. 128, August 1, 2011, No. 8)
Pub: Penton Media Inc.
Description: Board of Directors of the Mailing and Fulfillment Service Association (MFSA) voted to support the US Postal Service's move to five-day delivery service.

20676 ■ "New Approach to Mechanical Binding" in *American Printer* (Vol. 128, July 1, 2011, No. 7)
Pub: Penton Media Inc.
Description: EcoBinder coil binding system from Kugler-Womako eliminates traditional plastic combs or wire spiral with the use of 22-mm wide printable paper rings.

20677 ■ "OCE Boosts JetStream Productivity" in *American Printer* (Vol. 128, August 1, 2011, No. 8)
Pub: Penton Media Inc.
Description: New Oce JetStream 1400 and 3000 digital full-color inkjet presses are profiled. The new models promise higher speed to grow print volume.

20678 ■ "One World" in *American Printer* (Vol. 128, August 1, 2011, No. 8)
Pub: Penton Media Inc.
Description: Graph Expo will highlight entrepreneurs focused on the connection between content, technology and business models.

20679 ■ "Paper a la Carte" in *American Printer* (Vol. 128, June 1, 2011, No. 6)
Pub: Penton Media Inc.
Description: Blurb, the online publishing platform, launched ProLine which features Mohawk Superfine and Mohawk proPhoto papers. ProLine papers offer two finishes: Pearl Photo and Uncoated.

20680 ■ "Paper Choices Made Simple" in *American Printer* (Vol. 128, June 1, 2011, No. 6)
Pub: Penton Media Inc.
Description: Choices, a new initiative by Boise, provides professional guidance to help customers and consumers make informed, effective choices for using paper.

20681 ■ "Paper Replaces PVC for Gift Cards" in *American Printer* (Vol. 128, June 1, 2011, No. 6)
Pub: Penton Media Inc.
Description: Monadnock Envi Card Stock replaces paper for gift cards, loyalty cards, membership cards, hotel keys and durable signage. This renewable wood fiber alternative to PVC card materials comes from Monadock Paper Mills.

20682 ■ "Prices Continue to Rise" in *American Printer* (Vol. 128, June 1, 2011, No. 6)
Pub: Penton Media Inc.
Description: Prices were increased by both Flint Group and Ashland Performance Materials by 7-10 percent and 5-15 percent respectively.

20683 ■ "Printers to the Trade" in *American Printer* (Vol. 128, July 1, 2011, No. 7)
Pub: Penton Media Inc.
Description: Wholesale printing is discussed. Two wholesale printers share insight into their success, from business philosophies in general to practices that build strong relationships.

20684 ■ "QR Codes: OK, I Get It Now" in *American Printer* (Vol. 128, July 1, 2011, No. 7)
Pub: Penton Media Inc.
Description: QR Code technology is discussed. It is up to the user to enter the proper QR Code.

20685 ■ "Reducing the Book's Carbon Footpring" in *American Printer* (Vol. 128, July 1, 2011, No. 7)
Pub: Penton Media Inc.
Description: Green Press Initiative's Book Industry Environmental Council is working to achieve a 20 percent reduction in the book industry's carbon footprint by 2020. The Council is made up of publishers, printers, paper suppliers, and non-governmental organizations.

20686 ■ "Root, Root, Root for the P.A. Hutchison Co." in *American Printer* (Vol. 128, August 1, 2011, No. 8)
Pub: Penton Media Inc.
Description: The P.A. Hutchison Company celebrate 100 years in the printing business. President and CEO Chris Hutchison presented awards to employees, however employees also presented awards to Chris and his father as Employer of the Century.

20687 ■ "Sappi Awards Gold NA Printers of the Year Winners" in *American Printer* (Vol. 128, July 1, 2011, No. 7)
Pub: Penton Media Inc.
Description: Sappi Fine Paper North America honored ten gold winners of its 14th North American Printers of the Year awards. Each gold winning printer will receive $20,000 to support marketing and brand initiatives.

20688 ■ "Seeing the Light" in *American Printer* (Vol. 128, July 1, 2011, No. 7)
Pub: Penton Media Inc.
Description: Four printing demos on sheetfed, digital, label and pad printing equipment were highlighted at the Fifth UV Days held in Stuttgart, Germany in May 2011.

20689 ■ "Seven Tips for Continuous Improvement" in *American Printer* (Vol. 128, July 1, 2011, No. 7)
Pub: Penton Media Inc.
Description: Seven tips are given to help any graphic arts or printing company improve by integrating lean manufacturing into operations.

20690 ■ "Something Old and Something New" in *American Printer* (Vol. 128, August 1, 2011, No. 8)
Pub: Penton Media Inc.
Description: Trade journalists and industry analysts were invited to Fujifilm North America Corporation's Hanover Park, Illinois facility to view it's sheetfed inkjet press. The JPress 720 is the first and only of its kind in the world.

20691 ■ "Successful First Year for Twin Rivers" in *American Printer* (Vol. 128, June 1, 2011, No. 6)
Pub: Penton Media Inc.
Description: Profile of Twin Rivers located in Maine. The firm manufactured 380,000 tons of free sheet and hybrid-groundwood papers in its first year.

20692 ■ "Tic-Tac-Show" in *American Printer* (Vol. 128, August 1, 2011, No. 8)
Pub: Penton Media Inc.
Description: Graph Expo has become the US print industry's main event. There will be as many as 500 exhibitors at this year's event and the Graphic Arts Show Company lists over 30 co-located events as well as 53 new sessions in the seminar program's 28 education categories.

20693 ■ "Transcontinental to Exchange Assets with Quad/Graphics" in *American Printer* (Vol. 128, August 1, 2011, No. 8)
Pub: Penton Media Inc.
Description: Transcontinental Inc. and Quad/Graphics Inc. entered into an agreement where Transcontinental will indirectly acquire all shares of Quad Graphics Canada Inc.

20694 ■ "Try a Little Social Media" in *American Printer* (Vol. 128, June 1, 2011, No. 6)
Pub: Penton Media Inc.
Description: Social media helps keep Ussery Printing on customers radar. Jim David, VP of marketing for the firm, states that 350 people following them on Facebook are from the local area.

20695 ■ "Use Ink Presets to Minimize Makeready" in *American Printer* (Vol. 128, July 1, 2011, No. 7)
Pub: Penton Media Inc.
Description: Automatic registration systems enable most printers to be in register very quickly after press startup. If the paper, ink and press time wasted during makeready can be reduced, these savings will flow directly to the bottom line. Ink presetting as an economical solution to set color quickly is a trend that continues to gain momentum.

20696 ■ "UV Suppliers Form Strategic Alliance" in *American Printer* (Vol. 128, June 1, 2011, No. 6)
Pub: Penton Media Inc.
Description: British ultra-violent curing systems developer Integration Technology Ltd. formed a strategic alliance with UV technology provider IST Metz GmbH of Germany in order to offer a complete line of UV solutions for the printing industry.

20697 ■ "Web to Print" in *American Printer* (Vol. 128, August 1, 2011, No. 8)
Pub: Penton Media Inc.
Description: Jerry Kennelly, CEO and founder of Tweak.com believes that Web-to-Design is middleware with no content. His firm offers an easy to use interface that flows right into the printer's workflow with no additional costs.

STATISTICAL SOURCES

20698 ■ *RMA Annual Statement Studies*
Pub: Robert Morris Associates (RMA)
Released: Annual. **Price:** $175.00 2006-07 edition, $105.00. **Description:** Contains composite balance sheets and income statements for more than 360 industries, including the accounting, auditing, and bookkeeping industries. Also contains five years of comparative historical data for discerning trends. Includes 16 commonly used ratios, computed for most of the size groupings for nearly every industry.

TRADE PERIODICALS

20699 ■ *American Typecasting Fellowship Newsletter*
Pub: American Typecasting Fellowship
Ed: Richard L. Hopkins, Editor. **Released:** Periodic. **Description:** Devoted to conveying information on the preservation of equipment and technology related to metal typecasting. Covers type founding, type design, matrix making, and letterpress printing. Recurring features include letters to the editor and news of members.

20700 ■ *Imaging News*
Pub: Diamond Research Corp.
Contact: Arthur S. Diamond, Editor & Publisher
Released: Monthly. **Price:** $175. **Description:** Trade magazine covering imaging materials, technologies, and markets. Available online only.

TRADE SHOWS AND CONVENTIONS

20701 ■ Graphics of the Americas
Printing Association of Florida, Inc.
6275 Hazeltine National Dr.
Orlando, FL 32822
Ph:(407)240-8009
Free: 800-749-4855
Fax:(407)240-8333
Co. E-mail: agaither@pafgraf.org
URL: http://www.pafgraf.org
Released: Annual. **Audience:** Graphics arts trade. **Principal Exhibits:** Graphic arts and specialty printing equipment, supplies, and services.

LIBRARIES

20702 ■ Carnegie-Mellon University–University Libraries I Special Collections
Hunt Library
4909 Frew St.
Pittsburgh, PA 15213-3890
Ph:(412)268-6622
Fax:(412)268-6945
Co. E-mail: mj0g@andrew.cmu.edu
URL: http://www.library.cmu.edu
Contact: Mary Kay Johnsen, Spec.Coll.Libn.
Scope: History of printing, 19th-century English literature, landmark books of science. **Services:** Library open to the public. **Holdings:** 12,000 books.

20703 ■ Cleveland Public Library–Literature Department
Main Bldg., 2nd Fl.
325 Superior Ave.
Cleveland, OH 44114-1271
Ph:(216)623-2881
Co. E-mail: literature@cpl.org
URL: http://www.cpl.org/TheLibrary/SubjectsCollections/Literature.aspx
Contact: Ron Antonucci, Mgr.
Scope: Fiction, drama and theater, film, radio, television, poetry, essays, humor, oratory and public speaking, craft of writing, literary criticism and biography, classical Greek and Latin, linguistics, journalism, book trade, printing, publishing, Library and information science. **Services:** Department open to the public. **Holdings:** 500,000 volumes; 11,368 bound periodical volumes; 23,000 theater programs and playbills; 16,000 titles of microform editions of plays and miscellanea; 190 vertical files. **Subscriptions:** 825 journals and other serials.

20704 ■ Free Library of Philadelphia–Social Science & History Department
1901 Vine St.
Philadelphia, PA 19103
Ph:(215)686-5396
Fax:(215)563-3628
URL: http://www.freelibrary.org
Contact: Jim DeWalt, Hd.
Scope: History, biography, social sciences, law, travels and geography, archeology, anthropology, sports and games. **Services:** Interlibrary loan. **Holdings:** 228,000 volumes; 53,900 pamphlets; 35 VF drawers of clippings. **Subscriptions:** 610 journals and other serials.

20705 ■ Grolier Club of New York Library
47 E. 60th St.
New York, NY 10022
Ph:(212)838-6690
Fax:(212)838-2445
Co. E-mail: ejh@grolierclub.org
URL: http://www.grolierclub.org
Contact: Eric Holzenberg, Dir.
Scope: Bibliography, history of printing, book-collecting, bookselling, arts of the book. **Services:** Library open to the public with restrictions. **Holdings:** 100,000 volumes; 5000 prints and portraits; bookplates. **Subscriptions:** 100 journals and other serials.

20706 ■ Rochester Institute of Technology–Melbert B. Cary, Jr. Graphic Arts Collection
Wallace Memorial Library
90 Lomb Memorial Dr.
Rochester, NY 14623-5604
Ph:(585)475-2408
Fax:(585)475-6900
Co. E-mail: dppwml@rit.edu
URL: http://library.rit.edu/cary
Contact: David Pankow, Cur.
Scope: Printing history, type specimens, typography, book arts, press books, calligraphy, papermaking, graphic arts, bookbinding. **Services:** Copying (limited); collection open to the public. **Holdings:** 50,000 books; 20 VF drawers of clippings; ephemera; pamphlets; 50 boxes of posters, broadsides, drawings; 400 boxes of correspondence and manuscript material. **Subscriptions:** 20 journals and other serials.

20707 ■ Yale University–Arts Library I Special Collections
Robert B. Haas Family Arts Library, Lower Level
180 York St.
PO Box 208318
New Haven, CT 06520-8318
Ph:(203)432-4439
Fax:(203)432-0549
Co. E-mail: jae.rossman@yale.edu
URL: http://www.library.yale.edu/arts/specialcollections
Contact: Jae Jennifer Rossman, Asst.Dir., Spec.Coll.
Scope: Typography, book illustration and design, bookbinding, papermaking, bookplates, private presses, artists' books, conceptual books, and fine printing. **Services:** Collection open to the public. **Holdings:** 20,000 books; prints and broadsides; type specimens; archive of student printing, including masters' theses from School of Graphic Design and School of Photography at Yale; 1 million bookplates; Japanese prints; stage and costume designs. **Subscriptions:** 20 journals and other serials.

ASSOCIATIONS AND OTHER ORGANIZATIONS

20708 ■ AFL-CIO I SEIU I District 925
1914 N 34th St., Ste. 100
Seattle, WA 98103
Ph:(206)322-3010
Free: (866)734-8925
Fax:(206)547-5581
Co. E-mail: khart@seiu925.org
URL: http://www.seiu925.org
Contact: Karen Hart, Pres.

Description: National union of secretaries, stenographers, typists, clerks, and other office, technical, and professional workers in the U.S. Promotes collective bargaining for office workers and sponsors research and educational programs on pay equality, automation, and career advancement. Seeks to organize the nearly 20 million office workers in the U.S.; compiles statistics. .

20709 ■ National Association of Legal Secretaries International
8159 E 41st St.
Tulsa, OK 74145-3312
Ph:(918)582-5188
Fax:(918)582-5907
Co. E-mail: info@nals.org
URL: http://www.nals.org
Contact: Doris T. Compton PP, Pres.-Elect

Description: Legal secretaries and others employed in work of a legal nature in law offices, banks, and courts. Sponsors legal secretarial training courses and awards those passing a two-day examination the rating of Certified Professional Legal Secretary. **Publications:** *Career Legal Secretary*; *Manual for Lawyer's Assistant* .

20710 ■ National Court Reporters Association
8224 Old Courthouse Rd.
Vienna, VA 22182-3808
Ph:(703)556-6272
Free: 800-272-6272
Fax:(703)556-6291
Co. E-mail: melanie@sonntagreporting.com
URL: http://www.ncraonline.org
Contact: Melanie Humphrey-Sonntag RDR, Pres.

Description: Represents Independent state, regional, and local associations. Verbatim court reporters who work as official reporters for courts and government agencies, as freelance reporters for independent contractors, and as captioners for television programming; retired reporters, teachers of court reporting, and school officials; student court reporters. Conducts research; compiles statistics; offers several certification programs; and publishes journal. **Publications:** *National Court Reporters Association—The Court Reporters Sourcebook* (annual).

20711 ■ Society of Corporate Secretaries and Governance Professionals
521 5th Ave.
New York, NY 10175
Ph:(212)681-2000
Fax:(212)681-2005
Co. E-mail: research@governanceprofessionals.org
URL: http://www.governanceprofessionals.org
Contact: Kenneth A. Bertsch, Pres./CEO

Description: Corporate secretaries, assistant secretaries, officers and executives of corporations and others interested in corporate practices and procedures. Conducts surveys and research. Sponsors educational programs for members. Maintains a central information and reference service. **Publications:** *The Corporate Secretary* (10/year).

DIRECTORIES OF EDUCATIONAL PROGRAMS

20712 ■ *Directory of Private Accredited Career Schools and Colleges of Technology*
Pub: Accrediting Commission of Career Schools and Colleges of Technology
Contact: Michale S. McComis, Exec. Dir.

Released: On web page. **Price:** Free. **Description:** Covers 3900 accredited post-secondary programs that provide training programs in business, trade, and technical fields, including various small business endeavors. Entries offer school name, address, phone, description of courses, job placement assistance, and requirements for admission. Arrangement is alphabetical.

TRADE SHOWS AND CONVENTIONS

20713 ■ National Association of Executive Secretaries Annual Conference
National Association of Executive Secretaries and Administrative Assistants
900 S. Washington St., No. G-13
Falls Church, VA 22046
Ph:(703)237-8616
Fax:(703)533-1153
Co. E-mail: Headquarters@naesaa.com
URL: http://www.naesaa.com

Released: Annual. **Principal Exhibits:** Business education products and services.

ASSOCIATIONS AND OTHER ORGANIZATIONS

20714 ■ Canadian Carpet Institute–Institut Canadien du Tapis
200-435 St. Laurent Blvd.
Ottawa, ON, Canada K1K 2Z8
Ph:(613)749-3265
Fax:(613)745-8753
Co. E-mail: info@canadiancarpet.org
URL: http://www.canadiancarpet.org
Contact: Raymonde Lemire, Admin. Mgr.
Description: Carpet manufacturers and suppliers. Seeks to advance the carpet and related industries. Facilitates exchange of information among members; serves as a clearinghouse on technical, regulatory, and maintenance issues relevant to carpeting; represents members' commercial and regulatory interests.

20715 ■ Society of Cleaning and Restoration Technicians
234 Cedric St.
Leesburg, GA 31763
Ph:(229)883-1202
Free: 800-949-4728
Fax:(229)438-7512
Co. E-mail: info@scrt.org
URL: http://www.scrt.org
Contact: Gary Glenn, Pres.
Description: Professional on-site carpet and upholstery cleaners, firms, and suppliers. Provides a forum for the exchange of technical and procedural information, including catastrophe restoration data, updates on new chemicals and processes, and technical, management, sales, and production materials. Monitors and reports on events affecting the carpet cleaning industry. Conducts workshops. **Publications:** *Technical* (5/year).

DIRECTORIES OF EDUCATIONAL PROGRAMS

20716 ■ *Directory of Private Accredited Career Schools and Colleges of Technology*
Pub: Accrediting Commission of Career Schools and Colleges of Technology
Contact: Michale S. McComis, Exec. Dir.
Released: On web page. **Price:** Free. **Description:** Covers 3900 accredited post-secondary programs that provide training programs in business, trade, and technical fields, including various small business endeavors. Entries offer school name, address, phone, description of courses, job placement assistance, and requirements for admission. Arrangement is alphabetical.

REFERENCE WORKS

20717 ■ *Carpet Cleaners Institute of the Northwest—Membership Roster*
Pub: Carpet Cleaners Institute of the Northwest
Contact: Thea Sanda, President
Released: Annual, May. **Covers:** Approximately 330 member companies involved in the carpet cleaning industry in Alberta, British Columbia, Idaho, Oregon, and Washington. **Entries Include:** Company name, address, phone, owner name.

TRADE PERIODICALS

20718 ■ *Cleaning & Restoration*
Pub: Restoration Industry Association
Contact: Tony Greenfield, Sales Mgr
E-mail: ria@rcn.com
Released: Monthly. **Price:** $69 nonmembers; $79 nonmembers Canada; $99 nonmembers international; $49 members; $59 members Canada; $79 members international. **Description:** Journal covering drapery, rug, upholstery, and carpet cleaning; fire and water damage; and disaster restoration and mechanical systems cleaning and inspection.

20719 ■ *ICS Cleaning Specialist*
Pub: Business News Publishing Company II L.L.C.
Contact: Phil Johnson, Gp. Publisher
E-mail: johnsonp@bnpmedia.com
Released: Monthly. **Description:** Trade magazine for the floor care and service industry.

20720 ■ *National Floor Trends Magazine*
Pub: Business News Publishing Company II L.L.C.
Contact: Michael Chmielecki, Assoc. Ed.
E-mail: chmieleckim@bnpmedia.com
Released: Monthly. **Description:** Trade magazine for the floor covering industry.

VIDEOCASSETTES/ AUDIOCASSETTES

20721 ■ *Upholstering a Dining Room Chair*
RMI Media
1365 N. Winchester St.
Olathe, KS 66061-5880
Ph:(913)768-1696
Free: 800-745-5480
Fax:800-755-6910
Co. E-mail: actmedia@act.org
URL: http://www.actmedia.com
Released: 1987. **Description:** Bonnie Enault demonstrates how to upholster two different types of dining room chairs. Specific instructions include how to remove old upholstering and how to measure, cut, and attach new fabric. **Availability:** VHS; 3/4U.

CONSULTANTS

20722 ■ Cleaning Consultant Services Inc.
3693 E Marginal Way S
PO Box 1273
Seattle, WA 98134
Ph:(206)682-9748
Fax:(206)622-6876
Co. E-mail: ccs@cleaningconsultants.com
URL: http://www.cleaningconsultants.com
Contact: Wm. R. Griffin, President
E-mail: wgriffin@cleaningconsultants.com
Scope: Management consultants to cleaning and maintenance contractors, property managers, hospitals, schools, hotels, building owners, facility directors, and small business owners in the cleaning industry. Services are designed to increase efficiency and profit through training and the use of time-saving techniques on the job; increase the useful life of building surfaces and equipment; encourage self development of cleaning and maintenance professionals; and make the world a clean and safe place to live. Specific consulting services are related to cleaning contract specifications development and negotiation, claim and dispute resolution, certified carpet and floor covering inspection and corrections, expert court testimony, independent certified cleaning and maintenance inspections, training program and materials development, building startup and long-range maintenance planning, architect and engineering services regarding cleaning, and building maintenance. Serves all industries in need of cleaning and maintenance services. **Publications:** "Raising the Bar with Science, Training and Upward Mobility," Jan, 2010; "Technology Revolutionizes the Cleaning Process "Cleaning for Health" is the New Mantra," Distribution Sales and Management Magazine, May, 2003; "Bill Griffin's Crystal Balls-Cleaning Trends in the Usa 2001," Floor Care is Hot in 2001," Mar, 2001; "In-clean Magazine (Australia), Feb, 2001; "Maintaining Swimming Pools, Spas, Whirlpool Tubs and Saunas," Executive House keeping, Feb, 2001; "Whats New with Floor Care," 2001. **Seminars:** Stone Maintenance Technician (SMT) IICRC Certification Course; Carpet Cleaning Technician; Apprentice/Basic Skills; Organizing Custodial Operations for Maximum Efficiency: How to Sell & Price Contract Cleaning; Starting a House cleaning Business; Rugs & Carpet Cleaning; How to Start and Operate a Successful Cleaning Business; Cleaning Schools in the 2000and Beyond; Bringing About and Working Through Change; Organizing Custodial Operations for Maximum Efficiency; Floor Care Technician (FCT)11 CPC Certified Course; Administering Cleaning Service Contracts.

20723 ■ Surface Technologies Inc.
18 Willotta Dr.
Suisun City, CA 94534-1446
Ph:(707)864-6313
Free: 800-241-2982
Fax:(707)864-6313
Contact: Richard E. Larson, President
Scope: Specializes in carpet, tile, wood, stone, and vinyl floor covering inspection and testing. Evaluates floor covering samples for durability, clean ability, and longevity of appearance. Trains hotel and other institutional personnel to maintain, clean, and repair floor coverings. Industries served include floor and wall covering and upholstery fabric manufacturers, as well as producers of all types of architectural surfaces. **Seminars:** Complaint Reduction Program; Selling Floor Covering Defensively; Turn Complaints into More Business; Presented to department stores and floor covering specialty stores.

FRANCHISES AND BUSINESS OPPORTUNITIES

20724 ■ Chem-Dry Carpet Drapery & Upholstery Cleaning
1530 N 1000 West
Logan, UT 84321

Free: 877-307-8233
Fax:(435)890-1091
Co. E-mail: charlie@chemdry.com
URL: http://www.chemdry.com
No. of Franchise Units: 2,165. **Founded:** 1977. **Franchised:** 1978. **Description:** They offer carpet cleaning service. **Equity Capital Needed:** $27,850-$122,650. **Franchise Fee:** $10,950-$12,950. **Royalty Fee:** $350/month. **Financial Assistance:** Limited in-house financing assistance available. **Training:** Provides 5 days at headquarters, video training and ongoing support.

20725 ■ Chem-Dry Carpet and Upholstery Cleaning
Harris Research, Inc.
1530 N 1000 W
Logan, UT 84321
Ph:(435)890-1051
Free: 877-307-8233
Fax:(435)755-8490
Co. E-mail: sales@chemdry.com
URL: http://www.chemdry.com
No. of Franchise Units: 4,500. **Founded:** 1977. **Franchised:** 1978. **Description:** Specializes in the care of carpet, drapery, upholstery and most fabrics. **Equity Capital Needed:** $25,000-$175,000, initial down payment $8,495. **Franchise Fee:** $12,950-$34,850. **Financial Assistance:** In-house financing available. Single and Multi-Unit packages available. **Training:** 5 days in-house training, yearly National Convention, and ongoing operational support.

20726 ■ ChemDry Canada Ltd.
8472 Harvard Pl.
Chilliwack, BC, Canada V2P 7Z5
Free: 888-243-6379
Fax:(604)795-7-71
Co. E-mail: franchisesales@chemdry.ca
URL: http://www.franchisedirectory.ca
No. of Franchise Units: 77. **Description:** Carpet and upholstery cleaning service. **Equity Capital Needed:** $20,000-$60,000 total investment; $20,000 startup capital required. **Franchise Fee:** $815/month. **Financial Assistance:** Yes. **Managerial Assistance:** Manuals and computer software provided. **Training:** Provides training and ongoing support by technical and commercial support staff who make oneon-one visits, and run scheduled Business Development Events and Seminars, an annual convention and a regular program of specialist courses.

20727 ■ Coit Cleaning and Restoration Services
897 Hinckley Rd.
Burlingame, CA 94010
Free: 800-243-8797
Fax:(650)692-8397
Co. E-mail: franchise@coit.com
URL: http://www.coit.com
No. of Franchise Units: 42. **No. of Company-Owned Units:** 8. **Founded:** 1950. **Franchised:** 1962. **Description:** Coit is a multi-service cleaning company, offering drapery cleaning, carpet cleaning, upholstery cleaning, area rug cleaning, air duct cleaning and more. **Equity Capital Needed:** $50,000-$145,000. **Franchise Fee:** $24,000-$40,000. **Financial Assistance:** Limited financing available. **Training:** Includes 10 days in corporate office.

20728 ■ Creative Colors International
19015 S Jodi Rd., Ste. E
Mokena, IL 60448
Ph:(708)478-1437
Free: 800-933-2656
Fax:(708)478-1636
Co. E-mail: campaign65@creativecolorsintl.com
URL: http://www.creativecolorsintl.com
No. of Franchise Units: 68. **No. of Company-Owned Units:** 3. **Founded:** 1980. **Franchised:** 1991. **Description:** Specializes in providing services for the repair, coloring, cleaning, and restoration of leather, vinyl, cloth, velour, plastics and other upholstery surfaces and related services on a mobile basis primarily to commercial customers. These customers include auto dealerships, hotels, airports, and individuals. **Equity Capital Needed:** Franchise fee and $10,000 in supplies; total investment under $50,000. **Franchise Fee:** $29,500. **Financial Assistance:** Financing is available on equipment and supplies, up to $8,000. **Managerial Assistance:** Franchisee will have onsite support and detailed Operations Manual, toll-free support and monthly newsletter. **Training:** An initial training course of 3 weeks is conducted at National Headquarters. In addition, a field representative will spend 1 week with franchise owner when business commences operation to establish accounts.

20729 ■ Duraclean International, Inc.
220 Campus Dr.
Arlington Heights, IL 60004
Ph:(847)704-7100
Free: 800-251-7070
Fax:(847)704-7101
Co. E-mail: info@duraclean.com
URL: http://www.duraclean.com
No. of Franchise Units: 374. **No. of Company-Owned Units:** 20. **Founded:** 1930. **Franchised:** 1945. **Description:** Carpet cleaning, ceiling & wall cleaning, water/fire/smoke damage restoration, janitorial, hard surface floor care, ventilation duct cleaning, high pressure washing, ultrasonic blind cleaning, mold remediation. **Equity Capital Needed:** $32,599-$88,999. **Franchise Fee:** $17,500. **Financial Assistance:** Financing arrangements available from Duraclean International. Lease packages on vans are also available. **Managerial Assistance:** Assists franchisees on an ongoing basis in technical, marketing and managerial areas. **Training:** Initial training provides training manuals, videotapes, schools, local hands-on assistance, magazines, bulletins, conventions and area meetings and ongoing support.

20730 ■ Heaven's Best Carpet & Upholstery Cleaning
M-CO Inc.
247 N 1st E
Rexburg, ID 83440
Ph:(208)359-1106
Free: 800-568-3605
Fax:(208)359-1236
No. of Franchise Units: 1,264. **Founded:** 1983. **Franchised:** 1983. **Description:** Heaven's Best is a unique, low-moisture cleaning process which provides a great alternative to the traditional total saturation methods of cleaning. Our customers love our dry-in-one-hour process. All aspects of the business are covered during the training. All franchisees must attend the training. **Equity Capital Needed:** $28,900-$65,000. **Franchise Fee:** $14,450. **Financial Assistance:** Yes. **Training:** Yes.

20731 ■ Interior Magic International, LLC
211 Cotton Grove Rd.
Lexington, NC 27292
Ph:(336)249-9976
Fax:(336)249-9978
Co. E-mail: info@myinteriormagic.com
URL: http://www.myinteriormagic.com
No. of Franchise Units: 40. **Founded:** 2001. **Franchised:** 2004. **Description:** Mobile business system that includes the most desirable combination of services available in the automotive reconditioning industry. We offer expert repair and re-dyeing of leather, vinyl, plastic, velour and carpet, as well as vapor steam cleaning, permanent odor elimination, stain removal, and a specialized carpet protection system. Our customers include auto dealers, restaurants, hotels, other commercial clients and individuals. **Equity Capital Needed:** $33,050-$100,060. **Franchise Fee:** $14,900-$39,900. **Financial Assistance:** Limited in-house financing available. **Managerial Assistance:** Additional guidance in accounting and marketing, a toll-free help line and operations manual also provided. **Training:** 3 weeks of instruction at our corporate headquarters, both in our training center and onsite with a field representative. Plus, we will assist you for 1 week to begin business in your chosen territory.

20732 ■ Langenwalter Carpet Dyeing
Lagenwalter Industries, Inc.
1111 Richfield Rd.
Placentia, CA 92670
Ph:(714)528-7610
Free: 800-422-4370
No. of Franchise Units: 65. **No. of Company-Owned Units:** 2. **Founded:** 1972. **Franchised:** 1980. **Description:** Complete carpet color correction, including bleach spots, sun fading, pet stains, food stains, punch and other discolorations. Also, complete color changes and full wall-to-wall carpet dyeing. **Equity Capital Needed:** $42,000 Minimum. **Franchise Fee:** $12,500. **Financial Assistance:** No. **Training:** Yes.

20733 ■ Modernistic Cleaning Services
Koppang Franchise Development Co.
1460 Rankin St.
Troy, MI 48083
Ph:(248)589-1700
Free: 877-567-7264
Fax:(248)589-2660
No. of Franchise Units: 4. **Founded:** 1972. **Franchised:** 1999. **Description:** Full service carpet and upholstery cleaning company. **Equity Capital Needed:** $65,000. **Franchise Fee:** $30,000. **Financial Assistance:** Yes. **Training:** Yes.

20734 ■ Professional Carpet Systems, Inc.
4211 Atlantic Ave.
Raleigh, NC 27604
Ph:(919)875-8871
Free: 800-925-5055
Fax:(919)875-9855
Co. E-mail: info@procarpetssys.com
URL: http://www.procarpetsys.com
No. of Franchise Units: 70. **Founded:** 1978. **Franchised:** 1982. **Description:** Onsite carpet re-dyeing, servicing thousands of apartment complexes, hotels and motels worldwide. Other services include carpet cleaning, rejuvenation, repair, water and flood damage restoration and odor control. **Equity Capital Needed:** $20,000. **Franchise Fee:** $9,995. **Financial Assistance:** Financing offered on equipment and territory fees above minimum to qualified individuals. **Training:** 2 weeks in Raleigh, NC for initial training. Eleven 2 day sessions are held every year for additional training, most with industry certification available. In addition, we have periodic workshops and an annual convention. During the training program, franchisees gain hands-on experience.

20735 ■ Servpro
Servpro Industries, Inc.
801 Industrial Blvd.
Gallatin, TN 37066
Ph:(615)451-0600
Free: 800-826-9586
Fax:(615)451-1602
Co. E-mail: franchise@servpronet.com
URL: http://www.servpro.com
No. of Franchise Units: 1,500+. **Founded:** 1967. **Franchised:** 1969. **Description:** A completely diversified cleaning & restoration business, with multiple income opportunities. The insurance restoration market (fire, smoke and water damage) is their main focus. Specialize in commercial & residential cleaning. **Equity Capital Needed:** $132,050-$180,450. **Franchise Fee:** $41,000. **Financial Assistance:** May offer partial financing in addition to assisting with2third party lenders. **Training:** Intensive home study curriculum, manuals and videos. Provides 2 weeks training in state of the art national training facility, 1 week set up/opening assistance, and trainer assistance. Ongoing support, convention, regional and area meetings, formal business reviews, newsletters, bulletins, and more.

20736 ■ Sparkle Carpet Cleaning
Sparkle Development Co.
1222 S Main Ave.
Scranton, PA 18504
Ph:(570)344-4660
Free: 800-298-4660
Fax:(570)344-7076
No. of Franchise Units: 2. **No. of Company-Owned Units:** 5. **Founded:** 1981. **Description:** Cleaners of carpet and upholstery. **Equity Capital Needed:** $10,000-$15,000. **Franchise Fee:** $5,000-$9,000. **Royalty Fee:** $75-150/month. **Financial Assistance:** Limited inhouse financing available. **Training:** Yes.

20737 ■ Stanley Steemer Carpet Cleaner
Stanley Steemer International, Inc.
5800 Innovation Dr.
Dublin, OH 43016
Ph:(614)764-2007
Free: 800-848-7496

No. of Franchise Units: 223. **No. of Company-Owned Units:** 73. **Description:** Carpet and upholstery cleaning and other related services. **Equity Capital Needed:** $93,690-$221,175. **Franchise Fee:** $20,000-$100,000. **Royalty Fee:** 7%. **Financial Assistance:** Limited financial assistance available. **Training:** Provides 2 weeks training at headquarters, as well as various training offered throughout the year and ongoing support.

20738 ■ Steam Brothers Professional Cleaning and Restoration
Steam Brothers Inc.
P.O. Box 3036
Bismarck, ND 58502
Ph:(701)222-1263
Free: 800-767-5064
Fax:(701)222-1372

No. of Franchise Units: 23. **Founded:** 1977. **Franchised:** 1983. **Description:** Offers services such as carpet, drapery and upholstery cleaning; fire, smoke and water damage restoration; furnace and air-duct cleaning; and acoustical ceiling cleaning. **Equity Capital Needed:** $5,000+ equipment. **Franchise Fee:** $16,000. **Financial Assistance:** No. **Managerial Assistance:** Provides manuals, seminars, field representatives, newsletters, troubleshooting hotlines, monthly advertising material and suggested uses, promotional recommendations, ongoing new product and services packages and more. **Training:** Offers training at headquarters in Bismarck, ND for 5 days. Training at franchisees location is for 2 days.

START-UP INFORMATION

20739 ■ "A Self-Serving Opportunity" in *Black Enterprise* (Vol. 37, February 2007, No. 7, pp. 52)
Pub: Earl G. Graves Publishing Co. Inc.
Ed: James C. Johnson. **Description:** Questions are answered regarding the startup of a vending machine business.

ASSOCIATIONS AND OTHER ORGANIZATIONS

20740 ■ Canadian Automatic Merchandising Association–Association Canadienne d'Auto Distribution
2233 Argentia Rd., Ste. 100
Mississauga, ON, Canada L5N 2X7
Ph:(905)826-7695
Free: 888-849-2262
Fax:(905)826-4873
Co. E-mail: info@vending-cama.com
URL: http://www.vending-cama.com
Contact: Amanda Curtis, Exec. Dir.
Description: Corporations and individuals engaged in the vending industry. Promotes growth and development of the automatic merchandising market. Represents members' interests before industrial organizations, government agencies, and the public. **Telecommunication Services:** electronic mail, acurtis@vending-cama.com.

20741 ■ National Automatic Merchandising Association
20 N Wacker Dr., Ste. 3500
Chicago, IL 60606-3102
Ph:(312)346-0370
Free: 888-337-8363
Fax:(312)704-4140
Co. E-mail: rgeerdes@vending.org
URL: http://www.vending.org
Contact: Richard M. Geerdes, Pres./CEO
Description: Manufacturing and operating companies in the automatic vending machine industry; food service management firms; office coffee machine operators; suppliers of products and services. Compiles industry statistics. **Publications:** *National Automatic Merchandising Association—Directory of Members* (annual); *National Automatic Merchandising Association-In Touch* (quarterly).

20742 ■ National Bulk Vendors Association
3240 E Union Hills Dr., Ste. 129
Phoenix, AZ 85050
Free: 888-NBV-AUSA
Fax:(480)302-5108
Co. E-mail: admin@nbva.org
URL: http://www.nbva.info
Contact: Bernie Schwarzli, Pres.
Description: Manufacturers, distributors, and operators of bulk vending merchandise and equipment. .

REFERENCE WORKS

20743 ■ *Automatic Merchandiser—Blue Book Buyer's Guide Issue*
Pub: Cygnus Business Media
Contact: Michael Martin, President
Released: Annual. **Publication Includes:** Suppliers of products, services, and equipment to the merchandise vending, contract foodservice, and office coffee service industries. **Entries Include:** Company name, address, phone, names of executives, trade and brand names, and products or services offered. **Arrangement:** Classified by type of business. **Indexes:** Alphabetical, product.

20744 ■ "AVT Featured on TD Waterhouse Market News Website and in Vending Times Magazine" in *Benzinga.com* (August 17, 2011)
Pub: Benzinga.com
Ed: Benzinga Staff. **Description:** AVT Inc. was featured online and in an article reporting the firm's plan to install automated vending machines in high-profile areas including malls, office buildings, stadiums and arenas.

20745 ■ "AVT Launches New ExpressPay Vending Systems" in *Benzinga.com* (July 13, 2011)
Pub: Benzinga.com
Ed: Benzinga Staff. **Description:** AVT Inc. has developed a new high-tech vending system that features a touch screen interface and a cashless payment system so users can find what they want easily and pay using a credit card.

20746 ■ "Buck-ing the Trend?" in *Baltimore Business Journal* (Vol. 28, August 13, 2010, No. 14, pp. 1)
Pub: Baltimore Business Journal
Ed: Gary Haber. **Description:** Baltimore Orioles' new manager Buck Showalter has managed to win games for fans. However, not all businesses around Camden Yards were boosted by the Orioles' surge as street vendors complained of worsening business.

20747 ■ "Cannabis Science Signs Exclusive and Non-Exclusive Agreement with Prescription Vending Machines" in *Benzinga.com* (October 29, 2011)
Pub: Benzinga.com
Ed: Benzinga Staff. **Description:** Cannabis Science Inc., a biotech company developing pharmaceutical cannabis products has partnered with Prescription Vending Machines Inc. and its principal Vincent Meddizadeh to provide industry specific consulting and advisory services to Cannabis Science.

20748 ■ "Eagle's Wine Kiosk Is Area's 1st" in *Pittsburgh Post-Gazette* (October 28, 2010)
Pub: Pittsburgh-Post Gazette
Ed: Bob Batz Jr. **Description:** Giant Eagle Market District store at Settlers Ridge opened the first self-serve wine kiosk in Western Pennsylvania. The kiosk will have a built-in breathalyzer panel to ensure safety.

20749 ■ "Effort Is Growing to Offer Healthier Choices in Vending Machines" in *Philadelphia Inquirer* (July 29, 2011)
Pub: Philadelphia Media Network Inc.
Ed: Don Sapatkin. **Description:** Since Boston's mayor announced a ban on the sale of all sugar sweetened beverages on city properties, it seems more cities, states, hospitals, businesses, and even park systems are following suit. Thus, vending machines are beginning to offer healthier snacks and drinks to consumers.

20750 ■ "Essentially Organic Vending Takes Healthy Snacks to Ohio High School" in *Entertainment Close-Up* (September 13, 2011)
Pub: Close-Up Media
Description: Essentially Organic Vending is offering students a healthy alternative for their snacking. The vending machines will be stocked with nutritious energy options.

20751 ■ "EX3D to Launch In-Theater Vending Machines for Stylish RealD 3D Glasses" in *Entertainment Close-Up* (August 16, 2011)
Pub: Close-Up Media
Description: Marchon3d has partnered with Cinemark and UltraStar Cinemas to install vending machines selling Marchon3D's line of patented, curved RealD 3D compatible eyeglasses.

20752 ■ "H.I.G. Capital Announces Acquisition of Next Generation Vending" in *Benzinga.com* (October 29, 2011)
Pub: Benzinga.com
Ed: Benzinga Staff. **Description:** H.I.G. Capital LLC, a leader in global private investments, acquired Next Generation Vending and Food Service Inc.. Next Generation is a provider of vending services for corporate and institutional clients in Northeastern United States.

20753 ■ "High-Tech Machines Show a New Age of Vending" in *Wisconsin State Journal* (October 14, 2011)
Pub: Wisconsin State Journal
Ed: Barry Adams. **Description:** Vending machines are looking more like an iPad than the machines of the past. These high tech machines are seeing sharp rises in use.

20754 ■ "IF Challenges Atlanta's Vending Monopoly" in *Benzinga.com* (July 28, 2011)
Pub: Benzinga.com
Ed: Benzinga Staff. **Description:** A lawsuit was filed by The Institute for Justice to challenge Atlanta's unconstitutional vending monopoly on behalf of two Atlanta street vendors.

20755 ■ "LCB Turning Off Wine Vending Machines" in *Pittsburgh Post-Gazette* (September 20, 2011)
Pub: PG Publishing Company
Ed: Tracie Mauriello. **Description:** Grocery store shoppers will no longer be able to purchase a bottle of wine from wine kiosks in Pennsylvania.

20756 ■ "Moooove Over, Sodas: Okaloosa to Get Dairy Vending Machines for Two Schools" in *Northwest Florida Daily News* (September 27, 2001)
Pub: Freedom Communications
Ed: Katie Tammen. **Description:** Two Okaloosa County high schools will be offering more lunch options by installing refrigerated vending machines featuring dairy-related food.

20757 ■ "National Automatic Merchandising Association Takes Vending on the Road" in *Food and Beverage Close-Up* (September 6, 2011)
Pub: Close-Up Media
Description: National Automatic Merchandising Association launched the new age of vending and is taking its machines, products and technology on the road to say thank you to loyal users of vending machines.

20758 ■ "A Parisian Vending Machine for Baguettes 24/7" in *Benzinga.com* ()
Pub: Benzinga.com
Ed: Benzinga Staff. **Description:** Jean-Louis Hecht has created a vending machine that offers fresh baguettes 24 hours a day, seven days a week.

20759 ■ "Research and Markets Adds Report: Vending Machines" in *Travel and Leisure Close-Up* (October 20, 2011)
Pub: Close-Up Media
Description: Research and Markets has added "Vending Machines – Global Strategic Business Report" to its lineup. The report analyzes globally installed vending machines in US million dollars by the following product types: Beverage, Food, Cigarette, and Other Products (includes personal and health care products, contraceptives, books, magazines).

20760 ■ "Sheets Energy Strips Unveils New Vending Machines" in *Food and Beverage Close-Up* (August 12, 2011)
Pub: Close-Up Media
Description: Sheets Energy Strips is installing vending machines in malls, office buildings, stadiums and arenas in New York, New Jersey, Connecticut and Florida. These machines will offer 4 packs, 10 packs and Sheets branded hats and T-shirts.

20761 ■ "Sodexo Updates Healthy Vending Program" in *Entertainment Close-Up* (September 25, 2011)
Pub: Close-Up Media
Description: Sodexo launched its Your Health Your Way On-the-Go program for its vending machines across the nation.

20762 ■ "The Ultimate Vending Machine" in *Benzinga.com* (August 15, 2011)
Pub: Benzinga.com
Ed: Benzinga Staff. **Description:** Louis Hecht, a baker from Hombourg-Haut, France is selling fresh-baked bread in vending machines. Each machine holds 90 pre-cooked loaves which are warmed before being delivered to the customer.

20763 ■ *Vending Times—Buyers Guide and Directory Issue*
Pub: Vending Times Inc.
Contact: Alicia Lavay-Kertes, Pres./Publisher
E-mail: alicia@vendingtimes.net
Released: Annual, Latest edition 2009. **Price:** $40, individuals includes shipping and handling. **Publication Includes:** Lists of manufacturers and suppliers of equipment and products used by vending machine industry operators, including product venders, juke boxes, pinball and other games; industry trade associations. **Entries Include:** Company name, address, phone, names of key personnel, description of products. **Arrangement:** Classified by product or service.

20764 ■ "Vista-Based NCV Bought by Canteen Vending" in *North County Times* (October 18, 2011)
Ed: Pat Maio. **Description:** Details of North Carolina-based Canteen Vending Services' acquisition of NCV Refreshment Services, are given.

20765 ■ "Working the Streets" in *Baltimore Business Journal* (Vol. 28, July 30, 2010, No. 12, pp. 1)
Pub: Baltimore Business Journal
Ed: Amanda Pino. **Description:** Reports show that street vendors are popping up on new corners in Baltimore, Maryland, with city-inspected stainless steel food carts in tow. Applications for street vending licenses shot up at the end of 2009 and into this summer. It is believed that pinning down the exact number of vendors operating at any one point is difficult.

STATISTICAL SOURCES

20766 ■ *RMA Annual Statement Studies*
Pub: Robert Morris Associates (RMA)
Released: Annual. **Price:** $175.00 2006-07 edition, $105.00. **Description:** Contains composite balance sheets and income statements for more than 360 industries, including the accounting, auditing, and bookkeeping industries. Also contains five years of comparative historical data for discerning trends. Includes 16 commonly used ratios, computed for most of the size groupings for nearly every industry.

20767 ■ *The Vended Foods Market*
Pub: Rector Press, Ltd.
Contact: Lewis Sckolnick, Pres
Released: 2009. **Price:** Contact Rector Press.

TRADE PERIODICALS

20768 ■ *Automatic Merchandiser*
Pub: Cygnus Business Media
Contact: Emily Refermat, Managing Editor
E-mail: emily.refermat@vendingmarketwatch.com
Released: Monthly. **Description:** Vending and office coffee service industry trade magazine.

TRADE SHOWS AND CONVENTIONS

20769 ■ Atlantic Coast Exposition - Showcasing the Vending and Food Service Industry
IMI Association Executives Inc.
2501 Aerial Center Pkwy.
Suite 103
Morrisville, NC 27560
Ph:(919)459-2070
Free: 800-729-2776
Fax:(919)459-2075
Co. E-mail: info@imiae.com
URL: http://www.imiae.com
Released: Annual. **Audience:** Vending, food service, and OCS personnel. **Principal Exhibits:** Vending machines, office coffee service equipment, food stuffs, and related goods and services.

FRANCHISES AND BUSINESS OPPORTUNITIES

20770 ■ Protocol, LLC.
2110 Cheshire Way, Ste. A
Greensboro, NC 27405
Ph:(651)454-0518
Free: 800-227-5336
Fax:(651)454-9542
No. of Franchise Units: 40,000. **Founded:** 1987. **Franchised:** 1996. **Description:** Business opportunity in vending machine distributorships. **Equity Capital Needed:** $10,000. **Franchise Fee:** $500. **Financial Assistance:** No. **Training:** Yes.

ASSOCIATIONS AND OTHER ORGANIZATIONS

20771 ■ Entertainment Merchants Association
16530 Ventura Blvd., Ste. 400
Encino, CA 91436-4551
Ph:(818)385-1500
Free: 800-955-8732
Fax:(818)385-0567
Co. E-mail: emaoffice@entmerch.org
URL: http://www.vsda.org
Contact: Bob Geistman, Chm.
Description: Retailers and distributors of videocassettes and videodiscs; associate members are major studios or independent companies that produce video programming and manufacturers of video games, accessories, and other goods and services for the video software industry. Represents and acts as spokesperson for the video software merchandising industry. Conducts statistical survey of video retailing; offers legal counsel representing members' interests in Washington, DC. Offers seminars on management and inventory control. **Publications:** *VSDA Video Voice* (monthly).

20772 ■ InfoComm International
11242 Waples Mill Rd., Ste. 200
Fairfax, VA 22030
Ph:(703)273-7200
Free: 800-659-7469
Co. E-mail: customerservice@infocomm.org
URL: http://www.infocomm.org
Contact: Randal A. Lemke PhD, Exec. Dir.
Purpose: Represents for-profit individuals and organizations that derive revenue from the commercialization or utilization of communications technology. Ensures the credibility and desirability of its members' products and services by representing the communications industry to the public, business, education, and governments. **Publications:** *ICIA Membership Directory* (annual); *InfoCommunity News* (quarterly).

REFERENCE WORKS

20773 ■ "Are Movie Theaters Doomed?" in *Business Horizons* (November-December 2007, pp. 491)
Pub: Elsevier Technology Publications
Ed: Jon Silver, John McDonnell. **Description:** Theater operators must embrace new technologies and more diverse target markets if they are to stem the decline in theatergoers. Movie theaters remain highly vulnerable to trends in the home entertainment industry.

20774 ■ "Beyond YouTube: New Uses for Video, Online and Off" in *Inc.* (October 2007, pp. 53-54)
Pub: Gruner & Jahr USA Publishing
Ed: Leah Hoffmann. **Description:** Small companies are using video technology for embedding messages into email, broadcasting live interactive sales and training seminars, as well as marketing campaigns. Experts offer insight into producing and broadcasting business videos.

20775 ■ "Blockbuster Launches Internet Movie Downloads to Compete Against Netflix, Others" in *Chicago Tribune* (December 3, 2008)
Pub: McClatchy-Tribune Information Services
Ed: Eric Benderoff. **Description:** Blockbuster Inc., the DVD rental giant, has launched a new service that delivers movies to their customer's homes via the Internet in an attempt to compete against Netflix and other competitors.

20776 ■ *Bowker's Complete Video Directory*
Pub: R.R. Bowker L.L.C.
Released: Annual, Latest edition March, 2011. **Price:** $595, individuals hardcover. **Covers:** In four volumes, over 250,000 theatrical and nontheatrical videocassette titles (Vols. 1 and 2: Entertainment, Vols. 3 and 4 educational special interest). **Entries Include:** Video title, date released, supplier name, cast, producer/director name, suggested list price, description of contents. **Arrangement:** Alphabetical. **Indexes:** Volumes 1-3—Title; Volumes 1 and 2—Genre, series, laser or videodisc, 8mm, closed-caption video, international standards, manufacturers and distributors, services and suppliers, entertainment; Volume 1—Spanish-language video, award-winning video, cast/director; Volumes 3 and 4—Education/special interest.

20777 ■ *Exceptional Service, Exceptional Profit: The Secrets of Building a Five-Star Customer Service Organization*
Pub: AMACOM
Ed: Leonard Inghilleri, Micah Solomon. **Released:** April 1, 2010. **Price:** $21.95. **Description:** Team of insiders share exclusive knowledge of the loyalty-building techniques pioneered by the world's most successful service leaders, including brick-and-mortar stars such as The Ritz-Carlton and Lexus and online success stories such as Netflix and CD Baby.

20778 ■ "For DVD Company, No Extra Innings: Capturing a Season Takes Fast Work" in *Boston Business Journal* (Vol. 27, December 7, 2007)
Pub: American City Business Journals Inc.
Ed: Terry Lefton. **Description:** Details of the development of MLB's annual World Series film by MLB Productions are discussed. The company is compelled to produce the film in a short period of time due to a promised November 27, 2007 delivery date. According to Elizabeth Scott, MLB vice president of programming and business affairs, she was concerned about the things that could directly affect sales.

20779 ■ "iMozi Integrates Esprida LiveControl for Advanced DVD Kiosk Hardware" in *Wireless News* (December 20, 2010)
Pub: Close-Up Media Inc.
Description: Provider of self-service entertainment technology, iMozi Canada has partnered with Esprida to make its automated DVD Kiosk solutions Esprida-enabled. Esprida develops remote device management solutions and will offer enhanced capabilities and to improve customer experience for users.

20780 ■ *International Television and Video Almanac*
Pub: Quigley Publishing Company Inc.
Ed: Eileen Quigley, Editor. **Released:** Annual, January; latest edition 2011. **Price:** $235, individuals. **Covers:** "Who's Who in Motion Pictures and Television and Home Video," television networks, major program producers, major group station owners, cable television companies, distributors, firms serving the television and home video industry, equipment manufacturers, casting agencies, literary agencies, advertising and publicity representatives, television stations, associations, list of feature films produced for television; statistics, industry's year in review, award winners, satellite and wireless cable provider, primetime programming, video producers, distributors, wholesalers. **Entries Include:** Generally, company name, address, phone; manufacturer and service listings may include description of products and services and name of contact; producing, distributing, and station listings include additional detail, and contacts for cable and broadcast networks. **Arrangement:** Classified by service or activity. **Indexes:** Full.

20781 ■ "Netflix Gets No Respect" in *Barron's* (Vol. 89, July 27, 2009, No. 30, pp. 26)
Pub: Dow Jones & Co., Inc.
Ed: Tiernan Ray. **Description:** Netflix met expectations when they announced their second quarter sales but their shares still fell by almost 10 percent. Analysts say their entry into the "streaming video" business is a mixed bag since customers are increasingly buying the cheaper monthly plan and this is dragging the economics of the business.

20782 ■ "Netflix vs. Blockbuster" in *Inc.* (October 2007, pp. 32)
Pub: Gruner & Jahr USA Publishing
Description: Nexflix, the mail-order DVD rental service, is losing market share to Blockbuster, even after matching prices to that of its competitors. Entrepreneurs are asked how they would run Netflix to gain back market share.

20783 ■ "Public Media Works to Launch DVD Kiosk Operations in Toronto, Canada" in *Internet Wire* (November 15, 2010)
Pub: Comtex
Description: Public Media Works Inc. along with its EntertainmentXpress Inc., have partnered with Spot Venture Distribution Inc. and Signifi Solutions Inc., both headquartered in Toronto, Canada, to manage and expand the Spot DVD movie and game kiosk business in greater Toronto and other Canadian locations.

20784 ■ *Video Source Book*
Pub: Gale
Released: Annual, Latest edition 48th; October, 2011. **Price:** $825, individuals. **Covers:** Approximately 160,000 videos covering more than 130,000 complete programs available from more than 2,100 distribu-

tors. **Entries Include:** Video title, release year, description, run time, format, audience, MPAA rating, credits, producer, awards, distributor, price. Distributor's address and phone are given in a separate list. **Arrangement:** Alphabetical. **Indexes:** Subject, cast, special formats, distributor, awards, alternate title.

STATISTICAL SOURCES

20785 ■ *RMA Annual Statement Studies*
Pub: Robert Morris Associates (RMA)
Released: Annual. **Price:** $175.00 2006-07 edition, $105.00. **Description:** Contains composite balance sheets and income statements for more than 360 industries, including the accounting, auditing, and bookkeeping industries. Also contains five years of comparative historical data for discerning trends. Includes 16 commonly used ratios, computed for most of the size groupings for nearly every industry.

TRADE PERIODICALS

20786 ■ *Home Media Retailing*
Pub: Questex Media Group
Contact: Thomas K. Arnold, Publisher
Released: Weekly. **Price:** $49.99 print; $79.99 Canada and Mexico print; $99.99 elsewhere print. **Description:** Business magazine for retailers of prerecorded video software, blank tapes, and accessories.

20787 ■ *Variety*
Pub: Reed Business Information
Ed: Dana Harris, Editor, dana.harris@variety.com. **Released:** Weekly, 50/yr. **Price:** $259; $25 monthly. **Description:** Newspaper (tabloid) reporting on theatre, television, radio, music, records, and movies.

20788 ■ *Video Watchdog*
Pub: Video Watchdog
Contact: Tim Lucas, Editor & Publisher
Released: Monthly. **Price:** $48 bulk mail - U.S.; $57 1st class - U.S.; $69 other countries economy; $78 other countries airmail. **Description:** Video, DVD, and movie magazine.

TRADE SHOWS AND CONVENTIONS

20789 ■ VSDA's Home Entertainment
Home Entertainment Events
201 Sandpointe Ave., Ste. 500
Santa Ana, CA 92707
Free: 800-854-3112
Fax:(714)513-8848
URL: http://www.homemediaexpo.com
Released: Annual. **Audience:** Video/DVD retailers (trade only). **Principal Exhibits:** Re-recorded video software, computer software for video retailers, accessory products for retailers and manufacturers, and trade publications.

COMPUTERIZED DATABASES

20790 ■ *BaselineFT's In Production Database*
New York Times Media Group
3415 S Sepulveda Blvd., Ste. 200
Los Angeles, CA 90034
Ph:(310)482-3400
Free: 800-858-3669
Fax:(310)393-7799
URL: http://www.baselineresearch.com
Description: Lists more than 5000 film and television projects that are either announced, in pre-production, production, post-production, or awaiting release. Monitors activity in the entertainment industry through press releases, local film commissions, industry sources, and phone calls to producers. **Availability:** Online: New York Times Media Group. **Type:** Full text.

20791 ■ *Mini Movie Reviews*
Cineman Syndicate L.L.C.
31 Purchase St., Ste. 203
Rye, NY 10580
Ph:(914)582-8906
Fax:(914)967-5588
Co. E-mail: cinemansyndicate@verizon.net
URL: http://www.minireviews.com
Description: Contains movie reviews written for syndication by film critic Jay A. Brown. Each review includes a 60- to 90-word summary, a list of principal stars, and a rating (Great, Good, Fair, Boring, or Poor). A coming-attractions column is included every other week. The reviews are published in more than 60 newspapers worldwide. Reviews are divided into 3 categories: New movie Releases; DVD Movie Guide (with reviews of new releases and top rentals of major movies available on DVD and videocassette); and MiniReviews of Top Playing Films. **Availability:** Online: Cineman Syndicate L.L.C., Cengage Learning Inc., LexisNexis Group, Dow Jones & Company Inc. **Type:** Directory; Full text.

LIBRARIES

20792 ■ American Film Institute–Louis B. Mayer Library
2021 N. Western Ave.
Box 27999
Los Angeles, CA 90027-1657
Ph:(323)856-7654
Fax:(323)467-4578
URL: http://www.afi.com/about/library.aspx
Contact: Caroline Sisneros, Libn.
Scope: Moving pictures, television, video, cable, satellite. **Services:** Copying; Library open to the public. Indexing Service (microfiche); Film Production Index, 1930-1969 (card). **Holdings:** 14,000 books; 900 bound periodical volumes; 6000 motion picture and television scripts; 44 oral history transcripts; 535 seminar transcripts; 600 seminar audiotapes; 75 reels of microfilm. **Subscriptions:** 100 journals and other serials (approximately); 5 newspapers.

20793 ■ Hollywood Film Archive Library
8391 Beverly Blvd. PMB 321
Hollywood, CA 90048
Ph:(323)655-4968
Co. E-mail: cabaret66@aol.com
Contact: D. Richard Baer, Dir.
Scope: Motion pictures, television, video. **Services:** Library open to the public by appointment only. **Holdings:** 2400 volumes; 6000 motion picture stills; Monthly Film Bulletin, 1934 to present; Motion Picture Exhibitor, 1931-1972; Motion Picture Herald, 1944-1960; Boxoffice, 1960 to present.

20794 ■ Jerome Hill Library
32 2nd Ave.
New York, NY 10003-8631
Ph:(212)505-5181
Fax:(212)477-2714
Co. E-mail: robert@anthologyfilmarchives.org
URL: http://anthologyfilmarchives.org
Contact: Robert Haller, Dir. of Coll.
Scope: History of cinema, avant-garde film, video, performance art. **Services:** Copying; Library open to the public by appointment. **Holdings:** 10,000 books; 250 bound periodical series; 650 magnetic tapes; 1100 stills files (arranged by director); 450 film and video vertical Organization files; 2600 individual vertical files; audiotapes of lectures; International publications and periodicals. **Subscriptions:** 300 journals and other serials.

ASSOCIATIONS AND OTHER ORGANIZATIONS

20795 ■ Accreditation Council on Optometric Education
243 N Lindbergh Blvd., 1st Fl.
St. Louis, MO 63141-7881
Ph:(314)991-4100
Fax:(314)991-4101
Co. E-mail: acoe@aoa.org
URL: http://www.aoa.org/x5153.xml
Contact: J. Bart Campbell OD, Chm.

Description: Accrediting body for professional Optometric Degree (O.D.) programs (examination, diagnosis, and treatment and management of diseases and disorders of the vision system, the eyes and associated structures as well as diagnosis of related systemic conditions), paraoptometric educational programs, and optometric residency programs. Members are appointed by the president of the American Optometric Association. Works to ensure the quality of optometric education by establishing and applying valid educational standards and announces list of accredited programs. .

20796 ■ American Academy of Optometry
6110 Executive Blvd., Ste. 506
Rockville, MD 20852
Ph:(301)984-1441
Fax:(301)984-4737
Co. E-mail: aaoptom@aaoptom.org
URL: http://www.aaopt.org
Contact: Dr. Karla Zadnik, Pres./CEO

Description: Represents optometrists, educators, and scientists interested in optometric education, and standards of care in visual problems. Conducts continuing education for optometrists and visual scientists. Sponsors 4-day annual meeting. **Publications:** *Eye Mail Monthly* (monthly); *Optometry and Vision Science* (monthly).

20797 ■ American Board of Opticianry
6506 Loisdale Rd., Ste. 209
Springfield, VA 22150
Ph:(703)719-5800
Free: 800-296-1379
Fax:(703)719-9144
Co. E-mail: mail@abo-ncle.org
URL: http://www.abo-ncle.org

Description: Provides uniform standards for dispensing opticians by administering the National Opticianry Competency Examination and by issuing the Certified Optician Certificate to those passing the exam. Administers the Master in Ophthalmic Optics Examination and issues certificates to opticians at the advanced level passing the exam. Maintains records of persons certified for competency in eyeglass dispensing. Adopts and enforces continuing education requirements; assists and encourages state licensing boards in the use of the National Opticianry Competency Examination for licensure purposes. .

20798 ■ American Optometric Association
243 N Lindbergh Blvd.
St. Louis, MO 63141
Ph:(314)991-4100
Free: 800-365-2219
Fax:(314)991-4101
Co. E-mail: dmcarlson@aoa.org
URL: http://www.aoa.org
Contact: Dori M. Carlson OD, Pres.

Description: Professional association of optometrists, students of optometry, and paraoptometric assistants and technicians. Purposes are: to improve the quality, availability, and accessibility of eye and vision care; to represent the optometric profession; to help members conduct their practices; to promote the highest standards of patient care. Monitors and promotes legislation concerning the scope of optometric practice, alternate health care delivery systems, health care cost containment, Medicare, and other issues relevant to eye/vision care. Supports the International Library, Archives and Museum of Optometry which includes references on ophthalmic and related sciences with emphasis on the history and socioeconomic aspects of optometry. Operates Vision U.S.A. program, which provides free eye care to the working poor, and the InfantSEE program, which provides free vision assessments for infants between six and twelve months of age. Conducts specialized education programs; operates placement service; compiles statistics. Maintains museum. Conducts Seal of Acceptance Program. **Publications:** *Optometry: Journal of the American Optometric Association* (monthly).

20799 ■ American Optometric Foundation
6110 Executive Blvd., Ste. 506
Rockville, MD 20852
Ph:(301)984-4734
Fax:(301)984-4737
Co. E-mail: aof@aaoptom.org
URL: http://www.aaopt.org/aof/about/index.asp
Contact: Catherine S. Amos, Pres.

Description: Optometrists, optometric organizations, corporations, and the public. Promotes research, education, literature, and professional advancement in the visual sciences. Supports fellowships in graduate research. **Publications:** *The Torch* (quarterly).

20800 ■ American Optometric Student Association
243 N Lindbergh Blvd.
St. Louis, MO 63141
Ph:(314)983-4321
Co. E-mail: mburle@theaosa.org
URL: http://www.theaosa.org
Contact: Marlene Burle CMP, Exec. Dir.

Description: Optometric students, state optometric associations, and family members of optometric students. Collects updated information on progress in the optometry field. Provides members with opportunities to work in areas of health care need such as local community health projects, school curriculum changes, and health manpower legislation. Works to improve optometric education and health care for the general population. Maintains active liaison with other optometric associations. Conducts communications program. **Publications:** *AOSA Foresight: Optometry Looking Forward* (semiannual); *Communicator* (9/year).

20801 ■ Association of Regulatory Boards of Optometry
200 S College St., Ste. 1630
Charlotte, NC 28202
Ph:(704)970-2710
Fax:(704)970-2720
Co. E-mail: arbo@arbo.org
URL: http://www.arbo.org
Contact: Jerry Ritch OD, Chm.

Description: Represents the North American regulatory boards of optometry. Works to assist member licensing agencies in regulating the practice of optometry for the public welfare. **Publications:** *Directory of Boards of Optometry* (annual).

20802 ■ Association of Schools and Colleges of Optometry
6110 Executive Blvd., Ste. 420
Rockville, MD 20852
Ph:(301)231-5944
Fax:(301)770-1828
Co. E-mail: mwall@opted.org
URL: http://www.opted.org
Contact: Martin A. Wall CAE, Exec. Dir.

Description: Works to achieve excellence in optometric education and to helping its member schools/colleges prepare well-qualified graduates for entrance into the profession of optometry. Aims to serve the American public through the continued advancement and promotion of all aspects of academic optometry. **Publications:** *Faculty Survey Report* (annual); *Optometric Education* (quarterly); *Residency Online Directory*; *Student Survey Report* (annual).

20803 ■ Association of Vision Science Librarians
University of Michigan
1000 Wall St.
Ann Arbor, MI 48105
Ph:(734)763-9468
Fax:(734)936-9050
Co. E-mail: goren@umich.edu
URL: http://www.avsl.org
Contact: Ms. Gale Oren MILS, Chair

Description: Works to foster collective and individual acquisition and dissemination of vision science information. Improves services for persons seeking vision science information. Develops standards among member-affiliated libraries. **Publications:** *Guidelines for Vision Science Libraries* (annual); *International Directory of Members* (3/year); *Opening Day Book, Journal and Media Collection: Vision Science* (triennial); *Union List of Vision-Related Serials* .

20804 ■ Better Vision Institute
225 Reinekers Ln., Ste. 700
Alexandria, VA 22314
Ph:(703)548-4560

Fax:(703)548-4580
Co. E-mail: ezb@thevisioncouncil.org
URL: http://www.thevisioncouncil.org/bvi
Contact: W. Lee Ball Jr., Chm.
Description: Advisory council of the Vision Council of America. Carried out in consultation with a board of eye care professionals who inform the public of the need for more adequate vision care. **Publications:** *Perspective* .

20805 ■ Canadian Association of Optometrists–Association Canadienne des Optometristes
234 Argyle Ave.
Ottawa, ON, Canada K2P 1B9
Free: 888-263-4676
Fax:(613)235-2025
Co. E-mail: info@opto.ca
URL: http://www.opto.ca
Contact: Glenn Campbell, Exec. Dir.
Description: The mission of the Canadian Association of Optometrists is to represent the profession of Optometry; to enhance the quality, availability, and accessibility of eye, vision, and related health care; to enhance and promote the independent, and ethical decision-making of its members; and to assist Doctors of Optometry in practicing successfully in accordance with the highest standards of patient care. **Publications:** *CJO* (quarterly); *In Touch* (monthly).

20806 ■ Canadian Ophthalmological Society–Societe Canadienne d'Ophthalmologie
610-1525 Carling Ave.
Ottawa, ON, Canada K1Z 8R9
Ph:(613)729-6779
Fax:(613)729-7209
Co. E-mail: cos@eyesite.ca
URL: http://www.eyesite.ca
Contact: Jennifer Brunet-Colvey, Exec. Dir.
Description: Works to ensure the provision of optimal eye care to all Canadians by promoting excellence in ophthalmology and providing services to support its members in practice. **Publications:** *Canadian Journal of Ophthalmology* (bimonthly).

20807 ■ College of Optometrists in Vision Development
215 W Garfield Rd., Ste. 200
Aurora, OH 44202
Ph:(330)995-0718
Free: 888-268-3770
Fax:(330)995-0719
Co. E-mail: info@covd.org
URL: http://www.covd.org
Contact: Ms. Pamela R. Happ CAE, Exec. Dir.
Description: Optometrists involved in developmental vision care and vision therapy with emphasis on visual information processing in visually related learning problems. Seeks to establish a body of practitioners who are knowledgeable in functional and developmental concepts of vision, to insure that the public will receive continually improving vision care; to enable members to maintain the highest standards of professional knowledge and competency; to educate and encourage optometrists to qualify for membership and fellowship in the college; to certify optometrists skilled in this specialty. Conducts national educational programs and public information programs. **Publications:** *E-mail Newsletter Briefs* (weekly); *Membership Directory and Desk Reference* (annual); *Optometry and Vision Development Journal* (quarterly); *Visions Newsletter* (bimonthly).

20808 ■ Contact Lens Manufacturers Association
PO Box 29398
Lincoln, NE 68529
Ph:(402)465-4122
Free: 800-344-9060
Fax:(402)465-4187
Co. E-mail: c_pantle@sbcglobal.net
URL: http://www.clma.net
Contact: Mr. Al Vaske, Pres.
Description: Represents contact lens laboratories, material, solution and equipment manufacturers in the United States and abroad. Aims to increase awareness and utilization of custom-manufactured contact lenses. .

20809 ■ National Academy of Opticianry
8401 Corporate Dr., Ste. 605
Landover, MD 20785
Free: 800-229-4828
Fax:(301)577-3880
Co. E-mail: info@nao.org
URL: http://www.nao.org
Contact: Danne Ventura, Pres.
Description: Offers review courses for national certification and state licensure examinations to members. Maintains speakers' bureau and Career Progression Program. **Publications:** *Academy Newsletter* (quarterly); *Ophthalmic Dispensing Review Book* .

20810 ■ National Association of Vision Professionals
1775 Church St. NW
Washington, DC 20036
Ph:(202)234-1010
Fax:(202)234-1020
Co. E-mail: mhartlove@usa.net
URL: http://visionpros.org
Contact: Linda Pinnell, Pres.
Description: Individuals responsible for or connected with vision conservation and eye health programs in public or private agencies and institutions. Serves as a forum for ideas and programs, cooperates with other agencies, and promotes professional standards. Certifies vision screening personnel. .

20811 ■ National Board of Examiners in Optometry
200 S College St., No. 1920
Charlotte, NC 28202
Ph:(704)332-9565
Free: 800-969-EXAM
Fax:(704)332-9568
Co. E-mail: nbeo@optometry.org
URL: http://www.optometry.org
Contact: Jack Terry PhD, Exec. Dir.
Description: Administers entry-level criterion-referenced credentialing examinations to students and graduates of accredited schools and colleges of optometry for use by individual state licensing boards. Provides other evaluation, assessment, and survey services to the profession. **Publications:** *Test Points* (3/year).

20812 ■ National Contact Lens Examiners
6506 Loisdale Rd., Ste. 209
Springfield, VA 22150
Ph:(703)719-5800
Fax:(703)719-9144
Co. E-mail: mail@abo-ncle.org
URL: http://www.abo.org
Description: Serves as National certifying agency promoting continued development of opticians and technicians as contact lens fitters by formulating standards and procedures for determination of entry-level competency. Assists in the continuation, development, administration, and monitoring of a national Contact Lens Registry Examination (CLRE), which verifies entry-level competency of contact lens fitters. Issues certificates. Activities include: maintaining records of those certified in contact lens fitting; encouraging state occupational licensing and credentialing agencies to use the CLRE for licensure purposes; identifying contact lens dispensing education needs as a result of findings of examination programs; disseminating information to sponsors of contact lens continuing education programs. .

20813 ■ National Optometric Association
PO Box 198959
Chicago, IL 60619-8959
Free: 877-394-2020
Fax:(773)721-7351
Co. E-mail: info@nationaloptometricassociation.com
URL: http://www.natoptassoc.org
Contact: Dr. Vicki L. Hughes, Pres.
Description: Represents optometrists dedicated to increasing awareness of the status of eye/vision health in the minority community and the national community at-large. Strives to make known the impact of the eye/vision dysfunction on the effectiveness and productivity of citizens and the academic proficiency of students. Conducts national minority recruiting programs, job placement, assistance programs for graduates, practitioners, and optometric organizations, and the promotion of delivery of care. Maintains speakers' bureau. Offers specialized education program. .

20814 ■ Optical Laboratories Association
11096 Lee Hwy., Ste. A-101
Fairfax, VA 22030-5039
Ph:(703)359-2830
Free: 800-477-5652
Fax:(703)359-2834
Co. E-mail: ola@ola-labs.org
URL: http://www.ola-labs.org
Contact: Robert L. Dziuban CAE
Description: Represents independent, wholesale ophthalmic laboratories and suppliers serving the ophthalmic field. .

20815 ■ Opticians Association of America
4064 E Fir Hill Dr.
Lakeland, TN 38002
Ph:(901)388-2423
Fax:(901)388-2348
Co. E-mail: oaa@oaa.org
URL: http://www.oaa.org
Contact: Christopher M. Allen, Exec. Dir.
Description: Retail dispensing opticians who fill prescriptions for glasses or contact lenses written by a vision care specialist. Works to advance the science of ophthalmic optics. Conducts research and educational programs. Maintains museum and speakers' bureau. Compiles statistics. **Publications:** *American Optician* (quarterly).

20816 ■ Opticians Association of Canada–Association des Opticiens du Canada
2706-83 Garry St.
Winnipeg, MB, Canada R3C 4J9
Ph:(204)982-6060
Free: 800-847-3155
Fax:(204)947-2519
Co. E-mail: canada@opticians.ca
URL: http://www.opticians.ca
Contact: Dalie Schellen, Pres.
Description: Dispensing opticians. Promotes advancement of opticianry. Works to safeguard members' economic and professional interests. Conducts educational programs. **Publications:** *Vision* (bimonthly).

20817 ■ Vision Council
225 Reinekers Ln., Ste. 700
Alexandria, VA 22314
Ph:(703)548-4560
Free: (866)826-0290
Fax:(703)548-4580
Co. E-mail: info@thevisioncouncil.org
URL: http://www.thevisioncouncil.org
Contact: Edward E. Greene, CEO
Description: Trade association of optical industry companies that sponsor exhibits at industry trade shows. Works to serve the collective interests of the ophthalmic community; encourages the public to visit eye care practitioners regularly. Seeks to produce top quality trade shows. Conducts public educational programs. .

DIRECTORIES OF EDUCATIONAL PROGRAMS

20818 ■ *Directory of Private Accredited Career Schools and Colleges of Technology*
Pub: Accrediting Commission of Career Schools and Colleges of Technology
Contact: Michale S. McComis, Exec. Dir.
Released: On web page. **Price:** Free. **Description:** Covers 3900 accredited post-secondary programs that provide training programs in business, trade, and technical fields, including various small business endeavors. Entries offer school name, address, phone, description of courses, job placement assistance, and requirements for admission. Arrangement is alphabetical.

REFERENCE WORKS

20819 ■ *Contact Lens Manufacturers Association—Member Directory*
Pub: Contact Lens Manufacturers Association
Released: Annual, March. **Entries Include:** Company name, address, phone, name and title of contact. **Arrangement:** Alphabetical within membership categories. **Indexes:** Geographical.

20820 ■ "SEEing an Opportunity; Golden's Eyewear Chain Has a National Vision" in *Crain's Detroit Business* (Vol. 24, January 7, 2008, No. 1)
Pub: Crain Communications Inc. - Detroit
Ed: Sheena Harrison. **Description:** Richard Golden, who recently sold D.O.C. Optics Corporation is planning to build a new national eyewear chain called SEE Inc., which stands for Selective Eyewear Elements. SEE will sell expensive-looking glasses at lower prices than designer styles.

20821 ■ "Visionary Riches" in *Small Business Opportunities* (Winter 2009)
Pub: Entrepreneur Media Inc.
Description: Profile of Sterling Optical, which was included in a recent listing of 25 franchise high performers in The Wall Street Journal and is poised for mega-growth due to its offerings of professional eye exams, impeccable customer service, convenient locations and a great selection of eyewear.

STATISTICAL SOURCES

20822 ■ *RMA Annual Statement Studies*
Pub: Robert Morris Associates (RMA)
Released: Annual. **Price:** $175.00 2006-07 edition, $105.00. **Description:** Contains composite balance sheets and income statements for more than 360 industries, including the accounting, auditing, and bookkeeping industries. Also contains five years of comparative historical data for discerning trends. Includes 16 commonly used ratios, computed for most of the size groupings for nearly every industry.

TRADE PERIODICALS

20823 ■ *AAO News*
Pub: Alberta Association of Optometrists (AAO)
Released: Bimonthly. **Price:** Included in membership. **Description:** Covers news of interest in the field of optometry in Canada.

20824 ■ *AOA News*
Pub: American Optometric Association
Released: 18/yr. **Description:** Magazine of news and events for the American Optometric Association.

20825 ■ *Eyecare Business*
Pub: Lippincott Williams & Wilkins VisionCare Group
Contact: Stephenie K. De Long, Editor-in-Chief
E-mail: delongsk@lwwvisioncare.com
Released: Monthly. **Description:** Magazine for eyecare professionals.

20826 ■ *Eyewitness*
Pub: Contact Lens Society of America
Ed: Ledonna buckner, Editor. **Released:** Quarterly. **Price:** Included in membership. **Description:** Informs members of developments in the contact lens industry. Also reports on related educational information and technical papers. Recurring features include news of research, calendar of events, reports of meetings, and associate member listing.

20827 ■ *Gleams*
Pub: Glaucoma Research Foundation
Contact: Catalina San Agustin
Ed: Catalina San Agustin, Editor, catalinas@glaucoma.org. **Released:** Quarterly, 3/year. **Price:** Free. **Description:** Examines the results of clinical and basic research on glaucoma. Seeks to increase public knowledge of the eye disease and discusses prevention of blindness from the disease. Contains articles on glaucoma research, treatment updates and tips on living with glaucoma.

20828 ■ *National Glaucoma Research Report*
Pub: American Health Assistance Foundation
Released: 3/year. **Price:** Free. **Description:** Highlights the work of glaucoma researchers and provides tips for individuals with glaucoma. Recurring features include news of research and columns titled From the Presidents and Ask the Experts.

20829 ■ *Optometric Education*
Pub: Association of Schools & Colleges of Optometry
Contact: Dominick M. Maino, Co-Ed.
Ed: Elizabeth Hoppe, Editor. **Released:** 3/yr. **Price:** $30; $40 other countries. **Description:** Optometric journal.

TRADE SHOWS AND CONVENTIONS

20830 ■ Annual Meeting of the American Academy of Ophthalmology
American Academy of Ophthalmology
655 Beach St.
PO Box 7424
San Francisco, CA 94120-7424
Ph:(415)561-8500
Fax:(415)561-8533
Co. E-mail: aaoe@aao.org
URL: http://www.aao.org
Released: Annual. **Audience:** Ophthalmologists and related trade professionals. **Principal Exhibits:** Ophthalmic equipment and instruments. **Dates and Locations:** 2011 Oct 22-25.

20831 ■ California Optometric Association OptoWest
California Optometric Association
2415 K St.
Sacramento, CA 95816
Ph:(916)441-3990
Free: 800-877-5738
Fax:(916)448-1423
Co. E-mail: contact@coavision.org
URL: http://www.coavision.org
Released: Annual. **Principal Exhibits:** Optometric equipment, supplies, and services. **Dates and Locations:** 2011 Apr 07-10, Indian Wells, CA.

20832 ■ International Vision Expo and Conference/West
Reed Exhibitions Contemporary Forums
11900 Silvergate Dr.
Dublin, CA 94568
Ph:(925)828-7100
Fax:800-329-9923
Co. E-mail: info@cforums.com
URL: http://www.contemporaryforums.com
Released: Annual. **Audience:** Industry buyers, opticians, and optometrists. **Principal Exhibits:** Contact lenses, solutions, and care kits; frames; glass and plastic ophthalmic lenses; plano sunglasses; specialty lenses; business and record management systems; computer systems; dispensing, display, and examination equipment; laboratory systems; office furniture and design services; training programs; vision aids. **Dates and Locations:** 2011 Sep 21-24, Las Vegas, NV.

20833 ■ MOA Fall Seminar
Michigan Optometric Association
530 W. Ionia St.
Lansing, MI 48933
Ph:(517)482-0616
Fax:(517)482-1611
URL: http://www.michigan.aoa.org
Released: Annual. **Audience:** Professional optometrists, optometric technicians and assistants, and ophthalmic suppliers. **Principal Exhibits:** Ophthalmic supplies and services. **Dates and Locations:** 2011 Oct 05-06, Lansing, MI.

FRANCHISES AND BUSINESS OPPORTUNITIES

20834 ■ Pearle Vision, Inc.
Cole National Corp.
4000 Luxottica Pl.
Mason, OH 45040
Ph:(513)765-3327
Free: 800-732-7531
Fax:(513)492-3462
Co. E-mail: opportunities@pearlevision.com
URL: http://www.pearlevison.com/fh.htm
No. of Franchise Units: 346. **No. of Company-Owned Units:** 322. **Founded:** 1961. **Franchised:** 1980. **Description:** Eyewear and eye-care stores. **Equity Capital Needed:** $202,258-$577,103. **Franchise Fee:** $30,000. **Royalty Fee:** 5.5
%. **Financial Assistance:** Third party financing available. **Training:** Offers 1 week at headquarters, 1 week at franchisees location, at company-owned location (optional) 1 week and ongoing support.

20835 ■ Sterling Optical
Emerging Vision, Inc.
520 8th Ave., Rm. 2300
New York, NY 10018
Ph:(516)390-2133
Fax:(516)320-8073
URL: http://www.sterlingoptical.com
No. of Franchise Units: 180. **No. of Company-Owned Units:** 10. **Founded:** 1919. **Franchised:** 1992. **Description:** Franchises optic centers. **Equity Capital Needed:** $100,000-$660,000. **Franchise Fee:** $20,000. **Financial Assistance:** No. **Training:** Ongoing training programs with initial focus on in-store operation and business operating systems. Continuing education through onsite visits.

LIBRARIES

20836 ■ American Academy of Optometry Library
6110 Executive Blvd., Ste. 506
Rockville, MD 20852
Ph:(301)984-1441
Fax:(301)984-4737
Co. E-mail: aaoptom@aaoptom.org
URL: http://www.aaopt.org
Contact: Lois Schoenbrun, Exec.Dir.
Scope: Optometry, physiological optics, ocular pathology. **Services:** Library not open to the public. **Holdings:** Optometry & Vision Science (formerly the American Journal of Optometry & Physiological Optics). **Subscriptions:** 12 journals and other serials.

20837 ■ American Optometric Association–International Library, Archives & Museum of Optometry
243 N. Lindbergh Blvd.
St. Louis, MO 63141
Ph:(314)991-4100
Free: 800-365-2219
Fax:(314)991-4101
Co. E-mail: ilamo@aoa.org
URL: http://www.aoa.org/x11718.xml
Contact: Linda Draper, Spec.Coll.Libn.
Scope: Vision, optometry, ophthalmology, optics. **Services:** Interlibrary loan; copying; Library open to the public. **Holdings:** 10,000 books; 400 feet of archives. **Subscriptions:** 300 journals and other serials.

20838 ■ Florida Ophthalmic Institute Library
7106 NW 11th Pl.
Gainesville, FL 32605-3140
Ph:(352)331-2020
Fax:(352)331-2019
Contact: Norman S. Levy, Dr. of Opthalmology
Scope: Ophthalmology, visual sciences. **Services:** Library not open to the public. **Holdings:** 104 books; 14 bound periodical volumes. **Subscriptions:** 14 journals and other serials.

20839 ■ National Eye Research Foundation Library
9461 Harrison St.
Des Plaines, IL 60016-1542
Ph:800-621-2258
Fax:(847)564-0807
Co. E-mail: info@nerf.org
URL: http://www.nerf.org
Scope: Optometry. **Services:** Library open to the public for reference use only.

20840 ■ Pennsylvania College of Optometry–Gerard Cottet Library
8360 Old York Rd.
Elkins Park, PA 19027
Ph:(215)780-1260
Free: 800-824-6262
Co. E-mail: keith@pco.edu
URL: http://www.salus.edu/facilities/library.html
Contact: Keith Lammers, Dir.

Scope: Optometry, ophthalmology, optics theory, ophthalmic optics, contact lenses, low vision rehabilitation. **Services:** Interlibrary loan; copying; Library open to the public with restrictions. **Holdings:** 8000 books; 21,000 bound periodical volumes; 2 VF drawers of old instruments pamphlets; 125 videocassettes; 9650 audiocassettes; 100 slides; 160 CD-ROMs; CD-ROM. **Subscriptions:** 280 journals and other serials.

20841 ■ Southern California College of Optometry–M.B. Ketchum Memorial Library
2575 Yorba Linda Blvd.
Fullerton, CA 92831-1699
Ph:(714)449-7440
Fax:(714)879-0481
Co. E-mail: library@scco.edu
URL: http://www.scco.edu/library
Contact: D. J. Matthews, Dir. of Lib.Svcs.

Scope: Optometry, optics, ophthalmology; vision. **Services:** Interlibrary loan; copying; Library open to the public with restrictions. **Holdings:** 10,000 books; 6000 bound periodical volumes; 450 theses; 500 AV programs. **Subscriptions:** 360 serials.

RESEARCH CENTERS

20842 ■ Dry Eye and Tear Research Center
Regions Hospital
640 Jackson St.
St. Paul, MN 55101
Ph:(651)254-1001
Fax:(651)254-1480
Co. E-mail: j.d.nelson@healthpartners.com
Contact: Dr. J. Daniel Nelson, Dir.
E-mail: j.d.nelson@healthpartners.com

Scope: Basic and clinical studies of dry eye and tearing disorders, focusing on ocular surface diseases, the effects of chemicals and nutrients on corneal epithelium, and the role of hormones in the development of dry eye states.

20843 ■ Duke University–Eye Center
PO Box 3802
Durham, NC 27710
Ph:(919)684-6611
Free: 800—422-1575
Fax:(919)681-6343
Co. E-mail: info@dukeeye.org
URL: http://www.dukehealth.org/eye_center
Contact: Dr. David L. Epstein, Ch.
E-mail: info@dukeeye.org

Scope: Eye disorders, with special focus on retinal detachment, corneal diseases, and proliferative diabetic retinopathy.

20844 ■ University of Calgary–Vision and Aging Laboratory
Department of Psychology
2500 University Dr. NW
Calgary, AB, Canada T2N 1N4
Ph:(403)220-5561
Fax:(403)282-8249
Co. E-mail: donkline@ucalgary.ca
URL: http://www.psych.ucalgary.ca/PACE/VA-Lab/
Contact: Prof. Donald Kline PhD, Dir.
E-mail: donkline@ucalgary.ca

Scope: Aging effects on vision, optical and neural aspects of visual aging, visual aging, visual human factors and everyday tasks; visual health, refractive surgery, vision change and quality-of-life, visual testing. **Services:** Gerontological vision testing and correction. **Educational Activities:** Public presentations. **Awards:** Graduate awards.

20845 ■ University of California, Los Angeles–Jules Stein Eye Institute
100 Stein Plz.
Los Angeles, CA 90095-7000
Ph:(310)206-7202
Fax:(310)794-7906
Co. E-mail: mondinopatients@jsei.ucla.edu
URL: http://www.jsei.org
Contact: Bartly J. Mondino MD, Dir.
E-mail: mondinopatients@jsei.ucla.edu

Scope: Research and study in sciences related to vision, care of patients with eye disease, and education in ophthalmology. **Services:** UCLA Mobile Eye Clinic. **Publications:** Annual report; Clinical Update (3/year); EYE (3/year). **Educational Activities:** Grand Rounds (weekly); Jules Stein Eye Institute Seminar.

20846 ■ University of Texas—Houston Health Science Center–Cizik Eye Clinic
Memorial Hermann Medical Plz., 18th Fl.
6400 Fannin St.
Houston, TX 77030
Ph:(713)559-5200
Fax:(713)795-0733
Co. E-mail: richard.s.ruiz@uth.tms.edu
URL: http://www.cizikeye.org
Contact: Dr. Richard S. Ruiz
E-mail: richard.s.ruiz@uth.tms.edu

Scope: Cataracts, corneal disease, glaucoma, neuroophthalmology, ophthalmic surgery, pediatric ophthalmology, strabismus, and retinal disease. Additional studies include ocular melanoma, retinitis pigmentosa, diabetes, retinal pigment epithelial transplantation, ischemic optic neuropathy decompression, and pattern electrogram in Alzheimer's disease. **Services:** Hermann Eye Fund, provides help for indigent patients and funds for research and teaching. **Educational Activities:** Courses and seminars; Postdoctoral degree program.

ASSOCIATIONS AND OTHER ORGANIZATIONS

20847 ■ Association of Teleservices International
12 Academy Ave.
Atkinson, NH 03811
Ph:(603)362-9489
Free: (866)896-ATSI
Fax:(603)362-9486
Co. E-mail: admin@atsi.org
URL: http://www.atsi.org
Contact: Mike Fultz, Pres.

Description: Telephone answering and voice message service providers. Seeks to foster growth and development in the industry. Represents the industry before Congress and regulatory agencies; negotiates with telephone companies. Holds seminars and workshops on the latest telecommunications technology; compiles statistics. Maintains hall of fame. **Publications:** *Connections* (bimonthly); *TeleCommunicator* (biweekly).

20848 ■ Canadian Call Management Association
24 Olive St., Unit 10
Grimsby, ON, Canada L3M 2B6
Ph:(905)309-0224
Free: 800-896-1054
Fax:(905)309-0225
Co. E-mail: info@camx.ca
URL: http://www.camx.ca/call-center/index_ang.cfm
Contact: Linda Osip, Exec. Dir.

Description: Call centers and message exchanges. Promotes excellence in the handling of voice and electronic messages. Represents members' interests; facilitates technical advancement in the field of telecommunications. **Publications:** *Advisor* (bimonthly).

20849 ■ Telecommunications Industry Association
2500 Wilson Blvd., Ste. 300
Arlington, VA 22201-3834
Ph:(703)907-7700
Fax:(703)907-7727
Co. E-mail: gseiffert@tiaonline.org
URL: http://www.tiaonline.org
Contact: Grant Seiffert, Pres.

Description: Serves the communications and IT industry, with proven strengths in standards development, domestic and international public policy, and trade shows. Facilitates business development and opportunities and a competitive market environment; provides a forum for member companies, the manufacturers and suppliers of products and services used in global communications. Represents the communications sector of the Electronic Industries Alliance. **Publications:** *Channel Intelligence Report*; *Industry Beat* (weekly); *PulseOnline* (monthly); *TIA Network* (weekly).

REFERENCE WORKS

20850 ■ *Telecommunications Directory*
Pub: Gale

Released: Annual, Latest edition 23rd; April, 2012. **Price:** $993, individuals. **Covers:** Two volumes-North America and International, Cover approximately 6,000 national and international voice and data communications networks, electronic mail services, teleconferencing facilities and services, facsimile services, Internet access providers, videotex and teletext operations, transactional services, local area networks, audiotex services, microwave systems/networkers, satellite facilities, and others involved in telecommunications, including related consultants, advertisers/marketers; associations, regulatory bodies, and publishers. **Entries Include:** Company or organization name, address, phone, fax, year established, name and title of contact, executive officers and board of directors, function or type of service; geographical area served; NAICS and SIC codes; number of employees; general description, including telecommunications-related activities; product/service; specific applications; means of access and equipment required; publications; intended market and availability; pricing; stock exchanges traded and ticker symbols; financial figures. **Arrangement:** Alphabetical by company name; within geographic region. **Indexes:** Name of firm/acronym, personal name, geographical (with name, address, phone, and director), and function/type of service (with name, address, phone). Indexes are cumulative.

TRADE PERIODICALS

20851 ■ *Audiotex Update*
Pub: Worldwide Videotex
Contact: Mark Wright

Ed: Mark Wright, Editor, markedit@juno.com. **Released:** Monthly. **Price:** $165, U.S. and Canada; $180, elsewhere. **Description:** Provides the latest news and information on the audiotex industry. Discusses voice processing/information products, services, companies, marketing strategies, and research and development. Recurring features include news of research and book reviews.

CONSULTANTS

20852 ■ Network Consulting & Associates Inc.
1626 S Luther Ave.
Oakbrook Terrace, IL 60181-5254
Ph:(630)424-1600
Fax:(630)424-1650
Contact: Dave Keating, President

Scope: Project management specialists with expertise in design, development, installation and ongoing operation of telecommunications systems including private networks, corporate voice networks, telephone systems, videoconferencing, voice mail systems, bypass systems, fiber optics, microwave, facsimile and premise distribution systems. Specialty areas include requirements definitions, RFP's, proposal evaluations, feasibility studies and system cut-overs. **Seminars:** Getting Started - Your Own In-house Project; IBM Midrange AS400 Support; Network Evaluations.

20853 ■ Reston Consulting Group Inc.
462 Herndon Pky., Ste. 203
Herndon, VA 20170-5234
Ph:(703)834-1155
Fax:(703)834-3086
Co. E-mail: info@rcg.com
URL: http://www.rcg.com
Contact: Brij Bhushan, President
E-mail: brijb@atsrcg.com

Scope: Provides consulting services for voice, data, video and integrated communication networks; develops plans for networks. Also provides network design, engineering and integration services. Serves private industries as well as government agencies.

LIBRARIES

20854 ■ Alcatel Network Systems Library
2912 Wake Forest Rd.
Raleigh, NC 27609
Ph:(919)850-6414
Fax:(919)850-5131
Co. E-mail: joan.viscounty@usa.alcatel.com
URL: http://www.alcatel.com
Contact: Joan Viscounty, Libn.

Scope: Telecommunications, electronics, computers, business management. **Services:** Library open to the public by appointment. **Holdings:** 3000 books; 120 bound periodical volumes; 175 proceedings of conferences and symposia; 200 engineering reports. **Subscriptions:** 225 journals and other serials.

20855 ■ GTE Telephone Operations Headquarters Library
600 Hidden Ridge
MCF04P01
Irving, TX 75038
Ph:(972)718-5549
Fax:(214)718-2399
Contact: Charlotte Wixx Clark, Lib.Hd.

Scope: Market research, telecommunications, technology, business telecommunication-related products. **Services:** Interlibrary loan; Library not open to the public. **Holdings:** 450 books; 8 CD-ROM; 10,000 studies; reports; manuscripts. **Subscriptions:** 152 journals and other serials.

20856 ■ Pitney Bowes Information Center
35 Waterview Dr., No. 26-33
Shelton, CT 06484-4301
Ph:(203)924-3235
URL: http://www.pb.com

Scope: Computers, software engineering, printing technology, inks, adhesives, physics, postal service, telecommunications. **Services:** Interlibrary loan; Center not open to the public. **Holdings:** 3000 books. **Subscriptions:** 300 journals and other serials.

RESEARCH CENTERS

20857 ■ University of Louisville–Information Technology Resource Center
Shelby Campus
9001 Shelbyville Rd.
Louisville, KY 40222
Ph:(502)852-0900
Fax:(502)852-4701
Co. E-mail: graham@louisville.edu
Contact: James H. Graham Jr., Dir.
E-mail: graham@louisville.edu
Scope: Applied information technology. Research focuses on the effects of information technology on the workplace, including assistance to start-up and existing businesses on leveraging emerging technologies, proof-of-concept, and application development. **Services:** New technology testing; Support, to local and commonwealth economic agencies. **Educational Activities:** Seminars and product demonstrations.

ASSOCIATIONS AND OTHER ORGANIZATIONS

20858 ■ International Desalination Association
PO Box 387
Topsfield, MA 01983
Ph:(978)887-0410
Fax:(978)887-0411
Co. E-mail: info@idadesal.org
URL: http://www.idadesal.org
Contact: Dr. Corrado Sommariva, Pres.
Description: Users and suppliers of desalination equipment; water reuse and reclamation consultants. Seeks to develop and promote worldwide application of desalination and desalination technology in maintaining water supplies, controlling water pollution, and purifying, treating, and reusing water. Disseminates information on desalination-related subjects and water reuse. Encourages the establishment of standards, specifications, procedures, and the efficient use of water for energy. Conducts seminars and workshops. **Publications:** *Conference Proceedings* (biennial); *IDA Desalination and Water Reuse Quarterly* (quarterly); *IDA Membership Directory* (annual); *IDA Newsletter* (bimonthly).

20859 ■ National Utility Contractors Association I Clean Water Council
3925 Chain Bridge Rd., Ste. 301
Fairfax, VA 22030
Ph:(703)358-9300
Fax:(703)358-9307
Co. E-mail: bill@nuca.com
URL: http://www.nuca.com
Contact: Bill Hillman, CEO
Description: Construction, engineering, manufacturing, distribution, labor, and general business associations. Promotes increased federal funding for water quality infrastructure. Conducts educational programs to raise public awareness of water quality issues; conducts lobbying activities. .

20860 ■ Ocean Futures Society
325 Chapala St.
Santa Barbara, CA 93101
Ph:(805)899-8899
Fax:(805)899-8898
Co. E-mail: contact@oceanfutures.org
URL: http://www.oceanfutures.org
Contact: Jean-Michel Cousteau, Pres./Chm.
Description: Provides the global community with a forum for exploring issues affecting the ocean, its inhabitants, and its habitats. **Publications:** *Jean-Michel Cousteau Dispatch* (monthly).

20861 ■ Water Quality Association
4151 Naperville Rd.
Lisle, IL 60532-1088
Ph:(630)505-0160
Fax:(630)505-9637
Co. E-mail: info@wqa.org
URL: http://www.wqa.org
Contact: Peter J. Censky, Exec. Dir.
Description: Individuals or firms engaged in the manufacture and/or assembly and distribution and/or retail selling of water treatment equipment, supplies, and services. Promotes the acceptance and use of industry equipment, products, and services. Provides activities, programs, and services designed to improve economy and efficiency within the industry. Conducts expositions and certification and equipment validation programs. Compiles statistics. **Publications:** *Water Treatment Fundamentals*; *Water Treatment Fundamentals Seminar Audio Cassette Series*; *WQA NewsFax* (bimonthly).

REFERENCE WORKS

20862 ■ "Blackwater is LEED Golden for Port of Portland Building" in *Contractor* (Vol. 56, October 2009, No. 10, pp. 3)
Pub: Penton Media, Inc.
Ed: Robert P. Mader. **Description:** Worrel Water Technologies' Tidal Wetlands Living Machine recycles blackwater from the toilets and sends it right back to flush the toilets. The Technology is being installed in the new headquarters of the Port of Portland which aims to get awarded a gold certificate from the Leadership in Energy and Environmental Design.

20863 ■ "Corporate Park Retrofits for Water Savings" in *Contractor* (Vol. 56, October 2009, No. 10, pp. 5)
Pub: Penton Media, Inc.
Description: Merrit Corporate Park in Norwalk, Connecticut has been interested in improving building efficiency and one of their buildings has been retrofitted with water-efficient plumbing systems which will allow them to save as much as two million gallons of water. ADP Service Corp. helped the park upgrade their plumbing system.

20864 ■ "More Than 1,000 Attend Second WaterSmart" in *Contractor* (Vol. 56, November 2009, No. 11, pp. 3)
Pub: Penton Media, Inc.
Description: Over 1,000 plumbing and water conservation professionals attended the second WaterSmart Innovations Conference and Exposition in Las Vegas. Plumbing industry personalities made presentations during the conference and several innovative products were displayed at the trade show.

20865 ■ "Next Stage of Green Building will be Water Efficiency" in *Contractor* (Vol. 56, July 2009, No. 7, pp. 41)
Pub: Penton Media, Inc.
Description: One market report says that water efficiency and conservation will become critical factors in green design, construction, and product selection in the next five years from 2009. The report outlines how critical it will be for the construction industry to address responsible water practices in the future.

20866 ■ "Snow Melt Systems Offer Practical Solutions" in *Contractor* (Vol. 56, October 2009, No. 10, pp. S6)
Pub: Penton Media, Inc.
Ed: Lisa Murton Beets. **Description:** Cases are discussed in which the installation of a snow melt system becomes a necessity. One example describes how limited space means there would be no place to put plowed snow; snow melt systems can also resolve problems that arise due to an excess of melting snow.

20867 ■ "Water Company Eyeing Region for a New Plant" in *Charlotte Business Journal* (Vol. 25, December 10, 2010, No. 38, pp. 1)
Pub: Charlotte Business Journal
Ed: Ken Elkins. **Description:** California-based Niagara Bottling Company is hoping to find a site in Charlotte, North Carolina where it can build a water bottling plant that would employ 70 workers. The investment is expected to cost about $25 million to $40 million.

20868 ■ *Water Conditioning & Purification—Buyers Guide Issue*
Pub: Publicom, Inc.
Contact: Kurt C. Peterson, Publisher
E-mail: kcpeterson@wcponline.com
Released: Continuous. **Price:** Free. **Publication Includes:** List of about 800 manufacturers and suppliers in the water treatment and purification industry. **Entries Include:** Company name, address, phone, name of contact, line of business. **Arrangement:** Classified by product/service, then alphabetical. **Indexes:** Brand and trade names, product.

20869 ■ *Water Quality Association—Membership Directory*
Pub: Water Quality Association
Contact: Margit Fotre, Dir. of Membership & Marketing
E-mail: mfotre@wqa.org
Released: Annual, July. **Covers:** About 1,860 retailer, individual, and allied members, and about 540 member manufacturers and suppliers and 450 international members. **Entries Include:** For manufacturers and suppliers—Company name, address, phone, names and titles of key personnel, description of products and services. For retailers—Member name, company name, address, phone. For others—Member name, company name (if any), address. **Arrangement:** Manufacturers and suppliers are alphabetical; others are geographical in separate lists. **Indexes:** Member company listing.

20870 ■ "WQA Develops Certification Program" in *Contractor* (Vol. 57, January 2010, No. 1, pp. 56)
Pub: Penton Media, Inc.
Description: Water Quality Association is now offering a new certification program for companies that may be affected by California's law that prohibits any products intended to convey or dispense water for human consumption that is not lead-free. All pipe or plumbing fixtures must be certified by a third party certification body.

20871 ■ "WQA's Leadership Conference Tackles Industry Issues" in *Contractor* (Vol. 56, October 2009, No. 10, pp. 3)
Pub: Penton Media, Inc.
Ed: Candace Roulo. **Description:** Water Quality Association's Mid-Year Leadership Conference held in Bloomingdale, Illinois in September 2009 tackled lead

regulation, water softeners, and product efficiency. The possibility of a WQA green seal was discussed by the Water Sciences Committee and the Government Relations Committee meeting.

STATISTICAL SOURCES

20872 ■ *The U.S. Market for Bottled, Enhanced and Flavored Water - 3rd Edition*
Pub: MarketResearch.com

Released: 2003. **Price:** $2250.00. **Description:** *The U.S. Market for Bottled and Enhanced Edition Water* is a brand-new report that offers a unique perspective on the changing market for bottled spring and fortified waters. No other market research report provides both the comprehensive analysis and extensive data that The U.S. Market for Bottled and Enhanced Water offers.

TRADE PERIODICALS

20873 ■ *Drinking Water & Backflow Prevention*
Pub: IAPMO

Ed: Krystal Renea Garza, Editor. **Released:** Monthly. **Price:** $45, U.S. year; $53 Canada and Mexico.; $59, elsewhere year. **Description:** Presents articles directed toward "individuals, companies, organizations, agencies, and municipalities with an interest in drinking water protection and backflow prevention." Contains information on safety standards, water system protection, training programs, cross-connection control, and all issues related to preventing the contamination of potable drinking water supplies with backflow prevention devices. Recurring features include case studies, letters to the editor, news of research, columns titled Test Your Investigative Skills and Backflow Prevention Device Repairs, and reports of meetings. Also carries news of educational opportunities, job listings, notices of publications available, and a calendar of events.

20874 ■ *MainStream–Streamline*
Pub: American Water Works Association (AWWA)
Contact: Mary A. Parmelee

Ed: Mary A. Parmelee, Editor, mparmele@awwa.org. **Released:** Biweekly, online; print issue is published quarterly. **Price:** Included in membership; $16, nonmembers U.S. and Canada; $22, nonmembers elsewhere. **Description:** Carries news of the Association and features about the drinking water industry, including regulations, legislation, conservation, treatment, quality, distribution, management, and utility operations. Recurring features include letters to the editor, a calendar of events, reports of meetings, news of educational opportunities, notices of publications available, education and job opportunities in the industry and legislative news.

20875 ■ *Operations Forum*
Pub: Water Environment Federation

Released: Monthly. **Price:** $79 nonmembers. **Description:** Magazine covering operation/maintenance of WWTPs and wastewater collections systems.

20876 ■ *Water Conditioning & Purification*
Pub: Publicom, Inc.
Contact: Kurt C. Peterson, Publisher
E-mail: kcpeterson@wcponline.com

Released: Monthly. **Description:** Magazine on residential and commercial water conditioning and purification.

20877 ■ *Water Desalination Report*
Pub: Maria C. Smith

Ed: Tom Pankratz, Editor. **Released:** Weekly. **Price:** $500, U.S. **Description:** Concentrates on the activities of government and industry worldwide concerning the desalination of seawater and brackish water. Discusses such topics as problems with water supply and reuse, resource planning, and pollution control. Reports on federal budgets, regulation, new and future programs, opportunities in business, and research. Recurring features include book reviews and a schedule of activities.

20878 ■ *Water Policy Report*
Pub: Inside Washington Publishers
Contact: Charlie Mitchell, Chief Editor

Released: Biweekly, every other Monday. **Price:** $650, U.S. and Canada; $700, elsewhere. **Description:** Reports on federal water quality programs and policies. Covers topics such as drinking water, toxics, enforcement, monitoring, and state/EPA relations.

20879 ■ *Water Technology*
Pub: National Trade Publications Inc.
Contact: Phil Arndt, Publisher
E-mail: parndt@watertechonline.com

Released: Monthly. **Description:** Magazine focusing on point of use water treatment.

VIDEOCASSETTES/ AUDIOCASSETTES

20880 ■ *Natural Waste Water Treatment*
Bullfrog Films, Inc.
PO Box 149
Oley, PA 19547
Ph:(610)779-8226
Free: 800-543-3764
Fax:(610)370-1978
Co. E-mail: video@bullfrogfilms.com
URL: http://bullfrogfilms.com

Released: 1987. **Description:** A look at small decentralized sewage treatment plants that use the natural purifying characteristics of marsh plants. **Availability:** VHS; 3/4U.

20881 ■ *Wastewater Treatment*
Practicing Law Institute
810 7th Ave., 21st Fl.
New York, NY 10019-5818
Ph:(212)824-5700
Free: 800-260-4PLI
Co. E-mail: info@pli.edu
URL: http://www.pli.edu

Released: 1988. **Description:** Be sure to run your wastewater system correctly, because no one wants to end up with second-rate bilge as a finished product. **Availability:** VHS; 3/4U.

TRADE SHOWS AND CONVENTIONS

20882 ■ Environmex/Watermex South China - International Environment & Water Management Technology, Equipment & Control Systems Exhibition
Hong Kong Exhibition Services Ltd.
Units 2010, 20/F
China Resources Bldg.
26 Harbour Rd.
Wanchai, People's Republic of China
Ph:852 2804 1500
Fax:852 2528 3103
Co. E-mail: exhibit@hkesallworld.com
URL: http://www.hkesallworld.com

Released: Biennial. **Audience:** Trade professionals. **Principal Exhibits:** Environment and water management equipment, supplies, and services.

CONSULTANTS

20883 ■ Frank Thatcher Associates Inc.
564 Market St., Ste. 612
San Francisco, CA 94104-5414
Ph:(415)956-6118
Fax:(415)956-3228
Contact: Gregory J. Forrest, President

Scope: Firm provides professional telecommunications engineering services, specializing in microwave radio, transit and public safety radio, 911 and computer-aided dispatch systems, and radio data transmission. Industries served: private microwave companies, public safety agencies, public transit agencies, government agencies, water and wastewater treatment and distribution agencies.

FRANCHISES AND BUSINESS OPPORTUNITIES

20884 ■ Culligan International Company
9399 West Higgins Rd., No. 1100
Rosemont, IL 60018
Ph:(847)430-2800
Fax:(847)430-2357
URL: http://www.culligan.com

No. of Franchise Units: 549. **No. of Company-Owned Units:** 71. **Founded:** 1936. **Franchised:** 1939. **Description:** Water treatment devices, softeners, filters, drinking water units and bottled water. **Equity Capital Needed:** Minimum $103,000-$342,000 to invest. **Franchise Fee:** $25,000. **Financial Assistance:** No. **Training:** Yes.

COMPUTERIZED DATABASES

20885 ■ *WATERNET Bibliographic Database*
American Water Works Association
6666 W Quincy Ave.
Denver, CO 80235
Ph:(303)794-7711
Free: 800-926-7337
Fax:(303)347-0804
URL: http://www.awwa.org

Description: Contains more than 50,000 citations, with abstracts, to literature on water quality, water utility management, analytical procedures for water quality testing, energy-related economics, water system materials, water and wastewater treatment and reuse, industrial and potable uses of water, and environmental issues related to water. Typical data elements include author name, article title, journal title, publication date, volume and issue numbers, page numbers, availability, ISSN, language, document type, and abstract. Items are selected from books, conference proceedings, journals, newsletters, standards, handbooks, water quality standard test methods, and all AWWA and AWWA Research Foundation (AWWARF) publications, e.g., *Annual Conference Proceedings*, *Water Quality Technology Conference Proceedings*, *Distribution System Symposium Proceedings*, and *Conference Seminars*. Also covers selected non-AWWA items. Corresponds to the online WATERNET database. **Availability:** CD-ROM: American Water Works Association. **Type:** Bibliographic.

LIBRARIES

20886 ■ Arizona Department of Environmental Quality Library
1110 W. Washington St.
Phoenix, AZ 85007
Ph:(602)771-2217
Fax:(602)771-2399
Co. E-mail: cona.lorraine@azdeq.gov
URL: http://www.azdeq.gov
Contact: Lorraine Cona, Libn.

Scope: Water quality, hazardous waste, wastewater, water pollution, air quality, solid waste. **Services:** Library open to the public. **Holdings:** 1500 books.

20887 ■ CDM–Herman G. Dresser Library
50 Hampshire St.
Cambridge, MA 02139
Ph:(617)452-6000
Fax:(617)452-8000
Co. E-mail: infocenter@cdm.com
URL: http://www.cdm.com
Contact: Stacie Cohen, Libn.

Scope: Environmental engineering, waste disposal, wastewater and solid waste management, water supply, water resources, hazardous wastes, infrastructure management. **Services:** Interlibrary loan; Library open to the public by appointment only. **Holdings:** 13000 books; 900 bound periodical volumes; 4000 reports; 5000 report data/computations; 2500 pamphlets; 4000 reprints of articles written by employees; 4000 microfiche. **Subscriptions:** 100 journals and other serials.

20888 ■ Clough Harbor & Associates Library
III Winners Circle
PO Box 5269
Albany, NY 24060
Ph:(518)453-4500
Fax:(518)458-1735
Co. E-mail: info@chacompanies.com
URL: http://www.chacompanies.com
Contact: Kathy Gale, Dir./Libn.
Scope: The environment, sewage, wastewater. **Services:** Library not open to the public. **Holdings:** 2000 books; 50 bound periodical volumes; 1000 reports; 1500 catalogs. **Subscriptions:** 35 journals and other serials; 3 newspapers.

20889 ■ EIMCO Baker Process Equipment Company Technical Library
669 W. 200 S.
Salt Lake City, UT 84110-0300
Ph:(801)526-2000
Fax:(801)526-2435
Scope: Water treatment, waste management, solid/liquid separation technology. **Holdings:** 1550 books; 500 bound periodical volumes; 500 documents; 40 VF drawers of technical files.

20890 ■ Greeley and Hansen LLC Library
100 S. Wacker Dr., Ste. 1400
Chicago, IL 60606-4004
Ph:(312)558-9000
Fax:(312)558-1986
Co. E-mail: bgoeser@greeley-hansen.com
Contact: Bonnie C. Goeser, Libn.
Scope: Wastewater and water treatment, solid waste disposal, sewerage, flood control, hydraulics. **Services:** Interlibrary loan; copying; Library open to the public with restrictions. **Holdings:** 2000 books; 14,000 internal reports and drawings; 30,000 microforms. **Subscriptions:** 10 journals and other serials.

20891 ■ Kentucky Department for Environmental Protection–EPIC Library
14 Reilly Rd.
Frankfort, KY 40601
Ph:(502)564-2150
Fax:(502)564-4245
Co. E-mail: lance.burk@mail.state.ky.us
URL: http://www.dep.ky.gov
Scope: Water quality, air quality, waste management, environmental law. **Services:** Interlibrary loan; copying. **Holdings:** 480 monographs; 7500 reports on paper and microfiche. **Subscriptions:** 150 journals and other serials.

20892 ■ Malcolm Pirnie Virtual Library/LSSI
20250 Century Blvd., Ste. 200
Germantown, MD 20874-1114
Ph:888-909-1020
Fax:(301)540-0903
Co. E-mail: lenoreg@lssi.com
URL: http://www.lssi.com/pirnie/about.html
Contact: Lenore Grossinger, Proj.Mgr./Libn.
Scope: Environmental engineering, water, wastewater, air pollution, hazardous waste and solid waste management. **Services:** Interlibrary loan; copying; Library not open to the public. **Holdings:** 7000 volumes; 1000 U.S. Environmental Protection Agency reports. **Subscriptions:** 200 journals and other serials.

20893 ■ Massachusetts Water Resources Authority Library
100 1st Ave.
Boston, MA 02129
Ph:(617)305-5583
Fax:(617)371-1610
Co. E-mail: mwralib@mwra.state.ma.us
URL: http://www.mwra.com
Contact: Mary E. Lydon, Lib. and Rec.Mgr.
Scope: Water, wastewater, law. **Services:** Interlibrary loan; copying; Library open to the public by appointment. **Holdings:** 4000 books; 1300 reports; microfilm; videos; CDs. **Subscriptions:** 20 journals and other serials.

20894 ■ Nalco Company Library
1601 W. Diehl Rd.
Naperville, IL 60563-1198
Ph:(630)305-1000
Free: 800-265-5059
Fax:(630)305-2900
URL: http://www.nalco.com
Contact: Maureen Livingston
Scope: Chemistry, water treatment, polymer science. **Services:** Interlibrary loan; services open to the public by appointment. **Holdings:** 25,000 books; 10,000 bound periodical volumes; 28 VF drawers of bulletins, reprints; 20 VF drawers of technical data; 4000 unbound journals; microfilm. **Subscriptions:** 400 journals and other serials.

20895 ■ Oklahoma State University–Ecotoxicology and Water Quality Research Laboratory Library
430 Life Sciences, W.
Stillwater, OK 74078
Ph:(405)744-9691
Fax:(405)744-7824
Co. E-mail: bidwelj@okstate.edu
URL: http://zoology.okstate.edu/zoo_affl/ewqrl/ecotoxlb.htm
Contact: Dr. Joseph R. Bidwell, Dir.
Scope: Water pollution. **Holdings:** 8000 volumes of reprints.

20896 ■ University of District of Columbia–D.C. Water Resources Research Center Library
4340 Connecticut Ave. NW, Bldg. 52 R 416G
Washington, DC 20008
Ph:(202)274-7139
URL: http://www.udc.edu/wrri
Contact: William W. Hare, Dir.
Scope: Water - quality, quantity, problems, planning and policy, conservation; groundwater. **Services:** Center open to faculty members and students. **Holdings:** 4000 volumes.

20897 ■ University of Hawaii at Manoa–Water Resources Research Center Library
Holmes Hall 285
2540 Dole St.
Honolulu, HI 96822
Ph:(808)956-7298
Fax:(808)956-5044
Co. E-mail: rbabcock@hawaii.edu
URL: http://www.wrrc.hawaii.edu/index.html
Contact: Roger W. Babcock, Assoc.Res.
Scope: Water - cycles, supply, quantity, quality, management, protection, planning. **Services:** Library open to the University community. **Holdings:** 6500 volumes; 400 reports. **Subscriptions:** 10 journals and other serials.

RESEARCH CENTERS

20898 ■ Central State University–International Center for Water Resources Management
1400 Brush Row Rd.
PO Box 1004
Wilberforce, OH 45384-1004
Ph:(937)376-6212
Fax:(937)376-6257
Co. E-mail: sri@centralstate.edu
URL: http://www.centralstate.edu/academics/bus_ind/water_res/index.html
Contact: Prof. Subramania I. Sritharan PhD, Ch./Dir.
E-mail: sri@centralstate.edu
Scope: Water resources management, including water quality, hydrology, hydraulics, remote sensing, irrigation and drainage, socio-economic issues; agricultural water management; water resources economics, effects of water quality on the management of water resources, hydrogeology, geophysics, and geochemical modeling. **Services:** Advisory services (occasionally). **Publications:** Annual reports. **Educational Activities:** Short courses on Water Management Topics (occasionally); Undergraduate programs, includes education and research in environmental engineering, water resources management, geology and earth science; Workshops (occasionally).

20899 ■ Cooling Technology Institute
PO Box 73383
Houston, TX 77273-3383
Ph:(281)583-4087
Fax:(281)537-1721
Co. E-mail: vmanser@cti.org
URL: http://www.cti.org
Contact: Virginia A. Manser, Admin.
E-mail: vmanser@cti.org
Scope: Investigates ways to improve technology, design, performance, and maintenance of water-cooling towers. Works to reduce water and air pollution. **Services:** Speakers' Bureau. **Publications:** CTI Journal (semiannually); CTI Manual; CTI News (semiannually). **Educational Activities:** Summer Work Meetings (annually); Summer Workshop; Workshops and seminars.

20900 ■ Environmental Research Foundation
6513 N Christiana Ave.
Lincolnwood, IL 60712
Ph:(732)828-9995
Free: 888—272-2435
Fax:(732)791-4603
Co. E-mail: info@rachel.org
URL: http://www.rachel.org
Contact: Peter Montague, Exec.Dir.
E-mail: info@rachel.org
Scope: Toxic, hazardous, and solid waste problems, including management, incineration, and landfills. **Publications:** Rachel's Environment & Health Weekly.

20901 ■ Grand Valley State University–Robert B. Annis Water Resources Institute
Lake Michigan Center
740 W Shoreline Dr.
Muskegon, MI 49441
Ph:(616)331-3749
Fax:(616)331-3864
Co. E-mail: steinmaa@gvsu.edu
URL: http://www.gvsu.edu/wri
Contact: Alan D. Steinman PhD, Dir.
E-mail: steinmaa@gvsu.edu
Scope: Aquatic ecology, ecosystem restoration, education and outreach, environmental toxicology, fisheries, hydrology, limnology, microbial ecology, molecular ecology, pollution prevention, stream ecology, watershed ecology and management, wetland ecology. **Services:** Information resource, for government units and consulting engineers. **Publications:** Water Resources Review (semiannually). **Educational Activities:** Educational programs and cruises, for the public, K-12 students, and college students; Hazardous Waste Management Workshop, for government units and consulting engineers; Periodic workshops, on groundwater, surface water, and regional GIS systems; Project WET (Water Education for Teachers).

20902 ■ McGill University–Environmental Engineering Laboratory
Macdonald Engineering Bldg., Rm. 492
Department of Civil Engineering & Applied Mechanics
817 Sherbrooke St. W
Montreal, QC, Canada H3A 2K6
Ph:(514)398-6861
Fax:(514)398-7361
Co. E-mail: ronald.gehr@mcgill.ca
URL: http://www.mcgill.ca/civil/grad/areas/environmental
Contact: Prof. Ronald Gehr PhD, Dir.
E-mail: ronald.gehr@mcgill.ca
Scope: Water and wastewater treatment, including wastewater disinfection, bioremediation, sludge processing, odor characterization, enzyme processes, carbon dioxide sequestration, and site remediation. **Educational Activities:** Graduate research training in engineering.

20903 ■ Morehead State University–Water Testing Laboratory
150 University Blvd.
Morehead, KY 40351
Ph:(606)783-2962

Fax:(606)783-5045
Co. E-mail: t.pass@moreheadstate.edu
URL: http://www2.moreheadstate.edu/wtl
Contact: Dr. Ted Pass, Dir.
E-mail: t.pass@moreheadstate.edu
Scope: Conducts water quality testing for sewage contamination and the presence of bacteria and fungi in drinking water, recreation water, and water utilized by hemodialysis units. Also performs soil assays for Histoplama Capsulation and Cryptococcus Neoformans and performs analysis for Cryptosporidium Parvum and Giardia in raw and treated water.

20904 ■ Ohio State University–Water Resources Center
311 Hitchcock Hall
2070 Neil Ave.
Columbus, OH 43210
Ph:(614)292-2771
Fax:(614)292-3780
Co. E-mail: walker.455@osu.edu
URL: http://wrc.osu.edu
Contact: Dr. Harold Walker, Co-Dir.
E-mail: walker.455@osu.edu
Scope: Administers and coordinates research in the University and within the state on water and water-related problems, including water quality, hydrology, water and wastewater treatment, industrial waste treatment, and water resource economics. Trains scientists and engineers in water management. **Educational Activities:** Seminars; Symposium (annually).

20905 ■ Oklahoma State University–Ecotoxicology and Water Quality Research Laboratory
430 Life Sciences W
Stillwater, OK 74078
Ph:(405)744-9691
Fax:(405)744-7824
Co. E-mail: bidwelj@okstate.edu
URL: http://zoology.okstate.edu/zoo_affl/ewqrl/ecotoxlb.htm
Contact: Dr. Joseph R. Bidwell, Dir.
E-mail: bidwelj@okstate.edu
Scope: Biological aspects of water and soil pollution, including transport, fate, and effect of water pollutants, ecotoxicology, analysis of pollutants with gas chromatography, atomic absorption, and bioassays with aquatic organisms.

20906 ■ South Dakota State University–South Dakota Water Resources Research Institute
SAE 211, Box 2120
Brookings, SD 57007
Ph:(605)688-4910
Fax:(605)688-4917
Co. E-mail: van.kelley@sdstate.edu
URL: http://wri.sdstate.edu
Contact: Dr. Van C. Kelley, Dir.
E-mail: van.kelley@sdstate.edu
Scope: Conducts and coordinates University research in water and related resources, especially those concerned with the agricultural effect on lakes, streams, and groundwater including the plant, soil, and groundwater continuum. Specific concerns include irrigation technology, water management, water supply (hydrologic quantity and quality), water use, non-point source pollution, lake management, watershed studies, and water treatment. **Services:** Interpretation and Consultation Service, for use of waters analyzed through the Water Quality and Water Pesticide Lab. **Publications:** Brochure; Water News (quarterly). **Educational Activities:** Big Sioux Water Festival (annually); Lake Water Quality Workshop (annually), designed for teachers, extension educators and lake residents; Lakes are Cool Festival; Northern Prairie Water Festival (annually).

20907 ■ Tennessee Technological University–Center for the Management, Utilization and Protection of Water Resources
PO Box 5033
Cookeville, TN 38505
Ph:(931)372-3507
Fax:(931)372-6346
Co. E-mail: dgeorge@tntech.edu
URL: http://www.tntech.edu/wrc/home
Contact: Dr. Dennis B. George, Dir.
E-mail: dgeorge@tntech.edu
Scope: Water use, water availability, wastewater treatment and disposal, and toxic substance identification, focusing on management and protection of water resources to provide sustainable water supplies and habitat for fisheries, including resource management, environmental aquatic hazards, and watershed analysis.

20908 ■ Texas State University-San Marcos–Edwards Aquifer Research and Data Center
Freeman Aquatic Science Bldg.
San Marcos, TX 78666
Ph:(512)245-2329
Fax:(512)245-2669
Co. E-mail: glennlongley@txstate.edu
URL: http://www.eardc.txstate.edu
Contact: Dr. Glenn Longley, Dir.
E-mail: glennlongley@txstate.edu
Scope: Groundwater ecosystem studies, focusing on the Edwards Aquifer, water quality, and groundwater modeling. **Services:** Laboratory services. **Publications:** Newsletter (online) (semiannually). **Educational Activities:** Ten aquatic studies summer camps, aquatic studies field days, educational presentations, seminars and workshops.

20909 ■ University of Massachusetts at Amherst–Massachusetts Water Resources Research Center
Blaisdell House
310 Hicks Way
Amherst, MA 01003
Ph:(413)545-2842
Fax:(413)545-2304
Co. E-mail: rees@ecs.umass.edu
URL: http://www.umass.edu/tei/wrrc
Contact: Paula Rees, Dir.
E-mail: rees@ecs.umass.edu
Scope: Water and water-related resources, including basic and applied studies on acid deposition in soil and water, supply and demand problems, quality of water, drinking water treatment, and management and development of water resources for all uses. Research projects on lakes, streams, groundwater, and estuaries involve problems of engineering, resource planning and management, economics, geohydrology, ecology, and social sciences. Specific studies include an assessment of non-point sources dissolved of organic matter contributions to the coastal zone; enhanced recovery of hydrocarbons by soil flushing with nonionic surfactants; long-term assessment of acid rain impacts of surface waters; and creation of a citizen volunteer river and lake monitoring network. Established under the Water Resources Research Act of 1965, Public Law 88-379, to conduct and coordinate research on water and water-related resources at the University and within the state and to provide training of scientists and graduate students through research investigations and experiments. **Services:** Coordination of lake and river citizen monitoring. **Publications:** Technical reports. **Educational Activities:** Water Resources Research Conference (annually), in late October; Workshops (occasionally), in Massachusetts and New England.

START-UP INFORMATION

20910 ■ *Design and Launch Your eCommerce Business in a Week*
Pub: Entrepreneur Press
Ed: Jason R. Rich. **Released:** July 2008. **Price:** $17. 95. **Description:** Guide to help anyone start an online business in one week; included tips for Website design.

20911 ■ *E-Preneur*
Pub: Career Press, Inc.
Ed: Richard Goossen. **Released:** April 2008. **Price:** $15.99. **Description:** Entrepreneurs in the new virtual marketplace are examined. The book surveys and explains the field of Web 2.0 and entrepreneurs successfully using the virtual marketplace.

20912 ■ "Five Low-Cost Home Based Startups" in *Women Entrepreneur* (December 16, 2008)
Pub: Entrepreneur Media Inc.
Ed: Lesley Spencer Pyle. **Description:** During tough economic times, small businesses have an advantage over large companies because they can adjust to economic conditions more easily and without having to go through corporate red tape that can slow the implementation process. A budding entrepreneur may find success by taking inventory of his or her skills, experience, expertise and passions and utilizing those qualities to start a business. Five low-cost home-based startups are profiled. These include starting an online store, a virtual assistant service, web designer, sales representative and a home staging counselor.

20913 ■ *How to Start a Home-Based Web Design Business, 4th Edition*
Pub: Globe Pequot Press
Ed: Jim Smith. **Released:** July 1, 2010. **Price:** $18. 95. **Description:** Comprehensive guide contains all the necessary tools and strategies required to successfully launch and grow a Web design business.

20914 ■ "A Matter of Online Trust" in *Entrepreneur* (Vol. 37, August 2009, No. 8, pp. 35)
Pub: Entrepreneur Media, Inc.
Ed: Mikal E. Belicove. **Description:** Startup websites should make their potential customers feel confident to do business with them. To build customer's trust, the website should have an attractive and professional design, clear and simple navigation, error-free copy, and physical address, telephone number, and e-mail address.

20915 ■ "Online Fortunes" in *Small Business Opportunities* (Fall 2008)
Pub: Entrepreneur Media Inc.
Description: Fifty hot, e-commerce enterprises for the aspiring entrepreneur to consider are featured; virtual assistants, marketing services, party planning, travel services, researching, web design and development, importing as well as creating an online store are among the businesses featured.

20916 ■ *Start Your Own Net Services Business*
Pub: Entrepreneur Press
Released: February 1, 2009. **Price:** $17.95. **Description:** Web design, search engine marketing, new-media online, and blogging, are currently the four most popular web services available. This book provides information to start a net service business.

20917 ■ *Starting an iPhone Application Business for Dummies*
Pub: Wiley Publishing
Ed: Aaron Nicholson, Joel Elad, Damien Stolarz. **Released:** October 26, 2009. **Price:** $24.99. **Description:** Ways to create a profitable, sustainable business developing and marketing iPhone applications are profiled.

20918 ■ *Starting a Yahoo! Business For Dummies*
Pub: John Wiley & Sons, Incorporated
Ed: Rob Snell. **Released:** May 27, 2006. **Price:** $24. 99. **Description:** Advice helps turn Web browsers into buyers, boost online traffic, and information to launch a profitable online business.

20919 ■ "Startup Aims to Cut Out Coupon Clipping" in *The Business Journal-Serving Metropolitan Kansas City* (Vol. 26, August 15, 2008, No. 49)
Pub: American City Business Journals, Inc.
Ed: Suzanna Stagemeyer. **Description:** TDP Inc., who started operations 18 months ago, aims to transform stale coupon promotions using technology by digitizing the entire coupon process. The process is expected to enable consumers to hunt coupons online where they will be automatically linked to loyalty cards. Other views and information on TDP and its services are presented.

20920 ■ "Truthfully Speaking" in *Entrepreneur* (Vol. 35, November 2007, No. 11, pp. 118)
Pub: Entrepreneur Media Inc.
Ed: Amanda C. Kooser. **Description:** Internet startup guru Guy Kawasaki talks about his new Web venture Truemors and shares tips on creating a successful Web-based company.

20921 ■ *Web Design Business*
Pub: Globe Pequot Press
Ed: Jim Smith. **Released:** January 2007. **Price:** $18. 95. **Description:** Information for starting a home-based Web design firm is given.

ASSOCIATIONS AND OTHER ORGANIZATIONS

20922 ■ IDEAlliance - International Digital Enterprise Alliance
1421 Prince St., Ste. 230
Alexandria, VA 22314-2805
Ph:(703)837-1070
Fax:(703)837-1072
Co. E-mail: dsteinhardt@idealliance.org
URL: http://www.idealliance.org
Contact: David J. Steinhardt, Pres./CEO
Description: Works to advance user-driven, cross-industry solutions for all publishing and content-related processes by developing standards fostering business alliances and identifying best practices. .

EDUCATIONAL PROGRAMS

20923 ■ Active Server Pages I
EEI Communications
66 Canal Center Plz., Ste. 200
Alexandria, VA 22314
Ph:(703)683-0683
Free: 888-253-2762
Fax:(703)683-4915
Co. E-mail: train@eeicom.com
URL: http://www.eeicom.com/training
Price: $745.00. **Description:** Covers Active Server Pages (ASP) basics and development, building an ASP dictionary object, utilizing text files, researching and installing third-party ASP components, and writing advanced database queries. **Locations:** Silver Spring, MD; Alexandria, VA; Hunt Valley, MD; and Columbia, MD.

20924 ■ Adobe ColdFusion I
EEI Communications
66 Canal Center Plz., Ste. 200
Alexandria, VA 22314
Ph:(703)683-7453
Free: 888-253-2762
Fax:(703)683-7310
Co. E-mail: train@eeicom.com
URL: http://www.eeicom.com/training
Price: $745.00. **Description:** Geared towards experienced Web designers, this seminar covers creating databases and Web sites utilizing ColdFusion. **Remarks:** Formerly known as Macromedia Authorware. **Locations:** Alexandria, VA.

20925 ■ Adobe Dreamweaver I
EEI Communications
66 Canal Center Plz., Ste. 200
Alexandria, VA 22314
Ph:(703)683-7453
Free: 888-253-2762
Fax:(703)683-7310
Co. E-mail: train@eeicom.com
URL: http://www.eeicom.com/training
Price: $745.00. **Description:** Covers utilizing Dreamweaver's page-layout capabilities, site management tools, and support for dynamic HTML to create Web pages. **Remarks:** Formerly known as Macromedia Authorware. **Locations:** Silver Spring, MD; Alexandria, VA; and Hunt Valley, MD.

20926 ■ Adobe Dreamweaver II
EEI Communications
66 Canal Center Plz., Ste. 200
Alexandria, VA 22314
Ph:(703)683-7453
Free: 888-253-2762

Fax:(703)683-7310
Co. E-mail: train@eeicom.com
URL: http://www.eeicom.com/training

Price: $745.00. **Description:** This seminar covers advanced Web page development focusing on CSS Layout, advanced site building features, site management, behaviors, interactivity, and customization. **Remarks:** Formerly known as Macromedia Authorware. **Locations:** Silver Spring, MD; and Alexandria, VA.

20927 ■ Adobe Dreamweaver III
EEI Communications
66 Canal Center Plz., Ste. 200
Alexandria, VA 22314
Ph:(703)683-7453
Free: 888-253-2762
Fax:(703)683-7310
Co. E-mail: train@eeicom.com
URL: http://www.eeicom.com/training

Price: $745.00. **Description:** Learn how to set up and use Dreamweaver to build serverside scripting (ASP, ColdFusion, or PHP) in order to manage database content on the Web. **Remarks:** Formerly known as Macromedia Authorware. **Locations:** Alexandria, VA.

20928 ■ Adobe Fireworks I
EEI Communications
66 Canal Center Plz., Ste. 200
Alexandria, VA 22314
Ph:(703)683-7453
Free: 888-253-2762
Fax:(703)683-7310
Co. E-mail: train@eeicom.com
URL: http://www.eeicom.com/training

Price: $745.00. **Description:** Covers utilizing Fireworks and drawing tools, photo editing tools, and optimization features to create Web graphics. **Remarks:** Formerly known as Macromedia Authorware. **Locations:** Silver Spring, MD.

20929 ■ Adobe GoLive
EEI Communications
66 Canal Center Plz., Ste. 200
Alexandria, VA 22314
Ph:(703)683-7453
Free: 888-253-2762
Fax:(703)683-7310
Co. E-mail: train@eeicom.com
URL: http://www.eeicom.com/training

Price: $745.00. **Description:** Covers utilizing GoLive, a visual Web design program, to create complex Web pages. **Locations:** Silver Spring, MD; Alexandria, VA; Hunt Valley, MD; and Columbia, MD.

20930 ■ Cascading Style Sheets (CSS) I
EEI Communications
66 Canal Center Plz., Ste. 200
Alexandria, VA 22314
Ph:(703)683-7453
Free: 888-253-2762
Fax:(703)683-7310
Co. E-mail: train@eeicom.com
URL: http://www.eeicom.com/training

Price: $745.00. **Description:** Building upon Web Page Development I and II, this seminar covers the introduction of Document Object Module (DOM) and working with cascading style sheets. **Locations:** Alexandria, VA.

20931 ■ JavaScript for Non-Programmers
EEI Communications
66 Canal Center Plz., Ste. 200
Alexandria, VA 22314
Ph:(703)683-7453
Free: 888-253-2762
Fax:(703)683-7310
Co. E-mail: train@eeicom.com
URL: http://www.eeicom.com/training

Price: $1,065.00. **Description:** Covers creating and applying JavaScript to a Web site. **Locations:** Silver Spring, MD; Alexandria, VA; Hunt Valley, MD; and Columbia, MD.

REFERENCE WORKS

20932 ■ "The 40-Year-Old Intern" in *Entrepreneur* (Vol. 37, October 2009, No. 10, pp. 90)
Pub: Entrepreneur Media, Inc.

Ed: Kristin Ladd. **Description:** Brian Kurth's VocationVacation is an internship program aimed at helping people experience their dream job. The website, launched in January 2004, matches people with businesses that allow them to experience their fantasy jobs.

20933 ■ "352 Media Group Opens New Tampa Web Design and Digital Marketing Office" in *Entertainment Close-Up* (May 2, 2011)
Pub: Close-Up Media

Description: 352 Media Group opened its newest office in Tampa, Florida in May 2011. The firm is noted for its achievements in Web design and digital marketing.

20934 ■ "529.com Wins Outstanding Achievement in Web Development" in *Investment Weekly* (November 14, 2009, pp. 152)
Pub: Investment Weekly News

Description: Web Marketing Association's 2009 WebAward for Financial Services Standard of Excellence and Investment Standard of Excellence was won by 529.com, the website from Upromise Investments, Inc., the leading administrator of 529 college savings plans.

20935 ■ "Aiming at a Moving Web Target" in *Entrepreneur* (Vol. 37, August 2009, No. 8, pp. 30)
Pub: Entrepreneur Media, Inc.

Ed: Dan O'Shea. **Description:** Rapidly increasing numbers of businesspeople are web surfing on mobile phones. To make a website that is accessible to people on the move, the main page should be light on images and graphics and the most important information should be put near the top. A more intensive route is to create a separate mobile-specific website.

20936 ■ "Analyzing the Analytics" in *Entrepreneur* (Vol. 37, October 2009, No. 10, pp. 42)
Pub: Entrepreneur Media, Inc.

Ed: Mikal E. Belicove. **Description:** Startups can maximize Web analytics by using them to monitor traffic sources and identify obstacles to converting them into targeted behaviors . Startups should set trackable Web site goals and continuously track traffic and conversion rates.

20937 ■ "Apparel Apparatchic at Kmart" in *Barron's* (Vol. 88, March 17, 2008, No. 11, pp. 16)
Pub: Dow Jones & Company, Inc.

Description: Kmart began a nationwide search for women to represent the company in a national advertising campaign. Contestants need to upload their photos to Kmart's website and winners will be chosen by a panel of celebrity judges. The contest aims to reverse preconceived negative notions about the store's quality and service.

20938 ■ "Attention, Please" in *Entrepreneur* (Vol. 36, April 2008, No. 4, pp. 52)
Pub: Entrepreneur Media, Inc.

Ed: Andrea Cooper. **Description:** Gurbaksh Chahal created his own company ClickAgents at the age of 16, and sold it two years later for $40 million to ValueClick. He then founded BlueLithium, an online advertising network on behavioral targeting, which Yahoo! Inc. bought in 2007 for $300 million. Chahal, now 25, talks about his next plans and describes how BlueLithium caught Yahoo's attention.

20939 ■ "Attorney Internet Marketing Services Launched by SEO Advantage at SEOLegal.com" in *Internet Wire* (October 5, 2009)
Pub: Comtex News Network, Inc.

Description: SEO Advantage, an Internet marketing and website designer firm, has extended its services to the legal industry.

20940 ■ "Attract More Online Customers: Make Your Website Work Harder for You" in *Black Enterprise* (Vol. 37, November 2006, No. 4, pp. 66)
Pub: Earl G. Graves Publishing Co. Inc.

Ed: Description: Having an impressive presence on the Internet has become crucial. Detailed advice on making your website serve your business in the best way possible is included.

20941 ■ "Auctions and Bidding: a Guide for Computer Scientists" in *ACM Computing Surveys* (Vol. 43, Summer 2011, No. 2, pp. 10)
Pub: Association for Computing Machinery

Ed: Simon Parsons, Juan A. Rodriguez-Aguilar, Mark Klein. **Description:** There are various actions: single dimensional, multi-dimensional, single-sided, double-sided, first-price, second-price, English, Dutch, Japanese, sealed-bid, and these have been extensively discussed and analyzed in economics literature. This literature is surveyed from a computer science perspective, primarily from the viewpoint of computer scientists who are interested in learning about auction theory, and to provide pointers into the economics literature for those who want a deeper technical understanding. In addition, since auctions are an increasingly important topic in computer science, the article also looks at work on auctions from the computer science literature. The aim is to identify what both bodies of work tell us about creating electronic auctions.

20942 ■ "Auto Show Taps Moms" in *Marketing to Women* (Vol. 21, April 2008, No. 4, pp. 3)
Pub: EPM Communications, Inc.

Description: Teamed with Mother Proof, an online site which features automotive content aimed at moms, the Chicago Auto Show will present a full day of programming with the emphasis on mom.

20943 ■ "avVaa World Health Care Products Rolls Out Internet Marketing Program" in *Health and Beauty Close-Up* (September 18, 2009)
Pub: Close-Up Media

Description: avVaa World Health Care Products, Inc., a biotechnology company, manufacturer and distributor of nationally branded therapeutic, natural health care and skin products, has signed an agreement with Online Performance Marketing to launch of an Internet marketing campaign in order to broaden its presence online. The impact of advertising on the Internet to generate an increase in sales is explored.

20944 ■ "The Bankrate Double Pay" in *Barron's* (Vol. 88, March 24, 2008, No. 12, pp. 27)
Pub: Dow Jones & Company, Inc.

Ed: Neil A. Martin. **Description:** Shares of Bankrate may rise as much as 25 percent from their level of $45.08 a share due to a strong cash flow and balance sheet. The company's Internet business remains strong despite weakness in the online advertising industry and is a potential takeover target.

20945 ■ "Banks Fall Short in Online Services for Savvy Traders" in *Barron's* (Vol. 88, March 17, 2008, No. 11, pp. 35)
Pub: Dow Jones & Company, Inc.

Ed: Theresa W. Carey. **Description:** Banc of America Investment Services, WellsTrade, and ShareBuilder are at the bottom of the list of online brokerages because they offer less trading technologies and product range. Financial shoppers miss out on a lot of customized tools and analytics when using these services.

20946 ■ "Be Wary of Legal Advice on Internet, Lawyers Warn" in *Crain's Detroit Business* (Vol. 24, September 22, 2008, No. 38, pp. 16)
Pub: Crain Communications, Inc.

Ed: Harriet Tramer. **Description:** While some lawyers feel that the proliferation of legal information on the Internet can point people in the right direction, others maintain that it simply results in giving false hope, may bring about confusion or worse yet, it sometimes makes their jobs even harder.

20947 ■ "Boom has Tech Grads Mulling Their Options" in *Globe & Mail* (March 14, 2006, pp. B1)
Pub: CTVglobemedia Publishing Inc.
Ed: Grant Robertson. **Description:** Internet giant Google Inc. has stepped up its efforts to hire the talented people, in Canada, at Waterloo University in southern Ontario, to expand its operations. The details of the job market and increasing salaries are analyzed.

20948 ■ "Borders Previews New Web Site" in *Crain's Detroit Business* (Vol. 23, October 8, 2007, No. 41, pp. 4)
Pub: Crain Communications Inc. - Detroit
Ed: Sheena Harrison. **Description:** Borders Group Inc. previewed its new Website that allows customers to buy items that include the Magic Shelf, a virtual bookcase that displays available recommended books, movies and music.

20949 ■ "Bottoms Up!" in *Entrepreneur* (Vol. 36, April 2008, No. 4, pp. 128)
Pub: Entrepreneur Media, Inc.
Ed: Amanda C. Kooser. **Description:** Jill Bernheimer launched her online alcohol business Domaine547 in 2007, and encountered challenges as legal issues over the licensing and launching of the business took about seven months to finish. Domain547 features blog and forum areas. Marketing strategy that connects to the social community is one of the ways to reach out to customers.

20950 ■ "Building a Better Twitter Brand: My Foray Into Social Analytics" in *Inc.* (Vol. , pp.)
Pub: Inc. Magazine
Ed: John Brandon. **Description:** A small business using Twitter to research and promote the firm decided to test some Web-based dashboards that allow you to manage and analyze accounts on multiple social media networks including Facebook, Twitter, and LinkedIn.

20951 ■ "Building Your Business: A Strong Web Presence Is a Must" in *Black Enterprise* (Vol. 38, December 2007, No. 5, pp. 74)
Pub: Earl G. Graves Publishing Co. Inc.
Ed: Tennille M. Robinson. **Description:** Building a strong presence on the Internet is crucial to any growing business. Websites can provide information or sell merchandise, but the site must also make sure the customer knows how to use and navigate around within the site. Common mistakes to avoid when designing a small business Website are outlined.

20952 ■ "BusinessOnLine Launches a New Web-Based Search Engine Optimization Tool" in *Internet Wire* (October 19, 2009)
Pub: Comtex News Network, Inc.
Description: First Link Checker, a complimentary new search engine optimization tool that helps site owners optimize their on-page links by understanding which of those links are actually being counted in Google's relevancy algorithm, was developed by BusinessOnLine, a rapidly growing Internet marketing agency. This tool will make it easy for the average web master to ensure that their internal link structure is optimized.

20953 ■ "Can You Say $1 Million? A Language-Learning Start-Up Is Hoping That Investors Can" in *Inc.* (Vol. 33, November 2011, No. 9, pp. 116)
Pub: Inc. Magazine
Ed: April Joyner. **Description:** Startup, Verbling is a video platform that links language learners and native speakers around the world. The firm is working to raise money to hire engineers in order to build the product and redesign their Website.

20954 ■ "CarTango Lauches Site for Women" in *Marketing to Women* (Vol. 21, April 2008, No. 4, pp. 5)
Pub: EPM Communications, Inc.
Description: CarTango.com is an Internet site that seeks to overcome what women say are dismissive or pushy salespeople by allowing the shoppers the chance to decide what they want before inviting dealers to compete for their business.

20955 ■ "Chamber Offers Seminar on Web Design" in *Charlotte Observer* (February 6, 2007)
Pub: Knight-Ridder/Tribune Business News
Ed: Joe DePriest. **Description:** Belmont Chamber of Commerce and Gaston College Small Business Center will offer seminars on online Web design.

20956 ■ "Chris Curtis Preaches the Gospel of Internet Success" in *Black Enterprise* (Vol. 38, March 2008, No. 8, pp. 56)
Pub: Earl G. Graves Publishing Co. Inc.
Ed: Anthony Calypso. **Description:** Profile of the Web Business Ownership Series, a collection of 20 free seminars that help small businesses learn about the Web development process.

20957 ■ "A Class Act" in *Hawaii Business* (Vol. 53, March 2008, No. 9, pp. 25)
Pub: Hawaii Business Publishing
Ed: Cathy S. Cruz-George. **Description:** UBoost is a startup company that offers online content for the educational magazine 'Weekly Reader'. The website features quizzes and allows users to accumulate points and redeem rewards afterward. Other details about the company are discussed.

20958 ■ "Click Here to Book" in *Caterer & Hotelkeeper* (October 28, 2011, No. 288)
Pub: Reed Reference Publishing
Ed: Ross Bentley. **Description:** Customers expectations are determined by the quality of a Website when booking hotel rooms.

20959 ■ "A Click In the Right Direction: Website Teaches Youth Financial Literacy" in *Black Enterprise* (Vol. 38, December 2007, No. 5)
Pub: Earl G. Graves Publishing Co. Inc.
Ed: Nicole Norfleet. **Description:** Profile of Donald Lee Robinson who launched SkillsThatClick, a Website that teaches young individuals ages 12 to 15 about money management. Robinson shares how he used his Navy career as a model for designing the site.

20960 ■ *Clicking Through: A Survival Guide for Bringing Your Company Online*
Pub: Bloomberg Press
Ed: Jonathan I. Ezor. **Released:** October 1999. **Description:** Summary of legal compliance issues faced by small companies doing business on the Internet, including copyright and patent laws.

20961 ■ "Clicks For Cash: Earning More From Your Website" in *Inc.* (December 2007, pp. 64-65)
Pub: Gruner & Jahr USA Publishing
Ed: Michael Fitzgerald. **Description:** Ways to use a company's Website to generate revenue are discussed. Free services for placing ads include Google AdSense, AdBrite, AuctionAds, Chitkia eMiniMalls, Vizu Answers, and Value Click; profiles of each service are presented.

20962 ■ *The Complete Guide to Google Adwords: Secrets, Techniques, and Strategies You Can Learn to Make Millions*
Pub: Atlantic Publishing Company
Released: December 1, 2010. **Price:** $24.95. **Description:** Google AdWords, when it launched in 2002 signaled a fundamental shift in what the Internet was for so many individuals and companies. Learning and understanding how Google AdWords operates and how it can be optimized for maximum exposure, boosting click through rates, conversions, placement, and selection of the right keywords, can be the key to a successful online business.

20963 ■ "Consumer Electronics: Brick and Mortar Vs. Online" in *Retail Merchandiser* (Vol. 51, September-October 2011, No. 5, pp. 15)
Pub: Phoenix Media Corporation
Description: Brick and mortar retailers with Websites are discovering that the Internet is used more for research than purchasing when it comes to electronics products. According to a recent study conducted by The NPD Group shows that 56 percent of consumers research televisions online before purchasing, but only 19 percent actually buy them online.

20964 ■ "Contec Innovations Inc.: MovieSet.com First to Mobilize Content Using BUZmob" in *Canadian Corporate News* (May 16, 2007)
Pub: Comtex News Network Inc.
Description: Contec Innovations Inc., a provider of mobile infrastructure software, announced that MovieSet.com is the first Internet portal to mobilize their content using BUZmob, the company's new mobile publishing service that allows content publishers to enable mobile access to their feed-based content on any mobile device or network in real-time.

20965 ■ *Content Rich: Writing Your Way to Wealth on the Web*
Pub: 124 S Mercedes Rd.
Ed: Jon Wuebben. **Released:** April 2008. **Price:** $19. 95. **Description:** A definitive search engine optimization (SEO) copywriting guide for search engine rankings and sales conversion. It includes topics not covered in other books on the subject and targets the small to medium sized business looking for ways to maximize online marketing activities as well as designers and Web developers seeking to incorporate more SEO techniques into design and content.

20966 ■ "Conversations with Customers" in *Business Journal Serving Greater Tampa Bay* (Vol. 31, December 31, 2010, No. 1, pp. 1)
Pub: Tampa Bay Business Journal
Description: Tampa Bay, Florida-based businesses have been using social media to interact with customers. Forty percent of businesses have been found to have at least one social media platform to reach customers and prospects.

20967 ■ "Coping with the Web" in *Agency Sales Magazine* (Vol. 39, December 2009, No. 11, pp. 52)
Pub: MANA
Ed: Karen Saunders. **Description:** When branding your company on the Internet, strategy should first be discussed with the website designer and the target and niche audience should also be defined. Describing "what" and "how" the product or service is offering is also important. In addition, perception, the logo, and the tag line are some elements that are needed to create a brand.

20968 ■ *Crush It!*
Pub: HarperStudio/HarperCollins
Ed: Gary Vaynerchuk. **Released:** 2009. **Price:** $19. 99. **Description:** Ways the Internet can help entrepreneurs turn their passions into successful companies.

20969 ■ "Cyber Thanksgiving Online Shopping a Growing Tradition" in *Marketing Weekly News* (December 12, 2009, pp. 137)
Pub: Investment Weekly News
Description: According to e-commerce analysts, Thanksgiving day is becoming increasingly important to retailers in terms of online sales. Internet marketers are realizing that consumers are already searching for Black Friday sales and if they find deals on the products they are looking for, they are highly likely to make their purchase on Thanksgiving day instead of waiting.

20970 ■ "DCAA-Compliant Accounting Solution Provider Intros Redesign of Website at sympaq.com" in *Entertainment Close-Up* (April 18, 2011)
Pub: Close-Up Media
Description: Aldebaron Inc., developer of DCAA-compliant accounting solution SYMPAQ SQL, launched a new Website that will assist government contractors access information about their products and services.

20971 ■ *Design and Launch an Online Travel Business in a Week*
Pub: Entrepreneur Press
Ed: Charlene Davis. **Released:** May 1, 2009. **Price:** $17.95. **Description:** Guide providing techniques and professional advice for starting an online travel business. Tips are given to build a Website, find qualified providers and to set up a payment system.

20972 ■ *Design and Launch Your Online Boutique in a Week*
Pub: Entrepreneur Press
Ed: Melissa Campanelli. **Released:** June 2008. **Price:** $17.95. **Description:** Guide to start an online boutique includes information on business planning, Website design and funding.

20973 ■ "Designing Events Updates Online Suite" in *Wireless News* (October 25, 2009)
Pub: Close-Up Media
Description: Designing Events, an outsourcing and consulting firm for conferences and meetings, announced the release of an update to its Designing Events Online suite of web-based management and marketing tools; features include enhanced versions of online registration and collaboration, content management, session development, social media and conference websites.

20974 ■ *Designing Websites for Every Audience*
Pub: F & W Publications, Incorporated
Ed: Ilise Benun. **Released:** January 2003. **Description:** Twenty-five case studies targeting six difference audiences are used to help a business design, or make over, a Website.

20975 ■ "Do-It-Yourself Portfolio Management" in *Barron's* (Vol. 89, July 13, 2009, No. 28, pp. 25)
Pub: Dow Jones & Co., Inc.
Ed: Mike Hogan. **Description:** Services of several portfolio management web sites are presented. These web sites include MarketRiders E.Adviser, TD Ameritrade and E*Trade.

20976 ■ "Dots Sings To New Tune With Its Radio Station" in *Crain's Cleveland Business* (Vol. 30, June 15, 2009, No. 23, pp. 7)
Pub: Crain Communications, Inc.
Description: Dots LLC, a women's clothing retailer, has launched an online radio station on its Website. The station plays the in-store music to customers while they are shopping online.

20977 ■ "Drive Traffic To Your Blog" in *Women Entrepreneur* (January 13, 2009)
Pub: Entrepreneur Media Inc.
Ed: Lesley Spencer Pyle. **Description:** Internet social networking has become a vital component to marketing one's business. Tips are provided on how to establish a blog that will attract attention to one's business and keep one's customers coming back for more.

20978 ■ *eBay Business the Smart Way*
Pub: AMACOM
Ed: Joseph T. Sinclair. **Released:** June 6, 2007. **Price:** $17.95. **Description:** eBay commands ninety percent of all online auction business. Computer and software expert and online entrepreneur shares information to help online sellers get started and move merchandise on eBay. Tips include the best ways to build credibility, find products to sell, manage inventory, create a storefront Website, and more.

20979 ■ *EBay Income: How ANYONE of Any Age, Location, and/or Background Can Build a Highly Profitable Online Business with eBay (Revised 2nd Edition)*
Pub: Atlantic Publishing Company
Released: December 1, 2010. **Price:** $24.95. **Description:** A complete overview of eBay is given and guides any small company through the entire process of creating the auction and auction strategies, photography, writing copy, text and formatting, multiple sales, programming tricks, PayPal, accounting, creating marketing, merchandising, managing email lists, advertising plans, taxes and sales tax, best time to list items and for how long, sniping programs, international customers, opening a storefront, electronic commerce, buy-it now pricing, keywords, Google marketing and eBay secrets.

20980 ■ *Effective Web Presence Solutions for Small Businesses: Strategies for Successful Implementation*
Pub: IGI Global
Ed: Stephen Burgess,, Carmine Sellitto, Stergios Karanasio, Stan Karanasios. **Released:** March 1, 2009. **Price:** $165.00. **Description:** Business strategies to implement a Web presence for any small business, is examined, focusing on website development.

20981 ■ *Electronic Commerce*
Pub: Course Technology
Ed: Gary Schneider, Bryant Chrzan, Charles McCormick. **Released:** May 1, 2010. **Price:** $117.95. **Description:** E-commerce can open the door to more opportunities than ever before for small business. Packed with real-world examples and cases, the book delivers comprehensive coverage of emerging online technologies and trends and their influence on the electronic marketplace. It details how the landscape of online commerce is evolving, reflecting changes in the economy and how business and society are responding to those changes. Balancing technological issues with the strategic business aspects of successful e-commerce, the new edition includes expanded coverage of international issues, social networking, mobile commerce, Web 2.0 technologies, and updates on spam, phishing, and identity theft.

20982 ■ *Emerging Business Online: Global Markets and the Power of B2B Internet Marketing*
Pub: FT Press
Ed: Lara Fawzy, Lucas Dworksi. **Released:** October 1, 2010. **Price:** $49.99. **Description:** An introduction into ebocube (emerging business online), a comprehensive proven business model for Internet B2B marketing in emerging markets.

20983 ■ "Empire of Pixels" in *Entrepreneur* (Vol. 37, September 2009, No. 9, pp. 50)
Pub: Entrepreneur Media, Inc.
Ed: Jason Daley. **Description:** Entrepreneur Jack Levin has successfully grown Imageshack, an image-hosting Web service. The Website currently gets 50 million unique visitors a month. Levin has launched Y-Frog, an application that uses Imageshack to allow Twitter users to add images to their posts.

20984 ■ "Entrepreneur Column" in *Entrepreneur* (September 24, 2009)
Pub: Entrepreneur Media, Inc.
Ed: Allen Moon. **Description:** In an attempt to compete with Google, Microsoft and Yahoo have entered a partnership to merge their search services; advice on the best ways to get noticed on this new search engine entitled Bing, is provided.

20985 ■ *The Essential Online Solution: The 5-Step Formula for Small Business Success*
Pub: John Wiley & Sons, Incorporated
Ed: Rick Segel; Barbara Callan-Bogia. **Released:** October 2006. **Price:** $22.95. **Description:** Strategies to help any small business increase its online presence and compete with big retail chains. Tips for success Web design are included.

20986 ■ *The Facebook Effect: The Inside Story of the Company That Is Connecting the World*
Pub: Simon & Shuster
Ed: David Kirkpatrick. **Released:** June 8, 2010. **Price:** $26.00. **Description:** There's never been a Website like Facebook: more than 350 million people have accounts, and if the growth rate continues, by 2013 every Internet user worldwide will have his or her own page. No one's had more access to the inner workings of the phenomenon than Kirkpatrick, a senior tech writer at Fortune magazine. Written with the full cooperation of founder Mark Zuckerberg, the book follows the company from its genesis in a Harvard dorm room through its successes over Friendster and MySpace, the expansion of the user base, and Zuckerberg's refusal to sell.

20987 ■ *The Facebook Era: Tapping Online Social Networks to Build Better Products, Reach New Audiences, and Sell More Stuff*
Pub: Prentice Hall
Ed: Clara Shih. **Price:** $24.99. **Description:** The '90s were about the World Wide Web of information and the power of linking Web pages. Today it's about the World Wide Web of people and the power of the social graph. Online social networks are fundamentally changing the way we live, work, and interact. They offer businesses immense opportunities to transform customer relationships for profit: opportunities that touch virtually every business function, from sales and marketing to recruiting, collaboration to executive decision-making, product development to innovation.

20988 ■ "Fast Fact: Women's Online Habits" in *Marketing to Women* (Vol. 22, July 2009, No. 7, pp. 1)
Pub: EPM Communications, Inc.
Description: Lists the Internet habits of women. Statistical data included.

20989 ■ "Financo Panel Lauds Product, Online Marketing" in *Home Textiles Today* (Vol. 31, January 25, 2010, No. 3, pp. 1)
Pub: Reed Business Information, Inc.
Ed: James Mammarella. **Description:** Overview of the Financo Annual Merchandising Industry Chief Executives Event during which there was much discussion on the merits of e-commerce, online marketing as well as the traditional methods of brand recognition and retailing.

20990 ■ "Fitter from Twitter" in *Boston Business Journal* (Vol. 30, December 17, 2010, No. 47, pp. 1)
Pub: Boston Business Journal
Ed: Lisa van der Pool. **Description:** Small businesses are increasing their use of the Twitter microblogging platform to attract and retain customers. Lisa Johnson, who owns Modern Pilates studios, managed to raise awareness of her personal brand nationally through the social media platform.

20991 ■ "For MySpace, A Redesign to Entice Generation Y" in *The New York Times* (October 27, 2010, pp. B3)
Pub: The New York Times Company
Ed: Miguel Helft. **Description:** MySpace is redesigning its Website in order to attract individuals from the Generation Y group.

20992 ■ "ForeSee Finds Satisfaction On Web Sites, Bottom Line" in *Crain's Detroit Business* (Vol. 24, February 25, 2008, No. 8, pp. 3)
Pub: Crain Communications Inc. - Detroit
Ed: Tom Henderson. **Description:** Ann Arbor-based ForeSee Results Inc. evaluates user satisfaction on Web sites. The company expects to see an increase of 40 percent in revenue for 2008 with plans to expand to London, Germany, Italy and France by the end of 2009.

20993 ■ "Forsys Metals Corporation Goes "Live" With Q4's On-Demand Disclosure Management Software" in *Canadian Corporate News* (May 16, 2007)
Pub: Comtex News Network Inc.
Description: Forsys Metals Corp. selected Q4 Web Systems to automate its corporate website disclosure with Q4's software platform which also automates and simplifies many of the administrative tasks that Forsys was doing manually, allowing them to focus their internal resources on the business.

20994 ■ "Fresh Direct's Crisis" in *Crain's New York Business* (Vol. 24, January 14, 2008, No. 2, pp. 3)
Pub: Crain Communications, Inc.
Ed: Lisa Fickenscher. **Description:** Freshdirect, an Internet grocery delivery service, finds itself under siege from federal immigration authorities, customers and labor organizations due to its employment practice of hiring illegals. At stake is the grocer's reputation as well as its ambitious growth plans, including an initial public offering of its stock.

20995 ■ "The Frugal Billionaire" in *Canadian Business* (Vol. 79, Winter 2006, No. 24, pp. 63)
Pub: Rogers Media
Ed: Joe Castaldo. **Description:** The achievements of David Cheriton are described, along with his investments in various firms, including Google Inc.

20996 ■ "Funbrain Launches Preschool Content" in *Marketing to Women* (Vol. 21, March 2008, No. 3, pp. 3)
Pub: EPM Communications, Inc.
Description: Funbrain.com launches The Moms and Kids Playground, a section of the website devoted to activities and games for moms and kids aged 2 to 6; content aims at building early computer skills and to teach basic concepts such as counting and colors.

20997 ■ "Get Online or Be Left Behind" in *Women In Business* (Vol. 61, August-September 2009, No. 4, pp. 33)
Pub: American Business Women's Association
Ed: Diane Stafford. **Description:** Technology's significance for the connectivity purposes among business people is discussed. Details on the use of wireless tools and online social media to boost technology IQ are presented.

20998 ■ "Get Online Quick in the Office Or in the Field" in *Contractor* (Vol. 56, October 2009, No. 10, pp. 47)
Pub: Penton Media, Inc.
Ed: William Feldman; Patti Feldman. **Description:** Contractors can set up a web site in minutes using the www.1and1.com website. Verizon's Novatel MIFI 2372 HSPA personal hotspot device lets contractors go online in the field. The StarTech scalable business management system helps contractors manage daily operations.

20999 ■ *Getting Clients and Keeping Clients for Your Service Business*
Pub: Atlantic Publishing Company
Ed: Anne M. Miller; Gail Brett Levine. **Released:** August 28, 2008. **Price:** $24.95 paperback. **Description:** Tips are offered to help any small service business identify customers, brand and grow the business, as well as development of logos, brochures and Websites.

21000 ■ "Google Edges into Wireless E-Mail" in *Globe & Mail* (February 19, 2007, pp. B5)
Pub: CTVglobemedia Publishing Inc.
Ed: Simon Avery. **Description:** Google Inc. has introduced a free mobile e-mail service in Canada. The mobile users can read, send, and search messages using the new software.

21001 ■ "Google's Next Stop: Below 350?" in *Barron's* (Vol. 88, March 10, 2008, No. 10, pp. 17)
Pub: Dow Jones & Company, Inc.
Ed: Jacqueline Doherty. **Description:** Share prices of Google Inc. are expected to drop from their level of $433 each to below $350 per share. The company is expected to miss its earnings forecast for the first quarter of 2008, and its continued aggressive spending on non-core areas will eventually bring down earnings.

21002 ■ "Graceful Landing" in *Entrepreneur* (Vol. 37, November 2009, No. 11, pp. 59)
Pub: Entrepreneur Media, Inc.
Ed: Mikal E. Belicove. **Description:** Successful marketers regularly use Website landing pages to capture qualified leads and make sales. It is believed that an effective landing page devoted to a single product or service offering can significantly boost leads and conversion rates. Organizations can create a top-notch landing page by anticipating customer expectations and focusing on a clear call to action.

21003 ■ "Growth of Free Dailies Dropping" in *Globe & Mail* (March 24, 2007, pp. B7)
Pub: CTVglobemedia Publishing Inc.
Ed: Grant Robertson. **Description:** The decrease in the readership of free newspapers in Canada, in view of growing preference for online news, is discussed.

21004 ■ "A Hacker in India Hijacked His Website Design and Was Making Good Money Selling It" in *Inc.* (December 2007, pp. 77-78, 80)
Pub: Gruner & Jahr USA Publishing
Ed: Darren Dahl. **Description:** John Anton, owner of an online custom T-shirt business and how a company in India was selling software Website templates identical to his firm's Website.

21005 ■ "Happy Blogging" in *Black Enterprise* (Vol. 38, January 2008, No. 6, pp. 47)
Pub: Earl G. Graves Publishing Co. Inc.
Ed: Sonya A. Donaldson. **Description:** Individual seeks advice for setting up a Website and starting a blog; Squarespace and Weebly both offer Web design.

21006 ■ "Harlequin Leads the Way" in *Marketing to Women* (Vol. 22, July 2009, No. 7, pp. 1)
Pub: EPM Communications, Inc.
Description: Although the publishing industry has been slow to embrace new media options, the Internet is now a primary source for reaching women readers. Harlequin has been eager to court their female consumers over the Internet and often uses women bloggers in their campaigns strategies.

21007 ■ "Harley-Davidson Moves to Unconventional Marketing Plan" in *Business Journal-Milwaukee* (Vol. 28, November 26, 2010, No. 8, pp. A1)
Pub: Milwaukee Business Journal
Ed: Rich Rovito. **Description:** Harley Davidson Inc. hired Boulder, Colorado-based Victors & Spoils, an agency that specializes in crowdsourcing, to implement a new creative marketing model. Under the plan, Harley Davidson will draw on the ideas of its brand enthusiasts to help guide the brand's marketing direction.

21008 ■ "Harnessing the Wisdom of Crowds" in *Entrepreneur* (Vol. 37, September 2009, No. 9, pp. 74)
Pub: Entrepreneur Media, Inc.
Ed: Mark Henricks. **Description:** Online customer service business Get Satisfaction has registered growth. The business enables customers to search for answers to common product questions. Customers use the service to post questions, complaints, and even product ideas.

21009 ■ "Has Microsoft Found a Way to Get at Yahoo?" in *Advertising Age* (Vol. 79, July 7, 2008, No. 26, pp. 4)
Pub: Crain Communications, Inc.
Ed: Abbey Klaassen. **Description:** Microsoft's attempt to acquire Yahoo's search business is discussed as is Yahoo's plans for the future at a time when the company's shares have fallen dangerously low.

21010 ■ "A Home's Identity in Black and White" in *Crain's Chicago Business* (Vol. 31, April 21, 2008, No. 16, pp. 35)
Pub: Crain Communications, Inc.
Ed: Lisa Bertagnoli. **Description:** Real estate agents are finding that showing customers a written floor plan is a trend that is growing since many buyers feel that Online virtual tours distort a room. Although floor plans cost up to $500 to have drawn up, they clearly show potential buyers the exact dimensions of rooms and how they connect.

21011 ■ *How to Make Money with Social Media: Using New and Emerging Media to Grow Your Business*
Pub: FT Press
Ed: Jamie Turner, Reshma Shah. **Released:** October 1, 2010. **Price:** $24.99. **Description:** Marketers, executives, entrepreneurs are shown more effective ways to utilize Internet social media to make money. This guide brings together both practical strategies and proven execution techniques for driving maximum value from social media marketing.

21012 ■ "How to Make Your Website Really Sell" in *Entrepreneur* (Vol. 37, September 2009, No. 9, pp. 79)
Pub: Entrepreneur Media, Inc.
Ed: David Port. **Description:** Advice on how to succeed in Internet marketing is presented. Offering visitors purchase incentives on the home page is encouraged. Delivery of customized landing pages and content is also recommended.

21013 ■ "How Marketers Can Tap the Web" in *Sales and Marketing Management* (November 12, 2009)
Pub: Nielsen Business Media, Inc.
Description: Internet marketing strategies require careful planning and tools in order to track success. Businesses are utilizing this trend to attract new clients as well as keep customers they already have satisfied. Advice on website development and design is provided.

21014 ■ "How Not to Build a Website" in *Women Entrepreneur* (December 24, 2008)
Pub: Entrepreneur Media Inc.
Ed: Erica Ruback; Joanie Reisen. **Description:** Tips for producing a unique and functional Website are given as well as a number of lessons a pair of entrepreneurs learned while trying to launch their networking website, MomSpace.com.

21015 ■ *How to Open and Operate a Financially Successful Bookstore on Amazon and Other Web Sites: With Companion CD-ROM*
Pub: Atlantic Publishing Company
Released: December 1, 2010. **Price:** $39.95. **Description:** This book was written for every used book aficionado and bookstore owner who currently wants to take advantage of the massive collection of online resources available to start and run your own online bookstore business.

21016 ■ *How to Use the Internet to Advertise, Promote, and Market Your Business or Web Site: With Little or No Money*
Pub: Atlantic Publishing Company
Released: December 1, 2010. **Price:** $24.95. **Description:** Information is given to help build, promote, and make money from your Website or brick and mortar store using the Internet, with minimal costs.

21017 ■ "Hunter and the Hunted" in *Canadian Business* (Vol. 81, Summer 2008, No. 9, pp. 12)
Pub: Rogers Media Ltd.
Ed: Thomas Watson. **Description:** Brian Hunter, a partner in oil and gas engineering firm Montane Resources, invested his life savings in Vancouver-based Canacord Capital Corp. Details of the asset-backed commercial paper fiasco and Hunter's use of Facebook to encourage other investors to participate in his claim against the mortgage company are presented.

21018 ■ *I'm on LinkedIn - Now What? (Second Edition): A Guide to Getting the Most Out of LinkedIn*
Pub: Happy About
Ed: Diane Danielson. **Released:** January 7, 2009. **Price:** $19.95. **Description:** Designed to help get the most out of LinkedIn, the popular business networking site and follows the first edition and includes the latest and great approaches using LinkedIn. With over 32 million members there is a lot of potential to find and develop relationships to help in your business and personal life, but many professionals find themselves wondering what to do once they sign up. This book explains the different benefits of the system and recommends best practices (including LinkedIn Groups) so that you get the most out of LinkedIn.

21019 ■ "Image Conscious" in *Canadian Business* (Vol. 81, March 17, 2008, No. 4, pp. 36)
Pub: Rogers Media
Ed: Andrew Wahl. **Description:** Idee Inc. is testing an Internet search engine for images that does not rely on tags but compares its visual data to a database of other images. The company was founded and managed by Leila Boujnane as an off-shoot of their risk-management software firm. Their software has already been used by image companies to track copyrighted images and to find images within their own archives.

21020 ■ "In Print and Online" in *Marketing to Women* (Vol. 22, August 2009, No. 8, pp. 3)
Pub: EPM Communications, Inc.
Description: Seventeen magazine is unifying its print and Online editions with complementary content, a strategy that seems to be working as every aspect of Seventeen drives the reader to another component.

21021 ■ *Information Industry Directory*
Pub: Gale
Released: Annual, Latest edition 36th; April, 2011. **Price:** $1105, individuals. **Covers:** Approximately 12,000 organizations, systems, and services involved in the production and distribution of information in electronic form: database producers and their products online host services, transactional services, library and information networks, bibliographic utilities, library management systems, information retrieval software, mailing list services, fee-based information on demand services, document delivery sources, data collection and analysis centers and firms, and related consultants, service companies, professional and trade associations, publishers, and research activities. **Entries Include:** Name of parent organization, name of system of service, address, phone, toll-free phone, fax, telex, email address, year founded name of unit head, size of staff, names of any affiliated organizations, financial information. Internet access information, general description of electronic product, system, or service, subjects covered or areas of service offered, sources of data for the system, type and quantity of stored information in all forms, publications and microform products and services, computer-based products and services, other services, clientele served, availability and restrictions, name of contact. **Arrangement:** Alphabetical. **Indexes:** Master, database name, software name, publication/microform title, function/service, personal name, subject, geographical.

21022 ■ "Inside Intel's Effectiveness System for Web Marketing" in *Advertising Age* (Vol. 81, January 25, 2010, No. 4, pp. 4)
Pub: Crain's Communications
Ed: Beth Snyder Bulik. **Description:** Overview of Intel's internally developed program called Value Point System in which the company is using in order to evaluate and measure online marketing effectiveness.

21023 ■ "Inside an Online Bazaar" in *Entrepreneur* (Vol. 37, September 2009, No. 9, pp. 38)
Pub: Entrepreneur Media, Inc.
Ed: Kara Ohngren. **Description:** Etsy.com is a website that provides a marketplace for handmade products. The site has attracted more than 250,000 sellers since its launch in 2005. Site features and services are also supplied.

21024 ■ "Internet Marketing 2.0: Closing the Online Chat Gap" in *Agent's Sales Journal* (November 2009, pp. 14)
Pub: Summit Business Media
Ed: Jeff Denenholz. **Description:** Advice regarding the implementation of an Internet marketing strategy for insurance agencies includes how and why to incorporate a chat feature in which a sales agent can communicate in real-time with potential or existing customers. It is important to understand if appropriate response mechanisms are in place to convert leads into actual sales.

21025 ■ "Internet Marketing Agency .Com Marketing Wins National Awards for Web Design and SEO" in *Marketing Weekly News* (Jan. 2, 2010)
Pub: Investment Weekly News
Description: Internet marketing agency .Com Marketing has won two bronze awards for its exceptional quality web services; the company is a full-service interactive marketing and advertising agency that specializes in a variety of online services including web design, social media marketing and press releases.

21026 ■ "It's a Hit" in *Entrepreneur* (Vol. 36, March 2008, No. 3, pp. 110)
Pub: Entrepreneur Media Inc.
Ed: John Jantsch. **Description:** Entrepreneurs use the Web to market business and keeping relevant content in the Website is important to address questions from customers. Other considerations in marketing businesses online include: interacting with site visitors, using Web applications for project collaboration and file storage, and encouraging customers to post reviews.

21027 ■ "It's a New Game: Killerspin Pushes Table Tennis to Extreme Heights" in *Black Enterprise* (Vol. 37, October 2006, No. 3, pp. 73)
Pub: Earl G. Graves Publishing Co. Inc.
Ed: Bridget McCrea. **Description:** Profile of Robert Blackwell and his company Killerspin L.L.C., which is popularizing the sport of table tennis. Killerspin has hit $1 million in revenues due to product sales primarily generated through the company's website, magazines, DVDs, and event ticket sales.

21028 ■ "Johnson's Taps Online Animation" in *Marketing to Women* (Vol. 21, April 2008, No. 4, pp. 3)
Pub: EPM Communications, Inc.
Description: Johnson's has launched a new integrated campaign for its baby lotion in an effort to appeal to the growing number of moms online.

21029 ■ "JumpTV to Hold Conference Call to Discuss Q1 Results and Annual General Meeting" in *Canadian Corporate News* (May 16, 2007)
Pub: Comtex News Network Inc.
Description: Profile of JumpTv, the world's leading broadcaster of ethnic television over the Internet, and the results of a conference that discussed their first quarter 2007 financial report as well as the company's business goals. Statistical data included.

21030 ■ "Kawasaki's New Top Gun" in *Brandweek* (Vol. 49, April 21, 2008, No. 16, pp. 18)
Pub: VNU Business Media, Inc.
Description: Discusses Kawasaki's marketing plan which included designing an online brochure in which visitors could create a video by building their own test track on a grid and then selecting visual special effects and musical overlay. This engaging and innovative marketing technique generated more than 166,000 unique users within the first three months of being launched.

21031 ■ "Keep Them Posted" in *Entrepreneur* (Vol. 35, October 2007, No. 10, pp. 39)
Pub: Entrepreneur Media Inc.
Ed: Gwen Moran. **Description:** Survey by the Pew Internet and American Life Project found that 12 million American adults maintain blogs, which are created for personal and business reasons. Blogs are effective in giving a business a personal touch while informing the public about its operations and products. Tips on how to create an effective business blog are presented.

21032 ■ "Kid-Friendly Business Sources" in *Black Enterprise* (Vol. 37, January 2007, No. 6, pp. 40)
Pub: Earl G. Graves Publishing Co. Inc.
Ed: Carolyn M. Brown. **Description:** Financial or business camps are a great way to encourage a child who interested in starting his or her own business. A number of these camps are available each year including Kidpreneurs Conference and Bull and Bear Investment Camp. Other resources are available online. Resources included.

21033 ■ "Kuno Creative to Present B2B Social Media Campaign Webinar" in *Entertainment Close-Up* (August 25, 2011)
Pub: Close-Up Media
Description: Kuno Creative, an inbound marketing agency, will host Three Steps of a Successful B2B Social Media Campaign. The firm is a provider of Website development, branding, marketing strategy, public relations, Internet marketing, and inbound marketing.

21034 ■ "Last Founder Standing" in *Conde Nast Portfolio* (Vol. 2, June 2008, No. 6, pp. 124)
Pub: Conde Nast Publications, Inc.
Ed: Kevin Maney. **Description:** Interview with Amazon CEO Jeff Bezos in which he discusses the economy, the company's new distribution center and the hiring of employees for it, e-books, and the overall vision for the future of the firm.

21035 ■ "Laterooms and Octopus Travel Top Greenlight's Integrated Search Report for the Hotel Sector" in *Internet Wire* (October 23, 2009)
Pub: Comtex News Network, Inc.
Description: According to a research report conducted by Greenlight, the UK's leading independent Internet search marketing agency, the most visible hotel websites in natural search during June 2009 are premierinn.com, booking.com and laterooms.com; OctopusTravel.com generated the greatest share of the paid search section with 21 percent visibility. The report is focused on the hotel sector and covers the second quarter of 2009. Statistical data included.

21036 ■ "Lavante, Inc. Joins Intersynthesis, Holistic Internet Marketing Company" in *Internet Wire* (November 5, 2009)
Pub: Comtex News Network, Inc.
Description: Lavante, Inc., the leading provider of on-demand vendor information and profit recovery audit solutions for Fortune 1000 companies has chosen Intersynthesis, a new holistic Internet marketing firm, as a provider of pay for performance services. Lavante believes that Intersynthesis' expertise and knowledge combined with their ability to develop integrated strategies, will help them fuel more growth.

21037 ■ "Legal Aid: Sample Legal Documents can Lower Your Attorney Fees" in *Black Enterprise* (Vol. 37, October 2006, No. 3, pp. 210)
Pub: Earl G. Graves Publishing Co. Inc.
Ed: Tamara E. Holmes. **Description:** FreeLegalForms.net provides thousands of free legal forms. These forms are not a substitute for consultation with an attorney but the sample documents can help save you time and money.

21038 ■ "Legislating the Cloud" in *Information Today* (Vol. 28, October 2011, No. 9, pp. 1)
Pub: Information Today, Inc.
Description: Internet and telecommunications industry leaders are asking for legislation to address the emerging market in cloud computing. Existing communications laws do not adequately govern the modern Internet.

21039 ■ "A Life of Spice" in *Entrepreneur* (Vol. 37, September 2009, No. 9, pp. 46)
Pub: Entrepreneur Media, Inc.
Ed: Jason Daley. **Description:** Matt and Bryan Walls have successfully grown their Atlanta, Georgia-based Snorg Tees T-shirt company. The company has expanded its product offering and redesigned its Website to be more user-friendly. The company has registered between $5 and 10 million in 2008.

21040 ■ "Lights, Camera, Action: Tools for Creating Video Blogs" in *Inc.* (Volume 32, December 2010, No. 10, pp. 57)
Pub: Inc. Magazine
Ed: John Brandon. **Description:** A video blog is a good way to spread company news, talk about products, and stand out among traditional company blogs. New editing software can create two- to four-minute blogs using a webcam and either Windows Live Essentials, Apple iLife 2011, Powerdirector 9 Ultra, or Adobe Visual Communicator 3.

21041 ■ "MaggieMoo's Ice Cream and Treatery" in *Ice Cream Reporter* (Vol. 23, September 20, 2010, No. 10, pp. 7)
Pub: Ice Cream Reporter
Description: MaggieMoo's Ice Cream and Treatery has launched a new Website where visitors can learn about the brands newest ice cream innovations.

21042 ■ "Make It Easy" in *Entrepreneur* (Vol. 36, May 2008, No. 5, pp. 49)
Pub: Entrepreneur Media, Inc.
Ed: Mike Hogan. **Description:** Zoho has a Planner that keep contacts, notes and reminders and a DB & Reports feature for reports, data analysis and pricing comparisons. WebEx WebOffice Workgroup supports

document management and templates for contacts lists, time sheets and sales tracking. Other online data manages are presented.

21043 ■ "Marketing Management Analytics Announces MMA Digital" in *Internet Wire* (January 26, 2010)
Pub: Comtex News Network, Inc.
Description: Innovator and pioneer in marketing effectiveness, Marketing Management Analytics, is offering a new service called MMA Digital; using this service companies will be able to more accurately measure the effects of digital media alongside other marketing tools in order to better understand and leverage the drivers of online marketing success.

21044 ■ "McD's Warms Up For Olympics Performance" in *Advertising Age* (Vol. 79, July 7, 2008, No. 26, pp. 8)
Pub: Crain Communications, Inc.
Ed: Description: Overview of McDonald's marketing plans for the company's sponsorship of the Olympics which includes a website, an alternate-reality game, names featured on U.S. athletes and on-the-ground activities.

21045 ■ "Milk Producers Target Moms" in *Marketing to Women* (Vol. 21, January 2008, No. 1, pp. 3)
Pub: EPM Communications, Inc.
Description: In an attempt to encourage moms to serve milk with meals, the American Dairy Association partners with the New York State Dietetic Association to promote milk via a new logo, website and contest.

21046 ■ *Million Dollar Website: Simple Steps to Help You Compete with the Big Boys-Even on a Small Business Budget*
Pub: Prentice Hall Press
Ed: Lori Culwell. **Released:** May 9, 2010. **Price:** $19. 95. **Description:** Resource for any small business owner wishing to build a successful Website in order to compete with big box stores.

21047 ■ "Mobile Presence, in a Flash: DIY Tools for Creating Smartphone-Friendly Websites" in *Inc.* (Vol. 33, November 2011, No. 9, pp. 50)
Pub: Inc. Magazine
Ed: John Brandon. **Description:** DudaMobile and FiddleFly convert regular Websites into mobile sites that work on most smartphones. Profiles of both apps services are included.

21048 ■ "Most Viewed Stories, Videos on farmindustrynews.com in 2010" in *Farm Industry News* (January 4, 2011)
Pub: Penton Business Media Inc.
Description: The top ten most popularly viewed stories and videos presented on farmindustrynews. com Website are listed.

21049 ■ "The Neighborhood Watch" in *Hawaii Business* (Vol. 53, March 2008, No. 9, pp. 36)
Pub: Hawaii Business Publishing
Ed: David K. Choo. **Description:** OahuRe.com offers information on Hawaii real estate market, with spreadsheets and comparative market analysis page, which shows properties that are active, sold, or in escrow. Other details about OahuRe.com are discussed. A list of other top real estate websites in Hawaii and in the U.S. in general is provided.

21050 ■ "Net Connections" in *Black Enterprise* (Vol. 38, July 2008, No. 12, pp. 28)
Pub: Earl G. Graves Publishing Co. Inc.
Ed: Anthony S. Calypso. **Description:** Marketers are making strategic partnerships with online social networks in an attempt to gain further market reach. The value of these networks appears to be on the rise forcing media companies to recalculate their strategies for delivering products to customers.

21051 ■ "Networking Web Sites: a Two-Edged Sword" in *Contractor* (Vol. 56, October 2009, No. 10, pp. 52)
Pub: Penton Media, Inc.
Ed: H. Kent Craig. **Description:** People need to be careful about the information that they share on social networking Web sites. They should realize that future bosses, coworkers, and those that might want to hire them might read those information. Posting on these sites can cost career opportunities and respect.

21052 ■ "The New Basics of Marketing" in *Inc.* (February 2008, pp. 75-81)
Pub: Gruner & Jahr USA Publishing
Ed: Leigh Buchanan. **Description:** New tools for marketing a business or service include updating or upgrading a Website, using email or texting, or advertising on a social Internet network.

21053 ■ "New Recession-Proof Internet Marketing Package Allows Businesses to Ramp Up Web Traffic and Profits" in *PR Newswire* (Jan. 25, 2010)
Pub: PR Newswire Association, LLC
Description: Profile of Reel Web Design, a leading marketing firm in New York City that caters to small to medium sized businesses with smaller budgets that need substantial return on investment; Reel Web Design offers video production and submission, web design and maintenance and press release writing among additional services.

21054 ■ "New TurnHere Survey Reveals Online Video Trends" in *Internet Wire* (October 22, 2009)
Pub: Comtex News Network, Inc.
Description: TurnHere, Inc., the leading online video marketing services company, released the findings of its recent survey regarding current and future trends in online video among marketing agencies and brand recognition; the report found that online video has and will continue to play a prominent role in the realm of marketing edging out both search and email marketing campaigns. Additional highlights and statistical data included.

21055 ■ "A New Way to Tell When to Fold" in *Barron's* (Vol. 88, July 7, 2008, No. 27, pp. 27)
Pub: Dow Jones & Co., Inc.
Ed: Theresa W. Carey. **Description:** Overview of the Online trading company SmartStops, a firm that aims to tell investors when to sell the shares of a particular company. The company's Web site categorizes stocks as moving up, down, or sideways, and calculates exit points for individual stocks based on an overall market trend.

21056 ■ "Norvax University Health Insurance Sales Training and Online Marketing Conference" in *Internet Wire* (January 27, 2010)
Pub: Comtex News Network, Inc.
Description: Overview of the Norvax University Marketing and Sales Success Conference Tour which includes insurance sales training seminars, proven and innovative online marketing techniques and a host of additional information and networking opportunities.

21057 ■ "Oh, Behave!" in *Entrepreneur* (Vol. 36, April 2008, No. 4, pp. 87)
Pub: Entrepreneur Media, Inc.
Ed: Gwen Moran. **Description:** Online social networks can pose awkward situations for users. These include instances such as getting a link request from someone you do not know, having a contact post embarrassing information on your site, and a contact asking you to be refer him to one of your business contacts. Tips on how to deal with these situations are discussed.

21058 ■ "Omniture's Next Version of SearchCenter Delivers Landing Page Optimization" in *Internet Wire* (September 24, 2009)
Pub: Comtex News Network, Inc.
Description: Omniture, Inc., a leading provider of online business optimization software, has announced a new release of Omniture SearchCenter; this latest version will allow search engine marketers to test landing pages across campaigns and ad groups.

21059 ■ "On Target" in *Canadian Business* (Vol. 81, July 22, 2008, No. 12-13, pp. 45)
Pub: Rogers Media Ltd.
Ed: Calvin Leung. **Description:** Companies such as LavalifePRIME, a dating website devoted to singles 45 and older, discuss the value of marketing and services aimed at Canada's older consumers. One-third of Canada's 33 million people are 50-plus, controlling 77 percent of the countries wealth.

21060 ■ "Online Forex Broker Tadawul FX Intros Arabic Website" in *Entertainment Close-Up* (June 23, 2011)
Pub: Close-Up Media
Description: Online forex broker, Tadawul FX, launched its Arabic language Website, noting that the Middle East is a key market for the investment firm.

21061 ■ "Online Marketing and Promotion of Canadian Films via Social Media Tools" in *CNW Group* (January 27, 2010)
Pub: Comtex News Network, Inc.
Description: Telefilm Canada announced the launch of a pilot initiative aimed at encouraging the integration of online marketing and the use of social media tools into means of distribution ahead of a films' theatrical release. During this pilot phase Web-Cine 360 will target French-language feature films.

21062 ■ "Online Postings Really Influence Older Women" in *Marketing to Women* (Vol. 22, July 2009, No. 7, pp. 8)
Pub: EPM Communications, Inc.
Description: Women over the age of 55 are more likely to be swayed to purchase a product by referrals from others, including Online postings by strangers. Another key influence is associated with the brand's ability to address their lifestyle needs.

21063 ■ "Online Self-Publishing Services" in *Black Enterprise* (Vol. 37, November 2006, No. 4, pp. 90)
Pub: Earl G. Graves Publishing Co. Inc.
Description: Profiles of five online self-publishing services.

21064 ■ "Orbitz Adds Parent Panel" in *Marketing to Women* (Vol. 21, March 2008, No. 3, pp. 5)
Pub: EPM Communications, Inc.
Description: Orbitz introduces the Orbitz Parent Panel in an attempt to better connect with traveling families.

21065 ■ "Ordering Pizza Hut From Your Facebook Page?" in *Advertising Age* (Vol. 79, November 10, 2008, No. 42, pp. 50)
Pub: Crain Communications, Inc.
Ed: Emily Bryson York. **Description:** Fast-food chains are experimenting with delivery/takeout services via social networks such as Facebook and iPhone applications. This also allows the chains to build valuable databases of their customers.

21066 ■ "Our Gadget of the Week: Mostly, I Liked It" in *Barron's* (Vol. 88, July 14, 2008, No. 28, pp. 31)
Pub: Dow Jones & Co., Inc.
Ed: Jay Palmer. **Description:** Review of the Apple iPhone 3G, which costs $199, has better audio and is slightly thicker than its predecessor; using the 3G wireless connection makes going online faster but drains the battery faster too.

21067 ■ "Our World with Black Enterprise" in *Black Enterprise* (Vol. 37, February 2007, No. 7, pp. 145)
Pub: Earl G. Graves Publishing Co. Inc.
Description: Our World with Black Enterprise is a television broadcast that features roundtable discussions and interviews with important African American figures.

21068 ■ "Pagetender LLC Releases Website Design Package for HubSpot Users" in *Internet Wire* (September 30, 2009)
Pub: Comtex News Network, Inc.
Description: Profile of Pagetender LLC, a Certified HubSpot partner, who announced a Website Design Package marketed specifically for HubSpot Owner and Marketer users. This packaged was developed for small to medium sized businesses that want a website designed or their current site redesigned on

HubSpot's Content Management System. Companies that would like a more robust site have the option of adding Flash development, ecommerce and photo galleries.

21069 ■ "P&G to Mine E-Commerce Potential" in *Business Courier* (Vol. 26, September 18, 2009, No. 21, pp. 1)
Pub: American City Business Journals, Inc.
Ed: Lisa Biank Fasig. **Description:** Procter & Gamble (P&G) is looking to turn the hits to the company's Websites into increased sales. The program will include a shop now option to track all emerging sales.

21070 ■ "Paterson Plots Comeback With Internet IPO" in *Globe & Mail* (February 20, 2006, pp. B1)
Pub: CTVglobemedia Publishing Inc.
Ed: Grant Robertson. **Description:** The initial public offering plans of chief executive officer Scott Paterson of JumpTV.com are presented.

21071 ■ "Pet-Food Crisis a Boon to Organic Players" in *Advertising Age* (Vol. 78, April 9, 2007, No. 15, pp. 3)
Pub: Crain Communications, Inc.
Ed: Jack Neff. **Description:** In the wake of the pet-food recall crisis, the natural-and-organic segment of the market is gaining recognition and sales; one such manufacturer, Blue Buffalo, has not only seen huge sale increases but also has witnessed a 50-60 percent increase in traffic to the brand's website which has led to the decision to move up the timetable for the brand's first national ad campaign.

21072 ■ "Play By Play: These Video Products Can Add New Life to a Stagnant Website" in *Black Enterprise* (Vol. 41, December 2010, No. 5)
Pub: Earl G. Graves Publishing Co. Inc.
Ed: Marcia Wade Talbert. **Description:** Web Visible, provider of online marketing products and services, cites video capability as the fastest-growing Website feature for small business advertisers. Profiles of various devices for adding video to a Website are included.

21073 ■ "The Power of Negative Thinking" in *Inc.* (Volume 32, December 2010, No. 10, pp. 43)
Pub: Inc. Magazine
Ed: Jason Fried. **Description:** A Website is software and most businesses have and need a good Website to generate business. Understanding for building a powerful Website is presented.

21074 ■ "Pretentious and Loving It" in *Entrepreneur* (Vol. 37, August 2009, No. 8, pp. 34)
Pub: Entrepreneur Media, Inc.
Ed: Eric Mahoney. **Description:** Pitchfork.com features reviews of albums from independent artists. Their most innovative section is Pitchfork.tv, featuring videos of bands, and Forkcast along with their Features section that contains articles about bands and their histories.

21075 ■ "Pro Livestock Launches Most Comprehensive Virtual Sales Barn for Livestock and Breed Stock" in *Benzinga.com* (October 29, 2011)
Pub: Benzinga.com
Ed: Benzinga Staff. **Description:** Pro Livestock Marketing launched the first online sales portal for livestock and breed stock. The firm has designed a virtual sales barn allowing individuals to purchase and sell cattle, swine, sheep, goats, horses, rodeo stock, show animals, specialty animals, semen and embryos globally. It is like an eBay for livestock and will help ranchers and farmers grow.

21076 ■ "Recalls Cause Consumers to Put More Stock in Online Reviews" in *Crain's Cleveland Business* (Vol. 28, November 12, 2007, No. 45)
Pub: Crain Communications, Inc.
Ed: Jack Neff. **Description:** Due to the string of product recalls over the last year, consumers are looking at online product reviews to help them make purchasing decisions which could reshape marketing for a wide range of products.

21077 ■ "Recovery2.0: a Work in Progress" in *Tampa Bay Business Journal* (Vol. 30, December 18, 2009, No. 52, pp. 3)
Pub: American City Business Journals
Ed: Margaret Cashill. **Description:** The debut of the Recovery.gov 2.0 version has raised questions regarding the Website's price tag, which will cost nearly $18 million. Tampa, Florida-based GSL Solutions Inc. president Michael Gaines believes the Websites created with existing technologies tend to cost less than custom development. The difference between Recovery.org and Recovery.gov are explained.

21078 ■ "Reportlinker Adds Report: Social Networks: Five Consumer Trends for 2009" in *Wireless News* (October 23, 2009)
Pub: Close-Up Media
Description: "Social Networks: Five Consumer Trends for 2009," a new market research report by Reportlinker.com found that in the countries of Italy and Spain lag behind their European neighbors in Internet development. Since large numbers of consumers in these two countries remain offline, only a minimal portion of total advertising spending goes into Internet marketing, and those advertising campaigns are directed at the relatively young, affluent users. Statistical data included.

21079 ■ "Reportlinker.com Adds Report: GeoWeb and Local Internet Markets: 2008 Edition" in *Entertainment Close-Up* (September 11, 2009)
Pub: Close-Up Media
Description: Reportlinker.com is adding a new market research report that is available in its catalogue: GeoWeb and Local Internet Markets - 2008 Edition; highlights include the outlook for consumer mapping services and an examination of monetizing services and an analysis the development outlook for geospacial Internet market, also referred to as the Geoweb.

21080 ■ "Research Reports: How Analysts Size Up Companies" in *Barron's* (Vol. 88, March 17, 2008, No. 11, pp. M13)
Pub: Dow Jones & Company, Inc.
Ed: Anita Peltonen. **Description:** Shares of Applied Industrial Technologies are ranked Market Perform while the shares of Google get a buy rating. Salix Pharmaceuticals gets a Sell/Above-Average risk rating. The shares of Dune Energy, Franklin Resources, Internet Brands, Piper Jaffray, and Texas Instruments are also rated.

21081 ■ "Resource Line" in *Black Enterprise* (Vol. 37, January 2007, No. 6, pp. 6)
Pub: Earl G. Graves Publishing Co. Inc.
Description: Interactive Media Editor, Philana Patterson, writes a column for blackenterprise.com that offers advice and provides resources for entrepreneurs, corporate executives, business owners, and budding investors.

21082 ■ "Retail Franchises to Start Now" in *Entrepreneur* (Vol. 37, August 2009, No. 8, pp. 88)
Pub: Entrepreneur Media, Inc.
Ed: Tracy Stapp. **Description:** Listing of retail franchises is presented and is categorized based on their products sold. The total cost of the franchise and the website are also included as well as additional statistical data.

21083 ■ "The Right Time for REITs" in *Barron's* (Vol. 88, July 14, 2008, No. 28, pp. 32)
Pub: Dow Jones & Co., Inc.
Ed: Mike Hogan. **Description:** Discusses the downturn in U.S. real estate investment trusts so these are worth considering for investment. Several Websites that are useful for learning about real estate investment trusts for investment purposes are presented.

21084 ■ "Rise Interactive, Internet Marketing Agency, Now Offers Social Media Training and Advisory Services" in *Internet Wire* (Nov. 4, 2009)
Pub: Comtex News Network, Inc.
Description: Profile of Rise Interactive, a full-service Internet marketing agency which has recently added social media to its list of offerings; the agency touts that its newest service gives their clients the power to have ongoing communication with current and potential customers on the sites they are most actively visiting.

21085 ■ "ROIonline Announces Streaming Video Products" in *Marketing Weekly News* (December 5, 2009, pp. 155)
Pub: Investment Weekly News
Description: ROIonline LLC, an Internet marketing firm serving business-to-business and the industrial marketplace, has added streaming video options to the Internet solutions it offers its clients; due to the huge increase of broadband connections, videos are now commonplace on the Internet and can often convey a company's message in a must more efficient, concise and effective way that will engage a website's visitor thus delivering a high return on a company's investment.

21086 ■ "Rumor Has It" in *Entrepreneur* (Vol. 35, October 2007, No. 10, pp. 30)
Pub: Entrepreneur Media Inc.
Ed: Chris Penttila. **Description:** Some entrepreneurs like Ren Moulton and Dan Scudder regard rumor sites and product blogs as great sources of market research. However, there are legal issues that must be studied before using these Internet sites in marketing and product development. The use and limitations of rumor sites and product blogs are provided.

21087 ■ "Schipul Enhances Website Via Tendenci 5" in *Entertainment Close-Up* (March 30, 2011)
Pub: Close-Up Media
Description: Schipul, Website marketing and design firm, upgraded their Website using Tendenci 5 which features capabilities that cater to the interests of the user. Tendenci 5 also powers Websites for Houston Technology Center, Discovery Green, Tendenci and YMCA Houston.

21088 ■ *The Search: How Google and Its Rival Rewrote the Rules of Business and Transformed Our Culture*
Pub: Penguin Group Incorporated
Ed: John Battelle. **Released:** October 3, 2006. **Price:** $14.95. **Description:** Provides a history of Internet search technology.

21089 ■ *The SEO Manifesto: A Practical and Ethical Guide to Internet Marketing and Search Engine Optimization*
Pub: Cape Project Management Inc.
Ed: Dan Tousignant, Pamela Gobiel. **Released:** December 5, 2011. **Price:** $14.99. **Description:** Comprehensive guide for each phase of launching an online business; chapters include checklists, process descriptions, and examples.

21090 ■ "Sharing the Micro Wealth" in *Entrepreneur* (Vol. 37, July 2009, No. 7, pp. 46)
Pub: Entrepreneur Media, Inc.
Ed: Jennie Dorris. **Description:** Step-by-step guide is presented on how Kiva.org, a website which allows people to make microloans to entrepreneurs across the world, works. The website, founded by Matt Flannery, raises $1 million weekly and it will add U.S. entrepreneurs to its list of loan recipients in June 2010. Other features of Kiva.org are discussed.

21091 ■ "Shipping 2.0" in *Entrepreneur* (Vol. 36, April 2008, No. 4, pp. 54)
Pub: Entrepreneur Media, Inc.
Ed: Heather Clancy. **Description:** Doggypads.com contacted with Web 2.0 service provider Shipwire to handle its warehouse concerns. The service works by paying a rent to Shipwire and they will store the client's items. The client's customers can continue to order from the client's website and Shipwire will take care of delivery. Doggypads was able to save up on costs by using Shipwire.

21092 ■ "Shoestring-Budget Marketing" in *Women Entrepreneur* (January 5, 2009)
Pub: Entrepreneur Media Inc.
Ed: Maria Falconer. **Description:** Pay-per-click search engine advertising is the traditional type of e-marketing that may not only be too expensive for

certain kinds of businesses but also may not attract the quality customer base a business looking to grow needs to find. Social networking websites have become a mandatory marketing tool for business owners who want to see growth in their sales; tips are provided for utilizing these networking websites in order to gain more visibility on the Internet which can, in turn, lead to the more sales.

21093 ■ "Siteworx Earns 4 Interactive Media Awards in Q1 of 2011" in *Entertainment Close-Up* (, 2011)
Pub: Close-Up Media
Description: Details of the four awards Siteworx earned for its achievements in Web development and design are outlined.

21094 ■ *The Small Business Owner's Manual: Everything You Need to Know to Start Up and Run Your Business*
Pub: Career Press, Incorporated
Ed: Joe Kennedy. **Released:** June 2005. **Price:** $19.99 (US), $26.95 (Canadian). **Description:** Comprehensive guide for starting a small business, focusing on twelve ways to obtain financing, business plans, selling and advertising products and services, hiring and firing employees, setting up a Web site, business law, accounting issues, insurance, equipment, computers, banks, financing, customer credit and collection, leasing, and more.

21095 ■ "Social Media: Communicate the Important Stuff" in *Agency Sales Magazine* (Vol. 39, November 2009, No. 10, pp. 52)
Pub: MANA
Ed: Jack Foster. **Description:** Social media such as Twitter or Facebook allows businesses to communicate with their customers over great distances but this technology can take away from the personal touch. For those that want to implement these tools in their marketing plans, they should first find out which social media networks their target audience use and give their customers reasons to become fans.

21096 ■ "Social Media, E-Mail Remain Challenging for Employees" in *Workforce Management* (Vol. 88, December 14, 2009, No. 13, pp. 4)
Pub: Crain Communications, Inc.
Ed: Ed Frauenheim. **Description:** Examining the impact of Internet social networking and the workplace; due to the power of these new technologies, it is important that companies begin to set clear policies regarding Internet use and employee privacy.

21097 ■ "Social Networkers for Hire" in *Black Enterprise* (Vol. 40, December 2009, No. 5, pp. 56)
Pub: Earl G. Graves Publishing Co., Inc.
Ed: Brittany Hutson. **Description:** Companies are utilizing social networking sites in order to market their brand and personally connect with consumers and are increasingly looking to social media specialists to help with this task. Aliya S. King is one such web strategist, working for ICED Media by managing their Twitter, Facebook, YouTube and Flickr accounts for one of their publicly traded restaurant clients.

21098 ■ "Social Networking Butterfly" in *Entrepreneur* (Vol. 37, September 2009, No. 9, pp. 48)
Pub: Entrepreneur Media, Inc.
Ed: Jason Daley. **Description:** Entrepreneur Ashley Qualls has successfully grown Whateverlife.com. The site was originally created to share Qualls' custom MySpace.com templates with friends and family. Qualls is planning to redesign the site as a social network focused on Web design.

21099 ■ "Social Networking Site for Moms" in *Marketing to Women* (Vol. 21, March 2008, No. 3, pp. 3)
Pub: EPM Communications, Inc.
Description: The Cradle is a social networking site devoted to pregnancy and new parenthood.

21100 ■ "Sometimes, Second Impressions Count Most" in *Canadian Business* (Vol. 83, October 12, 2010, No. 17, pp. 11)
Pub: Rogers Media Ltd.
Ed: Richard Branson. **Description:** Developing a favorable impression at the first point of contact is imperative for businesses. Managers who want their organizations to make positive first and second impressions need to learn to balance the Web's labor-saving efficiencies with human assistants. The importance of considering the customer relations value in company Websites is also explained.

21101 ■ "Sticking to Stories; Havey Ovshinksy Changes Method, Keeps the Mission" in *Crain's Detroit Business* (Vol. 24, March 31, 2008)
Pub: Crain Communications, Inc.
Ed: Daniel Duggan. **Description:** Profile of Harvey Ovshinsky, an award-winning documentary filmmaker who has reinvented his work with corporations who want to market themselves with the transition to digital media. His company, HKO Media, takes Ovshinsky's art of storytelling and enhances it through multimedia operations on the Internet through a joint venture with a man he once mentored, Bob Kernen.

21102 ■ "Stimulating Fare at the SBA" in *Barron's* (Vol. 89, July 20, 2009, No. 29, pp. 12)
Pub: Dow Jones & Co., Inc.
Ed: Jim McTague. **Description:** Internet access at the Small Business Administration slowed down on 7 July 2009, apparently caused by employees streaming videos of the Michael Jackson tribute. The agency claims that the event did not disrupt its operations.

21103 ■ "Success Products" in *Black Enterprise* (Vol. 37, February 2007, No. 7, pp. 135)
Pub: Earl G. Graves Publishing Co. Inc.
Ed: Tanisha A. Sykes. **Description:** Using innovative resources that are already at your fingertips instead of trying to reach out to companies first is a great way to discover whether you have a viable idea or product. Be motivated to start an e-newsletter letting people know about your products and attend conferences like The Motivation Show, the world's largest exhibition of motivational products and services related to performance in business.

21104 ■ *Success Secrets of Social Media Marketing Superstars*
Pub: Entrepreneur Press
Ed: Mitch Meyerson. **Released:** June 1, 2010. **Price:** $21.95. **Description:** Provides access to the playbooks of social media marketers who reveal their most valuable strategies and tactics for standing out in the new online media environment.

21105 ■ "Suncoast Pest Control Introduces New Website" in *Entertainment Close-Up* (March 16, 2011)
Pub: Close-Up Media
Description: Florida pest control company, Suncoast Pest Control, launched a new Website to better serve their customers. The new Website will allow users to reach local Florida pest control professionals 24 hours a day.

21106 ■ "A Taxing Proposition" in *Black Enterprise* (Vol. 37, January 2007, No. 6, pp. 6)
Pub: Earl G. Graves Publishing Co. Inc.
Description: Learn how to avoid tax problems on Black Enterprise's website, blackenterprise.com.

21107 ■ "Tee Off Online" in *Black Enterprise* (Vol. 37, January 2007, No. 6, pp. 52)
Pub: Earl G. Graves Publishing Co. Inc.
Ed: James C. Johnson. **Description:** The E-Com Resource Center is one of many resources that are available for those interested in starting an e-commerce business. One of the first steps is to create a business plan, of which there are free samples available at BPlans.com.

21108 ■ "Texas Fold 'Em" in *Canadian Business* (Vol. 79, October 9, 2006, No. 20, pp. 44)
Pub: Rogers Media
Ed: John Gray. **Description:** New policies of the United States law makers for the online casino industries that could force many of them out of business are discussed.

21109 ■ "The Way I Work" in *Inc.* (March 2008, pp. 102-104, 106)
Pub: Gruner & Jahr USA Publishing
Ed: Hannah Clark Steiman. **Description:** Profile of Howard Lefkowitz, CEO of Vegas.com, a Website that allows visitors to book flights, reserve hotel rooms, buy show tickets, make spa appointments, and coordinate any and all aspects of a trip to Las Vegas. The firm also runs brick-and-mortar box offices and concierge desks at various cities.

21110 ■ "Things Really Clicking for Macy's Online" in *Business Courier* (Vol. 24, November 30, 2008, No. 33, pp. 1)
Pub: American City Business Journals, Inc.
Ed: Lisa Biank Fasig. **Description:** Retailer Macy's online division Macys.com are projecting sales at $1billion in 2007, compared to $620 million in 2006. Macy's new online features and products and the growth of online retail sector are also discussed.

21111 ■ "Thomas Industrial Network Unveils Custom SPEC" in *Entertainment Close-Up* (March 3, 2011)
Pub: Close-Up Media
Description: Thomas Industrial Network assists custom manufacturers and industrial service providers a complete online program called Custom SPEC which includes Website development and Internet exposure.

21112 ■ "Tim Armstrong" in *Canadian Business* (Vol. 81, July 21, 2008, No. 11, pp. 10)
Pub: Rogers Media Ltd.
Ed: Calvin Leung. **Description:** Interview with Tim Armstrong who is the president of advertising and commerce department of Google Inc. for North America; the information technology company executive talked about the emerging trends and changes to YouTube made by the company since its acquisition in 2006.

21113 ■ "To Blog, Or Not To Blog" in *Canadian Business* (Vol. 80, December 25, 2006, No. 1, pp. 15)
Pub: Rogers Media
Ed: Andy Holloway. **Description:** The growing use of weblogs for internet marketing by business enterprises is discussed.

21114 ■ "The Top Mistakes of Social Media Marketing" in *Agency Sales Magazine* (Vol. 39, November 2009, No. 9, pp. 42)
Pub: MANA
Ed: Pam Lontos; Maurice Ramirez. **Description:** One common mistake in social media marketing is having more than one image on the Internet because this ruins a business' credibility. Marketers need to put out messages that are useful to their readers and to keep messages consistent.

21115 ■ "Traffic's Up: Website's Down Preventing Costly Crashes" in *Inc.* (March 2008, pp. 55-56)
Pub: Gruner & Jahr USA Publishing
Ed: Darren Dahl. **Description:** Grid Web hosting protects a small company's Website when a sudden burst of Internet traffic hits enabling it to continue rather than be crippled. Options can vary in cost from $4 to $1,000 monthly and include using a shared server, grid server, virtual private server, or a dedicated server. The article explains each option.

21116 ■ "Traits that Makes Blogs Attractive to Book Publishers" in *Marketing to Women* (Vol. 22, July 2009, No. 7, pp. 1)
Pub: EPM Communications, Inc.
Description: Book publishers are finding a beneficial relationship between themselves and women bloggers on the Internet. A high visitor count, frequent

updates and active readership are criteria for identifying the blogs with the most clout and therefore providing the greatest benefit to publishers.

21117 ■ "Transform Your Life" in *Black Enterprise* (Vol. 37, January 2007, No. 6, pp. 14)
Pub: Earl G. Graves Publishing Co. Inc.
Description: Through the magazine, television and radio programs, events, and the website, the various platforms of Black Enterprise will provide the tools necessary to achieve success in business ventures, career aspirations, and personal goals.

21118 ■ "The Twittering Class" in *Entrepreneur* (Vol. 37, September 2009, No. 9, pp. 40)
Pub: Entrepreneur Media, Inc.
Ed: Mikal E. Belicove. **Description:** Advice on how entrepreneurs can use online social networks to promote their businesses is presented. Facebook offers applications and advertising solutions to promote Websites, products and services. Twitter, on the other hand, provides instant messaging, which can be done through computer or cell phone.

21119 ■ *Twitterville: How Businesses Can Thrive in the New Global Neighborhoods*
Pub: Portfolio Hardcover
Ed: Shel Israel. **Price:** $23.95. **Description:** Twitter is the most rapidly adopted communication tool in history, going from zero to ten million users in just over two years. On Twitter, word can spread faster than wildfire. Companies no longer have the option of ignoring the conversation. Unlike other hot social media spaces, Twitterville is dominated by professionals, not students. And despite its size, it still feels like a small town. Twitter allows people to interact much the way they do face-to-face, honestly and authentically.

21120 ■ "Unlimited Priorities Strengthens Executive Team" in *Entertainment Close-Up* (November 1, 2011)
Pub: Close-Up Media
Description: Founder and president of Unlimited Priorities Corporation, Iris L. Hanney, added two executive level professionals to her team. The new employees will help increase the firm's capabilities in social media and information technology.

21121 ■ "Up To Code? Website Eases Compliance Burden for Entrepreneurs" in *Black Enterprise* (Vol. 38, March 2008, No. 8, pp. 48)
Pub: Earl G. Graves Publishing Co. Inc.
Ed: Robin White-Goode. **Description:** Business.gov is a presidential E-government project created to help small businesses easily find, understand, and comply with laws and regulations pertaining to a particular industry.

21122 ■ "Utah Technology Council: Social Media Is Here to Stay; Embrace It" in *Wireless News* (December 14, 2009)
Pub: Close-Up Media
Description: Social media outlets such as Facebook and Twitter are blurring the lines between advertising, public relations, branding and marketing; businesses must stop thinking in terms of traditional marketing versus Internet marketing if they want to succeed in today's marketing climate.

21123 ■ "A View to a Killer Business Model" in *Black Enterprise* (Vol. 40, December 2009, No. 5, pp. 50)
Pub: Earl G. Graves Publishing Co., Inc.
Ed: Sonya A. Donaldson. **Description:** Profile of Gen2Media Corp., a production, technology and Internet marketing firm based in Florida with offices in New York; Gen2Media is utilizing the advances in technology to now include video in its online marketing offerings.

21124 ■ "Virtus.com Wins 'Best of Industry' WebAward for Excellence in Financial Services" in *Investment Weekly News* (October 24, 2009)
Pub: Investment Weekly News
Description: Web Marketing Association honored Virtus.com, the Website of Virtus Investment Partners, Inc., for Outstanding Achievement in Web Development and Acsys Interactive was awarded the Financial Services Standard of Excellence Award for developing the site. The site was part of a rebranding effort and is a one-stop portal for both financial advisors and their investors.

21125 ■ "Web-Based Solutions Streamline Operations" in *Contractor* (Vol. 56, December 2009, No. 12, pp. 28)
Pub: Penton Media, Inc.
Ed: William Feldman; Patti Feldman. **Description:** Sage Project Lifecycle Management is a Web-based service platform for plumbing and HVAC contractors. It enables effective workflow and document management. Projectmates, on the other hand, is a Web-based enterprise-wide solution for managing both commercial plumbing and HVAC projects.

21126 ■ "Web Biz Brulant Surfing for Acquisition Candidates" in *Crain's Cleveland Business* (Vol. 28, December 3, 2007, No. 48, pp. 6)
Pub: Crain Communications, Inc.
Ed: Chuck Soder. **Description:** Brulant Inc., a provider of web development and marketing services, is looking to acquire other companies after growing for five years straight. The company is one of the largest technology firms in Northeast Ohio.

21127 ■ "Web-Preneuring" in *Small Business Opportunities* (May 2008)
Pub: Harris Publications Inc.
Description: 1&1 Internet provides known servers with more than 6.84 million customers through contracts with both consumer and business users. It operates five secure data centers housing 40,000 servers that process more than 5 billion monthly emails.

21128 ■ "Web to Print" in *American Printer* (Vol. 128, August 1, 2011, No. 8)
Pub: Penton Media Inc.
Description: Jerry Kennelly, CEO and founder of Tweak.com believes that Web-to-Design is middleware with no content. His firm offers an easy to use interface that flows right into the printer's workflow with no additional costs.

21129 ■ "Web Sight: Do You See What I See?" in *Entrepreneur* (Vol. 35, October 2007, No. 10, pp. 58)
Pub: Entrepreneur Media Inc.
Ed: Heather Clancy. **Description:** Owners of Trunkt, a boutique in New York that showcases independent designs, have created a new style of Website called Trunkt.org. The Website allows buyers to select the products they want to see and designers can choose anytime which of their items will be displayed on the site. An explanation of the strategy that helped bring Trunkt closer to its clients is presented.

21130 ■ "Web Site Design, Content Can Boost Diversity" in *HRMagazine* (Vol. 53, August 2008, No. 8, pp. 20)
Pub: Society for Human Resource Management
Description: Design and content of an employer's Website influences prospective young job candidates, especially young black job seekers, a new academic study has found. The findings appear in Black and White and Read All Over: Race Differences in Reactions To Recruitment Web Sites, published in the summer 2008 issue of the Human Resource Management Journal.

21131 ■ "Web Site Focuses on Helping People Find Jobs, Internships with Area Businesses" in *Crain's Detroit Business* (Vol. 26, Jan. 4, 2010)
Pub: Crain Communications, Inc.
Ed: Dustin Walsh. **Description:** DetroitIntern.com, LLC is helping metro Detroit college students and young professionals find career-advancing internships or jobs with local businesses.

21132 ■ "Web Traffic Numbers Facing Scrutiny" in *Boston Business Journal* (Vol. 27, November 2, 2007, No. 40, pp. 1)
Pub: American City Business Journals Inc.
Ed: Jesse Noyes. **Description:** Interactive Advertising Bureau (IAB) held a summit meeting with major industry players in an effort to create more transparent standards for measuring Internet traffic. The terms at issue were registered users, unique visitors, time spent and retention.

21133 ■ "Web Translation Made Simple" in *Inc.* (Vol. 33, October 2011, No. 8, pp. 44)
Pub: Inc. Magazine
Ed: Adam Baer. **Description:** Smartling is a Web-based service that translates sites into more than 50 foreign languages. The software will begin translation right after setting up the account.

21134 ■ "Webadvertising" in *MarketingMagazine* (Vol. 115, September 27, 2010, No. 13, pp. 70)
Pub: Rogers Publishing Ltd.
Description: Website advertising in Canada is examined.

21135 ■ "Website Backup Made Simple" in *Inc.* (Vol. 33, September 2011, No. 7, pp. 52)
Pub: Inc. Magazine
Ed: John Brandon. **Description:** Tools to back up content on a Website are profiled. Vaultpress works only with sites that run on the WordPress publishing platform and CodeGuard works with a variety of publishing platforms and hosting services.

21136 ■ "Website Triples Traffic in Three Weeks Using Press Releases" in *PR Newswire* (January 5, 2010)
Pub: PR Newswire Association, LLC
Description: Irbtrax, an Internet marketing firm, concluded a comprehensive study revealing that online press release submission services offer measurable Website traffic-building results.

21137 ■ "Website for Women 50+ Launches" in *Marketing to Women* (Vol. 21, April 2008, No. 4, pp. 5)
Pub: EPM Communications, Inc.
Description: Vibrantnation.com is an online community targeting women over age 50; members can share recommendations on a variety of topics such as vacation spots, retailers and financial issues.

21138 ■ "Wendy Turner; Vice-President and General Manager, Vocalo.org" in *Crain's Chicago Business* (Vol. 31, May 5, 2008, No. 18, pp. 22)
Pub: Crain Communications, Inc.
Ed: Kevin McKeough. **Description:** Profile of Wendy Turner who is a leader at Vocalo, a combination of talk radio and Web site, where listeners can set up profile pages similar to those on Facebook.

21139 ■ "What You Look Like Online" in *Black Enterprise* (Vol. 37, January 2007, No. 6, pp. 56)
Pub: Earl G. Graves Publishing Co. Inc.
Ed: Marcia A. Reed-Woodard. **Description:** Of 100 executive recruiters 77 percent stated that they use search engines to check the backgrounds of potential job candidates, according to a survey conducted by ExecuNet. Of those surveyed 35 percent stated that they eliminate potential candidates based on information they find online so it is important to create a positive Web presence which highlights professional image qualities.

21140 ■ "What's In Your Toolbox" in *Women In Business* (Vol. 61, August-September 2009, No. 4, pp. 7)
Pub: American Business Women's Association
Ed: Mimi Kopulos. **Description:** Business owners are increasingly turning to using social networking websites, such as Facebook, LinkedIn and Twitter, to promote their companies. The number of adult social media users has increased from 8 percent in 2005 to 35 percent in 2009.

21141 ■ "Why-Max?" in *Canadian Business* (Vol. 81, July 22, 2008, No. 12-13, pp. 19)
Pub: Rogers Media Ltd.
Ed: Andrew Wahl. **Description:** Nascent technology known as LTE (Long Term Evolution) is expected to challenge Intel's WiMax wireless technology as the wireless broadband standard. LTE , which is believed to be at least two years behind WiMax in develop-

ment, is likely to be supported by wireless and mobile-phone carriers. Views and information on WiMax and LTE are presented.

21142 ■ "Why Some Get Shaften By Google Pricing" in *Advertising Age* (Vol. 79, July 14, 2008, No. 7, pp. 3)
Pub: Crain Communications, Inc.
Ed: Abbey Klaassen. **Description:** Google's search advertising is discussed as well as the company's pricing structure for these ads.

21143 ■ "Why Women Blog and What They Read" in *Marketing to Women* (Vol. 22, July 2009, No. 7, pp. 8)
Pub: EPM Communications, Inc.
Description: Listing of topics that are visited the most by female Internet users. Statistical data included.

21144 ■ "Will the Force Be With Salesforce?" in *Barron's* (Vol. 88, March 24, 2008, No. 12, pp. 20)
Pub: Dow Jones & Company, Inc.
Ed: Mark Veverka. **Description:** Shares of Salesforce.com are likely to drop from the $44.83-a-share level in the face of a deteriorating economy and financial sector and thus lower demand for business software. The company is unlikely to deliver on its ambitious earnings forecasts for 2008 especially with strengthening competition from Oracle.

21145 ■ "Winner: Private Company, Less Than $100M" in *Crain's Detroit Business* (Vol. 25, June 22, 2009, No. 25)
Pub: Crain Communications Inc. - Detroit
Ed: Tom Henderson. **Description:** Profile of ForeSee Results, an Ann Arbor, Michigan-based firm that uses the University of Michigan American Consumer Satisfaction Index to help businesses measure satisfaction with their Websites.

21146 ■ "Women Clicking to Earn Virtual Dollars" in *Sales and Marketing Management* (November 11, 2009)
Pub: Nielsen Business Media, Inc.
Ed: Stacy Straczynski. **Description:** According to a new report from Internet marketing firm Q Interactive, women are increasingly playing social media games where they are able to click on an ad or sign up for a promotion to earn virtual currency. Research is showing that this kind of marketing may be a potent tool, especially for e-commerce and online stores.

21147 ■ "WordStream Announces a Pair of Firsts for SEO and PPC Keyword Research Tools" in *Internet Wire* (November 10, 2009)
Pub: Comtex News Network, Inc.
Description: WordSteam, Inc., a provider of pay-per-click (PPC) and search engine optimization (SEO) solutions for continuously expanding and optimizing search marketing efforts has released two new features in their flagship Keyword Management solution; these tools will allow marketers to analyze data from paid search, organic search and estimated totals from keyword suggestion tools side-by-side.

21148 ■ "Work Smarter" in *Entrepreneur* (Vol. 36, April 2008, No. 4, pp. 70)
Pub: Entrepreneur Media, Inc.
Ed: Amanda C. Kooser. **Description:** Online applications that address a business' particular needs are presented. These web applications offer email services, collaboration services of sharing and editing documents and presentations, and tie-ups with online social networking sites. Details on various web applications are provided.

21149 ■ "The Yahoo Family Tree" in *Conde Nast Portfolio* (Vol. 2, June 2008, No. 6, pp. 34)
Pub: Conde Nast Publications, Inc.
Ed: Blaise Zerega. **Description:** Yahoo, founded in 1994 by Stanford students Jerry Yang and David Filo, is still an Internet powerhouse. The company's history is also outlined as well as the reasons in which Microsoft desperately wants to acquire the firm.

21150 ■ "You Are What They Click" in *Entrepreneur* (Vol. 37, July 2009, No. 7, pp. 43)
Pub: Entrepreneur Media, Inc.
Ed: Mikal Belicove. **Description:** Hiring the right website design firm is the first stage in building an online business, and this involves various factors such as price, technical expertise, and talent. Writing a request for proposal (RFP) detailing the website's details, which include purpose, budget and audience, is the first step the process. Other tips in finding the right web designer are given.

21151 ■ "Your Annual Business Tune-Up" in *Business Week* (December 28, 2006)
Pub: McGraw-Hill Companies
Ed: Karen E. Klein. **Description:** Interview with entrepreneurial expert, Ty Freyvogel, founder of EntrpreneursLab.com. Freyvogel gives tips on how a thorough review of existing systems, vendors, customers, and employees could help keep an entrepreneur's business not only safe but highly successful in the upcoming year.

21152 ■ "Your Turn in the Spotlight" in *Inc.* (Volume 32, December 2010, No. 10, pp. 57)
Pub: Inc. Magazine
Ed: John Brandon. **Description:** Examples of three video blogs created by entrepreneurs to promote their businesses and products are used to show successful strategies. Wine Library TV promotes a family's wine business; SHAMA.TV offers marketing tips and company news; and Will It Blend? promotes sales of a household blender.

21153 ■ "Zen and the Art of Twitter Maintenance" in *Agency Sales Magazine* (Vol. 39, September-October 2009, No. 9, pp. 48)
Pub: MANA
Ed: Terry Brock. **Description:** Online social networks such as Twitter, LinkedIn, and Facebook should be used to stay in touch with business relationships, especially customers. There should be a focus on making customers happy and building the bottomline when using these tools.

21154 ■ "Zeon Solutions Teams with Endeca for SaaS Version of Endeca InFront" in *Entertainment Close-Up* (October 25, 2011)
Pub: Close-Up Media
Description: Zeon Solutions, an enterprise e-commerce and Website development firm announced a special licensing partnership with Endecca Technologies. Endeca is an information management software company that provides small and mid-size retailers with high-performance Customer Experience Management technology.

TRADE PERIODICALS

21155 ■ *Digital Design Newsletter*
Pub: Step-By-Step Publishing
Contact: Kathy Vonachen
Ed: Sara Booth, Editor, booth@dgusa.com. **Released:** Monthly. **Price:** $48, U.S.; $83.46, Canada. **Description:** Contains how-to articles on electronic illustration, graphic design, and production via real-world projects.

21156 ■ *Mastering CorelDRAW Newsletter*
Pub: Kazak Communications
Ed: Chris Dickman, Editor. **Released:** 10/year. **Price:** $47. **Description:** Covers CorelDRAW graphics applications. Offers tips and tricks with a hands-on focus. Remarks: Also available on diskette.

21157 ■ *Online*
Pub: Online, A Division of Information Today Inc.
Ed: Marydee Ojala, Editor, marydee@infotoday.com. **Released:** Bimonthly. **Price:** $129.50; $243 two years; $145 Canada and Mexico; $172 other countries. **Description:** Professional magazine covering online and CD-ROM databases with practical how-to articles covering the entire online industry.

CONSULTANTS

21158 ■ Construction Computing Solutions Inc.
40 Orchard Ct.
Brick, NJ 08724-4396
Ph:(732)899-4319
Fax:(732)899-1921
Co. E-mail: constructioncomputing@comcast.net
URL: http://www.ccspcs.com
Contact: Gerry Bierbrauer, President
E-mail: gerryb@ccswebservices.com
Scope: Links home and small business customers, contractors and engineers with their PC system's hardware and software to achieve the maximum productivity that the hardware and software allow. Offers individual and network PC consulting services for home users, small (0-10 user) to medium (10-50 user) businesses, and construction and engineering companies in the tri-state area in the following general areas: Evaluation of computer needs, hardware, software and training, sales and installation of hardware and software as needed, sales, set up and training on construction specific software, training for and/or administration of software and network functions, internet sales, set up, access, email, and web pages.

21159 ■ Creative Computer Resources Inc.
5001 Horizons Dr., Ste. 200
Columbus, OH 43220-5291
Ph:(614)384-7557
Free: (866)720-0209
Fax:(614)573-6331
Co. E-mail: team@planet-ccr.com
URL: http://www.planet-ccr.com
Contact: M. Erik Mueller, President
E-mail: merikm@atsplanet-ccr.com
Scope: Firm offers information systems support, custom software development, website design, development and implementation. Provides information technology support and management services to small and mid-size businesses.

FRANCHISES AND BUSINESS OPPORTUNITIES

21160 ■ TruePresence
1401 Russell St.
Baltimore, MD 21230
Ph:(410)649-2160
Fax:(410)649-2166
No. of Franchise Units: 17. **Founded:** 2003. **Franchised:** 2005. **Description:** Web design/development & internet marketing. **Equity Capital Needed:** $48,000. **Franchise Fee:** $35,000. **Royalty Fee:** 6%. **Financial Assistance:** No. **Training:** Offers 5 days at headquarters, 3 days at franchisees location with ongoing support.

LIBRARIES

21161 ■ District of Columbia Public Library–Technology and Science Division
Martin Luther King Memorial Library
901 G St., NW, Rm. 107
Washington, DC 20001
Ph:(202)727-1175
Fax:(202)727-1129
Co. E-mail: commentssuggestions.dcpl@dc.gov
URL: http://dclibrary.org
Contact: Lessie O. Mtewa, Asst.Libn.
Scope: Automobile and appliance repair, botany, cookery, general science, geology, genetics, manufacturing, nutrition, paleontology, pet care, printing, zoology, mathematics, computer science, biology, domestic arts, earth science, chemistry and chemical technology, physics, engineering, agriculture, gardening, medicine, psychiatry, astronomy, consumer information, health, veterinary science, physical anthropology. **Services:** Interlibrary loan; copying; Library open to the public. **Holdings:** 92,127 books; 2500 bound periodical volumes; 5755 microforms; 65 VF drawers. **Subscriptions:** 300 journals and other serials.

21162 ■ NORTEL–Information Resource Network
5945 Airport Rd. Ste. 360
Mississauga, ON, Canada L4V 1R9
Ph:(905)863-7000

Free: 800-466-7835
URL: http://www.nortel.com
Contact: John M. Doolittle, Sr.VP, Corp.Svcs.
Scope: Telecommunications, computer science, electronics, systems engineering. **Services:** Center not open to the public. **Holdings:** 12,000 books; 3000 bound periodical volumes; 8000 conferences; reports. **Subscriptions:** 800 journals and other serials; 15 newspapers.

RESEARCH CENTERS

21163 ■ Design Management Institute
101 Tremont St., Ste. 300
Boston, MA 02108
Ph:(617)338-6380
Fax:(617)338-6570
Co. E-mail: jtobin@dmi.org
URL: http://www.dmi.org/dmi/html/index.htm
Contact: John Tobin, VP
E-mail: jtobin@dmi.org
Scope: Conducts field studies on the management of design in products, communications, and environments in industry, business, and public institutions, emphasizing industrial design in product development. Activities are carried out through the Center for Research and the Design Management Education and Research Forum. The Center for Research directs the TRIAD Design Project, a multi-year international research effort on the management of design resources in numerous industries in Japan, Europe, and the U.S. The Design Management Education and Research Forum is an international group of academics who chart the course for further research in design management. **Services:** Environmental information for design managers. **Publications:** The Design Management Journal. **Educational Activities:** Seminars and symposia, through its Center for Education.

START-UP INFORMATION

21164 ■ *Becoming a Personal Trainer for Dummies*
Pub: John Wiley & Sons, Incorporated
Ed: Melyssa Michael, Linda Formichelli. **Released:** October 2004. **Price:** $19.99 (US), $25.99 (Canadian). **Description:** Legal and tax issues involved in starting and running a personal trainer firm. The book offers suggestions for incorporating massage and nutritional services.

ASSOCIATIONS AND OTHER ORGANIZATIONS

21165 ■ American Society of Bariatric Physicians
2821 S Parker Rd., Ste. 625
Aurora, CO 80014
Ph:(303)770-2526
Fax:(303)779-4834
Co. E-mail: info@asbp.org
URL: http://www.asbp.org
Contact: Laurie Traetow CPA, Exec. Dir.
Description: Physicians with a special interest in the study and treatment of obesity and associated conditions. Encourages excellence in the practice of bariatric medicine through exchange of information, research, and continuing education. Sponsors regional courses and clinical research programs. Offers a physician referral service. **Publications:** *The Bariatrician* (quarterly); *News from ASBP* (bimonthly).

21166 ■ Overeaters Anonymous World Service Office
PO Box 44020
Rio Rancho, NM 87174-4020
Ph:(505)891-2664
Fax:(505)891-4320
Co. E-mail: info@oa.org
URL: http://www.oa.org
Contact: Naomi Lippel, Managing Dir.
Description: Individuals who have a desire to stop eating compulsively. Program is a twelve-step self-help fellowship patterned after that of Alcoholics Anonymous. **Publications:** *Lifeline* (monthly).

21167 ■ Take Off Pounds Sensibly
PO Box 070360
Milwaukee, WI 53207
Ph:(414)482-4620
Free: 800-932-8677
Co. E-mail: topsinteractive@tops.org
URL: http://www.tops.org
Contact: Barb Cady, Pres.
Description: Weight control self-help association using group dynamics, competition, and recognition to help members lose weight. Advocates physician-approved individual programs, and physician-set weight goals. **Publications:** *TOPS News* (monthly).

REFERENCE WORKS

21168 ■ *Everything is Possible: Life and Business Lessons from a Self-Made Billionaire and the Founder of Slim-Fast*
Pub: Newmarket Press
Ed: S. Daniel Abraham. **Released:** February 10, 2010. **Price:** $24.95. **Description:** A profile of the founder of Slim-Fast nutritional diet drink used to help people lose weight.

TRADE PERIODICALS

21169 ■ *Calorie Control Commentary*
Pub: Calorie Control Council
Contact: Judy Rogers
Ed: Released: 2/year. **Price:** Free; $10 international subscriptions.. **Description:** Focuses on the scientific and regulatory status of diet sweeteners, fat substitutes, and low-calorie and reduced-fat foods and beverages. Includes articles and statistics concerning dieting in the U.S.

21170 ■ *Shape*
Pub: Weider Publications
Contact: Barbara S. Harris MA, Editor-in-Chief
Released: Monthly. **Price:** $14.97 print; $29.97 Canada; $41.97 other countries; $14.97 digital. **Description:** Magazine for women covering nutrition, weight control, physical fitness, psychology, fashion, beauty and travel.

TRADE SHOWS AND CONVENTIONS

21171 ■ California Dietetic Association Meeting
California Dietetic Association
7740 Manchester Ave., Ste. 102
Playa Del Rey, CA 90293-8499
Ph:(310)822-0177
Fax:(310)823-0264
Co. E-mail: bridget@dietitian.org
URL: http://www.dietitian.org
Released: Annual. **Audience:** Nutrition and dietetic professionals. **Principal Exhibits:** Food and nutrition services. **Dates and Locations:** 2011 Apr 28-30, Pasadena, CA.

CONSULTANTS

21172 ■ Center for Lifestyle Enhancement - Columbia Medical Center of Plano
3901 W 15th St.
Plano, TX 75075
Ph:(972)596-6800
Fax:(972)519-1299
Co. E-mail: mcp.cle@hcahealthcare.com
URL: http://www.medicalcenterofplano.com
Contact: Doug Browning, Vice President
E-mail: boesdorfer@hcahealthcare.com
Scope: Provides professional health counseling in the areas of general nutrition for weight management, eating disorders, diabetic education, cholesterol reduction and adolescent weight management. Offers work site health promotion and preventive services. Also coordinates speaker's bureau, cooking classes and physician referrals. Industries served: education, insurance, healthcare, retail or wholesale, data processing and manufacturing throughout Texas. **Seminars:** Rx Diet and Exercise; Smoking Cessation; Stress Management; Health Fairs; Fitness Screenings; Body Composition; Nutrition Analysis; Exercise Classes; Prenatal Nutrition; SHAPEDOWN; Successfully Managing Diabetes; Gourmet Foods for Your Heart; The Aging Heart; Heart Smart Saturday featuring Day of Dance; Weight-Loss Management Seminars; The Right Stroke for Men; Peripheral Artery Disease Screening; Menstruation: The Cycle Begins; Boot Camp for New Dads; Grand parenting 101: Caring for Kids Today; Teddy Bear Camp; New Baby Day Camp; Safe Sitter Baby-Sitting Class.

FRANCHISES AND BUSINESS OPPORTUNITIES

21173 ■ Curves
Curves International
100 Ritchie Rd.
Waco, TX 76712
Free: 800-848-1096
Fax:(254)399-8004
No. of Franchise Units: 6,385. **Founded:** 1995. **Franchised:** 1995. **Description:** Fitness and weight loss center for women. **Equity Capital Needed:** $29,900-$65,000. **Franchise Fee:** $29,900, including equipment. **Financial Assistance:** No. **Training:** Yes.

21174 ■ DIET CENTER
Health Management Group, Inc.
395 Springside Dr.
Akron, OH 44333-2496
Ph:(330)665-5861
Free: 800-656-3294
Fax:(330)666-2197
Co. E-mail: tziegler@hmgmail.com
URL: http://www.dietcenter.com
No. of Franchise Units: 98. **Founded:** 1970. **Franchised:** 1973. **Description:** Diet Center counselors work one-on-one with clients, helping develop a personalized, low-fat eating style and a more active lifestyle. With the aid of a new behavior-management program, clients design their own practical solutions for losing and maintaining weight, learning to improve their health and appearance by focusing on reducing body fat areas. **Equity Capital Needed:** $50,000, liquidity. **Franchise Fee:** $25,000. **Financial Assistance:** No. **Training:** Training is provided both at the home office and in regional. Includes nutritional training.

21175 ■ Jenny Craig Weight Loss & Management Centres
Jenny Craig International, Inc.
5770 Fleet St.
Carlsbad, CA 92008

Free: 888-848-8885
Co. E-mail: franchising@jennycraig.com
URL: http://www.jennycraig.com/franchising

No. of Franchise Units: 216. **No. of Company-Owned Units:** 431. **Founded:** 1983. **Franchised:** 1987. **Description:** Offers a weight loss program in the U.S. and Canada featuring personal counseling, low-calorie Jenny's Cuisine, and a supportive and motivating environment. **Equity Capital Needed:** $165,600-$349,500. **Franchise Fee:** $25,000. **Financial Assistance:** No. **Training:** Yes.

21176 ■ L.A. Weight Loss Centers
420 Dresher Rd., Ste. 200
Horsham, PA 19044
Ph:(215)246-4302
Free: 888-258-7099
Fax:(215)346-8810

No. of Franchise Units: 373. **No. of Company-Owned Units:** 437. **Founded:** 1989. **Franchised:** 1998. **Description:** Personalized weight management. **Equity Capital Needed:** $84,600-$149,800. **Franchise Fee:** $20,000. **Royalty Fee:** 7%. **Financial Assistance:** Limited third party financing and in-house assistance. **Training:** 4 weeks at headquarters, 3 weeks at franchisee's location and ongoing support.

21177 ■ Lite For Life
Lite for Life Franchise Corp., Inc.
398 Main St.
Los Altos, CA 94022
Ph:(650)941-3200
Fax:(650)559-3111

No. of Franchise Units: 2 **No. of Company-Owned Units:** 4. **Founded:** 1978. **Franchised:** 2003. **Description:** Weight loss and nutritional consulting. **Equity Capital Needed:** $75,000+/-. **Franchise Fee:** $20,000. **Financial Assistance:** No. **Training:** Yes.

21178 ■ Lucille Roberts Fitness Express
4 E 80th St.
New York, NY 10021
Free: 888-582-4553
Fax:(212)734-4151
No. of Company-Owned Units: 47. **Founded:** 1970. **Franchised:** 2005. **Description:** Women's fitness & weight-loss center. **Equity Capital Needed:** $271,850-$402,400. **Franchise Fee:** $25,000. **Royalty Fee:** 6%. **Financial Assistance:** Third party financing available. **Training:** Offers 1 week at headquarters with ongoing support.

21179 ■ SureSlim Wellness Clinic
Sure Slim Holdings Inc.
4632 Boulderwood Dr.
Victoria, BC, Canada V8Y 3G5
Ph:(250)995-0482
Free: (866)773-0177
Fax:(866)595-4003
Co. E-mail: Gerald@sureslim.ca
URL: http://www.sureslim.ca
No. of Franchise Units: 14. **No. of Company-Owned Units:** 1. **Founded:** 2000. **Franchised:** 2002. **Description:** The franchise offers successful weight loss system. **Equity Capital Needed:** $135,000. **Franchise Fee:** $35,000. **Training:** Yes.

LIBRARIES

21180 ■ American Dietetic Association–Knowledge Center
120 S. Riverside Plaza, Ste. 20000
Chicago, IL 60606-6995
Ph:(312)877-1600, x4864
Free: 800-877-1600
Co. E-mail: knowledge@eatright.org
URL: http://www.eatright.org/
Contact: Margaret Williams, Info.Spec./Libn.
Scope: Nutrition, dietetics, food service. **Services:** Interlibrary loan; copying; Library open to the public by appointment. **Holdings:** 3000 books. **Subscriptions:** 60 journals and other serials; 4 newspapers.

21181 ■ National Eating Disorder Information Centre
ES 7-421
200 Elizabeth St.
Toronto, ON, Canada M5G 2C4
Ph:(416)340-4156
Free: (866)633-4220
Fax:(416)340-4736
Co. E-mail: nedic@uhn.on.ca
URL: http://www.nedic.ca
Contact: Merryl Bear, Dir.
Scope: Eating disorders, food preoccupation, weight preoccupation, support groups. **Services:** Centre open to the public. **Holdings:** 50 books. **Subscriptions:** 250 journals and other serials.

RESEARCH CENTERS

21182 ■ Columbia University–New York Obesity Research Center–Centro de Investigacion sobre Obesidad
College of Physicians & Surgeons
St. Luke's-Roosevelt Hospital
1090 Amsterdam Ave., 14th Fl.
New York, NY 10025
Ph:(212)523-4196
Fax:(212)523-3416
Co. E-mail: fxp1@columbia.edu
URL: http://www.nyorc.org/
Contact: Dr. F. Xavier Pi-Sunyer, Dir.
E-mail: fxp1@columbia.edu
Scope: Obesity, including molecular genetics, regulation of food intake, nutrient uptake and oxidation, body composition, stable isotope methodology, exercise physiology, diabetes, and insulin resistance. **Educational Activities:** Postdoctoral training program; Predoctoral training, for PhD candidates of the university's Institute of Human Nutrition; Seminars (weekly); Symposia (semiannually).

FRANCHISES AND BUSINESS OPPORTUNITIES

21183 ■ Housewarmers
6500 Greenville Ave.
Dallas, TX 75206
Ph:(214)534-5041
Free: (866)241-8065
Fax:(404)235-0702

No. of Franchise Units: 50. **No. of Company-Owned Units:** 7. **Founded:** 1999. **Franchised:** 2002. **Description:** Neighborhood welcoming service. **Equity Capital Needed:** $15,200-$55,900. **Franchise Fee:** $12,500-$50,000. **Royalty Fee:** 12%. **Financial Assistance:** No. **Training:** Offers 3-4 days training at headquarters, 2 visits at franchisee's location, and ongoing support.

21184 ■ Newcomers Welcome Service
900 Victors Way, Ste. 200
Ann Arbor, MI 48108
Ph:(734)994-9199
Fax:(734)994-9323

No. of Company-Owned Units: 7. **Founded:** 1960. **Franchised:** 2007. **Description:** Welcome service. **Equity Capital Needed:** $15,000-$20,000. **Franchise Fee:** $25,000. **Royalty Fee:** $75+/week. **Financial Assistance:** No.

Window Dressing Business

SOURCES OF SUPPLY

21185 ■ *Visual Merchandising & Store Design—Buyers' Guide Issue*
Pub: ST Media Group International Inc.
Released: Annual, Latest edition 2009. **Publication Includes:** Over 1,300 manufacturers and distributors of retail display equipment and products; nearly 600 store design, lighting, and visual merchandising firms; related trade and professional associations. **Entries Include:** For manufacturers and service firms—Company name, address, phone, name and title of contact, number of employees, sales volume, products. Similar data given for associations. **Arrangement:** Alphabetical. **Indexes:** Product, fax number.

TRADE PERIODICALS

21186 ■ *Creative*
Pub: Magazines/Creative Inc.
Released: Bimonthly. **Price:** $30; $50 other countries; $4 single issue; $20 illustrated guide; $44 two years. **Description:** Magazine reporting on point of purchase displays; exhibits; premiums and incentives; audio-visual techniques; direct marketing; and sales promotion materials.

21187 ■ *Stores*
Pub: NRF Enterprises Inc.
Contact: Susan Reda, Exec. Dir.
Released: Monthly. **Price:** $120 nonmembers. **Description:** Magazine for retail traders.

21188 ■ *Visual Merchandising and Store Design*
Pub: ST Media Group International Inc.
Contact: Kristin Godsey, Assoc. Publisher
E-mail: kristin.godsey@stmediagroup.com
Ed: Steve Kaufman, Editor, steve.kaufman@stmediagroup.com. **Released:** Monthly. **Price:** $42 U.S.; $66 2 years, U.S.; $62 Canada (surface); $100 2 years, Canada (surface); $65 Mexico/Foreign (surface); $105 2 years, Mexico/Foreign (surface); $100 Mexico, 1st Class; $175 2 years, Mexico 1st Class; $115 Central/South America; $205 2 years, Central/South America. **Description:** The leading magazine of the retail design industry covering the latest trends in retail design, store planning, and merchandise presentation.

VIDEOCASSETTES/ AUDIOCASSETTES

21189 ■ *Home Decorating Combo*
Nancy's Notions Ltd.
333 Beichl Ave.
P.O. Box 683
Beaver Dam, WI 53916-0683
Ph:(920)887-7321
Free: 800-725-0361
Fax:800-255-8119
Co. E-mail: customerservice@nancysnotions.com
URL: http://www.nancysnotions.com
Released: 1987. **Description:** This video contains two programs on fabric-based home decoration: "Window Treatments" and "Instant Decorating." **Availability:** VHS.

TRADE SHOWS AND CONVENTIONS

21190 ■ Global Shop - Tradeshow and Seminars for Visual Merchandiser
VNU Expositions
14685 Avion Pkwy., Ste. 400
Chantilly, VA 20151
Ph:(703)488-2700
Free: 800-765-7615
Fax:(703)488-2725
URL: http://www.vnuexpo.com
Released: Annual. **Audience:** Trade only; retailers, store designers, operations and construction professionals, brand marketers, visual merchandisers. **Principal Exhibits:** Retail display props and decorations.

FRANCHISES AND BUSINESS OPPORTUNITIES

21191 ■ Blind Brokers Network
23052 Alicia Pky., Ste. H202
Mission Viejo, CA 92692
Ph:(949)768-6695
Free: 888-922-5463
No. of Franchise Units: 301. **No. of Company-Owned Units:** 1. **Founded:** 1985. **Franchised:** 2006. **Description:** Discount blinds, shades and shutters. **Equity Capital Needed:** $1,495-$4,995. **Financial Assistance:** No. **Training:** Offers 3 days at headquarters, by phone & vendor training and ongoing support.

21192 ■ Gotcha Covered
1611 N Stemmons Fwy., Ste. 318
Carrollton, TX 75006
Ph:(972)466-2544
Fax:(972)446-6774
URL: http://www.gotchacoveredblinds.com
No. of Franchise Units: 125. **Founded:** 1995. **Franchised:** 1999. **Description:** Blinds, shades, shutters and draperies. **Equity Capital Needed:** $50,100-$82,300 total investment; $65,000 cash liquidity. **Franchise Fee:** $39,900-$59,900. **Royalty Fee:** 4-8%. **Financial Assistance:** Financing available. **Training:** Offers 2 weeks at headquarters, 19 weeks at franchisees location, annual 2 day seminar, 2 day trimester business development review and ongoing support provided.

21193 ■ The Screenmobile
The Screenmobile Corp.
72050A Corporate Way
Thousand Palms, CA 92276
Free: 800-775-7795
Fax:(760)343-7543
No. of Franchise Units: 94. **No. of Company-Owned Units:** 1. **Founded:** 1980. **Franchised:** 1982. **Description:** Window and door screening. **Equity Capital Needed:** $90,000. **Franchise Fee:** $35,500-$69,500. **Financial Assistance:** No. **Training:** Yes.

21194 ■ Today's Window Fashions
5519 S Mission Rd., No. E
Bonsall, CA 92003
Ph:(760)630-8119
Free: 877-998-6329
Fax:(760)923-7234
Co. E-mail: todaysblinds1@aol.com
URL: http://www.todaysblinds.com
No. of Franchise Units: 32. **No. of Company-Owned Units:** 1. **Founded:** 1993. **Franchised:** 1997. **Description:** Custom window coverings. **Equity Capital Needed:** $52,000-$59,000. **Franchise Fee:** $49,000. **Royalty Fee:** 4%. **Financial Assistance:** Third party financing available. **Training:** Offers 5 days at corporate headquarters, 3 days of onsite, and ongoing support.

21195 ■ V2K Window Decor & More
7853 E Arapahoe Ct., Ste. 3100
Centennial, CO 80112
Ph:(303)202-1120
Free: 800-200-0835
Fax:(303)202-5201
Co. E-mail: roy@v2k.com
URL: http://www.franchiseV2k.com
No. of Franchise Units: 186. **Founded:** 1996. **Franchised:** 1997. **Description:** Window treatments/digital design services. **Franchise Fee:** $59,900. **Financial Assistance:** No. **Training:** Offers 2 weeks training followed by 1 week advanced training after 4 months in the field.

LIBRARIES

21196 ■ Art Institute of Philadelphia Library
1610 Chestnut St.
Philadelphia, PA 19103
Ph:(215)405-6402
Co. E-mail: rschachter@aii.edu
URL: http://rs185.aisites.com
Contact: Ruth Schachter, Dir.
Scope: Visual communications, interior design, industrial design, animation, fashion marketing, fashion design, visual merchandising, photography, website design, multimedia. **Services:** Interlibrary loan; Library not open to the public (circulation services provided for students and faculty). **Holdings:** 31,000 volumes; 2000 videocassettes; audiocassettes. **Subscriptions:** 170 print subscriptions and other serials.

ASSOCIATIONS AND OTHER ORGANIZATIONS

21197 ■ Business Technology Association
12411 Wornall Rd., Ste. 200
Kansas City, MO 64145
Ph:(816)941-3100
Free: 800-505-2821
Fax:(816)941-4838
Co. E-mail: info@bta.org
URL: http://www.bta.org
Contact: Tom Ouellette, Pres.
Description: Dealers and resellers of office equipment and networking products and services. Offers 60 seminars on management, service, technology, and business systems. Conducts research, provides business-supporting services and benefits, including insurance, and legal counsel. **Publications:** *BTA Membership Directory* (annual); *Business Owner* (bimonthly); *Office Technology* (monthly).

DIRECTORIES OF EDUCATIONAL PROGRAMS

21198 ■ *Directory of Private Accredited Career Schools and Colleges of Technology*
Pub: Accrediting Commission of Career Schools and Colleges of Technology
Contact: Michale S. McComis, Exec. Dir.
Released: On web page. **Price:** Free. **Description:** Covers 3900 accredited post-secondary programs that provide training programs in business, trade, and technical fields, including various small business endeavors. Entries offer school name, address, phone, description of courses, job placement assistance, and requirements for admission. Arrangement is alphabetical.

TRADE PERIODICALS

21199 ■ *Scroll*
Pub: Wordstar Processing Users' Group Inc.
Ed: Dr. David M. Rafky, Editor. **Released:** Bimonthly. **Price:** Included in membership. **Description:** Provides news regarding various aspects of word processing with WordStar software, includes reviews of word processing software, computer tips, a glossary of terms used in each issue, and information for writers. Recurring features include letters to the editor, news of research, and book reviews. Regular columns titled Fade-In, In Response, and Computers and the Disabled.

Accounting

START-UP INFORMATION

21200 ■ *The Small Business Start-Up Kit*
Pub: NOLO
Ed: Peri Pakroo. **Released:** January 2008. **Price:** $29.99. **Description:** Entrepreneurial advice for launching a new business. Topics include compliance with state regulations, sole proprietorships, partnerships, corporations, limited liability companies, as well as accounting and tax information.

21201 ■ *Start and Run a Bookkeeping Business*
Pub: Self-Counsel, Incorporated
Ed: Angie Mohr. **Released:** October 2005. **Price:** $17.95 (US), $22.95 (Canadian). **Description:** Advice for starting and running a bookkeeping service business. Includes MS Word and PDF formats for use in Windows-based PC.

ASSOCIATIONS AND OTHER ORGANIZATIONS

21202 ■ Accountants Global Network
2851 S Parker Rd., Ste. 850
Aurora, CO 80014
Ph:(303)743-7880
Free: 800-782-2272
Fax:(303)743-7660
Co. E-mail: rhood@agn.org
URL: http://www.agn-na.org
Contact: Rita J. Hood, Exec. Dir.
Description: Represents and promotes the fields of separate and independent accounting and consulting firms serving business organizations. .

21203 ■ Canadian Payroll Association–Association canadienne de la paie
250 Bloor St. E, Ste. 1600
Toronto, ON, Canada M4W 1E6
Ph:(416)487-3380
Free: 800-387-4693
Fax:(416)487-3384
Co. E-mail: membership@payroll.ca
URL: http://www.payroll.ca
Contact: Patrick Culhane, Pres./CEO
Description: Represents the payroll community in Canada; offers education programs, advocacy efforts, products and services to help members enhance and adapt payroll operations, meet new legislative requirements, address changing workplace needs and take advantage of emerging technologies. **Publications:** *CPA E-Source* (bimonthly); *Dialogue Magazine* (bimonthly).

21204 ■ Community Banking Advisory Network
624 Grassmere Park Dr., Ste. 15
Nashville, TN 37211
Ph:(615)377-3392
Free: 800-231-2524
Fax:(615)377-7092
Co. E-mail: info@bankingcpas.com
URL: http://www.bankingcpas.com
Contact: Patrick Pruett, Exec. Dir.
Description: Certified Public Accounting (CPA) firms providing financial and consulting services to community banks. Seeks to advance CPA services to the community banking industry. Sponsors continuing education and training courses; conducts industry and member surveys; facilitates formation of joint ventures; makes available marketing assistance; facilitates resource sharing among members. **Publications:** *Community Banking Advisor* (quarterly).

21205 ■ Construction Industry CPAs/ Consultants Association
15011 E Twilight View Dr.
Fountain Hills, AZ 85268
Ph:(480)836-0300
Free: 800-864-0491
Fax:(480)836-0400
Co. E-mail: jcorcoran@cicpac.com
URL: http://www.cicpac.com
Contact: John J. Corcoran CPA, Exec. Dir.
Description: Certified Public Accounting (CPA) firms providing financial and consulting services to construction companies. Seeks to advance CPA services to the construction industries. Sponsors continuing education and training courses; conducts industry and member surveys; facilitates formation of joint ventures; makes available marketing assistance; facilitates resource sharing among members. .

21206 ■ CPA Auto Dealer Consultants Association
624 Grassmere Park Dr., Ste. 15
Nashville, TN 37211
Ph:(615)377-3392
Free: 800-231-2524
Fax:(615)377-7092
Co. E-mail: info@autodealercpas.net
URL: http://www.autodealercpas.net
Contact: Patrick Pruett, Exec. Dir.
Description: Certified Public Accounting (CPA) firms providing financial and consulting services to automobile dealers. Seeks to advance CPA services to automobile dealers. Sponsors continuing education and training courses; conducts industry and member surveys; facilitates formation of joint ventures; makes available marketing assistance; facilitates resource sharing among members. **Publications:** *Auto Focus* (quarterly).

21207 ■ CPA Manufacturing Services Association
624 Grassmere Park Dr., Ste. 15
Nashville, TN 37211
Ph:(615)377-3392
Free: 800-231-2524
Fax:(615)377-7092
Co. E-mail: info@manufacturingcpas.com
URL: http://www.manufacturingcpas.com
Contact: Patrick Pruett, Exec. Dir.
Description: Certified Public Accounting (CPA) firms providing financial and consulting services to the manufacturing industries. Seeks to advance CPA services to manufacturers. Sponsors continuing education and training courses; conducts industry and member surveys; facilitates formation of joint ventures; makes available marketing assistance; facilitates resource sharing among members. **Publications:** *Client* (periodic);Membership Directory (periodic).

21208 ■ IGAF Worldwide
3235 Satellite Blvd., Bldg. 400, Ste. 300
Duluth, GA 30096
Ph:(678)417-7730
Fax:(678)999-3959
Co. E-mail: kmead@igafworldwide.org
URL: http://www.igaf.org
Contact: Kevin Mead, Pres./Exec. Dir.
Description: Works to ensure that the standard for accounting, auditing, and management services are maintained. .

21209 ■ International Budget Partnership
820 1st St. NE, Ste. 510
Washington, DC 20002
Ph:(202)408-1080
Fax:(202)408-8173
Co. E-mail: info@internationalbudget.org
URL: http://www.internationalbudget.org
Contact: Warren Krafchik, Dir.
Description: Works to assist civil society organizations globally to improve budget policies and decision-making processes. **Publications:** *A Guide to Budget Work for NGOs*; *Budgeting for the Future, Building another Europe*; *IBP Newsletter* (bimonthly).

21210 ■ Society of Depreciation Professionals
347 5th Ave., Ste. 703
New York, NY 10016
Ph:(646)417-6378
Co. E-mail: admin@depr.org
URL: http://www.depr.org
Contact: Rob Pierce CDP, Pres.
Description: Accountants and other individuals with an interest in the depreciation of assets. Promotes "professionalism and ethics within the art of depreciation." Serves as a forum for the discussion of issues affecting depreciation; sponsors continuing professional development courses for members. .

EDUCATIONAL PROGRAMS

21211 ■ Accounting's New Guidelines: From GAAP to IFRS
AMA
600 AMA Way
Saranac Lake, NY 12983-5534
Ph:(212)586-8100
Free: 877-566-9441
Fax:(518)891-0368
Co. E-mail: customerservice@amanet.org
URL: http://www.amaseminars.org
Price: $2,095.00 for non-members; $1,895.00 for AMA members and $1,623 for General Services Administration (GSA) members. **Description:** Understand the complexities of the coming GAAP-to-IFRS

changeover in this two-day course. **Locations:** Arlington, VA,; DC; Atlanta, GA; Chicago, IL; New York, NY; and San Francisco, CA.

21212 ■ AMA's Budgeting Workshop
American Management Association
600 AMA Way
Saranac Lake, NY 12983-5534
Ph:(212)586-8100
Free: 877-566-9441
Fax:(518)891-0368
Co. E-mail: customerservice@amanet.org
URL: http://www.amaseminars.org
Price: $2,345.00 for non-members; $2,095.00 for AMA members; and $1,794.00 for General Services Administration (GSA) members. **Description:** Two-day seminar covering the budgeting process from fundamentals through development and how to measure performance. **Locations:** New York, NY; Washington, DC; Arlington, VA; Atlanta, GA; and San Francisco, CA.

21213 ■ AMA's Course on Financial Analysis
American Management Association
600 AMA Way
Saranac Lake, NY 12983-5534
Ph:(212)586-8100
Free: 877-566-9441
Fax:(518)891-0368
Co. E-mail: customerservice@amanet.org
URL: http://www.amaseminars.org
Price: $2,545.00 for non-members; $2,295.00 for AMA members; and $1,965.00 for General Services Administration (GSA) members. **Description:** Three-day seminar for managers with budget responsibilities; covers corporate planning, capital investments, cash flow, balance sheets, mergers and acquisitions, and other financial aspects of business. **Locations:** New York, NY; Atlanta, GA; Chicago, IL; Arlington, VA; Washington, DC; and San Francisco, CA.

21214 ■ Budgeting for Publications
EEI Communications
66 Canal Ctr. Plz., Ste. 200
Alexandria, VA 22314-5507
Ph:(703)683-7453
Free: 888-253-2762
Fax:(703)683-7310
Co. E-mail: train@eeicom.com
URL: http://www.eeicom.com/training
Price: $425.00. **Description:** Seminar that covers the basics of developing and monitoring budgets for the publications department, including types of publications departments, profit and cost centers, defining profit, margins, revenues, and analysis, budgeting traps, and what you can and cannot control. **Locations:** Alexandria, VA.

21215 ■ Debits and Credits: How Accounting Really Works
Canadian Management Centre
150 York St., 5th Fl.
Toronto, ON, Canada M5H 3S5
Free: 800-262-2519
Fax:(416)214-6047
Co. E-mail: cmcinfo@cmctraining.org
URL: http://www.cmctraining.org
Price: $2,195.00 for members; $2,395.00 for non-members. **Description:** Developed for business professional with no accounting skills. Master the essentials of accounting and put yourself in a position to succeed. **Locations:** Toronto, ON.

21216 ■ Financial Analysis (Canada)
Canadian Management Centre
150 York St., 5th Fl.
Toronto, ON, Canada M5H 3S5
Ph:(416)214-5678
Free: 877-262-2519
Fax:(416)214-6047
Co. E-mail: cmcinfo@cmctraining.org
URL: http://www.cmctraining.org
Price: $2,195.00 Canadian for non-members; $1,995.00 Canadian for CMC members. **Description:** Two-day seminar for managers with budget responsibilities; covers corporate planning, capital investments, cash flow, balance sheets, mergers and acquisitions, and other financial aspects of business. **Locations:** Toronto, ON.

21217 ■ Fixed Asset Accounting
American Management Association
600 AMA Way
Saranac Lake, NY 12983-5534
Ph:(212)586-8100
Free: 877-566-9441
Fax:(518)891-0368
Co. E-mail: customerservice@amanet.org
URL: http://www.amaseminars.org
Price: $2,095.00 for non-members; $1,895.00 for AMA members; and $1,623.00 for General Services Administration (GSA) members. **Description:** Two-day seminar for accountants and managers with less than two years of experience in fixed asset accounting; covers tax benefits, transitioning to a computerized system, and getting started with paperwork. **Locations:** Arlington, DC; New York, NY; and Washington, DC.

21218 ■ Fundamentals of Cost Accounting
American Management Association
600 AMA Way
Saranac Lake, NY 12983-5534
Ph:(212)586-8100
Free: 877-566-9441
Fax:(518)891-0368
Co. E-mail: customerservice@amanet.org
URL: http://www.amaseminars.org
Price: $2,195.00 for non-members; $1,995.00 for AMA members; and $1,708.00 for General Services Administration (GSA) members. **Description:** Covers the use of cost accounting, analyzing reports, choosing a cost system, and measuring results. **Locations:** Atlanta, GA; New York, NY; Chicago, IL; San Francisco, CA; Arlington, VA; and Washington, DC.

21219 ■ Fundamentals of Finance and Accounting for Administrative Professionals
American Management Association
600 AMA Way
Saranac Lake, NY 12983-5534
Ph:(212)586-8100
Free: 877-566-9441
Fax:(518)891-0368
Co. E-mail: customerservice@amanet.org
URL: http://www.amaseminars.org
Price: $1,895.00; $1,695.00 for AMA members; and $1,451.00 for General Services Administration (GSA) members. **Description:** Covers basic accounting principles, cash flow accounting, and learning to understand various financial documents. **Locations:** New York, NY; Washington, DC; Arlington, VA; and San Francisco, CA.

21220 ■ Government Contract Accounting
Seminar Information Service, Inc.
20 Executive Park, Ste. 120
Irvine, CA 92614
Ph:(949)261-9104
Free: 877-SEM-INFO
Fax:(949)261-1963
Co. E-mail: info@seminarinformation.com
URL: http://www.seminarinformation.com
Price: $995.00. **Description:** Accounting principles as they relate to procurement activities with the Federal Government, with focus on Government forms and formats, direct and indirect cost rate submissions, cost principles, dealing with Government auditors, changes and delay claims and terminations. **Locations:** La Jolla, CA; Hilton Head Island, SC; Washington, DC; Las Vegas, NV; and Dulles, VA.

21221 ■ How to Develop and Administer a Budget
Fred Pryor Seminars & CareerTrack
5700 Broadmoor St., Ste. 300
Mission, KS 66202
Free: 800-944-8503
Fax:(913)967-8849
Co. E-mail: customerservice@pryor.com
URL: http://www.careertrack.com
Price: $179.00; $169.00 for groups of 5 or more. **Description:** Covers the benefits of budgeting, budgeting concepts, templates, and methods for evaluating budgets. **Locations:** Cities throughout the United States.

21222 ■ How to Use Crystal Reports
Fred Pryor Seminars & CareerTrack
5700 Broadmoor St., Ste. 300
Mission, KS 66202
Free: 800-780-8476
Fax:(913)967-8849
Co. E-mail: customerservice@pryor.com
URL: http://www.pryor.com
Price: $199.00; $189.00 for groups of 5 or more. **Description:** Learn effective data management, including financial, sales, and personal presentation and distribution. **Locations:** Cities throughout the United States.

21223 ■ How to Use QuickBooks
Fred Pryor Seminars & CareerTrack
5700 Broadmoor St., Ste. 300
Mission, KS 66202
Free: 800-780-8476
Fax:(913)967-8849
Co. E-mail: customerservice@pryor.com
URL: http://www.pryor.com
Price: $199.00; $189.00 for groups of 5 or more. **Description:** Learn how to manage your inventory, track costs of your business, generate professional invoices and purchase orders, manage accounts payables and receivables and more. **Locations:** Cities throughout the United States.

21224 ■ Organizing and Managing Accounts Payable
Padgett-Thompson Seminars
Rockhurst University CEC
14502 W. 105th St.
Lenexa, KS 66215
Free: 800-349-1935
URL: http://www.findaseminar.com/tpd/Padgett-Thompson-Seminars.asp
Price: $199.00. **Description:** Seminar promotes the latest proven techniques and best practices to improve accuracy and save money for your company. **Locations:** Cherry Hill, NJ; Arlington, VA.

21225 ■ Organizing and Managing Accounts Payable (Onsite)
Seminar Information Service, Inc.
20 Executive Park, Ste. 120
Irvine, CA 92614
Ph:(949)261-9104
Free: 877-SEM-INFO
Fax:(949)261-1963
Co. E-mail: info@seminarinformation.com
URL: http://www.seminarinformation.com
Price: $199.00. **Description:** Comprehensive seminar where you'll learn the best practices guaranteed to improve your accuracy, as well as techniques, tips and shortcuts that will help you get more done in less time. **Locations:** Cities throughout the United States.

21226 ■ Project Cost Management: Estimating, Budgeting and Earned Value Analysis
Canadian Management Centre
150 York St., 5th Fl.
Toronto, ON, Canada M5H 3S5
Free: 800-262-2519
Fax:(416)214-6047
Co. E-mail: cmcinfo@cmctraining.org
URL: http://www.cmctraining.org
Price: $1,845.00 for members; $1,995.00 for non-members. **Description:** Learn how to apply proven methods, tools, and techniques to prepare estimates, develop and monitor budgets, manage cash flow, and use earned value analysis. **Locations:** Toronto, ON.

21227 ■ The Sales And Use Tax Seminar
Seminar Information Service, Inc.
20 Executive Park, Ste. 120
Irvine, CA 92614
Ph:(949)261-9104
Free: 877-SEM-INFO

Fax:(949)261-1963
Co. E-mail: info@seminarinformation.com
URL: http://www.seminarinformation.com

Price: $199.00. **Description:** Learn how to determine which transactions are taxable, find exemptions you may not be aware of, and handle business partners who aren't in compliance with new tax laws. **Locations:** Cities throughout the United States.

21228 ■ Super-Effective Techniques for Collecting Accounts Receivable
Padgett-Thompson Seminars
Rockhurst University CEC
14502 W. 105th St.
Lenexa, KS 66215
Free: 800-349-1935
URL: http://www.findaseminar.com/tpd/Padgett-Thompson-Seminars.asp

Price: $179.00. **Description:** Designed to get participants up to speed on the basic issues involved with collecting overdue money. **Locations:** Boston, MA.

REFERENCE WORKS

21229 ■ "2011 Tax Information of Interest" in *Business Owner* (Vol. 35, November-December 2011, No. 6, pp. 10)
Pub: DL Perkins Company

Description: Compilation of 2011 tax information to help small business take advantage of all tax incentives.

21230 ■ "Accountants Get the Hook" in *Canadian Business* (Vol. 80, October 22, 2007, No. 21, pp. 19)
Pub: Rogers Media

Ed: John Gray. **Description:** Chartered Accountants of Ontario handed down the decision on Douglas Barrington, Anthony Power and Claudio Russo's professional misconduct case. The three accountants of Deloitte & Touche LLP must pay C$100,000 in fines and C$417,000 in costs. Details of the disciplinary case are presented.

21231 ■ *Accounting and Finance for Your Small Business*
Pub: John Wiley & Sons, Incorporated

Ed: Steven M. Bragg; E. James Burton. **Released:** April 2006. **Price:** $49.00. **Description:** Financial procedures and techniques for establishing and maintaining a profitable small company are outlined.

21232 ■ "Accrual vs. Cash Accounting, Explained" in *Business Owner* (Vol. 35, July-August 2011, No. 4, pp. 13)
Pub: DL Perkins Company

Description: Cash method versus accrual accounting methods are examined, using hypothetical situations.

21233 ■ "Adler Blanchard & Freeman Reports New SmartKeeper Bookkeeping Service" in *Professional Services Close-Up* (March 24, 2011)
Pub: Close-Up Media

Description: Profile of Adler Blanchard & Freeman (AB&F) accountants and business advisors. The firm has expanded its client offerings to include their new SmartKeeper Business and Personal Bookkeeping Service for small to mid-sized companies and individuals.

21234 ■ "Bar Hopping: Your Numbers At a Glance" in *Inc.* (January 2008, pp. 44-45)
Pub: Gruner & Jahr USA Publishing

Ed: Michael Fitzgerald. **Description:** Software that helps any company analyze data include Crystal Xcelsius, a program that takes data from Excel documents and turns them into animated gauges, charts and graphs; CashView, a Web-based application that tracks receivables and payables; iDashboards, a Web-based programs that produces animated gauges, maps, pie charts and graphs; Corda Human Capital Management, that transforms stats like head count, productivity, and attrition into graphs and dials; NetSuite, a Web-based application that tracks key indicators; and Cognos Now, that gauges, dials, and graphs data.

21235 ■ "Battling Back from Betrayal" in *Harvard Business Review* (Vol. 88, December 2010, No. 12, pp. 130)
Pub: Harvard Business School Publishing

Ed: Daniel McGinn. **Description:** Stephen Greer's scrap metal firm, Hartwell Pacific, lost several million dollars due to a lack of efficient and appropriate inventory audits, accounting procedures, and new-hire reference checks for his foreign operations. Greer believes that balancing growth with control is a key component of success.

21236 ■ *Beat the Taxman: Easy Ways to Tax Save in Your Small Business*
Pub: John Wiley & Sons, Incorporated

Ed: Stephen Thompson. **Released:** May 2008. **Price:** $26.95. **Description:** Concise tax planner to help entrepreneurs take advantage of current tax laws.

21237 ■ "A Bigger Deal" in *Crain's Cleveland Business* (Vol. 28, November 12, 2007, No. 45, pp. 1)
Pub: Crain Communications, Inc.

Ed: Shawn A. Turner. **Description:** In an attempt to boost its revenue CBiz Inc., a provider of accounting and business services, is looking to balance its acquisitions of smaller companies with larger ones as part of its overall growth strategy.

21238 ■ "Book of Lists 2010" in *Philadelphia Business Journal* (Vol. 28, December 25, 2009, No. 45, pp. 1)
Pub: American City Business Journals

Description: Rankings of companies and organizations within the banking, biotechnology, economic development, healthcare, hospitality, law and accounting, marketing and media, real estate, and technology industries in the Philadelphia, Pennsylvania area are presented. Rankings are based on sales, business size, and more.

21239 ■ "Bookkeeping Service Opens First Sacramento Franchise" in *Sacramento Bee* (April 13, 2011)
Pub: Sacramento Bee

Ed: Mark Glover. **Description:** Franchise bookkeeping service called BookKeeping Express opened its new office in Roseville, California; its first shop in the area.

21240 ■ "Businesses Balk at 1099 Provision in Health Reform Law" in *Baltimore Business Journal* (Vol. 28, August 13, 2010, No. 14, pp. 1)
Pub: Baltimore Business Journal

Ed: Scott Dance. **Description:** Small business advocates and accountants have criticized the Internal Revenue Service Form 1099 provision in the health care reform law as not worth the cost of time and money. Critics believe the policy would create a deluge of the documents that is too much for the companies or the IRS to handle. Details of the provision are also discussed.

21241 ■ "Cautions On Loans With Your Business" in *Business Owner* (Vol. 35, July-August 2011, No. 4, pp. 5)
Pub: DL Perkins Company

Description: Caution must be used when borrowing from or lending to any small business. Tax guidelines for the borrowing and lending practice are also included.

21242 ■ "Changing the Rules of the Accounting Game" in *Canadian Business* (Vol. 81, December 8, 2008, No. 21, pp. 19)
Pub: Rogers Media Ltd.

Ed: Al Rosen. **Description:** Interference from world politicians in developing accounting standards is believed to have resulted in untested rules that are inferior to current standards. European lawmakers have recently asked to change International Financial Reporting Standards.

21243 ■ *The Complete Startup Guide for the Black Entrepreneur*
Pub: Career Press Inc.

Ed: Bill Boudreaux. **Description:** President and founder of a consulting firm for home-based entrepreneurs share information to help minorities start their own companies. Tips to create a business plan, buy essential equipment, price products and services, pay the bills, and set up a work space are covered.

21244 ■ *Computer Accounting Essentials with Microsoft Office Accounting 2010*
Pub: McGraw-Hill Higher Education

Ed: Carol Yacht, Susan Crosson. **Released:** March 10, 2010. **Description:** Step-by-step guide to using Microsoft's Office Professional 2007 Accounting program.

21245 ■ "Convergence Collaboration: Revising Revenue Recognition" in *Management Accounting Quarterly* (Vol. 12, Spring 2011, No. 3, pp. 18)
Pub: Management Accounting Quarterly

Ed: Jack T. Ciesielski, Thomas R. Weirich. **Description:** While revenue recognition is critical, regulations have been developed on an ad hoc basis until now. The joint FASB/IASB proposed accounting standard on revenue recognition is a meaningful convergence of standards that will require a major adjustment for financial statement preparers. The proposal is a radical departure from the way revenue has been recognized by the U.S. GAAP. For industries such as consulting, engineering, construction, and technology, it could dramatically change revenue recognition, impacting the top line. The new proposed standard, its potential impact, and the critical role that contracts play is examined thoroughly.

21246 ■ *Deduct It!: Lower Your Small Business Taxes*
Pub: NOLO

Ed: Stephen Fishman. **Released:** November 2009. **Price:** $34.99. **Description:** Ways to maximize business tax deductions for any type of small business owner (sole proprietor, partnership, LLC, corporation).

21247 ■ *Directory of Global Professional Accounting and Business Certifications*
Pub: John Wiley & Sons, Incorporated

Ed: Lal Balkaran. **Released:** February 9, 2007. **Price:** $35.00. **Description:** Resource for international accounting, auditing, and business professions.

21248 ■ "Do Fair Value Adjustments Influence Dividend Policy?" in *Accounting and Business Research* (Vol. 41, Spring 2011, No. 2, pp. 51)
Pub: American Institute of CPAs

Ed: Igor Goncharov, Sander van Triest. **Description:** The impact of positive fair value adjustments on corporate distributions is examined using a Russian setting that requires disclosure of unrealized fair value adjustments in income. It was found that there is no rise in dividends due to positive fair value adjustments and that on the contrary, a negative relationship exists between adjustments and dividend changes.

21249 ■ *EBay Income: How ANYONE of Any Age, Location, and/or Background Can Build a Highly Profitable Online Business with eBay (Revised 2nd Edition)*
Pub: Atlantic Publishing Company

Released: December 1, 2010. **Price:** $24.95. **Description:** A complete overview of eBay is given and guides any small company through the entire process of creating the auction and auction strategies, photography, writing copy, text and formatting, multiple sales, programming tricks, PayPal, accounting, creating marketing, merchandising, managing email lists, advertising plans, taxes and sales tax, best time to list items and for how long, sniping programs, international customers, opening a storefront, electronic commerce, buy-it now pricing, keywords, Google marketing and eBay secrets.

21250 ■ "Economic Crisis and Accounting Evolution" in *Accounting and Business Research* (Vol. 41, Summer 2011, No. 3, pp. 2159)
Pub: American Institute of CPAs
Ed: Gregory Waymire, Sudipta Basu. **Description:** Financial reporting changes at the face of economic crises are studied using a punctuated equilibrium evolution. Findings show that financial reporting has a minor impact but may amplify economic crises. Attempts to enhance accounting amid economic crises may not be as beneficial as planned.

21251 ■ *Electronic Commerce: Technical, Business, and Legal Issues*
Pub: Prentice Hall PTR
Ed: Oktay Dogramaci; Aryya Gangopadhyay; Yelena Yesha; Nabil R. Adam. **Released:** August 1998. **Description:** Provides insight into the goals of using the Internet to grow a business in the areas of networking and telecommunication, security, and storage and retrieval; business areas such as marketing, procurement and purchasing, billing and payment, and supply chain management; and legal aspects such as privacy, intellectual property, taxation, contractual and legal settlements.

21252 ■ *Employer Legal Forms Simplified*
Pub: Nova Publishing Company
Ed: Daniel Sitarz. **Released:** August 2007. **Price:** $24.95. **Description:** Business reference containing the following forms needed to handle employees in any small business environment: application, notice, confidentiality, absence, federal employer forms and notices, and many payroll forms. All forms are included on a CD that comes in both PDF and text formats. Adobe Acrobat Reader software is also included on the CD. The forms are valid in all fifty states and Washington, DC.

21253 ■ "Ethics Commission May Hire Collection Agency" in *Tulsa World* (August 21, 2010)
Pub: World Publishing
Ed: Barbara Hoberock. **Description:** Oklahoma Ethics Commission is considering a more to hire a collection agency or law firm in order to collect fees from candidates owing money for filing late financial reports.

21254 ■ "Final State Budget Is a Mixed Bag of Key Industries" in *The Business Journal - Serving Phoenix and the Valley of the Sun* (Vol. 28, July 4, 2008, No. 44, pp. 3)
Pub: American City Business Journals, Inc.
Ed: Mike Sunnucks; Patrick O'Grady. **Description:** Approved by Governor Janet Napolitano and passed by the Arizona Legislature, the $9.9 billion state budget is beneficial to some industries in the business community. The tax cap for on Arizona Lottery has been removed which is beneficial to the industry, while the solar energy industry and real estate developers stand to lose from the spending bill. Other details of the finance budget are presented.

21255 ■ "Finally, Justice" in *Canadian Business* (Vol. 82, April 27, 2009, No. 7, pp. 12)
Pub: Rogers Media
Ed: John Gray. **Description:** Former investment adviser Alex Winch feels that he was vindicated with the Canadian Court's ruling that Livent Inc. founders Garth Drabinsky and Myron Gottlieb were guilty of fraud. Drabinsky filed a libel case on Winch over Winch's letter that complained over Livent's accounting procedures. Winch also criticized the inconsistent accounting during Drabinsky's term as chief executive of another firm.

21256 ■ *Finance & Accounting: How to Keep Your Books and Manage Your Finances with an MBA, a CPA, or a Ph.D*
Pub: Adams Media Corporation
Ed: Suzanne Caplan. **Price:** $19.95.

21257 ■ "The Finance Function In A Global Corporation" in *Harvard Business Review* (Vol. 86, July-August 2008, No. 8, pp. 108)
Pub: Harvard Business School Press
Ed: Mihir A. Desai. **Description:** Designing and implementing a successful finance function in a global setting is discussed. Additional topics include the internal capital market, managing risk and budgeting capital internationally.

21258 ■ *Financial Management 101: Get a Grip on Your Business Numbers*
Pub: Self-Counsel Press, Incorporated
Ed: Angie Mohr. **Released:** November 2007. **Price:** $16.95. **Description:** An overview of business planning, financial statements, budgeting and advertising for small businesses. s.

21259 ■ *Financial Times Guide to Business Start Up 2007*
Pub: Pearson Education, Limited
Ed: Sara Williams; Jonquil Lowe. **Released:** November 2006. **Price:** $52.50. **Description:** Guide for starting and running a new business is presented. Sections include ways to get started, direct marketing, customer relations, management and accounting.

21260 ■ *The Flaw of Averages: Why We Underestimate Risk in the Face of Uncertainty*
Pub: John Wiley & Sons, Inc.
Ed: Sam L. Savage. **Released:** June 3, 2009. **Price:** $22.95. **Description:** Personal and business plans are based on uncertainties on a daily basis. The common avoidable mistake individuals make in assessing risk in the face of uncertainty is defined. The explains why plans based on average assumptions are wrong, on average, in areas as diverse as finance, healthcare, accounting, the war on terror, and climate change.

21261 ■ "Function Over Forms?" in *Barron's* (Vol. 88, June 30, 2008, No. 26, pp. 17)
Pub: Dow Jones & Co., Inc.
Ed: Eric Savitz. **Description:** Securities and Exchange Commission (SEC) chairman Christopher Cox wants the SEC to consider an overhaul of the forms used to meet the agency's disclosure requirements. Cox also said that the U.S. Generally Accepted Accounting Standards has too many rules with exceptions and alternative interpretations.

21262 ■ *Getting Rich In Your Underwear: How To Start and Run a Profitable Home-Based Business*
Pub: HCM Publishing
Ed: Peter I. Hupalo. **Released:** April 1, 2005. **Price:** $17.95. **Description:** Book offers insight into starting a home-based business. Entrepreneurs will learn about business models and the home business; distribution and fulfillment of product or service; marketing and sales; how to overcome the fear of starting a business; personal success characteristics; naming a business; zoning and insurance; intellectual capital; copyrights, trademarks, and patents; limited liability companies and S-corporations; business expenses and accounting; taxes; fifteen basic steps for starting a home-based business, state resources for starting a home company; and seven home-based business ideas.

21263 ■ "Give Until It Works" in *Hispanic Business* (Vol. 30, March 2008, No. 3, pp. 26)
Pub: Hispanic Business
Ed: Rick Munarriz. **Description:** Donating to qualified charities and non-profit organizations for maximizing tax advantage to be availed on the income tax bill is examined. The amount that can be deducted from the total taxable amount is usually less then the actual amount donated and must be made during that calendar year.

21264 ■ "Growing Strong" in *Entrepreneur* (Vol. 35, November 2007, No. 11, pp. 36)
Pub: Entrepreneur Media Inc.
Ed: Nichole L. Torres. **Description:** Amy Langer founded Salo LL with partner John Folkestad. The company is growing fast since its 2002 launch, with over $40 million in projections for 2007. The finance and accounting staffing company tops the list of the fastest-growing women-led companies in North America.

21265 ■ "Handle With Care" in *Hawaii Business* (Vol. 53, October 2007, No. 5, pp. 66)
Pub: Hawaii Business Publishing
Ed: Kenneth Sheffield. **Description:** Discusses a fiduciary, who may be a board member, business owner, or a trustee, and is someone who supervises and manages the affairs and the resources of a principal. Fiduciary duties, which include accounting, cost review and risk management, must be served with the benefit of the principal as the priority. Ways of breaching fiduciary duties and how to avoid them are discussed.

21266 ■ "The Hidden Tax" in *Canadian Business* (Vol. 81, April 14, 2008, No. 6, pp. 28)
Pub: Rogers Media
Ed: Al Rosen. **Description:** Accounting fraud could take out a sizable sum from one's retirement fund when computed over a long period of time. The much bigger tax on savings is the collective impact of the smaller losses that do not attract the attention they deserve. Ensuring that investors are not unnecessarily taxed 2 percent of their total investments every year outweighs the benefit of a 2 percent reduction in personal tax rates.

21267 ■ *How to Start an Internet Sales Business*
Pub: Lulu.com
Ed: Dan Davis. **Released:** August 2005. **Price:** $19. 95. **Description:** Small business guide for launching an Internet sales company. Topics include business structure, licenses, and taxes.

21268 ■ *How to Start and Run a Small Book Publishing Company: A Small Business Guide to Self-Publishing and Independent Publishing*
Pub: HCM Publishing
Ed: Peter I. Hupalo. **Released:** August 30, 2002. **Price:** $18.95. **Description:** The book teaches all aspects of starting and running a small book publishing company. Topics covered include: inventory accounting in the book trade, just-in-time inventory management, turnkey fulfillment solutions, tax deductible costs, basics of sales and use tax, book pricing, standards in terms of the book industry, working with distributors and wholesalers, cover design and book layout, book promotion and marketing, how to select profitable authors to publish, printing process, printing on demand, the power of a strong backlist, and how to value copyright.

21269 ■ "How To: Manage Your Cash Better" in *Inc.* (Volume 32, December 2010, No. 10, pp. 69)
Pub: Inc. Magazine
Description: A monthly guide to policies, procedures and practices for managing cash for a small business.

21270 ■ "IFRS Monopoly: the Pied Piper of Financial Reporting" in *Accounting and Business Research* (Vol. 41, Summer 2011, No. 3, pp. 291)
Pub: American Institute of CPAs
Ed: Shyam Sunder. **Description:** The disadvantages of granting monopoly to the international financial reporting standards (IFRS) are examined. Results indicate that an IFRS monopoly removes the chances for comparing alternative practices and learning from them. An IFRS monopoly also eliminates customization of financial reporting to fit local differences in governance, business, economic, and legal conditions.

21271 ■ "Internal Auditor Wants Ethics Review of City's Casper Golf Contract" in *Business Courier* (Vol. 27, September 10, 2010, No. 19, pp. 1)
Pub: Business Courier
Ed: Dan Monk. **Description:** Mark Ashworth, an internal auditor for Cincinnati, Ohio is pushing for an ethics review of management contract for seven city-owned golf courses. Ashworth wants the Ohio Ethics

Commission to investigate family ties between a superintendent for the Cincinnati Recreation Commission and Billy Casper Golf.

21272 ■ "IRS Announces New Standards for Tax Preparers" in *Bellingham Business Journal* (Vol. February 2010, pp. 9)
Pub: Sound Publishing Inc.
Ed: Isaac Bonnell. **Description:** A new oversight plan was announced by the Internal Revenue Services (IRS) that will require tax professionals to pass a competency test and register with the government in order to ensure greater accountability in the industry.

21273 ■ "Kaboom!" in *Canadian Business* (Vol. 81, November 10, 2008, No. 19, pp. 18)
Pub: Rogers Media Ltd.
Ed: Al Rosen, Mark Rosen. **Description:** International Financial Reporting Standards (IFRS) is a good idea in theory but was implemented in a hurry and had poor quality standards from the beginning.

21274 ■ "Know Your Numbers" in *Inc.* (Volume 32, December 2010, No. 10, pp. 39)
Pub: Inc. Magazine
Ed: Norm Brodsky. **Description:** Ways to maximize profit and minimize tax burden are presented.

21275 ■ "Lifesavers" in *Black Enterprise* (Vol. 41, December 2010, No. 5, pp. 38)
Pub: Earl G. Graves Publishing Co. Inc.
Ed: Tamara E. Holmes. **Description:** Profile of Interventional Nephrology Specialists Access Center and founders Dr. Omar Davis and Dr. Natarsha Grant; the center generated $5.5 million in revenue for 2009. Details on how they run their successful center are included.

21276 ■ "Living in a 'Goldfish Bowl'" in *WorkingUSA* (Vol. 11, June 2008, No. 2, pp. 277)
Pub: Blackwell Publishers Ltd.
Ed: John Lund. **Description:** Recent changes in laws, regulations and even the reporting format of labor organization annual financial reports in both the U.S. and Australia have received surprisingly little attention, yet they have significantly increased the amount of information available both to union members and the public in general, as reports in both countries are available via government Websites. While such financial reporting laws are extremely rare in European countries, with the exception of the UK and Ireland, the U.S. and Australian reporting systems have become among the most detailed in the world. After reviewing these changes in financial reporting and the availability of these reports, as well as comparing and contrasting the specific reporting requirements of each country, this paper then examines the cost-benefit impact of more detailed financial reporting.

21277 ■ "Market Volatility and Your Retirement" in *Agency Sales Magazine* (Vol. 39, August 2009, No. 8, pp. 48)
Pub: MANA
Ed: Joshua D. Mosshart. **Description:** Strategies for retirees in managing investments amid market volatility are presented. Retirees should keep their withdrawal assumptions conservative, maintain sensible asset allocation, review and rebalance their portfolio and allow a financial professional to guide them. Insights on market volatility are also given.

21278 ■ "May I Handle That For You?" in *Inc.* (March 2008, pp. 40, 42)
Pub: Gruner & Jahr USA Publishing
Ed: Taylor Mallory. **Description:** According to a recent survey, 53 percent of all companies outsource a portion of their human resources responsibilities. Ceridian, Administaff, Taleo, KnowledgeBank, and CheckPoint HR are among the companies profiled.

21279 ■ *MBA In a Day*
Pub: John Wiley and Sons, Inc.
Ed: Steven Stralser, PhD. **Released:** 2004. **Price:** $34.95. **Description:** Management professor presents important concepts, business topics and strategies that can be used by anyone to manage a small business or professional practice. Topics covered include: human resources and personal interaction, ethics and leadership skills, fair negotiation tactics, basic business accounting practices, project management, and the fundamentals of economics and marketing.

21280 ■ "Merger Mania: Regional Snaps Up HVS" in *The Business Journal-Serving Greater Tampa Bay* (Vol. 28, September 26, 2008, No. 40, pp. 1)
Pub: American City Business Journals, Inc.
Ed: Alexis Muellner. **Description:** It was reported that Harper Van Scoik & Co. LLP has finalized a merger with Carr Riggs & Ingram LLC. The agreement, effective October 1, 2008, is a merger of HVS assets into CRI. Bill Carr, a managing partner, revealed that HVS' $5 million in revenue will take CRI from $78 million to $82 million in revenue.

21281 ■ *Mergers and Acquisitions from A to Z*
Pub: Amacom
Ed: Andrew J. Sherman, Milledge A. Hart. **Released:** January 2006. **Price:** $35.00. **Description:** Guide for the entire process of mergers and acquisitions, including taxes, accounting, laws, and projected financial gain.

21282 ■ *Microfinance*
Pub: Palgrave Macmillan
Ed: Mario La Torre; Gianfranco A. Vento; Philip Molyneux. **Released:** October 2006. **Price:** $80.00. **Description:** Microfinance involves the analysis of operational, managerial and financial aspects of a small business.

21283 ■ *Minding Her Own Business, 4th Ed.*
Pub: Sphinx Publishing
Ed: Jan Zobel. **Released:** January 1, 2005. **Price:** $16.95. **Description:** A guide to taxes and financial records for women entrepreneurs is presented.

21284 ■ "My Favorite Tool for Managing Expenses" in *Inc.* (Volume 32, December 2010, No. 10, pp. 60)
Pub: Inc. Magazine
Ed: J.J. McCorvey. **Description:** Web-based service called Expensify is outlined. The service allows companies to log expenses while away from the office using the service's iPhone application.

21285 ■ "New Century's Fall Has a New Culprit" in *Barron's* (Vol. 88, March 31, 2008, No. 13, pp. 20)
Pub: Dow Jones & Company, Inc.
Ed: Jonathan R. Laing. **Description:** Court examiner Michael Missal reports that New Century Financial's auditor contributed to New Century's demise by its negligence in permitting improper and imprudent practices related to New Century's accounting processes. New Century's bankruptcy filing is considered the start of the subprime-mortgage crisis.

21286 ■ "New Institutional Accounting and IFRS" in *Accounting and Business Research* (Vol. 41, Summer 2011, No. 3, pp. 309)
Pub: American Institute of CPAs
Ed: Peter Wysocki. **Description:** A new framework for institutional accounting research is presented. It has five fundamental components – efficient versus inefficient results, interdependencies, causation, level of analysis, and institutional structure. The use of the framework for evaluation accounting institutions such as the international financial reporting standards is discussed.

21287 ■ "New Money" in *Entrepreneur* (Vol. 36, February 2008, No. 2, pp. 62)
Pub: Entrepreneur Media Inc.
Ed: C.J. Prince. **Description:** Tips on how to handle business finance, with regard to the tightened credit standards imposed by leading institutions, are provided. These include: selling receivables, margining blue chips, and selling purchase orders.

21288 ■ "Olympus is Urged to Revise Board" in *Wall Street Journal Eastern Edition* (November 28, 2011, pp. B3)
Pub: Dow Jones & Company Inc.
Ed: Phred Dvorak. **Description:** Koji Miyata, once a director on the board of troubled Japanese photographic equipment company, is urging the company to reorganize its board, saying the present group should resign their board seats but keep their management positions. The company has come under scrutiny for its accounting practices and costly acquisitions.

21289 ■ *The One Minute Entrepreneur*
Pub: Doubleday
Ed: Ken Blanchard; assisted by Don Hutson and Ethan Willis. **Released:** 2008. **Price:** $19.95. **Description:** Four traditional business ideas are covered including: revenue needs to exceed expenses, bill collection, customer service, and employee motivation in order to be successful.

21290 ■ *Open Source Solutions for Small Business Problems*
Pub: Charles River Media
Ed: John Locke. **Released:** May 2004. **Price:** $35.95. **Description:** Open source software provides solutions to many small business problems such as tracking electronic documents, scheduling, accounting functions, managing contact lists, and reducing spam.

21291 ■ *Outfoxing the Small Business Owner*
Pub: Adams Media Corporation
Ed: Gene Marks. **Released:** January 2005. **Description:** Special skill sets are required to sell, service or deal with small business customers.

21292 ■ "Paperless Bookkeeping Program" in *Fleet Owner Online* (February 15, 2011)
Pub: Penton Business Media Inc.
Description: TruckTax launched its new paperless bookkeeping system to help manage bookkeeping tasks, accounting and business tax information and filings for truckers.

21293 ■ "Pick and Save" in *Entrepreneur* (Vol. 36, April 2008, No. 4, pp. 66)
Pub: Entrepreneur Media, Inc.
Ed: C.J. Prince. **Description:** Business owners can purchase the needed big equipment to offset this year's expected profit. They can also switch to annualized computing of quarterly income and estimated tax payments to pay less estimated taxes for the first half of the year. Other tips on tax planning are provided.

21294 ■ "Piece of Health Law 'A Goner'" in *Baltimore Business Journal* (Vol. 28, November 19, 2010, No. 28, pp. 1)
Pub: Baltimore Business Journal
Ed: Kent Hoover. **Description:** Montana Senator Max Baucus, a Democrat who heads the Senate Finance Committee, has revealed his plan to push legislation that would repeal the 1099 IRS provision that was created by the health care reform law and will result in more paperwork for small businesses when it goes into effect in 2012.

21295 ■ "Place Restrictions on Your Stock Shares" in *Business Owner* (Vol. 35, July-August 2011, No. 4, pp. 14)
Pub: DL Perkins Company
Description: It is critical for any small business owner to be certain that the buyer or recipient of any part of the company represents that the stock is being acquired or given for investment purposes only.

21296 ■ "Proposed Accounting Changes Could Complicate Tenant's Leases" in *Baltimore Business Journal* (Vol. 28, July 2, 2010, No. 8, pp. 1)
Pub: Baltimore Business Journal
Ed: Daniel J. Sernovitz. **Description:** The Financial Accounting Standards Board has proposed that companies must indicate the value of real estate leases as assets and liabilities on balance sheets instead of expenses. The proposals could cause some companies to document millions of dollars in charges on their books or find difficulty in getting loans.

21297 ■ "Prosecutors Dish Sordid AIPC Story" in *The Business Journal-Serving Metropolitan Kansas City* (Vol. 27, September 19, 2008, No. 1)
Pub: American City Business Journals, Inc.
Ed: Suzanna Stagemeyer. **Description:** Prosecutors in the American Italian Pasta Co.'s accounting fraud case have revealed evidence on the schemes used

by then-officers of the company to commit fraud. District attorney John Wood has dubbed the case as the largest corporate fraud lawsuit in the history of the district of Missouri. How AIPC fell from being an industry leader is also discussed.

21298 ■ *QuickBooks All-in-One Desk Reference for Dummies*
Pub: John Wiley & Sons, Incorporated
Ed: Stephen L. Nelson. **Released:** January 2007. **Price:** $29.99 (US), $42.99 (Canadian). **Description:** Compilation of nine self-contained minibooks to get the most from QuickBooks accounting software. Companion Web site with sample business plan workbook and downloadable profit-volume cost analysis workbook included.

21299 ■ *QuickBooks for the New Bean Counter: Business Owner's Guide 2006*
Pub: Wheatmark
Ed: Joseph L. Catallini. **Released:** July 2006. **Price:** $21.95. **Description:** Profile of QuickBooks software, offering insight into using the software's accounting and bookkeeping functions.

21300 ■ *QuickBooks Simple Start for Dummies*
Pub: John Wiley & Sons, Incorporated
Ed: Stephen L. Nelson. **Released:** October 2004. **Price:** $21.99. **Description:** Profile of Intuits new accounting software geared to micro businesses. Advice is offered on daily, monthly, and yearly accounting activities covering records, sales tax, and reports.

21301 ■ *QuickBooks X on Demand*
Pub: Que
Ed: Gail Perry. **Released:** December 2006. **Price:** $34.99. **Description:** Step-by-step training for using various small business financial software programs; includes illustrated, full color explanations.

21302 ■ *QuickBooks X for Dummies*
Pub: John Wiley & Sons, Incorporated
Ed: Stephen L. Nelson. **Released:** November 2006. **Price:** $21.99. **Description:** Key features of QuickBooks software for small business are introduced. Invoicing and credit memos, recoding sales receipts, accounting, budgeting, taxes, payroll, financial reports, job estimating, billing, tracking, data backup, are among the features.

21303 ■ "Quicken Starter Edition 2008" in *Black Enterprise* (Vol. 38, March 2008, No. 8, pp. 54)
Pub: Earl G. Graves Publishing Co. Inc.
Ed: Sonya A. Donaldson. **Description:** Profile of Quicken Starter Edition 2008 offering programs that track spending; it will also categorize tax deductible expenses.

21304 ■ *Reading Financial Reports for Dummies*
Pub: John Wiley and Sons, Inc.
Ed: Lita Epstein. **Released:** January 2009. **Price:** $21.99. **Description:** This second edition contains more new and updated information, including new information on the separate accounting and financial reporting standards for private/small businesses versus public/large businesses; updated information reflecting 2007 laws on international financial reporting standards; new content to match SEC and other governmental regulatory changes over the last three years; new information about how the analyst-corporate connection has changed the playing field; the impact of corporate communications and new technologies; new examples that reflect the current trends; and updated Websites and resources.

21305 ■ "Reform or Perish" in *Canadian Business* (Vol. 82, April 27, 2009, No. 7, pp. 20)
Pub: Rogers Media
Ed: Al Rosen. **Description:** It is believed that Canada needs to fix its financial regulatory framework in order to provide more oversight on accounting procedures that is often left up to auditors. While the U.S. has constantly rebuilt its regulatory framework, Canada has not instituted reforms on its regulations. Canada entered the recession with a strong system but needs to build more substance into it.

21306 ■ *Sarbanes-Oxley for Dummies, 2nd Ed.*
Pub: John Wiley and Sons, Inc.
Ed: Jill Gilbert Welytok. **Released:** February 2008. **Price:** $21.99. **Description:** Provides the latest Sarbanes-Oxley (SOX) legislation with procedures to safely and effectively reduce compliance costs. Topics include way to: establish SOX standards for IT professionals, minimize compliances costs for every aspect of a business, survive a Section 404 audit, avoid litigation under SOX, anticipate future rules and trends, create a post-SOX paper trail, increase a company's standing and reputation, work with SOX in a small business, meet new SOX standards, build a board that can't be bought, and to comply with all SOX management mandates.

21307 ■ *Schaum's Outline Financial Management, Third Edition*
Pub: McGraw-Hill
Ed: Jae K. Shim; Joel G. Siegel. **Released:** May 2007. **Price:** $22.95 (CND). **Description:** Rules and regulations governing corporate finance, including the Sarbanes-Oxley Act are discussed.

21308 ■ "SEC Extends Small Business Deadline for SOX Audit Requirement" in *HRMagazine* (Vol. 53, August 2008, No. 8, pp. 20)
Pub: Society for Human Resource Management
Description: Securities and Exchange Commission has approved a one-year extension of the compliance date for smaller public companies to meet the Section 404(b) auditor attestation requirement of the Sarbanes-Oxley Act.

21309 ■ *Self-Employed Tax Solutions: Quick, Simple, Money-Saving, Audit-Proof Tax and Recordkeeping Basics*
Pub: The Globe Pequot Press
Ed: June Walker. **Released:** January 1, 2009. **Price:** $17.95. **Description:** A simple system for maintaining tax records and filing tax forms for any small business is explored.

21310 ■ *Six SIGMA for Small Business*
Pub: Entrepreneur Press
Ed: Greg Brue. **Released:** October 2005. **Price:** $19.95 (US), $26.95 (Canadian). **Description:** Jack Welch's Six SIGMA approach to business covers accounting, finance, sales and marketing, buying a business, human resource development, and new product development.

21311 ■ "Small is Bountiful for Intuit" in *Barron's* (Vol. 90, September 13, 2010, No. 37, pp. 22)
Pub: Barron's Editorial & Corporate Headquarters
Ed: Mark Veverka. **Description:** Finance software maker Intuit wants to tap the underserved small business market. One analyst sees Intuit's shares rising 25 percent to 55 percent in the next 12 months from September 2010.

21312 ■ *The Small Business Bible: Everything You Need to Know to Succeed in Your Small Business*
Pub: John Wiley & Sons, Incorporated
Ed: Steven D. Strauss. **Released:** September 2008. **Price:** $19.95 (US), $28.99 (Canadian). **Description:** Comprehensive guide to starting and running a successful small business. Topics include bookkeeping and financial management, marketing, publicity, and advertising.

21313 ■ *Small Business Desk Reference*
Pub: Penguin Books (USA) Incorporated
Ed: Gene Marks. **Released:** December 2004. **Description:** Comprehensive guide for starting or running a successful small business, focusing on buying a business or franchise, writing a business plan, financial management, accounting, legal issues, human resources management, operations, marketing, sales, customer service, taxes, insurance, and ethics. Information for launching a restaurant, property management firm, retail outlet, consulting firm, and service business is included.

21314 ■ *Small Business for Dummies, 3rd Ed.*
Pub: John Wiley and Sons, Inc.
Ed: Eric Tyson; Jim Schell. **Released:** March 2008. **Price:** $21.99. **Description:** Guidebook for anyone wanting to start or grow a small business; topics include information financing, budgeting, marketing, management and more.

21315 ■ *The Small Business Owner's Manual: Everything You Need to Know to Start Up and Run Your Business*
Pub: Career Press, Incorporated
Ed: Joe Kennedy. **Released:** June 2005. **Price:** $19.99 (US), $26.95 (Canadian). **Description:** Comprehensive guide for starting a small business, focusing on twelve ways to obtain financing, business plans, selling and advertising products and services, hiring and firing employees, setting up a Web site, business law, accounting issues, insurance, equipment, computers, banks, financing, customer credit and collection, leasing, and more.

21316 ■ *Small Business Survival Guide*
Pub: Adams Media Corporation
Ed: Cliff Ennico. **Price:** $12.95. **Description:** Small business expert provides strategies to start a company and survive in the 21st Century. He shows small business owners how to succeed despite challenges that can defeat any firm. His advice covers suppliers; customers and contractors; competitors and creditors; spouses, family and friends; as well as the ways lawyers, accountants and other can steal an entrepreneur's success. Ennico also describes how startups can comply with local regulations.

21317 ■ *Small Business Survival Guide: Starting, Protecting, and Securing Your Business for Long-Term Success*
Pub: Adams Media Corporation
Ed: Cliff Ennico. **Released:** September 2005. **Price:** $12.95 (US), $17.95 (Canadian). **Description:** Entrepreneurship in the new millennium. Topics include creditors, taxes, competition, business law, and accounting.

21318 ■ *Smart Tax Write-Offs, 5th Ed.*
Pub: Rayve Productions, Inc.
Ed: Norm Ray. **Released:** February 2008. **Price:** $15.95. **Description:** Guidebook to help small business owners take advantage of legitimate tax deductions for home-based and other entrepreneurial businesses.

21319 ■ "Smart Year-End Tax Moves" in *Business Owner* (Vol. 35, November-December 2011, No. 6, pp. 8)
Pub: DL Perkins Company
Description: Managing small business and individual taxes is more important in a bad economy. It is imperative to seek all tax incentives that apply to your business.

21320 ■ "Spotlight on Pensions" in *Business Horizons* (Vol. 51, March-April 2008, No. 2, pp. 105)
Pub: Elsevier Advanced Technology Publications
Ed: Laureen A. Maines. **Description:** Perceptions of pension burden and risk among financial statement users is likely to increase with changes in pension accounting. These perceptions might affect decisions on pension commitments and investments.

21321 ■ "Spotlight on Principles-based Financial Reporting" in *Business Horizons* (September-October 2007, pp. 359)
Pub: Elsevier Technology Publications
Ed: Laureen A. Maines. **Description:** Employment of principles-based standards in order to generate reliable financial reporting and to reduce misrepresentations is discussed. Rules-based standards are distinguished from principles-based standards.

21322 ■ "Staffing Firm Grows by Following Own Advice-Hire a Headhunter" in *Crain's Detroit Business* (Vol. 24, October 6, 2008, No. 40, pp. 1)
Pub: Crain Communications, Inc.
Ed: Sherri Begin. **Description:** Profile of Venator Holdings L.L.C., a staffing firm that provides searches for companies in need of financial-accounting and

technical employees; the firm's revenue has increased from $1.1 million in 2003 to a projected $11.5 million this year due to a climate in which more people are exiting the workforce than are coming in with those particular specialized skills and the need for a temporary, flexible workforce for contract placements at companies that do not want to take on the legacy costs associated with permanent employees. The hiring of an external headhunter to find the right out-of-state manager for Venator is also discussed.

21323 ■ "State Budget Woes Hurt Many Vendors, Senior Services" in *Sacramento Business Journal* (Vol. 25, August 15, 2008, No. 24, pp. 1)
Pub: American City Business Journals, Inc.
Ed: Melanie Turner. **Description:** Delays in the passage of the California state budget have adversely affected the health care industry. The Robertson Adult Day Health Care had taken out loans to keep the business afloat. The state Legislature has reduced Medi-Cal reimbursement to health care providers by 10 percent.

21324 ■ *Streetwise Finance and Accounting for Entrepreneurs: Set Budgets, Manage Costs, Keep Your Business Profitable*
Pub: Adams Media Corporation
Ed: Suzanne Caplan. **Released:** November 2006. **Price:** $25.95. **Description:** Book offers a basic understanding of accounting and finance for small businesses, including financial statements, credits and debits, as well as establishing a budget. Strategies for small companies in financial distress are included.

21325 ■ *Streetwise Small Business Book of Lists: Hundreds of Lists to Help You Reduce Costs, Increase Revenues, and Boost Your Profits!*
Pub: Adams Media Corporation
Ed: Gene Marks. **Released:** September 2006. **Price:** $25.95. **Description:** Strategies to help small business owners locate services, increase sales, and lower expenses.

21326 ■ *Tactical Entrepreneur: The Entrepreneur's Game Plan*
Pub: Sortis Publishing
Ed: Brian J. Hazelgren. **Released:** September 2005. **Price:** $14.95. **Description:** A smart, realistic business plan is essential for any successful entrepreneur. Besides offering products or services, small business owners must possess skills in accounting, planning, human resources management, marketing, and information technology.

21327 ■ "Take Control of Your Company's Finances" in *Green Industry Pro* (Vol. 23, March 2011, No. 3, pp. 24)
Pub: Cygnus Business Media
Ed: Gregg Wartgow. **Description:** Understanding that when certain leading indicators that affect the outcome of certain lagging indicators are aligned, companies will be able to take control of their firm's finances. Ways to improve the processes that drive financial performance for landscape firms are outlined.

21328 ■ "Technology and Returnable Asset Management" in *Canadian Electronics* (Vol. 23, February 2008, No. 1, pp. 6)
Pub: CLB Media Inc.
Ed: Mark Borkowski. **Description:** Peter Kastner, president of Vestigo Corporation, believes that public companies without an asset track, trace, and control system in place could face Sarbanes-Oakley liability if error-prone processes result to misstatements of asset inventory positions. He also thinks that the system can improve return on assets by increasing the utilization of returnables.

21329 ■ "Test Your Structural Integrity" in *Entrepreneur* (Vol. 37, August 2009, No. 8, pp. 60)
Pub: Entrepreneur Media, Inc.
Ed: Jennifer Lawler. **Description:** Tax considerations can be important when choosing a business structure. For example, profits are taxed to the corporation in a C corp while profits are taxed only once at an S corp or a limited liability company. Meeting a tax professional should be done prior to switching to a different structure.

21330 ■ "Throughput Metrics Meet Six Sigma" in *Management Accounting Quarterly* (Vol. 12, Spring 2011, No. 3, pp. 12)
Pub: Management Accounting Quarterly
Ed: Shaun Aghili. **Description:** Throughput accounting (TA) metrics can be combined with six sigma's DMAIC methodology and various time-tested analysis and measurement tools for added effectiveness in resolving resource constraint issues. The goal is to optimize not only the output of a specific department but that of the entire system, by implementing a cost accounting system that is conducive to system optimization while increasing product quality, process integrity, or ideally, both.

21331 ■ "ValienteHernandez Acquired" in *The Business Journal-Serving Greater Tampa Bay* (Vol. 28, September 12, 2008, No. 38, pp. 1)
Pub: American City Business Journals, Inc.
Ed: Alexis Muellner. **Description:** Minnesota accounting firm LarsonAllen LLP has acquired Florida-based ValienteHernandez PA, creating a company with 35 employees to be based in ValienteHernandez's newly built office in Tampa Bay Area. Other details about the merger are provided.

21332 ■ "Welcome Back" in *Canadian Business* (Vol. 82, April 27, 2009, No. 7, pp. 25)
Pub: Rogers Media
Ed: Sarka Halas. **Description:** Some Canadian companies such as Gennum Corporation have taken advantage of corporate sale-leasebacks to raise money at a time when credit is hard to acquire. Corporate sale-leasebacks allow companies to sell their property assets while remaining as tenants of the building. Sale-leasebacks allow firms to increase capital while avoiding the disruptions that may result with moving.

21333 ■ "Where Women Work" in *Marketing to Women* (Vol. 21, April 2008, No. 4, pp. 8)
Pub: EPM Communications, Inc.
Description: According to the U.S. Census Bureau, 60 percent of America's professional tax preparers are women. Also features additional trends concerning women in the workplace. Statistical data included.

21334 ■ *Working Papers, Chapters 1-14 for Needles/Powers/Crosson's Financial and Managerial Accounting*
Pub: Cengage South-Western
Ed: Belverd E. Needles, Marian Powers, Susan V. Crosson. **Released:** May 10, 2010. **Price:** $62.95. **Description:** Appropriate accounting forms for completing all exercises, problems and cases in the text are provided for financial management of a small company.

TRADE PERIODICALS

21335 ■ *Keep Up to Date on Accounts Payable*
Pub: Progressive Business Publications
Ed: Nathan Hall, Editor, nhall@pbp.com. **Released:** 23/year. **Price:** $230, individuals. **Description:** Supplies updates on state and local sales use taxes, plus IRS 1099 regulations and best practices in accounts payable. Recurring features include interviews, news of research, a calendar of events, and a column titled Sharpen Your Judgment.

VIDEOCASSETTES/ AUDIOCASSETTES

21336 ■ *CPE Network: Accounting and Auditing Report*
Bisk Education
9417 Princess Palm Ave.
Tampa, FL 33619
Free: 800-874-7877
Co. E-mail: info@bisk.com
URL: http://www.bisk.com
Released: 1994. **Price:** $799.00. **Description:** Outlines informaton on current industry issues, pronouncements, new standards, recent decisions, insider reports on exposure drafts, and other early indicators of upcoming changes in the accounting and auditing areas. Video newsletter published 11 times per year. **Availability:** VHS.

21337 ■ *Small Business Accounting Systems*
Instructional Video
2219 C St.
Lincoln, NE 68502
Ph:(402)475-6570
Free: 800-228-0164
Fax:(402)475-6500
Co. E-mail: feedback@insvideo.com
URL: http://www.insvideo.com
Price: $19.95. **Description:** Illustrates basic small business accounting, providing instruction on recording transactions, the balance sheet, and the income statement. **Availability:** VHS.

TRADE SHOWS AND CONVENTIONS

21338 ■ National Society of Public Accountants Annual Convention
National Society of Public Accountants
1010 N. Fairfax St.
Alexandria, VA 22314-1574
Ph:(703)549-6400
Free: 800-966-6679
Fax:(703)549-2984
Co. E-mail: NSA@wizard.net
URL: http://www.nsa.org
Released: Annual. **Principal Exhibits:** Exhibits related to public accounting.

CONSULTANTS

21339 ■ American Topical Association, Americana Unit
17 Peckham Rd.
Poughkeepsie, NY 12603-2018
Ph:(845)452-2126
Fax:(781)459-0392
Co. E-mail: info@americanaunit.org
URL: http://www.americanaunit.org
Contact: Dennis M. Dengel, Treasurer
E-mail: dennisdengel@yahoo.com
Scope: Philatelic club devoted to the collecting of stamps, covers and other philatelic material related to the topic of Americana. **Publications:** "The Tragedy at the World Trade Center," 2001; "Abraham Lincoln on Worldwide Stamps," 1998; "George Washington on Stamps," 1997; "J F K & his Family on Stamps," 1995; "Ronald Wilson Reagan and First Lady Nancy Reagan on World Wide Stamps"; "The Roosevelt's on Worldwide Stamps"; "St. Thomas & Prince Islands"; "The SS President Adams"; "Collecting the Presidents"; "Americana New Issues Listing".

21340 ■ Arnold S. Goldin & Associates Inc.
5030 Champion Blvd., Ste. G-6231
Boca Raton, FL 33496
Ph:(561)994-5810
Fax:(561)994-5860
Co. E-mail: arnold@goldin.com
URL: http://www.goldin.com
Contact: Arnold S. Goldin, Principle
E-mail: arnold@goldin.com
Scope: An accounting and management consulting firm. Serves clients worldwide. Provides management services. Handles monthly write-ups and tax returns.

21341 ■ Avery, Cooper & Co.
4918-50th St.
PO Box 1620
Yellowknife, NT, Canada X1A 2P2
Ph:(867)873-3441
Free: 800-661-0787

Fax:(867)873-2353
Co. E-mail: gerry@averyco.nt.ca
URL: http://www.averyco.nt.ca
Contact: Theresa Slator, Mgr
E-mail: theresa@atsaveryco.nt.ca
Scope: Accounting and management consulting firm. **Seminars:** Sage Software Training. **Special Services:** ACCPAC Plus; Sage Accpac ERP.

21342 ■ Business Learning Center
2206 SE Washington St.
Portland, OR 97222
Ph:(503)653-7108
Fax:(503)786-6064
Co. E-mail: blcmay19@msn.com
Contact: Richard J. Wood, Owner
Scope: Provides every type of business service for small businesses, including accounting and tax services, business forms and systems, and investment counseling.

21343 ■ Century Business Services Inc.
6050 Oak Tree Blvd. S, Ste. 500
Cleveland, OH 44131-6951
Ph:(216)525-1947
Fax:(216)447-9007
Co. E-mail: info@cbiz.com
URL: http://www.cbiz.com
Contact: Steven L. Gerard, CEO
E-mail: gdufour@cbiz.com
Scope: A business consulting and tax services firm providing financial, consulting, tax and business services through seven groups: Financial management, tax advisory, construction and real estate, health-care, litigation support, capital resource and CEO outsource. **Publications:** "FAS 154: Changes in the Way We Report Changes," 2006; "Equity-Based Compensation: How Much Does it Really Cost Your Business," 2006; "Preventing Fraud - Tips for Nonprofit Organizations"; "Today's Workforce and Nonprofit Organizations: Meeting a Critical Need"; "IRS Highlights Top Seven Form 990 Errors". **Seminars:** Health Care - What the Future Holds; Consumer Driven Health Plans; Executive Plans; Health Savings Accounts; Healthy Wealthy and Wise; Legislative Update; Medicare Part D; Retirement Plans.

21344 ■ Charles A. Krueger
1908 Innsbrooke Dr.
Sun Prairie, WI 53590
Ph:(608)837-5247
Fax:(608)825-7538
Co. E-mail: ckrueger@bus.wisc.edu
E-mail: ckrueger@bus.wisc.edu
Scope: Financial management consultant specializing in professional education programs for managers and executives. Programs include: Finance and accounting for nonfinancial executives, financial management for executives, and developing and using financial information for decision making. Major industries served include manufacturing, service, healthcare and insurance. **Publications:** "Monitoring Financial Results, chapter in Corporate Controllers Manual," Warren Gorham and Lamont. **Seminars:** Finance and Accounting for Nonfinancial Executives; Financial Management for Health Care Executives; Financial Management for Insurance Executives; Direct Costing; Flexible Budgeting; Contribution Reporting; Building Value and Driving Profits - A Business Simulation.

21345 ■ CheckMark Software Inc.
724 Whalers Way, Bldg. H, Ste. 101
Fort Collins, CO 80525-7578
Ph:(970)225-0522
Free: 800-444-9922
Fax:(970)225-0611
Co. E-mail: info@checkmark.com
URL: http://www.checkmark.com
Contact: Terry Stone, Dir of Sales
E-mail: rgilmore@checkmark.com
Scope: Developer of accounting software tools for small businesses and provides fast, easy to use, affordable accounting and payroll solutions to small and medium sized businesses. Provides payroll software and multiledger integrated accounting software. **Special Services:** MultiLedger™; Payroll.

21346 ■ Comprehensive Professional Management Inc.
222 E Dundee Rd.
Wheeling, IL 60090-3009
Ph:(847)520-1301
Fax:(847)520-0372
Co. E-mail: bob@cpmincfs.com
Contact: Kathy Rathunde, Principle
E-mail: mkstumpf@atsaol.com
Scope: Services include accounting, financial planning, litigation support, pension profit sharing administration, practice surveys, professional corporation issues, retirement and estate planning and tax advice.

21347 ■ DacEasy Inc.
1715 N Brown Rd.
Lawrenceville, GA 30043
Ph:(770)492-6414
Free: 800-322-3279
Fax:(770)724-2874
Co. E-mail: sales@daceasy.com
URL: http://www.daceasy.com
Contact: Marchell Gillis
E-mail: marchell.gillis@sage.com
Scope: Develops an accounting system for small businesses that integrates accounting, invoicing, payroll, communications, and management software into a single package. **Seminars:** DacEasy Training. **Special Services:** DacEasy.

21348 ■ Donald C. Wright
3906 Lawndale Ln. N
Plymouth, MN 55446-2940
Ph:(763)478-6999
Co. E-mail: donaldwright@compuserve.com
URL: http://www.donaldwrightcpa.com
Contact: Donald C. Wright, President
E-mail: donaldwright@compuserve.com
Scope: Offers accounting, tax, and small business consulting services. Services include cash flow and budgeting analysis; financial forecast and projections; financial statements; reviews and compilations; tax planning, tax preparation; IRS and state/local representation; international taxation; estate, gift and trust tax return preparation; benefit plan services; business succession planning; estate planning; financial planning; management advisory services, pension and profit sharing plans, retirement planning, expert witness services and employee benefits plans. Serves individuals, corporations, partnerships, and non-profit organizations. **Seminars:** Qualified pension plans and employee welfare benefit plans.

21349 ■ Dorn & Associates Inc.
8506 Bass Lake Rd.
Minneapolis, MN 55428-5304
Ph:(763)533-7689
Fax:(763)533-1143
Contact: Chad L. Dorn, Vice President
E-mail: chad@dorn-associates.com
Scope: Services include accounting, marketing, employment partnership, new doctor agreements, personnel issues and human resources assessment, practice management, practice merger acquisition sale and liquidation, practice surveys and valuation, staff development and training.

21350 ■ Doyle & Dulaney
41 Sutter St.
San Francisco, CA 94104-4903
Ph:(415)398-3140
Contact: Thomas Doyle, Director
Scope: Business and financial consultants specializing in manual and computer bookkeeping and accounting systems. Expertise in fund accounting, business methods and procedures, reports and other written communications such as manuals, handbooks, and procedure guides. Also skilled in forms design, records management, and instructional material development. Serving nonprofit organizations, the professions, and smaller service-oriented businesses.

21351 ■ Earl Rodney CPA.
5787 W Sunrise Blvd.
Plantation, FL 33313-6269
Ph:(954)583-3635
Fax:(954)321-0532
Co. E-mail: earl3@usa.com
E-mail: earl3@usa.com
Scope: Business and finance consultant serving all industries, nonprofit, and government in Florida. Activities include public accounting, auditing, taxation, expert witness, management advisory services, governmental audits, nonprofit audits, and financial statement disclosures. Also conducts peer reviews of CPA firms. **Publications:** "Depreciation in the Practical Accountant". **Seminars:** Off site Peer Reviews; Classes in accounting disclosures and in how to audit non profit organizations.

21352 ■ Frankel and Topche P.C.
1700 Galloping Hill Rd.
Kenilworth, NJ 07033
Ph:(908)298-7700
Fax:(908)298-7701
Co. E-mail: info@frankelandtopche.com
URL: http://www.frankelandtopche.com
Contact: Aaron Saiewitz, Principle
E-mail: gtopche@atsfrankelandtopche.com
Scope: Offers financial consulting for closely held businesses. Assists in mergers and acquisitions, tax planning, strategic business planning, family succession planning, accounting, auditing, and obtaining financing. The firm serves small businesses in the service, retail, wholesale, and manufacturing industries. Specializes in real estate, lumber and building materials, and service businesses. **Seminars:** Annual Tax Seminar.

21353 ■ Gates, Moore & Co.
3340 Peachtree Rd. NE, Tower Pl. 100, Ste. 600
Atlanta, GA 30326
Ph:(404)266-9876
Fax:(404)266-2669
Co. E-mail: postmaster@gatesmoore.com
URL: http://www.gatesmoore.com
Contact: Lori Foley, Principle
E-mail: lfoley@atsgatesmoore.com
Scope: Firm provides management consulting and accounting services to medical practices, hospital owned practices, staff model managed care organizations, IPAs, MSOs, PO, and PHOs. Services include comprehensive operational assessments, managed care negotiations, practice start-ups and expansion, development of MSOs, strategic planning, mergers, cost accounting analysis, practice valuations, income division plans, medical record documentation and coding reviews, expert witness testimony, patient satisfaction surveys and corporate compliance planning. **Publications:** "Practicing Medicine in the 21st Century"; "Physicians, Dentists and Veterinarians"; "Insurance Portability and Accountability Act Privacy Manual"; "How To Guide for your Medical Practice and Health Insurance Portability and Accountability Act Security Manual"; "A How To Guide for your Medical Practice"; "Cost Analysis Made Simple: A Step by Step Guide to Using Cost Accounting to Ensure Practice Profitability"; "Cost Cutting Strategies for Medical Practices"; "Cost Cutting Strategies for Medical Practices"; "Getting the Jump on Year-End Tax Planning"; "New 401(k) Safe Harbor Option: Increased Opportunities for the Physician and Practice"; "Not All Tax News is Bad News"; "Shareholder Agreements: Identifying and Addressing Five Risk Areas"; "Surprise - Your Practice has a Deferred Income Tax Liability". **Seminars:** Documenting and Billing High Risk Codes, 2010; Current Challenges in Ob/Gyn Recruiting, 2010; Planning for Physician Wind-down & Retirement, 2010; HITECH "How To" - Opportunities & Risks, 2010; Pediatric Coding and Audits; Recruiting and Retaining Physicians; How to Prepare for the Recovery Audit Contractors - RAC, 2010; Meaningful Use Rule, 2010; The Revenue Stream in Practice, Apr, 2008; Improving Efficiencies in a Small Family Medicine Practice, Oct, 2007; Using Compensation Models to Improve Performance, Sep, 2007; The Financial Side of Personnel Management, Sep, 2007; Pay for Performance-Is it Really Contracting for Quality?, New York State Ophthalmological Society, Sep, 2007; Beyond the Class Action Settlement Payments-Looking Prospectively at Managed Care Companies Behavior, New York State Ophthalmological Society, Sep, 2007; Protecting your clients from Embezzlement, Jun, 2007; What P4P Means to Your Medical Practice, May, 2007; Finance for the

Practicing Physician, May, 2007; Trashing, Dipping and Ghosts in Medical Practices: Protecting your clients from Embezzlement, Apr, 2006.

21354 ■ Horwath International Association
420 Lexington Ave., Ste. 526
New York, NY 10170-0526
Ph:(212)808-2000
Fax:(212)808-2020
Co. E-mail: contactus@horwath.com
URL: http://www.horwath.com
Contact: Mark Hildebrand, CEO
E-mail: mhildebrand@atshorwath.com
Scope: Services include: Accounting, auditing, tax and management consulting. Provides innovative business solutions in the area of assurance, business services, consulting, corporate finance, risk management, tax and technology. **Publications:** "Does Your Business Have an E-Commerce Strategy"; "Americas Tax Facts," 2007; "Caring Sharing Investing Growing: The Story of Horwath International," Nov, 2006; "How To Franchise Internationally"; "International Tax Planning Manual: Expatriates and Migrants"; "Americas Tax Facts 2007"; "European and Middle East Tax Facts 2008"; "International Offshore Financial Services"; "International Tax Planning Manual: Corporations"; "Asia or Pacific Tax News 2008: Issue 2"; "FOMB: A Quiz for Business Owners". **Seminars:** Demand Creation Training, Dec, 2006; Marketing, Dec, 2006.

21355 ■ Kroll Zolfo Cooper L.L.C.
777 S Figueroa St., 24th Fl.
Los Angeles, CA 90017
Ph:(212)561-4000
Fax:(212)948-4226
Co. E-mail: mwyse@krollzolfocooper.com
URL: http://www.krollzolfocooper.com
Contact: Stephen F. Cooper, Principal
E-mail: scooper@kroll.com
Scope: Firm provides accounting consulting services to businesses. Specializes in restructuring and turnaround consulting; interim and crisis management; performance improvement; creditor advisory; cross-border restructuring and corporate finance.

21356 ■ Larry J. Anderson Insurance
1200 35th St., Ste. 206-4
West Des Moines, IA 50266-1958
Ph:(515)221-1973
Fax:(515)221-0074
Co. E-mail: andy4021@aol.com
Contact: Larry J. Anderson, Owner
E-mail: andy4021@aol.com
Scope: Offers business consulting services including temporary technical aid in accounting, turn around and cash management, and bail-out assistance. Also provides operations research, models, forecasting, project scheduling, and economic forecasting services. Provides assistance in group health insurance in both fully insured groups and self-funded groups.

21357 ■ Marion S. Rice
5281 Pinnacle Rd.
Dayton, OH 45417
Ph:(937)859-7763
Fax:(937)847-0046
Scope: Provides consultation to individuals and small businesses on tax management and bookkeeping activities.

21358 ■ Mitchell & Titus L.L.P.
1101 New York Ave. NW
Washington, DC 20005
Ph:(212)709-4500
Fax:(212)709-4680
Co. E-mail: newyork.office@mitchelltitus.com
URL: http://www.mitchelltitus.com
Contact: Ronald Benjamin, Partner
E-mail: ronald.benjamin@mitchelltitus.com
Scope: Firm provides assurance, advisory business services, transaction support and tax services. Specializes in auditing and accounting services, tax planning and preparation services management and business advisory services. **Publications:** "ITEM Club Budget preview report," 2010; "Year end personal planning," 2010; "Steering towards the future using the Pre Budget Report to help the UK rebound," 2009; "Be careful what you wish for," 2009; "Year end personal planning," 2009. **Seminars:** Budget Seminar 2010, Mar, 2010.

21359 ■ Penny & Associates Inc.
166 Water St., Ste. 3
Port Perry, ON, Canada L9L 1C4
Ph:(905)985-0712
Free: 800-699-6190
Fax:(905)985-9461
Co. E-mail: mail@pennyinc.com
URL: http://www.pennyinc.com
Contact: Tracey Hepburn, Principle
E-mail: sbaylis@atspennyinc.com
Scope: Accounting and management firm that offers accounting and business solutions. Assistance in preparation of financial reports, reconciliation of inter company accounts, foreign currency transactions, investment trades and auditor working paper files and assistance in developing accounting policies and procedures. Provides part-time controllers to prepare financial statements, cash flow management, credit negotiations and give financial management advice or oversee accounting staff. **Seminars:** Quick Books, Aug, 2001; How to Stand Up to People Without Being a Jerk; How to Build Influence and Rapport With Almost Anyone; Dealing With Dissatisfied, Different and Difficult People; Effective Public Speaking; How to Incorporate Yourself; Company Perks: Attracting & Retaining Good People; FIRST AID. **Special Services:** Quickbooks[R].

21360 ■ The Stillwater Group
920 E Shore Dr.
PO Box 168
Stillwater, NJ 07875
Ph:(973)579-7080
Fax:(973)579-7970
Co. E-mail: education@stillwater.com
URL: http://www.stillwater.com
Contact: David Woodward, COO
E-mail: gfinch@atsstillwater.com
Scope: Provides strategic planning, budget and financial management, process improvement, organizational design and assessment, and college student services operations. **Publications:** "Integrated Resource Planning (Irp)," Business Officer Magazine, 2005; "The Economic Risk Conundrum," University Business Magazine; "Revenue Analysis and Tuition Strategy"; "Managing Advancement Services: Processes and Paper".

COMPUTERIZED DATABASES

21361 ■ *e-JEP*
American Economic Association
2014 Broadway, Ste. 305
Nashville, TN 37203
Ph:(615)322-2595
Fax:(615)343-7590
Co. E-mail: aeainfo@vanderbilt.edu
URL: http://www.vanderbilt.edu/AEA
Description: Contains the full text of the *Journal of Economic Perspectives.* Includes articles, reports, and other material for economists and economics professionals. Features analysis and critiques of recent research findings and developments in public policy. Includes coverage of global economics issues and developments. Features articles on education in economics, employment issues for economists, and other issues of concern to professional economists. **Availability:** Online: American Economic Association, Thomson Reuters; CD-ROM: American Economic Association. **Type:** Full text.

COMPUTER SYSTEMS/ SOFTWARE

21362 ■ Aatrix Top Pay
Aatrix Software
2100 Library Cir.
Grand Forks, ND 58201
Ph:(701)746-6017
Free: 800-426-0854
Fax:(701)787-0594
URL: http://www.aatrix.com
Price: Contact Aatrix. **Description:** Handles payroll calculations and tax deductions for both salaried and hourly employees.

21363 ■ Argos Software–ABECAS Insight
Argos Computers
5737 N Fresno St.
Fresno, CA 93710
Ph:(559)227-1000
Fax:(559)227-9644
Co. E-mail: info@argosoftware.com
URL: http://www.argosoftware.com
Description: Available for MS-DOS operating system. Payroll system for agricultural employees.

LIBRARIES

21364 ■ Buffalo & Erie County Public Library–Business, Science & Technology
1 Lafayette Sq.
Buffalo, NY 14203
Ph:(716)858-8900
Fax:(716)858-6211
Co. E-mail: muellern@buffalolib.org
URL: http://www.buffalolib.org
Contact: Nancy Mueller, Div.Mgr.
Scope: Investments, real estate, economics, marketing, engineering, computer science, technology, medical information for laymen, consumer information, automotive repair. **Services:** Interlibrary loan; copying; Library open to the public. **Holdings:** 312,916 books; 60,516 bound periodical volumes. **Subscriptions:** 2908 journals and other serials; 4 newspapers.

21365 ■ Carnegie Library of Pittsburgh–Downtown & Business
612 Smithfield St.
Pittsburgh, PA 15222-2506
Ph:(412)281-7141
Fax:(412)471-1724
Co. E-mail: business@carnegielibrary.org
Contact: Karen Rossi, Br.Mgr.
Scope: Investments, small business, entrepreneurship, management, marketing, insurance, advertising, personal finance, accounting, real estate, job and career, International business. **Services:** Library open to the public. **Holdings:** 13,000 business volumes; VF materials; microfilm; looseleaf services; AV materials.

21366 ■ Napier University–Craiglockhart Campus Library
219 Colinton Rd.
Edinburgh EH14 1DJ, United Kingdom
Ph:(44)131 4554260
Fax:(44)131 4554276
Co. E-mail: craiglockhartlc@napier.ac.uk
URL: http://staff.napier.ac.uk/services/library/about/Pages/default.aspx
Contact: Catherine Walker, Campus Lib.Mgr.
Scope: Accounting, economics, finance, hospitality and tourism, languages, law, management, marketing, statistics. **Holdings:** Books; videos.

21367 ■ Nichols College–Conant Library
124 Center Rd.
Dudley, MA 01571
Ph:(508)213-2222
Free: 877-266-2681
Co. E-mail: reference@nichols.edu
URL: http://www.nichols.edu/library
Contact: Jim Douglas, Lib.Dir.
Scope: Management, advertising, finance and accounting, small business, marketing, taxation, economics, International trade, humanities. **Services:** Interlibrary loan; copying; information service to groups; document delivery; Library open to Dudley and Webster residents. **Holdings:** 48,000 volumes; 1677 audio/visual titles; 3804 reels of microfilm. **Subscriptions:** 278 journals and electronic subscriptions.

21368 ■ University of Kentucky–Business & Economics Information Center
B&E Info. Ctr., Rm. 116
335-BA Gatton College of Business & Economics
Lexington, KY 40506-0034
Ph:(859)257-5868
Fax:(859)323-9496
Co. E-mail: mrazeeq@pop.uk.edu
URL: http://www.uky.edu//Provost/academicprograms.html
Contact: Michael A. Razeeq, Bus.Ref.Libn.

Scope: Business, economics, business management, marketing, finance, accounting. **Services:** Library open to the public for reference use only.

Agribusiness

START-UP INFORMATION

21369 ■ "Drink Up" in *Black Enterprise* (Vol. 38, March 2008, No. 8, pp. 50)
Pub: Earl G. Graves Publishing Co. Inc.
Ed: Tennille H. Robinson. **Description:** Advice is given to an individual seeking to start a natural juice small business, along with information for finding a bottling company.

21370 ■ "Fixing Up the Area: Leo Piatz Opens General Repair Business" in *The Dickinson Press* (November 16, 2010)
Pub: Dickinson Press
Ed: Ashley Martin. **Description:** Profile of Leo Piatz, owner of Leo's Repair in Dickinson, North Dakota; Piatz provides welding and fabricating services to farmers and ranchers in the area.

21371 ■ "Local Flavor" in *Entrepreneur* (Vol. 35, November 2007, No. 11, pp. 110)
Pub: Entrepreneur Media Inc.
Ed: Nichole L. Torres. **Description:** Local food products are growing in the market today as consumers are becoming interested in where their food comes; you can start a business by investigating the kinds of foods popular in your region.

21372 ■ *Starting and Running Your Own Horse Business*
Pub: Storey Publishing, LLC
Ed: Mary Ashby McDonald. **Released:** November 1, 2009. **Price:** $19.95. **Description:** Insight into starting and running a successful equestrian business is given. The book covers safety, tips for operating a riding school or horse camp, strategies for launching a carriage business, along with tax and insurance advice.

ASSOCIATIONS AND OTHER ORGANIZATIONS

21373 ■ ACDI/VOCA
50 F St. NW, Ste. 1075
Washington, DC 20001
Ph:(202)469-6000
Free: 800-929-8622
Fax:(202)469-6257
Co. E-mail: webmaster@acdivoca.org
URL: http://www.acdivoca.org
Contact: Carl H. Leonard, Pres./CEO
Description: Agricultural cooperatives, agribusinesses, farmers' organizations, and farm credit banks in the United States. Assists in organizing and providing technical assistance for cooperatives and agribusinesses in developing countries, usually under contract with the Agency for International Development. Advises governmental and other agencies in agricultural marketing, supply, and credit; carries out feasibility studies for specific agribusiness ventures; arranges formal and on-the-job training in cooperative practices for government officials, cooperative functionaries, and rural leaders; conducts short- and long-term technical assistance programs. Conducts extensive global volunteer programs that introduce American agricultural and financial know-how to developing economies, an exchange that furthers international cooperation and fellowship and promotes global business. Invites resumes of U.S. agriculture, business, and finance experts who are willing to serve overseas on short-term assignments.
.

21374 ■ Agri-Energy Roundtable
PO Box 5565
Washington, DC 20016
Ph:(202)887-0528
Co. E-mail: agenergy@aol.com
URL: http://www.agribusinesscouncil.org/aer.htm
Contact: Nicholas E. Hollis, Exec. Dir.
Description: International association that includes oil company executives and leaders of international agribusinesses. Serves as an information clearinghouse to improve dialogue on cooperative energy-agricultural development among the industrialized and developing nations. Attempts to bridge the gap on food and energy issues through cooperation between the oil exporting countries and western technology in the private sector. Sponsors trade missions. **Publications:** *Agri-Energy Report* (quarterly); *Agri-Enterprise in Development: New Leadership and Technology for Food Security*; *Beyond Food and Energy Security: New Agribusiness Markets and Technologies*; *Food and Energy Security: Managing the New Technologies*; *Managing Agro-Economic Peacekeeping: Trade and Development Realities for Food Security*; *Regional Africa Bulletin* .

21375 ■ Agribusiness Council
3312 Porter St. NW
Washington, DC 20008
Ph:(202)296-4563
Fax:(202)887-9178
Co. E-mail: agenergy@aol.com
URL: http://agribusinesscouncil.org
Contact: Nicholas E. Hollis, Pres./CEO
Description: Business organizations, universities and foundations, and individuals interested in stimulating and encouraging agribusiness in cooperation with the public sector, both domestic and international. Seeks to aid in relieving the problems of world food supply. Supports coordinated agribusiness in the developing nations by identifying opportunities for investment of U.S. private-sector technology management and financial resources. Advises agribusiness leaders about selected developing countries with good investment climates; brings potential investment opportunities to the attention of U.S. agribusiness firms; coordinates informal network of state agribusiness councils and grassroots organization; encourages companies to make investment feasibility studies in agribusiness; provides liaison and information exchange between agribusiness firms, governments, international organizations, universities, foundations, and other groups with the objective of identifying areas of cooperation and mutual interest; encourages projects geared to the conversion of subsistence farming to intensive, higher income agriculture in order to bring the world's rural populations, wherever feasible, into the market economy. .

21376 ■ Agricultural Groups Concerned About Resources and the Environment
100 Stone Rd. W, Ste. 106
Guelph, ON, Canada N1G 5L3
Ph:(519)837-1326
Fax:(519)837-3209
Co. E-mail: agcare@agcare.org
URL: http://www.agcare.org
Contact: Paul Wettlaufer, Chm.
Description: Farmers and agricultural industries. Promotes environmentally sustainable food production. Facilitates communication among members; serves as a clearinghouse on sustainable agriculture. **Publications:** *AGCare Update* (quarterly); *Project Report* (periodic).

21377 ■ American Brahmousin Council
PO Box 88
Whitesboro, TX 76273
Ph:(903)564-3995
Co. E-mail: info@brahmousin.org
URL: http://www.brahmousin.org
Contact: Bob Cummins, Interim Dir.
Description: Breeders of Brahmousin cattle. **Publications:** *Brahmousin Connection* (quarterly).

21378 ■ American Society of Agricultural Consultants
N78W14573 Appleton Ave., No. 287
Menomonee Falls, WI 53051
Ph:(262)253-6902
Fax:(262)253-6903
Co. E-mail: cmerry@countryside-marketing.com
URL: http://www.agconsultants.org
Contact: Paige Gilligan, Pres.
Description: Members are independent, full-time consultants in many specialty areas serving agribusiness interests throughout the world. Strives to maintain high standards of ethics and competence in the consulting field. Provides referral service to agribusiness interests seeking consultants having specific knowledge, experience, and expertise. Maintains liaison with governmental agencies utilizing consultants and with legislative and administrative acts affecting consultants. .

21379 ■ Canadian Consulting Agrologists Association
510, 5920-1A St. SW
Calgary, AB, Canada T2H 0G3
Fax:(403)255-4592
Co. E-mail: terry.betker@mnp.ca
URL: http://www.ccaa.bz
Contact: Terry Betker, Pres.
Description: Agrologists and other agricultural consultants. Seeks to advance the science and practice of agriculture; promotes professional development of members. Makes available support and services to farmers; conducts research and educational programs.

21380 ■ Canadian Society for Bioengineering–La Societe Canadienne de Genie Agroalimentaire et de Bioingenierie
PO Box 23101
RPO McGillivray
Winnipeg, MB, Canada R3T 5S3

Ph:(204)233-1881
Fax:(204)231-8282
Co. E-mail: bioeng@shaw.ca
URL: http://www.bioeng.ca
Contact: Ali Madani, Sec./Mgr.
Description: Individuals engaged in the practice of agricultural and biosystems engineering; agricultural and biosystems engineering educators and students. Seeks to advance the study and practice of agricultural engineering and bioengineering. Conducts research; makes available continuing professional development programs for members. **Publications:** *Canadian Biosystems Engineering*; *Perspectives* (quarterly).

21381 ■ Communicating for America
PO Box 677
Fergus Falls, MN 56538-0677
Ph:(218)739-3241
Free: 800-432-3276
Fax:(218)739-3832
Co. E-mail: caep@caep.org
URL: http://www.communicatingforamerica.org
Contact: Wayne Nelson, Pres.
Description: Promotes the general health, well being and advancement of people in agriculture and agribusiness. Participates in federal and state issues that affect the quality of life in rural America and provides members with a variety of money-saving benefit programs. Conducts grants program, research on rural issues, and international exchange programs with an agricultural focus. **Publications:** *CA Highlights* (monthly); *CAEP In Touch* (quarterly); *Smart Choices* (quarterly).

21382 ■ National Council of Agricultural Employers
8233 Old Courthouse Rd., Ste. 200
Vienna, VA 22182
Ph:(703)790-9039
Co. E-mail: matt@ncaeonline.org
URL: http://www.ncaeonline.org
Contact: Frank Gasperini CAE, Exec. VP
Description: Growers of agricultural commodities who employ hand labor for field crops; processors and handlers, farm and commodity organizations, and others whose business is related to labor-intensive farming in the U.S. Aims to improve the position and image of U.S. agriculture as an employer of labor and to facilitate and encourage the establishment and maintenance of an adequate force of agricultural employees. Serves as clearinghouse for exchange of information on labor supply, length of employment, and other conditions of work. Does not engage in recruitment, housing, supplying, or employment of agricultural workers, and does not represent its members or others in negotiating with labor unions or other organizations, or in agreeing to any contract relating to hours, wages, or working conditions. Keeps member abreast of national legislation affecting agricultural labor. .

21383 ■ Organization for Competitive Markets
PO Box 6486
Lincoln, NE 68506
Ph:(402)817-4443
Fax:(360)237-8784
Co. E-mail: ocm@competitivemarkets.com
URL: http://www.competitivemarkets.com
Contact: Randy Stevenson, Pres.
Description: Works for increased competition and protection for the agricultural marketplace. Works against "abuse of corporate power and consolidation of the agricultural market". **Publications:** *OCM Newsletter* .

21384 ■ United Agribusiness League
54 Corporate Park
Irvine, CA 92606-5105
Ph:(949)975-1424
Free: 800-223-4590
Fax:(949)975-1573
Co. E-mail: info@aul.org
URL: http://www.ual.org
Contact: Richard Schmidt, Pres./CEO
Description: Agricultural industries and businesses. Promotes the development and common interest of the agricultural industry. Works to coordinate members' activities to advance agribusiness in general; provides services and benefits to enable members to realize greater productive efficiency. Serves as a clearinghouse on international agribusiness. Provides employee health care plans and other insurance to agribusinesses. **Publications:** *Ag Crime Prevention Brochures*; *Crime Prevention* (quarterly); *Healthy Times* (monthly).

REFERENCE WORKS

21385 ■ "14 Tips to Tune Up Your Self-Propelled Sprayer" in *Farm Industry News* (November 3, 2010)
Pub: Penton Business Media Inc.
Description: Tips for maintaining a self-propelled sprayer used to apply farm chemicals and fertilizers are listed.

21386 ■ "100-BU. Beans" in *Farm Industry News* (Vol. 42, January 1, 2009, No. 1)
Pub: Penton Media, Inc.
Ed: Lynn Grooms. **Description:** Demand for soybeans has increased and growers are seeing an increase in yields as well due to breeders that are using molecular-assisted selection; other aspects of the soybean market are presented.

21387 ■ "100 Percent Equipment Tax Deduction Deadline Nears" in *Farm Industry News* (December 1, 2010)
Pub: Penton Business Media Inc.
Description: Farmers and small business owners are warned that the first deadline for taking advantage of the tax code provision that allows them to deduct the full purchase price of qualified capital expenditures up to $500,000 during the tax year is nearing.

21388 ■ "$550 Cash Rent on 330 Acres in Iowa" in *Farm Industry News* (November 30, 2011)
Pub: Penton Business Media Inc.
Ed: Karen McMahon. **Description:** A farmer in Iowa accepted a bid for $550/acre for his 330-acre farm for one year. The next closest bid was $350/acre. This rent will amount to more than the farmer paid for all of his land in the 1960s and 1970s. High rents are not alarming because of the high profitability farmers are currently receiving from crops.

21389 ■ "2011 FinOvation Awards" in *Farm Industry News* (January 19, 2011)
Pub: Penton Business Media Inc.
Ed: Jodie Wehrspann. **Description:** The 2011 FinOvation Award winners are announced, covering new products that growers need for corn and soybean crops. Winners range from small turbines and a fuel-efficient pickup to a Class 10 combine and drought-tolerant hybrids.

21390 ■ *Ag Equipment Power*
Pub: Clintron Publishers
Contact: Craig Withers, Editor & Publisher
E-mail: craig@agpowermag.com
Released: Monthly, Latest edition 2010. **Price:** $12, individuals. **Publication Includes:** Featuring news agricultural equipment and technology for growers in Washington, Idaho, and Oregon. List of about 750 manufacturers, distributors, dealers, and suppliers of new and used farm machinery and chemicals; coverage limited to Washington, Oregon, and Idaho. **Entries Include:** Company name, address, product lines. **Arrangement:** Classified by for subscribers.

21391 ■ "Ag Firms Harvest Revenue Growth" in *The Business Journal-Serving Metropolitan Kansas City* (Vol. 26, July 18, 2008, No. 45, pp. 1)
Pub: American City Business Journals, Inc.
Ed: Steve Vockrodt. **Description:** Five of the biggest agricultural companies in the Kansas City area, except one, reported multibillion-dollar revenue increases in 2007. The companies, which include Lansing Trade Group, posted a combined $9.5 billion revenue growth. The factors that affected the revenue increase in the area's agricultural companies, such as prices and high demand, are also examined.

21392 ■ "Ag Officials Employ Preventive Pest Control" in *Yakima Herald-Republic* (June 24, 2011)
Pub: Yakima Herald-Republic
Ed: Ross Courtney. **Description:** Washington State Department of Agriculture is placing vineyard traps for the European grapevine moth, an invasive species whose larvae eat grape buds and fruit clusters, thus exposing the vines to diseases that could destroy them.

21393 ■ *Agri Marketing—Marketing Services Guide Issue*
Pub: Doane Agricultural Services
Contact: William Schuermann, VP, Ag Svcs.
E-mail: bschuermann@doane.com
Released: Annual, latest edition Oct 2004. **Publication Includes:** Lists over 1400 top agricultural companies in the United States, leading agricultural advertisers (for past five years), marketing services firms (including public relations, photography, editorial, art and graphics, audiovisual, marketing research, marketing consultants), and United States and Canadian radio and television broadcasting stations, advertising and public relations agencies, network programming, and publications. Agriculture-related associations are included. **Entries Include:** For leading companies—Logo, name, address, phone, names of key personnel, products, marketing area, fiscal year, name and city of advertising and/or public relations agency handling account. For leading print advertisers—Company name, address, phone, key personnel, publication unit, sales representative firm, full-page space and cost for advertising. For agencies—Company name, address, name and phone of contact, year established, total agency billings, breakdown of billings by type of activity fo **Arrangement:** Alphabetical. **Indexes:** Service company's service, publication location.

21394 ■ *Agri Marketing—The Top 50*
Pub: Doane Agricultural Services
Contact: Bill Schuermann, Editorial Dir., Publisher
Released: Annual, April or May. **Publication Includes:** List of the top 50 U.S. and Canadian advertising agencies and public relations firms, chosen on the basis of agricultural business income. **Entries Include:** Agency name, location, income for agricultural accounts in most recent year, branch offices, major clients served. **Arrangement:** Alphabetical.

21395 ■ "Agribusiness: How to Get Rich in Farming" in *Canadian Business* (Vol. 80, January 29, 2007, No. 3, pp. 42)
Pub: Rogers Media
Ed: Peter Shawn Taylor. **Description:** The trends pertaining to the income of Canadian farmers are examined. The methods of increasing the profits of Canadian agribusinesses are discussed.

21396 ■ "Agricharts Launches New Mobile App for Ag Market" in *Farm Industry News* (December 1, 2011)
Pub: Penton Business Media Inc.
Description: AgriCharts provides market data, agribusiness Website hosting and technology solutions for the agricultural industry. AgriCharts is a division of Barchart.com Inc. and announced the release of a new mobile applications that offers real-time or delayed platform for viewing quotes, charts and analysis of grains, livestock and other commodity markets.

21397 ■ "Allowing Ethanol Tax Incentive to Expire Would Risk Jobs, RFAas Dinneen Says" in *Farm Industry News* (November 3, 2010)
Pub: Penton Business Media Inc.
Description: Jobs would be at risk if the ethanol tax incentive expires.

21398 ■ "Alternative Energy is a Major Topic at Agritechnica 2011" in *Farm Industry News* (November 16, 2011)
Pub: Penton Business Media Inc.
Ed: Mark Moore. **Description:** Sustainable agricultural systems were a hot topic at this year's Agritechnia 2011, held in Germany. Germany is a leader in the development of on-farm biogas systems.

21399 ■ "Apples, Decoded: WSU Scientist Unraveling the Fruit's Genetics" in *Puget Sound Business Journal* (Vol. 29, September 5, 2008, No. 20)
Pub: American City Business Journals
Ed: Clay Holtzman. **Description:** Washington State University researcher is working to map the apple's genome in order to gain information about how the fruit grows, looks and tastes. His work, funded by a research grant from the US Department of Agriculture and the Washington Apple Commission is crucial to improving the state's position as an apple-producing region.

21400 ■ "Art of the Online Deal" in *Farm Industry News* (March 25, 2011)
Pub: Penton Business Media Inc.
Description: Farmers share advice for shopping online for machinery; photos, clean equipment, the price, equipment details, and online sources topped their list.

21401 ■ "Atlantis-Resistant Figures on the Up" in *Farmer's Weekly* (March 28, 2008, No. 320)
Pub: Reed Business Information
Description: Researches are studying the number of cases in which blackgrass became resistant to Atlantis to determine if the resistance is due mainly to the ALS target-site mechanism or enhanced metabolism.

21402 ■ "Autumn Rat Control Essential for Poultry Units" in *Poultry World* (Vol. 165, September 2011, No. 9, pp. 32)
Pub: Reed Business Information Inc.
Description: Dr. Alan Buckle discusses the use of rodenticides control, focusing on poultry units.

21403 ■ "The Bear Arrives - With Bargain Hunters" in *Barron's* (Vol. 88, July 7, 2008, No. 27, pp. M3)
Pub: Dow Jones & Co., Inc.
Ed: Kopin Tan. **Description:** US stock markets have dropped 20 percent below their highs, entering the bear market at the end of June 2008. It was also the worst performance of the stock markets during June. Wine maker Constellation Brands, however, reported a 50 percent rise in net income for the first quarter of 2008.

21404 ■ "Because He Is Still Growing: Horst Rechelbacher: Intelligent Nutrients Minneapolis" in *Inc.* (Volume 32, December 2010, No. 10)
Pub: Inc. Magazine
Ed: Mike Hoffman. **Description:** Horst Rechelbacher, founder of hair care company Aveda, and after selling Aveda to Estee Lauder, he is expanding into a nutraceuticals company offering hair care products that are organically grown.

21405 ■ "The Believer" in *Inc.* (December 2007, pp. 130-138)
Pub: Gruner & Jahr USA Publishing
Ed: Leigh Buchanan. **Description:** Profile of Selena Cuffe, wine importer and socially conscious woman entrepreneur, who is focusing her talents on helping South Africa get wine products to America.

21406 ■ "Bertha's Birth Stirs Juice" in *Barron's* (Vol. 88, July 14, 2008, No. 28, pp. M11)
Pub: Dow Jones & Co., Inc.
Ed: Tom Sellen. **Description:** Price of frozen concentrated orange juice, which has risen to four-month highs of $1.3620 in July 2008 is due, in part, to the hurricane season that has come earlier than normal in the far eastern Atlantic thereby possibly harming the 2008-2009 Florida orange crop. Future tropical-storm development will affect the prices of this commodity.

21407 ■ "Best Turnaround Stocks" in *Canadian Business* (Vol. 82, Summer 2009, No. 8, pp. 32)
Pub: Rogers Media
Ed: Calvin Leung. **Description:** Canadian companies that are believed to have the potential for the best turnaround stocks are presented. Suggested stocks include those of Migao Corporation, which is rated by most research firms as a Buy. Migao produces potash-based fertilizers for the Chinese market.

21408 ■ "Beverage Brand Vies To Be the Latest Purple Prince" in *Brandweek* (Vol. 49, April 21, 2008, No. 16, pp. 20)
Pub: VNU Business Media, Inc.
Ed: Becky Ebenkamp. **Description:** Profile on the new beverage product Purple and its founder, Ted Farnsworth; Purple is a drink that blends seven antioxidant-rich juices to create what Mr. Farnsworth calls a "Cascade Effect" that boosts antioxidants' effectiveness. Mr. Farnsworth is marketing the brand's Oxygen Radical Absorbance Capability (ORAC) which is a value of 7,600 compared with orange juice's 1,200.

21409 ■ "Biodiesel Poised to Regain Growth" in *Farm Industry News* (January 21, 2011)
Pub: Penton Business Media Inc.
Description: According to Gary Haer, vice president of sales and marketing for Renewable Energy Group, the biodiesel industry is positioned to regain growth in 2011 with the reinstatement of the biodiesel blendersa tax credt of $1 per gallon.

21410 ■ "Bottler Will Regain Its Pop" in *Barron's* (Vol. 88, March 17, 2008, No. 11, pp. 56)
Pub: Dow Jones & Company, Inc.
Ed: Alexander Eule. **Description:** Discusses he 30 percent drop in the share price of PepsiAmericas Inc. from their 2007 high which presents an opportunity to buy into the company's dependable U.S. market and fast growing Eastern European business. The bottler's Eastern European operating profits in 2007 grew to $101 million from $21 million in 2006.

21411 ■ "Brazil's New King of Food" in *Barron's* (Vol. 89, July 13, 2009, No. 28, pp. 28)
Pub: Dow Jones & Co., Inc.
Ed: Kenneth Rapoza. **Description:** Perdigao and Sadia's merger has resulted in the creation of Brasil Foods and the shares of Brasil Foods provides a play on both Brazil's newly energized consumer economy and its role as a major commodities exporter. Brasil Foods shares could climb as much as 36 percent.

21412 ■ "Brewing National Success" in *Hawaii Business* (Vol. 53, November 2007, No. 5, pp. 46)
Pub: Hawaii Business Publishing
Ed: Alex Salkever. **Description:** Kona Brewing Co. (KBC) is already selling its brews in four cities in Florida and 17 other states and Japan as well. KBC is currently forming a deal with Red Hook to produce Longboard Lager and other KBC brews at Red Hooks' brewery in New Hampshire. KBC's chief executive officer Mattson Davis shares KBC's practices for success.

21413 ■ "Buhler Versatile Launches Next Generation of Equipment" in *Farm Industry News* (November 23, 2011)
Pub: Penton Business Media Inc.
Ed: Jodie Wehrspann. **Description:** Canadian owned Versatile is expanding its four-wheel drive tractor division with sprayers, tillage, and seeding equipment.

21414 ■ "Building Portfolios for a World of 2.5 Percent Gains" in *Barron's* (Vol. 88, July 7, 2008, No. 27, pp. L9)
Pub: Dow Jones & Co., Inc.
Ed: Karen Hube. **Description:** Interview with Harold Evenski whom is a financial planner running a fee-only planning practice; he continues to caution investors against pursuing short-term gains and focusing on long-term trends. He advises investors against investing in commodity and real estate stocks and is concerned about the possible effects of high inflation.

21415 ■ *Business Management for Tropical Dairy Farmers*
Pub: CSIRO Publishing
Ed: John Moran. **Released:** August 1, 2009. **Price:** $33.95. **Description:** Business management skills required for dairy farmers are addressed, focusing on financial management and ways to improve cattle housing and feeding systems.

21416 ■ "Businessman Legend Passes: Charles H. James II Credited With Transforming Family Business" in *Black Enterprise* (December 2007)
Pub: Earl G. Graves Publishing Co. Inc.
Ed: Tara C. Walker. **Description:** Profile of Charles H. James II, president and chairman of The James Corporation, a family-owned multigenerational food distribution company that started as a produce firm.

21417 ■ "A Busy Little Parasite" in *Hawaii Business* (Vol. 53, March 2008, No. 9, pp. 1)
Pub: Hawaii Business Publishing
Ed: Jason Ubay. **Description:** Bee mites were first sighted in Hawaii by Michael Kliks on April 6, 2007 and have since been a cause of concern for the beekeeping industry and pollinated-dependent crop industry. Hawaii's agricultural industry estimates that the losses due to bee mites may amount to between $42 million and $62 million. Steps taken to address the issue are discussed.

21418 ■ "Buying Seed by Weight or By Count" in *Farm Industry News* (October 20, 2010)
Pub: Penton Business Media Inc.
Ed: Mark Moore. **Description:** Soybean producers have the option of buying seeds by count or by weight; tips for either method of purchase are outlined.

21419 ■ "Buzz Kill" in *Canadian Business* (Vol. 83, August 17, 2010, No. 13-14, pp. 24)
Pub: Rogers Media Ltd.
Ed: Rachel Mendleson. **Description:** Beekeeping industry has been plagued by a massive wave of honeybee deaths since 2006, which pushed upward the cost of per hive-rental. The death of honeybees has put the food supply at risk since it jeopardized the growth of pumpkins, as well as other crops in large acreage. Insights on the Colony Collapse Disorder are outlined.

21420 ■ "Can Turfway Park Stay in the Race?" in *Business Courier* (Vol. 26, January 8, 2010, No. 38, pp. 1)
Pub: American City Business Journals, Inc.
Ed: Jon Newberry. **Description:** Legalization of slot machine gambling in Kentucky could affect raceway Turfway Park and the state's thoroughbred industry. Thousands of farms and jobs in the industry could be lost if slot machine gambling is approved.

21421 ■ "Careers in Organic Food Preparation" in *Occupational Outlook Quarterly* (Vol. 54, Fall 2010, No. 3, pp. 3)
Pub: U.S. Bureau of Labor Statistics
Ed: Adam Bibler. **Description:** Organic methods of food production, including methods that combine science with traditional farming practices, are outlined. Facts regarding careers in organic food preparation are presented.

21422 ■ "Case IH Announces Strategy to Meet 2014 Clean Air Standards" in *Farm Industry News* (September 15, 2011)
Pub: Penton Business Media Inc.
Ed: Jodie Wehrspann. **Description:** Case IH will meet EPA's stringent engine emissions limits imposed in 2014, called Tier 4. The limits call for a 90 percent reduction in particulate matter and nitrogen oxides (NOx) over the Tier 3 requirements from a few years ago.

21423 ■ "Cash Rents Reach Sky-High Levels" in *Farm Industry News* (November 23, 2011)
Pub: Penton Business Media Inc.
Ed: Karen McMahon. **Description:** Strong commodity prices are driving land values creating a hot rental market for farm land. Highest rents occur when farmers compete head-to-head for land.

21424 ■ "CGB Purchases Illinois Grain-Fertilizer Firm" in *Farm Industry News* (December 2, 2011)
Pub: Penton Business Media Inc.
Description: CGB Enterprises Inc. bought Twomey Company's grain and fertilizer assets. The purchase includes eight locations and a barge loading terminal near Gladstone, Illinois and storage capacity of 51 million bushels and 18,000 tons of liquid fertilizer.

21425 ■ "Cheese Spread Whips Up a Brand New Bowl" in *Brandweek* (Vol. 49, April 21, 2008, No. 16, pp. 17)
Pub: VNU Business Media, Inc.
Ed: Mike Beirne. **Description:** Mrs. Kinser's Pimento Cheese Spread is launching a new container for its product in order to attempt stronger brand marketing with a better bowl in order to win over the heads of households as young as in their 30s. The company also intends to begin distribution in Texas and the West Coast. Mrs. Kinser's is hoping that the new packaging will provide a more distinct branding and will help consumers distinguish what flavor they are buying.

21426 ■ "Chino Valley Ranches: a Family of Farmers" in *Retail Merchandiser* (Vol. 51, September-October 2011, No. 5, pp. 79)
Pub: Phoenix Media Corporation
Ed: Angela Forsyth. **Description:** Charles B. Nichols and his wife Isabella purchased their ranch in Beaumont, California in the early 1950s. The family has been raising their chickens, producing eggs with quality, integrity and honesty the foundation of their business.

21427 ■ "Chopping Option Added to Calmer Corn Head Kits" in *Farm Industry News* (January 16, 2011)
Pub: Penton Business Media Inc.
Description: New equipment for combines, called the BT Chopper option for Calmer Corn Heads, will chop and crust BT corn stalks into confetti-sized pieces for easier decomposition in the field.

21428 ■ "Coca-Cola Looks Ready to Pause" in *Barron's* (Vol. 88, March 10, 2008, No. 10, pp. 18)
Pub: Dow Jones & Company, Inc.
Ed: Michael Santoli. **Description:** Shares of Coca-Cola are expected to turn sideways or experience a slight drop from $59.50 each to the mid-50 level. The company has seen its shares jump 40 percent since 2006, when it was in a series of measures to improve profitability.

21429 ■ "Coming Soon: Electric Tractors" in *Farm Industry News* (November 21, 2011)
Pub: Penton Business Media Inc.
Ed: Jodie Wehrspann. **Description:** The agricultural industry is taking another look at electric farm vehicles. John Deere Product Engineering Center said that farmers can expect to see more diesel-electric systems in farm tractors, sprayers, and implements.

21430 ■ "Commodities: Who's Behind the Boom?" in *Barron's* (Vol. 88, March 31, 2008, No. 13, pp. 3)
Pub: Dow Jones & Company, Inc.
Ed: Gene Epstein. **Description:** Proliferation of mutual funds and exchange traded funds tied to commodities indexes has helped speculative buying reach unusual levels. Index funds are estimated to account for 40 percent of all bullish bets on commodities. Commodities could drop by 30 percent as speculators retreat. Statistical data included.

21431 ■ "Community Food Co-op Creates Revolving Loan Program for Local Farmers" in *Bellingham Business Journal* (Vol. February 2010, pp. 3)
Pub: Sound Publishing Inc.
Description: Community Food Co-op's Farm Fund received a $12,000 matching grant from the Sustainable Whatcom Fund of the Whatcom Community Foundation. The Farm Fund will create a new revolving loan program for local farmers committed to using sustainable practices.

21432 ■ "Company Severs Ties with Chiquita, Starts Own Brand" in *Business Journal-Serving Phoenix and the Valley of the Sun* (October 5, 2007)
Pub: American City Business Journals, Inc.
Ed: Mike Sunnucks. **Description:** Melones International is ending a deal with Chiquita Brands International Inc. Melones will now distribute its produce in the U.S. under its own brand, called Plain Jane. Alejandro N. Canelos Jr., head of the firm, stated their relationship with Chiquita was good, but wants to promote the Plain Jane brand name.

21433 ■ "Confidence High, But Lenders More Cautious" in *Farmer's Weekly* (March 28, 2008, No. 320)
Pub: Reed Business Information
Description: Discusses the effect of the global credit crunch on farmers as well as recent auctions which were timed to beat changes to capital gains tax.

21434 ■ "Corn Belt Farmland Prices Hit Record Levels" in *Farm Industry News* (December 1, 2011)
Pub: Penton Business Media Inc.
Ed: David Hest. **Description:** Farmland prices have set records over the last six months in Iowa. Farmland broker and auction company owner, Murray Wise, believes this is not a bubble, that the economics of this market are solid.

21435 ■ "Corn May Get Shucked By Soy" in *Barron's* (Vol. 88, March 31, 2008, No. 13, pp. M12)
Pub: Dow Jones & Company, Inc.
Ed: Angie Pointer. **Description:** Acreage allotted to soybeans could jump by 12 percent from 2007's 63.6 million as the price for soybeans reaches record highs. Corn acreage could drop by 6.7 percent as other crops expand and higher fertilizer prices shift farmers away from corn.

21436 ■ "Count Out The Consumer" in *Barron's* (Vol. 88, July 7, 2008, No. 27, pp. 10)
Pub: Dow Jones & Co., Inc.
Description: American consumers are not expected to give the US economy its much-needed boost as the rising food and energy prices are taking their toll. US consumers have cut spending on utilities and food and are increasing their use of credit cards.

21437 ■ "Crop Insurance Harvest Prices in 2011" in *Farm Industry News* (November 9, 2011)
Pub: Penton Business Media Inc.
Ed: Gary Schnitkey. **Description:** Risk Management Agency (RMA) reported harvest prices for corn and soybean grown in the Midwest with corn at $6.32 per bushel, 31 cents higher than the project $6.01; soybeans were at $12.14 per bushel, down $1.35 from the projected price of $13.49.

21438 ■ "Dean Foods" in *Ice Cream Reporter* (Vol. 23, November 20, 2010, No. 12, pp. 8)
Pub: Ice Cream Reporter
Description: The impact of higher commodity prices can be seen in the recent news from Dean Foods, the largest U.S. dairy company, which reported that rising butterfat and other dairy commodity costs have led to lower-than-expected quarterly profits after it cut prices to compete with private-label brands.

21439 ■ "Deere to Open Technology Center in Germany" in *Chicago Tribune* (September 3, 2008)
Pub: McClatchy-Tribune Information Services
Ed: James P. Miller. **Description:** Deere & Co. plans to open a technology and innovation center in Germany; details of the company's expansion plans are discussed.

21440 ■ "Department of Agriculture" in *Ice Cream Reporter* (Vol. 23, November 20, 2010, No. 12, pp. 8)
Pub: Ice Cream Reporter
Description: Department of Agriculture notes that food price inflation for 2010 will be at its lowest since 1992.

21441 ■ "Dick Haskayne" in *Canadian Business* (Vol. 81, March 31, 2008, No. 5, pp. 72)
Pub: Rogers Media
Ed: Andy Holloway. **Description:** Dick Haskayne says that he learned a lot about business from his dad who ran a butcher shop where they had to make a decision on buying cattle and getting credit. Haskayne says that family, friends, finances, career, health, and infrastructure are benchmarks that have to be balanced.

21442 ■ *Directory of American Agriculture*
Pub: Agricultural Resources & Communications Inc.
Contact: Chris Wilson, Publisher
Released: Irregular, Latest edition 2005. **Price:** $50, individuals. **Covers:** National and state agricultural organizations; federal and state agricultural departments, agencies, and programs; colleges of agriculture at land grant universities, state 4-H leaders, farm broadcasters and publications, farm credit councils, agricultural information services and other agricultural organizations, agencies and institutions. **Entries Include:** Organization name, address, phone, fax, name and title of contact. National organization entries include additional information. **Arrangement:** Alphabetical. **Indexes:** Categorical, by type of organization.

21443 ■ "Dividing to Conquer" in *Barron's* (Vol. 88, March 31, 2008, No. 13, pp. 22)
Pub: Dow Jones & Company, Inc.
Ed: Andrew Bary. **Description:** Altria's spin off of Philip Morris International could unlock substantial value for both domestic and international cigarette concerns. The strong brands and ample payouts from both companies will most likely impress investors.

21444 ■ "Don't Fall Foul of Farming's Workplace Killer" in *Farmer's Weekly* (March 28, 2008, No. 320)
Pub: Reed Business Information
Description: Discusses the Work at Height Regulations that were introduced to reduce the risk of injury and death caused by accidental falls in the workplace.

21445 ■ "Dow AgroSciences Buys Wheat Breeding Firm in Pacific Northwest" in *Farm Industry News* (July 29, 2011)
Pub: Penton Business Media Inc.
Description: Dow AgroSciences purchased Northwest Plant Breeding Company, a cereals breeding station in Washington in 2011. The acquisition will help Dow expand its Hyland Seeds certified wheat seed program foundation in the Pacific Northwest. Financial terms of the deal were not disclosed.

21446 ■ "Drought Takes Toll on Farmers, Restaurants" in *Saint Louis Business Journal* (Vol. 31, August 12, 2011, No. 51, pp. 1)
Pub: Saint Louis Business Journal
Ed: E.B. Solomont. **Description:** The drought in St. Louis, Missouri has adversely impacted farmers and restaurants in the areas. Diners can expect to lose some ingredients from their menus.

21447 ■ "DuPontas Pioneer Hi-Bred, Evogene to Develop Rust-Resistant Soybean Varieties" in *Farm Industry News* (November 22, 2011)
Pub: Penton Business Media Inc.
Ed: Karen McMahon. **Description:** DuPont and Evogene have signed a new contract to work together to develop resistance in soybeans to rust. Financial terms of the agreement were not disclosed.

21448 ■ "Eco-Preneuring" in *Small Business Opportunities* (Jan. 2008)
Pub: Harris Publications Inc.
Description: Iceland Naturally is a joint marketing effort among tourism and business interests hoping to increase demand for Icelandic products including frozen seafood, bottled water, agriculture, and tourism in North America.

21449 ■ "Egg Fight: The Yolk's on the Short" in *Barron's* (Vol. 88, July 7, 2008, No. 27, pp. 20)
Pub: Dow Jones & Co., Inc.
Ed: Christopher C. Williams. **Description:** Shares of Cal-Maine Foods, the largest egg producer and distributor in the US, are due for a huge rise because of the increase in egg prices. Short sellers, however, continue betting that the stock, priced at $31.84 each, will eventually go down.

21450 ■ "EPA Grants E15 Waiver for 2001-2006 Vehicles" in *Farm Industry News* (January 21, 2011)
Pub: Penton Business Media Inc.
Description: U.S. Environmental Protection Agency waived a limitation on selling gasoline that contains more than 10 percent ethanol for model year 2001-2006 cars and light trucks, allowing fuel to contain up to 15 percent ethanol (E15) for these vehicles.

21451 ■ *Equipment Marketing and Distribution Association—Membership Directory*
Pub: Equipment Marketing & Distribution Association
Contact: Jim Manke CAE, Exec. Dir.
E-mail: jrmanke@associationsolutionsinc.com
Released: Annual. **Covers:** 120 members; coverage includes Canada. **Entries Include:** Company name, address, phone, name of principal executive, territory covered. **Arrangement:** Alphabetical.

21452 ■ *Ethnic Solidarity for Economic Survival: Korean Greengrocers in New York City*
Pub: Russell Sage Foundation Publications
Ed: Pyong Gap Min. **Released:** August 2008. **Price:** $32.50. **Description:** Investigations into the entrepreneurial traditions of Korean immigrant families in New York City running ethnic businesses, particularly small grocery stores and produce markets. Social, cultural and economic issues facing these retailers are discussed.

21453 ■ "Every Year, Thousands of People Are Killed By Pathogens In Food. William Hanson Wants To Help" in *Inc.* (November 2007, pp. 46-47)
Pub: Gruner & Jahr USA Publishing
Ed: Dalia Fahmy. **Description:** OmniFresh 1000 System tests produce for pathogens such as E.coli and salmonella. The firm is able to test for these pathogens in two hours compared to traditional tests that take as many as three days. Each year some 5,000 Americans die from food-borne diseases.

21454 ■ "Experts Discuss New Tax Rules in Webinar to Help Farmers With Year-End Tax Planning" in *Farm Industry News* (November 22, 2011)
Pub: Penton Business Media Inc.
Description: Section 179 deductions and Bonus Depreciation tax rules for years 2011 and 2012 and how they impact farming operations are available at TractorLife.com. The Website helps farmers maintain and extend the operating lives of their tractors.

21455 ■ "Farm Aid" in *Canadian Business* (Vol. 80, November 5, 2007, No. 22, pp. 123)
Pub: Rogers Media
Ed: Calvin Leung. **Description:** Canadian farmers experiencing difficulties with increasing their earning as the price of production is greater than the amount they earn from produce. Government assistance programs, including the Canadian Agricultural Income Stabilization, are aimed at helping farmers mitigate the impacts of the high prices of production. The effectiveness of Canadian farm policies are evaluated.

21456 ■ "Farming Season Starts in December" in *Farm Industry News* (November 29, 2011)
Pub: Penton Business Media Inc.
Ed: Kent Lock. **Description:** One farmer suggests the season starts in December because one third of his seed and fertilizer for the following year has already been bought and paid for and his cropping mix changes little from one year to another.

21457 ■ "Fast-Release Calcium Could Help Control Club Root" in *Farmer's Weekly* (March 28, 2008, No. 320)
Pub: Reed Business Information
Description: According to initial observations from a new HGCA club root research study, applications of fertilizers that rapidly release calcium may help improve performance of both susceptible and resistant oilseed rape varieties.

21458 ■ "Feedback From Payers Will Be Vital For Future Developments" in *Farmer's Weekly* (March 28, 2008, No. 320)
Pub: Reed Business Information
Description: Potato Council staff will carry on working with levy payers to retain the same high caliber of marketing, research and other activities.

21459 ■ "Fertilizer for Growth" in *Canadian Business* (Vol. 83, September 14, 2010, No. 15, pp. 76)
Pub: Rogers Media Ltd.
Ed: Bryan Borzykowski. **Description:** Australian-based BHP Billiton launches a C$38.5 billion hostile takeover bid for Saskatchewan-based Potash Corporation and some investors immediately bought Potash stock at C$130. However, Potash has resisted BHP's offer and announced a plan to try to stop the deal.

21460 ■ "A Few Points of Contention" in *Barron's* (Vol. 88, July 14, 2008, No. 28, pp. 3)
Pub: Dow Jones & Co., Inc.
Ed: Michael Santoli. **Description:** Headline inflation tends to revert to the lower core inflation, which excludes food and energy in its calculation over long periods. Prominent private equity figures believe that regulators should allow more than the de facto 10 percent to 25 percent limit of commercial banks to hasten the refunding of the financial sector.

21461 ■ "The Final Frontier" in *Canadian Business* (Vol. 80, October 8, 2007, No. 20, pp. 127)
Pub: Rogers Media
Ed: Andy Holloway. **Description:** Effects of economic development in Northern Canada's natural environment are discussed. The caribou, which are still a primary source of food and clothing in the region, are dying. It is assumed that mining and petroleum projects are affecting the migration patterns of the animals inhabiting the region. The need to maintain a balance between the needs of resource companies and traditional businesses is also discussed.

21462 ■ "FinOvation 2009" in *Farm Industry News* (Vol. 42, January 1, 2009, No. 1)
Pub: Penton Media, Inc.
Ed: Karen McMahon; David Hest; Mark Moore. **Description:** New and innovative products and technologies are presented.

21463 ■ "First Impression of Robotic Farming Systems" in *Farm Industry News* (September 30, 2011)
Pub: Penton Business Media Inc.
Ed: Jodie Wehrspann. **Description:** Farm Science Review featured tillage tools and land rollers, including John Deere's GPS system where a cart tractor is automatically controlled as well as a new line of Kinze's carts and a video of their robotic system for a driver-less cart tractor.

21464 ■ "Five Ways to Make RTK Pay" in *Farm Industry News* (March 25, 2011)
Pub: Penton Business Media Inc.
Ed: David Hest. **Description:** It is important for farmers to decide whether they are seeking greater accuracy or faster payback when upgrading navigation systems. The trend towards higher accuracy continues to grow.

21465 ■ "Food & Wine Publisher Tries His Hand at Saber Rattling" in *Advertising Age* (Vol. 77, December 4, 2006, No. 49, pp. 16)
Pub: Crain Communications, Inc.
Description: French vineyards are facing a massive overproduction crisis due to a falling number in the amount of wine the French are drinking per week.

21466 ■ "For Going All Out to Transform the Way Our Food Is Grown: Chuck Lacy" in *Inc.* (Volume 32, December 2010, No. 10, pp. 94)
Pub: Inc. Magazine
Ed: Adam Bluestein. **Description:** Profile of Rotokawa Cattle Company and its mission to transform the business of beef and grow their herd of beef cattle.

21467 ■ "For Putting Down Roots in Business: Amy Norquist: Greensulate, New York City" in *Inc.* (Volume 32, December 2010, No. 10, pp. 106)
Pub: Inc. Magazine
Ed: Christine Lagorio. **Description:** Profile of Amy Norquist who left her position at an environmental nonprofit organization to found Greensulate. Her firm insulates rooftops with lavender, native grasses and succulents called sedum in order to eliminate carbon from the atmosphere.

21468 ■ "Fossil Fuel, Renewable Fuel Shares Expected to Flip Flop" in *Farm Industry News* (April 29, 2011)
Pub: Penton Business Media Inc.
Description: Total energy use of fossil fuels is predicted to fall 5 percent by the year 2035, with renewable fuel picking it up.

21469 ■ "Fries With That?" in *Canadian Business* (Vol. 81, September 29, 2008, No. 16, pp. 33)
Pub: Rogers Media Ltd.
Ed: Calvin Leung. **Description:** Profile of Toronto-based New York Fries, which has four stores in South Korea, is planning to expand further as well as into Hong Kong and Macau; the company also has a licensee in the United Arab Emirates whom is also planning to expand.

21470 ■ "Frosted Flakes Goes For Gold" in *Marketing to Women* (Vol. 21, April 2008, No. 4, pp. 3)
Pub: EPM Communications, Inc.
Description: Kellogg is appealing to health-conscious moms with its new product Frosted Flakes Gold.

21471 ■ "Fuel King: The Most Fuel-Efficient Tractor of the Decade is the John Deere 8295R" in *Farm Industry News* (November 10, 2011)
Pub: Penton Business Media Inc.
Description: Farm Industry News compiled a list of the most fuel-efficient tractors with help from the Nebraska Tractor Test Lab, with the John Deere 8295R PTO winner of the most fuel-efficient tractor of the decade.

21472 ■ *Fugitive Denim: A Moving Story of People and Pants in the Borderless World of Global Trade*
Pub: W.W. Norton & Company
Ed: Rachel Snyder. **Released:** April 2009. **Price:** $16.95. **Description:** In-depth study of the global production and processes of how jeans are designed, sewn, and transported as well as how the cotton for denim is grown, regulated, purchased and processed.

21473 ■ "Game On: The Hunt Is On for Nation's Top Keeper" in *Farmer's Weekly* (March 28, 2008, No. 320)
Pub: Reed Business Information
Description: Gamekeepers must strike the natural balance that encourages wildlife and protects game. CLA Game Fair and Farmer's Weekly are holding a competition for Gamekeeper of the Year 2008.

21474 ■ "General Clark Stresses Ethanols Role In National Security At Ag Connect" in *Farm Industry News* (January 11, 2011)
Pub: Penton Business Media Inc.
Description: General Clark stressed the role of ethanols in national security at the AgConnect.

21475 ■ "GL Homes Buys 1,000 Acres in Former Agricultural Reserve" in *Miami Daily Business Review* (March 26, 2008)
Pub: ALM Media Inc.
Ed: Polyana da Costa. **Description:** One of the nation's largest home builders, GL Homes, purchased over 1,000 acres of agricultural land in Southern Palm Beach County, Florida. Plans for 554 residential units are detailed.

21476 ■ "Good Things Happen When We Buy Local" in *Crain's Detroit Business* (Vol. 24, October 6, 2008, No. 40, pp. 7)
Pub: Crain Communications, Inc.
Description: Michigan is facing incredibly difficult economic times. One way in which each one of us can help the state and the businesses located here is by purchasing our goods and services from local vendors. The state Agriculture Department projected that if Michigan households earmarked $10 per week in their grocery purchases to made-in-Michigan products, this would generate $30 million a week in economic impact.

21477 ■ "Grape Expectations" in *Canadian Business* (Vol. 80, March 12, 2007, No. 6, pp. 55)
Pub: Rogers Media
Ed: Andrea Jezvovit. **Description:** The emergence of Nova Scotia as one of the leading wine-making places in Canada, in view of its favorable climate for growing grapes, is discussed.

21478 ■ "The Great Cleanup" in *Canadian Business* (Vol. 81, April 14, 2008, No. 6, pp. 50)
Pub: Rogers Media
Ed: Graham Silnicki. **Description:** China's rectification program includes the licensing of 100 percent of food producers and monitoring of 100 percent of raw materials for exports between August and December, 2007. There is a lot of money to be made for those who are willing to help China win its quality battle. PharmEng International Inc. is one of the companies that helps Chinese companies meet international quality standards.

21479 ■ "Grow-Ops" in *Canadian Business* (Vol. 81, October 27, 2008, No. 18, pp. 112)
Pub: Rogers Media Ltd.
Ed: Calvin Leung. **Description:** Canada's agriculture and agri-food industry is ripe for expansion and to meet global demand that is expected to double by 2050. Better water management and biotechnology are among the strategies that could help increase output of Canada's agricultural industry.

21480 ■ "Growers Urged to Allow for Soil Nutrients" in *Farmer's Weekly* (March 28, 2008, No. 320)
Pub: Reed Business Information
Ed: Andrew Blake. **Description:** Discusses the importance of taking in account soil nitrogen supplies when planning their remaining fertilizer applications.

21481 ■ "Growing Pains" in *Canadian Business* (Vol. 81, July 22, 2008, No. 12-13, pp. 35)
Pub: Rogers Media Ltd.
Ed: Alex Mylnek. **Description:** Laughing Stock Vineyards' Cynthia Enns and David Enns plan to target young buyers by using social media. The Enns however, are concerned that targeting younger buyers may affect Laughing Stock's image as a premium brand. Additional information regarding the company's future plans is presented.

21482 ■ "Half Empty or Half Full" in *Crain's Chicago Business* (Vol. 31, March 24, 2008, No. 12, pp. 4)
Pub: Crain Communications, Inc.
Ed: Meghan Streit. **Description:** Lifeway Foods Inc., the health food company which manufactures a yogurt-like drink called kefir, is being negatively affected by the soaring price of milk; however, the fact that probiotics are picking up in the market may mean that Lifeway stands a good chance of bouncing back and the company's lower share price could be an opportunity for long-term investors who have a tolerance for risk.

21483 ■ "Head of Horse Farmers and Owners Jockey for Saratoga Pastures, Breeder Awards" in *Business Review, Albany New York* (Nov. 23, 2007)
Pub: American City Business Journals, Inc.
Ed: Robin K. Cooper. **Description:** Trends in Saratoga County's equine industry are discussed. More than fifty horse farms and 11,000 horses are in Saratoga, which is more than any other county in New York. Joe McMahon, a horse breeder and also the vice president of New York Breeders Sales Company, plans to expand his business by tapping into a new market. He plans to build his stable of top registered New York stallions.

21484 ■ "Hello, Old Friends" in *Business Courier* (Vol. 24, October 12, 2008, No. 26, pp. 1)
Pub: American City Business Journals, Inc.
Ed: Jon Newberry. **Description:** Pittsburgh-based Iron City Brewing Co., a company born out of Pittsburgh Brewing Co.'s reorganization, is resuming the production of Wiedemann Bohemian Style Special Beer. Cincinnati-based Christian Moerlein Brewing Co. is also bringing back its famous Burger beer, which hasn't been available locally for a couple of years. The two companies' plans regarding the reintroduction of their beer products are discussed.

21485 ■ *A History of Small Business in America*
Pub: University of North Carolina Press
Ed: Mansel G. Blackford. **Released:** May 2003. **Price:** $22.95. **Description:** History of American small business from the colonial era to present, showing how it has played a role in the nation's economic, political, and cultural development across manufacturing, sales, services and farming.

21486 ■ "Hopes Grow for Milk Price Increase From Tesco" in *Farmer's Weekly* (March 28, 2008, No. 320)
Pub: Reed Business Information
Description: Farmers will see an increase in the price supermarket Tesco will pay for their milk.

21487 ■ "How Growers Buy" in *Farm Industry News* (Vol. 42, January 1, 2009, No. 1)
Pub: Penton Media, Inc.
Ed: Karen McMahon. **Description:** According to a survey regarding the buying habits among large commercial growers, most prefer to purchase from local retailers, customer service is important concerning their decision on who to buy products from, and price and convenience seem to be more important then brand.

21488 ■ "How High Can Soybeans Fly?" in *Barron's* (Vol. 88, March 10, 2008, No. 10, pp. M14)
Pub: Dow Jones & Company, Inc.
Ed: Kenneth Rapoza. **Description:** Prices of soybeans have risen to $14.0875 a bushel, up 8.3 percent for the week. Increased demand, such as in China and in other developing economies, and the investment-driven commodities boom are boosting prices.

21489 ■ "How Sweet It Will Be" in *Barron's* (Vol. 89, July 13, 2009, No. 28, pp. M13)
Pub: Dow Jones & Co., Inc.
Ed: Debbie Carlson. **Description:** Raw sugar experienced a rally in the first half of 2009 and the long term outlook for sugar prices is still good. However, there is a likely near-term correction due to the onset of Brazilian harvest that could be 20.7 percent higher for 2009 as compared to the previous year and October contracts could fall to 15.61 cents per pound.

21490 ■ "An Ill Wind: Icelandic Bank Failures Chill Atlantic Canada" in *Canadian Business* (Vol. 81, November 10, 2008, No. 19, pp. 10)
Pub: Rogers Media Ltd.
Ed: Charles Mandel. **Description:** Bank failures in Iceland have put a stop to flights ferrying Icelanders to Newfoundland to purchase Christmas gifts, thereby threatening Newfoundland's tourism industry. The credit of Newfoundland's fisheries is also being squeezed since most of Atlantic Canadian seafood processors hold lines of credit from Icelandic banks.

21491 ■ "Ill Winds; Cuba's Economy" in *The Economist* (Vol. 390, January 3, 2009, No. 8612, pp. 20)
Pub: The Economist Newspaper Inc.
Description: Cuba's long-term economic prospects remain poor with the economy forecasted to grow only 4.3 percent for the year, about half of the original forecast, due in part to Hurricane Gustav which caused $10 billion in damage and disrupted the food-supply network and devastated farms across the region; President Raul Castro made raising agricultural production a national priority and the rise in global commodity prices hit the country hard. The only bright spot has been the rise in tourism which is up 9.3 percent over 2007.

21492 ■ "Illinois Farmland Tops $11,000 Per Acre" in *Farm Industry News* (June 27, 2011)
Pub: Penton Business Media Inc.
Ed: Karen McMahon. **Description:** Farmland property in Illinois continues to grow in value, selling for $11,000 per acre. Statistical data included.

21493 ■ "Importers Share Safety Liability" in *Feedstuffs* (Vol. 80, January 21, 2008, No. 3, pp. 19)
Pub: Miller Publishing Company, Inc.
Description: Pet food and toys containing lead paint are among products from China being recalled due to safety concerns. American Society for Quality's list of measures that outsourcing companies can take to help ensure safer products being imported to the U.S.

21494 ■ "Investment Bank Predicts Shakeup in Farm Equipment Industry" in *Farm Industry News* (November 16, 2011)
Pub: Penton Business Media Inc.
Ed: Jodie Wehrspann. **Description:** Farming can expect to see more mergers and acquisitions in the agricultural equipment industry, as it appears to be in the early stages of growth over the next few years.

21495 ■ "Irene Rosenfeld; Chairman and CEO, Kraft Foods Inc." in *Crain's Chicago Business* (Vol. 31, May 5, 2008, No. 18, pp. 31)
Pub: Crain Communications, Inc.
Ed: David Sterrett. **Description:** Profile of Irene Rosenfeld who is the chairman and CEO of Kraft Foods Inc. and is entering the second year of a three-year plan to boost sales of well-known brands such as Oreo, Velveeta and Oscar Mayer while facing soaring commodity costs and a declining market-share. Ms. Rosenfeld's turnaround strategy also entails spending more on advertising and giving managers more control over their budgets and product development.

21496 ■ "Kraft Taps Cheese Head; Jordan Charged With Fixing Foodmaker's Signature Product" in *Crain's Chicago Business* (April 14, 2008)
Pub: Crain Communications, Inc.
Ed: David Sterrett. **Description:** Kraft Foods Inc. has assigned Rhonda Jordan, a company veteran, to take charge of the cheese and dairy division which has been losing market shares to cheaper store-brand cheese among cost-sensitive shoppers as Kraft and its competitors raise prices to offset soaring dairy costs.

21497 ■ "Land Agent Taken Over" in *Farmer's Weekly* (March 28, 2008, No. 320)
Pub: Reed Business Information
Description: Property business Smiths Gore will take over Cluttons' rural division, one of the oldest names in land agency. Cluttons said it had decided to sell its rural business as part of a strategic repositioning that would refocus the business on commercial, residential and overseas opportunities.

21498 ■ "The Latin Beat Goes On" in *Barron's* (Vol. 88, July 7, 2008, No. 27, pp. L5)
Pub: Dow Jones & Co., Inc.
Ed: Tom Sullivan. **Description:** Latin American stocks have outperformed other regional markets due to rising commodities prices and favorable economic climate. Countries such as Brazil, Mexico, Chile, and Peru provide investment opportunities, while Argentina and Venezuela are tougher places to invest.

21499 ■ "Leapin' Lizards, Does SoBe Have Some Work To Do On Life Water" in *Brandweek* (Vol. 49, April 21, 2008, No. 16, pp. 32)
Pub: VNU Business Media, Inc.
Ed: Amy Shea. **Description:** Discusses the competing marketing campaigns of both Vitaminwater, now owned by Coca-Cola, and SoBe Life Water which is

owned by Pepsi; also looks at the repositioning of Life Water as a thirst-quencher, rather than a green product as well as the company's newest advertising campaign.

21500 ■ "Leica Beefs Up Steering Options, Steering Display Features" in *Farm Industry News* (January 10, 2011)
Pub: Penton Business Media Inc.
Description: Leica Geosystems is offering a new hydraulic steering kit for older tractors, along with new steering patterns and other features on its Leica mojo3C and mojoMINI displays.

21501 ■ "Leinie's Charts National Craft Beer Rollout" in *The Business Journal-Milwaukee* (Vol. 25, August 29, 2008, No. 49, pp. A1)
Pub: American City Business Journals, Inc.
Ed: Rich Rovito. **Description:** Jacob Leinenkugel Brewing Co. is expected to complete the national rollout of its craft beer brands, while the launch of a new beer is prepared for this fall. The rollout is will likely benefit MillerCoors LLC, and will leave Alaska as the only state without Leinenkugel beer. Other views and information on Leinenkugel's national rollout are presented.

21502 ■ "Levy Boards: From Unity Comes Farming's Strength" in *Farmer's Weekly* (March 28, 2008, No. 320)
Pub: Reed Business Information
Description: Discusses the amalgamation of five farming levy boards to create the Agriculture and Horticulture Development Board.

21503 ■ "Li'l Guy Rolls Up Into Bigger Company" in *The Business Journal-Serving Metropolitan Kansas City* (Vol. 26, September 12, 2008)
Pub: American City Business Journals, Inc.
Ed: Suzanna Stagemeyer. **Description:** Li'l Guy Foods, a Mexican food company in Kansas City, Missouri, has merged with Tortilla King Inc. Li'l Guy's revenue in 2007 was $3.3 million, while a newspaper report said that Tortilla King's revenue in 2001 was $7.5 million. Growth opportunities for the combined companies and Li'l Guy's testing of the Wichita market are discussed.

21504 ■ "Lords Should Get Real About Food" in *Farmer's Weekly* (March 28, 2008, No. 320)
Pub: Reed Business Information
Description: Discusses the reasons why farming needs subsidies and suggests that the House of Lords should look at the way that grocery stores are operating.

21505 ■ "Making the Most of Milk to Revive a Falling Market" in *Farmer's Weekly* (March 28, 2008, No. 320)
Pub: Reed Business Information
Description: DairyCo, eight of whom are working dairy farmers, aim to promote a feeding campaign for better herd health, provide research into efficient labor use, and sponsor discussion groups to enhance business skills.

21506 ■ "Marketer Bets Big on U.S.'s Growing Canine Obsession" in *Advertising Age* (Vol. 79, April 14, 2008, No. 15, pp. 14)
Pub: Crain Communications, Inc.
Ed: Emily Bryson York. **Description:** Overview of FreshPet, a New Jersey company that began marketing two brands of refrigerated dog food-Deli Fresh and FreshPet Select-which are made from fresh ingredients such as beef, rice and carrots. The company projects continued success due to the amount of money consumers spend on their pets as well as fears derived from the 2007 recalls that inspired consumers to look for smaller, independent manufacturers that are less likely to source ingredients from China.

21507 ■ "Markets Defy the Doomsayers" in *Barron's* (Vol. 88, March 24, 2008, No. 12, pp. M5)
Pub: Dow Jones & Company, Inc.
Ed: Leslie P. Norton. **Description:** US stock markets registered strong gains, with the Dow Jones Industrial Average rising 3.43 percent on the week to close at 12,361.32, in a rally that may be seen as short-covering. Shares of Hansen Natural are poised for further drops with a slowdown in the energy drink market.

21508 ■ "Maternity Wear Goes Green" in *Marketing to Women* (Vol. 21, March 2008, No. 3, pp. 3)
Pub: EPM Communications, Inc.
Description: Mother's Work Inc. has launched a series of environmentally-friendly products made from such sustainable fibers as organic cotton and bamboo.

21509 ■ "McCormick Focuses on Customer, Dealer Service" in *Farm Industry News* (September 17, 2010)
Pub: Penton Business Media Inc.
Description: McCormick has developed a new plan that focuses on fast and complete service to both customers and dealers.

21510 ■ "Melamine Analytical Methods Released" in *Feedstuffs* (Vol. 80, October 6, 2008, No. 41, pp. 2)
Pub: Miller Publishing Company
Description: Romer Labs has released new validations for its AgraQuant Melamine enzyme-linked immunosorbent assay. The test kit screens for melamine in feed and diary products, including pet foods, milk and milk powder. Melamine by itself is nontoxic in low doses, but when combined with cyanuric acid it can cause fatal kidney stones. The Chinese dairy industry is in the midst of a huge melamine crisis; melamine-contaminated dairy and food products from China have been found in more than 20 countries.

21511 ■ "Milk Producers Target Moms" in *Marketing to Women* (Vol. 21, January 2008, No. 1, pp. 3)
Pub: EPM Communications, Inc.
Description: In an attempt to encourage moms to serve milk with meals, the American Dairy Association partners with the New York State Dietetic Association to promote milk via a new logo, website and contest.

21512 ■ "Minimizing Import Risks" in *Canadian Sailings* (July 7, 2008)
Pub: Commonwealth Business Media
Ed: Jack Kohane. **Description:** New food and product safety laws may be enacted by Canada's Parliament; importers, retailers and manufacturers could face huge fines if the new laws are passed.

21513 ■ "Minnesota Farms' Net Worth Grows 10 Percent Each Year for 15 Years" in *Farm Industry News* (August 22, 2011)
Pub: Penton Business Media Inc.
Ed: Dale Nordquist. **Description:** The average value of farms in Minnesota is growing at a fast pace. Total assets per farm have increased by more than $1.1 million over the past 15 years. Statistical data included.

21514 ■ "Monsanto's Next Single-Bag Refuge Product Approved" in *Farm Industry News* (December 5, 2011)
Pub: Penton Business Media Inc.
Description: Monsanto's refuge-in-a-bag (RIB) product was approved for commercialization in 2012. The Genuity VT Double Pro RIB Complete is a blend of 95 percent Genuity VT Double Pro and 5 percent refuge (non-Bt) seed and provides above-ground pest control and not corn rootworm protection.

21515 ■ "The Mood of a Nation" in *Canadian Business* (Vol. 81, April 14, 2008, No. 6, pp. 56)
Pub: Rogers Media
Ed: Joe Castaldo. **Description:** Independent Fish Harvesters Inc. processes more kilograms a year and has had to hire more workers but its managers worry about how a slowdown in the U.S. economy will affect his business. A planned shopping complex in Mirabel Quebec, the manufacturing industry in Kitchener, Ontario, and a cattle farming business in Sarnia, Ontario are discussed to provide a snapshot of the challenges that business in Canada are facing as recession looms.

21516 ■ "More Cuts On the Way At Ag School" in *Business First-Columbus* (December 14, 2007, pp. A1)
Pub: American City Business Journals, Inc.
Ed: Carrie Ghose. **Description:** Program cuts at Ohio State University's Agriculture School are discussed. A voluntary retirement incentive to reduce staff was approved by the University's trustees. Since 2000, the College of Food, Agricultural and Environmental Sciences' staff have decreased by 21 percent, while the faculty experienced a 25 percent reduction. According to Bobby Moser, the college's dean, the institution is looking for other ways to generate income.

21517 ■ "Most Viewed Stories, Videos on farmindustrynews.com in 2010" in *Farm Industry News* (January 4, 2011)
Pub: Penton Business Media Inc.
Description: The top ten most popularly viewed stories and videos presented on farmindustrynews.com Website are listed.

21518 ■ *National Agri-Marketing Association—Directory of Members*
Pub: National Agri-Marketing Association
Contact: Jenny Pickett, Exec. VP/CEO
E-mail: jennyp@nama.org
Released: Annual, January. **Price:** $150. **Covers:** 2,500 persons active in agricultural advertising and marketing for manufacturers, advertising agencies, and media. Published as part of the Agri-Marketing Marketing Services Guide. **Entries Include:** Member name and position, company name, address, phone. **Arrangement:** Geographical, alphabetical.

21519 ■ "National Cattlemen's Beef Association" in *Retail Merchandiser* (Vol. 51, September-October 2011, No. 5, pp. 77)
Pub: Phoenix Media Corporation
Description: National Cattlemen's Beef Association offers a wide range of tools and information to keep its members informed regarding the state of the beef industry. Their Website provides tools to help cattle producers improve operations.

21520 ■ "The New Alchemists" in *Canadian Business* (Vol. 81, October 27, 2008, No. 18, pp. 22)
Pub: Rogers Media Ltd.
Ed: Joe Castaldo. **Description:** Ethanol industry expects second-generation ethanol or cellulosic biofuels to provide ecologically friendly technologies than the ethanol made from food crops. Government and industries are investing on producing cellulosic biofuels.

21521 ■ "New Crop Protection Products from Monsanto, Valent, DuPont, FMC, BASF" in *Farm Industry News* (December 17, 2010)
Pub: Penton Business Media Inc.
Ed: Mark Moore. **Description:** Glyphosate-dominated herbicides are declining because a more diversified market for corn and soybeans is available. New crop care includes old chemistries, new formulations and unique combinations of both giving farmers more choices to protect the yield potential of their corn and soybean crops. Profiles of new products are included.

21522 ■ "New Ethanol Plant Planned In Iowa to Use Corn Stover" in *Farm Industry News* (June 27, 2011)
Pub: Penton Business Media Inc.
Ed: Lynn Grooms. **Description:** DuPont Danisco Cellulosic Ethanol (DDCE) will buy land next to the Lincolnway Energy corn-based ethanol plant in Nevada, Iowa in order to produce ethanol from corn stover at the location.

21523 ■ "New Life for Old Chemistries" in *Farm Industry News* (Vol. 42, January 1, 2009, No. 1)
Pub: Penton Media, Inc.
Ed: Mark Moore. **Description:** To expand the uses of familiar crop protection products, chemical companies are utilizing biotechnology research and develop-

ment tools; many off-patent products are being rejuvenated with small changes to make the product even better than it was when originally conceived.

21524 ■ "New Yetter Stubble Solution Prevents Tire, Track Damage" in *Farm Industry News* (November 21, 2011)
Pub: Penton Business Media Inc.
Description: The new Yetter 5000 Stalk Devastator helps prevent premature tire and track wear and damage caused by crop stubble.

21525 ■ "The Next Big Thing" in *Farm Industry News* (Vol. 42, January 1, 2009, No. 1)
Pub: Penton Media, Inc.
Ed: David Hest. **Description:** Communication technology that allows farmers to detect equipment location, travel speed and real-time fuel and sprayer/combine tank levels will pay off with better machine use efficiency, improved maintenance and reduced downtime. These telemetry systems will be widely available in the next few years.

21526 ■ "Nonstop Round Baler Earns Top International Award for Krone" in *Farm Industry News* (November 18, 2011)
Pub: Penton Business Media Inc.
Ed: Karen McMahon. **Description:** The new Ultima baler from Krone can make and net a bale in 40 seconds without stopping, thus producing 90 bales an hour. The new baler, still in test stage, won top honors at the Agritechnica farm equipment show in Hannover, Germany.

21527 ■ "Numerous Changes Made to Crop Production and Consumption Forecasts" in *Farm Industry News* (November 9, 2011)
Pub: Penton Business Media Inc.
Ed: Darrel Good. **Description:** USDA November Crop Production and WASDE reports contained various changes in production and consumption forecasts for corn, soybeans, and what for the current marketing year. A brief summary for each crop is included.

21528 ■ "Ocean of Opportunity" in *Hawaii Business* (Vol. 53, October 2007, No. 4, pp. 61)
Pub: Hawaii Business Publishing
Ed: Mike Markrich. **Description:** Brew Moon owner Marcus Bender and former Coca-Cola Enterprises Inc. executive Jim Stevens have introduced Kai Vodka in June 2007. The new drink is being marketed to professional women, the number of which is increasing based on a research by the Queens College Department of Sociology. The development process of the new product is also discussed.

21529 ■ "One-Pass Tillage" in *Farm Industry News* (Vol. 42, January 1, 2009, No. 1)
Pub: Penton Media, Inc.
Description: Bigham Brothers Inc.'s One Pass Terr-Till, a tool that breaks up compacted soil while cutting heavy residue, is reviewed.

21530 ■ "OPEC Exposed" in *Hawaii Business* (Vol. 54, September 2008, No. 3, pp. 2)
Pub: Hawaii Business Publishing
Ed: Serena Lim. **Description:** Organization of the Petroleum Exporting Countries (OPEC) has said that their effort in developing an alternative energy source has driven prices up. The biofuel sector is criticizing the statement, saying that a research study found that biofuels push petroleum prices down by 15 percent. Details on the effect of rising petroleum prices are discussed.

21531 ■ "Org to Moms: Eat Your Veggies" in *Marketing to Women* (Vol. 21, April 2008, No. 4, pp. 3)
Pub: EPM Communications, Inc.
Description: In order to increase the purchase and consumption of fruit and vegetables to moms, the non profit Produce for Better Health Foundation is launching a series of initiatives.

21532 ■ "Outlook for Montana Agriculture" in *Montana Business Quarterly* (Vol. 49, Spring 2011, No. 1, pp. 26)
Pub: Bureau of Business & Economic Research
Ed: George Haynes. **Description:** Montana farmers and ranchers are rebounding from lower prices and production to higher prices and record production in 2010. The state has limited dairy and hog production, but farm income is still likely rise between 15 to 25 percent in 2010 over previous year.

21533 ■ "Perry's Goes Organic" in *Ice Cream Reporter* (Vol. 22, December 20, 2008, No. 1, pp. 1)
Pub: Ice Cream Reporter
Description: Family-owned Perry's Ice Cream is starting a new line of organic ice cream in both vanilla and chocolate flavors. All Perry's products are made with milk and cream from local dairy farmers.

21534 ■ "Pet-Food Industry Too Slow" in *Advertising Age* (Vol. 78, March 26, 2007, No. 13, pp. 29)
Pub: Crain Communications, Inc.
Ed: Description: Many crisis-communications experts believe that the pet-food industry mishandled the problem by waiting almost a month to recall the 60 million "wet-food" products after numerous consumer complaints. Experts site that the first 24 to 49 hours are the most important in dealing with a crisis of this nature.

21535 ■ "Pioneer Unveils Drought-Tolerant Hybrids" in *Farm Industry News* (January 6, 2011)
Pub: Penton Business Media Inc.
Description: Eight new drought-tolerant hybrids are now available across five genetic platforms from Pioneer. The new hybrids, marketed under the Optimum AQUAmax brand name (previously announced as Drought Tolerant 1 Hybrids), contain a collection of native corn traits that improve water access and utilization.

21536 ■ "Playing Defense" in *Crain's Chicago Business* (Vol. 31, November 10, 2008, No. 45, pp. 4)
Pub: Crain Communications, Inc.
Ed: Monee Fields-White. **Description:** Chicago's money managers are increasingly investing in local companies such as Caterpillar Inc., a maker of construction and mining equipment, Kraft Foods Inc. and Baxter International Inc., a manufacturer of medical products, in an attempt to bolster their portfolios. These companies have a history of surviving tough economic times.

21537 ■ "Potash Sale Must Be Blocked" in *Canadian Business* (Vol. 83, October 12, 2010, No. 17, pp. 24)
Pub: Rogers Media Ltd.
Ed: Kasey Coholan. **Description:** Chief executive officers (CEOs) and corporate leaders in Canada are concerned about the possible sale of Potash Corporation to foreign buyers. A Compas Inc. poll recently asked CEOs whether the Canadian Government should step in to block the sale of the country's largest fertilizer firm.

21538 ■ "Precision Crop Control with Valley Irrigation/CropMetrics Partnership" in *Farm Industry News* (January 6, 2011)
Pub: Penton Business Media Inc.
Description: Irrigation systems have become a precision farming tool since partnering with agronomic software systems to apply products across the field by prescription. Valley Irrigation and CropMetrics have partnered in order to variably control water, fertilizer and other crop management products through a center pivot irrigation system.

21539 ■ "Precision Fertilizer Spreading Shown at Agritechnica" in *Farm Industry News* (November 23, 2011)
Pub: Penton Business Media Inc.
Ed: Karen McMahon. **Description:** Rauch, the German firm, introduced a new system that precisely spreads fertilizer on crops. The new product was shown at Agritechnica.

21540 ■ "Preparing for Weed Control" in *Farmer's Weekly* (March 28, 2008, No. 320)
Pub: Reed Business Information
Description: Profile of Richard Beachell who farms in a joint venture with his neighbor. Beachell discusses nitrogen applications, fungicides and the reduction of pesticides.

21541 ■ "Presidential Address: Innovation in Retrospect and Prospect" in *Canadian Journal of Electronics* (Vol. 43, November 2010, No. 4)
Pub: Journal of the Canadian Economics Association
Ed: James A. Brander. **Description:** Has innovation slowed in recent decades? While there has been progress in information and communications technology, the recent record of innovation in agriculture, energy, transportation and healthcare sectors is cause for concern.

21542 ■ "Press Release: New Corn Hybrid from Seed Consultants" in *Farm Industry News* (January 6, 2011)
Pub: Penton Business Media Inc.
Description: Seed Consultants Inc. is releasing its first proprietary corn line called SC 1101. The product was developed, bred, and tested for the eastern Corn Belt diseases, soils, and growing conditions.

21543 ■ "Press Release: New Trough Drinker From Pride of the Farm" in *Farm Industry News* (January 5, 2011)
Pub: Penton Business Media Inc.
Description: Model WPO70 is a 90-inch long trough drinker designed for high-capacity feedyard applications and features foam-filly poly construction and a rib-reinforced trough. A description of this new offering from Pride of the Farm is included.

21544 ■ "Press Release: Revolver Grain Auger End from Mauer Manufacturing" in *Farm Industry News* (December 17, 2010)
Pub: Penton Business Media Inc.
Description: Profile of the Revolver Grain Auger End from Mauer Manufacturing is presented. The new design eliminates grain loss/dribble, reduces grain in the next year's crop, and has a greater clearance for combine unloading auger.

21545 ■ "Press Release: Trimble Introduces CFX-750 Display" in *Farm Industry News* (January 4, 2011)
Pub: Penton Business Media Inc.
Description: Trimble is offering a touch screen display called the CFX-750. The new 8-inch full-color display allows farmers to choose the specific guidance, steering and precision agriculture capabilities that best fit their farm's particular needs. The display can be upgraded as business needs change, including the addition of GLONASS capabilities, or the addition of section and rate control for crop inputs such as seed, chemicals and fertilizer.

21546 ■ "Pressure Growing on Processors" in *Farmer's Weekly* (March 28, 2008, No. 320)
Pub: Reed Business Information
Description: Increasing milk prices may be inevitable in order to stop more farmers from leaving the industry and encourage them to produce more milk.

21547 ■ "Prison Farms are Closing, but the Manure Remains" in *Canadian Business* (Vol. 83, August 17, 2010, No. 13-14, pp. 9)
Pub: Rogers Media Ltd.
Ed: Steve Maich. **Description:** The explanation given by Canada's government ministers on planned closure of the prison farms and scrapping of the long form census are designed by mixing of spin, argument and transparent justification. The defense should have been plausible but the ministers could not handle the simple questions about statistics and prison job training with pretense.

21548 ■ "Pro Livestock Launches Most Comprehensive Virtual Sales Barn for Livestock and Breed Stock" in *Benzinga.com* (October 29, 2011)
Pub: Benzinga.com
Ed: Benzinga Staff. **Description:** Pro Livestock Marketing launched the first online sales portal for livestock and breed stock. The firm has designed a

virtual sales barn allowing individuals to purchase and sell cattle, swine, sheep, goats, horses, rodeo stock, show animals, specialty animals, semen and embryos globally. It is like an eBay for livestock and will help ranchers and farmers grow.

21549 ■ "Prosecutors Dish Sordid AIPC Story" in *The Business Journal-Serving Metropolitan Kansas City* (Vol. 27, September 19, 2008, No. 1)
Pub: American City Business Journals, Inc.
Ed: Suzanna Stagemeyer. **Description:** Prosecutors in the American Italian Pasta Co.'s accounting fraud case have revealed evidence on the schemes used by then-officers of the company to commit fraud. District attorney John Wood has dubbed the case as the largest corporate fraud lawsuit in the history of the district of Missouri. How AIPC fell from being an industry leader is also discussed.

21550 ■ "Purdue Agronomist: Consider Costs Before Tilling" in *Farm Industry News* (November 8, 2011)
Pub: Penton Business Media Inc.
Ed: Lisa Schluttenhofer. **Description:** Farmers consider soil drainage, fertilizer and planting needs as well as economic thresholds before making tillage decisions, according to a Purdue extension agronomist.

21551 ■ "The Quality Revolution" in *Canadian Business* (Vol. 81, November 10, 2008, No. 19, pp. 128)
Pub: Rogers Media Ltd.
Ed: Andrew Nikiforuk. **Description:** John Volpe believes that the pursuit of quantity of food choices leads to tasteless meals, expanding waistlines, and food poisoning and stresses emphasis on food quality and food security.

21552 ■ "R&D Will Remain a Key Priority" in *Farmer's Weekly* (March 28, 2008, No. 320)
Pub: Reed Business Information
Description: Executives as well as the board of the new Horticultural Development Company (HDC) remain committed to the efficient delivery of research and development, a promotional drive and communications over the coming year.

21553 ■ "Recipe for Disaster?" in *Sacramento Business Journal* (Vol. 25, July 4, 2008, No. 18, pp. 1)
Pub: American City Business Journals, Inc.
Ed: Mark Anderson. **Description:** Restaurateurs are challenged with balancing rising operating costs and what customers are willing to pay for their services. Flour prices in 2008 have increased by 46 percent from April 2007. Other views on the situation, as well as trends, forecasts and statistics on sales, outlook on economic conditions, consumer price index, and the typical split of restaurant revenue, are presented.

21554 ■ "Red Diesel Cost Sparks a Move to Home-Grown Fuel" in *Farmer's Weekly* (March 28, 2008, No. 320)
Pub: Reed Business Information
Description: Due to the rising cost of red diesel, the idea of growing one's own tractor fuel has an undeniable attraction for many farmers. A growing pressure is weighing on engine manufacturers to produce designs that can run on both SVO as well as biodiesel.

21555 ■ "Red, Pink and More: Cause Marketing Surges as a Prime Tactic to Reach Female Customers" in *Marketing to Women* (April 2008)
Pub: EPM Communications, Inc.
Description: According to the American Marketing Association, forty percent of women say they are more likely to purchase a product or service if they know a certain amount of the price is being donated directly to a cause or campaign that they believe in supporting.

21556 ■ "Report: McD's Pepsi Score Best With Young Hispanics" in *Brandweek* (Vol. 49, April 21, 2008, No. 16, pp. 8)
Pub: VNU Business Media, Inc.
Ed: Della de Lafuente. **Description:** According to a new report, in order to reach Hispanic Gen Yers, marketing strategists need to understand this demographic's "bi-dentity," something which has proved an elusive task to many marketers. Another trend is the emergence of Latinas who have careers, as opposed to just jobs. There is an opportunity to tap this new, young and empowered female market with innovative messaging. Statistical data included.

21557 ■ "Roll Your Own" in *Business North Carolina* (Vol. 28, March 2008, No. 3, pp. 66)
Pub: Business North Carolina
Ed: Amanda Parry. **Description:** Profile of U.S. Flue-Cured Tobacco Growers who process tobacco and make cigarettes. Details of the program are outlined.

21558 ■ "Roseville Investing Big in Downtown" in *Sacramento Business Journal* (Vol. 28, September 2, 2011, No. 27, pp. 1)
Pub: Sacramento Business Journal
Ed: Michael Shaw. **Description:** The city of Roseville, California is planning to invest in downtown development projects. The plan includes a new town square, a venue for a farmers market and an interactive water fountain.

21559 ■ "Russian Renaissance" in *Chicago Tribune* (September 22, 2008)
Pub: McClatchy-Tribune Information Services
Ed: Alex Rodriguez. **Description:** Winemakers from Russia are returning to the craft and quality of winemaking now that they are free from Soviet restraints.

21560 ■ "Safer Ammonium-Nitrate-Based Fertilizer" in *Farm Industry News* (Vol. 42, January 1, 2009, No. 1)
Pub: Penton Media, Inc.
Description: Honeywell has patented a new technology which it will use to develop a highly effective, safer ammonium-nitrate-based fertilizer that has a significantly lower potential for explosion.

21561 ■ "Salary Hike for Managers Reflects Demand" in *Farmer's Weekly* (March 28, 2008, No. 320)
Pub: Reed Business Information
Description: Discusses the Institute of Agricultural Management and its survey of farm managers' pay and conditions; farm managers are getting paid 25 percent more than in 2003.

21562 ■ "SCPA Members Seek Senate Support for H.R. 872" in *Farm Industry News* (May 26, 2011)
Pub: Penton Business Media Inc.
Ed: Forrest Laws. **Description:** U.S. House of Representatives passed legislation, H.R. 872 the Reducing Regulatory Burdens Act that frees pesticide applicators from having to obtain NPDES permits for applications over or near water.

21563 ■ "The Second Most Fuel-Efficient Tractor of the Decade: John Deere 8320R" in *Farm Industry News* (November 10, 2011)
Pub: Penton Business Media Inc.
Description: John Deere's 8320R Tractor was ranked second in the Farm Industry News listing of the top 40 most fuel-efficient tractors of the decade, following the winner, John Deere's 8295R PTO tractor.

21564 ■ "Seed-Count Labeling" in *Farm Industry News* (October 20, 2010)
Pub: Penton Business Media Inc.
Ed: Mark Moore. **Description:** National Conference on Weights and Measures voted to standardize testing methods and procedures that will verify seed-count labeling.

21565 ■ "Self-Employment in the United States" in *Montly Labor Review* (Vol. 133, September 2010, No. 9, pp. 17)
Pub: Bureau of Labor Statistics
Description: Self employment in 2009 in the U.S. continued to be more common among men, Whites, Asians, and older workers and in the agriculture, construction, and services industries.

21566 ■ "Shear Profit" in *Crain's Cleveland Business* (Vol. 28, October 29, 2007, No. 43, pp. 3)
Pub: Crain Communications, Inc.
Ed: David Bennett. **Description:** Alpaca farms are becoming a very profitable business for a number of Northeast Ohio entrepreneurs due to the high return on initial investments, tax incentives and the rise in demand for the animals. Ohio leads the country in the number of alpaca farms with roughly one-third located in Northeast Ohio.

21567 ■ "A Simple Old Reg that Needs Dusting Off" in *Barron's* (Vol. 88, June 30, 2008, No. 26, pp. 35)
Pub: Dow Jones & Co., Inc.
Ed: Gene Epstein. **Description:** Senator Joe Lieberman has a point when he accused speculators of inflating the prices of food and fuel futures but introducing legislation to address speculation has an alternative. The senator's committee should instead demand that the Commodity Futures Trading Commission enforce position limits on the maximum number of contracts in a given market per speculative entity.

21568 ■ "Sleep It Off In a Silo B & B" in *Chicago Tribune* (December 14, 2008)
Pub: McClatchy-Tribune Information Services
Ed: Bill Daley. **Description:** Profile of Oregon's Abbey Road Farm bed-and-breakfast which is located on an 82-acre working farm; guests stay in shiny metal farm silos which have been converted into luxury rooms with views of the farm.

21569 ■ "A Soggy Harvest" in *Business Journal-Portland* (Vol. 24, October 5, 2007, No. 32, pp. 1)
Pub: American City Business Journals, Inc.
Ed: Robin J. Moody. **Description:** Vintners in Willamette Valley are facing a tough challenge with a rainy wine harvest season and a delay in the ripening of grapes due to a cool spring and August. Rain decreased the sugar content of grapes and poses a danger with molds. The economic impact of the rainy harvest season in wine making is discussed.

21570 ■ "Sole Proprietorship Returns, 2008 Part 2" in *SOI Bulletin* (Vol. 30, Summer 2010, No. 1, pp. 27)
Pub: Government Printing Office
Description: Table of Nonfarm Sole Proprietorships is presented. Statistics are broken down by sector reporting all nonfarm industries as well as agriculture, forestry, hunting and fishing.

21571 ■ "Spend Wisely on Managing Your Hedgerows" in *Farmer's Weekly* (March 28, 2008, No. 320)
Pub: Reed Business Information
Ed: Richard Winspear. **Description:** Discusses the importance of a well-managed hedge which should gradually grow upwards and outwards where eventually it would reach the point when rejuvenation by coppicing or laying was needed to restart the cycle.

21572 ■ "State Investment Goes Sour" in *Business Journal Portland* (Vol. 26, December 4, 2009, No. 39, pp. 1)
Pub: American City Business Journals Inc.
Ed: Erik Siemers. **Description:** Oregon might recoup only $500,000 of a $20 million loan to Vancouver-based Cascade Grain Products LLC. Cascade Grain's ethanol plant in Clatskanie, OR will be put into auction under the supervision of a bankruptcy court.

21573 ■ "Stone to Run Hickory Farmer's Market" in *Charlotte Observer* (January 31, 2007)
Pub: Knight-Ridder/Tribune Business News
Ed: Jen Aronoff. **Description:** Betty Stone has been hired to manage the Downtown Hickory Farmers Market. The market will run from May 5 through October 6, 2007.

21574 ■ "Stronger Corn? Take It Off Steroids, Make It All Female" in *Farm Industry News* (December 5, 2011)
Pub: Penton Business Media Inc.
Ed: Brian Wallheimer. **Description:** Purdue University researcher found that higher improvements in corn crops, and possibly other crops, were yielded when steroids were discontinued.

21575 ■ "Taking the 'Comprehensive' Out of Immigration Reform" in *Hispanic Business* (September 2007, pp. 8)
Pub: Hispanic Business
Ed: Patricia Guadalupe. **Description:** Information about the AgJOBS bill, legislation that would grant legal residency to migrant agricultural workers is discussed.

21576 ■ "Temporary Measures" in *Occupational Outlook Quarterly* (Vol. 54, Fall 2010, No. 3, pp. 36)
Pub: U.S. Bureau of Labor Statistics
Description: Data on temporary help services employment from the U.S. Bureau of Labor Statistics suggests good news for all nonfarm workers. The data had been rising steadily for most of 2009.

21577 ■ "The Trouble With $150,000 Wine" in *Barron's* (Vol. 88, July 7, 2008, No. 27, pp. 33)
Pub: Dow Jones & Co., Inc.
Ed: Orley Ashenfelter. **Description:** Review of the book, "The Billionaire's Vinegar: The Mystery of the World's Most Expensive Bottle of Wine," which discusses vintners along with the marketing and distribution of wine as well as the winemaking industry as a whole.

21578 ■ "Time to Leave the Party?" in *Barron's* (Vol. 88, March 24, 2008, No. 12, pp. M16)
Pub: Dow Jones & Company, Inc.
Ed: Andrea Hotter. **Description:** Prices of commodities such as gold, copper, crude oil, sugar, cocoa, and wheat have fallen from their all-time highs set in the middle of March 2008. Analysts, however, caution that this decline in prices may be temporary, and that a banking crisis may trigger new price rises in commodities.

21579 ■ "Too Much Precaution About Biotech Corn" in *Barron's* (Vol. 88, March 17, 2008, No. 11, pp. 54)
Pub: Dow Jones & Company, Inc.
Ed: Mark I. Schwartz. **Description:** In the U.S., 90 percent of cultivated soybeans are biotech varietals as well as 60 percent of the corn. Farmers have significantly reduced their reliance on pesticides in the growing of biotech corn. Biotech cotton cultivation has brought hundreds of millions of dollars in net financial gains to farmers. The European Union has precluded the cultivation or sale of biotech crops within its border.

21580 ■ "Top 50 Exporters" in *Hispanic Business* (Vol. 30, July-August 2008, No. 7-8, pp. 42)
Pub: Hispanic Business, Inc.
Ed: Hildy Medina. **Description:** Increases in exports revenues reported by food exporters and green companies in a time of economic slowdown in the U.S are described. Food exporters have benefited from the growth of high-volume grocery stores in underdeveloped countries and the German governments' promotion of solar energy has benefited the U.S. solar heating equipment and solar panel manufactures.

21581 ■ "Top Design Award for Massey Ferguson 7624 Dyna-VT" in *Farm Industry News* (November 14, 2011)
Pub: Penton Business Media Inc.
Description: Massey Ferguson won top honors for its MF 7624 Dyna-VT as the Golden Tractor for Design award in the 2012 Tractor of the Year competition. The award is presented annually by journalists from 22 leading farming magazines in Europe and manufacturers have to be nominated to enter.

21582 ■ "Top Worst Weeds in Corn" in *Farm Industry News* (November 29, 2011)
Pub: Penton Business Media Inc.
Ed: John Pocock. **Description:** Effective weed control for profitable crops is discussed with information from leading weed scientists from the University of Illinois Extension. It is important for farmers to know what their worst weed is in order to choose the best product, or mix of products, to control them.

21583 ■ "Trading Down at the Supermarket" in *Barron's* (Vol. 88, July 14, 2008, No. 28, pp. 36)
Pub: Dow Jones & Co., Inc.
Ed: Alexander Eule. **Description:** Shares of Ralcorp Holdings are cheap at around $49.95 after slipping 20 percent prior to their acquisition of Post cereals from Kraft. Some analysts believe its shares could climb over 60 percent to $80 as value-seeking consumers buy more private label products.

21584 ■ "Tri-State to Get New Headquarters" in *Business Courier* (Vol. 27, October 22, 2010, No. 25, pp. 1)
Pub: Business Courier
Ed: James Ritchie. **Description:** Hong Kong-based corn processing firm Global Bio-Chem Technology is set to choose Greater Cincinnati, Ohio as a location of its North American headquarters. The interstate access, central location, and low labor and property costs might have enticed Global Bio-Chem to invest in the region. Statistics on Chinese direct investment in U.S. are also presented.

21585 ■ "Trouble With Transport" in *Farmer's Weekly* (March 28, 2008, No. 320)
Pub: Reed Business Information
Description: Profile of Richard Crewe and his wife Jane who farm alongside a main trans-Canadian railway line but keep getting pushed back on their delivery of malt barley.

21586 ■ "Truffled Ahead: Farms for Rare Delicacy Gain Ground In State" in *Puget Sound Business Journal* (Vol. 29, December 26, 2008, No. 36)
Pub: American City Business Journals
Ed: Steve Wilhelm. **Description:** Twenty farmers in Washington started small plots for truffles, which are irregular fungi growing around tree roots and are considered restaurant delicacies. These truffles could generate $35,000 per acre, although they need a decade to mature.

21587 ■ "Turfway Slowing its Gait" in *Business Courier* (Vol. 26, November 6, 2009, No. 28, pp. 1)
Pub: American City Business Journals, Inc.
Ed: Jon Newberry. **Description:** Kentucky's Turfway Park will be decreasing its weekly race schedule from five days to three days in the first two months of 2010, and to four days in March 2010. The decision to make reductions in the schedule is attributed to the relocation of thoroughbred racing to states that allow casino gambling. As a result, Turfway Park's resources and purse money would be focused on less days.

21588 ■ "Up on the Farm" in *Canadian Business* (Vol. 81, October 27, 2008, No. 18, pp. 119)
Pub: Rogers Media Ltd.
Ed: Sean Silcoff. **Description:** Investing in Saskatchewan's agricultural land is explored. Calvert government's lifting of restrictions on ownership of land have enabled Doug Emsley and Brad Farquhar to invest in farmlands in the area. Emsley and Farquhar lease the farmlands they own, enabling farmers to buy equipment and improve crop yields.

21589 ■ "Up On The Farm" in *Canadian Business* (Vol. 81, March 31, 2008, No. 5, pp. 23)
Pub: Rogers Media
Ed: John Gray. **Description:** Agricultural products have outperformed both energy and metal and even the prospect of a global economic slowdown does not seem to hinder its prospects. The Organization for Economic Cooperation and Development sees prices above historic equilibrium levels during the next ten years given that fuel and fertilizers remain high and greater demand from India and China remain steady

21590 ■ "Versatile's Back" in *Farm Industry News* (Vol. 42, January 1, 2009, No. 1)
Pub: Penton Media, Inc.
Ed: Jodie Wehrspann. **Description:** Overview of Winnipeg, Manitoba's tractor manufacturer Versatile's strategy to rebrand its tractor segment; the strategy comes a year after Russian Combine Factory Rostselmash Ltd. bought the majority share of common stock from the Canadian business.

21591 ■ "A Very Good Year for Beer" in *Entrepreneur* (Vol. 37, October 2009, No. 10, pp. 18)
Pub: Entrepreneur Media, Inc.
Ed: Jennie Dorris. **Description:** Americans are shifting to craft beers, as shown by the almost 6 percent rise in craft beer sales in 2008. Mass-market domestic brand sales grew 0.6 percent while imported beer sales declined by 3.4 percent.

21592 ■ "Virus Threatens WNY Peach Industry" in *Business First Buffalo* (October 12, 2007, pp. 1)
Pub: American City Business Journals, Inc.
Ed: Thomas Hartley. **Description:** Plum pox virus, which first appeared in Niagara County, Buffalo, New York in 2005, attacks peaches and there is no known cure to date. The $2 million peach industry in West New York can be destroyed by this virus, which is safe for humans, but makes peaches unmarketable. Other information about plum pox virus and the potential economic damage it can cause is discussed.

21593 ■ "We All Scream for Ice Cream" in *Crain's Chicago Business* (Vol. 31, April 28, 2008, No. 17, pp. 48)
Pub: Crain Communications, Inc.
Ed: Phuong Ly. **Description:** Profile of Oberweis' ice cream shops which has expanded its business by delivering dairy products to grocery stores.

21594 ■ "Welch's Uses Taste Strips in Ads" in *Marketing to Women* (Vol. 21, April 2008, No. 4, pp. 3)
Pub: EPM Communications, Inc.
Description: Welch's is positioning its 139-year-old brand in a new and inventive way with a new marketing campaign in which print ads will feature a tamper-evident flavor pouch that contains a dissolving taste strip flavored with Welch's grape juice.

21595 ■ "Welsh Meat Sales on the Rise" in *Farmer's Weekly* (March 28, 2008, No. 320)
Pub: Reed Business Information
Description: Due, in part, to marketing efforts, retail sales of Welsh lamb and beef rose significantly in the first two months of 2008.

21596 ■ "What'll You Have Tonight?" in *Barron's* (Vol. 88, July 4, 2008, No. 28, pp. 22)
Pub: Dow Jones & Co., Inc.
Ed: Neil A. Martin. **Description:** Shares of Diageo could rise by 30 percent a year from June 2008 after it slipped due to U.S. sales worries. The company also benefits from the trend toward more premium alcoholic beverage brands worldwide especially in emerging markets.

21597 ■ "What's In a Name?" in *Barron's* (Vol. 88, March 17, 2008, No. 11, pp. 7)
Pub: Dow Jones & Company, Inc.
Ed: Alan Abelson. **Description:** Eliot Spitzer's resignation incidentally caused the stock market to go up by 400 points. The Federal Reserve Board's new Term Securities Lending Facility provides liquidity to the big lenders by funneling $200 billion in the form of 28-day loans of Treasuries. The analysis of Paul Brodsky and Lee Quaintance of QB Partners on the demand for commodities is also discussed.

21598 ■ "Where Canada Meets the World" in *Canadian Business* (Vol. 80, October 8, 2007, No. 20, pp. 86)
Pub: Rogers Media
Ed: Zena Olijnyk. **Description:** An overview of facilities within Canada's borders that contributes to the country's economy is presented. The facilities include

fishing vessels and seaports. Agencies that regulate the borders such as the Canada Border Services Agency and the Department of Fisheries and Oceans are also presented.

21599 ■ "Which Direction are Herbicides Heading?" in *Farm Industry News* (October 11, 2011)
Pub: Penton Business Media Inc.
Ed: Jennifer Shike. **Description:** Currently, one of the best solutions for growers fighting weed resistance may be 2,4-D or other auxin herbicides.

21600 ■ "The Whole Package" in *Entrepreneur* (Vol. 36, February 2008, No. 2, pp. 24)
Pub: Entrepreneur Media Inc.
Description: Holy Bohn, owner of The Honest Statute, developed an environmentally-friendly packaging for her pet food products. The company hired a packaging consultant and spent $175,000. Big corporations also spend money and plunge into the latest trends in packaging ranging from lighter and flexible to temperature-sensitive labels.

21601 ■ "Why Nestle Should Sell Alcon" in *Barron's* (Vol. 88, March 17, 2008, No. 11, pp. M12)
Pub: Dow Jones & Company, Inc.
Ed: Sean Walters. **Description:** Nestle should sell Alcon because Nestle can't afford to be complacent as its peers have made changes to their portfolios to boost competitiveness. Nestle's stake in Alcon and L'Oreal have been ignored by investors and Nestle could realize better value by strengthening its nutrition division through acquisitions.

21602 ■ "The Worm Lady" in *Hawaii Business* (Vol. 53, October 2007, No. 4, pp. 57)
Pub: Hawaii Business Publishing
Ed: Jolyn Okimoto Rosa. **Description:** Mindy Jaffe, also known as the worm lady, founded the Waikiki Worm Company in 2004 and sells composting worms. The company, which received much attention from the media, has earned $54,000 in revenue in 2004, and $92,000 and $120,000 in 2005 and 2006, respectively. Jaffe's past ventures and the challenges she is facing with her new company are discussed.

21603 ■ "Wrigley's a Rich Meal for Mars" in *Crain's Chicago Business* (Vol. 31, May 5, 2008, No. 18, pp. 2)
Pub: Crain Communications, Inc.
Ed: Steven R. Strahler. **Description:** Mars Inc. will have to manage wisely in order to make their acquisition of Wm. Wrigley Jr. Co. profitable due to the high selling price of Wrigley which far exceeds the industry norm. Statistical data included.

TRADE PERIODICALS

21604 ■ *Agri Marketing*
Pub: Doane Agricultural Services
Contact: Judy Knoll, Customer Service managing editorager
E-mail: judyk@agrimarketing.com
Released: Monthly. **Price:** $42 U.S. and Canada; $72 U.S. and Canada two years; $70 other countries; $120 other countries two years. **Description:** Magazine covering marketing, sales, and communications news for agribusiness professionals.

21605 ■ *Agribusiness*
Pub: John Wiley & Sons Inc.
Contact: Harry M. Kaiser, Assoc. Ed.
Ed: Ronald W. Cotterill, Editor, fmpc@canr.cag.uconn.edu. **Released:** Quarterly. **Price:** $1,749 institutions print only; $1,805 institutions, Canada print only; $1,833 institutions rest of world, print only; $1,924 institutions print with online; $1,980 institutions, Canada print with online; $2,008 institutions rest of world, print with online. **Description:** Publication focusing on applied research in agribusiness, including agricultural inputs, agricultural production, commodity processing, food manufacturing, and food distribution.

21606 ■ *American Journal of Agricultural Economics*
Pub: John Wiley & Sons Inc.
Ed: Paul V. Preckel, Editor. **Released:** 5/yr. **Price:** $301 institutions print & online; $273 institutions print, online; $314 institutions print & online; $285 institutions print, online; $314 institutions, other countries print & online; $285 institutions, other countries print, online. **Description:** Journal of agricultural and resource economics.

21607 ■ *Arizona Farm Bureau News*
Pub: Arizona Farm Bureau Federation
Released: Semimonthly. **Price:** $25, U.S.. **Description:** Covers the agricultural industry with an emphasis on Arizona. Specializes in issue specific and regulatory news.

21608 ■ *Canola Digest*
Pub: Canola Council of Canada
Contact: Kelly Funke, Assoc. Ed.
E-mail: funkek@canola-council.org
Ed: Dave Wilkins, Editor, wilkinsd@canola-council.org. **Released:** 4x/yr. **Price:** $35, U.S. and Canada. **Description:** Provides information on canola and related interests. Recurring features include on farm articles, market reports analysis, news of research, a calendar of events, reports of meetings, and news of educational opportunities, industry news and issues.

21609 ■ *Composting News*
Pub: McEntee Media Corp.
Ed: Ken McEntee, Editor, ken@recycle.cc. **Released:** Monthly. **Price:** $83, individuals; $93, Canada and Mexico; $105, other countries. **Description:** Covers news and trends in the composting industry. Also reports on compost product prices. Recurring features include letters to the editor, interviews, news of research, a calendar of events, reports of meetings, and notices of publications available.

21610 ■ *The Davlin Report*
Pub: The Davlin Report Inc.
Ed: Andrew Davlin, Jr., Editor, aquaandy@aol.com. **Released:** Periodic. **Price:** $39.95, U.S. 4 issues; $59.95, U.S. 8 issues. **Description:** Reports on the aquaculture industry & companies, oil & gas companies & attractive common stocks.

21611 ■ *Farm Bureau News*
Pub: American Farm Bureau Federation
Contact: Phyllis Brown, Assistant Editor
Ed: Lynne Finnerty, Editor, lynnef@fb.org. **Released:** Bimonthly, except monthly in August & December. **Price:** $10, individuals $10/year; $30, individuals first class delivery; $48, elsewhere surface mail; $63, elsewhere airmail. **Description:** Discusses current legislation, court decisions, trade issues, and the use of innovative production methods. Recurring features include editorials, commentaries and the President's Column.

21612 ■ *Farm Industry News*
Pub: Southwest Farm Press
Contact: Karen McMahon, Editor-in-Chief
E-mail: karen.mcmahon@penton.com
Released: 12/yr. **Description:** Agriculture trade magazine covering new products and technology.

21613 ■ *Farm and Ranch News*
Pub: Farm & Ranch News
Contact: George Parker Jr., Editor & Publisher
E-mail: george@farmandranchnews.com
Released: Monthly. **Price:** $12.50 in Florida; $15 out of state. **Description:** Trade publication covering agribusiness issues for commercial farmers and ranchers.

21614 ■ *Farming Uncle*
Pub: TORO
Contact: Louis Toro III, Editor & Publisher
Released: Quarterly. **Price:** $10; $18 two years; $15 other countries; $3 single issue. **Description:** Agricultural magazine.

21615 ■ *Fastline—Illinois Farm Edition*
Pub: Fastline
Released: 13/yr. **Price:** $18; $30 two years; $45 Canada and Mexico; $95 other countries. **Description:** Illustrated buying guide for the farming industry.

21616 ■ *Fastline—Indiana Farm Edition*
Pub: Fastline
Released: 13/yr. **Price:** $35 3 years; $30 two years; $18; $45 Canada and Mexico; $95 other countries. **Description:** Illustrated buying guide for the farming industry.

21617 ■ *Fastline—Iowa Farm Edition*
Pub: Fastline
Released: 13/yr. **Price:** $35 3 years; $30 two years; $18; $45 Canada and Mexico; $95 other countries. **Description:** Illustrated buying guide for the farming industry.

21618 ■ *Fastline—Kansas Farm Edition*
Pub: Fastline
Released: 13/yr. **Price:** $18; $30 two years; $45 Canada and Mexico; $95 other countries; $35 3 years. **Description:** Illustrated buying guide for the farming industry.

21619 ■ *Fastline—Kentucky Farm Edition*
Pub: Fastline
Released: 13/yr. **Price:** $18; $30 two years; $45 Canada and Mexico; $95 other countries; $35 3 years. **Description:** Illustrated buying guide for the farming industry.

21620 ■ *Fastline—Mid-Atlantic Farm Edition*
Pub: Fastline
Released: 13/yr. **Price:** $18; $30 two years; $45 Canada and Mexico; $95 other countries; $35 3 years. **Description:** Illustrated buying guide for the farming industry.

21621 ■ *Fastline—Mid-South Farm Edition*
Pub: Fastline
Released: 13/yr. **Price:** $18; $30 two years; $45 Canada and Mexico; $95 other countries; $35 3 years. **Description:** Illustrated buying guide for the farming industry.

21622 ■ *Fastline—Minnesota Farm Edition*
Pub: Fastline
Released: 13/yr. **Price:** $18; $30 two years; $45 Canada and Mexico; $95 other countries. **Description:** Illustrated buying guide for the farming industry.

21623 ■ *Fastline—Missouri Farm Edition*
Pub: Fastline
Released: 13/yr. **Price:** $18; $30 two years; $45 Canada and Mexico; $95 other countries. **Description:** Illustrated buying guide for the farming industry.

21624 ■ *Fastline—Nebraska Farm Edition*
Pub: Fastline
Released: 13/yr. **Price:** $18; $30 two years; $45 Canada and Mexico; $95 other countries; $35 3 years. **Description:** Illustrated buying guide for the farming industry.

21625 ■ *Fastline—Northeast Farm Edition*
Pub: Fastline
Released: 13/yr. **Price:** $35 3 years; $30 two years; $18; $45 Canada and Mexico; $95 other countries. **Description:** Illustrated buying guide for the farming industry.

21626 ■ *Fastline—Ohio Farm Edition*
Pub: Fastline
Released: 13/yr. **Price:** $18; $30 two years; $45 Canada and Mexico; $95 other countries; $35 3 years. **Description:** Illustrated buying guide for the farming industry.

21627 ■ *Fastline—Oklahoma Farm Edition*
Pub: Fastline
Released: 13/yr. **Price:** $18; $30 two years; $45 Canada and Mexico; $95 other countries; $35 3 years. **Description:** Illustrated buying guide for the farming industry.

21628 ■ *Fastline—Rocky Mountain Farm Edition*
Pub: Fastline
Released: 13/yr. **Price:** $35 3 years; $30 two years; $18; $45 Canada and Mexico; $95 other countries. **Description:** Illustrated buying guide for the farming industry.

21629 ■ *Fastline—Southeast Farm Edition*
Pub: Fastline
Released: 13/yr. **Price:** $18; $30 two years; $45 Canada and Mexico; $95 other countries. **Description:** Illustrated buying guide for the farming industry.

21630 ■ *Fastline—Tennessee Farm Edition*
Pub: Fastline
Released: 13/yr. **Price:** $35 3 years; $30 two years; $45 Canada and Mexico; $95 other countries; $18. **Description:** Illustrated buying guide for the farming industry.

21631 ■ *Fastline—Texas Farm Edition*
Pub: Fastline
Released: 13/yr. **Price:** $18; $30 two years; $45 Canada and Mexico; $95 other countries. **Description:** Illustrated buying guide for the farming industry.

21632 ■ *Fastline—Wisconsin Farm Edition*
Pub: Fastline
Released: 13/yr. **Price:** $35 3 years; $30 two years; $18; $45 Canada and Mexico; $95 other countries. **Description:** Illustrated buying guide for the farming industry.

21633 ■ *Grainews*
Pub: Agricore United
Ed: Lyndsey Smith, Editor, lyndsey@fbcpublishing.com. **Released:** 17/yr (plus specials). **Price:** $41.10 Canada; $67.27 two years. **Description:** A "how-to" paper for Western Canadian farmers and their families.

21634 ■ *Journal of International Food and Agribusiness Marketing*
Pub: Routledge Journals
Contact: Erdener Kaynak, Editor-in-Chief
Released: Quarterly. **Price:** $118 online only; $124 print & online. **Description:** Journal studying food and agribusiness marketing systems in a variety of socioeconomic and political systems around the world.

21635 ■ *The Leader for Agriculture*
Pub: NYFEA—The Association for Educating Agricultural Leaders
Ed: Gordon Stone, Editor, gordonstone@nyfea.org. **Released:** Semiannual. **Price:** $15, individuals. **Description:** Serves as a communications link between state associations. Provides information on state and national educational programs, activities, and meetings. Recurring features include interviews, reports of meetings, and news of educational opportunities.

21636 ■ *Pulse Newsletter*
Pub: Saskatchewan Pulse Corp.
Contact: Donald Jaques, Administrator
Released: Bimonthly. **Price:** $10.70, U.S. and Canada. **Description:** Provides information on the Saskatchewan pulse crop development board, as well as research and marketing of pulses. Recurring features include news of research, a calendar of events, and reports of meetings.

VIDEOCASSETTES/ AUDIOCASSETTES

21637 ■ *The Agricultural Marketplace*
American Management Association
1601 Broadway
New York, NY 10087-7327
Ph:877-566-9441
Free: 800-262-9699
Fax:(518)891-0368
Co. E-mail: customerservice@amanet.org
URL: http://www.amanet.org
Description: Provides information on livestock futures and options in an easily understood language. **Availability:** VHS.

TRADE SHOWS AND CONVENTIONS

21638 ■ Mid-South Farm and Gin Supply Exhibit
Southern Cotton Ginners Association
874 Cotton Gin Pl.
Memphis, TN 38106
Ph:(901)947-3104
Fax:(901)947-3103
Co. E-mail: mary.stice@southerncottonginners.org
URL: http://www.southerncottonginners.org
Released: Annual. **Audience:** Agribusiness professionals. **Principal Exhibits:** Agricultural equipment, supplies and services.

21639 ■ Spokane Ag Expo
Spokane Regional Chamber of Commerce
AG Bureau
801 W. Riverside, Ste. 100
Spokane, WA 99201
Ph:(509)624-1393
Free: 800-776-5263
Fax:(509)747-0077
Co. E-mail: info@chamber.spokane.net
URL: http://www.spokanechamber.org
Released: Annual. **Audience:** Farmers, ranchers, agribusiness professionals, and general public. **Principal Exhibits:** Farm machinery, technology, and services.

21640 ■ VIV Poultry Yutav
Royal Dutch Jaarbeurs
Jaarbeursplein 6
NL-3521 AL Utrecht, Netherlands
Ph:31 30 2955911
Fax:31 30 2940379
Co. E-mail: info@jaarbeursutrecht.nl
URL: http://www.jaarbeursutrecht.nl
Released: Annual. **Principal Exhibits:** Poultry farming, breeding, feed, and processing.

21641 ■ World AgExpo
International Agri-Center, Inc.
4450 S. Laspina St.
PO Box 1475
Tulare, CA 93274-9539
Ph:(559)688-1751
Free: 800-999-9186
Fax:(559)686-5065
Co. E-mail: info@farmshow.org
URL: http://www.farmshow.org
Released: Annual. **Audience:** Farmers, dairymen and international buyers. **Principal Exhibits:** Agricultural equipment, supplies, and services.

CONSULTANTS

21642 ■ Adayana Healthcare Group
3905 Vincennes Rd., Ste. 402
Indianapolis, IN 46268
Ph:(317)415-0500
Free: 800-285-8859
Fax:(317)415-0501
Co. E-mail: editor@adayana.com
URL: http://www.adayana.com
Contact: Brett Hall, CFO
E-mail: swilson@atsadayana.com
Scope: Provides custom designed training programs in the following areas: sales, sales management, coaching, market research, strategic planning, and mergers and acquisition consulting. Also provides technical training and product launch support in the areas of agricultural inputs, equipment, distribution and technology. **Seminars:** Strategies for Meeting the Expectations of Tomorrow's Workforce, Feb, 2010; Fundamentals of Agriculture; Managing Target Marketing Strategies; Developing a Marketing Mindset; Building a Value Proposition; Defining, Delivering, and Capturing Value; Handling Objections and Closing the Sale; Territory Management and Key Account Planning; Motivation and Performance Management.

21643 ■ Agland Investment Services Inc.
900 Larkspur Landing Cir., Ste. 205
Larkspur, CA 94939
Ph:(415)461-5820
Fax:(415)461-5821
Co. E-mail: agland@aglandinvest.com
URL: http://www.aglandinvest.com
Contact: Flavio Feferman, Director
E-mail: wmott@atsaglandinvest.com
Scope: An agribusiness consulting and investment company which provides a wide range of economic, marketing, technical and investment consultation to agricultural producers, agribusiness companies and government agencies in the Western United States and in many countries around the world. The firm tends to concentrate on high-value specialty crops, including fruits, vegetables and cut flowers. **Seminars:** Agribusiness Training Programs; Financial Analysis Training.

21644 ■ Agpro Inc.
859 Airport Rd.
Paris, TX 75462-7151
Ph:(903)785-5531
Free: 800-527-1030
Fax:(903)784-7895
Co. E-mail: info@agprousa.com
URL: http://www.agprousa.com
Contact: Tracy Crawford, Principle
E-mail: agpro@neto.com
Scope: Offers agricultural engineering design consultation for animal raising facilities including dairies, beef feedlots, swine operations and embryo transplant facilities. Services include land utilization, plot plans, building design, equipment selection, integration with other farm and commercial activities, pollution control systems, genetic engineering systems and computer applications. Also offers computer control and automation consultation, as well as consultation for waste management and control for food processing plants. Expertise in dairy, swine manure handling and their processing needs. **Publications:** "PD Exclusive: Progressivedairy.com," Jul, 2008; "ANM: Industry Insights," Mar, 2007.

21645 ■ Agri-Business Consultants Inc.
911 Edison Ave.
Lansing, MI 48910-3339
Ph:(517)482-7506
Fax:(517)482-7506
Co. E-mail: maotto@ameritech.net
Contact: Matt Duchrow, Principal
E-mail: swwagner@atscomcast.net
Scope: Agricultural consultants providing fertilizer recommendations, crop protection recommendations, soil fertility and crop protection consulting, irrigation scheduling, educational sessions, contract research and expert witness services. Industries served: Farmers and ag chemical companies.

21646 ■ Agri-Personnel
5120 Old Bill Cook Rd.
Atlanta, GA 30349-0319
Ph:(404)768-5701
Fax:(404)768-5705
Contact: David J. Wicker, Owner
Scope: Agribusiness consultants active in executive/professional/technical recruitment and placement, and in mergers, acquisitions, and divestitures in various industries including dairy, feed, food, fertilizer, farm chemicals, poultry and egg, animal health, and pulp and paper.

21647 ■ AgriCapital Corp.
1410 Broadway, Ste. 1802
New York, NY 10018-5018
Ph:(212)944-9500
Fax:(212)944-9525
Co. E-mail: info@agricapital.com
URL: http://www.agricapital.com
Contact: David J. Repking Jr., Principle
E-mail: repking@atsagricapital.com
Scope: Provides investment banking services for agribusiness clients in the United States and abroad, including financial consulting, debt and equity placements and joint ventures, and mergers and acquisitions. Industries served: Agribusiness and food companies. **Publications:** "Seed world"; "Strategic Agribusiness Review," Dec, 2003; "Yield," Jun, 2003; "Feed Management," May, 2002. **Seminars:** Thoughts on Private Equity and Agribusiness, Sep, 2009; Capital Markets and the Crop Input Sector, Oct, 2006; Views on the Crop Protection Industry, Sep, 2005; Mergers and Acquisitions in the US Food and Agribusiness Industry, Sep, 2002.

21648 ■ Agricultural Consulting Services Inc.
1634 Monroe Ave.
Rochester, NY 14618-9769
Ph:(585)473-1100
Free: 877-310-1100

Fax:877-315-2200
Co. E-mail: acs@acsoffice.com
URL: http://www.acsoffice.com
Contact: Sarah Walker, Engineering Manager
E-mail: swalker@atsacsoffice.com
Scope: Provides farm business management services including business and economic analysis, computer hardware and software installation and training, and enterprise budgets and analysis. Also offers crop production management, monitoring, and advises in the areas of crop nutrition, pest management, weed control, tillage practices, and irrigation scheduling. Environmental work includes complete analytical and monitoring services for soil, wastewater, sludge, and groundwater. Serves farms and agribusiness. **Publications:** "Forage - Timing of First Cutting".

21649 ■ Agricultural Engineering Associates
1000 Promontory Dr.
PO Box 4
Uniontown, KS 66779
Ph:(620)756-1000
Free: 800-499-5893
Fax:(620)756-4600
Co. E-mail: johng@agengineering.com
URL: http://www.agengineering.com
Contact: William Sympson, Principle
E-mail: william@atsagengineering.com
Scope: Agricultural engineering consultants offering guidance on the design of swine production facilities, beef feedlots, dairy facilities, waste management systems, soil and water conservation design and resource development including watershed planning, dam design and irrigation supply dam design, grain and feed storage, drying and processing facilities, irrigation system evaluation and design, rural water district system design, land leveling design for irrigation and drainage and land surveying. Industries served: production and commercial agriculture, research, demonstration and test facilities, government agencies and in-house materials testing laboratories.

21650 ■ Agricultural Investment Associates Inc.
1000 Skokie Blvd., Ste. 358
Wilmette, IL 60091
Ph:(847)251-8822
Fax:(847)251-8876
Co. E-mail: johncottingham@att.net
Contact: William B. Sayre, President
E-mail: johncala@aol.com
Scope: Investment consultant to domestic and foreign institutions, corporations and individuals covering investments in farms, ranches and agri businesses. Services include feasibility studies, appraisals, management, analysis and negotiations.

21651 ■ Agrisoft
9130 Anaheim Pl., Ste. 120
Rancho Cucamonga, CA 91730
Ph:(909)980-5338
Fax:(909)987-3154
Co. E-mail: info@agrisoftsolutions.com
URL: http://www.agrisoftcmc.com
Contact: Jim Brashears, Vice President
E-mail: ctorres@atsagrisoftsolutions.com
Scope: Provides turnkey software and hardware solutions for the animal agricultural industry. Other software solutions include business process consulting, custom application development, software installation and maintenance and equipment configuration. Industries served: chicken, egg, turkey and swine industries. **Seminars:** AgriSoft CMCs Client Seminar, Oct, 2008. **Special Services:** Agrisoft ERP; Agrisoft AIM.

21652 ■ AgriSolutions Inc.
31832 Delhi Rd.
Brighton, IL 62012
Ph:(618)372-3000
Free: 888-486-2208
Fax:(618)372-4000
Co. E-mail: internetmail@agrisolutions.com
URL: http://www.agrisolutions.com
Contact: Daryl Pohlman, Accounting Manager
E-mail: dmpohlma@atsagrisolutions.com
Scope: Offers agricultural consulting services including business planning and growth, historical performance analysis, strategic planning assistance, planning for financial success, CFO financial assistance, project consulting, entity consolidation, credit sourcing, budgeting, business succession, and estate and retirement planning. Other services provided are benchmarking comparisons, accounting and tax services and education and training to manage businesses. Serves the agricultural sector including farmers, non-farm entrepreneurs, financial institutions and agribusinesses. Clients range from local farmers to multinational agribusinesses. **Special Services:** Ag-Manager[R].

21653 ■ AgriTech Inc.
2775 Oakridge Ct.
Upper Arlington, OH 43221-2526
Ph:(614)488-0841
Co. E-mail: agritech@iwaynet.net
Contact: Dr. William E. Riddle, President
Scope: A consulting research organization dedicated to serving agribusiness; food, beverage, and dairy processing industries; and government agencies. The client's technology base is used to identify new markets, improve existing markets, develop targeted business and technology plans, and improve operational activities. Specializes in market research, value-added market assessments, feasibility studies, and the evaluation of business and technology plans and strategies. In addition, the firm matches agricultural resources with potential markets to identify value added products that can promote economic growth.

21654 ■ Agvise Laboratories Inc.
604 Hwy. 15
PO Box 510
Northwood, ND 58267-4412
Ph:(701)587-6010
Fax:(701)587-6013
Co. E-mail: agvise@polarcomm.com
URL: http://www.agviselabs.com
Contact: Robert Deutsch, President
E-mail: agvise@atspolarcomm.com
Scope: Provides agriculture testing services such as soil testing and plant analysis including, GLP and Non-GLP analysis to crop consultants, fertilizer retailers, producers, engineering firms and pesticide registration companies. **Publications:** "Manure and Nematode Test Results on the Internet"; "Sampling and Submitting Livestock Waste for Analysis"; "Precision Ag Helpers"; "New Minnesota Corn Nitrogen Fertilizer Guidelines"; "Zone Nutrient Management in Sugar beet Production"; "Reducing Soybean Cyst Nematode with Crop Rotation"; "Fall Strip Tillage: More and More Each Year"; "High Soil Nitrates Following Drought!"; "High Soil pH-Can we Fix this Problem?". **Seminars:** Precision Ag-Update 2009, 2009; Rock Rolling-Is It For You?, 2009; Seed Placed Fertilizer Limits, 2009; Precision Soil Testing, 2008; Soil Fertility Seminars; Tornado Tale; Compaction Update; Delta Yield; Phosphorus for Soybean; Soil Amendments; Strip Tillage Update; Sulfur for Corn.

21655 ■ Ascheman Associates Inc.
2921 Beverly Dr.
Des Moines, IA 50322-4255
Ph:(515)276-7371
Fax:(515)276-8707
Co. E-mail: rascheman@aol.com
Contact: Robert E. Ascheman, President
E-mail: rascheman@aol.com
Scope: Provides consulting, expert witness and related agribusiness services to agricultural-oriented businesses including: producers; agrochemical; fertilizer, seed and equipment companies; the insurance industry; the legal profession and government agencies. **Seminars:** Value of Grid Soil Sampling; Liming by the Grid System; Integrated Crop Management Services.

21656 ■ Ben Felt & Associates
120 N Elm St.
Escondido, CA 92025
Ph:(760)480-0785
Contact: Ben Felt, Owner
Scope: Advises lenders, owners and managers of agricultural enterprises on matters of financial administration. Also provides expertise in structuring international merger and acquisition opportunities. Concentrates in the following areas: investment capital; expert witness testimony; general financial management advice; preparation of cash flow projections and budgets; provides problem loan administration and negotiates debt restructure; and analyzes the financial impact that economic and political trends may have upon the enterprise.

21657 ■ Buzz Me
5206 Pear Butte Dr.
Yakima, WA 98901-1667
Ph:(509)452-6555
Fax:(509)452-6555
Co. E-mail: bugoff95@aol.com
Contact: Dr. Daniel F. Mayer, Owner
Scope: Provides consulting services dealing with entomology (insects). Provides pest control recommendations, research with new pesticides and chemical testing and expert witness services. **Publications:** "Pollinator Protection: A Bee and Pesticide Handbook," Wicwas Press.

21658 ■ C.C. Canada Forestry & Realty Co.
819 Mill St.
PO Box 337
Camden, SC 29020-4416
Ph:(803)432-9780
Fax:(803)432-0232
Co. E-mail: cclandman@aol.com
Contact: Clarence C. Canada, President
E-mail: cclandman@bellsouth.net
Scope: Provides consulting services in forest management and appraisal. Services include financial counsel especially in the agricultural field and timberland; and aid in securing loans with major insurance companies for agricultural and agribusiness loans. Also advises large corporations, as well as individuals, on real estate investments and acquisitions. Works with government agencies.

21659 ■ Clark Consulting International Inc.
435 Root St.
PO Box 68
Park Ridge, IL 60068-0068
Ph:(847)836-5100
Fax:(847)589-8889
Co. E-mail: warren.clark@ccimarketing.com
URL: http://www.ccimarketing.com
Contact: Warren E. Clark, President
E-mail: warren.clark@atsccimarketing.com
Scope: Multipurpose agri marketing communications consulting firm including public relations; market research; advertising and direct mail expertise. Serves the seed; chemical; machinery; computer and agricultural futures industries. Internet promotion and product marketing in agriculture. **Seminars:** Managing Your Consulting Practice Using Computers; Winning Ag PR Programs That Produce Results; Ag Targeted Direct Mail Niche Marketing. **Special Services:** AgPR online.

21660 ■ Custom Forestry Inc.
16798 Claridon Troy Rd.
Burton, OH 44021-9606
Ph:(440)834-1680
Fax:(440)834-1680
Co. E-mail: lynneebel@hotmail.com
Contact: Ralph Hershberger, Owner
E-mail: l.ebel@att.net
Scope: Offers forestry consulting services that include forest management, timber sales, valuations, timber trespass valuations and litigation, advice on federal assistance programs, Christmas tree plantation management, multiple use land management, shelter-belts, silviculture, and insect management.

21661 ■ DPRA Inc.
200 Research Dr.
Manhattan, KS 66503
Ph:(785)539-3565

Fax:(785)539-5353
Co. E-mail: info@dpra.com
URL: http://www.dpra.com
Contact: Dr. Peter Homenuck, Principal
E-mail: paul.garcia@atsdpra.com
Scope: Consultants on a variety of environmental problems and situations. Experience includes agriculture, agribusiness, water pollution control, and hazardous and municipal waste management. Activities emphasize litigation support, data management, and information services, as well as international programs. Serves private industries as well as government agencies. **Special Services:** TALIRA[R].

21662 ■ Eastern Laboratory Service Associates
517 N George St.
York, PA 17404-2765
Ph:(717)846-4953
Fax:(717)846-4986
Contact: T. F. Lagattuta, Director
Scope: Provides technical counsel on chemical and microbiological testing, evaluation and quality control services primarily for environmental, agribusiness, feed industry and food manufacturing. Offers consultation, advisory services, research and development on technical problems, new product formulation, and product or process improvement. Also performs general testing of refrigerants, food products, solid waste, water and waste water for compliance with EPA, DER, FDA and other governmental agencies.

21663 ■ G.V. Olsen Associates
123 Picketts Ridge Rd.
Redding, CT 06896
Ph:(203)770-3433
Fax:(203)938-4186
Contact: Gustav Olsen, President
E-mail: gusolsen@hotmail.com
Scope: Provides agribusiness research, analysis and report writing services, focusing on farm input products such as seed, fertilizer, chemicals, and machinery, as well as production, storage, transportation, and marketing of food and fiber products. Also identifies and evaluates new market and product opportunities. Industries served: Agribusiness, biotechnology, food and agriculture.

21664 ■ Indiana Design Consortium Inc.
416 Main St.
PO Box 180
Lafayette, IN 47902-0180
Ph:(765)423-5469
Fax:(765)423-4440
Co. E-mail: idc@idc-marketing.com
URL: http://www.idc-marketing.com
Contact: Brian Koning, Editor
E-mail: barb@atsidc-marketing.com
Scope: Provides marketing and marketing communications services for industrial, service oriented, and agribusiness clients. Also involved in industrial product design for industry and agribusiness.

21665 ■ INTRANCO Inc.
1825 I St. NW, Ste. 400
Washington, DC 20006-5403
Ph:(202)429-6820
Fax:(703)978-8335
Contact: William Lake, President
Scope: Provides management consulting for agribusinesses, primarily enterprises in the Third World. Works with private entrepreneurs and government-sponsored institutions. Has experience with livestock, fruits, vegetables, field crops, small animals, fisheries and poultry. Engages in the international trade of agricultural equipment, machinery and raw products. Industries served: Food and feed industries and government agencies. **Seminars:** Mold Inhibitors in the 1990 Decade; Agribusiness in West Africa - Is It Possible?; Poultry in Nigeria - The Challenge.

21666 ■ J. Stewart Murray Agency
639 Borebank St.
Winnipeg, MB, Canada R3N 1G1
Ph:(204)488-3885
Fax:(204)489-0129
Co. E-mail: smurray6@shaw.ca
Contact: Stewart J. Murray, President
E-mail: smurray6@shaw.ca
Scope: Marketing and sales consultants for agri-industrial automotive. Industries served: Agriculture-agribusiness, industrial supply trades and government agencies in Canada.

21667 ■ J.H. Hare & Associates Ltd.
270 Roslyn Rd., Ste. 1
Winnipeg, MB, Canada R3L 0H3
Ph:(204)477-0066
Free: 800-661-4273
Fax:(204)488-0051
Co. E-mail: john@hareman.com
URL: http://www.hyper-egg.com
Contact: Shelagh Hare, Principle
E-mail: shelagh@atshareman.com
Scope: Agribusiness management consultants with extensive experience in: Animal nutrition and feed formulation, agri marketing, technical services to agribusiness, agricultural promotion, and sales and sales training. Serves the agriculture and food and beverage industries, as well as government agencies. **Special Services:** X-CEL; X-Change; X-Change Plus.

21668 ■ Keck & Co.
410 Walsh Rd.
Atherton, CA 94027
Ph:(650)854-9588
Fax:(650)854-7240
Co. E-mail: info@kecko.com
Contact: Barbara Keck, Owner
E-mail: info@kecko.com
Scope: Conducts management services nationally, focusing on strategic research, marketing, and planning for businesses involved in the packaging container and equipment industry, food processing, and related technology suppliers. Develops feasibility studies to assess the possible success or failure of entering a new market, introducing a new product or product line extension, or starting a new venture; primary market research to determine what motivates consumers/buyers, and best "positioning" for product in the marketplace; business development programs; promotional programs to differentiate client company from competitors; vertical/horizontal marketing audits; technology acceptance assessments; due diligence for investors; and management assistance with investment issues. **Seminars:** Taking the Failure Factors Out of New Product Introductions; Introduction to Marketing for Food Manufacturing Personnel; New Product Development Workshop: Plans and Elements; Starting Your Own Consulting Business; The Marketing Plan.

21669 ■ McKinnon, Allen & Associates Western Ltd.
1115 46th Ave. SE
Calgary, AB, Canada T2G 2A5
Ph:(403)243-4345
Fax:(403)228-3767
Contact: S. Douglas Allen, President
Scope: The firms multidisciplinary work team provides independent opinions and practical solutions to a variety of problems in the areas of agribusiness, farm and ranch management, agricultural environmental consulting and rural land use. Specific areas of expertise are as follows: Financial advisory consulting, agricultural environmental monitoring, general agricultural management consulting, economic evaluation, land use planning, land valuation, surface rights disputes and expropriations, farm management for absentee owners, and damage claims. **Publications:** "Observations of pH in field soils near a sour gas plant in Alberta," Springer Netherlands, 1983.

21670 ■ Micro-Macro International Inc.
183 Paradise Blvd., Ste. 108
Athens, GA 30607
Ph:(706)548-4557
Free: 800-837-8664
Fax:(706)548-4891
Co. E-mail: pamaaron@mmilabs.com
URL: http://www.mmilabs.com
Contact: Dr. Zana C. Somda, Mgr
E-mail: zanasomda@atsmmilabs.com
Scope: Offers consultation on agricultural production field, container, greenhouse and hydroponic systems. Provides analytical services for the analysis of water, waste water, soil, plant tissue and other biological substances for their element content. Industries served: Agricultural producers, research institutes and individuals, fertilizer manufacturers and government agencies. **Publications:** "Plant Analysis Handbook," 1991; "Diagnosis and Recommendation Integrated Systems (Dris)"; "Kjeldahl Method for Nitrogen Determination"; "Plant Nutrition Manual". **Seminars:** Techniques of soil testing and plant analysis; Laboratory instruction on methods of analysis.

21671 ■ Miller Agricultural Consulting Services
10967 County Rd. 19
Lawton, ND 58345-9661
Ph:(701)655-3591
Contact: Judith Miller, Principle
Scope: Agricultural consultant working with clients in the area of machine design and safety as it pertains to machines used in the production of agricultural crops. Crops include wheat, barley, corn, sunflowers, sugar beets, and potatoes. Special emphasis on farm safety issues, crop drying systems, and forensic evaluation.

21672 ■ Pest Pros Inc.
10086 1st St.
PO Box 188
Plainfield, WI 54966-0188
Ph:(715)335-4046
Fax:(715)335-4746
Co. E-mail: pestpros@uniontel.net
URL: http://www.pestprosinc.com
Contact: Randy M. Van Haren, President
E-mail: pestpros@uniontel.net
Scope: Offers agricultural consulting involving fertility and pesticide recommendations, soil microbe assay and contract research.

21673 ■ Ralph E. Williams & Associates
c/o Purdue University, 901 W State St.
West Lafayette, IN 47907
Ph:(765)494-4560
Fax:(765)494-2152
Co. E-mail: rew@purdue.edu
Contact: Dr. Ralph E. Williams, President
E-mail: ralph_williams@entm.purdue.edu
Scope: Offers services in forensic entomology, use of insects in crime scene investigations. Serves prosecuting attorneys, law enforcement agencies, state and local coroners and medical examiners. Also provides training and consulting services in livestock and poultry pest control and public health pest control. Serves agribusiness, local and state public health agencies and individuals. **Publications:** "Modern Gas Processing Methods," Artech House Publishers, Jul, 1990. **Seminars:** Forensic Entomology Training Session; Livestock and Poultry Pest Management.

21674 ■ SEA-ARM Consulting Associates
640 Line St.
Hollister, CA 95023
Ph:(831)637-1468
Fax:(831)637-4377
Contact: Samuel Armstrong, President
Scope: Offers expertise regarding financial restructuring (including start-ups and spin-offs) and technology transfer, relating to agriculture production, processing and marketing. Special emphasis on cooperatives. Industries served: Agriculture, agribusiness, cooperatives and government. **Seminars:** Starting a New Business; Strawberry Production, Organic farm productions, Marketing.

21675 ■ Sobek Engineering
51492 Sobek Rd. E
PO Box 7
Edwall, WA 99008-9703
Ph:(509)236-2371

Fax:(509)236-2426
Co. E-mail: sobekeng@aol.com
Contact: Irvin G. Sobek, President
Scope: Provides consulting engineering service in the food processing field and associated agribusiness areas. Has served in the frozen food, flour milling, and freeze-drying areas, as well as agricultural and industrial accident investigation. Also conducts noise surveys and noise abatement engineering.

21676 ■ Southern Plantations Group Inc.
2410 Westgate Dr., Ste. 101
PO Box 70967
Albany, GA 31708
Ph:(229)439-0012
Fax:(229)883-8881
Co. E-mail: spg@splantations.com
URL: http://www.splantations.com
Contact: Jeffery D. Peterson, Senior VP
E-mail: jpeterson@atssplantations.com
Scope: Provides appraisal and counseling services for investors and lenders in farm land, timberland and agribusiness projects across the Southern U.S.; and farm planning, budgeting, management, and accounting services for farmers near its area of activity. Specific services include establishing and reviewing investment criteria, investment selection and negotiation, alternative investment analysis and review, management and operations audits, appraisals, problem investments, and management of property investment and divestment. Industries served: investors, lenders, government agencies, agribusinesses in production, agriculture, input, and marketing sectors. U.S., southeast Asia and Latin America.

21677 ■ Sterling Executive Counselors Inc.
516 S Pokegama Ave.
Grand Rapids, MN 55744-3838
Ph:(218)326-4421
Free: 888-326-4421
Fax:(218)326-4430
Contact: Marsha Kelly, Principal
Scope: Public affairs and management consultants offering reputation and issue management, public relations, and government relations counsel. Industries served: agribusiness, pet, gaming, forest products, natural resources and energy.

21678 ■ Trenna R. Grabowski CPA Ltd.
15 N 12th & Broadway
PO Box 38
Du Bois, IL 62831
Ph:(618)787-4430
Fax:(618)787-4460
Co. E-mail: trenna@agcpa.net
URL: http://www.theagcpa.com
Contact: Trenna R. Grabowski, Owner
E-mail: grabeau@midwest.net
Scope: Offers financial management, strategic planning, and budgeting for agribusiness and small and family-owned firms. Heavily involved in tax planning and research. Consulting on choosing hardware and software for agribusiness. Related experience in personal financial planning, tax planning, and projections. Speaking and teaching a specialty, seminars, workshops, and conference presentations available. **Publications:** "Refund Anticipation Loans-Do They Make Sense," Jan, 2010; "Employee Turnover and Corporate Culture," Jan, 2010; "Stock Market: A New Year Sparks Optimism," Jan, 2010; "Tax Organizers-Friend or Foe," Jan, 2010. **Seminars:** Agribusiness Tax Seminar; Tax Planning; Incorporating the Farm; Alternative Forms of Business Organization; Estate and Financial Planning; The Farm Business Plan.

COMPUTERIZED DATABASES

21679 ■ *AGRICOLA Database*
U.S. Department of Agriculture
Abraham Lincoln Bldg.
10301 Baltimore Ave.
Beltsville, MD 20705
Ph:(301)504-5755
Fax:(301)504-6927
Co. E-mail: webmaster@nal.usda.gov
URL: http://www.nalusda.gov
Description: Contains more than 3.5 million records from journal literature, government reports, serials, monographs, theses, patents, audiovisual resources, and technical reports in agriculture and related areas that have been acquired by the National Agricultural Library (NAL) as well as citations contributed by cooperating institutions. Includes agricultural economics and rural sociology, agricultural production, animal sciences, chemistry, entomology, food and human nutrition, forestry, natural resources, pesticides, plant science, soils and fertilizers, and water resources. Also covers related areas such as biology and biotechnology, botany, ecology, and natural history. Contributing agencies include land grant institutions, the NAL Food and Nutrition Information Center (abstracts available from 1973 to date), and the Arid Lands Information Center. Corresponds in part to *Bibliography of Agriculture.* **Availability:** Online: ProQuest LLC, DIMDI, the German Institute of Medical Documentation and Information, STN International, EBSCO Publishing, Wolters Kluwer Health, ProQuest LLC, ProQuest LLC, EBSCO Publishing; CD-ROM: Wolters Kluwer Health. **Type:** Bibliographic.

LIBRARIES

21680 ■ Albany Historical Society, Inc.–Library/Special Collections
c/o Doyle Bechtelheimer
415 Grant
Sabetha, KS 66534
Ph:(913)284-3446
URL: http://www.albanydays.org
Contact: Daryl Bechtelheimer, Pres.
Scope: Agricultural equipment, railroads one-room schools. **Services:** Library open to the public. **Holdings:** 200 books.

21681 ■ Alberta Agriculture and Food–Crop Diversification Centre South–Branch Library (301 H)
301 Horticultural Station Road East
Brooks, AB, Canada T1R 1E6
Ph:(403)362-1308
Fax:(403)362-1306
Co. E-mail: shelley.barkley@gov.ab.ca
URL: http://www1.agric.gov.ab.ca/$department/deptdocs.nsf/all/opp4386
Contact: Shelley Barkley, Info.Off.
Scope: Plants, pathology, horticulture, entomology, special crops. **Services:** Interlibrary loan; copying; Library open to the public. **Holdings:** Figures not available.

21682 ■ Alberta - Agriculture, Food and Rural Development–Business Management Innovations Branch Library
201 Provincial Bldg.
5030-50 St.
Olds, AB, Canada T4H 1S1
Ph:(403)556-4328
Fax:(403)556-7545
URL: http://www.agric.gov.ab.ca/app21/rtw/index.jsp
Scope: Agriculture, economics, technology, agricultural economics, farm management, finance, computer. **Services:** Interlibrary loan. **Holdings:** Figures not available.

21683 ■ Booz Allen Hamilton–Research Services and Information Center
225 W. Wacker Dr.
Chicago, IL 60606
Ph:(312)419-8100
Fax:(312)578-4667
URL: http://www.boozallen.com
Scope: Management, agribusiness, finance, marketing, manufacturing, retailing, information management, consumer products, healthcare, telecommunications, food retailing, consulting, electronic commerce. **Services:** Interlibrary loan; Center not open to the public. **Holdings:** 5000 books; client reports; company Annual reports. **Subscriptions:** 300 serials.

21684 ■ Canada - Agriculture and Agri-Food Canada–Dairy and Swine Research and Development Centre Lennoxville–Canadian Agriculture Library (2000)
2000 College St.
PO Box 90
Sherbrooke, QC, Canada J1M 1Z3
Ph:(819)565-9174
Fax:(819)564-5507
Co. E-mail: info@agr.gc.ca
URL: http://www4.agr.gc.ca
Contact: Josee Toulouse, Chf.
Scope: Dairy cattle, pigs. **Services:** Interlibrary loan; Library provides limited on-site consultation to the public. **Holdings:** 5000 books; 6000 e-books. **Subscriptions:** 3750 journals and other serials.

21685 ■ Canadian Grain Commission Library
303 Main St., Rm. 801
Winnipeg, MB, Canada R3C 3G8
Ph:(204)983-0878
Fax:(204)983-6098
Co. E-mail: library-bibliotheque@grainscanada.gc.ca
URL: http://www.grainscanada.gc.ca
Contact: Dawn Bassett, Coord., Lib.Svcs.
Scope: Cereal chemistry, cereals, oilseeds, grain industry and trade, baking, brewing, milling. **Services:** Interlibrary loan; copying; SDI; Library open to the public for reference use only. **Holdings:** 5000 books; 10,000 bound periodical volumes; 1000 pamphlets; 1500 reports. **Subscriptions:** 200 journals and other serials; 10 newspapers.

21686 ■ Cargill, Incorporated Information Center
PO Box 9300
Minneapolis, MN 55440
Ph:(952)742-5224
Free: 800-227-4455
Fax:(952)742-6062
Co. E-mail: peter_sidney@cargill.com
URL: http://www.cargill.com
Contact: Gregory R. Page, Chm./CEO
Scope: Food ingredients and systems, grain storage and handling, commodity trading, agribusiness, finance, marketing, biochemistry, hybrid corn breeding and genetics, animal feeding and nutrition, vegetable oil processing and chemistry, agricultural and food products, market research. **Services:** Center not open to the public. **Holdings:** 10,000 books; 500 bound periodical volumes; 250 other cataloged items; 10,000 internal research reports; 2000 general information files; 16,000 documents. **Subscriptions:** 750 journals and other serials; 20 newspapers.

21687 ■ Delaware Valley College of Science and Agriculture–Joseph Krauskopf Memorial Library
700 E. Butler Ave.
Doylestown, PA 18901-2697
Ph:(215)489-2953
Co. E-mail: library@delval.edu
URL: http://www.delval.edu/library
Contact: Peter Kupersmith, Lib.Dir.
Scope: Agribusiness, agronomy, large animal science, biology, communication, computer and business information systems, criminal justice administration, dairy science, English literature, equine science, food industry, horticulture, ornamental horticulture, chemistry, business administration, small animal science, turf management, wildlife conservation, zoo biology. **Services:** Interlibrary loan; copying; Library open to the public for reference use only. **Holdings:** 55,000 volumes; 4520 bound periodical volumes; 1525 reels of microfilm; 50,650 microfiche. **Subscriptions:** 13,000 journals.

21688 ■ Illinois Agricultural Association–Illinois Farm Bureau Information Research Center
1701 Towanda Ave.
Box 2901
Bloomington, IL 61701
Ph:(309)557-2534

Fax:(309)557-3185
Co. E-mail: eculver@iflb.org
URL: http://www.ilfb.org/
Contact: Ellen Culver, Dir.

Scope: Agriculture - economics, marketing, cooperatives, management, insurance, environment. **Services:** Interlibrary loan; copying; subscriptions; Internet training; abstracting; Library open to the public for reference use only. **Holdings:** 5000 volumes; 100 microforms; 500 audio/visual materials. **Subscriptions:** 500 journals and other serials; 7 newspapers.

21689 ■ International Fertilizer Development Center–Travis P. Hignett Memorial Library
PO Box 2040
Muscle Shoals, AL 35662
Ph:(256)381-6600
Fax:(256)381-7408
Co. E-mail: cbennett@ifdc.org
URL: http://www.ifdc.org/About/Library
Contact: Cheryl Bennett, Libn.

Scope: Fertilizers, agricultural economics, nutrient management, agribusiness, training. **Services:** Interlibrary loan; literature searching; Library not open to the public; document delivery. **Holdings:** 20,000 books; 4365 bound periodical volumes; 468 pamphlets; 337 AV programs; 20,000 patents. **Subscriptions:** 200 journals and other serials.

21690 ■ International Food Policy Research Institute Library
2033 K St., NW
Washington, DC 20006
Ph:(202)862-5614
Fax:(202)467-4439
Co. E-mail: ifpri-library@cgiar.org
URL: http://www.ifpri.org/resources
Contact: Luz Marina Alvare, Hd.

Scope: Food policy and research, developmental economics, International trade, food security, agricultural economics and statistics, food safety. **Services:** Interlibrary loan; copying; Library open to the public by appointment. **Holdings:** 3000 books; 4000 research reports. **Subscriptions:** 120 journals and other serials.

21691 ■ Mississippi State University–Agricultural & Forestry Experiment Station–Delta Research and Extension Center (82 St)
82 Stoneville Rd.
PO Box 197
Stoneville, MS 38776
Ph:(662)686-3261
Fax:(662)686-7336
Co. E-mail: rhwatson@drec.msstate.edu
URL: http://msucares.com/drec
Contact: Rhonda H. Watson, Libn.

Scope: Agriculture, botany, agricultural economics, mathematics, agricultural engineering, meteorology. **Services:** Interlibrary loan; Library open to the public. **Holdings:** 14,500 books; 6000 bound periodical volumes; 348 reels of microfilm; 50,000 pamphlets. **Subscriptions:** 225 journals and other serials; 10 newspapers.

21692 ■ Pioneer Hi-Bred International, Inc.–Library Resources Group
7300 NW 62nd Ave.
PO Box 1004
Johnston, IA 50131-1004
Ph:(515)270-4199
Fax:(515)253-2184
Co. E-mail: dana.smith@pioneer.com
URL: http://www.pioneer.com
Contact: Dana Smith, Corp.Libn.

Scope: Plant genetics, agriculture, agribusiness, law, taxation, business. **Services:** Interlibrary loan; Library not open to the public. **Holdings:** 1480 books. **Subscriptions:** 180 journals and other serials.

21693 ■ Purdue University Libraries—KRAN–Management and Economics Library
504 W. State St.
West Lafayette, IN 47907-2058
Ph:(765)494-2920
Co. E-mail: kranlib@purdue.edu
URL: http://www.lib.purdue.edu/mel
Contact: Tomalee Doan, Hd.

Scope: Business Organization and management; economics - applied, history, principles, theory, systems; industrial relations; agricultural economics; business statistics and mathematics; marketing; taxation; real estate; finance; accounting. **Services:** Interlibrary loan; copying; Library open to the public. **Holdings:** 115,485 volumes; 5067 bound Annual reports to stockholders; 112,953 microforms; newspaper clippings. **Subscriptions:** 1028 journals and other serials.

21694 ■ Sandoz Agro Corporate Library
1100 E Woodfield Rd., No. 500
Schaumburg, IL 60173-5116
Ph:(847)390-3600
Fax:(847)390-3945
Contact: Candy J. Ortman, Libn./Archv.

Scope: Pesticides, herbicides, organic chemistry, entomology, botany, agribusiness. **Services:** Interlibrary loan. **Holdings:** 7500 books; 7000 bound periodical volumes; 7000 reels of microfilm. **Subscriptions:** 180 journals and other serials.

21695 ■ Tennessee Valley Authority–TVA Environmental Research Center–TVA Research Library (PO Box)
PO Box 1010
Muscle Shoals, AL 35662-1010
Free: 800-831-5744
Co. E-mail: resmg@tva.com
URL: http://www.tva.gov

Scope: Environmental sciences, biomass, chemistry, chemical engineering, competitive business marketing, environmental sciences, waste management. **Services:** Interlibrary loan. **Holdings:** 600 volumes; government documents. **Subscriptions:** 6 journals and other serials.

21696 ■ U.S.D.A.–Economic Research Service–ERS Reference Center (1800)
1800 M St. NW, Rm. 3050
Washington, DC 20036-5831
Ph:(202)694-5058
Fax:(202)694-5757
Co. E-mail: mgraham@ers.usda.gov
URL: http://www.ers.usda.gov
Contact: Marilynn Graham, Dir.

Scope: Agricultural economics. **Services:** Copying (limited); Center open to the public by appointment. **Holdings:** 16,000 monographs; 10,000 microforms; microfiche; archives. **Subscriptions:** 318 journals and other serials.

21697 ■ University of California, Berkeley–Giannini Foundation of Agricultural Economics–Research Library (248 G)
248 Giannini Hall, No. 3310
Berkeley, CA 94720-3310
Ph:(510)642-7121
Fax:(510)643-8911
Co. E-mail: gflibrary@are.berkeley.edu
URL: http://are.berkeley.edu/library/
Contact: Susan Garbarino, Hd.Libn.

Scope: Agriculture - economics, labor, land utilization, valuation and tenure, marketing and transportation problems, cost of production and marketing studies; agricultural economic developments in Lesser Developed Countries; environmental economics; water resources economics; conservation of natural resources. **Services:** Interlibrary loan; copying; Library open to qualified researchers for reference use only. **Holdings:** 21,000 volumes; 153,000 pamphlets; 3900 microforms; 150 maps; 540 microfiche titles, 3400 reels of microfilm. **Subscriptions:** 3000 journals and other serials.

21698 ■ University of California, Davis–Agricultural and Resource Economics Library
Social Sciences & Humanities Bldg., Rm. 4101
One Shields Ave.
Davis, CA 95616-8512
Ph:(530)752-1540
Fax:(530)752-5614
Co. E-mail: arel@primal.ucdavis.edu
URL: http://arelibrary.ucdavis.edu
Contact: Barbara Hegenbart, Libn.

Scope: Agricultural economics; agricultural business; land, resource, environmental and consumer economics. **Services:** Interlibrary loan; document delivery; copying; Library open to the public for reference use only. **Holdings:** 7000 volumes; 150,000 pamphlets; 2600 serials. **Subscriptions:** 8580 journals and other serials.

21699 ■ University of Illinois at Urbana-Champaign–Isaac Funk Family Library of Agricultural, Consumer and Environmental Sciences Library
200 ACES Library, Information and Alumni Ctr.
1101 S. Goodwin, MC-633
Urbana, IL 61801
Ph:(217)333-2416
Fax:(217)333-0558
Co. E-mail: allen2@uiuc.edu
URL: http://www.library.illinois.edu/agx/
Contact: Robert S. Allen, Hd.Libn.

Scope: Agricultural economics, animal science, agricultural engineering, crops, biotechnology, family and consumer economics, foods and nutrition, human development and family ecology, textiles, horticulture, food science and technology, environmental science, agricultural history, forestry, soils. **Services:** Interlibrary loan; copying; Library open to the public. **Holdings:** 97,000 volumes; 12,000 microforms; CD-ROMs; reports; patents; microfiche. **Subscriptions:** 3200 journals and other serials.

21700 ■ University of Minnesota, St. Paul–Magrath Library
1984 Buford Ave.
St. Paul, MN 55108
Ph:(612)624-2233
Fax:(612)626-7585
Co. E-mail: magrath@umn.edu
URL: http://magrath.lib.umn.edu/
Contact: Wendy Pradt Lougee, Univ.Libn.

Scope: Agricultural and applied economics; agricultural engineering; agricultural education; home economics; agronomy and plant genetics; animal science; horticultural sciences; biological sciences; food science and nutrition; plant pathology; soil science; biochemistry; family social science; adult education; social work; Vo-Tech education; design; housing; apparel. **Services:** Interlibrary loan; copying; document delivery; Library open to the public for reference use only. **Holdings:** 441,420 volumes; 437,283 documents; 208 AV programs; 977 CD-ROMs; 55,367 microfiche; 1937 microfilm; 3111 maps. **Subscriptions:** 3208 journals and other serials.

21701 ■ University of Wisconsin—Madison–Land Tenure Collection
550 N. Park St.
Madison, WI 53706
Ph:(608)262-8029
Fax:(608)262-2141
Co. E-mail: kdbrown@wisc.edu
URL: http://www.nelson.wisc.edu/ltc/resources/ltc_collection.html
Contact: Kurt Brown, Comm.Dir.

Scope: Land tenure, agrarian reform, agricultural economics, Latin America, Asia, Africa, Eastern Europe, rural development, developing countries. **Services:** Interlibrary loan; copying; Library open to the public. **Holdings:** 30,000 books; 1200 bound periodical volumes; 36,000 unbound reports, manuscripts, clippings, pamphlets, documents; 8 VF drawers of microfilm and microfiche; 100 titles of Economic Development Plans; 250 titles of dissertations. **Subscriptions:** 350 journals and other serials.

21702 ■ University of Wisconsin—Madison–Steenbock Memorial Library
550 Babcock Dr.
Madison, WI 53706-1293
Ph:(608)262-9635

Fax:(608)263-3221
URL: http://steenbock.library.wisc.edu
Contact: Jean Gilbertson, Dir.
Scope: Life sciences, agriculture, veterinary medicine, biotechnology, food and dairy science, family studies, consumer science, agricultural economics. **Services:** Interlibrary loan; copying; document delivery; Library open to the public. **Holdings:** 124,000 books; 121,582 monographs; 73,607 bound periodical volumes; 472,556 documents; 90,221 microforms; 765 AV programs. **Subscriptions:** 2503 journals and other serials.

21703 ■ Vermont Community and Technical Colleges Library
Hartness Library System
Main St.
Randolph Center, VT 05061
Ph:(802)728-1237
Free: 800-431-0025
Fax:(802)728-1506
Co. E-mail: library@vtc.edu
URL: http://hartness.vsc.edu/rework/index.php
Contact: David Sturges, Lib.Dir.
Scope: Engineering technologies architectural, civil, computer, electrical, electronics, mechanical; architecture and building technology; automotive technology; business technology; construction management; landscape development; semi-conductor processing; veterinary technology; nursing; science fiction; dairy management; agribusiness. **Services:** Copying; workstations; Library open to the public with restrictions. **Holdings:** 56,000 books; 5000 e-books. **Subscriptions:** 200 journals and other serials; 8 newspapers.

21704 ■ Western Maryland Public Libraries–Regional Library
100 S. Potomac St.
Hagerstown, MD 21740
Ph:(301)739-3250
Fax:(301)739-5839
Co. E-mail: jthompson@washcolibrary.org
URL: http://www.westmdlib.info
Contact: Joe Thompson, Assoc.Dir.
Scope: Small business; antiques and collectibles; Civil Service and vocational tests; small scale farming. **Services:** Interlibrary loan; copying; Library open to the public with restrictions. **Holdings:** 62,000 books; 2500 audiovisuals. **Subscriptions:** 3 newspapers.

RESEARCH CENTERS

21705 ■ Agricultural Utilization Research Institute
PO Box 599
Crookston, MN 56716-0599
Ph:(218)281-7600
Free: 800—279-5010
Fax:(218)281-3759
Co. E-mail: tspaeth@auri.org
URL: http://www.auri.org
Contact: Teresa Spaeth, Exec.Dir.
E-mail: tspaeth@auri.org
Scope: Agriculture products from state, including research projects to convert corn to ethanol and biodegradable plastics, and to pelletize soybeans for export. Seeks to identify and create new markets and expand existing markets for new or existing commodities, ingredients, and products; develop energy efficient, natural resource-saving production practice; and develop alternative crops and products for emerging markets. **Services:** Technical assistance to farmers, agribusinesses, and producer groups (daily), New product development, feasibility testing, technology development. **Publications:** Ag Innovation News (quarterly).

21706 ■ American Seed Research Foundation
225 Reinekers Ln., Ste. 650
Alexandria, VA 22314-2875
Ph:(703)837-8140
Fax:(703)837-9365
URL: http://www.amseed.com/asrf/index.html
Contact: Suzanne Nicolas, Dir.
Scope: Seeds, including technology advancement in the seed industry.

21707 ■ Arizona State University–Sustainable Technologies, Agribusiness Resource Center
Mail Code 0180
Bldg. 340, EAP Rm. 121 & 123
Mesa, AZ 85212
Ph:(480)727-1240
Fax:(480)727-1801
Co. E-mail: john.brock@asu.edu
URL: http://www.poly.asu.edu/star
Contact: Dr. John H. Brock, Coord.
E-mail: john.brock@asu.edu
Scope: Agribusiness policy studies, including research and development related to arid zone requirements, including projects in emerging democracies, economic development, technology, high valued products or industrial product potential, biomass utilization, and specialized instrument development. **Services:** Transfers technology from the University to start-up companies, Biotechnology electronics and other materials. **Publications:** Working Treatise Series. **Educational Activities:** Graduate training.

21708 ■ California Institute for Rural Studies
221 G St., Ste. 204
Davis, CA 95616
Ph:(530)756-6555
Co. E-mail: info@cirsinc.org
URL: http://www.cirsinc.org
Contact: Gail Wadsworth, Exec.Dir.
E-mail: info@cirsinc.org
Scope: Rural community ethnography and demographics; rural poverty; hired farm labor; labor contractors; pesticide use and sustainable agriculture; land ownership and farm structure; water law, transfers, and distribution; various agricultural health and safety topics. **Services:** Consulting, on a contract basis. **Publications:** Reports and Working Papers; Rural California Report (quarterly). **Educational Activities:** Leadership and liaison training.

21709 ■ California State University, Fresno–Center for Agricultural Business
2910 E Barstow Ave.
Fresno, CA 93740-0115
Ph:(559)278-4405
Fax:(559)278-6032
Co. E-mail: mpaggi@csufresno.edu
URL: http://cab.cati.csufresno.edu
Contact: Mechel Paggi PhD, Dir.
E-mail: mpaggi@csufresno.edu
Scope: Agribusiness in California, especially the San Joaquin Valley. Studies concentrate on farm business planning and other related labor issues, labor supply and demand (migrant workers and immigration law), computer applications in agriculture, water supply and its environmental consequences, agricultural exports, enhancement of markets and alternatives to traditional export markets, food and fiber industry management, and agricultural process, including processing, brokerage, wholesaling, and agricultural safety issues. **Publications:** Conference proceedings (annually). **Educational Activities:** Seminars in personnel management and labor laws, in English and Spanish; Seminars in business planning and agricultural trade.

21710 ■ George Morris Centre
225-150 Research Ln.
Guelph, ON, Canada N1G 4T2
Ph:(519)822-3929
Fax:(519)837-8721
Co. E-mail: info@georgemorris.org
URL: http://www.georgemorris.org
Contact: Robert (Bob) Seguin, Exec.Dir.
E-mail: info@georgemorris.org
Scope: Agricultural policies and marketing strategies, including policy positions and alternatives, agricultural and agrifood industry competitiveness, international trade policies, product standards regulation, marketing boards, and commodity value versus income stabilization. **Publications:** Market reports; Newsletter; Research reports. **Educational Activities:** Canadian Agri-Food Executive Development Program; Canadian Total Excellence in Agricultural Management Program (CTEAM); Courses, on futures and options trading.

21711 ■ Indiana Agricultural Leadership Institute
72 W Main St.
Danville, IN 46122
Ph:(317)745-0947
Fax:(317)745-0956
Co. E-mail: beth@agriinstitute.org
URL: http://www.agriinstitute.org
Contact: Beth Archer, Exec.Dir.
E-mail: beth@agriinstitute.org
Scope: Agribusiness development. **Services:** Agricultural Leadership Development Program; Resource for Developing Community Leadership Program. **Publications:** Newsletter (bimonthly). **Educational Activities:** Indiana Agricultural Forum; Indiana Agricultural Leadership Program.

21712 ■ Institute for Agriculture and Trade Policy
2105 1st Ave. S
Minneapolis, MN 55404
Ph:(612)870-0453
Fax:(612)870-4846
Co. E-mail: iatp@iatp.org
URL: http://www.iatp.org
Contact: Jim Harkness, Pres.
E-mail: iatp@iatp.org
Scope: Food, trade, agriculture, land, rural affairs, environmental issues, and sustainable development.

21713 ■ Iowa State University of Science and Technology–Midwest Agribusiness Trade Research and Information Center
578 Heady Hall
Ames, IA 50011-1070
Ph:(515)294-1183
Fax:(515)294-6336
Co. E-mail: babcock@iastate.edu
URL: http://www.matric.iastate.edu
Contact: Prof. Bruce A. Babcock PhD, Exec.Dir.
E-mail: babcock@iastate.edu
Scope: Expands international trade in agribusiness products produced in the Midwest by small and medium sized businesses. Focuses on export markets, market impediments, trade agreements, trade policies, and technologies that improve competitiveness in international markets. Market studies focus on geographical markets and value-added and niche markets for non-commodity products. **Services:** Consulting with non-university organizations and agribusinesses to discover and fulfill research and informational needs. **Publications:** Working papers and research papers. **Educational Activities:** Conferences, seminars, on policy and trade issues for agricultural products.

21714 ■ New Mexico State University–Agricultural Experiment Station
PO Box 30003, MSC 3BF
Las Cruces, NM 88003-8003
Ph:(575)646-3125
Fax:(575)646-5975
Co. E-mail: sloring@nmsu.edu
URL: http://aces.nmsu.edu/aes
Contact: Dr. Steven Loring, Assoc.Dir.
E-mail: sloring@nmsu.edu
Scope: New Mexico and western U.S. agriculture; natural and human resources, especially as it applies to livestock, crops, soils, and improvement of rural living. Conducts studies in agricultural economics, agricultural business, economic development, agricultural and extension education, agronomy, animal science, clothing/textile/fashion marketing, entomology, environmental science, family and consumer science, fishery and wildlife sciences, forestry, human nutrition and food science, hotel and restaurant management, horticulture, molecular biology, plant breeding, plant pathology, plant physiology, range science, recreational areas management, soil science, and weed science. **Services:** Science-based information service, to citizens of New Mexico, via the Cooperative Extension Service; Technology transfer (annually), for producers, consumers, and environmentalists of the state. **Publications:** Agricultural Experi-

ment Station Research Bulletins (occasionally). **Educational Activities:** Conferences, workshops, short courses, field days (annually), for farmers, cattlemen, conservationists, and homemakers of the state.

21715 ■ North Carolina State University–Research Stations Division
1001 Mail Service Center
Raleigh, NC 27699-1001
Ph:(919)733-3236
Fax:(919)733-1754
Co. E-mail: eddie.pitzer@ncagr.gov
URL: http://www.ncagr.com/research/
Contact: Edward Pitzer, Dir.
E-mail: eddie.pitzer@ncagr.gov
Scope: Crops, forestry, aquaculture, livestock, and poultry.

21716 ■ Prairie Agricultural Machinery Institute
Hwy. 5 W, Box 1150
Humboldt, SK, Canada S0K 2A0
Ph:(306)682-2555
Free: 800—567-7264
Fax:(306)682-5080
Co. E-mail: humboldt@pami.ca
URL: http://www.pami.ca
Contact: Sharon Doepker, Res.Libn.
E-mail: humboldt@pami.ca
Scope: Component machinery testing. **Publications:** Research reports (occasionally).

21717 ■ Purdue University–Center for Food and Agricultural Business
Krannert Bldg., Rm. 781
403 W State St.
West Lafayette, IN 47907-2056
Ph:(765)494-4247
Fax:(765)494-4333
Co. E-mail: gray@purdue.edu
URL: http://www.agecon.purdue.edu/cab
Contact: Dr. Allan Gray, Dir.
E-mail: gray@purdue.edu
Scope: Agribusiness, including the use of operations research techniques for solving agribusiness problems; analysis of the specialized marketing, management and finance problems of agricultural businesses; buying behaviors of agricultural producers; risk management strategies of food and agribusiness firms; and evaluation of agribusiness marketing strategies. **Publications:** Articles. **Educational Activities:** Food and agribusiness management education programs, including programs that focus on specific functional management areas such as marketing, finance, personnel management, sales management, and relationship marketing.

21718 ■ University of Delaware–Halophyte Biotechnology Center
College of Earth, Ocean, & Environment
700 Pilottown Rd.
Lewes, DE 19958
Ph:(302)645-4264
Fax:(302)645-4028
Co. E-mail: jackg@udel.edu
URL: http://www.ceoe.udel.edu/halophyte
Contact: Prof. John L. Gallagher PhD, Co-Dir.
E-mail: jackg@udel.edu
Scope: Sustainable saline agriculture and wetlands restoration, including improvement of salt-tolerant crops and development of plants that will drive high productivity ecosystems without continual human input. **Publications:** Newsletter. **Educational Activities:** Degree and non-degree programs, in halophyte agronomy and biology, comparative wetland ecology, plant nutrition in saline soils, and salt tolerance mechanisms.

21719 ■ University of Florida–Institute of Food and Agricultural Sciences
1008 McCarty Hall
PO Box 110180
Gainesville, FL 32611-0180
Ph:(352)392-1971
Fax:(352)265-6932
Co. E-mail: jackpayne@ufl.edu
URL: http://www.ifas.ufl.edu
Contact: Dr. Jack Payne, Sen.VP
E-mail: jackpayne@ufl.edu
Scope: Food and agriculture sciences, natural resources, and renewable resources. **Publications:** Faculty Directory (semiannually); Impact Magazine (semiannually); Inside IFAS Newsletter (monthly); Newsline Newsletter (quarterly).

Bartering

ASSOCIATIONS AND OTHER ORGANIZATIONS

21720 ■ International Reciprocal Trade Association
524 Middle St.
Portsmouth, VA 23704
Ph:(757)393-2292
Fax:(757)257-4014
Co. E-mail: ron@irta.com
URL: http://www.irta.com
Contact: Ron D. Whitney, Exec. Dir.

Description: Individuals, partnerships, corporations, and firms that engage in the commercial barter industry worldwide, including local trade exchanges which act as clearinghouses, and corporate trade companies which arrange domestic and international barter transactions. Works to foster and promote the interests of the commercial barter industry through the establishment of ethical standards and self-regulation; to represent members before government agencies in matters affecting the industry; to introduce firms engaged in bartering activities; to resolve disputes between members; influence public laws and regulations affecting the industry; disseminate information and conduct public relations programs. Serves as a clearinghouse for industry and public inquiries. Compiles statistics on the segment of commercial barter accounted for by organized trade exchanges and corporate trade companies. Conducts consumer protection, educational, and training programs. Operates Corporate Barter Council as a self-governing body for the corporate trade sector. Awards professional accreditation; operates referral and placement services; maintains speakers' bureau; supports charitable programs. **Publications:** *IRTA Dialogue* (quarterly).

21721 ■ The Waterfront Center
PO Box 53351
Washington, DC 20009
Ph:(202)337-0356
Fax:(202)986-0448
Co. E-mail: mail@waterfrontcenter.org
URL: http://www.waterfrontcenter.org
Contact: Ann E. Breen, Co-Dir./Co-Founder

Description: State and local governments; architectural, engineering, and design firms; developers; educational institutions; persons in the boating industry; interested others. Helps communities develop waterfronts that facilitate economic growth while providing for public access and recreation. Conducts forums that address problems and opportunities in a particular community; provides on-site analyses and consulting; offers slide presentations; conducts research. **Publications:** *Caution: Working Waterfront: The Impact of Change on Marine Businesses*; *Urban Waterfront Resource List* (periodic); *The Waterfront: A Worldwide Urban Success Story* (annual); *Waterfront World Spotlight* (quarterly); *Waterfronts: Cities Reclaim Their Edge* .

REFERENCE WORKS

21722 ■ "Age-Old System of Bartering Is Being Revolutionized by Phoenix Company, Premier Barter" in *Internet Wire* (July 12, 2010)
Pub: Comtex
Description: Premier Barter is helping entrepreneurs rediscover the system of bartering as a method of exchanging goods and services without cash or credit.

21723 ■ "Area Small Businesses Enjoy Benefits of Bartering Group" in *News-Herald* (August 22, 2010)
Pub: The News-Herald
Ed: Brandon C. Baker. **Description:** ITEX is a publicly traded firm that spurs cashless, business-to-business transactions within its own marketplace. Details of the bartering of goods and services within the company are outlined.

21724 ■ "Bartering, Browsing, Borrowing to Save" in *Reading Eagle* (July 20, 2010)
Pub: Reading Eagle/Reading Times
Ed: Jessica Bakeman. **Description:** Various forms of bartering are outlined to help small companies as well as individuals.

21725 ■ "Bartering is Local Club's Stock in Trade" in *Pueblo Chieftain* (September 6, 2010)
Pub: The Pueblo Chieftain
Ed: Loretta Sword. **Description:** As the economy waivers, a barter club in Pueblo, Colorado thrives. An examination of the club and the way it operates is included.

21726 ■ "Bartering Makes a Return in Hard Times" in *Atlanta Journal-Constitution* (October 2, 2010, pp. A15)
Pub: Atlanta Journal-Constitution
Ed: Bill York. **Description:** The advantages of bartering are explored.

21727 ■ "Bartering Takes Businesses Back to Basics: Broker's Exchange Helps Members to Reach New Customers" in *Buffalo News* (July 9, 2010)
Pub: The Buffalo News
Ed: Dino Grandoni. **Description:** Bartering clubs can help small businesses reach new customers and to expand their business.

21728 ■ "Bartering Trades on Talents" in *Reading Eagle* (June 20, 2010)
Pub: Reading Eagle/Reading Times
Ed: Tony Lucia. **Description:** Bartering is not just a way of trading goods and services, it can be an essential tool for small business to survive in a bad economy.

21729 ■ "Beat the Buck: Bartering Tips from In-The-Know Authors" in (June 23, 2010)
Pub: The Telegraph
Ed: Jill Moon. **Description:** The Art of Barter is a new book to help small businesses learn this art form in order to expand customer base and reserve cash flow.

21730 ■ "Benefits of Bartering" in *Mail Tribune* (November 22, 2010)
Pub: Mail Tribune
Ed: Damian Mann. **Description:** Various people discuss the use of bartering for their small companies in order to improve business.

21731 ■ "Businesses Band Together in Destin Bartering to Keep Heads Above Water" in *Destin Log* (July 24, 2010)
Pub: The Destin Log
Ed: Andrew Metz. **Description:** Profile of The Barter Company located in Destin, Florida, whose owner believes that bartering for goods and services can help small companies in a down economy.

21732 ■ "Fair Exchange" in *Food and Drink* (Winter 2010, pp. 84)
Pub: Schofield Media Group
Ed: Don Mardak. **Description:** Bartering can assist firms in the food and beverage industry to attract new customers, maximize resources, and reduce cash expenses.

21733 ■ "A Family's Fortune" in *Canadian Business* (Vol. 80, Winter 2007, No. 24, pp. 103)
Pub: Rogers Media
Ed: Graham F. Scott. **Description:** James Richardson started as a tailor before moving into the grain business because his clients paid him in sacks of wheat and barley. The James Richardson and Sons Ltd. entered the radio business in 1927 but later sold it off in 1951.

21734 ■ "International Monetary Barter Helps Discretionary Industry" in *Benzinga.com* (January 24, 2011)
Pub: Benzinga.com
Ed: Benzinga Staff. **Description:** International Monetary Systems Limited, a business-to-business bartering firm, is helping wedding and event planners close deals with customers with bartering solutions.

21735 ■ "Poor Economy Inspires Rich Alternatives In a Modern, and Tax-Free, Twist on Bartering" in *Houston Chronicle* (June 7, 2010)
Pub: Houston Chronicle Publishing Company
Ed: Michael Rubinkam. **Description:** Time banking helps individuals and firms receive goods or services by depositing time dollars into a bank reserved for receipt of goods and services.

21736 ■ "Will Work for Equity" in *Inc.* (March 2008, pp. 50, 52)
Pub: Gruner & Jahr USA Publishing
Ed: Ryan McCarthy. **Description:** Profile of Dave Graham and his information technology company; Graham built his business by taking equity in client firms rather than charging fees. Four tips to consider before signing a work-for-equity business deal are outlined.

ASSOCIATIONS AND OTHER ORGANIZATIONS

21737 ■ American Mutual Life Association
19424 S Waterloo Rd.
Cleveland, OH 44119
Ph:(216)531-1900
Fax:(216)531-8123
Co. E-mail: amla@americanmutual.org
URL: http://americanmutual.org
Description: Fraternal benefit life insurance society. Maintains recreation center. **Publications:** *Our Voice* (biweekly).

21738 ■ American Society of Pension Professionals and Actuaries
4245 N Fairfax Dr., Ste. 750
Arlington, VA 22203
Ph:(703)516-9300
Fax:(703)516-9308
Co. E-mail: asppa@asppa.org
URL: http://www.asppa.org
Contact: Brian H. Graff Esq., Exec. Dir./CEO
Description: Aims to educate pension actuaries, consultants, administrators, and other benefits professionals. Seeks to preserve and enhance the private pension system as part of the development of a cohesive and coherent national retirement income policy. .

21739 ■ Council on Employee Benefits
1311 King St.
Alexandria, VA 22314
Ph:(703)549-6025
Fax:(703)549-6027
Co. E-mail: scanfield@ceb.org
URL: http://www.ceb.org
Contact: Shane Canfield, Exec. Dir.
Description: Employers seeking informal exchange of experiences and information on the design, financing, and administration of employee benefit programs, both domestic and international. Provides a medium for the exchange of ideas, information, and statistics; sponsors or conducts research projects on benefits; makes known its views on legislative matters affecting employee benefits. Conducts research. .

21740 ■ Employee Benefit Research Institute
1100 13th St. NW, Ste. 878
Washington, DC 20005-4058
Ph:(202)659-0670
Fax:(202)775-6312
Co. E-mail: info@ebri.org
URL: http://www.ebri.org
Contact: Dallas L. Salisbury, Pres./CEO
Description: Corporations, consulting firms, banks, insurance companies, unions, and others with an interest in the future of employee benefit programs. Purpose is to contribute to the development of effective and responsible public policy in the field of employee benefits through research, publications, educational programs, seminars, and direct communication. Sponsors a broad range of studies on retirement income, health, disability, and other benefit programs; disseminates study results. Maintains research library with information on employee benefit programs. **Publications:** *EBRI Databook on Employee Benefits* (periodic); *EBRI Issue Brief* (monthly); *EBRI Notes* (monthly); *EBRI Pension Investment Report* (periodic); *Washington Bulletin* (biweekly).

21741 ■ Employers Council on Flexible Compensation
927 15th St. NW, Ste. 1000
Washington, DC 20005
Ph:(202)659-4300
Fax:877-747-3539
Co. E-mail: david@ecfc.org
URL: http://www.ecfc.org
Contact: Mr. Dennis Triplett, Chm.
Description: Represents employers and service providers who have implemented or are interested in flexible compensation plans allowing employees to choose from a variety of benefits packages. Promotes flexible compensation plans including cafeteria plans, health reimbursement arrangements, cash-or-deferred plans and other defined contribution plans. Monitors legislation and represents members' interests before Congress. Lobbies to preserve and simplify the flexible compensation provisions of the Internal Revenue Code. .

21742 ■ ERISA Industry Committee
1400 L St. NW, Ste. 350
Washington, DC 20005
Ph:(202)789-1400
Fax:(202)789-1120
Co. E-mail: mugoretz@eric.org
URL: http://www.eric.org
Contact: Mark J. Ugoretz, Pres.
Description: Large corporations that sponsor employee pension, health, and other benefit programs. Represents the concerns of major employers regarding policy, legislative, judicial, and regulatory matters involving the administration of private retirement, health, and other employee benefit plans. Issues briefings to members' congressional representatives. Operates speakers' bureau. (ERISA is an acronym for the Employee Retirement Income Security Act of 1974). .

21743 ■ International Foundation of Employee Benefit Plans
PO Box 69
Brookfield, WI 53008-0069
Ph:(262)786-6700
Free: 888-334-3327
Fax:(262)786-8670
Co. E-mail: membership@ifebp.org
URL: http://www.ifebp.org
Contact: John J. Simmons, Pres./Chm.
Description: Provides sources for employee benefits and compensation information and education, including seminars and conferences, books and an information center, CEBS and Certificate Series. Conducts more than 100 educational programs. Provides Internet job and resume posting service. **Publications:** *Benefits & Compensation Digest* (monthly).

21744 ■ International Society of Certified Employee Benefit Specialists
PO Box 209
Brookfield, WI 53008-0209
Ph:(262)786-8771
Fax:(262)786-8650
Co. E-mail: iscebs@iscebs.org
URL: http://www.iscebs.org
Contact: Steven E. Grieb, Pres.
Description: Graduates of the Certified Employee Benefit Specialist Program, co-sponsored by the International Foundation of Employee Benefit Plans and the Wharton School of the University of Pennsylvania. Promotes continuing education and professional development of employee benefit practitioners through courses and seminars. **Publications:** *International Society of Certified Employee Benefit Specialists—Membership Directory* (annual).

21745 ■ National Coordinating Committee for Multi-employer Plans
815 16th St. NW
Washington, DC 20006
Ph:(202)737-5315
Fax:(202)737-1308
Co. E-mail: nccmp@nccmp.org
URL: http://www.nccmp.org
Contact: Randy G. DeFrehn, Exec. Dir.
Description: International trade unions and jointly administered employee benefit trust funds. Promotes the interests of organizations that provide retirement security, health, and other welfare benefits to individuals working in industries that, due to their structure, would not otherwise provide sufficient pension and welfare benefits. Lobbies before Congress and federal regulatory agencies and participates in judicial proceedings affecting multiemployer plans and participants. .

21746 ■ National Institute of Pension Administrators
401 N Michigan Ave., Ste. 2200
Chicago, IL 60611
Free: 800-999-6472
Fax:(312)673-6609
Co. E-mail: nipa@nipa.org
URL: http://www.nipa.org
Contact: Laura J. Rudzinski, Exec. Dir.
Description: Individuals with at least a year of experience in pension administration, full-time pension administration employees, and interested individuals. Sponsors educational program for the accreditation of pension administrators and a series of regional programs relative to pension/profit-sharing programs and administration. **Publications:** *PLAN Horizons* (quarterly).

21747 ■ Woman's Life Insurance Society
PO Box 5020
Port Huron, MI 48061-5020
Ph:(810)985-5191
Free: 800-521-9292
Co. E-mail: website@womanslife.org
URL: http://www.womanslife.org
Contact: Janice U. Whipple, Natl. Pres./Chm.
Description: Fraternal benefit life insurance society focusing on the needs of women. Each review or lo-

cal club engages in local charitable community projects. **Publications:** *Woman's Life* (quarterly).

21748 ■ Workmen's Benefit Fund of the U.S.A.
399 Conklin St., Ste. 310
Farmingdale, NY 11735-2614
Ph:(516)938-6060
Fax:(516)706-9020
Co. E-mail: info@wbfusa.org
URL: http://www.wbfusa.org
Description: Serves as a fraternal benefit life insurance society. **Publications:** *WBF in Action* (quarterly).

REFERENCE WORKS

21749 ■ "16 Creative and Cheap Ways to Say 'Thank You'" in *HR Specialist* (Vol. 8, September 2010, No. 9, pp. 8)
Pub: Capitol Information Group Inc.
Description: Tips for starting an employee appreciation program for a small company are presented.

21750 ■ *101 Businesses You Can Start with Less Than One Thousand Dollars: for Retirees*
Pub: Atlantic Publishing Company
Ed: Heather Lee Shepherd. **Released:** October 2007. **Price:** $21.95. **Description:** According to a study by the U.S. Department of Health and Human Resources, people starting their work careers will face the following situation when they retire at the age of 65: they will have annual incomes between $4,000 and $26,000. According to the Social Security Administration, today's retirees can count on corporate pensions and Social Security for 61 percent of their retirement income. The remainder must come from other sources. Therefore, if this holds true for the future, today's workers need to accumulate enough in personal savings to make up the 39 percent shortfall in retirement income. The solution for many will be to start a small part-time business.

21751 ■ "401(k) Keys to Stable Value" in *Barron's* (Vol. 88, March 10, 2008, No. 10, pp. 40)
Pub: Dow Jones & Company, Inc.
Ed: Tom Sullivan. **Description:** Stable-value funds offer investors stability in a period of volatility in financial markets, attracting $888 million in funds. The Securities and Exchange Commission approved the launch of actively managed exchange-traded funds.

21752 ■ "Amount Md. Pays to Unemployed Dips to Lowest Level Since '08" in *Baltimore Business Journal* (Vol. 28, November 12, 2010, No. 27)
Pub: Baltimore Business Journal
Ed: Scott Dance. **Description:** Maryland paid out $50 million for unemployment benefits in September 2010 for its lowest payout since 2008. The drop in unemployment payout could mean lower taxes for employers who pay for the benefits. The unemployment rate in Maryland, however, increased to 7.5 percent.

21753 ■ "The Annual Entitlement Lecture: Trustees of Medicare and Social Security Issue Another Dismal Report" in *Barron's* (March 31, 2008)
Pub: Dow Jones & Company, Inc.
Ed: Thomas G. Donlan. **Description:** Expenditures on Medicare hospital insurance and the revenues available to pay for it have led to a gap of capital valued at $38.6 trillion. Slashing the benefits or raising taxes will not solve the gap which exists unless the government saves the money and invests it in private markets.

21754 ■ "An Apple a Day" in *Entrepreneur* (Vol. 36, February 2008, No. 2, pp. 19)
Pub: Entrepreneur Media Inc.
Ed: Mark Henricks. **Description:** Businesses are handling rising health coverage costs by providing employees with wellness programs, which include smoking-cessation programs, consumer-directed plans for savings on premiums, and limited medical care plans. Details on the growing trend regarding employee health coverage are discussed.

21755 ■ "Are Prepaid Legal Services Worthwhile?" in *Contractor* (Vol. 56, December 2009, No. 12, pp. 31)
Pub: Penton Media, Inc.
Ed: Susan Linden McGreevy. **Description:** Companies' provision of legal insurance as an employee benefit in the United States is discussed. Stoppage of premium payment halts employee coverage. It also does not cover all kinds of personal issues.

21756 ■ "At Your Service: Corporate Concierges Come in Three Varieties" in *Incentive* (August 25, 2008)
Pub: Nielson Business Media
Ed: Nathan Adkisson. **Description:** Companies are offering corporate concierge services to handle tasks for new employees as a sign-on benefit. Concierge of Boston has six employees that focus on fulfilling the needs of individuals.

21757 ■ "Bank on It" in *Hawaii Business* (Vol. 53, November 2007, No. 5, pp. 60)
Pub: Hawaii Business Publishing
Ed: Kathleen Bryan. **Description:** Many Baby Boomers that are preparing to retire would like to give back and make a difference. One way is to make gifts of Individual Retirement Assets (IRA). During 2007 people over 70 years can make withdrawals from an IRA and donate it without realizing the income as taxable.

21758 ■ "Banks Fret About Gist Of Bailout" in *The Business Journal-Serving Metropolitan Kansas City* (Vol. 27, September 26, 2008, No. 2)
Pub: American City Business Journals, Inc.
Ed: James Dornbrook. **Description:** Banks from the Kansas City area hope that the proposed $700 billion bailout will not send the wrong message. UMB Financial Corp. chairman says that he hopes that the bailout would benefit companies that were more risk restrained and punish those that took outsized risk. Other bank executives' perceptions on the planned bailout are given.

21759 ■ "The Best Option for All" in *American Executive* (Vol. 7, September 2009, No. 5, pp. 170)
Pub: RedCoat Publishing, Inc.
Ed: Ashley McGown. **Description:** Plaza Associates, a collections agency that conducts business primarily in the accounts receivable management sector, is the first in the industry to purchase 100 percent of the company from the founders through the formation of a leveraged Employee Stock Ownership Plan (ESOP).

21760 ■ "Best Practices: Developing a Rewards Program" in *Franchising World* (Vol. 42, September 2010, No. 9, pp. 13)
Pub: International Franchise Association
Ed: Leah Templeton. **Description:** Rewards for a job well done are examined in order to recognize franchisees for outstanding performance. Ways to customize a rewards program are outlined.

21761 ■ "Bills Raise Blues Debate; An Unfair Edge or Level Playing Field?" in *Crain's Detroit Business* (Vol. 24, January 21, 2008, No. 3)
Pub: Crain Communications Inc. - Detroit
Ed: Sherri Begin. **Description:** Changes in Michigan state law would change the way health insurance can be sold to individuals. Michigan Blue Cross Blue Shield is working to keep its tax-exempt status while staying competitive against for-profit insurers and nonprofit HMOs.

21762 ■ "Boosting Corporate Entrepreneurship Through HRM Practices" in *Human Resource Management* (Vol. 49, July-August 2010, No. 4)
Pub: John Wiley
Ed: Ralf Schmelter, Rene Mauer, Christiane Borsch, Malte Brettel. **Description:** A study was conducted to determine which human resource management (HRM) practices promote corporate entrepreneurship (CE) in small and medium-sized enterprises (SMEs). Findings indicate that staff selection, staff development, training, and staff rewards on CE have a strong impact on SMEs.

21763 ■ "Both Eyes on the Prize" in *Canadian Business* (Vol. 83, September 14, 2010, No. 15, pp. 42)
Pub: Rogers Media Ltd.
Ed: Jacqueline Nelson. **Description:** North American executive compensation has fundamentally shifted partly due to pressure from the US government and recent adjustments in the way CEO pay packages are structured. The changes have also become common practice in Canada and helped in scrutinizing the executive pay.

21764 ■ "Build a Better Bonus" in *Canadian Business* (Vol. 80, January 15, 2007, No. 2, pp. 65)
Pub: Rogers Media
Ed: John Gray. **Description:** The use of employee performance incentives to enhance employee productivity is discussed. Tips for employers, on how to creative an effective bonus plan, are presented.

21765 ■ "Builders, Unions Aim to Cut Costs; Pushing Changes to Regain Share of Residential Market; Seek Council's Help" in *Crain's New York Business*
Pub: Crain Communications, Inc.
Ed: Erik Engquist. **Description:** Union contractors and workers are worried about a decline in their market share for housing so they intend to ask the City Council to impose new safety and benefit standards on all contractors to avoid being undercut by nonunion competitors.

21766 ■ *Business Owner's Toolkit Tax Guide*
Pub: Toolkit Media Group
Released: January 2009. **Price:** $17.95. **Description:** Resource addresses the tax-filing process while helping to minimize bills. Discussions are focused on important issues pertaining to the small business owner. Topics cover include: personal and business expenses and how they are differentiated, how employee benefit plans are handled on tax returns, and what the IRS looks for when conducting audits. Free online information and support is also included.

21767 ■ "Businesses Keep a Watchful Eye on Worker's Comp" in *The Business Journal-Serving Greater Tampa Bay* (September 5, 2008)
Pub: American City Business Journals, Inc.
Ed: Jane Meinhardt. **Description:** Pending a ruling from the Florida Supreme Court that could uphold the 2003 changes on workers' compensation law, the outcome would include restrictions on claimant attorneys' fees and allow the competitive workers' compensation insurance rates to remain low. However, insurance rates are expected to go up if the court overturns the changes.

21768 ■ "CEO Pay: Best Bang for Buck" in *Philadelphia Business Journal* (Vol. 30, September 30, 2011, No. 33, pp. 1)
Pub: American City Business Journals Inc.
Ed: Jeff Blumenthal. **Description:** A study by Strategic Research Solutions on the compensation of chief executive officers in Philadelphia, Pennsylvania-based public companies reveals that only a few of them performed according to expectations. These include Brian Roberts of Comcast, John Conway of Crown Holdings, and Frank Hermance of Ametek Inc.

21769 ■ "CEO Pay: The Details" in *Crain's Detroit Business* (Vol. 25, June 22, 2009, No. 25, pp.)
Pub: Crain Communications Inc. - Detroit
Description: Total compensation packages for CEOs at area companies our outlined. These packages include salary, bonuses, stock awards, and options.

21770 ■ "Change of Plans" in *Entrepreneur* (Vol. 35, November 2007, No. 11, pp. 74)
Pub: Entrepreneur Media Inc.
Ed: C.J. Prince. **Description:** Companies should provide 401K plans that meet employee needs and

demographics, with new technology allowing providers to lower their own costs. Details on finding a plans that appeal to employees are examined.

21771 ■ "Connecting the Dots Between Wellness and Elder Care" in *Benefits and Compensation Digest* (Vol. 47, August 2010, No. 8, pp. 18)
Pub: International Foundation of Employee Benefit Plans
Ed: Sandra Timmermann. **Description:** Employees caring for aged and infirm parents deal with time and financial issues and other stresses. The connection between health status of caregivers and employers' health care costs could be aided by linking programs and benefits with wellness and caregiving.

21772 ■ "Consulting Firm Goes Shopping" in *Crain's Chicago Business* (Vol. 31, April 28, 2008, No. 17, pp. 45)
Pub: Crain Communications, Inc.
Ed: Phuong Ly. **Description:** Clark & Wamberg LLC was created last year after the merger of Clark Inc. to a Dutch insurance conglomerate. Clark Inc. was a life insurance and benefits consultancy which had been on a downslide, returning just 5.6 percent a year to shareholders. In contrast Clark & Wamberg posted first-year revenue of $106.8 million, fueled by business from its executive compensation and health care clients.

21773 ■ "Corporate Canada Eyes Retiree Benefit Cuts" in *Globe & Mail* (March 8, 2006, pp. B3)
Pub: CTVglobemedia Publishing Inc.
Ed: Virginia Galt. **Description:** A survey on Canadian companies reveals that due to rising health care costs and increasing number of baby boomer retirements, these companies are to cut down on health benefits they are providing to these retired employees.

21774 ■ *Create Your Own Employee Handbook: A Legal and Practical Guide*
Pub: NOLO
Ed: Amy DelPo, Lisa Guerin. **Released:** June 2009. **Price:** $49.99. **Description:** Information for business owners to develop an employee handbook that covers company benefits, policies, procedures, and more.

21775 ■ "CreFirst To Reward Doctors for Reducing Costs, Improving Care" in *Baltimore Business Journal* (Vol. 28, June 4, 2010, No. 4, pp. 1)
Pub: Baltimore Business Journal
Ed: Scott Graham. **Description:** CareFirst Blue Cross Blue Shield plans to introduce a program that dangles big financial rewards to physicians who change the way they deliver primary care by improving the health of their sickest patients while reducing costs. The company will soon begin recruiting primary care physicians in Maryland, Washington DC, and Northern Virginia.

21776 ■ "Crouching Tigers Spring to Life" in *Globe & Mail* (April 14, 2007, pp. B1)
Pub: CTVglobemedia Publishing Inc.
Ed: Grant Robertson. **Description:** The prospects of the acquisition of BCE Inc, by Canadian pension funds are discussed. The effect of the growth of these pension funds on the Canadian economy is described.

21777 ■ "Cutting Health Care Costs: the 3-Legged Stool" in *HR Specialist* (Vol. 8, September 2010, No. 9, pp. 1)
Pub: Capitol Information Group Inc.
Description: Employer spending on health insurance benefits to employees is investigated.

21778 ■ "Desk-Bound No More" in *Charlotte Business Journal* (Vol. 25, August 13, 2010, No. 21, pp. 1)
Pub: Charlotte Business Journal
Ed: Adam O' Daniel. **Description:** Bank of America has launched a program that encourages employees to work on their own schedules. The program encourages productivity and health work-life balance. A survey has also revealed that employees feel more productive under the program.

21779 ■ "Discount Shopping: Holiday Shopping Meets Social Media" in *Employee Benefit News* (Vol. 25, December 1, 2011, No. 15)
Pub: SourceMedia Inc.
Ed: Rob J. Thurston. **Description:** Offering employees access to discount shopping using social media sites for Christmas bonuses, could be the gift that keeps on giving.

21780 ■ "Discovery Communications" in *Workforce Management* (Vol. 88, December 14, 2009, No. 13, pp. 17)
Pub: Crain Communications, Inc.
Ed: Jeremy Smerd. **Description:** Discovery Communications provides its employees a wealth of free health services via a comprehensive work-site medical clinic that is available to its employees and their dependents. Overview of the company's innovative approach to healthcare is presented.

21781 ■ "Do You Have A Retirement Parachute?" in *Barron's* (Vol. 88, July 7, 2008, No. 27, pp. 32)
Pub: Dow Jones & Co., Inc.
Ed: Jane White. **Description:** The idea that American companies should emulate the Australian retirement system which implements a forced contribution rate for all employers regarding an adequate retirement plan for their employees is discussed.

21782 ■ "DoEs and DonEts" in *Canadian Business* (Vol. 79, July 17, 2006, No. 14-15, pp. 29)
Pub: Rogers Media
Ed: Andy Holloway; Erin Pooley; Thomas Watson. **Description:** Strategic tips for planning systematic investments, in order to make life more enjoyable after retirement, are elucidated.

21783 ■ "Doing the Right Thing" in *Black Enterprise* (Vol. 38, July 2008, No. 12, pp. 50)
Pub: Earl G. Graves Publishing Co. Inc.
Ed: Tamara E. Holmes. **Description:** More business owners are trying to become more environmentally friendly, either due to their belief in social responsibility or for financial incentives or for both reasons. Tips for making one's business more environmentally responsible are included as well as a listing of resources that may be available to help owners in their efforts.

21784 ■ "Doing Without" in *Baltimore Business Journal* (Vol. 28, June 11, 2010, No. 5, pp. 1)
Pub: Baltimore Business Journal
Ed: Scott Graham. **Description:** Maryland Health Care Commission report figures have shown only 47,661 small businesses provided some level of health coverage to 381,517 employees in 2009. These numbers are down from 51,283 employers who offered benefits to 407,983 employees in 2008 to highlight a disturbing trend in Maryland's small-group insurance market. Reasons for the drop are discussed.

21785 ■ "Don't Try This Offshore" in *Harvard Business Review* (Vol. 86, September 2008, No. 9, pp. 39)
Pub: Harvard Business School Press
Ed: Description: Fictitious outsourcing scenario is presented, with contributors offering advice. The suggestions address the ease or complexity of offshoring business creativity, along with challenges and benefits.

21786 ■ "Elder Care At Work" in *HRMagazine* (Vol. 53, September 2008, No. 9, pp. 111)
Pub: Society for Human Resource Management
Ed: Pamela Babcock. **Description:** Many employers are helping workers who face sudden, short-term elder care needs.

21787 ■ "Employee Motivation: A Powerful New Model" in *Harvard Business Review* (Vol. 86, July-August 2008, No. 8, pp. 78)
Pub: Harvard Business School Press
Ed: Nitin Nohria; Boris Groysbert; Linda Eling Lee. **Description:** Four drives underlying employee motivation are discussed as well as processes for leveraging these drives through corporate culture, job design, reward systems, and resource-allocation priorities.

21788 ■ "Expert Sees No Radical Reform of 401(K) System" in *Workforce Management* (Vol. 88, November 16, 2009, No. 12, pp. 12)
Pub: Crain Communications, Inc.
Ed: Ed Frauenheim. **Description:** Although many would like to see an overhaul of the 401(k) retirement system, it is unlikely to occur anytime soon; however, the drastic stock market drop of 2008 has raised pointed questions about the 401(k) system and if it enables a secure retirement for American workers.

21789 ■ "Experts Take the Temp of Obama Plan" in *The Business Journal-Serving Metropolitan Kansas City* (Vol. 27, November 14, 2008, No. 10)
Pub: American City Business Journals, Inc.
Ed: Rob Roberts. **Description:** Kansas City, Missouri-based employee benefits experts say president-elect Barack Obama's health care reform plan is on track. Insurance for children and capitalization for health information technology are seen as priority areas. The plan is aimed at reducing the number of uninsured people in the United States.

21790 ■ "Exposed?" in *Mergers & Acquisitions: The Dealmaker's Journal* (March 1, 2008)
Pub: SourceMedia, Inc.
Ed: Jerry Abejo. **Description:** State-run pension plans' contributions are declining due to a loss of tax revenue from plummeting home values.

21791 ■ "Facilitating and Rewarding Creativity During New Product Development" in *Journal of Marketing* (Vol. 75, July 2011, No. 4, pp. 53)
Pub: American Marketing Association
Ed: James E. Burroughs, Darren W. Dahl, C. Page Moreau, Amitava Chattopadhay, Gerald J. Gorn. **Description:** A study to determine the effects of rewards to creativity in the process of new product development is presented. The findings show that the effect of rewards can be made positive if combined with appropriate creativity training.

21792 ■ "Falling Local Executive Pay Could Suggest a Trend" in *Tampa Bay Business Journal* (Vol. 30, January 15, 2010, No. 4, pp. 1)
Pub: American City Business Journals
Ed: Margie Manning. **Description:** Tampa Bay, Florida-based Raymond James Financial Inc. and MarineMax Inc.'s proxy statements have shown the decreasing compensation of the companies' highest paid executives. The falling trend in executive compensation was a result of intensified shareholder scrutiny and the economy.

21793 ■ "The Final Say" in *Hispanic Business* (Vol. 30, March 2008, No. 3, pp. 52)
Pub: Hispanic Business
Ed: Hildy Medina. **Description:** Vice-Chairwoman of the pensions and investments committee and Illinois State Senator Iris Martinez is the first Hispanic woman to be elected Senator and is advocating for pension funds to include Hispanic money managers and minority- and female-owned businesses in the investment plans.

21794 ■ "Financial Education: Boomer's Spending Hurts Retirement" in *Employee Benefit News* (Vol. 25, November 1, 2011, No. 14, pp. 18)
Pub: SourceMedia Inc.
Ed: Ann Marsh. **Description:** Financial planners and employers need to educate clients and employees about retirement planning. Boomers are spending money that should be saved for their retirement.

21795 ■ "Get More Time Off" in *Canadian Business* (Vol. 80, March 12, 2007, No. 6, pp. 32)
Pub: Rogers Media
Ed: June Morrow. **Description:** Expert advice to employees to make use of leaves of absence to improve their career instead of working continuously for a long period is presented.

21796 ■ "Give a Little Back" in *Canadian Business* (Vol. 79, November 20, 2006, No. 23, pp. 17)
Pub: Rogers Media
Ed: Jack Mintz. **Description:** The plans of Jim Flaherty, Canada's minister of finance, to remove the corporate tax bias on income paid to pension plans are discussed.

21797 ■ "Glossary of Health Benefit Terms" in *HRMagazine* (Vol. 53, August 2008, No. 8, pp. 78)
Pub: Society for Human Resource Management
Description: Glossary of health benefit terms is presented to help when choosing a health benefits package.

21798 ■ "A Golden Retirement?" in *Canadian Business* (Vol. 81, December 8, 2008, No. 21, pp. 7)
Pub: Rogers Media Ltd.
Ed: Paul Webster. **Description:** Canada Pension Plan Investment Board (CPPIB) is believed to have suffered heavy losses in global stock markets. CPPIB has moved aggressively into stock markets after independent managers started handling the funds in 2000.

21799 ■ "Good Decisions. Bad Outcomes" in *Harvard Business Review* (Vol. 88, December 2010, No. 12, pp. 40)
Pub: Harvard Business School Publishing
Ed: Dan Ariely. **Description:** Suggestions are provided for developing and implementing improved reward systems that in turn produce better decision-making processes. These include documenting critical assumptions and changing mind sets.

21800 ■ *Greening Your Small Business: How to Improve Your Bottom Line, Grow Your Brand, Satisfy Your Customers and Save the Planet*
Pub: Prentice Hall Press
Ed: Jennifer Kaplan. **Released:** November 3, 2009. **Price:** $19.95. **Description:** A definitive resource for anyone who wants their small business to be cutting-edge, competitive, profitable, and eco-conscious. Stories from small business owners address every aspect of going green, from basics such as recycling waste, energy efficiency, and reducing information technology footprint, to more in-depth concerns such as green marketing and communications, green business travel, and green employee benefits.

21801 ■ "Healthcare: How To Get a Better Deal" in *Inc.* (November 2007, pp. 34)
Pub: Gruner & Jahr USA Publishing
Ed: Sarah Goldstein. **Description:** Things to consider when choosing an insurance carrier for your employees are explored.

21802 ■ "Help Employees Give Away Some Of That Bonus" in *Harvard Business Review* (Vol. 86, July-August 2008, No. 8, pp. 1)
Pub: Harvard Business School Press
Ed: Michael I. Norton; Elizabeth W. Dunn. **Description:** Research indicates that how employees spend their bonuses is key to their resultant happiness, rather than simply receiving the bonus itself. Firms that offer donation options can thereby increase employee satisfaction.

21803 ■ "Hire Power" in *Entrepreneur* (Vol. 35, November 2007, No. 11, pp. 105)
Pub: Entrepreneur Media Inc.
Ed: Mark Henricks. **Description:** Companies with big resources may hire human resource (HR) consultants to help with writing manuals, drafting policies and designing benefits for employees. HR consultants may also be hired to assist with specific functions or other strategic aspects.

21804 ■ "How to Avoid the Three Big Mistakes" in *Barron's* (Vol. 88, March 10, 2008, No. 10, pp. 30)
Pub: Dow Jones & Company, Inc.
Ed: Karen Hube. **Description:** Investors, particularly those having retirement investments, are advised to diversify their investments, refrain from market timing, and minimize payments to maximize investment gains. An investor committing these mistakes could lose as much as $375,000 dollars over ten years.

21805 ■ "How Much is Too Much?" in *Canadian Business* (Vol. 79, July 17, 2006, No. 14-15, pp. 55)
Pub: Rogers Media
Ed: John Gray. **Description:** Elucidates the emphasis on the need for companies to analyze the executive pay packages designed by compensation consultants.

21806 ■ *How to Start and Run Your Own Corporation: S-Corporations For Small Business Owners*
Pub: HCM Publishing
Ed: Peter I. Hupalo. **Released:** March 6, 2003. **Price:** $22.95. **Description:** Basics of corporate business structure are explained. Topics include discovering the best business structure for your company; how to decided between an S-Corporation and LLC; choosing the state in which to incorporate, how to form a corporation, angel investing, special issues for one-person corporations, the role of bylaws and corporate minutes, board of directors, taxes, workers' compensation issues, retirement plans, and more.

21807 ■ "Inch by Inch, Employees Lose Ground" in *Business Courier* (Vol. 26, November 13, 2009, No. 29, pp. 1)
Pub: American City Business Journals, Inc.
Ed: James Ritchie. **Description:** Employees in Ohio who retained their jobs have suffered losses in salary and other benefits, as companies exert efforts to save money. Thirty-four percent of employees experienced pay cuts. Statistical data included.

21808 ■ "Insurers Warn Brokers" in *Sacramento Business Journal* (Vol. 25, August 22, 2008, No. 25, pp. 1)
Pub: American City Business Journals, Inc.
Ed: Kathy Robertson. **Description:** Sacramento, California-based health plans have warned insurance brokers not to combine two different kinds of insurance products or they will be stricken from the sales network. The health plans also asked employers to promise not to combine plans with self-insurance. Such schemes are seen to destroy lower-premium health products.

21809 ■ "International Benefits Roundup" in *Employee Benefit News* (Vol. 25, December 1, 2011, No. 15)
Pub: SourceMedia Inc.
Description: Employee contributions to an employer-sponsored defined contribution plan in Japan will allowed on a tax-deductible basis; however, currently employee contributions are not allowed. The defined contribution plan is outlined for better understanding.

21810 ■ "Investigation Hints at Workers' Comp Trouble" in *Sacramento Business Journal* (Vol. 25, July 4, 2008, No. 18, pp. 1)
Pub: American City Business Journals, Inc.
Ed: Kelly Johnson. **Description:** In 500 California firms, a survey of worker compensation revealed that 38 percent of the companies had problems with required coverage. Government investigators are bothered that 107 companies did not respond to the official inquiry. Other views and information on the survey and on the expected economic implications of the findings are presented.

21811 ■ "Is Raising CPP Premiums a Good Idea?" in *Canadian Business* (Vol. 83, July 20, 2010, No. 11-12, pp. 37)
Pub: Rogers Media Ltd.
Description: Big labor is pushing for an increase in Canada Pension Plan premiums but pension consultants believe this system is not broken and that the government needs to focus on addressing the low rate of personal retirement savings. If the premiums go up, even those with high savings will be forced to pay more and it could block other plans that really address the real issue.

21812 ■ "Is There a Doctor In the House?" in *Black Enterprise* (Vol. 41, December 2010, No. 5, pp. 42)
Pub: Earl G. Graves Publishing Co. Inc.
Ed: Renita Burns. **Description:** Health insurance premiums have increased between 15 percent and 20 percent for small business owners, making it one of the most expensive costs. Ways to evaluate a health plan's costs and effectiveness are examined.

21813 ■ "Kids in Crisis" in *Employee Benefit News* (Vol. 25, November 1, 2011, No. 14, pp. 26)
Pub: SourceMedia Inc.
Ed: Lisa V. Gillespie. **Description:** Employers and vendor are taking more aggressive steps to help battle childhood obesity.

21814 ■ "Labor Pains" in *Canadian Business* (Vol. 79, August 14, 2006, No. 16-17, pp. 80)
Pub: Rogers Media
Description: Canada's employment insurance is analyzed in view of the growing shortage of labor.

21815 ■ "Leave Policies: How to Avoid Leave-Related Lawsuits" in *Employee Benefit News* (Vol. 25, December 1, 2011, No. 15, pp. 12)
Pub: SourceMedia Inc.
Ed: John F. Galvin. **Description:** Tips for employers when adding disability and maternity leave benefits to workers are outlined, with focus on ways to avoid leave-related lawsuits.

21816 ■ "Legg's Compensation Committee Chair Defends CEO Fetting's Pay" in *Boston Business Journal* (Vol. 29, July 22, 2011, No. 11, pp. 1)
Pub: American City Business Journals Inc.
Ed: Gary Haber. **Description:** Legg Mason Inc. CEO Mark R. Fetting has been awarded $5.9 million pay package and he expects to receive questions regarding it in the coming shareholders meeting. However, Baltimore, Maryland-based RKTL Associates chairman emeritus Harold R. Adams believes Fetting has done a tremendous job in bringing Legg's through a tough market.

21817 ■ "Legislators Must Cut Cost of Government" in *Crain's Detroit Business* (Vol. 24, October 6, 2008, No. 40, pp. 6)
Pub: Crain Communications, Inc.
Description: Southeast and West Michigan business leaders are setting aside their differences and have proposed clear agendas, ranging from eliminating the Michigan Business Tax to overhauling public employee and retiree benefits and pensions. Lawmakers must also come together to find solutions for the state's economy and discover an entirely new vision for the future of Michigan business.

21818 ■ "Like Mom and Apple Pie" in *Canadian Business* (Vol. 79, October 9, 2006, No. 20, pp. 19)
Pub: Rogers Media
Ed: Peter Shawn Taylor. **Description:** Impact of paying huge tax bills on the social benefits of family income is discussed. Income splitting as an effective way to lower household's overall tax bill is presented.

21819 ■ "Looking For Financing?" in *Hispanic Business* (Vol. 30, July-August 2008, No. 7-8, pp. 16)
Pub: Hispanic Business, Inc.
Ed: Frank Nelson. **Description:** Investment firms want to know about businesses that need funding for either expansion or acquisition; companies fitting this profile are interviewed and their perceptions are discussed. Investment firms need businesses to be realistic in their expectations and business plans which show spending of funds and expected benefits, long term goals, track record and strong management teams.

21820 ■ *Managing Health Benefits in Small and Mid-Sized Organizations*
Pub: Amacom
Ed: Patricia Halo. **Released:** July 1999. **Description:** Comprehensive guide for developing health care plans for companies employing between 50 and 5,000 employees in order to provide employees with better health care at lower prices.

21821 ■ "M&I Execs May Get Golden Parachutes" in *Business Journal-Milwaukee* (Vol. 28, December 31, 2010, No. 14, pp. A3)
Pub: Milwaukee Business Journal
Ed: Rich Kirchen. **Description:** Marshall and Isley Corporation's top executives have a chance to receive golden-parachute payments it its buyer, BMO Financial Group, repays the Troubled Asset Relief Program (TARP) loan on behalf of the company. One TARP rule prevents golden-parachute payments to them and the next five most highly paid employees of TARP recipients.

21822 ■ "The Massachusetts Mess: Good Health Care Is Expensive" in *Barron's* (Vol. 89, July 27, 2009, No. 30, pp. 39)
Pub: Dow Jones & Co., Inc.
Ed: Thomas G. Donlan. **Description:** Massachusetts' mandatory health insurance has produced the highest rate of insurance coverage among the states but the state is now unable to afford its dream of universal coverage just three years after they enacted it. This supposed model for federal health-care reform is turning out to be a joke.

21823 ■ "Md. Tries to Recoup $73M from Actuary" in *Baltimore Business Journal* (Vol. 28, June 11, 2010, No. 5, pp. 1)
Pub: Baltimore Business Journal
Ed: Gary Haber. **Description:** Maryland State Retirement and Pension System has won nearly $73 million in administrative ruling against Milliman Inc. over pension loss miscalculations. However, Milliman filed two court cases seeking to reverse the decision and to recoup to the state any money a court orders.

21824 ■ "Medicare Plans Step Up Battle for Subscribers" in *Sacramento Business Journal* (Vol. 28, October 21, 2011, No. 34, pp. 1)
Pub: Sacramento Business Journal
Ed: Kathy Robertson. **Description:** California's market for health plans have become increasingly competitive as more than 313,000 seniors try to figure out the best plans to meet their needs for 2012. Health plans are rated on Medicare materials to help consumers distinguish among the Medicare health maintenance organizations (HMOs).

21825 ■ "Mettle Detector" in *Canadian Business* (Vol. 79, July 17, 2006, No. 14-15, pp. 63)
Pub: Rogers Media
Ed: Calvin Leung. **Description:** The difficulties faced in completing the Certified Financial Analyst course, and the rewards one can expect after its completion, are discussed.

21826 ■ "Monaco Pay Cut Draws Attention" in *The Business Journal-Portland* (Vol. 25, August 8, 2008, No. 22, pp. 1)
Pub: American City Business Journals, Inc.
Ed: Erik Siemers. **Description:** Monaco Coach Corp. cut the salaries of five top executives in an effort to reduce the company's $178 million worth of inventory. The executives can earn the lost salary back if the inventory is reduced by $58 million a year after August 2008.

21827 ■ "The Moody Blues" in *Entrepreneur* (Vol. 36, April 2008, No. 4, pp. 87)
Pub: Entrepreneur Media, Inc.
Ed: Mark Henricks. **Description:** Depression among employees can affect their productivity and cost the company. Businesses with a workforce that is likely to have depression should inform their employees about the health benefits covered by insurance. Other details on how to address depression concerns among employees are discussed.

21828 ■ "More Businesses Will Shift Health Costs to Workers" in *Business Review, Albany New York* (Vol. 34, November 16, 2007, No. 33, pp. 1)
Pub: American City Business Journals, Inc.
Ed: Barbara Pinckney. **Description:** Survey conducted by consulting firm Benetech Inc. showed that sixty percent of employers are planning to increase payroll deductions to pay for health insurance premiums. More than ninety percent of the employers prefer HMO plans, followed by Preferred Provider Organizations. Other details of the survey are discussed.

21829 ■ "More Small Businesses Willing to Fund Employees' Benefits" in *Baltimore Business Journal* (Vol. 28, June 18, 2010, No. 6, pp. 1)
Pub: Baltimore Business Journal
Ed: Scott Graham. **Description:** An increasing number of small businesses in Maryland are tapping into potentially cheaper self-funded health plans instead of providing fully insured benefits to employees through traditional health plans. Self-funded health plans charge employers for health care up to a specified level. Economic implications of self-funded plans to small businesses are discussed.

21830 ■ "New Year, New Estate Plan" in *Hawaii Business* (Vol. 53, February 2008, No. 8, pp. 54)
Pub: Hawaii Business Publishing
Ed: Antony M. Orme. **Description:** Discusses the start of the new year which can be a time to revise wills and estate plans as failure to do so may create problems of unequal inheritance and increase in estate tax exemption, which could disinherit beneficiaries. Other circumstances that can prompt changes in wills and estate plans are presented.

21831 ■ "Nobel Winners Provide Insight on Outsourcing, Contract Work" in *Workforce Management* (Vol. 88, November 16, 2009, No. 12, pp. 11)
Pub: Crain Communications, Inc.
Ed: Jeremy Smerd. **Description:** Insights into such workforce management issues as bonuses, employee contracts and outsourcing has been recognized by the Nobel Prize winners in economics whose research sheds a light on the way economic decisions are made outside markets.

21832 ■ "OMERS Labors With Troubles at the Top" in *Globe & Mail* (February 26, 2007, pp. B3)
Pub: CTVglobemedia Publishing Inc.
Ed: Elizabeth Church. **Description:** The trouble over fund management and leadership change in the Ontario Municipal Employees Retirement System is discussed.

21833 ■ "Open Enrollment: Staying Healthy During Enrollment Season" in *Employee Benefit News* (Vol. 25, November 1, 2011, No. 14, pp. 41)
Pub: SourceMedia Inc.
Ed: Shana Sweeney. **Description:** Tips for staying healthy during your benefit open enrollment period are outlined.

21834 ■ *Overcoming Barriers to Entrepreneurship in the United States*
Pub: Lexington Books
Ed: Diana Furchtgott-Roth. **Released:** March 28, 2008. **Price:** $24.95. **Description:** Real and perceived barriers to the founding and running of small businesses in America are discussed. Each chapter outlines how policy and economic environments can hinder business owners and offers tips to overcome these obstacles. Starting with venture capital access in Silicon Valley during the Internet bubble, the book goes on to question the link between personal wealth and entrepreneurship, examines how federal tax rates affect small business creation and destruction, explains the low rate of self-employment among Mexican immigrants, and suggests ways pension coverage can be increased in small businesses.

21835 ■ "Paychecks of Some Bank CEOs Have a Pre-Recession Look" in *Boston Business Journal* (Vol. 29, May 13, 2011, No. 1, pp. 1)
Pub: American City Business Journals Inc.
Ed: Gary Haber. **Description:** The salaries of United States-based bank chief executive officers have increased to pre-recession levels. Wells Fargo and Company's John G. Stumpf received $17.6 million in 2010. Community bank executives, on the other hand, have seen minimal increases.

21836 ■ "Penny Chief Shops For Shares" in *Barron's* (Vol. 88, July 7, 2008, No. 27, pp. 29)
Pub: Dow Jones & Co., Inc.
Ed: Teresa Rivas. **Description:** Myron Ullman III, chairman and chief executive officer of J.C. Penney, purchased $1 million worth of shares of the company. He now owns 393,140 shares of the company and an additional 1,282 on his 401(k) plan.

21837 ■ "The People Puzzle; Re-Training America's Workers" in *The Economist* (Vol. 390, January 3, 2009, No. 8612, pp. 32)
Pub: The Economist Newspaper Inc.
Description: With thousands of workers losing their jobs, America is now facing the task of getting them back to work. With an overall unemployment rate of 6.7 percent, the federal government has three main ways for leading workers back to employment: training them for new jobs, providing unemployment insurance in order to replace lost wages during the period of job-hunting; and matching employers who desire a skill with workers who have that skill. Specialized staffing agencies provide employers and potential employees with the help necessary to find a job in some of the more niche markets.

21838 ■ "Perks Still Popular: Jets May be Out, but CEO Benefits Abound" in *Crain's Detroit Business* (Vol. 25, June 22, 2009)
Pub: Crain Communications Inc. - Detroit
Ed: Ryan Beene. **Description:** Benefits packages of local CEOs are outlined. Statistical data included.

21839 ■ "Picking a 529 College Savings Plan" in *Black Enterprise* (Vol. 37, February 2007, No. 7, pp. 46)
Pub: Earl G. Graves Publishing Co. Inc.
Ed: Carolyn M. Brown. **Description:** Advice is given to help choose the right college savings plan.

21840 ■ "A Piece of the Action" in *Black Enterprise* (Vol. 38, January 2008, No. 6, pp. 42)
Pub: Earl G. Graves Publishing Co. Inc.
Ed: Alan Hughes. **Description:** Andre Williams, owner of Kaze Sushi restaurant, offered generous incentive plan-equity in the business in order to acquire Chef Kaze Chan and Chef Hari Chan. Williams' entrepreneurial pursuits are discussed.

21841 ■ *PPC's Guide to Choosing Retirement Plans for Small Businesses*
Pub: Practitioners Publishing Company
Released: June 2004. **Price:** $119.00. **Description:** Guide to evaluate and select retirement plans for small business.

21842 ■ *PPC's Guide to Compensation Planning for Small Business*
Pub: Practitioners Publishing Company
Released: September 2004. **Price:** $119.00. **Description:** Technical guide for developing a compensation system for small business. Forms and letters included.

21843 ■ "Prescription for Health: Choosing the Best Healthcare Plan" in *Black Enterprise* (Vol. 38, July 2008, No. 12, pp. 48)
Pub: Earl G. Graves Publishing Co. Inc.
Ed: Tamara E. Holmes. **Description:** According to a survey of small-business owners conducted by SurePayroll Inc., 20 percent of respondents have had a prospective employee refuse a job offer because healthcare benefits did not come with it. Cost is not the only reason many small-business owners do not offer these benefits. Guidelines to help take some of the confusion out of the guesswork that comes with trying to find the proper fit concerning healthcare benefits are outlined.

21844 ■ "The Price of Citizenship" in *Canadian Business* (Vol. 79, August 14, 2006, No. 16-17, pp. 13)
Pub: Rogers Media
Ed: Jack Mintz. **Description:** Safety and insurance benefits provided by the Canadian government to Canadian passport holders returning from Lebanon, is discussed.

21845 ■ "Recession Drags Down CEO Pay; Full Impact May Not Have Played Out" in *Crain's Detroit Business* (Vol. 25, June 22, 2009, No. 25)
Pub: Crain Communications Inc. - Detroit
Ed: Ryan Beene. **Description:** Median overall compensation package for Detroit's top-compensated 50 CEOs was down 10.67 percent from $2.3 million in 2007 to $2.06 million in 2008. Statistical data included.

21846 ■ *Retire Dollar Smart*
Pub: Trafford Publishing
Ed: Jim Miller. **Released:** July 2006. **Price:** $25.99. **Description:** The difference between savings and investments and their importance is examined, along with four rules for converting good investments into even greater ones. Contingency plans for healthcare costs as well as ways to manage taxes on investments are discussed. Five methods to control the costs of investing and saving include the use of smart strategies; getting independent, accurate, complete information; investing passively; asking for a discount; and taking off your blinders. Ten steps for designing a foolproof retirement investment portfolio are also provided.

21847 ■ "Retirement Barriers: Lowering Retirement System Barriers for Women" in *Employee Benefit News* (Vol. 25, December 1, 2011, No. 15)
Pub: SourceMedia Inc.
Ed: Mary Nell Billings. **Description:** Challenges faced by small business for lowering retirement benefits barriers for women and minorities, which is difficult to put into practice, is discussed.

21848 ■ "Retirement Plan Disclosures: Prepare Now for Fiduciary Rules" in *Employee Benefit News* (Vol. 25, November 1, 2011, No. 14, pp. 24)
Pub: SourceMedia Inc.
Ed: Brian M. Pinheiro, Kurt R. Anderson. **Description:** Department of Labor has delayed the deadlines on new affirmative obligations for fiduciaries of retirement plans subject to the Employee Retirement Income Security Act. Details included.

21849 ■ "RIM Rocks Out: Billionaire Bosses Sponsor a Free Concert for Deserving Staff" in *Canadian Business* (Vol. 80, Winter 2007, No. 24)
Pub: Rogers Media
Ed: Joe Castaldo. **Description:** Jim Balsillie and Mike Lazaridis of Research in Motion Ltd. (RIM) rented out the Air Canada Centre in Toronto to give their employees a free concert that features performances by the Tragically Hip and Van Halen on November 15, 2007. RIM has sponsored concerts by Aerosmith, Tom Cochrane, and the Barenaked Ladies in past parties that only shows how far the company goes in terms of employee appreciation.

21850 ■ "Running On Empty" in *The Business Journal-Milwaukee* (Vol. 25, July 4, 2008, No. 41, pp. A1)
Pub: American City Business Journals, Inc.
Ed: David Doege. **Description:** Employers are more engaged in offering incentives designed to offset commuting costs. Among the incentives offered are gas cards, parking reimbursement and midyear wage increases. The other efforts to help employees with the costs of going to work are discussed.

21851 ■ "A Safety Net in Need of Repair" in *The Economist* (Vol. 390, January 3, 2009, No. 8612, pp. 33)
Pub: The Economist Newspaper Inc.
Description: America's unemployment-insurance scheme is outdated and skimpy compared to other industrialized countries despite the fact that Americans tend to work harder at returning to the job market; the benefits are lower and available for a smaller amount of time and less unemployed workers are even able to collect these benefits. Statistical data included.

21852 ■ "Sales of Pension Income Targeted by Senator" in *Wall Street Journal Eastern Edition* (November 21 , 2011, pp. C7)
Pub: Dow Jones & Company Inc.
Ed: Leslie Scism. **Description:** Senator Tom Harkin is concerned about a widening business in which retirees and veterans sell pension income to investors in the secondary market. The business provides major profits for middlemen. Harkin wants those who are considering such a sale to have adequate information provided and knowledge in order to avoid unscrupulous dealings.

21853 ■ "A Say on Pay" in *Canadian Business* (Vol. 82, April 27, 2009, No. 7, pp. 14)
Pub: Rogers Media
Ed: Joe Castaldo. **Description:** A COMPAS Inc. survey of 134 Canadian chief executive officers found that 44 percent agree that CEO compensation should be subject to a non-binding vote. The respondents were also divided on whether to allow shareholders to exercise retroactive clawbacks on executive compensation if firm performance turns out to be worse than projected.

21854 ■ "Shopping Around for New Ideas" in *Canadian Business* (Vol. 79, July 17, 2006, No. 14-15, pp. 76)
Pub: Rogers Media
Description: Pensions should be a win-win situation for both the employer and the employee. The perspective of both parties concerning pension plans is explored as well as the need to amend laws in order to make sure that one class of merchant does not suffer at the cost of another.

21855 ■ "Small Biz Owners Are Tapping Into Health Savings Plans" in *Small Business Opportunities* (Fall 2007)
Pub: Harris Publications Inc.
Ed: Michael L. Corne. **Description:** Health savings accounts were developed by Golden Rule, a United Healthcare company. Today, more than 40 percent of the company's customers are covered by health savings account plans.

21856 ■ "Small Business Compensation" in *Small Business Economic Trends* (March 2008, pp. 10)
Pub: National Federation of Independent Business
Ed: William C. Dunkelberg, Holly Wade. **Description:** Graphs and tables that present compensation plans and compensation changes of small businesses in the U.S. are provided. The figures include data from 1968 to 2008.

21857 ■ "Small Businesses Changing Their Health Plan Preferences" in *Boston Business Journal* (Vol. 29, June 24, 2011, No. 7, pp. 1)
Pub: American City Business Journals Inc.
Ed: Scott Dance. **Description:** Small businesses in Maryland are shifting from traditional health plans to the consumer-oriented health savings accounts or HSAs. Health insurance industry experts say the change is indicative of the insurance buyers' desire to be more thrifty and discerning in their health care purchases.

21858 ■ "Small Businesses Get Creative to Retain Workers" in *Crain's Detroit Business* (Vol. 24, March 17, 2008, No. 11, pp. 21)
Pub: Crain Communications, Inc.
Ed: Nancy Kaffer. **Description:** Small businesses are often unable to compete with larger firms when it comes to offering employees fringe benefits and such perks as a company gym or an in-house chef; however, many smaller companies have found that the key to gaining employee loyalty lies in creating an atmosphere in which employees feel job satisfaction. Also provides tips on how to keep employees.

21859 ■ "Small, But Mighty" in *Employee Benefit News* (Vol. 25, November 1, 2011, No. 14, pp. 32)
Pub: SourceMedia Inc.
Ed: Andrea Davis. **Description:** Three consulting firms are facing the challenge of helping clients understand the new health care reform in a tight economy.

21860 ■ "Something Different in the Air? The Collapse of the Schwarzenegger Health Plan in California" in *WorkingUSA* (June 2008)
Pub: Blackwell Publishers Ltd.
Ed: Daniel J.B. Mitchell. **Description:** In January 2007, California Governor Arnold Schwarzenegger proposed a state universal health care plan modeled after the Massachusetts individual mandate program. A year later, the plan was dead. Although some key interest groups eventually backed the plan, it was overwhelmed by a looming state budget crisis and a lack of gubernatorial focus. Although much acclaimed for his stance on greenhouse gases, stem cells, hydrogen highways, and other Big Ideas, diffused gubernatorial priorities and a failure to resolve California's chronic fiscal difficulties let the clock run out on universal health care.

21861 ■ "Spotlight on Pensions" in *Business Horizons* (Vol. 51, March-April 2008, No. 2, pp. 105)
Pub: Elsevier Advanced Technology Publications
Ed: Laureen A. Maines. **Description:** Perceptions of pension burden and risk among financial statement users is likely to increase with changes in pension accounting. These perceptions might affect decisions on pension commitments and investments.

21862 ■ "Spread Your Wings" in *Canadian Business* (Vol. 81, March 17, 2008, No. 4, pp. 31)
Pub: Rogers Media
Ed: Megan Harman. **Description:** Financing from angel investors is one avenue that should be explored by startups. Angel investors are typically affluent individuals who invest their own money. Angel investors usually want at least 10 times their initial investment within eight years but they benefit the businesses through their help in decision-making and the industry expertise they provide.

21863 ■ "State Expects Increase of $50 Million from Film Bills; Come Back, Al Roker" in *Crain's Detroit Business* (March 24, 2008)
Pub: Crain Communications, Inc.
Ed: Bill Shea. **Description:** Overview of the new film initiative and its incentives designed to entice more film work to Michigan; the measures could bring $50 million to $100 million in movie production work for the rest of this year compared to the $4 million total the state saw last year. Also discusses the show "DEA" which was filmed in Detroit and stars Al Roker.

21864 ■ "Steeling for Battle" in *Crain's Chicago Business* (Vol. 31, April 21, 2008, No. 16, pp. 3)
Pub: Crain Communications, Inc.
Ed: Bob Tita. **Description:** Discusses contract negotiations between the United Steelworkers union and ArcelorMittal USA Inc., the nation's largest steelmaker, and U.S. Steel Corp., the third-largest; the union sees these negotiations as the best chance in two decades to regain lost ground but industry experts predict the companies will try to reduce benefits, demand a separate, lower wage scale for new hires and look for relief from the rising costs for retirees' health insurance coverage.

21865 ■ "Surprise Package" in *Business Courier* (Vol. 27, June 25, 2010, No. 8, pp. 1)
Pub: Business Courier
Ed: Dan Monk, Jon Newberry, Steve Watkins. **Description:** More than 60 percent of the chief executive officers (CEOs) in Greater Cincinnati's 35 public companies took a salary cut in 2009, but stock grants resulted in large paper gains for the CEOs. The salary cuts show efforts of boards of directors to observe austerity. Statistics on increased values of stock awards for CEOs, median pay for CEOs, and median shareholder return are also presented.

21866 ■ "Survey Finds State Execs Cool On Climate Change" in *The Business Journal-Milwaukee* (Vol. 25, August 8, 2008, No. 46, pp. A1)
Pub: American City Business Journals, Inc.
Ed: David Doege. **Description:** According to a survey of business executives in Wisconsin, business leaders do not see climate change as a press-

ing concern, but businesses are moving toward more energy-efficient operations. The survey also revealed that executives believe that financial incentives can promote energy conservation. Other survey results are provided.

21867 ■ "Survivorship Policies: Planning a Policy for Two" in *Employee Benefit News* (Vol. 25, November 1, 2011, No. 14, pp. 20)
Pub: SourceMedia Inc.
Ed: Marli D. Riggs. **Description:** Survivorship insurance is becoming an added benefit high net worth individuals and executives should consider when evaluating life insurance policies.

21868 ■ "Swinging For the Fences" in *Academy of Management Journal* (October 2007, pp. 1055)
Pub: Academy of Management
Ed: William Gerard Sanders, Donald C. Hambrick. **Description:** Study examines managerial risk-taking vis-a-vis stock options of the company; results reveal that stock options instigate CEOs to take unwise risks that could bring huge losses to the company.

21869 ■ "Take the Wheel: the Pension Protection Act Doesn't Mean You Can Sit Back and Relax" in *Black Enterprise* (October 2007)
Pub: Earl G. Graves Publishing Co. Inc.
Ed: Mellody Hobson. **Description:** Pension Protection Act provides multiple benefits and tax advantages for retirement, however the investment options and contribution rates are very conservative.

21870 ■ "Taking Full Advantage: What You Need To Know During Open-Enrollment Season" in *Black Enterprise* (Vol. 38, November 2007, No. 4)
Pub: Earl G. Graves Publishing Co. Inc.
Ed: Donald Jay Korn. **Description:** Employees can change or enroll in new insurance benefits during the fall season. It is important to assess each plan offered and to determine your deductible. Statistical data included.

21871 ■ "Tax Reform Analysis: Reforms Equal Smaller 401(k)s" in *Employee Benefit News* (Vol. 25, December 1, 2011, No. 15, pp. 19)
Pub: SourceMedia Inc.
Ed: Lisa V. Gillespie. **Description:** According to a new analysis by the Employee Benefit Research Institute, two recent proposals to change existing tax treatment of 401(k) retirement plans could cost workers because they would lower their account balances towards retirement.

21872 ■ "Teachers, U.S. Fund Providence Made Moves On BCE Buyout" in *Globe & Mail* (April 10, 2007, pp. B17)
Pub: CTVglobemedia Publishing Inc.
Ed: Boyd Erman; Sinclair Stewart; Jacquie McNish. **Description:** The Ontario Teachers Pension Plan, the largest shareholder of telecommunications firm BCE Inc., has called for a partnership with buyout firm Providence Equity Partners Inc. in order to acquire BCE Inc.

21873 ■ *This Is Not Your Parents' Retirement: A Revolutionary Guide for a Revolutionary Generation*
Pub: Entrepreneur Press
Ed: Patrick P. Astre. **Released:** July 2005. **Price:** $19.95 (US), $26.95 (Canadian). **Description:** Mutual funds, stocks, bonds, insurance products, and tax strategies for retirement planning.

21874 ■ "Tied to Home: Female Owned Businesses Export Less, And It's Not Just Because They're Smaller" in *Canadian Business* (April 14, 2008)
Pub: Rogers Media
Ed: Lauren McKeon. **Description:** Only 12 percent of small and midsized enterprises that are run by women export their products and services. Government agencies can be more proactive in promoting the benefits of exporting by including women in case studies and recruiting women as mentors. Exporting provides great growth potential especially for the service sector where women have an advantage.

21875 ■ "To Thine Own Self" in *Entrepreneur* (Vol. 35, November 2007, No. 11, pp. 50)
Pub: Entrepreneur Media Inc.
Ed: Torabi Farnoosh. **Description:** Self-directed individual retirement account (IRA) provides more investment options as payoff from this can be higher than an average mutual fund. Details on how to manage self-directed IRAs are discussed.

21876 ■ "Tradeshow Attendance Incentives Add Up" in *Pet Product News* (Vol. 64, December 2010, No. 12, pp. 14)
Pub: BowTie Inc.
Ed: Mark E. Battersby. **Description:** Pointers on how pet specialty retailers can claim business travel tax and income tax deductions for expenses paid or incurred in participation at tradeshows, conventions, and meetings are presented. Incentives in form of these deductions could allow pet specialty retailers to gain business benefits, aside from the education and enjoyment involved with the travel.

21877 ■ "Trust But Verify: FMLA Software Isn't Foolproof, So Apply a Human Touch" in *HR Specialist* (Vol. 8, September 2010, No. 9, pp. 3)
Pub: Capitol Information Group Inc.
Description: Employers are using software to track FMLA information, however, it is important for employers to review reasons for eligibility requirements, particularly when an employee is reportedly overstepping the bounds within leave regulations due to software error.

21878 ■ "Types of Health Plans" in *HRMagazine* (Vol. 53, August 2008, No. 8, pp. 72)
Pub: Society for Human Resource Management
Description: Definitions are given for various types of health care coverage available. Fee-for-service (FFS), health maintenance organization (HMO), preferred provider organization (PPO), point of service (POS) and consumer-directed health plan (CDHP) are outlined.

21879 ■ "Uncashed Checks: Retirement Plans in a Quandry" in *Employee Benefit News* (Vol. 25, December 1, 2011, No. 15, pp. 18)
Pub: SourceMedia Inc.
Ed: Terry Dunne. **Description:** Complex issues arise when employees don't cash their 401(k) balance checks. The US Department of Labor permits plans to cash out accounts of former employees with less than $1,000 to reduce the cost and time required to manage them.

21880 ■ *Understanding Workers Compensation*
Pub: Government Institutes
Contact: Kenneth Wolff DC, Medical Examiner/Disability Evaluator
Price: $72, individuals. **Publication Includes:** Listing of state and provincial workers compensation administrators. **Entries Include:** Name, address, phone. Principal content of publication is explanation of the Workers Compensation System.

21881 ■ "Unions and Upward Mobility for Low-Wage Workers" in *WorkingUSA* (Vol. 11, September 2008, No. 3, pp. 337)
Pub: Blackwell Publishers Ltd.
Ed: John Schmitt, Margy Waller, Shawn Fremstad, Ben Zipperer. **Description:** Examination of the impact of unionization on the pay and benefits in fifteen important low-wage occupations is outlined. Even after controlling for important differences between union and nonunion workers, including such factors as age and education level, unionization improves the pay and benefits offered in what are otherwise low-paying occupations.

21882 ■ "Use a Benefits Checklist to Ease New-Hire Onboarding" in *HR Specialist* (Vol. 8, September 2010, No. 9, pp. 4)
Pub: Capitol Information Group Inc.
Description: Checklist to help employees enroll in a company's benefit offerings is provided, courtesy of Wayne State University in Detroit, Michigan.

21883 ■ "Wal-Mart Expansion Plans Hit Roadblock" in *Crain's Chicago Business* (Vol. 31, March 24, 2008, No. 12, pp. 2)
Pub: Crain Communications, Inc.
Ed: Monee Fields-White. **Description:** Wal-Mart Stores Inc.'s expansion plans in Chicago have suffered a series of setbacks due to a shifting political landscape in which may require the company to pay higher wages. Wal-Mart claims that its hourly pay and benefits are fair; however, the labor force does not agree.

21884 ■ "W&S to Trim Rich Retirement Plan" in *Business Courier* (Vol. 27, October 15, 2010, No. 24, pp. 1)
Pub: Business Courier
Ed: Dan Monk. **Description:** Insurance firm Western & Southern Financial Group announced that it will reduce the pension benefits of its 4,000 associates by more than 30 percent starting January 1, 2011. The move is expected to reduce annual retirement payments by several thousand dollars per associate. Western is a Fortune 500 company and has $34 billion in total assets.

21885 ■ "We Have a Budget, Too" in *Entrepreneur* (Vol. 37, October 2009, No. 10, pp. 89)
Pub: Entrepreneur Media, Inc.
Ed: Craig Matsuda. **Description:** One human resources executive at a financial services company claims that health care issues are as costly and irritating for companies as they are for the employees. Health care vendors and insurers try as much as possible to maximize profits, while companies exert much effort to maximize benefits for their workers.

21886 ■ "What Choice Did I Have?" in *Entrepreneur* (Vol. 37, October 2009, No. 10, pp. 88)
Pub: Entrepreneur Media, Inc.
Ed: Craig Matsuda. **Description:** Profile of a worker at a financial services company who acquired first hand knowledge concerning the relationship between health insurance costs and coverage. The worker's son got severely ill, forcing the worker to spend above what is covered by health insurance.

21887 ■ "What You Should Know About Signing Bonuses" in *Black Enterprise* (Vol. 38, October 2007, No. 3, pp. 70)
Pub: Earl G. Graves Publishing Co. Inc.
Ed: Marcia Reed-Woodard. **Description:** High-level corporate executives are receiving sign-on bonuses. According to a study conducted by World@Work, nearly 70 percent of employers signing bonuses attract key employees.

21888 ■ "Winners and Losers" in *Crain's Detroit Business* (Vol. 25, June 22, 2009, No. 25, pp. 18)
Pub: Crain Communications Inc. - Detroit
Description: Rankings for Detroit's 50 top-compensated CEOs has changed due to the economic recession. The biggest changes are discussed.

21889 ■ "Women Draw Less Pension Income" in *Marketing to Women* (Vol. 21, March 2008, No. 3, pp. 6)
Pub: EPM Communications, Inc.
Description: According to a study by the Employee Benefit Research Institute, women over the age of 50 are much less likely to receive annuity and/or pension income. Statistical data included.

21890 ■ "Work At It!" in *Hawaii Business* (Vol. 53, October 2007, No. 4, pp. 44)
Pub: Hawaii Business Publishing
Ed: Cathy S. Cruz-George. **Description:** Employers in Hawaii are mitigating the effects of rising health-care costs by giving their employees health insurance and offering wellness programs. Employer-based health insurance has increases by 87 percent in the United States over the 2000-2006 period. Wellness programs that address different aspects of employees' health, such as food consumption, drug compliance and smoking habits, are discussed.

TRADE PERIODICALS

21891 ■ *Benefits Law Journal*
Pub: Aspen Publishers Inc.
Released: Quarterly. **Price:** $450. **Description:** Journal covering the welfare benefits field, including new types, delivery methods, and legal requirements.

21892 ■ *Benefits Quarterly*
Pub: International Society of Certified Employee Benefit Specialists
Contact: Paul Fronstin PhD, Assoc. Ed.
Ed: Jack L. VanDerhei, PhD, Editor. **Released:** Quarterly. **Price:** $125; $95 students. **Description:** Journal for human resources professionals.

21893 ■ *BNA Pension & Benefits Reporter*
Pub: Bureau of National Affairs Inc.
Contact: D. Sayre
Ed: David A. Sayre, Editor. **Price:** $1811, individual; online two users $2730. **Description:** Covers pension developments stemming from the passage of the Employee Retirement Income Security Act of 1974 (ERISA) and its amendments. Discusses pension and welfare benefit regulations, standards, enforcement actions, court decisions, legislative and administrative actions, agency options, and employee benefit trust fund requirements.

21894 ■ *EBRI Issue Brief*
Pub: Employee Benefit Research Institute
Contact: Steve Blakely
E-mail: blakely@ebri.org
Ed: Dallas Salisbury, Editor, salisbury@ebri.org. **Released:** Monthly. **Price:** Included in membership; $224, nonmembers; $25, single issue. **Description:** Examines, analyzes, and interprets key issues and trends in the employee benefits field. Covers one topic in-depth in each issue. Remarks: Price includes subscription to the newsletter Employee Benefit Notes.

21895 ■ *EBRI Notes*
Pub: Employee Benefit Research Institute
Contact: Martha Bobbino, Dir. Library Resources
E-mail: blakely@ebri.org
Ed: Dallas Salisbury, Editor, salisbury@ebri.org. **Released:** Monthly. **Price:** Included in membership; $199, nonmembers. **Description:** "Analyzes and discusses newly released employee benefits data and reviews a wide range of policy issues, research and publications." Recurring features include news of research, legal analysis, legislative updates. Remarks: Subscription includes EBRI Issue Brief.

21896 ■ *Employee Benefit Plan Review*
Pub: Aspen Publishers, Inc. (Frederick, Maryland)
Contact: Sue Burzawa, Assoc. Ed.
Released: Monthly. **Price:** $295. **Description:** Magazine serving decision-makers who administer, design, install, and service employee benefit plans.

21897 ■ *Employee Benefits Cases*
Pub: Bureau of National Affairs Inc.
Contact: David A. Sayre, Managing Editor
Released: Weekly, 50/year. **Price:** $1,141. **Description:** Reports full text of federal and state court opinions and selected decisions of arbitrators and the National Labor Relations Board on employee benefits issues. Recurring features include a cumulative index digest, tables of cases, a topical index, and a classification guide.

21898 ■ *Employee Benefits Management Directions*
Pub: CCH Inc.
Released: Biweekly. **Price:** $299. **Description:** Considers new trends in employee benefits management, including 401k plans, family leave programs, health insurance, retirement plans, and relocation assistance. Provides tax information and news of legislation and court cases. Recurring features include news of educational opportunities and conferences. Remarks: Included with subscription to Employee Benefits Management.

21899 ■ *Employee Relations Law Journal*
Pub: Aspen Publishers Inc.
Released: Quarterly. **Price:** $439 single issue. **Description:** Journal for employers and legal advisors covering problems with equal employment opportunity, occupational health and safety, labor-management relations, and employee benefits and compensation.

21900 ■ *Employee Services Management*
Pub: ESM Association
Contact: Patrick B. Stinson, Publisher
Ed: Renee M. Mula, Editor, reneemula@esmassn.org. **Released:** Quarterly. **Price:** $52; $74 two years; $67 other countries; $6 single issue. **Description:** Trade magazine focusing on employee services, fitness, and recreation programming.

21901 ■ *Employment Relations Today*
Pub: John Wiley & Sons Inc.
Contact: Thomas D. Cairns, Editorial Advisory Board
Ed: Carol DiPaolo, Editor. **Released:** Quarterly. **Price:** $770 print; $770 Canada print; $794 other countries print; $770 institutions print; $770 institutions, Canada print, for Canada add 5%GST; $794 institutions, other countries print. **Description:** Journal for senior human resources executives covering HR strategies and best practices.

21902 ■ *Flexible Benefits*
Pub: Aspen Publishers Inc.
Ed: Gregory E. Matthews, Editor. **Released:** Monthly. **Price:** $290, individuals. **Description:** Features news and research of interest to benefit managers and consultants. Focus is on employee benefits that involve choice. Recurring features include news of research, reports of meetings, news of educational opportunities, and original analysis of regulations affecting benefits.

21903 ■ *Journal of Compensation and Benefits*
Pub: RIA Group
Ed: Jeffrey D. Mamorsky, Editor. **Released:** Bimonthly. **Price:** $498. **Description:** Magazine offering practical guidance on compensation and employee benefits issues.

21904 ■ *Journal of Deferred Compensation*
Pub: Aspen Publishers Inc.
Released: 4/yr. **Price:** $339. **Description:** Journal covering analysis, strategies, and advice for executive retirement and compensation professionals.

21905 ■ *Journal of Pension Benefits*
Pub: Aspen Publishers Inc.
Ed: Ilene Ferenczy, Editor. **Released:** Quarterly. **Price:** $290. **Description:** Journal covering pension issues for pension professionals.

21906 ■ *Journal of Pension Planning and Compliance*
Pub: Aspen Publishers Inc.
Contact: Bruce J. McNeil, Editor-in-Chief
Released: 4/yr. **Price:** $369. **Description:** Journal covering pension compliance and design issues for professionals.

21907 ■ *Medical Benefits*
Pub: Aspen Publishers Inc.
Ed: Margaret Mucklo, Editor. **Released:** Semimonthly. **Price:** $385. **Description:** Focuses on key developments, statistics, and studies relating to the health care system. Covers eight major topic areas: cost containment, employee benefits, employee health/wellness, quality of care, delivery systems, government in health care, legal issues, and health care expenditure data.

21908 ■ *Pension Plan Guide*
Pub: CCH Inc.
Released: Weekly. **Price:** $2,099 print and CD-ROM. **Description:** Loose leaf series on pension plans.

21909 ■ *Pension Plan Guide—Summary*
Pub: CCH Inc.
Contact: Theodore Simons
Ed: Theodore Simons, Editor. **Released:** Weekly. **Price:** $139. **Description:** Focuses on pension nondiscrimination rules, benefit trends, court decisions, IRS and ERISA regulation and releases, withdrawal liability, and Supreme Court actions regarding pension plans.

21910 ■ *What's New in Benefits & Compensation*
Pub: Progressive Business Publications
Ed: John T. Hiatt, Editor. **Released:** Semimonthly. **Price:** $299, individuals. **Description:** Communicates the latest legal, tax and policy developments that help benefits executives address cost concerns while meeting complex needs of employees. Recurring features include interviews, news of research, and a column titled Sharpen Your Judgment.

21911 ■ *Work/Life Today*
Pub: National Institute of Business Management
Ed: Sharon O'Malley, Editor. **Released:** Monthly. **Price:** $355, individuals. **Description:** Provides information on family-friendly benefit programs.

21912 ■ *Work Span*
Pub: WorldatWork
Ed: Jean Christ-Offerson, Editor, jchristofferson@worldatwork.org. **Released:** 10/year. **Description:** Concentrates on issues in the fields of compensation and benefits and human resource management. Includes legislative updates, resources, and case studies.

21913 ■ *WorldatWork Journal*
Pub: WorldatWork
Ed: Dan Cafaro, Editor, dcafaro@worldatwork.org. **Released:** 4/year. **Price:** $210, Included in membership; $85, nonmembers U.S. and U.S. territories; $120, nonmembers other countries. **Description:** Offers strategic-focused articles dealing with topics such as compensation, benefits, and human resources management.

CONSULTANTS

21914 ■ Aaron Deitsch, F.S.A.
107-23 71st Rd., Ste. 231
Forest Hills, NY 11375-0366
Ph:(718)793-9885
Fax:(718)793-9888
Co. E-mail: ad2@pensionconsultant.com
URL: http://www.pensionconsultant.com
E-mail: ad2@pensionconsultant.com
Scope: Pension consultant and actuary providing consulting services in the employee benefits field, specializing in retirement plans. **Publications:** "Retirement Plan Basics"; "Retirement Plan Tips, Retirement Plan Traps"; "Profit Sharing Plan Tips, Profit Sharing Plan Traps"; "Defined Benefit Pension Plan Tips, Defined Benefit Pension Plan Traps"; "401(K) Plan Tips, 401(K) Plan Traps"; "401(K) Plans-Tips on Controlling 401(K) Plan Costs". **Seminars:** Pension Plan Library; Pension Plan Tools/Applications; Pension Plan and Retirement Plan Assistance.

21915 ■ Abacus Benefit Consultants Inc.
55 Stamp Farm Rd.
Cranston, RI 02921-3401
Ph:(401)942-4900
Fax:(401)942-8989
Co. E-mail: info@abacusbci.com
URL: http://www.abacusbci.com
Contact: Donald Powers, Principle
E-mail: dpowers@atsabacusbci.com
Scope: Administrators and consultants for employee benefit plans. Offers clients a menu of services in the traditional full service approach and coordinate with insurance companies and/or mutual fund companies with unbundled service package for 401(k) plans.

21916 ■ Advanced Benefits & Human Resources
9350-F Snowden River Pky., Ste. 222
Columbia, MD 21045
Ph:(410)290-9037
Fax:(410)740-2568
Co. E-mail: hrb@abhr.com
Contact: Linda Polacek, President
Scope: Provides human resource consulting to high technology businesses. Offers services in the areas of human resources, benefits, and training. Creates, maintains, or updates current human resource functions.

21917 ■ A.E. Roberts Co.
11490 Xeon St. NW, Ste. 200
Coon Rapids, MN 55448-3111
Ph:(763)757-5119
Free: 800-486-4585
Fax:(413)215-6877
Co. E-mail: info@aeroberts.com
URL: http://www.aeroberts.com
Contact: Mark Mosiman, Principle
E-mail: bizdev@aeroberts.com
Scope: Specializes in compliance training, focusing on regulatory compliance and human resource management issues. **Seminars:** ADA Seminar; COBRA Seminar; FMLA Seminar; HIPAA Privacy Seminar; HIPAA Portability Seminar; Section 125 Cafeteria Plans Seminar.

21918 ■ Aldrich & Cox Inc.
3075 Southwestern Blvd., Ste. 202
Orchard Park, NY 14127-1287
Ph:(716)675-6300
Fax:(716)675-2098
Co. E-mail: consult@aldrichandcox.com
URL: http://www.aldrichandcox.com
Contact: Charles H. Cox, President
E-mail: cox@atsaldrichandcox.com
Scope: Offers insurance and risk management counseling for all lines of insurance and self insurance to business, industry, institutions, political subdivisions, and utilities. Serves on a continuing basis but is also available for special projects, such as risk management audits in the Eastern United States and Canada.

21919 ■ AmeriFlex Financial Services
3700 State St., Ste. 310
PO Box 30340
Santa Barbara, CA 93105
Ph:(805)898-0893
Free: 800-425-1522
Fax:(805)898-0759
Co. E-mail: ameriflex@ameriflex.com
URL: http://www.ameriflex.com
Contact: Troy Hammond, President
E-mail: troy.hammond@atsameriflex.com
Scope: Develops and markets retirement and employee benefit programs to businesses, schools districts, hospitals, non-profit organizations and individual investors. **Publications:** "Women and Retirement Planning," Jul, 2006; "Top Ten Financial Planning Tips for Women," Coastal Woman Magazine, 2005. **Special Services:** AmeriFlex[R]; CFP[R].

21920 ■ Aon Hewitt
100 Half Day Rd.
Lincolnshire, IL 60069-3342
Ph:(847)295-5000
Free: 800-332-2111
Fax:(847)295-7634
Co. E-mail: info@hewittassociates.com
URL: http://www.hewittassociates.com
Contact: Vince Coppola, Senior VP
Scope: Offers services covering human resources, employee benefits, compensation, financial management and administration. **Publications:** "Lessons Uncovered: it Makes a Difference: Change Management and Hr Bpo"; "What Makes a Sourcing Advisor a Good Sourcing Advisor?". **Seminars:** How Do You Prepare and Educate Plan Participants, Nov, 2006. **Special Services:** Rapid eMerge[TM]; M&A Management Center[TM].

21921 ■ Benefit Communications Inc.
2126 21st Ave. S
PO Box 120789
Nashville, TN 37212-4318
Ph:(615)292-3786
Free: 800-489-3786
Fax:(615)383-7917
Co. E-mail: info@benefitcommunications.com
URL: http://www.benefitcommunications.com
Contact: Pride Scanlan, Principle
E-mail: pscanlan@atsbenefitcommunications.com
Scope: An employee benefit communications and servicing company that specializes in three areas voluntary products, employee communications and open enrollment outsourcing.

21922 ■ Benefit Partners Inc.
363 Falconbridge Rd.
Sudbury, ON, Canada P3A 5K5
Ph:(705)524-1559
Free: 800-461-6326
Fax:(705)524-5553
Co. E-mail: peter.d@benefitpartners.com
URL: http://www.benefitpartners.com
Contact: Vic Skot, Principle
E-mail: vic.skot@atsbenefitpartners.com
Scope: Services include employee benefits, pension, executive compensation, human resources and financial management. Industries served: Corporate and personal insurance planning and private wealth management.

21923 ■ Benefit Sources & Solutions
1952 US Hwy. 22
Bound Brook, NJ 08805
Ph:(732)560-1010
Fax:(732)560-1049
Co. E-mail: srappoport@benefitsource.com
URL: http://www.benefitsource.com
Contact: Tanya Pridgeon, Principle
E-mail: srappoport@benefitsource.com
Scope: Provides business leaders and human resource professionals at emerging companies and established global corporations with a personalized multi-faceted approach to manage their employee benefit programs. Designs, implements and administers employee benefit plans that are integrated in an employer's compensation package.

21924 ■ Benefits Dynamics Inc.
89 N Haddon Ave., Ste. D
Haddonfield, NJ 08033-2473
Ph:(856)616-1400
Fax:(856)616-1401
Co. E-mail: benefit@benefitdynamics.com
Contact: Mark Moran, Vice President
E-mail: joannm@benefitdynamics.com
Scope: A full service employee benefit, record keeping consultant and outsourcing organization. Provides pension consulting, administration and actuarial services, cafeteria and flexible benefit plans, human resource systems outsourcing, interactive voice-response systems, electronic employee benefit enrollment and transportation plans.

21925 ■ Benetech Inc.
3947 Lennane Dr., Ste. 250
Sacramento, CA 95834
Ph:(916)484-6811
Free: 800-285-7526
Fax:(916)488-1743
Co. E-mail: db@benetechinc.com
URL: http://www.benetechinc.com
Contact: Robert L. Brandon, President
E-mail: robb@benetechinc.com
Scope: An actuarial consulting and administration firm specializing in retirement plans for small and medium-size businesses. Offers plan design, record keeping and consulting services. Consulting services in plan design options for Profit Sharing, 401(k), and Defined Benefit Plans.

21926 ■ C F Services Group Inc.
9083 Shady Grove Ct.
Gaithersburg, MD 20877
Ph:(301)963-8820
Fax:(301)963-3733
Co. E-mail: jill@cfservicesgroup.com
URL: http://www.cfservicesgroup.com
Contact: Lenard S. Cohen, Owner
E-mail: len@atscfservicesgroup.com
Scope: Provides advice, information and comparisons regarding life insurance, mutual funds, limited partnerships, and other securities. Emphasis is on employee benefit planning and financial advice for businesses and key executives. Industries served: small businesses and professional practices. **Publications:** "Whole Life Insurance"; "Term Life Insurance"; "Universal Life Insurance"; "Variable Life Insurance"; "Auto Insurance"; "Insurance Claims"; "Maximizing Insurance Benefits"; "Insuring Your Future"; "Assessing Disability Insurance"; "Types of Health Care"; "Protecting Your Home"; "Additional Liability Coverage"; "Planning Options"; "Future of Social Security"; "Social Security Income"; "Keogh Plans"; "Equity-Indexed Annuities"; "Retirement Plan Distributions"; "Cash Management Basics".

21927 ■ Chernoff Diamond & Company L.L.C.
990 Stewart Ave., Ste. 520
Garden City, NY 11530-4869
Ph:(516)683-6100
Fax:(516)683-6163
Co. E-mail: mail@chernoffdiamond.com
URL: http://www.chernoffdiamond.com
Contact: Gladys Ahrens, Director
E-mail: gahrens@atschernoffdiamond.com
Scope: Provides comprehensive services and design; implementation and administration of employee benefit plans, pension, profit sharing and 401(k) plans; programs of executive and deferred compensation and sophisticated life insurance plans. Provides specialized advisory support in the areas of health and welfare, retirement and estate trust planning.

21928 ■ Compliance Consulting Corp.
406 Marquis St.
PO Box 13673
Jackson, MS 39236
Ph:(601)982-1219
Free: 800-435-1266
Fax:(601)982-1220
Co. E-mail: admin@cobracompliance.com
URL: http://www.cobracompliance.com
Contact: Keith Hughes, Mgr
E-mail: khughes@atscobracompliance.com
Scope: Provide clients with administration that meets all of the COBRA regulatory requirements. Offers critical functions necessary for a comprehensive COBRA and HIPAA administration program.

21929 ■ Comprehensive Professional Management Inc.
222 E Dundee Rd.
Wheeling, IL 60090-3009
Ph:(847)520-1301
Fax:(847)520-0372
Co. E-mail: bob@cpmincfs.com
Contact: Kathy Rathunde, Principle
E-mail: mkstumpf@atsaol.com
Scope: Services include accounting, financial planning, litigation support, pension profit sharing administration, practice surveys, professional corporation issues, retirement and estate planning and tax advice.

21930 ■ CONEXIS Benefits Administrators L.P.
6191 N State Highway 161, Ste. 400
Irving, TX 75038
Ph:(214)596-6919
Free: 877-266-3947
Fax:877-353-2948
Co. E-mail: sales@conexis.org
URL: http://www.conexis.org
Contact: Gordon Albury, Vice President
E-mail: agehrki@complink.biz
Scope: Provides web based COBRA HIPAA FSA direct bill compliance and administration services. Texas based outsourcing solution offers automated benefit administration for all-sized type of business. **Seminars:** COBRA/HPAA Compliance; FSA - What's new; Comparing FSA, HRA and HSA Programs.

21931 ■ Counts Benefit Services Inc.
2634 Mosby Ct.
Frederick, MD 21701
Ph:(301)694-3009
Fax:(301)694-3066
Co. E-mail: jcounts@countsbenefits.us
URL: http://www.countsfinancial.com
Contact: James E. Counts, Owner
E-mail: jcounts@countsbenefits.us
Scope: Consulting services include evaluation of employer's benefit plans as to cost vs. benefits, self insured benefits as well as fully insured welfare plans, and defined contribution/defined benefit plans. Also designs executive compensation programs and salary continuation benefits. Active with wide variety of industries. **Publications:** "Eighty percent of Americans agree they would benefit from having basic financial education and information". **Seminars:** The Financial Alternative to Success Seminar.

21932 ■ Donald C. Wright
3906 Lawndale Ln. N
Plymouth, MN 55446-2940
Ph:(763)478-6999
Co. E-mail: donaldwright@compuserve.com
URL: http://www.donaldwrightcpa.com
Contact: Donald C. Wright, President
E-mail: donaldwright@compuserve.com
Scope: Offers accounting, tax, and small business consulting services. Services include cash flow and budgeting analysis; financial forecast and projections; financial statements; reviews and compilations; tax planning, tax preparation; IRS and state/local representation; international taxation; estate, gift and trust tax return preparation; benefit plan services; business succession planning; estate planning; financial planning; management advisory services, pension and profit sharing plans, retirement planning, expert witness services and employee benefits plans. Serves individuals, corporations, partnerships, and non-profit organizations. **Seminars:** Qualified pension plans and employee welfare benefit plans.

21933 ■ Dorn & Associates Inc.
8506 Bass Lake Rd.
Minneapolis, MN 55428-5304
Ph:(763)533-7689
Fax:(763)533-1143
Contact: Chad L. Dorn, Vice President
E-mail: chad@dorn-associates.com
Scope: Services include accounting, marketing, employment partnership, new doctor agreements, personnel issues and human resources assessment, practice management, practice merger acquisition sale and liquidation, practice surveys and valuation, staff development and training.

21934 ■ Employee Benefit Research Institute
1100 13th St. NW, Ste. 878
Washington, DC 20005-4051
Ph:(202)659-0670
Fax:(202)775-6312
Co. E-mail: info@ebri.org
URL: http://www.ebri.org
Contact: Young Park, Principle
E-mail: park@atsebri.org
Scope: A public policy research organization serving as an employee benefits information source on health, welfare and retirement issues. Services include: basic benefit program descriptions, legislation analysis, media coverage and interpretation and long-range planning. Specializes in research on pensions, social security, health care, Medicare, long-term care, and flexible benefits. Serves government, academic consumers, consultants, banks, insurance companies, investment managers, law and accounting firms, corporations, and individuals. **Publications:** "Retirement Security in the United States-Current Sources, Future Prospects, and Likely Outcomes of Current Trends," 2006; "Estimating the Value of Changes in OASI Benefits Under Social Security Reforms," Jun, 2006; "Will Wider Use of Evidence-Based Medicine Significantly Enhance Healthcare Quality and Affordability? Implications for Consumer-Driven Health Benefits," 2003; "Consumer Driven Health Benefits: A Continuing Evolution," 2002; "The Economic Costs of the Uninsured Implications for Business and Government," 2000; "The Future of Private Retirement Plans," 2000; "EBRI Issue Briefs"; "EBRI Notes"; "Pension Investment Report PIR"; "EBRI Data book on Employee Benefits"; "Fundamentals of Employee Benefits Programs". **Seminars:** Policy Forums, Congressional Briefings.

21935 ■ Employee Benefits of St. Cloud Inc.
940 Industrial Dr. S, Ste. 111
Sauk Rapids, MN 56379-1272
Ph:(320)251-0034
Fax:(320)251-0340
Co. E-mail: nfo@ebsc-online.org
URL: http://www.ebsc-online.org
Contact: Sue Mohs, Mgr
E-mail: smohs@atsebsc-online.org
Scope: Consulting firm offers employee benefit planning services. Provider of plan design, administration and consulting services for small to middle-market employers. Expertise in qualified retirement plans, fringe benefit and flexible benefit plans, and non-qualified deferred compensation plans.

21936 ■ Employee Services Management Association
568 Spring Rd., Ste. D
Elmhurst, IL 60126-3896
Ph:(630)559-0020
Fax:(630)559-0025
Co. E-mail: esmahq@esmassn.org
URL: http://www.esmassn.org
Contact: Dorothy McGuire, Editor
E-mail: dorothymcguire@atsesmassn.org
Scope: Offers counsel on employee recreation/leisure activities and services for industry, business and government agencies. It provides an information and communication center for persons responsible for administering employee services, recreation and fitness programs. **Publications:** "Employee Services Management"; "A Strategic Component of Business". **Seminars:** Leadership Workshop.

21937 ■ The Epler Co.
450 B St., Ste. 750
San Diego, CA 92101
Ph:(619)239-0831
Fax:(619)239-0807
Co. E-mail: consultants@eplercompany.com
URL: http://www.eplercompany.com
Contact: Barbara Craven, Principal
E-mail: bcraven@atseplercompany.com
Scope: Offers actuarial and consulting services for employee benefits specializing in retirement plans, health, life, accidental death and dismemberment, long-term disability insurance plans, and executive compensation. Administers retiree health studies, AB1200 studies for schools, and merger studies on benefits. Conducts base pay, bonus and benefit surveys. Designs total compensation programs.

21938 ■ First Health
2610 Decker Lake Ln.
Salt Lake City, UT 84119
Ph:(801)954-6550
URL: http://www.firsthealth.coventryhealthcare.com
Contact: David A. Kreager, Vice President
Scope: Consultants active in the areas of retirement and savings plan design and administration, welfare plan design, and employee benefit communication.

21939 ■ Flex-Plan Services Inc.
11400 SE 6th St., Ste. 125
PO Box 53250
Bellevue, WA 98004-6423
Ph:(425)452-3500
Free: 800-669-3539
Fax:(425)451-7002
Co. E-mail: flexplan@flex-plan.com
URL: http://www.flex-plan.com
Contact: Bob Aitken, Secretary
E-mail: maitken@atsflex-plan.com
Scope: Flexible benefit plan design and administration for cafeteria-type plans, form 5500 preparation and employee benefit statements. Also assists with the design and administration of retirement plans. Offers customized Windows-based software systems that allow employers to communicate with and to enroll employees electronically for all employee benefit plans. Provides employee self service via internet and/or intranet. Industries served: All.

21940 ■ Franklin F. Beach & Co.
5478 N Rolling Oaks Dr.
Memphis, TN 38119
Ph:(901)763-4082
Fax:(901)767-1533
Contact: Franklin F. Beach, President
Scope: The firm offers counseling, estate planning and employee benefit planning including pension planning, profit sharing, executive compensation, health and welfare plans, business organization and management expertise.

21941 ■ A Friend of the Family
1 Huntington Rd., Ste. 702
Athens, GA 30606
Ph:(770)725-2748
Fax:(706)725-1650
Co. E-mail: info@afriend.com
URL: http://www.afriend.com
Contact: Abena Muhammad, Mgr
E-mail: crd@atsafriend.com
Scope: Human resource development consultants for personal care services as part of employee benefit programs. Programs include: Childcare, elder care, home secretaries, shopping and errand services. Serves private industries as well as government agencies.

21942 ■ Gallagher Benefit Services Inc.
2 Pierce Pl.
Itasca, IL 60143-1203
Ph:(630)773-3800
Fax:(630)285-4000
Co. E-mail: gbswebmaster@gallagherbenefits.com
URL: http://www.gallagherbenefits.com
Contact: William Ziebell, Exec VP
Scope: Offers consultation in areas of benefits planning, delivery, and administration. Services include executive benefits programs, health and welfare schemes, healthcare analytics, human resource services, international benefits services, retirement plan services and voluntary benefits services. Industries served: healthcare, higher education, hospitality and restaurant, transportation and non profit organizations. **Publications:** "Final HIPAA Nondiscrimination and Wellness Plan Rules Issued," 2007; "Using Electronic Media For Employee Benefit Elections and Notices," 2006. **Seminars:** Safety By Design, Marina Center, South Sioux City, NE, Nov, 2008; Hospitality Loss Prevention, DFW Radisson South Hotel, Irving, TX, Mar, 2006.

21943 ■ Health Insurance Specialists Inc.
17620A Redland Rd.
Rockville, MD 20855
Ph:(301)590-0006
Fax:(301)590-0661
Co. E-mail: info@his-inc.com
URL: http://www.his-inc.com
Contact: Jon S. Belinkie, President
E-mail: jbelinkie@atshis-inc.com
Scope: Serves a wide variety of businesses and individuals by designing comprehensive insurance packages and benefit plans, full service insurance and financial services firm, third party administration, human resources outsourcing.

21944 ■ HealthChoice
583 D'Onofrio Dr., Ste. 101
Madison, WI 53719
Ph:(608)833-7988
Free: 800-334-7988
Fax:(608)833-7540
Co. E-mail: info@healthchoice.com
URL: http://www.healthchoice.com
Contact: Clifford Morris, President
E-mail: info@healthchoice.com
Scope: Firm provides employee assistance program which concentrates on to reduce employer productivity loses. **Publications:** "Graduating From Child Care to Elder Care".

21945 ■ Healy & Associates Inc.
3033 W Jefferson St., Apt. W
Joliet, IL 60435-6449
Ph:(815)741-0102
Fax:(815)744-5412
Contact: Richard Kelling, President
Scope: Personal development consultant with experience in alcoholism and family treatment; employee assistance program consultation and implementation; health promotion programming on stress, smoking cessation, weight control; alcohol and drug related prevention and educational programming; and individual, group and family counseling. Serves private industries as wells government agencies. **Seminars:** Assertive Communication; Alcohol and Drug Problems in the Workplace; Chemical Dependency: Enabling vs. Intervention; Stress Management; Employee Assistance Programs; Smoking Cessation in the Workplace; Eating and Weight Issues; Cultural Diversity Training; Adapting to Change in the Workplace; Adapting to Shift Work.

21946 ■ Hooker & Holcombe Inc.
65 LaSalle Rd., Ste. 402
West Hartford, CT 06107-2397
Ph:(860)521-8400
Free: 800-457-1245
Fax:(860)521-3742
Co. E-mail: info@hhconsultants.com
URL: http://www.hhconsultants.com/HH
Contact: Rodger K. Metzger, Principle
E-mail: ddunn@atshhconsultants.com
Scope: Offers employee benefit services in the areas of pension plans, 401(k) plans, profit sharing, ESOP, thrift and savings plans, retirement plan outsourcing services and actuarial consulting.

21947 ■ In Plain English
14501 Antigone Dr.
PO Box 3300
Gaithersburg, MD 20885-3300
Ph:(301)340-2821
Free: 800-274-9645
Fax:(301)279-0115
Co. E-mail: rwohl@inplainenglish.com
URL: http://www.inplainenglish.com
Contact: Ronald H. Wohl, CEO
E-mail: rwohl@inplainenglish.com
Scope: Management consultants helping government and businesses research, design, write and produce user oriented management information for human resources, employee benefits, business process, corporate and marketing needs. Services include: GSA mob is schedule for consulting to the government; employee benefit communications, plain English business writing workshops for print and electronic media; communicating strategy and tactics; marketing research, business planning and communications; readability testing; usability testing and monitoring strategy. **Publications:** "The Benefits Communication"; "The Employee Benefits Communication ToolKit," Commerce Clearinghouse; "Benefits Communication," Business and Legal Reports. **Seminars:** Plain English Writing Training; Summary Plan Description Compliance workshops; Re-Humanizing the Corporation, Human Resources and Employee Benefits Communication Workshop; 21 Writing Tips for the 21st Century; Make the Write Impression; Writing to Inform and Instruct; The Dreaded Nuts and Bolts; Writing to Persuade; Writing Policy and Procedure Manuals In Plain English; Writing for Accountants and Auditors In Plain English. **Special Services:** In Plain English[R].

21948 ■ Infinisource
5210 N Main
PO Box 5818
Dayton, OH 45415
Ph:(937)275-6280
Free: 800-779-6384
Fax:(937)275-6065
Co. E-mail: benefits@aurorasolutions.com
URL: http://www.aurorasolutions.com
Contact: Nancy L. Lee, Owner
E-mail: nlee@atsaurorasolutions.com
Scope: Provides employee benefit administrative services to the outsourcing marketplace. Concentrates resources on the administration and compliance of employee benefit plans. Concentrate resources on the administration and compliance of employee benefit plans. Provides services no matter where medical claims are paid, where trustee services are located, or where record keeping is originated.

21949 ■ John Chute & Associates
150 Consumers Rd., Ste. 508
Toronto, ON, Canada M2J 1P9
Ph:(416)250-8600
Free: 800-565-2488
Fax:(416)250-8605
Co. E-mail: postmaster@jchute.com
URL: http://www.jchute.com
Contact: Susan Pucci, Principle
E-mail: gene.tomsic@atsjchute.com
Scope: Provides counsel in the design, costing and communication of all forms of employee benefit plans. Human resource consulting skills, training, team building, job evaluation, performance appraisal, labor relations. Also provides professional advice in corporate human resource and organizational development matters.

21950 ■ JPMorgan Compensation and Benefit Strategies
216 S Jefferson St., Ste. 600
Chicago, IL 60661
Ph:(312)454-3222
Fax:(312)454-1213
Co. E-mail: support@jpmorgan.com
URL: http://www.jpmorgan.com/cbs
Contact: Tom Terry, Managering Director
Scope: Provider of compensation, retirement plan and health care consulting services. Areas of expertise include: Compliance, employee communication, executive compensation, financial modeling, health and welfare, health improvement programs and retirement plans. **Seminars:** Computershare The Source 2006: Inspiration and Insight; The PDP Advantage for Public Sector plans; National Municipal OPEB Liabilities Conference; Fourth Annual New England Public Finance Conference. Computershare The Source 2006: Inspiration and Insight; The PDP Advantage for Public Sector plans; National Municipal OPEB Liabilities Conference; Fourth Annual New England Public Finance Conference.

21951 ■ Kevin L. Pohle P.L.L.C.
5820 Main St., Ste. 316-317
Williamsville, NY 14221
Ph:(716)565-0565
Fax:(716)568-8384
Co. E-mail: klpohle@pohlecpa.com
URL: http://www.pohlecpa.com
Contact: Kevin L. Pohle, President
E-mail: klpohle@pohlecpa.com
Scope: Offers tax planning, preparation and representation services, investigative accounting and compliance and other management consulting services. Serves small local manufacturing and service companies, individual accounts, non-profit agencies as well as large, publicly held companies.

21952 ■ Larry W. Buck & Associates Inc.
710 N Post Oak Rd., Ste. 101
Houston, TX 77024
Ph:(713)278-0200
Fax:(713)278-0202
Co. E-mail: lbuck@lbuckassociates.com
Contact: N. Richard Magel, VP of Operations
E-mail: lbuck@lbuckassociates.com
Scope: Consulting firm active in risk management and employee benefit planning.

21953 ■ Managing Work and Family Inc.
1625 Sheridan Rd.
Wilmette, IL 60091
Ph:(847)308-0919
Fax:(661)885-7865
Co. E-mail: mwfam@aol.com
URL: http://www.mwfam.com
Contact: Bonnie Michaels, President
E-mail: mwfam@aol.com
Scope: The firm was designed for employers interested in creating a culture and work environment conducive to loyalty and productivity from employees with family responsibilities. The firm offers consulting, organizational assessments, flexible work option design, training for managers and employees, child and elder care services, videos, books and family days. Representative client industries include: Advertising, banking and finance, electronic communications, data processing, education, government, health care, hospitality, manufacturing, pharmaceutical and service industries. **Publications:** "Living Well, Tuning Out the Every Day Stresses on Vacation," Aug, 2006; "A Journey of Work-Life Renewal: The Power to Recharge & Rekindle Passion in Your Life," 2003; "Managing Work and Family Kopy kit"; "Solving the Work/Family Puzzle". **Seminars:** Building Resilience During Turbulent Times; Managing Employees During Stressful Times; WHAT'S YOUR RQ; Leadership Renewal for Work-Life Professionals; Leadership Renewal for Work-Life Professionals; Beyond Sensitivity and Diversity Training; Beyond balance For individuals newly displaced; Employee Information & Training; Beyond balance for individuals in stressful work life situations.

21954 ■ Money Source Financial Services Inc.
1328 S Main St.
Ann Arbor, MI 48104
Ph:(734)213-0300
Fax:(734)213-5900
Co. E-mail: info@msfs.com
URL: http://www.msfs.com
Contact: Kaci Sichender, Mgr of Bus Devel
E-mail: kacis@atsmsfs.com
Scope: Provides clients with access to employee benefit programs. Offers access to nearly any investment or insurance products. Provides experience in the design, implementation, and funding of 401k plans, Simplified Employee Pension Plan SEP, profit sharing plans, money purchase plans, and IRA's and rollover plans.

21955 ■ New England Human Resource Group
36 Cedar Pond Dr.
Warwick, RI 02886
Ph:(401)732-8877
Contact: Ronald G. Snyder, President
Scope: Firm specializes in compensation systems, benefits, legal compliance, personnel policies, resources, employee relations law, safety and risk management, training and development, continuous improvement, career management, organizational change, strategic planning, human resource audits, ISO 9000 and QS 9000, professional development, financial planning, staffing, and executive development.

21956 ■ New Ways to Work Inc.
103 Morris St., Ste. A
Sebastopol, CA 95472-3858
Ph:(707)824-4000
Fax:(707)824-4410
Co. E-mail: newways@newwaystowork.org
URL: http://www.newwaystowork.org
Contact: Steve Trippe, President
E-mail: sgtrippe@atsnewwaystowork.org
Scope: Focuses on improving the lives of the nations youth. helps communities build systems that connect schools, community organizations and businesses, and improve the services, educational programs and support the community provides for its youth. creates the environment and guides a process that brings the right people together with customized tools for powerful learning and dramatic change. **Publications:** "A Guide to Career Development Opportunities in California's High Schools". **Seminars:** Career pathways; building local intermediary organizations; strengthening youth councils; increasing youth involvement; creating quality work-based learning systems; All Youth-One Systems.

21957 ■ PAR Enterprises Inc.
1845 Summer St., Dept. lt97
Stamford, CT 06905-5034
Ph:(203)973-0366
Free: 888-333-5727
Fax:(203)973-0366
Co. E-mail: par@par-ent.com
URL: http://www.par-ent.com
Contact: Dr. Paul A. Rivera, Principle
Scope: Assists in design, implementation and communication of healthcare, retirement, other welfare benefit programs, real estate needs, insurance and pension plans. **Publications:** "Official Compendium Of Inner City Street Games".

21958 ■ Princeton Health Systems Inc.
9 Mercer St.
Princeton, NJ 08540
Ph:(609)924-7799
Free: 800-437-6668
Fax:(609)497-0739
Co. E-mail: byoung23@aol.com
URL: http://www.princetonhealthsystems.com
Contact: Beth Young, President
E-mail: byoung23@aol.com
Scope: Offers consulting services in the evaluation, planning, implementation and assessment of medical care services to employees, including cost containment strategies and health and fitness programs. **Publications:** "Certain Solutions Administrator's

Guide," Johnson & Johnson Health Management Inc., 1992; "Sports Medicine Up-Date," New Jersey Medicine, 1991; "The Wrestlers' Nutrition Manual," Bucknell University, 1990.

21959 ■ Ralph Moss Ltd.
200 Town Centre Blvd., Ste. 102
Markham, ON, Canada L3R 8G5
Ph:(905)513-9868
Free: 888-667-7583
Fax:(905)513-9893
Co. E-mail: info@ralphmossltd.on.ca
URL: http://www.ralphmoss.ca
Contact: Dr. Ralph W. Moss, Principle
E-mail: moss@atsralphmossltd.on.ca
Scope: Acts as benefit consultants on projects, reviewing and making recommendations, not only on existing benefit programs, but also commenting on the taxability of benefits, legal issues and industry standards, as well as financial underwriting arrangements and other various cost factors. **Publications:** "Financial Planning Report".

21960 ■ The Segal Group Inc.
1 Park Ave., 8th Fl.
Manhattan, NY 10016-5895
Ph:(212)251-5000
Fax:(212)251-5490
URL: http://www.segalco.com
Contact: Robert D. Krinsky, Chairman of the Board
E-mail: jmazo@atssegalco.com
Scope: A leading, independent firm of benefit, compensation and human resources consultants. In January 2002, Segal acquired Sibson Consulting, a human capital consulting firm. The combined organization, with more than 1, 000employees is headquartered in Mew York and has offices throughout the United States, in Canada and the United Kingdom. Clients include corporations, non-profit organizations, professional service firms, state and local governments and joint boards of trustees administering pension, health and welfare plans under the Taft-Hartley Act.

21961 ■ Siebrand-Wilton Associates Inc.
PO Box 369
Marlboro, NJ 07746-0369
Ph:(732)917-0239
Fax:(732)972-0214
Co. E-mail: clientsvcs@s-wa.com
URL: http://www.s-wa.com
Contact: John S. Sturges, President
E-mail: bencomp@s-wa.com
Scope: Assesses, plans and implements human resources aspects of mergers and acquisitions. Offers human resources consulting in compensation and benefit plan design, mergers and acquisitions (HR aspects), business ethics assessment and development, editing, writing and association management services, and contract professionals and interim executives. **Publications:** "Should Government or Business Try to Save Medicare," HR News; "Executive Temping," HR Horizons; "When is an Employee Truly an Employee," HR Magazine; "Examining Your Insurance Carrier," HR Magazine.

21962 ■ The Stoller Co.
190 N Wiget Ln., Ste. 110
Walnut Creek, CA 94598
Ph:(925)932-1800
Free: 800-207-3674
Fax:(925)932-1869
Co. E-mail: info@stollerco.com
URL: http://www.stollerco.com
Contact: J. Curtis Stoller, President
E-mail: curtstoller@stollerco.com
Scope: Specializes in retirement and 401K plans, human resources, compensation, systems consulting, and workplace compliance.

21963 ■ Swartzbaugh-Farber & Associates Inc.
1015 N 98th St., Westroads Pointe, Ste. 221
Omaha, NE 68114-2357
Ph:(402)397-5800
Fax:(402)397-5424
Co. E-mail: securefuture@swartzbaugh.com
URL: http://www.swartzbaugh.com
Contact: Marsha J. Anzalone, Principle
E-mail: marsha.anzalone@atsswartzbaugh.com
Scope: Specializes in group employee benefits and executive benefits compensation. **Seminars:** Health care Boot Camp, Aug, 2007; Benchmarking Seminar, 2007; Understanding HIPAA Seminar, Mar, 2006; HR - Developing a Profit Center, Nov, 2005.

21964 ■ TRI-AD Actuaries Inc.
221 W Crest St., Ste. 300
Escondido, CA 92025-1737
Ph:(760)743-7555
Free: 800-733-7555
Fax:(760)489-9343
Co. E-mail: info@tri-ad.com
URL: http://www.tri-ad.com
Contact: George Naset, Principal
E-mail: chamilton@tri-ad.com
Scope: A full service human resources consulting and administration firm. Specializes in outsourcing benefit administration, designing comprehensive compensation and benefit programs, automating the HR department, reshaping your corporate culture and employee communication. Services include 401k Choice daily record keeping, actuarial services, COBRA Administration, Flexible spending, account administration, health and welfare benefit consulting, human resources effectiveness, organization effectiveness and retirement plans. **Publications:** "A Complete Chart of the 2008 Cost of Living Adjustments," Oct, 2007; "Check the Rollover Chart to See Which Types of Plans Will Accept Your Rollover," Aug, 2006; "A Complete Chart of the 2006 Cost of Living Adjustments," Jan, 2006; "Valerie Gieseke in Compensation and Benefits Review: Automating Benefits Administration," Nov, 2005. **Seminars:** Beyond COBRA: Offering More Comprehensive Post-Employment Benefits, Aug, 2009; Primer on Providers: Who Does What for Your 401(k) Plan, Jul, 2009; Refresher Course on the Basics of FSA Plan Administration, Jun, 2009; Found Money in Your 401(k) Plans, May, 2009; Found Money in Your Health & Welfare Benefit Plans, Apr, 2009; 401(k) Loans: Deal or No Deal?, Apr, 2008; COBRA 101: What You Need to Know About COBRA, Apr, 2007; An Update on Automatic Enrollment, Mar, 2007; Preparing for COBRA Open Enrollment, Oct, 2006.

COMPUTERIZED DATABASES

21965 ■ *ABI/INFORM*
ProQuest LLC
789 E Eisenhower Pky.
PO Box 1346
Ann Arbor, MI 48106-1346
Ph:(734)761-4700
Free: 800-521-0600
Fax:(734)761-6450
Co. E-mail: info@proquest.com
URL: http://www.proquest.com
Description: Contains approximately 6 million full text or bibliographic citations to articles from more than 800 business and management publications worldwide. **Availability:** Online: Wolters Kluwer Health, ProQuest LLC, ProQuest LLC, Questel SA, STN International, Colorado Alliance of Research Libraries, Financial Times Ltd., LexisNexis Group, ProQuest LLC. **Type:** Full text; Bibliographic; Image.

21966 ■ *Business Insurance*
Crain Communications Inc.
1155 Gratiot Ave.
Detroit, MI 48207
Ph:(313)446-6000
Free: 800-678-2427
Fax:(313)446-1616
Co. E-mail: info@crain.com
URL: http://www.crain.com
Description: Contains the complete text of *Business Insurance*, a newspaper providing information on the purchase and administration of corporate insurance and self-insurance programs, including property and liability insurance, reinsurance, and employee benefit and risk management programs. Includes reports on major commercial insurance claim settlements, legal and regulatory developments affecting the industry, and major losses resulting from fires, explosions, natural disasters, and litigation. Also includes analyses of industry issues and state, national, and international news. **Availability:** Online: Crain Communications Inc., LexisNexis Group, ProQuest LLC, Thomson Reuters. **Type:** Full text.

21967 ■ *Compliance Guide for Plan Administrators*
Wolters Kluwer Law & Business
2700 Lake Cook Rd.
Riverwoods, IL 60015
Ph:(847)267-7000
Free: 800-525-3335
Fax:(847)866-3095
URL: http://www.cch.com
Description: Contains detailed instructions and guidance for pension plan administrators. Includes information on complying with pension and welfare benefit law reporting and disclosure requirements. Focuses on retirement plans subject to ERISA and the Internal Revenue Code. Covers numerous types of retirement plans, fiduciary rules, compliance with the terms of a plan, and plan termination. Includes step-by-step procedures for complying with pension plan laws and regulations. **Availability:** Online: Wolters Kluwer Law & Business. **Type:** Full text.

21968 ■ *Employee Benefits Cases*
The Bureau of National Affairs Inc.
1801 S Bell St.
Arlington, VA 22202
Free: 800-372-1033
Co. E-mail: customercare@bna.com
URL: http://www.bna.com
Description: Contains the complete text of more than 6000 precedent-setting federal and state court decisions and significant employee benefits rulings of arbitrators. Subjects include reporting and disclosure, funding, participation, deductibility of contributions, preemption of state laws, qualification of employee benefits, plans, taxation of participants, vesting, collective bargaining, fiduciary responsibility, veterans rights, public employee plans, and termination insurance. Listings are arranged in alphabetical order by subject. Also includes a classification guide, topical index, and cumulative digest and index. **Availability:** Online: The Bureau of National Affairs Inc., Thomson Reuters. **Type:** Full text.

21969 ■ *Employee Benefits Infosource*
International Foundation of Employee Benefit Plans
18700 W Bluemound Rd.
PO Box 69
Brookfield, WI 53008-0069
Ph:(262)786-6710
Free: 888-334-3327
Fax:(262)786-8670
Co. E-mail: ebinfo@ifebp.org
URL: http://www.ifebp.org
Description: Contains more than 86,000 citations, with abstracts, to the worldwide literature on employee benefit plans. Covers surveys, statistics, trends, and background information in these areas: corporate, union, and public employee benefit plans, group insurance, international benefits, pension investments, health care, compensation, human resources, and benefit plan service providers. Sources include some 250 periodicals, newsletters, books, research reports, news releases, and proceedings. **Availability:** Online: International Foundation of Employee Benefit Plans, ProQuest LLC. **Type:** Bibliographic.

21970 ■ *Pension & Benefits Daily*
The Bureau of National Affairs Inc.
1801 S Bell St.
Arlington, VA 22202
Free: 800-372-1033
Co. E-mail: customercare@bna.com
URL: http://www.bna.com
Description: Contains current information on significant judicial, legislative, and regulatory developments affecting employee benefits and pension planning. Covers federal and state court decisions, legislation, and regulations relating to health insurance, tax reform, benefits, and pensions. Covers such topics as age discrimination, employee stock options, col-

lective bargaining, executive compensation, investments, tax policies and guidance, Social Security, and more. **Availability:** Online: Thomson Reuters, The Bureau of National Affairs Inc. **Type:** Full text.

21971 ■ *Pension & Benefits Reporter*
The Bureau of National Affairs Inc.
1801 S Bell St.
Arlington, VA 22202
Free: 800-372-1033
Co. E-mail: customercare@bna.com
URL: http://www.bna.com
Description: Contains up-to-date reporting and coverage of state and federal legislative, regulatory, and judicial activities related to pensions and benefits. Includes coverage of IRS and Labor Department regulations and enforcement issues, tax legislation, health care reform, and developments within industry. Includes taxation of benefits, individual retirement accounts, and fringe benefits. **Availability:** Online: Thomson Reuters, The Bureau of National Affairs Inc. **Type:** Full text.

LIBRARIES

21972 ■ AIAS Library
PO Box 521
Logandale, NV 89021
Ph:(702)398-3701
Fax:(702)398-3700
Contact: D.K. Smith, Libn.
Scope: Employee stock ownership plans. **Services:** Library open to members only. **Holdings:** 2955 books; 2006 reports; 54 manuscripts. **Subscriptions:** 205 journals and other serials; 13 newspapers.

21973 ■ Employee Services Management Association Information Center
568 Spring Rd., Ste. D
Elmhurst, IL 60126-3896
Ph:(630)559-0020
Fax:(630)559-0025
Co. E-mail: esmahq@esmassn.org
URL: http://www.esmassn.org
Contact: Renee M. Mula, Exec.Dir.
Scope: Employees - activities, sports, recreation, facilities, travel, fitness, wellness, pre-retirement planning, assistance programs, productivity, day care, eldercare. **Services:** Center open to the public for reference use only. **Holdings:** 50 volumes; archives.

21974 ■ Ivins, Phillips, Barker Library
1700 Pennsylvania Ave. NW, Ste. 600
Washington, DC 20006
Ph:(202)662-3443
Fax:(202)393-7601
Co. E-mail: jefff@ipbtax.com
URL: http://ipbtax.com
Contact: Jeffrey T. Freilich, Libn.
Scope: Pensions, taxation. **Services:** Interlibrary loan; copying; Library not open to the public. **Holdings:** 1000 volumes; technical reports; CD-ROMs.

21975 ■ Towers Perrin–Western Canada Information Centre
3700, 150 - 6 Ave., SW
Calgary, AB, Canada T2P 3Y7
Ph:(403)261-1432
Fax:(403)237-6733
Co. E-mail: val.ward@towers.com
Contact: Val Ward
Scope: Human resource management, total rewards, pensions, employee benefits, executive compensation, employee communications, pension and benefits administration services, pension fund asset management. **Services:** Interlibrary loan. **Holdings:** 1000 books. **Subscriptions:** 100 journals and other serials; 4 newspapers.

21976 ■ Towers Watson Information Centre
1100 Melville St., Ste. 1600
Vancouver, BC, Canada V6E 4A6
Ph:(604)691-1000
Fax:(604)691-1062
URL: http://www.towerswatson.com/
Scope: Actuarial science, employee benefits, compensation, human resources. **Holdings:** Figures not available.

RESEARCH CENTERS

21977 ■ Pennsylvania State University–Risk Management Research Center
310F Smeal College of Business
University Park, PA 16802
Ph:(814)865-3961
Fax:(814)865-6284
Co. E-mail: afs1@psu.edu
URL: http://www.smeal.psu.edu/rmrc
Contact: Prof. Arnold F. Shapiro PhD, Dir.
E-mail: afs1@psu.edu
Scope: Encourages and conducts research on the design and funding of employee benefit plans, including pensions and group health insurance, and actuarial studies.

21978 ■ University of North Carolina at Chapel Hill–Cecil G. Sheps Center for Health Services Research
CB No. 7590
725 Martin Luther King Jr. Blvd.
Chapel Hill, NC 27599
Ph:(919)966-5011
Fax:(919)966-5764
Co. E-mail: timothy_carey@med.unc.edu
URL: http://www.shepscenter.unc.edu
Contact: Timothy S. Carey MD, Dir.
E-mail: timothy_carey@med.unc.edu
Scope: Aging, disability, and long-term care; child health services; health care economics and finance; health care organization; medical practice; mental health and substance abuse services and systems research; health professions and primary care; preventive health services; rural health research; women's health research; and minority health disparity research. **Services:** Technical assistance, for a number of state agencies. **Publications:** Consensus in DHHS Region IV: Women and Infant Health Indicators for Planning and Evaluation; North Carolina Health Professions Data Book; North Carolina Health Professions Fact Sheet. **Educational Activities:** Annual DHHS Region IV Conference on Maternal and Child Health, Family Planning, and Services for Children With Special Health Needs; Annual DHHS Region IV Workshop on the Collection and Use of Data for MCH and Women's Health Planning and Evaluation; Seminars and training programs.

21979 ■ University of Pennsylvania–Pension Research Council
3000 Steinberg Hall - Dietrich Hall
The Wharton School
3620 Locust Walk
Philadelphia, PA 19104-6302
Ph:(215)898-7620
Fax:(215)573-3418
Co. E-mail: mitchelo@wharton.upenn.edu
URL: http://www.pensionresearchcouncil.org
Contact: Prof. Olivia S. Mitchell PhD, Exec.Dir.
E-mail: mitchelo@wharton.upenn.edu
Scope: Private sector and public employee pension and benefits plans and social insurance to the extent to which it influences employer-sponsored arrangements. Seeks to strengthen institutional arrangements designed to provide financial resources for a secure old age through basic research into their social, economic, legal, actuarial, and financial foundations. **Publications:** Newsletter; Working paper series. **Educational Activities:** Symposium (annually).

21980 ■ West Virginia University–Institute for Labor Studies and Research
Knapp Hall, Rm. 709
Extension Service
PO Box 6031
Morgantown, WV 26506-6031
Ph:(304)293-3323
Free: 800—626-4748
Fax:(304)293-3395
Co. E-mail: tony.michael@mail.wvu.edu
URL: http://laborstudiesandresearch.ext.wvu.edu
Contact: David Anthony (Tony) Michael, Prog.Ldr.
E-mail: tony.michael@mail.wvu.edu
Scope: Labor, including studies on employee benefits, labor-management cooperation, and industrial safety. **Educational Activities:** Residential programs and conferences.

Budgets/Budgeting

ASSOCIATIONS AND OTHER ORGANIZATIONS

21981 ■ American Association for Budget and Program Analysis
PO Box 1157
Falls Church, VA 22041
Ph:(703)941-4300
Fax:(703)941-1535
Co. E-mail: aabpa@aabpa.org
URL: http://www.aabpa.org
Contact: Jon Stehle, Pres.

Description: Professionals in budgeting, policy analysis, and program & management analysis evaluation who are employed by the federal government, state and local agencies, private companies, and academic institutions. Seeks to advance knowledge in budgeting management and program analysis. Promotes the exchange of ideas and information. Conducts monthly program with guest speakers from government agencies, congress, and institutions. **Publications:** *Public Budgeting and Finance* (quarterly).

21982 ■ International Budget Partnership
820 1st St. NE, Ste. 510
Washington, DC 20002
Ph:(202)408-1080
Fax:(202)408-8173
Co. E-mail: info@internationalbudget.org
URL: http://www.internationalbudget.org
Contact: Warren Krafchik, Dir.

Description: Works to assist civil society organizations globally to improve budget policies and decision-making processes. **Publications:** *A Guide to Budget Work for NGOs*; *Budgeting for the Future, Building another Europe*; *IBP Newsletter* (bimonthly).

EDUCATIONAL PROGRAMS

21983 ■ Project Scheduling and Budgeting - Achieving Cost-Effective and Timely Delivery (Onsite)
Seminar Information Service, Inc.
20 Executive Park, Ste. 120
Irvine, CA 92614
Ph:(949)261-9104
Free: 877-SEM-INFO
Fax:(949)261-1963
Co. E-mail: info@seminarinformation.com
URL: http://www.seminarinformation.com

Price: $2,490.00. **Description:** Learn how to: Build schedules and budgets that transform project constraints into project success; Construct Work Breakdown Structures (WBS) and network diagrams and estimate task durations; Calculate Critical Path and optimize your project plan; Allocate costs and chart expected cash flow; Assign resources effectively and respond to end-date changes; Perform Earned Value Analysis (EVA) to keep the project on track. **Locations:** Reston, VA; and New York, NY.

REFERENCE WORKS

21984 ■ "2009: A Call For Vision" in *Women Entrepreneur* (January 28, 2009)
Pub: Entrepreneur Media Inc.

Ed: Elinor Robin. **Description:** Providing exemplary customer service, reducing expenses and creating an out-of-the-box niche are three key factors that will help business survive during this economic crisis. Business owners must see potential where others see failure in order to create new opportunities that may not only allow their business to survive during these times but may actually cause some businesses to thrive despite this economic downturn.

21985 ■ "Another Baby Step" in *Canadian Business* (Vol. 81, March 31, 2008, No. 5, pp. 32)
Pub: Rogers Media

Ed: Andrew Wahl. **Description:** Discusses the Canadian government's federal budget which makes it easier to tap into tax credits for corporate research and development. However, these steps do not really go far enough to boost industrial research levels in Canada. Making these incentives at least partially refundable could help during tough economic times.

21986 ■ "Budget Strategically to Stay on Course" in *Entrepreneur* (August 28, 2008)
Pub: Entrepreneur Media Inc.

Ed: Tim Berry. **Description:** Budgeting is one of the most valuable tools in a manager's arsenal. The importance of budgeting is discussed and tips for surviving an economic recession are provided.

21987 ■ "Business Must Stand Up And Be Counted" in *Crain's Detroit Business* (Vol. 24, October 6, 2008, No. 40, pp. 6)
Pub: Crain Communications, Inc.

Description: Discusses the challenges that the new mayor of Detroit faces concerning business, the state of the economy and the exceptionally tight budget the city is running on, which includes a lot of red ink. It is very likely that the city is going to see tax revenues fall substantially in the next few months and business leaders may find it in their favor to lend their support to the new mayor as well as provide him with the executive talent necessary to overcome some of these crucial issues.

21988 ■ "Business Stands Firm for Reform" in *Crain's Detroit Business* (Vol. 26, January 4, 2010, No. 1, pp. 3)
Pub: Crain Communications, Inc.

Ed: Amy Lane. **Description:** As Michigan faces a new year of budgetary problems, many business groups are preparing to hold firm against tax increases and instead push for enacting spending reforms.

21989 ■ "Different Aspects of Project Management" in *Contractor* (Vol. 57, February 2010, No. 2, pp. 30)
Pub: Penton Media, Inc.

Ed: H. Kent Craig. **Description:** There are differences when managing a two-man crew as a foreman and a 2,000 employee company as a corporate president. A project manager should have good skills in human psychology, accounting, and the knowledge of a mechanical engineer, architect, civil engineer, and also the meditative skills of a Zen master.

21990 ■ "Dream On: California's Budget Fix may not Last for Long." in *Barron's* (Vol. 89, July 27, 2009, No. 30, pp. 21)
Pub: Dow Jones & Co., Inc.

Ed: Jonathan R. Laing. **Description:** California's budget agreement which purports to eliminate a $26 billion deficit is discussed. The frequent budgetary dustups in the state calls for several reforms including a rainy day fund of 15 percent of any budget and a constitutional convention. Other reform suggestions are discussed.

21991 ■ "Efficient Cash Management Essential To Be Competitive" in *Crain's Cleveland Business* (Vol. 28, November 12, 2007, No. 45, pp. 25)
Pub: Crain Communications, Inc.

Ed: Ken Moultrie. **Description:** In order to sustain a business it is important to organize cash-management efforts around three core areas: cash in, static cash and cash out. Tips for the successful management of these areas are provided.

21992 ■ *Entrepreneurial Finance*
Pub: Pearson Education, Limited

Ed: Philip J. Adelman; Alan M. Marks. **Released:** July 2006. **Price:** $87.35. **Description:** Financial aspects of running a small business are covered; topics include sole proprietorships, partnerships, limited liability companies, and private corporations.

21993 ■ "Exit Strategy" in *Barron's* (Vol. 89, July 6, 2009, No. 27, pp. 3)
Pub: Dow Jones & Co., Inc.

Ed: Alan Abelson. **Description:** US Federal Reserve is not likely to change its easy-money strategy in the short term. States such as California are suffering from spiraling costs and declining revenues and are struggling to balance their budgets. The US unemployment rate climbed to 9.5 percent in June 2009.

21994 ■ "Facebook: A Promotional Budget's Best Friend" in *Women Entrepreneur* (February 1, 2009)
Pub: Entrepreneur Media Inc.

Ed: Tamara Monosoff. **Description:** Facebook began as a social networking website but has become a valuable marketing tool for all types of businesses, organizations and causes. Tips are provided for creating a Facebook account and growing one's network on Facebook.

21995 ■ *Financial Management 101: Get a Grip on Your Business Numbers*
Pub: Self-Counsel Press, Incorporated

Ed: Angie Mohr. **Released:** November 2007. **Price:** $16.95. **Description:** An overview of business planning, financial statements, budgeting and advertising for small businesses. s.

21996 ■ "Get Back To Business Planning Fundamentals" in *Entrepreneur* (October 24, 2008)
Pub: Entrepreneur Media Inc.
Ed: Tim Berry. **Description:** During a recession it is important to know what adjustment to make to your business plan. Some fundamentals to remember include: watching things more closely by tracking progress on cash, sales, new projects, customer satisfaction, ad spending and expenses; looking for built-in indicators such as what drives sales or expenses; watching what drives cash flow; and do not make mistakes such as laying off experienced employees too soon.

21997 ■ "Handle With Care" in *Hawaii Business* (Vol. 53, October 2007, No. 5, pp. 66)
Pub: Hawaii Business Publishing
Ed: Kenneth Sheffield. **Description:** Discusses a fiduciary, who may be a board member, business owner, or a trustee, and is someone who supervises and manages the affairs and the resources of a principal. Fiduciary duties, which include accounting, cost review and risk management, must be served with the benefit of the principal as the priority. Ways of breaching fiduciary duties and how to avoid them are discussed.

21998 ■ "Inch by Inch, Employees Lose Ground" in *Business Courier* (Vol. 26, November 13, 2009, No. 29, pp. 1)
Pub: American City Business Journals, Inc.
Ed: James Ritchie. **Description:** Employees in Ohio who retained their jobs have suffered losses in salary and other benefits, as companies exert efforts to save money. Thirty-four percent of employees experienced pay cuts. Statistical data included.

21999 ■ "Insurers No Longer Paying Premium for Advertising" in *Brandweek* (Vol. 49, April 21, 2008, No. 16, pp. SR3)
Pub: VNU Business Media, Inc.
Ed: Eric Newman. **Description:** Insurance companies are cutting their advertising budgets after years of accelerated double-digit growth in spending due to the economic downturn, five years of record-breaking ad spend and a need to cut expenditures as claims costs rise and a competitive market keeps premiums in place. Statistical data included.

22000 ■ "Irene Rosenfeld; Chairman and CEO, Kraft Foods Inc." in *Crain's Chicago Business* (Vol. 31, May 5, 2008, No. 18, pp. 31)
Pub: Crain Communications, Inc.
Ed: David Sterrett. **Description:** Profile of Irene Rosenfeld who is the chairman and CEO of Kraft Foods Inc. and is entering the second year of a three-year plan to boost sales of well-known brands such as Oreo, Velveeta and Oscar Mayer while facing soaring commodity costs and a declining market-share. Ms. Rosenfeld's turnaround strategy also entails spending more on advertising and giving managers more control over their budgets and product development.

22001 ■ "Key Budgeting Tips: For Your Management Team" in *Agency Sales Magazine* (Vol. 39, December 2009, No. 11, pp. 49)
Pub: MANA
Ed: Gene Siciliano. **Description:** Constructing a budget must be the result of coordinated input and effort. Practice is also important in creating a budget and accurately predicting actual results is not the objective but giving the company a direction for course correction.

22002 ■ "Life's Work: Oliver Sacks" in *Harvard Business Review* (Vol. 88, November 2010, No. 11, pp. 152)
Pub: Harvard Business School Publishing
Ed: Lisa Burrell. **Description:** Neurologist and author Oliver Sacks discusses whether different types of minds tend toward certain skills, physician-patient communication, and his own perspectives from being a patient himself.

22003 ■ "Local Hotels Brace for Downturn" in *Crain's Chicago Business* (Vol. 31, March 31, 2008, No. 13, pp. 3)
Pub: Crain Communications, Inc.
Ed: Bob Tita. **Description:** Chicago hotels are seeing a noticeable drop in business-related guests so far this year due to a slumping national economy, tighter corporate expense budgets and higher airfares.

22004 ■ *Million Dollar Website: Simple Steps to Help You Compete with the Big Boys-Even on a Small Business Budget*
Pub: Prentice Hall Press
Ed: Lori Culwell. **Released:** May 9, 2010. **Price:** $19.95. **Description:** Resource for any small business owner wishing to build a successful Website in order to compete with big box stores.

22005 ■ "Pick and Save" in *Entrepreneur* (Vol. 36, April 2008, No. 4, pp. 66)
Pub: Entrepreneur Media, Inc.
Ed: C.J. Prince. **Description:** Business owners can purchase the needed big equipment to offset this year's expected profit. They can also switch to annualized computing of quarterly income and estimated tax payments to pay less estimated taxes for the first half of the year. Other tips on tax planning are provided.

22006 ■ "Pro Teams Shift Ad Budgets; Naming Rights Deals Near $1 Billion" in *Brandweek* (Vol. 49, April 21, 2008, No. 16, pp. 18)
Pub: VNU Business Media, Inc.
Ed: Barry Janoff. **Description:** More and more professional sports marketers are spending less of their advertising budgets on traditional media outlets such as television, print and radio; the growing trend in sports marketing is in utilizing new media venues such as the Internet in which innovative means are used to encourage interaction with fans.

22007 ■ *QuickBooks X for Dummies*
Pub: John Wiley & Sons, Incorporated
Ed: Stephen L. Nelson. **Released:** November 2006. **Price:** $21.99. **Description:** Key features of QuickBooks software for small business are introduced. Invoicing and credit memos, recoding sales receipts, accounting, budgeting, taxes, payroll, financial reports, job estimating, billing, tracking, data backup, are among the features.

22008 ■ *Small Business Cash Flow: Strategies for Making Your Business a Financial Success*
Pub: John Wiley & Sons, Incorporated
Ed: Denise O'Berry. **Released:** October 2006. **Price:** $19.95. **Description:** Tips to help small businesses manage money are given.

22009 ■ *Small Business Clustering Technology: Applications in Marketing, Management, Finance, and IT*
Pub: Idea Group Publishing
Ed: Robert C. MacGregor; Ann Hodgkinson. **Released:** June 2006. **Description:** An overview of the development and role of small business clusters in disciplines that include economics, marketing, management and information systems.

22010 ■ *Small Business for Dummies, 3rd Ed.*
Pub: John Wiley and Sons, Inc.
Ed: Eric Tyson; Jim Schell. **Released:** March 2008. **Price:** $21.99. **Description:** Guidebook for anyone wanting to start or grow a small business; topics include information financing, budgeting, marketing, management and more.

22011 ■ *Small Business Management*
Pub: John Wiley & Sons, Incorporated
Ed: Margaret Burlingame. **Released:** March 2007. **Price:** $44.95. **Description:** Advice for starting and running a small business as well as information on the value and appeal of small businesses, is given. Topics include budgets, taxes, inventory, ethics, e-commerce, and current laws.

22012 ■ *The Small Business Savings Plan: 101 Tactics for Controlling Costs and Boosting the Bottom Line*
Pub: Kaplan Books
Ed: Timothy R. Gase. **Released:** May 2007. **Price:** $28.00. **Description:** Strategies for small business owners to develop a savings plan and increase profits are outlined.

22013 ■ *Streetwise Finance and Accounting for Entrepreneurs: Set Budgets, Manage Costs, Keep Your Business Profitable*
Pub: Adams Media Corporation
Ed: Suzanne Caplan. **Released:** November 2006. **Price:** $25.95. **Description:** Book offers a basic understanding of accounting and finance for small businesses, including financial statements, credits and debits, as well as establishing a budget. Strategies for small companies in financial distress are included.

22014 ■ *Streetwise Small Business Book of Lists: Hundreds of Lists to Help You Reduce Costs, Increase Revenues, and Boost Your Profits!*
Pub: Adams Media Corporation
Ed: Gene Marks. **Released:** September 2006. **Price:** $25.95. **Description:** Strategies to help small business owners locate services, increase sales, and lower expenses.

22015 ■ "Stretch Your Advertising Dollars" in *Women Entrepreneur* (January 27, 2009)
Pub: Entrepreneur Media Inc.
Ed: Rosalind Resnick. **Description:** During such poor economic times, most businesses are having to cut their advertising budgets; tips for targeting your advertising dollars toward the customer base most likely to buy your product are given.

22016 ■ "Taking a Pounding; Recession Fears Weigh Down Steakhouse Operator Morton's" in *Crain's Chicago Business* (March 31, 2008)
Pub: Crain Communications, Inc.
Ed: Monee Fields-White. **Description:** Morton's Restaurant Group Inc. has seen a 50 percent drop in shares in the past six months due to the economy and cutbacks in corporate expense accounts; business customers provide the restaurant about 80 percent of its revenue.

22017 ■ "Ten Ways to Save on Business Travel" in *Women Entrepreneur* (November 21, 2008)
Pub: Entrepreneur Media Inc.
Ed: Julie Moline. **Description:** Advice regarding ways in which to save money when traveling for business is given.

22018 ■ "Travel Leery" in *Crain's Chicago Business* (Vol. 31, March 31, 2008, No. 13, pp. 3)
Pub: Crain Communications, Inc.
Description: Due to the rise in airline prices and a possible recession, many companies are starting to change their travel policies and limit travel spending.

22019 ■ *Valuing the Closely Held Firm*
Pub: Oxford University Press
Ed: Michael S. Long; Thomas A. Bryant. **Released:** March 2007. **Price:** $65.00. **Description:** The differences between a large and small firm and their ability to generate future cash flow are discussed.

22020 ■ "Watchful Eye: Entrepreneur Protects Clients and His Bottom Line" in *Black Enterprise* (Vol. 38, March 2008, No. 8, pp. 46)
Pub: Earl G. Graves Publishing Co. Inc.
Ed: Tennille M. Robinson. **Description:** Profile of Elijah Shaw, founder of Icon Services Corporation, a full service security and investigative service; Shaw shares his plans to protect clients while growing his business.

22021 ■ "What Are You, A Bank? You Probably Lend Your Customers More Money Than You Realize." in *Inc.* (November 2007, pp. 81)
Pub: Gruner & Jahr USA Publishing
Ed: Norm Brodsky. **Description:** Small business owners don't realize when that when customers do not pay on time, it is the same as lending them money. Tips to get customers to pay on time are listed.

22022 ■ "Your Bottom Line: How To Bring In Dollars When Times Are Tough" in *Small Business Opportunities* (November 2007)
Pub: Harris Publications Inc.
Ed: Description: Adding a new product or promoting a product in a new way can help any small business during hard economic times.

TRADE PERIODICALS

22023 ■ *OMB Watcher*
Pub: OMB Watch
Contact: Brian Gumm, Communications Dir.
Ed: . **Released:** Bimonthly. **Price:** individuals. **Description:** Summarizes initiatives and other administrative issues of the White House Office of Management and Budget (OMB). Frequently includes short analyses of the federal budget and regulatory processes as well as related issues.

22024 ■ *Public Budgeting and Finance*
Pub: North-South Center Press at the University of Miami
Contact: John L. Mikesell, Editor-in-Chief
E-mail: mikesell@indiana.edu
Released: Quarterly. **Price:** $93 print & online; $138 Europe, print & online; $91 out of country print & online; $74 members Americas, print & online; $110 members Europe, print & online; $74 members and other countries, print & online; $446 institutions print online; $687 institutions, other countries print online; $446 institutions Europe, print online. **Description:** Journal exploring theory and practice in financial management and budgeting at all levels of public sector government.

VIDEOCASSETTES/ AUDIOCASSETTES

22025 ■ *Budgeting*
Video Arts, Inc.
c/o Aim Learning Group
8238-40 Lehigh
Morton Grove, IL 60053-2615
Free: 877-444-2230
Fax:(416)252-2155
Co. E-mail: service@aimlearninggroup.com
URL: http://www.aimlearninggroup.com
Released: 1986. **Price:** $790.00. **Description:** An illustrative program for the business owner in how to balance the company's budget so as to move onto an upward course. **Availability:** VHS; 8mm; 3/4U; Special order formats.

22026 ■ *Doing More with Less*
Educational Activities, Inc.
PO Box 87
Baldwin, NY 11510
Free: 800-797-3223
Fax:(516)623-9282
URL: http://www.edact.com
Price: $99.00. **Description:** Part of the Management Speaks Series. Discusses ways to maximize business resources without increasing costs. **Availability:** VHS.

22027 ■ *FASB 95: Statement of Cash Flows*
Bisk Education
9417 Princess Palm Ave.
Tampa, FL 33619
Free: 800-874-7877
Co. E-mail: info@bisk.com
URL: http://www.bisk.com
Price: $199.00. **Description:** Profiles accounting techniques centering on the assessment of current and future cash inflows, outflows, and cash flow problems that lead to business failure. Includes workbook and quizzer. **Availability:** VHS.

CONSULTANTS

22028 ■ AMC International Inc.
864 S Robertson Blvd., Ste. 207
PO Box 11292
Los Angeles, CA 90035
Ph:(310)652-5620
Fax:(310)652-6709
Co. E-mail: inquiry@amcusa.com
Contact: Abe Moradian, President
Scope: Offers day to day business management, business turn around, marketing strategies, development or refinement of corporate mission, and merger and acquisition evaluations. Industries served all.

22029 ■ Automated Accounting
23325 Gerbera St.
Moreno Valley, CA 92553
Ph:(951)653-5053
Co. E-mail: autoacc@earthlink.net
Contact: Gary Capolino, Owner
Scope: A business management consulting firm that caters to small businesses. Offers software installation services, tax preparation services and business plan advisory services. **Publications:** "Inflated Real Estate Prices. . .How Did This Happen," Moreno Valley Magazine, Aug, 2005.

22030 ■ Business Methods Corp.
503 Rte. 10 E
Randolph, NJ 07869
Ph:(973)703-2022
Fax:(973)328-4584
Co. E-mail: businessmethods@aol.com
URL: http://www.bmclogo.com
Contact: Dr. Kevin Chen, CEO
E-mail: kchenbmc@aol.com
Scope: Specialty advertising business which includes custom imprinted promotional product promotions.

22031 ■ Expenses Limited Inc.
2204 Morris Ave., Ste. 104
Union, NJ 07083-5914
Ph:(908)688-9080
Fax:(908)688-5045
Contact: Robert J. Giardina, President
Scope: Provides expense reduction services for general and administrative expense areas. Focuses on all type of industries.

22032 ■ Harvey C. Skoog
7151 E Addis Ave.
Prescott Valley, AZ 86314
Ph:(928)772-1448
Co. E-mail: hskoog@pvaz.net
E-mail: hskoog@pvaz.net
Scope: Firm has expertise in taxes, payroll, financial planning, budgeting, buy/sell planning, business start-up, fraud detection, troubled business consulting, acquisition, and marketing. Serves the manufacturing, construction, and retailing industries in Arizona.

22033 ■ Larry J. Anderson Insurance
1200 35th St., Ste. 206-4
West Des Moines, IA 50266-1958
Ph:(515)221-1973
Fax:(515)221-0074
Co. E-mail: andy4021@aol.com
Contact: Larry J. Anderson, Owner
E-mail: andy4021@aol.com
Scope: Offers business consulting services including temporary technical aid in accounting, turn around and cash management, and bail-out assistance. Also provides operations research, models, forecasting, project scheduling, and economic forecasting services. Provides assistance in group health insurance in both fully insured groups and self-funded groups.

22034 ■ Mark Vanderstelt
9831 Gulfstream Ct.
Fishers, IN 46037
Ph:(317)576-9328
Fax:(317)576-9328
Scope: Consulting services include financial planning and analysis, inventory control, cash management, return on investment, budgeting, pricing, system design and analysis, mergers and acquisitions, feasibility studies, data processing, cost systems and controls, and performance measurement. Also performs operational and financial reviews.

FRANCHISES AND BUSINESS OPPORTUNITIES

22035 ■ Leadership Management, Inc.
4567 Lake Shore Dr.
Waco, TX 76710
Free: 800-568-1241
Fax:(254)722-9588
No. of Franchise Units: 195. **Founded:** 1965. **Franchised:** 1965. **Description:** The franchise provides business aids and services. **Equity Capital Needed:** $35,000-$42,500. **Franchise Fee:** $30,000. **Royalty Fee:** 6%. **Financial Assistance:** No. **Training:** Includes 2 days training at headquarters, 2 days at franchisee's location and ongoing support.

COMPUTER SYSTEMS/ SOFTWARE

22036 ■ Aatrix Top Pay
Aatrix Software
2100 Library Cir.
Grand Forks, ND 58201
Ph:(701)746-6017
Free: 800-426-0854
Fax:(701)787-0594
URL: http://www.aatrix.com
Price: Contact Aatrix. **Description:** Handles payroll calculations and tax deductions for both salaried and hourly employees.

22037 ■ Argos Software–ABECAS Insight
Argos Computers
5737 N Fresno St.
Fresno, CA 93710
Ph:(559)227-1000
Fax:(559)227-9644
Co. E-mail: info@argosoftware.com
URL: http://www.argosoftware.com
Description: Available for MS-DOS operating system. Payroll system for agricultural employees.

ASSOCIATIONS AND OTHER ORGANIZATIONS

22038 ■ Association for Business Communication
PO Box 6143
Nacogdoches, TX 75962-0001
Ph:(936)468-6280
Fax:(936)468-6281
Co. E-mail: abcjohnson@sfasu.edu
URL: http://www.businesscommunication.org
Contact: Dr. Betty S. Johnson, Exec. Dir.
Description: College teachers of business communication; management consultants in business communications; training directors and correspondence supervisors of business firms, direct mail copywriters, public relations writers, and others interested in communication for business. **Publications:** *Business Communication Quarterly* (quarterly); *Journal of Business Communication* (quarterly); *Making Communication Requirements More Explicit in the AACSB Standards for MBA Programs* .

22039 ■ International Association of Business Communicators
601 Montgomery St., Ste. 1900
San Francisco, CA 94111
Ph:(415)544-4700
Free: 800-776-4222
Fax:(415)544-4747
Co. E-mail: member_relations@iabc.com
URL: http://www.iabc.com
Contact: Julie Freeman, Pres.
Description: Represents Communication managers, public relations directors, writers, editors, audiovisual specialists, and others in the public relations and organizational communication field that use a variety of media to communicate with internal audiences (employees, management, association members, and leaders) and external audiences (media, customers, dealers, investors, and government). Conducts research in the communication field and encourages establishment of college-level programs in organizational communication. Offers accreditation program; conducts surveys on employee communication effectiveness and media trends. **Publications:** *Essentials of Employee Communication*; *The Human Element*; *The Truth About B2B Marketing ROI*;Newsletter (monthly).

22040 ■ Society for Technical Communication
9401 Lee Hwy., Ste. 300
Fairfax, VA 22031
Ph:(703)522-4114
Fax:(703)522-2075
Co. E-mail: stc@stc.org
URL: http://www.stc.org
Contact: Dr. Hillary Hart, Pres.
Description: Writers, editors, educators, scientists, engineers, artists, publishers, and others professionally engaged in or interested in the field of technical communication; companies, corporations, organizations and agencies interested in the aims of the society. Seeks to advance the theory and practice of technical communication in all media. Sponsors high school writing contests. **Publications:** *Technical Communication* (quarterly).

EDUCATIONAL PROGRAMS

22041 ■ Adobe Captivate 3
EEI Communications
66 Canal Ctr. Plz., Ste. 200
Alexandria, VA 22314-5507
Ph:(703)683-7453
Free: 888-253-2762
Fax:(703)683-7310
Co. E-mail: train@eeicom.com
URL: http://www.eeicom.com/training
Price: $745.00. **Description:** Seminar that teaches how to create professional quality, interactive simulations and software demonstrations without any programming or multimedia knowledge, including basics, captions and timelines, images, pointer paths, buttons, and highlight boxes, movies, rollover captions and rollover images, slide labels and notes, audio, animation, and question slides. **Remarks:** Formerly known as Macromedia Authorware. **Locations:** Alexandria, VA.

22042 ■ Advanced Editing
EEI Communications
66 Canal Center Plz., Ste. 200
Alexandria, VA 22314
Ph:(703)683-7453
Free: 888-253-2762
Fax:(703)683-7310
Co. E-mail: train@eeicom.com
URL: http://www.eeicom.com/training
Price: $745.00. **Description:** Covers advanced editing techniques, including copyediting, substantive editing, style sheets, English grammar, and query lists. **Locations:** Alexandria, VA.

22043 ■ Advanced Leadership Communication Strategies
American Management Association
600 AMA Way
Saranac Lake, NY 12983-5534
Ph:(212)586-8100
Free: 877-566-9441
Fax:(518)891-0368
Co. E-mail: customerservice@amanet.org
URL: http://www.amaseminars.org
Price: $2,645.00 for non-members; $2,395.00 for AMA members; and $2,051.00 for General Services Administration (GSA) members. **Description:** Three-day seminar to build on current strong leadership skills and influence across the board. **Locations:** San Francisco, CA; Washington, DC; Chicago, IL; and Arlington, VA.

22044 ■ Assertive Communication - Essential Skills for Successful Women
Padgett-Thompson Seminars
Rockhurst University CEC
14502 W. 105th St.
Lenexa, KS 66215
Free: 800-349-1935
URL: http://www.findaseminar.com/tpd/Padgett-Thompson-Seminars.asp
Price: $199.00. **Description:** Assertiveness training for today's business woman. **Locations:** Cities throughout the United States and Canada.

22045 ■ Assertiveness Skills: Communicating With Authority and Impact
Learning Tree International
1805 Library St.
Reston, VA 20190-5630
Ph:(703)709-9019
Free: 888-843-8733
URL: http://www.learningtree.com
Price: $1,890.00. **Description:** Develop a positive, assertive style and build a skill set that will enable you to react positively in demanding situations. **Locations:** Reston, VA; Toronto, ON; Ottawa, ON; New York, NY; Rockville, MD; and Washington, DC.

22046 ■ Assertiveness Training for Managers (Canada)
Canadian Management Centre
150 York St., 5th Fl.
Toronto, ON, Canada M5H 3S5
Ph:(416)214-5678
Free: 877-262-2519
Fax:(416)214-6047
Co. E-mail: cmcinfo@cmctraining.org
URL: http://www.cmctraining.org
Price: $2,295.00 Canadian for non-members; $2,095.00 Canadian for CMC members. **Description:** Covers using assertive behavior professionally, requesting change, managing conflict, and defining objectives. **Locations:** Toronto, ON; and Calgary, AB.

22047 ■ Assertiveness Training for Women in Business
American Management Association
600 AMA Way
Saranac Lake, NY 12983-5534
Ph:(212)586-8100
Free: 877-566-9441
Fax:(518)891-0368
Co. E-mail: customerservice@amanet.org
URL: http://www.amaseminars.org
Price: $2,345.00 for non-members; $2,095.00 for AMA members; and $1,794.00 for General Services Administration (GSA) members. **Description:** Covers self-image, stress management, various communication techniques for assertiveness, and male and female workplace attitudes. **Locations:** Cities throughout the United States.

22048 ■ Assertiveness Training for Women in Business (Canada)
Canadian Management Centre
150 York St., 5th Fl.
Toronto, ON, Canada M5H 3S5
Ph:(416)214-5678
Free: 877-262-2519

Fax:(416)214-6047
Co. E-mail: cmcinfo@cmctraining.org
URL: http://www.cmctraining.org
Price: $2,295.00 Canadian for non-members; $2,095.00 Canadian for CMC members. **Description:** Covers self-image, stress management, various communication techniques for assertiveness, and male and female workplace attitudes. **Locations:** Toronto, ON.

22049 ■ Bargaining With Vendors and Suppliers
Padgett-Thompson Seminars
Rockhurst University CEC
14502 W. 105th St.
Lenexa, KS 66215
Free: 800-349-1935
URL: http://www.findaseminar.com/tpd/Padgett-Thompson-Seminars.asp
Price: $249.00. **Description:** A one-day seminar that teaches practical bargaining skills that will help a company come out of every negotiation a winner. **Locations:** Cities throughout the United States.

22050 ■ Business Conversation for Sales and Service (Onsite)
Seminar Information Service, Inc.
20 Executive Park, Ste. 120
Irvine, CA 92614
Ph:(949)261-9104
Free: 877-SEM-INFO
Fax:(949)261-1963
Co. E-mail: info@seminarinformation.com
URL: http://www.seminarinformation.com
Price: $225.00 for non-members; $165.00 for The Management Association, Inc. members. **Description:** Participants will learn practical tips and practice conversation. Build common ground with colleagues, customers, and senior managers, including methods to develop a repertoire of topics, make skillful transitions, develop confidence and draw people to you. **Locations:** Waukesha, WI.

22051 ■ Business Conversation Skills for the Multilingual Professional
American Management Association
600 AMA Way
Saranac Lake, NY 12983-5534
Ph:(212)586-8100
Free: 877-566-9441
Fax:(518)891-0368
Co. E-mail: customerservice@amanet.org
URL: http://www.amaseminars.org
Price: $1,995.00 for non-members; $1,795.00 for AMA members; and $1,537.00 for General Services Administration (GSA) members. **Description:** Comprehensive two-day workshop will improve your conversation skills on all levels to achieve your professional and organizational goals. **Locations:** New York, NY; Chicago, IL; Arlington, VA; Washington, DC; and San Francisco, CA.

22052 ■ Communicating Change
Canadian Management Centre
150 York St., 5th Fl.
Toronto, ON, Canada M5H 3S5
Free: 800-262-2519
Fax:(416)214-6047
Co. E-mail: cmcinfo@cmctraining.org
URL: http://www.cmctraining.org
Price: $945.00 for members; $1,095.00 for non-members. **Description:** Learn how to leverage communication as a critical vehicle for enabling change in an organization. **Locations:** Toronto, ON.

22053 ■ Communicating Effectively in Your Corporate Culture (Onsite)
Seminar Information Service, Inc.
20 Executive Park, Ste. 120
Irvine, CA 92614
Ph:(949)261-9104
Free: 877-SEM-INFO
Fax:(949)261-1963
Co. E-mail: info@seminarinformation.com
URL: http://www.seminarinformation.com
Price: $370.00 for non-members; $275.00 for The Management Association, Inc. members. **Description:** Gives participants a sound understanding of the principles of effective communication and the skill to recognize and resolve communication breakdowns in the workplace. Attendees learn the objectives of communication, gain active listening skills and how to give directions that get results. **Locations:** Waukesha, WI.

22054 ■ Communicating with a Multigenerational Workforce–AMA's Myers-Briggs Type Indicator (MBTI) Certification Program
600 AMA Way
Saranac Lake, NY 12983-5534
Ph:(212)586-8100
Free: 877-566-9441
Fax:(518)891-0368
Co. E-mail: customerservice@amanet.org
URL: http://www.amaseminars.org
Price: $1,695.00 for non-members; $1,495.00 for AMA members; and $1,280.00 for General Services Administration (GSA) members. **Description:** Workshop that focuses on the key MBTI applications of team building, leadership and individual development. **Locations:** San Francisco, CA; Arlington, VA; and New York, NY.

22055 ■ Communication Boot Camp
American Management Association
600 AMA Way
Saranac Lake, NY 12983-5534
Ph:(212)586-8100
Free: 877-566-9441
Fax:(518)891-0368
Co. E-mail: customerservice@amanet.org
URL: http://www.amaseminars.org
Price: $2,195.00 for non-members; $1,995.00 for AMA members; and $1,708.00 for General Services Administration (GSA) members. **Description:** Three-day seminar to assess your communication skills, develop listening competencies, increase cognitive skills, and roadmap for clearer communication. **Locations:** Washington, DC; Arlington, VA; New York, NY; Chicago, IL; and San Francisco, CA.

22056 ■ Communication and Interpersonal Skills: A Seminar for IT and Technical Professionals
American Management Association
600 AMA Way
Saranac Lake, NY 12983-5534
Ph:(212)586-8100
Free: 877-566-9441
Fax:(518)891-0368
Co. E-mail: customerservice@amanet.org
URL: http://www.amaseminars.org
Price: $2,095.00 for non-members; $1,895.00 for AMA members; and $1,623.00 for General Services Administration (GSA) members. **Description:** Learn how to combine your interpersonal communication skills effectively with your technical skills to get results. **Locations:** New York, NY; Washington, DC; Arlington, VA; Dallas, TX, Chicago, IL; and San Francisco, CA.

22057 ■ Communication and Interpersonal Skills for IT & Technical Professionals (Canada)
Canadian Management Centre
150 York St., 5th Fl.
Toronto, ON, Canada M5H 3S5
Ph:(416)214-5678
Free: 877-262-2519
Fax:(416)214-6047
Co. E-mail: cmcinfo@cmctraining.org
URL: http://www.cmctraining.org
Price: $1,995.00 Canadian for non-members; $1,845.00 Canadian for CMC members. **Description:** Covers effective communication skills, prioritizing, and dealing with various types of communication styles. **Locations:** Toronto, ON.

22058 ■ Communication Skills: Results Through Collaboration
Learning Tree International
1805 Library St.
Reston, VA 20190-5630
Ph:(703)709-9019
Free: 888-843-8733
URL: http://www.learningtree.com
Price: $2,490.00. **Description:** Learn to achieve results in your communications with others and build collaborative relationships. **Locations:** Cities throughout the United States and Canada.

22059 ■ Communication Skills: Results Through Collaboration (Onsite)
Seminar Information Service, Inc.
20 Executive Park, Ste. 120
Irvine, CA 92614
Ph:(949)261-9104
Free: 877-SEM-INFO
Fax:(949)261-1963
Co. E-mail: info@seminarinformation.com
URL: http://www.seminarinformation.com
Price: $2,490. **Description:** Learn how to: Achieve results in your communications with others; Build collaborative relationships that emphasize trust and respect; Communicate effectively using simple, concise and direct language; Enhance your active listening skills; Foster cross-cultural understanding in your workplace; Eliminate the roadblocks that undermine your ability to communicate effectively. **Locations:** Cities throughout the United States.

22060 ■ Communication Skills for Women
Fred Pryor Seminars & CareerTrack
5700 Broadmoor St., Ste. 300
Mission, KS 66202
Free: 800-780-8476
Fax:(913)967-8849
Co. E-mail: customerservice@pryor.com
URL: http://www.pryor.com
Price: $99.00; $89.00 for groups of 5 or more. **Description:** Covers valuable insights women can use to enhance their communication style while earning the respect and cooperation of others, including how to control your emotions and stay composed and effective while under pressure. **Locations:** Cities throughout the United States.

22061 ■ Communication Techniques That Get Results: A Course for Administrative Professionals
AMA
600 AMA Way
Saranac Lake, NY 12983-5534
Ph:(212)586-8100
Free: 877-566-9441
Fax:(518)891-0368
Co. E-mail: customerservice@amanet.org
URL: http://www.amaseminars.org
Price: $1,545.00 for non-members; $1,395.00 for AMA members. **Description:** Meet changing job demands and deliver optimum results through better communication in this two-day course. **Locations:** Washington, DC; Chicago, IL.

22062 ■ Comprehensive Proofreading
EEI Communications
66 Canal Center Plz., Ste. 200
Alexandria, VA 22314
Ph:(703)683-7453
Free: 888-253-2762
Fax:(703)683-7310
Co. E-mail: train@eeicom.com
URL: http://www.eeicom.com/training
Price: $745.00. **Description:** Covers creating proofreading checklists, using style guides, and proofreading electronic documents. **Locations:** Silver Spring, MD; and Alexandria, VA.

22063 ■ Conflict Communications
EEI Communications
66 Canal Center Plz., Ste. 200
Alexandria, VA 22314
Ph:(703)683-7453
Free: 888-253-2762
Fax:(703)683-7310
Co. E-mail: train@eeicom.com
URL: http://www.eeicom.com/training
Price: $425.00. **Description:** Learn to coach people through conflict, identify different levels and forms of conflict and why people react differently to conflict. **Locations:** Silver Spring, MD; Hunt Valley, MD; Columbia, MD; and Alexandria, VA.

22064 ■ Conflict Management Skills for Women
Seminar Information Service, Inc.
20 Executive Park, Ste. 120
Irvine, CA 92614
Ph:(949)261-9104
Free: 877-SEM-INFO
Fax:(949)261-1963
Co. E-mail: info@seminarinformation.com
URL: http://www.seminarinformation.com
Price: $99.00; $89.00 for four or more. **Description:** Learn how to keep unmanaged conflicts, disagreements and out-of-control emotions from harming your important working and personal relationships. **Locations:** Cities throughout the United States.

22065 ■ Critical Business Communication Skills
Padgett-Thompson Seminars
Rockhurst University CEC
14502 W. 105th St.
Lenexa, KS 66215
Free: 800-349-1935
URL: http://www.findaseminar.com/tpd/Padgett-Thompson-Seminars.asp
Price: $249.00. **Description:** A one-day seminar to help participants gain the critical skills needed to deliver engaging presentations. **Locations:** Mission, KS.

22066 ■ Critical Thinking and Out-of-the-Box Problem Solving (Onsite)
Seminar Information Service, Inc.
20 Executive Park, Ste. 120
Irvine, CA 92614
Ph:(949)261-9104
Free: 877-SEM-INFO
Fax:(949)261-1963
Co. E-mail: info@seminarinformation.com
URL: http://www.seminarinformation.com
Price: $2,490.00. **Description:** Learn how to: Make better decisions through critical thinking and creative problem solving; Adapt to different thinking styles in group and team environments; Foster an innovative environment in your workplace; Recognize and remove barriers to individual and group creativity; Systematically analyze a target problem; Present your ideas clearly and concisely for maximum stakeholder buy-in; Transform your creativity into practical business solutions. **Locations:** Rockville, MD; Philadelphia, PA; Irving, TX; Toronto, CN; Roseland, NJ; New York, NY; and Waltham, MA.

22067 ■ Customer Focused Telephone Techniques
Seminar Information Service, Inc.
20 Executive Park, Ste. 120
Irvine, CA 92614
Ph:(949)261-9104
Free: 877-SEM-INFO
Fax:(949)261-1963
Co. E-mail: info@seminarinformation.com
URL: http://www.seminarinformation.com
Price: $370.00. **Description:** Participants learn the importance of telephone and acquire professional skills for better business practice, including calming angry clients and projecting a confident business image. **Locations:** Palatine, IL; and Waukesha, WI.

22068 ■ Designing for Diversity
EEI Communications
66 Canal Center Plz., Ste. 200
Alexandria, VA 22314
Ph:(703)683-7453
Free: 888-253-2762
Fax:(703)683-7310
Co. E-mail: train@eeicom.com
URL: http://www.eeicom.com/training
Price: $425.00. **Description:** Workshop to help you connect with all your audiences utilizing the appropriate visual imagery and words, including when not to send ethnically targeted messages, and designing "one size fits all" publications when your budget won't permit targeted publications, and the effects of visual imagery on attitudes and behavior. **Locations:** Alexandria, VA.

22069 ■ Developing Diversity Communication and Messaging
Seminar Information Service, Inc.
20 Executive Park, Ste. 120
Irvine, CA 92614
Ph:(949)261-9104
Free: 877-SEM-INFO
Fax:(949)261-1963
Co. E-mail: info@seminarinformation.com
URL: http://www.seminarinformation.com
Price: $795.00. **Description:** Covers basic concepts of developing a diversity communication strategy and key techniques for communicating a diversity crisis. **Locations:** New York, NY.

22070 ■ Developing Dynamic Presentation Skills (Onsite)
Seminar Information Service, Inc.
20 Executive Park, Ste. 120
Irvine, CA 92614
Ph:(949)261-9104
Free: 877-SEM-INFO
Fax:(949)261-1963
Co. E-mail: info@seminarinformation.com
URL: http://www.seminarinformation.com
Price: $1,890.00. **Description:** Learn how to prepare an effective presentation by organizing key points into a coherent story; Capture and maintain audience interest and attention using interactive techniques. **Locations:** Reston, VA; Toronto, CN; and New York, NY.

22071 ■ Developing Effective Business Conversation Skills
American Management Association
600 AMA Way
Saranac Lake, NY 12983-5534
Ph:(212)586-8100
Free: 877-566-9441
Fax:(518)891-0368
Co. E-mail: customerservice@amanet.org
URL: http://www.amaseminars.org
Price: $2,095.00 for non-members; $1,895.00 for AMA members; and $1,623.00 for General Services Administration (GSA) members. **Description:** Learn effective business communication skills. **Locations:** Chicago, IL; New York, NY; Atlanta, GA; and San Francisco, CA.

22072 ■ Developing Effective Communications Skills
Seminar Information Service, Inc.
20 Executive Park, Ste. 120
Irvine, CA 92614
Ph:(949)261-9104
Free: 877-SEM-INFO
Fax:(949)261-1963
Co. E-mail: info@seminarinformation.com
URL: http://www.seminarinformation.com
Price: $1,495.00. **Description:** learn skills for communicating powerfully, sending clear messages, and conducting challenging conversations while maintaining effective working relationships with supervisors and co-workers. **Locations:** New York, NY.

22073 ■ Dynamic Listening Skills for Successful Communication
American Management Association
600 AMA Way
Saranac Lake, NY 12983-5534
Ph:(212)586-8100
Free: 877-566-9441
Fax:(518)891-0368
Co. E-mail: customerservice@amanet.org
URL: http://www.amaseminars.org
Price: $1,995.00 for non-members; $1,795.00 for AMA members; and $1,537.00 for General Services Administration (GSA) members. **Description:** Develop listening skills that encourage productive interactions. **Locations:** New York, NY; Chicago, IL; and San Francisco, CA.

22074 ■ Editorial Skills for Non-Editors
EEI Communications
66 Canal Center Plz., Ste. 200
Alexandria, VA 22314
Ph:(703)683-7453
Free: 888-253-2762
Fax:(703)683-7310
Co. E-mail: train@eeicom.com
URL: http://www.eeicom.com/training
Price: $425.00. **Description:** Covers punctuation and grammar, usage, and proofreading marks. **Locations:** Silver Spring, MD; and Alexandria, VA.

22075 ■ Effective Briefings
EEI Communications
66 Canal Center Plz., Ste. 200
Alexandria, VA 22314
Ph:(703)683-7453
Free: 888-253-2762
Fax:(703)683-7310
Co. E-mail: train@eeicom.com
URL: http://www.eeicom.com/training
Price: $425.00. **Description:** Hands-on course where you explore elements, principles, and guidelines of effective briefings, including how to deliver vocally, verbally, and visually, find the focus and the right tone, organize your message, create slides and handouts that support your message, and customize the message and delivery for your various audiences. **Locations:** Alexandria, VA.

22076 ■ Effective Business Writing
EEI Communications
66 Canal Center Plz., Ste. 200
Alexandria, VA 22314
Ph:(703)683-7453
Free: 888-253-2762
Fax:(703)683-7310
Co. E-mail: train@eeicom.com
URL: http://www.eeicom.com/training
Price: $425.00. **Description:** Covers the basic elements of writing effective business letters, e-mails, and memos, including grammar, audience analysis, persuasion, and usage problems. **Locations:** Silver Spring, MD; and Alexandria, VA.

22077 ■ Effective Communication and Motivation
Seminar Information Service, Inc.
20 Executive Park, Ste. 120
Irvine, CA 92614
Ph:(949)261-9104
Free: 877-SEM-INFO
Fax:(949)261-1963
Co. E-mail: info@seminarinformation.com
URL: http://www.seminarinformation.com
Price: $580.00 for non-members; $415.00 for The Management Association, Inc. members. **Description:** Gives managerial personnel a sound understanding of the principles of effective communication and the skill to recognize and to resolve communication breakdowns in the workplace. Participants learn to apply communication skills to problem solving, employee relations and performance appraisal. **Locations:** Waukesha, WI; and Palatine, IL.

22078 ■ Effective Executive Speaking
American Management Association
600 AMA Way
Saranac Lake, NY 12983-5534
Ph:(212)586-8100
Free: 877-566-9441
Fax:(518)891-0368
Co. E-mail: customerservice@amanet.org
URL: http://www.amaseminars.org
Price: $2,345.00 for non-members; $2,095.00 for AMA members; and $1,794.00 for General Services Administration (GSA) members. **Description:** Learn to speak, present, and communicate effectively. **Locations:** New York, NY; Chicago, IL; San Francisco, CA; Washington, DC; Arlington, VA; and Atlanta, GA.

22079 ■ Effective Presentation Techniques: Public Speaking
EEI Communications
66 Canal Center Plz., Ste. 200
Alexandria, VA 22314
Ph:(703)683-7453
Free: 888-253-2762
Fax:(703)683-7310
Co. E-mail: train@eeicom.com
URL: http://www.eeicom.com/training
Price: $425.00. **Description:** Covers assessing the audience, organizational skills, and effective delivery styles. **Locations:** Alexandria, VA.

22080 ■ Effective Technical Writing
American Management Association
600 AMA Way
Saranac Lake, NY 12983-5534
Ph:(212)586-8100
Free: 877-566-9441
Fax:(518)891-0368
Co. E-mail: customerservice@amanet.org
URL: http://www.amaseminars.org
Price: $2,195.00 for non-members; $1,995.00 for AMA members; and $1,708.00 for General Services Administration (GSA) members. **Description:** Covers the basics of writing technical documents such as reports, manuals, specifications, proposals, and instructions. **Locations:** Cities throughout the United States.

22081 ■ Enhancing Your People Skills
Seminar Information Service, Inc.
20 Executive Park, Ste. 120
Irvine, CA 92614
Ph:(949)261-9104
Free: 877-SEM-INFO
Fax:(949)261-1963
Co. E-mail: info@seminarinformation.com
URL: http://www.seminarinformation.com
Price: $1,495.00. **Description:** Build awareness and skill in the areas of team dynamics, group problem solving, and group decision making. The critical structural and behavioral dimensions of building and leading an effective work team or task force are fully explored. You will develop leadership skills applicable to many areas, but especially suited to self-directed work teams, employee participation teams, interdepartmental task groups, and other group situations where combined efforts are needed to reach optimal performance levels. **Locations:** New York, NY.

22082 ■ Essential Skills of Dynamic Public Speaking
Padgett-Thompson Seminars
Rockhurst University CEC
14502 W. 105th St.
Lenexa, KS 66215
Free: 800-349-1935
URL: http://www.findaseminar.com/tpd/Padgett-Thompson-Seminars.asp
Price: $249.00. **Description:** Workshop provides face-saving techniques that will make any business presentation easier. **Locations:** Cities throughout the United States.

22083 ■ The Essentials of Communicating With Diplomacy and Professionalism
Seminar Information Service, Inc.
20 Executive Park, Ste. 120
Irvine, CA 92614
Ph:(949)261-9104
Free: 877-SEM-INFO
Fax:(949)261-1963
Co. E-mail: info@seminarinformation.com
URL: http://www.seminarinformation.com
Price: $299.00; $269.00 for 4 or more. **Description:** Learn techniques to handle even the most difficult situations and difficult people with confidence. **Locations:** Cities throughout the United States.

22084 ■ The Essentials of Communication and Collaboration
Padgett-Thompson Seminars
Rockhurst University CEC
14502 W. 105th St.
Lenexa, KS 66215
Free: 800-349-1935
URL: http://www.findaseminar.com/tpd/Padgett-Thompson-Seminars.asp
Price: $249.00. **Description:** Seminar teaches the essential communication techniques that facilitate cooperation and collaboration at work. **Locations:** Cities throughout the United States.

22085 ■ Exceptional Presentation Training
Baker Communications, Inc.
10101 SW Freeway, Ste. 630
Houston, TX 77074
Ph:(713)627-7700
Fax:(713)587-2051
Co. E-mail: info@bakercommunications.com
URL: http://www.bakercommunications.com
Price: $1,700.00. **Description:** This workshop will aid all participants in helping to deliver their intended message to both internal and external clients. **Locations:** Calgary, AB; Chicago, IL; Dallas, TX; Houston, TX; and New York, NY.

22086 ■ Facilitation Skills
Learning Tree International
1805 Library St.
Reston, VA 20190-5630
Ph:(703)709-9019
Free: 888-843-8733
URL: http://www.learningtree.com
Price: $2,490.00. **Description:** For managers, supervisors, project managers, business analysts, and others who want to improve team performance and solve business problems. **Locations:** Toronto, ON; New York, NY; Washington, DC; Rockville, MD; and Ottawa, ON.

22087 ■ Geometric Dimensioning and Tolerancing, Level 1 (Onsite)
Seminar Information Service, Inc.
20 Executive Park, Ste. 120
Irvine, CA 92614
Ph:(949)261-9104
Free: 877-SEM-INFO
Fax:(949)261-1963
Co. E-mail: info@seminarinformation.com
URL: http://www.seminarinformation.com
Price: $1,695.00. **Description:** Learn how to improve your effectiveness at communicating and interpreting specifications on engineering drawings. **Locations:** Troy, MI.

22088 ■ Getting Better Results Through Conversations
Canadian Management Centre
150 York St., 5th Fl.
Toronto, ON, Canada M5H 3S5
Free: 800-262-2519
Fax:(416)214-6047
Co. E-mail: cmcinfo@cmctraining.org
URL: http://www.cmctraining.org
Price: $495.00 for members; $545.00 for non-members. **Description:** A half-day business communication workshop offering a concentrated blast of practical knowledge. **Locations:** Toronto, ON.

22089 ■ High Performance Business Writing (Canada)
Canadian Management Centre
150 York St., 5th Fl.
Toronto, ON, Canada M5H 3S5
Ph:(416)214-5678
Free: 877-262-2519
Fax:(416)214-6047
Co. E-mail: cmcinfo@cmctraining.org
URL: http://www.cmctraining.org
Price: $1,995.00 Canadian for non-members; $1,845.00 Canadian for CMC members. **Description:** Covers improving business writing skills, focusing on documents, letters, e-mails, reports, and memos. **Locations:** Toronto, ON; and Ottawa, ON.

22090 ■ How to Be an Outstanding Communicator
Padgett-Thompson Seminars
Rockhurst University CEC
14502 W. 105th St.
Lenexa, KS 66215
Free: 800-349-1935
URL: http://www.findaseminar.com/tpd/Padgett-Thompson-Seminars.asp
Price: $179.00. **Description:** One-day seminar that teaches how to get support from employees and co-workers, project a confident image, and master the key communication skills that you will need to succeed in the workplace. **Locations:** Cities throughout the United States and Canada.

22091 ■ How to Build Strategic Thinking Skills
Seminar Information Service, Inc.
20 Executive Park, Ste. 120
Irvine, CA 92614
Ph:(949)261-9104
Free: 877-SEM-INFO
Fax:(949)261-1963
Co. E-mail: info@seminarinformation.com
URL: http://www.seminarinformation.com
Price: $199.00. **Description:** Learn how to view challenges or problems in a totally new way and the effective strategies that follow to ensure a positive outcome. **Locations:** Cities throughout the United States.

22092 ■ How to Communicate with Tact & Professionalism
Fred Pryor Seminars & CareerTrack
5700 Broadmoor St., Ste. 300
Mission, KS 66202
Free: 800-780-8476
Fax:(913)967-8849
Co. E-mail: customerservice@pryor.com
URL: http://www.pryor.com
Price: $299.00; $279.00 for groups of 3 or more. **Description:** Learn to become a polished, persuasive communicator and express your thoughts and ideas with clarity and diplomacy, including how to decode body language to understand what people are really saying. **Locations:** Cities throughout the United States.

22093 ■ How to Deliver Presentations with Ease & Confidence
Fred Pryor Seminars & CareerTrack
5700 Broadmoor St., Ste. 300
Mission, KS 66202
Free: 800-780-8476
Fax:(913)967-8849
Co. E-mail: customerservice@pryor.com
URL: http://www.pryor.com
Price: $179.00; $169.00 for groups of 5 or more. **Description:** Improve and enhance your effectiveness in every speaking situation without fear and anxiety. **Locations:** Cities throughout the United States.

22094 ■ How to Design Eye-Catching Brochures, Newspapers, Ads, Reports
Fred Pryor Seminars & CareerTrack
5700 Broadmoor St., Ste. 300
Mission, KS 66202
Free: 800-944-8503
Fax:(913)967-8849
Co. E-mail: customerservice@pryor.com
URL: http://www.careertrack.com
Price: $99.00; $89.00 for groups of 5 or more. **Description:** Covers basic design and layout skills for headlines, text, and graphics for printed documents. **Locations:** Cities throughout the United States.

22095 ■ How to Manage Conflict and Confrontation
Fred Pryor Seminars & CareerTrack
5700 Broadmoor St., Ste. 300
Mission, KS 66202
Free: 800-780-8476
Fax:(913)967-8849
Co. E-mail: customerservice@pryor.com
URL: http://www.pryor.com
Price: $149.00; $139.00 for groups of 5 or more. **Description:** Learn practical and proven techniques for managing workplace conflict. **Locations:** Cities throughout the United States.

22096 ■ How to Present Online: A Skills-Based Workshop (Live Online)
American Management Association
600 AMA Way
Saranac Lake, NY 12983-5534
Ph:(212)586-8100
Free: 877-566-9441
Fax:(518)891-0368
Co. E-mail: customerservice@amanet.org
URL: http://www.amaseminars.org
Price: $2,345.00 for non-members; $2,095.00 for AMA members; and $1,794.00 for General Services Administration (GSA) members. **Description:** Learn how to conduct presentations to online audiences with successful techniques.

22097 ■ How to Work Most Effectively with Your Boss (Onsite)
American Management Association
600 AMA Way
Saranac Lake, NY 12983-5534
Ph:(212)586-8100
Free: 877-566-9441
Fax:(518)891-0368
Co. E-mail: customerservice@amanet.org
URL: http://www.amaseminars.org
Price: $1,695.00 for non-members; $1,495.00 for AMA members. **Description:** Covers effective communication and problem solving teamwork skills. **Locations:** Atlanta, GA; and San Francisco, CA.

22098 ■ How to Work With Difficult, Demanding, and Inconsiderate People
Padgett-Thompson Seminars
Rockhurst University CEC
14502 W. 105th St.
Lenexa, KS 66215
Free: 800-349-1935
URL: http://www.findaseminar.com/tpd/Padgett-Thompson-Seminars.asp
Price: $79.00. **Description:** Learn what it takes to defuse angry coworkers and how to keep emotions in check. **Locations:** Cities throughout the United States.

22099 ■ Improving Your Communication Skills for Success
Seminar Information Service, Inc.
20 Executive Park, Ste. 120
Irvine, CA 92614
Ph:(949)261-9104
Free: 877-SEM-INFO
Fax:(949)261-1963
Co. E-mail: info@seminarinformation.com
URL: http://www.seminarinformation.com
Price: $249.00. **Description:** Learn the essential communication skills you need to handle any situation that arises with confidence. **Locations:** Cities throughout the United States.

22100 ■ Indexing I
EEI Communications
66 Canal Center Plz., Ste. 200
Alexandria, VA 22314
Ph:(703)683-7453
Free: 888-253-2762
Fax:(703)683-7310
Co. E-mail: train@eeicom.com
URL: http://www.eeicom.com/training
Price: $745.00. **Description:** Covers indexing for websites and books, including determining key words, categorizing information, and using cross-references. **Locations:** Silver Spring, MD; Alexandria, VA; Hunt Valley, MD; and Columbia, MD.

22101 ■ Indexing II
EEI Communications
66 Canal Center Plz., Ste. 200
Alexandria, VA 22314
Ph:(703)683-7453
Free: 888-253-2762
Fax:(703)683-7310
Co. E-mail: train@eeicom.com
URL: http://www.eeicom.com/training
Price: $425.00. **Description:** Covers editing and evaluating indices. **Locations:** Silver Spring, MD; Alexandria, VA; Hunt Valley, MD; and Columbia, MD.

22102 ■ Influence Skills: Getting Results Without Direct Authority (Onsite)
Seminar Information Service, Inc.
20 Executive Park, Ste. 120
Irvine, CA 92614
Ph:(949)261-9104
Free: 877-SEM-INFO
Fax:(949)261-1963
Co. E-mail: info@seminarinformation.com
URL: http://www.seminarinformation.com
Price: $2,890.00. **Description:** Learn how to: Apply influence strategies to gain commitment from others and foster collaboration; Define desired outcomes for win-win results; Dynamically adjust your approach to others to gain buy-in; Achieve goals by enhancing trust and cooperation; Deal effectively with challenging behaviors to overcome resistance and inertia in others; Use knowledge and competence rather than position and status to influence others. **Locations:** Cities throughout the United States Ottawa and Toronto, CN.

22103 ■ Influence Strategies
Seminar Information Service, Inc.
20 Executive Park, Ste. 120
Irvine, CA 92614
Ph:(949)261-9104
Free: 877-SEM-INFO
Fax:(949)261-1963
Co. E-mail: info@seminarinformation.com
URL: http://www.seminarinformation.com
Price: $795.00. **Description:** Provides you with a greater understanding of your personal motive preferences, the preferences of others, and application of this dynamic toward becoming more effective in specific work situations. **Locations:** New York, NY.

22104 ■ Interactive Training Techniques for the Classroom
Seminar Information Service, Inc.
20 Executive Park, Ste. 120
Irvine, CA 92614
Ph:(949)261-9104
Free: 877-SEM-INFO
Fax:(949)261-1963
Co. E-mail: info@seminarinformation.com
URL: http://www.seminarinformation.com
Price: $370.00. **Description:** Participants prepare themselves to be both presenter and discussion leader. **Locations:** Waukesha, WI.

22105 ■ Interpersonal Skills for Managers (Canada)
Canadian Management Centre
150 York St., 5th Fl.
Toronto, ON, Canada M5H 3S5
Ph:(416)214-5678
Free: 877-262-2519
Fax:(416)214-6047
Co. E-mail: cmcinfo@cmctraining.org
URL: http://www.cmctraining.org
Price: $2,195.00 Canadian for non-members; $1,995.00 Canadian for CMC members. **Description:** Covers problem solving, negotiation, motivating and creating enthusiasm, dealing with conflict, and tactics for working with difficult employees. **Locations:** Toronto, ON; Ottawa, ON; and Calgary, AB.

22106 ■ Introduction to Information Design
EEI Communications
66 Canal Center Plz., Ste. 200
Alexandria, VA 22314
Ph:(703)683-7453
Free: 888-253-2762
Fax:(703)683-7310
Co. E-mail: train@eeicom.com
URL: http://www.eeicom.com/training
Price: $745.00. **Description:** Topics include defining information design, understanding how users process information, techniques for information design, information graphics, and presenting Web information. **Locations:** Alexandria, VA.

22107 ■ Keeping the Team on Track (Onsite)
Seminar Information Service, Inc.
20 Executive Park, Ste. 120
Irvine, CA 92614
Ph:(949)261-9104
Free: 877-SEM-INFO
Fax:(949)261-1963
Co. E-mail: info@seminarinformation.com
URL: http://www.seminarinformation.com
Price: $370.00 for non-members; $275.00 for The Management Association, Inc. members. **Description:** Learn to recognize the signs of ineffective meetings and learn the formal tools to accomplish expected results with particular focus on managing the meeting process and techniques to keep the team on track. **Locations:** Waukesha, WI.

22108 ■ Managing Difficult and Sensitive Conversations
Canadian Management Centre
150 York St., 5th Fl.
Toronto, ON, Canada M5H 3S5
Free: 800-262-2519
Fax:(416)214-6047
Co. E-mail: cmcinfo@cmctraining.org
URL: http://www.cmctraining.org
Price: $495.00 for members; $545.00 for non-members. **Description:** Learn to confront others who are not performing and get them to change. **Locations:** Toronto, ON.

22109 ■ Managing Emotions under Pressure
Fred Pryor Seminars & CareerTrack
5700 Broadmoor St., Ste. 300
Mission, KS 66202
Free: 800-780-8476
Fax:(913)967-8849
Co. E-mail: customerservice@pryor.com
URL: http://www.pryor.com
Price: $79.00; $74.00 for groups of 5 or more. **Description:** Learn to develop self-discipline and manage your emotions in the workplace. **Locations:** Cities throughout the United States.

22110 ■ Managing Emotions and Thriving Under Pressure
Seminar Information Service, Inc.
20 Executive Park, Ste. 120
Irvine, CA 92614
Ph:(949)261-9104
Free: 877-SEM-INFO
Fax:(949)261-1963
Co. E-mail: info@seminarinformation.com
URL: http://www.seminarinformation.com
Price: $249.00; $139.00 each for 4 or more. **Description:** Learn self-discipline skills and rid yourself of unproductive behaviors. **Locations:** Cities throughout the United States.

22111 ■ Managing Emotions in the Workplace: Strategies for Success
American Management Association
600 AMA Way
Saranac Lake, NY 12983-5534
Ph:(212)586-8100
Free: 877-566-9441
Fax:(518)891-0368
Co. E-mail: customerservice@amanet.org
URL: http://www.amaseminars.org
Price: $2,095.00 for non-members; $1,895.00 for AMA members; and $1,623.00 for General Services (GSA) members. **Description:** Covers methods for effectively and professionally communicating emotion, creating positive work environments, and emotional control. **Locations:** New York, NY; Atlanta, GA; Chicago, IL; San Francisco, CA; and Washington, DC.

22112 ■ Managing Successful Negotiations
Seminar Information Service, Inc.
20 Executive Park, Ste. 120
Irvine, CA 92614
Ph:(949)261-9104
Free: 877-SEM-INFO
Fax:(949)261-1963
Co. E-mail: info@seminarinformation.com
URL: http://www.seminarinformation.com
Price: $1,595.00. **Description:** Designed to help you acquire the necessary concept, skills, and techniques to prepare for and to conduct successful negotiations. **Locations:** Boston, MA.

22113 ■ Mistake-Free Grammar & Proofreading
Fred Pryor Seminars
5700 Broadmoor St., Ste. 300
Mission, KS 66202
Free: 800-944-8503
Fax:(913)967-8849
Co. E-mail: customerservice@pryor.com
URL: http://www.careertrack.com
Price: $149.00; $139.00 for groups of 5 or more. **Description:** Covers grammar and usage in business writing, including punctuation, capitalization, quotations, spelling, sentence structure, and related topics. **Locations:** Cities throughout the United States.

22114 ■ Negotiating Effectively
Seminar Information Service, Inc.
20 Executive Park, Ste. 120
Irvine, CA 92614
Ph:(949)261-9104
Free: 877-SEM-INFO
Fax:(949)261-1963
Co. E-mail: info@seminarinformation.com
URL: http://www.seminarinformation.com
Price: $1,495.00. **Description:** Learn basic negotiation techniques by focusing on the dynamics of interpersonal and group conflict; differing styles and approaches to negotiation; the negotiation process; and negotiating to achieve mutual benefit. **Locations:** New York, NY.

22115 ■ Negotiating to Win
American Management Association
600 AMA Way
Saranac Lake, NY 12983-5534
Ph:(212)586-8100
Free: 877-566-9441
Fax:(518)891-0368
Co. E-mail: customerservice@amanet.org
URL: http://www.amaseminars.org
Price: $2,345.00 for non-members; $2,095.00 for AMA members; and $1,794.00 for General Services Administration (GSA) members. **Description:** Covers appropriate scenarios for negotiation, persuasion skills, and strategies for oral and written negotiations. **Locations:** Cities throughout the Unite States.

22116 ■ Negotiating to Win (Canada)
Canadian Management Centre
150 York St., 5th Fl.
Toronto, ON, Canada M5H 3S5
Ph:(416)214-5678
Free: 877-262-2519
Fax:(416)214-6047
Co. E-mail: cmcinfo@cmctraining.org
URL: http://www.cmctraining.org
Price: $2,195.00 Canadian for non-members; $1,995.00 Canadian for CMC members. **Description:** Covers techniques for successful negotiations, in every industry and at every level; includes the negotiation process, overcoming people problems, and improving negotiation strategies. **Locations:** Calgary, AB; Ottawa, ON; and Toronto, ON.

22117 ■ Negotiation Skills: Achieving Successful Outcomes (Onsite)
Seminar Information Service, Inc.
20 Executive Park, Ste. 120
Irvine, CA 92614
Ph:(949)261-9104
Free: 877-SEM-INFO
Fax:(949)261-1963
Co. E-mail: info@seminarinformation.com
URL: http://www.seminarinformation.com
Price: $2,490.00. **Description:** Learn how to: Conduct principled negotiations that result in wise agreements; Incorporate a process approach into your negotiation skill set; Formulate principled communication strategies and styles to deflect 'hardball' tactics; Apply psychology principles to negotiate effectively; Enhance your negotiation skills by applying best practices in a real-world setting. **Locations:** New York, NY; Ottawa, CN; and Toronto, CN.

22118 ■ The Outstanding Receptionist
Fred Pryor Seminars & CareerTrack
5700 Broadmoor St., Ste. 300
Mission, KS 66202
Free: 800-780-8476
Fax:(913)967-8849
Co. E-mail: customerservice@pryor.com
URL: http://www.pryor.com
Price: $99.00; $89.00 for groups of 5 or more. **Description:** Learn how to improve your skills and better support everyone in your organization. **Locations:** Cities throughout the United States.

22119 ■ Perfecting Your Presentation Skills
Seminar Information Service, Inc.
20 Executive Park, Ste. 120
Irvine, CA 92614
Ph:(949)261-9104
Free: 877-SEM-INFO
Fax:(949)261-1963
Co. E-mail: info@seminarinformation.com
URL: http://www.seminarinformation.com
Price: $1,495.00. **Description:** Learn how to manage anxiety; develop dynamic delivery skills; connect with/focus on listeners; and how to gain confidence and comfort when presenting. **Locations:** New York, NY.

22120 ■ Performance Measurement Analysis
EEI Communications
66 Canal Center Plz., Ste. 200
Alexandria, VA 22314
Ph:(703)683-7453
Free: 888-253-2762
Fax:(703)683-7310
Co. E-mail: train@eeicom.com
URL: http://www.eeicom.com/training
Price: $1,065.00. **Description:** Through communication, integration, and alignment with objectives, Performance Measurement can help employees realize the value of their contributions to the organization. **Locations:** Silver Spring, MD; Hunt Valley, MD; Columbia, MD; and Alexandria, VA.

22121 ■ Persuasive Communications in Marketing and Public Relations
EEI Communications
66 Canal Center Plz., Ste. 200
Alexandria, VA 22314
Ph:(703)683-7453
Free: 888-253-2762
Fax:(703)683-7310
Co. E-mail: train@eeicom.com
URL: http://www.eeicom.com/training
Price: $1,065.00. **Description:** Course designed for department heads and project managers, as well as mid-level communications professionals who want to expand their public relations and marketing skills. **Locations:** Alexandria, VA.

22122 ■ Persuasive Leadership: Storytelling that Inspires (Onsite)
Seminar Information Service, Inc.
20 Executive Park, Ste. 120
Irvine, CA 92614
Ph:(949)261-9104
Free: 877-SEM-INFO
Fax:(949)261-1963
Co. E-mail: info@seminarinformation.com
URL: http://www.seminarinformation.com
Price: $1,499.00. **Description:** Participants develop their storytelling abilities and learn how to use humor to persuade and motivate others, as well as polish their existing speaking skills and develop powerful new ones. **Locations:** Cleveland, OH.

22123 ■ The Power of Listening: Unlocking Your Communication Potential
Seminar Information Service, Inc.
20 Executive Park, Ste. 120
Irvine, CA 92614
Ph:(949)261-9104
Free: 877-SEM-INFO
Fax:(949)261-1963
Co. E-mail: info@seminarinformation.com
URL: http://www.seminarinformation.com
Price: $1,495.00. **Description:** Examine the listening process and assess your listening strengths and needs to develop effective listening techniques and strategies. **Locations:** New York, NY.

22124 ■ Powerful Communication Skills for Women
Padgett-Thompson Seminars
Rockhurst University CEC
14502 W. 105th St.
Lenexa, KS 66215
Free: 800-349-1935
URL: http://www.findaseminar.com/tpd/Padgett-Thompson-Seminars.asp
Price: $139.00. **Description:** A workshop designed specifically for professional women. **Locations:** Cities throughout the United States.

22125 ■ Professional Communication: What Message Are You Sending?
Fred Pryor Seminars & CareerTrack
5700 Broadmoor St., Ste. 300
Mission, KS 66202
Free: 800-780-8476
Fax:(913)967-8849
Co. E-mail: customerservice@pryor.com
URL: http://www.pryor.com
Price: $149.00; $139.00 for groups of 5 or more. **Description:** Learn to communicate with confidence and credibility. **Locations:** Cities throughout the United States.

22126 ■ Resolving Conflict
Seminar Information Service, Inc.
20 Executive Park, Ste. 120
Irvine, CA 92614
Ph:(949)261-9104
Free: 877-SEM-INFO
Fax:(949)261-1963
Co. E-mail: info@seminarinformation.com
URL: http://www.seminarinformation.com
Price: $1,495.00 **Description:** Provide you with an understanding of the nature of conflict in organizations, key approaches to managing conflict, and an insight into your style of handling conflict and ways to enhance your conflict resolution effectiveness. **Locations:** New York, NY.

22127 ■ Responding to Conflict: Strategies for Improved Communication
American Management Association
600 AMA Way
Saranac Lake, NY 12983-5534
Ph:(212)586-8100
Free: 877-566-9441
Fax:(518)891-0368
Co. E-mail: customerservice@amanet.org
URL: http://www.amaseminars.org
Price: $2,345.00 for non-members; $2,095.00 for AMA members; and $1,794.00 for General Services Administration (GSA) members. **Description:** Covers effective communication, diffusing misunderstanding, creating open and honest work environments, dealing with conflict, and improving listening skills. **Locations:** Arlington, VA; Chicago, IL; Atlanta, GA; San Diego, CA; San Francisco, CA; and New York, NY.

22128 ■ Responding to Conflict: Strategies for Improved Communication (Canada)
Canadian Management Centre
150 York St., 5th Fl.
Toronto, ON, Canada M5H 3S5
Ph:(416)214-5678
Free: 877-262-2519
Fax:(416)214-6047
Co. E-mail: cmcinfo@cmctraining.org
URL: http://www.cmctraining.org
Price: $2,395.00 Canadian for non-members; $2,195.00 Canadian for CMC members. **Description:** Covers effective communication, diffusing misunderstanding, creating open and honest work environments, dealing with conflict, and improving listening skills. **Locations:** Toronto, ON.

22129 ■ Sensitivity Skills in Working with Others
Seminar Information Service, Inc.
20 Executive Park, Ste. 120
Irvine, CA 92614
Ph:(949)261-9104
Free: 877-SEM-INFO
Fax:(949)261-1963
Co. E-mail: info@seminarinformation.com
URL: http://www.seminarinformation.com
Price: $275.00 for MRA members; $370.00 for non-members. **Description:** Learn the difference between behaviors that are appropriate, inappropriate, and perhaps illegal, and improve skills in communicating across cultures. **Locations:** Waukesha, WI; and Palatine, IL.

22130 ■ Speak! Present! Influence! (Onsite)
Seminar Information Service, Inc.
20 Executive Park, Ste. 120
Irvine, CA 92614
Ph:(949)261-9104

Free: 877-SEM-INFO
Fax:(949)261-1963
Co. E-mail: info@seminarinformation.com
URL: http://www.seminarinformation.com
Price: $1,399.00. **Description:** Participants learn to overcome fear and relax under pressure; to become more dynamic and persuasive; to improve voice quality and speak without strain; to organize material for clear, effective delivery; and to make a personal connection with the audience. **Locations:** Cleveland, OH.

22131 ■ Speaking Skills for Professionals (Onsite)
Seminar Information Service, Inc.
20 Executive Park, Ste. 120
Irvine, CA 92614
Ph:(949)261-9104
Free: 877-SEM-INFO
Fax:(949)261-1963
Co. E-mail: info@seminarinformation.com
URL: http://www.seminarinformation.com
Price: $580.00 for non-members; $435.00 for The Management Association, Inc. members. **Description:** Learn the techniques and practices of expert speakers. Participants will learn how to gain people's attention, how to project an image of authority and competence, and how to speak with confidence. **Locations:** Waukesha, WI.

22132 ■ Strategies for Developing Effective Presentation Skills
American Management Association
600 AMA Way
Saranac Lake, NY 12983-5534
Ph:(212)586-8100
Free: 877-566-9441
Fax:(518)891-0368
Co. E-mail: customerservice@amanet.org
URL: http://www.amaseminars.org
Price: $2,195.00 for non-members; $1,995.00 for AMA members; and $1,708.00 for General Services Administration (GSA) members. **Description:** Covers overcoming stage fright, various types of presentations, developing a full presentation, and techniques for delivering a presentation, including answering questions and interacting with the audience. **Locations:** San Francisco, CA; Washington, DC; Atlanta, GA; Chicago, IL; and New York, NY.

22133 ■ Strategies of Effective Writing
EEI Communications
66 Canal Center Plz., Ste. 200
Alexandria, VA 22314
Ph:(703)683-7453
Free: 888-253-2762
Fax:(703)683-7310
Co. E-mail: train@eeicom.com
URL: http://www.eeicom.com/training
Price: $745.00. **Description:** Covers basic writing skills, including effective planning as a means of saving time, generating ideas, organizing ideas, writing concisely and clearly, and attracting and holding readers' interest. **Locations:** Alexandria, VA.

22134 ■ Strengthening Your People Skills in the Workplace
Padgett-Thompson Seminars
Rockhurst University CEC
14502 W. 105th St.
Lenexa, KS 66215
Free: 800-349-1935
URL: http://www.findaseminar.com/tpd/Padgett-Thompson-Seminars.asp
Price: $229.00. **Description:** A one-day workshop to gain the essential people skills needed to push your career ahead. **Locations:** Colorado Springs, CO; Albuquerque, NM; Salt Lake City, UT; Boise, ID.

22135 ■ Substantive Editing I
EEI Communications
66 Canal Center Plz., Ste. 200
Alexandria, VA 22314
Ph:(703)683-7453
Free: 888-253-2762
Fax:(703)683-7310
Co. E-mail: train@eeicom.com
URL: http://www.eeicom.com/training
Price: $745.00. **Description:** Covers editing for clarity and meaning, including reworking vague or inappropriate phrases, untangling muddled language, posing effective questions to the author, and revising with a purpose. **Locations:** Silver Spring, MD; and Alexandria, VA.

22136 ■ Successful Meeting Planning (Onsite)
American Management Association
600 AMA Way
Saranac Lake, NY 12983-5534
Ph:(212)586-8100
Free: 877-566-9441
Fax:(518)891-0368
Co. E-mail: customerservice@amanet.org
URL: http://www.amaseminars.org
Price: $1,545.00 for non-members; $1,395.00 for AMA members; and $1,195.00 for General Services Administration (GSA) members. **Description:** Covers all aspects of successfully planning a meeting, including objectives, budget, site selection, and working with vendors. **Locations:** Washington, DC; and New York, NY.

22137 ■ TechConnect (Onsite)
Seminar Information Service, Inc.
20 Executive Park, Ste. 120
Irvine, CA 92614
Ph:(949)261-9104
Free: 877-SEM-INFO
Fax:(949)261-1963
Co. E-mail: info@seminarinformation.com
URL: http://www.seminarinformation.com
Price: $1,399.00. **Description:** Learn how to put technical information into language a lay audience can understand, including how to organize information so it flows smoothly and leads to action and how to deliver information at the appropriate level of audience understanding and to be concise, to the point, and eliminate data dump. **Locations:** Cleveland, OH.

22138 ■ Technical Writing
EEI Communications
66 Canal Center Plz., Ste. 200
Alexandria, VA 22314
Ph:(703)683-7453
Free: 888-253-2762
Fax:(703)683-7310
Co. E-mail: train@eeicom.com
URL: http://www.eeicom.com/training
Price: $745.00. **Description:** Covers the technical writing process from analyzing an audience and developing a purpose to laying out a document with both text and graphics. **Locations:** Silver Spring, MD; and Alexandria, VA.

22139 ■ Training Difficult Issues in Diversity
Seminar Information Service, Inc.
20 Executive Park, Ste. 120
Irvine, CA 92614
Ph:(949)261-9104
Free: 877-SEM-INFO
Fax:(949)261-1963
Co. E-mail: info@seminarinformation.com
URL: http://www.seminarinformation.com
Price: $1,295.00. **Description:** Provides trainers with a step-by-step curriculum for delivering training and education on the tougher issues, including racism, privilege, religion, sexual orientation, gender identity, and oppression. Explore training techniques and models that get diversity messages across. **Locations:** New York, NY.

22140 ■ Webinars with a WOW Factor: Creating Memorable Meeting Across the Globe
Seminar Information Service, Inc.
20 Executive Park, Ste. 120
Irvine, CA 92614
Ph:(949)261-9104
Free: 877-SEM-INFO
Fax:(949)261-1963
Co. E-mail: info@seminarinformation.com
URL: http://www.seminarinformation.com
Price: $1,495.00. **Description:** Discover techniques that will make your material come to life on the screen and over the phone. **Locations:** Minneapolis, MN.

22141 ■ Writing Statements of Work: The Heart of Any Contract
Seminar Information Service, Inc.
20 Executive Park, Ste. 120
Irvine, CA 92614
Ph:(949)261-9104
Free: 877-SEM-INFO
Fax:(949)261-1963
Co. E-mail: info@seminarinformation.com
URL: http://www.seminarinformation.com
Price: $1,995.00. **Description:** Provides the essential information you'll need, including basic contract management concepts, to consistently develop and administer effective Statements of Work. **Locations:** Victoria, CN; Washington, DC; Atlanta, GA; Seattle, WA; Chicago, IL; Dallas, TX; and Morristown, NJ.

22142 ■ Writing for the Web II
EEI Communications
66 Canal Ctr. Plz., Ste. 200
Alexandria, VA 22314-5507
Ph:(703)683-7453
Free: 888-253-2762
Fax:(703)683-7310
Co. E-mail: train@eeicom.com
URL: http://www.eeicom.com/training
Price: $745.00. **Description:** Seminar for persons with 3-5 years' experience as a Web writer or editor, or have completed Writing for the Web I, covering how to define your genre and audience, develop a structure for your Web content, working with subject matter experts who aren't writers, making the most of your writing project, giving and getting feedback, writing links that work for your client, how to write menus so clients can use them, and recasting a print article for the Web. **Locations:** Silver Spring, MD; and Alexandria, VA.

22143 ■ XML Web Services
EEI Communications
66 Canal Center Plz., Ste. 200
Alexandria, VA 22314
Ph:(703)683-7453
Free: 888-253-2762
Fax:(703)683-7310
Co. E-mail: train@eeicom.com
URL: http://www.eeicom.com/training
Price: $1,065.00. **Description:** Learn how Web services can enhance your Web site and communication with other companies. **Locations:** Alexandria, VA.

REFERENCE WORKS

22144 ■ *10 Make-or-Break Career Moments: Navigate, Negotiate, and Communicate for Success*
Pub: Crown Business Books
Ed: Casey Hawley. **Released:** May 4, 2010. **Price:** $13.99. **Description:** Communication consultant, Casey Hawley, provides a guide to smart communication for any business setting.

22145 ■ *10 Steps to Successful Social Networking for Business*
Pub: American Society for Training and Development
Ed: Darin Hartley. **Released:** July 1, 2010. **Price:** $19.95. **Description:** Designed for today's fast-paced, need-it-yesterday business environment and for the thousands of workers who find themselves faced with new assignments, responsibilities, and requirements and too little time to learn what they must know.

22146 ■ *The 29 Percent Solution*
Pub: Greenleaf Book Group Press
Ed: Ivan Misner, Michele Donovan. **Released:** 2008. **Price:** $21.95. **Description:** It is true that some people are better connected than others. That means

that connecting is a skill that can be acquired. Networking skills used to increase business connections are highlighted.

22147 ■ "The 40-Year-Old Intern" in *Entrepreneur* (Vol. 37, October 2009, No. 10, pp. 90)
Pub: Entrepreneur Media, Inc.
Ed: Kristin Ladd. **Description:** Brian Kurth's VocationVacation is an internship program aimed at helping people experience their dream job. The website, launched in January 2004, matches people with businesses that allow them to experience their fantasy jobs.

22148 ■ "2010 American Business Woman of ABWA" in *Women In Business* (Vol. 61, October-November 2009, No. 5, pp. 22)
Pub: American Business Women's Association
Ed: Doris Brown. **Description:** Achievements of Doris Brown are presented in light of her being named as the 2010 American Business Woman of American Business Women's Association (ABWA). She specializes in the field of client and customer satisfaction for Avue Technologies. Brown believes that her involvement in the ABWA has helped her to see the importance of being a resource for other people.

22149 ■ "Ace Every Introduction" in *Women Entrepreneur* (September 10, 2008)
Pub: Entrepreneur Media Inc.
Ed: Cynthia McKay. **Description:** Making a powerful first impression is one of the most important marketing tools a business owner can possess. Advice about meeting new business contacts is given.

22150 ■ "All In Good Fun" in *Entrepreneur* (Vol. 36, May 2008, No. 5, pp. 22)
Pub: Entrepreneur Media, Inc.
Ed: Christopher Percy Collier. **Description:** According to a study conducted in 2007, humor in the workplace helps people communicate effectively and improves camaraderie. Company leaders and entrepreneurs can also tell humorous stories about themselves, but must also set lines that should not be crossed. The humorous atmosphere in the company YouSendIt is presented.

22151 ■ "All Those Applications, and Phone Users Just Want to Talk" in *Advertising Age* (Vol. 79, August 11, 2008, No. 31, pp. 18)
Pub: Crain Communications, Inc.
Ed: Mike Vorhaus. **Description:** Although consumers are slowly coming to text messaging and other data applications, a majority of those Americans surveyed stated that they simply want to use their cell phones to talk and do not care about other activities. Statistical data included.

22152 ■ "The Americans Are Coming" in *The Economist* (Vol. 390, January 3, 2009, No. 8612, pp. 44)
Pub: The Economist Newspaper Inc.
Description: Student recruitment consultancies, which help place international students at universities in other countries and offer services such as interpreting or translating guidelines, are discussed; American universities who have shunned these agencies in the past; the result has been that America underperforms in relation to its size with a mere 3.5 percent of students on its campuses that are from abroad.

22153 ■ "Anytime Access" in *Crain's Cleveland Business* (Vol. 28, October 22, 2007, No. 42, pp. 17)
Pub: Crain Communications, Inc.
Ed: Brad Dicken. **Description:** Technology continues to evolve in the competitive world of mobile communications in which the phone has become a sleek multitool that can take a call, send and e-mail, calculate the tip after dinner and snap a photograph.

22154 ■ "The Art and Business of Motivation Speaking: Your Guide" in *Inc.* (Volume 32, December 2010, No. 10, pp. 124)
Pub: Inc. Magazine
Ed: Leigh Buchanan. **Description:** Profile of Josh Shipp that discusses his career as a motivational speaker.

22155 ■ "The Art of Persuasion: How You Can Get the Edge You Need To Reach Every Goal" in *Small Business Opportunities* (November 2007)
Pub: Harris Publications Inc.
Ed: Paul Endress. **Description:** Expert in the field of psychology to business in the areas of communication, hiring and retention discusses a unique approach to solving business problems.

22156 ■ "Attorney Internet Marketing Services Launched by SEO Advantage at SEOLegal.com" in *Internet Wire* (October 5, 2009)
Pub: Comtex News Network, Inc.
Description: SEO Advantage, an Internet marketing and website designer firm, has extended its services to the legal industry.

22157 ■ *Awesomely Simple: Essential Business Strategies for Turning Ideas Into Action*
Pub: Jossey-Bass
Ed: John Spence. **Released:** September 8, 2009. **Price:** $24.95. **Description:** Six key strategies that create a foundation for achieving business excellence include: vivid vision, best people, a performance-oriented culture, robust communication, a sense of urgency, and extreme customer focus.

22158 ■ *Be a Brilliant Business Writer: Write Well, Write Fast, and Whip the Competition*
Pub: Crown Business Books
Ed: Jane Curry, Diana Young. **Released:** October 5, 2010. **Price:** $13.99. **Description:** Tools for mastering the art of persuasive writing in every document created, from email and client letters to reports and presentations, this book will help any writer convey their message with clarity and power, increase productivity by reducing rewrites, and provide the correct tone for navigating office politics.

22159 ■ "Blog Buzz Heralds Arrival of IPhone 2.0" in *Advertising Age* (Vol. 79, June 9, 2008, No. 40, pp. 8)
Pub: Crain Communications, Inc.
Ed: Abbey Klaasen. **Description:** Predictions concerning the next version of the iPhone include a global-positioning-system technology as well as a configuration to run on a faster, 3G network.

22160 ■ "Book Smart" in *Hawaii Business* (Vol. 53, December 2007, No. 6, pp. 39)
Pub: Hawaii Business Publishing
Ed: David K. Choo. **Description:** Different parts of a biography entry in the Black Book are examined in relation to their usage in starting a conversation with an executive. The second part, which is the educational background, is considered the most significant of all, due to the amount of information given. The importance of making connections in Hawaii is discussed.

22161 ■ "Bridging the Gap: Contextualing Professional Ethics in Collaborative Writing Projects" in *Business Communication Quarterly* (Dec.2007)
Pub: Sage Publications USA
Ed: J.A. Rice. **Description:** A classroom activity for business management students integrates ethical concepts with business writing strategies, while increasing understanding of writing ethics by emphasizing its rhetorical, contingent, and public nature.

22162 ■ "The Business Value of Social Networks" in *Agency Sales Magazine* (Vol. 39, July 2009, No. 7, pp. 44)
Pub: MANA
Ed: Daniel Burrus. **Description:** Personal and business uses of several Web 2.0 tools for salespeople are discussed. Leading questions which will guide salespeople in finding out if one particular tool will benefit them are presented.

22163 ■ "Can We Talk?" in *Canadian Business* (Vol. 79, September 11, 2006, No. 18, pp. 131)
Pub: Rogers Media
Ed: Sarah B. Hood. **Description:** The importance of informal communications and steps to build strong social networks within the organizations are discussed.

22164 ■ "Can You Hear Me Now?" in *Harvard Business Review* (Vol. 86, July-August 2008, No. 8, pp. 23)
Pub: Harvard Business School Press
Ed: Katharina Pick. **Description:** Tips for improving communication among boardroom members are presented. These include encouraging frankness via in-meeting leaders, and the ability of directors to meet without managers.

22165 ■ "Canadians Keep Memories in 'Inboxes' Instead of Shoe Boxes; MSN Canada" in *Canadian Corporate News* (May 14, 2007)
Pub: Comtex News Network Inc.
Description: According to an MSN Canada online poll, 76 percent of Canadians are creating 'virtual shoeboxes' with their email inboxes and archiving important messages, photos, and documents.

22166 ■ "Charlotte Pipe Launches Satirical Campaign" in *Contractor* (Vol. 57, January 2010, No. 1, pp. 6)
Pub: Penton Media, Inc.
Description: Charlotte Pipe and Foundry Co. launched an advertising campaign that uses social media and humor to make a point about how it can be nearly impossible to determine if imported cast iron pipes and fittings meet the same quality standards as what is made in the U.S. The campaign features 'pipe whisperers' and also spoofs pipe sniffing dogs.

22167 ■ *Common Sense Purchasing: Hard Knock Lessons Learned from a Purchasing Pro*
Pub: Booksurge, LLC
Ed: Tom DePaoli. **Released:** February 2004. **Price:** $9.99. **Description:** Guide to purchasing and negotiating deals.

22168 ■ "Competing for Jobs" in *Women In Business* (Vol. 63, Summer 2011, No. 2, pp. 37)
Pub: American Business Women's Association
Ed: Leigh Elmore. **Description:** Job hunting tips for women in the US in relation to generation demographic groups are presented. Effective communications and positive interactions are essential to career development. Generation groups' strengths and weaknesses as job seekers are also given.

22169 ■ "Conferencing Takes on High-Tech Futuristic Feel" in *Crain's Cleveland Business* (Vol. 28, October 29, 2007, No. 43, pp. 17)
Pub: Crain Communications, Inc.
Ed: Chuck Soder. **Description:** Overview of the newest technologies which are making local company's meetings more effective including: tele-presence, a videoconferencing technology, as well as virtual flip charts.

22170 ■ "Conversations with Customers" in *Business Journal Serving Greater Tampa Bay* (Vol. 31, December 31, 2010, No. 1, pp. 1)
Pub: Tampa Bay Business Journal
Description: Tampa Bay, Florida-based businesses have been using social media to interact with customers. Forty percent of businesses have been found to have at least one social media platform to reach customers and prospects.

22171 ■ "The Copyright Evolution" in *Information Today* (Vol. 28, November 2011, No. 10, pp. 1)
Pub: Information Today, Inc.
Ed: Nancy Davis Kho. **Description:** For information professionals, issues surrounding copyright compliance have traditionally been on the consumption side. However, today, content consumption is only half the program because blogging, tweeting, and commenting is a vital part of more standard duties for workers as corporations aim to create authentic communications with customers.

22172 ■ "Creative Marketing: How to Cultivate a Network of Endless Referrals" in *Agency Sales Magazine* (Vol. 39, July 2009, No. 7, pp. 38)
Pub: MANA
Ed: Bob Burg. **Description:** Tips on how a salesperson can build a network of people that will bring them referrals are presented. Asking a person about their business and re-introducing one's self to an earlier acquaintance while remembering their names are some elements in the process of building this network.

22173 ■ "Deals Still Get Done at Drake's Coq d'Or" in *Crain's Chicago Business* (Vol. 31, November 17, 2008, No. 46, pp. 35)
Pub: Crain Communications, Inc.
Ed: Shia Kapos. **Description:** Chicago's infamous Coq d'Or, a restaurant and lounge located at the Drake Hotel, is still a favorite establishment for noted executives but the eatery is now trying to cater to younger professionals through marketing and offering new beverages that appeal to that demographic. Many find it the perfect environment in which to close deals, relax or network.

22174 ■ "Does Rudeness Really Matter?" in *Academy of Management Journal* (October 2007, pp. 1181)
Pub: Academy of Management
Ed: Christine L. Porath, Amir Erez. **Description:** Study assessing the effect of impoliteness on performance and helpfulness showed rude behavior lowered performance levels and also decreased attitude of helpfulness.

22175 ■ "The Don't Do Lists" in *Inc.* (Vol. 33, October 2011, No. 8, pp. 65)
Pub: Inc. Magazine
Ed: Jennifer Alsever, Adam Bluestein. **Description:** Ten business leaders and experts share their don't do lists, the things that should be avoided when going on sales calls, planning business lunches, motivating employees and more are presented.

22176 ■ "Don't Leave Employees on the Outside Looking In" in *Canadian Business* (Vol. 83, July 20, 2010, No. 11-12, pp. 13)
Pub: Rogers Media Ltd.
Ed: Richard Branson. **Description:** Managers should be careful with employee's tendencies to use the word 'they' when problems occur since this shows that employees are not associating themselves with their company. Employees should be involved in the development of the company and improving the flow of information is important in overcoming this communication challenge.

22177 ■ "Drive Traffic To Your Blog" in *Women Entrepreneur* (January 13, 2009)
Pub: Entrepreneur Media Inc.
Ed: Lesley Spencer Pyle. **Description:** Internet social networking has become a vital component to marketing one's business. Tips are provided on how to establish a blog that will attract attention to one's business and keep one's customers coming back for more.

22178 ■ *e-Riches 2.0: Next-Generation Marketing Strategies for Making Million Online*
Pub: AMACOM
Ed: Scott Fox. **Released:** May 27, 2009. **Price:** $25.00. **Description:** Beginner's guide to using the Internet to help grow business, including the best ways to use email lists and newsletters, RSS feeds, online viral marketing, social networking, microblogging, online video and radio/podcasts, tele-seminars and webinars, search engine keyword advertising and affiliate program advertising.

22179 ■ *Electronic Commerce*
Pub: Course Technology
Ed: Gary Schneider, Bryant Chrzan, Charles McCormick. **Released:** May 1, 2010. **Price:** $117.95. **Description:** E-commerce can open the door to more opportunities than ever before for small business. Packed with real-world examples and cases, the book delivers comprehensive coverage of emerging online technologies and trends and their influence on the electronic marketplace. It details how the landscape of online commerce is evolving, reflecting changes in the economy and how business and society are responding to those changes. Balancing technological issues with the strategic business aspects of successful e-commerce, the new edition includes expanded coverage of international issues, social networking, mobile commerce, Web 2.0 technologies, and updates on spam, phishing, and identity theft.

22180 ■ "Elemental Nabs $5.5 Million" in *The Business Journal-Portland* (Vol. 25, July 18, 2008, No. 19, pp. 1)
Pub: American City Business Journals, Inc.
Ed: Aliza Earnshaw. **Description:** Elemental Technologies Inc., a Portland, Oregon-based software company got $5.5 million in new funding, bringing its total invested capital to $7.1 million in nine months since October 2008. The company plans to launch Badaboom, software for converting video into various formats, later in 2008.

22181 ■ *Emerging Business Online: Global Markets and the Power of B2B Internet Marketing*
Pub: FT Press
Ed: Lara Fawzy, Lucas Dworksi. **Released:** October 1, 2010. **Price:** $49.99. **Description:** An introduction into ebocube (emerging business online), a comprehensive proven business model for Internet B2B marketing in emerging markets.

22182 ■ "Empire of Pixels" in *Entrepreneur* (Vol. 37, September 2009, No. 9, pp. 50)
Pub: Entrepreneur Media, Inc.
Ed: Jason Daley. **Description:** Entrepreneur Jack Levin has successfully grown Imageshack, an image-hosting Web service. The Website currently gets 50 million unique visitors a month. Levin has launched Y-Frog, an application that uses Imageshack to allow Twitter users to add images to their posts.

22183 ■ "Entrepreneur Column" in *Entrepreneur* (September 24, 2009)
Pub: Entrepreneur Media, Inc.
Ed: Allen Moon. **Description:** In an attempt to compete with Google, Microsoft and Yahoo have entered a partnership to merge their search services; advice on the best ways to get noticed on this new search engine entitled Bing, is provided.

22184 ■ "Etiquette, Common Sense Often Lag Behind Smarter Devices" in *Crain's Cleveland Business* (Vol. 28, October 22, 2007, No. 42, pp. 21)
Pub: Crain Communications, Inc.
Ed: Chrissy Kadleck. **Description:** Discusses the importance of good etiquette in regards to electronic communication both within as well as outside the business world.

22185 ■ "Extreme Negotiations" in *Harvard Business Review* (Vol. 88, November 2010, No. 11, pp. 66)
Pub: Harvard Business School Publishing
Ed: Jeff Weiss, Aram Donigian, Jonathan Hughes. **Description:** Examination of military negotiation skills that are applicable in business situations. Skills include soliciting others' perspectives, developing and proposing multiple solutions, and inviting others to assess them.

22186 ■ "Facebook: A Promotional Budget's Best Friend" in *Women Entrepreneur* (February 1, 2009)
Pub: Entrepreneur Media Inc.
Ed: Tamara Monosoff. **Description:** Facebook began as a social networking website but has become a valuable marketing tool for all types of businesses, organizations and causes. Tips are provided for creating a Facebook account and growing one's network on Facebook.

22187 ■ *The Facebook Effect: The Inside Story of the Company That Is Connecting the World*
Pub: Simon & Shuster
Ed: David Kirkpatrick. **Released:** June 8, 2010. **Price:** $26.00. **Description:** There's never been a Website like Facebook: more than 350 million people have accounts, and if the growth rate continues, by 2013 every Internet user worldwide will have his or her own page. No one's had more access to the inner workings of the phenomenon than Kirkpatrick, a senior tech writer at Fortune magazine. Written with the full cooperation of founder Mark Zuckerberg, the book follows the company from its genesis in a Harvard dorm room through its successes over Friendster and MySpace, the expansion of the user base, and Zuckerberg's refusal to sell.

22188 ■ *The Facebook Era: Tapping Online Social Networks to Build Better Products, Reach New Audiences, and Sell More Stuff*
Pub: Prentice Hall
Ed: Clara Shih. **Price:** $24.99. **Description:** The '90s were about the World Wide Web of information and the power of linking Web pages. Today it's about the World Wide Web of people and the power of the social graph. Online social networks are fundamentally changing the way we live, work, and interact. They offer businesses immense opportunities to transform customer relationships for profit: opportunities that touch virtually every business function, from sales and marketing to recruiting, collaboration to executive decision-making, product development to innovation.

22189 ■ "Fast Fact: Women's Online Habits" in *Marketing to Women* (Vol. 22, July 2009, No. 7, pp. 1)
Pub: EPM Communications, Inc.
Description: Lists the Internet habits of women. Statistical data included.

22190 ■ "Faster and Shorter" in *Canadian Business* (Vol. 81, October 13, 2008, No. 17, pp. 25)
Pub: Rogers Media Ltd.
Ed: Terri Goveia. **Description:** Study revealed that instant messaging (IM) technologies are slowly becoming legitimate in the corporate world. IM is traditionally considered as a distraction, but it was found to let workers make targeted inquiries that gives them what they need in an instant. Other views and information about IMs is included.

22191 ■ *Fierce Conversations*
Pub: Berkley Trade
Ed: Susan Scott. **Released:** January 6, 2004. **Price:** $15.00. **Description:** Seven Principles of Fierce Conversations are addressed to help readers become effective conversationalists in both business and social settings.

22192 ■ "Five Steps to an Effective Business Call" in *Hawaii Business* (Vol. 53, October 2007, No. 4, pp. 64)
Pub: Hawaii Business Publishing
Ed: Matthew K. Ing. **Description:** University of Hawaii professor Libda Patrylak believes that communication skills are integral to business success, which is why businesses should know how to properly handle phone conversations. Presented are five ways of achieving effective business phone calls, such as setting rules for employees to follow with regards to answering calls and providing undivided attention to the other speaker.

22193 ■ "Five Things" in *Hawaii Business* (Vol. 53, November 2007, No. 5, pp. 20)
Pub: Hawaii Business Publishing
Ed: Jason Ubay. **Description:** Discusses products that are allowed to be carried on board airplane flights by business travelers.

22194 ■ "Five Tips for New Managers" in *Hawaii Business* (Vol. 53, November 2007, No. 5, pp. 59)
Pub: Hawaii Business Publishing
Ed: Jason Ubay. **Description:** New managers should remember to know what their roles are, learn from others, build an infrastructure according to the customer's needs, communicate professionally and have consideration.

22195 ■ *The Game-Changer: How Every Leader Can Drive Everyday Innovation*
Pub: Crown Business
Ed: A.G. Lafley, Ram Charan. **Price:** $27.50. **Description:** Management guru Charan and Proctor & Gamble CEO Lafley provide lessons to encourage in-

novation at all levels, including how to hire for and encourage an environment of communication and tangible work processes.

22196 ■ "Get on the Green" in *Entrepreneur* (Vol. 35, November 2007, No. 11, pp. 44)
Pub: Entrepreneur Media Inc.
Ed: James Park. **Description:** Golf is a sport where business people are provided with a casual atmosphere where they can open a conversation regarding business topics. Details on how spending time on the course provides a good environment for business discussions.

22197 ■ "Get Online or Be Left Behind" in *Women In Business* (Vol. 61, August-September 2009, No. 4, pp. 33)
Pub: American Business Women's Association
Ed: Diane Stafford. **Description:** Technology's significance for the connectivity purposes among business people is discussed. Details on the use of wireless tools and online social media to boost technology IQ are presented.

22198 ■ "Get Personal" in *Entrepreneur* (Vol. 36, April 2008, No. 4)
Pub: Entrepreneur Media, Inc.
Ed: Romanus Wolter. **Description:** Customers appreciate personal contact, and communicating with them can help business owners' customer relations. Some ways on how to keep a personal touch with customers and improve business dealings include blending technology with personal interaction and knowing what the customers want. Other tips are provided.

22199 ■ "Getting Drowned Out by the Brainstorm" in *Canadian Business* (Vol. 83, June 15, 2010, No. 10, pp. 91)
Pub: Rogers Media Ltd.
Ed: Joe Castaldo. **Description:** A study reveals that people generate more ideas when they do it alone rather than as part of a brainstorming group. The limited range of ideas is due to the fixation of group members on the first idea that gets offered.

22200 ■ "Getting Inventive With...Richard Brindisi and Gregory Vittardi" in *Crain's Cleveland Business* (Vol. 28, October 22, 2007, No. 42)
Pub: Crain Communications, Inc.
Ed: Kimberly Bonvissuto. **Description:** Profile of the SmartShopper, a handheld, voice-recognition device for dictating shopping and errand lists, and its creators, Richard G. Brindisi and Gregory Vittardi.

22201 ■ *Getting More: How to Negotiate to Achieve Your Goals in the Real World*
Pub: Crown Business Books
Ed: Stuart Diamond. **Released:** December 28, 2010. **Price:** $26.00. **Description:** When negotiating, people fail to meet their goals due to focusing on power and the 'win-win' instead of on relationships and perceptions, thus not finding enough things to trade. They think others should be rational when they are dealing with emotions and they get distracted from the real goal.

22202 ■ *Getting to Yes: Negotiating Agreement Without Giving In*
Pub: Penguin Books (USA) Incorporated
Ed: Roger Fisher, William L. Ury, Bruce Patton. **Released:** December 1991. **Price:** $15.00. **Description:** Strategies for negotiating mutually acceptable agreements in all types of conflict.

22203 ■ *The Golden 120 Seconds of Every Sales Call: A Fresh Innovative Look at the Sales Process*
Pub: NorlightsPress.com
Ed: Peter G. Dennis. **Released:** October 28, 2009. **Price:** $15.95. **Description:** Salespeople who want to find their personal style, gain confidence, and avoid deal-killing mistakes must read this book. It will show both new and experienced sales professionals how to use key fundamentals with every call, every selling interaction, and every opportunity to make something happen. Anyone who sells for a living has experienced the magic moments that can make or break a sales. Advice is given to help recognize, and learn to cultivate, this vital part of the sales process.

22204 ■ "Grooming Your Online Persona" in *Women In Business* (Vol. 62, June 2010, No. 2, pp. 36)
Pub: American Business Women's Association
Ed: Diane Stafford. **Description:** Employees' use of online social networks could become a basis on how their employers, clients, or business partners would judge them. Personal details, pictures and other online data should be filtered to avoid inappropriate or uncomfortable situations and distinguish personal from professional or work life.

22205 ■ *Groundswell: Winning in a World Transformed by Social Technologies*
Pub: Harvard Business School Press
Ed: Charlene Li, Josh Bernoff. **Released:** 2008. **Price:** $29.95. **Description:** Corporate executives are struggling with a new trend: people using online social technologies (blogs, social networking sites, YouTube, podcasts) to discuss products and companies, write their own news, and find their own deals.

22206 ■ *Groups in Context: Leadership and Participation in Small Groups*
Pub: McGraw-Hill Companies
Ed: Gerald L. Wilson. **Released:** June 2004. **Price:** $62.98. **Description:** Small group communication skills for the workplace, in churches, social groups, or civic organizations.

22207 ■ *Guide to Business Information on Central and Eastern Europe*
Pub: Taylor and Francis Group Ltd
Contact: Tania Koon, Author
Released: Latest edition June, 2000. **Price:** $75, individuals hardback. **Covers:** Twelve countries of Central and Eastern Europe. **Entries Include:** Country overview; current developments; company name, address, phone, fax; names and titles of key personnel; industries and services; legislation; and organizations.

22208 ■ *Guide to Business Information on Russia, the NIS, and the Baltic States*
Pub: Taylor and Francis Group Ltd
Contact: Tania Koon, Author
Released: Latest edition November, 2000. **Price:** $45, individuals. **Covers:** Fifteen countries of Russia, the NIS, and the Baltic States. **Entries Include:** Current developments; company name, address, phone, fax; industries and services; legislation; and organizations.

22209 ■ "Harlequin Leads the Way" in *Marketing to Women* (Vol. 22, July 2009, No. 7, pp. 1)
Pub: EPM Communications, Inc.
Description: Although the publishing industry has been slow to embrace new media options, the Internet is now a primary source for reaching women readers. Harlequin has been eager to court their female consumers over the Internet and often uses women bloggers in their campaigns strategies.

22210 ■ "Help for Job Seekers" in *Crain's Detroit Business* (Vol. 26, January 18, 2010, No. 3, pp. 14)
Pub: Crain Communications, Inc.
Description: CareerWorks is aimed at helping those who are in career transition or are looking for new jobs; this weekly collection of news, advertising and information includes weekly stories, events and the highlighting of a person who has successfully made the transition from one profession to another. On the Website, readers are welcome to post an anonymous resume in order to attract employers.

22211 ■ *High Trust Selling: Make More Money, in Less Time, with Less Stress*
Pub: Nelson Business
Ed: Todd Duncan. **Released:** April 2007. **Price:** $14.99. **Description:** Laws governing salesmanship are divided into two sections. The first deals with attitudes, aptitudes, and abilities required for successful selling; the second with communication, courtship, camaraderie and commitments between salespeople and their clients.

22212 ■ "Holidays Should Foster Mutual Respect" in *Women In Business* (Vol. 61, October-November 2009, No. 5, pp. 33)
Pub: American Business Women's Association
Ed: Diane Stafford. **Description:** Workplaces have modified the way year-end holiday celebrations are held in an effort to promote mutual respect. The workers' varying religious beliefs, political affiliations, and other differences have brought about the modifications. The importance of developing mutual understanding is emphasized as a mechanism to stimulate successful business ties.

22213 ■ "How Anger Poisons Decision Making" in *Harvard Business Review* (Vol. 88, September 2010, No. 9, pp. 26)
Pub: Harvard Business School Publishing
Ed: Jennifer S. Lerner, Katherine Shonk. **Description:** Importance of accountability in mitigating the negative effects of anger on the decision making process is stressed.

22214 ■ "How to Do the Business Dinner" in *Business Owner* (Vol. 35, March-April 2011, No. 2, pp. 7)
Pub: DL Perkins Company
Description: Dining with others, whether client of employee, it is important to use this as an opportunity to develop relationships. Tips are given to help make the best of a dining experience are provided.

22215 ■ "How the Generation Gap Can Hurt Your Business" in *Agency Sales Magazine* (Vol. 39, November 2009, No. 10, pp. 16)
Pub: MANA
Ed: Jack Foster. **Description:** Now that there are four generations of people in the workplace, there is a need to add flexibility to communications for independent manufacturers representatives. Managers can encourage the younger generations to do the research and the boomers to process information and let each side report to the other.

22216 ■ *How to Make Money with Social Media: Using New and Emerging Media to Grow Your Business*
Pub: FT Press
Ed: Jamie Turner, Reshma Shah. **Released:** October 1, 2010. **Price:** $24.99. **Description:** Marketers, executives, entrepreneurs are shown more effective ways to utilize Internet social media to make money. This guide brings together both practical strategies and proven execution techniques for driving maximum value from social media marketing.

22217 ■ "How to Make Your Website Really Sell" in *Entrepreneur* (Vol. 37, September 2009, No. 9, pp. 79)
Pub: Entrepreneur Media, Inc.
Ed: David Port. **Description:** Advice on how to succeed in Internet marketing is presented. Offering visitors purchase incentives on the home page is encouraged. Delivery of customized landing pages and content is also recommended.

22218 ■ "How Not to Build a Website" in *Women Entrepreneur* (December 24, 2008)
Pub: Entrepreneur Media Inc.
Ed: Erica Ruback; Joanie Reisen. **Description:** Tips for producing a unique and functional Website are given as well as a number of lessons a pair of entrepreneurs learned while trying to launch their networking website, MomSpace.com.

22219 ■ "How Pixar Fosters Collective Creativity" in *Harvard Business Review* (Vol. 86, September 2008, No. 9, pp. 64)
Pub: Harvard Business School Press
Ed: Ed Catmull. **Description:** Pixar Animation Studios illustrates peer-culture methods for fostering product development. These include allowing any employee to communicate with any other employee, providing a safe environment for new ideas, and watching the academic community closely for innovations.

22220 ■ "How to Plan and Execute Effective Sales Meetings" in *Agency Sales Magazine* (Vol. 39, August 2009, No. 8, pp. 8)
Pub: MANA
Ed: Jack Foster. **Description:** Basic guide to successful representative-manufacturer sales meetings based on effective planning is presented. The representative and the manufacturer will reap the benefits of a productive meeting only when they both focus on what's going to transpire before, during and after the event. Insights from industry players are also presented.

22221 ■ "HR Tech on the Go" in *Workforce Management* (Vol. 88, November 16, 2009, No. 12, pp. 1)
Pub: Crain Communications, Inc.
Ed: Ed Frauenheim. **Description:** Examination of the necessity of mobile access of human resources software applications that allow managers to recruit, schedule and train employees via their mobile devices; some industry leaders believe that mobile HR applications are vital while others see this new technology as hype.

22222 ■ "Hunter and the Hunted" in *Canadian Business* (Vol. 81, Summer 2008, No. 9, pp. 12)
Pub: Rogers Media Ltd.
Ed: Thomas Watson. **Description:** Brian Hunter, a partner in oil and gas engineering firm Montane Resources, invested his life savings in Vancouver-based Canacord Capital Corp. Details of the asset-backed commercial paper fiasco and Hunter's use of Facebook to encourage other investors to participate in his claim against the mortgage company are presented.

22223 ■ "I Can Make Your Brain Look Like Mine" in *Harvard Business Review* (Vol. 88, December 2010, No. 12, pp. 32)
Pub: Harvard Business School Publishing
Description: Psychology professor Uri Hasson discusses findings that the brain waves of a speaker and a listener become similar as the listener's comprehension increases.

22224 ■ "Ideas at Work: Total Communicator" in *Business Strategy Review* (Vol. 21, Autumn 2010, No. 3, pp. 10)
Pub: Blackwell Publishers Ltd.
Ed: Stuart Crainer. **Description:** Vittorio Colao has been chief executive of Vodafone Group for two years. He brings to the company special experience as CEO of RCS MediaGroup in Milan, which publishes newspapers, magazines and books in Italy, Spain and France. Prior to RCS, he held other positions within Vodaphone. Colao shares his views on business, the global economy and leading Vodafone.

22225 ■ *If You Have to Cry, Go Outside: And Other Things Your Mother Never Told You*
Pub: HarperOne
Ed: Kelly Cutrone. **Released:** February 2, 2010. **Price:** $22.99. **Description:** Women's mentor advices on how to make it in one of the most competitive industries in the world, fashion. She has kicked people out of fashion shows, forced some of reality television's shiny start to fire their friends, and built her own company which is one of the most powerful public relations firms in the fashion business.

22226 ■ *I'm on LinkedIn - Now What? (Second Edition): A Guide to Getting the Most Out of LinkedIn*
Pub: Happy About
Ed: Diane Danielson. **Released:** January 7, 2009. **Price:** $19.95. **Description:** Designed to help get the most out of LinkedIn, the popular business networking site and follows the first edition and includes the latest and great approaches using LinkedIn. With over 32 million members there is a lot of potential to find and develop relationships to help in your business and personal life, but many professionals find themselves wondering what to do once they sign up. This book explains the different benefits of the system and recommends best practices (including LinkedIn Groups) so that you get the most out of LinkedIn.

22227 ■ "The 'In-Crowd' Online: Professionals Take Networking To New Levels" in *Black Enterprise* (Vol. 38, January 2008, No. 6, pp. 47)
Pub: Earl G. Graves Publishing Co. Inc.
Ed: Alwin A.D. Jones. **Description:** The Internet is providing new ways for professionals to network with others. New sites like LinkedIn.com provide entrepreneurs with access to others with a business life similar to theirs.

22228 ■ "In the Know?" in *Entrepreneur* (Vol. 37, July 2009, No. 7, pp. 30)
Pub: Entrepreneur Media, Inc.
Ed: Brad Feld. **Description:** Tips on what entrepreneurs should and should not share with their venture capitalists (VCs) are given. Entrepreneurs must be transparent with their VCs, but they should not bombard VCs with too many details. The aspect of a business that a VC is concerned with varies from one VC to another, and it is important that entrepreneurs understand the best way to communicate with their VC.

22229 ■ *Information Technology for the Small Business: How to Make IT Work For Your Company*
Pub: TAB Computer Systems, Incorporated
Ed: T.J. Benoit. **Released:** June 2006. **Price:** $17. 95. **Description:** Basics of information technology to help small companies maximize benefits are covered. Topics include pitfalls to avoid, email and Internet use, data backup, recovery and overall IT organization.

22230 ■ "Integrating Business Core Knowledge through Upper Division Report Composition" in *Business Communication Quarterly* (December 2007)
Pub: Sage Publications USA
Ed: Joy Roach, Daniel Tracy, Kay Durden. **Description:** An assignment that integrates subjects and encourages the use of business communication report-writing skills is presented. This assignment is designed to complement business school curricula and help develop critical thinking and organizational skills.

22231 ■ "Internet Marketing 2.0: Closing the Online Chat Gap" in *Agent's Sales Journal* (November 2009, pp. 14)
Pub: Summit Business Media
Ed: Jeff Denenholz. **Description:** Advice regarding the implementation of an Internet marketing strategy for insurance agencies includes how and why to incorporate a chat feature in which a sales agent can communicate in real-time with potential or existing customers. It is important to understand if appropriate response mechanisms are in place to convert leads into actual sales.

22232 ■ "An Introvert's Guide to Schmoozing" in *Canadian Business* (Vol. 83, July 20, 2010, No. 11-12, pp. 73)
Pub: Rogers Media Ltd.
Ed: Jasmine Budak. **Description:** Writer Nancy Ankowitz says that introverts seem to get grouped with social misfits but introverts are people who recharge by spending time alone. Ankowitz advises introverts to use their strengths in quiet strengths such as writing and listening as well as learning to speak in public.

22233 ■ "IPhone 3G" in *Advertising Age* (Vol. 79, November 17, 2008, No. 43, pp. 15)
Pub: Crain Communications, Inc.
Ed: Beth Snyder Bulik. **Description:** Review of Apple's new iPhone 3G which includes the addition of smart-phone applications as well as a price drop; the new functionalities as well as the lower price seems to be paying off for Apple who reported sales of 6.9 million iPhones in its most recent quarter, in which the 3G hit store shelves.

22234 ■ "Is It Time to Ban Swearing at Work?" in *HR Specialist* (Vol. 8, September 2010, No. 9, pp. 2)
Pub: Capitol Information Group Inc.
Description: Screening software has been developed to identify profanity used in business correspondence.

22235 ■ "Israeli Spam Law May Have Global Impact" in *Information Today* (Vol. 26, February 2009, No. 2, pp. 28)
Pub: Information Today, Inc.
Ed: David Mirchin. **Description:** Israels new law, called Amendment 40 of the Communications Law, will regulate commercial solicitations including those sent without permission via email, fax, automatic phone dialing systems, or short messaging technologies.

22236 ■ "It's Not About You" in *Entrepreneur* (Vol. 35, November 2007, No. 11, pp. 102)
Pub: Entrepreneur Media Inc.
Ed: Barry Farber. **Description:** Companies should focus on the customers' need and show them that they care about them. Listening to and learning about your customers can make selling easier; tips on how to stay focused on the customers' needs are outlined.

22237 ■ *It's Not Just Who You Know: Transform Your Life (and Your Organization) by Turning Colleagues and Contacts into Lasting Relationships*
Pub: Crown Business Books
Ed: Tommy Spaulding. **Released:** August 10, 2010. **Price:** $23.00. **Description:** Tommy Spaulding teaches the reader how to reach out to others in order to create lasting relationships that go beyond superficial contacts.

22238 ■ *It's Not Who You Know - It's Who Knows You!: The Small Business Guide to Raising Your Profits by Raising Your Profile*
Pub: John Wiley & Sons, Inc.
Ed: David Avrin. **Released:** November 9, 2010. **Price:** $24.95. **Description:** When it comes to promoting a small business or a brand, it is essential to know how valuable high-profile attention can be. But for most small companies, the cost of hiring an outside firm to increase attention can be too expensive.

22239 ■ "Jay Berkowitz to Present Making Social Media Money Seminar at Affiliate Summit West" in *Entertainment Close-Up* (January 15, 2010)
Pub: Close-Up Media
Description: Highlights of Jay Berkowitz's conference, "Making Social Media Make Money" include ways in which to develop Internet marketing strategies that will maximize Website traffic and convert that traffic to sales.

22240 ■ "Just Shut The Hell Up" in *Canadian Business* (Vol. 81, July 22, 2008, No. 12-13, pp. 33)
Pub: Rogers Media Ltd.
Ed: Jane Bao. **Description:** Employees desire better communication as opposed to more communication from their managers. Advice regarding managing communication in the workplace is given including ways in which speakers can say more with fewer words.

22241 ■ "Keep Them Posted" in *Entrepreneur* (Vol. 35, October 2007, No. 10, pp. 39)
Pub: Entrepreneur Media Inc.
Ed: Gwen Moran. **Description:** Survey by the Pew Internet and American Life Project found that 12 million American adults maintain blogs, which are created for personal and business reasons. Blogs are effective in giving a business a personal touch while informing the public about its operations and products. Tips on how to create an effective business blog are presented.

22242 ■ "Keys to Overcome Fear of Follow-Up" in *Agency Sales Magazine* (Vol. 39, December 2009, No. 11, pp. 26)
Pub: MANA
Ed: Judy Garmaise. **Description:** In order to be more successful at making follow-up calls, salespeople should not take rejection personally and never assume that they are going to annoy prospects if they follow-up. Those that follow-up with prospects stand out among others since few salespeople do this.

22243 ■ *The Language of Success: Business Writing That Informs, Persuades, and Gets Results*
Pub: AMACOM

Ed: Tom Sant. **Released:** January 2008. **Price:** $15. 00. **Description:** The damage that can be done when words are used ineffectively and the power to be gained when they are used well in business.

22244 ■ "Learning by Doing: Engaging Students through Learner-Centered Activities" in *Business Communication Quarterly* (Dec. 2007, pp. 451)
Pub: Sage Publications USA

Ed: Karl L. Smart, Nancy Csapo. **Description:** Active learning techniques, such as the Puzzle Brain Spark activity, allow students to engage in learning activities that allow deeper thinking, critical thinking, and problem solving ability that develop business management skills.

22245 ■ "Lessons Learned from Instructional Design Theory" in *Business Communication Quarterly* (December 2007, pp. 414)
Pub: Sage Publications USA

Ed: Lisa A. Burke. **Description:** Instructors should present course information to business students in a way that enhances understanding and should use presentation techniques that students may eventually use; course materials should be kept relevant and simple.

22246 ■ *Liespotting: Proven Techniques to Detect Deception*
Pub: St. Martins Press/Macmillan

Ed: Pamela Meyer. **Released:** July 20, 2010. **Price:** $24.99. **Description:** Liespotting links three disciplines: facial recognition training, interrogation training, and a comprehensive survey of research in the field - into a specialized body of information developed specifically to help business leaders detect deception and get the information they need to successfully conduct their most important interactions and transactions.

22247 ■ *Life's a Game So Fix the Odds: How to Be More Persuasive and Influential in Your Personal and Business*
Pub: John Wiley & Sons, Incorporated

Ed: Philip Hesketh. **Released:** September 2005. **Price:** $24.95 (US), $31.00 (Canadian). **Description:** Seven psychological reasons behind why and how people are persuaded and how to use these reasons to your advantage in both your personal and business life.

22248 ■ "Like Being There" in *Canadian Business* (Vol. 79, August 14, 2006, No. 16-17, pp. 77)
Pub: Rogers Media

Ed: Gerry Blackwell. **Description:** Latest video conferencing facilities at the Halo Collaboration Studio, are discussed.

22249 ■ "Lines of Communication" in *Entrepreneur* (Vol. 37, October 2009, No. 10, pp. 80)
Pub: Entrepreneur Media, Inc.

Ed: Brad Feld. **Description:** Entrepreneurial companies should establish a clear and open communication culture between their management teams and their venture capital backers. Chief executive officers should trust their leadership teams when it comes to communicating with venture capitalists.

22250 ■ "Listen Up: There's a Revolution in the Cubicle" in *Barron's* (Vol. 89, July 27, 2009, No. 30, pp. 18)
Pub: Dow Jones & Co., Inc.

Ed: Jay Palmer. **Description:** Plantronics will be among the first beneficiaries when the unified communications revolution arrives in the office. Plantronics' shares could rise to around 30 in 2009 from the 20s as of July 2009. Unified communications could create a huge new multimillion-dollar market for Plantronics.

22251 ■ "Local Knowledge" in *Hawaii Business* (Vol. 53, December 2007, No. 6, pp. 40)
Pub: Hawaii Business Publishing

Ed: David K. Choo. **Description:** Rules and facts business professionals need to know about the local life in Hawaii are presented. The important components in island life include knowledge Hawaiian high schools' histories and image, the local sports scene, special events, potluck ethics, and locals' favorite destination, which is Las Vegas.

22252 ■ "Looking Out for the Little Guys" in *Black Enterprise* (Vol. 38, October 2007, No. 3, pp. 58)
Pub: Earl G. Graves Publishing Co. Inc.

Ed: Kaylyn Kendall Dines. **Description:** Biz Tech-Connect is a Web portal that offers free online and social networking, along with four modules that help small businesses with marketing and advertising, communications and mobility, financial management, and customer relationship management.

22253 ■ *Made to Stick: Why Some Ideas Survive and Others Die*
Pub: Doubleday Broadway Publishing Group

Ed: Chip Heath; Dan Heath. **Released:** January 2, 2007. **Price:** $26.00. **Description:** Entertaining, practical guide to effective business communication; information is derived form psychosocial studies on memory, emotion and motivation.

22254 ■ "Making Diverse Teams Click" in *Harvard Business Review* (Vol. 86, July-August 2008, No. 8, pp. 20)
Pub: Harvard Business School Press

Ed: Jeffrey T. Polzer. **Description:** 360-degree feedback to increase the efficacy of diverse-member workplace teams, which involves each member providing feedback to the others on the team is discussed.

22255 ■ "Managing Corporate Social Networks" in *Harvard Business Review* (Vol. 86, July-August 2008, No. 8, pp. 26)
Pub: Harvard Business School Press

Ed: Adam M. Kleinbaum; Michael L. Tushman. **Description:** Tips on how to promote business creativity and foster knowledge building through business social networks are given.

22256 ■ "Managing the Facebookers; Business" in *The Economist* (Vol. 390, January 3, 2009, No. 8612, pp. 10)
Pub: Economist Newspaper Ltd.

Description: According to a report from PricewaterhouseCoopers, a business consultancy, workers from Generation Y, also known as the Net Generation, are more difficult to recruit and integrate into companies that practice traditional business acumen. 61 percent of chief executive managers say that they have trouble with younger employees who tend to be more narcissistic and more interested in personal fulfillment with a need for frequent feedback and an over-precise set of objectives on the path to promotion which can be hard for managers who are used to a different relationship with their subordinates. Older bosses should prepare to make some concessions to their younger talent since some of the issues that make them happy include cheaper online ways to communicate and additional coaching, both of which are good for business.

22257 ■ "Marketers Push for Mobile Tuesday as the New Black Friday" in *Advertising Age* (Vol. 79, December 1, 2008, No. 44, pp. 21)
Pub: Crain Communications, Inc.

Ed: Natalie Zmuda. **Description:** Marketers are using an innovative approach in an attempt to stimulate business on the Tuesday following Thanksgiving by utilizing consumer's cell phones to alert them of sales or present them with coupons for this typically slow retail business day; with this campaign both advertisers and retailers are hoping to start Mobile Tuesday, another profitable shopping day in line with Black Friday and Cyber Monday.

22258 ■ *Marketing 2.0: Bridging the Gap between Seller and Buyer through Social Media Marketing*
Pub: Wheatmark

Ed: Bernie Borges. **Released:** July 14, 2009. **Price:** $22.95. **Description:** Winning strategies to attract people to your company and your employees using social media site on the Internet are outlined.

22259 ■ "Marketing Scholarship 2.0" in *Journal of Marketing* (Vol. 75, July 2011, No. 4, pp. 225)
Pub: American Marketing Association

Ed: Richard J. Lutz. **Description:** A study of the implications of changing environment and newer collaborative models for marketing knowledge production and dissemination is presented. Crowdsourcing has become a frequently employed strategy in industry. Academic researchers should collaborate more as well as the academe and industry, to make sure that important problems are being investigated.

22260 ■ *Mastering Business Negotiation*
Pub: Jossey Bass

Ed: Roy J. Lewicki; Alexander Hiam. **Released:** July 21, 2006. **Price:** $24.95. **Description:** Resource guide for any manager requiring practical strategies and ideas for negotiating in business; the book shows how to understand the game to better control the situation, predict the sequence of negotiations, identify tactics of others, and to apply the rules of the game.

22261 ■ *Mastering Business Negotiation: A Working Guide to Making Deals and Resolving Conflict*
Pub: Jossey-Bass Publishers

Ed: Roy J. Lewicki; Alexander Hiam. **Released:** July 21, 2006. **Price:** $24.95. **Description:** Provides extensive insight into practical strategies and ideas for conducting business negotiations.

22262 ■ *Masters of Sales: Secrets from Top Sales Professionals That Will Transform You Into a World Class Salesman*
Pub: Entrepreneur Press

Ed: Ivan R. Misner; Don Morgan. **Released:** August 15, 2007. **Price:** $19.95. **Description:** Eighty successful salespeople share insight into selling.

22263 ■ *MBA In a Day*
Pub: John Wiley and Sons, Inc.

Ed: Steven Stralser, PhD. **Released:** 2004. **Price:** $34.95. **Description:** Management professor presents important concepts, business topics and strategies that can be used by anyone to manage a small business or professional practice. Topics covered include: human resources and personal interaction, ethics and leadership skills, fair negotiation tactics, basic business accounting practices, project management, and the fundamentals of economics and marketing.

22264 ■ "Meetings Go Virtual" in *HRMagazine* (Vol. 54, January 2009, No. 1, pp. 74)
Pub: Society for Human Resource Management

Ed: Elizabeth Agnvall. **Description:** Microsoft Office Live Meeting conferencing software allows companies to schedule meetings from various company locations, thus saving travel costs.

22265 ■ "Mobile Security for Business V5" in *SC Magazine* (Vol. 20, August 2009, No. 8, pp. 55)
Pub: Haymarket Media, Inc.

Description: Review of F-Secure's Mobile Security for Business v5 which offers protection for business smartphones that can be centralized for protection monitoring by IT administrators.

22266 ■ "The Mobile Workforce Revolution" in *Canadian Business* (Vol. 81, March 31, 2008, No. 5, pp. 28)
Pub: Rogers Media

Ed: Diane Horton. **Description:** Diane Horton explains how a mobile workforce helps companies cut costs, increase productivity, and boost employee motivation. Horton says that employees believe they usually become more productive by 15 to 30 percent after their companies go mobile.

22267 ■ "More Power to Your Presentation" in *Business Strategy Review* (Vol. 21, Spring 2010, No. 1, pp. 50)
Pub: Wiley-Blackwell
Ed: Roly Grimshaw. **Description:** You might wonder what similarities there can be between a Russian oligarch and an entrepreneur. When it comes to persuading people to invest, there are plenty.

22268 ■ "Mosaid Grants First Wireless Parent License To Matsushita" in *Canadian Electronics* (Vol. 23, June-July 2008, No. 5, pp. 1)
Pub: Action Communication Inc.
Description: Matsushita Electric Industrial Co. Ltd. has been granted a six-and-a-half-year license by Mosaid Technologies Inc. to manufacture the latter's products. The patent portfolio license agreement covers Mosaid's Wi-Fi, Wi-Max, CDMA-enabled notebook computers and other products.

22269 ■ "'Mr. CEO, Please Do Elaborate On Your Firm's Metrics'" in *Business Courier* (Vol. 24, February 29, 2008, No. 47, pp. 1)
Pub: American City Business Journals, Inc.
Ed: Jon Newberry. **Description:** Discusses a rogue caller who goes by the name of Joe Herrick, Steven Nissan and Joe Harris has joined in over a dozen conference calls, asking chief executive officers on their plans and commenting on the companies' operations. The mystery caller attempts to pass himself off as a financial analyst. Transcripts of some conference calls, in which the rogue caller is involved, are provided.

22270 ■ "Negotiating Muscle" in *Black Enterprise* (Vol. 38, February 2008, No. 7, pp. 70)
Pub: Earl G. Graves Publishing Co. Inc.
Ed: Sonia Alleyne. **Description:** Negotiating historically has been a barrier for women in business, the book, "Ask For It: How Women Can Use the Power of Negotiation to Get What They Really Want" helps professional females identify and create great business opportunities.

22271 ■ "Net Profits: Get a Social Life" in *Entrepreneur* (Vol. 35, October 2007, No. 10, pp. 140)
Pub: Entrepreneur Media Inc.
Ed: Amanda C. Kooser. **Description:** Social networking sites such as Facebook and MySpace have millions of users, a sign that social networking is a growing industry. One way to enter this industry is target marketing, like Med3Q, a site for health-conscious individuals had done. How Med3q is earning through online advertising and sponsors is explained.

22272 ■ "Networking Web Sites: a Two-Edged Sword" in *Contractor* (Vol. 56, October 2009, No. 10, pp. 52)
Pub: Penton Media, Inc.
Ed: H. Kent Craig. **Description:** People need to be careful about the information that they share on social networking Web sites. They should realize that future bosses, coworkers, and those that might want to hire them might read those information. Posting on these sites can cost career opportunities and respect.

22273 ■ "The New Guard" in *Entrepreneur* (Vol. 36, February 2008, No. 2, pp. 46)
Pub: Entrepreneur Media Inc.
Ed: Amanda C. Kooser. **Description:** A natural language search engine is being developed by Powerset for better online searching. Zannel Inc. offers Instant Media Messaging platform, which allows for social networking using phones. Ning is an online platform that allows users to customize and control their social networks.

22274 ■ "New Sprint Phone Whets Appetite for Applications" in *The Business Journal-Serving Metropolitan Kansas City* (Vol. 26, July 25, 2008)
Pub: American City Business Journals, Inc.
Ed: Suzanna Stagemeyer. **Description:** Firms supporting the applications of the new Samsung Instinct, which was introduced by Sprint Nextel Corp. in June 2008, have reported usage rates increase for their products. Handmark, whose mobile services Pocket Express comes loaded with Instinct, has redirected employees to meet the rising demand for the services. Other views and information on Instinct, are presented.

22275 ■ "The Next Big Thing" in *Farm Industry News* (Vol. 42, January 1, 2009, No. 1)
Pub: Penton Media, Inc.
Ed: David Hest. **Description:** Communication technology that allows farmers to detect equipment location, travel speed and real-time fuel and sprayer/combine tank levels will pay off with better machine use efficiency, improved maintenance and reduced downtime. These telemetry systems will be widely available in the next few years.

22276 ■ "The Next Generation of Bluetooth Headsets" in *Inc.* (Vol. 31, January-February 2009, No. 1, pp. 41)
Pub: Mansueto Ventures LLC
Ed: Mark Spoonauer. **Description:** Information on the latest Bluetooth headsets that allow users to talk hands-free and the new technology that blocks ambient sounds is given. Aliph Jawbone, Plantronics Voyager Jabra BT530, and Motorola Motopure H15 are profiled.

22277 ■ "'No Snitch' Culture in American Business" in *Business Owner* (Vol. 35, September-October 2011, No. 5, pp. 7)
Pub: DL Perkins Company
Description: It is important to make known the fact that a businessman is performing unethical or illegal activities in his firm.

22278 ■ "Nortel Makes Customers Stars in New Campaign" in *Brandweek* (Vol. 49, April 21, 2008, No. 16, pp. 8)
Pub: VNU Business Media, Inc.
Ed: Mike Beirne. **Description:** Nortel has launched a new television advertising campaign in which the business-to-business communications technology provider cast senior executives in 30-second TV case studies that show how Nortel's technology helped their businesses innovate.

22279 ■ "Not Your Dad's Business Card" in *Small Business Opportunities* (July 2008)
Pub: Entrepreneur Media Inc.
Ed: Rob Schlacter. **Description:** Provides tips on how to effectively design and use business cards.

22280 ■ "Office Party Attire" in *Women In Business* (Vol. 61, October-November 2009, No. 5, pp. 27)
Pub: American Business Women's Association
Ed: Leigh Elmore. **Description:** Office holiday party attire should conform to factors such as time, location, scheduled events, and other company-furnished details. Observing this guideline can help in upholding the business nature of the party. Party attendees are also encouraged to network with other attendees, while tips on how to behave during the party are also presented.

22281 ■ "Oh, Behave!" in *Entrepreneur* (Vol. 36, April 2008, No. 4, pp. 87)
Pub: Entrepreneur Media, Inc.
Ed: Gwen Moran. **Description:** Online social networks can pose awkward situations for users. These include instances such as getting a link request from someone you do not know, having a contact post embarrassing information on your site, and a contact asking you to be refer him to one of your business contacts. Tips on how to deal with these situations are discussed.

22282 ■ "On Beyond Powerpoint: Presentations Get a Wake-Up Call" in *Inc.* (November 2007, pp. 58-59)
Pub: Gruner & Jahr USA Publishing
Ed: Michael Fitzgerald. **Description:** New software that allows business presentations to be shared online are profiled, including ProfCast, audio podcasts for sales, marketing, and training; SmartDraw2008, software that creates professional graphics; Dimdim, an open-Web conferencing tool; Empressr, a hosted Web service for creating, managing, and sharing multimedia presentations; Zentation, a free tool that allows users to watch slides and a videos of presenter; Spresent, a Web-based presentation tool for remote offices or conference calls.

22283 ■ "The One Thing You Must Get Right When Building a Brand" in *Harvard Business Review* (Vol. 88, December 2010, No. 12, pp. 80)
Pub: Harvard Business School Publishing
Ed: Patrick Barwise, Sean Meehan. **Description:** Four uses for new media include: communicating a clearly defined customer promise, creating trust via delivering on the promise, regularly improving on the promise, and innovating past what is familiar.

22284 ■ "Online Postings Really Influence Older Women" in *Marketing to Women* (Vol. 22, July 2009, No. 7, pp. 8)
Pub: EPM Communications, Inc.
Description: Women over the age of 55 are more likely to be swayed to purchase a product by referrals from others, including Online postings by strangers. Another key influence is associated with the brand's ability to address their lifestyle needs.

22285 ■ *Open Source Solutions for Small Business Problems*
Pub: Charles River Media
Ed: John Locke. **Released:** May 2004. **Price:** $35. 95. **Description:** Open source software provides solutions to many small business problems such as tracking electronic documents, scheduling, accounting functions, managing contact lists, and reducing spam.

22286 ■ *The Orange Revolution*
Pub: Free Press
Ed: Adrian Gostick, Chester Elton. **Released:** September 21, 2010. **Price:** $25.00. **Description:** Based on a 350,000-person study by the Best Companies Group, as well as research into exceptional teams at leading companies, including Zappos.com, Pepsi Beverages Company, and Madison Square Garden, the authors have determined a key set of characteristics displayed by members of breakthrough teams, and have identified a set of rules great teams live by, which generate a culture of positive teamwork and led to extraordinary results. Using specific stories from the teams they studied, they reveal in detail how these teams operate and how managers can transform their own teams into such high performers by fostering: stronger clarity of goals, greater trust among team members, more open and honest dialogue, stronger accountability for all team members, and purpose-based recognition of team member contributions.

22287 ■ "Ordering Pizza Hut From Your Facebook Page?" in *Advertising Age* (Vol. 79, November 10, 2008, No. 42, pp. 50)
Pub: Crain Communications, Inc.
Ed: Emily Bryson York. **Description:** Fast-food chains are experimenting with delivery/takeout services via social networks such as Facebook and iPhone applications. This also allows the chains to build valuable databases of their customers.

22288 ■ "OtherInbox Ready for Revenue: Software Startup Expects Profits in '09" in *Austin Business JournalInc.* (Vol. 28, January 2, 2009)
Pub: American City Business Journals
Ed: Christopher Calnan. **Description:** Founder of Austin, Texas-based OtherBox Inc. expects the company to generate revenue through subscriptions and advertising and also reach profitability in 2009. The company's email management tool sends secondary mail to an alternate location thereby freeing up the work inbox for more urgent messages.

22289 ■ "Our Gadget of the Week: Business Buddy" in *Barron's* (Vol. 88, July 7, 2008, No. 27, pp. 26)
Pub: Dow Jones & Co., Inc.
Ed: Jay Palmer. **Description:** Review and evaluation of the Lenovo X300 laptop computer which offers executives a variety of features despite its smaller

size and weight. The laptop is about 0.73 inch thick, comes with a 64-gigabyte solid-state drive from Samsung, and weighs less than three pounds.

22290 ■ "Our Gadget of the Week: Mostly, I Liked It" in *Barron's* (Vol. 88, July 14, 2008, No. 28, pp. 31)
Pub: Dow Jones & Co., Inc.
Ed: Jay Palmer. **Description:** Review of the Apple iPhone 3G, which costs $199, has better audio and is slightly thicker than its predecessor; using the 3G wireless connection makes going online faster but drains the battery faster too.

22291 ■ *Outsourcing: Information Technology, Original Equipment Manufacturer, Leo, Oursourcing, Offshoring Research Network, Crowdsourcing*
Pub: General Books LLC
Released: May 1, 2010. **Price:** $14.14. **Description:** Chapters include information for outsourcing firms and how to maintain an outsourcing business.

22292 ■ *The Owners Manual for Small Business*
Pub: Planning Shop
Ed: Rhonda Abrams. **Released:** December 2005. **Price:** $19.95. **Description:** Reference book offering tips for starting a small business, low-cost marketing, and communicating effectively.

22293 ■ "PDAs Are Great - As Long As You Can Find Them" in *Crain's Chicago Business* (Vol. 31, May 5, 2008, No. 18, pp. 41)
Pub: Crain Communications, Inc.
Ed: Jennifer Olvera. **Description:** Discusses a new service from Global Lost & Found Inc. in which after paying a one-time fee, customers receive a label with an identification number and a toll free phone number so if they lose a gadget such as a cell phone, PDA or laptop the finder can return the device and are rewarded with a gift card.

22294 ■ "People Often Trust Eloquence More Than Honesty" in *Harvard Business Review* (Vol. 88, November 2010, No. 11, pp. 36)
Pub: Harvard Business School Publishing
Ed: Todd Rogers, Michael I. Norton. **Description:** The article shows how deftly side-stepping a question in an eloquent manner generates a more positive response in an audience than does a direct answer that is ineffectively delivered. Implications for both politics and business are discussed.

22295 ■ *Persuasive Business Proposals*
Pub: AMACOM
Ed: Tom Sant. **Released:** December 2003. **Price:** $17.95. **Description:** Writing to win more customers, clients, and contracts.

22296 ■ "Pet-Food Industry Too Slow" in *Advertising Age* (Vol. 78, March 26, 2007, No. 13, pp. 29)
Pub: Crain Communications, Inc.
Ed: Description: Many crisis-communications experts believe that the pet-food industry mishandled the problem by waiting almost a month to recall the 60 million "wet-food" products after numerous consumer complaints. Experts site that the first 24 to 49 hours are the most important in dealing with a crisis of this nature.

22297 ■ "Pioneering Strategies for Entrepreneurial Success" in *Business Horizons* (Vol. 51, January-February 2008, No. 1, pp. 21)
Pub: Elsevier Advanced Technology Publications
Ed: Candida G. Brush. **Description:** Entrepreneurs are known for new products, services, processes, markets and industries. In order to achieve success, they have to develop a clear vision, creatively manage finances, and use social skills to persuade others to commit to the venture. Pioneering strategies and their implementation are examined.

22298 ■ *The Power of Body Language*
Pub: Simon & Schuster Inc.
Ed: Tonya Reiman. **Released:** 2008. **Price:** $15.00. **Description:** Body language expert describes the hidden meaning behind specific gestures, facial cues, stances, and body movements to help anyone communicate in business.

22299 ■ *The Power of Nice: How to Conquer the Business World with Kindness*
Pub: Doubleday
Ed: Linda Kaplan Thaler; Robin Koval. **Released:** September 19, 2006. **Price:** $17.95. **Description:** The key principles to running a business through thoughtfulness and kindness are exhibited with the use of success stories.

22300 ■ *The Power of a Positive No: How to Say No and Still Get to Yes*
Pub: Random Housing Publishing Group
Ed: William Ury. **Released:** December 2007. **Price:** $16.00. **Description:** According to the author, a positive no begins with yes and ends with yes.

22301 ■ *PPC's Guide to Small Business Consulting Engagements*
Pub: Practitioners Publishing Company
Released: March 2004. **Price:** $226.00. **Description:** Technical guide for conducting consulting engagements for small business.

22302 ■ "Pressed for Time" in *Marketing to Women* (Vol. 21, March 2008, No. 3, pp. 1)
Pub: EPM Communications, Inc.
Description: Statistical data concerning the tools women use for time management which include gadgets as well as traditional media such as calendars.

22303 ■ "Rapport Overhaul" in *Small Business Opportunities* (Winter 2009)
Pub: Entrepreneur Media Inc.
Ed: Laurie Brown. **Description:** Advice concerning ways in which to build customer rapport is provided.

22304 ■ *Reading Financial Reports for Dummies*
Pub: John Wiley and Sons, Inc.
Ed: Lita Epstein. **Released:** January 2009. **Price:** $21.99. **Description:** This second edition contains more new and updated information, including new information on the separate accounting and financial reporting standards for private/small businesses versus public/large businesses; updated information reflecting 2007 laws on international financial reporting standards; new content to match SEC and other governmental regulatory changes over the last three years; new information about how the analyst-corporate connection has changed the playing field; the impact of corporate communications and new technologies; new examples that reflect the current trends; and updated Websites and resources.

22305 ■ "Real-Time Computer-Mediated Communication" in *Business Communication Quarterly* (December 2007, pp. 466)
Pub: Sage Publications USA
Ed: Amy Newman. **Description:** Technology-based simulation for business students to respond to emails and instant messages is presented. The simulation allows students to handle volume business correspondence at work with organizational context and under real-word business situations.

22306 ■ "Reinventing Your Rep Training Program" in *Agency Sales Magazine* (Vol. 39, August 2009, No. 8, pp. 40)
Pub: MANA
Description: Tips on how to encourage manufacturer's representatives to attend scheduled training sessions are given. Manufacturers should learn the value of keeping the training program up-to-date and communicate with the sales team to know what needs to be revamped. Problems faced by representatives with inside sales staff should also be addressed by the manufacturer.

22307 ■ "Relationship "Farming" Tools" in *Agency Sales Magazine* (Vol. 39, August 2009, No. 8, pp. 46)
Pub: MANA
Ed: Terry L. Brock. **Description:** Manufacturer's representatives should spend time, money and effort in establishing and maintaining relationships; one tool to help is the new Fujitsu S1500 scanner. The scanner can accomplish critical tasks, quickly, easily and at low cost. Other suggestions to help build better business relationships are given.

22308 ■ "Research and Markets Adds Report: The U.S. Mobile Web Market" in *Entertainment Close-Up* (December 10, 2009)
Pub: Close-Up Media
Description: Highlights of the new Research and Markets report "The U.S. Mobile Web Market: Taking Advantage of the iPhone Phenomenon" include: mobile Internet marketing strategies; the growth of mobile web usage; the growth of revenue in the mobile web market; and a look at Internet business communications, social media and networking.

22309 ■ "Rethinking the Organization" in *Strategy & Leadership* (Vol. 38, September-October 2010, No. 5, pp. 13-19)
Pub: Emerald Inc.
Ed: Stephen Denning. **Description:** A study identifies the changes needed to be adopted by top managers to achieve game-changing innovation at an organization-wide level. Findings indicate that CEOs should practice pull management in order to nurture fruitful communication between employees and customers and achieve organizational involvement of customers.

22310 ■ "Rise Interactive, Internet Marketing Agency, Now Offers Social Media Training and Advisory Services" in *Internet Wire* (Nov. 4, 2009)
Pub: Comtex News Network, Inc.
Description: Profile of Rise Interactive, a full-service Internet marketing agency which has recently added social media to its list of offerings; the agency touts that its newest service gives their clients the power to have ongoing communication with current and potential customers on the sites they are most actively visiting.

22311 ■ "The Rise of Pompei" in *Retail Merchandiser* (Vol. 51, September-October 2011, No. 5, pp. 13)
Pub: Phoenix Media Corporation
Description: Soho creative consulting group follows its C3 philosophy to create an invigorated brand experience that transforms customers from consumers to empowered buyers. Pompei AD is a leading creative consultancy that specializes in design and branding for retail, museum, hospitality, and other sectors.

22312 ■ "Rule of Thumb" in *Entrepreneur* (Vol. 36, May 2008, No. 5, pp. 44)
Pub: Entrepreneur Media, Inc.
Ed: Guy Kawasaki. **Description:** Business presentations using PowerPoint are recommended to have no more than 10 slides, last no longer than 20 minutes and have font no smaller than 30 points. Topics covered should include problem, solution, business model, underlying technology, and projections among others.

22313 ■ "Rumor Has It" in *Entrepreneur* (Vol. 35, October 2007, No. 10, pp. 30)
Pub: Entrepreneur Media Inc.
Ed: Chris Penttila. **Description:** Some entrepreneurs like Ren Moulton and Dan Scudder regard rumor sites and product blogs as great sources of market research. However, there are legal issues that must be studied before using these Internet sites in marketing and product development. The use and limitations of rumor sites and product blogs are provided.

22314 ■ "The Rypple Effect; Performance Management" in *The Economist* (Vol. 390, January 3, 2009, No. 8612, pp. 48)
Pub: The Economist Newspaper Inc.
Description: New companies such as Rypple, a new, web-based service, claim that they can satisfy the Net Generation's need for frequent assessments while easing the burden this creates for management.

22315 ■ "Sales Communications in a Mobile World" in *Business Communication Quarterly* (December 2007, pp. 492)
Pub: Sage Publications USA
Ed: Daniel T. Norris. **Description:** Salespeople can take advantage of the latest mobile technologies while maintaining a personal touch with clients and

customers through innovation, formality in interactions, client interactions, and protection and security of mobile data.

22316 ■ "Saving Face Time" in *Canadian Business* (Vol. 81, December 8, 2008, No. 21, pp. 21)
Pub: Rogers Media Ltd.
Ed: Calvin Leung. **Description:** Landing business deals in China requires fostering informal relationships as well as avoiding offensive gestures. Canadians planning to do business in China should be aware of the Chinese concept of 'face'. Other tips for doing business in China are listed.

22317 ■ *The Savvy Gal's Guide to Online Networking (Or What Would Jane Austen Do?)*
Pub: Booklocker.com Inc.
Ed: Diane K. Daneilson, Lindsey Pollak. **Released:** August 10, 2007. **Price:** $14.95. **Description:** It is a truth universally acknowledged that a woman in search of a fabulous career must be in want of networking opportunities. Or so Jane Austen would say if she were writing, or more likely, blogging today. So begins the must-read guide to networking in the 21st Century. Authors and networking experts share the nuts, bolts and savvy secrets that businesswomen need in order to use technology to build professional relationships.

22318 ■ *The Savvy Girl's Guide to Online Networking (Or What Would Jane Austen Do?)*
Pub: Booklocker.com Inc.
Ed: Diane K. Danielson; Lindsey Pollak. **Released:** August 10, 2007. **Price:** $14.95. **Description:** The book offers tips, tactics and etiquette for businesswomen wishing to build professional relationships via email, online networks, blogs, and message boards.

22319 ■ *Say Everything: How Blogging Began, What It's Becoming, and Why It Matters*
Pub: Crown Business
Ed: Scott Rosenberg. **Released:** 2009. **Price:** $26. 00. **Description:** A history of Internet blogs that explains how they started and why they matter to any small business.

22320 ■ "Say Goodbye to Shy" in *Canadian Business* (Vol. 79, September 11, 2006, No. 18, pp. 125)
Pub: Rogers Media
Ed: Alex Mlynek. **Description:** Tips and practices for effective communications at workplaces are presented.

22321 ■ "Say Goodbye to Voicemail" in *Agency Sales Magazine* (Vol. 39, November 2009, No. 10, pp. 3)
Pub: MANA
Description: Salespeople should think twice before leaving a voicemail. The emerging modern etiquette is to send a text message or to e-mail the customer or client. Communication suggestions for both salespeople and their principals are presented.

22322 ■ "Scientific American Builds Novel Blog Network" in *Information Today* (Vol. 28, September 2011, No. 8, pp. 12)
Pub: Information Today, Inc.
Ed: Kurt Schiller. **Description:** Scientific American launched a new blog network that joins a diverse lineup of bloggers cover various scientific topics under one banner. The blog network includes 60 bloggers providing insights into the ever-changing world of science and technology.

22323 ■ "The Secret Strategy for Meaningful Sales Meetings" in *Agency Sales Magazine* (Vol. 39, December 2009, No. 11, pp. 40)
Pub: MANA
Ed: Dave Kahle. **Description:** Sales meetings can be made more meaningful by focusing on the end results that the meeting seeks to achieve. Describing the changed behavior that is sought from the sales force and working backwards from there also help make a sales meeting more meaningful.

22324 ■ "Secrets To Trade Show Success" in *Women Entrepreneur* (September 12, 2008)
Pub: Entrepreneur Media Inc.
Ed: Lesley Spencer Pyle. **Description:** Trade shows require an enormous amount of work, but they are an investment that can pay off handsomely because they allow a business to get their product or service in front of their target market. Advice regarding trade shows is given including selecting the correct venue, researching the affair and following up on leads obtained at the event.

22325 ■ "Shoestring-Budget Marketing" in *Women Entrepreneur* (January 5, 2009)
Pub: Entrepreneur Media Inc.
Ed: Maria Falconer. **Description:** Pay-per-click search engine advertising is the traditional type of e-marketing that may not only be too expensive for certain kinds of businesses but also may not attract the quality customer base a business looking to grow needs to find. Social networking websites have become a mandatory marketing tool for business owners who want to see growth in their sales; tips are provided for utilizing these networking websites in order to gain more visibility on the Internet which can, in turn, lead to the more sales.

22326 ■ "Six Tips To Maximize Networking Opportunities" in *Women Entrepreneur* (November 3, 2008)
Pub: Entrepreneur Media Inc.
Ed: Tamara Monosoff. **Description:** Networking events fall into the realm of business development as opposed to immediate sales opportunities. It is important to remember that these events provide a chance to build relationships that may someday help one's business. Tips to help make the most out of networking events are provided.

22327 ■ "Size Matters" in *Entrepreneur* (Vol. 36, April 2008, No. 4, pp. 44)
Pub: Entrepreneur Media, Inc.
Ed: Robert Kiyosaki. **Description:** Entrepreneurs planning to expand their business face challenges when it comes to employing more people and addressing internal relationships, communications and procedures. People skills, organizational skills and leadership skills are some of the things to consider before adding employees.

22328 ■ "Slow but Steady into the Future" in *Barron's* (Vol. 88, July 7, 2008, No. 27, pp. M)
Pub: Dow Jones & Co., Inc.
Ed: Mark Veverka. **Description:** Investors are advised to maintain their watch on the shares of business software company NetSuite. The company's chief executive officer, Zach Nelson, claims that the company has a 10-year lead on its competitors with the development of software-as-a service.

22329 ■ *The Social Media Bible: Tactics, Tools, and Strategies for Business Success*
Pub: John Wiley & Sons, Inc.
Ed: Lon Safko, David Brake. **Released:** June 17, 2009. **Price:** $29.95. **Description:** Information is given to build or transform a business into social media, where customers, employees, and prospects connect, collaborate, and champion products and services in order to increase sales and to beat the competition.

22330 ■ "Social Media: Communicate the Important Stuff" in *Agency Sales Magazine* (Vol. 39, November 2009, No. 10, pp. 52)
Pub: MANA
Ed: Jack Foster. **Description:** Social media such as Twitter or Facebook allows businesses to communicate with their customers over great distances but this technology can take away from the personal touch. For those that want to implement these tools in their marketing plans, they should first find out which social media networks their target audience use and give their customers reasons to become fans.

22331 ■ "Social Media, E-Mail Remain Challenging for Employees" in *Workforce Management* (Vol. 88, December 14, 2009, No. 13, pp. 4)
Pub: Crain Communications, Inc.
Ed: Ed Frauenheim. **Description:** Examining the impact of Internet social networking and the workplace; due to the power of these new technologies, it is important that companies begin to set clear policies regarding Internet use and employee privacy.

22332 ■ "Social Networkers for Hire" in *Black Enterprise* (Vol. 40, December 2009, No. 5, pp. 56)
Pub: Earl G. Graves Publishing Co., Inc.
Ed: Brittany Hutson. **Description:** Companies are utilizing social networking sites in order to market their brand and personally connect with consumers and are increasingly looking to social media specialists to help with this task. Aliya S. King is one such web strategist, working for ICED Media by managing their Twitter, Facebook, YouTube and Flickr accounts for one of their publicly traded restaurant clients.

22333 ■ "Social Networking Butterfly" in *Entrepreneur* (Vol. 37, September 2009, No. 9, pp. 48)
Pub: Entrepreneur Media, Inc.
Ed: Jason Daley. **Description:** Entrepreneur Ashley Qualls has successfully grown Whateverlife.com. The site was originally created to share Qualls' custom MySpace.com templates with friends and family. Qualls is planning to redesign the site as a social network focused on Web design.

22334 ■ "Social Networking Site for Moms" in *Marketing to Women* (Vol. 21, March 2008, No. 3, pp. 3)
Pub: EPM Communications, Inc.
Description: The Cradle is a social networking site devoted to pregnancy and new parenthood.

22335 ■ "Social Networks in the Workplace" in *Strategy & Leadership* (Vol. 38, July-August 2010, No. 4, pp. 50-53)
Pub: Emerald Inc.
Ed: Daniel Burrus. **Description:** The opinions of futurist Daniel Burrus on a novel trend called 'Business 2.0', which involves the use of social networking applications as business tools, are presented. His suggestion that personal social networking technology can be used by businesses to improve collaboration, problem solving, and leadership communications to achieve continuous value innovation is discussed.

22336 ■ "Sometimes, Second Impressions Count Most" in *Canadian Business* (Vol. 83, October 12, 2010, No. 17, pp. 11)
Pub: Rogers Media Ltd.
Ed: Richard Branson. **Description:** Developing a favorable impression at the first point of contact is imperative for businesses. Managers who want their organizations to make positive first and second impressions need to learn to balance the Web's labor-saving efficiencies with human assistants. The importance of considering the customer relations value in company Websites is also explained.

22337 ■ "Sound Check" in *Agency Sales Magazine* (Vol. 39, August 2009, No. 8, pp. 14)
Pub: MANA
Ed: Dave Kahle. **Description:** Most customers believe salespersons are unable to do well in terms of listening, which is one of the four fundamental competencies of a sales person. Listening is the primary tool to uncover deeper and more powerful needs and motivations of the customer. A guide on how to listen better and improve listening effectiveness is presented.

22338 ■ "Speak Better: Five Tips for Polished Presentations" in *Women Entrepreneur* (September 19, 2008)
Pub: Entrepreneur Media Inc.
Ed: Suzannah Baum. **Description:** Successful entrepreneurs agree that exemplary public speaking skills are among the core techniques needed to propel their business forward. A well-delivered presentation can result in securing a new distribution channel, gaining new customers, locking into a new referral stream or receiving extra funding.

22339 ■ *The Speed of Trust*
Pub: Simon & Schuster, Inc.
Ed: Stephen M.R. Covey with Rebecca R. Merrill. **Description:** Advice is given to help cultivate trust in business, politics and personal relationships.

22340 ■ "Spell It Out" in *Entrepreneur* (Vol. 36, April 2008, No. 4, pp. 123)
Pub: Entrepreneur Media, Inc.
Ed: Emily Weisberg. **Description:** IM:It is an apparel and accessories company that markets products with instant messaging (IM) acronyms and emoticons. Examples of these are "LOL" and "GTG". Other details on IM:It products are discussed.

22341 ■ *Start Your Own Blogging Business, Second Edition*
Pub: Entrepreneur Press
Released: July 1, 2010. **Price:** $17.95. **Description:** Interviews with professional bloggers from some of the most popular blogs on the Internet will help anyone interested in starting their own blogging business.

22342 ■ "Staying Engaged" in *Black Enterprise* (Vol. 38, February 2008, No. 7, pp. 64)
Pub: Earl G. Graves Publishing Co. Inc.
Ed: Sonia Alleyne. **Description:** Rules to help business leaders construct networking contacts in order to maximize professional success are outlined.

22343 ■ "Study: Instant Messaging Can Benefit Workplaces" in *HRMagazine* (Vol. 53, August 2008, No. 8, pp. 20)
Pub: Society for Human Resource Management
Description: Using text messaging at work is less, not more disruptive, even as it promotes more frequent communication, according to a study published in the Journal of Compute-Mediated Communication.

22344 ■ "Stylish Successes" in *Women In Business* (Vol. 61, October-November 2009, No. 5, pp. 12)
Pub: American Business Women's Association
Ed: Leigh Elmore; Megan L. Reese. **Description:** Amanda Horan Kennedy, Angela Samuels, Barbara Nast Saletan, and Patty Nast Canton are career women who ventured into entrepreneurship. They are deemed to possess networking and teamwork skills that ensured their success in the garment industry.

22345 ■ "Sunbrella Engages Consumers Via Social Media" in *Home Textiles Today* (Vol. 31, May 24, 2011, No. 13, pp. 4)
Pub: Reed Business Information
Description: Performance fabric brand Sunbrella is marketing to social media, such as Facebook and Twitter, in order to boost consumer interest and retailer support.

22346 ■ *Table Talk: The Savvy Girl's Alternative to Networking*
Pub: AuthorHouse
Ed: Diane Danielson. **Released:** April 1, 2003. **Price:** $17.50. **Description:** Let's face it. Women and men are different. So why should we all have to network in the same way? And, why should women have to 'network' at all? Between family and work responsibilities, the idea of pressing flesh at some not-very-festive cocktail party is right up there in appeal with a root canal. But what if women could find a way to make career boosting connections that are actually fun? Enter 'table talk', a new way to network for time-pressed, professional women.

22347 ■ "Team Bonding for Fun and Profit" in *Women Entrepreneur* (December 3, 2008)
Pub: Entrepreneur Media Inc.
Ed: Eve Gumpel. **Description:** Discusses the benefits that competitions such as the 2008 BG U.S. Challenge in Lake Placid, New York, can offer in terms of team building and employee motivation as well as networking and the development of a positive working relationship with partners and competitors alike.

22348 ■ "The File On...Jenne Distributors" in *Crain's Cleveland Business* (Vol. 28, October 8, 2007, No. 40, pp. 26)
Pub: Crain Communications, Inc.
Ed: Kimberly Bonvissuto. **Description:** Overview of the telecommunications equipment company, Jenne Distributors, a firm that is projecting more than $125 million in revenue for 2007.

22349 ■ "The Simon Cowell of Sales" in *Inc.* (March 2008, pp. 81-82)
Pub: Gruner & Jahr USA Publishing
Ed: Norm Brodsky. **Description:** Successful selling tips to help anyone trying to close a deal are examined.

22350 ■ "Tired of PowerPoint? Try This Instead" in *Harvard Business Review* (Vol. 88, September 2010, No. 9, pp. 30)
Pub: Harvard Business School Publishing
Ed: Daniel McGinn, Stephanie Crowley. **Description:** Usefulness of graphic recording, also known as storyboarding or visual facilitation, during client meetings is illustrated.

22351 ■ "Top IPhone Apps" in *Advertising Age* (Vol. 79, December 15, 2008, No. 46, pp. 17)
Pub: Crain Communications, Inc.
Ed: Marissa Miley. **Description:** Free and low cost applications for the iPhone are described including Evernote, an application that allows users to outsource their memory to keep track of events, notes, ides and more; Handshake, a way for users to exchange business cards and pictures across Wi-Fi and 3G; CityTransit, an interactive map of the New York subway system that uses GPS technology to find nearby stations and also tells the user if a train is out of commission that day; and Stage Hand which allows users to deliver a presentation, control timing and slide order on the spot.

22352 ■ "The Top Mistakes of Social Media Marketing" in *Agency Sales Magazine* (Vol. 39, November 2009, No. 9, pp. 42)
Pub: MANA
Ed: Pam Lontos; Maurice Ramirez. **Description:** One common mistake in social media marketing is having more than one image on the Internet because this ruins a business' credibility. Marketers need to put out messages that are useful to their readers and to keep messages consistent.

22353 ■ "Tracking Your Fleet Can Increase Bottom Line" in *Contractor* (Vol. 56, November 2009, No. 11, pp. 26)
Pub: Penton Media, Inc.
Ed: Candace Roulo. **Description:** GPS fleet management system can help boost a contractor's profits, employee productivity, and efficiency. These are available as a handheld device or a cell phone that employees carry around or as a piece of hardware installed in a vehicle. These lets managers track assets and communicate with employees about jobs.

22354 ■ "Traits that Makes Blogs Attractive to Book Publishers" in *Marketing to Women* (Vol. 22, July 2009, No. 7, pp. 1)
Pub: EPM Communications, Inc.
Description: Book publishers are finding a beneficial relationship between themselves and women bloggers on the Internet. A high visitor count, frequent updates and active readership are criteria for identifying the blogs with the most clout and therefore providing the greatest benefit to publishers.

22355 ■ "The Twittering Class" in *Entrepreneur* (Vol. 37, September 2009, No. 9, pp. 40)
Pub: Entrepreneur Media, Inc.
Ed: Mikal E. Belicove. **Description:** Advice on how entrepreneurs can use online social networks to promote their businesses is presented. Facebook offers applications and advertising solutions to promote Websites, products and services. Twitter, on the other hand, provides instant messaging, which can be done through computer or cell phone.

22356 ■ *Twitterville: How Businesses Can Thrive in the New Global Neighborhoods*
Pub: Portfolio Hardcover
Ed: Shel Israel. **Price:** $23.95. **Description:** Twitter is the most rapidly adopted communication tool in history, going from zero to ten million users in just over two years. On Twitter, word can spread faster than wildfire. Companies no longer have the option of ignoring the conversation. Unlike other hot social media spaces, Twitterville is dominated by professionals, not students. And despite its size, it still feels like a small town. Twitter allows people to interact much the way they do face-to-face, honestly and authentically.

22357 ■ "Understanding Persuasive Online Sales Messages from eBay Auctions" in *Business Communication Quarterly* (December 2007, pp. 482)
Pub: Sage Publications USA
Ed: Barbara Jo White, Daniel Clapper, Rita Noel, Jenny Fortier, Pierre Grabolosa. **Description:** eBay product listings were studied to determine the requirements of persuasive sales writing. Potential sellers should use the proper keywords and make an authentic description with authentic photographs of the item being auctioned.

22358 ■ "Urban Tree Service" in *New Hampshire Business Review* (Vol. 33, March 25, 2011, No. 6, pp. 35)
Pub: Business Publications Inc.
Description: Urban Tree Service received the Professional Communications Award from the Tree Care Industry Association for excellence in marketing and communications.

22359 ■ "Use Common Sense in Office Gift-Giving" in *Women In Business* (Vol. 61, October-November 2009, No. 5, pp. 32)
Pub: American Business Women's Association
Ed: Maureen Sullivan. **Description:** Tips on office gift-giving during the Christmas season are discussed. Aside from ensuring appropriateness of the gift with respect to the recipient, a fixed giving budget must be adhered to. Gifts that can be used by anyone may be selected and those with religious overtones must be avoided.

22360 ■ "Use Social Media to Enhance Brand, Business" in *Contractor* (Vol. 56, December 2009, No. 12, pp. 14)
Pub: Penton Media, Inc.
Ed: Elton Rivas. **Description:** Advice on how plumbing contractors should use online social networks to increase sales is presented including such issues as clearly defining goals and target audience. An additional advantage to this medium is that advertisements can easily be shared with other users.

22361 ■ "Using Teaching Teams to Encourage Active Learning" in *Business Communication Quarterly* (December 2007, pp. 457)
Pub: Sage Publications USA
Ed: Lisa E. Gueldenzoph. **Description:** The practice of dividing classes into teaching teams to encourage active learning is studied. Students in business management courses become more involved in the learning process with this technique and collaborate to enhance better understanding of course content.

22362 ■ "The Value of Conversations With Employees; Talk Isn't Cheap" in *Gallup Management Journal* (June 30, 2011)
Pub: Gallup
Ed: Jessica Tyler. **Description:** When managers have meaningful exchanges with their employees, they don't only show they care, they also add value to their organization's bottom line.

22363 ■ "Vistaprint Survey Indicates that Online Marketing Taking Hold Among Small Businesses" in *Internet Wire* (December 10, 2009)
Pub: Comtex News Network, Inc.
Description: According to a comprehensive survey from Vistaprint N.V., small businesses are very likely to increase their use of Internet marketing strategies such as paid and organic search, email marketing, social media networking and custom websites over the next year. Trends continue to show that more small businesses are indeed adapting to the changing marketplace and are more willing to diversify their marketing strategies than ever before.

22364 ■ "Wait a Minute!" in *Entrepreneur* (Vol. 37, September 2009, No. 9, pp. 76)
Pub: Entrepreneur Media, Inc.
Ed: Jennifer Wang. **Description:** Advice on how entrepreneurs in the United States should secure funding in view of the economic crisis is presented.

Enough interest should be stimulated so as to secure a follow-up meeting. Investors should be asked questions that would encourage them to tell stories related to the downturn.

22365 ■ "We Move Forward as a Team" in *Women In Business* (Vol. 61, December 2009, No. 6, pp. 6)
Pub: American Business Women's Association
Ed: Rene Street. **Description:** Based on her experiences in ABWA's National Board of Directors retreat, an executive director of the American Business Women's Association, shares her belief that interaction is necessary for a successful business enterprise. She believes that the problems presented in the retreat's team-building exercises are similar to challenges which are faced in ABWA, in the workplace, and in the marketplace.

22366 ■ "The Web Gets Real" in *Canadian Business* (Vol. 79, July 17, 2006, No. 14-15, pp. 19)
Pub: Rogers Media
Ed: Andrew Wahl. **Description:** Ron Lake's efforts of bringing the virtual and physical worlds more closely together by using Geographic Markup Language (GML) are presented.

22367 ■ *What Men Don't Tell Woman about Business: Opening Up the Heavily Guarded Alpha Male Playbook*
Pub: John Wiley and Sons, Inc.
Ed: Christopher V. Fleet. **Released:** October 26, 2007. **Description:** Valuable guide for any woman in business, this book helps reveal everything a woman needs to know in order to understand, communicate, and compete with men in business.

22368 ■ "What's In Your Toolbox" in *Women In Business* (Vol. 61, August-September 2009, No. 4, pp. 7)
Pub: American Business Women's Association
Ed: Mimi Kopulos. **Description:** Business owners are increasingly turning to using social networking websites, such as Facebook, LinkedIn and Twitter, to promote their companies. The number of adult social media users has increased from 8 percent in 2005 to 35 percent in 2009.

22369 ■ "What's Your Social Media Strategy?" in *Black Enterprise* (Vol. 41, November 2010, No. 4, pp. 75)
Pub: Earl G. Graves Publishing Co. Inc.
Ed: Denise Campbell. **Description:** Advice for using social media sites such as Twitter, Facebook and LinkedIn as a professional networking tool is given.

22370 ■ *When Family Businesses are Best*
Pub: Palgrave Macmillan
Ed: Randel S. Carlock, John L. Ward. **Released:** March 1, 2010. **Price:** $45.00. **Description:** An exploration into effective planning and communication to help small businesses grow into multigeneration family enterprises.

22371 ■ "When Good Deals Go Bad: How to Renegotiate a Contract" in *Inc.* (November 2007, pp. 33-34)
Pub: Gruner & Jahr USA Publishing
Ed: Dee Gill. **Description:** Ways to renegotiate contracts are discussed. Robb Corwin of Gorilla Fuel discusses how he was able to renegotiate contracts in order to save his business.

22372 ■ "Why LinkedIn is the Social Network that Will Never Die" in *Advertising Age* (Vol. 81, December 6, 2010, No. 43, pp. 2)
Pub: Crain Communications, Inc.
Ed: Irina Slutsky. **Description:** Despite the popularity of Facebook, LinkIn in will always be a source for professionals who wish to network.

22373 ■ "Why Mumbai at 1PM is the Center of the Business World" in *Harvard Business Review* (Vol. 88, October 2010, No. 10, pp. 38)
Pub: Harvard Business School Publishing
Ed: Michael Segalla. **Description:** A time zone chart is presented for assisting in the planning of international conference calls.

22374 ■ "Why Women Blog and What They Read" in *Marketing to Women* (Vol. 22, July 2009, No. 7, pp. 8)
Pub: EPM Communications, Inc.
Description: Listing of topics that are visited the most by female Internet users. Statistical data included.

22375 ■ "Wi-Fi Finds Its Way Despite Nixed Plan for Free System" in *Crain's Cleveland Business* (Vol. 28, November 12, 2007, No. 45, pp. 3)
Pub: Crain Communications, Inc.
Ed: Jay Miller. **Description:** Discusses the issues facing Cleveland and Northeast Ohio concerning their proposal to offer citizens wireless Internet services for free or a small fee.

22376 ■ "The Wiki-Powered Workplace" in *Workforce Management* (Vol. 88, November 16, 2009, No. 12, pp. 8)
Pub: Crain Communications, Inc.
Description: Many organizations are successfully using wikis inside the corporate structure for business communications and knowledge sharing. Wikis can be a very powerful tool due to the inherent transparency that comes with allowing everything to be edited with the accountability of seeing who is doing the editing. A brilliant employee may be noticed sooner because they are doing work in the wiki and the work is being judged on its own merit.

22377 ■ "Windstream Expands Business Service Into Monroe" in *Marketing Weekly News* (January 23, 2010, pp. 77)
Pub: Investment Weekly News
Description: Windstream Corp. announces the expansion of its data and voice services into Monroe, N.C., which will give local businesses a new choice for advanced communication services and network security.

22378 ■ "Wise Guy: Get In Good" in *Entrepreneur* (Vol. 35, October 2007, No. 10, pp. 46)
Pub: Entrepreneur Media Inc.
Ed: Guy Kawasaki. **Description:** Good public relations are a requirement for business entrepreneurs, and it can be achieved through proper communication. Giving of and asking for favors are some of the ways to build relationships in the business world. Other tips on how to build good business relationships are provided.

22379 ■ "Words at Work" in *Information Today* (Vol. 26, February 2009, No. 2, pp. 25)
Pub: Information Today, Inc.
Description: Current new buzzwords include the following: digital amnesia, or overload by availability, speed and volume of digital information; maternal profiling, a form a discrimination against women; recipe malpractice, a reminder that just because you can turn on a stove it doesn't make you a chef; ringxiety, the act when everyone reaches for their cell phone when one rings; verbing, the practice of turning good nouns into verbs.

22380 ■ "Work Smarter" in *Entrepreneur* (Vol. 36, April 2008, No. 4, pp. 70)
Pub: Entrepreneur Media, Inc.
Ed: Amanda C. Kooser. **Description:** Online applications that address a business' particular needs are presented. These web applications offer email services, collaboration services of sharing and editing documents and presentations, and tie-ups with online social networking sites. Details on various web applications are provided.

22381 ■ "The Workplace Generation Gaps" in *Women In Business* (Vol. 62, June 2010, No. 2, pp. 8)
Pub: American Business Women's Association
Ed: Leigh Elmore. **Description:** Generation gaps among baby boomers, Generation X and Generation Y in the workplace are attributed to technological divides and differences in opinions. These factors could lead to workplace misunderstandings, employee turnover and communication difficulties. Details on managing such workplace gaps are discussed.

22382 ■ "Yammer Gets Serious" in *Inc.* (Volume 32, December 2010, No. 10, pp. 58)
Pub: Inc. Magazine
Ed: Eric Markowitz. **Description:** Yammer, an internal social network for companies, allows coworkers to share ideas and documents in real-time. Details of this service are included.

22383 ■ "Your First 100 Days on Your New Job" in *Women In Business* (Vol. 63, Spring 2011, No. 1, pp. 28)
Pub: American Business Women's Association
Ed: Diane Stafford. **Description:** The first 100 days on the job are crucial if the person's permanent hiring is conditional on surviving a probationary period. The new hire must do more than just master the job's technical details to maximize the chance of success. Details of some basic tips to fit into the corporate culture and get along with coworkers are also discussed.

TRADE PERIODICALS

22384 ■ *Corporate Writer and Editor*
Pub: Lawrence Ragan Communications Inc.
Contact: Sharon Pryer
Released: Monthly. **Price:** $209, U.S.; $239, other countries. **Description:** Presents information designed to help corporate writers and editors create successful company publications. Topics include writing, design, finding the right outside designers and freelancers, and others.

22385 ■ *The Facilitator*
Pub: Nurre Ink
Contact: Susan M. Nurre, Editor & Publisher
E-mail: snurre@thefacilitator.com
Released: Quarterly. **Price:** $35, U.S.; $35, institutions; $40, out of country. **Description:** Provides articles written by facilitators that are designed to link facilitators from around the world in a forum of sharing, networking, and communicating. Includes updates on training, automated meeting tools, and resources. Recurring features include tips and techniques, a calendar of events, reports of meetings, news of educational opportunities, book reviews, and notices of publications available.

22386 ■ *The Gauge*
Pub: Delahaye Medialink
Contact: Katharine Delahaye Paine, Publisher
E-mail: kpaine@delahaye.com
Ed: William Teunis Paarlberg, Editor, wpaarlberg@aol.com. **Released:** Bimonthly. **Price:** $75. **Description:** Provides information on and evaluates marketing communications activities of companies. Recurring features include interviews, news of research, and a calendar of events.

22387 ■ *Harvard Management Communication Letter*
Pub: Harvard Business School Publishing
Ed: Nick Morgan, Editor, nmorgan@hbsp.harvard.edu. **Released:** Monthly. **Price:** $99, U.S.; $119, Canada and Mexico; $139, elsewhere; $169, two years in USA. **Description:** Provides information and techniques for managers on effective communication.

22388 ■ *Journal of Employee Communication Management–Reagan Report*
Pub: Lawrence Ragan Communications Inc.
Ed: David Murray, Editor, dmurrayil@earthlink.net. **Released:** Bimonthly. **Price:** $249, U.S.; $279, other countries. **Description:** Covers corporate communications issues, such as increasing retention, developing measurement tools, and addressing issues such as mergers, downsizing, and branding.

22389 ■ *The Nash & Cibinic Report*
Pub: West Group
Ed: Ralph Nash, Editor. **Released:** Monthly. **Price:** $1,706.88. **Description:** Discusses government contracts analysis and reporting. Topics include procurement management, contractor claims, and competition and awards.

22390 ■ *The Retort*
Pub: The Chemists' Club Library
Released: Bimonthly. **Description:** Highlights the Club's services and resources about chemistry and the chemical business, as well as membership news and events. Recurring features include a collection and a column titled President's Message.

22391 ■ *Women Chemists*
Pub: American Chemical Society
Ed: Teri Quinn Gray, Editor. **Released:** Semiannual. **Description:** Aims "to be leaders in attracting, developing, and promoting women in the chemical sciences." Reports on women's achievements in the chemical sciences, as well as grants available, symposiums, and current events.

VIDEOCASSETTES/ AUDIOCASSETTES

22392 ■ *The Art of Telecommunication*
Film Ideas, Inc.
308 N. Wolf Rd.
Wheeling, IL 60090
Ph:(874)419-0255
Free: 800-475-3456
Fax:(874)419-8933
Co. E-mail: info@filmideas.com
URL: http://www.filmideas.com
Price: $49.95. **Description:** Describes the telephone skills that are an integral part of the business world today. Also discusses office protocol, basic telecommunications equipment, and the facsimile machine. **Availability:** VHS.

22393 ■ *Communicate!*
Axzo Press
Thomson Course Technology
25 Thomson Pl.
Boston, MA 02210
Free: 888-534-5556
Fax:888-715-0220
Co. E-mail: customerservice@axzopress.com
URL: http://www.axzopress.com
Price: $98. **Description:** This video helps you and your associates learn what good communication is, analyze your own communication skills, and add to your existing skills. **Availability:** VHS.

22394 ■ *Communication*
American Media, Inc.
4621 121st St.
Urbandale, IA 50323-2311
Ph:(515)224-0919
Free: 888-776-8268
Fax:(515)327-2555
Co. E-mail: custsvc@ammedia.com
URL: http://www.ammedia.com
Released: 1989. **Price:** $1485.00. **Description:** Communication, in the form of memos, phone calls, and presentations are essential to business success. **Availability:** VHS; 3/4U.

22395 ■ *Effective Presentations: How to Make Powerhouse Presentations That Get the Results You Want*
Instructional Video
2219 C St.
Lincoln, NE 68502
Ph:(402)475-6570
Free: 800-228-0164
Fax:(402)475-6500
Co. E-mail: feedback@insvideo.com
URL: http://www.insvideo.com
Price: $69.95. **Description:** Describes effective presentation methods, including how to understand and evaluate your listeners' expectations, how to organize your ideas and make them interesting, and how to create your own style. Includes guidebook. **Availability:** VHS.

22396 ■ *How to Deal with the Foreign Accent: Diversity on the Phone*
Excellence in Training Corp.
c/o ICON Training
804 Roosevelt St.
Polk City, IA 50226
Free: 800-609-0479
Co. E-mail: info@icontraining.com
URL: http://www.icontraining.com
Released: 1991. **Price:** $375.00. **Description:** A guide to communicating with people whose first language is other than English. **Availability:** VHS; 3/4U; Special order formats.

22397 ■ *Introduction to Technical and Business Communication*
GPN Educational Media
1550 Executive Drive
Elgin, IL 60123
Ph:(402)472-2007
Free: 800-228-4630
Fax:800-306-2330
Co. E-mail: askgpn@smarterville.com
URL: http://www.shopgpn.com
Released: 1983. **Price:** $300.00. **Description:** This course teaches businessmen the fundamentals of technical writing and business communication. **Availability:** VHS; 3/4U; Special order formats.

22398 ■ *Listening Skills*
Video Arts, Inc.
c/o Aim Learning Group
8238-40 Lehigh
Morton Grove, IL 60053-2615
Free: 877-444-2230
Fax:(416)252-2155
Co. E-mail: service@aimlearninggroup.com
URL: http://www.aimlearninggroup.com
Released: 1991. **Price:** $200.00. **Description:** The skill of listening is demonstrated using clips that show how people feel when they are not listened to. **Availability:** VHS; 8mm; 3/4U; Special order formats.

22399 ■ *Manners at Work*
American Media, Inc.
4621 121st St.
Urbandale, IA 50323-2311
Ph:(515)224-0919
Free: 888-776-8268
Fax:(515)327-2555
Co. E-mail: custsvc@ammedia.com
URL: http://www.ammedia.com
Released: 1990. **Price:** $395.00. **Description:** The basics of corporate etiquette, including introductions, handshakes, and professional conduct, are covered. **Availability:** VHS; 3/4U; 8mm.

TRADE SHOWS AND CONVENTIONS

22400 ■ Alliance Texas
Showorks Inc.
1205 N. Napa St.
Spokane, WA 99202
Ph:(509)838-8755
Fax:(509)838-2838
Co. E-mail: showorks@showorksinc.com
URL: http://www.showorksinc.com
Audience: Buyers and contracting officers from military bases. **Principal Exhibits:** Small business procurement opportunities.

22401 ■ Association for Business Communication Annual Convention
Association for Business Communication
PO Box 6143
Nacogdoches, TX 75962-6143
Ph:(936)468-6280
Fax:(936)468-6281
Co. E-mail: abcjohnson@fasu.edu
URL: http://www.businesscommunication.org
Released: Annual. **Audience:** College business communication teachers. **Principal Exhibits:** Books and communication technology products.

22402 ■ Texas Press Association Annual Midwinter Conference and Trade Show
Texas Press Association
718 W. 5th St., Ste. 100
Austin, TX 78701
Ph:(512)477-6755
Fax:(512)477-6759
URL: http://www.texaspress.com
Released: Annual. **Audience:** Newspaper publishers, editors, and members of corporate communications departments. **Principal Exhibits:** Equipment, supplies, and services for newspapers and corporate communication departments.

CONSULTANTS

22403 ■ American English Academy
111 N Atlantic Blvd., Ste. 112
Monterey Park, CA 91754
Ph:(626)457-2800
Fax:(626)457-2808
Co. E-mail: admission@aea-usa.com
URL: http://www.aea-usa.com
Contact: Charles Policky, President
Scope: Specializes in providing on-site English language and communication development for corporations and individuals. Also develops and delivers training in speaking, writing, pronunciation, grammar, and idioms with an emphasis on business communication. Offers individual, small group, intensive, and long-distance learning. Programs tailor-made for each client.

22404 ■ Ann Welsh Communications Inc.
1110 Yonge St., Ste. 301
Toronto, ON, Canada M4W 2L6
Ph:(416)972-1930
Fax:(416)972-6494
Co. E-mail: ann@annwelsh.com
URL: http://www.annwelsh.com
Contact: Ann Welsh, President
E-mail: ann@annwelsh.com
Scope: Change management facilitation and communications, executive writing services.

22405 ■ Beeline Learning Solutions
14911 Quorum Dr., Ste. 120
Dallas, TX 75254
Ph:(972)813-0465
Fax:(972)386-8667
Co. E-mail: info@consultingpartners.com
URL: http://www.beeline.com
Contact: Debra Gann, Managering Director
E-mail: gann@atsconsultingpartners.com
Scope: Consulting firm offering technology, content, and services addressing recruitment and sourcing, talent management, and learning and performance optimization. Solutions offered include contingent workforce solutions, vendor management software, talent management solutions, recruitment process outsourcing, performance management, applicant tracking, learning management and eLearning. **Special Services:** Beeline[R].

22406 ■ BeeWall Diversity
22136 Westheimer Pky., Ste. 313
Katy, TX 77450-8296
Ph:(281)500-6000
Fax:(281)395-6095
Co. E-mail: info@beewalldiversity.com
Contact: Stephanie Thibeaux, President
E-mail: sthibeaux@beewalldiversity.com
Scope: A diversity, organizational development, and human resource consulting and training firm. Provides services in change management, conflict resolution, emotional intelligence, and organizational development.

22407 ■ Beverly Hyman and Associates
23 E 10 St., Ste. 212
New York, NY 10003
Ph:(212)983-6250
Fax:(212)983-6342
Co. E-mail: bevhyman@aol.com
URL: http://www.beverlyhyman.com
Contact: Beverly Hyman, President
E-mail: bevhyman@aol.com
Scope: Communication and training consultants offering such programs as training the trainer, communications skills, business (or technical) writing, public speaking, management skills or supervisory skills, negotiations, direct communication (assertiveness training), women in management, time management, and sales training. Serves private industries as

well as government agencies. **Publications:** "Training for Productivity"; "How Successful Women Manage"; "The Trainers Handbook The AMA Guide to Effective Training"; "The Heart of the Sale Making the Customers Need to Buy the Key to Successful Selling"; "How to Market by Telephone, How to Interview Effectively, Total Time Management and How to Motivate for Superior Performance". **Seminars:** Training the Trainer; Advanced Training the Trainer; Coaching and Counseling; Constructive Feedback; Supervisory Skills; Writing Skills; Interpersonal Communications; Leadership Skills; Presentation Skills; Customer Service; Communication Skills; Public Speaking; Negotiating Skills Women in Management; Time Management; Sales Training Skills; Assertiveness Skills; Executive Coaching.

22408 ■ Blackmon Roberts Group Inc.
4000 Ponce De Leon Blvd., Ste. 470
Coral Gables, FL 33145
Ph:(863)802-1280
Fax:(863)802-1290
Co. E-mail: dbeinformation@blackmonroberts.com
URL: http://www.blackmonroberts.com
Contact: Willie Barnes, Principal
Scope: Technical support consultant in technical writing, planning, research, needs analysis, marketing and training, offers training programs from cultural sensitivity issues to effective listening skills.

22409 ■ The Bosley Group
824 Heather Ln.
Charlotte, NC 28209-2428
Ph:(704)641-1334
Fax:(704)523-1282
Co. E-mail: info@theplainlanguagegroup.com
Contact: Deborah S. Bosley, Owner
E-mail: deborah@theplainlanguagegroup.com
Scope: Writing consultant delivering simplified communication training and documentation to corporations. Services include communication audits, document design, and business and technical writing and training.

22410 ■ Casino, Hotel & Resort Consultants L.L.C.
8100 Via Del Cerro Ct.
Las Vegas, NV 89117
Ph:(702)646-7200
Fax:(702)646-6680
Co. E-mail: info@hraba.com
URL: http://www.hraba.com
Contact: John S. Hraba, President
E-mail: jshraba@aol.com
Scope: Casino and hospitality industry consultants. Firm specializes in developing and implementing customized forecast and labor management control systems that deliver immediate, positive impact to the company's bottom line. Involved in production planning, employ surveys and communication, inventory management, business process reviews, audits, development and implementation of key management reports. **Seminars:** Payroll Cost Control; Effective Staff Scheduling.

22411 ■ Charismedia
610 W End Ave., Ste. B1
New York, NY 10001
Ph:(212)362-6808
Fax:(212)362-6809
Co. E-mail: charismedia@earthlink.net
URL: http://www.charismedia.net
Contact: Ying Jo Wong, Principle
E-mail: charismedia@earthlink.net
Scope: Offers speech and image training as well as speech writing services for effective presentation skills. Conducts workshops like anti-stage fright breathing, psychophysical exercises, transformational success imagery, face reading and body language, EMDR (Eye Movement Desensitization Re-Processing) for Permanent Trauma and Fear Removal, Bach Flower remedies, thought field therapy, cross-cultural communication, speech, voice and diction; regional and foreign accent elimination and acquisition, Positive Perception Management (P.P.M.), Ad-libbing, humor and spontaneity training, fast creative speech preparation, Neuro-Linguistic Programming and Hypnosis. **Publications:** "Flaunt It"; "Improve Your Sex Life"; "Phone Power"; "Train Your Voice"; "Turning Tinny, Tiny Tones To Gold"; "The New Secrets of Charisma: How to Discover and Unleash your Hidden Powers," McGraw-Hill, Jul, 1999. **Seminars:** Services for Comfortable Effective Speaking.

22412 ■ Communispond Inc.
5 Lauras Ln.
East Hampton, NY 11937-5916
Ph:(631)907-8010
Free: 800-529-5925
Fax:(631)907-8011
Co. E-mail: marketing@communispond.com
URL: http://www.communispond.com
Contact: Todd Wright, VP of Operations
Scope: Firm is a comprehensive communications and sales training resource. It partners with its clients to help them reach their strategic goals. The business communication curriculum includes executive presentation skills, senior executive, speaking on paper, communicating for improved performance, interviewing skills and media skills. The Socratic sales curriculum includes Socratic selling skills, sales presentation skills, Socratic negotiating skills, communicating for improved sales performance, selling on paper, hiring the right sales person and strategic account management. Special techniques include methods for handling confrontational situations, conferences, meetings, news briefings, media interviews, sales proposals and speaker's bureaus. **Publications:** "Socratic Selling Skills: The Discipline of Customer-Centered Sales"; "It's Not What You Say, But How It Sounds"; "Butt Heads With the Boss Without Getting Fired"; "Five Critical Aspects to Getting More Return from Employee Training"; "Building Your Case: Five Forms of Evidence Reps Should Use to Persuade the Doctor"; "The Full Force of Your Ideas: Mastering the Science of Persuasion". **Seminars:** Executive Presentation Skills; Persuasive Dialogue, Aug, 2008; Sales Presentation Skills; Selling by Phone; Senior Executive Presentation Skills; Write up Front on the Web; Mastering Interpersonal Communication; Call Centers: Solving Customers Problems.

22413 ■ COMsciences Inc.
4712 Admiralty Way, Ste. 870
Marina del Rey, CA 90292
Ph:(310)823-5257
Fax:(323)937-0160
Co. E-mail: info@comsciences.com
URL: http://www.comsciences.com
Contact: Jack Torobin, CEO
E-mail: jtorobin@comsciences.com
Scope: Firm offers research services to support public relations, corporate advertising, impact of new communications media, communication entertainment, and internet/web development. Also provides strategic management consulting on communications, marketing, opinion surveys, and organizational development and assessment. The company specializes in media campaigns and evaluation tools. Also conducts government sponsored and media sponsored surveys. Serves all industry sectors, especially. com, wireless telecommunications, interactive media, and consumer electronics. **Publications:** "Wanted: Radical Thinking," Pmg World Magazine, Mar, 2003. **Special Services:** iKIT[R]; imovio[R].

22414 ■ DDL OMNI
8260 Greensboro Dr., Ste. 600
McLean, VA 22102
Ph:(703)903-9777
Fax:(703)903-9745
Co. E-mail: info@ddlomni.com
URL: http://www.ddlomni.com
Contact: Thomas K. Cole, Vice President
E-mail: nancy.doolin@atsddlomni.com
Scope: Provides technical services in the core services of the defense core provides reengineering, defense reinvestment and technology transfer; test and evaluation engineering; analysis support; software test and evaluation and information management services. Transportation core provides logistics and analysis; public outreach team and consensus building program assessment and restructuring and information clearing house services. Health core provides technical information training and organizational development health-related research disability research and management and policy analysis services. Energy core provides technology transfer, modeling and simulation reengineering and information management services. Environment core provides environmental program support environmental communications and environmental technology. Also provides communications services, including conference design and management and technical documentation, program logistics and analysis motion picture and video tape production, and other outreach initiatives. **Publications:** "Configuration Management Reports"; "Functional Requirement Documents"; "Groom Reports"; "Maintenance Requirement Cards"; "Operation and Maintenance Manuals"; "Pre-Mission Check Out Procedures"; "Shipping Reports"; "TempAlt Documents"; "Training Publications".

22415 ■ Development Resource Consultants
PO Box 118
Rancho Cucamonga, CA 91729
Ph:(909)902-7655
Fax:(909)476-6942
Co. E-mail: drc@gotodrc.com
URL: http://www.gotodrc.com
Contact: Jerry R. Frey, Partner
E-mail: jfrey@atsgotodrc.com
Scope: Specializes in office re-organization, employee training in office organization, communication skills, sales training and career counseling. **Publications:** "Institute of Management Consultants Southern California Chapter," Jan, 2006.

22416 ■ Full Voice
3217 Broadway Ave., Ste. 300
Kansas City, MO 64111
Ph:(816)941-0011
Free: 800-684-8764
Fax:(816)931-8887
Co. E-mail: info@infullvoice.com
URL: http://www.fullvoice.us
Contact: Michienne Dixon, Principle
E-mail: garrett@infullvoice.com
Scope: Vocal performance training firm offering consulting services and personal training sessions in the implementation of effective vocal communication techniques for the development of business relationships and career enhancement. Formalizes a program of proven techniques into a practical method of helping individuals improve their ability to better present themselves when speaking in a professional situation. Industries served: All. **Publications:** "You Can Sound Like You Know What You're Saying". **Seminars:** You Can Sound Like You Know What You're Saying; The Psychology of Vocal Performance; Security. . .the Ability to Accept Change; Knowing. . .the Key to Relaxed Public Communication; The Effective Voice for Customer Service Enhancement; You Can Speak With Conviction; How To Make Yours a Championship Team; Functional English For Foreign Trade. **Special Services:** FULL VOICE[TM].

22417 ■ Germuska Communications
441 N Brockway St.
PO Box 426
Palatine, IL 60067
Ph:(847)934-1984
Co. E-mail: tom@germuska.com
Contact: Thomas A. Germuska Sr., President
E-mail: tom@germuska.com
Scope: Offers public relations and business communications consulting and services for corporations, organizations and individuals. Additional expertise in crisis communications; speech writing; grant writing annual report and newsletter production; as well as developing and executing successful print and broadcast public relations programs. Industries served: Advertising, consumer products, entertainment, recreation and travel, hospitality, individuals, manufacturing, nonprofit organization sand associations, service industries, and transportation. **Seminars:** Crisis Communications Planning; Newsletter Production; Public Relations for Not-for-Profit Organizations.

22418 ■ Great Western Association Management Inc.
7995 E Prentice Ave., Ste. 100
Greenwood Village, CO 80111
Ph:(303)770-2220

Fax:(303)770-1614
Co. E-mail: info83@gwami.com
URL: http://www.gwami.com
Contact: Sheryl Pitts, Principle
E-mail: kwojdyla@atsgwami.com
Scope: Provides clients with products and services to effectively manage existing and startup, for- and not-for-profit organizations. Clients select from a menu of services including association development and public relations, conferences and seminars, financial management, membership communications, and governance. Expertise also includes association strategic planning, compliance, lobbying, meeting planning, fundraising, marketing and communications. Serves national, regional and state organizations. **Seminars:** Site selection; Creative program development; Contract negotiations; On-site conference management; Trade show management; Travel and logistics.

22419 ■ The Handler Group Inc.
425 W End Ave., Apt. 3A
New York, NY 10024-5718
Ph:(212)873-1899
Contact: Mark Lambert Handler, President
E-mail: mlhandler@aol.com
Scope: Provides marketing, communication planning, and design services, specializing in development of internal and external business communications. Develops corporate identity, corporate literature, employee communications, sales promotion materials, consumer product packaging and information, brochures, annual reports, and presentation materials. Industries served: Cable/television, technology software, business information, hospitality, and banking.

22420 ■ Herrick International: Partners for Performance
1834 Ridge Ave.
Evanston, IL 60201
Ph:(847)274-9206
Co. E-mail: jherrick@herrickinternational.com
Contact: Dr. Penny Hirsch, Principle
E-mail: jherrick@herrickinternational.com
Scope: Firm partners with organizations to leverage employee performance. Areas of expertise include inter cultural communication, diversity, document design, leadership development and conflict resolution. **Publications:** "And Then She Said"; "How to Make Effective Business Presentation"; "Planning for Successful Interviews"; "It's Not What You Say"; "Cross-cultural issues with International LLM Students".

22421 ■ In Plain English
14501 Antigone Dr.
PO Box 3300
Gaithersburg, MD 20885-3300
Ph:(301)340-2821
Free: 800-274-9645
Fax:(301)279-0115
Co. E-mail: rwohl@inplainenglish.com
URL: http://www.inplainenglish.com
Contact: Ronald H. Wohl, CEO
E-mail: rwohl@inplainenglish.com
Scope: Management consultants helping government and businesses research, design, write and produce user oriented management information for human resources, employee benefits, business process, corporate and marketing needs. Services include: GSA mob is schedule for consulting to the government; employee benefit communications, plain English business writing workshops for print and electronic media; communicating strategy and tactics; marketing research, business planning and communications; readability testing; usability testing and monitoring strategy. **Publications:** "The Benefits Communication"; "The Employee Benefits Communication ToolKit," Commerce Clearinghouse; "Benefits Communication," Business and Legal Reports. **Seminars:** Plain English Writing Training; Summary Plan Description Compliance workshops; Re-Humanizing the Corporation, Human Resources and Employee Benefits Communication Workshop; 21 Writing Tips for the 21st Century; Make the Write Impression; Writing to Inform and Instruct; The Dreaded Nuts and Bolts; Writing to Persuade; Writing Policy and Procedure Manuals In Plain English; Writing for Accountants and Auditors In Plain English. **Special Services:** In Plain English[R].

22422 ■ James G. Patterson - The Cogent Communicator
9571 E Caldwell Dr.
Tucson, AZ 85747-9218
Ph:(520)574-9353
Fax:(520)574-0620
Co. E-mail: cogent@indirect.com
E-mail: cogent@indirect.com
Scope: Trainer and consultant in quality and communication. Specialties include ISO 9000, TQM, quality audits, communication audits, effective writing, presentation skills and negotiating. Actively promotes speaking and consulting to association groups. Serves corporate and government audiences worldwide. **Publications:** "Benchmarking Basics Crisp," Sep, 1995; "Supervisory Communication Ami," 1995; "Negotiating Amacom Work smart Series," 1995; "Intro to Iso 9000," Crisp Publications, 1994; "Leadership Development," Astd Info-Line, 1994; "How to Become a Better Negotiator". **Seminars:** Intro to ISO 9000; Implementing an Effective TQM Program; Team building; Leadership Development; Effective Writing; Presentation Skills for Executives; Negotiation Skills; Customer Service. **Special Services:** Maintains ISO 9000 Nicodemus software.

22423 ■ Kay Britten Communications Inc.
6057 Waterview Ct.
West Bloomfield, MI 48322
Ph:(248)592-0507
Contact: A. Britten Kay, Owner
Scope: Business communication master coach and motivator. Provides marketing and public relations consulting.

22424 ■ Komei Inc.
8910 Purdue Rd., Ste. 480
Indianapolis, IN 46268-1197
Ph:(317)616-1810
Fax:(317)616-1811
Co. E-mail: solutions@komei.com
URL: http://www.komei.com
Contact: Casey Davis, Vice President
E-mail: casey@atskomei.com
Scope: Global corporation dedicated to helping people and organizations change together, and reach their goals, through better communication. Offers customized in-house seminars, workshops, and coaching in writing, presentation skills, international and intercultural communication, and team and community building. **Publications:** "Written Communication Profiler"; "The McGraw-Hill 36-Hour Course in Business Writing and Communication"; "Mihaly Csikszentmihalyi: Good Business: Leadership, Flow, and the Making of Meaning"; "Richard Saul Wurman: Information Anxiety 2"; "The Brand You 50"; "The Cluetrain Manifesto: The End of Business"; "What to Say to Get What You Want". **Seminars:** Writing; Presentation Skills; International and Intercultural Communication.

22425 ■ Miller, Hellwig Associates
150 W End Ave.
New York, NY 10023-5713
Ph:(212)799-0471
Fax:(212)877-0186
Co. E-mail: millerhelwig@earthlink.net
Contact: Ernest C. Miller, President
Scope: Consulting services in the areas of start-up businesses; small business management; employee surveys and communication; performance appraisals; executive searches; team building; personnel policies and procedures; market research. Also involved in improving cross-cultural and multi-cultural relationships, particularly with Japanese clients. **Seminars:** Objectives and standards/recruiting for boards of directors.

22426 ■ Organization Counselors Inc.
44 W Broadway, Ste. 1102
PO Box 987
Salt Lake City, UT 84101
Ph:(801)363-2900
Fax:(801)363-0861
Co. E-mail: jpanos@xmission.com
Contact: John E. Panos, President
E-mail: jpanos@xmission.com
Scope: Organizational development; employee surveys and communication; outplacement; team building; total quality management and continuous improvement. **Seminars:** Correcting Performance Problems; Total Quality Management; Employee Selection; Performance Management.

22427 ■ ProActive English
4355 SE 29th Ave.
Portland, OR 97202
Ph:(503)231-2906
Co. E-mail: infopae@proactive-english.com
URL: http://www.proactive-english.com
Contact: David Kertzner, Managing Director
E-mail: dkertzner@atsproactive-english.com
Scope: Offers on-site individual and small group language and communication training. Sets up learning plans tailored to the needs and schedules of managers and executives who are non-native English speakers. Serves all industries. **Seminars:** Communicating in Business Situations; Presentations and Pronunciation; Tailored Curriculum; One-on-One Programs.

22428 ■ Reynolds Communication
184 Columbia Hts.
Brooklyn, NY 11201-2105
Ph:(718)625-6797
Fax:(212)509-4224
Co. E-mail: sreynold@stern.nyu.edu
Contact: Sana O. Reynolds, Principle
Scope: Consultant specializing in cross cultural and organizational communication. Areas of expertise include inter cultural communication, business and technical writing, presentation coaching, document design and plain language consulting. **Publications:** "Composing effective e-mail messages," Communication World, Jul, 1997; "Selling to another language," Communication World, Dec, 1996.

22429 ■ Roger S. Peterson Marketing & Communications
3090 Union St.
Rocklin, CA 95677-1837
Ph:(916)624-1894
Fax:(916)624-3069
Co. E-mail: peterson@sacramentowriters.com
URL: http://www.sacramentowriters.com/market_communication.asp
Contact: Roger S. Peterson, President
E-mail: peterson@sacramentowriters.com
Scope: Specializes in business-to-business marketing communications, marketing diagnostics and marketing strategy for small to mid sized firms. **Publications:** "The Secret to Incentive Program Success: Incentive ROI that makes bean counters smile!"; "The Magic Megaphone"; "Ama Handbook For: Managing Business-To-Business Marketing Communications," McGraw-Hill, Apr, 1997. **Seminars:** Essentials of Marketing; The Communications Audit; Survival Training for Product Managers; Marketing Positioning & Promotion; Marketing Tools and How to Use Them; Marketing for Small Business, various American Management Association Courses.

22430 ■ Syntaxis Inc.
2109 Broadway, Ste. 16-159
New York, NY 10023-2106
Ph:(212)799-3000
Fax:(212)799-3021
Co. E-mail: info@syntaxis.com
URL: http://www.syntaxis.com
Contact: Andrew Garman, Principal
E-mail: brandt.johnson@atssyntaxis.com
Scope: Firm trains business professionals to speak and write more powerfully. Areas include presentation skills, business writing, grammar, and e-mail etiquette. **Publications:** "Presentation Skills for Business Professionals"; "A Writing Guide for Business Professionals"; "E-Mail Etiquette for Business Professionals".

22431 ■ Tim W. Hrastar Associates
184 Abbey Dr.
Springboro, OH 45066
Ph:(937)886-0186
Fax:(937)886-0186
Co. E-mail: twh@rapportmarketing.com
URL: http://www.rapportmarketing.com
Contact: Tim W. Hrastar, Owner
E-mail: twh@rapportmarketing.com
Scope: Specializes in helping the accounting and legal professions improve their communications and client relations. Offers communications expertise with emphasis on interpersonal and organizational communications. Experienced in presentation skills coaching, meeting dynamics, counseling in marketing, and client relations communications for professional services field. Clients include Fortune 500 companies as well as small businesses, government agencies, and other organizations in such diverse fields as food service, finance, health care, travel, and consumer and industrial products. **Publications:** "A Plan to Increase Your Market Share hot," Sep, 2009; "Ask Your Client These Questions hot," Feb, 2009; "An Idea to Better Serve Your Small Business Client," 2009; "Ask Your Client These Questions," 2009; "Capturing Your Audience in Five Seconds," 2009; "Business Development in a Down Market," 2009; "Asking for the Business," 2009; "How Do You Look at the World," Jan, 2008; "Business Development Takes Patience, Persistence and a Plan," 2007; "How to Make Persuasive Presentations with Confidence"; "Returning Phone Calls, Why Its Important"; "Five Tips on Thinking Ahead of Your Clients"; "Rapport"; "Five Tips on Thinking Ahead of Your Clients"; "Returning Phone Calls, Why It's Important"; "The Eyes Have It!"; "Reducing Client Apprehension"; "How Would Your Clients Rate You in the Following Areas? Part I". **Seminars:** Business Development for Lawyers; Persuasive Communications in the Courtroom; How to Create and Deliver Persuasive Presentations; How to Create and Deliver Persuasive Presentations; Meeting Dynamics for Lawyers: Conducting and Participating in Effective Meetings; Cool Tools to Improve Client Communications. **Special Services:** Rapport Marketing[R].

22432 ■ Tom Shillock Consulting
5545 SW Windsor Ct.
Portland, OR 97221-2150
Ph:(503)291-7928
Fax:(503)221-2052
Co. E-mail: tomsh@qwest.net
Contact: Tom Shillock, Principle
E-mail: tomsh@qwest.net
Scope: Offers consulting services in marketing and communications including public relations and advertising. Industries served: high technology.

22433 ■ Trendzitions Inc.
25691 Atlantic Ocean Dr., Ste. B13
Lake Forest, CA 92630-8842
Ph:(949)727-9100
Free: 800-266-2767
Fax:(949)727-3444
Co. E-mail: ctooker@trendzitions.com
URL: http://www.trendzitions.com
Contact: Christian Tooker, President
E-mail: ctooker@atstrendzitions.com
Scope: Provides services in the areas of communications consulting, project management, construction management, and furniture procurement. Offers information on spatial uses, building codes, ADA compliance and city ordinances. Also offers budget projections.

22434 ■ The Watts Corp.
22117 161st Ave. SE
Monroe, WA 98272-9171
Ph:(425)941-6781
Fax:(360)805-5873
Contact: Jeffrey H. Watts, CEO
E-mail: jeffrey@wattslink.com
Scope: A profit coach with expertise in sales and profitability, general operations. Available as seminar presenter and venture turn-around. **Seminars:** Customized programs to address specific needs of your company.

22435 ■ Write Wise Communications L.L.C.
488 W 19th St., Ste. 359
Houston, TX 77008
Ph:(713)863-9140
Fax:(713)863-9140
Co. E-mail: contact@writewisecommunications.com
URL: http://www.writewisecommunications.com
Contact: Alise Isbell, Owner
E-mail: alise@writewisecommunications.com
Scope: Firm specializes in needs assessment, strategic planning, training, communication effectiveness surveys, instructional design, course development, writing, organizational development, business planning, virtual teaming, process improvement, online education planning and implementation, and performance improvement. **Seminars:** Grammar Refresher for Adults; Business Writing for Business Professionals; Technical Writing; Writing Effective Proposals; Service Spotlight! Effective Written Presentations; Service Spotlight! Effective Verbal Presentations; Service Spotlight! Effective Distance Presentations; Effective Teamwork over Distance; Time Management; More Productive Meetings; Managing the Strategic Planning Process.

FRANCHISES AND BUSINESS OPPORTUNITIES

22436 ■ Allegra Marketing *Print* Mail
Allegra Network LLC
47585 Galleon Dr.
Plymouth, MI 48170
Ph:(248)596-8600
Free: 800-726-9050
Fax:(248)596-8601
URL: http://www.allegranetwork.com
No. of Franchise Units: 300. **Founded:** 1976. **Franchised:** 1977. **Description:** Full service printing centers. **Equity Capital Needed:** $172,348-$520,814. **Franchise Fee:** $35,000 Start-up Model, $45,000 MatchMaker Model, $20,000 resale. **Financial Assistance:** Third party financing available. **Training:** Provides 2 weeks training at headquarters and 1 week onsite and ongoing support.

Business Correspondence

ASSOCIATIONS AND OTHER ORGANIZATIONS

22437 ■ Association for Business Communication
PO Box 6143
Nacogdoches, TX 75962-0001
Ph:(936)468-6280
Fax:(936)468-6281
Co. E-mail: abcjohnson@sfasu.edu
URL: http://www.businesscommunication.org
Contact: Dr. Betty S. Johnson, Exec. Dir.
Description: College teachers of business communication; management consultants in business communications; training directors and correspondence supervisors of business firms, direct mail copywriters, public relations writers, and others interested in communication for business. **Publications:** *Business Communication Quarterly* (quarterly); *Journal of Business Communication* (quarterly); *Making Communication Requirements More Explicit in the AACSB Standards for MBA Programs* .

22438 ■ International Association of Business Communicators
601 Montgomery St., Ste. 1900
San Francisco, CA 94111
Ph:(415)544-4700
Free: 800-776-4222
Fax:(415)544-4747
Co. E-mail: member_relations@iabc.com
URL: http://www.iabc.com
Contact: Julie Freeman, Pres.
Description: Represents Communication managers, public relations directors, writers, editors, audiovisual specialists, and others in the public relations and organizational communication field that use a variety of media to communicate with internal audiences (employees, management, association members, and leaders) and external audiences (media, customers, dealers, investors, and government). Conducts research in the communication field and encourages establishment of college-level programs in organizational communication. Offers accreditation program; conducts surveys on employee communication effectiveness and media trends. **Publications:** *Essentials of Employee Communication*; *The Human Element*; *The Truth About B2B Marketing ROI*;Newsletter (monthly).

EDUCATIONAL PROGRAMS

22439 ■ Advanced Copyediting
EEI Communications
66 Canal Center Plz., Ste. 200
Alexandria, VA 22314
Ph:(703)683-7453
Free: 888-253-2762
Fax:(703)683-7310
Co. E-mail: train@eeicom.com
URL: http://www.eeicom.com/training
Price: $745.00. **Description:** This course will help you develop and enhance both knowledge and skills in the editing and production process. **Locations:** Alexandria, VA.

22440 ■ Advanced Writing and Editing for Government Proposals
EEI Communications
66 Canal Center Plz., Ste. 200
Alexandria, VA 22314
Ph:(703)683-7453
Free: 888-253-2762
Fax:(703)683-7310
Co. E-mail: train@eeicom.com
URL: http://www.eeicom.com/training
Price: $745.00. **Description:** Developed for anyone who regularly writes, edits, or manages government proposals to explore proposal-specific writing and editing challenges, including how to ensure consistent voice no matter how many writers are involved. **Locations:** Alexandria, VA.

22441 ■ AMA's 2-Day Business Writing Workshop
American Management Association
600 AMA Way
Saranac Lake, NY 12983-5534
Ph:(212)586-8100
Free: 877-566-9441
Fax:(518)891-0368
Co. E-mail: customerservice@amanet.org
URL: http://www.amaseminars.org
Price: $1,995.00 for non-members; $1,795.00 for AMA members; and $1,537.00 for General Services Administration (GSA) members. **Description:** Learn basic formats and formulas to compose documents and communicate what your readers need to know. **Locations:** Cities throughout the United States.

22442 ■ Basics of Government Contract Administration
Seminar Information Service, Inc.
20 Executive Park, Ste. 120
Irvine, CA 92614
Ph:(949)261-9104
Free: 877-SEM-INFO
Fax:(949)261-1963
Co. E-mail: info@seminarinformation.com
URL: http://www.seminarinformation.com
Price: $1,095.00. **Description:** Designed to show you how to fill out the most common standard forms, where the forms are found, and how proper forms preparation avoids administration pitfalls. **Locations:** Las Vegas, NV; Arlington, VA; Orlando, FL; and Long Beach, CA;.

22443 ■ Business English and Grammar Review
Arizona Government Training Center
530 E McDowell Rd., Ste. 107-483
Phoenix, AZ 85004
Ph:(480)967-7544
Free: 800-970-1270
Fax:(480)966-6325
Co. E-mail: help@agts.com
URL: http://www.agts.com
Price: $229.00 for non-members; $189.00 for AGTS members. **Description:** Covers grammatical errors, punctuation, sentence structure, spelling, and plurals and possessives. **Locations:** Phoenix, AZ.

22444 ■ Business Grammar and Proofreading
Padgett-Thompson Seminars
Rockhurst University CEC
14502 W. 105th St.
Lenexa, KS 66215
Free: 800-349-1935
URL: http://www.findaseminar.com/tpd/Padgett-Thompson-Seminars.asp
Price: $199.00. **Description:** A one-day workshop that features a "no-fear" approach to dealing with spelling and grammar. **Locations:** Cities throughout the United States.

22445 ■ Business Grammar & Proofreading (Onsite)
Seminar Information Service, Inc.
20 Executive Park, Ste. 120
Irvine, CA 92614
Ph:(949)261-9104
Free: 877-SEM-INFO
Fax:(949)261-1963
Co. E-mail: info@seminarinformation.com
URL: http://www.seminarinformation.com
Price: $199.00. **Description:** Designed for busy professionals who want to brush up on grammar, spelling, proofreading and business usage. **Locations:** Cities throughout the United States.

22446 ■ Business Writing for Administrative Professionals
American Management Association
600 AMA Way
Saranac Lake, NY 12983-5534
Ph:(212)586-8100
Free: 877-566-9441
Fax:(518)891-0368
Co. E-mail: customerservice@amanet.org
URL: http://www.amaseminars.org
Price: $1,895.00 for non-members; $1,695.00 for AMA members; and $1,451.00 for General Services Administration (GSA) members. **Description:** Learn the skills and techniques you need to write and edit various documents. **Locations:** Washington, DC; Arlington, VA; San Francisco, CA; Washington, DC; New York, NY; and Morristown, NJ.

22447 ■ Business Writing and Grammar Skills
Padgett-Thompson Seminars
Rockhurst University CEC
14502 W. 105th St.
Lenexa, KS 66215
Free: 800-349-1935
URL: http://www.findaseminar.com/tpd/Padgett-Thompson-Seminars.asp
Price: $299.00. **Description:** Developed exclusively for business professionals, this two-day workshop delivers tools and techniques that will add clarity and power to business documents. **Locations:** Cities throughout the United States.

22448 ■ Business Writing and Grammar Skills Made Easy and Fun!
Seminar Information Service, Inc.
20 Executive Park, Ste. 120
Irvine, CA 92614
Ph:(949)261-9104
Free: 877-SEM-INFO
Fax:(949)261-1963
Co. E-mail: info@seminarinformation.com
URL: http://www.seminarinformation.com
Price: $299.00; $269.00 for 4 or more. **Description:** Learn how to project your ideas effectively and clearly through proven techniques. **Locations:** Cities throughout the United States.

22449 ■ Business Writing for the Multilingual Professional
American Management Association
600 AMA Way
Saranac Lake, NY 12983-5534
Ph:(212)586-8100
Free: 877-566-9441
Fax:(518)891-0368
Co. E-mail: customerservice@amanet.org
URL: http://www.amaseminars.org
Price: $2,195.00 for non-members; $1,995.00 for AMA members; and $1,708.00 for General Services Administration (GSA) members. **Description:** Learn practical techniques for creating effective business documents, with focus on correct English grammar and usage. **Locations:** New York, NY; Washington, DC; Arlington, VA; and Chicago, IL.

22450 ■ Business Writing for Results
Fred Pryor Seminars & CareerTrack
5700 Broadmoor St., Ste. 300
Mission, KS 66202
Free: 800-780-8476
Fax:(913)967-8849
Co. E-mail: customerservice@pryor.com
URL: http://www.pryor.com
Price: $199.00; $189.00 for groups of 5 or more. **Description:** Learn to write powerful letters, memos, reports, and proposals that get results. **Locations:** Cities throughout the United States.

22451 ■ Clear Business, Technical, and E-mail Writing (Onsite)
Seminar Information Service, Inc.
20 Executive Park, Ste. 120
Irvine, CA 92614
Ph:(949)261-9104
Free: 877-SEM-INFO
Fax:(949)261-1963
Co. E-mail: info@seminarinformation.com
URL: http://www.seminarinformation.com
Price: $500.00. **Description:** This workshop provides a step-by-step process for designing and writing a clear document, e-mail message, or report with the use of writing, revising, and editing exercises. **Locations:** Redwood City, CA.

22452 ■ Communicating Up, Down and Across the Organization (Canada)
Canadian Management Centre
150 York St., 5th Fl.
Toronto, ON, Canada M5H 3S5
Ph:(416)214-5678
Free: 877-262-2519
Fax:(416)214-6047
Co. E-mail: cmcinfo@cmctraining.org
URL: http://www.cmctraining.org
Price: $1,995.00 Canadian for non-members; $1,845.00 Canadian for CMC members. **Description:** Seminar that encourages dialogue throughout the organization and between different departments, including gaining self-esteem, targeting your message by knowing your audience, building team commitment, develop interpersonal techniques for influencing, build persuasive business cases, and constructing an informative, attention getting project update. **Locations:** Toronto, ON; and Ottawa, ON.

22453 ■ Developing Procedures, Policies and Documentation (Onsite)
Seminar Information Service, Inc.
20 Executive Park, Ste. 120
Irvine, CA 92614
Ph:(949)261-9104
Free: 877-SEM-INFO
Fax:(949)261-1963
Co. E-mail: info@seminarinformation.com
URL: http://www.seminarinformation.com
Price: $1,555.00. **Description:** Learn how to define audience information needs and requirements and how to design information that meets user needs, including how to develop information that is user-friendly and accessible and how to organized information in modular and flexible units for later re-use. **Locations:** Cities throughout the United States.

22454 ■ E-mail and Business Writing
Fred Pryor Seminars & CareerTrack
5700 Broadmoor St., Ste. 300
Mission, KS 66202
Free: 800-780-8476
Fax:(913)967-8849
Co. E-mail: customerservice@pryor.com
URL: http://www.pryor.com
Price: $99.00; $89.00 for groups of 5 or more. **Description:** Learn how to craft e-mail messages that are grammatically correct, concise, and to the point. **Locations:** Cities throughout the United States.

22455 ■ The E-Mail and Business Writing Workshop
Padgett-Thompson Seminars
Rockhurst University CEC
14502 W. 105th St.
Lenexa, KS 66215
Free: 800-349-1935
URL: http://www.findaseminar.com/tpd/Padgett-Thompson-Seminars.asp
Price: $199.00. **Description:** A one-day seminar that offers tips and techniques to guarantee that every message written will be polished and on target. **Locations:** Cities throughout the United States.

22456 ■ Effective Business Writing
Baker Communications, Inc.
10101 SW Freeway, Ste. 630
Houston, TX 77074
Ph:(713)627-7700
Fax:(713)587-2051
Co. E-mail: info@bakercommunications.com
URL: http://www.bakercommunications.com
Price: $695.00. **Description:** Participants learn to convey ideas and information with clarity and precision in memos, letters, reports, and other business correspondence. **Locations:** Boston, MA; Calgary, AB; and Houston, TX.

22457 ■ Effective Technical Writing
American Management Association
1601 Broadway
New York, NY 10019
Ph:(212)586-8100
Free: 800-262-9699
Fax:(212)903-8168
Co. E-mail: customerservice@amanet.org
URL: http://www.amanet.org
Price: $1,795.00 for non-members; $1,595.00 for AMA members. **Description:** Covers the basics of writing technical documents such as reports, manuals, specifications, proposals, and instructions. **Locations:** Atlanta, GA; Chicago, IL; and New York, NY.

22458 ■ Exceptional Business Writing and Goof-Proof Grammar
Fred Pryor Seminars & CareerTrack
5700 Broadmoor St., Ste. 300
Mission, KS 66202
Free: 800-780-8476
Fax:(913)967-8849
Co. E-mail: customerservice@pryor.com
URL: http://www.pryor.com
Price: $299.00; $279.00 for groups of 3 or more. **Description:** Learn how to communicate clearly and effectively so others view you as confident and capable. **Locations:** Cities throughout the United States.

22459 ■ Government Proposal Writing Basics
EEI Communications
66 Canal Center Plz., Ste. 200
Alexandria, VA 22314
Ph:(703)683-7453
Free: 888-253-2762
Fax:(703)683-7310
Co. E-mail: train@eeicom.com
URL: http://www.eeicom.com/training
Price: $745.00. **Description:** Designed for proposal novices at any level of writing ability, this course explains the unique features of government proposals and the government procurement process. **Locations:** Alexandria, VA.

22460 ■ Hands-On Business and Report Writing: The Art of Persuasion (Onsite)
Seminar Information Service, Inc.
20 Executive Park, Ste. 120
Irvine, CA 92614
Ph:(949)261-9104
Free: 877-SEM-INFO
Fax:(949)261-1963
Co. E-mail: info@seminarinformation.com
URL: http://www.seminarinformation.com
Price: $2,490.00. **Description:** Learn how to: Write compelling documents that focus your message; Compose targeted messages using a standard writing process; Improve document comprehension with polished grammar and punctuation; Produce winning proposals, recommendation reports and executive summaries; Create effective written communications that drive your business; Develop a clear, persuasive writing style. **Locations:** New York, NY; and Toronto, CN.

22461 ■ How to Communicate with Diplomacy, Tact and Credibility (Canada)
Canadian Management Centre
150 York St., 5th Fl.
Toronto, ON, Canada M5H 3S5
Ph:(416)214-5678
Free: 877-262-2519
Fax:(416)214-6047
Co. E-mail: cmcinfo@cmctraining.org
URL: http://www.cmctraining.org
Price: $1,995.00 Canadian for non-members; $1,845.00 Canadian for CMC members. **Description:** Seminar covering how to mold your communication style to meet the needs of individual situations, develop active listening and questioning strategies, gain cooperation and respect by promoting and modeling tolerance with politically correct attitudes and communication, break through communication gridlock, expand the communication network, and turn communication conflicts into opportunities for cooperation and growth. **Locations:** Toronto, ON; and Ottawa, ON.

22462 ■ How to Sharpen Your Business Writing Skills
American Management Association
600 AMA Way
Saranac Lake, NY 12983-5534
Ph:(212)586-8100
Free: 877-566-9441
Fax:(518)891-0368
Co. E-mail: customerservice@amanet.org
URL: http://www.amaseminars.org
Price: $2,445.00 for non-members; $2,195.00 for AMA members; and $1,880.00 for General Services Administration (GSA) members. **Description:** Covers how to solve common writing problems, various writing concepts, and how to write effective letters, memos, reports, and business proposals. **Locations:** San Francisco, CA; Arlington, VA; Washington, DC; Chicago, IL; Atlanta, GA; and New York, NY.

22463 ■ How to Write Effective Policies and Procedures
Seminar Information Service, Inc.
20 Executive Park, Ste. 120
Irvine, CA 92614
Ph:(949)261-9104
Free: 877-SEM-INFO
Fax:(949)261-1963
Co. E-mail: info@seminarinformation.com
URL: http://www.seminarinformation.com
Price: $249.00. **Description:** Covers rules, strategies, guidelines and shortcuts that will make your job easier and ensure you get the results of a well-written policies and procedures that are read and understood by all. **Locations:** Cities throughout the United States.

22464 ■ Mapping Business Communications (Onsite)
Seminar Information Service, Inc.
20 Executive Park, Ste. 120
Irvine, CA 92614
Ph:(949)261-9104
Free: 877-SEM-INFO
Fax:(949)261-1963
Co. E-mail: info@seminarinformation.com
URL: http://www.seminarinformation.com
Price: $995.00. **Description:** Learn to identify the purpose of each communication define the specific action required from the reader customize the message for different audiences to achieve greater results organize communications to make information quick and easy to find, and present information in the way that best suits the target audience. **Locations:** Waltham, MA.

22465 ■ Mistake-Free Grammar & Proofreading
Fred Pryor Seminars & CareerTrack
5700 Broadmoor St., Ste. 300
Mission, KS 66202
Free: 800-780-8476
Fax:(913)967-8849
Co. E-mail: customerservice@pryor.com
URL: http://www.pryor.com
Price: $149.00; $139.00 for groups of 5 or more. **Description:** Learn grammar rules and to proofread with perfection. **Locations:** Cities throughout the United States.

22466 ■ Records Retention and Destruction
Fred Pryor Seminars & CareerTrack
5700 Broadmoor St., Ste. 300
Mission, KS 66202
Free: 800-780-8476
Fax:(913)967-8849
Co. E-mail: customerservice@pryor.com
URL: http://www.pryor.com
Price: $149.00; $139.00 for groups of 5 or more. **Description:** Gain valuable information for successfully organizing, storing, archiving and destroying your organization's critical business documents while eliminating risk and ensuring compliance with the latest legal requirements. **Locations:** Cities throughout the United States.

22467 ■ Substantive Editing III
EEI Communications
66 Canal Center Plz., Ste. 200
Alexandria, VA 22314
Ph:(703)683-7453
Free: 888-253-2762
Fax:(703)683-7310
Co. E-mail: train@eeicom.com
URL: http://www.eeicom.com/training
Price: $425.00. **Description:** Evaluate your editing style, fine tune your ability to differentiate levels of edit, review documents at the appropriate level, learn to set clear expectations, find new ways to give constructive feedback to writers, and learn to coach, rather than edit, to encourage better writing. **Locations:** Alexandria, VA.

22468 ■ Technical Writing: A Comprehensive Hands-On Introduction (Onsite)
Seminar Information Service, Inc.
20 Executive Park, Ste. 120
Irvine, CA 92614
Ph:(949)261-9104
Free: 877-SEM-INFO
Fax:(949)261-1963
Co. E-mail: info@seminarinformation.com
URL: http://www.seminarinformation.com
Price: $2,890.00. **Description:** Learn how to: Write clear, effective technical = documents, including user manuals and technical reports; Assess your target audience and develop documents to meet their needs; Choose the appropriate writing style to communicate to specialized audiences; Build effective sentences, paragraphs and sections that explain information clearly; Employ diagrams, tables, charts and other graphical tools effectively; Create informative and interesting content that your readers will comprehend and utilize. **Locations:** Rockville, MD; Ottawa, CN; and Alexandria, VA.

22469 ■ Writing the Perfect Business E-Mail
EEI Communications
66 Canal Ctr. Plz., Ste. 200
Alexandria, VA 22314-5507
Ph:(703)683-7453
Free: 888-253-2762
Fax:(703)683-7310
Co. E-mail: train@eeicom.com
URL: http://www.eeicom.com/training
Price: $425.00. **Description:** Seminar that covers e-mails that get read and are understood, including keeping it short and simple, make it useful, spelling, grammar, and other problems, controlling emotion, writing attachments that get read, progress reports, instructions, and evaluations and recommendations. **Locations:** Silver Spring, MD; Alexandria, VA; Hunt Valley, MD; and Columbia, MD.

22470 ■ Writing for the Web
AMA
600 AMA Way
Saranac Lake, NY 12983-5534
Ph:(212)586-8100
Free: 877-566-9441
Fax:(518)891-0368
Co. E-mail: customerservice@amanet.org
URL: http://www.amaseminars.org
Price: $1,995.00 for non-members; $1,795.00 for AMA members; $1,537.00 for General Services Administration (GSA) members. **Description:** Create online content that connects with readers to achieve better results in this two-day course. **Locations:** New York, NY; Arlington, VA; and Washington, DC.

REFERENCE WORKS

22471 ■ "Ask Inc." in *Inc.* (January 2008, pp. 60)
Pub: Gruner & Jahr USA Publishing
Description: Ways to manage high volumes of email are examined.

22472 ■ *Be a Brilliant Business Writer: Write Well, Write Fast, and Whip the Competition*
Pub: Crown Business Books
Ed: Jane Curry, Diana Young. **Released:** October 5, 2010. **Price:** $13.99. **Description:** Tools for mastering the art of persuasive writing in every document created, from email and client letters to reports and presentations, this book will help any writer convey their message with clarity and power, increase productivity by reducing rewrites, and provide the correct tone for navigating office politics.

22473 ■ "Before You Hit Send: Crafting Workplace E-Mails to Avoid Mishaps" in *Black Enterprise* (Vol. 38, January 2008, No. 6, pp. 85)
Pub: Earl G. Graves Publishing Co. Inc.
Ed: Tennille M. Robinson. **Description:** Tips to use before sending an office email our presented. It is important to keep emails looking professional.

22474 ■ "Bridging the Gap: Contextualing Professional Ethics in Collaborative Writing Projects" in *Business Communication Quarterly* (Dec.2007)
Pub: Sage Publications USA
Ed: J.A. Rice. **Description:** A classroom activity for business management students integrates ethical concepts with business writing strategies, while increasing understanding of writing ethics by emphasizing its rhetorical, contingent, and public nature.

22475 ■ "Campaigner Survey: 46 Percent of Small Businesses Use Email Marketing" in *Wireless News* (November 21, 2009)
Pub: Close-Up Media
Description: Almost half (46 percent) of small businesses surveyed by Campaigner's 2009 State of Small Business Online Marketing, say that they rely on email marketing to help them find new customers, keep existing ones and grow their businesses. The survey also found that 36 percent of small businesses plan to begin using email marketing over the next year. The trend to utilize Internet marketing tools is allowing small businesses to grow faster and generate higher revenues than those that are not using these mediums.

22476 ■ "Canadians Keep Memories in 'Inboxes' Instead of Shoe Boxes; MSN Canada" in *Canadian Corporate News* (May 14, 2007)
Pub: Comtex News Network Inc.
Description: According to an MSN Canada online poll, 76 percent of Canadians are creating 'virtual shoeboxes' with their email inboxes and archiving important messages, photos, and documents.

22477 ■ "Conferencing Takes on High-Tech Futuristic Feel" in *Crain's Cleveland Business* (Vol. 28, October 29, 2007, No. 43, pp. 17)
Pub: Crain Communications, Inc.
Ed: Chuck Soder. **Description:** Overview of the newest technologies which are making local company's meetings more effective including: tele-presence, a videoconferencing technology, as well as virtual flip charts.

22478 ■ "Creative Marketing: How to Cultivate a Network of Endless Referrals" in *Agency Sales Magazine* (Vol. 39, July 2009, No. 7, pp. 38)
Pub: MANA
Ed: Bob Burg. **Description:** Tips on how a salesperson can build a network of people that will bring them referrals are presented. Asking a person about their business and re-introducing one's self to an earlier acquaintance while remembering their names are some elements in the process of building this network.

22479 ■ "Etiquette, Common Sense Often Lag Behind Smarter Devices" in *Crain's Cleveland Business* (Vol. 28, October 22, 2007, No. 42, pp. 21)
Pub: Crain Communications, Inc.
Ed: Chrissy Kadleck. **Description:** Discusses the importance of good etiquette in regards to electronic communication both within as well as outside the business world.

22480 ■ "Extreme Negotiations" in *Harvard Business Review* (Vol. 88, November 2010, No. 11, pp. 66)
Pub: Harvard Business School Publishing
Ed: Jeff Weiss, Aram Donigian, Jonathan Hughes. **Description:** Examination of military negotiation skills that are applicable in business situations. Skills include soliciting others' perspectives, developing and proposing multiple solutions, and inviting others to assess them.

22481 ■ "Facebook: A Promotional Budget's Best Friend" in *Women Entrepreneur* (February 1, 2009)
Pub: Entrepreneur Media Inc.
Ed: Tamara Monosoff. **Description:** Facebook began as a social networking website but has become a valuable marketing tool for all types of businesses, organizations and causes. Tips are provided for creating a Facebook account and growing one's network on Facebook.

22482 ■ "Faster and Shorter" in *Canadian Business* (Vol. 81, October 13, 2008, No. 17, pp. 25)
Pub: Rogers Media Ltd.
Ed: Terri Goveia. **Description:** Study revealed that instant messaging (IM) technologies are slowly becoming legitimate in the corporate world. IM is traditionally considered as a distraction, but it was found to let workers make targeted inquiries that gives them what they need in an instant. Other views and information about IMs is included.

22483 ■ "Five Steps to an Effective Business Call" in *Hawaii Business* (Vol. 53, October 2007, No. 4, pp. 64)
Pub: Hawaii Business Publishing
Ed: Matthew K. Ing. **Description:** University of Hawaii professor Libda Patrylak believes that communication skills are integral to business success,

which is why businesses should know how to properly handle phone conversations. Presented are five ways of achieving effective business phone calls, such as setting rules for employees to follow with regards to answering calls and providing undivided attention to the other speaker.

22484 ■ "Five Things...For Photo Fun" in *Hawaii Business* (Vol. 53, October 2007, No. 4, pp. 20)
Pub: Hawaii Business Publishing
Ed: Cathy S. Cruz-George. **Description:** Featured is a buyers guide of products used for capturing or displaying digital photos; products featured include the Digital Photo Wallet and Light Affection.

22485 ■ "Get Personal" in *Entrepreneur* (Vol. 36, April 2008, No. 4)
Pub: Entrepreneur Media, Inc.
Ed: Romanus Wolter. **Description:** Customers appreciate personal contact, and communicating with them can help business owners' customer relations. Some ways on how to keep a personal touch with customers and improve business dealings include blending technology with personal interaction and knowing what the customers want. Other tips are provided.

22486 ■ "Grooming Your Online Persona" in *Women In Business* (Vol. 62, June 2010, No. 2, pp. 36)
Pub: American Business Women's Association
Ed: Diane Stafford. **Description:** Employees' use of online social networks could become a basis on how their employers, clients, or business partners would judge them. Personal details, pictures and other online data should be filtered to avoid inappropriate or uncomfortable situations and distinguish personal from professional or work life.

22487 ■ "How to Boost Your Super Bowl ROI" in *Advertising Age* (Vol. 80, December 7, 2009, No. 41, pp. 3)
Pub: Crain's Communications
Ed: Abbey Klaassen. **Description:** Internet marketing is essential, even for the corporations that can afford to spend $3 million on a 30-second Super Bowl spot; last year, Super Bowl advertising reached an online viewership of 99.5 million while 98.7 million people watched the game on television validating the idea that public relations must go farther than a mere television ad campaign. Social media provides businesses with a longer shelf life for their ad campaigns. Advice is also given regarding ways in which to strategize a smart and well-thought plan for utilizing the online marketing options currently available.

22488 ■ "How Pixar Fosters Collective Creativity" in *Harvard Business Review* (Vol. 86, September 2008, No. 9, pp. 64)
Pub: Harvard Business School Press
Ed: Ed Catmull. **Description:** Pixar Animation Studios illustrates peer-culture methods for fostering product development. These include allowing any employee to communicate with any other employee, providing a safe environment for new ideas, and watching the academic community closely for innovations.

22489 ■ "How to Write a Report" in *Canadian Business* (Vol. 80, November 5, 2007, No. 22, pp. 41)
Pub: Rogers Media
Ed: Gabriel Fuchs. **Description:** Basic rule in writing a report is the so-called USNA, which stands for Use Synonyms, No Acronyms. Synonyms make the report seem more interesting while acronyms increase the chance of being misunderstood. Details of how to write an impressive business report are given.

22490 ■ "Hunter and the Hunted" in *Canadian Business* (Vol. 81, Summer 2008, No. 9, pp. 12)
Pub: Rogers Media Ltd.
Ed: Thomas Watson. **Description:** Brian Hunter, a partner in oil and gas engineering firm Montane Resources, invested his life savings in Vancouver-based Canacord Capital Corp. Details of the asset-backed commercial paper fiasco and Hunter's use of Facebook to encourage other investors to participate in his claim against the mortgage company are presented.

22491 ■ "I Can Make Your Brain Look Like Mine" in *Harvard Business Review* (Vol. 88, December 2010, No. 12, pp. 32)
Pub: Harvard Business School Publishing
Description: Psychology professor Uri Hasson discusses findings that the brain waves of a speaker and a listener become similar as the listener's comprehension increases.

22492 ■ *Information Technology for the Small Business: How to Make IT Work For Your Company*
Pub: TAB Computer Systems, Incorporated
Ed: T.J. Benoit. **Released:** June 2006. **Price:** $17. 95. **Description:** Basics of information technology to help small companies maximize benefits are covered. Topics include pitfalls to avoid, email and Internet use, data backup, recovery and overall IT organization.

22493 ■ "Integrating Business Core Knowledge through Upper Division Report Composition" in *Business Communication Quarterly* (December 2007)
Pub: Sage Publications USA
Ed: Joy Roach, Daniel Tracy, Kay Durden. **Description:** An assignment that integrates subjects and encourages the use of business communication report-writing skills is presented. This assignment is designed to complement business school curricula and help develop critical thinking and organizational skills.

22494 ■ "An Introvert's Guide to Schmoozing" in *Canadian Business* (Vol. 83, July 20, 2010, No. 11-12, pp. 73)
Pub: Rogers Media Ltd.
Ed: Jasmine Budak. **Description:** Writer Nancy Ankowitz says that introverts seem to get grouped with social misfits but introverts are people who recharge by spending time alone. Ankowitz advises introverts to use their strengths in quiet strengths such as writing and listening as well as learning to speak in public.

22495 ■ "Is It Time to Ban Swearing at Work?" in *HR Specialist* (Vol. 8, September 2010, No. 9, pp. 2)
Pub: Capitol Information Group Inc.
Description: Screening software has been developed to identify profanity used in business correspondence.

22496 ■ "Israeli Spam Law May Have Global Impact" in *Information Today* (Vol. 26, February 2009, No. 2, pp. 28)
Pub: Information Today, Inc.
Ed: David Mirchin. **Description:** Israels new law, called Amendment 40 of the Communications Law, will regulate commercial solicitations including those sent without permission via email, fax, automatic phone dialing systems, or short messaging technologies.

22497 ■ *The Language of Success: Business Writing That Informs, Persuades, and Gets Results*
Pub: AMACOM
Ed: Tom Sant. **Released:** January 2008. **Price:** $15. 00. **Description:** The damage that can be done when words are used ineffectively and the power to be gained when they are used well in business.

22498 ■ "Life's Work: Oliver Sacks" in *Harvard Business Review* (Vol. 88, November 2010, No. 11, pp. 152)
Pub: Harvard Business School Publishing
Ed: Lisa Burrell. **Description:** Neurologist and author Oliver Sacks discusses whether different types of minds tend toward certain skills, physician-patient communication, and his own perspectives from being a patient himself.

22499 ■ "Managing Corporate Social Networks" in *Harvard Business Review* (Vol. 86, July-August 2008, No. 8, pp. 26)
Pub: Harvard Business School Press
Ed: Adam M. Kleinbaum; Michael L. Tushman. **Description:** Tips on how to promote business creativity and foster knowledge building through business social networks are given.

22500 ■ "Meetings Go Virtual" in *HRMagazine* (Vol. 54, January 2009, No. 1, pp. 74)
Pub: Society for Human Resource Management
Ed: Elizabeth Agnvall. **Description:** Microsoft Office Live Meeting conferencing software allows companies to schedule meetings from various company locations, thus saving travel costs.

22501 ■ "Mosaid Grants First Wireless Parent License To Matsushita" in *Canadian Electronics* (Vol. 23, June-July 2008, No. 5, pp. 1)
Pub: Action Communication Inc.
Description: Matsushita Electric Industrial Co. Ltd. has been granted a six-and-a-half-year license by Mosaid Technologies Inc. to manufacture the latter's products. The patent portfolio license agreement covers Mosaid's Wi-Fi, Wi-Max, CDMA-enabled notebook computers and other products.

22502 ■ "'Mr. CEO, Please Do Elaborate On Your Firm's Metrics'" in *Business Courier* (Vol. 24, February 29, 2008, No. 47, pp. 1)
Pub: American City Business Journals, Inc.
Ed: Jon Newberry. **Description:** Discusses a rogue caller who goes by the name of Joe Herrick, Steven Nissan and Joe Harris has joined in over a dozen conference calls, asking chief executive officers on their plans and commenting on the companies' operations. The mystery caller attempts to pass himself off as a financial analyst. Transcripts of some conference calls, in which the rogue caller is involved, are provided.

22503 ■ "New Sprint Phone Whets Appetite for Applications" in *The Business Journal-Serving Metropolitan Kansas City* (Vol. 26, July 25, 2008)
Pub: American City Business Journals, Inc.
Ed: Suzanna Stagemeyer. **Description:** Firms supporting the applications of the new Samsung Instinct, which was introduced by Sprint Nextel Corp. in June 2008, have reported usage rates increase for their products. Handmark, whose mobile services Pocket Express comes loaded with Instinct, has redirected employees to meet the rising demand for the services. Other views and information on Instinct, are presented.

22504 ■ "Not Your Dad's Business Card" in *Small Business Opportunities* (July 2008)
Pub: Entrepreneur Media Inc.
Ed: Rob Schlacter. **Description:** Provides tips on how to effectively design and use business cards.

22505 ■ "Oh, Behave!" in *Entrepreneur* (Vol. 36, April 2008, No. 4, pp. 87)
Pub: Entrepreneur Media, Inc.
Ed: Gwen Moran. **Description:** Online social networks can pose awkward situations for users. These include instances such as getting a link request from someone you do not know, having a contact post embarrassing information on your site, and a contact asking you to be refer him to one of your business contacts. Tips on how to deal with these situations are discussed.

22506 ■ "OtherInbox Ready for Revenue: Software Startup Expects Profits in '09" in *Austin Business JournalInc.* (Vol. 28, January 2, 2009)
Pub: American City Business Journals
Ed: Christopher Calnan. **Description:** Founder of Austin, Texas-based OtherBox Inc. expects the company to generate revenue through subscriptions and advertising and also reach profitability in 2009. The company's email management tool sends secondary mail to an alternate location thereby freeing up the work inbox for more urgent messages.

22507 ■ "Our Gadget of the Week: Business Buddy" in *Barron's* (Vol. 88, July 7, 2008, No. 27, pp. 26)
Pub: Dow Jones & Co., Inc.
Ed: Jay Palmer. **Description:** Review and evaluation of the Lenovo X300 laptop computer which offers executives a variety of features despite its smaller size and weight. The laptop is about 0.73 inch thick, comes with a 64-gigabyte solid-state drive from Samsung, and weighs less than three pounds.

22508 ■ "Our Gadget of the Week: Mostly, I Liked It" in *Barron's* (Vol. 88, July 14, 2008, No. 28, pp. 31)
Pub: Dow Jones & Co., Inc.
Ed: Jay Palmer. **Description:** Review of the Apple iPhone 3G, which costs $199, has better audio and is slightly thicker than its predecessor; using the 3G wireless connection makes going online faster but drains the battery faster too.

22509 ■ "Partnering for Success" in *Art Business News* (Vol. 36, October 2009, No. 10, pp. 4)
Pub: Summit Business Media
Ed: Jennifer Dulin Wiley. **Description:** In such a volatile economy many savvy artists and gallery owners are turning to out-of-the-box partnerships for continued success; these partnerships are also pervading the Internet, especially with such social media networks as Facebook and Twitter where artists and businesses can develop a loyal following.

22510 ■ "People Often Trust Eloquence More Than Honesty" in *Harvard Business Review* (Vol. 88, November 2010, No. 11, pp. 36)
Pub: Harvard Business School Publishing
Ed: Todd Rogers, Michael I. Norton. **Description:** The article shows how deftly side-stepping a question in an eloquent manner generates a more positive response in an audience than does a direct answer that is ineffectively delivered. Implications for both politics and business are discussed.

22511 ■ *Persuasive Business Proposals*
Pub: AMACOM
Ed: Tom Sant. **Released:** December 2003. **Price:** $17.95. **Description:** Writing to win more customers, clients, and contracts.

22512 ■ "Pressed for Time" in *Marketing to Women* (Vol. 21, March 2008, No. 3, pp. 1)
Pub: EPM Communications, Inc.
Description: Statistical data concerning the tools women use for time management which include gadgets as well as traditional media such as calendars.

22513 ■ "A Proper Welcome" in *Canadian Business* (Vol. 79, July 17, 2006, No. 14-15, pp. 67)
Pub: Rogers Media
Ed: Graham Lowe. **Description:** New-employee orientation programs of various companies are highlighted. Useful practices to create a comfortable ambiance for new recruits are elucidated as well.

22514 ■ "Real-Time Computer-Mediated Communication" in *Business Communication Quarterly* (December 2007, pp. 466)
Pub: Sage Publications USA
Ed: Amy Newman. **Description:** Technology-based simulation for business students to respond to emails and instant messages is presented. The simulation allows students to handle volume business correspondence at work with organizational context and under real-word business situations.

22515 ■ "Research and Markets Adds Report: The U.S. Mobile Web Market" in *Entertainment Close-Up* (December 10, 2009)
Pub: Close-Up Media
Description: Highlights of the new Research and Markets report "The U.S. Mobile Web Market: Taking Advantage of the iPhone Phenomenon" include: mobile Internet marketing strategies; the growth of mobile web usage; the growth of revenue in the mobile web market; and a look at Internet business communications, social media and networking.

22516 ■ "The Rypple Effect; Performance Management" in *The Economist* (Vol. 390, January 3, 2009, No. 8612, pp. 48)
Pub: The Economist Newspaper Inc.
Description: New companies such as Rypple, a new, web-based service, claim that they can satisfy the Net Generation's need for frequent assessments while easing the burden this creates for management.

22517 ■ "Say Goodbye to Voicemail" in *Agency Sales Magazine* (Vol. 39, November 2009, No. 10, pp. 3)
Pub: MANA
Description: Salespeople should think twice before leaving a voicemail. The emerging modern etiquette is to send a text message or to e-mail the customer or client. Communication suggestions for both salespeople and their principals are presented.

22518 ■ "Shoestring-Budget Marketing" in *Women Entrepreneur* (January 5, 2009)
Pub: Entrepreneur Media Inc.
Ed: Maria Falconer. **Description:** Pay-per-click search engine advertising is the traditional type of e-marketing that may not only be too expensive for certain kinds of businesses but also may not attract the quality customer base a business looking to grow needs to find. Social networking websites have become a mandatory marketing tool for business owners who want to see growth in their sales; tips are provided for utilizing these networking websites in order to gain more visibility on the Internet which can, in turn, lead to the more sales.

22519 ■ "Social Media: Communicate the Important Stuff" in *Agency Sales Magazine* (Vol. 39, November 2009, No. 10, pp. 52)
Pub: MANA
Ed: Jack Foster. **Description:** Social media such as Twitter or Facebook allows businesses to communicate with their customers over great distances but this technology can take away from the personal touch. For those that want to implement these tools in their marketing plans, they should first find out which social media networks their target audience use and give their customers reasons to become fans.

22520 ■ "Social Networking Site for Moms" in *Marketing to Women* (Vol. 21, March 2008, No. 3, pp. 3)
Pub: EPM Communications, Inc.
Description: The Cradle is a social networking site devoted to pregnancy and new parenthood.

22521 ■ "Spell It Out" in *Entrepreneur* (Vol. 36, April 2008, No. 4, pp. 123)
Pub: Entrepreneur Media, Inc.
Ed: Emily Weisberg. **Description:** IM:It is an apparel and accessories company that markets products with instant messaging (IM) acronyms and emoticons. Examples of these are "LOL" and "GTG". Other details on IM:It products are discussed.

22522 ■ *Table Talk: The Savvy Girl's Alternative to Networking*
Pub: AuthorHouse
Ed: Diane Danielson. **Released:** April 1, 2003. **Price:** $17.50. **Description:** Let's face it. Women and men are different. So why should we all have to network in the same way? And, why should women have to 'network' at all? Between family and work responsibilities, the idea of pressing flesh at some not-very-festive cocktail party is right up there in appeal with a root canal. But what if women could find a way to make career boosting connections that are actually fun? Enter 'table talk', a new way to network for time-pressed, professional women.

22523 ■ "Understanding Persuasive Online Sales Messages from eBay Auctions" in *Business Communication Quarterly* (December 2007, pp. 482)
Pub: Sage Publications USA
Ed: Barbara Jo White, Daniel Clapper, Rita Noel, Jenny Fortier, Pierre Grabolosa. **Description:** eBay product listings were studied to determine the requirements of persuasive sales writing. Potential sellers should use the proper keywords and make an authentic description with authentic photographs of the item being auctioned.

22524 ■ "Vistaprint Survey Indicates that Online Marketing Taking Hold Among Small Businesses" in *Internet Wire* (December 10, 2009)
Pub: Comtex News Network, Inc.
Description: According to a comprehensive survey from Vistaprint N.V., small businesses are very likely to increase their use of Internet marketing strategies such as paid and organic search, email marketing, social media networking and custom websites over the next year. Trends continue to show that more small businesses are indeed adapting to the changing marketplace and are more willing to diversify their marketing strategies than ever before.

22525 ■ "Why Mumbai at 1PM is the Center of the Business World" in *Harvard Business Review* (Vol. 88, October 2010, No. 10, pp. 38)
Pub: Harvard Business School Publishing
Ed: Michael Segalla. **Description:** A time zone chart is presented for assisting in the planning of international conference calls.

22526 ■ "Wi-Fi Finds Its Way Despite Nixed Plan for Free System" in *Crain's Cleveland Business* (Vol. 28, November 12, 2007, No. 45, pp. 3)
Pub: Crain Communications, Inc.
Ed: Jay Miller. **Description:** Discusses the issues facing Cleveland and Northeast Ohio concerning their proposal to offer citizens wireless Internet services for free or a small fee.

22527 ■ "Words at Work" in *Information Today* (Vol. 26, February 2009, No. 2, pp. 25)
Pub: Information Today, Inc.
Description: Current new buzzwords include the following: digital amnesia, or overload by availability, speed and volume of digital information; maternal profiling, a form a discrimination against women; recipe malpractice, a reminder that just because you can turn on a stove it doesn't make you a chef; ringxiety, the act when everyone reaches for their cell phone when one rings; verbing, the practice of turning good nouns into verbs.

22528 ■ "Work Smarter" in *Entrepreneur* (Vol. 36, April 2008, No. 4, pp. 70)
Pub: Entrepreneur Media, Inc.
Ed: Amanda C. Kooser. **Description:** Online applications that address a business' particular needs are presented. These web applications offer email services, collaboration services of sharing and editing documents and presentations, and tie-ups with online social networking sites. Details on various web applications are provided.

22529 ■ "The Workplace Generation Gaps" in *Women In Business* (Vol. 62, June 2010, No. 2, pp. 8)
Pub: American Business Women's Association
Ed: Leigh Elmore. **Description:** Generation gaps among baby boomers, Generation X and Generation Y in the workplace are attributed to technological divides and differences in opinions. These factors could lead to workplace misunderstandings, employee turnover and communication difficulties. Details on managing such workplace gaps are discussed.

TRADE PERIODICALS

22530 ■ *Copy Editor*
Pub: Barbara Wallraff
Ed: Barbara Wallraff, Editor, barbaraw@copyeditor.com. **Released:** Bimonthly. **Price:** $69; $74, Canada and Mexico; $128, two years; $138, Canada and Mexico 2 years. **Description:** Covers new words, changes in usage, and reference books for editors.

22531 ■ *Writing That Works*
Pub: Communications Concepts Inc.
Contact: John De Lellis, Editor & Publisher
Released: Monthly. **Price:** $119 U.S., Canada and Mexico. **Description:** Advises corporate, nonprofit, agency and independent communicators on business

writing and publishing. Also covers writing techniques, style matters, publication management, and online publishing. Publisher also sponsors annual APEX Awards for Publication Excellence.

VIDEOCASSETTES/ AUDIOCASSETTES

22532 ■ *Basic Steps for Better Business Writing*
Encyclopedia Britannica
331 N. LaSalle St.
Chicago, IL 60654
Ph:(312)347-7159
Free: 800-323-1229
Fax:(312)294-2104
URL: http://www.britannica.com
Released: 1988. **Price:** $1995.00. **Description:** This package of five video-cassettes, including a Leader's Guide, shows employees how to cut their writing time in half while generating written communications that sell ideas, stimulate action and reduce confusion. **Availability:** VHS; 3/4U.

22533 ■ *Better Business Grammar*
Briefings Publishing Group
2807 N. Parham Rd., Ste. 200
Richmond, VA 23294
Free: 800-791-8699
Fax:(570)-320-2079
Co. E-mail: briefingsweborders@publishersservice-associates.com
URL: http://www.briefings.com
Released: 1991. **Price:** $79.00. **Description:** Basic tips for managers on how to get over common stumbling blocks of the English language when writing. **Availability:** VHS.

22534 ■ *Business Writing: Quick, Clear, Concise*
American Media, Inc.
4621 121st St.
Urbandale, IA 50323-2311
Ph:(515)224-0919
Free: 888-776-8268
Fax:(515)327-2555
Co. E-mail: custsvc@ammedia.com
URL: http://www.ammedia.com
Released: 1992. **Price:** $695.00. **Description:** Features tips on reducing writing time, improving clarity, and organizing ideas using a five-step method. Includes an instructor's guide, participant workbooks, an erase-board, and overhead transparencies. **Availability:** VHS; 3/4U; 8mm.

22535 ■ *Business Writing Skills Series*
Cambridge Educational
c/o Films Media Group
132 West 31st Street, 17th Floor
Ste. 124
New York, NY 10001
Free: 800-257-5126
Fax:(609)671-0266
Co. E-mail: custserve@films.com
URL: http://www.cambridgeol.com
Released: 199?. **Price:** $149.95. **Description:** Two tape series offers practical tips for organizing your thoughts effectively for written business communication. Includes advice on breaking writer's block, creating a strong opening and closing, choosing a formal versus an informal style, and more. **Availability:** VHS.

22536 ■ *Communication*
American Media, Inc.
4621 121st St.
Urbandale, IA 50323-2311
Ph:(515)224-0919
Free: 888-776-8268
Fax:(515)327-2555
Co. E-mail: custsvc@ammedia.com
URL: http://www.ammedia.com
Released: 1989. **Price:** $1485.00. **Description:** Communication, in the form of memos, phone calls, and presentations are essential to business success. **Availability:** VHS; 3/4U.

22537 ■ *Techniques to Improve Your Writing: Practical G/T Business Writing*
Instructional Video
2219 C St.
Lincoln, NE 68502
Ph:(402)475-6570
Free: 800-228-0164
Fax:(402)475-6500
Co. E-mail: feedback@insvideo.com
URL: http://www.insvideo.com
Price: $79.95. **Description:** Outlines techniques on how to write reports, memos, and letters more clearly. Also covers tough punctuation and grammar questions. Includes handbook. **Availability:** VHS.

CONSULTANTS

22538 ■ Alliance Management International Ltd.
PO Box 470691
Cleveland, OH 44147-0691
Ph:(440)838-1922
Fax:(440)740-1434
Co. E-mail: bob@bgruss.com
Contact: Ken Gruss, Mgr
E-mail: bgruss@cox.net
Scope: A consulting company that helps to form national and international strategic alliances. Handles alliances between companies forming joint ventures. Staff specialized in small company-large company alliance, alliance assessment and analysis, and alliance strategic planning. **Seminars:** Joint Business Planning; Developing a Shared Vision; Current and New/Prospective Partner Assessment; Customer Service; Sales Training; Leader and Management Skills.

22539 ■ American English Academy
111 N Atlantic Blvd., Ste. 112
Monterey Park, CA 91754
Ph:(626)457-2800
Fax:(626)457-2808
Co. E-mail: admission@aea-usa.com
URL: http://www.aea-usa.com
Contact: Charles Policky, President
Scope: Specializes in providing on-site English language and communication development for corporations and individuals. Also develops and delivers training in speaking, writing, pronunciation, grammar, and idioms with an emphasis on business communication. Offers individual, small group, intensive, and long-distance learning. Programs tailor-made for each client.

22540 ■ Beeline Learning Solutions
14911 Quorum Dr., Ste. 120
Dallas, TX 75254
Ph:(972)813-0465
Fax:(972)386-8667
Co. E-mail: info@consultingpartners.com
URL: http://www.beeline.com
Contact: Debra Gann, Managering Director
E-mail: gann@atsconsultingpartners.com
Scope: Consulting firm offering technology, content, and services addressing recruitment and sourcing, talent management, and learning and performance optimization. Solutions offered include contingent workforce solutions, vendor management software, talent management solutions, recruitment process outsourcing, performance management, applicant tracking, learning management and eLearning. **Special Services:** Beeline[R].

22541 ■ The Handler Group Inc.
425 W End Ave., Apt. 3A
New York, NY 10024-5718
Ph:(212)873-1899
Contact: Mark Lambert Handler, President
E-mail: mlhandler@aol.com
Scope: Provides marketing, communication planning, and design services, specializing in development of internal and external business communications. Develops corporate identity, corporate literature, employee communications, sales promotion materials, consumer product packaging and information, brochures, annual reports, and presentation materials. Industries served: Cable/television, technology software, business information, hospitality, and banking.

22542 ■ Navarro, Kim & Associates
529 N Charles St., Ste. 202
Baltimore, MD 21201
Ph:(410)837-6317
Fax:(410)837-6294
Co. E-mail: bnavarro@sprynet.com
Contact: Beltran Navarro, Director
E-mail: bnavarro@sprynet.com
Scope: Specializes in bridging the gap between firms and non-traditional ethnic communities, especially in community development and institutional building.

22543 ■ Turn of Phrase
2529 Meade Ct.
Ann Arbor, MI 48105
Ph:(734)995-1579
Fax:(734)995-1321
Contact: Sally Hanna, President
E-mail: sadlyhanne@aol.com
Scope: Offers professional writing and editing on business topics. For example, prepares reference manuals, user guides, learning guides, Microsoft Windows help systems, reports, white papers, and other types of documents. Specializes in writing about computer software, especially for non-technical readers. Industries served: engineering, computer, manufacturing.

22544 ■ Write It Well
5626 Estates Dr.
PO Box 13098
Oakland, CA 94601
Ph:(510)655-6477
Fax:(510)291-9744
Co. E-mail: info@writeitwell.com
URL: http://www.writeitwell.com
Contact: Diane Lutovich, Principle
E-mail: melaniewise@atswriteitwell.com
Scope: Develops training programs, instructional materials, and procedures manuals; conduct customized in house classes in communications skills and performance management. Offers Training for Letter Communication. **Publications:** "Professional Writing Skills: A Self-Paced Training Program"; "Grammar for Grown ups A Self-Paced Training Program"; "Writing Performance Documentation A Self-Paced Training Program"; "Report and Proposal Writing for Environmental Professionals A Self-Paced Training Program"; "How to Write Reports and Proposals A Self-Paced Training Program"; "Just Commas 9 Basic Rules to Master Comma Usage"; "E-Mail - a Write it a Well Guide". **Seminars:** Business Writing; Effective E-Mail; Grammar Fundamentals; Technical Writing.

COMPUTER SYSTEMS/ SOFTWARE

22545 ■ *Better Business Writing–Crisp Learning*
Chris Learning
PO Box 25690
Rochester, NY 14625
Ph:888-534-5556
Free: 800-442-7477
Fax:888-715-0220
Co. E-mail: courseiltcrisp@thomaslearning.com
URL: http://www.axzopress.com
Contact: John Winder, Pres
Price: $13.95 (VCI CD-ROM). **Description:** Based on the *Better Business Writing* video and book. Includes book and user's guide.

RESEARCH CENTERS

22546 ■ Colorado State University–Center for Research on Communication and Technology
C-229 Clark Bldg.
Fort Collins, CO 80523-1785
Ph:(970)491-5674

Fax:(970)491-2908
Co. E-mail: don.zimmerman@colostate.edu
URL: http://www.colostate.edu/Depts/CROWACT
Contact: Prof. Don Zimmerman
E-mail: don.zimmerman@colostate.edu
Scope: Health communication, risk communication, usability testing, diffusion of innovations, Web design, human factors, human computer interactions, interface design, writing, writing processes, online writing centers, technology transfer, science communication, legibility, tobacco and alcohol warnings, digital television, communicating risk of sexually transmitted diseases, communication history.

22547 ■ University of Notre Dame–Fanning Center for Business Communication
Mendoza College of Business
Notre Dame, IN 46556
Ph:(574)631-8397
Fax:(574)631-5255
Co. E-mail: james.s.orourke.2@nd.edu
URL: http://business.nd.edu/Fanning_Center_for_Business_Communication
Contact: Prof. James S. O'Rourke IV, Dir.
E-mail: james.s.orourke.2@nd.edu
Scope: Business communication, including writing, speaking, listening, persuasion and other communication behaviors in the workplace; corporate communication, including the production of case studies designed to support instruction; intercultural communication, including the production of books and learning materials designed to support instruction. **Services:** Instruction, counseling, and guidance, in management and corporate communication. **Publications:** Management and Corporate Communication Case Studies (semiannually). **Educational Activities:** Conference on Corporate Communication (annually); Management Development Seminars; Workshops. **Awards:** E.D. Fanning Award; L.B. Pilkinton Award.

START-UP INFORMATION

22548 ■ *Entrepreneurship Strategy: Changing Patterns in New Venture Creation, Growth, and Reinvention*
Pub: SAGE Publications, Incorporated
Ed: Lisa K. Gundry; Jill R. Kickul. **Released:** August 2006. **Price:** $69.95. **Description:** Entrepreneurial strategies that incorporate new venture emergence, early growth, and reinvention and innovation are examined.

22549 ■ *Going Solo: Developing a Home-Based Consulting Business from the Ground Up*
Pub: McGraw-Hill Companies Incorporated
Ed: William J. Bond. **Released:** January 1997. **Description:** Ways to turn specialized knowledge into a home-based successful consulting firm, focusing on targeting client needs, business plans, and growth.

ASSOCIATIONS AND OTHER ORGANIZATIONS

22550 ■ Association for Corporate Growth - Toronto Chapter
1 Concorde Gate, Ste. 802
Toronto, ON, Canada M3C 3N6
Ph:(416)868-1881
Fax:(416)391-3633
Co. E-mail: acgtoronto@acg.org
URL: http://www.acg.org/toronto/default.aspx
Contact: Stephen B. Smith, Pres.
Description: Professionals with a leadership role in strategic corporate growth. Seeks to facilitate the professional advancement of members, and the practice of corporate growth management. Fosters communication and cooperation among members; conducts continuing professional education programs. **Publications:** *Mergers & Acquisitions - The Dealmaker's Journal* (monthly).

EDUCATIONAL PROGRAMS

22551 ■ Total Productive Maintenance (TPM) & 5S
American Trainco
9785 S Maroon Cir., Ste. 300
PO Box 3397
Englewood, CO 80112
Ph:(303)531-4560
Free: 877-978-7246
Fax:(303)531-4565
Co. E-mail: Sales@AmericanTrainco.com
URL: http://www.americantrainco.com
Price: $990.00. **Description:** Two-day seminar that focuses on getting managers, maintenance personnel and equipment users all working together to prevent equipment problems and reduce expenditures. **Locations:** Cities throughout the United States.

REFERENCE WORKS

22552 ■ "3CDC's Biggest Year" in *Business Courier* (Vol. 26, December 18, 2009, No. 34, pp. 1)
Pub: American City Business Journals, Inc.
Ed: Lucy May. **Description:** Cincinnati Center City Development Corporation (3CDC) will make 2010 its biggest year with nearly $164 million projects in the works. Historic tax credits and continued help from the city have allowed the private nonprofit organization to finance mega projects such as the $43 million renovation and expansion of Washington Park. Other projects that 3CDC will start or complete in 2010 are presented.

22553 ■ *The 7 Irrefutable Rules of Small Business Growth*
Pub: John Wiley & Sons, Incorporated
Ed: Steven S. Little. **Released:** February 2005. **Price:** $18.95. **Description:** Proven strategies to maintain small business growth are outlined, covering topics such as technology, business plans, hiring, and more.

22554 ■ *10 Steps to Successful Social Networking for Business*
Pub: American Society for Training and Development
Ed: Darin Hartley. **Released:** July 1, 2010. **Price:** $19.95. **Description:** Designed for today's fast-paced, need-it-yesterday business environment and for the thousands of workers who find themselves faced with new assignments, responsibilities, and requirements and too little time to learn what they must know.

22555 ■ *The 29 Percent Solution*
Pub: Greenleaf Book Group Press
Ed: Ivan Misner, Michele Donovan. **Released:** 2008. **Price:** $21.95. **Description:** It is true that some people are better connected than others. That means that connecting is a skill that can be acquired. Networking skills used to increase business connections are highlighted.

22556 ■ "$49M Defense Contracts Hits Austin" in *Austin Business JournalInc.* (Vol. 28, August 8, 2008, No. 21, pp. A1)
Pub: American City Business Journals
Ed: Laura Hipp. **Description:** BAE Systems PLC has landed a $49 million contract to build thermal cameras, which are expected to be installed on tanks in 2009 and 2010. BAE is expected to land other defense contracts and is likely to add employees in order to meet production demands.

22557 ■ "100-BU. Beans" in *Farm Industry News* (Vol. 42, January 1, 2009, No. 1)
Pub: Penton Media, Inc.
Ed: Lynn Grooms. **Description:** Demand for soybeans has increased and growers are seeing an increase in yields as well due to breeders that are using molecular-assisted selection; other aspects of the soybean market are presented.

22558 ■ "The 100 Fastest-Growing Companies" in *Hispanic Business* (Vol. 30, July-August 2008, No. 7-8, pp. 22)
Pub: Hispanic Business, Inc.
Ed: Michael Bowker. **Description:** CEO's of the five fastest growing Hispanic-owned companies discuss the success of their companies; most of them attribute their success to proper investment and diversification, effective innovations and seeing growth opportunities where others see roadblocks.

22559 ■ "The 100 Most Bullish Stocks" in *Canadian Business* (Vol. 81, Summer 2008, No. 9, pp. 81)
Pub: Rogers Media Ltd.
Ed: Megan Harman; Lauren McKeon. **Description:** 100 of the most bullish stocks are taken from the list of the 500 best-performing stocks. The idea is to narrow the list help investors in their investment decisions since it is difficult to choose from a large list. Analysts rate the companies with 5 being the most bullish and 1 the least. Other details of the roster are presented.

22560 ■ *101 Secrets to Building a Winning Business*
Pub: Allen & Unwin
Ed: Andrew Griffiths. **Released:** September 1, 2009. **Price:** $14.95. **Description:** Provides expert information for running and growing a small business.

22561 ■ "352 Media Group Opens New Tampa Web Design and Digital Marketing Office" in *Entertainment Close-Up* (May 2, 2011)
Pub: Close-Up Media
Description: 352 Media Group opened its newest office in Tampa, Florida in May 2011. The firm is noted for its achievements in Web design and digital marketing.

22562 ■ "2009: A Call For Vision" in *Women Entrepreneur* (January 28, 2009)
Pub: Entrepreneur Media Inc.
Ed: Elinor Robin. **Description:** Providing exemplary customer service, reducing expenses and creating an out-of-the-box niche are three key factors that will help business survive during this economic crisis. Business owners must see potential where others see failure in order to create new opportunities that may not only allow their business to survive during these times but may actually cause some businesses to thrive despite this economic downturn.

22563 ■ "2011 a Record Year for New Wind Energy Installations in Canada" in *CNW Group* (September 26, 2011)
Pub: CNW Group
Description: Canada reports a record for new wind energy projects in 2011 with about 1,338 MW of newly installed wind energy capacity expected to come on line, compared to 690 MW installed in 2010. Statistical data included.

22564 ■ "ABB Could Still Engineer an Upside" in *Barron's* (Vol. 89, July 20, 2009, No. 29, pp. M6)
Pub: Dow Jones & Co., Inc.
Ed: Goran Mijuk. **Description:** Swiss engineering company ABB can remain profitable as its power transmission and distribution activities continue to generate earnings. The company is also benefiting from increased exposure in emerging markets.

22565 ■ "ACE Back in Unfriendly Skies" in *Globe & Mail* (February 14, 2006, pp. B17)
Pub: CTVglobemedia Publishing Inc.
Ed: Brent Jang. **Description:** ACE Aviation Holdings Inc. reported $258 million profit for 2005. The opinions of analysts on the share price of the company for 2006 are presented.

22566 ■ "Achieving Greatness" in *Black Enterprise* (Vol. 38, January 2008, No. 6, pp. 50)
Pub: Earl G. Graves Publishing Co. Inc.
Description: Randall Pinkett, winner of a reality show on television and chairman of BCT Partners, insists that a business cannot survive by doing just enough or more of the same. Pinkett's New Jersey company provides management, technology and consulting to other firms.

22567 ■ "Actions to Implement Three Potent Post-Crisis Strategies" in *Strategy & Leadership* (Vol. 38, September-October 2010, No. 5)
Pub: Emerald Inc.
Ed: Saul J. Berman, Richard Christner, Ragna Bell. **Description:** The need for organizations to design and implement strategies to cope with the possible situations in the post-economic crisis environment is emphasized. The plans that organizations should implement to successfully manage uncertainty and complexity and to foster their eventual growth are discussed.

22568 ■ "Add Aquatics to Boost Business" in *Pet Product News* (Vol. 64, December 2010, No. 12, pp. 20)
Pub: BowTie Inc.
Ed: David Lass. **Description:** Pet stores are encouraged to add aquatics departments to increase profitability through repeat sales. This goal can be realized by sourcing, displaying, and maintaining high quality live fish. Other tips regarding the challenges associated with setting up an aquatics department are presented.

22569 ■ "Adidas' Brand Ambitions" in *Business Journal Portland* (Vol. 27, December 10, 2010, No. 41, pp. 1)
Pub: Portland Business Journal
Ed: Erik Siemers. **Description:** Adidas AG, the second-largest sporting goods brand in the world, hopes to increase global revenue by 50 percent by 2015. The German company, which reported $14.5 billion sales, plans to improve its U.S. market. The U.S. is Adidas' largest, but also the most underperforming market for the firm.

22570 ■ "AdvacePierre Heats Up" in *Business Courier* (Vol. 27, October 29, 2010, No. 26, pp. 1)
Pub: Business Courier
Ed: John Newberry. **Description:** Bill Toler, chief executive officer of AdvancePierre Foods, is aiming for more growth and more jobs. The company was formed after the merger of Pierre Foods with two Oklahoma-based food processing companies. Toler wants to expand production and is set to start adding employees in the next 6-12 months.

22571 ■ "Advancing the Ball" in *Inside Healthcare* (Vol. 6, December 2010, No. 7, pp. 31)
Pub: RedCoat Publishing Inc.
Ed: Michelle McNickle. **Description:** Profile of Medicalodges an elder-care specialty company that provides both patient care and technology development. President and CEO of the firm believes that hiring good employees is key to growth for any small business.

22572 ■ *Advancing Research on Minority Entrepreneurship*
Pub: SAGE Publications, Inc.
Ed: James H. Johnson Jr.; Timothy Bates; William E. Jackson III; James H. Johnson; William E. Jackson. **Released:** September 2007. **Price:** $34.00. **Description:** Although minorities are more likely to engage in start-up businesses than others, minority entrepreneurs are less likely to get their enterprises off the ground or succeed in growing their businesses. The higher failure rates, lower sales and profits and less employment are among topics discussed.

22573 ■ "Ag Firms Harvest Revenue Growth" in *The Business Journal-Serving Metropolitan Kansas City* (Vol. 26, July 18, 2008, No. 45, pp. 1)
Pub: American City Business Journals, Inc.
Ed: Steve Vockrodt. **Description:** Five of the biggest agricultural companies in the Kansas City area, except one, reported multibillion-dollar revenue increases in 2007. The companies, which include Lansing Trade Group, posted a combined $9.5 billion revenue growth. The factors that affected the revenue increase in the area's agricultural companies, such as prices and high demand, are also examined.

22574 ■ "Agribusiness: How to Get Rich in Farming" in *Canadian Business* (Vol. 80, January 29, 2007, No. 3, pp. 42)
Pub: Rogers Media
Ed: Peter Shawn Taylor. **Description:** The trends pertaining to the income of Canadian farmers are examined. The methods of increasing the profits of Canadian agribusinesses are discussed.

22575 ■ "AIC To Buy $350M of Real Estate" in *Austin Business JournalInc.* (Vol. 28, November 14, 2008, No. 35, pp. 1)
Pub: American City Business Journals
Ed: Kate Harrington. **Description:** Austin-based AIC Ventures LP is planning to buy $350 million worth of commercial real estate. The company's move will double its acquisitions. It is also planning to acquire 30 assets for its eight fun in 2009 from middle-market companies.

22576 ■ "Air Canada, WestJet Fill More Seats" in *Globe & Mail* (January 6, 2006, pp. B3)
Pub: CTVglobemedia Publishing Inc.
Ed: Brent Jang. **Description:** The reasons behind the increase in passenger for Air Canada and WestJet Airlines Ltd. are presented.

22577 ■ "Airing It Out" in *The Business Journal-Serving Greater Tampa Bay* (Vol. 28, July 11, 2008, No. 29, pp. 1)
Pub: American City Business Journals, Inc.
Ed: Jane Meinhardt. **Description:** Flanders Corp. is planning to expand its business in Europe and Southeast Asia. The St. Petersburg, Florida-based company has about 2,800 employees and manufactures air filtration products for industrial and residential applications.

22578 ■ "Akerman Senterfitt Merger Deal Close" in *The Business Journal-Serving Greater Tampa Bay* (Vol. 28, July 18, 2008, No. 30, pp. 1)
Pub: American City Business Journals, Inc.
Ed: Jeff Blumenthal. **Description:** Sources familiar to the negotiations of Akerman Senterfitt's planned merger with Wolf Block has disclosed that executive committees of both firms have approved the deal. They expect to create an 800-lawyer firm with a significant presence in the U.S. East Coast. Other views and information on the deal and its expected impact on law practice in Florida are presented.

22579 ■ "Alberta's Runaway Train" in *Canadian Business* (Vol. 80, December 25, 2006, No. 1, pp. 17)
Pub: Rogers Media
Ed: Andrew Nikiforuk. **Description:** The high revenue brought about by the growth in the number of oil sand plants in Canada and the simultaneous burden on infrastructure and housing is discussed.

22580 ■ "Algoma Shares Soar on Growing Sale Rumors" in *Globe & Mail* (February 13, 2007, pp. B1)
Pub: CTVglobemedia Publishing Inc.
Ed: Andrew Willis; Greg Keenan. **Description:** The stock prices of Algoma Steel Inc. have touched record high of $40 on the Toronto Stock Exchange. The growing rumors about the possible takeover bid is the major reason for the stock price growth.

22581 ■ "All In The Family" in *Canadian Business* (Vol. 79, September 25, 2006, No. 19, pp. 75)
Pub: Rogers Media
Ed: Zena Olijnyk. **Description:** Continuing ownership of Weston dynasty on Canada's largest chain Loblaw Co. is discussed.

22582 ■ "All Indicators in Michigan Innovation Index Drop in 4Q" in *Crain's Detroit Business* (Vol. 25, June 22, 2009, No. 25, pp. 9)
Pub: Crain Communications Inc. - Detroit
Ed: Ryan Beene. **Description:** Economic indicators that rate Michigan's innovation fell in the fourth quarter of 2008. The index of trademark applications, SBA loans, venture capital funding, new incorporations and other indicators traced dropped 12.6 points.

22583 ■ "All Revved Up" in *Barron's* (Vol. 90, September 13, 2010, No. 37, pp. 18)
Pub: Barron's Editorial & Corporate Headquarters
Ed: Christopher C. Williams. **Description:** Shares of Advance Auto Parts has returned 55 percent in a span of three years and the stock could still reach the mid-60s by 2011 from its price of 46.07 in the second week of September 2010. The shares are trading at just 13 times the 2011 earnings.

22584 ■ "Allen Tate Expanding to Research Triangle Park: Firm Expects Raleigh Market to Grow Faster" in *Charlotte Observer* (January 31, 2007)
Pub: Knight-Ridder/Tribune Business News
Ed: Doug Smith; Dudley Price. **Description:** Allen Tate Realtors expanded its operations to the Research Triangle area. The firm is predicting a strong market and growth in Charlotte, North Carolina.

22585 ■ "AllHipHop.com's Founders Thought a Weeklong Event Would Raise the Company'" in *Inc.* (February 2008, pp. 48-51)
Pub: Gruner & Jahr USA Publishing
Ed: Kermit Pattison. **Description:** Co-founders Greg Watkins and Chuck Creekmur, planned a weeklong festival to promote their company, AllHipHop.com; the event nearly ruined the firm. The online firm provides news about hip hop artists and the industry and is updated daily.

22586 ■ "Amcon Distributing Co." in *Arkansas Business* (Vol. 26, November 9, 2009, No. 45, pp. 13)
Pub: Journal Publishing Inc.
Description: Amcon Distributing Co., a consumer products company, has bought the convenience store distribution assets of Discount Distributors from its parent, Harps Food Stores Inc., significantly increasing its wholesale distribution presence in the northwest Arkansas market. The acquisition will be funded through Amcon's existing credit facilities.

22587 ■ "Americhem to Shutter Maryland Operation" in *Crain's Cleveland Business* (Vol. 28, October 29, 2007, No. 43, pp. 14)
Pub: Crain Communications, Inc.
Description: Americhem Inc., a manufacturer of colors and additives for polymer products has announced plans to expand two plants in Cuyahoga Falls while phasing out its operations in Salisbury, Maryland.

22588 ■ "Analyzing the Analytics" in *Entrepreneur* (Vol. 37, October 2009, No. 10, pp. 42)
Pub: Entrepreneur Media, Inc.
Ed: Mikal E. Belicove. **Description:** Startups can maximize Web analytics by using them to monitor traffic sources and identify obstacles to converting

them into targeted behaviors . Startups should set trackable Web site goals and continuously track traffic and conversion rates.

22589 ■ "Ann Arbor Google's Growth Dips" in *Crain's Detroit Business* (Vol. 25, June 8, 2009, No. 23, pp. 3)
Pub: Crain Communications Inc. - Detroit
Ed: Bill Shea. **Description:** Global recession has slowed the growth of Google Inc. Three years ago, when Google moved to Ann Arbor, Michigan it estimated it would provide 1,000 new jobs within five years, so far the firm employs 250.

22590 ■ "Are You Ignoring Trends That Could Shake Up Your Business?" in *Harvard Business Review* (Vol. 88, July-August 2010, No. 7-8, pp. 124)
Pub: Harvard Business School Publishing
Ed: Elie Ofek, Luc Wathieu. **Description:** Ways for firms to capitalize on trends that might otherwise negatively affect their business are spotlighted. These include using certain aspects of the trend to augment traditional product/service offerings, and combining the trend with the offerings to transcend its traditional category.

22591 ■ "Arizona Firms In Chicago Go For Gold With '08 Games" in *The Business Journal - Serving Phoenix and the Valley of the Sun* (Vol. 28, August 8, 2008, No. 49, pp. 1)
Pub: American City Business Journals, Inc.
Ed: Patrick O'Grady. **Description:** More than 20 U.S. athletes will wear Arizona-based eSoles LLC's custom-made insoles to increase their performance at the 2008 Beijing Olympics making eSoles one of the beneficiaries of the commercialization of the games. Translation software maker Auralog Inc saw a 60 percent jump in sales from its Mandarin Chinese language applications.

22592 ■ "Art Institute of Chicago Goes Green" in *Contractor* (Vol. 56, July 2009, No. 7, pp. 1)
Pub: Penton Media, Inc.
Ed: Candace Roulo. **Description:** Art Institute of Chicago's Modern Wing museum addition will receive a certification that makes them one of the most environmentally sound museum expansions in the U.S. A modified variable-air-volume system is being used to meet temperature and humidity requirements in the building and it also has a double curtain wall to capture summer heat.

22593 ■ "At 5-Year Mark, News 9 Makes Presence Felt in Competition for Ad Dollars" in *Business Review, Albany New York* (October 5, 2007)
Pub: American City Business Journals, Inc.
Ed: Barbara Pinckney. **Description:** The 24-hour news channel Capital News 9 can be watched live by viewers on their cell phones beginning late 2007 or early 2008 as part of a deal between Time Warner Cable and Sprint Nextel Corporation to bring Sprint's Pivot technology. News 9 marked its fifth year and plans to continue expanding coverage and provide better services to viewers.

22594 ■ "Athletes' Performance Building $10 Million Facility In ASU Park" in *The Business Journal - Serving Phoenix and the Valley of the Sun* (Vol. 28, August 8, 2008, No. 49, pp. 1)
Pub: American City Business Journals, Inc.
Ed: Jan Buchholz. **Description:** Athletes' Performance's planned facility at Arizona State University is scheduled to begin in November 2008 and expected to be completed by September 2009. The new building will almost double the company's training space as it will expand from around 19,000 square feet to 35,000 square feet.

22595 ■ "ATI Now Ready to Pounce on Biotech" in *Austin Business JournalInc.* (Vol. 28, August 22, 2008, No. 23, pp. 1)
Pub: American City Business Journals
Ed: Laura Hipp. **Description:** Austin Technology Incubator has entered the biotechnology sector through a program of the University of Texas incubator. The company's bioscience program was set off by a grant from the City of Austin worth $125,000. The growth of Austin's biotechnology sector is examined.

22596 ■ "ATS Secures Investment From Goldman Sachs" in *The Business Journal - Serving Phoenix and the Valley of the Sun* (Vol. 29, September 26, 2008, No. 4, pp. 1)
Pub: American City Business Journals, Inc.
Ed: Patrick O'Grady. **Description:** Goldman Sachs made an investment to American Traffic Solutions Inc. (ATS) which will allow it to gain two seats on the board of the red-light and speed cameras maker. The investment will help ATS maintain its rapid growth which is at 83 percent over the past 18 months leading up to September 2008.

22597 ■ "Auction Company Grows with Much Smaller Sites" in *Automotive News* (Vol. 86, October 31, 2011, No. 6488, pp. 23)
Pub: Crain Communications Inc.
Ed: Arlena Sawyers. **Description:** Auction Broadcasting Company has launched auction sites and is expanding into new areas. The family-owned business will provide auctions half the size traditionally used. The firm reports that 40 percent of the General Motors factory-owned vehicles sold on consignment were purchased by online buyers, up 30 percent over 2010.

22598 ■ "Austin's GMP Growth Top in Nation" in *Austin Business JournalInc.* (Vol. 29, January 8, 2010, No. 44, pp. 1)
Pub: American City Business Journals
Ed: Jacob Dirr. **Description:** Austin's gross metropolitan product (GMP) has grown by 2 percent, putting it in the top 5 for GMP growth among the largest 100 American metropolitan areas. Insights into the area's business and technology services are examined.

22599 ■ "Australian Firm Buys Off Sands Engineering Company for $1 Billion" in *Globe & Mail* (February 8, 2007, pp. B3)
Pub: CTVglobemedia Publishing Inc.
Ed: David Ebner. **Description:** Australia's WorleyParson Ltd. acquires Colt Engineering Corp., a private petroleum company, for $1 billion. The acquision will provide WorleyParson an opportunity to expand its operations in Australia.

22600 ■ "Avnet Inc.'s Expansion Fueled By Mergers and Acquisitions" in *The Business Journal - Serving Phoenix and the Valley of the Sun* (Vol. 28, September 12, 2008, No. 53, pp. 1)
Pub: American City Business Journals, Inc.
Ed: Patrick O'Grady. **Description:** Avnet Inc. has grown and has nearly tripled its revenue in the past ten years through the company's acquisitions and consolidation. The company's revenue in 2008 is $17.9 billion. Other details about the company's growth are discussed.

22601 ■ "Awaiting a Call from Deutsche Telekom" in *Barron's* (Vol. 90, September 6, 2010, No. 36, pp. M5)
Pub: Barron's Editorial & Corporate Headquarters
Ed: Vito J. Racanelli. **Description:** Deutsche Telekom's (DT) T-Mobile USA Unit has settled in the number four position in the market and the parent company will need to decide if it will hold onto the company in the next 12-18 months from September 2010. T-Mobile's rivals will make critical improvements during this time and DT has the option to upgrade T-Mobile at the cost of improvements to its other units.

22602 ■ *Awesomely Simple: Essential Business Strategies for Turning Ideas Into Action*
Pub: Jossey-Bass
Ed: John Spence. **Released:** September 8, 2009. **Price:** $24.95. **Description:** Six key strategies that create a foundation for achieving business excellence include: vivid vision, best people, a performance-oriented culture, robust communication, a sense of urgency, and extreme customer focus.

22603 ■ "Back to Business for Bishop Museum" in *Hawaii Business* (Vol. 54, August 2008, No. 2, pp. 53)
Pub: Hawaii Business Publishing
Ed: Shara Enay. **Description:** Bishop Museum, ranked 224 in Hawaii Business' top 250 companies for 2008, had $29.5 million in gross sales for 2007, up 52.8 percent from the $19.3 million gross sales in 2006. The company has cut 24 positions in a restructuring effort for the museum's sustainability. Grants, artifacts and plans for sustainable operations are discussed.

22604 ■ "Bagging Profits; High-End Grocers Expand Despite Stale Economy" in *Crain's Detroit Business* (Vol. 24, March 24, 2008, No. 12, pp. 1)
Pub: Crain Communications, Inc.
Ed: Nancy Kaffer. **Description:** Discusses the expansion plans of several high-end grocery stores in the Detroit area and the reasons why, despite the poor economy, these gourmet grocers are doing well. Statistical data included.

22605 ■ "The Balancing Act: How Busy Executives Make Their Lives Work" in *Black Enterprise* (Vol. 37, February 2007, No. 7, pp. 118)
Pub: Earl G. Graves Publishing Co. Inc.
Ed: Marcia A. Reed-Woodard. **Description:** More than 70 percent of women with children work outside the home, according to a 2005 survey conducted by the U.S. Department of Labor Bureau. One of the biggest struggles these women face is balancing family with career aspirations and climbing the corporate ranks.

22606 ■ "Baldwin Connelly Partnership Splits" in *Business Journal Serving Greater Tampa Bay* (Vol. 30, November 19, 2010, No. 48, pp. 1)
Pub: Tampa Bay Business Journal
Ed: Alexis Muellner. **Description:** The fast-growing insurance brokerage Baldwin Connelly is now breaking up after five years. Two different entrepreneurial visions have developed within the organization and founders Lowry Baldwin and John Connell will not take separate tracks. Staffing levels in the firm are expected to remain the same.

22607 ■ "BancVue to Expand" in *Austin Business JournalInc.* (Vol. 29, November 27, 2009, No. 38, pp. 1)
Pub: American City Business Journals
Ed: Kate Harrington. **Description:** Significant growth of BancVue in the past six years has prompted the company to look for a site that could increase its office space from 25,000 square feet to 65,000 square feet. BancVue offers bank and credit union software solutions and is planning to lease or buy a property in Austin, Texas.

22608 ■ "Bank Bullish on Austin" in *Austin Business JournalInc.* (Vol. 29, November 13, 2009, No. 36, pp. A1)
Pub: American City Business Journals
Ed: Kate Harrington. **Description:** American Bank's presence in Austin, Texas has been boosted by new management and a new 20,000 square foot building. This community bank intends to focus on building relationship with commercial banking customers. American Bank also plans to extend investment banking, treasury management, and commercial lending services.

22609 ■ "A Banking Play Without Banking Plagues" in *Barron's* (Vol. 88, March 31, 2008, No. 13, pp. 26)
Pub: Dow Jones & Company, Inc.
Ed: Jack Willoughby. **Description:** Fiserv's shares have been dragged down by about 20 percent which presents an appealing entry point since the shares could rise by 30 percent or more by 2009. The company enables banks to post and open new checks and keeps track of loans which are not discretionary processes of banks.

22610 ■ "Bargain Hunting In Vietnam" in *Barron's* (Vol. 88, July 14, 2008, No. 28, pp. M6)
Pub: Dow Jones & Co., Inc.

Ed: Elliot Wilson. **Description:** Vietnam's economy grew by just 6.5 percent for the first half of 2008 and its balance of payments ballooned to $14.4 billion. The falling stock prices in the country is a boon for bargain hunters and investing in the numerous domestic funds is one way of investing in the country. Some shares that investors are taking an interest in are also discussed.

22611 ■ "Bark Up The Right Tree" in *Small Business Opportunities* (Winter 2009)
Pub: Entrepreneur Media Inc.

Description: Profile of Central Bark, a daycare company catering to pets that offers franchise opportunities and is expanding rapidly despite the economic downturn; the company's growth strategy is also discussed.

22612 ■ "Bartering Takes Businesses Back to Basics: Broker's Exchange Helps Members to Reach New Customers" in *Buffalo News* (July 9, 2010)
Pub: The Buffalo News

Ed: Dino Grandoni. **Description:** Bartering clubs can help small businesses reach new customers and to expand their business.

22613 ■ "Bartering Trades on Talents" in *Reading Eagle* (June 20, 2010)
Pub: Reading Eagle/Reading Times

Ed: Tony Lucia. **Description:** Bartering is not just a way of trading goods and services, it can be an essential tool for small business to survive in a bad economy.

22614 ■ "Basel3 Quick Fix Actually Neither" in *Canadian Business* (Vol. 83, October 12, 2010, No. 17, pp. 19)
Pub: Rogers Media Ltd.

Ed: Thomas Watson. **Description:** Information about the so-called Basel 3 standards, which will require banks to hold top-quality capital totaling at least 7 percent of their risk-bearing assets is provided. The rules' supporters believe that a good balance has been reached between improving the Basel 2 framework and maintaining enough lending capital to stimulate an economic growth.

22615 ■ "Baskin-Robbins Expanding in China and U.S." in *Ice Cream Reporter* (Vol. 21, August 20, 2008, No. 9, pp. 1)
Pub: Ice Cream Reporter

Description: Baskin-Robbins will open its first store in Shanghai, China along with plans for 100 more shops in that country. They will also be expanding their market in the Dallas/Fort Worth, Texas area as well as Greater Cincinnati/Northern Kentucky regions.

22616 ■ "Baskin-Robbins Expanding to South Texas" in *Ice Cream Reporter* (Vol. 23, July 20, 2010, No. 8, pp. 4)
Pub: Ice Cream Reporter

Description: Baskin-Robbins will develop six new shops in south Texas after signing agreements with two franchisees.

22617 ■ "Baskin-Robbins: New in U.S., Old in Japan" in *Ice Cream Reporter* (Vol. 23, August 20, 2010, No. 9, pp. 2)
Pub: Ice Cream Reporter

Description: Baskin-Robbins is celebrating its first franchise in Japan.

22618 ■ "Baskin-Robbins Reopens in New Orleans" in *Ice Cream Reporter* (Vol. 23, September 20, 2010, No. 10, pp. 3)
Pub: Ice Cream Reporter

Description: Baskin-Robbins will open its first shop in New Orleans, Louisiana after Hurricane Katrina in 2005. The shop stands in the exact location of a Baskin-Robbins shop destroyed by Katrina.

22619 ■ "Baskin-Robbins Tests New Upscale Concept" in *Ice Cream Reporter* (Vol. 21, September 20, 2008, No. 10, pp. 1)
Pub: Ice Cream Reporter

Description: Baskin-Robbins is opening its new upscale store, Cafe 31 in an effort to invigorate its brand. The shop will serve fondues, cakes and other treats prepared by an in-store chef.

22620 ■ "Battling Back from Betrayal" in *Harvard Business Review* (Vol. 88, December 2010, No. 12, pp. 130)
Pub: Harvard Business School Publishing

Ed: Daniel McGinn. **Description:** Stephen Greer's scrap metal firm, Hartwell Pacific, lost several million dollars due to a lack of efficient and appropriate inventory audits, accounting procedures, and new-hire reference checks for his foreign operations. Greer believes that balancing growth with control is a key component of success.

22621 ■ "BCE Mulls Radical Changes With Industry Under Pressure" in *Globe & Mail* (March 30, 2007, pp. B1)
Pub: CTVglobemedia Publishing Inc.

Ed: Andrew Willis; Jacquie McNish; Catherine McLean. **Description:** An account on the expansion plans of BCE Inc., which plans to acquire TELUS Corp., is presented.

22622 ■ "BCE Wireless Growth Flags in Fourth Quarter" in *Globe & Mail* (February 8, 2007, pp. B5)
Pub: CTVglobemedia Publishing Inc.

Ed: Catherine McLean. **Description:** BCE Inc., the largest telecommunications provider in Canada, reported $699 million profit in the final quarter of 2006. The company signed up 169,000 wireless customers in the important holiday season.

22623 ■ *Be the Elephant: Build a Bigger, Better Business*
Pub: Workman Publishing Company

Ed: Steve Kaplan. **Price:** $19.95. **Description:** Entrepreneur and author sets out an accessible, no-frills plan for business owners, managers, and other industrialists to grow their businesses into elephants: big and strong but also smart. Advice is given on fostering a growth mind-set, assessing risk, and creating unique selling propositions.

22624 ■ *Beans: Four Principles for Running a Business in Good Times or Bad*
Pub: John Wiley & Sons, Incorporated

Ed: Leslie Yerkes, Charles Decker, Bob Nelson **Released:** June 2003. **Price:** $19.95. **Description:** Profile of Monorail Espresso, the popular Seattle coffee company that has become prosperous by intentionally staying small and building a strong customer service program.

22625 ■ "The Bear Arrives - With Bargain Hunters" in *Barron's* (Vol. 88, July 7, 2008, No. 27, pp. M3)
Pub: Dow Jones & Co., Inc.

Ed: Kopin Tan. **Description:** US stock markets have dropped 20 percent below their highs, entering the bear market at the end of June 2008. It was also the worst performance of the stock markets during June. Wine maker Constellation Brands, however, reported a 50 percent rise in net income for the first quarter of 2008.

22626 ■ "Become A Brand" in *Women Entrepreneur* (September 14, 2008)
Pub: Entrepreneur Media Inc.

Ed: Suzy Girard-Ruttenberg. **Description:** Powerful brands are effective, innovative, exclusive or even socially conscious; it is important for small businesses to understand the power of becoming a brand since it is one of the best ways in which to position one's company and drive its growth.

22627 ■ "Bedding a Leader in Kohl's Q1 Gains" in *Home Textiles Today* (Vol. 31, May 24, 2011, No. 13, pp. 1)
Pub: Reed Business Information

Description: Kohl's credited home furnishings, particularly bedding, as the leading source of its first-quarter sales and profit gains in 2011. Statistical data included.

22628 ■ "Beer Drinkers Wanted More. The Brewer Had No Room to Expand. How Could It Keep the Taps Flowing?" in *Inc.* (October 2007, pp. 65-66)
Pub: Gruner & Jahr USA Publishing

Ed: Alex Salkever. **Description:** Profile of John McDonald, founder of Boulevard, the second-largest beer company located in Kansas City, Missouri. McDonald tells how he was able to expand his turn-of-the-century brick building he had imported from Bavaria by developing a 70,000-square-foot building on four acres adjacent to his existing location rather move to a suburb.

22629 ■ "Beer Stocks Rally on Anheuser, InBev Report" in *Globe & Mail* (February 16, 2007, pp. B3)
Pub: CTVglobemedia Publishing Inc.

Ed: Keith McArthur. **Description:** The stock prices of beer manufacturing industries have increased considerably after impressive profit reports from Anheuser Busch Cos Inc. and InBev SA. Complete analysis in this context is presented.

22630 ■ *The Beermat Entrepreneur: Turn Your Good Idea Into a Great Business*
Pub: Pearson Education, Ltd.

Ed: Mike Southon, Andrew Leigh, Chris West. **Released:** March 1, 2009. **Price:** $39.50. **Description:** Information to help start, maintain and grow a small business is given, along with suggestions for working with a bank.

22631 ■ "Behind the Numbers: When It Comes to Earnings, Look for Quality, Not Just Quantity" in *Black Enterprise* (July 2008, pp. 35)
Pub: Earl G. Graves Publishing Co. Inc.

Ed: Chris Keenan. **Description:** It is important for investors to examine the quality of a company's earnings rather than fixate on the quantity of those earnings. Advice is given regarding issues investors can look at when trying to determine the potential growth of a firm.

22632 ■ "Being Big By Design" in *Canadian Business* (Vol. 82, April 27, 2009, No. 7, pp. 39)
Pub: Rogers Media

Ed: Andrew Wahl. **Description:** Gennum expects that its planned acquisition of Tundra Semiconductor will expand its market presence and leverage its research and development better than working alone. The proposed friendly acquisition could challenge Zarlink Semiconductor as the largest Canadian semiconductor firm in terms of revenue. The merger could expand Gennum's addressable market to about $2 billion.

22633 ■ "Benchmark Makes Granduca Entrance" in *Houston Business Journal* (Vol. 40, January 8, 2010, No. 35, pp. 2)
Pub: American City Business Journals

Ed: Jennifer Dawson. **Description:** Houston, Texas-based Interfin Company, owner of the Hotel Granduca, has tapped the services of Benchmark Hospitality International to manage the property. The hiring of Benchmark is part of Interfin's efforts to develop Granduca hotels in other markets. Statistical data included.

22634 ■ "Best Cash Flow Generators" in *Canadian Business* (Vol. 81, Summer 2008, No. 9, pp. 73)
Pub: Rogers Media Ltd.

Ed: Calvin Leung. **Description:** Table showing the five-year annualized growth rate and one-year stock performance of companies that have grown their cash flow per share at an annualized rate of 15 percent or more over the past five years. Analysts project that the cash flow trend will continue. Other details of the stock performance index are presented.

22635 ■ "Best Defensive Stocks" in *Canadian Business* (Vol. 81, Summer 2008, No. 9, pp. 67)
Pub: Rogers Media Ltd.

Ed: Calvin Leung. **Description:** Stocks of the companies presented have market capitalization of greater than $1 billion and dividend gains of at least 2 percent. A table showing the average one-year total return of the stocks is provided.

22636 ■ "Best Growth Stocks" in *Canadian Business* (Vol. 81, Summer 2008, No. 9, pp. 61)
Pub: Rogers Media Ltd.
Ed: Calvin Leung. **Description:** Table showing the one-year performance of growth stocks is presented. Edmonton-based Stantec Inc. expects to advance its sales and profits by 15 percent to 20 percent per year through tapping international markets and acquisitions. Analysts forecast a 17.1 percent growth rate annually over the next 3 to 5 years.

22637 ■ "Best Income Trust" in *Canadian Business* (Vol. 81, Summer 2008, No. 9, pp. 69)
Pub: Rogers Media Ltd.
Ed: Calvin Leung. **Description:** Table showing five-year annualized growth rate and one-year stock performance of real estate investment trusts firms in Canada is presented. Calgary-based Boardwalk REIT is projected to grow the fastest among North American REITs over the next two years. Other details on the stock performance analysis are presented.

22638 ■ "Best Managed Companies (Canada)" in *Canadian Business* (Vol. 82, Summer 2009, No. 8, pp. 38)
Pub: Rogers Media
Ed: Calvin Leung. **Description:** Agrium Inc. and Barrick Gold Corporation are among those that are found to be the best managed companies in Canada. Best managed companies also include software firm Open Text Corporation, which has grown annual sales by 75 percent and annual profits by 160 percent since 1995. Open Text markets software that allow firms to manage word-based data, and has 46,000 customers in 114 countries.

22639 ■ "Best Managed Companies" in *Canadian Business* (Vol. 81, Summer 2008, No. 9, pp. 71)
Pub: Rogers Media Ltd.
Ed: Calvin Leung. **Description:** Table showing the five-year annualized growth rate and one-year stock performance of companies that have grown their cash flow per share at an annualized rate of 15 percent or more over the past five years. Analysts project that the cash flow trend will continue. Other details of the stock performance index are presented.

22640 ■ "Best Turnaround Stocks" in *Canadian Business* (Vol. 81, Summer 2008, No. 9, pp. 65)
Pub: Rogers Media Ltd.
Ed: Calvin Leung. **Description:** Share prices of Sierra Wireless Inc. and EXFO Electro Optical Engineering Inc. have fallen over the past year but have good chance at a rebound considering that the companies have free cash flow and no long-term debt. One-year stock performance analysis of the two companies is presented.

22641 ■ "Best Value Stocks" in *Canadian Business* (Vol. 81, Summer 2008, No. 9, pp. 63)
Pub: Rogers Media Ltd.
Ed: Calvin Leung. **Description:** Table showing the one-year performance of bargain or best-value stocks is presented. These stocks are undervalued compared to their North American peers, but it is projected that their five-year average return on equity is greater.

22642 ■ "Better Card Collecting" in *Canadian Business* (Vol. 80, January 15, 2007, No. 2, pp. 66)
Pub: Rogers Media
Ed: Sarah B. Hood. **Description:** Tips on how to collect business cards and use them for enhancing one's business performance are presented. Targeting specific people, taking notes and giving follow ups are some suggestions.

22643 ■ "Better Made's Better Idea: Diversify Despite Rising Costs" in *Crain's Detroit Business* (Vol. 24, September 22, 2008, No. 38, pp. 18)
Pub: Crain Communications, Inc.
Ed: Nathan Skid. **Description:** Better Made Snack Foods Inc. is planning to expand its product lines and market reach as well as boost manufacturing capability during a time in which the company is being buffeted by rising commodity and fuel costs. The company feels that diversification is the key to maintain sales and growth.

22644 ■ "Betting on the Glitz" in *Canadian Business* (Vol. 79, October 9, 2006, No. 20, pp. 104)
Pub: Rogers Media
Ed: Zena Olijnyk. **Description:** Holt, Renfrew & Co-many's expansion plans to cash on the booming demand for high end retail luxury markets are discussed.

22645 ■ "Beyond Auto; Staffing Firm Malace Grabs Revenue Jump" in *Crain's Detroit Business* (Vol. 26, January 18, 2010, No. 3, pp. 3)
Pub: Crain Communications, Inc.
Ed: Sherri Welch. **Description:** Malace & Associates Inc., the Troy-based human resources management company, expects its diversification into nonautomotive industries to help double its revenues this year. Due to the automotive downturn, between October 2008 and March 2009 the company lost approximately 48 percent of its business.

22646 ■ *Beyond Booked Solid: Your Business, Your Life, Your Way-It's All Inside*
Pub: John Wiley and Sons, Inc.
Ed: Michael Port. **Released:** April 2008. **Price:** $24. 95. **Description:** Professional service providers and small business owners will discover tactics and strategies for growing and expanding their companies while allowing them to find time to relax and enjoy their lives. Owners will learn to attract new clients and grow profits.

22647 ■ "The Big 50" in *Canadian Business* (Vol. 81, Summer 2008, No. 9, pp. 125)
Pub: Rogers Media Ltd.
Description: Large publicly held corporations are ranked based on market capitalization and stock performance. Potash Corp. of Saskatchewan topped the roster with 169.3 percent of return and even surpassing its 2007 result of 107 percent. A table showing the 2008 rankings of the companies is presented.

22648 ■ "Big Energy Deals Power OptiSolar's Local Growth" in *Sacramento Business Journal* (Vol. 25, August 22, 2008, No. 25, pp. 1)
Pub: American City Business Journals, Inc.
Ed: Celia Lamb. **Description:** Solar energy projects are driving Sacramento, California-based OptiSolar's growth. The company is set to begin construction of its first photovoltaic project in Ontario. It also plans to build the world largest photovoltaic project in San Luis Obispo County.

22649 ■ "A Bigger Deal" in *Crain's Cleveland Business* (Vol. 28, November 12, 2007, No. 45, pp. 1)
Pub: Crain Communications, Inc.
Ed: Shawn A. Turner. **Description:** In an attempt to boost its revenue CBiz Inc., a provider of accounting and business services, is looking to balance its acquisitions of smaller companies with larger ones as part of its overall growth strategy.

22650 ■ *Bigger Isn't Always Better*
Pub: AMACOM
Ed: Robert M. Tomasko. **Price:** $24.95.

22651 ■ "Bigger TIF Makes Development Inroads" in *The Business Journal-Serving Metropolitan Kansas City* (Vol. 26, July 11, 2008, No. 44)
Pub: American City Business Journals, Inc.
Ed: Rob Roberts. **Description:** On July 9, 2008 the Tax Increment Financing Commission voted to expand a TIF district to Tiffany Springs Road. The plan for the TIF district close to Kansas City International Airport is to include a-half mile of the road. The impacts of the expansion on construction projects and on the road network are analyzed.

22652 ■ "Biodiesel Poised to Regain Growth" in *Farm Industry News* (January 21, 2011)
Pub: Penton Business Media Inc.
Description: According to Gary Haer, vice president of sales and marketing for Renewable Energy Group, the biodiesel industry is positioned to regain growth in 2011 with the reinstatement of the biodiesel blendersa tax credt of $1 per gallon.

22653 ■ "BK Menu Gives Casual Dining Reason to Worry" in *Advertising Age* (Vol. 79, November 17, 2008, No. 43, pp. 12)
Pub: Crain Communications, Inc.
Ed: Emily Bryson York. **Description:** Burger King is beginning to compete with such casual dining restaurants as Applebees and the Cheesecake Factory with new premium menu items, including thicker burgers and ribs; statistical data regarding the casual dining segment which continues to fall and Burger King, whose sales continue to rise is included.

22654 ■ "Black On Black Business: Moorehead Buys Hank Aaron's Toyota Dealership" in *Black Enterprise* (Vol. 38, February 2008, No. 7, pp. 28)
Pub: Earl G. Graves Publishing Co. Inc.
Ed: Brenda Porter. **Description:** In a move to expand his automotive business, Thomas A. Moorehead, CEO of BMW/MINI of Sterling, Georgia bought Hank Aaron's Toyota automobile dealership in McDonough, Georgia. Moorehead stated that he will call the new store Toyota of McDonough.

22655 ■ "Blacks Go Broadband: High Speed Internet Adoption Grows Among African Americans" in *Black Enterprise* (Vol. 38, February 2008)
Pub: Earl G. Graves Publishing Co. Inc.
Ed: Cliff Hocker. **Description:** Number of black households using broadband Internet services tripled since 2005 according to a survey conducted by Pew Internet and American Life Project.

22656 ■ "A Bleak Earnings View" in *Barron's* (Vol. 88, March 10, 2008, No. 10, pp. 15)
Pub: Dow Jones & Company, Inc.
Description: Analysts expect consumer discretionary profits in the S&P 500 to drop 8.4 percent in the first quarter of 2008. A less confident consumer is expected to pull profits down, putting forecasts of earnings growth in the S&P 500 at risk. Statistical data included.

22657 ■ "Blockbuster Launches Internet Movie Downloads to Compete Against Netflix, Others" in *Chicago Tribune* (December 3, 2008)
Pub: McClatchy-Tribune Information Services
Ed: Eric Benderoff. **Description:** Blockbuster Inc., the DVD rental giant, has launched a new service that delivers movies to their customer's homes via the Internet in an attempt to compete against Netflix and other competitors.

22658 ■ "Blue Bell Breaks Ground in South Carolina" in *Ice Cream Reporter* (Vol. 23, August 20, 2010, No. 9, pp. 3)
Pub: Ice Cream Reporter
Description: Texas-based Blue Bell Creameries will open a new 2,000 square foot transfer facility in North Charleston, South Carolina. The facility will expand Blue Bell's distribution efforts in the state.

22659 ■ "BofA Cutting 70 Charlotte Tech Jobs" in *Charlotte Observer* (January 31, 2007)
Pub: Knight-Ridder/Tribune Business News
Ed: Rick Rothacker. **Description:** Bank of America announced the elimination of 70 technology positions at their Charlotte, North Carolina facility. The move is part of the company's effort to increase efficiency.

22660 ■ "The Book On Indigo" in *Canadian Business* (Vol. 81, July 22, 2008, No. 12-13, pp. 29)
Pub: Rogers Media Ltd.
Ed: Thomas Watson. **Description:** Indigo Books & Music Inc. reported record sales of $922 million resulting in a record net profit of $52.8 million for the

2008 fiscal year ended March 29, 2008. Earnings per share were $2.13, greater than Standard & Poor's expected $1.70 per share. Additional information concerning Indigo Books is presented.

22661 ■ "Book Publishing is Growing" in *Information Today* (Vol. 28, October 2011, No. 9, pp. 10)
Pub: Information Today, Inc.
Ed: Paula J. Hane. **Description:** U.S. book publishing industry is reporting growth in its sector, despite the poor economy. BookStats, a comprehensive statistical survey conducted on the modern publishing industry in the U.S. reported Americans are reading in all print and digital formats. In 2011, 114 million ebooks were sold and now account for 13.6 percent of revenue from adult fiction. In contrast, 603 million trade hardcover books (fiction and nonfiction) were sold in 2011, a 5.8 percent increase over 2008.

22662 ■ "Boom has Tech Grads Mulling Their Options" in *Globe & Mail* (March 14, 2006, pp. B1)
Pub: CTVglobemedia Publishing Inc.
Ed: Grant Robertson. **Description:** Internet giant Google Inc. has stepped up its efforts to hire the talented people, in Canada, at Waterloo University in southern Ontario, to expand its operations. The details of the job market and increasing salaries are analyzed.

22663 ■ "Bottler Will Regain Its Pop" in *Barron's* (Vol. 88, March 17, 2008, No. 11, pp. 56)
Pub: Dow Jones & Company, Inc.
Ed: Alexander Eule. **Description:** Discusses he 30 percent drop in the share price of PepsiAmericas Inc. from their 2007 high which presents an opportunity to buy into the company's dependable U.S. market and fast growing Eastern European business. The bottler's Eastern European operating profits in 2007 grew to $101 million from $21 million in 2006.

22664 ■ "Bottom-Fishing and Speed-Dating in India" in *Barron's* (Vol. 88, March 24, 2008, No. 12, pp. M12)
Pub: Dow Jones & Company, Inc.
Ed: Elliot Wilson. **Description:** Indian stocks have fallen hard in 2008, with Mumbai's Sensex 30 down 30 percent from its January 2008 peak of 21,000 to 14,995 in March. The India Private Equity Fair 2008 attracted 140 of the world's largest private equity firms and about 24 of India's fastest-growing corporations. Statistical data included.

22665 ■ "Bountiful Barrels: Where to Find $140 Trillion" in *Barron's* (Vol. 88, July 14, 2008, No. 28, pp. 40)
Pub: Dow Jones & Co., Inc.
Ed: Andrew Bary. **Description:** Surge in oil prices has caused a large transfer of wealth to oil-producing countries thereby reshaping the global economy. Oil reserves of oil exporting countries are now valued at $140 trillion. Economist Stephen Jen believes that this wealth will be transformed into paper assets as these countries invest in global stocks and bonds.

22666 ■ "Brad Wall" in *Canadian Business* (Vol. 82, April 27, 2009, No. 7, pp. 9)
Pub: Rogers Media
Ed: Joe Castaldo. **Description:** Saskatchewan Premier Brad Wall believes that the mood in the province is positive, as its economy is one of the few that is expected to post growth in 2009. Wall actively promotes the province in job fairs, offering $20,000 in tuition for recent college and university graduates that relocate in the province for seven years. Wall's views on the province's economy and challenges are presented.

22667 ■ "Branching Out" in *Canadian Business* (Vol. 79, July 17, 2006, No. 14-15, pp. 41)
Pub: Rogers Media
Description: Visa selected this narrative in an attempt to show the company's usefulness.

22668 ■ "Breaking Through" in *Inc.* (January 2008, pp. 90-93)
Pub: Gruner & Jahr USA Publishing
Ed: Mike Hofman. **Description:** Entrepreneur Keith R. McFarland, shares insight into why most successful companies eventually plateau, while others keep on growing.

22669 ■ *The Breakthrough Company*
Pub: Crown Publishing/Random House
Ed: Keith McFarland. **Released:** September 1, 2009. **Price:** $16.00 paperback. **Description:** Traits of high-growth players that actually make it in business.

22670 ■ *The Breakthrough Company: How Everyday Companies Become Extraordinary Performers*
Pub: Crown Business
Ed: Keith McFarland. **Released:** January 2008. **Price:** $27.50. **Description:** Why do some entrepreneurial enterprises become successful while others fail? After years of studying and analyzing successful growth companies, the author sets out a strategy and destroys myths about how to make it to the next level.

22671 ■ "Brewed to Succeed; Mokarbia Perks Up Sales for King Coffee" in *Crain's Detroit Business* (Vol. 24, March 17, 2008, No. 11, pp. 3)
Pub: Crain Communications, Inc.
Ed: Brent Snavely. **Description:** Profile of King Coffee Tea Services, Royal Oak-based company, whose distributing deal with Mokarabia coffee has generated an increase in sales.

22672 ■ "Brewing National Success" in *Hawaii Business* (Vol. 53, November 2007, No. 5, pp. 46)
Pub: Hawaii Business Publishing
Ed: Alex Salkever. **Description:** Kona Brewing Co. (KBC) is already selling its brews in four cities in Florida and 17 other states and Japan as well. KBC is currently forming a deal with Red Hook to produce Longboard Lager and other KBC brews at Red Hooks' brewery in New Hampshire. KBC's chief executive officer Mattson Davis shares KBC's practices for success.

22673 ■ "Briarcliff Office Building Fills Up Fast" in *The Business Journal-Serving Metropolitan Kansas City* (Vol. 26, Sept. 5, 2008, pp. 1)
Pub: American City Business Journals, Inc.
Ed: Rob Roberts. **Description:** Prior to its opening the Hilltop Office Building in Kansas City Missouri has attained 80 percent occupancy. FCStone Group Inc.'s plan to move to the building has boosted the facility's occupancy. Description and dimensions of the office building are also provided.

22674 ■ *Bridging the Equity Gap for Innovative SMEs*
Pub: Palgrave Macmillan
Ed: Elisabetta Gualandri. **Released:** December 1, 2009. **Price:** $85.00. **Description:** This book addresses the evaluation of financial constraints faced by innovative and startup companies and explores ways for bridging the financing and equity gap faced by small to medium business enterprises.

22675 ■ "Broadband Reaches Access Limits in Europe" in *Information Today* (Vol. 26, February 2009, No. 2, pp. 22)
Pub: Information Today, Inc.
Ed: Jim Ashling. **Description:** Eurostat (the Statistical Office of the European communities) reports results from is survey regarding Internet use by businesses throughout its 27-member states. Iceland, Finland and the Netherlands provide the most access at broadband speeds, followed by Belgium, Spain and France.

22676 ■ "Building His Dream" in *Business Courier* (Vol. 24, January 25, 2008, No. 42, pp. 1)
Pub: American City Business Journals, Inc.
Ed: Laura Baverman. **Description:** Technology entrepreneur Mahendra Vora plans to build a more than $100 million local IT headquarters for VTech Holdings Ltd by 2010. Acquisition of four $5 million companies within 2008 are part of the owner's plan to expand the office equipment company. Other plans for the IT company are discussed.

22677 ■ "Building Your Business: A Strong Web Presence Is a Must" in *Black Enterprise* (Vol. 38, December 2007, No. 5, pp. 74)
Pub: Earl G. Graves Publishing Co. Inc.
Ed: Tennille M. Robinson. **Description:** Building a strong presence on the Internet is crucial to any growing business. Websites can provide information or sell merchandise, but the site must also make sure the customer knows how to use and navigate around within the site. Common mistakes to avoid when designing a small business Website are outlined.

22678 ■ "Burger Market Sizzling with Newcomers" in *Boston Business Journal* (Vol. 29, June 10, 2011, No. 5, pp. 1)
Pub: American City Business Journals Inc.
Ed: Ryan Sharrow. **Description:** The burger trend in Maryland is on the rise with burger joints either opening up or expanding into several branches. Startup costs for this kind of business range between $250,000 to $400,000. With a growth rate of roughly 17 percent in 2009, this so-called better burger segment of the burger categories is expected to dominate the market for quite some time.

22679 ■ "Business Diary" in *Crain's Detroit Business* (Vol. 24, October 6, 2008, No. 40, pp. 23)
Pub: Crain Communications, Inc.
Description: Detailed listing of acquisitions, expansions, new products, new services, business contracts and startups from the Detroit area is provided.

22680 ■ *Business Plans to Game Plans*
Pub: John Wiley and Sons, Inc.
Ed: Jan B. King. **Released:** 2003. **Price:** $27.50. **Description:** Information for running a small business are examined, focusing on action plans and ways to avoid the pitfalls of strategic planning. The book describes how entrepreneurs should set standards, lead by example, look to the future, focus on important details, face reality, grow profitability, and take action.

22681 ■ "Business Still Expected to Take Hit in 2008" in *Business Journal-Serving Phoenix and the Valley of the Sun* (December 28, 2007)
Pub: American City Business Journals, Inc.
Ed: Ty Young. **Description:** Semiconductor industry is forecasting a slow first quarter for 2008 and industry analysts believe there will be decreased growth for the rest of the year. The impending recession in the U.S. will lead to a fall in consumer spending, which will in turn drive down the demand for electronics. The semiconductor revenue forecast for 2010 is also discussed.

22682 ■ *Business Vision: Beyond the Horizon, 2nd Ed.*
Pub: Business Vision Group
Ed: Dennis Wengert. **Released:** January 2009. **Description:** Challenges small business owners face when running their companies are addressed in order to position themselves for the future. The book teaches how to envision future direction and measure personal and business activities that provide an indication of personal progress in achieving visionary business leadership.

22683 ■ "Businesses Owned by Minorities Proliferate" in *MMR* (Vol. 27, November 29, 2010, No. 18, pp. 33)
Pub: Mass Market Retailers
Description: Ethnic minorities are launching new businesses faster than the general population of the U.S. Statistical data included.

22684 ■ "Buying Power of Hispanics Growing" in *Austin Business JournalInc.* (Vol. 29, November 27, 2009, No. 38, pp. 1)
Pub: American City Business Journals
Ed: Sandra Zaragoza. **Description:** Hispanic Marketing Symposium presented a report stating that the buying power of Hispanics of Austin, Texas has grown

by 54 percent in last five years to $9.4 billion in 2009. Details on the projected growth of the Hispanic market in the are is covered.

22685 ■ "Cadillac Tower Largest to Start in a Decade" in *Globe & Mail* (March 28, 2006, pp. B5)
Pub: CTVglobemedia Publishing Inc.
Ed: Elizabeth Church. **Description:** The plans of Cadillac Fairview Corporation Ltd. to build office towers, in downtown Canada, are presented.

22686 ■ "Campaigner Survey: 46 Percent of Small Businesses Use Email Marketing" in *Wireless News* (November 21, 2009)
Pub: Close-Up Media
Description: Almost half (46 percent) of small businesses surveyed by Campaigner's 2009 State of Small Business Online Marketing, say that they rely on email marketing to help them find new customers, keep existing ones and grow their businesses. The survey also found that 36 percent of small businesses plan to begin using email marketing over the next year. The trend to utilize Internet marketing tools is allowing small businesses to grow faster and generate higher revenues than those that are not using these mediums.

22687 ■ "Can America Invent Its Way Back?" in *Business Week* (September 22, 2008, No. 4100, pp. 52)
Pub: McGraw-Hill Companies, Inc.
Description: Business leaders as well as economists agree that innovative new products, services and ways of doing business may be the only way in which America can survive the downward spiral of the economy; innovation economics may be the answer and may even provide enough growth to enable Americans to prosper in the years to come.

22688 ■ "Can a Brazilian SUV Take On the Jeep Wrangler?" in *Business Week* (September 22, 2008, No. 4100, pp. 50)
Pub: McGraw-Hill Companies, Inc.
Ed: Helen Walters. **Description:** Profile of the Brazilian company TAC as well as the flourishing Brazilian car market; TAC has launched a new urban vehicle, the Stark, which has won prizes for innovation; the company uses local technology and manufacturing expertise.

22689 ■ "Can Brewer Make Cheap Seats Pay?" in *Globe & Mail* (January 7, 2006, pp. B4)
Pub: CTVglobemedia Publishing Inc.
Ed: Brent Jang. **Description:** The plans of chief executive officer Montie Brewer of Air Canada to upgrade airplanes are presented.

22690 ■ "Can This Duo be Saved? Renovating 2 Tallest Edifices Downtown Will Be Costly, Owner Says" in *Charlotte Observer* (February 4, 2007)
Pub: Knight-Ridder/Tribune Business News
Ed: Jefferson George. **Description:** Gastonia, North Carolina city leaders are making plans to renovate the Lawyers Building and the Commercial Building in an effort to revitalize the downtown area.

22691 ■ "Can You Hear Them Now?" in *Hawaii Business* (Vol. 54, August 2008, No. 2, pp. 48)
Pub: Hawaii Business Publishing
Ed: Jason Ubay. **Description:** Coral Wireless LLC (dba Mobi PCS) is ranked 237 in Hawaii Business' list of the state's top 250 companies for 2008. The company is a local wireless phone provider, which has expanded its market to Oahu, Maui and the Big Island since opening in 2006, offering 13 phones and unlimited texts and calls. Details on the company's sales are provided.

22692 ■ "Canada, Not China, Is Partner In Our Economic Prosperity" in *Crain's Chicago Business* (Vol. 31, April 14, 2008, No. 15, pp. 14)
Pub: Crain Communications, Inc.
Ed: Paul O'Connor. **Description:** In 2005 more than $500 billion in two-way trade crossed the friendly border between the Great Lakes states and Canadian provinces and for decades Canada is every Great Lakes State's number one and growing export market.

22693 ■ "Canada's Oil Rush" in *Canadian Business* (Vol. 81, October 13, 2008, No. 17, pp. 58)
Pub: Rogers Media Ltd.
Description: Excerpt from Andrew Nikiforuk's 'Tar Sands' details the exploration and development of oil sands in Alberta, Canada and its significance to the U.S. Canada has been the United State's largest supplier of oil since 2002, accounting for 18 percent of U.S. oil imports. Details regarding Canada's oil sand are examined.

22694 ■ "Canadian Patients Give Detroit Hospitals a Boost" in *Crain's Detroit Business* (Vol. 24, April 14, 2008, No. 15, pp. 10)
Pub: Crain Communications, Inc.
Ed: Jay Greene. **Description:** Each year thousands of Canadians travel to Detroit area hospitals seeking quicker solutions to medical problems or access to services that are limited or unavailable in Canada.

22695 ■ "Canadian Research Generates Innovation and Prosperity" in *Canadian Business* (Vol. 81, October 27, 2008, No. 18, pp. 87)
Pub: Rogers Media Ltd.
Description: Universities play a key role in helping Canadians achieve prosperity, competitiveness, and quality of life by conducting more than a third of Canada's research. Research in universities help train graduates to apply sophisticated knowledge to real problems.

22696 ■ "CanWEA Unveils WindVision for BC: 5,250 MW of Wind Energy by 2025" in *CNW Group* (October 4, 2011)
Pub: CNW Group
Description: Wind industry leaders are asking British Columbia, Canada policy makers to created conditions to further develop and integrate wind energy in accordance with greenhouse gas emission targets and projected economic growth. Statistical data included.

22697 ■ "Cash-Heavy Biovail on the Prowl for Deals" in *Globe & Mail* (March 24, 2006, pp. B1)
Pub: CTVglobemedia Publishing Inc.
Ed: Leonard Zehr. **Description:** Biovail Corp. posted 48 percent rise in profits for 2005. The business growth plans of the company through acquisitions are presented.

22698 ■ *Cash In a Flash*
Pub: Crown Business Books
Ed: Robert G. Allen, Mark Victor Hansen. **Released:** December 28, 2010. **Price:** $15.00. **Description:** Proven, practical advice and techniques are given to help entrepreneurs make money quickly using skills and resources known to generate permanent and recurring income.

22699 ■ "Caterpillar to Expand Research, Production in China" in *Chicago Tribune* (August 27, 2008)
Pub: McClatchy-Tribune Information Services
Ed: James P. Miller. **Description:** Caterpillar Inc., the Peoria-based heavy-equipment manufacturer, plans to establish a new research-and-development center at the site of its rapidly growing campus in Wuxi.

22700 ■ "A Cautionary Tale for Emerging Market Giants" in *Harvard Business Review* (Vol. 88, September 2010, No. 9, pp. 99)
Pub: Harvard Business School Publishing
Ed: J. Stewart Black, Allen J. Morrison. **Description:** Key factors that negatively affected Japan corporate growth and organizational effectiveness include: devotion to established path, isolated domestic markets, homogenous executive teams, and a non-contentious labor force. Solutions include leadership development programs, multicultural input, and cross-cultural training.

22701 ■ "Cemex Paves a Global Road to Solid Growth" in *Barron's* (Vol. 88, March 10, 2008, No. 10, pp. 24)
Pub: Dow Jones & Company, Inc.
Ed: Sandra Ward. **Description:** Shares of Cemex are expected to perform well with the company's expected strong performance despite fears of a US recession. The company has a diverse geographical reach and benefits from a strong worldwide demand for cement.

22702 ■ "Centrue Sets Down New Roots in St. Louis; Bank Looks to Expand in Exurbs of Chicago" in *Crain's Chicago Business* (May 5, 2008)
Pub: Crain Communications, Inc.
Ed: H. Lee Murphy. **Description:** Centrue Financial Corp. has moved its headquarters from Ottawa to suburban St. Louis in search of higher-growth markets. The banks acquisitions and expansion plans are also discussed.

22703 ■ "The Challenges of Commercial Work" in *Indoor Comfort Marketing* (Vol. 70, May 2011, No. 5, pp. 14)
Pub: Industry Publications Inc.
Ed: Matt Spink. **Description:** The challenges faced by heating, ventilation, cooling small businesses expanding into commercial accounts are discussed.

22704 ■ "Champion Enterprises Buys UK Company" in *Crain's Detroit Business* (Vol. 24, March 17, 2008, No. 11, pp. 4)
Pub: Crain Communications, Inc.
Ed: Daniel Duggan. **Description:** With the acquisition of ModularUK Building Systems Ltd., a steel-frame modular manufacturer, Champion Enterprises has continued its expansion outside the United States.

22705 ■ "The Changing Face of the U.S. Consumer" in *Advertising Age* (Vol. 79, July 7, 2008, No. 26, pp. 1)
Pub: Crain Communications, Inc.
Ed: Peter Francese. **Description:** It is essential for marketers to examine demographic shifts when looking at ways in which to market brands. The average head-of-households is aging and marketers must not continue to ignore them. Statistical data included.

22706 ■ "Channeling for Growth" in *The Business Journal-Serving Greater Tampa Bay* (Vol. 28, July 11, 2008, No. 29, pp. 1)
Pub: American City Business Journals, Inc.
Ed: Margie Manning. **Description:** HSN Inc., one of the largest employers in Tampa Bay, Florida, is expected to spend an additional $9.7 million annually as it plans to hire more accounting, internal audit, legal, treasury and tax personnel after its spin-off to a public company. Details on the company's sales growth are provided.

22707 ■ "Cheap Thrills: Where to Look When You're Craving a Low-Price Wine" in *Chicago Tribune* (January 12, 2009)
Pub: McClatchy-Tribune Information Services
Ed: Bill Daley. **Description:** Wines priced $15 and above are being hit the hardest by the economic downturn while cheaper wines, specifically those priced between $3 and $6, are seeing a growth in sales.

22708 ■ "Chiefs Hope Renovations Score Big With Sponsors" in *The Business Journal-Serving Metropolitan Kansas City* (Vol. 26, July 11, 2008)
Pub: American City Business Journals, Inc.
Ed: James Dornbrook. **Description:** Kansas City Chiefs officials expect to obtain 12 to 14 new major sponsors with the completion of the Arrowhead Stadium renovations. The new sponsorship opportunities will include naming rights for the stadium and practice facility. The team's marketing strategies are discussed.

22709 ■ "Children's Hospital to Grow" in *Austin Business Journal* (Vol. 31, July 22, 2011, No. 20, pp. A1)
Pub: American City Business Journals Inc.
Ed: Sandra Zaragoza. **Description:** Austin, Texas-based Dell Children's Medical Center is set to embark

on a tower expansion. The plan will accommodate more patients and make room for the hospital's growing specialty program.

22710 ■ "Children's Products Maker Not the New Kid on the Block" in *Crain's Cleveland Business* (Vol. 28, November 26, 2007, No. 47, pp. 3)
Pub: Crain Communications, Inc.
Ed: David Bennett. **Description:** Discusses the business model employed by Shamrock Industries Inc., a rising star in the competitive world of children's products; the company, which does business as Foundations Quality Children's Products, has expanded into a 63,000-square-foot distribution center which has boosted its local profile significantly.

22711 ■ "The China Syndrome" in *Canadian Business* (Vol. 79, July 17, 2006, No. 14-15, pp. 25)
Pub: Rogers Media
Ed: Peter Diekmeyer. **Description:** Contrasting pace of growth in China and India are presented. Reasons for the slow pace of growth of Canadian companies like CAE Inc. and Magna in India are also discussed.

22712 ■ "China's ZTE in Hunt for Partners" in *Globe & Mail* (February 27, 2006, pp. B1)
Pub: CTVglobemedia Publishing Inc.
Ed: Gordon Pitts. **Description:** The business growth plans of ZTE Corp. in Canada, through partnership, are presented.

22713 ■ "Chris Curtis Preaches the Gospel of Internet Success" in *Black Enterprise* (Vol. 38, March 2008, No. 8, pp. 56)
Pub: Earl G. Graves Publishing Co. Inc.
Ed: Anthony Calypso. **Description:** Profile of the Web Business Ownership Series, a collection of 20 free seminars that help small businesses learn about the Web development process.

22714 ■ "Christ Hospital to Expand" in *Business Courier* (Vol. 27, June 25, 2010, No. 8, pp. 3)
Pub: Business Courier
Ed: Dan Monk, James Ritchie. **Description:** Christ Hospital intends to invest more than $300 million and generate 200 jobs in an expansion of its Mount Auburn campus in Cincinnati, Ohio. About $22 million in retail activity can be created by the hospital expansion, which will also include a replacement garage and new surgery facilities.

22715 ■ "Chuy's Gears Up to Serve Atlants, Other Untapped Cities" in *Austin Business Journal* (Vol. 31, June 17, 2011, No. 15, pp. 1)
Pub: American City Business Journals Inc.
Ed: Cody Lyon. **Description:** Chuy's Holdings Inc. plans to expand into the Southeastern United States, particularly in Atlanta, Georgia. The restaurant, which secured $67.5 million in debt financing in May 2011, added 20 stores in five years and plans to open eight locations in 2011.

22716 ■ "CIBC Spends $1.1 Billion on Caribbean Expansion" in *Globe & Mail* (March 14, 2006, pp. B1)
Pub: CTVglobemedia Publishing Inc.
Ed: Sinclair Stewart. **Description:** Canadian Imperial Bank of Commerce (CIBC), the fifth-largest bank of Canada, is planning to spend $1.1billion to buy major share of Barbados-based First Caribbean International Bank. The details of the acquisition plan are presented.

22717 ■ "Cineplex Sees Past the Big Picture" in *Globe & Mail* (February 8, 2007, pp. B9)
Pub: CTVglobemedia Publishing Inc.
Ed: Shirley Won. **Description:** Cineplex Entertainment LP reported $4.6 million profit in the final quarter of 2006. The movie chain is introducing video-game tournaments and live rock concerts to improve sales.

22718 ■ "Clean Bathrooms Are Big Key to Convenience Store's Success" in *Marketing to Women* (Vol. 23, January 2010, No. 1, pp. 3)
Pub: EPM Communications, Inc.
Description: Buc-ee's, a Texas-based convenience store chain, is attributing its large female consumer base to the cleanliness of its bathrooms. The chain actually markets itself specifically to female consumers.

22719 ■ "Clean-Tech Focus Sparks Growth" in *Philadelphia Business Journal* (Vol. 28, January 15, 2010, No. 48, pp. 1)
Pub: American City Business Journals
Ed: Peter Key. **Description:** Keystone Redevelopment Group and economic development organization Ben Franklin Technology Partners of Southeastern Pennsylvania have partnered in supporting the growth of new alternative energy and clean technology companies. Keystone has also been developing the Bridge Business Center.

22720 ■ "ClearEdge Hums Along" in *Business Journal Portland* (Vol. 26, December 18, 2009, No. 41, pp. 1)
Pub: American City Business Journals Inc.
Ed: Erik Siemers. **Description:** Hillsboro-based ClearEdge Power Inc. expanded its workforce and facilities with $15M capital from investors. Since May 2009, the number of employees increased from 40 to 150 and headquarters expanded from 5,000 to 80,000 square feet.

22721 ■ "ClickFuel Unveils Internet Marketing Tools for Small Businesses" in *Internet Wire* (October 19, 2009)
Pub: Comtex News Network, Inc.
Description: ClickFuel, a firm that manages, designs and tracks marketing campaigns has unveiled a full software suite of affordable services and technology solutions designed to empower small business owners and help them promote and grow their businesses through targeted Internet marketing campaigns.

22722 ■ "Clicks From Round the World: Simplifying International E-Commerce" in *Inc.* (Volume 32, December 2010, No. 10, pp. 146)
Pub: Inc. Magazine
Ed: Ryan Underwood. **Description:** By 2014, global e-commerce spending is expected to increase more than 90 percent, with much of that growth coming from Latin America.

22723 ■ "Climate Right Systems Provides Pre-Assembled Equipment Packages" in *Contractor* (Vol. 56, July 2009, No. 7, pp. 1)
Pub: Penton Media, Inc.
Description: Climate Right Systems offers completely engineered, assembled, and tested equipment packages for hydronic heating and cooling. This package does away with the need to custom fabricate on-site and lets mechanical and plumbing contractors expand their offerings without added overhead and risk.

22724 ■ "CN Profit a Boon for Top Brass" in *Globe & Mail* (March 23, 2007, pp. B5)
Pub: CTVglobemedia Publishing Inc.
Ed: Brent Jang. **Description:** Canadian National Railway Co., Montreal-based freight carrier, paid $7.3 million in compensation to its top five executives. The company has posted a record $2.1 billion profits in 2006.

22725 ■ "CNinsure Offers Safety in Numbers" in *Barron's* (Vol. 90, September 13, 2010, No. 37, pp. 29)
Pub: Barron's Editorial & Corporate Headquarters
Ed: Teresa Rivas. **Description:** China's insurance holding company CNinsure has a long growth future due to the nascent insurance market in the country. It has also been diversifying its offerings and it has a broad network in the nation. The shares of the company are trading cheaply at nearly 14 times its 2011 earnings, and is considered a good point for investors.

22726 ■ "Coca-Cola Looks Ready to Pause" in *Barron's* (Vol. 88, March 10, 2008, No. 10, pp. 18)
Pub: Dow Jones & Company, Inc.
Ed: Michael Santoli. **Description:** Shares of Coca-Cola are expected to turn sideways or experience a slight drop from $59.50 each to the mid-50 level. The company has seen its shares jump 40 percent since 2006, when it was in a series of measures to improve profitability.

22727 ■ "Cogeco Profit Jumps 47 Percent in First Quarter" in *Globe & Mail* (January 13, 2006, pp. B3)
Pub: CTVglobemedia Publishing Inc.
Ed: Catherine McLean. **Description:** The reasons behind 47 percent increase in first quarter 2006 profits for Cogeco Inc. are presented.

22728 ■ "Coherent Laying Off 144 As It Prepares To Shut Auburn Plant" in *Sacramento Business Journal* (Vol. 25, August 1, 2008, No. 22, pp. 1)
Pub: American City Business Journals, Inc.
Ed: Melanie Turner. **Description:** Sacramento, California-based Coherent Inc. is planning to lay off 144 workers at its Auburn facility. Coherent has been cutting payroll and its real estate holdings. Statistics on the company's earnings are also provided.

22729 ■ "Cold Stone Creamery" in *Ice Cream Reporter* (Vol. 22, January 20, 2009, No. 2, pp. 8)
Pub: Ice Cream Reporter
Description: Franchise News reports that Cold Stone Creamery is looking for master franchisees to support its expansion into the North German market. The report notes that following its successful launch in Denmark, the firm is also preparing for expansion into France.

22730 ■ "Collection Agencies Industry Rankings" in *Collections and Credit Risk* (Vol. 14, September 1, 2009, No. 8, pp. 18)
Pub: SourceMedia, Inc.
Description: Ranking of the top collection agencies in the United States in terms of the revenue generated in 2007 and 2088; statistical data included.

22731 ■ "Commensurate with Experience" in *Entrepreneur* (Vol. 37, October 2009, No. 10, pp. 84)
Pub: Entrepreneur Media, Inc.
Ed: Carol Tice. **Description:** RingRevenue, a firm that specializes in pay-per-call technology that allows affiliate networks and advertising agencies to track purchases, began a funding round in June 2009 which it closed quickly after obtaining $3.5 million in venture capital. The round was closed earlier than the projections of its owners due to their track record.

22732 ■ "Commentary: US Economic Recovery and Policy" in *Small Business Economic Trends* (July 2010, pp. 3)
Pub: National Federation of Independent Business
Description: U.S. Government is making economic recovery difficult, with one of the largest tax increases in history arriving in six months. Meanwhile, Congress is looking into taxing successful businesses, which will potentially hamper growth and real investment. Other insights on the government's role in the country's economic growth are presented.

22733 ■ "Commercial Water Efficiency Initiatives Announced" in *Contractor* (Vol. 56, November 2009, No. 11, pp. 5)
Pub: Penton Media, Inc.
Ed: Robert P. Mader. **Description:** Plumbing engineers John Koeller and Bill Gauley are developing a testing protocol for commercial toilets. The team said commercial toilets should have a higher level of flush performance than residential toilets for certification. The Environmental Protection Agency's WaterSense program wants to expand the program into the commercial/institutional sector.

22734 ■ *Common Sense Business: Starting, Operating, and Growing Your Small Business-In Any Economy!*
Pub: HarperCollins Publishers, Inc.
Ed: Steve Gottry. **Released:** July 2006. **Price:** $13. 95. **Description:** Ideas are offered to help entrepreneurs start and manage a company.

22735 ■ "Companies Must Innovate, Regardless of Economy" in *Crain's Detroit Business* (Vol. 25, June 1, 2009, No. 22, pp. M007)
Pub: Crain Communications Inc. - Detroit
Ed: Sherri Begin Welch. **Description:** Despite the economy, leaders of Michigan's successful companies stress that small businesses must innovate in order to grow.

22736 ■ "Company Hopes To Pack Profits With Self-Storage" in *Crain's Detroit Business* (Vol. 24, February 18, 2008, No. 7, pp. 15)
Pub: Crain Communications Inc. - Detroit
Ed: Daniel Duggan. **Description:** Storage Opportunity Partners has purchased a vacant building to convert into a self-storage facility.

22737 ■ "Competitors' Resource-Oriented Strategies" in *Academy of Management Review* (January 2008, pp. 97)
Pub: ScholarOne, Inc.
Ed: Laurence Capron, Olivier Chatain. **Description:** Firms can maintain a competitive advantage by implementing competitor's' resource-oriented strategies to combat the resources of rivals in factor markets as well as political markets.

22738 ■ *The Complete Idiot's Guide to Starting and Running a Thrift Store*
Pub: Alpha Publishing House
Ed: Ravel Buckley, Carol Costa. **Released:** January 5, 2010. **Price:** $18.95. **Description:** Thrift stores saw a 35 percent increase in sales during the falling economy in 2008. Despite the low startup costs, launching and running a thrift store is complicated. Two experts cover the entire process, including setting up a store on a nonprofit basis, choosing a location, funding, donations for saleable items, recruiting and managing staff, sorting items, pricing, and recycling donations.

22739 ■ "Computer Forensics Firms Get Boost From New Evidence Rules" in *Crain's Detroit Business* (Vol. 24, March 24, 2008, No. 12, pp. 28)
Pub: Crain Communications, Inc.
Ed: Chad Halcom. **Description:** Computer forensics is a growing niche for firms such as the Center for Computer Forensics in Southfield; driving some of the growth are new amendments to the Federal Rules of Civil Procedure, which took effect about a year ago and address standards of evidence for electronic records, or "e-discovery," that are admissible for civil cases in federal courts.

22740 ■ *The Connection Key: Seven Ways the World's Most Successful Entrepreneurs Trounce the Competition and How You Can, Too*
Pub: John Wiley & Sons, Inc.
Ed: Maribeth Kuzmeski. **Released:** September 22, 2009. **Price:** $22.95. **Description:** The book is written under the premise that getting ahead in business does not come down to smarts, guts, rare talent, or plain old luck. While those things are helpful, the real missing ingredient is the ability to meaningfully connect with others.

22741 ■ "Contracting Firm Sees Timing Right for Expansion" in *Tampa Bay Business Journal* (Vol. 29, November 13, 2009, No. 47, pp. 1)
Pub: American City Business Journals
Ed: Janet Leiser. **Description:** Construction management company Moss & Associates LLC of Fort Lauderdale, Florida has launched its expansion to Tampa Bay. Moss & Associates has started the construction of the Marlins stadium in Miami, Florida's Little Havana section. It also plans to diversify by embarking on other government development, such as health care facilities and airports.

22742 ■ "Conversation" in *Harvard Business Review* (Vol. 86, September 2008, No. 9, pp. 32)
Pub: Harvard Business School Press
Ed: Susan Donovan. **Description:** Danish software entrepreneur Thorkil Sonne has helped improve employment for individuals with autism after discovering the perception of detail and remarkable memory skills in his own son, who has autism. His company, Specialisterne, was built via focusing on these strengths.

22743 ■ "Coping With a Shrinking Planet" in *Agency Sales Magazine* (Vol. 39, December 2009, No. 11, pp. 46)
Pub: MANA
Ed: Mark Young. **Description:** China and India are forcing big changes in the world and are posing a huge threat to U.S. manufacturers and their sales representatives. Reps may want to consider expanding into these territories. Helping sell American products out of the country presents an opportunity for economic expansion.

22744 ■ *Corporate Entrepreneurship: Top Managers and New Business Creation*
Pub: Cambridge University Press
Ed: Vijay Sathe. **Released:** February 2007. **Price:** $35.00. **Description:** Studies covering entrepreneurship and business growth are examined.

22745 ■ "Cost Cuts Lead Dealers to Record Profits" in *Globe & Mail* (March 24, 2006, pp. B3)
Pub: CTVglobemedia Publishing Inc.
Ed: Omar El Akkad. **Description:** The reasons behind posting of $4.3 billion profit by Canadian securities sector, for 2005, are presented.

22746 ■ "Counting on Engagement at Ernst and Young" in *Workforce Management* (Vol. 88, November 16, 2009, No. 12, pp. 25)
Pub: Crain Communications, Inc.
Ed: Ed Frauenheim. **Description:** Employee engagement has been difficult to maintain through the recession but firms such as Ernst & Young have found that the effort to keep their employees loyal has paid off.

22747 ■ "Courier 250 Companies Hope to Rebound From 2009" in *Business Courier* (Vol. 27, July 16, 2010, No. 11, pp. 1)
Pub: Business Courier
Ed: Dan Monk, Jon Newberry. **Description:** Private companies that are featured in the Courier 250 publication have lost almost $4 billion in revenue, while combined sales dropped by 11 percent to 32 billion in 2009. Courier 250 is a guide to public companies, large nonprofits, private firms, and other related entities in Ohio's Cincinnati region.

22748 ■ "Craig Muhlhauser" in *Canadian Business* (Vol. 81, September 15, 2008, No. 14-15, pp. 6)
Pub: Rogers Media Ltd.
Ed: Andrew Wahl. **Description:** Interview with Craig Muhlhauser who is the CEO of Celestica, a manufacturing company that provides services for the electronics sector; Muhlhauser discusses the company's restructuring program, which he feels was the secret to their surprising first-quarter results. Muhlhauser states that the company is operating with more forward visibility and that understanding the opportunities during the current economic situation presents the biggest challenge.

22749 ■ "Creativity: A Key Link to Entrepreneurial Behavior" in *Business Horizons* (September-October 2007, pp. 365)
Pub: Elsevier Technology Publications
Ed: Stephen Ko, John E. Butler. **Description:** Importance of creativity and its link to entrepreneurial behavior is examined. In a study of various entrepreneurs, studies concluded that a solid knowledge base, a well-developed social network, and a strong focus on identifying opportunities are relevant to entrepreneurial behavior.

22750 ■ *Creativity and Innovation: Breaking New Ground...Without Breaking the Bank*
Pub: A & C Black
Ed: Janice Armstrong. **Released:** March 1, 2009. **Price:** $12.95. **Description:** Advice is given to help small business owners be creative in order to compete in their sector.

22751 ■ "Criticare Sees Rapid Expansion" in *Business Journal-Milwaukee* (Vol. 28, December 31, 2010, No. 14, pp. A1)
Pub: Milwaukee Business Journal
Ed: Rich Rovito. **Description:** Criticare Systems Inc. expanded its distribution network, added customers, launched two new products and transferred into a new building in Pewaukee, Wisconsin at the start of their fiscal year. Criticare expanded its workforce and now has nearly 140 full time employees.

22752 ■ "A Crowd for the Cloud" in *CIO* (Vol. 24, October 2, 2010, No. 1, pp. 16)
Pub: CIO
Ed: Stephanie Overby. **Description:** Information about a project which aimed to implement a cloud-based crowdsourcing platform and innovation-management process is provided. Chubb Group of Insurance Companies wanted to mine revenue-generating ideas from its 10,400 employees and hundreds of thousands of external agents. The company hosted its first innovation event using its new system in October 2008.

22753 ■ "Cruising In Choppy Water" in *The Business Journal-Portland* (Vol. 25, August 22, 2008, No. 24, pp. 1)
Pub: American City Business Journals, Inc.
Ed: Erik Siemers. **Description:** Yacht builder Christensen Shipyards Inc. is experiencing robust business despite the slowing US economy, building four yachts a year as of 2008. The company expects revenues to hit $90 million and is opening a 500,000-square-foot plant in Tennessee.

22754 ■ "Cupcake Maker Grabs Outpost" in *Crain's New York Business* (Vol. 27, August 15, 2011, No. 33, pp. 16)
Pub: Crain Communications Inc.
Ed: Jermaine Taylor. **Description:** Family-owned miniature cupcake maker, Baked by Melissa, singed a ten-year lease, expanding their stores to five. The business was started three years ago by advertising executive Melissa Bushell.

22755 ■ "Customer Loyalty: Making Your Program Excel" in *Franchising World* (Vol. 42, August 2010, No. 8, pp. 47)
Pub: International Franchise Association
Ed: Steve Baxter. **Description:** Customer loyalty is key to any franchise operation's growth. Tips for identifying preferred customers are outlined.

22756 ■ "Customers Turned Off? Not at Best Buy" in *Barron's* (Vol. 88, March 24, 2008, No. 12, pp. 29)
Pub: Dow Jones & Company, Inc.
Ed: Sandra Ward. **Description:** Shares of Best Buy, trading at $42.41 each, are expected to rise to an average of $52 a share due to the company's solid fundamentals. The company's shares have fallen 20 percent from their 52-week high and are attractive given the company's bright prospects in the video game sector and high-definition video.

22757 ■ *Cute Little Store: Between the Entrepreneurial Dream and Business Reality*
Pub: Outskirts Press, Incorporated
Ed: Adeena Mignogna. **Released:** May 2006. **Price:** $11.95. **Description:** Challenges of starting and growing a retail business are profiled.

22758 ■ "Cutting Credit Card Processing Costs" in *Hawaii Business* (Vol. 53, March 2008, No. 9, pp. 56)
Pub: Hawaii Business Publishing
Ed: Robert K.O. Lum. **Description:** Accepting credit card payments offers businesses with profits from the discount rate. The discount rate includes processing fee, VISA & MasterCard assessment and interchange. Details regarding merchant service cost and discount rate portions are discussed. Statistical data included.

22759 ■ "Data Center Plan Bearing Fruit From Apple, Spec Center" in *Charlotte Business Journal* (Vol. 25, October 15, 2010, No. 30, pp. 1)
Pub: Charlotte Business Journal
Ed: Ken Elkins. **Description:** Apple Inc. is planning to expand its server farm at the North Carolina Data Center Corridor in Catawba County. T5 Partners, on the other hand, will build a shell building to house a server on the site. Infocrossing Inc. will also build an open data center in the area.

22760 ■ "Data Firm Growth 'Opportunistic'" in *Tampa Bay Business Journal* (Vol. 30, January 29, 2010, No. 6, pp. 1)
Pub: American City Business Journals
Ed: Michael Hinman. **Description:** E Solutions Corporation is experiencing growth amid the economic downturn, with its Park Tower data center occupancy in Tampa Florida expanding from 14,000 square feet to 20,000 square feet. Details on the increased operations fueled by demand for information storage and management services offered by the company are discussed.

22761 ■ "Daycare Dollars" in *Small Business Opportunities* (Winter 2009)
Pub: Entrepreneur Media Inc.
Description: Profile of Maui Playcare, a franchise that provides parents drop-in daycare for their children without having to purchase a membership, make reservations or pay costly dues; the company is expanding beyond its Hawaiian roots onto the mainland and is expected to have between 40 and 50 locations signed by the end of 2010.

22762 ■ "Deal Braces Cramer for Growth Run" in *The Business Journal-Serving Metropolitan Kansas City* (Vol. 26, July 4, 2008, No. 43, pp. 1)
Pub: American City Business Journals, Inc.
Ed: James Dornbook. **Description:** Gardner, Kansas-based Cramer Products Inc. bought 100 percent of the stocks of Louisville, Kentucky-based Active Ankle Inc. from 26 private investors increasing its revenue by 20 percent. The latter is the second largest vendor of Cramer. Other details of the merger are presented.

22763 ■ "Dealer Gets a Lift with Acquisitions at Year's End" in *Crain's Detroit Business* (Vol. 26, January 11, 2010, No. 2, pp. 3)
Pub: Crain Communications, Inc.
Ed: Ryan Beene. **Description:** Alta Equipment Co., a forklift dealer, closed 2009 with a string of acquisitions expecting to double the firm's employee headcount and triple its annual revenue. Alta Lift Truck Services, Inc., as the company was known before the acquisitions, was founded in 1984 as Michigan's dealer for forklift manufacturer Yale Materials Handling Corp.

22764 ■ "Debt Buyers Industry Rankings" in *Collections and Credit Risk* (Vol. 14, September 1, 2009, No. 8, pp. 19)
Pub: SourceMedia, Inc.
Description: Ranking of the top debt buyers in the United States in terms of the revenue generated in 2007 and 2088; statistical data included.

22765 ■ "Debutante NYSE Soars 20 Percent" in *Globe & Mail* (March 9, 2006, pp. B1)
Pub: CTVglobemedia Publishing Inc.
Ed: John Partridge. **Description:** The debutant share trading of NYSE Group Inc. is discussed. The prices rose by 20 percent before closing.

22766 ■ "December 19 Is a Great Day to be Terrible" in *Internet Wire* (December 15, 2009)
Pub: Comtex News Network, Inc.
Description: Overview of the plans to market the grand opening of the newest Terrible Herbst location in Las Vegas, Nevada. Terrible Herbst is a complete convenience destination offering a gas station, convenience store, car wash and lube center.

22767 ■ "A Decent Proposal" in *Hawaii Business* (Vol. 53, March 2008, No. 9, pp. 52)
Pub: Hawaii Business Publishing
Ed: Jacy L. Youn. **Description:** Bonnie Cooper and Brian Joy own Big Rock Manufacturing Inc., a stone manufacturing company, which sells carved rocks and bowls, lava benches, waterfalls, and Buddhas. Details about the company's growth are discussed.

22768 ■ "Deere to Open Technology Center in Germany" in *Chicago Tribune* (September 3, 2008)
Pub: McClatchy-Tribune Information Services
Ed: James P. Miller. **Description:** Deere & Co. plans to open a technology and innovation center in Germany; details of the company's expansion plans are discussed.

22769 ■ "Defense Contractor May Expand Locally; BAE Systems Ramps Up Vehicle Prototypes" in *Crain's Detroit Business* (March 24, 2008)
Pub: Crain Communications, Inc.
Ed: Chad Halcom. **Description:** Profile of BAE Systems, a defense contractor, that has built a prototype in the highly competitive Joint Light Tactical Vehicle project; the company has also completed its prototype RG33L Mine Resistant Recovery Maintenance Vehicle and has plans for expansion.

22770 ■ "Detroit Residential Market Slows; Bright Spots Emerge" in *Crain's Detroit Business* (Vol. 24, October 6, 2008, No. 40, pp. 11)
Pub: Crain Communications, Inc.
Ed: Daniel Duggan. **Description:** Discusses the state of the residential real estate market in Detroit; although condominium projects receive the most attention, deals for single-family homes are taking place in greater numbers due to financing issues. Buyers can purchase a single family home with a 3.5 percent down payment compared to 20 percent for some condo deals because of the number of first-time homebuyer programs under the Federal Housing Administration.

22771 ■ "Deutsche Bank Joins the Club" in *Barron's* (Vol. 88, March 31, 2008, No. 13, pp. M6)
Pub: Dow Jones & Company, Inc.
Ed: Arindam Nag. **Description:** Deutsche Bank's tangible leverage has worsened sharply in the past year from 2.1 percent to 2.3 percent during 2002-2006 to only 1.6 percent. The bank has also been accumulating a lot of illiquid assets and its Level-3 assets are three times its tangible equity.

22772 ■ "Developers Await Hotel" in *The Business Journal-Portland* (Vol. 25, July 11, 2008, No. 18, pp. 1)
Pub: American City Business Journals, Inc.
Ed: Wendy Culverwell. **Description:** Developers are eager to start the construction of a new hotel at the Oregon Convention Center in Portland, Oregon as hey say that the project will help boost the convention center neighborhood. The project, called The Westin Portland at the Convention Center, is partly handled by Ashforth Pacific Inc.

22773 ■ "Developers Poised to Pull Trigers" in *Boston Business Journal* (Vol. 30, November 12, 2010, No. 42, pp. 1)
Pub: Boston Business Journal
Ed: Craig M. Douglas. **Description:** Large residential projects are expected to break ground in Boston, Massachusetts in 2011, as real estate developers expect growth for the industry. Real estate experts expect more than 2,000 rental units to be available by 2011. Information on key real estate projects in Boston is presented.

22774 ■ "Diamond in the Rough" in *Canadian Business* (Vol. 79, October 23, 2006, No. 21, pp. 71)
Pub: Rogers Media
Ed: Mark Brown. **Description:** The opening of a new mine 420 kilometers northeast of Yellowknife in Northwest Territories by Tahera Diamond Corp. is discussed.

22775 ■ "Digital Duplication" in *Crain's Cleveland Business* (Vol. 28, October 1, 2007, No. 39, pp. 3)
Pub: Crain Communications, Inc.
Ed: David Bennett. **Description:** Profile of the business plan of eBlueprint Holdings LLC, a reprographics company that found success by converting customers' paper blueprints to an electronic format; the company plans to expand into other geographic markets by acquiring solid reprographics companies and converting their computer systems so that customers' blueprints can be managed electronically.

22776 ■ "A Direct Approach" in *Business Journal-Portland* (Vol. 24, November 9, 2007, No. 36, pp. 1)
Pub: American City Business Journals, Inc.
Ed: Matthew Kish. **Description:** Respond 2 LLC's annual revenue has increased from $14.2 million in 2004 to almost $50 million in 2007. The growth is attributed to a $100 million contract with Vonage. The role of the popularity of infomercials on the success of the Portland-based marketing company is evaluated.

22777 ■ "Discovery Networks" in *Brandweek* (Vol. 49, April 21, 2008, No. 16, pp. SR9)
Pub: VNU Business Media, Inc.
Ed: Anthony Crupi. **Description:** Provides contact information for sales and marketing personnel for the Discovery networks as well as a listing of the station's top programming and an analysis of the current season and the target audience for those programs running in the current season. The networks flagship station returned to the top 10 in 2007, averaging 1.28 million viewers.

22778 ■ "The Display Group Is Super-Sized" in *Michigan Vue* (Vol. 13, July-August 2008, No. 4, pp. 34)
Pub: Entrepreneur Media Inc.
Description: Profile of the Display Group, located in downtown Detroit, this company provides custom designed mobile marketing displays as well as special event production services for trade show displays. The rental house and design service is also beginning to see more business due to the film initiative, which provides incentives for films that are shooting in Michigan.

22779 ■ "Dodge Frets Over Flood of Fast Money" in *Globe & Mail* (May 2, 2007, pp. B1)
Pub: CTVglobemedia Publishing Inc.
Ed: Heather Scoffield. **Description:** The concern of governor of Bank of Canada, David Dodge, over the increase in global liquidity due to growth in the business of private equity, is discussed.

22780 ■ "The Dogs of the TSX" in *Canadian Business* (Vol. 82, Summer 2009, No. 8, pp. 42)
Pub: Rogers Media
Ed: Calvin Leung. **Description:** David Stanley revealed in an analysis of the ten companies on the S&P/TSX 60 index with the highest dividend yields, known as the Dogs of TSX, the dogs delivered an annual return of 13 percent between 1987 to 2005. The Dogs is a stock-picking method that involves buying the ten companies on the S&P/TSX 60 index with the highest dividend yields, and then selling them a year later.

22781 ■ "Dollar Tree Store To Open Mid-July in Shelby Mall" in *La Crosse Tribune* (June 20, 2010)
Pub: La Crosse Tribune
Ed: Steve Cahalan. **Description:** Dollar Tree Inc. plans to open a new store in the location formerly occupied by Family Dollar.

22782 ■ *Don't Bitch, Just Get Rich*
Pub: Simon and Schuster Incorporated
Ed: Toney Fitzgerald. **Released:** June 2006. **Price:** $16.00. **Description:** Advice is given to business leaders to help them shift from the position whereby money has power over you to taking responsibility for life choices in order to meet new challenges.

22783 ■ "Down by the Bay" in *Canadian Business* (Vol. 81, December 8, 2008, No. 21, pp. 15)
Pub: Rogers Media Ltd.
Ed: Calvin Leung. **Description:** Hudsons Bay Company chief executive Jeffrey Sherman believes that his vast experience in retail will help him find the company's customer base. Sales are estimated to increase 3.6 percent in 2009 after posting average annual retail sales increases of 5 percent between 2006 and 2008.

22784 ■ "Dreyer's Grand Ice Cream" in *Ice Cream Reporter* (Vol. 23, September 20, 2010, No. 10, pp. 8)
Pub: Ice Cream Reporter
Description: Dreyer's Grand Ice Cream will add one hundred new manufacturing jobs at its plant in Laurel, Maryland and another 65 new hires before the end of 2010 and another 35 in 2011.

22785 ■ "Drilling Deep and Flying High" in *Barron's* (Vol. 88, June 30, 2008, No. 26, pp. 34)
Pub: Dow Jones & Co., Inc.
Ed: Kenneth Rapoza. **Description:** Shares of Petrobras could rise another 25 percent if the three deepwater wells that the company has found proves as lucrative as some expect. Petrobras will become an oil giant if the reserves are proven.

22786 ■ *Duct Tape Marketing: The World's Most Practical Small Business Marketing Guide*
Pub: Thomas Nelson Inc.
Ed: John Jantsch. **Released:** May 2008. **Price:** $14.99. **Description:** Small business owners are provided the tools and tactics necessary to market and grow a business.

22787 ■ "Dunkin' Donuts Franchise Looking Possible for 2011" in *Messenger-Inquirer* (January 2, 2010)
Pub: Messenger-Inquirer
Ed: Joy Campbell. **Description:** Dunkin' Donuts has approved expansion of their franchises in the Owensboro, Kentucky region.

22788 ■ "Duro Bag to Expand, Add 130 Jobs" in *Business Courier* (Vol. 27, August 6, 2010, No. 14, pp. 1)
Pub: Business Courier
Ed: Jon Newberry. **Description:** Duro Bag Manufacturing Company will expand capacity at its Florence, Kentucky plant and will add around 130 jobs over the next few years. The state of Kentucky has given preliminary approval for up to $1 million in tax incentives over 10 years, tied to the creation of new jobs. The company's investment will include new production and packaging equipment and building improvements.

22789 ■ "Dynamic Duo" in *Barron's* (Vol. 88, March 10, 2008, No. 10, pp. 45)
Pub: Dow Jones & Company, Inc.
Ed: Shirley A. Lazo. **Description:** General Dynamics, the world's sixth-largest military contractor, raised its dividend payout by 20.7 percent from 29 cents to 35 cents a share. Steel Dynamics, producer of structural steel and steel bar products, declared a 2-for-1 stock split and raised its quarterly dividend by 33 percent to a split-adjusted 10 cents a share.

22790 ■ *E-Commerce in Regional Small to Medium Enterprises*
Pub: Idea Group Publishing
Ed: Robert MacGregor. **Released:** July 2007. **Price:** $99.95. **Description:** Strategies small to medium enterprises (SMEs) need to implement in order to compete with larger, global businesses and the role electronic commerce plays in this process are outlined. Studies of e-commerce in multiple regional areas, focusing on the role of business size, business sector, market focus, gender of CEO, and education level of the CEO are discussed.

22791 ■ *E-Myth Mastery: The Seven Essential Disciplines for Building a World Class Company*
Pub: HarperCollins Publishers Inc.
Ed: Michael E. Gerber. **Released:** March 2007. **Price:** $16.95. **Description:** Leadership, marketing, money, management, lead conversion, lead generation, client fulfillment are the seven keys to successful entrepreneurship.

22792 ■ *The E Myth Revisited: Why Most Small Businesses Don't Work and What to Do*
Pub: HarperCollins Publishers
Ed: Michael E. Gerber. **Released:** January 18, 2010. **Price:** $11.10. **Description:** The book dispels the myths surrounding starting a business and shows how traditional assumptions can get in the way of running a small company. Topics cover entrepreneurship from infancy to growth and covers franchising.

22793 ■ *The E-Myth Revisited: Why Most Small Businesses Don't Work and What to Do About It*
Pub: HarperInformation
Ed: Michael E. Gerber. **Released:** November 2005. **Price:** $39.00. **Description:** Keys for developing a prosperous small business is presented in an updated version of the author's best-seller published in the nineties.

22794 ■ "Eastland Future Unclear: Local Merchants Say They're OK Amid Closings of 4 More Stores" in *Charlotte Observer* (February 8, 2007)
Pub: Knight-Ridder/Tribune Business News
Ed: Nichole Monroe Bell. **Description:** Retailers in the Eastland Mall that market goods to shoppers looking for the urban, hip-hop look are most successful.

22795 ■ "Eckerd Sales Spell Relief for Coutu" in *Globe & Mail* (January 18, 2006, pp. B4)
Pub: CTVglobemedia Publishing Inc.
Ed: Bertrand Marotte. **Description:** The details on Eckerd Corp., which posted rise in sales by 2.7 percent in December 2005, are presented. Eckerd Corp. is a unit of Jean Coutu Group (PJC) Inc.

22796 ■ "Eclipse to Hire 50 for Airp;ort Hangar" in *Business Review, Albany New York* (Vol. 34, November 9, 2007, No. 32, pp. 3)
Pub: American City Business Journals, Inc.
Ed: Robin K. Cooper. **Description:** Eclipse Aviation, a jet manufacturer will hire fifty workers who will operate its new maintenance hangar at Albany International Airport. The company was expected to hire around twenty-five employees after it announced its plan to open one of the seven U.S. Factory Service Centers in 2005. Denise Zieske, the airport Economic Development Manager, expects the hangar construction to be completed by December 2007.

22797 ■ "Eco-Preneuring" in *Small Business Opportunities* (July 2008)
Pub: Entrepreneur Media Inc.
Ed: Mary C. Pearl. **Description:** Profile of Wildlife Trust, a rapidly growing global organization dedicated to innovative conservation science linking health and ecology. With partners in nearly twenty countries, Wildlife Trust draws on global strengths in order to respond to well-defined local needs. In the Dominican Republic, they are working with the community and local biologists in order to restore fishing and create jobs in the field of ecotourism.

22798 ■ "Economy Peddles Rent In This Cycle" in *The Business Journal-Serving Metropolitan Kansas City* (Vol. 26, August 8, 2008, No. 48)
Pub: American City Business Journals, Inc.
Ed: Ashlee Kieler. **Description:** Rental demand for apartment units in downtown Kansas City, Missouri, is increasing due to the housing crisis, lack of real estate development, and increasing popularity of the downtown area. The downtown area has 7,378 multifamily units as of June 2008, of which 4,114 are rentals.

22799 ■ "An Educated Play on China" in *Barron's* (Vol. 88, June 30, 2008, No. 26, pp. M6)
Pub: Dow Jones & Co., Inc.
Ed: Mohammed Hadi. **Description:** New Oriental Education & Technology Group sells English-language courses to an increasingly competitive Chinese workforce that values education. The shares in this company have been weighed down by worries on the impact of the Beijing Olympics on enrollment and the Sichuan earthquake. These shares could be a great way to get exposure to the long-term growth in China.

22800 ■ *Effective Small Business Management: An Entrepreneurial Approach*
Pub: Prentice Hall Higher Education
Ed: Norman M. Scarborough; Thomas W. Zimmerer; Douglas L. Wilson. **Released:** March 2006. **Price:** $178.33. **Description:** Provides undergraduate and graduate entrepreneurship and/or small business management courses with information to successfully launch a new company. The books offers entrepreneurs the tools required to develop staying power to succeed and grow their new business.

22801 ■ "Efficient Cash Management Essential To Be Competitive" in *Crain's Cleveland Business* (Vol. 28, November 12, 2007, No. 45, pp. 25)
Pub: Crain Communications, Inc.
Ed: Ken Moultrie. **Description:** In order to sustain a business it is important to organize cash-management efforts around three core areas: cash in, static cash and cash out. Tips for the successful management of these areas are provided.

22802 ■ "El Paso Firm Rides Boom to the Top" in *Hispanic Business* (Vol. 30, July-August 2008, No. 7-8, pp. 28)
Pub: Hispanic Business, Inc.
Ed: Jeremy Nisen. **Description:** VEMAC, a commercial construction management and general contracting firm that is experiencing success despite the plummeting construction market is discussed. VEMAC's success is attributed to the Pentagons' $5 billion investment in construction for the benefit of new personnel and their families to be transferred to Fort Bliss, a U.S. army base adjacent to El Paso.

22803 ■ "Elements For Success" in *Small Business Opportunities* (November 2008)
Pub: Entrepreneur Media Inc.
Description: Profile of Elements, a physical fitness club that approach a healthy lifestyle for women, which includes the components of body, beauty and mind; the network of upscale, boutique style health clubs differ from other providers in its "balanced lifestyle" approach to a healthy lifestyle. This unique niche is gaining in popularity despite the faltering economy.

22804 ■ "Elevated Status" in *Business Courier* (Vol. 24, March 21, 2008, No. 50, pp. 1)
Pub: American City Business Journals, Inc.
Ed: James Ritchie. **Description:** Overview of Tri-Health Inc.'s growth is presented. Currently, the company's revenue is estimated to be around $1 billion. Since 2004, the company was able to build patient towers, an outpatient facility in Lebanon, and was able to acquire the Group Health Associates physician practice. TriHealth recently hired 500 nurses in order to meet its needs.

22805 ■ *Email Marketing by the Numbers: How to Use the World's Greatest Marketing Tool to Take Any Organization to the Next Level*
Pub: John Wiley and Sons Inc.
Ed: Chris Baggott. **Released:** April 2007. **Price:** $29.99 (CND). **Description:** Tips for using email to market small business products and services are provided.

22806 ■ *The Emerging Markets Century: How a New Breed of World-Class Companies is Overtaking the World*
Pub: Free Press/Simon & Schuster Inc.
Ed: Antoine van Agtmael. **Released:** 2007. **Price:** $29.00. **Description:** An exploration of how companies like Lenovo and Haier who are presently in emerging economies are already competing with household name brands like Ford and Sony, thus proving globalization is here to stay.

22807 ■ "Emerging Tech Fund Strong in 2009" in *Austin Business JournalInc.* (Vol. 29, December 25, 2009, No. 42, pp. 1)
Pub: American City Business Journals
Ed: Christopher Calnan. **Description:** Texas' Emerging Technology Fund (ETF) has seen an increase in applications from the state's technology companies in 2009. ETF received 87 applications in 2009 from Central Texas companies versus 50 during 2008 while $10.5 million was given to seven Texas companies compared with $10.6 million to ten companies in 2008.

22808 ■ "The Emperor Strikes Back" in *Canadian Business* (Vol. 80, March 26, 2007, No. 7, pp. 48)
Pub: Rogers Media
Ed: Rachel Pulfer. **Description:** The financial performance of Fairfax Financial Holdings Ltd. in 2006 is presented. The efforts of chief executive Prem Watsa to lead the company towards growth track are also presented.

22809 ■ "Employers Plan to Fill Jobs" in *Philadelphia Business Journal* (Vol. 28, February 5, 2010, No. 51, pp. 1)
Pub: American City Business Journals
Ed: Peter van Allen. **Description:** Philadelphia, Pennsylvania's largest employers have openings for at least 6,000 jobs. But businesses remain cautious and are selective in hiring or waiting to see what happens to federal policy changes.

22810 ■ "EnCana Surpasses All Canadian Profit Records" in *Globe & Mail* (February 16, 2007, pp. B5)
Pub: CTVglobemedia Publishing Inc.
Ed: David Ebner. **Description:** Canada-based energy giant EnCana Corp. has reported $5.65 billion profits for the fiscal year 2006. The company has outpaced expectations by this impressive figure.

22811 ■ "Endeca Gears Up for Likely IPO Bid" in *Boston Business Journal* (Vol. 31, July 1, 2011, No. 23, pp. 1)
Pub: Boston Business Journal
Ed: Kyle Alspach. **Description:** Endeca Inc. is readying itself for its plans to register as a public company. The search engine technology leader is enjoying continued growth with revenue up by 30 percent in 2010 while its expansion trend makes it an unlikely candidate for an acquisition.

22812 ■ "The Endless Flow of Russell Simmons" in *Entrepreneur* (Vol. 37, September 2009, No. 9, pp. 24)
Pub: Entrepreneur Media, Inc.
Ed: Josh Dean. **Description:** Entrepreneur Russell Simmons has successfully grown his businesses by focusing on underserved markets. Simons has never given up on any business strategy. He has also entered the music, clothing and television industries.

22813 ■ "Energy Consulting Company to Expand" in *Austin Business JournalInc.* (Vol. 28, November 7, 2008, No. 34, pp. A1)
Pub: American City Business Journals
Ed: Kate Harrington. **Description:** CLEAResult Consulting Inc. is planning to increase its workforce and move its headquarters to a larger office. The company has posted 1,000 percent increase in revenues. The company's adoption of best practices and setting of benchmark goals are seen as the reason for its growth.

22814 ■ "Energy Sparks Job Growth" in *The Business Journal-Serving Greater Tampa Bay* (Vol. 28, August 8, 2008, No. 33, pp. 1)
Pub: American City Business Journals, Inc.
Ed: Margie Manning. **Description:** Energy infrastructure projects in Tampa Bay, Florida, are increasing the demand for labor in the area. Energy projects requiring an increase in labor include TECO Energy Inc.'s plan for a natural gas pipeline in the area and the installation of energy management system in Bank of America's branches in the area.

22815 ■ *The Engine of America: The Secrets to Small Business Success from Entrepreneurs Who Have Made It!*
Pub: John Wiley and Sons, Inc.
Ed: Hector Barreto; Robert J. Wagman (As told to). **Released:** September 2007. **Price:** $24.95. **Description:** Successful business strategies from CEOs of fifty small businesses (some of which are now large corporations) are shared to help entrepreneurs start or grow an existing company.

22816 ■ "Engine of Growth: U.S. Industry Funk hasn't Hurt Cummins or Its Investors" in *Barron's* (Vol. 88, July 14, 2008, No. 28, pp. 43)
Pub: Dow Jones & Co., Inc.
Ed: Shirley A. Lazo. **Description:** Engine maker Cummins increased its quarterly common dividend by 40 percent to 17.5 cents per share from 12.5 cents. CVS Caremark's dividend saw a hike of 18.4 percent from 9.5 cents to 11.25 cents per share while its competitor Walgreen is continuing its 75th straight year of dividend distribution and its 33rd straight year of dividend hikes.

22817 ■ *Enterprise, Entrepreneurship and Innovation: Concepts, Context and Commercialization*
Pub: Elsevier Science and Technology Books
Ed: Robin Lowe, Sue Marriott. **Released:** June 2006. **Price:** $39.95. **Description:** Application of enterprise, innovation and entrepreneurship are discussed to help companies grow.

22818 ■ *Entrepreneurial Strategies: New Technologies and Emerging Markets*
Pub: Blackwell Publishing Limited
Ed: Arnold Cooper; Sharon Alvarez; Alejandro Carrera; Luiz Mesquita; Robert Vassolo. **Released:** August 2006. **Price:** $69.95. **Description:** Ideas to help a small business expand into emerging market economies (EMEs) are discussed. Despite the high failure rate, this book helps a small firm develop a successful plan.

22819 ■ *Entrepreneurial Strategy Emerging Businesses in Declining Industries*
Pub: Edward Elgar Publishing, Incorporated
Ed: Cassia. **Released:** July 2006. **Price:** $110.00. **Description:** Role of entrepreneurship in context of older and declining industries is explored. The book offers insight into entrepreneurial dynamics behind emerging businesses in declining industries, especially the roles of resources processes and people.

22820 ■ *The Entrepreneur's Guide to Managing Growth and Handling Crisis*
Pub: Greenwood Publishing Group, Inc.
Ed: Theo J. Van Dijk. **Released:** December 2007. **Price:** $39.95. **Description:** The author explains how entrepreneurs can overcome crisis by changing the way they handle customers, by putting new processes and procedures in place, and managing employees in a professional manner. The book includes appendices with tips for hiring consultants, creating job descriptions, and setting up systems to chart cash flow as well as worksheets, tables and figures and a listing of resources.

22821 ■ *Entrepreneurship: A Process Perspective*
Pub: Thomson South-Western
Ed: Robert A. Baron; Scott A. Shane. **Released:** February 2007. **Price:** $137.95. **Description:** Entrepreneurial process covering team building, finances, business plan, legal issues, marketing, growth and exit strategies.

22822 ■ "Entrepreneurship: As Cool As It Gets" in *Canadian Business* (Vol. 80, January 29, 2007, No. 3, pp. 10)
Pub: Rogers Media
Ed: Norman de Bono. **Description:** The proposed construction of a restaurant with ice in Dubai by the Canadian firm Iceculture Inc. for the Sharaf Group is discussed. The growth of the clientele of Iceculture Inc. is described.

22823 ■ *Entrepreneurship and Economic Growth*
Pub: Edward Elgar Publishing, Incorporated
Ed: Carree. **Released:** October 2006. **Price:** $195.00. **Description:** Historic and country-specific studies and articles regarding entrepreneurship and innovation, growth models, competition and productivity, and empirical evidence.

22824 ■ *Entrepreneurship and the Financial Community Starting Up and Growing New Businesses*
Pub: Edward Elgar Publishing, Incorporated
Ed: Clarysse. **Released:** November 2006. **Price:** $75.00. **Description:** Understanding the role of private equity providers in the development and growth processes of small business.

22825 ■ *Entrepreneurship and the Growth of Firms*
Pub: Edward Elgar Publishing, Incorporated
Ed: Davidsson. **Released:** December 2006. **Price:** $100.00. **Description:** Relationships between entrepreneurial skills and business growth are explored.

22826 ■ *Entrepreneurship, Innovation and Economic Growth*
Pub: Edward Elgar Publishing, Incorporated
Ed: David B. Audretsch. **Released:** July 2006. **Price:** $145.00. **Description:** Links between entrepreneurship, innovation and economic growth are examined.

22827 ■ *Entrepreneurship, Innovation and the Growth Mechanism of the Free-Enterprise Economies*
Pub: Princeton University Press
Ed: Eytan Sheshinski; William J. Baumol. **Released:** January 2007. **Price:** $65.00. **Description:** Scholars address the free-enterprise Western economies.

22828 ■ *Entrepreneurship: The Engine of Growth*
Pub: Greenwood Publishing Group, Incorporated
Ed: Maria Minniti; Andrew Zacharakis; Stephen Spinelli; Mark P. Rice; Timothy G. Habbershon. **Released:** November 2006. **Price:** $300.00. **Description:** Dynamics of entrepreneurship are examined.

22829 ■ *Entrepreneurship in the U.S.: The 2005 Assessment*
Pub: Springer
Ed: Paul Reynolds. **Released:** March 2007. **Price:** $79.95. **Description:** Entrepreneurship and its role in the U.S. economy is discussed, examining new business creation and its impact on job growth, productivity enhancements, innovation, and social mobility.

22830 ■ "eResearch Issues Initiating Report on Aldershot Resources Ltd." in *Canadian Corporate News* (May 14, 2007)
Pub: Comtex News Network Inc.
Description: Overview of Bob Weir and Michael Wood's Initiating Report on Aldershot Resources Ltd., a junior Canadian-based uranium exploration company with prospective projects in Canada, Zambia, Australia, and a base metals project in Chile.

22831 ■ "Essential Releases Record First Quarter Results" in *Canadian Corporate News* (May 14, 2007)
Pub: Comtex News Network Inc.
Description: The first quarter of 2007 saw record financial performance despite numerous challenges for Essential Energy Services Trust. Statistical data included.

22832 ■ *Exceptional Service, Exceptional Profit: The Secrets of Building a Five-Star Customer Service Organization*
Pub: AMACOM
Ed: Leonard Inghilleri, Micah Solomon. **Released:** April 1, 2010. **Price:** $21.95. **Description:** Team of insiders share exclusive knowledge of the loyalty-building techniques pioneered by the world's most successful service leaders, including brick-and-mortar stars such as The Ritz-Carlton and Lexus and online success stories such as Netflix and CD Baby.

22833 ■ "Executive Decision: Lead a Double Life for Geac's Sake" in *Globe & Mail* (January 21, 2006, pp. B4)
Pub: CTVglobemedia Publishing Inc.
Ed: Simon Avery. **Description:** The details of growth of Geac Computer Corporation Ltd., under chief executive officer Charles Jones, are presented.

22834 ■ "Executive Decision: To Make Inroads Against RIM, Palm Steals Its Strategy" in *Globe & Mail* (March 25, 2006, pp. B3)
Pub: CTVglobemedia Publishing Inc.
Ed: Simon Avery. **Description:** The Palm Inc., global leader in portable device manufacturing, is looking forward to improve its sales of Palm Treos, a wireless portable device that connects to internet and email. Palm is also planning to build partnerships, under the efficient management of Michael Moskow-

itz, general manager and vice-president of Palm Inc., with the other companies to increase the sales of its wireless devices.

22835 ■ "Executive Interview: Arturo Elias" in *Canadian Business* (Vol. 80, January 29, 2007, No. 3, pp. 16)
Pub: Rogers Media
Ed: Thomas Watson. **Description:** The views of Arturo Elias, the president of General Motors Canada Limited, on the prospects of the growth of the company revenues during the year 2007 are presented.

22836 ■ "Expanding Middleby's Food Processing Biz" in *Crain's Chicago Business* (Vol. 31, April 21, 2008, No. 16, pp. 6)
Pub: Crain Communications, Inc.
Ed: David Sterrett. **Description:** Profile of the executive vice-president of the food processing company, Middleby Corp, whose business plan is to develop new products, begin looking for acquisitions and simplify operations in order to expand the firm.

22837 ■ "Expansions Signal Growing Interest in Waste-to-Energy Plants" in *Crain's Cleveland Business* (Vol. 28, November 5, 2007, No. 44)
Pub: Crain Communications, Inc.
Ed: Bruce Geiselman. **Description:** According to industry insiders, concerns about greenhouse gas emissions as well as escalating energy and waste disposal prices are fueling increased interest in waste-to-energy plants. Many plants are expanding and considering building new trash-burning plants; this marks the first growth in capacity in more than a decade.

22838 ■ "Explore New Avenues to Success...Boldly!" in *Indoor Comfort Marketing* (Vol. 70, May 2011, No. 5, pp. 18)
Pub: Industry Publications Inc.
Ed: Rich Rutigliano. **Description:** Strategies to help fuel companies succeed in today's market are explored.

22839 ■ "Exxon Braving the Danger Zones" in *Globe & Mail* (March 8, 2007, pp. B1)
Pub: CTVglobemedia Publishing Inc.
Ed: Shawn McCarthy. **Description:** The plans of Exxon Mobil Corp. to increase its revenues through the expansion of its operations in Asia, Africa, and the Middle East are discussed.

22840 ■ "Eyes to the Sky" in *Canadian Business* (Vol. 80, March 26, 2007, No. 7, pp. 33)
Pub: Rogers Media
Ed: Joe Castaldo. **Description:** The growth and prices of condominium market in the Canada are analyzed.

22841 ■ "Face Values: Going for Global Growth" in *Business Strategy Review* (Vol. 21, Autumn 2010, No. 3, pp. 60)
Pub: Blackwell Publishers Ltd.
Ed: Laura Tyson. **Description:** Global economic issues are examined with Laura Tyson, former Dean of London Business School, Professor at University of California Berkeley, and current advisor to President Obama.

22842 ■ "Face Values: Responsibility Inc" in *Business Strategy Review* (Vol. 21, Summer 2010, No. 2, pp. 66)
Pub: Wiley-Blackwell
Ed: John Connolly. **Description:** Investment and growth in emerging markets will bring new opportunities, but with them added responsibility. Will companies be able to rise to meet the new responsibility agenda?

22843 ■ "Face Values: Responsibility Inc." in *Business Strategy Review* (Vol. 21, Summer 2010, No. 2, pp. 66)
Pub: Blackwell Publishers Ltd.
Ed: John Connolly. **Description:** Investment and growth in emerging markets will bring new opportunities, but added responsibility comes with it. Will companies be able to rise to meet the new responsibility agenda?

22844 ■ *The Facebook Effect: The Inside Story of the Company That Is Connecting the World*
Pub: Simon & Shuster
Ed: David Kirkpatrick. **Released:** June 8, 2010. **Price:** $26.00. **Description:** There's never been a Website like Facebook: more than 350 million people have accounts, and if the growth rate continues, by 2013 every Internet user worldwide will have his or her own page. No one's had more access to the inner workings of the phenomenon than Kirkpatrick, a senior tech writer at Fortune magazine. Written with the full cooperation of founder Mark Zuckerberg, the book follows the company from its genesis in a Harvard dorm room through its successes over Friendster and MySpace, the expansion of the user base, and Zuckerberg's refusal to sell.

22845 ■ "Familiar Fun" in *Crain's Cleveland Business* (Vol. 28, October 22, 2007, No. 42, pp. 3)
Pub: Crain Communications Inc.
Ed: John Booth. **Description:** Marketing for the 2007 holiday season has toy retailers focusing on American-made products because of recent recalls of toys produced in China that do not meet U.S. safety standards.

22846 ■ "Family Throne" in *Hawaii Business* (Vol. 53, March 2008, No. 9, pp. 51)
Pub: Hawaii Business Publishing
Ed: Cathy S. Cruz-George. **Description:** Jeanette and George Grace inherited Paradise Lua Inc., a portable toilet company founded by George's father. The toilets are rented by Aloha Stadium during football season and St. Patrick's Day block party among others. The company has 2,500 toilets and 20 pumping trucks and had earnings of $1.3 million in 2007.

22847 ■ "Fashion Forward - Frugally" in *Entrepreneur* (Vol. 37, July 2009, No. 7, pp. 18)
Pub: Entrepreneur Media, Inc.
Ed: Jason Daley. **Description:** Staci Deal, a Fayetteville-based franchisee of fashion brand Plato's Closet, shares her experiences on the company's growth. Deal believes that the economy, and the fact that Fayetteville is a college town, played a vital role in boosting the used clothing store's popularity. Her thoughts on being a young business owner, and the advantages of running a franchise are also given.

22848 ■ *Faster Cheaper Better*
Pub: Crown Business Books
Ed: Michael Hammer. **Released:** December 28, 2010. **Price:** $27.50. **Description:** Nine levels for transforming work in order to achieve business growth are outlined. The book helps small business compete against the low-wage countries.

22849 ■ "Female Hispanic Professionals by the Number" in *Hispanic Business* (Vol. 30, April 2008, No. 4, pp. 8)
Pub: Hispanic Business
Description: More executive opportunities are presenting themselves for future generations of Hispanic women who are more frequently being found in high-level positions. Statistical data included.

22850 ■ "Fewer People Dying At Work" in *Sacramento Business Journal* (Vol. 25, August 29, 2008, No. 26, pp. 1)
Pub: American City Business Journals, Inc.
Ed: Kathy Robertson. **Description:** Statistics show that workplace deaths in California dropped by 24 percent in 2007 compared with the previous year. Much of the decline was observed in the construction industry, where a slowing economy affected employment and dangerous work. The number of workplace deaths in the state also declined in all major categories except fires and explosions.

22851 ■ "Fifth Third CEO Kabat: A World of Difference" in *Business Courier* (Vol. 26, January 1, 2010, No. 37, pp. 1)
Pub: American City Business Journals, Inc.
Ed: Steve Watkins. **Description:** CEO Kevin Kabat of Cincinnati-based Fifth Third Bancorp believes that the bank's assets of $111 billion and stock value of more than $10 indicate the recovery from the low stock prices posted in February 2009. He attributes the recovery from the federal government's stress test finding in May 2009 that Fifth Third needs to generate $1.1 billion.

22852 ■ "Fifth Third Spinoff" in *Business Courier* (Vol. 27, July 16, 2010, No. 11, pp. 1)
Pub: Business Courier
Ed: Dan Monk, Steve Watkins. **Description:** Electronic-funds transfer company Fifth Third Solutions (FTPS), a spinoff of Fifth Third Bancorp, is seeking as much as 200,000 square feet of new office space in Ohio. The bank's sale of 51 percent ownership stake to Boston-based Advent International Corporation has paved the way for the growth of FTPS. How real estate brokers' plans have responded to FTPS' growth mode is discussed.

22853 ■ "Filling the Gap" in *Canadian Business* (Vol. 80, March 12, 2007, No. 6, pp. 62)
Pub: Rogers Media
Ed: Andrew Wahl. **Description:** The chief executive officer of GAP, Bruce Poon Tip, shares his experience and efforts in the growth of the company to a leading position in Canada.

22854 ■ "Finalist: Private Company, Less Than $100M" in *Crain's Detroit Business* (Vol. 25, June 22, 2009, No. 25)
Pub: Crain Communications Inc. - Detroit
Ed: Nancy Kaffer. **Description:** Profile of W3R Consulting and CFO Patrick Tom= ina. The company offers information technology consulting. Tomina discusses the company's 505 strategy: to grow its annual revenue to $50 million in five years.

22855 ■ *Financing Growth: Strategies, Capital Structure, and M and A Transactions*
Pub: John Wiley & Sons, Inc.
Ed: Kenneth H. Marks, Larry E. Robbins, Gonzalo Fernandez, John P. Funkhouser, D.L. Williams. **Released:** September 1, 2009. **Price:** $95.00. **Description:** Guide for emerging growth and middle market companies includes information to help understand and apply the basics of corporate finance using empirical data and actual company cases to illustrate capital structures and financing approaches.

22856 ■ "Finding A Higher Gear" in *Harvard Business Review* (Vol. 86, July-August 2008, No. 8, pp. 68)
Pub: Harvard Business School Press
Ed: Thomas A. Stewart; Anand P. Raman. **Description:** Anand G. Mahindra, the chief executive officer of Mahindra and Mahindra Ltd., discusses how his company fosters innovation, drawn from customer centricity, and how this will grow the company beyond India's domestic market.

22857 ■ "Finding a Way to Continue Growing" in *Green Industry Pro* (Vol. 23, March 2011, No. 3, pp. 31)
Pub: Cygnus Business Media
Description: Profile of Brett Lemcke, VP of R.M. Landscape located in Rochester, New York. Lemcke tells how his Landscape Industry Certified credentials helped him to grow his business and beat out his competition.

22858 ■ "FirstMerit's Top Executive Turns Around Credit Quality" in *Crain's Cleveland Business* (Vol. 28, October 15, 2007, No. 41, pp. 3)
Pub: Crain Communications, Inc.
Ed: Shawn A. Turner. **Description:** Discusses the ways in which chairman and CEO Paul Greig has been able to improve FirstMerit Corp.'s credit quality and profit margin. Strategies included selling more than $70 million in bad loans, hiring a new chief credit officer and redirecting its focus on cross-selling its wealth and investment services to its commercial customers. Statistical data included.

22859 ■ "Fiscally Fit" in *Entrepreneur* (Vol. 37, October 2009, No. 10, pp. 130)
Pub: Entrepreneur Media, Inc.
Ed: Jason Daley. **Description:** Landrie Peterman, owner of an Anytime Fitness franchise in Oregon,

describes how she turned her business around. The franchise, located in an industrial park, saw growth after six months with the help of corporate clients.

22860 ■ "Five-Ring Circus" in *Entrepreneur* (Vol. 35, November 2007, No. 11, pp. 76)
Pub: Entrepreneur Media Inc.
Ed: Scott Bernard Nelson. **Description:** China's economy is growing and is expected to do well even after the 2008 Olympics, but growth could slow from eleven percent to eight or nine percent. Chinese portfolio concerns with regard to health and environmental records and bureaucratic fraud are discussed.

22861 ■ "Food Fight" in *Canadian Business* (Vol. 79, November 6, 2006, No. 22, pp. 18)
Pub: Rogers Media
Ed: Zena Olijnyk. **Description:** The war between Canadian grocers and Wal-Mart due to its plans for opening new stores is analyzed.

22862 ■ "For Gilead, Growth Beyond AIDS" in *Barron's* (Vol. 88, June 30, 2008, No. 26, pp. 18)
Pub: Dow Jones & Co., Inc.
Ed: Jay Palmer. **Description:** First-quarter 2008 revenue for Gilead Sciences grew by 22 percent and an earnings gain of 19 percent thanks to their HIV-treatment drugs that comprised over two-thirds of the company's sales in 2007. An analyst has a 12-month target from June, 2008 of 65 per share. The factors behind the company's prospects are also discussed.

22863 ■ "Ford, Chrysler Dinged as Little Cars Rule Road" in *Globe & Mail* (March 2, 2007, pp. B3)
Pub: CTVglobemedia Publishing Inc.
Ed: Greg Keenan. **Description:** The Ford Motor Co. and the Chrysler Group posted a decline in automobile sales in the first two months of 2007. The sales statistics of other automobile companies in Canada are also presented.

22864 ■ "ForeSee Finds Satisfaction On Web Sites, Bottom Line" in *Crain's Detroit Business* (Vol. 24, February 25, 2008, No. 8, pp. 3)
Pub: Crain Communications Inc. - Detroit
Ed: Tom Henderson. **Description:** Ann Arbor-based ForeSee Results Inc. evaluates user satisfaction on Web sites. The company expects to see an increase of 40 percent in revenue for 2008 with plans to expand to London, Germany, Italy and France by the end of 2009.

22865 ■ "Formulating Policy With a Parallel Organization" in *Strategy & Leadership* (Vol. 38, September-October 2010, No. 5, pp. 33-38)
Pub: Emerald Inc.
Ed: Dale E. Zand, Thomas F. Hawk. **Description:** A study analyzes a case to examine the parallel organization concept and its successful implementation by a CEO to integrate independent divisions of a firm. Findings reveal that the implementation of the parallel organization improved the policy formulation, strategic planning profitability of the firm while also better integrating its independent divisions.

22866 ■ "Franchising Lures Boomers" in *Business Journal-Portland* (Vol. 24, November 9, 2007, No. 36, pp. 1)
Pub: American City Business Journals, Inc.
Ed: Wendy Culverwell. **Description:** Popularity of franchising has increased, and investors belonging to the baby boom generation contribute largely to this growth. The number of aging baby boomers is also increasing, particularly in Oregon, which means further growth of franchises can be expected. Reasons why franchising is a good investment for aging baby boomers are given.

22867 ■ "Free Fall" in *Canadian Business* (Vol. 79, September 11, 2006, No. 18, pp. 28)
Pub: Rogers Media
Ed: Zena Olijnyk. **Description:** Second quarter results of Imax Corp are reviewed. The company's performance and its future prospects are also presented.

22868 ■ "Fresh Direct's Crisis" in *Crain's New York Business* (Vol. 24, January 14, 2008, No. 2, pp. 3)
Pub: Crain Communications, Inc.
Ed: Lisa Fickenscher. **Description:** Freshdirect, an Internet grocery delivery service, finds itself under siege from federal immigration authorities, customers and labor organizations due to its employment practice of hiring illegals. At stake is the grocer's reputation as well as its ambitious growth plans, including an initial public offering of its stock.

22869 ■ "Fries With That?" in *Canadian Business* (Vol. 81, September 29, 2008, No. 16, pp. 33)
Pub: Rogers Media Ltd.
Ed: Calvin Leung. **Description:** Profile of Toronto-based New York Fries, which has four stores in South Korea, is planning to expand further as well as into Hong Kong and Macau; the company also has a licensee in the United Arab Emirates whom is also planning to expand.

22870 ■ "From Craft Biz To Wholesale Giant" in *Women Entrepreneur* (January 19, 2009)
Pub: Entrepreneur Media Inc.
Ed: Maria Falconer. **Description:** Advice is given on how to turn a small craft business into a full-time venture; tips to help one transition from a part-time designer to a full-time wholesaler and brand are also included.

22871 ■ "From Fat to Fit" in *Canadian Business* (Vol. 79, September 25, 2006, No. 19, pp. 100)
Pub: Rogers Media
Ed: Graham Scott. **Description:** The increase in physical fitness clubs across Canada is discussed.

22872 ■ "From Malls to Steel Plants" in *Crain's Chicago Business* (Vol. 31, April 28, 2008, No. 17, pp. 30)
Pub: Crain Communications, Inc.
Ed: Samantha Stainburn. **Description:** Profile of the company Graycor Inc. which started out as a sand-blasting and concrete-breaking firm but has grown into four businesses due to innovation and acquisitions. Graycor's businesses include: Graycor Industrial Constructors Inc., which builds and renovates power plants and steel mills; Graycor Construction Co., which erects stores, medical centers and office buildings; Graycor Blasting Co., which uses explosives and blasts tunnels for industrial cleaning, and Graycor International Inc., which provides construction services in Mexico.

22873 ■ "From OTC Sellers to Surgeons, Healthcare Marketers Target Women to Achieve Growth" in *Marketing to Women* (February 2008)
Pub: EPM Communications, Inc.
Description: Healthcare companies are targeting women with ad campaigns, new product development and new technology in order to reach and develop brand loyalty.

22874 ■ "Fromm Family Foods Converts Old Feed Mill Into Factory for Gourmet Pet Food" in *Wisconsin State Journal* (August 3, 2011)
Pub: Capital Newspapers
Ed: Barry Adams. **Description:** Fromm Family Foods, a gourmet cat and dog food company spent $10 million to convert an old feed mill into a pet food manufacturing facility. The owner forecasts doubling or tripling its production of 600 tons of feed per week in about five years.

22875 ■ "Frozen Dessert Year in Review..." in *Ice Cream Reporter* (Vol. 22, January 20, 2009, No. 2, pp. 1)
Pub: Ice Cream Reporter
Description: Falling economy caused the closing of several ice cream plants across the U.S. in 2008. Top stories of interest to the industry are presented.

22876 ■ "Frozen Yogurt Market Heats Up Again" in *Houston Business Journal* (Vol. 40, November 27, 2009, No. 29, pp. 1)
Pub: American City Business Journals
Ed: Allison Wollam. **Description:** Frozen yogurt stores are being reestablished or expanding in new sites throughout Houston, Texas due to presumed oversupply of ice cream stores in the market. Among these stores are Berripop, BlueBerryHill, Fruituzy, and Tasti D-Lite. Suggestions for these stores to focus on frozen yogurts in order to distinguish them from stores offering other products such as specialty drink items and sandwiches are outlined.

22877 ■ "Funeral Directors Get Creative As Boomers Near Great Beyond" in *Advertising Age* (Vol. 79, October 13, 2008, No. 38, pp. 30)
Pub: Crain Communications, Inc.
Ed: Lenore Skenazy. **Description:** Despite the downturn in the economy, the funeral business is thriving due to the number of baby boomers who realize the importance of making preparations for their death. Marketers are getting creative in their approach and many companies have taken into consideration the need for a more environmental friendly way to dispose of bodies and thus have created innovative businesses that reflect this need.

22878 ■ "Gail Lissner; Vice-President, Appraisal Research Counselors" in *Crain's Chicago Business* (Vol. 31, May 5, 2008, No. 18, pp. 28)
Pub: Crain Communications, Inc.
Ed: Phuong Ly. **Description:** Profile of Gail Lissner who is the vice-president of the Appraisal Research Counselors, a company that puts out the quarterly "Residential Benchmark Report," in which Ms. Lissner co-authors and is considered a must-read in the industry. Ms. Lissner has risen to become one of the most sought-after experts on the Chicago market considering real estate.

22879 ■ "Gallery Street Launches ArtCandy" in *Art Business News* (Vol. 34, November 2007, No. 11, pp. 8)
Pub: Pfingsten Publishing, LLC
Description: Fine-art reproduction house Gallery Street recently launched its new division, ArtCandy Editions; the division was created in order to help a network of artists expand the distribution of their work.

22880 ■ *The Game-Changer: How You Can Drive Revenue and Profit Growth with Innovation*
Pub: Crown Business
Ed: A.G. Lafley, Ram Charan. **Released:** 2009. **Price:** $27.50. **Description:** Former Proctor and Gamble CEO A.G. Lafley outlines principles of innovation that turned the company around and shows how that strategy can work for any business.

22881 ■ "The Game of Operation" in *Crain's Chicago Business* (Vol. 31, April 28, 2008, No. 17, pp. 26)
Pub: Crain Communications, Inc.
Ed: Samantha Stainburn. **Description:** Revenue at Medline Industries Inc., a manufacturer of medical products, has risen 12 percent a year since 1976, reaching $2.81 billion last year. Growth at the company is due to new and increasingly sophisticated operations by surgeons which brings about the need for more specialized tools.

22882 ■ "Games Gone Wild: City's Newest Public Company Aims for the Sky" in *Business Courier* (Vol. 27, September 24, 2010, No. 21, pp. 1)
Pub: Business Courier
Ed: Dan Monk. **Description:** Video game company Zoo Entertainment Inc., which is based in Norwood near Cincinnati, Ohio aims to build a strong company and to position itself for future growth. The company reported $27.6 million in revenue for the first half of 2010 and analysts project $100 million in sales for 2011.

22883 ■ "GE Looking to Extend Hot Streak" in *Business Courier* (Vol. 24, January 25, 2008, No. 42, pp. 1)
Pub: American City Business Journals, Inc.
Ed: John Newberry. **Description:** GE Aviation has enjoyed strong revenues and sales due to increase aircraft engine orders. It has an engine backlog order

of $19 million as of the end of 2007. Data on the aviation company's revenues, operating profit and total engine orders for the year 2004 to 2007 are presented.

22884 ■ "GE Milestone: 1,000th Wind Turbine Installed in Canada" in *CNW Group* (October 4, 2011)
Pub: CNW Group
Description: GE installed its 1,000th wind turbine in Canada at Cartier Wind Energy's Gros Morne project in the Gaspesie Region of Quebec, Canada. As Canada continues to expand its use of wind energy, GE plans to have over 1,100 wind turbines installed in the nation by the end of 2011.

22885 ■ "Generational Savvy" in *Hawaii Business* (Vol. 54, August 2008, No. 2, pp. 135)
Pub: Hawaii Business Publishing
Ed: Jolyn Okimoto Rosa. **Description:** Lawrence Takeo Kagawa founded Security Insurance Agency, later renamed Occidental Underwriters of Hawaii Ltd., in 1933 to provide insurance to Asian-Americans in Hawaii at lower premiums. Details on the company's history, growth investment products and Transamerica Life products and 75 years of family-run business are discussed.

22886 ■ "Genzyme: Underrated Oversold" in *Barron's* (Vol. 88, March 24, 2008, No. 12, pp. 58)
Pub: Dow Jones & Company, Inc.
Ed: Johanna Bennett. **Description:** Shares of biotechnology company Genzyme appear oversold and underrated at their $71.86 level. The company's finances are on a solid foundation, with revenues over $3.8 billion in 2007 and forecasts of $4.5-4.7 billion in revenue for 2008.

22887 ■ *Get Your Business to Work!: 7 Steps to Earning More, Working Less and Living the Life You Want*
Pub: BenBella Books
Ed: George Hedley. **Released:** June 9, 2010. **Price:** $24.95. **Description:** Complete step-by-step guide for the small business owner to realize profits, wealth and freedom.

22888 ■ *Getting to Scale: Growing Your Business Without Selling Out*
Pub: Berrett-Koehler Publishers, Incorporated
Ed: Jill Bamburg. **Released:** July 2006. **Price:** $14. 95. **Description:** Ways for entrepreneurs to preserve the value of their company while maintaining growth and competitiveness.

22889 ■ "Getting in Shape" in *Crain's Cleveland Business* (Vol. 28, December 3, 2007, No. 48, pp. 13)
Pub: Crain Communications, Inc.
Ed: Chrissy Kadleck. **Description:** According to the Medical Fitness Association, the number of medically integrated health and fitness centers has grown from 79 centers in 1985 to 875 in 2006. Summa Wellness Institute, the 65,000-square-foot health-and-fitness facility which opened next to Summa Health Systems's outpatient medical center is discussed.

22890 ■ "Giants Now Admit They Roam Planet Earth; Time To Buy?" in *Barron's* (Vol. 88, March 31, 2008, No. 13, pp. 39)
Pub: Dow Jones & Company, Inc.
Ed: Eric J. Savitz. **Description:** Oracle's third-quarter results showed that top-line growth fell short of expectations but the company is expected to fare better than most applications companies in the downturn. Google had a flat growth in the number of people who click their online ads. The time for investors in the tech sector with a long-term horizon has arrived.

22891 ■ *The Girl's Guide to Building a Million-Dollar Business*
Pub: AMACOM
Ed: Susan Wilson Solovic. **Released:** 2008. **Price:** $21.95. **Description:** Success plan for women business owners; the book includes tips for determination, managing changing relationships, keeping employees and customers happy, getting and maintaining credit, overcoming gender bias, and creating a good business plan and solid brand.

22892 ■ "The Global Economy, the Labor Force and Franchising's Future" in *Franchising World* (Vol. 42, September 2010, No. 9, pp. 35)
Pub: International Franchise Association
Ed: Jeffrey A. Rosensweig. **Description:** Point forecasting and the methodology called scenario analysis are presented looking at the global economy and future of franchising in the U.S. and abroad.

22893 ■ "Golden Spoon Accelerates Expansion Here and Abroad" in *Ice Cream Reporter* (Vol. 22, December 20, 2008, No. 1, pp. 2)
Pub: Ice Cream Reporter
Description: Golden Spoon frozen yogurt franchise chain is developing 35 more locations in the Phoenix, Arizona area along with plans to open a store in Japan.

22894 ■ *Good Capitalism, Bad Capitalism, and the Economics of Growth and Prosperity*
Pub: Yale University Press
Ed: William J. Baumol, Robert E. Litan, Carl J. Schramm. **Released:** October 1, 2009. **Price:** $22. 00. **Description:** The book identifies the conditions that characterize good capitalism and discusses capitalist economies.

22895 ■ *Good to Great: Why Some Companies Make the Leap...and Others Don't*
Pub: HarperInformation
Ed: Jim Collins. **Released:** October 2001. **Price:** $29.99. **Description:** Management styles for growing a modern business.

22896 ■ "A Good Sign for Commercial Real Estate" in *Austin Business JournalInc.* (Vol. 29, December 18, 2009, No. 41, pp. 1)
Pub: American City Business Journals
Ed: Kate Harrington. **Description:** Factors that could contribute to the reemergence of the commercial mortgage-backed securities market in Texas are discussed. These securities can potentially boost the commercial real estate market statewide as well as nationwide. Commercial mortgage-backed securities origination in 2009 is worth less that $1 billion, compared with $238 billion in 2008.

22897 ■ *The Google Story: Inside the Hottest Business, Media, and Technology Success of Our Time*
Pub: Random Housing Publishing Group
Ed: David A. Vise; Mark Malseed. **Price:** $26.00.

22898 ■ "Graduates to the TSX in 2008" in *Canadian Business* (Vol. 81, Summer 2008, No. 9, pp. 79)
Pub: Rogers Media Ltd.
Ed: Calvin Leung. **Description:** Table showing the market capitalization and stock performance of the companies that jumped to the TSX Venture Exchange is presented. The 17 companies that made the leap to the list will have an easier time raising capital, although leeway must be made in investing since they are still new businesses.

22899 ■ "Grand Action Makes Grand Changes in Grand Rapids" in *Crain's Detroit Business* (Vol. 25, June 1, 2009, No. 22, pp. M012)
Pub: Crain Communications Inc. - Detroit
Ed: Amy Lane. **Description:** Businessman Dick DeVos believes that governments are not always the best to lead certain initiatives. That's why, in 1991, he gathered 50 west Michigan community leaders and volunteers to look consider the construction of an arena and expanding or renovating local convention operations. Grand Action has undertaken four major projects in the city.

22900 ■ "Green Clean Machine" in *Small Business Opportunities* (Winter 2010)
Pub: Harris Publications Inc.
Description: Eco-friendly maid franchise plans to grow its $62 million sales base. Profile of Maid Brigade, a green-cleaning franchise is planning to expand across the country.

22901 ■ "Green Light" in *The Business Journal-Portland* (Vol. 25, July 11, 2008, No. 18, pp. 1)
Pub: American City Business Journals, Inc.
Ed: Erik Siemers. **Description:** Ecos Consulting, a sustainability consulting company based in Portland, Oregon, is seeing a boost in revenue as more businesses turn to sustainable practices. The company's revenue rose by 50 percent in 2007 and employees increased from 57 to 150. Other details about Ecos' growth are discussed.

22902 ■ *Greening Your Small Business: How to Improve Your Bottom Line, Grow Your Brand, Satisfy Your Customers and Save the Planet*
Pub: Prentice Hall Press
Ed: Jennifer Kaplan. **Released:** November 3, 2009. **Price:** $19.95. **Description:** A definitive resource for anyone who wants their small business to be cutting-edge, competitive, profitable, and eco-conscious. Stories from small business owners address every aspect of going green, from basics such as recycling waste, energy efficiency, and reducing information technology footprint, to more in-depth concerns such as green marketing and communications, green business travel, and green employee benefits.

22903 ■ "Groomers Eye Profit Growth Through Services" in *Pet Product News* (Vol. 64, December 2010, No. 12, pp. 26)
Pub: BowTie Inc.
Ed: Kathleen M. Mangan. **Description:** Pet groomers can successfully offer add-on services by taking into account insider customer knowledge, store image, and financial analysis in the decision-making process. Many pet groomers have decided to add services such as spa treatments and training due to a slump in the bathing and grooming business. How some pet groomers gained profitability through add-on services is explored.

22904 ■ "Ground Floor Opportunity" in *Small Business Opportunities* (July 2008)
Pub: Entrepreneur Media Inc.
Description: Profile of Doug Disney, the founder of the booming franchise Tile Outlet Always in Stock, which sells ceramic and porcelain tile and stone products at wholesale prices; Disney found inspiration in a book he read in two days and that motivated him to expand his venture into a huge franchise opportunity.

22905 ■ "Grow-Ops" in *Canadian Business* (Vol. 81, October 27, 2008, No. 18, pp. 112)
Pub: Rogers Media Ltd.
Ed: Calvin Leung. **Description:** Canada's agriculture and agri-food industry is ripe for expansion and to meet global demand that is expected to double by 2050. Better water management and biotechnology are among the strategies that could help increase output of Canada's agricultural industry.

22906 ■ *Growing Business Handbook: Inspirational Advice from Successful Entrepreneurs and Fast-Growing UK Companies*
Pub: Kogan Page, Limited
Ed: Adam Jolly. **Released:** February 2007. **Price:** $49.95. **Description:** Tips for growing and running a successful business are covered, focusing on senior managers in middle market and SME companies.

22907 ■ "A Growing Concern" in *Canadian Business* (Vol. 79, October 9, 2006, No. 20, pp. 90)
Pub: Rogers Media
Ed: Jeff Sanford. **Description:** With rich dividends being harvested by companies producing ethanol, after ethanol became a petrol additive, is discussed.

22908 ■ "A Growing Dilemma" in *Crain's Cleveland Business* (Vol. 28, October 8, 2007, No. 40, pp. 19)
Pub: Crain Communications, Inc.
Ed: Kimberly Bonvissuto. **Description:** Discusses small business owners who often have to grapple with the decision on whether or not to expand their operations and the importance of a business plan which may help owners with that decision.

22909 ■ "Growing Field" in *Crain's Detroit Business* (Vol. 26, January 11, 2010, No. 2, pp. 3)
Pub: Crain Communications, Inc.
Description: Detroit's TechTown was awarded a combination loan and grant of $4.1 million from the U.S. Department of Housing and Urban Development to build a 15,000-square-foot stem cell center, a collection of laboratories that will be available to both for-profit companies and university researchers.

22910 ■ *Growing and Managing a Small Business: An Entrepreneurial Perspective*
Pub: Houghton Mifflin College Division
Ed: Kathleen R. Allen. **Released:** July 2006. **Price:** $105.27. **Description:** Introduction to business ownership and management from startup through growth.

22911 ■ "Growing at the Margins" in *Business Journal Serving Greater Tampa Bay* (Vol. 30, November 5, 2010, No. 46, pp. 1)
Pub: Tampa Bay Business Journal
Ed: Margie Manning. **Description:** Jabil Circuit Inc. has reported an increase in revenues from its smart phones and medical devices. The company has been focusing on its core services such as making smart phone parts and medical devices.

22912 ■ "Growing Subscriber Base Fuels Roger's Rosy Outlook for 2007" in *Globe & Mail* (February 16, 2007, pp. B3)
Pub: CTVglobemedia Publishing Inc.
Ed: Catherine McLean. **Description:** Canada-based Rogers Communications Inc. has projected increased profits for the 2007 fiscal year. The company has increased its market share by 14 percent with fourth quarter revenues of $176 million.

22913 ■ *Growing Your Business*
Pub: Routledge Inc.
Ed: Burke. **Released:** December 2006. **Price:** $150. 00. **Description:** Growth strategies for small businesses are presented.

22914 ■ "Growing Your Business Through BPI Certification" in *Indoor Comfort Marketing* (Vol. 70, May 2011, No. 5, pp. 12)
Pub: Industry Publications Inc.
Ed: Scott Vadino. **Description:** Profile of the Building Performance Institute and the ways BPI certification will help grow a heating, ventilation, cooling firm.

22915 ■ "Growth Back on CIBC's Agenda" in *Globe & Mail* (March 3, 2006, pp. B1)
Pub: CTVglobemedia Publishing Inc.
Ed: Sinclair Stewart. **Description:** The details on business growth of Canadian Imperial Bank of Commerce, which posted $547 million profit for first quarter 2006, are presented.

22916 ■ *Guerrilla Marketing, 4th Edition: Easy and Inexpensive Strategies for Making Big Profits from Your Small Business*
Pub: Houghton Mifflin Company
Ed: Jay Conrad Levinson. **Released:** May 2007. **Price:** $19.95. **Description:** Marketing strategies for small businesses is designed to revolutionize, expand and grow businesses. .

22917 ■ "Habitat, Home Depot Expand Building Programs" in *Contractor* (Vol. 56, September 2009, No. 9, pp. 16)
Pub: Penton Media, Inc.
Description: Habitat for Humanity International and The Home Depot Foundation are planning to expand their Partners in Sustainable Building program. The program will provide funds to help Habitat affiliates build 5,000 homes. Comments from executives are also included.

22918 ■ "Halls Give Hospital Drive $11 Million Infusion" in *The Business Journal-Serving Metropolitan Kansas City* (Vol. 26, July 18, 2008)
Pub: American City Business Journals, Inc.
Ed: Rob Roberts. **Description:** Don Hall, chairman of Hallmark Cards Inc., and eight family members have announced that they will give $11 million to Children's Mercy Hospitals and Clinics for its $800 million expansion plan. Hall Family Foundation president Bill Hall that contributions such as that for Children's Mercy reflect the charitable interests of the foundation's board and founders. The possible impacts of the Hall's donation are analyzed.

22919 ■ *The Handbook of Financing Growth: Strategies and Capital Structure*
Pub: John Wiley & Sons, Incorporated
Ed: Kenneth H. Marks, John P. Funkhouser, Larry E. Robbins. **Released:** March 2005. **Price:** $85.00 (US), $123.95 (Canadian). **Description:** Using empirical data and actual case studies, strategies are presented to illustrate capital structures and fund raising techniques for emerging growth and middle-market companies.

22920 ■ "Happy Trails: RV Franchiser Gives Road Traveling Enthusiasts a Lift" in *Black Enterprise* (Vol. 38, July 2008, No. 12, pp. 47)
Pub: Earl G. Graves Publishing Co. Inc.
Ed: Tamara E. Holmes. **Description:** Overview of Bates International Motor Home Rental Systems Inc., a growing franchise that gives RV owners the chance to rent out their big-ticket purchases to others when they are not using them; Sandra Williams Bate launched the company as a franchise in July 1997 and now has a fleet of 30 franchises across the country. She expects the company to reach 2.2 million for 2008 due to a marketing initiative that will expand the company's presence.

22921 ■ "Harleysville Eyes Growth After Nationwide Deal" in *Philadelphia Business Journal* (Vol. 30, October 7, 2011, No. 34, pp. 1)
Pub: American City Business Journals Inc.
Ed: Jeff Blumenthal. **Description:** Harleysville Group announced growth plans after the company was sold to Columbus, Ohio-based Nationwide Mutual Insurance Company for about $1.63 billion. Nationwide gained an independent agency platform in 32 states with the Harleysville deal.

22922 ■ "Harnessing the Wisdom of Crowds" in *Entrepreneur* (Vol. 37, September 2009, No. 9, pp. 74)
Pub: Entrepreneur Media, Inc.
Ed: Mark Henricks. **Description:** Online customer service business Get Satisfaction has registered growth. The business enables customers to search for answers to common product questions. Customers use the service to post questions, complaints, and even product ideas.

22923 ■ "Haute Flyers" in *Canadian Business* (Vol. 80, November 19, 2007, No. 23, pp. 68)
Pub: Rogers Media
Ed: Rachel Pulfer. **Description:** Duckie Brown has been nominated by the Council of Fashion Designers of America as best menswear designer in the U.S. for 2007, along with leaders Calvin Klein and Ralph Lauren. The New York-based company was formed the day after September 11, 2001, but the timing did not hamper its growth. The works and plans of owners Steven Cox and Daniel Silver are described.

22924 ■ "Have I Got a Deal For You" in *Canadian Business* (Vol. 83, October 12, 2010, No. 17, pp. 65)
Pub: Rogers Media Ltd.
Ed: Bryan Borzykowski. **Description:** U.S. automobile market currently has more than three players, providing investors with a number of investment options. The sector is still mired in uncertainty, but people believe that these companies can only grow from this point forward. However, investors should use due diligence before jumping into the market.

22925 ■ "Hawaii Business 2008 SB Success Awards" in *Hawaii Business* (Vol. 53, February 2008, No. 8, pp. 43)
Pub: Hawaii Business Publishing
Description: Winners in the Hawaii Business 2008 SB Success Awards are presented; the awards give recognition for Hawaii small businesses with less than 100 employees and are based on four criteria, namely: unique service or product; rapid expansion or sales growth; longevity; and competency in overcoming challenges.

22926 ■ "Hayes Lemmerz Reports Some Good News Despite Losses" in *Crain's Detroit Business* (Vol. 24, April 14, 2008, No. 15, pp. 4)
Pub: Crain Communications, Inc.
Ed: Nancy Kaffer. **Description:** Hayes Lemmerz International Inc., a wheel manufacturer from Northville that has reported a positive free cash flow for the first time in years, a narrowed net loss in the fourth quarter and significant restructuring of the company's debt.

22927 ■ "Head of Horse Farmers and Owners Jockey for Saratoga Pastures, Breeder Awards" in *Business Review, Albany New York* (Nov. 23, 2007)
Pub: American City Business Journals, Inc.
Ed: Robin K. Cooper. **Description:** Trends in Saratoga County's equine industry are discussed. More than fifty horse farms and 11,000 horses are in Saratoga, which is more than any other county in New York. Joe McMahon, a horse breeder and also the vice president of New York Breeders Sales Company, plans to expand his business by tapping into a new market. He plans to build his stable of top registered New York stallions.

22928 ■ *Heads in Beds*
Pub: Prentice Hall PTR
Ed: Ivo Raza. **Released:** May 28, 2004. **Description:** Advice is given to help build brands, generate sales and grow profits through marketing for any hospitality or tourism business.

22929 ■ "Health Care Leads Sectors Attracting Capital" in *Hispanic Business* (Vol. 30, March 2008, No. 3, pp. 14)
Pub: Hispanic Business
Ed: Scott Williams. **Description:** Discusses the capital gains of Hispanic-owned companies and other Hispanic leaders in the investment and retail fields in the year 2007. Sectors like health care, media, food and technology saw a healthy flow of capital due to successful mergers, acquisitions and increased private equity investments.

22930 ■ "Health Centers Plan Expansion" in *Crain's Detroit Business* (Vol. 25, June 15, 2009, No. 24, pp. 3)
Pub: Crain Communications Inc. - Detroit
Ed: Jay Greene. **Description:** Detroit has five federally qualified health centers that plan to receive over $3 million in federal stimulus money that will be used to expand projects that will care for uninsured patients.

22931 ■ "Healthy Dose of Vitality" in *Business Courier* (Vol. 24, February 29, 2008, No. 47, pp. 1)
Pub: American City Business Journals, Inc.
Ed: Dan Monk. **Description:** Healthy Advice plans to become a leading consumer brand and expand to pharmacies and hospitals. The growth opportunities for healthy Advice are discussed.

22932 ■ "Helping Customers Fight Pet Waste" in *Pet Product News* (Vol. 64, November 2010, No. 11, pp. 52)
Pub: BowTie Inc.
Ed: Sandy Robins. **Description:** Pet cleaning products manufacturers have been enjoying high sales figures by paying attention to changing pet ownership trends and environmental awareness. Meanwhile, the inclusion of user-friendly features in these products has also been boosted by the social role of pets and the media attention to pet waste. How manufacturers have been responding to this demand is explored.

22933 ■ "Helping Women Grow Their Businesses One Entrepreneur at a Time" in *Hispanic Business* (July-August 2007, pp. 56-57)
Pub: Hispanic Business
Ed: Hildy Medina. **Description:** American Express OPEN is a program focusing on women business owners whose companies report revenues of

$200,000 or more. The program offers the chance to win a free year of mentoring, marketing and technology assistance along with a $50,000 line of credit.

22934 ■ "High Energy: Gaurdie Banister Joins Aera As President and CEO" in *Black Enterprise* (Vol. 38, July 2008, No. 12, pp. 30)
Pub: Earl G. Graves Publishing Co. Inc.

Ed: Brenda Porter. **Description:** Gaurdie Banister Jr. has been appointed president and CEO of Aera Energy L.L.C., becoming one of the first African Americans in the nation to run a major energy corporation. His plans for the firm include utilizing new, sophisticated technologies in order to unlock the 3-1/2 billion barrels of resources the company has on their books in a safe and environmentally friendly way. He also hopes to increase production and maintain cost leadership.

22935 ■ "High Hopes: Ralph Mitchell's Picks Have Growth Potential" in *Black Enterprise* (Vol. 37, February 2007, No. 7, pp. 42)
Pub: Earl G. Graves Publishing Co. Inc.

Ed: Carolyn M. Brown. **Description:** Ralph Mitchell, president and senior financial advisor of Braintree-Carthage Financial Group, offers three recommendations: Toll Brothers, Home Depot, and Lowe's.

22936 ■ "The High-Intensity Entrepreneur" in *Harvard Business Review* (Vol. 88, September 2010, No. 9, pp. 74)
Pub: Harvard Business School Publishing

Ed: Anne S. Habiby, Deirdre M. Coyle Jr. **Description:** Examination of the role of small companies in promoting global economic growth is presented. Discussion includes identifying entrepreneurial capability.

22937 ■ "High Marks; Parker Hannifin's Stock Lauded by Wall Street Journal" in *Crain's Cleveland Business* (Vol. 28, November 5, 2007, No. 44)
Pub: Crain Communications, Inc.

Description: According to The Wall Street Journal, Parker Hannifin Corp., a manufacturer of motion and control equipment, is one of eight stocks that are attractively priced and continuously showing growth.

22938 ■ "His Place in the Sun" in *Canadian Business* (Vol. 79, October 23, 2006, No. 21, pp. 77)
Pub: Rogers Media

Ed: Zena Olijnyk. **Description:** The business interests of Canadian real estate developer Derek Elliott in the Dominican Republic, is discussed.

22939 ■ "Hispanic Business 100 Fastest-Growing Companies" in *Hispanic Business* (July-August 2007, pp. 28, 30, 32, 36)
Pub: Hispanic Business

Description: Top 100 Hispanic businesses are ranked by sales growth 2002-2006, gross sales, profit ranges, number of employees, and year the firm was founded.

22940 ■ "Hispanic Executives Continue Their Rise to Prominence Amid a Shaky Economy" in *Hispanic Business* (January-February 2009, pp. 12-14)
Pub: Hispanic Business

Ed: Michael Bowker. **Description:** Hispanic Business Media's 2009 Corporate Elite winners defied expectations and a tough economy and rose to the top of their industries; innovation being cited as key to growth of Hispanic-owned companies.

22941 ■ "Hispantelligence Report" in *Hispanic Business* (January-February 2008, pp. 8)
Pub: Hispanic Business

Description: Presentation of the Hispanic Business Stock Index shows the current value of fifteen Hispanic companies through December 2007. Forecasts showing increased growth for Hispanic-owned companies are also included.

22942 ■ *History of Canadian Business 1867-1914*
Pub: University of Toronto Press
Ed: R.T. Naylor. **Released:** 1975. **Description:** Covers the growth of business in Canada.

22943 ■ "Hola and Aloha" in *Hawaii Business* (Vol. 53, December 2007, No. 6, pp. 131)
Pub: Hawaii Business Publishing
Ed: Jason Ubay. **Description:** Juan Carlos Bianchetti is the trilingual owner of Ole Tours Hawaii, a travel wholesaler that targets Portuguese and Spanish-speaking visitors. The competition for American and Japanese tourists is already tight, which is why Bianchetti opted to target a different segment of the Hawaii tourism market. Plans for the company's expansion in Kauai, Brazil, and Argentina, are mentioned.

22944 ■ "Hollander 95 Project Getting Bigger" in *Boston Business Journal* (Vol. 29, September 23, 2011, No. 20, pp. 1)
Pub: American City Business Journals Inc.
Ed: Gary Haber. **Description:** Hollander 95 Business Park is in for a huge change as its new owners plan a $50 million expansion which calls for building as many as eight more buildings or a total of more than 500,000 square feed. FRP Development bought the site for $4.35 million at a foreclosure sale in July 2010 and is now seeking city approval for an Industrial Planned Unit Development designation.

22945 ■ "Home Depot Eyes Wholesale Spinoff" in *Globe & Mail* (February 13, 2007, pp. B13)
Pub: CTVglobemedia Publishing Inc.
Description: Home Depot Inc. is planning to sell or spinoff its professional supply business to focus on retail stores. The weakening sales and profits are the main driving force behind the company's decision.

22946 ■ "A Home of Her Own" in *Hawaii Business* (Vol. 53, October 2007, No. 4, pp. 51)
Pub: Hawaii Business Publishing
Ed: Maria Torres-Kitamura. **Description:** It was observed that the number of single women in Hawaii purchasing their own home has increased, as that in the whole United States where the percentage has increased from 14 percent in 1995 to 22 percent in 2006. However, First Hawaiian Bank's Wendy Lum thinks that the trend will not continue in Hawaii due to lending restrictions. The factors that women consider in buying a home of their own are presented.

22947 ■ "Homelessness, Hair Care and 12,000 Bottles of Tequila" in *Entrepreneur* (Vol. 37, July 2009, No. 7, pp. 5)
Pub: Entrepreneur Media, Inc.
Ed: Dennis Romero. **Description:** John Paul DeJoria believes that the biggest hurdle he has faced in business is rejection, and that the successful people will do whatever is required in order to succeed. DeJoria is the man behind Paul Mitchell Systems and Patron Tequila. He was recently included in Forbes magazine's list of global billionaires.

22948 ■ "Hospital Errors Made Public" in *Sacramento Business Journal* (Vol. 25, August 8, 2008, No. 23, pp. 1)
Pub: American City Business Journals, Inc.
Ed: Kathy Robertson. **Description:** California hospitals reported 1,224 serious and preventable errors for the fiscal year ended June 30, 2008. Consumer groups have expressed concerns at the number and level of violations. Views and information on the errors, as well as a table detailing the number of hospital errors classified by error type, are presented.

22949 ■ "Hospital Revenue Healthier in 2009" in *Orlando Business Journal* (Vol. 26, February 5, 2010, No. 36, pp. 1)
Pub: American City Business Journals
Ed: Melanie Stawicki Azam. **Description:** Orlando Health, Health Central and Adventist Health System are Florida-based hospital systems that generated the most profits in 2009. Orlando Health had the highest profit in 2009 at $73.3 million, contrary to about $31 million in losses in 2008. The increased profits are attributed to stock market recovery, cost-cutting initiatives, and rising patient volumes.

22950 ■ "Hospitals See Major Shift To Outpatient Care" in *The Business Journal-Milwaukee* (Vol. 25, September 12, 2008, No. 51, pp. A1)
Pub: American City Business Journals, Inc.
Ed: Corrinne Hess. **Description:** Statistics show that the revenue of Wisconsin hospitals from outpatient medical care is about to surpass revenue from hospital patients who stay overnight. This revenue increase is attributed to new technology and less-invasive surgery. Trends show that the shift toward outpatient care actually started in the late 1980s and early 1990s.

22951 ■ "Hotels Seeking Room Downtown" in *Crain's New York Business* (Vol. 24, January 14, 2008, No. 2, pp. 32)
Pub: Crain Communications, Inc.
Ed: Laura Koss-Feder. **Description:** In a rush to expand capacity in New York City, particularly lower Manhattan, the hotel industry plans to more than double the existing rooms in the area.

22952 ■ "How Exports Could Save America" in *Barron's* (Vol. 89, July 20, 2009, No. 29, pp. 15)
Pub: Dow Jones & Co., Inc.
Ed: Jonathan R. Laing. **Description:** Increase in US exports should help drive up the nation's economic growth, according to Wells Capital Management strategist Jim Paulsen. He believes US gross domestic product could grow by 3-3.5 percent annually starting in 2010 due to a more favorable trade balance.

22953 ■ "How Hard Could It Be? The Four Pillars of Organic Growth" in *Inc.* (January 2008, pp. 69-70)
Pub: Gruner & Jahr USA Publishing
Ed: Joel Spolsky. **Description:** Revenue, head count, public relations, and quality are the four most important aspects of any growing business.

22954 ■ "How High Can Soybeans Fly?" in *Barron's* (Vol. 88, March 10, 2008, No. 10, pp. M14)
Pub: Dow Jones & Company, Inc.
Ed: Kenneth Rapoza. **Description:** Prices of soybeans have risen to $14.0875 a bushel, up 8.3 percent for the week. Increased demand, such as in China and in other developing economies, and the investment-driven commodities boom are boosting prices.

22955 ■ *How to Make Big Money in Your Own Small Business: Unexpected Rules Every Small Business Owner Needs to Know*
Pub: Hyperion Press
Ed: Jeffrey J. Fox. **Released:** May 2004. **Price:** $16. 95. **Description:** Former sales and marketing pro offers advice on growing a small business.

22956 ■ *How to Make Money with Social Media: Using New and Emerging Media to Grow Your Business*
Pub: FT Press
Ed: Jamie Turner, Reshma Shah. **Released:** October 1, 2010. **Price:** $24.99. **Description:** Marketers, executives, entrepreneurs are shown more effective ways to utilize Internet social media to make money. This guide brings together both practical strategies and proven execution techniques for driving maximum value from social media marketing.

22957 ■ *How to Open and Operate a Financially Successful Construction Company*
Pub: Atlantic Publishing Group, Inc.
Ed: Tanya R. Davis. **Released:** April 2008. **Price:** $39.95 paperback. **Description:** Construction businesses are predicted to be one of the fastest growing industries in the U.S. economy, according to the U.S. Bureau of Labor Statistics. A comprehensive guide is offered detailing the practical side of starting and growing a construction firm. The step-by-step guide

provides sample business forms, leases, contracts, worksheets and checklists for planning and running the day-to-day operations.

22958 ■ *How to Open and Operate a Financially Successful Private Investigation Business: With Companion CD-ROM*
Pub: Atlantic Publishing Company
Released: December 1, 2010. **Price:** $39.95. **Description:** With a massive upside and potential for growth the private investigation sector is growing. The book will teach everything needed to know about working in the private investigation field, starting with the basics of what you can expect and what preconceptions that may just be Hollywood. Information is given to help choose a niche of investigation and hot to start thinking in the abstract, questioning everything but recognizing facts for what they are, as well as the differences between a private investigator and a police officer.

22959 ■ "How to Secure U.S. Jobs" in *Gallup Management Journal* (October 27, 2011)
Pub: Gallup
Ed: Jim Clifton. **Description:** If America doubled its number of engaged customers globally, it could triple exports, which would create more good jobs and put the US economy back on track.

22960 ■ "How To Live To Be 100; John E. Green Co. Grows Through Diversification" in *Crain's Detroit Business* (February 18, 2008)
Pub: Crain Communications Inc. - Detroit
Ed: Chad Halcom. **Description:** Continuity, name recognition, and inventiveness are keys to continuing growth for Highland Park, Michigan's John E. Green Company, designer of pipe systems and mechanical contractor.

22961 ■ "How Two Flourishing Exporters Did It" in *Hispanic Business* (Vol. 30, July-August 2008, No. 7-8, pp. 46)
Pub: Hispanic Business, Inc.
Ed: Richard Kaplan. **Description:** Vigorous growth in export revenues posted by two Hispanic-owned export companies Compasa LLC and Ametza LLC is discussed; both firms have benefited from their closer locations to major Mexican markets, superior quality of their products, market knowledge and the relationships of trust developed with key business partners.

22962 ■ "HP Eats Into Rival Dell Sales as Profits Soar" in *Globe & Mail* (February 21, 2007, pp. B15)
Pub: CTVglobemedia Publishing Inc.
Ed: Connie Guglielmo. **Description:** The world's largest personal computer maker Hewlett Packard Co. has reported increased profits by 26 percent to $1.55 billion during the first quarter. The company has outpaced its competitor Dell Inc. by offering low priced personal computers during this period.

22963 ■ "HSBC Canada Posts 8.8 Percent Profit Gain in 2006" in *Globe & Mail* (February 20, 2007, pp. B14)
Pub: CTVglobemedia Publishing Inc.
Ed: Andrew Willis. **Description:** HSBC Bank Canada reported profits of $497 million in 2006. The financial results of the company for 2006 are presented.

22964 ■ "Huntington's Future At a Crossroads" in *Crain's Cleveland Business* (Vol. 30, June 22, 2009, No. 24, pp. 1)
Pub: Crain Communications, Inc.
Ed: Arielle Kass. **Description:** Despite Huntington Bancshares plans to expand in the Cleveland, Ohio area, experts wonder if the bank will be able to take advantage of the area's growth in the long run. Statistical data included.

22965 ■ "Husky Proceeds on Heavy-Oil Expansion" in *Globe & Mail* (March 21, 2006, pp. B1)
Pub: CTVglobemedia Publishing Inc.
Ed: Patrick Brethour. **Description:** Canadian energy giant Husky Energy Inc. has started its $90 million engineering effort to determine the cost of the $2.3 billion heavy-oil up gradation expansion plan. Details of the project are elaborated upon.

22966 ■ "Hyde Park Hungry for Expansion at Cap" in *Business First-Columbus* (October 12, 2007, pp. A1)
Pub: American City Business Journals, Inc.
Ed: Dan Eaton. **Description:** The Cap, an area developed for the retail and restaurant industry, is experiencing major changes such as Hyde Park Restaurant System's planned expansion, and the expected departure of other tenants. The expansion of Hyde Park will lead to the relocation of Schakolad Chocolate Factory.

22967 ■ "Hyundai's Hitting Its Stride" in *Barron's* (Vol. 89, July 20, 2009, No. 29, pp. M7)
Pub: Dow Jones & Co., Inc.
Ed: Assif Shameen. **Description:** Hyundai Motors has kept growing by producing better products, enabling it to increase its sales and market share despite the weaker automotive market. The shares of Hyundai and Kia are poised to rise due to their improved finances.

22968 ■ "IBM's Best-Kept Secret" in *Canadian Business* (Vol. 79, September 25, 2006, No. 19, pp. 19)
Pub: Rogers Media
Ed: Andrew Wahl. **Description:** The contribution of IBM vice-president Steve Mills in company's development is discussed.

22969 ■ "An Ice Boost in Revenue; Wings Score With Expanded Corporate Sales" in *Crain's Detroit Business* (Vol. 25, June 1, 2009, No. 22)
Pub: Crain Communications Inc. - Detroit
Ed: Bill Shea. **Description:** Stanley Cup finals always boost business for the Detroit area, even during a recession. The Red Wings corporate office reported corporate sponsorship revenue luxury suite rentals, Legends Club seats and advertising were up 40 percent this year over 2008.

22970 ■ "Ideas at Work: The Reality of Costs" in *Business Strategy Review* (Vol. 21, Summer 2010, No. 2, pp. 40)
Pub: Wiley-Blackwell
Ed: Jules Goddard. **Description:** If you think that cost cutting is the surest way to business success, the author wants to challenge every assumption you hold. Costs are an outcome of sound strategy, never the goal of strategy. He offers a new perspective on what counts when it comes to costs.

22971 ■ "Identify and Conquer" in *Black Enterprise* (Vol. 38, December 2007, No. 5, pp. 76)
Pub: Earl G. Graves Publishing Co. Inc.
Ed: Tennille M. Robinson. **Description:** Twenty-two-year-old entrepreneur wants to expand her wholesale body oil and skincare products business.

22972 ■ "Illinois Bets On Recycling Program" in *Chicago Tribune* (November 29, 2008)
Pub: McClatchy-Tribune Information Services
Ed: Joel Hood. **Description:** Traditionally the holiday gift-giving season is one of the most wasteful times of year and the state of Illinois is granting $760,000 to small businesses and cities in an attempt to expand curbside recycling programs and hire additional workers to address electronic waste.

22973 ■ "Illinois Farmland Tops $11,000 Per Acre" in *Farm Industry News* (June 27, 2011)
Pub: Penton Business Media Inc.
Ed: Karen McMahon. **Description:** Farmland property in Illinois continues to grow in value, selling for $11,000 per acre. Statistical data included.

22974 ■ "Imax Becomes Toast of Movie Industry" in *Globe & Mail* (January 10, 2006, pp. B2)
Pub: CTVglobemedia Publishing Inc.
Ed: Grant Robertson. **Description:** The United States-based mainstream theatres company Imax Corp., has reported a 35 percent rise in its ticket sales, showing the growing interest of the American audience in the Imax formatted films. A complete focus on this trend is presented.

22975 ■ *Import/Export for Dummies*
Pub: John Wiley and Sons, Inc.
Ed: John J. Capela. **Released:** June 2008. **Price:** $19.99. **Description:** Provides entrepreneurs and small- to medium-size businesses with information required to start exporting products globally and importing goods to the U.S. Topics covered include the ins and outs of developing or expanding operations to gain market share, with details on the top ten countries in which America trades, from Canada to Germany to China.

22976 ■ "Impressive Numbers: Companies Experience Substantial Increases in Dollars, Employment" in *Hispanic Business* (July-August 2007)
Pub: Hispanic Business
Ed: Derek Reveron. **Description:** Profiles of five fastest growing Hispanic companies reporting increases in revenue and employment include Brightstar, distributor of wireless products; Greenway Ford Inc., a car dealership; Fred Loya Insurance, auto insurance carrier; and Group O, packaging company; and Diverse Staffing, Inc., an employment and staffing firm.

22977 ■ "IMRA's Ultrafast Lasers Bring Precision, profits; Ann Arbor Company Eyes Expansion" in *Crain's Detroit Business* (March 10, 2008)
Pub: Crain Communications, Inc.
Ed: Tom Henderson. **Description:** IMRA America Inc. plans to expand its headquarters and has applied for permits to build a fourth building that will house research and development facilities and allow the company more room for manufacturing; the company plans to add about 20 more employees that would include research scientists, manufacturing and assembly workers, engineers and salespeople. The growth is due mainly to a new technology of ultrafast fiber lasers that reduce side effects for those getting eye surgeries and help manufacturers of computer chips to reduce their size and cost.

22978 ■ "In Addition, Pinkberry Reports It Is Opening a New Shop in Sunnyvale, CA" in *Ice Cream Reporter* (Vol. 23, October 20, 2010)
Pub: Ice Cream Reporter
Description: Pinkberry opened a new shop in Sunnyvale, California, its fourth opening in the South Bay and its 101st location worldwide.

22979 ■ "Inc. 500: the Class of 2011" in *Inc.* (Vol. 33, September 2011, No. 7, pp. 71)
Pub: Inc. Magazine
Description: A listing of the Inc. 500 businesses that are rebuilding the economy and changing the world is presented.

22980 ■ "Incubator Cooking Up Expansion Plans" in *Business First Columbus* (Vol. 25, December 5, 2008, No. 15, pp.)
Pub: American City Business Journals
Ed: Kevin Kemper. **Description:** United States-based Science and Technology Campus Corporation is planning to build additional office space in Columbus, Ohio. The site is designed to accommodate three large tenants. Comment from company executives are presented.

22981 ■ "Indian Buyer Gives Life to Algoma Expansion" in *Globe & Mail* (April 17, 2007, pp. B1)
Pub: CTVglobemedia Publishing Inc.
Ed: Greg Keenan. **Description:** The proposed capacity expansion of Algoma Steel Inc. after its acquisition by Essar Global Ltd. is discussed.

22982 ■ "Industrial Evolution" in *Entrepreneur* (Vol. 35, November 2007, No. 11, pp. 142)
Pub: Entrepreneur Media Inc.
Ed: Nichole L. Torres. **Description:** Businesses often target specific customer bases, but it is possible that your business does not fit a particular industry as

your services may also be needed in other fields. Details with regard to expanding businesses into other industries are discussed.

22983 ■ "Industrial RE Market Shows Signs of Health" in *Business Courier* (Vol. 27, August 20, 2010, No. 16, pp. 1)
Pub: Business Courier
Ed: Jon Newberry. **Description:** Cincinnati, Ohio's industrial real estate sector has experienced growth during the first half of 2010. The industry has seen a large net loss of occupied space in 2009.

22984 ■ "Inn at Saratoga Owners Buy Caribbean Hotel" in *Business Review, Albany New York* (Vol. 34, November 2, 2007, No. 31, pp. 3)
Pub: American City Business Journals, Inc.
Ed: Robin K. Cooper. **Description:** Bob Israel, owner of the Inn at Saratoga in Saratoga Springs, New York, made a $3 million to $4 million acquisition of the 22-room Mafolie Hotel and Restaurant in the Island of St. Thomas in the Caribbean. This is Israel's first real estate venture out of Saratoga Springs.

22985 ■ "Innovating Globally" in *Business Strategy Review* (Vol. 21, Spring 2010, No. 1, pp. 24)
Pub: Wiley-Blackwell
Ed: Costas Markides, Stuart Crainer. **Description:** Costas Markides has spent over two decades studying business strategy and innovation. Recently, he has been focusing on the bigger picture of how people can address major social problems. Can the techniques used by managers to create innovation inside organizations work with global change?

22986 ■ *Innovative Approaches to Global Sustainability*
Pub: Palgrave Macmillan
Ed: Charles Wankel, James A.F. Stoner. **Released:** April 13, 2010. **Price:** $30.00. **Description:** Examples are given to help businesses become sustainable as we move towards a sustainable world.

22987 ■ "Innovative Growth" in *Small Business Opportunities* (March 2008)
Pub: Harris Publications Inc.
Ed: Peter Erickson. **Description:** Nine tips are outlined to help small companies and entrepreneurs to partner with larger companies.

22988 ■ "Insider" in *Canadian Business* (Vol. 81, March 31, 2008, No. 5, pp. 76)
Pub: Rogers Media
Ed: John Gray. **Description:** Discusses a comparison of an average Canadian family's finances in 1990 with the data from 2007. The average family in 2007 has over $80,000 in debt compared to just under $52,000 in 1990. However, Canadians have also been accumulating solid assets such as homes and stocks. This means that Canadian debt load has fallen from 22 percent in 1990 to 20 percent in 2007 when taken as a percentage of total net worth.

22989 ■ *Instant Cashflow: Hundreds of Proven Strategies to Win Customers, Boost Margins and Take More Money Home*
Pub: McGraw-Hill Companies
Ed: Bradley J. Sugars. **Released:** December 2005. **Price:** $17.95 (US), $22.95 (Canadian). **Description:** Nearly 300 proven marketing and sales strategies are shared by the author, a self-made millionaire. Advice on creating the proper mindset, generating new leads, boosting the conversion rate of leads to sales, maximizing the value of the average sale, and measuring results is included.

22990 ■ *Instant Profit: Successful Strategies to Boost Your Margin and Increase the Profitability of Your Business*
Pub: McGraw-Hill Companies
Ed: Bradley J. Sugars. **Released:** December 2005. **Price:** $16.95 (US), $22.95 (Canadian). **Description:** Advice on management, money, marketing, and merchandising a successful small business is offered.

22991 ■ "Insuraprise Growing Fast" in *Austin Business Journal* (Vol. 31, April 22, 2011, No. 7, pp. 1)
Pub: American City Business Journals Inc.
Ed: Sandra Zaragoza. **Description:** Austin, Texas-based Insuraprise Inc. is finalizing the purchase of a 24,000-square-foot office at 12116 Jekel Circle. The firm, with 23 salespeople and sales that are growing nearly 300 percent over the past 18 months, will now have room to grow. Insuraprise plans to hire 35 new salespersons for its call center.

22992 ■ "Insurers No Longer Paying Premium for Advertising" in *Brandweek* (Vol. 49, April 21, 2008, No. 16, pp. SR3)
Pub: VNU Business Media, Inc.
Ed: Eric Newman. **Description:** Insurance companies are cutting their advertising budgets after years of accelerated double-digit growth in spending due to the economic downturn, five years of record-breaking ad spend and a need to cut expenditures as claims costs rise and a competitive market keeps premiums in place. Statistical data included.

22993 ■ "Intangible Assets" in *Canadian Business* (Vol. 79, July 17, 2006, No. 14-15, pp. 17)
Pub: Rogers Media
Ed: Al Rosen. **Description:** Need for investors to check the actual worth of a company and not to get carried away by the inflated claims made by the company is emphasized.

22994 ■ "International Dairy Queen" in *Ice Cream Reporter* (Vol. 23, October 20, 2010, No. 11, pp. 7)
Pub: Ice Cream Reporter
Description: International Dairy Queen will open more than 100 new outlets in China in 2011, adding to the current level of more than 300 outlets in that country.

22995 ■ *International Entrepreneurship in Small and Medium Size Enterprises: Orientation, Environment and Strategy*
Pub: Edward Elgar Publishing, Incorporated
Ed: Hamid Etemad. **Released:** October 2004. **Price:** $130.00. **Description:** Issues involved in internationalizing small and medium sized (SME) businesses. Topics include an investigation into the emerging patterns of SME growth and international expansion in response to the changing competitive environment, dynamics of competitive behavior, entrepreneurial processes and a formulation of strategy.

22996 ■ *International Growth of Small and Medium Enterprises*
Pub: Routledge
Ed: Nina Nummela. **Released:** February 10, 2010. **Price:** $110.00. **Description:** This volume focuses on how companies expand their operations across borders through opportunity exploration and exploitation, and identification and development of innovations.

22997 ■ "Internationalization of Australian Family Businesses" in *Family Business Review* (Vol. 19, September 2006)
Pub: Family Firm Institute Inc.
Ed: Chris Graves, Jill Thomas. **Description:** Concept that managerial capabilities of family firms lag behind those of non-family counterparts as they expand is discussed.

22998 ■ "Invacare Plans '08 Release for Portable Oxygen Product" in *Crain's Cleveland Business* (Vol. 28, October 22, 2007, No. 42, pp. 5)
Pub: Crain Communications, Inc.
Ed: Chuck Soder. **Description:** Invacare Corp., an Elyria-based maker of home health care equipment, plans the release of a new "extremely portable" oxygen concentration machine in 2008. The XP02 is expected to increase sales due to the popularity of portable oxygen concentrators.

22999 ■ "Investors Finding Bay Area Deals" in *Tampa Bay Business Journal* (Vol. 29, November 6, 2009, No. 46, pp. 1)
Pub: American City Business Journals
Ed: Margie Manning. **Description:** Private equity investors have found dozens of privately held companies in Tampa Bay area in Florida in which to invest $84 million fresh equity. Revenue generation, growth, solid management teams are some of the factors found by the investors on these companies which span a range of sizes and industries.

23000 ■ "An Investor's Guide to This Year's Inc. 500" in *Inc.* (October 2007, pp. 34)
Pub: Gruner & Jahr USA Publishing
Description: Three investment firms specializing in growth companies provide insight into today's market.

23001 ■ "IPhone 3G" in *Advertising Age* (Vol. 79, November 17, 2008, No. 43, pp. 15)
Pub: Crain Communications, Inc.
Ed: Beth Snyder Bulik. **Description:** Review of Apple's new iPhone 3G which includes the addition of smart-phone applications as well as a price drop; the new functionalities as well as the lower price seems to be paying off for Apple who reported sales of 6.9 million iPhones in its most recent quarter, in which the 3G hit store shelves.

23002 ■ "Is 'Tsunami' of Freight in our Future?" in *Business Courier* (Vol. 26, November 27, 2009, No. 31, pp. 1)
Pub: American City Business Journals, Inc.
Ed: Dan Monk. **Description:** Freight companies are planning for cargo-container shipping facilities on the riverfront of Cincinnati in light of the completion of the $5 billion Panama Canal expansion in 2015. The city's capability to utilize the growth in freight has been under investigation by authorities.

23003 ■ "Is Your Company Ready to Succeed?" in *Business Strategy Review* (Vol. 21, Spring 2010, No. 1, pp. 68)
Pub: Wiley-Blackwell
Ed: Srikumar Rao. **Description:** The author asked thousands of students about the ideal company of the future, the kind of place where they would want to spend their lives.

23004 ■ *Island of Profit in a Sea of Red Ink Why 40 Percent of Your Business Is Unprofitable and How to Fix It*
Pub: Portfolio
Ed: Jonathan L.S. Byrnes. **Released:** October 14, 2010. **Price:** $27.95. **Description:** Top companies from around the world turn to Jonathan Byrnes to figure out where to find profit for their companies. He shows which parts of a business are worth expanding, and which are just a drain on resources. He has found that roughly 40 percent of any new client's business is unprofitable, and that profit increases of thirty percent or more are within reach.

23005 ■ "It's In the Bag" in *Entrepreneur* (Vol. 36, April 2008, No. 4, pp. 122)
Pub: Entrepreneur Media, Inc.
Ed: Celeste Hoang. **Description:** Sandy Stein launched Alexx Inc in 2004, which markets keychains, called Finders Key Purse, with unique designs to help find keys easier inside the purse. Some of the key ring designs are hearts, sandals, and crowns. The company has approximately $6 million worth of sales in 2007.

23006 ■ "It's Not Perfect; But Illinois a Good Home for Business" in *Crain's Chicago Business* (Vol. 34, October 24, 2011, No. 42, pp. 18)
Pub: Crain Communications Inc.
Description: Focusing on all factors that encompass Illinois' business environment, findings show that Illinois is a good place to start and grow a business. The study focused on corporate income tax rates and the fact that talent, access to capital and customers along with transportation connections are among the important factors the state has for small businesses.

23007 ■ *It's Not Who You Know - It's Who Knows You!: The Small Business Guide to Raising Your Profits by Raising Your Profile*
Pub: John Wiley & Sons, Inc.

Ed: David Avrin. **Released:** November 9, 2010. **Price:** $24.95. **Description:** When it comes to promoting a small business or a brand, it is essential to know how valuable high-profile attention can be. But for most small companies, the cost of hiring an outside firm to increase attention can be too expensive.

23008 ■ "It's What You Know. It's Who You Know. It's China" in *Inc.* (Vol. 33, October 2011, No. 8, pp. 80)
Pub: Inc. Magazine

Ed: David H. Freedman. **Description:** Michael Lee will be the first American entrepreneur to build big in China. The company is piloting two large commercial real estate developments, one in New York City the other in Nanjing, China.

23009 ■ "ITT Places Its Bet With Defense Buy; Selling Equipment to Army Pays Off" in *Crain's New York Business* (Vol. 24, January 7, 2008)
Pub: Crain Communications, Inc.

Description: ITT Corp.'s revenue has jumped by 20 percent in each of the past three years due to demand for the company's radio sets and night-vision goggles. The firm has acquired EDO Corp., which specializes in battlefield communications systems, in an attempt to expand its defense-industry division.

23010 ■ "Ivorydale Looks to Clean Up" in *Business Courier* (Vol. 26, January 15, 2010, No. 39, pp. 1)
Pub: American City Business Journals, Inc.

Ed: Jon Newberry. **Description:** Cincinnati-based St. Bernard Soap Company plans to focus on new services such as product development and logistics and to continue growth and put excess capacity to work. The unit of Ontario, Canada-based Trillium Health Care Products Inc. is the largest contract manufacturer of bar soap in North America.

23011 ■ "Jacksonville-based Interline Expanding in Janitorial-Sanitation Market" in *Florida Times-Union* (May 10, 2011)
Pub: Florida Times-Union

Ed: Mark Basch. **Description:** Interline Brands Inc., located in Jacksonville, Florida, aims to grow its business with two recent acquisitions of firms that distribute janitorial and sanitation products. Interline markets and distributes maintenance, repair and operations products.

23012 ■ *Jan and Jeannie Levinson's Startup Guide to Guerilla Marketing: A Simple Battle Plan for Boosting Profits*
Pub: Entrepreneur Press

Ed: Jay Conrad Levinson; Jeannie Levinson. **Released:** January 2008. **Price:** $21.95. **Description:** Primer for marketing a new or existing business.

23013 ■ "J&J Snack Rakes in Sales" in *Philadelphia Business Journal* (Vol. 28, September 25, 2009, No. 32, pp. 1)
Pub: American City Business Journals

Ed: Peter van Allen. **Description:** Analysts expect J&J Snack Foods Corporation to boost earnings by 48 percent for fiscal year ending September 2009. Stable commodity prices have benefited the company.

23014 ■ "Janitorial Equipment and Supplies US Market" in *PR Newswire* (October 24, 2011)
Pub: PR Newswire

Description: United States demand for janitorial equipment and supplies (excluding chemical products) is predicted to rise 2.4 percent per year to $7.6 billion in 2013. New product development will lead to increased sales of higher-value goods in the industry.

23015 ■ "J.C. Watts First Black John Deere Dealer" in *Black Enterprise* (Vol. 37, November 2006, No. 4, pp. 36)
Pub: Earl G. Graves Publishing Co. Inc.

Ed: Kiara Ashanti. **Description:** Profile of former Congressman J.C. Watts Jr., a man who grew up in rural America and is the first African American to own a John Deere Dealership.

23016 ■ "Jean Coutu Resuscitates Bottom Line" in *Globe & Mail* (January 11, 2006, pp. B5)
Pub: CTVglobemedia Publishing Inc.

Ed: Bertrand Marotte. **Description:** The details on Jean Coutu Group (PJC) Inc., which posted $30.8 million profits for second quarter 2005, are presented.

23017 ■ "Jet Sales Put Bombardier Back in Black" in *Globe & Mail* (March 30, 2006, pp. B1)
Pub: CTVglobemedia Publishing Inc.

Ed: Bertrand Morotte. **Description:** The details on Bombardier Inc., which posted 20 percent rise in shares following $86 million profit for fourth quarter 2005, are presented.

23018 ■ "Jobs Data Show A Slow Leak" in *Barron's* (Vol. 88, July 7, 2008, No. 27, pp. 34)
Pub: Dow Jones & Co., Inc.

Ed: Gene Epstein. **Description:** In June 2008, the United States manufacturing sector showed an expansion, with the purchasing managers' index rising to 50.2 from 49.6; the unemployment rate in the US, which stayed steady at 5.5 percent in June 2008 is also discussed. Statistical data included.

23019 ■ "Johnson Publishing Expands: Moving Into Television and Internet To Extend Brand" in *Black Enterprise* (October 2007)
Pub: Earl G. Graves Publishing Co. Inc.

Ed: Tamara E. Holmes. **Description:** Johnson Publishing Company has followed the lives of black families in both Ebony and Jet magazines. The media firm has expanded its coverage by developing entertainment content for television, the Internet and other digital arenas.

23020 ■ *Jump Start Your Business Brain*
Pub: Brain Brew Books

Ed: Doug Hall, Tom Peters. **Released:** 2005. **Price:** $16.99 paperback. **Description:** Author focuses on helping small business owners to become more successful using simple tools that help them discover, develop, and identify great ideas.

23021 ■ *Jump Start Your Business Brain: Ideas, Advice and Insights for Immediate Marketing and Innovation Success*
Pub: Emmis Books

Ed: Doug Hall. **Released:** April 2005. **Price:** $23.99. **Description:** Strategies to improve sales, marketing, and business development.

23022 ■ "JumpTV to Hold Conference Call to Discuss Q1 Results and Annual General Meeting" in *Canadian Corporate News* (May 16, 2007)
Pub: Comtex News Network Inc.

Description: Profile of JumpTv, the world's leading broadcaster of ethnic television over the Internet, and the results of a conference that discussed their first quarter 2007 financial report as well as the company's business goals. Statistical data included.

23023 ■ "KC Presents Healthy Market for Medical REIT" in *Business Journal-Serving Metropolitan Kansas City* (Vol. 26, November 30, 2007)
Pub: American City Business Journals, Inc.

Ed: Rob Roberts. **Description:** Medical Properties Trust, the only real estate investment trust that specializes in buying hospitals, is planning to invest in Kansas City due to its fast growing hospital market. The company owns 29 properties nationwide and is still planning to increase its portfolio.

23024 ■ "Keep On Truckin'" in *Boston Business Journal* (Vol. 31, August 5, 2011, No. 28, pp. 3)
Pub: Boston Business Journal

Ed: Lisa van der Pool. **Description:** Food truck business is booming in Boston with more than 25 trucks dotting the area including 15 new truck locations approved by the city in July 2011. The business is rather costly to start because it requires more than $100,000 capital and the food truck can run between $50,000 to $100,000.

23025 ■ "Keeping Tabs" in *Entrepreneur* (Vol. 36, February 2008, No. 2, pp. 38)
Pub: Entrepreneur Media Inc.

Ed: Robert Kiyosaki. **Description:** Measuring and reporting the number of customers being served by a business can help in the company's growth. Details on this idea are discussed.

23026 ■ "Kid Rock" in *Canadian Business* (Vol. 81, Summer 2008, No. 9, pp. 54)
Pub: Rogers Media Ltd.

Ed: John Gray. **Description:** Damien Reynolds is the founder, chairman and chief executive officer of Vancouver-based Longview Capital Partners. The investment bank, founded in 2005, is one of the fastest-growing companies in British Columbia. The recent economic downturn has battered the stocks of the company and its portfolio of junior miners.

23027 ■ "Kinetico Exec Going Global to Increase Growth Flow" in *Crain's Cleveland Business* (Vol. 28, October 1, 2007, No. 39, pp. 5)
Pub: Crain Communications, Inc.

Ed: David Bennett. **Description:** Shamus Hurley, the new CEO and president of Kinetico Inc., a manufacturer of water filtering and softening equipment for residential, commercial and municipal use, plans to expand the company to target markets overseas.

23028 ■ "King of the Crib: How Good Samaritan Became Ohio's Baby HQ" in *Business Courier* (Vol. 27, June 18, 2010, No. 7, pp. 1)
Pub: Business Courier

Ed: James Ritchie. **Description:** Cincinnati's Good Samaritan hospital had 6,875 live births in 2009, which is more than any other hospital in Ohio. They specialize in the highest-risk pregnancies and deliveries and other hospitals are trying to grab Good Samaritan's share in this niche.

23029 ■ "Knowing Is Growing: Five Strategies To Develop You and Your Business" in *Black Enterprise* (Vol. 38, November 2007, No. 4, pp. 106)
Pub: Earl G. Graves Publishing Co. Inc.

Ed: Erinn R. Johnson. **Description:** Five strategies for growing a small business are listed by Andrew Morrison, founder of the Small Business Camp. The camp provides training, coaching, and marketing services to entrepreneurs.

23030 ■ "Kodiak Bucks Bear Market" in *Austin Business JournalInc.* (Vol. 29, December 18, 2009, No. 41, pp. 1)
Pub: American City Business Journals

Ed: Kate Harrington. **Description:** Austin, Texas-based Kodiak Assembly Solutions LLC, a company that installs components into printed circuit boards for product or evaluation tool kit prototyping purposes, will expand despite the recession. It will relocate from a 28,000 square foot space to a 42,000 square foot space in North Austin. The firm will also increase its workforce by 20 employees.

23031 ■ "Labor of Love" in *Green Industry Pro* (Vol. 23, March 2011, No. 3, pp. 14)
Pub: Cygnus Business Media

Ed: Gregg Wartgow. **Description:** Profile of CLS Landscape Management in Chino, California and its owner who started the company when he was 21 years old. Kevin Davis built his landscape firm into a $20 million a year business without using any dedicated salesperson.

23032 ■ "LaSalle Street Firms Cherry-Pick Talent As Wall Street Tanks" in *Crain's Chicago Business* (Vol. 31, November 17, 2008, No. 46)
Pub: Crain Communications, Inc.

Ed: H. Lee Murphy. **Description:** Many local businesses are taking advantage of the lay offs that many major Wall Street firms are undergoing in their workforces; these companies see the opportunity to woo talent and expand their staff with quality executives.

23033 ■ "Last Founder Standing" in *Conde Nast Portfolio* (Vol. 2, June 2008, No. 6, pp. 124)
Pub: Conde Nast Publications, Inc.
Ed: Kevin Maney. **Description:** Interview with Amazon CEO Jeff Bezos in which he discusses the economy, the company's new distribution center and the hiring of employees for it, e-books, and the overall vision for the future of the firm.

23034 ■ "Lathrop Finds Partner In LA" in *The Business Journal-Serving Metropolitan Kansas City* (Vol. 27, November 21, 2008, No. 11, pp. 1)
Pub: American City Business Journals, Inc.
Ed: Steve Vockrodt. **Description:** Kansas, Missouri-based Lathrop and Gage LLP is planning to merge with Spillane Shaeffer Aronoff Bandlow LLP. The merging of the business law firms will add entertainment clients to Lathrop's fold. Comments from executives are also presented.

23035 ■ "Lavante, Inc. Joins Intersynthesis, Holistic Internet Marketing Company" in *Internet Wire* (November 5, 2009)
Pub: Comtex News Network, Inc.
Description: Lavante, Inc., the leading provider of on-demand vendor information and profit recovery audit solutions for Fortune 1000 companies has chosen Intersynthesis, a new holistic Internet marketing firm, as a provider of pay for performance services. Lavante believes that Intersynthesis' expertise and knowledge combined with their ability to develop integrated strategies, will help them fuel more growth.

23036 ■ "Law Firms Troll for Complaints Among Disgruntled Workers" in *The Business Journal-Serving Greater Tampa Bay* (Vol. 28, July 11, 2008)
Pub: American City Business Journals, Inc.
Ed: Jane Meinhardt. **Description:** Economic slowdown has affected businesses as they downsize, seeing an increase in wage and hour complaints using loopholes in the Fair Labor Standards Act, from which several law firms are recently generating revenue. Federal judges notice the increase in lawsuits and ordered that law firms show cause for non-compliance.

23037 ■ *Law for the Small and Growing Business*
Pub: Jordans Publishing Limited
Ed: P. Bohm. **Released:** February 2007. **Price:** $59. 98. **Description:** Legal and regulatory issues facing small businesses, including employment law, health and safety, commercial property, company law and finance are covered.

23038 ■ "Leading Ohio Internet Marketing Firm Announces Growth in September" in *Marketing Weekly News* (September 26, 2009, pp. 24)
Pub: Investment Weekly News
Description: Despite a poor economy, Webbed Marketing, a leading social media marketing and search engine optimization firm in the Midwest, has added five additional professionals to its fast-growing team. The company continues to win new business, provide more services and hire talented employees.

23039 ■ *Leap! 101 Ways to Grow Your Business*
Pub: Career Press, Inc.
Ed: Stephanie Chandler. **Released:** August 8, 2010. **Price:** $15.99. **Description:** Business growth requires more than a business plan and a dream. Tools and techniques to take a small company to the next level are outlined.

23040 ■ "Leaps and Bounds: Liberty Power, Force 3 Ride Rapid Expansion to the Top" in *Hispanic Business* (July-August 2007, pp. 20-22, 24)
Pub: Hispanic Business
Ed: Derek Reveron. **Description:** Profiles of Liberty Power Corporation, a Florida supplier of retail electricity and Force 3 Inc. of Maryland, network infrastructure developer are two of the 100 fastest growing Hispanic businesses recognized in 2007.

23041 ■ "Lenders" in *The Business Journal - Serving Phoenix and the Valley of the Sun* (Vol. 28, July 25, 2008, No. 47, pp. 1)
Pub: American City Business Journals, Inc.
Ed: Jan Buchholz. **Description:** Private equity lender Investor Mortgage Holdings Inc. has continued growing despite the crisis surrounding the real estate and financial industries and has accumulated a $700 million loan portfolio. Private lending has become increasingly important in financing real estate deals as commercial credit has dried up.

23042 ■ *Let's Buy a Company: How to Accelerate Growth Through Acquisitions*
Pub: Career Press, Incorporated
Ed: H. Lee Rust. **Released:** January 2006. **Price:** $18.99 (US), $25.95 (Canadian). **Description:** Advice for negotiating terms and pricing as well as other aspects of mergers and acquisitions in small companies.

23043 ■ "Life Sciences Become State's Growth Powerhouse" in *Crain's Detroit Business* (Vol. 25, June 1, 2009, No. 22, pp. M008)
Pub: Crain Communications Inc. - Detroit
Ed: Amy Lane. **Description:** According to a study conducted by Anderson Economic Group, Michigan's University Research Corridor has helped grow the life sciences industry. Statistical details included.

23044 ■ "A Life of Spice" in *Entrepreneur* (Vol. 37, September 2009, No. 9, pp. 46)
Pub: Entrepreneur Media, Inc.
Ed: Jason Daley. **Description:** Matt and Bryan Walls have successfully grown their Atlanta, Georgia-based Snorg Tees T-shirt company. The company has expanded its product offering and redesigned its Website to be more user-friendly. The company has registered between $5 and 10 million in 2008.

23045 ■ "Life's Work: Ben Bradlee" in *Harvard Business Review* (Vol. 88, September 2010, No. 9, pp. 128)
Pub: Harvard Business School Publishing
Ed: Alison Beard. **Description:** Newspaper publisher Ben Bradlee discusses factors that lead to success, including visible supervisors, enthusiasm, appropriate expansion, and the importance in truth in reporting.

23046 ■ "Li'l Guy Rolls Up Into Bigger Company" in *The Business Journal-Serving Metropolitan Kansas City* (Vol. 26, September 12, 2008)
Pub: American City Business Journals, Inc.
Ed: Suzanna Stagemeyer. **Description:** Li'l Guy Foods, a Mexican food company in Kansas City, Missouri, has merged with Tortilla King Inc. Li'l Guy's revenue in 2007 was $3.3 million, while a newspaper report said that Tortilla King's revenue in 2001 was $7.5 million. Growth opportunities for the combined companies and Li'l Guy's testing of the Wichita market are discussed.

23047 ■ "Liquor Stores Sips on Growth Cocktail" in *Globe & Mail* (February 6, 2006, pp. B5)
Pub: CTVglobemedia Publishing Inc.
Ed: Omar El Akkad. **Description:** The business growth plans of Liquor Stores Income Fund are presented.

23048 ■ "The Little Biotech that Could" in *Barron's* (Vol. 89, July 27, 2009, No. 30, pp. 19)
Pub: Dow Jones & Co., Inc.
Ed: Christopher C. Williams. **Description:** OSI Pharmaceuticals' shares is a compelling investment bet among small biotech firms due to its Tarceva anticancer drug which has a 23 percent market share as well as their strong balance sheet. OSI is planning to expand the use of Tarceva which could re-ignite sales and one analyst expects the shares to trade in the 40s one year from July 2009.

23049 ■ "Live and Learn: Lionel Hurtubise" in *Canadian Business* (Vol. 80, January 29, 2007, No. 3, pp. 64)
Pub: Rogers Media
Ed: Andy Holloway. **Description:** The views of Lionel Hurtubise, the chairman of SR Telecom, PolarSat, and STP, on his life and the growth of the Canadian telecommunications industry are presented.

23050 ■ "Local Auto Suppliers Upbeat as Detroit 3's Prospects Trend Up" in *Crain's Cleveland Business* (Vol. 30, June 8, 2009, No. 22, pp. 1)
Pub: Crain Communications, Inc.
Ed: Dan Shingler. **Description:** According to the Center for Automotive Research located in Ann Arbor, Michigan, if Detroit automakers can hold their market share, they will end up producing more vehicles as the market recovers.

23051 ■ *Local Enterprises in the Global Economy: Issues of Governance and Upgrading*
Pub: Edward Elgar Publishing, Incorporated
Ed: Hubert Schmitz. **Released:** November 2004. **Price:** $35.00 (soft cover), $110.00 (hard bound). **Description:** Examination of the relationships between globalization, corporate governance, and the economic performance of small businesses and local enterprises.

23052 ■ "Local Outlook: Stronger Growth Ahead" in *Montana Business Quarterly* (Vol. 49, Spring 2011, No. 1, pp. 10)
Pub: Bureau of Business & Economic Research
Ed: Paul E. Polzin. **Description:** Local economic growth is broken down into three areas: fastest growing in Richland, Gallatin and Flathead Counties; the second growth group consists of Yellowstone, Silver Bow, and Lewis and Clark Counties, which all grew at rates higher than the statewide average; slowest growth was seen in Missoula, Ravalli, Cascade, and Custer Counties. Statistical data included.

23053 ■ "Locally Based Stocks Escape Worst of Market's Turmoil" in *Crain's Detroit Business* (Vol. 24, September 22, 2008, No. 38, pp. 4)
Pub: Crain Communications, Inc.
Ed: Daniel Duggan. **Description:** Locally-based companies did not take as big a hit as might be expected with the shock to the financial markets last week; this is due mainly to the fact that the region does not have heavy exposure to energy or capital markets.

23054 ■ "Lombard Leaves Starbucks" in *Black Enterprise* (Vol. 38, July 2008, No. 12, pp. 28)
Pub: Earl G. Graves Publishing Co. Inc.
Ed: Tamara E. Holmes. **Description:** Ken Lombard stepped down from his position as head of Starbuck's entertainment division; the company is restructuring its entertainment unit in an attempt to revitalize sales and reduce costs.

23055 ■ "Long - And Leery" in *Barron's* (Vol. 88, March 31, 2008, No. 13, pp. 47)
Pub: Dow Jones & Company, Inc.
Ed: Jack Willoughby. **Description:** Tom Claugus' Bay Resource Partners hedge fund has returned 20 percent annually since it started in 1993. Claugus says that he is as aggressively long as he has ever been despite the dangers of the U.S. market. Claugus' stock picks include Canadian Natural Resources, NII Holdings, and Discover Financial.

23056 ■ "Looking For Financing?" in *Hispanic Business* (Vol. 30, July-August 2008, No. 7-8, pp. 16)
Pub: Hispanic Business, Inc.
Ed: Frank Nelson. **Description:** Investment firms want to know about businesses that need funding for either expansion or acquisition; companies fitting this profile are interviewed and their perceptions are discussed. Investment firms need businesses to be realistic in their expectations and business plans which show spending of funds and expected benefits, long term goals, track record and strong management teams.

23057 ■ "Loop Hotel Plan Locks Up Funding" in *Crain's Chicago Business* (Vol. 31, March 24, 2008, No. 12, pp. 2)
Pub: Crain Communications, Inc.
Ed: Eddie Baeb. **Description:** Signaling further expansion in the downtown hotel market, the secured

$395 million in financing will fund a 610-room luxury hotel operated by J.W. Marriott, a more upscale brand in the Marriott line.

23058 ■ "Lots More Mr. Nice Guy" in *Canadian Business* (Vol. 80, October 22, 2007, No. 21, pp. 58)
Pub: Rogers Media
Ed: Zena Olijnyk. **Description:** Galen Weston Jr., executive chairman of Loblaw and heir to the Weston family business, has his hands full running the company. Details of his turnaround strategies and ambitious plans to increase profitability of the business are discussed.

23059 ■ *Low Risk, High Reward*
Pub: R & R Publishing
Ed: Bob Reiss with Jeffrey L. Cruikshank. **Released:** 2000. **Price:** $19.95. **Description:** Successful entrepreneur teaches others about creating, growing and maintaining a successful business venture. The book offers a step-by-step approach to helping entrepreneurs minimize the risk involved in a new business while examining the skills and resources needed to succeed.

23060 ■ "Loyalty Cards Score Points" in *Crain's Cleveland Business* (Vol. 30, June 8, 2009, No. 22, pp. 1)
Pub: Crain Communications, Inc.
Ed: Chuck Soder. **Description:** Northeast Ohio retailers are promoting loyalty and rewards programs in order to attract and maintain loyal customers.

23061 ■ "Lumber Rebounds" in *Business Journal Portland* (Vol. 26, December 11, 2009, No. 40, pp. 1)
Pub: American City Business Journals Inc.
Ed: Erik Siemers. **Description:** Oregon's lumber industry could be boosted as wood consumption across the country is expected to increase by 11 percent or 34.5 billion board feet in 2010.

23062 ■ "The Macomb Group: Bigger Can Be Better" in *Crain's Detroit Business* (Vol. 24, September 29, 2008, No. 39, pp. 34)
Pub: Crain Communications, Inc.
Ed: Chad Halcom. **Description:** Overview of the plan of The Macomb Group includes a strategy of growing from a small supplier to a medium-sized regional distributor of valves, pipes and fittings.

23063 ■ *Macrowikinomics: Rebooting Business and the World*
Pub: Portfolio Hardcover
Ed: Don Tapscott, Anthony D. Williams. **Released:** September 28, 2010. **Price:** $27.95. **Description:** Wikinomics Don Tapscott and Anthony Williams showed how mass collaboration was changing the way businesses communicate, create value,, and compete in the new global marketplace in 2007. Now, in the wake of the global financial crisis, the principles of wikinomics have become more powerful than ever.

23064 ■ "Made In Canada" in *Canadian Business* (Vol. 80, March 12, 2007, No. 6, pp. 11)
Pub: Rogers Media
Ed: Ian Harvey. **Description:** The devision of Christie Digital Systems Canada Inc. to increase production of its DLP projectors, in view of high demand from the United States, is discussed.

23065 ■ "Magna Nears Top of Auto Parts Heap" in *Globe & Mail* (May 1, 2007, pp. B4)
Pub: CTVglobemedia Publishing Inc.
Ed: Greg Keenan. **Description:** Magna International Inc. is poised to become the largest automobile parts supplier in North America. The state of the automobile parts industry in Canada is also discussed.

23066 ■ "The Main Event" in *Canadian Business* (Vol. 80, November 19, 2007, No. 23, pp. 28)
Pub: Rogers Media
Ed: Zena Olijnyk. **Description:** U.S.-based Lowe's Companies, Inc. will be opening three stores in Canada in December 2007 and another three in 2008. The housing market crisis in the U.S. is the reason behind the home improvement store's Canadian expansion. The impacts of the expansion on Canadian home care stores and on the market competition are evaluated.

23067 ■ *Make Your Business Survive and Thrive! 100+ Proven Marketing Methods to Help You Beat the Odds*
Pub: John Wiley & Sons, Incorporated
Ed: Priscilla Y. Huff. **Released:** December 2006. **Price:** $19.95. **Description:** Small business and entrepreneurial expert gives information to help small and home-based businesses grow.

23068 ■ "Making the Cut; Osprey Takes Undervalued Courses to the Leader Board" in *Crain's Detroit Business* (Vol. 24, April 7, 2008, No. 14)
Pub: Crain Communications, Inc.
Ed: Jason Deegan. **Description:** Profile of Osprey Management Co., a diverse real estate company that continues to expand its golf portfolio through the company's recreation division; although many developers are getting out of the field due to Michigan's sluggish golf industry, Osprey has found success by purchasing properties in turmoil for more affordable prices.

23069 ■ "The Man Behind Brascan" in *Canadian Business* (Vol. 79, Winter 2006, No. 24, pp. 64)
Pub: Rogers Media
Ed: Andy Holloway. **Description:** The role of Jack Cockwell in the growth of Brookfield Asset Management Inc., is described.

23070 ■ "Management Matters with Mike Myatt: Are You Creating Growth in a Down Economy?" in *Commercial Property News* (March 17, 2008)
Pub: Nielsen Company
Ed: Mike Myatt. **Description:** Senior executives are expected to create growth for their company regardless of recession, economic slowdown, inflation, or tight credit and capital markets.

23071 ■ *Managing Business Growth: Get a Grip on the Numbers That Count*
Pub: Self-Counsel Press, Incorporated
Ed: Angie Mohr. **Released:** October 2004. **Price:** $14.95. **Description:** Fourth book in the Numbers 101 for Small Business Series, teaches how small company owners can expand their businesses using sound financial planning.

23072 ■ *Managing Economies, Trade and International Business*
Pub: Palgrave Macmillan
Ed: Aidan O'Connor. **Released:** January 19, 2010. **Price:** $90.00. **Description:** An in-depth look at the areas that affect and influence international business, exploring specific issues businesses face in terms of economic development, trade law, and international marketing and management.

23073 ■ "M&T On the March?" in *Baltimore Business Journal* (Vol. 28, November 12, 2010, No. 27, pp. 1)
Pub: Baltimore Business Journal
Ed: Gary Haber. **Description:** Information on the growth of M&T Bank, as well as its expansion plans are presented. M&T recently acquired Wilmington Trust and took over $500 million in deposits from the failed K Bank. Analysts believe that M&T would continue its expansion through Washington DC and Richmond, Virginia, especially after a bank executive acknowledged that the markets in those areas are attractive.

23074 ■ "A Manufacturing Revival" in *Boston Business Journal* (Vol. 31, May 27, 2011, No. 18, pp. 1)
Pub: Boston Business Journal
Ed: Kyle Alspach. **Description:** Massachusetts' manufacturing sector has grown despite the high cost of labor, real estate and electricity. Manufacturing jobs in the state have increased to 2,800 in April 2011.

23075 ■ "Manulife Posts Billion-Dollar Profit" in *Globe & Mail* (February 14, 2007, pp. B7)
Pub: CTVglobemedia Publishing Inc.
Ed: Andrew Willis. **Description:** Manulife Financial Corp., Canada's largest insurer, reported $1.1 billion profit in the fourth quarter of 2006. The financial results of Manulife reflected a 39 percent rise in quarterly profit at the nation's wealth management division.

23076 ■ "Marathon Money" in *Hawaii Business* (Vol. 53, December 2007, No. 6, pp. 127)
Pub: Hawaii Business Publishing
Ed: Jolyn Okimoto Rosa. **Description:** Discusses the effects of the Honolulu Marathon on small businesses' sales. The Running Room, for instance, experience growth in sales starting from the training season up to the end of the race, as a surge of Hawaiian residents and tourists come into the store for items such as running shoes and blister kits. The marathon's impact on Hawaii's tourism is examined as well.

23077 ■ "Marine Act Amendments Gain Parliamentary Approval" in *Canadian Sailings* (July 7, 2008)
Pub: Commonwealth Business Media
Ed: Alex Binkley. **Description:** Changes to the Canada Marine Act provides better borrowing deals as well as an ability to tap into federal infrastructure funding for environmental protection measures, security improvements and other site enhancements.

23078 ■ "Marketer Bets Big on U.S.'s Growing Canine Obsession" in *Advertising Age* (Vol. 79, April 14, 2008, No. 15, pp. 14)
Pub: Crain Communications, Inc.
Ed: Emily Bryson York. **Description:** Overview of FreshPet, a New Jersey company that began marketing two brands of refrigerated dog food-Deli Fresh and FreshPet Select-which are made from fresh ingredients such as beef, rice and carrots. The company projects continued success due to the amount of money consumers spend on their pets as well as fears derived from the 2007 recalls that inspired consumers to look for smaller, independent manufacturers that are less likely to source ingredients from China.

23079 ■ "The Market's (Very) Tender Spring Shoots" in *Barron's* (Vol. 88, March 31, 2008, No. 13, pp. M3)
Pub: Dow Jones & Company, Inc.
Ed: Kopin Tan. **Description:** Expansion in price-earnings multiples and a lower credit-default risk index has encouraged fans of the spring-awakening theory. Shares of industrial truckers have gone up 32 percent in 2008 and some shares are pushing five-year highs brought on by higher efficiency and earnings from more load carried. The prospects of the shares of Foot Locker are also discussed.

23080 ■ "Martin Marietta Expands Rock Solid Port Manatee Presence" in *Tampa Bay Business Journal* (Vol. 30, January 8, 2010, No. 3, pp. 1)
Pub: American City Business Journals
Ed: Jane Meinhardt. **Description:** Raleigh, North Carolina-based Martin Marietta Materials Inc. has been granted by Florida's Manatee County Port Authority with a 30-year, $42 million contract. Through the contract, an aggregate terminal will be built by Martin Marietta at the port. Construction work is anticipated to start in earl 2010 with terminal operations commencing by late summer 2010.

23081 ■ *Mastering Business Growth and Change Made Easy*
Pub: Entrepreneur Press
Ed: Jeffrey A. Hansen. **Released:** October 2005. **Price:** $19.95 (US), $26.95 (Canadian). **Description:** Tips for growing a small business, regardless of state or environment.

23082 ■ "Mattel's Got a Monster Holiday Hit, But Will Franchise Have Staying Power?" in *Advertising Age* (Vol. 81, December 6, 2010, No. 43)
Pub: Crain Communications, Inc.
Ed: Beth Snyder Bulik. **Description:** Monster High transmedia play expands beyond dolls to merchandise, apparel and entertainment.

23083 ■ "A Matter of Interest" in *Canadian Business* (Vol. 79, July 17, 2006, No. 14-15, pp. 21)
Pub: Rogers Media
Ed: Jeff Sanford. **Description:** With the steady decrease in savings, the need for growth in Canada's payloan industry is discussed. Also emphasized are the challenges faced by payloan operators.

23084 ■ "Maximizing the Success of New Products" in *Black Enterprise* (Vol. 38, October 2007, No. 3, pp. 70)
Pub: Earl G. Graves Publishing Co. Inc.
Description: New product development drives business growth and profitability. University of Chicago offers a weeklong New Product Development in Innovation class for executive training.

23085 ■ *Maximum Marketing, Minimum Dollars: The Top 50 Ways to Grow Your Small Business*
Pub: Kaplan Books
Ed: Kim Gordon. **Released:** April 2006. **Price:** $24. 00. **Description:** Marketing tips to increase sales are presented. Small business owners will learn to maximize marketing with 50 innovative and affordable methods, including online marketing.

23086 ■ "MBA Project Turns on Tastebuds" in *The Business Journal - Serving Phoenix and the Valley of the Sun* (Vol. 28, August 15, 2008, No. 50)
Pub: American City Business Journals, Inc.
Ed: Angela Gonzales. **Description:** Amol Khade, Venkat Nallapati and Govind Arora, master of businesss administration graduates from Thunderbird School of Global Management, have opened an Indian restaurant, called The Daba, in Tempe, Arizona. The Indian name of the restaurant means 'a place for travelers to stop for rest and food'. Franchise plans for the restaurant are discussed.

23087 ■ "MBAs Plus Designers Equals New Life for Business" in *Globe & Mail* (April 24, 2007, pp. B1)
Pub: CTVglobemedia Publishing Inc.
Ed: Gordon Pitts. **Description:** The need for Canadian companies to combine the skills of management graduates and designers to achieve corporate growth is discussed.

23088 ■ "Meadowbrook CEO Sees 20 Percent Growth With New Acquisition" in *Crain's Detroit Business* (Vol. 24, March 10, 2008, No. 10, pp. 4)
Pub: Crain Communications, Inc.
Ed: Jay Greene. **Description:** Discusses the major turnaround of Meadowbrook Insurance Group after Robert Cubbin became CEO and implemented a new business strategy.

23089 ■ "Meadowbrook To Acquire ProCentury in $272.6 Million Deal" in *Crain's Detroit Business* (Vol. 24, February 25, 2008, No. 8, pp. 4)
Pub: Crain Communications Inc. - Detroit
Description: Meadowbrook Insurance Group, based in Southfield, Michigan reports its proposed acquisition of ProCentury Corporation based in Columbus, Ohio. Meadowbrook provides risk-management to agencies, professional and trade associations and small-to-midsize businesses.

23090 ■ "Medicaid Insurers See Growth in Small Business Market" in *Boston Business Journal* (Vol. 31, July 15, 2011, No. 25, pp. 1)
Pub: Boston Business Journal
Ed: Julie M. Donnelly. **Description:** BMC HealthNet Plan announced plans to launch small business products to serve small businesses that are priced out of rising premium rates at large Massachusetts insurers. BMC joined competitors CeltiCare Health Plan and Neighborhood Health Plan in augmenting its core business.

23091 ■ "The Medium 150" in *Canadian Business* (Vol. 81, Summer 2008, No. 9, pp. 129)
Pub: Rogers Media Ltd.
Description: Medium-sized companies are ranked based on market capitalization and stock performance. Timminico Ltd. topped the roster with 1,294.2 percent returns, while Petrominerales Ltd. ranked second with 325.4 percent. A table showing the 2008 rankings of the companies is presented.

23092 ■ *Medium Sized Firms and Economics Growth*
Pub: Nova Science Publishers, Incorporated
Ed: Janez Prasniker. **Released:** April 2005. **Price:** $130.00. **Description:** Medium sized companies should have a more definitive presence in modern microeconomic theory, the theory of entrepreneurship, and the theory of financial markets.

23093 ■ "Meet Joe Fresh" in *Canadian Business* (Vol. 79, November 6, 2006, No. 22, pp. 49)
Pub: Rogers Media
Ed: Calvin Leung. **Description:** The efforts of Joseph Mimran, a fashion designer, in improving the business of Joe Fresh style products are analyzed.

23094 ■ "Members Make Sacrifices for a World-Class Course" in *Crain's Detroit Business* (Vol. 24, April 7, 2008, No. 14, pp. 21)
Pub: Crain Communications, Inc.
Ed: Jason Deegan. **Description:** Rees Jones Inc. completed a $1.8 million redesign of the Oakland Hills Country Club golf course last year. By all indications, the redesign has been a success since it is among the handful of courses good enough to host future majors which is beneficial for the local economy.

23095 ■ *Memos to the Prime Minister: What Canada Could Be in the 21st Century*
Pub: John Wiley & Sons, Incorporated
Ed: Harvey Schacter. **Released:** April 11, 2003. **Price:** $16.95. **Description:** A look into the business future of Canada. Topics include business, healthcare, think tanks, policy groups, education, the arts, economy, and social issues.

23096 ■ "Menchie's Tops Restaurant Business' Future 50 List" in *Ice Cream Reporter* (Vol. 23, August 20, 2010, No. 9, pp. 4)
Pub: Ice Cream Reporter
Description: Menchie's, frozen yogurt shop, announced it placed first in the Restaurant Business Magazine's Future 50, ranking the franchise the fastest-growing in the food industry.

23097 ■ "Mercy Parent Nets Almost $1B in 2011" in *Sacramento Business Journal* (Vol. 28, September 30, 2011, No. 31, pp. 1)
Pub: Sacramento Business Journal
Ed: Kathy Robertson. **Description:** Catholic Healthcare West has reported almost $1 billion in profits for 2010. The company has reported a profit margin of 8.7 percent. It also absorbed more than $1 billion in costs from charity care and government programs.

23098 ■ "Merger Mania: Regional Snaps Up HVS" in *The Business Journal-Serving Greater Tampa Bay* (Vol. 28, September 26, 2008, No. 40, pp. 1)
Pub: American City Business Journals, Inc.
Ed: Alexis Muellner. **Description:** It was reported that Harper Van Scoik & Co. LLP has finalized a merger with Carr Riggs & Ingram LLC. The agreement, effective October 1, 2008, is a merger of HVS assets into CRI. Bill Carr, a managing partner, revealed that HVS' $5 million in revenue will take CRI from $78 million to $82 million in revenue.

23099 ■ "Mexican Companies to Rent Space in TechTown, Chinese Negotiating" in *Crain's Detroit Business* (Vol. 24, September 29, 2008, No. 39)
Pub: Crain Communications, Inc.
Ed: Tom Henderson. **Description:** Wayne State University's TechTown, the business incubator and research park, has signed an agreement with the Mexican government that will provide temporary office space to 25 Mexican companies looking to find customers or establish partnerships in Michigan. TechTown's executive director is negotiating with economic development officials from China. To accommodate foreign visitors the incubator is equipping offices with additional equipment and resources.

23100 ■ "Michigan Institute of Urology Grows in Expertise, Services" in *Crain's Detroit Business* (Vol. 24, April 7, 2008, No. 14, pp. 13)
Pub: Crain Communications, Inc.
Ed: Jay Greene. **Description:** One of the nation's largest urology groups, the Michigan Institute of Urology, plans to continue its growth by adding doctors and offering new treatment options. The growth is financially beneficial to the group, but it also cuts down on health care costs since the group can perform procedures for a lesser rate than at a hospital.

23101 ■ "Micro-Cap Companies" in *Canadian Business* (Vol. 81, Summer 2008, No. 9, pp. 157)
Pub: Rogers Media Ltd.
Description: Micro-cap companies have lower than $221 million in terms of market capitalization. Burnaby, British Columbia-based Fancamp Exploration Ltd. topped the roster with 1,116.7 percent in return. A table showing the 2008 rankings of the companies is presented.

23102 ■ "MicroTech: No. 1 Fastest-Growing Company" in *Hispanic Business* (July-August 2009, pp. 20, 22)
Pub: Hispanic Business
Ed: Suzanne Heibel. **Description:** Profile of Tony Jimenez, former lieutenant colonel in the Army and CEO and founder of Virginia-based information technology firm, Micro Tech LLC. Jimenez was named Latinos in Information Science and Technology Association's CEO of the Year for 2008.

23103 ■ "Millennials: The Great White Hope for Wine Industry" in *Advertising Age* (Vol. 81, December 6, 2010, No. 43, pp. 2)
Pub: Crain Communications, Inc.
Ed: E.J. Shultz. **Description:** Generation offers category of most growth potential in 30 years and 7-Eleven and vintner are taking notice.

23104 ■ "Million-Dollar Babies" in *Black Enterprise* (Vol. 38, January 2008, No. 6, pp. 64)
Pub: Earl G. Graves Publishing Co. Inc.
Ed: Tennille M. Robinson. **Description:** Books and programs to help any small business grow to the $1 million mark are outlined.

23105 ■ "Mimosa Systems Gains 150,000 New NearPoint Users" in *Information Today* (Vol. 26, February 2009, No. 2, pp. 31)
Pub: Information Today, Inc.
Description: Mimosa System's NearPoint archive solution features email and file archiving, e-discovery, archive virtualization, and disaster recovery capabilities.

23106 ■ "Minnesota Farms' Net Worth Grows 10 Percent Each Year for 15 Years" in *Farm Industry News* (August 22, 2011)
Pub: Penton Business Media Inc.
Ed: Dale Nordquist. **Description:** The average value of farms in Minnesota is growing at a fast pace. Total assets per farm have increased by more than $1.1 million over the past 15 years. Statistical data included.

23107 ■ "MIR Growing With Help From Former Pfizer Workers" in *Crain's Detroit Business* (Vol. 24, January 28, 2008, No. 4, pp. 33)
Pub: Crain Communications Inc. - Detroit
Ed: Tom Henderson. **Description:** Molecular Imaging Research Inc. helps fund research at its parent firm, Molecular Therapeutics Inc. The company provides imaging services and other in vivo and in vitro services to help pharmaceutical companies test new compounds.

23108 ■ *The Mirror Test: How to Breathe New Life Into Your Business*
Pub: Grand Central Publishing

Ed: Jeffrey W. Hayzlett. **Released:** May 10, 2010. **Price:** $24.99. **Description:** Consultant and author, Jeffrey Hayzlett, explains why a business is not doing well and asks the questions that most business managers are afraid to ask.

23109 ■ "Mission: Poach California" in *Business Journal Portland* (Vol. 26, December 11, 2009, No. 40, pp. 1)
Pub: American City Business Journals Inc.

Ed: Andy Giegerich. **Description:** Leaders of Greenlight Greater Portland, a privately funded economic development organization, will visit California five times in 2010 in an attempt to lure California businesses to expand or relocate in Oregon.

23110 ■ "A Mixed-Bag Quarter" in *Barron's* (Vol. 88, July 7, 2008, No. 27, pp. 19)
Pub: Dow Jones & Co., Inc.

Ed: Shirley A. Lazo. **Description:** Seven component companies of the Dow Jones Industrial Average increased their dividend payouts in the second quarter of 2008 despite the weak performance of the index. Five companies in the Dow Jones Transportation index and three in the Dow Jones Utilities also increased their dividends.

23111 ■ "Mobile: Juanes Fans Sing for Sprint" in *Advertising Age* (Vol. 79, November 3, 2008, No. 41, pp. 22)
Pub: Crain Communications, Inc.

Ed: Laurel Wentz. **Description:** Marketers are appealing to the Hispanic market since they are more prone to use their cell phones to respond to contests, download videos, ringtones, or other data activity. Sprint recently sponsored a contest inviting people to sing like Colombian megastar Juanes; the participants filmed and sent their videos using their cell phones rather than laptops or camcorders illustrating the Hispanic overindex on mobile-phone technology. The contest generated hundreds of thousands of dollars in additional fee revenue, as monthly downloads increased 63 percent.

23112 ■ "Mobile Marketing Grows With Size of Cell Phone Screens" in *Crain's Detroit Business* (Vol. 24, January 14, 2008, No. 2, pp. 13)
Pub: Crain Communications Inc. - Detroit

Ed: Bill Shea. **Description:** Experts are predicting increased marketing for cell phones with the inception of larger screens and improved technology.

23113 ■ "The Mobile Workforce Revolution" in *Canadian Business* (Vol. 81, March 31, 2008, No. 5, pp. 28)
Pub: Rogers Media

Ed: Diane Horton. **Description:** Diane Horton explains how a mobile workforce helps companies cut costs, increase productivity, and boost employee motivation. Horton says that employees believe they usually become more productive by 15 to 30 percent after their companies go mobile.

23114 ■ "The Molson Way" in *Canadian Business* (Vol. 80, April 9, 2007, No. 8, pp. 36)
Pub: Rogers Media

Ed: Andy Holloway. **Description:** The success of the seventh generation of Molson family in running the Molson Coors Brewing Co. since it was established 221 years ago by John Molson is discussed.

23115 ■ "Money and the Mayhem" in *Canadian Business* (Vol. 83, September 14, 2010, No. 15, pp. 52)
Pub: Rogers Media Ltd.

Ed: Greg Hudson. **Description:** Ultimate Fighting Championship (UFC) has hired Tom Wright as director of operations for Canada, who finally managed to get mixed martial arts sanctioned in Ontario. Canada is UFC's largest market after the US and accounting for about 15-20 percent in annual revenue.

23116 ■ "Montana Outlook: Stronger Growth Ahead" in *Montana Business Quarterly* (Vol. 49, Spring 2011, No. 1, pp. 7)
Pub: Bureau of Business & Economic Research

Ed: Patrick M. Barkey. **Description:** A look at Montana's economy and future growth is given. Experts are predicting that the state will experience new growth in 2011, with 2012 showing its best growth since 2006. Statistical data included.

23117 ■ "Montana's Manufacturing Industry" in *Montana Business Quarterly* (Vol. 49, Spring 2011, No. 1, pp. 29)
Pub: Bureau of Business & Economic Research

Ed: Todd A. Morgan, Charles E. Keegan III, Colin B. Sorenson. **Description:** Manufacturing remains a vital part of Montana's economy despite the recession and decline in the production of wood products. Statistical data included.

23118 ■ "MooBella Adds Two Airports" in *Ice Cream Reporter* (Vol. 23, November 20, 2010, No. 12, pp. 5)
Pub: Ice Cream Reporter

Description: MooBella Inc. has placed MooBella Ice Creamery machines in New England's Logan International Airport in Boston and in New Hampshire's Manchester-Boston Regional Airport.

23119 ■ "More Jobs Heading to Suburb" in *Austin Business JournalInc.* (Vol. 29, November 20, 2009, No. 37, pp. 1)
Pub: American City Business Journals

Ed: Kate Harrington. **Description:** Site of Advanced Integration Technologies (AIT) in Pflugerville, Texas might increase its workforce to 80 employees in the next six months due to the creation of an incentive package. Funds from the Pflugerville Community Development Corporation have been helping AIT's initiative to hire more workers. The firm receives $2,000 from the plan for every new employee it hires.

23120 ■ "More Sales Leads, Please: Or, What Happened When Frontline Selling Started Practicing What It Preaches" in *Inc.* (November 2007)
Pub: Gruner & Jahr USA Publishing

Description: Frontline Selling located in Oakland, New Jersey helps train sales teams to generate and convert sales leads. The consulting firm doubled their marketing budget to increase their own sales.

23121 ■ "More SouthPark Shopping" in *Charlotte Business Journal* (Vol. 25, July 16, 2010, No. 17, pp. 1)
Pub: Charlotte Business Journal

Ed: Will Boye. **Description:** Charlotte, North Carolina-based Bissel Companies has announced plans to expand its retail presence at the Siskey and Sharon properties in SouthPark. Bissel Companies has requested a rezoning to a mixed-use development classification so that it can utilize the entire ground floor of the Siskey building for restaurant and retail uses.

23122 ■ *More Than a Pink Cadillac*
Pub: McGraw-Hill

Ed: Jim Underwood. **Released:** 2002. **Price:** $23.95. **Description:** Profile of Mary Kay Ash who turned her $5,000 investment into a billion-dollar corporation. Ash's nine principles that form the foundation of her company's global success are outlined. Stories from her sales force leaders share ideas for motivating employees, impressing customers and building a successful company. The book emphasizes the leadership skills required to drive performance in any successful enterprise.

23123 ■ "MPI Expansion Goes Back to Family Roots" in *Crain's Detroit Business* (Vol. 25, June 1, 2009, No. 22, pp. M007)
Pub: Crain Communications Inc. - Detroit

Ed: Sherri Begin Welch. **Description:** William Parfet, grandson of Upjohn Company founder, is expanding MPI Research's clinical and early clinical research operations into two buildings in Kalamazoo, land which was once part of his grandfather's farm.

23124 ■ *The Multinational Enterprise Revisited: The Essential Buckley and Casson*
Pub: Palgrave Macmillan

Ed: Peter J. Buckley, Mark Casson. **Released:** January 5, 2010. **Price:** $95.00. **Description:** A compilation of essays gathered from over thirty years discussing the future of the multinational enterprise, and includes a new introduction and conclusion to bond the pieces together in a comprehensive overview of the theory of the multinational enterprise.

23125 ■ "MV Transportation Winds $133M Contract" in *Black Enterprise* (Vol. 38, November 2007, No. 4, pp. 30)
Pub: Earl G. Graves Publishing Co. Inc.

Ed: Marcia A. Wade. **Description:** MV Transportation won a $133 million contract to operate 139 fixed-route buses in the San Gabriel and Pomona valley areas of California.

23126 ■ "Myths of Deleveraging" in *Barron's* (Vol. 90, August 23, 2010, No. 34, pp. M14)
Pub: Barron's Editorial & Corporate Headquarters

Ed: Gene Epstein. **Description:** The opposite is true against reports about deleveraging or the decrease in credit since inflation-adjusted-investment factories and equipment rose 7.8 percent in the first quarter of 2010. On consumer deleveraging, sales of homes through credit is weak but there is a trend towards more realistic homeownership and consumer spending on durable goods rose 8.8 percent.

23127 ■ "NBC Universal Cable" in *Brandweek* (Vol. 49, April 21, 2008, No. 16, pp. SR11)
Pub: VNU Business Media, Inc.

Ed: Anthony Crupi. **Description:** Provides contact information for sales and marketing personnel for the NBC Universal Cable networks as well as a listing of the station's top programming and an analysis of the current season and the target audience for those programs running in the current season. The network's stations include USA, Sci Fi and Bravo. Ad revenue for the network grew 30 percent in the first quarter.

23128 ■ "Neurosciences, Orthopedics Push Mease Dunedin Plan" in *Tampa Bay Business Journal* (Vol. 29, October 30, 2009, No. 45, pp. 1)
Pub: American City Business Journals

Ed: Margie Manning. **Description:** Mease Dunedin Hospital has pushed with a $19 million renovation and expansion plan that would triple the space in its operating suites, in line with its effort to become a center of excellence focused on neurosciences, orthopedics and the spine. The hospital expects these kinds of specialties will help offset the cost of less profitable services.

23129 ■ "Never Boring: Ad Agencies' Big Changes" in *Business Courier* (Vol. 24, February 8, 2008, No. 44, pp. 1)
Pub: American City Business Journals, Inc.

Ed: Dan Monk. **Description:** Many changes are occurring in Cincinnati's advertising industry, including new clients, acquisitions, and market leaders, and an increase in employment. Bridge Worldwide passed Northlich LLC as the city's largest advertising agency.

23130 ■ "New Beginnings for VIBE" in *Black Enterprise* (Vol. 37, November 2006, No. 4, pp. 34)
Pub: Earl G. Graves Publishing Co. Inc.

Ed: Mashaun D. Simon. **Description:** Danyel Smith replaced Mimi Valdes as editor-in-chief of VIBE magazine after the Wicks Group, private equity firm focused on selected segments of the media, communications, and information industries, purchased the magazine.

23131 ■ "New Drug Could Revitalize Amgen" in *Barron's* (Vol. 88, July 7, 2008, No. 27, pp. 23)
Pub: Dow Jones & Co., Inc.

Ed: Johanna Bennett. **Description:** Shares of the biotechnology company Amgen could receive a boost from the release of the anti-osteoporosis drug denosumab. The shares, priced at $48.84 each, are trading at 11 times expected earnings for 2008 and could also be boosted by cost cutting measures.

23132 ■ "New Health Care Sector" in *Hispanic Business* (July-August 2009, pp. 10-12)
Pub: Hispanic Business
Ed: Rob Kuznia. **Description:** Despite the recession and reform, the health care sector continues to grow at a fast rate. The top ten health care organizations are outlined.

23133 ■ "New-Home Sales Grab a Foothold With Q2 Boost" in *Sacramento Business Journal* (Vol. 25, July 11, 2008, No. 19, pp. 1)
Pub: American City Business Journals, Inc.
Ed: Michael Shaw. **Description:** Statistics show that homebuilders in Sacramento, California experienced an increase in new-home sales during the second quarter of 2008. It was also reported that builders moved more homes without slashing prices significantly. Barry Grant, president of KB Home's Sacramento division, believes that the improvement is caused by the stability in the supply of resale homes.

23134 ■ "New King Top the Charts" in *The Business Journal-Portland* (Vol. 25, August 8, 2008, No. 22, pp. 1)
Pub: American City Business Journals, Inc.
Ed: Andy Giegerich. **Description:** Spanish-language KRYP-FM station's spring 2008 ratings soared to 6.4 from 2.8 for the previous year. The station timing is flawless given the fact that one of every three new Portland-area residents between 2002 and 2007 were Latino.

23135 ■ "New Kittinger Showroom Twice the Size of the Last One" in *Business First Buffalo* (December 7, 2007, pp. 4)
Pub: American City Business Journals, Inc.
Ed: Tracey Drury. **Description:** Kittinger Furniture Company, an upscale furniture maker, has opened a 6,000 square foot retail outlet at the Transit Road, New York. The company's moved to attract suburban and affluent customers for its high-end furniture products.

23136 ■ "New Leadership Panel Has Advice for Collins" in *Business First Buffalo* (November 23, 2007, pp. 1)
Pub: American City Business Journals, Inc.
Ed: David Bertola. **Description:** Business First and Leadership Buffalo sponsored a meeting that convened business and civic leaders to discuss issues important to the economic growth and development of Western New York. The panel made recommendations to the County Executive-elect Christopher Collins. Details of the forum are included.

23137 ■ "New Life for Old Chemistries" in *Farm Industry News* (Vol. 42, January 1, 2009, No. 1)
Pub: Penton Media, Inc.
Ed: Mark Moore. **Description:** To expand the uses of familiar crop protection products, chemical companies are utilizing biotechnology research and development tools; many off-patent products are being rejuvenated with small changes to make the product even better than it was when originally conceived.

23138 ■ "A New Reality; There are Some Signs of Hope Amid 2009's Darkness" in *Crain's Cleveland Business* (Vol. 30, June 29, 2009, No. 25)
Pub: Crain Communications, Inc.
Ed: John Booth. **Description:** Despite all the pessimism, there are some signs that the economy is slowly stabilizing.

23139 ■ *The New Role of Regional Management*
Pub: Palgrave Macmillan
Ed: Bjorn Ambos, Bodo B. Schlegelmilch. **Released:** January 19, 2010. **Price:** $95.00. **Description:** Regional management is becoming more important to companies as they expand globally. This book explores the challenges of European, United States and Asian companies and outlines how regional headquarters can develop into Dynamic Competence Relay centers to master these issues.

23140 ■ "New Sprint Phone Whets Appetite for Applications" in *The Business Journal-Serving Metropolitan Kansas City* (Vol. 26, July 25, 2008)
Pub: American City Business Journals, Inc.
Ed: Suzanna Stagemeyer. **Description:** Firms supporting the applications of the new Samsung Instinct, which was introduced by Sprint Nextel Corp. in June 2008, have reported usage rates increase for their products. Handmark, whose mobile services Pocket Express comes loaded with Instinct, has redirected employees to meet the rising demand for the services. Other views and information on Instinct, are presented.

23141 ■ "New Stores, New Headquarters in Schenectady for Golub Corporation" in *Business Review, Albany New York* (November 23, 2007)
Pub: American City Business Journals, Inc.
Ed: Michael DeMasi. **Description:** Details of Golub Corporation's expansion plan are presented. The supermarket chain, which has 116 stores in six northeastern states, plans to open thirty more stores within the next three or four years. The company will also build 524,000 square feet of warehouse space which will help in supplying new stores. Its corporate headquarters will also move to a vacant lot in Schenectady, New York.

23142 ■ *New Technology-Based Firms in the New Millennium, Volume 5*
Pub: Elsevier Science and Technology Books
Ed: Ray Oakey; Saleema Kauser; Aard Groen; Peter van der Sijde. **Released:** November 2006. **Price:** $145.00. **Description:** Papers from the Annual High Technology Smal Firms conference are presented. Experts address strategic growth for these small firms.

23143 ■ "New Technology, Growing Fan Base Fuel Truck Trend" in *Nation's Restaurant News* (Vol. 45, June 13, 2001, No. 12, pp. 16)
Pub: Penton Media Inc.
Ed: Ron Ruggless. **Description:** Food trucks drove more interest at this year's National Restaurant Association Restaurant Hotel-Motel Show in Chicago. The trend continues to show long-term growth.

23144 ■ "New Year's Resolutions: How Three Companies Came Up With Their 2008 Growth Strategies" in *Inc.* (January 2008, pp. 47-49)
Pub: Gruner & Jahr USA Publishing
Ed: Martha C. White. **Description:** Three companies share 2008 growth strategies; companies include a candle company, a voice mail and text messaging marketer, and hotel supplier of soap and shampoo.

23145 ■ "Newcomers Join Roster of Indoor Sports Venues" in *Business Review, Albany New York* (Vol. 34, October 12, 2007, No. 28, pp. 1)
Pub: American City Business Journals, Inc.
Ed: Adam Sichko. **Description:** Indoor sports scene in Albany, New York is growing, with several indoor training facilities with a special attention to baseball and softball being built. These facilities include the $2.2 million Extra Innings facility in Ballston Corporate Technology Park and the Warning Track facility on Route 9 in Malta. The market for indoor sports, which is seen as saturated, is analyzed.

23146 ■ "Nine Sectors to Watch: Biotech" in *Canadian Business* (Vol. 81, December 24, 2007, No. 1, pp. 48)
Pub: Rogers Media
Ed: Calvin Leung. **Description:** Forecasts on the Canadian biotechnology sector for 2008 are presented. Details on the increase in the number of biotechnology companies and prediction on the government's plan for business incentives are discussed.

23147 ■ "Nine Sectors to Watch: Construction" in *Canadian Business* (Vol. 81, December 24, 2007, No. 1, pp. 48)
Pub: Rogers Media
Ed: Jeff Sanford. **Description:** Infrastructure deficit of C$123 billion, and still growing, was recently reported by the Federation of Canadian Municipalities. Details on plans for infrastructure projects and forecasts on the construction sector for 2008 are discussed.

23148 ■ "Nine Sectors to Watch: Energy" in *Canadian Business* (Vol. 81, December 24, 2007, No. 1, pp. 54)
Pub: Rogers Media
Ed: Jeff Sanford. **Description:** One of the concerns in the petroleum industry is the fear of decline in production in many oilfields, as analysts predict the world will be pumping 17 percent less by 2025. Details on the continuing rise in demand and increase in prices are discussed.

23149 ■ "Nine Sectors to Watch: Gold" in *Canadian Business* (Vol. 81, December 24, 2007, No. 1, pp. 53)
Pub: Rogers Media
Ed: John Gray. **Description:** Turmoil in the financial markets, triggered by the meltdown in subprime mortgages, has pushed the price of gold to more than $840 an ounce in November 2007. Details on investor interest in gold and prediction on price trends in trade are discussed.

23150 ■ "Nine Sectors to Watch: Metals" in *Canadian Business* (Vol. 81, December 24, 2007, No. 1, pp. 46)
Pub: Rogers Media
Ed: John Gray. **Description:** Forecasts on the Canadian metal industries for 2008 are discussed. Details on mine production and the rise in prices are also presented.

23151 ■ "Nine Sectors to Watch: Retail" in *Canadian Business* (Vol. 81, December 24, 2007, No. 1, pp. 56)
Pub: Rogers Media
Ed: Zena Olijnyk. **Description:** Canadian consumers are expected to spend more in 2008 as the Canadian dollar hit par with the U.S. greenback after the slowdown in the U.S. economy. Forecasts on retail sales growth are presented.

23152 ■ "Nine Sectors to Watch: Telecom" in *Canadian Business* (Vol. 81, December 24, 2007, No. 1, pp. 44)
Pub: Rogers Media
Ed: Andrew Wahl. **Description:** Forecasts on the Canadian telecommunications industry for 2008 are presented. Details on consumer spending growth, the popularity of broadband, and activities in the wireless sector are also discussed.

23153 ■ "No Frills - And No Dodge" in *Crain's Detroit Business* (Vol. 24, September 22, 2008, No. 38, pp. 3)
Pub: Crain Communications, Inc.
Ed: Bradford Wernie. **Description:** Chrysler LLC is in the middle of a business plan known as Project Genesis, a five-year strategy in which the company will reduce the dealer count by combining its Jeep, Chrysler and Dodge brands under one rooftop wherever possible. Not every dealer will be able to arrange this deal because of the investment required to expand stores in which have low-overhead; many of these stores feel that low-overhead structures are more likely to survive difficult times than the larger stores in which the Genesis consolidation plan intends to implement.

23154 ■ "No Lines, No Waiting" in *The Business Journal-Serving Greater Tampa Bay* (Vol. 28, August 15, 2008, No. 34, pp. 1)
Pub: American City Business Journals, Inc.
Ed: Jane Meinhardt. **Description:** Voda LLC, which was founded to commercialize developments by David Fries, develops outdoor sensor networks used for environmental monitoring by markets like research, the security industry, and the government.

Fries already licensed 12 technologies for clients for about $130,000 per technology. Other information on Voda LLC is presented.

23155 ■ *No Man's Land: What to Do When Your Company Is Too Big to Be Small but Too Small to Be Big*
Pub: Portfolio Publishing
Ed: Doug Tatum. **Released:** September 13, 2007. **Price:** $24.95. **Description:** Insight to help fast-growing companies navigate the fatal trap of no-man's land, a perilous zone where they have outgrown the habits and practices that fueled their early growth but have not yet adopted new practices and resources in order to cope with new situations and challenges.

23156 ■ "No Rooms for the Inn In This High-Rise" in *Chicago Tribune* (October 4, 2008)
Pub: McClatchy-Tribune Information Services
Ed: Ameet Sachdev; Jim Kirk. **Description:** Construction has stalled for several hotel expansion projects due to the economy which has caused a decline in occupancy and little growth in average daily room rates in downtown Chicago because consumers and businesses are becoming more cautious in the amount of money they spend on travel.

23157 ■ "No Surprises" in *Canadian Business* (Vol. 79, September 25, 2006, No. 19, pp. 49)
Pub: Rogers Media
Ed: Jeff Sanford. **Description:** The increasing income trust sector in Canada is discussed.

23158 ■ "Nonprofit to Grow" in *Austin Business JournalInc.* (Vol. 29, January 22, 2010, No. 46, pp. 1)
Pub: American City Business Journals
Ed: Sandra Zaragoza. **Description:** Southwest Key Programs Inc. received a $2.1 million grant from the U.S. Economic Development Administration to help finance the building of a $3.6 million 'Social Enterprise Complex'. The complex is expected to create at least 100 jobs in East Austin, Texas. Details of the plan for the complex are presented.

23159 ■ "Northern Kentucky Adds 1,355 Jobs in '07" in *Business Courier* (Vol. 24, February 15, 2008, No. 45, pp. 3)
Pub: American City Business Journals, Inc.
Ed: Lucy May. **Description:** Jobs generated by new and expanding businesses in Northern Kentucky in 2007 totaled to 1,355, which boosted total business sales to $410 million. The ripple effects of the businesses are expected to create 5,432 new jobs and increase business sales to more than $888 million.

23160 ■ "The Numbers Speak For Themselves" in *Barron's* (Vol. 88, July 14, 2008, No. 28, pp. 16)
Pub: Dow Jones & Co., Inc.
Ed: Bill Alpert. **Description:** Discusses quant fund managers versus traditional long-short equity funds after quants outperformed traditional funds in the year 2000. Causes for the underperformance are outlined and statistical data is included.

23161 ■ "Office Leasing Gains Ground" in *Sacramento Business Journal* (Vol. 25, July 18, 2008, No. 20, pp. 1)
Pub: American City Business Journals, Inc.
Ed: Michael Shaw. **Description:** There were at least 84,000 square feet leased to companies in the Sacramento area in the three months prior to August 2008. This development is good news considering that overall vacant leases were around 247,000 square feet for the previous quarter.

23162 ■ "Oh, Grow Up!" in *Entrepreneur* (Vol. 35, October 2007, No. 10, pp. 120)
Pub: Entrepreneur Media Inc.
Ed: Mark Henricks. **Description:** Most entrepreneurs are overwhelmed with the idea of expanding their business, forgetting to strategically plan the process of business growth. However, there are certain steps entrepreneurs must take in turning a startup business into a bigger venture. Eight steps to growing a business, such as asking for advice and deciding on a focus are presented.

23163 ■ "Ohio Commerce Draws Closer to Profitability" in *Crain's Cleveland Business* (Vol. 28, October 29, 2007, No. 43, pp. 14)
Pub: Crain Communications, Inc.
Ed: Shawn A. Turner. **Description:** Overview of the business plan of Ohio Commerce Bank, a de novo, or startup bank that is close to turning the corner to profitability. The bank opened in November 2006 and focuses on dealing with small businesses totaling $5 million or less in annual revenues.

23164 ■ "Ohio Franchise Buys 21 Jacksonville Area Papa John's" in *Florida Times-Union* (December 20, 2010)
Pub: Florida Times-Union
Ed: Mark Basch. **Description:** Ohio-based Papa John's pizza franchise acquired 21 of the restaurants in Duval, Clay and St. Johns counties in Jacksonville, Florida.

23165 ■ "Oil Patch Expects Richer Shell Offer" in *Globe & Mail* (January 3, 2006, pp. B1)
Pub: CTVglobemedia Publishing Inc.
Ed: Andrew Willis; Patrick Brethour. **Description:** The concerns investors over the feasibility of Royal Dutch Shell PLC's acquisition of Shell Canada Ltd., for $7.6 billion, are presented. Shell Canada Ltd. reports rise in shares by ten percent.

23166 ■ "OK, Bring in the Lawyers" in *Crain's Chicago Business* (Vol. 31, November 17, 2008, No. 46, pp. 26)
Pub: Crain Communications, Inc.
Ed: Daniel Rome Levine. **Description:** Bankruptcy attorneys are finding the economic and credit crisis a benefit for their businesses due to the high number of business owners and mortgage holders that are need of their services. One Chicago firm is handling ten times the number of cases they did the previous year and of that about 80 percent of their new clients are related to the real estate sector.

23167 ■ "On Growth Path of Rising Star" in *Boston Business Journal* (Vol. 31, June 24, 2011, No. 22, pp. 3)
Pub: Boston Business Journal
Ed: Kyle Alspach. **Description:** 1366 Technologies Inc. of Lexington, Massachusetts is considered a rising solar power technology company. The firm secured $150 million loan guarantee from the US Department of Energy that could go to the construction of a 1,000 megawatt solar power plant.

23168 ■ "On the High Road" in *Crain's Cleveland Business* (Vol. 28, October 8, 2007, No. 40, pp. 2)
Pub: Crain Communications, Inc.
Description: According to the American Public Transportation Association, the Greater Cleveland Regional Transit Authority is the best public transit system in North America. Ridership has increased steadily in the last few years. Statistical data included.

23169 ■ "On Hire Ground" in *Entrepreneur* (Vol. 36, February 2008, No. 2, pp. 19)
Pub: Entrepreneur Media Inc.
Description: ADP Small Business Services, an economic consulting firm, showed that small businesses had increased employment rates in 2007 and added 77,000 jobs in November 2007. Entrepreneurial employment and data showing the contribution of small businesses to job growth are presented.

23170 ■ "On a Roll" in *Canadian Business* (Vol. 79, Winter 2006, No. 24, pp. 49)
Pub: Rogers Media
Ed: Thomas Watson. **Description:** The efforts of the Canadian automobile spare parts manufacturer, Magna International Inc., to expand into the the Russian market, are described.

23171 ■ "One on One With SEIA's President, CEO" in *Contractor* (Vol. 57, January 2010, No. 1, pp. 40)
Pub: Penton Media, Inc.
Ed: Dave Yates. **Description:** Solar Energy Industries Association President and CEO Rhone Resch says that the deployment of solar systems in the U.S. has exploded since 2005 and that there is a need to make inroads for shaping the U.S. energy policy. Resch says one of the hurdles they face is that there are no universal standards.

23172 ■ "Online All the Time" in *Retail Merchandiser* (Vol. 51, July-August 2011, No. 4, pp. 18)
Pub: Phoenix Media Corporation
Description: Ecommerce sales are rising at a steady pace and for cross-channel retailers it is boosting sales in the weak economy. Online sales are expected to reach $188 billion in 2011, boasting a 13.7 rate of growth.

23173 ■ "Optimism Index" in *Black Enterprise* (Vol. 41, September 2010, No. 2, pp. 24)
Pub: Earl G. Graves Publishing Co. Inc.
Description: According to a Pew Research Center report, 81 percent of African Americans expect to improve their finances in 2011. Blacks have carried a disproportionate share of job losses and housing foreclosures in the recession that began in 2007.

23174 ■ "Oracle: No Profit of Doom" in *Barron's* (Vol. 88, March 31, 2008, No. 13, pp. 40)
Pub: Dow Jones & Company, Inc.
Ed: Mark Veverka. **Description:** Oracle's revenues grew by 21 percent but fell short of expectation and their profits came in at the low-end of expectations. The company's shares dropped 8 percent but investors are advised to pay more attention to the company's earnings expansion rather than revenue growth in a slow economy. Nokia's Rick Simonson points out that their markets in Asia and particularly India is growing so they are not as affected by the U.S. economic conditions.

23175 ■ "O'Reilly Will Soup Up KC Warehouse" in *The Business Journal-Serving Metropolitan Kansas City* (Vol. 26, August 15, 2008, No. 49)
Pub: American City Business Journals, Inc.
Ed: Rob Roberts. **Description:** O'Reilly Automotive Inc. plans to construct a 215,000-square foot warehouse in Kansas City. The move is expected to triple the size of the company's distribution center. Other views and information on the planned warehouse construction, are presented.

23176 ■ "Organic Dairy Farmers Wanted" in *Canadian Business* (Vol. 80, April 23, 2007, No. 9, pp. 11)
Pub: Rogers Media
Ed: Wendy Glauser. **Description:** The growth of the Harmony Organic due to demand for organic dairy products is presented.

23177 ■ *Organizations Alive!: Six Things That Challenge - Seven That Bring Success*
Pub: Yuill & Associates
Ed: Jan Yuill. **Released:** January 2005. **Price:** $35.12 for book and guide. **Description:** New insight into understanding how organizations function as individuals is presented by an international consultant. Customer service, resource management, outsourcing, and management are among the issues covered.

23178 ■ "Out to Draw Work, Talent" in *Crain's Detroit Business* (Vol. 24, April 14, 2008, No. 15, pp. 3)
Pub: Crain Communications, Inc.
Ed: Bill Shea. **Description:** Profile of Southfield-based Kinetic Post Inc., a growing post-production house that offers video, audio, animation, print, online and related services to corporations and advertising agencies.

23179 ■ "Out of Fashion" in *Barron's* (Vol. 88, March 17, 2008, No. 11, pp. 48)
Pub: Dow Jones & Company, Inc.
Ed: Robin Goldwyn Blumenthal. **Description:** Shares of Perry Ellis International and G-III Apparel Group have taken some beating in the market despite good growth earnings prospects. Perry Ellis sees earnings growth of 8 to 11 percent for fiscal 2009, while G-III Apparel expects earnings growth of 25 percent.

23180 ■ "The Outcome of an Organization Overhaul" in *Black Enterprise* (Vol. 41, December 2010, No. 5)
Pub: Earl G. Graves Publishing Co. Inc.
Ed: Tamara E. Holmes. **Description:** Savvy business owners understand the need for change in order to stay competitive and be successful. This article examines how to manage change as well as what strategies can help employees to get with the program faster.

23181 ■ "Outlook for Montana Agriculture" in *Montana Business Quarterly* (Vol. 49, Spring 2011, No. 1, pp. 26)
Pub: Bureau of Business & Economic Research
Ed: George Haynes. **Description:** Montana farmers and ranchers are rebounding from lower prices and production to higher prices and record production in 2010. The state has limited dairy and hog production, but farm income is still likely rise between 15 to 25 percent in 2010 over previous year.

23182 ■ *Outsmart! How to Do What Your Competitors Can't*
Pub: FT Press
Ed: Jim Champy. **Released:** March 7, 2008. **Price:** $22.99. **Description:** Small business growth can be achieved through outsmarting your competition. The author identifies eight powerful ways to compete in the toughest marketplace.

23183 ■ "Overview - Small Business Optimism" in *Small Business Economic Trends* (July 2010, pp. 4)
Pub: National Federation of Independent Business
Description: An optimism index among small businesses surveyed in the U.S. from 1986 to 2010 is presented in graph form. A small business optimism index from January 2005 to June 2010 is also given in tabular form. The index value was seasonally adjusted at 1986=100.

23184 ■ *The Oz Principle*
Pub: Prentice Hall Press
Ed: Roger Connors. **Released:** 1994. **Price:** $24.95. **Description:** The role of personal and organizational accountability in getting business results is profiled.

23185 ■ *The Pampered Chef*
Pub: Doubleday Broadway Publishing Group
Ed: Doris Christopher. **Description:** The Pampered Chef has been selling high quality kitchen tools through in-home cooking demonstration for twenty-five years. CEO and founder explains how she turned her one woman company into a business with sales approaching $1 billion. Christopher shares her story by providing the foundation, strategies for entrepreneurs, setting priorities, knowing when to expand and when to slow growth, and dealing with adversity.

23186 ■ "P&G's Iams Finds Itself in a Pet-Food Dogfight" in *Advertising Age* (Vol. 78, March 5, 2007, No. 10, pp. 6)
Pub: Crain Communications, Inc.
Ed: Jack Neff. **Description:** Proctor & Gamble Co.'s Iams has been slow to embrace the trend toward foods for pets that appear fit for human consumption. Competitors such as Nestle Purina have made big gains with its colorful premium Beneful brand and dry nuggets that look like chunks of vegetables and meat. Statistical data included.

23187 ■ "Parent Firm's Global Reach, Stricter Air Quality Rules Have Stock Smiling" in *Crain's Cleveland Business* (October 15, 2007)
Pub: Crain Communications, Inc.
Ed: David Bennett. **Description:** Since Stock Equipment Co., a firm that makes industrial pollution control equipment, was acquired by Schenck Process Group, a diversified global manufacturer based in Germany, the company's orders from abroad have been on the rise. The purchase has opened the doors to regions such as Eastern and Central Europe, Latin America and Australia.

23188 ■ "PD Targeting Audience Growth with Web Initiatives" in *Crain's Cleveland Business* (Vol. 30, June 29, 2009, No. 25, pp. 1)
Pub: Crain Communications, Inc.
Ed: Kathy Ames Carr. **Description:** Plain Dealer's publisher C.Z. Egger has his news organization focusing on online offerings in order to build circulation of its newspaper. The 167-year-old paper boasts 1,305,203 readers in print and online weekly.

23189 ■ "PDX Bucks National Trend" in *The Business Journal-Portland* (Vol. 25, August 1, 2008, No. 21, pp. 1)
Pub: American City Business Journals, Inc.
Ed: Erik Siemers. **Description:** Portland International Airport could face problems as air carriers are planning to reduce capacity at the airport. The airport is showing signs of growth despite the slowdown in the airline industry. Other airlines that are planning to reduce seating capacity at the airport are also presented.

23190 ■ "Peak Show" in *Canadian Business* (Vol. 81, December 24, 2007, No. 1, pp. 28)
Pub: Rogers Media
Ed: Thomas Watson. **Description:** Factors affecting oil prices could include political instability and economic slowdown, but peak oil is not one of them as it is believed there is still plenty of oil in supply. Details on the oil supply and demand, trend for higher prices, and peak oil expert Matthew Simmons' prediction on the issue are discussed.

23191 ■ "Penney's Buys Wal-Mart Site" in *Crain's Chicago Business* (Vol. 31, March 31, 2008, No. 13, pp. 13)
Pub: Crain Communications, Inc.
Ed: Eddie Baeb. **Description:** J.C. Penny Co. bought the closed Wal-Mart location in Crystal Lake and plans to open a store next year in its push to become more prominent in non-mall locations; Penney plans to expand and renovate the store.

23192 ■ "Penske Opens Its First Smart Car Dealership In Bloomfield Hills" in *Crain's Detroit Business* (Vol. 24, January 21, 2008, No. 3)
Pub: Crain Communications Inc. - Detroit
Ed: Sheena Harrison. **Description:** Information about Penske Automotive Group's Smart Car addition to its dealership lineup. Smart Car pricing starts at $11,590, with more than 30,000 individuals reserving vehicles.

23193 ■ "Perfecting the Process: Creating a Move Efficient Organization On Your Terms" in *Black Enterprise* (Vol. 41, October 2010, No. 3)
Pub: Earl G. Graves Publishing Co. Inc.
Ed: Tamara E. Holmes. **Description:** More than ever, entrepreneurs need to identify new ways of doing business in a cost-effective manner in order to expand their companies, while remaining true to their customer demands.

23194 ■ "Pet-Food Crisis a Boon to Organic Players" in *Advertising Age* (Vol. 78, April 9, 2007, No. 15, pp. 3)
Pub: Crain Communications, Inc.
Ed: Jack Neff. **Description:** In the wake of the pet-food recall crisis, the natural-and-organic segment of the market is gaining recognition and sales; one such manufacturer, Blue Buffalo, has not only seen huge sale increases but also has witnessed a 50-60 percent increase in traffic to the brand's website which has led to the decision to move up the timetable for the brand's first national ad campaign.

23195 ■ "PetSmart: A Barking Buy" in *Barron's* (Vol. 89, July 6, 2009, No. 27, pp. 15)
Pub: Dow Jones & Co., Inc.
Ed: Jay Palmer. **Description:** Shares of PetSmart could climb from $21.70 to about $28 due to the company's improving profits, cash flow, and product portfolio. The company's shares are trading at 14 times projected 2010 earnings of $1.64 a share.

23196 ■ "PGA Tourney Drives Area Economy, Image" in *Crain's Detroit Business* (Vol. 24, April 7, 2008, No. 14, pp. 22)
Pub: Crain Communications, Inc.
Ed: Jason Deegan. **Description:** Discusses the major economic impact the 2008 PGA Championship will have when it visits the south course at Oakland Hills Country Club August 4-10.

23197 ■ "Phoenix Company Realizing Dream of Global Growth" in *The Business Journal - Serving Phoenix and the Valley of the Sun* (Vol. 28, July 18, 2008, No. 46, pp. 1)
Pub: American City Business Journals, Inc.
Ed: Chris Casacchia. **Description:** Phoenix, Arizona-based lubricant maker DreamBrands Inc. is realizing global growth. The company, which has been generating interest from institutional investors, is seeking a second round of funding. Details of the company's products and marketing plans are also discussed.

23198 ■ "Pinellas Leaders Want First Leg of Light Rail" in *The Business Journal-Serving Greater Tampa Bay* (Vol. 28, August 8, 2008, No. 33)
Pub: American City Business Journals, Inc.
Ed: Larry Halstead. **Description:** Proposed routes for the first leg of the planned light railway system in the Tampa Bay, Florida area are being presented as the Tampa Bay Area Regional Transportation Authority is about to make its master plan for the project. A sales tax for transit is being proposed to fund the project, as well as an expansion of the accompanying bus system.

23199 ■ "Pioneer Bank Ready to Expand" in *Austin Business JournalInc.* (Vol. 28, December 19, 2008, No. 40, pp. 1)
Pub: American City Business Journals
Ed: Christopher Calnan. **Description:** Pioneer Bank, an 18-month old community bank based in Dripping Springs, Texas is planning to raise $6 million to open branches in the Austin area, including Hays County locations such as San Marcos, Buda, and Kyle. Pioneer's deposits have growing from $2.2 million to $54 million in 18 months.

23200 ■ "A Pioneer of Paying With Plastic" in *Crain's Chicago Business* (Vol. 31, April 28, 2008, No. 17, pp. 39)
Pub: Crain Communications, Inc.
Ed: Phuong Ly. **Description:** Profile of Perfect Plastic Printing Corp., a family-owned company which manufactures credit cards, bank cards and gift cards and whose sales hit $50.1 million last year, a 16 percent jump from 2006.

23201 ■ "Pitch for SPX Expansion was Full of Energy" in *Charlotte Business Journal* (Vol. 25, November 19, 2010, No. 35, pp. 1)
Pub: Charlotte Business Journal
Ed: John Downey. **Description:** SPX Corporation announced that it will expand their headquarters in Ballantyne after Charlotte and North Carolina leaders made an aggressive push to retain the company. SPX Corporation is expected to invest $70 million for the expansion, which would mean 180 new jobs in Charlotte.

23202 ■ "Playboy to Target Lucrative India Market With No-Nudes Version" in *Globe & Mail* (January 2, 2006, pp. B2)
Pub: CTVglobemedia Publishing Inc.
Ed: Anand Giridharadas. **Description:** The planning of Chicago based Playboy Enterprises Inc. to target lucrative India market with no nudes version, in order to increase its market shares is discussed.

23203 ■ "Playing Citigroup's Woes" in *Barron's* (Vol. 88, March 31, 2008, No. 13, pp. M7)
Pub: Dow Jones & Company, Inc.
Ed: Steven M. Sears. **Description:** Citigroup's first-quarter earnings estimate was slashed to a $1.15-per-share-loss from 28 cents. A strategist recommends buying the company's shares at Sept. 20, 2008 put and selling a Sept. 17.50 put with a maximum profit of $166 if the shares is at or below $17.50 at expiration.

23204 ■ "Playing to Win" in *Entrepreneur* (Vol. 36, May 2008, No. 5, pp. 40)
Pub: Entrepreneur Media, Inc.
Ed: Robert Kiyosaki. **Description:** Four personality types needed by entrepreneurs to drive their leadership in business are given. 'I must be liked' are social directors and go-betweens; 'I must be comfortable' are those who seek job security and are not at ease with deadlines; I must be right are those strong in opinion; and 'I must win' are people in charge.

23205 ■ "Point, Click, Buy" in *Barron's* (Vol. 90, September 6, 2010, No. 36, pp. 11)
Pub: Barron's Editorial & Corporate Headquarters
Ed: Vito J. Racanelli. **Description:** Non-travel online retail sales from January to July 2010 increased nine percent which indicates that online shopping for the coming holidays will be good. Online sales are outpacing traditional shopping, but pricing is still critical.

23206 ■ "PopCap Games Achieves Significant Increase in Return on Ad Spend With Omniture SearchCenter" in *Internet Wire* (September 15, 2009)
Pub: Comtex News Network, Inc.
Description: PopCap Games, a leading computer games provider, is using Omniture SearchCenter together with Omniture SiteCatalyst to increase revenue from its search engine marketing campaign. Omniture, Inc. is a leading provider of Internet business optimization software.

23207 ■ "Port Metro Vancouver Unveiled" in *Canadian Sailings* (July 7, 2008)
Pub: Commonwealth Business Media
Description: Vancouver Fraser Port Authority is marketing the port as Port Metro Vancouver; Along with the new name the port has announced additional strategies for continued growth and launched a new logo.

23208 ■ "Portfolio Recovery Associates Expands Its Hampton Call Center" in *Internet Wire* (January 20, 2010)
Pub: Comtex News Network, Inc.
Description: Entering into a lease amendment in order to expand its Hampton, Virginia call center and extend its lease agreement, Portfolio Recovery Associates, Inc., a company that collects, purchases and manages defaulted consumer debt, plans to upgrade the existing space enabling them to draw on local talent.

23209 ■ "Portland Wooing Under Armour to West Coast Facility" in *Baltimore Business Journal* (Vol. 27, January 29, 2010, No. 39, pp. 1)
Pub: American City Business Journals
Ed: Andy Giegerich. **Description:** Baltimore, Maryland sports apparel maker, Under Armour, is planning a west coast expansion with Portland, Oregon among the sites considered to house its apparel and footwear design center. Portland officials counting on the concentration of nearly 10,000 activewear workers in the city will help lure the company to the city.

23210 ■ "The Power Brokers" in *Crain's Chicago Business* (Vol. 31, April 28, 2008, No. 17, pp. 41)
Pub: Crain Communications, Inc.
Ed: Samantha Stainburn. **Description:** Profile of BlueStar Energy Services Inc., one of the first suppliers to cash in on the deregulation f the electricity market by the Illinois Legislature; last year BlueStar's revenue was $171.1 million, up from $600,000 in 2002, the year the company was founded.

23211 ■ "Power Partnerships" in *Business Courier* (Vol. 27, October 22, 2010, No. 25, pp. 1)
Pub: Business Courier
Ed: Lucy May. **Description:** The $400 million Harrah's casino and the $47 million redevelopment and expansion of Washington Park are project aimed at boosting the economy in downtown Cincinnati, Ohio. These projects will be done in cooperation with the National Association for the Advancement of Colored People. Insights into the role of minority-owned businesses in regional economic development are explored.

23212 ■ *The Power of Social Networking: Using the Whuffie Factor to Build Your Business*
Pub: Crown Business Books
Ed: Tara Hunt. **Released:** May 4, 2010. **Price:** $15.00. **Description:** This book shows how any small business can harness its power by increasing whuffie, the store of social capital that is the currency of the digital world. Blogs and social networks such as Facebook and Twitter are used to help grow any small firm.

23213 ■ "Price War: Managerial Salaries Are Beating the National Average, But Maybe Not for Long" in *Canadian Business* (March 31, 2008)
Pub: Rogers Media
Ed: Megan Harman. **Description:** Real average hourly earnings of managers increase by 20 percent in ten years as companies increase wages to avoid the risk of losing key managers to the competition and in preparation for the retirement of baby boomers. Tough market conditions affect management more since their incentives are tied to individual and corporate performance.

23214 ■ *Principled Profit: Marketing that Puts People First*
Pub: Accurate Writing & More
Ed: Shel Horowitz. **Price:** $17.50. **Description:** The importance for companies to market ethically and honestly is stressed. Quality marketing will build customer loyalty and that will translate into new customers and repeat business. A customer-retention strategy is outlined along with ideas to increase profits of any small business.

23215 ■ "Principles for Creating Growth in Challenging Times" in *Agency Sales Magazine* (Vol. 39, September-October 2009, No. 9, pp. 35)
Pub: MANA
Ed: Robert Goshen. **Description:** Creating a productive environment is one vital key for businesses to utilize during the challenging times that arise due to a weak economy; other important factors include maintaining a good relationship with the staff, responding appropriately to challenges and keeping a sense of humor.

23216 ■ "Priority: Recessionade" in *Inc.* (February 2008, pp. 19-20)
Pub: Gruner & Jahr USA Publishing
Ed: Amy Feldman. **Description:** Despite signs of inflation, entrepreneurs see these tough economic times as an opportunity to start or grow their businesses. Five entrepreneurs share insight into ways this economic downturn can work to grow their businesses.

23217 ■ "Private Label Manufacturers Association" in *Ice Cream Reporter* (Vol. 23, July 20, 2010, No. 8, pp. 7)
Pub: Ice Cream Reporter
Description: Branded frozen dessert manufacturers sold more frozen desserts in terms of sales volume and revenue and market share in 2009. Statistical details included.

23218 ■ "Procter & Gamble Boosts Bet on Exclusive Brands" in *Business Courier* (Vol. 27, July 9, 2010, No. 10, pp. 1)
Pub: Business Courier
Ed: Jon Newberry. **Description:** Procter & Gamble is creating more special versions of its brands such as Pringles and Pampers exclusively for retail partners such as Tesco in the U.K. The greater push towards this direction is seen as a way to regain market share.

23219 ■ "Profit Predictions Look Too Plump" in *Barron's* (Vol. 88, March 31, 2008, No. 13, pp. 37)
Pub: Dow Jones & Company, Inc.
Ed: Johanna Bennett. **Description:** Full-year forecast points to a 14 percent gain for 2008 but the second-half profit increases would have to grow at a fast rate and peak at 61 percent in the fourth quarter to achieve this. Trends in the U.S. economic conditions are also discussed.

23220 ■ "Profit Strong Rona to Maintain Acquisition Strategy" in *Globe & Mail* (February 22, 2007, pp. B14)
Pub: CTVglobemedia Publishing Inc.
Description: Canada-based Rona Inc., home improvement retailer that reported record annual profit in 2006, will continue its strategy of acquisitions. The company has reported profits of $190.6 million in 2006.

23221 ■ "The Profitability of Mobility" in *Entrepreneur* (Vol. 37, September 2009, No. 9, pp. 98)
Pub: Entrepreneur Media, Inc.
Ed: John Daley. **Description:** Wireless Zone franchisee Jonah Engler says he manages the business by hiring managers that could do the job. He has given his employees small equity ownership in the company. He also says great service and referrals have contributed to his business' growth.

23222 ■ *Profits Aren't Everything. They're the Only Thing: No-Nonsense Rules from the Ultimate Contrarian and Small Business Guru*
Pub: HarperCollins Publishers
Ed: George Cloutier. **Released:** September 9, 2010. **Price:** $24.99. **Description:** In difficult economic times, the only way for small businesses to survive is to maximize profits. Thirteen steps to maximize profits in a slow economy are outlined.

23223 ■ "Project Could Forge Path to Jobs, Growth" in *Business Courier* (Vol. 26, September 11, 2009, No. 20, pp. 1)
Pub: American City Business Journals, Inc.
Ed: Lucy May. **Description:** The planned 13.5 mile Mill Creek Greenway Trail extension could create 445 jobs and bring $52 million to the economy of Cincinnati, Ohio. The trail extension would cost $24 million and would be used for recreational purposes.

23224 ■ "PRWT Service Acquires Pharmaceutical Plant: Firm Wins Multimillion-Dollar Contract with Merck" in *Black Enterprise* (March 2008)
Pub: Earl G. Graves Publishing Co. Inc.
Ed: Tamara E. Holmes. **Description:** PRWT Services Inc. expanded through its acquisition of a chemical manufacturing plant in New Jersey. The Whitehouse Station, part of Merck & Co. Inc. produces active pharmaceutical ingredients for antibiotics, making PRWT the first minority-owned company in the U.S. to manufacture active pharmaceutical ingredients.

23225 ■ "Public Media Works to Launch DVD Kiosk Operations in Toronto, Canada" in *Internet Wire* (November 15, 2010)
Pub: Comtex
Description: Public Media Works Inc. along with its EntertainmentXpress Inc., have partnered with Spot Venture Distribution Inc. and Signifi Solutions Inc., both headquartered in Toronto, Canada, to manage and expand the Spot DVD movie and game kiosk business in greater Toronto and other Canadian locations.

23226 ■ "Public Opinion" in *Entrepreneur* (Vol. 36, April 2008, No. 4, pp. 28)
Pub: Entrepreneur Media, Inc.
Ed: Aliza Sherman. **Description:** According to a 2007 report from Group and Organization Management, women in top positions can lead publicly traded companies to stock price and earnings growth. Some women business owners say that going public has provided them with the capital to grow. Details on the potential of women-managed publicly traded companies are discussed.

23227 ■ "Pumping in Africa" in *Canadian Business* (Vol. 79, October 23, 2006, No. 21, pp. 162)
Pub: Rogers Media
Ed: Jeff Sanford. **Description:** EastCoast Energy Corp.'s business venture of opening a natural gas company based in Tanzania and marketing of natural gas to expanding markets in East Africa is discussed.

23228 ■ "Putting 'Extra' in Extra-Silky Shampoo" in *Crain's Chicago Business* (Vol. 31, April 28, 2008, No. 17, pp. 37)
Pub: Crain Communications, Inc.
Ed: Phuong Ly. **Description:** Profile of HallStar Co., a Chicago-based company which develops and manufactures specialty chemicals to upgrade existing products such as hair dye, lotion and deodorant. HallStar has seen its annual earnings rise more than 30 percent since 2002.

23229 ■ "Putting 'Great' Back Into A&P" in *Crain's New York Business* (Vol. 24, January 7, 2008, No. 1, pp. 3)
Pub: Crain Communications, Inc.
Description: After five straight years ending in 2005, A&P Grocery lost revenue; due to a sweeping plan to freshen up its supermarkets the company returned to growth mode and was able to acquire longtime competitor Pathmark Stores.

23230 ■ "Putting the Service-Profit Chain to Work" in *Harvard Business Review* (Vol. 86, July-August 2008, No. 8, pp. 118)
Pub: Harvard Business School Press
Ed: James L. Heskett; Thomas O. Jones; Gary W. Loveman; W. Earl Sasser Jr.; Leonard A. Schlesinger. **Description:** Advice is given on how to foster profitability in service businesses. Topics include the link between employee satisfaction and customer satisfaction, internal service quality, external service value, and revenue growth.

23231 ■ "The Puzzle of Our Productivity" in *Canadian Business* (Vol. 83, September 14, 2010, No. 15, pp. 22)
Pub: Rogers Media Ltd.
Ed: Rachel Madison. **Description:** Industry Canada economist Annette Ryan revealed in a presentation to the Canadian Association for Business Economics that growth in Canadian labor productivity has steadily declined since the 1980s. Ryan believes that business decisions have played an important role in the poor productivity results. Other details of the findings are presented.

23232 ■ "Qualcomm Could Win Big as the IPhone 3G Calls" in *Barron's* (Vol. 88, July 4, 2008, No. 28, pp. 30)
Pub: Dow Jones & Co., Inc.
Ed: Eric J. Savitz. **Description:** Apple iPhone 3G's introduction could widen the smartphone market thereby benefiting handset chipmaker Qualcomm in the process. Qualcomm Senior V.P., Bill Davidson sees huge potential for his company's future beyond phones with their Snapdragon processor. The prospects of Sun Microsystems' shares are also discussed.

23233 ■ "Quantivo Empowers Online Media Companies to Immediately Expand Audiences and Grow Online Profits" in *Internet Wire* (Nov. 18, 2009)
Pub: Comtex News Network, Inc.
Description: Quantivo, the leader in on-demand Behavioral Analytics, has launched a new solution that includes 22 of the most critical Internet audience behavior insights as out-of-the-box reports; Internet marketers need to understand their audience, what they want and how often to offer it to them in order to gain successful branding and campaigns online.

23234 ■ *Raising Capital*
Pub: Kiplinger Books and Tapes
Ed: Andrew J. Sherman. **Price:** $34.95. **Description:** Corporate attorney provides a comprehensive guide using in-depth, practical advice on raising money to start and grow a business. A 115-page appendix contains samples of financing agreements, forms and questionnaires.

23235 ■ "R&R Ice Cream" in *Ice Cream Reporter* (Vol. 23, November 20, 2010, No. 12, pp. 8)
Pub: Ice Cream Reporter
Description: R&R Ice Cream, the United Kingdom's largest ice cream manufacturer, has completed a private offering of senior secured notes that has raised 298 million (pounds sterling) to fund expansion and acquisitions.

23236 ■ "R&R Launches Upscale Spoony's and Low Fat Dragon's Den" in *Ice Cream Reporter* (Vol. 23, August 20, 2010, No. 9, pp. 3)
Pub: Ice Cream Reporter
Description: European ice cream manufacturer R&R has acquired French ice cream maker Rolland and will position itself as an upscale challenger to brands like Ben & Jerry's.

23237 ■ "The RBC Dynasty Continues" in *Globe & Mail* (January 30, 2006, pp. B1)
Pub: CTVglobemedia Publishing Inc.
Ed: Gordon Pitts. **Description:** The details on business growth of Royal Bank of Canada, under chief executive officer Gordon Nixon, are presented.

23238 ■ "RBC's Hot Foreign Operations Contribute to Record Profit" in *Globe & Mail* (March 3, 2007, pp. B3)
Pub: CTVglobemedia Publishing Inc.
Ed: Andrew Willis. **Description:** Royal Bank of Canada posted 27.6 percent growth in the final quarter of 2006. The bank posted $1.49 billion in profits.

23239 ■ "Ready To Take Your Business Global?" in *Black Enterprise* (Vol. 41, August 2010, No. 1, pp. 89)
Pub: Earl G. Graves Publishing Co. Inc.
Ed: Alan Hughes. **Description:** The 2010 Black Enterprise Entrepreneurs Conference held in May stressed the need for all small firms to promote a global agenda in order to stay competitive.

23240 ■ "Real Estate Wheeling and Dealing Picks Up" in *Business Journal Portland* (Vol. 27, October 29, 2010, No. 35, pp. 1)
Pub: Portland Business Journal
Ed: Wendy Culverwell. **Description:** LoopNet has listed 33 prominent commercial properties for sale in Portland, Oregon's real estate market. However, reasons for the sales rush are not totally clear, but speculations point to the end of the Bush tax cuts in 2010 that prompted real estate investors to close the deals and avoid the increase in capital gains taxes.

23241 ■ "Recent Deals Signal an M&A Resurgence" in *Austin Business JournalInc.* (Vol. 29, January 22, 2010, No. 46, pp. 1)
Pub: American City Business Journals
Ed: Jacob Dirr. **Description:** The acquisition of at least six Austin, Texas technology companies reflects the growing acquisition activity in the US. Corporations have bought 86 companies and spent $7.3 billion during the fourth quarter of 2009. Insights into the impact of the acquisition activity to Austin's entrepreneurial energy are also given.

23242 ■ "Red Mango Set to Grow in Florida" in *Ice Cream Reporter* (Vol. 23, September 20, 2010, No. 10, pp. 2)
Pub: Ice Cream Reporter
Description: Red Mango will add 12 new locations throughout Florida. The stores offer healthy, nutritious frozen yogurt, smoothies and parfaits.

23243 ■ "Rediscovering the Land of Opportunity" in *Green Industry Pro* (July 2011)
Pub: Cygnus Business Media
Ed: Gregg Wartgow. **Description:** Landscape contractors need to discover new strategies that will generate leads and convert those leads into sales.

23244 ■ "Remodeled Stores Help Fabric Retailer Stitch Up Profit Growth" in *Investor's Business Daily* (January 7, 2010, pp. A06)
Pub: Investor's Business Daily
Ed: Marilyn Much. **Description:** Overview of the successful plan implemented by Darrell Webb for Jo-Ann Fabric and Craft stores to stimulate growth and generate revenue; changes include better inventory controls and remodeling; statistical data included.

23245 ■ "A Renewal in Rentals" in *Barron's* (Vol. 88, March 17, 2008, No. 11, pp. 17)
Pub: Dow Jones & Company, Inc.
Ed: Description: Discusses the projected entry of the estimated 82 million echo-boomers into the rentals market and the influx of immigrants and displaced homeowners which could turn apartments into lucrative investments again. While apartment-building completions rose slowly since 2003, demand is expected to increase steeply until 2015.

23246 ■ "Renewed Vision" in *Hawaii Business* (Vol. 54, August 2008, No. 2, pp. 49)
Pub: Hawaii Business Publishing
Ed: Jason Ubay. **Description:** Saint Francis Healthcare System of Hawaii, ranked 81 in Hawaii's top 250 companies for 2008, has been rebranding to focus on senior community healthcare and sold some of its operations, which explains the decline in gross sales from $219.5M in 2006 to $122.7M in 2007. The system's senior services and home hospice service expansion are provided.

23247 ■ *Renovate Before You Innovate: Why Doing the New Thing Might Not Be the Right Thing*
Pub: Portfolio Publishing
Ed: Sergio Zyman, with Armin A Brott. **Released:** Octobr 4, 2004. **Description:** The author uses his experience as the manager behind the introduction to the New Coke as an example of a lazy business growth strategy. He offers insight into successful growth strategies for any small business owner.

23248 ■ "Rental Demand Boosts Revenue for Sun Communities Inc." in *Crain's Detroit Business* (Vol. 24, March 24, 2008, No. 12, pp. 4)
Pub: Crain Communications, Inc.
Ed: Daniel Duggan. **Description:** Despite the decline in sales of manufactured homes, demand for rental units and rent-to-own programs have brought Sun Communities Inc. increased revenue. The real estate investment trust, based in Southfield, owns, operates, finances and develops manufactured home communities in the Midwest and Southeast. Statistical data included.

23249 ■ "Reply! Grows at Unprecedented Rate, Rips Beta Off Its Marketplace" in *Marketing Weekly News* (September 19, 2009, pp. 149)
Pub: Investment Weekly News
Description: Profile of Reply.com, a leader in locally-targeted Internet marketing, announced significant growth in terms of revenue, enhanced features and services and new categories since launching its beta Reply! Marketplace platform. Even in the face of an economic downturn, the company has posted over 50 percent revenue growth in the Real Estate and Automotive categories.

23250 ■ "Retail in Austin Strong, Will Continue to Be" in *Austin Business JournalInc.* (Vol. 29, January 22, 2010, No. 46, pp. 1)
Pub: American City Business Journals
Ed: Jacob Dirr. **Description:** Retail sector in Austin, Texas has outpaced the national average in value, mid-tier, high-end and drugs retail sectors, according to a report by Pitney Bowes. The national consulting firm's report has projected growth in every sector until the end of fiscal 2012. Data regarding other sectors is also included.

23251 ■ "Retail Franchises to Start Now" in *Entrepreneur* (Vol. 37, August 2009, No. 8, pp. 88)
Pub: Entrepreneur Media, Inc.
Ed: Tracy Stapp. **Description:** Listing of retail franchises is presented and is categorized based on their products sold. The total cost of the franchise and the website are also included as well as additional statistical data.

23252 ■ "Retail Slump Deflates Local Development" in *Business Courier* (Vol. 24, February 29, 2008, No. 47, pp. 1)
Pub: American City Business Journals, Inc.
Ed: Lisa Biank Fasig. **Description:** 2007 sales of the retail industry are the slowest since the year 2003, driving retail stores to reconsider their expansion plans for 2008. A number of retail projects have been delayed, cancelled or altered, including Newport

Pavilion, Rivers Crossing, Wal-Mart Supercenters, Legacy Place and Millworks. The impacts of retail slowdown on development projects are analyzed further.

23253 ■ "Ric Elis/Dan Feldstein" in *Charlotte Business Journal* (Vol. 25, December 31, 2010, No. 41, pp. 6)
Pub: Charlotte Business Journal
Ed: Ken Elkins. **Description:** Charlotte, North Carolina-based Internet marketing firm Red Ventures has grown significantly. General Atlantic has purchased stakes in Red Ventures.

23254 ■ *Riches in Niches: How to Make It Big in a Small Market*
Pub: Career Press, Inc.
Ed: Susan Friedmann. **Released:** May 10, 2007. **Price:** $21.99. **Description:** The multiple factors that separate the experts from the service professionals who may actually have betters skills, but are never heard about, are discussed. The seven secrets every entrepreneur should know are listed.

23255 ■ "Riding High" in *Small Business Opportunities* (November 2008)
Pub: Entrepreneur Media Inc.
Ed: Stan Roberts. **Description:** Profile of David Sanborn who found a way to turn his passion for biking into a moneymaking opportunity by opening his own bicycle shops; Sanborn's goal is to become the largest independent bike retailer in the United States.

23256 ■ "Right From the Start" in *Small Business Opportunities* (July 2010)
Pub: Harris Publications Inc.
Ed: Ed Krug. **Description:** Ed Krug from Pitch Blue provides sales support services by partnering with small and mid-sized companies to set and reach new revenue targets.

23257 ■ "RIM's Test of Faith" in *Canadian Business* (Vol. 80, April 9, 2007, No. 8, pp. 29)
Pub: Rogers Media
Ed: Joe Castaldo. **Description:** The growth of Research In Motion Ltd. in terms of its sales and profits despite a patent suit on it and competition of rivals is discussed.

23258 ■ "Rise in Occupancy Rate Fuels Area Hotel Building Boom" in *Crain's Detroit Business* (Vol. 24, March 10, 2008, No. 10, pp. 14)
Pub: Crain Communications, Inc.
Ed: Jonathan Eppley. **Description:** Due to a rise in the region's yearly occupancy rate, a number of new hotel construction and renovation projects are slated for the Detroit area.

23259 ■ "Rising in the East; Research and Development" in *The Economist* (Vol. 390, January 3, 2009, No. 8612, pp. 47)
Pub: The Economist Newspaper Inc.
Description: Impressive growth of the technological research and development in Asian countries is discussed. Statistical data included.

23260 ■ *Risk Takers and Innovators, Great Canadian Business Ventures Since 1950*
Pub: Altitude Publishing
Ed: Sandra Phinney. **Released:** June 15, 2004. **Price:** $7.95. **Description:** Successful business leaders share their creativity, technology skills, and entrepreneurship.

23261 ■ "The Road Map for Scotiabank's Asian Expansion" in *Globe & Mail* (April 7, 2007, pp. B3)
Pub: CTVglobemedia Publishing Inc.
Ed: Tara Perkins. **Description:** Executive vice-president of Bank of Nova Scotia, Rob Pitfield shares his plan to expand the bank's Asian market.

23262 ■ "Roger Rechler Played Major Role in Long Island's Evolution" in *Commercial Property News* (March 17, 2008)
Pub: Nielsen Company
Description: Profile of Roger Rechler, real estate developer on Long Island, New York, is presented. Rechler, who died in March 2008, was instrumental in the development, ownership and operations of the largest commercial real estate portfolio on Long Island.

23263 ■ "The Role of Human and Financial Capital in the Profitability and Growth of Women-Owned Small Firms" in *Journal of Small Business Management*
Pub: Blackwell Publishing, Inc.
Ed: Susan Coleman. **Description:** Examines the relationship between the human and financial capital in both men and women-owned businesses and firm performance in the service and retail sectors.

23264 ■ "Roseville Ob-Gyn Group Grows With Patient Focus, Diverse Services" in *Crain's Detroit Business* (Vol. 24, April 7, 2008, No. 14)
Pub: Crain Communications, Inc.
Ed: Christine Snyder. **Description:** According to the American Medical Association, the number of medical groups of 10 or more physicians has been growing. Eastside Gynecology Obstetrics is one such group which has seen its yearly revenue grow due to a good business plan and a diversity of services and doctors.

23265 ■ "Roundy' Pushing Chicago Expansion" in *Milwaukee Business Journal* (Vol. 27, February 12, 2010, No. 20, pp. A1)
Pub: American City Business Journals
Ed: Rich Kirchen. **Description:** Roundy Supermarkets Inc. is expanding in Chicago, Illinois as the Milwaukee-based company is set to open one store in downtown Chicago and another in the Arlington suburb. The store openings have been pushed back to spring and early summer in 2010 due to the economic downturn.

23266 ■ "Rule of the Masses: Reinventing Fashion Via Crowdsourcing" in *WWD* (Vol. 200, July 26, 2010, No. 17, pp. 1)
Pub: Conde Nast Publications Inc.
Ed: Cate T. Corcoran. **Description:** Large apparel brands and retailers are crowdsourcing as a way to increase customer loyalty and to build their businesses.

23267 ■ "S2C Global Installs Its First Mass Production Aquaduct Unit in North America" in *Canadian Corporate News* (May 16, 2007)
Pub: Comtex News Network Inc.
Description: S2C Global Systems, a leader of distributing 5-gallon bottled water units to the consumer, has announced the installation of its first mass production Aquaduct in Surrey, British Columbia.

23268 ■ "Sabathia Deal Makes Dollars and Sense" in *The Business Journal-Milwaukee* (Vol. 25, July 11, 2008, No. 42, pp. A1)
Pub: American City Business Journals, Inc.
Ed: Mark Kass. **Description:** It was reported that the Milwaukee Brewers' acquisition of CC Sabathia will mean that the team will pick up an estimated $5 million in salary that Sabathia is owed for the remainder of the season. Because of this, the team will not make a profit in 2008. The acquisition of Sabathia is expected to cause an increase in attendance and merchandise revenue over the remainder of the season.

23269 ■ "Salad Creations To Open 2nd Location" in *Crain's Detroit Business* (Vol. 24, March 3, 2008, No. 9, pp. 26)
Pub: Crain Communications Inc. - Detroit
Ed: Brent Snavely. **Description:** Salad Creations, a franchise restaurant that allows customers to create their own salads and also offers soups and sandwiches; Salad Creations plans to open a total of five locations by the end of 2008.

23270 ■ "Sales Gave W&S Record '07" in *Business Courier* (Vol. 24, March 14, 2008, No. 49, pp. 1)
Pub: American City Business Journals, Inc.
Ed: Jon Newberry. **Description:** Western & Southern Financial Group was able to achieve a record $365 million in net income thanks in large part to the double-digit increases in profits by its W&S Agency Group field offices and non-insurance businesses. The sale of their Integrated Investment Services Subsidiary and shares in several Marriot hotels also added to the record profit.

23271 ■ *Salesforce.com Secrets of Success: Best Practices for Growth and Profitability*
Pub: Prentice Hall Business Publishing
Ed: David Taber. **Released:** May 15, 2009. **Price:** $34.99. **Description:** Guide for using Salesforce.com; it provides insight into navigating through user groups, management, sales, marketing and IT departments in order to achieve the best results.

23272 ■ "Samsung's Metamorphosis" in *Austin Business Journal* (Vol. 31, May 20, 2011, No. 11, pp. 1)
Pub: American City Business Journals Inc.
Ed: Christopher Calnan. **Description:** Samsung Austin Semiconductor LP, a developer of semiconductors for smartphones and tablet computers, plans to diversify its offerings to include niche products: flash memory devices and microprocessing devices. In light of this strategy, Samsung Austin will be hiring 300 engineers as part of a $3.6 billion expansion of its plant.

23273 ■ "Saratoga Eagle Project Quenches Thirst To Grow" in *Business Review, Albany New York* (Vol. 34, November 30, 2007, No. 35, pp. 3)
Pub: American City Business Journals, Inc.
Ed: Robin K. Cooper. **Description:** Saratoga Eagle Sales and Service will be searching for contractors for the construction of its new beverage distribution center at the WJ Grande Industrial Park in Saratoga Springs, New York. The $8 million, 107,000 square foot facility is part of Saratoga Eagle's expansion plan. The company's growth in the Capital Region market and $1.3 million tax break are discussed.

23274 ■ "Saudi Overtures" in *The Business Journal-Portland* (Vol. 25, August 15, 2008, No. 23, pp. 1)
Pub: American City Business Journals, Inc.
Ed: Aliza Earnshaw. **Description:** Saudi Arabia's huge revenue from oil is creating opportunities for Oregon companies as the country develops new cities, industrial zones, and tourism centers. Oregon exported only $46.8 million worth of goods to Saudi Arabia in 2007 but the kingdom is interested in green building materials and methods, renewable energy and water quality control, and nanotechnology all of which Oregon has expertise in.

23275 ■ "Scotiabank Targets More Baby Boomers" in *Globe & Mail* (March 4, 2006, pp. B5)
Pub: CTVglobemedia Publishing Inc.
Ed: Elizabeth Church. **Description:** Bank of Nova Scotia posted $844 million profit for first quarter 2006. The plans of the bank to achieve baby boomer client base are presented.

23276 ■ "Scripps' Dinner Bell" in *Business Courier* (Vol. 24, October 19, 2008, No. 27, pp. 1)
Pub: American City Business Journals, Inc.
Ed: Dan Monk. **Description:** Discusses the split of E.W. Scripps Co.'s Food Network into a separate publicly traded company Scripps Networks Interactive could produce expansion into Asia and Europe.

23277 ■ "Sean Durfy" in *Canadian Business* (Vol. 80, April 23, 2007, No. 9, pp. 14)
Pub: Rogers Media
Ed: Michelle Magnan. **Description:** Sean Durfy, president of WestJet Airlines Ltd., feels that marketing is essential factor for growth of airline industry.

23278 ■ "Sears' Profit Result Puts Ball in Parent's Court" in *Globe & Mail* (February 3, 2006, pp. B4)
Pub: CTVglobemedia Publishing Inc.
Ed: Marina Strauss. **Description:** Sears Canada Inc. achieved $783.4 million in profits for fourth quarter 2005. The financial performance of the company paves way for the acquisition of Sears Holdings Corp.

23279 ■ "Second to None" in *Crain's Detroit Business* (Vol. 26, January 18, 2010, No. 3, pp. 9)
Pub: Crain Communications, Inc.
Ed: Nancy Kaffer. **Description:** Second-stage companies are beginning to attract more attention from government entities and the business community

alike, due in part to their ability to create jobs more rapidly than their counterparts both smaller and larger. Second-stage companies have between 10-99 employees and consistently have supplied the most jobs, despite overall job declines in recent years.

23280 ■ "Secret Ingredient" in *Entrepreneur* (Vol. 35, November 2007, No. 11, pp. 172)
Pub: Entrepreneur Media Inc.
Ed: Sara Wilson. **Description:** Ojon Corporation in Burlington, Ontario, Canada has developed a natural hair- and skin-care line from ojon oil. The oil, which has very good restorative effects on hair, is extracted from nuts found in ojon trees in the rainforests of Honduras. Details on how Ojon Corporation started and its growing venture in the market are outlined.

23281 ■ "Secrets To Trade Show Success" in *Women Entrepreneur* (September 12, 2008)
Pub: Entrepreneur Media Inc.
Ed: Lesley Spencer Pyle. **Description:** Trade shows require an enormous amount of work, but they are an investment that can pay off handsomely because they allow a business to get their product or service in front of their target market. Advice regarding trade shows is given including selecting the correct venue, researching the affair and following up on leads obtained at the event.

23282 ■ "Sedo Keeps Trucking in Good Times and Bad" in *Crain's Chicago Business* (Vol. 31, April 28, 2008, No. 17, pp. 35)
Pub: Crain Communications, Inc.
Ed: Samantha Stainburn. **Description:** Discusses Seko Worldwide Inc., an Itasca-based freight forwarder, and its complicated road to growth and expansion on a global scale.

23283 ■ "SEEing an Opportunity; Golden's Eyewear Chain Has a National Vision" in *Crain's Detroit Business* (Vol. 24, January 7, 2008, No. 1)
Pub: Crain Communications Inc. - Detroit
Ed: Sheena Harrison. **Description:** Richard Golden, who recently sold D.O.C. Optics Corporation is planning to build a new national eyewear chain called SEE Inc., which stands for Selective Eyewear Elements. SEE will sell expensive-looking glasses at lower prices than designer styles.

23284 ■ "Seeking Local SBA Loan?" in *Business Courier* (Vol. 26, October 16, 2009, No. 25, pp. 1)
Pub: American City Business Journals, Inc.
Ed: Steve Watkins. **Description:** The largest banks in Greater Cincinnati reduced Small Business Administration (SBA) lending by 41 percent for the fiscal year ended September 2009. For the year, local SBA loans from all banks in the area declined 25 percent. The importance of SBA loans for growth of small business is examined.

23285 ■ "Sense of Discovery" in *Business Journal Portland* (Vol. 27, November 19, 2010, No. 38, pp. 1)
Pub: Portland Business Journal
Ed: Erik Siemers. **Description:** Tigard, Oregon-based Exterro Inc. CEO Bobby Balachandran announced plans to go public without the help of an institutional investor. Balachandran believes Exterro could grow to a $100 million legal compliance software company in the span of three years. Insights on Exterro's growth as market leader in the $1 billion legal governance software market are also given.

23286 ■ "Seton Grows Heart Institute" in *Austin Business Journal* (Vol. 31, July 15, 2011, No. 19, pp. A1)
Pub: American City Business Journals Inc.
Ed: Sandra Zaragoza. **Description:** Seton Heart Institute experienced significant growth in the last six months. The organization added physicians, specialists and outreach offices across Central Texas.

23287 ■ "A Shallow Pool" in *Canadian Business* (Vol. 81, Summer 2008, No. 9, pp. 44)
Pub: Rogers Media Ltd.
Ed: Joe Castaldo. **Description:** Bank of Canada projected in its 'Monetary Policy Report' a growth rate of 1.4 percent in 2008 and does not expect the economy to fully recover until mid-2010. The Canadian stock market has been recovering although slowly with just a 1.6 percent gain by April 30. Other details on the Canadian equity market are presented.

23288 ■ "Shear Profit" in *Crain's Cleveland Business* (Vol. 28, October 29, 2007, No. 43, pp. 3)
Pub: Crain Communications, Inc.
Ed: David Bennett. **Description:** Alpaca farms are becoming a very profitable business for a number of Northeast Ohio entrepreneurs due to the high return on initial investments, tax incentives and the rise in demand for the animals. Ohio leads the country in the number of alpaca farms with roughly one-third located in Northeast Ohio.

23289 ■ "Shell Profit Top $2 Billion as Oil Sands Output Surges" in *Globe & Mail* (January 26, 2006, pp. B6)
Pub: CTVglobemedia Publishing Inc.
Ed: Patrick Brethour. **Description:** The reasons behind posting of $2 billion profits for 2005, by Shell Canada Ltd. are presented.

23290 ■ "Shoestring-Budget Marketing" in *Women Entrepreneur* (January 5, 2009)
Pub: Entrepreneur Media Inc.
Ed: Maria Falconer. **Description:** Pay-per-click search engine advertising is the traditional type of e-marketing that may not only be too expensive for certain kinds of businesses but also may not attract the quality customer base a business looking to grow needs to find. Social networking websites have become a mandatory marketing tool for business owners who want to see growth in their sales; tips are provided for utilizing these networking websites in order to gain more visibility on the Internet which can, in turn, lead to the more sales.

23291 ■ "Shopped Out; Retailing Gloom" in *The Economist* (Vol. 390, January 3, 2009, No. 8612, pp. 26)
Pub: The Economist Newspaper Inc.
Description: Economic volatility in the retail sector is having an impact on a number of countries around the globe. Europe is experiencing hard economic times as well and unless businesses have a strong business plan banks feel unable to lend the money necessary to tide the retailers over. The falling pound has increased the cost of imported goods and small to midsize retail chains may not be able to weather such an unforgiving economic climate.

23292 ■ "Should You Invest in the Long Tail?" in *Harvard Business Review* (Vol. 86, July-August 2008, No. 8, pp. 88)
Pub: Harvard Business School Press
Ed: Anita Elberse. **Description:** Relevance of the long tail, or the sustainability of sales after a given product's launch is examined. It is posited that niche sales are not as sustainable as those for products with broader appeal.

23293 ■ "Show Me the Love" in *Canadian Business* (Vol. 79, November 6, 2006, No. 22, pp. 77)
Pub: Rogers Media
Ed: Jeannette Hanna. **Description:** The strategies to improve brand image with relation to success of Tim Horton's brand are presented.

23294 ■ "Sign Up To Grow Your Business, Generate Jobs" in *Women Entrepreneur* (November 25, 2008)
Pub: Entrepreneur Media Inc.
Ed: Eve Gumpel. **Description:** Nell Merlino has announced the new Make Mine A Million-Dollar Race, which aims to encourage hundreds of thousands of women entrepreneurs to grow their business to revenue goals of $250,00, $500,000 or $1 million and more as well as create 800,000 new jobs in an attempt to stimulate the nation's economy.

23295 ■ "The Silvery Moon Moves to Larger Space" in *Bellingham Business Journal* (Vol. March 2010, pp. 5)
Pub: Sound Publishing Inc.
Description: Jewelry store, the Silvery Moon, moved to a larger location in order to expand its business. The new location was chosen because it offers the firm more visibility. The store offers find silver and gold pieces and specializes in Pacific Northwest native jewelry.

23296 ■ "Six Leading Economists on What to Expect in the Year Ahead: Glen Hodgson; Canada in Depth" in *Canadian Business* (December 24, 2007)
Pub: Rogers Media
Ed: Glen Hodgson. **Description:** Western Canada is expected to have the best economic performance for 2008 among all of the country's regions with a growth rate of 3.6 percent for Alberta and three percent for British Columbia. Details on the country's growth in real income, trends in the labor market, and the effect of Canadian dollar's parity with the U.S. dollar on exports are discussed.

23297 ■ "Six Leading Economists on What to Expect in the Year Ahead: Peter Buchanan" in *Canadian Business* (December 24, 2007)
Pub: Rogers Media
Ed: Peter Buchanan. **Description:** The world economy is expected to grow by five percent in 2008, which is below the pace of the previous two years. Details on the U.S. credit crunch, the U.S. dollar's depreciation, and the economic expansion of developing economies are discussed.

23298 ■ "Size Matters" in *Entrepreneur* (Vol. 36, April 2008, No. 4, pp. 44)
Pub: Entrepreneur Media, Inc.
Ed: Robert Kiyosaki. **Description:** Entrepreneurs planning to expand their business face challenges when it comes to employing more people and addressing internal relationships, communications and procedures. People skills, organizational skills and leadership skills are some of the things to consider before adding employees.

23299 ■ "Skinner's No Drive-Thru CEO" in *Crain's Chicago Business* (Vol. 31, April 28, 2008, No. 17, pp. 1)
Pub: Crain Communications, Inc.
Ed: David Sterrett. **Description:** Profile of James Skinner who was named CEO for McDonald's Corp. in November 2004 and has proved to be a successful leader despite the number of investors who doubted him when he came to the position. Mr. Skinner has overseen three years of unprecedented sales growth and launched the biggest menu expansion in 30 years.

23300 ■ "The Skype's the Limit" in *Canadian Business* (Vol. 80, February 12, 2007, No. 4, pp. 70)
Pub: Rogers Media
Ed: Gerry Blackwell. **Description:** The increase in the market share of Skype Technologies S.A.'s Internet phone service to 171 million users is discussed.

23301 ■ "The Small 300" in *Canadian Business* (Vol. 81, Summer 2008, No. 9, pp. 137)
Pub: Rogers Media Ltd.
Description: Small cap-companies are ranked based on market capitalization and stock performance. Calgary-based Grande Cache Coal Corp. topped the roster with 1,000 percent of return resulting from strong sales. A table showing the 2008 rankings of the companies is presented.

23302 ■ "Small Business Capital Outlays" in *Small Business Economic Trends* (January 2008, pp. 16)
Pub: National Federation of Independent Business
Description: Graph representing actual and planned capital expenditures among small businesses surveyed in the U.S. from January 1986 to December 2007 is given. Tables showing actual capital expenditures, type of capital expenditures made, amount of capital expenditures made, and capital expenditure plans are also presented.

23303 ■ *Small Business Cash Flow: Strategies for Making Your Business a Financial Success*
Pub: John Wiley & Sons, Incorporated
Ed: Denise O'Berry. **Released:** October 2006. **Price:** $19.95. **Description:** Tips to help small businesses manage money are given.

23304 ■ *Small Business for Dummies, 3rd Ed.*
Pub: John Wiley and Sons, Inc.

Ed: Eric Tyson; Jim Schell. **Released:** March 2008. **Price:** $21.99. **Description:** Guidebook for anyone wanting to start or grow a small business; topics include information financing, budgeting, marketing, management and more.

23305 ■ "Small Business Earnings" in *Small Business Economic Trends* (March 2008, pp. 6)
Pub: National Federation of Independent Business

Ed: William C. Dunkelberg, Holly Wade. **Description:** Two tables and a graph representing the earnings of small businesses in the U.S. are presented. Statistics for actual earnings changes are provided. The figures in the graph include data from 1986 to 2008.

23306 ■ *Small Business: Innovation, Problems and Strategies*
Pub: Nova Science Publishers, Inc.

Ed: John E. Michaels, Leonardo F. Piraro. **Released:** April 1, 2009. **Price:** $89.00. **Description:** Innovation is a fundamental determinant of value creation in businesses and can also be a key to successful economic growth. The innovative process and innovative effort of small companies are examined and evaluated, along with alternative strategies.

23307 ■ "Small Business Outlook" in *Small Business Economic Trends* (July 2010, pp. 4)
Pub: National Federation of Independent Business

Description: A graph representing outlook among small businesses surveyed in the U.S. from January 1986 to June 2010 is presented. Tables showing small business outlook for expansion and outlook for general business conditions from January 2005 to June 2010, and most important reasons for expansion outlook are also given.

23308 ■ "Small Business Prices" in *Small Business Economic Trends* (July 2010, pp. 8)
Pub: National Federation of Independent Business

Description: A graph from a survey of small businesses in the U.S. is given representing business prices from January 1986 to June 2010. Actual prices (last three months) and planned prices (next three months) were compared in the graph. Tables of actual price changes and price plans from January 2005 to June 2010 are also supplied.

23309 ■ "Small Business Sales" in *Small Business Economic Trends* (July 2010, pp. 7)
Pub: National Federation of Independent Business

Description: A graph from a survey of small businesses in the U.S. is given representing sales from January 1986 to June 2010. Actual sales (prior three months) and expected sales (next three months) were compared in the graph. Tables of actual sales changes and sales expectations from January 2005 to June 2010 are also given.

23310 ■ *Small Business Savvy*
Pub: Adams Media Corporation

Ed: Norma J. Rist; Katina Z. Jones. **Released:** 2002. **Description:** Advice is given to women wishing to start their own companies using guidance and real-world examples to help position themselves for future growth. Tips to survive through a bad economic environment, breaking into a market, working with less money, accepting change, and ways to balance success with personal life are explored.

23311 ■ *Small Business Sourcebook*
Pub: Cengage Gale

Released: July 2009. **Price:** $578.00. **Description:** Two-volume guide to more than 27,300 listings of live and print sources for small business startups as well as small business growth and development. Over 30,500 topics are included.

23312 ■ *Small Business Turnaround*
Pub: Adams Media Corporation

Ed: Marc Kramer. **Price:** $17.95 paperback.

23313 ■ *Small Giants: Companies That Choose to Be Great Instead of Big*
Pub: Penguin Group

Ed: Bo Burlingame. **Released:** March 27, 2007. **Price:** $16.00. **Description:** Profiles of privately held companies that have become huge in their field without becoming large corporations.

23314 ■ "Small Wind Power Market to Double by 2015 at $634 Million" in *Western Farm Press* (September 30, 2011)
Pub: Penton Media Inc.

Description: Small wind power provides cost-effective electricity on a highly localized level, in both remote settings as well as in conjunction with power from the utility grid. Government incentives are spurring new growth in the industry.

23315 ■ "Smith Fuels BNE Drive to Grow Job Market" in *Business First Buffalo* (November 2, 2007, pp. 1)
Pub: American City Business Journals, Inc.

Ed: James Fink. **Description:** David Smith is taking on the role as the new chairman of Buffalo Niagara Enterprise. He aims to market the Buffalo Niagara region to attract new businesses and help existing companies retain workers.

23316 ■ "Solar Credit Lapse Spur Late Demand" in *The Business Journal - Serving Phoenix and the Valley of the Sun* (Vol. 28, July 18, 2008)
Pub: American City Business Journals, Inc.

Ed: Patrick O'Grady. **Description:** Businesses looking to engage in the solar energy industry are facing the problems of taxation and limited solar panel supply. Solar panels manufacturers are focusing more on the European market. Political issues surrounding the federal tax credit policy on solar energy users are also discussed.

23317 ■ "Sophia Siskel; CEO, Chicago Botanic Garden" in *Crain's Chicago Business* (Vol. 31, May 5, 2008, No. 18, pp. 36)
Pub: Crain Communications, Inc.

Ed: John Rosenthal. **Description:** Profile of Sophia Siskel who is the CEO of the Chicago Botanic Garden and is overseeing the $100 million expansion which will put the Botanic Garden at the forefront of plant conservation science; Ms. Siskel is also an efficient marketer and researcher.

23318 ■ "A Sound Setup" in *Black Enterprise* (Vol. 38, November 2007, No. 4, pp. 100)
Pub: Earl G. Graves Publishing Co. Inc.

Ed: Anthony Calypso. **Description:** Choosing the right corporate identity can ensure that a business has the right foundation on which to build and grow.

23319 ■ "The Spark's Back in Sanyo" in *Barron's* (Vol. 88, March 31, 2008, No. 13, pp. M9)
Pub: Dow Jones & Company, Inc.

Ed: Jay Alabaster. **Description:** Things are looking up for Sanyo Electric after its string of calamities that range from major losses brought on by earthquake damage to its semiconductor operations and its near collapse and bailout. The company looks poised for a rebound as they are on track for their first net profit since 2003 and could beat its earnings forecast for 2008.

23320 ■ "Speak Better: Five Tips for Polished Presentations" in *Women Entrepreneur* (September 19, 2008)
Pub: Entrepreneur Media Inc.

Ed: Suzannah Baum. **Description:** Successful entrepreneurs agree that exemplary public speaking skills are among the core techniques needed to propel their business forward. A well-delivered presentation can result in securing a new distribution channel, gaining new customers, locking into a new referral stream or receiving extra funding.

23321 ■ "A Sports Extravaganza - To Go" in *Canadian Business* (Vol. 79, June 19, 2006, No. 13, pp. 21)
Pub: Rogers Media

Ed: Andy Holloway. **Description:** Television broadcasting industry in Canada utilizing advanced technologies like mobile television and internet protocol television in broadcasting major sports events. Large number of new technologies are being invented to support increasing demand.

23322 ■ "Sprint Tries to Wring Out Positives" in *The Business Journal-Serving Metropolitan Kansas City* (Vol. 26, August 8, 2008, No. 48)
Pub: American City Business Journals, Inc.

Ed: Suzanna Stagemeyer. **Description:** Sprint Nextel Corp. reported that 901,000 subscribers left the company in the quarter ending June 30, 2008; fewer than the nearly 1.1 million it lost in the previous quarter. Customer turnover also dropped to just less than 2 percent, compared to 2.45 percent in the first quarter of 2008.

23323 ■ "Staffing Firm Grows by Following Own Advice-Hire a Headhunter" in *Crain's Detroit Business* (Vol. 24, October 6, 2008, No. 40, pp. 1)
Pub: Crain Communications, Inc.

Ed: Sherri Begin. **Description:** Profile of Venator Holdings L.L.C., a staffing firm that provides searches for companies in need of financial-accounting and technical employees; the firm's revenue has increased from $1.1 million in 2003 to a projected $11.5 million this year due to a climate in which more people are exiting the workforce than are coming in with those particular specialized skills and the need for a temporary, flexible workforce for contract placements at companies that do not want to take on the legacy costs associated with permanent employees. The hiring of an external headhunter to find the right out-of-state manager for Venator is also discussed.

23324 ■ "STAR TEC Incubator's Latest Resident Shows Promise" in *The Business Journal-Serving Greater Tampa Bay* (August 8, 2008)
Pub: American City Business Journals, Inc.

Ed: Jane Meinhardt. **Description:** Field Forensics Inc., a resident of the STAR Technology Enterprise Center, has grown after being admitted into the business accelerator. The producer of defense and security devices and equipment has doubled 2007 sales as of 2008.

23325 ■ "Starbucks Drive-Throughs: Can the Cafe Keep Its Cool?" in *Globe & Mail* (January 6, 2006, pp. B7)
Pub: CTVglobemedia Publishing Inc.

Ed: Steven Gray. **Description:** The feasibility of Starbucks Corp.'s plans to introduce drive-through cafes is discussed.

23326 ■ *The Starbucks Experience*
Pub: McGraw-Hill

Ed: Joseph A. Michelli. **Released:** September 14, 2006. **Price:** $24.95. **Description:** Boardroom strategies, employee motivation tips, community involvement, and customer satisfaction are issues addressed, using Starbucks as a model.

23327 ■ *The Starbucks Experience: 5 Principles for Turing Ordinary into Extraordinary*
Pub: McGraw-Hill

Ed: Joseph A. Michelli. **Released:** November 2006.

23328 ■ *Start, Run, and Grow a Successful Small Business, 2nd Edition*
Pub: CCH, Inc.

Ed: Susan M. Jacksack. **Price:** $24.95.

23329 ■ *Start Small, Finish Big*
Pub: Warner Business Books

Ed: Fred DeLuca. **Price:** $14.95.

23330 ■ "State Film Business Tops $1.3 Billion" in *The Business Journal-Portland* (Vol. 25, August 22, 2008, No. 24, pp. 1)
Pub: American City Business Journals, Inc.

Ed: Andy Giegerich. **Description:** Oregon's film industry has generated $1.39 billion in direct and indirect economic impact in 2007, a 55 percent rise from 2005 levels. The growth of the industry is attributed to tax incentives issued in 2007, which attracted film production companies from other states.

23331 ■ "State of Play" in *Canadian Business* (Vol. 79, June 19, 2006, No. 13, pp. 25)
Pub: Rogers Media
Ed: Andrew Wahl; Zena Olijnyk; Jeff Sanford. **Description:** Top 100 information technology companies in Canada are ranked by their market capitalization as of June 1. The statistics that show the revenues of these companies are also presented.

23332 ■ "State Shock Prices Take Large Tumble" in *The Business Journal-Milwaukee* (Vol. 25, September 12, 2008, No. 51, pp. A1)
Pub: American City Business Journals, Inc.
Ed: Rich Rovito. **Description:** Weak economic times have caused the stocks of most publicly traded companies in Wisconsin to dip in 2008. Companies that appeared on the worst performing stocks list also experienced drops in share price to as much as 70 percent. Information about the companies that experienced increases in stock prices is also presented. Statistical data included.

23333 ■ "Steady Spending in Retail" in *Business Week* (September 22, 2008, No. 4100, pp. 13)
Pub: McGraw-Hill Companies, Inc.
Ed: Tara Kalwarski. **Description:** Retail jobs have begun to decline on the national level despite the two percent growth in the industry over the last year; much of the growth has been attributed to the sales of higher-priced oil products.

23334 ■ *The Sticking Point Solution: 9 Ways to Move Your Business from Stagnation to Stunning Growth in Tough Economic Times*
Pub: Vanguard Press
Ed: Jay Abraham. **Released:** May 10, 2010. **Price:** $25.95. **Description:** Renowned business consultant, Jay Abraham, reveals the nine ways even successful businesses get stuck, hit plateaus, and fail to achieve their dreams and he explains how to get unstuck and create exponential growth.

23335 ■ "Still Looking Good" in *Canadian Business* (Vol. 80, March 26, 2007, No. 7, pp. 29)
Pub: Rogers Media
Ed: Andy Holloway. **Description:** The real estate prices in various parts of Canada are analyzed. The future growth potential of the industry is forecasted.

23336 ■ "Still Stretching" in *Business Courier* (Vol. 24, December 28, 2008, No. 37, pp. 1)
Pub: American City Business Journals, Inc.
Ed: Lucy May. **Description:** Minority-owned businesses have experienced growth in 2007 as Cincinnati and Hamilton County used a workforce development and economic inclusion policy. Kroger Co., for example, has been inducted to the Billion Dollar Roundtable in 2007 for attaining $1 billion in annual spending with suppliers that are minority- owned. The need for more progress within the minority-owned enterprises is discussed.

23337 ■ "Stone Company Slated to Expand Here" in *Austin Business JournalInc.* (Vol. 28, September 12, 2008, No. 26, pp. 1)
Pub: American City Business Journals
Ed: Jean Kwon. **Description:** Architectural Granite & Marble Inc. has a $6 million investment that moved the company from 2,500 square feet of space to a 10,000 square foot office in Southwest Austin, Texas. The investment will also provide for the company's expansion in Nashville, Tennessee and San Antonio, Texas.

23338 ■ "Stop the Innovation Wars" in *Harvard Business Review* (Vol. 88, July-August 2010, No. 7-8, pp. 76)
Pub: Harvard Business School Publishing
Ed: Vijay Govindarajan, Chris Trimble. **Description:** Methods for managing conflicts between partners during the innovation initiative process are highlighted. These include dividing the labor, assembling a dedicated team, and mitigating likelihood for any potential conflict.

23339 ■ *Straight Talk About Small Business Success in New Jersey: How to Maximize the Growth, Cash Flow and Profitability of Your Small Business*
Pub: Business Success Systems, Incorporated
Ed: Salim Omar. **Released:** April 2004. **Description:** Small business information geared to new and existing small businesses in New Jersey.

23340 ■ *Strategies for Growth in SMEs: The Role of Information and Information Systems*
Pub: Elsevier Science & Technology Books
Ed: Margi Levy, Philip Powell. **Released:** December 2004. **Price:** $62.95. **Description:** Role of information and information systems in the growth of small and medium-sized enterprises in the U.S.

23341 ■ *Streetwise Small Business Book of Lists: Hundreds of Lists to Help You Reduce Costs, Increase Revenues, and Boost Your Profits!*
Pub: Adams Media Corporation
Ed: Gene Marks. **Released:** September 2006. **Price:** $25.95. **Description:** Strategies to help small business owners locate services, increase sales, and lower expenses.

23342 ■ *Streetwise Small Business Turnaround: Revitalizing Your Struggling or Stagnant Enterprise*
Pub: Adams Media Corporation
Ed: Marc Kramer. **Released:** November 1999. **Description:** Practical tips and advice are provided for rejuvenating an existing small business.

23343 ■ "Substantial Deal Expected to Create Jobs, Help Industrial Market" in *Tampa Bay Business Journal* (Vol. 30, January 8, 2010, No. 3)
Pub: American City Business Journals
Ed: Janet Leiser. **Description:** Food distribution firm Gordon Food Service (GFS) is on the brink of purchasing Albertson's million-square-foot warehouse along with 158 acres of space. The deal between GFS and Albertson's could expand GFS' presence in west Central Florida. A history of GFS' growth is included

23344 ■ "Success Coach: Dare to Dream" in *Entrepreneur* (Vol. 35, October 2007, No. 10, pp. 146)
Pub: Entrepreneur Media Inc.
Ed: Romaus Wolter. **Description:** Business goals that are seemingly impossible to reach can actually be achieved through careful planning. Making the goals clear is the first step toward achievement. Details for setting goals and how to attain them are presented.

23345 ■ *Success Secrets to Maximize Business in Canada (Culture Shock! Success Secrets to Maximize Business)*
Pub: Graphic Arts Center Publishing Company
Ed: Ken Coates. **Released:** October 5, 2000. **Description:** Part of the Culture Shock! Series that helps companies maximize business opportunities in Canada.

23346 ■ *A Successful Family Business*
Pub: Penguin Group USA Inc.
Ed: Neil Pahel, Janis Raye. **Released:** August 1, 2009. **Price:** $18.95. **Description:** Guide to running a family business includes information for expanding beyond the original family firm and family versus hired management.

23347 ■ "SunBank Plans Expansion Via Wall-Mart" in *Business Journal-Serving Phoenix and the Valley of the Sun* (Vol. 10, November 9, 2007)
Pub: American City Business Journals, Inc.
Ed: Chris Casacchia. **Description:** SunBank plans to install 12 to 14 branches in Wal-Mart stores in Arizona and hire 100 bankers by the end of 2008. Wal-Mart also offers financial products at other stores through partnerships with other banks.

23348 ■ "Super Success" in *Small Business Opportunities* (November 2008)
Pub: Entrepreneur Media Inc.
Description: Profile of PromoWorks LLC, a company founded by Michael Kent, that distributes samples of food at grocery stores for clients like Kraft Foods, Inc. and Kellogg Co. and also handles the logistics, provides the employees and tracks the products' sales.

23349 ■ *SuperCorp: How Vanguard Companies Create Innovation, Profits, Growth, and Social Good*
Pub: Crown Business
Ed: Rosabeth Moss Kanter. **Released:** 2009. **Price:** $27.50. **Description:** Harvard professor makes a persuasive case showing how social good is good for any company's bottom line.

23350 ■ "Suppliers Look to Rack Up Big Sales to Distributors" in *The Business Journal-Serving Metropolitan Kansas City* (August 15, 2008)
Pub: American City Business Journals, Inc.
Ed: James Dornbrook. **Description:** Suppliers of shelving units, conveyor systems and other equipment used in distribution facilities are expecting new business opportunities along with the planned intermodal projects in the Kansas City area. Suppliers have already observed that small distributors have started to relocate to the city because of the intermodal projects. Demand for shelves and lifts have also increased.

23351 ■ "The Sure Thing That Flopped" in *Harvard Business Review* (Vol. 86, July-August 2008, No. 8, pp. 29)
Pub: Harvard Business School Press
Ed: Gerald Zaltman; Lindsay Zaltman. **Description:** Fictitious brand extension scenario is presented, with contributors providing suggestions and advice. The company's struggles with expanding the brand may be alleviated by improving consumer research, focusing on emotional responses to products and services.

23352 ■ "Survey: More Buyers Expect to Spend Less in Most Media" in *Advertising Age* (Vol. 79, July 7, 2008, No. 26, pp. 3)
Pub: Crain Communications, Inc.
Ed: Megan McIlroy. **Description:** Marketers are decreasing their budgets for advertising in television, radio, newspaper and outdoor due to the economic downturn. Statistical data concerning advertising agencies and marketers included.

23353 ■ "The Survey Says" in *Collections and Credit Risk* (Vol. 14, September 1, 2009, No. 8, pp. 16)
Pub: SourceMedia, Inc.
Ed: Bill Grabarek; Darren Waggoner. **Description:** Revenue for the top accounts receivable management firms rose nearly 20 percent in 2008 despite lower liquidation rates, a poor economy and riskier, albeit cheaper debt portfolios; the trend may continue this year as collection agencies expect revenue, on average, to increase 5.8 percent. Debt buyers, however, found that their revenue fell nearly 7 percent in 2008 and expect it to fall another 12 percent this year.

23354 ■ "Survive the Small-to-Big Transition" in *Entrepreneur* (November 4, 2008)
Pub: Entrepreneur Media Inc.
Ed: Elizabeth Wilson. **Description:** Transitioning a small company to a large company can be a challenge, especially during the time when it is too big to be considered small and too small to be considered big. Common pitfalls during this time are discussed as well as techniques business owners should implement when dealing with this transitional period.

23355 ■ "Susan Leger Ferraro Built a $7.2 Million Day Care Business. Now She Wants To Expand-And Cash Out" in *Inc.* (January 2008, pp. 50-53)
Pub: Gruner & Jahr USA Publishing
Ed: Dalia Fahmy. **Description:** Profile of Susan Leger Ferraro who wants to expand her chain of day care centers into Florida and California and sell part of her 87 percent stake to reduce financial risk.

23356 ■ "Swedes Swoop In To Save Time4" in *Advertising Age* (Vol. 78, January 29, 2007, No. 5, pp. 4)
Pub: Crain Communications, Inc.
Ed: Nat Ives. **Description:** Overview of Stockholm's Bonnier Group, a family-owned publisher that is looking to expand its U.S. presence; Bonnier recently acquired a number of Time Inc. magazines.

23357 ■ "Sweet Tea; Neil Golden" in *Advertising Age* (Vol. 79, November 17, 2008, No. 43, pp. 4)
Pub: Crain Communications, Inc.
Ed: Emily Bryson York. **Description:** McDonald's launch of iced coffee and sweat tea, which were promoted via price cuts over the summer, helped to boost sales at the fast-food chain.

23358 ■ "Sykes Group Targets GunnAllen" in *The Business Journal-Serving Greater Tampa Bay* (Vol. 28, September 5, 2008, No. 37, pp. 1)
Pub: American City Business Journals, Inc.
Ed: Margie Manning. **Description:** GAH Holdings LLC. a newly formed investment company by John H. Sykes of Sykes Enterprises Inc., will add capital to Tampa Bay Area investment banking firm GunnAllen Holdings Inc. The capital infusion is to aid GunnAllen Holdings in expanding and diversifying as GAH becomes its largest shareholder.

23359 ■ "Table Games Get a Leg Up" in *Philadelphia Business Journal* (Vol. 28, January 15, 2010, No. 48, pp. 1)
Pub: American City Business Journals
Ed: Athena Merritt, Peter Van Allen. **Description:** Casino operators expect the addition of live table games such as poker and blackjack at existing and planned casinos in Philadelphia will generate 1,000 new jobs. Most of the jobs will be dealers and floor supervisors.

23360 ■ "Taco Bell; David Ovens" in *Advertising Age* (Vol. 79, November 17, 2008, No. 43, pp. S2)
Pub: Crain Communications, Inc.
Ed: Emily Bryson York. **Description:** Due to the addition of new products such as a low-calorie, low-fat Fresco menu; a fruity iced beverage; and a value initiative, Taco Bell now accounts for half of Yum Brands' profits. The chain has also benefited from a new chief marketing officer, David Ovens, who oversees ad support.

23361 ■ "Taiwan Technology Initiatives Foster Growth" in *Canadian Electronics* (Vol. 23, February 2008, No. 1, pp. 28)
Pub: CLB Media Inc.
Description: A study conducted by the Market Intelligence Center shows that currently, Taiwan is the world's larges producer of information technology products such as motherboards, servers, and LCD monitors. In 2006, Taiwan's LED industry reached a production value of NTD 21 billion. This push into the LED sector shows the Ministry of Economic Affairs' plan to target industries that are environmentally friendly.

23362 ■ "Taking a Chance" in *Baltimore Business Journal* (Vol. 28, July 16, 2010, No. 10, pp. 1)
Pub: Baltimore Business Journal
Ed: Scott Dance. **Description:** North Avenue in Baltimore, Maryland is considered a rough neighborhood due to the dangers of prostitution and drug dealing. However, some entrepreneurs have taken the risk of building their businesses on North Avenue as revitalization efforts grow. One of the challenges for businesses in rough neighborhoods is bringing customers to their stores or offices.

23363 ■ "Taking Collections" in *Investment Dealers' Digest* (Vol. 75, October 9, 2009, No. 38, pp. 19)
Pub: SourceMedia, Inc.
Ed: Aleksandrs Rozens. **Description:** Although the nation's debt-collection industry has grown with increased reliance by consumers on credit, valuations of these firms have lessened due to the economy which has hurt some of the success of these firms in obtaining the debt back from consumers who are experiencing trying economic times.

23364 ■ "Taking the Right Road" in *Entrepreneur* (Vol. 37, October 2009, No. 10, pp. 104)
Pub: Entrepreneur Media, Inc.
Ed: Jason Daley. **Description:** Joe Grubb's franchise of BrightStar Healthcare, a home health care provider, in Knoxville, Tennessee has grown into a $1 million business. Grubb, a former sales agent, experienced slow growth for his franchise and had to deal with cash flow issues during its first few months.

23365 ■ "Tanganyika Announces First Quarter 2007 Results" in *Canadian Corporate News* (May 14, 2007)
Pub: Comtex News Network Inc.
Description: Tanganyika Oil Company Ltd., announced the interim operating and financial results for the first quarter ending March 31, 2007. Statistical data included.

23366 ■ "Tax Deal Yields Polaris Offices" in *Business First-Columbus* (October 26, 2007, pp. A1)
Pub: American City Business Journals, Inc.
Ed: Brian R. Ball. **Description:** Speculation on a possible office building construction is increasing with the expansion of tax incentives to build at the Polaris Centers of Commerce. Details of community reinvestment in the Columbus, Ohio area along with possible 15-year 100 percent tax abatements for Polaris office buildings are discussed.

23367 ■ "Tea for 33 Million" in *Canadian Business* (Vol. 80, March 12, 2007, No. 6, pp. 10)
Pub: Rogers Media
Ed: Wendy Glauser. **Description:** The plan of owner of Cargo & James Tea, Tim Grover, to expand his business in North America to reach about 33 million, is discussed.

23368 ■ "The Tea Bag Test" in *Canadian Business* (Vol. 79, October 23, 2006, No. 21, pp. 83)
Pub: Rogers Media
Ed: Clive Mather. **Description:** Tips for business executives, on how to manage leadership skills to attain optimal business growth, are presented.

23369 ■ "A Team Sport" in *Business Courier* (Vol. 26, October 2, 2009, No. 23, pp. 1)
Pub: American City Business Journals, Inc.
Ed: Lisa Biank Fasig. **Description:** Procter & Gamble (P&G) revised the way it works with marketing, design and public relations firms. Creative discussions will be managed by only two representatives, the franchise leader and the brand agency leader in order for P&G to simplify operations as it grows larger and more global.

23370 ■ "The Tech 100" in *Canadian Business* (Vol. 81, July 21, 2008, No. 11, pp. 48)
Pub: Rogers Media Ltd.
Ed: Calvin Leung. **Description:** Absolute Software Corp. Day4 Energy Inc., Sandvine Corp., Norsat International Inc. and Call Genie Inc. are the five technology firms included in the annual ranking of top companies in Canada by market capitalization. The services and the one-year total return potential of the companies are presented.

23371 ■ "Teeling and Gallagher: A Textbook for Success" in *Agency Sales Magazine* (Vol. 39, September-October 2009, No. 9, pp. 20)
Pub: MANA
Ed: Jack Foster. **Description:** Profile of Teeling & Gallagher, a manufacturing firm that was founded in 1946 as the D.G. Teeling Company and continued as a one-person agency until 1960 when Tom Gallagher joined the company. Tom Gallagher talks about how things have changed and his work with his son Bob in the agency.

23372 ■ "TELUS Drawing More Power From Its Wireless Operations" in *Globe & Mail* (February 17, 2007, pp. B3)
Pub: CTVglobemedia Publishing Inc.
Ed: Catherine McLean. **Description:** TELUS Corp., the fast-growing wireless business company, posted tripled profits in the fourth quarter of 2006. The revenues of the company increased 8 percent in the same period.

23373 ■ "Telus Tunes in to the TV Revolution" in *Globe & Mail* (February 18, 2006, pp. B4)
Pub: CTVglobemedia Publishing Inc.
Ed: Eric Reguly. **Description:** The business growth plans of chief executive officer Darren Entwistle of Telus Corp. are presented.

23374 ■ "Tempel Steel To Expand Its Chicago Plant" in *Chicago Tribune* (August 22, 2008)
Pub: McClatchy-Tribune Information Services
Ed: James P. Miller. **Description:** Tempel Steel Co. is no longer considering transferring a Libertyville factory's production to Mexico; the company has responded to government incentives and will instead shift that work to its plant on Chicago's North Side.

23375 ■ "Testing Firm to Add Jobs" in *Business Courier* (Vol. 26, December 11, 2009, No. 33, pp. 1)
Pub: American City Business Journals, Inc.
Ed: Dan Monk. **Description:** Cincinnati-based Q Laboratories announced plans to add dozens of jobs with the $1.6 million stimulus assisted expansion. The company hired Michael Lichtenberg & Sons Construction Co. to build a new 9,000 square foot laboratory building.

23376 ■ "Texas State Poised for Boom" in *Austin Business JournalInc.* (Vol. 29, January 29, 2010, No. 47, pp. 1)
Pub: American City Business Journals
Ed: Sandra Zaragoza. **Description:** Texas State University, San Marcos has seen its student population grow to 30,800 and the university is set for $633 million in construction projects to address demand for student housing and building expansions and renovations. Details on the buildings and student housing plans for the projects are provided.

23377 ■ "Thai Ice Cream Cremo Expanding to Middle East" in *Ice Cream Reporter* (Vol. 23, September 20, 2010, No. 10, pp. 3)
Pub: Ice Cream Reporter
Description: Thai-based frozen dessert manufacturer Chomthana, maker of Cremo brand ice cream, is expanding into the Middle East.

23378 ■ "The End of the Line for Line Extensions?" in *Advertising Age* (Vol. 79, July 7, 2008, No. 26, pp. 3)
Pub: Crain Communications, Inc.
Ed: Description: After years of double-digit growth, some of the most heavily extended personal-care products have slowed substantially or even declined in the U.S. Unilever's Dove and P&G's Pantene and Olay are two such brands that have been affected. Statistical data included.

23379 ■ "The File On...Jenne Distributors" in *Crain's Cleveland Business* (Vol. 28, October 8, 2007, No. 40, pp. 26)
Pub: Crain Communications, Inc.
Ed: Kimberly Bonvissuto. **Description:** Overview of the telecommunications equipment company, Jenne Distributors, a firm that is projecting more than $125 million in revenue for 2007.

23380 ■ "The File On...Skoda Minotti" in *Crain's Cleveland Business* (Vol. 28, October 8, 2007, No. 40, pp. 26)
Pub: Crain Communications, Inc.
Ed: Kimberly Bonvissuto. **Description:** Overview of Skoda Minotti, the accounting and financial services firm located in Mayfield Village; the company has 140 employees and an expanded slate of services.

23381 ■ "The Next 20 Years: How Customer and Workforce Attitudes Will Evolve" in *Harvard Business Review* (Vol. 85, July-August 2007, No. 7-8)
Pub: Harvard Business School Publishing
Ed: Neil Howe, William Strauss. **Description:** Identification of social categories inhabited by age groups is used to calculate how consumer and employee opinions and behavior will change, and how this will impact economic development and corporate growth.

23382 ■ *There's a Business In Every Woman: A 7-Step Guide to Discovering, Starting, and Building the Business of Your Dreams*
Pub: Ballantine/Random House
Ed: Ann M. Holmes. **Released:** 2008. **Price:** $15.00 paperback. **Description:** Economist and workplace expert provides a no-nonsense guide detailing seven steps to creating a successful business, based on her own experiences and on those of her employees. She highlights the importance of understanding and using your core competencies, building an organized infrastructure from the start, and planning for and managing your growth.

23383 ■ *The Thin Book of Naming Elephants: How to Surface Undiscussables for Greater Organizational Success*
Pub: Thin Book Publishing Company
Ed: Sue Annis Hammond; Andrea B. Mayfield. **Released:** January 2004. **Price:** $10.95. **Description:** Organizational success is of upmost importance to today's entrepreneurs and organizations. The hierarchal system in which people are afraid to speak up in organizations is discussed. The points of view and inability to see things from an overall perspective can cause insecurity among employees. The three elephants present in every organization include: arrogance, hubris, and screamers and the damage caused by these elephants in any organization is examined.

23384 ■ "Thirsty Lion on the Prowl" in *Business Journal Portland* (Vol. 27, November 5, 2010, No. 36, pp. 1)
Pub: Portland Business Journal
Ed: Wendy Culverwell. **Description:** Concept Entertainment Inc.'s impending launch of the Thirsty Lion Pub and Grill at the Washington Square in downtown Portland, Oregon is part of its West Coast expansion plan. A discussion of the planning involved in realizing Thirsty Lion is discussed, along with pub offerings that are expected to be enjoyed by customers.

23385 ■ "Thomas Morley; President, The Lube Stop Inc., 37" in *Crain's Cleveland Business* (Vol. 28, November 19, 2007, No. 46, pp. F-12)
Pub: Crain Communications, Inc.
Ed: David Bennett. **Description:** Profile of Thomas Morley, president of The Lube Stop Inc., who is dedicated to promoting the company's strong environmental record as an effective way to differentiate Lube Stop from its competition. Since Mr. Morley came to the company in 2004, Lube Stop has increased sales by 10 percent and has boosted its operating profits by 30 percent.

23386 ■ "Thomson Eyes Asia for Expansion" in *Globe & Mail* (February 10, 2006, pp. B4)
Pub: CTVglobemedia Publishing Inc.
Ed: Grant Robertson. **Description:** The business growth plans of Thomson Corp., in Asia, are presented.

23387 ■ "Time for a Little Pruning" in *Barron's* (Vol. 89, July 6, 2009, No. 27, pp. 13)
Pub: Dow Jones & Co., Inc.
Ed: Dimitra DeFotis. **Description:** Investors are advised to avoid the shares of Whole Foods, American Tower, T. Rowe Price, Iron Mountain, Intuitive Surgical, Salesforce.com, and Juniper Networks due to their high price to earnings ratios. The shares of Amazon.com, Broadcom, and Expeditors International of Washington remain attractive to investors despite their high price to earnings ratios due to their strong growth.

23388 ■ "Timken's Bearings Rolling in China, India" in *Crain's Cleveland Business* (Vol. 28, October 29, 2007, No. 43, pp. 14)
Pub: Crain Communications, Inc.
Ed: David Bennett. **Description:** Canton-based Timken Co., a manufacturer of bearings and specialty metals, is seeing growing demand for its line of tapered roller bearings, which allow rail users to carry heavy car loads. The company is finding significant growth in China and India due to their rapidly growing rail markets.

23389 ■ "Tips From a Turnaround Expert" in *Business Owner* (Vol. 35, July-August 2011, No. 4, pp. 8)
Pub: DL Perkins Company
Description: The book, 'The Six Month Fix: Adventures in Rescuing Failing Companies' by Gary Sutton is summarized. It provides lessons for finding and building profits in failing firms.

23390 ■ "TiVo, Domino's Team to Offer Pizza Ordering by DVR" in *Advertising Age* (Vol. 79, November 17, 2008, No. 43, pp. 48)
Pub: Crain Communications, Inc.
Ed: Brian Steinberg. **Description:** Domino's Pizza and TiVo are teaming up to make it possible for customers to order from the restaurant straight from their DVR. The companies see that this kind of interactive television and consumer experience will only serve to generate more sales as the customer can be exposed to a fuller range of menu selections and will not have to interrupt their viewing, while workers can spend more time making the product.

23391 ■ "TMC Development Closes $1.1 Million Real Estate Purchase" in *Internet Wire* (September 17, 2009)
Pub: Comtex News Network, Inc.
Description: TMC Development announced the closing of a $1.1 million real estate purchase for Mansa, LLC dba Kwikee Mart, a Napa-based convenience store; TMC helped the company secure a Small Business Administration 504 loan in order to purchase the acquisition of a 3,464 square foot building. SBA created the 504 loan program to provide financing for growing small and medium-sized businesses.

23392 ■ "Toes for Business" in *Hispanic Business* (October 2007, pp. 10, 12)
Pub: Hispanic Business
Ed: Gabriel Rodriguez. **Description:** Prima ballerinas, Lorena and Lorna Feijoo, have increased box office sales by at least 30 to 40 percent. A discussion with Pedro Pablo Pena, artistic director of the Miami Hispanic Ballet Corps and founder of the first Choreographic Workshop of Havana is included.

23393 ■ "Tofutti Brands" in *Ice Cream Reporter* (Vol. 23, September 20, 2010, No. 10, pp. 6)
Pub: Ice Cream Reporter
Description: Tofutti Brands announced net sales at $4.5 million for second quarter 2010.

23394 ■ "Top 49ers Alphabetical Listing with Five Years Rank and Revenue" in *Alaska Business Monthly* (Vol. 27, October 2011, No. 10, pp. 100)
Pub: Alaska Business Publishing Company
Description: A listing of Alaska's top 49 performing companies ranked by revenue for years 2010 and 2011.

23395 ■ "Top 50 By 1-Year Return" in *Canadian Business* (Vol. 81, Summer 2008, No. 9, pp. 121)
Pub: Rogers Media Ltd.
Description: Table showing the top 50 Canadian companies ranked in terms of one-year return is presented. Toronto, Canada-based Timminco Ltd. topped the roster with a 1,294.2 percent in one-year return. However, the share prices of the company were affected by the recent controversy in its silicon purification process.

23396 ■ "Top 50 By 5-Year Return" in *Canadian Business* (Vol. 81, Summer 2008, No. 9, pp. 123)
Pub: Rogers Media Ltd.
Description: Table showing the rankings of the top 50 Canadian companies in terms of five-year return is presented. Silver Wheaton Corp. topped the roster with a 178.5 percent in five-year return. The company's share prices have skyrocketed despite increasing silver prices.

23397 ■ "Top 50 in the Capital Market" in *Canadian Business* (Vol. 81, Summer 2008, No. 9, pp. 117)
Pub: Rogers Media Ltd.
Description: Research in Motion Ltd. topped the list of companies in Canada in terms of market capitalization. The company's share prices surge to 119.8 percent in the year ended April 4. A table showing the top 50 Canadian companies in terms of market capitalization is presented.

23398 ■ "Top 50" in *Entrepreneur* (Vol. 35, November 2007, No. 11, pp. 38)
Pub: Entrepreneur Media Inc.
Description: List of the 50 fastest-growing women-led businesses in North America is presented.

23399 ■ "Top 50 Exporters" in *Hispanic Business* (Vol. 30, July-August 2008, No. 7-8, pp. 42)
Pub: Hispanic Business, Inc.
Ed: Hildy Medina. **Description:** Increases in exports revenues reported by food exporters and green companies in a time of economic slowdown in the U.S are described. Food exporters have benefited from the growth of high-volume grocery stores in underdeveloped countries and the German governments' promotion of solar energy has benefited the U.S. solar heating equipment and solar panel manufactures.

23400 ■ "Top 50 In Profits" in *Canadian Business* (Vol. 81, Summer 2008, No. 9, pp. 116)
Pub: Rogers Media Ltd.
Description: Royal Bank of Canada topped the Investor 500 by profits list despite the slower economic growth in Canada and the U.S. The bank was in the runner-up position in the 2007. RBC's growth strategy is through hefty acquisitions in the U.S. A table ranking the top 50 companies in Canada in terms of profits is presented.

23401 ■ "Top 50 In Total Revenue" in *Canadian Business* (Vol. 81, Summer 2008, No. 9, pp. 119)
Pub: Rogers Media Ltd.
Description: Table showing the top 50 Canadian companies in terms of total revenue is presented. Manulife Financial Corp. topped the list with revenue of 34.5 billion. The financial services firm is the 6th largest provider of life insurance in the world and the second largest in North America.

23402 ■ "Top 100 Consolidate Gains" in *Hispanic Business* (Vol. 30, July-August 2008, No. 7-8, pp. 30)
Pub: Hispanic Business, Inc.
Ed: Richard Kaplan. **Description:** Data developed by HispanTelligence on the increase in revenue posted by the top 100 fastest-growing U.S. Hispanic firms over the last five years is reported. Despite the economic downturn, the service sector, IT and health suppliers showed an increase in revenue whereas construction companies showed a marginal slump in revenue growth.

23403 ■ "Top Private Companies" in *Baltimore Business Journal* (Vol. 28, August 27, 2010, No. 16, pp. 1)
Pub: Baltimore Business Journal
Ed: Gary Haber. **Description:** The combined revenue of the 100 largest private firms in Maryland's Baltimore region dropped from about $22.7 billion in 2008 to $21 billion in 2009, an annual decrease of more than 7 percent. To survive the recession's impact, these firms resorted to strategies such as government contracting and overseas expansion.

23404 ■ "Top Twenty Wealthiest Landowners" in *Hawaii Business* (Vol. 53, November 2007, No. 5, pp. 34)
Pub: Hawaii Business Publishing
Description: Provided is a table of the wealthiest landowners in Hawaii. Their assessed value, total acres owned, prominent holdings, other notable holdings and years of presence in Hawaii are also provided. Statistical data included.

23405 ■ "A Torch in the Darkness" in *Canadian Business* (Vol. 83, August 17, 2010, No. 13-14, pp. 66)
Pub: Rogers Media Ltd.
Ed: Joe Castaldo. **Description:** Research In Motion (RIM) unveiled the BlackBerry Touch, featuring a touch screen as well as a physical keyboard, in an attempt to repel competitors and expand share in the consumer smart phone market. RIM shares have fallen 43 percent from its peak in 2009.

23406 ■ "Tough-Love Boss at BMO Demands Retail Turnaround" in *Globe & Mail* (March 2, 2007, pp. B13)
Pub: CTVglobemedia Publishing Inc.
Ed: Andrew Willis. **Description:** William Downe, the newly appointed chief executive of Bank of Montreal (BMO), discusses strategies to improve the number of retail customers. The BMO reported $292 million profits in the first quarter of 2007.

23407 ■ "Toyota Expected to Construct Two N.A. Plants" in *Globe & Mail* (February 14, 2007, pp. B4)
Pub: CTVglobemedia Publishing Inc.
Description: Toyota Motor Corp. is planning to construct two vehicle assembly plants in North America and one more plant in Canada. The company is also planning to sell 208,000 vehicles in 2007.

23408 ■ "Toyota Marks Record Profit Sales" in *Globe & Mail* (February 7, 2007, pp. B10)
Pub: CTVglobemedia Publishing Inc.
Ed: Martin Fackler. **Description:** The record quarterly sales and earnings reported by Japanese automaker Toyota Motor Corp. are discussed. The company sold 2.16 million vehicles during the quarter while registering 426.8 billion yen in profits.

23409 ■ "Toyota Tops GM in Global Sales" in *Globe & Mail* (April 25, 2007, pp. B1)
Pub: CTVglobemedia Publishing Inc.
Ed: Greg Keenan. **Description:** The success of Toyota Motor Corp. in surpassing General Motors Corp. in its global sales is discussed.

23410 ■ *Trading Places: SMEs in the Global Economy, A Critical Research Handbook*
Pub: Edward Elgar Publishing, Incorporated
Ed: Lloyd-Reason. **Released:** September 2006. **Price:** $110.00. **Description:** An overview of international research for small and medium-sized companies wishing to expand in the global economy.

23411 ■ "Traffic Slows at O'Hare; As Airlines Cut Flights, City Tries to Push Expansion Forward" in *Crain's Chicago Business* (April 28, 2008)
Pub: Crain Communications, Inc.
Ed: Paul Merrion; John Pletz. **Description:** O'Hare International Airport is seeing a decline in passenger traffic just as the city of Chicago presses cash-strapped airlines to fund the second phase of the airport's expansion which would include the extension of one runway, the relocation of two others and the construction of a new western terminal.

23412 ■ "Tragedies Add Demand for Inspiron's Alert System" in *Crain's Cleveland Business* (Vol. 28, October 29, 2007, No. 43, pp. 5)
Pub: Crain Communications, Inc.
Ed: Chuck Soder. **Description:** Inspiron Logistics Corp. has seen huge growth over the past months for its Wireless Emergency Notification System which colleges and universities have rushed to buy since the April 16 shootings at Virginia Tech. The company now makes more than half of its revenue by selling the systems to colleges whereas previous to the shootings the academic market accounted for just 20 percent of the company's sales.

23413 ■ "Training Essential For Growth; It Doesn't Have To Cost Much" in *Crain's Detroit Business* (Vol. 24, January 21, 2008, No. 3, pp. 14)
Pub: Crain Communications Inc. - Detroit
Ed: Sheena Harrison. **Description:** Employee training is essential for small companies to achieve growth.

23414 ■ "Training the Troops: Battlefield Simulations Bring Growth to UNITECH" in *Black Enterprise* (Vol. 38, February 2008, No. 7, pp. 30)
Pub: Earl G. Graves Publishing Co. Inc.
Ed: Cliff Hocker. **Description:** Universal Systems and Technology (UNITECH) received a total of over $45 million U.S. Department of Defense orders during September and October 2007. UNITECH designs and manufactures battlefield simulation devices used to train troops in the Army and Marine Corps.

23415 ■ "Transportation: Laidlaw's Chief Driver" in *Canadian Business* (Vol. 80, January 29, 2007, No. 3, pp. 14)
Pub: Rogers Media
Ed: Michelle Magnan. **Description:** The role of Kevin Benson in the restructuring and growth of the bankrupt transportation company Laidlaw Inc. is described. The increase in the revenues of the restructures company is discussed.

23416 ■ "Trisun Healthcare Eager to Add Centers" in *Austin Business JournalInc.* (Vol. 28, August 22, 2008, No. 23, pp. 1)
Pub: American City Business Journals
Ed: Kate Harrington. **Description:** Austin-based nursing and rehabilitation centers operator Trisun Healthcare plans to build more facilities as part of a growth strategy that can expand beyond Texas. Trisun has 16 facilities along the corridor from San Antonio to Temple, and projects to have three more in Texas in 2008.

23417 ■ "Troy Brewer Opens Own Bottling Operation" in *Business Review, Albany New York* (Vol. 34, November 16, 2007, No. 33, pp. 3)
Pub: American City Business Journals, Inc.
Ed: Michael DeMasi. **Description:** Brown Brewing Company's owner Peter Martin invested in $100,000 worth of bottling equipment and has now doubled his production capacity to 3,000 barrels. Davidson Brothers, another brewery that bottles its own beer, sells 3,000 to 5,000 cases of beer annually. Industry sales of draft breweries are presented.

23418 ■ *True to Yourself: Leading a Values-Based Business*
Pub: Berrett-Koehler Publishers, Incorporated
Ed: Mark S. Albion. **Released:** June 2006. **Price:** $14.95. **Description:** Pressures faced by entrepreneurs running small companies are discussed. Advice is offered to help grow and maintain a profitable business.

23419 ■ "Tulsa-Based Dollar Thrifty Adds Franchises" in *Journal Record* (December 7, 2010)
Pub: Dolan Media Newswires
Ed: D. Ray Tuttle. **Description:** Dollar Thrifty Automotive Group Inc. opened 31 franchise locations in 2010 as part of its expansion plan in the U.S.

23420 ■ "Turfway Slowing its Gait" in *Business Courier* (Vol. 26, November 6, 2009, No. 28, pp. 1)
Pub: American City Business Journals, Inc.
Ed: Jon Newberry. **Description:** Kentucky's Turfway Park will be decreasing its weekly race schedule from five days to three days in the first two months of 2010, and to four days in March 2010. The decision to make reductions in the schedule is attributed to the relocation of thoroughbred racing to states that allow casino gambling. As a result, Turfway Park's resources and purse money would be focused on less days.

23421 ■ "A Turn in the South" in *The Economist* (Vol. 390, January 3, 2009, No. 8612, pp. 34)
Pub: The Economist Newspaper Inc.
Description: Overview of Charleston, South Carolina, a region that lost its navy base in 1996, which had provided work for more than 22,000 people; the city developed a plan called Noisette in order to redevelop the area and today the economy is healthier and more diversified than it was a decade ago. Charleston was described as among the best cities for doing business by Inc. Magazine and seems to be handling the downturn of the economy fairly well. Statistical data regarding growth, business and population is included.

23422 ■ "Twenty Years of Advocacy and Education" in *Women Entrepreneur* (January 18, 2009)
Pub: Entrepreneur Media Inc.
Ed: Eve Gumpel. **Description:** Profile of Sharon Hadary who served as executive director of the Center for Women's Business Research for two decades; Hadary discusses what she has learned about women business owners, their impact on the economy and what successful business owners share in common.

23423 ■ *Twitterville: How Businesses Can Thrive in the New Global Neighborhoods*
Pub: Portfolio Hardcover
Ed: Shel Israel. **Price:** $23.95. **Description:** Twitter is the most rapidly adopted communication tool in history, going from zero to ten million users in just over two years. On Twitter, word can spread faster than wildfire. Companies no longer have the option of ignoring the conversation. Unlike other hot social media spaces, Twitterville is dominated by professionals, not students. And despite its size, it still feels like a small town. Twitter allows people to interact much the way they do face-to-face, honestly and authentically.

23424 ■ "Two Local Firms Make Inc. List: Minority Business" in *Indianapolis Business Journal* (Vol. 31, August 30, 2010, No. 26, pp. 13A)
Pub: Indianapolis Business Journal Corporation
Description: Smart IT staffing agency and Entap Inc., an IT outsourcing firm were among the top ten fastest growing black-owned businesses in the U.S. by Inc. magazine.

23425 ■ "U-Swirl To Open in Salt Lake City Metro Market" in *Ice Cream Reporter* (Vol. 23, November 20, 2010, No. 12, pp. 4)
Pub: Ice Cream Reporter
Description: Healthy Fast Food Inc., parent company to U-SWIRL International Inc., the owner and franchisor of U-SWIRL Frozen Yogurt cafes signed a franchising area development agreement for the Salt Lake City metropolitan area with Regents Management and will open 5 cafes over a five year period.

23426 ■ "UC's Goering Center to Get New Director" in *Business Courier* (Vol. 24, February 15, 2008, No. 45, pp. 3)
Pub: American City Business Journals, Inc.
Ed: Dan Monk. **Description:** Kent Lutz, director of University of Cincinnati Goering (UC) Center for Family & Private Business is to leave the resource center in June 2008 after nine years of service. Changes in the UC-affiliated institute include the expansion of the board from three to seven members and developing new programs related to family businesses.

23427 ■ "The Ultimate Business Tune-Up: For Times Like These" in *Inc.* (Vol. 31, January-February 2009, No. 1, pp. 70)
Pub: Mansueto Ventures LLC
Description: Twenty-three things do energize a small business in tough economic times are outlined with insight from successful entrepreneurs.

23428 ■ "The Ultimate Cure" in *Conde Nast Portfolio* (Vol. 2, June 2008, No. 6, pp. 110)
Pub: Conde Nast Publications, Inc.
Ed: David Ewing Duncan. **Description:** Small upstarts as well as pharmaceutical giants are developing drugs for the neurotechnology industry; these

firms are attempting to adapt groundbreaking research into the basic workings of the brain to new drugs for ailments ranging from multiple sclerosis to dementia to insomnia.

23429 ■ *Ultimate Homebased Business Handbook: How to Start, Run, and Grow Your Own Profitable Business*
Pub: Entrepreneur Press
Ed: James Stephenson. **Released:** June 2008. **Price:** $29.95 (US), $34.95 (Canadian). **Description:** Detailed information for anyone wanting to start a home-based business. Topics include how-to tips, ideas, tools, and print and online resources.

23430 ■ "UMKC, Hospital Drill Down on Deal" in *The Business Journal-Serving Metropolitan Kansas City* (Vol. 26, July 18, 2008, No. 45, pp. 1)
Pub: American City Business Journals, Inc.
Ed: Rob Roberts. **Description:** University of Missouri Kansas City and Children's Mercy Hospital are negotiating the hospital's potential acquisition of the university's School of Dentistry building. The deal would transfer the 240,000-square foot dental school building to Children's Mercy. Plans for a new dental school building for the UMKC are also presented.

23431 ■ "An Unfair Knock on Nokia" in *Barron's* (Vol. 88, March 10, 2008, No. 10, pp. 36)
Pub: Dow Jones & Company, Inc.
Ed: Mark Veverka. **Description:** Discusses the decision by the brokerage house Exane to recommend a Sell on Nokia shares, presumably due to higher inventories, which is unfounded. The news that the company's inventories are rising is not an indicator of falling demand for its products. The company is also benefiting from solid management and rising market share.

23432 ■ "Unify Corp. Back in the Black, Poised to Grow" in *Sacramento Business Journal* (Vol. 25, August 29, 2008, No. 26, pp. 1)
Pub: American City Business Journals, Inc.
Ed: Melanie Turner. **Description:** It was reported that Unify Corp. returned to profitability in the fiscal year ended April 30, 2008 with a net income of $1.6 million, under the guidance of Todd Wille. Wille, who took over as the company's chief executive officer in October 2000, was named as Turnaround CEO of the Year in June 2008 for his efforts.

23433 ■ "United Insurance To Grow St. Pete's Corporate Base" in *The Business Journal-Serving Greater Tampa Bay* (August 29, 2008)
Pub: American City Business Journals, Inc.
Ed: Margie Manning. **Description:** United Insurance Holdings LC is on its way to becoming a public company by agreeing in a reverse merger with FMG Acquisition Corp. The $104.3 million agreement will provide the company's St. Petersburg operations the opportunity to grow. The other impacts of the proposed reverse merger are examined.

23434 ■ "U.S. Retailer Eyes 'Tween' Market" in *Globe & Mail* (January 30, 2007, pp. B1)
Pub: CTVglobemedia Publishing Inc.
Ed: Marina Strauss. **Description:** The decision of Tween Brands Inc. (Too Incorporated) to open 100 new stores in Canada as part of its expansion is discussed. The company's focus on targeting girls for its products is detailed.

23435 ■ "U.S. Savvy Helps Fuel TD's Fortunes" in *Globe & Mail* (February 23, 2007, pp. B1)
Pub: CTVglobemedia Publishing Inc.
Ed: Andrew Willis; Tavia Grant. **Description:** The rise in the revenues of Toronto-Dominion Bank due to its acquisition of American financial service providers and the rise in its domestic retail banking revenues are disussed.

23436 ■ "Universal Energy Group Releases March 31, 2007 Financial Statements" in *Canadian Corporate News* (May 14, 2007)
Pub: Comtex News Network Inc.
Description: Universal Energy Group Ltd., a company that sells electricity and natural gas to small to mid-size commercial and small industrial customers as well as residential customers, announced the release of its March 31, 2007 financial statements. Management's analysis and discussion of the company's financial condition and results of operations are listed. Statistical data included.

23437 ■ "Uptick in Clicks: Nordstrom's Online Sales Surging" in *Puget Sound Business Journal* (Vol. 29, August 22, 2008, No. 18, pp. 1)
Pub: American City Business Journals
Ed: Gregg Lamm. **Description:** Nordstrom Inc.'s online division grew its sales by 15 percent in the second quarter of 2008, compared to 2007's 4.3 percent in overall decline. The company expects their online net sales to reach $700 million in 2008 capturing eight percent of overall sales.

23438 ■ "USAmeriBank Deals for Growth" in *The Business Journal-Serving Greater Tampa Bay* (Vol. 28, September 26, 2008, No. 40, pp. 1)
Pub: American City Business Journals, Inc.
Ed: Margie Manning. **Description:** It is believed that the pending $14.9 million purchase of Liberty Bank by USAmeriBank could be at the forefront of a trend. Executives of both companies expect the deal to close by the end of 2008. USAmeriBank will have $430 million in assets and five offices in Pinellas, Florida once the deal is completed.

23439 ■ "Utilities Report Lower Customer Growth Rate, Power Use" in *The Business Journal - Serving Phoenix and the Valley of the Sun* (Vol. 28, August 8, 2008, No. 49, pp. 1)
Pub: American City Business Journals, Inc.
Ed: Patrick O'Grady. **Description:** Arizona Public Service Co. and Salt River Project are experiencing sharp decrease in customer growth rates due to less movement of people to the Valley. Arizona Public Service Co. expects a further decline of just 1 percent customer growth by the end of 2008 while Salt River Project expects this to grow between 1 to 2 percent for the two years ahead of 2008.

23440 ■ "V&J Scores Partnership with Shaq" in *Business Journal-Milwaukee* (Vol. 25, October 12, 2007, No. 2, pp. A1)
Pub: American City Business Journals, Inc.
Ed: Rich Kirchen. **Description:** O'Neal Franchise Group has agreed to a partnership with V&J Foods of Milwaukee to handle Auntie Anne's shops in New York, South Africa, Michigan, and the Caribbean. V&J O'Neal Enterprises will open six Auntie Anne's soft pretzel shops in Detroit towards the end of 2007. Planned international ventures of the partnership are presented.

23441 ■ "VC Boosts WorkForce; Livonia Software Company to Add Sales, Marketing Staff" in *Crain's Detroit Business* (March 24, 2008)
Pub: Crain Communications, Inc.
Ed: Tom Henderson. **Description:** WorkForce Software Inc., a company that provides software to manage payroll processes and oversee compliance with state and federal regulations and with union rules, plans to use an investment of $5.5 million in venture capital to hire more sales and marketing staff.

23442 ■ "The VC Shakeout" in *Harvard Business Review* (Vol. 88, July-August 2010, No. 7-8, pp. 21)
Pub: Harvard Business School Publishing
Ed: Joseph Ghalbouni, Dominque Rouzies. **Description:** Authors argue that in order to be successful, venture capital needs to focus less on how to sell a newly acquired investment and more on ways to grow a good company.

23443 ■ *The Venture Cafe*
Pub: Business Plus
Ed: Teresa Esser. **Released:** 2002. **Description:** Research covering the types of entrepreneurs who build new, high-technology ventures from the ground up. Author interviewed over 150 high-tech professionals in order to gather information to help others start high-tech companies.

23444 ■ "VeriFone Announces Global Security Solutions Business" in *Marketing Weekly News* (October 3, 2009)
Pub: Investment Weekly News
Description: Focused on delivering innovative security solutions, VeriFone Holdings, Inc. announced the formation of its Global Security Solutions Business Unit, including VeriShield Protect, an end-to-end encryption to protect cardholder data throughout the merchant and processor systems. The business will focus on consulting, sales and implementation of these new products in order to help retailers and processors protect customer data.

23445 ■ "Verizon Comes Calling With 500 Jobs" in *Business First Columbus* (Vol. 25, September 15, 2008, No. 4, pp. 1)
Pub: American City Business Journals
Ed: Brian R. Ball. **Description:** Hilliard, Ohio offered Verizon Wireless a 15-year incentive package worth $3.4 million for the company to move 300 customer financial services jobs to the city in addition to the 200 jobs from their facility in Dublin, Ohio. The incentives include a return of 15 percent of the income tax generated by the jobs.

23446 ■ "Vernon Revamp" in *Business Courier* (Vol. 26, October 9, 2009, No. 24, pp. 1)
Pub: American City Business Journals, Inc.
Ed: Dan Monk. **Description:** Al Neyer Inc. will redevelop the Vernon Manor Hotel as an office building for the Cincinnati Children's Hospital Medical Center. The project will cost $35 million and would generate a new investment vehicle for black investors who plan to raise $2.7 million in private offerings to claim majority ownership of the property after its renovations.

23447 ■ "Virgin Mobile has Big Plans for Year Two" in *Globe & Mail* (March 6, 2006, pp. B5)
Pub: CTVglobemedia Publishing Inc.
Ed: Catherine McLean. **Description:** The business growth plans of Virgin Mobile Canada are presented.

23448 ■ "VISA: Canadians Spend $97 Million on Mom This Mother's Day" in *Canadian Corporate News* (May 16, 2007)
Pub: Comtex News Network Inc.
Description: Visa Canada finds that Canadians are spending more on Mother's Day in recent years. Since 2002, sales of jewelry, flowers, and cards have climbed steadily in the week before Mother's Day weekend.

23449 ■ "Vision for Camden in Better Focus" in *Philadelphia Business Journal* (Vol. 30, September 30, 2011, No. 33, pp. 1)
Pub: American City Business Journals Inc.
Ed: Natalie Kostelni. **Description:** More than $500 million worth of projects aimed at redeveloping the downtown and waterfront areas of Camden, New Jersey are being planned. These include the construction of residential, commercial, and education buildings.

23450 ■ "Visionary Riches" in *Small Business Opportunities* (Winter 2009)
Pub: Entrepreneur Media Inc.
Description: Profile of Sterling Optical, which was included in a recent listing of 25 franchise high performers in The Wall Street Journal and is poised for mega-growth due to its offerings of professional eye exams, impeccable customer service, convenient locations and a great selection of eyewear.

23451 ■ "Wachovia Gears Up for Major Arizona Expansion" in *Business Journal-Serving Phoenix and the Valley of the Sun* (Vol. 5, Oct. 5, 2007)
Pub: American City Business Journals, Inc.
Ed: Chris Casacchia. **Description:** Wachovia, America's fourth-largest bank is finalizing a deal to build its Arizona headquarters in downtown Phoenix. The bank plans to add an additional 100 employees

by June 2008 and double its financial network to 30 offices in four years. Wachovia will also convert fifteen World Savings Bank branches it acquired in 2006 through Golden West Financial Corporation.

23452 ■ *Wake Up and Smell the Zeitgeist*
Pub: Basic Books
Ed: Grand McCracken. **Released:** 2010. **Price:** $26. 95. **Description:** Insight is given into an element of corporate success that's often overlooked and valuable suggestions are offered for any small business to pursue.

23453 ■ "'Wal-Mart Effect' Feeds Grocer Price Wars" in *Globe & Mail* (March 15, 2007, pp. B14)
Pub: CTVglobemedia Publishing Inc.
Ed: Marina Strauss. **Description:** The decrease in profit reports by Canadian grocery giants amidst high expansion plans by Wal-Mart Stores Inc. are discussed. This industry is witnessing the most severe pricing competitions in recent times.

23454 ■ "Wal-Mart Expansion Plans Hit Roadblock" in *Crain's Chicago Business* (Vol. 31, March 24, 2008, No. 12, pp. 2)
Pub: Crain Communications, Inc.
Ed: Monee Fields-White. **Description:** Wal-Mart Stores Inc.'s expansion plans in Chicago have suffered a series of setbacks due to a shifting political landscape in which may require the company to pay higher wages. Wal-Mart claims that its hourly pay and benefits are fair; however, the labor force does not agree.

23455 ■ "Wal-Mart Proposed for Timmerman Plaza" in *Business Journal-Milwaukee* (Vol. 28, December 31, 2010, No. 14, pp. A1)
Pub: Milwaukee Business Journal
Ed: Sean Ryan. **Description:** Dickson, Tennessee-based Gatlin Development Company Inc. owner Franklin C. Gatlin III revealed plans for a new Wal-Mart store in Timmerman Plaza in Milwaukee, Wisconsin. Wal-Mart plans to open up approximately 18 new stores in southeast Wisconsin in 2012 and the Timmerman project is the first of four that Gatlin will submit for city approval.

23456 ■ "Wal-Mart Takes Expansion Up a Notch" in *Globe & Mail* (March 21, 2007, pp. B8)
Pub: CTVglobemedia Publishing Inc.
Ed: Shirley Won. **Description:** Retail giant Wal-Mart Canada Corp. is planning to invest $500 million for expanding its business in Ontario region. It will open 21 new outlets by the end of 2007.

23457 ■ "Walgreen Takes Up Doctoring" in *Crain's Chicago Business* (Vol. 31, March 31, 2008, No. 13, pp. 18)
Pub: Crain Communications, Inc.
Ed: Mark Bruno. **Description:** Walgreen Co. has agreed to acquire two firms that provide on-site medical and pharmaceutical services to large companies. Walgreen feels that these facilities mark the future of health care for a number of large corporations.

23458 ■ "Walk This Way" in *Barron's* (Vol. 90, August 23, 2010, No. 34, pp. 13)
Pub: Barron's Editorial & Corporate Headquarters
Ed: Christopher C. Williams. **Description:** Crocs and Skechers are selling very popular shoes and sales show no signs of winding down. The shares of both companies are attractively prices.

23459 ■ *The Wall Street Journal. Complete Small Business Guidebook*
Pub: Three Rivers Press
Ed: Colleen DeBaise. **Released:** December 29, 2009. **Price:** $15.00. **Description:** The mechanics of building, running and growing a profitable business are outlined, teaching how to write a business plan, ways to finding money during lean years, how to keep stress in check, time management, investment in technology, hiring, marketing, management basics, angel investing and venture capital, as well as an exit strategy.

23460 ■ "Walmart, Target Moving to Convenience Store Near You" in *Hardware Retailing* (Vol. 199, November 2010, No. 5, pp. 60)
Pub: North American Retail Hardware Association
Description: Walmart has plans to move into small convenience stores in Chicago, Detroit, San Francisco, and Los Angeles.

23461 ■ "The War for Good Jobs; The World Will IBe Led with Economic Force" in *Gallup Management Journal* (September 7, 2011)
Pub: Gallup
Ed: Jim Clifton. **Description:** Gallup's chairman believes the next world war will be for good jobs and the winner will triumph with economic force, driven primarily by job creation and quality GDP growth.

23462 ■ "Watchful Eye: Entrepreneur Protects Clients and His Bottom Line" in *Black Enterprise* (Vol. 38, March 2008, No. 8, pp. 46)
Pub: Earl G. Graves Publishing Co. Inc.
Ed: Tennille M. Robinson. **Description:** Profile of Elijah Shaw, founder of Icon Services Corporation, a full service security and investigative service; Shaw shares his plans to protect clients while growing his business.

23463 ■ "Wattles Plugs Back Into State" in *Business Journal Portland* (Vol. 27, November 19, 2010, No. 38, pp. 1)
Pub: Portland Business Journal
Ed: Wendy Culverwell. **Description:** Denver, Colorado-based Ultimate Electronics Inc.'s first store in Oregon was opened in Portland and the 46th store in the chain of electronic superstores is expected to employ 70-80 workers. The venture is the latest for Mark Wattles, one of Oregon's most successful entrepreneurs, who acquired Ultimate from bankruptcy.

23464 ■ "We All Scream for Ice Cream" in *Crain's Chicago Business* (Vol. 31, April 28, 2008, No. 17, pp. 48)
Pub: Crain Communications, Inc.
Ed: Phuong Ly. **Description:** Profile of Oberweis' ice cream shops which has expanded its business by delivering dairy products to grocery stores.

23465 ■ *We Are Smarter Than Me: How to Unleash the Power of Crowds in Your Business*
Pub: Wharton School Publishing
Ed: Barry Libert; Jon Spector; Don Tapscott. **Released:** October 5, 2007. **Price:** $21.99. **Description:** Ways to use social networking and community in order to make decisions and plan your business, with a focus on product development, manufacturing, marketing, customer service, finance, management, and more.

23466 ■ "Wear More Hats" in *Canadian Business* (Vol. 80, March 12, 2007, No. 6, pp. 39)
Pub: Rogers Media
Ed: Michael Stern. **Description:** The need on the part of managers to volunteer to accept more responsibilities for their growth as well as that of company's is discussed.

23467 ■ "Web Biz Brulant Surfing for Acquisition Candidates" in *Crain's Cleveland Business* (Vol. 28, December 3, 2007, No. 48, pp. 6)
Pub: Crain Communications, Inc.
Ed: Chuck Soder. **Description:** Brulant Inc., a provider of web development and marketing services, is looking to acquire other companies after growing for five years straight. The company is one of the largest technology firms in Northeast Ohio.

23468 ■ "Welcome to the Neighborhood" in *Hawaii Business* (Vol. 53, October 2007, No. 4, pp. 48)
Pub: Hawaii Business Publishing
Ed: Jolyn Okimoto Rosa. **Description:** Finance Factors is planning to build branches in Manoa, and Liliha, as part of its strategy to position itself in high-yield areas. The company chose Manoa and Liliha due to thee sites' rich deposits. Its strategy with regards to the branches' location and to the building design is discussed.

23469 ■ "Wells Fargo Will Soon Lead Local Banks in Deposits" in *Austin Business JournalInc.* (Vol. 28, December 5, 2008, No. 38, pp. A1)
Pub: American City Business Journals
Ed: Christopher Calnan. **Description:** Acquisition of Wachovia Corporation by Wells Fargo and Company will leave the latter as the top bank for deposits in Austin, Texas. The merged bank will have deposits of more than $ billion, more than the $3.9 billion deposits Bank of America maintains in the area.

23470 ■ "Welsh Meat Sales on the Rise" in *Farmer's Weekly* (March 28, 2008, No. 320)
Pub: Reed Business Information
Description: Due, in part, to marketing efforts, retail sales of Welsh lamb and beef rose significantly in the first two months of 2008.

23471 ■ "Wendy's Mulls Total Hortons Selloff" in *Globe & Mail* (January 7, 2006, pp. B5)
Pub: CTVglobemedia Publishing Inc.
Ed: Sinclair Stewart; Omar El Akkad. **Description:** The plans of Wendy's International Inc. to spin off Tim Hortons are presented.

23472 ■ "WestJet Ponders Growth Plan Following Record Profit" in *Globe & Mail* (February 15, 2007, pp. B15)
Pub: CTVglobemedia Publishing Inc.
Ed: Brent Jang. **Description:** The Calgary-based WestJet Airlines Ltd., which reported a record $114.7 million profit last year, is planning to expand its operations by 2010. The airline is planning new services and carriers.

23473 ■ *What Works: Success in Stressful Times*
Pub: Harper Press
Ed: Hamish McRae. **Released:** January 21, 2010. **Price:** $30.12. **Description:** Exploration of success stories from across the glove, and what Michelle Obama referred to as 'the flimsy difference between success and failure.' Why do some initiatives take off while others flounder? How have communities managed to achieve so much while others struggle? What distinguishes the good companies from the bad? What lessons can be learned from the well-ordered Mumbai community made famous by 'Slumdog Millionaire'? Why have Canadian manners helped Whistler become the most popular ski resort in North America?

23474 ■ "What'll You Have Tonight?" in *Barron's* (Vol. 88, July 4, 2008, No. 28, pp. 22)
Pub: Dow Jones & Co., Inc.
Ed: Neil A. Martin. **Description:** Shares of Diageo could rise by 30 percent a year from June 2008 after it slipped due to U.S. sales worries. The company also benefits from the trend toward more premium alcoholic beverage brands worldwide especially in emerging markets.

23475 ■ "What's Holding Down Small Business?" in *Business Owner* (Vol. 35, November-December 2011, No. 6, pp. 3)
Pub: DL Perkins Company
Description: According to a recent survey conducted by the National Federation of Independent Business, demand is the number one reason for slow growth to any small business in today's economy.

23476 ■ "What's Next, Pup Tents in Bryant Park?" in *Advertising Age* (Vol. 78, January 29, 2007, No. 5, pp. 4)
Pub: Crain Communications, Inc.
Ed: Stephanie Thompson. **Description:** Designers such as Ralph Lauren, Juicy Couture, Burberry and Kiehl's have been expanding their businesses with new clothing lines for pets. Packaged Facts, a division of MarketResearch.com, predicts that pet expenditures will continue to grow in the years to come.

23477 ■ *When Family Businesses are Best*
Pub: Palgrave Macmillan

Ed: Randel S. Carlock, John L. Ward. **Released:** March 1, 2010. **Price:** $45.00. **Description:** An exploration into effective planning and communication to help small businesses grow into multi-generation family enterprises.

23478 ■ *When Growth Stalls: How It Happens, Why You're Stuck, and what To Do About It*
Pub: John Wiley & Sons, Inc.

Ed: Steve McKee. **Released:** March 1, 2009. **Price:** $27.95. **Description:** Marketing expert presents evidence that demonstrates that slow growth experienced by a firm is usually not the cause of mismanagement or blundering, but by natural market forces and destructive internal dynamics that are often unrecognized.

23479 ■ "When Success Isn't Enough" in *Entrepreneur* (Vol. 35, November 2007, No. 11, pp. 78)
Pub: Entrepreneur Media Inc.

Ed: Chris Penttila. **Description:** Companies that achieve success can often times continue to push for more growth. Details on planning expansion and boosting sales of several companies are explored.

23480 ■ "Where Next?" in *Business Strategy Review* (Vol. 21, Summer 2010, No. 2, pp. 20)
Pub: Wiley-Blackwell

Description: The emergence of large, vibrant and seemingly unstoppable new markets has been the good news story of the past decade. Brazil, Russia, India and China (BRIC) are among those who have emerged blinking into the new economy.

23481 ■ "Where's the Lava" in *Hawaii Business* (Vol. 53, November 2007, No. 5, pp. 18)
Pub: Hawaii Business Publishing

Ed: Jason Ubay. **Description:** Hawaii Volcanoes National Park used to allow visitors to drive to the end of the paved coastal park road and view flowing lava that came from Kilauea until it reached the sea. On Father's Day morning in June 2007, Kilauea began erupting outside the park and the lava flows inland to Kahaualea and Wao Kele O Puna natural area reserves. In July 2007 321,217 visitors came to the park, a 14 percent increase compared to the same month in 2006.

23482 ■ "While Competitors Shut Doors, Subway Is Still Growing" in *Advertising Age* (Vol. 79, July 21, 2008, No. 28, pp. 4)
Pub: Crain Communications, Inc.

Ed: Emily Bryson York. **Description:** Subway, the largest fast-food chain, with 22,000 U.S. locations, is adding 800 this year, despite the economic downturn that has caused competitors such as Starbucks to close stores and McDonald's to focus its expansion abroad.

23483 ■ "Whopper; Russ Klein" in *Advertising Age* (Vol. 79, November 17, 2008, No. 43, pp. S10)
Pub: Crain Communications, Inc.

Ed: Emily Bryson York. **Description:** Burger King has seen a double digit increase in the sales of its Whopper hamburger despite the economic recession that has hit many in the restaurant industry particularly hard. For most of the spring, U.S. same-store-sales gains beat McDonald's.

23484 ■ "Why the Rout in Financials Isn't Over" in *Barron's* (Vol. 88, June 30, 2008, No. 26, pp. 23)
Pub: Dow Jones & Co., Inc.

Ed: Robin Goldwyn Blumenthal. **Description:** Top market technician Louise Yamada warns that the retreat in the shares of financial services is not yet over based on her analysis of stock charts. Yamada's analysis of the charts of Citigroup, Fifth Third Bancorp and Merrill Lynch are discussed together with the graphs for these shares. Statistical data included.

23485 ■ "Why We'll Never Escape Facebook" in *Canadian Business* (Vol. 83, June 15, 2010, No. 10, pp. 28)
Pub: Rogers Media Ltd.

Ed: James Cowan, Tamara Shopsin, Jason Fulford. **Description:** Facebook users are growing in numbers despite criticism of the site's privacy policies that have put the onus of keeping anonymous to the user. Facebook's business model and its growing influence on the Internet are discussed.

23486 ■ "William Barr III; President, Co-Founder, Universal Windows Direct, 33" in *Crain's Cleveland Business* (November 19, 2007)
Pub: Crain Communications, Inc.

Ed: David Bennett. **Description:** Profile of William Barr III, the president and co-founder of Universal Windows Direct, a manufacturer of vinyl windows and siding, whose successful salesmanship and leadership has propelled his company forward.

23487 ■ "Winburn's Big Idea" in *Business Courier* (Vol. 27, October 8, 2010, No. 23, pp. 1)
Pub: Business Courier

Ed: Dan Monk, Lucy May. **Description:** Cincinnati Councilman Charlie Winburn proposed the creation of Cincinnati Competitive Edge Division and to remake a small-business division of the city in order to start a job-creation program. The new division will monitor compliance to the city's small business inclusion regulations, as well as to help small business owners grow.

23488 ■ "Windstream Expands Business Service Into Monroe" in *Marketing Weekly News* (January 23, 2010, pp. 77)
Pub: Investment Weekly News

Description: Windstream Corp. announces the expansion of its data and voice services into Monroe, N.C., which will give local businesses a new choice for advanced communication services and network security.

23489 ■ "Winner: Nonprofit, Human Services" in *Crain's Detroit Business* (Vol. 25, June 22, 2009, No. 25, pp. E002)
Pub: Crain Communications Inc. - Detroit

Ed: Sherri Begin Welch. **Description:** Profile of Lighthouse of Oakland County, located in Pontiac, Michigan. The nonprofit and its three subsidiaries are operating on a consolidated 2009 budget of $8.5 million.

23490 ■ "The Winner's Circle" in *Hispanic Business* (Vol. 30, April 2008, No. 4, pp. 20)
Pub: Hispanic Business

Ed: Hildy Medina. **Description:** Although there has been progress concerning Hispanic women professionals who are growing in numbers in the upper echelons of the corporate arena, many still find that they face discrimination when it comes to pay and promotions. Statistical data included.

23491 ■ "Wireless Provider's Star Grows $283 Million Brighter" in *Hispanic Business* (July-August 2007, pp. 60)
Pub: Hispanic Business

Description: Profile of Brightstar Corporation, the world's largest wireless phone distribution and supply chain reported record growth in 2007.

23492 ■ "Wirtz Partners With California Liquor Wholesaler To Expand Reach" in *Chicago Tribune* (December 17, 2008)
Pub: McClatchy-Tribune Information Services

Ed: Mike Hughlett. **Description:** Young's Market Co. and Wirtz Beverage Group have tentatively agreed to a joint venture that will give both companies a larger reach in the wine and liquor distribution business.

23493 ■ "WNY Casing In On Loonie's Climb" in *Business First Buffalo* (November 23, 2007, pp. 1)
Pub: American City Business Journals, Inc.

Ed: Scott Thomas. **Description:** Economy of Western New York has rebounded since the 9/11 recession and the rise of the Canadian dollar, which has contributed to the areas economic growth. Canadian shoppers are frequenting markets in the area due to the parity of the U.S. and Canadian dollar. Details of the cross-border shopping and its impact in WNY are discussed.

23494 ■ "Women Clicking to Earn Virtual Dollars" in *Sales and Marketing Management* (November 11, 2009)
Pub: Nielsen Business Media, Inc.

Ed: Stacy Straczynski. **Description:** According to a new report from Internet marketing firm Q Interactive, women are increasingly playing social media games where they are able to click on an ad or sign up for a promotion to earn virtual currency. Research is showing that this kind of marketing may be a potent tool, especially for e-commerce and online stores.

23495 ■ "Women Inch Forward on Corporate Boards" in *Marketing to Women* (Vol. 21, April 2008, No. 4, pp. 6)
Pub: EPM Communications, Inc.

Description: According to the latest study by Inter-Organization Network, few huge leaps of progress and in some cases backsliding has taken place in regards to gender diversity on corporate boards. Statistical data included.

23496 ■ "Work/Family Balance Boosts Business" in *Marketing to Women* (Vol. 21, February 2008, No. 2, pp. 8)
Pub: EPM Communications, Inc.

Description: Flexibility in the workplace is becoming a more important issue to both women and men. Statistical data included.

23497 ■ "The World Is Your Hospital" in *Canadian Business* (Vol. 81, July 22, 2008, No. 12-13, pp. 62)
Pub: Rogers Media Ltd.

Ed: Sharda Prashad. **Description:** Medical tourism is seen as a booming industry around the world and is expected to grow to around $40 billion in 2010. Key information regarding medical tourism and services are presented. Views on the possible impact of medical tourism on Canada's health care industry, as well as medical tourism opportunities in Canada, are also given.

23498 ■ "A World of Opportunity: Foreign Markets Offer Diversity to Keen Investors" in *Canadian Business* (Vol. 81, Summer 2008, No. 9)
Pub: Rogers Media Ltd.

Ed: Andrew Wahl. **Description:** International Monetary Fund projected in its 'World Economy Outlook' that there is a 25 percent chance that a global recession will occur in 2008 and 2009. Global growth rate is forecasted at 3.7 percent in 2008. Inflation in Asia emerging markets and forecasts on stock price indexes are presented.

23499 ■ "The World Tomorrow" in *Canadian Business* (Vol. 81, December 24, 2007, No. 1, pp. 35)
Pub: Rogers Media

Ed: Zena Olijnyk. **Description:** Global economy is predicted to be in a difficult period as analysts expect a slowdown in economic growth. Germany's Deutsche Bank wrote in a report about 'growth recession' that the chances of the world growth falling below two percent being one in three. Forecasts on other global economic aspects are explored.

23500 ■ "World Wide Technology Expands" in *Black Enterprise* (Vol. 37, December 2006, No. 5, pp. 34)
Pub: Earl G. Graves Publishing Co. Inc.

Ed: Marcia A. Wade. **Description:** World Wide Technology Inc. opened a streamlined, higher capacity 12,000-square-foot Integration Technology Center near its corporate headquarters in St. Louis. The new venture will transfer lower costs to customers.

23501 ■ "Wowing Her Customers" in *Women In Business* (Vol. 61, August-September 2009, No. 4, pp. 34)
Pub: American Business Women's Association

Ed: Kathleen Leighton. **Description:** Gail Worth, together with her brother, bought her parents' Harley-Davidson motorcycle dealership in Grandview, Missouri. She eventually had the dealership to herself when her brother broke out of the partnership. Gail says she is comfortable in a man's world kind of business and has expanded the business with a 10-acre site.

23502 ■ "Wrigley's Newest Taste: Wolfberry" in *Crain's Chicago Business* (Vol. 31, March 31, 2008, No. 13, pp. 1)
Pub: Crain Communications, Inc.

Ed: David Sterrett. **Description:** Wm. Wrigley Jr. Co. has introduced a gum line in China that touts the medicinal advantages of aloe vera to improve skin and wolfberry to boost energy in an attempt to keep the company positioned as the top candy firm in China.

23503 ■ "The Wrong Tune" in *The Business Journal-Portland* (Vol. 25, July 25, 2008, No. 20, pp. 1)
Pub: American City Business Journals, Inc.

Ed: Robin J. Moody. **Description:** Views and information on turnaround management and recovery plans of the Oregon Symphony, are presented. The nonprofit organization has lost a total of $5.1 million between 2002 and 2008, and $400,000 annual interest payments for a $7 million bank loan. Increased ticket sales, as well as cost cutting measures, are helping improve the finance of the organization.

23504 ■ "Yamana's Golden Boy" in *Canadian Business* (Vol. 80, November 19, 2007, No. 23, pp. 49)
Pub: Rogers Media

Ed: John Gray. **Description:** Profile of Peter Marrone, founder of the gold-producing company Yamana Gold Inc. in 2003. Yamana has grown since its 2003 launch, with $110 million reported earnings for the first three quarters in 2007. Marrone's career and how he built Yamana are discussed.

23505 ■ "A Year After Fiorina's Exit, Hurd Makes His Mark" in *Globe & Mail* (February 8, 2006, pp. B9)
Pub: CTVglobemedia Publishing Inc.

Ed: Shawn McCarthy. **Description:** The business growth strategies of chief executive officer Mark Hurd of Hewlett-Packard Co. are presented.

23506 ■ "YoCream" in *Ice Cream Reporter* (Vol. 23, September 20, 2010, No. 10, pp. 6)
Pub: Ice Cream Reporter

Description: YoCream reported a sales increase for third quarter 2010 at 15.6 percent and net income increasing 25 percent to $2,141,000 for that quarter.

23507 ■ "Yogun Fruz Adds First Location in Southern New York State" in *Ice Cream Reporter* (Vol. 23, September 20, 2010, No. 10, pp. 2)
Pub: Ice Cream Reporter

Description: Yogen Fruz signed a master franchise agreement to expand into the southern counties of New York State. The firm offers a healthy and beneficial option to fast food and typical dessert choices.

23508 ■ "Yogurtini" in *Ice Cream Reporter* (Vol. 23, September 20, 2010, No. 10, pp. 7)
Pub: Ice Cream Reporter

Description: Self-serve frozen yogurt chain, Yogurtini has opened its second store in Kansas City, Missouri.

23509 ■ "You Won't Go Broke Filling Up On These Stocks" in *Barron's* (Vol. 88, July 14, 2008, No. 28, pp. 38)
Pub: Dow Jones & Co., Inc.

Ed: Assif Shameen. **Description:** Due to high economic growth, pro-business policies and a consumption boom, the Middle East is a good place to look for equities. The best ways in which to gain exposure to this market include investing in the real estate industry and telecommunications markets as well as large banks that serve corporations and consumers.

23510 ■ "Your Big Give" in *Small Business Opportunities* (September 2008)
Pub: Entrepreneur Media Inc.
Ed: Michael Guld. **Description:** Cause related marketing is beneficial to businesses as well as the communities they inhabit; three small businesses that are elevating their standing in the community while at the same time increasing their customer base are profiled.

23511 ■ "Your Booming Business: How You Can Align Sales and Marketing for Dynamic Growth" in *Small Business Opportunities* (Spring 2008)
Pub: Harris Publications Inc.
Ed: Voss W. Graham. **Description:** Voss Graham, founder and CEO of Inneractive Consulting Group Inc., works with companies to develop and hire successful sales teams. A checklist from the American Bankers Association to help write a business plan is included.

23512 ■ *Your Business, Your Future: How to Predict and Harness Growth*
Pub: Allen and Unwin Pty., Limited
Ed: Linda Hailey. **Released:** January 2007. **Price:** $16.95. **Description:** Four distinct phases every small companies faces during growth are profiled.

23513 ■ *Your First Business Plan: A Simple Question-and-Answer Format Designed to Help You Write Your Own Plan*
Pub: Sourcebooks, Incorporated
Ed: Joseph A. Covello. **Released:** May 2005. **Price:** $14.95. **Description:** Writing a good first business plan outlines successful business growth.

23514 ■ "Zakkamono Taps Growing Market for Collectibles" in *Hawaii Business* (Vol. 54, September 2008, No. 3, pp. 68)
Pub: Hawaii Business Publishing
Ed: Casey Chin. **Description:** Profile of Zakkamono, a business that designs and sells designer toys, shirts and other collectibles; the first toys being Mousubi and Miao figurines. Owners Zakka and Rae Huo say that one of the business' challenges is finding manufacturing resources. Other details about Zakkamono are discussed.

23515 ■ "Zebra's Changing Stripes" in *Crain's Chicago Business* (Vol. 31, November 17, 2008, No. 46, pp. 4)
Pub: Crain Communications, Inc.
Ed: John Pletz. **Description:** Zebra Technologies Corp., the world's largest manufacturer of bar-code printers is profiled; the company's stock has plunged with shares declining 40 percent in the past three months grinding the firm's growth to a halt. Zebra's plans to regain revenue growth are also discussed.

23516 ■ "ZF Revving Up Jobs, Growth" in *Business Courier* (Vol. 26, November 6, 2009, No. 28, pp. 1)
Pub: American City Business Journals, Inc.
Ed: Jon Newberry. **Description:** Proposed $96 million expansion of German-owned automotive supplier ZF Steering systems LLC is anticipated to generate 299 jobs in Boone County, Kentucky. ZF might invest $90 million in equipment, while the rest will go to building and improvements.

TRADE PERIODICALS

23517 ■ *Expansion Management*
Pub: Penton Media Inc.
Contact: Ron Lowy, Publisher
E-mail: ron.lowy@penton.com
Ed: Josh Cable, Editor, josh.cable@penton.com. **Released:** 6/yr. **Price:** $50 Canada; $68 institutions international. **Description:** Magazine assisting executives and managers worldwide in planning and overseeing their companies' facilities development and other expansion and relocation activities.

23518 ■ *NACOMEX Insider*
Pub: NACOMEX USA Inc.
Contact: Robert Zises
Ed: Robert Zises, Editor, zises@nacomex.com. **Released:** Quarterly. **Price:** $199, U.S.. **Description:** Provides information on historical values, current tactics, and residual value forecasting for ad valorem tax, bankruptcy, loss compensation, and related purposes. Recurring features include news of research and a column titled Industry Round-up.

VIDEOCASSETTES/ AUDIOCASSETTES

23519 ■ *Growing Your Company*
Instructional Video
2219 C St.
Lincoln, NE 68502
Ph:(402)475-6570
Free: 800-228-0164
Fax:(402)475-6500
Co. E-mail: feedback@insvideo.com
URL: http://www.insvideo.com
Price: $99.00. **Description:** Offers advise on issues affecting business owners and managers, such as financial strategy, employee motivation, outselling the competition, and quality. **Availability:** VHS.

23520 ■ *The Ten Commandments of Networking*
Encyclopedia Britannica
331 N. LaSalle St.
Chicago, IL 60654
Ph:(312)347-7159
Free: 800-323-1229
Fax:(312)294-2104
URL: http://www.britannica.com
Released: 1994. **Price:** $39.95. **Description:** One-part seminar and one-part live demonstration of various networking situations, geared toward the entrepreneur who wants to expand and cultivate personal and business relationships. **Availability:** VHS.

CONSULTANTS

23521 ■ BPT Consulting Associates Ltd.
12 Parmenter Rd., Ste. B-6
Londonderry, NH 03053
Ph:(603)437-8484
Free: 888-278-0030
Fax:(603)434-5388
Co. E-mail: bptcons@tiac.net
Contact: John Kuczynski, President
E-mail: bptcons@tiac.net
Scope: Provides management consulting expertise and resources to cross-industry clients with services for: Business Management consulting, People/Human Resources Transition and Training programs, and a full cadre of multi-disciplined Technology Computer experts. Virtual consultants with expertise in e-commerce, supply chain management, organizational development, and business application development consulting.

23522 ■ Flor & Associates
179 Schan Dr.
Churchville, PA 18966-1619
Ph:(215)355-7466
Fax:(215)355-7464
Co. E-mail: fredflor@msn.com
Contact: Frederick Flor, President
Scope: Offers business development consulting helping companies increase the value of their businesses. Services include: market development for technologies sand products; product positioning strategies; technology assessment; competitive intelligence and analysis; team augmentation and facilitation; business growth strategies including acquisitions, licensing, and partnerships.

23523 ■ Herpers Gowling L.L.P.
4 Hughson St. S, Ste. 300
Hamilton, ON, Canada L8N 3Z1
Ph:(905)529-3328
Free: 888-735-9909
Fax:(905)529-3980
Co. E-mail: dgowling@herpersgowling.com
URL: http://www.herpersgowling.com
Contact: David Gowling, President
E-mail: dgowling@atsherpersgowling.com
Scope: Provides services to small and medium size businesses in the areas of financial management,

strategic planning, mergers and acquisitions and re-engineering/restructuring. **Special Services:** 310 DEBT[R].

23524 ■ McMann & Ransford
1 Sugar Creek Center Blvd., Ste. 300
Sugar Land, TX 77478
Free: (866)267-0299
URL: http://www.mcmannransford.com
Contact: Dean E. McMann, CEO
E-mail: dmcmann@mcmannransford.com
Scope: Provides of management consulting, training, executive recruiting and market research services specializing in the professional services industry.

23525 ■ Norman A. Robins Consulting
5127 S Cornell Ave.
Chicago, IL 60615-4215
Ph:(773)667-6463
Contact: S. R. Robins, Principle
Scope: Helps companies develop strategic plans that will improve profits, reduce costs, and accelerate growth.

23526 ■ Plans and Solutions Inc.
7823 Mistic View Ct.
PO Box 8905
Derwood, MD 20855
Ph:(301)947-8150
Fax:(240)525-5601
Co. E-mail: info@plansandsolutions.com
URL: http://www.plansandsolutions.com
Contact: Kenneth D. Weiss, President
E-mail: kw@plansandsolutions.com
Scope: Market research and competitive analysis; marketing and promotion planning, and executing promotion plans. Specializes in registration and problem solving services that include food canning establishment and process registration, registration under the terrorism act, assistance in case of detention of shipments, and on-site inspection of processing plants and records. Most clients are minority-owned businesses in the USA and companies overseas that want to begin or increase exports to the United States and Canada. **Publications:** "Building an Import/Export Business," John Wiley & Sons, 2002; "How to Conquer the U.S. Market "; "Going Global (Getting Started in International Trade)". **Seminars:** U.S. Import Regulations on Food Products.

23527 ■ The Sanderson Group Inc.
515 E 85 St., Ste. 4E
New York, NY 10028
Ph:(212)249-2556
Fax:(212)249-2557
Co. E-mail: robin@thesandersongroup.com
URL: http://www.thesandersongroup.com
Contact: Robin Sanderson, President
E-mail: robin@thesandersongroup.com
Scope: Offers marketing consulting; communications and event/promotion marketing; develops objectives, establishes strategies and tactics to capitalize on the opportunities, and executes programs. Services provided include: strategic and marketing planning, target marketing with expertise in college or teen markets, integrated marketing programs, sampling, event marketing, new product development, corporate communications, strategic alliance formation, website strategic partnerships, website development and marketing, new business development, market research, sales and field force creation and management and customer acquisition.

23528 ■ Stillman H. Publishers Inc.
21405 Woodchuck Ln.
Boca Raton, FL 33428
Ph:(561)482-6343
Contact: Herbert Stillman, President
Scope: Offers consulting services in the following areas: management, start ups, profit maximization, world wide negotiating, interim management, corporate debt resolution.

LIBRARIES

23529 ■ Buffalo & Erie County Public Library–Business, Science & Technology
1 Lafayette Sq.
Buffalo, NY 14203
Ph:(716)858-8900
Fax:(716)858-6211
Co. E-mail: muellern@buffalolib.org
URL: http://www.buffalolib.org
Contact: Nancy Mueller, Div.Mgr.
Scope: Investments, real estate, economics, marketing, engineering, computer science, technology, medical information for laymen, consumer information, automotive repair. **Services:** Interlibrary loan; copying; Library open to the public. **Holdings:** 312,916 books; 60,516 bound periodical volumes. **Subscriptions:** 2908 journals and other serials; 4 newspapers.

23530 ■ U.S. Dept. of Commerce–Library and Information Center
1401 Constitution Ave., NW
Washington, DC 20230
Ph:(202)482-5511
Fax:(202)482-5685
Co. E-mail: lawlibrary@doc.gov
URL: http://www.osec.doc.gov/lib/
Contact: Vera E. Whisenton, Dir.
Scope: Economics, export-import, foreign trade, business, economic theory, economic conditions, statistics, marketing, industry, finance, management, telecommunications. **Services:** Interlibrary loan; copying; Library open to the public for reference use only. **Holdings:** 45,000 books and bound periodical volumes; 4300 reels of microfilm; 250,000 volumes of microfiche; CD-ROMs. **Subscriptions:** 625 journals and other serials.

23531 ■ University of South Carolina–The Moore School of Business–Elliot White Springs Business Library (Franc)
Francis M. Hipp Bldg., 2nd Fl.
1705 College St.
Columbia, SC 29208
Ph:(803)777-6032
Fax:(803)777-6876
URL: http://www.sc.edu/library/pubserv/business.html
Contact: Dwight Gardner, Hd.Bus.Libn.
Scope: Corporations. **Services:** Interlibrary loan; copying; Library open to the public with restrictions. **Holdings:** 30,000 books; 4000 bound periodical volumes. **Subscriptions:** 350 journals and other serials; 5 newspapers.

RESEARCH CENTERS

23532 ■ Minnesota Labor and Industry Department–Policy Development, Research and Statistics Unit
443 Lafayette Rd. N
St. Paul, MN 55155
Ph:(651)284-5025
Free: 800—342-5354
Fax:(651)284-5726
Co. E-mail: dli.research@state.mn.us
URL: http://www.dli.mn.gov/Research.asp
Contact: Dr. David Berry
E-mail: dli.research@state.mn.us
Scope: Workers' compensation system and occupational safety and health programs in Minnesota. **Publications:** Minnesota Minimum Wage Report (annually); Minnesota Worker's Compensation System Report (annually); Minnesota Workplace Safety Report (annually).

Business Law

START-UP INFORMATION

23533 ■ *Becoming a Personal Trainer for Dummies*
Pub: John Wiley & Sons, Incorporated
Ed: Melyssa Michael, Linda Formichelli. **Released:** October 2004. **Price:** $19.99 (US), $25.99 (Canadian). **Description:** Legal and tax issues involved in starting and running a personal trainer firm. The book offers suggestions for incorporating massage and nutritional services.

23534 ■ *Enterprise Planning and Development: Small Business and Enterprise Start-Up Survival and Growth*
Pub: Elsevier Science and Technology Books
Ed: David Butler. **Released:** August 2006. **Price:** $42.95. **Description:** Innovation, intellectual property, and exit strategies are among the issues discussed in this book involving current entrepreneurship.

23535 ■ *How to Start, Operate and Market a Freelance Notary Signing Agent Business*
Pub: Gom Publishing, LLC
Ed: Victoria Ring. **Released:** September 2004. **Price:** $8.18. **Description:** Due to the changes in the 2001 Uniform Commercial Code allowing notary public agents to serve as a witness to mortgage loan closings (eliminating the 2-witness requirement under the old code), notaries are working directly for mortgage, title and signing companies as mobile notaries.

23536 ■ *Legal Guide for Starting and Running a Small Business*
Pub: NOLO
Ed: Fred Steingold. **Released:** April 2008. **Price:** $34.99. **Description:** Information for starting a new business focusing on choosing a business structure, taxes, employees and independent contractors, trademark and service marks, licensing and permits, leasing and improvement of commercial space, buying and selling a business, and more.

23537 ■ *Partnership: Small Business Start-Up Kit*
Pub: Nova Publishing Company
Ed: Daniel Sitarz. **Released:** November 2005. **Price:** $29.95. **Description:** Guidebook detailing partnership law by state covering the formation and use of partnerships as a business form. Information on filing requirements, property laws, legal liability, standards, and the new Revised Uniform Partnership Act is covered.

23538 ■ *Raising Capital*
Pub: Kiplinger Books and Tapes
Ed: Andrew J. Sherman. **Price:** $34.95. **Description:** Corporate attorney provides a comprehensive guide using in-depth, practical advice on raising money to start and grow a business. A 115-page appendix contains samples of financing agreements, forms and questionnaires.

23539 ■ *Small Business Legal Tool Kit*
Pub: Entrepreneur Press
Ed: Ira Nottonson; Theresa A. Pickner. **Released:** May 2007. **Price:** $36.95. **Description:** Legal expertise is provided by two leading entrepreneurial attorneys. Issues covered include forming and operating a business: taxes, contracts, leases, bylaws, trademarks, small claims court, etc.

23540 ■ *The Small Business Owner's Manual: Everything You Need to Know to Start Up and Run Your Business*
Pub: Career Press, Incorporated
Ed: Joe Kennedy. **Released:** June 2005. **Price:** $19.99 (US), $26.95 (Canadian). **Description:** Comprehensive guide for starting a small business, focusing on twelve ways to obtain financing, business plans, selling and advertising products and services, hiring and firing employees, setting up a Web site, business law, accounting issues, insurance, equipment, computers, banks, financing, customer credit and collection, leasing, and more.

23541 ■ *Working for Yourself: An Entrepreneur's Guide to the Basics*
Pub: Kogan Page, Limited
Ed: Jonathan Reuvid. **Released:** September 2006. **Description:** Guide for starting a new business venture, focusing on raising financing, legal and tax issues, marketing, information technology, and site location.

23542 ■ *Your First Business Plan: A Simple Question-and-Answer Format Designed to Help You Write Your Own Plan*
Pub: Sourcebooks, Incorporated
Ed: Joseph A. Covello. **Released:** May 2005. **Price:** $14.95. **Description:** Writing a good first business plan outlines successful business growth.

EDUCATIONAL PROGRAMS

23543 ■ Advanced Section 1031 Exchanges (Onsite)
Seminar Information Service, Inc.
20 Executive Park, Ste. 120
Irvine, CA 92614
Ph:(949)261-9104
Free: 877-SEM-INFO
Fax:(949)261-1963
Co. E-mail: info@seminarinformation.com
URL: http://www.seminarinformation.com
Price: $379.00. **Description:** This advanced seminar will provide you with practical tools and strategies you can use when participating in more complicated exchanges. **Locations:** Cincinnati, OH.

23544 ■ The Basic of HR Law
Padgett-Thompson Seminars
Rockhurst University CEC
14502 W. 105th St.
Lenexa, KS 66215
Free: 800-349-1935
URL: http://www.findaseminar.com/tpd/Padgett-Thompson-Seminars.asp
Price: $249.00. **Description:** A one-day seminar covering the basics of human resources law. **Locations:** Worcester, MA; Providence, RI; Boston, MA.

23545 ■ Collections Laws
Fred Pryor Seminars & CareerTrack
5700 Broadmoor St., Ste. 300
Mission, KS 66202
Free: 800-780-8476
Fax:(913)967-8849
Co. E-mail: customerservice@pryor.com
URL: http://www.pryor.com
Price: $149.00; $139.00 for groups of 5 or more. **Description:** Learn to collect money effectively and legally with an understanding of the Fair Debt Collection Practices Act (FDCPA). **Locations:** Cities throughout the United States.

23546 ■ Commercial and Real Estate Loan Documents: More than Just Papers (Onsite)
Seminar Information Service, Inc.
20 Executive Park, Ste. 120
Irvine, CA 92614
Ph:(949)261-9104
Free: 877-SEM-INFO
Fax:(949)261-1963
Co. E-mail: info@seminarinformation.com
URL: http://www.seminarinformation.com
Price: $429.00. **Description:** Seminar designed to provide you with the key information you need to increase your working knowledge and understanding of the key legal and non-legal issues related to commercial loan documentation, including the meaning of loan documents, common documentation mistakes, more effective methods to replace existing lenders and deal with third parties, and collateral. **Locations:** Fayetteville, AR.

23547 ■ Concentrated Course in Construction Contracts
Seminar Information Service, Inc.
20 Executive Park, Ste. 120
Irvine, CA 92614
Ph:(949)261-9104
Free: 877-SEM-INFO
Fax:(949)261-1963
Co. E-mail: info@seminarinformation.com
URL: http://www.seminarinformation.com
Price: $1,195.00. **Description:** Seven-day practical education in construction operations and construction law, including job set-up, claims avoidance, bonds, liens and insurance, specifications and bidding, labor relations, subcontracting, and more. **Locations:** Las Vegas, NV.

23548 ■ Data Analysis for EEO Professionals (Onsite)
Seminar Information Service, Inc.
20 Executive Park, Ste. 120
Irvine, CA 92614
Ph:(949)261-9104
Free: 877-SEM-INFO
Fax:(949)261-1963
Co. E-mail: info@seminarinformation.com
URL: http://www.seminarinformation.com
Price: $1,195.00. **Description:** Provides a solid understanding of the effective use of statistical analysis in EEO management and legal proceedings. Topics covered include: the legal basis for the use of

statistics in EEO; which analytical tools are appropriate; how to interpret the results; when to conduct additional investigation; and strategies for presenting findings to management, agencies, and the courts. **Locations:** New York, NY.

23549 ■ Employment Discrimination Law Update
Seminar Information Service, Inc.
20 Executive Park, Ste. 120
Irvine, CA 92614
Ph:(949)261-9104
Free: 877-SEM-INFO
Fax:(949)261-1963
Co. E-mail: info@seminarinformation.com
URL: http://www.seminarinformation.com

Price: $895.00. **Description:** Covers changes in EEO law and enforcement, sexual harassment, resolving claims and implementing ADA, and the FMLA. **Locations:** San Francisco, CA; Chicago, IL; and Washington, DC.

23550 ■ The Essentials of Collections Law
Padgett-Thompson Seminars
Rockhurst University CEC
14502 W. 105th St.
Lenexa, KS 66215
Free: 800-349-1935
URL: http://www.findaseminar.com/tpd/Padgett-Thompson-Seminars.asp

Price: $179.00. **Description:** A one-day training session for accounts receivable professionals at all levels. **Locations:** Cities throughout the United States.

23551 ■ Harassment Prevention in the Workplace
Seminar Information Service, Inc.
20 Executive Park, Ste. 120
Irvine, CA 92614
Ph:(949)261-9104
Free: 877-SEM-INFO
Fax:(949)261-1963
Co. E-mail: info@seminarinformation.com
URL: http://www.seminarinformation.com

Price: $795.00. **Description:** Explore the legal and policy concerns related to this complex workplace issue, including review and explore the guidelines for identifying inappropriate behavior; the laws, agency interpretations and court cases; and the key elements necessary for writing and implementing policies and procedures. **Locations:** New York, NY.

23552 ■ How to Legally Terminate Employees With Attitude Problems
Padgett-Thompson Seminars
Rockhurst University CEC
14502 W. 105th St.
Lenexa, KS 66215
Free: 800-349-1935
URL: http://www.findaseminar.com/tpd/Padgett-Thompson-Seminars.asp

Price: $199.00. **Description:** Learn how to act with confidence as you terminate problem employees who are damaging productivity and the company's effectiveness. **Locations:** Cities throughout the United States.

23553 ■ How to Manage an Information Security Program
Seminar Information Service, Inc.
20 Executive Park, Ste. 120
Irvine, CA 92614
Ph:(949)261-9104
Free: 877-SEM-INFO
Fax:(949)261-1963
Co. E-mail: info@seminarinformation.com
URL: http://www.seminarinformation.com

Price: $2,050.00. **Description:** Learn the components of a comprehensive plan, covering access control software applications; telecom/network security measures; physical protection of the computer facility; and the legal and regulatory aspects of information security. **Locations:** New York, NY; and Orlando, FL.

23554 ■ Human Resources and the Law
Seminar Information Service, Inc.
20 Executive Park, Ste. 120
Irvine, CA 92614
Ph:(949)261-9104
Free: 877-SEM-INFO
Fax:(949)261-1963
Co. E-mail: info@seminarinformation.com
URL: http://www.seminarinformation.com

Price: $1,995.00. **Description:** Provides the human resources professional with an understanding of the laws that obligate employers, recent legislation and court cases defining employer/employee rights and obligations, legal and business considerations bearing on employer decisions, practical implications of the laws in day-to-day human resources operations, impact of the laws on the development of policies and procedures, and alternatives for minimizing the company's exposure to employee lawsuits and administrative charges. **Locations:** New York, NY.

23555 ■ Introduction to Human Resources Law
Seminar Information Service, Inc.
20 Executive Park, Ste. 120
Irvine, CA 92614
Ph:(949)261-9104
Free: 877-SEM-INFO
Fax:(949)261-1963
Co. E-mail: info@seminarinformation.com
URL: http://www.seminarinformation.com

Price: $995.00. **Description:** Overview of the legal issues associated with day-to-day employment-related decisions and actions. **Locations:** New York, NY.

23556 ■ Legal Issues in Real Estate Foreclosure (Onsite)
Seminar Information Service, Inc.
20 Executive Park, Ste. 120
Irvine, CA 92614
Ph:(949)261-9104
Free: 877-SEM-INFO
Fax:(949)261-1963
Co. E-mail: info@seminarinformation.com
URL: http://www.seminarinformation.com

Price: $369.00. **Description:** Gain practical procedural pointers on how to assertively protect your clients' financial interests through an in-depth understanding of the foreclosure process. **Locations:** Memphis, TN.

23557 ■ Payroll Law
Seminar Information Service, Inc.
20 Executive Park, Ste. 120
Irvine, CA 92614
Ph:(949)261-9104
Free: 877-SEM-INFO
Fax:(949)261-1963
Co. E-mail: info@seminarinformation.com
URL: http://www.seminarinformation.com

Price: $199.00. **Description:** Learn exactly where you're vulnerable in complying with complex FLSA mandates, identify common mistakes that get most companies hauled into court, and ensure 100 percent accuracy and compliance, as well as examine special payroll situations like garnishments and levies and involuntary deductions. **Locations:** Cities throughout the United States.

23558 ■ Payroll Law 2011
Fred Pryor Seminars & CareerTrack
5700 Broadmoor St., Ste. 300
Mission, KS 66202
Free: 800-780-8476
Fax:(913)967-8849
Co. E-mail: customerservice@pryor.com
URL: http://www.pryor.com

Price: $199.00; $189.00 for groups of 5 or more. **Description:** Learn to handle payroll accurately, legally, and with confidence. **Locations:** Cities throughout the United States.

23559 ■ Practical Construction Law
Seminar Information Service, Inc.
20 Executive Park, Ste. 120
Irvine, CA 92614
Ph:(949)261-9104
Free: 877-SEM-INFO
Fax:(949)261-1963
Co. E-mail: info@seminarinformation.com
URL: http://www.seminarinformation.com

Price: $995.00. **Description:** Covers factors that must be considered at every stage of the construction process, including contracts, bidding for private and public work and Uniform Commercial Code. **Locations:** Las Vegas, NV.

23560 ■ A Practical Guide to the Davis-Bacon Act
Seminar Information Service, Inc.
20 Executive Park, Ste. 120
Irvine, CA 92614
Ph:(949)261-9104
Free: 877-SEM-INFO
Fax:(949)261-1963
Co. E-mail: info@seminarinformation.com
URL: http://www.seminarinformation.com

Price: $595.00; $349.00 for four or more. **Description:** Discussions of what the Act requires of contractors, special problem areas, overtime matters and calculations, sanctions for violations, how to develop on-going compliance procedures and more. **Locations:** Las Vegas, NV.

23561 ■ Property Condition Assessments Featuring E2018 Standard Guide (Onsite)
Seminar Information Service, Inc.
20 Executive Park, Ste. 120
Irvine, CA 92614
Ph:(949)261-9104
Free: 877-SEM-INFO
Fax:(949)261-1963
Co. E-mail: info@seminarinformation.com
URL: http://www.seminarinformation.com

Price: $895.00. **Description:** Two-day course with focus of the ASTM Property Condition Assessment standard and explains why it was developed. **Locations:** Chicago, IL; Las Vegas, NV; and Orlando, FL.

23562 ■ Property Taking Through Eminent Domain: What You Need to Know (Onsite)
Seminar Information Service, Inc.
20 Executive Park, Ste. 120
Irvine, CA 92614
Ph:(949)261-9104
Free: 877-SEM-INFO
Fax:(949)261-1963
Co. E-mail: info@seminarinformation.com
URL: http://www.seminarinformation.com

Price: $365.00. **Description:** Get the knowledge you need to exert the municipality's rights and achieve the best outcome possible, including how the Kelo ruling will affect your organization when considering a taking and get clear explanations of the parameters guiding the action. **Locations:** Oklahoma City, OK.

23563 ■ Real Estate Law: Advanced Issues and Answers (Onsite)
Seminar Information Service, Inc.
20 Executive Park, Ste. 120
Irvine, CA 92614
Ph:(949)261-9104
Free: 877-SEM-INFO
Fax:(949)261-1963
Co. E-mail: info@seminarinformation.com
URL: http://www.seminarinformation.com

Price: $399.00. **Description:** Go beyond the basics for an advanced look at complicated real estate concerns like resolving title defects, finding practical solutions to environmental conflicts, clearing difficult liens from titles, and dealing properly with property affected by a bankruptcy. **Locations:** Mission, KS; Topeka, KS; and Wichita, KS.

23564 ■ Resolving Real Estate Title Defects
Seminar Information Service, Inc.
20 Executive Park, Ste. 120
Irvine, CA 92614
Ph:(949)261-9104
Free: 877-SEM-INFO

Fax:(949)261-1963
Co. E-mail: info@seminarinformation.com
URL: http://www.seminarinformation.com
Price: $369.00. **Description:** Learn to recognize and resolve title problems that may arise during real estate transactions; Apply the standards of title examination effectively to uncover problems and prevent them whenever possible; Confidently take the next step when you recognize a defect and ensure the transaction goes smoothly. **Locations:** Tampa, FL.

23565 ■ Writing Effective EEO Investigative Reports
Seminar Information Service, Inc.
20 Executive Park, Ste. 120
Irvine, CA 92614
Ph:(949)261-9104
Free: 877-SEM-INFO
Fax:(949)261-1963
Co. E-mail: info@seminarinformation.com
URL: http://www.seminarinformation.com
Price: $1,195.00. **Description:** Focuses exclusively on the written product of an effective investigation. Topics include understanding the Faragher-Ellert Affirmative Defense and addressing credibility. **Locations:** New York, NY.

DIRECTORIES OF EDUCATIONAL PROGRAMS

23566 ■ *Bond's Franchise Guide 2009*
Pub: Source Book Publications
Ed: Robert E. Bond, Michelle Yang. **Released:** April 7, 2009. **Description:** Comprehensive directory offering prospective franchise owners a current and detailed profile of 1,000 franchises, as well as supplemental profiles of franchise attorneys and consultants; companies are divided into 45 categories for easy comparison.

23567 ■ *Neal-Schuman Guide to Finding Legal and Regulatory Information on the Internet*
Pub: Neal-Schuman Publishers Inc.
Ed: Yvonne J. Chandler, Editor. **Released:** new edition expected 2005. **Price:** $135, individuals. **Covers:** 900 Internet sites offering local, state, and federal legal and government information. **Entries Include:** Title, publishing agency, URL, brief description of the site.

REFERENCE WORKS

23568 ■ "11th Circuit: Don't Break the Law to Comply with It" in *Miami Daily Business Review* (October 21, 2009)
Pub: Incisive Media Ltd.
Ed: Janet L. Conley. **Description:** Niagara Credit Solutions argued with a three-judge panel that the company broke the rule saying debt collectors must identify themselves so that they could comply with a rule barring debt collectors from communicating about a debt with third parties.

23569 ■ "13D Filings" in *Barron's* (Vol. 88, March 24, 2008, No. 12, pp. M13)
Pub: Dow Jones & Company, Inc.
Description: HealthCor Management called as problematic the plan of Magellan Health Services to use its high cash balances for acquisitions. Carlson Capital discussed with Energy Partners possible changes in the latter's board. Investor Carl Icahn suggested that Enzon Pharmaceuticals consider selling itself or divest some of its assets.

23570 ■ "13D Filings: Investors Report to the SEC" in *Barron's* (Vol. 88, March 31, 2008, No. 13, pp. M10)
Pub: Dow Jones & Company, Inc.
Description: Obrem Capital Management wants Micrel to rescind Micrel's shareholder-rights plan and to boost its board to six members from five. Patricia L. Childress plans to nominate herself to the board of Sierra Bancorp, and Luther King Capital Management may consider a competing acquisition proposal for Industrial Distribution Group.

23571 ■ *The 30-Second Commute*
Pub: McGraw-Hill
Ed: Beverley Williams; Don Cooper. **Released:** 2004. **Price:** $19.95. **Description:** Home-based business owners explain how entrepreneurs can avoid long commutes and high costs of working outside the home by starting a home-based company. Essential steps for launching a successful home-based business are covered, including type of business, legal issues, and writing a business plan.

23572 ■ "$3.5 Million Lawsuit Points Finger at Black Firm" in *Black Enterprise* (Vol. 38, March 2008, No. 8)
Pub: Earl G. Graves Publishing Co. Inc.
Ed: Cliff Hocker. **Description:** World Wide Technology, the world's largest black-owned company is being sued by a former employee for racial discrimination and retaliation. Details of the lawsuit are outlined.

23573 ■ *365 Answers about Human Resources for the Small Business Owner: What Every Manager Needs to Know about Work Place Law*
Pub: Atlantic Publishing Company
Ed: Mary Holihan. **Released:** June 2006. **Price:** $21. 95. **Description:** Common questions employers ask about employees and the law are answered.

23574 ■ "Accountants Get the Hook" in *Canadian Business* (Vol. 80, October 22, 2007, No. 21, pp. 19)
Pub: Rogers Media
Ed: John Gray. **Description:** Chartered Accountants of Ontario handed down the decision on Douglas Barrington, Anthony Power and Claudio Russo's professional misconduct case. The three accountants of Deloitte & Touche LLP must pay C$100,000 in fines and C$417,000 in costs. Details of the disciplinary case are presented.

23575 ■ "After the Storm: Following a Tragic Loss, the Chambers Family Is Starting To See the Light" in *Black Enterprise* (November 2007)
Pub: Earl G. Graves Publishing Co. Inc.
Ed: Sheryl Nance Nash. **Description:** A family law firm filed bankruptcy after the death of a daughter.

23576 ■ "AG Warns Slots MBE Plan Risky" in *Boston Business Journal* (Vol. 29, May 27, 2011, No. 3, pp. 1)
Pub: American City Business Journals Inc.
Ed: Scott Dance. **Description:** Attorney General Doug Gansler states that the law extending the minority business program on slots parlors contracting through 2018 could be open to lawsuits. He recommended that the state should conduct a study proving that minority- and women-owned businesses do not get a fair share in the gaming industry before it signs the bill to avoid lawsuits from majority-owned firms.

23577 ■ "Akerman Senterfitt Merger Deal Close" in *The Business Journal-Serving Greater Tampa Bay* (Vol. 28, July 18, 2008, No. 30, pp. 1)
Pub: American City Business Journals, Inc.
Ed: Jeff Blumenthal. **Description:** Sources familiar to the negotiations of Akerman Senterfitt's planned merger with Wolf Block has disclosed that executive committees of both firms have approved the deal. They expect to create an 800-lawyer firm with a significant presence in the U.S. East Coast. Other views and information on the deal and its expected impact on law practice in Florida are presented.

23578 ■ "All About The Benjamins" in *Canadian Business* (Vol. 81, September 29, 2008, No. 16, pp. 92)
Pub: Rogers Media Ltd.
Ed: David Baines. **Description:** Discusses real estate developer Royal Indian Raj International Corp., a company that planned to build a $3 billion "smart city" near the Bangalore airport; to this day nothing has ever been built. The company was incorporated in 1999 by Manoj C. Benjamin one investor, Bill Zack, has been sued by the developer for libel due to his website that calls the company a scam. Benjamin has had a previous case of fraud issued against him as well as a string of liabilities and lawsuits.

23579 ■ "American Axle Sues to Force Steelmaker to Resume Suspended Parts Shipment" in *Crain's Detroit Business* (Vol. 25, June 15, 2009)
Pub: Crain Communications Inc. - Detroit
Ed: Robert Sherefkin. **Description:** American Axle & Manufacturing Holdings Inc. is facing a shutdown if a Michigan court does not force Republic Engineered Products Inc., a specialty steelmaker, to ship parts. If the parts are not shipped, it could cause assembly plants to shutdown.

23580 ■ *American Bar Association Legal Guide for Small Business: Everything You Need to Know About Small Business*
Pub: Random House Information Group
Ed: American Bar Association. **Released:** June 10, 2010. **Description:** The American Bar Association provides insight into financial, health and family issues affecting small business, including start up issues, employment laws, financing a business, and selling a business.

23581 ■ "Ann Alexander; Senior Attorney, Natural Resources Defense Council" in *Crain's Chicago Business* (Vol. 31, May 5, 2008, No. 18)
Pub: Crain Communications, Inc.
Ed: Emily Stone. **Description:** Profile of Ann Alexander who is the senior attorney at the Natural Resources Defense Council and is known for her dedication to the environment and a career spent battling oil companies, steelmakers and the government to change federal regulations. One recent project aims to improve the Bush administration's fuel economy standards for SUVs. Past battles include her work to prevent permits from slipping through the cracks such as the proposal by London-based BP PLC to dump 54 percent more ammonia and 35 percent more suspended solids from its Whiting, Indiana refinery into Lake Michigan-the source of drinking water for Chicago and its surrounding communities.

23582 ■ *Antitrust Law: Economic Theory and Common Law Evolution*
Pub: Cambridge University Press
Ed: Keith N. Hylton. **Released:** January 22, 2010. **Price:** $39.99. **Description:** A consolidation of various perspectives on antitrust law and its evolution.

23583 ■ "Antwerpen Takes on Chrysler Financial Over Foreclosure Sales" in *Baltimore Business Journal* (Vol. 28, July 30, 2010, No. 12, pp. 1)
Pub: Baltimore Business Journal
Ed: Gary Haber. **Description:** Antwerpen Motorcars Ltd. aims to fight the scheduled foreclosure sale of real estate it leases in Baltimore County, including the showroom for its Hyundai dealership on Baltimore National Pike in Catonsville, Maryland. The company is planning to file papers in court to stop the scheduled August 11, 2010 auction sought by Chrysler Financial Services Americas LLC.

23584 ■ *Are Government Purchasing Policies Failing Small Business?: Congressional Hearing*
Pub: DIANE Publishing Company
Ed: John F. Kerry. **Released:** September 2002. **Price:** Paperback $35.00. **Description:** Covers Congressional hearing: Steven App, Treasury Department; Fred Armendariz and Major Clark, Small Business Administration; Susan Allen, Pan Asian American Chamber of Commerce; Stephen Denlinger, Latin American Management Association; Charles Henry, National Veteran's Business Development Corporation; Morris Hudson, MO Procurement Technology Assistance Centers; Bar Kasoff, Women Impact, Public Policy; Pam Mazza, Piliero, Massa and Pargament; Ron Newlan, HubZone Contract National Council; Pat Parker, Native American Management Service; Joann Payne, Women First National Legislative Commission; Mike Robinson, MA Small Business Development Centers; Ramon Rodriguez, Hispanic

Chamber of Commerce; Angela Styles, Office of Management and Budget; Ralph Thomas, NASA; John Turner, MN Business Enterprise Legal Defense Fund; James Turpin, American Subcontractor's Association, Inc.; and Henry Wilfong, National Association of Small Disadvantaged Business.

23585 ■ *Atiyah's Accidents, Compensation and the Law*
Pub: Cambridge University Press
Ed: Peter Cane, Patrick Atiyah. **Released:** January 22, 2010. **Price:** $56.00. **Description:** Leading authority on the law of personal injuries compensation and the social, political and economic issues surrounding it.

23586 ■ "Attend To Your Corporate Housekeeping" in *Women Entrepreneur* (December 4, 2008)
Pub: Entrepreneur Media Inc.
Ed: Nina Kaufman. **Description:** Business owners can lose all the benefits and privileges of the corporate form if they do not follow proper corporate formalities such as holding an annual meeting, electing officers and directors and adopting or passing corporate resolutions. Creditors are able to take from one's personal assets if such formalities have not been followed.

23587 ■ "Attorney Covers Climate in Copenhagen" in *Houston Business Journal* (Vol. 40, December 25, 2009, No. 33, pp. 1)
Pub: American City Business Journals
Ed: Ford Gunter. **Description:** Houston environmental attorney Richard Faulk talks to the United Nations Climate Change Conference in Copenhagen, Denmark. Faulk believes the conference failed due to political differences between countries like US and China. Faulk believed the discussion of developed and developing countries on verification and limits on carbon emissions is something good that came from the conference.

23588 ■ "Attorney Guides Biotech Company in $6 Million Initial Public Offering" in *Miami Daily Business Review* (March 26, 2008)
Pub: ALM Media Inc.
Description: In order to raise capital to engage in a full-scale trial of MyoCell to receive clinical approval, Bioheart Inc., launched an initial public offering. Bioheart researches and develops cell therapies to treat heart damage.

23589 ■ "Attorney Internet Marketing Services Launched by SEO Advantage at SEOLegal.com" in *Internet Wire* (October 5, 2009)
Pub: Comtex News Network, Inc.
Description: SEO Advantage, an Internet marketing and website designer firm, has extended its services to the legal industry.

23590 ■ "Attorney Panel Tackles Contract Questions" in *Agency Sales Magazine* (Vol. 39, September-October 2009, No. 9, pp. 8)
Pub: MANA
Ed: Jack Foster. **Description:** MANAfest conference tackled issues regarding a sales representative's contract. One attorney from the panel advised reps to go through proposed agreements with attorneys who are knowledgeable concerning rep laws. Another attorney advised reps to communicate with a company to ask about their responsibilities if that company is facing financial difficulty.

23591 ■ "Auto Repair Business Owner Sentenced" in *Ventura County Star* (November 20, 2010)
Pub: Ventura County Star
Ed: Raul Hernandez. **Description:** Oxnard, California auto repair business owner was sentenced to jail for grand theft and falsification of smog certificate information.

23592 ■ "Balancing Freedom of Speech with the Right To Privacy" in *Pace Law Review* (Fall 2007)
Pub: American Society on Aging
Ed: Anna Zwierz Messa. **Description:** Information is offered to help authorities and funeral directors cope with protests occurring during a funeral.

23593 ■ "Banking on Twitter" in *Baltimore Business Journal* (Vol. 27, February 6, 2010, No. 40, pp. 1)
Pub: American City Business Journals
Ed: Gary Haber. **Description:** Ways that banks are using Twitter, Facebook and other social networking sites to provide customer services is discussed. First Mariner Bank is one of those banks that are finding the social media platform as a great way to reach customers. Privacy issues regarding this marketing trend are examined.

23594 ■ "Bankruptcies" in *Crain's Detroit Business* (Vol. 26, January 4, 2010, No. 1, pp. 5)
Pub: Crain Communications, Inc.
Ed: Dustin Walsh. **Description:** Listing of local businesses that filed for Chapter 7 or 11 protection in U.S. Bankruptcy Court in Detroit December 11-28. Under Chapter 11, a company files for reorganization. Chapter 7 involves total liquidation.

23595 ■ "Bankruptcies Shoot Up 68 Percent" in *Sacramento Business Journal* (Vol. 25, July 18, 2008, No. 20, pp. 1)
Pub: American City Business Journals, Inc.
Ed: Kathy Robertson. **Description:** Personal bankruptcy in the Sacramento area rose by 88 percent for the first half of 2008 while business bankruptcies rose by 50 percent for the same period. The numbers of consumer bankruptcy reflects the effect of high debt, rising mortgage costs, and declining home values on U.S. households.

23596 ■ "Bankruptcies Soar As Market Takes a Tumble" in *The Business Journal - Serving Phoenix and the Valley of the Sun* (Vol. 28, August 22, 2008, No. 51, pp. 1)
Pub: American City Business Journals, Inc.
Ed: Chris Casacchia. **Description:** Chapter 7 and Chapter 13 bankruptcy filings have increased 112 percent in July 2008, for a total of 1,225 filings in Phoenix. Chapter 11 business reorganizations also increased by 86 percent compared to 2007 figures because of the challenging national economy. Other views and information on the rise in bankruptcy filings in Phoenix are presented.

23597 ■ "Bankruptcies Swell" in *The Business Journal-Portland* (Vol. 25, July 4, 2008, No. 17, pp. 1)
Pub: American City Business Journals, Inc.
Ed: Andy Giegerich. **Description:** Individual and business bankruptcy filings in Portland, Oregon had increased. The rising gas and food prices, mortgage crisis and tightening lending standards are seen as causes of bankruptcies. Statistics on bankruptcy filings are also provided.

23598 ■ "Bankruptcy Blowback" in *Business Week* (September 22, 2008, No. 4100, pp. 36)
Pub: McGraw-Hill Companies, Inc.
Ed: Jessica Silver-Greenberg. **Description:** Changes to bankruptcy laws which were enacted in 2005 after banks and other financial institutions lobbied hard for them are now suffering the consequences of the laws which force more troubled borrowers to let their homes go into foreclosure; lenders suffer financially every time they have to take on a foreclosure and the laws in which they lobbied so hard to see enacted are now becoming a problem for these lending institutions. Details of the changes in the laws are outlined as are the affects on the consumer, the economy and the lenders.

23599 ■ "Bankruptcy Claims Brooke, Gives Franchisees Hope" in *The Business Journal-Serving Metropolitan Kansas City* (October 31, 2008)
Pub: American City Business Journals, Inc.
Ed: James Dornbrook; Steve Vockrodt. **Description:** Insurer Brooke Corp. was required to file for Chapter 11 bankruptcy for a deal to sell all of its assets to businessmen Terry Nelson and Lysle Davidson. The new Brooke plans to share contingency fees with franchisees. The impacts of the bankruptcy case on Brooke franchisees are discussed.

23600 ■ *Bankruptcy for Small Business*
Pub: Sphinx Publishing
Ed: Wendell Schollander. **Released:** July 1, 2008. **Price:** $22.95 paperback. **Description:** Bankruptcy laws can be used to save a small business, homes or other property. The book provides general information for small business owners regarding the reasons for money problems, types of bankruptcy available and their alternatives, myths about bankruptcy, and the do's and don'ts for filing for bankruptcy.

23601 ■ *Bankruptcy for Small Business, 2E: Know Your Legal Rights and Recover from Mistakes and Start Over Successfully*
Pub: Sourcebooks, Inc.
Ed: Wendell Schollander; Wes Schollander. **Released:** July 2008. **Price:** $22.95. **Description:** Bankruptcy laws can actually help small business owners save their companies, homes and other property. This book offers general information regarding reasons for money problems, types of bankruptcy available to small business owners as well as alternatives to bankruptcy and more.

23602 ■ "Barred Collection Agency Sued by Colorado AG" in *Collections & Credit Risk* (Vol. 15, August 1, 2010, No. 7, pp. 7)
Pub: SourceMedia Inc.
Description: Collection agency run by Chad Lee received notice that it is barred from collecting in the State of Colorado by Attorney General John Suther's office. A ruling cited that the firm engages in harassment or abuse and/or threats of violence, made false representations as to its legal status of debts, made false and misleading representations of nonpayment of debts that would result in arrest, and that Lee failed to disclose his previous felony conviction.

23603 ■ "Battling Back from Betrayal" in *Harvard Business Review* (Vol. 88, December 2010, No. 12, pp. 130)
Pub: Harvard Business School Publishing
Ed: Daniel McGinn. **Description:** Stephen Greer's scrap metal firm, Hartwell Pacific, lost several million dollars due to a lack of efficient and appropriate inventory audits, accounting procedures, and new-hire reference checks for his foreign operations. Greer believes that balancing growth with control is a key component of success.

23604 ■ "Be Proactive - Closely Review Contracts" in *Contractor* (Vol. 56, July 2009, No. 7, pp. 19)
Pub: Penton Media, Inc.
Ed: Al Schwartz. **Description:** Contract disputes can make subcontractors suffer big financial losses or even cause a new subcontractor to fail. Subcontractors should scour the plans and specifications for any references to work that might remotely come under their scope and to cross out any line in the contract that does not accurately reflect the work that they agreed to.

23605 ■ "Be Wary of Legal Advice on Internet, Lawyers Warn" in *Crain's Detroit Business* (Vol. 24, September 22, 2008, No. 38, pp. 16)
Pub: Crain Communications, Inc.
Ed: Harriet Tramer. **Description:** While some lawyers feel that the proliferation of legal information on the Internet can point people in the right direction, others maintain that it simply results in giving false hope, may bring about confusion or worse yet, it sometimes makes their jobs even harder.

23606 ■ "Beer Sales 'Foament' a Dispute" in *Philadelphia Business Journal* (Vol. 28, October 9, 2009, No. 34, pp. 1)
Pub: American City Business Journals
Ed: Peter van Allen. **Description:** Malt Beverages Distributors Association of Pennsylvania filed a case against the Liquor Control Board (LCB) at the Pennsylvania Supreme Court in order to further restrict store sales. The dispute stems from the supermarket chains circumventing the liquor law with the blessings of LCB.

23607 ■ *The Big Squeeze: Tough Times for the American Workers*
Pub: Pantheon Books
Ed: Steven Greenhouse. **Released:** 2009. **Price:** $25.95. **Description:** Labor correspondent for the New York Times reports on the bleak condition of the current workplace environment, citing violations of child labor laws and forced slave labor conditions in third world countries and robber baron era occurring often here in America that are expanding the number of working poor.

23608 ■ "Bills Would Regulate Mortgage Loan Officers" in *Crain's Detroit Business* (Vol. 24, February 25, 2008, No. 8, pp. 9)
Pub: Crain Communications Inc. - Detroit
Ed: Amy Lane. **Description:** New legislation in Michigan, if passed, would create a registration process for mortgage loan officers in the state in order to address the mortgage loan crisis.

23609 ■ "BIM: The Risks You Need to Watch Out For" in *Contractor* (Vol. 57, February 2010, No. 2, pp. 28)
Pub: Penton Media, Inc.
Ed: Susan Linden McGreevy. **Description:** Legal and risk management issues surrounding Building Information Modeling (BIM) can be divided into three categories namely; intellectual property, liability for content, and the responsibility for the inputs into the model. The agreement should be done in a way that protects the intellectual rights of the authors when using BIM.

23610 ■ "BIM and You: Know Its Benefits and Risks" in *Contractor* (Vol. 57, January 2010, No. 1, pp. 46)
Pub: Penton Media, Inc.
Ed: Susan Linden McGreevy. **Description:** Building Information Modeling is intended to be "collaborative" and this could raise legal issues if a contractor sends an electronic bid and it is filtered out. Other legal issues that mechanical contractors need to consider before using this technology are discussed.

23611 ■ "Biovail Hits SAC With $4.6 Billion Suit" in *Globe & Mail* (February 23, 2006, pp. B1)
Pub: CTVglobemedia Publishing Inc.
Ed: Shawn McCarthy. **Description:** The details of Biovail Corp.'s securities fraud case against SAC Management LLC are presented.

23612 ■ "BK Franchisees Lose Sleep Over Late-Night Rule" in *Advertising Age* (Vol. 79, August 11, 2008, No. 31, pp. 1)
Pub: Crain Communications, Inc.
Ed: Emily Bryson York. **Description:** Burger King's corporate headquarters mandates that franchisees remain open until at least 2 a.m. Three Miami operators have filed a lawsuit that alleges the extended hours can be dangerous, do not make money and overtax the workforce.

23613 ■ "Black's Truth: Will a Prison Stay Change the Way Conrad Black Operates?" in *Canadian Business* (Vol. 81, March 31, 2008, No. 5)
Pub: Rogers Media
Ed: Matthew McClearn. **Description:** Conrad Black will serve a 6 and a half years in prison but he asserts that his successors at Hollinger International and Hollinger Inc. grossly mismanaged and unjustly enriched themselves. Black also asserts that International violated the so-called November Agreement and that he is the aggrieved party. Black's assertions show a character flaw that cannot be corrected in prison.

23614 ■ "Blast Blame" in *The Business Journal-Milwaukee* (Vol. 25, September 5, 2008, No. 50, pp. 1)
Pub: American City Business Journals, Inc.
Description: Rexnord Industries LLC and J.M. Brennan Inc.'s property damage trial in connection with the explosion at the Falk Corp. plant in Menomonee Valley, Wisconsin is set to begin. Lawyers for the two companies have failed to reach a settlement. A leaking propane line was seen as the cause of the blast.

23615 ■ "Blood Diamonds are Forever" in *Canadian Business* (Vol. 83, August 17, 2010, No. 13-14, pp. 59)
Pub: Rogers Media Ltd.
Ed: Matthew McClearn. **Description:** The failed case against Donald McKay who was found in possession of rough diamonds in a raid by Royal Canadian Mounted Police has raised doubts about Kimberley Process (KP) attempts to stop the illicit global trade in diamonds. KP has managed to reduce total global trade of blood diamonds by 1 percent in mid-2000.

23616 ■ "Bloomberg Law Upgraded Its Online Legal Research Platform" in *Information Today* (Vol. 28, September 2011, No. 8, pp. 28)
Pub: Information Today, Inc.
Description: Bloomberg Law upgraded its online legal research platform for law practices. The new services includes a redesigned interface, improved search capabilities, and expanded collaboration and workflow features, while maintaining it comprehensive law resources such as mergers and acquisitions, antitrust, and securities.

23617 ■ "Boeing's Next Flight May Well Be to the South" in *Puget Sound Business Journal* (Vol. 29, November 21, 2008, No. 31, pp.)
Pub: American City Business Journals
Ed: Steve Wilhelm. **Description:** Southern states in the U.S. are luring Boeing Company to locate a new plant in their region which is experiencing a growing industrial base while offering permissive labor laws as selling points.

23618 ■ "Book of Lists 2010" in *Philadelphia Business Journal* (Vol. 28, December 25, 2009, No. 45, pp. 1)
Pub: American City Business Journals
Description: Rankings of companies and organizations within the banking, biotechnology, economic development, healthcare, hospitality, law and accounting, marketing and media, real estate, and technology industries in the Philadelphia, Pennsylvania area are presented. Rankings are based on sales, business size, and more.

23619 ■ "Border Boletin: UA to Take Lie-Detector Kiosk to Poland" in *Arizona Daily Star* (September 14, 2010)
Pub: Arizona Daily Star
Ed: Brady McCombs. **Description:** University of Arizona's National Center for Border Security and Immigration Research will send a team to Warsaw, Poland to show border guards from 27 European Union countries the center's Avatar Kiosk. The Avatar technology is designed for use at border ports and airports to assist Customs officers detect individuals who are lying.

23620 ■ "Bottoms Up!" in *Entrepreneur* (Vol. 36, April 2008, No. 4, pp. 128)
Pub: Entrepreneur Media, Inc.
Ed: Amanda C. Kooser. **Description:** Jill Bernheimer launched her online alcohol business Domaine547 in 2007, and encountered challenges as legal issues over the licensing and launching of the business took about seven months to finish. Domain547 features blog and forum areas. Marketing strategy that connects to the social community is one of the ways to reach out to customers.

23621 ■ "Bountiful Exterminator Indicted for Unlawful Pesticide Use" in *Standard-Examiner* (February 3, 2011)
Pub: Standard-Examiner
Ed: Bryon Saxton. **Description:** Bugman Pest and Lawn Inc. indicted Coleman Nocks and his business, Bugman Pest and Lawn Inc. for three counts of unlawful use of the pesticide Fumitoxin, resulting in the death of two little girls.

23622 ■ "Breaking Up" in *Canadian Business* (Vol. 80, March 12, 2007, No. 6, pp. 34)
Pub: Rogers Media
Ed: John Gray. **Description:** The need for business partners to draft a shareholder agreement in the beginning of their business to make it easier to break their relationship in case of disputes later is discussed.

23623 ■ "Brief: Janitorial Company Must Pay Back Wages" in *Buffalo News* (September 24, 2011)
Pub: The Buffalo News
Ed: Jonathan D. Epstein. **Description:** Knights Facilities Management, located in Michigan, provides grounds maintenance and janitorial services at the Ralph Wilson Stadium in Buffalo, New York. The US Department of Labor ordered the firm to pay $22,000 in back wages and damages to 26 employees for overtime and minimum wage compensation. Details of the company's violation of the Fair Labor Standards Act are included.

23624 ■ "Bristol-Myers Close to Settling Lawsuit" in *Globe & Mail* (January 23, 2006, pp. B6)
Pub: CTVglobemedia Publishing Inc.
Ed: Barbara Martinez. **Description:** The details of shareholder case against Bristol-Myers Squibb Co. are presented. The dispute is over the company's claim on the efficiency of Vanlev drug.

23625 ■ "Brooke Agents Claim Mistreatment" in *The Business Journal-Serving Metropolitan Kansas City* (Vol. 27, October 24, 2008, No. 7, pp. 1)
Pub: American City Business Journals, Inc.
Ed: James Dornbrook. **Description:** Franchisees of Brooke Corp., an insurance franchise, face uncertainty as their bills remain unpaid and banks threaten to destroy their credit. The company bundled and sold franchisee loans to different banks, but the credit crunch left the company with massive debts and legal disputes.

23626 ■ "Burger Heirs' Long-Bottled Fight Plays Out" in *Business Courier* (Vol. 24, January 11, 2008, No. 40, pp. 1)
Pub: American City Business Journals, Inc.
Ed: Dan Monk. **Description:** Discussion of an heir to the Burger Brewing Co. Michael Cundall who has filed for permission to pursue efforts to question the legality of a 1984 transaction in which the Cundall family sold its share of the Central Investment Corp. (CIC). The court ruled that Cundall may continue fighting for his claim that his uncle, John Koons, breached fiduciary duties by pressuring the family to sell its CIC stake. Details of the court rulings are given.

23627 ■ "Burned Investors Fire Back" in *Canadian Business* (Vol. 80, April 23, 2007, No. 9, pp. 12)
Pub: Rogers Media
Ed: Geoff Kirbyson; Dan Lett. **Description:** The details of the oppression remedy suit filed by investors on Maple Leaf Distillers Inc. and Protos International are presented.

23628 ■ "Business Diary" in *Crain's Detroit Business* (Vol. 24, October 6, 2008, No. 40, pp. 23)
Pub: Crain Communications, Inc.
Description: Detailed listing of acquisitions, expansions, new products, new services, business contracts and startups from the Detroit area is provided.

23629 ■ "Business Looks for Results in Congress" in *Baltimore Business Journal* (Vol. 28, November 5, 2010, No. 26, pp. 1)
Pub: Baltimore Business Journal
Ed: Kent Hoover. **Description:** Republican candidates in the 2010 Congressional elections were overwhelmingly supported by the business community. Republican John Boehner, who will be the next Speaker of the House, says that the party's victory would end economic uncertainty and would assist small businesses to rehire workers.

23630 ■ "Business Owners Lien Trinity Project" in *The Business Journal-Serving Greater Tampa Bay* (Vol. 28, July 25, 2008, No. 31, pp. 1)
Pub: American City Business Journals, Inc.
Ed: Janet Leiser. **Description:** The Internal Revenue Service is trying to collect $2.9 million from the developer of the Trinity Town Center, William Plaines, due to the delays in the project. This is in addition to a $5.2 million lien by the project's subcontractors.

23631 ■ "Business Put Cash Behind Bernstein" in *Baltimore Business Journal* (Vol. 28, August 20, 2010, No. 15, pp. 1)
Pub: Baltimore Business Journal
Ed: Scott Dance. **Description:** Baltimore, Maryland-based businesses have invested $40,000 to support lawyer Gregg L. Bernstein in the 2010 State Attorney election. The election campaign is being fueled by fear of a crime surge. Many businesses have been dealing with crimes such as muggings, shootings, and car break-ins.

23632 ■ "Business as Usual at RIM, Balsillie Says" in *Globe & Mail* (March 6, 2007, pp. B1)
Pub: CTVglobemedia Publishing Inc.
Ed: Simon Avery. **Description:** The continuation of normal business at Research In Motion Ltd., after the resignation of Jim Balsillie from the chairman's post, is described. The investigation of securities fraud at Research In Motion Ltd., and the continuation of Jim Balsillie as the co-chief executive officer of the company is discussed.

23633 ■ "Businesses Keep a Watchful Eye on Worker's Comp" in *The Business Journal-Serving Greater Tampa Bay* (September 5, 2008)
Pub: American City Business Journals, Inc.
Ed: Jane Meinhardt. **Description:** Pending a ruling from the Florida Supreme Court that could uphold the 2003 changes on workers' compensation law, the outcome would include restrictions on claimant attorneys' fees and allow the competitive workers' compensation insurance rates to remain low. However, insurance rates are expected to go up if the court overturns the changes.

23634 ■ "Businesses Need to Know State, Federal Laws for Employing Minors" in *Crain's Detroit Business* (Vol. 25, June 15, 2009, No. 24)
Pub: Crain Communications Inc. - Detroit
Ed: Nancy Kaffer. **Description:** Small business owners must know the law before employing minors. According to Steven Fishman, partner with Bodman LLP, who practices workplace law, most small business owners are not aware of laws regarding employment of minors.

23635 ■ "California Company Suing City's Lupin Over its Generic Diabetes Drug" in *Baltimore Business Journal* (Vol. 27, January 1, 2010)
Pub: American City Business Journals
Ed: Gary Haber. **Description:** California-based Depomed Inc. is suing Baltimore, Maryland-based Lupin Pharmaceuticals Inc. and its parent company in India over the patents to a diabetes drug. Lupin allegedly infringed on Depomed's four patents for Glumetza when it filed for permission to sell its own version of the drug with the US Food and Drug Administration. Details on generic pharmaceutical manufacturer tactics are discussed.

23636 ■ "Can He Win the Patent Game?" in *Globe & Mail* (February 20, 2006, pp. B1)
Pub: CTVglobemedia Publishing Inc.
Ed: Simon Avery; Paul Waldie. **Description:** A profile on managerial abilities of chief executive officer Jim Balsillie of Research In Motion Ltd., who will face the patent case with NTP Inc., is presented.

23637 ■ *Canadian Small Business Kit for Dummies*
Pub: John Wiley & Sons, Incorporated
Ed: Margaret Kerr; JoAnn Kurtz. **Released:** May 2006. **Price:** $28.99. **Description:** Resources include information on changes to laws and taxes for small businesses in Canada.

23638 ■ "Canadian Wind Farm Sued Due to Negative Health Effects" in *PC Magazine Online* (September 22, 2011)
Pub: PC Magazine
Description: Suncor Energy is being sued by a family in Ontario, Canada. The family claims that Suncor's wind turbines have created health problems for them, ranging from vertigo and sleep disturbance to depression and suicidal thoughts. The family's home is over 1,000 meters from the eight wind turbines, and according to Ontario officials, wind turbines must be a minimum of 550 meters from existing homes.

23639 ■ "Carvel" in *Ice Cream Reporter* (Vol. 23, September 20, 2010, No. 10, pp. 7)
Pub: Ice Cream Reporter
Description: Pamela Carvel, niece of Carvel founding soft serve has been barred from bringing any more lawsuits against her uncle's estate.

23640 ■ "The Case for Treating the Sex Trade as an Industry" in *Canadian Business* (Vol. 83, October 12, 2010, No. 17, pp. 9)
Pub: Rogers Media Ltd.
Ed: Steve Maich. **Description:** It is believed that the worst aspects of prostitution in Canada are exacerbated by the fact that it must take place in secret. The laws that deal with the market for sex have led to an unsafe working environment. Prostitutes believe their industry needs to be sanctioned and regulated rather than ignored and reviled.

23641 ■ "Catch the Wind Announces Filing of Injunction Against Air Data Systems LLC and Philip Rogers" in *CNW Group* (September 30, 2011)
Pub: CNW Group
Description: Catch the Wind, providers of laser-based wind sensor products and technology, filed an injunction against Optical Air Data Systems (OADS) LLC and its former President and CEO Philip L. Rogers. The complaint seeks to have OADS and Rogers return tangible and intangible property owned by Catch the Wind, which the firm believes to be critical to the operations of their business.

23642 ■ "Cautions on Negotiating Business and Personal Contracts" in *Business Owner* (Vol. 35, March-April 2011, No. 2, pp. 12)
Pub: DL Perkins Company
Description: Information is provided to help small business owners protect themselves during contract discussions, whether business or personal. A negotiating checklist is provided.

23643 ■ "Centerpoint Funding In Limbo" in *The Business Journal - Serving Phoenix and the Valley of the Sun* (Vol. 28, August 1, 2008, No. 48)
Pub: American City Business Journals, Inc.
Ed: Jan Buchholz. **Description:** Avenue Communities LLC has threatened to file a case against Mortgages Ltd. over the finance of the Centerpoint development project in Tempe, Arizona. Avenue Communities want Mortgages Ltd. to file a motion with the U.S. Bankruptcy Court so that it can secure financing for the project. Other views and information on the finance of Centerpoint, are presented.

23644 ■ "CEOs Divided About Census" in *Canadian Business* (Vol. 83, August 17, 2010, No. 13-14, pp. 20)
Pub: Rogers Media Ltd.
Ed: Jacqueline Nelson. **Description:** A Compass poll of Canadian CEOs on what the government should do with controversial long-form census is presented. The poll results show that 30 percent believe the government should remove any threat of punishment for failure to complete the survey. The CEOs also believe the law must be enforced by the government to encourage participation.

23645 ■ "The CEO's New Armor" in *Conde Nast Portfolio* (Vol. 2, June 2008, No. 6, pp. 56)
Pub: Conde Nast Publications, Inc.
Ed: John Cassidy. **Description:** Due to a new breed in C.E.O.'s contracts it is nearly impossible to fire them regardless of their performance. Despite the Sarbanes-Oxley Act in which attempted to codify C.E.O. responsibilities, corporate bosses responded by quietly demanding individual contracts, which, in many cases, were drawn up by their own lawyers and accepted by company boards with no outside oversight or review.

23646 ■ "Changes Sought to Health Law" in *Baltimore Business Journal* (Vol. 28, July 30, 2010, No. 12, pp. 1)
Pub: Baltimore Business Journal
Ed: Kent Hoover. **Description:** Business groups that opposed health care reform are working to undo parts of the new laws even before they go into effect. Business groups are gaining support for one legislative fix, which is repealing the law's provision that requires all businesses to file 1099 forms with the IRS any time they pay more than $600 a year to another business.

23647 ■ "Channelside On the Blocks" in *The Business Journal-Serving Greater Tampa Bay* (Vol. 28, August 29, 2008, No. 36, pp. 1)
Pub: American City Business Journals, Inc.
Ed: Michael Hinman. **Description:** In a bankruptcy auction for The Place, one of the more visible condominium projects at Channelside, the lowest bid is just below $73 a square foot. KeyBank National Association, the Key Developers Group LLC's lender, leads the auction planned for October 15, 2008. The reason behind the low minimum bid required to participate in the said action is discussed.

23648 ■ "Chesley Fighting Ky. Disbarment" in *Business Courier* (Vol. 27, September 10, 2010, No. 19, pp. 1)
Pub: Business Courier
Ed: Jon Newberry. **Description:** Stan Chesley, a Cincinnati attorney, has been accused of making false statements to the courts and bar officials, self-dealing in violation of the bar's conflict of interest rules, and failing to adequately inform clients. Kentucky Bar Association officials will seek to have Chesley permanently disbarred.

23649 ■ "Child-Care Policy and the Labor Supply of Mothers with Young Children" in *University of Chicago Press* (Vol. 26, July 2008, No. 3)
Pub: University of Chicago Press
Ed: Pierre Lefebvre, Philip Merrigan. **Description:** In 1997, the provincial government of Quebec, the second most populous province in Canada, initiated a new childcare policy. Licensed childcare service providers began offering day care spaces at the reduced fee of $5 per day per child for children aged four. By 2000, the policy applied to all children not in kindergarten. Using annual data (1993-2002) drawn from Statistics Canada's Survey of Labour and Income Dynamics, the results show that the policy had a large and statistically significant impact on the labor supply of mothers with preschool children.

23650 ■ "China Vs. the World: Whose Technology Is It?" in *Harvard Business Review* (Vol. 88, December 2010, No. 12, pp. 94)
Pub: Harvard Business School Publishing
Ed: Thomas M Hout, Pankaj Ghemawat. **Description:** Examination of the regulation the Chinese government is implementing that require foreign corporations wishing to do business in the country to give up their new technologies. These regulations avoid World Trade Organization technology transfer provisions and complicate the convergence of socialism and capitalism.

23651 ■ *Choosing the Right Legal Form of Business: The Complete Guide to Becoming a Sole Proprietor, Partnership, LLC, or Corporation*
Pub: Atlantic Publishing Company
Ed: Pat Mitchell. **Released:** January 1, 2009. **Price:** $24.95. **Description:** According to the U.S. Small Business Administration, nearly 250,000 new businesses start up annually; currently there are over nine million small companies in the nation. The importance of choosing the proper legal form of business is stressed.

23652 ■ "Citi Ruling Could Chill SEC, Street Legal Pacts" in *Wall Street Journal Eastern Edition* (November 29, 2011, pp. C1)
Pub: Dow Jones & Company Inc.
Ed: Jean Eaglesham, Chad Bray. **Description:** A $285 million settlement was reached between the Securities and Exchange Commission and Citigroup

Inc. over allegations the bank misled investors over a mortgage-bond deal. Now, Judge Jed S. Rakoff has ruled against the settlement, a decision that will affect the future of such attempts to prosecute Wall Street fraud. Rakoff said that the settlement was "neither fair, nor reasonable, nor adequate, nor in the public interest."

23653 ■ "CityLink Project On Hold" in *Business Courier* (Vol. 24, November 9, 2008, No. 30, pp. 3)
Pub: American City Business Journals, Inc.
Ed: Dan Monk. **Description:** Developers of the CityLink project have indicated that it will be at least a year before they start the planned social services mall at 800 Bank West End. According to Tim Senff, Citylink CEO, the company wants to build bridges before constructing the buildings. The project's critics are still considering whether to appeal a court ruling regarding the facility's compliance with the city's zoning code.

23654 ■ *Clicking Through: A Survival Guide for Bringing Your Company Online*
Pub: Bloomberg Press
Ed: Jonathan I. Ezor. **Released:** October 1999. **Description:** Summary of legal compliance issues faced by small companies doing business on the Internet, including copyright and patent laws.

23655 ■ "Climate Law Could Dig into our Coal-Dusted Pockets" in *Business Courier* (Vol. 26, November 20, 2009, No. 30, pp. 1)
Pub: American City Business Journals, Inc.
Ed: Lucy May. **Description:** Passage of federal climate legislation into law is set to increase household cost for Greater Cincinnati, according to the calculation by the Brookings Institute. The increase for residents of the area will amount to $244 in 2020 and the city was ranked the sixth-highest rate in the nation, behind Indianapolis.

23656 ■ "Collateral Damage" in *Business Courier* (Vol. 26, October 16, 2009, No. 25, pp. 1)
Pub: American City Business Journals, Inc.
Ed: Jon Newberry. **Description:** Non-union construction firms representing Ohio Valley Associated Builders and Contractors Inc. have filed cases against unionized shops claiming violations of wage law in Ohio. Defendants say the violations are minor, however, they believe they are caught in the middle of the group's campaign to change the state's wage law.

23657 ■ "Collection Agency Issues Whitepaper on Legal and Ethical Methods of Collecting on Overdue Accounts" in *Internet Wire* (July 20, 2009)
Pub: Comtex News Network, Inc.
Description: American Profit Recovery, a collection agency based in Massachusetts and Michigan, has updated and reissued a whitepaper on what businesses can and cannot do regarding conversing with their customers in an attempt to collect on overdue accounts and payments. A detailed summary on the federal laws associated with collecting on overdue accounts is outlined in such a way that any business owner, manager, or responsible party can easily understand.

23658 ■ "Combat Mission: Rebuffed, BAE Systems Fights Army Contract Decision" in *Business Courier* (Vol. 26, September 25, 2009)
Pub: American City Business Journals, Inc.
Ed: Jon Newberry. **Description:** BAE Systems filed a complaint with the US Government Accountability Office after the US Army issued an order to BAE's competitor for armoured trucks which is potentially worth over $3 billion. Hundreds of jobs in Butler County, Ohio hinge on the success of the contract protest.

23659 ■ *Complete Employee Handbook: A Step-by-Step Guide to Create a Custom Handbook That Protects Both the Employer and the Employee*
Pub: Moyer Bell
Ed: Michael A. Holzschu. **Released:** August 2007. **Description:** Comprehensive guide book helps employers deal with basic personnel issues. Details for creating a cohesive personnel program to meet specific needs and goals are addressed. Topics covered include employment-at-will practices, equal opportunity, sexual harassment, disabled and immigrant and legal alien workers in lay terms and stresses the dangers of oversight. The book includes a CD that contains sample employee handbooks, federal regulations and laws, forms for complying with government programs and worksheets for assessing personnel needs and goals.

23660 ■ *The Complete Guide to Buying a Business*
Pub: NOLO
Ed: Fred S. Steingold. **Released:** November 2007. **Price:** $24.99. **Description:** Key steps in buying a business are highlighted, focusing on legal issues, tax considerations, approaches for valuing a business, financing, structuring the deal, along with forms and documents for taking ownership are included.

23661 ■ "Computer Forensics Firms Get Boost From New Evidence Rules" in *Crain's Detroit Business* (Vol. 24, March 24, 2008, No. 12, pp. 28)
Pub: Crain Communications, Inc.
Ed: Chad Halcom. **Description:** Computer forensics is a growing niche for firms such as the Center for Computer Forensics in Southfield; driving some of the growth are new amendments to the Federal Rules of Civil Procedure, which took effect about a year ago and address standards of evidence for electronic records, or "e-discovery," that are admissible for civil cases in federal courts.

23662 ■ "Contract Design as a Firm Capability" in *Academy of Management Review* (October 2007, pp. 1060)
Pub: ScholarOne, Inc.
Ed: Nicholas Argyres, Kyle J. Mayer. **Description:** A firm's capabilities for designing detailed contracts and the role of managers, engineers, and lawyers in the design of such contracts is highlighted.

23663 ■ "Contract Reveals Details of ACE Jet Deals" in *Globe & Mail* (January 24, 2006, pp. B3)
Pub: CTVglobemedia Publishing Inc.
Ed: Brent Jang. **Description:** The details of contract between Boeing Co. and Air Canada are presented.

23664 ■ "Contracts" in *Agency Sales Magazine* (Vol. 39, September-October 2009, No. 9, pp. 7)
Pub: MANA
Description: One session at the MANAfest conference provided suggestions to sales representatives when negotiating a contract with their principals. New sales representatives need to stand their ground and to negotiate a fair and balanced contract with every principal that they sign on with.

23665 ■ "A Conversation With Steven Hilfinger, Foley & Lardner L.L.P." in *Crain's Detroit Business* (Vol. 24, March 24, 2008, No. 12, pp. 1)
Pub: Crain Communications, Inc.
Description: Interview with Steven Hilfinger who is a member of Foley & Lardner L.L.P.'s mergers and acquisitions practice and is co-chair of its automotive industry team. Hilfinger discusses such issues as the role a board of directors can play in the M&A process and the future of the auto market.

23666 ■ "Corporex in Battle With Hedge Fund" in *Business Courier* (Vol. 24, December 21, 2008, No. 36, pp. 1)
Pub: American City Business Journals, Inc.
Ed: Jon Newberry. **Description:** Discusses a breach of contract complaint that was filed by Apollo Real Estate Advisors against Corporex Companies Inc. but Corporex said that the lawsuit was intended to counter an arbitration complaint filed by Corporex against Apollo, which seeks $11 million in termination fees. The issue is in relation to the acquisition of Eagle Hospitality by Apollo earlier in 2007.

23667 ■ "Crash Pads" in *Business Courier* (Vol. 24, November 2, 2008, No. 29, pp. 1)
Pub: American City Business Journals, Inc.
Ed: Jon Newberry. **Description:** Francisca Webster accumulated $4 million in mortgage debt in about 2 months. She filed a lawsuit against her tax preparer and her mortgage broker contending that the defendants had breached their fiduciary duties to her and made fraudulent misrepresentations to her. The other details of the case are supplied.

23668 ■ "Credit Crunch Gives, Takes Away" in *The Business Journal-Serving Metropolitan Kansas City* (Vol. 27, October 17, 2008, No. 5, pp. 1)
Pub: American City Business Journals, Inc.
Ed: Suzanna Stagemeyer. **Description:** Although many Kansas City business enterprises have been adversely affected by the U.S. credit crunch, others have remained relatively unscathed. Examples of how local businesses are being impacted by the crisis are provided including: American Trailer & Storage Inc., which declared bankruptcy after failing to pay a long-term loan; and NetStandard, a technology firm who, on the other hand, is being pursued by prospective lenders.

23669 ■ "Crime and Punishment" in *Canadian Business* (Vol. 81, December 24, 2007, No. 1, pp. 21)
Pub: Rogers Media
Ed: Joe Castaldo. **Description:** Cmpass Inc.'s survey of 137 Canadian chief executive officers showed that they want tougher imposition of sentences on white-collar criminals, as they believe that the weak enforcement of securities laws gives an impression that Canada is a country where it is easy to get away with fraud.

23670 ■ "Critics Target Bribery Law" in *Wall Street Journal Eastern Edition* (November 28, 2011, pp. B1)
Pub: Dow Jones & Company Inc.
Ed: Joe Palazzuolo. **Description:** Concern about how the Foreign Corrupt Practices Act, the United States' anti-bribery law, is enforced has drawn the focus of corporate lobbyists. Corporations have paid some $4 billion in penalties in cases involving the law, which prohibits companies from paying foreign officials bribes. The US Chamber of Commerce believes amending the act should be a priority.

23671 ■ "Crowdsourcing the Law" in *LJN's Legal Tech Newsletter* (October 1, 2010)
Pub: ALM
Ed: Robert J. Ambrogi. **Description:** Spindle Law strives to make legal research faster and smarter using crowdsourcing as one means to reach users.

23672 ■ "Currency: I'm Otta Here" in *Entrepreneur* (Vol. 35, October 2007, No. 10, pp. 72)
Pub: Entrepreneur Media Inc.
Ed: C.J. Prince. **Description:** Liberum Research revealed that 193 chief financial officers (CFOs) at small companies have either resigned or retired during the first half of 2007. A survey conducted by Tatum found that unreasonable expectations from the management and compliance to regulations are the main reasons why CFOs are leaving small firms. The chief executive officer's role in making CFOs stay is also discussed.

23673 ■ "D.A.G. Sues to Stay on Job" in *Business Courier* (Vol. 24, November 9, 2008, No. 30, pp. 4)
Pub: American City Business Journals, Inc.
Ed: Jon Newberry. **Description:** D.A.G. Construction Co. filed a breach of contract lawsuit against the Cincinnati Metropolitan Housing Authority. The company asked the Hamilton County Pleas Court to stop the housing authority from taking over a $10 million senior housing project. According to the company, the agency displaced D.A.G. and its subcontractors without warning.

23674 ■ "Dairy Queen Aims to Blitz Blizzberry" in *Ice Cream Reporter* (Vol. 23, August 20, 2010, No. 9, pp. 1)
Pub: Ice Cream Reporter
Description: International Diary Queens has filed a lawsuit to stop Yogubliz Inc. from using Blizzberry

and Blizz Frozen Yogurt as the name of its shops because the name is so close to Dairy Queen's Blizzard frozen dessert.

23675 ■ "Day-Care Center Owner to Argue Against Liquor Store Opening Nearby" in *Chicago Tribune* (March 13, 2008)
Pub: McClatchy-Tribune Information Services
Ed: Matthew Walberg. **Description:** NDLC's owner feels that Greenwood Liquors should not be granted its liquor license due to the claim that the NDLC is not only a day-care center but also a school that employs state-certified teachers.

23676 ■ "Deal With Tribes Revives Revenue Stream" in *Crain's Detroit Business* (Vol. 24, March 24, 2008, No. 12, pp. 6)
Pub: Crain Communications, Inc.
Ed: Amy Lane. **Description:** Michigan Bureau of State Lottery's 2003 launch of its Club Keno game caused the Little River Band of Ottawa Indians and the Little Traverse Bay Bands of Odawa Indians to halt payments of shared casino revenue with the state. The federal lawsuit that resulted has now been settled and tribal revenue-sharing will resume as well as $26 million in previous payments to the state of Michigan that the tribes had put into escrow.

23677 ■ "Decorated Marine Sues Contractor" in *Wall Street Journal Eastern Edition* (November 29, 2011, pp. A4)
Pub: Dow Jones & Company Inc.
Ed: Julian E. Barnes. **Description:** Marine Devon Maylie, who was awarded the Congressional Medal of Honor for bravery, has filed a lawsuit against defense contractor BAE Systems PLC claiming that the company prevented his hiring by another firm by saying he has a mental condition and a drinking problem. Maylie says that this was in retaliation for his objections to the company's plan to sell the Pakistani military high-tech sniper scopes.

23678 ■ "Defensive Training" in *Crain's Detroit Business* (Vol. 24, September 22, 2008, No. 38, pp. 11)
Pub: Crain Communications, Inc.
Ed: Robert Ankeny. **Description:** Rising retaliation claims in regards to discrimination complaints are creating an atmosphere in which managers must learn how to avoid or deal with these lawsuits as well as the retaliation that often follows. Examples of cases are given as well as advice for dealing with such problems that may arise in the workplace.

23679 ■ "Developer Wins Bout with Bank in Roundabout Way" in *Tampa Bay Business Journal* (Vol. 30, January 29, 2010, No. 6, pp. 1)
Pub: American City Business Journals
Ed: Janet Leiser. **Description:** Developer Donald E. Phillips of Phillips Development and Realty LLC won against the foreclosure filed by First Horizon National Corporation, which is demanding the company to fully pay its $2.9 million loan. Phillips requested that his company pay monthly mortgage and extend the loan's maturity date.

23680 ■ "Developers Compete for APG Project" in *Baltimore Business Journal* (Vol. 27, October 16, 2009, No. 23, pp. 1)
Pub: American City Business Journals
Ed: Daniel J. Sernovitz. **Description:** Corporate Office Properties Trust has lost the case in Delaware bankruptcy court to prevent rival St. John Properties Inc. from going ahead with its plans to develop the 400 acres at Aberdeen Proving Ground (APG) in Maryland. Both developers have competed for the right to develop the two million square foot business park in APG.

23681 ■ "DHS Finalizes Rules Allowing Electronic I-9s" in *HR Specialist* (Vol. 8, September 2010, No. 9, pp. 5)
Pub: Capitol Information Group Inc.
Description: U.S. Department of Homeland Security issued regulations that give employers more flexibility to electronically sing and store I-9 employee verification forms.

23682 ■ *Dictionary of Real Estate Terms*
Pub: Barron's Educational Series, Incorporated
Ed: Jack P. Friedman, Jack C. Harris, J. Bruce Lindeman. **Released:** October 2008. **Price:** $13.99. **Description:** More than 2,500 real estate terms relating to mortgages and financing, brokerage law, architecture, rentals and leases, property insurance, and more.

23683 ■ "Direct Recovery Associates Debt Collection Agency Beats Industry Record" in *Internet Wire* (June 24, 2010)
Pub: Comtex
Description: Direct Recovery Associates Inc. was named as one of the highest collection records in the industry, which has consistently improved over 18 years. The firm is an international attorney-based debt collection agency.

23684 ■ *The Diversity Code: Unlocking the Secrets to Making Differences Work in the Real World*
Pub: AMACOM
Ed: Michelle T. Johnson. **Released:** September 8, 2010. **Price:** $19.95. **Description:** The most diligent compliance with laws and regulations can't foster true work place diversity. The best organizations have become genuine cross-cultural communities that believe equality in reconciling difference and valuing them. The book promotes understanding by answering many of the toughest questions that professionals and their employers are afraid to ask.

23685 ■ "DOL Sets Stiff New Child Labor Penalties" in *HR Specialist* (Vol. 8, September 2010, No. 9, pp. 2)
Pub: Capitol Information Group Inc.
Description: U.S. Department of Labor (DOL) will impose new penalties for employers that violate U.S. child labor laws. Details of the new law are included.

23686 ■ "easyhome Ltd. Discovers Employee Fraud at an Easyfinancial Kiosk Company" in *Internet Wire* (October 14, 2010)
Pub: Comtex
Description: Canada's leading merchandise leasing company and provider of financial services, easyhome Ltd., reported employee fraud totaling $3.4 million that was perpetrated against the firm's easyfinancial services business.

23687 ■ "The Economic Loss Rule and Franchise Attorneys" in *Franchise Law Journal* (Vol. 27, Winter 2008, No. 3, pp. 192)
Pub: American Bar Association
Ed: Christian C. Burden, Sean Trende. **Description:** Economic loss rule prohibits recovery of damages in tort when the subject injury is unaccompanied by either property damage or personal injury.

23688 ■ "EEOC Sues Charlotte-Based Lebo's" in *Charlotte Observer* (February 7, 2007)
Pub: Knight-Ridder/Tribune Business News
Ed: Mike Drummond. **Description:** The U.S. Equal Employment Opportunity Commission filed a pregnancy discrimination lawsuit against Lebo's Shoe Stores, located in Charlotte, North Carolina. The suit alleges the store withdrew an offer to hire a woman after finding out she was pregnant.

23689 ■ *Effect of the Overvalued Dollar on Small Exporters: Congressional Hearing*
Pub: DIANE Publishing Company
Ed: Donald Manzullo. **Released:** September 2002. **Price:** $30.00. **Description:** Congressional hearing: Witnesses: Dr. Lawrence Chimerine, Economist; Tony Raimondo, President and CEO, Behlen Manufacturing Company; Robert J. Weskamp, President, Wes-Tech, Inc.; Wayne Dollar, President, Georgia Farm Bureau; and Vargese George, President and CEO, Westex International, Inc. Appendix includes correspondence sent to committee on the overvalued dollar.

23690 ■ *Electronic Commerce: Technical, Business, and Legal Issues*
Pub: Prentice Hall PTR
Ed: Oktay Dogramaci; Aryya Gangopadhyay; Yelena Yesha; Nabil R. Adam. **Released:** August 1998. **Description:** Provides insight into the goals of using the Internet to grow a business in the areas of networking and telecommunication, security, and storage and retrieval; business areas such as marketing, procurement and purchasing, billing and payment, and supply chain management; and legal aspects such as privacy, intellectual property, taxation, contractual and legal settlements.

23691 ■ "Eminent Domain Fight Looks Imminent" in *The Business Journal-Serving Metropolitan Kansas City* (Vol. 26, August 1, 2008, No. 47)
Pub: American City Business Journals, Inc.
Ed: Rob Roberts. **Description:** Views and information on the proposed constitutional amendments that will limit the use of eminent domain in Missouri, are presented. The proposals are expected to largely ban the taking of private property for private development. It may be included in a November 4,2008 statewide vote for approval.

23692 ■ "Employee Called for Jury Duty" in *Business Owner* (Vol. 35, March-April 2011, No. 2, pp. 14)
Pub: DL Perkins Company
Description: State laws govern small business rights and obligations regarding employee jury duty obligations. All states do require that employers allow employees to fulfill their jury duty obligations and retaliation, demotion, discipline or termination resulting from jury duty is illegal.

23693 ■ "Employees Can't Be Punished for Refusing to Work Due to Safety Concerns" in *HR Specialist* (Vol. 8, September 2010, No. 9, pp. 1)
Pub: Capitol Information Group Inc.
Description: Whistle-blower provisions in several federal laws make it illegal for employers to retaliate against employees who raise safety concerns to their employer or the government.

23694 ■ "Employees Change Clothes at Work? Heed New Pay Rules" in *HR Specialist* (Vol. 8, September 2010, No. 9, pp. 1)
Pub: Capitol Information Group Inc.
Description: U.S. Department of Labor issued a new interpretation letter that states times spent changing in and out of 'protective clothing' (e.g., helmets, smocks, aprons, gloves, etc.) is considered paid time. It also says time spent changing 'ordinary clothes' (i. e., uniform) may not be compensable itself, but could start the clock on the workday, meaning all activities after - such as walking to the workstation - would be paid time. More details and a link to the DOL are included.

23695 ■ *Employer Legal Forms Simplified*
Pub: Nova Publishing Company
Ed: Daniel Sitarz. **Released:** August 2007. **Price:** $24.95. **Description:** Business reference containing the following forms needed to handle employees in any small business environment: application, notice, confidentiality, absence, federal employer forms and notices, and many payroll forms. All forms are included on a CD that comes in both PDF and text formats. Adobe Acrobat Reader software is also included on the CD. The forms are valid in all fifty states and Washington, DC.

23696 ■ *The Employer's Legal Advisor*
Pub: AMACOM
Ed: Thomas M. Hanna. **Released:** April 30, 2007. **Price:** $24.00. **Description:** Attorney provides tips for reducing the possibility of a lawsuit and winning a case if one does go to court.

23697 ■ "Employers See Workers' Comp Rates Rising" in *Sacramento Business Journal* (Vol. 28, April 8, 2011, No. 6, pp. 1)
Pub: Sacramento Business Journal
Ed: Kelly Johnson. **Description:** Employers in California are facing higher workers compensation costs. Increased medical costs and litigation are seen to drive the trend.

23698 ■ *Enabling Environments for Jobs and Entrepreneurship: The Role of Policy and Law in Small Enterprise Employment*
Pub: International Labour Office
Ed: Gerhard Reinecke. **Released:** February 2004. **Price:** $83.25. **Description:** National policies, laws and regulations governing workplace safety.

23699 ■ "Enforcer In Fantasyland" in *Crain's New York Business* (Vol. 24, February 25, 2008, No. 8, pp. 10)
Pub: Crain Communications Inc.
Ed: Hilary Potkewitz. **Description:** Patent law, particularly in the toy and game industry, is recession-proof according to Barry Negrin, partner at Pryor Cashman. Negrin co-founded his patent practice group. Despite massive recalls of toys and the concern over toxic toys, legal measures are in place in this industry.

23700 ■ *Entrepreneurship: A Process Perspective*
Pub: Thomson South-Western
Ed: Robert A. Baron; Scott A. Shane. **Released:** February 2007. **Price:** $137.95. **Description:** Entrepreneurial process covering team building, finances, business plan, legal issues, marketing, growth and exit strategies.

23701 ■ "Estate Tax Problems may Soon Disappear" in *Contractor* (Vol. 56, September 2009, No. 9, pp. 60)
Pub: Penton Media, Inc.
Ed: Irv Blackman. **Description:** Advice on how to effectively plan estate tax in the United States. Pending changes to US estate tax laws are seen to resolve inheritance problems. Captive insurance firms can lower property and casualty insurance costs to transfer businesses to children.

23702 ■ "Ethics Commission May Hire Collection Agency" in *Tulsa World* (August 21, 2010)
Pub: World Publishing
Ed: Barbara Hoberock. **Description:** Oklahoma Ethics Commission is considering a more to hire a collection agency or law firm in order to collect fees from candidates owing money for filing late financial reports.

23703 ■ "Exxon Braving the Danger Zones" in *Globe & Mail* (March 8, 2007, pp. B1)
Pub: CTVglobemedia Publishing Inc.
Ed: Shawn McCarthy. **Description:** The plans of Exxon Mobil Corp. to increase its revenues through the expansion of its operations in Asia, Africa, and the Middle East are discussed.

23704 ■ "Fair Play? China Cheats, Carney Talks and Rankin Walks; Here's the Latest" in *Canadian Business* (Vol. 81, March 17, 2008, No. 4)
Pub: Rogers Media
Description: Discusses the World Trade Organization which says that China is breaking trade rules by taxing imports of auto parts at the same rate as foreign-made finished cars. Mark Carney first speech as the governor of the Bank of Canada made economists suspect a rate cut on overnight loans. Andre Rankin was ordered by the Ontario Securities Commission to pay $250,000 in investigation costs.

23705 ■ *Family Limited Partnership Deskbook*
Pub: American Bar Association
Ed: David T. Lewis; Andrea C. Chomakos. **Released:** March 25, 2008. **Price:** $169.95. **Description:** Forming and funding a family limited partnership or limited liability company is complicated. In-depth analysis of all facets of this business entity are examined using detailed guidance on the basic principles of drafting, forming, funding, and valuing an FLP or LLC and also covers tax concerns. Examples and extensive sample forms are included on a CD-ROM included with the book.

23706 ■ "Family Takes Wind Turbine Companies to Court Over Gag Clauses on Health Effects of Turbines" in *CNW Group* (September 12, 2011)
Pub: CNW Group
Description: Shawn and Trisha Drennan are concerned about the negative experiences other have had with wind turbines close to their homes, including adverse health effects. The couple's home will be approximately 650 meters from the Kingsbridge II wind farm project in Ontario, Canada.

23707 ■ "FBI Initiates Fraud Inquiry Into Mortgage Lenders" in *Miami Daily Business Review* (March 26, 2008)
Pub: ALM Media Inc.
Description: FBI has launched investigations into Countrywide Financial, the nation's largest mortgage lender, along with sixteen other firms, tied to the subprime mortgage crisis.

23708 ■ "Fed May Ban Amphibian Trade" in *Pet Product News* (Vol. 64, November 2010, No. 11, pp. 13)
Pub: BowTie Inc.
Description: U.S. Fish and Wildlife Service is seeking public input on a petition submitted by the conservation activist group Defenders of Wildlife. The petition involves possible classification of chytrid fungus-infected amphibians and amphibian eggs as 'injurious wildlife' under the Lacey Act. Interstate trading or importation of injurious wildlife into the U.S. is not allowed.

23709 ■ "Federal Fund Valuable Tool For Small-Biz Innovators" in *Crain's Detroit Business* (Vol. 24, September 29, 2008, No. 39, pp. 42)
Pub: Crain Communications, Inc.
Ed: Nancy Kaffer. **Description:** Grants from the Small Business Innovation Research Program, or SBIR grants, are federal funds that are set aside for 11 federal agencies to allocate to tech-oriented small-business owners. Firms such as Biotechnology Business Consultants help these companies apply for SBIR grants.

23710 ■ "Feds to Pay University $20M" in *Business Courier* (Vol. 27, July 23, 2010, No. 12, pp. 3)
Pub: Business Courier
Ed: James Ritchie. **Description:** The U.S. government is set to pay University Hospital and medical residents who trained there $20 million as part of a tax dispute settlement. Around 1,000 former residents are to receive tax refunds. But the hospital must provide the U.S. Internal Revenue Service with extensive documentation.

23711 ■ "The Fences of a Patent" in *Information Today* (Vol. 26, February 2009, No. 2, pp. 13)
Pub: Information Today, Inc.
Ed: George H. Pike. **Description:** Patent law is examined using the Blackboard course management software used by many colleges and universities as its example.

23712 ■ "Fight Against Fake" in *The Business Journal-Portland* (Vol. 25, July 18, 2008, No. 19, pp. 1)
Pub: American City Business Journals, Inc.
Ed: Erik Siemers. **Description:** Companies, such as Columbia Sportswear Co. and Nike Inc., are fighting the counterfeiting of their sportswear and footwear products through the legal process of coordinating with law enforcement agencies to raid factories. Most of the counterfeiting factories are in China and India. Other details on the issue are discussed.

23713 ■ "Fight Ensues Over Irreplaceable Gowns" in *Tampa Bay Business Journal* (Vol. 30, January 15, 2010, No. 4, pp. 1)
Pub: American City Business Journals
Ed: Janet Leiser. **Description:** People's Princess Charitable Foundation Inc. founder Maureen Rorech Dunkel has sought Chapter 11 bankruptcy protection before a state court decides on the fate of the five of 13 Princess Diana Gowns. Dunkel and the nonprofit were sued by Patricia Sullivan of HRH Venture LLC who claimed they defaulted on $1.5 million in loans.

23714 ■ "Fighting Detroit" in *Baltimore Business Journal* (Vol. 27, January 22, 2010, No. 38, pp. 1)
Pub: American City Business Journals
Ed: Daniel J. Sernovitz. **Description:** Baltimore, Maryland-based car dealers could retrieve their franchises from car manufacturers, Chrysler LLC and General Motors Corporation, through a forced arbitration. A provision in a federal budget mandates the arbitration. The revoking of franchises has been attributed to the car manufacturers' filing of bankruptcy protection.

23715 ■ "Final Player In Big Mortgage Fraud Operation Gets Jail Time" in *Boston Business Journal* (Vol. 31, May 27, 2011, No. 18, pp. 3)
Pub: Boston Business Journal
Ed: Galen Moore. **Description:** Real estate broker Ralp Appolon has been sentenced to 70 months in prison for wire fraud. Appolon was part of a group that falsified information about property purchase prices. A total of ten mortgage lenders have become victims of the group.

23716 ■ "Finally, Justice" in *Canadian Business* (Vol. 82, April 27, 2009, No. 7, pp. 12)
Pub: Rogers Media
Ed: John Gray. **Description:** Former investment adviser Alex Winch feels that he was vindicated with the Canadian Court's ruling that Livent Inc. founders Garth Drabinsky and Myron Gottlieb were guilty of fraud. Drabinsky filed a libel case on Winch over Winch's letter that complained over Livent's accounting procedures. Winch also criticized the inconsistent accounting during Drabinsky's term as chief executive of another firm.

23717 ■ "Firms Sue Doracon to Recoup More Than $1M in Unpaid Bills" in *Baltimore Business Journal* (Vol. 28, July 9, 2010, No. 9, pp. 1)
Pub: Baltimore Business Journal
Ed: Scott Dance. **Description:** Concrete supplier Paul J. Rach Inc., Selective Insurance Company, and equipment leasing firm Colonial Pacific Leasing Corporation intend to sue Baltimore, Maryland-based Doracon Contracting Inc. for $1 million in unpaid bills. Doracon owed Colonial Pacific $794,000 and the equipment is still in Doracon's possession. Selective Insurance and Paul J. Rach respectively seek $132,000 and $88,000.

23718 ■ "Five-Ring Circus" in *Entrepreneur* (Vol. 35, November 2007, No. 11, pp. 76)
Pub: Entrepreneur Media Inc.
Ed: Scott Bernard Nelson. **Description:** China's economy is growing and is expected to do well even after the 2008 Olympics, but growth could slow from eleven percent to eight or nine percent. Chinese portfolio concerns with regard to health and environmental records and bureaucratic fraud are discussed.

23719 ■ "Follow the ABCs of Buying a Business" in *Women Entrepreneur* (September 10, 2008)
Pub: Entrepreneur Media Inc.
Ed: Nina Kaufman. **Description:** Buying a business will likely result in the largest single asset one will ever own. A list of steps one can take in order to educate and protect themselves is provided.

23720 ■ "For Baxter, A Lingering PR Problem; Ongoing Focus On Heparin Deaths Ups Heat On CEO" in *Crain's Chicago Business* (April 21, 2008)
Pub: Crain Communications, Inc.
Ed: Mike Colias. **Description:** Baxter International Inc.'s recall of the blood-thinning medication heparin has exposed the company to costly litigation and put the perils of overseas drug manufacturing in the spotlight. Wall Street investors predict that an indefinite halt in production of the drug should not hurt the company's bottom line since heparin represents a tiny sliver of the business. Since Baxter began recalling the drug in January its shares have continued to outpace most other medical stocks.

23721 ■ "Former Synthes Officers Receive Prison Sentences" in *Wall Street Journal Eastern Edition* (November 22 , 2011, pp. B4)
Pub: Dow Jones & Company Inc.
Ed: Peter Loftus. **Description:** Michael D. Huggins, formerly chief operating officer of medical-device maker Synthes Ltd., and Thomas B. Higgins, formerly the president of Synthes spine unit, were given prison

sentences of nine months while a third executive, John J. Walsh, formerly director of regulatory and clinical affairs in the spine division, was given a five-month sentence for their involvement in the promotion of the unauthorized use of a bone cement produced by the company.

23722 ■ "Franchise Law in China: Law, Regulations, and Guidelines" in *Franchise Law Journal* (Vol. 27, Summer 2007, No. 1, pp. 57)

Pub: American Bar Association

Ed: Paul Jones, Erik Wulff. **Description:** Issues faced by foreign franchising are discussed, with a focus on China.

23723 ■ "Franchisees Lose Battle Against BK" in *Advertising Age* (Vol. 79, June 2, 2008, No. 22, pp. 46)

Pub: Crain Communications, Inc.

Ed: Emily Bryson York. **Description:** Burger King has had continuing litigation with former franchisees from New York, Luan and Elizabeth Sadik, who claim that Burger King's double cheeseburger, along with additional problems, created the environment for their eventual insolvency. Burger King has since terminated its test of selling the double cheeseburger for $1, although the company declined to comment on the reason for this decision.

23724 ■ "Fraud Alleged at Norshield; Investors Out $215 Million" in *Globe & Mail* (March 8, 2007, pp. B1)

Pub: CTVglobemedia Publishing Inc.

Ed: Paul Waldie. **Description:** The investigation of the diversion of $215 million in investors' money by the management of Norshield Asset Management (Canada) Ltd. is described.

23725 ■ "Free Speech Vs. Privacy in Data Mining" in *Information Today* (Vol. 28, September 2011, No. 8, pp. 22)

Pub: Information Today, Inc.

Ed: George H. Pike. **Description:** The U.S. Constitution does not explicitly guarantee the right of privacy. Organizations and businesses that require obtaining and disseminating information can be caught in the middle of privacy rights. The long-term impact on data mining, Internet marketing, and Internet privacy issues are examined.

23726 ■ "From Buyout to Busted" in *Business Week* (September 22, 2008, No. 4100, pp. 18)

Pub: McGraw-Hill Companies, Inc.

Ed: Emily Thornton; Deborah Stead. **Description:** Bankruptcy filings by private equity-backed companies are at a record high with 134 American firms taken private (or invested in) by buyout firms that have filed for protection this year under Chapter 11; this is 91 percent higher than the previous year, which had set a record when 70 of such companies filed for protection under Chapter 11.

23727 ■ "FTC Takes Aim At Foreclosure 'Rescue' Firm" in *The Business Journal-Serving Greater Tampa Bay* (Vol. 28, September 19, 2008, No. 39)

Pub: American City Business Journals, Inc.

Ed: Michael Hinman. **Description:** United Home Savers LLP has been ordered to halt its mortgage foreclosure rescue services after the Federal Trade Commission accused it of deceptive advertising. The company is alleged to have charged customers $1,200 in exchange for unfulfilled promises to keep them in their homes.

23728 ■ "Full-Court Press for Apple" in *Barron's* (Vol. 88, March 24, 2008, No. 12, pp. 47)

Pub: Dow Jones & Company, Inc.

Ed: Mark Veverka. **Description:** Apple Inc. is facing more intellectual property lawsuits in 2008, with 30 patent lawsuits filed compared to 15 in 2007 and nine in 2006. The lawsuits, which involve products such as the iPod and the iPhone, present some concern for Apple's shareholders.

23729 ■ "Funeral Picketing Laws and Free Speech" in *Kansas Law Review* (Vol. 55, April 2007, No. 3, pp. 575-627)

Pub: American Society on Aging

Ed: Stephen R. McAllister. **Description:** In-depth information covering laws governing protests and freedom of speech during funerals is presented.

23730 ■ "Get Fit On a Dine: Resolve To Be Healthy-and Wealthy-This New Year" in *Black Enterprise* (Vol. 38, January 2008, No. 6, pp. 86)

Pub: Earl G. Graves Publishing Co. Inc.

Ed: Angela P. Moore-Thorpe. **Description:** According to International Health, Racquet, and Sportsclub Association, nearly 43 million people are members of health clubs in the U.S. Corporate wellness programs as well as laws and your rights as a club member are explained.

23731 ■ "Get Prepared for New Employee Free Choice Act" in *HRMagazine* (Vol. 53, December 2008, No. 12, pp. 22)

Pub: Society for Human Resource Management

Ed: Allen Smith. **Description:** According to the director of global labor and employee relations with Ingersoll Rand Company, unions may have started having employees signing authorization cards in anticipation of the Employee Free Choice Act. Once signed, the cards are good for one year and employers would have only ten days in which to prepare for bargaining with unions over the first labor contract. The Act also requires these negotiations be subject to mandatory arbitration if a contract is not reached within 120 days of negotiations with unions, resulting in employers' wage rates, health insurance, retirement benefits and key language about flexibility would be determined by an arbitrator with no vested interest in the success of the company.

23732 ■ "Getting Out of an IRS Mess" in *Black Enterprise* (Vol. 37, December 2006, No. 5, pp. 53)

Pub: Earl G. Graves Publishing Co. Inc.

Ed: Carolyn M. Brown. **Description:** Owing back taxes to the IRS can lead to huge penalties and interest. Here are some tips on how to handle paying the IRS what you owe them.

23733 ■ "The GHG Quandary: Whose Problem Is It Anyway?" in *Canadian Business* (Vol. 81, September 15, 2008, No. 14-15, pp. 72)

Pub: Rogers Media Ltd.

Ed: Matthew McClearn. **Description:** Nongovernmental organizations were able to revoke the permit for Imperial Oil Ltd's Kearl oilsands project on the grounds of its expected greenhouse gas emission but the court's ruling was rendered irrelevant by bureaucratic paper-shuffling shortly after. The idea of an environmental impact assessment as a guide to identify the consequences of a project is also discussed.

23734 ■ "Green Shift Sees Red" in *Canadian Business* (Vol. 81, September 29, 2008, No. 16)

Pub: Rogers Media Ltd.

Ed: Jeff Sanford. **Description:** Green Shift Inc. is suing the Liberal Party of Canada in an $8.5 million lawsuit for using the phrase "green shift" when they rolled out their carbon tax and climate change policy. The company has come to be recognized as a consultant and provider of green products such as non-toxic, biodegradable cups, plates, and utensils for events.

23735 ■ *Green Your Small Business: Profitable Ways to Become an Ecopreneur*

Pub: McGraw-Hill

Ed: Scott Cooney. **Released:** November 7, 2008. **Price:** $19.95 paperback. **Description:** Advice and guidance is given to help any entrepreneur start, build or grow a green business, focusing on green business basics, market research and financing, as well as handling legal and insurance issues.

23736 ■ "Greenberg Sues U.S. Over AIG Rescue" in *Wall Street Journal Eastern Edition* (November 22 , 2011, pp. C3)

Pub: Dow Jones & Company Inc.

Ed: Liam Pleven, Serena Ng. **Description:** Former Chief Executive Officer of American International Group Inc., Maurice R. 'Hank' Greenberg, has filed a lawsuit against the United States and the Federal Reserve Bank of New York on behalf of shareholders and his company, Starr International Company Inc., claiming that the government was wrong in taking control of the insurance giant and used it to move tens of millions of dollars to the trading partners of AIG.

23737 ■ "Hard Times for Hard Money" in *Sacramento Business Journal* (Vol. 25, July 18, 2008, No. 20, pp. 1)

Pub: American City Business Journals, Inc.

Ed: Michael Shaw. **Description:** Three private lenders who supplied $1 million sued VLD Realty, its associated companies and owners Volodymyr and Leonid Dubinsky accusing them of default after a plan to build two subdivisions fell through. Investigators are finding that borrowers and lenders ignored most rules on private investments on real estate.

23738 ■ "Hearing Damage Leads to Settlement" in *Register-Guard* (August 13, 2011)

Pub: The Register-Guard

Ed: Karen McCowan. **Description:** Cynergy Pest Control lost a court battle when a rural Cottage Grove man was granted a $37,000 settlement after his hearing was damaged by the pest control companies method to eradicate gophers, using blasts in his neighbor's yard.

23739 ■ *Here Come the Regulars: How to Run a Record Label on a Shoestring Budget*

Pub: Faber & Faber, Inc.

Ed: Ian Anderson. **Released:** October 1, 2009. **Price:** $15.00. **Description:** Author, Ian Anderson launched his own successful record label, Afternoon Records when he was 18 years old. Anderson shares insight into starting a record label, focusing on label image, budget, blogging, potential artists, as well as legal aspects.

23740 ■ "Hike in Md.'s Alcohol Tax May Be Hard For Lawmakers to Swallow" in *Baltimore Business Journal* (Vol. 28, November 19, 2010, No. 28)

Pub: Baltimore Business Journal

Ed: Emily Mullin. **Description:** Maryland's General Assembly has been reluctant to support a dime-per-drink increase in alcohol tax that was drafted in the 2009 bill if the tax revenue goes into a separate fund. The alcohol tax increase is considered unnecessary by some lawmakers and business leaders due to impending federal spending boosts.

23741 ■ "Hispanic Businesses Try to Drum Up Cash to Battle Crime Spree" in *Baltimore Business Journal* (Vol. 28, September 3, 2010, No. 17)

Pub: Baltimore Business Journal

Ed: Scott Dance. **Description:** Hispanic businesses in Baltimore, Maryland have been raising funds to pay off-duty police officers to patrol a few blocks of Broadway in Fells Point to help curb crime. Efforts to make the area a Latin Town have failed owing to muggings, prostitution and drug dealing. Comments from small business owners are also given.

23742 ■ "Home Builder, Four Others, Face Sentencing" in *Business Courier* (Vol. 27, November 26, 2010, No. 30, pp. 1)

Pub: Business Courier

Ed: Jon Newberry. **Description:** Home builder Bernie Kurlemann was convicted on November 10, 2010 on six felony counts and faces up to 65 years in prison due to his part in a 2006 Warren County mortgage fraud scheme. Four other business people have pleaded guilty to related charges, and all are awaiting sentencing in early 2011.

23743 ■ *House of Cards: A Tale of Hubris and Wretched Excess on Wall Street*
Pub: Anchor Press
Ed: William D. Cohan. **Released:** February 9, 2010. **Price:** $16.95. **Description:** A historical account of the events leading up to the Bear Stearns implosion.

23744 ■ *How to Form Your Own Corporation without a Lawyer for Under $75.00*
Pub: Dearborn Trade Publishing Inc.
Ed: Ted Nicholas; Sean P. Melvin. **Price:** $19.95.

23745 ■ *How to Start a Bankruptcy Forms Processing Service*
Pub: Graphico Publishing Company
Ed: Victoria Ring. **Released:** September 2004. **Price:** $39.00. **Description:** Due to the increase in bankruptcy filings, attorneys are outsourcing related jobs in order to reduce overhead.

23746 ■ *How to Start and Run Your Own Corporation: S-Corporations For Small Business Owners*
Pub: HCM Publishing
Ed: Peter I. Hupalo. **Released:** March 6, 2003. **Price:** $22.95. **Description:** Basics of corporate business structure are explained. Topics include discovering the best business structure for your company; how to decided between an S-Corporation and LLC; choosing the state in which to incorporate, how to form a corporation, angel investing, special issues for one-person corporations, the role of bylaws and corporate minutes, board of directors, taxes, workers' compensation issues, retirement plans, and more.

23747 ■ "Human Capital: When Change Means Terminating an Employee" in *Black Enterprise* (Vol. 41, November 2010, No. 4, pp. 40)
Pub: Earl G. Graves Publishing Co. Inc.
Ed: Tamara E. Holmes. **Description:** Covering successful business change strategies, this article focuses on how the law and nondiscrimination policies can affect this aspect of the workplace.

23748 ■ "Hunter and the Hunted" in *Canadian Business* (Vol. 81, Summer 2008, No. 9, pp. 12)
Pub: Rogers Media Ltd.
Ed: Thomas Watson. **Description:** Brian Hunter, a partner in oil and gas engineering firm Montane Resources, invested his life savings in Vancouver-based Canacord Capital Corp. Details of the asset-backed commercial paper fiasco and Hunter's use of Facebook to encourage other investors to participate in his claim against the mortgage company are presented.

23749 ■ "Identity Thieves Hit a New Low" in *Information Today* (Vol. 26, February 2009, No. 2, pp. 1)
Pub: Information Today, Inc.
Ed: Phillip Britt. **Description:** Identity thieves are opening credit lines after reading obituaries. Actual identity theft cases are examined.

23750 ■ "IF Challenges Atlanta's Vending Monopoly" in *Benzinga.com* (July 28, 2011)
Pub: Benzinga.com
Ed: Benzinga Staff. **Description:** A lawsuit was filed by The Institute for Justice to challenge Atlanta's unconstitutional vending monopoly on behalf of two Atlanta street vendors.

23751 ■ "If Just One Person Applies, Are You Required to Hire Him?" in *HR Specialist* (Vol. 8, September 2010, No. 9, pp. 7)
Pub: Capitol Information Group Inc.
Description: It is legal to decline hiring an applicant, or even promoting a current employee, if they are the only applicant for a particular position. It may be good choice to wait for more applicants or to change recruiting strategy.

23752 ■ "IFRS Monopoly: the Pied Piper of Financial Reporting" in *Accounting and Business Research* (Vol. 41, Summer 2011, No. 3, pp. 291)
Pub: American Institute of CPAs
Ed: Shyam Sunder. **Description:** The disadvantages of granting monopoly to the international financial reporting standards (IFRS) are examined. Results indicate that an IFRS monopoly removes the chances for comparing alternative practices and learning from them. An IFRS monopoly also eliminates customization of financial reporting to fit local differences in governance, business, economic, and legal conditions.

23753 ■ "Illinois Regulators Revoke Collection Agency's License" in *Collections & Credit Risk* (Vol. 15, August 1, 2010, No. 7, pp. 13)
Pub: SourceMedia Inc.
Description: Creditors Service Bureau of Springfield, Illinois had its license revoked by a state regulatory agency and was fined $55,000 because the owner and president, Craig W. Lewis, did not turn over portions of collected funds to clients.

23754 ■ "Immigrants Trapped in Forex Mess" in *Boston Business Journal* (Vol. 27, October 5, 2007, No. 36, pp. 1)
Pub: American City Business Journals Inc.
Ed: Jackie Noblett. **Description:** U. S. Commodity Futures Trading Commission and Swiss Federal Banking Commission are jointly working on the case of Tradex Swiss AG. Investors have filed lawsuits to recover their money. Details of the illegal operation of the Forex company are discussed.

23755 ■ "Immigration Issues Frustrate Owners From Overseas" in *The Business Journal-Serving Greater Tampa Bay* (Vol. 28, August 15, 2008)
Pub: American City Business Journals, Inc.
Ed: Margie Manning. **Description:** Investors who availed the E-2 visa program believe that the tightened restrictions on the visa program has trapped them in the United States. The E-2 investor visa program was designed to attract investors into the U.S., but restrictions were tightened after the September 11, 2001 attacks. Other views and information on E-2 and its impact on investors are presented.

23756 ■ *Incorporate Your Business: A 50 State Legal Guide to Forming a Corporation*
Pub: Nolo
Ed: Anthony Mancuso. **Released:** January 2004. **Description:** Legal guide to incorporating a business in the U.S., covering all 50 states.

23757 ■ "An Insurance Roll-Up In Danger of Unraveling" in *Barron's* (Vol. 88, March 17, 2008, No. 11, pp. 51)
Pub: Dow Jones & Company, Inc.
Ed: Bill Alpert. **Description:** Shares of National Financial Partners have fallen below their initial offering price as sputtering sales and management turnover leave many investors wondering. One of the company's star brokers is being sued for their "life settlement" contracts while another broker is being pursued by the IRS for unpaid taxes.

23758 ■ "An Integrative Model of Experiencing and Responding to Mistreatment at Work" in *Academy of Management Review* (January 2008, pp. 76)
Pub: ScholarOne, Inc.
Ed: Julie B. Olson-Buchanan, Wendy R. Boswell. **Description:** Integrative model with theoretical framework is presented to increase understanding of the effects of an individual's perceived experience of workplace mistreatment in dispute resolutions and the person's response to it.

23759 ■ "The Interview" in *Crain's Cleveland Business* (Vol. 30, June 22, 2009, No. 24, pp. 9)
Pub: Crain Communications, Inc.
Description: In an interview with Mary K. Whitmer, partner at Kohrman Jackson & Krantz, she addresses issues facing the Northeast Ohio legal community. Ms. Whitmer is the new president of the Cleveland Metropolitan Bar Association.

23760 ■ "Investment Firms Unite: Coalition Fights New Tax Law" in *Black Enterprise* (Vol. 38, December 2007, No. 5, pp. 52)
Pub: Earl G. Graves Publishing Co. Inc.
Ed: Joyce Jones. **Description:** Minorities working in private equity, real estate and investment management firms have united to form the Access to Capital Coalition to oppose legislation that they feel would adversely affect their ability to attract investments and executives. Details of the group are included.

23761 ■ "Investment Manager Disciplined" in *Sacramento Business Journal* (Vol. 25, July 4, 2008, No. 18, pp. 1)
Pub: American City Business Journals, Inc.
Ed: Mark Anderson. **Description:** Community Capital Management's David A. Zwick is permanently barred by the Securities and Exchange Commission (SEC) from associating with any broker or dealer, after investigations revealed that he took part in paying kickbacks to a bond trader. Other views and information on Community Capital, and on the SEC investigation on Zwick, are presented.

23762 ■ "Investors Sue Jackson Properties for Fraud, Breach of Contract" in *The Business Journal - Serving Phoenix and the Valley of the Sun* (Vol. 28, July 18, 2008, No. 46, pp. 1)
Pub: American City Business Journals, Inc.
Ed: Jan Buchholz. **Description:** Investors sued Jackson Properties EVB Inc. and Jackson Properties EVB LLC for fraud and breach of contract over a botched housing development deal. The investors also filed a complaint before the Arizona Corporation Commission. The investors stand to lose $8 million from the halted development deal.

23763 ■ "Israeli Spam Law May Have Global Impact" in *Information Today* (Vol. 26, February 2009, No. 2, pp. 28)
Pub: Information Today, Inc.
Ed: David Mirchin. **Description:** Israels new law, called Amendment 40 of the Communications Law, will regulate commercial solicitations including those sent without permission via email, fax, automatic phone dialing systems, or short messaging technologies.

23764 ■ "Jennifer Hernandez Helps Developers Transform Contaminated Properties" in *Hispanic Business* (Vol. 30, April 2008, No. 4, pp. 32)
Pub: Hispanic Business
Ed: Hildy Medina. **Description:** Jennifer Hernandez is a partner and head of the law firm of Holland & Knight's environmental practice which specializes in the restoration of polluted land where former industrial and commercial buildings once stood, known as brownfields. Brownfield redevelopment can be lucrative but costly due to the cleaning up of contaminated land and challenging because of federal and state environmental laws.

23765 ■ "Judge Gives RIM One Last Chance" in *Globe & Mail* (February 25, 2006, pp. B5)
Pub: CTVglobemedia Publishing Inc.
Ed: Barrie McKenna; Paul Waldie. **Description:** United States District Court Judge James Spencer offers more time for Research In Motion Ltd. (RIM) to settle the patent infringement dispute with NTP Inc. RIM's shares increase by 6.2 percent following the decision.

23766 ■ "Judgment Day" in *Canadian Business* (Vol. 79, September 11, 2006, No. 18, pp. 27)
Pub: Rogers Media
Ed: John Gray. **Description:** The long, drawn out legal proceedings carried out by Bre-X Minerals Ltd. whose case against its former vice chairman and chief geolist, John Felderhof are presented.

23767 ■ "Juicy Feud; Deal Caps Years of Rancor in Wrigley Gum Dynasty" in *Crain's Chicago Business* (Vol. 31, May 5, 2008, No. 18, pp. 1)
Pub: Crain Communications, Inc.
Ed: David Sterrett. **Description:** Discusses the sale of Wm. Wrigley Jr. Co. to Mars Inc. and Warren Buffett for $23 billion as well as the intra-family feuding which has existed for nearly a decade since William Wrigley Jr. took over as CEO of the company following his father's death.

23768 ■ "Kimball Hill Files for Chapter 11" in *Crain's Chicago Business* (Vol. 31, April 28, 2008, No. 17, pp. 12)
Pub: Crain Communications, Inc.
Description: Homebuilder Kimball Hill filed for Chapter 11 bankruptcy protection after months of negotiations with lenders. The firm plans to continue operations as it restructures its debt.

23769 ■ "Lathrop Finds Partner In LA" in *The Business Journal-Serving Metropolitan Kansas City* (Vol. 27, November 21, 2008, No. 11, pp. 1)
Pub: American City Business Journals, Inc.
Ed: Steve Vockrodt. **Description:** Kansas, Missouri-based Lathrop and Gage LLP is planning to merge with Spillane Shaeffer Aronoff Bandlow LLP. The merging of the business law firms will add entertainment clients to Lathrop's fold. Comments from executives are also presented.

23770 ■ "Law Firm Jones Day Coming to Boston" in *Boston Business Journal* (Vol. 30, November 19, 2010, No. 43, pp. 1)
Pub: Boston Business Journal
Ed: Lisa van der Pool. **Description:** Jones Day is set to open an office in Boston, Massachusetts. The company will be the largest law firm to enter Boston since 2007. The firm will open with at least three partners.

23771 ■ "Law Firms Plan Rate Bumps" in *Houston Business Journal* (Vol. 40, December 25, 2009, No. 33, pp. 1)
Pub: American City Business Journals
Ed: Ford Gunter. **Description:** Survey shows that Houston, Texas-based law firms were in line with a 3.2 percent average rate hike projected for 2010. The big firms were ready to offset some losses with a rate bump of 4 percent while smaller firms have been expecting an increase of about 3 percent.

23772 ■ "Law Firms See Improvement in Financing Climate" in *Sacramento Business Journal* (Vol. 28, October 14, 2011, No. 33, pp. 1)
Pub: Sacramento Business Journal
Ed: Kathy Robertson. **Description:** Sacramento, California-based Weintraub Genshlea Chediak Law Corporation has helped close 26 financing deals worth more than $1.6 billion in 2010, providing indication of improvement in Sacramento's economy. Lawyers have taken advantage of low interest rates to make refinancing agreements and help clients get new funds.

23773 ■ "Law Firms Troll for Complaints Among Disgruntled Workers" in *The Business Journal-Serving Greater Tampa Bay* (Vol. 28, July 11, 2008)
Pub: American City Business Journals, Inc.
Ed: Jane Meinhardt. **Description:** Economic slowdown has affected businesses as they downsize, seeing an increase in wage and hour complaints using loopholes in the Fair Labor Standards Act, from which several law firms are recently generating revenue. Federal judges notice the increase in lawsuits and ordered that law firms show cause for non-compliance.

23774 ■ *Law (in Plain English) for Small Business*
Pub: Sourcebooks, Incorporated
Ed: Leonard D. DuBoff. **Released:** November 2006. **Description:** Small business law is described in easy to read format.

23775 ■ "Law Reform, Collective Bargaining, and the Balance of Power: Results of an Empirical Study" in *WorkingUSA* (June 2008)
Pub: Blackwell Publishers Ltd.
Ed: Ellen Dannin, Michelle Dean, Gangaram Singh. **Description:** Despite Congress' having made clear policy statements in the National Labor Relations Act that the law was intended to promote equality of bargaining power between employers and employees, to promote the practice and procedure of collective bargaining as the method of setting workplace terms and conditions of employment, and forbidding construing the law "so as to either interfere with or impede or diminish in any way the right to strike," by early 1940, the courts had given employers the right to permanently replace strikers and implement their final offer at impasse. Judges have often justified these doctrines as promoting balance in bargaining. Critics contend that the doctrines have the capacity to destroy the right to strike, unbalance bargaining power, and divert parties from the process of bargaining collectively. Some have proposed allowing temporary but not permanent striker replacement. The article uses a bargaining simulation followed by a survey and debriefing comments to test these opposing claims.

23776 ■ *Law for the Small and Growing Business*
Pub: Jordans Publishing Limited
Ed: P. Bohm. **Released:** February 2007. **Price:** $59. 98. **Description:** Legal and regulatory issues facing small businesses, including employment law, health and safety, commercial property, company law and finance are covered.

23777 ■ "Lawyers Cash In On Alcohol" in *Business Journal Portland* (Vol. 27, November 19, 2010, No. 38, pp. 1)
Pub: Portland Business Journal
Ed: Andy Giegerich. **Description:** Oregon-based law firms have continued to corner big business on the state's growing alcohol industry as demand for their services increased. Lawyers, who represent wine, beer and liquor distillery interests, have seen their workload increased by 20 to 30 percent in 2009.

23778 ■ "Lawyers Lock Up Cops as Clients" in *Sacramento Business Journal* (Vol. 28, April 8, 2011, No. 6, pp. 1)
Pub: Sacramento Business Journal
Ed: Kathy Robertson. **Description:** Sacramento-based law firm Mastagni, Holstedt and Chiurazzi has grown its client base by specializing in law enforcement labor issues. The firm represents 80,000 public sector correctional officers in the US. The firm has been experiencing an increase in new business as public sector employers face huge budget deficits.

23779 ■ "Lawyers Sued Over Lapsed Lacrosse Patent" in *Crain's Detroit Business* (Vol. 25, June 8, 2009, No. 23, pp. 5)
Pub: Crain Communications Inc. - Detroit
Ed: Chad Halcom. **Description:** Warrior Sports Inc., a manufacturer of lacrosse equipment located in Warren, Michigan is suing the law firm Dickinson Wright PLLC and two of its intellectual property lawyers over patent rights to lacrosse equipment.

23780 ■ "Leaning Tower" in *Business Courier* (Vol. 27, June 4, 2010, No. 5, pp. 1)
Pub: Business Courier
Ed: Jon Newberry. **Description:** New York-based developer Armand Lasky, owner of Tower Place Mall in downtown Cincinnati, Ohio has sued Birmingham, Alabama-based Regions Bank to prevent the bank's foreclosure on the property. Regions Bank claims Lasky was in default on an $18 million loan agreement. Details on the mall's leasing plan is also discussed.

23781 ■ "Leave Policies: How to Avoid Leave-Related Lawsuits" in *Employee Benefit News* (Vol. 25, December 1, 2011, No. 15, pp. 12)
Pub: SourceMedia Inc.
Ed: John F. Galvin. **Description:** Tips for employers when adding disability and maternity leave benefits to workers are outlined, with focus on ways to avoid leave-related lawsuits.

23782 ■ "Legal Aid: Sample Legal Documents can Lower Your Attorney Fees" in *Black Enterprise* (Vol. 37, October 2006, No. 3, pp. 210)
Pub: Earl G. Graves Publishing Co. Inc.
Ed: Tamara E. Holmes. **Description:** FreeLegalForms.net provides thousands of free legal forms. These forms are not a substitute for consultation with an attorney but the sample documents can help save you time and money.

23783 ■ "Legalities of Diversity" in *Hispanic Business* (September 2007, pp. 26)
Pub: Hispanic Business
Ed: Francisco Ramos Jr., Bill Krutzen. **Description:** Most companies in America have diversity programs, however, critics believe diversity can be used as reverse discrimination because minorities are getting preferential treatment in hiring, promotion, and admissions.

23784 ■ "Legislating the Cloud" in *Information Today* (Vol. 28, October 2011, No. 9, pp. 1)
Pub: Information Today, Inc.
Description: Internet and telecommunications industry leaders are asking for legislation to address the emerging market in cloud computing. Existing communications laws do not adequately govern the modern Internet.

23785 ■ "The Letter of the Law" in *Collections and Credit Risk* (Vol. 14, November 1, 2009, No. 9, pp. 40)
Pub: SourceMedia, Inc.
Ed: Michelle Dunn. **Description:** Analyzes the regulatory landscape regarding debt collection and the ways in which those in the field are dealing with a tough economy, unclear laws and the newest regulations.

23786 ■ "Linens 'N Things, Dyson in Dust-Up" in *Crain's Chicago Business* (Vol. 31, March 24, 2008, No. 12, pp. 12)
Pub: Crain Communications, Inc.
Description: Linens 'N Things is being sued by vacuum-cleaner manufacturer Dyson who is alleging that it hasn't been paid some of the $1.3 million it says it is owed for merchandise.

23787 ■ "Local Manufacturers See Tax Proposal Hurting Global Operations" in *Crain's Cleveland Business* (Vol. 30, May 18, 2009, No. 20)
Pub: Crain Communications, Inc.
Ed: Dan Shingler. **Description:** New tax laws proposed by the Obama Administration could hinder the efforts of some Northeast Ohio industrial companies from expanding their overseas markets. The law is designed to prevent companies from moving jobs overseas.

23788 ■ "Look Before You Lease" in *Women Entrepreneur* (February 3, 2009)
Pub: Entrepreneur Media Inc.
Ed: Nina L. Kaufman. **Description:** Top issues to consider before leasing an office space are discussed including: additional charges that may be expected on top of the basic rental price; determining both short- and long-term goals; the cost of improvements to the space; the cost of upkeep; and the conditions of the lease.

23789 ■ "Look Out, Barbie, Bratz are Back" in *Canadian Business* (Vol. 83, August 17, 2010, No. 13-14, pp. 18)
Pub: Rogers Media Ltd.
Ed: Joe Castaldo. **Description:** California-based MGA Entertainment has wrestled back control over Bratz from Mattel after a six-year legal battle. However, MGA owner Isaac Larian could still face legal hurdles if Mattel pursues a retrial. He now has to revive the brand which virtually disappeared from stores when Mattel won the rights for Bratz.

23790 ■ "Making Factory Tours Count" in *Playthings* (Vol. 107, January 1, 2009, No. 1, pp. 14)
Pub: Reed Business Information
Ed: Malcolm Denniss. **Description:** The importance of touring an overseas toy supplier's manufacturing facility is stressed. Strategies for general factory visits are outlined in order to determine safety-related quality assurance issues in production.

23791 ■ *Managing Economies, Trade and International Business*
Pub: Palgrave Macmillan
Ed: Aidan O'Connor. **Released:** January 19, 2010. **Price:** $90.00. **Description:** An in-depth look at the areas that affect and influence international business,

exploring specific issues businesses face in terms of economic development, trade law, and international marketing and management.

23792 ■ "Market Recoups Its Losses - And Its Optimism" in *Barron's* (Vol. 89, July 20, 2009, No. 29, pp. M3)
Pub: Dow Jones & Co., Inc.
Ed: Kopin Tan. **Description:** US stock markets gained heavily in the third week of July 2009, rising by about 7 percent during the week. The shares of human resource management companies could be overpriced as they are trading at very high price-earnings multiples. Baxter International faces a class-action suit due to its alleged conspiracy with CSL to fix blood-plasma product prices.

23793 ■ "Market Squeezes Some Lawyers" in *Austin Business JournalInc.* (Vol. 28, December 12, 2008, No. 39, pp. 1)
Pub: American City Business Journals
Ed: Jean Kwon. **Description:** Austin, Texas-based lawyers have been adversely affected by the economic downtown. Fewer works for lawyers in mergers and acquisitions and other activities are being offered. Lawyers are refinancing debts and offering other services.

23794 ■ "Maryland Ready to Defend Slots Minority Policy" in *Boston Business Journal* (Vol. 29, July 8, 2011, No. 9, pp. 3)
Pub: American City Business Journals Inc.
Ed: Scott Dance. **Description:** The legality of Maryland's minority inclusion policy may be put under scrutiny once the lawsuit filed by rejected slots developer Baltimore City Entertainment Group on July 5, 2011 is heard in court. The lawsuit aims to stop the bidding process on a proposed casino in Baltimore because the minority policy amounts to reverse discrimination.

23795 ■ *McMafia: A Journey Through the Global Criminal Underworld*
Pub: Pantheon Books
Ed: Misha Glenny. **Released:** 2009. **Price:** $27.95. **Description:** Criminal entrepreneurs are using well-organized cosmopolitan networks to capitalize on globalization. Money from wars and illegal activities are being used to raise venture capital to finance criminal enterprises.

23796 ■ "Md. Tries to Recoup $73M from Actuary" in *Baltimore Business Journal* (Vol. 28, June 11, 2010, No. 5, pp. 1)
Pub: Baltimore Business Journal
Ed: Gary Haber. **Description:** Maryland State Retirement and Pension System has won nearly $73 million in administrative ruling against Milliman Inc. over pension loss miscalculations. However, Milliman filed two court cases seeking to reverse the decision and to recoup to the state any money a court orders.

23797 ■ "Meet Rebecca. She's Here to Fire You" in *Inc.* (November 2007, pp. 25-26)
Pub: Gruner & Jahr USA Publishing
Ed: Max Chafkin. **Description:** Amid liability concerns as well as CEO guilt, more and more firms are using consulting companies to fire workers. These outsourced firms help small companies structure severance and document information in order to limit legal liability when firing an employee.

23798 ■ "Melnyk Loses Round in Battle for Hemosol" in *Globe & Mail* (January 24, 2007, pp. B3)
Pub: CTVglobemedia Publishing Inc.
Ed: Leonard Zehr. **Description:** Biovail Corp. chairman Eugene Melnyk's loosing of the case against Catalyst Capital Group Inc. over the acquisition of Hemosol Corp. is discussed.

23799 ■ *Mergers and Acquisitions from A to Z*
Pub: Amacom
Ed: Andrew J. Sherman, Milledge A. Hart. **Released:** January 2006. **Price:** $35.00. **Description:** Guide for the entire process of mergers and acquisitions, including taxes, accounting, laws, and projected financial gain.

23800 ■ "MF Global Moved Clients' Funds to BNY Mellon" in *Wall Street Journal Eastern Edition* (November 19 , 2011, pp. B2)
Pub: Dow Jones & Company Inc.
Ed: Aaron Lucchetti. **Description:** Since the collapse of securities brokerage MF Global Holdings Ltd., one question has remained: where did the hundreds of millions of dollars in customers' accounts go? It has been revealed that MF Global moved those millions from its own brokerage unit to Bank of New York Mellon Corporation in August of this year, just two months before filing for bankruptcy protection.

23801 ■ "Midwest Looks 'Back to the Future" in *The Business Journal-Milwaukee* (Vol. 25, July 18, 2008, No. 43, pp. A1)
Pub: American City Business Journals, Inc.
Ed: Rich Rovito. **Description:** Midwest Air Group Inc. announced plans to reduce their work force by 40 percent or 1,200 employees after an earlier announcement of a drastic fleet reduction. These steps are being taken by the company in an effort to avoid filing bankruptcy since this would cost the airline millions of dollars in legal and other professional fees.

23802 ■ "Millions of Senior Citizens Swindled by Financial Fraud" in *Black Enterprise* (Vol. 41, September 2010, No. 2, pp. 24)
Pub: Earl G. Graves Publishing Co. Inc.
Description: One of every five citizens over the age of 65 have been victims of financial fraud. Statistical data included.

23803 ■ "Missing MF Global Funds Could Top $1.2 Billion" in *Wall Street Journal Eastern Edition* (November 22 , 2011, pp. A1)
Pub: Dow Jones & Company Inc.
Ed: Aaron Lucchetti, Dan Strumpf. **Description:** As the investigation into the collapse of securities brokerage MF Global Holdings Ltd. continues, the question of what happened to customers' funds has to be answered. Now, it is believed that the actual amount of missing funds is much more than the $600 million originally thought, and could be well over $1.2 billion.

23804 ■ "Monopoly Money Madness" in *Canadian Business* (Vol. 81, March 17, 2008, No. 4, pp. 9)
Pub: Rogers Media
Description: Enbridge was given permission by the Ontario Energy Board to collect $22 million it spent on an out-of-court settlement for charging unfair fees from 1994 to 2002. Customers are essentially being gouged twice in this scenario. The monopoly of Enbridge should end and the consumers should not have to pay for the system's faults.

23805 ■ "More Law Partners Jumping Ship" in *Boston Business Journal* (Vol. 27, October 5, 2007, No. 36, pp. 1)
Pub: American City Business Journals Inc.
Ed: Lisa van der Pool. **Description:** Boston lawyers are moving from one law firm to another, a practice becoming more prevalent than in recent times. Loss of revenue, clients and poor partner morale are some of the reasons for these actions. Details of this profound trend are discussed.

23806 ■ "Mosaid Grants First Wireless Parent License To Matsushita" in *Canadian Electronics* (Vol. 23, June-July 2008, No. 5, pp. 1)
Pub: Action Communication Inc.
Description: Matsushita Electric Industrial Co. Ltd. has been granted a six-and-a-half-year license by Mosaid Technologies Inc. to manufacture the latter's products. The patent portfolio license agreement covers Mosaid's Wi-Fi, Wi-Max, CDMA-enabled notebook computers and other products.

23807 ■ "Mulroney on the Record" in *Canadian Business* (Vol. 79, September 11, 2006, No. 18, pp. 43)
Pub: Rogers Media
Description: Canada's former prime minister and senior partner at the law firm Ogilvy Renault, Brain Mulroney speaks about the major policies and initiatives of the current government and its impact on the country's economy.

23808 ■ "A Nasty Russian Tale" in *Canadian Business* (Vol. 81, March 3, 2008, No. 3, pp. 85)
Pub: Rogers Media
Ed: Andrew Nikiforuk. **Description:** Billionaires Alex Shnaider and Michael Shtaif entered a partnership for an oil venture which ended in a slew of litigations. Cases of breach of contract, injurious falsehood and other related lawsuits were filed against Shnaider. Details of the lawsuits and the other parties involved in the disputes are presented.

23809 ■ "Natalie Peterson; Corporate Counsel, Steris Corp., 39" in *Crain's Cleveland Business* (Vol. 28, November 19, 2007, No. 46, pp. F-14)
Pub: Crain Communications, Inc.
Ed: Chuck Soder. **Description:** Profile of Natalie Peterson, corporate counsel for Steris Corp., a manufacturer of sterilization products; Peterson's blue-collar background did not detour her from her collegiate goals although she hardly knew how to fill out a college application. After graduating from Stanford Law School in 1997, she opted to return to Cleveland in lieu of more lucrative job offers in San Francisco. She has joined the school board and has participated in the 3Rs program, in which lawyers visit public schools in Cleveland to get students thinking about career choices and talk about constitutional law.

23810 ■ "New Century's Fall Has a New Culprit" in *Barron's* (Vol. 88, March 31, 2008, No. 13, pp. 20)
Pub: Dow Jones & Company, Inc.
Ed: Jonathan R. Laing. **Description:** Court examiner Michael Missal reports that New Century Financial's auditor contributed to New Century's demise by its negligence in permitting improper and imprudent practices related to New Century's accounting processes. New Century's bankruptcy filing is considered the start of the subprime-mortgage crisis.

23811 ■ "New Health Law, Lack of Docs Collide on Cape Cod" in *Boston Business Journal* (Vol. 27, October 12, 2007, No. 37, pp. 1)
Pub: American City Business Journals Inc.
Ed: Mark Hollmer. **Description:** There is a shortage of primary care providers at Outer Cape Health Services in Massachusetts, with the isolation of the area and as physicians look for higher paying careers in specialty positions. The Commonwealth Health Insurance Connector Authority is pushing for a new health insurance law and is working with Cape Cod Chamber of Commerce to conduct outreach programs.

23812 ■ "New ICA, Ex-Builder Tangle Over Construction" in *Boston Business Journal* (Vol. 27, October 12, 2007, No. 37, pp. 1)
Pub: American City Business Journals Inc.
Ed: Michelle Hillman. **Description:** Now-defunct George B.H. Macomber Company is suing the Institute of Contemporary Art (ICA) in Boston, Massachusetts as it believes that it has done extra work worth more than $6.6 million that was not included in the original contract with the construction of the museum. A series of setbacks and minor repairs has caused delays in the opening of the ICA, which was further complicated when Macomber began having financial difficulties.

23813 ■ "New Law Lets Shareholders Play Hardball With Firms" in *Globe & Mail* (January 2, 2006, pp. B1)
Pub: CTVglobemedia Publishing Inc.
Ed: Janet McFarland. **Description:** Business lawyer Wes Voorheis discusses about the launching of Bill 198 by plaintiffs' lawyers on behalf of ordinary retail investors.

23814 ■ "New Race Suit at Local Coke Plant" in *Business Courier* (Vol. 24, February 1, 2008, No. 43, pp. 1)
Pub: American City Business Journals, Inc.
Ed: Jon Newberry. **Description:** Another racial harassment lawsuit has been filed against the Coca-Cola Enterprises Inc. plant in Madisonville by its 23

black workers. The lawsuit alleges that the working environment at the plant continues to be offensive, abusive, intimidating and hostile. Details of the class-action suit are provided.

23815 ■ "New Rule Rankles In Jersey" in *Philadelphia Business Journal* (Vol. 30, September 16, 2011, No. 31, pp. 1)
Pub: American City Business Journals Inc.
Ed: Jeff Blumenthal. **Description:** A new rule in New Jersey which taxes out-of-state companies that conduct business in the state earned the ire of several banks, mortgage lenders and credit card companies and prompted opponents to threaten to file lawsuits. The new rule is an amendment to New Jersey Division of Taxation's corporate business tax regulation and is retroactive to 2002. Details are given.

23816 ■ *New Technology-Based Firms in the New Millennium, Volume 6*
Pub: Elsevier Science & Technology Books
Ed: Ray Oakey, R. Oakey. **Released:** May 2008. **Price:** $149.00. **Description:** Collection of papers from the Annual International High Technology Firms (HTSFs) Conference cover issues of importance to governments as they develop technological program. Papers are grouped into three sections: theory, strategy and clustering, and spin-off firms.

23817 ■ "New York Collection Agency's Bribery Case Resolved" in *Collections & Credit Risk* (Vol. 15, August 1, 2010, No. 7, pp. 19)
Pub: SourceMedia Inc.
Description: Criminal conviction and civil settlement in a bribery case and Medicaid scam involving H.I.S. Holdings Inc. and owner Deborah Kantor is examined.

23818 ■ "The Next Step in Patent Reform" in *Information Today* (Vol. 28, November 2011, No. 10, pp. 1)
Pub: Information Today, Inc.
Ed: George H. Pike. **Description:** The Leahy-Smith America Invents Act was signed into law in September 2011. The new act reformed the previous US patent system. Information involving the new patent law process is discussed.

23819 ■ "No Matter the Workplace Size, Handbooks Can Play a Vital Role" in *Crain's Cleveland Business* (Vol. 28, November 12, 2007, No. 45)
Pub: Crain Communications, Inc.
Ed: David Prizinsky. **Description:** Employee handbooks are important for even small businesses that wish to remain relatively informal since that documentation can help a company with a defense when confronted by employee or government lawsuits; they also demonstrate a consistency in policy which is a vital way in which employees, managers and owners remain focused on the company's prime goals.

23820 ■ "Nobel Winners Provide Insight on Outsourcing, Contract Work" in *Workforce Management* (Vol. 88, November 16, 2009, No. 12, pp. 11)
Pub: Crain Communications, Inc.
Ed: Jeremy Smerd. **Description:** Insights into such workforce management issues as bonuses, employee contracts and outsourcing has been recognized by the Nobel Prize winners in economics whose research sheds a light on the way economic decisions are made outside markets.

23821 ■ "Nortel Plays Big to Settle Lawsuits" in *Globe & Mail* (February 9, 2006, pp. B1)
Pub: CTVglobemedia Publishing Inc.
Ed: Catherine McLean. **Description:** The details on Nortel Networks Corp.'s settlement of cases with shareholders are presented.

23822 ■ "Not All Contracts a Good Fit for Fashion Reps" in *Agency Sales Magazine* (Vol. 39, September-October 2009, No. 9, pp. 10)
Pub: MANA
Ed: Jack Foster. **Description:** Difficult situations regarding the relationship between sales representatives and their principals in the fashion industry are presented and suggestions on how to create contracts that seek to prevent potential problems are provided. Sales reps should make sure that manufacturer has a viable business that is well thought-out and adequately financed.

23823 ■ "Not Enough To Go Around" in *The Business Journal-Milwaukee* (Vol. 25, August 15, 2008, No. 47, pp. A1)
Pub: American City Business Journals, Inc.
Ed: David Doege. **Description:** Most of the creditors of bankrupt real estate developer Scott Fergus are likely to remain unpaid as he only has an estimated $30,000 available for paying debts. Creditors, as of the 13 August 2008 deadline for filing claims, have filed a total of $79.1 million in claims.

23824 ■ "Not In Our Backyard" in *Canadian Business* (Vol. 80, October 22, 2007, No. 21, pp. 76)
Pub: Rogers Media
Ed: Anrew Nikiforuk. **Description:** Alberta Energy and Utilities Board's proposed construction of electric transmission line has let to protests by landowners. The electric utility was also accused of spying on ordinary citizens and violating impartiality rules. Details of the case between Lavesta Area Group and the Board are discussed.

23825 ■ "Oce Business Services: Discovery Made Easy" in *Information Today* (Vol. 26, February 2009, No. 2, pp. 31)
Pub: Information Today, Inc.
Ed: Barbara Brynko. **Description:** Oce Business Services provides document process management and electronic discovery through its CaseData repertoire of legal management solutions.

23826 ■ "Of Marks and Men" in *Canadian Business* (Vol. 80, March 12, 2007, No. 6, pp. 59)
Pub: Rogers Media
Ed: Andy Holloway. **Description:** The importance on the part of business enterprises to register for trademarks to avoid any threat of litigation in future is discussed.

23827 ■ "Ohio Collection Agency Settles Second Lawsuit" in *Collections & Credit Risk* (Vol. 15, July 1, 2010, No. 6, pp. 9)
Pub: SourceMedia Inc.
Description: National Enterprise Systems, will pay $75,000 for illegal and abusive collection charged in a lawsuit filed by West Virginia's Attorney General's office. Money will be used to reimburse students and consumers who paid the illegal fees to the company.

23828 ■ "OK, Bring in the Lawyers" in *Crain's Chicago Business* (Vol. 31, November 17, 2008, No. 46, pp. 26)
Pub: Crain Communications, Inc.
Ed: Daniel Rome Levine. **Description:** Bankruptcy attorneys are finding the economic and credit crisis a benefit for their businesses due to the high number of business owners and mortgage holders that are need of their services. One Chicago firm is handling ten times the number of cases they did the previous year and of that about 80 percent of their new clients are related to the real estate sector.

23829 ■ "Only in Canada, Eh?" in *Canadian Business* (Vol. 79, November 6, 2006, No. 22, pp. 17)
Pub: Rogers Media
Ed: Al Rosen. **Description:** The ethics of corporate spying with relation to competitive information leakage are analyzed.

23830 ■ "Open Price Agreements: Good Faith Pricing in the Franchise Relationship" in *Franchise Law Journal* (Vol. 27, Summer 2007, No. 1)
Pub: American Bar Association
Ed: Douglas C. Berry, David M. Byers, Daniel J. Oates. **Description:** Open price term contracts are important to franchise businesses. Details of open price contracts are examined.

23831 ■ "OSC Eyes New Tack on Litigation" in *Globe & Mail* (April 9, 2007, pp. B1)
Pub: CTVglobemedia Publishing Inc.
Ed: Janet McFarland. **Description:** The efforts of the Ontario Securities Commission to set up a tribunal for the investigation and control of securities fraud are described. The rate of the conviction of corporate officials in cases heard by the courts is discussed.

23832 ■ "Others' Economic Woes Bring Business to Bankruptcy Attorney" in *The Business Journal - Serving Phoenix and the Valley of the Sun* (Vol. 28, July 4, 2008, No. 44, pp. 7)
Pub: American City Business Journals, Inc.
Ed: Mike Sunnucks. **Description:** Economic slowdown has increased the demand for the services offered by law firms and bankruptcy attorneys. The number of small business and consumer bankruptcies has surged in 2005. Attorney Dan Gukeisen of Gukeisen Law Group PC has shifted his focus to handling bankruptcy filings and foreclosure matters.

23833 ■ "Paging Dr. Phil" in *Canadian Business* (Vol. 79, September 25, 2006, No. 19, pp. 21)
Pub: Rogers Media
Ed: John Gray. **Description:** Increasing corporate crimes in software industry is discussed by focusing on recent case of Hewlett and Packard.

23834 ■ "P&G vs. IRS: Split Decision" in *Business Courier* (Vol. 27, July 16, 2010, No. 11, pp. 1)
Pub: Business Courier
Ed: Jon Newberry. **Description:** Implications of a court ruling in a $435 million legal dispute between Procter & Gamble Company (P&G) and the Internal Revenue Service (IRS) are discussed. A $21 million win has been realized for P&G for its interpretation of research and development tax credits. However, the said case might involve more than $700 million in P&G tax deductions from 2001 through 2004 that the IRS had disallowed.

23835 ■ "Patently Absurd" in *Globe & Mail* (January 28, 2006, pp. B4)
Pub: CTVglobemedia Publishing Inc.
Ed: Barrie McKenna; Paul Waldie; Simon Avery. **Description:** An overview of facts about patent dispute between Research In Motion Ltd. and NTP Inc. is presented.

23836 ■ "PBSJ Launches Internal Probe" in *Tampa Bay Business Journal* (Vol. 30, January 8, 2010, No. 3, pp. 1)
Pub: American City Business Journals
Ed: Margie Manning. **Description:** Florida-based engineering firm PBSJ Corporation has started an internal investigation into possible violations of any laws, including the Foreign Corrupt Practices Act. Projects handled by subsidiary PBS&J International in foreign countries are the focus of the investigation.

23837 ■ "Perspective: Borderline Issues" in *Entrepreneur* (Vol. 35, October 2007, No. 10, pp. 48)
Pub: Entrepreneur Media Inc.
Ed: Joshua Kurlantzick. **Description:** Failure of the immigration reform bill is expected to result in increased difficulty in finding workers that would take on the dirty and perilous jobs, which are usually taken by immigrants. Regularizing immigration on the other hand will cost business owners money by making them spend for the legality of their employees' stay in the U.S. Other effects of immigration laws on entrepreneurs are discussed.

23838 ■ "Pet Food Insider Sold Shares Before Recall" in *Globe & Mail* (April 10, 2007, pp. B1)
Pub: CTVglobemedia Publishing Inc.
Ed: Keith McArthur. **Description:** The issue related the selling of share units by Mark Weins, chief financial officer of pet food firm Menu Foods Income Fund, just before the recall of contaminated pet food is discussed.

23839 ■ "Piece of Health Law 'A Goner'" in *Baltimore Business Journal* (Vol. 28, November 19, 2010, No. 28, pp. 1)
Pub: Baltimore Business Journal

Ed: Kent Hoover. **Description:** Montana Senator Max Baucus, a Democrat who heads the Senate Finance Committee, has revealed his plan to push legislation that would repeal the 1099 IRS provision that was created by the health care reform law and will result in more paperwork for small businesses when it goes into effect in 2012.

23840 ■ "Pioneers Get All The Perks" in *Canadian Business* (Vol. 81, March 3, 2008, No. 3, pp. 18)
Pub: Rogers Media

Description: Suncor Energy Inc. will face royalty payments from 25% to 30% of net profits as it signs a new deal with Alberta. Biovail Corp., meanwhile, is under a U.S. grand jury investigation for supposed improprieties in Cardizem LA heart drug launch. The Conference Board of Canada's proposal to impose taxes on greenhouse gas emissions and other developments in the business community are discussed.

23841 ■ "Pipe Show Finds a Way for Smokers to Light Up" in *Crain's Chicago Business* (Vol. 31, April 28, 2008, No. 17, pp. 57)
Pub: Crain Communications, Inc.

Ed: H. Lee Murphy. **Description:** With the help of attorneys within its local membership of 150 pipe collectors, the Chicagoland Pipe Collectors Club will be allowed to smoke at its 13th International Pipe & Tobacciana Show at Pheasant Run Resort. The event is expected to draw 4,000 pipe enthusiasts from as far as China and Russia.

23842 ■ "Plans for Coal-Fired Electricity Could Go Up in Smoke" in *Globe & Mail* (March 5, 2007, pp. B7)
Pub: CTVglobemedia Publishing Inc.

Ed: Steve James. **Description:** The coal-fired power project initiated by Texas-based utility company TXU Corp. is receiving legal challenges from green groups. The possible disasters caused by the coal-fired plant are presented.

23843 ■ "Play It Safe" in *Entrepreneur* (Vol. 35, November 2007, No. 11, pp. 26)
Pub: Entrepreneur Media Inc.

Ed: Gwen Moran. **Description:** U.S.-based toy manufacturers find opportunity from concerns regarding the recent recalls of toys that are made in China. The situation can provide better probability of parents buying toys made in the U.S. or Europe, where manufacturing standards are stricter.

23844 ■ "Porsche Raises VW Stake, Makes Bid for Firm" in *Globe & Mail* (March 26, 2007, pp. B5)
Pub: CTVglobemedia Publishing Inc.

Ed: Chad Thomas. Jeremy Van Logan. **Description:** Automobile giant Porsche AG has increased its stake in Volkswagen AG to $54 billion recently. The company is planning a merger by claiming 30%stake under German law.

23845 ■ *PPC's Small Business Tax Guide*
Pub: Practitioners Publishing Company

Ed: Douglas L. Weinbrenner, Virginia R. Bergman, Toni M. Greenwall, James A. Keller, Scott Mayfield, Linda A. Markwood. **Released:** January 2005. **Price:** $189.00. **Description:** Business tax laws are covered in an easy to understand format.

23846 ■ *PPC's Small Business Tax Guide, Vol. 2*
Pub: Practitioners Publishing Company

Ed: Douglas L. Weinbrenner, Virginia R. Bergman, Toni M. Greenwall, James A. Keller, Scott Mayfield, Linda A. Markwood. **Released:** January 2005. **Price:** $189.00. **Description:** Second volume containing technical guide covering business tax laws.

23847 ■ "A Practical Approach to Addressing Holdover Ex-Franchisee Trademark Issues" in *Franchise Law Journal* (Vol. 27, Summer 2007, No. 1)
Pub: American Bar Association

Ed: Christopher P. Bussert, William M. Bryner. **Description:** Franchisor-franchisee relationships can become legally complicated when they are terminated. Laws governing trademarks and other proprietary materials are examined.

23848 ■ "Practice Problems" in *Crain's Cleveland Business* (Vol. 30, June 22, 2009, No. 24, pp. 9)
Pub: Crain Communications, Inc.

Ed: Arielle Kass. **Description:** Many laid off attorneys are finding few options in the down economy and some are setting up their own practices.

23849 ■ "Prepaid Cards and State Unclaimed Property Laws" in *Franchise Law Journal* (Vol. 27, Summer 2007, No. 1, pp. 23)
Pub: American Bar Association

Ed: Phillip W. Bohl, Kathryn J. Bergstrom, Kevin J. Moran. **Description:** Unredeemed value of electronic prepaid stored-value credit cards for retail purchases is known as breakage. Laws governing unclaimed property as it relates to these gift cards is covered.

23850 ■ *Prepare to Be a Teen Millionaire*
Pub: Health Communications, Inc.

Ed: Robyn Collins; Kimberly Spinks Burleson. **Released:** April 1, 2008. **Price:** $16.95. **Description:** Business reference for any teenager wishing to become a successful entrepreneur; advice is given from successful teenage millionaires. Topics covered include: choosing a business name, type, and location; use of the Internet; legal issues; branding, sales, and marketing; funding and financial management; return on investment; retirement; development of a sound business plan; and certification for minority or women-owned companies.

23851 ■ "Prichard the Third" in *Canadian Business* (Vol. 83, October 12, 2010, No. 17, pp. 34)
Pub: Rogers Media Ltd.

Ed: Thomas Watson. **Description:** Robert Prichard, the new chair of international business law firm Torys, talks about his current role; his job involved advising clients, representing the firm, being part of the leadership team, and recruiting talent. He considers 'Seven Days in Tibet' as the first book to have an influence on his world view.

23852 ■ "Privacy Concern: Are 'Group' Time Sheets Legal?" in *HR Specialist* (Vol. 8, September 2010, No. 9, pp. 4)
Pub: Capitol Information Group Inc.

Description: Under the Fair Labor Standards Act (FLSA) employers are required to maintain and preserve payroll or other records, including the number of hours worked, but it does not prescribe a particular order or form in which these records must be kept.

23853 ■ "Prosecutors Dish Sordid AIPC Story" in *The Business Journal-Serving Metropolitan Kansas City* (Vol. 27, September 19, 2008, No. 1)
Pub: American City Business Journals, Inc.

Ed: Suzanna Stagemeyer. **Description:** Prosecutors in the American Italian Pasta Co.'s accounting fraud case have revealed evidence on the schemes used by then-officers of the company to commit fraud. District attorney John Wood has dubbed the case as the largest corporate fraud lawsuit in the history of the district of Missouri. How AIPC fell from being an industry leader is also discussed.

23854 ■ "Protection, Flexibility Make Single-Member LLCs Attractive" in *Crain's Cleveland Business* (Vol. 28, November 12, 2007, No. 45)
Pub: Crain Communications, Inc.

Ed: Peter DeMarco. **Description:** Discusses the reasons why single-member limited liability companies are gaining popularity; LLC structure allows a great deal of flexibility and protects the owner from liability.

23855 ■ "Quicksilver Resources Receives Favorable Judgement" in *Canadian Corporate News* (May 16, 2007)
Pub: Comtex News Network Inc.

Description: The 236th Judicial District Court of Texas ruled in favor of Quicksilver Resources Inc., a crude oil and natural gas exploration and production company, in the litigation between Quicksilver and CMS Marketing Services and Trading Company regarding the sale and purchase of 10,000 million British thermal units of natural gas per day at a minimum price of $2.47 per MMbtu, with the condition that the parties share any upside equally. The Court has rescinded the contract, rendering it void.

23856 ■ "The Rage Offstage at Marvel" in *Barron's* (Vol. 88, June 30, 2008, No. 26, pp. 19)
Pub: Dow Jones & Co., Inc.

Ed: Bill Alpert. **Description:** Lawsuits against Marvel Entertainment and Stan Lee are pushing the claims from Peter F. Paul that Stan Lee Media was undone by the actions of the accused. Paul's associates argue that Stan Lee Media owns rights to Marvel characters and that they want half the profits that Marvel is making.

23857 ■ "Ralcorp Investigated for Rejecting ConAgra Bid" in *Saint Louis Business Journal* (Vol. 32, September 16, 2011, No. 3, pp. 1)
Pub: Saint Louis Business Journal

Ed: Evan Binns. **Description:** New York-based Levi & Korsinsky started investigating Ralcorp Holidngs Inc. after it rejected ConAgra Foods Inc.'s third and latest takeover bid of $5.17 billion. The investigation would determine whether Ralcorp's directors had acted on behalf of shareholders' best interest.

23858 ■ "Recovery on Tap for 2010?" in *Orlando Business Journal* (Vol. 26, January 1, 2010, No. 31, pp. 1)
Pub: American City Business Journals

Ed: Melanie Stawicki Azam, Richard Bilbao, Christopher Boyd, Anjali Fluker. **Description:** Economic forecasts for Central Florida's leading business sectors in 2010 are presented. These sectors include housing, film and TV, sports business, law, restaurants, aviation, tourism and hospitality, banking and finance, commercial real estate, retail, health care, insurance, higher education, and manufacturing. According to some local executives, Central Florida's economy will slowly recover in 2010.

23859 ■ "Reform Law Spares Community Banks from FDIC Fee Hike" in *Baltimore Business Journal* (Vol. 28, July 23, 2010, No. 11, pp. 1)
Pub: Baltimore Business Journal

Ed: Gary Haber. **Description:** A new financial regulator bill has exempted community banks from increased Federal Insurance Deposit Corporation fees. Large banks with assets of $10 billion and above will be required to pay the higher fee in 2010. Small banks are seen to hold bank fees at bay owing to the exemption.

23860 ■ "Regulation Papered Over" in *Charlotte Business Journal* (Vol. 25, November 5, 2010, No. 33, pp.)
Pub: Charlotte Business Journal

Ed: Adam O'Daniel. **Description:** County courts in North Carolina are having challenges coping with its oversight and regulation duties as it becomes too busy with foreclosure cases. Clerks in some county courts have presided over foreclosure hearings because of the flooding of foreclosure cases.

23861 ■ "Regulators Revoke Mann Bracken's Collection Agency Licenses" in *Collections & Credit Risk* (Vol. 15, September 1, 2010, No. 8, pp. 19)
Pub: SourceMedia Inc.

Description: Maryland regulators have revoked the collections licenses of defunct law firm Mann Bracken LLP.

23862 ■ "Retailers, Your Will, and More" in *Agency Sales Magazine* (Vol. 39, July 2009, No. 7, pp. 46)
Pub: MANA
Ed: Melvin H. Daskal. **Description:** IRS audit guide for small retail businesses is presented. Tips on how to make a will with multiple beneficiaries are discussed together with medical expenses that can not be deducted.

23863 ■ "Revocable, Irrevocable and Living Trusts" in *Business Owner* (Vol. 35, September-October 2011, No. 5, pp. 5)
Pub: DL Perkins Company
Description: Comprehensive guide is offered to provide information on all forms of trusts.

23864 ■ "RIM Allegedly Caused 'Substantial Harm'" in *Globe & Mail* (January 18, 2006, pp. B6)
Pub: CTVglobemedia Publishing Inc.
Ed: Simon Avery. **Description:** The details of dispute between Research In Motion Ltd. and NTP Inc. are presented.

23865 ■ "RIM Says It's Willing to Cut a Check" in *Globe & Mail* (February 24, 2006, pp. B1)
Pub: CTVglobemedia Publishing Inc.
Ed: Simon Avery. **Description:** The settlement terms proposed by Research In Motion Ltd. in a patent infringement case with NTP Inc. are presented.

23866 ■ "RIM's Options Story Under Fire" in *Globe & Mail* (March 16, 2007, pp. B1)
Pub: CTVglobemedia Publishing Inc.
Ed: Janet McFarland. **Description:** The investigation of the backdating of options by Research In Motion Ltd. is discussed. The analysis of the backdating of company's options issues by Professor Erik Lie from the University of Iowa is presented.

23867 ■ "A Road Map to the New FTC Franchise Rule" in *Franchise Law Journal* (Vol. 27, Fall 2007, No. 2, pp. 105)
Pub: American Bar Association
Ed: Gerald C. Wells, Dennis E. Wieczorek. **Description:** Information about the Federal Trade Commission's revised Franchise Rule (16 C.F.R. Part 436 Disclosure Requirements and Prohibitions Concerning Franchising) (the New Rule) which replaces the original 1978 Franchise Rule (the Old Rule) is given; a comprehensive overview of the New Rule and its implications for the franchise industry is included.

23868 ■ "'Rocket Docket' Leaves Memphis Debtors Behind" in *Commercial Appeal* (November 28, 2009)
Pub: Commercial Appeal
Ed: Bartholomew Sullivan. **Description:** According to an investigation by the Scripps Howard News Service, Memphians lodged 807 formal complaints about debt-collection practices to the Federal Trade Commission in a 2 1/2 -year period ending in July; Nearly 1/3 of the complaints involved some type of error with the debt in question. The majority of the complaints were leveled at NCO Group, which also generated the most complaints around the country.

23869 ■ "RPA Preps for Building Radiant Conference, Show" in *Contractor* (Vol. 57, January 2010, No. 1, pp. 5)
Pub: Penton Media, Inc.
Description: Radiant Panel Association is accepting registrations for its Building Radiant 2010 Conference and Trade Show. The conference will discuss radiant heating as well as insurance and other legal matters for mechanical contractors.

23870 ■ "Rumor Has It" in *Entrepreneur* (Vol. 35, October 2007, No. 10, pp. 30)
Pub: Entrepreneur Media Inc.
Ed: Chris Penttila. **Description:** Some entrepreneurs like Ren Moulton and Dan Scudder regard rumor sites and product blogs as great sources of market research. However, there are legal issues that must be studied before using these Internet sites in marketing and product development. The use and limitations of rumor sites and product blogs are provided.

23871 ■ "Sabia Signals a Bold, New Course for BCE" in *Globe & Mail* (February 2, 2006, pp. B1)
Pub: CTVglobemedia Publishing Inc.
Ed: Catherine McLean. **Description:** The reasons behind the decision of chief executive officer Michael Sabia to streamline operations of BCE Inc. are presented.

23872 ■ "SEC Doesn't Buy Biovail's Claims" in *Barron's* (Vol. 88, March 31, 2008, No. 13, pp. 20)
Pub: Dow Jones & Company, Inc.
Ed: Bill Alpert. **Description:** Overstatement of earnings and chronic fraudulent conduct has led the SEC to file a stock fraud suit against Biovail, Eugene Melnyk and three others present or former employees of Biovail. Melnyk had the firm file suit in 2006 that blames short-sellers and stock researchers for the company's drop in share price.

23873 ■ *Selling the Invisible: A Field Guide to Modern Marketing*
Pub: Business Plus
Ed: Harry Beckwith. **Price:** $22.95. **Description:** Tips for marketing and selling intangibles such as health care, entertainment, tourism, legal services, and more are provided.

23874 ■ "Senators Predict Online School Changes" in *Puget Sound Business Journal* (Vol. 29, September 19, 2008, No. 22, pp. 1)
Pub: American City Business Journals
Ed: Clay Holtzman. **Description:** State senators promise to create new legislation that would tighten the monitoring and oversight of online public schools. The officials are concerned about the lack of oversight of the programs as well as lack of knowledge about content of the lessons.

23875 ■ "Sense of Discovery" in *Business Journal Portland* (Vol. 27, November 19, 2010, No. 38, pp. 1)
Pub: Portland Business Journal
Ed: Erik Siemers. **Description:** Tigard, Oregon-based Exterro Inc. CEO Bobby Balachandran announced plans to go public without the help of an institutional investor. Balachandran believes Exterro could grow to a $100 million legal compliance software company in the span of three years. Insights on Exterro's growth as market leader in the $1 billion legal governance software market are also given.

23876 ■ "Shaky on Free Trade" in *Canadian Business* (Vol. 81, December 24, 2007, No. 1, pp. 29)
Pub: Rogers Media
Ed: Rachel Pulfer. **Description:** Rhetoric at the U.S. presidential elections seems to be pointing toward a weaker free trade consensus, with Democratic candidates being against the renewal of free trade deals, while Republican candidates seem to be for free trade.

23877 ■ "Shopping Around for New Ideas" in *Canadian Business* (Vol. 79, July 17, 2006, No. 14-15, pp. 76)
Pub: Rogers Media
Description: Pensions should be a win-win situation for both the employer and the employee. The perspective of both parties concerning pension plans is explored as well as the need to amend laws in order to make sure that one class of merchant does not suffer at the cost of another.

23878 ■ "Sign of Progress" in *Playthings* (Vol. 106, October 1, 2008, No. 9, pp. 4)
Pub: Reed Business Information
Ed: Cliff Annicelli. **Description:** The ramifications of the toy recalls in 2007 are discussed. Mandates for lead-free toys and other safety issues are having an impact on the American toy industry.

23879 ■ "Sign of the Times: Temp-To-Perm Attorneys" in *HRMagazine* (Vol. 54, January 2009, No. 1, pp. 24)
Pub: Society for Human Resource Management
Ed: Bill Leonard. **Description:** A growing number of law firms are hiring professional staff on a temp-to-perm basis according to the president of Professional Placement Services in Florida. Firms can save money while testing potential employees on a temporary basis.

23880 ■ "A Simple Old Reg that Needs Dusting Off" in *Barron's* (Vol. 88, June 30, 2008, No. 26, pp. 35)
Pub: Dow Jones & Co., Inc.
Ed: Gene Epstein. **Description:** Senator Joe Lieberman has a point when he accused speculators of inflating the prices of food and fuel futures but introducing legislation to address speculation has an alternative. The senator's committee should instead demand that the Commodity Futures Trading Commission enforce position limits on the maximum number of contracts in a given market per speculative entity.

23881 ■ "Six Leading Economists on What to Expect in the Year Ahead: Derek Holt; Housing" in *Canadian Business* (December 24, 2007)
Pub: Rogers Media
Ed: Derek Holt. **Description:** The Canadian subprime mortgage market could take a different turn from that of the U.S. as laws governing Canada's mortgage market indirectly limit the probability of a slowdown. Details on how Canada avoided the slowdown in the housing market and forecasts of new homes for 2008 are discussed.

23882 ■ *Small Business Access to Health Care: Congressional Hearing*
Pub: DIANE Publishing Company
Ed: Donald A. Manzullo. **Released:** 2001. **Price:** $20. 00. **Description:** Congressional hearing held at Crystal Lake, Illinois. Witnesses: Mary Blankenbaker, Co-Owner, Benjamin's Restaurant; Ryan Brauns, Senior Vice President, Rockford Consulting and Brokerage; Scott Shalek, RHU, Shalek Financial Services; Brad Close, National Federation of Independent Businesses; Ken Koehler, Flowerwood, Inc.; Brad Buxton, Vice President of Networks and Medical Management, Blue Cross and Blue Shield of Illinois; Isabella Wilson, Chief Financial Office, Illinois Blower, Inc.; and James Milam, Illinois State Medical Society.

23883 ■ *Small Business Desk Reference*
Pub: Penguin Books (USA) Incorporated
Ed: Gene Marks. **Released:** December 2004. **Description:** Comprehensive guide for starting or running a successful small business, focusing on buying a business or franchise, writing a business plan, financial management, accounting, legal issues, human resources management, operations, marketing, sales, customer service, taxes, insurance, and ethics. Information for launching a restaurant, property management firm, retail outlet, consulting firm, and service business is included.

23884 ■ *Small Business Legal Strategies*
Pub: Aspatore Books, Incorporated
Released: July 2004. **Price:** $37.95. **Description:** Corporate Chairs and Partners from top firms in the U.S. offering insight into selecting, engaging, employing, and benefiting from external corporate counsel for the small business owner or executive.

23885 ■ *Small Business Management*
Pub: John Wiley & Sons, Incorporated
Ed: Margaret Burlingame. **Released:** March 2007. **Price:** $44.95. **Description:** Advice for starting and running a small business as well as information on the value and appeal of small businesses, is given. Topics include budgets, taxes, inventory, ethics, e-commerce, and current laws.

23886 ■ *Small Business Survival Guide*
Pub: Adams Media Corporation
Ed: Cliff Ennico. **Price:** $12.95. **Description:** Small business expert provides strategies to start a company and survive in the 21st Century. He shows small business owners how to succeed despite challenges that can defeat any firm. His advice covers suppliers; customers and contractors; competitors and creditors; spouses, family and friends; as well as the ways

lawyers, accountants and other can steal an entrepreneur's success. Ennico also describes how startups can comply with local regulations.

23887 ■ *Small Business Survival Guide: Starting, Protecting, and Securing Your Business for Long-Term Success*
Pub: Adams Media Corporation
Ed: Cliff Ennico. **Released:** September 2005. **Price:** $12.95 (US), $17.95 (Canadian). **Description:** Entrepreneurship in the new millennium. Topics include creditors, taxes, competition, business law, and accounting.

23888 ■ *Small Time Operator: How to Start Your Own Business, Keep Your Books, Pay Your Taxes, and Stay Out of Trouble*
Pub: Bell Springs Publishing
Ed: Bernard B. Kamoroff. **Released:** January 2008. **Price:** $18.95. **Description:** Comprehensive guide for starting any kind of business.

23889 ■ "Snatching Talent: Local Law Firms Quietly Boost Poaching" in *Boston Business Journal* (Vol. 31, July 29, 2011, No. 27, pp. 3)
Pub: Boston Business Journal
Ed: Lisa van der Pool. **Description:** National law firms Jones Day and Latham & Watkins LLP set up offices in Boston, Massachusetts. Their move also created an upswing on confidential conversation as both firms are aggressively poaching lawyers from Boston's other top firms.

23890 ■ "Soldiering On to Remake the SBA" in *Inc.* (February 2008, pp. 21)
Pub: Gruner & Jahr USA Publishing
Description: Steven Preston discusses efforts to improve the Small Business Administration's processes to improve services to small businesses. Topics covered include customer service issues, loans, and fraud.

23891 ■ "Sorry: Good Defense for Mal Offense" in *The Business Journal-Serving Metropolitan Kansas City* (Vol. 26, July 4, 2008, No. 43, pp. 1)
Pub: American City Business Journals, Inc.
Ed: Rob Roberts. **Description:** According to a survey conducted by the Kansas City Business Journal, ten hospitals in Kansas City showed that they have adopted disclosure policies that include prompt apologies and settlement offers. The policy is effective in minimizing medical malpractice lawsuits. Other details of the survey are presented.

23892 ■ "Soured Relationship Plays Out in Courts" in *The Business Journal-Serving Greater Tampa Bay* (Vol. 28, September 19, 2008, No. 39)
Pub: American City Business Journals, Inc.
Ed: Janet Leiser. **Description:** Heirs of developer Julian Hawthorne Lifset won a court battle to end a 50-year lease with Specialty Restaurants Corp. in Rocky Point. The decision opens the Tampa Bay prime waterfront property for new development.

23893 ■ "Speedway Explored Sale" in *Business Courier* (Vol. 24, October 12, 2008, No. 26, pp. 1)
Pub: American City Business Journals, Inc.
Ed: Jon Newberry. **Description:** Court records revealed that Kentucky Speedway discussed a possible sale of its Gallatin County track to International Speedway Corp. (ISC) before it sued NASCAR and ISC in 2005 for monopolizing bigtime racing. Kentucky Speedway chairman Jerry Carroll explained in a sworn statement that ISC was only interested in the sale if it can buy the track for a cheap price. The court proceedings and the sale allegations are discussed.

23894 ■ "State Democrats Push for Changes to Plant Security Law" in *Chemical Week* (Vol. 172, July 19, 2010, No. 17, pp. 8)
Pub: Access Intelligence
Ed: Kara Sissell. **Description:** Legislation has been introduced to revise the existing U.S. Chemical Facility Anti-Terrorism Standards (CFATS) that would include a requirement for facilities to use inherently safer technology (IST). The bill would eliminate the current law's exemption of water treatment plants and certain port facilities and preserve the states' authority to establish stronger security standards.

23895 ■ "State Reaps $440M with Small-Biz Tax Crackdown" in *Boston Business Journal* (Vol. 27, October 19, 2007, No. 38, pp. 1)
Pub: American City Business Journals Inc.
Ed: Lisa van der Pool. **Description:** Massachusetts Department of Revenue has generated $440 million from businesses who have not filed or paid enough taxes. Discover Tax is a database program that targets tax evaders. Small businesses are impacted by this system most.

23896 ■ "State Unemployment Fraud Rising Sharply" in *Sacramento Business Journal* (Vol. 28, October 21, 2011, No. 34, pp. 1)
Pub: Sacramento Business Journal
Ed: Michael Shaw. **Description:** California's Employment Development Department has reported that overpayments, especially due to fraud or misrepresentation, have increased from $88 million in 2008 to more than $250 million in 2010. However, criminal prosecutions in 2010 were fewer than in 2008 as the agency struggles to recover the money.

23897 ■ *Stay Out of Court: The Small Business Owners Guide to Prevent or Resolve Disputes and Avoid Lawsuit Hell*
Pub: Entrepreneur Press
Ed: Andrew A. Caffey. **Released:** January 24, 2005. **Price:** $17.95. **Description:** Business law attorney offers tools to help small company owners to solve disputes without going to court.

23898 ■ "Stelco Investors Told Their Stock Now Worthless" in *Globe & Mail* (January 23, 2006, pp. B4)
Pub: CTVglobemedia Publishing Inc.
Ed: Greg Keenan. **Description:** The reasons behind Ontario Superior Court's approval of Stelco Inc.'s restructuring proposal are presented.

23899 ■ "Stikemans' Ascent, Its Legacy, and Its Future" in *Globe & Mail* (January 29, 2007, pp. B2)
Pub: CTVglobemedia Publishing Inc.
Ed: Jacquie McNish. **Description:** Pierre Raymond, chairman of legal firm Stikeman Elliott LLP, talks about his strategies to handle competition, his challenges, and about Canada's present mergers and acquisition scenario. Stikeman achieved the first place in 2006 M&A legal rankings.

23900 ■ "Stock Car Racing" in *Canadian Business* (Vol. 81, September 15, 2008, No. 14-15, pp. 29)
Pub: Rogers Media Ltd.
Ed: Thomas Watson. **Description:** Some analysts predict a Chapter 11-style tune-up making GM and Ford a speculative turnaround stock. However, the price of oil could make or break the shares of the Big Three U.S. automobile manufacturers and if oil goes up too high then a speculative stock to watch is an electric car company called Zenn Motor Co.

23901 ■ "Success Fees" in *Canadian Business* (Vol. 80, March 12, 2007, No. 6, pp.)
Pub: Rogers Media
Ed: David Baines. **Description:** Legal issues regarding payment of lawyer fees termed 'fair fee' in Canada are discussed with an instance of Inmet Mining Corp.'s dealing with lawyer Irwin Nathanson.

23902 ■ "Suits Keep Flying in Wireless Service Marketing Wars" in *Globe & Mail* (March 22, 2007, pp. B3)
Pub: CTVglobemedia Publishing Inc.
Ed: Catherine McLean. **Description:** The suit filed by Telus Corp. against BCE Mobile Communications Inc. over the latter's alleged misleading advertisement in the press is discussed.

23903 ■ "The Suits Look Better Than the Shares" in *Barron's* (Vol. 88, March 31, 2008, No. 13, pp. 25)
Pub: Dow Jones & Company, Inc.
Ed: Bill Alpert. **Description:** Jos. A. Bank's inventory has increased sharply raising questions about the company's growth prospects. The company's shares have already dropped significantly from 46 to 23 and could still continue its slide. The company is also battling a class action suit where plaintiffs allege that the Bank inventories were bloated.

23904 ■ "Sundt, DPR Score $470 Million Biotech Project" in *The Business Journal - Serving Phoenix and the Valley of the Sun* (Vol. 29, September 19, 2008, No. 3, pp. 1)
Pub: American City Business Journals, Inc.
Ed: Jan Buchholz. **Description:** Sundt Inc. and DPR Construction Inc. were awarded the winning joint-venture contract to develop the second phase of the Arizona Biomedical Collaborative on the Phoenix Biomedical Campus. Both firms declined to comment, but an employee of the Arizona Board of Regents confirmed that the firms won the bidding. Views and information on the development project are presented.

23905 ■ "Sunwest Vies To Stave Off Bankruptcy" in *The Business Journal-Portland* (Vol. 25, August 15, 2008, No. 23, pp. 1)
Pub: American City Business Journals, Inc.
Ed: Robin J. Moody. **Description:** Sunwest Management Inc. is teetering on the edge of bankruptcy as creditors start foreclosure on nine of their properties. This could potentially displace residents of the assisted living operator. Sunwest is trying to sell smaller packages of properties to get a $100 million bridge loan to maintain operations.

23906 ■ "Sutter, CHW Reject Blue Cross Deal" in *Sacramento Business Journal* (Vol. 25, August 15, 2008, No. 24, pp. 1)
Pub: American City Business Journals, Inc.
Ed: Kathy Robertson. **Description:** California-based Sutter Health and Catholic Healthcare West have rejected the $11.8 million class action settlement in connection with contract rescissions between California hospitals and Anthem Blue Cross. Blue Cross can halt the settlement if not enough hospitals accept it. The deal covers all hospitals that owe money due to rescinded Blue Cross coverage.

23907 ■ "Take on an Elephant Without Getting Trampled" in *Globe & Mail* (March 17, 2007, pp. B3)
Pub: CTVglobemedia Publishing Inc.
Ed: Grant Robertson. **Description:** The plan of chief executive officer of Canpages Inc. Olivier Vincent to beat the profit margin and market share of Yellow Pages Group is discussed.

23908 ■ *Tax Savvy for Small Business: Year-Round Tax Strategies to Save You Money*
Pub: NOLO
Ed: Frederick W. Daily, Bethany K. Laurence. **Released:** September 2005. **Price:** $36.99. **Description:** Tax strategies for small business. Includes the latest tax numbers and laws as well as current Internal Revenue Service forms and publications.

23909 ■ "The Ten Commandments of Legal Risk Management" in *Business Horizons* (Vol. 51, January-February 2008, No. 1, pp. 13)
Pub: Elsevier Advanced Technology Publications
Ed: Michael B. Metzger. **Description:** Effective legal risk management is tightly linked with ethical and good management, and managers' behaviors have to be professional and based on ethically defensible principles of action. Basic human tendencies cannot be used in justifying questionable decisions in court. Guidelines for legal risk management are presented.

23910 ■ "This Just In" in *Crain's Detroit Business* (Vol. 25, June 22, 2009, No. 25, pp. 1)
Pub: Crain Communications Inc. - Detroit
Description: Yamasaki Associates, an architectural firm has been sued for non payment of wages to four employees. Yamasaki spokesperson stated the economy has affected the company and it is focusing marketing efforts on areas encouraged by recovery funding.

23911 ■ "Thousands Balk at Health Law Sign-Up Mandate" in *Boston Business Journal* (Vol. 27, November 9, 2007, No. 41, pp. 1)
Pub: American City Business Journals Inc.
Ed: Mark Hollmer. **Description:** About 100,000 Massachusetts residents have not signed up for insurance plans created as part of the state's health care reform law. Insurers have underestimated the number of new customers signing up for insurance and come close to risking penalties if they do not get insurance by the end of 2007. The Commonwealth Health Insurance Connector Authority's deadline to buy insurance before penalties kick in is November 15, 2007.

23912 ■ "TIA Wrestles with Procurement Issues" in *Business Journal Serving Greater Tampa Bay* (Vol. 30, November 12, 2010, No. 47, pp. 1)
Pub: Tampa Bay Business Journal
Ed: Mark Holan. **Description:** Tampa International Airport (TIA) has been caught in conflict of interest and procurement policy issues after the Hillsborough County Aviation Authority learned of the spousal relationship of an employee with his wife's firm, Gresham Smith and Partners. Gresham already won contracts with TIA and was ahead of other firms in a new contract.

23913 ■ "A 'To Do' List" in *Playthings* (Vol. 107, January 1, 2009, No. 1, pp. 9)
Pub: Reed Business Information
Ed: Richard Gottlieb. **Description:** Profile of the Building Our Future Toy Conference held in October 2008. Participants discussed the industry's future and is seeking ways to understand the toys children want in today's society.

23914 ■ "'Tone-Deaf' Suitor or True Harasser: How to Tell" in *HR Specialist* (Vol. 8, September 2010, No. 9, pp. 1)
Pub: Capitol Information Group Inc.
Description: Details are critical to any harassment charge in the workplace. Courts now list factors employers should consider when trying to determine whether an employee has been sexually harassed at work.

23915 ■ "Top Law Firms Join Forces" in *Business Journal Portland* (Vol. 27, December 3, 2010, No. 40, pp. 1)
Pub: Portland Business Journal
Ed: Andy Giegerich. **Description:** Law Firms Powell PC and Roberts Kaplan LLP will forge a collaboration, whereby 17 Roberts Kaplan attorneys will join the Portland, Oregon-based office of Lane Powell. The partnership is expected to strengthen the law firms' grip on Portland's banking clients.

23916 ■ "Trial of Enron Ex-Bosses to Begin Today" in *Globe & Mail* (January 30, 2006, pp. B1)
Pub: CTVglobemedia Publishing Inc.
Ed: Shawn McCarthy. **Description:** The details of the case against former executives Kenneth L. Lay and Jeffrey Skilling of Enron Corp. are presented.

23917 ■ "The Trials of Brian Hunter" in *Canadian Business* (Vol. 81, March 3, 2008, No. 3, pp. 64)
Pub: Rogers Media
Ed: Thomas Watson. **Description:** Brian Hunter was a considered a brilliant trader in Wall Street before he was blamed for the fall of the Amaranth hedge fund. Some people blame Hunter for placing bets based on unpredictable weather when he was a trader for Amaranth Advisors LLC. The accusation against Hunter that he conspired to manipulate natural gas prices is also discussed.

23918 ■ "Tripped by Trump?" in *The Business Journal-Serving Greater Tampa Bay* (Vol. 28, July 25, 2008, No. 31, pp. 1)
Pub: American City Business Journals, Inc.
Ed: Michael Hinman. **Description:** Jean Shahnasarian, a buyer of the Trump Tower Tampa, filed cases against Donald Trump, The Trump Organization Inc., and Trump Tower Tampa for giving misleading information about Trump's involvement in the project. She wants a return of her $278,000 deposit and does not want to take part in the sale of the project.

23919 ■ "Troubled Project In Court" in *The Business Journal-Portland* (Vol. 25, July 25, 2008, No. 20, pp. 1)
Pub: American City Business Journals, Inc.
Ed: Wendy Culverwell. **Description:** Views and information on Salpare Bay's Hayden Island project, as well as on financing problems and cases associated with the project, are presented. Construction of luxurious waterside condominiums stopped last fall, after the discovery of financing problems and subcontractors and other parties started filing claims and counterclaims.

23920 ■ "Troy Patent Law Firm Launches Rent-Free Tech Incubator" in *Crain's Detroit Business* (Vol. 25, June 8, 2009, No. 23, pp. 4)
Pub: Crain Communications Inc. - Detroit
Ed: Tom Henderson. **Description:** Young Basile Hanlon MacFarlane & Helmholdt PC, a patent law firm located in Troy, Michigan has created a small, rent-free technology incubator on site. The incubator will be called North Woodward Tech Incubator and has room for four or five startups. The incubator is for the earliest or pre-seed stage for entrepreneurs who have not yet gotten significant investment capital.

23921 ■ "Truckers Walk Strike Line" in *Puget Sound Business Journal* (Vol. 29, October 24, 2008, No. 27, pp. 1)
Pub: American City Business Journals
Ed: Steve Wilhelm. **Description:** Teamsters Local 174 went on strike against Oak Harbor Freight Lines Inc. over alleged company violations of federal labor laws. The union also accuses the company of engaging directly with employees and holding mandatory meetings about contract negotiations.

23922 ■ "Trust But Verify: FMLA Software Isn't Foolproof, So Apply a Human Touch" in *HR Specialist* (Vol. 8, September 2010, No. 9, pp. 3)
Pub: Capitol Information Group Inc.
Description: Employers are using software to track FMLA information, however, it is important for employers to review reasons for eligibility requirements, particularly when an employee is reportedly overstepping the bounds within leave regulations due to software error.

23923 ■ "Trust Distrust" in *Canadian Business* (Vol. 79, July 17, 2006, No. 14-15, pp. 61)
Pub: Rogers Media
Ed: John Gray. **Description:** The need to frame better trust deeds in order to protect the investor's money as well as their returns is examined.

23924 ■ *Ultimate Guide to Project Management*
Pub: Entrepreneurial Press
Ed: Sid Kemp. **Released:** October 2005. **Price:** $29.95 (US), $39.95 (Canadian). **Description:** Project management strategies including writing a business plan and developing a good advertising campaign.

23925 ■ *Ultimate Small Business Advisor*
Pub: Entrepreneur Press
Ed: Andi Axman. **Released:** May 2007. **Price:** $30. 95. **Description:** Tip for starting and running a small business, including new tax rulings and laws affecting small business, are shared.

23926 ■ *Ultimate Startup Directory: Expert Advice and 1,500 Great Startup Ideas*
Pub: Entrepreneur Press
Ed: James Stephenson. **Released:** February 2007. **Price:** $30.95 (CND). **Description:** Startup opportunities in over 30 industries are given, along with information on investment, earning potential, skills, legal requirements and more.

23927 ■ "Under Fire, Sabia Triggers Battle for BCE" in *Globe & Mail* (April 14, 2007, pp. B1)
Pub: CTVglobemedia Publishing Inc.
Ed: Boyd Erman. **Description:** The announcement of negotiations for the sale of BCE Inc. by its chief executive officer Michael Sabia is discussed. The efforts of Ontario Teachers Pension Plan to submit its proposal for the sale are described.

23928 ■ *Understanding Small Business*
Pub: Tate Publishing and Enterprises, LLC
Ed: Edward McMahon. **Released:** May 2006. **Price:** $20.95. **Description:** Three step process to help an entrepreneur build a basic business plan and an effective cash flow statement to minimize risk.

23929 ■ "Unfair Distraction of Employees" in *Business Owner* (Vol. 35, March-April 2011, No. 2, pp. 8)
Pub: DL Perkins Company
Description: Fair Credit Collection Practices Act makes it illegal for collectors to contact a debtor at his or her place of employment if the collector is made aware that it is against personnel policy of the employer for the worker to take such a call.

23930 ■ "Union, Heal Thyself" in *Canadian Business* (Vol. 81, July 21, 2008, No. 11, pp. 9)
Pub: Rogers Media Ltd.
Description: General Motors Corp. was offered by the federal government a $250 million fund after the company declared plans to close its facility in Ontario. The government move is geared towards supporting the workers who have refused to support the automotive company. Details of the labor contract between General Motors and the Canadian Auto Workers are presented.

23931 ■ "Union Questions Patrick Cudahy Layoffs" in *Business Journal-Milwaukee* (Vol. 28, December 3, 2010, No. 9, pp. A1)
Pub: Milwaukee Business Journal
Ed: Rich Ravito. **Description:** United Food and Commercial Workers Local 1473 is investigating Patrick Cudahy Inc.'s termination of 340 jobs. The union said the company has violated the law for failing to issue proper notice of a mass layoff.

23932 ■ "U.S. Attorney Post the Latest Twist" in *The Business Journal-Serving Greater Tampa Bay* (Vol. 28, July 25, 2008, No. 31, pp. 1)
Pub: American City Business Journals, Inc.
Ed: Jane Meinhardt. **Description:** Tampa, Florida-based lawyer A. Brian Albritton has been nominated to be the U.S. Attorney for the Middle District of Florida. He is an expert in cases involving white-collar crime, secret theft, noncompete agreements, and other agreements.

23933 ■ "U.S. Trade Body Clears Apple in Patent Case" in *Wall Street Journal Eastern Edition* (November 23 , 2011, pp. C1)
Pub: Dow Jones & Company Inc.
Ed: Matt Jarzemsky, Paul Mozur. **Description:** HTC Corporation alleged in its patent-infringement case against Apple Inc. that Apple violated patents of S3 Graphics Inc., a company which was acquired by HTC Corporation. Now the International Trade Commission has issued a ruling saying that Apple did not violate the patents.

23934 ■ "Universal Music Sues Grooveshark's Parent" in *Wall Street Journal Eastern Edition* (November 22 , 2011, pp. B5)
Pub: Dow Jones & Company Inc.
Ed: Ethan Smith. **Description:** Escape Media Group Inc., the parent company of online-music service Grooveshark, and seven of its executives have been sued by Universal Music Group, which alleges patent infringement involving its sound recordings. The executives are alleged to have uploaded thousands of songs onto Grooveshark.

23935 ■ "Unlicensed Utah Collection Agency Settles with Idaho Department of Finance" in *Idaho Business Review, Boise* (July 15, 2010)
Pub: Idaho Business Review
Description: Federal Recovery Acceptance Inc., doing business as Paramount Acceptance in Utah, agreed to pay penalties and expenses after the firm was investigated by the state for improprieties. The firm was charged with conducting unlicensed collection activity.

23936 ■ "Unpleasant Surprise" in *Barron's* (Vol. 88, March 24, 2008, No. 12, pp. 60)
Pub: Dow Jones & Company, Inc.
Ed: Shirley A. Lazo. **Description:** Discusses the $175 million that footwear company Genesco received in a settlement with Finish Line and UBS is considered as a stock distribution and is taxable as dividend income. Railroad company CSX raised its quarterly common payout from 15 cents to 18 cents.

23937 ■ "Unwanted News for Hospitals" in *Business Courier* (Vol. 24, October 26, 2008, No. 28, pp. 1)
Pub: American City Business Journals, Inc.
Ed: Description: Christ and St. Luke Hospital might be sharing responsibility costs on the $207 million hospital being built by Health Alliance, the group they are parting with. Christ and St. Lu ke hospitals will be paying $60 million and $25 miilion for partial liability res pectively because the plans for the said project were already underway before they decided to withdraw. Christ Hospital is involved in a whistleblower case that might cause $424 million in liability across the group.

23938 ■ "Up To Code? Website Eases Compliance Burden for Entrepreneurs" in *Black Enterprise* (Vol. 38, March 2008, No. 8, pp. 48)
Pub: Earl G. Graves Publishing Co. Inc.
Ed: Robin White-Goode. **Description:** Business.gov is a presidential E-government project created to help small businesses easily find, understand, and comply with laws and regulations pertaining to a particular industry.

23939 ■ "Valuation of Intangible Assets in Franchise Companies and Multinational Groups" in *Franchise Law Journal* (Winter 2008)
Pub: American Bar Association
Ed: Bruce S. Schaeffer, Susan J. Robins. **Description:** Intangible assets, also known as intellectual properties are the most valuable assets for companies today. Legal intellectual property issues faced by franchises firms are discussed.

23940 ■ "Verdict: Few Legal Jobs" in *Boston Business Journal* (Vol. 31, June 17, 2011, No. 21, pp. 1)
Pub: Boston Business Journal
Ed: Lisa van der Pool. **Description:** Law school graduates in Massachusetts are finding it harder to find work as the legal job market remains weak. The national employment rate for the 2010 law school class fell to 87.6 percent, while only 68.4 percent held jobs that require passing the bar examination.

23941 ■ "Voices: Breaking the Corruption Habit" in *Business Strategy Review* (Vol. 21, Autumn 2010, No. 3, pp. 67)
Pub: Wiley-Blackwell
Ed: David De Cremer. **Description:** In times of crisis, it seems natural that people will work together for the common good. David De Cremer cautions that, on the contrary, both economic and social research prove otherwise. He proposes steps for organizations to take to prevent corrupt behaviors.

23942 ■ "VPA to Pay $9.5 Million to Settle Whistle-Blower Lawsuits" in *Crain's Detroit Business* (Vol. 26, January 11, 2010, No. 2, pp. 13)
Pub: Crain Communications, Inc.
Ed: Jay Greene. **Description:** According to Terrence Berg, first assistant with the U.S. Attorney's Office in Detroit, Voluntary Physicians Association, a local home health care company, has agreed to pay $9.5 million to settle four whistle-blower lawsuits; the agreement settles allegations that VPA submitted claims to TriCare, the Michigan Medicaid program and Medicare for unnecessary home visits, tests and procedures.

23943 ■ "What Enforcement?" in *Canadian Business* (Vol. 81, December 24, 2007, No. 1, pp. 26)
Pub: Rogers Media
Ed: Al Rosen. **Description:** Securities enforcement in Canada needs to be improved in order to tackle white collar crimes that influence investors' opinion of the country. There have been high-profile cases where investigations have not been initiated. Details on the responsibilities of the securities commissions and the need for enforcement mandate in a separate agency are discussed.

23944 ■ "What's Good Faith Got to Do With Contracts?" in *Contractor* (Vol. 56, November 2009, No. 11, pp. 41)
Pub: Penton Media, Inc.
Ed: Susan Linden McGreevy. **Description:** Uniform Commercial Code makes the obligation to act in good faith a term of every commercial transaction. The code generally applies to the sale of goods and not to construction contracts but parties to a construction contract have the right to expect people to act in good faith and forego actions not related to the contract itself.

23945 ■ "When Are Sales Representatives Also Franchisees?" in *Franchise Law Journal* (Vol. 27, Winter 2008, No. 3, pp. 151)
Pub: American Bar Association
Ed: John R.F. Baer, David A. Beyer, Scott P. Weber. **Description:** Review of the traditional definitions of sales representatives along with information on how these distribution models could fit into various legal tests for a franchise.

23946 ■ "When Worlds Collide: The Enforceability of Arbitration Agreements in Bankruptcy" in *Franchise Law Journal* (Summer 2007)
Pub: American Bar Association
Ed: Mark A. Salzberg, Gary M. Zinkgraf. **Description:** Most franchise agreements carry broad arbitration clauses requiring arbitration of nearly all disputes between franchisor and franchisee; how these clauses govern issues of bankruptcy are explored.

23947 ■ "Whistleblower or Manipulator?" in *Canadian Business* (Vol. 81, July 22, 2008, No. 12-13, pp. 11)
Pub: Rogers Media Ltd.
Ed: John Gray. **Description:** Discusses Maria Messina who is portrayed by prosecutors of the Livent Inc. trial as a whistleblower, while defense lawyers insist that she is a manipulator. Defense lawyers allege that Messina, who was Livent's chief financial officer, is a character assassin that made money out of Livent's bankruptcy. Other views on Messina, as well as information on the case, are presented.

23948 ■ "Who's Next?" in *Boston Business Journal* (Vol. 27, November 16, 2007, No. 42, pp. 1)
Pub: American City Business Journals Inc.
Ed: Lisa van der Pool. **Description:** Boston, Massachusetts' burgeoning technology and biotech industries along with rising billing rates make it a unique legal market. Law firms cross the threshold either by merging with or acquiring a smaller law firm. Boston as a unique legal market is discussed.

23949 ■ "Why Copyright Isn't Property" in *Information Today* (Vol. 26, February 2009, No. 2, pp. 18)
Pub: Information Today, Inc.
Ed: K. Matthew Dames. **Description:** An overview of intellectual property is presented. Intellectual property refers to "creations of the mind: inventions, literary and artistic works, and symbols, names, and designs used in commerce", according to the World Intellectual Property Organization (WIPO). WIPO divides intellectual property into two categories: industrial property consisting of patents, trademarks, and industrial designs; and copyright: literary, artistic, creative, and aesthetic works.

23950 ■ "Will Focus on Business Continue?" in *Baltimore Business Journal* (Vol. 28, November 5, 2010, No. 26, pp. 1)
Pub: Baltimore Business Journal
Ed: Scott Dance. **Description:** The 2010 election may call for new efforts to teach new lawmakers to assure that the viewpoints of businesses are considered and accurately delivered. The Greater Baltimore Committee and similar groups have gathered reports on the competitiveness of Maryland and are planning to use them to make a case of keeping business a top priority.

23951 ■ *Work at Home Now*
Pub: Career Press, Inc.
Ed: Christine Durst, Michael Haaren. **Released:** October 9, 2010. **Price:** $14.99. **Description:** There are legitimate home-based jobs and projects that can be found on the Internet, but trustworthy guidance is scarce. There is a 58 to 1 scam ratio in work at-home advertising filled with fraud.

23952 ■ "Workers' Comp System Cuts Through Paper" in *Sacramento Business Journal* (Vol. 25, July 11, 2008, No. 19, pp. 1)
Pub: American City Business Journals, Inc.
Ed: Kelly Johnson. **Description:** California has started testing a new paperless system for handling disputed workers' compensation claims. It is believed that the shift will affect people both inside and outside of the state Division of Workers' Compensation and the state Workers' Compensation Appeals Board. The other details of the planned system are also presented.

23953 ■ "Working His Magic at Home" in *Business Courier* (Vol. 24, February 22, 2008, No. 46, pp. 1)
Pub: American City Business Journals, Inc.
Ed: Lucy May. **Description:** Rob Portman has left his position at the White House as budget director and decided to practice law at Squire, Sanders & Dempsey in Cincinnati. However, analysts believe that Portman's political career is not finished yet, as some expect him to become a gubernatorial or senatorial candidate in 2010. Portman's impacts on Cincinnati's business community are also evaluated.

23954 ■ *Working for Yourself: Law and Taxes for Independent Contractors, Freelancers and Consultants*
Pub: NOLO Publications
Ed: Stephen Fishman. **Released:** March 2008. **Price:** $39.99 paperback. **Description:** In-depth information is shared for contractors, freelancers and consultants involving business law and small business taxes.

23955 ■ *Your Lawyer: An Owner's Manual*
Pub: Agate Publishing, Incorporated
Ed: Henry C. Krasnow. **Released:** November 2005. **Price:** $14.00. **Description:** Small business guide that assists owners and managers to find, work with, and inspire attorneys. Includes an overview of the legal processes involved in running a small company.

23956 ■ "Your Lawyer: An Owner's Manual, a Business Owner's Guide to Managing Your Lawyer" in *Family Business Review* (June 2006)
Pub: Family Firm Institute Inc.
Ed: Jane Hilburt-Davis. **Description:** Profile of the guide for managing a lawyer for a family-owned small business.

TRADE PERIODICALS

23957 ■ *Association Law and Policy*
Pub: American Society of Association Executives
Price: Included in membership. **Description:** Internet newsletter providing information on antitrust, tax, employment, and other legal issue affecting associations and association executives.

23958 ■ *The Business Torts Reporter*
Pub: Aspen Publishers
Ed: Richard E. Kaye, Editor. **Released:** Monthly, 12/yr. **Price:** $525 with free standard shipping on U.S prepaid orders. **Description:** Journal covering business tort law for legal professionals.

23959 ■ *California Labor and Employment ALERT Newsletter*
Pub: Castle Publications Ltd.
Contact: Richard Simmons, President
Released: Bimonthly. **Price:** $90; $105 includes 3-ring binder. **Description:** Reports on current developments in California and federal laws concerning personnel and employment issues. Recurring features include notices of publications available.

23960 ■ *Insights*
Pub: Aspen Publishers
Contact: Amy L. Goodman
Released: Monthly. **Price:** $680 with free standard shipping on U.S prepaid orders. **Description:** Journal covering legal developments in corporate and securities law on the state, national and worldwide levels.

23961 ■ *International Journal of Franchising and Distribution Law*
Pub: Kluwer Academic/Plenum Publishing Corp.
Ed: Martin Mendelsohn, Editor. **Released:** Quarterly. **Description:** Journal covering franchise law worldwide.

23962 ■ *Laborwatch*
Pub: Berens & Tate, P.C.
Ed: Released: Monthly. **Price:** $167; $277, two years. **Description:** Monthly report on the developments in labor relations, employment litigation, and human resource management.

23963 ■ *Legislative Watch*
Pub: American Tort Reform Association
Ed: Released: Weekly. **Price:** Included in membership. **Description:** Membership newsletter of the American Tort Reform Association.

VIDEOCASSETTES/ AUDIOCASSETTES

23964 ■ *Business Litigation*
National Institute for Trial Advocacy (NITA)
361 Centennial Pkwy., Ste. 220
Louisville, CO 80027-1281
Ph:(720)890-4860
Free: 800-225-6482
Fax:(720)890-7069
Co. E-mail: customerservice@nita.org
URL: http://www.nita.org/
Released: 1987. **Price:** $1995.00. **Description:** Provides a practical primer to business litigation with an emphasis on the prevention of disputes, the effect they have on the client's business, and alternatives to going to court. Since many disputes do end up in civil court, the series covers pretrial and trial strategies, the examining of friendly and hostile witnesses, and closing statements. **Availability:** VHS; 3/4U.

CONSULTANTS

23965 ■ Comprehensive Professional Management Inc.
222 E Dundee Rd.
Wheeling, IL 60090-3009
Ph:(847)520-1301
Fax:(847)520-0372
Co. E-mail: bob@cpmincfs.com
Contact: Kathy Rathunde, Principle
E-mail: mkstumpf@atsaol.com
Scope: Services include accounting, financial planning, litigation support, pension profit sharing administration, practice surveys, professional corporation issues, retirement and estate planning and tax advice.

23966 ■ donphin.com Inc.
1001 B Ave., Ste. 200
Coronado, CA 92118
Ph:(619)550-3533
Free: 800-234-3304
Fax:(619)600-0096
Co. E-mail: inquiry@donphin.com
URL: http://www.donphin.com
Contact: Donald A. Phin, CEO
E-mail: don@donphin.com
Scope: Offers a comprehensive approach to understanding and applying a broad range of business principles: legal compliance issues, management concerns, health and safety, customer service, marketing, information management. Industries served: All developing small businesses. **Publications:** "Doing Business Right!"; "HR That Works!"; "Lawsuit Free! How to Prevent Employee Lawsuits"; "Building Powerful Employment Relationships!"; "Victims, Villains and Heroes: Managing Emotions in The Workplace". **Seminars:** Doing Business Right!; HR That Works!; Building Powerful Employment Relationships; Lawsuit Free!.

23967 ■ Equity Partners of America Ltd.
1450 W Long Lake Rd., Ste. 340
Troy, MI 48098-6351
Ph:(248)952-0300
Fax:(248)952-0314
Co. E-mail: equitypartners@email.msn.com
Contact: Albert A. Koch, Managing Director
Scope: Private investment bank specializing in debt and equity capital procurement; buying and selling businesses; shareholder value enhancement strategies; and litigation and alternative dispute resolution assistance; including expert witness assistance. Serves manufacturing, distribution and service industries. **Seminars:** Preparation of a business plan; Use of financial statements in damage claims; Determining the value of a business; When to sell a family business.

23968 ■ Invent Resources Inc.
PO Box 548
Lexington, MA 02420-0005
Ph:(781)862-0200
Fax:(781)721-2300
Co. E-mail: pavelle@comcast.net
URL: http://www.weinvent.com
Contact: Sol Aisenberg, Principle
E-mail: pavelle@comcast.net
Scope: Provides consultancy services to provide support in developing and prototyping new, proprietary products. Offer inventory services on demand. Assist clients who need innovations in product lines, have hit technical bottlenecks, or need improvements in manufacturing processes. Provide assistance to individuals and clients in obtaining, reviewing, and strengthening patents.

23969 ■ Juroviesky and Ricci L.L.P.
410 Park Ave., 15th Fl., Ste. 697
New York, NY 10022
Ph:(416)481-0718
Free: 877-578-7529
Fax:(416)481-1792
Co. E-mail: hjuroviesky@jruslaw.com
URL: http://www.jruslaw.com
Contact: Henry Juroviesky, Managing Partner
E-mail: hjuroviesky@jruslaw.com
Scope: A law firm providing legal services on both sides of the United States/Canadian border. Practice areas include international business and corporate law, corporate governance, U.S./Canadian litigation, U.S. and Canadian corporate tax planning; state, provincial, and local tax planning; and international tax planning. **Publications:** "Is the United States the Next Great Tax Haven," Feb, 2005; "Under What Circumstances may Canadian Citizens Enter the United States as a Business Visitor," Feb, 2005; "Massachusetts Unsuccessful in its Sales and Use Tax Revenue Grab Against Drop Shippers," Feb, 2005; "Tax and Legal Hiccups in the Course of a US Acquisition," Feb, 2005; "Do I Need To Worry About Collecting and Remitting Sales/Use Tax When I Sell to US Customers," Jan, 2005.

23970 ■ Law Offices of David Bow Woo
700 S Flower St., Ste. 1100
Los Angeles, CA 90017-4113
Ph:(213)892-6309
Fax:(213)892-2215
Co. E-mail: david.woo@azbar.org
Contact: David Bow Woo, Owner
E-mail: david.woo@azbar.org
Scope: Attorney specializing in business litigation and transactions. Emphasis is on financial motivation and import and export trade financing.

23971 ■ Nixon Peabody L.L.P.
100 Summer St.
Boston, MA 02110-2106
Ph:(617)345-1000
Fax:(617)345-1300
URL: http://www.nixonpeabody.com
Contact: Yolanda Jones, Editor
E-mail: yljones@atsnixonpeabody.com
Scope: Multi-practice law firm serving business, industry and individuals. Practice areas include antitrust, class actions, corporate governance and regulatory, corporate transactions, corporate trust, environmental, equipment finance, FDA regulatory, financial restructuring and bankruptcy, franchise and distribution, global finance, government contracts, government investigations and white collar defense, immigration, intellectual property, international, international arbitration, labor and employment, litigation and dispute resolution, private clients, private equity, products liability, mass and complex tort, project finance, public finance, real estate, securities, syndication, and tax. **Publications:** "Passage to India: Ensuring 'safe travels' in business," Dec, 2008; "The Deputization of State AGs Under CPSIA," Dec, 2008; "New Rules Mandating the Disclosure of Consumer Complaints," Dec, 2008.

23972 ■ Ruf & Associates L.L.C.
510 East 770 North
Orem, UT 84097
Ph:(801)764-9100
Free: (866)589-8871
Fax:(866)589-8871
Co. E-mail: info@rufassociates.com
URL: http://www.rufassociates.com
Contact: Steven H. Ruf, COO
E-mail: steve@atsrufassociates.com
Scope: Provides consulting services for construction claims, cost segregation studies, litigation support, insurance claims, insurance claim appraisals, construction management and financial management. **Publications:** "The Cash Benefits of Cost Segregation," Jul, 2007.

FRANCHISES AND BUSINESS OPPORTUNITIES

23973 ■ AAA Franchise Legal Help Hotline
Franchise Foundations
4157 23rd St.
San Francisco, CA 94114
Free: 800-942-4402
Founded: 1980. **Description:** Advice on franchise legal issues.

23974 ■ Angiuli Katkin & Gentile, LLP
60 Bay St., PH Ste.
Staten Island, NY 10301
Ph:(718)816-0005
Fax:(718)816-4660
Founded: 1985. **Description:** Provide legal services for franchise operation.

23975 ■ Carter & Tani
402 E Roosevelt Rd., Ste. 206
Wheaton, IL 60187
Ph:(630)668-2135
Founded: 1977. **Description:** Assist start-up franchisees and franchisors.

23976 ■ Dickinson & Wheelock P.C.
7660 Woodway Dr., Ste. 460
Houston, TX 77063
Ph:(713)722-8118
Free: 800-727-3458
Fax:(713)722-9688
Description: Franchise and business attorneys.

23977 ■ Franchise Law Team
30021 Tomas, Ste. 260
Rancho Santa Margarita, CA 92688
Ph:(949)459-7474
Free: 888-276-2976
Fax:(949)459-7772
Founded: 1985. **Description:** Registration, advice, and dispute resolution.

23978 ■ Friedman, Rosenwasser & Goldbaum, P.A.
The Plaza
5355 Town Center Rd., Ste. 801
Boca Raton, FL 33486
Ph:(561)395-5511
Fax:(561)395-2648
Founded: 1986. **Description:** International and domestic franchise services.

23979 ■ Gowling Lafleur Henderson LLP
550 Burrard St., Ste. 2300
PO Box 30
Vancouver, BC, Canada V6C 2B5
Ph:(604)683-6498
Fax:(604)683-3558
Founded: 1877. **Description:** Full service law firm for franchisors.

23980 ■ Harold L. Kestenbaum, Esq.
90 Merrick Ave., Ste. 601
East Meadow, NY 11559
Ph:(516)745-0099
Fax:(516)745-0293
Founded: 1977. **Description:** Franchise attorney and consultant.

23981 ■ iFranchise Group
905 W 175th St., 2nd Fl.
Homewood, IL 60430
Ph:(708)957-2300
Fax:(708)957-2395
Co. E-mail: info@ifranchise.net
URL: http://www.ifranchise.com
Description: Offers services on strategic planning, franchise law, operations documentation, marketing and sales, and executive recruiting for franchisors.

23982 ■ James B. Sheets, Attorney at Law
One Summit Ave., Ste. 304
Fort Worth, TX 76102
Ph:(817)335-6040
Fax:(817)335-2503
Description: Legal services.

23983 ■ Joseph J. Walczak, P.C.
14045 S 88th Ave.
Orland Park, IL 60462
Ph:(708)349-6908
Fax:(708)349-2438
Founded: 1988. **Description:** Franchise and trademark law.

23984 ■ Kanouse & Walker, P.A.
2255 Glades Rd., Ste. 324
Boca Raton, FL 33431
Ph:(561)451-8090
Fax:(561)451-8089
Founded: 1974. **Description:** Represents franchisees in buying a franchise.

23985 ■ Law Offices of Suzanne C. Cummings & Associates, P.C.
Two Main St., Ste. 300
Stoneham, MA 02180
Ph:(781)481-9090
Free: 800-982-9636
Fax:(781)481-9191
Description: Franchise law and business advisors.

23986 ■ Marks & Klein, LLP, Attorneys-at-Law
63 Riverside Ave.
Red Bank, NJ 07701
Ph:(732)747-7100
Fax:(732)219-0625
Founded: 1971. **Description:** Franchisee and franchisor representation.

23987 ■ Mitchell J. Kassoff, Esq. (Attorney)
2 Foster Ct.
South Orange, NJ 07079-1002
Ph:(973)762-1776
Founded: 1979. **Description:** Nationwide legal representation.

23988 ■ Peter C. Lagarias, Esq.
The Legal Solutions Group, L.L.P.
1629 Fifth Ave.
San Rafael, CA 94901-1828
Ph:(415)460-0100
Fax:(415)460-1099
Description: Franchise litigation and service.

23989 ■ Zarco Einhorn Salkowski & Brito, P.A.
International Pl.
100 SE 2nd St., 27th Fl.
Miami, FL 33131
Ph:(305)374-5418
Fax:(305)374-5428
Founded: 1992. **Description:** Franchise and commercial litigation.

COMPUTERIZED DATABASES

23990 ■ *ABA/BNA Lawyers' Manual on Professional Conduct*
The Bureau of National Affairs Inc.
1801 S Bell St.
Arlington, VA 22202
Free: 800-372-1033
Co. E-mail: customercare@bna.com
URL: http://www.bna.com
Description: Contains news and advice on attorney conduct. Contains full text of the ABA Model Rules of Professional Conduct and Responsibility, ABA ethics opinions, state ethics rule comparisons with ABA models, and other relevant model standards. Includes issues relating to conflicts of interest, client confidences, advertising, fees, discipline, malpractice and related topics. Also includes biweekly reports on recent court decisions, ethics opinions, disciplinary actions and news. **Availability:** Online: The Bureau of National Affairs Inc., Thomson Reuters. **Type:** Full text.

23991 ■ *American Journey: The Constitution and Supreme Court*
Cengage Learning Inc.
27500 Drake Rd.
Farmington Hills, MI 48331-3535
Ph:(248)699-4253
Free: 800-877-4253
Fax:(248)699-8069
Co. E-mail: galeord@gale.com
URL: http://gale.cengage.com
Description: Contains Supreme Court decisions that interpreted it and the enduring issues that contribute to the public debate in America. Major themes include: the Constitutional Convention and James Madison's detailed debate notes, the role of the Supreme Court, including complete decisions and dissenting opinions on a wide range of constitutional questions, state's rights, original intent, separation of powers, and republican government and a hyperlinked version of the Constitution. Corresponds to the online database of the same name. **Availability:** CD-ROM: Cengage Learning Inc. **Type:** Full text; Audio; Image.

23992 ■ *Atlantic Provinces Reports*
Maritime Law Book Ltd.
PO Box 302
Fredericton, NB, Canada E3B 4Y9
Ph:(506)453-9921
Free: 800-561-0220
Fax:(506)453-9525
Co. E-mail: service@mlb.nb.ca
URL: http://www.mlb.nb.ca
Description: Contains headnotes of selected judicial decisions of the courts of New Brunswick, Nova Scotia, Newfoundland, and Prince Edward Island. Also includes decisions of the Supreme Court of Canada on appeals from these provincial courts. Corresponds to *New Brunswick Reports* (2d Series), *Nova Scotia Reports* (2d Series), and *Newfoundland and Prince Edward Island Reports.* **Availability:** Online: LexisNexis Canada Inc. **Type:** Bibliographic.

23993 ■ *Bankruptcy Law Reporter*
The Bureau of National Affairs Inc.
1801 S Bell St.
Arlington, VA 22202
Free: 800-372-1033
Co. E-mail: customercare@bna.com
URL: http://www.bna.com
Description: Contains coverage of every aspect of bankruptcy law. Subjects encompass bankruptcy jury trials, bankruptcy fraud and abuse, bad faith filings, exemptions, executory contracts, home mortgage cramdowns, judicial liens, lender liability, lien stripping, trustees' duties, and related topics. **Availability:** Online: The Bureau of National Affairs Inc., Thomson Reuters. **Type:** Full text.

23994 ■ *The Bar Register of Preeminent Lawyers*
LexisNexis Martindale-Hubbell
121 Chanlon Rd.
New Providence, NJ 07974
Ph:(908)464-6800
Free: 800-526-4902
Fax:(908)771-8704
Co. E-mail: info@martindale.com
URL: http://www.martindale.com
Description: Contains information on more than 8900 law practices rated in the *Martindale-Hubbell Law Directory.* Includes names of members of the firm; names of associates and "of counsel"; full contact information, including address, telephone numbers and email; representative clients; and additional branch office locations. Listings are arranged by state and city under 66 areas of practice—from administrative law and general practice to transportation and tax law. Also contains an index by firm name. **Availability:** Online: LexisNexis Group. **Type:** Directory.

23995 ■ *Canadian Law List*
Thomson Reuters Canada Ltd.
1 Corporate Plz.
2075 Kennedy Rd.
Toronto, ON, Canada M1T 3V4
Ph:(416)609-3800
Free: 800-387-5351
Fax:(416)298-5082
URL: http://www.canadalawbook.ca
Description: Contains a listing of 59,000 lawyers and 20,000 legal firms, judges and government offices in Canada. Includes law firm profiles, worldwide affiliations, personal biographical information and listings of government departments, plus related legal services. Searchable by title, year called to the bar, law firm, telephone and fax numbers, and email addresses. **Availability:** Online: Thomson Reuters Canada Ltd; CD-ROM: Thomson Reuters Canada Ltd. **Type:** Directory.

23996 ■ *CCH Tax Protos*
CCH Canadian Ltd.
90 Sheppard Ave. E, Ste. 300
Toronto, ON, Canada M2N 6X1
Ph:(416)224-2224
Free: 800-268-4522
Fax:(416)224-2243
Co. E-mail: cservice@cch.ca
URL: http://www.cch.ca
Description: Contains current information on taxes in Canada. Includes updates on legislation, interpretation bulletins, information circulars, rulings, Department of Finance releases, Revenue Canada releases, court cases, Internal Revenue Canada documents, draft legislation and explanatory notes, CCH Tax newsletters, and more. **Availability:** Online: CCH Canadian Ltd. **Type:** Bulletin board.

23997 ■ *Class Action Litigation Report*
The Bureau of National Affairs Inc.
1801 S Bell St.
Arlington, VA 22202

Free: 800-372-1033
Co. E-mail: customercare@bna.com
URL: http://www.bna.com
Description: Contains information on all aspects of class action litigation. Subjects include class certification, class actions filed, antitrust, consumer issues, rule reform, verdicts and settlements, attorney fees, employment and discrimination, health care, mass torts, securities, and products issues. Includes highlights of the top reports, brief descriptions of other prominent developments, summaries of case filings, new reports, conference reports, analysis and perspective, and practice tips. Arranged by topical list, litigation subjects, and alphabetical table of cases. **Availability:** Online: The Bureau of National Affairs Inc., Thomson Reuters. **Type:** Full text.

23998 ■ *Computer Technology Law Report*
The Bureau of National Affairs Inc.
1801 S Bell St.
Arlington, VA 22202
Free: 800-372-1033
Co. E-mail: customercare@bna.com
URL: http://www.bna.com
Description: Contains news and developments in the field of computer technology law. Subjects include antitrust issues; computer technology exports; contract liability; design patents; digital assets; network security; "open source" software licensing and development; patent protection; reverse engineering; tort liability; trademark protection; the Uniform Computer Transaction Act; liability for defective computer hardware and software products; insurance coverage for computer-related liabilities; patent protection for software and computer-related products and services; software licensing and piracy; and software copyright protection. Includes summaries of the most important developments in the field; brief descriptions of other important issues; court proceedings of related cases and decision; news of non-judicial developments; lists of conferences, seminars and related events; and a list of related websites. Enables users to access by alphabetical list of topics and by issue date. **Availability:** Online: The Bureau of National Affairs Inc., Thomson Reuters. **Type:** Full text.

23999 ■ *Corporate Law Daily*
The Bureau of National Affairs Inc.
1801 S Bell St.
Arlington, VA 22202
Free: 800-372-1033
Co. E-mail: customercare@bna.com
URL: http://www.bna.com
Description: Contains the full spectrum of judicial, legislative, regulatory, and tax issues that affect corporate practice. Subjects include antitrust, corporate criminal liability, international trade, litigation, occupational safety and health, product liability, professional responsibility, securities, corporate law, corporate governance, employment discrimination, environmental enforcement, and intellectual property. **Availability:** Online: The Bureau of National Affairs Inc., Thomson Reuters. **Type:** Full text.

24000 ■ *Criminal Law Reporter*
The Bureau of National Affairs Inc.
1801 S Bell St.
Arlington, VA 22202
Free: 800-372-1033
Co. E-mail: customercare@bna.com
URL: http://www.bna.com
Description: Contains reports on news and court proceedings in the field of criminal law. Subjects include appeals, arrest, capital punishment, civil liability, civil rights, confrontation and cross-examination, defenses, double jeopardy, drugs, driving, electronic surveillance and wiretapping, police misconduct, prisons and jails, racketeering, representation by counsel, search and seizure, self-incrimination, sentencing, sex offenses, state constitutional law, statutory interpretation, witnesses, entrapment, evidence, firearms, forfeiture, fraud, grand juries, guilty pleas, habeas corpus, immunity, interrogation and confessions, jury trial, money laundering, and obscenity. Sections include Highlights, In This Issue, Table of Cases, Court Decision, In Brief, News, Conference Reports, Special Reports, Circuit Split Roundup, Supreme Court Proceedings, and Index and Table of Cases. **Availability:** Online: The Bureau of National Affairs Inc., Thomson Reuters. **Type:** Full text.

24001 ■ *DART: British Columbia Statute Service*
Thomson Reuters Canada Ltd.
1 Corporate Plz.
2075 Kennedy Rd.
Toronto, ON, Canada M1T 3V4
Ph:(416)609-3800
Free: 800-387-5351
Fax:(416)298-5082
URL: http://www.canadalawbook.ca
Description: Contains all British Columbia Statutes from the 1996 consolidation, including all new Acts, the British Columbia Statute Citator, and the Annotations of British Columbia and Supreme Court of Canada Decisions reported in the *British Columbia Decisions Statute Citator*. Includes complete amendment history for each statute, including amendments that have received Royal Assent but are not yet in force. **Availability:** Online: Thomson Reuters Canada Ltd; CD-ROM: Thomson Reuters Canada Ltd. **Type:** Full text.

24002 ■ *DART: Western Decisions*
Thomson Reuters Canada Ltd.
1 Corporate Plz.
2075 Kennedy Rd.
Toronto, ON, Canada M1T 3V4
Ph:(416)609-3800
Free: 800-387-5351
Fax:(416)298-5082
URL: http://www.canadalawbook.ca
Description: Covers British Columbia decisions, civil and criminal cases since 1979; Manitoba decisions, civil and criminal cases since 1980; Saskatchewan decisions, civil and criminal cases since 1980; and Alberta decisions, civil and criminal cases since 1980. **Availability:** Online: Thomson Reuters Canada Ltd; CD-ROM: Thomson Reuters Canada Ltd. **Type:** Full text.

24003 ■ *EIU ViewsWire*
The Economist Group
26 Red Lion Sq.
London WC1R 4HQ, United Kingdom
Ph:44 20 7576 8181
Fax:44 20 7576 8476
Co. E-mail: london@eiu.com
URL: http://www.eiu.com
Description: Provides up to 150 articles daily covering practical business intelligence, including key events, market issues, impending crises, and the business and regulatory environment in emerging and International markets. Covers information from more than 195 countries. Includes: Briefings: critical political, economic, and business changes around the world organized by the topics of company, economy, finance, politics, regulations, and industry. Forecasts: Country updates-continuously updated overviews of GDP, inflation, demand, investment, fiscal policy, interest rates, currency, external accounts, and the political scene in more than 190 countries. Consensus forecasts-monthly currency, interest rate, and equity market short-term outlooks provided by multinational companies and investment banks. Country risk summary-political and credit risk ratings and analysis for 100 countries. Five-year forecasts—quarterly growth, inflation, and trade indicators for 60 countries. Forecast summaries—quarterly key economic indicators and business watchlist. Background: facts and figures on current conditions in more than 190 countries. Key economic indicators—quarterly statistics on growth, trade, reserves, and currencies. Basic data and country fact sheet-population data, per capita GDP, political structure, taxes, foreign trade and policy issues. Trade, tax and forex regulations-Connecticut updated full regulatory profiles on 60 countries. **Availability:** Online: The Economist Group, Thomson Reuters, Financial Times Ltd., LexisNexis Group. **Type:** Full text; Numeric.

24004 ■ *Electronic Commerce & Law Report*
The Bureau of National Affairs Inc.
1801 S Bell St.
Arlington, VA 22202
Free: 800-372-1033
Co. E-mail: customercare@bna.com
URL: http://www.bna.com
Description: Contains news and developments in the field of electronic commerce law. Topics include consumer protection laws, copyright and trademark issues, cryptography, database protection, defamation, domain name disputes, electronic signatures, free speech/First Amendment issues, information licensing, Internet governance, Internet-related telecommunications regulation, jurisdiction, network security, online contracting, online gambling, online marketing, privacy, and trade regulation. Covers summaries of the most significant developments in e-commerce law; e-commerce news from legislatures, agencies, and industry; and court proceedings. Enables users to search by topic, state, company and medium. **Availability:** Online: The Bureau of National Affairs Inc., Thomson Reuters. **Type:** Full text.

24005 ■ *Family Law Reporter*
The Bureau of National Affairs Inc.
1801 S Bell St.
Arlington, VA 22202
Free: 800-372-1033
Co. E-mail: customercare@bna.com
URL: http://www.bna.com
Description: Contains information on family law. Includes new state and federal legislative developments, appellate court family cases, and monitors new trends and issues. Subjects include adoption, alimony, child custody, bankruptcy and marital debts, child abduction, domestic partnership and non-marital relationships, domestic torts, equitable distribution, grandparents' rights, joint tenancy, military benefits, prenuptial agreements, joint tenancy, paternity, visitation rights, child support, domestic torts, IRS rulings, separation agreemtns, surrogate parenthood and assisted conception, taxes and divorce planning, Uniform Child Custody Jurisdiction Enforcement Act, Uniform Interstate Family Support Act, visitation, pensions, and property rights. Information is organized by topic or by state. **Availability:** Online: The Bureau of National Affairs Inc., Thomson Reuters. **Type:** Full text.

24006 ■ *Florida Jurisprudence on Westlaw*
Thomson Reuters
610 Opperman Dr.
Eagan, MN 55123
Ph:(651)687-7000
Free: 800-344-5008
Fax:(651)687-5827
Co. E-mail: west.customer.service@thomsonreuters.com
URL: http://www.westlaw.com
Description: Contains the complete text of the multi-volume encyclopedia of Florida law, *Florida Jurisprudence, Second Edition*. Includes supplementary materials as part of updated documents. Organized into 220 topics including Table of statutes and Table of Cases. **Availability:** Online: Thomson Reuters. **Type:** Full text.

24007 ■ *A Guide to Federal Sector Equal Employment Opportunity (EEO) Law and Practice*
Dewey Publications Inc.
2009 N 14th St., Ste. 705
Arlington, VA 22201
Ph:(703)524-1355
Fax:(703)524-1463
Co. E-mail: deweypublications@gmail.com
URL: http://www.deweypub.com
Description: Provides references to thousands of decisions of the EEOC Office of Federal Operations, along with procedural and practice guidance. Integrates the new civil rights laws and updated EEOC Part 1614 regulations for Federal sector employees. Corresponds to the print version of *A Guide to Federal Sector Equal Employment Law and Practice*. **Availability:** CD-ROM: Dewey Publications Inc. **Type:** Full text.

24008 ■ *A Guide to Merit Systems Protection Board (MSPB) Law and Practice*
Dewey Publications Inc.
2009 N 14th St., Ste. 705
Arlington, VA 22201

Ph:(703)524-1355
Fax:(703)524-1463
Co. E-mail: deweypublications@gmail.com
URL: http://www.deweypub.com
Description: Analyzes thousands of published decisions of the MSPB, the courts, and nonprecedential decisions of the U.S. Court of Appeals for the Federal Court. Includes the latest revisions in statutes, regulations, and case decisions. Corresponds to the print version of *A Guide to Merit Systems Protection Board Law and Practice*. **Availability:** CD-ROM: Dewey Publications Inc. **Type:** Full text.

24009 ■ *Industrial Patent Activity in the United States Parts 1 and 2, 1974-1998*
U.S. Patent and Trademark Office
Madison Bldgs. (East & West)
600 Dulany St.
PO Box 1450
Alexandria, VA 22314
Ph:(703)308-4357
Free: 800-786-9199
Fax:(703)306-2737
Co. E-mail: usptoinfo@uspto.gov
URL: http://www.uspto.gov
Description: Provides information on the activity, ownership, and National origin of utility Patents granted by the U.S. Patent and Trademark Office. Part 1, Time Series Profile by Company and Country of Origin, 1974-1998, covers ownership and national origin of patents granted by U.S. Patent Office between 1974 and 1998. Includes list of more than 8500 corporations, universities, Government agencies, and other businesses that received patents, ranked by degree of activity. Part 2, Alphabetical Listing by Company, 1974-1998, contains alphabetical list of every U.S. and foreign organization that was granted five or more U.S. patents between 1974 and 1998. **Availability:** CD-ROM: U.S. Department of Commerce. **Type:** Patents/Trademarks.

24010 ■ *IRS Publication 334: Tax Guide for Small Business*
U.S. Department of the Treasury
1111 Constitution Ave. NW
Washington, DC 20224
Ph:(202)622-2000
Free: 800-829-3676
Fax:(202)622-6642
URL: http://www.irs.ustreas.gov
Description: Contains the complete text of the 2009 edition of *IRS Publication 334 (Tax Guide for Small Business)*, covering information on U.S. federal tax law and tax return preparation for small businesses. Enables the user to search by topic and to retrieve IRS listings of technical authorities. **Availability:** Online: U.S. Department of the Treasury. **Type:** Full text; Directory.

24011 ■ *KeyCite*
Thomson Reuters
610 Opperman Dr.
Eagan, MN 55123
Ph:(651)687-7000
Free: 800-344-5008
Fax:(651)687-5827
Co. E-mail: west.customer.service@thomsonreuters.com
URL: http://www.westlaw.com
Description: Contains citing references, including case law and secondary law. Provides direct history, negative indirect history, and related references to the history of a case. **Availability:** Online: Thomson Reuters. **Type:** Bibliographic; Full text.

24012 ■ *Labor and Employment Law Library*
The Bureau of National Affairs Inc.
1801 S Bell St.
Arlington, VA 22202
Free: 800-372-1033
Co. E-mail: customercare@bna.com
URL: http://www.bna.com
Description: Contains information on all aspects of labor and employment law. Includes news summaries and analysis of developments; full text of federal and summaries of state statutes, regulations, and policy statements regarding fair employment practices; full text of significant federal and state decisions regarding fair employment practices from 1965 to the present; full text of federal and summaries of state statutes, regulations, and policy statements regarding individual employment rights; full text of significant federal and state decisions regarding individual employment rights from 1986 to the present; full text of federal and summaries of state statutes, regulations, and policy statements regarding wages and hours; full text of significant federal and state decisions regarding wages and hours from 1959 to the present; full text of federal and summaries of state statutes, regulations, and policy statements regarding Americans with Disabilities Act cases; full text of significant federal and state decisions regarding Americans with Disabilities Act cases from 1974 to the present; full text of labor arbitration and dispute decisions, arbitration rules and procedures; full text of significant federal and state decisions regarding labor-management decisions from 1984 to the present; and state laws. Subjects include discrimination, wages and hours, sexual harassment, absenteeism and turnover, affirmative action/diversity, age bias and compulsory retirement, Americans with disabilities, benefit plans, collective bargaining, contract negotiation and enforcement, drug and alcohol testing, employment-at-will, employment testing, fair employment practices, family and medical leave, fetal protection, handling grievances, hiring, hours of work, independent contractors, individual employment rights, jurisdiction and procedure, labor arbitration, labor-management relations, layoffs and shutdowns, leave rights, overtime pay, pay equity, workers' compensation, work rules and discipline, wages and hours, union organizing, termination, temporary and leased workers, strikes and slowdowns, smoking in the workplace, safety and health, right to information, privacy, political activies, pension law/ERISA, and minimum wage. **Availability:** Online: The Bureau of National Affairs Inc; CD-ROM: The Bureau of National Affairs Inc. **Type:** Full text.

24013 ■ *The Law Digest*
LexisNexis Martindale-Hubbell
121 Chanlon Rd.
New Providence, NJ 07974
Ph:(908)464-6800
Free: 800-526-4902
Fax:(908)771-8704
Co. E-mail: info@martindale.com
URL: http://www.martindale.com
Description: Contains summaries of statutory law worldwide. Includes up-to-date digests of laws of the 50 states, the District of Columbia, Puerto Rico and the U.S. Virgin Islands; English-language summaries of the laws of 80 countries, including new sections on Vietnam, the Slovak Republic, the Republic of Latvia, and the Island of Guernsey; complete texts of over 50 Uniform and Model Acts and International Conventions; and information on the Federal Judiciary and the Rules of Conduct of the American Bar Association. Listings are classified under more than 100 topics and 700 subheadings, including Absentees, Frauds, Motor Vehicles, Trade Secrets and Witnesses. **Availability:** Online: LexisNexis Group. **Type:** Full text.

24014 ■ *Lawyer Locator*
LexisNexis Martindale-Hubbell
121 Chanlon Rd.
New Providence, NJ 07974
Ph:(908)464-6800
Free: 800-526-4902
Fax:(908)771-8704
Co. E-mail: info@martindale.com
URL: http://www.martindale.com
Description: Contains information on more than one million lawyers and law firms in 160 countries. Enables the user to search by name, geographic location, area of practice, firm size and languages. **Availability:** Online: LexisNexis Martindale-Hubbell. **Type:** Directory.

24015 ■ *LexisNexis Personal Injury NetLetter*
LexisNexis Canada Inc.
123 Commerce Valley Dr. E, Ste. 700
Markham, ON, Canada L3T 7W8
Ph:(905)479-2665
Free: 800-668-6481
Co. E-mail: service@lexisnexis.ca
URL: http://www.lexisnexis.ca
Description: Provides access to the newsletter by Professor Gerald Robertson, University of Alberta. **Availability:** Online: LexisNexis Canada Inc. **Type:** Full text.

24016 ■ *Mergers Unleashed*
Investcorp International Inc.
1 State St. Plaza, 27th Fl.
New York, NY 10004
Ph:(212)803-8200
Free: 800-221-1809
Co. E-mail: custserv@sourcemedia.com
URL: http://www.sourcemedia.com
Description: Contains the complete text of *Mergers & Acquisitions Report* and *Mergers & Acquisitions Journal*. Covers pending and ongoing deals as well as insights into industry trends, strategies, and the firms and individuals involved. **Availability:** Online: LexisNexis Group, Investcorp International Inc. **Type:** Full text.

24017 ■ *The National Law Journal*
ALM Media Properties LLC
120 Broadway, 5th Fl.
New York, NY 10271
Ph:(212)457-9400
Free: 800-888-8300
Fax:(646)417-7705
Co. E-mail: customercare@alm.com
URL: http://www.alm.com
Description: Contains the complete text of *The National Law Journal*, a weekly newspaper for the legal profession. Feature articles cover trends in case law, employment, criminal investigations, and law office management techniques. Also covers major legal events and personalities, with analyses of their social and legal impact. **Availability:** Online: ALM Media Properties LLC, LexisNexis Group, Thomson Reuters. **Type:** Full text.

24018 ■ *New York Jurisprudence, 2d, LawDesk CD-ROM ed.*
Thomson Reuters
610 Opperman Dr.
Eagan, MN 55123
Ph:(651)687-7000
Free: 800-344-5008
Fax:(651)687-5827
Co. E-mail: west.customer.service@thomsonreuters.com
URL: http://www.westlaw.com
Description: Provides the full text of the multi-volume encyclopedia of New York law, *New York Jurisprudence, Second Edition*. Supplementary materials are included as part of any updated document. **Availability:** CD-ROM: Thomson Reuters. **Type:** Full text.

24019 ■ *Ohio Jurisprudence on Westlaw*
Thomson Reuters, West
610 Opperman Dr.
Eagan, MN 55123
Ph:(651)687-7000
Free: 800-344-5008
Fax:800-340-9378
Co. E-mail: west.customer.service@thomsonreuters.com
URL: http://west.thomson.com
Description: Contains a comprehensive encyclopedia of civil and criminal Ohio law, substantive and procedural. Organized into 400 topics, including: Table of Statutes and Table of Cases with Annotation References to specific provisions of the Ohio Constitution, statutes, and regulations. Also includes references to other Westlaw sources; Indexing by descriptions or legal concept for fast referencing; and Footnotes citing cases, statutes, and law review articles. **Availability:** Online: Thomson Reuters, West. **Type:** Full text.

24020 ■ *Pharmaceutical Law & Industry Report*
The Bureau of National Affairs Inc.
1801 S Bell St.
Arlington, VA 22202

Free: 800-372-1033
Co. E-mail: customercare@bna.com
URL: http://www.bna.com
Description: Contains news on federal and state laws and regulations regarding the pharmaceutical and biotech industries. Also includes federal and state legislative, regulatory, and legal developments that affect drug costs, pharmaceutical pricing and reimbursement. Topics include antitrust enforcement actions, fraud and abuse investigations, drug formularies, state discount/rebate programs, generics vs. brand name drugs, reforms to the Hatch Waxman Act governing generic drugs, pharmacy benefit management regulation, lawsuits involving patent issues or Food and Drug Administration regulations, health insurance plans, patents on drugs, manufacturing costs, pricing, regulation of drug company advertising, International price regulation, and product liability of drug manufacturers. Sections include Highlights, Index, Lead Report, News, Analysis & Perspective, and Regulatory Calendar. **Availability:** Online: The Bureau of National Affairs Inc. **Type:** Full text.

24021 ■ *State Tax Notes*
Tax Analysts
400 S Maple Ave., Ste. 400
Falls Church, VA 22046
Ph:(703)533-4400
Free: 800-955-2444
Co. E-mail: cservice@tax.org
URL: http://www.taxanalysts.com
Description: Follows tax developments in every state, and keeps track of interstate trends. Covers multi-state Organizations, state tax conferences, tax decisions from courts nationwide, rulings and regulations from revenue departments, and legislation from all 50 states each week. **Availability:** Online: LexisNexis Group. **Type:** Full text.

24022 ■ *State Tax Today*
Tax Analysts
400 S Maple Ave., Ste. 400
Falls Church, VA 22046
Ph:(703)533-4400
Free: 800-955-2444
Co. E-mail: cservice@tax.org
URL: http://www.taxanalysts.com
Description: Covers tax news and documents from every state, the District of Columbia, and all U.S. possessions, complete with summaries and full text of legislation. Includes proposed and finalized regulations, *Revenue Rulings & Procedures*, supreme, appellate, and tax court opinions, and private letter rulings. **Availability:** Online: Tax Analysts. **Type:** Full text.

24023 ■ *The Tax Directory*
Tax Analysts
400 S Maple Ave., Ste. 400
Falls Church, VA 22046
Ph:(703)533-4400
Free: 800-955-2444
Co. E-mail: cservice@tax.org
URL: http://www.taxanalysts.com
Description: Contains information on more than 20,000 tax professionals. Vol. One Government Officials Worldwide including state and federal officials, including taxwriting committees U.S. Department of Treasury and IRS, Tax Court Judges, International Financial Specialists, Tax and Business Journalists, Professional Associations, and Tax Groups and Coalitions. Vol. Two Corporate Tax Managers including names and contact information for tax managers in largest U.S corporations. Entries including industry description derived from the Securities and Exchange Commission's four-digit Standard Industry Classification code used by the listed companies for filing purposes. **Availability:** Online: LexisNexis Group; CD-ROM: Tax Analysts. **Type:** Directory.

24024 ■ *Texas Jurisprudence on Westlaw*
Thomson Reuters
610 Opperman Dr.
Eagan, MN 55123
Ph:(651)687-7000
Free: 800-344-5008
Fax:(651)687-5827
Co. E-mail: west.customer.service@thomsonreuters.com
URL: http://www.westlaw.com
Description: Provides the full text of *Texas Jurisprudence, Third Edition*. Contains a comprehensive encyclopedia of Texas law. **Availability:** Online: Thomson Reuters; CD-ROM: Thomson Reuters. **Type:** Full text.

24025 ■ *TOMES Plus System*
Thomson Reuters
6200 S Syracuse Way, Ste. 300
Greenwood Village, CO 80111-4740
Ph:(303)486-6444
Free: 800-525-9083
Fax:(303)486-6460
Co. E-mail: mdx.info@thomson.com
URL: http://www.micromedex.com
Description: Contains chemical, medical, and toxicological information for the industrial and occupational medicine markets. Covers clinical effects, range of toxicity, workplace standards, kinetics, and physiochemical standards. Comprises 16 files: MEDITEXT Medical Managements—contains protocols on the evaluation, medical response, and treatment of individuals acutely exposed to industrial chemicals. Includes Occupational Safety and Health Administration (OSHA) occupational exposure standards. HAZARDTEXT Hazard Managements—contains initial response protocols to incidents involving hazardous materials (e.g., fires, spills, leaks). Includes Occupational Safety and Health Administration (OSHA) occupational exposure standards. Hazardous Substances Data Bank (HSDB)—contains data on more than 4200 chemical substances that are of known or potential toxicity and to which substantial populations are exposed. OHM/TADS (Oil and Hazardous Materials/Technical Assistance Data System)—contains data gathered from published literature on 1402 materials that have been designated oil or hazardous materials. Provides technical support for dealing with potential or actual dangers resulting from the discharge of oil or hazardous substances. Up to 126 data fields, some textual and some numeric, may be present for each record (i.e., one material). A record includes identification of the substance (CAS Registry Number, common and trade names, and chemical formula), physical properties, uses, toxicity, handling procedures, and suggested methods for disposing of spilled materials. Produced by the U.S. Environmental Protection Agency (EPA). Corresponds to the OHM-TADS online database. Chemical Hazards Response Information System (CHRIS)—contains information on approximately 1200 chemical substances for use in spill situations. Includes chemical names and synonyms, molecular formula, biological and fire hazard potential, and chemical and physical properties. Also includes information on water pollution and toxicity of chemicals to aquatic life. Produced by the U.S. Coast Guard. Corresponds to the Chemical Hazards Response Information System (CHRIS) online database. IRIS (Integrated Risk Information System)—contains information on the health risk assessment of more than 450 hazardous substances. Covers toxicity, carcinogenicity, chemical and physical properties, and applicable regulations. Includes reference doses (i.e., concentrations of substances below which adverse health effects are not expected to occur), and carcinogenic risk assessment of varying concentrations of substances in air and drinking water. Also includes summaries of EPA regulatory actions. Produced by the U.S. Environmental Protection Agency (EPA). Corresponds to the IRIS online database. INFOTEXT Documents—provides general health and safety data on nonchemical-specific topics such as ergonomics and human health risk assessments. Registry of Toxic Effects of Chemical Substances (RTECS)—offers toxicity data on more than 135,000 substances, extracted from scientific literature worldwide, includes specifics on mutagenicity, carcinogenicity, reproductive hazards, and acute and chronic toxicity of hazardous substances. 1996 North American Emergency Response Guidebook (NAERG). NIOSH (National Institute for Occupational Safety and Health) Pocket Guide—contains critical industrial hygiene data for approximately 675 chemicals with information on exposure limits, U.S. IDLH concentrations, incompatibilities and reactivities, personal protection, and recommendations for respirator selection. New Jersey Fact Sheets from the N.J. Department of Health—offers employee-oriented exposure risk information useful when addressing worker right-to-know issues and developing training programs. Includes generic, non-technical worker safety and training information, frequently asked questions & answers, and a glossary of terms for more than 700 hazardous substances. **Availability:** Online: Thomson Reuters. **Type:** Bibliographic; Full text; Numeric.

24026 ■ *Toxics Law Reporter*
The Bureau of National Affairs Inc.
1801 S Bell St.
Arlington, VA 22202
Free: 800-372-1033
Co. E-mail: customercare@bna.com
URL: http://www.bna.com
Description: Contains news, developments, and federal and state actions in the field of toxic tort, hazardous waste, and related insurance litigation. Subjects include allocation issues, business and real estate transactions, CERCLA/superfund, contribution protection, cost recovery and cleanup litigation, due diligence, environmental exposure, government enforcement actions, hazardous waste law, liability insurance, occupational exposure, parent/subsidiary petroleum exclusion, personal injury, product liability, property damage, RCRA citizen suits, residential exposure, spills, state suits, and tort reform. Includes highlights of the week's most significant developments in the field; list of reports grouped by subject; reports on pending litigation, court decisions, verdicts and settlements and procedural developments; lists of meetings and conferences related to the field; table of cases in alphabetical order, and cumulative index of articles and cases. **Availability:** Online: Thomson Reuters, The Bureau of National Affairs Inc. **Type:** Full text.

LIBRARIES

24027 ■ Alberta Securities Commission Library
300-5th Ave. SW, 4th Fl.
Calgary, AB, Canada T2P 3C4
Ph:(403)297-6454
Free: 877-355-0585
Fax:(403)297-6156
Co. E-mail: inquiries@asc.ca
URL: http://www.albertasecurities.com
Contact: Yanming Fei, Libn.
Scope: Securities legislation, corporate law. **Services:** Library not open to the public. **Holdings:** Figures not available.

24028 ■ Arnold & Porter LLP Library
399 Park Ave.
New York, NY 10022-4690
Ph:(212)715-1382
Fax:(212)715-1399
Co. E-mail: kim.fenty@aporter.com
Contact: Kim R. Fenty, Lib.Mgr.
Scope: Litigation; law - tax, corporate, and environmental. **Services:** Interlibrary loan; Library not open to the public. **Holdings:** 20,000 books; 400 bound periodical volumes. **Subscriptions:** 205 journals and other serials; 15 newspapers.

24029 ■ Bryan Cave LLP Law Library
1155 F St., NW
Washington, DC 20004
Ph:(202)508-6000
Fax:(202)508-6200
Co. E-mail: laura.green@bryancave.com
URL: http://www.bryancave.com
Contact: Laurie Green, Mgr., Lib. & Res.Svcs.
Scope: Government and politics; law - commercial, corporate, environmental, intellectual property, taxation. **Services:** Interlibrary loan; copying; faxing; Library open to the public with restrictions. **Holdings:** 11,000 volumes. **Subscriptions:** 200 journals and other serials.

24030 ■ Hewlett-Packard Company–Legal/Tax Library
3000 Hanover St.
M/S 1069
Palo Alto, CA 94304-1112
Ph:(650)857-1501
Fax:(650)857-5518
URL: http://www.hp.com
Contact: Emily Morris, Info.Anl.
Scope: Legal topics, intellectual property, taxation. **Services:** Library not open to the public. **Holdings:** 2000 books. **Subscriptions:** 160 journals and other serials; 6 newspapers.

24031 ■ Lang Michener LLP Library
1500 Royal Centre
1055 W. Georgia St.
PO Box 11117
Vancouver, BC, Canada V6E 4N7
Ph:(604)689-9111
Fax:(604)685-7084
URL: http://www.langmichener.ca/
Scope: Law - tax, mining; litigation; corporate securities. **Services:** Library not open to the public. **Holdings:** Figures not available.

24032 ■ LECG, LLC Library
2000 Powell St., Ste. 600
Emeryville, CA 94608
Ph:(510)985-6700
Fax:(510)653-9898
Co. E-mail: nadams@lecg.com
URL: http://www.lecg.com
Contact: Nancy Adams, Libn.
Scope: Economics, business, antitrust. **Services:** Library open to the public by appointment only. **Holdings:** 2500 books. **Subscriptions:** 50 journals and other serials; 4 newspapers.

24033 ■ Long & Levit Library
465 California St., 5th Fl.
San Francisco, CA 94104
Ph:(415)397-2222
Fax:(415)397-6392
Co. E-mail: info@longlevit.com
URL: http://www.longlevit.com
Contact: Holly Mohler, Libn.
Scope: Insurance, environmental, professional liability, construction. **Services:** Interlibrary loan; copying; Library open to the public at librarian's discretion. **Holdings:** 10,000 books. **Subscriptions:** 75 journals and other serials; 4 newspapers.

24034 ■ McCarthy Tetrault Library
PO Box 10424, Pacific Centre
777 Dunsmuir St., Ste. 1300
Vancouver, BC, Canada V7Y 1K2
Ph:(604)643-7100
Free: (87)
Fax:(604)643-7900
Co. E-mail: jlecky@mccarthy.ca
URL: http://www.mccarthy.ca
Contact: Joanne Lecky, Dir., Lib.Svcs.
Scope: Law, corporate law, securities. **Services:** Library not open to the public. **Holdings:** Figures not available.

24035 ■ Miller Thomson LLP Library
Scotia Plaza
40 King St. W., Ste. 5800
Toronto, ON, Canada M5H 3S1
Ph:(416)595-8500
Fax:(416)595-8695
Co. E-mail: ifreeman@millerthomson
URL: http://www.millerthomson.com
Contact: Ines Freeman, Libn.
Scope: Law - labor, estate, tax, corporate, commercial, environmental. **Services:** Interlibrary loan; copying; Library not open to the public. **Holdings:** 2000 books. **Subscriptions:** 20 journals and other serials; 6 newspapers.

24036 ■ University of Hawaii at West O'ahu–Center for Labor Education and Research I CLEAR Labor Law Library
96-043 Ala Ike, Bldg. 400, Rm. 402
Pearl City, HI 96782
Ph:(808)454-4774
Fax:(808)454-4776
Co. E-mail: clear@hawaii.edu
URL: http://clear.uhwo.hawaii.edu/library.html
Contact: Dr. William Puette, Dir.
Scope: Labor law. **Services:** Library open to the public for reference use only. **Holdings:** Law manuals, reports, and materials; article files.

RESEARCH CENTERS

24037 ■ Boston University–Center for Law, Business and Technology
School of Law, 8th Fl.
765 Commonwealth Ave.
Boston, MA 02215
Ph:(617)353-3112
Fax:(617)353-3077
Co. E-mail: meurer@bu.edu
URL: http://www.bu.edu/law
Contact: Prof. Michael Meurer, Dir.
E-mail: meurer@bu.edu
Scope: Law and technology issues, with recent focus on new biotechnology products for gene therapy and transgenic agriculture, and other applications. Other subjects include expert systems software and legal and professional responsibility issues, corporate management of environmental risk and self-auditing, multinational corporations and environmental protection, chemical industry initiatives for preventing accident hazards, right-to-know as a regulatory alternative for protecting health, safety, and environment, and telecom/internet legal issues. **Educational Activities:** Seminars, symposia, conferences and speakers.

START-UP INFORMATION

24038 ■ *Become Your Own Boss in 12 Months: A Month-by-Month Guide to a Business that Works*
Pub: Adams Media Corporation
Ed: Melinda F. Emerson. **Released:** March 10, 2010. **Price:** $14.95. **Description:** Realistic planning guide to help would-be entrepreneurs transition from working for someone else to working for themselves is given. The key to successfully starting a new company lies in thoughtful preparation at least a year and a half before quitting a job.

24039 ■ *Becoming a Personal Trainer for Dummies*
Pub: John Wiley & Sons, Incorporated
Ed: Melyssa Michael, Linda Formichelli. **Released:** October 2004. **Price:** $19.99 (US), $25.99 (Canadian). **Description:** Legal and tax issues involved in starting and running a personal trainer firm. The book offers suggestions for incorporating massage and nutritional services.

24040 ■ *Building a Dream: A Canadian Guide to Starting Your Own Business*
Pub: McGraw-Hill Ryerson Ltd.
Ed: Walter S. Good. **Released:** 2005. **Description:** Topics covered include evaluating business potential, new business ideas, starting or buying a business, franchise opportunities, business organization, protecting an idea, arranging financing, and developing a business plan.

24041 ■ *Design and Launch Your Online Boutique in a Week*
Pub: Entrepreneur Press
Ed: Melissa Campanelli. **Released:** June 2008. **Price:** $17.95. **Description:** Guide to start an online boutique includes information on business planning, Website design and funding.

24042 ■ *EBay Income: How ANYONE of Any Age, Location, and/or Background Can Build a Highly Profitable Online Business with eBay (Revised 2nd Edition)*
Pub: Atlantic Publishing Company
Released: December 1, 2010. **Price:** $24.95. **Description:** A complete overview of eBay is given and guides any small company through the entire process of creating the auction and auction strategies, photography, writing copy, text and formatting, multiple sales, programming tricks, PayPal, accounting, creating marketing, merchandising, managing email lists, advertising plans, taxes and sales tax, best time to list items and for how long, sniping programs, international customers, opening a storefront, electronic commerce, buy-it now pricing, keywords, Google marketing and eBay secrets.

24043 ■ *The Elements of Small Business*
Pub: Silver Lake Publishing
Ed: John Thaler. **Released:** October 2004. **Price:** $12.95. **Description:** Concepts, markets, worksheets, letters, business plans, and sample legal forms for starting and running a small business are included.

24044 ■ *Entrepreneurial Itch: What No One Tells You About Starting Your Own Business*
Pub: Self-Counsel Press Inc.
Ed: David Trahair. **Released:** December 2006. **Price:** $13.95. **Description:** Small business accountant shares a plan for starting a business.

24045 ■ *Entrepreneurship*
Pub: John Wiley and Sons Inc.
Ed: William D. Bygrave; Andrew Zacharakis. **Released:** March 2007. **Price:** $115.95. **Description:** Information for starting a new business is shared, focusing on marketing and financing a product or service.

24046 ■ *Entrepreneurship Strategy: Changing Patterns in New Venture Creation, Growth, and Reinvention*
Pub: SAGE Publications, Incorporated
Ed: Lisa K. Gundry; Jill R. Kickul. **Released:** August 2006. **Price:** $69.95. **Description:** Entrepreneurial strategies that incorporate new venture emergence, early growth, and reinvention and innovation are examined.

24047 ■ "Follow the Numbers: It's the Best Way To Spot Problems Before They Become Life-Threatening" in *Inc.* (January 2008, pp. 63-64)
Pub: Gruner & Jahr USA Publishing
Ed: Norm Brodsky. **Description:** It is important for any small business to track monthly sales and gross margins by hand for the first year or two. When writing the numbers, be sure to break them out by product category or service type and by customer.

24048 ■ "Getting Others To Take Your Startup Seriously" in *Women Entrepreneur* (August 1, 2008)
Pub: Entrepreneur Media Inc.
Ed: Tamara Monosoff. **Description:** Writing a serious business plan is essential if you want others to take your startup endeavor seriously. As friends, family and acquaintances see you taking positive steps toward your goal they will begin to lend their support and may even help get the business off the ground.

24049 ■ *Getting Rich In Your Underwear: How To Start and Run a Profitable Home-Based Business*
Pub: HCM Publishing
Ed: Peter I. Hupalo. **Released:** April 1, 2005. **Price:** $17.95. **Description:** Book offers insight into starting a home-based business. Entrepreneurs will learn about business models and the home business; distribution and fulfillment of product or service; marketing and sales; how to overcome the fear of starting a business; personal success characteristics; naming a business; zoning and insurance; intellectual capital; copyrights, trademarks, and patents; limited liability companies and S-corporations; business expenses and accounting; taxes; fifteen basic steps for starting a home-based business, state resources for starting a home company; and seven home-based business ideas.

24050 ■ *Going Solo: Developing a Home-Based Consulting Business from the Ground Up*
Pub: McGraw-Hill Companies Incorporated
Ed: William J. Bond. **Released:** January 1997. **Description:** Ways to turn specialized knowledge into a home-based successful consulting firm, focusing on targeting client needs, business plans, and growth.

24051 ■ *How to Get the Financing for Your New Small Business: Innovative Solutions from the Experts Who Do It Every Day*
Pub: Atlantic Publishing Company
Ed: Sharon L. Fullen. **Released:** May 2006. **Price:** $39.95, includes companion CD-Rom. **Description:** Ready capital is essential for starting and expanding a small business. Topics include traditional financing methods, financial statements, and a good business plan.

24052 ■ *How to Open and Operate a Financially Successful Private Investigation Business: With Companion CD-ROM*
Pub: Atlantic Publishing Company
Released: December 1, 2010. **Price:** $39.95. **Description:** With a massive upside and potential for growth the private investigation sector is growing. The book will teach everything needed to know about working in the private investigation field, starting with the basics of what you can expect and what preconceptions that may just be Hollywood. Information is given to help choose a niche of investigation and hot to start thinking in the abstract, questioning everything but recognizing facts for what they are, as well as the differences between a private investigator and a police officer.

24053 ■ "Oh, Grow Up!" in *Entrepreneur* (Vol. 35, October 2007, No. 10, pp. 120)
Pub: Entrepreneur Media Inc.
Ed: Mark Henricks. **Description:** Most entrepreneurs are overwhelmed with the idea of expanding their business, forgetting to strategically plan the process of business growth. However, there are certain steps entrepreneurs must take in turning a startup business into a bigger venture. Eight steps to growing a business, such as asking for advice and deciding on a focus are presented.

24054 ■ "Rehab Will Turn Hospital Into Incubator" in *The Business Journal-Serving Metropolitan Kansas City* (Vol. 26, September 12, 2008)
Pub: American City Business Journals, Inc.
Ed: Rob Roberts. **Description:** Independence Regional Health Center will be purchased by CEAH Realtors and be converted into the Independence Regional Entrepreneurial Center, a business incubator that will house startups and other tenants. Other details about the planned entrepreneurial center are provided.

24055 ■ *The Small Business Owner's Manual: Everything You Need to Know to Start Up and Run Your Business*
Pub: Career Press, Incorporated
Ed: Joe Kennedy. **Released:** June 2005. **Price:** $19.99 (US), $26.95 (Canadian). **Description:**

Comprehensive guide for starting a small business, focusing on twelve ways to obtain financing, business plans, selling and advertising products and services, hiring and firing employees, setting up a Web site, business law, accounting issues, insurance, equipment, computers, banks, financing, customer credit and collection, leasing, and more.

24056 ■ *Start and Run a Delicatessen: Small Business Starters Series*
Pub: How To Books

Ed: Deborah Penrith. **Released:** November 9, 2010. **Price:** $30.00. **Description:** Information for starting and running a successful delicatessen is provided. Insight is offered into selecting a location, researching the market, writing a business plan and more.

24057 ■ *Starting Green: An Ecopreneur's Guide to Starting a Green Business from Business Plans to Profits*
Pub: Entrepreneur Press

Ed: Glenn E. Croston. **Released:** September 9, 2010. **Price:** $21.95. **Description:** Entrepreneur and scientist outlines green business essentials and helps uncover eco-friendly business opportunities, build a sustainable business plan, and gain the competitive advantage.

24058 ■ "Startup Aims to Cut Out Coupon Clipping" in *The Business Journal-Serving Metropolitan Kansas City* (Vol. 26, August 15, 2008, No. 49)
Pub: American City Business Journals, Inc.

Ed: Suzanna Stagemeyer. **Description:** TDP Inc., who started operations 18 months ago, aims to transform stale coupon promotions using technology by digitizing the entire coupon process. The process is expected to enable consumers to hunt coupons online where they will be automatically linked to loyalty cards. Other views and information on TDP and its services are presented.

24059 ■ *Swimming Against the Stream: Launching Your Business and Making Your Life*
Pub: Macmillan Publishers Limited

Ed: Tim Waterstone. **Released:** March 2007. **Price:** $17.99. **Description:** Ten rules for launching a new business are outlined using real-life experiences.

24060 ■ "Three Weeks To Startup" in *Entrepreneur* (December 19, 2008)
Pub: Entrepreneur Media Inc.

Ed: Tim Berry; Sabrina Parsons. **Description:** Breakdown for realistically starting a business in three weeks is provided in detail.

24061 ■ *The Toilet Paper Entrepreneur: The Tell-It-Like-It-Is Guide to Cleaning Up In Business, Even If You Are At the End of Your Roll*
Pub: Obsidian Launch LLC

Ed: Mike Michalowicz. **Price:** $24.95. **Description:** The founder of three multimillion-dollar companies, including Obsidian Launch, a company that partners with first-time entrepreneurs to grow their concepts into industry leaders.

24062 ■ *The Unofficial Guide to Starting a Small Business*
Pub: John Wiley & Sons, Incorporated

Ed: Marcia Layton Turner. **Released:** October 2004. **Price:** $16.99. **Description:** Information and tools for starting a small business, covering the start-up process, from market research, to business plans, to marketing programs.

24063 ■ *What No One Ever Tells You About Starting Your Own Business: Real-Life Start-Up Advice from 101 Successful Entrepreneurs*
Pub: Kaplan Publishing

Ed: Jan Norman. **Released:** July 2004. **Price:** $18.95 (US), $28.95 (Canadian). **Description:** From planning to marketing, advice is given to entrepreneurs starting new companies. s.

ASSOCIATIONS AND OTHER ORGANIZATIONS

24064 ■ Auto Suppliers Benchmarking Association
4606 FM 1960 W, Ste. 250
Houston, TX 77069-9949
Ph:(281)440-5044
Fax:(281)440-6677
URL: http://www.asbabenchmarking.com
Description: Automotive supplier firms with an interest in benchmarking. Promotes the use of benchmarking, wherein businesses compare their processes with those of their competitors, as a means of improving corporate efficiency and profitability. Facilitates exchange of information among members; conducts target operations, procurement, development, and maintenance studies; identifies model business practices. .

EDUCATIONAL PROGRAMS

24065 ■ Design Reviews for Effective Product Development (Onsite)
Seminar Information Service, Inc.
20 Executive Park, Ste. 120
Irvine, CA 92614
Ph:(949)261-9104
Free: 877-SEM-INFO
Fax:(949)261-1963
Co. E-mail: info@seminarinformation.com
URL: http://www.seminarinformation.com
Price: $725.00. **Description:** Seminar covering how formal design reviews can improve products by uncovering potential problems before they are discovered at a latter stage of development when the costs of correction are much higher, as well as the requirements for successful reviews. **Locations:** Troy, MI.

24066 ■ Disaster Recovery Planning: Ensuring Business Continuity
Learning Tree International
1805 Library St.
Reston, VA 20190-5630
Ph:(703)709-9019
Free: 888-843-8733
URL: http://www.learningtree.com
Price: $2,890.00. **Description:** Create, document, and test continuity arrangements for the organization. This course is valuable for those managing and maintaining the continuity of an organization's critical processes. **Locations:** Cities throughout the United States.

24067 ■ Maintenance Planning & Scheduling
American Trainco
9785 S Maroon Cir., Ste. 300
PO Box 3397
Englewood, CO 80112
Ph:(303)531-4560
Free: 877-978-7246
Fax:(303)531-4565
Co. E-mail: Sales@AmericanTrainco.com
URL: http://www.americantrainco.com
Price: $990.00. **Description:** Learn to reduce maintenance costs by better planning with your existing workforce. **Locations:** Cities throughout the United States.

24068 ■ Project Management: Skills for Success (Onsite)
Seminar Information Service, Inc.
20 Executive Park, Ste. 120
Irvine, CA 92614
Ph:(949)261-9104
Free: 877-SEM-INFO
Fax:(949)261-1963
Co. E-mail: info@seminarinformation.com
URL: http://www.seminarinformation.com
Price: $2,890.00. **Description:** Learn how to: Produce a project plan for successful delivery; Plan and run projects using best practices in a 6-step project management process; Implement risk management techniques and mitigation strategies; Estimate and schedule task work and duration with confidence; Implement monitoring tools and controls to keep you fully in command of the project; Recognize and practice the leadership skills needed to run a motivated team. **Locations:** Ottawa, CN; and Philadelphia, PA.

24069 ■ Project Quality Management for Project Managers - Delivering Consistent Quality (Onsite)
Seminar Information Service, Inc.
20 Executive Park, Ste. 120
Irvine, CA 92614
Ph:(949)261-9104
Free: 877-SEM-INFO
Fax:(949)261-1963
Co. E-mail: info@seminarinformation.com
URL: http://www.seminarinformation.com
Price: $2,490.00. **Description:** Learn how to: Implement effective project quality management best practices; Apply a proven analysis method to identify stakeholder quality expectations and refine project scope; Leverage an industry standard template to create a project Quality Management Plan (QMP); Generate a quality assurance task list that incorporates project, product and process; Transform quality assurance recommendations into corrective and improvement actions; Design and implement quality control gates throughout the project and product life cycles. **Locations:** New York, NY; Ottawa, CN; Reston, VA; and Toronto, CN.

24070 ■ Strategic Marketing: Concepts and Strategies
Seminar Information Service, Inc.
20 Executive Park, Ste. 120
Irvine, CA 92614
Ph:(949)261-9104
Free: 877-SEM-INFO
Fax:(949)261-1963
Co. E-mail: info@seminarinformation.com
URL: http://www.seminarinformation.com
Price: $1,595.00. **Description:** Topics include the marketing process, defining the competition, and the marketing mix. **Locations:** Chelmsford, MA.

24071 ■ Strategic Planning for Organizational Success (Onsite)
Learning Tree International
1805 Library St.
Reston, VA 20190-5630
Ph:(703)709-9019
Free: 888-843-8733
URL: http://www.learningtree.com
Price: $2,490.00. **Description:** Learn to formulate strategic plans to help the organization advance and grow. **Locations:** Toronto, ON; Reston, VA.

REFERENCE WORKS

24072 ■ *The 7 Irrefutable Rules of Small Business Growth*
Pub: John Wiley & Sons, Incorporated
Ed: Steven S. Little. **Released:** February 2005. **Price:** $18.95. **Description:** Proven strategies to maintain small business growth are outlined, covering topics such as technology, business plans, hiring, and more.

24073 ■ "13D Filings" in *Barron's* (Vol. 88, March 10, 2008, No. 10, pp. M11)
Pub: Dow Jones & Company, Inc.
Description: Barington Capital and Clinton Group sent a letter to Dillard's demanding a list of the company's stockholders. Elliott Associates announced that it is prepared to take over Packeteer for $5.50 a share. Strongbow capital suggested a change in leadership in Duckwall-ALCO Stores.

24074 ■ "13D Filings: Investors Report to the SEC" in *Barron's* (Vol. 88, March 31, 2008, No. 13, pp. M10)
Pub: Dow Jones & Company, Inc.
Description: Obrem Capital Management wants Micrel to rescind Micrel's shareholder-rights plan and to boost its board to six members from five. Patricia L. Childress plans to nominate herself to the board of Sierra Bancorp, and Luther King Capital Management may consider a competing acquisition proposal for Industrial Distribution Group.

24075 ■ *The 30-Second Commute*
Pub: McGraw-Hill
Ed: Beverley Williams; Don Cooper. **Released:** 2004. **Price:** $19.95. **Description:** Home-based business owners explain how entrepreneurs can avoid long commutes and high costs of working outside the home by starting a home-based company. Essential steps for launching a successful home-based business are covered, including type of business, legal issues, and writing a business plan.

24076 ■ "$50 Million Project for West Chester" in *Business Courier* (Vol. 24, December 14, 2008, No. 35, pp. 1)
Pub: American City Business Journals, Inc.
Ed: Laura Baverman. **Description:** Commercial developer Scott Street Partners is planning to invest $50 million for the development of a site south of the Streets of West Chester retail center. The 31-acre project will generate 1,200 jobs, and will bring in offices, restaurants and a hotel. The development plans and the features of the site are discussed as well.

24077 ■ *101 Internet Businesses You Can Start from Home: How to Choose and Build Your Own Successful E-Business*
Pub: Maximum Press
Ed: Susan Sweeney. **Released:** June 2006. **Price:** $29.95. **Description:** Guide for starting and growing an Internet business; information for developing a business plan, risk levels, and promotional techniques are included.

24078 ■ "Adapt or Die" in *Black Enterprise* (Vol. 38, July 2008, No. 12, pp. 27)
Pub: Earl G. Graves Publishing Co. Inc.
Ed: Oguntoyinbo Lekan. **Description:** Turbulence in the domestic auto industry is hitting auto suppliers hard and black suppliers, the majority of whom contract with the Big Three, are just beginning to establish relationships with import car manufacturers. The more savvy CEOs are adopting new technologies in order to weather the downturn in the economy and in the industry as a whole.

24079 ■ "Aeronautics Seeking New HQ Site" in *The Business Journal-Milwaukee* (Vol. 25, September 5, 2008, No. 50, pp. 1)
Pub: American City Business Journals, Inc.
Ed: Rich Kirchen. **Description:** Milwaukee, Wisconsin-based Aeronautics Corp. of America is planning to move its headquarters to a new site. The company has started to search for a new site. It also plans to consolidate its operations under one roof.

24080 ■ "The Agency Model Is Bent But Not Broken" in *Advertising Age* (Vol. 79, July 7, 2008, No. 26, pp. 17)
Pub: Crain Communications, Inc.
Ed: Stephen Fajen. **Description:** In the new-media environment, advertising agencies must change the way in which they do business and receive payment.

24081 ■ "The Agency-Selection Process Needs Fixing Now" in *Advertising Age* (Vol. 79, July 7, 2008, No. 26, pp. 18)
Pub: Crain Communications, Inc.
Ed: Avi Dan. **Description:** Marketers are facing increased challenges in this sagging economic climate and must realize the importance of choosing the correct advertising agency for their company in order to benefit from a more-stable relationship that yields better business results. Advice for marketers regarding the best way to choose an agency is included.

24082 ■ "Air Canada to Slash 600 Non-Union Jobs" in *Globe & Mail* (February 11, 2006, pp. B3)
Pub: CTVglobemedia Publishing Inc.
Ed: Brent Jang. **Description:** The reasons behind workforce reduction by ACE Aviation Holdings Inc. at Air Canada are presented.

24083 ■ "Airlines Mount PR Push to Win Public Support Against Big Oil" in *Advertising Age* (Vol. 79, July 14, 2008, No. 7, pp. 1)
Pub: Crain Communications, Inc.
Ed: Michael Bush. **Description:** Top airline executives from competing companies have banded together in a public relations plan in which they are sending e-mails to their frequent fliers asking for aid in lobbying legislators to put a restriction on oil speculation.

24084 ■ "All Fired Up!" in *Small Business Opportunities* (November 2008)
Pub: Entrepreneur Media Inc.
Ed: Stan Roberts. **Description:** Profile of Brixx Wood Fired Pizza, which has launched a franchising program due to the amount of interest the company's founders received over the years; franchisees do not need experience in the food industry or pizza restaurant service business in order to open a franchise of their own because all franchisees receive comprehensive training in which they are educated on all of the necessary tools to effectively run the business.

24085 ■ "All Options Open On Chrysler: Magna" in *Globe & Mail* (February 28, 2007, pp. B3)
Pub: CTVglobemedia Publishing Inc.
Ed: Greg Keenan. **Description:** The 65 percent drop in the profits of Magna International Inc. and the plans of its chief executive officer Don Walker to make the company more competitive are discussed.

24086 ■ "Americhem to Shutter Maryland Operation" in *Crain's Cleveland Business* (Vol. 28, October 29, 2007, No. 43, pp. 14)
Pub: Crain Communications, Inc.
Description: Americhem Inc., a manufacturer of colors and additives for polymer products has announced plans to expand two plants in Cuyahoga Falls while phasing out its operations in Salisbury, Maryland.

24087 ■ "An Amazing Race" in *Canadian Business* (Vol. 81, March 3, 2008, No. 3, pp. 25)
Pub: Rogers Media
Ed: Rachel Pulfer. **Description:** U.S. presidential candidates Barack Obama and Hilary Clinton lead the Democratic Part primaries while John McCain is a frontrunner at the Republican Party. These leading candidates have different plans for the U.S. economy which will affect Canada's own economy particularly concerning trade policies. The presidential candidates' proposals and the impacts of U.S. economic downturn on Canada are examined.

24088 ■ "Analyst Questions CanWest Papers' Viability" in *Globe & Mail* (January 14, 2006, pp. B3)
Pub: CTVglobemedia Publishing Inc.
Ed: Grant Robertson. **Description:** The opinions of analyst Tim Casey of BMO Nesbitt Burns Inc. over the prospects of two newspapers Dose and National Post of CanWest Global Communications Corp., which planned cost restructuring efforts, are presented.

24089 ■ "Are You Ready for a Transformation?" in *Women Entrepreneur* (November 28, 2008)
Pub: Entrepreneur Media Inc.
Ed: Aliza Sherman. **Description:** Marlene J. Waldock, an expert in women's empowerment and reinvention, discusses brand modification and what a business owner should consider before attempting to change or modify their brand.

24090 ■ "Are Your Goals Hitting the Right Target?" in *Business Strategy Review* (Vol. 21, Autumn 2010, No. 3, pp. 46)
Pub: Wiley-Blackwell
Ed: Alan Meekings, Steve Briault, Andy Neely. **Description:** Setting targets is normal in most organizations. The authors think such a practice can cause more ham than good. They offer a better plan.

24091 ■ *The Art of the Start*
Pub: Portfolio Publishing
Ed: Guy Kawasaki. **Price:** $26.95. **Description:** Apple's Guy Kawasaki offers information to help would-be entrepreneurs create new enterprises. As founder and CEO of Garage Technology Ventures, he has field-tested his ideas with newly hatched companies and he takes readers through every phase of creating a business, from the very basics of raising money and designing a business model through the many stages that eventually lead to success and thus giving back to society.

24092 ■ "Attend To Your Corporate Housekeeping" in *Women Entrepreneur* (December 4, 2008)
Pub: Entrepreneur Media Inc.
Ed: Nina Kaufman. **Description:** Business owners can lose all the benefits and privileges of the corporate form if they do not follow proper corporate formalities such as holding an annual meeting, electing officers and directors and adopting or passing corporate resolutions. Creditors are able to take from one's personal assets if such formalities have not been followed.

24093 ■ "Auction-Rate Cash Frees Up" in *The Business Journal-Portland* (Vol. 25, August 15, 2008, No. 23, pp. 1)
Pub: American City Business Journals, Inc.
Ed: Aliza Earnshaw. **Description:** FEI Co. and RadiSys Corp. have received notices that UBS AG will buy back the auction-rate securities that were sold to them in around two years from 2008. FEI had $110.1 million invested in auction-rate securities while RadiSys holds $62.8 million of these securities.

24094 ■ "Automaker Foundations Run Leaner" in *Crain's Detroit Business* (Vol. 26, January 11, 2010, No. 2, pp. 1)
Pub: Crain Communications, Inc.
Ed: Sherri Welch. **Description:** Overview of the Detroit automobile industry includes restoring profitability, smarter marketing strategies and philanthropy. Each company comprising the Big 3 is examined, as is their vision for the future.

24095 ■ "Avnet Inc.'s Expansion Fueled By Mergers and Acquisitions" in *The Business Journal - Serving Phoenix and the Valley of the Sun* (Vol. 28, September 12, 2008, No. 53, pp. 1)
Pub: American City Business Journals, Inc.
Ed: Patrick O'Grady. **Description:** Avnet Inc. has grown and has nearly tripled its revenue in the past ten years through the company's acquisitions and consolidation. The company's revenue in 2008 is $17.9 billion. Other details about the company's growth are discussed.

24096 ■ "Back to Business for Bishop Museum" in *Hawaii Business* (Vol. 54, August 2008, No. 2, pp. 53)
Pub: Hawaii Business Publishing
Ed: Shara Enay. **Description:** Bishop Museum, ranked 224 in Hawaii Business' top 250 companies for 2008, had $29.5 million in gross sales for 2007, up 52.8 percent from the $19.3 million gross sales in 2006. The company has cut 24 positions in a restructuring effort for the museum's sustainability. Grants, artifacts and plans for sustainable operations are discussed.

24097 ■ "Back in the Race" in *Barron's* (Vol. 88, March 17, 2008, No. 11, pp. 43)
Pub: Dow Jones & Company, Inc.
Ed: Leslie P. Norton. **Description:** Katherine Schapiro was able to get Sentinel International Equity's Morningstar classification to blended fund from a value fund rating after joining Sentinel from her former jobs at Strong Overseas Fund. Schapiro aims to benefit from the global rebalancing as the U.S.'s share of the world economy shrinks.

24098 ■ "The Balanced Business" in *Women In Business* (Vol. 63, Spring 2011, No. 1, pp. 14)
Pub: American Business Women's Association
Ed: Leigh Elmore. **Description:** The balance scoreboard has developed to a full strategic planning and management system from its early use as a simple performance measurement network. Executives are able to execute their strategies by using information from the balance scoreboard. Insights on Mayer Group Inc. executive Ken Mayer's view of the balance scorecard are also shared.

24099 ■ "Bankruptcy Claims Brooke, Gives Franchisees Hope" in *The Business Journal-Serving Metropolitan Kansas City* (October 31, 2008)
Pub: American City Business Journals, Inc.
Ed: James Dornbrook; Steve Vockrodt. **Description:** Insurer Brooke Corp. was required to file for Chapter 11 bankruptcy for a deal to sell all of its assets to businessmen Terry Nelson and Lysle Davidson. The new Brooke plans to share contingency fees with franchisees. The impacts of the bankruptcy case on Brooke franchisees are discussed.

24100 ■ "Bark Up The Right Tree" in *Small Business Opportunities* (Winter 2009)
Pub: Entrepreneur Media Inc.
Description: Profile of Central Bark, a daycare company catering to pets that offers franchise opportunities and is expanding rapidly despite the economic downturn; the company's growth strategy is also discussed.

24101 ■ "Barnes Shakes Up Sara Lee Exec Suite" in *Crain's Chicago Business* (Vol. 31, April 21, 2008, No. 16, pp. 1)
Pub: Crain Communications, Inc.
Ed: David Sterrett. **Description:** In an attempt to cut costs and boost profits, Sara Lee Corp.'s CEO Brenda Barnes is restructuring the company's management team.

24102 ■ "BASF Launches $4.9 Billion Bid for Rival Engelhard" in *Globe & Mail* (January 4, 2006, pp. B7)
Pub: CTVglobemedia Publishing Inc.
Ed: Mike Esterl; Steve Levine. **Description:** The plans of BASF AG, to acquire Engelhard Corp. for $4.9 billion, are presented.

24103 ■ "Bayer Job Cuts to Hit Canada" in *Globe & Mail* (March 3, 2007, pp. B7)
Pub: CTVglobemedia Publishing Inc.
Description: Bayer AG, German drug maker, planned cut of 6,100 jobs as a part of their cost-cutting strategies. The company, which plans to save 700 million euros by the end of 2007, may eliminate some positions in Canadian branches.

24104 ■ "BCE Mulls Radical Changes With Industry Under Pressure" in *Globe & Mail* (March 30, 2007, pp. B1)
Pub: CTVglobemedia Publishing Inc.
Ed: Andrew Willis; Jacquie McNish; Catherine McLean. **Description:** An account on the expansion plans of BCE Inc., which plans to acquire TELUS Corp., is presented.

24105 ■ "Best Growth Stocks" in *Canadian Business* (Vol. 81, Summer 2008, No. 9, pp. 61)
Pub: Rogers Media Ltd.
Ed: Calvin Leung. **Description:** Table showing the one-year performance of growth stocks is presented. Edmonton-based Stantec Inc. expects to advance its sales and profits by 15 percent to 20 percent per year through tapping international markets and acquisitions. Analysts forecast a 17.1 percent growth rate annually over the next 3 to 5 years.

24106 ■ "The Best Option for All" in *American Executive* (Vol. 7, September 2009, No. 5, pp. 170)
Pub: RedCoat Publishing, Inc.
Ed: Ashley McGown. **Description:** Plaza Associates, a collections agency that conducts business primarily in the accounts receivable management sector, is the first in the industry to purchase 100 percent of the company from the founders through the formation of a leveraged Employee Stock Ownership Plan (ESOP).

24107 ■ "Better Made's Better Idea: Diversify Despite Rising Costs" in *Crain's Detroit Business* (Vol. 24, September 22, 2008, No. 38, pp. 18)
Pub: Crain Communications, Inc.
Ed: Nathan Skid. **Description:** Better Made Snack Foods Inc. is planning to expand its product lines and market reach as well as boost manufacturing capability during a time in which the company is being buffeted by rising commodity and fuel costs. The company feels that diversification is the key to maintain sales and growth.

24108 ■ "Beyond Auto; Staffing Firm Malace Grabs Revenue Jump" in *Crain's Detroit Business* (Vol. 26, January 18, 2010, No. 3, pp. 3)
Pub: Crain Communications, Inc.
Ed: Sherri Welch. **Description:** Malace & Associates Inc., the Troy-based human resources management company, expects its diversification into nonautomotive industries to help double its revenues this year. Due to the automotive downturn, between October 2008 and March 2009 the company lost approximately 48 percent of its business.

24109 ■ "A Big Dream That 'Was Going Nowhere'" in *Globe & Mail* (February 4, 2006, pp. B4)
Pub: CTVglobemedia Publishing Inc.
Ed: Konrad Yakabuski. **Description:** The reasons behind the decision of Bombardier Inc. to terminate its plans to develop jet airplanes are presented.

24110 ■ "Big Sell-Off At Sunwest" in *The Business Journal-Portland* (Vol. 25, July 25, 2008, No. 20, pp. 1)
Pub: American City Business Journals, Inc.
Ed: Robin J. Moody. **Description:** Oregon's largest operator of assisted living facilities Sunwest Management Inc. is expected to sell 132 of its properties. The planned sale, which is believed to be worth more than $1 billion, will help Sunwest pay creditors and investors. Other views and information on the planned sale, as well as on Sunwest's services which include adult day care, are presented.

24111 ■ *Big Vision, Small Business*
Pub: Ivy Sea, Inc.
Ed: Jamie S. Walters. **Released:** October 10, 2002. **Price:** $17.95. **Description:** The power of the small enterprise is examined. The author shares her expertise as an entrepreneur and founder of a business consulting firm to help small business owners successfully run their companies. Interviews with more than seventy small business owners provide insight into visioning, planning, and establishing a small company, as well as strategies for good employee and customer relationships.

24112 ■ "A Bigger Deal" in *Crain's Cleveland Business* (Vol. 28, November 12, 2007, No. 45, pp. 1)
Pub: Crain Communications, Inc.
Ed: Shawn A. Turner. **Description:** In an attempt to boost its revenue CBiz Inc., a provider of accounting and business services, is looking to balance its acquisitions of smaller companies with larger ones as part of its overall growth strategy.

24113 ■ "Blackstone Set to Sell Stake" in *Globe & Mail* (March 17, 2007, pp. B6)
Pub: CTVglobemedia Publishing Inc.
Ed: Tennille Tracy. **Description:** The plan of Blackstone Group to sell 10 percent of its stake to raise $4 billion and its proposal to go for initial public offering is discussed.

24114 ■ "Block Plans Office Park Along K-10 Corridor" in *The Business Journal-Serving Metropolitan Kansas City* (Vol. 27, October 3, 2008)
Pub: American City Business Journals, Inc.
Ed: Rob Roberts. **Description:** Kansas City, Missouri-based Block and Co. is planning to build four office buildings at the corner of College Boulevard and Ridgeview Road in Olathe. Features of the planned development are provided. Comments from executives are also presented.

24115 ■ "Blood Bank" in *Canadian Business* (Vol. 80, February 12, 2007, No. 4, pp. 36)
Pub: Rogers Media
Ed: Erin Pooley. **Description:** The plan of Insception Biosciences to popularize stem cell banks, which can store stem cells, is discussed.

24116 ■ *Blue Ocean Strategy: How to Create Uncontested Market Space and Make Competition Irrelevant*
Pub: Harvard Business School Publishing
Ed: W. Chan Kim. **Released:** January 2005. **Price:** $29.95.

24117 ■ "The Board Shorts Executive" in *Hawaii Business* (Vol. 53, January 2008, No. 7, pp. 33)
Pub: Hawaii Business Publishing
Ed: Mike Markrich. **Description:** Vans Triple Crown of Surfing executive director Randy Rarick believes that the surfing business requires knowledge of the sport and integity to the game's lifestyle and spirit. His organization manages surfing events, and has generated jobs for the locals. Plans for Vans Triple Crown are supplied.

24118 ■ "Bovie Medical Makes Electrosurgical Strike" in *The Business Journal-Serving Greater Tampa Bay* (Vol. 28, August 22, 2008, No. 35)
Pub: American City Business Journals, Inc.
Ed: Margie Manning. **Description:** Bovie Medical Group, which manufactures electrosurgical products, is planning to sell its manufacturing plant in the Tyrone Industrial Park and to purchase the former Harland Clarke facility. The moves are expected to boost the efficiency and the development of new products. Other information on Bovie Medical Group is presented.

24119 ■ "Bracing for Impact" in *Playthings* (Vol. 106, September 1, 2008, No. 8, pp. 15)
Pub: Reed Business Information
Ed: J. Tol Broome Jr. **Description:** A good risk management plan for any company consists of making correct decisions in the following six key areas: operational, reputation, regulatory, legal, liquidity, and disaster.

24120 ■ "Brewing National Success" in *Hawaii Business* (Vol. 53, November 2007, No. 5, pp. 46)
Pub: Hawaii Business Publishing
Ed: Alex Salkever. **Description:** Kona Brewing Co. (KBC) is already selling its brews in four cities in Florida and 17 other states and Japan as well. KBC is currently forming a deal with Red Hook to produce Longboard Lager and other KBC brews at Red Hooks' brewery in New Hampshire. KBC's chief executive officer Mattson Davis shares KBC's practices for success.

24121 ■ "Briarcliff Office Building Fills Up Fast" in *The Business Journal-Serving Metropolitan Kansas City* (Vol. 26, Sept. 5, 2008, pp. 1)
Pub: American City Business Journals, Inc.
Ed: Rob Roberts. **Description:** Prior to its opening the Hilltop Office Building in Kansas City Missouri has attained 80 percent occupancy. FCStone Group Inc.'s plan to move to the building has boosted the facility's occupancy. Description and dimensions of the office building are also provided.

24122 ■ "Bringing Big Guns" in *Business Courier* (Vol. 24, January 18, 2008, No. 41, pp. 1)
Pub: American City Business Journals, Inc.
Ed: Lucy May. **Description:** Chief executive officer of Nidland Co. John Hayden was assigend as Cincinnati USA Partnership chairman. Hayden will bring his expertise to help the partnership drive economic development in the Greater Cincinnati area. Details of the parntership's plans are suplied.

24123 ■ "Budget Strategically to Stay on Course" in *Entrepreneur* (August 28, 2008)
Pub: Entrepreneur Media Inc.
Ed: Tim Berry. **Description:** Budgeting is one of the most valuable tools in a manager's arsenal. The importance of budgeting is discussed and tips for surviving an economic recession are provided.

24124 ■ "Building Alexian Brothers' Clinical Reputation" in *Crain's Chicago Business* (Vol. 31, May 5, 2008, No. 18, pp. 6)
Pub: Crain Communications, Inc.
Ed: Mike Colias. **Description:** Profile of the CEO of Alexian Brothers Medical Center in Elk Grove Village who plans to stabilize Alexian Brothers' financial performance in part by eliminating $20 million in annual costs.

24125 ■ "Building His Dream" in *Business Courier* (Vol. 24, January 25, 2008, No. 42, pp. 1)
Pub: American City Business Journals, Inc.
Ed: Laura Baverman. **Description:** Technology entrepreneur Mahendra Vora plans to build a more than $100 million local IT headquarters for VTech Holdings Ltd by 2010. Acquisition of four $5 million companies within 2008 are part of the owner's plan to expand the office equipment company. Other plans for the IT company are discussed.

24126 ■ "Bumpy Ride Ahead for United" in *Crain's Chicago Business* (Vol. 31, May 5, 2008, No. 18, pp. 3)
Pub: Crain Communications, Inc.
Ed: John Pletz. **Description:** Continental Airlines Inc. walked away from merger talks with United Airlines last week. Now the choices facing United boil down to going it alone in an increasingly stormy airline business or a less-desirable merger with US Airways Group Inc. Analysts expect United to lose $977 million this year due, mainly, to the high price of fuel.

24127 ■ "Burdened by Debt, Borders Group Suspends Dividends, May Be Sold" in *Crain's Detroit Business* (Vol. 24, March 24, 2008, No. 12)
Pub: Crain Communications, Inc.
Ed: Nancy Kaffer. **Description:** Ann Arbor-based Borders Group Inc. is exploring its options and may put itself up for sale due to its declining stock price and mounting debt. The company's fiscal year was capped by poor holiday sales and Borders does not have the cash on hand to meet the 2009 goals set in its strategic plan.

24128 ■ *A Business of My Own? 21 Steps to Successfully Starting and Running a Small Business*
Pub: Enfield Publishing
Ed: Marjorie Cleveland Fisher. **Released:** January 2005. **Description:** New ideas to start or grow a small business, including ideas for writing business plans with examples, adopting a business structure, and setting goals and objectives.

24129 ■ "Business Plan Refines Focus" in *Business Journal Portland* (Vol. 27, December 10, 2010, No. 41, pp. 1)
Pub: Portland Business Journal
Ed: Wendy Culverwell. **Description:** Organizers of the Oregon Business Plan's Leadership Summit 2010 seek the opinions of nearly 1,000 business, education, political, and civic leaders in an effort to address how to rehabilitate Oregon's economy. The opinion-seeking actions recognize the organizers' belief that the economic fate of the state depends on rural Oregon.

24130 ■ *Business Plans to Game Plans*
Pub: John Wiley and Sons, Inc.
Ed: Jan B. King. **Released:** 2003. **Price:** $27.50. **Description:** Information for running a small business are examined, focusing on action plans and ways to avoid the pitfalls of strategic planning. The book describes how entrepreneurs should set standards, lead by example, look to the future, focus on important details, face reality, grow profitability, and take action.

24131 ■ *Business Plans Handbook*
Pub: Gale
Released: Annual, Latest edition 9th; Published May, 2002. **Price:** $231, individuals. **Publication Includes:** 24 actual business plans, including executive summaries, market profiles and analyses, product and production information, and management, personnel, and financial data. Appendix includes a sample business plan template; two fictional plans; listings of small business associations, consultants, venture capital/finance companies; SBA and SBDC offices; SCORE offices; small business term glossary; and a cumulative index.

24132 ■ *Business Plans Kit for Dummies, 2nd Edition*
Pub: John Wiley and Sons Inc.
Released: September 2005.

24133 ■ *Business Plans That Work: A Guide for Small Business*
Pub: McGraw-Hill Companies
Ed: Jeffry A. Timmons, Stephen Spinelli, Andrew Zacharakis. **Released:** April 2004. **Price:** $12.89 (US), $24.95 (Canadian). **Description:** Guide for preparing a small business plan along with an analysis of potential business opportunities.

24134 ■ "Business Succession Planning" in *New Jersey Law Review* (December 7, 2007)
Pub: New Jersey Law Journal
Ed: Robert W. Cockren, Elga A. Goodman. **Description:** Ninety percent of American businesses are family-owned. The importance of estate planning for family-owned or controlled firms is covered.

24135 ■ *Business Vision: Beyond the Horizon, 2nd Ed.*
Pub: Business Vision Group
Ed: Dennis Wengert. **Released:** January 2009. **Description:** Challenges small business owners face when running their companies are addressed in order to position themselves for the future. The book teaches how to envision future direction and measure personal and business activities that provide an indication of personal progress in achieving visionary business leadership.

24136 ■ "Businesses Still on the Mend" in *Boston Business Journal* (Vol. 29, September 9, 2011, No. 18, pp. 1)
Pub: American City Business Journals Inc.
Ed: Scott Dance. **Description:** The 9/11 terrorist attacks have caused many companies in the US to dramatically shift course in response to changes in the economy. The concern that the cost of being unprepared for future disasters could be larger has remained among many companies.

24137 ■ "Cadillac Tower Largest to Start in a Decade" in *Globe & Mail* (March 28, 2006, pp. B5)
Pub: CTVglobemedia Publishing Inc.
Ed: Elizabeth Church. **Description:** The plans of Cadillac Fairview Corporation Ltd. to build office towers, in downtown Canada, are presented.

24138 ■ "Calming Customers" in *The Business Journal-Portland* (Vol. 25, August 29, 2008, No. 25, pp. 1)
Pub: American City Business Journals, Inc.
Ed: Kirsten Grind; Rob Smith. **Description:** Credit unions and banks in the Portland area are reaching out to clients in an effort to reassure them on the security of their money and the firms' financial stability. Roy Whitehead of Washington Federal Savings, for instance, wrote 41,000 customers of the bank to reassure them. The strategies of different banks and credit unions to answer their client's worries are discussed

24139 ■ "Can Brewer Make Cheap Seats Pay?" in *Globe & Mail* (January 7, 2006, pp. B4)
Pub: CTVglobemedia Publishing Inc.
Ed: Brent Jang. **Description:** The plans of chief executive officer Montie Brewer of Air Canada to upgrade airplanes are presented.

24140 ■ "Carveouts Back in Vogue" in *Mergers & Acquisitions: The Dealmaker's Journal* (March 1, 2008)
Pub: SourceMedia, Inc.
Ed: Ken MacFadyen. **Description:** Discusses ways in which companies look for hidden assets that they can exploit in worsening economic times; oftentimes firms try to sell off assets or in other instances they will look to unlock value through public spinoffs or through internal reorganizations.

24141 ■ "A Case Study: Real-Life Business Planning" in *Entrepreneur* (February 3, 2009)
Pub: Entrepreneur Media Inc.
Ed: Tim Berry. **Description:** Provides a case study of a two-day planning meeting for Palo Alto Software in which the executives of the company met for their annual planning cycle and discussed ways in which the company needed to change in order to stay viable in today's tough economic climate.

24142 ■ "Casinos See College as Job Jackpot" in *The Business Journal-Serving Metropolitan Kansas City* (Vol. 26, August 1, 2008, No. 47)
Pub: American City Business Journals, Inc.
Ed: Suzanna Stagemeyer. **Description:** Wyandotte County casino managers revealed plans to develop partnerships with Kansas City Kansas Community College. The planned partnership is expected to include curriculum development and degree programs that would help train employees for the planned casinos. Other views and information on the project are presented.

24143 ■ "The Caterer and Hotelkeeper Interview Patrick Harbour and Nathan Jones" in *Caterer & Hotelkeeper* (October 28, 2011, No. 288)
Pub: Reed Reference Publishing
Description: Profiles of Patrick Harbour and Nathan Jones who quit their jobs to start their own catering business. The partners discuss their business strategy when launching their boutique catering firm and ways they are adapting to the slow economy in order to remain successful.

24144 ■ "CAW Boss Troubled Over 'Vulnerable' Ford Plants" in *Globe & Mail* (January 19, 2006, pp. B6)
Pub: CTVglobemedia Publishing Inc.
Ed: Greg Keenan. **Description:** The concerns of president Buzz Hargrove of Canadian Auto Workers on the impact of Ford Motor Co.'s restructuring efforts on closure of automotive plants in Canada, are presented.

24145 ■ "Centerra Caught in Kyrgyzstan Dispute" in *Globe & Mail* (April 19, 2007, pp. B5)
Pub: CTVglobemedia Publishing Inc.
Ed: Andy Hoffman. **Description:** The details of the demonstrations carried against government proposal to nationalize Centerra Gold Inc.'s assets are presented.

24146 ■ *The Checklist Manifesto: How to Get Things Right*
Pub: Metropolitan Books
Ed: Dr. Atul Gawande. **Price:** $24.50. **Description:** How tragic errors can be sharply reduced with a piece of paper, hand-drawn boxes, and a pencil.

24147 ■ "Chelsea Community Hospital to Merge with St. Joseph Mercy Health" in *Crain's Detroit Business* (Vol. 24, March 24, 2008, No. 12)
Pub: Crain Communications, Inc.
Ed: Jay Greene. **Description:** Chelsea Community Hospital has signed a letter of intent to merge with St. Joseph Mercy Health System and will negotiate merger terms, including a plan to fund an unspecified amount of facility improvements and equipment purchases at Chelsea.

24148 ■ "Children's Products Maker Not the New Kid on the Block" in *Crain's Cleveland Business* (Vol. 28, November 26, 2007, No. 47, pp. 3)
Pub: Crain Communications, Inc.
Ed: David Bennett. **Description:** Discusses the business model employed by Shamrock Industries Inc., a rising star in the competitive world of children's products; the company, which does business as

Foundations Quality Children's Products, has expanded into a 63,000-square-foot distribution center which has boosted its local profile significantly.

24149 ■ "China's ZTE in Hunt for Partners" in *Globe & Mail* (February 27, 2006, pp. B1)
Pub: CTVglobemedia Publishing Inc.
Ed: Gordon Pitts. **Description:** The business growth plans of ZTE Corp. in Canada, through partnership, are presented.

24150 ■ "Choosing Strategies For Change" in *Harvard Business Review* (Vol. 86, July-August 2008, No. 8, pp. 130)
Pub: Harvard Business School Press
Ed: John P. Kotter; Leonard A. Schlesinger. **Description:** Methods for implementing organizational change include identifying potential areas of resistance, providing the necessary skills and information to counteract resistance, and assessing situational factors that may influence results.

24151 ■ "CIBC Spends $1.1 Billion on Caribbean Expansion" in *Globe & Mail* (March 14, 2006, pp. B1)
Pub: CTVglobemedia Publishing Inc.
Ed: Sinclair Stewart. **Description:** Canadian Imperial Bank of Commerce (CIBC), the fifth-largest bank of Canada, is planning to spend $1.1billion to buy major share of Barbados-based First Caribbean International Bank. The details of the acquisition plan are presented.

24152 ■ "Citadel Hires Three Lehman Execs" in *Chicago Tribune* (October 2, 2008)
Pub: McClatchy-Tribune Information Services
Ed: James P. Miller. **Description:** Citadel Investment Group LLC, Chicago hedge-fund operator, has hired three former senior executives of bankrupt investment banker Lehman Brothers Holding Inc. Citadel believes that the company's hiring spree will help them to further expand the firm's capabilities in the global fixed income business.

24153 ■ "City Struggles to Iron Out Tangled Transportation" in *Crain's New York Business* (Vol. 24, January 14, 2008, No. 2, pp. 33)
Pub: Crain Communications, Inc.
Ed: Judith Messina. **Description:** Discusses the possible solutions to improve lower Manhattan's transportation infrastructure including the construction of three new transit centers, an expansion in ferry service and the plan to get parked buses off the street.

24154 ■ "CityLink Project On Hold" in *Business Courier* (Vol. 24, November 9, 2008, No. 30, pp. 3)
Pub: American City Business Journals, Inc.
Ed: Dan Monk. **Description:** Developers of the CityLink project have indicated that it will be at least a year before they start the planned social services mall at 800 Bank West End. According to Tim Senff, Citylink CEO, the company wants to build bridges before constructing the buildings. The project's critics are still considering whether to appeal a court ruling regarding the facility's compliance with the city's zoning code.

24155 ■ "Civil Council Almost On Board With Light Rail Plan" in *The Business Journal-Serving Metropolitan Kansas City* (September 5, 2008)
Pub: American City Business Journals, Inc.
Ed: Steve Vockrodt. **Description:** Civic Council of Greater Kansas City has taken back its demand for the city to show a 10-year financial plan to win its endorsement of a light rail plan. The council said it will accept a five-year financial plan for the project. Details of the light rail plan are also presented.

24156 ■ "Cleanup to Polish Plating Company's Bottom Line" in *Crain's Cleveland Business* (Vol. 28, October 29, 2007, No. 43, pp. 4)
Pub: Crain Communications, Inc.
Ed: Jay Miller. **Description:** Barker Products Co, a manufacturer of nuts and bolts, is upgrading its aging facility which will allow them to operate at capacity and will save the company several hundred thousand dollars a year in operating costs. The new owners secured a construction loan from the county's new Commercial Redevelopment Fund which will allow them to upgrade the building which was hampered by years of neglect.

24157 ■ "Clothier Delays Opening" in *The Business Journal-Serving Metropolitan Kansas City* (Vol. 27, November 14, 2008, No. 10, pp. 1)
Pub: American City Business Journals, Inc.
Ed: Suzanna Stagemeyer. **Description:** Jos A. Bank Clothiers Inc. has delayed the opening of its store at the Kansas City Power and Light District in Missouri for the first quarter of 2009. The company is still waiting for other tenants to open shop in the district. Comments from officials concerning the retail sector are also presented.

24158 ■ "Comcast Networks" in *Brandweek* (Vol. 49, April 21, 2008, No. 16, pp. SR9)
Pub: VNU Business Media, Inc.
Ed: Anthony Crupi. **Description:** Provides contact information for sales and marketing personnel for the Comcast networks as well as a listing of the station's top programming and an analysis of the current season and the target audience for those programs running in the current season. Experts believe Comcast will continue to acquire more stations into their portfolio.

24159 ■ "Companies Must Set Goals for Diversity" in *Crain's Detroit Business* (Vol. 24, April 14, 2008, No. 15, pp. 16)
Pub: Crain Communications, Inc.
Ed: Laura Weiner. **Description:** Diversity programs should start with a plan that takes into account exactly what the company wants to accomplish; this may include wanting to increase the bottom line with new contracts or wanting a staff that is more innovative in their ideas due to their varied backgrounds.

24160 ■ *The Company We Keep: Reinventing Small Business for People, Community, and Place*
Pub: Chelsea Green Publishing
Ed: John Abrams, William Grieder. **Released:** June 2006. **Price:** $18.00. **Description:** The new business trend in social entrepreneurship as a business plan enables small business owners to meet the triple bottom line of profits for people (employees and owners), community, and the environment.

24161 ■ *The Complete Startup Guide for the Black Entrepreneur*
Pub: Career Press Inc.
Ed: Bill Boudreaux. **Description:** President and founder of a consulting firm for home-based entrepreneurs share information to help minorities start their own companies. Tips to create a business plan, buy essential equipment, price products and services, pay the bills, and set up a work space are covered.

24162 ■ *Contingency Planning and Disaster Recovery: A Small Business Guide*
Pub: John Wiley & Sons, Incorporated
Ed: Donna R. Childs, Stefan Dietrich. **Released:** October 2002. **Description:** Four keys issues to help a business plan for disasters include: preparation, response, recovery, and sample IT solutions in order to secure property and confidential data files and covers the six types of disasters: human errors, equipment failures, third-party failures, environmental hazards, fires and other structural catastrophes, and terrorism and sabotage.

24163 ■ "Continuously Monitoring Workers' Comp Can Limit Costs" in *Crain's Cleveland Business* (Vol. 28, October 8, 2007, No. 40, pp. 21)
Pub: Crain Communications, Inc.
Ed: Michael Lagnoni. **Description:** When operating without a plan for managing its workers' compensation program, a company risks losing money. For most companies workers' compensation insurance premiums are often reduced to an annual budget entry but employers who are actively involved in the management of their programs are more likely to experience reductions in premiums and limit indirect costs associated with claims.

24164 ■ "Copper Giant to Spin Off Silver Assets" in *Globe & Mail* (February 27, 2006, pp. B1)
Pub: CTVglobemedia Publishing Inc.
Ed: Sinclair Stewart; Andrew Willis. **Description:** The reasons behind the sale of silver mining assets by Codelco are presented.

24165 ■ "Copycat" in *Canadian Business* (Vol. 79, October 23, 2006, No. 21, pp. 53)
Pub: Rogers Media
Ed: Andrew Wahl. **Description:** The conversion of BCE Inc. into an income trust for tax advantages, soon after the transition of its business rival Telus Corp. into an income trust, is discussed.

24166 ■ "CP Rail Cuts Jobs to Keep Pace With CN" in *Globe & Mail* (January 16, 2006, pp. B1)
Pub: CTVglobemedia Publishing Inc.
Ed: Brent Jang. **Description:** Canadian Pacific Railway Ltd. (CPR) reduces workforce in order to remain competitive with Canadian National Railway Co. The details of CPR's proposal are presented.

24167 ■ "CPR Signals a Switch in Strategy to Narrow Competitive Gap With CN" in *Globe & Mail* (January 20, 2006, pp. B3)
Pub: CTVglobemedia Publishing Inc.
Ed: Brent Jang. **Description:** The reasons behind the restructuring efforts of Canadian Pacific Railway Ltd. are presented.

24168 ■ *Craft, Inc.*
Pub: Chronicle Books LLC
Ed: Meg Mateo Ilasco. **Released:** August 2007. **Price:** $16.95. **Description:** Business primer for entrepreneurial crafters wishing to turn their hobbies into a small business, including tips for developing products, naming the company, writing a business plan, applying for licenses, and paying taxes.

24169 ■ "Craig Muhlhauser" in *Canadian Business* (Vol. 81, September 15, 2008, No. 14-15, pp. 6)
Pub: Rogers Media Ltd.
Ed: Andrew Wahl. **Description:** Interview with Craig Muhlhauser who is the CEO of Celestica, a manufacturing company that provides services for the electronics sector; Muhlhauser discusses the company's restructuring program, which he feels was the secret to their surprising first-quarter results. Muhlhauser states that the company is operating with more forward visibility and that understanding the opportunities during the current economic situation presents the biggest challenge.

24170 ■ "Creativity: A Key Link to Entrepreneurial Behavior" in *Business Horizons* (September-October 2007, pp. 365)
Pub: Elsevier Technology Publications
Ed: Stephen Ko, John E. Butler. **Description:** Importance of creativity and its link to entrepreneurial behavior is examined. In a study of various entrepreneurs, studies concluded that a solid knowledge base, a well-developed social network, and a strong focus on identifying opportunities are relevant to entrepreneurial behavior.

24171 ■ "Credit Unions Cast Wary Eye at Paulson Plan, But Not Panicking Yet" in *The Business Review Albany* (Vol. 35, April 11, 2008, No. 1)
Pub: The Business Review
Ed: Barbara Pinckney. **Description:** Credit unions are suspicious of US Treasury Secretary Henry Paulson's plan to establish a single federally insured depository institution charter for all institutions covered by federal deposit insurance. The charter would replace national banks, federal savings associations, and federal credit union charters.

24172 ■ "Cruising In Choppy Water" in *The Business Journal-Portland* (Vol. 25, August 22, 2008, No. 24, pp. 1)
Pub: American City Business Journals, Inc.
Ed: Erik Siemers. **Description:** Yacht builder Christensen Shipyards Inc. is experiencing robust business despite the slowing US economy, building four yachts a year as of 2008. The company expects revenues to hit $90 million and is opening a 500,000-square-foot plant in Tennessee.

24173 ■ "DaimlerChrysler Bears Down on Smart" in *Globe & Mail* (March 27, 2006, pp. B11)
Pub: CTVglobemedia Publishing Inc.
Ed: Oliver Suess. **Description:** DaimlerChrysler AG, German automobile industry giant, is planning to cut down its workforce its Smart division. The Chrysler is also planning to stop the production of its four-seater models, to end losses at Smart division.

24174 ■ "Danger, Will Robinson!" in *Business Owner* (Vol. 35, July-August 2011, No. 4, pp. 3)
Pub: DL Perkins Company
Description: Critical measures each small business owner must take to ensure the success of their company are outlined.

24175 ■ *Dare to Prepare - How to Win Before You Begin*
Pub: Crown Publishing/Random House
Ed: Ronald M. Shapiro; Gregory Jordan. **Released:** February 24, 2009. **Price:** $14.95 paperback. **Description:** Shapiro uses his experience as one of America's top negotiators and lawyers to show how meticulous planning can raise the odds of success in business as well as in life.

24176 ■ "Deals Still Get Done at Drake's Coq d'Or" in *Crain's Chicago Business* (Vol. 31, November 17, 2008, No. 46, pp. 35)
Pub: Crain Communications, Inc.
Ed: Shia Kapos. **Description:** Chicago's infamous Coq d'Or, a restaurant and lounge located at the Drake Hotel, is still a favorite establishment for noted executives but the eatery is now trying to cater to younger professionals through marketing and offering new beverages that appeal to that demographic. Many find it the perfect environment in which to close deals, relax or network.

24177 ■ "December 19 Is a Great Day to be Terrible" in *Internet Wire* (December 15, 2009)
Pub: Comtex News Network, Inc.
Description: Overview of the plans to market the grand opening of the newest Terrible Herbst location in Las Vegas, Nevada. Terrible Herbst is a complete convenience destination offering a gas station, convenience store, car wash and lube center.

24178 ■ "Decline in Assets Is Costly for Advisers" in *The Business Journal-Serving Metropolitan Kansas City* (Vol. 27, October 24, 2008)
Pub: American City Business Journals, Inc.
Ed: James Dornbrook. **Description:** Financial advisers in the Kansas City, Missouri area are forced to cut costs as their assets have decreased sharply due to the huge drop in stock prices. American Century Investments was forced to diversify into foreign assets and cut 90 jobs as its assets dropped to $84 billion. Diversification has softened the impact of the steep decline in stock prices for Waddell & Reed Financial Inc.

24179 ■ "Deere to Open Technology Center in Germany" in *Chicago Tribune* (September 3, 2008)
Pub: McClatchy-Tribune Information Services
Ed: James P. Miller. **Description:** Deere & Co. plans to open a technology and innovation center in Germany; details of the company's expansion plans are discussed.

24180 ■ "Digital Duplication" in *Crain's Cleveland Business* (Vol. 28, October 1, 2007, No. 39, pp. 3)
Pub: Crain Communications, Inc.
Ed: David Bennett. **Description:** Profile of the business plan of eBlueprint Holdings LLC, a reprographics company that found success by converting customers' paper blueprints to an electronic format; the company plans to expand into other geographic markets by acquiring solid reprographics companies and converting their computer systems so that customers' blueprints can be managed electronically.

24181 ■ "Dividing to Conquer" in *Barron's* (Vol. 88, March 31, 2008, No. 13, pp. 22)
Pub: Dow Jones & Company, Inc.
Ed: Andrew Bary. **Description:** Altria's spin off of Philip Morris International could unlock substantial value for both domestic and international cigarette concerns. The strong brands and ample payouts from both companies will most likely impress investors.

24182 ■ "Diving for the Next Big Gold Rush" in *Canadian Business* (Vol. 80, February 12, 2007, No. 4, pp. 28)
Pub: Rogers Media
Ed: Thomas Watson. **Description:** The interest of Canadian mining companies led by Nautilus Minerals to invest in mining for deep sea-floor massive sulphide deposits, which have several minerals, is discussed.

24183 ■ "Do You Have A Retirement Parachute?" in *Barron's* (Vol. 88, July 7, 2008, No. 27, pp. 32)
Pub: Dow Jones & Co., Inc.
Ed: Jane White. **Description:** The idea that American companies should emulate the Australian retirement system which implements a forced contribution rate for all employers regarding an adequate retirement plan for their employees is discussed.

24184 ■ "Doctors Eye Rating Plan With Caution" in *The Business Journal-Portland* (Vol. 25, July 4, 2008, No. 17, pp. 1)
Pub: American City Business Journals, Inc.
Ed: Robin J. Moody. **Description:** Doctors in Portland, Oregon are wary of a new Providence Health Plan system that rates their performance on patients with certain medical conditions. The system is expected to discourage wasteful procedures, thereby, saving employers' money. Other mechanics of the rating system are also discussed.

24185 ■ "The Dogs of TSX" in *Canadian Business* (Vol. 81, Summer 2008, No. 9, pp. 77)
Pub: Rogers Media Ltd.
Ed: Calvin Leung. **Description:** Table showing the one-year stock performance of the ten highest dividend-yielding stocks on the S&P/TSX 60 Composite Index is presented. This technique is similar to the 'Dogs of the Dow' approach. The idea in this investment strategy is to buy equal amounts of stocks from these companies and selling them a year later, and then repeat the process.

24186 ■ *Doing Business Anywhere: The Essential Guide to Going Global*
Pub: John Wiley and Sons, Inc.
Ed: Tom Travis. **Released:** 2007. **Price:** $24.95. **Description:** Plans are given for new or existing businesses to organize, plan, operate and execute a business on a global basis. Trade agreements, brand protection and patents, ethics, security as well as cultural issues are among the issues addressed.

24187 ■ "Don't Quit When The Road Gets Bumpy" in *Women Entrepreneur* (November 25, 2008)
Pub: Entrepreneur Media Inc.
Ed: Bonnie Price. **Description:** Discusses techniques four women entrepreneurs are utilizing to keep their businesses successful despite the credit crunch and the economic downturn.

24188 ■ "Don't Try This Offshore" in *Harvard Business Review* (Vol. 86, September 2008, No. 9, pp. 39)
Pub: Harvard Business School Press
Ed: Description: Fictitious outsourcing scenario is presented, with contributors offering advice. The suggestions address the ease or complexity of offshoring business creativity, along with challenges and benefits.

24189 ■ "Doyle: Domino's New Pizza Seasoned with Straight Talk" in *Crain's Detroit Business* (Vol. 26, January 11, 2010, No. 2, pp. 1)
Pub: Crain Communications, Inc.
Ed: Nathan Skid. **Description:** Interview with J. Patrick Doyle, the CEO of Domino's Pizza, Inc.; the company has launched a new marketing campaign that focuses on its bold new vision.

24190 ■ *Dreams with a Deadline: How to Turn a Strategy for Tomorrow Into a Plan for Today*
Pub: Pearson Education, Limited
Ed: Jacques Horovitz; Anne-Valerie Ohlsson-Corboz. **Released:** November 2006. **Price:** $54.00. **Description:** Tips for successful entrepreneurship are covered.

24191 ■ "Economic Crises Calls For Better Marketing Plans" in *Entrepreneur* (October 1, 2008)
Pub: Entrepreneur Media Inc.
Ed: Tim Berry. **Description:** Revising one's business plan is essential, especially during times of economic crisis; sales and marketing plans should be reviewed, analyzed and changed in an attempt to survive the economic downturn.

24192 ■ "Economic Outlook 2009" in *Hispanic Business* (January-February 2009, pp. 30, 32)
Pub: Hispanic Business
Ed: Dr. Juan Solana. **Description:** Successful business policies of the past no longer work in this economic climate. New tools and initiatives regarding monetary policy, fiscal policy and a higher multiplier are required to survive the crisis.

24193 ■ "Economic Stimulus Plan Needs Scrutiny" in *Crain's Detroit Business* (Vol. 24, April 7, 2008, No. 14, pp. 8)
Pub: Crain Communications, Inc.
Description: Overview of Mayor Kwame Kilpatrick's economic stimulus package which many believe needs to be scrutinized closely since the true financial status of Detroit is unclear.

24194 ■ "Efficient Cash Management Essential To Be Competitive" in *Crain's Cleveland Business* (Vol. 28, November 12, 2007, No. 45, pp. 25)
Pub: Crain Communications, Inc.
Ed: Ken Moultrie. **Description:** In order to sustain a business it is important to organize cash-management efforts around three core areas: cash in, static cash and cash out. Tips for the successful management of these areas are provided.

24195 ■ "The Emperor Strikes Back" in *Canadian Business* (Vol. 80, March 26, 2007, No. 7, pp. 48)
Pub: Rogers Media
Ed: Rachel Pulfer. **Description:** The financial performance of Fairfax Financial Holdings Ltd. in 2006 is presented. The efforts of chief executive Prem Watsa to lead the company towards growth track are also presented.

24196 ■ "EnCana Axes Spending on Gas Wells" in *Globe & Mail* (February 16, 2006, pp. B1)
Pub: CTVglobemedia Publishing Inc.
Ed: Dave Ebner. **Description:** The reasons behind EnCana Corp.'s cost spending measures by $300 million on natural gas wells are presented. The company projects 2 percent cut in gas and oil sales for 2006.

24197 ■ "Energy Sparks Job Growth" in *The Business Journal-Serving Greater Tampa Bay* (Vol. 28, August 8, 2008, No. 33, pp. 1)
Pub: American City Business Journals, Inc.
Ed: Margie Manning. **Description:** Energy infrastructure projects in Tampa Bay, Florida, are increasing the demand for labor in the area. Energy projects requiring an increase in labor include TECO Energy

Inc.'s plan for a natural gas pipeline in the area and the installation of energy management system in Bank of America's branches in the area.

24198 ■ *Entrepreneurial Management*
Pub: McGraw-Hill
Ed: Robert J. Calvin. **Description:** Starting a new business takes careful consideration, determined preparation and a well-developed plan president of an international company that helps startups offers strategies, tools, techniques, models and methodologies for starting a new business. This guidebook covers all aspects of launching a new company as well as hands-on business skills and the motivation to keep new business owners moving towards success while conquering the entrepreneurial challenges along with way.

24199 ■ "Entrepreneurial Orientation and Firm Performance" in *Journal of Small Business and Entrepreneurship* (Vol. 23, Winter 2010, No. 1)
Pub: Canadian Council for Small Business and Entrepreneurship
Description: The article develops a theoretical model of the relationship between firm-level entrepreneurship and firm performance. This model is intended to further clarify the consequences of an 'entrepreneurial orientation', paying particular attention to the differential relationship that exists between the three sub-dimensions of entrepreneurial orientation and firm performance. Included in the theoretical model are other important variables (such as organizational structure and environmental characteristics) that may impact the EO-performance relationship. Propositions are developed regarding the various configurations of the sub-dimensions of EO and organizational structure that would be most appropriate in a given environmental context. Future research may also benefit from considering the important role that organizational strategy and life cycle stage play in this model. The implications of this model for both researchers and managers are discussed.

24200 ■ *The Entrepreneur's Strategy Guide: Ten Keys for Achieving Marketplace Leadership*
Pub: Greenwood Publishing Group, Incorporated
Ed: Tom Cannon. **Released:** September 2006. **Price:** $44.95. **Description:** Ten principles of marketplace leadership are explored. The book provides a plan for small businesses, including diagnostics, checklists, and other interactive exercises to study both external and internal principles.

24201 ■ *Entrepreneurship*
Pub: McGraw-Hill Higher Education
Ed: Robert D. Hisrich; Michael P. Peters; Dean A. Shepherd. **Released:** October 2006. **Price:** $106.50. **Description:** Advice is offered to entrepreneurs in formulating, planning, and implementing a business plan.

24202 ■ *Entrepreneurship: A Process Perspective*
Pub: Thomson South-Western
Ed: Robert A. Baron; Scott A. Shane. **Released:** February 2007. **Price:** $137.95. **Description:** Entrepreneurial process covering team building, finances, business plan, legal issues, marketing, growth and exit strategies.

24203 ■ *Essentials of Entrepreneurship and Small Business Management*
Pub: Prentice Hall PTR
Ed: Thomas W. Zimmerer; Norman M. Scarborough; Doug Wilson. **Released:** February 2007. **Price:** $106. 67. **Description:** New venture creation and the knowledge required to start a new business are shared. The challenges of entrepreneurship, business plans, marketing, e-commerce, and financial considerations are explored.

24204 ■ *Everything I Know About Business I Learned at McDonald's: The 7 Leadership Principles that Drive Break Out Success*
Pub: The McGraw-Hill Companies
Ed: Paul Facella. **Released:** 2009. **Price:** $24.95. **Description:** McDonald's management philosophy is as simple as its menu, but don't underestimate the effectiveness of founder Ray Kroc's business plan.

24205 ■ "Executive Decision: Damn the Profit Margins, Sleeman Declares War on Buck-a-Beer Foes" in *Globe & Mail* (January 28, 2006, pp. B3)
Pub: CTVglobemedia Publishing Inc.
Ed: Andy Hoffman. **Description:** The cost savings plans of chief executive officer John Sleeman of Sleeman Breweries Ltd. are presented.

24206 ■ "Executive Decision: Lead a Double Life for Geac's Sake" in *Globe & Mail* (January 21, 2006, pp. B4)
Pub: CTVglobemedia Publishing Inc.
Ed: Simon Avery. **Description:** The details of growth of Geac Computer Corporation Ltd., under chief executive officer Charles Jones, are presented.

24207 ■ "Executive Decision: To Make Inroads Against RIM, Palm Steals Its Strategy" in *Globe & Mail* (March 25, 2006, pp. B3)
Pub: CTVglobemedia Publishing Inc.
Ed: Simon Avery. **Description:** The Palm Inc., global leader in portable device manufacturing, is looking forward to improve its sales of Palm Treos, a wireless portable device that connects to internet and email. Palm is also planning to build partnerships, under the efficient management of Michael Moskowitz, general manager and vice-president of Palm Inc., with the other companies to increase the sales of its wireless devices.

24208 ■ "Executive Training" in *Black Enterprise* (Vol. 37, December 2006, No. 5, pp. 70)
Pub: Earl G. Graves Publishing Co. Inc.
Ed: Marcia A. Reed-Woodard. **Description:** Roy N. Gundy Jr. was preparing to introduce a new strategic plan within his division and understood that his plan may fail if not executed properly. He discusses his experience in the Wharton School's executive education workshop Implementing Strategy, at the University of Pennsylvania and gives tips on putting strategy into action.

24209 ■ "Expanding Middleby's Food Processing Biz" in *Crain's Chicago Business* (Vol. 31, April 21, 2008, No. 16, pp. 6)
Pub: Crain Communications, Inc.
Ed: David Sterrett. **Description:** Profile of the executive vice-president of the food processing company, Middleby Corp, whose business plan is to develop new products, begin looking for acquisitions and simplify operations in order to expand the firm.

24210 ■ "Experts Take the Temp of Obama Plan" in *The Business Journal-Serving Metropolitan Kansas City* (Vol. 27, November 14, 2008, No. 10)
Pub: American City Business Journals, Inc.
Ed: Rob Roberts. **Description:** Kansas City, Missouri-based employee benefits experts say president-elect Barack Obama's health care reform plan is on track. Insurance for children and capitalization for health information technology are seen as priority areas. The plan is aimed at reducing the number of uninsured people in the United States.

24211 ■ "Familiar Face Aims to Rebuild Distributor's Once-Strong Local Ties" in *Crain's Cleveland Business* (December 3, 2007)
Pub: Crain Communications, Inc.
Ed: David Bennett. **Description:** Phillips Contractors Supply, a tool distributor, has a new president and co-owner, James Beckett. Beckett was once vice president of operations so he knows the company well and has plans to re-establish the firm's presence in the region.

24212 ■ "Family Feud: Pawn Shop Empire Stalls with Transition to Second Generation" in *Billings Gazette* (December 19, 2010)
Pub: Billings Gazette
Ed: Jan Falstad. **Description:** Profile of Ben L. Brown Sr. and his pawn shop located in Billings, Montana is presented. Brown discusses his plan to transition his business to his children.

24213 ■ *Family Limited Partnership Deskbook*
Pub: American Bar Association
Ed: David T. Lewis; Andrea C. Chomakos. **Released:** March 25, 2008. **Price:** $169.95. **Description:** Forming and funding a family limited partnership or limited liability company is complicated. In-depth analysis of all facets of this business entity are examined using detailed guidance on the basic principles of drafting, forming, funding, and valuing an FLP or LLC and also covers tax concerns. Examples and extensive sample forms are included on a CD-ROM included with the book.

24214 ■ "The Family-Run Business" in *Small Business Opportunities* (Get Rich At Home 2010)
Pub: Harris Publications Inc.
Ed: Gene Siciliano. **Description:** The good, the bad and the ugly of succession planning for any small business is spotlighted.

24215 ■ "Film Giants Disney, Pixar Talk Marriage" in *Globe & Mail* (January 19, 2006, pp. B1)
Pub: CTVglobemedia Publishing Inc.
Ed: Merissa Marr; Nick Wingfield. **Description:** The plans of Walt Disney Co. to acquire Pixar Animation Studios are presented.

24216 ■ "Finalist: Private Company, Less Than $100M" in *Crain's Detroit Business* (Vol. 25, June 22, 2009, No. 25)
Pub: Crain Communications Inc. - Detroit
Ed: Nancy Kaffer. **Description:** Profile of W3R Consulting and CFO Patrick Tom= ina. The company offers information technology consulting. Tomina discusses the company's 505 strategy: to grow its annual revenue to $50 million in five years.

24217 ■ *Financing Growth: Strategies, Capital Structure, and M and A Transactions*
Pub: John Wiley & Sons, Inc.
Ed: Kenneth H. Marks, Larry E. Robbins, Gonzalo Fernandez, John P. Funkhouser, D.L. Williams. **Released:** September 1, 2009. **Price:** $95.00. **Description:** Guide for emerging growth and middle market companies includes information to help understand and apply the basics of corporate finance using empirical data and actual company cases to illustrate capital structures and financing approaches.

24218 ■ "Financing for NNSA Plant Is a Work in Progress" in *The Business Journal-Serving Metropolitan Kansas City* (October 24, 2008)
Pub: American City Business Journals, Inc.
Ed: Rob Roberts. **Description:** The Kansas City Council approved a development plan for a $500 million nuclear weapons parts plant in south Kansas City. The US Congress approved a $59 million annual lease payment to the plant's developer. Financing for the construction of the plant remains in question as the plant's developers have to shoulder construction costs.

24219 ■ "Finding the Voice of the Marketplace" in *Mergers & Acquisitions: The Dealmaker's Journal* (March 1, 2008)
Pub: SourceMedia, Inc.
Description: Companies oftentimes are unable to achieve their strategic goals through acquisition due, in part, to not understanding the target's market and its position in the marketplace.

24220 ■ "Five Steps to Killer Business Ideas" in *Hawaii Business* (Vol. 53, December 2007, No. 6, pp. 135)
Pub: Hawaii Business Publishing
Ed: Jason Ubay. **Description:** Five ways to formulating good business concepts are presented. The importance of keeping an open mind and analyzing the market is discussed.

24221 ■ "Follow the ABCs of Buying a Business" in *Women Entrepreneur* (September 10, 2008)
Pub: Entrepreneur Media Inc.
Ed: Nina Kaufman. **Description:** Buying a business will likely result in the largest single asset one will ever own. A list of steps one can take in order to educate and protect themselves is provided.

24222 ■ "For Going All Out to Transform the Way Our Food Is Grown: Chuck Lacy" in *Inc.* (Volume 32, December 2010, No. 10, pp. 94)
Pub: Inc. Magazine
Ed: Adam Bluestein. **Description:** Profile of Rotokawa Cattle Company and its mission to transform the business of beef and grow their herd of beef cattle.

24223 ■ "Ford Fix Requires 'Painful' Remedy" in *Globe & Mail* (January 9, 2006, pp. B1)
Pub: CTVglobemedia Publishing Inc.
Ed: Greg Keenan. **Description:** The plans of Ford Motor Co. to streamline Canadian operations are presented.

24224 ■ "Forget the Elaborate Business Plans, Kids With Passion Are Our Next Great Entrepreneurs" in *Inc.* (October 2007, pp. 87-88)
Pub: Gruner & Jahr USA Publishing
Description: George Gendron, founder and executive director of the Innovation and Entrepreneurship Program at Clark University, stresses the importance of encouraging business students in his entrepreneurial program to follow their passion. The program is dedicated to real-world entrepreneurship by creating businesses rather than business plans.

24225 ■ "Former Chrysler Dealers Build New Business Model" in *Crain's Detroit Business* (Vol. 25, June 22, 2009, No. 25, pp. 3)
Pub: Crain Communications Inc. - Detroit
Ed: Daniel Duggan. **Description:** Joe Ricci is one of 14 Detroit area dealerships whose franchises have been terminated. Ricci and other Chrysler dealers in the area are starting new businesses or switching to new franchises.= Ricci's All American Buyer's Service will be located in Dearborn and will sell only used cars.

24226 ■ "Formulating Policy With a Parallel Organization" in *Strategy & Leadership* (Vol. 38, September-October 2010, No. 5, pp. 33-38)
Pub: Emerald Inc.
Ed: Dale E. Zand, Thomas F. Hawk. **Description:** A study analyzes a case to examine the parallel organization concept and its successful implementation by a CEO to integrate independent divisions of a firm. Findings reveal that the implementation of the parallel organization improved the policy formulation, strategic planning profitability of the firm while also better integrating its independent divisions.

24227 ■ "Founding Family Acquires Airport Marriott" in *Crain's Cleveland Business* (Vol. 28, November 5, 2007, No. 44, pp. 3)
Pub: Crain Communications, Inc.
Ed: Stan Bullard. **Description:** Big River Real Estate LLC, part of the Marriott family's investment fund, is the new owner of the Cleveland Airport Marriott; renovations estimated at about $11 million will ensure that the hotel meets Marriott's standards.

24228 ■ "Four Big Fat Business Plan Lies" in *Entrepreneur* (December 11, 2008)
Pub: Entrepreneur Media Inc.
Ed: Tim Berry. **Description:** Business plans are essential for every business and do not necessarily have to be a complex document containing a full list of components. Other misconceptions concerning business plans are also discussed.

24229 ■ "Franchisees Lose Battle Against BK" in *Advertising Age* (Vol. 79, June 2, 2008, No. 22, pp. 46)
Pub: Crain Communications, Inc.
Ed: Emily Bryson York. **Description:** Burger King has had continuing litigation with former franchisees from New York, Luan and Elizabeth Sadik, who claim that Burger King's double cheeseburger, along with additional problems, created the environment for their eventual insolvency. Burger King has since terminated its test of selling the double cheeseburger for $1, although the company declined to comment on the reason for this decision.

24230 ■ "Fries With That?" in *Canadian Business* (Vol. 81, September 29, 2008, No. 16, pp. 33)
Pub: Rogers Media Ltd.
Ed: Calvin Leung. **Description:** Profile of Toronto-based New York Fries, which has four stores in South Korea, is planning to expand further as well as into Hong Kong and Macau; the company also has a licensee in the United Arab Emirates whom is also planning to expand.

24231 ■ "From Craft Biz To Wholesale Giant" in *Women Entrepreneur* (January 19, 2009)
Pub: Entrepreneur Media Inc.
Ed: Maria Falconer. **Description:** Advice is given on how to turn a small craft business into a full-time venture; tips to help one transition from a part-time designer to a full-time wholesaler and brand are also included.

24232 ■ "From War Zone to Franchise Zone" in *Entrepreneur* (Vol. 37, August 2009, No. 8, pp. 104)
Pub: Entrepreneur Media, Inc.
Ed: Jason Daley. **Description:** Ross Paterson says that he realized that the material he used in the Growth Coach franchise could give the people of Afghanistan the systematic model they need. Paterson says that the Afghans are very business-oriented people but that they work in a different system than Americans.

24233 ■ "Gail Mukaihata Hannemann" in *Hawaii Business* (Vol. 53, January 2008, No. 7, pp. 24)
Pub: Hawaii Business Publishing
Ed: Cathy S. Cruz-George. **Description:** Discusses the Girl Scouts of Hawaii which has altered its business model to become more appealing to young girls in the 21st century. Gail Mukaihata Hanneman, the chief executive officer of the nonprofit organization, states that the Girl Scouts has consolidated some of its operations to increase efficiency. Her views on what employers must learn about the youth and on the adults' roles in developing the younger generation are given.

24234 ■ "Game On" in *Canadian Business* (Vol. 80, February 12, 2007, No. 4, pp. 15)
Pub: Rogers Media
Ed: Calvin Leung. **Description:** The plan of president of TransGaming Vikas Gupta to create innovative software programs for games that can be played in different operating systems is discussed.

24235 ■ "Game Plan" in *Canadian Business* (Vol. 79, September 11, 2006, No. 18, pp. 50)
Pub: Rogers Media
Ed: Joe Castaldo. **Description:** Strategies adopted by gaming companies to revitalize their business and give a stimulus to their falling resources are presented.

24236 ■ "Get Back To Business Planning Fundamentals" in *Entrepreneur* (October 24, 2008)
Pub: Entrepreneur Media Inc.
Ed: Tim Berry. **Description:** During a recession it is important to know what adjustment to make to your business plan. Some fundamentals to remember include: watching things more closely by tracking progress on cash, sales, new projects, customer satisfaction, ad spending and expenses; looking for built-in indicators such as what drives sales or expenses; watching what drives cash flow; and do not make mistakes such as laying off experienced employees too soon.

24237 ■ "Get Off The Rollercoaster" in *Michigan Vue* (Vol. 13, July-August 2008, No. 4, pp. 19)
Pub: Entrepreneur Media Inc.
Ed: Donald N. Hobley Jr. **Description:** Benefits of creating and implementing a solid financial plan during these rocky economic times are examined. Things to keep in mind before meeting with a financial planner include risk assessment, investment goals, the length of time required to meet those goals and the amount of money one has available to invest.

24238 ■ "Get Over Your Fear of Change" in *Canadian Business* (Vol. 83, June 15, 2010, No. 10, pp. 38)
Pub: Rogers Media Ltd.
Ed: Michelle Magnan. **Description:** Organizational behavior professor Chip Heath says that resistance to change is based on the conflict between our analytical, rational side and our emotional side that is in love with comfort. Heath states that businesses tend to focus on the negatives during an economic crisis while they should be focusing on what is working and ways to do more of that.

24239 ■ *The Girl's Guide to Building a Million-Dollar Business*
Pub: AMACOM
Ed: Susan Wilson Solovic. **Released:** 2008. **Price:** $21.95. **Description:** Success plan for women business owners; the book includes tips for determination, managing changing relationships, keeping employees and customers happy, getting and maintaining credit, overcoming gender bias, and creating a good business plan and solid brand.

24240 ■ "GM Axing Prices; Kerkorian Calls for Crisis Plan" in *Globe & Mail* (January 11, 2006, pp. B1)
Pub: CTVglobemedia Publishing Inc.
Ed: Greg Keenan. **Description:** The financial restructuring proposal of investor Kirk Kerkorian for General Motors Corp. is presented.

24241 ■ "Gold Medal" in *Canadian Business* (Vol. 79, October 9, 2006, No. 20, pp. 57)
Pub: Rogers Media
Ed: Andrew Wahl. **Description:** Creativity skills and management strategies of Rob McEwen, founder and chief executive officer of Goldcorp Inc., are presented.

24242 ■ "Grace Puma; Senior Vice-President of Strategic Sourcing, United Airlines" in *Crain's Chicago Business* (May 5, 2008)
Pub: Crain Communications, Inc.
Ed: John Rosenthal. **Description:** Profile of Grace Puma who is the senior vice-president of strategic sourcing at United Airlines and is responsible for cutting costs at the company in a number of ways including scheduling safety inspections at the same time as routine maintenance, thereby reducing the downtime of each aircraft by five days as well as replacing a third of her staff with outside talent.

24243 ■ "A Graceful (and Lucrative) Exit" in *Black Enterprise* (Vol. 38, November 2007, No. 4, pp. 108)
Pub: Earl G. Graves Publishing Co. Inc.
Ed: Tamara E. Holmes. **Description:** BlueKey Business Brokerage helps clients buy, grow or sell a business. Four key points are examined in order to successfully exit a business.

24244 ■ "Grave Concerns" in *Canadian Business* (Vol. 81, July 21 2008, No. 11, pp. 25)
Pub: Rogers Media Ltd.
Ed: Andrew Nikiforuk. **Description:** Air pollution control regulations to reduce greenhouse gasses have been implemented by the Canadian government. The federal government is planning to construct a carbon funeral industry that will store the global warming gases, however the expenditure for the project will be shifted to the taxpayers. Details of the Bruce Peachy's initiative on how to reduce GHGs are presented.

24245 ■ "Great Canadian's President Folds His Cards" in *Globe & Mail* (February 21, 2006, pp. B4)
Pub: CTVglobemedia Publishing Inc.
Ed: Peter Kennedy. **Description:** The reasons behind the resignation of Anthony Martin as president of Great Canadian Gaming Corp. are presented.

24246 ■ "Green Acres" in *Hawaii Business* (Vol. 54, September 2008, No. 3, pp. 48)
Pub: Hawaii Business Publishing
Ed: Jan Tenbruggencate. **Description:** Bill Cowern's Hawaiian Mahogany is a forestry business that processes low-value trees to be sold as wood chips, which can be burned to create biodiesel. Cowern is

planning to obtain certification to market carbon credits and is also working with Green Energy Hawaii for the permit of a biomass-fueled power plant. Other details about Cowern's business are discussed.

24247 ■ "The Green Conversation" in *Harvard Business Review* (Vol. 86, September 2008, No. 9, pp. 58)
Pub: Harvard Business School Press
Description: Six guidelines are presented for addressing and benefiting from environmentally conscious corporate decision making and practices. Topics covered include marketing, supply chain, and leadership.

24248 ■ "'Groundhog Day' B & B Likely Will Be Converted Into One In Real Life" in *Chicago Tribune* (October 21, 2008)
Pub: McClatchy-Tribune Information Services
Ed: Carolyn Starks. **Description:** Everton Martin and Karla Stewart Martin have purchased the Victorian house that was featured as a bed-and-breakfast in the 1993 hit move "Groundhog Day"; the couple was initially unaware of the structure's celebrity status when they purchased it with the hope of fulfilling their dream of owning a bed-and-breakfast.

24249 ■ "Growers Urged to Allow for Soil Nutrients" in *Farmer's Weekly* (March 28, 2008, No. 320)
Pub: Reed Business Information
Ed: Andrew Blake. **Description:** Discusses the importance of taking in account soil nitrogen supplies when planning their remaining fertilizer applications.

24250 ■ "A Growing Dilemma" in *Crain's Cleveland Business* (Vol. 28, October 8, 2007, No. 40, pp. 19)
Pub: Crain Communications, Inc.
Ed: Kimberly Bonvissuto. **Description:** Discusses small business owners who often have to grapple with the decision on whether or not to expand their operations and the importance of a business plan which may help owners with that decision.

24251 ■ "Growing Pains" in *Canadian Business* (Vol. 81, July 22, 2008, No. 12-13, pp. 35)
Pub: Rogers Media Ltd.
Ed: Alex Mylnek. **Description:** Laughing Stock Vineyards' Cynthia Enns and David Enns plan to target young buyers by using social media. The Enns however, are concerned that targeting younger buyers may affect Laughing Stock's image as a premium brand. Additional information regarding the company's future plans is presented.

24252 ■ "Handleman Liquidation Leaves Questions For Shareholders" in *Crain's Detroit Business* (Vol. 24, October 6, 2008, No. 40, pp. 4)
Pub: Crain Communications, Inc.
Ed: Nancy Kaffer. **Description:** Discusses Handleman Co., a Troy-based music distribution company, and their plan of liquidation and dissolution as well as how shareholders will be affected by the company's plan. Handleman filed its plan to liquidate and dissolve assets with the Securities and Exchange Commission in mid-August, following several quarters of dismal earnings.

24253 ■ "Has Microsoft Found a Way to Get at Yahoo?" in *Advertising Age* (Vol. 79, July 7, 2008, No. 26, pp. 4)
Pub: Crain Communications, Inc.
Ed: Abbey Klaassen. **Description:** Microsoft's attempt to acquire Yahoo's search business is discussed as is Yahoo's plans for the future at a time when the company's shares have fallen dangerously low.

24254 ■ "HBC Sets Friday as Deadline to Trump Zucker Takeover Bid" in *Globe & Mail* (January 18, 2006, pp. B1)
Pub: CTVglobemedia Publishing Inc.
Ed: Marina Strauss. **Description:** The reasons behind Hudson's Bay Co.'s decision to seek alternative bids on the company are presented. Investor Jerry Zucker earlier offered $1.1 billion for the company.

24255 ■ "Hello, Old Friends" in *Business Courier* (Vol. 24, October 12, 2008, No. 26, pp. 1)
Pub: American City Business Journals, Inc.
Ed: Jon Newberry. **Description:** Pittsburgh-based Iron City Brewing Co., a company born out of Pittsburgh Brewing Co.'s reorganization, is resuming the production of Wiedemann Bohemian Style Special Beer. Cincinnati-based Christian Moerlein Brewing Co. is also bringing back its famous Burger beer, which hasn't been available locally for a couple of years. The two companies' plans regarding the reintroduction of their beer products are discussed.

24256 ■ "High Energy: Gaurdie Banister Joins Aera As President and CEO" in *Black Enterprise* (Vol. 38, July 2008, No. 12, pp. 30)
Pub: Earl G. Graves Publishing Co. Inc.
Ed: Brenda Porter. **Description:** Gaurdie Banister Jr. has been appointed president and CEO of Aera Energy L.L.C., becoming one of the first African Americans in the nation to run a major energy corporation. His plans for the firm include utilizing new, sophisticated technologies in order to unlock the 3-1/2 billion barrels of resources the company has on their books in a safe and environmentally friendly way. He also hopes to increase production and maintain cost leadership.

24257 ■ "Higher Freight Rates Keep CPR Rolling in Profit" in *Globe & Mail* (February 1, 2006, pp. B3)
Pub: CTVglobemedia Publishing Inc.
Ed: Brent Jang. **Description:** Canadian Pacific Railway Ltd. posted $135.4 million in revenues for fourth quarter 2005. The company's earnings projections for 2006 and workforce reduction plans are presented.

24258 ■ "His Place in the Sun" in *Canadian Business* (Vol. 79, October 23, 2006, No. 21, pp. 77)
Pub: Rogers Media
Ed: Zena Olijnyk. **Description:** The business interests of Canadian real estate developer Derek Elliott in the Dominican Republic, is discussed.

24259 ■ "Historic Glenview Homes Could Be Torn Down" in *Chicago Tribune* (September 25, 2008)
Pub: McClatchy-Tribune Information Services
Ed: Courtney Flynn. **Description:** Leaders of the Glenview New Church would like to see a buyer emerge who would move and restore two historic homes sitting on the church's property. If a buyer does not come forward the church plans to demolish the homes to make room for condominiums and the expansion of their school.

24260 ■ "Hit the Green" in *Canadian Business* (Vol. 79, August 14, 2006, No. 16-17, pp. 73)
Pub: Rogers Media
Ed: Andrew Wahl. **Description:** Reorganization of the bankrupt 4everSports golf company in the United States is discussed.

24261 ■ "HOK Sport May Build Own Practice" in *The Business Journal-Serving Metropolitan Kansas City* (Vol. 26, August 29, 2008, No. 51, pp. 1)
Pub: American City Business Journals, Inc.
Ed: Rob Roberts. **Description:** HOK Sport Venue Event is considering a spin-off from its parent company, HOK Group Inc. HOK Sport spokeswoman Gina Leo confirms that the firm is exploring structures, including a management buyout. Some of HOK Sport Venue Event's Minnesota projects are discussed.

24262 ■ "How I Did It: Laurel Touby Mediabistro" in *Inc.* (March 2008, pp. 124-126)
Pub: Gruner & Jahr USA Publishing
Ed: Eric Schine. **Description:** Profile of Laurel Touby and her business plan; Touby started Mediabistro as a series of parties that turned into an influential job listing and training Website for journalists. Last year she sold it for $23 million.

24263 ■ "How to Keep Your Sales from Running Out of Gas" in *Agency Sales Magazine* (Vol. 39, July 2009, No. 7, pp. 30)
Pub: MANA
Ed: John Graham. **Description:** Salespeople can let the good times deceive them into thinking that success will go on forever. Salespeople and businesses should see prospecting as a strategy for creating a continuing flow of business.

24264 ■ *How to Make Big Money*
Pub: Hyperion Books
Ed: Jeffrey J. Fox. **Released:** May 19, 2004. **Price:** $16.95. **Description:** Entrepreneur and consultant offers advice to help others create successful startups and prosper. Fox directs new business owners with a counterintuitive style and describes essential methods that beat the competition. Tips include: setting priorities, getting a personal driver, creating a contingency plan for employees, pricing to value, saving money, and getting an office outside of the home.

24265 ■ "How Not to Build a Website" in *Women Entrepreneur* (December 24, 2008)
Pub: Entrepreneur Media Inc.
Ed: Erica Ruback; Joanie Reisen. **Description:** Tips for producing a unique and functional Website are given as well as a number of lessons a pair of entrepreneurs learned while trying to launch their networking website, MomSpace.com.

24266 ■ *How to Start a Home-Based Craft Business, 5th Edition*
Pub: Globe Pequot Press
Ed: Kenn Oberrecht. **Released:** July 2007. **Price:** $18.95. **Description:** Advice for starting a home-based craft business is given, including sources for finding supplies on the Internet, writing a business plan, publicity, zoning ordinances, and more.

24267 ■ *How to Start and Run Your Own Corporation: S-Corporations For Small Business Owners*
Pub: HCM Publishing
Ed: Peter I. Hupalo. **Released:** March 6, 2003. **Price:** $22.95. **Description:** Basics of corporate business structure are explained. Topics include discovering the best business structure for your company; how to decided between an S-Corporation and LLC; choosing the state in which to incorporate, how to form a corporation, angel investing, special issues for one-person corporations, the role of bylaws and corporate minutes, board of directors, taxes, workers' compensation issues, retirement plans, and more.

24268 ■ "How Will You Ever Replace Yourself?" in *Canadian Business* (Vol. 83, August 17, 2010, No. 13-14, pp. 77)
Pub: Rogers Media Ltd.
Ed: Jacqueline Nelson. **Description:** SoftBank founder and CEO masayoshi Son created his very own school called SoftBank Academia in order to pick a successor that will follow his footprint. Son's strategy is extreme but other corporate leaders should pay attention to succession planning.

24269 ■ *How to Write a Business Plan*
Pub: Kogan Page, Limited
Ed: Brian Finch. **Released:** February 10, 2010. **Price:** $17.95. **Description:** Starting with the premise that there's only one chance to make a good impression, this book covers all the issues involved in producing a successful business plan, from profiling competitors to forecasting marketing development.

24270 ■ *How to Write a Great Business Plan for Your Small Business in 60 Minutes or Less*
Pub: Atlantic Publishing
Ed: Sharon L. Fullen. **Released:** January 2006. **Price:** $39.95 includes CD-Rom. **Description:** A good business plan outlines goals and works as a company's resume to obtain funding, credit from suppliers, management of the operations and finances, promotion and marketing, and more.

24271 ■ "Husky Proceeds on Heavy-Oil Expansion" in *Globe & Mail* (March 21, 2006, pp. B1)
Pub: CTVglobemedia Publishing Inc.
Ed: Patrick Brethour. **Description:** Canadian energy giant Husky Energy Inc. has started its $90 million engineering effort to determine the cost of the $2.3 billion heavy-oil up gradation expansion plan. Details of the project are elaborated upon.

24272 ■ "Ian Gordon" in *Canadian Business* (Vol. 81, Summer 2008, No. 9, pp. 10)
Pub: Rogers Media Ltd.
Ed: Matthew McClearn. **Description:** Bolder Investment Partners' Ian Gordon discussed the economic theory promulgated by Russian economist Nikolai Kondratieff. The cycle begins with a rising economy then followed by deflationary depression. Details of his views on the Kondratieff cycle and its application to the current economy are presented.

24273 ■ "Ideas at Work: The Reality of Costs" in *Business Strategy Review* (Vol. 21, Summer 2010, No. 2, pp. 40)
Pub: Wiley-Blackwell
Ed: Jules Goddard. **Description:** If you think that cost cutting is the surest way to business success, the author wants to challenge every assumption you hold. Costs are an outcome of sound strategy, never the goal of strategy. He offers a new perspective on what counts when it comes to costs.

24274 ■ "Ill Winds; Cuba's Economy" in *The Economist* (Vol. 390, January 3, 2009, No. 8612, pp. 20)
Pub: The Economist Newspaper Inc.
Description: Cuba's long-term economic prospects remain poor with the economy forecasted to grow only 4.3 percent for the year, about half of the original forecast, due in part to Hurricane Gustav which caused $10 billion in damage and disrupted the food-supply network and devastated farms across the region; President Raul Castro made raising agricultural production a national priority and the rise in global commodity prices hit the country hard. The only bright spot has been the rise in tourism which is up 9.3 percent over 2007.

24275 ■ "In Puerto Rico, Slow and Steady Wins Race" in *Globe & Mail* (February 24, 2007, pp. B3)
Pub: CTVglobemedia Publishing Inc.
Ed: Andrew Willis. **Description:** The plan of Scotiabank de Puerto Rico's chief executive officer Richard Waugh to improve its market presence using its international banking relations is discussed.

24276 ■ "Inland Snaps Up Rival REITs" in *Crain's Chicago Business* (Vol. 31, November 17, 2008, No. 46, pp. 3)
Pub: Crain Communications, Inc.
Ed: Alby Gallun. **Description:** Discusses Inland American Real Estate Trust Inc., a real estate investment trust that is napping up depressed shares of publicly traded competitors, a possible first step toward taking over these companies; however, with hotel and retail properties accounting for approximately 70 percent of its portfolio, the company could soon face its own difficulties.

24277 ■ "Innovating Globally" in *Business Strategy Review* (Vol. 21, Spring 2010, No. 1, pp. 24)
Pub: Wiley-Blackwell
Ed: Costas Markides, Stuart Crainer. **Description:** Costas Markides has spent over two decades studying business strategy and innovation. Recently, he has been focusing on the bigger picture of how people can address major social problems. Can the techniques used by managers to create innovation inside organizations work with global change?

24278 ■ "Inside the New Nortel" in *Canadian Business* (Vol. 79, November 6, 2006, No. 22, pp. 93)
Pub: Rogers Media
Ed: Andrew Wahl. **Description:** The team plans of Nortel Networks to improve its technology market by appointing new team are analyzed.

24279 ■ *Instinct: Tapping Your Entrepreneurial DNA to Achieve Your Business Goals*
Pub: Warner Books, Incorporated
Ed: Mary H. Frakes; Thomas L. Harrison. **Released:** September 2006. **Price:** $15.99. **Description:** Research shows that entrepreneurs may attribute their success to genetics.

24280 ■ "Insurers No Longer Paying Premium for Advertising" in *Brandweek* (Vol. 49, April 21, 2008, No. 16, pp. SR3)
Pub: VNU Business Media, Inc.
Ed: Eric Newman. **Description:** Insurance companies are cutting their advertising budgets after years of accelerated double-digit growth in spending due to the economic downturn, five years of record-breaking ad spend and a need to cut expenditures as claims costs rise and a competitive market keeps premiums in place. Statistical data included.

24281 ■ "Integrating Your Compliance Program" in *Franchising World* (Vol. 42, November 2010, No. 11, pp. 49)
Pub: International Franchise Association
Ed: Melanie Bergeron. **Description:** Compliance is integral to every part of any business operation and it is necessary for a company to make standards and compliance to those standards a priority.

24282 ■ "The Intrawest Empire" in *Canadian Business* (Vol. 79, October 9, 2006, No. 20, pp. 27)
Pub: Rogers Media
Ed: Erik Heinrich. **Description:** The future development plans of Intrawest Corp., are discussed. Strategic plans of Joe Houssian, the chairman, president and chief executive officer of Intrawest Corp., are also presented.

24283 ■ "Intrawest Puts Itself on Market" in *Globe & Mail* (March 1, 2006, pp. B1)
Pub: CTVglobemedia Publishing Inc.
Ed: Elizabeth Church. **Description:** The reasons behind the decision of Intrawest Corp. to go for sale or seek partnerships are presented. The company appointed Goldman Sachs & Co. to meet the purpose.

24284 ■ "Investing in the IT that Makes a Competitive Difference" in *Harvard Business Review* (Vol. 86, July-August 2008, No. 8, pp. 98)
Pub: Harvard Business School Press
Ed: Andrew McAfee; Erik Brynjolfsson. **Description:** Components of a successful information technology management strategy are examined. These techniques are broad in spectrum, produce immediate results, are consistent and precise, facilitate monitoring, and promote enforceability.

24285 ■ "Iogen, VW Look to Build Ethanol Plant" in *Globe & Mail* (January 9, 2006, pp. B3)
Pub: CTVglobemedia Publishing Inc.
Ed: Simon Tuck. **Description:** Iogen Corp. and Volkswagen AG plan cellulose ethanol plant in Germany. The details of the project are presented.

24286 ■ "Irene Rosenfeld; Chairman and CEO, Kraft Foods Inc." in *Crain's Chicago Business* (Vol. 31, May 5, 2008, No. 18, pp. 31)
Pub: Crain Communications, Inc.
Ed: David Sterrett. **Description:** Profile of Irene Rosenfeld who is the chairman and CEO of Kraft Foods Inc. and is entering the second year of a three-year plan to boost sales of well-known brands such as Oreo, Velveeta and Oscar Mayer while facing soaring commodity costs and a declining market-share. Ms. Rosenfeld's turnaround strategy also entails spending more on advertising and giving managers more control over their budgets and product development.

24287 ■ "Jamieson Eyes $175 Million Trust IPO" in *Globe & Mail* (March 7, 2006, pp. B1)
Pub: CTVglobemedia Publishing Inc.
Ed: Sinclair Stewart; Leonard Zehr. **Description:** The reasons behind $175 million initial public offering plans of Jamieson Laboratories Ltd. are presented.

24288 ■ "Just Add Water and Lily Pads" in *Crain's Chicago Business* (Vol. 31, April 28, 2008, No. 17, pp. 50)
Pub: Crain Communications, Inc.
Ed: Phuong Ly. **Description:** Aquascape Inc., a major manufacturer of pond-building supplies, is using the recent drought in the South which hurt its business significantly to create a new product: an upscale, decorative version of the rain barrel which will collect rainwater to circulate through a pond or a fountain.

24289 ■ "Just Hang Up" in *Barron's* (Vol. 88, March 10, 2008, No. 10, pp. 45)
Pub: Dow Jones & Company, Inc.
Ed: Tiernan Ray. **Description:** Sprint's shares are expected to continue falling while the company attempts to attract subscribers by cutting prices, cutting earnings in the process. The company faces tougher competition from better-financed AT&T and Verizon Communications.

24290 ■ "Kawasaki's New Top Gun" in *Brandweek* (Vol. 49, April 21, 2008, No. 16, pp. 18)
Pub: VNU Business Media, Inc.
Description: Discusses Kawasaki's marketing plan which included designing an online brochure in which visitors could create a video by building their own test track on a grid and then selecting visual special effects and musical overlay. This engaging and innovative marketing technique generated more than 166,000 unique users within the first three months of being launched.

24291 ■ "Keeping Railcars 'Busy At All Times' At TTX" in *Crain's Chicago Business* (Vol. 31, April 28, 2008, No. 17, pp. 6)
Pub: Crain Communications, Inc.
Ed: Bob Tita. **Description:** Profile of the president of Chicago railcar pool operator TTX Co. and his business plan for the company which includes improving fleet management and car purchasing through better use of data on railroad demand.

24292 ■ "Kinetico Exec Going Global to Increase Growth Flow" in *Crain's Cleveland Business* (Vol. 28, October 1, 2007, No. 39, pp. 5)
Pub: Crain Communications, Inc.
Ed: David Bennett. **Description:** Shamus Hurley, the new CEO and president of Kinetico Inc., a manufacturer of water filtering and softening equipment for residential, commercial and municipal use, plans to expand the company to target markets overseas.

24293 ■ "Kroger Girds for Invasion of U.K. Chain" in *Business Courier* (Vol. 24, November 2, 2008, No. 29, pp. 1)
Pub: American City Business Journals, Inc.
Ed: Jon Newberry. **Description:** Tesco PLC will be opening its first Fresh & Easy Neighborhood Markets in Southern California. The company has committed $500 million per year to get a share of the $500 billion US food retailing market and will be opening more stores in quick succession. Tesco's arrival can be difficult for Kroger because Kroger had obtained much of its success by using Tesco's UK model.

24294 ■ "Lafley Gives Look At His Game Plan" in *Business Courier* (Vol. 24, March 21, 2008, No. 50, pp. 1)
Pub: American City Business Journals, Inc.
Ed: Lisa Biank Fasig. **Description:** Overview of A.G. Lafley's book entitled 'The Game-Changer', is presented. Lafley, Procter & Gamble Co.'s chief executive officer, documented his philosophy and strategy in his book. His work also includes Procter & Gamble's hands-on initiatives such as mock-up grocery stores and personal interviews with homeowners.

24295 ■ "Land Agent Taken Over" in *Farmer's Weekly* (March 28, 2008, No. 320)
Pub: Reed Business Information
Description: Property business Smiths Gore will take over Cluttons' rural division, one of the oldest names in land agency. Cluttons said it had decided to sell its

rural business as part of a strategic repositioning that would refocus the business on commercial, residential and overseas opportunities.

24296 ■ "Land on Boardwalk" in *Canadian Business* (Vol. 82, April 27, 2009, No. 7, pp. 19)
Pub: Rogers Media
Ed: Calvin Leung. **Description:** Boardwalk REIT remains as one of the most attractive real estate investment trusts in Canada, with 73 percent of analysts rating the firm a Buy. Analyst Neil Downey believes that good management, as well as a good business model, makes Boardwalk a good investment. Downey is concerned however, that a worsening of Alberta's economy could significantly impact Boardwalk.

24297 ■ "Last Founder Standing" in *Conde Nast Portfolio* (Vol. 2, June 2008, No. 6, pp. 124)
Pub: Conde Nast Publications, Inc.
Ed: Kevin Maney. **Description:** Interview with Amazon CEO Jeff Bezos in which he discusses the economy, the company's new distribution center and the hiring of employees for it, e-books, and the overall vision for the future of the firm.

24298 ■ "Lathrop Finds Partner In LA" in *The Business Journal-Serving Metropolitan Kansas City* (Vol. 27, November 21, 2008, No. 11, pp. 1)
Pub: American City Business Journals, Inc.
Ed: Steve Vockrodt. **Description:** Kansas, Missouri-based Lathrop and Gage LLP is planning to merge with Spillane Shaeffer Aronoff Bandlow LLP. The merging of the business law firms will add entertainment clients to Lathrop's fold. Comments from executives are also presented.

24299 ■ *Leap! 101 Ways to Grow Your Business*
Pub: Career Press, Inc.
Ed: Stephanie Chandler. **Released:** August 8, 2010. **Price:** $15.99. **Description:** Business growth requires more than a business plan and a dream. Tools and techniques to take a small company to the next level are outlined.

24300 ■ "Leaving a Legacy: Patricia Latimore and Bourdi Apreala Build a Comprehensive Estate Plan" in *Black Enterprise* (January 2008)
Pub: Earl G. Graves Publishing Co. Inc.
Ed: Cliff Hocker. **Description:** Estate planning is critical for anyone, especially small business owners.

24301 ■ "Lehman's Hail Mary Pass" in *Business Week* (September 22, 2008, No. 4100, pp. 28)
Pub: McGraw-Hill Companies, Inc.
Ed: Matthew Goldstein; David Henry; Ben Levison. **Description:** Overview of Lehman Brothers' CEO Richard Fuld's plan to keep the firm afloat and end the stock's plunge downward; Fuld's strategy calls for selling off a piece of the firm's investment management business.

24302 ■ "Like Father?" in *Canadian Business* (Vol. 79, Winter 2006, No. 24, pp. 38)
Pub: Rogers Media
Ed: Zena Olijnyk. **Description:** The achievements of the chairman of Thomson Corp., David Thomson, are discussed. The plans of David Thomson to diversify into different areas of business are discussed.

24303 ■ "Listen to Bond Market on Tembec" in *Globe & Mail* (January 25, 2006, pp. B1)
Pub: CTVglobemedia Publishing Inc.
Ed: Derek DeCloet. **Description:** The feasibility of Tembec Inc.'s restructuring efforts is discussed.

24304 ■ "Lombard Leaves Starbucks" in *Black Enterprise* (Vol. 38, July 2008, No. 12, pp. 28)
Pub: Earl G. Graves Publishing Co. Inc.
Ed: Tamara E. Holmes. **Description:** Ken Lombard stepped down from his position as head of Starbuck's entertainment division; the company is restructuring its entertainment unit in an attempt to revitalize sales and reduce costs.

24305 ■ "Looking Back" in *Entrepreneur* (Vol. 36, March 2008, No. 3, pp. 118)
Pub: Entrepreneur Media Inc.
Ed: Romanus Wolter. **Description:** Entrepreneurs can learn from their mistakes and improve current operations by documenting new strategies and ideas from them, evaluating information and its possible effects, and integrating what has been learned with future plans.

24306 ■ "Looking For Financing?" in *Hispanic Business* (Vol. 30, July-August 2008, No. 7-8, pp. 16)
Pub: Hispanic Business, Inc.
Ed: Frank Nelson. **Description:** Investment firms want to know about businesses that need funding for either expansion or acquisition; companies fitting this profile are interviewed and their perceptions are discussed. Investment firms need businesses to be realistic in their expectations and business plans which show spending of funds and expected benefits, long term goals, track record and strong management teams.

24307 ■ "Losses Threaten Comp Care's Future Viability" in *The Business Journal-Serving Greater Tampa Bay* (Vol. 28, August 15, 2008, No. 34)
Pub: American City Business Journals, Inc.
Ed: Margie Manning. **Description:** Comprehensive Care Corp. expressed that it may have to cease or drastically curtail its operations if it won't be able to raise additional funding in the next two or three months. The firm, which provides managed behavioral health care services, is also believed to be exploring a sale. Other views and information on Comprehensive Care's finances and plans are presented.

24308 ■ "Lotus Starts Slowly, Dodges Subprime Woes" in *Crain's Detroit Business* (Vol. 24, April 14, 2008, No. 15, pp. 3)
Pub: Crain Communications, Inc.
Ed: Tom Henderson. **Description:** Discusses Lotus Bancorp Inc. and their business plan, which although is not right on target due to the subprime mortgage meltdown, is in a much better position than its competitors due to the quality of their loans.

24309 ■ "Loyalty Pays" in *Entrepreneur* (Vol. 36, February 2008, No. 2, pp. 63)
Pub: Entrepreneur Media Inc.
Ed: David Worrell. **Description:** Michael Vadini, chief executive officer of Titan Technology Partners looks after his stockholders and investors by making sure that they are protected from risk. Having been affected by the downturn in the technology industry between 2001 and 2004, Vadini granted his investors a liquidity preference. Details regarding his actions to retain investor loyalty are discussed.

24310 ■ "The Macomb Group: Bigger Can Be Better" in *Crain's Detroit Business* (Vol. 24, September 29, 2008, No. 39, pp. 34)
Pub: Crain Communications, Inc.
Ed: Chad Halcom. **Description:** Overview of the plan of The Macomb Group includes a strategy of growing from a small supplier to a medium-sized regional distributor of valves, pipes and fittings.

24311 ■ "Magna Stalwart to Push for Product Coups" in *Globe & Mail* (April 9, 2007, pp. B1)
Pub: CTVglobemedia Publishing Inc.
Ed: Greg Keenan. **Description:** The resignation of Fred Gingl from the vice-chairmanship of the board of directors of Magna International Inc. is described. Mr. Gingl's plans to create wealth for Magna International Inc. through the development of new products are discussed.

24312 ■ "Magna in Talks on Building Cars for DaimlerChrysler" in *Globe & Mail* (February 27, 2007, pp. B1)
Pub: CTVglobemedia Publishing Inc.
Ed: Greg Keenan. **Description:** The plans of Magna International Inc. to purchase securities of Chrysler Corp. are discussed. The possibility of the manufacture of cars by Magna International Inc. for DaimlerChrysler AG is discussed.

24313 ■ "Magna Wants to Help Chrysler, but a Takeover's Not on the Cards" in *Globe & Mail* (March 1, 2007, pp. B1)
Pub: CTVglobemedia Publishing Inc.
Ed: Greg Keenan. **Description:** The plans of Magna International Inc. to help Chrysler Corp. to overcome its financial problems are discussed. The appointment of Michael Neuman as the chief executive officer of Magna International Inc. is described.

24314 ■ "Major Tech Employers Pulling Out" in *Sacramento Business Journal* (Vol. 25, August 1, 2008, No. 22, pp. 1)
Pub: American City Business Journals, Inc.
Ed: Celia Lamb. **Description:** Biotechnology company Affymetrix Inc. is planning to close its West Sacramento, California plant and lay off 110 employees. The company said it will expand a corporate restructuring plan. Affymetrix also plans to lease out or sell its building at Riverside Parkway.

24315 ■ "Managers as Visionaries: a Skill That Can Be Learned" in *Strategy and Leadership* (Vol. 39, September-October 2011, No. 5, pp. 56-58)
Pub: Emerald Group Publishing Inc.
Ed: Stephen M. Millett. **Description:** A study uses research findings to examine whether visionary management can be learned. Results conclude that managers can learn visionary management through intuitive pattern recognition of trends and by using scenarios for anticipating and planning for likely future occurrences.

24316 ■ "Managing the Facebookers; Business" in *The Economist* (Vol. 390, January 3, 2009, No. 8612, pp. 10)
Pub: Economist Newspaper Ltd.
Description: According to a report from PricewaterhouseCoopers, a business consultancy, workers from Generation Y, also known as the Net Generation, are more difficult to recruit and integrate into companies that practice traditional business acumen. 61 percent of chief executive managers say that they have trouble with younger employees who tend to be more narcissistic and more interested in personal fulfillment with a need for frequent feedback and an over-precise set of objectives on the path to promotion which can be hard for managers who are used to a different relationship with their subordinates. Older bosses should prepare to make some concessions to their younger talent since some of the issues that make them happy include cheaper online ways to communicate and additional coaching, both of which are good for business.

24317 ■ "Mandel Site Favored For UWM Hall" in *The Business Journal-Milwaukee* (Vol. 25, September 19, 2008, No. 52, pp. A1)
Pub: American City Business Journals, Inc.
Description: University of Wisconsin-Milwaukee student residence hall's leading location is a site pushed by Mandel Group Inc. Real estate sources say that the developer's proposal offers the best opportunity for business development and the least conflict with nearby neighborhoods. Plans for the Mandel site are presented.

24318 ■ "Many Roads Lead to Value" in *Barron's* (Vol. 88, March 10, 2008, No. 10, pp. 46)
Pub: Dow Jones & Company, Inc.
Ed: Lawrence C. Strauss. **Description:** David J. Williams, lead manager of Excelsior Value & Restructuring Fund, invests in struggling companies and those companies whose turnarounds show promise. Morgan Stanley, Lehman Brothers, and Petroleo Brasileiro are some of the companies he holds shares in, while he has unloaded shares of Citigroup, Freddie Mac, and Sallie Mae.

24319 ■ "Marriott Checks Out Hotel Prospect" in *The Business Journal-Serving Metropolitan Kansas City* (Vol. 27, November 14, 2008, No. 10)
Pub: American City Business Journals, Inc.
Description: Marriott International Inc. is planning to operate a hotel in Kansas City, Missouri and may take over the Kansas City Marriot Downtown although other hotel operators are interested in bidding on the project.

24320 ■ "Massive Ford Restructuring to Cut 1,200 More Canadian Jobs" in *Globe & Mail* (January 24, 2006, pp. B1)
Pub: CTVglobemedia Publishing Inc.
Ed: Greg Keenan. **Description:** The details on streamlining of operations of Ford Motor Co., in Canada, are presented.

24321 ■ "Mayfair Considers Moving Boston Store" in *The Business Journal-Milwaukee* (Vol. 25, September 5, 2008, No. 50, pp. 1)
Pub: American City Business Journals, Inc.
Ed: Rich Kirchen. **Description:** Milwaukee, Wisconsin-based Bon-Ton Stores is planning to relocate its Boston Store at the Mayfair Mall. The existing store is to be redeveloped into smaller specialty shops. Details of the new facility are also presented.

24322 ■ "MBA Project Turns on Tastebuds" in *The Business Journal - Serving Phoenix and the Valley of the Sun* (Vol. 28, August 15, 2008, No. 50)
Pub: American City Business Journals, Inc.
Ed: Angela Gonzales. **Description:** Amol Khade, Venkat Nallapati and Govind Arora, master of business administration graduates from Thunderbird School of Global Management, have opened an Indian restaurant, called The Daba, in Tempe, Arizona. The Indian name of the restaurant means 'a place for travelers to stop for rest and food'. Franchise plans for the restaurant are discussed.

24323 ■ "McCormick Focuses on Customer, Dealer Service" in *Farm Industry News* (September 17, 2010)
Pub: Penton Business Media Inc.
Description: McCormick has developed a new plan that focuses on fast and complete service to both customers and dealers.

24324 ■ "Meadowbrook CEO Sees 20 Percent Growth With New Acquisition" in *Crain's Detroit Business* (Vol. 24, March 10, 2008, No. 10, pp. 4)
Pub: Crain Communications, Inc.
Ed: Jay Greene. **Description:** Discusses the major turnaround of Meadowbrook Insurance Group after Robert Cubbin became CEO and implemented a new business strategy.

24325 ■ "Measure Your Business Plan Results" in *Entrepreneur* (January 6, 2009)
Pub: Entrepreneur Media Inc.
Ed: Tim Berry. **Description:** Although no business plan is ever right on target, it is still essential for every business owner to create one; the way in which to analyze the actual results compared to the plan are discussed.

24326 ■ "Microsoft's Big Gamble" in *Canadian Business* (Vol. 81, March 3, 2008, No. 3, pp. 13)
Pub: Rogers Media
Ed: Andrew Wahl. **Description:** Microsoft Corp. is taking a big risk in buying Yahoo, as it is expected to pay more than $31 a share to finalize the acquisition. The deal would be seven and a half times bigger than any other that Microsoft has entered before, an execution of such deal is also anticipated to become a challenge for Microsoft. Recommendations on how Microsoft should handle the integration of the two businesses are given.

24327 ■ "Midtown Tampa Bay Taking Shape" in *The Business Journal-Serving Greater Tampa Bay* (Vol. 28, September 12, 2008, No. 38, pp. 1)
Pub: American City Business Journals, Inc.
Ed: Janet Leiser. **Description:** Midtown Tampa Bay's 610,000 square foot shopping and entertainment center is being planned in Florida and is to replace the Tampa Bay One project proposed years earlier. The retail center is to be developed by Bromley Cos. and Opus South Corp. and is expected to have five buildings. Other details about the plan are discussed.

24328 ■ "Midwest Looks 'Back to the Future" in *The Business Journal-Milwaukee* (Vol. 25, July 18, 2008, No. 43, pp. A1)
Pub: American City Business Journals, Inc.
Ed: Rich Rovito. **Description:** Midwest Air Group Inc. announced plans to reduce their work force by 40 percent or 1,200 employees after an earlier announcement of a drastic fleet reduction. These steps are being taken by the company in an effort to avoid filing bankruptcy since this would cost the airline millions of dollars in legal and other professional fees.

24329 ■ "Midwest Seeks Concessions From Creditors" in *The Business Journal-Milwaukee* (Vol. 25, July 25, 2008, No. 44, pp. A1)
Pub: American City Business Journals, Inc.
Ed: Rich Rovito. **Description:** Midwest Airlines Inc. is turning to creditors and lease holders for the financial aspect of its restructuring, which involves going back to serving popular business destinations. Chief executive officer Timothy believes that the company can survive in a niche market as long as it provides quality service. He discusses Midwest's restructuring plan.

24330 ■ "Million-Dollar Babies" in *Black Enterprise* (Vol. 38, January 2008, No. 6, pp. 64)
Pub: Earl G. Graves Publishing Co. Inc.
Ed: Tennille M. Robinson. **Description:** Books and programs to help any small business grow to the $1 million mark are outlined.

24331 ■ "Modern-Day Midas Hasn't Lost Touch" in *Globe & Mail* (January 19, 2006, pp. B4)
Pub: CTVglobemedia Publishing Inc.
Ed: Shirley Won. **Description:** The investment plans of chief executive officer Rob McEwen of U.S. Gold Corp. are presented.

24332 ■ "Monaco Pay Cut Draws Attention" in *The Business Journal-Portland* (Vol. 25, August 8, 2008, No. 22, pp. 1)
Pub: American City Business Journals, Inc.
Ed: Erik Siemers. **Description:** Monaco Coach Corp. cut the salaries of five top executives in an effort to reduce the company's $178 million worth of inventory. The executives can earn the lost salary back if the inventory is reduced by $58 million a year after August 2008.

24333 ■ "More Manufacturers Scout Military Contracts As Auto Industry Lags" in *Crain's Detroit Business* (Vol. 24, September 29, 2008, No. 39)
Pub: Crain Communications, Inc.
Ed: Chad Halcom. **Description:** Many Michigan manufacturers are looking to grow with new military contracts now that the reality of the auto industry is becoming more clear; these companies see that the government contracts may be the only way in which they will be able to stay in business through these rough economic times.

24334 ■ "A Motorola Spinoff Is No Panacea" in *Barron's* (Vol. 88, March 31, 2008, No. 13, pp. 19)
Pub: Dow Jones & Company, Inc.
Ed: Mark Veverka. **Description:** Motorola's plan to try and spinoff their handset division is bereft of details as to how or specifically when in 2009 the spinoff would occur. There's no reason to buy the shares since there's a lot of execution risk to the plan. Motorola needs to hire a proven cellphone executive and develop a compelling new cellphone platform.

24335 ■ "'Mr. CEO, Please Do Elaborate On Your Firm's Metrics'" in *Business Courier* (Vol. 24, February 29, 2008, No. 47, pp. 1)
Pub: American City Business Journals, Inc.
Ed: Jon Newberry. **Description:** Discusses a rogue caller who goes by the name of Joe Herrick, Steven Nissan and Joe Harris has joined in over a dozen conference calls, asking chief executive officers on their plans and commenting on the companies' operations. The mystery caller attempts to pass himself off as a financial analyst. Transcripts of some conference calls, in which the rogue caller is involved, are provided.

24336 ■ "Mr. Deeds" in *Canadian Business* (Vol. 81, March 31, 2008, No. 5, pp. 24)
Pub: Rogers Media
Ed: Thomas Watson. **Description:** Ron Sandler has the right experience to save Northern Rock PLC get through its liquidity problems. Sandler is known for saving Lloyd's of London in the mid-90's and he is not afraid to make enemies. Ron Sandler's assignment to help Northern Rock comes at a time when the health of the U.K. housing is not great.

24337 ■ "Muddy Portfolio Raises a Question: Just What Is National City Worth?" in *Crain's Detroit Business* (Vol. 24, April 7, 2008, No. 14)
Pub: Crain Communications, Inc.
Ed: Jay Miller. **Description:** National City Bank is looking at strategies to help it deal with its credit and loan problems which are reflected in its falling stock price. One possible solution is a merger with another bank, however most national banks are facing their own home-loan portfolio issues and may be unable to tackle another company's unresolved problems. Statistical data included.

24338 ■ "Museum Center to Exhibit New Look" in *Business Courier* (Vol. 24, February 22, 2008, No. 46, pp. 1)
Pub: American City Business Journals, Inc.
Ed: Dan Monk. **Description:** Discusses a $120 million renovation is being planned for the Cincinnati Museum Center complex at Union Terminal. The project aims to build a 14-acre park and office spaces in the area. Details of the Museum Center's renovation plans are given.

24339 ■ "NBC" in *Brandweek* (Vol. 49, April 21, 2008, No. 16, pp. SR6)
Pub: VNU Business Media, Inc.
Ed: John Consoli. **Description:** Provides contact information for sales and marketing personnel for the NBC network as well as a listing of the station's top programming and an analysis of the current season and the target audience for those programs running in the current season. NBC also devised a new strategy of announcing its prime-time schedule 52 weeks in advance which was a hit for advertisers who felt this gave them a better opportunity to plan for product placement. Even with the station's creative sales programs, they could face a challenge from Fox in terms of upfront advertisement purchases.

24340 ■ "Needed: A Strategy; Banking In China" in *The Economist* (Vol. 390, January 3, 2009, No. 8612, pp. 54)
Pub: The Economist Newspaper Inc.
Description: International banks are competing for a role in China but are finding obstacles in their paths such as a reduction in the credit their operations may receive from Chinese banks and the role they can play in the public capital markets which remain limited.

24341 ■ "Net Connections" in *Black Enterprise* (Vol. 38, July 2008, No. 12, pp. 28)
Pub: Earl G. Graves Publishing Co. Inc.
Ed: Anthony S. Calypso. **Description:** Marketers are making strategic partnerships with online social networks in an attempt to gain further market reach. The value of these networks appears to be on the rise forcing media companies to recalculate their strategies for delivering products to customers.

24342 ■ *Never Bet the Farm: How Entrepreneurs Take Risks, Make Decisions and How You Can, Too*
Pub: Jossey Bass
Ed: Anthony Iaquinto; Stephen Spinelli Jr. **Released:** March 17, 2006. **Price:** $19.95. **Description:** Two successful entrepreneurs offer advice for others launching new businesses. The authors show that preparing for setbacks and using a framework to reduce risks and simplify decision making can increase chances for success.

24343 ■ "The New Arsenal of Risk Management" in *Harvard Business Review* (Vol. 86, September 2008, No. 9, pp. 92)
Pub: Harvard Business School Press
Ed: Kevin Bueler; Andrew Freeman; Ron Hulme. **Description:** Goldman Sachs Group Inc. is used to illustrate methods for successful risk management. The investment bank's business principles, partnerships, and oversight practices are discussed.

24344 ■ "A New Perspective On the Development Model for Family Business" in *Family Business Review* (Vol. 19, December 2006, No. 4, pp. 317)
Pub: Family Firm Institute Inc.
Ed: Matthew W. Rutherford, Lori A. Muse, Sharon L. Oswald. **Description:** Empirical test model of the developmental model for family business is proposed and owner, firm and family characteristics which have an impact on the development model are examined.

24345 ■ "A New Will to Win" in *Harvard Business Review* (Vol. 88, September 2010, No. 9, pp. 110)
Pub: Harvard Business School Publishing
Ed: Daniel McGinn. **Description:** Importance of succession and contingency planning are emphasized in this account of Rick Hendrick's response to business loss coupled with personal tragedy. Focus and determination in leadership are also discussed.

24346 ■ "New Year, New Estate Plan" in *Hawaii Business* (Vol. 53, February 2008, No. 8, pp. 54)
Pub: Hawaii Business Publishing
Ed: Antony M. Orme. **Description:** Discusses the start of the new year which can be a time to revise wills and estate plans as failure to do so may create problems of unequal inheritance and increase in estate tax exemption, which could disinherit beneficiaries. Other circumstances that can prompt changes in wills and estate plans are presented.

24347 ■ "Nexen, OPTI Boost Oil Sands Spending" in *Globe & Mail* (February 18, 2006, pp. B5)
Pub: CTVglobemedia Publishing Inc.
Ed: Dave Ebner. **Description:** The reasons behind the decision of Nexen Inc. and OPTI Canada Inc., to allocate 10 percent more funding on oil sands, are presented.

24348 ■ "Nike's Next Splash" in *The Business Journal-Portland* (Vol. 25, August 22, 2008, No. 24, pp. 1)
Pub: American City Business Journals, Inc.
Ed: Erik Siemers. **Description:** Business analysts expect Nike to bid for the endorsement services of swimmer Michael Phelps after the swimmer's contract with Speedo expires. The company, however, is a lightweight in the swimming apparel market and is not focusing on swimming as a growth sector.

24349 ■ "No Frills - And No Dodge" in *Crain's Detroit Business* (Vol. 24, September 22, 2008, No. 38, pp. 3)
Pub: Crain Communications, Inc.
Ed: Bradford Wernie. **Description:** Chrysler LLC is in the middle of a business plan known as Project Genesis, a five-year strategy in which the company will reduce the dealer count by combining its Jeep, Chrysler and Dodge brands under one rooftop wherever possible. Not every dealer will be able to arrange this deal because of the investment required to expand stores in which have low-overhead; many of these stores feel that low-overhead structures are more likely to survive difficult times than the larger stores in which the Genesis consolidation plan intends to implement.

24350 ■ "No Risk? No Reward" in *Canadian Business* (Vol. 79, September 11, 2006, No. 18, pp. 93)
Pub: Rogers Media
Ed: Dennis Seguin. **Description:** Box office performances of the Canadian films are presented. Strategies to revitalize the film businesses in Canada are suggested.

24351 ■ "Nobody Knows What To Do" in *Barron's* (Vol. 88, March 17, 2008, No. 11, pp. 40)
Pub: Dow Jones & Company, Inc.
Ed: Mark Veverka. **Description:** Attendees of the South by Southwest Interactive conference failed to get an insight on how to make money on the Web from former Walt Disney CEO Michael Eisner when Eisner said there's no proven business model for financing projects. Eisner said he finances his projects with the help of his connections to get product-placement deals.

24352 ■ "Nortel Starting From Scratch" in *Globe & Mail* (February 24, 2006, pp. B3)
Pub: CTVglobemedia Publishing Inc.
Ed: Catherine McLean. **Description:** The restructuring efforts of chief executive officer Mike Zafirovski of Nortel Networks Corp. are presented.

24353 ■ "Not the Six O'Clock News" in *Canadian Business* (Vol. 80, January 15, 2007, No. 2, pp. 10)
Pub: Rogers Media
Ed: Marlene Rego. **Description:** The proposal by Paul Jay, the chief executive officer of Independent World Television, to launch The Real News Project, is discussed. The objective of the project is to establish an independent news and current affairs network solely through viewers.

24354 ■ "Nursing Home Group Put on the Block" in *Globe & Mail* (February 23, 2006, pp. B1)
Pub: CTVglobemedia Publishing Inc.
Ed: Elizabeth Church. **Description:** The reasons behind the decision of Exetendicare Inc. to go for sale are presented.

24355 ■ "N.Y. Investors Reject AnorMed Board Proposal" in *Globe & Mail* (February 21, 2006, pp. B11)
Pub: CTVglobemedia Publishing Inc.
Ed: Leonard Zehr. **Description:** The reasons behind the denial of investors over the restructuring plans of AnorMed are presented.

24356 ■ "Ohio Commerce Draws Closer to Profitability" in *Crain's Cleveland Business* (Vol. 28, October 29, 2007, No. 43, pp. 14)
Pub: Crain Communications, Inc.
Ed: Shawn A. Turner. **Description:** Overview of the business plan of Ohio Commerce Bank, a de novo, or startup bank that is close to turning the corner to profitability. The bank opened in November 2006 and focuses on dealing with small businesses totaling $5 million or less in annual revenues.

24357 ■ "Olympus is Urged to Revise Board" in *Wall Street Journal Eastern Edition* (November 28, 2011, pp. B3)
Pub: Dow Jones & Company Inc.
Ed: Phred Dvorak. **Description:** Koji Miyata, once a director on the board of troubled Japanese photographic equipment company, is urging the company to reorganize its board, saying the present group should resign their board seats but keep their management positions. The company has come under scrutiny for its accounting practices and costly acquisitions.

24358 ■ "OMERS Joins Bid for U.K. Port Giant" in *Globe & Mail* (March 28, 2006, pp. B1)
Pub: CTVglobemedia Publishing Inc.
Ed: Paul Waldie. **Description:** The plans of Ontario Municipal Employees Retirement Board to partner with Goldman Sachs Group Inc., in order to acquire Associated British Ports PLC, are presented.

24359 ■ "On a Mission: Ginch Gonch Wants You to Get Rid of Your Tighty Whities" in *Canadian Business* (Vol. 81, September 29, 2008, No. 16)
Pub: Rogers Media Ltd.
Ed: Michelle Magnan. **Description:** New Equity Capital acquired underwear maker Ginch Gonch in July 2008; founder Jason Sutherland kept his position as creative director of the company and will retain his title as 'director of stitches and inches'. The company is known for its products, which are reminiscent of the days when people wore underwear covered in cowboys and stars as kids. The company also claims that Nelly, Justin Timberlake, and Hilary Duff have worn their products.

24360 ■ "On a Roll" in *Canadian Business* (Vol. 79, Winter 2006, No. 24, pp. 49)
Pub: Rogers Media
Ed: Thomas Watson. **Description:** The efforts of the Canadian automobile spare parts manufacturer, Magna International Inc., to expand into the the Russian market, are described.

24361 ■ "One Paddle, Two Paddle" in *Hawaii Business* (Vol. 53, October 2007, No. 4, pp. 65)
Pub: Hawaii Business Publishing
Ed: Kyle Galdeira. **Description:** Oiwi Ocean Gear's strategy may not give instant profits, but it works well for the company's goal of providing high-quality apparel for paddlers. The apparel company produces and markets swimwear, paddling jerseys and active wear. The company's strategy is compared with the selling of mass-produced clothes lower prices.

24362 ■ "Open Skies: Opportunity, Challenge for Airlines" in *Crain's Chicago Business* (April 21, 2008)
Pub: Crain Communications, Inc.
Ed: Paul Merrion. **Description:** Discusses the new aviation agreement between Europe and the United States known as Open Skies; the pact creates opportunities for U.S. carriers to fly to new destinations in Europe from more U.S. cities; it also allows carriers to fly between European cities, something they have not been able to do until now.

24363 ■ "O'Reilly Will Soup Up KC Warehouse" in *The Business Journal-Serving Metropolitan Kansas City* (Vol. 26, August 15, 2008, No. 49)
Pub: American City Business Journals, Inc.
Ed: Rob Roberts. **Description:** O'Reilly Automotive Inc. plans to construct a 215,000-square foot warehouse in Kansas City. The move is expected to triple the size of the company's distribution center. Other views and information on the planned warehouse construction, are presented.

24364 ■ "Organization Redesign and Innovative HRM" in *Human Resource Management* (Vol. 49, July-August 2010, No. 4, pp. 809-811)
Pub: John Wiley
Ed: Pat Lynch. **Description:** An overview of the book, 'Organization Redesign and Innovative HRM' is presented.

24365 ■ "Organizing for Disaster: Lessons from the Military" in *Business Horizons* (November-December 2007, pp. 479)
Pub: Elsevier Technology Publications
Ed: Michael R. Weeks. **Description:** Design of resilient and robust organizational structures for disaster management is discussed. These structures must be planned before disasters in order to be more effective and efficient.

24366 ■ "The Outcome of an Organization Overhaul" in *Black Enterprise* (Vol. 41, December 2010, No. 5)
Pub: Earl G. Graves Publishing Co. Inc.
Ed: Tamara E. Holmes. **Description:** Savvy business owners understand the need for change in order to stay competitive and be successful. This article examines how to manage change as well as what strategies can help employees to get with the program faster.

24367 ■ "Paramount Said to be Working on Sale of Oil Sands Assets" in *Globe & Mail* (April 24, 2007, pp. B1)
Pub: CTVglobemedia Publishing Inc.
Ed: Norval Scott. **Description:** The proposed sale of oil sands in Surmont and the shares of North American Oil Sands Corp. by Paramount Resources Ltd. is discussed.

24368 ■ "Patricia Hemingway Hall; President, Chief Operating Officer, Health Care Service Corp." in *Crain's Chicago Business* (May 5, 2008)
Pub: Crain Communications, Inc.
Ed: Mike Colias. **Description:** Profile of Patricia Hemingway Hall who is the president and chief operating officer of Health Care Service Corp., a new strategy launched by Blue Cross & Blue Shield of Illinois; the new endeavor will emphasize wellness rather than just treatment across its four health plans.

24369 ■ "Pavilions Poised for Image Overhaul" in *The Business Journal - Serving Phoenix and the Valley of the Sun* (Vol. 28, August 22, 2008)
Pub: American City Business Journals, Inc.
Ed: Jan Buchholz. **Description:** DeRitto Partners Inc. is expected to push through with plans for a major renovation of the 1.1 million-square foot Scottsdale Pavilions in Scottsdale, Arizona. An aggressive marketing campaign is planned to be included in the renovation, which aims to address high vacancy rates and competition. Views and information on the planned renovation are presented.

24370 ■ "PDX Bucks National Trend" in *The Business Journal-Portland* (Vol. 25, August 1, 2008, No. 21, pp. 1)
Pub: American City Business Journals, Inc.
Ed: Erik Siemers. **Description:** Portland International Airport could face problems as air carriers are planning to reduce capacity at the airport. The airport is showing signs of growth despite the slowdown in the airline industry. Other airlines that are planning to reduce seating capacity at the airport are also presented.

24371 ■ "People; E-Commerce, Online Games, Mobile Apps" in *Advertising Age* (Vol. 80, October 19, 2009, No. 35, pp. 14)
Pub: Crain's Communications
Ed: Nat Ives. **Description:** Profile of People Magazine and the ways in which the publisher is moving its magazine forward by exploring new concepts in a time of declining newsstand sales and advertising pages; among the strategies are e-commerce such as the brand People Style Watch in which consumers are able highlight clothing and jewelry and then connect to retailers' sites and a channel on Taxi TV, the network of video-touch screens in New Your City taxis.

24372 ■ "People; E-Commerce, Online Games, Mobile Apps: This Isn't Your Mom's People" in *Advertising Age* (Vol. 80, October 19, 2009, No. 35)
Pub: Crain's Communications
Ed: Nat Ives. **Description:** Profile of People Magazine and the ways in which the publisher is moving its magazine forward by exploring new concepts in a time of declining newsstand sales and advertising pages; among the strategies are e-commerce such as the brand People Style Watch in which consumers are able highlight clothing and jewelry and then connect to retailers' sites and a channel on Taxi TV, the network of video-touch screens in New Your City taxis.

24373 ■ "Perfecting the Process: Creating a Move Efficient Organization On Your Terms" in *Black Enterprise* (Vol. 41, October 2010, No. 3)
Pub: Earl G. Graves Publishing Co. Inc.
Ed: Tamara E. Holmes. **Description:** More than ever, entrepreneurs need to identify new ways of doing business in a cost-effective manner in order to expand their companies, while remaining true to their customer demands.

24374 ■ "Peter Gilgan" in *Canadian Business* (Vol. 82, April 27, 2009, No. 7, pp. 58)
Pub: Rogers Media
Ed: Calvin Leung. **Description:** Mattamy Homes Ltd. president and chief executive officer Peter Gilgan believes that their business model of building communities in an organized way brings advantages to the firm and for their customers. He also believes in adopting their product prices to new market realities. Gilgan considers the approvals regime in Ontario his biggest challenge in the last 20 years.

24375 ■ "Pinellas Leaders Want First Leg of Light Rail" in *The Business Journal-Serving Greater Tampa Bay* (Vol. 28, August 8, 2008, No. 33)
Pub: American City Business Journals, Inc.
Ed: Larry Halstead. **Description:** Proposed routes for the first leg of the planned light railway system in the Tampa Bay, Florida area are being presented as the Tampa Bay Area Regional Transportation Authority is about to make its master plan for the project. A sales tax for transit is being proposed to fund the project, as well as an expansion of the accompanying bus system.

24376 ■ *Planet Google: One Company's Audacious Plan to Organize Everything We Know*
Pub: Free Press
Ed: Randall Stross. **Released:** 2009. **Price:** $26.00. **Description:** The book examines Google, the leader in Internet search engines.

24377 ■ "The Play's the Thing" in *Business Strategy Review* (Vol. 21, Summer 2010, No. 2, pp. 58)
Pub: Wiley-Blackwell
Ed: Michael G. Jacobides. **Description:** Those who study and plan strategies risk falling into the traps that maps, graphs, charts and matrices present. The author feels that strategy might best be cast as a dramatic playscript that can reveal the unfolding plots of business far better than traditional strategic tools, as the landscape shifts around us.

24378 ■ "Portfolio Recovery Associates Expands Its Hampton Call Center" in *Internet Wire* (January 20, 2010)
Pub: Comtex News Network, Inc.
Description: Entering into a lease amendment in order to expand its Hampton, Virginia call center and extend its lease agreement, Portfolio Recovery Associates, Inc., a company that collects, purchases and manages defaulted consumer debt, plans to upgrade the existing space enabling them to draw on local talent.

24379 ■ *The Power of Pull: How Small Moves, Smartly Made, Can Set Big Things in Motion*
Pub: Basic Books
Ed: John Hagel III, Seely Brown, Lang Divison. **Released:** April 13, 2010. **Description:** Examination of how we can effectively address the most pressing challenges in a rapidly changing and increasingly interdependent world is addressed. New ways in which passionate thinking, creative solutions, and committed action can and will make it possible for small businesses owners to seize opportunities and remain in step with change.

24380 ■ *Prepare to Be a Teen Millionaire*
Pub: Health Communications, Inc.
Ed: Robyn Collins; Kimberly Spinks Burleson. **Released:** April 1, 2008. **Price:** $16.95. **Description:** Business reference for any teenager wishing to become a successful entrepreneur; advice is given from successful teenage millionaires. Topics covered include: choosing a business name, type, and location; use of the Internet; legal issues; branding, sales, and marketing; funding and financial management; return on investment; retirement; development of a sound business plan; and certification for minority or women-owned companies.

24381 ■ "Profico Takes Itself Off the Market" in *Globe & Mail* (March 14, 2006, pp. B1)
Pub: CTVglobemedia Publishing Inc.
Ed: Deborah Yedlin; Dave Ebner. **Description:** Profico Energy Management Ltd., Canada's largest junior energy explorer, has backed off its potential acquisition plans. The decreased prices of the natural gas are the main reasons that caused Profico to back off from the acquisition plan.

24382 ■ "Purdue Agronomist: Consider Costs Before Tilling" in *Farm Industry News* (November 8, 2011)
Pub: Penton Business Media Inc.
Ed: Lisa Schluttenhofer. **Description:** Farmers consider soil drainage, fertilizer and planting needs as well as economic thresholds before making tillage decisions, according to a Purdue extension agronomist.

24383 ■ "Q&A: Joseph Ribkoff" in *Canadian Business* (Vol. 81, March 31, 2008, No. 5, pp. 4)
Pub: Rogers Media
Ed: Zena Olijnyk. **Description:** Joseph Ribkoff started his career in the garment trade by sweeping floors and running deliveries for a dress manufacturer called Town & Country and earned $16 a week. Ribkoff says that the key to controlling costs in Canada is to invest in the latest equipment and technology to stay competitive.

24384 ■ "Quarreling Parties Keep Schenectady Redevelopment Plan In Limbo" in *The Business Review Albany* (Vol. 35, April 4, 2008, No. 53)
Pub: The Business Review
Ed: Michael DeMasi. **Description:** First National Bank of Scotia chairman Louis H. Buhrmaster opposes the Erie Boulevard design project. as it could negatively affect access to the bank. Buhrmaster, aslo a vice president for Schenectady Industrial Corp, prohibits environmental assessment at the former American Locomotive property. The issues affecting the progress of the planned redevelopment at Schenectady are analyzed

24385 ■ "Ready for the Worst? How to Disaster-Proof Your Business" in *Inc.* (Vol. 33, September 2011, No. 7, pp. 38)
Pub: Inc. Magazine
Ed: J.J. McCorvey, Dave Smith. **Description:** Twelve products to and services designed to help small businesses run smoothly in the event of a disaster are outlined.

24386 ■ "Realities May Blur Vision" in *The Business Journal-Serving Metropolitan Kansas City* (Vol. 27, September 19, 2008, No. 1, pp. 1)
Pub: American City Business Journals, Inc.
Ed: Rob Roberts. **Description:** Vision Metcalf is a study by Kansas City that depicts how Metcalf Avenue could look like if redeveloped. Redevelopment plans for the Metcalf corridor include a 20-story mixed-use building on a vacant car dealership. The challenges that the redevelopment plans will face are also analyzed.

24387 ■ "The Rebranding Game: If at First You Pick the Wrong Name, You Can Always Try, Try Again" in *Inc.* (Vol. 30, December 2008, No. 12)
Pub: Mansueto Ventures LLC
Ed: Ryan McCarthy. **Description:** Many entrepreneurs discover their firm's name can be too limiting or outdated. The process for rebranding a company is outlined.

24388 ■ "Recession-Proof Your Startup" in *Crain's Chicago Business* (Vol. 31, November 10, 2008, No. 45, pp. 24)
Pub: Crain Communications, Inc.
Description: Detailed information concerning ways in which to start a business during an economic crisis is provided. Ways in which to find financing, the importance of a solid business plan, customer service, problem-solving and finding the right niche for the region are also discussed.

24389 ■ "Recession Survival Tip: Less Is More" in *Women Entrepreneur* (December 31, 2008)
Pub: Entrepreneur Media Inc.
Ed: Suzy Girard-Ruttenberg. **Description:** These trying economic times can be an opportunity to make bold changes in one's business that may yield lasting

results, not just short-term survival; simplification, accountability and shoring up one's margins are things to look at when determining the goals of the company.

24390 ■ "Red Tape Ties Detroit Housing Rehab Plan" in *Crain's Detroit Business* (Vol. 24, September 22, 2008, No. 38, pp. 1)
Pub: Crain Communications, Inc.

Ed: Ryan Beene. **Description:** Venture-capital firm Wilherst Oxford LLC is a Florida-based company that has purchased 300 inner-city homes which were in foreclosure in Detroit. Wilherst Oxford is asking the city to forgive the existing tax and utility liens so the firm can utilize the money for home improvements. The city, however, is reluctant but has stated that they are willing to negotiate.

24391 ■ "Refreshing" in *Canadian Business* (Vol. 79, September 11, 2006, No. 18, pp. 22)
Pub: Rogers Media

Ed: Joe Castaldo. **Description:** Turnaround strategies and initiatives adopted by Canadian Beverage Corp. to boost its declining sales are presented.

24392 ■ "The Relationship Between Boards and Planning In Family Businesses" in *Family Business Review* (Vol. 19, March 2006, No. 1, pp. 65)
Pub: Family Firm Institute Inc.

Ed: Timothy Blumentritt. **Description:** Study determining the extent of control exercised by board of directors and advisory boards on business planning within family-owned businesses is covered.

24393 ■ "Renewed Vision" in *Hawaii Business* (Vol. 54, August 2008, No. 2, pp. 49)
Pub: Hawaii Business Publishing

Ed: Jason Ubay. **Description:** Saint Francis Healthcare System of Hawaii, ranked 81 in Hawaii's top 250 companies for 2008, has been rebranding to focus on senior community healthcare and sold some of its operations, which explains the decline in gross sales from $219.5M in 2006 to $122.7M in 2007. The system's senior services and home hospice service expansion are provided.

24394 ■ "Retail: Loblaw Goes for Broke" in *Canadian Business* (Vol. 80, January 29, 2007, No. 3, pp. 7)
Pub: Rogers Media

Ed: Zena Oiljnyk. **Description:** The efforts of Loblaw Companies Limited to reduce its operational expenses are described. The company's decision to reduce the number of employees at its national and regional offices, besides closing some of its facilities, is discussed.

24395 ■ "Retiring Baby Boomers and Dissatisfied Gen-Xers Cause...Brain Drain" in *Agency Sales Magazine* (Vol. 39, November 2009, No. 10)
Pub: MANA

Ed: Denise Kelly. **Description:** Due to the impending retirement of the baby boomers a critical loss of knowledge and experience in businesses will result. Creating a plan to address this loss of talent centered on the development of the younger generation is discussed.

24396 ■ "Return to Wealth; Bank Strategy" in *The Economist* (Vol. 390, January 3, 2009, No. 8612, pp. 56)
Pub: The Economist Newspaper Inc.

Description: UBS' strategy to survive these trying economic times is presented. Statistical data included. UBS has a stronger balance-sheet than most of its investment-banking peers and has reduced its portfolio.

24397 ■ *Rework*
Pub: Crown Business

Ed: Jason Fried, David Heinemeier Hansson. **Released:** March 9, 2010. **Price:** $22.00. **Description:** Works to help entrepreneurs and business owners to rethink strategy, customers, and getting things accomplished.

24398 ■ "The Road Map for Scotiabank's Asian Expansion" in *Globe & Mail* (April 7, 2007, pp. B3)
Pub: CTVglobemedia Publishing Inc.

Ed: Tara Perkins. **Description:** Executive vice-president of Bank of Nova Scotia, Rob Pitfield shares his plan to expand the bank's Asian market.

24399 ■ "Roadside Attraction" in *Hawaii Business* (Vol. 53, January 2008, No. 7, pp. 39)
Pub: Hawaii Business Publishing

Ed: Jason Ubay. **Description:** Businesses beside the Kamehameha Highway find ways to survive in a rural community. Sunshine Arts Hawaii, for instance, uses a bright-colored and huge mural to attract tourists who drive along the highway. Other techniques employed by businesses in the aforementioned are des cribed.

24400 ■ "Rock Hall Shifts Advertising to 'Significant Markets' in Region" in *Crain's Cleveland Business* (Vol. 28, July 23, 2007, No. 29, pp. 6)
Pub: Crain Communications, Inc.

Ed: John Booth. **Description:** Cleveland's Rock and Roll Hall of Fame and Museum is attempting a different marketing strategy this year with aims of reaching a broader audience in the Midwest and Great Lakes regions.

24401 ■ "'Rocket Docket' Leaves Memphis Debtors Behind" in *Commercial Appeal* (November 28, 2009)
Pub: Commercial Appeal

Ed: Bartholomew Sullivan. **Description:** According to an investigation by the Scripps Howard News Service, Memphians lodged 807 formal complaints about debt-collection practices to the Federal Trade Commission in a 2 1/2 -year period ending in July; Nearly 1/3 of the complaints involved some type of error with the debt in question. The majority of the complaints were leveled at NCO Group, which also generated the most complaints around the country.

24402 ■ "Roseville Ob-Gyn Group Grows With Patient Focus, Diverse Services" in *Crain's Detroit Business* (Vol. 24, April 7, 2008, No. 14)
Pub: Crain Communications, Inc.

Ed: Christine Snyder. **Description:** According to the American Medical Association, the number of medical groups of 10 or more physicians has been growing. Eastside Gynecology Obstetrics is one such group which has seen its yearly revenue grow due to a good business plan and a diversity of services and doctors.

24403 ■ "Rule of Thumb" in *Entrepreneur* (Vol. 36, May 2008, No. 5, pp. 44)
Pub: Entrepreneur Media, Inc.

Ed: Guy Kawasaki. **Description:** Business presentations using PowerPoint are recommended to have no more than 10 slides, last no longer than 20 minutes and have font no smaller than 30 points. Topics covered should include problem, solution, business model, underlying technology, and projections among others.

24404 ■ "St. Rose Professor Builds Contractors and Micro-Doctors" in *Business Review, Albany New York* (Vol. 34, December 28, 2007, No. 39)
Pub: American City Business Journals, Inc.

Ed: Robin K. Cooper. **Description:** Mike Mathews is an associate professor at the College of Saint Rose School of Business and one of the founders of the Center for Micro Enterprises Development, which provides training programs on business planning and management. Details of the business school's curricula and foundations are discussed.

24405 ■ "Sandi Jackson; Alderman, 7th Ward, City of Chicago" in *Crain's Chicago Business* (Vol. 31, May 5, 2008, No. 18, pp. 31)
Pub: Crain Communications, Inc.

Ed: Sarah A. Klein. **Description:** Profile of Sandi Jackson who is an alderman of the 7th ward of the city of Chicago and is addressing issues such as poverty and crime as well as counting on a plan to develop the former USX Corp. steel mill to revitalize the area's economic climate.

24406 ■ "Satellite Down, Stock Up: Raytheon Is On Target With Ten Percent Dividend Increase" in *Barron's* (Vol. 88, March 31, 2008, No. 13)
Pub: Dow Jones & Company, Inc.

Ed: Shirley A. Lazo. **Description:** Raytheon hiked their quarterly dividend to 28 cents per share from 25.5 cents. Aircastle slashed their quarterly common dividend by 64 percent for them to retain additional capital that can be used to increase their liquidity position.

24407 ■ *Save Your Small Business: 10 Crucial Strategies to Survive Hard Times or Close Down and Move On*
Pub: NOLO

Ed: Ralph Warner, Bethany Laurence. **Released:** August 1, 2009. **Price:** $29.99. **Description:** According to a study among 500 businesses, 44 percent used credit cards in order to meet their firm's needs in the previous six months. Written by a business owner, this book provides twelve strategies to protect personal assets from creditors and survive the current recession.

24408 ■ "Savvas Chamberlain" in *Canadian Business* (Vol. 81, March 17, 2008, No. 4, pp. 92)
Pub: Rogers Media

Ed: Andrew Wahl. **Description:** Savvas Chamberlain says he feels cheated during his teenage years because life was not normal for him growing up in Cyprus with all the uprisings against Britain. Chamberlain says he runs Dalsa like he plays chess because all his positions are shown all the time but he keeps his strategy to himself.

24409 ■ "Scanning Dell's Shopping List" in *Barron's* (Vol. 89, July 13, 2009, No. 28, pp. 24)
Pub: Dow Jones & Co., Inc.

Ed: Mark Veverka. **Description:** It is believed that Dell will be looking for companies to acquire since they poached an experienced mergers-and-acquisitions executive. In addition Dell's CEO is reportedly telling people he plans to go shopping. Dell executives have also stated an interest in data storage.

24410 ■ "Scotiabank Targets More Baby Boomers" in *Globe & Mail* (March 4, 2006, pp. B5)
Pub: CTVglobemedia Publishing Inc.

Ed: Elizabeth Church. **Description:** Bank of Nova Scotia posted $844 million profit for first quarter 2006. The plans of the bank to achieve baby boomer client base are presented.

24411 ■ "The Search for Big Oil" in *Canadian Business* (Vol. 80, April 9, 2007, No. 8, pp. 10)
Pub: Rogers Media

Ed: Joe Castaldo. **Description:** The continuing effort of Canmex Minerals Corp. to explore for oil in Somalia despite the failure of several other companies is discussed.

24412 ■ "The Seat-Of-The-Pants School of Marketing" in *Brandweek* (Vol. 49, April 21, 2008, No. 16, pp. 24)
Pub: VNU Business Media, Inc.

Ed: David Vinjamuri. **Description:** Excerpt from the book "Accidental Branding: How Ordinary People Build Extraordinary Brands," by David Vinjamuri, discusses six shared principles for creating a brand that is unique and will be successful over the long-term.

24413 ■ "A Security Risk?" in *Canadian Business* (Vol. 80, October 22, 2007, No. 21, pp. 36)
Pub: Rogers Media

Ed: Joe Castaldo. **Description:** Garda World Security Corporation declared a C$1.5 million loss in the second quarter of 2007. The company's securities have been falling since June and hit a 52-week low of $15.90 in September. Details of the physical and cash-handling firm's strategy to integrate its acquisitions are discussed.

24414 ■ "Shell Venture Aims at 'Oil Rocks'" in *Globe & Mail* (March 22, 2006, pp. B1)
Pub: CTVglobemedia Publishing Inc.
Ed: Patrick Brethour. **Description:** Royal Dutch Shell PLC is all set to launch its Alberta's operations in bitumen deposits trapped in limestone. Details of the new venture are analyzed.

24415 ■ "Shermag Plans Two Shutdowns, 300 More Layoffs" in *Globe & Mail* (February 13, 2007, pp. B5)
Pub: CTVglobemedia Publishing Inc.
Ed: Bertrand Marotte. **Description:** Shermag Inc., Canada's largest publicly traded furniture company, is permanently closing two plants and eliminating 300 jobs. The mounting losses and deteriorating stock prices are stated as main reasons for plant shutdowns.

24416 ■ "Shermag Says Refinishing Not Complete" in *Globe & Mail* (February 14, 2006, pp. B3)
Pub: CTVglobemedia Publishing Inc.
Ed: Bertrand Marotte. **Description:** The details on restructuring efforts of Shermag Inc. are presented.

24417 ■ "Shorts Story" in *Barron's* (Vol. 89, July 6, 2009, No. 27, pp. 16)
Pub: Dow Jones & Co., Inc.
Ed: Gene Epstein. **Description:** Shares of Compass Minerals, J2 Global Communications, K12, Middleby, and Pactiv should be shorted by investors. These companies suffer from weaknesses in their business models, making them vulnerable to a share price decline.

24418 ■ "Should You Go Into Business With Your Spouse?" in *Women Entrepreneur* (September 1, 2008)
Pub: Entrepreneur Media Inc.
Ed: Tamara Monosoff. **Description:** Things to consider before starting a business with one's spouse are discussed. Compatible work ethics, clear expectations of one another, long-term goals for the company and the status of the relationship are among the things to consider before starting a business endeavor with a spouse.

24419 ■ "Sixty-Acre Vision for North Suburbs" in *Business Courier* (Vol. 24, April 4, 2008, No. 52, pp. 1)
Pub: American City Business Journals, Inc.
Ed: Laura Baverman. **Description:** Al Neyer Inc. plans for a mixed-use development at the 60-acre site it has recently purchased. The mixed-use project could cost up to $100 million, and will include medical offices, residential buildings, and corporate offices. Details of Al Neyer's plans for the site are given.

24420 ■ "Skinner's No Drive-Thru CEO" in *Crain's Chicago Business* (Vol. 31, April 28, 2008, No. 17, pp. 1)
Pub: Crain Communications, Inc.
Ed: David Sterrett. **Description:** Profile of James Skinner who was named CEO for McDonald's Corp. in November 2004 and has proved to be a successful leader despite the number of investors who doubted him when he came to the position. Mr. Skinner has overseen three years of unprecedented sales growth and launched the biggest menu expansion in 30 years.

24421 ■ "Sleeman Cuts Again as Cheap Suds Bite" in *Globe & Mail* (March 3, 2006, pp. B3)
Pub: CTVglobemedia Publishing Inc.
Ed: Andy Hoffman. **Description:** The details on 5 percent employee reduction at Sleeman Breweries Ltd., which posted 86 percent decline in profits for fourth quarter 2005, are presented.

24422 ■ "Slimmed-Down Supplier TI Automotive Relaunches" in *Crain's Detroit Business* (Vol. 26, January 11, 2010, No. 2, pp. 14)
Pub: Crain Communications, Inc.
Ed: Robert Sherefkin. **Description:** TI Automotive Ltd., one of the world's largest suppliers of fuel storage and delivery systems, has reorganized the company by splitting it into five global divisions and is relaunching its brand which is now more focused on new technology.

24423 ■ *Small Business: An Entrepreneur's Business Plan*
Pub: South-Western
Ed: J.D Ryan, Gail P. Hiduke. **Released:** October 2008. **Price:** $119.95. **Description:** Assistance in preparing a business plan that identifies opportunities and ways to target a customer market.

24424 ■ *Small Business Desk Reference*
Pub: Penguin Books (USA) Incorporated
Ed: Gene Marks. **Released:** December 2004. **Description:** Comprehensive guide for starting or running a successful small business, focusing on buying a business or franchise, writing a business plan, financial management, accounting, legal issues, human resources management, operations, marketing, sales, customer service, taxes, insurance, and ethics. Information for launching a restaurant, property management firm, retail outlet, consulting firm, and service business is included.

24425 ■ *Small Business Management*
Pub: John Wiley and Sons Inc.
Ed: Margaret Burlingame; Don Gulbrandsen; Richard M. Hodgetts; Donald F. Kuratko. **Released:** March 2007. **Price:** $44.95. **Description:** Tips for starting and running a successful small business are given, including advice on writing a business plan, financing, and the law.

24426 ■ "Small is the New Big in Autos" in *Globe & Mail* (February 16, 2006, pp. B3)
Pub: CTVglobemedia Publishing Inc.
Ed: Greg Keenan. **Description:** The reasons behind the introduction of subcompact cars by companies such as Ford Motor Co. are presented. The automobiles were unveiled at Canadian International Auto Show in Toronto.

24427 ■ "So You Want to Start a Business?" in *Women Entrepreneur* (August 5, 2008)
Pub: Entrepreneur Media Inc.
Ed: Cynthia McKay. **Description:** Advice for taking an idea and turning it into a legitimate business is given.

24428 ■ "A Socko Payout Menu: Rural Phone Carrier Plots to Supercharge Its Shares" in *Barron's* (Vol. 88, June 30, 2008, No. 26, pp. M5)
Pub: Dow Jones & Co., Inc.
Ed: Shirley A. Lazo. **Description:** CenturyTel boosted its quarterly common payout to 70 cents from 6.75 cents per share die to its strong cash flows and solid balance sheet. Eastman Kodak's plan for a buyback will be partially funded by its $581 million tax refund. CME Group will buyback stocks through 2009 worth $1.1 billion.

24429 ■ "Somanetics to Buy Back Up to $15 Million of Common Shares" in *Crain's Detroit Business* (Vol. 24, April 7, 2008, No. 14, pp. 4)
Pub: Crain Communications, Inc.
Ed: Tom Henderson. **Description:** Somanetics Corp., a company that manufactures and markets noninvasive devices for monitoring blood oxygen levels in the brain and elsewhere in the body during surgery, plans to buy back up to $15 million worth of its common shares. Statistical data included on the company's current and past earnings and stock prices as well as its plans to increase revenue.

24430 ■ "Sorrell Digs Deep to Snag TNS" in *Advertising Age* (Vol. 79, July 14, 2008, No. 7, pp. 1)
Pub: Crain Communications, Inc.
Ed: Michael Bush. **Description:** Martin Sorrell's strategic vision for expansion in order to become the largest ad-agency holding company in the world is discussed.

24431 ■ "Sorry: Good Defense for Mal Offense" in *The Business Journal-Serving Metropolitan Kansas City* (Vol. 26, July 4, 2008, No. 43, pp. 1)
Pub: American City Business Journals, Inc.
Ed: Rob Roberts. **Description:** According to a survey conducted by the Kansas City Business Journal, ten hospitals in Kansas City showed that they have adopted disclosure policies that include prompt apologies and settlement offers. The policy is effective in minimizing medical malpractice lawsuits. Other details of the survey are presented.

24432 ■ "A Sound Setup" in *Black Enterprise* (Vol. 38, November 2007, No. 4, pp. 100)
Pub: Earl G. Graves Publishing Co. Inc.
Ed: Anthony Calypso. **Description:** Choosing the right corporate identity can ensure that a business has the right foundation on which to build and grow.

24433 ■ "Special Sector" in *Crain's Cleveland Business* (Vol. 28, November 5, 2007, No. 44, pp. 3)
Pub: Crain Communications, Inc.
Ed: David Bennett. **Description:** Specialty Metals Processing Inc. is investing more than $6 million to amp up productions; the company believes this big investment will pay off due to the company's ability to process complex metal alloys, such as titanium, in a region where there is a small number of competitors.

24434 ■ "Spend Wisely on Managing Your Hedgerows" in *Farmer's Weekly* (March 28, 2008, No. 320)
Pub: Reed Business Information
Ed: Richard Winspear. **Description:** Discusses the importance of a well-managed hedge which should gradually grow upwards and outwards where eventually it would reach the point when rejuvenation by coppicing or laying was needed to restart the cycle.

24435 ■ "Stadium Developers Seek a Win With the State" in *The Business Journal-Serving Metropolitan Kansas City* (Vol. 26, August 22, 2008)
Pub: American City Business Journals, Inc.
Ed: Rob Roberts. **Description:** Three Trails Redevelopment LLC is hoping to win $30 million in state tax credits from the Missouri Development Finance Board for the construction of an 18,500-seat Wizards stadium. The project is contingent on state tax incentives and the company remains optimistic about their goal.

24436 ■ "Staffing Firm Grows by Following Own Advice-Hire a Headhunter" in *Crain's Detroit Business* (Vol. 24, October 6, 2008, No. 40, pp. 1)
Pub: Crain Communications, Inc.
Ed: Sherri Begin. **Description:** Profile of Venator Holdings L.L.C., a staffing firm that provides searches for companies in need of financial-accounting and technical employees; the firm's revenue has increased from $1.1 million in 2003 to a projected $11.5 million this year due to a climate in which more people are exiting the workforce than are coming in with those particular specialized skills and the need for a temporary, flexible workforce for contract placements at companies that do not want to take on the legacy costs associated with permanent employees. The hiring of an external headhunter to find the right out-of-state manager for Venator is also discussed.

24437 ■ "Starbucks Drive-Throughs: Can the Cafe Keep Its Cool?" in *Globe & Mail* (January 6, 2006, pp. B7)
Pub: CTVglobemedia Publishing Inc.
Ed: Steven Gray. **Description:** The feasibility of Starbucks Corp.'s plans to introduce drive-through cafes is discussed.

24438 ■ "Starbucks' Wheel Strategy" in *Puget Sound Business Journal* (Vol. 29, October 3, 2008, No. 24, pp. 1)
Pub: American City Business Journals
Ed: Greg Lamm. **Description:** Starbuck Corporation has placed drive-through windows in nearly 50 percent of its locations. Dorothy Kim, executive vice president of global strategy, revealed that the firm's transformation strategy includes the addition of even more drive-through windows since people want the car-friendly conveniences.

24439 ■ "Stelco Investors Told Their Stock Now Worthless" in *Globe & Mail* (January 23, 2006, pp. B4)
Pub: CTVglobemedia Publishing Inc.
Ed: Greg Keenan. **Description:** The reasons behind Ontario Superior Court's approval of Stelco Inc.'s restructuring proposal are presented.

24440 ■ "Stelco Seeks to Shave Its Fixed Costs" in *Globe & Mail* (March 8, 2007, pp. B1)
Pub: CTVglobemedia Publishing Inc.
Ed: Greg Keenan. **Description:** The plans of Stelco Inc. to control its fixed costs in order to protect itself from economic downturns are discussed.

24441 ■ "Still Unprepared For Natural Disasters" in *Black Enterprise* (Vol. 38, January 2008, No. 6, pp. 28)
Pub: Earl G. Graves Publishing Co. Inc.
Ed: Alexis McCombs. **Description:** According to a study conducted by the American Red Cross, 19 percent of African Americans are not prepared for a natural disaster, compared to 10 percent of white Americans.

24442 ■ "Stock Car Racing" in *Canadian Business* (Vol. 81, September 15, 2008, No. 14-15, pp. 29)
Pub: Rogers Media Ltd.
Ed: Thomas Watson. **Description:** Some analysts predict a Chapter 11-style tune-up making GM and Ford a speculative turnaround stock. However, the price of oil could make or break the shares of the Big Three U.S. automobile manufacturers and if oil goes up too high then a speculative stock to watch is an electric car company called Zenn Motor Co.

24443 ■ "Strategic Issue Management as Change Catalyst" in *Strategy and Leadership* (Vol. 39, September-October 2011, No. 5, pp. 20-29)
Pub: Emerald Group Publishing Inc.
Ed: Bruce E. Perrott. **Description:** A study analyzes the case of a well-known Australian healthcare organization to examine how a company's periodic planning cycle is supplemented with a dynamic, real-time, strategic-issue-management system under high turbulence conditions. Findings highlight the eight steps that a company's management can use in its strategic issue management (SIM) process to track, monitor and manage strategic issues so as to ensure that the corporate, strategy, and capability are aligned with one another in turbulent times.

24444 ■ *Strategizing, Disequilibrium, and Profit*
Pub: Stanford University Press
Ed: John A. Mathews. **Released:** June 2006. **Price:** $24.95. **Description:** Author proposes the use of a conceptual framework that is consistent with real economies instead of equilibrium-based foundations when creating a business strategy.

24445 ■ "Strategy: Hurry Up and Wait" in *Business Courier* (Vol. 24, February 1, 2008, No. 43, pp. 50)
Pub: American City Business Journals, Inc.
Ed: Dan Monk. **Description:** It has taken years for Enerfab Inc. chairman Dave Herche to develop new product lines, form an expert management group and come up with a strategic-planning approach. However, his patience has paid off since Enerfab's revenue has grown by 93 percent since 2005. Herche's strategy for Enerfab and its impacts on the company are analyzed further.

24446 ■ "Stung by Recession, Hemmer Regroups with New Strategy" in *Business Courier* (Vol. 27, June 4, 2010, No. 5, pp. 1)
Pub: Business Courier
Ed: Lucy May. **Description:** Paul Hemmer Companies reduced its work force and outsourced operations such as marketing and architecture, in order for the commercial and construction firm to survive the recession. Hammer's total core revenue in 2009 dropped to less than $30 million forcing the closure of its Chicago office.

24447 ■ "Success Coach: Dare to Dream" in *Entrepreneur* (Vol. 35, October 2007, No. 10, pp. 146)
Pub: Entrepreneur Media Inc.
Ed: Romaus Wolter. **Description:** Business goals that are seemingly impossible to reach can actually be achieved through careful planning. Making the goals clear is the first step toward achievement. Details for setting goals and how to attain them are presented.

24448 ■ "Suitors Circling Chrysler as Sale Likely" in *Globe & Mail* (February 19, 2007, pp. B1)
Pub: CTVglobemedia Publishing Inc.
Ed: Jason Singer. **Description:** DaimlerChrysler AG is planning to sell or spin-off the Chrysler Group, as a cost cutting strategy. Chrysler reported a 40 percent drop in fourth quarter profit because of the $1.5 billion operating loss.

24449 ■ "Sunriver Venture Hits Snag" in *The Business Journal-Portland* (Vol. 25, August 1, 2008, No. 21, pp. 1)
Pub: American City Business Journals, Inc.
Ed: Robin J. Moody. **Description:** Portland, Oregon based-Sunwest Management Inc. has divided its Sunriver resort community to make way for a redevelopment plan. Sunwest owner Jon Harder and three partners formed SilverStar Destinations LLC to broker the purchase and redevelopment of the property. Details and description of the redevelopment project are also presented.

24450 ■ "Sunwest Vies To Stave Off Bankruptcy" in *The Business Journal-Portland* (Vol. 25, August 15, 2008, No. 23, pp. 1)
Pub: American City Business Journals, Inc.
Ed: Robin J. Moody. **Description:** Sunwest Management Inc. is teetering on the edge of bankruptcy as creditors start foreclosure on nine of their properties. This could potentially displace residents of the assisted living operator. Sunwest is trying to sell smaller packages of properties to get a $100 million bridge loan to maintain operations.

24451 ■ "Suppliers Look to Rack Up Big Sales to Distributors" in *The Business Journal-Serving Metropolitan Kansas City* (August 15, 2008)
Pub: American City Business Journals, Inc.
Ed: James Dornbrook. **Description:** Suppliers of shelving units, conveyor systems and other equipment used in distribution facilities are expecting new business opportunities along with the planned intermodal projects in the Kansas City area. Suppliers have already observed that small distributors have started to relocate to the city because of the intermodal projects. Demand for shelves and lifts have also increased.

24452 ■ "Survive the Small-to-Big Transition" in *Entrepreneur* (November 4, 2008)
Pub: Entrepreneur Media Inc.
Ed: Elizabeth Wilson. **Description:** Transitioning a small company to a large company can be a challenge, especially during the time when it is too big to be considered small and too small to be considered big. Common pitfalls during this time are discussed as well as techniques business owners should implement when dealing with this transitional period.

24453 ■ *Tactical Entrepreneur: The Entrepreneur's Game Plan*
Pub: Sortis Publishing
Ed: Brian J. Hazelgren. **Released:** September 2005. **Price:** $14.95. **Description:** A smart, realistic business plan is essential for any successful entrepreneur. Besides offering products or services, small business owners must possess skills in accounting, planning, human resources management, marketing, and information technology.

24454 ■ "Take 'Em Out of the Ball Game" in *Canadian Business* (Vol. 79, November 20, 2006, No. 23, pp. 19)
Pub: Rogers Media
Ed: Andy Holloway. **Description:** Strategies adopted by retailers to retain profitable customers are discussed.

24455 ■ "Talisman CEO Touts Benefits of Going It Alone" in *Globe & Mail* (March 22, 2006, pp. B1)
Pub: CTVglobemedia Publishing Inc.
Ed: Dave Ebner. **Description:** The opinions of chief executive officer Jim Buckee of Talisman Energy Inc. on the benefits for the company to remain autonomous are presented.

24456 ■ "Tea for 33 Million" in *Canadian Business* (Vol. 80, March 12, 2007, No. 6, pp. 10)
Pub: Rogers Media
Ed: Wendy Glauser. **Description:** The plan of owner of Cargo & James Tea, Tim Grover, to expand his business in North America to reach about 33 million, is discussed.

24457 ■ *Technology Ventures: From Idea to Enterprise*
Pub: McGraw-Hill Higher Education
Ed: Thomas Byers, Richard Dorf, Andrew Nelson. **Released:** January 10, 2010. **Description:** An action-approached through the use of examples, exercises, cases, sample business plans, and recommended sources helps entrepreneurs start and run a technology-base small business.

24458 ■ "Tee Off Online" in *Black Enterprise* (Vol. 37, January 2007, No. 6, pp. 52)
Pub: Earl G. Graves Publishing Co. Inc.
Ed: James C. Johnson. **Description:** The E-Com Resource Center is one of many resources that are available for those interested in starting an e-commerce business. One of the first steps is to create a business plan, of which there are free samples available at BPlans.com.

24459 ■ "Telesat's New Rocket Man" in *Canadian Business* (Vol. 80, January 29, 2007, No. 3, pp. 21)
Pub: Rogers Media
Ed: Andrew Wahl. **Description:** The plans of Dan Goldberg, the chief executive officer of Telesat Canada, for the enhancement of the company's services are discussed.

24460 ■ "Test Your Structural Integrity" in *Entrepreneur* (Vol. 37, August 2009, No. 8, pp. 60)
Pub: Entrepreneur Media, Inc.
Ed: Jennifer Lawler. **Description:** Tax considerations can be important when choosing a business structure. For example, profits are taxed to the corporation in a C corp while profits are taxed only once at an S corp or a limited liability company. Meeting a tax professional should be done prior to switching to a different structure.

24461 ■ *There's a Business In Every Woman: A 7-Step Guide to Discovering, Starting, and Building the Business of Your Dreams*
Pub: Ballantine/Random House
Ed: Ann M. Holmes. **Released:** 2008. **Price:** $15.00 paperback. **Description:** Economist and workplace expert provides a no-nonsense guide detailing seven steps to creating a successful business, based on her own experiences and on those of her employees. She highlights the importance of understanding and using your core competencies, building an organized infrastructure from the start, and planning for and managing your growth.

24462 ■ "Thirsty Lion on the Prowl" in *Business Journal Portland* (Vol. 27, November 5, 2010, No. 36, pp. 1)
Pub: Portland Business Journal
Ed: Wendy Culverwell. **Description:** Concept Entertainment Inc.'s impending launch of the Thirsty Lion Pub and Grill at the Washington Square in downtown Portland, Oregon is part of its West Coast expansion plan. A discussion of the planning involved in realizing Thirsty Lion is discussed, along with pub offerings that are expected to be enjoyed by customers.

24463 ■ "Thomson Eyes Asia for Expansion" in *Globe & Mail* (February 10, 2006, pp. B4)
Pub: CTVglobemedia Publishing Inc.
Ed: Grant Robertson. **Description:** The business growth plans of Thomson Corp., in Asia, are presented.

24464 ■ "A Timely Matter" in *Canadian Business* (Vol. 81, March 31, 2008, No. 5, pp. 12)
Pub: Rogers Media
Description: Discusses the committee responsible for restructuring $33 billion of asset-backed commercial paper which has moved back their implemen-

tation plan by a month citing complexities. British Columbia has surpassed the $1 billion mark in fiscal '07-'08 from their oil and gas rights. Biovail Corp. founder Eugene Melnyk said he had lost confidence in the management of the company.

24465 ■ "Tom Gaglardi" in *Canadian Business* (Vol. 82, April 27, 2009, No. 7, pp. 56)
Pub: Rogers Media
Ed: Calvin Leung. **Description:** Northland Properties Corporation president Tom Gaglardi believes that their business model of keeping much of operations in-house allows the firm to crate assets at a lesser price while commanding higher margins than their competitors. He believes that it is an ideal time to invest in the hospitality industry because of opportunities to purchase properties at low prices.

24466 ■ "Top 50 In Profits" in *Canadian Business* (Vol. 81, Summer 2008, No. 9, pp. 116)
Pub: Rogers Media Ltd.
Description: Royal Bank of Canada topped the Investor 500 by profits list despite the slower economic growth in Canada and the U.S. The bank was in the runner-up position in the 2007. RBC's growth strategy is through hefty acquisitions in the U.S. A table ranking the top 50 companies in Canada in terms of profits is presented.

24467 ■ "Transportation Enterprise" in *Advertising Age* (Vol. 79, June 9, 2008, No. 23, pp. S10)
Pub: Crain Communications, Inc.
Ed: Jean Halliday. **Description:** Overview of Enterprise rent-a-car's plan to become a more environmentally-friendly company. The family-owned business has spent $1 million a year to plant trees since 2006 and has added more fuel-efficient cars, hybrids and flex-fuel models.

24468 ■ "Transportation: Laidlaw's Chief Driver" in *Canadian Business* (Vol. 80, January 29, 2007, No. 3, pp. 14)
Pub: Rogers Media
Ed: Michelle Magnan. **Description:** The role of Kevin Benson in the restructuring and growth of the bankrupt transportation company Laidlaw Inc. is described. The increase in the revenues of the restructures company is discussed.

24469 ■ "Turmoil Means Changes For Retailers" in *The Business Journal-Serving Metropolitan Kansas City* (Vol. 27, October 10, 2008, No. 4)
Pub: American City Business Journals, Inc.
Ed: Suzanna Stagemeyer. **Description:** Impacts of the financial crisis on Kansas Metropolitan Area retailers are varied. Rob Dalzell, for instance, found it difficult to secure a loan for his new self-serve yogurt store Yummo. The trends in retailing in the area are examined further as well as ways in which local businesses are changing in an attempt to stay solvent during the economic downturn.

24470 ■ *The Ultimate Competitive Advantage*
Pub: Berrett-Koehler Publishers
Ed: Donald Mitchell; Carol Coles; B. Thomas Golisano. **Released:** March 12, 2003. **Price:** $36.95. **Description:** Results of a ten year study of companies that experienced fast growth over a three year period shows that while unsuccessful companies apply outdated business models, the successful ones improve their business models every two to four years.

24471 ■ *Ultimate Guide to Buying or Selling Your Business*
Pub: Entrepreneur Press
Ed: Ira N. Nottonson. **Released:** September 2004. **Price:** $24.95 (US), $35.95 (Canadian). **Description:** Proven strategies to evaluate, negotiate, and buy or sell a small business. Franchise and family business succession planning is included.

24472 ■ "UMKC, Hospital Drill Down on Deal" in *The Business Journal-Serving Metropolitan Kansas City* (Vol. 26, July 18, 2008, No. 45, pp. 1)
Pub: American City Business Journals, Inc.
Ed: Rob Roberts. **Description:** University of Missouri Kansas City and Children's Mercy Hospital are negotiating the hospital's potential acquisition of the university's School of Dentistry building. The deal would transfer the 240,000-square foot dental school building to Children's Mercy. Plans for a new dental school building for the UMKC are also presented.

24473 ■ "Unilever's CMO Finally Gets Down To Business" in *Advertising Age* (Vol. 79, July 7, 2008, No. 26, pp. 11)
Pub: Crain Communications, Inc.
Ed: Jack Neff. **Description:** Overview of Unilever's chief marketing officer Simon Clift's strategy for promoting its products; now that the company has restructured, Clift is able to focus all of his energy on the challenges of the new-media climate that marketers are having to face.

24474 ■ "Union, Heal Thyself" in *Canadian Business* (Vol. 81, July 21, 2008, No. 11, pp. 9)
Pub: Rogers Media Ltd.
Description: General Motors Corp. was offered by the federal government a $250 million fund after the company declared plans to close its facility in Ontario. The government move is geared towards supporting the workers who have refused to support the automotive company. Details of the labor contract between General Motors and the Canadian Auto Workers are presented.

24475 ■ "United Insurance To Grow St. Pete's Corporate Base" in *The Business Journal-Serving Greater Tampa Bay* (August 29, 2008)
Pub: American City Business Journals, Inc.
Ed: Margie Manning. **Description:** United Insurance Holdings LC is on its way to becoming a public company by agreeing in a reverse merger with FMG Acquisition Corp. The $104.3 million agreement will provide the company's St. Petersburg operations the opportunity to grow. The other impacts of the proposed reverse merger are examined.

24476 ■ "U.S. Playing Card Might Shuffle HQ" in *Business Courier* (Vol. 24, March 21, 2008, No. 50, pp. 1)
Pub: American City Business Journals, Inc.
Ed: Jon Newberry. **Description:** United States Playing Card Co. is considering the possibility of relocating. It is expected that the company will finalize its decision by June 2008. According to Phil Dolci, the company's president, the firm is looking at certain locations in Ohio, Kentucky, and Indiana. He also revealed that the plan to relocate was prompted by the desire to improve the company's manufacturing facilities.

24477 ■ "The Urge to Converge" in *Canadian Business* (Vol. 79, October 9, 2006, No. 20, pp. 41)
Pub: Rogers Media
Ed: Andy Holloway. **Description:** Arthur Griffiths, chief executive officer of Infotec Business Systems Inc., decision to diversify into broad brand business is discussed.

24478 ■ "The Value of Human Resource Management for Organizational Performance" in *Business Horizons* (November-December 2007, pp. 503)
Pub: Elsevier Technology Publications
Ed: Yongmei Liu, James G. Combs, David J. Ketchen, R. Duane Ireland. **Description:** Benefits of human resource management for business are studied using date from 19,000 organizations. Human resource management adds value to business, especially when it is integrated with business strategy and when human resource systems are emphasized.

24479 ■ "Versatile's Back" in *Farm Industry News* (Vol. 42, January 1, 2009, No. 1)
Pub: Penton Media, Inc.
Ed: Jodie Wehrspann. **Description:** Overview of Winnipeg, Manitoba's tractor manufacturer Versatile's strategy to rebrand its tractor segment; the strategy comes a year after Russian Combine Factory Rostselmash Ltd. bought the majority share of common stock from the Canadian business.

24480 ■ "Virgin Mobile has Big Plans for Year Two" in *Globe & Mail* (March 6, 2006, pp. B5)
Pub: CTVglobemedia Publishing Inc.
Ed: Catherine McLean. **Description:** The business growth plans of Virgin Mobile Canada are presented.

24481 ■ "Voices: Breaking the Corruption Habit" in *Business Strategy Review* (Vol. 21, Autumn 2010, No. 3, pp. 67)
Pub: Blackwell Publishers Ltd.
Ed: David De Cremer. **Description:** In times of crisis, it seems natural that people will work together for the common good. The author cautions that, on the contrary, both economic and social research proves otherwise. Steps for organizations to take to prevent corrupt behaviors are investigated.

24482 ■ "Wal-Mart Relaunches Private Brand, Reimagines Stores Layout" in *Marketing to Women* (Vol. 22, July 2009, No. 7, pp. 5)
Pub: EPM Communications, Inc.
Description: Wal-Mart is focusing its strategies by centering on new store layouts that they believe will match their new branding of "fast, friendly, and clean" and enable mothers to "just get on with what they need to do."

24483 ■ "Walker Seeks More Business Participation" in *Business Journal-Milwaukee* (Vol. 28, December 10, 2010, No. 10, pp. A1)
Pub: Milwaukee Business Journal
Ed: Rich Kirchen. **Description:** Wisconsin governor Scott Walker is seeking the aid of Milwaukee business leaders to participate in resolving the challenges posed by the economic crisis. Walker is aiming to create 250,000 jobs. He is also planning to call a special session of the legislature to enact strategies to jumpstart the economy.

24484 ■ *The Wall Street Journal. Complete Small Business Guidebook*
Pub: Three Rivers Press
Ed: Colleen DeBaise. **Released:** December 29, 2009. **Price:** $15.00. **Description:** The mechanics of building, running and growing a profitable business are outlined, teaching how to write a business plan, ways to finding money during lean years, how to keep stress in check, time management, investment in technology, hiring, marketing, management basics, angel investing and venture capital, as well as an exit strategy.

24485 ■ *We Are Smarter Than Me: How to Unleash the Power of Crowds in Your Business*
Pub: Wharton School Publishing
Ed: Barry Libert; Jon Spector; Don Tapscott. **Released:** October 5, 2007. **Price:** $21.99. **Description:** Ways to use social networking and community in order to make decisions and plan your business, with a focus on product development, manufacturing, marketing, customer service, finance, management, and more.

24486 ■ "Weathering the Economic Storm" in *Playthings* (Vol. 107, January 1, 2009, No. 1, pp. 10)
Pub: Reed Business Information
Ed: J. Tol Broome Jr. **Description:** Six steps for toy companies to survive the economic turndown are outlined: Outline your business model; seek professional input; meet with your banker; cut your costs; manage your inventory; and use your trade credit.

24487 ■ "Welcome to the Neighborhood" in *Hawaii Business* (Vol. 53, October 2007, No. 4, pp. 48)
Pub: Hawaii Business Publishing
Ed: Jolyn Okimoto Rosa. **Description:** Finance Factors is planning to build branches in Manoa, and Liliha, as part of its strategy to position itself in high-yield areas. The company chose Manoa and Liliha due to thee sites' rich deposits. Its strategy with regards to the branches' location and to the building design is discussed.

24488 ■ "Wendy's Mulls Total Hortons Selloff" in *Globe & Mail* (January 7, 2006, pp. B5)
Pub: CTVglobemedia Publishing Inc.
Ed: Sinclair Stewart; Omar El Akkad. **Description:** The plans of Wendy's International Inc. to spin off Tim Hortons are presented.

24489 ■ "Weyerhaeuser's REIT Decision Shouldn't Scare Investors Away" in *Barron's* (Vol. 88, June 30, 2008, No. 26, pp. 18)
Pub: Dow Jones & Co., Inc.
Ed: Christopher Williams. **Description:** Weyerhaeuser Co.'s management said that a conversion to a real estate investment trust was not likely in 2009 since the move is not tax-efficient as of the moment and would overload its non-timber assets with debt. The company's shares have fallen by 19.5 percent. However, the company remains an asset-rich outfit and its activist shareholder is pushing for change.

24490 ■ "What Are You Doing Differently?" in *Agency Sales Magazine* (Vol. 39, December 2009, No. 11, pp. 3)
Pub: MANA
Ed: Bryan C. Shirley. **Description:** Strategies that sales representatives can do to plan for a good year include professional development, networking with other reps, and making more sales calls and seeing more people. The end of the year is the perfect time for reps to write or re-write their mission statement and to conduct line profitability.

24491 ■ "What Are Your Party's Legislative Priorities for 2008?" in *Hawaii Business* (Vol. 53, January 2008, No. 7, pp. 22)
Pub: Hawaii Business Publishing
Description: Discusses the Democratic Party of Hawaii which will prioritize giving more opportunities to earn a living a wage in 2008, according to the party chairwoman Jeani Withington. The Republican Party chairman Willes K. Lee, meanwhile, states that his party will seek to enhance the local business climate. The political parties' plans for Hawaii for the year 2008 are presented in detail.

24492 ■ "What Homes Do Retirees Want?" in *Canadian Business* (Vol. 79, July 17, 2006, No. 14-15, pp.)
Pub: Rogers Media
Ed: Joe Cataldo. **Description:** The obstacles and challenges faced by homebuilders in Canada as well as the approach adopted by them to appeal to the mature homebuilders segment, is discussed.

24493 ■ "What Players in the Midmarket Are Talking About" in *Mergers & Acquisitions: The Dealmaker's Journal* (March 1, 2008)
Pub: SourceMedia, Inc.
Description: Sports Properties Acquisition Corp. went public at the end of January; according to the company's prospectus, it is not limiting its focus to just teams, it is also considering deals for stadium construction companies, sports leagues, facilities, sports-related advertising and licensing of products, in addition to other related segments.

24494 ■ *What Self-Made Millionaires Really Think, Know and Do: A Straight-Talking Guide to Business Success and Personal Riches*
Pub: John Wiley & Sons, Incorporated
Ed: Richard Dobbins; Barrie Pettman. **Released:** September 2006. **Price:** $24.95. **Description:** Guide for understanding the concepts of entrepreneurial success; the book offers insight into bringing an idea into reality, marketing, time management, leadership skills, and setting clear goals.

24495 ■ "What's Cooking?" in *Entrepreneur* (Vol. 36, April 2008, No. 4, pp. 98)
Pub: Entrepreneur Media, Inc.
Ed: Eileen Figure Sandlin. **Description:** Unique and unusual restaurants have the potential to attract customers and provide them with fresh menu options. Outlining goals, strategies and details on proposed concept and target market can also help in restaurant planning. Other tips on how to plan launching your own restaurant are provided.

24496 ■ *When Family Businesses are Best*
Pub: Palgrave Macmillan
Ed: Randel S. Carlock, John L. Ward. **Released:** March 1, 2010. **Price:** $45.00. **Description:** An exploration into effective planning and communication to help small businesses grow into multi-generation family enterprises.

24497 ■ "Why Intel Should Dump Its Flash-Memory Business" in *Barron's* (Vol. 88, March 10, 2008, No. 10, pp. 35)
Pub: Dow Jones & Company, Inc.
Ed: Eric J. Savitz. **Description:** Intel Corp. must sell its NAND flash-memory business as soon as it possibly can to the highest bidder to focus on its PC processor business and take advantage of other business opportunities. Apple should consider a buyback of 10 percent of the company's shares to lift its stock.

24498 ■ "Worth His Salt" in *Hawaii Business* (Vol. 53, January 2008, No. 7, pp. 45)
Pub: Hawaii Business Publishing
Ed: Jolyn Okimoto Rosa. **Description:** Bryan Zada owns three PretzelMaker franchises, whose total loss amounted to $40,000 in 2003. Zada believes that listening to employees was one of the key steps in turning the business around. The efforts made to improve the franchises' products are also given.

24499 ■ "The Wrong Tune" in *The Business Journal-Portland* (Vol. 25, July 25, 2008, No. 20, pp. 1)
Pub: American City Business Journals, Inc.
Ed: Robin J. Moody. **Description:** Views and information on turnaround management and recovery plans of the Oregon Symphony, are presented. The non-profit organization has lost a total of $5.1 million between 2002 and 2008, and $400,000 annual interest payments for a $7 million bank loan. Increased ticket sales, as well as cost cutting measures, are helping improve the finance of the organization.

24500 ■ "Xerox's Former CEO On Why Succession Shouldn't Be a Horse Race" in *Harvard Business Review* (Vol. 88, October 2010, No. 10, pp. 47)
Pub: Harvard Business School Publishing
Ed: Anne Mulcahy. **Description:** The importance of beginning talks between chief executive officers and boards of directors as early as possible to ensure a smooth transition is stressed. This can also prevent turning successions into competitions, with the resultant loss of talent when other candidates 'lose'.

24501 ■ "A Year After Fiorina's Exit, Hurd Makes His Mark" in *Globe & Mail* (February 8, 2006, pp. B9)
Pub: CTVglobemedia Publishing Inc.
Ed: Shawn McCarthy. **Description:** The business growth strategies of chief executive officer Mark Hurd of Hewlett-Packard Co. are presented.

24502 ■ "Young Entrepreneur's Business Plan? An Ice Cream Boat? Really Floats: Maine at Work" in *Portland Press Herald* (August 9, 2010)
Pub: Portland Press Herald
Ed: Ray Routhier. **Description:** Profile of Jake Viola, founder of and ice cream boat located near Portland, Maine. Viola is a sophomore at Yale University and sells ice cream from his pontoon boat on Little Sebago lake.

24503 ■ "Young Millionaires" in *Entrepreneur* (Vol. 35, October 2007, No. 10, pp. 76)
Pub: Entrepreneur Media Inc.
Ed: Jessica Chen, Lindsay Hollway, Amanda C. Kooser, Kim Orr, James Park, Nichole L. Torres, and Sarah Wilson. **Description:** Young successful entrepreneurs of 2007 were chosen to talk about their success story and their business strategies in the past and those for the future. Among those featured are Kelly Flatley, Brendan Synnott, Herman Flores, Myles Kovacs, Haythem Haddad, Jim Wetzel, Lance Lawson, Jacob DeHart, Jake Nickell, Tim Vanderhook, Chris Vanderhook, Russell Vanderhook, Megan Duckett, Brad Sugars, John Vechey, Brian Fiete, Jason Kapalka, Nathan Jones, Devon Rifkin, Ryan Black, Ed Nichols, Jeremy Black, Amy Smilovic, Bob Shallenberger, and John Cavanagh.

24504 ■ "Your Booming Business: How You Can Align Sales and Marketing for Dynamic Growth" in *Small Business Opportunities* (Spring 2008)
Pub: Harris Publications Inc.
Ed: Voss W. Graham. **Description:** Voss Graham, founder and CEO of Inneractive Consulting Group Inc., works with companies to develop and hire successful sales teams. A checklist from the American Bankers Association to help write a business plan is included.

24505 ■ *Your Guide to Preparing a Plan to Raise Money for Your Own Business*
Pub: Productive Publications
Ed: Iain Williamson. **Released:** June 1991. **Description:** A good business plan is essential for raising money for any small business.

24506 ■ "Zebra's Changing Stripes" in *Crain's Chicago Business* (Vol. 31, November 17, 2008, No. 46, pp. 4)
Pub: Crain Communications, Inc.
Ed: John Pletz. **Description:** Zebra Technologies Corp., the world's largest manufacturer of bar-code printers is profiled; the company's stock has plunged with shares declining 40 percent in the past three months grinding the firm's growth to a halt. Zebra's plans to regain revenue growth are also discussed.

24507 ■ "Zell Takes a Gamble on Tribune" in *Globe & Mail* (April 3, 2007, pp. B1)
Pub: CTVglobemedia Publishing Inc.
Ed: Sinclair Stewart. **Description:** The purchase of the majority share in Tribune Co. by Samuel Zell is described. Samuel Zell's plans to keep the company's assets intact are discussed.

24508 ■ "Zucker's HBC Shakeup Imminent" in *Globe & Mail* (February 20, 2006, pp. B3)
Pub: CTVglobemedia Publishing Inc.
Ed: Marina Strauss. **Description:** The plans of investor Jerry Zucker to revamp Hudson's Bay Co., upon its acquisition, are presented.

TRADE PERIODICALS

24509 ■ *Enrich!*
Pub: National Chamber of Commerce for Women
Contact: Jay Orson, Ad.Mgr.
Ed: R. Wright, Editor. **Released:** Bimonthly. **Price:** $96. **Description:** Strives to assist readers on business-plan, career-path, and pay-comparison goals.

VIDEOCASSETTES/ AUDIOCASSETTES

24510 ■ *Managing the Emerging Company*
Leslie T. McClure
PO Box 1223
Pebble Beach, CA 93953
Ph:(831)656-0553
Fax:(831)656-0555
Co. E-mail: leslie@411videoinfo.com
URL: http://www.411videoinfo.com
Released: 1997. **Price:** $990.00. **Description:** Ten-volume set deals with the functions of developing and running a business. **Availability:** VHS.

24511 ■ *Product Strategy: All the Right Moves*
RMI Media
1365 N. Winchester St.
Olathe, KS 66061-5880
Ph:(913)768-1696
Free: 800-745-5480
Fax:800-755-6910
Co. E-mail: actmedia@act.org
URL: http://www.actmedia.com
Released: 1991. **Price:** $89.95. **Description:** Presents a case study of Carushka, a dance and exercise wear manufacturer, to demonstrate success-

ful methods for increasing product use and customers; finding new uses for existing products; and broadening the product appeal to old and new markets. **Availability:** VHS.

CONSULTANTS

24512 ■ Ameriwest Business Consultants Inc.
3725 E Wade Ln.
PO Box 26266
Colorado Springs, CO 80917-5852
Ph:(719)380-7096
Fax:(719)380-7096
Co. E-mail: email@abchelp.com
URL: http://www.abchelp.com
Contact: Rodd Brechtl, President
E-mail: rodb@abchelp.com
Scope: Specializes in assisting start up businesses and those with sales of 5million dollars or less and those who have 50 employees or less. Services and products offered include written business plans; do it yourself business plan kits; business valuations; do it yourself business start up kits; written loan packages; do it yourself loan packaging guides; business analysis; do it yourself financial projections software; do it yourself complete financial analysis; website development assistance; general consulting.

24513 ■ Beacon Management Group Inc.
1000 W McNab Rd., Ste. 150
Pompano Beach, FL 33069-4719
Ph:(954)782-1119
Free: 800-771-8721
Fax:(954)969-2566
Co. E-mail: md@beaconmgmt.com
URL: http://www.beaconmgmt.com
Contact: Chris Roy, Treasurer
E-mail: md@beaconmgmt.com
Scope: Specializes in change management, organized workplaces, multicultural negotiations and dispute resolutions and internet based decision making.

24514 ■ Biomedical Management Resources
PO Box 10977
Conway, AR 72034
Ph:(801)272-4668
Fax:(801)277-3290
Co. E-mail: SeniorManagement@BiomedicalManagement.com
URL: http://www.biomedicalmanagement.com
Contact: Ping Fong Jr., President
E-mail: pingfong@biomedicalmanagement.com
Scope: Provides business development, interim management, and executive search services. Assists companies in strategic alliances, corporate partnering, business acquisition. Demonstrated success in identifying recruiting, and placing key managers in difficult to hire positions.

24515 ■ BPT Consulting Associates Ltd.
12 Parmenter Rd., Ste. B-6
Londonderry, NH 03053
Ph:(603)437-8484
Free: 888-278-0030
Fax:(603)434-5388
Co. E-mail: bptcons@tiac.net
Contact: John Kuczynski, President
E-mail: bptcons@tiac.net
Scope: Provides management consulting expertise and resources to cross-industry clients with services for: Business Management consulting, People/Human Resources Transition and Training programs, and a full cadre of multi-disciplined Technology Computer experts. Virtual consultants with expertise in e-commerce, supply chain management, organizational development, and business application development consulting.

24516 ■ Bran Management Services Inc.
2106 High Ridge Rd.
Louisville, KY 40207-1128
Ph:(502)896-1632
Contact: Robert C. Braverman, CEO
Scope: Offers management consulting services to companies in manufacturing, distribution and services to help them cope with growth and change. Helps small businesses create and identify product strategies. Services include developing international business opportunities; turnaround management; sales and marketing development; business planning; acquisitions and mergers.

24517 ■ Business Development Group Inc.
17340 W 12 Mile Rd., Ste. 101
Southfield, MI 48076
Ph:(248)552-0821
Fax:(248)552-1924
Co. E-mail: info@busdevgroup.com
URL: http://www.busdevgroup.com
Contact: Fred Zimmer, Partner
E-mail: njsimon@aol.com
Scope: Consulting firm expertise in leadership development; strategic thinking; organizational transformation; team-based work systems; organizational learning; rapid change; knowledge management; competitive intelligence; crisis management; merger and acquisition integration; product integration and new product development. **Publications:** "Navigating in the Sea of Change," Competitive Intelligence Review Journal; "The Influence of Cultural Aspects of Strategic Information, Analysis and Delivery"; "What Leadership Needs From Competitive Intelligence Professionals," Journal of Association for Global and Strategic Information. **Seminars:** Process of Self-Design for the Evolving Organization; Large System Change Intervention; Self Assessment and the Transformational Process; The Knowledge Exchange - Shared Practices Workshop.

24518 ■ Business Resource Software Inc.
1779 Wells Branch Pky.
Austin, TX 78728
Ph:(512)251-7541
Free: 800-423-1228
Fax:(512)251-4401
Co. E-mail: sales@brs-inc.com
URL: http://www.brs-inc.com
Contact: Larry Nesbit, President
E-mail: brown@brs-inc.com
Scope: Provides marketing and business planning software. Provides an evaluation of business conditions and advises the users about situations in their specific business. **Special Services:** Plan Write[R]; Quick Insight[R]; Business Insight[R].

24519 ■ BusinessPlanWorld.com
PO Box 1322, Sta. B
Mississauga, ON, Canada L4Y 4B6
Ph:(709)643-8544
Co. E-mail: theboss@businessplanworld.com
URL: http://www.businessplanworld.com
Contact: Wanda Keough, CFO
E-mail: support@atscansombodyhelpme.com
Scope: Services include business plan creation, complete website development services and educational software development. **Publications:** "How to open a Bed and Breakfast"; "How to open a Bookstore"; "How to open a Restaurant"; "How to open a Youth Center"; "How to open a Rough Collie Kennel"; "How to open a Video Store"; "How to open a Confectionery Store"; "How to open a Night Club/Bar".

24520 ■ CAST Management Consultants Inc.
700 S Flower St., Ste. 1900
Los Angeles, CA 90017
Ph:(213)614-8066
Fax:(213)614-0760
Co. E-mail: info@castconsultants.com
URL: http://www.castconsultants.com
Contact: Greg Ball, Exec VP
Scope: Management consultants active in the following areas: business strategy formulation, market analysis, business plan formulation, competitive advantage analysis, information technology development, organizational development, financial analysis and planning, strategic planning, entry strategies into new markets, implementation of strategy, international strategic planning, international marketing, and international joint venture. Serves private industries as well as government agencies.

24521 ■ CEA Investments Corp.
301-2210 W 40th Ave.
Vancouver, BC, Canada V6M 1W6
Ph:(604)689-5547
Fax:(604)689-5567
Co. E-mail: info@ceainvestment.com
URL: http://www.ceainvestment.com
Contact: Emmanuel B. Nicolas, Principle
Scope: Specializes in strategic planning, mergers and acquisitions, and operations consulting, to mid-sized corporations. Areas of expertise include corporate planning, financial engineering, joint venture structuring, international corporate networking, identifying acquisition opportunities, locating investment partners, corporate evaluations, negotiating buy/sell agreements, business planning, markets studies and products evaluation, and outsourcing.

24522 ■ CFO Service
112 Chester Ave.
Saint Louis, MO 63122
Ph:(314)757-2940
Contact: John D. Skae, President
E-mail: jds217@aol.com
Scope: A group of professional executives that provide upper management services to companies that cannot support a full time COO or CFO. Provides clients in the areas of business planning, company policies, contract negotiations, safety policies, product and service pricing, loans management, taxes, cost analysis, loss control and budgeting.

24523 ■ Chamberlain & Cansler Inc.
2251 Perimeter Park Dr.
Atlanta, GA 30341
Ph:(770)457-5699
Contact: Charles L. Cansler, Owner
Scope: Firm specializes in strategic planning; profit enhancement; small business management; interim management; crisis management; turnarounds.

24524 ■ Clayton/Curtis/Cottrell
1722 Madison Ct.
Louisville, CO 80027-1121
Ph:(303)665-2005
Contact: Robert Cottrell, President
Scope: Market research firm specializes in providing consultations for packaged goods, telecommunications, direct marketing and printing, and packaging industries. Services include strategic planning; profit enhancement; startup businesses; mergers and acquisitions; joint ventures; divestitures; interim management; crisis management; turnarounds; market size, segmentation and rates of growth; competitor intelligence; image and reputation, and competitive analysis. **Publications:** "Turn an attitude into a purchase," Jul, 1995; "Mixed results for private label; price assaults by the national brands are getting heavy, but there's still a place for private label," Jun, 1995; "In-store promotion goes high-tech: is the conventional coupon destined for obsolescence?," Jun, 1995.

24525 ■ Comprehensive Business Services
3201 Lucas Cir.
Lafayette, CA 94549
Ph:(925)283-8272
Fax:(925)283-8272
Contact: Walter H. Diebold, President
Scope: Business/financial consultants with related experience in marketing, finance, organization, business planning, and profit development. Industries served include construction, manufacturing, and wholesale.

24526 ■ CRO Engineering Ltd.
1895 William Hodgins Ln.
Carp, ON, Canada K0A 1L0
Ph:(613)839-1108
Fax:(613)839-1406
Co. E-mail: grefford@ieee.org
Contact: John Grefford, Principle
E-mail: grefford@ieee.org
Scope: Specializes in management services, contract R and D, risk analysis, business services. technology assessment, independent engineering verification and validation, audit services, project or program

management, engineering cost analysis, technology research. Engineering review, business plan analysis and development.

24527 ■ DRI Consulting
2 Otter Ln.
North Oaks, MN 55127-6436
Ph:(651)415-1400
Free: (866)276-4600
Fax:(651)415-9968
Co. E-mail: dric@dric.com
URL: http://www.dric.com
Contact: Dr. Heather Mortensen, Principle
E-mail: heathermortensen@atsdric.com
Scope: Licensed psychologists providing organization and management consulting. Developing leaders, managers and individuals through coaching, business strategy, career development, crisis management, policy consultation and technology optimization.

24528 ■ Elizabeth Capen
27 E 95th St., Apt. 5E
New York, NY 10128-0824
Ph:(212)427-7654
Fax:(212)876-3190
Scope: Focuses on strategic marketing planning and positioning. Identifies effective marketing tools; plans and reviews advertising and collateral materials; writes business plans; and performs secondary research and competitive analysis. Industries served: services, small businesses, and entrepreneurial ventures in northeastern and middle Atlantic regions. **Seminars:** Handling Issues of Growth; Using Published Information as a Marketing Tool.

24529 ■ Entrepreneurial Strategies
107 S Yellowstone Ave., Ste. C
Bozeman, MT 59715
Ph:(406)587-5664
Fax:(406)586-0396
Co. E-mail: nfkrueger@rocketmail.com
Contact: Norris F. Krueger, Principle
E-mail: nfkrueger@hotmail.com
Scope: Academic consultants helping organizations become more entrepreneurial; helping communities become more entrepreneurial; providing market assessments for 'really new' products and technologies; offering strategic planning and marketing planning.

24530 ■ FCP Consulting
500 Sutter St., Ste. 507
San Francisco, CA 94102-1114
Ph:(415)956-5558
Fax:(415)956-5722
Contact: Cox Ferrall, President
Scope: Management consulting in Business-To-Business sales.

24531 ■ Fogg Management Consulting
80 Shadow Farm Way
Wakefield, RI 02879-3635
Ph:(401)789-9511
Fax:(401)789-8544
Contact: C. Davis Fogg, President
E-mail: davis.fogg@foggmgt.com
Scope: Provides strategic planning and implementation services. Serves all industries, coaches CEO' s and senior executives. **Publications:** "Implementing Your Strategic Plan"; "Team Based Strategic Planning".

24532 ■ Frankel and Topche P.C.
1700 Galloping Hill Rd.
Kenilworth, NJ 07033
Ph:(908)298-7700
Fax:(908)298-7701
Co. E-mail: info@frankelandtopche.com
URL: http://www.frankelandtopche.com
Contact: Aaron Saiewitz, Principle
E-mail: gtopche@atsfrankelandtopche.com
Scope: Offers financial consulting for closely held businesses. Assists in mergers and acquisitions, tax planning, strategic business planning, family succession planning, accounting, auditing, and obtaining financing. The firm serves small businesses in the service, retail, wholesale, and manufacturing industries. Specializes in real estate, lumber and building materials, and service businesses. **Seminars:** Annual Tax Seminar.

24533 ■ Gerson Goodson Inc.
2451 McMullen Booth Rd., Ste. 201
Clearwater, FL 33759
Ph:(727)726-7619
Free: 888-237-7424
Fax:(727)726-2406
Co. E-mail: getrich@richgerson.com
URL: http://www.richgerson.com
Contact: Richard F. Gerson, Principal
E-mail: richard.gerson@atsrichgerson.com
Scope: Independent consulting firm provides performance management solutions to improve performance and maximize productivity in organizations. Provides assistance to organizations in talent and performance management, leadership development, selection and hiring practices, employee and customer retention, and customer service. Conducts a systematic needs analysis of the entire marketing, sales and customer service operations of the company. Identifies hidden, neglected and underutilized marketing, sales and customer service assets. **Publications:** "Winning The Inner Game Of Selling," 1999; "Marketing Strategies for Small Businesses," 1994; "Measuring Customer Satisfaction," 1993; "Beyond Customer Service," 1992; "Achieving High Performance"; "Guaranteeing Performance Improvement"; "The Executive Athlete"; "Positive Performance Improvement". **Seminars:** Marketing Real Estate Services Management Development, Oct, 2007; Presentation Skills, Oct, 2007; From Member Service to Sales, Sep, 2007; Leadership Development, Sep, 2007; The Marketing Difference That Makes The Difference: How To Position Your Company For Rapid Growth Regardless Of The Economy Or The Competition; Growing Your Business With What You Already Have: How To Identify And Profit From The Hidden Marketing Assets That Are Currently Costing You Money; The R Factor In Customer Service: 5Ways To Grow Your Business For Little Or No Cost.

24534 ■ Great Lakes Consulting Group Inc.
54722 Little Flower Trl.
Mishawaka, IN 46545
Ph:(574)287-4500
Fax:(574)233-2688
Contact: James E. Schrager, President
Scope: Provides consulting services in the areas of strategic planning; feasibility studies; start-up businesses; small business management; mergers and acquisitions; joint ventures; divestitures; interim management; crisis management; turnarounds; business process re-engineering; venture capital; and international trade.

24535 ■ The Greystone Group Inc.
440 N Wells, Ste. 570
Chicago, IL 60610
Ph:(616)451-8880
Fax:(616)451-9180
Co. E-mail: consult@greystonegp.com
E-mail: consult@greystonegp.com
Scope: Firm specializes in strategic planning and communications; organizational development; start-up businesses; business management; mergers and acquisitions; joint ventures; divestitures; business process re-engineering.

24536 ■ Grimmick Consulting Services
455 Donner Way
San Ramon, CA 94582
Ph:(925)735-1036
Fax:(925)735-1100
Co. E-mail: hank@grimmickconsulting.com
URL: http://www.grimmickconsulting.com
Contact: Henry Grimmick, President
E-mail: hank@grimmickconsulting.com
Scope: Provides consulting services in the areas of strategic planning; organizational assessment; organizational development; leadership and management development Baldridge criteria, process improvement and balanced scorecards and team dynamics.

24537 ■ Health Strategy Group Inc.
46 River Rd.
Chatham, NY 12037
Ph:(518)392-6770
Contact: John Fiorillo, Principle
Scope: Provides consulting services in the areas of strategic planning, feasibility studies, start-up businesses, organizational development, market research, customer service audits, new product development, marketing, public relations. **Publications:** "Online Consumer Surveys as a Methodology for Assessing the Quality of the United States Health Care System," 2004.

24538 ■ Healthscope Inc.
400 Lancaster Ave.
Devon, PA 19333
Ph:(610)687-6199
Fax:(610)687-6376
Co. E-mail: health@voicenet.com
Contact: Brian King, President
E-mail: dmking47@hotmail.com
Scope: An independent health care management and consulting firm. Provides business planning, decision making and implementation support. Specialties include strategic business consulting, business plan development focused on bottom line improvement, revenue enhancement expense reduction planning and implementation, practice expansion consolidation, feasibility studies and decision making, new site service start-up planning and implementation practice valuation and transition, physician group mergers and affiliations, joint ventures, MSO planning, start up and management, IPA PO development support, physician network reengineering, medical practice management, baseline operational and financial assessment, managed care contracting support, personnel management, physician compensation planning, fee schedule development, day-to-day operations management supervision, financial management, clinical protocols development, customized management report development, physician and staff education; performance monitoring, billing system evaluation, planning and selection, interim or ongoing management support, practice reorganization, patient accounts management, practice marketing.

24539 ■ Hewitt Development Enterprises
18 Lindley Ave.
North Kingstown, RI 02852
Ph:(305)372-0941
Free: 800-631-3098
Fax:(305)372-0941
Co. E-mail: info@hewittdevelopment.com
URL: http://www.hewittdevelopment.com
Contact: Robert G. Hewitt, Principal
E-mail: bob@hewittdevelopment.com
Scope: Specializes in strategic planning; profit enhancement; start-up businesses; interim management; crisis management; turnarounds; production planning; just-in-time inventory management; and project management. Serves senior management (CEOs, CFOs, division presidents, etc.) and acquirers of distressed businesses.

24540 ■ Horizon Consulting Services
1315 Garthwick Dr.
Los Altos, CA 94024-6147
Ph:(650)967-0906
Fax:(650)967-0906
Contact: Wendy Marshall Grossman, President
Scope: Assists start-up to mid-sized businesses to grow and increase profits through effective business plans and operational programs. Areas of expertise include business plans and strategies; market evaluations; competitive analysis; pricing; financial plans and budgets; financial management; marketing strategies; product positioning and introduction, forecasting and analysis; and business policies and procedures. Concentrates on providing practical results, customized to the needs and budget of its clients. Industries served: high-technology industries including computers, software, communications, other electronic products and components, and other manufacturing and service industries.

24541 ■ Jerome W. McGee & Associates
7826 Eastern Ave. NW, Ste. 300
Washington, DC 20012
Ph:(202)726-7272
Fax:(202)726-2946
Contact: Bruce W. McGee, President
Scope: Business consultants experienced in office automation, small business management, invention and patent counseling, technology commercialization, loan packaging and business plan development. **Seminars:** Marketing Research for the High-Technology Business; Introduction to Microcomputers; Marketing Technological Products to Industry; How to Evaluate Your Technical Idea; Patenting Your Own Invention.

24542 ■ John Alan Cohan
433 N Camden Dr., Ste. 100
Beverly Hills, CA 90210
Ph:(310)278-0203
Free: 800-255-1529
Fax:(310)859-8656
Co. E-mail: johnalancohan@aol.com
URL: http://www.johnalancohan.com
Contact: Cohan John Alan, Principle
Scope: Consultant assists in the development of business plans for startups in the fields of livestock, horses, farming, or aviation. Also provides tax consultations and tax opinion letters to support deductions.

24543 ■ K & T Training
103 Greenville St.
Newnan, GA 30263
Ph:(770)253-5870
Fax:(770)253-8866
Contact: J. R. Tumperi, President
Scope: Specializes in strategic planning; profit enhancement; organizational development; start-up businesses; interim management; crisis management; turnarounds; business process re-engineering; team building; cost controls.

24544 ■ Keck & Co.
410 Walsh Rd.
Atherton, CA 94027
Ph:(650)854-9588
Fax:(650)854-7240
Co. E-mail: info@kecko.com
Contact: Barbara Keck, Owner
E-mail: info@kecko.com
Scope: Conducts management services nationally, focusing on strategic research, marketing, and planning for businesses involved in the packaging container and equipment industry, food processing, and related technology suppliers. Develops feasibility studies to assess the possible success or failure of entering a new market, introducing a new product or product line extension, or starting a new venture; primary market research to determine what motivates consumers/buyers, and best "positioning" for product in the marketplace; business development programs; promotional programs to differentiate client company from competitors; vertical/horizontal marketing audits; technology acceptance assessments; due diligence for investors; and management assistance with investment issues. **Seminars:** Taking the Failure Factors Out of New Product Introductions; Introduction to Marketing for Food Manufacturing Personnel; New Product Development Workshop: Plans and Elements; Starting Your Own Consulting Business; The Marketing Plan.

24545 ■ Keiei Senryaku Corp.
19191 S Vermont Ave., Ste. 530
Torrance, CA 90502-1049
Ph:(310)366-3331
Free: 800-951-8780
Fax:(310)366-3330
Co. E-mail: takenakaes@earthlink.net
Contact: Kurt Miyamoto, President
Scope: Offers consulting services in the areas of strategic planning; feasibility studies; profit enhancement; organizational development; start-up businesses; mergers and acquisitions; joint ventures; divestitures; executive searches; sales management; and competitive analysis.

24546 ■ Key Communications Group Inc.
5617 Warwick Pl.
Chevy Chase, MD 20815-5503
Ph:(301)656-0450
Free: 800-705-5353
Fax:(301)656-4554
Co. E-mail: mr.dm@verizon.net
Contact: Carol A. Jason, Principle
E-mail: mr.dm@verizon.net
Scope: Direct marketing and publishing consultants specializing in subscriber and member acquisition for newsletters and other niche B2B publications, organizations and associations. Specialties: small and start-up businesses; mergers and acquisitions; joint ventures; divestitures; product development; employee surveys and communication; market research; customer service audits; new product development; direct marketing and competitive intelligence. **Publications:** "How I Tripled Site License Sales in One Year," Pma, Jul, 2004.

24547 ■ Management Strategies
1000 S Old Woodward, Ste. 105
Birmingham, MI 48009
Ph:(248)258-2756
Fax:(248)258-3407
Co. E-mail: bob@hois.com
Contact: Robert E. Hoisington, President
E-mail: bob@hois.com
Scope: Firm specializes in strategic planning; feasibility studies; profit enhancement; organizational studies; start up businesses; turnarounds; business process re engineering; industrial engineering; marketing; ecommerce.

24548 ■ Market Focus
12 Maryland Rd.
PO Box 402
Maplewood, NJ 07040
Ph:(973)378-2470
Fax:(973)378-2470
Co. E-mail: mcss66@marketfocus.com
Contact: Daniel A. Zaslow, President
E-mail: dakaslow@comcast.net
Scope: Offers advisory services to executives of corporate business units and mid-sized companies in the development and implementation of corporate and market strategies. Studies relate to business planning, new market/product entry, acquisitions and industry/competitive profiles for firms in advanced technology, business and financial services and basic industry. Projects focus on practical, effective approaches to maximizing the potential of existing operations and exploiting future growth opportunities. Practice philosophy emphasizes close client relationships, active management participation and senior consultant involvement. **Publications:** "Surviving in Hard Times," NJ Contractor. **Seminars:** Charting a Course for Future Company Growth; Marketing Planning; Construction Marketing in the 90's; Marketing and The CFO.

24549 ■ Marketing Leverage Inc.
2022 Laurel Oak
Palm City, FL 34990
Free: 800-633-1422
Fax:(772)659-8664
Co. E-mail: lkelly@marketingleverage.com
URL: http://www.marketingleverage.com
Contact: Genina Gravlin, Principle
E-mail: davery@atsmarketingleverage.com
Scope: Consulting and research firm focusing on the targeting, retention and satisfaction of customers. Consulting is offered for due diligence; marketing and customer retention strategy; program design and implementation. Research services offered help clients determine service improvements that increase customer loyalty; boosting sales through better understanding buyer motivations; increasing the odds of product acceptance through new product concept testing; and improving the effectiveness of advertising, collateral, publications through audience evaluation. Clients include top financial services, insurance, health care, technology and management services organizations. **Publications:** "Creating Strategic Leverage"; "Exploring Corporate Strategy"; "Competitive Advantage"; "Breakpoint and Beyond "; "Competitive Strategy ". **Seminars:** Best Practices in Brainstorming; Getting Results in the Real World; Finding the Leverage in Your Customer Strategy; The Role of Communications in Building Customer Loyalty; Building a Customer Centered Relationship and Making it Pay. **Special Services:** The Marketing Leverage Win/Loss Tracking System™.

24550 ■ McCreight & Company Inc.
36 Grove St., Ste. 4
New Canaan, CT 06840-5329
Ph:(203)801-5000
Fax:(866)646-8339
Co. E-mail: roc@implementstrategy.com
URL: http://www.implementstrategy.com
Contact: Laraine Mehr-Turlis, CFO
E-mail: jas@atsimplementstrategy.com
Scope: The firm assist the global clients with strategy implementation involving large scale change, including mergers, divestitures, alliances, and new business launches. Along with the alliance partners, focus on issues that energize or constrain strategic change including: plans and goals; transition design; management competence; organization structure, effectiveness, and staffing; roles and responsibilities; management processes; information management and technology; and change management effectiveness. **Publications:** "The Board's Role in Strengthening M&A Success," Boardroom Briefing, 2008; "Creating the Future," Ask Magazine, 2007; "Strategy Implementation Insights," Mccreight and Company Inc., Oct, 2007; "Sustaining Growth," Deloitte and Ct Technology Council, Jul, 2006; "A Four Phase Approach to Succession Planning," Southern Connecticut Newspapers Inc., 2005; E perspective; Board Effectiveness Insights; and Information Technology Insights. **Seminars:** Successful Mergers and Acquisitions - An Implementation Guide; Global 100One-Face-to-the-Customer; Implementation of Strategic Change.

24551 ■ McDonald Consulting Group Inc.
1900 W Park Dr., Ste. 280
Westborough, MA 01581
Ph:(952)841-6357
Fax:(507)664-9389
Co. E-mail: rmcdonald@mcdonaldconsultinggroup.com
URL: http://www.mcdonaldconsultinggroup.com
Contact: Ron A. McDonald, President
E-mail: rmcdonald@mcdonaldconsultinggroup.com
Scope: A management consulting firm specializing in assisting insurance companies improve operations. Provides services in the areas of strategic planning; profit enhancement; organizational development; interim management; crisis management; turnarounds; business process re-engineering; benefits and compensation planning and total quality management. **Publications:** "Improving Customer Focus through Organizational Structure," AASCIF News; "Changing Strategies in Hard Markets," The National Underwriter; "Moving Beyond Management 101: Postgraduate Time Management for Executives," The National Underwriter; "A New Attitude: 3 Clients Improved Results Through Our Fundamental Change Process," Bests Review; "How to Organize Your Company Around Your Customers," Bests Review. **Seminars:** How to establish "expense allowable"; How to design an incentive compensation plan around a units core success measures.

24552 ■ McShane Group Inc.
2345 York Rd., Ste. 102
Timonium, MD 21093
Ph:(410)560-0077
Fax:(410)560-2718
Co. E-mail: tmcshane@mcshanegroup.com
URL: http://www.mcshanegroup.com
Contact: Richard D. Montgomery, Principle
E-mail: rdm@atsmcshanegroup.com
Scope: Turnaround consulting and crisis management firm. Specializes in due diligence services, interim management, strategic business realignments, business sale and asset depositions and debt restructuring. Industries served: technology, financial, retail, distribution, medical, educational, manufacturing, contracting, environmental and health care.

24553 ■ Mefford, Knutson & Associates Inc.
6437 Lyndale Ave. S, Ste. 103
Richfield, MN 55423-1465
Ph:(612)869-8011
Free: 800-831-0228
Fax:(612)869-8004
Co. E-mail: info@mkaonline.net
URL: http://www.mkaonline.net
Contact: Jennifer Thompson, Director
E-mail: jthompson@atsmkaonline.com
Scope: A consulting and licensed business brokerage firm specializing in start-up businesses; strategic planning; mergers and acquisitions; joint ventures; divestitures; business process re-engineering; personnel policies and procedures; market research; new product development and cost controls.

24554 ■ Milestone Inc.
PO Box 630
Dedham, MA 02027
Ph:(781)467-1200
Fax:(781)467-0299
Co. E-mail: bob@milestoneideas.com
URL: http://www.milestoneideas.com
Contact: William J. Heater, Mgr
E-mail: bob@milestoneideas.com
Scope: Facilitates 100 business creativity and innovation growth sessions per year. Assists to: Discover new growth strategies and planning options; create new ideas, new promises, value propositions, products and programs; identify and integrate customer passions in new and surprising ways; realize higher returns on involvement, interest and investment; refine processes, accelerate innovative growth and build better teams. **Publications:** "Can your brand tell a bigger story". **Seminars:** Ideas in Action; Double-Gesturing; Growth in a period of no growth; Strike while the iron is cold; Natural Creative Strategies; The Enduring Power of Open Ended Creativity; Ideation Techniques to Drive Brand Value. **Special Services:** Milestone[R]; IMMERgENT[R]; SmartAlec.

24555 ■ MoneySoft Inc.
1 E Camelback Rd., Ste. 550
Phoenix, AZ 85012-1650
Ph:(602)266-7710
Free: 800-966-7797
Fax:(602)230-1864
Co. E-mail: info@moneysoft.com
URL: http://www.moneysoft.com
Contact: Michael Bray, Principle
E-mail: mbray@moneysoft.com
Scope: Specializes in the publication of software for the corporate acquisition and development community. Assists businesses develop acquisition goals and criteria that build shareholder value; determine whether an acquisition candidate meets their criteria; conduct analysis of the candidate's historic performance and position; estimate the candidate's future earning capacity; prepare professional-quality valuations and appraisal reports for tax, business planning or litigation related matters; determine purchase price and optimal terms. Prepare a detailed plan to finance the acquisition; estimate the future earnings of the candidate after the acquisition; generate fact-filled acquisition proposals for presentation to management and funding sources; and manage and track fixed assets and depreciation. **Publications:** "The Price is Right- Or is It?"; "Preparing Financial Projections and Valuations"; "Negotiating Business Acquisitions"; "Managing the Process of Buying a Business"; "The Overpayment Trap"; "Strategies to Avoid the Overpayment Trap"; "The Value, Price and Cost of an Acquisition"; "The Trouble with EBITDA". **Special Services:** Corporate Valuation Professional[TM]; DealSense[R]; Buy-OutPlan[R]; Corporate Valuation[TM]; Lightning Deal Reviewer[R]; Fixed Asset Pro[TM]; Benchmark Pro 2006[TM]; DealSense Plus; Mergerstat[R].

24556 ■ New Commons
545 Pawtucket Ave., Studio 106A
PO Box 116
Pawtucket, RI 02860
Ph:(401)351-7110
Fax:(401)351-7158
Co. E-mail: info@newcommons.com
URL: http://www.newcommons.com
Contact: Robert Leaver, Principal
E-mail: rleaver@atsnewcommons.com
Scope: Builder of agile human networks to champion innovation and mobilize change; to pursue business opportunities; to custom design agile organizations and communities, to foster civic engagement. Clients include organizations on-profits, corporations, government agencies, educational institutions; networks-Trade/professional groups, IT services collaborations, service-sharing collectives; and communities- municipalities, states and statewide agencies, regional collaborations. **Publications:** "Plexus Imperative," Sep, 2005; "Creating 21st Century Capable Innovation Systems," Aug, 2004; "Call to Action: Building Providences Creative and Innovative Economy"; "Getting Results from Meetings"; "The Entrepreneur as Artist," Commonwealth Publications; "Leader and Agent of Change," Commonwealth Publications; "Achieving our Providence: Lessons of City-Building," Commonwealth Publications. **Seminars:** Introduction to Social Computing (Web 2.0), Jan, 2009; Every Company Counts, Jun, 2009; Facilitating for Results; Story-Making and Story-Telling.

24557 ■ Nightingale Associates
7445 Setting Sun Way
Columbia, MD 21046-1261
Ph:(410)381-4280
Fax:(410)381-4280
Co. E-mail: fredericknightingale@nightingaleassociates.net
URL: http://www.nightingaleassociates.net
Contact: Frederick C. Nightingale, Managing Director
E-mail: fredericknightingale@nightingaleassociates.net
Scope: Management training and consulting firm offering the following skills: productivity and accomplishment; leadership skills for the experienced manager; management skills for the new manager; leadership and teambuilding; supervisory development; creative problem solving; real strategic planning; providing superior customer service; international purchasing and supply chain management; negotiation skills development and fundamentals of purchasing. **Seminars:** Productivity and Accomplishment Management Skills for the New Manager; Leadership and Team building; Advanced Management; Business Process Re engineering; Strategic Thinking; Creative Problem Solving; Customer Service; International Purchasing and Materials Management; Fundamentals of Purchasing; Negotiation Skills Development; Providing superior customer service; Leadership skills for the experienced manager.

24558 ■ P2C2 Group Inc.
4101 Denfeld Ave.
Kensington, MD 20895-1514
Ph:(301)942-7985
Fax:(301)942-7986
Co. E-mail: info@p2c2group.com
URL: http://www.p2c2group.com
Contact: Jim Kendrick, President
E-mail: kendrick@p2c2group.com
Scope: Works with clients on the business side of federal program and project management. Services include program/project planning and optimization; acquisition strategy and work statements; IT Capital Planning and Investment Control (CPIC); business cases - new, revisions, critiques; budget analysis - cost benefits- alternatives; CPIC, SELC, and security documentation; research, metrics, analysis, and case studies. Consulting support helping to: Define or redefine programs; strengthen portfolio management; identify alternatives for lean budgets; improve capital planning and investment; develop better plans and documentation, and evaluate performance of existing program investments. **Publications:** "OMB 300s Go Online," Federal Sector Report, Mar, 2007; "Using Risk-Adjusted Costs for Projects," Federal Sector Report, Feb, 2007; "Make Better Decisions Using Case Studies," Federal Sector Report, Jan, 2007; "PMO Performance Measurement & Metrics"; "Executive Sponsors for Projects"; "ABCs of the Presidential Transition"; "Financial Systems and Enterprise Portfolio Management"; "The Future of CPIC"; "Critical Factors for Program and Project Success"; "Using Risk-Adjusted Costs for Projects"; "Tactics for a Successful Year of CPIC"; "Operational Analysis Reviews"; "Successful IT Strategic Planning"; "Information Technology Investment Management". **Seminars:** How to Hire a Management Consultant and Get the Results You Expect.

24559 ■ Performance Consulting Associates Inc.
3700 Crestwood Pky., Ste. 100
Duluth, GA 30096
Ph:(770)717-2737
Fax:(770)717-7014
Co. E-mail: info@pcaconsulting.com
URL: http://www.pcaconsulting.com
Contact: Robert Wilson, Mgr
E-mail: wilson@atspcaconsulting.com
Scope: Maintenance consulting and engineering firm specializing in production planning, project management, team building, and re-engineering maintenance. **Publications:** "Does Planning Pay," Plant Services, Nov, 2000; "Asset Reliability Coordinator," Maintenance Technology, Oct, 2000; "Know What it is You Have to Maintain," Maintenance Technology; May, 2000; "Does Maintenance Planning Pay," Maintenance Technology, Nov, 2000.; "What is Asset Management?"; "Implementing Best Business Practices".

24560 ■ Performance Consulting Group Inc.
8031 SW 35th Terr.
Miami, FL 33155-3443
Ph:(305)264-5577
Fax:(305)264-9079
Contact: Patrick J. O'Brien, President
Scope: Firm provides consulting services in the areas of strategic planning; profit enhancement; product development; and production planning.

24561 ■ Pioneer Business Consultants
9042 Garfield Ave., Ste. 312
Huntington Beach, CA 92646
Ph:(714)964-7600
Fax:(714)962-6585
Contact: Ron von Freyman, Mgr
Scope: Offers general management consulting specializing in business acquisitions, tax and business planning, cash flow analyses, business valuations and business sales and expert witness court testimony regarding business sales, valuations and accounting.

24562 ■ Plans and Solutions Inc.
7823 Mistic View Ct.
PO Box 8905
Derwood, MD 20855
Ph:(301)947-8150
Fax:(240)525-5601
Co. E-mail: info@plansandsolutions.com
URL: http://www.plansandsolutions.com
Contact: Kenneth D. Weiss, President
E-mail: kw@plansandsolutions.com
Scope: Market research and competitive analysis; marketing and promotion planning, and executing promotion plans. Specializes in registration and problem solving services that include food canning establishment and process registration, registration under the terrorism act, assistance in case of detention of shipments, and on-site inspection of processing plants and records. Most clients are minority-owned businesses in the USA and companies overseas that want to begin or increase exports to the United States and Canada. **Publications:** "Building an Import/Export Business," John Wiley & Sons, 2002; "How to Conquer the U.S. Market "; "Going Global (Getting Started in International Trade)". **Seminars:** U.S. Import Regulations on Food Products.

24563 ■ Rothschild Strategies Unlimited L.L.C.
19 Thistle Rd.
PO Box 7568
Norwalk, CT 06851-1909
Ph:(203)846-6898

Fax:(203)847-1426
Co. E-mail: bill@strategyleader.com
URL: http://www.strategyleader.com
Contact: William Rothchild, CEO
E-mail: billrothschild@atsoptonline.net
Scope: Consults with senior management and business level strategy teams to develop overall strategic direction, set priorities and creates sustainable competitive advantages and differentiators. Enables organizations to enhance their own strategic thinking and leadership skills so that they can continue to develop and implement profitable growth strategies. **Publications:** "Putting It All Together-a guide to strategic thinking"; "Competitive Advantage"; "Ristaker, Caretaker, Surgeon & Undertaker four faces of strategic leadership"; "The Secret to GE's Success"; "Having the Right Strategic Leader and Team". **Seminars:** Who is going the WRONG way?; Learning from your Successes and Failures. **Special Services:** StrategyLeader[R].

24564 ■ Sklar and Associates Inc.
242 Laurel Bay Dr.
Murrells Inlet, SC 29576
Ph:(202)257-5061
Fax:(843)651-3090
Co. E-mail: sklarincdc@aol.com
URL: http://www.sklarinc.com
Contact: Tim Sklar, President
Scope: Provides consulting services for business acquisitions, business development and project finance. Provides audit oversight services to listed corporations on Sarbanes-Oxley compliance. Services include: Due diligence analyses and corporate governance. Industries served: transportation sectors, energy sector and commercial real estate industries. **Seminars:** Financial Analysis in MBA; Emerging Company Finance; Due Diligence in Business Acquisition; Business Valuation.

24565 ■ Staubs Business Services
23320 S Vermont Ave.
Torrance, CA 90502-2940
Ph:(310)830-9128
Fax:(310)830-9128
Co. E-mail: harry_l_staubs@lamg.com
Contact: Harry L. Staubs, Principle
Scope: Provides business consulting support to new product development and business plans.

24566 ■ Strategic MindShare Consulting
1401 Brickell Ave., Ste. 640
Miami, FL 33131
Ph:(305)377-2220
Fax:(305)377-2280
Co. E-mail: dee@strategicmindshare.com
URL: http://www.strategicmindshare.com
Contact: Cynthia R. Cohen, President
E-mail: cohen@strategicmindshare.com
Scope: Firm specializes in strategic planning; feasibility studies; profit enhancement; organizational development; start-up businesses; mergers and acquisitions; joint ventures; divestitures; interim management; crisis management; turnarounds; new product development and competitive analysis. **Publications:** "Top Ten CEO Burning Issues for 2005"; "Top Ten Consumer Behavioral Trends for 2005"; "The Influence Factors"; "New Profit Opportunities for Retailers and Consumer Product Companies".

24567 ■ Tamayo Consulting Inc.
169 Saxony Rd., Ste. 112
Encinitas, CA 92024-6779
Ph:(760)479-1352
Free: 800-580-9606
Fax:(760)479-1465
Co. E-mail: info@tamayoconsulting.com
URL: http://www.tamayoconsulting.com
Contact: Diane West, Principal
E-mail: jdreyer@atsearthlink.net
Scope: Training and consulting firm specializing in leadership and team development. Industries served: private, non-profit, government, educational. **Seminars:** Presentation AdvantEdge Program; Lead point Development Program; Supervisor Development Programs.

24568 ■ ValueNomics Value Specialists
50 W San Fernando St., Ste. 600
San Jose, CA 95113
Ph:(408)200-6400
Fax:(408)200-6401
Co. E-mail: info@amllp.com
Contact: Jeff A. Stegner, Partner
Scope: Consulting is offered in the areas of financial management, process re-engineering, growth business services; governance, risk/compliance, SOX readiness and compliance, SAS 70, enterprise risk management, system security, operational and internal audit; business advisory services; valuation services; CORE assessment; contract assurance; transaction advisory services, IT solutions and litigation support services. **Publications:** "Dueling Appraisers: How Differences in Input and Assumptions May Control the Value," Apr, 2005; "The Business of Business Valuation and the CPA as an expert witness"; "The Business of Business Valuation," McGraw-Hill Professional Publishers Inc.

24569 ■ VenturEdge Corp.
4711 Yonge St., Ste. 1105
Toronto, ON, Canada M2N 6K8
Ph:(416)224-2000
Fax:(416)224-2376
Co. E-mail: info@venturedge.com
URL: http://www.venturedge.com
Contact: David Chung-Ki Hui, Principle
E-mail: hui@atsventuredge.com
Scope: Provides services including strategy formulation; business planning; financial management; business coaching; performance improvement; information management; merger, acquisitions and divestitures; family succession planning; competitive intelligence. **Publications:** "Reputation," Harvard Business School Press, 1996; "Competing for the Future," Harvard Business School Press, 1994; "The Fifth Discipline," 1990.

24570 ■ Vision Management
149 Meadows Rd.
Lafayette, NJ 07848-3120
Ph:(973)702-1116
Fax:(973)702-8311
Contact: Norman L. Naidish, President
Scope: Firm specializes in profit enhancement; strategic planning; business process reengineering; industrial engineering; facilities planning; team building; inventory management; and total quality management (TQM). **Publications:** "To increase profits, improve quality," Manufacturing Engineering, May, 2000.

24571 ■ Weich & Bilotti Inc.
600 Worcester Rd., 4th Fl.
Framingham, MA 01702
Ph:(508)663-1600
Fax:(508)663-1682
Co. E-mail: info@weich-bilotti.com
URL: http://www.weich-bilotti.com
Contact: Mervyn D. Weich, President
E-mail: mweich@weich-bilotti.com
Scope: Specializes in business plans, venture capital, computer information systems, turnaround/ interim management, retail consulting, start-up process, college recruiting and IS and IT personnel.

24572 ■ Western Capital Holdings Inc.
10050 E Applwood Dr.
Parker, CO 80138
Ph:(303)841-1022
Fax:(303)770-1945
Contact: Patrick T. Frasco, President
Scope: Specialists in all phases of financial and management consulting. Provide strong emphasis in strategic planning and corporate development, financial analysis, acquisitions, investment banking and corporate finance. Projects range in size and duration to fit clients needs. Services can be applied to many diverse financial projects that may include the following: Business plan development, budgeting and forecasting, strategic planning, cash flow analysis, cash flow management, corporate development, banking relations, asset management, and financial analysis. Industries served: Food industry, manufacturing, distribution, retailing, computer services, agribusiness, financial services, insurance, and government agencies. **Seminars:** Buy Low, Sell High, Collect Early and Pay Late; Preparing Your Company for Sale; Venture Capital - Finding an Angel.

COMPUTER SYSTEMS/ SOFTWARE

24573 ■ Automate Your Business Plan 2009
Out of Your Mind ... and Into the Marketplace
13381 White Sand Dr.
Tustin, CA 92780-4565
Ph:(714)544-0248
Free: 800-419-1513
Fax:(714)730-1414
Co. E-mail: lpinson@business-plan.com
URL: http://www.business-plan.com
Price: $95.00. **Description:** A computer program designed to help prepare a business plan.

RESEARCH CENTERS

24574 ■ Chadron State College–Nebraska Business Development Center
Burhkiser Technology Complex, Rm. 120
1000 Main St.
Chadron, NE 69337
Ph:(308)432-6282
Fax:(308)432-6430
Co. E-mail: jkoehn@csc.edu
URL: http://www.csc.edu/business/nbdc/about.csc
Contact: James Koehn, Asst.Dir.
E-mail: jkoehn@csc.edu
Scope: Management education, market research, marketing plans, strategic planning, financial planning, cash flow budgeting, capital budgeting, loan packaging, rural development, and business plans. **Services:** Consulting. **Publications:** NBDC Business Calendar (annually). **Educational Activities:** Continuing education programs.

24575 ■ University of Nebraska at Omaha–Nebraska Business Development Center
Mammel Hall, Ste. 200
College of Business Administration
Omaha, NE 68182-0248
Ph:(402)554-2521
Fax:(402)554-3473
Co. E-mail: rbernier@unomaha.edu
URL: http://nbdc.unomaha.edu
Contact: Robert Bernier, Dir.
E-mail: rbernier@unomaha.edu
Scope: Management education, market research, marketing plans, strategic planning, financial planning, cash flow budgeting, capital budgeting, loan packaging, and rural development. **Services:** Business consulting; Government procurement assistance; Manufacturing assistance. **Publications:** Keys to Successful Business Start-Up in Nebraska; NBDC Business Calendar (annually). **Educational Activities:** Computer training and business education programs (weekly), for corporate managers.

Business Relocation

START-UP INFORMATION

24576 ■ "Head West, Young Startup?" in *Boston Business Journal* (Vol. 30, October 22, 2010, No. 39, pp. 1)
Pub: Boston Business Journal
Ed: Galen Moore. **Description:** Startup companies Lark Technologies, Baydin and E la Cart Inc. are planning to leave Boston, Massachusetts for Silicon Valley. Lark has developed a vibrating wrist strap that syncs with a mobile phone's alarm clock.

REFERENCE WORKS

24577 ■ "1Q Office Vacancies Mainly Up; Class A Space Bucks Trend, Falls" in *Crain's Detroit Business* (Vol. 24, April 14, 2008, No. 15)
Pub: Crain Communications, Inc.
Ed: Daniel Duggan. **Description:** Although more office space became vacant in the first quarter, Class A space went in the opposite direction with several local businesses are moving from less-desirable to more desirable areas.

24578 ■ "Aeronautics Seeking New HQ Site" in *The Business Journal-Milwaukee* (Vol. 25, September 5, 2008, No. 50, pp. 1)
Pub: American City Business Journals, Inc.
Ed: Rich Kirchen. **Description:** Milwaukee, Wisconsin-based Aeronautics Corp. of America is planning to move its headquarters to a new site. The company has started to search for a new site. It also plans to consolidate its operations under one roof.

24579 ■ "Affordable Again" in *The Business Journal-Serving Greater Tampa Bay* (Vol. 28, July 18, 2008, No. 30, pp. 1)
Pub: American City Business Journals, Inc.
Ed: Janet Leiser. **Description:** Rental rates for office space in the Tampa Bay area has dropped to $21.68 a foot, after demand for the second quarter of 2008 has remained low. Commercial real estate experts say that the industry can easily rebound from what is believed to be the weakest demand in 20 years. Other views, information and statistics on real estate demand and prices in Tampa Bay are, are presented.

24580 ■ "Aircraft Maker May Land Here" in *Austin Business Journal* (Vol. 31, April 15, 2011, No. 6, pp. 1)
Pub: American City Business Journals Inc.
Ed: Jacob Dirr. **Description:** Icon Aircraft Inc. is planning to build a manufacturing facility in Austin, Texas. The company needs 100,000 square feet of space in a new or renovated plant. Executive comments are included.

24581 ■ "Airmall Mulls I-95 Travel Plazas Bid" in *Boston Business Journal* (Vol. 29, September 2, 2011, No. 17, pp. 3)
Pub: American City Business Journals Inc.
Ed: Alexander Jackson. **Description:** Airmall USA is planning to move its food courts from the Baltimore/ Washington International Thurgood Marshall Airport to the new travel plazas on Interstate 95. The plazas are up for bid.

24582 ■ "Another California Firm On Way" in *Austin Business Journal* (Vol. 31, May 6, 2011, No. 9, pp. 1)
Pub: American City Business Journals Inc.
Ed: Christopher Calnan. **Description:** Main Street Hub Inc. is planning to build a facility in Austin, Texas. The company helps businesses manage their online reputations. Main Street has selected Aquila Commercial LLC as its real estate broker.

24583 ■ "BancVue to Expand" in *Austin Business JournalInc.* (Vol. 29, November 27, 2009, No. 38, pp. 1)
Pub: American City Business Journals
Ed: Kate Harrington. **Description:** Significant growth of BancVue in the past six years has prompted the company to look for a site that could increase its office space from 25,000 square feet to 65,000 square feet. BancVue offers bank and credit union software solutions and is planning to lease or buy a property in Austin, Texas.

24584 ■ "Bank Bullish on Austin" in *Austin Business JournalInc.* (Vol. 29, November 13, 2009, No. 36, pp. A1)
Pub: American City Business Journals
Ed: Kate Harrington. **Description:** American Bank's presence in Austin, Texas has been boosted by new management and a new 20,000 square foot building. This community bank intends to focus on building relationship with commercial banking customers. American Bank also plans to extend investment banking, treasury management, and commercial lending services.

24585 ■ "Bellingham Boatbuilder Norstar Yachts Maintains Family Tradition" in *Bellingham Business Journal* (Vol. February 2010, pp. 12)
Pub: Sound Publishing Inc.
Ed: Isaac Bonnell. **Description:** Profile of Norstar Yachts and brothers Gary and Steve Nordtvedt who started the company in 1994. The company recently moved its operations to a 12,000 square foot space in the Fairhaven Marine Industrial Park.

24586 ■ "Boeing's Next Flight May Well Be to the South" in *Puget Sound Business Journal* (Vol. 29, November 21, 2008, No. 31, pp.)
Pub: American City Business Journals
Ed: Steve Wilhelm. **Description:** Southern states in the U.S. are luring Boeing Company to locate a new plant in their region which is experiencing a growing industrial base while offering permissive labor laws as selling points.

24587 ■ "Bond Hill Cinema Site To See New Life" in *Business Courier* (Vol. 27, October 29, 2010, No. 26, pp. 1)
Pub: Business Courier
Ed: Dan Monk. **Description:** Avondale, Ohio's Corinthian Baptist Church will redevelop the 30-acre former Showcase Cinema property to a mixed-use site that could feature a college, senior home, and retail. Corinthian Baptist, which is one of the largest African-American churches in the region, is also planning to relocate the church.

24588 ■ "Bovie Medical Makes Electrosurgical Strike" in *The Business Journal-Serving Greater Tampa Bay* (Vol. 28, August 22, 2008, No. 35)
Pub: American City Business Journals, Inc.
Ed: Margie Manning. **Description:** Bovie Medical Group, which manufactures electrosurgical products, is planning to sell its manufacturing plant in the Tyrone Industrial Park and to purchase the former Harland Clarke facility. The moves are expected to boost the efficiency and the development of new products. Other information on Bovie Medical Group is presented.

24589 ■ "Cal-ISO Plans $125 Million Facility" in *Sacramento Business Journal* (Vol. 25, August 1, 2008, No. 22, pp. 1)
Pub: American City Business Journals, Inc.
Ed: Celia Lamb; Michael Shaw. **Description:** Sacramento, California-based nonprofit organization California Independent System Operator (ISO) is planning to build a new headquarters in Folsom. The new building would double its current leased space to 227,000 square feet. The ISO will seek tax-exempt bond financing for the project.

24590 ■ *Catawba County Chamber of Commerce—Membership Directory/ Relocation Guide*
Pub: Catawba County Chamber of Commerce
Covers: Chamber members. **Entries Include:** Contact details.

24591 ■ "Centrue Sets Down New Roots in St. Louis; Bank Looks to Expand in Exurbs of Chicago" in *Crain's Chicago Business* (May 5, 2008)
Pub: Crain Communications, Inc.
Ed: H. Lee Murphy. **Description:** Centrue Financial Corp. has moved its headquarters from Ottawa to suburban St. Louis in search of higher-growth markets. The banks acquisitions and expansion plans are also discussed.

24592 ■ "Chuy's Gears Up to Serve Atlants, Other Untapped Cities" in *Austin Business Journal* (Vol. 31, June 17, 2011, No. 15, pp. 1)
Pub: American City Business Journals Inc.
Ed: Cody Lyon. **Description:** Chuy's Holdings Inc. plans to expand into the Southeastern United States, particularly in Atlanta, Georgia. The restaurant, which secured $67.5 million in debt financing in May 2011, added 20 stores in five years and plans to open eight locations in 2011.

24593 ■ "Cities Work to Attract Small Biz" in *Crain's Detroit Business* (Vol. 25, June 8, 2009, No. 23, pp. 20)
Pub: Crain Communications Inc. - Detroit
Ed: Nancy Kaffer. **Description:** Royal Oak and other metropolitan cities are trying to attract small companies to their towns.

24594 ■ "City, County May Kill VC Tax" in *Business Journal-Portland* (Vol. 24, October 12, 2007, No. 33, pp. 1)
Pub: American City Business Journals, Inc.
Ed: Aliza Earnshaw. **Description:** City of Portland and Multnomah County in Oregon may soon kill taxes levied on venture capital (VC) firms, which is expected to take place in late October 2007. Capitalists have long been saying that taxation is driving them out of town, but this change is expected to generate more investments and persuade VC firms to relocate within city limits.

24595 ■ "City Wooing Red Roof Inn for Return of Corporate HQ" in *Business First-Columbus* (October 19, 2007, pp. A1)
Pub: American City Business Journals, Inc.
Ed: Description: Department of Development of Columbus, Ohio offered Red Roof Inns Inc. a four-year, 40 percent jobs growth initiative to entice the company to move its corporate headquarters into the city from Dallas, Texas. The Watermark Island office building off Dublin Road and Grandview Avenue will be the headquarters of the company if it accepts the offer.

24596 ■ "Clinic to Use Medical Summit to Pump Up Cardiology Center" in *Crain's Cleveland Business* (Vol. 28, October 1, 2007, No. 39, pp. 6)
Pub: Crain Communications, Inc.
Ed: Chuck Soder. **Description:** Overview of the Medical Innovation Summit, sponsored by the Cleveland Clinic and regional business recruitment group Team NEO, whose theme was cardiology. The goal for this year's summit went beyond finding companies for the cardiovascular center, it also looked to market the region to other industries with growth potential.

24597 ■ "Creativity is Essential in Sagging Relocation Market" in *Crain's Cleveland Business* (Vol. 28, November 5, 2007, No. 44, pp. 19)
Pub: Crain Communications, Inc.
Ed: Christine Gordillo. **Description:** Since Northeast Ohio was headquarters to a number of Fortune 500 companies, residential real estate builders and brokers could count on corporate relocation clients for a steady stream of business. Today, corporations have become more cautious when relocating talent due to the costs involved which has forced industry experts to be more patient and more creative in the ways they attract out-of-town buyers who are likely to be a sure sell.

24598 ■ "Criticare Sees Rapid Expansion" in *Business Journal-Milwaukee* (Vol. 28, December 31, 2010, No. 14, pp. A1)
Pub: Milwaukee Business Journal
Ed: Rich Rovito. **Description:** Criticare Systems Inc. expanded its distribution network, added customers, launched two new products and transferred into a new building in Pewaukee, Wisconsin at the start of their fiscal year. Criticare expanded its workforce and now has nearly 140 full time employees.

24599 ■ "Delaware Diaper Maker Wanting To Expand Less Than a Year After Move" in *Business First-Columbus* (December 7, 2007, pp. A6)
Pub: American City Business Journals, Inc.
Ed: Dan Eaton. **Description:** Duluth, Georgia-based Associated Hygienic Products LLC is planning to expand its production operations by 20 percent and hire new workers. The diaper maker was awarded state incentives to facilitate its transfer from Marion to Delaware. Details are included.

24600 ■ "Delta Looks at Downtown Departure" in *Business Courier* (Vol. 27, October 1, 2010, No. 22, pp. 1)
Pub: Business Courier
Ed: Dan Monk. **Description:** Delta Air Lines Inc. has been looking for a smaller office for its reservations center in downtown Cincinnati, Ohio. Delta has informed the city of its plan to seek proposals on office space alternatives in advance of the 2011 lease expiration. Insights on the current employment status at the reservations center are also given.

24601 ■ "Dollar Doldrums; How American Companies are Beating the Currency Crunch" in *Inc.* (March 2008, pp. 45-46)
Pub: Gruner & Jahr USA Publishing
Ed: Sarah Goldstein. **Description:** Despite the low American dollar, some exporters are seeing a growth in their businesses, while other have had to relocate operations and switch to U.S. supplier. Four business owners tell how they are dealing with the current economic conditions.

24602 ■ "Downtown Evens Tenant Ledger" in *The Business Journal-Serving Metropolitan Kansas City* (Vol. 26, July 11, 2008, No. 44, pp. 1)
Pub: American City Business Journals, Inc.
Ed: Rob Roberts. **Description:** Financial services company PricewaterhouseCoopers will relocate its office from the Broadway Square building, but it will not leave downtown as it signs a long-term lease for a 27,000 square feet of space in Town Pavilion. Town Pavilion is the biggest multitenant office building in downtown. Downtown's market competitiveness is also examined.

24603 ■ "Exxon Mobil Campus 'Clearly Happening'" in *Houston Business Journal* (Vol. 40, January 15, 2010, No. 36, pp. 1)
Pub: American City Business Journals
Ed: Jennifer Dawson. **Description:** Oil and gas company Exxon Mobil intends to relocate its employees from Houston, Texas and Fairfax, Virginia into a 400-acre site near the town of Spring, Texas. Meanwhile, Exxon Mobil has refused to disclose further details of the relocation plan. Insights from real estate professionals on this relocation plan are examined.

24604 ■ "FIS-Metavante Deal Paying Off for Many" in *Business Journal-Milwaukee* (Vol. 28, December 17, 2010, No. 11, pp. A1)
Pub: Milwaukee Business Journal
Ed: Rich Kirchen. **Description:** Jacksonville, Florida-based Fidelity National Information Services Inc., also known as FIS, has remained committed to Milwaukee, Wisconsin more than a year after purchasing Metavante Technologies Inc. FIS has transferred several operations into Metropolitan Milwaukee and has continued its contribution to charitable organizations in the area.

24605 ■ "Formaspace Finds a Bigger Home" in *Austin Business JournalInc.* (Vol. 29, December 4, 2009, No. 39, pp. 1)
Pub: American City Business Journals
Ed: Kate Harrington. **Description:** Formaspace Technical Furniture has signed a lease for 56,700 square feet in Harris Ridge Business Center at Northeast Austin, Texas, which represents one of the area's largest leases for 2009. The new lease enables Formaspace to hire new employees, invest in new equipment, and take advantage of a taxing designation created for manufacturers.

24606 ■ "Good for Business: Houston is a Hot Spot for Economic Growth" in *Black Enterprise* (Vol. 37, October 2006, No. 3, pp. 216)
Pub: Earl G. Graves Publishing Co. Inc.
Ed: Jeanette Valentine. **Description:** Fast-growing sectors in the biotechnology and healthcare industries are among the driving forces of Houston's economic growth. More than 76,000 small businesses in the area employ about one in four area workers, according to the Small Business Administration. Housing and business costs are 26 and 11 percent below the national average, respectively, garnering the attention of corporate giants.

24607 ■ "Hyde Park Hungry for Expansion at Cap" in *Business First-Columbus* (October 12, 2007, pp. A1)
Pub: American City Business Journals, Inc.
Ed: Dan Eaton. **Description:** The Cap, an area developed for the retail and restaurant industry, is experiencing major changes such as Hyde Park Restaurant System's planned expansion, and the expected departure of other tenants. The expansion of Hyde Park will lead to the relocation of Schakolad Chocolate Factory.

24608 ■ "Insurance Firm Consolidates Offices; Integro Finds the Right Price Downtown" in *Crain's New York Business* (January 14, 2008)
Pub: Crain Communications, Inc.
Description: Integro insurance brokers is relocating its headquarters to 1 State Street Plaza, where it will consolidate its operations in March. The firm feels that the upscale design will provide an appropriate setting for entertaining clients and an engaging work environment for employees.

24609 ■ "Insurer Buys Foundation's Uptown HQ" in *Charlotte Business Journal* (Vol. 25, December 17, 2010, No. 39, pp. 1)
Pub: Charlotte Business Journal
Ed: Will Boye. **Description:** Charlotte, North Carolina-based Synergy Coverage Solutions has purchased the three-story building owned by Foundations For the Carolinas for slightly more than $3 million. Synergy plans to relocate its operation in the uptown building by August 2011.

24610 ■ "Is It Time to Move to a Real Office?" in *Women Entrepreneur* (December 30, 2008)
Pub: Entrepreneur Media Inc.
Ed: Aliza Sherman. **Description:** Before moving a company from a home-office to a real office it is important to make sure that the additional overhead that will be incurred by the move is comfortably covered and that the move is being done for the right reasons. Several women entrepreneurs who have moved their businesses from their homes to an actual rental space are profiled.

24611 ■ "Kodiak Bucks Bear Market" in *Austin Business JournalInc.* (Vol. 29, December 18, 2009, No. 41, pp. 1)
Pub: American City Business Journals
Ed: Kate Harrington. **Description:** Austin, Texas-based Kodiak Assembly Solutions LLC, a company that installs components into printed circuit boards for product or evaluation tool kit prototyping purposes, will expand despite the recession. It will relocate from a 28,000 square foot space to a 42,000 square foot space in North Austin. The firm will also increase its workforce by 20 employees.

24612 ■ "KXAN Seeks Larger Studio, Office Space" in *Austin Business Journal* (Vol. 31, May 27, 2011, No. 12, pp. A1)
Pub: American City Business Journals Inc.
Ed: Cody Lyon. **Description:** Austin NBC affiliate KXAN Television is opting to sell its property north of downtown and relocate to another site. The station is now inspecting possible sites to house its broadcasting facility and employees totaling as many as 200 people. Estimated cost of the construction of the studios and offices is $13 million plus another million in moving the equipment.

24613 ■ "Lack of Support Drives Scientists Away from Valley" in *The Business Journal - Serving Phoenix and the Valley of the Sun* (Vol. 28, August 1, 2008, No. 48, pp. 1)
Pub: American City Business Journals, Inc.
Ed: Angela Gonzales. **Description:** Lack of support for scientists has caused scientists like Dietrich Stephan to depart from the city. Stephan is expected to relocate to California where he has found funding for his company Navigenics. Other views and information on the rising rate of the departure of scientists are presented.

24614 ■ "LatinWorks Cozies Up to Chevy in Detroit" in *Austin Business Journal* (Vol. 31, August 12, 2011, No. 23, pp. A1)
Pub: American City Business Journals Inc.
Ed: Sandra Zaragoza. **Description:** Hispanic marketing agency LatinWorks opened an office in Detroit to better serve its client Chevrolet and to potentially secure more contracts from its parent company General Motors, whose offices are located nearby.

24615 ■ "Law Firm Jones Day Coming to Boston" in *Boston Business Journal* (Vol. 30, November 19, 2010, No. 43, pp. 1)
Pub: Boston Business Journal
Ed: Lisa van der Pool. **Description:** Jones Day is set to open an office in Boston, Massachusetts. The

company will be the largest law firm to enter Boston since 2007. The firm will open with at least three partners.

24616 ■ "Look Before You Lease" in *Women Entrepreneur* (February 3, 2009)
Pub: Entrepreneur Media Inc.
Ed: Nina L. Kaufman. **Description:** Top issues to consider before leasing an office space are discussed including: additional charges that may be expected on top of the basic rental price; determining both short- and long-term goals; the cost of improvements to the space; the cost of upkeep; and the conditions of the lease.

24617 ■ "Mayfair Considers Moving Boston Store" in *The Business Journal-Milwaukee* (Vol. 25, September 5, 2008, No. 50, pp. 1)
Pub: American City Business Journals, Inc.
Ed: Rich Kirchen. **Description:** Milwaukee, Wisconsin-based Bon-Ton Stores is planning to relocate its Boston Store at the Mayfair Mall. The existing store is to be redeveloped into smaller specialty shops. Details of the new facility are also presented.

24618 ■ "MBT Add On: Gone by 2012?" in *Crain's Detroit Business* (Vol. 24, October 6, 2008, No. 40, pp. 1)
Pub: Crain Communications, Inc.
Ed: Amy Lane. **Description:** Discusses the Michigan Business Tax (MBT), which has angered many businesses in the state due to the addition of a 21.99 percent surcharge. Although the tax policy will cut taxes on 63 percent of businesses in the state and represent no tax liability change for another nine percent of firms, other businesses will see increases of 100 percent or more. This increase means that many business owners will be forced to relocate or close their establishment and others will have to eliminate jobs. Lawmakers are attempting to find a solution to this problem.

24619 ■ "Mission: Poach California" in *Business Journal Portland* (Vol. 26, December 11, 2009, No. 40, pp. 1)
Pub: American City Business Journals Inc.
Ed: Andy Giegerich. **Description:** Leaders of Greenlight Greater Portland, a privately funded economic development organization, will visit California five times in 2010 in an attempt to lure California businesses to expand or relocate in Oregon.

24620 ■ "More Jobs Moving Out of City" in *Business Courier* (Vol. 24, March 14, 2008, No. 49, pp. 1)
Pub: American City Business Journals, Inc.
Ed: Steve Watkins; Laura Baverman. **Description:** UBS Financial Services Inc. is moving Gradison to Kenwood Town Place in Sycamore Township a year after UBS acquired Gradison. The township does not have a tax on earnings so the move will save Gradison's employees the 2.1 percent Cincinnati tax.

24621 ■ "Move South Could Bring Big Benefits" in *Business Journal-Portland* (Vol. 24, November 9, 2007, No. 36, pp. 1)
Pub: American City Business Journals, Inc.
Ed: Matthew Kish. **Description:** Freightliner LLC has announced that it would move around one-tenth of its jobs to Fort Mill, South Carolina, but stated that immediate plans for headquarters relocation have not been made. The relocation of its headquarters is expected to earn $100 million in economic incentives. The benefits of moving to the area, aside from the economic incentives, are discussed.

24622 ■ "Moving On: What's It Worth?" in *Entrepreneur* (Vol. 36, February 2008, No. 2, pp. 32)
Pub: Entrepreneur Media Inc.
Ed: Jacquelyn Lynn. **Description:** An area's cost of living should be considered by business owners when relocating, as it can affect operating costs and salary expenses, among other issues. Details on how to decide on business relocation with regard to cost of living concerns are examined.

24623 ■ "NEMRA Announces Headquarters Move" in *Agency Sales Magazine* (Vol. 39, September-October 2009, No. 9, pp. 53)
Pub: MANA
Description: NEMRA, the National Electrical Manufacturers' Representatives Association is moving their headquarters to 28 Deer Street, Suite 302, Portsmouth, New Hampshire. The association has also added Michelle Rivers-Jameson as their manager of operations and Kirsty Stebbins as their manager of marketing and member services.

24624 ■ "A New Mix of Tenants Settles In" in *Crain's New York Business* (Vol. 24, January 14, 2008, No. 2, pp. 26)
Pub: Crain Communications, Inc.
Ed: Andrew Marks. **Description:** More and more nonfinancial firms are relocating downtown due to the new retailers and restaurants that are reshaping the look and feel of lower Manhattan.

24625 ■ "Office Leasing Gains Ground" in *Sacramento Business Journal* (Vol. 25, July 18, 2008, No. 20, pp. 1)
Pub: American City Business Journals, Inc.
Ed: Michael Shaw. **Description:** There were at least 84,000 square feet leased to companies in the Sacramento area in the three months prior to August 2008. This development is good news considering that overall vacant leases were around 247,000 square feet for the previous quarter.

24626 ■ "Opportunity Knocks" in *Small Business Opportunities* (September 2008)
Pub: Entrepreneur Media Inc.
Description: Profile of YourOffice USA, a franchise that provides home-based and small businesses cost-effective and efficient support through "virtual" offices that are available as much or as little as the client needs it; they also supply necessary tools such as a professional business address, private mailbox service, personalized telephone answering and more that supports clients who want to look, act and operate with an advanced business image.

24627 ■ "Penney's Buys Wal-Mart Site" in *Crain's Chicago Business* (Vol. 31, March 31, 2008, No. 13, pp. 13)
Pub: Crain Communications, Inc.
Ed: Eddie Baeb. **Description:** J.C. Penny Co. bought the closed Wal-Mart location in Crystal Lake and plans to open a store next year in its push to become more prominent in non-mall locations; Penney plans to expand and renovate the store.

24628 ■ "Portland Wooing Under Armour to West Coast Facility" in *Baltimore Business Journal* (Vol. 27, January 29, 2010, No. 39, pp. 1)
Pub: American City Business Journals
Ed: Andy Giegerich. **Description:** Baltimore, Maryland sports apparel maker, Under Armour, is planning a west coast expansion with Portland, Oregon among the sites considered to house its apparel and footwear design center. Portland officials counting on the concentration of nearly 10,000 activewear workers in the city will help lure the company to the city.

24629 ■ "Race Benefits: Changes Afoot for Ironman" in *Business Journal Serving Greater Tampa Bay* (Vol. 30, October 29, 2010, No. 45, pp. 1)
Pub: Tampa Bay Business Journal
Ed: Margaret Cashill. **Description:** World Triatholon Corporation, organizer of the Ironman World Championship 70.3, will move the sports event from Florida to Nevada in 2011. A replacement event, the 5150 Triathlon Series, will be held in 2011 and the series finale will be staged in Florida's Clearwater Beach. How hotels and motels in the area will benefit from the 5150 Triathlon Series is discussed.

24630 ■ "RES Stakes Its Claim in Area" in *Philadelphia Business Journal* (Vol. 28, January 29, 2010, No. 50, pp. 1)
Pub: American City Business Journals
Ed: Peter Key. **Description:** RES Software Company Inc. of Amsterdam, Netherlands appointed Jim Kirby as president for the Americas and Klaus Besier as chairman in an effort to boost the firm's presence in the US. Brief career profiles of Kirby and Besier are included. RES develops software that allows management of information flow between an organization and its employees regardless of location.

24631 ■ "Retail News: Children's Boutique Relocates to Conway" in *Sun News* (June 4, 2010)
Pub: The Sun News
Description: Little Angel's Children's Boutique and Big Oak Frame Shop have moved to downtown locations in Conway, South Carolina. Little Angel's will sell children's clothing and accessories, shoes and gifts, while the frame shop will offer custom framing along with the sale of stationary, invitations and local prints.

24632 ■ "Search Engine: GE Looks Around" in *Business Courier* (Vol. 24, March 7, 2008, No. 48, pp. 1)
Pub: American City Business Journals, Inc.
Ed: Laura Baverman. **Description:** GE Aviation, an aircraft engine company, could move about 1,500 Tri-employees to its new office in West Chester, Liberty Township, Northern Kentucky, as its leases are set to expire in 2009 and 2010. The company revealed that developers are prompting the firm to send out a request-for-proposal to choose development companies in 2008.

24633 ■ "Shire Seeking New Digs for Headquarters" in *Philadelphia Business Journal* (Vol. 30, September 2, 2011, No. 29, pp. 1)
Pub: American City Business Journals Inc.
Ed: Natalie Kostelni. **Description:** Dublin, Ireland-based Shire PLC announced plans to relocate its North American headquarters from Chesterbrook Corporate Center in Wayne, Pennsylvania and currently evaluating their options. The specialty biopharmaceutical firm is also considering a move to New Jersey or Delaware.

24634 ■ "The Silvery Moon Moves to Larger Space" in *Bellingham Business Journal* (Vol. March 2010, pp. 5)
Pub: Sound Publishing Inc.
Description: Jewelry store, the Silvery Moon, moved to a larger location in order to expand its business. The new location was chosen because it offers the firm more visibility. The store offers find silver and gold pieces and specializes in Pacific Northwest native jewelry.

24635 ■ "Sobering Consequences" in *The Business Journal-Milwaukee* (Vol. 25, July 11, 2008, No. 42, pp. A1)
Pub: American City Business Journals, Inc.
Ed: Rich Rovito. **Description:** Milwaukee Mayor Tom Barrett and Wisconsin Governor Jim Doyle met with MillerCoors management in an effort to convince the company to locate its corporate headquarters in the city. The company is expected to announce its decision by mid-July 2008. It was revealed that the decision-making process is focusing on determining an optimal location for the headquarters.

24636 ■ "State Printing Plant on the Move" in *Sacramento Business Journal* (Vol. 25, August 29, 2008, No. 26, pp. 1)
Pub: American City Business Journals, Inc.
Ed: Michael Shaw; Celia Lamb. **Description:** California is planning to replace its printing plant on Richards Boulevard and 7th Street with a newly built or leased facility in the Sacramento area. It was revealed that the project will meet the state's standards for new buildings. It is believed that the new site will require 15 acres or more depending on requirements.

24637 ■ "Suppliers Look to Rack Up Big Sales to Distributors" in *The Business Journal-Serving Metropolitan Kansas City* (August 15, 2008)
Pub: American City Business Journals, Inc.
Ed: James Dornbrook. **Description:** Suppliers of shelving units, conveyor systems and other equipment used in distribution facilities are expecting new business opportunities along with the planned inter-

modal projects in the Kansas City area. Suppliers have already observed that small distributors have started to relocate to the city because of the intermodal projects. Demand for shelves and lifts have also increased.

24638 ■ "Sykes Shift from GunnAllen to New Venture" in *Tampa Bay Business Journal* (Vol. 30, December 18, 2009, No. 52, pp. 1)
Pub: American City Business Journals
Ed: Margie Manning. **Description:** Tampa, Florida's entrepreneur John H. Sykes acquired Pointe Capital Inc., a GunnAllen Holdings Inc. subsidiary, through his JHS Capital Holdings Inc. and changed the name to JHS Capital Advisors Inc. Sykes will become president and CEO of JHS Capital Advisors and will relocate its corporate headquarters to Tampa, Florida.

24639 ■ "Taking the Over-the-Counter Route to US" in *Barron's* (Vol. 88, July 7, 2008, No. 27, pp. 24)
Pub: Dow Jones & Co., Inc.
Ed: Eric Uhlfelder. **Description:** Many multinational companies have left the New York Stock Exchange and allowed their shares to trade over-the-counter. The companies have taken advantage of a 2007 SEC rule allowing publicly listed foreign companies to change trading venues if less than 5 percent of global trading volume in the past 12 months occurred in the US.

24640 ■ "Tecumseh Products to Begin Moving HQ" in *Crain's Detroit Business* (Vol. 24, March 31, 2008, No. 13, pp. 35)
Pub: Crain Communications, Inc.
Ed: Chad Halcom. **Description:** Tecumseh Products Co., a manufacturer of compressor products, will transfer its headquarters to Pittsfield Township near Ann Arbor.

24641 ■ "Tri-State to Get New Headquarters" in *Business Courier* (Vol. 27, October 22, 2010, No. 25, pp. 1)
Pub: Business Courier
Ed: James Ritchie. **Description:** Hong Kong-based corn processing firm Global Bio-Chem Technology is set to choose Greater Cincinnati, Ohio as a location of its North American headquarters. The interstate access, central location, and low labor and property costs might have enticed Global Bio-Chem to invest in the region. Statistics on Chinese direct investment in U.S. are also presented.

24642 ■ "UC May Expand into Old Ford Plant" in *Business Courier* (Vol. 26, December 25, 2009, No. 35, pp. 1)
Pub: American City Business Journals, Inc.
Ed: Dan Monk. **Description:** Developer Stuart Lichter is planning to acquire University of Cincinnati (UC) as a tenant at a two-story office building on a 132-acre site where a vacant Ford transmission plant is located. Details of the transaction are outlined.

24643 ■ "U.S. Playing Card Might Shuffle HQ" in *Business Courier* (Vol. 24, March 21, 2008, No. 50, pp. 1)
Pub: American City Business Journals, Inc.
Ed: Jon Newberry. **Description:** United States Playing Card Co. is considering the possibility of relocating. It is expected that the company will finalize its decision by June 2008. According to Phil Dolci, the company's president, the firm is looking at certain locations in Ohio, Kentucky, and Indiana. He also revealed that the plan to relocate was prompted by the desire to improve the company's manufacturing facilities.

24644 ■ "Viewing Ironman As Gold, R.I. Firm Buys Its Parent" in *The Business Journal-Serving Greater Tampa Bay* (Vol. 28, September 19, 2008)
Pub: American City Business Journals, Inc.
Ed: Pete Williams. **Description:** Providence Equity Partners purchased World Triathlon Corp., parent company of the Ironman Triathlon, for an undisclosed sum. The acquisition means that the World Triathlon Headquarters will move to Tampa, Florida, and allows Providence Equity Partners to stage or license rights to Ironman and half-Ironman distance events.

24645 ■ "'We Are Not a Marketing Company'" in *Boston Business Journal* (Vol. 31, June 10, 2011, No. 20, pp. 1)
Pub: Boston Business Journal
Ed: Julie M. Donnelly. **Description:** Vertex Pharmaceuticals Inc. is marketing its new Hepatitis C treatment, Incivek. The company hired people to connect patients to the drug. Vertex is also set to move to a new facility in Boston, Massachusetts.

24646 ■ "Welcome: From the Chamber of Commerce" in *Inside Business* (Vol. 13, September-October 2011, No. 5, pp. SS5)
Pub: Great Lakes Publishing Company
Ed: Diane Helbig. **Description:** Diane Helbig, Chairperson for the Lakewood Chamber of Commerce in Ohio touts the areas as the best place to start and run a small company. Two colleges, real estate, and culture are among the reasons cited.

24647 ■ "What City is the No. 1 Destination for Residents Moving From WNY?" in *Business First Buffalo* (October 26, 2007, pp. 1)
Pub: American City Business Journals, Inc.
Ed: G. Scott Thomas. **Description:** IRS records reveal that 2,639 people moved from the Buffalo County Region of New York to the Rochester area from 2005 to 2006. Family considerations and career opportunities are the main factors for the almost reciprocal migration of people from Rochester to Buffalo, New York.

TRADE PERIODICALS

24648 ■ *Expansion Management*
Pub: Penton Media Inc.
Contact: Ron Lowy, Publisher
E-mail: ron.lowy@penton.com
Ed: Josh Cable, Editor, josh.cable@penton.com. **Released:** 6/yr. **Price:** $50 Canada; $68 institutions international. **Description:** Magazine assisting executives and managers worldwide in planning and overseeing their companies' facilities development and other expansion and relocation activities.

CONSULTANTS

24649 ■ The Boyd Company Inc.
301 N Harrison St., Ste. 415
Princeton, NJ 08540-3512
Ph:(609)890-0726
Free: 800-974-2693
Fax:(609)920-0266
Co. E-mail: contact@theboydcompany.com
URL: http://www.theboydcompany.com
Contact: John H. Boyd, President
E-mail: jhb@theboydcompany.com
Scope: Provides site selection services to corporate clients expanding or relocating manufacturing, office, and distribution warehousing facilities. Provides corporate management with objective and authoritative analyzes of all geographically variable costs and other quantitative and qualitative location factors affecting optimum site selection. Firm works throughout the 50 states on behalf of leading United States corporations and overseas companies planning direct investment in the United States. **Special Services:** BizCosts[R].

24650 ■ C.D.S. Building Movers
8 Sweetnam Dr.
Ottawa, ON, Canada K2S 1G2
Ph:(613)836-1215
Free: 800-267-5516
Fax:(613)831-0240
Co. E-mail: info@cdsmovers.com
URL: http://www.cdsmovers.com
Contact: John Sweetman, President
E-mail: john@atscdsmovers.com
Scope: Structural engineering and building relocation consultants providing appraisals and feasibility studies for the relocation of large buildings and structures. Specializing in historic and heritage masonry buildings.

24651 ■ Daniel Bloom and Associates Inc.
11517 128th Ave. N
PO Box 1233
Largo, FL 33779
Ph:(727)581-6216
Fax:(727)216-8532
Co. E-mail: dan@dbaiconsulting.com
URL: http://www.dbaiconsulting.com
Contact: Sharon Megiel, Principle
E-mail: dan@dbaiconsulting.com
Scope: Human resources management consultant with a specialization in corporate relocation. Offers clients a turn key service aimed at meeting the unique relocation needs of their employees. Develops and implements training programs within the relocation industry. **Publications:** "Where Have All the Elders Gone," Aug, 2002; "Recoup Your Hiring Investment," Brainbuzz.com, Aug, 2000; "Managing Your Lump Sum Program," Brainbuzz.com, Jun, 2000; "Buyer Value Options," Brainbuzz.com, Apr, 2000; "Just Get Me There". **Seminars:** Chaos in the Workplace: Multiple Generational Interactions; Training Effectiveness: Is the Cost Justified?; Human Capital Resource Management: A Six-Sigma Based Approach to Paving Your Way to the Table; Welcome to My World.

24652 ■ The Foster Group
13321 Purple Sage Rd.
Dallas, TX 75240
Ph:(972)690-4041
Fax:(972)692-7042
Contact: Mary Sue Foster, President
E-mail: marysue@earthlink.net
Scope: Provides services including leadership development, team building, appreciative inquiry, conflict solution for managers and executive. Involves in fund raising, grant uniting for non-profits. **Publications:** "Move It! Relocating Your Business with No Downtime".

24653 ■ Hartford Despatch International
225 Prospect St.
PO Box 280271
East Hartford, CT 06128-1654
Ph:(860)528-9551
Free: 800-678-9000
Fax:(860)282-1224
Co. E-mail: custsvc@hartforddespatch.com
URL: http://www.hartforddespatch.com
Contact: Sandra Silva, Mgr
E-mail: smolloy@atshartforddespatch.com
Scope: Domestic and international relocation services company. An independent provider of worldwide moving and storage services.

24654 ■ International Management Consulting Group Inc.
1309 Harlan Dr., Ste. 205
Bellevue, NE 68005
Ph:(402)291-4545
Free: 800-665-4624
Fax:(402)291-4343
Co. E-mail: imcg@neonramp.com
Contact: Shawn Bengston, Mgr
Scope: Offers the following operational effectiveness programs: productivity improvement programs directed toward any sized business; business and strategic planning for executives; executive and employee seminars; work measurement and performance accounting; relocation planning and management services; job design, job analysis and human resources selection consulting; executive out placement services; and total quality management business processes re-engineering, procurement and purchasing practices. Also provides analysis of business problems faced by entrepreneurs and small business owners. Consultants seek cost savings for clients while expanding into new markets and managed growth opportunities for any sized businesses. Industries served: nearly all; but specialize in the following: insurance, transportation (passenger), family-owned businesses, and light manufacturing heavy production environment and wholesale/retail. **Publications:** "Why Every Executive Needs a Coach," 1997; "The Professional Job Finding System," 1997; "Why Small Business Is Where It's AT in the 1990's"; "It's All in the Plan," Small Business Reports, Jun, 1994; "Six Tips for Picking a Consultant," Small Busi-

ness Reports, Jan, 1994. **Seminars:** Why Every Executive Needs a Coach; Strategic Planning for the 21st Century Executive; Mistakes Managers Make: And How to Avoid Them; Entrepreneurship in the 1990's; How to Start a Small Business and Survive; Time Management for Business Owners; Stress Management: How to Live With Stress; How to Select a Consultant in the 1990's; Total Quality Management: What's It All About; Business Process Reengineering; Activity-Based Learning. **Special Services:** Activity-based learning^{TM}.

24655 ■ NRI Relocation Inc.
195 Arlington Heights Rd., Ste. 101
Buffalo Grove, IL 60089
Ph:(847)215-5000
Free: 800-598-8887
Fax:(847)215-7633
Co. E-mail: nri@nrirelocation.com
URL: http://www.nrirelocation.com
Contact: Karin Schroeder, Principle
E-mail: kschroeder@atsnrirelocation.com
Scope: A full service relocation management company. Assists corporations in the creation and execution of relocation programs. Services include developing, updating and implementing relocation policies for employees, new hires and special group moves; design and implementation of in-house or modified in-house relocation management; appraisal, marketing and acquisition of residential property; home finding; temporary living; household goods transportation; policy counseling and spouse assistance. International services include language and cultural training; freight forwarding; destination services; Visa; repatriation and spouse assistance.

24656 ■ Overland, Pacific & Cutler Inc.
3750 Schaufele Ave., Ste. 150
Long Beach, CA 90808
Ph:(562)304-2000
Free: 800-400-7356
Fax:(562)304-2020
Co. E-mail: info@pacrelo.com
URL: http://www.opcservices.com
Contact: John Cutler, Principle
E-mail: rarmstrong@atsoverland-resources.com
Scope: A full-service relocation assistance, inspection, and property management firm providing services to Redevelopment Agencies, School Districts, Housing Authorities, Transportation Authorities, other public agencies and private sector clients. Demonstrated consistent on-time, on-budget performance in hundreds of successful residential tenant, homeowner, commercial, industrial and mobile home park projects using federal (HUD, FAA, DOT, CDBG, HOME) or state relocation guidelines. Specific services include: on-site project administration with bilingual staff, comprehensive initial project planning, analysis and budgeting, preparation of Relocation and Replacement Housing Plans, administration of temporary moves for housing rehabilitation projects, public housing/Section 8 HQS inspection services, liaison work with community groups, social service agencies and legislative bodies, and support in eminent domain litigation and expert witness testimony. **Seminars:** Right of Way Acquisition for Engineers, 2008; Commercial Relocations, 2008; Relax, It's Only Business Relocation, Dec, 2007; Relocation Nightmares, Aug, 2007; Relax. . . It's Only Residential Relocation, Mar, 2007.

24657 ■ Prudential Relocation Intercultural Services
2555 55th St., Ste. 201D
Boulder, CO 80301
Ph:(303)449-8440
Free: 800-622-6722
Fax:(303)449-1064
Contact: Evelyn Hu-Dehart, Principle
Scope: Provides senior level consulting services specializing in cross cultural aspects of international business. Focuses on corporate image overseas, foreign business practices and structures, multicultural management team building, development of off shore joint ventures, alliances and supplier networks, inter-cultural negotiations, global strategic planning, analysis of power structures in foreign business communities, and coaching of top level international business travelers.

24658 ■ Renal Center
12 Chelsea Ct.
Hillsdale, NJ 07642-1227
Ph:(201)664-4451
Fax:(201)664-1267
Co. E-mail: cncarson@msn.com
Contact: Christopher N. Carson, Principle
Scope: Construction Consulting, Construction Management, Building Management Consulting, Provide Expert Witness Testimony in Dispute Matters. Arbitrator for Alternate Dispute Resolution cases.

24659 ■ Wadley-Donovan GrowthTech L.L.C.
150 Morris Ave., Ste. 203
Springfield, NJ 07081
Ph:(973)379-7700
Free: 800-929-5622
Fax:(973)379-7771
Co. E-mail: info@wadley-donovan.com
URL: http://www.wdgtech.com
Contact: Dennis J. Donovan, Director
E-mail: ddonovan@atswadley-donovan.com
Scope: Business location/relocation specialists, from strategic planning through decision and implementation. Services include: Definition of strategic issues for the geographic deployment of people and facilities; delineating alternatives to the current geographic configuration; relocation feasibility analyses; identification and evaluation of locations for new facilities, or relocating operations; site identification and evaluation; economic development incentive negotiations; and relocation implementation services. Services extend to detailed planning, employee surveys, attrition management, and recruitment and training strategies at the new location. **Publications:** "Benefits from Economic and Workforce Development Collaboration"; "Finger lakes WiB transformation and integration of Workforce and Economic Development". **Seminars:** Corporate Location Trends in the Mid 1990s; Labor Challenges Facing Corporate America; Labor Quality Challenges and Employment Growth Opportunities for Center Cities.

ASSOCIATIONS AND OTHER ORGANIZATIONS

24660 ■ BBB Wise Giving Alliance
4200 Wilson Blvd., Ste. 800
Arlington, VA 22203-1838
Ph:(703)276-0100
Fax:(703)525-8277
Co. E-mail: give@council.bbb.org
URL: http://www.bbb.org/us/Wise-Giving
Contact: H. Art Taylor, Pres./CEO
Description: Supported by companies and local Better Business Bureaus operated autonomously in the United States and Puerto Rico, which are in turn supported by 270,000 local business members. Seeks to promote and foster the highest ethical relationship between businesses and the public through voluntary self-regulation, consumer and business education, and service excellence. Provides support to local Better Business Bureaus. Administers the advertising industry's self-regulatory program that monitors and investigates the truth and accuracy of national advertising claims; monitors and pre-screens advertising directed towards children. Develops information on national charitable organizations and whether they meet voluntary ethical standards for soliciting organizations. Provides information to help consumers and businesses make informed purchasing decisions and avoid costly scams and frauds; and settles consumer complaints through arbitration and other means. Operates BBB AUTO LINE, a national mediation and arbitration service providing an independent forum to resolve consumer complaints involving 32 participating auto manufacturers; Local Better Business Bureaus respond to more than 23 million requests for service annually, fielding 20 million pre-purchase inquiries and 3 million complaints. **Publications:** Annual Report (annual).

REFERENCE WORKS

24661 ■ "All About The Benjamins" in *Canadian Business* (Vol. 81, September 29, 2008, No. 16, pp. 92)
Pub: Rogers Media Ltd.
Ed: David Baines. **Description:** Discusses real estate developer Royal Indian Raj International Corp., a company that planned to build a $3 billion "smart city" near the Bangalore airport; to this day nothing has ever been built. The company was incorporated in 1999 by Manoj C. Benjamin one investor, Bill Zack, has been sued by the developer for libel due to his website that calls the company a scam. Benjamin has had a previous case of fraud issued against him as well as a string of liabilities and lawsuits.

24662 ■ "Avoiding Invention Scams" in *Black Enterprise* (Vol. 37, January 2007, No. 6, pp. 46)
Pub: Earl G. Graves Publishing Co. Inc.
Ed: James C. Johnson. **Description:** Invention promotion firms provide inventors assistance in developing a prototype for product development. It is important to research these companies before making a commitment to work with them because there are a number of these firms that are not legitimate and have caused independent inventors to lose thousands of dollars by making false claims as to the market potential of the inventions.

24663 ■ "Black's Truth: Will a Prison Stay Change the Way Conrad Black Operates?" in *Canadian Business* (Vol. 81, March 31, 2008, No. 5)
Pub: Rogers Media
Ed: Matthew McClearn. **Description:** Conrad Black will serve a 6 and a half years in prison but he asserts that his successors at Hollinger International and Hollinger Inc. grossly mismanaged and unjustly enriched themselves. Black also asserts that International violated the so-called November Agreement and that he is the aggrieved party. Black's assertions show a character flaw that cannot be corrected in prison.

24664 ■ "Dating Games" in *Canadian Business* (Vol. 79, September 25, 2006, No. 19, pp. 23)
Pub: Rogers Media
Ed: John Gray. **Description:** Increasing stock option scandals in Canada and American companies is discussed.

24665 ■ "Do the Math" in *Canadian Business* (Vol. 79, October 9, 2006, No. 20, pp. 17)
Pub: Rogers Media
Ed: Al Rosen. **Description:** Faulty practices followed by regulators in Canadian stock market are discussed. The need for authorities to protect investors against these frauds are emphasized.

24666 ■ "FTC Takes Aim At Foreclosure 'Rescue' Firm" in *The Business Journal-Serving Greater Tampa Bay* (Vol. 28, September 19, 2008, No. 39)
Pub: American City Business Journals, Inc.
Ed: Michael Hinman. **Description:** United Home Savers LLP has been ordered to halt its mortgage foreclosure rescue services after the Federal Trade Commission accused it of deceptive advertising. The company is alleged to have charged customers $1,200 in exchange for unfulfilled promises to keep them in their homes.

24667 ■ "The Hidden Tax" in *Canadian Business* (Vol. 81, April 14, 2008, No. 6, pp. 28)
Pub: Rogers Media
Ed: Al Rosen. **Description:** Accounting fraud could take out a sizable sum from one's retirement fund when computed over a long period of time. The much bigger tax on savings is the collective impact of the smaller losses that do not attract the attention they deserve. Ensuring that investors are not unnecessarily taxed 2 percent of their total investments every year outweighs the benefit of a 2 percent reduction in personal tax rates.

24668 ■ "A History of Neglect" in *Canadian Business* (Vol. 79, September 11, 2006, No. 18, pp. 21)
Pub: Rogers Media
Ed: Al Rosen. **Description:** Faulty practices being followed by auditors and regulators of Canada are discussed. The need for appropriate steps to protect investors against these frauds are emphasized.

24669 ■ "Identity Crisis: The Battle For Your Data" in *Canadian Business* (Vol. 81, March 17, 2008, No. 4, pp. 12)
Pub: Rogers Media
Description: Nigel Brown explains that businesses must protect their data through encryption and tightening up access to data. Brown also points out that banks and merchants bear most of the costs for identity fraud and leaves individuals with a lot of pain and heartache in clearing their name.

24670 ■ "'Mr. CEO, Please Do Elaborate On Your Firm's Metrics'" in *Business Courier* (Vol. 24, February 29, 2008, No. 47, pp. 1)
Pub: American City Business Journals, Inc.
Ed: Jon Newberry. **Description:** Discusses a rogue caller who goes by the name of Joe Herrick, Steven Nissan and Joe Harris has joined in over a dozen conference calls, asking chief executive officers on their plans and commenting on the companies' operations. The mystery caller attempts to pass himself off as a financial analyst. Transcripts of some conference calls, in which the rogue caller is involved, are provided.

24671 ■ "A Nasty Russian Tale" in *Canadian Business* (Vol. 81, March 3, 2008, No. 3, pp. 85)
Pub: Rogers Media
Ed: Andrew Nikiforuk. **Description:** Billionaires Alex Shnaider and Michael Shtaif entered a partnership for an oil venture which ended in a slew of litigations. Cases of breach of contract, injurious falsehood and other related lawsuits were filed against Shnaider. Details of the lawsuits and the other parties involved in the disputes are presented.

24672 ■ "New Ways to Catch a Thief" in *Barron's* (Vol. 88, March 10, 2008, No. 10, pp. 37)
Pub: Dow Jones & Company, Inc.
Ed: Theresa W. Carey. **Description:** Online brokerage firms employ different methods to protect the accounts of their customers from theft. These methods include secure Internet connections, momentary passwords, and proprietary algorithms.

24673 ■ "One-Time Area Trust Executive Finds Trouble in N.H." in *The Business Journal-Serving Metropolitan Kansas City* (September 12, 2008)
Pub: American City Business Journals, Inc.
Ed: Steve Vockrodt. **Description:** About 200 investors, some from Missouri's Kansas City area, claim that they had conducted business with Noble Trust Co.. The trust company was placed under New Hampshire Banking Department's conservatorship after $15 million was discovered to be missing from its account. It is alleged that the money was lost in a Colorado Ponzi scheme.

24674 ■ "Prosecutors Dish Sordid AIPC Story" in *The Business Journal-Serving Metropolitan Kansas City* (Vol. 27, September 19, 2008, No. 1)
Pub: American City Business Journals, Inc.
Ed: Suzanna Stagemeyer. **Description:** Prosecutors in the American Italian Pasta Co.'s accounting fraud

case have revealed evidence on the schemes used by then-officers of the company to commit fraud. District attorney John Wood has dubbed the case as the largest corporate fraud lawsuit in the history of the district of Missouri. How AIPC fell from being an industry leader is also discussed.

24675 ■ "Retailers Report 'Shrinkage' of Inventory on the Rise" in *Arkansas Business* (Vol. 26, September 28, 2009, No. 39, pp. 17)
Pub: Journal Publishing Inc.

Ed: Mark Friedman. **Description:** According to a National Retail Security Survey report released last June, retailers across the country have lost about $36.5 billion in shrinkage, most of it at the hands of employees and shoplifters alike. Statistical data included.

24676 ■ "The Trials of Brian Hunter" in *Canadian Business* (Vol. 81, March 3, 2008, No. 3, pp. 64)
Pub: Rogers Media

Ed: Thomas Watson. **Description:** Brian Hunter was a considered a brilliant trader in Wall Street before he was blamed for the fall of the Amaranth hedge fund. Some people blame Hunter for placing bets based on unpredictable weather when he was a trader for Amaranth Advisors LLC. The accusation against Hunter that he conspired to manipulate natural gas prices is also discussed.

24677 ■ "U.S. Attorney Post the Latest Twist" in *The Business Journal-Serving Greater Tampa Bay* (Vol. 28, July 25, 2008, No. 31, pp. 1)
Pub: American City Business Journals, Inc.
Ed: Jane Meinhardt. **Description:** Tampa, Florida-based lawyer A. Brian Albritton has been nominated to be the U.S. Attorney for the Middle District of Florida. He is an expert in cases involving white-collar crime, secret theft, noncompete agreements, and other agreements.

TRADE PERIODICALS

24678 ■ *Consumer Protection Report*
Pub: National Association of Attorneys General
Ed: Sarah Reznek, Editor, sreznek@naag.org. **Released:** Bimonthly. **Description:** Seeks to protect citizens from consumer frauds. Reports on legislation, regulations, the Federal Trade Commission, and on state activities such as consumer information and complaint programs. Examines consumer fraud lawsuits throughout the country, covering cases involving such matters as false advertising, fraudulent billing, and regulation of charitable trusts and organizations. Recurring features include announcements and news of publications.

24679 ■ *Homecare Administrative HORIZONS*
Pub: Beacon Health Corp.
Contact: Diane J. Omdahl RN, MS, Editor-in-Chief
Released: Monthly. **Price:** $347, individuals. **Description:** Provides homecare agency management information on all kinds of business and personnel topics. Incorporates comprehensive how-to information, current regulatory requirements, and documentation strategies. Runs a series of articles, including how to move into managed care, how to manage and measure outcomes, how to survive scrutiny by medicare's fraud squad, strengthening agency/physician relationships, and personnel issues. Recurring features include columns titled Peaks & Valleys, Fine-tuning the Fundamentals, Clearing the Fog, and Higher Ground.

VIDEOCASSETTES/ AUDIOCASSETTES

24680 ■ *LBOs and Fraudulent Conveyances*
Practicing Law Institute
810 7th Ave., 21st Fl.
New York, NY 10019-5818
Ph:(212)824-5700
Free: 800-260-4PLI
Co. E-mail: info@pli.edu
URL: http://www.pli.edu
Released: 1988. **Price:** $24.95. **Description:** Defines state and federal laws regarding fradulent conveyances following a leverage buy-out. **Availability:** VHS.

ASSOCIATIONS AND OTHER ORGANIZATIONS

24681 ■ Caribbean-Central American Action
1710 Rhode Island Ave., NW, Ste. 300
Washington, DC 20036
Ph:(202)331-9467
Fax:(202)785-0376
Co. E-mail: info@c-caa.org
URL: http://www.c-caa.org
Contact: Anton E. Edmunds, Sr. Consultant

Description: Promotes private-sector-led economic development in the Caribbean Basin and throughout the hemisphere; facilitates trade and investment in the region by stimulating a constructive dialogue between the private and public sectors to improve the policy and regulatory environments for business on both international and local levels; conducts policy-oriented programs in sectors such as financial services, transportation, energy, agriculture, textiles, intellectual property rights, tourism, telecommunications, and information technology. **Publications:** *Caribbean Region Profile* (annual); *CCAA Quarterly* (quarterly).

24682 ■ European Travel Commission
50 W 23rd St., 11th Fl.
New York, NY 10010
Co. E-mail: etc@spring-obrien.com
URL: http://www.VisitEurope.com/us
Contact: Robert K. Franklin, Exec. Dir.

Purpose: Represents government tourism organizations cooperating to promote travel to Europe and further international goodwill and economic prosperity. **Publications:** *VisitEurope* (monthly).

24683 ■ International Business Aviation Council
999 Rue University, Ste. 16-33
Montreal, QC, Canada H3C 5J9
Ph:(514)954-8054
Fax:(514)954-6161
Co. E-mail: info@ibac.org
URL: http://www.ibac.org
Contact: Donald D. Spruston, Dir. Gen.

Description: International business aircraft associations; national and regional business aviation organizations or subgroups. Aims to provide information on all aspects of international business aircraft operations; ensure that the interests of international business aviation are brought to the attention of and understood by authorities; improve the safety, efficiency and economic use of business aircraft operating internationally. Stresses the importance of business aviation to the economy and to the well-being of all nations. Maintains liaison with international aviation organizations to ensure safe and orderly growth of international business aviation throughout the world. Compiles statistics. **Publications:** *IBAC Update* (quarterly). **Telecommunication Services:** electronic mail, dspruston@ibac.org; electronic mail, plessard@ibac.org.

24684 ■ National Business Travel Association
110 N Royal St., 4th Fl.
Alexandria, VA 22314
Ph:(703)684-0836
Fax:(703)684-0263
Co. E-mail: info@gbta.org
URL: http://www2.nbta.org/usa/Pages/default.aspx
Contact: Craig Banikowski CCTE, Pres./CEO
Description: Travel managers and providers. Works to enhance the educational advancement and image of the profession and membership; enhance the value of the travel manager in meeting corporate travel needs and financial goals; provide education to members about industry matters, issues and technology; cultivate a positive public image of the corporate travel industry; advocate and protect the interests of members and their corporations on legislative and regulatory matters; promote safety, security, efficiency and quality travel; and enhance professionalism and recognition of the industry and individual members. Provides a forum for the constructive exchange of information and ideas among members. .

REFERENCE WORKS

24685 ■ "Advertising May Take a Big Hit in Southwest/AirTran Merger" in *Baltimore Business Journal* (Vol. 28, October 1, 2010, No. 21, pp. 1)
Pub: Baltimore Business Journal
Ed: Gary Haber. **Description:** Advertising on television stations and the publishing industry in Baltimore could drop as a result of the merger between rival discount airlines Southwest Airlines and AirTran Airways. Southwest is among the top advertisers in the U.S., spending $126 million in 2009. No local jobs are expected to be affected because neither airline uses a local advertising firm.

24686 ■ "Airlines Mount PR Push to Win Public Support Against Big Oil" in *Advertising Age* (Vol. 79, July 14, 2008, No. 7, pp. 1)
Pub: Crain Communications, Inc.
Ed: Michael Bush. **Description:** Top airline executives from competing companies have banded together in a public relations plan in which they are sending e-mails to their frequent fliers asking for aid in lobbying legislators to put a restriction on oil speculation.

24687 ■ "Airmall Mulls I-95 Travel Plazas Bid" in *Boston Business Journal* (Vol. 29, September 2, 2011, No. 17, pp. 3)
Pub: American City Business Journals Inc.
Ed: Alexander Jackson. **Description:** Airmall USA is planning to move its food courts from the Baltimore/Washington International Thurgood Marshall Airport to the new travel plazas on Interstate 95. The plazas are up for bid.

24688 ■ "Are Your Goals Hitting the Right Target?" in *Business Strategy Review* (Vol. 21, Autumn 2010, No. 3, pp. 46)
Pub: Wiley-Blackwell
Ed: Alan Meekings, Steve Briault, Andy Neely. **Description:** Setting targets is normal in most organizations. The authors think such a practice can cause more ham than good. They offer a better plan.

24689 ■ "Around the World in a Day" in *Agency Sales Magazine* (Vol. 39, August 2009, No. 8, pp. 36)
Pub: MANA
Ed: Jack Foster. **Description:** Highlights of Manufacturer's Agents National Association (MANA) member Les Rapchak one-day visit to Basra, Iraq are presented. Rapchak completed the trip via Frankfurt, Germany and Kuwait with a stop afterwards in Istanbul, Turkey. His purpose for the trip was to take part in a seminar at the State Company for Petrochemical Industries.

24690 ■ "Behind the Scenes: Companies At the Heart of Everyday Life" in *Inc.* (February 2008, pp. 26-27)
Pub: Gruner & Jahr USA Publishing
Ed: Athena Schindelheim. **Description:** Profiles of companies providing services to airports, making the environment safer and more efficient, as well as more comfortable for passengers and workers. Centerpoint Manufacturing provides garbage bins that can safely contain explosions producing thousands of pounds of pressure; Infax, whose software displays arrival and departure information on 19-foot-wide screens; Lavi Industries, whose products include security barricades, hostess stands, and salad-bar sneeze guards; and SATech maker of rubber flooring that helps ease discomfort for workers having to stand for long periods of time.

24691 ■ *Being Self-Employed: How to Run a Business Out of Your Home, Claim Travel and Depreciation and Earn a Good Income Well into Your 70s or 80s*
Pub: Allyear Tax Guides
Ed: Holmes F. Crouch, Irma Jean Crouch, Barbara J. MacRae. **Released:** September 2004. **Price:** $24.95 (US), $37.95 (Canadian). **Description:** Guide for small business to keep accurate tax records.

24692 ■ "Best Cash Flow Generators" in *Canadian Business* (Vol. 82, Summer 2009, No. 8, pp. 40)
Pub: Rogers Media
Ed: Calvin Leung. **Description:** Agrium Inc. and FirstService Corporation are in the list of firms that are found to have the potential to be the best cash flow generators in Canada. The list also includes WestJet Airlines Ltd., which accounts for 385 flights each day. More than 80 percent of analysts rate the airline stocks a Buy.

24693 ■ "Bigger TIF Makes Development Inroads" in *The Business Journal-Serving Metropolitan Kansas City* (Vol. 26, July 11, 2008, No. 44)
Pub: American City Business Journals, Inc.
Ed: Rob Roberts. **Description:** On July 9, 2008 the Tax Increment Financing Commission voted to expand a TIF district to Tiffany Springs Road. The plan for the TIF district close to Kansas City Interna-

tional Airport is to include a-half mile of the road. The impacts of the expansion on construction projects and on the road network are analyzed.

24694 ■ "Boeing Scores $21.7 Billion Order in Indonesia" in *Wall Street Journal Eastern Edition* (November 18 , 2011, pp. B6)
Pub: Dow Jones & Company Inc.

Ed: David Kesmodel, Laura Meckler. **Description:** Boeing has garnered a large contract to deliver Boeing 737 jets to Indonesia's Lion Air. There are those who are lobbying against the US government's practice of subsidizing foreign companies that make contracts with American aerospace companies.

24695 ■ "Border Boletin: UA to Take Lie-Detector Kiosk to Poland" in *Arizona Daily Star* (September 14, 2010)
Pub: Arizona Daily Star

Ed: Brady McCombs. **Description:** University of Arizona's National Center for Border Security and Immigration Research will send a team to Warsaw, Poland to show border guards from 27 European Union countries the center's Avatar Kiosk. The Avatar technology is designed for use at border ports and airports to assist Customs officers detect individuals who are lying.

24696 ■ "The Business Owner's Flight Plan" in *Entrepreneur* (Vol. 37, July 2009, No. 7, pp. 22)
Pub: Entrepreneur Media, Inc.

Description: Greg Rosner, author of 'The Road Warrior Survival Guide: Practical Tips for the Business Traveler,' shares insights on the stages of a typical business trip. Delegating a trusted colleague who can assume certain tasks that you cannot deal with remotely, expecting that the trip is not a vacation, and taking a Thursday night flight are some of the tips given to business travelers.

24697 ■ "Business Start-Up a Learning Experience for Young Bellingham Entrepreneur" in *Bellingham Herald* (July 18, 2010)
Pub: Bellingham Herald

Ed: Dave Gallagher. **Description:** Profile of 21-year-old entrepreneur, Chase Larabee, who developed an online program that helps airport fixed-based operators handle refueling, hotel and transportation reservations and other requests from private airplane pilots.

24698 ■ "Business Travel Can be a Trip if Structured Right" in *Globe & Mail* (February 3, 2007, pp. B11)
Pub: CTVglobemedia Publishing Inc.

Ed: Roma Luciw. **Description:** The importance of arranging a proper business trip for executives by employers, in order to achieve good benefits for the company, is discussed.

24699 ■ "By Land, Air, and Sea: New Passport Rules in Effect" in *Black Enterprise* (Vol. 37, January 2007, No. 6., pp. 101)
Pub: Earl G. Graves Publishing Co. Inc.

Ed: Stephanie Young. **Description:** As part of a new security measure by the Western Hemisphere Travel Initiative, a passport will now be required for U.S. citizens traveling by air between Mexico, Canada, South and Central America, and the Caribbean. This initiative, designed to easily identify travelers and enforce border security, will most likely extend to land or sea travel no later than January 1, 2008.

24700 ■ "Cell Phone the Ticket on American Airlines" in *Chicago Tribune* (November 14, 2008)
Pub: McClatchy-Tribune Information Services

Ed: Julie Johnsson. **Description:** American Airlines is testing a new mobile boarding pass at O'Hare International Airport. Travelers on American can board flights and get through security checkpoints by flashing a bar code on their phones. Passengers must have an Internet-enabled mobile device and an active e-mail address in order to utilize this service.

24701 ■ "City a Pawn in Airlines' Chess Game" in *Business Courier* (Vol. 24, January 18, 2008, No. 41, pp. 1)
Pub: American City Business Journals, Inc.

Ed: Lisa Biank Fasig. **Description:** Delta Air Lines is under negotitaions with Northwest Airlines and UAL Corp. for a proposed merger. The deal will have a negative impact on Cincinnati as a hub regardless whether it goes to UAL or Northwest. The impacts of the planned merger on Cincinnati's labor market and airport traffic are discussed.

24702 ■ "City Plans Downtown Congestion Fees" in *Crain's Chicago Business* (Vol. 31, May 5, 2008, No. 18, pp. 12)
Pub: Crain Communications, Inc.

Description: By penalizing downtown drivers and rewarding public-transit users, Chicago officials plan to unclog Loop streets. The $153 million federal grant would establish a pilot network of express bus routes and set up a peak-period pricing system for city, street and private garage parking and for building loading zones.

24703 ■ "City Struggles to Iron Out Tangled Transportation" in *Crain's New York Business* (Vol. 24, January 14, 2008, No. 2, pp. 33)
Pub: Crain Communications, Inc.

Ed: Judith Messina. **Description:** Discusses the possible solutions to improve lower Manhattan's transportation infrastructure including the construction of three new transit centers, an expansion in ferry service and the plan to get parked buses off the street.

24704 ■ "Civil Council Almost On Board With Light Rail Plan" in *The Business Journal-Serving Metropolitan Kansas City* (September 5, 2008)
Pub: American City Business Journals, Inc.

Ed: Steve Vockrodt. **Description:** Civic Council of Greater Kansas City has taken back its demand for the city to show a 10-year financial plan to win its endorsement of a light rail plan. The council said it will accept a five-year financial plan for the project. Details of the light rail plan are also presented.

24705 ■ "Columbia Sale Narrowed To Two Developers" in *The Business Journal-Milwaukee* (Vol. 25, July 18, 2008, No. 43, pp. A1)
Pub: American City Business Journals, Inc.

Ed: Corrinne Hess. **Description:** Officials of Columbia St. Mary's Inc plan to pick one of two real-estate developers who will buy the 8-acre property of the Columbia Hospital which the company will move away from when their new hospital has been constructed. The hospital on Newport Ave. has been on the market since 2001.

24706 ■ "Congestion Relief" in *Canadian Business* (Vol. 80, February 12, 2007, No. 4, pp. 31)
Pub: Rogers Media

Ed: Andrea Jezovit. **Description:** The development of a satellite-based system for traffic management including paying for parking fees by Skymeter Corp. is discussed.

24707 ■ "Daley's Efforts to Ease Traffic Woes Fall Short" in *Crain's Chicago Business* (Vol. 31, May 5, 2008, No. 18, pp. 18)
Pub: Crain Communications, Inc.

Description: Discusses some of the inherent problems of Mayor Daley's plan to reduce traffic congestion by creating a tax on drivers who park their cars downtown during peak traffic periods and putting articulated buses on new bus-only lanes on major arterial streets leading into the Loop.

24708 ■ "Debut Year Brings Success for Bike-Trail Boosters" in *Business Courier* (Vol. 24, January 4, 2008, No. 39, pp. 4)
Pub: American City Business Journals, Inc.

Ed: Dan Monk. **Description:** Discusses the first year of Cincinnati's Trail Yeah has brought in success as five local government boards approve the bike-trail enthusiast group's endorsement of a cycling path that would connect the city's downtown to the Loveland Bike Trail. The group is planning to raise $3 million to $5 million for the trails first phase.

24709 ■ "Defying Gravity?" in *Canadian Business* (Vol. 81, October 13, 2008, No. 17, pp. 17)
Pub: Rogers Media Ltd.

Ed: Joe Castaldo. **Description:** Airlines around the world are expected to lose $4.1 billion in 2009, but experts believe Canadian airlines will be able to survive the economic challenges. Lower demand for air travel and uncertainty on oil prices are also expected to make the conditions more challenging. Views and key information on airlines in Canada and around the world are cited.

24710 ■ "Delta Looks at Downtown Departure" in *Business Courier* (Vol. 27, October 1, 2010, No. 22, pp. 1)
Pub: Business Courier

Ed: Dan Monk. **Description:** Delta Air Lines Inc. has been looking for a smaller office for its reservations center in downtown Cincinnati, Ohio. Delta has informed the city of its plan to seek proposals on office space alternatives in advance of the 2011 lease expiration. Insights on the current employment status at the reservations center are also given.

24711 ■ "Developers Await Hotel" in *The Business Journal-Portland* (Vol. 25, July 11, 2008, No. 18, pp. 1)
Pub: American City Business Journals, Inc.

Ed: Wendy Culverwell. **Description:** Developers are eager to start the construction of a new hotel at the Oregon Convention Center in Portland, Oregon as hey say that the project will help boost the convention center neighborhood. The project, called The Westin Portland at the Convention Center, is partly handled by Ashforth Pacific Inc.

24712 ■ "Doctor On the Go: Concessions International Founder Opens Airport Clinic" in *Black Enterprise* (Vol. 38, October 2007, No. 3, pp. 34)
Pub: Earl G. Graves Publishing Co. Inc.

Ed: Tara C. Walker. **Description:** Aero Clinic is an onsite healthcare facility designed to care for travelers. Located at Atlanta's Hartsfield-Jackson International Airport, the clinic is the first of its kind.

24713 ■ "Don Bell" in *Canadian Business* (Vol. 80, November 5, 2007, No. 22, pp. 164)
Pub: Rogers Media

Ed: Michelle Magnan. **Description:** Don Bell was not able to finish his degree at University of Calgary, however, he managed to build companies such as WestJet. Bell hates bureaucracy and believes in the importance of a good corporate culture. Details on his life as a father and a pilot along with his advice for entrepreneurs are given.

24714 ■ "Don't Touch My Laptop, If You Please Mr. Customs Man" in *Canadian Electronics* (Vol. 23, June-July 2008, No. 4, pp. 6)
Pub: Action Communication Inc.

Ed: Mark Borkowski. **Description:** Canadian businessmen bringing electronic devices to the US can protect the contents of their laptops by hiding their data from US border agents. They can also choose to clean up the contents of their laptop using file erasure programs.

24715 ■ "Doubletree Finds a Niche for Giving Back" in *Hotel and Motel Management* (Vol. 225, July 2010, No. 8, pp. 6)
Pub: Questex Media Group Inc.

Ed: Paul J. Heney. **Description:** Profile of Doubletree Hotel's community outreach programs that help employee volunteers work to educate children and the public about issues important to the environment.

24716 ■ "Empowered" in *Harvard Business Review* (Vol. 88, July-August 2010, No. 7-8, pp. 94)
Pub: Harvard Business School Publishing

Ed: Josh Bernoff, Ted Schadler. **Description:** HERO concept (highly empowered and resourceful operative) which builds a connection between employees, managers, and IT is outlined. The resultant additional experience and knowledge gained by employees improves customer relationship management.

24717 ■ "Entrepreneurs: Search Party" in *Business Strategy Review* (Vol. 21, Autumn 2010, No. 3, pp. 30)
Pub: Wiley-Blackwell
Ed: Georgina Peters. **Description:** Entrepreneurs tend to be fixated on coming up with a foolproof idea for a new business and then raising money to start it. Raising startup funds is difficult, but it doesn't have to be that way. Search funds offers an innovative alternative, and the results are often impressive.

24718 ■ "First Airport Location for Paciugo Gelato" in *Ice Cream Reporter* (Vol. 23, October 20, 2010, No. 11, pp. 2)
Pub: Ice Cream Reporter
Description: Paciugo Gelato and Caffee has partnered with airport concessions developer Airmail to open a shop in the Cleveland Hopkins International Airport. The firm will create a wide variety of choices for travelers.

24719 ■ "Five Things" in *Hawaii Business* (Vol. 53, November 2007, No. 5, pp. 20)
Pub: Hawaii Business Publishing
Ed: Jason Ubay. **Description:** Discusses products that are allowed to be carried on board airplane flights by business travelers.

24720 ■ "Flights of Fancy" in *Crain's Chicago Business* (Vol. 31, April 21, 2008, No. 16, pp. 27)
Pub: Crain Communications, Inc.
Ed: Sarah A. Klein. **Description:** Due to the competition for business travelers, who account for 30 percent of airline revenue, airlines are offering a number of luxury amenities, especially on long-haul routes.

24721 ■ "Flying High Down Under" in *Entrepreneur* (Vol. 37, August 2009, No. 8, pp. 16)
Pub: Entrepreneur Media, Inc.
Ed: Dan Oko. **Description:** V Australia offers direct flights from Los Angeles International Airport to Brisbane, Melbourne, and Sydney in Australia. Their Boeing 777-300ER aircrafts has a fully stocked sit-down bar in the business class, touch screens with audio and video on demand and passengers get to perk up with Bulgari toiletries kits.

24722 ■ "Flying the Unfriendly Skies" in *Crain's Chicago Business* (Vol. 31, April 21, 2008, No. 16, pp. 26)
Pub: Crain Communications, Inc.
Ed: Sarah A. Klein. **Description:** Due to the number of Chicago companies and entrepreneurs who are traveling overseas more frequently in order to strengthen ties with customers, companies and oftentimes even business partners, the number of flights leaving O'Hare International Airport for destinations abroad has surged; In 2007, international passengers departing O'Hare totaled 5.7 million, up from 2.4 million in 1990.

24723 ■ "For Going All Out to Transform the Way Our Food Is Grown: Chuck Lacy" in *Inc.* (Volume 32, December 2010, No. 10, pp. 94)
Pub: Inc. Magazine
Ed: Adam Bluestein. **Description:** Profile of Rotokawa Cattle Company and its mission to transform the business of beef and grow their herd of beef cattle.

24724 ■ "Fuel for Thought" in *Canadian Business* (Vol. 81, April 14, 2008, No. 6, pp. 18)
Pub: Rogers Media
Ed: John Gray. **Description:** Discusses a web poll of 133 CEOs and other business leaders that shows that they predict oil prices to increase to US $113 per barrel over the 2008 to 2010 timeframe. Most of the respondents did not favor cutting gas taxes but this group wants the government to cut taxes on fuel-efficient vehicles and increase subsidies to local transit systems.

24725 ■ "Full Speed Ahead: How to Get the Most Out of Your Company Vehicles" in *Entrepreneur* (Vol. 37, October 2009, No. 10, pp. 78)
Pub: Entrepreneur Media, Inc.
Ed: Jill Amadio. **Description:** Methods of saving costs on purchasing and maintaining vehicles are described. Tips include shopping online, choosing hybrid vehicles, and choosing cars with incentives and lower insurance costs.

24726 ■ "Glendale Pumping $29 Million Into Redevelopment" in *The Business Journal - Serving Phoenix and the Valley of the Sun* (Vol. 28, August 1, 2008, No. 48, pp. 1)
Pub: American City Business Journals, Inc.
Ed: Mike Sunnucks. **Description:** Glendale City is planning to invest $29 million to improve city infrastructure like roadways and water and sewer lines over the next five years. Glendale's city council is also planning to hold a workshop on the redevelopment projects in September 2008. Other views and information on the redevelopment project, are presented.

24727 ■ *Greening Your Small Business: How to Improve Your Bottom Line, Grow Your Brand, Satisfy Your Customers and Save the Planet*
Pub: Prentice Hall Press
Ed: Jennifer Kaplan. **Released:** November 3, 2009. **Price:** $19.95. **Description:** A definitive resource for anyone who wants their small business to be cutting-edge, competitive, profitable, and eco-conscious. Stories from small business owners address every aspect of going green, from basics such as recycling waste, energy efficiency, and reducing information technology footprint, to more in-depth concerns such as green marketing and communications, green business travel, and green employee benefits.

24728 ■ "'Groundhog Day' B & B Likely Will Be Converted Into One In Real Life" in *Chicago Tribune* (October 21, 2008)
Pub: McClatchy-Tribune Information Services
Ed: Carolyn Starks. **Description:** Everton Martin and Karla Stewart Martin have purchased the Victorian house that was featured as a bed-and-breakfast in the 1993 hit move "Groundhog Day"; the couple was initially unaware of the structure's celebrity status when they purchased it with the hope of fulfilling their dream of owning a bed-and-breakfast.

24729 ■ "Have Tag, Will Travel" in *Inc.* (Vol. 33, November 2011, No. 9, pp. 48)
Pub: Inc. Magazine
Ed: Abram Brown. **Description:** Truleytag and Boomerangit are provide services to protect luggage while traveling. Turlytag provides brightly colored ID tags and stickers that attach to any item and feature words Return Me along with the company's contact information. Boomerangit's ID tags and labels feature the words Return for Reward along with their information.

24730 ■ "Heavy Duty: The Case Against Packing Lightly" in *Crain's Chicago Business* (Vol. 31, April 21, 2008, No. 16, pp. 29)
Pub: Crain Communications, Inc.
Ed: Sarah A. Klein. **Description:** Penelope Biggs, a Northern Trust executive who manages sales teams in North America, Europe and Asia gives advice on traveling abroad for business including time management skills, handling time-zone hops and avoiding jet-lag.

24731 ■ "Honest Harry" in *Hawaii Business* (Vol. 53, November 2007, No. 5, pp. 39)
Pub: Hawaii Business Publishing
Ed: David K. Choo. **Description:** Mayor Harry Kim testified in support of the Superferry controversial in Hawaii last September 2007. Kim says that the Superferry would allow local business and families to have more opportunities for commerce and recreation. Kim's testimony was not persuasive enough for Maui Circuit Judge Joseph Cardoza who ruled that the Superferry may not operate while an environmental assessment is being completed.

24732 ■ "Hotel Tax Eyed For Waukesha" in *The Business Journal-Milwaukee* (Vol. 25, August 29, 2008, No. 49, pp. A1)
Pub: American City Business Journals, Inc.
Ed: Rich Kirchen. **Description:** Midwest Airlines Center chairman Frank Gimbel wants Waukesha County to help in the funding of the $200-million expansion of the convention center through a hotel room tax. The Waukesha hotel industry is expected to oppose the new room tax. Other views and information on the planned new room tax in Waukesha are presented.

24733 ■ "Hotels Get a Fill-Up" in *Crain's Detroit Business* (Vol. 25, June 1, 2009, No. 22, pp. 1)
Pub: Crain Communications Inc. - Detroit
Ed: Daniel Duggan. **Description:** Hot Rod Power Tour will have a $1 million economic impact on the area when it arrives in June 2009; the tour will bring 3,500 out-of-state custom vehicles to the event, whose owners will be needing hotel rooms.

24734 ■ "Hotels' Healthy Finish in '07" in *Crain's Chicago Business* (Vol. 31, March 24, 2008, No. 12, pp. 16)
Pub: Crain Communications, Inc.
Ed: Alby Gallun. **Description:** Chicago's hotel market saw mostly rising occupancies and room rates in the fourth quarter of 2007, reflecting continued strong demand from leisure and business travelers; however, due to the current state of the economy hoteliers face an increasingly uncertain outlook.

24735 ■ "How Hierarchy Can Hurt Strategy Execution" in *Harvard Business Review* (Vol. 88, July-August 2010, No. 7-8, pp. 74)
Pub: Harvard Business School Publishing
Description: A series of charts illustrate Harvard Business Review's Advisory Council survey results regarding perceptions of strategy development and execution identifying obstacles and key factors affecting implementation.

24736 ■ "Huberman Failing to Keep CTA on Track" in *Crain's Chicago Business* (Vol. 31, April 21, 2008, No. 16, pp. 22)
Pub: Crain Communications, Inc.
Description: Discusses the deplorable service of CTA, the Chicago Transit Authority, as well as CTA President Ron Huberman who, up until last week had riders hoping he had the management skills necessary to fix the system's problems; Tuesday's event left hundreds of riders trapped for hours and thousands standing on train platforms along the Blue Line waiting for trains that never came.

24737 ■ "I-5 Bridge Funding Unclear" in *The Business Journal-Portland* (Vol. 25, July 11, 2008, No. 18, pp. 1)
Pub: American City Business Journals, Inc.
Ed: Andy Giegerich. **Description:** Financing for a new Interstate 5 bridge is unclear as Washington lawmakers identify two priority projects other than the planned bridge, which is shared with Oregon. An estimate says that the two states could pay between $487.6 million and $1.5 billion for the new bridge. Other details on the financing of the project are discussed.

24738 ■ "Ideas at Work: The Reality of Costs" in *Business Strategy Review* (Vol. 21, Summer 2010, No. 2, pp. 40)
Pub: Wiley-Blackwell
Ed: Jules Goddard. **Description:** If you think that cost cutting is the surest way to business success, the author wants to challenge every assumption you hold. Costs are an outcome of sound strategy, never the goal of strategy. He offers a new perspective on what counts when it comes to costs.

24739 ■ "Immigration Issues Frustrate Owners From Overseas" in *The Business Journal-Serving Greater Tampa Bay* (Vol. 28, August 15, 2008)
Pub: American City Business Journals, Inc.
Ed: Margie Manning. **Description:** Investors who availed the E-2 visa program believe that the tightened restrictions on the visa program has trapped

them in the United States. The E-2 investor visa program was designed to attract investors into the U.S., but restrictions were tightened after the September 11, 2001 attacks. Other views and information on E-2 and its impact on investors are presented.

24740 ■ "In China, Railways to Riches" in *Barron's* (Vol. 88, July 7, 2008, No. 27, pp. M9)
Pub: Dow Jones & Co., Inc.
Ed: Assif Shameen. **Description:** Shares of Chinese railway companies look to benefit from multimillion-dollar investments aimed at upgrading the Chinese railway network. Investment in the sector is expected to reach $210 billion for the 2006-2010 period.

24741 ■ "Innovating Globally" in *Business Strategy Review* (Vol. 21, Spring 2010, No. 1, pp. 24)
Pub: Wiley-Blackwell
Ed: Costas Markides, Stuart Crainer. **Description:** Costas Markides has spent over two decades studying business strategy and innovation. Recently, he has been focusing on the bigger picture of how people can address major social problems. Can the techniques used by managers to create innovation inside organizations work with global change?

24742 ■ "Innovation's Holy Grail" in *Harvard Business Review* (Vol. 88, July-August 2010, No. 7-8, pp. 132)
Pub: Harvard Business School Publishing
Ed: C.K. Prahalad, R.A. Mashelkar. **Description:** Three forms of business innovation are presented, inspired by the tenets of Mahatma Gandhi. They are: changing organizational capabilities, sourcing or creating new capabilities, and disrupting conventional business models. Illustrations for these methods are also included.

24743 ■ *The Itty Bitty Guide to Business Travel*
Pub: Chronicle Books LLC
Ed: Stacie Krajchir, Carrie Rosten. **Released:** April 2004. **Description:** Advice on all aspects of business travel, including low-price airfare, packing and coping with stress.

24744 ■ "Just Following Directions" in *Entrepreneur* (Vol. 36, February 2008, No. 2, pp. 56)
Pub: Entrepreneur Media Inc.
Ed: Amanda C. Kooser. **Description:** Buyer's guide for purchasing Global Positioning System units is presented.

24745 ■ "Keeping Railcars 'Busy At All Times' At TTX" in *Crain's Chicago Business* (Vol. 31, April 28, 2008, No. 17, pp. 6)
Pub: Crain Communications, Inc.
Ed: Bob Tita. **Description:** Profile of the president of Chicago railcar pool operator TTX Co. and his business plan for the company which includes improving fleet management and car purchasing through better use of data on railroad demand.

24746 ■ "Leave It Behind; Novel Packing Strategy" in *Crain's Chicago Business* (Vol. 31, April 21, 2008, No. 16, pp. 32)
Pub: Crain Communications, Inc.
Ed: Sarah A. Klein. **Description:** Patrick Brady who investigates possible violations of the Foreign Corrupt Practices Act has a novel approach when traveling to frequent destinations which allows him to travel with only a carry-on piece of luggage: he leaves suits at dry cleaners in the places he visits most often and since he mainly stays at the same hotels, he also leaves sets of workout clothes and running shoes with hotel staff.

24747 ■ "Lightening the Load" in *Crain's Cleveland Business* (Vol. 28, October 8, 2007, No. 40, pp. 3)
Pub: Crain Communications, Inc.
Ed: Jay Miller. **Description:** Companies reliant on barge deliveries are running well below capacity due to both the building up of silt at the bottom of the Cuyahoga River as well as the lower water levels which are causing a number of problems for the barges and big boats that deliver goods to the region.

24748 ■ "Local Hotels Brace for Downturn" in *Crain's Chicago Business* (Vol. 31, March 31, 2008, No. 13, pp. 3)
Pub: Crain Communications, Inc.
Ed: Bob Tita. **Description:** Chicago hotels are seeing a noticeable drop in business-related guests so far this year due to a slumping national economy, tighter corporate expense budgets and higher airfares.

24749 ■ "Location, Location" in *Black Enterprise* (Vol. 38, February 2008, No. 7, pp. 64)
Pub: Earl G. Graves Publishing Co. Inc.
Ed: Marcia Reed-Woodard. **Description:** Overseas work assignments are increasing, especially for workers in the U.S., Canada and Latin America.

24750 ■ "The Long Game" in *Business Strategy Review* (Vol. 21, Summer 2010, No. 2, pp. 36)
Pub: Wiley-Blackwell
Ed: Stuart Crainer. **Description:** Profile of Alibab.com and its CEO David Wei.

24751 ■ "The Lords of Ideas" in *Business Strategy Review* (Vol. 21, Autumn 2010, No. 3, pp. 57)
Pub: Wiley-Blackwell
Ed: Stuart Crainer. **Description:** True originators of modern business strategy are interviewed.

24752 ■ "Luxe Hotels on a Budget" in *Inc.* (Volume 32, December 2010, No. 10, pp. 60)
Pub: Inc. Magazine
Ed: Adam Baer. **Description:** Off & Away Website allows users to vie for discounted hotel rooms at more than 100 luxury properties. To compete, uses buy $1 bids and each time an individual bids the price of the room goes up by 10 cents.

24753 ■ "Making Visitors Out Of Listeners" in *Hawaii Business* (Vol. 54, July 2008, No. 1, pp. 18)
Pub: Hawaii Business Publishing
Ed: Casey Chin. **Description:** Japanese workers are subscribing to the Official Hawaii Podcast in iTunes, which offers a free 20-minute, Japanese-language audio content on different topics, such as dining reviews and music from local artists. The concept is a way to attract Japanese travelers to come to Hawaii.

24754 ■ "Mass-Transit Backers: Change in State Funding Needed" in *Crain's Detroit Business* (Vol. 24, October 6, 2008, No. 40, pp. 19)
Pub: Crain Communications, Inc.
Ed: Bill Shea. **Description:** Options to reform transportation and infrastructure funding in the state of Michigan are examined. Transit revitalization investment zones are also discussed.

24755 ■ "Meetings Go Virtual" in *HRMagazine* (Vol. 54, January 2009, No. 1, pp. 74)
Pub: Society for Human Resource Management
Ed: Elizabeth Agnvall. **Description:** Microsoft Office Live Meeting conferencing software allows companies to schedule meetings from various company locations, thus saving travel costs.

24756 ■ "Mergers Mean Woe for Fliers; Airline Hookups Boost Fares, Diminish Service" in *Crain's Chicago Business* (April 21, 2008)
Pub: Crain Communications, Inc.
Ed: John Pletz. **Description:** Discusses the impact airline mergers will have on customer service, pricing and business travel, particularly at Chicago's O'Hare International Airport.

24757 ■ "Military Center a Go" in *Austin Business JournalInc.* (Vol. 29, December 11, 2009, No. 40, pp. 1)
Pub: American City Business Journals
Ed: Kate Harrington. **Description:** The $40 million Armed Forces Guard and Reserve Center project at Austin-Bergstrom International Airport has resumed work after a delay of several years. The project is in both the House and Senate versions of the fiscal 2010 Military Construction and Veterans Appropriations Bill that would earmark $16.5 million for the center and $5.7 million for the maintenance facility. Details of construction plans are covered.

24758 ■ "The Money Train: How Public Projects Shape Our Economic Future" in *Hawaii Business* (Vol. 54, September 2008, No. 3, pp. 31)
Pub: Hawaii Business Publishing
Ed: Jason Ubay. **Description:** Public projects impact the construction industry as such projects create jobs and new infrastructure that can lead to private developments. Details on the government contracts and construction projects in Hawaii and their rising costs and impact on the state's economy are discussed.

24759 ■ "MooBella Adds Two Airports" in *Ice Cream Reporter* (Vol. 23, November 20, 2010, No. 12, pp. 5)
Pub: Ice Cream Reporter
Description: MooBella Inc. has placed MooBella Ice Creamery machines in New England's Logan International Airport in Boston and in New Hampshire's Manchester-Boston Regional Airport.

24760 ■ "Muirhead Farmhouse B & B Owners Get Hospitality Right" in *Chicago Tribune* (July 31, 2008)
Pub: McClatchy-Tribune Information Services
Ed: Glenn Jeffers. **Description:** Profile of the Muirhead Farmhouse, a bed-and-breakfast owned by Mike Petersdorf and Sarah Muirhead Petersdorf; Frank Lloyd Wright designed the historic farmhouse which blends farm life and history into a unique experience that is enhanced by the couple's hospitality.

24761 ■ "Nighttime Shuttle to Connect Detroit, Ferndale, Royal Oak" in *Crain's Detroit Business* (Vol. 24, October 6, 2008, No. 40, pp. 24)
Pub: Crain Communications, Inc.
Ed: Nancy Kaffer. **Description:** With hopes of bridging the social gap between the cities and suburbs, Chris Ramos has launched The Night Move, a new shuttle service that will ferry passengers between Royal Oak, Ferndale and downtown Detroit. The cost for a round trip ticket is $12.

24762 ■ "No Rooms for the Inn In This High-Rise" in *Chicago Tribune* (October 4, 2008)
Pub: McClatchy-Tribune Information Services
Ed: Ameet Sachdev; Jim Kirk. **Description:** Construction has stalled for several hotel expansion projects due to the economy which has caused a decline in occupancy and little growth in average daily room rates in downtown Chicago because consumers and businesses are becoming more cautious in the amount of money they spend on travel.

24763 ■ "On the Go: a Busy Executive Is Always Well-Equipped for Travel" in *Black Enterprise* (Vol. 40, July 2010, No. 12, pp. 106)
Pub: Earl G. Graves Publishing Co. Inc.
Ed: Sonia Alleyne. **Description:** Successful sales executive, Henry Watkins, shares tips on business travel.

24764 ■ "On the High Road" in *Crain's Cleveland Business* (Vol. 28, October 8, 2007, No. 40, pp. 2)
Pub: Crain Communications, Inc.
Description: According to the American Public Transportation Association, the Greater Cleveland Regional Transit Authority is the best public transit system in North America. Ridership has increased steadily in the last few years. Statistical data included.

24765 ■ "Orbitz Adds Parent Panel" in *Marketing to Women* (Vol. 21, March 2008, No. 3, pp. 5)
Pub: EPM Communications, Inc.
Description: Orbitz introduces the Orbitz Parent Panel in an attempt to better connect with traveling families.

24766 ■ "Our Gadget of the Week: Business Buddy" in *Barron's* (Vol. 88, July 7, 2008, No. 27, pp. 26)
Pub: Dow Jones & Co., Inc.
Ed: Jay Palmer. **Description:** Review and evaluation of the Lenovo X300 laptop computer which offers executives a variety of features despite its smaller size and weight. The laptop is about 0.73 inch thick, comes with a 64-gigabyte solid-state drive from Samsung, and weighs less than three pounds.

24767 ■ "Pack Mentality" in *Crain's Chicago Business* (Vol. 31, April 21, 2008, No. 16, pp. 31)
Pub: Crain Communications, Inc.
Ed: Sarah A. Klein. **Description:** Jill Smart, the head of human resources for a company with 170,000 employees worldwide, frequently travels to India, London and Singapore; Ms. Smart provides advice concerning efficiency, time management and avoiding jet-lag.

24768 ■ "Packing Chic" in *Black Enterprise* (Vol. 38, February 2008, No. 7, pp. 154)
Pub: Earl G. Graves Publishing Co. Inc.
Ed: Sonai Alleyne. **Description:** Profile of Angela Theodora's leather overnight bags that offer a variety of smart compartments for the business traveler.

24769 ■ "PDX Bucks National Trend" in *The Business Journal-Portland* (Vol. 25, August 1, 2008, No. 21, pp. 1)
Pub: American City Business Journals, Inc.
Ed: Erik Siemers. **Description:** Portland International Airport could face problems as air carriers are planning to reduce capacity at the airport. The airport is showing signs of growth despite the slowdown in the airline industry. Other airlines that are planning to reduce seating capacity at the airport are also presented.

24770 ■ "Pinellas Leaders Want First Leg of Light Rail" in *The Business Journal-Serving Greater Tampa Bay* (Vol. 28, August 8, 2008, No. 33)
Pub: American City Business Journals, Inc.
Ed: Larry Halstead. **Description:** Proposed routes for the first leg of the planned light railway system in the Tampa Bay, Florida area are being presented as the Tampa Bay Area Regional Transportation Authority is about to make its master plan for the project. A sales tax for transit is being proposed to fund the project, as well as an expansion of the accompanying bus system.

24771 ■ "The Play's the Thing" in *Business Strategy Review* (Vol. 21, Summer 2010, No. 2, pp. 58)
Pub: Wiley-Blackwell
Ed: Michael G. Jacobides. **Description:** Those who study and plan strategies risk falling into the traps that maps, graphs, charts and matrices present. The author feels that strategy might best be cast as a dramatic playscript that can reveal the unfolding plots of business far better than traditional strategic tools, as the landscape shifts around us.

24772 ■ "Portion of Silver Line Will Run By Year's End" in *Crain's Cleveland Business* (Vol. 28, November 5, 2007, No. 44, pp. 6)
Pub: Crain Communications, Inc.
Ed: Jay Miller. **Description:** Cleveland's new Silver Line rapid transit will board its first passengers before the end of the year. The project is expected to spur economic development in the area and will speed transportation along Euclid Avenue.

24773 ■ "Possible Green Light On Transit" in *The Business Journal-Milwaukee* (Vol. 25, July 25, 2008, No. 44, pp. A1)
Pub: American City Business Journals, Inc.
Ed: David Doege. **Description:** $50 million in federal funding is being sought by Wisconsin's Milwaukee County Executive Scott Walker for the creation of two bus rapid transit lines, and is to be added to the unspent Milwaukee area federal funds worth $91.5 million. The new transit line will have new higher-speed buses and fewer stops than the traditional line.

24774 ■ "Power Play" in *Harvard Business Review* (Vol. 88, July-August 2010, No. 7-8, pp. 84)
Pub: Harvard Business School Publishing
Ed: Jeffrey Pfeffer. **Description:** Guidelines include in-depth understanding of resources at one's disposal, relentlessness that still provides opponents with opportunities to save face, and a determination not to be put off by the processes of politics.

24775 ■ "Pride Lands Janitorial Work at New Terminal" in *Sacramento Business Journal* (Vol. 28, June 10, 2011, No. 15, pp. 1)
Pub: Sacramento Business Journal
Ed: Kelly Johnson. **Description:** Pride Industries Inc. won the five-year $9.4 million contract to clean the Sacramento International Airport's new Terminal B, which will open in fall 2011. The nonprofit organization posts a revenue of $191 million for 2011 and currently employs more than 2,400 people with disabilities. The contract is expected to provide savings of over $3 million a year to the airport.

24776 ■ "Proposed Transit Legislation" in *Crain's Detroit Business* (Vol. 24, October 6, 2008, No. 40, pp. 19)
Pub: Crain Communications, Inc.
Description: Breakdown of state Representative Marie Donigan's proposed transit legislation includes tax increment financing. Other pieces of the proposed legislation are examined.

24777 ■ "Put It In Drive" in *Entrepreneur* (Vol. 36, April 2008, No. 4, pp. 31)
Pub: Entrepreneur Media, Inc.
Ed: Jill Amadio. **Description:** Commercial vehicle models for 2008 are presented. These new models are more user- and environment-friendly. Features and prices of car models and tips to consider before purchasing are presented.

24778 ■ "Road Warriors: How To Survive Business Travel" in *Crain's Detroit Business* (Vol. 24, February 4, 2008, No. 5, pp. 11)
Pub: Crain Communications Inc. - Detroit
Description: Entrepreneurs share tips that help save time and energy at airports when traveling for business.

24779 ■ "Route Optimization Impacts the Bottom Line" in *Contractor* (Vol. 56, November 2009, No. 11, pp. 48)
Pub: Penton Media, Inc.
Ed: Dave Beaudry. **Description:** Plumbing and HVAC businesses can save a significant amount of money from route optimization. The process begins with gathering information on a fleet and a routing software tool can determine the effectiveness of current route configurations and identify preferable route plans.

24780 ■ "RT Seeking Ways to Finance Expansion" in *Sacramento Business Journal* (Vol. 28, July 29, 2011, No. 22, pp. 1)
Pub: Sacramento Business Journal
Ed: Melanie Turner. **Description:** Sacramento Regional Transit District is considering ways to finance all its capital projects outlined in a 30-year transit master plan which would cost more than $7 billion to complete. Current funding sources include developer fees and state and federal assistance and fares. Part of the master plan is a light-rail line to Sacramento International Airport.

24781 ■ "Running On Empty" in *The Business Journal-Milwaukee* (Vol. 25, July 4, 2008, No. 41, pp. A1)
Pub: American City Business Journals, Inc.
Ed: David Doege. **Description:** Employers are more engaged in offering incentives designed to offset commuting costs. Among the incentives offered are gas cards, parking reimbursement and midyear wage increases. The other efforts to help employees with the costs of going to work are discussed.

24782 ■ "Save Money on Travel With These Websites for Frequent Fliers" in *Inc.* (Vol. 31, January-February 2009, No. 1, pp. 44)
Pub: Mansueto Ventures LLC
Description: Four Websites offering services to the business traveler are profiled: MissRefund.com will get the taxes and fuel surcharges back to any traveler canceling a flight; Vayama.com is a booking site focused on routes and destinations not generally available online; Airfarewatchdog.com searches for listing sites for best travel deals; and Yapta alerts users to good prices for particular flights.

24783 ■ "Scanning the Field" in *Business Courier* (Vol. 26, January 8, 2010, No. 38, pp. 1)
Pub: American City Business Journals, Inc.
Ed: Jon Newberry. **Description:** Anti-terror detection systems developer Valley Force Composite Technologies Inc. of Kentucky plans to enter the market with its high-resolution ODIN and Thor-LVX screening systems. These systems are expected to meet the increasing demand for airport security equipment.

24784 ■ "Singapore Airlines' Balancing Act" in *Harvard Business Review* (Vol. 88, July-August 2010, No. 7-8, pp. 145)
Pub: Harvard Business School Publishing
Ed: Loizos Heracleous, Jochen Wirtz. **Description:** Singapore Airlines is used as an illustration of organizational effectiveness. The article includes the firm's 4-3-3 rule of spending, its promotion of centralized as well as decentralized innovation, use of technology, and strategic planning.

24785 ■ "Sleep It Off In a Silo B & B" in *Chicago Tribune* (December 14, 2008)
Pub: McClatchy-Tribune Information Services
Ed: Bill Daley. **Description:** Profile of Oregon's Abbey Road Farm bed-and-breakfast which is located on an 82-acre working farm; guests stay in shiny metal farm silos which have been converted into luxury rooms with views of the farm.

24786 ■ "Small Dutch Islands Saba, Statia Content With Low-Key Niche" in *Travel Weekly* (Vol. 69, August 16, 2010, No. 33, pp. 22)
Pub: NorthStar Travel Media LLC
Ed: Gay Nagle Myers. **Description:** Small Caribbean islands market and promote their region for tourism by never competing with the bigger destinations. Saba and Statia are the two smallest islands in the Caribbean and rely on repeat guests, word-of-mouth recommendations and travel agents willing to promote them.

24787 ■ "The Solution" in *Entrepreneur* (Vol. 37, October 2009, No. 10, pp. 71)
Pub: Entrepreneur Media, Inc.
Ed: Jennifer Wang. **Description:** Ford's 2010 Transit Connect is a compact commercial van developed specifically for small business owners. The compact van offers an integrated in-dash computer system providing a cellular broadband connection.

24788 ■ "Sometimes You Have to Ignore the Rule Book" in *Canadian Business* (Vol. 83, September 14, 2010, No. 15, pp. 13)
Pub: Rogers Media Ltd.
Ed: Richard Branson. **Description:** The rule book has provided a clear framework for employees particularly when cash and accounting are at issue. However, sometimes rules were made to be broken and the rule book should not become an excuse for poor customer service or hinder great service. How Virgin Atlantic practices this type of corporate culture is discussed.

24789 ■ "Sound Advice From Dr. Sleep" in *Crain's Chicago Business* (Vol. 31, April 21, 2008, No. 16, pp. 30)
Pub: Crain Communications, Inc.
Ed: Sarah A. Klein. **Description:** James K. Wyatt, the director of the Sleep Disorders Centers at Rush University Medical Center in Chicago, gives advice to business executives concerning what to eat, how to nap and which drugs to take or avoid in order to ease the strain of air travel, particularly on overseas flights.

24790 ■ "South Lake Tahoe B & B Blocks Out Neveda's Neon" in *Chicago Tribune* (May 18, 2008)
Pub: McClatchy-Tribune Information Services
Ed: Randall Weissman. **Description:** Profile of the Black Bear Inn, a small bed-and-breakfast in South Lake Tahoe owned by Jerry Birdwell and Kevin

Chandler; the welcoming ambience is a delightful departure from ski resort hotel rooms. Pricing and further details of the various rooms are described.

24791 ■ "State Aviation Fuel Tax Proposal Runs Into Turbulence" in *Crain's Detroit Business* (Vol. 25, June 15, 2009, No. 24, pp. 5)
Pub: Crain Communications Inc. - Detroit
Ed: Amy Lane. **Description:** Delta Airlines Inc. is concerned about a proposal that would change the way Michigan taxes aviation fuel. The plan would go from the current cents-per-gallon tax to a percentage tax on the wholesale price of fuel, which would raise the taxes significantly.

24792 ■ "State Weighs Tearing Down Hoan" in *The Business Journal-Milwaukee* (Vol. 25, August 22, 2008, No. 48, pp. A1)
Pub: American City Business Journals, Inc.
Ed: Pete Millard. **Description:** Department of Transportation of Wisconsin is studying the feasibility of tearing the Daniel Hoan Memorial Bridge down because rehabilitating the bridge is costly. Rebuilding the Interstate 794 at street level could be less expensive. The potential plans for the bridge are discussed further.

24793 ■ "Stay in Touch, Wherever You Roam: Smartphones for Overseas Travel" in *Inc.* (Volume 32, December 2010, No. 10, pp. 60)
Pub: Inc. Magazine
Description: International cell phones services are profiled, including HTC Aria, Nokia E73 Mode, Samsung Captivate, and Blackberry Bold 9650.

24794 ■ "Still in the Jet Set" in *Barron's* (Vol. 89, July 13, 2009, No. 28, pp. 13)
Pub: Dow Jones & Co., Inc.
Ed: Brad Davis. **Description:** Coastal Jet Service will be offering coast-to-coast flights and a one way ride on their Cessna Citation X will cost $4,600 plus tax. The service is a compromise between a corporate jet and a first-class seat on a commercial flight and the jets fly out of Westchester County, New York and land in Burbank, California.

24795 ■ "Strictly Business" in *Black Enterprise* (Vol. 38, October 2007, No. 3, pp. 62)
Pub: Earl G. Graves Publishing Co. Inc.
Description: Profile of the HP iPAQ hw6925 smartphone suited to small business use. The phone offers mobile word processing and messaging features great for the tech-savvy business traveler.

24796 ■ "Ten Ways to Save on Business Travel" in *Women Entrepreneur* (November 21, 2008)
Pub: Entrepreneur Media Inc.
Ed: Julie Moline. **Description:** Advice regarding ways in which to save money when traveling for business is given.

24797 ■ "TIA Wrestles with Procurement Issues" in *Business Journal Serving Greater Tampa Bay* (Vol. 30, November 12, 2010, No. 47, pp. 1)
Pub: Tampa Bay Business Journal
Ed: Mark Holan. **Description:** Tampa International Airport (TIA) has been caught in conflict of interest and procurement policy issues after the Hillsborough County Aviation Authority learned of the spousal relationship of an employee with his wife's firm, Gresham Smith and Partners. Gresham already won contracts with TIA and was ahead of other firms in a new contract.

24798 ■ "Tightening Economy Squeezes Business Travel" in *HRMagazine* (Vol. 53, August 2008, No. 8, pp. 19)
Pub: Society for Human Resource Management
Ed: Kathy Gurchiek. **Description:** New surveys show that some companies are not cutting out business travel, they are using cheaper hotels and cutting back on trade shows and conference travel. Statistical data included.

24799 ■ "To Build for the Future, Reach Beyond the Skies" in *Canadian Business* (Vol. 83, June 15, 2010, No. 10, pp. 11)
Pub: Rogers Media Ltd.
Ed: Richard Branson. **Description:** Richard Branson says that tackling an engineering challenge or a scientific venture is a real adventure for an entrepreneur. Branson discusses Virgin's foray into the aviation business and states that at Virgin, they build for the future.

24800 ■ "TomTom GO910: On the Road Again" in *Black Enterprise* (Vol. 37, January 2007, No. 6, pp. 52)
Pub: Earl G. Graves Publishing Co. Inc.
Ed: Stephanie Young. **Description:** TomTom GO 910 is a GPS navigator that offers detailed maps of the U.S., Canada, and Europe. Consumers view their routes by a customizable LCD screen showing everything from the quickest to the shortest routes available or how to avoid toll roads. Business travelers may find this product invaluable as it also functions as a cell phone and connects to a variety of other multi-media devices.

24801 ■ "Top IPhone Apps" in *Advertising Age* (Vol. 79, December 15, 2008, No. 46, pp. 17)
Pub: Crain Communications, Inc.
Ed: Marissa Miley. **Description:** Free and low cost applications for the iPhone are described including Evernote, an application that allows users to outsource their memory to keep track of events, notes, ides and more; Handshake, a way for users to exchange business cards and pictures across Wi-Fi and 3G; CityTransit, an interactive map of the New York subway system that uses GPS technology to find nearby stations and also tells the user if a train is out of commission that day; and Stage Hand which allows users to deliver a presentation, control timing and slide order on the spot.

24802 ■ "Tradeshow Attendance Incentives Add Up" in *Pet Product News* (Vol. 64, December 2010, No. 12, pp. 14)
Pub: BowTie Inc.
Ed: Mark E. Battersby. **Description:** Pointers on how pet specialty retailers can claim business travel tax and income tax deductions for expenses paid or incurred in participation at tradeshows, conventions, and meetings are presented. Incentives in form of these deductions could allow pet specialty retailers to gain business benefits, aside from the education and enjoyment involved with the travel.

24803 ■ "Traffic Slows at O'Hare; As Airlines Cut Flights, City Tries to Push Expansion Forward" in *Crain's Chicago Business* (April 28, 2008)
Pub: Crain Communications, Inc.
Ed: Paul Merrion; John Pletz. **Description:** O'Hare International Airport is seeing a decline in passenger traffic just as the city of Chicago presses cash-strapped airlines to fund the second phase of the airport's expansion which would include the extension of one runway, the relocation of two others and the construction of a new western terminal.

24804 ■ "A Train of Our Own" in *Canadian Business* (Vol. 79, July 17, 2006, No. 14-15, pp. 71)
Pub: Rogers Media
Ed: Victor Dwyer. **Description:** The luxuries and pleasure of traveling in private rail road cars are discussed.

24805 ■ "Travel In Style, Or Not: Finding a Company Travel Service for Every Budget" in *Inc.* (January 2008, pp. 36-37)
Pub: Gruner & Jahr USA Publishing
Ed: Larry Olmsted. **Description:** Profiles of various travel services to help small businesses. Firms profiled include Cassis Travel Services, providing first class bookings; Open from American Express, specializing in business class travel; Travelocity business, providing travel agents with 24/7 services; Diners Club Corporate Card, with many features; and Expedia Corporate Travel, allowing users to compare prices for airline tickets, hotels, and car rentals.

24806 ■ "Travel Leery" in *Crain's Chicago Business* (Vol. 31, March 31, 2008, No. 13, pp. 3)
Pub: Crain Communications, Inc.
Description: Due to the rise in airline prices and a possible recession, many companies are starting to change their travel policies and limit travel spending.

24807 ■ "Travel Rewards Take Off" in *Inc.* (Vol. 33, October 2011, No. 8, pp. 46)
Pub: Inc. Magazine
Ed: Matthew DeLuca. **Description:** Credit card companies are offering travel reward cards with special perks, including sign-up bonuses; three such cards are described.

24808 ■ "Travel Tears" in *Crain's Chicago Business* (Vol. 31, November 17, 2008, No. 46, pp. 3)
Pub: Crain Communications, Inc.
Ed: Bob Tita. **Description:** Hotels, restaurants and conventions are seeing a decline in profits due to corporate travel cutbacks and the sagging economy. City and state revenues derived from taxes on tourism-related industries are also suffering.

24809 ■ "The Traveler's Traveler" in *Entrepreneur* (Vol. 37, September 2009, No. 9, pp. 22)
Pub: Entrepreneur Media, Inc.
Ed: Kim Orr. **Description:** Business travel columnist Joe Sharkey says technology may someday replace business travel. Airlines are realizing that a part of the business travel market has disappeared. Sharkey also says airlines can never get those customers back.

24810 ■ "Turbulent Times and Golden Opportunity" in *Business Strategy Review* (Vol. 21, Spring 2010, No. 1, pp. 34)
Pub: Wiley-Blackwell
Ed: Don Sull. **Description:** For those feeling storm-tossed by today's economy, the author believes there's much to learn from Carnival Cruise Lines, a company that discovered that turbulence often has an upside.

24811 ■ "TW Trade Shows to Offer Seminars On Niche Selling, Social Media" in *Travel Weekly* (Vol. 69, October 4, 2010, No. 40, pp. 9)
Pub: NorthStar Travel Media LLC
Description: Travel Weekly's Leisure World 2010 and Fall Home Based Travel Agent Show focused on niche selling, with emphasis on all-inclusives, young consumers, groups, incentives, culinary vacations, and honeymoon or romance travel.

24812 ■ "Vacation, What Vacation?" in *Black Enterprise* (Vol. 41, August 2010, No. 1, pp. 36)
Pub: Earl G. Graves Publishing Co. Inc.
Description: Nearly 50 percent of employers expect employees to check in with the office while they are away on vacation.

24813 ■ "Virgin America Flies with V&S on Web" in *ADWEEK* (Vol. 51, July 12 2010, No. 27, pp. 31)
Pub: Nielsen Business Media Inc.
Description: Victors & Spoils, a crowdsourcing agency is examined.

24814 ■ "Vonage V-Phone: Use Your Laptop to Make Calls Via the Internet" in *Black Enterprise* (Vol. 37, January 2007, No. 6, pp. 52)
Pub: Earl G. Graves Publishing Co. Inc.
Ed: James C. Johnson. **Description:** Overview of the Vonage V-Phone, which is small flash drive device that lets you make phone calls through a high-speed Internet connection and plugs into any computer's USB port. Business travels may find this product to be a wonderful solution as it includes 250MB of memory and can store files, digital photos, MP3s, and more.

24815 ■ "'We Had to Won the Mistakes'" in *Harvard Business Review* (Vol. 88, July-August 2010, No. 7-8, pp. 108)
Pub: Harvard Business School Publishing
Ed: Adi Ignatius. **Description:** Interview with Howard Schultz, CEO of Starbucks, covers topics that include investment in retraining, the impact of competition, premium quality, authenticity, customer services, strategy development, work-and-life issues, and international presence.

24816 ■ "What's the Black Travel Market Worth?" in *Black Enterprise* (Vol. 38, January 2008, No. 6, pp. 54)
Pub: Earl G. Graves Publishing Co. Inc.
Ed: Aisha Sylvester. **Description:** African American travel market, both business and pleasure, is one of the top three fastest growing markets in the industry. Hugh Riley, director of marketing for the Caribbean Tourism Organization shares his ideas on the relationship between African American travelers and the Caribbean tourism industry.

24817 ■ "Wisdom from the Mountaintops" in *Canadian Business* (Vol. 83, October 12, 2010, No. 17, pp. 91)
Pub: Rogers Media Ltd.
Ed: Matthew McClearn. **Description:** Techniques used to save lives on the world's highest mountains could make companies more creative. Mountaineers have time to talk to one another, and the resulting flow of ideas help climbers reach the summit. Organizations are expected to foster communication both internally and externally.

TRADE PERIODICALS

24818 ■ *Better Business Traveling*
Pub: Traveling Times Inc.
Ed: Mirko A. Ilich, Editor. **Released:** Monthly. **Description:** Provides news and information of interest to business travelers.

24819 ■ *Business Travel News*
Pub: Nielsen Business Media
Contact: David Meyer, Editor-in-Chief
E-mail: dmeyer@btnonline.com
Released: Weekly. **Description:** Tabloid newspaper covering business travel.

24820 ■ *Corporate Meetings & Incentives*
Pub: Primedia Business Magazines & Media
Contact: Melissa Fromento, Gp. Publisher
E-mail: mfromento@meetingsnet.com
Ed: Barbara Scofidio, Editor, bscofidio@meetingsnet.com. **Released:** Monthly. **Price:** $97 Canada; $123 Free to qualified subscribers in USA; $123 other countries. **Description:** Magazine for executives and travel professionals responsible for choosing sites and destinations for meeting and incentive travel programs.

24821 ■ *Runzheimer Reports on Travel Management*
Pub: Runzheimer International
Ed: Phyllis Schumann, Sr., Editor, ps@runzheimer.com. **Released:** Quartely. **Price:** Free Web Service. **Description:** Intended to help control business travel costs. Covers travel budgets, corporate arrangements with travel agencies, in-house travel departments, and travel policies for business firms. Also discusses negotiation of special rates/services with travel suppliers. Recurring features include a profile of a major city, with information on car rentals, hotels, and special attractions. Remarks: Also available via e-mail.

24822 ■ *Southern Festivals*
Pub: Southern Festivals
Contact: Jim Taylor
Released: Bimonthly. **Description:** A statewide newspaper covering travel and tourism.

CONSULTANTS

24823 ■ CM Uberman Enterprises Inc.
444 N Frederick Ave., Ste. L304
Gaithersburg, MD 20877
Ph:(301)417-0030
Fax:(301)417-0507
Co. E-mail: reuberman@aol.com
Contact: Rudy Uberman, Vice President
E-mail: reuberman@aol.com
Scope: Conference and meeting management assistance offered to nonprofit institutions and agencies. Maintains a discount travel network covering hotels, airline flights, and care rentals. Serves all travelers: Corporate, nonprofit and personal.

24824 ■ Global Experts in Travel Inc.
1441 E Maple Rd.
Troy, MI 48083
Ph:(248)528-6911
Free: 888-886-8864
Fax:(248)528-3774
Co. E-mail: sales@ttm.com
Contact: Amy Smith, Mgr
E-mail: asmith@atsttm.com
Scope: Travel consultant in developing and renewing corporate travel policies, as well as negotiating special air, hotel, and car rental rates.

24825 ■ Off the Beaten Path L.L.C.
7 E Beall St.
Bozeman, MT 59715
Ph:(406)586-1311
Free: 800-445-2995
Fax:(406)587-4147
Co. E-mail: travel@offthebeatenpath.com
URL: http://www.offthebeatenpath.com
Contact: William L. Bryan Jr., Chairman of the Board
E-mail: billb@atsoffthebeatenpath.com
Scope: A travel planning services consultancy and consulting on ecotourism; positioning of one's lodge and business in the marketplace, pricing, marketing plans and strategic planning. **Seminars:** Soil to Bottle.

24826 ■ Trans-Research International Inc.
2320 Clifftops Ave.
PO Box 1178
Monteagle, TN 37356-2007
Ph:(931)924-7280
Fax:(931)924-7279
Co. E-mail: chuckontrucks@yahoo.com
Contact: Carl Connell, VP of Operations
E-mail: chuckclowdis@aol.com
Scope: Transportation consultant in corporate transportation cost reduction and management, third party logistics evaluations and private fleet analysis. **Seminars:** Negotiating for Profit.

LIBRARIES

24827 ■ Maritz Travel Company Resource Center
1375 N. Highway Dr.
Fenton, MO 63099
Ph:(636)827-4000
Free: 877-462-7489
URL: http://www.maritz.com
Contact: Steve Maritz, Chm./CEO
Scope: Travel data - hotels, restaurants, sightseeing, steamships, countries and cities. **Services:** Interlibrary loan; Library not open to the public. **Holdings:** 300 books; 177 bound periodical volumes; 95 VF drawers of travel-related brochures and reports; 2200 videotapes. **Subscriptions:** 35 journals and other serials.

24828 ■ Nadasdy Ferenc Museum Library
Varkerulet 1
H-9600 Sarvar, Hungary
Ph:(36)95 320158
Fax:(36)95 320158
Co. E-mail: nadasdy.sarvar@museum.hu
URL: http://www.museum.hu/museum/index_hu.php?ID=669
Contact: Takacs Zoltan, Dir.
Scope: Regional history. **Services:** Library open to the public with restrictions. **Holdings:** 4000 volumes.

24829 ■ Travel Industry Association of America Library
1100 New York Ave. NW, Ste. 450
Washington, DC 20005-3934
Ph:(202)408-8422
Fax:(202)408-1255
URL: http://www.tia.org
Contact: Suzanne D. Cook, Sr. VP, Res.
Scope: Travel and tourism. **Services:** Library not open to the public. **Holdings:** 3000 research documents; 3800 government documents; 250 unpublished travel research reports; 15,000 clippings; 20 tapes. **Subscriptions:** 27 journals and other serials.

Business Vision/Goals

START-UP INFORMATION

24830 ■ *A Business of My Own? 21 Steps to Successfully Starting and Running a Small Business*
Pub: Enfield Publishing
Ed: Marjorie Cleveland Fisher. **Released:** January 2005. **Description:** New ideas to start or grow a small business, including ideas for writing business plans with examples, adopting a business structure, and setting goals and objectives.

24831 ■ "Rehab Will Turn Hospital Into Incubator" in *The Business Journal-Serving Metropolitan Kansas City* (Vol. 26, September 12, 2008)
Pub: American City Business Journals, Inc.
Ed: Rob Roberts. **Description:** Independence Regional Health Center will be purchased by CEAH Realtors and be converted into the Independence Regional Entrepreneurial Center, a business incubator that will house startups and other tenants. Other details about the planned entrepreneurial center are provided.

24832 ■ "Startup Aims to Cut Out Coupon Clipping" in *The Business Journal-Serving Metropolitan Kansas City* (Vol. 26, August 15, 2008, No. 49)
Pub: American City Business Journals, Inc.
Ed: Suzanna Stagemeyer. **Description:** TDP Inc., who started operations 18 months ago, aims to transform stale coupon promotions using technology by digitizing the entire coupon process. The process is expected to enable consumers to hunt coupons online where they will be automatically linked to loyalty cards. Other views and information on TDP and its services are presented.

24833 ■ "Three Weeks To Startup" in *Entrepreneur* (December 19, 2008)
Pub: Entrepreneur Media Inc.
Ed: Tim Berry; Sabrina Parsons. **Description:** Breakdown for realistically starting a business in three weeks is provided in detail.

EDUCATIONAL PROGRAMS

24834 ■ 2011 National Electrical Code (NEC)
American Trainco
9785 S Maroon Cir., Ste. 300
PO Box 3397
Englewood, CO 80112
Ph:(303)531-4560
Free: 877-978-7246
Fax:(303)531-4565
Co. E-mail: Sales@AmericanTrainco.com
URL: http://www.americantrainco.com
Price: $990.00. **Description:** Provides anyone working with electricity the most up-to-date, best practices for safe installation and maintenance of electrical systems and equipment, including the new 2011 Code changes. **Locations:** Cities throughout the United States.

24835 ■ Advanced Critical Thinking Applications Workshop
American Management Association
600 AMA Way
Saranac Lake, NY 12983-5534
Ph:(212)586-8100
Free: 877-566-9441
Fax:(518)891-0368
Co. E-mail: customerservice@amanet.org
URL: http://www.amaseminars.org
Price: $2,445.00 for non-members; $2,195.00 for AMA members; and $1,880.00 for General Services Administration (GSA) members. **Description:** Two-day seminar applying critical thinking skills and how they influence challenges in the work environment. **Locations:** San Francisco, CA; New York, NY; Atlanta, GA; Washington, DC; and Arlington, VA.

24836 ■ Air Conditioning & Refrigeration
American Trainco
9785 S Maroon Cir., Ste. 300
PO Box 3397
Englewood, CO 80112
Ph:(303)531-4560
Free: 877-978-7246
Fax:(303)531-4565
Co. E-mail: Sales@AmericanTrainco.com
URL: http://www.americantrainco.com
Price: $990.00. **Description:** Course designed for anyone who needs to understand basic operation, maintenance, and troubleshooting of air conditioning and refrigeration systems in order to improve efficiencies and uptime at their industrial plants and large building facilities. **Locations:** Cities throughout the United States.

24837 ■ AMA's Financial Modeling and Forecasting Workshop
American Management Association
600 AMA Way
Saranac Lake, NY 12983-5534
Ph:(212)586-8100
Free: 877-566-9441
Fax:(518)891-0368
Co. E-mail: customerservice@amanet.org
URL: http://www.amaseminars.org
Price: $2,545.00 for non-members; $2,295.00 for AMA members; and $1,965.00 for General Services Administration (GSA) members. **Description:** Three-day seminar that covers advanced Excel modeling techniques, creating your own model from real-world examples, and analyzing and applying findings to confirm your forecast. **Locations:** New York, NY; Atlanta, GA; Washington, DC; Arlington, VA; San Diego, CA; San Francisco, CA; and Chicago, IL.

24838 ■ Arc Flash Protection & Electrical Safety 70E
American Trainco
9785 S Maroon Cir., Ste. 300
PO Box 3397
Englewood, CO 80112
Ph:(303)531-4560
Free: 877-978-7246
Fax:(303)531-4565
Co. E-mail: Sales@AmericanTrainco.com
URL: http://www.americantrainco.com
Price: $990.00. **Description:** Training course designed to save lives, prevent disabling injuries, and prevent damage to plants, buildings and equipment. Participants learn about personal safety for working on or around electrical systems and equipment, how to use proper materials and procedures for doing electrical work, and the potential consequences for themselves and others if they don't. **Locations:** Cities throughout the United States.

24839 ■ Auditing the Manufacturing Process
Seminar Information Service, Inc.
20 Executive Park, Ste. 120
Irvine, CA 92614
Ph:(949)261-9104
Free: 877-SEM-INFO
Fax:(949)261-1963
Co. E-mail: info@seminarinformation.com
URL: http://www.seminarinformation.com
Price: $2,195.00. **Description:** Learn how to identify key manufacturing data to help objectively perform risk assessment of the conversion cycle, while discovering how to analyze the impact of shop floor activities on the balance sheet and income statement, and review the audit concerns in implementing new technologies. **Locations:** Boston, MA; and Chicago, IL.

24840 ■ Basic Electricity for the Non Electrician
American Trainco
9785 S Maroon Cir., Ste. 300
PO Box 3397
Englewood, CO 80112
Ph:(303)531-4560
Free: 877-978-7246
Fax:(303)531-4565
Co. E-mail: Sales@AmericanTrainco.com
URL: http://www.americantrainco.com
Price: $990.00. **Description:** Understanding and working with industrial electricity. **Locations:** Cities throughout the United States.

24841 ■ Boiler Operation, Maintenance & Safety
American Trainco
9785 S Maroon Cir., Ste. 300
PO Box 3397
Englewood, CO 80112
Ph:(303)531-4560
Free: 877-978-7246
Fax:(303)531-4565
Co. E-mail: Sales@AmericanTrainco.com
URL: http://www.americantrainco.com
Price: $990.00. **Description:** Seminar designed to teach building and facility maintenance personnel how to service their own boiler safely reducing the need for outside service contractors, while at the same time increases your confidence and comfort level in operating and maintaining your own broilers. **Locations:** Cities throughout the United States.

24842 ■ Building a Strategy Focused Organization
EEI Communications
66 Canal Center Plz., Ste. 200
Alexandria, VA 22314
Ph:(703)683-7453
Free: 888-253-2762
Fax:(703)683-7310
Co. E-mail: train@eeicom.com
URL: http://www.eeicom.com/training
Price: $1,625.00. **Description:** Identifies strategies that can help your organization meet the challenges of the competitive environment and improve overall effectiveness across organizational boundaries. **Locations:** Silver Spring, MD; Hunt Valley, MD; Columbia, MD; and Alexandria, VA.

24843 ■ Business Analysis Fundamentals
600 AMA Way
Saranac Lake, NY 12983-5534
Ph:(212)586-8100
Free: 877-566-9441
Fax:(518)891-0368
Co. E-mail: customerservice@amanet.org
URL: http://www.amaseminars.org
Price: $2,095.00 for non-members; $1,895.00 for AMA members; and $1,623.00 for General Services Administration (GSA) members. **Description:** Hands-on seminar can help ensure that you and your company choose and implement the right solutions for all future projects and initiatives. **Locations:** Atlanta, GA; Arlington, VA; San Francisco, CA; Washington, DC; Chicago, IL; and New York, NY.

24844 ■ Chilled Water Systems
American Trainco
9785 S Maroon Cir., Ste. 300
PO Box 3397
Englewood, CO 80112
Ph:(303)531-4560
Free: 877-978-7246
Fax:(303)531-4565
Co. E-mail: Sales@AmericanTrainco.com
URL: http://www.americantrainco.com
Price: $990.00. **Description:** Learn to control your systems and properly maintain them, getting the most out of them. **Locations:** Cities throughout the United States.

24845 ■ The Conference on Social Media
Seminar Information Service, Inc.
20 Executive Park, Ste. 120
Irvine, CA 92614
Ph:(949)261-9104
Free: 877-SEM-INFO
Fax:(949)261-1963
Co. E-mail: info@seminarinformation.com
URL: http://www.seminarinformation.com
Price: $249.00. **Description:** Learn how to make social media link your organization, including new tools and ways to grow your business, and how to define your strategy and create your plan prior to taking the leap into social media. **Locations:** Cities throughout the United States.

24846 ■ Developing a Balanced Scorecard for Business & Government
EEI Communications
66 Canal Center Plz., Ste. 200
Alexandria, VA 22314
Ph:(703)683-7453
Free: 888-253-2762
Fax:(703)683-7310
Co. E-mail: train@eeicom.com
URL: http://www.eeicom.com/training
Price: $1,065.00. **Description:** The Balanced ScoreCard evaluates performance from four basic perspectives, Customer, Financial, Internal Processes and Learning and Growth. By utilizing Key Performance Indicators (KPIs) to reflect the performance of the organization at a variety of levels, the Balanced ScoreCard allows organizations to better understand, communicate and improve on organizational performance. **Locations:** Silver Spring, MD; Hunt Valley, MD; Columbia, MD; and Alexandria, VA.

24847 ■ Electrical Ladder Drawings, Schematics & Design
American Trainco
9785 S Maroon Cir., Ste. 300
PO Box 3397
Englewood, CO 80112
Ph:(303)531-4560
Free: 877-978-7246
Fax:(303)531-4565
Co. E-mail: Sales@AmericanTrainco.com
URL: http://www.americantrainco.com
Price: $990.00. **Description:** Training will include exercises where participants create schematic diagrams based on circuit descriptions, as well as interpreting schematic drawings so that they can provide verbal or written circuit descriptions and an understanding of several types of drawings and diagrams including Block, Pictorial, One-line, Wiring, Terminal, and Schematic. **Locations:** Cities throughout the United States.

24848 ■ Generators & Emergency Power
American Trainco
9785 S Maroon Cir., Ste. 300
PO Box 3397
Englewood, CO 80112
Ph:(303)531-4560
Free: 877-978-7246
Fax:(303)531-4565
Co. E-mail: Sales@AmericanTrainco.com
URL: http://www.americantrainco.com
Price: $990.00. **Description:** Learn what you can do, and should do with generators, to make sure your facility will keep running even when the electricity to your facility doesn't. **Locations:** Cities throughout the United States.

24849 ■ How to Conduct Your Own Energy Audit
American Trainco
9785 S Maroon Cir., Ste. 300
PO Box 3397
Englewood, CO 80112
Ph:(303)531-4560
Free: 877-978-7246
Fax:(303)531-4565
Co. E-mail: Sales@AmericanTrainco.com
URL: http://www.americantrainco.com
Price: $990.00. **Description:** Two-day hands-on seminar shows you how to find quick and inexpensive ways to immediately cut energy costs at your plant or facility. **Locations:** Orange County, CA; and Orlando, FL.

24850 ■ HVAC Controls & Air Distribution
American Trainco
9785 S Maroon Cir., Ste. 300
PO Box 3397
Englewood, CO 80112
Ph:(303)531-4560
Free: 877-978-7246
Fax:(303)531-4565
Co. E-mail: Sales@AmericanTrainco.com
URL: http://www.americantrainco.com
Price: $990.00. **Description:** Learn how to "control" their controls, and how to use fundamental air distribution principles for achieving consistent HVAC comfort and efficiency in buildings, plants and facilities. **Locations:** Cities throughout the United States.

24851 ■ Improve Your Analytical Skills: Making Information Work for You
American Management Association
600 AMA Way
Saranac Lake, NY 12983-5534
Ph:(212)586-8100
Free: 877-566-9441
Fax:(518)891-0368
Co. E-mail: customerservice@amanet.org
URL: http://www.amaseminars.org
Price: $1,995.00 for non-members; $1,795.00 for AMA members; and $1,537.00 for General Services Administration (GSA) members. **Description:** Learn how to assimilate, assess, organize, and analyze information. **Locations:** Cities throughout the United States

24852 ■ Instrumentation, Process Measurement & Control
American Trainco
9785 S Maroon Cir., Ste. 300
PO Box 3397
Englewood, CO 80112
Ph:(303)531-4560
Free: 877-978-7246
Fax:(303)531-4565
Co. E-mail: Sales@AmericanTrainco.com
URL: http://www.americantrainco.com
Price: $990.00. **Description:** Learn why it is necessary to measure what is going on with your systems and equipment, how to measure it, and what those measurements may mean in terms of action that should be taken to eliminate future downtime and unnecessary expense. **Locations:** Ontario, CA; Kansas City, MO; Philadelphia, PA; Salt Lake, UT; and Arlington, VA.

24853 ■ Inventory Control for Maintenance
American Trainco
9785 S Maroon Cir., Ste. 300
PO Box 3397
Englewood, CO 80112
Ph:(303)531-4560
Free: 877-978-7246
Fax:(303)531-4565
Co. E-mail: Sales@AmericanTrainco.com
URL: http://www.americantrainco.com
Price: $990.00. **Description:** Focus on building an inventory management system that will lead to better control through optimization of inventory quantities, organization of inventory and access to inventory. **Locations:** Orange County, CA; and Orlando, FL.

24854 ■ Maintenance Planning & Scheduling
American Trainco
9785 S Maroon Cir., Ste. 300
PO Box 3397
Englewood, CO 80112
Ph:(303)531-4560
Free: 877-978-7246
Fax:(303)531-4565
Co. E-mail: Sales@AmericanTrainco.com
URL: http://www.americantrainco.com
Price: $990.00. **Description:** Learn to reduce maintenance costs by better planning with your existing workforce. **Locations:** Cities throughout the United States.

24855 ■ Maintenance Welding
American Trainco
9785 S Maroon Cir., Ste. 300
PO Box 3397
Englewood, CO 80112
Ph:(303)531-4560
Free: 877-978-7246
Fax:(303)531-4565
Co. E-mail: Sales@AmericanTrainco.com
URL: http://www.americantrainco.com
Price: $990.00. **Description:** Learn welding techniques, welding processes, metal and filler selection, cutting processes, new fabrications, troubleshooting defects, welding repair, personal safety, managing costs, record keeping and more. **Locations:** Cities throughout the United States.

24856 ■ Motor Selection, Maintenance, Testing & Replacement
American Trainco
9785 S Maroon Cir., Ste. 300
PO Box 3397
Englewood, CO 80112
Ph:(303)531-4560
Free: 877-978-7246
Fax:(303)531-4565
Co. E-mail: Sales@AmericanTrainco.com
URL: http://www.americantrainco.com
Price: $495.00. **Description:** Seminar designed for anyone whose work is affected by motors at their facility, whether they are mechanics doing the work, a supervisor in charge of fixing problems, or purchasing agents responsible for saving money. **Locations:** Anchorage, AK; and Honolulu, HI.

24857 ■ PLC Programming & Applications
American Trainco
9785 S Maroon Cir., Ste. 300
PO Box 3397
Englewood, CO 80112
Ph:(303)531-4560
Free: 877-978-7246
Fax:(303)531-4565
Co. E-mail: Sales@AmericanTrainco.com
URL: http://www.americantrainco.com
Price: $990.00. **Description:** Provides skills needed to organize, plan, write, enter, test, and document SLC500 programs using the basic programming instructions and RSLogix software. **Locations:** Cities throughout the United States.

24858 ■ PLCs for Non-Programmers
American Trainco
9785 S Maroon Cir., Ste. 300
PO Box 3397
Englewood, CO 80112
Ph:(303)531-4560
Free: 877-978-7246
Fax:(303)531-4565
Co. E-mail: Sales@AmericanTrainco.com
URL: http://www.americantrainco.com
Price: $990.00. **Description:** Seminar designed for maintenance technicians, electricians, or other non-programmers who need a general understanding of automation and Programmable Logic Controllers. **Locations:** Cities throughout the United States.

24859 ■ Plumbing & Pipefitting for Plants & Buildings
American Trainco
9785 S Maroon Cir., Ste. 300
PO Box 3397
Englewood, CO 80112
Ph:(303)531-4560
Free: 877-978-7246
Fax:(303)531-4565
Co. E-mail: Sales@AmericanTrainco.com
URL: http://www.americantrainco.com
Price: $990.00. **Description:** Covers the necessary requirements to follow code and safety regulations while providing the student with a practical foundation to quickly identify problems and solve them on their own, whether it's a low-pressure water supply line problem, drippy valve or a clogged drain trap. **Locations:** Phoenix, AZ; Orange County, CA; Sacramento, CA; and Denver, CO.

24860 ■ Predictive Maintenance and Condition Monitoring
American Trainco
9785 S Maroon Cir., Ste. 300
PO Box 3397
Englewood, CO 80112
Ph:(303)531-4560
Free: 877-978-7246
Fax:(303)531-4565
Co. E-mail: Sales@AmericanTrainco.com
URL: http://www.americantrainco.com
Price: $990.00. **Description:** Provides the fundamentals of PdM and condition monitoring applicable to plants, facilities, and manufacturing lines. **Locations:** Orange County, CA; and Orlando, FL.

24861 ■ The Proactive Leader I: Develop an Effective Agenda, Build Support, and Gain Traction
Seminar Information Service, Inc.
20 Executive Park, Ste. 120
Irvine, CA 92614
Ph:(949)261-9104
Free: 877-SEM-INFO
Fax:(949)261-1963
Co. E-mail: info@seminarinformation.com
URL: http://www.seminarinformation.com
Price: $1,495.00. **Description:** Learn to identify and prioritize arenas where you can effect change in your organization, including the skills of political competence to take the next steps toward building support and gaining traction for your idea. **Locations:** New York, NY.

24862 ■ Project Initiation and Planning
EEI Communications
66 Canal Center Plz., Ste. 200
Alexandria, VA 22314
Ph:(703)683-7453
Free: 888-253-2762
Fax:(703)683-7310
Co. E-mail: train@eeicom.com
URL: http://www.eeicom.com/training
Price: $1,065.00. **Description:** Learn how to incorporate project charter, work breakdown structure, a risk and change management plan, communications plan, schedule and budget to guarantee a successful project. **Locations:** Silver Spring, MD; Hunt Valley, MD; Columbia, MD; and Alexandria, VA.

24863 ■ Project Quality Management for Project Managers - Delivering Consistent Quality (Onsite)
Seminar Information Service, Inc.
20 Executive Park, Ste. 120
Irvine, CA 92614
Ph:(949)261-9104
Free: 877-SEM-INFO
Fax:(949)261-1963
Co. E-mail: info@seminarinformation.com
URL: http://www.seminarinformation.com
Price: $2,490.00. **Description:** Learn how to: Implement effective project quality management best practices; Apply a proven analysis method to identify stakeholder quality expectations and refine project scope; Leverage an industry standard template to create a project Quality Management Plan (QMP); Generate a quality assurance task list that incorporates project, product and process; Transform quality assurance recommendations into corrective and improvement actions; Design and implement quality control gates throughout the project and product life cycles. **Locations:** New York, NY; Ottawa, CN; Reston, VA; and Toronto, CN.

24864 ■ Project Scheduling and Budgeting - Achieving Cost-Effective and Timely Delivery (Onsite)
Seminar Information Service, Inc.
20 Executive Park, Ste. 120
Irvine, CA 92614
Ph:(949)261-9104
Free: 877-SEM-INFO
Fax:(949)261-1963
Co. E-mail: info@seminarinformation.com
URL: http://www.seminarinformation.com
Price: $2,490.00. **Description:** Learn how to: Build schedules and budgets that transform project constraints into project success; Construct Work Breakdown Structures (WBS) and network diagrams and estimate task durations; Calculate Critical Path and optimize your project plan; Allocate costs and chart expected cash flow; Assign resources effectively and respond to end-date changes; Perform Earned Value Analysis (EVA) to keep the project on track. **Locations:** Reston, VA; and New York, NY.

24865 ■ Pump Repair & Maintenance
American Trainco
9785 S Maroon Cir., Ste. 300
PO Box 3397
Englewood, CO 80112
Ph:(303)531-4560
Free: 877-978-7246
Fax:(303)531-4565
Co. E-mail: Sales@AmericanTrainco.com
URL: http://www.americantrainco.com
Price: $990.00. **Description:** Learn common sense pump maintenance and repair techniques to keep facilities and equipment up and running. **Locations:** Cities throughout the United States.

24866 ■ Pumps & Pump Systems
American Trainco
9785 S Maroon Cir., Ste. 300
PO Box 3397
Englewood, CO 80112
Ph:(303)531-4560
Free: 877-978-7246
Fax:(303)531-4565
Co. E-mail: Sales@AmericanTrainco.com
URL: http://www.americantrainco.com
Price: $990.00. **Description:** From the pump and pump system, to the people who operate, maintain and design the pump system, this seminar will teach students how to identify the real problems causing pump failure, and how to avoid repeating those problems in the future. **Locations:** Cities throughout the United States.

24867 ■ Steam Systems Maintenance, Safety & Optimization
American Trainco
9785 S Maroon Cir., Ste. 300
PO Box 3397
Englewood, CO 80112
Ph:(303)531-4560
Free: 877-978-7246
Fax:(303)531-4565
Co. E-mail: Sales@AmericanTrainco.com
URL: http://www.americantrainco.com
Price: $990.00. **Description:** This course will teach you how to keep your steam system working efficiently and how to fix common problems and work safely reducing energy loss. **Locations:** Cities throughout the United States.

24868 ■ Strategic Planning for Organizational Success (Onsite)
Seminar Information Service, Inc.
20 Executive Park, Ste. 120
Irvine, CA 92614
Ph:(949)261-9104
Free: 877-SEM-INFO
Fax:(949)261-1963
Co. E-mail: info@seminarinformation.com
URL: http://www.seminarinformation.com
Price: $2,390.00. **Description:** Learn how to: Formulate strategic plans to help your organization advance and grow; Detect the strengths, weaknesses, opportunities and threats (SWOT) that drive strategy; Identify strategies to better position your organization for long-term competitive advantage; Translate strategy into action; Execute strategy and deliver results through people and processes; Establish strategic planning, monitoring and controlling mechanisms that ensure positive results. **Locations:** Toronto, CN; and Reston, VA.

24869 ■ Troubleshooting Mechanical Drive Systems & Rotating Equipment
American Trainco
9785 S Maroon Cir., Ste. 300
PO Box 3397
Englewood, CO 80112
Ph:(303)531-4560
Free: 877-978-7246
Fax:(303)531-4565
Co. E-mail: Sales@AmericanTrainco.com
URL: http://www.americantrainco.com
Price: $990.00. **Description:** Provide a new perspective on troubleshooting mechanical and rotating equipment and learn about basic mechanical applications, failures, life expectancy and maintenance shafts, bearings, couplings, chains, sprockets, bushings, gears, belts, sheaves and other mechanical components. You'll learn what data to measure, track and trend so that when equipment fails you can get quick answers to what is wrong, as well as fix the real problems with your equipment and not just the symptoms. **Locations:** Cities throughout the United States.

24870 ■ Understanding & Troubleshooting Hydraulics
American Trainco
9785 S Maroon Cir., Ste. 300
PO Box 3397
Englewood, CO 80112
Ph:(303)531-4560
Free: 877-978-7246
Fax:(303)531-4565
Co. E-mail: Sales@AmericanTrainco.com
URL: http://www.americantrainco.com
Price: $990.00. **Description:** Provides the basic building blocks and information you need to become proficient in working with industrial hydraulics and

fluid power, whether a small mobile unit or large industrial installation. **Locations:** Cities throughout the United States.

24871 ■ Uninterruptable Power Supply (UPS) Maintenance and Readiness
American Trainco
9785 S Maroon Cir., Ste. 300
PO Box 3397
Englewood, CO 80112
Ph:(303)531-4560
Free: 877-978-7246
Fax:(303)531-4565
Co. E-mail: Sales@AmericanTrainco.com
URL: http://www.americantrainco.com
Price: $495.00. **Description:** Seminar designed for personnel responsible for the UPS systems in industrial plants, public facilities, and commercial buildings. **Locations:** Sacramento, CA; and San Diego, CA.

24872 ■ Variable Frequency Drives
American Trainco
9785 S Maroon Cir., Ste. 300
PO Box 3397
Englewood, CO 80112
Ph:(303)531-4560
Free: 877-978-7246
Fax:(303)531-4565
Co. E-mail: Sales@AmericanTrainco.com
URL: http://www.americantrainco.com
Price: $990.00. **Description:** Learn how to troubleshoot common VFD problems, take care of your own equipment, and avoid costly repairs or service repairs, including how to identify hazards associated with working on VFDs, an understanding of the importance of safe work practices, recognition of the main components of a VFD system, and the different methods of controlling a VFD. **Locations:** Cities throughout the United States.

24873 ■ Water Treatment for Boilers, Chillers & Cooling Towers
American Trainco
9785 S Maroon Cir., Ste. 300
PO Box 3397
Englewood, CO 80112
Ph:(303)531-4560
Free: 877-978-7246
Fax:(303)531-4565
Co. E-mail: Sales@AmericanTrainco.com
URL: http://www.americantrainco.com
Price: $495.00. **Description:** One-day seminar to take the mystery out of creating, and stabilizing high water quality for your HVAC systems. **Locations:** Cities throughout the United States.

REFERENCE WORKS

24874 ■ "13D Filings" in *Barron's* (Vol. 88, March 24, 2008, No. 12, pp. M13)
Pub: Dow Jones & Company, Inc.
Description: HealthCor Management called as problematic the plan of Magellan Health Services to use its high cash balances for acquisitions. Carlson Capital discussed with Energy Partners possible changes in the latter's board. Investor Carl Icahn suggested that Enzon Pharmaceuticals consider selling itself or divest some of its assets.

24875 ■ "13D Filings: Investors Report to the SEC" in *Barron's* (Vol. 88, July 4, 2008, No. 28, pp. M10)
Pub: Dow Jones & Co., Inc.
Description: Robino Stortini Holdings will seek control of Investors Capital Holdings either alone or with members of the company's management. Discovery Group I will withhold its votes at the nomination of directors for TESSCO Technologies while JMB Capital Partners Master Fund plans to nominate a slate of candidates to the board of Maguire Properties.

24876 ■ *The 100 Best Businesses to Start When You Don't Want To Work Hard Anymore*
Pub: Career Press Inc.
Ed: Lisa Rogak. **Price:** $16.99. **Description:** Author helps burned-out workers envision a new future as a small business owner. Systems analysis, adventure travel outfitting, bookkeeping, food delivery, furniture making, and software development are among the industries examined.

24877 ■ "ACE Aims High With Spinoff of Repair Unit" in *Globe & Mail* (January 31, 2007, pp. B15)
Pub: CTVglobemedia Publishing Inc.
Ed: Brent Jang. **Description:** The decision of ACE Aviation Holdings Inc. to sell its aircraft maintenance division and add workforce at its El Salvador plant is discussed.

24878 ■ "Acquisition of a Uranium Exploration Project, Laguiche Basin, Opinaca Area, Quebec" in *Canadian Corporate News* (May 16, 2007)
Pub: Comtex News Network Inc.
Description: Dios Exploration Inc. negotiated an option agreement with Sirios Resources Inc. to explore the Opinaca Nord Property with a project that comprises one main anomaly cluster for gold in association with arsenic and two detailed uranium anomaly clusters.

24879 ■ "The Agency Model Is Bent But Not Broken" in *Advertising Age* (Vol. 79, July 7, 2008, No. 26, pp. 17)
Pub: Crain Communications, Inc.
Ed: Stephen Fajen. **Description:** In the new-media environment, advertising agencies must change the way in which they do business and receive payment.

24880 ■ "The Agency-Selection Process Needs Fixing Now" in *Advertising Age* (Vol. 79, July 7, 2008, No. 26, pp. 18)
Pub: Crain Communications, Inc.
Ed: Avi Dan. **Description:** Marketers are facing increased challenges in this sagging economic climate and must realize the importance of choosing the correct advertising agency for their company in order to benefit from a more-stable relationship that yields better business results. Advice for marketers regarding the best way to choose an agency is included.

24881 ■ "Air Canada to Slash 600 Non-Union Jobs" in *Globe & Mail* (February 11, 2006, pp. B3)
Pub: CTVglobemedia Publishing Inc.
Ed: Brent Jang. **Description:** The reasons behind workforce reduction by ACE Aviation Holdings Inc. at Air Canada are presented.

24882 ■ "Air Canada's Flight Plan for 777s Excludes India" in *Globe & Mail* (March 28, 2007, pp. B5)
Pub: CTVglobemedia Publishing Inc.
Ed: Brent Jang. **Description:** The decision of Air Canada to exclude India and to fly its Boeing 777s due to poor economic returns is discussed.

24883 ■ "All Eyes On Iris" in *Canadian Business* (Vol. 81, July 22, 2008, No. 12-13, pp. 20)
Pub: Rogers Media Ltd.
Ed: Jack Mintz. **Description:** Provincial governments in Canada are believed to be awaiting Alberta Finance Minister Iris Evans' financial and investment policies as well as Evans' development of a new saving strategy. Alberta is the only Canadian province that is in position to invest in sovereign wealth funds after it eliminated its debt in 2005.

24884 ■ "All Fired Up!" in *Small Business Opportunities* (November 2008)
Pub: Entrepreneur Media Inc.
Ed: Stan Roberts. **Description:** Profile of Brixx Wood Fired Pizza, which has launched a franchising program due to the amount of interest the company's founders received over the years; franchisees do not need experience in the food industry or pizza restaurant service business in order to open a franchise of their own because all franchisees receive comprehensive training in which they are educated on all of the necessary tools to effectively run the business.

24885 ■ "All In Good Fun" in *Entrepreneur* (Vol. 36, May 2008, No. 5, pp. 22)
Pub: Entrepreneur Media, Inc.
Ed: Christopher Percy Collier. **Description:** According to a study conducted in 2007, humor in the workplace helps people communicate effectively and improves camaraderie. Company leaders and entrepreneurs can also tell humorous stories about themselves, but must also set lines that should not be crossed. The humorous atmosphere in the company YouSendIt is presented.

24886 ■ "All Options Open On Chrysler: Magna" in *Globe & Mail* (February 28, 2007, pp. B3)
Pub: CTVglobemedia Publishing Inc.
Ed: Greg Keenan. **Description:** The 65 percent drop in the profits of Magna International Inc. and the plans of its chief executive officer Don Walker to make the company more competitive are discussed.

24887 ■ "Analyst Questions CanWest Papers' Viability" in *Globe & Mail* (January 14, 2006, pp. B3)
Pub: CTVglobemedia Publishing Inc.
Ed: Grant Robertson. **Description:** The opinions of analyst Tim Casey of BMO Nesbitt Burns Inc. over the prospects of two newspapers Dose and National Post of CanWest Global Communications Corp., which planned cost restructuring efforts, are presented.

24888 ■ "Analysts Not Fazed By Constellation's Halt to New Nuclear Plants" in *Baltimore Business Journal* (Vol. 28, October 22, 2010, No. 24)
Pub: Baltimore Business Journal
Ed: Scott Dance. **Description:** Wall Street analysts believe that Constellation Energy Group Inc.'s decision to pull out of the nuclear construction business would not change their outlook on the company. New nuclear power had been one of Constellation's long-term goals, but the company pulled the plug on the project. It is believed that most investors were not expecting any payoff from the venture.

24889 ■ "Are You Ready for a Transformation?" in *Women Entrepreneur* (November 28, 2008)
Pub: Entrepreneur Media Inc.
Ed: Aliza Sherman. **Description:** Marlene J. Waldock, an expert in women's empowerment and reinvention, discusses brand modification and what a business owner should consider before attempting to change or modify their brand.

24890 ■ "Are Your Goals Hitting the Right Target?" in *Business Strategy Review* (Vol. 21, Autumn 2010, No. 3, pp. 46)
Pub: Blackwell Publishers Ltd.
Ed: Alan Meekings, Steve Briault, Andy Neely. **Description:** Setting targets is normal in most organizations. The authors think such a practice can cause more harm than good and offer a better strategy.

24891 ■ "Australian Firm Buys Off Sands Engineering Company for $1 Billion" in *Globe & Mail* (February 8, 2007, pp. B3)
Pub: CTVglobemedia Publishing Inc.
Ed: David Ebner. **Description:** Australia's WorleyParson Ltd. acquires Colt Engineering Corp., a private petroleum company, for $1 billion. The acquision will provide WorleyParson an opportunity to expand its operations in Australia.

24892 ■ "Automaker Foundations Run Leaner" in *Crain's Detroit Business* (Vol. 26, January 11, 2010, No. 2, pp. 1)
Pub: Crain Communications, Inc.
Ed: Sherri Welch. **Description:** Overview of the Detroit automobile industry includes restoring profitability, smarter marketing strategies and philanthropy. Each company comprising the Big 3 is examined, as is their vision for the future.

24893 ■ "Avnet Inc.'s Expansion Fueled By Mergers and Acquisitions" in *The Business Journal - Serving Phoenix and the Valley of the Sun* (Vol. 28, September 12, 2008, No. 53, pp. 1)
Pub: American City Business Journals, Inc.
Ed: Patrick O'Grady. **Description:** Avnet Inc. has grown and has nearly tripled its revenue in the past ten years through the company's acquisitions and consolidation. The company's revenue in 2008 is $17.9 billion. Other details about the company's growth are discussed.

24894 ■ *Awesomely Simple: Essential Business Strategies for Turning Ideas Into Action*
Pub: Jossey-Bass
Ed: John Spence. **Released:** September 8, 2009. **Price:** $24.95. **Description:** Six key strategies that create a foundation for achieving business excellence include: vivid vision, best people, a performance-oriented culture, robust communication, a sense of urgency, and extreme customer focus.

24895 ■ "Back to Business for Bishop Museum" in *Hawaii Business* (Vol. 54, August 2008, No. 2, pp. 53)
Pub: Hawaii Business Publishing
Ed: Shara Enay. **Description:** Bishop Museum, ranked 224 in Hawaii Business' top 250 companies for 2008, had $29.5 million in gross sales for 2007, up 52.8 percent from the $19.3 million gross sales in 2006. The company has cut 24 positions in a restructuring effort for the museum's sustainability. Grants, artifacts and plans for sustainable operations are discussed.

24896 ■ "The Balanced Business" in *Women In Business* (Vol. 63, Spring 2011, No. 1, pp. 14)
Pub: American Business Women's Association
Ed: Leigh Elmore. **Description:** The balance scoreboard has developed to a full strategic planning and management system from its early use as a simple performance measurement network. Executives are able to execute their strategies by using information from the balance scoreboard. Insights on Mayer Group Inc. executive Ken Mayer's view of the balance scorecard are also shared.

24897 ■ "Baldwin Connelly Partnership Splits" in *Business Journal Serving Greater Tampa Bay* (Vol. 30, November 19, 2010, No. 48, pp. 1)
Pub: Tampa Bay Business Journal
Ed: Alexis Muellner. **Description:** The fast-growing insurance brokerage Baldwin Connelly is now breaking up after five years. Two different entrepreneurial visions have developed within the organization and founders Lowry Baldwin and John Connell will not take separate tracks. Staffing levels in the firm are expected to remain the same.

24898 ■ "Bark Up The Right Tree" in *Small Business Opportunities* (Winter 2009)
Pub: Entrepreneur Media Inc.
Description: Profile of Central Bark, a daycare company catering to pets that offers franchise opportunities and is expanding rapidly despite the economic downturn; the company's growth strategy is also discussed.

24899 ■ "Battered Loblaw Makes Deep Job Cuts" in *Globe & Mail* (January 23, 2007)
Pub: CTVglobemedia Publishing Inc.
Description: Loblaw Companies Ltd., supermarket giant, is eliminating up to 1,000 administrative jobs and shifting more buying responsibilities to its suppliers. The grocer will also introduce a national inventory strategy called "category management".

24900 ■ *Battling Big Box: How Nimble Niche Companies Can Outmaneuver Giant Companies*
Pub: Career Press, Inc.
Ed: Henry Dubroff, Susan J. Marks. **Released:** January 1, 2009. **Price:** $15.99. **Description:** Small companies can compete with larger firms through agility, adaptability, customer service, and credibility. Topics include information to help empower employees, build a powerful brand, manage cash flow, and maintaining a business vision.

24901 ■ "BCE Mulls Radical Changes With Industry Under Pressure" in *Globe & Mail* (March 30, 2007, pp. B1)
Pub: CTVglobemedia Publishing Inc.
Ed: Andrew Willis; Jacquie McNish; Catherine McLean. **Description:** An account on the expansion plans of BCE Inc., which plans to acquire TELUS Corp., is presented.

24902 ■ "Best Growth Stocks" in *Canadian Business* (Vol. 81, Summer 2008, No. 9, pp. 61)
Pub: Rogers Media Ltd.
Ed: Calvin Leung. **Description:** Table showing the one-year performance of growth stocks is presented. Edmonton-based Stantec Inc. expects to advance its sales and profits by 15 percent to 20 percent per year through tapping international markets and acquisitions. Analysts forecast a 17.1 percent growth rate annually over the next 3 to 5 years.

24903 ■ "Better Made's Better Idea: Diversify Despite Rising Costs" in *Crain's Detroit Business* (Vol. 24, September 22, 2008, No. 38, pp. 18)
Pub: Crain Communications, Inc.
Ed: Nathan Skid. **Description:** Better Made Snack Foods Inc. is planning to expand its product lines and market reach as well as boost manufacturing capability during a time in which the company is being buffeted by rising commodity and fuel costs. The company feels that diversification is the key to maintain sales and growth.

24904 ■ "Betting on the Glitz" in *Canadian Business* (Vol. 79, October 9, 2006, No. 20, pp. 104)
Pub: Rogers Media
Ed: Zena Olijnyk. **Description:** Holt, Renfrew & Comany's expansion plans to cash on the booming demand for high end retail luxury markets are discussed.

24905 ■ "A Big Dream That 'Was Going Nowhere'" in *Globe & Mail* (February 4, 2006, pp. B4)
Pub: CTVglobemedia Publishing Inc.
Ed: Konrad Yakabuski. **Description:** The reasons behind the decision of Bombardier Inc. to terminate its plans to develop jet airplanes are presented.

24906 ■ *Big Vision, Small Business*
Pub: Ivy Sea, Inc.
Ed: Jamie S. Walters. **Released:** October 10, 2002. **Price:** $17.95. **Description:** The power of the small enterprise is examined. The author shares her expertise as an entrepreneur and founder of a business consulting firm to help small business owners successfully run their companies. Interviews with more than seventy small business owners provide insight into visioning, planning, and establishing a small company, as well as strategies for good employee and customer relationships.

24907 ■ "A Bigger Deal" in *Crain's Cleveland Business* (Vol. 28, November 12, 2007, No. 45, pp. 1)
Pub: Crain Communications, Inc.
Ed: Shawn A. Turner. **Description:** In an attempt to boost its revenue CBiz Inc., a provider of accounting and business services, is looking to balance its acquisitions of smaller companies with larger ones as part of its overall growth strategy.

24908 ■ "Blackstone Set to Sell Stake" in *Globe & Mail* (March 17, 2007, pp. B6)
Pub: CTVglobemedia Publishing Inc.
Ed: Tennille Tracy. **Description:** The plan of Blackstone Group to sell 10 percent of its stake to raise $4 billion and its proposal to go for initial public offering is discussed.

24909 ■ "Brewing National Success" in *Hawaii Business* (Vol. 53, November 2007, No. 5, pp. 46)
Pub: Hawaii Business Publishing
Ed: Alex Salkever. **Description:** Kona Brewing Co. (KBC) is already selling its brews in four cities in Florida and 17 other states and Japan as well. KBC is currently forming a deal with Red Hook to produce Longboard Lager and other KBC brews at Red Hooks' brewery in New Hampshire. KBC's chief executive officer Mattson Davis shares KBC's practices for success.

24910 ■ "Budget Strategically to Stay on Course" in *Entrepreneur* (August 28, 2008)
Pub: Entrepreneur Media Inc.
Ed: Tim Berry. **Description:** Budgeting is one of the most valuable tools in a manager's arsenal. The importance of budgeting is discussed and tips for surviving an economic recession are provided.

24911 ■ *Building a Business the Buddhist Way*
Pub: Celestial Arts Publishing Company
Ed: Geri Larkin. **Released:** September 2004. **Price:** $11.67 (Canadian). **Description:** Principles of entrepreneurship for starting and growing a business while maintaining a balance between business goals and spiritual goals.

24912 ■ "Calming Customers" in *The Business Journal-Portland* (Vol. 25, August 29, 2008, No. 25, pp. 1)
Pub: American City Business Journals, Inc.
Ed: Kirsten Grind; Rob Smith. **Description:** Credit unions and banks in the Portland area are reaching out to clients in an effort to reassure them on the security of their money and the firms' financial stability. Roy Whitehead of Washington Federal Savings, for instance, wrote 41,000 customers of the bank to reassure them. The strategies of different banks and credit unions to answer their client's worries are discussed

24913 ■ "Can Brewer Make Cheap Seats Pay?" in *Globe & Mail* (January 7, 2006, pp. B4)
Pub: CTVglobemedia Publishing Inc.
Ed: Brent Jang. **Description:** The plans of chief executive officer Montie Brewer of Air Canada to upgrade airplanes are presented.

24914 ■ "CanWest Plotting Buyback of Newspaper Income Trust" in *Globe & Mail* (February 7, 2007, pp. B1)
Pub: CTVglobemedia Publishing Inc.
Ed: Sinclair Stewart; Boyd Erman; Grant Robertson. **Description:** The CanWest Global Communications Corp.'s decision to sell its media assets in Australia and New Zealand in order to finance its plans of repurchasing its newspaper income trust CanWest MediaWorks Income Fund is discussed.

24915 ■ "Carveouts Back in Vogue" in *Mergers & Acquisitions: The Dealmaker's Journal* (March 1, 2008)
Pub: SourceMedia, Inc.
Ed: Ken MacFadyen. **Description:** Discusses ways in which companies look for hidden assets that they can exploit in worsening economic times; oftentimes firms try to sell off assets or in other instances they will look to unlock value through public spinoffs or through internal reorganizations.

24916 ■ "A Case Study: Real-Life Business Planning" in *Entrepreneur* (February 3, 2009)
Pub: Entrepreneur Media Inc.
Ed: Tim Berry. **Description:** Provides a case study of a two-day planning meeting for Palo Alto Software in which the executives of the company met for their annual planning cycle and discussed ways in which the company needed to change in order to stay viable in today's tough economic climate.

24917 ■ "CAW Boss Troubled Over 'Vulnerable' Ford Plants" in *Globe & Mail* (January 19, 2006, pp. B6)
Pub: CTVglobemedia Publishing Inc.
Ed: Greg Keenan. **Description:** The concerns of president Buzz Hargrove of Canadian Auto Workers

on the impact of Ford Motor Co.'s restructuring efforts on closure of automotive plants in Canada, are presented.

24918 ■ "Children's Products Maker Not the New Kid on the Block" in *Crain's Cleveland Business* (Vol. 28, November 26, 2007, No. 47, pp. 3)
Pub: Crain Communications, Inc.
Ed: David Bennett. **Description:** Discusses the business model employed by Shamrock Industries Inc., a rising star in the competitive world of children's products; the company, which does business as Foundations Quality Children's Products, has expanded into a 63,000-square-foot distribution center which has boosted its local profile significantly.

24919 ■ "Choosing Strategies For Change" in *Harvard Business Review* (Vol. 86, July-August 2008, No. 8, pp. 130)
Pub: Harvard Business School Press
Ed: John P. Kotter; Leonard A. Schlesinger. **Description:** Methods for implementing organizational change include identifying potential areas of resistance, providing the necessary skills and information to counteract resistance, and assessing situational factors that may influence results.

24920 ■ "Cineplex Sees Past the Big Picture" in *Globe & Mail* (February 8, 2007, pp. B9)
Pub: CTVglobemedia Publishing Inc.
Ed: Shirley Won. **Description:** Cineplex Entertainment LP reported $4.6 million profit in the final quarter of 2006. The movie chain is introducing video-game tournaments and live rock concerts to improve sales.

24921 ■ "Citadel Hires Three Lehman Execs" in *Chicago Tribune* (October 2, 2008)
Pub: McClatchy-Tribune Information Services
Ed: James P. Miller. **Description:** Citadel Investment Group LLC, Chicago hedge-fund operator, has hired three former senior executives of bankrupt investment banker Lehman Brothers Holding Inc. Citadel believes that the company's hiring spree will help them to further expand the firm's capabilities in the global fixed income business.

24922 ■ "Civil Council Almost On Board With Light Rail Plan" in *The Business Journal-Serving Metropolitan Kansas City* (September 5, 2008)
Pub: American City Business Journals, Inc.
Ed: Steve Vockrodt. **Description:** Civic Council of Greater Kansas City has taken back its demand for the city to show a 10-year financial plan to win its endorsement of a light rail plan. The council said it will accept a five-year financial plan for the project. Details of the light rail plan are also presented.

24923 ■ "Clothier Delays Opening" in *The Business Journal-Serving Metropolitan Kansas City* (Vol. 27, November 14, 2008, No. 10, pp. 1)
Pub: American City Business Journals, Inc.
Ed: Suzanna Stagemeyer. **Description:** Jos A. Bank Clothiers Inc. has delayed the opening of its store at the Kansas City Power and Light District in Missouri for the first quarter of 2009. The company is still waiting for other tenants to open shop in the district. Comments from officials concerning the retail sector are also presented.

24924 ■ "CN to Webcast 2007 Analyst Meeting in Toronto May 23-24" in *Canadian Corporate News* (May 16, 2007)
Pub: Comtex News Network Inc.
Description: Canadian National Railway Company (CN) broadcast its analyst meeting in Toronto with a webcast which focused on CN's opportunities, strategies, and financial outlook through the year 2010.

24925 ■ "Connie Ozan; Founder, Design Director, Twist Creative, 37" in *Crain's Cleveland Business* (Vol. 28, November 19, 2007, No. 46)
Pub: Crain Communications, Inc.
Ed: John Booth. **Description:** Profile of Connie Ozan, design director and founder of Twist Creative, an advertising agency that she runs with her husband, Michael; Ms. Ozan credits her husband's business sense in bringing a more strategic side to the company in which to complement her art direction.

24926 ■ "Copper Giant to Spin Off Silver Assets" in *Globe & Mail* (February 27, 2006, pp. B1)
Pub: CTVglobemedia Publishing Inc.
Ed: Sinclair Stewart; Andrew Willis. **Description:** The reasons behind the sale of silver mining assets by Codelco are presented.

24927 ■ "Copycat" in *Canadian Business* (Vol. 79, October 23, 2006, No. 21, pp. 53)
Pub: Rogers Media
Ed: Andrew Wahl. **Description:** The conversion of BCE Inc. into an income trust for tax advantages, soon after the transition of its business rival Telus Corp. into an income trust, is discussed.

24928 ■ "Corporate Diversity Driving Profits" in *Hispanic Business* (Vol. 30, September 2008, No. 9, pp. 12)
Pub: Hispanic Business, Inc.
Ed: Michael Bowker. **Description:** U.S. businesses are beginning to appreciate the importance of diversity and are developing strategies to introduce a diverse workforce that reflects the cultural composition of their customers. The realization that diversity increases profits and the use of professional networks to recruit and retain skilled minority employees are two other new trends impacting corporate diversity in the U.S.

24929 ■ "CP Rail Cuts Jobs to Keep Pace With CN" in *Globe & Mail* (January 16, 2006, pp. B1)
Pub: CTVglobemedia Publishing Inc.
Ed: Brent Jang. **Description:** Canadian Pacific Railway Ltd. (CPR) reduces workforce in order to remain competitive with Canadian National Railway Co. The details of CPR's proposal are presented.

24930 ■ "CPR Signals a Switch in Strategy to Narrow Competitive Gap With CN" in *Globe & Mail* (January 20, 2006, pp. B3)
Pub: CTVglobemedia Publishing Inc.
Ed: Brent Jang. **Description:** The reasons behind the restructuring efforts of Canadian Pacific Railway Ltd. are presented.

24931 ■ "Craig Muhlhauser" in *Canadian Business* (Vol. 81, September 15, 2008, No. 14-15, pp. 6)
Pub: Rogers Media Ltd.
Ed: Andrew Wahl. **Description:** Interview with Craig Muhlhauser who is the CEO of Celestica, a manufacturing company that provides services for the electronics sector; Muhlhauser discusses the company's restructuring program, which he feels was the secret to their surprising first-quarter results. Muhlhauser states that the company is operating with more forward visibility and that understanding the opportunities during the current economic situation presents the biggest challenge.

24932 ■ "The Data Drivers" in *Canadian Business* (Vol. 81, September 15, 2008, No. 14-15, pp. 1)
Pub: Rogers Media Ltd.
Ed: Andrew Wahl. **Description:** Canadian regulators hope that an auction of telecommunications companies will inject more competition into the industry; however, newcomers may not be able to rely on lower prices in order to gain market share from the three major telecommunications companies that already have a stronghold on the market. Analysts feel that providing additional data service is the key to surviving market disruptions.

24933 ■ "Deals Still Get Done at Drake's Coq d'Or" in *Crain's Chicago Business* (Vol. 31, November 17, 2008, No. 46, pp. 35)
Pub: Crain Communications, Inc.
Ed: Shia Kapos. **Description:** Chicago's infamous Coq d'Or, a restaurant and lounge located at the Drake Hotel, is still a favorite establishment for noted executives but the eatery is now trying to cater to younger professionals through marketing and offering new beverages that appeal to that demographic. Many find it the perfect environment in which to close deals, relax or network.

24934 ■ "Decline in Assets Is Costly for Advisers" in *The Business Journal-Serving Metropolitan Kansas City* (Vol. 27, October 24, 2008)
Pub: American City Business Journals, Inc.
Ed: James Dornbrook. **Description:** Financial advisers in the Kansas City, Missouri area are forced to cut costs as their assets have decreased sharply due to the huge drop in stock prices. American Century Investments was forced to diversify into foreign assets and cut 90 jobs as its assets dropped to $84 billion. Diversification has softened the impact of the steep decline in stock prices for Waddell & Reed Financial Inc.

24935 ■ "Deep Thoughts: Getting Employees to Think Better Requires a Bit of Creative Thinking Itself" in *Canadian Business* (March 17, 2008)
Pub: Rogers Media
Ed: Lauren McKeon. **Description:** Discusses the reason a company needs to make their employees understand that ideas are the stuff of life. For employees to be more creative, they need to cultivate spark moments, play with possibilities, and venture into the unknown.

24936 ■ "Deja Vu" in *Canadian Business* (Vol. 81, July 22, 2008, No. 12-13, pp. 38)
Pub: Rogers Media Ltd.
Ed: Joe Castaldo. **Description:** Laurent Beaudoin has retired as chief executive officer for Bombardier Inc.'s, a manufacturer of regional and business aircraft, but kept a role in the firm as a non-executive chairman. Beaudoin first resigned from the company in 1999, but had to return in 2004 to address challenging situations faced by the company. Beaudoin's views on management and the company are presented.

24937 ■ "Desmarais Makes Move into U.S." in *Globe & Mail* (February 2, 2007, pp. B1)
Pub: CTVglobemedia Publishing Inc.
Ed: Andrew Willis. **Description:** The decision of Desmarais family, which runs Great-West Lifeco Inc., to acquire Putnam Investment Trust for $4.6 billion to enter the United States market, is discussed.

24938 ■ "Dividing to Conquer" in *Barron's* (Vol. 88, March 31, 2008, No. 13, pp. 22)
Pub: Dow Jones & Company, Inc.
Ed: Andrew Bary. **Description:** Altria's spin off of Philip Morris International could unlock substantial value for both domestic and international cigarette concerns. The strong brands and ample payouts from both companies will most likely impress investors.

24939 ■ "Diving for the Next Big Gold Rush" in *Canadian Business* (Vol. 80, February 12, 2007, No. 4, pp. 28)
Pub: Rogers Media
Ed: Thomas Watson. **Description:** The interest of Canadian mining companies led by Nautilus Minerals to invest in mining for deep sea-floor massive sulphide deposits, which have several minerals, is discussed.

24940 ■ "Don't Quit When The Road Gets Bumpy" in *Women Entrepreneur* (November 25, 2008)
Pub: Entrepreneur Media Inc.
Ed: Bonnie Price. **Description:** Discusses techniques four women entrepreneurs are utilizing to keep their businesses successful despite the credit crunch and the economic downturn.

24941 ■ "Don't Try This Offshore" in *Harvard Business Review* (Vol. 86, September 2008, No. 9, pp. 39)
Pub: Harvard Business School Press
Ed: Description: Fictitious outsourcing scenario is presented, with contributors offering advice. The suggestions address the ease or complexity of offshoring business creativity, along with challenges and benefits.

24942 ■ "Doyle: Domino's New Pizza Seasoned with Straight Talk" in *Crain's Detroit Business* (Vol. 26, January 11, 2010, No. 2, pp. 1)
Pub: Crain Communications, Inc.
Ed: Nathan Skid. **Description:** Interview with J. Patrick Doyle, the CEO of Domino's Pizza, Inc.; the company has launched a new marketing campaign that focuses on its bold new vision.

24943 ■ "Economic Crises Calls For Better Marketing Plans" in *Entrepreneur* (October 1, 2008)
Pub: Entrepreneur Media Inc.
Ed: Tim Berry. **Description:** Revising one's business plan is essential, especially during times of economic crisis; sales and marketing plans should be reviewed, analyzed and changed in an attempt to survive the economic downturn.

24944 ■ "EnCana Axes Spending on Gas Wells" in *Globe & Mail* (February 16, 2006, pp. B1)
Pub: CTVglobemedia Publishing Inc.
Ed: Dave Ebner. **Description:** The reasons behind EnCana Corp.'s cost spending measures by $300 million on natural gas wells are presented. The company projects 2 percent cut in gas and oil sales for 2006.

24945 ■ "Entrepreneurial Orientation and Firm Performance" in *Journal of Small Business and Entrepreneurship* (Vol. 23, Winter 2010, No. 1)
Pub: Canadian Council for Small Business and Entrepreneurship
Description: The article develops a theoretical model of the relationship between firm-level entrepreneurship and firm performance. This model is intended to further clarify the consequences of an 'entrepreneurial orientation', paying particular attention to the differential relationship that exists between the three sub-dimensions of entrepreneurial orientation and firm performance. Included in the theoretical model are other important variables (such as organizational structure and environmental characteristics) that may impact the EO-performance relationship. Propositions are developed regarding the various configurations of the sub-dimensions of EO and organizational structure that would be most appropriate in a given environmental context. Future research may also benefit from considering the important role that organizational strategy and life cycle stage play in this model. The implications of this model for both researchers and managers are discussed.

24946 ■ "Executive Decision: Damn the Profit Margins, Sleeman Declares War on Buck-a-Beer Foes" in *Globe & Mail* (January 28, 2006, pp. B3)
Pub: CTVglobemedia Publishing Inc.
Ed: Andy Hoffman. **Description:** The cost savings plans of chief executive officer John Sleeman of Sleeman Breweries Ltd. are presented.

24947 ■ "Executive Decision: Lead a Double Life for Geac's Sake" in *Globe & Mail* (January 21, 2006, pp. B4)
Pub: CTVglobemedia Publishing Inc.
Ed: Simon Avery. **Description:** The details of growth of Geac Computer Corporation Ltd., under chief executive officer Charles Jones, are presented.

24948 ■ "Expanding Middleby's Food Processing Biz" in *Crain's Chicago Business* (Vol. 31, April 21, 2008, No. 16, pp. 6)
Pub: Crain Communications, Inc.
Ed: David Sterrett. **Description:** Profile of the executive vice-president of the food processing company, Middleby Corp, whose business plan is to develop new products, begin looking for acquisitions and simplify operations in order to expand the firm.

24949 ■ "Exxon Braving the Danger Zones" in *Globe & Mail* (March 8, 2007, pp. B1)
Pub: CTVglobemedia Publishing Inc.
Ed: Shawn McCarthy. **Description:** The plans of Exxon Mobil Corp. to increase its revenues through the expansion of its operations in Asia, Africa, and the Middle East are discussed.

24950 ■ "Film Giants Disney, Pixar Talk Marriage" in *Globe & Mail* (January 19, 2006, pp. B1)
Pub: CTVglobemedia Publishing Inc.
Ed: Merissa Marr; Nick Wingfield. **Description:** The plans of Walt Disney Co. to acquire Pixar Animation Studios are presented.

24951 ■ "Find Your Marketing Mojo" in *Business Owner* (Vol. 35, July-August 2011, No. 4, pp. 14)
Pub: DL Perkins Company
Description: Marketing and branding a small business can be learned and implemented by following a process that begins with setting and creating the vision that every successful venture requires: a crystal-clear vision for who you are, what you stand for, and why customers will come to you rather than competitors.

24952 ■ "Finding the Voice of the Marketplace" in *Mergers & Acquisitions: The Dealmaker's Journal* (March 1, 2008)
Pub: SourceMedia, Inc.
Description: Companies oftentimes are unable to achieve their strategic goals through acquisition due, in part, to not understanding the target's market and its position in the marketplace.

24953 ■ "FirstMerit's Top Executive Turns Around Credit Quality" in *Crain's Cleveland Business* (Vol. 28, October 15, 2007, No. 41, pp. 3)
Pub: Crain Communications, Inc.
Ed: Shawn A. Turner. **Description:** Discusses the ways in which chairman and CEO Paul Greig has been able to improve FirstMerit Corp.'s credit quality and profit margin. Strategies included selling more than $70 million in bad loans, hiring a new chief credit officer and redirecting its focus on cross-selling its wealth and investment services to its commercial customers. Statistical data included.

24954 ■ "Five Steps to Killer Business Ideas" in *Hawaii Business* (Vol. 53, December 2007, No. 6, pp. 135)
Pub: Hawaii Business Publishing
Ed: Jason Ubay. **Description:** Five ways to formulating good business concepts are presented. The importance of keeping an open mind and analyzing the market is discussed.

24955 ■ "Flat or Slight Decline Seen for Nortel 2007 Revenue" in *Globe & Mail* (March 17, 2007, pp. B3)
Pub: CTVglobemedia Publishing Inc.
Ed: Catherine McLean. **Description:** The forecast about Nortel Network Corp's decrease in the 2007 revenue and its restructuring to reduce costs is discussed.

24956 ■ "Follow the ABCs of Buying a Business" in *Women Entrepreneur* (September 10, 2008)
Pub: Entrepreneur Media Inc.
Ed: Nina Kaufman. **Description:** Buying a business will likely result in the largest single asset one will ever own. A list of steps one can take in order to educate and protect themselves is provided.

24957 ■ "Ford Fix Requires 'Painful' Remedy" in *Globe & Mail* (January 9, 2006, pp. B1)
Pub: CTVglobemedia Publishing Inc.
Ed: Greg Keenan. **Description:** The plans of Ford Motor Co. to streamline Canadian operations are presented.

24958 ■ "Ford's $12.7 Billion Loss Signals End of an Era" in *Globe & Mail* (January 26, 2007, pp. B1)
Pub: CTVglobemedia Publishing Inc.
Ed: Greg Keenan. **Description:** The loss of $12.7 billion incurred by Ford Motors Co., and its decision to close down several of its plants, cut thousands of jobs and focus on passenger cars, is discussed.

24959 ■ "Founding Family Acquires Airport Marriott" in *Crain's Cleveland Business* (Vol. 28, November 5, 2007, No. 44, pp. 3)
Pub: Crain Communications, Inc.
Ed: Stan Bullard. **Description:** Big River Real Estate LLC, part of the Marriott family's investment fund, is the new owner of the Cleveland Airport Marriott; renovations estimated at about $11 million will ensure that the hotel meets Marriott's standards.

24960 ■ "Four Big Fat Business Plan Lies" in *Entrepreneur* (December 11, 2008)
Pub: Entrepreneur Media Inc.
Ed: Tim Berry. **Description:** Business plans are essential for every business and do not necessarily have to be a complex document containing a full list of components. Other misconceptions concerning business plans are also discussed.

24961 ■ "Franchisees Lose Battle Against BK" in *Advertising Age* (Vol. 79, June 2, 2008, No. 22, pp. 46)
Pub: Crain Communications, Inc.
Ed: Emily Bryson York. **Description:** Burger King has had continuing litigation with former franchisees from New York, Luan and Elizabeth Sadik, who claim that Burger King's double cheeseburger, along with additional problems, created the environment for their eventual insolvency. Burger King has since terminated its test of selling the double cheeseburger for $1, although the company declined to comment on the reason for this decision.

24962 ■ "Free Fall" in *Canadian Business* (Vol. 79, September 11, 2006, No. 18, pp. 28)
Pub: Rogers Media
Ed: Zena Olijnyk. **Description:** Second quarter results of Imax Corp are reviewed. The company's performance and its future prospects are also presented.

24963 ■ "Fries With That?" in *Canadian Business* (Vol. 81, September 29, 2008, No. 16, pp. 33)
Pub: Rogers Media Ltd.
Ed: Calvin Leung. **Description:** Profile of Toronto-based New York Fries, which has four stores in South Korea, is planning to expand further as well as into Hong Kong and Macau; the company also has a licensee in the United Arab Emirates whom is also planning to expand.

24964 ■ "From Craft Biz To Wholesale Giant" in *Women Entrepreneur* (January 19, 2009)
Pub: Entrepreneur Media Inc.
Ed: Maria Falconer. **Description:** Advice is given on how to turn a small craft business into a full-time venture; tips to help one transition from a part-time designer to a full-time wholesaler and brand are also included.

24965 ■ "From War Zone to Franchise Zone" in *Entrepreneur* (Vol. 37, August 2009, No. 8, pp. 104)
Pub: Entrepreneur Media, Inc.
Ed: Jason Daley. **Description:** Ross Paterson says that he realized that the material he used in the Growth Coach franchise could give the people of Afghanistan the systematic model they need. Paterson says that the Afghans are very business-oriented people but that they work in a different system than Americans.

24966 ■ "Gail Mukaihata Hannemann" in *Hawaii Business* (Vol. 53, January 2008, No. 7, pp. 24)
Pub: Hawaii Business Publishing
Ed: Cathy S. Cruz-George. **Description:** Discusses the Girl Scouts of Hawaii which has altered its business model to become more appealing to young girls in the 21st century. Gail Mukaihata Hanneman, the chief executive officer of the nonprofit organization, states that the Girl Scouts has consolidated some of its operations to increase efficiency. Her views on what employers must learn about the youth and on the adults' roles in developing the younger generation are given.

24967 ■ *Get Your Business to Work!: 7 Steps to Earning More, Working Less and Living the Life You Want*
Pub: BenBella Books

Ed: George Hedley. **Released:** June 9, 2010. **Price:** $24.95. **Description:** Complete step-by-step guide for the small business owner to realize profits, wealth and freedom.

24968 ■ "GM Axing Prices; Kerkorian Calls for Crisis Plan" in *Globe & Mail* (January 11, 2006, pp. B1)
Pub: CTVglobemedia Publishing Inc.

Ed: Greg Keenan. **Description:** The financial restructuring proposal of investor Kirk Kerkorian for General Motors Corp. is presented.

24969 ■ "Gold Medal" in *Canadian Business* (Vol. 79, October 9, 2006, No. 20, pp. 57)
Pub: Rogers Media

Ed: Andrew Wahl. **Description:** Creativity skills and management strategies of Rob McEwen, founder and chief executive officer of Goldcorp Inc., are presented.

24970 ■ "Grace Puma; Senior Vice-President of Strategic Sourcing, United Airlines" in *Crain's Chicago Business* (May 5, 2008)
Pub: Crain Communications, Inc.

Ed: John Rosenthal. **Description:** Profile of Grace Puma who is the senior vice-president of strategic sourcing at United Airlines and is responsible for cutting costs at the company in a number of ways including scheduling safety inspections at the same time as routine maintenance, thereby reducing the downtime of each aircraft by five days as well as replacing a third of her staff with outside talent.

24971 ■ "The Grass is Greener" in *Canadian Business* (Vol. 79, August 14, 2006, No. 16-17, pp. 43)
Pub: Rogers Media

Ed: Thomas Watson. **Description:** Owner of New Image Plans LLC, Joe White, shares his views on the Canadian market for the marijuana drug.

24972 ■ "Green Acres" in *Hawaii Business* (Vol. 54, September 2008, No. 3, pp. 48)
Pub: Hawaii Business Publishing

Ed: Jan Tenbruggencate. **Description:** Bill Cowern's Hawaiian Mahogany is a forestry business that processes low-value trees to be sold as wood chips, which can be burned to create biodiesel. Cowern is planning to obtain certification to market carbon credits and is also working with Green Energy Hawaii for the permit of a biomass-fueled power plant. Other details about Cowern's business are discussed.

24973 ■ "The Green Conversation" in *Harvard Business Review* (Vol. 86, September 2008, No. 9, pp. 58)
Pub: Harvard Business School Press

Description: Six guidelines are presented for addressing and benefiting from environmentally conscious corporate decision making and practices. Topics covered include marketing, supply chain, and leadership.

24974 ■ "'Groundhog Day' B & B Likely Will Be Converted Into One In Real Life" in *Chicago Tribune* (October 21, 2008)
Pub: McClatchy-Tribune Information Services

Ed: Carolyn Starks. **Description:** Everton Martin and Karla Stewart Martin have purchased the Victorian house that was featured as a bed-and-breakfast in the 1993 hit move "Groundhog Day"; the couple was initially unaware of the structure's celebrity status when they purchased it with the hope of fulfilling their dream of owning a bed-and-breakfast.

24975 ■ "Growing Pains" in *Canadian Business* (Vol. 81, July 22, 2008, No. 12-13, pp. 35)
Pub: Rogers Media Ltd.

Ed: Alex Mylnek. **Description:** Laughing Stock Vineyards' Cynthia Enns and David Enns plan to target young buyers by using social media. The Enns however, are concerned that targeting younger buyers may affect Laughing Stock's image as a premium brand. Additional information regarding the company's future plans is presented.

24976 ■ "Handleman Liquidation Leaves Questions For Shareholders" in *Crain's Detroit Business* (Vol. 24, October 6, 2008, No. 40, pp. 4)
Pub: Crain Communications, Inc.

Ed: Nancy Kaffer. **Description:** Discusses Handleman Co., a Troy-based music distribution company, and their plan of liquidation and dissolution as well as how shareholders will be affected by the company's plan. Handleman filed its plan to liquidate and dissolve assets with the Securities and Exchange Commission in mid-August, following several quarters of dismal earnings.

24977 ■ "Hartco Income Fund Announces the Completion of the CompuSmart Strategic Review" in *Canadian Corporate News* (May 14, 2007)
Pub: Comtex News Network Inc.

Description: Hartco Income Fund announced that it has completed the process of exploring strategic options for CompuSmart and found that it should implement a plan to sell select stores and assets while consolidating remaining CompuSmart locations over the next sixty days.

24978 ■ "Hawaii Business 2008 SB Success Awards" in *Hawaii Business* (Vol. 53, February 2008, No. 8, pp. 43)
Pub: Hawaii Business Publishing

Description: Winners in the Hawaii Business 2008 SB Success Awards are presented; the awards give recognition for Hawaii small businesses with less than 100 employees and are based on four criteria, namely: unique service or product; rapid expansion or sales growth; longevity; and competency in overcoming challenges.

24979 ■ "HBC Sets Friday as Deadline to Trump Zucker Takeover Bid" in *Globe & Mail* (January 18, 2006, pp. B1)
Pub: CTVglobemedia Publishing Inc.

Ed: Marina Strauss. **Description:** The reasons behind Hudson's Bay Co.'s decision to seek alternative bids on the company are presented. Investor Jerry Zucker earlier offered $1.1 billion for the company.

24980 ■ "High Energy: Gaurdie Banister Joins Aera As President and CEO" in *Black Enterprise* (Vol. 38, July 2008, No. 12, pp. 30)
Pub: Earl G. Graves Publishing Co. Inc.

Ed: Brenda Porter. **Description:** Gaurdie Banister Jr. has been appointed president and CEO of Aera Energy L.L.C., becoming one of the first African Americans in the nation to run a major energy corporation. His plans for the firm include utilizing new, sophisticated technologies in order to unlock the 3-1/2 billion barrels of resources the company has on their books in a safe and environmentally friendly way. He also hopes to increase production and maintain cost leadership.

24981 ■ "Hit the Green" in *Canadian Business* (Vol. 79, August 14, 2006, No. 16-17, pp. 73)
Pub: Rogers Media

Ed: Andrew Wahl. **Description:** Reorganization of the bankrupt 4everSports golf company in the United States is discussed.

24982 ■ "HOK Sport May Build Own Practice" in *The Business Journal-Serving Metropolitan Kansas City* (Vol. 26, August 29, 2008, No. 51, pp. 1)
Pub: American City Business Journals, Inc.

Ed: Rob Roberts. **Description:** HOK Sport Venue Event is considering a spin-off from its parent company, HOK Group Inc. HOK Sport spokeswoman Gina Leo confirms that the firm is exploring structures, including a management buyout. Some of HOK Sport Venue Event's Minnesota projects are discussed.

24983 ■ "Home Depot Eyes Wholesale Spinoff" in *Globe & Mail* (February 13, 2007, pp. B13)
Pub: CTVglobemedia Publishing Inc.

Description: Home Depot Inc. is planning to sell or spinoff its professional supply business to focus on retail stores. The weakening sales and profits are the main driving force behind the company's decision.

24984 ■ *Hoover's Vision*
Pub: Cengage Learning

Ed: Gary Hoover. **Description:** Founder of Bookstop Inc. and Hoover's Inc. provides a plan to turn an enterprise into a success by showing entrepreneurs how to address inputs with an open mind in order to see more than what other's envision. Hoover pushes business owners to create and feed a clear and consistent vision by recognizing the importance of history and trends, then helps them find the essential qualities of entrepreneurial leadership.

24985 ■ *Hoover's Vision: Original Thinking for Business Success*
Pub: Thomson South-Western/Texere

Ed: Gary Hoover. **Released:** October 15, 2001. **Description:** Three keys to business success are to observe and understand other people, serve others while making their lives better, and develop a business style that expresses your5 own passions while serving others.

24986 ■ "How to Keep Your Sales from Running Out of Gas" in *Agency Sales Magazine* (Vol. 39, July 2009, No. 7, pp. 30)
Pub: MANA

Ed: John Graham. **Description:** Salespeople can let the good times deceive them into thinking that success will go on forever. Salespeople and businesses should see prospecting as a strategy for creating a continuing flow of business.

24987 ■ "Husky Proceeds on Heavy-Oil Expansion" in *Globe & Mail* (March 21, 2006, pp. B1)
Pub: CTVglobemedia Publishing Inc.

Ed: Patrick Brethour. **Description:** Canadian energy giant Husky Energy Inc. has started its $90 million engineering effort to determine the cost of the $2.3 billion heavy-oil up gradation expansion plan. Details of the project are elaborated upon.

24988 ■ "Ideas at Work: The Reality of Costs" in *Business Strategy Review* (Vol. 21, Summer 2010, No. 2, pp. 40)
Pub: Blackwell Publishers Ltd.

Ed: Jules Goddard. **Description:** If you think that cost cutting is the surest way to business success, the author will challenge every assumption held. Costs are an outcome of a sound strategy. A new perspective on handling costs is outlined.

24989 ■ "In Puerto Rico, Slow and Steady Wins Race" in *Globe & Mail* (February 24, 2007, pp. B3)
Pub: CTVglobemedia Publishing Inc.

Ed: Andrew Willis. **Description:** The plan of Scotiabank de Puerto Rico's chief executive officer Richard Waugh to improve its market presence using its international banking relations is discussed.

24990 ■ "Inland Snaps Up Rival REITs" in *Crain's Chicago Business* (Vol. 31, November 17, 2008, No. 46, pp. 3)
Pub: Crain Communications, Inc.

Ed: Alby Gallun. **Description:** Discusses Inland American Real Estate Trust Inc., a real estate investment trust that is napping up depressed shares of publicly traded competitors, a possible first step toward taking over these companies; however, with hotel and retail properties accounting for approximately 70 percent of its portfolio, the company could soon face its own difficulties.

24991 ■ "Inside the New Nortel" in *Canadian Business* (Vol. 79, November 6, 2006, No. 22, pp. 93)
Pub: Rogers Media

Ed: Andrew Wahl. **Description:** The team plans of Nortel Networks to improve its technology market by appointing new team are analyzed.

24992 ■ "Intangible Assets" in *Canadian Business* (Vol. 79, July 17, 2006, No. 14-15, pp. 17)
Pub: Rogers Media
Ed: Al Rosen. **Description:** Need for investors to check the actual worth of a company and not to get carried away by the inflated claims made by the company is emphasized.

24993 ■ "International Nickel Ventures Corporation Reports Results for the First Quarter 2007" in *Canadian Corporate News* (May 16, 2007)
Pub: Comtex News Network Inc.
Description: Profile of International Nickel Ventures Corporation (INV) including its financial report for the first quarter of fiscal 2007, its partnership and possible acquisition of Teck Cominco Limited, and its plans for the future. Statistical data included.

24994 ■ "The Intrawest Empire" in *Canadian Business* (Vol. 79, October 9, 2006, No. 20, pp. 27)
Pub: Rogers Media
Ed: Erik Heinrich. **Description:** The future development plans of Intrawest Corp., are discussed. Strategic plans of Joe Houssian, the chairman, president and chief executive officer of Intrawest Corp., are also presented.

24995 ■ "Intrawest Puts Itself on Market" in *Globe & Mail* (March 1, 2006, pp. B1)
Pub: CTVglobemedia Publishing Inc.
Ed: Elizabeth Church. **Description:** The reasons behind the decision of Intrawest Corp. to go for sale or seek partnerships are presented. The company appointed Goldman Sachs & Co. to meet the purpose.

24996 ■ "Iogen, VW Look to Build Ethanol Plant" in *Globe & Mail* (January 9, 2006, pp. B3)
Pub: CTVglobemedia Publishing Inc.
Ed: Simon Tuck. **Description:** Iogen Corp. and Volkswagen AG plan cellulose ethanol plant in Germany. The details of the project are presented.

24997 ■ "It's Not About the G1; Google Just Wants You to Use the Mobile Web" in *Advertising Age* (Vol. 79, September 29, 2008, No. 36, pp. 32)
Pub: Crain Communications, Inc.
Ed: Abbey Klaassen. **Description:** Google's Android is the first serious competitor to Apple's iPhone; the company says that its goal is to simplify the mobile market and get wireless subscribers to use the mobile Internet and purchase smartphones.

24998 ■ "J.C. Watts First Black John Deere Dealer" in *Black Enterprise* (Vol. 37, November 2006, No. 4, pp. 36)
Pub: Earl G. Graves Publishing Co. Inc.
Ed: Kiara Ashanti. **Description:** Profile of former Congressman J.C. Watts Jr., a man who grew up in rural America and is the first African American to own a John Deere Dealership.

24999 ■ "Just Be Nice" in *Canadian Business* (Vol. 79, October 9, 2006, No. 20, pp. 141)
Pub: Rogers Media
Ed: Joe Castaldo. **Description:** The customer relationship management strategies on customer retention and satisfaction adopted by WestJet are discussed.

25000 ■ "KC Plants Downshift" in *The Business Journal-Serving Metropolitan Kansas City* (Vol. 27, November 7, 2008, No. 9, pp. 1)
Pub: American City Business Journals, Inc.
Ed: James Dornbrook. **Description:** Discusses Ford Motor Co. and General Motors' factories in the region; Ford Motor Co. removed the second shift on the F-150 line at the Kansas City Assembly Plant but added a shift to the production of the Ford Escape and Mercury Mariner in an attempt to avoid layoffs. One spokesman for General Motors, however, states that they cannot guarantee that they won't make any production cuts and layoffs in the future.

25001 ■ "Kodak Cuts Deep in Effort to Change Focus" in *Globe & Mail* (February 9, 2007, pp. B8)
Pub: CTVglobemedia Publishing Inc.
Ed: Gillian Wee. **Description:** Eastman Kodak Co., the world's largest photography company, is eliminating 5,000 more jobs than the originally planned 28,000 jobs. The job cuts are being driven by the sale of Kodak's health-imaging unit.

25002 ■ "Labatt to Swallow Lakeport" in *Globe & Mail* (February 2, 2007, pp. B1)
Pub: CTVglobemedia Publishing Inc.
Ed: Keith McArthur. **Description:** The decision of Labatt Brewing Company Ltd. to acquire Lakeport Brewing Income Fund for $201.4 million is discussed.

25003 ■ "Lafley Gives Look At His Game Plan" in *Business Courier* (Vol. 24, March 21, 2008, No. 50, pp. 1)
Pub: American City Business Journals, Inc.
Ed: Lisa Biank Fasig. **Description:** Overview of A.G. Lafley's book entitled 'The Game-Changer', is presented. Lafley, Procter & Gamble Co.'s chief executive officer, documented his philosophy and strategy in his book. His work also includes Procter & Gamble's hands-on initiatives such as mock-up grocery stores and personal interviews with homeowners.

25004 ■ "Land Agent Taken Over" in *Farmer's Weekly* (March 28, 2008, No. 320)
Pub: Reed Business Information
Description: Property business Smiths Gore will take over Cluttons' rural division, one of the oldest names in land agency. Cluttons said it had decided to sell its rural business as part of a strategic repositioning that would refocus the business on commercial, residential and overseas opportunities.

25005 ■ "Last Founder Standing" in *Conde Nast Portfolio* (Vol. 2, June 2008, No. 6, pp. 124)
Pub: Conde Nast Publications, Inc.
Ed: Kevin Maney. **Description:** Interview with Amazon CEO Jeff Bezos in which he discusses the economy, the company's new distribution center and the hiring of employees for it, e-books, and the overall vision for the future of the firm.

25006 ■ "Lathrop Finds Partner In LA" in *The Business Journal-Serving Metropolitan Kansas City* (Vol. 27, November 21, 2008, No. 11, pp. 1)
Pub: American City Business Journals, Inc.
Ed: Steve Vockrodt. **Description:** Kansas, Missouri-based Lathrop and Gage LLP is planning to merge with Spillane Shaeffer Aronoff Bandlow LLP. The merging of the business law firms will add entertainment clients to Lathrop's fold. Comments from executives are also presented.

25007 ■ *The Leader of the Future 2*
Pub: Jossey Bass
Ed: Frances Hesselbein; Marshall Goldsmith. **Released:** September 18, 2006. **Price:** $27.95. **Description:** Wisdom is lent to any small business owner or leader of a nonprofit organization.

25008 ■ *Leadership 101: What Every Leader Needs to Know*
Pub: Nelson Business
Ed: John C. Maxwell. **Released:** September 2002. **Price:** $9.99. **Description:** Ways to enhance leadership skills focusing on following a vision and bringing others along.

25009 ■ *Leap! 101 Ways to Grow Your Business*
Pub: Career Press, Inc.
Ed: Stephanie Chandler. **Released:** August 8, 2010. **Price:** $15.99. **Description:** Business growth requires more than a business plan and a dream. Tools and techniques to take a small company to the next level are outlined.

25010 ■ "Lehman's Hail Mary Pass" in *Business Week* (September 22, 2008, No. 4100, pp. 28)
Pub: McGraw-Hill Companies, Inc.
Ed: Matthew Goldstein; David Henry; Ben Levison. **Description:** Overview of Lehman Brothers' CEO Richard Fuld's plan to keep the firm afloat and end the stock's plunge downward; Fuld's strategy calls for selling off a piece of the firm's investment management business.

25011 ■ "Loblaw Posts 40 Percent Profit Drop as it Scrambles to Lower Costs" in *Globe & Mail* (February 9, 2006, pp. B1)
Pub: CTVglobemedia Publishing Inc.
Ed: Marina Strauss. **Description:** The reasons behind 40 percent decline in profits for Lobalaw Companies Ltd., for fourth quarter 2005, are presented.

25012 ■ "Lombard Leaves Starbucks" in *Black Enterprise* (Vol. 38, July 2008, No. 12, pp. 28)
Pub: Earl G. Graves Publishing Co. Inc.
Ed: Tamara E. Holmes. **Description:** Ken Lombard stepped down from his position as head of Starbuck's entertainment division; the company is restructuring its entertainment unit in an attempt to revitalize sales and reduce costs.

25013 ■ "Looking For Financing?" in *Hispanic Business* (Vol. 30, July-August 2008, No. 7-8, pp. 16)
Pub: Hispanic Business, Inc.
Ed: Frank Nelson. **Description:** Investment firms want to know about businesses that need funding for either expansion or acquisition; companies fitting this profile are interviewed and their perceptions are discussed. Investment firms need businesses to be realistic in their expectations and business plans which show spending of funds and expected benefits, long term goals, track record and strong management teams.

25014 ■ "The Lords of Ideas" in *Business Strategy Review* (Vol. 21, Autumn 2010, No. 3, pp. 57)
Pub: Blackwell Publishers Ltd.
Ed: Stuart Crainer. **Description:** True originators of modern strategy are profiled.

25015 ■ "Losses Threaten Comp Care's Future Viability" in *The Business Journal-Serving Greater Tampa Bay* (Vol. 28, August 15, 2008, No. 34)
Pub: American City Business Journals, Inc.
Ed: Margie Manning. **Description:** Comprehensive Care Corp. expressed that it may have to cease or drastically curtail its operations if it won't be able to raise additional funding in the next two or three months. The firm, which provides managed behavioral health care services, is also believed to be exploring a sale. Other views and information on Comprehensive Care's finances and plans are presented.

25016 ■ "The Macomb Group: Bigger Can Be Better" in *Crain's Detroit Business* (Vol. 24, September 29, 2008, No. 39, pp. 34)
Pub: Crain Communications, Inc.
Ed: Chad Halcom. **Description:** Overview of the plan of The Macomb Group includes a strategy of growing from a small supplier to a medium-sized regional distributor of valves, pipes and fittings.

25017 ■ "Magna Stalwart to Push for Product Coups" in *Globe & Mail* (April 9, 2007, pp. B1)
Pub: CTVglobemedia Publishing Inc.
Ed: Greg Keenan. **Description:** The resignation of Fred Gingl from the vice-chairmanship of the board of directors of Magna International Inc. is described. Mr. Gingl's plans to create wealth for Magna International Inc. through the development of new products are discussed.

25018 ■ "Magna in Talks on Building Cars for DaimlerChrysler" in *Globe & Mail* (February 27, 2007, pp. B1)
Pub: CTVglobemedia Publishing Inc.
Ed: Greg Keenan. **Description:** The plans of Magna International Inc. to purchase securities of Chrysler Corp. are discussed. The possibility of the manufacture of cars by Magna International Inc. for DaimlerChrysler AG is discussed.

25019 ■ "Magna Wants to Help Chrysler, but a Takeover's Not on the Cards" in *Globe & Mail* (March 1, 2007, pp. B1)
Pub: CTVglobemedia Publishing Inc.
Ed: Greg Keenan. **Description:** The plans of Magna International Inc. to help Chrysler Corp. to overcome its financial problems are discussed. The appointment of Michael Neuman as the chief executive officer of Magna International Inc. is described.

25020 ■ "Major Tech Employers Pulling Out" in *Sacramento Business Journal* (Vol. 25, August 1, 2008, No. 22, pp. 1)
Pub: American City Business Journals, Inc.
Ed: Celia Lamb. **Description:** Biotechnology company Affymetrix Inc. is planning to close its West Sacramento, California plant and lay off 110 employees. The company said it will expand a corporate restructuring plan. Affymetrix also plans to lease out or sell its building at Riverside Parkway.

25021 ■ "Marriott Checks Out Hotel Prospect" in *The Business Journal-Serving Metropolitan Kansas City* (Vol. 27, November 14, 2008, No. 10)
Pub: American City Business Journals, Inc.
Description: Marriott International Inc. is planning to operate a hotel in Kansas City, Missouri and may take over the Kansas City Marriot Downtown although other hotel operators are interested in bidding on the project.

25022 ■ "MBA Essentials: Real-Life Instruction" in *Women In Business* (Vol. 61, October-November 2009, No. 5, pp. 28)
Pub: American Business Women's Association
Ed: Leigh Elmore. **Description:** University of Kansas School of Business allied itself with the American Business Women's Association (ABWA) which led to the formation of the ABWA-KU MBA essentials program. With this program, ABWA members are exposed to graduate-level coursework that delves on business topics, such as strategy and operations.

25023 ■ "MBA Project Turns on Tastebuds" in *The Business Journal - Serving Phoenix and the Valley of the Sun* (Vol. 28, August 15, 2008, No. 50)
Pub: American City Business Journals, Inc.
Ed: Angela Gonzales. **Description:** Amol Khade, Venkat Nallapati and Govind Arora, master of businesss administration graduates from Thunderbird School of Global Management, have opened an Indian restaurant, called The Daba, in Tempe, Arizona. The Indian name of the restaurant means 'a place for travelers to stop for rest and food'. Franchise plans for the restaurant are discussed.

25024 ■ "Measure Your Business Plan Results" in *Entrepreneur* (January 6, 2009)
Pub: Entrepreneur Media Inc.
Ed: Tim Berry. **Description:** Although no business plan is ever right on target, it is still essential for every business owner to create one; the way in which to analyze the actual results compared to the plan are discussed.

25025 ■ "Meet Joe Fresh" in *Canadian Business* (Vol. 79, November 6, 2006, No. 22, pp. 49)
Pub: Rogers Media
Ed: Calvin Leung. **Description:** The efforts of Joseph Mimran, a fashion designer, in improving the business of Joe Fresh style products are analyzed.

25026 ■ "Mentoring Support" in *Black Enterprise* (Vol. 38, July 2008, No. 12, pp. 64)
Pub: Earl G. Graves Publishing Co. Inc.
Description: With his relocation from his multicultural team in New York to the less diverse Scripps Networks' headquarters in Knoxville, Earl Cokley has made it a top priority to push for more diversity and mentoring opportunities within the management of the media and marketing company.

25027 ■ "Mettle Detector" in *Canadian Business* (Vol. 79, July 17, 2006, No. 14-15, pp. 63)
Pub: Rogers Media
Ed: Calvin Leung. **Description:** The difficulties faced in completing the Certified Financial Analyst course, and the rewards one can expect after its completion, are discussed.

25028 ■ "Microsoft Clicks Into High Speed" in *Hispanic Business* (Vol. 30, July-August 2008, No. 7-8, pp. 54)
Pub: Hispanic Business, Inc.
Ed: Derek Reveron. **Description:** Microsoft's diversity hiring and vendor diversity program to capture more Hispanic consumer and business-to-business market is described. One of the main goals of these programs is to hire more Hispanic executives and managers who will help the company develop and market products and services that will appeal and benefit Hispanic consumers.

25029 ■ "Microsoft's Big Gamble" in *Canadian Business* (Vol. 81, March 3, 2008, No. 3, pp. 13)
Pub: Rogers Media
Ed: Andrew Wahl. **Description:** Microsoft Corp. is taking a big risk in buying Yahoo, as it is expected to pay more than $31 a share to finalize the acquisition. The deal would be seven and a half times bigger than any other that Microsoft has entered before, an execution of such deal is also anticipated to become a challenge for Microsoft. Recommendations on how Microsoft should handle the integration of the two businesses are given.

25030 ■ "Midtown Tampa Bay Taking Shape" in *The Business Journal-Serving Greater Tampa Bay* (Vol. 28, September 12, 2008, No. 38, pp. 1)
Pub: American City Business Journals, Inc.
Ed: Janet Leiser. **Description:** Midtown Tampa Bay's 610,000 square foot shopping and entertainment center is being planned in Florida and is to replace the Tampa Bay One project proposed years earlier. The retail center is to be developed by Bromley Cos. and Opus South Corp. and is expected to have five buildings. Other details about the plan are discussed.

25031 ■ "Midwest Looks 'Back to the Future" in *The Business Journal-Milwaukee* (Vol. 25, July 18, 2008, No. 43, pp. A1)
Pub: American City Business Journals, Inc.
Ed: Rich Rovito. **Description:** Midwest Air Group Inc. announced plans to reduce their work force by 40 percent or 1,200 employees after an earlier announcement of a drastic fleet reduction. These steps are being taken by the company in an effort to avoid filing bankruptcy since this would cost the airline millions of dollars in legal and other professional fees.

25032 ■ "Midwest Seeks Concessions From Creditors" in *The Business Journal-Milwaukee* (Vol. 25, July 25, 2008, No. 44, pp. A1)
Pub: American City Business Journals, Inc.
Ed: Rich Rovito. **Description:** Midwest Airlines Inc. is turning to creditors and lease holders for the financial aspect of its restructuring, which involves going back to serving popular business destinations. Chief executive officer Timothy believes that the company can survive in a niche market as long as it provides quality service. He discusses Midwest's restructuring plan.

25033 ■ "Milton Touts ACE Unit to Would-Be Buyers" in *Globe & Mail* (February 10, 2007, pp. B6)
Pub: CTVglobemedia Publishing Inc.
Ed: Brent Jang. **Description:** The decision of Air Canada chairman Robert Milton to sell Air Canada Technical Services unit is presented. ACE Aviation Holdings Inc. is the parent company of Air Canada.

25034 ■ "Modern-Day Midas Hasn't Lost Touch" in *Globe & Mail* (January 19, 2006, pp. B4)
Pub: CTVglobemedia Publishing Inc.
Ed: Shirley Won. **Description:** The investment plans of chief executive officer Rob McEwen of U.S. Gold Corp. are presented.

25035 ■ "More Manufacturers Scout Military Contracts As Auto Industry Lags" in *Crain's Detroit Business* (Vol. 24, September 29, 2008, No. 39)
Pub: Crain Communications, Inc.
Ed: Chad Halcom. **Description:** Many Michigan manufacturers are looking to grow with new military contracts now that the reality of the auto industry is becoming more clear; these companies see that the government contracts may be the only way in which they will be able to stay in business through these rough economic times.

25036 ■ *More Than a Pink Cadillac*
Pub: McGraw-Hill
Ed: Jim Underwood. **Released:** 2002. **Price:** $23.95. **Description:** Profile of Mary Kay Ash who turned her $5,000 investment into a billion-dollar corporation. Ash's nine principles that form the foundation of her company's global success are outlined. Stories from her sales force leaders share ideas for motivating employees, impressing customers and building a successful company. The book emphasizes the leadership skills required to drive performance in any successful enterprise.

25037 ■ *Navigating Your Way to Business Success: An Entrepreneur's Journey*
Pub: FreeBridge Publishing, Inc.
Ed: Kathryn B. Freeland. **Released:** January 10, 2010. **Price:** $24.95. **Description:** Learn first-hand from a successful entrepreneur about assessing skills and talent, envisioning your company, planning a path to success, and then tapping into available government agencies to make your business become a reality.

25038 ■ "NBC" in *Brandweek* (Vol. 49, April 21, 2008, No. 16, pp. SR6)
Pub: VNU Business Media, Inc.
Ed: John Consoli. **Description:** Provides contact information for sales and marketing personnel for the NBC network as well as a listing of the station's top programming and an analysis of the current season and the target audience for those programs running in the current season. NBC also devised a new strategy of announcing its prime-time schedule 52 weeks in advance which was a hit for advertisers who felt this gave them a better opportunity to plan for product placement. Even with the station's creative sales programs, they could face a challenge from Fox in terms of upfront advertisement purchases.

25039 ■ "Needed: A Strategy; Banking In China" in *The Economist* (Vol. 390, January 3, 2009, No. 8612, pp. 54)
Pub: The Economist Newspaper Inc.
Description: International banks are competing for a role in China but are finding obstacles in their paths such as a reduction in the credit their operations may receive from Chinese banks and the role they can play in the public capital markets which remain limited.

25040 ■ "Net Connections" in *Black Enterprise* (Vol. 38, July 2008, No. 12, pp. 28)
Pub: Earl G. Graves Publishing Co. Inc.
Ed: Anthony S. Calypso. **Description:** Marketers are making strategic partnerships with online social networks in an attempt to gain further market reach. The value of these networks appears to be on the rise forcing media companies to recalculate their strategies for delivering products to customers.

25041 ■ "New Beginnings for VIBE" in *Black Enterprise* (Vol. 37, November 2006, No. 4, pp. 34)
Pub: Earl G. Graves Publishing Co. Inc.
Ed: Mashaun D. Simon. **Description:** Danyel Smith replaced Mimi Valdes as editor-in-chief of VIBE magazine after the Wicks Group, private equity firm focused on selected segments of the media, communications, and information industries, purchased the magazine.

25042 ■ "New BMO Boss Set to Cut 1,000 Jobs" in *Globe & Mail* (February 1, 2007, pp. B3)
Pub: CTVglobemedia Publishing Inc.
Ed: Andrew Willis. **Description:** The decision of the new chief executive officer of the Bank of Montreal, Bill Downe, to cut down 1,000 jobs, to boost the company's performance is discussed.

25043 ■ "Nexen, OPTI Boost Oil Sands Spending" in *Globe & Mail* (February 18, 2006, pp. B5)
Pub: CTVglobemedia Publishing Inc.
Ed: Dave Ebner. **Description:** The reasons behind the decision of Nexen Inc. and OPTI Canada Inc., to allocate 10 percent more funding on oil sands, are presented.

25044 ■ "No Frills - And No Dodge" in *Crain's Detroit Business* (Vol. 24, September 22, 2008, No. 38, pp. 3)
Pub: Crain Communications, Inc.
Ed: Bradford Wernie. **Description:** Chrysler LLC is in the middle of a business plan known as Project Genesis, a five-year strategy in which the company will reduce the dealer count by combining its Jeep, Chrysler and Dodge brands under one rooftop wherever possible. Not every dealer will be able to arrange this deal because of the investment required to expand stores in which have low-overhead; many of these stores feel that low-overhead structures are more likely to survive difficult times than the larger stores in which the Genesis consolidation plan intends to implement.

25045 ■ "No Secrets; Businesses Find It Pays to Open Books to Employees" in *Crain's Detroit Business* (Vol. 26, January 18, 2010, No. 3)
Pub: Crain Communications, Inc.
Ed: Dustin Walsh. **Description:** Many businesses are finding that practicing an open-book management wherein employees share financial and decision-making duties that are usually left up to executives of firms creates a transparency within a company that eliminates the us versus them mentality between management and employees. Another benefit to this business model is that employees get to really participate in the business, learning to manage money and run a business entity.

25046 ■ "Nortel Starting From Scratch" in *Globe & Mail* (February 24, 2006, pp. B3)
Pub: CTVglobemedia Publishing Inc.
Ed: Catherine McLean. **Description:** The restructuring efforts of chief executive officer Mike Zafirovski of Nortel Networks Corp. are presented.

25047 ■ "Not Just for Kids: ADHD can be Debilitating for an Employee, and Frustrating for Bosses" in *Canadian Business* (April 14, 2008)
Pub: Rogers Media
Ed: Andy Holloway. **Description:** Up to four percent of North American adults continue to feel the effects of Attention Deficit Hyperactivity Disorder or Attention Deficit Disorder. Explaining the value of the task at hand to people who are afflicted with these conditions is one way to keep them engaged in the workplace. Giving them opportunities to create their own working structure is another strategy to manage these people.

25048 ■ "Not the Six O'Clock News" in *Canadian Business* (Vol. 80, January 15, 2007, No. 2, pp. 10)
Pub: Rogers Media
Ed: Marlene Rego. **Description:** The proposal by Paul Jay, the chief executive officer of Independent World Television, to launch The Real News Project, is discussed. The objective of the project is to establish an independent news and current affairs network solely through viewers.

25049 ■ "Numerous Changes Made to Crop Production and Consumption Forecasts" in *Farm Industry News* (November 9, 2011)
Pub: Penton Business Media Inc.
Ed: Darrel Good. **Description:** USDA November Crop Production and WASDE reports contained various changes in production and consumption forecasts for corn, soybeans, and what for the current marketing year. A brief summary for each crop is included.

25050 ■ "On a Mission: Ginch Gonch Wants You to Get Rid of Your Tighty Whities" in *Canadian Business* (Vol. 81, September 29, 2008, No. 16)
Pub: Rogers Media Ltd.
Ed: Michelle Magnan. **Description:** New Equity Capital acquired underwear maker Ginch Gonch in July 2008; founder Jason Sutherland kept his position as creative director of the company and will retain his title as 'director of stitches and inches'. The company is known for its products, which are reminiscent of the days when people wore underwear covered in cowboys and stars as kids. The company also claims that Nelly, Justin Timberlake, and Hilary Duff have worn their products.

25051 ■ "On a Roll" in *Canadian Business* (Vol. 79, October 9, 2006, No. 20, pp. 51)
Pub: Rogers Media
Ed: Joe Castaldo. **Description:** Corporate management strategies of Denis Turcotte, chief executive officer of Algoma Steel Inc., are presented.

25052 ■ "One Paddle, Two Paddle" in *Hawaii Business* (Vol. 53, October 2007, No. 4, pp. 65)
Pub: Hawaii Business Publishing
Ed: Kyle Galdeira. **Description:** Oiwi Ocean Gear's strategy may not give instant profits, but it works well for the company's goal of providing high-quality apparel for paddlers. The apparel company produces and markets swimwear, paddling jerseys and active wear. The company's strategy is compared with the selling of mass-produced clothes lower prices.

25053 ■ "Ontario Keeps Bleeding Jobs as Michelin Closes Tire Plant" in *Globe & Mail* (February 3, 2006, pp. B1)
Pub: CTVglobemedia Publishing Inc.
Ed: Greg Keenan; Heather Scoffield. **Description:** The reasons behind facility shutdown and workforce reduction by Michelin SA, in Ontario, are presented.

25054 ■ "Open Skies: Opportunity, Challenge for Airlines" in *Crain's Chicago Business* (April 21, 2008)
Pub: Crain Communications, Inc.
Ed: Paul Merrion. **Description:** Discusses the new aviation agreement between Europe and the United States known as Open Skies; the pact creates opportunities for U.S. carriers to fly to new destinations in Europe from more U.S. cities; it also allows carriers to fly between European cities, something they have not been able to do until now.

25055 ■ "Paramount Said to be Working on Sale of Oil Sands Assets" in *Globe & Mail* (April 24, 2007, pp. B1)
Pub: CTVglobemedia Publishing Inc.
Ed: Norval Scott. **Description:** The proposed sale of oil sands in Surmont and the shares of North American Oil Sands Corp. by Paramount Resources Ltd. is discussed.

25056 ■ "Patricia Hemingway Hall; President, Chief Operating Officer, Health Care Service Corp." in *Crain's Chicago Business* (May 5, 2008)
Pub: Crain Communications, Inc.
Ed: Mike Colias. **Description:** Profile of Patricia Hemingway Hall who is the president and chief operating officer of Health Care Service Corp., a new strategy launched by Blue Cross & Blue Shield of Illinois; the new endeavor will emphasize wellness rather than just treatment across its four health plans.

25057 ■ "People; E-Commerce, Online Games, Mobile Apps" in *Advertising Age* (Vol. 80, October 19, 2009, No. 35, pp. 14)
Pub: Crain's Communications
Ed: Nat Ives. **Description:** Profile of People Magazine and the ways in which the publisher is moving its magazine forward by exploring new concepts in a time of declining newsstand sales and advertising pages; among the strategies are e-commerce such as the brand People Style Watch in which consumers are able highlight clothing and jewelry and then connect to retailers' sites and a channel on Taxi TV, the network of video-touch screens in New Your City taxis.

25058 ■ "People; E-Commerce, Online Games, Mobile Apps: This Isn't Your Mom's People" in *Advertising Age* (Vol. 80, October 19, 2009, No. 35)
Pub: Crain's Communications
Ed: Nat Ives. **Description:** Profile of People Magazine and the ways in which the publisher is moving its magazine forward by exploring new concepts in a time of declining newsstand sales and advertising pages; among the strategies are e-commerce such as the brand People Style Watch in which consumers are able highlight clothing and jewelry and then connect to retailers' sites and a channel on Taxi TV, the network of video-touch screens in New Your City taxis.

25059 ■ "Perfecting the Process: Creating a Move Efficient Organization On Your Terms" in *Black Enterprise* (Vol. 41, October 2010, No. 3)
Pub: Earl G. Graves Publishing Co. Inc.
Ed: Tamara E. Holmes. **Description:** More than ever, entrepreneurs need to identify new ways of doing business in a cost-effective manner in order to expand their companies, while remaining true to their customer demands.

25060 ■ "Playboy to Target Lucrative India Market With No-Nudes Version" in *Globe & Mail* (January 2, 2006, pp. B2)
Pub: CTVglobemedia Publishing Inc.
Ed: Anand Giridharadas. **Description:** The planning of Chicago based Playboy Enterprises Inc. to target lucrative India market with no nudes version, in order to increase its market shares is discussed.

25061 ■ "The Play's the Thing" in *Business Strategy Review* (Vol. 21, Summer 2010, No. 2, pp. 58)
Pub: Blackwell Publishers Ltd.
Ed: Michael G. Jacobides. **Description:** Those who study and plan strategies risk falling into the traps that maps, graphs, charts and matrices present. A better strategy might be using a playscript that can reveal the unfolding plots of business far better than traditional strategic tools as the landscapes shifts.

25062 ■ "Profit Strong Rona to Maintain Acquisition Strategy" in *Globe & Mail* (February 22, 2007, pp. B14)
Pub: CTVglobemedia Publishing Inc.
Description: Canada-based Rona Inc., home improvement retailer that reported record annual profit in 2006, will continue its strategy of acquisitions. The company has reported profits of $190.6 million in 2006.

25063 ■ "Ratio-Cination" in *Canadian Business* (Vol. 79, October 23, 2006, No. 21, pp. 164)
Pub: Rogers Media
Ed: Ian McGugan. **Description:** Tips for investors, on how to make market observations before selecting companies for purchasing stocks, are presented.

25064 ■ "Realities May Blur Vision" in *The Business Journal-Serving Metropolitan Kansas City* (Vol. 27, September 19, 2008, No. 1, pp. 1)
Pub: American City Business Journals, Inc.
Ed: Rob Roberts. **Description:** Vision Metcalf is a study by Kansas City that depicts how Metcalf Avenue could look like if redeveloped. Redevelopment plans for the Metcalf corridor include a 20-story mixed-use building on a vacant car dealership. The challenges that the redevelopment plans will face are also analyzed.

25065 ■ "Recession Survival Tip: Less Is More" in *Women Entrepreneur* (December 31, 2008)
Pub: Entrepreneur Media Inc.
Ed: Suzy Girard-Ruttenberg. **Description:** These trying economic times can be an opportunity to make bold changes in one's business that may yield lasting results, not just short-term survival; simplification, accountability and shoring up one's margins are things to look at when determining the goals of the company.

25066 ■ "Refreshing" in *Canadian Business* (Vol. 79, September 11, 2006, No. 18, pp. 22)
Pub: Rogers Media
Ed: Joe Castaldo. **Description:** Turnaround strategies and initiatives adopted by Canadian Beverage Corp. to boost its declining sales are presented.

25067 ■ "The Reinvention of Management" in *Strategy and Leadership* (Vol. 39, March-April 2011, No. 2, pp. 9)
Pub: Emerald Group Publishing Inc.
Ed: Stephen Denning. **Description:** An examination found that critical changes in management practice involves five shifts. These shifts involve the firm's goals, model of coordination, the role of managers and values practiced. Other findings of the study are discussed.

25068 ■ "Retail: Loblaw Goes for Broke" in *Canadian Business* (Vol. 80, January 29, 2007, No. 3, pp. 7)
Pub: Rogers Media
Ed: Zena Oiljnyk. **Description:** The efforts of Loblaw Companies Limited to reduce its operational expenses are described. The company's decision to reduce the number of employees at its national and regional offices, besides closing some of its facilities, is discussed.

25069 ■ "Return to Wealth; Bank Strategy" in *The Economist* (Vol. 390, January 3, 2009, No. 8612, pp. 56)
Pub: The Economist Newspaper Inc.
Description: UBS' strategy to survive these trying economic times is presented. Statistical data included. UBS has a stronger balance-sheet than most of its investment-banking peers and has reduced its portfolio.

25070 ■ *Rework*
Pub: Crown Business
Ed: Jason Fried, David Heinemeier Hansson. **Released:** March 9, 2010. **Price:** $22.00. **Description:** Works to help entrepreneurs and business owners to rethink strategy, customers, and getting things accomplished.

25071 ■ "Right From the Start" in *Small Business Opportunities* (July 2010)
Pub: Harris Publications Inc.
Ed: Ed Krug. **Description:** Ed Krug from Pitch Blue provides sales support services by partnering with small and mid-sized companies to set and reach new revenue targets.

25072 ■ "The Road Map for Scotiabank's Asian Expansion" in *Globe & Mail* (April 7, 2007, pp. B3)
Pub: CTVglobemedia Publishing Inc.
Ed: Tara Perkins. **Description:** Executive vice-president of Bank of Nova Scotia, Rob Pitfield shares his plan to expand the bank's Asian market.

25073 ■ "Roadside Attraction" in *Hawaii Business* (Vol. 53, January 2008, No. 7, pp. 39)
Pub: Hawaii Business Publishing
Ed: Jason Ubay. **Description:** Businesses beside the Kamehameha Highway find ways to survive in a rural community. Sunshine Arts Hawaii, for instance, uses a bright-colored and huge mural to attract tourists who drive along the highway. Other techniques employed by businesses in the aforementioned are des cribed.

25074 ■ "Rule of Thumb" in *Entrepreneur* (Vol. 36, May 2008, No. 5, pp. 44)
Pub: Entrepreneur Media, Inc.
Ed: Guy Kawasaki. **Description:** Business presentations using PowerPoint are recommended to have no more than 10 slides, last no longer than 20 minutes and have font no smaller than 30 points. Topics covered should include problem, solution, business model, underlying technology, and projections among others.

25075 ■ "Sabia Signals a Bold, New Course for BCE" in *Globe & Mail* (February 2, 2006, pp. B1)
Pub: CTVglobemedia Publishing Inc.
Ed: Catherine McLean. **Description:** The reasons behind the decision of chief executive officer Michael Sabia to streamline operations of BCE Inc. are presented.

25076 ■ "Samsung's Metamorphosis" in *Austin Business Journal* (Vol. 31, May 20, 2011, No. 11, pp. 1)
Pub: American City Business Journals Inc.
Ed: Christopher Calnan. **Description:** Samsung Austin Semiconductor LP, a developer of semiconductors for smartphones and tablet computers, plans to diversify its offerings to include niche products: flash memory devices and microprocessing devices. In light of this strategy, Samsung Austin will be hiring 300 engineers as part of a $3.6 billion expansion of its plant.

25077 ■ "Savvas Chamberlain" in *Canadian Business* (Vol. 81, March 17, 2008, No. 4, pp. 92)
Pub: Rogers Media
Ed: Andrew Wahl. **Description:** Savvas Chamberlain says he feels cheated during his teenage years because life was not normal for him growing up in Cyprus with all the uprisings against Britain. Chamberlain says he runs Dalsa like he plays chess because all his positions are shown all the time but he keeps his strategy to himself.

25078 ■ "Scouting and Keeping Good Talent in the Workplace" in *Hawaii Business* (Vol. 53, January 2008, No. 7, pp. 50)
Pub: Hawaii Business Publishing
Ed: Christie Dermegian. **Description:** Tips on improving employee selection and retention are presented. The strategies in choosing and keeping the right employees include identifying which type of people the company needs and improving the workplace environment.

25079 ■ "The Seat-Of-The-Pants School of Marketing" in *Brandweek* (Vol. 49, April 21, 2008, No. 16, pp. 24)
Pub: VNU Business Media, Inc.
Ed: David Vinjamuri. **Description:** Excerpt from the book "Accidental Branding: How Ordinary People Build Extraordinary Brands," by David Vinjamuri, discusses six shared principles for creating a brand that is unique and will be successful over the long-term.

25080 ■ "Shermag Plans Two Shutdowns, 300 More Layoffs" in *Globe & Mail* (February 13, 2007, pp. B5)
Pub: CTVglobemedia Publishing Inc.
Ed: Bertrand Marotte. **Description:** Shermag Inc., Canada's largest publicly traded furniture company, is permanently closing two plants and eliminating 300 jobs. The mounting losses and deteriorating stock prices are stated as main reasons for plant shutdowns.

25081 ■ "Shermag Says Refinishing Not Complete" in *Globe & Mail* (February 14, 2006, pp. B3)
Pub: CTVglobemedia Publishing Inc.
Ed: Bertrand Marotte. **Description:** The details on restructuring efforts of Shermag Inc. are presented.

25082 ■ "Shoppers Targets an Upscale Move" in *Globe & Mail* (January 19, 2007, pp. B4)
Pub: CTVglobemedia Publishing Inc.
Ed: Marina Strauss. **Description:** Shoppers Drug Mart Corp.'s plan to boost sales of cosmetics and take up global sourcing to offer new products is discussed.

25083 ■ "Should You Go Into Business With Your Spouse?" in *Women Entrepreneur* (September 1, 2008)
Pub: Entrepreneur Media Inc.
Ed: Tamara Monosoff. **Description:** Things to consider before starting a business with one's spouse are discussed. Compatible work ethics, clear expectations of one another, long-term goals for the company and the status of the relationship are among the things to consider before starting a business endeavor with a spouse.

25084 ■ "Sign Up To Grow Your Business, Generate Jobs" in *Women Entrepreneur* (November 25, 2008)
Pub: Entrepreneur Media Inc.
Ed: Eve Gumpel. **Description:** Nell Merlino has announced the new Make Mine A Million-Dollar Race, which aims to encourage hundreds of thousands of women entrepreneurs to grow their business to revenue goals of $250,00, $500,000 or $1 million and more as well as create 800,000 new jobs in an attempt to stimulate the nation's economy.

25085 ■ "Sleeman Cuts Again as Cheap Suds Bite" in *Globe & Mail* (March 3, 2006, pp. B3)
Pub: CTVglobemedia Publishing Inc.
Ed: Andy Hoffman. **Description:** The details on 5 percent employee reduction at Sleeman Breweries Ltd., which posted 86 percent decline in profits for fourth quarter 2005, are presented.

25086 ■ "Slimmed-Down Supplier TI Automotive Relaunches" in *Crain's Detroit Business* (Vol. 26, January 11, 2010, No. 2, pp. 14)
Pub: Crain Communications, Inc.
Ed: Robert Sherefkin. **Description:** TI Automotive Ltd., one of the world's largest suppliers of fuel storage and delivery systems, has reorganized the company by splitting it into five global divisions and is relaunching its brand which is now more focused on new technology.

25087 ■ *Small Business, Big Life: Five Steps to Creating a Great Life with Your Own Small Business*
Pub: Thomas Nelson Inc.
Ed: Louis Barajas. **Price:** $22.99. **Description:** Barajas describes his and his father's independent entrepreneurial paths and suggests an inspirational approach to business that relies on four personal greatness cornerstones: truth, responsibility, awareness, and courage, and on keeping in mind your vision and your team's needs. The book provides a new look at achieving a work/life balance.

25088 ■ "Small is the New Big in Autos" in *Globe & Mail* (February 16, 2006, pp. B3)
Pub: CTVglobemedia Publishing Inc.
Ed: Greg Keenan. **Description:** The reasons behind the introduction of subcompact cars by companies such as Ford Motor Co. are presented. The automobiles were unveiled at Canadian International Auto Show in Toronto.

25089 ■ "So You Want to Start a Business?" in *Women Entrepreneur* (August 5, 2008)
Pub: Entrepreneur Media Inc.
Ed: Cynthia McKay. **Description:** Advice for taking an idea and turning it into a legitimate business is given.

25090 ■ "Sorrell Digs Deep to Snag TNS" in *Advertising Age* (Vol. 79, July 14, 2008, No. 7, pp. 1)
Pub: Crain Communications, Inc.
Ed: Michael Bush. **Description:** Martin Sorrell's strategic vision for expansion in order to become the largest ad-agency holding company in the world is discussed.

25091 ■ "Stadium Developers Seek a Win With the State" in *The Business Journal-Serving Metropolitan Kansas City* (Vol. 26, August 22, 2008)
Pub: American City Business Journals, Inc.
Ed: Rob Roberts. **Description:** Three Trails Redevelopment LLC is hoping to win $30 million in state tax credits from the Missouri Development Finance Board for the construction of an 18,500-seat Wizards stadium. The project is contingent on state tax incentives and the company remains optimistic about their goal.

25092 ■ "Starbucks Drive-Throughs: Can the Cafe Keep Its Cool?" in *Globe & Mail* (January 6, 2006, pp. B7)
Pub: CTVglobemedia Publishing Inc.
Ed: Steven Gray. **Description:** The feasibility of Starbucks Corp.'s plans to introduce drive-through cafes is discussed.

25093 ■ "Stelco Investors Told Their Stock Now Worthless" in *Globe & Mail* (January 23, 2006, pp. B4)
Pub: CTVglobemedia Publishing Inc.
Ed: Greg Keenan. **Description:** The reasons behind Ontario Superior Court's approval of Stelco Inc.'s restructuring proposal are presented.

25094 ■ "Stelco Seeks to Shave Its Fixed Costs" in *Globe & Mail* (March 8, 2007, pp. B1)
Pub: CTVglobemedia Publishing Inc.
Ed: Greg Keenan. **Description:** The plans of Stelco Inc. to control its fixed costs in order to protect itself from economic downturns are discussed.

25095 ■ "Stepping Up" in *Baltimore Business Journal* (Vol. 28, October 22, 2010, No. 24, pp. 1)
Pub: Baltimore Business Journal
Ed: Erik Siemers. **Description:** Uner Armour Inc. will release its Micro G line of four basketball sneakers on October 23, 2010. The company's executives mentioned that Under Armour's goal is to appeal to customers, and not to chip away at Nike Inc.'s supremacy in basketball shoes. The new sneakers will range from $80 to $110.

25096 ■ "Stikemans' Ascent, Its Legacy, and Its Future" in *Globe & Mail* (January 29, 2007, pp. B2)
Pub: CTVglobemedia Publishing Inc.
Ed: Jacquie McNish. **Description:** Pierre Raymond, chairman of legal firm Stikeman Elliott LLP, talks about his strategies to handle competition, his challenges, and about Canada's present mergers and acquisition scenario. Stikeman achieved the first place in 2006 M&A legal rankings.

25097 ■ "Stock Car Racing" in *Canadian Business* (Vol. 81, September 15, 2008, No. 14-15, pp. 29)
Pub: Rogers Media Ltd.
Ed: Thomas Watson. **Description:** Some analysts predict a Chapter 11-style tune-up making GM and Ford a speculative turnaround stock. However, the price of oil could make or break the shares of the Big Three U.S. automobile manufacturers and if oil goes up too high then a speculative stock to watch is an electric car company called Zenn Motor Co.

25098 ■ "Stockgroup Completes US $4.5 Million Financing" in *Canadian Corporate News* (May 16, 2007)
Pub: Comtex News Network Inc.
Description: Stockgroup, a financial media company focused on collaborative technologies and user-generated content, will use the proceeds of the private placement for acquisitions and general working capital.

25099 ■ "Stoneham Drilling Trust Announces Cash Distribution for May 2007" in *Canadian Corporate News* (May 16, 2007)
Pub: Comtex News Network Inc.
Description: Stoneham Drilling Trust, an income trust that provides contract drilling services to natural gas and oil exploration and production companies operating in western Canada, announced that its cash distribution for the period from May 1, 2007 to May 31, 2007 will be $0.15 per trust unit ($1.80 per annum).

25100 ■ "Strategy: Hurry Up and Wait" in *Business Courier* (Vol. 24, February 1, 2008, No. 43, pp. 50)
Pub: American City Business Journals, Inc.
Ed: Dan Monk. **Description:** It has taken years for Enerfab Inc. chairman Dave Herche to develop new product lines, form an expert management group and come up with a strategic-planning approach. However, his patience has paid off since Enerfab's revenue has grown by 93 percent since 2005. Herche's strategy for Enerfab and its impacts on the company are analyzed further.

25101 ■ *Streetwise Small Business Turnaround: Revitalizing Your Struggling or Stagnant Enterprise*
Pub: Adams Media Corporation
Ed: Marc Kramer. **Released:** November 1999. **Description:** Practical tips and advice are provided for rejuvenating an existing small business.

25102 ■ "Success Coach: Dare to Dream" in *Entrepreneur* (Vol. 35, October 2007, No. 10, pp. 146)
Pub: Entrepreneur Media Inc.
Ed: Romaus Wolter. **Description:** Business goals that are seemingly impossible to reach can actually be achieved through careful planning. Making the goals clear is the first step toward achievement. Details for setting goals and how to attain them are presented.

25103 ■ "Suitors Circling Chrysler as Sale Likely" in *Globe & Mail* (February 19, 2007, pp. B1)
Pub: CTVglobemedia Publishing Inc.
Ed: Jason Singer. **Description:** DaimlerChrysler AG is planning to sell or spin-off the Chrysler Group, as a cost cutting strategy. Chrysler reported a 40 percent drop in fourth quarter profit because of the $1.5 billion operating loss.

25104 ■ "Sunriver Venture Hits Snag" in *The Business Journal-Portland* (Vol. 25, August 1, 2008, No. 21, pp. 1)
Pub: American City Business Journals, Inc.
Ed: Robin J. Moody. **Description:** Portland, Oregon based-Sunwest Management Inc. has divided its Sunriver resort community to make way for a redevelopment plan. Sunwest owner Jon Harder and three partners formed SilverStar Destinations LLC to broker the purchase and redevelopment of the property. Details and description of the redevelopment project are also presented.

25105 ■ "Suppliers Look to Rack Up Big Sales to Distributors" in *The Business Journal-Serving Metropolitan Kansas City* (August 15, 2008)
Pub: American City Business Journals, Inc.
Ed: James Dornbrook. **Description:** Suppliers of shelving units, conveyor systems and other equipment used in distribution facilities are expecting new business opportunities along with the planned intermodal projects in the Kansas City area. Suppliers have already observed that small distributors have started to relocate to the city because of the intermodal projects. Demand for shelves and lifts have also increased.

25106 ■ "Survive the Small-to-Big Transition" in *Entrepreneur* (November 4, 2008)
Pub: Entrepreneur Media Inc.
Ed: Elizabeth Wilson. **Description:** Transitioning a small company to a large company can be a challenge, especially during the time when it is too big to be considered small and too small to be considered big. Common pitfalls during this time are discussed as well as techniques business owners should implement when dealing with this transitional period.

25107 ■ "Take on an Elephant Without Getting Trampled" in *Globe & Mail* (March 17, 2007, pp. B3)
Pub: CTVglobemedia Publishing Inc.
Ed: Grant Robertson. **Description:** The plan of chief executive officer of Canpages Inc. Olivier Vincent to beat the profit margin and market share of Yellow Pages Group is discussed.

25108 ■ "Talisman CEO Touts Benefits of Going It Alone" in *Globe & Mail* (March 22, 2006, pp. B1)
Pub: CTVglobemedia Publishing Inc.
Ed: Dave Ebner. **Description:** The opinions of chief executive officer Jim Buckee of Talisman Energy Inc. on the benefits for the company to remain autonomous are presented.

25109 ■ "Tate & Lyle to Sell Redpath Division to American Sugar" in *Globe & Mail* (February 15, 2007, pp. B15)
Pub: CTVglobemedia Publishing Inc.
Description: American Sugar Refining has agreed to acquire the Canadian sugar unit of Tate & Lyle PLC for $301.9 million. Tate & Lyle PLC has been selling off businesses and closing plants in order to focus on starches and Splenda.

25110 ■ "TD Pares in U.S., Still Aims for Growth" in *Globe & Mail* (March 24, 2007, pp. B6)
Pub: CTVglobemedia Publishing Inc.
Ed: Tara Perkins. **Description:** The decision of TD Banknorth Inc. to close some of its branches and remove 400 jobs, with a view to cutting down operational expenses, is discussed.

25111 ■ "Tea for 33 Million" in *Canadian Business* (Vol. 80, March 12, 2007, No. 6, pp. 10)
Pub: Rogers Media
Ed: Wendy Glauser. **Description:** The plan of owner of Cargo & James Tea, Tim Grover, to expand his business in North America to reach about 33 million, is discussed.

25112 ■ "Telus Tunes in to the TV Revolution" in *Globe & Mail* (February 18, 2006, pp. B4)
Pub: CTVglobemedia Publishing Inc.
Ed: Eric Reguly. **Description:** The business growth plans of chief executive officer Darren Entwistle of Telus Corp. are presented.

25113 ■ "Thomson Eyes Asia for Expansion" in *Globe & Mail* (February 10, 2006, pp. B4)
Pub: CTVglobemedia Publishing Inc.
Ed: Grant Robertson. **Description:** The business growth plans of Thomson Corp., in Asia, are presented.

25114 ■ "Top 50 In Profits" in *Canadian Business* (Vol. 81, Summer 2008, No. 9, pp. 116)
Pub: Rogers Media Ltd.
Description: Royal Bank of Canada topped the Investor 500 by profits list despite the slower economic growth in Canada and the U.S. The bank was in the runner-up position in the 2007. RBC's growth strategy is through hefty acquisitions in the U.S. A table ranking the top 50 companies in Canada in terms of profits is presented.

25115 ■ "Tough-Love Boss at BMO Demands Retail Turnaround" in *Globe & Mail* (March 2, 2007, pp. B13)
Pub: CTVglobemedia Publishing Inc.
Ed: Andrew Willis. **Description:** William Downe, the newly appointed chief executive of Bank of Montreal (BMO), discusses strategies to improve the number of retail customers. The BMO reported $292 million profits in the first quarter of 2007.

25116 ■ "Toyota Expected to Construct Two N.A. Plants" in *Globe & Mail* (February 14, 2007, pp. B4)
Pub: CTVglobemedia Publishing Inc.
Description: Toyota Motor Corp. is planning to construct two vehicle assembly plants in North America and one more plant in Canada. The company is also planning to sell 208,000 vehicles in 2007.

25117 ■ "Transportation Enterprise" in *Advertising Age* (Vol. 79, June 9, 2008, No. 23, pp. S10)
Pub: Crain Communications, Inc.
Ed: Jean Halliday. **Description:** Overview of Enterprise rent-a-car's plan to become a more environmentally-friendly company. The family-owned business has spent $1 million a year to plant trees since 2006 and has added more fuel-efficient cars, hybrids and flex-fuel models.

25118 ■ "Transportation: Laidlaw's Chief Driver" in *Canadian Business* (Vol. 80, January 29, 2007, No. 3, pp. 14)
Pub: Rogers Media
Ed: Michelle Magnan. **Description:** The role of Kevin Benson in the restructuring and growth of the

bankrupt transportation company Laidlaw Inc. is described. The increase in the revenues of the restructures company is discussed.

25119 ■ "Tri-State Lags Peer Cities in Jobs, Human Capital, Study Says" in *Business Courier* (Vol. 27, September 24, 2010, No. 21, pp. 1)
Pub: Business Courier
Ed: Dan Monk, Lucy May. **Description:** Greater Cincinnati, Ohio has ranked tenth overall in the 'Agenda 360/Vision 2015 Regional Indicators Project' report. The study ranked 12-city-peer groups in categories such as job indicators standing and people indicators standing. The ranking of jobs and human capital study is topped by Minneapolis, followed by Denver, Raleigh, and Austin.

25120 ■ "Trilogy Metals Inc.: Private Placement" in *Canadian Corporate News* (May 16, 2007)
Pub: Comtex News Network Inc.
Description: Trilogy Metals Inc. announces a private placement of 10,000,000 units at $0.08 per unit in an effort to raise total gross proceeds of $800,000 which will be allocated to working capital, new acquisitions, and to service existing debt.

25121 ■ "Turmoil Means Changes For Retailers" in *The Business Journal-Serving Metropolitan Kansas City* (Vol. 27, October 10, 2008, No. 4)
Pub: American City Business Journals, Inc.
Ed: Suzanna Stagemeyer. **Description:** Impacts of the financial crisis on Kansas Metropolitan Area retailers are varied. Rob Dalzell, for instance, found it difficult to secure a loan for his new self-serve yogurt store Yummo. The trends in retailing in the area are examined further as well as ways in which local businesses are changing in an attempt to stay solvent during the economic downturn.

25122 ■ "UMKC, Hospital Drill Down on Deal" in *The Business Journal-Serving Metropolitan Kansas City* (Vol. 26, July 18, 2008, No. 45, pp. 1)
Pub: American City Business Journals, Inc.
Ed: Rob Roberts. **Description:** University of Missouri Kansas City and Children's Mercy Hospital are negotiating the hospital's potential acquisition of the university's School of Dentistry building. The deal would transfer the 240,000-square foot dental school building to Children's Mercy. Plans for a new dental school building for the UMKC are also presented.

25123 ■ "Under Fire, Sabia Triggers Battle for BCE" in *Globe & Mail* (April 14, 2007, pp. B1)
Pub: CTVglobemedia Publishing Inc.
Ed: Boyd Erman. **Description:** The announcement of negotiations for the sale of BCE Inc. by its chief executive officer Michael Sabia is discussed. The efforts of Ontario Teachers Pension Plan to submit its proposal for the sale are described.

25124 ■ "Unify Corp. Back in the Black, Poised to Grow" in *Sacramento Business Journal* (Vol. 25, August 29, 2008, No. 26, pp. 1)
Pub: American City Business Journals, Inc.
Ed: Melanie Turner. **Description:** It was reported that Unify Corp. returned to profitability in the fiscal year ended April 30, 2008 with a net income of $1.6 million, under the guidance of Todd Wille. Wille, who took over as the company's chief executive officer in October 2000, was named as Turnaround CEO of the Year in June 2008 for his efforts.

25125 ■ "Unilever's CMO Finally Gets Down To Business" in *Advertising Age* (Vol. 79, July 7, 2008, No. 26, pp. 11)
Pub: Crain Communications, Inc.
Ed: Jack Neff. **Description:** Overview of Unilever's chief marketing officer Simon Clift's strategy for promoting its products; now that the company has restructured, Clift is able to focus all of his energy on the challenges of the new-media climate that marketers are having to face.

25126 ■ "United Insurance To Grow St. Pete's Corporate Base" in *The Business Journal-Serving Greater Tampa Bay* (August 29, 2008)
Pub: American City Business Journals, Inc.
Ed: Margie Manning. **Description:** United Insurance Holdings LC is on its way to becoming a public company by agreeing in a reverse merger with FMG Acquisition Corp. The $104.3 million agreement will provide the company's St. Petersburg operations the opportunity to grow. The other impacts of the proposed reverse merger are examined.

25127 ■ "U.S. Retailer Eyes 'Tween' Market" in *Globe & Mail* (January 30, 2007, pp. B1)
Pub: CTVglobemedia Publishing Inc.
Ed: Marina Strauss. **Description:** The decision of Tween Brands Inc. (Too Incorporated) to open 100 new stores in Canada as part of its expansion is discussed. The company's focus on targeting girls for its products is detailed.

25128 ■ "The Urge to Converge" in *Canadian Business* (Vol. 79, October 9, 2006, No. 20, pp. 41)
Pub: Rogers Media
Ed: Andy Holloway. **Description:** Arthur Griffiths, chief executive officer of Infotec Business Systems Inc., decision to diversify into broad brand business is discussed.

25129 ■ "Virgin Mobile has Big Plans for Year Two" in *Globe & Mail* (March 6, 2006, pp. B5)
Pub: CTVglobemedia Publishing Inc.
Ed: Catherine McLean. **Description:** The business growth plans of Virgin Mobile Canada are presented.

25130 ■ "Wal-Mart Relaunches Private Brand, Reimagines Stores Layout" in *Marketing to Women* (Vol. 22, July 2009, No. 7, pp. 5)
Pub: EPM Communications, Inc.
Description: Wal-Mart is focusing its strategies by centering on new store layouts that they believe will match their new branding of "fast, friendly, and clean" and enable mothers to "just get on with what they need to do."

25131 ■ "Walker Seeks More Business Participation" in *Business Journal-Milwaukee* (Vol. 28, December 10, 2010, No. 10, pp. A1)
Pub: Milwaukee Business Journal
Ed: Rich Kirchen. **Description:** Wisconsin governor Scott Walker is seeking the aid of Milwaukee business leaders to participate in resolving the challenges posed by the economic crisis. Walker is aiming to create 250,000 jobs. He is also planning to call a special session of the legislature to enact strategies to jumpstart the economy.

25132 ■ "Welcome to the Neighborhood" in *Hawaii Business* (Vol. 53, October 2007, No. 4, pp. 48)
Pub: Hawaii Business Publishing
Ed: Jolyn Okimoto Rosa. **Description:** Finance Factors is planning to build branches in Manoa, and Liliha, as part of its strategy to position itself in high-yield areas. The company chose Manoa and Liliha due to thee sites' rich deposits. Its strategy with regards to the branches' location and to the building design is discussed.

25133 ■ "Wendy's Mulls Total Hortons Selloff" in *Globe & Mail* (January 7, 2006, pp. B5)
Pub: CTVglobemedia Publishing Inc.
Ed: Sinclair Stewart; Omar El Akkad. **Description:** The plans of Wendy's International Inc. to spin off Tim Hortons are presented.

25134 ■ "WestJet Ponders Growth Plan Following Record Profit" in *Globe & Mail* (February 15, 2007, pp. B15)
Pub: CTVglobemedia Publishing Inc.
Ed: Brent Jang. **Description:** The Calgary-based WestJet Airlines Ltd., which reported a record $114.7 million profit last year, is planning to expand its operations by 2010. The airline is planning new services and carriers.

25135 ■ "Weyerhaeuser's REIT Decision Shouldn't Scare Investors Away" in *Barron's* (Vol. 88, June 30, 2008, No. 26, pp. 18)
Pub: Dow Jones & Co., Inc.
Ed: Christopher Williams. **Description:** Weyerhaeuser Co.'s management said that a conversion to a real estate investment trust was not likely in 2009 since the move is not tax-efficient as of the moment and would overload its non-timber assets with debt. The company's shares have fallen by 19.5 percent. However, the company remains an asset-rich outfit and its activist shareholder is pushing for change.

25136 ■ "What Are You Doing Differently?" in *Agency Sales Magazine* (Vol. 39, December 2009, No. 11, pp. 3)
Pub: MANA
Ed: Bryan C. Shirley. **Description:** Strategies that sales representatives can do to plan for a good year include professional development, networking with other reps, and making more sales calls and seeing more people. The end of the year is the perfect time for reps to write or re-write their mission statement and to conduct line profitability.

25137 ■ "What Players in the Midmarket Are Talking About" in *Mergers & Acquisitions: The Dealmaker's Journal* (March 1, 2008)
Pub: SourceMedia, Inc.
Description: Sports Properties Acquisition Corp. went public at the end of January; according to the company's prospectus, it is not limiting its focus to just teams, it is also considering deals for stadium construction companies, sports leagues, facilities, sports-related advertising and licensing of products, in addition to other related segments.

25138 ■ "What's Cooking?" in *Entrepreneur* (Vol. 36, April 2008, No. 4, pp. 98)
Pub: Entrepreneur Media, Inc.
Ed: Eileen Figure Sandlin. **Description:** Unique and unusual restaurants have the potential to attract customers and provide them with fresh menu options. Outlining goals, strategies and details on proposed concept and target market can also help in restaurant planning. Other tips on how to plan launching your own restaurant are provided.

25139 ■ "Why Intel Should Dump Its Flash-Memory Business" in *Barron's* (Vol. 88, March 10, 2008, No. 10, pp. 35)
Pub: Dow Jones & Company, Inc.
Ed: Eric J. Savitz. **Description:** Intel Corp. must sell its NAND flash-memory business as soon as it possibly can to the highest bidder to focus on its PC processor business and take advantage of other business opportunities. Apple should consider a buyback of 10 percent of the company's shares to lift its stock.

25140 ■ "Winning Gold" in *The Business Journal-Milwaukee* (Vol. 25, August 8, 2008, No. 46, pp. A1)
Pub: American City Business Journals, Inc.
Ed: Rich Rovito. **Description:** Johnson Controls Inc. of Milwaukee, Wisconsin is taking part in the 2008 Beijing Olympics with the installation of its sustainable control equipment and technology that monitor over 58,000 points in 18 Olympic venues. Details of Johnson Controls' green products and sustainable operations in China are discussed.

25141 ■ "Worth His Salt" in *Hawaii Business* (Vol. 53, January 2008, No. 7, pp. 45)
Pub: Hawaii Business Publishing
Ed: Jolyn Okimoto Rosa. **Description:** Bryan Zada owns three PretzelMaker franchises, whose total loss amounted to $40,000 in 2003. Zada believes that listening to employees was one of the key steps in turning the business around. The efforts made to improve the franchises' products are also given.

25142 ■ "A Year After Fiorina's Exit, Hurd Makes His Mark" in *Globe & Mail* (February 8, 2006, pp. B9)
Pub: CTVglobemedia Publishing Inc.
Ed: Shawn McCarthy. **Description:** The business growth strategies of chief executive officer Mark Hurd of Hewlett-Packard Co. are presented.

25143 ■ "Your Annual Business Tune-Up" in *Business Week* (December 28, 2006)
Pub: McGraw-Hill Companies
Ed: Karen E. Klein. **Description:** Interview with entrepreneurial expert, Ty Freyvogel, founder of EntrpreneursLab.com. Freyvogel gives tips on how a thorough review of existing systems, vendors, customers, and employees could help keep an entrepreneur's business not only safe but highly successful in the upcoming year.

25144 ■ "Zell Takes a Gamble on Tribune" in *Globe & Mail* (April 3, 2007, pp. B1)
Pub: CTVglobemedia Publishing Inc.
Ed: Sinclair Stewart. **Description:** The purchase of the majority share in Tribune Co. by Samuel Zell is described. Samuel Zell's plans to keep the company's assets intact are discussed.

25145 ■ "Zucker's HBC Shakeup Imminent" in *Globe & Mail* (February 20, 2006, pp. B3)
Pub: CTVglobemedia Publishing Inc.
Ed: Marina Strauss. **Description:** The plans of investor Jerry Zucker to revamp Hudson's Bay Co., upon its acquisition, are presented.

VIDEOCASSETTES/ AUDIOCASSETTES

25146 ■ *Action Plans for Implementing Quality and Productivity*
Lucerne Media
37 Ground Pine Rd.
Morris Plains, NJ 07950
Free: 800-341-2293
Fax:(973)538-0855
Co. E-mail: lucernemedia@optonline.net
URL: http://www.lucernemedia.com
Released: 1988. **Price:** $1400.00. **Description:** Dr. Myron Tribus suggests that American companies start planning ahead for the future instead of just shooting for the "quick fix." **Availability:** VHS; 3/4U.

25147 ■ *Goal Setting*
1st Financial Training Services
1515 E. Woodfield Rd., Ste. 345
Schaumburg, IL 60173
Ph:(847)969-0900
Free: 800-442-8662
Fax:(847)969-0521
URL: http://www.1stfinancialtraining.com
Released: 1987. **Price:** $150.00. **Description:** The importance of goals is discussed as well as types of goals, and characteristics of effective goals. **Availability:** VHS; 3/4U.

25148 ■ *Goals and Objectives*
1st Financial Training Services
1515 E. Woodfield Rd., Ste. 345
Schaumburg, IL 60173
Ph:(847)969-0900
Free: 800-442-8662
Fax:(847)969-0521
URL: http://www.1stfinancialtraining.com
Released: 1987. **Price:** $150.00. **Description:** Supervisors are the ones who have to tell the workers just what it is exactly that the top brass wants from them. **Availability:** VHS; 3/4U.

25149 ■ *Goals: Setting and Achieving Them on Schedule*
Cambridge Educational
c/o Films Media Group
132 West 31st Street, 17th Floor
Ste. 124
New York, NY 10001
Free: 800-257-5126
Fax:(609)671-0266
Co. E-mail: custserve@films.com
URL: http://www.cambridgeol.com
Released: 1986. **Price:** $49.95. **Description:** Setting realistic goals is one way for a person to get ahead, in either business or school. Ziglar shows you how. **Availability:** VHS.

25150 ■ *Make More Money by Setting Goals/ Rick Barrera*
Instructional Video
2219 C St.
Lincoln, NE 68502
Ph:(402)475-6570
Free: 800-228-0164
Fax:(402)475-6500
Co. E-mail: feedback@insvideo.com
URL: http://www.insvideo.com
Price: $95.00. **Description:** Rick Barrera offers his program developing the proper goals to increase business and income. Available only in the U.S. **Availability:** VHS.

CONSULTANTS

25151 ■ Adventure Learning Associates Inc.
567 Hale Rd.
PO Box 6062
Brattleboro, VT 05302
Ph:(802)254-6160
Free: 800-551-3210
Fax:(802)254-3852
Co. E-mail: info@alrna.com
URL: http://www.alrna.com
Contact: Paul A. Kidder, President
Scope: Provides consulting services and training in experiential training and development. Specifically provides team building, communications skills and empowerment skill sessions. Also focuses on needs analysis, strategic planning and visioning for newly developing groups. Firm specializes in training trainers in experiential outdoor programming. Industries served: all including government and can work with intact groups at all levels from line staff to boards and executive committees. **Seminars:** Train the Adventure Trainer.

25152 ■ AMC International Inc.
864 S Robertson Blvd., Ste. 207
PO Box 11292
Los Angeles, CA 90035
Ph:(310)652-5620
Fax:(310)652-6709
Co. E-mail: inquiry@amcusa.com
Contact: Abe Moradian, President
Scope: Offers day to day business management, business turn around, marketing strategies, development or refinement of corporate mission, and merger and acquisition evaluations. Industries served all.

25153 ■ Ameriwest Business Consultants Inc.
3725 E Wade Ln.
PO Box 26266
Colorado Springs, CO 80917-5852
Ph:(719)380-7096
Fax:(719)380-7096
Co. E-mail: email@abchelp.com
URL: http://www.abchelp.com
Contact: Rodd Brechtl, President
E-mail: rodb@abchelp.com
Scope: Specializes in assisting start up businesses and those with sales of 5million dollars or less and those who have 50 employees or less. Services and products offered include written business plans; do it yourself business plan kits; business valuations; do it yourself business start up kits; written loan packages; do it yourself loan packaging guides; business analysis; do it yourself financial projections software; do it yourself complete financial analysis; website development assistance; general consulting.

25154 ■ Blue Garnet Associates L.L.C.
8055 W Manchester Ave., Ste. 430
Playa del Rey, CA 90293
Ph:(310)439-1930
Fax:(310)388-1657
Co. E-mail: information@bluegarnet.net
URL: http://www.bluegarnet.net
Contact: Cassie Walker, Principle
E-mail: cassie@atsbluegarnet.net
Scope: A business strategy consulting firm that provides expertise in organizational visioning, strategic and business planning, market opportunity and growth strategy, impact assessment, and leadership and governance.

25155 ■ BroadVision Inc.
1600 Seaport Blvd., Ste. 550, North Bldg.
Redwood City, CA 94063-5589
Ph:(650)331-1000
Fax:(650)364-3425
Co. E-mail: info@broadvision.com
URL: http://www.broadvision.com
Contact: William E. Meyer, CFO
Scope: Firm delivers a combination of technologies and services in to the global market that enable its customers to power mission-critical web initiatives that ultimately deliver high-value to their bottom line. Areas of expertise include strategic services, interactive services, content and creative services and client services. Services include business planning, application strategy, ROI analysis, organization and business process consulting, building and deploying applications, content management, sourcing and workflow processes.

25156 ■ CFO Service
112 Chester Ave.
Saint Louis, MO 63122
Ph:(314)757-2940
Contact: John D. Skae, President
E-mail: jds217@aol.com
Scope: A group of professional executives that provide upper management services to companies that cannot support a full time COO or CFO. Provides clients in the areas of business planning, company policies, contract negotiations, safety policies, product and service pricing, loans management, taxes, cost analysis, loss control and budgeting.

25157 ■ Claude Hayes & Associates
9259 Hunterboro Dr.
Brentwood, TN 37027-6118
Ph:(615)377-0743
Fax:(615)370-8106
Contact: Claude W. Hayes Jr., Owner
Scope: Provides services in the areas of turnarounds, reengineering, restructuring, reorganization, startups, high profile growth, acquisitions, divestitures, due diligence, strategic/business (marketing/sales) plans, inventory control and management, cost pricing and control, market management, demand forecasting.

25158 ■ Flor & Associates
179 Schan Dr.
Churchville, PA 18966-1619
Ph:(215)355-7466
Fax:(215)355-7464
Co. E-mail: fredflor@msn.com
Contact: Frederick Flor, President
Scope: Offers business development consulting helping companies increase the value of their businesses. Services include: market development for technologies sand products; product positioning strategies; technology assessment; competitive intelligence and analysis; team augmentation and facilitation; business growth strategies including acquisitions, licensing, and partnerships.

25159 ■ Jarlett Consulting
3634 Tierra De Dios
Escondido, CA 92025
Ph:(760)745-1090
Fax:(760)741-2863
Co. E-mail: jarlett@earthlink.net
Contact: Frank E. Jarlett, President
Scope: Offers a comprehensive, integrated approach to successfully managing the future by understanding trends, setting goals, evaluating options, planning and managing. Includes analysis of global, national, state and local trends on technological, social, political and management issues. Provides products and services that meet future business goals, management of research and development, evaluating customers and competition, and writing winning proposals. **Publications:** "Making the Right Choices of Future Change and Growth".

25160 ■ J.B. Geller Consulting Inc.
9 Ridgedale Ln.
West Dennis, MA 02670-2545
Ph:(508)760-0044

Fax:(508)943-4122
Co. E-mail: jbgeller@capecod.net
Contact: Judith B. Geller, President
E-mail: jbgeller@attbi.com
Scope: A full service human resources consulting firm whose purpose is to empower leaders, managers and employees to welcome changes created by internal and external forces such as employment laws, mergers, acquisition, re-engineering, change in management, etc. Specific services include: management development, organizational development, visioning, personnel policy development and communication, recruitment, employee relations, team building, and career development. Industries served: Financial services, manufacturing, high-tech, health care, retail services, and government agencies. **Publications:** "Making Diversity Work"; "A Managers Guide to Human Behavior," American Management Association, 1994; "How to Comply with the Americans with Disabilities Act," American Management Association, 1992. **Seminars:** Visioning for Leaders: How to create and communicate a vision, purpose admission; Training Needs Assessment; How to Conduct Focus Groups; Interviewing Skills for Supervisors; Employment Laws for Supervisors; Disability Awareness Training; Prevention of Sexual Harassment; How to Comply with the Americans with Disabilities Act; Fearless Firing; Performance Management; How to Write Effective Job Descriptions; Diversity in the Workplace; Disability Awareness.

25161 ■ Lippert/Heilshorn and Associates Inc.
800 3rd Ave., Ste. 1701
New York, NY 10022-7649
Ph:(212)838-3777
Fax:(212)838-4568
Co. E-mail: keith@lhai.com
URL: http://www.lhai.com
Contact: Carolyn M. Capaccio, Vice President
E-mail: jcain@atslhai.com
Scope: An independent investor relations firm creating and supporting practices investor and media relations programs. Focuses on the development of public company identity and the communication of strategic vision. Strategic investor relations counsel provides companies with a tactical plan that integrates finance, communication, marketing, and securities law compliance. Corporate communications capabilities include handling situations; develops and executing media programs specially tailored to clients' needs, opportunities, and corporate objectives. Message positioning, counsel and press outreach are designed to help attain strategic IR goals.

25162 ■ Persephone C. Agrafiotis
302 N Bay St.
Manchester, NH 03104-2324
Ph:(603)625-8446
Fax:(603)625-8446
Co. E-mail: persephonea@webtv.com
E-mail: persephonea@webtv.com
Scope: Provides Record Review and Medical Expert Witness for Medical Legal cases in Medical Case Review, Nursing, Health Administration, Gerontology, Pediatrics and other clinical areas. Offers Health Care Management Consultation in Home Care, Long Term Care and General Management. Provides expertise in Preferred Provider Contracting Negotiations, Accrediting Processed to include JCAHO, Operations Review, Operations Auditing, Strategic Planning, Business Ethics Review and Implementation. Policy and Procedure, Strategies for the Future Planning, Review/Revision/Implementation, and Educational Programming. Industries Served: health care, human services, government and educational institutions. **Publications:** "In service Education and Training"; "The American Journal of Nursing"; "An Analysis of the Curriculum of Moral Education of Baccalaureate Nursing Students in New England". **Seminars:** Organizational Development; Group Dynamics; Leadership; Motivation; Assertiveness and Change; Performance Appraisals; Principles of Management; Marketing Educational Programs; Rag Quilt Technique; Quilting 101; Sewing 101; Sampler Quilt Hand Pieced; UFO (Unfinished Object) Finishing; Individualized Project; Learn to Knit and/or Crochet.

25163 ■ ReCourses Inc.
6101 Stillmeadow Dr.
Nashville, TN 37211-6518
Ph:(615)831-2277
Free: 888-476-5884
Fax:(615)831-2212
Co. E-mail: info@recourses.com
URL: http://www.recourses.com
Contact: David C. Baker, Principle
E-mail: david@recourses.com
Scope: A management consulting firm that works exclusively with small service providers in the communications industry, including public relations firms, advertising agencies, interactive companies and design studios. Services include Total Business Review, a complete examination of your business starting with an on site examination or discussion, followed by written recommendations and then supplemented with six months of implementation guidance. Areas reviewed include positioning, marketing, management, personnel, structure, finance, retirement, technology and specific growth issues. **Publications:** "Managing (Right) for the First Time". **Seminars:** Managing Client Relationships; Research and Strategy; Financial Management: Measuring and Enhancing Performance in a Marketing Firm, Sep, 2009; Building and Leading a Staff: The When, How, and What of Growth and Culture, Sep, 2009; Doing Effective Work: Adding Significance to the Strategic Portion of Your Work for Clients, Sep, 2009; Resourcing the Creative Process: Managing Pricing, Deadlines, Budgets, Quality, and Capacity, Apr, 2009. **Special Services:** ReCourses[R].

LIBRARIES

25164 ■ University of South Carolina–The Moore School of Business–Elliot White Springs Business Library (Franc)
Francis M. Hipp Bldg., 2nd Fl.
1705 College St.
Columbia, SC 29208
Ph:(803)777-6032
Fax:(803)777-6876
URL: http://www.sc.edu/library/pubserv/business.html
Contact: Dwight Gardner, Hd.Bus.Libn.
Scope: Corporations. **Services:** Interlibrary loan; copying; Library open to the public with restrictions. **Holdings:** 30,000 books; 4000 bound periodical volumes. **Subscriptions:** 350 journals and other serials; 5 newspapers.

Buying a Business

START-UP INFORMATION

25165 ■ *Legal Guide for Starting and Running a Small Business*
Pub: NOLO
Ed: Fred Steingold. **Released:** April 2008. **Price:** $34.99. **Description:** Information for starting a new business focusing on choosing a business structure, taxes, employees and independent contractors, trademark and service marks, licensing and permits, leasing and improvement of commercial space, buying and selling a business, and more.

ASSOCIATIONS AND OTHER ORGANIZATIONS

25166 ■ Institute of Certified Business Counselors
18831 Willamette Dr.
West Linn, OR 97068
Free: 877-422-2674
Fax:(503)635-1340
Co. E-mail: membership@i-cbc.org
URL: http://www.i-cbc.org
Contact: David Finsterwald
Description: Bankers, consultants, accountants, attorneys, appraisers, merger and acquisition specialists, estate planners, financial consultants and business brokers active in the continuation, evaluation, financing, or marketing of privately-held businesses. Offers training and advice on how to buy or sell a business, including information on what to look for in a prospective deal. Maintains speakers' bureau. **Publications:** *The Certified Business Counselor* (bimonthly).

REFERENCE WORKS

25167 ■ "Analysts: More Mergers for the Region's Hospitals" in *Boston Business Journal* (Vol. 30, October 15, 2010, No. 36, pp. 1)
Pub: Boston Business Journal
Ed: Julie M. Donnelly. **Description:** A number of hospitals in Boston, Massachusetts are engaging in mergers and acquisitions. Caritas Christi Health Care is set to be purchased by Cerberus Capital Management. The U.S. healthcare reform law is seen to drive the development.

25168 ■ "Are You Looking for an Environmentally Friendly Dry Cleaner?" in *Inc.* (Vol. 30, December 2008, No. 12, pp. 34)
Pub: Mansueto Ventures LLC
Ed: Shivani Vora. **Description:** Greenopia rates the greenness of 52 various kinds of businesses, including restaurants, nail salons, dry cleaners, and clothing stores. The guidebooks are sold through various retailers including Barnes & Noble and Amazon.com.

25169 ■ "Ask Inc." in *Inc.* (November 2007, pp. 70)
Pub: Gruner & Jahr USA Publishing
Description: Advice is given for any entrepreneur considering the sale of a company.

25170 ■ "Austin Energy May Build $2.3B Biomass Plant" in *Austin Business JournalInc.* (Vol. 28, July 25, 2008, No. 19, pp. A1)
Pub: American City Business Journals
Ed: Kate Harrington. **Description:** An approval from the Austin City Council is being sought by Austin Energy for a 20-year supply contract with Nacogdoches Power LLC to build a $2.3 billion biomass plant in East Texas. The 100-megawatt biomass plant, which is to run on waste wood, will have Austin Energy as its sole buyer.

25171 ■ "Black On Black Business: Moorehead Buys Hank Aaron's Toyota Dealership" in *Black Enterprise* (Vol. 38, February 2008, No. 7, pp. 28)
Pub: Earl G. Graves Publishing Co. Inc.
Ed: Brenda Porter. **Description:** In a move to expand his automotive business, Thomas A. Moorehead, CEO of BMW/MINI of Sterling, Georgia bought Hank Aaron's Toyota automobile dealership in McDonough, Georgia. Moorehead stated that he will call the new store Toyota of McDonough.

25172 ■ *Building a Dream: A Canadian Guide to Starting Your Own Business*
Pub: McGraw-Hill Ryerson Ltd.
Ed: Walter S. Good. **Released:** 2005. **Description:** Topics covered include evaluating business potential, new business ideas, starting or buying a business, franchise opportunities, business organization, protecting an idea, arranging financing, and developing a business plan.

25173 ■ *Buying and Selling a Business*
Pub: Entrepreneur Press
Ed: Ira Nottonson. **Released:** April 2008. **Price:** $32. 95. **Description:** Tips for negotiating sales are presented. Attorney, Ira Nottonson presents both sides of negotiations by presenting the both buyer's and seller's perspectives. Critical steps in the sale process, including presentation, negotiation and documentations are discussed. The book teaches how to gain the upper hand, minimize financial risk and be a winner regardless of side.

25174 ■ "Calista Sells Rural Newspapers" in *Alaska Business Monthly* (Vol. 27, October 2011, No. 10, pp. 8)
Pub: Alaska Business Publishing Company
Ed: Nancy Pounds. **Description:** Calista sold its six newspapers, a magazine, shoppers and its printing house. Details of the sales are given.

25175 ■ "CanWest Plotting Buyback of Newspaper Income Trust" in *Globe & Mail* (February 7, 2007, pp. B1)
Pub: CTVglobemedia Publishing Inc.
Ed: Sinclair Stewart; Boyd Erman; Grant Robertson. **Description:** The CanWest Global Communications Corp.'s decision to sell its media assets in Australia and New Zealand in order to finance its plans of repurchasing its newspaper income trust CanWest MediaWorks Income Fund is discussed.

25176 ■ "Capital Position" in *Business Journal-Milwaukee* (Vol. 28, December 24, 2010, No. 12, pp. A1)
Pub: Milwaukee Business Journal
Ed: Rich Kirchen. **Description:** Canada-based BMO Financial Group has purchased Marshall and Isley Corporation (M and I), which dominated lending among Wisconsin businesses for decades. The sale of M and I will enable other banks to recruit M and I's customers but BMO Financial remains a stronger competitor since it possesses a more potent capital position.

25177 ■ "CGB Purchases Illinois Grain-Fertilizer Firm" in *Farm Industry News* (December 2, 2011)
Pub: Penton Business Media Inc.
Description: CGB Enterprises Inc. bought Twomey Company's grain and fertilizer assets. The purchase includes eight locations and a barge loading terminal near Gladstone, Illinois and storage capacity of 51 million bushels and 18,000 tons of liquid fertilizer.

25178 ■ "Competitive Restaurant Scene Lures Buyers to Saratoga Springs" in *Business Review, Albany New York* (Vol. 34, October 26, 2007)
Pub: American City Business Journals, Inc.
Ed: Robin K. Cooper. **Description:** Restaurant industry in Saratoga Springs, New York, a competitive market, with the city having 102 licensed restaurants and 28,499 residents in 2006. Buyers tend to acquire restaurants in Saratoga Springs, New York due to its good market condition. Examples of restaurant acquisitions in Saratoga Springs are given.

25179 ■ *The Complete Guide to Buying a Business*
Pub: NOLO
Ed: Fred S. Steingold. **Released:** November 2007. **Price:** $24.99. **Description:** Key steps in buying a business are highlighted, focusing on legal issues, tax considerations, approaches for valuing a business, financing, structuring the deal, along with forms and documents for taking ownership are included.

25180 ■ *The Complete Guide to Selling a Business*
Pub: NOLO
Ed: Fred S. Steingold. **Released:** November 2007. **Price:** $34.99. **Description:** When selling a business it is critical that a sales agreement covers all key concerns from price and payment terms to liability protection and restrictions on future competition.

25181 ■ "A Counter Offer" in *Inc.* (February 2008, pp.)
Pub: Gruner & Jahr USA Publishing
Ed: Elaine Appleton Grant. **Description:** Online retailer offering a line of kitchen and home products has upgraded its Website in order to make the business more attractive to possible buyers of the company. The firm is asking $9.9 million and reported

gross revenue of $12.7 in 2007. The owner suggests that a buyer add product lines geared towards more rooms of the home than currently offer on the retail site.

25182 ■ "The Data Drivers" in *Canadian Business* (Vol. 81, September 15, 2008, No. 14-15, pp. 1)
Pub: Rogers Media Ltd.
Ed: Andrew Wahl. **Description:** Canadian regulators hope that an auction of telecommunications companies will inject more competition into the industry; however, newcomers may not be able to rely on lower prices in order to gain market share from the three major telecommunications companies that already have a stronghold on the market. Analysts feel that providing additional data service is the key to surviving market disruptions.

25183 ■ "Dow AgroSciences Buys Wheat Breeding Firm in Pacific Northwest" in *Farm Industry News* (July 29, 2011)
Pub: Penton Business Media Inc.
Description: Dow AgroSciences purchased Northwest Plant Breeding Company, a cereals breeding station in Washington in 2011. The acquisition will help Dow expand its Hyland Seeds certified wheat seed program foundation in the Pacific Northwest. Financial terms of the deal were not disclosed.

25184 ■ "Downtown Bank Got High Marks for Irwin Purchase, Is Looking For More" in *Business Courier* (Vol. 27, September 3, 2010, No. 18, pp. 1)
Pub: Business Courier
Ed: Steve Watkins. **Description:** First Financial Bancorp is looking to acquire more troubled banks following its purchase of Irwin Union Bank. The bank has reported a $383 million bargain purchase gain during the third quarter of 2009.

25185 ■ "Facebook Purchased Push Pop Press" in *Information Today* (Vol. 28, October 2011, No. 9, pp. 12)
Pub: Information Today, Inc.
Description: Facebook purchased Push Pop Press, a digital publishing company that developed a multi-touch interface for ebook publishing on the iPad.

25186 ■ "First Financial Aiming for Banking Big Leagues" in *Business Courier* (Vol. 26, December 4, 2009, No. 32, pp. 1)
Pub: American City Business Journals, Inc.
Ed: Steve Watkins. **Description:** First Financial Bancorp could dominate the community banking market of Greater Cincinnati after buying failed banks with the supervision of the FDIC. Details of the transactions are presented.

25187 ■ "First U.S. :M-Press Tiger with Inline Screen Printing" in *American Printer* (Vol. 128, June 1, 2011, No. 6)
Pub: Penton Media Inc.
Description: Graphic Tech located in California bought :M-Press Tiger, the first in North America with an inline screen printing unit.

25188 ■ "FIS-Metavante Deal Paying Off for Many" in *Business Journal-Milwaukee* (Vol. 28, December 17, 2010, No. 11, pp. A1)
Pub: Milwaukee Business Journal
Ed: Rich Kirchen. **Description:** Jacksonville, Florida-based Fidelity National Information Services Inc., also known as FIS, has remained committed to Milwaukee, Wisconsin more than a year after purchasing Metavante Technologies Inc. FIS has transferred several operations into Metropolitan Milwaukee and has continued its contribution to charitable organizations in the area.

25189 ■ "Follow the ABCs of Buying a Business" in *Women Entrepreneur* (September 10, 2008)
Pub: Entrepreneur Media Inc.
Ed: Nina Kaufman. **Description:** Buying a business will likely result in the largest single asset one will ever own. A list of steps one can take in order to educate and protect themselves is provided.

25190 ■ "For Hospitals, a Dating Game" in *Business Courier* (Vol. 26, December 4, 2009, No. 32, pp. 1)
Pub: American City Business Journals, Inc.
Ed: James Ritchie. **Description:** Drake Center, Fort Hamilton Hospital, and West Chester Medical Center are among the members of Cincinnati's Health Alliance looking for potential buyers or partners. Meanwhile, Jewish Hospital, another member of the Alliance, will be bought by Mercy Health Partners by January 7, 2010.

25191 ■ "For the Seasoned Buyer" in *Inc.* (Vol. 30, November 2008, No. 11, pp. 32)
Pub: Mansueto Ventures LLC
Ed: Darren Dahl. **Description:** Dominick Fimiano shares his plans to sell his ten-year-old business that manufactures and sells frozen pizza dough and crusts as well as a variety of topped pizzas. Products are purchased by schools, hospitals, bowling alleys and amusement parks. The business sale includes the buyer's taking on Fimiano's son the firm's most senior employee.

25192 ■ "Former Gov. Fletcher Starts Blue Ash Firm" in *Business Courier* (Vol. 26, October 9, 2009, No. 24, pp. 1)
Pub: American City Business Journals, Inc.
Ed: Lucy May. **Description:** Former Kentucky Governor Ernie Fletcher partnered with Belcan Corporation founder Ralph Anderson to purchase Blue Ash, Ohio-based Virtual Medical Network and form Alton Healthcare LLC. The company's goal is to increase practice revenues by adapting technology to reinvent clinical practices and deliver best possible care to more patients.

25193 ■ "The Furniture Company Wanted to Sell Him Its Buildings-And Close Down. Should He Buy the Company, Too?" in *Inc.* (November 2007)
Pub: Gruner & Jahr USA Publishing
Ed: Alex Salkever. **Description:** Rick Detkowski, real estate investor, discusses his decision to purchase the furniture company housed in the buildings he was interested in buying. The property would have cost him between $500,000 to $1 million, he was able to purchase the property and business with its entire inventory of furniture, vehicles, and machinery for $1.8 million.

25194 ■ "'Green' Cleaner Buys Local Firm" in *Puget Sound Business Journal* (Vol. 29, December 19, 2008, No. 35, pp. 3)
Pub: American City Business Journals
Ed: Greg Lamm. **Description:** Washington-based Blue Sky Cleaners has purchased Four Seasons Cleaners. The green company also purchased Queen Anne store and Four Seasons' routes fro Snohomish County through Seattle.

25195 ■ "Harleysville Eyes Growth After Nationwide Deal" in *Philadelphia Business Journal* (Vol. 30, October 7, 2011, No. 34, pp. 1)
Pub: American City Business Journals Inc.
Ed: Jeff Blumenthal. **Description:** Harleysville Group announced growth plans after the company was sold to Columbus, Ohio-based Nationwide Mutual Insurance Company for about $1.63 billion. Nationwide gained an independent agency platform in 32 states with the Harleysville deal.

25196 ■ "Hedge-Fund Titan Cohen Plans Bid for Dodgers" in *Wall Street Journal Eastern Edition* (November 25 , 2011, pp. C3)
Pub: Dow Jones & Company Inc.
Ed: Matthew Futterman, Gregory Zuckerman. **Description:** Steven A. Cohen, the founder and head of hedge-fund SAC Capital Advisors LLC is looking to make an offer at the bankruptcy auction for the financially-troubled Los Angeles Dodgers baseball team.

25197 ■ "Higher Thread Count for Metropole" in *Business Courier* (Vol. 26, September 25, 2009, No. 22, pp. 1)
Pub: American City Business Journals, Inc.
Ed: Lisa Biank Fasig, Lucy May. **Description:** Cincinnati Center City Development Corporation is under contract to buy the 225-unit apartment building called Metropole Apartments and 21c Museum Hotel is the lead candidate for the space. Advocates of some residents of the low-income rental complex complain that this move could leave them homeless.

25198 ■ *How to Buy and/or Sell a Small Business for Maximum Profit: A Step-by-Step Guide*
Pub: Atlantic Publishing Company
Ed: Rene V. Richards. **Released:** January 2006. **Price:** $24.95. **Description:** Suggestions, insights and techniques for buying and selling small businesses, includes advice on when to buy or sell, how to market the business, explanation of legal and financial documents involved in the sale and closing of a deal.

25199 ■ "Intel to Buy McAfee Security Business for 768B" in *eWeek* (August 19, 2010)
Pub: Ziff Davis Enterprise
Description: Intel will acquire security giant McAfee for approximately $7.68 billion, whereby McAfee would become a wholly owned subsidiary of Intel and would report to Intel's Software and Services Group.

25200 ■ *Let's Buy a Company: How to Accelerate Growth Through Acquisitions*
Pub: Career Press, Incorporated
Ed: H. Lee Rust. **Released:** January 2006. **Price:** $18.99 (US), $25.95 (Canadian). **Description:** Advice for negotiating terms and pricing as well as other aspects of mergers and acquisitions in small companies.

25201 ■ "Local Firm Snaps up 91 Area Pizza Huts" in *Orlando Business Journal* (Vol. 26, January 8, 2010, No. 32, pp. 1)
Pub: American City Business Journals
Ed: Alexis Muellner, Anjali Fluker. **Description:** Orlando, Florida-based CFL Pizza LLC bought the 91 Orlando-area Pizza Hut restaurants for $35 million from parent company Yum! Brands Inc. CFL Pizza plans to distribute parts of the business to Central Florida vendors and the first business up for grabs is the advertising budget.

25202 ■ "M&I Execs May Get Golden Parachutes" in *Business Journal-Milwaukee* (Vol. 28, December 31, 2010, No. 14, pp. A3)
Pub: Milwaukee Business Journal
Ed: Rich Kirchen. **Description:** Marshall and Isley Corporation's top executives have a chance to receive golden-parachute payments it its buyer, BMO Financial Group, repays the Troubled Asset Relief Program (TARP) loan on behalf of the company. One TARP rule prevents golden-parachute payments to them and the next five most highly paid employees of TARP recipients.

25203 ■ *Mergers and Acquisitions from A to Z*
Pub: Amacom
Ed: Andrew J. Sherman, Milledge A. Hart. **Released:** January 2006. **Price:** $35.00. **Description:** Guide for the entire process of mergers and acquisitions, including taxes, accounting, laws, and projected financial gain.

25204 ■ "Monsanto Acquires Targeted-Pest Control Technology Start-Up; Terms Not Disclosed" in *Benzinga.com* (, 2011)
Pub: Benzinga.com
Ed: Benzinga Staff. **Description:** Monsanto Company acquired Beelogics, a firm that researches and develops biological tools that control pests and diseases. Research includes a product that will help protect bee health.

25205 ■ "Murdock Carrousel Sold" in *Charlotte Observer* (January 31, 2007)
Pub: Knight-Ridder/Tribune Business News
Ed: Bob Fliss. **Description:** Details on the sale of the Murdock Carrousel shopping center are highlighted. The deal was reported at $281 million.

25206 ■ "The Next Chapter" in *Business Courier* (Vol. 26, November 20, 2009, No. 30, pp. 1)
Pub: American City Business Journals, Inc.
Ed: Lucy May. **Description:** Eric Browne and Mel Gravely purchased controlling interest in TriVersity Construction Group from CM-GC CEO Schulyler Murdoch and MBJ Consultants President Monroe Barnes. One third of the company was still owned by Cincinnati-based Messer and TriVersity and will continue to be a certified minority business enterprise.

25207 ■ "P/Kaufmann Sells Bennettsville" in *Home Textiles Today* (Vol. 31, May 24, 2011, No. 13, pp. 6)
Pub: Reed Business Information
Description: Decorative Screen Printers purchased the printing and finishing facility of P/Kaufmann in Bennettsville, South Carolina. However, the firm will continue its focus on its core business, a vat printing facility for home furnishings fabrics.

25208 ■ "Points of Light Sells MissionFish to eBay" in *Non-Profit Times* (Vol. 25, May 15, 2011, No. 7, pp. May 15, 2011)
Pub: NPT Publishing Group Inc.
Description: eBay purchased MissionFish, a subsidiary of Points of Light Institute for $4.5 million. MissionFish allows eBay sellers to give proceeds from sales to their favorite nonprofit organization and helps nonprofits raise funds by selling on eBay.

25209 ■ "Portland's Hilton For Sale" in *Business Journal Portland* (Vol. 27, October 22, 2010, No. 34, pp. 1)
Pub: Portland Business Journal
Ed: Wendy Culverwell. **Description:** Hilton Portland & Executive Tower, Portland's biggest hotel, is being sold by Cornerstone Real Estate Advisers LLC. Cornerstone hopes to close the deal for the 782-room complex by the end of 2010. Cornerstone contracted Jones Lang LaSalle to manage the sale, but terms to the deal are not available.

25210 ■ "Ric Elis/Dan Feldstein" in *Charlotte Business Journal* (Vol. 25, December 31, 2010, No. 41, pp. 6)
Pub: Charlotte Business Journal
Ed: Ken Elkins. **Description:** Charlotte, North Carolina-based Internet marketing firm Red Ventures has grown significantly. General Atlantic has purchased stakes in Red Ventures.

25211 ■ "Rosewood Site Faces Big Cleanup" in *Baltimore Business Journal* (Vol. 27, February 6, 2010, No. 40, pp. 1)
Pub: American City Business Journals
Ed: Daniel J. Sernovitz. **Description:** Environmental assessment report states that Maryland's Rosewood Center for the Developmentally Disabled has significant amounts of toxic chemicals, which could impact Stevenson University's decision to purchase the property. Senator Robert A. Zirkin believes that the state should pay for the cleanup, which is expected to cost millions.

25212 ■ "RS Information Systems Signs Buyout Deal" in *Black Enterprise* (February 2008)
Pub: Earl G. Graves Publishing Co. Inc.
Ed: Alan Hughes. **Description:** Details of the RS Information Systems buyout by Wyle, a privately held provider of high-tech aerospace engineering, testing, and research services.

25213 ■ "Sale of Solo Cup Plant Pending" in *Boston Business Journal* (Vol. 29, June 17, 2011, No. 6, pp. 1)
Pub: American City Business Journals Inc.
Ed: Daniel J. Sernovitz. **Description:** Baltimore developers Vanguard Equities Inc. and Greenberg Gibbons Commercial have contracted to buy the Solo Cup Company facility in Owing Mills and are now considering several plans for the property. Sale should be completed by September 2011 but no proposed sale terms are disclosed.

25214 ■ "A Second Chance to Make a Living" in *The Business Journal-Milwaukee* (Vol. 25, September 19, 2008, No. 52, pp. A1)
Pub: American City Business Journals, Inc.
Description: Unemployed workers and baby boomers are driving interest in purchasing small businesses. BizBuySell general manager Mike Handelsman reveals that the supply of small businesses for sale is decreasing due to the increased demand. The trends in the small business market are analyzed.

25215 ■ *The Secret of Exiting Your Business Under Your Terms!*
Pub: Outskirts Press, Incorporated
Ed: Gene H. Irwin. **Released:** August 2005. **Price:** $29.95. **Description:** Topics include how to sell a business for the highest value, tax laws governing the sale of a business, finding the right buyer, mergers and acquisitions, negotiating the sale, and using a limited auction to increase future value of a business.

25216 ■ *Six SIGMA for Small Business*
Pub: Entrepreneur Press
Ed: Greg Brue. **Released:** October 2005. **Price:** $19.95 (US), $26.95 (Canadian). **Description:** Jack Welch's Six SIGMA approach to business covers accounting, finance, sales and marketing, buying a business, human resource development, and new product development.

25217 ■ "Skype Ltd. Acquired GroupMe" in *Information Today* (Vol. 28, October 2011, No. 9, pp. 12)
Pub: Information Today, Inc.
Description: Skype Ltd. acquired GroupMe, a group messaging company that allows users to form impromptu groups where they can text message, share data, and make conference calls for free and is supported on Android, iPhone, BlackBerry, and Windows phones.

25218 ■ *Small Business Desk Reference*
Pub: Penguin Books (USA) Incorporated
Ed: Gene Marks. **Released:** December 2004. **Description:** Comprehensive guide for starting or running a successful small business, focusing on buying a business or franchise, writing a business plan, financial management, accounting, legal issues, human resources management, operations, marketing, sales, customer service, taxes, insurance, and ethics. Information for launching a restaurant, property management firm, retail outlet, consulting firm, and service business is included.

25219 ■ "Start or Buy? It's a Tough Question for Eager Entrepreneurs" in *Crain's Cleveland Business* (Vol. 28, October 8, 2007, No. 40)
Pub: Crain Communications, Inc.
Ed: David Prizinsky. **Description:** Discusses different approaches to becoming a small business owner.

25220 ■ "Symantic Completes Acquisition of VeriSign's Security Business" in *Internet Wire* (August 9, 2010)
Pub: Comtex
Description: Symantec Corporation acquired VeriSign's identity and authentication business, which includes Secure Sockets Layer (SSL) and Code Signing Certificate Services, the Managed Public Key Infrastructure (MPKI) Services, the VeriSign Trust Seal, the VeriSign Identity Protection (VIP) Authentication Service and the VIP Fraud Protection Service (FDS). The agreement also included a majority stake in VeriSign Japan.

25221 ■ "Tektronix Buys Arbor Networks for Security Business" in *eWeek* (August 9, 2010)
Pub: Ziff Davis Enterprise
Description: Tektronix Communications, provider of communications test and network intelligence solutions will acquire Arbor Networks. The deal will help Tektronix build a brand in security. Details of the transaction are included.

25222 ■ "Today's Business Sale Climate" in *Business Owner* (Vol. 35, September-October 2011, No. 5, pp. 10)
Pub: DL Perkins Company
Description: Despite the weak economy, there is a surplus of individuals wanting to purchase a small business. The Small Business Administration loan guarantees program helps with its loans for purchase/sale of business assistance.

25223 ■ *Ultimate Guide to Buying or Selling Your Business*
Pub: Entrepreneur Press
Ed: Ira N. Nottonson. **Released:** September 2004. **Price:** $24.95 (US), $35.95 (Canadian). **Description:** Proven strategies to evaluate, negotiate, and buy or sell a small business. Franchise and family business succession planning is included.

25224 ■ "Unexpected Guest" in *Business Journal-Milwaukee* (Vol. 28, November 19, 2010, No. 7, pp. A1)
Pub: Milwaukee Business Journal
Ed: Rich Rovito. **Description:** Caterpillar has agreed to purchase Bucyrus for $92 per share. The deal, which is subjected to a $200 million termination fee, is expected to close in mid-2011.

25225 ■ "Vista-Based NCV Bought by Canteen Vending" in *North County Times* (October 18, 2011)
Ed: Pat Maio. **Description:** Details of North Carolina-based Canteen Vending Services' acquisition of NCV Refreshment Services, are given.

25226 ■ "Welcome Back" in *Canadian Business* (Vol. 82, April 27, 2009, No. 7, pp. 25)
Pub: Rogers Media
Ed: Sarka Halas. **Description:** Some Canadian companies such as Gennum Corporation have taken advantage of corporate sale-leasebacks to raise money at a time when credit is hard to acquire. Corporate sale-leasebacks allow companies to sell their property assets while remaining as tenants of the building. Sale-leasebacks allow firms to increase capital while avoiding the disruptions that may result with moving.

25227 ■ "With New Listings, Business Brokers See Hope" in *Business Courier* (Vol. 27, September 3, 2010, No. 18, pp. 1)
Pub: Business Courier
Ed: Lucy May. **Description:** Business brokers in Cincinnati, Ohio are expecting better prices in view of the strengthening economy.

25228 ■ "Your Turn in the Spotlight" in *Inc.* (March 2008, pp. 30)
Pub: Gruner & Jahr USA Publishing
Ed: Elaine Appleton Grant. **Description:** Profile of a Tennessee business that produces events and concerts. The company offers a complete package of services handling staging, lighting, video, musical instrument rentals, and audio support. The founder has decided to sell the business and details of the asking price, price rationale, the pros and cons of buying the firm and its bottom line are examined.

TRADE PERIODICALS

25229 ■ *Venture Capital Journal*
Pub: Venture Economics Inc.
Contact: Kathleen Devlin, Editor-in-Chief
E-mail: Lawrence.Aragon@thomson.com
Released: Monthly. **Price:** $960, U.S. first year; $1650, elsewhere for combination of print and online edition. **Description:** Hard news, analysis and data on the North American private equity market.

VIDEOCASSETTES/ AUDIOCASSETTES

25230 ■ *How to Buy a Good Business with No Cash*
Cambridge Educational
c/o Films Media Group
132 West 31st Street, 17th Floor
Ste. 124
New York, NY 10001

Free: 800-257-5126
Fax:(609)671-0266
Co. E-mail: custserve@films.com
URL: http://www.cambridgeol.com
Released: 1987. **Price:** $39.95. **Description:** Successful venture capitalist Lionel Haines shows how someone can purchase a business without any cash. **Availability:** VHS; 3/4U.

25231 ■ *New or Used? Buying a Firm or Starting Your Own*
Instructional Video
2219 C St.
Lincoln, NE 68502
Ph:(402)475-6570
Free: 800-228-0164
Fax:(402)475-6500
Co. E-mail: feedback@insvideo.com
URL: http://www.insvideo.com
Price: $99.00. **Description:** Details the different options open to anyone wanting to start or obtain their own business. Discusses the various factors to be considered when putting a value on a company, negotiating price and terms, and closing the deal. **Availability:** VHS.

25232 ■ *Understanding Business Valuation*
Chesney Communications
2302 Martin St., Ste. 125
Irvine, CA 92612
Ph:(949)263-5500
Free: 800-223-8878
Fax:(949)263-5506
Co. E-mail: videocc@aol.com
URL: http://www.videocc.com
Released: 1987. **Description:** A look for the small businessman at how to plan the future of his company-growth, reinvestment and possible sale. **Availability:** VHS; 3/4U.

CONSULTANTS

25233 ■ BPT Consulting Associates Ltd.
12 Parmenter Rd., Ste. B-6
Londonderry, NH 03053
Ph:(603)437-8484
Free: 888-278-0030
Fax:(603)434-5388
Co. E-mail: bptcons@tiac.net
Contact: John Kuczynski, President
E-mail: bptcons@tiac.net
Scope: Provides management consulting expertise and resources to cross-industry clients with services for: Business Management consulting, People/Human Resources Transition and Training programs, and a full cadre of multi-disciplined Technology Computer experts. Virtual consultants with expertise in e-commerce, supply chain management, organizational development, and business application development consulting.

25234 ■ Business Team
1901 S Bascom Ave., Ste. 400
Campbell, CA 95008
Ph:(408)246-1102
Fax:(408)246-2219
Co. E-mail: sanjose@business-team.com
URL: http://www.business-team.com
Contact: William L. Kramer, Vice President
E-mail: mani@atsbusiness-team.com
Scope: Business consulting services offered to companies looking for buyers. Specializes in mergers and acquisitions, business brokerage, and valuations. **Seminars:** Business Valuation Enhancing the Value of Your Company.

25235 ■ Country Squire Inc.
10400 Griffin Rd., Ste. 303B
Fort Lauderdale, FL 33328
Ph:(954)434-0200
Free: 800-887-4867
Fax:(954)434-0200
Co. E-mail: mike@thelandpro.com
URL: http://www.thelandpro.com
Contact: Edward K. Gould, Principle
E-mail: mike@thelandpro.com
Scope: Provides real estate service. Offers services in locating, pricing, and purchasing of real property as well as representation of both buyers and/or sellers in real estate transactions and the negotiation of sales or acquisitions of businesses. **Seminars:** Competitor Intelligence: How to Get It/How to Use It.

25236 ■ Equity Partners of America Ltd.
1450 W Long Lake Rd., Ste. 340
Troy, MI 48098-6351
Ph:(248)952-0300
Fax:(248)952-0314
Co. E-mail: equitypartners@email.msn.com
Contact: Albert A. Koch, Managing Director
Scope: Private investment bank specializing in debt and equity capital procurement; buying and selling businesses; shareholder value enhancement strategies; and litigation and alternative dispute resolution assistance; including expert witness assistance. Serves manufacturing, distribution and service industries. **Seminars:** Preparation of a business plan; Use of financial statements in damage claims; Determining the value of a business; When to sell a family business.

25237 ■ Hampton Group
7172 Regional St., Ste. 290
Dublin, CA 94568
Ph:(925)830-3447
Free: 800-820-6424
Fax:(925)831-8194
Co. E-mail: dataforpeter@hotmail.com
Contact: Peter Siegel, Owner
E-mail: dataforpeter@hotmail.com
Scope: Consults on the buying and selling of small and medium-sized businesses.

25238 ■ Harvey C. Skoog
7151 E Addis Ave.
Prescott Valley, AZ 86314
Ph:(928)772-1448
Co. E-mail: hskoog@pvaz.net
E-mail: hskoog@pvaz.net
Scope: Firm has expertise in taxes, payroll, financial planning, budgeting, buy/sell planning, business start-up, fraud detection, troubled business consulting, acquisition, and marketing. Serves the manufacturing, construction, and retailing industries in Arizona.

25239 ■ Pundmann & Company Inc.
PO Box 446
Saint Charles, MO 63302
Ph:(636)940-1111
Fax:(636)925-0000
Co. E-mail: pundmann@aol.com
URL: http://www.pundmann.com
Contact: William R. Pundmann, President
E-mail: will@pundmann.com
Scope: Merchant banking firm providing advice to companies concerning mergers and acquisitions, private financing and business strategy. Offers clients expert assistance in a wide range of financial activities, such as asset redeployments, private placements, recapitalizations, strategic financial counseling and venture capital investments. Also provides in-house venture capital to clients. Industries served: general.

25240 ■ Thomson Venture Economics Inc.
395 Hudson St., Ste. 3
New York, NY 10014
Ph:(212)807-5000
Free: 888-989-8373
Fax:(212)807-5122
Contact: Adam Reinebach, Vice President
E-mail: adam.reinebach@atstfn.com
Scope: Venture capital and business development specialists providing customized research for industrial and financial corporations. Services include: identification of high-potential companies for investment, alliance or acquisition; assistance in establishing venture capital or strategic alliance programs; and assistance with specific acquisition searches. Services for institutional investors in venture capital include: Basic education and due diligence evaluation of venture capital as an investment; development of venture capital investment strategy; and identification of investment opportunities, portfolio monitoring, analysis, performance; and benchmarking for the venture capital asset class. Serves private industries as well as government agencies. **Seminars:** Performance Monitoring Workshop.

Compensation

ASSOCIATIONS AND OTHER ORGANIZATIONS

25241 ■ Council on Employee Benefits
1311 King St.
Alexandria, VA 22314
Ph:(703)549-6025
Fax:(703)549-6027
Co. E-mail: scanfield@ceb.org
URL: http://www.ceb.org
Contact: Shane Canfield, Exec. Dir.
Description: Employers seeking informal exchange of experiences and information on the design, financing, and administration of employee benefit programs, both domestic and international. Provides a medium for the exchange of ideas, information, and statistics; sponsors or conducts research projects on benefits; makes known its views on legislative matters affecting employee benefits. Conducts research. .

25242 ■ Employee Benefit Research Institute
1100 13th St. NW, Ste. 878
Washington, DC 20005-4058
Ph:(202)659-0670
Fax:(202)775-6312
Co. E-mail: info@ebri.org
URL: http://www.ebri.org
Contact: Dallas L. Salisbury, Pres./CEO
Description: Corporations, consulting firms, banks, insurance companies, unions, and others with an interest in the future of employee benefit programs. Purpose is to contribute to the development of effective and responsible public policy in the field of employee benefits through research, publications, educational programs, seminars, and direct communication. Sponsors a broad range of studies on retirement income, health, disability, and other benefit programs; disseminates study results. Maintains research library with information on employee benefit programs. **Publications:** *EBRI Databook on Employee Benefits* (periodic); *EBRI Issue Brief* (monthly); *EBRI Notes* (monthly); *EBRI Pension Investment Report* (periodic); *Washington Bulletin* (biweekly).

25243 ■ Employers Council on Flexible Compensation
927 15th St. NW, Ste. 1000
Washington, DC 20005
Ph:(202)659-4300
Fax:877-747-3539
Co. E-mail: david@ecfc.org
URL: http://www.ecfc.org
Contact: Mr. Dennis Triplett, Chm.
Description: Represents employers and service providers who have implemented or are interested in flexible compensation plans allowing employees to choose from a variety of benefits packages. Promotes flexible compensation plans including cafeteria plans, health reimbursement arrangements, cash-or-deferred plans and other defined contribution plans. Monitors legislation and represents members' interests before Congress. Lobbies to preserve and simplify the flexible compensation provisions of the Internal Revenue Code. .

25244 ■ International Foundation of Employee Benefit Plans
PO Box 69
Brookfield, WI 53008-0069
Ph:(262)786-6700
Free: 888-334-3327
Fax:(262)786-8670
Co. E-mail: membership@ifebp.org
URL: http://www.ifebp.org
Contact: John J. Simmons, Pres./Chm.
Description: Provides sources for employee benefits and compensation information and education, including seminars and conferences, books and an information center, CEBS and Certificate Series. Conducts more than 100 educational programs. Provides Internet job and resume posting service. **Publications:** *Benefits & Compensation Digest* (monthly).

25245 ■ UWC: Strategic Services on Unemployment and Workers' Compensation
910 17th St. NW, Ste. 315
Washington, DC 20006
Ph:(202)223-8902
Fax:(202)783-1616
Co. E-mail: info@uwcstrategy.org
URL: http://www.uwcstrategy.org
Contact: Douglas J. Holmes, Pres.
Description: Works to serve the business community by promoting Unemployment Insurance (UI) and Workers' Compensation (WC) programs that provide fair benefits to workers at affordable cost to employers and the community. **Publications:** *Highlights of State Unemployment Compensation Laws* (annual).

25246 ■ WorldatWork
14040 N Northsight Blvd.
Scottsdale, AZ 85260
Ph:(480)951-9191
Free: 877-951-9191
Fax:(480)483-8352
Co. E-mail: customerrelations@worldatwork.org
URL: http://www.worldatwork.org
Contact: David Smith CCP, Chm.
Description: Dedicated to knowledge leadership in compensation, benefits and total rewards, focusing on disciplines associated with attracting, retaining and motivating employees. Offers CCP, CBP and GRP certification and education programs, conducts surveys, research and provides networking opportunities. **Publications:** *Salary Budget Survey*; *Workspan Global* (monthly); *WorldatWork Journal* (quarterly).

REFERENCE WORKS

25247 ■ "Both Eyes on the Prize" in *Canadian Business* (Vol. 83, September 14, 2010, No. 15, pp. 42)
Pub: Rogers Media Ltd.
Ed: Jacqueline Nelson. **Description:** North American executive compensation has fundamentally shifted partly due to pressure from the US government and recent adjustments in the way CEO pay packages are structured. The changes have also become common practice in Canada and helped in scrutinizing the executive pay.

25248 ■ "CEOs With Headsets" in *Harvard Business Review* (Vol. 88, September 2010, No. 9, pp. 21)
Pub: Harvard Business School Publishing
Ed: Andrew Zimbalist. **Description:** Placing a salary cap on college coaches' compensation would not significantly affect coaching quality or an institution's ability to obtain talent. A salary growth rate comparison between coaches, university presidents, and full professors for the period 1986 to 2007 is also presented.

25249 ■ "Fairness First" in *Canadian Business* (Vol. 80, April 23, 2007, No. 9, pp. 45)
Pub: Rogers Media
Ed: Erin Pooley. **Description:** The need for the fair treatment of employees from the perspective of employee compensation is discussed.

25250 ■ "How Much is Too Much?" in *Canadian Business* (Vol. 79, July 17, 2006, No. 14-15, pp. 55)
Pub: Rogers Media
Ed: John Gray. **Description:** Elucidates the emphasis on the need for companies to analyze the executive pay packages designed by compensation consultants.

25251 ■ "Is Raising CPP Premiums a Good Idea?" in *Canadian Business* (Vol. 83, July 20, 2010, No. 11-12, pp. 37)
Pub: Rogers Media Ltd.
Description: Big labor is pushing for an increase in Canada Pension Plan premiums but pension consultants believe this system is not broken and that the government needs to focus on addressing the low rate of personal retirement savings. If the premiums go up, even those with high savings will be forced to pay more and it could block other plans that really address the real issue.

25252 ■ "Labor Compensation and Collective Bargaining Data" in *Montly Labor Review* (Vol. 133, September 2010, No. 9, pp. 116)
Pub: Bureau of Labor Statistics
Description: Employment cost index is presented, citing compensation by occupation and industry group.

25253 ■ "Mismanaging Pay and Performance" in *Business Strategy Review* (Vol. 21, Summer 2010, No. 2, pp. 54)
Pub: Wiley-Blackwell
Ed: Rupert Merson. **Description:** Understanding the relationship between performance measurement and desired behaviors is an important element of a company's talent management.

25254 ■ "New Work Order" in *Black Enterprise* (Vol. 38, March 2008, No. 8, pp. 60)
Pub: Earl G. Graves Publishing Co. Inc.
Description: Today's management challenges includes issues of more competition, globalization, outsourcing and technological advances. Suggestions to help create progressive leadership in small business that sustains a competitive edge are listed.

25255 ■ "Notes on Current Labor Statistics" in *Montly Labor Review* (Vol. 133, September 2010, No. 9, pp. 75)
Pub: Bureau of Labor Statistics

Description: Principal statistics and calculated by the Bureau of Labor Statistics are presented. The series includes statistics on labor force; employment; unemployment; labor compensation; consumer, producer, and international prices; productivity; international comparisons; and injury and illness statistics.

25256 ■ "Pay Fell for Many Local Execs in '09" in *Baltimore Business Journal* (Vol. 28, July 2, 2010, No. 8, pp. 1)
Pub: Baltimore Business Journal

Ed: Gary Haber. **Description:** Compensation for the 100 highest-paid executives in the Baltimore, Maryland area decreased in 2009, compared with 2008. At least $1 million were received by 59 out of 100 executives in 2009, while 75 earned the said amount in 2008. Factors that contributed to the executives' decisions to take pay cuts are discussed.

25257 ■ "Productivity Data" in *Montly Labor Review* (Vol. 133, September 2010, No. 9, pp. 137)
Pub: Bureau of Labor Statistics

Description: Productivity data is presented through indexes of productivity, hourly compensation and unit costs in 2007.

25258 ■ "Small Business Compensation" in *Small Business Economic Trends* (July 2010, pp. 10)
Pub: National Federation of Independent Business

Description: A graph from a survey of small businesses in the U.S. is given representing small business compensation from January 1986 to June 2010. Tables showing actual compensation changes and compensation plans are also presented. A graph comparing small business prices and labor compensation is supplied.

TRADE PERIODICALS

25259 ■ *Benefits & Compensation Digest–Benefits and Compensation Digest*
Pub: International Foundation of Employee Benefit Plans
Contact: Lauri Ludwig
E-mail: ronaellec@ifebp.org

Released: Monthly. **Price:** $100. **Description:** Covers the field of employee benefits. Recurring features include notices of publications and educational opportunities, news and announcements for members, and a review of current literature. Formerly *Employee Benefits Digest*.

25260 ■ *BNA Pension & Benefits Reporter*
Pub: Bureau of National Affairs Inc.
Contact: D. Sayre

Ed: David A. Sayre, Editor. **Price:** $1811, individual; online two users $2730. **Description:** Covers pension developments stemming from the passage of the Employee Retirement Income Security Act of 1974 (ERISA) and its amendments. Discusses pension and welfare benefit regulations, standards, enforcement actions, court decisions, legislative and administrative actions, agency options, and employee benefit trust fund requirements.

25261 ■ *EBRI Issue Brief*
Pub: Employee Benefit Research Institute
Contact: Steve Blakely
E-mail: blakely@ebri.org

Ed: Dallas Salisbury, Editor, salisbury@ebri.org. **Released:** Monthly. **Price:** Included in membership; $224, nonmembers; $25, single issue. **Description:** Examines, analyzes, and interprets key issues and trends in the employee benefits field. Covers one topic in-depth in each issue. Remarks: Price includes subscription to the newsletter Employee Benefit Notes.

25262 ■ *EBRI Notes*
Pub: Employee Benefit Research Institute
Contact: Martha Bobbino, Dir. Library Resources
E-mail: blakely@ebri.org

Ed: Dallas Salisbury, Editor, salisbury@ebri.org. **Released:** Monthly. **Price:** Included in membership; $199, nonmembers. **Description:** "Analyzes and discusses newly released employee benefits data and reviews a wide range of policy issues, research and publications." Recurring features include news of research, legal analysis, legislative updates. Remarks: Subscription includes EBRI Issue Brief.

25263 ■ *Employee Benefits Cases*
Pub: Bureau of National Affairs Inc.
Contact: David A. Sayre, Managing Editor

Released: Weekly, 50/year. **Price:** $1,141. **Description:** Reports full text of federal and state court opinions and selected decisions of arbitrators and the National Labor Relations Board on employee benefits issues. Recurring features include a cumulative index digest, tables of cases, a topical index, and a classification guide.

25264 ■ *Employee Benefits Review*
Pub: S. Harman & Associates Inc.

Ed: Saundra K. Harman, Editor. **Released:** Monthly, 12/year. **Description:** Covers labor, personnel, and technical issues in the federal personnel area. Lists upcoming conferences, workshops, and training seminars. Remarks: Also available via e-mail.

25265 ■ *Legal-Legislative Reporter*
Pub: International Foundation of Employee Benefit Plans
Contact: Mary Jo Brzezinski

Ed: Harry W. Burton, Editor. **Released:** Monthly. **Price:** $110 as part of publication package. **Description:** Presents news of court and legislative actions pertinent to employee benefit plans.

25266 ■ *Retirement Plans Report*
Pub: Western League of Savings Institutions

Ed: Gloria Sewell-Hacko, Editor. **Released:** Quarterly. **Description:** Reports on tax reform laws affecting retirement plan benefits. Covers IRAs (Individual Retirement Accounts) as well as the Basic Plan. Includes a question-and-answer column.

25267 ■ *Wages and Hours*
Pub: Bureau of National Affairs Inc.
Contact: Nancy J. Sedmak, Managing Editor

Released: Weekly. **Price:** $611. **Description:** Provides a guide to compliance with federal and state regulation of wages, hours, and child labor. Covers such topics as hours of work; minimum wage and overtime pay; equal pay; notice posting, reporting, and recordkeeping; enforcement and administration; exemptions; home work rules; public contracts; and industry and occupation checklists. Part of the BNA Policy and Practice Series, Wages and Hours can be purchased separately or in any combination with other binder publications entitled Compensation, Fair Employment Practices, Labor Relations, or Personnel Management.

25268 ■ *Work Span*
Pub: WorldatWork

Ed: Jean Christ-Offerson, Editor, jchristofferson@worldatwork.org. **Released:** 10/year. **Description:** Concentrates on issues in the fields of compensation and benefits and human resource management. Includes legislative updates, resources, and case studies.

CONSULTANTS

25269 ■ The Epler Co.
450 B St., Ste. 750
San Diego, CA 92101
Ph:(619)239-0831
Fax:(619)239-0807
Co. E-mail: consultants@eplercompany.com
URL: http://www.eplercompany.com
Contact: Barbara Craven, Principal
E-mail: bcraven@atseplercompany.com

Scope: Offers actuarial and consulting services for employee benefits specializing in retirement plans, health, life, accidental death and dismemberment, long-term disability insurance plans, and executive compensation. Administers retiree health studies, AB1200 studies for schools, and merger studies on benefits. Conducts base pay, bonus and benefit surveys. Designs total compensation programs.

25270 ■ Fox Lawson & Associates L.L.C.
1335 County Road D, Cir. E
Saint Paul, MN 55109-5260
Ph:(651)635-0976
Free: 800-383-0976
Fax:(651)635-0980
Co. E-mail: jfox@foxlawson.com
URL: http://www.foxlawson.com
Contact: Chelsea Christie, Principle
E-mail: jfox@atsfoxlawson.com

Scope: A compensation and human resources consulting firm, provides services to businesses of all sizes including finance, manufacturing, high tech, software development, food, retail, wholesale trade, communications, transportation, service, not-for-profit and education. **Seminars:** Compensation Strategies - Not Having a Plan Could Break the Bank.

25271 ■ Harvey C. Skoog
7151 E Addis Ave.
Prescott Valley, AZ 86314
Ph:(928)772-1448
Co. E-mail: hskoog@pvaz.net
E-mail: hskoog@pvaz.net

Scope: Firm has expertise in taxes, payroll, financial planning, budgeting, buy/sell planning, business start-up, fraud detection, troubled business consulting, acquisition, and marketing. Serves the manufacturing, construction, and retailing industries in Arizona.

25272 ■ Kevin L. Pohle P.L.L.C.
5820 Main St., Ste. 316-317
Williamsville, NY 14221
Ph:(716)565-0565
Fax:(716)568-8384
Co. E-mail: klpohle@pohlecpa.com
URL: http://www.pohlecpa.com
Contact: Kevin L. Pohle, President
E-mail: klpohle@pohlecpa.com

Scope: Offers tax planning, preparation and representation services, investigative accounting and compliance and other management consulting services. Serves small local manufacturing and service companies, individual accounts, non-profit agencies as well as large, publicly held companies.

COMPUTERIZED DATABASES

25273 ■ *Compensation Planning Journal*
The Bureau of National Affairs Inc.
1801 S Bell St.
Arlington, VA 22202
Free: 800-372-1033
Co. E-mail: customercare@bna.com
URL: http://www.bna.com/tax-accounting-t5000

Description: Reviews news developments which affect tax planning in major areas of specialized tax practice. Includes professional practitioners' commentary as well as reviews of actual or model benefit plans. Provides information on compensation related matters in Congress, the U.S. Treasury, Internal Revenue Service (IRS), the U.S. Labor Department, and the Pension Benefit Guaranty Corporation (PBGC). **Availability:** Online: The Bureau of National Affairs Inc. **Type:** Full text.

25274 ■ *LexisNexis Personal Injury NetLetter*
LexisNexis Canada Inc.
123 Commerce Valley Dr. E, Ste. 700
Markham, ON, Canada L3T 7W8
Ph:(905)479-2665
Free: 800-668-6481
Co. E-mail: service@lexisnexis.ca
URL: http://www.lexisnexis.ca

Description: Provides access to the newsletter by Professor Gerald Robertson, University of Alberta. **Availability:** Online: LexisNexis Canada Inc. **Type:** Full text.

25275 ■ *Pension & Benefits Reporter*
The Bureau of National Affairs Inc.
1801 S Bell St.
Arlington, VA 22202
Free: 800-372-1033
Co. E-mail: customercare@bna.com
URL: http://www.bna.com
Description: Contains up-to-date reporting and coverage of state and federal legislative, regulatory, and judicial activities related to pensions and benefits. Includes coverage of IRS and Labor Department regulations and enforcement issues, tax legislation, health care reform, and developments within industry. Includes taxation of benefits, individual retirement accounts, and fringe benefits. **Availability:** Online: Thomson Reuters, The Bureau of National Affairs Inc. **Type:** Full text.

25276 ■ *State Health Care Regulatory Developments*
The Bureau of National Affairs Inc.
1801 S Bell St.
Arlington, VA 22202
Free: 800-372-1033
Co. E-mail: customercare@bna.com
URL: http://www.bna.com
Description: Contains information on health care regulatory news and developments in the United States. Subjects include community-based care, home care, emergency care, infectious diseases, managed care, insurance, laboratories, Medicaid, mental health, medical waste, nursing homes, pharmaceuticals, physician services, professional licensing, provider relationships, worker protection and compensation. Entries are organized by state, topic, and register citation. **Availability:** Online: The Bureau of National Affairs Inc., Thomson Reuters. **Type:** Full text.

LIBRARIES

25277 ■ Towers Watson Information Centre
1100 Melville St., Ste. 1600
Vancouver, BC, Canada V6E 4A6
Ph:(604)691-1000
Fax:(604)691-1062
URL: http://www.towerswatson.com/
Scope: Actuarial science, employee benefits, compensation, human resources. **Holdings:** Figures not available.

START-UP INFORMATION

25278 ■ *The Art of the Start: The Time-Tested, Battle-Hardened Guide for Anyone Starting Anything*
Pub: Penguin Books (USA) Incorporated
Ed: Guy Kawasaki **Released:** September 2004. **Price:** $26.95. **Description:** Advice for someone starting a new business covering topics such as hiring employees, building a brand, business competition, and management.

25279 ■ *Small Business Survival Guide*
Pub: Adams Media Corporation
Ed: Cliff Ennico. **Price:** $12.95. **Description:** Small business expert provides strategies to start a company and survive in the 21st Century. He shows small business owners how to succeed despite challenges that can defeat any firm. His advice covers suppliers; customers and contractors; competitors and creditors; spouses, family and friends; as well as the ways lawyers, accountants and other can steal an entrepreneur's success. Ennico also describes how startups can comply with local regulations.

REFERENCE WORKS

25280 ■ "3Par: Storing Up Value" in *Barron's* (Vol. 90, August 30, 2010, No. 35, pp. 30)
Pub: Barron's Editorial & Corporate Headquarters
Ed: Mark Veverka. **Description:** Dell and Hewlett Packard are both bidding for data storage company 3Par. The acquisition would help Dell and Hewlett Packard provide customers with a one-stop shop as customers move to a private cloud in the Internet.

25281 ■ "13D Filings: Investors Report to the SEC" in *Barron's* (Vol. 88, March 31, 2008, No. 13, pp. M10)
Pub: Dow Jones & Company, Inc.
Description: Obrem Capital Management wants Micrel to rescind Micrel's shareholder-rights plan and to boost its board to six members from five. Patricia L. Childress plans to nominate herself to the board of Sierra Bancorp, and Luther King Capital Management may consider a competing acquisition proposal for Industrial Distribution Group.

25282 ■ "The 490 Made Chevy a Bargain Player" in *Automotive News* (Vol. 86, October 31, 2011, No. 6488, pp. S22)
Pub: Crain Communications Inc.
Ed: David Phillips. **Description:** The first Chevrolet with the 490 engine was sold in 1913, but it was too expensive for masses. In 1914 the carmaker launched a lower-priced H-series of cars competitively priced. Nameplates such as Corvette, Bel Air, Camaro and Silverado have defined Chevrolet through the years.

25283 ■ "2007 Fittest CEOs" in *Hawaii Business* (Vol. 53, October 2007, No. 4, pp. 40)
Pub: Hawaii Business Publishing
Description: Discusses the outcome of the fittest chief executive officers in Hawaii competition for 2007. Hawaii Capital Management's David Low leads the list while Group Pacific (Hawaii) Inc.'s Chip Doyle and Greater Good Inc.'s Kari Leong placed second and third, respectively. The CEO's routines, eating habits, and inspirations for staying fit are provided.

25284 ■ "A&E Networks" in *Brandweek* (Vol. 49, April 21, 2008, No. 16, pp. SR9)
Pub: VNU Business Media, Inc.
Ed: Anthony Crupi. **Description:** Provides contact information for sales and marketing personnel for the A&E Networks as well as a listing of the station's top programming and an analysis of the current season and the target audience for those programs running in the current season. A&E has reinvented itself as a premium entertainment brand over the last five years and with its $2.5 million per episode acquisition of The Sopranos, the station signaled that it was serious about getting back into the scripted programming business. The acquisition also helped the network compete against other cable networks and led to a 20 percent increase in prime-time viewers.

25285 ■ "Achieving Sustained Competitive Advantage: A Family Capital Theory" in *Family Business Review* (Vol. 19, June 2006, No. 2, pp. 135)
Pub: Family Firm Institute Inc.
Ed: James Hoffman, Mark Hoelscher, Ritch Sorenson. **Description:** Impact of capital assets on performance of family businesses is discussed.

25286 ■ "After Price Cuts, Competition GPS Makers Lose Direction" in *Brandweek* (Vol. 49, April 21, 2008, No. 16, pp. 16)
Pub: VNU Business Media, Inc.
Ed: Steve Miller. **Description:** Garmin and TomTom, two of the leaders in portable navigation devices, have seen lowering revenues due to dramatic price cuts and unexpected competition from the broadening availability of personal navigation on mobile phones. TomTom has trimmed its sales outlook for its first quarter while Garmin's stock dropped 40 percent since February.

25287 ■ "The AHA Moment" in *Hispanic Business* (December 2010)
Pub: Hispanic Business
Ed: Rebecca Vallaneda. **Description:** An interview with Gisela Girard on how competitive market conditions push buttons. Girard stepped down from her 18-month position as chairwoman the Association of Hispanic Advertising Agencies. She has more than 20 years of experience in advertising and research marketing.

25288 ■ "Airlines Mount PR Push to Win Public Support Against Big Oil" in *Advertising Age* (Vol. 79, July 14, 2008, No. 7, pp. 1)
Pub: Crain Communications, Inc.
Ed: Michael Bush. **Description:** Top airline executives from competing companies have banded together in a public relations plan in which they are sending e-mails to their frequent fliers asking for aid in lobbying legislators to put a restriction on oil speculation.

25289 ■ "All For One, None for All?" in *Canadian Business* (Vol. 83, October 12, 2010, No. 17, pp. 60)
Pub: Rogers Media Ltd.
Ed: Michael McCullogh. **Description:** The effect of the growth of Canada's overseas provincial trade offices on Canadian trade is discussed. Economic development commissions in the country have devised a single 'Consider Canada' campaign to pitch foreign investors. It is hoped that large cities will gain from banding together rather than competing against one another.

25290 ■ "All Options Open On Chrysler: Magna" in *Globe & Mail* (February 28, 2007, pp. B3)
Pub: CTVglobemedia Publishing Inc.
Ed: Greg Keenan. **Description:** The 65 percent drop in the profits of Magna International Inc. and the plans of its chief executive officer Don Walker to make the company more competitive are discussed.

25291 ■ *Alpha Dogs: How Your Small Business Can Become a Leader of the Pack*
Pub: HarperInformation
Ed: Donna Fenn. **Released:** May 2007. **Price:** $14. 95. **Description:** Ways for an entrepreneur to outsmart competitors in the marketplace, to generate higher sales, and earn lasting customer and employee loyalty.

25292 ■ "American Chemistry Council Launches Flagship Blog" in *Ecology,Environment & Conservation Business* (October 29, 2011, pp. 5)
Pub: HighBeam Research
Description: American Chemistry Council (ACC) launched its blog, American Chemistry Matters, where interactive space allows bloggers to respond to news coverage and to discuss policy issues and their impact on innovation, competitiveness, job creation and safety.

25293 ■ "The Anatomy of a High Potential" in *Business Strategy Review* (Vol. 21, Autumn 2010, No. 3, pp. 52)
Pub: Wiley-Blackwell
Ed: Doug Ready, Jay Conger, Linda Hill, Emily Stecker. **Description:** Companies have long been interested in identifying high-potential employees, but few firms know how to convert top talent into game changers - people who can shape the future of the business. The authors have found the x-factors that can make the high-potential list into a strong competitive advantage.

25294 ■ "Anytime Access" in *Crain's Cleveland Business* (Vol. 28, October 22, 2007, No. 42, pp. 17)
Pub: Crain Communications, Inc.
Ed: Brad Dicken. **Description:** Technology continues to evolve in the competitive world of mobile communications in which the phone has become a sleek multitool that can take a call, send and e-mail, calculate the tip after dinner and snap a photograph.

25295 ■ "Are Movie Theaters Doomed?" in *Business Horizons* (November-December 2007, pp. 491)
Pub: Elsevier Technology Publications
Ed: Jon Silver, John McDonnell. **Description:** Theater operators must embrace new technologies and more diverse target markets if they are to stem the decline in theatergoers. Movie theaters remain highly vulnerable to trends in the home entertainment industry.

25296 ■ "As Technology Changes, So Must African American Business" in *Black Enterprise* (Vol. 41, August 2010, No. 1, pp. 61)
Pub: Earl G. Graves Publishing Co. Inc.
Ed: Sonya A. Donaldson. **Description:** Social media is essential to compete in today's business environment, especially for African American firms.

25297 ■ "At the Drugstore, the Nurse Will See You Now" in *Globe & Mail* (April 13, 2007, pp. B1)
Pub: CTVglobemedia Publishing Inc.
Ed: Marina Strauss. **Description:** The appointment of several health professionals including nurse, podiatrists, etc. by Rexall Co. at its drugstores to face competition from rivals, is discussed.

25298 ■ "Awaiting a Call from Deutsche Telekom" in *Barron's* (Vol. 90, September 6, 2010, No. 36, pp. M5)
Pub: Barron's Editorial & Corporate Headquarters
Ed: Vito J. Racanelli. **Description:** Deutsche Telekom's (DT) T-Mobile USA Unit has settled in the number four position in the market and the parent company will need to decide if it will hold onto the company in the next 12-18 months from September 2010. T-Mobile's rivals will make critical improvements during this time and DT has the option to upgrade T-Mobile at the cost of improvements to its other units.

25299 ■ *Balls!: 6 Rules for Winning Today's Business Game*
Pub: John Wiley & Sons, Incorporated
Ed: Alexi Venneri. **Released:** January 2005. **Price:** $29.95. **Description:** In order to be successful business leaders must be brave, authentic, loud, lovable, and spunky and they need to lead their competition.

25300 ■ "Bark and Bite" in *Canadian Business* (Vol. 81, March 31, 2008, No. 5, pp. 20)
Pub: Rogers Media
Ed: Rachel Pulfer. **Description:** Hillary Clinton and Barack Obama both want to renegotiate NAFTA but the most job losses in the American manufacturing industry is caused by technological change and Asian competition than with NAFTA. The risk of protectionist trade policies has increased given the political atmosphere.

25301 ■ "BASF Launches $4.9 Billion Bid for Rival Engelhard" in *Globe & Mail* (January 4, 2006, pp. B7)
Pub: CTVglobemedia Publishing Inc.
Ed: Mike Esterl; Steve Levine. **Description:** The plans of BASF AG, to acquire Engelhard Corp. for $4.9 billion, are presented.

25302 ■ "Battle of the Titans" in *Canadian Business* (Vol. 81, March 17, 2008, No. 4, pp. 15)
Pub: Rogers Media
Ed: Rachel Pulfer. **Description:** Regulatory authorities in Canada gave Thomson Corp and Reuters Group PLC the permission to go ahead with their merger. The merged companies could eclipse Bloomberg LP's market share of 33 percent. Authorities also required Thomson and Reuters to sell some of their databases to competitors.

25303 ■ *Battling Big Box: How Nimble Niche Companies Can Outmaneuver Giant Companies*
Pub: Career Press, Inc.
Ed: Henry Dubroff, Susan J. Marks. **Released:** January 1, 2009. **Price:** $15.99. **Description:** Small companies can compete with larger firms through agility, adaptability, customer service, and credibility. Topics include information to help empower employees, build a powerful brand, manage cash flow, and maintaining a business vision.

25304 ■ *Be a Brilliant Business Writer: Write Well, Write Fast, and Whip the Competition*
Pub: Crown Business Books
Ed: Jane Curry, Diana Young. **Released:** October 5, 2010. **Price:** $13.99. **Description:** Tools for mastering the art of persuasive writing in every document created, from email and client letters to reports and presentations, this book will help any writer convey their message with clarity and power, increase productivity by reducing rewrites, and provide the correct tone for navigating office politics.

25305 ■ "Being Big By Design" in *Canadian Business* (Vol. 82, April 27, 2009, No. 7, pp. 39)
Pub: Rogers Media
Ed: Andrew Wahl. **Description:** Gennum expects that its planned acquisition of Tundra Semiconductor will expand its market presence and leverage its research and development better than working alone. The proposed friendly acquisition could challenge Zarlink Semiconductor as the largest Canadian semiconductor firm in terms of revenue. The merger could expand Gennum's addressable market to about $2 billion.

25306 ■ *The Big Switch*
Pub: W. W. Norton & Company, Inc.
Ed: Nicholas Carr. **Released:** January 19, 2009. **Price:** $16.95 paperback. **Description:** Today companies are dismantling private computer systems and tapping into services provided via the Internet. This shift is remaking the computer industry, bringing competitors such as Google to the forefront ant threatening traditional companies like Microsoft and Dell. The book weaves together history, economics, and technology to explain why computing is changing and what it means for the future.

25307 ■ "BK Menu Gives Casual Dining Reason to Worry" in *Advertising Age* (Vol. 79, November 17, 2008, No. 43, pp. 12)
Pub: Crain Communications, Inc.
Ed: Emily Bryson York. **Description:** Burger King is beginning to compete with such casual dining restaurants as Applebees and the Cheesecake Factory with new premium menu items, including thicker burgers and ribs; statistical data regarding the casual dining segment which continues to fall and Burger King, whose sales continue to rise is included.

25308 ■ "Blockbuster Launches Internet Movie Downloads to Compete Against Netflix, Others" in *Chicago Tribune* (December 3, 2008)
Pub: McClatchy-Tribune Information Services
Ed: Eric Benderoff. **Description:** Blockbuster Inc., the DVD rental giant, has launched a new service that delivers movies to their customer's homes via the Internet in an attempt to compete against Netflix and other competitors.

25309 ■ *Blue Ocean Strategy: How to Create Uncontested Market Space and Make Competition Irrelevant*
Pub: Harvard Business School Publishing
Ed: W. Chan Kim. **Released:** January 2005. **Price:** $29.95.

25310 ■ "Blueprint for Profit: Family-Run Lumberyard Sets Sites On Sales of $100 Million a Year" in *Small Business Opportunities* (Jan. 2008)
Pub: Harris Publications Inc.
Ed: Stan Roberts. **Description:** Profile of family-run lumberyard whose owner shares insight into the challenges of competing with big box operations like Home Depot and Lowe's.

25311 ■ "Boston Scientific Makes Formal Offer for Guidant, Possibly Thwarting J&J" in *Globe & Mail* (January 9, 2006, pp. B6)
Pub: CTVglobemedia Publishing Inc.
Ed: Silvia Pagan Westphal; Thomas M. Burton; Dennis Berman. **Description:** The details on Boston Scientific Corp.'s $25 billion bid on Guidant Corp. are presented. The company makes the move to outbid Johnson & Johnson.

25312 ■ "Bring It On" in *Entrepreneur* (Vol. 35, November 2007, No. 11, pp. 52)
Pub: Entrepreneur Media Inc.
Ed: Guy Kawasaki. **Description:** Tips on managing corporate competition in order to drive a company to success are presented.

25313 ■ "Builders, Unions Aim to Cut Costs; Pushing Changes to Regain Share of Residential Market; Seek Council's Help" in *Crain's New York Business*
Pub: Crain Communications, Inc.
Ed: Erik Engquist. **Description:** Union contractors and workers are worried about a decline in their market share for housing so they intend to ask the City Council to impose new safety and benefit standards on all contractors to avoid being undercut by nonunion competitors.

25314 ■ *Building Buzz to Beat the Big Boys*
Pub: Greenwood Publishing Group, Inc.
Ed: Steve O'Leary; Kim Sheehan. **Released:** March 30, 2008. **Price:** $39.95. **Description:** Seventy to eighty percent of small retail stores fail within the first five years of opening due to competition from big-box retailers and online stores. Service providers and small retailers should capitalize on the fact that they are local and can connect on a personal level with customers in a way the big stores cannot. Word of mouth marketing methods are very critical to any small retail or service company. This book is designed to help any small business compete against large competitors.

25315 ■ *Business Warrior: Strategy for Entrepreneurs*
Pub: Clearbridge Publishing
Ed: Sun Tzu. **Released:** September 2006. **Price:** $19.95. **Description:** Advice to help entrepreneurs understand competitive strategies in order to succeed, focusing on sales, marketing, and personnel management.

25316 ■ "Businesses Keep a Watchful Eye on Worker's Comp" in *The Business Journal-Serving Greater Tampa Bay* (September 5, 2008)
Pub: American City Business Journals, Inc.
Ed: Jane Meinhardt. **Description:** Pending a ruling from the Florida Supreme Court that could uphold the 2003 changes on workers' compensation law, the outcome would include restrictions on claimant attorneys' fees and allow the competitive workers' compensation insurance rates to remain low. However, insurance rates are expected to go up if the court overturns the changes.

25317 ■ *Busting the Myth of the Heroic CEO*
Pub: Cornell University Press
Ed: Michel Villette, Catherine Vuillermot. **Released:** 2010. **Price:** $24.95. **Description:** According to the authors, corporate leaders do not get ahead through productive risk-taking and innovation, but through ruthless exploitation of market imperfections and rivals.

25318 ■ "Can a Brazilian SUV Take On the Jeep Wrangler?" in *Business Week* (September 22, 2008, No. 4100, pp. 50)
Pub: McGraw-Hill Companies, Inc.
Ed: Helen Walters. **Description:** Profile of the Brazilian company TAC as well as the flourishing Brazilian car market; TAC has launched a new urban vehicle, the Stark, which has won prizes for innovation; the company uses local technology and manufacturing expertise.

25319 ■ "Canadian Research Generates Innovation and Prosperity" in *Canadian Business* (Vol. 81, October 27, 2008, No. 18, pp. 87)
Pub: Rogers Media Ltd.
Description: Universities play a key role in helping Canadians achieve prosperity, competitiveness, and quality of life by conducting more than a third of

Canada's research. Research in universities help train graduates to apply sophisticated knowledge to real problems.

25320 ■ "Capital Position" in *Business Journal-Milwaukee* (Vol. 28, December 24, 2010, No. 12, pp. A1)
Pub: Milwaukee Business Journal
Ed: Rich Kirchen. **Description:** Canada-based BMO Financial Group has purchased Marshall and Isley Corporation (M and I), which dominated lending among Wisconsin businesses for decades. The sale of M and I will enable other banks to recruit M and I's customers but BMO Financial remains a stronger competitor since it possesses a more potent capital position.

25321 ■ "Car Trouble" in *Canadian Business* (Vol. 80, October 22, 2007, No. 21, pp. 27)
Pub: Rogers Media
Ed: Thomas Watson. **Description:** Contract between General Motors Corporation and the United Auto Workers Union has created a competitive arm for the U.S. Big Three automakers. Data on the market and production data of car companies are presented.

25322 ■ "CarTango Lauches Site for Women" in *Marketing to Women* (Vol. 21, April 2008, No. 4, pp. 5)
Pub: EPM Communications, Inc.
Description: CarTango.com is an Internet site that seeks to overcome what women say are dismissive or pushy salespeople by allowing the shoppers the chance to decide what they want before inviting dealers to compete for their business.

25323 ■ "CBC Chief: Future is Now" in *Business Courier* (Vol. 27, August 13, 2010, No. 15, pp. 1)
Pub: Business Courier
Ed: Lucy May. **Description:** Tom Williams, chairman of the Cincinnati Business Committee (CBC), maintains that politicians and business leaders must cooperate to ensure the competitiveness of the city for the 21st Century. Under Williams' leadership, the CBC has put emphasis on initiatives related to government efficiency, economic development, and public education. Williams' views on a proposed inland port are given.

25324 ■ "Challenges Await Quad in Going Public" in *Milwaukee Business Journal* (Vol. 27, January 29, 2010, No. 18, pp. A1)
Pub: American City Business Journals
Ed: Rich Rovito. **Description:** Sussex, Wisconsin-based Quad/Graphics Inc.'s impending acquisition of rival Canadian World Color Press Inc. will transform it into a publicly held entity for the first time. Quad has operated as a private company for nearly 40 years and will need to adjust to changes, such as the way management shares information with Quad/Graphics' employees. Details of the merger are included.

25325 ■ *Change in SMEs: The New European Capitalism*
Pub: Palgrave Macmillan
Ed: Katharina Bluhm; Rudi Schmidt. **Released:** October 2008. **Price:** $95.00. **Description:** Effects of global change on corporate governance, management, competitive strategies and labor relations in small-to-medium sized enterprises in various European countries are discussed.

25326 ■ "Characteristics of Great Salespeople" in *Agency Sales Magazine* (Vol. 39, November 2009, No. 10, pp. 40)
Pub: MANA
Ed: Paul Pease. **Description:** Tips for managers in order to maximize the performance of their sales personnel are presented through several vignettes. Using performance based commission that rewards success, having business systems that support sales activity, and having an organizational culture that embraces sales as a competitive edge are some suggestions.

25327 ■ "Cheese Spread Whips Up a Brand New Bowl" in *Brandweek* (Vol. 49, April 21, 2008, No. 16, pp. 17)
Pub: VNU Business Media, Inc.
Ed: Mike Beirne. **Description:** Mrs. Kinser's Pimento Cheese Spread is launching a new container for its product in order to attempt stronger brand marketing with a better bowl in order to win over the heads of households as young as in their 30s. The company also intends to begin distribution in Texas and the West Coast. Mrs. Kinser's is hoping that the new packaging will provide a more distinct branding and will help consumers distinguish what flavor they are buying.

25328 ■ "Children's Products Maker Not the New Kid on the Block" in *Crain's Cleveland Business* (Vol. 28, November 26, 2007, No. 47, pp. 3)
Pub: Crain Communications, Inc.
Ed: David Bennett. **Description:** Discusses the business model employed by Shamrock Industries Inc., a rising star in the competitive world of children's products; the company, which does business as Foundations Quality Children's Products, has expanded into a 63,000-square-foot distribution center which has boosted its local profile significantly.

25329 ■ "Chinese Solar Panel Manufacturer Scopes Out Austin" in *Austin Business JournalInc.* (Vol. 29, October 30, 2009, No. 34, pp. 1)
Pub: American City Business Journals
Ed: Jacob Dirr. **Description:** China's Yingli Green Energy Holding Company Ltd. is looking for a site in order to construct a $20 million photovoltaic panel plant. Both Austin and San Antonio are vying to house the manufacturing hub. The project could create about 300 jobs and give Austin a chance to become a player in the solar energy market. Other solar companies are also considering Central Texas as an option to set up shop.

25330 ■ "Citadel Hires Three Lehman Execs" in *Chicago Tribune* (October 2, 2008)
Pub: McClatchy-Tribune Information Services
Ed: James P. Miller. **Description:** Citadel Investment Group LLC, Chicago hedge-fund operator, has hired three former senior executives of bankrupt investment banker Lehman Brothers Holding Inc. Citadel believes that the company's hiring spree will help them to further expand the firm's capabilities in the global fixed income business.

25331 ■ "Clash of the Titans" in *Canadian Business* (Vol. 80, March 12, 2007, No. 6, pp. 27)
Pub: Rogers Media
Ed: Andrew Wahl. **Description:** The frequent allegations of Google Inc. and Microsoft Corp. against each other over copyright and other legal issues, with a view to taking away other's market share, is discussed.

25332 ■ "Closures Pop Cork on Wine Bar Sector Consolidation" in *Houston Business Journal* (Vol. 40, January 22, 2010, No. 37, pp. A2)
Pub: American City Business Journals
Ed: Allison Wollam. **Description:** Wine bar market in Houston, Texas is in the midst of a major shift and heads toward further consolidation due to the closure of pioneering wine bars that opened in the past decade. The Corkscrew owner, Andrew Adams, has blamed the creation of competitive establishments to the closure which helped wear out his concept.

25333 ■ "Cloudy Future for VMware?" in *Barron's* (Vol. 90, September 13, 2010, No. 37, pp. 21)
Pub: Barron's Editorial & Corporate Headquarters
Ed: Jonathan R. Laing. **Description:** VMWare dominated the virtualization market for years, but it may be ending as it faces more competition from rivals that offer cloud computing services. The company's stocks are also expensive and are vulnerable to the smallest mishap.

25334 ■ "Coca-Cola Bottler Up for Sale: CEO J. Bruce Llewellyn Seeks Retirement" in *Black Enterprise* (Vol. 37, December 2006, No. 5, pp. 31)
Pub: Earl G. Graves Publishing Co. Inc.
Ed: Marcia A. Wade. **Description:** J. Bruce Llewellyn of Brucephil Inc., the parent company of the Philadelphia Coca-Cola Bottling Co. has agreed to sell its remaining shares to Coca-Cola Co., which previously owned 31 percent of Philly Coke. Analysts believe that Coca-Cola will eventually sell its shares to another bottler.

25335 ■ "Columbia Sale Narrowed To Two Developers" in *The Business Journal-Milwaukee* (Vol. 25, July 18, 2008, No. 43, pp. A1)
Pub: American City Business Journals, Inc.
Ed: Corrinne Hess. **Description:** Officials of Columbia St. Mary's Inc plan to pick one of two real-estate developers who will buy the 8-acre property of the Columbia Hospital which the company will move away from when their new hospital has been constructed. The hospital on Newport Ave. has been on the market since 2001.

25336 ■ "Combat Mission: Rebuffed, BAE Systems Fights Army Contract Decision" in *Business Courier* (Vol. 26, September 25, 2009)
Pub: American City Business Journals, Inc.
Ed: Jon Newberry. **Description:** BAE Systems filed a complaint with the US Government Accountability Office after the US Army issued an order to BAE's competitor for armoured trucks which is potentially worth over $3 billion. Hundreds of jobs in Butler County, Ohio hinge on the success of the contract protest.

25337 ■ "Companies Urged to Take Steps to Replenish Work Force" in *Crain's Cleveland Business* (Vol. 28, October 29, 2007, No. 43, pp. 9)
Pub: Crain Communications, Inc.
Ed: Mike Verespej. **Description:** If America wants to stay competitive in the global marketplace, experts say that the education system will need serious improvements. According to Thomas J. Donahue, president and CEO of the U.S. Chamber of Commerce, one-third of the K-through-12 students in the United States don't graduate from high school.

25338 ■ *Competing in Emerging Markets*
Pub: Taylor and Francis Group
Ed: Hemant Merchant. **Released:** October 2007. **Price:** $62.95. **Description:** Understanding the perils and promises of emerging markets to the growth of companies is discussed. Readings and case studies focus on the strategic and operational challenges companies face while competing in emerging markets.

25339 ■ "Competing On Resources" in *Harvard Business Review* (Vol. 86, July-August 2008, No. 8, pp. 140)
Pub: Harvard Business School Press
Ed: David J. Collis; Cynthia A. Montgomery. **Description:** Guidelines regarding assessing the value of resources, such as slow depreciation and superiority to competitors' similar resources are discussed.

25340 ■ "Competing on Talent Analytics" in *Harvard Business Review* (Vol. 88, October 2010, No. 10, pp. 52)
Pub: Harvard Business School Publishing
Ed: Thomas H. Davenport, Jeanne Harris, Jeremy Shapiro. **Description:** Six ways to use talent analytics to obtain the highest level of value from employees are listed. These include human-capital investment analysis, talent value models, workforce forecasts, and talent supply chains.

25341 ■ "Competition At Last?" in *Canadian Business* (Vol. 81, July 22, 2008, No. 12-13, pp. 7)
Pub: Rogers Media Ltd.
Description: Competition Policy Review Panel's 'Compete to Win' report revealed that Canada is being 'hollowed-out' by foreign acquisitions. The panel investigated competition and foreign investment policies in Canada. Key information on the report, as well as views on the Investment Canada Act and the Competition Act, is presented.

25342 ■ "Competition Qualms Overblown: Inco" in *Globe & Mail* (February 15, 2006, pp. B1)
Pub: CTVglobemedia Publishing Inc.
Ed: Wendy Stueck. **Description:** Inco Ltd. plans the acquisition of Falconbridge Ltd., for $12.5 billion. The advantages of the acquisition for Inco Ltd. are presented.

25343 ■ "Competition To Provide Liquidity on the New York Stock Exchange" in *Business Horizons* (November-December 2007, pp. 513)
Pub: Elsevier Technology Publications
Ed: Robert Battalio, Robert Jennings. **Description:** Provision of liquidity at the New York Stock Exchange is studied. On-floor traders enjoy some advantages in providing liquidity compared to off-floor traders. The NYSE is justified in implementing measures designed to level the playing field between on- and off-floor traders.

25344 ■ "The Competitive Imperative Of Learning" in *Harvard Business Review* (Vol. 86, July-August 2008, No. 8, pp. 60)
Pub: Harvard Business School Press
Ed: Amy C. Edmondson. **Description:** Experimentation and reflection are important components for maintaining success in the business world and are the kind of character traits that can help one keep his or her competitive edge.

25345 ■ "Competitive Restaurant Scene Lures Buyers to Saratoga Springs" in *Business Review, Albany New York* (Vol. 34, October 26, 2007)
Pub: American City Business Journals, Inc.
Ed: Robin K. Cooper. **Description:** Restaurant industry in Saratoga Springs, New York, a competitive market, with the city having 102 licensed restaurants and 28,499 residents in 2006. Buyers tend to acquire restaurants in Saratoga Springs, New York due to its good market condition. Examples of restaurant acquisitions in Saratoga Springs are given.

25346 ■ "Competitors Line Up to Save Failing Banks" in *The Business Journal - Serving Phoenix and the Valley of the Sun* (Vol. 28, July 25, 2008, No. 47, pp. 1)
Pub: American City Business Journals, Inc.
Ed: Chris Casacchia. **Description:** Financial institutions in Arizona are positioning themselves as possible buyers in the event of failure of one of their competitors. These banks have already approached the Federal Deposit Insurance Corp. about their ability to take over their more troubled competitors.

25347 ■ "Competitors' Resource-Oriented Strategies" in *Academy of Management Review* (January 2008, pp. 97)
Pub: ScholarOne, Inc.
Ed: Laurence Capron, Olivier Chatain. **Description:** Firms can maintain a competitive advantage by implementing competitor's' resource-oriented strategies to combat the resources of rivals in factor markets as well as political markets.

25348 ■ *The Complete Guide to Selling a Business*
Pub: NOLO
Ed: Fred S. Steingold. **Released:** November 2007. **Price:** $34.99. **Description:** When selling a business it is critical that a sales agreement covers all key concerns from price and payment terms to liability protection and restrictions on future competition.

25349 ■ *The Connection Key: Seven Ways the World's Most Successful Entrepreneurs Trounce the Competition and How You Can, Too*
Pub: John Wiley & Sons, Inc.
Ed: Maribeth Kuzmeski. **Released:** September 22, 2009. **Price:** $22.95. **Description:** The book is written under the premise that getting ahead in business does not come down to smarts, guts, rare talent, or plain old luck. While those things are helpful, the real missing ingredient is the ability to meaningfully connect with others.

25350 ■ "Construction Companies Think Smaller, Find Niches as Projects Become Fewer" in *Crain's Detroit Business* (March 10, 2008)
Pub: Crain Communications, Inc.
Ed: Daniel Duggan. **Description:** Due to the decline in development projects, construction firms are facing stronger competition for bids and are relying on their good track records or developing expertise in specific niches to get the job.

25351 ■ "Contractors Should Expand Their Services" in *Contractor* (Vol. 56, July 2009, No. 7, pp. 34)
Pub: Penton Media, Inc.
Ed: Steven Scandaliato. **Description:** All single family homes will be required to have fire sprinkler systems installed when the 2009 International Residential Code arrives. This presents an opportunity for plumbing contractors and they can be competitively priced against a fire protection contractor if they train their workforce to install sprinklers.

25352 ■ *Corporate Entrepreneurship & Innovation*
Pub: Thomson South-Western
Ed: Michael H. Morris; Donald F. Kuratko. **Released:** January 2007. **Price:** $104.95. **Description:** Innovation is the key to running a successful small business. The book helps entrepreneurs to develop the skills and business savvy to sustain a competitive edge.

25353 ■ "Cost of Md. Health Plan Not Known" in *Baltimore Business Journal* (Vol. 28, September 3, 2010, No. 17, pp. 1)
Pub: Baltimore Business Journal
Ed: Emily Mullin. **Description:** United States health reform is seen to result in increased health insurance prices in Maryland. However, health care reform advocates claim a new marketplace and increased competition will help keep costs down.

25354 ■ "CP Rail Cuts Jobs to Keep Pace With CN" in *Globe & Mail* (January 16, 2006, pp. B1)
Pub: CTVglobemedia Publishing Inc.
Ed: Brent Jang. **Description:** Canadian Pacific Railway Ltd. (CPR) reduces workforce in order to remain competitive with Canadian National Railway Co. The details of CPR's proposal are presented.

25355 ■ "CPR Signals a Switch in Strategy to Narrow Competitive Gap With CN" in *Globe & Mail* (January 20, 2006, pp. B3)
Pub: CTVglobemedia Publishing Inc.
Ed: Brent Jang. **Description:** The reasons behind the restructuring efforts of Canadian Pacific Railway Ltd. are presented.

25356 ■ "Crain's Nabs 15 Press Club Awards" in *Crain's Cleveland Business* (Vol. 30, June 29, 2009, No. 25, pp. 6)
Pub: Crain Communications, Inc.
Description: Crain's Cleveland Business was honored with 15 awards at the Ohio Excellence in Journalism competition conducted by the Press Club of Cleveland.

25357 ■ *Creativity and Innovation: Breaking New Ground...Without Breaking the Bank*
Pub: A & C Black
Ed: Janice Armstrong. **Released:** March 1, 2009. **Price:** $12.95. **Description:** Advice is given to help small business owners be creative in order to compete in their sector.

25358 ■ "Cupcake Eating Contest Draws World-Class Competitors" in *Waterloo Courier* (April 14, 2011)
Pub: Lee Enterprises
Ed: Amie Steffen. **Description:** World Cupcake Eating Championships were held at the Isle Casino Hotel Waterloo, Iowa, April 23, 2011. Major League Eating reports this to be the first time they've held a cupcake eating contest.

25359 ■ "Dairy Queen Ends Effort Against Yogubliz" in *Ice Cream Reporter* (Vol. 23, November 20, 2010, No. 12, pp. 1)
Pub: Ice Cream Reporter
Description: Dairy Queen has stopped demands that Yogubliz Inc. change its Blizzberry and Blizz Frozen Yogurt shops because they sound too much like Dairy Queen's Blizzard frozen dessert treat. Dairy Queen feared consumers would confuse the two brands.

25360 ■ "The Data Drivers" in *Canadian Business* (Vol. 81, September 15, 2008, No. 14-15, pp. 1)
Pub: Rogers Media Ltd.
Ed: Andrew Wahl. **Description:** Canadian regulators hope that an auction of telecommunications companies will inject more competition into the industry; however, newcomers may not be able to rely on lower prices in order to gain market share from the three major telecommunications companies that already have a stronghold on the market. Analysts feel that providing additional data service is the key to surviving market disruptions.

25361 ■ "David Low" in *Hawaii Business* (Vol. 53, October 2007, No. 4, pp. 38)
Pub: Hawaii Business Publishing
Ed: Cathy S. Cruz-George. **Description:** Hawaii Capital Management managing director David Low ranked first in the 2007 competition for fittest male executives in Hawaii. This 5-foot-9 executive, who weighed 225 lbs. in 2003, weighs 150 lbs. in 2007. The activities that improved Low's fitness, such as weight training, swimming, biking, and running, are discussed.

25362 ■ "The Dean of Design" in *Canadian Business* (Vol. 79, November 6, 2006, No. 22, pp. 42)
Pub: Rogers Media
Ed: Erin Pooley. **Description:** The need of a good business design to increase the business in saturated markets with relation to customer satisfaction is emphasized.

25363 ■ "Dean Foods" in *Ice Cream Reporter* (Vol. 23, November 20, 2010, No. 12, pp. 8)
Pub: Ice Cream Reporter
Description: The impact of higher commodity prices can be seen in the recent news from Dean Foods, the largest U.S. dairy company, which reported that rising butterfat and other dairy commodity costs have led to lower-than-expected quarterly profits after it cut prices to compete with private-label brands.

25364 ■ "Death of the PC" in *Canadian Business* (Vol. 83, October 12, 2010, No. 17, pp. 44)
Pub: Rogers Media Ltd.
Ed: Joe Castaldo. **Description:** The future of the personal computer (PC) is looking bleak as consumers are relying more on new mobile devices instead of their PC. A 'Wall Street Journal' article published in September 2010 reported that the iPad had cannibalized sales of laptops by as much as 50 percent. The emergence of tablet computers running alternative operating systems is also explained.

25365 ■ "Defense Contractor May Expand Locally; BAE Systems Ramps Up Vehicle Prototypes" in *Crain's Detroit Business* (March 24, 2008)
Pub: Crain Communications, Inc.
Ed: Chad Halcom. **Description:** Profile of BAE Systems, a defense contractor, that has built a prototype in the highly competitive Joint Light Tactical Vehicle project; the company has also completed its prototype RG33L Mine Resistant Recovery Maintenance Vehicle and has plans for expansion.

25366 ■ "Detroit Pawn Shop to be Reality TV Venue" in *UPI NewsTrack* (July 10, 2010)
Pub: United Press International-USA
Description: TruTV will present a new series called 'Hardcore Pawn' to compete with the History Channel's successful show 'Pawn Stars'. The show will feature American Jewelry and Loan in Detroit, Michigan and its owner Les Gold, who runs the store with his wife and children.

25367 ■ "Developers Compete for APG Project" in *Baltimore Business Journal* (Vol. 27, October 16, 2009, No. 23, pp. 1)
Pub: American City Business Journals
Ed: Daniel J. Sernovitz. **Description:** Corporate Office Properties Trust has lost the case in Delaware bankruptcy court to prevent rival St. John Properties Inc. from going ahead with its plans to develop the

400 acres at Aberdeen Proving Ground (APG) in Maryland. Both developers have competed for the right to develop the two million square foot business park in APG.

25368 ■ "Developers Vie for UWM Dorm" in *The Business Journal-Milwaukee* (Vol. 25, July 11, 2008, No. 42, pp. A1)
Pub: American City Business Journals, Inc.

Ed: Rich Kirchen. **Description:** Eight developers are competing to build a 500- to 700-student residence hall for the University of Wisconsin-Milwaukee. The residence hall will probably be developed within two miles of the main campus. It was revealed that the university's real estate foundation will select the successful bidder on July 25, 2008, and construction will begin by January 2009.

25369 ■ "The Digital Revolution is Over. Long Live the Digital Revolution!" in *Business Strategy Review* (Vol. 21, Spring 2010, No. 1, pp. 74)
Pub: Wiley-Blackwell

Ed: Gianvito Lanzolla, Jamie Anderson. **Description:** Many businesses are now involved in the digital marketplace. The authors argue that the new reality of numerous companies offering overlapping products means that it is critical for managers to understand digital convergence and to observe the imperatives for remaining competitive.

25370 ■ "Disney Has High Hopes for Duffy" in *Canadian Business* (Vol. 83, October 12, 2010, No. 17, pp. 14)
Pub: Rogers Media Ltd.

Ed: James Cowan. **Description:** The reintroduction of Duffy is expected to create a new, exclusive product line that distinguishes Disney's parks and stores from competitors. Duffy, a teddy bear, was first introduced at a Disney World store in Florida in 2002. The character was incorporated into the Disney mythology when its popularity grew in Japan.

25371 ■ "Diving Into Internet Marketing" in *American Agent and Broker* (Vol. 81, December 2009, No. 12, pp. 24)
Pub: Summit Business Media

Ed: Steve Anderson. **Description:** Internet marketing is becoming an essential tool for most businesses; advice is provided regarding the social networking opportunities available for marketing one's product or service on the Internet.

25372 ■ "Downtown Evens Tenant Ledger" in *The Business Journal-Serving Metropolitan Kansas City* (Vol. 26, July 11, 2008, No. 44, pp. 1)
Pub: American City Business Journals, Inc.

Ed: Rob Roberts. **Description:** Financial services company PricewaterhouseCoopers will relocate its office from the Broadway Square building, but it will not leave downtown as it signs a long-term lease for a 27,000 square feet of space in Town Pavilion. Town Pavilion is the biggest multitenant office building in downtown. Downtown's market competitiveness is also examined.

25373 ■ "Efficient Cash Management Essential To Be Competitive" in *Crain's Cleveland Business* (Vol. 28, November 12, 2007, No. 45, pp. 25)
Pub: Crain Communications, Inc.

Ed: Ken Moultrie. **Description:** In order to sustain a business it is important to organize cash-management efforts around three core areas: cash in, static cash and cash out. Tips for the successful management of these areas are provided.

25374 ■ "Elanco Challenges Bayer's Advantage, K9 Advantix Ad Claims" in *Pet Product News* (Vol. 64, November 2010, No. 11, pp. 11)
Pub: BowTie Inc.

Description: Elanco Animal Health has disputed Bayer Animal Health's print and Web advertising claims involving its flea, tick, and mosquito control products Advantage and K9 Advantix. The National Advertising Division of the Council of Better Business Bureaus recommended the discontinuation of ads, while Bayer Animal Health reiterated its commitment to self-regulation.

25375 ■ "Election Could Undo Renewable Energy Quotas" in *The Business Journal - Serving Phoenix and the Valley of the Sun* (Vol. 28, July 11, 2008, No. 45, pp. 1)
Pub: American City Business Journals, Inc.

Ed: Patrick O'Grady. **Description:** Competition for the three open seats in the Arizona Corporation Commission is intense, with 12 candidates contesting for the three slots. The commission's mandates for renewable energy and infrastructure investment will also be at stake.

25376 ■ *The Emerging Markets Century: How a New Breed of World-Class Companies is Overtaking the World*
Pub: Free Press/Simon & Schuster Inc.

Ed: Antoine van Agtmael. **Released:** 2007. **Price:** $29.00. **Description:** An exploration of how companies like Lenovo and Haier who are presently in emerging economies are already competing with household name brands like Ford and Sony, thus proving globalization is here to stay.

25377 ■ "Engine of Growth: U.S. Industry Funk hasn't Hurt Cummins or Its Investors" in *Barron's* (Vol. 88, July 14, 2008, No. 28, pp. 43)
Pub: Dow Jones & Co., Inc.

Ed: Shirley A. Lazo. **Description:** Engine maker Cummins increased its quarterly common dividend by 40 percent to 17.5 cents per share from 12.5 cents. CVS Caremark's dividend saw a hike of 18.4 percent from 9.5 cents to 11.25 cents per share while its competitor Walgreen is continuing its 75th straight year of dividend distribution and its 33rd straight year of dividend hikes.

25378 ■ *Entrepreneurship and Economic Growth*
Pub: Edward Elgar Publishing, Incorporated

Ed: Carree. **Released:** October 2006. **Price:** $195. 00. **Description:** Historic and country-specific studies and articles regarding entrepreneurship and innovation, growth models, competition and productivity, and empirical evidence.

25379 ■ "An Equity Fund of Their Own" in *Entrepreneur* (Vol. 35, October 2007, No. 10, pp. 68)
Pub: Entrepreneur Media Inc.

Ed: Lee Gimpel. **Description:** About 100 new private equity funds have formed since 2002, proof that private equity investing is becoming popular among companies. There is also an increase in competition to close deals owing to the large number of investors that companies can choose; advantages of smaller funds over the larger one is explained.

25380 ■ "Evaluate Your Process and Do It Better" in *Modern Machine Shop* (Vol. 84, October 2011, No. 5, pp. 34)
Pub: Gardner Publications

Ed: Wayne S. Chaneski. **Description:** In order to be more competitive, many machine shops owners are continually looking at their processes and procedures in order to be more competitive.

25381 ■ "Family Firm Performance: Further Evidence" in *Family Business Review* (Vol. 19, June 2006, No. 2, pp. 103)
Pub: Family Firm Institute Inc.

Ed: Jim Lee. **Description:** Empirical results of regression analysis, which is used to examine the competitiveness of family owned businesses and non-family firms are presented.

25382 ■ *Faster Cheaper Better*
Pub: Crown Business Books

Ed: Michael Hammer. **Released:** December 28, 2010. **Price:** $27.50. **Description:** Nine levels for transforming work in order to achieve business growth are outlined. The book helps small business compete against the low-wage countries.

25383 ■ "Film Incentives: A Hit or a Flop?" in *Michigan Vue* (Vol. 13, July-August 2008, No. 4, pp. 10)
Pub: Entrepreneur Media Inc.

Description: Michigan's new film incentive legislation is fulfilling its core purpose, according to Lisa Dancsok of the Michigan Economic Development Corp. (MEDC), by kickstarting the state's entry into the multi-billion dollar industry; the initiative is considered to be very competitive with other states and countries and is thought to be a way in which to help revitalize Michigan's struggling economy.

25384 ■ "Find Your Marketing Mojo" in *Business Owner* (Vol. 35, July-August 2011, No. 4, pp. 14)
Pub: DL Perkins Company

Description: Marketing and branding a small business can be learned and implemented by following a process that begins with setting and creating the vision that every successful venture requires: a crystal-clear vision for who you are, what you stand for, and why customers will come to you rather than competitors.

25385 ■ "Finding Competitive Advantage in Adversity" in *Harvard Business Review* (Vol. 88, November 2010, No. 11, pp. 102)
Pub: Harvard Business School Publishing

Ed: Bhaskar Chakravorti. **Description:** Four opportunities in adversity are identified and applied to business scenarios. These are matching unmet needs with unneeded resources, seeking collaboration from unlikely partners, developing small/appropriate solutions to large/complex issues, and focusing on the platform as well as the product.

25386 ■ "Finding a Way to Continue Growing" in *Green Industry Pro* (Vol. 23, March 2011, No. 3, pp. 31)
Pub: Cygnus Business Media

Description: Profile of Brett Lemcke, VP of R.M. Landscape located in Rochester, New York. Lemcke tells how his Landscape Industry Certified credentials helped him to grow his business and beat out his competition.

25387 ■ "Five Reasons Why the Gap Fell Out of Fashion" in *Globe & Mail* (January 27, 2007, pp. B4)
Pub: CTVglobemedia Publishing Inc.

Ed: Keith McArthur. **Description:** The five major market trends that have caused the decline of fashion clothing retailer Gap Inc.'s sales are discussed. The shift in brand, workplace fashion culture, competition, demographics, and consumer preferences have lead to the Gap's brand identity.

25388 ■ "Flights of Fancy" in *Crain's Chicago Business* (Vol. 31, April 21, 2008, No. 16, pp. 27)
Pub: Crain Communications, Inc.

Ed: Sarah A. Klein. **Description:** Due to the competition for business travelers, who account for 30 percent of airline revenue, airlines are offering a number of luxury amenities, especially on long-haul routes.

25389 ■ "Food Fight" in *Canadian Business* (Vol. 79, November 6, 2006, No. 22, pp. 18)
Pub: Rogers Media

Ed: Zena Olijnyk. **Description:** The war between Canadian grocers and Wal-Mart due to its plans for opening new stores is analyzed.

25390 ■ "For Bombardier, a Case of Deja Vu" in *Canadian Business* (Vol. 83, August 17, 2010, No. 13-14, pp. 28)
Pub: Rogers Media Ltd.

Ed: Laura Cameron. **Description:** Foreign competitors have accused the Quebec government and the Societe de transport de Montreal of giving Bombardier preferential treatment when it bids for contract to replace Montreal metro's rail cars. Bombardier was in a similar situation in 1974 when it won the contract to build the metro's second generation rail cars.

25391 ■ "Ford, Chrysler Dinged as Little Cars Rule Road" in *Globe & Mail* (March 2, 2007, pp. B3)
Pub: CTVglobemedia Publishing Inc.
Ed: Greg Keenan. **Description:** The Ford Motor Co. and the Chrysler Group posted a decline in automobile sales in the first two months of 2007. The sales statistics of other automobile companies in Canada are also presented.

25392 ■ "Forward Motion" in *Green Industry Pro* (July 2011)
Pub: Cygnus Business Media
Ed: Gregg Wartgow. **Description:** Several landscape contractors have joined this publication's Working Smarter Training Challenge over the last year. This process is helping them develop ways to improve work processes, boost morale, drive out waste, reduce costs, improve customer service, and be more competitive.

25393 ■ "Fox" in *Brandweek* (Vol. 49, April 21, 2008, No. 16, pp. SR3)
Pub: VNU Business Media, Inc.
Ed: John Consoli. **Description:** Provides contact information for sales and marketing personnel for the Fox network as well as a listing of the station's top programming and an analysis of the current season and the target audience for those programs running in the current season. In terms of upfront advertising dollars, it looks as if Fox will be competing against NBC for third place due to its success at courting the 18-49-year-old male demographic.

25394 ■ "Franchisees Lose Battle Against BK" in *Advertising Age* (Vol. 79, June 2, 2008, No. 22, pp. 46)
Pub: Crain Communications, Inc.
Ed: Emily Bryson York. **Description:** Burger King has had continuing litigation with former franchisees from New York, Luan and Elizabeth Sadik, who claim that Burger King's double cheeseburger, along with additional problems, created the environment for their eventual insolvency. Burger King has since terminated its test of selling the double cheeseburger for $1, although the company declined to comment on the reason for this decision.

25395 ■ *From Concept To Consumer: How to Turn Ideas Into Money*
Pub: Pearson Education Inc.
Ed: Phil Baker. **Released:** 2009. **Price:** $24.99. **Description:** Renowned product developer Phil Baker explains how a great idea accounts for only 5 percent of all the factors of success and why the majority of success is dependent upon a myriad of other factors, including the time it takes to get to market, price, marketing and distribution. By being their own best competition, a small company can stay one step ahead of competitors.

25396 ■ "The Future of Private Equity" in *Canadian Business* (Vol. 80, March 26, 2007, No. 7, pp. 19)
Pub: Rogers Media
Ed: Jack Mintz. **Description:** The impact growing Canadian economy and competition in global business on the performance of private equity funds is analyzed.

25397 ■ "Game On: The Hunt Is On for Nation's Top Keeper" in *Farmer's Weekly* (March 28, 2008, No. 320)
Pub: Reed Business Information
Description: Gamekeepers must strike the natural balance that encourages wildlife and protects game. CLA Game Fair and Farmer's Weekly are holding a competition for Gamekeeper of the Year 2008.

25398 ■ "Gatorade Loses Its Competitive Edge; Upstart Rivals Undercut Its Domination of Game" in *Crain's Chicago Business* (April 28, 2008)
Pub: Crain Communications, Inc.
Ed: Natalie Zmuda. **Description:** According to beverage-marketing experts, Gatorade is losing some of its market share to aggressive new rivals who are appealing to younger consumers.

25399 ■ *Getting to Scale: Growing Your Business Without Selling Out*
Pub: Berrett-Koehler Publishers, Incorporated
Ed: Jill Bamburg. **Released:** July 2006. **Price:** $14.95. **Description:** Ways for entrepreneurs to preserve the value of their company while maintaining growth and competitiveness.

25400 ■ "Give It Your All, and Don't Worry About the Rest" in *Inc.* (Vol. 33, November 2011, No. 9, pp. 37)
Pub: Inc. Magazine
Ed: Norm Brodsky. **Description:** In the early stage of a service company, the owners sell themselves to the customers.

25401 ■ "Gordon Nixon" in *Canadian Business* (Vol. 80, November 5, 2007, No. 22, pp. 9)
Pub: Rogers Media
Ed: Rachel Pulfer. **Description:** Royal Bank of Canada (RBC) CEO, Gordon Nixon, believes the Canadian financial services segment is heavily regulated. Nixon also feels that it has become difficult for local banks to enter the market since foreign banks can easily come in and compete with them. His views on RBC's success are provided.

25402 ■ "Gordon Nixon Q&A" in *Canadian Business* (Vol. 80, November 5, 2007, No. 22, pp. 9)
Pub: Rogers Media
Ed: Rachel Pulfer. **Description:** Royal Bank of Canada (RBC) chief executive officer Gordon Nixon believes that the Canadian financial services segment is heavily regulated. Nixon also feels that it has become difficult for local banks to enter the market since foreign banks can easily come in and compete with Canadian banks. His views on RBC's success are provided.

25403 ■ *Green to Gold*
Pub: Yale University Press
Ed: Daniel C. Esty; Andrew S. Winston. **Released:** January 2009. **Price:** $19.95. **Description:** Examples are given for small businesses to beat competition while tackling sustainability, engage stakeholders, develop NGO partnerships, and work environmental stewardship into corporate culture.

25404 ■ *Greening Your Small Business: How to Improve Your Bottom Line, Grow Your Brand, Satisfy Your Customers and Save the Planet*
Pub: Prentice Hall Press
Ed: Jennifer Kaplan. **Released:** November 3, 2009. **Price:** $19.95. **Description:** A definitive resource for anyone who wants their small business to be cutting-edge, competitive, profitable, and eco-conscious. Stories from small business owners address every aspect of going green, from basics such as recycling waste, energy efficiency, and reducing information technology footprint, to more in-depth concerns such as green marketing and communications, green business travel, and green employee benefits.

25405 ■ "Greg Stringham" in *Canadian Business* (Vol. 81, March 3, 2008, No. 3, pp. 8)
Pub: Rogers Media
Ed: Michelle Magnan. **Description:** Canadian Association of Petroleum Producers' Greg Stringham thinks that the new royalty plan will result in companies pulling out their investments for Alberta's conventional oil and gas sector. Stringham adds that Alberta is losing its competitive advantage and companies must study their cost profiles to retrieve that advantage. The effects of the royalty system on Alberta's economy are examined further.

25406 ■ "Guts Not Included" in *Canadian Business* (Vol. 81, March 31, 2008, No. 5, pp. 46)
Pub: Rogers Media
Ed: Andrew Wahl. **Description:** Executives need the vision to create a strategy that prepares for an uncertain future in light of growing global competition. Canadian business leaders have the right skills and education but do not have enough tolerance for risk.

25407 ■ "Hit the Books" in *Entrepreneur* (Vol. 36, April 2008, No. 4, pp. 74)
Pub: Entrepreneur Media, Inc.
Ed: Nichole L. Torres. **Description:** Lists of the top business schools in different U.S. universities are presented. These lists are categorized according to best professors, best classroom experience, most competitive students, greatest opportunity for women, and greatest opportunity for minority students. The lists, compiled by the Princeton Review, are based on student opinion.

25408 ■ "Hola and Aloha" in *Hawaii Business* (Vol. 53, December 2007, No. 6, pp. 131)
Pub: Hawaii Business Publishing
Ed: Jason Ubay. **Description:** Juan Carlos Bianchetti is the trilingual owner of Ole Tours Hawaii, a travel wholesaler that targets Portuguese and Spanish-speaking visitors. The competition for American and Japanese tourists is already tight, which is why Bianchetti opted to target a different segment of the Hawaii tourism market. Plans for the company's expansion in Kauai, Brazil, and Argentina, are mentioned.

25409 ■ "Hoover's Mobile, MobileSP Now Available" in *Information Today* (Vol. 26, February 2009, No. 2, pp. 29)
Pub: Information Today, Inc.
Description: Hoover's Inc. introduced its Hoover's Mobile for iPhone, BlackBerry and Windows Mobile smartphones along with Hoover's MobileSP for BlackBerry and Windows Mobile. Both products allow users to access customer, prospect, and partner information; analyze competitors; prepare for meetings; and find new opportunities. In addition, MobileSP adds one-click calling to executives, GPS-enabled location searches, advanced search and list building, and a custom call queue and a 'save to contacts' capabilities.

25410 ■ "Hopkins, UMd Worry Reduced NIH Budget Will Impact Research" in *Boston Business Journal* (Vol. 29, August 19, 2011, No. 15, pp. 1)
Pub: American City Business Journals Inc.
Ed: Scott Dance. **Description:** The budget for the National Institutes of Health (NIH) is slated to be cut by at least 7.9 percent to $2.5 billion in 2013. This will have a big negative effect on medical and biotech research in Maryland, especially Johns Hopkins University and University of Maryland, Baltimore which could face stiffer completion for grants from the NIH.

25411 ■ "Hostess Reveals Grand Prize Winner of 'CupCake Jackpot' Promotion" in *Entertainment Close-Up* (August 19, 2011)
Pub: Close-Up Media
Description: Tricia Botbyl was the grand prize winner of the Hostess 'CupCake Jackpot' promotion that asked consumers to 'spin' online to win $10,000. Consumers were asked to vote for their favorite Hostess Brand cupcake flavor.

25412 ■ *Housecleaning Business: Organize Your Business - Get Clients and Referrals - Set Rates and Services*
Pub: The Globe Pequot Press
Ed: Laura Jorstad, Melinda Morse. **Released:** June 1, 2009. **Price:** $18.95. **Description:** This book shares insight into starting a housecleaning businesses. It shows how to develop a service manual, screen clients, serve customers, select cleaning products, competition, how to up a home office, using the Internet to grow the business and offering green cleaning options to clients.

25413 ■ *How to Become a Great Boss: The Rules for Getting and Keeping the Best Employees*
Pub: Hyperion Special Markets
Ed: Jeffrey J. Fox. **Released:** May 15, 2002. **Price:** $16.95. **Description:** The book offers valuable advice to any manager or entrepreneur to improve leadership and management skills. Topics covered include:

hiring, managing, firing, partnership and competition, self and organization, employee performance, attitude, and priorities.

25414 ■ "How Dell Will Dial for Dollars" in *Austin Business JournalInc.* (Vol. 29, December 4, 2009, No. 39, pp. 1)
Pub: American City Business Journals
Ed: Christopher Calnan. **Description:** Dell Inc. revealed plans to launch a Mini3i smartphone in China which could enable revenue sharing by bundling with wireless service subscription. Dell's smartphone plan is similar to the netbook business, which Dell sold with service provided by AT&T Inc.

25415 ■ *How to Get Rich*
Pub: Ebury Press
Ed: Felix Dennis. **Released:** 2008. **Price:** $25.95. **Description:** Publisher of Maxim, The Week, and Stuff magazines, discusses the mistakes he made running his companies. He didn't understand that people who buy computer gaming magazines wanted a free game with each copy, as one of his rivals was offering. And he laments not diversifying into television and exploiting the Internet.

25416 ■ *How to Make Big Money*
Pub: Hyperion Books
Ed: Jeffrey J. Fox. **Released:** May 19, 2004. **Price:** $16.95. **Description:** Entrepreneur and consultant offers advice to help others create successful startups and prosper. Fox directs new business owners with a counterintuitive style and describes essential methods that beat the competition. Tips include: setting priorities, getting a personal driver, creating a contingency plan for employees, pricing to value, saving money, and getting an office outside of the home.

25417 ■ *How to Write a Business Plan*
Pub: Kogan Page, Limited
Ed: Brian Finch. **Released:** February 10, 2010. **Price:** $17.95. **Description:** Starting with the premise that there's only one chance to make a good impression, this book covers all the issues involved in producing a successful business plan, from profiling competitors to forecasting marketing development.

25418 ■ *How You Do...What You Do: Create Service Excellence That Wins Clients For Life*
Pub: McGraw-Hill
Ed: Bob Livingston. **Released:** June 6, 2008. **Price:** $27.95. **Description:** Today's marketplace has become a tougher place to do business because of new challenges such as escalating competition, well-informed clients, and dismal customer service. Clients now have more influence and choices than ever. Tips for achieving service excellence are provided.

25419 ■ "HP Eats Into Rival Dell Sales as Profits Soar" in *Globe & Mail* (February 21, 2007, pp. B15)
Pub: CTVglobemedia Publishing Inc.
Ed: Connie Guglielmo. **Description:** The world's largest personal computer maker Hewlett Packard Co. has reported increased profits by 26 percent to $1.55 billion during the first quarter. The company has outpaced its competitor Dell Inc. by offering low priced personal computers during this period.

25420 ■ *If You Have to Cry, Go Outside: And Other Things Your Mother Never Told You*
Pub: HarperOne
Ed: Kelly Cutrone. **Released:** February 2, 2010. **Price:** $22.99. **Description:** Women's mentor advices on how to make it in one of the most competitive industries in the world, fashion. She has kicked people out of fashion shows, forced some of reality television's shiny start to fire their friends, and built her own company which is one of the most powerful public relations firms in the fashion business.

25421 ■ "Inco's Takeover Offer Extended Four Months" in *Globe & Mail* (February 22, 2006, pp. B1)
Pub: CTVglobemedia Publishing Inc.
Ed: Wendy Stueck. **Description:** United States and Europe competition authorities wanted more time to investigate Inco Ltd.'s takeover of Falconbridge Ltd. and compelling Inco to extend its $12.5 billion offer for the third time.

25422 ■ "Increased Competition Prompts Detroit Hotels to Make Upgrades" in *Crain's Detroit Business* (Vol. 24, March 31, 2008, No. 13, pp. 1)
Pub: Crain Communications, Inc.
Ed: Daniel Duggan. **Description:** Five Detroit hotels have recently undergone upgrades or are preparing for major construction projects due to a more competitive hospitality market in the city.

25423 ■ "Inland Snaps Up Rival REITs" in *Crain's Chicago Business* (Vol. 31, November 17, 2008, No. 46, pp. 3)
Pub: Crain Communications, Inc.
Ed: Alby Gallun. **Description:** Discusses Inland American Real Estate Trust Inc., a real estate investment trust that is napping up depressed shares of publicly traded competitors, a possible first step toward taking over these companies; however, with hotel and retail properties accounting for approximately 70 percent of its portfolio, the company could soon face its own difficulties.

25424 ■ *Innovation and Its Discontents*
Pub: Princeton University Press
Ed: Josh Lerner, Adam B. Jaffe. **Released:** 2006. **Price:** $21.95 paperback. **Description:** According to the authors, America's patent system does not effectively serve as a generator and protector of patents and intellectual property.

25425 ■ *Innovation Nation: How America Is Losing Its Innovation Edge, Why It Matters, and How We Can Get It Back*
Pub: Free Press/Simon & Schuster
Ed: John Kao. **Released:** October 2, 2007. **Price:** $26.00. **Description:** Diagnoses of the lack of innovation being seen in the United States today is examined by a former Harvard Business School professor. He explains how innovation works and puts forth a strategy proposal in an attempt to help America regain its edge on innovation.

25426 ■ "Insurers No Longer Paying Premium for Advertising" in *Brandweek* (Vol. 49, April 21, 2008, No. 16, pp. SR3)
Pub: VNU Business Media, Inc.
Ed: Eric Newman. **Description:** Insurance companies are cutting their advertising budgets after years of accelerated double-digit growth in spending due to the economic downturn, five years of record-breaking ad spend and a need to cut expenditures as claims costs rise and a competitive market keeps premiums in place. Statistical data included.

25427 ■ *International Entrepreneurship in Small and Medium Size Enterprises: Orientation, Environment and Strategy*
Pub: Edward Elgar Publishing, Incorporated
Ed: Hamid Etemad. **Released:** October 2004. **Price:** $130.00. **Description:** Issues involved in internationalizing small and medium sized (SME) businesses. Topics include an investigation into the emerging patterns of SME growth and international expansion in response to the changing competitive environment, dynamics of competitive behavior, entrepreneurial processes and a formulation of strategy.

25428 ■ "International Growth" in *Black Enterprise* (Vol. 38, July 2008, No. 12, pp. 64)
Pub: Earl G. Graves Publishing Co. Inc.
Ed: Marcia A. Reed-Woodard. **Description:** Becoming an increasingly smaller portion of the global business environment is the U.S. economy. Christopher Catlin, an associate with Booz Allen Hamilton, a technology management and strategy-consulting firm, shares what he has learned about the global market.

25429 ■ "Into the Light: Making Our Way Through the Economic Tunnel" in *Agency Sales Magazine* (Vol. 39, August 2009, No. 8, pp. 26)
Pub: MANA
Ed: Michael Dotson. **Description:** Ways in which to avoid business stagnation brought about by the economic downturn, is presented. Being different, being a puzzle solver, and knowing the competition are among the things marketing personnel should do in order to wade through the economic downturn. Marketing via direct mail and the Internet also recommended.

25430 ■ "Investing in the IT that Makes a Competitive Difference" in *Harvard Business Review* (Vol. 86, July-August 2008, No. 8, pp. 98)
Pub: Harvard Business School Press
Ed: Andrew McAfee; Erik Brynjolfsson. **Description:** Components of a successful information technology management strategy are examined. These techniques are broad in spectrum, produce immediate results, are consistent and precise, facilitate monitoring, and promote enforceability.

25431 ■ "The iPhone Gets Some Competition" in *Inc.* (Vol. 31, January-February 2009, No. 1, pp. 42)
Pub: Mansueto Ventures LLC
Ed: Mark Spoonauer. **Description:** RIM's BlackBerry Storm and T-Mobile's G1 are competing with the iPhone 3G technology; the three systems are profiled.

25432 ■ "It's Not About the G1; Google Just Wants You to Use the Mobile Web" in *Advertising Age* (Vol. 79, September 29, 2008, No. 36, pp. 32)
Pub: Crain Communications, Inc.
Ed: Abbey Klaassen. **Description:** Google's Android is the first serious competitor to Apple's iPhone; the company says that its goal is to simplify the mobile market and get wireless subscribers to use the mobile Internet and purchase smartphones.

25433 ■ "Jack Be Nimble" in *Business Courier* (Vol. 24, October 26, 2008, No. 28, pp. 1)
Pub: American City Business Journals, Inc.
Ed: Laura Baverman. **Description:** Cincinnati Bell is losing around 47,000 phone lines a year due to the advent of wireless technology and increased competition from cable companies.

25434 ■ "Job Seeker's Readiness Guide: Unemployment's High and Competition is Tough" in *Black Enterprise* (Vol. 40, July 2010, No. 12, pp. 83)
Pub: Earl G. Graves Publishing Co. Inc.
Description: Five key areas to help someone seeking employment gain the competitive edge are listed.

25435 ■ "Joe Wikert, General Manager, O'Reilly Technology Exchange" in *Information Today* (Vol. 26, February 2009, No. 2, pp. 21)
Pub: Information Today, Inc.
Ed: Jamie Babbitt. **Description:** Joe Wikert, general manager of O'Reilly Technology Exchange discusses his plans to develop a free content model that will evolve with future needs. O'Reilly's major competitor is Google. Wikert plans to expand the firm's publishing program to include print, online, and in-person products and services.

25436 ■ "Just Hang Up" in *Barron's* (Vol. 88, March 10, 2008, No. 10, pp. 45)
Pub: Dow Jones & Company, Inc.
Ed: Tiernan Ray. **Description:** Sprint's shares are expected to continue falling while the company attempts to attract subscribers by cutting prices, cutting earnings in the process. The company faces tougher competition from better-financed AT&T and Verizon Communications.

25437 ■ "Kari Leong" in *Hawaii Business* (Vol. 53, October 2007, No. 4, pp. 39)
Pub: Hawaii Business Publishing
Ed: Cathy S. Cruz-George. **Description:** Greater Good Inc. president Kari Leong is the number 1 fittest female executive in Hawaii for 2007. Leong exercises at the gym and at her home, and carries her two children for strength training. The physical activities she had undergone during her college life at the Gonzaga University are discussed.

25438 ■ "Keep Customers Out of the Yellow Pages" in *Contractor* (Vol. 56, November 2009, No. 11, pp. 47)
Pub: Penton Media, Inc.
Ed: Matt Michel. **Description:** Mechanical contractors should keep customers away from the Yellow Pages where they could find their competition by putting stickers on the water heater or the front of the directory. Giving out magnets to customers and putting the company name on sink rings and invoices are other suggestions.

25439 ■ "Keeping the Faith in Fuel-Tech" in *Barron's* (Vol. 88, March 24, 2008, No. 12, pp. 20)
Pub: Dow Jones & Company, Inc.
Ed: Christopher C. Williams. **Description:** Shares of air pollution control company Fuel-Tech remain on track to reach $40 each from their $19 level due to a continued influx of contracts. The stock has suffered from lower-than-expected quarterly earnings and tougher competition but stand to benefit from increased orders.

25440 ■ "Kerkorian Shakes Up Chrysler Race" in *Globe & Mail* (April 6, 2007, pp. B1)
Pub: CTVglobemedia Publishing Inc.
Ed: Greg Keenan. **Description:** The bid of Kirk Kerkorian's Tracinda Corp. to acquire Daimler-Chrysler AG for $4.5 billion is discussed.

25441 ■ "King of the Crib: How Good Samaritan Became Ohio's Baby HQ" in *Business Courier* (Vol. 27, June 18, 2010, No. 7, pp. 1)
Pub: Business Courier
Ed: James Ritchie. **Description:** Cincinnati's Good Samaritan hospital had 6,875 live births in 2009, which is more than any other hospital in Ohio. They specialize in the highest-risk pregnancies and deliveries and other hospitals are trying to grab Good Samaritan's share in this niche.

25442 ■ *Knock Your Socks Off Selling*
Pub: Amacom
Ed: Jeffrey Gitomer. **Released:** May 1999. **Price:** $17.95. **Description:** Tips for salespeople to succeed in a competitive sales environment.

25443 ■ "Kraft Taps Cheese Head; Jordan Charged With Fixing Foodmaker's Signature Product" in *Crain's Chicago Business* (April 14, 2008)
Pub: Crain Communications, Inc.
Ed: David Sterrett. **Description:** Kraft Foods Inc. has assigned Rhonda Jordan, a company veteran, to take charge of the cheese and dairy division which has been losing market shares to cheaper store-brand cheese among cost-sensitive shoppers as Kraft and its competitors raise prices to offset soaring dairy costs.

25444 ■ "Kroger Girds for Invasion of U.K. Chain" in *Business Courier* (Vol. 24, November 2, 2008, No. 29, pp. 1)
Pub: American City Business Journals, Inc.
Ed: Jon Newberry. **Description:** Tesco PLC will be opening its first Fresh & Easy Neighborhood Markets in Southern California. The company has committed $500 million per year to get a share of the $500 billion US food retailing market and will be opening more stores in quick succession. Tesco's arrival can be difficult for Kroger because Kroger had obtained much of its success by using Tesco's UK model.

25445 ■ "Leapin' Lizards, Does SoBe Have Some Work To Do On Life Water" in *Brandweek* (Vol. 49, April 21, 2008, No. 16, pp. 32)
Pub: VNU Business Media, Inc.
Ed: Amy Shea. **Description:** Discusses the competing marketing campaigns of both Vitaminwater, now owned by Coca-Cola, and SoBe Life Water which is owned by Pepsi; also looks at the repositioning of Life Water as a thirst-quencher, rather than a green product as well as the company's newest advertising campaign.

25446 ■ "Lessons from Turnaround Leaders" in *Strategy and Leadership* (Vol. 39, May-June 2011, No. 3, pp. 36-43)
Pub: Emerald Group Publishing Inc.
Ed: David P. Boyd. **Description:** A study analyzes the cases of some successful turnaround leaders to present a strategic model to help firms tackle challenges such as employee inertia, competition and slow organizational renewal. It describes a change model consisting of five major steps to be followed by firms with environmental uncertainty for the purpose.

25447 ■ "Let the Big Fish Eat" in *Canadian Business* (Vol. 80, March 12, 2007, No. 6, pp. 4)
Pub: Rogers Media
Ed: Joe Chidley. **Description:** The need for profitable Canadian banks to go for mergers to enjoy the benefits of globalization and compete with global banks is discussed.

25448 ■ "Life After Cod" in *Globe & Mail* (March 18, 2006, pp. B1)
Pub: CTVglobemedia Publishing Inc.
Ed: Gordon Pitts. **Description:** Canadian fishing industry is under threat because of Chinese processing competition, high energy costs, rise of powerful retailers and the rise of Canadian dollar value. Fishing industry of Canada is analyzed.

25449 ■ "Lights, Camera, Action: Tools for Creating Video Blogs" in *Inc.* (Volume 32, December 2010, No. 10, pp. 57)
Pub: Inc. Magazine
Ed: John Brandon. **Description:** A video blog is a good way to spread company news, talk about products, and stand out among traditional company blogs. New editing software can create two- to four-minute blogs using a webcam and either Windows Live Essentials, Apple iLife 2011, Powerdirector 9 Ultra, or Adobe Visual Communicator 3.

25450 ■ "Linking Human Capital to Competitive Advantages" in *Human Resource Management* (Vol. 49, September-October 2010, No. 5)
Pub: John Wiley
Ed: Yan Jin, Margaret M. Hopkins, Jenell L.S. Wittmer. **Description:** A study was conducted to confirm the links among human capital, firm flexibility, and firm performance. The study also examines the emerging role of flexibility for a company's performance. A total of 201 senior supply chain management professionals from several manufacturing companies were included in the study.

25451 ■ "A Look At Three Gas-Less Cars" in *Hispanic Business* (Vol. 30, September 2008, No. 9, pp. 90)
Pub: Hispanic Business, Inc.
Ed: Daniel Soussa. **Description:** Three major car manufacturers, Chevrolet, BMW, and Honda, are giving market leader Toyota competition for the next generation of eco-friendly car. The latest and most advanced of the gasoline-less cars designed by the three firms, namely, the Chevrolet Volt, BMW's Hydrogen 7, and the Honda FCX Clarity, are reviewed.

25452 ■ "Look Who's Eating Loblaw's Lunch" in *Canadian Business* (Vol. 80, February 26, 2007, No. 5, pp. 44)
Pub: Rogers Media
Ed: Zena Olijnyk. **Description:** Loblaw Cos. Ltd. and Shoppers Drug Mart Corp. of Canada are finding increased competition from the global retail giant Wal-Mart Inc. The financial performance of the companies is analyzed.

25453 ■ "Lotus Starts Slowly, Dodges Subprime Woes" in *Crain's Detroit Business* (Vol. 24, April 14, 2008, No. 15, pp. 3)
Pub: Crain Communications, Inc.
Ed: Tom Henderson. **Description:** Discusses Lotus Bancorp Inc. and their business plan, which although is not right on target due to the subprime mortgage meltdown, is in a much better position than its competitors due to the quality of their loans.

25454 ■ *Macrowikinomics: Rebooting Business and the World*
Pub: Portfolio Hardcover
Ed: Don Tapscott, Anthony D. Williams. **Released:** September 28, 2010. **Price:** $27.95. **Description:** Wikinomics Don Tapscott and Anthony Williams showed how mass collaboration was changing the way businesses communicate, create value,, and compete in the new global marketplace in 2007. Now, in the wake of the global financial crisis, the principles of wikinomics have become more powerful than ever.

25455 ■ "The Main Event" in *Canadian Business* (Vol. 80, November 19, 2007, No. 23, pp. 28)
Pub: Rogers Media
Ed: Zena Olijnyk. **Description:** U.S.-based Lowe's Companies, Inc. will be opening three stores in Canada in December 2007 and another three in 2008. The housing market crisis in the U.S. is the reason behind the home improvement store's Canadian expansion. The impacts of the expansion on Canadian home care stores and on the market competition are evaluated.

25456 ■ *Making People Your Competitive Advantage*
Pub: Jossey Bass
Ed: Edward E. Lawler III. **Released:** 2008. **Price:** $29.95. **Description:** Competitive advantage in most organizations has shifted from reliability to innovation and flexibility. Organizations must combine the right structure with the right people to make it work.

25457 ■ *Marketing in a Web 2.0 World - Using Social Media, Webinars, Blogs, and More to Boost Your Small Business on a Budget*
Pub: Atlantic Publishing Company
Ed: Peter VanRysdam. **Released:** June 1, 2010. **Price:** $24.95. **Description:** Web 2.0 technologies have leveled the playing field for small companies trying to boost their presence by giving them an equal voice against larger competitors. Advice is given to help target your audience using social networking hubs.

25458 ■ "Marriott Checks Out Hotel Prospect" in *The Business Journal-Serving Metropolitan Kansas City* (Vol. 27, November 14, 2008, No. 10)
Pub: American City Business Journals, Inc.
Description: Marriott International Inc. is planning to operate a hotel in Kansas City, Missouri and may take over the Kansas City Marriot Downtown although other hotel operators are interested in bidding on the project.

25459 ■ *Mastering the Complex Sales: How to Compete and Win When the Stakes Are High!*
Pub: John Wiley & Sons, Incorporated
Ed: Jeff Thull. **Released:** May 2003. **Price:** $24.95. **Description:** Guide to compete for and win in complex selling, the business-to-business transactions involving multiple decisions by multiple people from multiple perspectives.

25460 ■ "McD's Picks a Soda Fight; Takes on 7-Eleven With $1 Pop as Economy Softens" in *Crain's Chicago Business* (April 14, 2008)
Pub: Crain Communications, Inc.
Ed: David Sterrett. **Description:** McDonald's Corp. is urging franchise owners to slash prices on large soft drinks to one dollar this summer to win customers from convenience store chains like 7-Eleven.

25461 ■ "McD's Tries to Slake Consumer Thirst for Wider Choice of Drinks" in *Advertising Age* (Vol. 79, June 9, 2008, No. 23, pp. 1)
Pub: Crain Communications, Inc.
Ed: Natalie Zmuda; Emily Bryson York. **Description:** McDonald's is testing the sale of canned and bottled drinks in about 150 locations in an attempt to offer more options to consumers who are going elsewhere for their beverage choices.

25462 ■ "Media Giant Remakes Itself: Job Cuts Signal Journal Sentinel's Focus on New Products" in *Business Journal-Milwaukee* (Oct. 12, 2007)
Pub: American City Business Journals, Inc.
Ed: Rich Kirchen. **Description:** Milwaukee Journal Sentinel is reducing its workforce by offering separation pay, and is willing to consider layoffs if the separation program fails. The downsizing is a result of lowered revenue, which was caused by the decline in printed news demand and increase in online competition. Strategies that the Journal Sentinel are employing, such as developing new products, to increase revenue are presented.

25463 ■ "Medicare Inc." in *Canadian Business* (Vol. 80, October 8, 2007, No. 20, pp. 160)
Pub: Rogers Media
Ed: Erin Pooley. **Description:** State of Canada's health care system is discussed. A report by the Fraser Institute in Vancouver predicts that public health spending in six of ten provinces in the country will use more than half the revenues from all sources by 2020. Experts believe competition in the health care industry will help solve the current problems in the sector.

25464 ■ "The Middle Ages" in *Hawaii Business* (Vol. 53, October 2007, No. 4, pp. 42)
Pub: Hawaii Business Publishing
Ed: Cathy S. Cruz-George. **Description:** Starcom Builders Inc.'s Theodore "Ted" Taketa, School Kine Cookies' Steven Gold And Sharon Serene of Sharon Serene Creative are among the participants in Hawaii's Fittest CEO competition for executives over 50 years old. Taketa takes yoga classes, and also goes to the gym while Serne has Mike Hann as her professional trainer. Eating habits of the aforementioned executives are also described.

25465 ■ "Miller's Crossroad" in *Canadian Business* (Vol. 83, September 14, 2010, No. 15, pp. 58)
Pub: Rogers Media Ltd.
Ed: Joe Castaldo. **Description:** Future Electronics founder and billionaire Robert Miller shares the secret of Future's unique operating model, which is based on inventory and market research. Miller attributes much of the company's success to its privately held status that enables quick movement against competitors.

25466 ■ *Million Dollar Website: Simple Steps to Help You Compete with the Big Boys-Even on a Small Business Budget*
Pub: Prentice Hall Press
Ed: Lori Culwell. **Released:** May 9, 2010. **Price:** $19. 95. **Description:** Resource for any small business owner wishing to build a successful Website in order to compete with big box stores.

25467 ■ "More Pain" in *Canadian Business* (Vol. 81, December 24, 2007, No. 1, pp. 12)
Pub: Rogers Media
Ed: Lauren McKeon. **Description:** Manufacturing sector in Canada is sinking with a forecast by as much as 23 percent for 2008, which can be offset as manufacturers say they plan to increase productivity by 25 percent. Details on the sector's competitiveness, workforce, importing of machinery from the U.S. and financial needs for research and development are examined.

25468 ■ "Most States Have High-Risk Health Insurance Pools" in *Crain's Detroit Business* (Vol. 24, March 24, 2008, No. 12, pp. 31)
Pub: Crain Communications, Inc.
Ed: Jay Greene. **Description:** High-risk health insurance pools, designed to cover individuals with medical conditions that essentially make them otherwise uninsurable, are being debated by the Senate Health Policy Committee; the pool concept is supported by Blue Cross Blue Shield of Michigan and contested by a number of consumer groups and competing health insurers.

25469 ■ "NBC" in *Brandweek* (Vol. 49, April 21, 2008, No. 16, pp. SR6)
Pub: VNU Business Media, Inc.
Ed: John Consoli. **Description:** Provides contact information for sales and marketing personnel for the NBC network as well as a listing of the station's top programming and an analysis of the current season and the target audience for those programs running in the current season. NBC also devised a new strategy of announcing its prime-time schedule 52 weeks in advance which was a hit for advertisers who felt this gave them a better opportunity to plan for product placement. Even with the station's creative sales programs, they could face a challenge from Fox in terms of upfront advertisement purchases.

25470 ■ "Needed: A Strategy; Banking In China" in *The Economist* (Vol. 390, January 3, 2009, No. 8612, pp. 54)
Pub: The Economist Newspaper Inc.
Description: International banks are competing for a role in China but are finding obstacles in their paths such as a reduction in the credit their operations may receive from Chinese banks and the role they can play in the public capital markets which remain limited.

25471 ■ "New Battle of Alberta: Pipelines" in *Globe & Mail* (February 3, 2006, pp. B1)
Pub: CTVglobemedia Publishing Inc.
Ed: Dave Ebner. **Description:** The details on stiffening competition between Enbridge Inc. and TransCanada Corp., to build petroleum pipeline from Alberta to Wisconsin, are presented.

25472 ■ "The Next Great Canadian Idea?" in *Canadian Business* (Vol. 81, July 21, 2008, No. 11, pp. 45)
Pub: Rogers Media Ltd.
Ed: Sharda Prashad. **Description:** Thane Heins has invented a generator that produces energy in an isolated system which contradicts the law of conservation of energy. Perepiteia generator is referred to as a 'perpetual motion machine.' Other inventions slated for the Canadian invention competition include Rob Matthies' batteries and Frank Naumann's Smart Trap.

25473 ■ *Niche and Grow Rich*
Pub: Entrepreneur Press
Ed: Jennifer Basye Sander; Peter Sander. **Released:** 2003. **Description:** Consultants share insight to entrepreneurs wishing to find a profitable niche market. Authors write that good niche businesses are easy to start and easy to defend from competitors. They also report that finding a successful niche can attract and maintain good customers who are willing to pay more for unique goods and services.

25474 ■ "A Novel Approach to the Market" in *Agency Sales Magazine* (Vol. 39, December 2009, No. 11, pp. 10)
Pub: MANA
Ed: Jack Foster. **Description:** R/B Sales created a "merchandising specialist" position that travels their territory and works with distributor counter sales teams. This puts them ahead of their competition as it increases their visibility, appeal and mix of products in their area.

25475 ■ "Office Supplier Won't Wait for Opportunity to Knock" in *Business Courier* (Vol. 24, December 28, 2008, No. 37, pp. 2)
Pub: American City Business Journals, Inc.
Ed: Lucy May. **Description:** Ace Products, an office supplier, stays competitive through its customer service and pricing.

25476 ■ "Omniplex on the Case" in *Black Enterprise* (Vol. 37, December 2006, No. 5, pp. 38)
Pub: Earl G. Graves Publishing Co. Inc.
Ed: Glenn Townes. **Description:** Office of Personnel Management in Washington D.C. recently awarded a service contract to Omniplex World Services Corp. Virginia-based, The Chantilly, will perform security investigations and background checks on current and prospective federal employees and military personnel and contractors.

25477 ■ "On tap: More Could Get MEGA Credits; Need to Look Outside State May Be Cut" in *Crain's Detroit Business* (April 7, 2008)
Pub: Crain Communications, Inc.
Ed: Amy Lane. **Description:** In order to qualify for Michigan Economic Growth Authority tax credits Michigan businesses may no longer have to shop outside the state due to a new bill which has already passed the state Senate and will move on to the House; the bill, along with further changes to the MEGA program, is designed to provide incentives for investments that would add relevance and make Michigan more competitive.

25478 ■ "Open Skies: Opportunity, Challenge for Airlines" in *Crain's Chicago Business* (April 21, 2008)
Pub: Crain Communications, Inc.
Ed: Paul Merrion. **Description:** Discusses the new aviation agreement between Europe and the United States known as Open Skies; the pact creates opportunities for U.S. carriers to fly to new destinations in Europe from more U.S. cities; it also allows carriers to fly between European cities, something they have not been able to do until now.

25479 ■ "An Opportunity for Patience" in *Barron's* (Vol. 88, June 30, 2008, No. 26, pp. M5)
Pub: Dow Jones & Co., Inc.
Ed: Fleming Meeks. **Description:** Shares of Louisiana-Pacific are near their 52-week low at $8.95 per share making them look like a better buy than they were at $11.51 in May, 2008. The company is a to player in a cyclical business and its balance sheet is sound compared to its peers with net debt at just $84 million or 20 percent of total capital.

25480 ■ *Outsmart! How to Do What Your Competitors Can't*
Pub: FT Press
Ed: Jim Champy. **Released:** March 7, 2008. **Price:** $22.99. **Description:** Small business growth can be achieved through outsmarting your competition. The author identifies eight powerful ways to compete in the toughest marketplace.

25481 ■ "Ownership Preferences, Competitive Heterogeneity, and Family-Controlled Businesses" in *Family Business Review* (June 2006)
Pub: Family Firm Institute Inc.
Ed: David G. Hoopes, Danny Miller. **Description:** Impact of ownership structure and corporate governance choices on competition among family-owned businesses is explored.

25482 ■ "P&G's Iams Finds Itself in a Pet-Food Dogfight" in *Advertising Age* (Vol. 78, March 5, 2007, No. 10, pp. 6)
Pub: Crain Communications, Inc.
Ed: Jack Neff. **Description:** Proctor & Gamble Co.'s Iams has been slow to embrace the trend toward foods for pets that appear fit for human consumption. Competitors such as Nestle Purina have made big gains with its colorful premium Beneful brand and dry nuggets that look like chunks of vegetables and meat. Statistical data included.

25483 ■ "Pavilions Poised for Image Overhaul" in *The Business Journal - Serving Phoenix and the Valley of the Sun* (Vol. 28, August 22, 2008)
Pub: American City Business Journals, Inc.
Ed: Jan Buchholz. **Description:** DeRitto Partners Inc. is expected to push through with plans for a major renovation of the 1.1 million-square foot Scottsdale Pavilions in Scottsdale, Arizona. An aggressive marketing campaign is planned to be included in the renovation, which aims to address high vacancy rates and competition. Views and information on the planned renovation are presented.

25484 ■ "Play By Play: These Video Products Can Add New Life to a Stagnant Website" in *Black Enterprise* (Vol. 41, December 2010, No. 5)
Pub: Earl G. Graves Publishing Co. Inc.
Ed: Marcia Wade Talbert. **Description:** Web Visible, provider of online marketing products and services, cites video capability as the fastest-growing Website feature for small business advertisers. Profiles of various devices for adding video to a Website are included.

25485 ■ *Playing Bigger Than You Are: How to Sell Big Accounts Even If You're David in a World of Goliaths*
Pub: John Wiley & Sons, Inc.
Ed: William T. Brooks, William P.G. Brooks. **Released:** November 1, 2009. **Price:** $18.99. **Description:** Small and mid-size companies are shown how to compete with larger firms and sell big accounts.

25486 ■ "Please Pass the Mayo" in *Crain's Chicago Business* (Vol. 31, April 28, 2008, No. 17, pp. 32)
Pub: Crain Communications, Inc.
Ed: Samantha Stainburn. **Description:** Fort Dearborn Co. has come a long way since it started as on one-press print shop; the family-owned company was struggling to keep up with the technology of making consumer product labels for curvy bottles of products like V8 V-Fusion juice and in 2006 sold off to Genstar Capital LLC which has pushed for acquisitions; last year, Fort Derborn bought its biggest competitor, Renaissance Mark Inc., doubling its size and adding spirit and wine makers to its client roster.

25487 ■ "Port in the Storm" in *Canadian Business* (Vol. 81, October 13, 2008, No. 17, pp. 101)
Pub: Rogers Media Ltd.
Ed: Calvin Leung. **Description:** Interport Inc.'s state-of-the-art studio complex in Toronto is discussed. The strong Canadian dollar, along with disputes within the movie industry, are creating challenges for the studio to secure Hollywood projects. Interport plans to compete for Hollywood projects based on quality.

25488 ■ "Pre-K Pressure" in *Hawaii Business* (Vol. 53, October 2007, No. 4, pp. 32)
Pub: Hawaii Business Publishing
Ed: David K. Choo. **Description:** Kindergarten admission in Hawaii is becoming more competitive. Parents, for example, prepare their children for the kindergarten admissions process by bringing them to the schools before the interview or by paying for tutorial services. The impacts of increased competition in school admissions on the life of Hawaiian children are discussed.

25489 ■ "Prepaid Phones Surge in Bad Economy" in *Advertising Age* (Vol. 79, November 17, 2008, No. 43, pp. 6)
Pub: Crain Communications, Inc.
Ed: Rita Chang. **Description:** Prepay cell phone offerings are becoming increasingly competitive amid a greater choice of plans and handsets. In an economic environment in which many consumers are unable to pass the credit checks required for traditional cell phone plans, the prepay market is surging.

25490 ■ "The Price of Profitability" in *Green Industry Pro* (Vol. 23, March 2011, No. 3, pp. 18)
Pub: Cygnus Business Media
Ed: Tony Bass. **Description:** Profit Builder Process is used to help landscaping companies be more competitive. Landscape contractors report pricing among their largest challenges and although the economy is improving, homeowners are paying closer attention to quality and service.

25491 ■ "Price War: Managerial Salaries Are Beating the National Average, But Maybe Not for Long" in *Canadian Business* (March 31, 2008)
Pub: Rogers Media
Ed: Megan Harman. **Description:** Real average hourly earnings of managers increase by 20 percent in ten years as companies increase wages to avoid the risk of losing key managers to the competition and in preparation for the retirement of baby boomers. Tough market conditions affect management more since their incentives are tied to individual and corporate performance.

25492 ■ "Procter & Gamble Boosts Bet on Exclusive Brands" in *Business Courier* (Vol. 27, July 9, 2010, No. 10, pp. 1)
Pub: Business Courier
Ed: Jon Newberry. **Description:** Procter & Gamble is creating more special versions of its brands such as Pringles and Pampers exclusively for retail partners such as Tesco in the U.K. The greater push towards this direction is seen as a way to regain market share.

25493 ■ "Putting 'Great' Back Into A&P" in *Crain's New York Business* (Vol. 24, January 7, 2008, No. 1, pp. 3)
Pub: Crain Communications, Inc.
Description: After five straight years ending in 2005, A&P Grocery lost revenue; due to a sweeping plan to freshen up its supermarkets the company returned to growth mode and was able to acquire longtime competitor Pathmark Stores.

25494 ■ "Q&A: Joseph Ribkoff" in *Canadian Business* (Vol. 81, March 31, 2008, No. 5, pp. 4)
Pub: Rogers Media
Ed: Zena Olijnyk. **Description:** Joseph Ribkoff started his career in the garment trade by sweeping floors and running deliveries for a dress manufacturer called Town & Country and earned $16 a week. Ribkoff says that the key to controlling costs in Canada is to invest in the latest equipment and technology to stay competitive.

25495 ■ "Queen Bees: All Sting, No Honey" in *Business Horizons* (September-October 2007, pp. 348)
Pub: Elsevier Technology Publications
Ed: Catherine M. Dalton. **Description:** Female rivalry or competition in the workplace and other domains are explained and compared to the behavior of honeybees. Novels and other works on the topic of competition among women are discussed.

25496 ■ "Quiznos Franchisees Walloped by Recession" in *Advertising Age* (Vol. 79, October 20, 2008, No. 39, pp. 3)
Pub: Crain Communications, Inc.
Ed: Emily Bryson York. **Description:** While the recession has taken a toll on the entire restaurant industry, a number of Quiznos franchisees claim to have been disproportionately affected due to lackluster marketing, higher-than-average commodity costs, competition with Subway and a premium-pricing structure that is incompatible with a tight economy.

25497 ■ *The Race for a New Game Machine: Creating the Chips Inside the Xbox 360 and the PlayStation 3*
Pub: Citadel Press
Ed: David Shippy, Mickie Phipps. **Released:** 2009. **Price:** $21.95. **Description:** The story of Microsoft and Sony's race to deliver the goods for the Xbox 360 and Playstation 3 is explored.

25498 ■ "R&R Launches Upscale Spoony's and Low Fat Dragon's Den" in *Ice Cream Reporter* (Vol. 23, August 20, 2010, No. 9, pp. 3)
Pub: Ice Cream Reporter
Description: European ice cream manufacturer R&R has acquired French ice cream maker Rolland and will position itself as an upscale challenger to brands like Ben & Jerry's.

25499 ■ "Ready To Take Your Business Global?" in *Black Enterprise* (Vol. 41, August 2010, No. 1, pp. 89)
Pub: Earl G. Graves Publishing Co. Inc.
Ed: Alan Hughes. **Description:** The 2010 Black Enterprise Entrepreneurs Conference held in May stressed the need for all small firms to promote a global agenda in order to stay competitive.

25500 ■ *Reality Check: The Irreverent Guide to Outsmarting, Outmanaging, and Outmarketing Your Competition*
Pub: Penguin Group USA Inc.
Ed: Guy Kawasaki. **Price:** $29.95. **Description:** Marketing guru and entrepreneur, Guy Kawasaki, provides a compilation of his blog posts on all aspects of starting and operating a business.

25501 ■ "Research and Markets Adds Report: Ghana: Convergence, Broadband and Internet Market" in *Wireless News* (September 4, 2009)
Pub: Close-Up Media
Description: Overview of a new report by Research and Markets entitled, "Ghana Convergence, Broadband and Internet Market - Overview, Statistics and Forecasts." Ghana was among the first countries in Africa connected to the Internet and to introduce ADSL broadband services; however, only 30 of the 140 licensed ISP's are operational making the sector highly competitive.

25502 ■ *Researching Company Financial Information*
Pub: MarketResearch.com
Released: Edition V. **Price:** $59, individuals. **Description:** Helps readers learn how to research and understand financial data from companies, as well as compile in-depth financial data on competitors in order to get a better picture of the competition. **Publication Includes:** A directory of corporate financial info sources.

25503 ■ "Retail Health Clinics Sprout in Area; Doctors Feel Threat, Have Concerns" in *Crain's Detroit Business* (April 7, 2008)
Pub: Crain Communications, Inc.
Ed: Mike Scott. **Description:** Competing with doctors' offices for routine patient visits are the retail health clinics which have made their way into the metro Detroit area. Physicians are concerned about the limited doctor supervision on site.

25504 ■ "Rich or Poor, Hospitals Must Work Together" in *Crain's Chicago Business* (Vol. 31, April 28, 2008, No. 17, pp. 22)
Pub: Crain Communications, Inc.
Description: Chicago=area safety-net hospitals that serve the poor, uninsured and underinsured are struggling to stay open while wealthier areas compete to build advanced facilities for the expensive surgical procedures their privately insured patients can afford. If these safety-net hospitals close, their patients, many of them in ambulances, will show up at the remaining hospitals resulting in a strain that will test the ability of hospitals across the region to care for all of their patients. Hospitals need to address the threats to the local health care system before it slips into crisis since the current every-hospital-for-itself approach that pays off big for some will eventually will make losers of everyone.

25505 ■ "RIM's Test of Faith" in *Canadian Business* (Vol. 80, April 9, 2007, No. 8, pp. 29)
Pub: Rogers Media
Ed: Joe Castaldo. **Description:** The growth of Research In Motion Ltd. in terms of its sales and profits despite a patent suit on it and competition of rivals is discussed.

25506 ■ "Rivals Blow In" in *Crain's Cleveland Business* (Vol. 30, June 1, 2009, No. 21, pp. 1)
Pub: Crain Communications, Inc.
Ed: Chuck Soder. **Description:** U.S. and Canadian competitors are hoping to start construction of offshore wind farm project proposed by Cuyahoga County's Great Lakes Energy Development Task Force. Details of the project are included.

25507 ■ "Safeway" in *Ice Cream Reporter* (Vol. 23, September 20, 2010, No. 10, pp. 8)
Pub: Ice Cream Reporter
Description: Safeway supermarkets have upsized their private label ice cream to a full half gallon, thus reversing the trend where most brands were shrinking their containers.

25508 ■ "St. Elizabeth Fights for Share at St. Lukes" in *Business Courier* (Vol. 27, November 12, 2010, No. 28, pp. 1)
Pub: Business Courier
Ed: James Ritchie. **Description:** Key information on how St. Elizabeth Healthcare helps partner St. Luke's Hospitals increase market share in the healthcare industry are presented. Some of St. Luke's hospitals, such as the St. Elizabeth Fort Thomas in Kentucky, are struggling with low occupancy rates, prompting St. Elizabeth to invest about $24 million to help St. Luke's increase its market share.

25509 ■ "Sales and the Absolute Power of Information" in *Agency Sales Magazine* (Vol. 39, July 2009, No. 7, pp. 16)
Pub: MANA
Ed: Dave Kahle. **Description:** Having good information can help a sales representative deliver effective sales performance. A process for collecting information about customers, prospects, and competitors is discussed.

25510 ■ "Sales Force Expertise: A Competitive Advantage" in *Agency Sales Magazine* (Vol. 39, November 2009, No. 10, pp. 10)
Pub: MANA
Ed: Ken Valla. **Description:** Maintaining an expert sales force is a competitive advantage that sales leaders can count on. The skills that the sales force need to have include "consultative selling" or the ability to understand and link to a customer's business priorities, conducting a process conversation, and asking discovery questions.

25511 ■ "Satellite Wars" in *Canadian Business* (Vol. 79, October 23, 2006, No. 21, pp. 35)
Pub: Rogers Media
Ed: Andy Holloway. **Description:** The strategies used by Sirius Canada Inc. and XM Canada, two major satellite radio companies to acquire more number of suscribers, are discussed.

25512 ■ *The Secret Language of Competitive Intelligence: How to See Through and Stay Ahead of Business Disruptions, Distortions, Rumors, and Smoke*
Pub: Crown Publishing Group
Ed: Leonard M. Fuld. **Released:** May 2006. **Price:** $24.95.

25513 ■ "Service With a Smile...And Comfy Chairs" in *Crain's Chicago Business* (Vol. 31, April 28, 2008, No. 17, pp. 46)
Pub: Crain Communications, Inc.
Ed: Phuong Ly. **Description:** O'Hare Auto Group has improved the experience of waiting for service on one's vehicle by offering wireless Internet, comfortable chairs and plasma TVs. The company also has long service hours, running from 6 a.m. to midnight Monday through Thursday so customers don't have to take time off work.

25514 ■ "Shaw, Telus Take Up Battle Positions" in *Globe & Mail* (January 1, 2006, pp. B1)
Pub: CTVglobemedia Publishing Inc.
Ed: Catherine McKLean. **Description:** The competition between Shaw Communications Inc. and Telus Corp. over voice over Internet protocol offer for customers is presented.

25515 ■ "Shipbuilding & Defence" in *Canadian Sailings* (July 7, 2008)
Pub: Commonwealth Business Media
Ed: Sharon Hobson. **Description:** Overview of the Joint Support Ship Project whose initial budget was set at $2.1 billion for the acquisition of the ships required for the Canadian navy; another $800 million was allotted for 20 years of in-service support. Four teams of competitors bid for the contract and the Department of National Defence decided to fund two teams for the project definition phase of the competition.

25516 ■ "Shout and Devour" in *Tulsa World* (November 7, 2009)
Pub: Tulsa World
Ed: Kyle Arnold. **Description:** Profile of convenience store Shout and Sack whose owners have distanced themselves from the corporate fray of the chain stores by offering homemade lunches served at a counter; the store recently gained national exposure that highlighted the popularity despite a market share heavily dominated by franchises and chains.

25517 ■ *Silos, Politics and Turf Wars: A Leadership Fable about Destroying the Barriers That Turn Colleagues Into Competitors*
Pub: Jossey Bass
Ed: Patrick M. Lencioni. **Released:** February 17, 2006. **Price:** $24.95. **Description:** The author addresses management problems through a fable that revolves around a self-employed consultant who has to dismantle silos at an upscale hotel, a technology company and a hospital. The story explains how organizations can use a collective operational vision in order to overcome pride, greed, and tribalism and work as a team with the same goal in mind.

25518 ■ "Sinai Doctor Seeks FDA OK for Drug" in *Baltimore Business Journal* (Vol. 28, July 16, 2010, No. 10, pp. 1)
Pub: Baltimore Business Journal
Ed: Emily Mullin. **Description:** Paul Gurbel, Sinai Hospital Center for Thrombosis Research director, is seeking an FDA approval of Brilinta, a drug which he helped create and test. Gurbel says that the approval could bring the drug to market as early as December 2010. The drug is expected to rival Bristol-Myers' Plavix, which generated almost $6.2 billion in 2009.

25519 ■ "Six Leading Economists on What to Expect in the Year Ahead: David Wolf" in *Canadian Business* (Dec. 24, 2007)
Pub: Rogers Media
Ed: David Wolf. **Description:** The Canadian dollar recently hit parity with the U.S. dollar, and the exchange rate is going fast and overvaluation of the Canadian dollar could bring in competition from U.S. products. Details on the impact of the slowdown of the U.S. economy on the exchange rate speed are discussed.

25520 ■ "Size Does Matter" in *International Journal of Globalisation and Small Business* (Vol. 4, September 21, 2010, No. 1, pp. 61)
Pub: Publishers Communication Group
Ed: Julia Cornnell, Ranjit Voola. **Description:** Examination of how members of an Australian-based manufacturing and engineering cluster share knowledge through networking as a means to improve competitive advantage.

25521 ■ "Slow but Steady into the Future" in *Barron's* (Vol. 88, July 7, 2008, No. 27, pp. M)
Pub: Dow Jones & Co., Inc.
Ed: Mark Veverka. **Description:** Investors are advised to maintain their watch on the shares of business software company NetSuite. The company's chief executive officer, Zach Nelson, claims that the company has a 10-year lead on its competitors with the development of software-as-a service.

25522 ■ *Small Business Survival Guide: Starting, Protecting, and Securing Your Business for Long-Term Success*
Pub: Adams Media Corporation
Ed: Cliff Ennico. **Released:** September 2005. **Price:** $12.95 (US), $17.95 (Canadian). **Description:** Entrepreneurship in the new millennium. Topics include creditors, taxes, competition, business law, and accounting.

25523 ■ "Small Businesses Get Creative to Retain Workers" in *Crain's Detroit Business* (Vol. 24, March 17, 2008, No. 11, pp. 21)
Pub: Crain Communications, Inc.
Ed: Nancy Kaffer. **Description:** Small businesses are often unable to compete with larger firms when it comes to offering employees fringe benefits and such perks as a company gym or an in-house chef; however, many smaller companies have found that the key to gaining employee loyalty lies in creating an atmosphere in which employees feel job satisfaction. Also provides tips on how to keep employees.

25524 ■ "Small Dutch Islands Saba, Statia Content With Low-Key Niche" in *Travel Weekly* (Vol. 69, August 16, 2010, No. 33, pp. 22)
Pub: NorthStar Travel Media LLC
Ed: Gay Nagle Myers. **Description:** Small Caribbean islands market and promote their region for tourism by never competing with the bigger destinations. Saba and Statia are the two smallest islands in the Caribbean and rely on repeat guests, word-of-mouth recommendations and travel agents willing to promote them.

25525 ■ *The Small-Mart Revolution: How Local Businesses Are Beating the Global Competition*
Pub: Berrett-Koehler Publishers, Incorporated
Ed: Michael H. Shuman. **Released:** July 2007. **Price:** $16.95. **Description:** Advice is given to help small businesses compete in a global environment.

25526 ■ "Smart Car Sales Take Big Hit in Recession" in *Business Journal-Milwaukee* (Vol. 28, December 10, 2010, No. 10, pp. A1)
Pub: Milwaukee Business Journal
Ed: Stacey Vogel Davis. **Description:** Sales of smart cars in Milwaukee declined in 2010. Smart Center Milwaukee sold only 52 new cars through October 2010. Increased competition is seen as a reason for the decline in sales.

25527 ■ "Snatching Talent: Local Law Firms Quietly Boost Poaching" in *Boston Business Journal* (Vol. 31, July 29, 2011, No. 27, pp. 3)
Pub: Boston Business Journal
Ed: Lisa van der Pool. **Description:** National law firms Jones Day and Latham & Watkins LLP set up offices in Boston, Massachusetts. Their move also created an upswing on confidential conversation as both firms are aggressively poaching lawyers from Boston's other top firms.

25528 ■ *The Social Media Bible: Tactics, Tools, and Strategies for Business Success*
Pub: John Wiley & Sons, Inc.
Ed: Lon Safko, David Brake. **Released:** June 17, 2009. **Price:** $29.95. **Description:** Information is given to build or transform a business into social media, where customers, employees, and prospects connect, collaborate, and champion products and services in order to increase sales and to beat the competition.

25529 ■ "Some Relief Possible Following Painful Week" in *Barron's* (Vol. 88, July 14, 2008, No. 28, pp. M3)
Pub: Dow Jones & Co., Inc.
Ed: Kopin Tan. **Description:** Dow Chemical is offering a 74 percent premium to acquire Rohm & Haas' coatings and electronics materials operations. Frontline amassed a 5.6 percent stake in rival Overseas Shipholding Group and a merger between the two would create a giant global fleet with pricing power. Highlights of the U.S. stock market during the week that ended in July 11, 2008 are discussed. Statistical data included.

25530 ■ "Special Sector" in *Crain's Cleveland Business* (Vol. 28, November 5, 2007, No. 44, pp. 3)
Pub: Crain Communications, Inc.
Ed: David Bennett. **Description:** Specialty Metals Processing Inc. is investing more than $6 million to amp up productions; the company believes this big investment will pay off due to the company's ability to process complex metal alloys, such as titanium, in a region where there is a small number of competitors.

25531 ■ "Staging a Martini-and-GQ Lifestyle; Faux Possessions Play to Buyer's Aspirations" in *Crain's Chicago Business* (April 21, 2008)
Pub: Crain Communications, Inc.
Ed: Kevin Davis. **Description:** Due to the competition of the slumping housing market, home stagers are becoming more prominent and are using creative

ways to make an impression beyond de-cluttering, painting and cleaning by using accents such as casually placed magazines, candles and table settings.

25532 ■ *The Starfish and the Spider: The Unstoppable Power of Leaderless Organizations*
Pub: Portfolio Publishing
Ed: Ori Brafman; Rod A. Beckstrom. **Released:** 2008. **Price:** $15.00 paperback. **Description:** Through their experiences promoting peace and economic development through decentralizing networking, the authors offer insight into ways that decentralizing can change organizations. Three techniques for combating a decentralized competitor are examined.

25533 ■ *Starting Green: An Ecopreneur's Guide to Starting a Green Business from Business Plans to Profits*
Pub: Entrepreneur Press
Ed: Glenn E. Croston. **Released:** September 9, 2010. **Price:** $21.95. **Description:** Entrepreneur and scientist outlines green business essentials and helps uncover eco-friendly business opportunities, build a sustainable business plan, and gain the competitive advantage.

25534 ■ "State Lawmakers Should Try Raising Jobs, Not Taxes" in *Crain's Chicago Business* (Vol. 31, March 24, 2008, No. 12, pp. 20)
Pub: Crain Communications, Inc.
Ed: Diug Whitley. **Description:** According to U.S. Department of Labor figures through December 2007, Illinois has ranked 45th in the nation in job growth for seven straight months. Many feel that the state would not need to raise taxes if they spent more time working to keep and attract employers that create jobs.

25535 ■ "State Wants to Add Escape Clause to Leases" in *Sacramento Business Journal* (Vol. 28, October 14, 2011, No. 33, pp. 1)
Pub: Sacramento Business Journal
Ed: Michael Shaw. **Description:** California Governor Jerry Brown's administration has decided to add escape clauses to new lease agreements, which created new worry for building owners and brokers in Sacramento, California. Real estate brokers believe the appropriation of funds clauses have been making the lenders nervous and would result in less competition.

25536 ■ "Stepping Up" in *Baltimore Business Journal* (Vol. 28, October 22, 2010, No. 24, pp. 1)
Pub: Baltimore Business Journal
Ed: Erik Siemers. **Description:** Uner Armour Inc. will release its Micro G line of four basketball sneakers on October 23, 2010. The company's executives mentioned that Under Armour's goal is to appeal to customers, and not to chip away at Nike Inc.'s supremacy in basketball shoes. The new sneakers will range from $80 to $110.

25537 ■ "Stikemans' Ascent, Its Legacy, and Its Future" in *Globe & Mail* (January 29, 2007, pp. B2)
Pub: CTVglobemedia Publishing Inc.
Ed: Jacquie McNish. **Description:** Pierre Raymond, chairman of legal firm Stikeman Elliott LLP, talks about his strategies to handle competition, his challenges, and about Canada's present mergers and acquisition scenario. Stikeman achieved the first place in 2006 M&A legal rankings.

25538 ■ "Stuck With Two Mortgages; The Nightmare When Buyers Upgrade" in *Crain's Chicago Business* (Vol. 31, April 21, 2008, No. 16)
Pub: Crain Communications, Inc.
Ed: Darci Smith. **Description:** Discusses the problem a number of people are facing due to the slump in the housing market: being stuck with two mortgages when they move because their former homes have not sold. Many thought they could afford to move to a larger home, anticipating significant equity appreciation that did not occur; now they are left with lowering their price and competing with the host of new developments.

25539 ■ "Suited for Success" in *Retail Merchandiser* (Vol. 51, July-August 2011, No. 4, pp. 6)
Pub: Phoenix Media Corporation
Description: MyBestFit is a size-matching body scanner that helps consumers find the perfect size clothing for themselves, giving brick and mortar retailers an edge on ecommerce competitors.

25540 ■ "Summit, Lions Gate are in Talks to Merge Studios" in *Wall Street Journal Eastern Edition* (November 29, 2011, pp. B2)
Pub: Dow Jones & Company Inc.
Ed: Erica Orden, Michelle Kung. **Description:** Movie studio Summit Entertainment LLC is in talks with television producer Lions Gate Entertainment Corporation about a possible merger. Previous talks have taken place, but no deal was ever reached. Such a deal would create a large, independent studio able to compete in the market with the big Hollywood giants.

25541 ■ "The Superpower Dilemma" in *Canadian Business* (Vol. 83, August 17, 2010, No. 13-14, pp. 42)
Pub: Rogers Media Ltd.
Description: Canada has been an energy superpower partly because it controls the energy source and the production means, particularly of fossil fuels. However, Canada's status as superpower could diminish if it replaces petroleum exports with renewable technology for using sources of energy available globally.

25542 ■ "Supply Chain Visibility A Two-Way Street" in *Canadian Sailings* (July 7, 2008)
Pub: Commonwealth Business Media
Ed: Jack Kohane. **Description:** Canada is experiencing unprecedented market pressures due to globalization. Competition from foreign countries, demand for better and faster service from customers and shorter innovation cycles are some of the problems the country is facing regarding trade and the importing and exporting industry.

25543 ■ "Surprise Offer for Dofasco Puts Heat on Arcelor" in *Globe & Mail* (January 16, 2006, pp. B1)
Pub: CTVglobemedia Publishing Inc.
Ed: Greg Keenan. **Description:** The details of competition between ThyssenKrupp AG and Arcelor SA to bid Dofasco Inc. are presented.

25544 ■ "Swift Shift" in *Crain's Cleveland Business* (Vol. 28, November 12, 2007, No. 45, pp. 1)
Pub: Crain Communications, Inc.
Ed: Shannon Mortland. **Description:** Discusses the ways in which Southwest General Health Center is working to stay competitive in a region that is highly saturated with health care providers.

25545 ■ "Tale of the Tape: IPhone Vs. G1" in *Advertising Age* (Vol. 79, October 27, 2008, No. 40, pp. 6)
Pub: Crain Communications, Inc.
Ed: Rita Chang. **Description:** T-Mobile's G1 has been positioned as the first serious competitor to Apple's iPhone. G1 is the first mobile phone to run on the Google-backed, open-source platform Android.

25546 ■ "Tamara Vrooman" in *Canadian Business* (Vol. 80, November 19, 2007, No. 23, pp. 9)
Pub: Rogers Media
Ed: Regan Ray. **Description:** Profile of Tamara Vrooman, newly appointed CEO of Canada's largest credit union, Vancity. Vrooman believes that Vancity has an advantage over big bank when it comes to the flexibility of products the company offers. The role of Vancity and credit unions in the banking sector of Canada is discussed.

25547 ■ "Team Bonding for Fun and Profit" in *Women Entrepreneur* (December 3, 2008)
Pub: Entrepreneur Media Inc.
Ed: Eve Gumpel. **Description:** Discusses the benefits that competitions such as the 2008 BG U.S. Challenge in Lake Placid, New York, can offer in terms of team building and employee motivation as well as networking and the development of a positive working relationship with partners and competitors alike.

25548 ■ "That Vision Thing" in *Canadian Business* (Vol. 80, December 25, 2006, No. 1, pp. 78)
Pub: Rogers Media
Description: Suggestions for better Canadian tax policy and making airspace competitive among other things, to improve the economy in 2007, are presented.

25549 ■ "Thomas Morley; President, The Lube Stop Inc., 37" in *Crain's Cleveland Business* (Vol. 28, November 19, 2007, No. 46, pp. F-12)
Pub: Crain Communications, Inc.
Ed: David Bennett. **Description:** Profile of Thomas Morley, president of The Lube Stop Inc., who is dedicated to promoting the company's strong environmental record as an effective way to differentiate Lube Stop from its competition. Since Mr. Morley came to the company in 2004, Lube Stop has increased sales by 10 percent and has boosted its operating profits by 30 percent.

25550 ■ "Tiny Telecom Big Prize in Bell Aliant Bid Battle" in *Globe & Mail* (April 4, 2007, pp. B1)
Pub: CTVglobemedia Publishing Inc.
Ed: Catherine McLean. **Description:** The competition between Bell Aliant Regional Communications Income Fund of BCE Inc. and Bragg Communications Inc. to bid for acquiring Amtelecom Income Fund is discussed.

25551 ■ "To Be Seen Is to Be Successful" in *Pet Product News* (Vol. 64, December 2010, No. 12, pp. 12)
Pub: BowTie Inc.
Ed: David Arvin. **Description:** Guidelines on how pet business retailers can boost customer visibility are described considering that complacency could hamper retailers' efforts to effectively market their businesses. To enhance customer base and stand out from competing businesses, being different, strategic, creative, and differentiated is emphasized.

25552 ■ "To Keep Freight Rolling, Springfield Must Grease the Hub" in *Crain's Chicago Business* (Vol. 31, April 21, 2008, No. 16, pp. 22)
Pub: Crain Communications, Inc.
Ed: Paul O'Connor. **Description:** Discusses the importance of upgrading Chicago's continental-hub freight rail system which is integral to moving international products as well as domestic ones. Global tonnage is expected to double by 2020 and unless more money is designated to upgrade the infrastructure the local and national economy will suffer.

25553 ■ "Tom Gaglardi" in *Canadian Business* (Vol. 82, April 27, 2009, No. 7, pp. 56)
Pub: Rogers Media
Ed: Calvin Leung. **Description:** Northland Properties Corporation president Tom Gaglardi believes that their business model of keeping much of operations in-house allows the firm to crate assets at a lesser price while commanding higher margins than their competitors. He believes that it is an ideal time to invest in the hospitality industry because of opportunities to purchase properties at low prices.

25554 ■ "Too Much too Soon" in *Barron's* (Vol. 89, July 27, 2009, No. 30, pp. 33)
Pub: Dow Jones & Co., Inc.
Ed: Leslie P. Norton. **Description:** Shares of hhgregg have risen 85 percent in the year leading up to July 2009 and analysts believe the stock could hit 25.

However, their 113 outlets are concentrated in states where unemployment is above 10 percent and expanding into areas already overstored. Competition is also rife and credit availability is still tight.

25555 ■ "Top Design Award for Massey Ferguson 7624 Dyna-VT" in *Farm Industry News* (November 14, 2011)
Pub: Penton Business Media Inc.
Description: Massey Ferguson won top honors for its MF 7624 Dyna-VT as the Golden Tractor for Design award in the 2012 Tractor of the Year competition. The award is presented annually by journalists from 22 leading farming magazines in Europe and manufacturers have to be nominated to enter.

25556 ■ "A Torch in the Darkness" in *Canadian Business* (Vol. 83, August 17, 2010, No. 13-14, pp. 66)
Pub: Rogers Media Ltd.
Ed: Joe Castaldo. **Description:** Research In Motion (RIM) unveiled the BlackBerry Touch, featuring a touch screen as well as a physical keyboard, in an attempt to repel competitors and expand share in the consumer smart phone market. RIM shares have fallen 43 percent from its peak in 2009.

25557 ■ "Tourism Bureau Seeks Hotel Tax Hike" in *Baltimore Business Journal* (Vol. 27, December 18, 2009, No. 32, pp. 1)
Pub: American City Business Journals
Ed: Rachel Bernstein. **Description:** Baltimore, Maryland's tourism agency, Visit Baltimore, has proposed a new hotel tax that could produce $2 million annually for its marketing budget, fund improvements to the city's 30-year-old convention center and help it compete for World Cup soccer games. Baltimore hotel leaders discuss the new tax.

25558 ■ "Train Now to Get the Competitive Edge" in *Contractor* (Vol. 56, October 2009, No. 10, pp. 58)
Pub: Penton Media, Inc.
Ed: Merry Beth Hall. **Description:** Due to the harsh economic climate, mechanical contractors would be well-served to train their employees while they have time to take them out of the field. This will help ensure that they are not behind when the economic recovery happens. Suggestions on how to choose the best type of training are presented.

25559 ■ "Travel Rewards Take Off" in *Inc.* (Vol. 33, October 2011, No. 8, pp. 46)
Pub: Inc. Magazine
Ed: Matthew DeLuca. **Description:** Credit card companies are offering travel reward cards with special perks, including sign-up bonuses; three such cards are described.

25560 ■ "TSX Linkup Sets Stage for Battle" in *Globe & Mail* (March 6, 2007, pp. B1)
Pub: CTVglobemedia Publishing Inc.
Ed: Boyd Erman; Sinclair Stewart. **Description:** The strategic alliance between TSX Group Inc. and International Securities Exchange Holdings Inc. for the establishment of a derivatives exchange in Canada is discussed. The prospects of competition between the new exchange and the Montreal Exchange are discussed.

25561 ■ "Turfway Slowing its Gait" in *Business Courier* (Vol. 26, November 6, 2009, No. 28, pp. 1)
Pub: American City Business Journals, Inc.
Ed: Jon Newberry. **Description:** Kentucky's Turfway Park will be decreasing its weekly race schedule from five days to three days in the first two months of 2010, and to four days in March 2010. The decision to make reductions in the schedule is attributed to the relocation of thoroughbred racing to states that allow casino gambling. As a result, Turfway Park's resources and purse money would be focused on less days.

25562 ■ "Two Local Bakers Winners of TV's 'Cupcake Wars'" in *Toledo Blade* (July 6, 2011)
Pub: Toledo Times
Description: Winners of cable network Food Channel's Cupcake Wars, Lori Jacobs and Dana Iliev own Cake in a Cup in Toledo, Ohio. The partners shop features creative cupcakes with names such as Monkey Business, Pretty in Pink, and Tropical Getaway.

25563 ■ *The Ultimate Competitive Advantage*
Pub: Berrett-Koehler Publishers
Ed: Donald Mitchell; Carol Coles; B. Thomas Golisano. **Released:** March 12, 2003. **Price:** $36.95. **Description:** Results of a ten year study of companies that experienced fast growth over a three year period shows that while unsuccessful companies apply outdated business models, the successful ones improve their business models every two to four years.

25564 ■ "Unfilled Hotels Go All Out for Business Meetings" in *Crain's Detroit Business* (Vol. 25, June 8, 2009, No. 23, pp. 9)
Pub: Crain Communications Inc. - Detroit
Ed: Daniel Duggan. **Description:** Hotels in Michigan are offering discounts to companies holding business meetings at their properties. Details of competition and plans are included.

25565 ■ "U.S. Attorney Post the Latest Twist" in *The Business Journal-Serving Greater Tampa Bay* (Vol. 28, July 25, 2008, No. 31, pp. 1)
Pub: American City Business Journals, Inc.
Ed: Jane Meinhardt. **Description:** Tampa, Florida-based lawyer A. Brian Albritton has been nominated to be the U.S. Attorney for the Middle District of Florida. He is an expert in cases involving white-collar crime, secret theft, noncompete agreements, and other agreements.

25566 ■ "U.S. Widens Rocket Field" in *Wall Street Journal Eastern Edition* (October 17 , 2011, pp. B4)
Pub: Dow Jones & Company Inc.
Ed: Andy Pasztor. **Description:** An agreement has been reached between National Aeronautics and Space Administration, the Department of Defense and the Air Force that will assist small commercial space ventures in bidding for profitable contracts for government launching. The program will give those companies a chance to compete against larger corporations.

25567 ■ "Warning Lights Flashing for Air Canada: Carty's Back" in *Globe & Mail* (February 22, 2006, pp. B1)
Pub: CTVglobemedia Publishing Inc.
Ed: Brent Jang. **Description:** Air Canada's rival, Donald Carty, former chief executive officer at American Airlines and new chairman of Toronto based Regco Holdings Inc., launches Porter Airlines Inc. out of Toronto City Center Airport this fall.

25568 ■ "Way More Than Mowing" in *Green Industry Pro* (Vol. 23, September 2011)
Pub: Cygnus Business Media
Ed: Rod Dickens. **Description:** Shipp Shape Lawn Services located in Sylvester, Georgia now offers aeration, fertilizing and weed control, mulching, yard renovation, flowerbed maintenance, landscaping, as well as irrigation repairs and installation in order to diversify the business and stay competitive.

25569 ■ *The Well-Timed Strategy: Managing Business Cycle for Competitive Advantage*
Pub: Wharton School Publishing
Ed: Peter Navarro. **Released:** January 23, 2006. **Price:** $34.99. **Description:** An overview of business cycles and risks is presented. Recession is a good time to find key personnel for a small business. Other issues addressed include investment, production, and marketing in order to maintain a competitive edge.

25570 ■ "Wells Fargo Will Soon Lead Local Banks in Deposits" in *Austin Business JournalInc.* (Vol. 28, December 5, 2008, No. 38, pp. A1)
Pub: American City Business Journals
Ed: Christopher Calnan. **Description:** Acquisition of Wachovia Corporation by Wells Fargo and Company will leave the latter as the top bank for deposits in Austin, Texas. The merged bank will have deposits of more than $ billion, more than the $3.9 billion deposits Bank of America maintains in the area.

25571 ■ "WestJet Gears Up for Domestic Dogfight" in *Globe & Mail* (May 1, 2007, pp. B6)
Pub: CTVglobemedia Publishing Inc.
Ed: Brent Jang. **Description:** The effort of WestJet Airlines Ltd. to compete with Air Canada for greater market share of passengers is discussed.

25572 ■ "What Makes for an Effective, Production-Oriented VMC?" in *Modern Machine Shop* (Vol. 84, November 2011, No. 6, pp. 24)
Pub: Gardner Publications
Ed: Derek Korn. **Description:** When a machine shop's existing VMC only offers a modest spindle performance and slow, non-cutting functions, the latest VMC technology for high-volume production that minimizes cycle times and maximizes competitiveness could be helpful. Makino's new Production Standard (PS) series of VMCs provides not only a number of standard features to shrink cycle times, but also design elements that can effectively support a shops production elements are defined.

25573 ■ *What Men Don't Tell Woman about Business: Opening Up the Heavily Guarded Alpha Male Playbook*
Pub: John Wiley and Sons, Inc.
Ed: Christopher V. Fleet. **Released:** October 26, 2007. **Description:** Valuable guide for any woman in business, this book helps reveal everything a woman needs to know in order to understand, communicate, and compete with men in business.

25574 ■ "While Competitors Shut Doors, Subway Is Still Growing" in *Advertising Age* (Vol. 79, July 21, 2008, No. 28, pp. 4)
Pub: Crain Communications, Inc.
Ed: Emily Bryson York. **Description:** Subway, the largest fast-food chain, with 22,000 U.S. locations, is adding 800 this year, despite the economic downturn that has caused competitors such as Starbucks to close stores and McDonald's to focus its expansion abroad.

25575 ■ "Why LinkedIn is the Social Network that Will Never Die" in *Advertising Age* (Vol. 81, December 6, 2010, No. 43, pp. 2)
Pub: Crain Communications, Inc.
Ed: Irina Slutsky. **Description:** Despite the popularity of Facebook, Linkln in will always be a source for professionals who wish to network.

25576 ■ "Why-Max?" in *Canadian Business* (Vol. 81, July 22, 2008, No. 12-13, pp. 19)
Pub: Rogers Media Ltd.
Ed: Andrew Wahl. **Description:** Nascent technology known as LTE (Long Term Evolution) is expected to challenge Intel's WiMax wireless technology as the wireless broadband standard. LTE , which is believed to be at least two years behind WiMax in development, is likely to be supported by wireless and mobile-phone carriers. Views and information on WiMax and LTE are presented.

25577 ■ "Why Nestle Should Sell Alcon" in *Barron's* (Vol. 88, March 17, 2008, No. 11, pp. M12)
Pub: Dow Jones & Company, Inc.
Ed: Sean Walters. **Description:** Nestle should sell Alcon because Nestle can't afford to be complacent as its peers have made changes to their portfolios to boost competitiveness. Nestle's stake in Alcon and L'Oreal have been ignored by investors and Nestle could realize better value by strengthening its nutrition division through acquisitions.

25578 ■ "Will Focus on Business Continue?" in *Baltimore Business Journal* (Vol. 28, November 5, 2010, No. 26, pp. 1)
Pub: Baltimore Business Journal
Ed: Scott Dance. **Description:** The 2010 election may call for new efforts to teach new lawmakers to assure that the viewpoints of businesses are considered and accurately delivered. The Greater Baltimore

Committee and similar groups have gathered reports on the competitiveness of Maryland and are planning to use them to make a case of keeping business a top priority.

25579 ■ "Will the Force Be With Salesforce?" in *Barron's* (Vol. 88, March 24, 2008, No. 12, pp. 20)
Pub: Dow Jones & Company, Inc.
Ed: Mark Veverka. **Description:** Shares of Salesforce.com are likely to drop from the $44.83-a-share level in the face of a deteriorating economy and financial sector and thus lower demand for business software. The company is unlikely to deliver on its ambitious earnings forecasts for 2008 especially with strengthening competition from Oracle.

25580 ■ *Win Government Contracts for Your Small Business*
Pub: CCH Incorporated
Ed: John Digiacomo. **Released:** June 2007. **Price:** $24.95 (US), $34.95 (Canadian). **Description:** Strategies to find, negotiate, and win government contracts, including the latest information for competing for these contracts. Tips for using the Internet, finding government buyers, and writing a winning proposal are included.

25581 ■ "Winburn's Big Idea" in *Business Courier* (Vol. 27, October 8, 2010, No. 23, pp. 1)
Pub: Business Courier
Ed: Dan Monk, Lucy May. **Description:** Cincinnati Councilman Charlie Winburn proposed the creation of Cincinnati Competitive Edge Division and to remake a small-business division of the city in order to start a job-creation program. The new division will monitor compliance to the city's small business inclusion regulations, as well as to help small business owners grow.

25582 ■ *Winner Take All: How Competitiveness Shapes the Fate of Nations*
Pub: Basic Books
Ed: Richard J. Elkus Jr. **Released:** 2009. **Price:** $27. 00. **Description:** American government and misguided business practices has allowed the U.S. to fall behind other countries in various market sectors such as cameras and televisions, as well as information technologies. It will take a national strategy to for America to regain its lead in crucial industries.

25583 ■ *Winner Takes All: Steve Wynn, Kirk Kerkorian, Gary Loveman, and the Race to Own Vegas*
Pub: Hyperion
Ed: Christina Binkley. **Released:** 2009. **Price:** $25. 95. **Description:** The story of three men, Steve Wynn, Kirk Kerkorian, and Gary Loveman, each with different backgrounds are reinventing Las Vegas.

25584 ■ "A Woman's Advantage" in *Black Enterprise* (Vol. 38, December 2007, No. 5, pp. 86)
Pub: Earl G. Graves Publishing Co. Inc.
Ed: Marcia Reed-Woodard. **Description:** Leadership development is essential for any small business. Simmons College's Strategic Leadership for Women educational course offers a five-day program for professional women teaching powerful strategies to perform, compete, and win in the workplace.

25585 ■ "Xerox's Former CEO On Why Succession Shouldn't Be a Horse Race" in *Harvard Business Review* (Vol. 88, October 2010, No. 10, pp. 47)
Pub: Harvard Business School Publishing
Ed: Anne Mulcahy. **Description:** The importance of beginning talks between chief executive officers and boards of directors as early as possible to ensure a smooth transition is stressed. This can also prevent turning successions into competitions, with the resultant loss of talent when other candidates 'lose'.

25586 ■ "XM Mulls Betting the Bank in Competitive Game of Subscriber Growth" in *Globe & Mail* (March 18, 2006, pp. B3)
Pub: CTVglobemedia Publishing Inc.
Ed: Grant Robertson. **Description:** Canadian Satellite Radio Inc., XM Canada, president and Chief Operating Officer Stephen Tapp feel that establishing a profile in satellite radio to attract subscribers is a very big challenge. His views on the Canadian radio market are detailed.

25587 ■ "Young-Kee Kim; Deputy Director, Fermi National Accelerator Laboratory" in *Crain's Chicago Business* (Vol. 31, May 5, 2008, No. 18)
Pub: Crain Communications, Inc.
Ed: Phuong Ly. **Description:** Profile of Young-Kee Kim who is the deputy director of Fermilab, a physics lab where scientists study the smallest particles in the universe; Ms. Kim was a researcher at Fermilab before becoming deputy director two years ago; Fermilab is currently home to the most powerful particle accelerator in the world and is struggling to compete with other countries despite cuts in federal funding.

25588 ■ *Your First Year in Real Estate: Making the Transition from Total Novice to Successful Professional*
Pub: Crown Business Books
Ed: Dirk Zeller. **Released:** $August 3, 2010. **Price:** $20.00. **Description:** Zeller helps new realtors to select the right company, develop mentor and client relationships, using the Internet and social networking to stay ahead of competition, to set and reach career goals, to stay current in the market, and more.

VIDEOCASSETTES/ AUDIOCASSETTES

25589 ■ *Building Strategic Relationships*
Educational Activities, Inc.
PO Box 87
Baldwin, NY 11510
Free: 800-797-3223
Fax:(516)623-9282
URL: http://www.edact.com
Price: $99.00. **Description:** Part of the Management Speaks Series. Details ways in which businesses can make use of their competition to help them better their chances for success. **Availability:** VHS.

25590 ■ *Competing for Customers*
Educational Activities, Inc.
PO Box 87
Baldwin, NY 11510
Free: 800-797-3223
Fax:(516)623-9282
URL: http://www.edact.com
Price: $99.00. **Description:** Part of the Management Speaks Series. Outlines how to win over the customer, customer relationships, new strategy for building customer loyalty, unsatisfied consumers, and the importance of customer service. **Availability:** VHS.

25591 ■ *Concerns Quarterly with Footage from CBS News: General Business*
Harcourt Brace College Publishers
301 Commerce, Ste. 3700
Fort Worth, TX 76102
Ph:(817)334-7500
Free: 800-237-2665
Fax:(817)334-0947
Co. E-mail: info@harcourt.com
URL: http://www.hmhco.com
Released: 1995. **Price:** $80.00. **Description:** Video newsletter containing footage from such CBS programs as CBS Evening News, 48 Hours, Street Stories, and CBS This Morning. Provides information on such topics as ethical responsibilities in business, people in business, competition, manufacturing, and marketing. Comes with instructor's guide. Available at an annual subscription rate of $300.00. **Availability:** VHS.

25592 ■ *Michael Porter on Competitive Strategy*
Harvard Business School
Soldiers Field
Boston, MA 02163
Ph:(617)495-6000
URL: http://www.hbs.edu
Released: 1989. **Price:** $1000.00. **Description:** The professor at Harvard Business School gives a few tips that will keep your business on top of its competition. **Availability:** VHS.

25593 ■ *Swim with the Sharks without Being Eaten Alive*
Instructional Video
2219 C St.
Lincoln, NE 68502
Ph:(402)475-6570
Free: 800-228-0164
Fax:(402)475-6500
Co. E-mail: feedback@insvideo.com
URL: http://www.insvideo.com
Price: $595.00. **Description:** Based on Harvey Mackay's best-selling book of the same name. Offers training advice on how to beat your competition, make the crucial sale, open the closed door, and swing the million-dollar deal at the last minute. **Availability:** VHS.

CONSULTANTS

25594 ■ ARDITO Information & Research Inc.
1019 Sedwick Dr., Ste. G
Wilmington, DE 19803
Ph:(302)479-5373
Free: 800-836-9068
Fax:(302)479-5375
Co. E-mail: sardito@ardito.com
URL: http://www.ardito.com
Contact: Stephanie C. Ardito, President
E-mail: sardito@ardito.com
Scope: A full-service information and research firm. Provides information in areas of financial data, published research, demographic data, industry-specific publications, competitor data, marketing and sales trends, new product developments, government relations, bibliographies. Industries served are pharmaceutical, health, publishing, and environment, and business. **Publications:** "The Swine flu pandemic: Authoritative information versus community gossip," Searcher, Oct, 2009; "The Medical blogosphere: How social networking platforms are changing medical searching," Searcher, May, 2009; "Social Networking and Video Web Sites: MySpace and YouTube Meet the Copyright Cops," Searcher, May, 2007; "Copyright Clearance Center raises transactional fees," Information Today, Jul, 2004.

25595 ■ Conor Environmental Services Inc.
282 County St., Ste. 519
Attleboro, MA 02703
Ph:(609)589-5475
Fax:(609)589-6037
Co. E-mail: consultces@usa.net
Contact: Lewis J. Corcoran, President
Scope: Firm provides a full range of environmental and engineering consulting services for both public and private organizations. Environmental company provides assessment, engineering, and remediation services, specializing in industrial and hazardous waste management. The integrated approach-combining scientific, engineering, and management services-provides cost-effective solutions to the complex scope of environmental problems. risk assessment and audit programs; and spill response management and planning services. Industries served: manufacturing, petroleum, power plants, utilities, wastewater treatment facilities, pipelines, landfills, banks, financial institutions, real estate developers, law firms, insurance companies, and government. **Seminars:** Beating the Competition: Winning with Better Information.

25596 ■ Queens Business Consulting
Queens School of Business, Goodes Hall, 143 Union St.
Kingston, ON, Canada K7L 3N6
Ph:(613)533-2309
Fax:(613)533-2370
Co. E-mail: qbc@business.queensu.ca
URL: http://www.qsbc.com
Contact: Amber Wallace, Principle
E-mail: awallace@atsbusiness.queensu.ca
Scope: Provides business plans, feasibility studies, financial planning, competitor analysis, market research, marketing strategies, production planning and systems implementation.

RESEARCH CENTERS

25597 ■ University of California, Los Angeles–Research Program in Takeovers and Corporate Restructuring
258 Tavistock Ave.
Los Angeles, CA 90049-3229
Ph:(310)472-5110
Fax:(310)472-9471
Co. E-mail: jweston@anderson.ucla.edu
URL: http://www.anderson.ucla.edu/faculty/john.weston
Contact: Prof. J. Fred Weston, Dir.
E-mail: jweston@anderson.ucla.edu
Scope: Diversification studies, pricing policies, economic implications of management of decentralized firms, industrial structure, regulated industries, corporate power, corporate governance, measurement of business risk, advertising and profits, concentration and inflation, mergers and acquisitions, corporate control, restructuring, antitrust, and case studies of individual industries and firms. **Publications:** Journal articles; Working papers. **Educational Activities:** Presentations to congressional committees.

Competitive Pricing

EDUCATIONAL PROGRAMS

25598 ■ How to Bargain & Negotiate with Vendors
Fred Pryor Seminars & CareerTrack
5700 Broadmoor St., Ste. 300
Mission, KS 66202
Free: 800-780-8476
Fax:(913)967-8849
Co. E-mail: customerservice@pryor.com
URL: http://www.pryor.com
Price: $179.00; $169.00 for groups of 5 or more. **Description:** Learn how to get lower prices, quicker delivery, higher quality and better service through negotiation. **Locations:** Cities throughout the United States.

REFERENCE WORKS

25599 ■ "The 490 Made Chevy a Bargain Player" in *Automotive News* (Vol. 86, October 31, 2011, No. 6488, pp. S22)
Pub: Crain Communications Inc.
Ed: David Phillips. **Description:** The first Chevrolet with the 490 engine was sold in 1913, but it was too expensive for masses. In 1914 the carmaker launched a lower-priced H-series of cars competitively priced. Nameplates such as Corvette, Bel Air, Camaro and Silverado have defined Chevrolet through the years.

25600 ■ "Advances in Pump Technology - Part Two" in *Contractor* (Vol. 57, February 2010, No. 2, pp. 22)
Pub: Penton Media, Inc.
Ed: Mark Eatherton. **Description:** Chinese and Japanese companies have come up with refrigerant based heat pump products that are air based which will significantly lower the installed cost of heat pump based systems. Some of these newer models have variable speed, soft start compressors and have the ability to perform high-efficiency heat pump operation on a modulating basis.

25601 ■ "After Price Cuts, Competition GPS Makers Lose Direction" in *Brandweek* (Vol. 49, April 21, 2008, No. 16, pp. 16)
Pub: VNU Business Media, Inc.
Ed: Steve Miller. **Description:** Garmin and TomTom, two of the leaders in portable navigation devices, have seen lowering revenues due to dramatic price cuts and unexpected competition from the broadening availability of personal navigation on mobile phones. TomTom has trimmed its sales outlook for its first quarter while Garmin's stock dropped 40 percent since February.

25602 ■ "Auctions and Bidding: a Guide for Computer Scientists" in *ACM Computing Surveys* (Vol. 43, Summer 2011, No. 2, pp. 10)
Pub: Association for Computing Machinery
Ed: Simon Parsons, Juan A. Rodriguez-Aguilar, Mark Klein. **Description:** There are various actions: single dimensional, multi-dimensional, single-sided, double-sided, first-price, second-price, English, Dutch, Japanese, sealed-bid, and these have been extensively discussed and analyzed in economics literature. This literature is surveyed from a computer science perspective, primarily from the viewpoint of computer scientists who are interested in learning about auction theory, and to provide pointers into the economics literature for those who want a deeper technical understanding. In addition, since auctions are an increasingly important topic in computer science, the article also looks at work on auctions from the computer science literature. The aim is to identify what both bodies of work tell us about creating electronic auctions.

25603 ■ "BK Menu Gives Casual Dining Reason to Worry" in *Advertising Age* (Vol. 79, November 17, 2008, No. 43, pp. 12)
Pub: Crain Communications, Inc.
Ed: Emily Bryson York. **Description:** Burger King is beginning to compete with such casual dining restaurants as Applebees and the Cheesecake Factory with new premium menu items, including thicker burgers and ribs; statistical data regarding the casual dining segment which continues to fall and Burger King, whose sales continue to rise is included.

25604 ■ "Blues Asking Price Out of Their League" in *Saint Louis Business Journal* (Vol. 32, September 23, 2011, No. 4, pp. 1)
Pub: Saint Louis Business Journal
Ed: Amy Kurtovic. **Description:** St. Louis Blues owner Dave Checketts wanted the hockey team sold before the start of the season and he believed the team could fetch $200 million or more. However, Hockey insiders believe the price was too high when considering the team's high debt ratio and several other National Hockey League teams on the market.

25605 ■ "Buick Prices Verano Below Rival Luxury Compacts" in *Automotive News* (Vol. 86, October 31, 2011, No. 6488, pp. 10)
Pub: Crain Communications Inc.
Ed: Mike Colias. **Description:** General Motors's Verano will compete with other luxury compacts such as the Lexus IS 250 and the Acura TSX, but will be prices significantly lower coming in with a starting price of $23,470, about $6,000 to $10,000 less than those competitors.

25606 ■ "Builders, Unions Aim to Cut Costs; Pushing Changes to Regain Share of Residential Market; Seek Council's Help" in *Crain's New York Business*
Pub: Crain Communications, Inc.
Ed: Erik Engquist. **Description:** Union contractors and workers are worried about a decline in their market share for housing so they intend to ask the City Council to impose new safety and benefit standards on all contractors to avoid being undercut by nonunion competitors.

25607 ■ "Businesses Keep a Watchful Eye on Worker's Comp" in *The Business Journal-Serving Greater Tampa Bay* (September 5, 2008)
Pub: American City Business Journals, Inc.
Ed: Jane Meinhardt. **Description:** Pending a ruling from the Florida Supreme Court that could uphold the 2003 changes on workers' compensation law, the outcome would include restrictions on claimant attorneys' fees and allow the competitive workers' compensation insurance rates to remain low. However, insurance rates are expected to go up if the court overturns the changes.

25608 ■ "Cash Rents Reach Sky-High Levels" in *Farm Industry News* (November 23, 2011)
Pub: Penton Business Media Inc.
Ed: Karen McMahon. **Description:** Strong commodity prices are driving land values creating a hot rental market for farm land. Highest rents occur when farmers compete head-to-head for land.

25609 ■ *Cheap: The High Cost of Discount Culture*
Pub: Penguin Group USA Inc.
Ed: Ellen Ruppel Shell. **Released:** July 2, 2009. **Price:** $25.95. **Description:** The American drive toward bargain-hunting and low-price goods has hidden costs in lower wages for workers and reduced quality of goods for consumers.

25610 ■ "Choice Bits" in *Crain's Cleveland Business* (Vol. 30, June 29, 2009, No. 25, pp. 19)
Pub: Crain Communications, Inc.
Description: Ross Farro, Cleveland area restaurateur who was featured in the New York Times story about casual dining chains competing over lunch traffic through pricing.

25611 ■ *Complete Idiot's Guide to Starting an Ebay Business*
Pub: Penguin Books (USA) Incorporated
Ed: Barbara Weltman, Malcolm Katt. **Released:** February 2008. **Price:** $19.95 (US), $29.00 (Canadian). **Description:** Guide for starting an eBay business includes information on products to sell, how to price merchandise, and details for working with services like PayPal, and how to organize fulfillment services.

25612 ■ *The Complete Idiot's Guide to Starting and Running a Thrift Store*
Pub: Alpha Publishing House
Ed: Ravel Buckley, Carol Costa. **Released:** January 5, 2010. **Price:** $18.95. **Description:** Thrift stores saw a 35 percent increase in sales during the falling economy in 2008. Despite the low startup costs, launching and running a thrift store is complicated. Two experts cover the entire process, including setting up a store on a nonprofit basis, choosing a location, funding, donations for saleable items, recruiting and managing staff, sorting items, pricing, and recycling donations.

25613 ■ *The Complete Startup Guide for the Black Entrepreneur*
Pub: Career Press Inc.
Ed: Bill Boudreaux. **Description:** President and founder of a consulting firm for home-based entrepreneurs share information to help minorities start their

own companies. Tips to create a business plan, buy essential equipment, price products and services, pay the bills, and set up a work space are covered.

25614 ■ "Construction Companies Think Smaller, Find Niches as Projects Become Fewer" in *Crain's Detroit Business* (March 10, 2008)
Pub: Crain Communications, Inc.
Ed: Daniel Duggan. **Description:** Due to the decline in development projects, construction firms are facing stronger competition for bids and are relying on their good track records or developing expertise in specific niches to get the job.

25615 ■ "Consumers Seek to Redo Rate Structure: Smaller Biz Paid Big Rates" in *Crain's Detroit Business* (Vol. 25, June 22, 2009)
Pub: Crain Communications Inc. - Detroit
Ed: Amy Lane. **Description:** Consumers Energy Company charged small business customers disproportionately higher rates on June 2009 electric bills than other consumers.

25616 ■ "Contractors Should Expand Their Services" in *Contractor* (Vol. 56, July 2009, No. 7, pp. 34)
Pub: Penton Media, Inc.
Ed: Steven Scandaliato. **Description:** All single family homes will be required to have fire sprinkler systems installed when the 2009 International Residential Code arrives. This presents an opportunity for plumbing contractors and they can bé competitively priced against a fire protection contractor if they train their workforce to install sprinklers.

25617 ■ "Corn Belt Farmland Prices Hit Record Levels" in *Farm Industry News* (December 1, 2011)
Pub: Penton Business Media Inc.
Ed: David Hest. **Description:** Farmland prices have set records over the last six months in Iowa. Farmland broker and auction company owner, Murray Wise, believes this is not a bubble, that the economics of this market are solid.

25618 ■ "COSE Turns On To Electricity Market" in *Crain's Cleveland Business* (Vol. 30, June 22, 2009, No. 24, pp. 4)
Pub: Crain Communications, Inc.
Ed: Jay Miller. **Description:** Council of Smaller Enterprises is working to offer small businesses and their employees electricity at discount prices set at auction by the Public Utilities Commission of Ohio and even lower prices from the Northern Ohio Public Energy Council. Details of the program are offered.

25619 ■ "Cost of Md. Health Plan Not Known" in *Baltimore Business Journal* (Vol. 28, September 3, 2010, No. 17, pp. 1)
Pub: Baltimore Business Journal
Ed: Emily Mullin. **Description:** United States health reform is seen to result in increased health insurance prices in Maryland. However, health care reform advocates claim a new marketplace and increased competition will help keep costs down.

25620 ■ "Crouser Offers UV Coating Price Report" in *American Printer* (Vol. 128, June 1, 2011, No. 6)
Pub: Penton Media Inc.
Description: Crouser and Associates will offer the 'Pricing Off-Line UV Coating' report that provides background information on all three types of protective printing coatings and price guidance. The report will also offer comparisons of four popular types of offline equipment.

25621 ■ "The Data Drivers" in *Canadian Business* (Vol. 81, September 15, 2008, No. 14-15, pp. 1)
Pub: Rogers Media Ltd.
Ed: Andrew Wahl. **Description:** Canadian regulators hope that an auction of telecommunications companies will inject more competition into the industry; however, newcomers may not be able to rely on lower prices in order to gain market share from the three major telecommunications companies that already have a stronghold on the market. Analysts feel that providing additional data service is the key to surviving market disruptions.

25622 ■ "Dean Foods" in *Ice Cream Reporter* (Vol. 23, November 20, 2010, No. 12, pp. 8)
Pub: Ice Cream Reporter
Description: The impact of higher commodity prices can be seen in the recent news from Dean Foods, the largest U.S. dairy company, which reported that rising butterfat and other dairy commodity costs have led to lower-than-expected quarterly profits after it cut prices to compete with private-label brands.

25623 ■ *The Designer's Guide to Marketing and Pricing: How to Win Clients and What to Charge Them*
Pub: F and W Publications, Inc.
Ed: Ilise Benun. **Released:** March 2008. **Price:** $19.99. **Description:** Guide to running a creative services business teaches designers how to be more effective, attract new clients, wages, and how to accurately estimate a project.

25624 ■ "Drop in the Bucket Makes a lot of Waves" in *Globe & Mail* (March 22, 2007, pp. B1)
Pub: CTVglobemedia Publishing Inc.
Ed: Greg Keenan. **Description:** The concern of several auto makers in Canada over the impact of providing heavy rebates to customers buying energy-efficient cars is discussed.

25625 ■ "Dropped Calls" in *Canadian Business* (Vol. 80, November 5, 2007, No. 22, pp. 34)
Pub: Rogers Media
Ed: Andrew Wahl. **Description:** Control over Canada's telecommunications market by Telus, Rogers and Bell Canada has resulted in a small number of innovations. The pricing regimes of these carriers have also stifled innovations in the telecommunications industry. The status of Canada's telecommunications industry is further analyzed.

25626 ■ *EBay Income: How ANYONE of Any Age, Location, and/or Background Can Build a Highly Profitable Online Business with eBay (Revised 2nd Edition)*
Pub: Atlantic Publishing Company
Released: December 1, 2010. **Price:** $24.95. **Description:** A complete overview of eBay is given and guides any small company through the entire process of creating the auction and auction strategies, photography, writing copy, text and formatting, multiple sales, programming tricks, PayPal, accounting, creating marketing, merchandising, managing email lists, advertising plans, taxes and sales tax, best time to list items and for how long, sniping programs, international customers, opening a storefront, electronic commerce, buy-it now pricing, keywords, Google marketing and eBay secrets.

25627 ■ "The Ethics of Price Discrimination" in *Business Ethics Quarterly* (Vol. 21, October 2011, No. 4, pp. 633)
Pub: Society for Business Ethics
Ed: Juan M. Elegido. **Description:** Price discrimination is the practice of charging different customers different prices for the same product. Many people consider price discrimination unfair, but economists argue that in many cases price discrimination is more likely to lead to greater welfare than is the uniform pricing alternative, sometimes even for every party in the transaction.

25628 ■ *Faster Cheaper Better*
Pub: Crown Business Books
Ed: Michael Hammer. **Released:** December 28, 2010. **Price:** $27.50. **Description:** Nine levels for transforming work in order to achieve business growth are outlined. The book helps small business compete against the low-wage countries.

25629 ■ "Flint Group Raises Prices" in *American Printer* (Vol. 128, August 1, 2011, No. 8)
Pub: Penton Media Inc.
Description: Due to the rising cost for raw materials, Flint Group is raising their prices for inks and coatings in North American.

25630 ■ "For His Bigness of Heart: Larry O'Toole: Gentle Giant Moving, Somerville, Massachusetts" in *Inc.* (Volume 32, December 2010)
Pub: Inc. Magazine
Description: Profile of Larry O'Toole, owners of Gentle Giant Moving Company, where his company charges more, but in return consumers receive a higher quality service.

25631 ■ "Fossil Fuel, Renewable Fuel Shares Expected to Flip Flop" in *Farm Industry News* (April 29, 2011)
Pub: Penton Business Media Inc.
Description: Total energy use of fossil fuels is predicted to fall 5 percent by the year 2035, with renewable fuel picking it up.

25632 ■ "Franchisees Lose Battle Against BK" in *Advertising Age* (Vol. 79, June 2, 2008, No. 22, pp. 46)
Pub: Crain Communications, Inc.
Ed: Emily Bryson York. **Description:** Burger King has had continuing litigation with former franchisees from New York, Luan and Elizabeth Sadik, who claim that Burger King's double cheeseburger, along with additional problems, created the environment for their eventual insolvency. Burger King has since terminated its test of selling the double cheeseburger for $1, although the company declined to comment on the reason for this decision.

25633 ■ *Free: The Future of a Radical Price*
Pub: Hyperion
Ed: Chris Anderson. **Released:** 2009. **Price:** $26.99. **Description:** A new trend shows companies using giveaways as a means to attract business and increase profits.

25634 ■ *From Concept To Consumer: How to Turn Ideas Into Money*
Pub: Pearson Education Inc.
Ed: Phil Baker. **Released:** 2009. **Price:** $24.99. **Description:** Renowned product developer Phil Baker explains how a great idea accounts for only 5 percent of all the factors of success and why the majority of success is dependent upon a myriad of other factors, including the time it takes to get to market, price, marketing and distribution. By being their own best competition, a small company can stay one step ahead of competitors.

25635 ■ "Get Sold On eBay" in *Entrepreneur* (Vol. 36, March 2008, No. 3, pp. 94)
Pub: Entrepreneur Media Inc.
Ed: Marcia Layton Turner. **Description:** Entrepreneurs are increasingly using eBay to sell products. Some tips to start selling products through eBay include: starting with used items, developing a niche to sell specific products, and researching product pricing. Other tips with regard to starting an eBay business are covered.

25636 ■ "Getting a Grip on the Saddle: Chasms or Cycles?" in *Journal of Marketing* (Vol. 75, July 2011, No. 4, pp. 21)
Pub: American Marketing Association
Ed: Deepa Chandrasekaran, Gerald J. Tellis. **Description:** A study of the saddle's generality across products and countries is presented. The saddle is fairly pervasive based on empirical analysis of historical sales data from ten products across 19 countries. The results indicate chasms and technological cycles for information/entertainment products while business cycles and technological cycles affect kitchen/laundry products.

25637 ■ "H&M Offers a Dress for Less" in *Canadian Business* (Vol. 83, September 14, 2010, No. 15, pp. 20)
Pub: Rogers Media Ltd.
Ed: Laura Cameron. **Description:** Swedish clothing company H&M has implemented loss leader strategy by pricing some dresses at extremely low prices. The economy has forced retailers to keep prices down despite the increasing cost of manufacturing, partly due to Chinese labor becoming more expensive. How the trend will affect apparel companies is discussed.

25638 ■ "High Anxiety" in *Canadian Business* (Vol. 80, November 19, 2007, No. 23, pp. 11)
Pub: Rogers Media
Ed: Zena Olijnyk. **Description:** Value of Canadian dollar continues to rise, and consumers are asking for lower prices of goods. Retailers, on the other hand, are facing concerns over losing sales. The impacts of the rising Canadian dollar on the business sector and consumer behavior are examined.

25639 ■ "Hospitals Face Big Whammy From State Fees" in *Business Courier* (Vol. 26, October 2, 2009, No. 23, pp. 1)
Pub: American City Business Journals, Inc.
Ed: James Ritchie. **Description:** Ohio hospitals are facing losses of nearly $145 million in franchise fees which are set to be levied by the state. Ohio hospitals will be responsible for a total of $718 million franchise fees as required by 2010-2011 state budget but will recover only 80 percent of the amount in increased Medicaid fees. Possible effects of anticipated losses to Ohio hospitals are examined.

25640 ■ *How to Get Rich*
Pub: Ebury Press
Ed: Felix Dennis. **Released:** 2008. **Price:** $25.95. **Description:** Publisher of Maxim, The Week, and Stuff magazines, discusses the mistakes he made running his companies. He didn't understand that people who buy computer gaming magazines wanted a free game with each copy, as one of his rivals was offering. And he laments not diversifying into television and exploiting the Internet.

25641 ■ "How Has City Golf Privatization Played?" in *Business Courier* (Vol. 27, September 10, 2010, No. 19, pp. 1)
Pub: Business Courier
Ed: Dan Monk. **Description:** It was reported that private contractors are getting more revenue from fewer golfers on city-owned courses in Cincinnati, Ohio. In 1998, the city handed over seven municipal courses to private management. However, some believe that the city has escalated a price war among the region's golf courses.

25642 ■ *How to Make Big Money*
Pub: Hyperion Books
Ed: Jeffrey J. Fox. **Released:** May 19, 2004. **Price:** $16.95. **Description:** Entrepreneur and consultant offers advice to help others create successful startups and prosper. Fox directs new business owners with a counterintuitive style and describes essential methods that beat the competition. Tips include: setting priorities, getting a personal driver, creating a contingency plan for employees, pricing to value, saving money, and getting an office outside of the home.

25643 ■ "How Much Profit is Enough?" in *Automotive News* (Vol. 86, October 31, 2011, No. 6488, pp. 12)
Pub: Crain Communications Inc.
Ed: Keith Crain. **Description:** Workers at the big three automobile companies are unhappy about the issues of class wealth, like the high compensations offered to CEOs.

25644 ■ *How to Start a Home-Based Senior Care Business: Develop a Winning Business Plan*
Pub: The Globe Pequot Press
Ed: James L. Ferry. **Released:** January 10, 2010. **Price:** $18.95. **Description:** Everything needed to know in order to start and run a profitable, ethical, and satisfying senior care business from your home. Information covers writing a good business plan, marketing services to families, creating a fee structure, and developing a network of trusted caregivers and service providers.

25645 ■ *How to Start and Run a Small Book Publishing Company: A Small Business Guide to Self-Publishing and Independent Publishing*
Pub: HCM Publishing
Ed: Peter I. Hupalo. **Released:** August 30, 2002. **Price:** $18.95. **Description:** The book teaches all aspects of starting and running a small book publishing company. Topics covered include: inventory accounting in the book trade, just-in-time inventory management, turnkey fulfillment solutions, tax deductible costs, basics of sales and use tax, book pricing, standards in terms of the book industry, working with distributors and wholesalers, cover design and book layout, book promotion and marketing, how to select profitable authors to publish, printing process, printing on demand, the power of a strong backlist, and how to value copyright.

25646 ■ "Innovating Low-Cost Business Models" in *Strategy and Leadership* (Vol. 39, March-April 2011, No. 2, pp. 43)
Pub: Emerald Group Publishing Inc.
Ed: Nicholas Kachaner, Zhenya Lindgardt, David Michael. **Description:** A process that can be used to implement low-cost innovation is presented. The process can be used to address the competitive challenges presented by multinationals' practice of presenting applications and price points that are intended for developing markets into developed markets. The process involves targeting large, and low-income segments of the market.

25647 ■ "Insurers No Longer Paying Premium for Advertising" in *Brandweek* (Vol. 49, April 21, 2008, No. 16, pp. SR3)
Pub: VNU Business Media, Inc.
Ed: Eric Newman. **Description:** Insurance companies are cutting their advertising budgets after years of accelerated double-digit growth in spending due to the economic downturn, five years of record-breaking ad spend and a need to cut expenditures as claims costs rise and a competitive market keeps premiums in place. Statistical data included.

25648 ■ "Is That the Best You Can Do?" in *Entrepreneur* (Vol. 37, October 2009, No. 10, pp. 85)
Pub: Entrepreneur Media, Inc.
Ed: Jennifer Wang. **Description:** Small business owners can deal with hagglers better by setting parameters in advance. They should convince hagglers by offering the best value and separating this from price.

25649 ■ "Just Hang Up" in *Barron's* (Vol. 88, March 10, 2008, No. 10, pp. 45)
Pub: Dow Jones & Company, Inc.
Ed: Tiernan Ray. **Description:** Sprint's shares are expected to continue falling while the company attempts to attract subscribers by cutting prices, cutting earnings in the process. The company faces tougher competition from better-financed AT&T and Verizon Communications.

25650 ■ "Law Firms Plan Rate Bumps" in *Houston Business Journal* (Vol. 40, December 25, 2009, No. 33, pp. 1)
Pub: American City Business Journals
Ed: Ford Gunter. **Description:** Survey shows that Houston, Texas-based law firms were in line with a 3.2 percent average rate hike projected for 2010. The big firms were ready to offset some losses with a rate bump of 4 percent while smaller firms have been expecting an increase of about 3 percent.

25651 ■ "Local Startup Hits Big Leagues" in *Austin Business Journallnc.* (Vol. 28, December 19, 2008, No. 40, pp. 1)
Pub: American City Business Journals
Ed: Christopher Calnan. **Description:** Qcue LLC, an Austin, Texas-based company founded in 2007 is developing a software system that can be used by Major League Baseball teams to change the prices of their single-game tickets based on variables affecting demand. The company recently completed a trial with the San Francisco Giants in 2008.

25652 ■ "Market Share" in *Business Journal-Milwaukee* (Vol. 28, December 3, 2010, No. 9, pp. A1)
Pub: Milwaukee Business Journal
Ed: Stacy Vogel Davis. **Description:** Roundy's Supermarkets' market share has decreased with the expansion of low-price grocery chains in Milwaukee, Wisconsin. Wal-Mart stores Inc., Aldi Inc., and Target Corporation have all opened new stores in the area.

25653 ■ "Medicaid Insurers See Growth in Small Business Market" in *Boston Business Journal* (Vol. 31, July 15, 2011, No. 25, pp. 1)
Pub: Boston Business Journal
Ed: Julie M. Donnelly. **Description:** BMC HealthNet Plan announced plans to launch small business products to serve small businesses that are priced out of rising premium rates at large Massachusetts insurers. BMC joined competitors CeltiCare Health Plan and Neighborhood Health Plan in augmenting its core business.

25654 ■ "Netflix vs. Blockbuster" in *Inc.* (October 2007, pp. 32)
Pub: Gruner & Jahr USA Publishing
Description: Nexflix, the mail-order DVD rental service, is losing market share to Blockbuster, even after matching prices to that of its competitors. Entrepreneurs are asked how they would run Netflix to gain back market share.

25655 ■ "Notes on Current Labor Statistics" in *Montly Labor Review* (Vol. 133, September 2010, No. 9, pp. 75)
Pub: Bureau of Labor Statistics
Description: Principal statistics and calculated by the Bureau of Labor Statistics are presented. The series includes statistics on labor force; employment; unemployment; labor compensation; consumer, producer, and international prices; productivity; international comparisons; and injury and illness statistics.

25656 ■ "Office Supplier Won't Wait for Opportunity to Knock" in *Business Courier* (Vol. 24, December 28, 2008, No. 37, pp. 2)
Pub: American City Business Journals, Inc.
Ed: Lucy May. **Description:** Ace Products, an office supplier, stays competitive through its customer service and pricing.

25657 ■ "Open Skies: Opportunity, Challenge for Airlines" in *Crain's Chicago Business* (April 21, 2008)
Pub: Crain Communications, Inc.
Ed: Paul Merrion. **Description:** Discusses the new aviation agreement between Europe and the United States known as Open Skies; the pact creates opportunities for U.S. carriers to fly to new destinations in Europe from more U.S. cities; it also allows carriers to fly between European cities, something they have not been able to do until now.

25658 ■ "Ownership Form, Managerial Incentives, and the Intensity of Rivalry" in *Academy of Management Journal* (Vol. 50, No. 4, August 2007)
Pub: Academy of Management
Ed: Govert Vroom, Javier Gimeno. **Description:** Ways in which differences in ownership form between franchised and company-owned units alter managerial incentives and competitive pricing in different oligopolistic contexts, or following competitors into foreign markets, is presented.

25659 ■ "Paying the Price" in *Baltimore Business Journal* (Vol. 28, July 9, 2010, No. 9, pp. 1)
Pub: Baltimore Business Journal
Ed: Emily Mullin. **Description:** Crab prices have never been higher in Baltimore, Maryland and businesses have been led to count on strengthening demand for seafood. For instance, the average price for a dozen large crabs has increased by 5 percent to $58.90. How restaurants have responded to the increase in prices is discussed, along with factors that might have caused the harvest of smaller crabs.

25660 ■ "Peter Gilgan" in *Canadian Business* (Vol. 82, April 27, 2009, No. 7, pp. 58)
Pub: Rogers Media
Ed: Calvin Leung. **Description:** Mattamy Homes Ltd. president and chief executive officer Peter Gilgan believes that their business model of building communities in an organized way brings advantages to the firm and for their customers. He also believes in adopting their product prices to new market realities. Gilgan considers the approvals regime in Ontario his biggest challenge in the last 20 years.

25661 ■ "Point, Click, Buy" in *Barron's* (Vol. 90, September 6, 2010, No. 36, pp. 11)
Pub: Barron's Editorial & Corporate Headquarters
Ed: Vito J. Racanelli. **Description:** Non-travel online retail sales from January to July 2010 increased nine percent which indicates that online shopping for the coming holidays will be good. Online sales are outpacing traditional shopping, but pricing is still critical.

25662 ■ "Prepaid Phones Surge in Bad Economy" in *Advertising Age* (Vol. 79, November 17, 2008, No. 43, pp. 6)
Pub: Crain Communications, Inc.
Ed: Rita Chang. **Description:** Prepay cell phone offerings are becoming increasingly competitive amid a greater choice of plans and handsets. In an economic environment in which many consumers are unable to pass the credit checks required for traditional cell phone plans, the prepay market is surging.

25663 ■ "Price Data" in *Montly Labor Review* (Vol. 133, September 2010, No. 9, pp. 128)
Pub: Bureau of Labor Statistics
Description: Consumer price indexes for all urban consumers and for urban wage earners and clerical workers is presented with U.S. city average, by expenditure category and commodity or service group.

25664 ■ "The Price of Profitability" in *Green Industry Pro* (Vol. 23, March 2011, No. 3, pp. 18)
Pub: Cygnus Business Media
Ed: Tony Bass. **Description:** Profit Builder Process is used to help landscaping companies be more competitive. Landscape contractors report pricing among their largest challenges and although the economy is improving, homeowners are paying closer attention to quality and service.

25665 ■ "Q&A: Joseph Ribkoff" in *Canadian Business* (Vol. 81, March 31, 2008, No. 5, pp. 4)
Pub: Rogers Media
Ed: Zena Olijnyk. **Description:** Joseph Ribkoff started his career in the garment trade by sweeping floors and running deliveries for a dress manufacturer called Town & Country and earned $16 a week. Ribkoff says that the key to controlling costs in Canada is to invest in the latest equipment and technology to stay competitive.

25666 ■ "Quiznos Franchisees Walloped by Recession" in *Advertising Age* (Vol. 79, October 20, 2008, No. 39, pp. 3)
Pub: Crain Communications, Inc.
Ed: Emily Bryson York. **Description:** While the recession has taken a toll on the entire restaurant industry, a number of Quiznos franchisees claim to have been disproportionately affected due to lackluster marketing, higher-than-average commodity costs, competition with Subway and a premium-pricing structure that is incompatible with a tight economy.

25667 ■ "Rough Q1 Begs Question: Is the Crocs Craze Over?" in *Brandweek* (Vol. 49, April 21, 2008, No. 16, pp. 16)
Pub: VNU Business Media, Inc.
Ed: Eric Newman. **Description:** Crocs, a rubber shoemaker, announced last week that it missed its expected first quarter revenues by 15 percent. The popular rubber sandals are suffering in sales due to a number of factors including a tougher economic environment, less expensive, knock-off brands, the cold weather delay of the spring season and fading consumer interest in plastic shoes.

25668 ■ "Rumors Kill Algoma Takeover Talks" in *Globe & Mail* (March 14, 2007, pp. B14)
Pub: CTVglobemedia Publishing Inc.
Ed: Tara Perkins. **Description:** Canada-based steel manufacturing giant Salzgitter AG has dropped its acquisition negotiations with Algoma Steel Inc. The decision comes after the secret price quotation was leaked to competitors.

25669 ■ "Small Business Compensation" in *Small Business Economic Trends* (September 2010, pp. 10)
Pub: National Federation of Independent Business
Ed: William C. Dunkelberg, Holly Wade. **Description:** A graph from a survey of small businesses in the U.S. is given, representing small business compensation from January 1986 to August 2010. Tables showing actual compensation changes and compensation plans are also presented. A graph comparing small business prices and labor compensation is supplied.

25670 ■ "Small Business Prices" in *Small Business Economic Trends* (July 2010, pp. 8)
Pub: National Federation of Independent Business
Description: A graph from a survey of small businesses in the U.S. is given representing business prices from January 1986 to June 2010. Actual prices (last three months) and planned prices (next three months) were compared in the graph. Tables of actual price changes and price plans from January 2005 to June 2010 are also supplied.

25671 ■ "Stepping Up" in *Baltimore Business Journal* (Vol. 28, October 22, 2010, No. 24, pp. 1)
Pub: Baltimore Business Journal
Ed: Erik Siemers. **Description:** Uner Armour Inc. will release its Micro G line of four basketball sneakers on October 23, 2010. The company's executives mentioned that Under Armour's goal is to appeal to customers, and not to chip away at Nike Inc.'s supremacy in basketball shoes. The new sneakers will range from $80 to $110.

25672 ■ "The Superpower Dilemma" in *Canadian Business* (Vol. 83, August 17, 2010, No. 13-14, pp. 42)
Pub: Rogers Media Ltd.
Description: Canada has been an energy superpower partly because it controls the energy source and the production means, particularly of fossil fuels. However, Canada's status as superpower could diminish if it replaces petroleum exports with renewable technology for using sources of energy available globally.

25673 ■ "Title Creep: The Chief Revenue Officer" in *Inc.* (March 2008, pp. 28)
Pub: Gruner & Jahr USA Publishing
Ed: The title, Chief Revenue Officer, is growing. The marketing function of the CRO is to oversee sales, new product development, and pricing.

25674 ■ "Unfilled Hotels Go All Out for Business Meetings" in *Crain's Detroit Business* (Vol. 25, June 8, 2009, No. 23, pp. 9)
Pub: Crain Communications Inc. - Detroit
Ed: Daniel Duggan. **Description:** Hotels in Michigan are offering discounts to companies holding business meetings at their properties. Details of competition and plans are included.

25675 ■ "Velvet Ice Cream" in *Ice Cream Reporter* (Vol. 21, July 20, 2008, No. 8, pp. 7)
Pub: Ice Cream Reporter
Description: Velvet Ice Cream is adding a $7 surcharge on deliveries of its products in order to offset rising fuel costs.

25676 ■ "'Wal-Mart Effect' Feeds Grocer Price Wars" in *Globe & Mail* (March 15, 2007, pp. B14)
Pub: CTVglobemedia Publishing Inc.
Ed: Marina Strauss. **Description:** The decrease in profit reports by Canadian grocery giants amidst high expansion plans by Wal-Mart Stores Inc. are discussed. This industry is witnessing the most severe pricing competitions in recent times.

25677 ■ "While Competitors Shut Doors, Subway Is Still Growing" in *Advertising Age* (Vol. 79, July 21, 2008, No. 28, pp. 4)
Pub: Crain Communications, Inc.
Ed: Emily Bryson York. **Description:** Subway, the largest fast-food chain, with 22,000 U.S. locations, is adding 800 this year, despite the economic downturn that has caused competitors such as Starbucks to close stores and McDonald's to focus its expansion abroad.

25678 ■ "With New Listings, Business Brokers See Hope" in *Business Courier* (Vol. 27, September 3, 2010, No. 18, pp. 1)
Pub: Business Courier
Ed: Lucy May. **Description:** Business brokers in Cincinnati, Ohio are expecting better prices in view of the strengthening economy.

VIDEOCASSETTES/ AUDIOCASSETTES

25679 ■ *Product Costs: What's In Them*
Phoenix Learning Group
2349 Chaffee Dr.
St. Louis, MO 63146-3306
Ph:(314)569-0211
Free: 800-221-1274
Fax:(314)569-2834
URL: http://www.phoenixlearninggroup.com
Released: 1979. **Description:** This show presents the factors that effect the final price of a product. **Availability:** VHS; 3/4U.

25680 ■ *Swim with the Sharks without Being Eaten Alive*
Instructional Video
2219 C St.
Lincoln, NE 68502
Ph:(402)475-6570
Free: 800-228-0164
Fax:(402)475-6500
Co. E-mail: feedback@insvideo.com
URL: http://www.insvideo.com
Price: $595.00. **Description:** Based on Harvey Mackay's best-selling book of the same name. Offers training advice on how to beat your competition, make the crucial sale, open the closed door, and swing the million-dollar deal at the last minute. **Availability:** VHS.

CONSULTANTS

25681 ■ Mark Vanderstelt
9831 Gulfstream Ct.
Fishers, IN 46037
Ph:(317)576-9328
Fax:(317)576-9328
Scope: Consulting services include financial planning and analysis, inventory control, cash management, return on investment, budgeting, pricing, system design and analysis, mergers and acquisitions, feasibility studies, data processing, cost systems and controls, and performance measurement. Also performs operational and financial reviews.

RESEARCH CENTERS

25682 ■ Weber State University–Center for Business and Economic Development
3815 University Cir.
Ogden, UT 84408-3815
Ph:(801)626-7232
Fax:(801)626-7423
Co. E-mail: bking1@weber.edu
URL: http://weber.edu/sbdc
Contact: Beverly King, Dir.
E-mail: bking1@weber.edu
Scope: Business development activities, market research, survey research, focus groups, and government feasibility studies. **Services:** Provides consulting and technical assistance for small businesses and contractual work for government and large businesses. **Educational Activities:** Courses on business planning and entrepreneurship and 40 annual training events; Scholarship (semiannually), for successful completion of entrepreneurship courses.

Consultants

START-UP INFORMATION

25683 ■ *Going Solo: Developing a Home-Based Consulting Business from the Ground Up*
Pub: McGraw-Hill Companies Incorporated
Ed: William J. Bond. **Released:** January 1997. **Description:** Ways to turn specialized knowledge into a home-based successful consulting firm, focusing on targeting client needs, business plans, and growth.

25684 ■ *How to Start a Home-Based Consulting Business: Define Your Specialty Build a Client Base Make Yourself Indispensable*
Pub: The Globe Pequot Press
Ed: Bert Holtje. **Released:** January 10, 2010. **Price:** $18.95. **Description:** Everything needed for starting and running a successful consulting business from home.

25685 ■ *Small Business Desk Reference*
Pub: Penguin Books (USA) Incorporated
Ed: Gene Marks. **Released:** December 2004. **Description:** Comprehensive guide for starting or running a successful small business, focusing on buying a business or franchise, writing a business plan, financial management, accounting, legal issues, human resources management, operations, marketing, sales, customer service, taxes, insurance, and ethics. Information for launching a restaurant, property management firm, retail outlet, consulting firm, and service business is included.

25686 ■ *Starting and Running a Coaching Business*
Pub: How To Books
Ed: Aryanne Oade. **Released:** August 9, 2010. **Price:** $26.00. **Description:** Guide for the comprehensive, practical and personalized process of starting and running a coaching business is presented.

25687 ■ *Starting Up On Your Own: How to Succeed as an Independent Consultant or Freelance*
Pub: FT Press
Ed: Mike Johnson. **Released:** February 1, 2010. **Price:** $24.99. **Description:** Concise guide for anyone wanting to start their own consulting firm is provided.

ASSOCIATIONS AND OTHER ORGANIZATIONS

25688 ■ Association of Independent Consultants
15 Wilson St.
Markham, ON, Canada L3P 1M9
Ph:(416)410-8163
Fax:(905)669-5233
Co. E-mail: info1@aiconsult.ca
URL: http://www.aiconsult.ca/en
Contact: Lawrence Fox, Pres.
Description: Independent consultants. Promotes professional advancement of members. Facilitates communication and cooperation among members; makes available volume discounts to members. Conducts business education courses; maintains speakers' bureau. **Publications:** *Thrive-on-Line* . **Telecommunication Services:** electronic mail, president1@aiconsult.ca.

25689 ■ Association of Management Consulting Firms
370 Lexington Ave., Ste. 2209
New York, NY 10017
Ph:(212)262-3055
Fax:(212)262-3054
Co. E-mail: info@amcf.org
URL: http://www.amcf.org/amcf
Contact: John Furth, Pres./CEO
Description: Trade association for consulting organizations that provide a broad range of managerial services to commercial, industrial, governmental, and other organizations and individuals. Seeks to unite management-consulting firms in order to develop and improve professional standards and practice in the field. Offers information and referral services on management consultants; administers public relations program. Conducts research. Monitors regulatory environment. **Publications:** *15th Annual Operating Ratios for Management Consulting Firms: A Resource for Benchmarking* (annual).

25690 ■ Association of Professional Computer Consultants
2323 Yonge St., Ste. 400
Toronto, ON, Canada M4P 2C9
Ph:(416)545-5275
Free: 888-487-2722
Co. E-mail: information@apcconline.com
URL: http://www.apcconline.com
Description: Promotes the interests of Independent Computer Consultants. **Publications:** *Gateway* (periodic).

25691 ■ Association of Proposal Management Professionals
PO Box 668
Dana Point, CA 92629-0668
Co. E-mail: memberservices@apmp.org
URL: http://www.apmp.org
Contact: Rick Harris, Exec. Dir.
Description: Proposal managers, proposal planners, proposal writers, consultants, desktop publishers and marketing managers. Encourages unity and cooperation among industry professionals. Seeks to broaden member knowledge and skills through developmental, educational and social activities. Maintains speakers' bureau. Provides current information and developments in the field. .

25692 ■ Canadian Association of International Development Consultants–Regroupement des consultants canadiens en developpement internationale
260 St. Patrick St., Ste. 101
Ottawa, ON, Canada K1N 5K5
Ph:(613)244-1050
Fax:(613)244-8315
Co. E-mail: caidc_rccdi@yahoo.ca
URL: http://www.caidc-rccdi.ca
Contact: Amitav Rath, Treas.
Description: Aims to provide services for, and to represent the interests of, Canadian international development consultants.

REFERENCE WORKS

25693 ■ *10 Make-or-Break Career Moments: Navigate, Negotiate, and Communicate for Success*
Pub: Crown Business Books
Ed: Casey Hawley. **Released:** May 4, 2010. **Price:** $13.99. **Description:** Communication consultant, Casey Hawley, provides a guide to smart communication for any business setting.

25694 ■ "A Conversation With; Ron Gatner, Jones Lang LaSalle" in *Crain's Detroit Business* (Vol. 24, October 6, 2008, No. 40, pp. 9)
Pub: Crain Communications, Inc.
Description: Interview with Ron Gatner who is a corporate real estate adviser with the real estate company Jones Lang LaSalle as well as the company's executive vice president and part of the tenant advisory team; Gatner speaks about the impact that the Wall Street crisis is having on the commercial real estate market in Detroit.

25695 ■ "Achieving Greatness" in *Black Enterprise* (Vol. 38, January 2008, No. 6, pp. 50)
Pub: Earl G. Graves Publishing Co. Inc.
Description: Randall Pinkett, winner of a reality show on television and chairman of BCT Partners, insists that a business cannot survive by doing just enough or more of the same. Pinkett's New Jersey company provides management, technology and consulting to other firms.

25696 ■ "AF Expands in New Green Building in Gothenburg" in *Ecology,Environment & Conservation Business* (September 24, 2011, pp. 2)
Pub: HighBeam Research
Description: AF signed a ten-year tenancy contract with Skanska for the premises of its new green building in Gothenburg, Sweden. AF offers qualified services and solutions for industrial processes, infrastructure projects and the development of products and IT systems.

25697 ■ "Altegrity Acquires John D. Cohen, Inc." in (November 19, 2009, pp. 14)
Pub: Investment Weekly News
Description: John D. Cohen, Inc., a contract provider of national security policy guidance and counsel to the federal government, was acquired by Altegrity, Inc., a global screening and security solutions provider; the company will become part of US

Investigations Services, LLC and operate under the auspices of Altegrity's new business, Altegrity Security Consulting.

25698 ■ "Alto Ventures Retains Investor Relations Professional" in *Canadian Corporate News* (May 16, 2007)
Pub: Comtex News Network Inc.

Description: Alto Ventures Ltd., a gold exploration and development company with a portfolio of eleven properties in the Canadian Shield, announced that it has engaged the consulting services of Mark Prosser in order to focus on increasing investor awareness and exposure to the investment community through the dissemination of corporate information to a network of North American and European institutions, retail brokerage firms, and private investors.

25699 ■ "The Americans Are Coming" in *The Economist* (Vol. 390, January 3, 2009, No. 8612, pp. 44)
Pub: The Economist Newspaper Inc.

Description: Student recruitment consultancies, which help place international students at universities in other countries and offer services such as interpreting or translating guidelines, are discussed; American universities who have shunned these agencies in the past; the result has been that America underperforms in relation to its size with a mere 3.5 percent of students on its campuses that are from abroad.

25700 ■ "Applying to Colleges? Consultants Can Demystify the Process" in *Palm Beach Post* (September 3, 2011)
Pub: Palm Beach Post

Ed: Susan Salisbury. **Description:** More parents are turning to college consultants to help guide them through the process of applying to and choosing the right college or university. These specialized consultants assist with every detail for several years and students can reach them 24/7; costs can vary from several hundred dollars to $10,000 depending on services.

25701 ■ "Ask Inc" in *Inc.* (February 2008, pp. 52)
Pub: Gruner & Jahr USA Publishing

Ed: James Dyson. **Description:** Owner of a consulting firm seeks advice to help his sales staff become more successful.

25702 ■ "Back Talk With Terrie M. Williams" in *Black Enterprise* (Vol. 38, December 2007, No. 5, pp. 204)
Pub: Earl G. Graves Publishing Co. Inc.

Ed: Tennille M. Robinson. **Description:** Profile of Terrie M. Williams, president of a public relations agency as well as founder of a youth empowerment organization called Stay Strong Foundation. Williams reflects on her bouts with depression and how the disease impacts sufferers and talks about her book that will inspire others dealing with depression.

25703 ■ "BDC Launches New Online Business Advice Centre" in *Internet Wire* (July 13, 2010)
Pub: Comtex

Description: The Business Development Bank of Canada (BDC) offers entrepreneurs the chance to use their new online BDC Advice Centre in order to seek advice regarding the challenges of entrepreneurship. Free online business tools and information to help both startups and established firms are also provided.

25704 ■ "Best Foot Forward" in *Canadian Business* (Vol. 80, October 22, 2007, No. 21, pp. 115)
Pub: Rogers Media

Ed: Jeremy Shinewald. **Description:** Jeremy Shinewald's mbaMission admissions consulting business helps prospective MBA students with essay writing, mock interview preparation and school selection. The consulting fee for application to one school is $2,250. Details of the business schools' MBA programs and tuition fees are explored.

25705 ■ *Big Vision, Small Business*
Pub: Ivy Sea, Inc.

Ed: Jamie S. Walters. **Released:** October 10, 2002. **Price:** $17.95. **Description:** The power of the small enterprise is examined. The author shares her expertise as an entrepreneur and founder of a business consulting firm to help small business owners successfully run their companies. Interviews with more than seventy small business owners provide insight into visioning, planning, and establishing a small company, as well as strategies for good employee and customer relationships.

25706 ■ *Birthing the Elephant: A Woman's Go-For-It Guide to Overcoming the Big Challenges of Launching a Business*
Pub: Ten Speed Press

Ed: Karin Abarbanel; Bruce Freeman. **Released:** 2008. **Price:** $15.95. **Description:** Consultants help women think like an entrepreneur in order to successfully launch any new business.

25707 ■ *Bond's Franchise Guide 2009*
Pub: Source Book Publications

Ed: Robert E. Bond, Michelle Yang. **Released:** April 7, 2009. **Description:** Comprehensive directory offering prospective franchise owners a current and detailed profile of 1,000 franchises, as well as supplemental profiles of franchise attorneys and consultants; companies are divided into 45 categories for easy comparison.

25708 ■ *Business Black Belt: Develop the Strength, Flexibility and Agility to Run Your Company*
Pub: Career Press, Inc.

Ed: Burke Franklin. **Released:** November 1, 2010. **Price:** $15.99. **Description:** Manual offering insights that will enable anyone to become successful in small business. Seventy short chapters included topics such as attitude, management, marketing, selling, employees, money, MBAs, lawyers, consultants, and investors.

25709 ■ *Business as Usual*
Pub: HarperBusiness

Ed: Anita Roddick. **Released:** 2005. **Price:** $12.95. **Description:** Founder of The Body Shop shares her story and gives her opinion on everything from cynical cosmetic companies to destructive consultants.

25710 ■ "Cannabis Science Signs Exclusive and Non-Exclusive Agreement with Prescription Vending Machines" in *Benzinga.com* (October 29, 2011)
Pub: Benzinga.com

Ed: Benzinga Staff. **Description:** Cannabis Science Inc., a biotech company developing pharmaceutical cannabis products has partnered with Prescription Vending Machines Inc. and its principal Vincent Meddizadeh to provide industry specific consulting and advisory services to Cannabis Science.

25711 ■ "CarBiz Inc. Speaking At NABD" in *Canadian Corporate News* (May 14, 2007)
Pub: Comtex News Network Inc.

Description: CarBiz Inc., a leading provider of software, consulting, and training solutions to the United States' automotive industry, had two of its executive officers speak at the National Alliance of Buy Here - Pay Here Dealers (NABD), a conference that draws over 2,000 dealers, service providers, and experts from across the United States.

25712 ■ "Certification Experts Germanischer Lloyd Wind Energy Assist NaiKun's Offshore Wind Project" in *Canadian Corporate News* (May 14, 2007)
Pub: Comtex News Network Inc.

Description: Germanischer Lloyd Wind Energy (GL Wind) will examine, inspect, and provide quality management services for the engineering, design, and construction of the offshore wind project planned by NaiKun Wind Development Inc. in northwest British Columbia.

25713 ■ *Chief Culture Officer: How to Create a Living, Breathing Corporation*
Pub: Basic Books

Ed: Grant McCracken. **Price:** $26.95. **Description:** Business consultant argues that corporations need to focus on 'reading' what's happening in the culture around them. Otherwise, companies will suffer the consequences, as Levi Strauss did when it missed out on the rise of hip-hop (and the baggy pants that are part of that lifestyle).

25714 ■ "Clean Wind Energy Tower Transitions from R&D Stage Company" in *Professional Services Close-Up* (September 30, 2011)
Pub: Close-Up Media

Description: Clean Wind Energy designed and is developing large downdraft towers that use benevolent, non-toxic natural elements to generate electricity and clean water. The firm is closing its internally staffed engineering office in Warrenton, Virginia and transitioning a development team to oversee and coordinate industry consultants and advisors to construct their first dual renewable energy tower.

25715 ■ *The Complete Startup Guide for the Black Entrepreneur*
Pub: Career Press Inc.

Ed: Bill Boudreaux. **Description:** President and founder of a consulting firm for home-based entrepreneurs share information to help minorities start their own companies. Tips to create a business plan, buy essential equipment, price products and services, pay the bills, and set up a work space are covered.

25716 ■ *Consultants and Consulting Organizations Directory*
Pub: Gale

Released: Annual, New edition expected 37th; February, 2012. **Price:** $1,392, individuals. **Covers:** Over 26,000 firms, individuals, and organizations active in consulting. **Entries Include:** Individual or organization name, address, phone, fax, e-mail, URL, specialties, founding date, branch offices, names and titles of key personnel, number of employees, financial data, publications, seminars and workshops. **Arrangement:** By broad subject categories. **Indexes:** Subject, geographical, organization name.

25717 ■ "Consulting Firm Goes Shopping" in *Crain's Chicago Business* (Vol. 31, April 28, 2008, No. 17, pp. 45)
Pub: Crain Communications, Inc.

Ed: Phuong Ly. **Description:** Clark & Wamberg LLC was created last year after the merger of Clark Inc. to a Dutch insurance conglomerate. Clark Inc. was a life insurance and benefits consultancy which had been on a downslide, returning just 5.6 percent a year to shareholders. In contrast Clark & Wamberg posted first-year revenue of $106.8 million, fueled by business from its executive compensation and health care clients.

25718 ■ "Cost Remains Top Factor In Considering Green Technology" in *Canadian Sailings* (June 30, 2008)
Pub: Commonwealth Business Media

Ed: Julie Gedeon. **Description:** Improving its environmental performance remains a priority in the shipping industry; however, testing new technologies can prove difficult due to the harsh conditions that ships endure as well as installation which usually requires a dry dock.

25719 ■ "Counting on Engagement at Ernst and Young" in *Workforce Management* (Vol. 88, November 16, 2009, No. 12, pp. 25)
Pub: Crain Communications, Inc.

Ed: Ed Frauenheim. **Description:** Employee engagement has been difficult to maintain through the recession but firms such as Ernst & Young have found that the effort to keep their employees loyal has paid off.

25720 ■ "Electronic Design and a Greener Environment" in *Canadian Electronics* (Vol. 23, June-July 2008, No. 4, pp. 6)
Pub: Action Communication Inc.

Ed: Nicholas Deeble. **Description:** Companies seeking to minimize their environmental impact are using

Design methodologies of Cadence Design Systems Ltd. The company's Low Power Format and Low Power Design Flow help reduce carbon dioxide emissions.

25721 ■ "Engineering Services Supplier Launches 'Robotic Renaissance'" in *Modern Machine Shop* (Vol. 84, September 2011, No. 4, pp. 46)
Pub: Gardner Publications
Description: Profile of Applied Manufacturing Technologies (AMT) new hiring initiative that supports continuing growth in the robotics industry. AMT is located in Orion, Michigan and supplies factory automation design, engineering and process consulting services.

25722 ■ *The Entrepreneur's Guide to Managing Growth and Handling Crisis*
Pub: Greenwood Publishing Group, Inc.
Ed: Theo J. Van Dijk. **Released:** December 2007. **Price:** $39.95. **Description:** The author explains how entrepreneurs can overcome crisis by changing the way they handle customers, by putting new processes and procedures in place, and managing employees in a professional manner. The book includes appendices with tips for hiring consultants, creating job descriptions, and setting up systems to chart cash flow as well as worksheets, tables and figures and a listing of resources.

25723 ■ "Finalist: Private Company, Less Than $100M" in *Crain's Detroit Business* (Vol. 25, June 22, 2009, No. 25)
Pub: Crain Communications Inc. - Detroit
Ed: Nancy Kaffer. **Description:** Profile of W3R Consulting and CFO Patrick Tom= ina. The company offers information technology consulting. Tomina discusses the company's 505 strategy: to grow its annual revenue to $50 million in five years.

25724 ■ "For Kenwood, Cavalry Could Be Close" in *Business Courier* (Vol. 26, October 2, 2009, No. 23, pp. 1)
Pub: American City Business Journals, Inc.
Ed: Dan Monk. **Description:** New York-based BlackRock Inc. is believed to be participating in the settlement liens at Kenwood Towne Place, a mixed-use development site in Cincinnati, Ohio. BlackRock may play a key role as an advisor or investor representative to an unnamed investors.

25725 ■ *Franchise: Freedom or Fantasy*
Pub: iUniverse
Ed: Mitchell York. **Released:** June 22, 2009. **Price:** $13.95. **Description:** Successful franchisee and professional certified coach guides individuals through the many steps involved in deciding whether or not to buy a franchise and how to do it correctly.

25726 ■ "Gail Lissner; Vice-President, Appraisal Research Counselors" in *Crain's Chicago Business* (Vol. 31, May 5, 2008, No. 18, pp. 28)
Pub: Crain Communications, Inc.
Ed: Phuong Ly. **Description:** Profile of Gail Lissner who is the vice-president of the Appraisal Research Counselors, a company that puts out the quarterly "Residential Benchmark Report," in which Ms. Lissner co-authors and is considered a must-read in the industry. Ms. Lissner has risen to become one of the most sought-after experts on the Chicago market considering real estate.

25727 ■ *Get Clients Now!, 2nd Edition: A 28-Day Marketing Program for Professionals, Consultants, and Coaches*
Pub: American Management Association
Ed: C.J. Hayden. **Released:** 2006. **Price:** $19.95.

25728 ■ "Grave Concerns" in *Canadian Business* (Vol. 81, July 21 2008, No. 11, pp. 25)
Pub: Rogers Media Ltd.
Ed: Andrew Nikiforuk. **Description:** Air pollution control regulations to reduce greenhouse gasses have been implemented by the Canadian government. The federal government is planning to construct a carbon funeral industry that will store the global warming gases, however the expenditure for the project will be shifted to the taxpayers. Details of the Bruce Peachy's initiative on how to reduce GHGs are presented.

25729 ■ "The Green Conversation" in *Harvard Business Review* (Vol. 86, September 2008, No. 9, pp. 58)
Pub: Harvard Business School Press
Description: Six guidelines are presented for addressing and benefiting from environmentally conscious corporate decision making and practices. Topics covered include marketing, supply chain, and leadership.

25730 ■ "Greg Lueck: Glass Blowing" in *Inc.* (Volume 32, December 2010, No. 10, pp. 36)
Pub: Inc. Magazine
Ed: April Joyner. **Description:** Profile of Greg Lueck, partner and COO of Centerstance, a tech consulting firm in Portland, Oregon. Lueck opened Firehouse Glass, a studio that provides workspace and equipment for glass blowers. He says glass blowing serves as a welcome counterbalance to the cerebral work he does at the office.

25731 ■ "Hire Power" in *Entrepreneur* (Vol. 35, November 2007, No. 11, pp. 105)
Pub: Entrepreneur Media Inc.
Ed: Mark Henricks. **Description:** Companies with big resources may hire human resource (HR) consultants to help with writing manuals, drafting policies and designing benefits for employees. HR consultants may also be hired to assist with specific functions or other strategic aspects.

25732 ■ "Housing Slide Picks Up Speed" in *Crain's Chicago Business* (Vol. 31, April 21, 2008, No. 16, pp. 2)
Pub: Crain Communications, Inc.
Ed: Eddie Baeb. **Description:** According to Tracy Cross & Associates Inc., a real estate consultancy, sales of new homes in the Chicago area dropped 61 percent from the year-earlier period which is more bad news for homebuilders, contractors and real estate agents who are eager for an indication that market conditions are improving.

25733 ■ *How to Make Big Money*
Pub: Hyperion Books
Ed: Jeffrey J. Fox. **Released:** May 19, 2004. **Price:** $16.95. **Description:** Entrepreneur and consultant offers advice to help others create successful startups and prosper. Fox directs new business owners with a counterintuitive style and describes essential methods that beat the competition. Tips include: setting priorities, getting a personal driver, creating a contingency plan for employees, pricing to value, saving money, and getting an office outside of the home.

25734 ■ "How Much is Too Much?" in *Canadian Business* (Vol. 79, July 17, 2006, No. 14-15, pp. 55)
Pub: Rogers Media
Ed: John Gray. **Description:** Elucidates the emphasis on the need for companies to analyze the executive pay packages designed by compensation consultants.

25735 ■ "Insider" in *Canadian Business* (Vol. 81, Summer 2008, No. 9, pp. 170)
Pub: Rogers Media Ltd.
Ed: Thomas Watson; Jeff Sanford. **Description:** Oil peak theory posits that the world has consumed half of the non-renewable resources is indicated by the surging oil prices. However, critics argued that the high oil prices are effects of market speculation and not the depletion of the supply. Ten reasons on why to buy and not buy peak oil are presented.

25736 ■ "Interbrand's Creative Recruiting" in *Business Courier* (Vol. 27, November 12, 2010, No. 28, pp. 1)
Pub: Business Courier
Ed: Dan Monk. **Description:** Global brand consulting firm Interbrand uses a creative recruitment agency to attract new employees into the company. Interbrand uses themed parties to attract prospective employees. The 'Alice In Wonderland' tea party for example, allowed the company to hire five new employees.

25737 ■ "Into the Groove: Fine-Tune Your Biz By Getting Into the Good Habit Groove" in *Small Business Opportunities* (Spring 2008)
Pub: Harris Publications Inc.
Description: Profile of Ty Freyvogel and his consulting firm Freyvogel Communications. Freyvogel serves the telecommunications need of Fortune 500 and mid-sized businesses.

25738 ■ *Kiss Theory Good Bye: Five Proven Ways to Get Extraordinary Results in Any Company*
Pub: Gold Pen Publishing
Ed: Bob Prosen. **Released:** August 2006. **Price:** $21.95. **Description:** Author provides wisdom from his career as a high-level executive at AT&T Global Information Solutions, Sabre, and Hitachi, as well as his consulting firm. The book focuses on business execution rather than processes or theory of business management and provides step-by-step instructions allowing organizations to maximize profitability and results.

25739 ■ "Knowing Is Growing: Five Strategies To Develop You and Your Business" in *Black Enterprise* (Vol. 38, November 2007, No. 4, pp. 106)
Pub: Earl G. Graves Publishing Co. Inc.
Ed: Erinn R. Johnson. **Description:** Five strategies for growing a small business are listed by Andrew Morrison, founder of the Small Business Camp. The camp provides training, coaching, and marketing services to entrepreneurs.

25740 ■ "Lifebank Grants Stock Options" in *Canadian Corporate News* (May 16, 2007)
Pub: Comtex News Network Inc.
Description: Lifebank, a biomedical service company that provides processing cryogenic storage of umbilical cord blood stem cells, announced that, under its stock option plan, it has granted incentive stock options to directors, officers, and consultants of the company.

25741 ■ "Making Your Mark: Five Steps To Brand Your Success" in *Black Enterprise* (Vol. 38, November 2007, No. 4, pp. 106)
Pub: Earl G. Graves Publishing Co. Inc.
Ed: Erinn R. Johnson. **Description:** Founder of Velvet Suite Marketing Consulting Group, Melissa D. Johnson, assists clients in building brands. Johnson offers tips to develop and build a sold brand in her new book, "Brand Me! Make Your Mark: Turn Passion Into Profit".

25742 ■ *The Management Myth: Why the "Experts" Keep Getting It Wrong*
Pub: W.W. Norton & Company
Ed: Matthew Stewart. **Released:** August 10, 2009. **Price:** $27.95. **Description:** An insider's perspective on the management consulting industry, which reveals the high fees and incompetent consultants.

25743 ■ "Managing the Facebookers; Business" in *The Economist* (Vol. 390, January 3, 2009, No. 8612, pp. 10)
Pub: Economist Newspaper Ltd.
Description: According to a report from PricewaterhouseCoopers, a business consultancy, workers from Generation Y, also known as the Net Generation, are more difficult to recruit and integrate into companies that practice traditional business acumen. 61 percent of chief executive managers say that they have trouble with younger employees who tend to be more narcissistic and more interested in personal fulfillment with a need for frequent feedback and an over-precise set of objectives on the path to promotion which can be hard for managers who are used to a different relationship with their subordinates. Older bosses should prepare to make some concessions to their younger talent since some of the issues that make them happy include cheaper online ways to communicate and additional coaching, both of which are good for business.

25744 ■ *Managing India's Small Industrial Economy: The Catalytic Role of Industrial Counselors and Policy Makers*
Pub: Sage Publications, Incorporated
Ed: V. Padmanand, V.G. Patel. **Released:** June 2004. **Price:** $35.95. **Description:** Case studies and

methodology are used to discuss the areas where industrial consultants are influencing sustainability and growth of small businesses in India's industrial economy.

25745 ■ *Marketing for Dummies*
Pub: John Wiley & Sons Inc.
Ed: Alexander Hiam, Editor. **Released:** latest edition 3rd; Published October, 2009. **Price:** $21.99, individuals paperback. **Publication Includes:** Marketing web sites, marketing consultants, trade associations, market researchers, and other experts. **Entries Include:** Individual or company name, address, phone number, web site address (where applicable). Principal content of publication is articles on marketing strategies.

25746 ■ "Meet Rebecca. She's Here to Fire You" in *Inc.* (November 2007, pp. 25-26)
Pub: Gruner & Jahr USA Publishing
Ed: Max Chafkin. **Description:** Amid liability concerns as well as CEO guilt, more and more firms are using consulting companies to fire workers. These outsourced firms help small companies structure severance and document information in order to limit legal liability when firing an employee.

25747 ■ *The Mirror Test: How to Breathe New Life Into Your Business*
Pub: Grand Central Publishing
Ed: Jeffrey W. Hayzlett. **Released:** May 10, 2010. **Price:** $24.99. **Description:** Consultant and author, Jeffrey Hayzlett, explains why a business is not doing well and asks the questions that most business managers are afraid to ask.

25748 ■ "More Sales Leads, Please: Or, What Happened When Frontline Selling Started Practicing What It Preaches" in *Inc.* (November 2007)
Pub: Gruner & Jahr USA Publishing
Description: Frontline Selling located in Oakland, New Jersey helps train sales teams to generate and convert sales leads. The consulting firm doubled their marketing budget to increase their own sales.

25749 ■ *My So-Called Freelance Life: How to Survive and Thrive as a Creative Professional for Hire*
Pub: Seal Press
Ed: Michelle Goodman. **Released:** October 1, 2008. **Price:** $15.95. **Description:** Guidebook for women wishing to start a freelancing business; tips, advice, how-to's and all the information needed to survive working from home are included.

25750 ■ "Nampa Police Department: Electronic Systems Just One Tool in Business Security Toolbox" in *Idaho Business Review* (October 29, 2010)
Pub: Dolan Media Newswires
Ed: Brad Carlson. **Description:** Police departments and private security firms can help small businesses with hard security and business consultants can assist with internal audit security and fraud prevention.

25751 ■ "New Database Brings Doctors Out of the Dark" in *Business Courier* (Vol. 26, October 23, 2009, No. 26, pp. 1)
Pub: American City Business Journals, Inc.
Ed: James Ritchie. **Description:** A database created by managed care consulting firm Praesentia allows doctors in Cincinnati to compare average reimbursements from health insurance companies to doctors in different areas. Specialist doctors in the city are paid an average of $172.25 for every office consultation.

25752 ■ *Niche and Grow Rich*
Pub: Entrepreneur Press
Ed: Jennifer Basye Sander; Peter Sander. **Released:** 2003. **Description:** Consultants share insight to entrepreneurs wishing to find a profitable niche market. Authors write that good niche businesses are easy to start and easy to defend from competitors. They also report that finding a successful niche can attract and maintain good customers who are willing to pay more for unique goods and services.

25753 ■ "Nothing But Net: Fran Harris Offers Advice On Winning the Game of Business" in *Black Enterprise* (Vol. 38, March 2008, No. 8, pp. 50)
Pub: Earl G. Graves Publishing Co. Inc.
Ed: Chana Garcia. **Description:** Fran Harris, certified life coach, business consultant, and CEO of her business, a multimedia development company, reveals five tips to ensure entrepreneurial success.

25754 ■ "On Hire Ground" in *Entrepreneur* (Vol. 36, February 2008, No. 2, pp. 19)
Pub: Entrepreneur Media Inc.
Description: ADP Small Business Services, an economic consulting firm, showed that small businesses had increased employment rates in 2007 and added 77,000 jobs in November 2007. Entrepreneurial employment and data showing the contribution of small businesses to job growth are presented.

25755 ■ "Outplacement Services" in *Black Enterprise* (Vol. 38, March 2008, No. 8, pp. 60)
Pub: Earl G. Graves Publishing Co. Inc.
Ed: Marcia Reed Woodard. **Description:** Tips to use while in career-transition are offered. Many times outplacement services are provided as part of a severance package to employees.

25756 ■ *PPC's Guide to Small Business Consulting Engagements*
Pub: Practitioners Publishing Company
Released: March 2004. **Price:** $226.00. **Description:** Technical guide for conducting consulting engagements for small business.

25757 ■ *PPC's Guide to Small Business Consulting Engagements, Vol. 2*
Pub: Practitioners Publishing Company
Released: March 2004. **Description:** Second volume of the technical guide for conducting consulting engagements for small business.

25758 ■ *PPC's Guide to Small Business Consulting Engagements, Vol. 3*
Pub: Practitioners Publishing Company
Released: March 2004. **Description:** Third volume of the technical guide for conducting consulting engagements for small business.

25759 ■ *Professional Services Marketing: How the Best Firms Build Premier Brands*
Pub: John Wiley & Sons, Inc.
Ed: Mike Schultz, John Doerr. **Released:** July 27, 2009. **Price:** $27.95. **Description:** Research based on best practices and processes for the professional services industry is presented. The book covers five key areas: creating a custom marketing and growth strategy, establishing a brand, implementing a marketing communications program, developing a lead strategy, and winning new clients.

25760 ■ "Provinces Tackle E-Waste Problem" in *Canadian Electronics* (Vol. 23, June-July 2008, No. 4, pp. 1)
Pub: Action Communication Inc.
Ed: Ken Manchen. **Description:** Canadian provinces are implementing measures concerning the safe and environmentally friendly disposal of electronic waste. Alberta, British Columbia, Nova Scotia, and Saskatchewan impose an e-waste recycling fee on electronic equipment purchases.

25761 ■ "Putting Vets to Work" in *Business Week* (September 22, 2008, No. 4100, pp. 18)
Pub: McGraw-Hill Companies, Inc.
Ed: Deborah Stead. **Description:** Advice is provided by former Marine Sal Cepeda, a consultant who advises employers on hiring veterans, for former military personnel coming back into the workforce.

25762 ■ *Raising Capital*
Pub: Greenwood Publishing Group, Inc.
Ed: David Nour. **Released:** March 1, 2009. **Price:** $39.95. **Description:** An overview to help entrepreneurs find capital for starting and maintaining a small business is presented. The author shows how to develop long-term relationships with financial partners and ways to attract financing to fund the startup and growth phases of any business. Entrepreneurs tell how they raised money from friends, family, angel investors, banks and venture capitalists and private equity firms.

25763 ■ "Raptor Opens Consultancy" in *Austin Business Journal* (Vol. 31, July 8, 2011, No. 18, pp. 1)
Pub: American City Business Journals Inc.
Ed: Christopher Calnan. **Description:** Boston hedge fund operator Raptor Group launched Raptor Accelerator, a consulting business providing sales and advisory services to early-stage companies in Central Texas. Aside from getting involved with the startups in which the Raptor Group invests, Raptor Accelerator will target firms operating in the sports, media, entertainment, and content technology sectors.

25764 ■ "Reduce the Risk of Failed Financial Judgments" in *Harvard Business Review* (Vol. 86, July-August 2008, No. 8, pp. 24)
Pub: Harvard Business School Press
Ed: Robert G. Eccles; Edward J. Fiedl. **Description:** Utilization of business consultants, evaluators, appraisers, and actuaries to decrease financial management risks is discussed.

25765 ■ "Restoring Grandeur" in *Business Courier* (Vol. 26, December 4, 2009, No. 32, pp. 1)
Pub: American City Business Journals, Inc.
Ed: Dan Monk. **Description:** Eagle Realty Group intends to spend more than $10 to restore the historic 12-story Phelps apartment building in Lytle Park in Cincinnati. Its president, Mario San Marco, expressed the need to invest in the building in order to maintain operations. The building could be restored into a hotel catering to executives and consultants.

25766 ■ "Retail in Austin Strong, Will Continue to Be" in *Austin Business JournalInc.* (Vol. 29, January 22, 2010, No. 46, pp. 1)
Pub: American City Business Journals
Ed: Jacob Dirr. **Description:** Retail sector in Austin, Texas has outpaced the national average in value, mid-tier, high-end and drugs retail sectors, according to a report by Pitney Bowes. The national consulting firm's report has projected growth in every sector until the end of fiscal 2012. Data regarding other sectors is also included.

25767 ■ "The Right Remedy: Entrepreneur's Success Is a Matter of Life and Death" in *Black Enterprise* (Vol. 38, February 2008, No. 7, pp. 46)
Pub: Earl G. Graves Publishing Co. Inc.
Ed: Tamara E. Holmes. **Description:** Profile of Leah Brown, whose company conducts clinical trials to determine if specific drugs will relieve particular symptoms. Her company will also visit physician's offices to make certain doctors are following proper protocol for a clinical trial or will collect data from patients.

25768 ■ "The Rise of Pompei" in *Retail Merchandiser* (Vol. 51, September-October 2011, No. 5, pp. 13)
Pub: Phoenix Media Corporation
Description: Soho creative consulting group follows its C3 philosophy to create an invigorated brand experience that transforms customers from consumers to empowered buyers. Pompei AD is a leading creative consultancy that specializes in design and branding for retail, museum, hospitality, and other sectors.

25769 ■ "The Secret Life of a Serial CEO" in *Inc.* (January 2008, pp. 80-88)
Pub: Gruner & Jahr USA Publishing
Ed: David H. Freedman. **Description:** Profile of Bob Cramer, who has lead six successful companies and is now searching for a new business venture and thinks he's found it. Cramer shares his journey from wooing venture capital, handling founders and his hunt for his newest venture.

25770 ■ "Security Alert: Data Server" in *Entrepreneur* (Vol. 36, February 2008, No. 2, pp. 28)
Pub: Entrepreneur Media Inc.
Ed: Amanda C. Kooser. **Description:** Michael Kogon is the founder of Definition 6, a technology consulting and interactive marking firm. He believes in the philosophy that the best way to keep sensitive data safe is not to store it. Details on the security policies of his firm are discussed.

25771 ■ "Selling Your Company" in *Inc.* (March 2008, pp. 78)
Pub: Gruner & Jahr USA Publishing
Ed: Myra Goodman. **Description:** Owner of a safety consulting company seeks advice for selling the firm.

25772 ■ "Sick of Trends? You Should Be" in *Brandweek* (Vol. 49, April 21, 2008, No. 16, pp. 22)
Pub: VNU Business Media, Inc.
Ed: Eric Zeitoun. **Description:** Eric Zeitoun, the president of Dragon Rouge, a global brand consultancy, discusses the importance of macrotrends as opposed to microtrends which he feels are often irrelevant, create confusion and cause marketers to lose site of the larger picture of their industry. Macrotrends, on the other hand, create a fundamental, societal shift that influences consumer attitudes over a long period of time.

25773 ■ *Silos, Politics and Turf Wars: A Leadership Fable about Destroying the Barriers That Turn Colleagues Into Competitors*
Pub: Jossey Bass
Ed: Patrick M. Lencioni. **Released:** February 17, 2006. **Price:** $24.95. **Description:** The author addresses management problems through a fable that revolves around a self-employed consultant who has to dismantle silos at an upscale hotel, a technology company and a hospital. The story explains how organizations can use a collective operational vision in order to overcome pride, greed, and tribalism and work as a team with the same goal in mind.

25774 ■ "Small, But Mighty" in *Employee Benefit News* (Vol. 25, November 1, 2011, No. 14, pp. 32)
Pub: SourceMedia Inc.
Ed: Andrea Davis. **Description:** Three consulting firms are facing the challenge of helping clients understand the new health care reform in a tight economy.

25775 ■ *The Sticking Point Solution: 9 Ways to Move Your Business from Stagnation to Stunning Growth in Tough Economic Times*
Pub: Vanguard Press
Ed: Jay Abraham. **Released:** May 10, 2010. **Price:** $25.95. **Description:** Renowned business consultant, Jay Abraham, reveals the nine ways even successful businesses get stuck, hit plateaus, and fail to achieve their dreams and he explains how to get unstuck and create exponential growth.

25776 ■ "Survey Finds State Execs Cool On Climate Change" in *The Business Journal-Milwaukee* (Vol. 25, August 8, 2008, No. 46, pp. A1)
Pub: American City Business Journals, Inc.
Ed: David Doege. **Description:** According to a survey of business executives in Wisconsin, business leaders do not see climate change as a pressing concern, but businesses are moving toward more energy-efficient operations. The survey also revealed that executives believe that financial incentives can promote energy conservation. Other survey results are provided.

25777 ■ "Tauri Group Partner Joining Homeland Security and Defense" in *Wireless News* (December 15, 2009)
Pub: Close-Up Media
Description: Managing partner Cosmo DiMaggio III of the Tauri Group, a provider of analytic consulting for homeland security, defense and space clients, has been elected to the Board of Directors at Homeland Security and Defense Business Council.

25778 ■ "Tech Deal Couples Homegrown Firms" in *The Business Journal-Serving Greater Tampa Bay* (Vol. 28, July 4, 2008, No. 28, pp. 1)
Pub: American City Business Journals, Inc.
Ed: Michael Hinman. **Description:** Tampa Bay, Florida-based Administrative Partners Inc. was acquired by Tribridge Inc. resulting in the strengthening of the delivery of Microsoft products to clients. Other details of the merger of the management consulting services companies are presented.

25779 ■ "Think Disruptive! How to Manage In a New Era of Innovation" in *Strategy & Leadership* (Vol. 38, July-August 2010, No. 4, pp. 5-10)
Pub: Emerald Inc.
Ed: Brian Leavy, John Sterling. **Description:** The views expressed by Scott Anthony, president of an innovation consultancy Innosight, on the need for corporate leaders to apply disruptive innovation in a recessionary environment are presented. His suggestion that disruptive innovation is the only way to survive during the economic crisis is discussed.

25780 ■ "Thomas Industrial Network Unveils Custom SPEC" in *Entertainment Close-Up* (March 3, 2011)
Pub: Close-Up Media
Description: Thomas Industrial Network assists custom manufacturers and industrial service providers a complete online program called Custom SPEC which includes Website development and Internet exposure.

25781 ■ *The Toilet Paper Entrepreneur: The Tell-It-Like-It-Is Guide to Cleaning Up In Business, Even If You Are At the End of Your Roll*
Pub: Obsidian Launch LLC
Ed: Mike Michalowicz. **Price:** $24.95. **Description:** The founder of three multimillion-dollar companies, including Obsidian Launch, a company that partners with first-time entrepreneurs to grow their concepts into industry leaders.

25782 ■ "Tool Time" in *Entrepreneur* (Vol. 36, March 2008, No. 3, pp. 90)
Pub: Entrepreneur Media Inc.
Ed: Nichole A. Torres. **Description:** DaVinci Institute holds an annual event in Colorado to display new products and inventions. Innovative Design Engineering Animation is a consulting company that helps inventors develop product through various stages. NineSigma Inc. has an online marketplace where inventors can post ideas for clients needing new products.

25783 ■ "Tough Sell" in *Black Enterprise* (Vol. 37, October 2006, No. 3, pp. 92)
Pub: Earl G. Graves Publishing Co. Inc.
Ed: Sonia Alleyne. **Description:** Career coaches can evaluate your talents and skills. In an era where more companies are downsizing a coach can help you decide if you are suited for your industry or should try switching careers.

25784 ■ "Trend: Tutors to Help You Pump Up the Staff" in *Business Week* (September 22, 2008, No. 4100, pp. 45)
Pub: McGraw-Hill Companies, Inc.
Ed: Reena Janaj. **Description:** High-level managers are turning to innovation coaches in an attempt to obtain advice on how to better sell new concepts within their companies. Individuals as well as consulting firms are now offering this service.

25785 ■ "Tweaking On-Board Activities, Equipment Saves Fuel, Reduces CO2" in *Canadian Sailings* (June 30, 2008)
Pub: Commonwealth Business Media
Description: Optimizing ship activities and equipment uses less fuel and therefore reduces greenhouse gas emissions. Ways in which companies are implementing research and development techniques in order to monitor ship performance and analyze data in an attempt to become more efficient are examined.

25786 ■ "Up Against the Ropes: A Professional Coach May Help" in *Black Enterprise* (Vol. 37, December 2006, No. 5, pp. 72)
Pub: Earl G. Graves Publishing Co. Inc.
Ed: Description: Executive coaching is now a $1 billion industry. The coaching process itself and traits to look for in a coach are discussed.

25787 ■ "VeriFone Announces Global Security Solutions Business" in *Marketing Weekly News* (October 3, 2009)
Pub: Investment Weekly News
Description: Focused on delivering innovative security solutions, VeriFone Holdings, Inc. announced the formation of its Global Security Solutions Business Unit, including VeriShield Protect, an end-to-end encryption to protect cardholder data throughout the merchant and processor systems. The business will focus on consulting, sales and implementation of these new products in order to help retailers and processors protect customer data.

25788 ■ "Water Works Spinoff Could Make Big Splash" in *Business Courier* (Vol. 24, October 19, 2008, No. 27, pp. 1)
Pub: American City Business Journals, Inc.
Ed: Dan Monk. **Description:** Cincinnati, Ohio city manager Milton Dohoney proposed to spin off the city-owned Greater Cincinnati Water Works into a regionally focused water district that could allow the city to receive millions of dollars in annual dividends. A feasibility study is to be conducted by a team of outside consultants and city staffers and is expected to be finished by summer of 2008.

25789 ■ *A Whack on the Side of the Head*
Pub: Business Plus
Ed: Roger von Oech. **Released:** May 2008. **Price:** $16.99. **Description:** The author, a consultant, shares insight into increasing entrepreneurial creativity.

25790 ■ "The Whole Package" in *Entrepreneur* (Vol. 36, February 2008, No. 2, pp. 24)
Pub: Entrepreneur Media Inc.
Description: Holy Bohn, owner of The Honest Statute, developed an environmentally-friendly packaging for her pet food products. The company hired a packaging consultant and spent $175,000. Big corporations also spend money and plunge into the latest trends in packaging ranging from lighter and flexible to temperature-sensitive labels.

25791 ■ "Winner: Private Company, Less Than $100M" in *Crain's Detroit Business* (Vol. 25, June 22, 2009, No. 25)
Pub: Crain Communications Inc. - Detroit
Ed: Tom Henderson. **Description:** Profile of ForeSee Results, an Ann Arbor, Michigan-based firm that uses the University of Michigan American Consumer Satisfaction Index to help businesses measure satisfaction with their Websites.

25792 ■ "Winning Gold" in *The Business Journal-Milwaukee* (Vol. 25, August 8, 2008, No. 46, pp. A1)
Pub: American City Business Journals, Inc.
Ed: Rich Rovito. **Description:** Johnson Controls Inc. of Milwaukee, Wisconsin is taking part in the 2008 Beijing Olympics with the installation of its sustainable control equipment and technology that monitor over 58,000 points in 18 Olympic venues. Details of Johnson Controls' green products and sustainable operations in China are discussed.

25793 ■ *Working for Yourself: Law and Taxes for Independent Contractors, Freelancers and Consultants*
Pub: NOLO Publications
Ed: Stephen Fishman. **Released:** March 2008. **Price:** $39.99 paperback. **Description:** In-depth information is shared for contractors, freelancers and consultants involving business law and small business taxes.

25794 ■ "Your Booming Business: How You Can Align Sales and Marketing for Dynamic Growth" in *Small Business Opportunities* (Spring 2008)
Pub: Harris Publications Inc.

Ed: Voss W. Graham. **Description:** Voss Graham, founder and CEO of Inneractive Consulting Group Inc., works with companies to develop and hire successful sales teams. A checklist from the American Bankers Association to help write a business plan is included.

TRADE PERIODICALS

25795 ■ *California Special Education Alert*
Pub: LRP Publications
Contact: Steve Bevilacquar, Editorial Dir.

Released: Monthly. **Price:** $260 plus $27 s/h. **Description:** Assists California special education administrators comply with changing special education laws, regulations, and policies on the state and federal level to avoid litigation. Recurring features include letters to the editor, interviews, and reports of meetings.

25796 ■ *SoloDining.com*
Pub: SoloDining.com
Contact: Marya Charles Alexander

Ed: Marya Charles Alexander, Editor. **Released:** Quarterly. **Price:** $25; $25, Canada plus $5 postage. **Description:** Provides strategies and tips on how to increase one's comfort and options when dining alone. Presents information on notable solo-friendly restaurants in the US and other countries. Describes solo-dining amenities to look for or suggest to restaurants. Now includes tips on solo travel.

VIDEOCASSETTES/ AUDIOCASSETTES

25797 ■ *How to Build a Profitable Consulting Practice 1 & 2*
Chesney Communications
2302 Martin St., Ste. 125
Irvine, CA 92612
Ph:(949)263-5500
Free: 800-223-8878
Fax:(949)263-5506
Co. E-mail: videocc@aol.com
URL: http://www.videocc.com

Released: 1987. **Price:** $59.95. **Description:** An entire Howard Shenson seminar about setting up a consulting practice, condensed into two hours. **Availability:** VHS; 3/4U.

CONSULTANTS

25798 ■ 2010 Fund 5
24351 Spartan St.
Mission Viejo, CA 92691-3920
Ph:(949)583-1992
Fax:(949)583-0474
Contact: Wally Eater, Principle

Scope: Funds in formation that will invest in technologies licensed from 30 universities.

25799 ■ ADG Group
4261 Northside Dr., Ste. 200
PO Box 52594
Atlanta, GA 30327
Ph:(404)264-9301
Fax:(404)261-3439
Contact: Cameron Adair, Chairman of the Board
E-mail: camadair@aol.com

Scope: Corporate finance advisory firm specializing in arranging venture capital financing for emerging companies. Assists with mergers, acquisitions, and divestitures. Offers balance sheet restructuring services for bankrupt and financially troubled companies. Also offers independent due diligence investigations.

25800 ■ Advanced Benefits & Human Resources
9350-F Snowden River Pky., Ste. 222
Columbia, MD 21045
Ph:(410)290-9037
Fax:(410)740-2568
Co. E-mail: hrb@abhr.com
Contact: Linda Polacek, President

Scope: Provides human resource consulting to high technology businesses. Offers services in the areas of human resources, benefits, and training. Creates, maintains, or updates current human resource functions.

25801 ■ The Advantage Group Inc.
38 Wellington St. E, Ste. 200
Toronto, ON, Canada M5E 1C7
Ph:(416)863-0685
Free: 800-671-1048
Fax:(416)863-0787
Co. E-mail: answers@advantagegroup.com
URL: http://www.advantagegroup.com
Contact: Ron Pirie, President
E-mail: ronpirie@atsadvantagegroup.com

Scope: Specializes in two key areas: performance benchmarking and pricing strategy. Each stream has developed a wide variety of customizable proprietary research tools to meet the needs of the clients. **Publications:** "7 Steps to building better customer relationships"; "How to Add Value to Customer Relationships"; "Top 10 Key Benefits of Building Business Relationships"; "Tips for Creating Better Relationships"; "Building Trust in Personal and Business Relationships"; "The Advantage Report Canadian Grocer"; "Customer Relationships"; "Customer Relationship Management: What it is and What it's not"; "The Advantage Report - Measuring the supplier-retailer relationship".

25802 ■ Advisory Management Services Inc.
9600 E 129th St., Ste. B
Kansas City, MO 64149-1025
Ph:(816)765-9611
Fax:(816)765-7447
Co. E-mail: amsi1@mindspring.com
Contact: Hal Wood, President

Scope: A management consulting and training firm specializing in employee relations, management and staff training, organizational development, strategic planning, and continuous quality improvement.

25803 ■ Aegis Communications Inc.
2 Greenwich Plz., Ste. 100
Greenwich, CT 06830-6353
Ph:(203)622-4944
Contact: David Bushko, CEO

Scope: Marketing firm specializing in using visualization tools to help clients define communication needs and develop communication strategies and plans.

25804 ■ The Alliance Management Group Inc.
38 Old Chester Rd., Ste. 300
Gladstone, NJ 07934
Ph:(908)234-2344
Fax:(908)234-0638
Co. E-mail: kathy@strategicalliance.com
URL: http://www.strategicalliance.com
Contact: Dan G. Watson, Senior Partner
E-mail: gene@atsstrategicalliance.com

Scope: The firm enables leading companies to maximize the value of their strategic alliances, mergers and acquisitions. Offers services in partner evaluation process, a planning and negotiating program, mergers and acquisition integration, management issues, the turnaround or termination of poorly performing alliances, and a competitive strategic analysis program. **Publications:** "Effective Practices For Sourcing Innovation," Jan-Feb, 2009; "Intellectual Property Issues in Collaborative Research Agreements," Nov-Dec, 2008; "Building University Relationships in China," Sep-Oct, 2008; "Reinventing Corporate Growth: Implementing the Transformational Growth Model"; "The Strongest Link"; "Allocating Patent Rights in Collaborative Research Agreements"; "Protecting Know-how and Trade Secrets in Collaborative Research Agreements," Aug, 2006; "Sourcing External Technology for Innovation," Jun, 2006. **Special Services:** "Want, Find, Get, Manage" Model[R]; "Want, Find, Get, Manage" Framework[R]; WFGM Framework[R]; The Alliance Implementation Program[R]; WFGM Paradigm[R]; WFGM Model[R]; "Want, Find, Get, Manage" Paradigm[R], Transformational Growth[R]; T-growth[R].

25805 ■ Alliance Management International Ltd.
PO Box 470691
Cleveland, OH 44147-0691
Ph:(440)838-1922
Fax:(440)740-1434
Co. E-mail: bob@bgruss.com
Contact: Ken Gruss, Mgr
E-mail: bgruss@cox.net

Scope: A consulting company that helps to form national and international strategic alliances. Handles alliances between companies forming joint ventures. Staff specialized in small company-large company alliance, alliance assessment and analysis, and alliance strategic planning. **Seminars:** Joint Business Planning; Developing a Shared Vision; Current and New/Prospective Partner Assessment; Customer Service; Sales Training; Leader and Management Skills.

25806 ■ Alternative Services Inc.
32625 7 Mile Rd., Ste. 10
Livonia, MI 48152-4269
Ph:(248)471-4880
Fax:(248)471-5230
URL: http://www.asi-mi.org
Contact: Arthur Mack, President
E-mail: bmcluckie@asi-mi.org

Scope: Provides social services management support to group homes for the mentally disabled. Also offers marketing, training, and financial services to businesses and nonprofit organizations.

25807 ■ Ambler Growth Strategy Consultants Inc.
3432 Reading Ave.
Hammonton, NJ 08037-8008
Ph:(609)567-9669
Free: 888-253-6662
Fax:(609)567-3810
Co. E-mail: thegrowthstrategist@ambler.com
URL: http://www.thegrowthstrategist.com
Contact: Melissa Norcross, Chief Marketing Officer
E-mail: melissa@atsambler.com

Scope: Growth strategies, strategic assessments, CEO coaching. **Publications:** "A joint venture can deliver more than growth"; "Achieving competitive advantage"; "Achieving resilience for your business during difficult times"; "Achieving resilient growth during challenging times"; "Acquisitions: A growth strategy to consider"; "Attracting and retaining long-term corporate sponsors"; "Celebrate Selling: The Consultative Relationship Way"; "A Joint Venture Can Deliver More Than Growth"; "Achieving Competitive Advantage"; "Achieving Resilience for Your Business During Difficult Times"; "Balancing Revenue Growth with Growth of a Business"; "Capture Your Competitive Advantage"; "Ease Succession Planning"; "Games Employees Play"; "How to Spark Innovation in an Existing Company"; "Managers demands must change with growth"; "Motivating Generation employees"; "Knowing when to hire ratios provide answers"; "Better customer service can bring black ink". **Seminars:** Strategic Leadership; Managing Innovation; Breaking Through Classic Barriers to Growth; Energize Your Enterprise; Capture Your Competitive Advantage; Four Entrepreneurial Styles; Perservance and Resilience; Real-Time Strategic Planning/RO1. **Special Services:** The Growth Strategist[TM].

25808 ■ American English Academy
111 N Atlantic Blvd., Ste. 112
Monterey Park, CA 91754
Ph:(626)457-2800
Fax:(626)457-2808
Co. E-mail: admission@aea-usa.com
URL: http://www.aea-usa.com
Contact: Charles Policky, President

Scope: Specializes in providing on-site English language and communication development for corporations and individuals. Also develops and delivers training in speaking, writing, pronunciation, grammar, and idioms with an emphasis on business communication. Offers individual, small group, intensive, and long-distance learning. Programs tailor-made for each client.

25809 ■ Anderson/Roethle Inc.
700 N Water St., Ste. 1100
Milwaukee, WI 53202-4221
Ph:(414)276-0070
Fax:(414)276-4364
Co. E-mail: info@anderson-roethle.com
URL: http://www.anderson-roethle.com
Contact: James H. Hunter, Managering Director
E-mail: jimh@atsanderson-roethle.com
Scope: Provides merger, acquisition and divestiture advisory services. Offers strategic planning, valuations and specialized M and A advisory services.

25810 ■ Apex Innovations Inc.
700 W 47th St., Ste. 300
PO Box 15208
Kansas City, MO 64112-1805
Ph:(913)254-0250
Fax:(913)254-0320
Co. E-mail: sales@apex-innovations.com
URL: http://www.apex-innovations.com
Contact: Connie Fox, Dir of Human Resources
Scope: A firm of business operations and technology professionals providing solutions nationwide for business needs. Provides a bridge between operations and technology for clients in manufacturing, insurance, banking and government. Offers services in business planning, assessment, education, business performance improvement, change management and the planning, and implementation management of solutions. **Special Services:** i-INFO.EPR™; i-INFO. WORKS™; i-INFO Classes™.

25811 ■ Arnold S. Goldin & Associates Inc.
5030 Champion Blvd., Ste. G-6231
Boca Raton, FL 33496
Ph:(561)994-5810
Fax:(561)994-5860
Co. E-mail: arnold@goldin.com
URL: http://www.goldin.com
Contact: Arnold S. Goldin, Principle
E-mail: arnold@goldin.com
Scope: An accounting and management consulting firm. Serves clients worldwide. Provides management services. Handles monthly write-ups and tax returns.

25812 ■ Association of Home-Based Women Entrepreneurs
PO Box 31561
Saint Louis, MO 63131-1561
Ph:(314)805-9519
Fax:(314)909-8179
Co. E-mail: aschaefer@advbizsol.com
URL: http://www.hbwe.org
Contact: Sue Lunnemann, Treasurer
E-mail: sue@atssl-solutions.biz
Scope: Organization dedicated to women working from home-based offices. Focuses on the needs and interests of women doing their own business. It also focuses on business-related programs and issues, networking, leads and mentoring for professional growth in a dynamic and friendly atmosphere. **Publications:** "Taking Your Business International"; "Dressing For Success"; "Web 2.0 The Future of the Internet"; "Assertiveness Skills for Women in Business". **Seminars:** Making Connections, Jul, 2008; One Inch Wide, One Mile Deep, Jun, 2008; Accelerating Your Business, May, 2008; Change is Good, Apr, 2008; Pyro Marketing, Jan, 2007; Twenty Five Key Steps To Maintaining A Successful Home-Based Business, Nov, 2006.

25813 ■ Aurora Management Partners Inc.
4485 Tench Rd., Ste. 340
Suwanee, GA 30024
Ph:(770)904-5209
Co. E-mail: rturcotte@auroramp.com
URL: http://www.auroramp.com
Contact: William A. Barbee, Director
E-mail: abarbee@atsauroramp.com
Scope: Firm specializes in turnaround management and reorganization consulting. Firm develop strategic initiatives, organize and analyze solutions, deal with creditor issues, review organizational structure and develop time frames for decision making. Turnaround services offered include Recovery plans and their implementation, Viability analysis, Crisis management, Financial restructuring, Corporate and organizational restructuring, Facilities rationalization, Liquidation management, Loan workout, Litigation support and Expert testimony, Contract renegotiation, Sourcing loan refinancing and Sourcing equity investment. **Publications:** "TMA Turnaround of the Year Award, Small Company, Honorable Mention," Nov, 2005; "Back From The Brink - Bland Farms," Progressive Farmer, Oct, 2004; "New Breed of Turnaround Managers," Catalyst Magazine, Aug, 2004; "Key Performance Drivers - Bland Farms," The Produce News, Apr, 2004; "Corporate Governance: Averting Crisis's Before They Happen," ABJ journal, Feb, 2004.

25814 ■ Automated Accounting
23325 Gerbera St.
Moreno Valley, CA 92553
Ph:(951)653-5053
Co. E-mail: autoacc@earthlink.net
Contact: Gary Capolino, Owner
Scope: A business management consulting firm that caters to small businesses. Offers software installation services, tax preparation services and business plan advisory services. **Publications:** "Inflated Real Estate Prices. . .How Did This Happen," Moreno Valley Magazine, Aug, 2005.

25815 ■ Bahr International Inc.
PO Box 795
Gainesville, TX 76241
Ph:(940)665-2344
Fax:(940)665-2359
Co. E-mail: info@bahrintl.com
URL: http://www.bahrintl.com
Contact: C. Charles Bahr III, Chairman of the Board
Scope: Offers consulting in general management, corporate polices and culture, and strategic and long-range planning. Provides management audits and reports and profit improvement programs. High level strategic marketing, advertising strategy/tactics, turnaround consulting and management.

25816 ■ Beacon Management Group Inc.
1000 W McNab Rd., Ste. 150
Pompano Beach, FL 33069-4719
Ph:(954)782-1119
Free: 800-771-8721
Fax:(954)969-2566
Co. E-mail: md@beaconmgmt.com
URL: http://www.beaconmgmt.com
Contact: Chris Roy, Treasurer
E-mail: md@beaconmgmt.com
Scope: Specializes in change management, organized workplaces, multicultural negotiations and dispute resolutions and internet based decision making.

25817 ■ Beeline Learning Solutions
14911 Quorum Dr., Ste. 120
Dallas, TX 75254
Ph:(972)813-0465
Fax:(972)386-8667
Co. E-mail: info@consultingpartners.com
URL: http://www.beeline.com
Contact: Debra Gann, Managering Director
E-mail: gann@atsconsultingpartners.com
Scope: Consulting firm offering technology, content, and services addressing recruitment and sourcing, talent management, and learning and performance optimization. Solutions offered include contingent workforce solutions, vendor management software, talent management solutions, recruitment process outsourcing, performance management, applicant tracking, learning management and eLearning. **Special Services:** Beeline[R].

25818 ■ Benchmark Consulting Group Inc.
283 Franklin St., Ste. 400
PO Box 126
Boston, MA 02110-3100
Ph:(617)482-7661
Fax:(617)423-2158
Co. E-mail: werobb35@aol.com
Contact: Walter E. Robb III, President
E-mail: werobb35@aol.com
Scope: Provides financial and management services to companies. Helps companies grow through debt, equity sourcing and restructuring, business valuation, acquisition and divestiture, computer information systems and improved operation profitability.

25819 ■ Bio-Technical Resources L.P.
1035 S 7th St.
Manitowoc, WI 54220-5301
Ph:(920)684-5518
Fax:(920)684-5519
Co. E-mail: info@biotechresources.com
URL: http://www.biotechresources.com
Contact: Tom Jerrell, President
E-mail: jerrell@atsbiotechresources.com
Scope: Services include strain improvement, process development and metabolic engineering. Solutions are also offered for the development of biotechnology products and processes through contract services in research and development, bio process scale-up, pilot scale manufacturing, technology and economic assessments. Target audience: pharmaceutical, biotechnology, chemical and food and feed industries. Client base may be global leaders as well as small companies and startups. **Publications:** "A Novel Fungus for the Production of Efficient Cellulases and Hemi-Cellulases," Jun, 2009; "Linoleic Acid Isomerase from Propionibacterium acnes: Purification, Characterization, Molecular Cloning, and Heterologous Expression," 2007; "Purification and Characterization of a Membrane-Bound Linoleic Acid Isomerase from Clostridium sporogenes," 2007; "Metabolic Engineering of Sesquiterpene Metabolism in Yeast," 2007; "Purification and Characterization of a Membrane-Bound Linoleic Acidlsomerase from Clostridium sporogenes," 2007; "Reduction of Background Interference in the Spectrophotometric Assay of Mevalonate Kinase," 2006; "A Soluble Form of Phosphatase in Saccharomyces cerevisiae Capable of Converting Farnesyl Diphosphate to E, E-Farnesol," 2006; "Ascorbate Biosynthesis: A Diversity of Pathways," BIOS Scientific Publishers, 2004; "The Biotechnology of Ascorbic Acid Manufacture," BIOS Scientific Publishers, 2004; "Detection of Farnesyl Diphosphate Accumulation in YeastERG9 Mutants," 2003; "Reverse Two-Hybrid System: Detecting Critical Interaction Domains and Screening for Inhibitors," Eaton Publishing, 2000. **Seminars:** Metabolic Engineering for Industrial Production of Glucosamine and N-Acetylglucosamine, Aug, 2003; Metabolic Engineering of E. coli for the Industrial Production of Glucosamine, Apr, 2003.

25820 ■ BioChem Technology Inc.
3620 Horizon Dr., Ste. 200
King of Prussia, PA 19406-2110
Ph:(610)768-9360
Fax:(610)768-9363
Co. E-mail: sales@biochemtech.com
URL: http://www.biochemtech.com
Contact: Allan Myers, Principle
E-mail: charlesxu@atsbiochemtech.com
Scope: A process consultation firm specializing in the monitoring, optimization and control of wastewater treatment processes. The technological optimization services include assessment of treatment capacities, facility re-rating, optimization services, de-bottlenecking services, flow dynamics/mixing pattern analysis. **Publications:** "A Novel Approach for Monitoring and Control of Denitrification in a Biological Nutrient Removal Facility," Oct, 1999; "A Unique Approach for Assessing the Capacity of a Biological Nutrient Removal Facility," Oct, 1999; "Enhancing Competitiveness of an Operations Staff: Five Years Experience with a BNR Wastewater Treatment Facility," Oct, 1998; "Optimization of Nitrification Process By On-Line Monitoring of Nitrification Time," Jun, 1997; "Monitoring and Control of the Nitrification Process Marine Park Water Reclamation Facility, City of Vancouver, WA," Oct, 1997; "Operational Improvements in a Biological Nutrient Removal Facility Using an Innovative Biological Activity Meter," May, 1996; "Operator Education and an Innovative Monitoring Technology Improve Performance of a Biological Nutrient Removal Facility," Oct, 1996; "Performance

Enhancement of a BNR Wastewater Treatment Facility Utilizing a Microcosm Reactor Equipped With a Biological Activity Meter," Oct, 1996; "Optimization of Biological Denitrification Through Biological Activity Monitoring: System Development," Jun, 1995. **Seminars:** A Five Year Case Study of a Feed Forward Nitrogen Reduction Process Control System, Jun, 2009; Alternate DO Control Based on On-line Ammonia Measurement, Jun, 2009.

25821 ■ BioSciCon Inc.
14905 Forest Landing Cir.
Rockville, MD 20850-3924
Ph:(301)610-9130
Fax:(301)610-7662
Co. E-mail: info@bioscicon.com
URL: http://www.bioscicon.com
Contact: Olivera Markovic, Director
E-mail: info@bioscicon.com
Scope: Sponsoring development of the technology of the Pap test accuracy via introduction of a new bio-marker that enhances visibility of abnormal cells on Pap smears or mono-layers of cervical cells obtained in solution. Conducts clinical trials for assessment of the test efficacy and safety, manufactures research tools for conduct of trials, and markets IP to license manufacturing, marketing, sales and distribution rights of the new technology line of products. **Publications:** "Cervical Acid Phosphates: A Biomarker of Cervical Dysplasia and Potential Surrogate Endpoint for Colposcopy," 2004; "Enhancing Pap test with a new biological marker of cervical dysplasia," 2004; "A cytoplasmic biomarker for liquid-based Pap," The FACEB Journal Experimental Biology, 2004; "Pap test and new biomarker-based technology for enhancing visibility of abnormal cells," 2004. **Special Services:** MarkPap[R]; PreservCyt[R].

25822 ■ Birchfield Jacobs Foodsystems Inc.
519 N Charles St., Ste. 350A
Baltimore, MD 21201-5022
Ph:(410)528-8700
Fax:(410)528-6060
URL: http://www.birchfieldjacobs.com
Contact: Robert Jacobs, Principle
E-mail: rjacobs@atsbirchfieldjacobs.com
Scope: Food facilities design consultants for colleges; universities; schools; healthcare facilities; government; military; correctional; country clubs and restaurants. Services include facilities design; feasibility studies; operations analysis and master planning.

25823 ■ Blankinship & Associates Inc.
322 C St.
Davis, CA 95616-7617
Ph:(530)757-0941
Fax:(530)757-0940
Co. E-mail: blankinship@envtox.com
URL: http://www.h2osci.com
Contact: Michael Blankinship, Principal
E-mail: mike@atsenvtox.com
Scope: Specializes in assisting water resource and conveyance, golf and production, protection and enhancement of natural resources. **Publications:** "Air Blast Sprayer Calibration and Chlorpyrifos Irrigation Study," Oct, 2007; "How Green is your golf course," Prosper Magazine, 2007. **Seminars:** CDFG Wildlands IPM Seminar, Oct, 2009.

25824 ■ BPT Consulting Associates Ltd.
12 Parmenter Rd., Ste. B-6
Londonderry, NH 03053
Ph:(603)437-8484
Free: 888-278-0030
Fax:(603)434-5388
Co. E-mail: bptcons@tiac.net
Contact: John Kuczynski, President
E-mail: bptcons@tiac.net
Scope: Provides management consulting expertise and resources to cross-industry clients with services for: Business Management consulting, People/Human Resources Transition and Training programs, and a full cadre of multi-disciplined Technology Computer experts. Virtual consultants with expertise in e-commerce, supply chain management, organizational development, and business application development consulting.

25825 ■ Bran Management Services Inc.
2106 High Ridge Rd.
Louisville, KY 40207-1128
Ph:(502)896-1632
Contact: Robert C. Braverman, CEO
Scope: Offers management consulting services to companies in manufacturing, distribution and services to help them cope with growth and change. Helps small businesses create and identify product strategies. Services include developing international business opportunities; turnaround management; sales and marketing development; business planning; acquisitions and mergers.

25826 ■ Business Consulting Services
207 Dickinson Ave.
PO Box 431
Swarthmore, PA 19081-1630
Ph:(610)328-9806
Contact: Thomas K. Casey, President
Scope: Management consulting organization dedicated to providing high quality, professional services to the business, government and non-profit communities. Specializes in the two key areas of business performance improvement and information technology consulting. Specifically for small business owners. **Publications:** "If You Fail To Plan"; "The True Cost Of Technology"; "Why Projects Fail"; "Planning For A Business Disruption". **Seminars:** How To Select, Manage and Contract Consultants, and Other Resources; How To Market Professional Services; Introduction To Management Consulting.

25827 ■ Business Education Associates
4 Long Hill Rd.
PO Box 4
Bethel, CT 06801
Ph:(203)798-6035
Contact: Robert J. Popp, President
E-mail: bob@ashfordgrp.com
Scope: Offers tailored management education programs. Has been designed to meet the business education needs of companies implementing new systems and companies to re-educate users of existing systems. **Publications:** "The Ashford Group and TQuist Partner to Provide High Impact Manufacturing Solutions"; "The Future of ERP"; "Winning the Implementation Game". **Special Services:** Building Manufacturing Excellence.

25828 ■ Business Improvement Architects
33 Riderwood Dr.
Toronto, ON, Canada M2L 2X4
Ph:(416)444-8225
Free: (866)346-3242
Fax:(416)444-6743
Co. E-mail: info@bia.ca
URL: http://www.bia.ca
Contact: Susan Lee, Principle
E-mail: slee@atsbia.ca
Scope: Provides the following services: strategic planning, leadership development, innovation and project and quality management. Specialize in strategic planning, change management, leadership assessment, and development of skills. **Publications:** "Avoiding Pit falls to Innovation"; "Create a New Dimension of Performance with Innovation"; "The Power of Appreciation in Leadership"; "Why It Makes Sense To Have a Strategic Enterprise Office"; "Burning Rubber at the Start of Your Project"; "Accounting for Quality"; "How Pareto Charts Can Help You Improve the Quality of Business Processes"; "Managing Resistance to Change". **Seminars:** The Innovation Process. . .From Vision to Reality, San Diego, Oct, 2007; Critical Thinking, Kuala Lump or, Sep, 2007; Critical Thinking, Brunei, Sep, 2007; Delivering Project Assurance, Auckland, Jun, 2007; From Crisis to Control: A New Era in Strategic Project Management, Prague, May, 2007; What Project Leaders Need to Know to Help Them Sleep Better At Night, London, May, 2007; Innovation Process. . .From Vision To Reality, Orlando, Apr, 2007. **Special Services:** Project Planning Tool[TM].

25829 ■ ByrneMRG
22 Isle of Pines Dr.
Hilton Head Island, SC 29928
Ph:(215)630-7411
Free: 888-816-8080
Co. E-mail: info@byrnemrg.com
URL: http://www.byrnemrg.com
Contact: Patrick J. Boyle, CEO
E-mail: pjboyle@byrnemrg.com
Scope: Firm specializes in management consulting, including department management, equipment evaluation and selection, project management, research and development planning; and database design and management. **Publications:** "Implementing Solutions to Everyday Issues".

25830 ■ C. Clint Bolte & Associates
809 Philadelphia Ave.
Chambersburg, PA 17201-1268
Ph:(717)263-5768
Fax:(717)263-8954
Co. E-mail: clint@clintbolte.com
URL: http://www.clintbolte.com
Contact: C. Clint Bolte, Principle
E-mail: cbolte3@comcast.net
Scope: Provides management consulting services to firms involved with the printing industry. Services include outsourcing studies, graphics supply chain management studies, company and equipment valuations, plant layout services, litigation support, fulfillment warehouse consulting and product development services. **Publications:** "UV Cost Savings Environmental Advantage"; "Possible Quebecor World Fall Out"; "80-20 Rule for Managing"; "Options Available in Starting Up a Mailing Operation"; "High Volume Print Buyers at Print 2009"; "Diversifying With Mailing & Fulfillment Services"; "New Business Model Needed for Magazine News stand Distribution"; "Purchasing Incentives Can Be Costly..".; "In-Plant New Product Opportunity for 2009: Tran promo Printing"; "Possible Quebecor World Fall Out"; "Offshore Print Evolution"; "Benefits of Third Party Lease Review"; "Unique Information Fulfillment Opportunities for In-Plant Printers"; "Tough Competition Forces New Strategic Realities for In-Plants"; "Direct Mail Industry Group Files Interpretive Ruling Requests with the Ssta"; "Interesting Opportunities Amid the Gray Clouds of 2007 Postal Rate Increases"; "Time to Break Through the Glass Ceiling," the Seybold Report, May, 2006; "Challenges and Opportunities Presented By Postal Rate Increases," the Seybold Report, May, 2006; "Packaging Roll Sheeting Comes of Age," the Seybold Report, May, 2006; "Diversifying with Mailing and Fulfillment Services," the Seybold Report, Jan, 2006. **Seminars:** How to compete with the majors.

25831 ■ Capell & Associates
601 Central Ave.
PO Box 742
Barnegat Light, NJ 08006
Ph:(202)572-8774
Fax:(609)494-7369
Co. E-mail: contact@capellandassociates.com
URL: http://www.capellandassociates.com
Contact: E. Daniel Capell, President
E-mail: dan_capell@att.net
Scope: Specialized consulting firm focused on direct marketing, magazine publishing and circulation. Consulting services include due diligence, circulation audits, benchmarking and list rental analysis. **Seminars:** Circulation for the Non-Circulator.

25832 ■ Casino, Hotel & Resort Consultants L.L.C.
8100 Via Del Cerro Ct.
Las Vegas, NV 89117
Ph:(702)646-7200
Fax:(702)646-6680
Co. E-mail: info@hraba.com
URL: http://www.hraba.com
Contact: John S. Hraba, President
E-mail: jshraba@aol.com
Scope: Casino and hospitality industry consultants. Firm specializes in developing and implementing customized forecast and labor management control systems that deliver immediate, positive impact to the company's bottom line. Involved in production planning, employ surveys and communication, inventory management, business process reviews, audits, development and implementation of key management reports. **Seminars:** Payroll Cost Control; Effective Staff Scheduling.

25833 ■ C.C. Comfort Consulting
3370 N Hayden Rd., Ste. 123-127
Scottsdale, AZ 85251
Ph:(480)483-8364
Contact: Clifton C. Comfort Jr., Principle
Scope: Evaluates, develops and implements financial, operational and compliance management systems strategies, programs and practices. Has professional recognition as certified public accountant, internal auditor, cost analyst and fraud examiner plus investigatory, law enforcement, and court experience ensure confidential handling of sensitive and legal matters. Works with management, audit, legal, security and outside personnel to evaluate and improve compliance, efficiency and effectiveness.

25834 ■ Center for Lifestyle Enhancement - Columbia Medical Center of Plano
3901 W 15th St.
Plano, TX 75075
Ph:(972)596-6800
Fax:(972)519-1299
Co. E-mail: mcp.cle@hcahealthcare.com
URL: http://www.medicalcenterofplano.com
Contact: Doug Browning, Vice President
E-mail: boesdorfer@hcahealthcare.com
Scope: Provides professional health counseling in the areas of general nutrition for weight management, eating disorders, diabetic education, cholesterol reduction and adolescent weight management. Offers work site health promotion and preventive services. Also coordinates speaker's bureau, cooking classes and physician referrals. Industries served: education, insurance, healthcare, retail or wholesale, data processing and manufacturing throughout Texas. **Seminars:** Rx Diet and Exercise; Smoking Cessation; Stress Management; Health Fairs; Fitness Screenings; Body Composition; Nutrition Analysis; Exercise Classes; Prenatal Nutrition; SHAPEDOWN; Successfully Managing Diabetes; Gourmet Foods for Your Heart; The Aging Heart; Heart Smart Saturday featuring Day of Dance; Weight-Loss Management Seminars; The Right Stroke for Men; Peripheral Artery Disease Screening; Menstruation: The Cycle Begins; Boot Camp for New Dads; Grand parenting 101: Caring for Kids Today; Teddy Bear Camp; New Baby Day Camp; Safe Sitter Baby-Sitting Class.

25835 ■ The Center for Organizational Excellence Inc.
15204 Omega Dr., Ste. 300
Rockville, MD 20850
Ph:(301)948-1922
Free: 877-674-3923
Fax:(301)948-2158
Co. E-mail: results@center4oe.com
URL: http://www.center4oe.com
Contact: Kirstin Austin, Mgr
E-mail: kaustin@atscenter4oe.com
Scope: An organizational effectiveness consulting firm specializing in helping organizations achieve results through people, process, and performance. Service areas include organizational performance systems, leadership systems, customer systems, and learning systems.

25836 ■ Center for Personal Empowerment
102 N Main St., Ste. 1
Columbia, IL 62236-1702
Ph:(618)281-3565
Free: 888-657-1530
Fax:(618)476-7083
Co. E-mail: personalempowerment@wholenet.net
Contact: Cherri Hendrix, Vice President
Scope: Private consultations and trainings to educate on how to determine which emotions, events, beliefs from the past prevent you from achieving success. Methods used include time line therapy, news linguistic programming and hypnosis. Behavior modification through NLP trainings. **Seminars:** NLP Practitioner Training; Hypnosis Certification Training; Lifemap Seminars.

25837 ■ Century Business Services Inc.
6050 Oak Tree Blvd. S, Ste. 500
Cleveland, OH 44131-6951
Ph:(216)525-1947
Fax:(216)447-9007
Co. E-mail: info@cbiz.com
URL: http://www.cbiz.com
Contact: Steven L. Gerard, CEO
E-mail: gdufour@cbiz.com
Scope: A business consulting and tax services firm providing financial, consulting, tax and business services through seven groups: Financial management, tax advisory, construction and real estate, health-care, litigation support, capital resource and CEO outsource. **Publications:** "FAS 154: Changes in the Way We Report Changes," 2006; "Equity-Based Compensation: How Much Does it Really Cost Your Business," 2006; "Preventing Fraud - Tips for Nonprofit Organizations"; "Today's Workforce and Nonprofit Organizations: Meeting a Critical Need"; "IRS Highlights Top Seven Form 990 Errors". **Seminars:** Health Care - What the Future Holds; Consumer Driven Health Plans; Executive Plans; Health Savings Accounts; Healthy Wealthy and Wise; Legislative Update; Medicare Part D; Retirement Plans.

25838 ■ CEO Advisors
848 Brickell Ave., Ste. 603
Miami, FL 33131
Ph:(305)371-8560
Fax:(305)371-8563
Co. E-mail: ciaizpurua@ceoadvisors.us
URL: http://www.ceoadvisors.us
Contact: Mario Castro, Vice President
E-mail: mcastro@atsceoadvisors.us
Scope: Business consulting firm offering clients services in strategy, mergers and acquisitions, corporate finance, corporate advisory, supply chain management, government relations and public affairs. Specializes in strategic planning, profit enhancement, start-up businesses, venture capital, appraisals and valuations.

25839 ■ CFI Group USA L.L.C.
625 Avis Dr.
Ann Arbor, MI 48108-9649
Ph:(734)930-9090
Free: 800-930-0933
Fax:(734)930-0911
Co. E-mail: askcfi@cfigroup.com
URL: http://www.cfigroup.com
Contact: Philip Doriot, Vice President, Public Relations
E-mail: mshelton@atscfigroup.com
Scope: Management consulting firm that helps its clients worldwide to maximize shareholder value by optimizing customer and employee satisfaction. Clients span a variety of industries, including manufacturing, telecommunications, retail and government. **Publications:** "Customer Satisfaction and Stock Prices: High Returns, Low Risk," American Marketing Association, Jan, 2006; "Customer Satisfaction Index Climbs," The Wall Street Journal, Feb, 2004; "What's Next? Customer Service is Key to Post-Boom Success," The Bottom Line, Mar, 2003; "Boost Stock Performance, Nation's Economy," Quality Progress, Feb, 2003.

25840 ■ CFO Service
112 Chester Ave.
Saint Louis, MO 63122
Ph:(314)757-2940
Contact: John D. Skae, President
E-mail: jds217@aol.com
Scope: A group of professional executives that provide upper management services to companies that cannot support a full time COO or CFO. Provides clients in the areas of business planning, company policies, contract negotiations, safety policies, product and service pricing, loans management, taxes, cost analysis, loss control and budgeting.

25841 ■ Chamberlain & Cansler Inc.
2251 Perimeter Park Dr.
Atlanta, GA 30341
Ph:(770)457-5699
Contact: Charles L. Cansler, Owner
Scope: Firm specializes in strategic planning; profit enhancement; small business management; interim management; crisis management; turnarounds.

25842 ■ Charismedia
610 W End Ave., Ste. B1
New York, NY 10001
Ph:(212)362-6808
Fax:(212)362-6809
Co. E-mail: charismedia@earthlink.net
URL: http://www.charismedia.net
Contact: Ying Jo Wong, Principle
E-mail: charismedia@earthlink.net
Scope: Offers speech and image training as well as speech writing services for effective presentation skills. Conducts workshops like anti-stage fright breathing, psychophysical exercises, transformational success imagery, face reading and body language, EMDR (Eye Movement Desensitization Re-Processing) for Permanent Trauma and Fear Removal, Bach Flower remedies, thought field therapy, cross-cultural communication, speech, voice and diction; regional and foreign accent elimination and acquisition, Positive Perception Management (P.P.M.), Ad-libbing, humor and spontaneity training, fast creative speech preparation, Neuro-Linguistic Programming and Hypnosis. **Publications:** "Flaunt It"; "Improve Your Sex Life"; "Phone Power"; "Train Your Voice"; "Turning Tinny, Tiny Tones To Gold"; "The New Secrets of Charisma: How to Discover and Unleash your Hidden Powers," McGraw-Hill, Jul, 1999. **Seminars:** Services for Comfortable Effective Speaking.

25843 ■ Chartered Management Co.
125 S Wacker Dr.
Chicago, IL 60606
Ph:(312)214-2575
Contact: William B. Avellone, President
Scope: Operations improvement consultants. Specializes in strategic planning; feasibility studies; management audits and reports; profit enhancement; start-up businesses; mergers and acquisitions; joint ventures; divestitures; interim management; crisis management; turnarounds; business process re-engineering; venture capital; and due diligence.

25844 ■ The Children's Psychological Trauma Center
2105 Divisadero St.
San Francisco, CA 94115
Ph:(415)292-7119
Fax:(415)749-2802
Co. E-mail: gil.kliman@cphc-sf.org
URL: http://www.cphc-sf.org
Contact: Charlotte E. Burchard, Managing Director
E-mail: charlotte.burchard@atscphn-sf.org
Scope: Treats those with psychological trauma claimed from stressors including institutional negligence, vehicular and aviation accidents, wrongful death in the family, rape, molestation, fire, explosion, flood, earthquake, loss of parents, terrorism, kidnapping, disfiguring events, emotional damage from social work, medical malpractice or defective products. Provides evaluation and reports to referring professionals. Experienced in forensic consultation and testimony. **Publications:** "My Personal Story About Tropical Storm Stan," Feb, 2006; "My Personal Story About Hurricanes Katrina and Rita: A guided activity workbook to help coping, learning and Healthy expression," Sep, 2005; "Helping Patients and their Families Cope in a National Disaster," Jan, 2002; "The practice of behavioral treatment in the acute rehabilitation setting".

25845 ■ Claremont Consulting Group
4525 Castle Ln.
La Canada, CA 91011-1436
Ph:(818)249-0584
Fax:(818)249-5811
Contact: Donald S. Remer, Partner
E-mail: amruskin@compuserve.com
Scope: Consulting, coaching, training, and litigation support in project management, engineering management, system engineering and cost estimating. **Publications:** "What Every Engineer Should Know About Project Management"; "100% product-oriented work breakdown structures and their importance to system engineering". **Seminars:** Project Management, System Engineering and Cost Estimating.

25846 ■ Clayton/Curtis/Cottrell
1722 Madison Ct.
Louisville, CO 80027-1121
Ph:(303)665-2005
Contact: Robert Cottrell, President
Scope: Market research firm specializes in providing consultations for packaged goods, telecommunications, direct marketing and printing, and packaging industries. Services include strategic planning; profit enhancement; startup businesses; mergers and acquisitions; joint ventures; divestitures; interim management; crisis management; turnarounds; market size, segmentation and rates of growth; competitor intelligence; image and reputation, and competitive analysis. **Publications:** "Turn an attitude into a purchase," Jul, 1995; "Mixed results for private label; price assaults by the national brands are getting heavy, but there's still a place for private label," Jun, 1995; "In-store promotion goes high-tech: is the conventional coupon destined for obsolescence?," Jun, 1995.

25847 ■ Colmen Menard Company Inc.
The Woods, 994 Old Eagle School Rd., Ste. 1000
Wayne, PA 19087
Ph:(484)367-0300
Fax:(484)367-0305
Co. E-mail: cmci@colmenmenard.com
URL: http://www.colmenmenard.com
Contact: David W. Menard, Managering Director
E-mail: dmenard@atscolmenmenard.com
Scope: Merger and acquisition corporate finance and business advisory services for public and private companies located in North America. **Publications:** "Success in Selling a Troubled Company," Nov, 2002; "Savvy Dealmakers," May, 2001; "Truisms," M&A Today, Nov, 2000.

25848 ■ Columbia Consultants
8950 Old Annapolis Rd., Rte. 108, Ste. 226
Columbia, MD 21045
Ph:(410)992-4700
Free: 800-783-7574
Fax:(410)992-4518
Contact: Anela Brooks, Principle
E-mail: abrooks@columbiaconsultants.net
Scope: A complete personnel service offering placement of both permanent and temporary employees. Provides professional services and integrated solutions.

25849 ■ Comer & Associates L.L.C.
5255 Holmes Pl.
Boulder, CO 80303
Ph:(303)786-7986
Free: 888-950-3190
Fax:(303)895-2347
URL: http://www.comerassociates.com
Contact: Jerry C. Comer, President
E-mail: jcomer@comer-associates.com
Scope: Specialize in developing markets and businesses. Marketing support includes: Developing and writing strategic and tactical business plans; developing and writing focused, effective market plans; researching market potential and competition; implementing targeted marketing tactics to achieve company objectives; conducting customer surveys to determine satisfaction and attitudes toward client. Organization development support includes: Executive/management training programs; executive coaching; team building; developing effective organization structures; and management of change in dynamic and competitive environments; individual coaching for management and leadership effectiveness. **Seminars:** Developing a Strategic Market Plan; Market Research: Defining Your Opportunity; Management and Leadership Effectiveness; Team Building; Developing a Business Plan; How to Close; Using Questions to Sell; Sales System Elements and Checklist; Working With Independent Reps; Features vs. Benefits; Overcoming Objections; Sales Force Automation.

25850 ■ Consultants National Resource Center
27-A Big Spring Rd.
PO Box 430
Clear Spring, MD 21722
Ph:(301)791-9332
Free: 800-290-3196
Fax:(301)582-3639
Co. E-mail: cnrc@erols.com
Contact: Lewis Williams, Director
E-mail: steve@mynabc.com
Scope: Provides marketing and strategic planning services for consultants. Also serves as membership center for the professional management institute. Industries served: all consulting disciplines. **Publications:** "Consulting Opportunities Journal"; "How to Master Continuous Learning". **Seminars:** How to Series on Starting and Building a Consulting Practice; Introduction to the Professional Management Institute; Consulting Boot camp; Planagement[R].

25851 ■ Consulting & Conciliation Service
2830 I St., Ste. 301
Sacramento, CA 95816
Ph:(916)396-0480
Free: 888-898-9780
Fax:(916)441-2828
Co. E-mail: service@azurewings.net
Contact: Jane A. McCluskey, Principle
E-mail: service@azurewings.net
Scope: Offers consulting and conciliation services. Provides pre-mediation counseling, training and research on preparing for a peaceful society, mediation and facilitation, and preparation for shifts in structure, policy and personnel. Offers sliding scale business rates and free individual consultation. **Publications:** "Native America and Tracking Shifts in US Policy"; "Biogenesis: A Discussion of Basic Social Needs and the Significance of Hope". **Seminars:** Positive Approaches to Violence Prevention: Peace building in Schools and Communities.

25852 ■ The Consulting Exchange
1770 Mass Ave., Ste. 288
PO Box 391050
Cambridge, MA 02140
Ph:(617)576-2100
Free: 800-824-4828
Co. E-mail: gday@consultingexchange.com
URL: http://www.cx.com
Contact: Geoffrey Day, President
E-mail: gday@consultingexchange.com
Scope: A consultant referral service for management and technical consultants. Serves a local, regional and international client base. **Publications:** "Looking for a Consultant? Success Points for Finding the Right One," Boston Business Journal, Jun, 2001; "Getting Full Value From Consulting is in Your Hands," Mass High Tech, May, 1998; "Developing Knowledge-Based Client Relationships, The Future of Professional Services"; "The Consultant's Legal Guide"; "The Business of Consulting: The Basics and Beyond".

25853 ■ The Consulting Source Inc.
1403 S Addison Ct.
Aurora, CO 80018-6003
Ph:(303)366-4800
Free: 800-520-1998
Fax:(303)366-4801
Co. E-mail: info@consultingsource.com
URL: http://www.consultingsource.com
Contact: Canfield Caryn, Principle
E-mail: msobey@consultingsource.com
Scope: A consultant search and referral service, helping companies identify the best professional expertise to meet their consulting requirements. Will find the most effective match from within its own database or will search national, regional and local consulting firms for the right fit. Services provided free of charge to client companies in all industries in the US fee based services provided for RFP development, reference checks and selection assistance.

25854 ■ The Corlund Group L.L.C.
101 Federal St., Ste. 310
Boston, MA 02110
Ph:(617)423-9364
Fax:(617)423-9371
Co. E-mail: info@corlundgroup.com
URL: http://www.corlundgroup.com
Contact: Deborah J. Cornwall, Managing Director
E-mail: dcornwall@atscorlundgroup.com
Scope: Boutique firm offering services in the areas of leadership, governance, and change with a particular focus on CEO and senior executive succession planning, including assessment, development, and orchestrating succession processes with management and Boards of Directors. Also Board governance effectiveness. **Publications:** "Are You Rolling the Dice on CEO Succession?" Center for Healthcare Governance, 2006; "Leadership Due Diligence: The Neglected Governance Frontier," Directorship, Sep, 2001; "Leadership Due Diligence: Managing the Risks," The Corporate Board, Aug, 2001; "Succession: The need for detailed insight," Directors and Boards, 2001; "CEO Succession: Who's Doing Due Diligence?," 2001.

25855 ■ Corporate Consulting Inc.
3333 Belcaro Dr.
Denver, CO 80209-4912
Ph:(303)698-9292
Fax:(303)698-9292
Co. E-mail: corpcons@compuserve.com
Contact: Devereux C. Josephs, President
E-mail: corpcons@compuserve.com
Scope: Specializes in feasibility studies, organizational development, small business management, mergers and acquisitions, joint ventures, divestitures, interim management, crisis management, turnarounds, financing, appraisals valuations and due diligence studies.

25856 ■ COTC Technologies Inc.
172 E Industrial Blvd.
PO Box 7615
Pueblo, CO 81007-4406
Ph:(719)547-0938
Free: 888-547-0938
Fax:(719)547-1105
Contact: Karen Renz, CFO
E-mail: karen@atscotc-consulting.com
Scope: Provides software consulting services to organizations that require assistance with their HP3000 computer system. Provides systems analysis, programming, operations support, and system management. Also provides PC software and hardware support and consulting. Additionally provides various training for the HP3000 computer system. Industries served: healthcare, aerospace procurement, aerospace proposal activities, and HP3000 computer systems.

25857 ■ Coyne Associates
4010 E Lake St.
Minneapolis, MN 55406-2201
Ph:(612)724-1188
Fax:(612)722-1379
Contact: Sandra Blanton, Principle
Scope: A marketing and public relations consulting firm that specializes in assisting architectural, engineering, and contractor/developer firms. Services include: marketing plains and audits, strategic planning, corporate identity, turnarounds, and sales training.

25858 ■ Creative Computer Resources Inc.
5001 Horizons Dr., Ste. 200
Columbus, OH 43220-5291
Ph:(614)384-7557
Free: (866)720-0209
Fax:(614)573-6331
Co. E-mail: team@planet-ccr.com
URL: http://www.planet-ccr.com
Contact: M. Erik Mueller, President
E-mail: merikm@atsplanet-ccr.com
Scope: Firm offers information systems support, custom software development, website design, development and implementation. Provides information technology support and management services to small and mid-size businesses.

25859 ■ Crystal Clear Communications Inc.
1633 W Winslow Dr., Ste. 210
Mequon, WI 53092
Ph:(262)240-0072
Fax:(262)240-0073
Co. E-mail: contact@crystalclear1.com
URL: http://www.crystalclear1.com
Contact: Chez Fogel, Principle
E-mail: chfogel@atscrystalclear.com
Scope: Specialize in helping executives identify impediments to success, and then develop strategies to surmount them. Serves to identify core problems,

suggest appropriate business changes, work with the organization to support these changes, and help executives articulate the behavior that will uphold these changes. Specializes in strategic planning; organizational development; small business management; executive coaching. **Publications:** "Weakest Link"; "Aware Leadership"; "Integrity"; "When Your Plate is Full"; "Problem Solving"; "Strategic Thinking".

25860 ■ David G. Schantz
29 Wood Run Cir.
Rochester, NY 14612-2271
Ph:(716)723-0760
Fax:(716)723-8724
Co. E-mail: daveschantz@yahoo.com
URL: http://www.daveschantz.freeservers.com
E-mail: daveschantz@yahoo.com
Scope: Provides industrial engineering services for photofinishing labs, including amateur-wholesale, professional, commercial, school, and package.

25861 ■ Development Resource Consultants
PO Box 118
Rancho Cucamonga, CA 91729
Ph:(909)902-7655
Fax:(909)476-6942
Co. E-mail: drc@gotodrc.com
URL: http://www.gotodrc.com
Contact: Jerry R. Frey, Partner
E-mail: jfrey@atsgotodrc.com
Scope: Specializes in office re-organization, employee training in office organization, communication skills, sales training and career counseling. **Publications:** "Institute of Management Consultants Southern California Chapter," Jan, 2006.

25862 ■ The Devine Group Inc.
7755 Montgomery Rd., Ste. 180
Cincinnati, OH 45236
Ph:(513)792-7500
Free: (866)792-7500
Fax:(513)793-8535
Co. E-mail: sales@devinegroup.com
URL: http://www.devinegroup.com
Contact: Dr. Syed Saad, VP of Research
E-mail: rwalker@atsdevinegroup.com
Scope: A human resource consulting company devoted to providing reliable and responsive information focusing on performance issues and answers. Dedicated to analyzing and enhancing job performance. Custom design and implement programs and workshops that will result in demonstrable behavior change on the job. Assist clients enhance their productivity via behavior analysis. **Publications:** "Leveraging Assessments for Enterprise Improvement," Oct, 2006; "Evaluation of Assessment Tools: The Five Criteria," Oct, 2006; "People Improvement Using Behavior Assessment," Aug, 2005; "Measuring Personality: The Good, the Bad and the Ugly," Jul, 25. **Special Services:** The Devine Inventory™.

25863 ■ Diamond Management & Technology Consultants Inc.
1101 Pennsylvania Ave. NW, Ste. 600
Washington, DC 20004
Ph:(312)255-5000
Fax:(312)255-6000
Co. E-mail: info@diamondcluster.com
URL: http://www.diamondconsultants.com
Contact: Melvyn E. Bergstein, Chairman of the Board
Scope: Provides business consulting services to help companies develop business strategies; information advantage services to help clients make better decisions about opportunities and risks by extracting the untapped value of data and by increasing the value of information management investments. Customer impact services help companies design and implement superior experiences across all interactions, which lead to passionate, profitable customer relationships; and execution services turn high-level strategies into measurable results. **Publications:** "Answer To a New Set of Shareholders," Jan, 2009; "Subprime Fallout: Investing in Data Management," Jun, 2008; "Billion-Dollar Lessons: What You Can Learn From the Most Inexcusable Business Failures of the Last 25 Years," Portfolio, 2008; "Unleashing the Killer App: Digital Strategies for Market Dominance," Harvard Business School Press, 1998; "The Compliance Conundrum: Guarding the Firm, Controlling Costs". **Seminars:** Banking for the Rural and the Underprivileged, Mumbai, Oct, 2007.

25864 ■ Dimond Hospitality Consulting Group Inc.
5710 Stoneway Trl.
Nashville, TN 37209
Ph:(615)353-0033
Fax:(615)352-5290
Co. E-mail: drew@dimondhotelconsulting.com
URL: http://www.dimondhotelconsulting.com
Contact: Drew W. Dimond, President
E-mail: drew@dimondhotelconsulting.com
Scope: Specializes in strategic planning; start-up businesses; business process re-engineering; team building; competitive analysis; venture capital; competitive intelligence; and due diligence. Offers litigation support. Comprehensive hospitality consulting firm that serves as an adviser to leading hotel companies, independent hotels, lending institutions, trustees, law firms, investment companies and municipalities in the areas of: Asset management, Acquisition due diligence, Arbitration, Disposition advisory services, Exit strategies, Financial review and analysis, Impact studies, Mediation. **Publications:** "The distressed debt conundrum," Jul, 2009; "How to buy distressed assets," Apr, 2009; "Cmbs Loans: A History and the Future," Apr, 2009; "Opportunity Knocks," Apr, 2009; "Another Reality Check," Mar, 2009; "An Inkling of Hope," Mar, 2009; "Strong World Tourism Growth in 2007," 2007; "Les U.S. Construction Pipeline Sets Another Record at 5011 Hotels with 654503 Rooms"; "Hotel Capitalization Rates Hold for Now"; "Winning Cornell Hotel and Restaurant Administration Quarterly Article Provides Hotel Brand Analysis"; "Breaking News for Lifestyle Hotels. Ian Schrager and Bill Marriott Announce Their Marriage Will the Schrager-Marriott Marriage Lead to Eternal Bliss Or End in Divorce What Will the M Hotels Children Be Named"; "Brands Vs Independents"; "Nyu Conf Takes Industry Temp"; "Economy Hotel Performance Indication of Travel Trends"; "Hotel Sales Continue at Brisk Pace"; "Fundamentals Strong, Weakening Undercurrent"; "Hotel Investments: Where Do We Go From Here"; "On the Road: Aahoa Panel Commits to Change"; "Cuba Not Ready, But Expecting U.S. Tourists".

25865 ■ Diversified Health Resources Inc.
875 N Michigan Ave., Ste. 3250
Chicago, IL 60611-1901
Ph:(312)266-0466
Fax:(312)266-0715
Contact: Andrea R. Rozran, President
E-mail: yablon@ix.netcom.com
Scope: Offers health care consulting for hospitals, nursing homes including homes for the aged, and other health related facilities and companies. Specializes in planning and marketing. Also conducts executive searches for top level health care administrative positions. Serves private industries as well as government agencies. **Publications:** "City Finance".

25866 ■ Donna Cornell Enterprises Inc.
68 N Plank Rd., Ste. 204
Newburgh, NY 12550-2122
Ph:(845)565-0088
Free: 888-769-3792
Fax:(845)565-0084
Co. E-mail: rc@cornellcareercenter.com
Contact: Donna Cornell, President
E-mail: rc@cornellcareercenter.com
Scope: Offers services in career consultant, professional search, job placement and national professional search. **Publications:** "The Power of the Woman Within"; "Juggling it All!"; "Journey: A Woman's Guide to Success"; "Shatter the Traditions".

25867 ■ DRI Consulting
2 Otter Ln.
North Oaks, MN 55127-6436
Ph:(651)415-1400
Free: (866)276-4600
Fax:(651)415-9968
Co. E-mail: dric@dric.com
URL: http://www.dric.com
Contact: Dr. Heather Mortensen, Principle
E-mail: heathermortensen@atsdric.com
Scope: Licensed psychologists providing organization and management consulting. Developing leaders, managers and individuals through coaching, business strategy, career development, crisis management, policy consultation and technology optimization.

25868 ■ Dropkin & Co.
390 George St.
New Brunswick, NJ 08901
Ph:(732)828-3211
Fax:(732)828-4118
Co. E-mail: murray@dropkin.com
URL: http://www.dropkin.com
Contact: Mel Nusbaum, Principle
E-mail: mel@atsdropkin.com
Scope: Firm specializes in feasibility studies; business management; business process re-engineering; and team building, health care and housing. **Publications:** "Bookkeeping for Nonprofits," Jossey Bass, 2005; "Guide to Audits of Nonprofit Organizations," PPC; "The Nonprofit Report," Warren, Gorham & Lamont; "The Budget Building Book for Nonprofits," Jossey-Bass; "The Cash Flow Management Book for Nonprofits," Jossey-Bass.

25869 ■ Dubuc Lucke & Company Inc.
120 W 5th St.
Cincinnati, OH 45202-2713
Ph:(513)579-8330
Fax:(513)241-6669
Contact: Kenneth E. Dubuc, President
Scope: Provides consulting services in the areas of profit enhancement; small business management; mergers and acquisitions; joint ventures; divestitures; interim management; crisis management; turnarounds; appraisals; valuations; due diligence; and international trade.

25870 ■ The DuMond Group
5282 Princeton Ave.
Westminster, CA 92683-2753
Ph:(714)373-0610
Contact: David L. Dumond, Principle
Scope: Human resources and executive search consulting firm that specializes in organizational development; small business management; employee surveys and communication; performance appraisals; and team building.

25871 ■ Dunelm International
437 Colebrook Ln.
Bryn Mawr, PA 19010-3216
Ph:(610)989-0144
Fax:(610)964-9524
Co. E-mail: jecdunelm@worldnet.att.net
Contact: John E. Crowther, President
E-mail: jecdunelm@dunelm.org.uk
Scope: Firm specializes in feasibility studies; start-up businesses; interim management; crisis management; turnarounds; business process re-engineering; sales forecasting; supply chain solution and project management.

25872 ■ Eastern Point Consulting Group Inc.
36 Glen Ave.
Newton, MA 02464
Ph:(617)965-4141
Fax:(617)965-4172
Co. E-mail: info@eastpt.com
URL: http://www.eastpt.com
Contact: Mary MacMahon, Principal
E-mail: kherzog@eastpt.com
Scope: Specializes in bringing practical solutions to complex challenges. Provides consulting and training in managing diversity; comprehensive sexual-harassment policies and programs; organizational development; benchmarks 360 skills assessment; executive coaching; strategic human resource planning; team building; leadership development for women; mentoring programs; and gender issues in the workplace. **Seminars:** Leadership Development for Women.

25873 ■ Education Development Center Inc.
55 Chapel St.
Newton, MA 02458-1060
Ph:(617)969-7100
Free: 800-225-4276

Fax:(617)969-5979
Co. E-mail: comment@edc.org
URL: http://www.edc.org
Contact: Luther Luedtke, President
E-mail: rrotner@atsedc.org
Scope: Services include research, training, educational materials and strategy, with activities ranging from seed projects to large-scale national and international initiatives. Specialize in program and fiscal management. Serves to design, deliver and evaluate innovative programs to address some of the world's most urgent challenges in education, health, and economic opportunity. Renders services to U.S. and foreign government agencies, private foundations, healthcare sectors, educational institutions, nonprofit organizations, universities, and corporations. **Publications:** "A Call to Action: HIV/AIDS, Health, Safety, and the Youth Employment Summit"; "A Case Against "Binge" as the Term of Choice: How to Get College Students to Personalize Messages about Dangerous Drinking"; "A Description of Foundation Skills Interventions for Struggling Middle-Grade Readers in Four Urban Northeast and Islands Region School Districts"; "A Guide to Facilitating Cases in Education"; "A Look at Social, Emotional, and Behavioral Screening Tools for Head Start and Early Head Start"; "A Multifaceted Social Norms Approach to Reduce High-Risk Drinking: Lessons from Hobart and William Smith Colleges"; "The New Media Literacy Handbook"; "Helping Children Outgrow War"; "Worms, Shadows, and Whirlpools: Science in the Early Childhood Classroom"; "Teacher Leadership in Mathematics and Science Casebook and Facilitator's Guide"; "Teachers' Professional Development and the Elementary Mathematics Classroom: Bringing Understandings to Light". **Seminars:** Designed to Introduce the Materials; To Guide Schools Through the Issues.

25874 ■ Effective Compensation Inc.
3609 S Wadsworth Blvd., Ste. 260
Lakewood, CO 80235
Ph:(303)854-1000
Free: 877-746-4324
Fax:(303)854-1030
Co. E-mail: eci@effectivecompensation.com
URL: http://www.effectivecompensation.com
Contact: Mike Sanchez, Principle
E-mail: tisselhardt@atseffectivecompensation.com
Scope: Independent compensation consulting firm specializing in working with clients on a collaborative basis to improve their organization's efficiency through competitive, focused total compensation processes. Helps organizations determine how to competitively pay their employees. Provides quality, culture sensitive, compensation consulting assistance to all types of employers. Specializes in surveys like drilling industry compensation surveys, environmental industry compensation surveys, liquid pipeline round table compensation surveys; and oil and gas E and P industry compensation surveys. **Publications:** "Alternative Job Evaluation Approaches"; "Broad Banding: A Management Overview"; "Job Evaluation: Understanding the Issues"; "Industry Compensation Surveys"; "Skill Based Pay"; "Four Levels of Team Membership"; "Factors in Designing an Incentive Plan"; "Key Stock Allocation Issues"; "Stock Plans Primer". **Seminars:** Alternative Job Evaluation Approaches; Broad Banding: A Management Overview; Skill Based Pay; Job Evaluation: Understanding the Issues; Designing Compensation Programs that Motivate Employees; Master the Compensation Maze; Base Salary Administration Manual.

25875 ■ Effective Resources Inc.
2655 Ulmerton Rd., Ste. 138
Clearwater, FL 33762
Ph:(865)622-7138
Free: 800-288-6044
Fax:800-409-2812
Co. E-mail: customerservice@effectiveresources.com
URL: http://www.effectiveresources.com
Contact: Barry L. Brown, President
E-mail: barry@effectiveresources.com
Scope: Human resource consulting firm helping clients in all aspects of planning and implementation, to assure the program meets their objectives and budget considerations. Can work with clients on an interim basis or as consultants on short term assignment. Products and services include salary and benefits surveys, employee satisfaction surveys, performance management, compensation administration, compliance assistance and personality profile testing. Specializes in compensation and incentive plans, performance appraisals, team building and personnel policies and procedures, affirmative action plan preparation. **Special Services:** DiSC[R] Personality Profile.

25876 ■ Effectiveness Resource Group Inc.
2529 170th Pl. SE
PO Box 7149
Bellevue, WA 98008-5520
Ph:(206)949-4171
Fax:(425)957-9186
Co. E-mail: don@consultdon.com
URL: http://www.consultdon.com
Contact: Donald H. Swartz, President
E-mail: dhsergsri@aol.com
Scope: Provides problem solving help to client organizations in public and private sectors so they can release and mobilize the full potential of their personnel to achieve productive and satisfying results. Emphasis is on technical or human productivity improvement projects and systems, total human resource systems design and implementation, and a whole systems approach to organizational change design and implementation. Serves private industries as well as government agencies. Consults with both internal and external consultants via e-mail and phone. Also offers executive coaching. **Seminars:** Life/Work Goals Exploration; Influencing Change Thru Consultation; Designing and Leading Participative Meetings; Designing, Leading and Managing Change; Project Management and Leadership; Performance Management; Productive Management of Differences; Performance Correction.

25877 ■ Environmental Health Science Inc.
418 Wall St.
Princeton, NJ 08540
Ph:(609)924-7616
Free: 800-841-8923
Fax:(609)924-0793
Co. E-mail: healthscience@comcast.net
URL: http://www.speechgeneratingdevices.com
Contact: Wilma Solomon, Principle
E-mail: davidg@atspatmedia.net
Scope: Specialists in rehabilitation technology for speech disorder and physically disabled persons. Offers demonstrations, evaluations and sales of the following types of equipment: augmentative speech communication systems, adaptive switches and specialty controls, and computer access devices. Industries served: hospitals and rehabilitation centers, schools, and special service organizations such as United Cerebral Palsy Association, Department of Human Services, etc. **Publications:** "Play & Learn"; "Bookworm Literacy Tool"; "Meville to Weville". **Seminars:** Augmentative Communication and Assistive Devices. **Special Services:** Boardmaker[R]; Dynamically Pro[R].

25878 ■ Everest Marketing
957 Ashland Ave.
Saint Paul, MN 55104-7019
Ph:(612)581-1333
Fax:(651)221-1978
Co. E-mail: aistrup@aistrup.com
Contact: Becky Aistrup, Principle
E-mail: mike@aistrup.com
Scope: Provides business-to-business marketing services including marketing plan development, marketing communications, market research and business intelligence. **Publications:** "Finding and Using Local Market Research To Improve Your Sales"; "Marketing to the Right People at the Right Time"; "Marketing in a Sales-Driven Environment"; "Money Well Spent! (Eight Steps to a successful consulting project)"; "Does this sound like you?"; "Marketing Quickies". **Seminars:** Market Research Basics for Managers; Profiting from Your Customer Database; Developing Your Strategic Marketing Plan from the Ground Up; A Team Process for Developing Your Marketing Plan; Developing a Commercialization Plan for Your SBIR (Small Business Innovation Research)Proposal; Using Marketing Strategies to Jump-Start Your Sales; Marketing in a Sales-Driven Environment and Marketing in a Technology-Driven Environment.

25879 ■ Everett & Co.
3126 S Franklin St.
Englewood, CO 80113
Ph:(303)761-7999
Fax:(303)781-8296
Contact: Wayne Everett, Principle
Scope: Provides strategic real estate solutions and project management.

25880 ■ Facility Directions Inc.
PO Box 761
Manchester, MO 63011
Ph:(636)256-4400
Free: 800-536-0044
Fax:(636)227-2868
Co. E-mail: walty@facilitydirections.com
URL: http://www.facilitydirections.com
Contact: Walter E. Yesberg, President
E-mail: walty@facilitydirections.com
Scope: Firm specializes in service to financial institutions; strategic planning; feasibility studies; facility and space planning; attitude surveys; site selection.

25881 ■ Family Resource Center on Disabilities
20 E Jackson Blvd., Ste. 300
Chicago, IL 60604-2265
Ph:(312)939-3513
Free: 800-952-4199
Fax:(312)939-7297
Co. E-mail: contact@frcd.org
URL: http://www.frcd.org
Contact: Charlotte des Jardins, Director
E-mail: contact@frcd.org
Scope: Provides consulting services to advocacy groups and individuals seeking support for children with disabilities. **Publications:** "How to Get Services By Being Assertive"; "How to Organize an Effective Parent/Advocacy Group and Move Bureaucracies"; "Main roads Travel to Tomorrow - a Road Map for the Future"; "Does Your Child Have Special Education Needs"; "How to Prepare for a Successful Due Process Hearing"; "How to Participate Effectively in Your Child's IEP Meeting"; "Tax Guide for Parents". **Seminars:** How to Support Parents as Effective Advocates; How to Get Services by Being Assertive; How to Develop an Awareness Program for Nondisabled Children; How to Organize a Parent Support Group; How to Move Bureaucratic Mountains; How to Raise Money Painlessly through Publishing; How to Use Humor in Public Presentations.

25882 ■ FCP Consulting
500 Sutter St., Ste. 507
San Francisco, CA 94102-1114
Ph:(415)956-5558
Fax:(415)956-5722
Contact: Cox Ferrall, President
Scope: Management consulting in Business-To-Business sales.

25883 ■ First Strike Management Consulting Inc.
401 Loblolly Ave.
PO Box 1188
Little River, SC 29566-1188
Ph:(843)385-6338
Fax:(843)390-1004
Co. E-mail: fsmc.hq@fsmc.com
URL: http://www.fsmc.com
Contact: J.D. Lewis, President
E-mail: jd.lewis@fsmc.com
Scope: Offers proposal management and program management services. Specializes in enterprise systems, management systems, and staff augmentation. Serves the following industries: Nuclear/Fossil Power, Petro-Chemical, Aerospace and Defense, Telecommunications, Engineering and Construction, Information Technology, Golf Course Construction/Management, Utility Engineering/Construction, Civil Works, and Housing Development. **Publications:** "Project Management for Executives"; "Project Risk Management"; "Project Communications Management"; "Winning Proposals, Four Computer Based

Training (CBT) courses"; "Principles of Program Management". **Seminars:** Preparing Winning Proposals in Response to Government RFPs.

25884 ■ Flett Research Ltd.
440 DeSalaberry Ave.
Winnipeg, MB, Canada R2L 0Y7
Ph:(204)667-2505
Fax:(204)667-2505
Co. E-mail: flett@flettresearch.ca
URL: http://www.flettresearch.ca
Contact: Dawn Gilbert, Principle
E-mail: flett@flettresearch.ca
Scope: Provides environmental audits and assessments. Offers contract research and consultation on environmental topics, specializing in limnology, with emphasis in microbiology, bio-geochemistry and radio-chemistry. Performs dating of sediments via Pb-210 and CS-137 methods, to determine sediment accumulation rates in lakes. One of a handful of labs in the world able to carry out total mercury and methyl mercury analyses at the sub-nanogram and L concentration in water.

25885 ■ Freese & Associates Inc.
PO Box 814
Chagrin Falls, OH 44022-0814
Ph:(440)564-9183
Fax:(440)564-7339
Co. E-mail: tfreese@freeseinc.com
URL: http://www.freeseinc.com
Contact: James H. Muir, Principle
E-mail: tfreese@freeseinc.com
Scope: A management consulting firm offering advice in all forms of business logistics. Consulting services are in the areas of strategic planning; network analysis, site selection, facility layout and design, outsourcing, warehousing, transportation and customer service. Typical projects include 3PL marketing surveys; third party outsourcing selection; operational audits; competitive analysis; inventory management; due diligence; and implementation project management. **Publications:** "Building Relationships is Key to Motivation," Distribution Center Management, Apr, 2006; "Getting Maximum Results from Performance Reviews," WERC Sheet, Oct, 2003; "SCM: Making the Vision a Reality," Supply Chain Management Review, Oct, 2003; "Contents Under Pressure," DC Velocity, Aug, 2003; "When Considering Outsourcing, It's Really a Financial Decision," Inventory Management Report, Mar, 2003. **Seminars:** WERC/CAWS Warehousing in China Conference, Sep, 2008; CSCMP Annual Conference, Denver, Oct, 2008; Keys to Retaining and Motivating Your Associates, Dallas, Mar, 2006; The Value and Challenges of Supply Chain Management, Dubai, Feb, 2006; Best Practices in Logistics in China, Jun, 2005; Keys to Motivating Associates, Dallas, May, 2005; The Goal and the Way of International Cooperation in Logistics, Jenobuk, Apr, 2005.

25886 ■ Full Voice
3217 Broadway Ave., Ste. 300
Kansas City, MO 64111
Ph:(816)941-0011
Free: 800-684-8764
Fax:(816)931-8887
Co. E-mail: info@infullvoice.com
URL: http://www.fullvoice.us
Contact: Michienne Dixon, Principle
E-mail: garrett@infullvoice.com
Scope: Vocal performance training firm offering consulting services and personal training sessions in the implementation of effective vocal communication techniques for the development of business relationships and career enhancement. Formalizes a program of proven techniques into a practical method of helping individuals improve their ability to better present themselves when speaking in a professional situation. Industries served: All. **Publications:** "You Can Sound Like You Know What You're Saying". **Seminars:** You Can Sound Like You Know What You're Saying; The Psychology of Vocal Performance; Security. . .the Ability to Accept Change; Knowing. . .the Key to Relaxed Public Communication; The Effective Voice for Customer Service Enhancement; You Can Speak With Conviction; How To Make Yours a Championship Team; Functional English For Foreign Trade. **Special Services:** FULL VOICE™.

25887 ■ GEC Consultants Inc.
4604 Birchwood Ave.
Skokie, IL 60076-3835
Ph:(847)674-6310
Fax:(847)674-3946
Co. E-mail: experts@gecconsultants.com
URL: http://www.gecconsultants.com
Contact: Lloyd M. Gordon, CEO
E-mail: legal@gecconsultants.com
Scope: Consulting in all areas of bar and restaurant operations. Restaurant manager development appraises existing locations or sites. Studies the feasibility of projects. Develop new concepts. Assist in expanding, existing food operations, marketing, expert witness (legal) for hospitality/restaurant industry. **Publications:** "How You Can Fight Back to Minimize This Recession!"; "New Thoughts On Leases"; "The Use of Job Analysis to Actually Reduce Payroll Costs"; "Do You Need a Feasibility Study?"; "Combat Negative Hospitality"; "How To Run A Successful Night club"; "Are Capitalists In Your Cabinet?"; "Marketing For The 21st Century"; "Profitability In The Banquet Industry"; "Starting a Restaurant, Bar or Catering Business"; "How To Find And Retain Suitable Employees"; "26 Things To Do To Plan A Restaurant"; "Wall Fabric or Paint: Decor Magic It's Your Call"; "The Art of Cafe Ambiance"; "Why You Need A Consultant". **Seminars:** How to increase restaurant profit, Member MSPC Speakers Bureau; Raising Capital for New Development and Expansion.

25888 ■ Gerson Goodson Inc.
2451 McMullen Booth Rd., Ste. 201
Clearwater, FL 33759
Ph:(727)726-7619
Free: 888-237-7424
Fax:(727)726-2406
Co. E-mail: getrich@richgerson.com
URL: http://www.richgerson.com
Contact: Richard F. Gerson, Principal
E-mail: richard.gerson@atsrichgerson.com
Scope: Independent consulting firm provides performance management solutions to improve performance and maximize productivity in organizations. Provides assistance to organizations in talent and performance management, leadership development, selection and hiring practices, employee and customer retention, and customer service. Conducts a systematic needs analysis of the entire marketing, sales and customer service operations of the company. Identifies hidden, neglected and underutilized marketing, sales and customer service assets. **Publications:** "Winning The Inner Game Of Selling," 1999; "Marketing Strategies for Small Businesses," 1994; "Measuring Customer Satisfaction," 1993; "Beyond Customer Service," 1992; "Achieving High Performance"; "Guaranteeing Performance Improvement"; "The Executive Athlete"; "Positive Performance Improvement". **Seminars:** Marketing Real Estate Services Management Development, Oct, 2007; Presentation Skills, Oct, 2007; From Member Service to Sales, Sep, 2007; Leadership Development, Sep, 2007; The Marketing Difference That Makes The Difference: How To Position Your Company For Rapid Growth Regardless Of The Economy Or The Competition; Growing Your Business With What You Already Have: How To Identify And Profit From The Hidden Marketing Assets That Are Currently Costing You Money; The R Factor In Customer Service: 5Ways To Grow Your Business For Little Or No Cost.

25889 ■ Global Business Consultants
200 Lake Hills Rd.
PO Box 776
Pinehurst, NC 28374-0776
Ph:(910)295-5991
Fax:(910)295-5991
Co. E-mail: gbc@pinehurst.net
Contact: Gerd Hofielen, Partner
E-mail: mcoin@atsyourculturecoach.com
Scope: Firm specializes in human resources management; project management; software development; and international trade. Offers litigation support. **Publications:** "Culture to Culture: Mission Trip Do's and Don'ts," Jul, 2005; "Rules of the Game: Global Business Protocol". **Seminars:** Cross-Cultural Training.

25890 ■ Global Technology Transfer L.L.C.
1500 Dixie Hwy.
Park Hills, KY 41011-2819
Ph:(859)431-1262
Fax:(859)431-5148
Co. E-mail: arzembrodt@worldnet.att.net
Contact: Michelle Hartley, CFO
Scope: Firm specializes in product development; quality assurance; new product development; and total quality management focusing on household chemical specialties, especially air fresheners. Utilizes latest technology from global resources. Specializes in enhancement products for home and automobile.

25891 ■ Goldore Consulting Inc.
120-5 St. NW, Ste. 1
PO Box 590
Linden, AB, Canada T0M 1J0
Ph:(403)546-4208
Fax:(403)546-4208
Co. E-mail: goldore@leadershipessentials.com
Contact: Robert A. Orr, President
E-mail: orr@leadershipessentials.com
Scope: Provides consulting service in leadership and management skills. Industries served: primarily charities, non-profits; some businesses. **Seminars:** The Challenge Of Leadership.

25892 ■ Great Lakes Consulting Group Inc.
54722 Little Flower Trl.
Mishawaka, IN 46545
Ph:(574)287-4500
Fax:(574)233-2688
Contact: James E. Schrager, President
Scope: Provides consulting services in the areas of strategic planning; feasibility studies; start-up businesses; small business management; mergers and acquisitions; joint ventures; divestitures; interim management; crisis management; turnarounds; business process re-engineering; venture capital; and international trade.

25893 ■ Great Western Association Management Inc.
7995 E Prentice Ave., Ste. 100
Greenwood Village, CO 80111
Ph:(303)770-2220
Fax:(303)770-1614
Co. E-mail: info83@gwami.com
URL: http://www.gwami.com
Contact: Sheryl Pitts, Principle
E-mail: kwojdyla@atsgwami.com
Scope: Provides clients with products and services to effectively manage existing and startup, for- and not-for-profit organizations. Clients select from a menu of services including association development and public relations, conferences and seminars, financial management, membership communications, and governance. Expertise also includes association strategic planning, compliance, lobbying, meeting planning, fundraising, marketing and communications. Serves national, regional and state organizations. **Seminars:** Site selection; Creative program development; Contract negotiations; On-site conference management; Trade show management; Travel and logistics.

25894 ■ The Greystone Group Inc.
440 N Wells, Ste. 570
Chicago, IL 60610
Ph:(616)451-8880
Fax:(616)451-9180
Co. E-mail: consult@greystonegp.com
E-mail: consult@greystonegp.com
Scope: Firm specializes in strategic planning and communications; organizational development; start-up businesses; business management; mergers and acquisitions; joint ventures; divestitures; business process re-engineering.

25895 ■ Grief Counseling & Support Services
8600 W Chester Pke., Ste. 304
Upper Darby, PA 19082
Ph:(610)789-7707

Fax:(610)469-9499
Contact: Jeffrey Kauffman, President
E-mail: jkharry@voicenet.com
Scope: Specializing in consulting and training services for organizations dealing with loss, trauma and grief issues. These services may include management consultations, crisis intervention, educational programming, policy development, program design, group process work, individual counseling or other support services. Training and support services also provided for loss issues for mental retardation service providers. Serves private industries as well as government agencies.

25896 ■ Grimmick Consulting Services
455 Donner Way
San Ramon, CA 94582
Ph:(925)735-1036
Fax:(925)735-1100
Co. E-mail: hank@grimmickconsulting.com
URL: http://www.grimmickconsulting.com
Contact: Henry Grimmick, President
E-mail: hank@grimmickconsulting.com
Scope: Provides consulting services in the areas of strategic planning; organizational assessment; organizational development; leadership and management development Baldridge criteria, process improvement and balanced scorecards and team dynamics.

25897 ■ Harding & Co.
511 Harvard Ave.
Swarthmore, PA 19081
Ph:(973)763-9284
Fax:(973)763-9347
Co. E-mail: fharding@hardingco.com
URL: http://www.hardingco.com
Contact: Gary Pines, Principle
E-mail: gpines@atshardingco.com
Scope: Firm specializes in sales management, client development and employee training. **Publications:** "Cross-Selling Success: A Rainmakers Guide to Professional Account Development," Aug, 2002; "Rain Making: The Professional's Guide to Attracting New Clients"; "Creating Rainmakers: The Managers Guide to Training Professionals to Attract New Clients".

25898 ■ Harris Advertising
G4162 Fenton Rd.
Flint, MI 48507-3637
Ph:(810)232-4120
Contact: Susan Kay Harris, President
Scope: Marketing and advertising firm provides advertisement services to private industries as well as government agencies.

25899 ■ Harvey A. Meier Co.
410 W Nevada St., Billings Ranch, Ste. 245
Ashland, OR 97520-1043
Ph:(509)458-3210
Fax:(541)488-7905
Co. E-mail: harvey@harveymeier.com
URL: http://www.harveymeier.com
Contact: Harvey A. Meier, President
E-mail: harvey@harveymeier.com
Scope: Firm provides service to chief executive officers and board of directors. Specializes in interim management, strategic planning, financial planning and organization governance. **Publications:** "The D'Artagnan Way".

25900 ■ Harvey C. Skoog
7151 E Addis Ave.
Prescott Valley, AZ 86314
Ph:(928)772-1448
Co. E-mail: hskoog@pvaz.net
E-mail: hskoog@pvaz.net
Scope: Firm has expertise in taxes, payroll, financial planning, budgeting, buy/sell planning, business start-up, fraud detection, troubled business consulting, acquisition, and marketing. Serves the manufacturing, construction, and retailing industries in Arizona.

25901 ■ Health Strategy Group Inc.
46 River Rd.
Chatham, NY 12037
Ph:(518)392-6770
Contact: John Fiorillo, Principle
Scope: Provides consulting services in the areas of strategic planning, feasibility studies, start-up businesses, organizational development, market research, customer service audits, new product development, marketing, public relations. **Publications:** "Online Consumer Surveys as a Methodology for Assessing the Quality of the United States Health Care System," 2004.

25902 ■ Hewitt Development Enterprises
18 Lindley Ave.
North Kingstown, RI 02852
Ph:(305)372-0941
Free: 800-631-3098
Fax:(305)372-0941
Co. E-mail: info@hewittdevelopment.com
URL: http://www.hewittdevelopment.com
Contact: Robert G. Hewitt, Principal
E-mail: bob@hewittdevelopment.com
Scope: Specializes in strategic planning; profit enhancement; start-up businesses; interim management; crisis management; turnarounds; production planning; just-in-time inventory management; and project management. Serves senior management (CEOs, CFOs, division presidents, etc.) and acquirers of distressed businesses.

25903 ■ Hickey & Hill Inc.
1009 Oak Hill Rd., Ste. 201
Lafayette, CA 94549-3812
Ph:(925)906-5331
Contact: Edwin L. Hill, CEO
Scope: Firm provides management consulting services to companies in financial distress. Expertise area: Corporate restructuring and turnaround.

25904 ■ hightechbiz.com
4209 Santa Monica Blvd., Ste. 201
PO Box 189
Los Angeles, CA 90029-3027
Ph:(323)913-3355
Free: 877-648-4753
Fax:(323)913-3355
Contact: Jack Potter, Principal
Scope: A full service marketing agency specializing in integrated marketing solutions. Services include: marketing surveys; positioning surveys; strategic and tactical plans; implementation plans; management consulting; product brochures; product catalogs; product packaging; product data sheets; direct mail programs; media research; competitive research; complete creative; production and film; media placement; corporate identity; in-house creative; public relations.

25905 ■ Hills Consulting Group Inc.
6 Partridge Ct.
Novato, CA 94945-1315
Ph:(415)898-3944
Contact: Michael R. Hills, President
Scope: Specializes in strategic planning; marketing surveys; market research; customer service audits; new product development; competitive analysis; and sales forecasting.

25906 ■ Holt Capital
1916 Pike Pl., Ste. 12-344
Seattle, WA 98101
Ph:(206)484-0403
Fax:(206)789-8034
Co. E-mail: info@holtcapital.com
URL: http://www.holtcapital.com
Contact: David Brazeau, Principle
E-mail: mjholt@holtcapital.com
Scope: Registered investment advisory firm. Services include: Debt planning, private equity, mergers, divestitures and acquisitions, transaction support services. Connects companies with capital. **Publications:** "Early Sales Key to Early-Stage Funding"; "Financial Transactions: Who Should Be At Your Table"; "Get the Deal Done: The Four Keys to Successful Mergers and Acquisitions"; "Is Your First Paragraph a Turn-off"; "Bubble Rubble: Bridging the Price Gap for an Early-Stage Business"; "Are You Ready For The new Economy"; "Could I Get Money or Jail Time With That The Sarbanes-Oxley Act Of 2002 gives early-stage companies More Risks". **Seminars:** Attracting Private Investors; Five Proven Ways to Finance Your Company; How to Get VC Financing; Venture Packaging; How to Finance Company Expansion.

25907 ■ Hornberger & Associates
1966 Lombard St.
San Francisco, CA 94123
Ph:(415)346-2106
Fax:(415)346-9993
Co. E-mail: info@hornbergerassociates.com
URL: http://www.hornbergerassociates.com
Contact: Deborah Hornberger, Principle
E-mail: deborah@hornbergerassociates.com
Scope: Specialized services include wealth management, retirement programs, small business banking, personal trust, investment management, brokerage services, mutual funds, relationship management, private banking and employee banking. Help clients by offering strategic marketing plans, market segmentation/niche marketing, website strategies and development; product development and introduction; client communications; product, sales and referral training; client retention programs and project management. **Publications:** "Establishing a Mini-trust Product," Bank Marketing, Oct, 1997. **Seminars:** Building a Marketing Plan Directed at Emerging Wealth Baby Boomers, Strategy Institute conference, Jun, 1999.

25908 ■ Human Resource Specialties Inc.
3 Monroe Pky., Ste. 900
PO Box 1733
Lake Oswego, OR 97035
Ph:(503)697-3329
Free: 800-354-3512
Fax:(503)636-1594
Co. E-mail: info@hrspecialties.com
URL: http://www.hrspecialties.com
Contact: Elaine W. Ankersen, Mgr
E-mail: elainea@atshrspecialties.com
Scope: Provides human resources assistance to organizations. Offers preparation of affirmative action plans, support documents, and adverse impact studies of personnel activities. Also offers customized consultations in small business services, diversity and discrimination, and investigations, complaints and grievances. Provides investigations, including allegations of unfair treatment, equal employment opportunity (EEO) and racial or sexual harassment. Offers customized web-based training (webinars) on a variety of HR, EEO and AAP-related topics.

25909 ■ I.H.R. Solutions
3333 E Bayaud Ave., Ste. 219
Denver, CO 80209
Ph:(303)588-4243
Fax:(303)978-0473
Co. E-mail: dhollands@ihrsolutions.com
Contact: Deborah Hollands, President
E-mail: dhollands@ihrsolutions.com
Scope: Provides joint-venture and start-up human resource consulting services as well as advice on organization development for international human capital. Industries served: high-tech and telecommunications.

25910 ■ IMC Consulting & Training
901 McHenry Ave., Ste. A
Modesto, CA 95350
Ph:(209)572-2271
Fax:(209)572-2862
Co. E-mail: info@imc-1.net
URL: http://www.imc-1.net
Contact: Ed Stout, Principle
E-mail: michael@imc-1.net
Scope: Firm helps businesses and professionals identify, develop and market their selling proposition to increase profits. Services include B-to-B surveys, direct marketing, media relations, planning and strategy, sales management, training and leadership coaching. **Publications:** "Consultant Earns Advanced Certificate," Hccsc Business Review, Dec, 2004; "Adapting to Change - the New Competitive Advantage," Business Journal, Jul, 2004; "Loyalty Marketing Can Divide New Business," Jun, 2004; "Eleven

Major Marketing Mistakes," Jul, 2003; "Planning to Win or Racing to Fail," Jun, 2003. **Seminars:** Negotiating High Profit Sales; How to Write Winning Proposals, Modesto Chamber of Commerce, Oct, 2007; Winning the 2nd Half: A 6-month Plan to Score New Customers and Profits.

25911 ■ In Plain English
14501 Antigone Dr.
PO Box 3300
Gaithersburg, MD 20885-3300
Ph:(301)340-2821
Free: 800-274-9645
Fax:(301)279-0115
Co. E-mail: rwohl@inplainenglish.com
URL: http://www.inplainenglish.com
Contact: Ronald H. Wohl, CEO
E-mail: rwohl@inplainenglish.com
Scope: Management consultants helping government and businesses research, design, write and produce user oriented management information for human resources, employee benefits, business process, corporate and marketing needs. Services include: GSA mob is schedule for consulting to the government; employee benefit communications, plain English business writing workshops for print and electronic media; communicating strategy and tactics; marketing research, business planning and communications; readability testing; usability testing and monitoring strategy. **Publications:** "The Benefits Communication"; "The Employee Benefits Communication ToolKit," Commerce Clearinghouse; "Benefits Communication," Business and Legal Reports. **Seminars:** Plain English Writing Training; Summary Plan Description Compliance workshops; Re-Humanizing the Corporation, Human Resources and Employee Benefits Communication Workshop; 21 Writing Tips for the 21st Century; Make the Write Impression; Writing to Inform and Instruct; The Dreaded Nuts and Bolts; Writing to Persuade; Writing Policy and Procedure Manuals In Plain English; Writing for Accountants and Auditors In Plain English. **Special Services:** In Plain English[R].

25912 ■ Innovative Scientific Analysis & Computing
6168 Flagstaff Rd.
PO Box 1636
Boulder, CO 80302
Ph:(303)440-7673
Fax:(303)545-6674
Co. E-mail: ros5e@isaac.com
URL: http://www.ros5e.com
Contact: Herrn C. Rose, Principle
E-mail: ros5e@isaac.com
Scope: Engineering services includes mathematical analysis specializing in optimal estimation, scientific programming, and database design and development, data encryption and security.

25913 ■ The Institute for Management Excellence
PO Box 5459
Lacey, WA 98509-5459
Ph:(360)412-0404
Co. E-mail: pwoc@itstime.com
URL: http://www.itstime.com
Contact: Michael Anthony, Director
E-mail: btaylor@itstime.com
Scope: Management consulting and training focuses on improving productivity, using practices and creative techniques. Practices based on the company's theme: It's time for new ways of doing business. Industries served: public sector, law enforcement, finance or banking, non profit, computers or high technology, education, human resources, utilities. **Publications:** "Income Without a Job," 2008; "The Other Side of Midnight, 2000: An Executive Guide to the Year 2000 Problem"; "Concordance to the Michael Teachings"; "Handbook of Small Business Advertising"; "The Personality Game"; "How to Market Yourself for Success". **Seminars:** The Personality Game; Power Path Seminars; Productivity Plus; Sexual Harassment and Discrimination Prevention; Worker's Comp Cost Reduction; Americans with Disabilities Act; In Search of Identify: Clarifying Corporate Culture.

25914 ■ Institute of Public Administration
411 Lafayette St., Ste. 303
New York, NY 10003
Ph:(212)992-9898
Free: 800-258-1102
Fax:(212)995-4876
Co. E-mail: p553@nyu.edu
URL: http://www.theipa.org
Contact: Yoshihiro Asano, Principle
Scope: A private nonprofit consulting, research and education organization experienced in management of governments and public enterprises. Firm's activities are directed toward the solution of emerging problems of government, organization, financial management and policies, and public enterprises in the United States and abroad. Programs are financed chiefly by contracts with local, state and federal governments, international aid agencies and foreign governments, public enterprises, and by foundation grants. Areas of concentration include personnel administration, structures and resources of local legislative bodies, training, structure and financing of public enterprises, public finance and fiscal reform, financial management and anti-corruption systems, sustainable urban development, urban and regional planning, organization and management, city/county charter revision, urban transportation, public sector ethics and citizenship, and management of government procurement systems. **Publications:** "Local Governance Approach to Social Reintegration and Economic Recovery in Post Conflict Countries: The Political Context for Programs of UNDP/UNCDF Assistance"; "Local Governance Approach to Social Reintegration and Economic Recovery in Post Conflict Countries: Programming Options for UNDP/ UNCDF Assistance"; "Local Governance Approach to Social Reintegration and Economic Recovery in Post Conflict Countries: The View from Mozambique"; "Local Governance Approach to Social Reintegration and Economic Recovery in Post Conflict Countries: Towards a Definition and a Rationale"; "Local Governance Approach to Post Conflict Recovery: Perspective from Cambodia"; "The Sustainable Human Development Strategy: A Proposal for Post Conflict Recovery Societies"; "Local Governance Approach to Post Conflict Recovery: Proceedings Report on the Workshop Organized by the Institute of Public Administration". **Seminars:** A Local Governance Approach to Post Conflict Recovery.

25915 ■ Interminds & Federer Resources Inc.
106 E 6th St., Ste. 310
Austin, TX 78701-3659
Ph:(512)476-8800
Fax:(512)476-8811
URL: http://www.interminds.com
Contact: Salvador Apud, Partner
E-mail: sapud@atsintegra100.com
Scope: Firm specializes in feasibility studies; startup businesses; small business management; mergers and acquisitions; joint ventures; divestitures; interim management; crisis management; turnarounds; production planning; team building; appraisals and valuations.

25916 ■ Interpersonal Coaching & Consulting
1516 W Lake St., Ste. 2000S
Minneapolis, MN 55408
Ph:(612)381-2494
Fax:(612)381-2494
Co. E-mail: mail@interpersonal-coaching.com
URL: http://www.interpersonal-coaching.com
Contact: Mary Belfry, Partner
E-mail: mail@interpersonal-coaching.com
Scope: Provides coaching and consulting to businesses and organizations. Assesses the interpersonal workplace through interviews, assessment instruments and individual group settings. Experienced as a therapist for over a decade. **Seminars:** Sexual harassment and discrimination issues.

25917 ■ Invent Resources Inc.
PO Box 548
Lexington, MA 02420-0005
Ph:(781)862-0200
Fax:(781)721-2300
Co. E-mail: pavelle@comcast.net
URL: http://www.weinvent.com
Contact: Sol Aisenberg, Principle
E-mail: pavelle@comcast.net
Scope: Provides consultancy services to provide support in developing and prototyping new, proprietary products. Offer inventory services on demand. Assist clients who need innovations in product lines, have hit technical bottlenecks, or need improvements in manufacturing processes. Provide assistance to individuals and clients in obtaining, reviewing, and strengthening patents.

25918 ■ Jest for the Health of It Services
PO Box 8484
Santa Cruz, CA 95061-8484
Ph:(831)425-8436
Fax:(831)425-8437
Co. E-mail: pwooten@jesthealth.com
URL: http://www.jesthealth.com
Contact: Shirley Trout, Mgr
E-mail: strout@atsnurseswhostay.com
Scope: Develops and presents seminars, keynotes and skill shops about the power of humor. Provides consulting services for development of humor rooms and comedy carts in hospitals. Conducts training for clowns to make visits in hospitals and nursing homes. Industries served: health professionals and businesses wishing to educate staff about healthy lifestyle choices. **Publications:** "Heart Humor and Healing"; "Compassionate Laughter: Jest for Your Health"; "The Hospital Clown: A Closer Look"; "Humor: An Antidote for Stress"; "Humor, Laughter and Play: Maintaining Balance in a Serious World"; "You've Got to Be Kidding: Humor Skills for Surviving Managed Care"; "Laughter as Therapy for Patient and Caregiver"; "Patty Wooten: Nurse Healer"; "Humor: An antidote for stress".

25919 ■ Jim Castello Marketing Communications Consultants
711 Red Wing Dr.
Lake Mary, FL 32746
Ph:(407)321-6322
Contact: James E. Castello Jr., President
Scope: Consultant develops creative ideas and marketing strategies, including collateral programs, public relations, advertising, and brochures. Industries served: All golf related industry/business, golf manufacturers, golf resorts, golf residential developments, golf professionals, golf clothing, golf accessories, golf associations, and golf travel. **Seminars:** How To Seminar for Family Fun Center Entrepreneurs; How To Seminar for Creativity in Golf Marketing; The Golf Business on the Internet.

25920 ■ Joel Greenstein & Associates
6212 Nethercombe Ct.
McLean, VA 22101
Ph:(703)893-1888
Co. E-mail: jgreenstein@contractmasters.com
Contact: Joel Greenstein, Principle
E-mail: jgreenstein@contractmasters.com
Scope: Provides services to minority and women-owned businesses and government agencies. Specializes in interpreting federal, agency-specific acquisition regulations and contract terms and conditions. Offers assistance with preparing technical, cost proposals and sealed bids.

25921 ■ Johnston Co.
1646 Massachusetts Ave., Ste. 22
Lexington, MA 02420
Ph:(781)862-7595
Fax:(781)862-9066
Co. E-mail: info@johnstoncompany.com
URL: http://www.johnstoncompany.com
Contact: Terry Sugrue, Mgr
E-mail: tzsugrue@atshotmail.com
Scope: Firm specializes in management audits and reports; start-up businesses; small business management; mergers and acquisitions; joint ventures; divestitures; interim management; crisis management; turnarounds; cost controls; financing; venture capital; controller services; financial management, strategic and advisory services. **Publications:** "Why are board meetings such a waste of time," Boston Business Journal, Apr, 2004.

25922 ■ K & T Training
103 Greenville St.
Newnan, GA 30263
Ph:(770)253-5870
Fax:(770)253-8866
Contact: J. R. Tumperi, President
Scope: Specializes in strategic planning; profit enhancement; organizational development; start-up businesses; interim management; crisis management; turnarounds; business process re-engineering; team building; cost controls.

25923 ■ Keck & Co.
410 Walsh Rd.
Atherton, CA 94027
Ph:(650)854-9588
Fax:(650)854-7240
Co. E-mail: info@kecko.com
Contact: Barbara Keck, Owner
E-mail: info@kecko.com
Scope: Conducts management services nationally, focusing on strategic research, marketing, and planning for businesses involved in the packaging container and equipment industry, food processing, and related technology suppliers. Develops feasibility studies to assess the possible success or failure of entering a new market, introducing a new product or product line extension, or starting a new venture; primary market research to determine what motivates consumers/buyers, and best "positioning" for product in the marketplace; business development programs; promotional programs to differentiate client company from competitors; vertical/horizontal marketing audits; technology acceptance assessments; due diligence for investors; and management assistance with investment issues. **Seminars:** Taking the Failure Factors Out of New Product Introductions; Introduction to Marketing for Food Manufacturing Personnel; New Product Development Workshop: Plans and Elements; Starting Your Own Consulting Business; The Marketing Plan.

25924 ■ Keiei Senryaku Corp.
19191 S Vermont Ave., Ste. 530
Torrance, CA 90502-1049
Ph:(310)366-3331
Free: 800-951-8780
Fax:(310)366-3330
Co. E-mail: takenakaes@earthlink.net
Contact: Kurt Miyamoto, President
Scope: Offers consulting services in the areas of strategic planning; feasibility studies; profit enhancement; organizational development; start-up businesses; mergers and acquisitions; joint ventures; divestitures; executive searches; sales management; and competitive analysis.

25925 ■ Key Communications Group Inc.
5617 Warwick Pl.
Chevy Chase, MD 20815-5503
Ph:(301)656-0450
Free: 800-705-5353
Fax:(301)656-4554
Co. E-mail: mr.dm@verizon.net
Contact: Carol A. Jason, Principle
E-mail: mr.dm@verizon.net
Scope: Direct marketing and publishing consultants specializing in subscriber and member acquisition for newsletters and other niche B2B publications, organizations and associations. Specialties: small and start-up businesses; mergers and acquisitions; joint ventures; divestitures; product development; employee surveys and communication; market research; customer service audits; new product development; direct marketing and competitive intelligence. **Publications:** "How I Tripled Site License Sales in One Year," Pma, Jul, 2004.

25926 ■ Koch Group Inc.
240 E Lake St., Ste. 300
Addison, IL 60101-2874
Ph:(630)941-1100
Free: 800-470-7845
Fax:(630)941-3865
Co. E-mail: info@kochgroup.com
URL: http://www.kochgroup.com
Contact: Charissa Pachucki, Treasurer
E-mail: rgg@atskochgroup.com
Scope: Provides industrial marketing consulting services to small to mid-sized manufacturers. Primary assistance includes industrial market research and analysis, identification of potential markets, strategic planning and plan implementation, market planning, sales analysis, competitor analysis. Specializes in assisting manufacturers identify, recruit, and manage agents and reps and developing website for business promotion. **Seminars:** Niche Marketing; Regional Industrial Association Recruiting; Strategic Marketing for Manufacturers; Strategic Marketing; How To Identify, Screen, Interview and Select High Quality Agents; Basics of Industrial Market Research; Elements of Industrial Marketing; Trade Adjustment Assistance For Firms; Developing New Business; Selecting An Industrial Web Site Developer; Strategic Selling; Pick Your Customer; Strategic and Tactical Marketing.

25927 ■ Kostka & Company Inc.
9 Wild Rose Ct.
Cromwell, CT 06416
Ph:(860)257-1045
Co. E-mail: mail@mmgnet.com
URL: http://www.mmgnet.com
Contact: Tom Steiner, Managing Partner
E-mail: peterpk@gmail.com
Scope: Areas of expertise: management consulting, global technology sourcing, complex project management, SKU management and new product introduction, application development, medical point-of-sale, multi-touch user interface, made-to-order management systems and Smartphone ERP connectivity. Clients include global fortune 500 companies as well as small and medium-sized businesses and startups.

25928 ■ Kroll Zolfo Cooper L.L.C.
777 S Figueroa St., 24th Fl.
Los Angeles, CA 90017
Ph:(212)561-4000
Fax:(212)948-4226
Co. E-mail: mwyse@krollzolfocooper.com
URL: http://www.krollzolfocooper.com
Contact: Stephen F. Cooper, Principal
E-mail: scooper@kroll.com
Scope: Firm provides accounting consulting services to businesses. Specializes in restructuring and turnaround consulting; interim and crisis management; performance improvement; creditor advisory; cross-border restructuring and corporate finance.

25929 ■ Kubba Consultants Inc.
1255 Montgomery Dr.
Deerfield, IL 60015
Ph:(847)729-0051
Fax:(847)729-8765
Co. E-mail: edkubba@aol.com
URL: http://www.kubbainc.com
Contact: Sam Sampat, Mgr
E-mail: edkubba@aol.com
Scope: Industrial and business-to-business marketing research and consulting. Services include new product research, new market evaluation, competitor analysis and customer value analysis.

25930 ■ L G Anthony Associates
40 Wellington Blvd.
Reading, PA 19610
Ph:(610)670-0477
Contact: Louis G. Anthony, Owner
Scope: Provides food service facility planning, layout and design, including equipment selection and specification. Also offers management systems and operations analysis, such as the development of operating policies and procedures. Firm can design menu planning and recipe development, food selection and specification, work simplification, service, and quality control around current concepts in the field. Industries served: hospital, nursing home, restaurant, group homes; commercial and institutional food service industries. **Seminars:** Food Service Sanitation; Menu Planning; Work Simplification; Quality Control in Food Service.

25931 ■ Liberty Business Strategies Ltd.
The Times Bldg., Ste. 400, Suburban Sq.
Ardmore, PA 19003
Ph:(610)649-3800
Fax:(610)649-0408
Co. E-mail: info@libertystrategies.com
URL: http://www.libertystrategies.com
Contact: Dr. Emmy S. Miller, President
E-mail: emmym@atslibertystrategies.com
Scope: Management consulting firm working with clients to gain speed and agility in driving their business strategy. The consulting model builds the alignment of strategy, organization commitment, and technology. Provides senior leader coaching and team development coaching. **Seminars:** Winning with Talent, Morison Annual Conference, Jul, 2009.

25932 ■ Linda Lipsky Restaurant Consultants Inc.
216 Foxcroft Rd.
PO Box 489
Broomall, PA 19008
Ph:(610)325-3663
Free: 877-425-3663
Fax:(610)325-3329
Co. E-mail: lipsky@restaurantconsult.com
URL: http://www.restaurantconsult.com
Contact: Linda J. Lipsky, President
E-mail: lipsky@restaurantconsult.com
Scope: Helps food and beverage operations achieve their highest level of profits, product consistency and service quality. Concentrates on implementing cost cutting measures, developing training programs for both front and heart of the house employees, engineering menus, performing Spotter's reports and creating organizational manuals and procedures for restaurant, bar, hotel, banquet facility, country clubs, or caterer. Key areas of specialization include on site operations evaluations to identify in effective cost controls, flaws in the organizational structure and inadequacies of management systems, policies and procedures; profit enhancement as a result of implementing cost-cutting measures in all prime cost areas; server training, sales incentive training, and management training and evaluation programs; recipe documentation, cost analysis, menu pricing and menu copy writing; competitive market surveys and market positioning analysis, and bridge management. **Seminars:** Designing Menus for Maximum Sales and Profits; How to Maximize Your Check Average; Going Beyond Your Customer's Expectations; Seeing Your Restaurant Through a Customer's Eyes; Making the Best First and Last Impression; Basic Training in Kitchen Management Techniques; Basic Training in Bar Management Techniques; Make Every Labor Dollar Count; Back to Basics/More Than Shift Management; Conducting Your Own In-House Inspection; Basics of Sanitation Training for Kitchen Employees; Basics of Sanitation Training for Dining Room Employees.

25933 ■ Lupfer & Associates
92 Glen St.
Natick, MA 01760-5646
Ph:(508)655-3950
Fax:(508)655-7826
Co. E-mail: donlupfer@aol.com
Contact: Donald Lupfer, President
E-mail: don.lupfer@lupferassociates.com
Scope: Assists off shore hi-tech companies in entering United States markets and specializes in channel development for all sorts of products. Perform MARCOM support for hi-tech United States clients. **Publications:** "What's Next For Distribution-Feast or Famine"; "The Changing Global Marketplace"; "Making Global Distribution Work". **Seminars:** How to do Business in the United States.

25934 ■ Management Resource Partners
181 2nd Ave., Ste. 542
San Mateo, CA 94401
Ph:(650)401-5850
Fax:(650)401-5850
Contact: John C. Roberts, Principle
Scope: Firm specializes in strategic planning; small business management; mergers and acquisitions; joint ventures; divestitures; interim management; crisis management; turn around; venture capital; appraisals and valuations.

25935 ■ Management Strategies
1000 S Old Woodward, Ste. 105
Birmingham, MI 48009
Ph:(248)258-2756
Fax:(248)258-3407
Co. E-mail: bob@hois.com
Contact: Robert E. Hoisington, President
E-mail: bob@hois.com
Scope: Firm specializes in strategic planning; feasibility studies; profit enhancement; organizational studies; start up businesses; turnarounds; business process re engineering; industrial engineering; marketing; ecommerce.

25936 ■ Mankind Research Foundation Inc.
1315 Apple Ave.
Silver Spring, MD 20910-3614
Ph:(301)587-8686
Fax:(301)585-8959
Contact: Carl Schleicher, CEO
Scope: Firm provide an organization for scientific development and application of technology that could have positive impact on the health, education, and welfare of mankind. Provide solution to seek and apply futuristic solutions to current problems. Provides services in the areas of advanced sciences, biotechnical, bionic, biocybernetic, biomedical, holistic health, bioimmunology, solar energy, accelerated learning, and sensory aids for handicapped. Current specific activities involve research in AIDS, drug abuse, affordable housing, food for the hungry, and literacy and remedial education.

25937 ■ Marketing Leverage Inc.
2022 Laurel Oak
Palm City, FL 34990
Free: 800-633-1422
Fax:(772)659-8664
Co. E-mail: lkelly@marketingleverage.com
URL: http://www.marketingleverage.com
Contact: Genina Gravlin, Principle
E-mail: davery@atsmarketingleverage.com
Scope: Consulting and research firm focusing on the targeting, retention and satisfaction of customers. Consulting is offered for due diligence; marketing and customer retention strategy; program design and implementation. Research services offered help clients determine service improvements that increase customer loyalty; boosting sales through better understanding buyer motivations; increasing the odds of product acceptance through new product concept testing; and improving the effectiveness of advertising, collateral, publications through audience evaluation. Clients include top financial services, insurance, health care, technology and management services organizations. **Publications:** "Creating Strategic Leverage"; "Exploring Corporate Strategy"; "Competitive Advantage"; "Breakpoint and Beyond "; "Competitive Strategy ". **Seminars:** Best Practices in Brainstorming; Getting Results in the Real World; Finding the Leverage in Your Customer Strategy; The Role of Communications in Building Customer Loyalty; Building a Customer Centered Relationship and Making it Pay. **Special Services:** The Marketing Leverage Win/Loss Tracking System^{TM}.

25938 ■ May Toy Lukens
3226 NE 26th Ct.
Renton, WA 98056
Ph:(425)891-3226
Contact: May T. Lukens, Principle
Scope: Provides training to teach people to think of ways to improve their operations continuously by changing the way they think. Industries served: All, particularly financial. Operational analysis and training. **Seminars:** Seminars and workshops in maximizing resource utilization and staff potential.

25939 ■ McCreight & Company Inc.
36 Grove St., Ste. 4
New Canaan, CT 06840-5329
Ph:(203)801-5000
Fax:(866)646-8339
Co. E-mail: roc@implementstrategy.com
URL: http://www.implementstrategy.com
Contact: Laraine Mehr-Turlis, CFO
E-mail: jas@atsimplementstrategy.com
Scope: The firm assist the global clients with strategy implementation involving large scale change, including mergers, divestitures, alliances, and new business launches. Along with the alliance partners, focus on issues that energize or constrain strategic change including: plans and goals; transition design; management competence; organization structure, effectiveness, and staffing; roles and responsibilities; management processes; information management and technology; and change management effectiveness. **Publications:** "The Board's Role in Strengthening M&A Success," Boardroom Briefing, 2008; "Creating the Future," Ask Magazine, 2007; "Strategy Implementation Insights," Mccreight and Company Inc., Oct, 2007; "Sustaining Growth," Deloitte and Ct Technology Council, Jul, 2006; "A Four Phase Approach to Succession Planning," Southern Connecticut Newspapers Inc., 2005; E perspective; Board Effectiveness Insights; and Information Technology Insights. **Seminars:** Successful Mergers and Acquisitions - An Implementation Guide; Global 100One-Face-to-the-Customer; Implementation of Strategic Change.

25940 ■ McDonald Consulting Group Inc.
1900 W Park Dr., Ste. 280
Westborough, MA 01581
Ph:(952)841-6357
Fax:(507)664-9389
Co. E-mail: rmcdonald@mcdonaldconsultinggroup.com
URL: http://www.mcdonaldconsultinggroup.com
Contact: Ron A. McDonald, President
E-mail: rmcdonald@mcdonaldconsultinggroup.com
Scope: A management consulting firm specializing in assisting insurance companies improve operations. Provides services in the areas of strategic planning; profit enhancement; organizational development; interim management; crisis management; turnarounds; business process re-engineering; benefits and compensation planning and total quality management. **Publications:** "Improving Customer Focus through Organizational Structure," AASCIF News; "Changing Strategies in Hard Markets," The National Underwriter; "Moving Beyond Management 101: Postgraduate Time Management for Executives," The National Underwriter; "A New Attitude: 3 Clients Improved Results Through Our Fundamental Change Process," Bests Review; "How to Organize Your Company Around Your Customers," Bests Review. **Seminars:** How to establish "expense allowable"; How to design an incentive compensation plan around a units core success measures.

25941 ■ McShane Group Inc.
2345 York Rd., Ste. 102
Timonium, MD 21093
Ph:(410)560-0077
Fax:(410)560-2718
Co. E-mail: tmcshane@mcshanegroup.com
URL: http://www.mcshanegroup.com
Contact: Richard D. Montgomery, Principle
E-mail: rdm@atsmcshanegroup.com
Scope: Turnaround consulting and crisis management firm. Specializes in due diligence services, interim management, strategic business realignments, business sale and asset depositions and debt restructuring. Industries served: technology, financial, retail, distribution, medical, educational, manufacturing, contracting, environmental and health care.

25942 ■ Medical Imaging Consultants Inc.
1037 US Highway 46, Ste. G-2
Clifton, NJ 07013-2445
Ph:(973)574-8000
Free: 800-589-5685
Fax:(973)574-8001
Co. E-mail: info@micinfo.com
URL: http://www.micinfo.com
Contact: Dr. Philip A. Femano, President
E-mail: phil@micinfo.com
Scope: Provides professional support services for radiology management and comprehensive continuing education programs for radiologic technologists. Management services include resource-critical database logistics; customer registration in educational programs; educational program development and Category A accreditation; national agency notification (e.g., ASRT, SNM-TS) of CE credits earned; meeting planning; manpower assessment; market research; expert witness; think-tank probes and executive summaries of industry issues. **Seminars:** Sectional Anatomy and Imaging Strategies; CT Cross-Trainer; CT Registry Review Program; MR Cross Trainer; MRI Registry Review Program; Digital Mammography Essentials for Technologists; Radiology Trends for Technologists.

25943 ■ Medical Outcomes Management Inc.
132 Central St., Ste. 215
Foxborough, MA 02035-2422
Ph:(508)543-0050
Fax:(508)543-1919
Co. E-mail: info@mom-inc.com
Contact: Vinit P. Nair, Mgr
E-mail: vinit@atsmom-inc.com
Scope: Management and technology consulting firm providing a specially focused group of services such as disease management programs and pharmacoeconomic studies. Services include clinical and educational projects, medical writing and editing, marketing and sales projects, disease registries, educational seminars, strategic planning projects, managed care organizations; and pharmaceutical and biotechnology companies. **Publications:** "Treatment of acute exacerbation's of chronic bronchitis in patients with chronic obstructive pulmonary disease: A retrospective cohort analysis logarithmically extended release vs. Azithromycin," 2003; "A retrospective analysis of cyclooxygenase-II inhibitor response patterns," 2002; "DUE criteria for use of regional urokinase infusion for deep vein thrombosis,"2002; "The formulary management system and decision-making process at Horizon Blue Cross Blue Shield of New Jersey," Pharmaco therapy, 2001. **Seminars:** Economic Modeling as a Disease Management Tool, Academy of Managed Care Pharmacy, Apr, 2005; Integrating Disease State Management and Economics, Academy of Managed Care Pharmacy, Oct, 2004; Clinical and economic outcomes in the treatment of peripheral occlusive diseases, Mar, 2003.

25944 ■ Mefford, Knutson & Associates Inc.
6437 Lyndale Ave. S, Ste. 103
Richfield, MN 55423-1465
Ph:(612)869-8011
Free: 800-831-0228
Fax:(612)869-8004
Co. E-mail: info@mkaonline.net
URL: http://www.mkaonline.net
Contact: Jennifer Thompson, Director
E-mail: jthompson@atsmkaonline.com
Scope: A consulting and licensed business brokerage firm specializing in start-up businesses; strategic planning; mergers and acquisitions; joint ventures; divestitures; business process re-engineering; personnel policies and procedures; market research; new product development and cost controls.

25945 ■ Midwest Computer Group L.L.C.
6060 Franks Rd.
House Springs, MO 63051-1101
Ph:(636)677-0287
Fax:(636)677-0287
Co. E-mail: sales@mcgcomputer.com
URL: http://www.mcgcomputer.com
Contact: Jeffrey A. Sanford, Mgr
E-mail: jeffrey@atsmcgcomputer.com
Scope: Firm specializes in helping businesses create accounting, marketing and business information systems; software development; and database design and management.

25946 ■ Midwest Research Institute
425 Volker Blvd.
Kansas City, MO 64110-2241
Ph:(816)753-7600
Fax:(816)753-8420
Co. E-mail: info@mriresearch.org
URL: http://www.mriresearch.org
Contact: Dr. William Hall, Chairman of the Board
E-mail: jshular@atsmriresearch.org
Scope: Independent not-for-profit research institute offering scientific services in the areas of national defense, health sciences, agriculture and food safety, engineering, energy, and infrastructure. Services include biomedical electronics, remote sensing, automation and control electromagnetic radiation, environmental sampling and analysis programs for industry and government, program management, engineering studies, exposure and risk assessment,

waste management strategies, contaminant identification, pollution prevention, and waste minimization. Expertise in highway safety/accident analysis, chemometrics/pattern recognition/neural networks, statistical support, process and product engineering.

25947 ■ Miller, Hellwig Associates
150 W End Ave.
New York, NY 10023-5713
Ph:(212)799-0471
Fax:(212)877-0186
Co. E-mail: millerhelwig@earthlink.net
Contact: Ernest C. Miller, President
Scope: Consulting services in the areas of start-up businesses; small business management; employee surveys and communication; performance appraisals; executive searches; team building; personnel policies and procedures; market research. Also involved in improving cross-cultural and multi-cultural relationships, particularly with Japanese clients. **Seminars:** Objectives and standards/recruiting for boards of directors.

25948 ■ National Center for Public Policy Research
501 Capitol Ct. NE
Washington, DC 20002
Ph:(202)543-4110
Fax:(202)543-5975
Co. E-mail: info@nationalcenter.org
URL: http://www.nationalcenter.org
Contact: Amy Moritz Ridenour, Principal
E-mail: aridenour@atsnationalcenter.org
Scope: A communications and research nonprofit organization offering advice and information on international affairs and United States domestic affairs. Sponsors Project 21. Gives special emphasis an environmental and regulatory issues and civil rights issues. **Publications:** "National Policy Analysis"; "Legal Briefs"; "White Paper: National Policy Analysis 523"; "Shattered Dreams: One Hundred Stories of Government Abuse"; "Shattered Lives: 100 Victims of Government Health Care".

25949 ■ Navarro, Kim & Associates
529 N Charles St., Ste. 202
Baltimore, MD 21201
Ph:(410)837-6317
Fax:(410)837-6294
Co. E-mail: bnavarro@sprynet.com
Contact: Beltran Navarro, Director
E-mail: bnavarro@sprynet.com
Scope: Specializes in bridging the gap between firms and non-traditional ethnic communities, especially in community development and institutional building.

25950 ■ New Commons
545 Pawtucket Ave., Studio 106A
PO Box 116
Pawtucket, RI 02860
Ph:(401)351-7110
Fax:(401)351-7158
Co. E-mail: info@newcommons.com
URL: http://www.newcommons.com
Contact: Robert Leaver, Principal
E-mail: rleaver@atsnewcommons.com
Scope: Builder of agile human networks to champion innovation and mobilize change; to pursue business opportunities; to custom design agile organizations and communities, to foster civic engagement. Clients include organizations on-profits, corporations, government agencies, educational institutions; networks-Trade/professional groups, IT services collaborations, service-sharing collectives; and communities- municipalities, states and statewide agencies, regional collaborations. **Publications:** "Plexus Imperative," Sep, 2005; "Creating 21st Century Capable Innovation Systems," Aug, 2004; "Call to Action: Building Providences Creative and Innovative Economy"; "Getting Results from Meetings"; "The Entrepreneur as Artist," Commonwealth Publications; "Leader and Agent of Change," Commonwealth Publications; "Achieving our Providence: Lessons of City-Building," Commonwealth Publications. **Seminars:** Introduction to Social Computing (Web 2.0), Jan, 2009; Every Company Counts, Jun, 2009; Facilitating for Results; Story-Making and Story-Telling.

25951 ■ The New Marketing Network Inc.
300 Park Ave., 17th Fl.
New York, NY 10022
Ph:(212)572-6392
Co. E-mail: info@newmarketingnetwork.com
URL: http://www.newmarketingnetwork.com
Contact: Sherri Coffelt, Vice President
E-mail: pwallace@newmarketingnetwork.com
Scope: Full service firm assisting companies in marketing, creative, research, branding and communications specialties. The firm assists companies achieve their growth initiatives, increase profits and establish a sustainable competitive advantage through successful new products, accurate trend identification; application; business and brand franchise expansion. Additional services include strategic planning and positioning; qualitative and quantitative research.

25952 ■ Nightingale Associates
7445 Setting Sun Way
Columbia, MD 21046-1261
Ph:(410)381-4280
Fax:(410)381-4280
Co. E-mail: fredericknightingale@nightingaleassociates.net
URL: http://www.nightingaleassociates.net
Contact: Frederick C. Nightingale, Managing Director
E-mail: fredericknightingale@nightingaleassociates.net
Scope: Management training and consulting firm offering the following skills: productivity and accomplishment; leadership skills for the experienced manager; management skills for the new manager; leadership and teambuilding; supervisory development; creative problem solving; real strategic planning; providing superior customer service; international purchasing and supply chain management; negotiation skills development and fundamentals of purchasing. **Seminars:** Productivity and Accomplishment Management Skills for the New Manager; Leadership and Team building; Advanced Management; Business Process Re engineering; Strategic Thinking; Creative Problem Solving; Customer Service; International Purchasing and Materials Management; Fundamentals of Purchasing; Negotiation Skills Development; Providing superior customer service; Leadership skills for the experienced manager.

25953 ■ Norman E Joe and Associates
700 - 6th Ave. SW, Ste. 100
Calgary, AB, Canada T2P 0T8
Ph:(952)595-8000
Fax:(952)595-0679
Co. E-mail: info@focustools.com
URL: http://www.focustools.com
E-mail: info@focustools.com
Scope: Consultants specializing in the development and implementation of problem-solving, decision-making and team processes for managers/supervisors and key people in a variety of organizations. Industries served: manufacturing, industrial, insurance/banking, healthcare and government. **Publications:** "What is the Decision Leader Review"; "Decision Focus Executive Learning". **Seminars:** How To Create Innovative Solutions On Demand, Jul, 2006; Essential tools to solve problems, make decisions and execute plans, faster and more effectively, Jul, 2006; Decision Focus; Creative Focus; The Focus; Team Focus. **Special Services:** Decision Focus 7.0[R].

25954 ■ North Carolina Fair Share
3824 Barrett Dr., Ste. 312
PO Box 12543
Raleigh, NC 27609
Ph:(919)786-7474
Fax:(919)786-7475
Co. E-mail: ncfslrw@aol.com
URL: http://www.ncfairshare.org
Contact: Lynice Williams, Principle
Scope: Social services firm consults on community organizing and lobbying for health issues.

25955 ■ Occupational & Environmental Health Consulting Services Inc.
635 Harding Rd.
Hinsdale, IL 60521-4814
Ph:(630)325-2083
Fax:(630)325-2098
Co. E-mail: bobb@safety-epa.com
URL: http://www.oehcs.com
Contact: Gail Brandys, Principle
E-mail: metromom@atssafety-epa.com
Scope: Provides consulting to industry on safety program development and implementation, industrial hygiene monitoring programs, occupational health nursing, wellness programs, medical monitoring, accident trending and statistics, emergency response planning, multilingual training, right-to-know compliance and training, hazardous waste management, random monitoring and mitigation, asbestos school inspection, and project management. Also offers indoor air quality, expert witnessing service. **Publications:** "Worldwide Exposure Standards for Mold and Bacteria"; "Global Occupational Exposure Limits for Over 5000 Specific Chemicals"; "Post-Remediation Verification and Clearance Testing for Mold and Bacteria Risk Based Levels of Cleanliness". **Seminars:** Right-To-Know Compliance; Setting Internal Exposure Standards; Hospital Right-to-Know and Contingency Response; Ethylene Oxide Control; Industrial Hygiene Training; Asbestos Worker Training; Biosafety; Asbestos Operations and Maintenance. **Special Services:** Safety Software Program, Audiogram Analysis, First Report of Injury Form, Human Resources Database; Material Safety Data Sheet (MSDS); NPDES Monthly Reports; Lockout/Tagout (LOTO) Procedure Software; VOC Usage Tracking and Reporting Software, Medical Department Patient Records Database, Pictorial Labels for Chemical Containers, TIER II Hazardous Material Inventory Form & Database.

25956 ■ Organization Counselors Inc.
44 W Broadway, Ste. 1102
PO Box 987
Salt Lake City, UT 84101
Ph:(801)363-2900
Fax:(801)363-0861
Co. E-mail: jpanos@xmission.com
Contact: John E. Panos, President
E-mail: jpanos@xmission.com
Scope: Organizational development; employee surveys and communication; outplacement; team building; total quality management and continuous improvement. **Seminars:** Correcting Performance Problems; Total Quality Management; Employee Selection; Performance Management.

25957 ■ Organizational Improvement Associates L.L.C.
40 Gilbert St.
Ridgefield, CT 06877
Ph:(203)417-4957
Fax:(203)244-5737
Co. E-mail: daveknibbe@oiaus.com
URL: http://www.oiaus.com
Contact: Valentina Espinosa-Shimizu, Principle
E-mail: daveknibbe@oiaus.com
Scope: Specializes in high-performance team development, executive coaching, employee development programs, performance management and reward systems and dispute mediation. Industries served: Consumer products, telecommunications, finance, health-care, amusement/leisure, hospitality/lodging, retail and pharmaceuticals.

25958 ■ P2C2 Group Inc.
4101 Denfeld Ave.
Kensington, MD 20895-1514
Ph:(301)942-7985
Fax:(301)942-7986
Co. E-mail: info@p2c2group.com
URL: http://www.p2c2group.com
Contact: Jim Kendrick, President
E-mail: kendrick@p2c2group.com
Scope: Works with clients on the business side of federal program and project management. Services include program/project planning and optimization; acquisition strategy and work statements; IT Capital Planning and Investment Control (CPIC); business cases - new, revisions, critiques; budget analysis - cost benefits- alternatives; CPIC, SELC, and security documentation; research, metrics, analysis, and case studies. Consulting support helping to: Define or redefine programs; strengthen portfolio management; identify alternatives for lean budgets; improve capital

planning and investment; develop better plans and documentation, and evaluate performance of existing program investments. **Publications:** "OMB 300s Go Online," Federal Sector Report, Mar, 2007; "Using Risk-Adjusted Costs for Projects," Federal Sector Report, Feb, 2007; "Make Better Decisions Using Case Studies," Federal Sector Report, Jan, 2007; "PMO Performance Measurement & Metrics"; "Executive Sponsors for Projects"; "ABCs of the Presidential Transition"; "Financial Systems and Enterprise Portfolio Management"; "The Future of CPIC"; "Critical Factors for Program and Project Success"; "Using Risk-Adjusted Costs for Projects"; "Tactics for a Successful Year of CPIC"; "Operational Analysis Reviews"; "Successful IT Strategic Planning"; "Information Technology Investment Management". **Seminars:** How to Hire a Management Consultant and Get the Results You Expect.

25959 ■ Papa and Associates Inc.
200 Consumers Rd., Ste. 305
Toronto, ON, Canada M2J 4R4
Ph:(416)512-7272
Fax:(416)512-2016
Co. E-mail: ppapa@papa-associates.com
URL: http://www.papa-associates.com
Contact: Roxanne Wilson, Mgr
E-mail: ppapa@atspapa-associates.com

Scope: Firm provides broad based management consulting services in the areas of quality assurance, environmental, health and safety and integrated management systems.

25960 ■ Parker Consultants Inc.
230 Mason St.
Greenwich, CT 06830-6633
Ph:(203)869-9400
Contact: William P. Hartl, Chairman of the Board

Scope: Firm specializes in strategic planning; organizational development; small business management; performance appraisals; executive searches; team building; and customer service audits.

25961 ■ Partners for Market Leadership Inc.
400 Galleria Pky., Ste. 1500
Atlanta, GA 30339
Ph:(770)850-1409
Free: 800-984-1110
Co. E-mail: dcarpenter@market-leadership.com
URL: http://www.market-leadership.com
Contact: Nancy Surdyka, Mgr
E-mail: nsurdyka@atsmarket-leadership.com

Scope: Boutique consulting firm focused on assisting clients to develop sustainable market leadership in geographic, practice area and/or industry markets. Provides consulting on market leadership, revenue enhancement, strategic development and change facilitation. Additional services are offered to legal, accounting, valuation and financial firms.

25962 ■ Pathways To Wellness
617 Everhart Rd.
Corpus Christi, TX 78411
Ph:(361)985-9642
Fax:(361)949-4627
Co. E-mail: path2wellness@earthlink.net
URL: http://www.path2wellness.com
Contact: Evy Coppola, Owner

Scope: Offer natural holistic health counseling, yoga and hatha yoga classes, teachers training and cookery classes for individuals and companies. Health counseling includes nutritional guidance, kinesiology, iridology, reflexology, energy healing, massage therapy, herbal and vitamin therapy, creative visualization and meditation. Provides supplements which bring about the same effects as that of natural sunshine. **Seminars:** Is It You Holding You Back?; The Balancing Act. . .Career. . . Family. . .and Self; Learning the Art of Friendly Persuasion; Stop Accepting What You Are Getting and Start Asking for What You Want!; Introduction to Natural Health and Healthy Living; Learn Why One Size Approaches to the Answers on Health Do Not Work; Introduction to Yoga. What is it? Who can do it? What can it do for you.

25963 ■ Performance Consulting Associates Inc.
3700 Crestwood Pky., Ste. 100
Duluth, GA 30096
Ph:(770)717-2737
Fax:(770)717-7014
Co. E-mail: info@pcaconsulting.com
URL: http://www.pcaconsulting.com
Contact: Robert Wilson, Mgr
E-mail: wilson@atspcaconsulting.com

Scope: Maintenance consulting and engineering firm specializing in production planning, project management, team building, and re-engineering maintenance. **Publications:** "Does Planning Pay," Plant Services, Nov, 2000; "Asset Reliability Coordinator," Maintenance Technology, Oct, 2000; "Know What it is You Have to Maintain," Maintenance Technology; May, 2000; "Does Maintenance Planning Pay," Maintenance Technology, Nov, 2000.; "What is Asset Management?"; "Implementing Best Business Practices".

25964 ■ Performance Consulting Group Inc.
8031 SW 35th Terr.
Miami, FL 33155-3443
Ph:(305)264-5577
Fax:(305)264-9079
Contact: Patrick J. O'Brien, President

Scope: Firm provides consulting services in the areas of strategic planning; profit enhancement; product development; and production planning.

25965 ■ Performance Dynamics Group L.L.C.
One Ridge Rd.
Green Brook, NJ 08812
Ph:(732)537-0381
Free: 888-720-7337
Co. E-mail: info@performance-dynamics.net
URL: http://www.performance-dynamics.net
Contact: Mark E. Green, President
E-mail: mark.green@atsperformance-dynamics.net

Scope: An organizational consulting group whose approach to learning and employee empowerment is designed to be both effective and efficient in achieving the specific knowledge and skill goals of a given program, in developing changes in thinking and behavior and also to foster and develop initiative, self confidence, creative problem-solving ability and interpersonal effectiveness of all participants. Brings improvement in areas of revenue growth, profitability, sales, marketing effectiveness, and employee and customer loyalty. **Seminars:** Accelerated Approach to Change; Commitment to Quality; Managing Cultural Diversity; The Corporate Energizer; The Power Pole Experience; Team Assessment; Self-Directed Work Teams.

25966 ■ Plans and Solutions Inc.
7823 Mistic View Ct.
PO Box 8905
Derwood, MD 20855
Ph:(301)947-8150
Fax:(240)525-5601
Co. E-mail: info@plansandsolutions.com
URL: http://www.plansandsolutions.com
Contact: Kenneth D. Weiss, President
E-mail: kw@plansandsolutions.com

Scope: Market research and competitive analysis; marketing and promotion planning, and executing promotion plans. Specializes in registration and problem solving services that include food canning establishment and process registration, registration under the terrorism act, assistance in case of detention of shipments, and on-site inspection of processing plants and records. Most clients are minority-owned businesses in the USA and companies overseas that want to begin or increase exports to the United States and Canada. **Publications:** "Building an Import/Export Business," John Wiley & Sons, 2002; "How to Conquer the U.S. Market "; "Going Global (Getting Started in International Trade)". **Seminars:** U.S. Import Regulations on Food Products.

25967 ■ Practice Development Counsel
60 Sutton Pl. S
New York, NY 10022
Ph:(212)593-1549
Fax:(212)980-7940
Co. E-mail: pwhaserot@pdcounsel.com
URL: http://www.pdcounsel.com
Contact: Steven A. Lauer, Mgr
E-mail: stevelauer@atssprintmail.com

Scope: Specializes in business development, service quality, retention, organizational development work/life excellence, and conflict resolution for professional firms. Provides coaching, client relationship management and quality service programs; strategic marketing planning/implementation; ancillary businesses/diversification; market research, trend watching, bench marking; facilitation and planning for retreats and creative decision making; new business proposals and presentations; marketing communications and public relations; and business development training, coaching, and materials. Also offers speaker's services - engagements, publicity, etc. Industries served: law, accounting, and financial services, executive search, design, architecture, real estate, and management consultants worldwide. **Publications:** "The Rainmaking Machine: Marketing Planning, Strategy and Management For Law Firms"; "The Marketer's Handbook of Tips & Checklists"; "Venturesome Questions: The Law Firms Guide to Developing a New Business Venture"; "Navigating the Whitewater of Internal Politics"; "Changing Attitudes on Firm Flexibility"; "Transition Planning: A Looming Challenge"; "Don't You Think the Solution Is to Bring In a Good Rainmaker?"; "Aligning Firm Culture with the Needs of the Times"; "What New Partners Need to Know"; "Dangers of Lack of Diversity"; "Learn to Respect Emotion in Business"; "What New Partners Need to Know"; "Taking Responsibility: Implementing Personal Marketing Plans"; "How to Change Unwritten Rules"; "Mentoring and Networking Converge"; "Integrating a New Practice into the Firm"; "Using Conflict Resolution Skills for Marketing Success"; "Sports Team Models for Law Firm Management". **Seminars:** Managing Work Expectations; Effective Coaching Skills; Service Quality; End-Running the Resistance Professionals Have to Getting Client Input; Ancillary Business Activities; Marketing for Professional Firms; Marketing Ethics; Business Development Training; Trends in Professional Services Marketing; Client Relationship Management; Collaborative Culture; Reaching Consensus; Conflict Resolution; Work life Balance; Generaltional Issues; Preparing New Partners; Becoming the Employer of Choice; A Marketing Approach to Recruiting; Implementing Workplace Flexibility; The Business Case for Flexible Work Arrangements.

25968 ■ Praxis Media Inc.
48 Harbourview Ave.
South Norwalk, CT 06854
Ph:(203)866-6666
Fax:(203)853-8299
Co. E-mail: aldo@praxismediainc.com
Contact: Deborah Winegrad, Vice President

Scope: Media needs analysis and project planning specialists provide services in product introductions, communications planning, technology application, promotion and marketing communications. Also assists with focus groups, research, concept development, creative development, scripting and executive speech coaching/training. Industries served: Financial services, high-tech, travel and leisure, health and pharmaceutical and telecommunications.

25969 ■ ProActive English
4355 SE 29th Ave.
Portland, OR 97202
Ph:(503)231-2906
Co. E-mail: infopae@proactive-english.com
URL: http://www.proactive-english.com
Contact: David Kertzner, Managing Director
E-mail: dkertzner@atsproactive-english.com

Scope: Offers on-site individual and small group language and communication training. Sets up learning plans tailored to the needs and schedules of managers and executives who are non-native English speakers. Serves all industries. **Seminars:** Communicating in Business Situations; Presentations and Pronunciation; Tailored Curriculum; One-on-One Programs.

25970 ■ Professional Counseling Centers Inc.
543 Coventry Way
Noblesville, IN 46062-9024
Ph:(317)877-3111
Contact: Margie Hanrahan, Owner
Scope: Business counselors offering services in the following areas: employee assistance, managed care, alcohol and drug treatment, labor and union consultation, and industrial mental health.

25971 ■ Public Administration Service
7927 Jones Branch Dr., Ste. 100 S
McLean, VA 22102-3322
Ph:(703)734-8970
Fax:(703)734-4965
Contact: Ramesh Khatiwada, Treasurer
Scope: Performs a variety of consulting and research work in serving the special needs of governments and other public service institutions. Services range from technical studies of central management problems to analyses of public policy issues, and in development administration water sewerage management and systems, rural development, and small farmer organization privatization, and management. Devoted exclusively to improving the conduct of public activities. Consulting services in the United States include organization and management, data processing and automation plans, position classification and compensation plans, police and fire service studies, public works and utilities studies, and parks management studies.

25972 ■ Public Policy Communications
4163 Dingman Dr.
Sanibel, FL 33957
Ph:(941)395-6773
Fax:(941)395-6779
Contact: Robert Schaeffer, President
E-mail: bobschaeffer@earthlink.net
Scope: Provides strategic communications for progressive causes, candidates and socially-responsible businesses. These include public relations strategies, political campaign planning, organizational development and training. Substantial work in report writing, editing and design as well as production of a full range of media materials. Industries served: nonprofit, social change organizations, foundations, political campaigns, environmentally and consumer-oriented businesses, government agencies. **Publications:** "Winning Local and State Elections," Free Press MacMillan; "Giving the Media Your Message, and The News Media and the Big Lie". **Seminars:** Giving the Media Your Message; Effective Public Relations Practices; Winning Your Election; Understanding the Government Budget Process; How to Be an Effective Advocate; Strategic Planning for Non-Profits; How to Run a News Conference: Ten Key Steps, 1998.

25973 ■ Public Sector Consultants Inc.
600 W St. Joseph St., Ste. 10
Lansing, MI 48933-2267
Ph:(517)484-4954
Fax:(517)484-6549
Co. E-mail: psc@pscinc.com
URL: http://www.pscinc.com
Contact: Julie Metty Bennett, Vice President
E-mail: jmettybennett@atspscinc.com
Scope: Offers policy research expertise, specializing in opinion polling, public relations, conference planning, and legislative and economic analysis. Industries served: Associations, education, environment, health-care, and public finance. **Publications:** "Ingham Community Voices Final Evaluation Report," Nov, 2008; "First Class Schools Analysis," Aug, 2008; "Opportunities for Achieving Efficiency in the Aging, Community Mental Health, Local Public Health, and Substance Abuse Coordinating Agency Networks," Aug, 2008; "Saginaw River Bay Area of Concern," Jun, 2008; "Portage Lake Water shed Forever Plan," May, 2008; "Smoke Free Workplaces," Apr, 2008; "Protecting and Restoring the Upper Looking Glass River," Feb, 2008; "Market Structures and the 21st Century Energy Plan," Sep, 2007; "The Growing Crisis of Aging Dams," Apr, 2007; "Financing Community Health Workers Why and How," Jan, 2007; "Hastings Area: Inter local Approaches to Growth Management," Jan, 2007; "Michigan's Part 201 Environmental Remediation Program Review," Jan, 2007.

25974 ■ The Purchasing Department
34 Claremont Ave.
Maplewood, NJ 07040-2118
Fax:(973)275-0749
Co. E-mail: eostpd@aol.com
Contact: James Thomas Milway, Principle
E-mail: jtmtpd@aol.com
Scope: Provides state of the art procurement arrangements, process re-engineering and outsourcing assistance to any business wishing to achieve purchasing savings and efficiencies to improve bottom line results. Available to provide contract services to businesses requiring specialized supplemental assistance to back up own personnel on special projects. **Seminars:** Green Purchasing: Buying Recycled Products; Ethics; Measuring Purchasing Performance; Supplier Teaming and Quality; Preparing for ISO 9000 in the Purchasing Department.

25975 ■ R.E. Moulton Inc.
50 Doaks Ln.
Marblehead, MA 01945
Ph:(781)631-1325
Fax:(781)631-2165
Co. E-mail: mike_lee@remoultoninc.com
URL: http://www.oneamerica.com/wps/wcm/connect/REMoulton
Contact: Reynolds E. Moulton Jr., Chairman of the Board
E-mail: dick@atsremoultoninc.com
Scope: Offers underwriting services, marketing solutions, claims administration and adjudication; policy and commission administration; and risk management solutions to clients. Supplementary service s include risk management and employee assistance. Clients include individuals, business men, employers and finance professionals.

25976 ■ Reed Royalty Public Affairs Inc.
30205 Hillside Terr.
San Juan Capistrano, CA 92675-1542
Ph:(949)240-2022
Fax:(949)240-0304
Co. E-mail: reed.royauy@home.com
Contact: Reed L. Royalty, President
E-mail: rroyalty@ocers.org
Scope: A governmental relations consultant who provides lobbying for changes in laws and government regulations, helps in obtaining licenses and permits, provides corporate training in governmental relations and assistance in winning government contracts. Services include crisis management, business association management and issue-specific community and media relations.

25977 ■ Rental Relocation Inc.
281 S Atlanta St.
Roswell, GA 30075
Ph:(770)641-8393
Free: 800-641-7368
Fax:(770)641-8607
Co. E-mail: ahlsinfo@rentalrelocation.com
URL: http://www.rentalrelocation.com
Contact: Christopher Bliss, President
E-mail: cbliss@atsrentalrelocation.com
Scope: Relocation firm offering services in corporate housing, rentals, free metro Atlanta apartment locating service, property management, house and condo rental relocation tours.

25978 ■ Rose & Crangle Ltd.
117 N 4th St.
PO Box 285
Lincoln, KS 67455
Ph:(785)524-5050
Fax:(785)524-3130
Co. E-mail: rcltd@nckcn.com
URL: http://www.roseandcrangle.com
Contact: Jeanne Crangle, Principle
E-mail: rcltd@nckcn.com
Scope: Firm provides evaluation, planning and policy analyzes for universities, associations, foundations, governmental agencies and private companies engaged in scientific, technological or educational activities. Special expertise in the development of new institutions. Special skills in providing planning and related group facilitation workshops. **Publications:** "Preface to Bulgarian Integration Into Europe and NATO: Issues of Science Policy And research Evaluation Practice," Ios Press, 2006; "Allocating Limited National Resources for Fundamental Research," 2005.

25979 ■ Rothschild Strategies Unlimited L.L.C.
19 Thistle Rd.
PO Box 7568
Norwalk, CT 06851-1909
Ph:(203)846-6898
Fax:(203)847-1426
Co. E-mail: bill@strategyleader.com
URL: http://www.strategyleader.com
Contact: William Rothchild, CEO
E-mail: billrothschild@atsoptonline.net
Scope: Consults with senior management and business level strategy teams to develop overall strategic direction, set priorities and creates sustainable competitive advantages and differentiators. Enables organizations to enhance their own strategic thinking and leadership skills so that they can continue to develop and implement profitable growth strategies. **Publications:** "Putting It All Together-a guide to strategic thinking"; "Competitive Advantage"; "Ristaker, Caretaker, Surgeon & Undertaker four faces of strategic leadership"; "The Secret to GE's Success"; "Having the Right Strategic Leader and Team". **Seminars:** Who is going the WRONG way?; Learning from your Successes and Failures. **Special Services:** StrategyLeader[R].

25980 ■ Sanford Consulting
52 Perry Corners Rd., RR 1
PO Box 314A
Amenia, NY 12501
Ph:(845)373-8960
Fax:(845)373-8961
Co. E-mail: sanford@mohawk.com
Contact: Anne Sanford, President
E-mail: sanford@mohawk.com
Scope: Helps businesses find, sell, to, and keep customers. Provides management and marketing services, including problem analysis and solution design for new business development, market analysis and segmentation, departmental organization and administrative policies and procedures. Industries served: small business, telecommunications, professional services, health care and nonprofits in the continental United States. **Seminars:** Trade show success; Finding customers; Business attitudes at not for profit and others.

25981 ■ SBR International
3 - 14 College St.
The Graeme Bldg.
Toronto, ON, Canada M5G 1K2
Ph:(416)962-7500
Fax:(416)962-7505
Co. E-mail: bizdev@sbr-global.com
URL: http://www.sbr-global.com
Contact: Chris Anstead, Managering Director
Scope: Specializes in the leasing of multi-disciplinary, high-performance work teams at customer in-house cost, under a mixed military/general contracting model. Engagements include BPR, IE, SA, market and competitor intelligence, logistics, strategy, audit, workouts/turnarounds, M and A support/targeting, statistics and micro-economic modeling, PMO support. **Seminars:** Electronic counter measures; Strategic planning; Project management.

25982 ■ Schneider Consulting Group Inc.
50 S Steele St., Ste. 390
Denver, CO 80209
Ph:(303)320-4413
Fax:(303)320-5795
Contact: Kim Schneider Malek, Vice President
E-mail: kim@atsscgfambus.com
Scope: Assists family-owned and privately-held business transition to the next generation and/or to a more professionally managed company, turn around consulting for small and medium size companies.

25983 ■ Scott Ashby Teleselling Inc.
1102 Ben Franklin Dr., Ste. 309
Sarasota, FL 34236
Ph:(941)388-4283
Fax:(941)388-5240
Co. E-mail: rscottashby@netscape.net
URL: http://www.scottashbyteleselling.com
Contact: R. Scott Ashby, Owner
E-mail: rscottashby@netscape.net
Scope: Provides consulting services and customized training programs that emphasize consultative telephone selling techniques. **Publications:** "How Will the Internet Affect Teleselling Programs?"; "When is Telemarketing Really Not Telemarketing?"; "The Future of Account Management Telesales". **Seminars:** Start-Up Educational, Planning and Strategy Development; Existing Program Audit, Evaluation, State-of-the-Art Best Practices Comparison, Tracking and Measurement Review, Systems and Procedures Analysis, and Optional Selling Skills; Develop New or Revised Consultative Telephone Selling; Helping Clients Build Relationship and Grow Their Business by Phone.

25984 ■ Sklar and Associates Inc.
242 Laurel Bay Dr.
Murrells Inlet, SC 29576
Ph:(202)257-5061
Fax:(843)651-3090
Co. E-mail: sklarincdc@aol.com
URL: http://www.sklarinc.com
Contact: Tim Sklar, President
Scope: Provides consulting services for business acquisitions, business development and project finance. Provides audit oversight services to listed corporations on Sarbanes-Oxley compliance. Services include: Due diligence analyses and corporate governance. Industries served: transportation sectors, energy sector and commercial real estate industries. **Seminars:** Financial Analysis in MBA; Emerging Company Finance; Due Diligence in Business Acquisition; Business Valuation.

25985 ■ Straightline Services Inc.
11 Centre St., Ste. 10
Salem, CT 06420-3845
Ph:(860)889-7929
Fax:(860)885-1894
Co. E-mail: straitln@aol.com
Contact: Wayne J. S. France CPCM, President
Scope: Design and implementation of organizational infrastructure, business plans and troubleshooting. Emphasizes on operations with a central and field or satellite offices. Industries served: Construction, resorts, Indian tribes, academies, small-medium sized business, mostly privately held.

25986 ■ Strategic MindShare Consulting
1401 Brickell Ave., Ste. 640
Miami, FL 33131
Ph:(305)377-2220
Fax:(305)377-2280
Co. E-mail: dee@strategicmindshare.com
URL: http://www.strategicmindshare.com
Contact: Cynthia R. Cohen, President
E-mail: cohen@strategicmindshare.com
Scope: Firm specializes in strategic planning; feasibility studies; profit enhancement; organizational development; start-up businesses; mergers and acquisitions; joint ventures; divestitures; interim management; crisis management; turnarounds; new product development and competitive analysis. **Publications:** "Top Ten CEO Burning Issues for 2005"; "Top Ten Consumer Behavioral Trends for 2005"; "The Influence Factors"; "New Profit Opportunities for Retailers and Consumer Product Companies".

25987 ■ TC International Marketing Inc.
11 Iliffe House, Iliffe Ave.
Leicester LE2 5LS, United Kingdom
Ph:(845)258-7482
Fax:(845)986-2130
Co. E-mail: tcintl@warwick.net
Contact: Graeme Wright, Partner
Scope: Business expansion consulting including feasibility studies, mergers and acquisitions, divestment, market research and strategizing.

25988 ■ Technology Management Group Co.
PO Box 3260
New Haven, CT 06515-0360
Ph:(203)387-1430
Fax:(203)387-1470
Co. E-mail: info@commtechsoftware.com
URL: http://www.ratafia.net
Contact: Manny Ratafia, President
E-mail: manny@commtechsoftware.com
Scope: Consulting services include analysis of market opportunities; product introductions; new ventures; acquisitions analysis; licensing, joint ventures, and OEM arrangements. Emphasis on polymers, medical devices, biotechnology, pharmaceuticals, and chemicals. **Special Services:** CommTechPowerSearch[R].

25989 ■ Trendzitions Inc.
25691 Atlantic Ocean Dr., Ste. B13
Lake Forest, CA 92630-8842
Ph:(949)727-9100
Free: 800-266-2767
Fax:(949)727-3444
Co. E-mail: ctooker@trendzitions.com
URL: http://www.trendzitions.com
Contact: Christian Tooker, President
E-mail: ctooker@atstrendzitions.com
Scope: Provides services in the areas of communications consulting, project management, construction management, and furniture procurement. Offers information on spatial uses, building codes, ADA compliance and city ordinances. Also offers budget projections.

25990 ■ Turnaround Inc.
3415 A St. NW
Gig Harbor, WA 98335
Ph:(253)857-6730
Fax:(253)857-6344
Co. E-mail: info@turnround-inc.com
URL: http://www.turnaround-inc.com
Contact: Miles Stover, President
E-mail: mstover@turnaround-inc.com
Scope: Firm provides interim executive management assistance and management advisory to small, medium and family-owned businesses that are not meeting their goals. Services include acting as an interim executive or on-site manager. Extensive practices in arena of bankruptcy management. **Publications:** "How to Identify Problem and Promising Management"; "How to Tell if Your Company is a Bankruptcy Candidate"; "Signs that Your Company is in Trouble"; "The Turnaround Specialist: How to File a Petition Under 11 USC 11". **Seminars:** Competitive Intelligence Gathering.

25991 ■ ValueNomics Value Specialists
50 W San Fernando St., Ste. 600
San Jose, CA 95113
Ph:(408)200-6400
Fax:(408)200-6401
Co. E-mail: info@amllp.com
Contact: Jeff A. Stegner, Partner
Scope: Consulting is offered in the areas of financial management, process re-engineering, growth business services; governance, risk/compliance, SOX readiness and compliance, SAS 70, enterprise risk management, system security, operational and internal audit; business advisory services; valuation services; CORE assessment; contract assurance; transaction advisory services, IT solutions and litigation support services. **Publications:** "Dueling Appraisers: How Differences in Input and Assumptions May Control the Value," Apr, 2005; "The Business of Business Valuation and the CPA as an expert witness"; "The Business of Business Valuation," McGraw-Hill Professional Publishers Inc.

25992 ■ Via Nova Consulting
1228 Winburn Dr.
Atlanta, GA 30344
Ph:(404)761-7484
Fax:(404)762-7123
Scope: Consulting services in the areas of strategic planning; privatization; executive searches; market research; customer service audits; new product development; competitive intelligence; and Total Quality Management (TQM).

25993 ■ Vision Management
149 Meadows Rd.
Lafayette, NJ 07848-3120
Ph:(973)702-1116
Fax:(973)702-8311
Contact: Norman L. Naidish, President
Scope: Firm specializes in profit enhancement; strategic planning; business process reengineering; industrial engineering; facilities planning; team building; inventory management; and total quality management (TQM). **Publications:** "To increase profits, improve quality," Manufacturing Engineering, May, 2000.

25994 ■ The Walk The Talk Co.
1100 Parker Sq., Ste. 250
Flower Mound, TX 75028-7458
Ph:(972)899-8300
Free: 800-888-2811
Fax:(972)899-9291
Co. E-mail: info@walkthetalk.com
URL: http://www.walkthetalk.com
Contact: Doug Westmoreland, VP of Operations
E-mail: ericharvey@walkthetalk.com
Scope: Assists a wide variety of organizations in implementing proprietary performance management system developed by the firm which concentrates on individual responsibility and decision making instead of disciplinary penalties. Helps organizations develop and implement peer review, a proven system that helps solve employee problems in a remarkable way-through employees and an evaluation process software is used whereby feedback is compiled from a full-range of sources, including a self-evaluation, leadership development workshops and keynote presentations and publications. **Publications:** "Positive Discipline"; "Leadership Secrets of Santa Claus"; "Start Right-Stay Right"; "Walk Awhile in My Shoes"; "Listen Up, Leader!"; "Five Star Teamwork"; "Ethics4Everyone"; "Leadership Courage"; "The Manager's Communication Handbook"; "180 Ways to Walk the Recognition Talk"; "The Manager's Coaching Handbook"; "The Best Leadership Advice I Ever Got"; "Power Exchange". **Seminars:** Walk the Talk; Coaching for Continuous Improvement; Managing Employee Performance; Customized Management Development Forums; Keynote presentations; Leadership Development Workshops; Consulting Services and Publications; Customer service training; Ethics and Values training.

25995 ■ Weich & Bilotti Inc.
600 Worcester Rd., 4th Fl.
Framingham, MA 01702
Ph:(508)663-1600
Fax:(508)663-1682
Co. E-mail: info@weich-bilotti.com
URL: http://www.weich-bilotti.com
Contact: Mervyn D. Weich, President
E-mail: mweich@weich-bilotti.com
Scope: Specializes in business plans, venture capital, computer information systems, turnaround/ interim management, retail consulting, start-up process, college recruiting and IS and IT personnel.

25996 ■ Wheeler and Young Inc.
33 Peter St.
Markham, ON, Canada L3P 2A5
Ph:(905)471-5709
Fax:(905)471-9989
Co. E-mail: wheeler@ericwheeler.ca
URL: http://www.ericwheeler.ca
Contact: Eric S. Wheeler, Managing Partner
E-mail: ewheeler@yorku.ca
Scope: Provides consulting services to high-tech companies on the implementation of software development processes; quality management systems (including ISO 9000 compliance) and business management systems. Offers business management and knowledge-management services to organizations. Industries served: Knowledge-based industries, including software and hardware development, medical and legal professionals, information service providers.

25997 ■ William E. Kuhn & Associates
234 Cook St.
Denver, CO 80206-5305
Ph:(303)322-8233

Fax:(303)331-9032
Co. E-mail: billkuhn1@cs.com
Contact: William E. Kuhn, Owner
E-mail: billkuhn1@cs.com
Scope: Firm specializes in strategic planning; profit enhancement; small business management; mergers and acquisitions; joint ventures; divestitures; human resources management; performance appraisals; team building; sales management; appraisals and valuations. **Publications:** "Creating a High-Performance Dealership," Office SOLUTIONS & Office DEALER, Jul-Aug, 2006.

25998 ■ ZS Engineering P.C.
99 Tulip Ave.
Floral Park, NY 11001
Ph:(516)328-3200
Fax:(516)328-6195
Co. E-mail: office@zsengineering.com
URL: http://www.zsengineering.com
Contact: Donna Conte, Mgr
E-mail: staszewski@atszsengineering.com
Scope: Offers engineering consulting services to building owners, building managers and contractors. Specializes in design and inspections of fire alarm systems, sprinkler systems, smoke control systems, building evaluations for fire code compliance, violations removal. **Seminars:** Fire protection courses for contractors and building management.

FRANCHISES AND BUSINESS OPPORTUNITIES

25999 ■ ABX-Associates Business Xchange
7604 Oak St.
Frisco, TX 75034
Ph:(214)850-6131
Fax:(866)462-7229
Founded: 1971. **Description:** Nationwide franchise brokers network.

26000 ■ American Franchise Consultants
520 W Gleneagles Dr.
Phoenix, AZ 85023
Free: 800-424-0749
Founded: 1995. **Description:** Business consultants.

26001 ■ Biga & Associates, Inc.
2415 E Kensington Rd.
Arlington Heights, IL 60004
Ph:(847)870-7521
Fax:(847)870-7553
Founded: 1989. **Description:** Franchise consultants.

26002 ■ Franchise Bancorp
294 Walker Dr., Ste. 2
Brampton, ON, Canada L6T 4Z2
Ph:(905)790-9023
Free: (866)463-4124
Fax:(905)790-7059
Co. E-mail: franchises@franchisebancorp.com
URL: http://www.franchisebancorp.com
No. of Company-Owned Units: 180. **Founded:** 1968. **Franchised:** 1968. **Description:** With a diverse combination of retail formats, Franchise Bancorp offers several business opportunities to satisfy various interests, lifestyles and investment levels. Living Lighting, Rafters, Panhandler, Rafters Home Stores and Global Ryan's Pet Foods forms the portfolio of franchises available through the Franchise Bancorp organization. **Equity Capital Needed:** $160,000-$470,000. **Franchise Fee:** $30,000.

26003 ■ Franchise Development International, LLC
370 SE 15 Ave.
Pompano Beach, FL 33060
Ph:(954)942-9424
Fax:(954)783-5177
Founded: 1991. **Description:** Franchise development and marketing.

26004 ■ Franchise Developments, Inc.
The Design Center, Ste. 660
5001 Baum Blvd.
Pittsburgh, PA 15213
Ph:(412)687-8484
Fax:(412)687-0541
Founded: 1970. **Description:** Develop, implement and launch franchise programs.

26005 ■ Franchise Foundations
4157 23rd St.
San Francisco, CA 94114
Free: 800-942-4402
Founded: 1980. **Description:** Franchise consulting.

26006 ■ Franchise Specialists, Inc.
1234 Maple St. Ext.
Moon Twp, PA 15108
Free: 800-261-5055
Founded: 1978. **Description:** Professional franchise development and sales.

26007 ■ Francorp, Inc.
20200 Governors Dr.
Olympia Fields, IL 60461
Ph:(708)481-2900
Free: 800-372-6244
Co. E-mail: info@francorp.com
URL: http://www.francorp.com
Founded: 1976. **Description:** Offers consultancy on franchising business. Consultants have provided full development programs, including feasibility studies, business plans, legal documents, operations manuals, and marketing materials for clients since 1976. **Training:** Provides post-development services for establishing franchisors, including lead generation programs, brochures, videotapes, international brokerage, PR, and expert witness service.

26008 ■ Jones & Co.
365 Bay St., 2nd Fl.
Toronto, ON, Canada M5H 2V1
Ph:(416)703-5716
Fax:(416)703-6180
Founded: 2004. **Description:** Law firm experienced in franchising and distribution.

26009 ■ Kaufman & Canoles, P.C.
150 W Main St., Ste. 2100
Norfolk, VA 23510
Ph:(757)624-3257
Fax:(757)624-3169
Founded: 1974. **Description:** Franchise attorneys.

26010 ■ L. Michael Schwartz, P.A.
10561 Barkley Pl., Ste. 510
Overland Park, KS 66212-1860
Ph:(913)341-1919
Fax:(913)341-0007
Description: Franchise consulting and full legal services.

26011 ■ Leon Gottlieb USA/Int'l Franchise/ Restaurant Consultants
Leon Gottlieb & Associates
4601 Sendero Pl.
Tarzana, CA 91356-4821
Ph:(818)757-1131
Fax:(818)757-1816
Founded: 1960. **Description:** Consultant, expert witness, arbitrator.

26012 ■ Lite For Life
Lite for Life Franchise Corp., Inc.
398 Main St.
Los Altos, CA 94022
Ph:(650)941-3200
Fax:(650)559-3111
No. of Franchise Units: 2 **No. of Company-Owned Units:** 4. **Founded:** 1978. **Franchised:** 2003. **Description:** Weight loss and nutritional consulting. **Equity Capital Needed:** $75,000+/-. **Franchise Fee:** $20,000. **Financial Assistance:** No. **Training:** Yes.

26013 ■ Marketing Resources Group
83-26 Lefferts Blvd.
Kew Gardens, NY 11415
Ph:(718)261-8882
Description: Franchise development, marketing, and sales.

26014 ■ McGrow Consulting
30 North St.
Hingham, MA 02043
Ph:(781)740-2211
Free: 800-358-8011
Founded: 1980. **Description:** Franchise consulting firm.

26015 ■ World Franchise Consultants
15965 Jeanette
Southfield, MI 48075
Ph:(248)559-1415
Free: 800-745-1415
Fax:(248)557-7931
Founded: 1973. **Description:** Franchise consulting and referral.

Credit and Collection

START-UP INFORMATION

26016 ■ *How to Start a Bankruptcy Forms Processing Service*
Pub: Graphico Publishing Company
Ed: Victoria Ring. **Released:** September 2004. **Price:** $39.00. **Description:** Due to the increase in bankruptcy filings, attorneys are outsourcing related jobs in order to reduce overhead.

ASSOCIATIONS AND OTHER ORGANIZATIONS

26017 ■ National Association of Credit Management
8840 Columbia 100 Pkwy.
Columbia, MD 21045-2158
Ph:(410)740-5560
Free: 800-955-8815
Fax:(410)740-5574
URL: http://www.nacm.org
Contact: Robin D. Schauseil CAE, Pres./COO
Description: Credit and financial executives representing manufacturers, wholesalers, financial institutions, insurance companies, utilities, and other businesses interested in business credit. Promotes sound credit practices and legislation. Conducts Graduate School of Credit and Financial Management at Dartmouth College, Hanover, NH. **Publications:** *Business Credit* (9/year); *Credit Executives Handbook*; *Manual of Credit and Commercial Laws* (annual).

EDUCATIONAL PROGRAMS

26018 ■ The Essentials of Collections Law
Seminar Information Service, Inc.
20 Executive Park, Ste. 120
Irvine, CA 92614
Ph:(949)261-9104
Free: 877-SEM-INFO
Fax:(949)261-1963
Co. E-mail: info@seminarinformation.com
URL: http://www.seminarinformation.com
Price: $179.00. **Description:** Get the essential facts for legally collecting accounts receivable, what violates the Fair Debt Collection Practices Act (FDCPA) and other laws that lead to costly fines and judgments. **Locations:** Cities throughout the United States.

REFERENCE WORKS

26019 ■ "A Conversation With; Ron Gatner, Jones Lang LaSalle" in *Crain's Detroit Business* (Vol. 24, October 6, 2008, No. 40, pp. 9)
Pub: Crain Communications, Inc.
Description: Interview with Ron Gatner who is a corporate real estate adviser with the real estate company Jones Lang LaSalle as well as the company's executive vice president and part of the tenant advisory team; Gatner speaks about the impact that the Wall Street crisis is having on the commercial real estate market in Detroit.

26020 ■ "A Good Step, But There's a Long Way to Go" in *Business Week* (September 22, 2008, No. 4100, pp. 10)
Pub: McGraw-Hill Companies, Inc.
Ed: James C. Cooper. **Description:** Despite the historic action by the U.S. government to nationalize the mortgage giants Freddie Mac and Fannie Mae, rising unemployment rates may prove to be an even bigger roadblock to bringing back the economy from its downward spiral. The takeover is meant to restore confidence in the credit markets and help with the mortgage crisis but the rising rate in unemployment may make many households unable to take advantage of any benefits which arise from the bailout. Statistical data included.

26021 ■ "Abroad, Not Overboard" in *Entrepreneur* (Vol. 36, April 2008, No. 4, pp. 68)
Pub: Entrepreneur Media, Inc.
Ed: Crystal Detamore-Rodman. **Description:** Export-Import Bank is an agency created by the U.S. government to help exporters get credit insurance and capital loans by providing them with loan guarantees. The bank, being criticized as supporting more the bigger exporters, has allotted to smaller businesses a bigger portion of the annual credit being approved.

26022 ■ "AIG Fixed; Is Michigan Next?" in *Crain's Detroit Business* (Vol. 24, September 22, 2008, No. 38, pp. 1)
Pub: Crain Communications, Inc.
Ed: Jay Greene. **Description:** Michigan's economic future is examined as is the mortgage buyout plan and American International Group Inc.'s takeover by the U.S. government.

26023 ■ *All About Credit*
Pub: Kaplan Publishing
Ed: Deborah McNaughton **Released:** April 1999. **Price:** $15.95. **Description:** Debt solution to specific credit problems for individuals denied credit, trying to mortgage a home, problems with creditors, and bankruptcy.

26024 ■ "All-Star Advice 2010" in *Black Enterprise* (Vol. 41, October 2010, No. 3, pp. 97)
Pub: Earl G. Graves Publishing Co. Inc.
Ed: Renita Burns, Sheiresa Ngo, Marcia Wade Talbert. **Description:** Financial experts share tips on real estate, investing, taxes, insurance and debt management.

26025 ■ "Apartment Market Down, Not Out" in *Crain's Detroit Business* (Vol. 24, October 6, 2008, No. 40, pp. 9)
Pub: Crain Communications, Inc.
Ed: Daniel Duggan. **Description:** Detroit's apartment market is considered to have some of the strongest fundamentals of any apartment market in the country with relatively low vacancy rates and a relatively low supply of new units compared with demand. Investors continue to show interest in the buildings but the national lending market is making it difficult to invest in the city.

26026 ■ "Are We There Yet?" in *Business Courier* (Vol. 24, April 4, 2008, No. 52, pp. 1)
Pub: American City Business Journals, Inc.
Ed: Lucy May; Dan Monk. **Description:** Groundbreaking for The Banks project happened in April 2, 2008, however, the future of the development remains uncertain due to some unresolved issues such as financing. Developers Harold A. Dawson Co. and Carter still have to pass final financing documents to Hamilton County and Cincinnati. The issue of financial commitment for the central riverfront project is examined.

26027 ■ "Asia Breathes a Sigh of Relief" in *Business Week* (September 22, 2008, No. 4100, pp. 32)
Pub: McGraw-Hill Companies, Inc.
Ed: Bruce Einhorn; Theo Francis; Chi-Chu Tschang; Moon Ihlwan; Hiroko Tashiro. **Description:** Foreign bankers, such as those in Asia, that had been investing heavily in the United States began to worry as the housing crisis deepened and the impact on Freddie Mac and Fannie Mae became increasingly clear. Due to the government bailout, however, central banks will most likely continue to buy American debt.

26028 ■ "Attend To Your Corporate Housekeeping" in *Women Entrepreneur* (December 4, 2008)
Pub: Entrepreneur Media Inc.
Ed: Nina Kaufman. **Description:** Business owners can lose all the benefits and privileges of the corporate form if they do not follow proper corporate formalities such as holding an annual meeting, electing officers and directors and adopting or passing corporate resolutions. Creditors are able to take from one's personal assets if such formalities have not been followed.

26029 ■ "Au Revoir Or Goodbye?" in *Barron's* (Vol. 88, July 14, 2008, No. 28, pp. 5)
Pub: Dow Jones & Co., Inc.
Ed: Alan Abelson. **Description:** Former Senator Phil Gramm's opinion that the U.S. is a "nation of whiners" as they moan about recession is another example of the disconnection between Washington and Wall Street on one hand and the real world on the other. It would be a catastrophe for most of the world if Fannie Mae and Freddie Mac were to go under and take their trillions of mortgage debt with them.

26030 ■ "B2B Commercial Collection Agency Accounts Fall" in *Managing Credit, Receivables & Collections* (November 2010, No. 10-11, pp. 9)
Pub: Institute of Management & Administration
Description: A fall in the number of Business-To-Business collection accounts reflects the pace of the global economic recovery.

26031 ■ "Back on Track-Or Off the Rails?" in *Business Week* (September 22, 2008, No. 4100, pp. 22)
Pub: McGraw-Hill Companies, Inc.
Ed: Peter Coy; Tara Kalwarski. **Description:** Discusses the possible scenarios the American economy may undergo due to the takeover of Fannie Mae and Freddie Mac. Statistical data included.

26032 ■ "Bad-Loan Bug Bites Mid-Tier Banks; More Pain, Tighter Lending Standards Ahead, CEOs Say" in *Crain's Chicago Business* (May 5, 2008)
Pub: Crain Communications, Inc.
Ed: Steve Daniels. **Description:** Mid-sized commercial banks form the bedrock of Chicago's financial-services industry and they are now feeling the results of the credit crisis that has engulfed the nation's largest banks and brokerages. Commercial borrowers are seeing tighter terms on loans and higher interest rates while bank investors are unable to forecast lenders' earnings performance from quarter to quarter. Statistical data included.

26033 ■ "Bad Loans Start Piling Up" in *Crain's New York Business* (Vol. 24, January 7, 2008, No. 1, pp. 2)
Pub: Crain Communications, Inc.
Ed: Tom Fredrickson. **Description:** Problems in the subprime mortgage industry have extended to other lending activities as evidenced by bank charge-offs on bad commercial and industrial loans which have more than doubled in the third quarter.

26034 ■ "Bailout May Force Cutbacks, Job Losses" in *The Business Journal - Serving Phoenix and the Valley of the Sun* (Vol. 29, September 26, 2008, No. 4, pp. 1)
Pub: American City Business Journals, Inc.
Ed: Mike Sunnucks. **Description:** Economists say the proposed $700 billion bank bailout could affect Arizona businesses as banks could be forced to reduce the amount and number of loans it has thereby forcing businesses to shrink capital expenditures and then jobs. However, the plan could also stimulate the economy by taking bad loans off banks balance sheets according to another economist.

26035 ■ "Bank Forces Brooke Founder To Sell His Holdings" in *The Business Journal-Serving Metropolitan Kansas City* (October 10, 2008)
Pub: American City Business Journals, Inc.
Ed: James Dornbrook. **Description:** Robert Orr who is the founder of Brooke Corp., a franchise of insurance agencies, says that he was forced to sell virtually all of his stocks in the company by creditors. First United Bank held the founder's stock as collateral for two loans worth $5 million and $7.9 million, which were declared in default in September 2008. Details of the selling of the company's stocks are provided.

26036 ■ "Bank Sticks to Rate Rise Script but 'Modest' is the Salient Word" in *Globe & Mail* (January 25, 2006, pp. B5)
Pub: CTVglobemedia Publishing Inc.
Ed: Heather Scoffield. **Description:** The reasons behind the decision of Bank of Canada to increase interest rate, which is posted at 3.5 percent, are presented.

26037 ■ "Bankruptcies Shoot Up 68 Percent" in *Sacramento Business Journal* (Vol. 25, July 18, 2008, No. 20, pp. 1)
Pub: American City Business Journals, Inc.
Ed: Kathy Robertson. **Description:** Personal bankruptcy in the Sacramento area rose by 88 percent for the first half of 2008 while business bankruptcies rose by 50 percent for the same period. The numbers of consumer bankruptcy reflects the effect of high debt, rising mortgage costs, and declining home values on U.S. households.

26038 ■ "Bankruptcies Swell" in *The Business Journal-Portland* (Vol. 25, July 4, 2008, No. 17, pp. 1)
Pub: American City Business Journals, Inc.
Ed: Andy Giegerich. **Description:** Individual and business bankruptcy filings in Portland, Oregon had increased. The rising gas and food prices, mortgage crisis and tightening lending standards are seen as causes of bankruptcies. Statistics on bankruptcy filings are also provided.

26039 ■ "Bankruptcy Blowback" in *Business Week* (September 22, 2008, No. 4100, pp. 36)
Pub: McGraw-Hill Companies, Inc.
Ed: Jessica Silver-Greenberg. **Description:** Changes to bankruptcy laws which were enacted in 2005 after banks and other financial institutions lobbied hard for them are now suffering the consequences of the laws which force more troubled borrowers to let their homes go into foreclosure; lenders suffer financially every time they have to take on a foreclosure and the laws in which they lobbied so hard to see enacted are now becoming a problem for these lending institutions. Details of the changes in the laws are outlined as are the affects on the consumer, the economy and the lenders.

26040 ■ "Banks, Retailers Squabble Over Fees" in *Baltimore Business Journal* (Vol. 28, June 18, 2010, No. 6, pp. 1)
Pub: Baltimore Business Journal
Ed: Gary Haber. **Description:** How an amendment to the financial regulatory reform bill would affect the bankers' and retailers' conflict over interchange fees is discussed. Interchange fees are paid for by retailers every time consumers make purchases through debit cards. Industry estimates indicate that approximately $50 million in such fees are paid by retailers.

26041 ■ "Banks Seeing Demand for Home Equity Loans Slowing" in *Crain's Cleveland Business* (Vol. 28, December 3, 2007, No. 48, pp. 1)
Pub: Crain Communications, Inc.
Ed: Shawn A. Turner. **Description:** Discusses the reasons for the decline in demand for home equity loans and lines of credit. Statistical data included.

26042 ■ "Barred Collection Agency Sued by Colorado AG" in *Collections & Credit Risk* (Vol. 15, August 1, 2010, No. 7, pp. 7)
Pub: SourceMedia Inc.
Description: Collection agency run by Chad Lee received notice that it is barred from collecting in the State of Colorado by Attorney General John Suther's office. A ruling cited that the firm engages in harassment or abuse and/or threats of violence, made false representations as to its legal status of debts, made false and misleading representations of nonpayment of debts that would result in arrest, and that Lee failed to disclose his previous felony conviction.

26043 ■ "The Best Option for All" in *American Executive* (Vol. 7, September 2009, No. 5, pp. 170)
Pub: RedCoat Publishing, Inc.
Ed: Ashley McGown. **Description:** Plaza Associates, a collections agency that conducts business primarily in the accounts receivable management sector, is the first in the industry to purchase 100 percent of the company from the founders through the formation of a leveraged Employee Stock Ownership Plan (ESOP).

26044 ■ "Best Turnaround Stocks" in *Canadian Business* (Vol. 81, Summer 2008, No. 9, pp. 65)
Pub: Rogers Media Ltd.
Ed: Calvin Leung. **Description:** Share prices of Sierra Wireless Inc. and EXFO Electro Optical Engineering Inc. have fallen over the past year but have good chance at a rebound considering that the companies have free cash flow and no long-term debt. One-year stock performance analysis of the two companies is presented.

26045 ■ "Beware the Ides of March" in *Canadian Business* (Vol. 81, April 14, 2008, No. 6, pp. 13)
Pub: Rogers Media
Ed: Jeff Sanford. **Description:** Financial troubles of Bear Stearns in March, 2008 was part of the credit crunch that started in the summer of 2007 in the U.S. when subprime mortgages that were written for people who could barely afford the payments started defaulting. The bankruptcy protection given to 20 asset backed commercial paper trusts is being fought by the investors in these securities who could stand to lose 40 percent of their money under the agreement.

26046 ■ "Big Sell-Off At Sunwest" in *The Business Journal-Portland* (Vol. 25, July 25, 2008, No. 20, pp. 1)
Pub: American City Business Journals, Inc.
Ed: Robin J. Moody. **Description:** Oregon's largest operator of assisted living facilities Sunwest Management Inc. is expected to sell 132 of its properties. The planned sale, which is believed to be worth more than $1 billion, will help Sunwest pay creditors and investors. Other views and information on the planned sale, as well as on Sunwest's services which include adult day care, are presented.

26047 ■ "Boosting Your Merchant Management Services With Wireless Technology" in *Franchising World* (Vol. 42, August 2010, No. 8, pp. 27)
Pub: International Franchise Association
Ed: Michael S. Slominski. **Description:** Franchises should have the capability to accept credit cards away from their businesses. This technology will increase sales.

26048 ■ "Boring Bonds Gain Pizzazz as Investors Flock to Debt Issues" in *Baltimore Business Journal* (Vol. 28, June 11, 2010, No. 5, pp. 1)
Pub: Baltimore Business Journal
Ed: Gary Haber. **Description:** Companies and nonprofit organizations have increased the pace of bond offerings in order to take advantage of the bonds' appeal among willing investors. Companies mostly issued corporate bonds to replace existing debt at lower interest rates and save them money from interest payments.

26049 ■ "Bracing for a Bear of a Week" in *Barron's* (Vol. 88, March 17, 2008, No. 11, pp. 24)
Pub: Dow Jones & Company, Inc.
Ed: Jacqueline Doherty. **Description:** JPMorgan Chase and the Federal Reserve Bank of New York's opening of a line of credit to Bear Stearns cut the stock price of Bear Stearns by 47 percent to 30 followed by speculation of an imminent sale. JP Morgan may be the only potential buyer for the firm and some investors say Bears could be sold at $20 to $30. Bears prime assets include its enormous asset base worth $395 billion.

26050 ■ "Branching Out" in *Canadian Business* (Vol. 79, July 17, 2006, No. 14-15, pp. 41)
Pub: Rogers Media
Description: Visa selected this narrative in an attempt to show the company's usefulness.

26051 ■ "Brooke Agents Claim Mistreatment" in *The Business Journal-Serving Metropolitan Kansas City* (Vol. 27, October 24, 2008, No. 7, pp. 1)
Pub: American City Business Journals, Inc.
Ed: James Dornbrook. **Description:** Franchisees of Brooke Corp., an insurance franchise, face uncertainty as their bills remain unpaid and banks threaten to destroy their credit. The company bundled and sold franchisee loans to different banks, but the credit crunch left the company with massive debts and legal disputes.

26052 ■ "Burdened by Debt, Borders Group Suspends Dividends, May Be Sold" in *Crain's Detroit Business* (Vol. 24, March 24, 2008, No. 12)
Pub: Crain Communications, Inc.
Ed: Nancy Kaffer. **Description:** Ann Arbor-based Borders Group Inc. is exploring its options and may put itself up for sale due to its declining stock price and mounting debt. The company's fiscal year was capped by poor holiday sales and Borders does not have the cash on hand to meet the 2009 goals set in its strategic plan.

26053 ■ "Can Your Business Still Land a Loan?" in *Entrepreneur* (Vol. 37, August 2009, No. 8, pp. 62)
Pub: Entrepreneur Media, Inc.
Ed: Carol Tice. **Description:** Banks are now sticking to the rules before making business loans. A business's existing bank should be the first place they should go to for a loan but if this fails, they should then look to smaller community and regional banks.

26054 ■ *Chain of Blame: How Wall Street Caused the Mortgage and Credit Crisis*
Pub: John Wiley & Sons, Inc.
Ed: Paul Muolo, Mathew Padilla. **Released:** 2009. **Price:** $27.95. **Description:** The book describes how risky loans given irresponsibly put big investment banks at the center of the subprime crisis.

26055 ■ "Chasing Credit" in *Canadian Business* (Vol. 81, November 10, 2008, No. 19, pp. 59)
Pub: Rogers Media Ltd.
Ed: Joe Castaldo. **Description:** Small and medium sized companies are dealing with tightening credit because they appear riskier than usual. Some of these businesses are turning to private investors, but this is not easy since many have invested everything in the stock market. The sector is expected to weaken with the broader Canadian market in the next six months from October 2008.

26056 ■ "China's Dagong Show" in *Canadian Business* (Vol. 83, August 17, 2010, No. 13-14, pp. 15)
Pub: Rogers Media Ltd.
Ed: Matthew McClearn. **Description:** Beijing, China-based Dagong Global Credit Rating has downgraded US credit ratings, as well as other developed countries such as Canada, while granting higher ratings to China, Russia and Brazil. However, there is a perceived disconnection between Dagong's ratings and its official pronouncements.

26057 ■ "Citizens Unveils Mobile App for Business Customers" in *New Hampshire Business Review* (Vol. 33, March 25, 2011, No. 6, pp. 27)
Pub: Business Publications Inc.
Description: Citizens Financial Group offers a new mobile banking application that allows business customers to manage cash and payments from a mobile device.

26058 ■ "Clock Ticks On Columbia Sussex Debt" in *Business Courier* (Vol. 27, July 30, 2010, No. 13, pp. 1)
Pub: Business Courier
Ed: Dan Monk. **Description:** Cincinnati, Ohio-based Columbia Sussex Corporation has made plans to restructure a $1 billion loan bundle that was scheduled to mature in October 2010. The privately held hotel has strived in a weak hotel market to keep pace with its $3 billion debt load.

26059 ■ "Collection Agencies Industry Rankings" in *Collections and Credit Risk* (Vol. 14, September 1, 2009, No. 8, pp. 18)
Pub: SourceMedia, Inc.
Description: Ranking of the top collection agencies in the United States in terms of the revenue generated in 2007 and 2088; statistical data included.

26060 ■ "Collection Agency Issues Whitepaper on Legal and Ethical Methods of Collecting on Overdue Accounts" in *Internet Wire* (July 20, 2009)
Pub: Comtex News Network, Inc.
Description: American Profit Recovery, a collection agency based in Massachusetts and Michigan, has updated and reissued a whitepaper on what businesses can and cannot do regarding conversing with their customers in an attempt to collect on overdue accounts and payments. A detailed summary on the federal laws associated with collecting on overdue accounts is outlined in such a way that any business owner, manager, or responsible party can easily understand.

26061 ■ "Collection Industry Fights Stigma, Lagging Payments" in *Crain's Cleveland Business* (Vol. 30, June 8, 2009, No. 22, pp. 15)
Pub: Crain Communications, Inc.
Ed: Joel Hammond. **Description:** John Murray, co-owner and president of JP Recovery Services Inc. in Rocky River, Ohio discusses the burden of the collection industry during a financial crisis like a recession. Statistical data included.

26062 ■ "Coming Soon: Bailouts of Fannie and Freddie" in *Barron's* (Vol. 88, July 14, 2008, No. 28, pp. 14)
Pub: Dow Jones & Co., Inc.
Ed: Jonathan R. Laing. **Description:** Assurances from the government that Fannie Mae and Freddie Mac are adequately capitalized and able to carry on their duties as guarantors or owners of over $5 trillion of U.S. home mortgages are designed to keep both entities afloat until they attempt to raise $10 billion in new equity. The government would assume any losses in a bailout and owners of the banks' papers would profit as yields drop.

26063 ■ "Companies Warned About California Collection Agency" in *Cardline* (Vol. 10, June 4, 2010, No. 23, pp. 3)
Pub: SourceMedia Inc.
Description: Maxwell, Turner & Associates has received an F-rating from the Better Business Bureau of Central California, citing 32 unanswered complaints in less than a year.

26064 ■ *Complete Idiot's Guide to Starting an Ebay Business*
Pub: Penguin Books (USA) Incorporated
Ed: Barbara Weltman, Malcolm Katt. **Released:** February 2008. **Price:** $19.95 (US), $29.00 (Canadian). **Description:** Guide for starting an eBay business includes information on products to sell, how to price merchandise, and details for working with services like PayPal, and how to organize fulfillment services.

26065 ■ "Condominium Sales Fall to a Seven-Year Low" in *Crain's Chicago Business* (Vol. 31, November 10, 2008, No. 45, pp. 2)
Pub: Crain Communications, Inc.
Ed: Alby Gallun. **Description:** Downtown Chicago condominium market is experiencing the lowest number of sales in years due to the tightening of the mortgage lending market, the Wall Street crisis and the downturn in the economy. The supply of new condos is soaring, the result of the building boom of 2005 and 2006; many developers are finding it difficult to pay off construction loans and fear foreclosure on their properties. Additional information and statistical data related to the downtown condominium market is provided.

26066 ■ "Confidence High, But Lenders More Cautious" in *Farmer's Weekly* (March 28, 2008, No. 320)
Pub: Reed Business Information
Description: Discusses the effect of the global credit crunch on farmers as well as recent auctions which were timed to beat changes to capital gains tax.

26067 ■ "Consumers Finding It Harder to Get and Keep Credit" in *Chicago Tribune* (January 10, 2009)
Pub: McClatchy-Tribune Information Services
Ed: Susan Chandler. **Description:** Five tips to maintain a good credit rating in these economic times are outlined and discussed.

26068 ■ "Contractors Fret Over Credit, People, Government" in *Contractor* (Vol. 57, February 2010, No. 2, pp. 7)
Pub: Penton Media, Inc.
Ed: Robert P. Mader. **Description:** Telephone interviews with 22 plumbing and HVAC contractors reveal that only two had sales increases for 2009 and that overall, contractors were down anywhere from seven to 25 percent. In the repair/service market, the residential sector was holding its own but the commercial portion was lagging behind.

26069 ■ "Cornered by Credit; As $1 Billion in Loans Come Due, Will Landlords Find Funds?" in *Crain's Detroit Business* (October 6, 2008)
Pub: Crain Communications, Inc.
Ed: Daniel Duggan. **Description:** Conduit loans are used by many real estate investors and are normally issued in 7- to 10-year terms with balloon payments due at the end, requiring the full balance to be paid upon maturity. Many building owners may find their properties going into foreclosure as these loans mature next year since these loans cannot be extended like typical loans and the credit crisis along with falling property values is making it more difficult to secure new sources of funding. Possible solutions to this problem are also explored.

26070 ■ "Cost of Business Banking May Soon Go Up" in *Baltimore Business Journal* (Vol. 28, October 29, 2010, No. 25, pp. 1)
Pub: Baltimore Business Journal
Ed: Gary Haber. **Description:** Experts in the financial industry expect banks to charge credit card transactions, especially to small business owners and consumers to recover about $11 million in lost revenue annually. Banks are expected to charge old fees and new ones, including $5 to $10 a month for a checking account.

26071 ■ "Count Out The Consumer" in *Barron's* (Vol. 88, July 7, 2008, No. 27, pp. 10)
Pub: Dow Jones & Co., Inc.
Description: American consumers are not expected to give the US economy its much-needed boost as the rising food and energy prices are taking their toll. US consumers have cut spending on utilities and food and are increasing their use of credit cards.

26072 ■ "Crash Pads" in *Business Courier* (Vol. 24, November 2, 2008, No. 29, pp. 1)
Pub: American City Business Journals, Inc.
Ed: Jon Newberry. **Description:** Francisca Webster accumulated $4 million in mortgage debt in about 2 months. She filed a lawsuit against her tax preparer and her mortgage broker contending that the defendants had breached their fiduciary duties to her and made fraudulent misrepresentations to her. The other details of the case are supplied.

26073 ■ "Credit Card Crackdown" in *Business Journal-Portland* (Vol. 24, November 23, 2007, No. 38, pp. 1)
Pub: American City Business Journals, Inc.
Ed: Andy Giegerich. **Description:** Oregon's U.S. Senator Ron Wyden is sponsoring Credit Card Safety Act of 2007, a bill that requires credit card companies to reduce the jargon of credit card agreements and require the Federal Reserve Board to launch a public education campaign among credit card users. The legislation will also impose a rating system for credit card contracts with five being the safest for consumers to use.

26074 ■ "The Credit Crisis Continues" in *Barron's* (Vol. 88, March 10, 2008, No. 10, pp. M12)
Pub: Dow Jones & Company, Inc.
Ed: Randall W. Forsyth. **Description:** Short-term Treasury yields dropped to new cyclical lows in early March 2008, with the yield for the two-year Treasury note falling to 1.532 percent. Spreads of the mortgage-backed securities of Fannie Mae and Freddie Mac rose on suspicion of collapses in financing.

26075 ■ "Credit Crisis Puts Market in Unprecedented Territory" in *Crain's New York Business* (Vol. 24, January 7, 2008, No. 1, pp. 14)
Pub: Crain Communications, Inc.
Ed: Aaron Elstein. **Description:** Banks are being forced to take enormous losses due to investors who are refusing to buy anything linked to subprime mortgages and associated securities.

26076 ■ "Credit Crunch Gives, Takes Away" in *The Business Journal-Serving Metropolitan Kansas City* (Vol. 27, October 17, 2008, No. 5, pp. 1)
Pub: American City Business Journals, Inc.
Ed: Suzanna Stagemeyer. **Description:** Although many Kansas City business enterprises have been adversely affected by the U.S. credit crunch, others

have remained relatively unscathed. Examples of how local businesses are being impacted by the crisis are provided including: American Trailer & Storage Inc., which declared bankruptcy after failing to pay a long-term loan; and NetStandard, a technology firm who, on the other hand, is being pursued by prospective lenders.

26077 ■ "Credit Crunch Takes Bite Out Of McDonald's" in *Advertising Age* (Vol. 79, September 29, 2008, No. 36, pp. 1)
Pub: Crain Communications, Inc.
Ed: Emily Bryson York. **Description:** McDonald's will delay its launch of coffee bars inside its restaurants due to the banking crisis which has prompted Bank of America to halt loans to the franchise chains.

26078 ■ "Credit-Market Crisis Batters Origen Financial's Bottom Line" in *Crain's Detroit Business* (Vol. 24, March 31, 2008, No. 13, pp. 4)
Pub: Crain Communications, Inc.
Ed: Description: Overview of the effect the credit-market crisis has had on Origen Financial Inc., a company that underwrites and services loans for manufactured housing. CEO Ronald Klein didn't think Origen would be affected by the collapse due to its sound operations but the company's share price dropped considerably causing its auditors to warn that the company's existence could be in jeopardy.

26079 ■ "Credit Reporting Myths and Reality" in *Black Enterprise* (Vol. 41, December 2010, No. 5, pp. 34)
Pub: Earl G. Graves Publishing Co. Inc.
Ed: Denise Campbell. **Description:** It is critical to understand all the factors affecting credit scores before making any major purchase.

26080 ■ "Curbing the Debt Collector" in *Business Journal-Portland* (Vol. 24, October 5, 2007, No. 32, pp. 1)
Pub: American City Business Journals, Inc.
Ed: Andy Giegerich. **Description:** Republican representative Sal Esquivel, who had a bad personal experience with a Houston collector, is developing legislation that would give the state attorney general's office enforcement powers over debt collecting agencies. The existing Oregon legislation concerning the debt collection industry is also discussed.

26081 ■ "Cutting Credit Card Processing Costs" in *Hawaii Business* (Vol. 53, March 2008, No. 9, pp. 56)
Pub: Hawaii Business Publishing
Ed: Robert K.O. Lum. **Description:** Accepting credit card payments offers businesses with profits from the discount rate. The discount rate includes processing fee, VISA & MasterCard assessment and interchange. Details regarding merchant service cost and discount rate portions are discussed. Statistical data included.

26082 ■ "Dealers Fight To Steer Course" in *The Business Journal-Serving Metropolitan Kansas City* (Vol. 27, November 7, 2008, No. 9, pp. 1)
Pub: American City Business Journals, Inc.
Ed: Steve Vockrodt. **Description:** One local automobile dealer says that their sales are down by 30 to 40 percent and that car financing is now in the low 60 percentile from 85 to 88 percent. The National Automobile Dealers Association says that 700 dealerships are likely to be lost for 2008.

26083 ■ "Death Spiral" in *Business Journal Serving Greater Tampa Bay* (Vol. 30, October 29, 2010, No. 45, pp. 1)
Pub: Tampa Bay Business Journal
Ed: Margie Manning. **Description:** Bay Cities Bank has started working on the loan portfolio of its acquisition, Progress Bank of Florida. Regulators closed Progress Bank in October 2010 after capital collapsed due to charge-offs and increases in the provision for future loan losses.

26084 ■ "Debt Buyers Industry Rankings" in *Collections and Credit Risk* (Vol. 14, September 1, 2009, No. 8, pp. 19)
Pub: SourceMedia, Inc.
Description: Ranking of the top debt buyers in the United States in terms of the revenue generated in 2007 and 2088; statistical data included.

26085 ■ "Debt-Collection Agency to Lay Off 368 in Hampton Center" in *Virginian-Pilot* (December 4, 2010)
Pub: Virginian-Pilot
Ed: Tom Shean. **Description:** NCO Financial Systems Inc., provider of debt-collection and outsourcing services will permanently lay off 368 workers at its Hampton call center in 2011.

26086 ■ "Delinquent Properties on the Rise" in *Business Courier* (Vol. 27, June 11, 2010, No. 6, pp. 1)
Pub: Business Courier
Ed: Dan Monk. **Description:** Reports show that Cincinnati now ranks in the U.S. Top 20 for its delinquency rate on securitized commercial real estate loans. In December 2009, the region ranked 28th out of 50 cities studied by Trepp LLC. As of May 30, 2010, more than $378 million in commercial mortgage-backed security loans were more than 60 days past due.

26087 ■ *Design and Launch an Online Travel Business in a Week*
Pub: Entrepreneur Press
Ed: Charlene Davis. **Released:** May 1, 2009. **Price:** $17.95. **Description:** Guide providing techniques and professional advice for starting an online travel business. Tips are given to build a Website, find qualified providers and to set up a payment system.

26088 ■ "Developer Wins Bout with Bank in Roundabout Way" in *Tampa Bay Business Journal* (Vol. 30, January 29, 2010, No. 6, pp. 1)
Pub: American City Business Journals
Ed: Janet Leiser. **Description:** Developer Donald E. Phillips of Phillips Development and Realty LLC won against the foreclosure filed by First Horizon National Corporation, which is demanding the company to fully pay its $2.9 million loan. Phillips requested that his company pay monthly mortgage and extend the loan's maturity date.

26089 ■ "Dick Haskayne" in *Canadian Business* (Vol. 81, March 31, 2008, No. 5, pp. 72)
Pub: Rogers Media
Ed: Andy Holloway. **Description:** Dick Haskayne says that he learned a lot about business from his dad who ran a butcher shop where they had to make a decision on buying cattle and getting credit. Haskayne says that family, friends, finances, career, health, and infrastructure are benchmarks that have to be balanced.

26090 ■ "Direct Recovery Associates Debt Collection Agency Beats Industry Record" in *Internet Wire* (June 24, 2010)
Pub: Comtex
Description: Direct Recovery Associates Inc. was named as one of the highest collection records in the industry, which has consistently improved over 18 years. The firm is an international attorney-based debt collection agency.

26091 ■ "Direct Recovery Associates, Inc. Debt Collection Agency Founder Featured in China Daily" in *Internet Wire* (November 9, 2010)
Pub: Comtex
Description: Richard Hart, founder of Direct Recovery Associates, was featured in an article published in the China Daily. The article discussed the increased credit and debt collection demands involving the U.S. and China.

26092 ■ "Doctors, Health Insurers Squabble Over Who Sends Patients the Bill" in *Baltimore Business Journal* (Vol. 27, February 6, 2010)
Pub: American City Business Journals
Ed: Scott Graham. **Description:** Issue of allowing patients to send reimbursement checks to physicians who are not part of their health insurer's provider network is being debated in Maryland. Details on the proposed Maryland bill and the arguments presented by doctors and insurers are outlined.

26093 ■ "Don't Count Your Millions Yet" in *Business Courier* (Vol. 24, January 11, 2008, No. 40, pp. 1)
Pub: American City Business Journals, Inc.
Ed: Steve Watkins. **Description:** Merger and acquisition deals have been difficult to complete since 2007 largely due to a weaker economy and the credit crunch. Buyers have become more cautious because of the state of the economy and capital has become tougher to obtain because of the credit market crisis. The trends in mergers and acquisitions are analyzed further.

26094 ■ "Don't Expect Quick Fix" in *The Business Journal-Serving Metropolitan Kansas City* (Vol. 27, October 3, 2008, No. 3, pp. 1)
Pub: American City Business Journals, Inc.
Ed: James Dornbrook. **Description:** United States governmental entities cannot provide a quick fix solution to the current financial crisis. The economy requires a systemic change in the way people think about credit. The financial services industry should also focus on core lending principles.

26095 ■ "Don't Quit When The Road Gets Bumpy" in *Women Entrepreneur* (November 25, 2008)
Pub: Entrepreneur Media Inc.
Ed: Bonnie Price. **Description:** Discusses techniques four women entrepreneurs are utilizing to keep their businesses successful despite the credit crunch and the economic downturn.

26096 ■ "DST Turns to Banks for Credit" in *The Business Journal-Serving Metropolitan Kansas City* (Vol. 27, October 3, 2008, No. 3, pp. 1)
Pub: American City Business Journals, Inc.
Ed: Rob Roberts. **Description:** Kansas City, Missouri-based DST Systems Inc., a company that provides sophisticated information processing, computer software services and business solutions, has secured a new five-year, $120 million credit facility from Enterprise Bank and Bank of the West. The deal is seen to reflect that the region and community-banking model remain stable. Comments from executives are also provided.

26097 ■ *EBay Income: How ANYONE of Any Age, Location, and/or Background Can Build a Highly Profitable Online Business with eBay (Revised 2nd Edition)*
Pub: Atlantic Publishing Company
Released: December 1, 2010. **Price:** $24.95. **Description:** A complete overview of eBay is given and guides any small company through the entire process of creating the auction and auction strategies, photography, writing copy, text and formatting, multiple sales, programming tricks, PayPal, accounting, creating marketing, merchandising, managing email lists, advertising plans, taxes and sales tax, best time to list items and for how long, sniping programs, international customers, opening a storefront, electronic commerce, buy-it now pricing, keywords, Google marketing and eBay secrets.

26098 ■ "eBay Inc. Completes Acquisition of Zong" in *Benzinga.com* (October 29, 2011)
Pub: Benzinga.com
Ed: Benzinga Staff. **Description:** eBay Inc. acquired Zong, a provider of payments through mobile carrier billing. Terms of the agreement are outlined.

26099 ■ "eBay Introduces Open Commerce Ecosystem" in *Entertainment Close-Up* (October 24, 2011)
Pub: Close-Up Media
Description: eBay's new X.commerce is an open commerce ecosystem that will arm developers and merchants with the technology tools required to keep pace with the ever-changing industry. X.commerce brings together the technology assets and developer communities of eBay, PayPal, Magento and partners to expand on eBays vision for enabling commerce.

26100 ■ "Economic Trends for Small Business" in *Small Business Economic Trends* (April 2008, pp. 1)
Pub: National Federation of Independent Business
Ed: William C. Dunkelberg, Holly Wade. **Description:** Summary of economic trends for small busi-

nesses in the U.S. is presented. Economic indicators such as capital spending, inventories and sales, inflation, and profits are given. Analysis of credit markets is also provided.

26101 ■ "End of the Beginning" in *Canadian Business* (Vol. 81, November 10, 2008, No. 19, pp. 17)
Pub: Rogers Media Ltd.
Ed: David Wolf. **Description:** The freeze in the money markets and historic decline in equity markets around the world finally forced governments into aggressive coordinated action. The asset price inflation brought on by cheap credit will now work in reverse and the tightening of credit will be difficult economically. Canada is exposed to the fallout everywhere, given that the U.S, the U.K. and Japan buy 30 percent of Canada's output.

26102 ■ "Ethics Commission May Hire Collection Agency" in *Tulsa World* (August 21, 2010)
Pub: World Publishing
Ed: Barbara Hoberock. **Description:** Oklahoma Ethics Commission is considering a more to hire a collection agency or law firm in order to collect fees from candidates owing money for filing late financial reports.

26103 ■ "Experts: Market Shaky But Resilient" in *The Business Journal-Serving Metropolitan Kansas City* (Vol. 27, September 19, 2008, No. 1)
Pub: American City Business Journals, Inc.
Ed: Steve Vockrodt. **Description:** Investment advisers believe that the local investors in Kansas City who have a long-term approach towards their portfolios may come out even or even experience gains despite the Wall Street financial crisis. The impacts of the crisis are expected to take time to reach the area of Kansas City. The potential impacts of the Wall Street meltdown are examined further.

26104 ■ "Fannie and Freddie: How They'll Change" in *Business Week* (September 22, 2008, No. 4100, pp. 30)
Pub: McGraw-Hill Companies, Inc.
Ed: Jane Sasseen. **Description:** Three possible outcomes of the fate of struggling mortgage giants Freddie Mac and Fannie Mae after the government bailout are outlined.

26105 ■ "Fewer Banks Offer Big Gifts to Lure Clients" in *Globe & Mail* (March 14, 2006, pp. D1)
Pub: CTVglobemedia Publishing Inc.
Ed: Chris Reidy. **Description:** Fewer banks are offering gifts to lure the customers in this year in the wake of less favorable interest rates in the spring season. The market climate is analyzed.

26106 ■ "Fifth Third Grapples With Account Snafu" in *Business Courier* (Vol. 24, December 7, 2008, No. 34, pp. 1)
Pub: American City Business Journals, Inc.
Ed: Jon Newberry. **Description:** Fifth Third Bank's vendor committed an error which led to a badly damaged credit score for Brett and Karen Reloka. The couple reported the incident to the bank and are still waiting for action to be taken. A major outourced services vendor caused paid-off mortgages to be reported delinquent.

26107 ■ "Fight Ensues Over Irreplaceable Gowns" in *Tampa Bay Business Journal* (Vol. 30, January 15, 2010, No. 4, pp. 1)
Pub: American City Business Journals
Ed: Janet Leiser. **Description:** People's Princess Charitable Foundation Inc. founder Maureen Rorech Dunkel has sought Chapter 11 bankruptcy protection before a state court decides on the fate of the five of 13 Princess Diana Gowns. Dunkel and the nonprofit were sued by Patricia Sullivan of HRH Venture LLC who claimed they defaulted on $1.5 million in loans.

26108 ■ "Financing for NNSA Plant Is a Work in Progress" in *The Business Journal-Serving Metropolitan Kansas City* (October 24, 2008)
Pub: American City Business Journals, Inc.
Ed: Rob Roberts. **Description:** The Kansas City Council approved a development plan for a $500 million nuclear weapons parts plant in south Kansas City. The US Congress approved a $59 million annual lease payment to the plant's developer. Financing for the construction of the plant remains in question as the plant's developers have to shoulder construction costs.

26109 ■ "Finger-Pointing Time" in *Barron's* (Vol. 88, March 10, 2008, No. 10, pp. 9)
Pub: Dow Jones & Company, Inc.
Ed: Michael Santoli. **Description:** Discusses who is to blame for the financial crisis brought about by the credit crunch in the United States; the country's financial markets will eventually digest this crisis but will bottom out first before the situation improves.

26110 ■ "Firms Sue Doracon to Recoup More Than $1M in Unpaid Bills" in *Baltimore Business Journal* (Vol. 28, July 9, 2010, No. 9, pp. 1)
Pub: Baltimore Business Journal
Ed: Scott Dance. **Description:** Concrete supplier Paul J. Rach Inc., Selective Insurance Company, and equipment leasing firm Colonial Pacific Leasing Corporation intend to sue Baltimore, Maryland-based Doracon Contracting Inc. for $1 million in unpaid bills. Doracon owed Colonial Pacific $794,000 and the equipment is still in Doracon's possession. Selective Insurance and Paul J. Rach respectively seek $132,000 and $88,000.

26111 ■ "FirstMerit's Top Executive Turns Around Credit Quality" in *Crain's Cleveland Business* (Vol. 28, October 15, 2007, No. 41, pp. 3)
Pub: Crain Communications, Inc.
Ed: Shawn A. Turner. **Description:** Discusses the ways in which chairman and CEO Paul Greig has been able to improve FirstMerit Corp.'s credit quality and profit margin. Strategies included selling more than $70 million in bad loans, hiring a new chief credit officer and redirecting its focus on cross-selling its wealth and investment services to its commercial customers. Statistical data included.

26112 ■ "A Flawed Yardstick for Banks" in *Barron's* (Vol. 88, July 14, 2008, No. 28, pp. M6)
Pub: Dow Jones & Co., Inc.
Ed: Arindam Nag. **Description:** Return on equity is no longer the best measure for investors to judge banks by in a post-subprime-crises world. Investors should consider the proportion of a bank's total assets that are considered risky and look out for any write-downs of goodwill when judging a bank's financial health.

26113 ■ "Florida's Housing Gloom May Add To Woes of National City" in *Crain's Cleveland Business* (Vol. 28, October 29, 2007, No. 43, pp. 1)
Pub: Crain Communications, Inc.
Ed: Shawn A. Turner. **Description:** Already suffering by bad loans in the troubled mortgage market, National City Corp. is attempting to diversify its geographic presence beyond the slow-growth industrial Midwest by acquiring two Florida firms. Analysts worry that the acquisitions may end up making National City vulnerable to a takeover if the housing slump continues and credit quality becomes more of an issue for the bank.

26114 ■ "Florin Car Dealers Drive Plan" in *Sacramento Business Journal* (Vol. 25, August 22, 2008, No. 25, pp. 1)
Pub: American City Business Journals, Inc.
Ed: Melanie Turner. **Description:** Automobile dealers in Sacramento, California are working with the city and the business district in planning for future redevelopment in Florin Road. The move stemmed from pressure from the Elk Grove Auto Mall, high fuel prices and the credit crunch. The area has suffered business closures recently.

26115 ■ "Former Mayor Driving $500 Million Real Estate Equity Fund" in *The Business Journal - Serving Phoenix and the Valley of the Sun* (Vol. 28, August 15, 2008, No. 50, pp. 1)
Pub: American City Business Journals, Inc.
Ed: Jan Buchholz. **Description:** Paul John, the former mayor of Phoenix, is establishing a $500 million real estate asset management fund. The fund is dubbed Southwest Next Capital Management and has attracted three local partners, namely Joseph Meyer, Jay Michalowski, and James Mullany, who all have background in finance and construction.

26116 ■ "Gateway Delays Start" in *The Business Journal-Serving Metropolitan Kansas City* (Vol. 27, October 31, 2008, No. 8, pp. 1)
Pub: American City Business Journals, Inc.
Ed: Rob Roberts. **Description:** Economic problems caused, in part, by the Wall Street crisis has resulted in the setback of a proposed mixed-use redevelopment project, The Gateway. The $307 million project, which includes the Kansas Aquarium, will be delayed due to financing problems. Details of the project are given.

26117 ■ "Get Paid and Get Moving" in *Entrepreneur* (Vol. 37, October 2009, No. 10, pp. 38)
Pub: Entrepreneur Media, Inc.
Description: GoPayments application from Intuit allows mobile telephones to process payments like credit card terminals. The application costs $19.95 a month and can be used on the Internet browsers of mobile telephones.

26118 ■ *Get Your Credit Straight: A Sister's Guide to Ditching Your Debt, Mending Your Credit, and Building a Strong Financial Future*
Pub: Broadway Books
Ed: Glinda Bridgforth. **Price:** $19.95. **Description:** Third book in the series is aimed primarily at African American women and offers helpful and understandable information for a larger audience. The sidebars on how women in particular tend to get into credit trouble and ways they can increase their financial knowledge and reign in their spending habits are especially notable.

26119 ■ "Goodwill Haunts Local Companies; Bad Buyouts During Boom Times Producing Big Writedowns" in *Crain's Chicago Business* (Apr. 28, 2008)
Pub: Crain Communications, Inc.
Ed: Ann Saphir. **Description:** Many companies are having to face the reality that they overpaid for acquisitions made in better economic times; investors often dismiss such one-time charges as mere accounting adjustments but writeoffs related to past acquisitions can signal future problems because they mean the expected profits that justified the purchase have not materialized. Writeoffs are particularly worrisome for firms with a lot of debt and whose banks require them to have enough assets to back up their borrowings.

26120 ■ "The Great Deleveraging" in *Canadian Business* (Vol. 81, October 13, 2008, No. 17, pp. 45)
Pub: Rogers Media Ltd.
Ed: Jeff Sanford. **Description:** 'Hell Week' of financial crisis on Wall Street is believed to have started with the downgrade of AIG Inc.'s credit rating. AIG is a major player in the credit derivatives market, and its bankruptcy would have affected firms on Wall Street.

26121 ■ "The Great Fall" in *Barron's* (Vol. 88, March 10, 2008, No. 10, pp. 5)
Pub: Dow Jones & Company, Inc.
Ed: Alan Abelson. **Description:** Discusses the US economy is considered to be in a recession, with the effects of the credit crisis expected to intensify as a result. Inflation is estimated at 4.3 percent in January 2008, while 63,000 jobs were lost in February 2008.

26122 ■ "Grin and Bear It" in *Canadian Business* (Vol. 81, March 3, 2008, No. 3, pp. 53)
Pub: Rogers Media
Ed: Jeff Sanford. **Description:** Discusses the United States economic downturn, caused by the credit market crisis, which is expected to affect the Canadian economy, as Canada depend on the U.S. for 80 percent of its exports. Economist David Rosenberg

thinks that in 2008, housing prices will decline by 15 percent and gross domestic product growth will slow to 0.8 percent. Other forecasts for Canadian economy are given.

26123 ■ *Grow Your Money: 101 Easy Tips to Plan, Save and Invest*
Pub: HarperBusiness
Ed: Jonathan D. Pond. **Released:** December 2007. **Price:** $26.95. **Description:** In what should be required reading for anyone entering the work world, the author offers helpful investment and financial definitions, debt-management strategies, retirement and home ownerships considerations and more.

26124 ■ "Hank Paulson On the Housing Bailout and What's Ahead" in *Business Week* (September 22, 2008, No. 4100, pp. 19)
Pub: McGraw-Hill Companies, Inc.
Ed: Maria Bartiromo. **Description:** Interview with Treasury Secretary Henry Paulson in which he discusses the bailout of Fannie Mae and Freddie Mac as well as the potential impact on the American economy and foreign interests and investments in the country. Paulson has faith that the government's actions will help to stabilize the housing market.

26125 ■ "Hard Times for Hard Money" in *Sacramento Business Journal* (Vol. 25, July 18, 2008, No. 20, pp. 1)
Pub: American City Business Journals, Inc.
Ed: Michael Shaw. **Description:** Three private lenders who supplied $1 million sued VLD Realty, its associated companies and owners Volodymyr and Leonid Dubinsky accusing them of default after a plan to build two subdivisions fell through. Investigators are finding that borrowers and lenders ignored most rules on private investments on real estate.

26126 ■ "Hastily Enacted Regulation Will Not Cure Economic Crisis" in *Crain's Chicago Business* (Vol. 31, May 5, 2008, No. 18, pp. 18)
Pub: Crain Communications, Inc.
Ed: Stephen P. D'Arcy. **Description:** Policymakers are looking for ways to respond to what is possibly the greatest financial crisis of a generation due to the collapse of the housing market, the credit crisis and the volatility of Wall Street.

26127 ■ "HBC Sells Credit Card Division" in *Globe & Mail* (February 8, 2006, pp. B1)
Pub: CTVglobemedia Publishing Inc.
Ed: Sinclair Stewart; Marina Strauss. **Description:** The details on General Electric Co.'s acquisition of Hudson's Bay Co.'s credit card division, for $370 million, are presented.

26128 ■ "Headwinds From the New Sod Slow Aer Lingus" in *Barron's* (Vol. 88, March 10, 2008, No. 10, pp. M6)
Pub: Dow Jones & Company, Inc.
Ed: Sean Walters; Arindam Nag. **Description:** Aer Lingus faces a drop in its share prices with a falling US market, higher jet fuel prices, and lower long-haul passenger load factors. British media companies Johnston Press and Yell Group are suffering from weaker ad revenue and heavier debt payments due to the credit crunch.

26129 ■ "Health Providers Throw Lifeline to Clinics" in *Sacramento Business Journal* (Vol. 25, July 25, 2008, No. 21, pp. 1)
Pub: American City Business Journals, Inc.
Ed: Kathy Robertson. **Description:** Health Net of California Inc., Catholic Healthcare West and Sutter Health are each providing up to $5 million in no-interest and low-interest loans to clinics in California, while the Sisters of Mercy of the Americas Burlingame Regional Community is offering $300,000. Other details on the short term loans are discussed.

26130 ■ "High-End Jeweler Loses Street Sparkle" in *Houston Business Journal* (Vol. 40, November 27, 2009, No. 29, pp. 1)
Pub: American City Business Journals
Ed: Allison Wollam. **Description:** High-end jeweler Bailey Banks & Biddle's 7,000 square foot prototype store in Houston, Texas' CityCentre will be ceasing operations despite its parent company's filing for Chapter 11 protection from creditors. According to the bankruptcy filing, parent company Finlay Enterprises Inc. of New York intends to auction off its business and assets. Finlay has 67 Bailey Banks locations throughout the US.

26131 ■ "Hit the Green" in *Canadian Business* (Vol. 79, August 14, 2006, No. 16-17, pp. 73)
Pub: Rogers Media
Ed: Andrew Wahl. **Description:** Reorganization of the bankrupt 4everSports golf company in the United States is discussed.

26132 ■ *Home-Based Business for Dummies*
Pub: John Wiley and Sons, Inc.
Ed: Paul Edwards, Sarah Edwards, Peter Economy. **Released:** February 25, 2005. **Price:** $19.99. **Description:** Provides all the information needed to start and run a home-based business. Topics include: selecting the right business; setting up a home office; managing money, credit, and financing; marketing; and ways to avoid distractions while working at home.

26133 ■ "A Home of Her Own" in *Hawaii Business* (Vol. 53, October 2007, No. 4, pp. 51)
Pub: Hawaii Business Publishing
Ed: Maria Torres-Kitamura. **Description:** It was observed that the number of single women in Hawaii purchasing their own home has increased, as that in the whole United States where the percentage has increased from 14 percent in 1995 to 22 percent in 2006. However, First Hawaiian Bank's Wendy Lum thinks that the trend will not continue in Hawaii due to lending restrictions. The factors that women consider in buying a home of their own are presented.

26134 ■ "Homes Stall As Owners Resist Major Price Cuts" in *Crain's Chicago Business* (Vol. 31, April 21, 2008, No. 16, pp. 38)
Pub: Crain Communications, Inc.
Ed: Kevin Davis. **Description:** Discusses the high-end housing market and the owners who are resisting major price cuts as well as the buyers who look at long market times as a sign that something is wrong with the property.

26135 ■ "Hospitals Feel Pain from Slow Economy" in *Business Courier* (Vol. 27, September 3, 2010, No. 18, pp. 1)
Pub: Business Courier
Ed: James Ritchie. **Description:** Hospitals in Cincinnati, Ohio have suffered from decreased revenues owing to the economic crises. Declining patient volumes and bad debt have also adversely impacted hospitals.

26136 ■ *How to Collect Debts (And Still Keep Your Customers)*
Pub: Amacom
Ed: David Sher, Martin Sher. **Released:** May 1999. **Description:** Suggestions for collecting as much money as possible, as quickly as possible, while maintaining customer goodwill, along with strategies for eliminating bad debt.

26137 ■ *How to Write a Great Business Plan for Your Small Business in 60 Minutes or Less*
Pub: Atlantic Publishing
Ed: Sharon L. Fullen. **Released:** January 2006. **Price:** $39.95 includes CD-Rom. **Description:** A good business plan outlines goals and works as a company's resume to obtain funding, credit from suppliers, management of the operations and finances, promotion and marketing, and more.

26138 ■ "If You Go Into the Market Today..." in *Canadian Business* (Vol. 82, Summer 2009, No. 8, pp. 18)
Pub: Rogers Media
Ed: Jeff Sanford. **Description:** Opinions of experts and personalities who are known to have bear attitudes towards the economy were presented in the event 'A Night with the Bears' in Toronto in April 2009. Known bears that served as resource persons in the event were Nouriel Roubini, Eric Sprott, Ian Gordon, and Meredith Whitney. The bears were observed to have differences regarding consumer debt.

26139 ■ "Illinois Regulators Revoke Collection Agency's License" in *Collections & Credit Risk* (Vol. 15, August 1, 2010, No. 7, pp. 13)
Pub: SourceMedia Inc.
Description: Creditors Service Bureau of Springfield, Illinois had its license revoked by a state regulatory agency and was fined $55,000 because the owner and president, Craig W. Lewis, did not turn over portions of collected funds to clients.

26140 ■ "Insider" in *Canadian Business* (Vol. 81, March 31, 2008, No. 5, pp. 76)
Pub: Rogers Media
Ed: John Gray. **Description:** Discusses a comparison of an average Canadian family's finances in 1990 with the data from 2007. The average family in 2007 has over $80,000 in debt compared to just under $52,000 in 1990. However, Canadians have also been accumulating solid assets such as homes and stocks. This means that Canadian debt load has fallen from 22 percent in 1990 to 20 percent in 2007 when taken as a percentage of total net worth.

26141 ■ "Karen Case; President of Commercial Real Estate Lending, Privatebancorp Inc." in *Crain's Chicago Business* (May 5, 2008)
Pub: Crain Communications, Inc.
Ed: Dee Gill. **Description:** Profile of Karen Case who was hired by PrivateBancorp Inc. to turn its minor share of the city's commercial real estate lending market into a major one.

26142 ■ "Kenosha 'Lifestyle Center' Delayed" in *The Business Journal-Milwaukee* (Vol. 25, August 8, 2008, No. 46, pp. A1)
Pub: American City Business Journals, Inc.
Ed: Rich Kirchen. **Description:** Quality Centers of Orlando, Florida has postponed construction plans for the Kenosha Town Center in Kenosha County, Wisconsin to 2009 due to the economic downturn and lending concerns. The $200-million, 750,000-square-foot retail and residential center will be located near the corner of Wisconsin Highway 50 and I-94.

26143 ■ "Kimball Hill Files for Chapter 11" in *Crain's Chicago Business* (Vol. 31, April 28, 2008, No. 17, pp. 12)
Pub: Crain Communications, Inc.
Description: Homebuilder Kimball Hill filed for Chapter 11 bankruptcy protection after months of negotiations with lenders. The firm plans to continue operations as it restructures its debt.

26144 ■ "Laugh or Cry?" in *Barron's* (Vol. 88, March 24, 2008, No. 12, pp. 7)
Pub: Dow Jones & Company, Inc.
Ed: Alan Abelson. **Description:** Discusses the American economy which is just starting to feel the effect of the credit and housing crises. JPMorgan Chase purchased Bear Stearns for $2 a share, much lower than its share price of $60, while quasi-government entities Fannie Mae and Freddie Mac are starting to run into trouble.

26145 ■ "Leaders Weigh In On Fannie Mae, Freddie Mac Failure, Fed Bailout" in *The Business Journal - Serving Phoenix and the Valley of the Sun* (Vol. 28, September 12, 2008, No. 53, pp. 1)
Pub: American City Business Journals, Inc.
Ed: Chris Casacchia; Mike Sunnucks; Jan Buchholz. **Description:** Fannie Mae and Freddie Mac's federal takeover was a move to help stabilize the financial market and it helped bring down interest rates in the past week. Local executives from Arizona's Phoenix area share their thoughts on the immediate effect of the takeover and its upside and downside.

26146 ■ "Lehman's Hail Mary Pass" in *Business Week* (September 22, 2008, No. 4100, pp. 28)
Pub: McGraw-Hill Companies, Inc.
Ed: Matthew Goldstein; David Henry; Ben Levison. **Description:** Overview of Lehman Brothers' CEO Richard Fuld's plan to keep the firm afloat and end

the stock's plunge downward; Fuld's strategy calls for selling off a piece of the firm's investment management business.

26147 ■ "Lenders" in *The Business Journal - Serving Phoenix and the Valley of the Sun* (Vol. 28, July 25, 2008, No. 47, pp. 1)
Pub: American City Business Journals, Inc.
Ed: Jan Buchholz. **Description:** Private equity lender Investor Mortgage Holdings Inc. has continued growing despite the crisis surrounding the real estate and financial industries and has accumulated a $700 million loan portfolio. Private lending has become increasingly important in financing real estate deals as commercial credit has dried up.

26148 ■ "Lending Door Slams" in *Puget Sound Business Journal* (Vol. 29, October 24, 2008, No. 27, pp. 1)
Pub: American City Business Journals
Ed: Jeanne Lang Jones, Kirsten Grind. **Description:** KeyBank's closure of its Puget Sound unit that services single-family homebuilders is part of a nationwide shutdown that includes similar closures in other cities. Bank of America is adopting more conservative terms for homebuilding loans while Union Bank of California is still offering credit for market rate housing.

26149 ■ "The Letter of the Law" in *Collections and Credit Risk* (Vol. 14, November 1, 2009, No. 9, pp. 40)
Pub: SourceMedia, Inc.
Ed: Michelle Dunn. **Description:** Analyzes the regulatory landscape regarding debt collection and the ways in which those in the field are dealing with a tough economy, unclear laws and the newest regulations.

26150 ■ "A Limited Sphere of Influence" in *Mergers & Acquisitions: The Dealmaker's Journal* (March 1, 2008)
Pub: SourceMedia, Inc.
Ed: Ken MacFadyen. **Description:** Changes to the interest rate has had little impact on the mergers and acquisitions market since the federal funds rate does not link directly to the liquidity available to the M&A market; lenders are looking at cash flows and are likely to remain cautious due to other factors impacting the market.

26151 ■ "Local Firms Will Feel Impact Of Wall St. Woes" in *The Business Journal-Milwaukee* (Vol. 25, September 19, 2008, No. 52, pp. A1)
Pub: American City Business Journals, Inc.
Ed: Rich Kirchen. **Description:** Wall Street's crisis is expected to affect businesses in Wisconsin, in terms of decreased demand for services and products and increased financing costs. Businesses in Milwaukee area may face higher interest rates and tougher loan standards. The potential impacts of the Wall Street crisis on local businesses are examined further.

26152 ■ "Local M&A Activity Sputters in 1Q" in *Crain's Chicago Business* (Vol. 31, April 21, 2008, No. 16, pp. 20)
Pub: Crain Communications, Inc.
Ed: H. Lee Murphy. **Description:** Local mergers-and-acquisitions activity is down by 34 percent in the first quarter compared to the fourth quarter of last year due to the credit crisis making financing harder to obtain.

26153 ■ "Marine Act Amendments Gain Parliamentary Approval" in *Canadian Sailings* (July 7, 2008)
Pub: Commonwealth Business Media
Ed: Alex Binkley. **Description:** Changes to the Canada Marine Act provides better borrowing deals as well as an ability to tap into federal infrastructure funding for environmental protection measures, security improvements and other site enhancements.

26154 ■ "Mass Mailers Try to Lick Rising Postal Rates" in *Crain's Detroit Business* (Vol. 24, March 10, 2008, No. 10, pp. 6)
Pub: Crain Communications, Inc.
Ed: Sherri Begin. **Description:** Discusses the ways in which companies are trying to mitigate the effect of rising postal costs.

26155 ■ "Measuring the Impact" in *Mergers & Acquisitions: The Dealmaker's Journal* (March 1, 2008)
Pub: SourceMedia, Inc.
Ed: Ken MacFadyen. **Description:** Discusses a new study out of Europe which contends that the private equity market does not have as much impact on the overall economy as critics contend.

26156 ■ "Media Industry Collection Agency Completes Acquisition" in *Collections & Credit Risk* (Vol. 15, December 1, 2010, No. 11, pp. 22)
Pub: SourceMedia Inc.
Description: Media Receivable Management Inc. (MRM) will take over the collection operations at Borden, Jones & Mitchell, in Miami, Florida. MRM clients are basically magazine and electronic media publishers.

26157 ■ "Midwest Seeks Concessions From Creditors" in *The Business Journal-Milwaukee* (Vol. 25, July 25, 2008, No. 44, pp. A1)
Pub: American City Business Journals, Inc.
Ed: Rich Rovito. **Description:** Midwest Airlines Inc. is turning to creditors and lease holders for the financial aspect of its restructuring, which involves going back to serving popular business destinations. Chief executive officer Timothy believes that the company can survive in a niche market as long as it provides quality service. He discusses Midwest's restructuring plan.

26158 ■ "More Ad Shops Link Payment to Results" in *Boston Business Journal* (Vol. 30, November 12, 2010, No. 42, pp. 1)
Pub: Boston Business Journal
Ed: Lisa van der Pool. **Description:** A growing number of advertising firms are proposing a 'value-based' payment scheme where they are paid a base fee plus a bonus if certain sales goals or other targets are met. The proposed shift in payment scheme is seen as reminiscent of the dot-com boom about ten years ago. Advertising firms are traditionally paid by the hour.

26159 ■ "Mortgage Securities Drop Hits Home" in *The Business Journal-Serving Metropolitan Kansas City* (Vol. 27, October 17, 2008, No. 5)
Pub: American City Business Journals, Inc.
Ed: Rob Roberts. **Description:** Sale of commercial mortgage-backed securities (CMBS) in Kansas City, Missouri have declined. The area may avoid layoffs if the United States government succeeds in stabilizing the economy. Major CMBS players in the area include Midland Loan Services Inc. and KeyBank Real Estate Capital.

26160 ■ "Mr. Deeds" in *Canadian Business* (Vol. 81, March 31, 2008, No. 5, pp. 24)
Pub: Rogers Media
Ed: Thomas Watson. **Description:** Ron Sandler has the right experience to save Northern Rock PLC get through its liquidity problems. Sandler is known for saving Lloyd's of London in the mid-90's and he is not afraid to make enemies. Ron Sandler's assignment to help Northern Rock comes at a time when the health of the U.K. housing is not great.

26161 ■ "Muddy Portfolio Raises a Question: Just What Is National City Worth?" in *Crain's Detroit Business* (Vol. 24, April 7, 2008, No. 14)
Pub: Crain Communications, Inc.
Ed: Jay Miller. **Description:** National City Bank is looking at strategies to help it deal with its credit and loan problems which are reflected in its falling stock price. One possible solution is a merger with another bank, however most national banks are facing their own home-loan portfolio issues and may be unable to tackle another company's unresolved problems. Statistical data included.

26162 ■ "Needed: A Strategy; Banking In China" in *The Economist* (Vol. 390, January 3, 2009, No. 8612, pp. 54)
Pub: The Economist Newspaper Inc.
Description: International banks are competing for a role in China but are finding obstacles in their paths such as a reduction in the credit their operations may receive from Chinese banks and the role they can play in the public capital markets which remain limited.

26163 ■ "A New Kid on the Block" in *Barron's* (Vol. 88, March 17, 2008, No. 11, pp. 58)
Pub: Dow Jones & Company, Inc.
Ed: Thomas G. Donlan. **Description:** Discusses the Federal Reserve which has offered to lend $100 billion in cash to banks and $200 billion in Treasuries to Wall Street investment banks that have problems with liquidity. The reluctance of the banks to lend money to meet a margin call on securities that could still depreciate is the reason why the agency is going into the direct loan business.

26164 ■ "New Money" in *Entrepreneur* (Vol. 36, February 2008, No. 2, pp. 62)
Pub: Entrepreneur Media Inc.
Ed: C.J. Prince. **Description:** Tips on how to handle business finance, with regard to the tightened credit standards imposed by leading institutions, are provided. These include: selling receivables, margining blue chips, and selling purchase orders.

26165 ■ "New York Collection Agency's Bribery Case Resolved" in *Collections & Credit Risk* (Vol. 15, August 1, 2010, No. 7, pp. 19)
Pub: SourceMedia Inc.
Description: Criminal conviction and civil settlement in a bribery case and Medicaid scam involving H.I.S. Holdings Inc. and owner Deborah Kantor is examined.

26166 ■ "The Next Government Bailout?" in *Barron's* (Vol. 88, March 10, 2008, No. 10, pp. 21)
Pub: Dow Jones & Company, Inc.
Ed: Jonathan Laing. **Description:** Fannie Mae may need a government bailout as it faces huge hits brought about by the effects of the housing crisis. The shares of the government-sponsored enterprise have dropped 65 percent since the housing crisis began.

26167 ■ "No More Debt" in *Black Enterprise* (Vol. 37, November 2006, No. 4, pp. 159)
Pub: Earl G. Graves Publishing Co. Inc.
Ed: Tanisha A. Sykes. **Description:** Eliminating debt is not necessarily easy and can be overwhelming. Here are some tips for reducing and eventually getting out of debt.

26168 ■ "Not Enough To Go Around" in *The Business Journal-Milwaukee* (Vol. 25, August 15, 2008, No. 47, pp. A1)
Pub: American City Business Journals, Inc.
Ed: David Doege. **Description:** Most of the creditors of bankrupt real estate developer Scott Fergus are likely to remain unpaid as he only has an estimated $30,000 available for paying debts. Creditors, as of the 13 August 2008 deadline for filing claims, have filed a total of $79.1 million in claims.

26169 ■ "A Novel Fix for the Credit Mess" in *Barron's* (Vol. 88, March 31, 2008, No. 13, pp. 10)
Pub: Dow Jones & Company, Inc.
Ed: Michael Santoli. **Description:** Due to the common bank-leverage factor of 10, the $250 billion of lost bank capital would have supported $2.5 trillion in lending capacity. Jeffrey Lewis suggests onerous regulations on bank-holding companies that own 10 to 25 percent, as they are partly to blame. Statistical data included.

26170 ■ "Ohio Collection Agency Settles Second Lawsuit" in *Collections & Credit Risk* (Vol. 15, July 1, 2010, No. 6, pp. 9)
Pub: SourceMedia Inc.
Description: National Enterprise Systems, will pay $75,000 for illegal and abusive collection charged in a lawsuit filed by West Virginia's Attorney General's office. Money will be used to reimburse students and consumers who paid the illegal fees to the company.

26171 ■ "OK, Bring in the Lawyers" in *Crain's Chicago Business* (Vol. 31, November 17, 2008, No. 46, pp. 26)
Pub: Crain Communications, Inc.
Ed: Daniel Rome Levine. **Description:** Bankruptcy attorneys are finding the economic and credit crisis a benefit for their businesses due to the high number of business owners and mortgage holders that are need of their services. One Chicago firm is handling ten times the number of cases they did the previous year and of that about 80 percent of their new clients are related to the real estate sector.

26172 ■ *The One Minute Entrepreneur*
Pub: Doubleday
Ed: Ken Blanchard; assisted by Don Hutson and Ethan Willis. **Released:** 2008. **Price:** $19.95. **Description:** Four traditional business ideas are covered including: revenue needs to exceed expenses, bill collection, customer service, and employee motivation in order to be successful.

26173 ■ "Opportunity Now Lies at Short End of the Market" in *Barron's* (Vol. 88, June 30, 2008, No. 26, pp. M9)
Pub: Dow Jones & Co., Inc.
Ed: Michael S. Derby. **Description:** Renewed credit concerns and the lesser chance of a Federal Reserve interest rate hike boosted the bond market. Some portfolio managers are more bullish on short-dated securities as they expect the market to adjust to a more appropriate outlook.

26174 ■ "Pay Me! How to Get the Money You're Owed When No One Seems to Have Any" in *Entrepreneur* (Vol. 37, July 2009, No. 7, pp. 49)
Pub: Entrepreneur Media, Inc.
Ed: Randy B. Hecht. **Description:** How certain collections scenarios with clients, who have already fallen behind on their payments, should be handled is discussed. During a down economy, business owners should properly manage collection and billing because this can actually strengthen client relationships. Insights on hiring a collections agency are also presented.

26175 ■ "A Pioneer of Paying With Plastic" in *Crain's Chicago Business* (Vol. 31, April 28, 2008, No. 17, pp. 39)
Pub: Crain Communications, Inc.
Ed: Phuong Ly. **Description:** Profile of Perfect Plastic Printing Corp., a family-owned company which manufactures credit cards, bank cards and gift cards and whose sales hit $50.1 million last year, a 16 percent jump from 2006.

26176 ■ "Placer Land Sells for $12 Million" in *Sacramento Business Journal* (Vol. 25, July 25, 2008, No. 21, pp. 1)
Pub: American City Business Journals, Inc.
Ed: Michael Shaw; Celia Lamb. **Description:** Reynen & Bardis Communities Inc., a Sacramento, California-based homebuilder, has purchased the Antonio Mountain Ranch in Placer County, California shortly before the property's scheduled foreclosure on June 27, 2008. Placer County Recorder's data show that the purchase price of the 808-acre wetland-rich property is $12 million.

26177 ■ "Port Authority Taking Heat in Kenwood Mess" in *Business Courier* (Vol. 26, September 18, 2009, No. 21, pp. 1)
Pub: American City Business Journals, Inc.
Ed: Dan Monk. **Description:** Port of Greater Cincinnati Development Authority is being criticized for not requiring payment and performance bonds to ensure that contractors would be paid. The criticism occurred after the general contractor for the project to build a parking garage at Kenwood Towne Plaza stopped paying its subcontractors.

26178 ■ "Portfolio Recovery Associates Expands Its Hampton Call Center" in *Internet Wire* (January 20, 2010)
Pub: Comtex News Network, Inc.
Description: Entering into a lease amendment in order to expand its Hampton, Virginia call center and extend its lease agreement, Portfolio Recovery Associates, Inc., a company that collects, purchases and manages defaulted consumer debt, plans to upgrade the existing space enabling them to draw on local talent.

26179 ■ *Practical Debt Collecting for Small Companies and Traders*
Pub: Meadow Books
Ed: Robin Evelegh. **Released:** December 2006. **Price:** $12.99. **Description:** Credit and collection guide for small companies.

26180 ■ "Prepaid Phones Surge in Bad Economy" in *Advertising Age* (Vol. 79, November 17, 2008, No. 43, pp. 6)
Pub: Crain Communications, Inc.
Ed: Rita Chang. **Description:** Prepay cell phone offerings are becoming increasingly competitive amid a greater choice of plans and handsets. In an economic environment in which many consumers are unable to pass the credit checks required for traditional cell phone plans, the prepay market is surging.

26181 ■ "Private Equity Firms Shopping Valley For Deals" in *The Business Journal - Serving Phoenix and the Valley of the Sun* (Vol. 29, September 19, 2008, No. 3, pp. 1)
Pub: American City Business Journals, Inc.
Ed: Mike Sunnucks. **Description:** Private equity firms from California, Boston, New York, and overseas are expected to invest in growth-oriented real estate markets that include Phoenix. Real estate experts revealed that privately held investment and acquisition firms are looking to invest in real estate markets hit by the housing crisis. Views and information on private equity firms' real estate investments are presented.

26182 ■ "Put It on MasterCard" in *Barron's* (Vol. 89, July 27, 2009, No. 30, pp. 16)
Pub: Dow Jones & Co., Inc.
Ed: Bill Alpert. **Description:** Shares of MasterCard trade at a discount at just 15 times its anticipated earnings and some believe that these shares may be a better play in an economic recovery. The prospects of these shares are compared with those of Visa.

26183 ■ "?Que Pasa? A Canadian-Cuban Credit Card Crisis" in *Canadian Business* (Vol. 81, March 31, 2008, No. 5, pp. 10)
Pub: Rogers Media
Ed: Geoff Kirbyson. **Description:** Discusses the acquisition of CUETS Financial Ltd. by the Bank of America which means that CUETS-issued credit cards in Cuba are worthless since U.S. laws prohibit transactions from Cuba and other sanctioned countries. CUETS members are advised to take multiple payment methods to Cuba.

26184 ■ "RBC Holds Inside Card With HBC Credit Assets" in *Globe & Mail* (January 25, 2006, pp. B1)
Pub: CTVglobemedia Publishing Inc.
Ed: Marina Strauss; Sinclair Stewart. **Description:** Hudson's Bay Co. (HBC) signed co-branding credit card agreement with Royal Bank of Canada are presented. The significance of the deal for HBC is discussed.

26185 ■ "Ready for a Rally?" in *The Economist* (Vol. 390, January 3, 2009, No. 8612, pp. 54)
Pub: The Economist Newspaper Inc.
Description: Analysts predict that the recession could end by 2010. The current economic crisis is presented in detail.

26186 ■ "Recession-Proof Your Startup" in *Crain's Chicago Business* (Vol. 31, November 10, 2008, No. 45, pp. 24)
Pub: Crain Communications, Inc.
Description: Detailed information concerning ways in which to start a business during an economic crisis is provided. Ways in which to find financing, the importance of a solid business plan, customer service, problem-solving and finding the right niche for the region are also discussed.

26187 ■ "Refi Requests Soar, But New Rules May Mean Fewer Closings" in *The Business Review Albany* (Vol. 35, April 4, 2008, No. 53, pp. 1)
Pub: The Business Review
Ed: Barbara Pinckney. **Description:** National refinancing applications grew by 82 percent in the week that ended March 21, 2008, due to the depressed real estate market and lower interest rates. Refinancing applicants, however, may be surprised with new rules on loan applications such as the required credit score of at least 720 in avoiding payment of extra fees. The developments in application standards for home loans are also examined.

26188 ■ "Regulators Revoke Mann Bracken's Collection Agency Licenses" in *Collections & Credit Risk* (Vol. 15, September 1, 2010, No. 8, pp. 19)
Pub: SourceMedia Inc.
Description: Maryland regulators have revoked the collections licenses of defunct law firm Mann Bracken LLP.

26189 ■ "Research and Markets Adds Report: Credit and Collection Practices 2009" in *Wireless News* (August 12, 2009)
Pub: Close-Up Media
Description: Research and Markets announced the addition of the "Credit and Collection Practices 2009" report which will highlight credit and collection industry practices and technologies. The report also includes an overview of the best practices in the field.

26190 ■ "Research Reports" in *Barron's* (Vol. 88, March 24, 2008, No. 12, pp. M10)
Pub: Dow Jones & Company, Inc.
Description: Investors are recommending purchasing shares of Ampco Pittsburgh due to an expected surge in earnings. Deteriorating credit quality presents problems for the shares of BankAtlantic Bancorp, whose price targets have been lowered from $7 to $5 each. Shares of Helicos Biosciences are expected to move sideways from their $6 level. Statistical data included.

26191 ■ "Return to Wealth; Bank Strategy" in *The Economist* (Vol. 390, January 3, 2009, No. 8612, pp. 56)
Pub: The Economist Newspaper Inc.
Description: UBS' strategy to survive these trying economic times is presented. Statistical data included. UBS has a stronger balance-sheet than most of its investment-banking peers and has reduced its portfolio.

26192 ■ "'Rocket Docket' Leaves Memphis Debtors Behind" in *Commercial Appeal* (November 28, 2009)
Pub: Commercial Appeal
Ed: Bartholomew Sullivan. **Description:** According to an investigation by the Scripps Howard News Service, Memphians lodged 807 formal complaints about debt-collection practices to the Federal Trade Commission in a 2 1/2 -year period ending in July; Nearly 1/3 of the complaints involved some type of error with the debt in question. The majority of the complaints were leveled at NCO Group, which also generated the most complaints around the country.

26193 ■ "Running the Numbers" in *Entrepreneur* (Vol. 37, July 2009, No. 7, pp. 87)
Pub: Entrepreneur Media, Inc.
Ed: Carol Tice. **Description:** Ways in which entrepreneurs can assess if they are ready to be a multi-unit franchisee are presented. Choosing the right locations, knowing how much assistance they can get from the franchisor, and financing are the key considerations when planning additional franchise units. Examples of success in multi-unit operations and multi-unit terms are also presented.

26194 ■ *Save Your Small Business: 10 Crucial Strategies to Survive Hard Times or Close Down and Move On*
Pub: NOLO
Ed: Ralph Warner, Bethany Laurence. **Released:** August 1, 2009. **Price:** $29.99. **Description:** According to a study among 500 businesses, 44 percent

used credit cards in order to meet their firm's needs in the previous six months. Written by a business owner, this book provides twelve strategies to protect personal assets from creditors and survive the current recession.

26195 ■ "SEC Report On Rating Agencies Falls Short" in *Barron's* (Vol. 88, July 14, 2008, No. 28, pp. 35)
Pub: Dow Jones & Co., Inc.
Ed: Jack Willoughby. **Description:** The Securities and Exchange Commissions report on credit-rating firms should have drawn attention to the slipshod practices in the offerings of collateralized debt obligations. The report fell short of prescribing correctives for the flawed system of these agencies' relationship with their clients.

26196 ■ "Sentiment Split on Financials" in *Barron's* (Vol. 88, March 24, 2008, No. 12, pp. M14)
Pub: Dow Jones & Company, Inc.
Ed: Steven M. Sears. **Description:** Experts in the financial sector are split as to whether or not the worst of the financial crisis brought on by the credit crunch is over. Some options traders are trading on are defensive puts, expecting the worst, while investors buying calls are considered as bullish.

26197 ■ "Shopped Out; Retailing Gloom" in *The Economist* (Vol. 390, January 3, 2009, No. 8612, pp. 26)
Pub: The Economist Newspaper Inc.
Description: Economic volatility in the retail sector is having an impact on a number of countries around the globe. Europe is experiencing hard economic times as well and unless businesses have a strong business plan banks feel unable to lend the money necessary to tide the retailers over. The falling pound has increased the cost of imported goods and small to midsize retail chains may not be able to weather such an unforgiving economic climate.

26198 ■ "'Short Sales,' A Sign of Housing Troubles, Start Popping Up" in *The Business Review Albany* (Vol. 35, April 11, 2008, No. 1, pp. 1)
Pub: The Business Review
Ed: Michael DeMasi. **Description:** Discusses the number of short sales, where homeowners ask banks to forgive part of their mortgages to sell the properties, which is starting to increase in the Albany, New York area. Real estate agents in the area are taking up crash courses in short selling.

26199 ■ "A Slice of Danish; Fixing Finance" in *The Economist* (Vol. 390, January 3, 2009, No. 8612, pp. 55)
Pub: The Economist Newspaper Inc.
Description: Denmark's mortgage-holders and the county's lending system is presented.

26200 ■ "Small Business Credit Conditions" in *Small Business Economic Trends* (April 2008, pp. 12)
Pub: National Federation of Independent Business
Ed: William C. Dunkelberg, Holly Wade. **Description:** Graphs and tables that present the credit conditions of small businesses in the U.S. are provided. The tables include figures on availability of loans, interest rates, and expected credit conditions.

26201 ■ *The Small Business Owner's Manual: Everything You Need to Know to Start Up and Run Your Business*
Pub: Career Press, Incorporated
Ed: Joe Kennedy. **Released:** June 2005. **Price:** $19.99 (US), $26.95 (Canadian). **Description:** Comprehensive guide for starting a small business, focusing on twelve ways to obtain financing, business plans, selling and advertising products and services, hiring and firing employees, setting up a Web site, business law, accounting issues, insurance, equipment, computers, banks, financing, customer credit and collection, leasing, and more.

26202 ■ *Small Business Survival Guide*
Pub: Adams Media Corporation
Ed: Cliff Ennico. **Price:** $12.95. **Description:** Small business expert provides strategies to start a company and survive in the 21st Century. He shows small business owners how to succeed despite challenges that can defeat any firm. His advice covers suppliers; customers and contractors; competitors and creditors; spouses, family and friends; as well as the ways lawyers, accountants and other can steal an entrepreneur's success. Ennico also describes how startups can comply with local regulations.

26203 ■ *Small Business Survival Guide: Starting, Protecting, and Securing Your Business for Long-Term Success*
Pub: Adams Media Corporation
Ed: Cliff Ennico. **Released:** September 2005. **Price:** $12.95 (US), $17.95 (Canadian). **Description:** Entrepreneurship in the new millennium. Topics include creditors, taxes, competition, business law, and accounting.

26204 ■ "Startup to Serve Bar Scene" in *Austin Business JournalInc.* (Vol. 29, December 18, 2009, No. 41, pp. 1)
Pub: American City Business Journals
Ed: Christopher Calnan. **Description:** Startup ATX Innovation Inc. of Austin, Texas has developed a test version of TabbedOut, a Web-based tool that would facilitate mobile phone-based restaurant and bar bill payment. TabbedOut has been tested by six businesses in Austin and will be available to restaurant and bar owners for free. Income would be generated by ATX through a 99-cent convenience charge per transaction.

26205 ■ "State Budget Woes Hurt Many Vendors, Senior Services" in *Sacramento Business Journal* (Vol. 25, August 15, 2008, No. 24, pp. 1)
Pub: American City Business Journals, Inc.
Ed: Melanie Turner. **Description:** Delays in the passage of the California state budget have adversely affected the health care industry. The Robertson Adult Day Health Care had taken out loans to keep the business afloat. The state Legislature has reduced Medi-Cal reimbursement to health care providers by 10 percent.

26206 ■ "State Targets Credit Fixers" in *Business Journal-Portland* (Vol. 24, October 12, 2007, No. 33, pp. 1)
Pub: American City Business Journals, Inc.
Ed: Andy Giegerich, Justin Matlick. **Description:** Number of companies that offer quick fix to consumers is growing; the State of Oregon is considering rules to target them. A group working on a study in the state's mortgage lending regulations could craft bills to be examined for legislative session in February 2008.

26207 ■ "Stuck With Two Mortgages; The Nightmare When Buyers Upgrade" in *Crain's Chicago Business* (Vol. 31, April 21, 2008, No. 16)
Pub: Crain Communications, Inc.
Ed: Darci Smith. **Description:** Discusses the problem a number of people are facing due to the slump in the housing market: being stuck with two mortgages when they move because their former homes have not sold. Many thought they could afford to move to a larger home, anticipating significant equity appreciation that did not occur; now they are left with lowering their price and competing with the host of new developments.

26208 ■ "Summary. Economic Trends for Small Business" in *Small Business Economic Trends* (February 2008, pp. 1)
Pub: National Federation of Independent Business
Ed: William C. Dunkelberg, Holly Wade. **Description:** Summary of economic trends for small businesses in the U.S. is provided. Economic indicators such as capital spending, inventories and sales, inflation, and profits are given. Analysis of credit markets is also provided.

26209 ■ "Sunwest Vies To Stave Off Bankruptcy" in *The Business Journal-Portland* (Vol. 25, August 15, 2008, No. 23, pp. 1)
Pub: American City Business Journals, Inc.
Ed: Robin J. Moody. **Description:** Sunwest Management Inc. is teetering on the edge of bankruptcy as creditors start foreclosure on nine of their properties. This could potentially displace residents of the assisted living operator. Sunwest is trying to sell smaller packages of properties to get a $100 million bridge loan to maintain operations.

26210 ■ "The Survey Says" in *Collections and Credit Risk* (Vol. 14, September 1, 2009, No. 8, pp. 16)
Pub: SourceMedia, Inc.
Ed: Bill Grabarek; Darren Waggoner. **Description:** Revenue for the top accounts receivable management firms rose nearly 20 percent in 2008 despite lower liquidation rates, a poor economy and riskier, albeit cheaper debt portfolios; the trend may continue this year as collection agencies expect revenue, on average, to increase 5.8 percent. Debt buyers, however, found that their revenue fell nearly 7 percent in 2008 and expect it to fall another 12 percent this year.

26211 ■ "Survival Guide: There Can Be an Upside to Managing a Downturn" in *Canadian Business* (Vol. 81, November 10, 2008, No. 19, pp. 54)
Pub: Rogers Media Ltd.
Ed: Sharda Prashad. **Description:** Canada-based Foxy is already limiting its exposure to retailers who could be a credit problem in case of recession. Retirement Life Communities is entering into fixed-rate and fixed-term loans for them to have sufficient financing to grow. Business owners need to realize that customers want more for less.

26212 ■ "Taking Collections" in *Investment Dealers' Digest* (Vol. 75, October 9, 2009, No. 38, pp. 19)
Pub: SourceMedia, Inc.
Ed: Aleksandrs Rozens. **Description:** Although the nation's debt-collection industry has grown with increased reliance by consumers on credit, valuations of these firms have lessened due to the economy which has hurt some of the success of these firms in obtaining the debt back from consumers who are experiencing trying economic times.

26213 ■ "Tampa Bay's CMBS Exposure Looms Large" in *Tampa Bay Business Journal* (Vol. 30, December 4, 2009, No. 50, pp. 1)
Pub: American City Business Journals
Ed: Margie Manning. **Description:** Tampa, Florida's metropolitan statistical area have listed 50 to 601 commercial mortgage-backed securities loans as delinquent with a total delinquent loan balance of $439 million. The total was 9.7 percent of the $4.5 billion loans outstanding and was higher than the delinquency rate in New York and Los Angeles.

26214 ■ "Too Much Information?" in *Black Enterprise* (Vol. 37, December 2006, No. 5, pp. 59)
Pub: Earl G. Graves Publishing Co. Inc.
Ed: James C. Johnson. **Description:** African American business owners often face the dilemma of whether or not to divulge their minority status when soliciting new customers and financial institutions. The quality of the products or services is always the key factor and race should never define one's business; however, it is appropriate to market oneself as a minority or women-owned business, especially if the company is in an industry where those clients are offered top-tier contracts.

26215 ■ "Too Much too Soon" in *Barron's* (Vol. 89, July 27, 2009, No. 30, pp. 33)
Pub: Dow Jones & Co., Inc.
Ed: Leslie P. Norton. **Description:** Shares of hhgregg have risen 85 percent in the year leading up to July 2009 and analysts believe the stock could hit 25. However, their 113 outlets are concentrated in states where unemployment is above 10 percent and expanding into areas already overstored. Competition is also rife and credit availability is still tight.

26216 ■ *The Trillion Dollar Meltdown: Easy Money, High Rollers, and the Great Credit Crash*
Pub: Public Affairs
Ed: Charles R. Morris. **Released:** 2009. **Price:** $22. 95. **Description:** Former banker believes that Wall Street and the financial community have too much

power in America. He estimates that writedowns and defaults of residential mortgages, commercial mortgages, junk bonds, leveraged loans, credit cards, and complex securitized bonds could reach $1 trillion.

26217 ■ "Troubled Project In Court" in *The Business Journal-Portland* (Vol. 25, July 25, 2008, No. 20, pp. 1)
Pub: American City Business Journals, Inc.
Ed: Wendy Culverwell. **Description:** Views and information on Salpare Bay's Hayden Island project, as well as on financing problems and cases associated with the project, are presented. Construction of luxurious waterside condominiums stopped last fall, after the discovery of financing problems and subcontractors and other parties started filing claims and counterclaims.

26218 ■ "Turmoil Means Changes For Retailers" in *The Business Journal-Serving Metropolitan Kansas City* (Vol. 27, October 10, 2008, No. 4)
Pub: American City Business Journals, Inc.
Ed: Suzanna Stagemeyer. **Description:** Impacts of the financial crisis on Kansas Metropolitan Area retailers are varied. Rob Dalzell, for instance, found it difficult to secure a loan for his new self-serve yogurt store Yummo. The trends in retailing in the area are examined further as well as ways in which local businesses are changing in an attempt to stay solvent during the economic downturn.

26219 ■ *Ultimate Credit and Collection Handbook*
Pub: Entrepreneur Press
Ed: Michelle Dunn. **Released:** August 2006. **Price:** $36.95. **Description:** Entrepreneurial experts offer advice for successful credit and collection procedures.

26220 ■ "Unfair Distraction of Employees" in *Business Owner* (Vol. 35, March-April 2011, No. 2, pp. 8)
Pub: DL Perkins Company
Description: Fair Credit Collection Practices Act makes it illegal for collectors to contact a debtor at his or her place of employment if the collector is made aware that it is against personnel policy of the employer for the worker to take such a call.

26221 ■ "U.S. Economy's Underlying Strengths Limit Recession Threat" in *Hispanic Business* (Vol. 30, April 2008, No. 4, pp. 14)
Pub: Hispanic Business
Ed: Dr. Juan B. Solana. **Description:** Large and small businesses as well as consumers and policymakers are attempting to identify the areas of risk and loss created by the economic crisis; analysts are now estimating that U.S. mortgage losses could reach the $380 to $400 billion mark. Also discusses the falling of wages and the rising of unemployment. Statistical data included.

26222 ■ "Unlicensed Utah Collection Agency Settles with Idaho Department of Finance" in *Idaho Business Review, Boise* (July 15, 2010)
Pub: Idaho Business Review
Description: Federal Recovery Acceptance Inc., doing business as Paramount Acceptance in Utah, agreed to pay penalties and expenses after the firm was investigated by the state for improprieties. The firm was charged with conducting unlicensed collection activity.

26223 ■ "Valenti: Roots of Financial Crisis Go Back to 1998" in *Crain's Detroit Business* (Vol. 24, October 6, 2008, No. 40, pp. 25)
Pub: Crain Communications, Inc.
Ed: Tom Henderson; Nathan Skid. **Description:** Interview with Sam Valenti III who is the chairman and CEO of Valenti Capital L.L.C., a wealth-management firm; Valenti discusses in detail the history that led up to the current economic crisis as well as his prediction for the future of the country.

26224 ■ *The Visa Approval Backlog and Its Impact on American Small Business: Congressional Hearing*
Pub: DIANE Publishing Company
Ed: Donald A. Manzullo. **Released:** July 2006. **Price:** $30.00. **Description:** Information regarding the Congressional hearing involving the Visa approval backlog is discussed.

26225 ■ "Welcome Back" in *Canadian Business* (Vol. 82, April 27, 2009, No. 7, pp. 25)
Pub: Rogers Media
Ed: Sarka Halas. **Description:** Some Canadian companies such as Gennum Corporation have taken advantage of corporate sale-leasebacks to raise money at a time when credit is hard to acquire. Corporate sale-leasebacks allow companies to sell their property assets while remaining as tenants of the building. Sale-leasebacks allow firms to increase capital while avoiding the disruptions that may result with moving.

26226 ■ "What Are You, A Bank? You Probably Lend Your Customers More Money Than You Realize." in *Inc.* (November 2007, pp. 81)
Pub: Gruner & Jahr USA Publishing
Ed: Norm Brodsky. **Description:** Small business owners don't realize when that when customers do not pay on time, it is the same as lending them money. Tips to get customers to pay on time are listed.

26227 ■ "What the Future Holds for Consumers" in *Black Enterprise* (Vol. 41, August 2010, No. 1, pp. 47)
Pub: Earl G. Graves Publishing Co. Inc.
Ed: Sheiresa Ngo. **Description:** The way people purchase goods and service has changed with technology. With an increased focus on security (as well as privacy and fairness) the U.S. Congress began regulating the credit card industry with the Fair Credit Reporting Act of 1970 and the Credit Card Accountability, Responsibility, and Disclosure (CARD) Act of 2009.

26228 ■ "When Dov Cries" in *Canadian Business* (Vol. 83, June 15, 2010, No. 10, pp. 71)
Pub: Rogers Media Ltd.
Ed: Joe Castaldo. **Description:** American Apparel disclosed that they will have problems meeting one of its debt covenants which could trigger a chain reaction that could lead to bankruptcy. The prospects look bleak, but eccentric company founder Dov Charney, has always defied expectations.

26229 ■ "Where to Stash Your Cash" in *Barron's* (Vol. 88, March 17, 2008, No. 11, pp. 41)
Pub: Dow Jones & Company, Inc.
Ed: Mike Hogan. **Description:** Investors are putting their money in money-market mutual funds seeking fractionally better yields and a safe haven from the uncertainties that was brought about by subprime lending. These funds, however, are hovering near 3.20 percent which is less than the 4 percent inflation rate.

26230 ■ "Wobbling Economy" in *The Business Journal-Serving Metropolitan Kansas City* (Vol. 27, September 26, 2008, No. 2, pp. 1)
Pub: American City Business Journals, Inc.
Ed: Rob Roberts. **Description:** Real estate developers in Kansas City Metropolitan Area are worried of the possible impacts of the crisis at Wall Street. They expect tightening of the credit market, which will result in difficulty of financing their projects. The potential effects of the Wall Street crisis are examined further.

26231 ■ "Woes Portend Consumer Shift" in *The Business Journal-Serving Metropolitan Kansas City* (Vol. 27, September 26, 2008, No. 2, pp. 1)
Pub: American City Business Journals, Inc.
Ed: Suzanna Stagemeyer. **Description:** Black Bamboo owner Tim Butt believes that prolonged tightening of the credit market will result in consumer spending becoming more cash-driven that credit card driven. The financial crisis has already constricted spending among consumers. Forecasts for the US economy are provided.

26232 ■ "The Worst Lies Ahead for Wall Street; More Losses Certain" in *Crain's New York Business* (Vol. 24, January 21, 2008, No. 3, pp. 1)
Pub: Crain Communications, Inc.
Ed: Aaron Elstein. **Description:** Due to the weakening economy, many financial institutions will face further massive losses forcing them to borrow more at higher interest rates and dragging down their earnings for years to come. The effects on commercial real estate and credit card loans are also discussed as well as the trend to investing in Asia and the Middle East.

26233 ■ "The Wrong Tune" in *The Business Journal-Portland* (Vol. 25, July 25, 2008, No. 20, pp. 1)
Pub: American City Business Journals, Inc.
Ed: Robin J. Moody. **Description:** Views and information on turnaround management and recovery plans of the Oregon Symphony, are presented. The non-profit organization has lost a total of $5.1 million between 2002 and 2008, and $400,000 annual interest payments for a $7 million bank loan. Increased ticket sales, as well as cost cutting measures, are helping improve the finance of the organization.

26234 ■ "Your Exposure to Bear Stearns" in *Barron's* (Vol. 88, March 17, 2008, No. 11, pp. 45)
Pub: Dow Jones & Company, Inc.
Ed: Tom Sullivan; Jack Willoughby. **Description:** Bear Stearns makes up 5.5 percent of Pioneer Independence's portfolio, 1.4 percent of Vanguard Windsor II's portfolio, 1.2 percent of Legg Mason Value Trust, about 1 percent of Van Kampen Equity & Income, and 0.79 percent of Putnam Fund for Growth & Income. Ginnie Mae securities are now trading at 1.78 percentage points over treasuries due to the mortgage crises.

26235 ■ "Your Startup may be Worth Less than You Think" in *Entrepreneur* (Vol. 37, October 2009, No. 10, pp. 96)
Pub: Entrepreneur Media, Inc.
Ed: Asheesh Advani. **Description:** Valuations of startups at the idea stage are dropping due to the effects of the recession. This drop is due to the decreasing availability of investment capital, the reduction in portfolio values of investors, and the increase in early stage startups.

TRADE PERIODICALS

26236 ■ *Collections & Credit Risk*
Pub: SourceMedia Inc.
Contact: Darren Waggoner, Editor-in-Chief
Released: Monthly. **Price:** $119; $148; $213 two years; $376 two years in Canada. **Description:** Business publication tracking trends in the credit and collections industry.

26237 ■ *What's Working in Credit & Collections*
Pub: Progressive Business Publications
Ed: Russell Case, Editor. **Released:** Semimonthly. **Price:** $253, individuals. **Description:** Teaches successful credit and collection techniques to build credit sales while avoiding losses. Recurring features include interviews, news of research, a calendar of events, and a column titled Sharpen Your Judgment.

VIDEOCASSETTES/ AUDIOCASSETTES

26238 ■ *It's in the Mail: Techniques for Collecting Debts*
Video Arts, Inc.
c/o Aim Learning Group
8238-40 Lehigh
Morton Grove, IL 60053-2615
Free: 877-444-2230
Fax:(416)252-2155
Co. E-mail: service@aimlearninggroup.com
URL: http://www.aimlearninggroup.com
Released: 1989. **Price:** $755.00. **Description:** A business guide to pressuring and applying legal leans on outstanding debtors. **Availability:** VHS; 3/4U.

CONSULTANTS

26239 ■ FinTrace Inc.
130 E 59th St., Ste. 1300
New York, NY 10022
Ph:(212)759-1688
Fax:(212)826-7019
Contact: Leonard Volodarsky, President
Scope: Firm conducts financial investigations. Specializes in locating missing property owners, unclaimed property, and assets, such as stocks, bonds, dividends, life insurance proceeds, mutual fund shares, bank accounts, oil and mineral royalties, and other tangible and financial instruments. Also purchases uncollected judicial judgments, investigates telecommunications and utility billing for surcharges, and obtains refunds. Industries served: All.

26240 ■ NetKnowledge Technologies L.L.C.
6565 N MacArthur Blvd.
Irving, TX 75039
Ph:(214)624-5122
Fax:(972)910-0069
Co. E-mail: aubrey.roberts@nksoft.com
URL: http://www.nktllc.com
Contact: John Chowdhury, Principle
E-mail: johnc@nktllc.com
Scope: Works with executives worldwide to solve pressing business problems through the integration of business strategy and operations; information technology; and change management.

LIBRARIES

26241 ■ Loan Brokers Association–Information Services
917 S. Park St.
Owosso, MI 48867-4422
Contact: Ben Campbell, Dir.
Scope: Loan brokers, loan consulting, credit repair, lending, credit cards, venture capital. **Services:** Copying; SDI; Library to members or by permission.

ASSOCIATIONS AND OTHER ORGANIZATIONS

26242 ■ Help Desk Institute
102 S Tejon St., Ste. 1200
Colorado Springs, CO 80903
Ph:(719)268-0174
Free: 800-248-5667
Fax:(719)268-0184
Co. E-mail: support@thinkhdi.com
URL: http://www.thinkhdi.com
Contact: Darien Chimoff, Chair
Description: Corporations, organizations, and agencies offering help desks or other customer or user information services. Promotes effective operation of help desks and related services. Facilitates exchange of information among members; evaluates and certifies support centers; conducts research and educational programs. **Publications:** *HDI Industry Insider* (biweekly); *Support and Service Suppliers Directory* (periodic); *SupportWorld* .

26243 ■ International Customer Service Association
1110 South Ave., Ste. No. 50
Staten Island, NY 10314
Ph:(374)273-1303
Co. E-mail: info@icsatoday.org
URL: http://www.icsa.com
Contact: Bill Gessert, Pres.
Description: Customer service professionals in public and private sectors united to develop the theory and understanding of customer service and management. Goals are to: promote professional development; standardize terminology and phrases; provide career counseling and placement services; establish hiring guidelines, performance standards and job descriptions. Provides a forum for shared problems and solutions. Compiles statistics. **Publications:** *ICSA News* (bimonthly).

EDUCATIONAL PROGRAMS

26244 ■ Achieving Excellence in Customer Service
Learning Tree International
1805 Library St.
Reston, VA 20190-5630
Ph:(703)709-9019
Free: 888-843-8733
URL: http://www.learningtree.com
Price: $2,490.00. **Description:** This course provides the tools and techniques to ensure you build and maintain mutually beneficial relationships with customers. **Locations:** Reston, VA; New York, NY; Washington, DC; and Rockville, MD.

26245 ■ The Conference on Customer Service
Seminar Information Service, Inc.
20 Executive Park, Ste. 120
Irvine, CA 92614
Ph:(949)261-9104
Free: 877-SEM-INFO
Fax:(949)261-1963
Co. E-mail: info@seminarinformation.com
URL: http://www.seminarinformation.com
Price: $149.00; $1399.00 for four or more. **Description:** Learn techniques and tips for effectively and successfully dealing with customers, including what customer service representatives need to stay motivated and productive. **Locations:** Cities throughout the United States.

26246 ■ Customer Satisfaction and Loyalty Research
Seminar Information Service, Inc.
20 Executive Park, Ste. 120
Irvine, CA 92614
Ph:(949)261-9104
Free: 877-SEM-INFO
Fax:(949)261-1963
Co. E-mail: info@seminarinformation.com
URL: http://www.seminarinformation.com
Price: $2,395.00. **Description:** Learn why it is important to assess customer satisfaction and the consequences of ignoring this vital area; how to design a study to measure customer satisfaction, how to structure and administer the survey questionnaire and how to select the sample; and how to implement results from the study to establish performance standards and goals for the future. **Locations:** San Francisco, CA; New York, NY; and Chicago, IL.

26247 ■ Customer Service Excellence: How to Win and Keep Customers
American Management Association
600 AMA Way
Saranac Lake, NY 12983-5534
Ph:(212)586-8100
Free: 877-566-9441
Fax:(518)891-0368
Co. E-mail: customerservice@amanet.org
URL: http://www.amaseminars.org
Price: $1,895.00 for non-members; $1,695.00 for AMA members; and $1,451.00 for General Services Administration (GSA) members. **Description:** Covers the skills needed to communicate professionalism, gain respect, improve customer relationships, and secure competitive advantage. **Locations:** New York, NY; San Francisco, CA; Arlington, VA; and Chicago, IL.

26248 ■ Customer Service That Wows!
Seminar Information Service, Inc.
20 Executive Park, Ste. 120
Irvine, CA 92614
Ph:(949)261-9104
Free: 877-SEM-INFO
Fax:(949)261-1963
Co. E-mail: info@seminarinformation.com
URL: http://www.seminarinformation.com
Price: $149.00. **Description:** Learn how to determine what the customer needs before they ask and giving them more than they expect. **Locations:** Raleigh, NC; Charlotte, NC; Orlando, FL; Tampa, FL; and Plantation, FL.

26249 ■ Exceptional Customer Service Leadership
Canadian Management Centre
150 York St., 5th Fl.
Toronto, ON, Canada M5H 3S5
Free: 800-262-2519
Fax:(416)214-6047
Co. E-mail: cmcinfo@cmctraining.org
URL: http://www.cmctraining.org
Price: $1,85.00 for members; $1,995.00 for non-members. **Description:** Guides you through proven approaches for excellent customer service leadership. **Locations:** Toronto, ON.

26250 ■ How to Collect Accounts Receivable
Fred Pryor Seminars & CareerTrack
5700 Broadmoor St., Ste. 300
Mission, KS 66202
Free: 800-780-8476
Fax:(913)967-8849
Co. E-mail: customerservice@pryor.com
URL: http://www.pryor.com
Price: $179.00; $169.00 for groups of 5 or more. **Description:** Learn to collect pastdue accounts without losing your customer. **Locations:** Cities throughout the United States.

REFERENCE WORKS

26251 ■ *101 Ways to Really Satisfy Your Customers: How to Keep Your Customers and Attract New Ones*
Pub: Allen & Unwin Pty., Limited
Ed: Andrew Griffiths. **Released:** April 2007. **Price:** $14.95. **Description:** Tips for providing excellent customer service that ensure loyalty and interest to a small business are examined.

26252 ■ "2009: A Call For Vision" in *Women Entrepreneur* (January 28, 2009)
Pub: Entrepreneur Media Inc.
Ed: Elinor Robin. **Description:** Providing exemplary customer service, reducing expenses and creating an out-of-the-box niche are three key factors that will help business survive during this economic crisis. Business owners must see potential where others see failure in order to create new opportunities that may not only allow their business to survive during these times but may actually cause some businesses to thrive despite this economic downturn.

26253 ■ "2010 American Business Woman of ABWA" in *Women In Business* (Vol. 61, October-November 2009, No. 5, pp. 22)
Pub: American Business Women's Association
Ed: Doris Brown. **Description:** Achievements of Doris Brown are presented in light of her being named as the 2010 American Business Woman of American Business Women's Association (ABWA). She specializes in the field of client and customer satisfaction for Avue Technologies. Brown believes that her involvement in the ABWA has helped her to see the importance of being a resource for other people.

26254 ■ *Alpha Dogs: How Your Small Business Can Become a Leader of the Pack*
Pub: HarperCollins Publishers
Ed: Donna Fenn. **Released:** May 2007. **Price:** $14. 95. **Description:** Eight entrepreneurs share insight into developing practical strategies in the areas of customer service, the use of technology and overcoming competition.

26255 ■ "Apparel Apparatchic at Kmart" in *Barron's* (Vol. 88, March 17, 2008, No. 11, pp. 16)
Pub: Dow Jones & Company, Inc.
Description: Kmart began a nationwide search for women to represent the company in a national advertising campaign. Contestants need to upload their photos to Kmart's website and winners will be chosen by a panel of celebrity judges. The contest aims to reverse preconceived negative notions about the store's quality and service.

26256 ■ "Applying Continuous Process Improvement for Managing Customer Loyalty" in *Agency Sales Magazine* (Vol. 39, November 2009, No. 10)
Pub: MANA
Ed: Bob Cicerone; Aaron Hekele; Jason Morado. **Description:** Steps in effective process improvement that reveals where opportunities exist to improve management practices and control customer loyalty are discussed. The process consists of thirteen factors grouped into three sets.

26257 ■ "Attention, Shoppers Take a Deep Breath: Why It Pays to Help Customers Relax" in *Inc.* (Vol. 33, November 2011, No. 9, pp. 26)
Pub: Inc. Magazine
Ed: J.J. McCorvey. **Description:** According to a current study, along with festive music and decorations for holiday shoppers, some merchants are considering back messages and pedicures to keep customers happy.

26258 ■ *Authenticity: What Consumers Really Want*
Pub: Harvard Business School Press
Ed: James H. Gilmore. **Released:** September 24, 2007. **Price:** $26.95. **Description:** In today's marketplace, consumers tend to buy based on how authentic a company's offer appears. A company's identity is explored through case studies and advertising slogans. The authors write from the theory that most everything is artificial, manmade, and fake.

26259 ■ *Awesomely Simple: Essential Business Strategies for Turning Ideas Into Action*
Pub: Jossey-Bass
Ed: John Spence. **Released:** September 8, 2009. **Price:** $24.95. **Description:** Six key strategies that create a foundation for achieving business excellence include: vivid vision, best people, a performance-oriented culture, robust communication, a sense of urgency, and extreme customer focus.

26260 ■ "Bad Client? Make Break Cleanly, Swiftly - and Based On Numbers" in *Crain's Detroit Business* (Vol. 23, November 19, 2007, No. 47)
Pub: Crain Communications Inc. - Detroit
Ed: Sheena Harrison. **Description:** Firing a difficult customer can be hard to do, but the best way to do it is cleanly and amicably.

26261 ■ "Bank Bullish on Austin" in *Austin Business JournalInc.* (Vol. 29, November 13, 2009, No. 36, pp. A1)
Pub: American City Business Journals
Ed: Kate Harrington. **Description:** American Bank's presence in Austin, Texas has been boosted by new management and a new 20,000 square foot building. This community bank intends to focus on building relationship with commercial banking customers. American Bank also plans to extend investment banking, treasury management, and commercial lending services.

26262 ■ "Banking on Twitter" in *Baltimore Business Journal* (Vol. 27, February 6, 2010, No. 40, pp. 1)
Pub: American City Business Journals
Ed: Gary Haber. **Description:** Ways that banks are using Twitter, Facebook and other social networking sites to provide customer services is discussed. First Mariner Bank is one of those banks that are finding the social media platform as a great way to reach customers. Privacy issues regarding this marketing trend are examined.

26263 ■ "Banks Deposit Reassurance, Calm Customers" in *The Business Journal-Serving Greater Tampa Bay* (Vol. 28, August 22, 2008)
Pub: American City Business Journals, Inc.
Ed: Margie Manning. **Description:** Community banks in the Tampa Bay Area are training tellers and other customer care workers to help reassure customers that their deposits are safe. Other measures to reassure depositors include joining a network that allows banks to share deposits. Additional information on moves community banks are making to reassure consumers is presented.

26264 ■ *Battling Big Box: How Nimble Niche Companies Can Outmaneuver Giant Companies*
Pub: Career Press, Inc.
Ed: Henry Dubroff, Susan J. Marks. **Released:** January 1, 2009. **Price:** $15.99. **Description:** Small companies can compete with larger firms through agility, adaptability, customer service, and credibility. Topics include information to help empower employees, build a powerful brand, manage cash flow, and maintaining a business vision.

26265 ■ "Be Innovative In Other Ways" in *Green Industry Pro* (Vol. 23, March 2011, No. 3, pp. 4)
Pub: Cygnus Business Media
Ed: Rod Dickens. **Description:** Emphasis is put on the importance of putting the customer first in order to successfully market any product or service. Six marketing ideas are presented to promote a landscaping business.

26266 ■ *Behind the Cloud*
Pub: Jossey-Bass
Ed: Marc Benioff, Carlye Adler. **Released:** 2010. **Price:** $27.95. **Description:** Salesforce.com is the world's most successful business-to-business cloud-computing company that sells an online service that helps businesses manage sales, customer service, and marketing functions.

26267 ■ "Best In Show" in *Pet Product News* (Vol. 64, November 2010, No. 11, pp. 20)
Pub: BowTie Inc.
Ed: Lizett Bond. **Description:** Cherrybrook Premium Pet Supplies offers an expanded array of quality holistic products and is staffed by people who possess wide knowledge of these products. Aside from receiving the Outstanding Holistic Approach award, Cherrybrook has opened three stores in New Jersey. How a holistic approach to service kept customers coming back is discussed.

26268 ■ "Best Practices: Just Say No" in *Entrepreneur* (Vol. 35, October 2007, No. 10, pp. 107)
Pub: Entrepreneur Media Inc.
Ed: Chris Penttila. **Description:** Customer service must have boundaries to prevent abuse by customers. Companies should learn to refuse unreasonable customer demands, set limitations and make customers understand and accept these limitations. Details on customer service policies are given.

26269 ■ "The Best and Worst Economic Times" in *Agency Sales Magazine* (Vol. 39, December 2009, No. 11, pp. 22)
Pub: MANA
Ed: Mark Young. **Description:** U.S. gross domestic product grew 3.5 percent and the stock market has improved but manufacturers are cutting commissions or dropping sales representatives. Despite these challenges, it can a good time for salespeople because clients need them more than ever. Salesmen should find new ways to do business for their clients during this current challenging environment.

26270 ■ *Beyond Booked Solid: Your Business, Your Life, Your Way-It's All Inside*
Pub: John Wiley and Sons, Inc.
Ed: Michael Port. **Released:** April 2008. **Price:** $24. 95. **Description:** Professional service providers and small business owners will discover tactics and strategies for growing and expanding their companies while allowing them to find time to relax and enjoy their lives. Owners will learn to attract new clients and grow profits.

26271 ■ *Beyond Buzz: The Next Generation of Word-of-Mouth Marketing*
Pub: AMACOM
Ed: Lois Kelly. **Released:** March 2007. **Price:** $24. 95. **Description:** The idea of buzz and marketing as fostering conversations is nothing new, but in this instructive book, the author (co-founder of a strategic-communications consulting firm), discusses various narrative frameworks often used to put products and services in context.

26272 ■ *Big Vision, Small Business*
Pub: Ivy Sea, Inc.
Ed: Jamie S. Walters. **Released:** October 10, 2002. **Price:** $17.95. **Description:** The power of the small enterprise is examined. The author shares her expertise as an entrepreneur and founder of a business consulting firm to help small business owners successfully run their companies. Interviews with more than seventy small business owners provide insight into visioning, planning, and establishing a small company, as well as strategies for good employee and customer relationships.

26273 ■ "Blockbuster Launches Internet Movie Downloads to Compete Against Netflix, Others" in *Chicago Tribune* (December 3, 2008)
Pub: McClatchy-Tribune Information Services
Ed: Eric Benderoff. **Description:** Blockbuster Inc., the DVD rental giant, has launched a new service that delivers movies to their customer's homes via the Internet in an attempt to compete against Netflix and other competitors.

26274 ■ "Boosting Worried Customers' Confidence" in *Gallup Management Journal* (November 8, 2011)
Pub: Gallup
Ed: Jessica Tyler, Patrick Whiston. **Description:** While customers fear a double-dip recession and US economic confidence is low, leading edge firms have found a timely and creative way to win customers: they are improving their wellbeing.

26275 ■ "Bottoms Up!" in *Entrepreneur* (Vol. 36, April 2008, No. 4, pp. 128)
Pub: Entrepreneur Media, Inc.
Ed: Amanda C. Kooser. **Description:** Jill Bernheimer launched her online alcohol business Domaine547 in 2007, and encountered challenges as legal issues over the licensing and launching of the business took about seven months to finish. Domain547 features blog and forum areas. Marketing strategy that connects to the social community is one of the ways to reach out to customers.

26276 ■ "Business Forecast: Stormy and Successful" in *Women In Business* (Vol. 62, June 2010, No. 2, pp. 12)
Pub: American Business Women's Association
Ed: Kathleen Leighton. **Description:** Stormy Simon, vice president of customer service at Overstock.com is a self-made career woman who started out as a temporary employee in the company in 2001. She was not able to attend college because she had two sons to care for after her divorce. Simon got involved in advertising and media buying and shares her love for business.

26277 ■ *Business Process Mapping Workbook: Improving Customer Satisfaction*
Pub: John Wiley & Sons, Inc.
Ed: J. Mike Jacka, Paulette J. Keller. **Released:** July 7, 2009. **Price:** $50.00. **Description:** The various steps involved in performing a business process map to achieve optimal customer satisfaction are outlined.

26278 ■ "Buying In" in *Harvard Business Review* (Vol. 86, September 2008, No. 9, pp. 36)

Pub: Harvard Business School Press

Ed: Andrew O'Connell. **Description:** Review of the book entitled, "Buying In: The Secret Dialogue between What We Buy and Who We Are" which offers tips that those in the field of marketing will find useful.

26279 ■ "Buying Power of Hispanics Growing" in *Austin Business JournalInc.* (Vol. 29, November 27, 2009, No. 38, pp. 1)

Pub: American City Business Journals

Ed: Sandra Zaragoza. **Description:** Hispanic Marketing Symposium presented a report stating that the buying power of Hispanics of Austin, Texas has grown by 54 percent in last five years to $9.4 billion in 2009. Details on the projected growth of the Hispanic market in the are is covered.

26280 ■ "Calming Customers" in *The Business Journal-Portland* (Vol. 25, August 29, 2008, No. 25, pp. 1)

Pub: American City Business Journals, Inc.

Ed: Kirsten Grind; Rob Smith. **Description:** Credit unions and banks in the Portland area are reaching out to clients in an effort to reassure them on the security of their money and the firms' financial stability. Roy Whitehead of Washington Federal Savings, for instance, wrote 41,000 customers of the bank to reassure them. The strategies of different banks and credit unions to answer their client's worries are discussed

26281 ■ "Cashing In: Gleaning an Education from Our Economic State" in *Agency Sales Magazine* (Vol. 39, August 2009, No. 8, pp. 22)

Pub: MANA

Ed: John Graham. **Description:** Businesses have learned that cutting price can kill business and being tough is normal. The recession has also taught that getting the right vision and gaining the confidence and trust of consumers are important.

26282 ■ "Certified Technicians can Increase Bottom Line" in *Contractor* (Vol. 56, September 2009, No. 9, pp. 37)

Pub: Penton Media, Inc.

Ed: Ray Isaac. **Description:** Certified technicians increase the value of HVAC firms, a survey by Service Round Table has reported. The increased value has been attributed to fewer callbacks, less warranty work and greater ability to educate consumers. Meanwhile, consumers are willing to pay more for the services of certified technicians.

26283 ■ "Changing Prescriptions" in *Business North Carolina* (Vol. 28, March 2008, No. 3, pp. 52)

Pub: Business North Carolina

Description: Profile of Moose Drug Company, founded by Archibald Walter Moose in 1882. Family owners share how they focus on pharmacoeconomics (cost-benefit analyses of drugs or drug therapy) and customer service.

26284 ■ *Cisco Network Design Solutions for Small-Medium Businesses*

Pub: Cisco Press

Ed: Peter Rybaczyk. **Released:** August 2004. **Price:** $55.00. **Description:** Solutions for computer networking professionals using computer networks within a small to medium-sized business. Topics cover not only core networking issues and solutions, but security, IP telephony, unified communications, customer relations management, wireless LANs, and more.

26285 ■ *Clued In*

Pub: Financial Times/Prentice Hall

Ed: Lewis Carbone. **Released:** May 24, 2004. **Price:** $34.99. **Description:** Tips for providing excellent customer service that keeps clients coming back are shared. Brand management and Experience Value Management are defined.

26286 ■ "Come Together" in *Pet Product News* (Vol. 64, December 2010, No. 12, pp. 28)

Pub: BowTie Inc.

Ed: Lizett Bond. **Description:** Pet supply retailers have posted improved sales and improved customer service by bundling their offerings. Bundling pertains to grouping related items such as collars and leashes into a single unit for marketing purposes. Aside from providing convenience and enhanced product information to customers, bundling has facilitated more efficient purchases.

26287 ■ *Consumer Behavior*

Pub: Prentice Hall Business Publishing

Ed: Leon Schiffman, Leslile Kanuk. **Released:** August 7, 2009. **Price:** $180.00. **Description:** Consumer behavior is central to the planning, development and implementation of marketing strategies.

26288 ■ "Conversations with Customers" in *Business Journal Serving Greater Tampa Bay* (Vol. 31, December 31, 2010, No. 1, pp. 1)

Pub: Tampa Bay Business Journal

Description: Tampa Bay, Florida-based businesses have been using social media to interact with customers. Forty percent of businesses have been found to have at least one social media platform to reach customers and prospects.

26289 ■ "Convert New Customers to Long Term Accounts" in *Indoor Comfort Marketing* (Vol. 70, February 2011, No. 2, pp. 22)

Pub: Industry Publications Inc.

Description: Marketing to new customers and suggestions for retaining them is covered.

26290 ■ "Courier Service Delivers Big Profits and Top-Notch Customer Service" in *Small Business Opportunities* (November 2007)

Pub: Harris Publications Inc.

Description: Profile of Relay Express, a courier franchising business started by three friends in 1986. The company focuses on customer service and calls them every 19 minutes to report on progress of a parcel until it is delivered.

26291 ■ "The Customer Is Right Even If He's Wrong" in *Contractor* (Vol. 57, February 2010, No. 2, pp. 12)

Pub: Penton Media, Inc.

Ed: Al Schwarz. **Description:** Mechanical contractors should note that customers will make a judgment based upon the impression that they form on their first meeting. Contractors can maintain a professional image by washing their trucks and having the personnel dress uniformly. Contractors have every right to demand that employees clean up and make a better impression on customers.

26292 ■ "Customer Loyalty: Making Your Program Excel" in *Franchising World* (Vol. 42, August 2010, No. 8, pp. 47)

Pub: International Franchise Association

Ed: Steve Baxter. **Description:** Customer loyalty is key to any franchise operation's growth. Tips for identifying preferred customers are outlined.

26293 ■ "Customer OKs on Press" in *American Printer* (Vol. 128, August 1, 2011, No. 8)

Pub: Penton Media Inc.

Description: Printers discuss the value of having customers meet at the plant in order to okay print colors for projects.

26294 ■ "Customer Preferences Control Skid Steer Choices" in *Rental Product News* (Vol. 33, June 2011)

Pub: Cygnus Business Media

Ed: Jenny Lescohier. **Description:** Understanding the types of controls available on skid steer equipment is essential. The article provides a comprehensive guide to using and maintaining skid steers for rental agencies.

26295 ■ "Customer Retention is Proportionate to Employee Retention" in *Green Industry Pro* (Vol. 23, September 2011)

Pub: Cygnus Business Media

Description: Presented in a question-answer format, information is provided to help retain customers as well as keeping workers happy.

26296 ■ "Customer Service Center Will Rise in Indian Land" in *Charlotte Observer* (February 4, 2007)

Pub: Knight-Ridder/Tribune Business News

Ed: Taylor Bright. **Description:** Kennametal is building a new customer service center in Lancaster County, North Carolina. Kennametal makes metal tools and parts, specializing in metals highly resistant to heat.

26297 ■ *Cute Little Store: Between the Entrepreneurial Dream and Business Reality*

Pub: Outskirts Press, Incorporated

Ed: Adeena Mignogna. **Released:** May 2006. **Price:** $11.95. **Description:** Challenges of starting and growing a retail business are profiled.

26298 ■ "The Dean of Design" in *Canadian Business* (Vol. 79, November 6, 2006, No. 22, pp. 42)

Pub: Rogers Media

Ed: Erin Pooley. **Description:** The need of a good business design to increase the business in saturated markets with relation to customer satisfaction is emphasized.

26299 ■ *Design and Launch Your Online Boutique in a Week*

Pub: Entrepreneur Press

Ed: Melissa Campanelli. **Released:** June 26, 2008. **Price:** $17.95. **Description:** Tips for starting an online boutique in a short amount of time are given. The books shows how to build the online boutique with designer goods or your own product, ways to create eye-catching content, online tools to handle payments and accept orders, marketing and advertising techniques, and customer service.

26300 ■ "Designing Solutions Around Customer Network Identity Goals" in *Journal of Marketing* (Vol. 75, March 2011, No. 2, pp. 36)

Pub: American Marketing Association

Ed: Amber M. Epp, Linda L. Price. **Description:** The role relational and collective goals in creating customer solutions is investigated using in-depth interviews with 21 families. Findings revealed four integration processes in customer networks, namely, offerings formed around individual coalitions, concurrent participation, alternate participation, and offerings formed around priority goals.

26301 ■ "Don't' Hate the Cable Guy" in *Saint Louis Business Journal* (Vol. 31, August 5, 2011, No. 50, pp. 1)

Pub: Saint Louis Business Journal

Ed: Angela Mueller. **Description:** Charter Communications named John Birrer as senior vice president of customer experience. The company experienced problems with its customer services.

26302 ■ "Down by the Bay" in *Canadian Business* (Vol. 81, December 8, 2008, No. 21, pp. 15)

Pub: Rogers Media Ltd.

Ed: Calvin Leung. **Description:** Hudsons Bay Company chief executive Jeffrey Sherman believes that his vast experience in retail will help him find the company's customer base. Sales are estimated to increase 3.6 percent in 2009 after posting average annual retail sales increases of 5 percent between 2006 and 2008.

26303 ■ "The Downside of Self-Management" in *Academy of Management Journal* (August 2007)

Pub: Academy of Management

Ed: Claus W. Langfred. **Description:** Study reveals that self-managing teams might accidentally restructure themselves inefficiently in response to conflict, thus the possible structure-related effects are analyzed.

26304 ■ "Dream Big! When the Going Gets Tough, Reps Work Harder and Smarter" in *Agency Sales Magazine* (Vol. 39, July 2009, No. 7, pp. 22)
Pub: MANA
Ed: John Chapin. **Description:** Sales representatives should use the tough economy as a warning and motivation to work harder and smarter. Reps should improve their selling by reading books, listening to tapes and CDs. They should also keep a good attitude and build relationships.

26305 ■ "eBay Business Looking Up" in *Zacks* (July 26, 2011)
Pub: Comtex News Network Inc.
Ed: Sejuti Banerjea. **Description:** eBay reported solid revenue growth for 2011 second quarter, keeping in line with the Zacks Consensus Estimate, and third quarter earnings are expected to be higher. eBay's new strategy is to direct traffic to bigger sellers with improved customer service, making this good for eBay businesses.

26306 ■ "Emack & Bolio" in *Ice Cream Reporter* (Vol. 23, October 20, 2010, No. 11, pp. 8)
Pub: Ice Cream Reporter
Description: Emack & Bolio's is engaging in scent marketing using various odors to help boost sales by attracting consumers with scents appropriate to their products.

26307 ■ "Empowered" in *Harvard Business Review* (Vol. 88, July-August 2010, No. 7-8, pp. 94)
Pub: Harvard Business School Publishing
Ed: Josh Bernoff, Ted Schadler. **Description:** HERO concept (highly empowered and resourceful operative) which builds a connection between employees, managers, and IT is outlined. The resultant additional experience and knowledge gained by employees improves customer relationship management.

26308 ■ *Exceptional Service, Exceptional Profit: The Secrets of Building a Five-Star Customer Service Organization*
Pub: AMACOM
Ed: Leonard Inghilleri, Micah Solomon. **Released:** April 1, 2010. **Price:** $21.95. **Description:** Team of insiders share exclusive knowledge of the loyalty-building techniques pioneered by the world's most successful service leaders, including brick-and-mortar stars such as The Ritz-Carlton and Lexus and online success stories such as Netflix and CD Baby.

26309 ■ "Experts Strive to Educate on Proper Pet Diets" in *Pet Product News* (Vol. 64, November 2010, No. 11, pp. 40)
Pub: BowTie Inc.
Ed: John Hustace Walker. **Description:** Pet supply manufacturers have been bundling small mammal food and treats with educational sources to help retailers avoid customer misinformation. This action has been motivated by the customer's quest to seek proper nutritional advice for their small mammal pets.

26310 ■ "Fast Fact: Quality of Foods, Cost Top Factors in Determining Where to Grocery Shop" in *Marketing to Women* (Vol. 22, August 2009)
Pub: EPM Communications, Inc.
Description: Efficient check-outs, customer service and a wide variety of products were all less important to female shoppers than the quality of food and value, which were seen as the ultimate factors in a woman's decision as to which grocery store they decide to frequent.

26311 ■ "Feet on the Street: Reps Are Ready to Hit the Ground Running" in *Agency Sales Magazine* (Vol. 39, July 2009, No. 7, pp. 12)
Pub: MANA
Ed: Jack Foster. **Description:** One of the major benefits to manufacturers in working with sales representatives is the concept of synergistic selling where the rep shows his mettle. The rep of today is a solution provider that anticipates and meets the customer's needs.

26312 ■ *Financial Times Guide to Business Start Up 2007*
Pub: Pearson Education, Limited
Ed: Sara Williams; Jonquil Lowe. **Released:** November 2006. **Price:** $52.50. **Description:** Guide for starting and running a new business is presented. Sections include ways to get started, direct marketing, customer relations, management and accounting.

26313 ■ "Five Tips for New Managers" in *Hawaii Business* (Vol. 53, November 2007, No. 5, pp. 59)
Pub: Hawaii Business Publishing
Ed: Jason Ubay. **Description:** New managers should remember to know what their roles are, learn from others, build an infrastructure according to the customer's needs, communicate professionally and have consideration.

26314 ■ "Forward Motion" in *Green Industry Pro* (July 2011)
Pub: Cygnus Business Media
Ed: Gregg Wartgow. **Description:** Several landscape contractors have joined this publication's Working Smarter Training Challenge over the last year. This process is helping them develop ways to improve work processes, boost morale, drive out waste, reduce costs, improve customer service, and be more competitive.

26315 ■ "Fresh Direct's Crisis" in *Crain's New York Business* (Vol. 24, January 14, 2008, No. 2, pp. 3)
Pub: Crain Communications, Inc.
Ed: Lisa Fickenscher. **Description:** Freshdirect, an Internet grocery delivery service, finds itself under siege from federal immigration authorities, customers and labor organizations due to its employment practice of hiring illegals. At stake is the grocer's reputation as well as its ambitious growth plans, including an initial public offering of its stock.

26316 ■ "FTC Takes Aim At Foreclosure 'Rescue' Firm" in *The Business Journal-Serving Greater Tampa Bay* (Vol. 28, September 19, 2008, No. 39)
Pub: American City Business Journals, Inc.
Ed: Michael Hinman. **Description:** United Home Savers LLP has been ordered to halt its mortgage foreclosure rescue services after the Federal Trade Commission accused it of deceptive advertising. The company is alleged to have charged customers $1,200 in exchange for unfulfilled promises to keep them in their homes.

26317 ■ "Get Back To Business Planning Fundamentals" in *Entrepreneur* (October 24, 2008)
Pub: Entrepreneur Media Inc.
Ed: Tim Berry. **Description:** During a recession it is important to know what adjustment to make to your business plan. Some fundamentals to remember include: watching things more closely by tracking progress on cash, sales, new projects, customer satisfaction, ad spending and expenses; looking for built-in indicators such as what drives sales or expenses; watching what drives cash flow; and do not make mistakes such as laying off experienced employees too soon.

26318 ■ "Get Personal" in *Entrepreneur* (Vol. 36, April 2008, No. 4)
Pub: Entrepreneur Media, Inc.
Ed: Romanus Wolter. **Description:** Customers appreciate personal contact, and communicating with them can help business owners' customer relations. Some ways on how to keep a personal touch with customers and improve business dealings include blending technology with personal interaction and knowing what the customers want. Other tips are provided.

26319 ■ *Getting Clients and Keeping Clients for Your Service Business*
Pub: Atlantic Publishing Company
Ed: Anne M. Miller; Gail Brett Levine. **Released:** August 28, 2008. **Price:** $24.95 paperback. **Description:** Tips are offered to help any small service business identify customers, brand and grow the business, as well as development of logos, brochures and Websites.

26320 ■ *The Girl's Guide to Building a Million-Dollar Business*
Pub: AMACOM
Ed: Susan Wilson Solovic. **Released:** 2008. **Price:** $21.95. **Description:** Success plan for women business owners; the book includes tips for determination, managing changing relationships, keeping employees and customers happy, getting and maintaining credit, overcoming gender bias, and creating a good business plan and solid brand.

26321 ■ "Give It Your All, and Don't Worry About the Rest" in *Inc.* (Vol. 33, November 2011, No. 9, pp. 37)
Pub: Inc. Magazine
Ed: Norm Brodsky. **Description:** In the early stage of a service company, the owners sell themselves to the customers.

26322 ■ "Good Price, Best Brands" in *Retail Merchandiser* (Vol. 51, July-August 2011, No. 4, pp. 58)
Pub: Phoenix Media Corporation
Description: Flemington Department Store has been a family-owned and operated retailer for over 50 years. Customer service is key to the store's success.

26323 ■ "Good Questions and the Basics of Selling" in *Agency Sales Magazine* (Vol. 39, September-October 2009, No. 9, pp. 14)
Pub: MANA
Ed: Dave Kahle. **Description:** Six basic elements to enhance the job of a sales person in regards to his relationship to a customer are presented.

26324 ■ *Greening Your Small Business: How to Improve Your Bottom Line, Grow Your Brand, Satisfy Your Customers and Save the Planet*
Pub: Prentice Hall Press
Ed: Jennifer Kaplan. **Released:** November 3, 2009. **Price:** $19.95. **Description:** A definitive resource for anyone who wants their small business to be cutting-edge, competitive, profitable, and eco-conscious. Stories from small business owners address every aspect of going green, from basics such as recycling waste, energy efficiency, and reducing information technology footprint, to more in-depth concerns such as green marketing and communications, green business travel, and green employee benefits.

26325 ■ "Harnessing the Wisdom of Crowds" in *Entrepreneur* (Vol. 37, September 2009, No. 9, pp. 74)
Pub: Entrepreneur Media, Inc.
Ed: Mark Henricks. **Description:** Online customer service business Get Satisfaction has registered growth. The business enables customers to search for answers to common product questions. Customers use the service to post questions, complaints, and even product ideas.

26326 ■ "Health Care Checkup" in *Business Courier* (Vol. 24, November 16, 2008, No. 31, pp. 1)
Pub: American City Business Journals, Inc.
Ed: James Ritchie. **Description:** Discusses a survey of 300 Greater Cincinnati residents about the quality of local health care and access to doctors indicates that there were improvements from five years ago. About 65 percent of those surveyed said the quality of their health care is good or excellent, a 12 percent improvement from a similar survey conducted five years ago. The other findings of the survey are also presented.

26327 ■ "Help Customers Choose Full Service Over Discount" in *Indoor Comfort Marketing* (Vol. 70, September 2011, No. 9, pp. 10)
Pub: Industry Publications Inc.
Ed: Richard Rutigliano. **Description:** Marketing strategies for HVAC/R firms to use in 2011 and 2012 heating seasons are outlined, focusing on oil heat.

26328 ■ "A Home's Identity in Black and White" in *Crain's Chicago Business* (Vol. 31, April 21, 2008, No. 16, pp. 35)
Pub: Crain Communications, Inc.
Ed: Lisa Bertagnoli. **Description:** Real estate agents are finding that showing customers a written floor plan is a trend that is growing since many buyers feel that Online virtual tours distort a room. Although floor plans cost up to $500 to have drawn up, they clearly show potential buyers the exact dimensions of rooms and how they connect.

26329 ■ "Hometown Value" in *Retail Merchandiser* (Vol. 51, July-August 2011, No. 4, pp. 50)
Pub: Phoenix Media Corporation
Ed: Todd Vowell. **Description:** Profile of family-owned Vowell's Marketplace located in Noxapater, Mississippi. The 10-store chain caters to its Southern roots and is run by the third generation of the Vowell family.

26330 ■ *Housecleaning Business: Organize Your Business - Get Clients and Referrals - Set Rates and Services*
Pub: The Globe Pequot Press
Ed: Laura Jorstad, Melinda Morse. **Released:** June 1, 2009. **Price:** $18.95. **Description:** This book shares insight into starting a housecleaning businesses. It shows how to develop a service manual, screen clients, serve customers, select cleaning products, competition, how to up a home office, using the Internet to grow the business and offering green cleaning options to clients.

26331 ■ *How to Collect Debts (And Still Keep Your Customers)*
Pub: Amacom
Ed: David Sher, Martin Sher. **Released:** May 1999. **Description:** Suggestions for collecting as much money as possible, as quickly as possible, while maintaining customer goodwill, along with strategies for eliminating bad debt.

26332 ■ *How Customers Think*
Pub: Harvard Business School Press
Ed: Gerald Zaltman. **Released:** February 21, 2003. **Price:** $32.95. **Description:** Despite marketing efforts and customer surveys, nearly eighty percent of all new products fail of fall short of prediction within the first six months after introduction. Consumer reactions to products and marketing programs are investigated.

26333 ■ "How Good Advice 'Online' Can Attract Customers" in *Indoor Comfort Marketing* (Vol. 70, August 2011, No. 8, pp. 20)
Pub: Industry Publications Inc.
Ed: Richard Rutigilano. **Description:** Online marketing tips for heating and cooling small businesses are explained.

26334 ■ "How Growers Buy" in *Farm Industry News* (Vol. 42, January 1, 2009, No. 1)
Pub: Penton Media, Inc.
Ed: Karen McMahon. **Description:** According to a survey regarding the buying habits among large commercial growers, most prefer to purchase from local retailers, customer service is important concerning their decision on who to buy products from, and price and convenience seem to be more important then brand.

26335 ■ "How He Thinks" in *Canadian Business* (Vol. 80, Winter 2007, No. 24, pp. 78)
Pub: Rogers Media
Ed: Roger Martin. **Description:** Isadore Sharp sought to combine the best of the small hotel with the best of the large hotel so that he could provide his guests with the sense of intimacy and personalized service while also bringing a wide array of amenities. Sharp decreed that there would be no customer service department at his hotel but every member of the staff are in charge of customer service.

26336 ■ "How to Make Marketing Work" in *Agency Sales Magazine* (Vol. 39, September-October 2009, No. 9, pp. 30)
Pub: MANA
Ed: John Graham. **Description:** Marketing's core concept is to focus total attention on the customer. Marketers should stop trying to manipulate customers and recognize that getting people through the door does not make them customers. Customer satisfaction is also important since even the most compelling marketing messages are worthless without this vital relationship.

26337 ■ "How to Manage Successful Crowdsourcing Projects" in *eWeek* (September 29, 2010)
Pub: Ziff Davis Enterprise
Description: The advantages, challenges and pitfalls faced when using crowdsourcing to improve a business are outlined. Crowdsourcing helps to eliminate the need to rely on an internal workforce and the need to forecast task volume.

26338 ■ "How to Protect Your Job in a Recession" in *Harvard Business Review* (Vol. 86, September 2008, No. 9, pp. 113)
Pub: Harvard Business School Press
Ed: Janet Banks; Diane Coutu. **Description:** Strategies are presented for enhancing one's job security. These include being a team player, empathizing with management, preserving optimism, and concentrating on the customer.

26339 ■ "How Two Flourishing Exporters Did It" in *Hispanic Business* (Vol. 30, July-August 2008, No. 7-8, pp. 46)
Pub: Hispanic Business, Inc.
Ed: Richard Kaplan. **Description:** Vigorous growth in export revenues posted by two Hispanic-owned export companies Compasa LLC and Ametza LLC is discussed; both firms have benefited from their closer locations to major Mexican markets, superior quality of their products, market knowledge and the relationships of trust developed with key business partners.

26340 ■ *How You Do...What You Do: Create Service Excellence That Wins Clients For Life*
Pub: McGraw-Hill
Ed: Bob Livingston. **Released:** June 6, 2008. **Price:** $27.95. **Description:** Today's marketplace has become a tougher place to do business because of new challenges such as escalating competition, well-informed clients, and dismal customer service. Clients now have more influence and choices than ever. Tips for achieving service excellence are provided.

26341 ■ *Hug Your Customers*
Pub: Hyperion Books
Ed: Jack Mitchell. **Price:** $19.95. **Description:** The CEO of Mitchells/Roberts, two very successful clothing stores, professes his belief in showering customers with attention. His secrets for long-term business success include advice about attracting a good staff, lowering marketing costs, and maintaining higher gross margins and revenues.

26342 ■ "The Human Approach" in *Entrepreneur* (Vol. 37, September 2009, No. 9, pp. 30)
Pub: Entrepreneur Media, Inc.
Description: Focusing on customer's needs is seen to result in better sales performance. Understanding customer needs is a question of emotional and social intelligence. Such sales competencies are seen as learned capabilities.

26343 ■ *I Love You More Than My Dog*
Pub: Portfolio
Ed: Jeanne Bliss. **Price:** $22.95. **Description:** Ways to win passionate, loyal and vocal customers in order to build a small business is outlined.

26344 ■ "iMozi Integrates Esprida LiveControl for Advanced DVD Kiosk Hardware" in *Wireless News* (December 20, 2010)
Pub: Close-Up Media Inc.
Description: Provider of self-service entertainment technology, iMozi Canada has partnered with Esprida to make its automated DVD Kiosk solutions Esprida-enabled. Esprida develops remote device management solutions and will offer enhanced capabilities and to improve customer experience for users.

26345 ■ *Instant Cashflow: Hundreds of Proven Strategies to Win Customers, Boost Margins and Take More Money Home*
Pub: McGraw-Hill Companies
Ed: Bradley J. Sugars. **Released:** December 2005. **Price:** $17.95 (US), $22.95 (Canadian). **Description:** Nearly 300 proven marketing and sales strategies are shared by the author, a self-made millionaire. Advice on creating the proper mindset, generating new leads, boosting the conversion rate of leads to sales, maximizing the value of the average sale, and measuring results is included.

26346 ■ "Insurance: Marathon Effort" in *Canadian Business* (Vol. 80, January 29, 2007, No. 3, pp. 11)
Pub: Rogers Media
Ed: Jeff Sanford. **Description:** The efforts of the insurance firm ING Canada Inc. to manage its relations with its customers are described. The enhancement of the insurance services provided by the company is discussed.

26347 ■ "Interchangeable or Irreplaceable?" in *American Printer* (Vol. 128, August 1, 2011, No. 8)
Pub: Penton Media Inc.
Description: Creating and maintaining customers is important for all graphic design and printing companies. Tips are shared to help maintain good customer satisfaction and repeat business.

26348 ■ "Is That the Best You Can Do?" in *Entrepreneur* (Vol. 37, October 2009, No. 10, pp. 85)
Pub: Entrepreneur Media, Inc.
Ed: Jennifer Wang. **Description:** Small business owners can deal with hagglers better by setting parameters in advance. They should convince hagglers by offering the best value and separating this from price.

26349 ■ "It's Not About You" in *Entrepreneur* (Vol. 35, November 2007, No. 11, pp. 102)
Pub: Entrepreneur Media Inc.
Ed: Barry Farber. **Description:** Companies should focus on the customers' need and show them that they care about them. Listening to and learning about your customers can make selling easier; tips on how to stay focused on the customers' needs are outlined.

26350 ■ "Just Be Nice" in *Canadian Business* (Vol. 79, October 9, 2006, No. 20, pp. 141)
Pub: Rogers Media
Ed: Joe Castaldo. **Description:** The customer relationship management strategies on customer retention and satisfaction adopted by WestJet are discussed.

26351 ■ "Keeping Customers Satisfied" in *Pet Product News* (Vol. 64, December 2010, No. 12, pp. 10)
Pub: BowTie Inc.
Ed: Devon McPhee. **Description:** Windsor, California-based Debbie's Pet Boutique, recipient of Pet Product News International's Outstanding Customer Service Award, has been dedicated to combining topnotch grooming services with a robust retail selection. These features might gain return customers for Debbie's Pet Boutique.

26352 ■ *The Kindess Revolution: The Company-Wide Culture Shift That Inspires Phenomenal Customer Service*
Pub: American Management Association
Ed: Ed Horrell. **Released:** 2006. **Price:** $23.00.

26353 ■ "Kubicki Juggles Lineup at Vianda" in *Business Courier* (Vol. 26, December 11, 2009, No. 33, pp. 1)
Pub: American City Business Journals, Inc.
Ed: Dan Monk. **Description:** Cincinnati real estate developer Chuck Kubicki replaced the management team of Vianda LLC and cancelled contracts with two vendors that caused a surge of customer complaints.

Vianda is a direct-response marketing firm that sells and distributes dietary supplements for wellness and sexual performance.

26354 ■ "Leadership Behavior and Employee Voice: Is the Door Really Open?" in *Academy of Management Journal* (August 2007)
Pub: Academy of Management
Ed: James R. Detert, Ethan R. Burris. **Description:** Relationships between two types of change-oriented leadership and subordinate improvement-oriented voice in a two-phase study are presented.

26355 ■ "Let Emerging Market Customers Be Your Teachers" in *Harvard Business Review* (Vol. 88, December 2010, No. 12, pp. 115)
Pub: Harvard Business School Publishing
Ed: Guillermo D'Andrea, David Marcotte, Gwen Dixon Morrison. **Description:** Examination of effective strategies for emerging markets is presented. These include helping educate customers as well as selling to them, adapting to customers' habits, and focusing brands appropriately. Magazine Luiza, a chain store in Brazil, is used to illustrate these points.

26356 ■ "Like a Business Militia" in *Crain's Detroit Business* (Vol. 25,
Pub: Crain Communications Inc. - Detroit
Ed: Daniel Duggan. **Description:** Hotel executives are forming hotel committees and associations in Southeastern Michigan in the hopes of drawing more visitors to the region. Meetings are encouraging the use of promoting specific regions in ways that will secure multi-hotel events.

26357 ■ "Looking Out for the Little Guys" in *Black Enterprise* (Vol. 38, October 2007, No. 3, pp. 58)
Pub: Earl G. Graves Publishing Co. Inc.
Ed: Kaylyn Kendall Dines. **Description:** Biz Tech-Connect is a Web portal that offers free online and social networking, along with four modules that help small businesses with marketing and advertising, communications and mobility, financial management, and customer relationship management.

26358 ■ "Loyalty Cards Score Points" in *Crain's Cleveland Business* (Vol. 30, June 8, 2009, No. 22, pp. 1)
Pub: Crain Communications, Inc.
Ed: Chuck Soder. **Description:** Northeast Ohio retailers are promoting loyalty and rewards programs in order to attract and maintain loyal customers.

26359 ■ "Luxe Men Are In Style" in *Brandweek* (Vol. 49, April 21, 2008, No. 16, pp. 12)
Pub: VNU Business Media, Inc.
Description: According to a recent survey by Unity Marketing, among 1,300 luxury shoppers found that men spent an average of $2,401 on fashion items over a three-month period which is nearly $1,000 more than women. Men also spring for more luxury items such as vehicles and memberships to exclusive clubs.

26360 ■ "Make Relationships Count: CRM Software That Works" in *Black Enterprise* (Vol. 38, February 2008, No. 7, pp. 60)
Pub: Earl G. Graves Publishing Co. Inc.
Ed: Fiona Haley. **Description:** Customer relationship management (CRM) software can help any small business keep track of clients. Descriptions of the latest CRM software offered are profiled, including Salesforce.com, Microsoft Dynamics, and Saga Software.

26361 ■ "Making Automated Royalty Payments Work for Your Franchise" in *Franchising World* (Vol. 42, October 2010, No. 10, pp. 30)
Pub: International Franchise Association
Ed: J.P. O'Brien. **Description:** In the past, royalty payments were sent by franchisees through regular postal mail and accompanied by a single slip of paper with handwritten notes indicating the month's revenue numbers and royalty amounts.

26362 ■ "Making It Click" in *Barron's* (Vol. 88, March 17, 2008, No. 11, pp. 31)
Pub: Dow Jones & Company, Inc.
Ed: Theresa W. Carey. **Description:** Listing of 23 online brokers that are evaluated based on their trade experience, usability, range of offerings, research amenities, customer service and access, and costs. TradeStation Securities takes the top spot followed by thinkorswim by just a fraction.

26363 ■ "Making It Work" in *Pet Product News* (Vol. 64, December 2010, No. 12, pp. S8)
Pub: BowTie Inc.
Ed: Kerri Chladnicek. **Description:** How focusing on service and flexibility allowed New Jersey-based pet supply store B.C. Woof to achieve success is discussed. B.C. Woof began as a pet-sitting business which eventually concentrated on natural foods. Aside from conducting a do-it-yourself approach in food formulation for customers, B.C. Woof has also been guiding customers on nutrients they need for their pets.

26364 ■ "Making It Work" in *Retail Merchandiser* (Vol. 51, July-August 2011, No. 4, pp. 43)
Pub: Phoenix Media Corporation
Ed: Anthony DiPaolo. **Description:** Profile of Anthony DiPaolo and his purchase of the Work 'N Gear retail store in 2002. The brick and mortar shop sells work wear and healthcare apparel and DiPaolo believes customer respect is essential to his success.

26365 ■ *Managing a Small Business Made Easy*
Pub: Entrepreneur Press
Ed: Martin E. Davis. **Released:** September 2005. **Price:** $19.95 (US), $26.95 (Canadian). **Description:** Examination of the essential elements for an entrepreneur running a business, including advice on leadership, customer service, financials, and more.

26366 ■ *Marketing 2.0: Bridging the Gap between Seller and Buyer through Social Media Marketing*
Pub: Wheatmark
Ed: Bernie Borges. **Released:** July 14, 2009. **Price:** $22.95. **Description:** Winning strategies to attract people to your company and your employees using social media site on the Internet are outlined.

26367 ■ "McCormick Focuses on Customer, Dealer Service" in *Farm Industry News* (September 17, 2010)
Pub: Penton Business Media Inc.
Description: McCormick has developed a new plan that focuses on fast and complete service to both customers and dealers.

26368 ■ "McD's Tries to Slake Consumer Thirst for Wider Choice of Drinks" in *Advertising Age* (Vol. 79, June 9, 2008, No. 23, pp. 1)
Pub: Crain Communications, Inc.
Ed: Natalie Zmuda; Emily Bryson York. **Description:** McDonald's is testing the sale of canned and bottled drinks in about 150 locations in an attempt to offer more options to consumers who are going elsewhere for their beverage choices.

26369 ■ "Mergers Mean Woe for Fliers; Airline Hookups Boost Fares, Diminish Service" in *Crain's Chicago Business* (April 21, 2008)
Pub: Crain Communications, Inc.
Ed: John Pletz. **Description:** Discusses the impact airline mergers will have on customer service, pricing and business travel, particularly at Chicago's O'Hare International Airport.

26370 ■ "Midwest Seeks Concessions From Creditors" in *The Business Journal-Milwaukee* (Vol. 25, July 25, 2008, No. 44, pp. A1)
Pub: American City Business Journals, Inc.
Ed: Rich Rovito. **Description:** Midwest Airlines Inc. is turning to creditors and lease holders for the financial aspect of its restructuring, which involves going back to serving popular business destinations. Chief executive officer Timothy believes that the company can survive in a niche market as long as it provides quality service. He discusses Midwest's restructuring plan.

26371 ■ *The Mom and Pop Store: How the Unsung Heroes of the American Economy Are Surviving and Thriving*
Pub: Walker & Company
Ed: Robert Spector. **Released:** September 1, 2009. **Price:** $26.00. **Description:** The history of small independent retail enterprises and how mom and pop stores in the U.S. continue to thrive through customer service and renewed community support for local businesses.

26372 ■ "Monopoly Money Madness" in *Canadian Business* (Vol. 81, March 17, 2008, No. 4, pp. 9)
Pub: Rogers Media
Description: Enbridge was given permission by the Ontario Energy Board to collect $22 million it spent on an out-of-court settlement for charging unfair fees from 1994 to 2002. Customers are essentially being gouged twice in this scenario. The monopoly of Enbridge should end and the consumers should not have to pay for the system's faults.

26373 ■ *More Than a Pink Cadillac*
Pub: McGraw-Hill
Ed: Jim Underwood. **Released:** 2002. **Price:** $23.95. **Description:** Profile of Mary Kay Ash who turned her $5,000 investment into a billion-dollar corporation. Ash's nine principles that form the foundation of her company's global success are outlined. Stories from her sales force leaders share ideas for motivating employees, impressing customers and building a successful company. The book emphasizes the leadership skills required to drive performance in any successful enterprise.

26374 ■ "Muirhead Farmhouse B & B Owners Get Hospitality Right" in *Chicago Tribune* (July 31, 2008)
Pub: McClatchy-Tribune Information Services
Ed: Glenn Jeffers. **Description:** Profile of the Muirhead Farmhouse, a bed-and-breakfast owned by Mike Petersdorf and Sarah Muirhead Petersdorf; Frank Lloyd Wright designed the historic farmhouse which blends farm life and history into a unique experience that is enhanced by the couple's hospitality.

26375 ■ "Multichannel Marketing: Mindset and Program Development" in *Business Horizons* (September-October 2007)
Pub: Elsevier Technology Publications
Ed: Bruce D. Weinberg, Salvatore Parise, Patricia J. Guinan. **Description:** Organizations should develop a multichannel mindset and design multichannel marketing programs in order to increase profitability and enhance customer satisfaction. Creating a holistic strategy, crating metrics that measure the impacts and overall performance, and designing organizational structure and incentives are key factors in implementing the marketing program.

26376 ■ "Network Like A Boy Scout" in *Women Entrepreneur* (January 15, 2009)
Pub: Entrepreneur Media Inc.
Ed: Merrily Orsini. **Description:** Marketing for businesses that provide products or services that people only seek during emergencies or natural disasters such as hurricanes can be a challenge; tips for branding such businesses, networking and establishing a strong customer base that will refer your business to others are given.

26377 ■ *Niche and Grow Rich*
Pub: Entrepreneur Press
Ed: Jennifer Basye Sander; Peter Sander. **Released:** 2003. **Description:** Consultants share insight to entrepreneurs wishing to find a profitable niche market. Authors write that good niche businesses are easy to start and easy to defend from competitors. They also report that finding a successful niche can attract and maintain good customers who are willing to pay more for unique goods and services.

26378 ■ "Office Supplier Won't Wait for Opportunity to Knock" in *Business Courier* (Vol. 24, December 28, 2008, No. 37, pp. 2)
Pub: American City Business Journals, Inc.

Ed: Lucy May. **Description:** Ace Products, an office supplier, stays competitive through its customer service and pricing.

26379 ■ *The One Minute Entrepreneur*
Pub: Doubleday

Ed: Ken Blanchard; assisted by Don Hutson and Ethan Willis. **Released:** 2008. **Price:** $19.95. **Description:** Four traditional business ideas are covered including: revenue needs to exceed expenses, bill collection, customer service, and employee motivation in order to be successful.

26380 ■ "The One Thing You Must Get Right When Building a Brand" in *Harvard Business Review* (Vol. 88, December 2010, No. 12, pp. 80)
Pub: Harvard Business School Publishing

Ed: Patrick Barwise, Sean Meehan. **Description:** Four uses for new media include: communicating a clearly defined customer promise, creating trust via delivering on the promise, regularly improving on the promise, and innovating past what is familiar.

26381 ■ *Organizations Alive!: Six Things That Challenge - Seven That Bring Success*
Pub: Yuill & Associates

Ed: Jan Yuill. **Released:** January 2005. **Price:** $35.12 for book and guide. **Description:** New insight into understanding how organizations function as individuals is presented by an international consultant. Customer service, resource management, outsourcing, and management are among the issues covered.

26382 ■ *Outfoxing the Small Business Owner*
Pub: Adams Media Corporation

Ed: Gene Marks. **Released:** January 2005. **Description:** Special skill sets are required to sell, service or deal with small business customers.

26383 ■ *Over the Counter*
Pub: The Mercier Press, Ltd.

Ed: Keogh. **Released:** January 1, 2009. **Price:** $54. 95. **Description:** An overview of the changing landscape of Cork, Ireland's retail stores is presented.

26384 ■ "Pay or Play: Do Nice (Sales) Guys Finish Last?" in *Agency Sales Magazine* (Vol. 39, August 2009, No. 8, pp. 8)
Pub: MANA

Ed: Julia M. Rahn. **Description:** How positive interpersonal relationships among salespersons, program coordinators, and other business-related professions will pay in terms of business success is presented. Business people should know the ideal customers, promise only what they can do, refer out when needed, and follow through with any stated promise. Further insight into these ideas is presented.

26385 ■ "The Perfect Formula to Build Your Brand" in *Entrepreneur* (Vol. 37, July 2009, No. 7, pp. 70)
Pub: Entrepreneur Media, Inc.

Ed: Susan J. Linder. **Description:** Combining a product with expertise and a promise is the formula in building a brand for startups. The product will not sell itself, so one must consider what makes the product truly unique. Meanwhile, establishing trust and a foundation for a brand can be achieved by making a promise to the consumer and fulfilling it.

26386 ■ "Perfecting Customer Services" in *Pet Product News* (Vol. 64, November 2010, No. 11, pp. 18)
Pub: BowTie Inc.

Description: Pet supply retailers are encouraged to emphasize customer experience and sales representatives' knowledge of the store's product offerings to foster repeat business. Employee protocols could be implemented to improve customer interaction. Other guidelines on developing a pet supply retail environment that advances repeat business are presented.

26387 ■ "Perfecting the Process: Creating a Move Efficient Organization On Your Terms" in *Black Enterprise* (Vol. 41, October 2010, No. 3)
Pub: Earl G. Graves Publishing Co. Inc.

Ed: Tamara E. Holmes. **Description:** More than ever, entrepreneurs need to identify new ways of doing business in a cost-effective manner in order to expand their companies, while remaining true to their customer demands.

26388 ■ "Peter Gilgan" in *Canadian Business* (Vol. 82, April 27, 2009, No. 7, pp. 58)
Pub: Rogers Media

Ed: Calvin Leung. **Description:** Mattamy Homes Ltd. president and chief executive officer Peter Gilgan believes that their business model of building communities in an organized way brings advantages to the firm and for their customers. He also believes in adopting their product prices to new market realities. Gilgan considers the approvals regime in Ontario his biggest challenge in the last 20 years.

26389 ■ "PGA Tour: Course Management" in *Retail Merchandiser* (Vol. 51, September-October 2011, No. 5, pp. 38)
Pub: Phoenix Media Corporation

Ed: Eric Slack. **Description:** PGA Tour must reach new customers and solidify relationships with its traditional base in order to continue its success. The PGA brand equity has translated into one of the largest retail licensing operations worldwide.

26390 ■ "The Phone-Service Test" in *Canadian Business* (Vol. 79, October 9, 2006, No. 20, pp. 137)
Pub: Rogers Media

Ed: Rachel Pulfer. **Description:** Suggestions to improve the customer services provided by airlines through call centers are discussed.

26391 ■ "The Price of Profitability" in *Green Industry Pro* (Vol. 23, March 2011, No. 3, pp. 18)
Pub: Cygnus Business Media

Ed: Tony Bass. **Description:** Profit Builder Process is used to help landscaping companies be more competitive. Landscape contractors report pricing among their largest challenges and although the economy is improving, homeowners are paying closer attention to quality and service.

26392 ■ *Principled Profit: Marketing that Puts People First*
Pub: Accurate Writing & More

Ed: Shel Horowitz. **Price:** $17.50. **Description:** The importance for companies to market ethically and honestly is stressed. Quality marketing will build customer loyalty and that will translate into new customers and repeat business. A customer-retention strategy is outlined along with ideas to increase profits of any small business.

26393 ■ "Putting the Service-Profit Chain to Work" in *Harvard Business Review* (Vol. 86, July-August 2008, No. 8, pp. 118)
Pub: Harvard Business School Press

Ed: James L. Heskett; Thomas O. Jones; Gary W. Loveman; W. Earl Sasser Jr.; Leonard A. Schlesinger. **Description:** Advice is given on how to foster profitability in service businesses. Topics include the link between employee satisfaction and customer satisfaction, internal service quality, external service value, and revenue growth.

26394 ■ "Q&A: David Labistour" in *Canadian Business* (Vol. 81, March 17, 2008, No. 4, pp. 10)
Pub: Rogers Media

Ed: Lauren McKeon. **Description:** David Labistour says that the difference between being a co-op retailer and a corporate-owned retailer in the case of Mountain Equipment Co-op (MEC) is that the company is owned by their customers and not by shareholders. Labistour also says that MEC works with their factories to ensure that these maintain ethical standards in the manufacturing process.

26395 ■ "The Question: Who Do You Think Is the Most Genuine?" in *Advertising Age* (Vol. 79, July 7, 2008, No. 26, pp. 4)
Pub: Crain Communications, Inc.

Ed: Ken Wheaton. **Description:** According to a survey conducted by Harris Interactive Reputation Quotient, Johnson & Johnson was deemed the most genuine brand. Google came in second followed by UPS.

26396 ■ "Rapport Overhaul" in *Small Business Opportunities* (Winter 2009)
Pub: Entrepreneur Media Inc.

Ed: Laurie Brown. **Description:** Advice concerning ways in which to build customer rapport is provided.

26397 ■ *Raving Fans: A Revolutionary Approach to Customer Service*
Pub: William Morrow

Ed: Ken Blanchard, Sheldon Bowles. **Released:** May 19, 1993. **Price:** $22.95. **Description:** Strategies to improve customer service in any industry are provided.

26398 ■ "Reaping Social-Media Rewards" in *Canadian Business* (Vol. 83, July 20, 2010, No. 11-12, pp. 19)
Pub: Rogers Media Ltd.

Ed: Lyndsie Bourgon. **Description:** Foursquare is a social network which provides benefits such as discounts to users who show loyalty to a business or a brand. One marketing executive believes Foursquare is a good platform for loyalty programs and is an inexpensive alternative to Aeroplan.

26399 ■ "Recession-Proof Your Startup" in *Crain's Chicago Business* (Vol. 31, November 10, 2008, No. 45, pp. 24)
Pub: Crain Communications, Inc.

Description: Detailed information concerning ways in which to start a business during an economic crisis is provided. Ways in which to find financing, the importance of a solid business plan, customer service, problem-solving and finding the right niche for the region are also discussed.

26400 ■ "Renters' Review – Secret Shoppers Strike Again" in *Rental Product News* (Vol. 33, June 2011)
Pub: Cygnus Business Media

Description: Staff of Rental Product News set out to rent various items from three different rental sources in order to evaluate the rental experience from the eyes of the average customer.

26401 ■ "Reps Have Needs Too!" in *Agency Sales Magazine* (Vol. 39, December 2009, No. 11, pp. 16)
Pub: MANA

Ed: Bill Heyden. **Description:** There is common information that a sales representatives needs to know prior to choosing a manufacturer to represent. Both parties must keep promises made to customers and prospects. Reps also need the support from the manufacturers and to clear matters regarding their commission. Interviewing tips for representatives to get this vital information are presented.

26402 ■ "Rethinking the Organization" in *Strategy & Leadership* (Vol. 38, September-October 2010, No. 5, pp. 13-19)
Pub: Emerald Inc.

Ed: Stephen Denning. **Description:** A study identifies the changes needed to be adopted by top managers to achieve game-changing innovation at an organization-wide level. Findings indicate that CEOs should practice pull management in order to nurture fruitful communication between employees and customers and achieve organizational involvement of customers.

26403 ■ *Rework*
Pub: Crown Business

Ed: Jason Fried, David Heinemeier Hansson. **Released:** March 9, 2010. **Price:** $22.00. **Description:** Works to help entrepreneurs and business owners to rethink strategy, customers, and getting things accomplished.

26404 ■ "RIM Opts to Be Little Less Open" in *Canadian Business* (Vol. 83, October 12, 2010, No. 17, pp. 13)
Pub: Rogers Media Ltd.
Ed: Joe Castaldo. **Description:** RIM is planning to stop releasing quarterly subscriber updates. However, some analysts are skeptical about the change due to the previous drop in company subscribers. The company also decided to stop reporting the average selling price of the BlackBerry, which analysts have also scrutinized.

26405 ■ "Roger Hickel Contracting: Smoothing the Road for Owners" in *Alaska Business Monthly* (Vol. 27, October 2011, No. 10, pp. 114)
Pub: Alaska Business Publishing Company
Ed: Gail West. **Description:** Profile of Roger Hickel and his contracting company that reports nearly $60 million annually in gross revenue. The firm focuses on customer service.

26406 ■ "Rule of the Masses: Reinventing Fashion Via Crowdsourcing" in *WWD* (Vol. 200, July 26, 2010, No. 17, pp. 1)
Pub: Conde Nast Publications Inc.
Ed: Cate T. Corcoran. **Description:** Large apparel brands and retailers are crowdsourcing as a way to increase customer loyalty and to build their businesses.

26407 ■ "Sales Force Expertise: A Competitive Advantage" in *Agency Sales Magazine* (Vol. 39, November 2009, No. 10, pp. 10)
Pub: MANA
Ed: Ken Valla. **Description:** Maintaining an expert sales force is a competitive advantage that sales leaders can count on. The skills that the sales force need to have include "consultative selling" or the ability to understand and link to a customer's business priorities, conducting a process conversation, and asking discovery questions.

26408 ■ "SEC Report On Rating Agencies Falls Short" in *Barron's* (Vol. 88, July 14, 2008, No. 28, pp. 35)
Pub: Dow Jones & Co., Inc.
Ed: Jack Willoughby. **Description:** The Securities and Exchange Commissions report on credit-rating firms should have drawn attention to the slipshod practices in the offerings of collateralized debt obligations. The report fell short of prescribing correctives for the flawed system of these agencies' relationship with their clients.

26409 ■ "Segmenting When It Matters" in *Business Strategy Review* (Vol. 21, Spring 2010, No. 1, pp. 46)
Pub: Wiley-Blackwell
Ed: Andreas Birnik, Richard Moat. **Description:** Authors argue that business complexity is directly linked to the degree of segmentation implemented by a company. They propose an approach to map business activities at the segment level to make sure that complexity is only introduced when it really matters.

26410 ■ *Sell More of Anything to Anyone: Sales Tips for Individuals, Business Owners and Sales Professionals*
Pub: Allen & Unwin
Ed: Andrew Griffiths. **Released:** May 10, 2010. **Price:** $16.95. **Description:** Tips are shared to help anyone improve sales skills while providing strong customer service.

26411 ■ *Serves You Right!*
Pub: Serves You Right!, Incorporated
Ed: Susan Brooks. **Released:** May 2004. **Price:** $15. 95. **Description:** Profile of excellence in customer service.

26412 ■ "Service With a Smile...And Comfy Chairs" in *Crain's Chicago Business* (Vol. 31, April 28, 2008, No. 17, pp. 46)
Pub: Crain Communications, Inc.
Ed: Phuong Ly. **Description:** O'Hare Auto Group has improved the experience of waiting for service on one's vehicle by offering wireless Internet, comfortable chairs and plasma TVs. The company also has long service hours, running from 6 a.m. to midnight Monday through Thursday so customers don't have to take time off work.

26413 ■ "Serving Unfair Customers" in *Business Horizons* (Vol. 51, January-February 2008, No. 1, pp. 29)
Pub: Elsevier Advanced Technology Publications
Ed: Leonard L. Berry, Kathleen Seiders. **Description:** Quality service is based on the maxim "the customer is always right", but customer behavior studies have revealed that customers can be glaringly unjust. These unfair customers exploit the customer service maxim, affecting both the company and other customers. Methods to effectively deal with unfair customers are explored.

26414 ■ "Show and Tell" in *Entrepreneur* (Vol. 36, May 2008, No. 5, pp. 54)
Pub: Entrepreneur Media, Inc.
Ed: Heather Clancy. **Description:** FreshStart Telephone uses recorded video testimonials of customers, by using Pure Digital Flip Video that downloads content directly to the computer, and uploads it in the company's website to promote their wireless phone service.

26415 ■ "Skinner's No Drive-Thru CEO" in *Crain's Chicago Business* (Vol. 31, April 28, 2008, No. 17, pp. 1)
Pub: Crain Communications, Inc.
Ed: David Sterrett. **Description:** Profile of James Skinner who was named CEO for McDonald's Corp. in November 2004 and has proved to be a successful leader despite the number of investors who doubted him when he came to the position. Mr. Skinner has overseen three years of unprecedented sales growth and launched the biggest menu expansion in 30 years.

26416 ■ *Small Business Desk Reference*
Pub: Penguin Books (USA) Incorporated
Ed: Gene Marks. **Released:** December 2004. **Description:** Comprehensive guide for starting or running a successful small business, focusing on buying a business or franchise, writing a business plan, financial management, accounting, legal issues, human resources management, operations, marketing, sales, customer service, taxes, insurance, and ethics. Information for launching a restaurant, property management firm, retail outlet, consulting firm, and service business is included.

26417 ■ *Small Business Survival Guide*
Pub: Adams Media Corporation
Ed: Cliff Ennico. **Price:** $12.95. **Description:** Small business expert provides strategies to start a company and survive in the 21st Century. He shows small business owners how to succeed despite challenges that can defeat any firm. His advice covers suppliers; customers and contractors; competitors and creditors; spouses, family and friends; as well as the ways lawyers, accountants and other can steal an entrepreneur's success. Ennico also describes how startups can comply with local regulations.

26418 ■ "Small Fish, Big Box Stores" in *Hawaii Business* (Vol. 53, November 2007, No. 5, pp. 55)
Pub: Hawaii Business Publishing
Ed: Jolyn Okimoto Rosa. **Description:** Ohana Seafoods can be found at big-box stores such as Costco, Marukai and Don Quijote. Owner Jeffrey Yee spends his weekend at a farmers market to have direct contact with his customers and get feedback right away. Ohana offers ready-to cook fish products, sauces and fish.

26419 ■ "Smarts Drive Sales" in *Pet Product News* (Vol. 64, December 2010, No. 12, pp. 1)
Pub: BowTie Inc.
Ed: Karen Shugart. **Description:** Retailers could make smart decisions by deciding how to best attract customers into their stores or resolving whether to nurture in-store or buy herps (reptiles) from suppliers. Paying attention to these smart decisions could help boost customer interest in herps and address customer demands.

26420 ■ *The Social Media Bible: Tactics, Tools, and Strategies for Business Success*
Pub: John Wiley & Sons, Inc.
Ed: Lon Safko, David Brake. **Released:** June 17, 2009. **Price:** $29.95. **Description:** Information is given to build or transform a business into social media, where customers, employees, and prospects connect, collaborate, and champion products and services in order to increase sales and to beat the competition.

26421 ■ "Solutions for the Frustrating Feline" in *Pet Product News* (Vol. 64, November 2010, No. 11, pp. 46)
Pub: BowTie Inc.
Ed: Lori Luechtefeld. **Description:** Products that can help customers deal with problematic cat behaviors, such as out-of-the-box urination and scratching are described. Information on such products including litter box deodorants and disposable scratchers is provided. Feline territorial behaviors can also be addressed by pheromone products that can calm hyperactive cats.

26422 ■ "Sometimes, Second Impressions Count Most" in *Canadian Business* (Vol. 83, October 12, 2010, No. 17, pp. 11)
Pub: Rogers Media Ltd.
Ed: Richard Branson. **Description:** Developing a favorable impression at the first point of contact is imperative for businesses. Managers who want their organizations to make positive first and second impressions need to learn to balance the Web's labor-saving efficiencies with human assistants. The importance of considering the customer relations value in company Websites is also explained.

26423 ■ "Sometimes You Have to Ignore the Rule Book" in *Canadian Business* (Vol. 83, September 14, 2010, No. 15, pp. 13)
Pub: Rogers Media Ltd.
Ed: Richard Branson. **Description:** The rule book has provided a clear framework for employees particularly when cash and accounting are at issue. However, sometimes rules were made to be broken and the rule book should not become an excuse for poor customer service or hinder great service. How Virgin Atlantic practices this type of corporate culture is discussed.

26424 ■ "Sound Check" in *Agency Sales Magazine* (Vol. 39, August 2009, No. 8, pp. 14)
Pub: MANA
Ed: Dave Kahle. **Description:** Most customers believe salespersons are unable to do well in terms of listening, which is one of the four fundamental competencies of a sales person. Listening is the primary tool to uncover deeper and more powerful needs and motivations of the customer. A guide on how to listen better and improve listening effectiveness is presented.

26425 ■ "Speakers Address Authenticity, R&D Evolution" in *Nation's Restaurant News* (Vol. 45, October 24, 2011, No. 32, pp. 32)
Pub: Penton Media Inc.
Ed: Bret Thorn. **Description:** Culinary trends are discussed, along with an examination of the food truck trend and how this small sector is creating a great influence on food and communication with customers and delivery expectations.

26426 ■ "Sponsorship, Booths Available for Spring Business Showcase" in *Bellingham Business Journal* (Vol. February 2010, pp. 3)
Pub: Sound Publishing Inc.
Description: Third Annual Spring Business Showcase still have space available for vendors and sponsors. The event gives local businesses the opportunity to increase their visibility and provides a means to increase sales and build relationships.

26427 ■ "The Start of a Beautiful Friendship: Partnering with Your Customers on R&D" in *Inc.* (March 2008, pp. 37-38)
Pub: Gruner & Jahr USA Publishing
Ed: Leigh Buchanan. **Description:** Joint research and development projects between customers and suppliers are a growing trend in the small business

community; these ventures can help keep new product development costs lower. Four tips to maintain a good working relationship in these ventures are outlined.

26428 ■ "State's Glass Ceiling Gets Higher" in *Business Journal-Milwaukee* (Vol. 25, October 5, 2007, No. 1, pp. A1)
Pub: American City Business Journals, Inc.
Ed: Jennifer Batog. **Description:** Report showed that more than a third of Wisconsin's fifty largest companies have no female executive officers, and the number of companies with at least one woman at top departments has also decreased since 2005. Companies lacking women at upper management levels risk jeopardizing their firms' vitality as diversity in executive offices leads to diverse ideas that can help in relating better to customers and clients.

26429 ■ "Stop Trying to Delight Your Customers" in *Harvard Business Review* (Vol. 88, July-August 2010, No. 7-8, pp. 116)
Pub: Harvard Business School Publishing
Ed: Matthew Dixon, Karen Freeman, Nicholas Toman. **Description:** Importance of resolving issues for customers is key to increasing their loyalty, rather than by exceeding customer expectations. Areas to address include decreasing customer need for follow-up calls, switching service channels, and the potential for negative emotional response.

26430 ■ "Stress-Test Your Strategy: the 7 Questions to Ask" in *Harvard Business Review* (Vol. 88, November 2010, No. 11, pp. 92)
Pub: Harvard Business School Publishing
Ed: Robert Simons. **Description:** Seven questions organizations should use to assess crisis management capabilities are: who is the primary customer, how do core values prioritize all parties, what performance variables are being tracked, what strategic boundaries have been set, how is creative tension being produced, how committed are workers to assisting each other, and what uncertainties are causing worry?

26431 ■ "Supply Chain Visibility A Two-Way Street" in *Canadian Sailings* (July 7, 2008)
Pub: Commonwealth Business Media
Ed: Jack Kohane. **Description:** Canada is experiencing unprecedented market pressures due to globalization. Competition from foreign countries, demand for better and faster service from customers and shorter innovation cycles are some of the problems the country is facing regarding trade and the importing and exporting industry.

26432 ■ "Take Out the Garbage" in *Entrepreneur* (Vol. 37, August 2009, No. 8, pp. 26)
Pub: Entrepreneur Media, Inc.
Ed: Michael Port. **Description:** Canned 1-2-3 sales tactics should be ditched since consumers express their values with the products and services they buy. Sales people should instead work their call list and become a masterful permission marketer, make relevant sales offers proportionate to the trust they have earned, and build credibility with the people they are meant to serve.

26433 ■ "Take This Job and Love It" in *Green Industry Pro* (Vol. 23, October 2011)
Pub: Cygnus Business Media
Ed: Gregg Wartgow. **Description:** Details of the lawsuit filed by the Professional Landcare Network (PLANET) against the U.S. Department of Labor are explained. Challenges faced by landscape firms because of employment costs are outlined. Statistical data included.

26434 ■ "Taking a Chance" in *Baltimore Business Journal* (Vol. 28, July 16, 2010, No. 10, pp. 1)
Pub: Baltimore Business Journal
Ed: Scott Dance. **Description:** North Avenue in Baltimore, Maryland is considered a rough neighborhood due to the dangers of prostitution and drug dealing. However, some entrepreneurs have taken the risk of building their businesses on North Avenue as revitalization efforts grow. One of the challenges for businesses in rough neighborhoods is bringing customers to their stores or offices.

26435 ■ "Tap the iPad and Mobile Internet Device Market" in *Franchising World* (Vol. 42, September 2010, No. 9, pp. 43)
Pub: International Franchise Association
Ed: John Thomson. **Description:** The iPad and other mobile Internet devices will help franchise owners interact with customers. It will be a good marketing tool for these businesses.

26436 ■ "Tapping the 'Well' in Wellness" in *Pet Product News* (Vol. 64, November 2010, No. 11, pp. 1)
Pub: BowTie Inc.
Ed: Wendy-Bedwell Wilson. **Description:** Healthy food and treats are among the leading wellness products being sought by customers from specialty retailers to keep their pets healthy. With this demand for pet wellness products, retailers suggest making sure that staff know key ingredients to emphasize to customers. Other insights into this trend and ways to engage customers are discussed.

26437 ■ "Teachable Moments: Worth Every Penny" in *Pet Product News* (Vol. 64, December 2010, No. 12, pp. 34)
Pub: BowTie Inc.
Ed: Cheryl Reeves. **Description:** Pet bird retailers can attain both outreach to customers and enhanced profitability by staging educational events such as the annual Parrot Palooza event of Burlington, New Jersey-based Bird Paradise. Aside from attracting a global audience, Parrot Palooza features seminars, workshops, classes, and bird-related contests.

26438 ■ "Technology: What Seems To Be the Problem? Self Service Gets a Tune-Up" in *Inc.* (February 2008, pp. 43-44)
Pub: Gruner & Jahr USA Publishing
Ed: Darren Dahl. **Description:** Self-service software can save companies money when responding to customer service phone calls, text or email messages. More companies are relying on alternatives such as automated Web-based self-service systems.

26439 ■ "Tell Us What You Really Think Collecting Customer Feedback" in *Inc.* (Vol. 30, December 2008, No. 12, pp. 52)
Pub: Mansueto Ventures LLC
Ed: Ryan Underwood. **Description:** According to a recent survey, nearly 77 percent of online shoppers review consumer-generated reviews of products before making a purchase.

26440 ■ *Thank God It's Monday! How to Create a Workplace You and Your Customers Love*
Pub: FT Press
Ed: Roxanne Emmerich. **Released:** April 18, 2009. **Price:** $19.99. **Description:** Tips on creating a positive environment for both employees and customers.

26441 ■ "The Next 20 Years: How Customer and Workforce Attitudes Will Evolve" in *Harvard Business Review* (Vol. 85, July-August 2007, No. 7-8)
Pub: Harvard Business School Publishing
Ed: Neil Howe, William Strauss. **Description:** Identification of social categories inhabited by age groups is used to calculate how consumer and employee opinions and behavior will change, and how this will impact economic development and corporate growth.

26442 ■ *Trade-Off: The Ever-Present Tension Between Quality and Conscience*
Pub: Crown Business Books
Ed: Kevin Maney. **Released:** August 17, 2010. **Price:** $15.00. **Description:** The tension between fidelity (the quality of a consumer's experience) and convenience (the ease of getting and paying for a product) are shown to be the forces that determine the success or failure of new products and services in the marketplace.

26443 ■ "The Transparent Supply Chain" in *Harvard Business Review* (Vol. 88, October 2010, No. 10, pp. 76)
Pub: Harvard Business School Publishing
Ed: Steve New. **Description:** Examination of the use of new technologies to create a transparent supply chain, such as next-generation 2D bar codes in clothing labels that can provide data on a garment's provenance.

26444 ■ *Treasure Hunt*
Pub: Penguin Group Incorporated
Ed: Michael J. Silverstein; John Butman. **Released:** May 4, 2006. **Description:** Explanation of people's spending habits and how to capitalize on retail sales.

26445 ■ "Turning Trust Into Success" in *Retail Merchandiser* (Vol. 51, July-August 2011, No. 4, pp. 52)
Pub: Phoenix Media Corporation
Ed: Karen Kondilis. **Description:** Shopko Stores employs tenured and trustworthy pharmacists and believes it is the core to their success.

26446 ■ *Up the Loyalty Ladder*
Pub: HarperCollins Publishers Inc.
Ed: Murray Rephel; Neil Raphel. **Released:** September 1996. **Description:** Marketing consultants share insight into growing any retail business and gain customer loyalty.

26447 ■ "Visionary Riches" in *Small Business Opportunities* (Winter 2009)
Pub: Entrepreneur Media Inc.
Description: Profile of Sterling Optical, which was included in a recent listing of 25 franchise high performers in The Wall Street Journal and is poised for mega-growth due to its offerings of professional eye exams, impeccable customer service, convenient locations and a great selection of eyewear.

26448 ■ *We Are Smarter Than Me: How to Unleash the Power of Crowds in Your Business*
Pub: Wharton School Publishing
Ed: Barry Libert; Jon Spector; Don Tapscott. **Released:** October 5, 2007. **Price:** $21.99. **Description:** Ways to use social networking and community in order to make decisions and plan your business, with a focus on product development, manufacturing, marketing, customer service, finance, management, and more.

26449 ■ "'We Had to Won the Mistakes'" in *Harvard Business Review* (Vol. 88, July-August 2010, No. 7-8, pp. 108)
Pub: Harvard Business School Publishing
Ed: Adi Ignatius. **Description:** Interview with Howard Schultz, CEO of Starbucks, covers topics that include investment in retraining, the impact of competition, premium quality, authenticity, customer services, strategy development, work-and-life issues, and international presence.

26450 ■ "A Weak Link Can Break the Chain of Good Service" in *Canadian Business* (Vol. 83, August 17, 2010, No. 13-14, pp. 11)
Pub: Rogers Media Ltd.
Ed: Richard Branson. **Description:** Good customer service is a practice that requires the efforts of the entire chain of coworkers that work as a team from beginning to end. The chain of assistance is only as strong as the weakest link when it comes to helping a customer.

26451 ■ "What Brain Science Tells Us About How to Excel" in *Harvard Business Review* (Vol. 88, December 2010, No. 12, pp. 123)
Pub: Harvard Business School Publishing
Ed: Edward M. Hallowell. **Description:** Relevant discoveries in brain research as they apply to boosting employee motivation and organizational effectiveness are explained. Included is a checklist of 15 items for use in assessing the fitness of a person for a particular job, focusing on the intersection of what one likes to do, what one does best, and what increases organizational value.

26452 ■ "What Most Banks Fail to See; New and Complex Financial Regulations Can be Daunting" in *Gallup Management Journal* (March 10, 2011)
Pub: Gallup
Ed: Sean Williams, Daniel Porcelli. **Description:** New financial regulations are complicated and politically charged. But banks that move beyond the fear of those regulations will find a new opportunity to engage customers.

26453 ■ "When Dov Cries" in *Canadian Business* (Vol. 83, June 15, 2010, No. 10, pp. 71)
Pub: Rogers Media Ltd.
Ed: Joe Castaldo. **Description:** American Apparel disclosed that they will have problems meeting one of its debt covenants which could trigger a chain reaction that could lead to bankruptcy. The prospects look bleak, but eccentric company founder Dov Charney, has always defied expectations.

26454 ■ *Who's Your Gladys?: How to Turn Even the Most Difficult Customer into Your Biggest Fan*
Pub: AMACOM
Ed: Marilyn Suttle, Lori Jo Vest. **Released:** September 9, 2009. **Price:** $22.95. **Description:** Every customer oriented business has a hard-to-satisfy client. This book shows how to serve customers who require a higher degree of skill to manage.

26455 ■ "Will Call Center Servicing Solve Labor's Customer Satisfaction Problems?" in *WorkingUSA* (Vol. 11, September 2008, No. 3, pp. 383)
Pub: Blackwell Publishers Ltd.
Ed: Steve Early. **Description:** Service Employees International Union (SEIU) has launched an ambitious plan to service hundreds of thousands of members through a network of Member Resource Centers (MRCs). This call center servicing strategy draws on the experience of unions in Australia and the customer service centers operated by major corporations. Call center critics fear the role of union stewards and shop floor activity will be undermined by the introduction of this system in SEIU workplaces in the U.S.

26456 ■ "Winner: Private Company, Less Than $100M" in *Crain's Detroit Business* (Vol. 25, June 22, 2009, No. 25)
Pub: Crain Communications Inc. - Detroit
Ed: Tom Henderson. **Description:** Profile of ForeSee Results, an Ann Arbor, Michigan-based firm that uses the University of Michigan American Consumer Satisfaction Index to help businesses measure satisfaction with their Websites.

26457 ■ "With a Smile: Customer Service Affects Every Aspect Of Your Business" in *Black Enterprise* (Vol. 38, January 2008, No. 6, pp. 43)
Pub: Earl G. Graves Publishing Co. Inc.
Ed: Ayana Dixon. **Description:** A good customer service program is essential for any small business; learning to anticipate what a customer needs before they even know they need it is key.

26458 ■ "You Can Rebuild It" in *Entrepreneur* (Vol. 37, July 2009, No. 7, pp. 28)
Pub: Entrepreneur Media, Inc.
Ed: Robert Kiyosaki. **Description:** Entrepreneurs, during tough times, should melt down old business strategies and start rebuilding the business. The business and its customers should be redefined in order to maximize marketing efforts and stay afloat when business slows down. Personal experiences in melting down a business and starting over are also given.

26459 ■ "You Can't Beat Habit" in *Entrepreneur* (Vol. 37, July 2009, No. 7, pp. 61)
Pub: Entrepreneur Media, Inc.
Ed: Neale Martin. **Description:** Customers are changing their spending behavior because of the financial meltdown, and this poses an opportunity for businesses to change their marketing practices in order to regain customers. Being flexible is one way to reestablish purchase behavior, along with paying attention to customer feedback.

26460 ■ "You Can't Fix It If You Don't Face It!" in *Indoor Comfort Marketing* (Vol. 70, June 2011, No. 6, pp. 14)
Pub: Industry Publications Inc.
Ed: John Levey. **Description:** Tips for avoiding repeat customer calls when installing or servicing HVAC/R equipment are provided.

26461 ■ "Your Guide to Local Style Business" in *Hawaii Business* (Vol. 53, December 2007, No. 6, pp. 36)
Pub: Hawaii Business Publishing
Ed: David K. Choo. **Description:** Discusses the importance of studying the Hawaiian culture when doing business locally. It was observed that geographical aspects increase emphasis on culture and lifestyle more than the need to rectify false imaging do. Details of how locals adhere to their culture are supplied.

26462 ■ "Zappo's CEO On Going to Extremes for Customers" in *Harvard Business Review* (Vol. 88, July-August 2010, No. 7-8, pp. 41)
Pub: Harvard Business School Publishing
Ed: Tony Hsieh. **Description:** Footwear firm Zappos.com Inc. improved corporate performance through enhanced customer service. Enhancements include highly visible phone numbers, avoidance of scripts, and viewing call centers as marketing departments.

26463 ■ "Zen and the Art of Twitter Maintenance" in *Agency Sales Magazine* (Vol. 39, September-October 2009, No. 9, pp. 48)
Pub: MANA
Ed: Terry Brock. **Description:** Online social networks such as Twitter, LinkedIn, and Facebook should be used to stay in touch with business relationships, especially customers. There should be a focus on making customers happy and building the bottomline when using these tools.

26464 ■ "Zeon Solutions Teams with Endeca for SaaS Version of Endeca InFront" in *Entertainment Close-Up* (October 25, 2011)
Pub: Close-Up Media
Description: Zeon Solutions, an enterprise e-commerce and Website development firm announced a special licensing partnership with Endecca Technologies. Endeca is an information management software company that provides small and mid-size retailers with high-performance Customer Experience Management technology.

TRADE PERIODICALS

26465 ■ *Customer Service Advantage*
Pub: Progressive Business Publications
Ed: Michele McGovern, Editor. **Released:** Semimonthly. **Price:** $253, individuals. **Description:** Presents practical methods for quantifying customer service benefits and motivating employees day in and day out. Recurring features include interviews, news of research, a calendar of events, news of educational opportunities, and a column titled Sharpen Your Judgment.

26466 ■ *First-Rate Customer Service*
Pub: Briefings Publishing Group
Ed: John McDonnel, Editor, edit@epinc.com. **Released:** Biweekly. **Description:** Offers customer contact personnel advice on enthusiasm and a service-oriented attitude on the job. Recurring features include feature titled A Case in Point. Remarks: Also available in Spanish.

26467 ■ *Journal of Relationship Marketing*
Pub: Routledge Journals
Contact: David Bejou PhD, Founding Ed.
Released: Quarterly. **Price:** $108 online; $113 print & online. **Description:** Journal on marketing.

26468 ■ *Smart Customer Service*
Pub: Clement Communications Inc.
Contact: Mike Johnson, Sr. Editor
Released: Biweekly. **Price:** $195. **Description:** Provides managers and supervisors with techniques and strategies to improve customer service and employee satisfaction. Includes information on recruiting higher quality employees.

VIDEOCASSETTES/ AUDIOCASSETTES

26469 ■ *Beyond Close to the Customer*
Phoenix Learning Group
2349 Chaffee Dr.
St. Louis, MO 63146-3306
Ph:(314)569-0211
Free: 800-221-1274
Fax:(314)569-2834
URL: http://www.phoenixlearninggroup.com
Released: 1989. **Price:** $895.00. **Description:** This is a three-part customer service enhancement program. **Availability:** VHS; 3/4U.

26470 ■ *Competing for Customers*
Educational Activities, Inc.
PO Box 87
Baldwin, NY 11510
Free: 800-797-3223
Fax:(516)623-9282
URL: http://www.edact.com
Price: $99.00. **Description:** Part of the Management Speaks Series. Outlines how to win over the customer, customer relationships, new strategy for building customer loyalty, unsatisfied consumers, and the importance of customer service. **Availability:** VHS.

26471 ■ *Competing Through Customer Service*
Video Arts, Inc.
c/o Aim Learning Group
8238-40 Lehigh
Morton Grove, IL 60053-2615
Free: 877-444-2230
Fax:(416)252-2155
Co. E-mail: service@aimlearninggroup.com
URL: http://www.aimlearninggroup.com
Released: 1989. **Price:** $730.00. **Description:** This video shows sure-fire methods for improving customer service by understanding and responding effectively to customer needs. **Availability:** VHS; 8mm; 3/4U; Special order formats.

26472 ■ *Customer Care Classic Moments*
Video Arts, Inc.
c/o Aim Learning Group
8238-40 Lehigh
Morton Grove, IL 60053-2615
Free: 877-444-2230
Fax:(416)252-2155
Co. E-mail: service@aimlearninggroup.com
URL: http://www.aimlearninggroup.com
Released: 1991. **Price:** $200.00. **Description:** Dealing with difficult customers is the focus of this video. Can be used to inject humor into a meeting, or as a meaningful exercise. **Availability:** VHS; 8mm; 3/4U; Special order formats.

26473 ■ *Customer Expectations*
1st Financial Training Services
1515 E. Woodfield Rd., Ste. 345
Schaumburg, IL 60173
Ph:(847)969-0900
Free: 800-442-8662
Fax:(847)969-0521
URL: http://www.1stfinancialtraining.com
Released: 1987. **Price:** $299.00. **Description:** Companies have to know what customers want before they can give it to them. **Availability:** VHS; 3/4U.

26474 ■ *Customer Retention/Service Quality*
1st Financial Training Services
1515 E. Woodfield Rd., Ste. 345
Schaumburg, IL 60173
Ph:(847)969-0900
Free: 800-442-8662

Fax:(847)969-0521
URL: http://www.1stfinancialtraining.com
Released: 1987. **Price:** $250.00. **Description:** Pope tells businesses how to keep their customers coming back. **Availability:** VHS; 3/4U.

26475 ■ *Customer Service or Else*
Enterprise Media
91 Harvey St.
Cambridge, MA 02140
Ph:(617)354-0017
Free: 800-423-6021
Fax:(617)354-1637
URL: http://www.enterprisemedia.com
Price: $795.00. **Description:** Peter Glen lectures on customer service issues. Full of funny, entertaining stories about customer service successes and nightmares. Comes with guide. **Availability:** VHS.

26476 ■ *Customer Service: It Pays to Please*
Phoenix Learning Group
2349 Chaffee Dr.
St. Louis, MO 63146-3306
Ph:(314)569-0211
Free: 800-221-1274
Fax:(314)569-2834
URL: http://www.phoenixlearninggroup.com
Released: 1985. **Description:** An instructional program that reveals the benefits and good business sense implicit in useful customer service. **Availability:** VHS; 3/4U.

26477 ■ *Customer Service: It's Good Business & It's Everybody's Business*
1st Financial Training Services
1515 E. Woodfield Rd., Ste. 345
Schaumburg, IL 60173
Ph:(847)969-0900
Free: 800-442-8662
Fax:(847)969-0521
URL: http://www.1stfinancialtraining.com
Released: 1987. **Price:** $325.00. **Description:** A demonstration of what some good workers have in common-good customer service skills. **Availability:** VHS; 3/4U.

26478 ■ *Dealing with the Irate Customer*
Advantage Media
c/o Kantola Productions
55 Sunnyside Ave.
Mill Valley, CA 94941
Ph:(415)381-9363
Free: 800-280-1180
Fax:(415)381-9801
Co. E-mail: kantola@kantola.com
URL: http://www.kantola.com/d/advantage.htm
Released: 1988. **Price:** $495.00. **Description:** Features role play as a model for dealing with the three types of anger. Good visual reinforcement. **Availability:** VHS.

26479 ■ *Doesn't Anybody Care?*
Direct Cinema Ltd.
PO Box 10003
Santa Monica, CA 90410-1003
Ph:(310)636-8200
Free: 800-525-0000
Fax:(310)636-8228
Co. E-mail: orders@directcinemalimited.com
URL: http://www.directcinema.com
Released: 1985. **Price:** $485.00. **Description:** A primer on customer service training. **Availability:** 3/4U; Special order formats.

26480 ■ *Don't Mind Him—He's Only a Customer*
Video Arts, Inc.
c/o Aim Learning Group
8238-40 Lehigh
Morton Grove, IL 60053-2615
Free: 877-444-2230
Fax:(416)252-2155
Co. E-mail: service@aimlearninggroup.com
URL: http://www.aimlearninggroup.com
Released: 1989. **Price:** $415.00. **Description:** Ideas are given as to how customers can be treated better. **Availability:** VHS; 3/4U.

26481 ■ *Effective Telephone Calling*
Encyclopedia Britannica
331 N. LaSalle St.
Chicago, IL 60654
Ph:(312)347-7159
Free: 800-323-1229
Fax:(312)294-2104
URL: http://www.britannica.com
Released: 1989. **Description:** This program demonstrates an easy-to-follow procedure for placing outgoing calls to reduce telephone cost, avoid misunderstandings and project a courteous, business-like image. **Availability:** VHS; 3/4U.

26482 ■ *The End of the Line*
American Media, Inc.
4621 121st St.
Urbandale, IA 50323-2311
Ph:(515)224-0919
Free: 888-776-8268
Fax:(515)327-2555
Co. E-mail: custsvc@ammedia.com
URL: http://www.ammedia.com
Released: 1992. **Price:** $495.00. **Description:** Teaches employees how to effectively deal with angry customers over the telephone. Includes a leader's guide. **Availability:** VHS; 3/4U; 8mm.

26483 ■ *The Good Old Days of Quality Service*
American Media, Inc.
4621 121st St.
Urbandale, IA 50323-2311
Ph:(515)224-0919
Free: 888-776-8268
Fax:(515)327-2555
Co. E-mail: custsvc@ammedia.com
URL: http://www.ammedia.com
Released: 1992. **Price:** $350.00. **Description:** A motivational program to teach employees about quality customer service through narrated musical vignettes. **Availability:** VHS; 3/4U; 8mm.

26484 ■ *Hot Under the Collar: Dealing with Angry Customers*
American Media, Inc.
4621 121st St.
Urbandale, IA 50323-2311
Ph:(515)224-0919
Free: 888-776-8268
Fax:(515)327-2555
Co. E-mail: custsvc@ammedia.com
URL: http://www.ammedia.com
Released: 1989. **Price:** $495.00. **Description:** Employees are taught how to properly deal with customers who are not happy. A leader's guide and reminder cards are available. **Availability:** VHS; 3/4U; Special order formats.

26485 ■ *How to Deliver Superior Customer Service*
Instructional Video
2219 C St.
Lincoln, NE 68502
Ph:(402)475-6570
Free: 800-228-0164
Fax:(402)475-6500
Co. E-mail: feedback@insvideo.com
URL: http://www.insvideo.com
Price: $99.00. **Description:** Offers advice from 15 experts on how to improve customer service, including how to perceive what the customer wants and motivating employees. **Availability:** VHS.

26486 ■ *How to Lose Customers without Really Trying (Attack & Defend)*
Video Arts, Inc.
c/o Aim Learning Group
8238-40 Lehigh
Morton Grove, IL 60053-2615
Free: 877-444-2230
Fax:(416)252-2155
Co. E-mail: service@aimlearninggroup.com
URL: http://www.aimlearninggroup.com
Released: 1988. **Price:** $790.00. **Description:** A two-pronged approach to customer service that helps to identify and eliminate the most common pitfalls in dealing with customers when things go wrong. **Availability:** VHS; 8mm; 3/4U; Special order formats.

26487 ■ *I Love People...It's Customers I Can't Stand*
Instructional Video
2219 C St.
Lincoln, NE 68502
Ph:(402)475-6570
Free: 800-228-0164
Fax:(402)475-6500
Co. E-mail: feedback@insvideo.com
URL: http://www.insvideo.com
Price: $98.00. **Description:** Discusses five different types of problem customers and procedures for dealing with them. **Availability:** VHS.

26488 ■ *It's Your Choice*
American Media, Inc.
4621 121st St.
Urbandale, IA 50323-2311
Ph:(515)224-0919
Free: 888-776-8268
Fax:(515)327-2555
Co. E-mail: custsvc@ammedia.com
URL: http://www.ammedia.com
Released: 1988. **Price:** $495.00. **Description:** A service manager is told that he can either change his attitude or find another job. The importance of treating customers politely is stressed. **Availability:** VHS; 3/4U.

26489 ■ *Managing for Customer Care*
American Media, Inc.
4621 121st St.
Urbandale, IA 50323-2311
Ph:(515)224-0919
Free: 888-776-8268
Fax:(515)327-2555
Co. E-mail: custsvc@ammedia.com
URL: http://www.ammedia.com
Released: 1990. **Price:** $495.00. **Description:** Aimed at managers and supervisors, this video tells how to deal with day-to-day customer service situations. Includes a trainer's guide, six overhead transparencies, and masters for photocopying. **Availability:** VHS; 3/4U; 8mm.

26490 ■ *Managing Difficult Customers 1...2...3*
SatNews Publishers
800 Siesta Way
Sonoma, CA 95476
Ph:(707)939-9306
Fax:(707)939-9235
Co. E-mail: design@satnews.com
URL: http://www.satnews.com
Released: 1990. **Price:** $495.00. **Description:** Gives tips on telephone skills as well as ideas for handling angry, talkative, and demanding customers. Skits show how to take charge of the situation. **Availability:** VHS; 3/4U.

26491 ■ *Objection Handling: Overcoming the Hurdles*
Aspen Publishers
7201 McKinney Circ.
Frederick, MD 21704
Ph:(301)698-7100
Free: 800-234-1660
Fax:800-901-9075
URL: http://www.aspenpublishers.com
Price: $495.00. **Description:** Suggests a five-step strategy to overcoming common customer objections. Unfortunately, the stiff actors provide poor examples. **Availability:** VHS.

26492 ■ *Oops! Time for Service Recovery*
SatNews Publishers
800 Siesta Way
Sonoma, CA 95476
Ph:(707)939-9306

Fax:(707)939-9235
Co. E-mail: design@satnews.com
URL: http://www.satnews.com

Released: 1991. **Price:** $650.00. **Description:** Discusses what to do when there is a service breakdown, disappointment, or misunderstanding with a customer. Available in two versions—one with stopping places with questions for dicussion and one with no stops. **Availability:** VHS; 3/4U.

26493 ■ *Partnering: The Heart of Selling Today*
American Media, Inc.
4621 121st St.
Urbandale, IA 50323-2311
Ph:(515)224-0919
Free: 888-776-8268
Fax:(515)327-2555
Co. E-mail: custsvc@ammedia.com
URL: http://www.ammedia.com

Price: $475.00. **Description:** Focuses on building lasting relationships with customers through partnering, a technique that helps customers solve their problems and questions. **Availability:** VHS; 3/4U; 8mm.

26494 ■ *The Power of Customer Service*
Nightingale-Conant Corp.
6245 W. Howard St.
Niles, IL 60714
Ph:(847)647-0300
Free: 800-560-6081
URL: http://www.nightingale.com

Released: 1991. **Price:** $95.00. **Description:** Customer-oriented service can be the greatest asset for any business. This video discusses the training and building of a service-oriented team. Includes an audio cassette and book. **Availability:** VHS.

26495 ■ *Quality Service: Frontline Commitment*
Phoenix Learning Group
2349 Chaffee Dr.
St. Louis, MO 63146-3306
Ph:(314)569-0211
Free: 800-221-1274
Fax:(314)569-2834
URL: http://www.phoenixlearninggroup.com

Price: $495.00. **Description:** Focuses on customer service breakdowns and the necessary skills to remedy the situation. One in a pair of videos using the same scenarios to illustrate different points. **Availability:** VHS.

26496 ■ *Quality Service: The Three R's for Managers*
Phoenix Learning Group
2349 Chaffee Dr.
St. Louis, MO 63146-3306
Ph:(314)569-0211
Free: 800-221-1274
Fax:(314)569-2834
URL: http://www.phoenixlearninggroup.com

Price: $495.00. **Description:** Focuses on customer service breakdowns and the necessary skills to remedy the situation. One of a pair of videos using the same scenarios to illustrate different points. **Availability:** VHS.

26497 ■ *Service Excellence*
Video Arts, Inc.
c/o Aim Learning Group
8238-40 Lehigh
Morton Grove, IL 60053-2615
Free: 877-444-2230
Fax:(416)252-2155
Co. E-mail: service@aimlearninggroup.com
URL: http://www.aimlearninggroup.com

Released: 1989. **Price:** $730.00. **Description:** This two-part video shows how your company can increase its profits by improving the three principal areas of customer service. At the end of the program is an opportunity to develop a customized strategy for customer service. **Availability:** VHS; 8mm; 3/4U; Special order formats.

26498 ■ *Service Sells/Phil Wexler*
Instructional Video
2219 C St.
Lincoln, NE 68502
Ph:(402)475-6570
Free: 800-228-0164
Fax:(402)475-6500
Co. E-mail: feedback@insvideo.com
URL: http://www.insvideo.com

Price: $395.00. **Description:** Phil Wexler offers tips on customer service and its effects on the success of the business. He covers the difference between operations-based thinking and market-based thinking, how the right choices can have an immediate impact on your business, targeting the needs of the customer, and minimizing customer complaints and objections. **Availability:** VHS.

26499 ■ *Service That Sells*
International Dairy-Deli-Bakery Association (IDDBA)
636 Science Dr.
PO Box 5528
Madison, WI 53705-0528
Ph:(608)310-5000
Fax:(608)238-6330
Co. E-mail: iddba@iddba.org
URL: http://www.iddba.org

Price: $160.00. **Description:** Bakery customer service training video. **Availability:** VHS.

26500 ■ *Take a Minute: The Organized Call*
SatNews Publishers
800 Siesta Way
Sonoma, CA 95476
Ph:(707)939-9306
Fax:(707)939-9235
Co. E-mail: design@satnews.com
URL: http://www.satnews.com

Price: $395.00. **Description:** Presents a four-step method to help employees prepare for and organize their outgoing calls. Creates a favorable impression with customers. **Availability:** VHS; 3/4U.

26501 ■ *Tony Alessandra, Ph.D.: On Customer-Driven Service*
Instructional Video
2219 C St.
Lincoln, NE 68502
Ph:(402)475-6570
Free: 800-228-0164
Fax:(402)475-6500
Co. E-mail: feedback@insvideo.com
URL: http://www.insvideo.com

Price: $95.00. **Description:** Part of the Tony Alessandra, Ph.D. Series. Outlines techniques to identify and exceed customer expectations and build strong, long-term customer relationships. **Availability:** VHS.

26502 ■ *Twelve Steps to Superior Customer Service*
Aspen Publishers
7201 McKinney Circ.
Frederick, MD 21704
Ph:(301)698-7100
Free: 800-234-1660
Fax:800-901-9075
URL: http://www.aspenpublishers.com

Released: 1986. **Price:** $495.00. **Description:** A manager's step-by-step guide to effective customer service. **Availability:** VHS; 3/4U; Special order formats.

26503 ■ *What Customers Want*
SatNews Publishers
800 Siesta Way
Sonoma, CA 95476
Ph:(707)939-9306
Fax:(707)939-9235
Co. E-mail: design@satnews.com
URL: http://www.satnews.com

Price: $525.00. **Description:** Six customers describe the kind of service they prefer so employees will have a better understanding of their customers' expectations. Includes skits to illustrate positive customer service. **Availability:** VHS; 3/4U.

26504 ■ *Who Killed Service?*
American Media, Inc.
4621 121st St.
Urbandale, IA 50323-2311
Ph:(515)224-0919
Free: 888-776-8268
Fax:(515)327-2555
Co. E-mail: custsvc@ammedia.com
URL: http://www.ammedia.com

Price: $1495.00. **Description:** Two programs, one for employees of all levels and one for management, discuss ways to provide top-notch customer service through a motivating and humorous video about a detective searching for the person who committed "servicide" at a company. **Availability:** VHS; 3/4U; 8mm.

CONSULTANTS

26505 ■ The Advantage Group Inc.
38 Wellington St. E, Ste. 200
Toronto, ON, Canada M5E 1C7
Ph:(416)863-0685
Free: 800-671-1048
Fax:(416)863-0787
Co. E-mail: answers@advantagegroup.com
URL: http://www.advantagegroup.com
Contact: Ron Pirie, President
E-mail: ronpirie@atsadvantagegroup.com

Scope: Specializes in two key areas: performance benchmarking and pricing strategy. Each stream has developed a wide variety of customizable proprietary research tools to meet the needs of the clients. **Publications:** "7 Steps to building better customer relationships"; "How to Add Value to Customer Relationships"; "Top 10 Key Benefits of Building Business Relationships"; "Tips for Creating Better Relationships"; "Building Trust in Personal and Business Relationships"; "The Advantage Report Canadian Grocer"; "Customer Relationships"; "Customer Relationship Management: What it is and What it's not"; "The Advantage Report - Measuring the supplier-retailer relationship".

26506 ■ Ann Arbor Consulting Associates Inc.
5204 Jackson Rd.
Ann Arbor, MI 48103-9625
Ph:(734)995-2404
Fax:(734)930-2018
Co. E-mail: philalexander@b2badvantage.net
URL: http://www.annarborconsulting.b2badvantage.net/
Contact: C. Philip Alexander, President
E-mail: philalexander@b2badvantage.net

Scope: Offers coaching and consulting to CEOs and top managers of smaller businesses in the areas of human resources development, total quality management, JP and R performance management systems, employee surveys, team building and strategic planning. **Publications:** "Jp&R System Manuals and Forms". **Special Services:** Beige Bag Software.

26507 ■ Asset Development Two
74 Blue Heron Dr.
Toms River, NJ 08753
Ph:(732)255-7855
Fax:(732)864-1816
Co. E-mail: bobsdoyle@comcast.net
URL: http://www.assetdevelopmenttwo.com
Contact: Robert S. Doyle, President
E-mail: bobsdoyle@comcast.net

Scope: A human resource consulting firm whose mission is twofold: to help people and their organizations to achieve their full potential and to help companies expand their strategic and financial perspectives. To this end, ADG develops programs that make significant and measurable improvements in productivity, profitability, customer satisfaction, operations, and in most areas of an organization. Specific areas include: sales and marketing, leadership and management development, customer service, critical thinking, strategic thinking and planning/selecting/assessing human resources, career management, and continuous process (quality) improvement.

26508 ■ Barclay Consulting Associates
44 Iselin Terr.
PO Box 1040
Larchmont, NY 10538
Ph:(914)834-9300
Fax:(914)834-9428
Co. E-mail: mjmargol@aol.com
Contact: Malcolm J. Margolis, President
E-mail: mjmargol@aol.com
Scope: Specializes in helping companies improve their logistics operations. The firm provides assistance in strategic planning, operations planning and productivity improvement in the following areas: Customer service, order processing, transportation, warehousing, inventory management, facilities network planning, procurement and forecasting. Serves private industries as well as government agencies.

26509 ■ Barker & Associates
1974 Wexford Cir.
Wheaton, IL 60187-6166
Ph:(630)260-9927
Fax:(630)260-9928
Contact: Patricia D. Barker, President
Scope: Consulting, training, and coaching firm specializing in providing human resource assessment, selection and development services focused primarily on people skills. Serves small, mid, and large-size organizations in both private industry and not-for-profit associations. **Seminars:** Strategic Marketing; Consultative Selling and Customer Service; From Hiring to Appraising - Developing Your Employees; Increased Productivity Through Managed Stress; Producing People Results Through Team building; Conflict Management; Communications, Managing Transition and Change; Creative Problem Solving.

26510 ■ The Benchmarking Network Inc.
4606 FM 1960 W, Ste. 300
Houston, TX 77069-9949
Ph:(281)440-5044
Fax:(281)440-6677
Co. E-mail: additional@benchmarkingnetwork.com
URL: http://www.benchmarkingnetwork.com
Contact: Alisa Beyer, Mgr
E-mail: jbowley@atsbenchmarkingnetwork.com
Scope: Firm leads benchmarking studies worldwide, as well as providing measures and metrics expertise, training, research, and implementation in support of process improvement, reengineering efforts and six sigma programs. Industries served: service, manufacturing, financial, retail, telecommunications, utilities, insurance, information systems, and healthcare. **Seminars:** Benchmarking - Introduction; Benchmarking - Advanced Topics; Customer Satisfaction Measurement; Total Quality Management; New Product Development as well as others. Over a dozen annual networking meetings targeting various industries or business processes.

26511 ■ Bill Johnson
1118 E Orangewood Ave.
Phoenix, AZ 85020-5029
Ph:(602)870-3333
Fax:(602)997-1676
Co. E-mail: bill@billjohnson.com
URL: http://www.billjohnson.com
Contact: Marjorie J. Johnson, Mgr
E-mail: bjcsp@aol.com
Scope: Advises in the areas of sales and sales management, focusing on customer service and telephone courtesy. Presents seminars on team building, management, sales and organization assessments, including retail distributor sales of tangibles, managing priorities, handling stress and time management. Also offers individual consulting. Industries served hospitality, automotive, banking and finance, entertainment, legal, nonprofit and retail and wholesale in public and private sector. **Publications:** "Managing Different People Differently," 1999; "Your Back Door To More Revenue"; "The Irate Customer: A Big Opportunity"; "Effective Priorities in Management and Life"; "Managing Multiple Priorities". **Seminars:** Managing and Selling Different People Differently; Will you be running with the Tall Dogs?; Customer Service and Telephone Courtesy; Managing Priorities and Stress; Building High Performing Teams; Ways to Keep Customers Coming Back; The Way Pros Sell Today. **Special Services:** FreedomMike[R].

26512 ■ Business Ventures Corp.
1650 Oakbrook Dr., Ste. 405
Norcross, GA 30093-1881
Ph:(770)729-8000
Fax:(770)729-8028
Co. E-mail: info@bventures.com
URL: http://www.bventures.com
Contact: Ruth A. King, CEO
E-mail: ruthking@bventures.com
Scope: Business development consultants specializing in construction industry. Works with HVAC, plumbing, and electrical contraction who need assistance in marketing, sales and promotion, operations management or finance. Also plan, execute, and monitor the marketing, sales, and promotional activities for new product introductions. Firm also writes business plans, monitors financial health of businesses, and performs operations management. **Publications:** "The Ugly Truth about Managing People," 2007; "The Ugly Truth about Small Business," 2006; "How to Write a Business Plan," Atlanta Business Chronicle; "Ask 10 Questions Before You Begin Your Business," Income Opportunities "HVAC Bookkeeping and Financial Statements"; "Service Manager's Guide to Running a Profitable Service Department"; "HVAC Career Training Manual"; "Technician's Procedures Manual"; "HVAC Residential Pricing Manual"; "21 Ways to Keep the Honest People Honest Manual"; "Keeping Score: Financial Management for Entrepreneurs"; "Keeping Score: Improving Contractor Productivity and Profitability"; "Keeping Score: Financial Management for Contractors". **Seminars:** The Seven Rules for Business Success; The Seven Greatest Lies of Small Business; Understanding the Financial Side of Business; Small Business Marketing; Strategic Business Planning.

26513 ■ Creative Communications International
1605 N Germantown Pky.
Cordova, TN 38016-5974
Ph:(901)755-2013
Free: 800-989-2013
Fax:(901)755-2228
Contact: Michael W. Hall, CEO
E-mail: mwhall@cci4pros.com
Scope: A communication consulting, training and publishing company. Trains customer service, teleservice, order fulfillment and reservation call center personnel on "developing a dynamic phone personality". **Publications:** "Becoming An Effective Storyteller".

26514 ■ Creative Concepts International Inc.
108 Eagle Glen Dr.
Woodstock, GA 30189
Ph:(770)926-1395
Fax:(770)926-1806
Co. E-mail: gene@geneswindell.com
URL: http://www.geneswindell.com
Contact: Gene Swindell, President
E-mail: gene@geneswindell.com
Scope: The firm provides companies with motivational keynotes and informative seminars on leadership, customer service, team building and consultative selling. **Seminars:** Leadership for Mastering Change; Quality Customer Service; Team building That Works; Coach Management; Customer Service is Your Only Business; Consultative Sales; Team Dynamics.

26515 ■ Cusato Ray & Associates Inc.
5676 Spinnaker Bay Dr.
Long Beach, CA 90802
Ph:(562)494-7896
Fax:(562)494-3403
Scope: Provides training materials to all industries in the areas of team building, customer service/contact, sales management, time management, and people selection. General management consultants.

26516 ■ David Herson Associates
524 Baldwin St.
Virginia Beach, VA 23452-7104
Ph:(757)463-7424
Contact: David Champion, Owner
Scope: Provides programs for organizations to increase understanding in various human resources areas. Specialty is customized training, that is, researching and developing programs with the purpose of meeting the program needs of the client. Industries served: Clients of all sizes in businesses, government agencies and associations. **Seminars:** Diversity; Sexual Harassment; Stress Management; Self Esteem; Conflict Management.

26517 ■ donphin.com Inc.
1001 B Ave., Ste. 200
Coronado, CA 92118
Ph:(619)550-3533
Free: 800-234-3304
Fax:(619)600-0096
Co. E-mail: inquiry@donphin.com
URL: http://www.donphin.com
Contact: Donald A. Phin, CEO
E-mail: don@donphin.com
Scope: Offers a comprehensive approach to understanding and applying a broad range of business principles: legal compliance issues, management concerns, health and safety, customer service, marketing, information management. Industries served: All developing small businesses. **Publications:** "Doing Business Right!"; "HR That Works!"; "Lawsuit Free! How to Prevent Employee Lawsuits"; "Building Powerful Employment Relationships!"; "Victims, Villains and Heroes: Managing Emotions in The Workplace". **Seminars:** Doing Business Right!; HR That Works!; Building Powerful Employment Relationships; Lawsuit Free!.

26518 ■ Dynamic Development
11 Bel Aire Dr.
Stamford, CT 06905
Ph:(203)329-0695
Fax:(203)329-1062
Contact: Paula Dangot, Principle
Scope: Offers a wide variety of customized training programs in management/supervisory, communication, interpersonal, customer service, and sales skills. Specializes in design of unique training, team building and other interactive learning solutions to organizational problems. Provides assessment services to diagnose training needs and organizational problems. Clients include major corporations in a wide range of industries, small companies, governmental and educational institutions. **Publications:** "The Dangers of Goals Setting," Supervisory Management, 1992; "Are You Stifling Your Employees?" Supervisory Management, 1992; "7 Ways Managers Undermine Teamwork," Supervisory Management, 1992. **Seminars:** Appraising Performance; Communicating Effectively; Cross-cultural Communication; Conducting Productive Meetings; Conflict Resolution; Customer Service Techniques; Decision Making; Delegating; Group Decision-Making; Interviewing Skills; Leadership Styles and Selection; Legal Issues in Human Resources; Listening Skills; Motivating and Rewarding Performance; Managing Change; Negotiation Skills; Networking Skills; Non-Verbal Communication; Problem-Solving; Proposal Writing; Public Speaking and Presentations; Sales Techniques; Supervising Employees; Stress Management; Team Building; Time Management; Training Trainers.

26519 ■ Enterprise Consulting Inc.
151 Fulton St.
PO Box 574
Norwood, MA 02062-2334
Ph:(781)762-4680
Co. E-mail: sales@eci-soft.com
Contact: Robert Calligan, Principle
E-mail: rcalligan@eci-soft.com
Scope: An independent consulting firm specializing in telecommunications analysis and design. Consulting services include: voice and data network analysis and design, PBX system analysis and design, voice processing system design, customer service/ACD design, development of in-house management teams, policy and procedures manuals, radio paging systems, health care communications systems design,

long distance optimization studies, development of strategic telecommunications plans, cable plant engineering analysis and design including fiber optic backbone design, local area network design and interconnection, CCTV and CATV network design, and development of cable plant Schematico via Auto Cad. Industries served: health care, college and university, manufacturing, financial services, state and municipal government agencies, utilities and professional service firms. **Seminars:** Voice Processing Systems Design; Basic Telecommunications for New Managers; Information Transport Network Design. **Special Services:** SMART.

26520 ■ Golden Eagle Business Services Inc.
PO Box 43447
Atlanta, GA 30336-0447
Ph:(404)881-6777
Fax:(770)944-9495
Co. E-mail: ivorydorsey@ivorydorsey.com
URL: http://www.ivorydorsey.com
Contact: Ivory J. Dorsey, President
E-mail: ivorydorsey@att.net
Scope: Provides sales, management, customer service change management and motivational training and consulting programs. Also public speaking engagements and special business projects. Serves private industries as well as government agencies. **Publications:** "Universal Appeal: The Bottom Line Benefit of Diversity"; "Winds of Change and the Business of Competition"; "Redefining Success"; "Personally Responding to the Challenge of Change"; "Diversity, Competition, and Your Bottom Line"; "E-Commerce and the Displacement Sales/Service Professional Eliminated or Empowered". **Seminars:** The Art of Delegation; The Winds of Change; Employee Motivation; Managing Diversity: Perception, Performance and Power; Developing a Sales Mentality in Customer Service.

26521 ■ Health Strategy Group Inc.
46 River Rd.
Chatham, NY 12037
Ph:(518)392-6770
Contact: John Fiorillo, Principle
Scope: Provides consulting services in the areas of strategic planning, feasibility studies, start-up businesses, organizational development, market research, customer service audits, new product development, marketing, public relations. **Publications:** "Online Consumer Surveys as a Methodology for Assessing the Quality of the United States Health Care System," 2004.

26522 ■ Hills Consulting Group Inc.
6 Partridge Ct.
Novato, CA 94945-1315
Ph:(415)898-3944
Contact: Michael R. Hills, President
Scope: Specializes in strategic planning; marketing surveys; market research; customer service audits; new product development; competitive analysis; and sales forecasting.

26523 ■ Hissong Associates Inc.
2335 Riviera Dr.
Vienna, VA 22181-3117
Ph:(703)281-2817
Fax:(703)242-8055
Co. E-mail: empower@hissong-inc.com
Contact: Robin Hissong, Mgr
E-mail: jerry@hissong-inc.com
Scope: Training consultants offering applied programs for organizational effectiveness, human resources development, and sales. Provides customized programs aimed at improving management, productivity, sales and harmony in the workplace. Primary focus is management and supervisory training, sales training and customer service training, team innovation, as well as consultation and personnel screening. Also offers a full range of videos, audio albums, training manuals, computer software and assessment instruments on many business subjects. Serves private industries, associations and government agencies. **Seminars:** Reading the Customer: A Differential Approach to Increased Sales; Teambuilding; The Empowered Manager; Presentation Excellence: People-Reading Secrets; Quality Customer Service; Customer Focused Selling; Time Management; Transcending the Recession on the Bridge of Eagles; Managing with Style.

26524 ■ Howick Associates
111 N Fairchild St.
Madison, WI 53703
Ph:(608)233-3377
Free: 800-236-3370
Fax:(608)233-1194
Co. E-mail: info@howickassociates.com
URL: http://www.howickassociates.com
Contact: Drew Howick, Bookkeeper
E-mail: dhowick@atsshowickassociates.com
Scope: Organizational development and training firm committed to helping organizations meet the demand for greater productivity by enhancing individual, team and organizational effectiveness. **Publications:** "The New Compleat Facilitator: A Handbook for Facilitators". **Seminars:** The Complete Virtual; Enhancing Your Presentation Style; Perceptive Communications; Listening; Effective Meeting Skills; Strategic Thinking and Planning; Performance Measurement; Facilitation Skills.

26525 ■ Impact Training Associates Inc.
320 Arden Ave., Ste. 240
Glendale, CA 91203
Ph:(818)241-3537
Free: 800-848-4333
Fax:(818)241-4416
Scope: Provides customized training that strengthens both individuals and organizations. This enables clients to better meet the changing requirements in the competitive market place of the 21st century. Focuses on accelerated learning and action-oriented training that can be applied immediately.

26526 ■ James P. Schiller
1621 N 50th Pl.
Milwaukee, WI 53208-2206
Ph:(414)771-3372
Fax:(414)771-8224
Co. E-mail: jschill12@aol.com
E-mail: jschill12@aol.com
Scope: Training consulting firm offers management research and training. Specializes in personal development programs, management and supervisory skills development. Focuses on performance, improvement, time strategies, mastering work skills, team building, leadership and effective communications. Systems used include: Performax Systems programs, profiles and assessment instruments. Serves corporate, nonprofit, and federal, state and local government employee audiences. **Seminars:** Time Management Strategies; Effective Listening; Improving Group Relationships; Innovation Seminar; Effective Management Strategies.

26527 ■ Joe Turner
3525 Sandybrook Ln., 2nd Fl.
Napa, CA 94558
Ph:(707)224-6344
Free: 888-754-6900
Fax:(707)224-6392
Co. E-mail: jmturner@joeturner.com
URL: http://www.joeturner.com
E-mail: jmturner@joeturner.com
Scope: Provides customer service consulting, materials, software and training for the new home industry. Specializes in construction defect litigation. Specific problem solving, including recruiting, validating employment information, meeting with homeowners and strategic assessment are available. Produces homeowner manuals for builders and developers. **Seminars:** TeamTraks.

26528 ■ Key Communications Group Inc.
5617 Warwick Pl.
Chevy Chase, MD 20815-5503
Ph:(301)656-0450
Free: 800-705-5353
Fax:(301)656-4554
Co. E-mail: mr.dm@verizon.net
Contact: Carol A. Jason, Principle
E-mail: mr.dm@verizon.net
Scope: Direct marketing and publishing consultants specializing in subscriber and member acquisition for newsletters and other niche B2B publications, organizations and associations. Specialties: small and start-up businesses; mergers and acquisitions; joint ventures; divestitures; product development; employee surveys and communication; market research; customer service audits; new product development; direct marketing and competitive intelligence. **Publications:** "How I Tripled Site License Sales in One Year," Pma, Jul, 2004.

26529 ■ Kutler Consultants
1420 Locust St., Ste. 35Q
Philadelphia, PA 19102
Ph:(215)732-2284
Contact: Edwin Kutler, Principal
Scope: Merchandise operations management consultants whose focus is on maximizing customer service and profitability through effective inventory management-assuring that quality merchandise, properly packaged, is in the right place at the right time, and to fill customer orders immediately. Specific areas of consulting include forecasting, inventory control, quality assurance and packaging, transportation and distribution, management information, order processing and fulfillment, statistical analysis, operations research and systems development. Industries served: Catalog, direct mail, television shopping, and home party plan.

26530 ■ Lieber & Associates
3740 N Lake Shore Dr., Ste. 15B-2
Chicago, IL 60613-4202
Ph:(773)325-9400
Fax:(773)325-0621
Co. E-mail: info@lieberandassociates.com
URL: http://www.lieberandassociates.com
Contact: Susan Helscher, Director
E-mail: m_lieber@lieberandassociates.com
Scope: Provides telephone marketing (inbound and outbound); database marketing; and telecommunications technology services for sales, customer service, and order departments. Also upgrades existing operations and start-ups. Performs strategic planning, facility design, equipment specification, network (telephone line) design, software recommendations, staff planning, database design, management systems development, program design, scripting, and project management to meet client requirements. Projects800 number call volumes. Industries served: Direct marketing, catalog order, customer service, utilities, cable television, travel and hospitality, advertising, broadcasting, general business and government in the United States and Worldwide. **Publications:** "BTB, Inbound Regulation on Horizon," DM News, May, 2006; "ATA Summit: Be Proactive on Regulation," DM News, Apr, 2006; "How to Integrate Telephone and Direct Marketing," 1993. **Seminars:** How to Integrate Telephone and Direct Marketing; Outsourcing Nuts and Bolts; How to Measure and Manage Telemarketing: How to Integrate Telephone, Direct and Internet Marketing-30 Ideas; Repackaging Tele services-A Public Image Make-Over; Transforming your Call Center into a Contact Center; Three Paradigm Shifts that are Changing Tele services Today.

26531 ■ Marketing Leverage Inc.
2022 Laurel Oak
Palm City, FL 34990
Free: 800-633-1422
Fax:(772)659-8664
Co. E-mail: lkelly@marketingleverage.com
URL: http://www.marketingleverage.com
Contact: Genina Gravlin, Principle
E-mail: davery@atsmarketingleverage.com
Scope: Consulting and research firm focusing on the targeting, retention and satisfaction of customers. Consulting is offered for due diligence; marketing and customer retention strategy; program design and implementation. Research services offered help clients determine service improvements that increase customer loyalty; boosting sales through better understanding buyer motivations; increasing the odds of product acceptance through new product concept testing; and improving the effectiveness of advertising, collateral, publications through audience evaluation. Clients include top financial services, insurance, health care, technology and management services organizations. **Publications:** "Creating Strategic Leverage"; "Exploring Corporate Strategy"; "Competi-

tive Advantage"; "Breakpoint and Beyond "; "Competitive Strategy ". **Seminars:** Best Practices in Brainstorming; Getting Results in the Real World; Finding the Leverage in Your Customer Strategy; The Role of Communications in Building Customer Loyalty; Building a Customer Centered Relationship and Making it Pay. **Special Services:** The Marketing Leverage Win/Loss Tracking System[TM].

26532 ■ McDargh Communications
33465 Dosinia Dr.
Dana Point, CA 92629-4488
Ph:(949)496-8640
Free: 877-477-4718
Fax:(949)248-7805
Co. E-mail: eileen@eileenmcdargh.com
URL: http://www.eileenmcdargh.com
Contact: Eileen McDargh, President
E-mail: eileen@eileenmcdargh.com
Scope: Provides management communications consulting for team building, management communication and training in a variety of communication related skills facilitates management retreats. **Publications:** "The Spirit of Nurse Leadership"; "Burn out, Balance & Bounty"; "Books: Work for a Living and Still Be Free to Live"; "The Resilient Spirit"; "Off the Chart Results"; "A Woman's Way to Incredible Success"; "Meditations for the Road Warrior"; "Talk Ain't Cheap...It's Priceless"; "Gifts from the Mountain". **Seminars:** Work for a Living and Still Be Free to Live; The Energy Connection.

26533 ■ onFocus Healthcare Inc.
5141 Virginia Way, Ste. 440
Brentwood, TN 37027
Ph:(615)871-4321
Free: 800-899-0021
Fax:(615)871-9821
Co. E-mail: info@m21partners.com
URL: http://www.onfocushealthcare.com
Contact: Dale Sargent, Senior Partner
E-mail: tian@m21partners.com
Scope: Training and consulting firm providing tested models for improving organizational and individual performance. Offers an architecture for organizational transformation that can involve a wide scope of dimensions including assessment of organizational effectiveness, strategic planning, assessment and development of leadership and consulting skills, role clarification, continuous improvement and customer satisfaction, and nontraditional selling. **Seminars:** Breakthrough Leadership Workshops; Organizational Transformation Architecture System; Design Your Future system; The Lifetime Customer process; Creating and Leading High Performance Teams; Role Clarification; Partnership Selling system. **Special Services:** Healthcare Alignment Solutions[TM]; Enterprise Performance Management.

26534 ■ Parker Consultants Inc.
230 Mason St.
Greenwich, CT 06830-6633
Ph:(203)869-9400
Contact: William P. Hartl, Chairman of the Board
Scope: Firm specializes in strategic planning; organizational development; small business management; performance appraisals; executive searches; team building; and customer service audits.

26535 ■ Personal Achievement Institute
1 Speaking Success Rd.
PO Box 6543
Kingman, AZ 86402-6543
Ph:(928)793-3303
Free: 800-793-3316
Fax:(928)753-7554
Co. E-mail: info@speakingbizsuccess.com
URL: http://www.speakingsuccess.com
Contact: Robert Milhander, Vice President
E-mail: burt@speakingsuccess.com
Scope: Consulting firm serves professional speakers, offering expertise in such areas as positioning, packaging, promotion, and presentation. **Publications:** "Speaking Success System: Professional Speakers Profit Letter"; "Burt Dubin Private Letter"; "Inner Circle Letter"; "Mission Possible"; "Positioning Magic"; "Selling to the Corporate Market"; "Positioning Magic Special Report"; "177 Wow! Wow! Showmanship Stratagems". **Seminars:** Speaking Success Boot Camps; Boot Camps-at-Sea, Inner Circle Retreats.

26536 ■ The Plotkin Group
5650 El Camino Real, Ste. 223
Carlsbad, CA 92008-7146
Ph:(760)603-8791
Free: 800-877-5685
Fax:(760)603-8570
Co. E-mail: info@plotkingroup.com
URL: http://www.plotkingroup.com
Contact: Mariel Moulton, Principle
E-mail: marie@atsplotkingroup.com
Scope: Employee testing and training organization offering pre-employment honesty, altitude, aptitude and skills tests; and past employment, 360degree assessments, behavior, style and communication tests by phone, paper and pencil, computers, the web, employee attitude surveys, customer service, sales, and management training. **Publications:** "Building a Winning Team"; "Achieving Above and Beyond Service"; "American Businesses Face Mountain of Problems"; "Appreciating the Richness of Cultural Diversity"; "Attitude is Everything"; "Club members spems are Driving Us All Crazy"; "Credibility and Trust"; "Crime Prevention: The Integrity Business"; "Employee Theft: Hidden Enemy"; "Empowering Employees Without Losing Control"; "How to Build Customer Loyalty"; "Hr Issues of the Millennium"; "Just the Facts (Honesty Testing)"; "Nation's Jobless Must Be Retrained, Put to Work"; "Phone Answering Systems: A Blessing Or a Curse?"; "Strive to Convert Poor Service Into Good Service"; "Tests are Best for Picking Best Worker for the Job"; "The Pre-Interview Hiring Process"; "Time Management"; "What Do Members Want"; "Who to Promote"; "You Can't Turn a Frog Into a Prince"; "Club members speak out about their dining room"; "Companies should stress attitudes over skills (SUN)"; "Companies will always need honest and dependable workers (SUN)"; "Dealing with the angry member"; "Employee selection: A key to member retention"; "Good customer service is the best route to profits (SUN)"; "Hiring, the key to profitability (SUN)"; "Honesty tests are legitimate tool for finding good employees (SUN)"; "How not to handle a crisis"; "How not to open a theater"; "How to determine an applicant's attitude"; "How to identify and develop leadership traits in employees"; "How to introduce pre-employment testing into an organization"; "Integrity among youth is on decline (SUN)"; "Issues of concern for owners"; "Issues of concern for golf companies"; "Ownership and empowerment"; "Road to success paved with customer satisfaction (SUN)"; "Screen applicants to weed out thieves (SUN)"; "When the going gets tough". **Seminars:** Building a Winning Team; Above and Beyond Customer Service Training; Taking the Guess Work Out of Hiring and Promoting.

26537 ■ Retail Management Consultants
2382 Camino Vita Roble, Ste. L
Carlsbad, CA 92011-1508
Ph:(760)431-2910
Free: 800-766-1908
Fax:(760)431-2915
Co. E-mail: info@whalinonretail.com
URL: http://www.whalinonretail.com
Contact: George Whalin, President
E-mail: george@atswhalinonretail.com
Scope: Specializes in helping retail organizations become more efficient, productive, and profitable. Consulting services include advertising and marketing, employee training programs, customer service improvement, and customer research. Industries served: All segments of the retail industry. **Seminars:** Retail Success!; Great Store Managers Make Great Stores!; Competition: Powerful trends that are changing what people buy, how they buy, and where they buy!; Stop, Look, Touch, and Buy: The Dynamics of Merchandising; Double Your Sales and Triple Your Profits with High-Impact Marketing and Promotions!; Every Customer Every Day; Customer Focused Selling; Competition? What Competition! Standing Out in Today's Competitive Retail Marketplace; How to Find an Eagle in a Flock of Turkeys! Finding, Hiring, and Keeping the BEST Retail Employees; Double Your Sales and Triple Your Profits with High-Impact Marketing and Promotions!; Customer-Direct Marketing: Increase Retail Sales with High-Impact Direct Mail & E-Mail; Power, Punch & Pizzazz! Create Advertising that Grabs Customer Attention and Sells More Merchandise; 12 Powerful Advertising Secrets Every Retailer Should Know; Great Store Managers Make Great Stores!; Into the Future! Powerful Trends Shaping the Future of Retailing.

26538 ■ Richard M. Harris Associates
255 Carlton Terr.
Teaneck, NJ 07666
Ph:(201)801-0087
Fax:(201)801-0087
Co. E-mail: rmharassoc@aol.com
URL: http://www.rmharrisassociates.com
Contact: Dr. Richard M. Harris, President
Scope: Offers small-group, customized workshops as well as one-on-one training in speaking skills and listening skills. Applications include: leadership development, management and sales presentation, meeting management, customer service, coaching and counseling and team building. Industries served: Drug and pharmaceutical, telecommunications, newspaper publishing, chemicals, advertising, printing and the military. **Publications:** "The Listening Leader: Powerful New Strategies for Becoming an Influential Communicator," Praeger Publishers, Apr, 2006; "Don't Get Emotional: A Crash Course on Listening," Feb, 2005. **Seminars:** Dialogues for Dating, Apr, 2007; The Advanced Persuasive Speaking; Persuasive Speaking Seminar; Selling Communications Skills; Listening to Lead; Executive Presentation Skills; Professional Communications Skills(PCS); A Practical Telephone-Skills Enhancement Workshop.

26539 ■ Service Quality Institute
9201 E Bloomington Fwy.
Minneapolis, MN 55420-3437
Ph:(952)884-3311
Free: 800-548-0538
Fax:(952)884-8901
Co. E-mail: quality@servicequality.com
URL: http://www.customer-service.com
Contact: Carman Velasco, Principal
Scope: Offers customer service training. It provides 30 customers service training programs that businesses can pick and choose from to improve the quality of customer care. **Publications:** "Achieving Excellence Through Customer Service," Bestsellers Publishers; "Ca$hing In: Get Promoted, Make More Money, Love Your Job," Bestsellers Publishing; "The Spirit of Excellence"; "Servicio Al Cliente". **Seminars:** E-Service; Achieving Excellence Through Customer Service; Cashing In Feelings; Leading Empowered Teams for Service Quality; Exceptional Service; Attaining Excellence by Keeping More Customers; Customer Service Excellence; Five Star Service; Creating a Service Culture Strategy; Leading Empowered Teams.

26540 ■ Your Writing Partner
2137 Mount Vernon Rd.
Atlanta, GA 30338
Ph:(770)395-7483
Free: 800-745-0494
Fax:(770)395-1931
Co. E-mail: kay@yourwritingpartner.net
URL: http://www.yourwritingpartner.net
Contact: M. Kay du Pont, Principle
E-mail: kay@atsyourwritingpartner.net
Scope: Human resource consultants who provide custom-designed and generic programs for clients. Services include customer analysis, instructional design, and training program design. Also provide performance improvement, editing, proofing, and rewriting services; meeting emceeing, planning and facilitation; conflict resolution; executive coaching. Industries served: banking, healthcare, hospitality, utilities, credit unions, insurance, food, and associations. **Publications:** "Writing for Big Results," Jan, 2008; "Writing Skills for the College-Bound Student "; "Don't Let Your Participles Dangle in Public," 2005; "Business Etiquette and Professionalism"; "Handling Diversity in the Workplace: Communication is the Key"; "How to Provide Excellent Service in Any Organization"; "Loving Mr. Lincoln". **Seminars:** Business Etiquette and Professionalism; Understanding and Communicating With Others; Politically Correct

and Profitable Writing Skills; Setting the Stage for Excellent Service; The Art of Successful Presentations; Friendly Fire: How Being Your Own Sweet Self Can Burn Others; Ideas Into Action: How to Keep All Those Good Conference Ideas From Going to Waste; Management and Supervisory Skills; How to Proofread Like a Pro; How to Excel at Editing; Grammar for Grownups; Writing for Today's Busy Readers (and Writers); Grammar For Youth; Writing Skills For College-Bound Students.

26541 ■ Ziglar Inc.
5055 W Park Blvd., Ste. 700
Plano, TX 75093
Ph:(972)233-9191
Free: 800-527-0306
Fax:(469)326-7556
Co. E-mail: info@ziglar.com
URL: http://www.ziglar.com
Contact: Gail Arnett, CFO
E-mail: info@ziglar.com
Scope: Offers management planning, strategic planning, teambuilding, skills assessment, and custom training to provide clients with the tools to build their business. **Publications:** "Better Than Good"; "Embrace the Struggle"; "God's Way Is Still the Best Way"; "Life Lifters"; "Secrets Of Closing The Sale"; "Raising Positive Kids In a Negative World"; "Ziglar on Selling"; "Over the Top"; "Qualities of Success"; "Changing the Picture"; "One Step at a Time". **Seminars:** Get Motivated, Salt Lake City, Jun, 2010; Get Motivated, Omaha, Jun, 2010; Born to win; Get Motivated; Ziglar Sales System; Essential Presentation Skills: Custom Curricula.

COMPUTER SYSTEMS/ SOFTWARE

26542 ■ *Measuring Customer Satisfaction–Crisp Learning–Thomson Learning (PO Bo)*
Chris Learning
PO Box 25690
Rochester, NY 14625
Ph:888-534-5556
Free: 800-442-7477
Fax:888-715-0220
Co. E-mail: customerservice@axzopress.com
URL: http://www.axzopress.com
Price: $13.95 **Description:** Based on the *Measuring Customer Satisfaction* video and book. Includes book and user's guide.

RESEARCH CENTERS

26543 ■ Purdue University–Center for Customer-Driven Quality
1262 Matthews Hall, Ste. 118
West Lafayette, IN 47907-1262
Ph:(765)494-9933
Fax:(765)494-0287
Co. E-mail: xdj1@cfs.purdue.edu
Contact: Dr. Richard Feinberg, Dir.
E-mail: xdj1@cfs.purdue.edu
Scope: Customer research, including basic design and implementation of inbound customer call-centers, customer privacy, complaint demographics, and customer satisfaction. **Educational Activities:** Call Center Certification Program; Courses and guest lectures; Quality customer service video training.

ASSOCIATIONS AND OTHER ORGANIZATIONS

26544 ■ Americans With Disabilities Act
9841 SW 100 Ave.
Miami, FL 33176
Ph:(305)271-0012
Fax:(305)273-1221
Co. E-mail: ergobob@consultant.com
URL: http://www.rehabserv.com
Contact: Robert L. Lessne PhD
Description: Individuals and organizations united to ensure compliance with the Americans With Disabilities Act of 1992. Compiles statistics; sponsors competitions; maintains speakers' bureau; and operates a museum with cones for visually impaired individuals. **Publications:** *ADA Compliance Kit*; *ADA Compliance Sourcebook* .

26545 ■ Common Destiny Alliance
University of Maryland
2110 Benjamin Bldg.
College Park, MD 20742
Ph:(301)405-0639
Fax:(301)405-3573
Co. E-mail: mh267@umail.umd.edu
URL: http://www.education.umd.edu/CODA/index.html
Contact: Walter Allen
Description: Organizations and scholars interested in working to end prejudice. Fosters the viewpoint that cultural diversity is "a resource that can help the nation attain goals such as improving economic productivity and the academic achievement of all children." Seeks to end racial isolation in schools, neighborhoods, and the work force. Promotes social policies, especially those related to education, that encourage racial and ethnic understanding and cooperation. Conducts research to identify the causes of racism and means to overcome racism. **Publications:** *Toward a Common Destiny: Improving Race and Ethnic Relations in America*; *Tracking, Diversity, and Educational Equity: What's New in the Research?* .

EDUCATIONAL PROGRAMS

26546 ■ Employment Discrimination Law Update
Seminar Information Service, Inc.
20 Executive Park, Ste. 120
Irvine, CA 92614
Ph:(949)261-9104
Free: 877-SEM-INFO
Fax:(949)261-1963
Co. E-mail: info@seminarinformation.com
URL: http://www.seminarinformation.com
Price: $895.00. **Description:** Covers changes in EEO law and enforcement, sexual harassment, resolving claims and implementing ADA, and the FMLA. **Locations:** San Francisco, CA; Chicago, IL; and Washington, DC.

26547 ■ Harassment Prevention in the Workplace
Seminar Information Service, Inc.
20 Executive Park, Ste. 120
Irvine, CA 92614
Ph:(949)261-9104
Free: 877-SEM-INFO
Fax:(949)261-1963
Co. E-mail: info@seminarinformation.com
URL: http://www.seminarinformation.com
Price: $795.00. **Description:** Explore the legal and policy concerns related to this complex workplace issue, including review and explore the guidelines for identifying inappropriate behavior; the laws, agency interpretations and court cases; and the key elements necessary for writing and implementing policies and procedures. **Locations:** New York, NY.

REFERENCE WORKS

26548 ■ "$3.5 Million Lawsuit Points Finger at Black Firm" in *Black Enterprise* (Vol. 38, March 2008, No. 8)
Pub: Earl G. Graves Publishing Co. Inc.
Ed: Cliff Hocker. **Description:** World Wide Technology, the world's largest black-owned company is being sued by a former employee for racial discrimination and retaliation. Details of the lawsuit are outlined.

26549 ■ "Barred Collection Agency Sued by Colorado AG" in *Collections & Credit Risk* (Vol. 15, August 1, 2010, No. 7, pp. 7)
Pub: SourceMedia Inc.
Description: Collection agency run by Chad Lee received notice that it is barred from collecting in the State of Colorado by Attorney General John Suther's office. A ruling cited that the firm engages in harassment or abuse and/or threats of violence, made false representations as to its legal status of debts, made false and misleading representations of nonpayment of debts that would result in arrest, and that Lee failed to disclose his previous felony conviction.

26550 ■ *Complete Employee Handbook: A Step-by-Step Guide to Create a Custom Handbook That Protects Both the Employer and the Employee*
Pub: Moyer Bell
Ed: Michael A. Holzschu. **Released:** August 2007. **Description:** Comprehensive guide book helps employers deal with basic personnel issues. Details for creating a cohesive personnel program to meet specific needs and goals are addressed. Topics covered include employment-at-will practices, equal opportunity, sexual harassment, disabled and immigrant and legal alien workers in lay terms and stresses the dangers of oversight. The book includes a CD that contains sample employee handbooks, federal regulations and laws, forms for complying with government programs and worksheets for assessing personnel needs and goals.

26551 ■ "Crafting Kinship at Home and Work: Women Miners in Wyoming" in *WorkingUSA* (Vol. 11, December 2008, No. 4, pp. 439)
Pub: Blackwell Publishers Ltd.
Ed: Jessica M. Smith. **Description:** Institutional policies and social dynamics shaping women working in the northeastern Wyoming mining industry are examined. Ethnographic research suggests that the women's successful integration into this nontraditional workplace is predicated on their ability to craft and maintain kin-like social relationships in two spheres. First, women miners have addressed the challenges of managing their home and work responsibilities by cultivating networks of friends and family to care for their children while they are at work. Second, women miners craft close relationships with coworkers in what are called 'crew families'. These relationships make their work more enjoyable and the ways in which they create camaraderie prompt a reconsideration of conventional accounts of sexual harassment in the mining industry.

26552 ■ "EEOC Sues Charlotte-Based Lebo's" in *Charlotte Observer* (February 7, 2007)
Pub: Knight-Ridder/Tribune Business News
Ed: Mike Drummond. **Description:** The U.S. Equal Employment Opportunity Commission filed a pregnancy discrimination lawsuit against Lebo's Shoe Stores, located in Charlotte, North Carolina. The suit alleges the store withdrew an offer to hire a woman after finding out she was pregnant.

26553 ■ "The Ethics of Price Discrimination" in *Business Ethics Quarterly* (Vol. 21, October 2011, No. 4, pp. 633)
Pub: Society for Business Ethics
Ed: Juan M. Elegido. **Description:** Price discrimination is the practice of charging different customers different prices for the same product. Many people consider price discrimination unfair, but economists argue that in many cases price discrimination is more likely to lead to greater welfare than is the uniform pricing alternative, sometimes even for every party in the transaction.

26554 ■ "Human Capital: When Change Means Terminating an Employee" in *Black Enterprise* (Vol. 41, November 2010, No. 4, pp. 40)
Pub: Earl G. Graves Publishing Co. Inc.
Ed: Tamara E. Holmes. **Description:** Covering successful business change strategies, this article focuses on how the law and nondiscrimination policies can affect this aspect of the workplace.

26555 ■ *It's Your Ship*
Pub: Warner Books Inc.
Ed: Michael Abrashoff. **Released:** May 1, 2002. **Price:** $24.95. **Description:** Naval Captain D. Michael Abrashoff shares management principles he used to shape his ship, the U.S.S. Benfold, into a model of progressive leadership. Abrashoff revolutionized ways to face the challenges of excessive costs, low morale, sexual harassment, and constant turnover.

26556 ■ "Less Than Zero" in *Canadian Business* (Vol. 80, November 5, 2007, No. 22, pp. 36)
Pub: Rogers Media
Ed: Andy Holloway. **Description:** Zero-tolerance policy with regards to discrimination and harassment at the workplace has been adopted by many compa-

nies. However, employers must exercise caution in terminating employees based on zero-tolerance policies since there are laws governing illegal dismissals. Important considerations employers should make in dismissing workers, such as proof of willful misconduct, are discussed.

26557 ■ "Looking To Hire Young? Be Careful" in *Boston Business Journal* (Vol. 30, November 19, 2010, No. 43, pp. 1)
Pub: Boston Business Journal
Ed: Lisa van der Pool. **Description:** The Massachusetts Commission Against Discrimination (MCAD) has been using undercover job applicants to expose discrimination. Cabot's Ice Cream and Restaurant has been accused of denying older workers equal employment opportunities. MCAD has discovered unfair hiring practices such as hiring high school and college students.

26558 ■ "Maryland Ready to Defend Slots Minority Policy" in *Boston Business Journal* (Vol. 29, July 8, 2011, No. 9, pp. 3)
Pub: American City Business Journals Inc.
Ed: Scott Dance. **Description:** The legality of Maryland's minority inclusion policy may be put under scrutiny once the lawsuit filed by rejected slots developer Baltimore City Entertainment Group on July 5, 2011 is heard in court. The lawsuit aims to stop the bidding process on a proposed casino in Baltimore because the minority policy amounts to reverse discrimination.

26559 ■ "Remind Managers to Avoid Talk of Employee Longevity" in *HR Specialist* (Vol. 8, September 2010, No. 9, pp. 3)
Pub: Capitol Information Group Inc.
Description: Supervisors need to understand that casual conversations can be used against an organization in law suits.

26560 ■ "Research: Mind the Gap" in *Business Strategy Review* (Vol. 21, Summer 2010, No. 2, pp. 84)
Pub: Wiley-Blackwell
Description: Isabel Fernandez-Mateo's cumulative gender disadvantage in contract employment is presented.

26561 ■ "Save the Date" in *Barron's* (Vol. 90, September 13, 2010, No. 37, pp. 35)
Pub: Barron's Editorial & Corporate Headquarters
Ed: Mark Veverka. **Description:** Mark Hurd is the new Co-President of Oracle after being forced out at Hewlett-Packard where he faced a harassment complaint. HP fired Hurd due to expense account malfeasance. Hurd is also set to speak at an Oracle trade show in San Francisco on September 20, 2010.

26562 ■ *Sexual Harassment*
Pub: ABC-CLIO
Ed: Lynn Eisaguirre, Editor. **Released:** Latest edition 2nd; December 1997. **Publication Includes:** List of agencies and organizations in the U.S. Concerned with sexual harassment. **Entries Include:** Organization name, address, phone. Principal content of publication is information on the history, social context, legal precedent, and legislative background of sexual harassment issues. Part of "Contemporary World Issues Series." **Arrangement:** Directory of organizations, selected print resources, film, Internet resources.

26563 ■ "Subprime Lenders Under Fire: Does the NAACP Have a Viable Case?" in *Black Enterprise* (Vol. 38, October 2007, No. 3, pp. 31)
Pub: Earl G. Graves Publishing Co. Inc.
Ed: Trevor Delaney. **Description:** NAACP filed a lawsuit charging a number of mortgage lenders with 'institutionalized systematic racism'. Lenders named in the suit include Accredited Home Lenders, Ameriquest Mortgage Company, BNC Mortgage, Citigroup, Encore Credit, First Franklin Financial Corporation, Fremont Investment and Loan, HSBC Finance Corporation, Long Beach Mortgage Company, Option One Mortgage Corporation, Washington Mutual Inc., and WMC Mortgage Corporation. Details of the lawsuit are included.

26564 ■ "'Tone-Deaf' Suitor or True Harasser: How to Tell" in *HR Specialist* (Vol. 8, September 2010, No. 9, pp. 1)
Pub: Capitol Information Group Inc.
Description: Details are critical to any harassment charge in the workplace. Courts now list factors employers should consider when trying to determine whether an employee has been sexually harassed at work.

26565 ■ "Unseen Injustice: Incivility as Modern Discrimination in Organizations" in *Academy of Management Review* (January 2008, pp. 55)
Pub: ScholarOne, Inc.
Ed: Lilia M. Cortina. **Description:** Analysis of social psychological research on modern discrimination to explain the theory of incivility used as part of sexism and racism in organizations. The selective incivility observed is discussed, as well as its implications and efforts to eliminate it.

26566 ■ "Words at Work" in *Information Today* (Vol. 26, February 2009, No. 2, pp. 25)
Pub: Information Today, Inc.
Description: Current new buzzwords include the following: digital amnesia, or overload by availability, speed and volume of digital information; maternal profiling, a form a discrimination against women; recipe malpractice, a reminder that just because you can turn on a stove it doesn't make you a chef; ringxiety, the act when everyone reaches for their cell phone when one rings; verbing, the practice of turning good nouns into verbs.

TRADE PERIODICALS

26567 ■ *The Columbus Times*
Pub: Columbus Times
Contact: Ophelia Devore Mitchell, Publisher Emeritus
Released: Weekly (Wed.). **Price:** $65.48; .50 single issue. **Description:** Black community newspaper.

26568 ■ *Manager's Legal Bulletin*
Pub: Alexander Hamilton Institute Inc.
Ed: Gloria Ju, Editor. **Released:** Semimonthly. **Price:** $72, individuals; $3.00, single issue. **Description:** Shows managers how to handle problems in the workplace without provoking lawsuits for illegal discrimination in hiring, firing, promotions, sexual harassment, or discipline decisions.

26569 ■ *Mealey's Emerging Insurance Disputes*
Pub: LexisNexis
Contact: A. Spencer
Ed: Steve Berstler, Editor. **Released:** Semimonthly. **Price:** $1,464, U.S. **Description:** Finds and tracks new areas of insurance litigation as they arise. Follows coverage actions involving underlying claims of sexual harassment and discrimination; sexual molestation and assault; attorney liability; patent and trademark infringement; construction defects, directors and officers claims; emotional distress; and intentional acts.

26570 ■ *The Webb Report*
Pub: Pacific Resource Development Group, Inc.
Ed: Released: Monthly. **Price:** Free; $10, single issue subscribers; $15, single issue non-subscribers. **Description:** Provides information on court cases and issues involving sexual harassment and guidelines concerning what is and what is not considered to be harassment and what to do about it. Recurring features include news of research and notices of publications available.

VIDEOCASSETTES/ AUDIOCASSETTES

26571 ■ *ADA: Commonsense Compliance*
Audio Graphics Training Systems
301 West Broome St., Suite 100
Lagrange, GA 30240
Ph:(404)507-2487
Free: 800-814-9792
Fax:(706)883-7136
Co. E-mail: customerservice@agts-web.com
URL: http://www.agts-web.com
Price: $695.00. **Description:** Illustrates the legal issues of the ADA through well-acted vignettes. Designed to be viewed in conjunction with "ADA: Understanding the Law." **Availability:** VHS.

26572 ■ *The ADA Maze: What You Can Do*
Commonwealth Films, Inc.
223 Commonwealth Ave.
Boston, MA 02116
Ph:(617)262-5634
Fax:(617)262-6948
Co. E-mail: info@commonwealthfilms.com
URL: http://www.commonwealthfilms.com
Released: 1991. **Price:** $425.00. **Description:** Defines the legal aspects of hiring according to the ADA through a combination of interviews and graphics. Aimed at managers, topics include the intent of the ADA, writing job descriptions, interviewing guidelines and more. **Availability:** VHS.

26573 ■ *ADA: Understanding the Law*
Audio Graphics Training Systems
301 West Broome St., Suite 100
Lagrange, GA 30240
Ph:(404)507-2487
Free: 800-814-9792
Fax:(706)883-7136
Co. E-mail: customerservice@agts-web.com
URL: http://www.agts-web.com
Price: $695.00. **Description:** Discusses the new ADA laws in a conference room setting. Confronts typical objections from management and gives clear information on legal requirements and ramifications. Designed to be viewed in conjunction with "ADA: Commonsense Compliance." **Availability:** VHS.

26574 ■ *Adjust Your Set: The Static Is Real*
University of Toronto
Media Commons
Robarts Library
130 St. George St., 3rd Fl.
Toronto, ON, Canada M5S 1A5
Ph:(416)978-6520
Fax:(416)978-8707
Co. E-mail: luke.dellcese@utoronto.ca
URL: http://www.utoronto.ca
Price: $79.95. **Description:** Addresses the issues that exist between men and women on the subject of sexual harassment. Contains vignettes on emotional manipulation, subtle threats of violence, heterosexism, feminist backlash in the classroom, harassment of disabled women, and battering in heterosexual relationships. Written and presented by students. **Availability:** VHS.

26575 ■ *The Americans with Disabilities Act: New Access to the Workplace*
Phoenix Learning Group
2349 Chaffee Dr.
St. Louis, MO 63146-3306
Ph:(314)569-0211
Free: 800-221-1274
Fax:(314)569-2834
URL: http://www.phoenixlearninggroup.com
Price: $495.00. **Description:** Covers a broad scope of information through interviews with government officials. Intended mainly for employers. **Availability:** VHS.

26576 ■ *Bridges: Skills to Manage a Diverse Workforce*
Learning Communications LLC
5520 Trabuco Rd.
Irvine, CA 92620
Free: 800-622-3610
Fax:(949)727-4323
Co. E-mail: sales@learncom.com
URL: http://www.learncomhr.com
Released: 1990. **Price:** $175.00. **Description:** An eight-part series designed to train supervisors and managers to deal with a culturally diverse workforce. The tapes are available individually or as a set. Trainer's manuals and participants manuals are included. **Availability:** VHS; 3/4U.

26577 ■ *Choices*
Learning Communications LLC
5520 Trabuco Rd.
Irvine, CA 92620
Free: 800-622-3610
Fax:(949)727-4323
Co. E-mail: sales@learncom.com
URL: http://www.learncomhr.com
Released: 1990. **Price:** $175.00. **Description:** A 12-part training course, designed to help train managers in EEO and affirmative action. Tapes are available as a set or individually. Trainer and participant manuals are included. **Availability:** VHS; 3/4U.

26578 ■ *Crossing the Line*
CA Working Group/We Do the Work
1611 Telegraph Ave Suite 1550
Oakland, CA 94612
Ph:(510)268-9675
Fax:(510)268-3606
Co. E-mail: info@theworkinggroup.org
URL: http://www.pbs.org/livelyhood
Price: $795.00. **Description:** Seven-part sexual harassment prevention training program that combines informed discussion of the legalities with seven real-life vignettes. Covers tips on how to identify behaviors that would be considered sexual harassment, how to differentiate between quid pro quo and hostile environments, and how to encourage environments that prevent sexual harassment. Includes participant and instructor's guides. **Availability:** VHS.

26579 ■ *Expanding Equal Opportunities—Implementing the Americans with Disabilities Act*
National Audiovisual Center
5301 Shawnee Rd.
Alexandria, VA 22312
Ph:(703)605-6000
Free: 800-553-6847
Fax:(703)321-8547
Co. E-mail: customerservice@ntis.gov
URL: http://www.ntis.gov/products/nac.aspx
Released: 1991. **Price:** $35.00. **Description:** Explains aspects of the Americans with Disabilities Act and how it affects the workplace. **Availability:** VHS.

26580 ■ *The Fairer Sex?*
corVISION Media, Inc.
872 S Milwaukee Ave. Ste. 295
Northbrook, IL 60062
Ph:877-364-7485
Free: 877-364-7485
Fax:(866)440-2614
Co. E-mail: corvision@aol.com
URL: http://www.corvision.com
Price: $295.00. **Description:** Tests whether women are truly discriminated in job market and in consumer purchasing situations. Intended to modify discriminatory behavior. **Availability:** VHS.

26581 ■ *Gateway to Opportunity: Interviewing Job Applicants with Disabilities*
Advantage Media
c/o Kantola Productions
55 Sunnyside Ave.
Mill Valley, CA 94941
Ph:(415)381-9363
Free: 800-280-1180
Fax:(415)381-9801
Co. E-mail: kantola@kantola.com
URL: http://www.kantola.com/d/advantage.htm
Released: 1992. **Price:** $495.00. **Description:** Illustrates detailed guidelines for interviewing according to the ADA through a combination of short scenarios and interviews. Note, however, that the guidelines don't necessarily address the legal issues per se. **Availability:** VHS.

26582 ■ *Given the Opportunity: Interacting with Individuals with Disabilities*
American Media, Inc.
4621 121st St.
Urbandale, IA 50323-2311
Ph:(515)224-0919
Free: 888-776-8268
Fax:(515)327-2555
Co. E-mail: custsvc@ammedia.com
URL: http://www.ammedia.com
Released: 1992. **Price:** $450.00. **Description:** A guide to interaction with the disabled in the workplace. Focuses primarily on four disabilities: hearing, sight, immobility, and the developmentally challenged, and the means of overcoming awkwardness when confronted with the disabled. **Availability:** VHS.

26583 ■ *Handling the Sexual Harassment Complaint*
Excellence in Training Corp.
c/o ICON Training
804 Roosevelt St.
Polk City, IA 50226
Free: 800-609-0479
Co. E-mail: info@icontraining.com
URL: http://www.icontraining.com
Released: 1991. **Price:** $495.00. **Description:** A program designed to train managers and supervisors how to avoid problems by the handling sexual harassment complaints correctly and legally. Includes a leader's guide and desk reminder cards. **Availability:** VHS; 3/4U; Special order formats.

26584 ■ *Intent vs. Impact*
Learning Communications LLC
5520 Trabuco Rd.
Irvine, CA 92620
Free: 800-622-3610
Fax:(949)727-4323
Co. E-mail: sales@learncom.com
URL: http://www.learncomhr.com
Released: 1991. **Price:** $175.00. **Description:** Two complete video training programs designed to help identify subtle forms of sexual harassment in the workplace. A trainer's manual and participants' manuals are included. **Availability:** VHS; 3/4U.

26585 ■ *It's Not Just Courtesy—It's the Law*
Excellence in Training Corp.
c/o ICON Training
804 Roosevelt St.
Polk City, IA 50226
Free: 800-609-0479
Co. E-mail: info@icontraining.com
URL: http://www.icontraining.com
Released: 1991. **Price:** $495.00. **Description:** A training program to raise awareness of sexual harassment among employees and teach them how to handle it. A leader's guide is included. **Availability:** VHS; 3/4U; Special order formats.

26586 ■ *Making the ADA Work for You*
American Media, Inc.
4621 121st St.
Urbandale, IA 50323-2311
Ph:(515)224-0919
Free: 888-776-8268
Fax:(515)327-2555
Co. E-mail: custsvc@ammedia.com
URL: http://www.ammedia.com
Released: 1992. **Price:** $595.00. **Description:** Aimed at supervisors and managers, this program features five narrators, each with a different disability, who present various scenarios. Interviewing, the definition of marginal functions, customer and employee reactions, and other topics are addressed. **Availability:** VHS.

26587 ■ *Preventing Sexual Harassment: A Management Responsibility*
Learning Communications LLC
5520 Trabuco Rd.
Irvine, CA 92620
Free: 800-622-3610
Fax:(949)727-4323
Co. E-mail: sales@learncom.com
URL: http://www.learncomhr.com
Released: 1992. **Description:** Training program consisting of two videotapes designed to show managers how to identify and prevent sexual harassement in the workplace and minimize liability. Defines sexual harassment, shows managers and supervisors how they can be held personally liable, presents practical steps to prevent harassment, details the elements of effective remedial action, and examines case studies. **Availability:** VHS; 3/4U.

26588 ■ *Preventing Sexual Harassment: A Shared Responsibility*
Learning Communications LLC
5520 Trabuco Rd.
Irvine, CA 92620
Free: 800-622-3610
Fax:(949)727-4323
Co. E-mail: sales@learncom.com
URL: http://www.learncomhr.com
Released: 1992. **Description:** Training program designed to prevent sexual harassment by employees and to minimize liability. Demonstrates the employer's prohibition against sexual harassment, highlights the availability of internal procedures for the resolution of complaints, and encourages employees to use internal procedures. **Availability:** VHS; 3/4U.

26589 ■ *Putting the ADA to Work for You*
American Occupational Therapy Association
4720 Montgomery Ln.
PO Box 31220
Bethesda, MD 20824-1220
Ph:(301)652-2682
Free: 800-377-8555
Fax:(301)652-7711
URL: http://www.aota.org
Released: 1992. **Price:** $50.00. **Description:** A real bargain for its low price and straight-forward approach. Combines interviews and short vignettes to suggest approaches to "reasonable accommodations." **Availability:** VHS.

26590 ■ *Sexual Harassment: Handling the Complaint*
Audio Graphics Training Systems
301 West Broome St., Suite 100
Lagrange, GA 30240
Ph:(404)507-2487
Free: 800-814-9792
Fax:(706)883-7136
Co. E-mail: customerservice@agts-web.com
URL: http://www.agts-web.com
Price: $1295.00. **Description:** Part two in a two-part series addressing the behavioral and legal issues surrounding sexual harassment. Directly confronts sensitive material in a constructive manner through well-acted vignettes. **Availability:** VHS.

26591 ■ *Sexual Harassment: Serious Business*
American Management Association
1601 Broadway
New York, NY 10087-7327
Ph:877-566-9441
Free: 800-262-9699
Fax:(518)891-0368
Co. E-mail: customerservice@amanet.org
URL: http://www.amanet.org
Price: $495.00. **Description:** Provides information on how to recognize and prevent sexual harassment in the workplace. **Availability:** VHS; CC.

26592 ■ *Sexual Harassment in the Workplace...Identify. Stop. Prevent.*
Excellence in Training Corp.
c/o ICON Training
804 Roosevelt St.
Polk City, IA 50226
Free: 800-609-0479
Co. E-mail: info@icontraining.com
URL: http://www.icontraining.com
Released: 1991. **Price:** $575.00. **Description:** A training program in the prevention and/or eliminating of sexual harassment in the workplace. A leader's guide and desk reminder cards are included. **Availability:** VHS; 3/4U; Special order formats.

26593 ■ *Welcome to the Team: Disability Etiquette in the Workplace*
Advantage Media
c/o Kantola Productions
55 Sunnyside Ave.
Mill Valley, CA 94941
Ph:(415)381-9363
Free: 800-280-1180

Fax:(415)381-9801
Co. E-mail: kantola@kantola.com
URL: http://www.kantola.com/d/advantage.htm
Released: 1992. **Price:** $495.00. **Description:** Illustrates the concept of "reasonable accommodations," through various examples and practical suggestions. Recommended for both managers and employees. Part one of a two part program. **Availability:** VHS.

CONSULTANTS

26594 ■ AIDS Partnership Michigan
2751 E Jefferson Ave., Ste. 301
Detroit, MI 48207
Ph:(313)446-9800
Free: 800-515-3434
Fax:(313)446-9839
Co. E-mail: info@aidspartnership.org
URL: http://www.aidspartnership.org
Contact: Barbara Murray, Managing Director
E-mail: murray@atsaidspartnership.org
Scope: Offers advice to corporations on the effects of HIV and AIDS in the workplace. Focus is on infected employee rights, co-worker rights, and employer responsibilities. Serves all industries.

26595 ■ Applied Personnel Research
62 Candlewood Rd.
Scarsdale, NY 10583
Ph:(617)244-8859
Fax:(617)244-8904
Co. E-mail: information@appliedpersonnelresearch.com
URL: http://www.appliedpersonnelresearch.com
Contact: Dr. Joel P. Wiesen, Director
E-mail: wiesen@appliedpersonnelresearch.com
Scope: Industrial psychology consulting services in the areas of personnel assessment and selection, and solution-oriented applied personnel research involving data collection and data analysis. Customized Consulting solutions can be provided. **Seminars:** The Recent Judicial Decision Concerning Two NYC Firefighter Exams, 2009; Possible New Approaches to Reduce Adverse Impact, 2007; Thinking Outside the Box in Merit Selection, Princeton, Nov, 2006; Limitations and Flaws in the Research Supporting Field Sobriety Tests, Las Vegas, Oct, 2006.

26596 ■ Coastal Training Technologies Corp.
500 Studio Dr.
Virginia Beach, VA 23452
Ph:(757)498-9014
Free: 800-861-7668
Fax:(757)498-3657
Co. E-mail: info@coastal.com
URL: http://www.coastalhr.com
Contact: Brett Fisher, Principle
E-mail: brettf@atscoastal.com
Scope: Provides consulting services and seminars on all aspects of management, human resources, and business, including customer relations and sexual harassment, works with managers one-on-one, implements programs, and presents seminars for entire departments. Serves private industries as well as government agencies. **Seminars:** Accounting and Corporate Finance; Americans with Disabilities Act (ADA); Business Meetings; Change Management; Coaching; Communication; Conflict Resolution; Creativity; Customer Service; Diversity; Drug-Free Workplace; Employee Development; Employee Retention; Government Employee; Group Dynamics; Harassment; Homeland Security; Interviewing Skills. **Special Services:** Coastal[R].

26597 ■ DiversityWorks
800 Heinz Ave., Ste. 14
Berkeley, CA 94710
Ph:(510)540-7008
Fax:(510)540-6976
Co. E-mail: mail@diversityworks.org
URL: http://www.diversityworks.org
Contact: Ariana Proehl, CEO
E-mail: arianap@atsdiversityworks.org
Scope: Offers diversity consulting to businesses, schools, youth groups, and a variety of organizations. Designs programs to suit to individual clients' needs. Areas of expertise include: Community-building (and team-building), consciousness-raising, skill building (leadership development, popular education, facilitation) and taking action. **Publications:** "Diversity Words"; "A Woman's Beauty"; "Youth Violence"; "Modern Day Minstrels"; "Love Makes the World Go Round"; "Glorification of White Supremacy through Movies".

26598 ■ DJT Consulting Group L.L.C.
2900 Sonoma Blvd., Ste. C
PO Box 6652
Vallejo, CA 94591
Ph:(707)674-0174
Fax:(707)638-0499
Co. E-mail: info@djtconsulting.com
URL: http://www.djtconsulting.com
Contact: Daniel I. Armenta, Principle
E-mail: dan@djtconsulting.com
Scope: Offers a range of grant management services including contract monitoring, research, grant writing, evaluation and project management. Specializes in grant proposal writing, project management and program development. Assists enhance financial resources, programs and services. **Seminars:** Finding and Winning Government Grants.

26599 ■ Dr. John A. Berger & Associates
2021 Midwest Rd., Ste. 200
Oak Brook, IL 60523
Ph:(630)953-8638
Fax:(630)953-8687
Contact: Dr. John A. Berger, Owner
Scope: Full service human resources consulting firm specializing in the practice of industrial/organizational psychology. Specializes in the areas of recruitment and selection; management continuity, development and succession planning; capability and performance testing and evaluation; organizational analysis and design, performance management; outplacement and terminations; turnarounds and crisis management; compensation; family owned business counseling - conflict resolution, management succession, and career planning for family members. Has developed structured hiring guides and selection systems; Has designed, developed and implemented a variety of performance appraisal systems both as part of total compensation projects and stand alone systems. Has served as an expert witness in a number of wrongful discharge and EEO discrimination cases. Industries served: manufacturing, financial services, high-tech, insurance, utilities, construction, retail, professional services, government, health care, publishing, leisure and food services.

26600 ■ D.R. Bennett & Associates
11846 Balboa Blvd., Ste. 298
Granada Hills, CA 91344
Ph:(818)360-2375
Fax:(818)366-7593
Co. E-mail: dbennett69@aol.com
Contact: Deborah R. Bennett, President
E-mail: dbennett69@aol.com
Scope: Human resources consultant who writes all human resources forms including employee handbooks and job descriptions; sets up employment applications, employee files and procedures to comply with regulations affecting employers; and finds and screens applicants and does the initial interviewing. Also offers management training in the areas of interviewing, employee evaluations, how to handle sexual harassment claims and progressive discipline and documentation. All services are tailored to meet EEOC and INS regulations as well as labor laws, to reduce exposure to worker's compensation stress claims, unemployment claims and wrongful termination suits. Industries served: small businesses with 25-100employees. **Seminars:** Interviewing Skills Seminar; Performance Appraisal Seminar.

26601 ■ Eastern Point Consulting Group Inc.
36 Glen Ave.
Newton, MA 02464
Ph:(617)965-4141
Fax:(617)965-4172
Co. E-mail: info@eastpt.com
URL: http://www.eastpt.com
Contact: Mary MacMahon, Principal
E-mail: kherzog@eastpt.com
Scope: Specializes in bringing practical solutions to complex challenges. Provides consulting and training in managing diversity; comprehensive sexual-harassment policies and programs; organizational development; benchmarks 360 skills assessment; executive coaching; strategic human resource planning; team building; leadership development for women; mentoring programs; and gender issues in the workplace. **Seminars:** Leadership Development for Women.

26602 ■ FW Consultants Ltd.
1025 W Glen Oaks Ln., Ste. 105
Mequon, WI 53092-3372
Ph:(262)241-8234
Fax:(262)241-8340
Co. E-mail: evelyn@fwcons.com
URL: http://www.fwcons.com
Contact: Evelyn S. Freeman, Principle
E-mail: evelyn@fwcons.com
Scope: Human resources consultants specializing in equal employment opportunity and affirmative action programs, demographic analyses, EEO/AA training, and statistical analyses to defend discrimination charges. Serves private industries as well as government agencies. **Seminars:** Affirmative Action Program Development; EEO/Affirmative Action Training.

26603 ■ Haight Consulting
1726 Palisades Dr.
Pacific Palisades, CA 90272-9867
Ph:(310)454-2988
Fax:(310)454-4516
Co. E-mail: haightcnsl@yahoo.com
Contact: Ralph Haight, Mgr
E-mail: haightcns@aol.com
Scope: Human Resources compliance: helping employers prevent and resolve issues on sexual harassment, disability discrimination, other forms of discrimination and harassment, retaliation, FMLA, and employee safety. Training (management, HR staff and internal investigators); policies and procedures; compliance program audits; expert witness/litigation consulting; and on-call consultation on individual issues and investigations. **Publications:** "Sexual Harassment Investigations Manual," CCH Inc, 2000; "The Federal Leave Compliance Kit," 1995; "Disability discrimination Reasonable Accommodation Kit," 1995; "Disability discrimination Administration Package"; "The Sexual Harassment Investigator's Kit"; "The California Sexual Harassment Compliance Kit". **Seminars:** Management and HR training on disability discrimination; sexual harassment; discrimination and harassment laws; FMLA; retaliation; recruiting and selection; preventing and resolving performance issues.

26604 ■ Human Resources Group Ltd.
4710 Lincoln Hwy., Ste. 233
Matteson, IL 60443
Ph:(708)946-9652
Fax:(708)946-9653
Co. E-mail: rorr@hrgroupltd.com
URL: http://www.hrgroupltd.com
Contact: Robert C. Orr, CEO
E-mail: rorr@hrgroupltd.com
Scope: Offers human resource consulting to small or medium-sized companies with limited human resource staff. Areas of expertise include sales and management training and development, employee opinion surveys, employee retention programs, customer service, communication strategies, and performance evaluation programs. Development of policies and procedures, employee handbooks, jobs compendium, and turnover reduction strategies. Provides training in legal compliance, i.e. Americans with Disabilities Act, sexual harassment, etc. Industries served: retail, casino gaming(including Indian gaming) and hospitality. **Publications:** "Employee Surveys: Being a "Mind Reader" Was never So Easy"; "Getting Over The "HR-Marketing Strange Bedfellows"; Underachievers"; "Employee Retention? No Problem!"; "Is Your Company The Employer Of Choice?"; "What is the Role of Your HR Department"; "Managing from A to Almost Z"; "The Top 10 Things HR Should be Doing"; "HR Department Assessment for the GM & HR Executive"; "Evaluating Executives"; "Economic Challenges - 11 Steps". **Seminars:** Effective Sales Management; Basics of Supervisory

Management; Human Resource Educational Program; Human Resources and the Small Business; Customer Service.

26605 ■ John Smithkey, III, RN
1271 Overland Ave. NE
North Canton, OH 44720-1731
Ph:(330)494-3729
Co. E-mail: schoolnurse007@aol.com
E-mail: schoolnurse007@aol.com

Scope: Specializes in public and occupational health, HIV/AIDS education and prevention programs, grant and proposal writing, and programs for businesses and employees. **Publications:** "The Strange World of Head Lice Information," Jun, 2003. **Seminars:** CPR; Communicable Diseases; Bloodborne Pathogen Training; Delegation of Nursing Tasks and Medication Administration Certification; Anaphylactic Shock and EpiPen Training.

26606 ■ The Kaleel Jamison Consulting Group Inc.
297 River St., Ste. 201
Troy, NY 12180
Ph:(518)271-7000
Free: 888-552-4662
Fax:(518)271-4400
Co. E-mail: kjcg411@kjcg.com
URL: http://www.kjcg.com
Contact: Catherine M. Volk, Principal
E-mail: catherinevolk@atskjcg.com

Scope: The firm creates high performing, worthy organizations through its unique brand of management consulting and strategic culture change, also assists organizations to become places where all people can do their work by shifting focus to business cultures that integrate individual and organizational needs and competencies, which improve productivity, product or service quality and bottom line performance. **Publications:** "Inclusion 3.5: Our Vision of the Future," Profiles in Diversity Journal, 2007; "The Next Leap Forward," 2007; "Tapping the Wisdom of the Ages: Ageism and the Need for Multi generational Organizations"; "Developing a Comprehensive Pipeline Strategy"; "White Awareness: Handbook for Anti-Racism Training," University of Oklahoma Press, 2003; "The Inclusion Breakthrough: Unleashing the Real Power of Diversity," Berrett-Koehler, 2002; "Eight Essential Axioms for Rapid Culture Change"; "The Need for Silence, Spontaneity and Thinking Time in 21st Century Organization"; "Road Map for the Path to Strategic Culture Change"; "Thee Path From Exclusive Club to Inclusive Organization". **Seminars:** Bring Your Whole Self To Life: Developing The Organizational And Personal Self (D/OPS), Potomac, Aug, 2008; D/Ops: Developing The Organizational And Personal Self; Dealing with Covert Processes.

26607 ■ Litigation Management & Training Services Inc.
301 E Ocean Blvd., Ste. 520
Long Beach, CA 90802-4862
Ph:(562)495-0098
Free: 800-548-6468
Fax:(562)495-1786
Co. E-mail: patricia@preventlitigation.com
URL: http://www.preventlitigation.com
Contact: Barbara S. Boarnet, Principle
E-mail: patricia@preventlitigation.com

Scope: Consults with private industry employers and government agencies on proactive legal management of the workplace, including sexual harassment prevention, legal aspects of human resources management, how to hire, fire and manage employees legally. Special programs for adopting and enforcing e-mail and internet abuse policies. Also trains on avoiding liabilities for design and delivery of training programs, health and safety regulatory compliance issues and legal aspects of violence prevention and workplace security. Personnel policy development, internal discrimination and misconduct investigations. **Publications:** "Heading off harassment. Effective training is critical to limiting legal exposure for workplace harassment".

26608 ■ Pacific Resource Development Group Inc.
1651 NE 185th St.
Seattle, WA 98155-3938
Ph:(206)367-1418
Free: 800-767-3062
Fax:(206)367-1418
Co. E-mail: pacres@shadesofgray.com
URL: http://www.shadesofgray.com
Contact: Susan L. Webb, President
E-mail: susan@shadesofgray.com

Scope: A consulting firm specializing in sexual harassment. Firm provides consulting and training services for managers, supervisors, general employees and individuals. Services include training, investigations, expert witness, training products and materials such as videos and books. **Publications:** "Training and Investigator Manuals," 2002; "Step Forward: Sexual Harassment in the Workplace," 1998; "Shockwaves: The Global Impact of Sexual Harassment," Master Media Ltd., Mar, 1994; "Step Forward," Mastermedia, 1991; "25 Things to Do If Sexual Harassment Happens to You"; "Six Simple Steps to Stop Sexual Harassment"; "How to Handle Sexual Harassment Complaints". **Seminars:** Sexual Harassment; Employee Training; Train-the-Trainer; Investigator Training; One-to-One Training. **Special Services:** Shades of Gray™.

26609 ■ Stier Associates
4 Dunellen
Cromwell, CT 06416-2702
Ph:(860)635-1590
Fax:(860)635-1591
Contact: Dr. Suzanne Stier, President

Scope: Offers personal development consulting. Services include: succession planning, executive coaching, strategic management, team building, and board development. Consulting services for public companies include: process consulting, team building, executive coaching, diversity management, strategic management and religious institutions.

26610 ■ The Training Station
5017 Dawnwood Ct.
PO Box 170536
Arlington, TX 76003
Ph:(817)683-2650
Free: 800-594-8181
Fax:(817)478-9816
Contact: Reginald Ferrell, Vice President
E-mail: reg_ferrell@yahoo.com

Scope: Training, human resource development, and marketing services consultants. Conducts needs analysis, program development, design, writing, execution, follow-up and assessment. Provides speaking engagements and seminars for all personnel. Specialize in sales and marketing, sexual harassment, recruiting, interviewing, selection and management skills. Management assessment tools and programs available. Standard or generic programs are available for immediate tailoring or modification, as well as custom developed materials and programs. Train-the-trainer methodology is also an option. Consulting on human resource issues are available upon request. Industries served: Chemical, food service, manufacturing, banking, medical, pharmaceutical, optical, and hard goods; also serve the electrical utility, retail, and power goods markets. **Seminars:** R.I.S.K.; S.H.A.M.E. (Sexual Harassment Awareness Managed Effectively); M.U.S.T. (Management Understanding of Sales and Training); Power Sales Management; Stress Management Training; Show Selling Seminar.

26611 ■ Vaccari & Associates Inc.
17 Cypress St. 1
Marblehead, MA 01945-1925
Ph:(781)639-0946
Fax:(781)639-0946
Co. E-mail: rvaccari1@verizon.net
Contact: Ralph J. Vaccari, President
E-mail: rvaccari@rcn.com

Scope: A provider of appraisals for primary and secondary mortgages, mortgage refinancing, employee relocation, private mortgage insurance removal, estate planning and divorce settlement.

COMPUTERIZED DATABASES

26612 ■ *Employment Discrimination Report*
The Bureau of National Affairs Inc.
1801 S Bell St.
Arlington, VA 22202
Free: 800-372-1033
Co. E-mail: customercare@bna.com
URL: http://www.bna.com

Description: Contains legislative, judicial and regulatory developments and news in the field of equal employment opportunity. Subjects cover age-based discrimination, appearance-based discrimination, class actions, damages and remedies, disabilities-based discrimination, national origin-based discrimination, race-based discrimination, religion-based discrimination, retaliation, rules of evidence, sexual harassment, sexual orientation-based discrimination, taxation, testers, discovery, employment practices liability insurance, family and medical leave, gender-based discrimination, glass ceiling, and jury practice. Sections include Highlights, Table of Contents, State Index, News, Table of Cases, Court Decisions, Verdicts & Settlements, State News, Arbitration, Interviews, Text, and Calendar of Events. **Availability:** Online: The Bureau of National Affairs Inc., Thomson Reuters. **Type:** Full text.

LIBRARIES

26613 ■ Tennessee Human Rights Commission–Resource Library
710 James Robertson Pkwy., Ste. 100
Corner of Rosa Parks Blvd.
Nashville, TN 37243-1219
Ph:(615)741-5825
Free: 800-251-3589
Fax:(615)532-2197
URL: http://www.state.tn.us/humanrights/mang_staff.html
Contact: Beverly L. Watts, Exec.Dir.

Scope: Race relations; discrimination in employment, housing, and public accommodations; legislation and decisions rendered in discrimination cases. **Services:** Library open to the public with restrictions. **Holdings:** 75 books; 500 bound periodical volumes; commission-related materials. **Subscriptions:** 10 journals and other serials.

26614 ■ U.S. Equal Employment Opportunity Commission Library
131 M Street, NE
Washington, DC 20507
Ph:(202)663-4900
Free: 800-669-6820
URL: http://www.eeoc.gov/
Contact: Susan D. Taylor, Dir., Lib./Info Svcs.

Scope: Employment discrimination, minorities, women, aged, persons with disabilities, labor law, civil rights. **Services:** Interlibrary loan; copying; Library open to the public by appointment. **Holdings:** 25,000 books. **Subscriptions:** 300 journals and other serials; 8 newspapers.

RESEARCH CENTERS

26615 ■ Center for Women Policy Studies
1776 Massachusetts Ave. NW, Ste. 450
Washington, DC 20036
Ph:(202)872-1770
Fax:(202)296-8962
Co. E-mail: cwps@centerwomenpolicy.org
URL: http://www.centerwomenpolicy.org
Contact: Dr. Leslie R. Wolfe, Pres.
E-mail: cwps@centerwomenpolicy.org

Scope: Public policy (federal, state, and global) that promotes women's human rights. Current key policy issues include access to education for low income women, the women's HIV/AIDS epidemic in the USA and worldwide, violence against women and girls, international trafficking of women and girls, work/family and workplace diversity, reproductive rights and justice, and the impact of US foreign policy on women worldwide. Designs model legislation and develops and disseminates research reports and policy papers.

Publications: E-News (monthly). **Educational Activities:** Foreign Policy Institute for State Legislators (annually), educates U.S. women state legislators on the impact of U.S. foreign policy on women worldwide and the role of state-level officials in influencing foreign policy.

ASSOCIATIONS AND OTHER ORGANIZATIONS

26616 ■ Canadian Association of Chemical Distributors–L'Association Canadienne des Distributeurs de Produits Chimiques
349 Davis Rd., Unit A
Oakville, ON, Canada L6J 5Z7
Ph:(905)844-9140
Fax:(905)844-5706
Co. E-mail: ccampbell@cacd.ca
URL: http://www.cacd.ca
Contact: Cathy Campbell, Exec. Dir.
Description: Chemical distributors in Canada. Represents members to governments, allied associations, and the public. **Publications:** *The Chemunicator* (quarterly).

26617 ■ Distribution Business Management Association
2938 Columbia Ave., Ste. 1102
Lancaster, PA 17603
Ph:(717)295-0033
Fax:(717)299-2154
Co. E-mail: dbminfo@dbm-assoc.com
URL: http://www.dcenter.com
Contact: Amy Z. Thorn, Exec. Dir.
Description: Management personnel in the wholesale distribution industries. Promotes education and continuing professional development in the materials handling, distribution, and supply chain industries. Conducts educational programs. **Publications:** *Distribution Business Management Journal* (semiannual).

26618 ■ Global Market Development Center
1275 Lake Plaza Dr.
Colorado Springs, CO 80906-3583
Ph:(719)576-4260
Fax:(719)576-2661
Co. E-mail: info@gmdc.org
URL: http://gmdc.com
Contact: David T. McConnell Jr., Pres./CEO
Description: General merchandise (nonfood) units of wholesale grocers, cooperatives, and voluntaries (110); chain food stores, service merchandisers, drug chains, mass merchandisers, wholesale drug companies, and wholesale clubs; manufacturers or suppliers of general merchandise (540) and health and beauty care products. Works to improve management operations, marketing programs, sales techniques, merchandising, and distribution functions of members; furthers management education and employee training; and promotes understanding and cooperation among members, the public, and government. Conducts research and compiles statistics. **Publications:** *Off the Shelf* (quarterly);Membership Directory (annual).

26619 ■ LTD Shippers Association
1230 Pottstown Pike, Ste. 6
Glenmoore, PA 19343
Ph:(610)458-3636
Fax:(610)458-8039
Co. E-mail: tomltd@aol.com
URL: http://www.ltdmgmt.com
Contact: Tom Craig, Pres.
Description: Works to leverage the buying power of the members for lower ocean freight prices. Has scope that includes ocean rates from Asia to United States, to Canada, Mexico, Puerto Rico and many other destinations; also rates to the U.S. and Canada from Brazil, the Mediterranean, India and other origins. Aims to design, develop, negotiate, implement and manage logistics or transportation programs for members. .

26620 ■ National Association of Wholesaler-Distributors
1325 G St. NW, Ste. 1000
Washington, DC 20005
Ph:(202)872-0885
Fax:(202)785-0586
Co. E-mail: naw@naw.org
URL: http://www.naw.org
Contact: Dirk Van Dongen, Pres.
Description: Federation of national, state, and regional associations, and individual wholesaler-distributor firms. Represents industry's views to the federal government. Analyzes current and proposed legislation and government regulations affecting the industry. Maintains public relations and media programs and a research foundation. Conducts wholesale executive management courses. **Publications:** *NAW Report* (bimonthly); *SmartBrief* .

26621 ■ National Convenience Store Distributors Association–Association nationale des distributeurs aux petites surfaces alimentaires
1695 Laval Blvd., Ste. 410
Laval, QC, Canada H7S 2M2
Ph:(450)967-3858
Free: 888-686-2823
Fax:(450)967-8839
Co. E-mail: nacda@nacda.ca
URL: http://www.nacda.ca
Contact: Raymond Bouchard, Chm.
Description: Assists members in providing dependable distribution of convenience products between suppliers and retailers. Represents member's interests with the government and other industry key players. Conducts educational seminars and programs relevant to member's business needs, thus contributing to the improvement of the convenience supply chain. **Publications:** *Distribution Management in the New Economy: A Blueprint for Success*; *Electronic-Commerce for Distribution Channels*; *Values Shift* .

26622 ■ NAW Institute for Distribution Excellence
1325 G St. NW, Ste. 1000
Washington, DC 20005
Ph:(202)872-0885
Fax:(202)785-0586
Co. E-mail: naw@naw.org
URL: http://www.naw.org/institute/iindex.php
Contact: Dirk Van Dongen, Pres.
Description: Firms that are members of the National Association of Wholesaler-Distributors, wholesalers, and trade associations. Seeks to advance knowledge in the field of wholesale distribution by means of long-range research projects. **Publications:** *Connect with Your Suppliers: A Wholesaler-Distributor's Guide to Electronic Communications Systems*; *Facing the Forces of Change: The Road to Opportunity* (triennial); *Price for Success: A Practical Guide for Improving Margins in Wholesale Distribution* .

REFERENCE WORKS

26623 ■ "Adapt or Die" in *Black Enterprise* (Vol. 38, July 2008, No. 12, pp. 27)
Pub: Earl G. Graves Publishing Co. Inc.
Ed: Oguntoyinbo Lekan. **Description:** Turbulence in the domestic auto industry is hitting auto suppliers hard and black suppliers, the majority of whom contract with the Big Three, are just beginning to establish relationships with import car manufacturers. The more savvy CEOs are adopting new technologies in order to weather the downturn in the economy and in the industry as a whole.

26624 ■ "Alliance Unit Signs Movie Distribution Deal" in *Globe & Mail* (January 24, 2006, pp. B6)
Pub: CTVglobemedia Publishing Inc.
Ed: Grant Robertson. **Description:** The details on the distribution agreement between Movie Distribution Income Fund and Weinstein Co. are presented. Movie Distribution Income Fund is a unit of Alliance Atlantis Communication Inc.

26625 ■ "Amcon Distributing Co." in *Arkansas Business* (Vol. 26, November 9, 2009, No. 45, pp. 13)
Pub: Journal Publishing Inc.
Description: Amcon Distributing Co., a consumer products company, has bought the convenience store distribution assets of Discount Distributors from its parent, Harps Food Stores Inc., significantly increasing its wholesale distribution presence in the northwest Arkansas market. The acquisition will be funded through Amcon's existing credit facilities.

26626 ■ *American Wholesalers and Distributors Directory*
Pub: Gale
Released: Annual, Latest edition 22nd; April, 2011. **Price:** $410, individuals. **Covers:** Name and address, fax number, SIC code, principal product lines, total number of employees, estimated annual sales volume and principal officers' information of 27,000 large and small wholesalers and distributors in the U.S. and Puerto Rico. **Arrangement:** By broad subject from principal product line, by Standard Industrial Classification code (SIC index), by state and city (geographical index), and by company name (alphabetic index). **Indexes:** SIC, geographical, alphabetical.

26627 ■ "ART Announces New Distribution Arrangement with GE Healthcare for eXplore Optix" in *Canadian Corporate News* (May 14, 2007)
Pub: Comtex News Network Inc.
Description: ART Advanced Research Technologies Inc., a medical device company and a leader in opti-

cal molecular imaging products for the pharmaceutical and healthcare industries, announced that it signed an agreement with GE Healthcare regarding worldwide distribution of its eXplore Optix preclinical optical molecular imaging system.

26628 ■ *Associated Equipment Distributors—Membership Directory*
Pub: Associated Equipment Distributors Inc.
Released: Annual, Latest edition 2011-2012. **Price:** $75, members single copy; $150, nonmembers single copy; $250, members 5 copies; $500, nonmembers 5 copies. **Covers:** Fifteen hundred U.S. and Canadian distributors. Available as a special issue of Construction Equipment Distribution magazine. **Entries Include:** Information on each company's branches, manufacturer members, banks, finance companies, specialized service firms and trade press, and AED contact person.

26629 ■ "Auto Supplier Stock Battered In Wake Of Wall Street Woes" in *Crain's Detroit Business* (Vol. 24, September 29, 2008, No. 39, pp. 4)
Pub: Crain Communications, Inc.
Ed: Ryan Beene. **Description:** Due to the volatility of the stock market and public perception of the $700 billion banking bailout, auto suppliers are now facing a dramatic drop in their shares. Statistical data included.

26630 ■ "AV Concept Expands Into Green Energy Storage" in *Wireless News* (January 25, 2010)
Pub: Close-Up Media
Description: Electronics distributor and manufacturer AV Concept Holdings Limited announced a marketing partnership with Boston-Power, a provider of lithium-ion batteries, with a focus in the Chinese and Korean markets.

26631 ■ "avVaa World Health Care Products Rolls Out Internet Marketing Program" in *Health and Beauty Close-Up* (September 18, 2009)
Pub: Close-Up Media
Description: avVaa World Health Care Products, Inc., a biotechnology company, manufacturer and distributor of nationally branded therapeutic, natural health care and skin products, has signed an agreement with Online Performance Marketing to launch of an Internet marketing campaign in order to broaden its presence online. The impact of advertising on the Internet to generate an increase in sales is explored.

26632 ■ "Beer Sales 'Foament' a Dispute" in *Philadelphia Business Journal* (Vol. 28, October 9, 2009, No. 34, pp. 1)
Pub: American City Business Journals
Ed: Peter van Allen. **Description:** Malt Beverages Distributors Association of Pennsylvania filed a case against the Liquor Control Board (LCB) at the Pennsylvania Supreme Court in order to further restrict store sales. The dispute stems from the supermarket chains circumventing the liquor law with the blessings of LCB.

26633 ■ "Black Diamond Holdings Corp. Receives SEC Approval" in *Canadian Corporate News* (May 16, 2007)
Pub: Comtex News Network Inc.
Description: Black Diamond Holdings, Corp., a British Columbia domiciled company and its two wholly owned subsidiaries are engaged in the bottling, importation, distribution, marketing, and brand creation of premium spirits and wines to worldwide consumers, announced that it has completed the SEC review process and has applied to list for trading in the United States on the OTC.BB.

26634 ■ "Blue Bell Breaks Ground in South Carolina" in *Ice Cream Reporter* (Vol. 23, August 20, 2010, No. 9, pp. 3)
Pub: Ice Cream Reporter
Description: Texas-based Blue Bell Creameries will open a new 2,000 square foot transfer facility in North Charleston, South Carolina. The facility will expand Blue Bell's distribution efforts in the state.

26635 ■ "Brewed to Succeed; Mokarbia Perks Up Sales for King Coffee" in *Crain's Detroit Business* (Vol. 24, March 17, 2008, No. 11, pp. 3)
Pub: Crain Communications, Inc.
Ed: Brent Snavely. **Description:** Profile of King Coffee Tea Services, Royal Oak-based company, whose distributing deal with Mokarabia coffee has generated an increase in sales.

26636 ■ "Brewing a Love-Haiti Relationship" in *The Business Journal - Serving Phoenix and the Valley of the Sun* (Vol. 28, July 4, 2008, No. 44)
Pub: American City Business Journals, Inc.
Ed: Yvonne Zusel. **Description:** Jean and Alicia Marseille have ventured into a coffee distribution company called Ka Bel LLC which markets Marabou brand of coffee imported from Haiti. Part of the proceeds of the business is donated to entrepreneurs from Jean's country, Haiti. Details of the Marseille's startup business and personal mission to help are discussed.

26637 ■ "Cannabis Science Signs Exclusive and Non-Exclusive Agreement with Prescription Vending Machines" in *Benzinga.com* (October 29, 2011)
Pub: Benzinga.com
Ed: Benzinga Staff. **Description:** Cannabis Science Inc., a biotech company developing pharmaceutical cannabis products has partnered with Prescription Vending Machines Inc. and its principal Vincent Meddizadeh to provide industry specific consulting and advisory services to Cannabis Science.

26638 ■ "CBC Eyes Partners for TV Downloads" in *Globe & Mail* (February 9, 2006, pp. B1)
Pub: CTVglobemedia Publishing Inc.
Ed: Grant Robertson. **Description:** The details on Canadian Broadcasting Corp.'s distribution agreement with Google Inc. and Apple Computer Inc. are presented.

26639 ■ "Cheese Spread Whips Up a Brand New Bowl" in *Brandweek* (Vol. 49, April 21, 2008, No. 16, pp. 17)
Pub: VNU Business Media, Inc.
Ed: Mike Beirne. **Description:** Mrs. Kinser's Pimento Cheese Spread is launching a new container for its product in order to attempt stronger brand marketing with a better bowl in order to win over the heads of households as young as in their 30s. The company also intends to begin distribution in Texas and the West Coast. Mrs. Kinser's is hoping that the new packaging will provide a more distinct branding and will help consumers distinguish what flavor they are buying.

26640 ■ "Children's Products Maker Not the New Kid on the Block" in *Crain's Cleveland Business* (Vol. 28, November 26, 2007, No. 47, pp. 3)
Pub: Crain Communications, Inc.
Ed: David Bennett. **Description:** Discusses the business model employed by Shamrock Industries Inc., a rising star in the competitive world of children's products; the company, which does business as Foundations Quality Children's Products, has expanded into a 63,000-square-foot distribution center which has boosted its local profile significantly.

26641 ■ "Chinese Fund Loans $33.5 Million to Prestolite" in *Crain's Detroit Business* (Vol. 26, January 18, 2010, No. 3, pp. 1)
Pub: Crain Communications, Inc.
Ed: Ryan Beene. **Description:** Prestolite Electric Inc., a distributor of alternators and starter motors for commercial and heavy-duty vehicles, looked to China for fresh capital in order to fund new product launches.

26642 ■ "Datran Media Executives to Lead Industry Debates Across Q1 Conferences" in *Internet Wire* (January 22, 2010)
Pub: Comtex News Network, Inc.
Description: Datran Media, an industry-leading digital marketing technology company, will be sending members of its management team to several conferences in the early part of the first quarter of 2010; discussions will include Internet marketing innovations, e-commerce and media distribution.

26643 ■ "Deal Braces Cramer for Growth Run" in *The Business Journal-Serving Metropolitan Kansas City* (Vol. 26, July 4, 2008, No. 43, pp. 1)
Pub: American City Business Journals, Inc.
Ed: James Dornbook. **Description:** Gardner, Kansas-based Cramer Products Inc. bought 100 percent of the stocks of Louisville, Kentucky-based Active Ankle Inc. from 26 private investors increasing its revenue by 20 percent. The latter is the second largest vendor of Cramer. Other details of the merger are presented.

26644 ■ "The Doomsday Scenario" in *Conde Nast Portfolio* (Vol. 2, June 2008, No. 6, pp. 91)
Pub: Conde Nast Publications, Inc.
Ed: Jeffrey Rothfeder. **Description:** Detroit and the U.S. auto industry are discussed as well as the ramifications of the demise of this manufacturing base. Similarities and differences between the downfall of the U.S. steel business and the impact it had on Pittsburg, Pennsylvania is also discussed.

26645 ■ "Egg Fight: The Yolk's on the Short" in *Barron's* (Vol. 88, July 7, 2008, No. 27, pp. 20)
Pub: Dow Jones & Co., Inc.
Ed: Christopher C. Williams. **Description:** Shares of Cal-Maine Foods, the largest egg producer and distributor in the US, are due for a huge rise because of the increase in egg prices. Short sellers, however, continue betting that the stock, priced at $31.84 each, will eventually go down.

26646 ■ "Energy Outfitter Wings Into Houston" in *Houston Business Journal* (Vol. 40, December 4, 2009, No. 30, pp. 2A)
Pub: American City Business Journals
Ed: Ford Gunter. **Description:** Red Wing Shoe Company Inc. has launched its personal protective equipment (PPE) line for oil and gas industry crewmen in North America by opening a 13,000 square foot distribution hub in Houston, Texas. The Houston facility was created to supply directly the oil and gas industry and to carry inventory for select distributors.

26647 ■ "Familiar Face Aims to Rebuild Distributor's Once-Strong Local Ties" in *Crain's Cleveland Business* (December 3, 2007)
Pub: Crain Communications, Inc.
Ed: David Bennett. **Description:** Phillips Contractors Supply, a tool distributor, has a new president and co-owner, James Beckett. Beckett was once vice president of operations so he knows the company well and has plans to re-establish the firm's presence in the region.

26648 ■ "Finalist: BlackEagle Partners L.L.C." in *Crain's Detroit Business* (Vol. 24, March 24, 2008, No. 12, pp. 12)
Pub: Crain Communications, Inc.
Ed: Brent Snavely. **Description:** Overview of private-equity firm, BlackEagle Partners L.L.C., an upstart that acquired Rockford Products Corp. in order to improve the performance of the company who does business with several major tier-one automotive suppliers; Rockford manufactures highly engineered chassis and suspension components for automakers and the automotive aftermarket.

26649 ■ "Fogg Planning Twinsburg Warehouse Project" in *Crain's Cleveland Business* (Vol. 28, November 26, 2007, No. 47, pp. 6)
Pub: Crain Communications, Inc.
Ed: Stan Bullard. **Description:** Discusses such projects as the proposed 205,000-square-foot distribution center in the works by Ray Fogg Corporate Properties LLC as well as other industrial real estate developments that are looking to target tenants that need larger spaces.

26650 ■ "Fraser and Neave Acquires King's Creameries" in *Ice Cream Reporter* (Vol. 23, November 20, 2010, No. 12, pp. 1)
Pub: Ice Cream Reporter
Description: Fraser and Neave Ltd., a Singapore-based consumer products marketer, has entered a conditional agreement to acquire all outstanding shares of King's Creameries, the leading manufacturer and distributor of frozen desserts.

26651 ■ *From Concept To Consumer: How to Turn Ideas Into Money*
Pub: Pearson Education Inc.
Ed: Phil Baker. **Released:** 2009. **Price:** $24.99. **Description:** Renowned product developer Phil Baker explains how a great idea accounts for only 5 percent of all the factors of success and why the majority of success is dependent upon a myriad of other factors, including the time it takes to get to market, price, marketing and distribution. By being their own best competition, a small company can stay one step ahead of competitors.

26652 ■ "Furniture Chain Moving to Harford" in *Baltimore Business Journal* (Vol. 27, January 22, 2010, No. 38, pp. 1)
Pub: American City Business Journals
Ed: David J. Sernovitz. **Description:** Manchester, Connecticut-based Bob's Discount Furniture signed a lease for 672,000 square feet of space in Harford County, Maryland. The site will become the discount furniture retailer's distribution center in mid-Atlantic US. As many as 200 jobs could be generated when the center opens.

26653 ■ "Gallery Street Launches ArtCandy" in *Art Business News* (Vol. 34, November 2007, No. 11, pp. 8)
Pub: Pfingsten Publishing, LLC
Description: Fine-art reproduction house Gallery Street recently launched its new division, ArtCandy Editions; the division was created in order to help a network of artists expand the distribution of their work.

26654 ■ "Handleman Liquidation Leaves Questions For Shareholders" in *Crain's Detroit Business* (Vol. 24, October 6, 2008, No. 40, pp. 4)
Pub: Crain Communications, Inc.
Ed: Nancy Kaffer. **Description:** Discusses Handleman Co., a Troy-based music distribution company, and their plan of liquidation and dissolution as well as how shareholders will be affected by the company's plan. Handleman filed its plan to liquidate and dissolve assets with the Securities and Exchange Commission in mid-August, following several quarters of dismal earnings.

26655 ■ *How to Start and Run a Small Book Publishing Company: A Small Business Guide to Self-Publishing and Independent Publishing*
Pub: HCM Publishing
Ed: Peter I. Hupalo. **Released:** August 30, 2002. **Price:** $18.95. **Description:** The book teaches all aspects of starting and running a small book publishing company. Topics covered include: inventory accounting in the book trade, just-in-time inventory management, turnkey fulfillment solutions, tax deductible costs, basics of sales and use tax, book pricing, standards in terms of the book industry, working with distributors and wholesalers, cover design and book layout, book promotion and marketing, how to select profitable authors to publish, printing process, printing on demand, the power of a strong backlist, and how to value copyright.

26656 ■ "Industry Escalates Lobbying Efforts For Loan Program" in *Crain's Detroit Business* (Vol. 24, September 22, 2008, No. 38, pp. 22)
Pub: Crain Communications, Inc.
Ed: Jay Greene; Ryan Beene; Harry Stoffer. **Description:** Auto suppliers such as Lear Corp., which is best known for vehicle seating, also supplies high-voltage wiring for Ford hybrids and is developing other hybrid components. These suppliers are joining automakers in lobbying for the loan program which would promote the accelerated development of fuel-efficient vehicles.

26657 ■ "Ingrian and Channel Management International Sign Distribution Agreement" in *Canadian Corporate News* (May 16, 2007)
Pub: Comtex News Network Inc.
Description: Channel Management International (CMI), a Canadian channel management and distribution company, and Ingrian Networks, Inc., the leading provider of data privacy solutions, announced a Canadian distribution agreement to resell Ingrian encryption solutions to the Canadian market.

26658 ■ "Jacksonville-based Interline Expanding in Janitorial-Sanitation Market" in *Florida Times-Union* (May 10, 2011)
Pub: Florida Times-Union
Ed: Mark Basch. **Description:** Interline Brands Inc., located in Jacksonville, Florida, aims to grow its business with two recent acquisitions of firms that distribute janitorial and sanitation products. Interline markets and distributes maintenance, repair and operations products.

26659 ■ "Kellog Pores Over KC Sites" in *Business Journal-Serving Metropolitan Kansas City* (Vol. 26, November 23, 2007, No. 11, pp. 1)
Pub: American City Business Journals, Inc.
Ed: Jim Davis. **Description:** Kellog Company is searching Kansas City for a parcel about 1.3 million square feet to build its product distribution center. According to brokers, a selection might come by end of November 2007. Some of the potential sites are detailed.

26660 ■ "Last Founder Standing" in *Conde Nast Portfolio* (Vol. 2, June 2008, No. 6, pp. 124)
Pub: Conde Nast Publications, Inc.
Ed: Kevin Maney. **Description:** Interview with Amazon CEO Jeff Bezos in which he discusses the economy, the company's new distribution center and the hiring of employees for it, e-books, and the overall vision for the future of the firm.

26661 ■ "Lightening the Load" in *Crain's Cleveland Business* (Vol. 28, October 8, 2007, No. 40, pp. 3)
Pub: Crain Communications, Inc.
Ed: Jay Miller. **Description:** Companies reliant on barge deliveries are running well below capacity due to both the building up of silt at the bottom of the Cuyahoga River as well as the lower water levels which are causing a number of problems for the barges and big boats that deliver goods to the region.

26662 ■ "Linens 'N Things, Dyson in Dust-Up" in *Crain's Chicago Business* (Vol. 31, March 24, 2008, No. 12, pp. 12)
Pub: Crain Communications, Inc.
Description: Linens 'N Things is being sued by vacuum-cleaner manufacturer Dyson who is alleging that it hasn't been paid some of the $1.3 million it says it is owed for merchandise.

26663 ■ "Lynn Johnson, President: Dowland-Bach" in *Alaska Business Monthly* (Vol. 27, October 2011, No. 10, pp. 11)
Pub: Alaska Business Publishing Company
Ed: Peg Stomierowski. **Description:** Profile of Lynn C. Johnson cofounder of Dowland-Bach Corporation, a manufacturing and distribution company is presented. The firms primary products are wellhead control and chemical injection systems for corrosion control, UL industrial control panels, and specialty stainless steel sheet metal fabrication.

26664 ■ "The Macomb Group: Bigger Can Be Better" in *Crain's Detroit Business* (Vol. 24, September 29, 2008, No. 39, pp. 34)
Pub: Crain Communications, Inc.
Ed: Chad Halcom. **Description:** Overview of the plan of The Macomb Group includes a strategy of growing from a small supplier to a medium-sized regional distributor of valves, pipes and fittings.

26665 ■ *Marketing for Entrepreneurs*
Pub: FT Press
Ed: Jurgen Wolff. **Released:** December 9, 2010. **Price:** $24.99. **Description:** This text identifies marketing as the entire process of researching, creating, distributing and selling a product or service. It isn't about theory and metrics, rather it is a practical guide that starts with the basics of all marketing aspects.

26666 ■ "Mexican Companies to Rent Space in TechTown, Chinese Negotiating" in *Crain's Detroit Business* (Vol. 24, September 29, 2008, No. 39)
Pub: Crain Communications, Inc.
Ed: Tom Henderson. **Description:** Wayne State University's TechTown, the business incubator and research park, has signed an agreement with the Mexican government that will provide temporary office space to 25 Mexican companies looking to find customers or establish partnerships in Michigan. TechTown's executive director is negotiating with economic development officials from China. To accommodate foreign visitors the incubator is equipping offices with additional equipment and resources.

26667 ■ "Mini Melts" in *Ice Cream Reporter* (Vol. 23, August 20, 2010, No. 9, pp. 8)
Pub: Ice Cream Reporter
Description: Mini Melts appointed David S. Tade to position of director of sales USA in order to cultivate existing distributors and add new partners to its distribution network.

26668 ■ "Minority Auto Suppliers Get Help Diversifying" in *Crain's Detroit Business* (Vol. 26, January 11, 2010, No. 2, pp. 3)
Pub: Crain Communications, Inc.
Ed: Sherri Welch. **Description:** Displaced minority auto suppliers are being given assistance by the Kauffman's Foundation Urban Entrepreneur Partnership Detroit program, a three-year effort to assist 150 of the region's suppliers into more diversified businesses.

26669 ■ "A Novel Approach to the Market" in *Agency Sales Magazine* (Vol. 39, December 2009, No. 11, pp. 10)
Pub: MANA
Ed: Jack Foster. **Description:** R/B Sales created a "merchandising specialist" position that travels their territory and works with distributor counter sales teams. This puts them ahead of their competition as it increases their visibility, appeal and mix of products in their area.

26670 ■ "Oakland County Hopes Auto Suppliers Can Drive Medical Industry Growth" in *Crain's Detroit Business* (March 10, 2008)
Pub: Crain Communications, Inc.
Ed: Chad Halcom. **Description:** Oakland County officials are hoping to create further economic development for the region by pairing health care companies and medical device makers with automotive suppliers in an attempt to discover additional crossover technology.

26671 ■ "Old Ford Plant to Sign New Tenants" in *Business Courier* (Vol. 27, August 13, 2010, No. 15, pp. 1)
Pub: Business Courier
Ed: Dan Monk. **Description:** Ohio Realty Advisors LLC, a company handling the marketing of the 1.9 million-square-foot former Ford Batavia plant is on the brink of landing one distribution and three manufacturing firms as tenants. These tenants are slated to occupy about 20 percent of the facility and generate as many as 250 jobs in Ohio.

26672 ■ "On the Itinerary: Your Future" in *Entrepreneur* (Vol. 37, October 2009, No. 10, pp. 92)
Pub: Entrepreneur Media, Inc.
Ed: Joel Holland. **Description:** Josh Hackler's Spanish Vines imports and distributes wines from Spain while using Spanish culture to help market the wines. The business was hatched after Hackler signed up for a study-abroad program in Spain.

26673 ■ "Online Marketing and Promotion of Canadian Films via Social Media Tools" in *CNW Group* (January 27, 2010)
Pub: Comtex News Network, Inc.
Description: Telefilm Canada announced the launch of a pilot initiative aimed at encouraging the integration of online marketing and the use of social media tools into means of distribution ahead of a films' theatrical release. During this pilot phase Web-Cine 360 will target French-language feature films.

26674 ■ "O'Reilly Will Soup Up KC Warehouse" in *The Business Journal-Serving Metropolitan Kansas City* (Vol. 26, August 15, 2008, No. 49)
Pub: American City Business Journals, Inc.
Ed: Rob Roberts. **Description:** O'Reilly Automotive Inc. plans to construct a 215,000-square foot warehouse in Kansas City. The move is expected to triple the size of the company's distribution center. Other views and information on the planned warehouse construction, are presented.

26675 ■ "Poisoning Relationships: Perceived Unfairness in Channels of Distribution" in *Journal of Marketing* (Vol. 75, May 2011, No. 3, pp. 99)
Pub: American Marketing Association
Ed: Stephen A. Samaha, Robert W. Palmatier, Rajiv P. Dant. **Description:** The effects of perceived unfairness on the relationships among members of distribution channels are examined. Perceived unfairness is found to directly damage relationships, aggravate the negative effects of conflict and opportunism, and undermine the benefits of the contract.

26676 ■ "Pop N Go Launching Into Dollar Store Market" in *Internet Wire* (July 14, 2009)
Pub: Comtex News Network, Inc.
Description: Pop N Go, Inc. announced that it will test the company's flagship popcorn vending machine in the rapidly growing dollar store distribution channel.

26677 ■ "Public Media Works to Launch DVD Kiosk Operations in Toronto, Canada" in *Internet Wire* (November 15, 2010)
Pub: Comtex
Description: Public Media Works Inc. along with its EntertainmentXpress Inc., have partnered with Spot Venture Distribution Inc. and Signifi Solutions Inc., both headquartered in Toronto, Canada, to manage and expand the Spot DVD movie and game kiosk business in greater Toronto and other Canadian locations.

26678 ■ "S3 Entertainment Group Partners with WFW International for Film Services in Michigan" in *Michigan Vue* (July-August 2008)
Pub: Entrepreneur Media Inc.
Description: William F. White (WFW), one of North America's largest production equipment providers has partnered with S3 Entertainment Group (S3EG), a Michigan-based full-service film production services company due to the new incentives package which currently offers the highest incentives in the United States, up to 42 percent. S3EG will actively store, lease, manage, distribute and sell WFW's equipment to the growing number of production teams that are filming in the state.

26679 ■ "Shipping 2.0" in *Entrepreneur* (Vol. 36, April 2008, No. 4, pp. 54)
Pub: Entrepreneur Media, Inc.
Ed: Heather Clancy. **Description:** Doggypads.com contacted with Web 2.0 service provider Shipwire to handle its warehouse concerns. The service works by paying a rent to Shipwire and they will store the client's items. The client's customers can continue to order from the client's website and Shipwire will take care of delivery. Doggypads was able to save up on costs by using Shipwire.

26680 ■ "Slimmed-Down Supplier TI Automotive Relaunches" in *Crain's Detroit Business* (Vol. 26, January 11, 2010, No. 2, pp. 14)
Pub: Crain Communications, Inc.
Ed: Robert Sherefkin. **Description:** TI Automotive Ltd., one of the world's largest suppliers of fuel storage and delivery systems, has reorganized the company by splitting it into five global divisions and is relaunching its brand which is now more focused on new technology.

26681 ■ "Sources" in *Canadian Electronics* (Vol. 23, August 2008, No. 5, pp. 12)
Pub: Action Communication Inc.
Description: Directory of electronic manufacturers, distributors and representatives in Canada is provided. The list presents distributors and representatives under each manufacturer.

26682 ■ "Speak Better: Five Tips for Polished Presentations" in *Women Entrepreneur* (September 19, 2008)
Pub: Entrepreneur Media Inc.
Ed: Suzannah Baum. **Description:** Successful entrepreneurs agree that exemplary public speaking skills are among the core techniques needed to propel their business forward. A well-delivered presentation can result in securing a new distribution channel, gaining new customers, locking into a new referral stream or receiving extra funding.

26683 ■ "Substantial Deal Expected to Create Jobs, Help Industrial Market" in *Tampa Bay Business Journal* (Vol. 30, January 8, 2010, No. 3)
Pub: American City Business Journals
Ed: Janet Leiser. **Description:** Food distribution firm Gordon Food Service (GFS) is on the brink of purchasing Albertson's million-square-foot warehouse along with 158 acres of space. The deal between GFS and Albertson's could expand GFS' presence in west Central Florida. A history of GFS' growth is included

26684 ■ "Super Success" in *Small Business Opportunities* (November 2008)
Pub: Entrepreneur Media Inc.
Description: Profile of PromoWorks LLC, a company founded by Michael Kent, that distributes samples of food at grocery stores for clients like Kraft Foods, Inc. and Kellogg Co. and also handles the logistics, provides the employees and tracks the products' sales.

26685 ■ "Suppliers Look to Rack Up Big Sales to Distributors" in *The Business Journal-Serving Metropolitan Kansas City* (August 15, 2008)
Pub: American City Business Journals, Inc.
Ed: James Dornbrook. **Description:** Suppliers of shelving units, conveyor systems and other equipment used in distribution facilities are expecting new business opportunities along with the planned intermodal projects in the Kansas City area. Suppliers have already observed that small distributors have started to relocate to the city because of the intermodal projects. Demand for shelves and lifts have also increased.

26686 ■ "Supply Chain Visibility A Two-Way Street" in *Canadian Sailings* (July 7, 2008)
Pub: Commonwealth Business Media
Ed: Jack Kohane. **Description:** Canada is experiencing unprecedented market pressures due to globalization. Competition from foreign countries, demand for better and faster service from customers and shorter innovation cycles are some of the problems the country is facing regarding trade and the importing and exporting industry.

26687 ■ "Sustaining Supply" in *Crain's Cleveland Business* (Vol. 28, November 19, 2007, No. 46, pp. 3)
Pub: Crain Communications, Inc.
Ed: David Bennett. **Description:** Local firms are playing key roles in preparing Wal-Mart suppliers to develop sustainable, or ecologically conscious, packaging. New products such as the innovative "eco-bottle" - a collapsed container made of recyclable plastic that will expand to its traditional size and shape once water is added and would transform to such items as window cleaner when the water mixes with the container's dry contents - are being designed by firms such as Nottingham Spirk.

26688 ■ "Tech Deal Couples Homegrown Firms" in *The Business Journal-Serving Greater Tampa Bay* (Vol. 28, July 4, 2008, No. 28, pp. 1)
Pub: American City Business Journals, Inc.
Ed: Michael Hinman. **Description:** Tampa Bay, Florida-based Administrative Partners Inc. was acquired by Tribridge Inc. resulting in the strengthening of the delivery of Microsoft products to clients. Other details of the merger of the management consulting services companies are presented.

26689 ■ "Technology Protects Lottery" in *Arkansas Business* (Vol. 26, September 28, 2009, No. 39, pp. 1)
Pub: Journal Publishing Inc.
Ed: George Waldon. **Description:** Arkansas Lottery Commission was initially criticized for what was seen as a major breach in security protocol by revealing the exact location of 26 million lottery tickets during a publicity stunt in which the media was invited to the main distribution center; however, due to the high-tech security that has been implemented the tickets are worthless until their status is changed after passing through multiple security scans.

26690 ■ "The Trouble With $150,000 Wine" in *Barron's* (Vol. 88, July 7, 2008, No. 27, pp. 33)
Pub: Dow Jones & Co., Inc.
Ed: Orley Ashenfelter. **Description:** Review of the book, "The Billionaire's Vinegar: The Mystery of the World's Most Expensive Bottle of Wine," which discusses vintners along with the marketing and distribution of wine as well as the winemaking industry as a whole.

26691 ■ "Top 50 Exporters" in *Hispanic Business* (Vol. 30, July-August 2008, No. 7-8, pp. 42)
Pub: Hispanic Business, Inc.
Ed: Hildy Medina. **Description:** Increases in exports revenues reported by food exporters and green companies in a time of economic slowdown in the U.S are described. Food exporters have benefited from the growth of high-volume grocery stores in underdeveloped countries and the German governments' promotion of solar energy has benefited the U.S. solar heating equipment and solar panel manufactures.

26692 ■ "Unilever Acquiring EVGA's Ice Cream Brands in Greece" in *Ice Cream Reporter* (Vol. 23, October 20, 2010, No. 11, pp. 1)
Pub: Ice Cream Reporter
Description: Unilever will acquire the ice cream brands and distribution network of the Greek frozen dessert manufacturer EVGA.

26693 ■ "US Cavalry Store" in *Retail Merchandiser* (Vol. 51, September-October 2011, No. 5, pp. 70)
Pub: Phoenix Media Corporation
Description: US Cavalry Store serves enlisted military members. The store has launched a newly upgraded Website and has expanded its distribution center.

26694 ■ *Values Sell: Transforming Purpose into Profit through Creative Sales and Distribution Strategies*
Pub: Berrett-Koehler Publishers, Incorporated
Ed: Nadine A. Thompson; Angela E. Soper. **Released:** March 28, 2007. **Price:** $16.95. **Description:** Sales and distribution are the lifeblood of any business, socially responsible businesses are no different.

26695 ■ "Vitabath: Sweet Smell of Success" in *Retail Merchandiser* (Vol. 51, September-October 2011, No. 5, pp. 82)
Pub: Phoenix Media Corporation
Description: After taking over at Vitabath, Rich Brands developed new scents and products and while discovering new channels to distribute these items.

26696 ■ "Web-Based Marketing Excites, Challenges Small Business Use" in *Colorado Springs Business Journal* (January 20, 2010)
Pub: Dolan Media Co.

Ed: Becky Hurley. **Description:** Business-to-business and consumer-direct firms alike are using the fast-changing Web technologies to increase sales, leads and track consumer behavior but once a company commits to an Online marketing plan, experts believe, they must be prepared to consistently tweak and overhaul content and distribution vehicles in order to keep up.

26697 ■ "The Wine Spectator" in *Business Courier* (Vol. 27, November 26, 2010, No. 30, pp. 1)
Pub: Business Courier

Ed: Dan Monk. **Description:** Vintner Select, a wine distributor, will introduce an internationally known portfolio of more than 50 German and Austrian wines. The company now distributes about 900 different wine labels from 220 producers in 10 countries to smaller, independent retailers in Indiana, Kentucky and Ohio.

26698 ■ "Wirtz Partners With California Liquor Wholesaler To Expand Reach" in *Chicago Tribune* (December 17, 2008)
Pub: McClatchy-Tribune Information Services

Ed: Mike Hughlett. **Description:** Young's Market Co. and Wirtz Beverage Group have tentatively agreed to a joint venture that will give both companies a larger reach in the wine and liquor distribution business.

26699 ■ "Worldwide Food Services (EREI) Tests Mini Dollar Store Program" in *Internet Wire* (August 6, 2009)
Pub: Comtex News Network, Inc.

Description: Mini Dollar Stores and Eagle View LLC, wholly-owned subsidiaries of Worldwide Food Services, Inc., recently met with government officials and purchasing agents to lay out a test program which would distribute Mini Dollar Store items into VA hospital gift shops.

TRADE PERIODICALS

26700 ■ *Distribution Center Management*
Pub: Alexander Research & Communications Inc.
Contact: Margaret DeWitt, Publisher

Ed: Troy Reynolds, Editor. **Released:** Monthly. **Price:** $199, individuals. **Description:** The monthly newsletter for distribution centers and warehouse managers with ideas and information on how to run their facilities more productively.

26701 ■ *Drop Shipping Marketing Methods*
Pub: Consolidated Marketing Services, Inc.

Ed: Nicholas T. Scheel, Editor, nscheel@drop-shipping-news.com. **Released:** Monthly. **Price:** $18, U.S. $25/year. **Description:** Supplies data on firms that drop ship their products as a means of distribution. Contains information on sources of consumer and industrial products, formulation of marketing policy, and on the pricing, ordering, packaging, and handling of drop shipments. Includes articles on uses of direct mail and direct-response advertising.

26702 ■ *Profiles in PDM*
Pub: Hunt Personnel Ltd.

Ed: Alex Metz, Editor. **Released:** Bimonthly. **Price:** Free. **Description:** Published as a series of bulletins on basic principles of physical distribution management. Carries articles written to highlight trends, provoke ideas or provide general information.

TRADE SHOWS AND CONVENTIONS

26703 ■ The FMI Show
International Foodservice Distributors Association
1410 Spring Hill Rd., Ste. 210
McLean, VA 22102
Ph:(703)532-9400
Fax:(703)538-4673
URL: http://www.ifdaonline.org
Released: Annual. **Audience:** Wholesale grocers, foodservice distributors, food industry executives, retail chains, and grocery manufacturers. **Principal Exhibits:** Material handling equipment, trucks, fork lifts, trailers, trucks, racks and pallets, computers and software, warehouse and fleet consultants and other services and equipment related to warehousing, distribution, human resources, information technology, logistics and transportation.

CONSULTANTS

26704 ■ Bavier, Bulger & Goodyear Inc.
270 Amity Rd., Ste. 224
Woodbridge, CT 06525-2236
Ph:(203)389-0001
Fax:(203)387-8558
URL: http://www.geomatrixproductions.com
Contact: Arthur C. Bulger, CEO
Scope: Specializes in all areas of manufacturing and distribution operations starting with facility planning, staffing and startup activities, and extending through organization, methods, processes and systems. Focuses on turnaround and improved management, performance measurement, controls, and disciplines. Specializes in operational due diligence of target companies in merger and acquisition transactions, as well as operations audits. Reports focus on identification of issues and solutions, heavy emphasis on controls, measurements, and profit improvement through cost reductions. Serves manufacturing and distribution clients; automotive primary, precious, and fabricated metals; rubber; plastics; electrical; electromechanical; electronic; ceramic; assembly; glass; chemical; synthetic materials; china; and printing industries.

26705 ■ Clear Light Books
823 Don Diego Ave.
Santa Fe, NM 87505
Ph:(505)989-9590
Free: 800-253-2747
Fax:(505)989-9519
Co. E-mail: info@clearlightbooks.com
URL: http://www.clearlightbooks.com
Contact: Harmon Houghton, Principle
E-mail: harmonhoughton@atsaol.com
Scope: Business management consulting specifically in the area of profit planning, as well as warehouse and distribution assistance. Additional expertise in computer system design. Industries served: small, medium-sized businesses and warehouse and distribution. **Special Services:** Warestudy™; Profit Planning™.

26706 ■ Compliance Systems Inc.
Hamilton House, 26 E Bryan St.
PO Box 9981
Savannah, GA 31401
Ph:(912)233-8181
Fax:(912)231-2938
Co. E-mail: csi@compliancesystemsinc.com
URL: http://www.compliancesystemsinc.com
Contact: Robbie Shea, Mgr
E-mail: rwigger@atscompliancesystemsinc.com
Scope: Marine consultants specializing in all areas of shipping and marine safety, including Port State Control Compliance, ISM Code Internal Auditing, and OPA 90 Compliance and Maritime Security. **Seminars:** Safety Training.

26707 ■ General Business Consultants Inc.
1502 Elmwood Ave.
Wilmette, IL 60091-1653
Ph:(847)256-3260
Fax:(847)256-1410
Co. E-mail: dick@genbuscon.com
URL: http://www.genbuscon.com
Contact: Dick Friedman, President
E-mail: dick@genbuscon.com
Scope: Specializes in helping wholesalers, distributors, supply houses and manufacturers acquire and use information technology more profitably. Firm services help avoid the pitfalls and problems of complex, confusing things such as: long range business or systems planning; system selection, contract negotiation and installation management of complete systems and warehouse management systems; do it yourself warehouse management systems. Business improvement services involve advanced recommendations for improving: profits and customer service; inventory management and warehouse operations; gross margins; business or systems continuity; ecommerce. **Publications:** "The Butler Did It: Errors That Get Customers Angry"; "Do You Really Need a New System"; "New Warehouse Management Technologies Beat the Old Ones"; "How to Avoid a Warehouse Management System Horror Story"; "Don't Sign That System Contract-Until Its Changed to Include Protections"; "Why Some Systems are Decreasing Customer Service, Margins and Inventory Profitability"; "How to Modify a System to Maximize Inventory-Based Customer Service and Roi"; "What Lists of Software Don't Show Can Kill a Distributor"; "Great Software Does Not Manage Inventory Effectively"; "System Contracts: Add Specific Performance Guarantees to Avoid Problems"; "RF, RFID, WMS, VDP, PTL: A Review of warehouse Technologies". **Seminars:** Tech Trends That Can Hurt Distributors And Wholesalers; Do you really need a new system?; Warehouse Management Systems (WMS): New Technologies, And Tips For A Successful WMS; Avoiding Excess Inventory And Shortages While Keeping Customer Service High; Why Some Systems Are Decreasing Customer Service, Margins And Return On Inventory Investment-And What To Do About It; Don't Sign That System Contract-Until You Change It To Protect Yourself; Talking Chips Replace Printed Bar Codes; Wireless Digital Networks Result in Go-Anywhere Data Communications; Warehouse Management Systems Become Affordable and Practical; Supply Chain Management Dramatically Alters Business Relationships; The Plot to Take Away Distributors Computers; Software Support Moves Overseas-the Pros and Cons.

26708 ■ Irving Shaw and Associates
417 C Andover Dr.
Monroe Township, NJ 08831-4304
Ph:(609)860-1122
Fax:(609)860-0996
Contact: Irving Shaw, President
E-mail: isa@nerc.com
Scope: Management consultants specializing in facilities design for factories and distribution centers. Consulting includes, but is not limited to, factory layout, distribution center planning, materials handling improvement, organization, planning, scheduling and controls. Active with a variety of manufacturers and distribution companies.

26709 ■ Myron I. Blumenfeld & Associates
303 E 83rd St., Ste. 16B
New York, NY 10028
Ph:(212)706-2112
Fax:(212)706-2118
Co. E-mail: mikeblumenfeld@myroniblumenfeld.com
URL: http://www.myroniblumenfeld.com
Contact: Myron I. Blumenfeld, President
E-mail: mike@myroniblumenfeld.com
Scope: Management specialists for consumer goods manufactures, wholesalers and retail in the areas of inventory management, strategic planning, logistics, merchandise planning, merchandise distribution and organization structure and development. **Seminars:** Starting Your Own Business. Business Planning. Inventory Management. New Innovations in Retail Distribution Technology. Bar Coding and Quick Response. Merchandise Planning for Quick Response. Global Marketing.

26710 ■ Wesley-Kind Associates Inc.
200 Old Country Rd., Ste. 364
Mineola, NY 11501-4235
Ph:(516)747-3434
Fax:(516)248-2728
Contact: Daniel A. Kind, President
Scope: Material handling and distribution consultants offering advice on plant and warehouse layouts and operating systems for the movement, storage and control of materials and products. Expertise includes materials and production management, advanced handling/storage systems, packaging and unitizing systems, capacity, productivity and customer service

audits, order filling systems, data processing control systems, transportation systems, site location analysis, facilities planning, and implementation. Industries served: manufacturing, distribution and retail corporations and state and U.S. Government agencies. **Publications:** "How to Reengineer the Storage Function," Penton Publishing, 1995.

RESEARCH CENTERS

26711 ■ National Association of Wholesaler-Distributors–NAW Institute for Distribution Excellence
1325 G St. NW, Ste. 1000
Washington, DC 20005
Ph:(202)872-0885
Fax:(202)785-0586
Co. E-mail: rschreibman@naw.org
URL: http://www.naw.org/institute/iindex.php
Contact: Ron Schreibman, Exec.Dir.
E-mail: rschreibman@naw.org
Scope: Wholesale distribution, focusing on long-range projects to advance knowledge in the field.

26712 ■ Texas A&M University–Thomas and Joan Read Center for Distribution Research and Education
3367 TAMU
College Station, TX 77843-3367
Ph:(979)845-4984
Free: (866)-260-2463
Fax:(979)845-4980
Co. E-mail: lawrence@entc.tamu.edu
URL: http://readcenter.tamu.edu/pages/index.php
Contact: Dr. F. Barry Lawrence, Dir.
E-mail: lawrence@entc.tamu.edu
Scope: Industrial distribution, sales force issues, quality assessment, logistics process design, e-commerce, distribution information systems interface, inventory management, supply chain management, financial analysis, organizational change, organizational culture, implementation of strategic plans, team building, benchmarking and gap analysis, developing core competencies, manufacturer-distributor relations, distributor profitability, purchasing, negotiations, distributor's asset management, financial transactions of the wholesaler-distributor, improving distributor return on investment, distribution operations management, product line profitability, trends, high-tech marketing, strategic alliances, strategic planning, market. **Publications:** E-newsletter (3/year). **Educational Activities:** Certificate in Distribution Management program; Continuing education programs for distributors and manufacturers; Distributor Management Development Seminars.

START-UP INFORMATION

26713 ■ *How to Start a Home-Based Mail Order Business*
Pub: Globe Pequot Press
Ed: Georganne Fiumara. **Released:** January 2005. **Price:** $17.95. **Description:** Step-by-step guide for starting and growing a home-based mail order business. Information about equipment, pricing, online marketing, are included along with worksheets and checklists for planning.

26714 ■ "Your Startup may be Worth Less than You Think" in *Entrepreneur* (Vol. 37, October 2009, No. 10, pp. 96)
Pub: Entrepreneur Media, Inc.
Ed: Asheesh Advani. **Description:** Valuations of startups at the idea stage are dropping due to the effects of the recession. This drop is due to the decreasing availability of investment capital, the reduction in portfolio values of investors, and the increase in early stage startups.

ASSOCIATIONS AND OTHER ORGANIZATIONS

26715 ■ Action for Enterprise
2009 N 14th St., Ste. 301
Arlington, VA 22201
Ph:(703)243-9172
Fax:(703)243-9123
Co. E-mail: info@actionforenterprise.org
URL: http://www.actionforenterprise.org
Contact: Frank Lusby, Exec. Dir./Founder
Description: Seeks to design and implement small enterprise development programs, based on a comprehensive analysis of business sectors and the interrelationships of enterprises that function with them. Initiates efforts to develop sustainable business development service providers at the local level.

26716 ■ Asia Pacific Foundation of Canada–Fondation Asie Pacifique du Canada
890 W Pender St., Ste. 220
Vancouver, BC, Canada V6C 1J9
Ph:(604)684-5986
Fax:(604)681-1370
Co. E-mail: info@asiapacific.ca
URL: http://www.asiapacific.ca
Contact: Mr. Yuen Pau Woo, Pres./CEO
Description: Seeks to remove barriers to international trade between Canada and Asia. Conducts applied research and policy analysis for issues related to Canada-Asia relations. Maintains network of study and research centers; works to improve access to information on Asian cultures and trade within Canada.

26717 ■ Brazil-Canada Chamber of Commerce
401 Bay St., Ste. 1608
Toronto, ON, Canada M5H 2Y4
Ph:(416)646-6770
Fax:(416)363-0406
Co. E-mail: info@brazcanchamber.org
URL: http://brazcanchamber.org
Contact: Raul Papaleo, Pres.
Description: Canadian corporations doing business in Brazil. Promotes increased trade between Canada and Brazil. Provides assistance to companies wishing to trade with Brazil. Represents members before international trade organizations and government agencies and lobbies for removal of statutory barriers to commerce.

26718 ■ British Canadian Chamber of Trade and Commerce–La Chambre de Commerce Canada - Grande Bretagne
Trust Tower
77 King St. W, Ste. 2401
Toronto, ON, Canada M5K 1G8
Ph:(416)816-9154
Fax:(647)435-3436
Co. E-mail: idalia@bcctc.ca
URL: http://bcctc.ca
Contact: Idalia Obregon, Exec. Dir.
Description: Canadian corporations doing business in the United Kingdom. Promotes increased trade between Britain and Canada. Represents members' interests; lobbies for removal of statutory impediments to trade. **Publications:** *Connections* (quarterly).

26719 ■ Canada-Czech Republic Chamber of Commerce
115 George St., Ste. 709
Oakville, ON, Canada L6J 0A2
Ph:(905)845-9606
Co. E-mail: admin@ccrcc.net
URL: http://www.ccrcc.net
Contact: Miroslav Princ
Description: Businesses in Canada and the Czech Republic. Promotes increased trade and investment between Canada and the Czech Republic. Promotes the Czech Republic as a gateway to Central and Eastern Europe, and Canada as a gateway to the North American Free Trade Agreement countries. Conducts educational programs.

26720 ■ Canada-Finland Chamber of Commerce
191 Eglinton Ave. E
Toronto, ON, Canada M4P 1K1
Ph:(416)486-1533
Fax:(416)486-1592
Co. E-mail: info@canadafinlandcc.com
URL: http://canadafinlandcc.com
Contact: Peter Auvinen, Pres.
Description: Canadian and Finnish businesses. Promotes increased trade between Canada and Finland. Provides information, assistance, and services to Finnish and Canadian corporations wishing to participate in international trade.

26721 ■ Canada-India Business Council–Conseil de Commerce Canada-Inde
1 St. Clair Ave. E, Ste. 302
Toronto, ON, Canada M4T 2V7
Ph:(416)214-5947
Fax:(416)214-9081
Co. E-mail: info@canada-indiabusiness.ca
URL: http://canada-indiabusiness.ca
Contact: Mr. Rana Sarkar, Pres./Exec. Dir.
Description: Canadian businesses trading with India. Promotes increased trade between Canada and India. Advocates for legislation conducive to trade; represents members before trade and industrial organizations and the public.

26722 ■ Canada-Pakistan Business Council
7825 Bayview Ave., Ste. 1311
Thornhill, ON, Canada L3T 7N2
Ph:(905)763-8281
Co. E-mail: info@cpbcoline.org
URL: http://www.cpbconline.org
Contact: Mr. Douglas Barker, Chm.
Description: Businesses and service providers. Promotes increased trade between Canada and Pakistan. Facilitates mutual economic development through transfer of technology; encourages and assists in the formation of joint ventures involving Canadian and Pakistani companies. Conducts educational programs. **Publications:** *Canada Pakistan Bulletin* (quarterly).

26723 ■ Canadian Association of Regulated Importers–Association Canadienne des Importateurs Reglementes
2525 St. Laurent Blvd., Ste. 203
Ottawa, ON, Canada K1H 8P5
Ph:(613)738-1729
Fax:(613)733-9501
Co. E-mail: devalk@magma.ca
URL: http://www.cariimport.org
Contact: Lucky Bilkhu, Chm.
Description: Companies engaged in the importation of goods into Canada. Promotes removal of international and domestic barriers to trade. Represents members before government agencies and international trade organizations.

26724 ■ Canadian Chamber of Commerce–La Chambre de Commerce du Canada
360 Albert St., Ste. 420
Ottawa, ON, Canada K1R 7X7
Ph:(613)238-4000
Fax:(613)238-7643
Co. E-mail: info@chamber.ca
URL: http://www.chamber.ca
Contact: Hon. Perin Beatty, Pres./CEO
Description: As Canada's largest and most influential business association, the Canadian Chamber of Commerce is the primary and vital connection between business and the federal government. It continually demonstrates impact on public policy and decision-making to the benefit of businesses, communities and families across Canada. Experience the power of a network of over 420 chambers of commerce and boards of trade, representing 192,000 businesses of all sizes in all sectors of the economy and in all regions.

26725 ■ Canadian Council for Aboriginal Business–Conseil Canadien pour le Commerce Autochtone
250 The Esplanade, Ste. 204
Toronto, ON, Canada M5A 1J2
Ph:(416)961-8663
Fax:(416)961-3995
Co. E-mail: info@ccab.com
URL: http://www.ccab.com
Contact: Clint Davis, Pres./CEO
Description: Promotes the full participation of aboriginal people in the Canadian economy. Seeks to connect aboriginal and non-aboriginal people and companies with the opportunities required to achieve personal and business success. Develops and operates the Progressive Aboriginal Relations (PAR) benchmarking and hallmarking program. Administers the Canadian Aboriginal Business Hall of Fame.

26726 ■ Canadian Council of Chief Executives–Conseil Canadien des Chefs d'Enterprise
99 Bank St., Ste. 1001
Ottawa, ON, Canada K1P 6B9
Ph:(613)238-3727
Fax:(613)238-3247
Co. E-mail: leaders@ceocouncil.ca
URL: http://www.ceocouncil.ca
Contact: John P. Manley, Pres./CEO
Description: Businesses and trade organizations. Promotes a healthy national economy. Conducts research; lobbies for legislation favorable to business; represents members' interests.

26727 ■ Canadian Federation of Independent Business–Federation Canadienne de l'Entreprise Independante
4141 Yonge St., Ste. 401
Toronto, ON, Canada M2P 2A6
Ph:(416)222-8022
Fax:(416)222-6103
Co. E-mail: cfib@cfib.ca
URL: http://www.cfib-fcei.ca/english/index.html
Contact: Catherine Swift, Chair/Pres./CEO
Description: Independent businesses. Promotes economic well-being of members and seeks to maintain a healthy domestic business climate. Represents members' interests before government agencies, labor and industrial organizations, and the public. **Publications:** *Mandate* (quarterly); *Quarterly Business Barometer* (3/year).

26728 ■ Canadian German Chamber of Industry and Commerce–La Chambre Canadienne Allemande de l'Industrie et du Commerce
480 University Ave., Ste. 1500
Toronto, ON, Canada M5G 1V2
Ph:(416)598-3355
Fax:(416)598-1840
Co. E-mail: info.toronto@germanchamber.ca
URL: http://kanada.ahk.de/en/home
Contact: Thomas Beck, Pres./CEO
Description: Canadian and German corporations and trade and industrial organizations. Promotes increased trade between Canada and Germany. Lobbies for removal of barriers to trade; represents the interests of business before government agencies, international trade organizations, and the public. **Publications:** *Canadian German Headlines* (monthly).

26729 ■ Canadian Labour Congress–Congres du travail du Canada
2841 Riverside Dr.
Ottawa, ON, Canada K1V 8X7
Ph:(613)521-3400
Fax:(613)521-4655
URL: http://www.canadianlabour.ca/home
Contact: Ken Georgetti, Pres.
Description: Works to ensure that all Canadians are able to find employment at fair wages, with union representation and the right to collective bargaining, in a safe environment. Seeks to create a just and equitable society. Joins with other organizations for advocacy and action on behalf of working Canadians. Facilitates establishment of grass roots organizations. Conducts research and educational programs; maintains speakers' bureau; compiles statistics. **Publications:** *C.L.C. Fax-Press* (weekly); *Sweatshop Alert* (periodic); *UI Bulletin* (periodic).

26730 ■ Canadian Netherlands Business and Professional Association
PO Box 5073
Sta. A
Toronto, ON, Canada M5W 1N4
Ph:(416)981-3424
Fax:(416)981-3424
Co. E-mail: info@cnbpa.ca
URL: http://www.cnbpa.ca
Contact: Tom Vandeloo, Pres.
Description: Business people and professionals in Canada and the Netherlands. Promotes increased trade and communication between Canada and the Netherlands. Serves as a forum for the exchange of information among members.

26731 ■ Committee for Economic Development
2000 L St. NW, Ste. 700
Washington, DC 20036
Ph:(202)296-5860
Free: 800-676-7353
Fax:(202)223-0776
Co. E-mail: info@ced.org
URL: http://www.ced.org
Contact: Charles E.M. Kolb, Pres.
Description: Trustees are heads of major corporations or university presidents. Works with expert advisers. Conducts research and formulates policy recommendations on national and international economic issues, including education, trade policy, U.S.-Japan economic relations, and problems of the inner city. Seeks to contribute to full employment, higher living standards, and increased opportunities for all through its studies and reports; promote economic growth and stability; strengthen the concepts and institutions essential to progress in a free society. **Publications:** *CED Forum* (semiannual).

26732 ■ Corporation for Enterprise Development
1200 G St. NW, Ste. 400
Washington, DC 20005
Ph:(202)408-9788
Fax:(202)408-9793
Co. E-mail: info@cfed.org
URL: http://cfed.org
Contact: Andrea Levere, Pres.
Description: Provides assistance to public and private organizations concerned with increasing economic opportunity of individuals through the encouragement and support of enterprise development; serves as a forum for the exchange of ideas. Strives to research, develop, and disseminate entrepreneurial policy initiatives at the local, state, and federal levels. Conducts consulting services and compiles statistics. **Publications:** *Accountability Newsletter* (monthly).

26733 ■ Council of Development Finance Agencies
85 E Gay St., Ste. 700
Columbus, OH 43215
Ph:(614)224-1300
Fax:(614)224-1343
Co. E-mail: info@cdfa.net
URL: http://www.cdfa.net
Contact: Toby Rittner, Pres./CEO
Description: Works for the advancement of development finance concerns and interests. Represents members of the development finance community from the public, private and non-profit sectors. **Publications:** *Development Finance Review Weekly* (weekly).

26734 ■ Dialogue on Diversity
1629 K St. NW, Ste. 300
Washington, DC 20006
Ph:(703)631-0650
Fax:(703)631-0617
Co. E-mail: dialog.div@prodigy.net
URL: http://www.dialogueondiversity.org
Contact: Ma. Cristina C. Caballero, Pres./CEO
Description: Promotes social and political advancement of women and men from diverse ethnic and national traditions; fosters increased economic empowerment; aims to promote and develop entrepreneurial excellence, technology, networking, and education. .

26735 ■ Edmonton Chamber of Commerce
700-9990 Jasper Ave.
Edmonton, AB, Canada T5J 1P7
Ph:(780)426-4620
Fax:(780)424-7946
Co. E-mail: info@edmontonchamber.com
URL: http://www.edmontonchamber.com
Contact: Mr. Martin Salloum, Pres./CEO
Description: Serves as the official voice of business in the Edmonton area. Provides networking opportunities via special events held during the year. Provides discount and affinity programs, business referrals and business resources. Owns and operates the World Trade Center Edmonton (WTCE), which is a member of the World Trade Centers Organization, a network of 300 centers in almost 100 countries worldwide. Assists businesses, professionals, and interested individuals in developing national and international trade by providing information and advice on new markets and products. Organizes trade missions to World Trade Centers and facilitates contact with government agencies. Offers research and information gathering on trade opportunities, educational programs, and consumer and business assistance. **Publications:** *Commerce News* (monthly); *Edmonton Commerce Directory* (annual).

26736 ■ I.E. Canada
160 Eglinton Ave. E, Ste. 300
Toronto, ON, Canada M4P 3B5
Ph:(416)595-5333
Fax:(416)595-8226
Co. E-mail: info@iecanada.com
URL: http://www.iecanada.com
Contact: John O'Reilly, Chm.
Description: Individuals and firms with an interest in Canada's international trade. Promotes increased participation by Canada in the global economy; seeks to maintain a business climate conducive to increased international trade. Represents members' interests before government agencies; prepares model trade programs, regulations, and policies. Provides advice and assistance to members; serves as a clearinghouse on international trade. **Publications:** *I.E. Global* (semiannual); *Importing into Canada*; *Tradeweek* (semimonthly).

26737 ■ Insight Center for Community Economic Development
2201 Broadway, Ste. 815
Oakland, CA 94612-3024
Ph:(510)251-2600
Fax:(510)251-0600
Co. E-mail: info@insightcced.org
URL: http://www.insightcced.org
Contact: Roger A. Clay Jr., Pres.
Description: Aims to build economic health in vulnerable communities. Develops and promotes innovative solutions that help people and communities become, and remain, economically secure. Collaborates with foundations, nonprofits, educational institutions, government and businesses to develop, strengthen and promote programs and public policy that: lead to good jobs, strengthen early care and education systems, and enable people and communities to build financial and educational assets. .

26738 ■ International Economic Development Council
734 15th St. NW, Ste. 900
Washington, DC 20005
Ph:(202)223-7800
Fax:(202)223-4745
Co. E-mail: kbielen@iedconline.org
URL: http://www.iedconline.org
Contact: Kelly Bielen
Description: Works to help economic development professionals improve the quality of life in their communities. Represents all levels of government, aca-

demia, and private industry; provides a broad range of member services including research, advisory services, conferences, professional certification, professional development, publications, legislative tracking and more. **Publications:** *Annual Federal Review and Budget Overview* (annual); *Economic Development Journal* (quarterly); *Economic Development Now* (bimonthly); *Federal Review* (annual).

26739 ■ International Finance Corporation
2121 Pennsylvania Ave. NW
Washington, DC 20433
Ph:(202)473-1000
Fax:(202)974-4384
URL: http://www.ifc.org
Contact: Lars Thunell, Exec. VP/CEO
Description: Promotes sustainable private sector investments in developing countries, as a way to reduce poverty and improve people's lives. .

26740 ■ National Association of Development Organizations Research Foundation
400 N Capitol St. NW, Ste. 390
Washington, DC 20001
Ph:(202)624-7806
Fax:(202)624-8813
Co. E-mail: info@nado.org
URL: http://www.nado.org
Contact: Matthew Chase, Exec. Dir.
Description: Identifies, studies and promotes regional solutions and approaches to improving local prosperity and services through the nationwide network of regional development organizations. Shares best practices and offers professional development training, analyzes the impact of federal policies and programs on regional development organizations, and examines the latest developments and trends in small metro and rural America. Provides federal advocacy, informative research, special reports and training to the nation's rural regional development organizations. .

26741 ■ National Development Council
708 Third Ave., Ste. 710
New York, NY 10017
Ph:(212)682-1106
Fax:(212)573-6118
Co. E-mail: training@nationaldevelopmentcouncil.org
URL: http://www.nationaldevelopmentcouncil.org
Contact: Robert W. Davenport, Pres.
Description: Brings innovative economic development financing programs to urban and rural communities interested in local business and industrial growth, commercial revitalization, and permanent job creation. Finances professionals' work with cities, counties, and states to: build permanent systems for developing financing; train local staff; structure and negotiate financing for development projects, local business development, and industrial expansion. Conducts intensive training program for economic development professionals with courses in business credit analysis, real estate financing, loan packaging, federal financing, and program management and implementation; has provided advice to congress and federal agencies that has helped create lending programs for job creation and small business investment; has initiated and managed presidential programs for Presidents Nixon, Ford, Carter, and Reagan. **Publications:** *Developments* (quarterly).

26742 ■ Pacific Basin Economic Council - Canadian Committee
890 W Pender St., Ste. 220
Vancouver, BC, Canada V6C 1J9
Ph:(604)684-5986
Fax:(604)681-1370
Co. E-mail: info@asiapacific.ca
URL: http://www.asiapacific.ca
Contact: John H. McArthur, Chm.
Description: Canadian corporations. Promotes increased trade between the countries bordering the Pacific Ocean. Gathers and disseminates information on international trade issues. **Publications:** *PBEC Report* (periodic). **Telecommunication Services:** electronic mail, communications@asiapacific.ca.

26743 ■ Sustainable Development Technology Canada–Technologies du Developpement Durable du Canada
45 O'Connor St., Ste. 1850
Ottawa, ON, Canada K1P 1A4
Ph:(613)234-6313
Fax:(613)234-0303
Co. E-mail: info@sdtc.ca
URL: http://www.sdtc.ca
Contact: Vicky J. Sharpe, Pres./CEO
Description: Seeks to promote a sustainable development technology infrastructure in Canada.

26744 ■ Swedish-Canadian Chamber of Commerce
2 Bloor St. W, Ste. 2109
Toronto, ON, Canada M4W 3E2
Ph:(416)925-8661
Fax:(416)929-8639
Co. E-mail: mglindmark@sccc.ca
URL: http://www.sccc.ca
Contact: Monika G. Lindmark, Exec. Dir.
Description: Facilitates business and cultural development between Sweden and Canada. Provides knowledge about both countries and promotes trade and business opportunities. Serves as a forum allowing Swedes and Canadians with mutual interests to connect at various levels, affords members' business and finds cultural and social opportunities.

26745 ■ USA Engage
1625 K St. NW, Ste. 200
Washington, DC 20006
Ph:(202)887-0278
Fax:(202)452-8160
Co. E-mail: nftcinformation@nftc.org
URL: http://www.usaengage.org
Contact: Jake Colvin, Dir.
Description: Promotes economic strength in America as integral to the nation's security and worldwide leadership. .

26746 ■ World Trade Centre Montreal
380 St. Antoine St. W, Ste. 6000
Montreal, QC, Canada H2Y 3X7
Ph:(514)871-4002
Free: 877-590-4040
Fax:(514)849-3813
Co. E-mail: wtcmontreal@ccmm.qc.ca
URL: http://www.ccmm.qc.ca/fr
Contact: Mr. Guy Jobin, Exec. Dir.
Description: Businesses, professionals, and interested individuals. Seeks to foster the export of products and services by supporting, training and advising companies, associations and economic development institutions and organizations on certain activities on international markets through an integrated programme of export solutions. **Telecommunication Services:** electronic mail, info@ccmm.qc.ca.

26747 ■ World Trade Centre Vancouver
999 Canada Pl., Ste. 400
Vancouver, BC, Canada V6C 3E1
Ph:(604)681-2111
Fax:(604)681-0437
Co. E-mail: contactus@boardoftrade.com
URL: http://www.boardoftrade.com
Contact: Tracy Campbell, Exec. Dir.
Description: Businesses, professionals, and interested individuals. Facilitates the development of national and international trade by providing traders and investors with information and advice on new markets and products. Organizes trade missions to World Trade Centers and facilitates contact with government agencies. Offers research and information gathering on trade opportunities, educational programs, and consumer and business assistance. **Publications:** *Sounding Board* (monthly).

26748 ■ World Trade and Convention Centre Halifax
1800 Argyle St.
PO Box 955
Halifax, NS, Canada B3J 2V9
Ph:(902)421-1302
Fax:(902)422-2922
Co. E-mail: paulc@tclns.com
URL: http://www.wtcchalifax.com
Contact: Mr. Paul A. Cody, Sr. Sales Mgr.
Description: Represents businesses, professionals, and interested individuals. Facilitates the development of national and international trade by providing traders and investors with information and advice on new markets and products. Organizes trade missions to World Trade Centers and facilitates contact with government agencies. Offers services such as research and information gathering on trade opportunities, educational programs, and consumer and business assistance.

REFERENCE WORKS

26749 ■ "$3 Million in Repairs Prep Cobo for Auto Show" in *Crain's Detroit Business* (Vol. 26, January 4, 2010, No. 1, pp. 1)
Pub: Crain Communications, Inc.
Ed: Nancy Kaffer. **Description:** Overview of the six projects priced roughly at $3 million which were needed in order to host the North American International Auto Show; show organizers stated that the work was absolutely necessary to keep the show in the city of Detroit.

26750 ■ "3CDC Investing $8 Million To Put New Life Into Old Homes" in *Globe & Mail* (February 28, 2006, pp. B1)
Pub: CTVglobemedia Publishing Inc.
Ed: Lucy May. **Description:** The Cincinnati Center City Development Corp. has bought more than 100 empty buildings and many around Washington Park in Over-the-Rhine. Its new project, called 3CDC, is to revitalize the historic neighborhood in the Washington Park area near Music Hall.

26751 ■ *The 5 Big Lies About American Business: Combating Smears Against the Free-Market Economy*
Pub: Crown Business Books
Ed: Michael Medved. **Released:** November 2, 2010. **Price:** $15.00. **Description:** Michael Medved, talk-radio personality and bestselling author, argues for capitalism. He presents popular myths about the free market system and discusses why each myth is instead good for Americans and our economy.

26752 ■ "$50 Million Project for West Chester" in *Business Courier* (Vol. 24, December 14, 2008, No. 35, pp. 1)
Pub: American City Business Journals, Inc.
Ed: Laura Baverman. **Description:** Commercial developer Scott Street Partners is planning to invest $50 million for the development of a site south of the Streets of West Chester retail center. The 31-acre project will generate 1,200 jobs, and will bring in offices, restaurants and a hotel. The development plans and the features of the site are discussed as well.

26753 ■ "217 Homes Planned for Former Crystal Cream Site" in *Sacramento Business Journal* (Vol. 25, August 8, 2008, No. 23, pp. 1)
Pub: American City Business Journals, Inc.
Ed: Michael Shaw. **Description:** MetroNova Development LLC plans to develop housing at the former Crystal Cream & Butter Co. site near downtown Sacramento. The developer expects to sell the new loft houses for about $300,000 without public subsidies. Views and other information on the planned development project, is presented.

26754 ■ "2009: A Call For Vision" in *Women Entrepreneur* (January 28, 2009)
Pub: Entrepreneur Media Inc.
Ed: Elinor Robin. **Description:** Providing exemplary customer service, reducing expenses and creating an out-of-the-box niche are three key factors that will help business survive during this economic crisis. Business owners must see potential where others see failure in order to create new opportunities that may not only allow their business to survive during these times but may actually cause some businesses to thrive despite this economic downturn.

26755 ■ "2010: Important Year Ahead for Waterfront" in *Bellingham Business Journal* (Vol. March 2010, pp. 2)
Pub: Sound Publishing Inc.
Ed: Isaac Bonnell. **Description:** A tentative timeline has been established for the environmental impact statement (EIS) slated for completion in May 2010. The plan for the Waterfront District includes detailed economic and architectural analysis of the feasibility of reusing remaining structures and retaining some industrial icons.

26756 ■ "A Conversation With; Ron Gatner, Jones Lang LaSalle" in *Crain's Detroit Business* (Vol. 24, October 6, 2008, No. 40, pp. 9)
Pub: Crain Communications, Inc.
Description: Interview with Ron Gatner who is a corporate real estate adviser with the real estate company Jones Lang LaSalle as well as the company's executive vice president and part of the tenant advisory team; Gatner speaks about the impact that the Wall Street crisis is having on the commercial real estate market in Detroit.

26757 ■ "A Good Step, But There's a Long Way to Go" in *Business Week* (September 22, 2008, No. 4100, pp. 10)
Pub: McGraw-Hill Companies, Inc.
Ed: James C. Cooper. **Description:** Despite the historic action by the U.S. government to nationalize the mortgage giants Freddie Mac and Fannie Mae, rising unemployment rates may prove to be an even bigger roadblock to bringing back the economy from its downward spiral. The takeover is meant to restore confidence in the credit markets and help with the mortgage crisis but the rising rate in unemployment may make many households unable to take advantage of any benefits which arise from the bailout. Statistical data included.

26758 ■ "According to the Chinese Zodiac, 2009 is the Year of the Ox" in *Canadian Business* (Vol. 81, December 8, 2008, No. 21, pp. 74)
Pub: Rogers Media Ltd.
Ed: Zarka Halas. **Description:** Forecasts for China in 2009 are presented. China is expected to maintain an 8 percent growth rate to keep the current labor market. A total of 68,000 companies have collapsed in China in the first half of 2008, while 2.5 million workers are likely to lose jobs in the Pearl River Delta by the end of 2008.

26759 ■ "Actions to Implement Three Potent Post-Crisis Strategies" in *Strategy & Leadership* (Vol. 38, September-October 2010, No. 5)
Pub: Emerald Inc.
Ed: Saul J. Berman, Richard Christner, Ragna Bell. **Description:** The need for organizations to design and implement strategies to cope with the possible situations in the post-economic crisis environment is emphasized. The plans that organizations should implement to successfully manage uncertainty and complexity and to foster their eventual growth are discussed.

26760 ■ "Active Sales" in *Green Industry Pro* (Vol. 23, September 2011)
Pub: Cygnus Business Media
Ed: Gregg Wartgow. **Description:** Craig den Hartog, owner of Emerald Magic Lawn Care located in Holtsville, New York, describes the various marketing tactics he has developed to increase sales in the current economic environment. Statistical data included.

26761 ■ "Adapt or Die" in *Black Enterprise* (Vol. 38, July 2008, No. 12, pp. 27)
Pub: Earl G. Graves Publishing Co. Inc.
Ed: Oguntoyinbo Lekan. **Description:** Turbulence in the domestic auto industry is hitting auto suppliers hard and black suppliers, the majority of whom contract with the Big Three, are just beginning to establish relationships with import car manufacturers. The more savvy CEOs are adopting new technologies in order to weather the downturn in the economy and in the industry as a whole.

26762 ■ "Affordable Again" in *The Business Journal-Serving Greater Tampa Bay* (Vol. 28, July 18, 2008, No. 30, pp. 1)
Pub: American City Business Journals, Inc.
Ed: Janet Leiser. **Description:** Rental rates for office space in the Tampa Bay area has dropped to $21.68 a foot, after demand for the second quarter of 2008 has remained low. Commercial real estate experts say that the industry can easily rebound from what is believed to be the weakest demand in 20 years. Other views, information and statistics on real estate demand and prices in Tampa Bay are, are presented.

26763 ■ "Affordable Housing on the Rise" in *Philadelphia Business Journal* (Vol. 28, October 23, 2009, No. 36, pp. 1)
Pub: American City Business Journals
Ed: Natalie Kostelni. **Description:** Philadelphia, Pennsylvania led an affordable housing boom with more than 800 new affordable housing units in the works in spite of the recession. The converging of developers and federal stimulus money has driven the sudden increase with the launching of several projects across the city.

26764 ■ "Aging Boomers to Slow Growth, Study Says" in *Globe & Mail* (March 15, 2006, pp. B5)
Pub: CTVglobemedia Publishing Inc.
Ed: Heather Scoffield. **Description:** Acording to a research study by economic forecasters at Global Insight (Canada) Inc., an issue about Canada controlling its economy, as the country's population is aging, is discussed.

26765 ■ "AIG Fixed; Is Michigan Next?" in *Crain's Detroit Business* (Vol. 24, September 22, 2008, No. 38, pp. 1)
Pub: Crain Communications, Inc.
Ed: Jay Greene. **Description:** Michigan's economic future is examined as is the mortgage buyout plan and American International Group Inc.'s takeover by the U.S. government.

26766 ■ "Ailing Economy Nibbling at Tech-Sector Jobs" in *Puget Sound Business Journal* (Vol. 29, November 7, 2008, No. 29, pp. 1)
Pub: American City Business Journals
Ed: Eric Engleman, John Cook. **Description:** Seattle-area tech start-up companies including Redfin, Zillow, WildTangent, Daptiv, Avelle, and Intrepid Learning Solutions have cut staff as the nation's economy staggers. The layoffs are reminiscent of the tech bubble era, but most startups these days have been more prudent about spending and hiring as compared to that period.

26767 ■ "Akerman Senterfitt Merger Deal Close" in *The Business Journal-Serving Greater Tampa Bay* (Vol. 28, July 18, 2008, No. 30, pp. 1)
Pub: American City Business Journals, Inc.
Ed: Jeff Blumenthal. **Description:** Sources familiar to the negotiations of Akerman Senterfitt's planned merger with Wolf Block has disclosed that executive committees of both firms have approved the deal. They expect to create an 800-lawyer firm with a significant presence in the U.S. East Coast. Other views and information on the deal and its expected impact on law practice in Florida are presented.

26768 ■ "Alberta: Help Wanted, Badly" in *Globe & Mail* (March 11, 2006, pp. B5)
Pub: CTVglobemedia Publishing Inc.
Ed: Patrick Brethour; Dawn Walton. **Description:** The issue of unemployment rate, which fell by 3.1 percent in Alberta, is discussed.

26769 ■ "Alberta Warns Ottawa On Taxes" in *Globe & Mail* (March 9, 2007, pp. B1)
Pub: CTVglobemedia Publishing Inc.
Ed: Steven Chase. **Description:** Ottawa's proposal to remove the tax break for oil sands projects has been criticized by Alberta finance minister Lyle Oberg. The cancelling of tax breaks could hamper development in oil sands and thus hit Alberta's economy.

26770 ■ "Alberta's Runaway Train" in *Canadian Business* (Vol. 80, December 25, 2006, No. 1, pp. 17)
Pub: Rogers Media
Ed: Andrew Nikiforuk. **Description:** The high revenue brought about by the growth in the number of oil sand plants in Canada and the simultaneous burden on infrastructure and housing is discussed.

26771 ■ "All Indicators in Michigan Innovation Index Drop in 4Q" in *Crain's Detroit Business* (Vol. 25, June 22, 2009, No. 25, pp. 9)
Pub: Crain Communications Inc. - Detroit
Ed: Ryan Beene. **Description:** Economic indicators that rate Michigan's innovation fell in the fourth quarter of 2008. The index of trademark applications, SBA loans, venture capital funding, new incorporations and other indicators traced dropped 12.6 points.

26772 ■ "Amid Recession, Companies Still Value Supplier Diversity Programs" in *Hispanic Business* (July-August 2009, pp. 34)
Pub: Hispanic Business
Ed: Joshua Molina. **Description:** The decline of traditionally strong industries, from automotive manufacturing to construction, has shaken today's economy and has forced small businesses, especially suppliers and minority-owned firms, turn to diversity programs in order to make changes.

26773 ■ "An Amazing Race" in *Canadian Business* (Vol. 81, March 3, 2008, No. 3, pp. 25)
Pub: Rogers Media
Ed: Rachel Pulfer. **Description:** U.S. presidential candidates Barack Obama and Hilary Clinton lead the Democratic Part primaries while John McCain is a frontrunner at the Republican Party. These leading candidates have different plans for the U.S. economy which will affect Canada's own economy particularly concerning trade policies. The presidential candidates' proposals and the impacts of U.S. economic downturn on Canada are examined.

26774 ■ "And In This Briefcase" in *Mergers & Acquisitions: The Dealmaker's Journal* (March 1, 2008)
Pub: SourceMedia, Inc.
Description: ACG San Diego decided to address the impact the changes in the economy will have on potential private equity transactions as well as what criteria private equity firms are looking for when assessing a company. At the opening of the chapter's 2008 breakfast meeting, real-world case studies were utilized with the audiences' participation in order to assess pre-deal risk scenarios.

26775 ■ "And The Winner Is..." in *Canadian Business* (Vol. 81, March 3, 2008, No. 3, pp. 21)
Pub: Rogers Media
Ed: Joe Castaldo. **Description:** Thirty out of 141 Canadian chief executive officers think that Hilary Clinton would be best for U.S.-Canada relations if elected as U.S. president. Findings also revealed that 60 respondents believe that presidential candidate John McCain would be best on handling issues of international military-security. Views on the candidates' performance and their ability to deal with the declining U.S. economy as well as international trade issues are also given.

26776 ■ *Animal Spirits: How Human Psychology Drives the Economy, and Why it Matters for Global Capitalism*
Pub: Princeton University Press
Ed: George A. Akerlof, Robert J. Shiller. **Released:** 2009. **Price:** $24.95. **Description:** Psychological factors that led to the depressed economy and how it may impede a turnaround.

26777 ■ "Another Baby Step" in *Canadian Business* (Vol. 81, March 31, 2008, No. 5, pp. 32)
Pub: Rogers Media
Ed: Andrew Wahl. **Description:** Discusses the Canadian government's federal budget which makes it easier to tap into tax credits for corporate research

and development. However, these steps do not really go far enough to boost industrial research levels in Canada. Making these incentives at least partially refundable could help during tough economic times.

26778 ■ "Another Man's Pain" in *Canadian Business* (Vol. 80, October 22, 2007, No. 21, pp. 33)
Pub: Rogers Media
Ed: Andy Holloway. **Description:** U.S. financial collapse can have a positive impact on Canadian investors. Graphs on the total number of home foreclosures in the U.S. from January to August 2007, as well as foreclosure market by type, are presented.

26779 ■ *Antitrust Law: Economic Theory and Common Law Evolution*
Pub: Cambridge University Press
Ed: Keith N. Hylton. **Released:** January 22, 2010. **Price:** $39.99. **Description:** A consolidation of various perspectives on antitrust law and its evolution.

26780 ■ "Apartment Ambitions" in *The Business Journal-Portland* (Vol. 25, August 8, 2008, No. 22, pp. 1)
Pub: American City Business Journals, Inc.
Ed: Wendy Culverwell. **Description:** Unico Properties LLC's Asa Flats+Lofts is one of the first of eight high-end apartment projects planned for Portland which will add a total of 2,130 new units to the Pearl District, South Waterfront, and downtown Portland. These apartments charge costs more than $1,600 or more per month over the average rent.

26781 ■ "Apartment Market Down, Not Out" in *Crain's Detroit Business* (Vol. 24, October 6, 2008, No. 40, pp. 9)
Pub: Crain Communications, Inc.
Ed: Daniel Duggan. **Description:** Detroit's apartment market is considered to have some of the strongest fundamentals of any apartment market in the country with relatively low vacancy rates and a relatively low supply of new units compared with demand. Investors continue to show interest in the buildings but the national lending market is making it difficult to invest in the city.

26782 ■ "Ardesta Venture-Capital Fund Folds" in *Crain's Detroit Business* (Vol. 24, September 22, 2008, No. 38, pp. 24)
Pub: Crain Communications, Inc.
Ed: Tom Henderson. **Description:** Due to the downturn in the local economy, Ann Arbor-based Ardesta LLC, a venture-capital firm specializing in micro- and nanotechnology research, has pulled the plug on its planned fund of $100 million and said no to an investment of up to $15 million from the state.

26783 ■ *Are the Rich Necessary? Great Economic Arguments and How They Reflect Our Personal Values*
Pub: Axios Press
Ed: Hunter Lewis. **Released:** 2007. **Price:** $20.00. **Description:** Investment advisor argues whether today's economic system promotes greed. Each chapter of the book poses a question and then he answers.

26784 ■ "Are You Ready for Dow 20,000?" in *Barron's* (Vol. 88, March 24, 2008, No. 12, pp. 26)
Pub: Dow Jones & Company, Inc.
Ed: Jonathan R. Laing. **Description:** Stock strategist James Finucane forecasts that the Dow Jones Industrial Average will rise from its 12,361 level to as high as 20,000 from 2008 to 2009. He believes that stock liquidation and a buildup of cash provide the perfect conditions for a huge rally.

26785 ■ "Are You Rich?" in *Barron's* (Vol. 88, March 10, 2008, No. 10, pp. 27)
Pub: Dow Jones & Company, Inc.
Ed: Tom Sullivan. **Description:** Discusses the minimum net worth of people considered as rich in America is now at $25 million. There are about 125,000 households in America that meet this threshold, while 49,000 households have a net worth between $25 million and $ 500 million, and about 1,400 US households have a net worth over $500 million.

26786 ■ "An Artwork in Progress" in *Hawaii Business* (Vol. 53, March 2008, No. 9, pp. 45)
Pub: Hawaii Business Publishing
Ed: Jolyn Okimoto Rosa. **Description:** Art galleries in Honolulu, Hawaii holds the First Friday Gallery Walk and other special events, which draw crowd to and increase sales activities in the city's downtown. The district also advocates for the reintroduction of Honolulu's Chinatown to the people. Details regarding the art galleries' Chinatown revival and its local economic impact are discussed.

26787 ■ "As Capital Gains Tax Hike Looms, Merger Activity Percolates" in *Baltimore Business Journal* (Vol. 28, August 27, 2010, No. 16, pp. 1)
Pub: Baltimore Business Journal
Ed: Scott Dance. **Description:** Concerns for higher capital gains taxes in 2011 have been provoking buyers and sellers to engage in mergers and acquisitions activity, which is expected to gain momentum before the end of 2010. Companies that had saved cash during the recession have been taking advantage of the buyer's market. Other trends in local and national mergers and acquisitions activity are presented.

26788 ■ *The Ascent of Money: A Financial History of the World*
Pub: Penguin Group USA Inc.
Ed: Niall Ferguson. **Released:** 2009. **Price:** $29.95. **Description:** How financial considerations prompted the Crusades and other surprising explanations of famous events are uncovered.

26789 ■ "Asia Breathes a Sigh of Relief" in *Business Week* (September 22, 2008, No. 4100, pp. 32)
Pub: McGraw-Hill Companies, Inc.
Ed: Bruce Einhorn; Theo Francis; Chi-Chu Tschang; Moon Ihlwan; Hiroko Tashiro. **Description:** Foreign bankers, such as those in Asia, that had been investing heavily in the United States began to worry as the housing crisis deepened and the impact on Freddie Mac and Fannie Mae became increasingly clear. Due to the government bailout, however, central banks will most likely continue to buy American debt.

26790 ■ *Asian Godfathers: Money and Power in Hong Kong and Southeast Asia*
Pub: Grove Atlantic
Ed: Joe Studwell. **Released:** September 2008. **Price:** $15.00 paperback. **Description:** Expose of some of Southeast Asia's top business moguls is highlighted, along with a look into the region's economic and social cultures.

26791 ■ "Athletes Face Wins and Losses After Pro Sport" in *The Business Journal - Serving Phoenix and the Valley of the Sun* (Vol. 29, September 19, 2008, No. 3, pp. 1)
Pub: American City Business Journals, Inc.
Ed: Chris Casacchia. **Description:** Professional athletes like hockey star Jeremy Roenick start businesses, while others like Joel Adamson work to boost local communities. Former athletes were found to be particularly interested with real estate businesses. Other views and information on former athletes and their life after sports are presented.

26792 ■ *Atiyah's Accidents, Compensation and the Law*
Pub: Cambridge University Press
Ed: Peter Cane, Patrick Atiyah. **Released:** January 22, 2010. **Price:** $56.00. **Description:** Leading authority on the law of personal injuries compensation and the social, political and economic issues surrounding it.

26793 ■ "Au Revoir Or Goodbye?" in *Barron's* (Vol. 88, July 14, 2008, No. 28, pp. 5)
Pub: Dow Jones & Co., Inc.
Ed: Alan Abelson. **Description:** Former Senator Phil Gramm's opinion that the U.S. is a "nation of whiners" as they moan about recession is another example of the disconnection between Washington and Wall Street on one hand and the real world on the other. It would be a catastrophe for most of the world if Fannie Mae and Freddie Mac were to go under and take their trillions of mortgage debt with them.

26794 ■ "Auctions and Bidding: a Guide for Computer Scientists" in *ACM Computing Surveys* (Vol. 43, Summer 2011, No. 2, pp. 10)
Pub: Association for Computing Machinery
Ed: Simon Parsons, Juan A. Rodriguez-Aguilar, Mark Klein. **Description:** There are various actions: single dimensional, multi-dimensional, single-sided, double-sided, first-price, second-price, English, Dutch, Japanese, sealed-bid, and these have been extensively discussed and analyzed in economics literature. This literature is surveyed from a computer science perspective, primarily from the viewpoint of computer scientists who are interested in learning about auction theory, and to provide pointers into the economics literature for those who want a deeper technical understanding. In addition, since auctions are an increasingly important topic in computer science, the article also looks at work on auctions from the computer science literature. The aim is to identify what both bodies of work tell us about creating electronic auctions.

26795 ■ "Austin on Verge of Losing 7,500 Jobs" in *Austin Business Journal* (Vol. 31, May 6, 2011, No. 9, pp. 1)
Pub: American City Business Journals Inc.
Ed: Jacob Dirr. **Description:** Proposed state budget cuts are seen to result in the loss of as many as 7,500 public and private sector jobs in Austin, Texas, with the private sector losing the majority of workers. Comments from analysts are included.

26796 ■ "Auto Sector's Outlook Dims, Survey Finds" in *Globe & Mail* (January 4, 2006, pp. B4)
Pub: CTVglobemedia Publishing Inc.
Ed: Greg Keenan. **Description:** The findings of KPMG's survey, on the opinions of chief executives of automotive sector on the impact of higher gas prices, are presented.

26797 ■ "Auto Show Aims to Electrify" in *Crain's Detroit Business* (Vol. 26, January 11, 2010, No. 2, pp. 1)
Pub: Crain Communications, Inc.
Ed: Ryan Beene. **Description:** Overview of the North American International Auto show include sixteen production and concept vehicles including eight from the Detroit 3. High-tech battery suppliers as well as hybrid and electric vehicles will highlight the show.

26798 ■ "Auto Supplier Stock Battered In Wake Of Wall Street Woes" in *Crain's Detroit Business* (Vol. 24, September 29, 2008, No. 39, pp. 4)
Pub: Crain Communications, Inc.
Ed: Ryan Beene. **Description:** Due to the volatility of the stock market and public perception of the $700 billion banking bailout, auto suppliers are now facing a dramatic drop in their shares. Statistical data included.

26799 ■ "Automotive Trouble" in *Canadian Business* (Vol. 82, April 27, 2009, No. 7, pp. 11)
Pub: Rogers Media
Ed: Thomas Watson. **Description:** The likely effects of a possible bailout of the U.S. automotive industry are examined. Some experts believe that a bailout will be good for the automotive industry and on the U.S. economy. Others argue however, that the nationalization may have a negative impact on the industry and on the economy.

26800 ■ "B2B Commercial Collection Agency Accounts Fall" in *Managing Credit, Receivables & Collections* (November 2010, No. 10-11, pp. 9)
Pub: Institute of Management & Administration
Description: A fall in the number of Business-To-Business collection accounts reflects the pace of the global economic recovery.

26801 ■ "BABs in Bond Land" in *Barron's* (Vol. 89, July 6, 2009, No. 27, pp. 14)
Pub: Dow Jones & Co., Inc.

Ed: Jim McTague. **Description:** American Recovery and Reinvestment Act has created taxable Build America Bonds (BAB) to finance new construction projects. The issuance of the two varieties of taxable BABs is expected to benefit the municipal bond market.

26802 ■ "A Baby Step to the South" in *Canadian Business* (Vol. 81, July 22, 2008, No. 12-13, pp. 21)
Pub: Rogers Media Ltd.

Ed: Jane Bao. **Description:** Canada's free trade agreement (FTA) with Colombia is seen as Canada's re-engagement with Latin America. Some politicians believe that the FTA is more of a political agreement than a trade agreement with Colombia. Key information on Canada's trade agreements, as well as trade with Colombia and Latin American countries, is presented.

26803 ■ "Back in the Race" in *Barron's* (Vol. 88, March 17, 2008, No. 11, pp. 43)
Pub: Dow Jones & Company, Inc.

Ed: Leslie P. Norton. **Description:** Katherine Schapiro was able to get Sentinel International Equity's Morningstar classification to blended fund from a value fund rating after joining Sentinel from her former jobs at Strong Overseas Fund. Schapiro aims to benefit from the global rebalancing as the U.S.'s share of the world economy shrinks.

26804 ■ "Back on Track-Or Off the Rails?" in *Business Week* (September 22, 2008, No. 4100, pp. 22)
Pub: McGraw-Hill Companies, Inc.

Ed: Peter Coy; Tara Kalwarski. **Description:** Discusses the possible scenarios the American economy may undergo due to the takeover of Fannie Mae and Freddie Mac. Statistical data included.

26805 ■ "Bad-Loan Bug Bites Mid-Tier Banks; More Pain, Tighter Lending Standards Ahead, CEOs Say" in *Crain's Chicago Business* (May 5, 2008)
Pub: Crain Communications, Inc.

Ed: Steve Daniels. **Description:** Mid-sized commercial banks form the bedrock of Chicago's financial-services industry and they are now feeling the results of the credit crisis that has engulfed the nation's largest banks and brokerages. Commercial borrowers are seeing tighter terms on loans and higher interest rates while bank investors are unable to forecast lenders' earnings performance from quarter to quarter. Statistical data included.

26806 ■ *Bad Money*
Pub: Viking Press/Penguin Group

Ed: Kevin Phillips. **Released:** April 15, 2008. **Description:** How the financial sector has hijacked the American economy, aided by Washington's ruinous faith in the efficiency of markets.

26807 ■ *Bad Samaritans: The Myth of Free Trade and the Secret History of Capitalism*
Pub: Bloomsbury USA

Ed: Ha-Joon Chang. **Released:** 2009. **Price:** $26.95. **Description:** Economist challenges open-market proponents and believes that free trade would do more harm than good.

26808 ■ "Bailout Forgets the 'Little Guys'" in *The Business Journal-Milwaukee* (Vol. 25, September 26, 2008, No. 53, pp. A1)
Pub: American City Business Journals, Inc.

Ed: Rich Kirchen. **Description:** Community Bankers of Wisconsin and the Wisconsin Bankers Association are urging members to approach congressional representatives and remind them to include local banks in building the $700 billion bailout plan. WBA president and CEO Kurt Bauer thinks that it is only fair to include smaller institutions in the bailout. The initial bailout plan and its benefit for the smaller banks are examined.

26809 ■ "Bailout May Force Cutbacks, Job Losses" in *The Business Journal - Serving Phoenix and the Valley of the Sun* (Vol. 29, September 26, 2008, No. 4, pp. 1)
Pub: American City Business Journals, Inc.

Ed: Mike Sunnucks. **Description:** Economists say the proposed $700 billion bank bailout could affect Arizona businesses as banks could be forced to reduce the amount and number of loans it has thereby forcing businesses to shrink capital expenditures and then jobs. However, the plan could also stimulate the economy by taking bad loans off banks balance sheets according to another economist.

26810 ■ "Baker Building A Snapshot Of Corridor's Future; Long-Empty Euclid Avenue Site Already Houses Two Tech Tenants" in *Crain's Cleveland Business*
Pub: Crain Communications, Inc.

Ed: Stan Bullard. **Description:** Due to a new transit line and the redevelopment of the old Baker Electric Building, the Euclid Ave. area of Cleveland is transforming from a known drug activity area to a new area for high-tech ventures.

26811 ■ "Bank Forces Brooke Founder To Sell His Holdings" in *The Business Journal-Serving Metropolitan Kansas City* (October 10, 2008)
Pub: American City Business Journals, Inc.

Ed: James Dornbrook. **Description:** Robert Orr who is the founder of Brooke Corp., a franchise of insurance agencies, says that he was forced to sell virtually all of his stocks in the company by creditors. First United Bank held the founder's stock as collateral for two loans worth $5 million and $7.9 million, which were declared in default in September 2008. Details of the selling of the company's stocks are provided.

26812 ■ "Bank Sticks to Rate Rise Script but 'Modest' is the Salient Word" in *Globe & Mail* (January 25, 2006, pp. B5)
Pub: CTVglobemedia Publishing Inc.

Ed: Heather Scoffield. **Description:** The reasons behind the decision of Bank of Canada to increase interest rate, which is posted at 3.5 percent, are presented.

26813 ■ "Banking Bailout: Boost or Bust?" in *Crain's Detroit Business* (Vol. 24, September 29, 2008, No. 39, pp. 1)
Pub: Crain Communications, Inc.

Ed: Amy Lane. **Description:** Economic insiders discuss the banking bailout and how it might impact the state of Michigan.

26814 ■ "Bankruptcies" in *Crain's Detroit Business* (Vol. 26, January 11, 2010, No. 2, pp. 7)
Pub: Crain Communications, Inc.

Ed: Dustin Walsh. **Description:** Listing of local businesses that filed for Chapter 7 or 11 protection in U.S. Bankruptcy Court in Detroit December 11-28. Under Chapter 11, a company files for reorganization. Chapter 7 involves total liquidation.

26815 ■ "Bankruptcies Shoot Up 68 Percent" in *Sacramento Business Journal* (Vol. 25, July 18, 2008, No. 20, pp. 1)
Pub: American City Business Journals, Inc.

Ed: Kathy Robertson. **Description:** Personal bankruptcy in the Sacramento area rose by 88 percent for the first half of 2008 while business bankruptcies rose by 50 percent for the same period. The numbers of consumer bankruptcy reflects the effect of high debt, rising mortgage costs, and declining home values on U.S. households.

26816 ■ "Bankruptcies Soar As Market Takes a Tumble" in *The Business Journal - Serving Phoenix and the Valley of the Sun* (Vol. 28, August 22, 2008, No. 51, pp. 1)
Pub: American City Business Journals, Inc.

Ed: Chris Casacchia. **Description:** Chapter 7 and Chapter 13 bankruptcy filings have increased 112 percent in July 2008, for a total of 1,225 filings in Phoenix. Chapter 11 business reorganizations also increased by 86 percent compared to 2007 figures because of the challenging national economy. Other views and information on the rise in bankruptcy filings in Phoenix are presented.

26817 ■ "Bankruptcies Swell" in *The Business Journal-Portland* (Vol. 25, July 4, 2008, No. 17, pp. 1)
Pub: American City Business Journals, Inc.

Ed: Andy Giegerich. **Description:** Individual and business bankruptcy filings in Portland, Oregon had increased. The rising gas and food prices, mortgage crisis and tightening lending standards are seen as causes of bankruptcies. Statistics on bankruptcy filings are also provided.

26818 ■ "Bankruptcy Blowback" in *Business Week* (September 22, 2008, No. 4100, pp. 36)
Pub: McGraw-Hill Companies, Inc.

Ed: Jessica Silver-Greenberg. **Description:** Changes to bankruptcy laws which were enacted in 2005 after banks and other financial institutions lobbied hard for them are now suffering the consequences of the laws which force more troubled borrowers to let their homes go into foreclosure; lenders suffer financially every time they have to take on a foreclosure and the laws in which they lobbied so hard to see enacted are now becoming a problem for these lending institutions. Details of the changes in the laws are outlined as are the affects on the consumer, the economy and the lenders.

26819 ■ "Banks Fret About Gist Of Bailout" in *The Business Journal-Serving Metropolitan Kansas City* (Vol. 27, September 26, 2008, No. 2)
Pub: American City Business Journals, Inc.

Ed: James Dornbrook. **Description:** Banks from the Kansas City area hope that the proposed $700 billion bailout will not send the wrong message. UMB Financial Corp. chairman says that he hopes that the bailout would benefit companies that were more risk restrained and punish those that took outsized risk. Other bank executives' perceptions on the planned bailout are given.

26820 ■ "Banks Lower Rates on CDs, Deposits" in *Baltimore Business Journal* (Vol. 27, January 1, 2010, No. 35, pp. 1)
Pub: American City Business Journals

Ed: Gary Haber. **Description:** Greater Baltimore area banks in Maryland have lowered their rates on certificates of deposits (CDs) and money market accounts, which could indicate the incoming trend for the first half of 2010. A banking industry forecast shows that lower Federal Funds rate, low inflation, and a new Federal Deposit Insurance Corporation (FDIC) rule might cause the rates to drop even further. Details on the FDIC rule are given.

26821 ■ "Bargain Hunting In Vietnam" in *Barron's* (Vol. 88, July 14, 2008, No. 28, pp. M6)
Pub: Dow Jones & Co., Inc.

Ed: Elliot Wilson. **Description:** Vietnam's economy grew by just 6.5 percent for the first half of 2008 and its balance of payments ballooned to $14.4 billion. The falling stock prices in the country is a boon for bargain hunters and investing in the numerous domestic funds is one way of investing in the country. Some shares that investors are taking an interest in are also discussed.

26822 ■ "Bark Up The Right Tree" in *Small Business Opportunities* (Winter 2009)
Pub: Entrepreneur Media Inc.

Description: Profile of Central Bark, a daycare company catering to pets that offers franchise opportunities and is expanding rapidly despite the economic downturn; the company's growth strategy is also discussed.

26823 ■ "Bartering is Local Club's Stock in Trade" in *Pueblo Chieftain* (September 6, 2010)
Pub: The Pueblo Chieftain

Ed: Loretta Sword. **Description:** As the economy waivers, a barter club in Pueblo, Colorado thrives. An examination of the club and the way it operates is included.

26824 ■ "Bartering Makes a Return in Hard Times" in *Atlanta Journal-Constitution* (October 2, 2010, pp. A15)
Pub: Atlanta Journal-Constitution
Ed: Bill York. **Description:** The advantages of bartering are explored.

26825 ■ "Bartering Trades on Talents" in *Reading Eagle* (June 20, 2010)
Pub: Reading Eagle/Reading Times
Ed: Tony Lucia. **Description:** Bartering is not just a way of trading goods and services, it can be an essential tool for small business to survive in a bad economy.

26826 ■ "Basel3 Quick Fix Actually Neither" in *Canadian Business* (Vol. 83, October 12, 2010, No. 17, pp. 19)
Pub: Rogers Media Ltd.
Ed: Thomas Watson. **Description:** Information about the so-called Basel 3 standards, which will require banks to hold top-quality capital totaling at least 7 percent of their risk-bearing assets is provided. The rules' supporters believe that a good balance has been reached between improving the Basel 2 framework and maintaining enough lending capital to stimulate an economic growth.

26827 ■ "The Bear Arrives - With Bargain Hunters" in *Barron's* (Vol. 88, July 7, 2008, No. 27, pp. M3)
Pub: Dow Jones & Co., Inc.
Ed: Kopin Tan. **Description:** US stock markets have dropped 20 percent below their highs, entering the bear market at the end of June 2008. It was also the worst performance of the stock markets during June. Wine maker Constellation Brands, however, reported a 50 percent rise in net income for the first quarter of 2008.

26828 ■ "Bear Market Tough On Investors" in *The Business Journal-Milwaukee* (Vol. 25, July 4, 2008, No. 41, pp. A1)
Pub: American City Business Journals, Inc.
Ed: Rich Kirchen. **Description:** Public companies and their investors in the Milwaukee area suffered as the bear market took hold of the Wisconsin stock market. There were 18 stocks out of the 36 publicly traded stocks that have fallen into the bear market, meaning a 20 percent decline from the market peak in the fall of 2007. The impacts of the bear market on investors are evaluated.

26829 ■ "The Bear's Back" in *Barron's* (Vol. 88, July 7, 2008, No. 27, pp. 17)
Pub: Dow Jones & Co., Inc.
Ed: Randall W. Forsyth; Vito Racanelli. **Description:** US stock markets have formally entered the bear market after the Dow Jones Industrial Average dropped 20 percent from its high as of June 2008. Investors remain uncertain as to how long the bear market will persist, especially with the US economy on the edge of recession.

26830 ■ "The Beauty of Banking's Big Ugly" in *Barron's* (Vol. 89, July 27, 2009, No. 30, pp. 31)
Pub: Dow Jones & Co., Inc.
Ed: Andrew Bary. **Description:** Appeal of the shares of Citigroup comes from its sharp discount to its tangible book value and the company's positive attributes include a strong capital position, high loan-loss reserves, and their appealing global-consumer. The shares have the potential to generate nice profits and decent stock gains as the economy turns.

26831 ■ "Bertha's Birth Stirs Juice" in *Barron's* (Vol. 88, July 14, 2008, No. 28, pp. M11)
Pub: Dow Jones & Co., Inc.
Ed: Tom Sellen. **Description:** Price of frozen concentrated orange juice, which has risen to four-month highs of $1.3620 in July 2008 is due, in part, to the hurricane season that has come earlier than normal in the far eastern Atlantic thereby possibly harming the 2008-2009 Florida orange crop. Future tropical-storm development will affect the prices of this commodity.

26832 ■ "Best Growth Stocks" in *Canadian Business* (Vol. 81, Summer 2008, No. 9, pp. 61)
Pub: Rogers Media Ltd.
Ed: Calvin Leung. **Description:** Table showing the one-year performance of growth stocks is presented. Edmonton-based Stantec Inc. expects to advance its sales and profits by 15 percent to 20 percent per year through tapping international markets and acquisitions. Analysts forecast a 17.1 percent growth rate annually over the next 3 to 5 years.

26833 ■ "Best Turnaround Stocks" in *Canadian Business* (Vol. 81, Summer 2008, No. 9, pp. 65)
Pub: Rogers Media Ltd.
Ed: Calvin Leung. **Description:** Share prices of Sierra Wireless Inc. and EXFO Electro Optical Engineering Inc. have fallen over the past year but have good chance at a rebound considering that the companies have free cash flow and no long-term debt. One-year stock performance analysis of the two companies is presented.

26834 ■ "Best Value Stocks" in *Canadian Business* (Vol. 81, Summer 2008, No. 9, pp. 63)
Pub: Rogers Media Ltd.
Ed: Calvin Leung. **Description:** Table showing the one-year performance of bargain or best-value stocks is presented. These stocks are undervalued compared to their North American peers, but it is projected that their five-year average return on equity is greater.

26835 ■ "The Best and Worst Economic Times" in *Agency Sales Magazine* (Vol. 39, December 2009, No. 11, pp. 22)
Pub: MANA
Ed: Mark Young. **Description:** U.S. gross domestic product grew 3.5 percent and the stock market has improved but manufacturers are cutting commissions or dropping sales representatives. Despite these challenges, it can a good time for salespeople because clients need them more than ever. Salesmen should find new ways to do business for their clients during this current challenging environment.

26836 ■ "Bet on China" in *Canadian Business* (Vol. 80, November 5, 2007, No. 22, pp. 30)
Pub: Rogers Media
Ed: Thomas Watson. **Description:** Former U.S. Federal Reserve Board head, Alan Greenspan, warns that contraction will happen in the Chinese market. However, the economic success of China does not seem to be at the point of ending, as the country remains the largest market for mobile telecommunications. Forecasts for Chinese trading and investments are provided.

26837 ■ "Bet on the Subcontinent" in *Canadian Business* (Vol. 81, April 14, 2008, No. 6, pp. 27)
Pub: Rogers Media
Ed: Calvin Leung. **Description:** Morgan Stanley Capital International India Index is down 28 percent for the first half of 2008 but this index rebounded 6 percent in 2002 then skyrocketed 65 percent in 2003. The economic reforms in the 1990's have created a growing middle class and households that can afford discretionary items will grow from eight million to 94 million by 2025. India's equity market could outperform developed markets if its economy grows at its current rate.

26838 ■ "Better Made's Better Idea: Diversify Despite Rising Costs" in *Crain's Detroit Business* (Vol. 24, September 22, 2008, No. 38, pp. 18)
Pub: Crain Communications, Inc.
Ed: Nathan Skid. **Description:** Better Made Snack Foods Inc. is planning to expand its product lines and market reach as well as boost manufacturing capability during a time in which the company is being buffeted by rising commodity and fuel costs. The company feels that diversification is the key to maintain sales and growth.

26839 ■ "Betting On Volatile Materials" in *Barron's* (Vol. 88, July 14, 2008, No. 28, pp. M11)
Pub: Dow Jones & Co., Inc.
Ed: John Marshall. **Description:** Economic slowdowns in the U.S., Europe and China could cause sharp short-term declines in the materials sector. The S&P Materials sector is vulnerable to shifts in the flow of funds. Statistical data included.

26840 ■ "Beware of Rotting Money" in *Barron's* (Vol. 89, July 13, 2009, No. 28, pp. 31)
Pub: Dow Jones & Co., Inc.
Ed: Thomas G. Donlan. **Description:** Inflation can take hold of a country and do it great harm; it is caused by people, most particularly central bankers in charge of the world's reserve currency. Arrogant economists pushed the belief that the government can engineer the economy and it is argued that there is trouble ahead when the government tries to control the economy.

26841 ■ *Big-Box Swindle: The True Cost of Mega-Retailers and the Fight for America's Independent Businesses*
Pub: Beacon Press
Ed: Stacy Mitchell. **Released:** October 2007. **Price:** $15.00. **Description:** Examination of the economic, environmental, and social damage done by big-box retailers like Wal-Mart, Costco, and Home Depot. Labor policies of these retailers, particularly those enforced by Wal-Mart, are discussed at length.

26842 ■ "Big Losses Mount for Hospitals" in *Baltimore Business Journal* (Vol. 27, October 23, 2009, No. 24, pp. 1)
Pub: American City Business Journals
Ed: Scott Graham. **Description:** Reported losses by nine of the 22 hospitals in the Greater Baltimore area during fiscal 2009 have proven that the health care industry is not immune to the recession. The rising costs of doing business and losses in the stock market have strongly affected the financial status of hospitals.

26843 ■ *The Big Squeeze: Tough Times for the American Workers*
Pub: Pantheon Books
Ed: Steven Greenhouse. **Released:** 2009. **Price:** $25.95. **Description:** Labor correspondent for the New York Times reports on the bleak condition of the current workplace environment, citing violations of child labor laws and forced slave labor conditions in third world countries and robber baron era occurring often here in America that are expanding the number of working poor.

26844 ■ *The Big Switch*
Pub: W. W. Norton & Company, Inc.
Ed: Nicholas Carr. **Released:** January 19, 2009. **Price:** $16.95 paperback. **Description:** Today companies are dismantling private computer systems and tapping into services provided via the Internet. This shift is remaking the computer industry, bringing competitors such as Google to the forefront ant threatening traditional companies like Microsoft and Dell. The book weaves together history, economics, and technology to explain why computing is changing and what it means for the future.

26845 ■ "'Biggest Loser' Adds Bit of Muscle to Local Economy" in *Crain's Detroit Business* (Vol. 26, January 4, 2010, No. 1, pp. 1)
Pub: Crain Communications, Inc.
Ed: Chad Halcom. **Description:** NBC's weight-loss reality show, "The Biggest Loser" has helped the local economy and generated a new crop of local startup businesses due to past contestants that were from the Detroit area.

26846 ■ "Bill Kaneko" in *Hawaii Business* (Vol. 53, December 2007, No. 6, pp. 32)
Pub: Hawaii Business Publishing
Ed: David K. Choo. **Description:** Hawaii Institute for Public Affairs chief executive officer and president Bill Kaneko believes that the Hawaiian economy is booming, however, he also asserts that the economy is too

focused on tourism and real estate. Kaneko has also realized the that the will of the people is strong while he was helping with the Hawaiian 2050 Sustainability Plan. The difficulties of making a sustainable Hawaii are discussed.

26847 ■ "Bill Lee's Auto Repair Business Chugs Along Despite Life's Obstacles" in *Bradenton Herald* (August 22, 2010)
Pub: Bradenton Herald
Ed: Grace Gagliano. **Description:** Profile of Bill Lee's Professional Automotive Services located in Bradenton, Florida. The auto repair business was opened 26 years ago and provides repair for an assortment of fleet vehicles, including truck repair.

26848 ■ "Biz Assesses 'Textgate' Fallout; Conventions, Smaller Deals Affected" in *Crain's Detroit Business* (Vol. 24, March 31, 2008)
Pub: Crain Communications, Inc.
Ed: Tom Henderson. **Description:** Businesspeople who were trying to measure the amount of economic damage is likely to be caused due to Mayor Kwame Kilpatrick's indictment on eight charges and found that: automotive and other large global deals are less likely to be affected than location decisions by smaller companies and convention site decisions. Also being affected are negotiations in which Mexican startup companies were planning a partnership with the TechTown incubator to pursue opportunities in the auto sector; those plans are being put on hold while they look at other sites.

26849 ■ "A Bleak Earnings View" in *Barron's* (Vol. 88, March 10, 2008, No. 10, pp. 15)
Pub: Dow Jones & Company, Inc.
Description: Analysts expect consumer discretionary profits in the S&P 500 to drop 8.4 percent in the first quarter of 2008. A less confident consumer is expected to pull profits down, putting forecasts of earnings growth in the S&P 500 at risk. Statistical data included.

26850 ■ "Block Plans Office Park Along K-10 Corridor" in *The Business Journal-Serving Metropolitan Kansas City* (Vol. 27, October 3, 2008)
Pub: American City Business Journals, Inc.
Ed: Rob Roberts. **Description:** Kansas City, Missouri-based Block and Co. is planning to build four office buildings at the corner of College Boulevard and Ridgeview Road in Olathe. Features of the planned development are provided. Comments from executives are also presented.

26851 ■ "Block Pulls Plug On Riverside Deal" in *The Business Journal-Serving Metropolitan Kansas City* (Vol. 27, October 10, 2008, No. 4)
Pub: American City Business Journals, Inc.
Ed: Rob Roberts. **Description:** Real estate developer Ken Block has backed out from a $300 million Riverside industrial project. Block says he has already invested $1 million of his own money into the deal. Details regarding the project are given.

26852 ■ "The Board Shorts Executive" in *Hawaii Business* (Vol. 53, January 2008, No. 7, pp. 33)
Pub: Hawaii Business Publishing
Ed: Mike Markrich. **Description:** Vans Triple Crown of Surfing executive director Randy Rarick believes that the surfing business requires knowledge of the sport and integity to the game's lifestyle and spirit. His organization manages surfing events, and has generated jobs for the locals. Plans for Vans Triple Crown are supplied.

26853 ■ "Boat Sales Sputter as Cash-Strapped Buyers Drift Away" in *Puget Sound Business Journal* (Vol. 29, August 15, 2008, No. 17, pp. 1)
Pub: American City Business Journals
Ed: Greg Lamm. **Description:** Boat sales in Washington fell by 44 percent in the second quarter of 2008. The decline is attributed to the soft economy, which has given customers second thoughts on purchasing recreational water vehicles.

26854 ■ "Bonds v. Stocks: Who's Right About Recession?" in *Barron's* (Vol. 90, August 23, 2010, No. 34, pp. M3)
Pub: Barron's Editorial & Corporate Headquarters
Ed: Kopin Tan. **Description:** The future of treasury securities and stocks should the U.S. enter or avoid a recession are discussed. The back to school business climate and BHP Billiton's bid for Potash Corporation of Saskatchewan are also discussed.

26855 ■ "Book of Lists 2010" in *Philadelphia Business Journal* (Vol. 28, December 25, 2009, No. 45, pp. 1)
Pub: American City Business Journals
Description: Rankings of companies and organizations within the banking, biotechnology, economic development, healthcare, hospitality, law and accounting, marketing and media, real estate, and technology industries in the Philadelphia, Pennsylvania area are presented. Rankings are based on sales, business size, and more.

26856 ■ "Boosting Worried Customers' Confidence" in *Gallup Management Journal* (November 8, 2011)
Pub: Gallup
Ed: Jessica Tyler, Patrick Whiston. **Description:** While customers fear a double-dip recession and US economic confidence is low, leading edge firms have found a timely and creative way to win customers: they are improving their wellbeing.

26857 ■ "Borrow For Tomorrow" in *Canadian Business* (Vol. 80, October 8, 2007, No. 20, pp. 193)
Pub: Rogers Media
Ed: David Wolf. **Description:** The possibility of running deficits in order to finance infrastructures in Canada is discussed. Statistics show that the country's net government debt is below 25 percent of GDP as of 2007, and that the government is spending less on public infrastructure. Based on these figures, it is expected that an increase in government debt could help in making infrastructure investments.

26858 ■ "Bottom-Fishing and Speed-Dating in India" in *Barron's* (Vol. 88, March 24, 2008, No. 12, pp. M12)
Pub: Dow Jones & Company, Inc.
Ed: Elliot Wilson. **Description:** Indian stocks have fallen hard in 2008, with Mumbai's Sensex 30 down 30 percent from its January 2008 peak of 21,000 to 14,995 in March. The India Private Equity Fair 2008 attracted 140 of the world's largest private equity firms and about 24 of India's fastest-growing corporations. Statistical data included.

26859 ■ "Bottom's Up" in *Barron's* (Vol. 88, July 14, 2008, No. 28, pp. 25)
Pub: Dow Jones & Co., Inc.
Ed: Jonathan R. Laing. **Description:** Economist Chip Case believes that home prices are nearing a bottom based on his analysis of the history of the housing market; surprisingly, in the past the housing market has rebounded after a quarter from a massive housing start drop. The drop in early stage delinquencies is another sign of the housing market's recovery.

26860 ■ "Bracing for a Bear of a Week" in *Barron's* (Vol. 88, March 17, 2008, No. 11, pp. 24)
Pub: Dow Jones & Company, Inc.
Ed: Jacqueline Doherty. **Description:** JPMorgan Chase and the Federal Reserve Bank of New York's opening of a line of credit to Bear Stearns cut the stock price of Bear Stearns by 47 percent to 30 followed by speculation of an imminent sale. JP Morgan may be the only potential buyer for the firm and some investors say Bears could be sold at $20 to $30. Bears prime assets include its enormous asset base worth $395 billion.

26861 ■ "Bracing for More Layoffs" in *Sacramento Business Journal* (Vol. 28, September 30, 2011, No. 31, pp. 1)
Pub: Sacramento Business Journal
Ed: Melanie Turner. **Description:** Sacramento, California workers are preparing for a fresh wave of layoffs. The weak economy is seen to drive the development.

26862 ■ "Brad Wall" in *Canadian Business* (Vol. 82, April 27, 2009, No. 7, pp. 9)
Pub: Rogers Media
Ed: Joe Castaldo. **Description:** Saskatchewan Premier Brad Wall believes that the mood in the province is positive, as its economy is one of the few that is expected to post growth in 2009. Wall actively promotes the province in job fairs, offering $20,000 in tuition for recent college and university graduates that relocate in the province for seven years. Wall's views on the province's economy and challenges are presented.

26863 ■ "Brazil's New King of Food" in *Barron's* (Vol. 89, July 13, 2009, No. 28, pp. 28)
Pub: Dow Jones & Co., Inc.
Ed: Kenneth Rapoza. **Description:** Perdigao and Sadia's merger has resulted in the creation of Brasil Foods and the shares of Brasil Foods provides a play on both Brazil's newly energized consumer economy and its role as a major commodities exporter. Brasil Foods shares could climb as much as 36 percent.

26864 ■ "Breadwinner Tries on Designer Jeans" in *Houston Business Journal* (Vol. 40, December 18, 2009, No. 32, pp. 1)
Pub: American City Business Journals
Ed: Allison Wollam. **Description:** Chuck Cain, the franchisee who introduced Panera Bread to Houston, Texas has partnered with tax accountant Jim Jacobsen to introduce custom-make Tattu Jeans. As more Tattu Jeans outlets are being planned, Cain is using entrepreneurial lessons learned from Panera Bread in the new venture. Both Panera Bread and Tattu Jeans were opened by Cain during economic downturns.

26865 ■ "Briarcliff Office Building Fills Up Fast" in *The Business Journal-Serving Metropolitan Kansas City* (Vol. 26, Sept. 5, 2008, pp. 1)
Pub: American City Business Journals, Inc.
Ed: Rob Roberts. **Description:** Prior to its opening the Hilltop Office Building in Kansas City Missouri has attained 80 percent occupancy. FCStone Group Inc.'s plan to move to the building has boosted the facility's occupancy. Description and dimensions of the office building are also provided.

26866 ■ "Bridging the Ingenuity Gap" in *Canadian Business* (Vol. 79, November 6, 2006, No. 22, pp. 12)
Pub: Rogers Media
Ed: Rachel Pulfer. **Description:** The views of Patrick Whitney, director of Illinois Institute of Technology's Institute of design, on globalization and business design methods are presented.

26867 ■ "BRIEF: Montana Street Pawn Shop Closing Doors" in *Montana Standard* (November 6, 2010)
Pub: Montana Standard
Ed: John Grant Emeigh. **Description:** First National Pawn located in Butte, Montana will close its doors after losing its lease. Co-owner Pat Evenson reported the lease situation coupled with the economy prompted the decision to close.

26868 ■ "Bringing Big Guns" in *Business Courier* (Vol. 24, January 18, 2008, No. 41, pp. 1)
Pub: American City Business Journals, Inc.
Ed: Lucy May. **Description:** Chief executive officer of Nidland Co. John Hayden was assigend as Cincinnati USA Partnership chairman. Hayden will bring his expertise to help the partnership drive economic development in the Greater Cincinnati area. Details of the parntership's plans are suplied.

26869 ■ "Bryan Berg" in *Hawaii Business* (Vol. 53, March 2008, No. 9, pp. 28)
Pub: Hawaii Business Publishing
Ed: David K. Choo. **Description:** Bryan Berg, senior vice president at Target Corp.'s Region 1, shares his thoughts about entering the Hawaiian market and Target representatives bringing malasadas when visiting a business in the state. Berg finds the state's

aloha spirit interesting and feels that it is important to be respectful of the Hawaiian culture and traditions in doing their business there.

26870 ■ "Budget Cuts Afflict Health Department" in *Business Courier* (Vol. 24, November 23, 2008, No. 32, pp. 1)
Pub: American City Business Journals, Inc.
Ed: Lucy May; James Ritchie. **Description:** Cincinnati must cut $25 million to balance its budget for 2008. As a result, the city will be cutting $704,000 from its Health Department's budget of $42 million, and will eliminate 31.6 positions by the end of 2007.

26871 ■ "Builder's Bankruptcy Fans Fears" in *Crain's Cleveland Business* (Vol. 28, October 22, 2007, No. 42, pp. 1)
Pub: Crain Communications, Inc.
Ed: Stan Bullard. **Description:** Whitlatch & Co., Northeast Ohio's largest builder by unit volume in the early 1990s, has filed for Chapter 11 bankruptcy. This is causing builders and others in the real estate industry to wonder how long and severe the housing slump will be and which companies will survive.

26872 ■ "Building Portfolios for a World of 2.5 Percent Gains" in *Barron's* (Vol. 88, July 7, 2008, No. 27, pp. L9)
Pub: Dow Jones & Co., Inc.
Ed: Karen Hube. **Description:** Interview with Harold Evenski whom is a financial planner running a fee-only planning practice; he continues to caution investors against pursuing short-term gains and focusing on long-term trends. He advises investors against investing in commodity and real estate stocks and is concerned about the possible effects of high inflation.

26873 ■ "Bumpy Ride Ahead for United" in *Crain's Chicago Business* (Vol. 31, May 5, 2008, No. 18, pp. 3)
Pub: Crain Communications, Inc.
Ed: John Pletz. **Description:** Continental Airlines Inc. walked away from merger talks with United Airlines last week. Now the choices facing United boil down to going it alone in an increasingly stormy airline business or a less-desirable merger with US Airways Group Inc. Analysts expect United to lose $977 million this year due, mainly, to the high price of fuel.

26874 ■ "Business Diary" in *Crain's Detroit Business* (Vol. 24, October 6, 2008, No. 40, pp. 23)
Pub: Crain Communications, Inc.
Description: Detailed listing of acquisitions, expansions, new products, new services, business contracts and startups from the Detroit area is provided.

26875 ■ "Business Must Stand Up And Be Counted" in *Crain's Detroit Business* (Vol. 24, October 6, 2008, No. 40, pp. 6)
Pub: Crain Communications, Inc.
Description: Discusses the challenges that the new mayor of Detroit faces concerning business, the state of the economy and the exceptionally tight budget the city is running on, which includes a lot of red ink. It is very likely that the city is going to see tax revenues fall substantially in the next few months and business leaders may find it in their favor to lend their support to the new mayor as well as provide him with the executive talent necessary to overcome some of these crucial issues.

26876 ■ "Business Plan Refines Focus" in *Business Journal Portland* (Vol. 27, December 10, 2010, No. 41, pp. 1)
Pub: Portland Business Journal
Ed: Wendy Culverwell. **Description:** Organizers of the Oregon Business Plan's Leadership Summit 2010 seek the opinions of nearly 1,000 business, education, political, and civic leaders in an effort to address how to rehabilitate Oregon's economy. The opinion-seeking actions recognize the organizers' belief that the economic fate of the state depends on rural Oregon.

26877 ■ "Business Stands Firm for Reform" in *Crain's Detroit Business* (Vol. 26, January 4, 2010, No. 1, pp. 3)
Pub: Crain Communications, Inc.
Ed: Amy Lane. **Description:** As Michigan faces a new year of budgetary problems, many business groups are preparing to hold firm against tax increases and instead push for enacting spending reforms.

26878 ■ "Business Still Expected To Take Hit In 2008" in *Business Journal-Serving Phoenix and the Valley of the Sun* (December 28, 2007)
Pub: American City Business Journals, Inc.
Ed: Chris Casacchia. **Description:** Community banks are expected to suffer through 2008 due to the subprime mortgage and credit crisis. Meanwhile, the asset devaluation of big banks and global investment companies are higher than that of smaller banks. Third and fourth quarter losses of banks, including Bear Sterns, are discussed.

26879 ■ "Business Through Hollywood's Lens" in *Harvard Business Review* (Vol. 88, October 2010, No. 10, pp. 146)
Pub: Harvard Business School Publishing
Ed: Batia Wiesnefeld, Gino Cattani. **Description:** The authors contend that businesses are likely to be portrayed as villains in movies because corruption has higher entertainment draw. However, movies also depict popular opinion, which encourages businesses to be accountable and to help build communities.

26880 ■ "The Business Value of Social Networks" in *Agency Sales Magazine* (Vol. 39, July 2009, No. 7, pp. 44)
Pub: MANA
Ed: Daniel Burrus. **Description:** Personal and business uses of several Web 2.0 tools for salespeople are discussed. Leading questions which will guide salespeople in finding out if one particular tool will benefit them are presented.

26881 ■ "Business Warns Against Tax Hike" in *Puget Sound Business Journal* (Vol. 29, November 14, 2008, No. 30, pp. 1)
Pub: American City Business Journals
Ed: Deirdre Gregg. **Description:** Washington-based businesses have warned state lawmakers against imposing new taxes because of the economic decline. They suggest the government should focus on spending cuts to address the $3 billion shortfall.

26882 ■ "Businesses Band Together in Destin Bartering to Keep Heads Above Water" in *Destin Log* (July 24, 2010)
Pub: The Destin Log
Ed: Andrew Metz. **Description:** Profile of The Barter Company located in Destin, Florida, whose owner believes that bartering for goods and services can help small companies in a down economy.

26883 ■ "Businesses Still on the Mend" in *Boston Business Journal* (Vol. 29, September 9, 2011, No. 18, pp. 1)
Pub: American City Business Journals Inc.
Ed: Scott Dance. **Description:** The 9/11 terrorist attacks have caused many companies in the US to dramatically shift course in response to changes in the economy. The concern that the cost of being unprepared for future disasters could be larger has remained among many companies.

26884 ■ "A Busy Little Parasite" in *Hawaii Business* (Vol. 53, March 2008, No. 9, pp. 1)
Pub: Hawaii Business Publishing
Ed: Jason Ubay. **Description:** Bee mites were first sighted in Hawaii by Michael Kliks on April 6, 2007 and have since been a cause of concern for the beekeeping industry and pollinated-dependent crop industry. Hawaii's agricultural industry estimates that the losses due to bee mites may amount to between $42 million and $62 million. Steps taken to address the issue are discussed.

26885 ■ "But Who's Counting..." in *Canadian Business* (Vol. 79, Winter 2006, No. 24, pp. 27)
Pub: Rogers Media
Ed: David Wolf. **Description:** The analysis of the debt management policies of the Canadian government is presented. The plans of the Canadian government to repay all of its debts by the year 2020 are discussed.

26886 ■ "Buy Now?" in *Hawaii Business* (Vol. 53, March 2008, No. 9, pp. 32)
Pub: Hawaii Business Publishing
Ed: David K. Choo. **Description:** Discusses the Honolulu Board of REALTORS which said that the last two months of 2007 saw double-digit housing sales drop, with December figures showing 30.6 percent and 22.9 percent decline in sales of single-family homes and condominiums, respectively. Forecasts on Hawaii's real estate market for 2008 are discussed.

26887 ■ "Calendar" in *Crain's Detroit Business* (Vol. 24, September 22, 2008, No. 38, pp. 17)
Pub: Crain Communications, Inc.
Description: Listing of events in the Detroit area include conferences addressing entrepreneurialism, economic development, and women business ownership.

26888 ■ "Calgary East" in *Canadian Business* (Vol. 80, January 15, 2007, No. 2, pp. 13)
Pub: Rogers Media
Ed: Charles Mandel. **Description:** The positive impact on the economy of Saint John city of New Brunswick province of Canada, due to the establishment of oil refineries by Irving Oil Ltd. in the area, is discussed.

26889 ■ "Call of Prepaid Heard by More" in *Chicago Tribune* (November 26, 2008)
Pub: McClatchy-Tribune Information Services
Ed: Wailin Wong. **Description:** Due to the economic downturn, more consumers are switching to no-contract, prepaid cell phone service. Customers find that the cost savings, flexibility and lack of contract are appealing in such uncertain times.

26890 ■ "Calling All Recruiters: Agent HR Puts Staffing Agents In Charge" in *Black Enterprise* (Vol. 38, December 2007, No. 5, pp. 72)
Pub: Earl G. Graves Publishing Co. Inc.
Ed: Chana Garcia. **Description:** Recruiting and staffing agencies are seeing a drop in services due to slow economic growth. AgentHR partners with full-service recruiters who have three to five year's experience-specialists soliciting their own clients, provide staffing services, and manage their own accounts, thus combining the roles of recruiter and salesperson.

26891 ■ "Calling An Audible" in *The Business Journal-Milwaukee* (Vol. 25, August 1, 2008, No. 45, pp. A1)
Pub: American City Business Journals, Inc.
Ed: David Dedge. **Description:** Tough economic conditions are forcing entertainment businesses in Milwaukee, Wisconsin, to try new business strategies to keep attracting customers. These strategies include keeping prices steady despite increasing costs and new sales promotions.

26892 ■ "Can America Invent Its Way Back?" in *Business Week* (September 22, 2008, No. 4100, pp. 52)
Pub: McGraw-Hill Companies, Inc.
Description: Business leaders as well as economists agree that innovative new products, services and ways of doing business may be the only way in which America can survive the downward spiral of the economy; innovation economics may be the answer and may even provide enough growth to enable Americans to prosper in the years to come.

26893 ■ "Can Avenue be Fashionable Again? Livernois Merchants, City Want Revival" in *Crain's Detroit Business* (March 10, 2008)
Pub: Crain Communications, Inc.
Ed: Nancy Kaffer. **Description:** Once a busy retail district, the Avenue of Fashion, a Livernois Avenue strip between Six Mile and Eight Mile roads, is facing a community business effort being backed by city support whose aim is to restore the area to its former glory.

26894 ■ "Can the State Afford a Big Time College Football Program?" in *Hawaii Business* (Vol. 53, March 2008, No. 9, pp. 26)
Pub: Hawaii Business Publishing
Description: Jill Nunokawa, civil rights at University of Hawaii, believes that athletics are extra-curricular and that the state needs to focus on priorities. State representative K. Mark Takai says that a football program brings pride and inspiration and can generate revenue and provide economic opportunities.

26895 ■ "Canada Nears European Trade Treaty" in *Globe & Mail* (February 5, 2007, pp. B1)
Pub: CTVglobemedia Publishing Inc.
Ed: Steven Chase. **Description:** The probable establishment of a treaty by Canada with Norway, Switzerland and Iceland for free-trade is discussed. The treaty will allow an annual business of $11 billion to take place in Canada.

26896 ■ "Canada, Not China, Is Partner In Our Economic Prosperity" in *Crain's Chicago Business* (Vol. 31, April 14, 2008, No. 15, pp. 14)
Pub: Crain Communications, Inc.
Ed: Paul O'Connor. **Description:** In 2005 more than $500 billion in two-way trade crossed the friendly border between the Great Lakes states and Canadian provinces and for decades Canada is every Great Lakes State's number one and growing export market.

26897 ■ "Canada Tomorrow" in *Canadian Business* (Vol. 80, October 8, 2007, No. 20, pp. 14)
Pub: Rogers Media
Ed: Donald J. Johnston. **Description:** An assessment of Canada's future in terms of its educational, social, and economic environment is presented. Concerns regarding the country's educational system such as the declining interest in science and technology and the possible lack of teachers in the future are discussed. In terms of its social and economic aspects, the need to support entrepreneurs and other qualified people is explained.

26898 ■ "Canada Tops Again in G7: Study" in *Globe & Mail* (March 22, 2006, pp. B8)
Pub: CTVglobemedia Publishing Inc.
Ed: Roma Luciw. **Description:** Canada is still the cheapest place to do business among G7 countries, even though the rising dollar has eroded some of its advantages over the United States. The survey is detailed.

26899 ■ "Canada's Uber-Wealthy" in *Canadian Business* (Vol. 80, Winter 2007, No. 24, pp. 16)
Pub: Rogers Media
Description: Statistics of the concentration of millionaire households around the world and the wealth of major cities in Canada are presented. The data reveals that Montreal has the highest concentration of billionaires and that the U.S. has the highest concentration of millionaire households.

26900 ■ "Canadian Research Generates Innovation and Prosperity" in *Canadian Business* (Vol. 81, October 27, 2008, No. 18, pp. 87)
Pub: Rogers Media Ltd.
Description: Universities play a key role in helping Canadians achieve prosperity, competitiveness, and quality of life by conducting more than a third of Canada's research. Research in universities help train graduates to apply sophisticated knowledge to real problems.

26901 ■ "Canadian Vehicle Sales Accelerate in April, but U.S. Goes on Bumpy Ride" in *Globe & Mail* (May 2, 2007, pp. B7)
Pub: CTVglobemedia Publishing Inc.
Ed: Greg Keenan. **Description:** The increase in Canadian vehicle sales to 169,280 in April 2007, but decline in their sales in the United States due to slump in housing sector are discussed.

26902 ■ "Candidates Differ On State's Green Streak" in *Business Journal Portland* (Vol. 27, October 22, 2010, No. 34, pp. 1)
Pub: Portland Business Journal
Ed: Andy Giegerich. **Description:** The views of Oregon gubernatorial candidates Chris Dudley and John Kitzhaber on the state's economy and on environmental policies are presented. Both Dudley, who is a Republican, and his Democratic challenger believe that biomass could help drive the state's economy. Both candidates also pledged changes in Oregon's business energy tax credit (BETC) program.

26903 ■ "Candidates Won't Bash Fed; Rate Cuts Bash Savers" in *Barron's* (Vol. 88, March 24, 2008, No. 12, pp. 31)
Pub: Dow Jones & Company, Inc.
Ed: Jim McTague. **Description:** Candidates in the 2008 US presidential election, like the current administration, do not and will not bash the Federal Reserve. The Federal Reserve's aggressive interest rate cuts hurt the incomes of people depending on their savings accounts.

26904 ■ "Capital Ideas: Regions to Lansing: Focus on Taxes, Reform, Keeping Talent" in *Crain's Detroit Business* (Vol. 24, October 6, 2008)
Pub: Crain Communications, Inc.
Ed: Amy Lane. **Description:** Michigan must make bold and dramatic changes in public policy regarding business legislation. The tax structure, unemployment issues and attracting and retaining talent are among the issues the state must confront, especially in this tough economic climate.

26905 ■ "The Carbon Equation" in *Canadian Business* (Vol. 81, October 27, 2008, No. 18, pp. 109)
Pub: Rogers Media Ltd.
Ed: Jack M. Mintz. **Description:** Economic and environmental impacts of the likely rejection of a carbon tax for the cap-and-trade system in Canada are discussed. The Conservative Party is expected tow in the 2008 elections and would likely pursue the cap-and-trade system.

26906 ■ "The Case of the Deflated IPO" in *Boston Business Journal* (Vol. 29, June 24, 2011, No. 7, pp. 1)
Pub: American City Business Journals Inc.
Ed: Scott Dance. **Description:** IPO market is on the rebound from the recession but for some companies in Maryland, the time is not yet ripe to go public. One of the companies that chooses to wait for better timing is SafeNet Inc. and it is eyeing some possible acquisitions while doing so.

26907 ■ "Cash for Appliances Targets HVAC Products, Water Heaters" in *Contractor* (Vol. 56, October 2009, No. 10, pp. 1)
Pub: Penton Media, Inc.
Ed: Candace Roulo. **Description:** States and territories would need to submit a full application that specifies their implementation plans if they are interested in joining the Cash for Appliances program funded by the American Recovery and Reinvestment Act. The Department of Energy urges states to focus on heating and cooling equipment, appliances and water heaters since these offer the greatest energy savings potential.

26908 ■ "Cashing In: Gleaning an Education from Our Economic State" in *Agency Sales Magazine* (Vol. 39, August 2009, No. 8, pp. 22)
Pub: MANA
Ed: John Graham. **Description:** Businesses have learned that cutting price can kill business and being tough is normal. The recession has also taught that getting the right vision and gaining the confidence and trust of consumers are important.

26909 ■ "Casinos See College as Job Jackpot" in *The Business Journal-Serving Metropolitan Kansas City* (Vol. 26, August 1, 2008, No. 47)
Pub: American City Business Journals, Inc.
Ed: Suzanna Stagemeyer. **Description:** Wyandotte County casino managers revealed plans to develop partnerships with Kansas City Kansas Community College. The planned partnership is expected to include curriculum development and degree programs that would help train employees for the planned casinos. Other views and information on the project are presented.

26910 ■ *The Catalyst Code: The Strategies Behind the World's Most Dynamic Companies*
Pub: Harvard Business School Press
Ed: David S. Evans; Richard Schmalensee. **Released:** May 9, 2007. **Price:** $29.95. **Description:** Economic catalysts businesses can bring consumers and merchants together in order to survive in an economy where markets, consumers and technology are always changing.

26911 ■ "Catching Creatives; Detroit Group Gets Grant to Attract 1,000 Design Pros" in *Crain's Detroit Business* (March 24, 2008)
Pub: Crain Communications, Inc.
Ed: Sherri Begin. **Description:** Design Detroit was given a $200,000 planning grant by the Knight Foundation, an organization that strives to back initiatives that leverage talent and resources in each of the 26 U.S. cities it funds, to inspire strategies to attract up to 1,000 creative professionals to live in Detroit.

26912 ■ "CBC Chief: Future is Now" in *Business Courier* (Vol. 27, August 13, 2010, No. 15, pp. 1)
Pub: Business Courier
Ed: Lucy May. **Description:** Tom Williams, chairman of the Cincinnati Business Committee (CBC), maintains that politicians and business leaders must cooperate to ensure the competitiveness of the city for the 21st Century. Under Williams' leadership, the CBC has put emphasis on initiatives related to government efficiency, economic development, and public education. Williams' views on a proposed inland port are given.

26913 ■ "CBC and Chrysler Strike Deal" in *Black Enterprise* (Vol. 37, December 2006, No. 5, pp. 36)
Pub: Earl G. Graves Publishing Co. Inc.
Ed: Kiara Ashanti. **Description:** Congressional Black Foundation and Chrysler Financial have partnered to provide financial education to students at historically black colleges and universities. The prime objective of the program is to reduce the number of college students that graduate with poor credit scores and high debt.

26914 ■ "Celebrate Success. Embrace Innovation" in *Black Enterprise* (Vol. 37, February 2007, No. 7, pp. 145)
Pub: Earl G. Graves Publishing Co. Inc.
Description: 2007 Women of Power Summit provides networking opportunities, empowerment sessions, and nightly entertainment. More than 500 executive women of color are expected to attend this inspiring summit in Phoenix, February 7-10.

26915 ■ "CEO Forecast" in *Hispanic Business* (January-February 2009, pp. 34, 36)
Pub: Hispanic Business
Ed: Jessica Haro, Richard Kaplan. **Description:** As economic uncertainty fogs the future, executives turn to government contracts in order to boost business. Revenue sources, health care challenges, environmental consulting and remediation services, as well as technological strides are discussed.

26916 ■ "C'est Bon" in *Canadian Business* (Vol. 79, September 25, 2006, No. 19, pp. 39)
Pub: Rogers Media
Ed: Benoit Aubin. **Description:** Economic development of Quebec City are evaluated on the eve of its formation anniversary.

26917 ■ "Challenges, Responses and Available Resources" in *Journal of Small Business and Entrepreneurship* (Vol. 23, Winter 2010, No. 1)
Pub: Canadian Council for Small Business and Entrepreneurship
Ed: Lynne Siemens. **Description:** Rural communities and their residents are exploring the potential of small business and entrepreneurship to address the

economic changes they are facing. While these rural areas present many opportunities, business people in these areas face challenges which they must navigate to operate successfully.

26918 ■ "Change Is in the Air" in *Agency Sales Magazine* (Vol. 39, August 2009, No. 8, pp. 30)
Pub: MANA
Ed: Jack Foster. **Description:** Highlights of the Power-Motion Technology Representatives Association (PTRA) 37th Annual Conference, which projected an economic upturn, are presented. Allan Bealulieu of the Institute for Trend Research gave the positive news while Manufacturer's Agents National Association (MANA) president Brain Shirley emphasized the need to take advantage of a turnaround.

26919 ■ "Channelside On the Blocks" in *The Business Journal-Serving Greater Tampa Bay* (Vol. 28, August 29, 2008, No. 36, pp. 1)
Pub: American City Business Journals, Inc.
Ed: Michael Hinman. **Description:** In a bankruptcy auction for The Place, one of the more visible condominium projects at Channelside, the lowest bid is just below $73 a square foot. KeyBank National Association, the Key Developers Group LLC's lender, leads the auction planned for October 15, 2008. The reason behind the low minimum bid required to participate in the said action is discussed.

26920 ■ "Chasing Credit" in *Canadian Business* (Vol. 81, November 10, 2008, No. 19, pp. 59)
Pub: Rogers Media Ltd.
Ed: Joe Castaldo. **Description:** Small and medium sized companies are dealing with tightening credit because they appear riskier than usual. Some of these businesses are turning to private investors, but this is not easy since many have invested everything in the stock market. The sector is expected to weaken with the broader Canadian market in the next six months from October 2008.

26921 ■ "Cheap Deposits Fuel Bank Profits" in *Boston Business Journal* (Vol. 31, July 29, 2011, No. 27, pp. 1)
Pub: Boston Business Journal
Ed: Tim MacLaughlin. **Description:** Massachusetts-are banks increased profits primarily due to inexpensive deposits. The cheaper deposits have provided profit stability and fuel loan growth in an environment of historically low interest rates and uncertain economic recovery. Details of the banks' move to shed the more expensive certificates of deposit in favor of money market accounts are discussed.

26922 ■ "Cheap Thrills: Where to Look When You're Craving a Low-Price Wine" in *Chicago Tribune* (January 12, 2009)
Pub: McClatchy-Tribune Information Services
Ed: Bill Daley. **Description:** Wines priced $15 and above are being hit the hardest by the economic downturn while cheaper wines, specifically those priced between $3 and $6, are seeing a growth in sales.

26923 ■ "The China Connection" in *Crain's Chicago Business* (Vol. 31, March 24, 2008, No. 12, pp. 26)
Pub: Crain Communications, Inc.
Ed: Samantha Stainburn. **Description:** Interview with Ben Munoz who studied abroad in Beijing, China for three months to study international economics, e-commerce and global leadership.

26924 ■ "China Pegs Surplus at $101.9 Billion" in *Globe & Mail* (January 12, 2006, pp. B1)
Pub: CTVglobemedia Publishing Inc.
Ed: Barrie McKenna. **Description:** The reasons behind the trade surplus of $101.9 billion, in China, are presented.

26925 ■ "China Trade Deficit Costs California Jobs" in *Sacramento Business Journal* (Vol. 25, August 8, 2008, No. 23, pp. 1)
Pub: American City Business Journals, Inc.
Ed: Melanie Turner. **Description:** California topped the ranking of states with job losses because of the rising trade deficit with China, losing 325,800 jobs between 2001-2007. The U.S. has lost 2.3 million workers within the period. Other views and information on the job loses because of the trade deficit with China, are presented.

26926 ■ "China's Dagong Show" in *Canadian Business* (Vol. 83, August 17, 2010, No. 13-14, pp. 15)
Pub: Rogers Media Ltd.
Ed: Matthew McClearn. **Description:** Beijing, China-based Dagong Global Credit Rating has downgraded US credit ratings, as well as other developed countries such as Canada, while granting higher ratings to China, Russia and Brazil. However, there is a perceived disconnection between Dagong's ratings and its official pronouncements.

26927 ■ *Chinese Ethnic Business: Global and Local Perspectives*
Pub: Routledge
Ed: Eric Fong; Chiu Luk. **Released:** May 2009. **Price:** $39.95 paperback. **Description:** Globalization impacts on the development of Chinese businesses are analyzed, focusing on economic globalization of the United States, Australia, and Canada. Information is focused on economic globalization and Chinese community development, transnational linkages, local urban structures, homogenization and place attachment, as well as methodology such as ethnographic studies, historical analysis, geographic studies and statistical analysis.

26928 ■ "City a Pawn in Airlines' Chess Game" in *Business Courier* (Vol. 24, January 18, 2008, No. 41, pp. 1)
Pub: American City Business Journals, Inc.
Ed: Lisa Biank Fasig. **Description:** Delta Air Lines is under negotitaions with Northwest Airlines and UAL Corp. for a proposed merger. The deal will have a negative impact on Cincinnati as a hub regardless whether it goes to UAL or Northwest. The impacts of the planned merger on Cincinnati's labor market and airport traffic are discussed.

26929 ■ "City Sets Yamhill Makeover" in *The Business Journal-Portland* (Vol. 25, July 4, 2008, No. 17, pp. 1)
Pub: American City Business Journals, Inc.
Ed: Andy Giegerich. **Description:** City government is scheduled to redevelop Peterson's property on Yamhill Street in Portland. The redevelopment is seen as a way to better developing commercial properties in the area. Problems associated with the project, which include cost and developer selection, are also discussed.

26930 ■ "City Slickers" in *Canadian Business* (Vol. 81, March 31, 2008, No. 5, pp. 36)
Pub: Rogers Media
Ed: Joe Castaldo. **Description:** Richard Florida believes that the creative class drives the economy and the prosperity of countries depends on attracting and retaining these people. Florida has brought attention to developing livable and economically vibrant cities thanks in part to his promotional skills. However, he has also drawn critics who see his data on his theories as flimsy and inadequate.

26931 ■ "Clean-Tech Focus Sparks Growth" in *Philadelphia Business Journal* (Vol. 28, January 15, 2010, No. 48, pp. 1)
Pub: American City Business Journals
Ed: Peter Key. **Description:** Keystone Redevelopment Group and economic development organization Ben Franklin Technology Partners of Southeastern Pennsylvania have partnered in supporting the growth of new alternative energy and clean technology companies. Keystone has also been developing the Bridge Business Center.

26932 ■ "Closed Minds and Open Skies" in *Barron's* (Vol. 88, March 10, 2008, No. 10, pp. 50)
Pub: Dow Jones & Company, Inc.
Ed: Thomas Donlan. **Description:** American politicians have closed minds when it comes to fair trade. The American government must not interfere with the country's manufacturing industries or worry about outsourcing defense contracts to European aerospace company Airbus.

26933 ■ "Clothier Delays Opening" in *The Business Journal-Serving Metropolitan Kansas City* (Vol. 27, November 14, 2008, No. 10, pp. 1)
Pub: American City Business Journals, Inc.
Ed: Suzanna Stagemeyer. **Description:** Jos A. Bank Clothiers Inc. has delayed the opening of its store at the Kansas City Power and Light District in Missouri for the first quarter of 2009. The company is still waiting for other tenants to open shop in the district. Comments from officials concerning the retail sector are also presented.

26934 ■ *Code of Federal Regulations: Title 13: Business Credit and Assistance*
Pub: United States Government Printing Office
Ed: Department of Commerce Staff. **Released:** May 2007. **Price:** $55.00. **Description:** Title 13 covers regulations governing the activities of the Small Business Administration and the Department of Commerce. Book covers information on business credit, finance, and economic development.

26935 ■ "Collection Industry Fights Stigma, Lagging Payments" in *Crain's Cleveland Business* (Vol. 30, June 8, 2009, No. 22, pp. 15)
Pub: Crain Communications, Inc.
Ed: Joel Hammond. **Description:** John Murray, co-owner and president of JP Recovery Services Inc. in Rocky River, Ohio discusses the burden of the collection industry during a financial crisis like a recession. Statistical data included.

26936 ■ *A Colossal Failure of Common Sense: The Inside Story of the Collapse of Lehman Brothers*
Pub: Crown Business
Ed: Lawrence G. McDonald, Patrick Robinson. **Released:** 2009. **Price:** $27.00. **Description:** Former employee of Lehman Brothers details the failure of leadership that led to the demise of the company.

26937 ■ "The Colt Effect" in *Hawaii Business* (Vol. 53, January 2008, No. 7, pp. 30)
Pub: Hawaii Business Publishing
Ed: David K. Choo. **Description:** Participation at the Bowl Championship Games can help the University of Hawaii financially. Playing at a prominent sports event could provoke donations from alumni and increase enrollment at the university. Examples of universities that earned generous income by becoming a part of prestigious sporting events are presented.

26938 ■ "Coming: Cheaper Oil and a Stronger Buck" in *Barron's* (Vol. 88, March 24, 2008, No. 12, pp. 53)
Pub: Dow Jones & Company, Inc.
Ed: Lawrence C. Strauss. **Description:** Carl C. Weinberg, the chief economist of High Frequency Economics, forecasts that Chinese economic growth will slow down and that oil prices will drop to $80 a barrel in 2008. He also believes that the US dollar will start rising the moment the Federal Reserve stops cutting interest rates.

26939 ■ "Coming Soon: Bailouts of Fannie and Freddie" in *Barron's* (Vol. 88, July 14, 2008, No. 28, pp. 14)
Pub: Dow Jones & Co., Inc.
Ed: Jonathan R. Laing. **Description:** Assurances from the government that Fannie Mae and Freddie Mac are adequately capitalized and able to carry on their duties as guarantors or owners of over $5 trillion of U.S. home mortgages are designed to keep both entities afloat until they attempt to raise $10 billion in new equity. The government would assume any losses in a bailout and owners of the banks' papers would profit as yields drop.

26940 ■ "Commentary. Economic Trends for Small Business" in *Small Business Economic Trends* (April 2008, pp. 3)
Pub: National Federation of Independent Business
Ed: William C. Dunkelberg, Holly Wade. **Description:** Commentary on the economic trends for small businesses in the U.S. is presented. Analysis of

recession possibilities is given. Reports indicate that the number of business owners citing inflation as their number one problem is at its highest point since 1982.

26941 ■ "Commentary. On Federal Reserve's Cut of Interest Rates" in *Small Business Economic Trends* (January 2008, pp. 3)
Pub: National Federation of Independent Business
Description: Federal Reserve cut interest rates and announced its economic outlook on September 18, 2007 to stimulate spending. The cut in interest rates, however, may not help in supporting consumer spending because savers may lose interest income. The expected economic impact of the interest rate cuts and the U.S. economic outlook are also discussed.

26942 ■ "Commentary" in *Small Business Economic Trends* (September 2010, pp. 3)
Pub: National Federation of Independent Business
Ed: William C. Dunkelberg, Holly Wade. **Description:** A commentary on the economic trends for small businesses in the U.S. is presented. An analysis of the unemployment rate and inflation is given. Economic growth is also expected to remain sub-par for some time, unless new policies are introduced.

26943 ■ "Commentary. Small Business Economic Trends" in *Small Business Economic Trends* (February 2008, pp. 3)
Pub: National Federation of Independent Business
Ed: William C. Dunkelberg, Holly Wade. **Description:** Commentary on the economic trends for small businesses in the U.S. is presented. Analysis of the U.S. Federal Reserve Board's efforts to prevent a recession is given. Reduction in business inventories is also discussed.

26944 ■ "Commentary: US Economic Recovery and Policy" in *Small Business Economic Trends* (July 2010, pp. 3)
Pub: National Federation of Independent Business
Description: U.S. Government is making economic recovery difficult, with one of the largest tax increases in history arriving in six months. Meanwhile, Congress is looking into taxing successful businesses, which will potentially hamper growth and real investment. Other insights on the government's role in the country's economic growth are presented.

26945 ■ "Commitment Issues" in *Workforce Management* (Vol. 88, November 16, 2009, No. 12, pp. 20)
Pub: Crain Communications, Inc.
Ed: Ed Frauenheim. **Description:** Employee engagement refers to how committed workers are to their company and how much extra effort they are willing to put in on the job; firms could find that they are having a more difficult time coming out of the recession if they lack this important feature in workplace relations.

26946 ■ *Common Sense Business: Starting, Operating, and Growing Your Small Business-In Any Economy!*
Pub: HarperInformation
Ed: Steve Gottry. **Released:** July 2005. **Price:** $19.95 (US), $26.95 (Canadian). **Description:** Strategies for starting, operating and growing a small business in any economy. .

26947 ■ "Companies Must Innovate, Regardless of Economy" in *Crain's Detroit Business* (Vol. 25, June 1, 2009, No. 22, pp. M007)
Pub: Crain Communications Inc. - Detroit
Ed: Sherri Begin Welch. **Description:** Despite the economy, leaders of Michigan's successful companies stress that small businesses must innovate in order to grow.

26948 ■ "Competition At Last?" in *Canadian Business* (Vol. 81, July 22, 2008, No. 12-13, pp. 7)
Pub: Rogers Media Ltd.
Description: Competition Policy Review Panel's 'Compete to Win' report revealed that Canada is being 'hollowed-out' by foreign acquisitions. The panel investigated competition and foreign investment policies in Canada. Key information on the report, as well as views on the Investment Canada Act and the Competition Act, is presented.

26949 ■ *The Complete Idiot's Guide to Starting and Running a Thrift Store*
Pub: Alpha Publishing House
Ed: Ravel Buckley, Carol Costa. **Released:** January 5, 2010. **Price:** $18.95. **Description:** Thrift stores saw a 35 percent increase in sales during the falling economy in 2008. Despite the low startup costs, launching and running a thrift store is complicated. Two experts cover the entire process, including setting up a store on a nonprofit basis, choosing a location, funding, donations for saleable items, recruiting and managing staff, sorting items, pricing, and recycling donations.

26950 ■ "Concierges Get New Marching Orders" in *New York Times* (Vol. 158, January 11, 2009, No. 54552, pp. 1)
Pub: New York Times Co./Globe Newspaper Co.
Ed: Vivian S. Toy. **Description:** Effects of the slowing economy are felt by individuals working as concierges.

26951 ■ "Condominium Sales Fall to a Seven-Year Low" in *Crain's Chicago Business* (Vol. 31, November 10, 2008, No. 45, pp. 2)
Pub: Crain Communications, Inc.
Ed: Alby Gallun. **Description:** Downtown Chicago condominium market is experiencing the lowest number of sales in years due to the tightening of the mortgage lending market, the Wall Street crisis and the downturn in the economy. The supply of new condos is soaring, the result of the building boom of 2005 and 2006; many developers are finding it difficult to pay off construction loans and fear foreclosure on their properties. Additional information and statistical data related to the downtown condominium market is provided.

26952 ■ "Confidence High, But Lenders More Cautious" in *Farmer's Weekly* (March 28, 2008, No. 320)
Pub: Reed Business Information
Description: Discusses the effect of the global credit crunch on farmers as well as recent auctions which were timed to beat changes to capital gains tax.

26953 ■ "Consumers Finding It Harder to Get and Keep Credit" in *Chicago Tribune* (January 10, 2009)
Pub: McClatchy-Tribune Information Services
Ed: Susan Chandler. **Description:** Five tips to maintain a good credit rating in these economic times are outlined and discussed.

26954 ■ "Contractors Fret Over Credit, People, Government" in *Contractor* (Vol. 57, February 2010, No. 2, pp. 7)
Pub: Penton Media, Inc.
Ed: Robert P. Mader. **Description:** Telephone interviews with 22 plumbing and HVAC contractors reveal that only two had sales increases for 2009 and that overall, contractors were down anywhere from seven to 25 percent. In the repair/service market, the residential sector was holding its own but the commercial portion was lagging behind.

26955 ■ "Conversation: Historian Geoffrey Jones On Why Knowledge Stays Put" in *Harvard Business Review* (Vol. 86, July-August 2008, No. 8)
Pub: Harvard Business School Press
Ed: Gardiner Morse. **Description:** Geoffrey Jones, Harvard Business School's professor of business history, discusses factors that cause knowledge to concentrate in particular regions, rather than disperse, such as the location of wealth.

26956 ■ "Conversation Starters for the Holiday" in *Barron's* (Vol. 89, July 6, 2009, No. 27, pp. 7)
Pub: Dow Jones & Co., Inc.
Ed: Michael Santoli. **Description:** Investors are concerned that the US will experience high inflation due to low interest rates and improved money supply. US consumer spending has increased to 70 percent of gross domestic product, brought by health-care spending increases, while savings rates have risen to 6.9 percent.

26957 ■ "A Conversation With Money Manager William Vellon" in *Crain's Chicago Business* (Vol. 31, November 17, 2008, No. 46, pp. 4)
Pub: Crain Communications, Inc.
Ed: Mike Colias. **Description:** Interview with William Vellon, the executive vice-president of Kingsbury Capital Investment Advisors; Vellon discusses ways in which the government can help the financial sector, his client base and bargains that investors should consider.

26958 ■ "A Conversation with; Renea Butler, Real Estate One Inc." in *Crain's Detroit Business* (Vol. 25, June 8, 2009, No. 23, pp. 12)
Pub: Crain Communications Inc. - Detroit
Ed: Ryan Beene. **Description:** Renea Butler, vice president of administration and human resources for Real Estate One Inc. in Southfield as well as vice president for public relations for the Human Resource Association of Greater Detroit, talks about how the economy has affected human resource services.

26959 ■ "A Conversation With Steven Hilfinger, Foley & Lardner L.L.P." in *Crain's Detroit Business* (Vol. 24, March 24, 2008, No. 12, pp. 1)
Pub: Crain Communications, Inc.
Description: Interview with Steven Hilfinger who is a member of Foley & Lardner L.L.P.'s mergers and acquisitions practice and is co-chair of its automotive industry team. Hilfinger discusses such issues as the role a board of directors can play in the M&A process and the future of the auto market.

26960 ■ "Cool Jobs in Hot Markets" in *Canadian Business* (Vol. 80, March 26, 2007, No. 7, pp. 66)
Pub: Rogers Media
Ed: Marlene Rego. **Description:** The growth in employment opportunities in various parts of the Canada is analyzed.

26961 ■ "Coping With a Shrinking Planet" in *Agency Sales Magazine* (Vol. 39, December 2009, No. 11, pp. 46)
Pub: MANA
Ed: Mark Young. **Description:** China and India are forcing big changes in the world and are posing a huge threat to U.S. manufacturers and their sales representatives. Reps may want to consider expanding into these territories. Helping sell American products out of the country presents an opportunity for economic expansion.

26962 ■ "Cornered by Credit; As $1 Billion in Loans Come Due, Will Landlords Find Funds?" in *Crain's Detroit Business* (October 6, 2008)
Pub: Crain Communications, Inc.
Ed: Daniel Duggan. **Description:** Conduit loans are used by many real estate investors and are normally issued in 7- to 10-year terms with balloon payments due at the end, requiring the full balance to be paid upon maturity. Many building owners may find their properties going into foreclosure as these loans mature next year since these loans cannot be extended like typical loans and the credit crisis along with falling property values is making it more difficult to secure new sources of funding. Possible solutions to this problem are also explored.

26963 ■ "Corporate Elite Show Resilience" in *The Business Journal-Serving Greater Tampa Bay* (Vol. 28, August 1, 2008, No. 32, pp. 1)
Pub: American City Business Journals, Inc.
Ed: Margie Manning; Alexis Muellner. **Description:** Stocks of the largest public companies in Tampa Bay, Florida, outperformed the S&P 500 index by 28 percent in the first half of 2008. The escalation is attributed to the growth orientation of the companies in the area and the lack of exposure to the real estate and financial services sectors.

26964 ■ "Corporation, Be Good! The Story of Corporate Social Responsibility" in *Business and Society* (December 2007, pp. 479-485)
Pub: Sage Publications USA
Ed: David M. Wasieleski. **Description:** Review of the book, "Corporation, Be Good! The Story of Corporate Social Responsibility" is presented. The book examines the importance of corporate responsibility and its economic impact.

26965 ■ "Council Power Shift Could Benefit Business" in *Business Courier* (Vol. 26, November 6, 2009, No. 28, pp. 1)
Pub: American City Business Journals, Inc.
Ed: Lucy May. **Description:** A majority in the Cincinnati City Council, which is comprised of reelected members, might be created by Charlie Winburn's impending return to the council. It would be empowered to decide on public safety, stock options taxes, and environmental justice. How the presumed majority would affect the city's economic progress is discussed.

26966 ■ "Count Out The Consumer" in *Barron's* (Vol. 88, July 7, 2008, No. 27, pp. 10)
Pub: Dow Jones & Co., Inc.
Description: American consumers are not expected to give the US economy its much-needed boost as the rising food and energy prices are taking their toll. US consumers have cut spending on utilities and food and are increasing their use of credit cards.

26967 ■ "Countdown" in *Canadian Business* (Vol. 81, March 3, 2008, No. 3, pp. 27)
Pub: Rogers Media
Ed: Al Rosen. **Description:** According to a recent poll only 42 percent of portfolio managers in Canada are aware that the country is planning to adopt the International Financial Reporting Standards beginning 2011. The shift to the new standards will have significant impacts on investment values and will be the biggest revolution in Canadian financial reporting. The effects of the transition on portfolio managers and investors are analyzed.

26968 ■ "Counting on Engagement at Ernst and Young" in *Workforce Management* (Vol. 88, November 16, 2009, No. 12, pp. 25)
Pub: Crain Communications, Inc.
Ed: Ed Frauenheim. **Description:** Employee engagement has been difficult to maintain through the recession but firms such as Ernst & Young have found that the effort to keep their employees loyal has paid off.

26969 ■ "Courier 250 Companies Hope to Rebound From 2009" in *Business Courier* (Vol. 27, July 16, 2010, No. 11, pp. 1)
Pub: Business Courier
Ed: Dan Monk, Jon Newberry. **Description:** Private companies that are featured in the Courier 250 publication have lost almost $4 billion in revenue, while combined sales dropped by 11 percent to 32 billion in 2009. Courier 250 is a guide to public companies, large nonprofits, private firms, and other related entities in Ohio's Cincinnati region.

26970 ■ "CPI, Coal Lead Local Stock Decline" in *Saint Louis Business Journal* (Vol. 32, October 14, 2011, No. 7, pp. 1)
Pub: Saint Louis Business Journal
Ed: Greg Edwards. **Description:** Coal companies and CPI Corporation were among those whose stocks have declined in St. Louis, Missouri. The stocks of local firms have plunged by 28 percent during the first nine months of 2011.

26971 ■ "Craig Muhlhauser" in *Canadian Business* (Vol. 81, September 15, 2008, No. 14-15, pp. 6)
Pub: Rogers Media Ltd.
Ed: Andrew Wahl. **Description:** Interview with Craig Muhlhauser who is the CEO of Celestica, a manufacturing company that provides services for the electronics sector; Muhlhauser discusses the company's restructuring program, which he feels was the secret to their surprising first-quarter results. Muhlhauser states that the company is operating with more forward visibility and that understanding the opportunities during the current economic situation presents the biggest challenge.

26972 ■ *Crash Proof 2.0: How to Profit From the Economic Collapse*
Pub: John Wiley & Sons, Inc.
Ed: Peter D. Schiff. **Released:** September 22, 2009. **Price:** $27.95. **Description:** Factors that will affect financial stability in the coming years are explained. A three step plan to battle the current economic downturn is also included.

26973 ■ "'Crazy' Or Not, Restaurateurs Are Finding Ways to Open New Eateries" in *Baltimore Business Journal* (Vol. 28, October 8, 2010)
Pub: Baltimore Business Journal
Ed: Joanna Sullivan. **Description:** New restaurants have been opening in Maryland. However, 515 restaurants have closed down due to the economic crisis. Comments from restaurateurs are also provided.

26974 ■ "The Credit Crisis Continues" in *Barron's* (Vol. 88, March 10, 2008, No. 10, pp. M12)
Pub: Dow Jones & Company, Inc.
Ed: Randall W. Forsyth. **Description:** Short-term Treasury yields dropped to new cyclical lows in early March 2008, with the yield for the two-year Treasury note falling to 1.532 percent. Spreads of the mortgage-backed securities of Fannie Mae and Freddie Mac rose on suspicion of collapses in financing.

26975 ■ "Credit Crisis Puts Market in Unprecedented Territory" in *Crain's New York Business* (Vol. 24, January 7, 2008, No. 1, pp. 14)
Pub: Crain Communications, Inc.
Ed: Aaron Elstein. **Description:** Banks are being forced to take enormous losses due to investors who are refusing to buy anything linked to subprime mortgages and associated securities.

26976 ■ "Credit Crunch Gives, Takes Away" in *The Business Journal-Serving Metropolitan Kansas City* (Vol. 27, October 17, 2008, No. 5, pp. 1)
Pub: American City Business Journals, Inc.
Ed: Suzanna Stagemeyer. **Description:** Although many Kansas City business enterprises have been adversely affected by the U.S. credit crunch, others have remained relatively unscathed. Examples of how local businesses are being impacted by the crisis are provided including: American Trailer & Storage Inc., which declared bankruptcy after failing to pay a long-term loan; and NetStandard, a technology firm who, on the other hand, is being pursued by prospective lenders.

26977 ■ "Credit Crunch Takes Bite Out Of McDonald's" in *Advertising Age* (Vol. 79, September 29, 2008, No. 36, pp. 1)
Pub: Crain Communications, Inc.
Ed: Emily Bryson York. **Description:** McDonald's will delay its launch of coffee bars inside its restaurants due to the banking crisis which has prompted Bank of America to halt loans to the franchise chains.

26978 ■ "Critics: Efforts to Fix Loans Won't Stop Foreclosure Wave" in *Business First Columbus* (Vol. 25, November 14, 2008, No. 12, pp. A1)
Pub: American City Business Journals
Ed: Adrian Burns. **Description:** Efforts by U.S. banks to help homeowners pay mortgages are seen to have little if any impact on foreclosures. Banks have announced plans to identify and aid troubled borrowers. Statistical data included.

26979 ■ "Crouching Tigers Spring to Life" in *Globe & Mail* (April 14, 2007, pp. B1)
Pub: CTVglobemedia Publishing Inc.
Ed: Grant Robertson. **Description:** The prospects of the acquisition of BCE Inc, by Canadian pension funds are discussed. The effect of the growth of these pension funds on the Canadian economy is described.

26980 ■ "Crude Awakening" in *Canadian Business* (Vol. 81, October 27, 2008, No. 18, pp. 14)
Pub: Rogers Media Ltd.
Ed: Jeff Sanford. **Description:** Jim Grays believes that a global liquid fuels crisis is coming and hopes the expected transition from oil dependence will be smooth. Charles Maxwell, on the other hand, predicts that a new world economy will arrive in three waves. Views of both experts are examined.

26981 ■ "Cruising In Choppy Water" in *The Business Journal-Portland* (Vol. 25, August 22, 2008, No. 24, pp. 1)
Pub: American City Business Journals, Inc.
Ed: Erik Siemers. **Description:** Yacht builder Christensen Shipyards Inc. is experiencing robust business despite the slowing US economy, building four yachts a year as of 2008. The company expects revenues to hit $90 million and is opening a 500,000-square-foot plant in Tennessee.

26982 ■ "The Cudgel of Samson" in *Barron's* (Vol. 88, March 24, 2008, No. 12, pp. 62)
Pub: Dow Jones & Company, Inc.
Ed: Thomas G. Donlan. **Description:** Discusses the Federal Reserve is jawboning businesses against inflation while inflation is starting to rise because of the abundance of cheap money. The practice of jawboning has been used by the administrations of past US presidents with limited effect.

26983 ■ "Daley's Efforts to Ease Traffic Woes Fall Short" in *Crain's Chicago Business* (Vol. 31, May 5, 2008, No. 18, pp. 18)
Pub: Crain Communications, Inc.
Description: Discusses some of the inherent problems of Mayor Daley's plan to reduce traffic congestion by creating a tax on drivers who park their cars downtown during peak traffic periods and putting articulated buses on new bus-only lanes on major arterial streets leading into the Loop.

26984 ■ "Darkness Falling..." in *Barron's* (Vol. 89, July 20, 2009, No. 29, pp. 13)
Pub: Dow Jones & Co., Inc.
Description: Newsletter writer Arch Crawford believes that market indicators signal a possible downturn in US stock markets. High risk areas also include China and Japan .

26985 ■ "Datebook" in *Crain's Chicago Business* (Vol. 31, April 28, 2008, No. 17, pp. 18)
Pub: Crain Communications, Inc.
Description: Listing of events in the Detroit area include conferences addressing entrepreneurialism, economic development, and women business ownership.

26986 ■ "David Azrieli" in *Canadian Business* (Vol. 82, April 27, 2009, No. 7, pp. 54)
Pub: Rogers Media
Ed: Alex Mlynek. **Description:** David Azrieli wants to take advantage of opportunities, revealing that he has increased his portfolio nearly every recession. Azrieli has recently purchased properties of General Electric near the Toronto airport for about $100 million. He believes the economy will rebound in the second half of 2009.

26987 ■ "Deal With Tribes Revives Revenue Stream" in *Crain's Detroit Business* (Vol. 24, March 24, 2008, No. 12, pp. 6)
Pub: Crain Communications, Inc.
Ed: Amy Lane. **Description:** Michigan Bureau of State Lottery's 2003 launch of its Club Keno game caused the Little River Band of Ottawa Indians and the Little Traverse Bay Bands of Odawa Indians to halt payments of shared casino revenue with the state. The federal lawsuit that resulted has now been settled and tribal revenue-sharing will resume as well as $26 million in previous payments to the state of Michigan that the tribes had put into escrow.

26988 ■ "Dealers Trying Not to Fold" in *Business First Columbus* (Vol. 25, December 5, 2008, No. 15, pp. A1)
Pub: American City Business Journals
Ed: Dan Eaton. **Description:** Increase in the number of automobile dealer closures in Ohio is seen to impact the state's economy. The trend of consolidation is forecasted to adversely affect employment and sales. Statistical data included.

26989 ■ "Debut Year Brings Success for Bike-Trail Boosters" in *Business Courier* (Vol. 24, January 4, 2008, No. 39, pp. 4)
Pub: American City Business Journals, Inc.
Ed: Dan Monk. **Description:** Discusses the first year of Cincinnati's Trail Yeah has brought in success as five local government boards approve the bike-trail enthusiast group's endorsement of a cycling path that would connect the city's downtown to the Loveland Bike Trail. The group is planning to raise $3 million to $5 million for the trails first phase.

26990 ■ "Decline in Assets Is Costly for Advisers" in *The Business Journal-Serving Metropolitan Kansas City* (Vol. 27, October 24, 2008)
Pub: American City Business Journals, Inc.
Ed: James Dornbrook. **Description:** Financial advisers in the Kansas City, Missouri area are forced to cut costs as their assets have decreased sharply due to the huge drop in stock prices. American Century Investments was forced to diversify into foreign assets and cut 90 jobs as its assets dropped to $84 billion. Diversification has softened the impact of the steep decline in stock prices for Waddell & Reed Financial Inc.

26991 ■ "Dedge Rejects Inflation Concerns" in *Globe & Mail* (January 26, 2007, pp. B3)
Pub: CTVglobemedia Publishing Inc.
Ed: Heather Scoffield. **Description:** The rejection of concern over inflation by Governor of the Bank of Canada David Dodge and his views on checking inflation in Alberta are discussed.

26992 ■ "Defying Gravity?" in *Canadian Business* (Vol. 81, October 13, 2008, No. 17, pp. 17)
Pub: Rogers Media Ltd.
Ed: Joe Castaldo. **Description:** Airlines around the world are expected to lose $4.1 billion in 2009, but experts believe Canadian airlines will be able to survive the economic challenges. Lower demand for air travel and uncertainty on oil prices are also expected to make the conditions more challenging. Views and key information on airlines in Canada and around the world are cited.

26993 ■ "Department of Agriculture" in *Ice Cream Reporter* (Vol. 23, November 20, 2010, No. 12, pp. 8)
Pub: Ice Cream Reporter
Description: Department of Agriculture notes that food price inflation for 2010 will be at its lowest since 1992.

26994 ■ "Despite Economic Upheaval Generation Y is Still Feeling Green: RSA Canada Survey" in *CNW Group* (October 28, 2010)
Pub: CNW Group
Description: Canadian Generation Y individuals believe it is important for their company to be environmentally-friendly and one-third of those surveyed would quit their job if they found their employer was environmentally irresponsible, despite the economy.

26995 ■ "Despite Gloom, Auto Sales Saw Gains in 2005" in *Globe & Mail* (January 5, 2006, pp. B1)
Pub: CTVglobemedia Publishing Inc.
Ed: Greg Keenan. **Description:** An overview of positve automotive sales in Canada, for 2005, is presented.

26996 ■ "Detroit 3's Fall Would Be a Big One in Ohio" in *Business First Columbus* (Vol. 25, November 28, 2008, No. 14, pp. A1)
Pub: American City Business Journals
Ed: Dan Eaton. **Description:** Ohio's economy will suffer huge negative effects in the event of a failure of one or more of the automotive companies, General Motors Corporation, Ford Motor Company, or Chrysler LLC. The state is home to 97,900 jobs in the automotive industry and is a vital link to the industry's supply network.

26997 ■ "Detroit Residential Market Slows; Bright Spots Emerge" in *Crain's Detroit Business* (Vol. 24, October 6, 2008, No. 40, pp. 11)
Pub: Crain Communications, Inc.
Ed: Daniel Duggan. **Description:** Discusses the state of the residential real estate market in Detroit; although condominium projects receive the most attention, deals for single-family homes are taking place in greater numbers due to financing issues. Buyers can purchase a single family home with a 3.5 percent down payment compared to 20 percent for some condo deals because of the number of first-time homebuyer programs under the Federal Housing Administration.

26998 ■ "Detroit Scores When Tigers Play; Studies Predict Winning Economy" in *Crain's Detroit Business* (Vol. 24, March 31, 2008, No. 13)
Pub: Crain Communications, Inc.
Ed: Bill Shea. **Description:** East Lansing-based Anderson Economic Group and the Detroit Regional Chamber predict that the economic impact of the Detroit Tigers will be very positive for the region due to an unexpected World Series trip two years ago followed by another strong season in 2007, player acquisitions and the popular Jim Leyland again managing the team. Statistical data included.

26999 ■ "Developer Banks On East Submarket, Slowdown Not a Hinderance" in *The Business Journal-Serving Greater Tampa Bay* (August 1, 2008)
Pub: American City Business Journals, Inc.
Ed: Janet Leiser. **Description:** CLW Industrial Group and Cobalt Industrial REIT II have teamed up to develop a 14-acre area in northeast Hillsborough County, Florida. The $15 million industrial park project includes the 175,000-square-foot New Tampa Commerce Center, scheduled for completion in the first quarter of 2009.

27000 ■ "Developers Await Hotel" in *The Business Journal-Portland* (Vol. 25, July 11, 2008, No. 18, pp. 1)
Pub: American City Business Journals, Inc.
Ed: Wendy Culverwell. **Description:** Developers are eager to start the construction of a new hotel at the Oregon Convention Center in Portland, Oregon as hey say that the project will help boost the convention center neighborhood. The project, called The Westin Portland at the Convention Center, is partly handled by Ashforth Pacific Inc.

27001 ■ *Developmental Entrepreneurship: Adversity, Risk, and Isolation*
Pub: Elsevier Science and Technology Books
Ed: Craig Galbraith. **Released:** August 2006. **Price:** $99.95. **Description:** Volume five of the series, this book focuses on the fields of entrepreneurship, sociology, and economics. Fifteen articles related to entrepreneurship and small business development within a global environment are included.

27002 ■ "Diary of a Short-Seller" in *Conde Nast Portfolio* (Vol. 2, June 2008, No. 6, pp. 44)
Pub: Conde Nast Publications, Inc.
Ed: Jesse Eisinger. **Description:** Profile of David Einhorn who is a fund manager that spoke out against finance company Allied Capital whose stock fell nearly 20 percent the day after Einhorn's critique; Einhorn subsequently had to contend with attacks against his credibility as well as investigations by the S.E.C.; Einhorn's experience illuminates our current economic crisis.

27003 ■ "Dick Evans" in *Canadian Business* (Vol. 82, April 27, 2009, No. 7, pp. 78)
Pub: Rogers Media
Ed: Sean Silcoff. **Description:** Former Rio Tinto Alcan chief executive officer Dick Evans believes that the 1982 downturn was worse than the current recession, at least for the mining sector. He also believes that while people are anxious, there is confidence that the economy will recover in two to three years. Key information on Evans, as well as his other views on being a CEO is presented.

27004 ■ "Different This Time?" in *Canadian Business* (Vol. 81, April 14, 2008, No. 6, pp. 38)
Pub: Rogers Media
Ed: Matthew McClearn. **Description:** Irving Fisher believed that the low interest rates of the 1920's spurred investors to borrow and use the money to speculate with the proceeds thereby increasing the debt to unmanageable levels prior to the stock market crash in Oct. 29, 1929. The U.S. economic conditions in 1929 and U.S. economic conditions in 2008 are discussed.

27005 ■ "Dirty Work Required" in *Workforce Management* (Vol. 88, November 16, 2009, No. 12, pp. 34)
Pub: Crain Communications, Inc.
Ed: John Hollon. **Description:** Due to salary freezes, pay cuts, layoffs, buyouts and a number of other stress factors brought about by the recession, employee engagement has been difficult to maintain by managers.

27006 ■ "Do You Have A Retirement Parachute?" in *Barron's* (Vol. 88, July 7, 2008, No. 27, pp. 32)
Pub: Dow Jones & Co., Inc.
Ed: Jane White. **Description:** The idea that American companies should emulate the Australian retirement system which implements a forced contribution rate for all employers regarding an adequate retirement plan for their employees is discussed.

27007 ■ "Dr. Mark Holder" in *Crain's Cleveland Business* (Vol. 30, June 29, 2009, No. 25, pp. 14)
Pub: Crain Communications, Inc.
Ed: Kathy Ames Carr. **Description:** Dr. Mark Holder is the director of the financial engineering program at Kent State University. Dr. Holder discusses his role to help teach his students how to market themselves for finance jobs in a down economy.

27008 ■ "Dodge Pushes Reform Agenda" in *Globe & Mail* (February 6, 2006, pp. B1)
Pub: CTVglobemedia Publishing Inc.
Ed: Heather Scoffield. **Description:** The impact of variations in global economy, on Canadian economy, is discussed. The recommendations of Governor David Dodge of Bank of Canada to resolve the issue are presented.

27009 ■ "Dodge Slashes Growth Estimate" in *Globe & Mail* (January 19, 2007, pp. B3)
Pub: CTVglobemedia Publishing Inc.
Ed: Heather Scoffield. **Description:** Bank of Canada Governor David Dodge decision to keep the interest rate 4.25 percent despite a slowdown in the economy is discussed.

27010 ■ "Does it Add Up?" in *Canadian Business* (Vol. 81, October 13, 2008, No. 17, pp. 18)
Pub: Rogers Media Ltd.
Ed: Jack Mintz. **Description:** Views on Canada's tax policy, as well as on tax reforms planned by major parties and their expected economic impact are discussed. The Tories' proposal to cut federal diesel fuel tax is seen as politically smart, but reforms on other taxes could help generate economic growth. High income tax rates are believed to discourage talented individuals from working in Canada.

27011 ■ "The Dogs of TSX" in *Canadian Business* (Vol. 81, Summer 2008, No. 9, pp. 77)
Pub: Rogers Media Ltd.
Ed: Calvin Leung. **Description:** Table showing the one-year stock performance of the ten highest dividend-yielding stocks on the S&P/TSX 60 Compos-

ite Index is presented. This technique is similar to the 'Dogs of the Dow' approach. The idea in this investment strategy is to buy equal amounts of stocks from these companies and selling them a year later, and then repeat the process.

27012 ■ "Dollar Daze: Canadian Businesses Must Adjust to a New Reality" in *Canadian Business* (Vol. 80, Winter 2007, No. 24, pp. 11)
Pub: Rogers Media
Ed: Jeff Sanford. **Description:** Several Canadian businessmen lost massive amounts in the Canadian value of their investments due to the volatility of the U.S. dollar. The factors that weighed down the value of the U.S. dollar include the announcement by China to diversify their currency reserves away from the U.S. dollar and concerns about the price of oil.

27013 ■ "Dollar Doldrums; How American Companies are Beating the Currency Crunch" in *Inc.* (March 2008, pp. 45-46)
Pub: Gruner & Jahr USA Publishing
Ed: Sarah Goldstein. **Description:** Despite the low American dollar, some exporters are seeing a growth in their businesses, while other have had to relocate operations and switch to U.S. supplier. Four business owners tell how they are dealing with the current economic conditions.

27014 ■ "Don't Bet Against The House" in *Barron's* (Vol. 88, July 14, 2008, No. 28, pp. 20)
Pub: Dow Jones & Co., Inc.
Ed: Sandra Ward. **Description:** Shares of Nasdaq OMX have lost more than 50 percent of their value from November 2007 to July 2008 but the value of these shares could climb 50 percent on the strength of world security exchanges. Only 15 percent of the company's revenues come from the U.S. and the shares are trading at 12.5 times the amount expected for 2008.

27015 ■ "Don't Expect Quick Fix" in *The Business Journal-Serving Metropolitan Kansas City* (Vol. 27, October 3, 2008, No. 3, pp. 1)
Pub: American City Business Journals, Inc.
Ed: James Dornbrook. **Description:** United States governmental entities cannot provide a quick fix solution to the current financial crisis. The economy requires a systemic change in the way people think about credit. The financial services industry should also focus on core lending principles.

27016 ■ "Don't Get Lulled by the Calm" in *Barron's* (Vol. 89, July 27, 2009, No. 30, pp. M13)
Pub: Dow Jones & Co., Inc.
Ed: Steven M. Sears. **Description:** Options traders expect volatility to return in the fall of 2009 and to bring correlation with it. September and October are typically the most volatile months and the trick is to survive earnings season.

27017 ■ "Don't Quit When The Road Gets Bumpy" in *Women Entrepreneur* (November 25, 2008)
Pub: Entrepreneur Media Inc.
Ed: Bonnie Price. **Description:** Discusses techniques four women entrepreneurs are utilizing to keep their businesses successful despite the credit crunch and the economic downturn.

27018 ■ "The Doomsday Scenario" in *Conde Nast Portfolio* (Vol. 2, June 2008, No. 6, pp. 91)
Pub: Conde Nast Publications, Inc.
Ed: Jeffrey Rothfeder. **Description:** Detroit and the U.S. auto industry are discussed as well as the ramifications of the demise of this manufacturing base. Similarities and differences between the downfall of the U.S. steel business and the impact it had on Pittsburg, Pennsylvania is also discussed.

27019 ■ "Doubtful Donors" in *Canadian Business* (Vol. 81, December 8, 2008, No. 21, pp. 8)
Pub: Rogers Media Ltd.
Ed: Dennis Seguin. **Description:** Key information on fundraising consultancy Inspire, as well as views and information on charitable organizations in Canada is presented. Inspire designs the financial architecture of charitable foundations in Canada, which was affected by the current financial crisis. Inspire advises foundations to keep existing donors.

27020 ■ "Down Mexico Way" in *Canadian Business* (Vol. 79, September 25, 2006, No. 19, pp. 27)
Pub: Rogers Media
Description: Presidential election in Mexico and its effects on its economy is discussed.

27021 ■ "Down a 'Peg" in *Canadian Business* (Vol. 79, September 25, 2006, No. 19, pp. 41)
Pub: Rogers Media
Ed: Bryan Borzykowski. **Description:** Economic development in Canada's Winnipeg city is evaluated.

27022 ■ "Down the Tracks, a Whistle Is a Blowin" in *Barron's* (Vol. 89, July 27, 2009, No. 30, pp. 36)
Pub: Dow Jones & Co., Inc.
Ed: Jim McTague. **Description:** Higher numbers of freight-rail carloads are a sign that the economy is improving and it is no stretch to imagine that this is aided by the American Recovery and Reinvestment Act. It is also predicted that 2009 municipal bond issuance will be above $373 billion with at least $55 billion of it made up of Buy America Bonds that are subsidized by the federal government.

27023 ■ "Downtown Detroit Needs More Retail" in *Crain's Detroit Business* (Vol. 24, March 10, 2008, No. 10, pp. 9)
Pub: Crain Communications, Inc.
Ed: Robin Boyle; James Bieri. **Description:** Although Detroit is doing well with event-driven traffic, the city remains far off the site selection rosters of major national retailers as well as smaller retail outlets.

27024 ■ "Downturn Tests HCL's Pledge to Employees" in *Workforce Management* (Vol. 88, November 16, 2009, No. 12, pp. 23)
Pub: Crain Communications, Inc.
Ed: Ed Frauenheim. **Description:** HCL Technologies has kept its promise to keep from laying any employees off during the recession which served as a test for the tech firm's Employee First program, which seeks to give workers greater income security as well as a stronger voice in the firm.

27025 ■ "Dream Big! When the Going Gets Tough, Reps Work Harder and Smarter" in *Agency Sales Magazine* (Vol. 39, July 2009, No. 7, pp. 22)
Pub: MANA
Ed: John Chapin. **Description:** Sales representatives should use the tough economy as a warning and motivation to work harder and smarter. Reps should improve their selling by reading books, listening to tapes and CDs. They should also keep a good attitude and build relationships.

27026 ■ "Dream On: California's Budget Fix may not Last for Long." in *Barron's* (Vol. 89, July 27, 2009, No. 30, pp. 21)
Pub: Dow Jones & Co., Inc.
Ed: Jonathan R. Laing. **Description:** California's budget agreement which purports to eliminate a $26 billion deficit is discussed. The frequent budgetary dustups in the state calls for several reforms including a rainy day fund of 15 percent of any budget and a constitutional convention. Other reform suggestions are discussed.

27027 ■ "Dreaming in Macau" in *Canadian Business* (Vol. 81, December 8, 2008, No. 21, pp. 65)
Pub: Rogers Media Ltd.
Ed: Joe Chidley. **Description:** Key information, as well as views on the economic aspects of Macau are presented. Macau was once monopolized by Stanley Ho's Sociedad de Turismo e Diversoes de Macau, but the government transformed the area into a leisure-and-entertainment spot. Details about Cirque de Soleil are also presented.

27028 ■ "Drug, Seed Firms Offer Antidote For Inflation" in *Crain's Chicago Business* (Vol. 31, April 21, 2008, No. 16, pp. 4)
Pub: Crain Communications, Inc.
Ed: Daniel Rome Levine. **Description:** Interview with Jerrold Senser, the CEO of Institutional Capital LLC in Chicago, in which he discusses the ways that the company is adjusting to the economic slowdown and rising inflation, his favorite firms for investment and his prediction of an economic turnaround; he also recommends five companies he feels are worth investing in.

27029 ■ "DST Turns to Banks for Credit" in *The Business Journal-Serving Metropolitan Kansas City* (Vol. 27, October 3, 2008, No. 3, pp. 1)
Pub: American City Business Journals, Inc.
Ed: Rob Roberts. **Description:** Kansas City, Missouri-based DST Systems Inc., a company that provides sophisticated information processing, computer software services and business solutions, has secured a new five-year, $120 million credit facility from Enterprise Bank and Bank of the West. The deal is seen to reflect that the region and community-banking model remain stable. Comments from executives are also provided.

27030 ■ "Dueling Visions" in *Barron's* (Vol. 89, July 27, 2009, No. 30, pp. 13)
Pub: Dow Jones & Co., Inc.
Ed: Michael Santoli. **Description:** Goldman Sachs' market strategists believe the stock market has entered a "sustained-rally" mode while Morgan Stanley's strategist believes this is a "rally to sell into". What is not known in the stock market is how much of a "V"-shaped recovery in earning the market rebound has already priced in.

27031 ■ "Early Spring Halts Drilling Season" in *Globe & Mail* (March 14, 2007, pp. B14)
Pub: CTVglobemedia Publishing Inc.
Ed: Norval Scott. **Description:** Decreased petroleum productivity in Canadian oil drilling rigs due to early spring season in western regions is discussed.

27032 ■ "Easy to be Queasy" in *Canadian Business* (Vol. 81, December 24, 2007, No. 1, pp. 25)
Pub: Rogers Media
Ed: Jack Mintz. **Description:** Canada could be facing a slowdown in economic growth for 2008 as the country's economy depends on the U.S. economy, which is still facing recession in the subprime market. Details on Canada's economic growth, the impact of the weak U.S. dollar, increase in the unemployment rate, and decline in tax revenue are explored.

27033 ■ "Economic Crises Calls For Better Marketing Plans" in *Entrepreneur* (October 1, 2008)
Pub: Entrepreneur Media Inc.
Ed: Tim Berry. **Description:** Revising one's business plan is essential, especially during times of economic crisis; sales and marketing plans should be reviewed, analyzed and changed in an attempt to survive the economic downturn.

27034 ■ "Economic Crisis and Accounting Evolution" in *Accounting and Business Research* (Vol. 41, Summer 2011, No. 3, pp. 2159)
Pub: Routledge
Ed: Gregory Waymire, Sudipta Basu. **Description:** Financial reporting changes at the face of economic crises are studied using a punctuated equilibrium evolution. Findings show that financial reporting has a minor impact but may amplify economic crises. Attempts to enhance accounting and economic crises may not be as beneficial as planned.

27035 ■ *Economic Development Administration—Annual Report*
Pub: U.S. Economic Development Administration
Contact: Sandi Walters, CFO
Released: Annual, Latest edition 2010. **Covers:** Recipients of grants, grant supplements, and loan guarantees from the Economic Development Administration under the Public Works and Economic

Development Act of 1965. Projects funded include public works, business development, research, planning, and disaster recovery. **Entries Include:** Recipient name, location, date of obligation, funds received by type of assistance, type of project, identification number. **Arrangement:** Geographical.

27036 ■ "Economic Distance and the Survival of Foreign Direct Investments" in *Academy of Management Journal* (Vol. 50, No. 5, October 2007)
Pub: Academy of Management
Ed: Eric W.K. Tsang, Paul S.L. Yip. **Description:** Study was undertaken to assess the relationship between economic disparities of various countries and foreign direct investments, focusing on Singapore. Results revealed that economic distance has a definite impact on foreign direct investment hazard rates.

27037 ■ *Economic Freedom and the American Dream*
Pub: Palgrave Macmillan
Ed: Joseph Shaanan. **Released:** January 5, 2010. **Price:** $55.00. **Description:** An exploration into the effects of economic freedom on American in several areas such as markets, politics, and opportunities for would-be entrepreneurs.

27038 ■ "Economic Outlook 2009" in *Hispanic Business* (January-February 2009, pp. 30, 32)
Pub: Hispanic Business
Ed: Dr. Juan Solana. **Description:** Successful business policies of the past no longer work in this economic climate. New tools and initiatives regarding monetary policy, fiscal policy and a higher multiplier are required to survive the crisis.

27039 ■ "Economic Prognosis" in *Barron's* (Vol. 89, July 13, 2009, No. 28, pp. 11)
Pub: Dow Jones & Co., Inc.
Ed: Karen Hube. **Description:** Loomis Sayles Bond Fund manager Dan Fuss believes that the economy is bottoming and that recovery will be long and drawn out. Fuss guesses that the next peak in 10-year Treasury yields will be about 6.25% in around 4 and a half or five years ahead of 2009.

27040 ■ "Economic Stimulus Plan Needs Scrutiny" in *Crain's Detroit Business* (Vol. 24, April 7, 2008, No. 14, pp. 8)
Pub: Crain Communications, Inc.
Description: Overview of Mayor Kwame Kilpatrick's economic stimulus package which many believe needs to be scrutinized closely since the true financial status of Detroit is unclear.

27041 ■ "Economic Trends for Small Business" in *Small Business Economic Trends* (April 2008, pp. 1)
Pub: National Federation of Independent Business
Ed: William C. Dunkelberg, Holly Wade. **Description:** Summary of economic trends for small businesses in the U.S. is presented. Economic indicators such as capital spending, inventories and sales, inflation, and profits are given. Analysis of credit markets is also provided.

27042 ■ *The Economics of Entrepreneurship*
Pub: Edward Elgar Publishing, Incorporated
Ed: Parker. **Released:** April 2006. **Price:** $240.00. **Description:** Previously published articles influencing research into the economic structure of entrepreneurship are examined.

27043 ■ *The Economics and Management of Small Business: An International Perspective*
Pub: Routledge
Ed: Graham Bannock. **Released:** May 2005. **Price:** $65.00. **Description:** International perspectives on the economics and management of small business, featuring case studies and empirical research.

27044 ■ *The Economics of Self-Employment and Entrepreneurship*
Pub: Cambridge University Press
Ed: Simon C. Parker. **Released:** July 2006. **Price:** $50.00. **Description:** The importance of self-employment and entrepreneurship in a modern economy is explored.

27045 ■ *The Economics of Small Firms*
Pub: Routledge Inc.
Ed: Johnson. **Released:** December 2006. **Price:** $41.95. **Description:** Introduction to the economics of small business, covering both theoretical and empirical issues.

27046 ■ "Economy Forcing Meeting Planners to Think Fast" in *Crain's Cleveland Business* (Vol. 30, June 15, 2009, No. 23, pp. 15)
Pub: Crain Communications, Inc.
Ed: Amy Ann Stoessel. **Description:** Meeting planners are working hard to meet lower corporate budgets when planning events.

27047 ■ "Economy Peddles Rent In This Cycle" in *The Business Journal-Serving Metropolitan Kansas City* (Vol. 26, August 8, 2008, No. 48)
Pub: American City Business Journals, Inc.
Ed: Ashlee Kieler. **Description:** Rental demand for apartment units in downtown Kansas City, Missouri, is increasing due to the housing crisis, lack of real estate development, and increasing popularity of the downtown area. The downtown area has 7,378 multifamily units as of June 2008, of which 4,114 are rentals.

27048 ■ "Economy Should Play Big Role When Presidential Spotlight Returns" in *Business First-Columbus* (November 9, 2007, pp. A1)
Pub: American City Business Journals, Inc.
Ed: Jeff Bell. **Description:** Ohio leaders, including the president of Columbus Chamber, Ty Marsh, suggests that Ohio has benefited from past campaigns as candidates spend money on advertising along with the media exposure the state received. The significance of Ohio in determining the winner in the 2008 presidential elections is discussed.

27049 ■ "Editor's Note" in *Canadian Business* (Vol. 81, March 17, 2008, No. 4, pp. 7)
Pub: Rogers Media
Ed: Joe Chidley. **Description:** Canadian Consolidated government expenditures increased by an average of 4.5 percent annually from 2003 to 2007. Health care, housing, and the environment were some of the areas which experienced higher spending. However, government spending in labor, employment, and immigration dropped 6.6 percent.

27050 ■ "Effect of Oil Prices on the Economy" in *Canadian Business* (Vol. 81, September 15, 2008, No. 14-15, pp. 5)
Pub: Rogers Media Ltd.
Ed: Joe Chidley. **Description:** Rise of oil prices above $100 in February 2008 and $140 in July signals the birth of a "new economy" according to commentators; this shift is causing uneasiness from oil industry professionals who are unsure of how this trend could be sustained. Oil dropped below $120 in August, which could slow down global economic growth followed by oil demand, then oil prices.

27051 ■ *Effect of the Overvalued Dollar on Small Exporters: Congressional Hearing*
Pub: DIANE Publishing Company
Ed: Donald Manzullo. **Released:** September 2002. **Price:** $30.00. **Description:** Congressional hearing: Witnesses: Dr. Lawrence Chimerine, Economist; Tony Raimondo, President and CEO, Behlen Manufacturing Company; Robert J. Weskamp, President, Wes-Tech, Inc.; Wayne Dollar, President, Georgia Farm Bureau; and Vargese George, President and CEO, Westex International, Inc. Appendix includes correspondence sent to committee on the overvalued dollar.

27052 ■ "Egg Fight: The Yolk's on the Short" in *Barron's* (Vol. 88, July 7, 2008, No. 27, pp. 20)
Pub: Dow Jones & Co., Inc.
Ed: Christopher C. Williams. **Description:** Shares of Cal-Maine Foods, the largest egg producer and distributor in the US, are due for a huge rise because of the increase in egg prices. Short sellers, however, continue betting that the stock, priced at $31.84 each, will eventually go down.

27053 ■ *Electronic Commerce*
Pub: Course Technology
Ed: Gary Schneider, Bryant Chrzan, Charles McCormick. **Released:** May 1, 2010. **Price:** $117.95. **Description:** E-commerce can open the door to more opportunities than ever before for small business. Packed with real-world examples and cases, the book delivers comprehensive coverage of emerging online technologies and trends and their influence on the electronic marketplace. It details how the landscape of online commerce is evolving, reflecting changes in the economy and how business and society are responding to those changes. Balancing technological issues with the strategic business aspects of successful e-commerce, the new edition includes expanded coverage of international issues, social networking, mobile commerce, Web 2.0 technologies, and updates on spam, phishing, and identity theft.

27054 ■ "Elements For Success" in *Small Business Opportunities* (November 2008)
Pub: Entrepreneur Media Inc.
Description: Profile of Elements, a physical fitness club that approach a healthy lifestyle for women, which includes the components of body, beauty and mind; the network of upscale, boutique style health clubs differ from other providers in its "balanced lifestyle" approach to a healthy lifestyle. This unique niche is gaining in popularity despite the faltering economy.

27055 ■ *The Elephant and the Dragon: The Rise of India and China and What It Means to All of Us*
Pub: W.W. Norton & Company
Ed: Robyn Meredith. **Released:** 2008. **Price:** $15. 95. **Description:** The author illustrates how both China and India have followed their own economic path, and examines the countries' similarities and considers the repercussions of their growing involvement in the world market.

27056 ■ *Elsewhere, U.S.A.: How We Got From the Company Man, Family Dinners, and the Affluent Society to the Home Office, Blackberry Moms, and Economic Anxiety*
Pub: Pantheon Books
Ed: Dalton Conley. **Released:** 2009. **Price:** $24.00. **Description:** The alienation of the working middle class in America and the downturned economy is examined.

27057 ■ "Embarq Sale Sets New Tone" in *The Business Journal-Serving Metropolitan Kansas City* (Vol. 27, October 31, 2008, No. 8, pp. 1)
Pub: American City Business Journals, Inc.
Ed: Suzsanna Stagemeyer. **Description:** CenturyTel Inc. has agreed to acquire Embarq Corp., a large phone company based in Overland Park. The acquisition deal is valued at $11.6 billion. The potential impacts of the deal on Kansas City's economy are analyzed.

27058 ■ *The Emerging Digital Economy: Entrepreneurship, Clusters, and Policy*
Pub: Springer
Ed: Borje Johansson; Charlie Karlsson; Roger Stough. **Released:** August 2006. **Price:** $119.00. **Description:** The new economy, or digital economy, and its impact on the way industries and firms choose to locate and cluster geographically.

27059 ■ *The Emerging Markets Century: How a New Breed of World-Class Companies is Overtaking the World*
Pub: Free Press/Simon & Schuster Inc.
Ed: Antoine van Agtmael. **Released:** 2007. **Price:** $29.00. **Description:** An exploration of how companies like Lenovo and Haier who are presently in emerging economies are already competing with household name brands like Ford and Sony, thus proving globalization is here to stay.

27060 ■ "Empathy: An Entrepreneur's Killer App" in *Women Entrepreneur* (February 3, 2009)
Pub: Entrepreneur Media Inc.
Ed: Kristi Hedges. **Description:** It is just as important to treat employees with courtesy and respect during bad economic times as it is in a good economy. Employers sometimes take advantage of such bad economic times since they realize that employees are grateful to have a job and cannot just quit and easily find work elsewhere. The importance of empathy in a company's leadership personnel is discussed.

27061 ■ "End of the Beginning" in *Canadian Business* (Vol. 81, November 10, 2008, No. 19, pp. 17)
Pub: Rogers Media Ltd.
Ed: David Wolf. **Description:** The freeze in the money markets and historic decline in equity markets around the world finally forced governments into aggressive coordinated action. The asset price inflation brought on by cheap credit will now work in reverse and the tightening of credit will be difficult economically. Canada is exposed to the fallout everywhere, given that the U.S, the U.K. and Japan buy 30 percent of Canada's output.

27062 ■ "End of an Era" in *Barron's* (Vol. 88, July 7, 2008, No. 27, pp. 3)
Pub: Dow Jones & Co., Inc.
Ed: Alan Abelson. **Description:** June 2008 was a very bad month for US stocks, with investors losing as much as 41.9 percent in the first half of 2008 signaling an end to the financial environment that prevailed around the world since the 1980's. The US job market lost 62,000 jobs in June 2008.

27063 ■ "Endowments for Colleges Hit Hard in '09" in *Milwaukee Business Journal* (Vol. 27, February 12, 2010, No. 20, pp. A1)
Pub: American City Business Journals
Ed: Corrinne Hess. **Description:** Southeast Wisconsin college endowments declined by as much as 35 percent in 2009 due to the economic downturn. A list of 2009 endowments to colleges in southeast Wisconsin and their percent change from 2008 is presented.

27064 ■ "Enforcer In Fantasyland" in *Crain's New York Business* (Vol. 24, February 25, 2008, No. 8, pp. 10)
Pub: Crain Communications Inc.
Ed: Hilary Potkewitz. **Description:** Patent law, particularly in the toy and game industry, is recession-proof according to Barry Negrin, partner at Pryor Cashman. Negrin co-founded his patent practice group. Despite massive recalls of toys and the concern over toxic toys, legal measures are in place in this industry.

27065 ■ *The Entrepreneurial Imperative: How America's Economic Miracle Will Reshape the World (And Change Your Life)*
Pub: HarperCollins Publishers, Inc.
Ed: Carl J. Schramm. **Released:** October 2006. **Price:** $24.95. **Description:** Carl Schramm, president of Kauffman Foundation discusses the secret to America's economy.

27066 ■ "Entrepreneurs Save the World" in *Women In Business* (Vol. 61, December 2009, No. 6, pp. 12)
Pub: American Business Women's Association
Ed: Leigh Elmore. **Description:** American economic growth is attributed to small businesses but more than one-third of these businesses have had to cut jobs in 2009, while only five percent have increased workforces. This trend motivated organizations, such as the Ewing Marion Kauffman Foundation, to bring together entrepreneurs and assist them in having greater participation in public dialogues about America's economy.

27067 ■ *Entrepreneurship and Economic Growth*
Pub: Edward Elgar Publishing, Incorporated
Ed: Carree. **Released:** October 2006. **Price:** $195. 00. **Description:** Historic and country-specific studies and articles regarding entrepreneurship and innovation, growth models, competition and productivity, and empirical evidence.

27068 ■ *Entrepreneurship and Economic Progress*
Pub: Routledge Inc.
Ed: Randall Holcombe. **Released:** October 2006. **Description:** Economic models of economic growth and the ways entrepreneurial progress are highlighted.

27069 ■ *Entrepreneurship, Geography, and American Economic Growth*
Pub: Cambridge University Press
Ed: Zoltan Acs; Catherine Armington. **Released:** June 2006. **Price:** $70.00. **Description:** Knowledge among college-educated workers was among the key reasons for economic growth throughout the U.S. in the 1990s.

27070 ■ *Entrepreneurship, Innovation and Economic Growth*
Pub: Edward Elgar Publishing, Incorporated
Ed: David B. Audretsch. **Released:** July 2006. **Price:** $145.00. **Description:** Links between entrepreneurship, innovation and economic growth are examined.

27071 ■ *Entrepreneurship, Innovation and the Growth Mechanism of the Free-Enterprise Economies*
Pub: Princeton University Press
Ed: Eytan Sheshinski; William J. Baumol. **Released:** January 2007. **Price:** $65.00. **Description:** Scholars address the free-enterprise Western economies.

27072 ■ *Entrepreneurship, Investment and Spatial Dynamics Lessons and Implications for an Enlarged EU*
Pub: Edward Elgar Publishing, Incorporated
Ed: Nijkamp. **Released:** September 2006. **Price:** $100.00. **Description:** Understanding the impact and interaction between investment, knowledge and entrepreneurship with an expanding European Union.

27073 ■ *Entrepreneurship in the U.S.: The 2005 Assessment*
Pub: Springer
Ed: Paul Reynolds. **Released:** March 2007. **Price:** $79.95. **Description:** Entrepreneurship and its role in the U.S. economy is discussed, examining new business creation and its impact on job growth, productivity enhancements, innovation, and social mobility.

27074 ■ "Evaluating the 1996-2006 Employment Projections" in *Montly Labor Review* (Vol. 133, September 2010, No. 9, pp. 33)
Pub: Bureau of Labor Statistics
Description: Bureau of Labor Statistics employment projections outperformed alternative naive models, but not projecting the housing bubble or the rise in oil prices caused some inaccuracies in the projects. These projections are used by policymakers, economists, and students.

27075 ■ "Even Gold Gets Tarnished When Everyone Wants Cash" in *Globe & Mail* (February 28, 2007, pp. B1)
Pub: CTVglobemedia Publishing Inc.
Ed: John Partridge. **Description:** The impact of fall in Chinese equities on the United States stock market and metal prices, including gold, is discussed.

27076 ■ "Even Money on Recession" in *Barron's* (Vol. 88, March 10, 2008, No. 10, pp. M9)
Pub: Dow Jones & Company, Inc.
Ed: Gene Epstein. **Description:** Discusses the US unemployment rate which was steady in February 2008 at 4.8 percent, while nonfarm payroll employment decreased by 63,000 in the same month, with the private sector losing 101,000 jobs. The economic indicators showed mixed signals on whether or not the US economy is in a recession.

27077 ■ "Event Stresses Cross-Border Cooperation" in *Crain's Detroit Business* (Vol. 24, March 31, 2008, No. 13, pp. 5)
Pub: Crain Communications, Inc.
Ed: Chad Halcom. **Description:** According to John Austin, a senior fellow of The Brookings Institution, open immigration policies, better transportation and trade across the border and a cleanup of the Great Lakes will bring economic resurgence to Midwestern states and Canadian provinces with manufacturing economies.

27078 ■ "Exit Strategy" in *Barron's* (Vol. 89, July 6, 2009, No. 27, pp. 3)
Pub: Dow Jones & Co., Inc.
Ed: Alan Abelson. **Description:** US Federal Reserve is not likely to change its easy-money strategy in the short term. States such as California are suffering from spiraling costs and declining revenues and are struggling to balance their budgets. The US unemployment rate climbed to 9.5 percent in June 2009.

27079 ■ "Experts: Market Shaky But Resilient" in *The Business Journal-Serving Metropolitan Kansas City* (Vol. 27, September 19, 2008, No. 1)
Pub: American City Business Journals, Inc.
Ed: Steve Vockrodt. **Description:** Investment advisers believe that the local investors in Kansas City who have a long-term approach towards their portfolios may come out even or even experience gains despite the Wall Street financial crisis. The impacts of the crisis are expected to take time to reach the area of Kansas City. The potential impacts of the Wall Street meltdown are examined further.

27080 ■ "Experts Take the Temp of Obama Plan" in *The Business Journal-Serving Metropolitan Kansas City* (Vol. 27, November 14, 2008, No. 10)
Pub: American City Business Journals, Inc.
Ed: Rob Roberts. **Description:** Kansas City, Missouri-based employee benefits experts say president-elect Barack Obama's health care reform plan is on track. Insurance for children and capitalization for health information technology are seen as priority areas. The plan is aimed at reducing the number of uninsured people in the United States.

27081 ■ "Export Opportunity" in *Business Journal-Portland* (Vol. 24, October 12, 2007, No. 33, pp. 1)
Pub: American City Business Journals, Inc.
Ed: Matthew Kish. **Description:** U.S. dollar is weak, hitting an all-time low against the Euro, while the Canadian dollar is also performing well it hit parity for the first time after more than thirty years. The weak U.S. dollar is making companies that sell overseas benefit as it makes their goods cheaper to buy.

27082 ■ "Face Values: Going for Global Growth" in *Business Strategy Review* (Vol. 21, Autumn 2010, No. 3, pp. 60)
Pub: Blackwell Publishers Ltd.
Ed: Laura Tyson. **Description:** Global economic issues are examined with Laura Tyson, former Dean of London Business School, Professor at University of California Berkeley, and current advisor to President Obama.

27083 ■ "Facebook: A Promotional Budget's Best Friend" in *Women Entrepreneur* (February 1, 2009)
Pub: Entrepreneur Media Inc.
Ed: Tamara Monosoff. **Description:** Facebook began as a social networking website but has become a valuable marketing tool for all types of businesses, organizations and causes. Tips are provided for creating a Facebook account and growing one's network on Facebook.

27084 ■ "Facing the Future" in *Canadian Business* (Vol. 81, March 31, 2008, No. 5, pp. 69)
Pub: Rogers Media
Ed: John Gray. **Description:** Discusses a web poll of 122 Canadian CEOs which shows that these leaders are convinced that the U.S. economy is slowing but are split on the impact that this will have on the Canadian economy. The aging and retiring workforce and the strong Canadian dollar are other concerns by these leaders.

27085 ■ "Fair Exchange" in *Food and Drink* (Winter 2010, pp. 84)
Pub: Schofield Media Group
Ed: Don Mardak. **Description:** Bartering can assist firms in the food and beverage industry to attract new customers, maximize resources, and reduce cash expenses.

27086 ■ *Falling Behind: How Rising Inequality Harms the Middle Class*
Pub: University of California Press
Ed: Robert H. Frank. **Released:** July 2007. **Price:** $21.95 paperback. **Description:** Economist argues that though middle-class American families aren't earning much more than they were a few decades ago, they are spending considerably more, a pattern attributed primarily to the context of seeing and emulating the spending habits of the rich.

27087 ■ "Falling Markets' Nastiest Habits" in *Barron's* (Vol. 88, July 7, 2008, No. 27, pp. 7)
Pub: Dow Jones & Co., Inc.
Ed: Michael Santoli. **Description:** US market conditions reflect a bear market, with the S&P 500 index falling 20 percent below its recent high as of June 2008. The bear market is expected to persist in the immediate future, although bear market rallies are likely to occur.

27088 ■ *False Economy: A Surprising Economic History of the World*
Pub: Riverhead Booksk
Ed: Alan Beattie. **Released:** 2009. **Price:** $26.95. **Description:** History shows that the choices made by countries, not luck, determine its economic fate.

27089 ■ "Familiar Fun" in *Crain's Cleveland Business* (Vol. 28, October 22, 2007, No. 42, pp. 3)
Pub: Crain Communications, Inc.
Ed: John Booth. **Description:** Northeast Ohio's toy manufacturers and stores are predicting a strong fourth quarter despite predictions for a low retail season. Toy industry insiders feel that new products with the benefit of the "Made in America" label will help them overcome the gloomy forecasts.

27090 ■ *Family Business*
Pub: Cengage South-Western
Ed: Ernesto J. Poza. **Released:** January 1, 2009. **Price:** $96.95. **Description:** Family-owned businesses face unique challenges in today's economy. This book provides the next generation of knowledge and skills required for profitable management and leadership in a family enterprise.

27091 ■ "Fannie and Freddie: How They'll Change" in *Business Week* (September 22, 2008, No. 4100, pp. 30)
Pub: McGraw-Hill Companies, Inc.
Ed: Jane Sasseen. **Description:** Three possible outcomes of the fate of struggling mortgage giants Freddie Mac and Fannie Mae after the government bailout are outlined.

27092 ■ "The Fed Still Has Ammunition" in *Barron's* (Vol. 90, August 30, 2010, No. 35, pp. M9)
Pub: Barron's Editorial & Corporate Headquarters
Ed: Randall W. Forsyth. **Description:** Federal Reserve chairman Ben Bernanke said the agency still has tools to combat deflation and a second downturn but these strategies are not needed at this time. The prospects of the Federal Open Market Committee's purchasing of treasuries are also discussed.

27093 ■ "Fed Tackles Bear of a Crisis" in *Barron's* (Vol. 88, March 17, 2008, No. 11, pp. M10)
Pub: Dow Jones & Company, Inc.
Ed: Randall W. Forsyth. **Description:** Emergency funding package for Bear Stearns from the Federal Reserve Bank of New York through JPMorgan Chase is one of the steps taken by the central bank shore up bank liquidity. Prior to the emergency funding, the central bank announced the Term Securities Lending Facility to allow dealers to borrow easily saleable Treasuries in exchange for less-liquid issues.

27094 ■ "Federal Bailout, Three Years Later" in *Business Owner* (Vol. 35, September-October 2011, No. 5, pp. 6)
Pub: DL Perkins Company
Description: State of the economy and small business sector three years after the government stimulus and bailout programs were instituted.

27095 ■ *Female Enterprise in the New Economy*
Pub: University of Toronto Press
Ed: Karen D. Hughes. **Released:** January 2006. **Price:** $67.00, paperback $27.50. **Description:** Examination of whether the increasingly entrepreneurial economy is offering women more opportunity or increases their risk for poverty and economic insecurity.

27096 ■ "Festivals Press on Despite Loss of Sponsors" in *Crain's Detroit Business* (Vol. 25, June 22, 2009, No. 25, pp. 3)
Pub: Crain Communications Inc. - Detroit
Ed: Sherri Began Welch. **Description:** Organizers of local festivals are experiencing a decrease in sponsorship this summer due to the slow economy. These events help keep areas vibrant and stress the importance of community and cultural events.

27097 ■ "A Few Points of Contention" in *Barron's* (Vol. 88, July 14, 2008, No. 28, pp. 3)
Pub: Dow Jones & Co., Inc.
Ed: Michael Santoli. **Description:** Headline inflation tends to revert to the lower core inflation, which excludes food and energy in its calculation over long periods. Prominent private equity figures believe that regulators should allow more than the de facto 10 percent to 25 percent limit of commercial banks to hasten the refunding of the financial sector.

27098 ■ "Fewer Banks Offer Big Gifts to Lure Clients" in *Globe & Mail* (March 14, 2006, pp. D1)
Pub: CTVglobemedia Publishing Inc.
Ed: Chris Reidy. **Description:** Fewer banks are offering gifts to lure the customers in this year in the wake of less favorable interest rates in the spring season. The market climate is analyzed.

27099 ■ "Fewer People Dying At Work" in *Sacramento Business Journal* (Vol. 25, August 29, 2008, No. 26, pp. 1)
Pub: American City Business Journals, Inc.
Ed: Kathy Robertson. **Description:** Statistics show that workplace deaths in California dropped by 24 percent in 2007 compared with the previous year. Much of the decline was observed in the construction industry, where a slowing economy affected employment and dangerous work. The number of workplace deaths in the state also declined in all major categories except fires and explosions.

27100 ■ "Fight Over Casino Funds Limits Kitty for MEDC" in *Crain's Detroit Business* (Vol. 24, January 21, 2008, No. 3, pp. 3)
Pub: Crain Communications Inc. - Detroit
Ed: Amy Lane. **Description:** Michigan Economic Development Corporation is facing uncertainty due to a Michigan American Indian tribe from the southwestern portion of the state withholding its 8 percent casino revenue share.

27101 ■ "Filling the Business Gap" in *Hispanic Business* (December 2010)
Pub: Hispanic Business
Ed: Richard Larsen. **Description:** New York group seeks to increase state diversity supplier spending to help create jobs and boost the economy. According to a recent study, six out of 10 small business owners will increase capital spending but delay hiring in 2011. However, potential job creation is good among businesses owned by women and minorities.

27102 ■ "Film Incentives: A Hit or a Flop?" in *Michigan Vue* (Vol. 13, July-August 2008, No. 4, pp. 10)
Pub: Entrepreneur Media Inc.
Description: Michigan's new film incentive legislation is fulfilling its core purpose, according to Lisa Dancsok of the Michigan Economic Development Corp. (MEDC), by kickstarting the state's entry into the multi-billion dollar industry; the initiative is considered to be very competitive with other states and countries and is thought to be a way in which to help revitalize Michigan's struggling economy.

27103 ■ "The Final Frontier" in *Canadian Business* (Vol. 80, October 8, 2007, No. 20, pp. 127)
Pub: Rogers Media
Ed: Andy Holloway. **Description:** Effects of economic development in Northern Canada's natural environment are discussed. The caribou, which are still a primary source of food and clothing in the region, are dying. It is assumed that mining and petroleum projects are affecting the migration patterns of the animals inhabiting the region. The need to maintain a balance between the needs of resource companies and traditional businesses is also discussed.

27104 ■ "Financing for NNSA Plant Is a Work in Progress" in *The Business Journal-Serving Metropolitan Kansas City* (October 24, 2008)
Pub: American City Business Journals, Inc.
Ed: Rob Roberts. **Description:** The Kansas City Council approved a development plan for a $500 million nuclear weapons parts plant in south Kansas City. The US Congress approved a $59 million annual lease payment to the plant's developer. Financing for the construction of the plant remains in question as the plant's developers have to shoulder construction costs.

27105 ■ "Find the Upside to a Down Economy" in *Women Entrepreneur* (September 30, 2008)
Pub: Entrepreneur Media Inc.
Ed: Tamara Monosoff. **Description:** Starting a new business in this economic crisis may not be as daunting of a pursuit as one might think. Aspiring entrepreneurs may find success by looking for opportunities in unusual places and relying on what they do best.

27106 ■ "Finding Competitive Advantage in Adversity" in *Harvard Business Review* (Vol. 88, November 2010, No. 11, pp. 102)
Pub: Harvard Business School Publishing
Ed: Bhaskar Chakravorti. **Description:** Four opportunities in adversity are identified and applied to business scenarios. These are matching unmet needs with unneeded resources, seeking collaboration from unlikely partners, developing small/appropriate solutions to large/complex issues, and focusing on the platform as well as the product.

27107 ■ "Finding Room for Financing" in *The Business Journal-Serving Metropolitan Kansas City* (Vol. 26, August 1, 2008, No. 47, pp. 1)
Pub: American City Business Journals, Inc.
Ed: Rob Roberts. **Description:** Kansas City officials are expecting to receive financing recommendations for a new 1,000-room convention headquarters hotel. The $300-million project could be financed either through private ownership with public subsidies, or through public ownership with tax-exempt bond financing. Other views and information on the project and its expected economic impact, are presented.

27108 ■ "Finger-Pointing Time" in *Barron's* (Vol. 88, March 10, 2008, No. 10, pp. 9)
Pub: Dow Jones & Company, Inc.
Ed: Michael Santoli. **Description:** Discusses who is to blame for the financial crisis brought about by the credit crunch in the United States; the country's financial markets will eventually digest this crisis but will bottom out first before the situation improves.

27109 ■ "First Franchising Census Report Highlights Industry's Economic Role" in *Franchising World* (Vol. 42, November 2010, No. 11, pp. 41)
Pub: International Franchise Association
Ed: John Reynolds. **Description:** Franchise businesses accounted for 10.5 percent of businesses with paid employees in the year 2007.

27110 ■ "Five Low-Cost Home Based Startups" in *Women Entrepreneur* (December 16, 2008)
Pub: Entrepreneur Media Inc.
Ed: Lesley Spencer Pyle. **Description:** During tough economic times, small businesses have an advantage over large companies because they can adjust to

economic conditions more easily and without having to go through corporate red tape that can slow the implementation process. A budding entrepreneur may find success by taking inventory of his or her skills, experience, expertise and passions and utilizing those qualities to start a business. Five low-cost home-based startups are profiled. These include starting an online store, a virtual assistant service, web designer, sales representative and a home staging counselor.

27111 ■ "A Flawed Yardstick for Banks" in *Barron's* (Vol. 88, July 14, 2008, No. 28, pp. M6)
Pub: Dow Jones & Co., Inc.

Ed: Arindam Nag. **Description:** Return on equity is no longer the best measure for investors to judge banks by in a post-subprime-crises world. Investors should consider the proportion of a bank's total assets that are considered risky and look out for any write-downs of goodwill when judging a bank's financial health.

27112 ■ "Florin Car Dealers Drive Plan" in *Sacramento Business Journal* (Vol. 25, August 22, 2008, No. 25, pp. 1)
Pub: American City Business Journals, Inc.

Ed: Melanie Turner. **Description:** Automobile dealers in Sacramento, California are working with the city and the business district in planning for future redevelopment in Florin Road. The move stemmed from pressure from the Elk Grove Auto Mall, high fuel prices and the credit crunch. The area has suffered business closures recently.

27113 ■ "Ford Canada's Edsel of a Year: Revenue Plummets 24 Percent in '05" in *Globe & Mail* (February 2, 2006, pp. B1)
Pub: CTVglobemedia Publishing Inc.

Ed: Greg Keenan. **Description:** Ford Motor Company of Canada Ltd. posted 24% decline in revenues for 2005. The drop in earnings is attributed to plant shutdown in Oaksville, Canada.

27114 ■ *Freakonomics: A Rogue Economist Explores the Hidden Side of Everything*
Pub: William Morrow

Ed: Steven D. Levitt; Stephen J. Dubner. **Price:** $25. 95.

27115 ■ "From Buyout to Busted" in *Business Week* (September 22, 2008, No. 4100, pp. 18)
Pub: McGraw-Hill Companies, Inc.

Ed: Emily Thornton; Deborah Stead. **Description:** Bankruptcy filings by private equity-backed companies are at a record high with 134 American firms taken private (or invested in) by buyout firms that have filed for protection this year under Chapter 11; this is 91 percent higher than the previous year, which had set a record when 70 of such companies filed for protection under Chapter 11.

27116 ■ "Fuel for Thought; Canadian Business Leaders on Energy Policy" in *Canadian Business* (Vol. 81, September 15, 2008, No. 14-15, pp. 12)
Pub: Rogers Media Ltd.

Ed: Joe Castaldo. **Description:** Most Canadian business leaders worry about the unreliability of the oil supply but feel that Canada is in a better position to benefit from the energy supply crisis than other countries. Many respondents also highlighted the need to invest in renewable energy sources.

27117 ■ "Funeral Directors Get Creative As Boomers Near Great Beyond" in *Advertising Age* (Vol. 79, October 13, 2008, No. 38, pp. 30)
Pub: Crain Communications, Inc.

Ed: Lenore Skenazy. **Description:** Despite the downturn in the economy, the funeral business is thriving due to the number of baby boomers who realize the importance of making preparations for their death. Marketers are getting creative in their approach and many companies have taken into consideration the need for a more environmental friendly way to dispose of bodies and thus have created innovative businesses that reflect this need.

27118 ■ "The Future Is Another Country; Higher Education" in *The Economist* (Vol. 390, January 3, 2009, No. 8612, pp. 43)
Pub: The Economist Newspaper Inc.

Description: Due to the growth of the global corporation, more ambitious students are studying at universities abroad; the impact of this trend is discussed.

27119 ■ "The Future of Private Equity" in *Canadian Business* (Vol. 80, March 26, 2007, No. 7, pp. 19)
Pub: Rogers Media

Ed: Jack Mintz. **Description:** The impact growing Canadian economy and competition in global business on the performance of private equity funds is analyzed.

27120 ■ "Futures Shock for the CME" in *Crain's Chicago Business* (Vol. 31, November 10, 2008, No. 45, pp. 8)
Pub: Crain Communications, Inc.

Ed: Ann Saphir. **Description:** Chicago-based CME Group Inc., the largest futures exchange operator in the U.S., is facing a potentially radically altered regulatory landscape as Congress weighs sweeping reform of financial oversight. The possible merger of the CFTC and the Securities and Exchange Commission are among CME's concerns. Other details of possible regulatory measures are provided.

27121 ■ "Game On! African Americans Get a Shot at $17.9 Billion Video Game Industry" in *Black Enterprise* (Vol. 38, July 2008, No. 12, pp. 56)
Pub: Earl G. Graves Publishing Co. Inc.

Ed: Carolyn M. Brown. **Description:** Despite the economic crisis, consumers are still purchasing the hottest video games and hardware. Tips for African American developers who want to become a part of this industry that lacks content targeting this demographic are offered.

27122 ■ "Gas Supplies Low Heading Into Summer Season" in *Globe & Mail* (April 13, 2007, pp. B6)
Pub: CTVglobemedia Publishing Inc.

Ed: Shawn McCarthy. **Description:** The decrease in the supply of gas due to maintenance problems at refineries in the United States and Canada is discussed.

27123 ■ "George Cohon" in *Canadian Business* (Vol. 79, November 20, 2006, No. 23, pp. 70)
Pub: Rogers Media

Ed: Zena Olijnyk. **Description:** George Cohon, the founder of McDonald's in Canada and Russia, speaks about the Canadian market and the experience of starting McDonald's in Canada.

27124 ■ "German Win Through Sharing" in *Canadian Business* (Vol. 83, September 14, 2010, No. 15, pp. 16)
Pub: Rogers Media Ltd.

Ed: Jordan Timm. **Description:** German economic historian Eckhard Hoffner has a two-volume work showing how German's relaxed attitude toward copyright and intellectual property helped it catch up to industrialized United Kingdom. Hoffner's research was in response to his interest in the usefulness of software patents. Information on the debate regarding Canada's copyright laws is given.

27125 ■ "Get Back To Business Planning Fundamentals" in *Entrepreneur* (October 24, 2008)
Pub: Entrepreneur Media Inc.

Ed: Tim Berry. **Description:** During a recession it is important to know what adjustment to make to your business plan. Some fundamentals to remember include: watching things more closely by tracking progress on cash, sales, new projects, customer satisfaction, ad spending and expenses; looking for built-in indicators such as what drives sales or expenses; watching what drives cash flow; and do not make mistakes such as laying off experienced employees too soon.

27126 ■ "Get in Line" in *Canadian Business* (Vol. 79, September 25, 2006, No. 19, pp. 43)
Pub: Rogers Media

Ed: Andy Holloway. **Description:** The needs of economically developing Canada's urban regions are discussed.

27127 ■ "Get Off The Rollercoaster" in *Michigan Vue* (Vol. 13, July-August 2008, No. 4, pp. 19)
Pub: Entrepreneur Media Inc.

Ed: Donald N. Hobley Jr. **Description:** Benefits of creating and implementing a solid financial plan during these rocky economic times are examined. Things to keep in mind before meeting with a financial planner include risk assessment, investment goals, the length of time required to meet those goals and the amount of money one has available to invest.

27128 ■ "Get Over Your Fear of Change" in *Canadian Business* (Vol. 83, June 15, 2010, No. 10, pp. 38)
Pub: Rogers Media Ltd.

Ed: Michelle Magnan. **Description:** Organizational behavior professor Chip Heath says that resistance to change is based on the conflict between our analytical, rational side and our emotional side that is in love with comfort. Heath states that businesses tend to focus on the negatives during an economic crisis while they should be focusing on what is working and ways to do more of that.

27129 ■ "Getting In on the Ground Floor" in *Barron's* (Vol. 89, July 27, 2009, No. 30, pp. 32)
Pub: Dow Jones & Co., Inc.

Ed: Jacqueline Doherty. **Description:** Shares of AvalonBay Communities have fallen 61 percent in the past two and a half years to July 2009 but at $56, the stock is trading near the asset value. The shares could rise as the economy improves and if the recovery takes longer, investors will be rewarded with a yield of 3.5 percent.

27130 ■ "Ghazi Insists Downtown Project Still On" in *The Business Journal-Milwaukee* (Vol. 25, August 1, 2008, No. 45, pp. A1)
Pub: American City Business Journals, Inc.

Ed: Rich Kirchen. **Description:** Afshin Ghazi remains confident that his $200 million Catalyst project in downtown Milwaukee, Wisconsin, will push through despite financial disputes delaying his EpiCentre project in Charlotte, North Carolina. He added that the Catalyst is on schedule for groundbreaking in the spring of 2009.

27131 ■ *Global Economic Crisis: Impact on Small Business*
Pub: Cengage South-Western

Ed: Global Economics Crisis Resource Center. **Released:** March 1, 2009. **Price:** $17.95. **Description:** A discussion of the historical context of the global economic crisis is presented, along with a discussion on the impact of this crisis on small businesses. It also provides learning goals, questions, key terms, and digital access to the Global Economic Crisis Resource Center.

27132 ■ "The Global Economy, the Labor Force and Franchising's Future" in *Franchising World* (Vol. 42, September 2010, No. 9, pp. 35)
Pub: International Franchise Association

Ed: Jeffrey A. Rosensweig. **Description:** Point forecasting and the methodology called scenario analysis are presented looking at the global economy and future of franchising in the U.S. and abroad.

27133 ■ "Global Market Could Be Silver Lining" in *Hispanic Business* (January-February 2008, pp. 14, 16, 18)
Pub: Hispanic Business

Description: Economic slowdown in the U.S. is expected to continue through 2008. However, the export sector should hold steady during the same period.

27134 ■ "Global Pain: Alberta's Gain" in *Canadian Business* (Vol. 79, August 14, 2006, No. 16-17, pp. 60)
Pub: Rogers Media
Ed: Jeff Sanford. **Description:** Political problems and conflicts in oil-rich countries like Iran, Venezuela, and Russia among others, which have benefited the petroleum industry in Alberta, is discussed.

27135 ■ "The Global Talent Hunt" in *Business Strategy Review* (Vol. 21, Spring 2010, No. 1, pp. 78)
Pub: Wiley-Blackwell
Ed: Richard Emerton. **Description:** Richard Emerton explains how the new 'triple context' of economy, environment and society will have profound implications for human resource practices. He suggests that viewing talent as abundant is the right perspective for a manager.

27136 ■ "Go Green Or Go Home" in *Black Enterprise* (Vol. 41, August 2010, No. 1, pp. 53)
Pub: Earl G. Graves Publishing Co. Inc.
Ed: Tennille M. Robinson. **Description:** The green economy has become an essential part of every business, however, small business owners need to learn how to participate, including minority owned entrepreneurs.

27137 ■ "Going Dutch" in *Canadian Business* (Vol. 81, October 27, 2008, No. 18, pp. 40)
Pub: Rogers Media Ltd.
Description: Experts like Philippe Bergevin suggest that current economic conditions in Canada are similar to those of the Netherlands in the 1970s. The Organisation for Economic Co-operation suggested that Canada should instead invest in sovereign wealth funds similar to Norway's policy.

27138 ■ "A Good Book Is Worth a Thousand Blogs" in *Barron's* (Vol. 88, July 14, 2008, No. 28, pp. 42)
Pub: Dow Jones & Co., Inc.
Ed: Gene Epstein. **Description:** Nine summer book suggestions on economics are presented. The list includes 'The Revolution' by Ron Paul, 'The Forgotten Man' by Amity Shales, 'The Commitments of Traders Bible' by Stephen Briese, and 'Economic Facts and Fallacies' by Thomas Sowell.

27139 ■ "Good for Business: Houston is a Hot Spot for Economic Growth" in *Black Enterprise* (Vol. 37, October 2006, No. 3, pp. 216)
Pub: Earl G. Graves Publishing Co. Inc.
Ed: Jeanette Valentine. **Description:** Fast-growing sectors in the biotechnology and healthcare industries are among the driving forces of Houston's economic growth. More than 76,000 small businesses in the area employ about one in four area workers, according to the Small Business Administration. Housing and business costs are 26 and 11 percent below the national average, respectively, garnering the attention of corporate giants.

27140 ■ *Good Capitalism, Bad Capitalism, and the Economics of Growth and Prosperity*
Pub: Yale University Press
Ed: William J. Baumol, Robert E. Litan, Carl J. Schramm. **Released:** October 1, 2009. **Price:** $22. 00. **Description:** The book identifies the conditions that characterize good capitalism and discusses capitalist economies.

27141 ■ "A Good Sign for Commercial Real Estate" in *Austin Business JournalInc.* (Vol. 29, December 18, 2009, No. 41, pp. 1)
Pub: American City Business Journals
Ed: Kate Harrington. **Description:** Factors that could contribute to the reemergence of the commercial mortgage-backed securities market in Texas are discussed. These securities can potentially boost the commercial real estate market statewide as well as nationwide. Commercial mortgage-backed securities origination in 2009 is worth less that $1 billion, compared with $238 billion in 2008.

27142 ■ "Good Things Happen When We Buy Local" in *Crain's Detroit Business* (Vol. 24, October 6, 2008, No. 40, pp. 7)
Pub: Crain Communications, Inc.
Description: Michigan is facing incredibly difficult economic times. One way in which each one of us can help the state and the businesses located here is by purchasing our goods and services from local vendors. The state Agriculture Department projected that if Michigan households earmarked $10 per week in their grocery purchases to made-in-Michigan products, this would generate $30 million a week in economic impact.

27143 ■ "Goodwill Haunts Local Companies; Bad Buyouts During Boom Times Producing Big Writedowns" in *Crain's Chicago Business* (Apr. 28, 2008)
Pub: Crain Communications, Inc.
Ed: Ann Saphir. **Description:** Many companies are having to face the reality that they overpaid for acquisitions made in better economic times; investors often dismiss such one-time charges as mere accounting adjustments but writeoffs related to past acquisitions can signal future problems because they mean the expected profits that justified the purchase have not materialized. Writeoffs are particularly worrisome for firms with a lot of debt and whose banks require them to have enough assets to back up their borrowings.

27144 ■ "Government Intervention" in *Canadian Business* (Vol. 79, November 6, 2006, No. 22, pp. 116)
Pub: Rogers Media
Description: The effects of income trust tax on economic conditions and investment of Canada are presented.

27145 ■ "Grainger Show Highlights Building Green, Economy" in *Contractor* (Vol. 57, February 2010, No. 2, pp. 3)
Pub: Penton Media, Inc.
Ed: Candace Roulo. **Description:** chief U.S. economist told attendees of the Grainger's 2010 Total MRO Solutions National Customer Show that the economic recovery would be subdued. Mechanical contractors who attended the event also learned about building sustainable, green products, and technologies, and economic and business challenges.

27146 ■ "Grand Letdown" in *The Business Journal-Milwaukee* (Vol. 25, September 12, 2008, No. 51, pp. A1)
Pub: American City Business Journals, Inc.
Ed: Rich Kirchen. **Description:** Overview of retail trade in Milwaukee, Wisconsin is presented. It has been observed that vacancies in storefronts both east and west of the Milwaukee River have increased, and the Shops of Grand Avenue has yet to attract new retailers or shoppers. The completion of the Marquette Interchange is also discussed.

27147 ■ "Gray, Gray, & Gray: a Difficult Year for Oilheat" in *Indoor Comfort Marketing* (Vol. 70, September 2011, No. 9, pp. 30)
Pub: Industry Publications Inc.
Description: According to the 20th Annual Oilheat Industry Survey, 2011 will be another dismal year for the industry sector.

27148 ■ "The Great Cleanup" in *Canadian Business* (Vol. 81, April 14, 2008, No. 6, pp. 50)
Pub: Rogers Media
Ed: Graham Silnicki. **Description:** China's rectification program includes the licensing of 100 percent of food producers and monitoring of 100 percent of raw materials for exports between August and December, 2007. There is a lot of money to be made for those who are willing to help China win its quality battle. PharmEng International Inc. is one of the companies that helps Chinese companies meet international quality standards.

27149 ■ "The Great Deleveraging" in *Canadian Business* (Vol. 81, October 13, 2008, No. 17, pp. 45)
Pub: Rogers Media Ltd.
Ed: Jeff Sanford. **Description:** 'Hell Week' of financial crisis on Wall Street is believed to have started with the downgrade of AIG Inc.'s credit rating. AIG is a major player in the credit derivatives market, and its bankruptcy would have affected firms on Wall Street.

27150 ■ "The Great Fall" in *Barron's* (Vol. 88, March 10, 2008, No. 10, pp. 5)
Pub: Dow Jones & Company, Inc.
Ed: Alan Abelson. **Description:** Discusses the US economy is considered to be in a recession, with the effects of the credit crisis expected to intensify as a result. Inflation is estimated at 4.3 percent in January 2008, while 63,000 jobs were lost in February 2008.

27151 ■ *The Great Inflation and Its Aftermath: The Past and Future of American Affluence*
Pub: Random House
Ed: Robert J. Samuelson. **Released:** 2009. **Price:** $26.00. **Description:** How inflation has shaped the economics in today's United States is examined.

27152 ■ "The Great Moderation" in *Canadian Business* (Vol. 80, February 12, 2007, No. 4, pp. 25)
Pub: Rogers Media
Ed: David Wolf. **Description:** Caution over the changes to stock inventory levels and their adverse impact on the Canadian economy is discussed.

27153 ■ *The Green Collar Economy: How One Solution Can Fix Our Two Biggest Problems*
Pub: HarperCollins Publishers
Ed: Van Jones. **Released:** November 1, 2009. **Price:** $14.99. **Description:** This book offers insight into rebuilding the nation's infrastructure and creating alternative energy sources that could boost the economy through increased employment and higher wages while decreasing our dependence on fossil fuels.

27154 ■ "Greg Stringham" in *Canadian Business* (Vol. 81, March 3, 2008, No. 3, pp. 8)
Pub: Rogers Media
Ed: Michelle Magnan. **Description:** Canadian Association of Petroleum Producers' Greg Stringham thinks that the new royalty plan will result in companies pulling out their investments for Alberta's conventional oil and gas sector. Stringham adds that Alberta is losing its competitive advantage and companies must study their cost profiles to retrieve that advantage. The effects of the royalty system on Alberta's economy are examined further.

27155 ■ *The Gridlock Economy: How Too Much Ownership Wrecks Markets, Stops Innovation, and Costs Lives*
Pub: Basic Books
Ed: Michael Heller. **Released:** 2009. **Price:** $26.00. **Description:** While private ownership generally creates wealth, the author believes that economic gridlock results when too many people own pieces of one thing, which results in too many people being able to block each other from creating or using a scarce source.

27156 ■ "Grin and Bear It" in *Canadian Business* (Vol. 81, March 3, 2008, No. 3, pp. 53)
Pub: Rogers Media
Ed: Jeff Sanford. **Description:** Discusses the United States economic downturn, caused by the credit market crisis, which is expected to affect the Canadian economy, as Canada depend on the U.S. for 80 percent of its exports. Economist David Rosenberg thinks that in 2008, housing prices will decline by 15 percent and gross domestic product growth will slow to 0.8 percent. Other forecasts for Canadian economy are given.

27157 ■ "Growing Field" in *Crain's Detroit Business* (Vol. 26, January 11, 2010, No. 2, pp. 3)
Pub: Crain Communications, Inc.
Description: Detroit's TechTown was awarded a combination loan and grant of $4.1 million from the U.S. Department of Housing and Urban Development to build a 15,000-square-foot stem cell center, a collection of laboratories that will be available to both for-profit companies and university researchers.

27158 ■ "Growing Pains" in *Crain's Cleveland Business* (Vol. 30, June 22, 2009, No. 24, pp. 3)
Pub: Crain Communications, Inc.
Ed: Shannon Mortland. **Description:** Judson's latest retirement community, called South Franklin Circle, is near completion despite a faltering economy and delays. Details of the project are explored.

27159 ■ "Growth in Fits and Starts" in *Canadian Business* (Vol. 83, July 20, 2010, No. 11-12, pp. 18)
Pub: Rogers Media Ltd.
Ed: James Cowan. **Description:** US home sales and manufacturing indicators have dropped and fears of a double-dip recession are widespread. However, a chief economist says that this is endemic to what can be seen after a recession caused by a financial crisis. In Canada, consumer optimism is rising and anxiety over losing one's job is waning.

27160 ■ "Growth Seen Climbing Out of a Trough" in *Globe & Mail* (March 3, 2007, pp. B5)
Pub: CTVglobemedia Publishing Inc.
Ed: Tavia Grant. **Description:** The economic condition of Canada in the fourth quarter 2006 is analyzed. The gross domestic product rose 1.4 percent in the fourth quarter.

27161 ■ *Guerrilla Marketing During Tough Times*
Pub: Morgan James Publishing, LLC
Ed: Jay Conrad Levinson. **Released:** November 2005. **Price:** $14.00. **Description:** Ways to market a small business during slow economic times.

27162 ■ "H&M Offers a Dress for Less" in *Canadian Business* (Vol. 83, September 14, 2010, No. 15, pp. 20)
Pub: Rogers Media Ltd.
Ed: Laura Cameron. **Description:** Swedish clothing company H&M has implemented loss leader strategy by pricing some dresses at extremely low prices. The economy has forced retailers to keep prices down despite the increasing cost of manufacturing, partly due to Chinese labor becoming more expensive. How the trend will affect apparel companies is discussed.

27163 ■ "Hank and Ben: Hedgies' BFFs" in *Barron's* (Vol. 88, March 31, 2008, No. 13, pp. 50)
Pub: Dow Jones & Company, Inc.
Ed: Tom Sullivan. **Description:** David Ballin of Alternative Investment Solutions says that everything in the financial markets is tainted and beaten-up which presents an extraordinary opportunity for hedge funds as long as they back up their decisions with sharp and intensive research. He adds that money managers should short suspect stocks and go long on undeservedly battered stocks in the same sector.

27164 ■ "Hank Paulson On the Housing Bailout and What's Ahead" in *Business Week* (September 22, 2008, No. 4100, pp. 19)
Pub: McGraw-Hill Companies, Inc.
Ed: Maria Bartiromo. **Description:** Interview with Treasury Secretary Henry Paulson in which he discusses the bailout of Fannie Mae and Freddie Mac as well as the potential impact on the American economy and foreign interests and investments in the country. Paulson has faith that the government's actions will help to stabilize the housing market.

27165 ■ "Has Daylight Savings Time Fuelled Gasoline Consumption" in *Globe & Mail* (April 14, 2007, pp. B1)
Pub: CTVglobemedia Publishing Inc.
Ed: Shawn McCarthy. **Description:** The prospects of the acquisition of BCE Inc, by Canadian pension funds are discussed. The effect of the growth of these pension funds on the Canadian economy is described.

27166 ■ "Hastily Enacted Regulation Will Not Cure Economic Crisis" in *Crain's Chicago Business* (Vol. 31, May 5, 2008, No. 18, pp. 18)
Pub: Crain Communications, Inc.
Ed: Stephen P. D'Arcy. **Description:** Policymakers are looking for ways to respond to what is possibly the greatest financial crisis of a generation due to the collapse of the housing market, the credit crisis and the volatility of Wall Street.

27167 ■ "Have High-Tech Tax Credits Helped or Hurt Hawaii?" in *Hawaii Business* (Vol. 53, December 2007, No. 6, pp. 28)
Pub: Hawaii Business Publishing
Description: Presents the opinons of Channel Capital LLC's Walter R. Roth and Hawaii Venture Capital Association's Bill Spencer concerning the impacts of tax credits. Roth thinks that Act 221 appeals to investors who can earn despite business failure while Spencer thinks that the legislation promotes investments in innovative technology firms. The need to support tax credits is also discussed.

27168 ■ "Hawaii's Identity Crisis" in *Hawaii Business* (Vol. 53, November 2007, No. 5, pp. 10)
Pub: Hawaii Business Publishing
Ed: Kelli Abe Trifonovitch. **Description:** Some Hawaiians have shown that the Superferry controversy makes it seem to the rest of the world as if they do not know what they are doing, and intensifies several issues regarding the stability of investing in Hawaii. With or without the Superferry, there is still no evidence that investors are afraid to put their money in Hawaii.

27169 ■ "Headwinds From the New Sod Slow Aer Lingus" in *Barron's* (Vol. 88, March 10, 2008, No. 10, pp. M6)
Pub: Dow Jones & Company, Inc.
Ed: Sean Walters; Arindam Nag. **Description:** Aer Lingus faces a drop in its share prices with a falling US market, higher jet fuel prices, and lower long-haul passenger load factors. British media companies Johnston Press and Yell Group are suffering from weaker ad revenue and heavier debt payments due to the credit crunch.

27170 ■ "A Heavy Burden" in *Crain's Cleveland Business* (Vol. 30, June 8, 2009, No. 22, pp. 13)
Pub: Crain Communications, Inc.
Ed: Chuck Soder. **Description:** Small business owners are making sacrifices in the tight economy. In a recent survey conducted by American Express, 30 percent of the 727 small business owners questioned said they no longer take salaries from their firms.

27171 ■ "Help for Job Seekers" in *Crain's Detroit Business* (Vol. 26, January 4, 2010, No. 1, pp. 14)
Pub: Crain Communications, Inc.
Description: CareerWorks is weekly paper targeting readers who are in a career transition or are looking for new employment.

27172 ■ "High Anxiety" in *Canadian Business* (Vol. 80, November 19, 2007, No. 23, pp. 11)
Pub: Rogers Media
Ed: Zena Olijnyk. **Description:** Value of Canadian dollar continues to rise, and consumers are asking for lower prices of goods. Retailers, on the other hand, are facing concerns over losing sales. The impacts of the rising Canadian dollar on the business sector and consumer behavior are examined.

27173 ■ "High-End Blunders" in *Crain's Chicago Business* (Vol. 31, April 21, 2008, No. 16, pp. 54)
Pub: Crain Communications, Inc.
Ed: Laura Bianchi. **Description:** Discusses some of the biggest errors sellers make that keep their homes from selling including: pricing too high; expecting to recoup the cost of very high-end amenities and decor; avant-garde decorating; owners that hover when the house is being shown; stripping the home of top-quality light fixtures and hardware and replacing them with inferior versions with the assumption that the new buyer will come in with their own decorator and redo it; and poorly maintained properties.

27174 ■ "The High-Intensity Entrepreneur" in *Harvard Business Review* (Vol. 88, September 2010, No. 9, pp. 74)
Pub: Harvard Business School Publishing
Ed: Anne S. Habiby, Deirdre M. Coyle Jr. **Description:** Examination of the role of small companies in promoting global economic growth is presented. Discussion includes identifying entrepreneurial capability.

27175 ■ *High Wire: The Precarious Financial Lives of American Families*
Pub: Basic Books
Ed: Peter Gosselin. **Released:** 2009. **Price:** $26.95. **Description:** Despite the general prosperity in America, household finances are growing more precarious making people more anxious about their economic prospects in the future.

27176 ■ "High-Yield Turns Into Road Kill" in *Barron's* (Vol. 88, July 7, 2008, No. 27, pp. M7)
Pub: Dow Jones & Co., Inc.
Ed: Emily Barrett. **Description:** High-yield bonds have returned to the brink of collapse after profits have recovered from the shock brought about by the collapse of Bear Stearns. The high-yield bond market could decline again due to weakness in the automotive sector, particularly in Ford and General Motors.

27177 ■ "Hispanic Business 100 Fastest-Growing Companies" in *Hispanic Business* (July-August 2009, pp. 16-18)
Pub: Hispanic Business
Ed: Joshua Molina. **Description:** Despite the recession, the 100 fastest growing companies profiled are able to maintain their competitive edge; federal contracts are key to their success. Service companies are at the top of the list and Texas and Florida are the states in which the top are located

27178 ■ "Hispanic Executives Continue Their Rise to Prominence Amid a Shaky Economy" in *Hispanic Business* (January-February 2009, pp. 12-14)
Pub: Hispanic Business
Ed: Michael Bowker. **Description:** Hispanic Business Media's 2009 Corporate Elite winners defied expectations and a tough economy and rose to the top of their industries; innovation being cited as key to growth of Hispanic-owned companies.

27179 ■ "Hispantelligence Report" in *Hispanic Business* (January-February 2009, pp. 10)
Pub: Hispanic Business
Description: U.S. Hispanic purchasing power is expected to reach $958 billion in 2009 and projected to reach $1.25 trillion by 2015, a rate of more than two times the overall national rate. Statistical data included.

27180 ■ *A History of Small Business in America*
Pub: University of North Carolina Press
Ed: Mansel G. Blackford. **Released:** May 2003. **Price:** $22.95. **Description:** History of American small business from the colonial era to present, showing how it has played a role in the nation's economic, political, and cultural development across manufacturing, sales, services and farming.

27181 ■ "Hitting Bottom?" in *Barron's* (Vol. 88, March 24, 2008, No. 12, pp. 21)
Pub: Dow Jones & Company, Inc.
Ed: Jacqueline Doherty. **Description:** Brokerage houses and banks may stabilize in 2008 as a result of regulatory responses brought about by the near-collapse of Bear Stearns. Some of their shares may rise by as much as 20 percent from 2008 to 2009.

27182 ■ "Ho, Ho, Ho!" in *Retail Merchandiser* (Vol. 51, September-October 2011, No. 5, pp. 10)
Pub: Phoenix Media Corporation
Ed: Ted Vaughan. **Description:** Despite consumer caution and economic woes, retail leaders are expecting a high volume holiday selling season for 2011 Christmas. Statistical data covering holiday sales expectations is included.

27183 ■ "Hobbies Hold Fast" in *Playthings* (Vol. 106, November 1, 2008, No. 1, pp. 6)
Pub: Reed Business Information
Ed: Karyn M. Peterson. **Description:** Profile of the 24th Annual iHobby Expo is presented. The event is a combined trade and consumer show offering a look

at the latest releases in die-cast collectibles, model railroads and aircraft, slot cars, remote control vehicles, rocketry, robotics, military toys, wood/plastic model kits, games, etc.

27184 ■ "Hold the McJobs: Canada's High-End Employment Boom" in *Globe & Mail* (February 17, 2006, pp. B1)
Pub: CTVglobemedia Publishing Inc.
Ed: Heather Scoffield. **Description:** A focus the increasing rate of high-end or professional jobs Canada and its negative influence on low-end and middle level jobs is presented.

27185 ■ "Hold Your Nose, Say 'Da'" in *Canadian Business* (Vol. 79, September 11, 2006, No. 18, pp. 151)
Pub: Rogers Media
Ed: Thomas Watson. **Description:** The changing business environment and investment opportunities in Russia despite its instable democracy are discussed. Russia's potential and its ability to attract productive investment are presented.

27186 ■ "Holiday Parties to Take a Hit in Hard Times" in *Philadelphia Business Journal* (Vol. 28, November 6, 2009, No. 38, pp. 1)
Pub: American City Business Journals
Ed: Peter van Allen. **Description:** Companies are cutting expenses in view of the economic downturn and are changing the way holiday parties will be held. Sixty-two percent of firms will still hold parties in 2009, but last minute decisions about reduced-cost parties are being made.

27187 ■ "Holiday Sales Look Uncertain for Microsoft and PC Sellers" in *Puget Sound Business Journal* (Vol. 29, November 28, 2008, No. 32)
Pub: American City Business Journals
Ed: Todd Bishop. **Description:** Personal computer makers face uncertain holiday sales for 2008 as a result of the weak U.S. economy and a shift toward low-cost computers. Personal computer shipments for the fourth quarter 2008 are forecast to drop 1 percent compared to the same quarter 2007.

27188 ■ "The Hollow Debate" in *Canadian Business* (Vol. 81, March 3, 2008, No. 3, pp. 26)
Pub: Rogers Media
Ed: Thomas Watson. **Description:** According to a report conducted by the Conference Board of Canada, the Canadian business community is not being hollowed out by acquisitions made by foreign companies. Findings further showed that local businesses are protected by dual shares and that the economy can benefit more from foreign acquisitions than local mergers. The need to relax foreign ownership restrictions and other recommendations are presented.

27189 ■ "The Home Game" in *Canadian Business* (Vol. 80, October 8, 2007, No. 20, pp. 68)
Pub: Rogers Media
Ed: Rachel Pulfer. **Description:** Analysis of Canada's banking industry is presented. Trends show that Canadian banks avoid risks in their investments, and usually choose to take safer paths. Experts believe these trends affect the country's economy and that Canadian banks do not play a significant role in economic development.

27190 ■ "A Home of Her Own" in *Hawaii Business* (Vol. 53, October 2007, No. 4, pp. 51)
Pub: Hawaii Business Publishing
Ed: Maria Torres-Kitamura. **Description:** It was observed that the number of single women in Hawaii purchasing their own home has increased, as that in the whole United States where the percentage has increased from 14 percent in 1995 to 22 percent in 2006. However, First Hawaiian Bank's Wendy Lum thinks that the trend will not continue in Hawaii due to lending restrictions. The factors that women consider in buying a home of their own are presented.

27191 ■ "Home Prices Sag" in *Crain's Chicago Business* (Vol. 31, April 28, 2008, No. 17, pp. 3)
Pub: Crain Communications, Inc.
Ed: Alby Gallun. **Description:** Since the slump in the housing market is continuing with no sign of recovery, Chicago-area home prices are poised for an even steeper drop this year. In 2007, the region's home prices fell nearly 5 percent and according to a forecast by Fiserv Inc., they will decline 8.1 percent this year and another 2.2 percent in 2009. Statistical data included.

27192 ■ "Homeownership: Still the American Dream?" in *Gallup Management Journal* (May 5, 2011)
Pub: Gallup
Description: The mortgage finance system is broken. Housing prices continue to fall. Foreclosures are expected to increase in the coming months. However, Gallup's chief economist does not believe this is the end of the American dream of owning one's own home.

27193 ■ "Homes, Not Bars, Stay Well Tended" in *Advertising Age* (Vol. 79, January 28, 2008, No. 4, pp. 8)
Pub: Crain Communications, Inc.
Ed: Jeremy Mullman. **Description:** Due to the downturn in the economy, consumers are drinking less at bars and restaurants; however, according to the Distilled Spirits Council of the United States, they are still purchasing expensive liquor to keep in their homes.

27194 ■ "Honest Harry" in *Hawaii Business* (Vol. 53, November 2007, No. 5, pp. 39)
Pub: Hawaii Business Publishing
Ed: David K. Choo. **Description:** Mayor Harry Kim testified in support of the Superferry controversial in Hawaii last September 2007. Kim says that the Superferry would allow local business and families to have more opportunities for commerce and recreation. Kim's testimony was not persuasive enough for Maui Circuit Judge Joseph Cardoza who ruled that the Superferry may not operate while an environmental assessment is being completed.

27195 ■ "Hospitals Feel Pain from Slow Economy" in *Business Courier* (Vol. 27, September 3, 2010, No. 18, pp. 1)
Pub: Business Courier
Ed: James Ritchie. **Description:** Hospitals in Cincinnati, Ohio have suffered from decreased revenues owing to the economic crises. Declining patient volumes and bad debt have also adversely impacted hospitals.

27196 ■ "Hot-Button Ordinances May Go Up for Review" in *Crain's Detroit Business* (Vol. 26, January 18, 2010, No. 3, pp. 1)
Pub: Crain Communications, Inc.
Ed: Nancy Kaffer. **Description:** Detroit's economic fate may be tied to the city's anti-privatization ordinance and its policy of giving contract preference to Detroit-based businesses. The new administration feels that it is time to put everything on the table in an attempt to look for ways in which to save the city money.

27197 ■ "Hot For All The Wrong Reasons" in *Canadian Business* (Vol. 81, March 31, 2008, No. 5, pp. 19)
Pub: Rogers Media
Ed: Andrea Jezovit. **Description:** Soaring platinum prices are due to South Africa's platinum mining industry's safety issues and power supply disruptions that exacerbate the metal's supply problems. South Africa supplies 80 percent of the world's platinum. South Africa's power utility has said that it cannot guarantee the industry's power needs until 2013.

27198 ■ "Hotel Woes Reflect Area Struggle" in *Business Journal Serving Greater Tampa Bay* (Vol. 30, December 3, 2010, No. 50, pp. 1)
Pub: Tampa Bay Business Journal
Ed: Mark Holan. **Description:** Quality Inn and Suites in East Tampa, Florida has struggled against the sluggish economy but remained open to guests despite facing a foreclosure. The hotel project is the center of East Tampa's redevelopment plans and public officials defend the $650,000 investment in public amenities near the building.

27199 ■ "Hotels' Healthy Finish in '07" in *Crain's Chicago Business* (Vol. 31, March 24, 2008, No. 12, pp. 16)
Pub: Crain Communications, Inc.
Ed: Alby Gallun. **Description:** Chicago's hotel market saw mostly rising occupancies and room rates in the fourth quarter of 2007, reflecting continued strong demand from leisure and business travelers; however, due to the current state of the economy hoteliers face an increasingly uncertain outlook.

27200 ■ *House of Cards*
Pub: Doubleday, a Division of Random House
Ed: William D. Cohan. **Released:** March 10, 2009. **Price:** $27.95. **Description:** The fall of Bear Stearns and the beginning of the Wall Street Collapse.

27201 ■ "House Prices Cooling Off, With Alberta Gearing Down" in *Globe & Mail* (February 9, 2007, pp. B4)
Pub: CTVglobemedia Publishing Inc.
Ed: Tavia Grant. **Description:** The house prices in Alberta, which are experiencing a torrid pace in price growth, are steady in the first month of 2007. The easing in house prices may show impact on inflation.

27202 ■ "Housing Market Dinged, But Not Done In, By Nationwide Slump" in *Business Review, Albany New York* (Vol. 34, December 21, 2007)
Pub: American City Business Journals, Inc.
Ed: Michael DeMasi. **Description:** Kirsten Keefe, a staff attorney of the Empire Justice Center, is questioning the validity of statistics that represent the number of home foreclosures in New York.

27203 ■ "Housing Markets Still Struggling" in *Montana Business Quarterly* (Vol. 49, Spring 2011, No. 1, pp. 17)
Pub: Bureau of Business & Economic Research
Ed: Scott Rickard. **Description:** Montana's economic conditions are a bit better than national averages. Data ranked by state, year-over-year price change, and total price peak is presented, along with statistical data for the entire nation.

27204 ■ "How Bad Is It?" in *Hawaii Business* (Vol. 54, July 2008, No. 1, pp. 35)
Pub: Hawaii Business Publishing
Ed: Jolyn Okimoto Rosa. **Description:** Donald G. Horner, chief executive officer of First Hawaiian Bank, says that the current Hawaiian economic situation is a cyclical slowdown. Maurice Kaya, an energy consultant, says the slowdown is due to overdependence on imported fuels. Other local leaders, such as Constance H. Lau, also discuss their view on the current economic situation in Hawaii.

27205 ■ "How to Beat the Pros" in *Canadian Business* (Vol. 81, Summer 2008, No. 9, pp. 59)
Pub: Rogers Media Ltd.
Ed: Calvin Leung. **Description:** Table showing the results of the Investor 500 beat the S&P/TSX composite index is presented. The average total return, best performing stocks and total return of the 2007 stock screen are provided.

27206 ■ "How Exports Could Save America" in *Barron's* (Vol. 89, July 20, 2009, No. 29, pp. 15)
Pub: Dow Jones & Co., Inc.
Ed: Jonathan R. Laing. **Description:** Increase in US exports should help drive up the nation's economic growth, according to Wells Capital Management strategist Jim Paulsen. He believes US gross domestic product could grow by 3-3.5 percent annually starting in 2010 due to a more favorable trade balance.

27207 ■ *How to Make Money in Stocks: A Winning System in Good Times and Bad*
Pub: The McGraw-Hill Companies
Ed: William J. O'Neil. **Released:** June 12. 2009. **Price:** $16.95. **Description:** The bestselling guide to buying stocks, from the founder of Investor's Busi-

ness Daily. The technique is based on a study of the greatest stock market winners dating back to 1953 and includes a seven-step process for minimizing risk, maximizing return, and finding stocks that are ready to perform.

27208 ■ "How Our Picks Beat The Bear" in *Barron's* (Vol. 88, July 14, 2008, No. 28, pp. 18)
Pub: Dow Jones & Co., Inc.
Ed: Andrew Bary. **Description:** Performance of the stocks that Barron's covered in the first half of 2008 is discussed; some of the worst picks and most rewarding pans have been in the financial sector while the best plays were in the energy, materials, and the transportation sectors.

27209 ■ "How to Ramp Up Marketing in a Downturn" in *Entrepreneur* (Vol. 37, July 2009, No. 7, pp. 55)
Pub: Entrepreneur Media, Inc.
Ed: Jeff Wuorio. **Description:** How businesses can save money while boosting their marketing efforts during a down economy is discussed. Using price-driven marketing, online social networks, and cause-driven marketing are among the suggested ways companies can attract more customers. Guarantees and warrantees, as well as contests, can also be used as marketing tools.

27210 ■ *How to Start Your Own Business for Entrepreneurs*
Pub: FT Press
Ed: Robert Ashton. **Released:** December 9, 2010. **Price:** $24.99. **Description:** More than 300,000 individuals start a business every year. That number will rise over the next year or two if the current economic downturn leads to widespread job losses.

27211 ■ "The HST Hornet's Nest" in *Canadian Business* (Vol. 83, September 14, 2010, No. 15, pp. 17)
Pub: Rogers Media Ltd.
Ed: Michael McCullough. **Description:** Canadian Premier Gordon Campbell's Harmonized Sales Tax (HST) initiative has left British Columbia's economic and political future stuck in uncertainty. The petition of a coalition group forced a bill to abolish the HST through legislation or referendum. How the HST's abolition will affect British Columbia's revenues is also discussed.

27212 ■ "The Human Factor" in *Canadian Business* (Vol. 80, October 8, 2007, No. 20, pp. 22)
Pub: Rogers Media
Ed: Alex Mynek. **Description:** David Foot, a demographer and an economics professor at the University of Toronto, talks about Canada's future, including economic and demographic trends. He discusses activities that should be done by businessmen in order to prepare for the future. He also addresses the role of the Canadian government in economic development.

27213 ■ "I-5 Bridge Funding Unclear" in *The Business Journal-Portland* (Vol. 25, July 11, 2008, No. 18, pp. 1)
Pub: American City Business Journals, Inc.
Ed: Andy Giegerich. **Description:** Financing for a new Interstate 5 bridge is unclear as Washington lawmakers identify two priority projects other than the planned bridge, which is shared with Oregon. An estimate says that the two states could pay between $487.6 million and $1.5 billion for the new bridge. Other details on the financing of the project are discussed.

27214 ■ "Idea Nation" in *Canadian Business* (Vol. 80, December 25, 2006, No. 1, pp. 57)
Pub: Rogers Media
Ed: Andy Holloway. **Description:** The potential of manufacturing companies and their innovations in the progress of the Canadian economy is discussed.

27215 ■ "Ideas at Work: Total Communicator" in *Business Strategy Review* (Vol. 21, Autumn 2010, No. 3, pp. 10)
Pub: Wiley-Blackwell
Ed: Stuart Crainer. **Description:** Vittorio Colao has been chief executive of Vodafone Group for two years. He brings to the company some special experience: from 2004-2006 he was CEO of RCS MediaGroup in Milan, which publishes newspapers, magazines and books in Italy, Spain and France. Colao shares his views on business, the global economy and leading Vodafone.

27216 ■ "If You Go Into the Market Today..." in *Canadian Business* (Vol. 82, Summer 2009, No. 8, pp. 18)
Pub: Rogers Media
Ed: Jeff Sanford. **Description:** Opinions of experts and personalities who are known to have bear attitudes towards the economy were presented in the event 'A Night with the Bears' in Toronto in April 2009. Known bears that served as resource persons in the event were Nouriel Roubini, Eric Sprott, Ian Gordon, and Meredith Whitney. The bears were observed to have differences regarding consumer debt.

27217 ■ "IFRS Monopoly: the Pied Piper of Financial Reporting" in *Accounting and Business Research* (Vol. 41, Summer 2011, No. 3, pp. 291)
Pub: American Institute of CPAs
Ed: Shyam Sunder. **Description:** The disadvantages of granting monopoly to the international financial reporting standards (IFRS) are examined. Results indicate that an IFRS monopoly removes the chances for comparing alternative practices and learning from them. An IFRS monopoly also eliminates customization of financial reporting to fit local differences in governance, business, economic, and legal conditions.

27218 ■ "An Ill Wind: Icelandic Bank Failures Chill Atlantic Canada" in *Canadian Business* (Vol. 81, November 10, 2008, No. 19, pp. 10)
Pub: Rogers Media Ltd.
Ed: Charles Mandel. **Description:** Bank failures in Iceland have put a stop to flights ferrying Icelanders to Newfoundland to purchase Christmas gifts, thereby threatening Newfoundland's tourism industry. The credit of Newfoundland's fisheries is also being squeezed since most of Atlantic Canadian seafood processors hold lines of credit from Icelandic banks.

27219 ■ "Ill Winds; Cuba's Economy" in *The Economist* (Vol. 390, January 3, 2009, No. 8612, pp. 20)
Pub: The Economist Newspaper Inc.
Description: Cuba's long-term economic prospects remain poor with the economy forecasted to grow only 4.3 percent for the year, about half of the original forecast, due in part to Hurricane Gustav which caused $10 billion in damage and disrupted the food-supply network and devastated farms across the region; President Raul Castro made raising agricultural production a national priority and the rise in global commodity prices hit the country hard. The only bright spot has been the rise in tourism which is up 9.3 percent over 2007.

27220 ■ *Immigrant, Inc.: Why Immigrant Entrepreneurs Are Driving the New Economy (and how they will save the American worker)*
Pub: John Wiley & Sons, Inc.
Ed: Richard T. Herman, Robert L. Smith. **Released:** November 9, 2009. **Price:** $19.77. **Description:** Immigrant entrepreneurs are driving the new economy and will play a role in saving American jobs.

27221 ■ "The Impact of Immigrant Entrepreneurs" in *Business Week* (February 7, 2007)
Pub: McGraw-Hill Companies
Ed: Kerry Miller. **Description:** Overview of immigrant entrepreneur's impact on economic development and their status as a driving force for the U.S. economy.

27222 ■ "In the Bag?" in *Canadian Business* (Vol. 81, March 3, 2008, No. 3, pp. 57)
Pub: Rogers Media
Ed: Calvin Leung. **Description:** American stocks are beginning to appear cheap amidst the threat of a worldwide economic slowdown, United States economic crisis and declining stock portfolios. Investors looking for bargain stocks should study the shares of Apple and Oshkosh Corp. Evaluation of other cheap-looking stocks such as the shares of Coach and 3M is also given.

27223 ■ *In Fed We Trust: Ben Bernanke's Ware on the Great Panic*
Pub: Crown Business
Ed: David Wessel. **Released:** 2009. **Price:** $27.99. **Description:** A look at the central bank's reaction to the crisis and Ben Bernanke has been forced to play the crisis by ear in order to keep the economy from imploding.

27224 ■ "In Search of the Next Big Thing: It's Out There - Just Waiting For You To Find It" in *Inc.* (Volume 32, December 2010, No. 10, pp. 34)
Pub: Inc. Magazine
Ed: April Joyner. **Description:** Innovation is the future for small business. A new book, Inside Real Innovation: How the Right Approach Can Move Ideas from R&D to Market - And Get the Economy Moving helps to break down the process by which innovation occurs.

27225 ■ "In Surging Oil Industry, Good Fortune Comes In Stages" in *Barron's* (Vol. 88, July 7, 2008, No. 27, pp. 12)
Pub: Dow Jones & Co., Inc.
Ed: Sandra Ward. **Description:** Shares of US land oil and gas driller Helmerich and Payne, priced at $69 each, are estimated to be at peak levels. The shares are trading at 17 times 2008 earnings and could be in for some profit taking.

27226 ■ "Incentives Debate Rages On Unabated" in *The Business Journal-Serving Metropolitan Kansas City* (Vol. 26, September 5, 2008, No. 52)
Pub: American City Business Journals, Inc.
Ed: Rob Roberts. **Description:** Debate on the new economic development and incentives policy adopted by the Kansas City Council is still on. The city's Planned Industrial Expansion Authority has rejected a standard property tax abatement proposal. The real estate development community has opposed the rejection of proposed the tax incentives policy.

27227 ■ "Inc. 500: the Class of 2011" in *Inc.* (Vol. 33, September 2011, No. 7, pp. 71)
Pub: Inc. Magazine
Description: A listing of the Inc. 500 businesses that are rebuilding the economy and changing the world is presented.

27228 ■ "Independence's Day Keeps on Getting Brighter" in *Business Courier* (Vol. 27, June 11, 2010, No. 6, pp. 1)
Pub: Business Courier
Ed: Lucy May. **Description:** Reports show that residential and commercial development continues in Independence, Kentucky despite the recession, with a 144-unit apartment complex under construction. The city recorded 152 new-home closings in 2009, or 25 percent of all new homes closed in Boone, Campbell, and Kenton counties.

27229 ■ "Indigenous Tourism Operators" in *International Journal of Entrepreneurship and Small Business* (Vol. 10, July 6, 2010, No. 4)
Pub: Publishers Communication Group
Ed: Andrews Cardow, Peter Wiltshier. **Description:** Emergent enthusiasm for tourism as a savior for economic development in the Chatham Islands of New Zealand is highlighted.

27230 ■ "Indulgent Parsimony: an Enduring Marketing Approach" in *Strategy and Leadership* (Vol. 39, March-April 2011, No. 2, pp. 36)
Pub: Emerald Group Publishing Inc.
Ed: Kenneth Alan Grossberg. **Description:** Indulgent parsimony (IP), a marketing strategy employed on consumers that are affected by recession, is found to be a relevant and appropriate approach that can help encourage buying. IP involves the selling of cheaper goods and services that allow consumers experience comfort and relief from stress.

27231 ■ "Industrial Vacancies Hit High; Economic Downturn Taking Toll on Area's Demand for Space" in *Crain's Chicago Business* (Apr. 21, 2008)
Pub: Crain Communications, Inc.
Ed: Alby Gallun. **Description:** Hitting its highest level in four years in the first quarter is the Chicago-area industrial vacancy rate, a sign that the slumping economy is depressing demand for warehouse and manufacturing space.

27232 ■ "The Influencers" in *Entrepreneur* (Vol. 36, March 2008, No. 3, pp. 66)
Pub: Entrepreneur Media Inc.
Ed: Andrea Cooper. **Description:** Among the 25 people, events, and trends that will influence business in 2008 are: the 2008 U.S. presidential elections, climate change, China, weakening U.S. dollar, mortgage crisis, generational shift, Bill Drayton, and Bill Gates. Other 2008 influencers are presented.

27233 ■ "Inland Snaps Up Rival REITs" in *Crain's Chicago Business* (Vol. 31, November 17, 2008, No. 46, pp. 3)
Pub: Crain Communications, Inc.
Ed: Alby Gallun. **Description:** Discusses Inland American Real Estate Trust Inc., a real estate investment trust that is napping up depressed shares of publicly traded competitors, a possible first step toward taking over these companies; however, with hotel and retail properties accounting for approximately 70 percent of its portfolio, the company could soon face its own difficulties.

27234 ■ *Innovate to Great: Re-Igniting Sustainable Innovation to Win in the Global Economy*
Pub: McGraw-Hill
Ed: Judy Estrin. **Released:** September 12, 2008. **Price:** $27.95. **Description:** The author explores innovation and creativity as a means for small companies to survive and expand in the global economy.

27235 ■ *Innovation and Entrepreneurship*
Pub: Collins Publications
Ed: Peter F. Drucker. **Released:** May 9, 2006. **Price:** $16.95. **Description:** Innovation and entrepreneurship are presented as a purposeful and systematic discipline to explain and analyze the challenges and opportunities of American's new entrepreneurial economy. The book explains the things established businesses, public service institutions, and new ventures need to know in order to succeed in today's economy.

27236 ■ "Innovation Station" in *Canadian Business* (Vol. 80, October 8, 2007, No. 20, pp. 42)
Pub: Rogers Media
Ed: Andrew Wahl. **Description:** Study and teaching of entrepreneurship at the University of Waterloo is discussed. Research projects in the university are expected to be influential in Canada's economic development. In spite of the success of these studies, financing is still a problem for the university, especially in technological innovations.

27237 ■ *Innovative Approaches to Global Sustainability*
Pub: Palgrave Macmillan
Ed: Charles Wankel, James A.F. Stoner. **Released:** April 13, 2010. **Price:** $30.00. **Description:** Examples are given to help businesses become sustainable as we move towards a sustainable world.

27238 ■ "Innovators Critical in Technical Economy" in *Crain's Cleveland Business* (Vol. 28, November 5, 2007, No. 44, pp. 10)
Pub: Crain Communications, Inc.
Ed: Peter Rea. **Description:** Discusses the importance to attract, develop and retain talented innovators on Ohio's economy. Also breaks down the four fronts on which the international battle for talent is being waged.

27239 ■ "The Ins and Outs of Unemployment in Canada, 1976-2008" in *Canadian Journal of Economics* (Vol. 44, November 2011, No. 4, pp. 1331)
Pub: Blackwell Publishers Ltd.
Ed: Michele Campolieti. **Description:** Flows into and out of unemployment in Canada at an aggregate and a number of disaggregated levels are studied.

27240 ■ "Insider" in *Canadian Business* (Vol. 81, March 31, 2008, No. 5, pp. 76)
Pub: Rogers Media
Ed: John Gray. **Description:** Discusses a comparison of an average Canadian family's finances in 1990 with the data from 2007. The average family in 2007 has over $80,000 in debt compared to just under $52,000 in 1990. However, Canadians have also been accumulating solid assets such as homes and stocks. This means that Canadian debt load has fallen from 22 percent in 1990 to 20 percent in 2007 when taken as a percentage of total net worth.

27241 ■ "Insitu Looks to Oregon" in *Business Journal Portland* (Vol. 27, October 29, 2010, No. 35, pp. 1)
Pub: Portland Business Journal
Ed: Erik Siemers. **Description:** Bingen, Washington-based Insitu Inc. announced that it has narrowed the search for a new corporate campus into five locations within the Columbia Gorge region. However, state economic development officials are curious whether the company will land in Oregon or Washington. Insights on economic impact of Insitu's decision are also given.

27242 ■ "Insurers No Longer Paying Premium for Advertising" in *Brandweek* (Vol. 49, April 21, 2008, No. 16, pp. SR3)
Pub: VNU Business Media, Inc.
Ed: Eric Newman. **Description:** Insurance companies are cutting their advertising budgets after years of accelerated double-digit growth in spending due to the economic downturn, five years of record-breaking ad spend and a need to cut expenditures as claims costs rise and a competitive market keeps premiums in place. Statistical data included.

27243 ■ *International Economic Development Council—Membership Directory*
Pub: International Economic Development Council
Contact: Jeffrey A. Finkle, Pres./CEO
Released: Irregular. **Covers:** Approximately 2,700 economic development professionals working in local and state governments; private sector professionals and corporations; local and community development corporations; neighborhood and manpower groups. **Entries Include:** For individual members—Name, address, phone. For corporations and community groups—Organization name, address, phone, fax, name and title of contact. **Arrangement:** Personal. **Indexes:** Geographical, Organizational.

27244 ■ "International ETFs: Your Passport to the World" in *Barron's* (Vol. 89, July 13, 2009, No. 28, pp. L10)
Pub: Dow Jones & Co., Inc.
Ed: John Hintze. **Description:** International exchange traded funds give investors more choices in terms of investment plays and there are 174 U.S. ETF listings worth $141 billion as of July 2009. Suggestions on how to invest in these funds based on one's conviction on how the global economy will unfold are presented.

27245 ■ "International Growth" in *Black Enterprise* (Vol. 38, July 2008, No. 12, pp. 64)
Pub: Earl G. Graves Publishing Co. Inc.
Ed: Marcia A. Reed-Woodard. **Description:** Becoming an increasingly smaller portion of the global business environment is the U.S. economy. Christopher Catlin, an associate with Booz Allen Hamilton, a technology management and strategy-consulting firm, shares what he has learned about the global market.

27246 ■ "Into the Light: Making Our Way Through the Economic Tunnel" in *Agency Sales Magazine* (Vol. 39, August 2009, No. 8, pp. 26)
Pub: MANA
Ed: Michael Dotson. **Description:** Ways in which to avoid business stagnation brought about by the economic downturn, is presented. Being different, being a puzzle solver, and knowing the competition are among the things marketing personnel should do in order to wade through the economic downturn. Marketing via direct mail and the Internet also recommended.

27247 ■ "Intrepid Souls: Meet a Few Who've Made the Big Leap" in *Crain's Chicago Business* (Vol. 31, November 10, 2008, No. 45, pp. 26)
Pub: Crain Communications, Inc.
Ed: Meredith Landry. **Description:** Advice is given from entrepreneurs who have launched businesses in the last year despite the economic crisis. Among the types of businesses featured are a cooking school, a child day-care center, a children's clothing store and an Internet-based company.

27248 ■ "Inventory Glut" in *Business Courier* (Vol. 24, March 28, 2008, No. 51, pp. 1)
Pub: American City Business Journals, Inc.
Ed: Laura Baverman. **Description:** Indian Hill and the downtown area have the highest monthly absorption rate for housing on a list of 42 Greater Cincinnati and Northern Kentucky neighborhoods. The two neighborhoods have 19 and 27 months of housing inventory respectively, which means home sellers need to either lower their prices or be very patient.

27249 ■ "Is this a Buying Opportunity?" in *Canadian Business* (Vol. 82, April 27, 2009, No. 7, pp. 46)
Pub: Rogers Media
Ed: Andy Holloway. **Description:** Home prices in Canada are down by as much as 14.2 percent in 2009 compared to prices in 2008, making homes more affordable now. Some housing experts believe that homes are still good investments as prices of rent and properties always recover. Meanwhile, a survey found that Canadians under 35 plan to buy a home within two years.

27250 ■ "Is Hawaii Ready for Universal Health Care?" in *Hawaii Business* (Vol. 53, February 2008, No. 8, pp. 26)
Pub: Hawaii Business Publishing
Description: Representative Lyn Finnegan does not believe that a universal health is good for Hawaii as health insurance for everyone will be difficult to achieve. Representative John M. Mizuno says that House Bill 1008 introduced in the state was a landmark for Hawaii as it will provide the people with health care insurance. Other details about their opinion on the topic are presented.

27251 ■ "Is the VIX in Denial?" in *Barron's* (Vol. 88, July 7, 2008, No. 27, pp. M12)
Pub: Dow Jones & Co., Inc.
Ed: Lawrence McMillan. **Description:** Volatility Index (VIX) of the Chicago Board Options Exchange did not rise significantly despite the drop in the US stock markets, rising to near 25. This market decline, however, will eventually result in investor panic and the rise of the VIX.

27252 ■ "It Could Be Worse" in *Barron's* (Vol. 89, July 27, 2009, No. 30, pp. 5)
Pub: Dow Jones & Co., Inc.
Ed: Alan Abelson. **Description:** Media sources are being fooled by corporate America who is peddling an economic recovery rather than reality as shown by the report of a rise in existing home sales which boosted the stock market even if it was a seasonal phenomenon. The phrase "things could be worse" sums up the reigning investment philosophy in the U.S. and this has been stirring up the market.

27253 ■ "It's Good to be Goldman" in *Barron's* (Vol. 89, July 20, 2009, No. 29, pp. 5)
Pub: Dow Jones & Co., Inc.
Ed: Randall W. Forsyth. **Description:** Profits of Goldman Sachs rose to $3.44 billion in the second quarter of 2009, aided by federal financial stimulus programs. CIT Group is facing bankruptcy and may need up to $6 billion to survive. The federal economic stimulus programs are benefiting Wall Street more than the US economy itself.

27254 ■ "It's Time To Swim" in *Canadian Business* (Vol. 81, March 3, 2008, No. 3, pp. 37)
Pub: Rogers Media
Ed: Megan Harman. **Description:** Canadian manufacturers should consider Asian markets such as India and the United Arab Emirates as the U.S.

economic downturn continues. Canada's shortage in skilled labor is also expected to negatively affect manufacturing industries. Ontario's plans to assist manufacturers are also presented.

27255 ■ "It's Time to Wise Up: Income Trusts" in *Canadian Business* (Vol. 79, November 6, 2006, No. 22, pp. 24)
Pub: Rogers Media
Ed: Mark Rosen. **Description:** The effects bogus financial reporting of income trusts on investors are analyzed.

27256 ■ "Janson: Duke's Dynamo, Regional President Focuses on Economic Development" in *Business Courier* (Vol. 27, July 9, 2010, No. 10, pp. 1)
Pub: Business Courier
Ed: Lucy May. **Description:** Duke Energy President Julie Janson is also chair of the Cincinnati USA Partnership for Economic Development and the co-chair of the Cincinnati Business Committee's Economic Development Task Force. Duke is launching a Site Readiness Pilot Program to help the region prepare for an economic recovery.

27257 ■ "J.C. Evans Seeks Bankruptcy Protection" in *Austin Business Journal* (Vol. 31, August 12, 2011, No. 23, pp. A1)
Pub: American City Business Journals Inc.
Ed: Vicky Garza. **Description:** J.C. Evans Construction Holdings Inc., as well as its affiliated companies, has filed for Chapter 11 bankruptcy following its continued financial breakdown which it blames on the tough economy. Details are included.

27258 ■ "Job Losses and Budget Shortfall Adding to Economic Woes" in *Sacramento Business Journal* (Vol. 25, July 11, 2008, No. 19, pp. 1)
Pub: American City Business Journals, Inc.
Ed: Kathy Robertson. **Description:** Budget cuts in California have been approved amid rising unemployment in a slowing economy. Statistics show that total industry employment in the Sacramento region decreased by 3,700 jobs from May 2007 to May 2008. Governor Arnold Schwarzenegger has ordered a 10 percent budget cut for state departments, but this cut will likely mean few layoffs.

27259 ■ "Jobless Rate Climbs Unexpectedly in December" in *Globe & Mail* (January 7, 2006, pp. B5)
Pub: CTVglobemedia Publishing Inc.
Description: The reasons behind increase in unemployment rate by 6.5 percent, in Canada, are presented.

27260 ■ "Jobs Boom Ramps Up in March" in *Globe & Mail* (April 7, 2007, pp. B1)
Pub: CTVglobemedia Publishing Inc.
Ed: Tara Perkins. **Description:** The increase in the number of jobs by 54,900 in Canada and 180,000 in the United States in March 2007 is discussed.

27261 ■ "Jobs Data Show A Slow Leak" in *Barron's* (Vol. 88, July 7, 2008, No. 27, pp. 34)
Pub: Dow Jones & Co., Inc.
Ed: Gene Epstein. **Description:** In June 2008, the United States manufacturing sector showed an expansion, with the purchasing managers' index rising to 50.2 from 49.6; the unemployment rate in the US, which stayed steady at 5.5 percent in June 2008 is also discussed. Statistical data included.

27262 ■ "Jobs, Export Surge Confirm Recovery" in *Globe & Mail* (March 10, 2007, pp. B5)
Pub: CTVglobemedia Publishing Inc.
Ed: Heather Scoffield. **Description:** The increase in the number of jobs and exports that is forecast to reverse the slowdown in the Canadian economy is discussed.

27263 ■ "The Judgment Deficit" in *Harvard Business Review* (Vol. 88, September 2010, No. 9, pp. 44)
Pub: Harvard Business School Publishing
Ed: Amar Bhide. **Description:** The importance of individual, decentralized initiative and judgment in the capitalist system is outlined. While financial models have their use, they cannot always account appropriately for the inherent uncertainty in economic decision making.

27264 ■ "KC Plants Downshift" in *The Business Journal-Serving Metropolitan Kansas City* (Vol. 27, November 7, 2008, No. 9, pp. 1)
Pub: American City Business Journals, Inc.
Ed: James Dornbrook. **Description:** Discusses Ford Motor Co. and General Motors' factories in the region; Ford Motor Co. removed the second shift on the F-150 line at the Kansas City Assembly Plant but added a shift to the production of the Ford Escape and Mercury Mariner in an attempt to avoid layoffs. One spokesman for General Motors, however, states that they cannot guarantee that they won't make any production cuts and layoffs in the future.

27265 ■ "Kenosha 'Lifestyle Center' Delayed" in *The Business Journal-Milwaukee* (Vol. 25, August 8, 2008, No. 46, pp. A1)
Pub: American City Business Journals, Inc.
Ed: Rich Kirchen. **Description:** Quality Centers of Orlando, Florida has postponed construction plans for the Kenosha Town Center in Kenosha County, Wisconsin to 2009 due to the economic downturn and lending concerns. The $200-million, 750,000-square-foot retail and residential center will be located near the corner of Wisconsin Highway 50 and I-94.

27266 ■ "Kent Officials Seek Further KSU, City Unity" in *Crain's Cleveland Business* (Vol. 28, December 3, 2007, No. 48, pp. 3)
Pub: Crain Communications, Inc.
Ed: Jay Miller. **Description:** Kent State University and Portage County are searching for a developer who will use a three-acre parcel to bring new life to the city's sagging downtown and create an area that will better link the town and the Kent State campus. The project will include a hotel and conference center as well as retail and restaurant space.

27267 ■ "Kid Rock" in *Canadian Business* (Vol. 81, Summer 2008, No. 9, pp. 54)
Pub: Rogers Media Ltd.
Ed: John Gray. **Description:** Damien Reynolds is the founder, chairman and chief executive officer of Vancouver-based Longview Capital Partners. The investment bank, founded in 2005, is one of the fastest-growing companies in British Columbia. The recent economic downturn has battered the stocks of the company and its portfolio of junior miners.

27268 ■ "The Kitchen is Closed; Eateries Forced Out by Soaring Rents, Declining Revenues" in *Crain's New York Business* (January 21, 2008)
Pub: Crain Communications, Inc.
Ed: Lisa Fickenscher. **Description:** Many restaurants have already closed in the area and experts expect many more will follow due to skyrocketing rents and declining revenues.

27269 ■ "Kodiak Bucks Bear Market" in *Austin Business JournalInc.* (Vol. 29, December 18, 2009, No. 41, pp. 1)
Pub: American City Business Journals
Ed: Kate Harrington. **Description:** Austin, Texas-based Kodiak Assembly Solutions LLC, a company that installs components into printed circuit boards for product or evaluation tool kit prototyping purposes, will expand despite the recession. It will relocate from a 28,000 square foot space to a 42,000 square foot space in North Austin. The firm will also increase its workforce by 20 employees.

27270 ■ "The Labor Crunch is Coming" in *Canadian Business* (Vol. 80, December 25, 2006, No. 1, pp. 74)
Pub: Rogers Media
Description: The need for skilled and educated workforce to meet labor shortage in future in Canada is discussed.

27271 ■ "Labor Pains" in *Canadian Business* (Vol. 79, August 14, 2006, No. 16-17, pp. 80)
Pub: Rogers Media
Description: Canada's employment insurance is analyzed in view of the growing shortage of labor.

27272 ■ "Laced Up and Ready to Run" in *Barron's* (Vol. 89, July 6, 2009, No. 27, pp. 12)
Pub: Dow Jones & Co., Inc.
Ed: Christopher C. Williams. **Description:** Shares of Foot Locker could raise from $10 to about $15 a share with the improvement of the economy. The company has benefited from prudent management and merchandising as well as better cost cutting, allowing it to better survive in a recession.

27273 ■ "Land on Boardwalk" in *Canadian Business* (Vol. 82, April 27, 2009, No. 7, pp. 19)
Pub: Rogers Media
Ed: Calvin Leung. **Description:** Boardwalk REIT remains as one of the most attractive real estate investment trusts in Canada, with 73 percent of analysts rating the firm a Buy. Analyst Neil Downey believes that good management, as well as a good business model, makes Boardwalk a good investment. Downey is concerned however, that a worsening of Alberta's economy could significantly impact Boardwalk.

27274 ■ "LaSalle Street Firms Cherry-Pick Talent As Wall Street Tanks" in *Crain's Chicago Business* (Vol. 31, November 17, 2008, No. 46)
Pub: Crain Communications, Inc.
Ed: H. Lee Murphy. **Description:** Many local businesses are taking advantage of the lay offs that many major Wall Street firms are undergoing in their workforces; these companies see the opportunity to woo talent and expand their staff with quality executives.

27275 ■ "Last Founder Standing" in *Conde Nast Portfolio* (Vol. 2, June 2008, No. 6, pp. 124)
Pub: Conde Nast Publications, Inc.
Ed: Kevin Maney. **Description:** Interview with Amazon CEO Jeff Bezos in which he discusses the economy, the company's new distribution center and the hiring of employees for it, e-books, and the overall vision for the future of the firm.

27276 ■ "The Latin Beat Goes On" in *Barron's* (Vol. 88, July 7, 2008, No. 27, pp. L5)
Pub: Dow Jones & Co., Inc.
Ed: Tom Sullivan. **Description:** Latin American stocks have outperformed other regional markets due to rising commodities prices and favorable economic climate. Countries such as Brazil, Mexico, Chile, and Peru provide investment opportunities, while Argentina and Venezuela are tougher places to invest.

27277 ■ "Laugh or Cry?" in *Barron's* (Vol. 88, March 24, 2008, No. 12, pp. 7)
Pub: Dow Jones & Company, Inc.
Ed: Alan Abelson. **Description:** Discusses the American economy which is just starting to feel the effect of the credit and housing crises. JPMorgan Chase purchased Bear Stearns for $2 a share, much lower than its share price of $60, while quasi-government entities Fannie Mae and Freddie Mac are starting to run into trouble.

27278 ■ "Law Firms See Improvement in Financing Climate" in *Sacramento Business Journal* (Vol. 28, October 14, 2011, No. 33, pp. 1)
Pub: Sacramento Business Journal
Ed: Kathy Robertson. **Description:** Sacramento, California-based Weintraub Genshlea Chediak Law Corporation has helped close 26 financing deals worth more than $1.6 billion in 2010, providing indication of improvement in Sacramento's economy. Lawyers have taken advantage of low interest rates to make refinancing agreements and help clients get new funds.

27279 ■ "Law Firms Troll for Complaints Among Disgruntled Workers" in *The Business Journal-Serving Greater Tampa Bay* (Vol. 28, July 11, 2008)
Pub: American City Business Journals, Inc.
Ed: Jane Meinhardt. **Description:** Economic slowdown has affected businesses as they downsize, seeing an increase in wage and hour complaints using loopholes in the Fair Labor Standards Act, from which

several law firms are recently generating revenue. Federal judges notice the increase in lawsuits and ordered that law firms show cause for non-compliance.

27280 ■ "Layoffs Continue to Be a Drag on Region's Recovery" in *Philadelphia Business Journal* (Vol. 28, January 22, 2010, No. 49, pp. 1)
Pub: American City Business Journals
Ed: Athena D. Merritt. **Description:** Mass layoffs continue to hamper Pennsylvania's economic recovery. Job losses are predicted to decline in 2010.

27281 ■ "Leaders and Lagards" in *Barron's* (Vol. 89, July 13, 2009, No. 28, pp. 14)
Pub: Dow Jones & Co., Inc.
Ed: J.R. Brandstrader. **Description:** Statistical table that shows the returns of different mutual funds in different categories that include U.S. stock funds, sector funds, world equity funds, and mixed equity funds is presented. The data presented is for the second quarter of 2009.

27282 ■ "Leaders Weigh In On Fannie Mae, Freddie Mac Failure, Fed Bailout" in *The Business Journal - Serving Phoenix and the Valley of the Sun* (Vol. 28, September 12, 2008, No. 53, pp. 1)
Pub: American City Business Journals, Inc.
Ed: Chris Casacchia; Mike Sunnucks; Jan Buchholz. **Description:** Fannie Mae and Freddie Mac's federal takeover was a move to help stabilize the financial market and it helped bring down interest rates in the past week. Local executives from Arizona's Phoenix area share their thoughts on the immediate effect of the takeover and its upside and downside.

27283 ■ *Leadership in the Era of Economic Uncertainty: Managing in a Downturn*
Pub: The McGraw-Hill Companies
Ed: Ram Charan. **Released:** December 2008. **Price:** $22.95. **Description:** Management consultant gives advice on how to weather the economic storm, focusing on cash flow and foregoing expansion.

27284 ■ "Leading Ohio Internet Marketing Firm Announces Growth in September" in *Marketing Weekly News* (September 26, 2009, pp. 24)
Pub: Investment Weekly News
Description: Despite a poor economy, Webbed Marketing, a leading social media marketing and search engine optimization firm in the Midwest, has added five additional professionals to its fast-growing team. The company continues to win new business, provide more services and hire talented employees.

27285 ■ "Legislators Must Cut Cost of Government" in *Crain's Detroit Business* (Vol. 24, October 6, 2008, No. 40, pp. 6)
Pub: Crain Communications, Inc.
Description: Southeast and West Michigan business leaders are setting aside their differences and have proposed clear agendas, ranging from eliminating the Michigan Business Tax to overhauling public employee and retiree benefits and pensions. Lawmakers must also come together to find solutions for the state's economy and discover an entirely new vision for the future of Michigan business.

27286 ■ "Legislature to Tackle Crisis in Jobless Fund" in *Baltimore Business Journal* (Vol. 27, December 18, 2009, No. 32, pp. 1)
Pub: American City Business Journals
Ed: Scott Dance. **Description:** Maryland's General Assembly is set to finalize changes to the state's unemployment insurance system as soon as it convenes for the 2010 session. The move was aimed to draw $127 million in stimulus money that can support the nearly depleted fund of unemployment benefits within 45 days.

27287 ■ "Legoland Plans Could Tumble After State's Modesa Denial" in *Business Journal-Serving Metropolitan Kansas City* (November 16, 2007)
Pub: American City Business Journals, Inc.
Ed: Jim Davis. **Description:** RED Development LLC's officials are not giving up after the Missouri Department of Economic Development said RED could not exploit the Missouri Downtown and Rural Economic Stimulus Act (Modesa) for the Legoland theme park development in Lee's Summit. Legoland's proposed site southeast of Interstate 470 and U.S. Highway 50 does not fit the Modesa because it is outside Lee's Summit.

27288 ■ "Lenders" in *The Business Journal - Serving Phoenix and the Valley of the Sun* (Vol. 28, July 25, 2008, No. 47, pp. 1)
Pub: American City Business Journals, Inc.
Ed: Jan Buchholz. **Description:** Private equity lender Investor Mortgage Holdings Inc. has continued growing despite the crisis surrounding the real estate and financial industries and has accumulated a $700 million loan portfolio. Private lending has become increasingly important in financing real estate deals as commercial credit has dried up.

27289 ■ "Lending Stays Down at Local Banks" in *Business Courier* (Vol. 27, October 1, 2010, No. 22, pp. 1)
Pub: Business Courier
Ed: Steve Watkins. **Description:** Greater Cincinnati's largest banks have experienced decreases in loans in the past year due to weak economy and sagging loan demands. Analysis of mid-year data has shown that loans drop by a total of $3.6 billion or 4 percent at the ten largest banks as of June 30, 2010 compared to same period in 2009.

27290 ■ "Lessons From My Father" in *Crain's Chicago Business* (Vol. 31, November 10, 2008, No. 45, pp. 28)
Pub: Crain Communications, Inc.
Ed: Rance Crain. **Description:** Rance Crain discusses his father, G.D. Crain Jr., who founded Crain Communications Inc. during the Great Depression. Advice is given for sustaining a business, even one that seems to be failing, during tough economic times.

27291 ■ "Let Markets Decide?" in *Canadian Business* (Vol. 80, October 8, 2007, No. 20, pp. 67)
Pub: Rogers Media
Ed: James Gillies. **Description:** Need to protect Canadian companies that could help boost the country's economy is discussed. It is expected that free markets alone will solve economic problems. Suggested policies that will discourage the takeover of major companies in the country, such as the organization of capitalization with multiple voting shares, are also presented.

27292 ■ "Let Us Count the Ways" in *Barron's* (Vol. 88, July 7, 2008, No. 27, pp. M10)
Pub: Dow Jones & Co., Inc.
Ed: Bennet Sedacca. **Description:** Investors are advised to remain cautious after the drop in stock prices in June 2008. The stock markets remain in the downtrend after reaching a peak in October 2007 and are on the verge of a collapse.

27293 ■ "The Letter of the Law" in *Collections and Credit Risk* (Vol. 14, November 1, 2009, No. 9, pp. 40)
Pub: SourceMedia, Inc.
Ed: Michelle Dunn. **Description:** Analyzes the regulatory landscape regarding debt collection and the ways in which those in the field are dealing with a tough economy, unclear laws and the newest regulations.

27294 ■ "Little Cheer in Holiday Forecast for Champagne" in *Advertising Age* (Vol. 88, November 17, 2008, No. 43, pp. 6)
Pub: Crain Communications, Inc.
Ed: Jeremy Mullman. **Description:** Due to a weak economy that has forced consumers to trade down from the most expensive alcoholic beverages as well as a weak U.S. dollar that has driven already lofty Champagne prices higher, makers of the French sparkling wine are anticipating a brutally slow holiday season.

27295 ■ "A Load of Bull?" in *Canadian Business* (Vol. 82, Summer 2009, No. 8, pp. 12)
Pub: Rogers Media
Ed: Joe Castaldo. **Description:** Some experts and analysts believe that the improvement of some economic indicators in Canada suggest an economic recovery. A survey of Russell Investment in March 2009 found that 60 percent of investment managers are bullish on Canadian stocks. Some experts like Mike Zyblock, however, remain cautious on the economy.

27296 ■ *Local Enterprises in the Global Economy: Issues of Governance and Upgrading*
Pub: Edward Elgar Publishing, Incorporated
Ed: Hubert Schmitz. **Released:** November 2004. **Price:** $35.00 (soft cover), $110.00 (hard bound). **Description:** Examination of the relationships between globalization, corporate governance, and the economic performance of small businesses and local enterprises.

27297 ■ "Local Firms Will Feel Impact Of Wall St. Woes" in *The Business Journal-Milwaukee* (Vol. 25, September 19, 2008, No. 52, pp. A1)
Pub: American City Business Journals, Inc.
Ed: Rich Kirchen. **Description:** Wall Street's crisis is expected to affect businesses in Wisconsin, in terms of decreased demand for services and products and increased financing costs. Businesses in Milwaukee area may face higher interest rates and tougher loan standards. The potential impacts of the Wall Street crisis on local businesses are examined further.

27298 ■ "Local Hotels Brace for Downturn" in *Crain's Chicago Business* (Vol. 31, March 31, 2008, No. 13, pp. 3)
Pub: Crain Communications, Inc.
Ed: Bob Tita. **Description:** Chicago hotels are seeing a noticeable drop in business-related guests so far this year due to a slumping national economy, tighter corporate expense budgets and higher airfares.

27299 ■ "Local Industrial Vacancies Climb" in *Crain's Chicago Business* (Vol. 31, November 17, 2008, No. 46, pp. 18)
Pub: Crain Communications, Inc.
Ed: Eddie Baeb. **Description:** Demand for local industrial real estate has declined dramatically as companies that use warehouse and factory space struggle to survive in an ailing economy. According to a report by Colliers Bennett & Kahnweiler Inc., a commercial real estate brokerage, the regional vacancy rate has risen to 9.86 percent in the third quarter, the fourth straight increase and the highest in the past 14 years.

27300 ■ "Local Knowledge" in *Hawaii Business* (Vol. 53, December 2007, No. 6, pp. 40)
Pub: Hawaii Business Publishing
Ed: David K. Choo. **Description:** Rules and facts business professionals need to know about the local life in Hawaii are presented. The important components in island life include knowledge Hawaiian high schools' histories and image, the local sports scene, special events, potluck ethics, and locals' favorite destination, which is Las Vegas.

27301 ■ "Local Lending Tumbles $10 Billion Since '08" in *Saint Louis Business Journal* (Vol. 31, August 26, 2011, No. 53, pp. 1)
Pub: Saint Louis Business Journal
Ed: Greg Edwards. **Description:** St. Louis, Missouri-based banks lending fell by more than 30 percent in less than three years, from about $30 billion in third and fourth quarters 2008 to about $20 billion in the most recent quarter. However, community banks revealed that they want to lend but there is no loan demand.

27302 ■ "Local M&A Activity Sputters in 1Q" in *Crain's Chicago Business* (Vol. 31, April 21, 2008, No. 16, pp. 20)
Pub: Crain Communications, Inc.
Ed: H. Lee Murphy. **Description:** Local mergers-and-acquisitions activity is down by 34 percent in the first quarter compared to the fourth quarter of last year due to the credit crisis making financing harder to obtain.

27303 ■ "Local Outlook: Stronger Growth Ahead" in *Montana Business Quarterly* (Vol. 49, Spring 2011, No. 1, pp. 10)
Pub: Bureau of Business & Economic Research
Ed: Paul E. Polzin. **Description:** Local economic growth is broken down into three areas: fastest growing in Richland, Gallatin and Flathead Counties; the second growth group consists of Yellowstone, Silver Bow, and Lewis and Clark Counties, which all grew at rates higher than the statewide average; slowest growth was seen in Missoula, Ravalli, Cascade, and Custer Counties. Statistical data included.

27304 ■ "Locally Based Stocks Escape Worst of Market's Turmoil" in *Crain's Detroit Business* (Vol. 24, September 22, 2008, No. 38, pp. 4)
Pub: Crain Communications, Inc.
Ed: Daniel Duggan. **Description:** Locally-based companies did not take as big a hit as might be expected with the shock to the financial markets last week; this is due mainly to the fact that the region does not have heavy exposure to energy or capital markets.

27305 ■ "Lofty Ambitions" in *Canadian Business* (Vol. 80, October 22, 2007, No. 21, pp. 26)
Pub: Rogers Media
Ed: Thomas Watson. **Description:** Canada has made its first trade deal in six years through the European Free Trade Agreement. This is a boost to the Canadian economy, but focus must be made on taking out internal barriers to inter-provincial trade and from third-party trade liberalization.

27306 ■ *The Logic of Life: The Rational Economics of an Irrational World*
Pub: Random House
Ed: Tim Harford. **Released:** February 2009. **Price:** $15.00 paperback. **Description:** Harford excels at making economists' studies palatable for discerning but non-expert readers. The uses hard data to show why promiscuous teens are actually health-conscious, divorce hasn't gotten a fair shake, corporate bosses will always be overpaid and job prospects for minorities continue to be grim.

27307 ■ "Long - And Leery" in *Barron's* (Vol. 88, March 31, 2008, No. 13, pp. 47)
Pub: Dow Jones & Company, Inc.
Ed: Jack Willoughby. **Description:** Tom Claugus' Bay Resource Partners hedge fund has returned 20 percent annually since it started in 1993. Claugus says that he is as aggressively long as he has ever been despite the dangers of the U.S. market. Claugus' stock picks include Canadian Natural Resources, NII Holdings, and Discover Financial.

27308 ■ "A Long Road to Recovery" in *Barron's* (Vol. 89, July 27, 2009, No. 30, pp. 37)
Pub: Dow Jones & Co., Inc.
Ed: Henry Kaufman. **Description:** United States' economy remains hobbled by some underlying constraint and real recovery remains ephemeral. Much of the financial problems could have been avoided if t he Federal Reserve was effectively guarding the financial system.

27309 ■ "A Look Ahead Into 2007" in *Canadian Business* (Vol. 80, December 25, 2006, No. 1, pp. 40)
Pub: Rogers Media
Description: The 2007 forecasts for various industrial sectors like telecom, information technology, manufacturing, retail, financial and energy among others is discussed.

27310 ■ "Looking For Good Buys" in *Black Enterprise* (Vol. 38, November 2007, No. 4, pp. 39)
Pub: Earl G. Graves Publishing Co. Inc.
Ed: Steve Garmhausen. **Description:** Lower interest rates mean consumers generally have more money to spend, which could spur economic growth in the retail sector of the U.S.

27311 ■ "Loonie Tunes: When Will the Dollar Rise Again?" in *Canadian Business* (Vol. 81, November 10, 2008, No. 19, pp. 62)
Pub: Rogers Media Ltd.
Ed: Joe Castaldo. **Description:** The Canadian dollar has weakened against the U.S. Dollar as the U.S. financial crisis rocked global markets. A currency strategist says that the strength of the U.S. dollar is not based on people's optimism on the U.S. economy but on a structural demand where U.S. non-financial corporations have been repatriating greenbacks from foreign subsidiaries.

27312 ■ "Loop 360 Offices Planned" in *Austin Business JournalInc.* (Vol. 28, December 5, 2008, No. 38, pp. A1)
Pub: American City Business Journals
Ed: Kate Harrington. **Description:** Nearly 356,000 square feet of office space is planned in the South Capital of Texas Highway Corridor, also known as Loop 360 in Austin. Riverside Developers plans to wait until the economy improves before starting construction.

27313 ■ "Lost in America" in *Canadian Business* (Vol. 79, October 23, 2006, No. 21, pp. 23)
Pub: Rogers Media
Ed: David Wolf. **Description:** The impact of a decline in the economy of the United States on global economy is analyzed.

27314 ■ *Macrowikinomics: Rebooting Business and the World*
Pub: Portfolio Hardcover
Ed: Don Tapscott, Anthony D. Williams. **Released:** September 28, 2010. **Price:** $27.95. **Description:** Wikinomics Don Tapscott and Anthony Williams showed how mass collaboration was changing the way businesses communicate, create value,, and compete in the new global marketplace in 2007. Now, in the wake of the global financial crisis, the principles of wikinomics have become more powerful than ever.

27315 ■ *Made in China: Secrets of China's Dynamic Entrepreneurs*
Pub: John Wiley & Sons, Inc.
Ed: Winter Nie, Katherine Xin. **Released:** March 1, 2009. **Price:** $24.95. **Description:** Insight and analysis of the strategies leading to China's rapidly growing economy are profiled.

27316 ■ "Making It Stick" in *Business Courier* (Vol. 24, November 9, 2008, No. 30, pp. 1)
Pub: American City Business Journals, Inc.
Ed: Lucy May. **Description:** Discusses a report by the Brookings Institution which shows the need for the U.S. government to offer greater support to the country's metro areas in order to excel globally. Ohio, which has seven of the country's 100 largest metropolitan areas, does not receive enough funds, due to the need to finance less populated areas. Because of this, Ohio politicians have to spread less funding in order to cover more constituents.

27317 ■ "Management Matters with Mike Myatt: Are You Creating Growth in a Down Economy?" in *Commercial Property News* (March 17, 2008)
Pub: Nielsen Company
Ed: Mike Myatt. **Description:** Senior executives are expected to create growth for their company regardless of recession, economic slowdown, inflation, or tight credit and capital markets.

27318 ■ *Managing Economies, Trade and International Business*
Pub: Palgrave Macmillan
Ed: Aidan O'Connor. **Released:** January 19, 2010. **Price:** $90.00. **Description:** An in-depth look at the areas that affect and influence international business, exploring specific issues businesses face in terms of economic development, trade law, and international marketing and management.

27319 ■ *Managing India's Small Industrial Economy: The Catalytic Role of Industrial Counselors and Policy Makers*
Pub: Sage Publications, Incorporated
Ed: V. Padmanand, V.G. Patel. **Released:** June 2004. **Price:** $35.95. **Description:** Case studies and methodology are used to discuss the areas where industrial consultants are influencing sustainability and growth of small businesses in India's industrial economy.

27320 ■ "Managing in Times of Uncertainty; What Leaders Can Learn From the Tumultuous Past Decade" in *Gallup Management Journal* (June 1, 2011)
Pub: Gallup
Description: Executives and managers have been facing a global financial meltdown for the past 10 years along with ongoing wars, an increase in terrorism, and epic natural disasters. The leadership lessons learned over this time are examined.

27321 ■ "Mandel Site Favored For UWM Hall" in *The Business Journal-Milwaukee* (Vol. 25, September 19, 2008, No. 52, pp. A1)
Pub: American City Business Journals, Inc.
Description: University of Wisconsin-Milwaukee student residence hall's leading location is a site pushed by Mandel Group Inc. Real estate sources say that the developer's proposal offers the best opportunity for business development and the least conflict with nearby neighborhoods. Plans for the Mandel site are presented.

27322 ■ "Manufacturing Jobs Go Begging in Downturn" in *Puget Sound Business Journal* (Vol. 29, December 26, 2008, No. 36, pp. 1)
Pub: American City Business Journals
Ed: Steve Wilhelm. **Description:** Trends show that skilled jobs in aerospace and other technology manufacturing industries are in a state of decline as layoffs hit broad sectors of the economy. Too few people are entering the field, prompting companies to try to maintain these skilled workers, thus creating problems that could affect the sector's vitality.

27323 ■ "Many Retailers Soften Return Policies" in *Austin Business JournalInc.* (Vol. 28, December 26, 2008, No. 41, pp. 1)
Pub: American City Business Journals
Ed: Jean Kwon. **Description:** National Retail Federation reported the percentage of retailers saying their holiday return policy in 2008 will slacken compared to last season has increased from 3.4 percent to 11 percent. An increasing percentage of retailers are also getting stingier, as 17.1 percent revealed that their return policies will be stricter.

27324 ■ "Many Sectors Lost Jobs In Detroit Area" in *Crain's Detroit Business* (Vol. 24, February 11, 2008, No. 6, pp. 3)
Pub: Crain Communications Inc. - Detroit
Ed: Amy Lane. **Description:** Southeast Michigan reported its highest jobless rate since 1992 in fourth quarter 2007. Statistical data included.

27325 ■ "Marathon Money" in *Hawaii Business* (Vol. 53, December 2007, No. 6, pp. 127)
Pub: Hawaii Business Publishing
Ed: Jolyn Okimoto Rosa. **Description:** Discusses the effects of the Honolulu Marathon on small businesses' sales. The Running Room, for instance, experience growth in sales starting from the training season up to the end of the race, as a surge of Hawaiian residents and tourists come into the store for items such as running shoes and blister kits. The marathon's impact on Hawaii's tourism is examined as well.

27326 ■ "Market Recoups Its Losses - And Its Optimism" in *Barron's* (Vol. 89, July 20, 2009, No. 29, pp. M3)
Pub: Dow Jones & Co., Inc.
Ed: Kopin Tan. **Description:** US stock markets gained heavily in the third week of July 2009, rising by about 7 percent during the week. The shares of human resource management companies could be overpriced as they are trading at very high price-

earnings multiples. Baxter International faces a class-action suit due to its alleged conspiracy with CSL to fix blood-plasma product prices.

27327 ■ "Market for Retail Space Flat, but Recovery Still Uncertain" in *Sacramento Business Journal* (Vol. 28, August 26, 2011, No. 26, pp. 1)
Pub: Sacramento Business Journal
Ed: Kelly Johnson. **Description:** The retail market in the Sacramento, California region remains challenged with the stock market volatility being the latest of its hurdles. The overall vacancy was 13.1 percent as of mid-2011, but retail real estate professionals express hopes that the worst is behind. A list and description of the region's winners and losers in retail vacancies is provided.

27328 ■ "Market Squeezes Some Lawyers" in *Austin Business JournalInc.* (Vol. 28, December 12, 2008, No. 39, pp. 1)
Pub: American City Business Journals
Ed: Jean Kwon. **Description:** Austin, Texas-based lawyers have been adversely affected by the economic downtown. Fewer works for lawyers in mergers and acquisitions and other activities are being offered. Lawyers are refinancing debts and offering other services.

27329 ■ "Market Watch" in *Barron's* (Vol. 89, July 20, 2009, No. 29, pp. M10)
Pub: Dow Jones & Co., Inc.
Ed: Peter Greene; Michael Darda; Ian Wyatt; Stephanie Pomboy. **Description:** Concerns about a possible increase in US inflation rates are overblown as the country remains in a deflationary environment. Goldman Sachs's second quarter 2009 earnings have already been priced in as its shares rose. Germany's plans of a possible dollar bond sale are in anticipation of a rise in the euro's value.

27330 ■ "Markets in Disarray...Fundamentals Still Strong?" in *Hispanic Business* (October 2007, pp. 14, 16, 18)
Pub: Hispanic Business
Ed: Dr. Juan B. Solana. **Description:** Quarterly economic forecast is presented, covering credit, interest rates, home prices, stock market, and what lies ahead.

27331 ■ "Marriott Checks Out Hotel Prospect" in *The Business Journal-Serving Metropolitan Kansas City* (Vol. 27, November 14, 2008, No. 10)
Pub: American City Business Journals, Inc.
Description: Marriott International Inc. is planning to operate a hotel in Kansas City, Missouri and may take over the Kansas City Marriot Downtown although other hotel operators are interested in bidding on the project.

27332 ■ "Mason Fashions Its Future" in *Business Courier* (Vol. 24, December 7, 2008, No. 34, pp. 1)
Pub: American City Business Journals, Inc.
Ed: Laura Baverman. **Description:** Economic Development Director Michele Blair contracted Cincinnati-based Jack Rouse & Associates to tap the remaining undeveloped land in Mason. The real estate firm is set to develop the 2,000 acres of undeveloped land.

27333 ■ "The Massachusetts Mess: Good Health Care Is Expensive" in *Barron's* (Vol. 89, July 27, 2009, No. 30, pp. 39)
Pub: Dow Jones & Co., Inc.
Ed: Thomas G. Donlan. **Description:** Massachusetts' mandatory health insurance has produced the highest rate of insurance coverage among the states but the state is now unable to afford its dream of universal coverage just three years after they enacted it. This supposed model for federal health-care reform is turning out to be a joke.

27334 ■ "Massive Ford Restructuring to Cut 1,200 More Canadian Jobs" in *Globe & Mail* (January 24, 2006, pp. B1)
Pub: CTVglobemedia Publishing Inc.
Ed: Greg Keenan. **Description:** The details on streamlining of operations of Ford Motor Co., in Canada, are presented.

27335 ■ "Maximize Your Marketing Results In a Down Economy" in *Franchising World* (Vol. 42, November 2010, No. 11, pp. 45)
Pub: International Franchise Association
Ed: Loren Rakich. **Description:** Strategies to help any franchisee to maximize their marketing efforts in a slow economy are outlined.

27336 ■ "Mayor Unveils Business Plan" in *Boston Business Journal* (Vol. 29, September 16, 2011, No. 19, pp. 1)
Pub: American City Business Journals Inc.
Ed: Gary Haber. **Description:** Mayor Stephanie Rawlings-Blake of Baltimore, Maryland unveiled her plan to push the economy forward. Her key objectives include giving more support for the city's technology companies and refocusing the Baltimore Development Corporation on job creation and retention.

27337 ■ "MBA Guide 2008" in *Canadian Business* (Vol. 81, November 10, 2008, No. 19, pp. 92)
Pub: Rogers Media Ltd.
Ed: Sharda Prashad. **Description:** Escalating tuition costs for an MBA degree means that the return on investment could take longer. One study found that MBA degree holders who graduated during recessionary times earned less than those who graduated during good economic times.

27338 ■ *MBA In a Day*
Pub: John Wiley and Sons, Inc.
Ed: Steven Stralser, PhD. **Released:** 2004. **Price:** $34.95. **Description:** Management professor presents important concepts, business topics and strategies that can be used by anyone to manage a small business or professional practice. Topics covered include: human resources and personal interaction, ethics and leadership skills, fair negotiation tactics, basic business accounting practices, project management, and the fundamentals of economics and marketing.

27339 ■ "MBT Add On: Gone by 2012?" in *Crain's Detroit Business* (Vol. 24, October 6, 2008, No. 40, pp. 1)
Pub: Crain Communications, Inc.
Ed: Amy Lane. **Description:** Discusses the Michigan Business Tax (MBT), which has angered many businesses in the state due to the addition of a 21.99 percent surcharge. Although the tax policy will cut taxes on 63 percent of businesses in the state and represent no tax liability change for another nine percent of firms, other businesses will see increases of 100 percent or more. This increase means that many business owners will be forced to relocate or close their establishment and others will have to eliminate jobs. Lawmakers are attempting to find a solution to this problem.

27340 ■ "McD's Dollar-Menu Fixation Sparks Revolt" in *Advertising Age* (Vol. 79, June 2, 2008, No. 22, pp. 1)
Pub: Crain Communications, Inc.
Ed: Emily Bryson York. **Description:** McDonald's franchisees say that low-cost dollar-menu offerings are impacting their bottom line and many have discontinued the dollar-menu altogether due to rising commodity costs, an increase in minimum wage and consumers trading down to the lower-price items.

27341 ■ "Measuring the Impact" in *Mergers & Acquisitions: The Dealmaker's Journal* (March 1, 2008)
Pub: SourceMedia, Inc.
Ed: Ken MacFadyen. **Description:** Discusses a new study out of Europe which contends that the private equity market does not have as much impact on the overall economy as critics contend.

27342 ■ *The Mechanics of Modernity in Europe and East Asia: Institutional Origins of Social Change and Stagnation*
Pub: Routledge
Ed: Erik Ringmar. **Released:** April 1, 2009. **Price:** $44.95. **Description:** Discussion of reasons why certain countries embarked on a path of sustained economic growth while others declined in Europe and East Asia.

27343 ■ "Medicare Inc." in *Canadian Business* (Vol. 80, October 8, 2007, No. 20, pp. 160)
Pub: Rogers Media
Ed: Erin Pooley. **Description:** State of Canada's health care system is discussed. A report by the Fraser Institute in Vancouver predicts that public health spending in six of ten provinces in the country will use more than half the revenues from all sources by 2020. Experts believe competition in the health care industry will help solve the current problems in the sector.

27344 ■ *Medium Sized Firms and Economics Growth*
Pub: Nova Science Publishers, Incorporated
Ed: Janez Prasniker. **Released:** April 2005. **Price:** $130.00. **Description:** Medium sized companies should have a more definitive presence in modern microeconomic theory, the theory of entrepreneurship, and the theory of financial markets.

27345 ■ "Members Make Sacrifices for a World-Class Course" in *Crain's Detroit Business* (Vol. 24, April 7, 2008, No. 14, pp. 21)
Pub: Crain Communications, Inc.
Ed: Jason Deegan. **Description:** Rees Jones Inc. completed a $1.8 million redesign of the Oakland Hills Country Club golf course last year. By all indications, the redesign has been a success since it is among the handful of courses good enough to host future majors which is beneficial for the local economy.

27346 ■ *Memos to the Prime Minister: What Canada Could Be in the 21st Century*
Pub: John Wiley & Sons, Incorporated
Ed: Harvey Schacter. **Released:** April 11, 2003. **Price:** $16.95. **Description:** A look into the business future of Canada. Topics include business, healthcare, think tanks, policy groups, education, the arts, economy, and social issues.

27347 ■ "Mequon Plan On Tracks, Bucks Housing Trend" in *The Business Journal-Milwaukee* (Vol. 25, September 26, 2008, No. 53, pp. A1)
Pub: American City Business Journals, Inc.
Ed: Pete Millard. **Description:** Insight Development Group plans to build condominium units and single-family homes despite the residential market downturn. The Orchard Glen project, a planned development in Mequon, is a $22 million project which will include 38 condos and 12 single-family homes. Details of the project are provided.

27348 ■ "Mexican Companies to Rent Space in TechTown, Chinese Negotiating" in *Crain's Detroit Business* (Vol. 24, September 29, 2008, No. 39)
Pub: Crain Communications, Inc.
Ed: Tom Henderson. **Description:** Wayne State University's TechTown, the business incubator and research park, has signed an agreement with the Mexican government that will provide temporary office space to 25 Mexican companies looking to find customers or establish partnerships in Michigan. TechTown's executive director is negotiating with economic development officials from China. To accommodate foreign visitors the incubator is equipping offices with additional equipment and resources.

27349 ■ "Michael Doesn't Live Here Anymore" in *Canadian Business* (Vol. 80, October 8, 2007, No. 20, pp. 52)
Pub: Rogers Media
Ed: Andrew Wahl. **Description:** Michael Treacy's career in the U.S. is discussed. Treacy, a Canadian entrepreneur, believes that Canada has few comparative advantages aside from its natural resources. Because of this, he also believes that it would not be feasible to do business in the country. Economic factors influenced him to do business in the U.S. instead.

27350 ■ "Micro-Finance Agencies and SMEs" in *International Journal of Entrepreneurship and Small Business* (Vol. 11, August 3, 2010)
Pub: Publishers Communication Group
Ed: Patricia A. Rowe, Michael J. Christie, Frank Hoy. **Description:** Institutional preparedness of economic development agencies for developing small and

medium-sized enterprises (SMEs) is discussed. The cases presented illustrate variations in the microfinance lender agency-enterprise development of processes for sharing vision and interdependence.

27351 ■ *Microtrends: The Small Forces Behind Tomorrow's Big Changes*
Pub: Business Plus
Ed: Mark J. Penn. **Released:** 2007. **Price:** $25.99. **Description:** Political pollster and lead presidential campaign strategist for Hillary Clinton, identifies seventy-five microtrends he believes are changing the social and cultural landscape in the U.S. and globally. The book covers the areas of health and wellness, technology, education and more.

27352 ■ "Midwest Seeks Concessions From Creditors" in *The Business Journal-Milwaukee* (Vol. 25, July 25, 2008, No. 44, pp. A1)
Pub: American City Business Journals, Inc.
Ed: Rich Rovito. **Description:** Midwest Airlines Inc. is turning to creditors and lease holders for the financial aspect of its restructuring, which involves going back to serving popular business destinations. Chief executive officer Timothy believes that the company can survive in a niche market as long as it provides quality service. He discusses Midwest's restructuring plan.

27353 ■ "Millions Needed To Finish First Place" in *The Business Journal-Milwaukee* (Vol. 25, August 15, 2008, No. 47, pp. A1)
Pub: American City Business Journals, Inc.
Ed: Rich Kirchen. **Description:** First Place on the River condominium project in Milwaukee, Wisconsin, needs $18.2 million before it can be completed. A total of $6.8 million have already been spent since the project went into receivership on 31 January 2008.

27354 ■ "Mine Woes Could Rouse Zinc" in *Barron's* (Vol. 88, July 7, 2008, No. 27, pp. M12)
Pub: Dow Jones & Co., Inc.
Ed: Andrea Hotter. **Description:** Prices of zinc could increase due to supply problems in producing countries such as Australia and China. London Metal Exchange prices for the metal have dropped about 36 percent in 2008.

27355 ■ *The Missing Class: Portraits of the Near Poor in America*
Pub: Houghton Mifflin
Ed: Katherine S. Newman; Victor Tan Chen. **Released:** 2007. **Description:** Information regarding the 57 million Americans existing on the razor-thin margin between poverty and middle class.

27356 ■ "Mitch D'Olier" in *Hawaii Business* (Vol. 53, November 2007, No. 5, pp. 27)
Pub: Hawaii Business Publishing
Ed: Cathy S. Cruz-George. **Description:** Mitch D'Olier chief executive officer of Kaneohe Ranch/ Harold K.L. Castle Foundation thinks that achievement gaps are a nationwide problem and that the Knowledge is Power Program is one of the programs that focuses on achievement gaps in some communities across the US. He also provides his insights on education in Hawaii and the current shortage of teachers.

27357 ■ "A Mixed-Bag Quarter" in *Barron's* (Vol. 88, July 7, 2008, No. 27, pp. 19)
Pub: Dow Jones & Co., Inc.
Ed: Shirley A. Lazo. **Description:** Seven component companies of the Dow Jones Industrial Average increased their dividend payouts in the second quarter of 2008 despite the weak performance of the index. Five companies in the Dow Jones Transportation index and three in the Dow Jones Utilities also increased their dividends.

27358 ■ "Mom Insight on Family, Current Affairs, and the Economy" in *Marketing to Women* (Vol. 23, November 2010, No. 11, pp. 5)
Pub: EPM Communications, Inc.
Description: Statistics regarding the way moms feel about current events, family and the economy are shared.

27359 ■ *The Mom and Pop Store: How the Unsung Heroes of the American Economy Are Surviving and Thriving*
Pub: Walker & Company
Ed: Robert Spector. **Released:** September 1, 2009. **Price:** $26.00. **Description:** The history of small independent retail enterprises and how mom and pop stores in the U.S. continue to thrive through customer service and renewed community support for local businesses.

27360 ■ *The Mommy Manifesto: How to Use Our Power to Think Big, Break Limitations and Achieve Success*
Pub: John Wiley & Sons, Inc.
Ed: Kim Lavine. **Released:** September 1, 2009. **Price:** $24.95. **Description:** A new women's revolution will help women take control of their careers, their lives, and their economic future. The book shows how mom's control the economy and have the power to become successful entrepreneurs.

27361 ■ "Moms Are Still Shopping" in *Marketing to Women* (Vol. 21, February 2008, No. 2, pp. 1)
Pub: EPM Communications, Inc.
Description: According to a monthly poll by Parenting Magazine, although the economic signs worsen many moms are still shopping. Statistical data included.

27362 ■ "Money Ball" in *Canadian Business* (Vol. 80, October 22, 2007, No. 21, pp. 40)
Pub: Rogers Media
Ed: Andy Holloway. **Description:** Rising Canadian dollar has a positive impact on the sports industry. Canadian team executives earn revenues in Canadian dollar, but pay expensive American dollar. Athletes who play in the Canadian Football Leagues benefit most from the increasing rate.

27363 ■ "The Money Train: How Public Projects Shape Our Economic Future" in *Hawaii Business* (Vol. 54, September 2008, No. 3, pp. 31)
Pub: Hawaii Business Publishing
Ed: Jason Ubay. **Description:** Public projects impact the construction industry as such projects create jobs and new infrastructure that can lead to private developments. Details on the government contracts and construction projects in Hawaii and their rising costs and impact on the state's economy are discussed.

27364 ■ "Montana Outlook: Stronger Growth Ahead" in *Montana Business Quarterly* (Vol. 49, Spring 2011, No. 1, pp. 7)
Pub: Bureau of Business & Economic Research
Ed: Patrick M. Barkey. **Description:** A look at Montana's economy and future growth is given. Experts are predicting that the state will experience new growth in 2011, with 2012 showing its best growth since 2006. Statistical data included.

27365 ■ "The Mood of a Nation" in *Canadian Business* (Vol. 81, April 14, 2008, No. 6, pp. 56)
Pub: Rogers Media
Ed: Joe Castaldo. **Description:** Independent Fish Harvesters Inc. processes more kilograms a year and has had to hire more workers but its managers worry about how a slowdown in the U.S. economy will affect his business. A planned shopping complex in Mirabel Quebec, the manufacturing industry in Kitchener, Ontario, and a cattle farming business in Sarnia, Ontario are discussed to provide a snapshot of the challenges that business in Canada are facing as recession looms.

27366 ■ "Moody and Paranoid" in *Barron's* (Vol. 88, March 10, 2008, No. 10, pp. M14)
Pub: Dow Jones & Company, Inc.
Ed: Steven M. Sears. **Description:** Discusses the options market which remains liquid but is cautious of possible failures, especially for financial companies. Investors are in absolute fear when trading with options involving the financial sector.

27367 ■ "More Callers Are Cutting Their Landlines" in *Chicago Tribune* (December 30, 2008)
Pub: McClatchy-Tribune Information Services
Ed: Eric Benderoff. **Description:** Despite sporadic outages for cell phone users, the trend for consumers to cut out the expense of a landline does not appear to be slowing; experts believe that the recession will further increase the number of consumers who decide to go completely wireless.

27368 ■ "More Manufacturers Scout Military Contracts As Auto Industry Lags" in *Crain's Detroit Business* (Vol. 24, September 29, 2008, No. 39)
Pub: Crain Communications, Inc.
Ed: Chad Halcom. **Description:** Many Michigan manufacturers are looking to grow with new military contracts now that the reality of the auto industry is becoming more clear; these companies see that the government contracts may be the only way in which they will be able to stay in business through these rough economic times.

27369 ■ "More Offices Planned For Percheron Square" in *The Business Journal-Milwaukee* (Vol. 25, August 22, 2008, No. 48, pp. A1)
Pub: American City Business Journals, Inc.
Ed: Pete Millard. **Description:** More office projects are under way at Percheron Square. Ryan Cos. US Inc., for example, plans to build over 200,000 square feet of office space at the area. Details of new office projects in Wisconsin are presented.

27370 ■ "More Pain" in *Canadian Business* (Vol. 81, December 24, 2007, No. 1, pp. 12)
Pub: Rogers Media
Ed: Lauren McKeon. **Description:** Manufacturing sector in Canada is sinking with a forecast by as much as 23 percent for 2008, which can be offset as manufacturers say they plan to increase productivity by 25 percent. Details on the sector's competitiveness, workforce, importing of machinery from the U.S. and financial needs for research and development are examined.

27371 ■ "Mortgage Securities Drop Hits Home" in *The Business Journal-Serving Metropolitan Kansas City* (Vol. 27, October 17, 2008, No. 5)
Pub: American City Business Journals, Inc.
Ed: Rob Roberts. **Description:** Sale of commercial mortgage-backed securities (CMBS) in Kansas City, Missouri have declined. The area may avoid layoffs if the United States government succeeds in stabilizing the economy. Major CMBS players in the area include Midland Loan Services Inc. and KeyBank Real Estate Capital.

27372 ■ "Most See Gloomy Year For Michigan Business" in *Crain's Detroit Business* (Vol. 24, October 6, 2008, No. 40, pp. 4)
Pub: Crain Communications, Inc.
Ed: Amy Lane. **Description:** Michigan residents are extremely concerned about the economic climate and business conditions in the state. According to the latest quarterly State of the State Survey, conducted by Michigan State University's Institute for Public Policy and Social Research, 63.9 percent of those surveyed anticipate bad times for Michigan businesses over the next year. Additional findings from the survey are also included.

27373 ■ "Move Over - Or Out" in *Puget Sound Business Journal* (Vol. 29, November 28, 2008, No. 32, pp. 1)
Pub: American City Business Journals
Ed: Kirsten Grind. **Description:** Real estate agents in the state of Washington are either moving to smaller real estate firms or quitting the industry due to the weak housing market. Lesser-known firms are experiencing an influx of experienced real estate agents, while 2,800 agents in the state have left the industry.

27374 ■ "Mover and Sheika" in *Conde Nast Portfolio* (Vol. 2, June 2008, No. 6, pp. 104)
Pub: Conde Nast Publications, Inc.
Ed: John Arlidge. **Description:** Profile of Princess Sheika Lubna who is the first female foreign trade minister in the Middle East, the United Arab Emirates biggest business envoy, paving the way for billions in new investment, and also a manufacturer of her own perfume line.

27375 ■ "Mr. Deeds" in *Canadian Business* (Vol. 81, March 31, 2008, No. 5, pp. 24)
Pub: Rogers Media
Ed: Thomas Watson. **Description:** Ron Sandler has the right experience to save Northern Rock PLC get through its liquidity problems. Sandler is known for saving Lloyd's of London in the mid-90's and he is not afraid to make enemies. Ron Sandler's assignment to help Northern Rock comes at a time when the health of the U.K. housing is not great.

27376 ■ "Mulroney on the Record" in *Canadian Business* (Vol. 79, September 11, 2006, No. 18, pp. 43)
Pub: Rogers Media
Description: Canada's former prime minister and senior partner at the law firm Ogilvy Renault, Brain Mulroney speaks about the major policies and initiatives of the current government and its impact on the country's economy.

27377 ■ "Myths of Deleveraging" in *Barron's* (Vol. 90, August 23, 2010, No. 34, pp. M14)
Pub: Barron's Editorial & Corporate Headquarters
Ed: Gene Epstein. **Description:** The opposite is true against reports about deleveraging or the decrease in credit since inflation-adjusted-investment factories and equipment rose 7.8 percent in the first quarter of 2010. On consumer deleveraging, sales of homes through credit is weak but there is a trend towards more realistic homeownership and consumer spending on durable goods rose 8.8 percent.

27378 ■ "Native Wisdom" in *Canadian Business* (Vol. 80, October 8, 2007, No. 20, pp. 121)
Pub: Rogers Media
Ed: Bernd Christmas. **Description:** Roles of Canadian indigenous peoples in the country's economic development are discussed. It is believed that empowering Canadian natives to contribute to the country's economy will positively affect the country's future. The need for education in preparing natives for the global economy is also tackled.

27379 ■ "New Chief Walking the Talk" in *Business Courier* (Vol. 27, August 27, 2010, No. 17, pp. 1)
Pub: Business Courier
Ed: Lucy May. **Description:** National Brand & Tag Company president, Eric Haas, has vowed to put his various work experiences when he assumes the presidency of North Kentucky Chamber of Commerce. Haas wants to help the Chamber influence government policies that could help various businesses through the economic depression.

27380 ■ "New Economy Initiative Gains Partners" in *Crain's Detroit Business* (Vol. 25, June 1, 2009, No. 22, pp. M014)
Pub: Crain Communications Inc. - Detroit
Ed: Sherri Begin Welch. **Description:** New Economy Initiative is a $100 million philanthropic initiative that focuses on regional economic development. Recent grants awarded to Michigan companies are outlined.

27381 ■ *The New Innovators: How Canadians are Shaping the Knowledge-Based Economy*
Pub: James Lorimer & Company Ltd.
Ed: Roger Voyer; Patti Ryan. **Released:** January 1, 1994. **Price:** $29.95. **Description:** Details are examined showing how the innovation process works and how ideas are successfully translated into marketable products.

27382 ■ "New Jobless Claims Filed in December Soar" in *Baltimore Business Journal* (Vol. 27, January 29, 2010, No. 39, pp. 1)
Pub: American City Business Journals
Ed: Scott Dance. **Description:** Maryland received 48,693 new claims for unemployment benefits in December 2009, reaching its highest monthly total since 1974. The number of claims was up 49 percent from November and 13 percent from the same period in 2008. Labor officials and economists discuss this trend.

27383 ■ "New King Top the Charts" in *The Business Journal-Portland* (Vol. 25, August 8, 2008, No. 22, pp. 1)
Pub: American City Business Journals, Inc.
Ed: Andy Giegerich. **Description:** Spanish-language KRYP-FM station's spring 2008 ratings soared to 6.4 from 2.8 for the previous year. The station timing is flawless given the fact that one of every three new Portland-area residents between 2002 and 2007 were Latino.

27384 ■ "New Leadership Panel Has Advice for Collins" in *Business First Buffalo* (November 23, 2007, pp. 1)
Pub: American City Business Journals, Inc.
Ed: David Bertola. **Description:** Business First and Leadership Buffalo sponsored a meeting that convened business and civic leaders to discuss issues important to the economic growth and development of Western New York. The panel made recommendations to the County Executive-elect Christopher Collins. Details of the forum are included.

27385 ■ "The New Orleans Saints" in *Entrepreneur* (Vol. 37, August 2009, No. 8, pp. 40)
Pub: Entrepreneur Media, Inc.
Ed: Jason Meyers. **Description:** Idea Village is a nonprofit group that fosters entrepreneurship in New Orleans, Louisiana. Entrepreneurship is indeed growing in the city during a time when the city is still recovering from the damage of hurricane Katrina.

27386 ■ "A New Reality; There are Some Signs of Hope Amid 2009's Darkness" in *Crain's Cleveland Business* (Vol. 30, June 29, 2009, No. 25)
Pub: Crain Communications, Inc.
Ed: John Booth. **Description:** Despite all the pessimism, there are some signs that the economy is slowly stabilizing.

27387 ■ "New Thinking for a New Financial Order" in *Harvard Business Review* (Vol. 86, September 2008, No. 9, pp. 26)
Pub: Harvard Business School Press
Ed: Diana Farell. **Description:** Factors driving the current global economy are analyzed with a focus on the influence of new public and private sectors and the impact of unregulated markets.

27388 ■ "A New World" in *Canadian Business* (Vol. 80, October 8, 2007, No. 20, pp. 136)
Pub: Rogers Media
Ed: Deborah Harford. **Description:** Effects of climate change in Canada's economy are presented. A report published by Natural Resources Canada's Climate Change Impacts and Adaptation Program shows severe weather events such as droughts and storms will cause severe economic problems. Canada's infrastructure could also be affected by the rise in sea level over the next century.

27389 ■ "Nexstar Super Meeting Breaks Business Barriers" in *Contractor* (Vol. 56, November 2009, No. 11, pp. 3)
Pub: Penton Media, Inc.
Ed: Candace Roulo. **Description:** Around 400 Nexstar members met to discuss the trends in the HVAC industry and the economic outlook for 2010. Former lead solo pilot John Foley for the Blue Angels made a presentation on how a business can increase overall productivity based on the culture of the Blue Angels. Some breakout sessions tackled how to optimize workflow and marketing.

27390 ■ "The Next Government Bailout?" in *Barron's* (Vol. 88, March 10, 2008, No. 10, pp. 21)
Pub: Dow Jones & Company, Inc.
Ed: Jonathan Laing. **Description:** Fannie Mae may need a government bailout as it faces huge hits brought about by the effects of the housing crisis. The shares of the government-sponsored enterprise have dropped 65 percent since the housing crisis began.

27391 ■ "The Next Waive" in *Hawaii Business* (Vol. 53, January 2008, No. 7, pp. 27)
Pub: Hawaii Business Publishing
Ed: Cathy S. Cruz-George. **Description:** Only 40,000 Koreans took a visit to Hawaii in 2007, a decline from the pre-September averages of 123,000 visits. The number of Korean visitors in Hawaii could increase if the visa waiver proposal is passed. Efforts to improve Hawaiian tourism are presented.

27392 ■ "Niche Markets, Green Will Be Okay in 2010" in *Contractor* (Vol. 57, January 2010, No. 1, pp. 1)
Pub: Penton Media, Inc.
Ed: Robert P. Mader . **Description:** Mechanical contractors will see most of their work stemming from niche markets, such as green work, as well as service work in 2010. It is said that things will turn around for the industry in 2012 and 2013 and one forecast believes that anything outside of the institutional or more public sector work could be down 15 to 30 percent.

27393 ■ "Nightmare on Wall Street" in *Canadian Business* (Vol. 81, October 13, 2008, No. 17, pp. 9)
Pub: Rogers Media Ltd.
Ed: Rachel Pulfer. **Description:** Information on events that happened on Wall Street on the week that started September 15, 2008, as well on its effect on financial markets around the world, are presented. Lehman Brothers filed for bankruptcy on September 15, 2008 after negotiations with Barclays Group and Bank of America failed. Details on AIG and Morgan Stanley are also presented.

27394 ■ "Nine Sectors to Watch: Metals" in *Canadian Business* (Vol. 81, December 24, 2007, No. 1, pp. 46)
Pub: Rogers Media
Ed: John Gray. **Description:** Forecasts on the Canadian metal industries for 2008 are discussed. Details on mine production and the rise in prices are also presented.

27395 ■ "Nine Sectors to Watch: Retail" in *Canadian Business* (Vol. 81, December 24, 2007, No. 1, pp. 56)
Pub: Rogers Media
Ed: Zena Olijnyk. **Description:** Canadian consumers are expected to spend more in 2008 as the Canadian dollar hit par with the U.S. greenback after the slowdown in the U.S. economy. Forecasts on retail sales growth are presented.

27396 ■ "Nine Sectors to Watch: Telecom" in *Canadian Business* (Vol. 81, December 24, 2007, No. 1, pp. 44)
Pub: Rogers Media
Ed: Andrew Wahl. **Description:** Forecasts on the Canadian telecommunications industry for 2008 are presented. Details on consumer spending growth, the popularity of broadband, and activities in the wireless sector are also discussed.

27397 ■ "No End to the Nightmare; America's Car Industry" in *The Economist* (Vol. 390, January 3, 2009, No. 8612, pp. 46)
Pub: The Economist Newspaper Inc.
Description: Detroit's struggling auto industry and the government loan package is discussed as well as the United Auto Worker union, which is loathed by Senate Republicans.

27398 ■ "No Rooms for the Inn In This High-Rise" in *Chicago Tribune* (October 4, 2008)
Pub: McClatchy-Tribune Information Services
Ed: Ameet Sachdev; Jim Kirk. **Description:** Construction has stalled for several hotel expansion projects due to the economy which has caused a decline in occupancy and little growth in average daily

room rates in downtown Chicago because consumers and businesses are becoming more cautious in the amount of money they spend on travel.

27399 ■ "No Shortage of Challenges for Cross-Border Trade" in *Canadian Sailings* (June 30, 2008)
Pub: Commonwealth Business Media
Ed: Kathlyn Horibe. **Description:** Pros and cons of the North American Free Trade Agreement are examined. The agreement between the U.S. and Canada concerning trade was an essential step toward securing economic growth for Canadian citizens. Two-way trade between the counties has tripled since the agreement and accounts for 7.1 million American and 3 million Canadian jobs.

27400 ■ "No Wild Highs Means No Wild Lows" in *Business Courier* (Vol. 24, January 18, 2008, No. 41, pp. 1)
Pub: American City Business Journals, Inc.
Ed: Laura Baverman. **Description:** Discusses a PMI Group report which revealed that the Greater Cincinnati area is in the lowest risk category for home value declines. The report forecast that the chance that housing prices in the area will fall below their current status by the year 2010 is less than 5 percent. Housing price forecasts for other areas are also provided.

27401 ■ "Nonprofits Hope Employees Dig Deep" in *Austin Business JournalInc.* (Vol. 28, December 5, 2008, No. 38, pp. A1)
Pub: American City Business Journals
Ed: Sandra Zaragoza. **Description:** Nonprofit organizations in Austin, Texas are stepping up workplace giving drives in the hope that workers will continue giving donations to them. Corporations are cutting costs due to the recession, reducing donations to nonprofit organizations in the process.

27402 ■ "Nonprofits Pressured to Rein in Fundraising Events" in *Crain's Detroit Business* (Vol. 25, June 15, 2009, No. 24, pp. 1)
Pub: Crain Communications Inc. - Detroit
Ed: Sherri Begin Welch. **Description:** Local corporations have asked nonprofit= s to limit fundraising events in order to cut costs during the recession.

27403 ■ "Northern Kentucky Adds 1,355 Jobs in '07" in *Business Courier* (Vol. 24, February 15, 2008, No. 45, pp. 3)
Pub: American City Business Journals, Inc.
Ed: Lucy May. **Description:** Jobs generated by new and expanding businesses in Northern Kentucky in 2007 totaled to 1,355, which boosted total business sales to $410 million. The ripple effects of the businesses are expected to create 5,432 new jobs and increase business sales to more than $888 million.

27404 ■ "Northern Overexposure" in *Canadian Business* (Vol. 79, August 14, 2006, No. 16-17, pp. 36)
Pub: Rogers Media
Description: Fall in revenue from foreign film productions in Canada due to its overexposure, and incentives offered by other nations to foreign film productions, are discussed.

27405 ■ "Not In My Backyard" in *Entrepreneur* (Vol. 36, May 2008, No. 5, pp. 42)
Pub: Entrepreneur Media, Inc.
Ed: Farnoosh Torabi. **Description:** More investors are turning to overseas real estate investments as the U.S. market sees a slowdown. Analysts say that risk-averse investors opt for funds with record of strong returns and U.S. real estate investment trusts that partner with foreign businesses for transparency purposes. Other details about foreign real estate investments are discussed.

27406 ■ "A Novel Fix for the Credit Mess" in *Barron's* (Vol. 88, March 31, 2008, No. 13, pp. 10)
Pub: Dow Jones & Company, Inc.
Ed: Michael Santoli. **Description:** Due to the common bank-leverage factor of 10, the $250 billion of lost bank capital would have supported $2.5 trillion in lending capacity. Jeffrey Lewis suggests onerous regulations on bank-holding companies that own 10 to 25 percent, as they are partly to blame. Statistical data included.

27407 ■ "Number of Mechanic's Liens Triple Since 2005" in *The Business Journal - Serving Phoenix and the Valley of the Sun* (Vol. 28, August 22, 2008, No. 51, pp. 1)
Pub: American City Business Journals, Inc.
Ed: Jan Buchholtz. **Description:** Experts are blaming the mortgage and banking industries for the tripling of mechanic's liens that were filed in Arizona from 2005 through August 6, 2008. The rise in mechanic's liens is believed to indicate stress in the real estate community. Other views and information on the rise of mechanic's liens filed in Arizona are presented.

27408 ■ "Numbers Game" in *Baltimore Business Journal* (Vol. 27, February 6, 2010, No. 40, pp. 1)
Pub: American City Business Journals
Ed: Scott Dance. **Description:** Doubts are being raised regarding the impact of the federal stimulus spending in addressing unemployment in Maryland, which has experienced 1,800 jobs created so far. Details on the view of companies and the insufficient amount of contracts that lead to the fewer number of workers being hired are discussed.

27409 ■ "Nvidia's Picture Brighter Than Stock Price Indicates" in *Barron's* (Vol. 88, March 24, 2008, No. 12, pp. 46)
Pub: Dow Jones & Company, Inc.
Ed: Eric J. Savitz. **Description:** Shares of graphics chip maker Nvidia, priced at $18.52 each, do not indicate the company's strong position in the graphics chip market. The company's shares have dropped due to fears of slower demand for PCs, but the company is not as exposed to broader economic forces.

27410 ■ "Oakland County Hopes Auto Suppliers Can Drive Medical Industry Growth" in *Crain's Detroit Business* (March 10, 2008)
Pub: Crain Communications, Inc.
Ed: Chad Halcom. **Description:** Oakland County officials are hoping to create further economic development for the region by pairing health care companies and medical device makers with automotive suppliers in an attempt to discover additional crossover technology.

27411 ■ "October 2009: Recovery Plods Along" in *Hispanic Business* (October 2009, pp. 10-11)
Pub: Hispanic Business
Ed: Dr. Juan Solana. **Description:** Economist reports on a possible economic recovery which will not be allowed to rely on a strong domestic demand in order to sustain it. Consumers, looking to counterbalance years of leverage financing based on unrealistic, ever-increasing home and portfolio valuations, are saving rather than spending money.

27412 ■ "Office Leasing Gains Ground" in *Sacramento Business Journal* (Vol. 25, July 18, 2008, No. 20, pp. 1)
Pub: American City Business Journals, Inc.
Ed: Michael Shaw. **Description:** There were at least 84,000 square feet leased to companies in the Sacramento area in the three months prior to August 2008. This development is good news considering that overall vacant leases were around 247,000 square feet for the previous quarter.

27413 ■ "Office Market May Turn Down" in *Crain's New York Business* (Vol. 24, January 14, 2008, No. 2, pp. 26)
Pub: Crain Communications, Inc.
Description: Although still dominated by Wall Street, the downturn in the economy is raising fears that the continuing fallout from the subprime mortgage crisis could result in layoffs that will derail the office market.

27414 ■ "Ohio's Reputation Lags Its Business Ranking" in *Business Courier* (Vol. 24, November 23, 2008, No. 32, pp. 1)
Pub: American City Business Journals, Inc.
Ed: Jon Newberry. **Description:** Site Selection magazine's annual ranking of the top states for new business facilities has ranked Ohio and Kentucky in seventh and eight place respectively, but an opinion survey of real estate executives had placed Ohio much lower at 14. The survey asked 6,000 executives if Ohio's conditions were best for new building projects.

27415 ■ "Oil Picks and Pans" in *Canadian Business* (Vol. 79, August 14, 2006, No. 16-17, pp. 67)
Pub: Rogers Media
Ed: Graham Scott. **Description:** A survey on investments in Canadian energy companies and the inflation caused by oil price hike, are discussed.

27416 ■ "OK, Bring in the Lawyers" in *Crain's Chicago Business* (Vol. 31, November 17, 2008, No. 46, pp. 26)
Pub: Crain Communications, Inc.
Ed: Daniel Rome Levine. **Description:** Bankruptcy attorneys are finding the economic and credit crisis a benefit for their businesses due to the high number of business owners and mortgage holders that are need of their services. One Chicago firm is handling ten times the number of cases they did the previous year and of that about 80 percent of their new clients are related to the real estate sector.

27417 ■ "On the Economic Dimensions of Corporate Social Responsibility" in *Business and Society* (December 2007, pp. 457-478)
Pub: Sage Publications USA
Ed: Fabienne Fortanier, Ans Kolk. **Description:** Economic impact of Fortune Global 250 firms analyzing concern for corporate social responsibility is discussed, focusing on an illustration of mechanisms by which multinational enterprises affect economic developed.

27418 ■ "On tap: More Could Get MEGA Credits; Need to Look Outside State May Be Cut" in *Crain's Detroit Business* (April 7, 2008)
Pub: Crain Communications, Inc.
Ed: Amy Lane. **Description:** In order to qualify for Michigan Economic Growth Authority tax credits Michigan businesses may no longer have to shop outside the state due to a new bill which has already passed the state Senate and will move on to the House; the bill, along with further changes to the MEGA program, is designed to provide incentives for investments that would add relevance and make Michigan more competitive.

27419 ■ *On the Wealth of Nations: Books That Changed the World*
Pub: Grove Atlantic
Ed: P.J. O'Rourke. **Released:** December 21, 2007. **Price:** $21.95. **Description:** Author defends the tenets of freedom of trade, the healthy pursuit of self-interest, and the importance of being a person who "adheres, on all occasions, steadily and resolutely to his maxims."

27420 ■ "Once More Into the Fray" in *Canadian Business* (Vol. 80, December 25, 2006, No. 1, pp. 13)
Pub: Rogers Media
Ed: Jack Mintz. **Description:** A forecast of slow down in the Canadian economy and an election year in 2007 is discussed.

27421 ■ *One Foot Out the Door: How to Combat the Psychological Recession That's Alienating Employees and Hurting American Business*
Pub: AMACOM
Ed: Judith M. Bardwick. **Released:** October 31, 2007. **Price:** $24.95. **Description:** Drawing on research that indicates Generation X and younger baby boomers feel disconnected from their jobs, the author explores the causes (bad management) of that

disengagement. Her pragmatic suggestions about how companies can prove their commitment to employees is beneficial.

27422 ■ "Online All the Time" in *Retail Merchandiser* (Vol. 51, July-August 2011, No. 4, pp. 18)
Pub: Phoenix Media Corporation
Description: Ecommerce sales are rising at a steady pace and for cross-channel retailers it is boosting sales in the weak economy. Online sales are expected to reach $188 billion in 2011, boasting a 13.7 rate of growth.

27423 ■ "OPEC Exposed" in *Hawaii Business* (Vol. 54, September 2008, No. 3, pp. 2)
Pub: Hawaii Business Publishing
Ed: Serena Lim. **Description:** Organization of the Petroleum Exporting Countries (OPEC) has said that their effort in developing an alternative energy source has driven prices up. The biofuel sector is criticizing the statement, saying that a research study found that biofuels push petroleum prices down by 15 percent. Details on the effect of rising petroleum prices are discussed.

27424 ■ "Optimism Index" in *Black Enterprise* (Vol. 41, September 2010, No. 2, pp. 24)
Pub: Earl G. Graves Publishing Co. Inc.
Description: According to a Pew Research Center report, 81 percent of African Americans expect to improve their finances in 2011. Blacks have carried a disproportionate share of job losses and housing foreclosures in the recession that began in 2007.

27425 ■ "Orders Up; Jobs Below Forecast" in *Charlotte Observer* (February 2, 2007)
Pub: Knight-Ridder/Tribune Business News
Ed: Kerry Hall. **Description:** U.S. Labor Department reported unemployment rates at 4.6 percent, up one-tenth of a percent. Economists had predicted 170,000 new jobs, but only 111,000 were created.

27426 ■ "Others' Economic Woes Bring Business to Bankruptcy Attorney" in *The Business Journal - Serving Phoenix and the Valley of the Sun* (Vol. 28, July 4, 2008, No. 44, pp. 7)
Pub: American City Business Journals, Inc.
Ed: Mike Sunnucks. **Description:** Economic slowdown has increased the demand for the services offered by law firms and bankruptcy attorneys. The number of small business and consumer bankruptcies has surged in 2005. Attorney Dan Gukeisen of Gukeisen Law Group PC has shifted his focus to handling bankruptcy filings and foreclosure matters.

27427 ■ "Ottawa to Push for Gas Deal Between Petrocan, Gazpron" in *Globe & Mail* (February 13, 2006, pp. B1)
Pub: CTVglobemedia Publishing Inc.
Ed: Greame Smith. **Description:** Jim Flaherty, finance minister of Canada is negotiating a 1.3 billion dollar deal between state owned Petro-Canada and Russia's OAO Gazprom. This once again highlighted the country's increasing dependence on Russia for its energy requirements.

27428 ■ "Ottawa's Real Estate Targets Exceed Market Appraisals" in *Globe & Mail* (March 19, 2007, pp. B1)
Pub: CTVglobemedia Publishing Inc.
Ed: Danier Leblanc. **Description:** The growth in the real estate market in Ottawa and the huge revenue the government is expecting from sale of nine buildings as part of its lease back plan is discussed.

27429 ■ "Outlook 2007" in *Canadian Business* (Vol. 80, December 25, 2006, No. 1, pp.)
Pub: Rogers Media
Ed: David Wolf. **Description:** Economists' 2007 forecast on global economy, particularly about Canada's housing and labor market among other sectors, is discussed.

27430 ■ "Outlook for Montana Agriculture" in *Montana Business Quarterly* (Vol. 49, Spring 2011, No. 1, pp. 26)
Pub: Bureau of Business & Economic Research
Ed: George Haynes. **Description:** Montana farmers and ranchers are rebounding from lower prices and production to higher prices and record production in 2010. The state has limited dairy and hog production, but farm income is still likely rise between 15 to 25 percent in 2010 over previous year.

27431 ■ "Over A Barrel" in *Canadian Business* (Vol. 81, July 21, 2008, No. 11, pp. 13)
Pub: Rogers Media Ltd.
Ed: Thomas Watson. **Description:** Analysts predict that the skyrocketing price of fuel will cause a crackdown in the market as purported in the peak oil theory. It is forecasted that the price of oil will reach $200 per barrel. Details of the effect of the increasing oil prices on the market are presented.

27432 ■ "Over a Barrel" in *Canadian Business* (Vol. 80, February 12, 2007, No. 4, pp. 52)
Pub: Rogers Media
Ed: Andrew Nikoforuk. **Description:** The potential of tar sands of Alberta in becoming the largest source of oil in the world and huge investments of Canadian companies to mine for the oil there are discussed.

27433 ■ *Overcoming Barriers to Entrepreneurship in the United States*
Pub: Lexington Books
Ed: Diana Furchtgott-Roth. **Released:** March 28, 2008. **Price:** $24.95. **Description:** Real and perceived barriers to the founding and running of small businesses in America are discussed. Each chapter outlines how policy and economic environments can hinder business owners and offers tips to overcome these obstacles. Starting with venture capital access in Silicon Valley during the Internet bubble, the book goes on to question the link between personal wealth and entrepreneurship, examines how federal tax rates affect small business creation and destruction, explains the low rate of self-employment among Mexican immigrants, and suggests ways pension coverage can be increased in small businesses.

27434 ■ "An Overview of Energy Consumption of the Globalized World Economy" in *Energy Policy* (Vol. 39, October 2011, No. 10, pp. 5920-2928)
Pub: Reed Elsevier Reference Publishing
Ed: Z.M. Chen, G.Q. Chen. **Description:** Energy consumption and its impact on the global world economy is examined.

27435 ■ "Overview - Small Business Optimism" in *Small Business Economic Trends* (September 2010, pp. 4)
Pub: National Federation of Independent Business
Ed: William C. Dunkelberg, Holly Wade. **Description:** An optimism index among small businesses surveyed in the U.S. from 1986 to 2010 is presented in a graph. A small business optimism index from 2005 to 2010 is also given in tabular form.

27436 ■ "Pain Ahead as Profit Pressure Increases" in *Crain's Chicago Business* (Vol. 31, May 5, 2008, No. 18, pp. 4)
Pub: Crain Communications, Inc.
Ed: Daniel Rome Levine. **Description:** Interview with David Klaskin, the chairman and chief investment officer at Oak Ridge Investments LLC, who discusses the outlook for the economy and corporate earnings, particularly in the housing and auto industries, the impact of economic stimulus checks, the weakness of the dollar and recommendations of stocks that individual investors may find helpful.

27437 ■ *Panic! The Story of Modern Financial Insanity*
Pub: W.W. Norton & Company
Ed: Michael Lewis. **Released:** 2009. **Price:** $27.95. **Description:** Two decades of stock market crashes are outlined.

27438 ■ *Paper Fortunes: Modern Wall Street: Where It's Been and Where It's Going*
Pub: St. Martin's Press LLC
Ed: Roy C. Smith. **Released:** 2010. **Price:** $35.00. **Description:** Comprehensive history of Wall Street and lessons learned with insight into ways Wall Street will reinvent itself in this new economy.

27439 ■ "Paper Tigers" in *Conde Nast Portfolio* (Vol. 2, June 2008, No. 6, pp. 84)
Pub: Conde Nast Publications, Inc.
Ed: Roger Lowenstein. **Description:** Newspapers are losing their advertisers and readers and circulation today is equal to that of 1950, a time when the U.S. population was half its present size.

27440 ■ "Past Promises Haunt Project" in *The Business Journal-Portland* (Vol. 25, August 1, 2008, No. 21, pp. 1)
Pub: American City Business Journals, Inc.
Ed: Aliza Earnshaw. **Description:** Oregon University System and Oregon Health and Science University will face the state Legislature to defend their request for a $250 million in state bonds to fund a life-sciences collaborative research building. The project is meant to help grow the Oregon bioscience industry. Comments from industry observers and legislators are also presented.

27441 ■ "Patchy Oil Profits" in *Canadian Business* (Vol. 80, February 12, 2007, No. 4, pp. 89)
Pub: Rogers Media
Ed: Michelle Magnan. **Description:** The fall in fourth-quarter earnings of several oil and gas companies in Canada, in view of rise in their expenditure, is discussed.

27442 ■ "Patients to Elect to Cut Care" in *The Business Journal-Serving Metropolitan Kansas City* (Vol. 27, November 21, 2008, No. 11, pp. 1)
Pub: American City Business Journals, Inc.
Ed: Rob Roberts. **Description:** Patients in Kansas City, Missouri are cutting down on health care services due to the economic crisis. A decline in diagnostic procedures has been observed at Northland Cardiology. Elective reconstructive procedures have also been reduced by 25 percent. Additional information and statistics regarding the healthcare sector is included.

27443 ■ "Paying for the Recession: Rebalancing Economic Growth" in *Montana Business Quarterly* (Vol. 49, Spring 2011, No. 1, pp. 2)
Pub: Bureau of Business & Economic Research
Ed: Patrick M. Barkey. **Description:** Four key issues required to address in order to rebalance economic growth in America are examined. They include: savings rates, global trade imbalances, government budgets and most importantly, housing price correction.

27444 ■ "PDX Bucks National Trend" in *The Business Journal-Portland* (Vol. 25, August 1, 2008, No. 21, pp. 1)
Pub: American City Business Journals, Inc.
Ed: Erik Siemers. **Description:** Portland International Airport could face problems as air carriers are planning to reduce capacity at the airport. The airport is showing signs of growth despite the slowdown in the airline industry. Other airlines that are planning to reduce seating capacity at the airport are also presented.

27445 ■ "Peak Show" in *Canadian Business* (Vol. 81, December 24, 2007, No. 1, pp. 28)
Pub: Rogers Media
Ed: Thomas Watson. **Description:** Factors affecting oil prices could include political instability and economic slowdown, but peak oil is not one of them as it is believed there is still plenty of oil in supply. Details on the oil supply and demand, trend for higher prices, and peak oil expert Matthew Simmons' prediction on the issue are discussed.

27446 ■ "The People Puzzle; Re-Training America's Workers" in *The Economist* (Vol. 390, January 3, 2009, No. 8612, pp. 32)
Pub: The Economist Newspaper Inc.
Description: With thousands of workers losing their jobs, America is now facing the task of getting them back to work. With an overall unemployment rate of 6.7 percent, the federal government has three main ways for leading workers back to employment: training them for new jobs, providing unemployment insurance in order to replace lost wages during the period of job-hunting; and matching employers who desire a skill with workers who have that skill. Specialized staffing agencies provide employers and potential employees with the help necessary to find a job in some of the more niche markets.

27447 ■ *Petty Capitalists and Globalization: Flexibility, Entrepreneurship, and Economic Development*
Pub: State University of New York Press
Ed: Alan Smart, Josephine Smart. **Released:** January 2006. **Price:** $26.95. **Description:** Investigation into ways small businesses in Europe, Asia, and Latin America are required to operate and compete in the fast-growing transnational economy.

27448 ■ "PGA Tourney Drives Area Economy, Image" in *Crain's Detroit Business* (Vol. 24, April 7, 2008, No. 14, pp. 22)
Pub: Crain Communications, Inc.
Ed: Jason Deegan. **Description:** Discusses the major economic impact the 2008 PGA Championship will have when it visits the south course at Oakland Hills Country Club August 4-10.

27449 ■ "A Place in the Sun" in *Canadian Business* (Vol. 81, July 22, 2008, No. 12-13, pp. 56)
Pub: Rogers Media Ltd.
Description: Experts believe that it is the best time for Canadians to own a retirement home in the U.S., where real estate prices are up to 50 percent below their peak. Other views concerning the economic conditions occurring in the United States, as well as on the implications for Canadians planning to invest in the country are presented.

27450 ■ "Planning Ahead" in *Crain's Cleveland Business* (Vol. 30, June 15, 2009, No. 23, pp. 12)
Pub: Crain Communications, Inc.
Ed: Shannon Mortland. **Description:** Cleveland area nonprofit organizations are developing new strategies for raising donations, while keeping costs down in the slow economy.

27451 ■ "Playing Defense" in *Crain's Chicago Business* (Vol. 31, November 10, 2008, No. 45, pp. 4)
Pub: Crain Communications, Inc.
Ed: Monee Fields-White. **Description:** Chicago's money managers are increasingly investing in local companies such as Caterpillar Inc., a maker of construction and mining equipment, Kraft Foods Inc. and Baxter International Inc., a manufacturer of medical products, in an attempt to bolster their portfolios. These companies have a history of surviving tough economic times.

27452 ■ "Polite Conversation" in *Mergers & Acquisitions: The Dealmaker's Journal* (March 1, 2008)
Pub: SourceMedia, Inc.
Description: In January, industry leaders and dealmakers met at Davos to discuss topics ranging from the possibility of a recession to what lies ahead in the deal market.

27453 ■ "Poor Economy Inspires Rich Alternatives In a Modern, and Tax-Free, Twist on Bartering" in *Houston Chronicle* (June 7, 2010)
Pub: Houston Chronicle Publishing Company
Ed: Michael Rubinkam. **Description:** Time banking helps individuals and firms receive goods or services by depositing time dollars into a bank reserved for receipt of goods and services.

27454 ■ "Population Growing Faster Than Retail, Service Sector" in *Crain's New York Business* (Vol. 24, January 14, 2008, No. 2, pp. 30)
Pub: Crain Communications, Inc.
Ed: Andrew Marks. **Description:** Downtown Manhattan is seeing more residential development; however, as more families call the area home the need for more retail and services is becoming evident.

27455 ■ "Portfolio: Written in the Polls" in *Entrepreneur* (Vol. 35, October 2007, No. 10, pp. 74)
Pub: Entrepreneur Media Inc.
Ed: Scott Bernard Nelson. **Description:** Ibbotsen Associates looked at trends in the U.S. presidential elections to see if the election has something to do with stock market behavior. It was found that election years beat non-election years in the stock market by nearly three percentage points each year. Details of the presidential elections' impact on the stock market are given.

27456 ■ "Portion of Silver Line Will Run By Year's End" in *Crain's Cleveland Business* (Vol. 28, November 5, 2007, No. 44, pp. 6)
Pub: Crain Communications, Inc.
Ed: Jay Miller. **Description:** Cleveland's new Silver Line rapid transit will board its first passengers before the end of the year. The project is expected to spur economic development in the area and will speed transportation along Euclid Avenue.

27457 ■ *The Post-American World*
Pub: W.W. Norton & Company
Ed: Fareed Zakaria. **Released:** 2009. **Price:** $25.95. **Description:** Analysis of the changes taking place as new countries are rising as status players challenging American dominance.

27458 ■ "The Power of Innovation" in *Canadian Business* (Vol. 81, March 17, 2008, No. 4, pp. 57)
Pub: Rogers Media
Ed: Andrew Wahl. **Description:** Canada ranks badly in terms innovation yardsticks that directly translate to economic growth such as business R&D as a percentage of GDP and R&D per capita. Canada's reliance on natural resources does not provide incentives to innovate unlike smaller countries with little natural resources. Canada could spur innovation through regulations that encourage industrial research.

27459 ■ "Power Partnerships" in *Business Courier* (Vol. 27, October 22, 2010, No. 25, pp. 1)
Pub: Business Courier
Ed: Lucy May. **Description:** The $400 million Harrah's casino and the $47 million redevelopment and expansion of Washington Park are project aimed at boosting the economy in downtown Cincinnati, Ohio. These projects will be done in cooperation with the National Association for the Advancement of Colored People. Insights into the role of minority-owned businesses in regional economic development are explored.

27460 ■ "Practice Problems" in *Crain's Cleveland Business* (Vol. 30, June 22, 2009, No. 24, pp. 9)
Pub: Crain Communications, Inc.
Ed: Arielle Kass. **Description:** Many laid off attorneys are finding few options in the down economy and some are setting up their own practices.

27461 ■ *Predictably Irrational: The Hidden Forces That Shape Our Decisions*
Pub: HarperCollins Publishers
Ed: Dan Ariely. **Released:** 2009. **Price:** $25.95. **Description:** Behaviorists are bringing the economics profession around to realizing that human beings are impulsive, shortsighted and procrastinating in behavior. Economists are using this information to market products to consumers.

27462 ■ "Pricey Oil, High Dollar Wipe Out Jobs" in *Globe & Mail* (February 11, 2006, pp. B6)
Pub: CTVglobemedia Publishing Inc.
Ed: Heather Scoffield. **Description:** The impact of higher oil prices and dollar value, on manufacturing jobs in Canada, is discussed.

27463 ■ "Principles for Creating Growth in Challenging Times" in *Agency Sales Magazine* (Vol. 39, September-October 2009, No. 9, pp. 35)
Pub: MANA
Ed: Robert Goshen. **Description:** Creating a productive environment is one vital key for businesses to utilize during the challenging times that arise due to a weak economy; other important factors include maintaining a good relationship with the staff, responding appropriately to challenges and keeping a sense of humor.

27464 ■ "Priority: Recessionade" in *Inc.* (February 2008, pp. 19-20)
Pub: Gruner & Jahr USA Publishing
Ed: Amy Feldman. **Description:** Despite signs of inflation, entrepreneurs see these tough economic times as an opportunity to start or grow their businesses. Five entrepreneurs share insight into ways this economic downturn can work to grow their businesses.

27465 ■ "Profit Predictions Look Too Plump" in *Barron's* (Vol. 88, March 31, 2008, No. 13, pp. 37)
Pub: Dow Jones & Company, Inc.
Ed: Johanna Bennett. **Description:** Full-year forecast points to a 14 percent gain for 2008 but the second-half profit increases would have to grow at a fast rate and peak at 61 percent in the fourth quarter to achieve this. Trends in the U.S. economic conditions are also discussed.

27466 ■ *Profits Aren't Everything. They're the Only Thing: No-Nonsense Rules from the Ultimate Contrarian and Small Business Guru*
Pub: HarperCollins Publishers
Ed: George Cloutier. **Released:** September 9, 2010. **Price:** $24.99. **Description:** In difficult economic times, the only way for small businesses to survive is to maximize profits. Thirteen steps to maximize profits in a slow economy are outlined.

27467 ■ "Program for Women Entrepreneurs: Tips for Surviving this Economy" in *Crain's Detroit Business* (Vol. 25, June 22, 2009, No. 25)
Pub: Crain Communications Inc. - Detroit
Description: Michigan Leadership Institute for Women Entrepreneurs will hold its third and final program, "Tough Times are Temporary, but Tough People are Permanent" at the Davenport University in Livonia, Michigan.

27468 ■ "Project Could Forge Path to Jobs, Growth" in *Business Courier* (Vol. 26, September 11, 2009, No. 20, pp. 1)
Pub: American City Business Journals, Inc.
Ed: Lucy May. **Description:** The planned 13.5 mile Mill Creek Greenway Trail extension could create 445 jobs and bring $52 million to the economy of Cincinnati, Ohio. The trail extension would cost $24 million and would be used for recreational purposes.

27469 ■ "PSU Launches $90 Million Project" in *The Business Journal-Portland* (Vol. 25, July 18, 2008, No. 19, pp. 1)
Pub: American City Business Journals, Inc.
Ed: Aliza Earnshaw. **Description:** Portland State University (PSU) has launched a $90-million project for a new business school building, which is to be located at Southwest Market and Southwest Park. The business school is expected to move in to its new 130,000-suqare-foot building by 2013. PSU business school needs to raise $30 million for the project.

27470 ■ "Push Is On To Build Region's Prospects In Film Industry" in *Crain's Cleveland Business* (Vol. 28, November 19, 2007, No. 46, pp. 1)
Pub: Crain Communications, Inc.
Ed: Jay Miller. **Description:** Overview of a bill that has been introduced by state Representative Thomas

Patton that would grant a 25 percent state income tax credit on investments of $300,000 or more in motion picture or television productions filmed in Ohio.

27471 ■ "Put It on MasterCard" in *Barron's* (Vol. 89, July 27, 2009, No. 30, pp. 16)
Pub: Dow Jones & Co., Inc.
Ed: Bill Alpert. **Description:** Shares of MasterCard trade at a discount at just 15 times its anticipated earnings and some believe that these shares may be a better play in an economic recovery. The prospects of these shares are compared with those of Visa.

27472 ■ "Putting the World at Your Fingertips" in *Barron's* (Vol. 88, July 7, 2008, No. 27, pp. L13)
Pub: Dow Jones & Co., Inc.
Ed: Neil A. Martin. **Description:** Currency-traded exchange funds allow investors to diversify their assets and take advantage of investment opportunities such as speculation and hedging. Investors can use these funds to build positions in favor of or against the US dollar.

27473 ■ "The Puzzle of Our Productivity" in *Canadian Business* (Vol. 83, September 14, 2010, No. 15, pp. 22)
Pub: Rogers Media Ltd.
Ed: Rachel Madison. **Description:** Industry Canada economist Annette Ryan revealed in a presentation to the Canadian Association for Business Economics that growth in Canadian labor productivity has steadily declined since the 1980s. Ryan believes that business decisions have played an important role in the poor productivity results. Other details of the findings are presented.

27474 ■ "Q&A" in *Canadian Business* (Vol. 81, July 22, 2008, No. 12-13, pp. 8)
Pub: Rogers Media Ltd.
Ed: Michelle Magnan. **Description:** Interview with Scott Saxberg who discusses Crescent Point Energy Trust's discovery of resources in Saskatchewan and believes that this is a once-in-a-lifetime type of event. Crescent Point holds 75 percent of its resources in Saskatchewan; this new finding being considered the second-largest pool discovered since the 1950s. Saxberg's other views as well as information on Crescent Point's services are presented.

27475 ■ "Q&A Interview With Perrin Beatty" in *Canadian Business* (Vol. 80, October 8, 2007, No. 20, pp. 13)
Pub: Rogers Media
Description: Perrin Beatty, president and chief executive officer of the Canadian Chamber of Commerce, talks about his move from the Canadian Manufacturers and Exporters to his current organization. He also discusses the state of Canada's economy, as well as the need for leadership.

27476 ■ "A Questionable Chemical Romance" in *Barron's* (Vol. 88, July 14, 2008, No. 28, pp. 28)
Pub: Dow Jones & Co., Inc.
Ed: Andrew Bary. **Description:** Dow Chemical paid $78-a-share for the surprise takeover of Rohm & Haas. The acquisition is reducing Dow Chemical's financial flexibility at a time when chemical companies are being affected by high costs and a weak U.S. economy.

27477 ■ "Quick Earnings Revival Unlikely" in *Barron's* (Vol. 88, June 30, 2008, No. 26, pp. 31)
Pub: Dow Jones & Co., Inc.
Ed: Johanna Bennett. **Description:** Analysts are pushing back their prediction of a U.S. economy turnaround to 2009. A recession in the first half of 2008 may not have happened but unemployment is rising and house prices continue to fall.

27478 ■ "Quiznos Franchisees Walloped by Recession" in *Advertising Age* (Vol. 79, October 20, 2008, No. 39, pp. 3)
Pub: Crain Communications, Inc.
Ed: Emily Bryson York. **Description:** While the recession has taken a toll on the entire restaurant industry, a number of Quiznos franchisees claim to have been disproportionately affected due to lackluster marketing, higher-than-average commodity costs, competition with Subway and a premium-pricing structure that is incompatible with a tight economy.

27479 ■ "The Racial Divide and the Class Struggle in the United States" in *WorkingUSA* (Vol. 11, September 2008, No. 3, pp. 311)
Pub: Blackwell Publishers Ltd.
Ed: Michael Goldfield. **Description:** An examination of questions of race that continue to play such a prominent role in contemporary society is presented, focusing on the undermining of potential solidarity and strength of the working class movement, what sustains racists attitudes, practices and institutions, especially in the face of trends in world economic development.

27480 ■ "Ready for the Back Burner" in *Barron's* (Vol. 88, March 17, 2008, No. 11, pp. 47)
Pub: Dow Jones & Company, Inc.
Ed: Vito J. Racanelli. **Description:** McDonald's has promised to return $15 billion to $17 billion to shareholders in 2007-2009 but headwinds are rising for the company. December, 2007 same-store sales were flat and the company's traffic growth in the U.S. is slowing. Its shares are likely to trade in tandem with the market until recession fears recede.

27481 ■ "Ready for a Rally?" in *The Economist* (Vol. 390, January 3, 2009, No. 8612, pp. 54)
Pub: The Economist Newspaper Inc.
Description: Analysts predict that the recession could end by 2010. The current economic crisis is presented in detail.

27482 ■ "Real Estate Market Still in a Slump" in *Montana Business Quarterly* (Vol. 49, Summer 2011, No. 2, pp. 15)
Pub: Bureau of Business & Economic Research
Ed: Patrick M. Barkey. **Description:** Montana's housing market is still in decline with no sign of improving in the near future. Statistical data included.

27483 ■ "Real Estate Vets Take Times In Stride" in *The Business Journal-Serving Metropolitan Kansas City* (Vol. 26, July 25, 2008, No. 46)
Pub: American City Business Journals, Inc.
Ed: Rob Roberts. **Description:** Kansas City, Missouri's real estate industry veterans like Allen Block believe that the challenges faced by the industry in the 1980s, when the Federal Reserve Board controlled the money supply to slow down inflation, were worse than the challenges faced today. Other views, trends and information on the real estate industry of the city, are presented.

27484 ■ "Realities May Blur Vision" in *The Business Journal-Serving Metropolitan Kansas City* (Vol. 27, September 19, 2008, No. 1, pp. 1)
Pub: American City Business Journals, Inc.
Ed: Rob Roberts. **Description:** Vision Metcalf is a study by Kansas City that depicts how Metcalf Avenue could look like if redeveloped. Redevelopment plans for the Metcalf corridor include a 20-story mixed-use building on a vacant car dealership. The challenges that the redevelopment plans will face are also analyzed.

27485 ■ "Realtors Signing Out" in *The Business Journal-Serving Metropolitan Kansas City* (Vol. 27, November 21, 2008, No. 11, pp. 1)
Pub: American City Business Journals, Inc.
Ed: Rob Roberts. **Description:** The Kansas City Regional Association of Realtors has lost 1,000 of its members due to the downturn in the housing market. Applications for realtor licenses have dropped by 159 percent. Changes in Missouri's licensing requirements are seen as additional reasons for the declines.

27486 ■ "Recession Fears Power Gold" in *Barron's* (Vol. 88, March 17, 2008, No. 11, pp. M14)
Pub: Dow Jones & Company, Inc.
Ed: Melanie Burton. **Description:** Gold prices have been more attractive as the U.S. dollar weakens and the Dow Jones Industrial Average has slipped almost 10 percent in 2008. The rate cuts from the Federal Reserve Board has also spurred inflation fears adding upward pressure to the price of the metal.

27487 ■ "Recession Management" in *Canadian Business* (Vol. 81, March 3, 2008, No. 3, pp. 62)
Pub: Rogers Media
Ed: Joe Castaldo. **Description:** Some companies such as Capital One Financial Corp. are managing their finances as if a recession has already taken place to prepare themselves for the looming economic downturn. Intel Corp., meanwhile shows how increasing its investments during a recession could be advantageous. Tips on how companies can survive a recession are provided.

27488 ■ "The Recession: Problem or Opportunity" in *Women In Business* (Vol. 61, October-November 2009, No. 5, pp. 34)
Pub: American Business Women's Association
Ed: J. Douglas Bate. **Description:** Business organizations' success during a recession is based on how management views the economic situation. The recession may be deemed as a setback or may be visualized as an opportunity that has to be grabbed for the organization. Suggestions on what management should do in the opportunity-creating or proactive approach are also highlighted.

27489 ■ "Recession-Proof Your Startup" in *Crain's Chicago Business* (Vol. 31, November 10, 2008, No. 45, pp. 24)
Pub: Crain Communications, Inc.
Description: Detailed information concerning ways in which to start a business during an economic crisis is provided. Ways in which to find financing, the importance of a solid business plan, customer service, problem-solving and finding the right niche for the region are also discussed.

27490 ■ "Recession Survival Tip: Less Is More" in *Women Entrepreneur* (December 31, 2008)
Pub: Entrepreneur Media Inc.
Ed: Suzy Girard-Ruttenberg. **Description:** These trying economic times can be an opportunity to make bold changes in one's business that may yield lasting results, not just short-term survival; simplification, accountability and shoring up one's margins are things to look at when determining the goals of the company.

27491 ■ "Recipe for Disaster?" in *Sacramento Business Journal* (Vol. 25, July 4, 2008, No. 18, pp. 1)
Pub: American City Business Journals, Inc.
Ed: Mark Anderson. **Description:** Restaurateurs are challenged with balancing rising operating costs and what customers are willing to pay for their services. Flour prices in 2008 have increased by 46 percent from April 2007. Other views on the situation, as well as trends, forecasts and statistics on sales, outlook on economic conditions, consumer price index, and the typical split of restaurant revenue, are presented.

27492 ■ "Recovery a Ruse?" in *Baltimore Business Journal* (Vol. 28, August 6, 2010, No. 13, pp. 1)
Pub: Baltimore Business Journal
Ed: Scott Dance. **Description:** Baltimore, Maryland-area businesses have remained cautious as their optimism faded along with the latest indicators on economic recovery. Economists believe they might be justified with their concern since sales were better, but there is no security that they will stay that way.

27493 ■ "Recovery on Tap for 2010?" in *Orlando Business Journal* (Vol. 26, January 1, 2010, No. 31, pp. 1)
Pub: American City Business Journals
Ed: Melanie Stawicki Azam, Richard Bilbao, Christopher Boyd, Anjali Fluker. **Description:** Economic forecasts for Central Florida's leading business sectors in 2010 are presented. These sectors include housing, film and TV, sports business, law, restaurants, aviation, tourism and hospitality, banking and finance, commercial real estate, retail, health care,

insurance, higher education, and manufacturing. According to some local executives, Central Florida's economy will slowly recover in 2010.

27494 ■ "Red Tape Ties Detroit Housing Rehab Plan" in *Crain's Detroit Business* (Vol. 24, September 22, 2008, No. 38, pp. 1)
Pub: Crain Communications, Inc.
Ed: Ryan Beene. **Description:** Venture-capital firm Wilherst Oxford LLC is a Florida-based company that has purchased 300 inner-city homes which were in foreclosure in Detroit. Wilherst Oxford is asking the city to forgive the existing tax and utility liens so the firm can utilize the money for home improvements. The city, however, is reluctant but has stated that they are willing to negotiate.

27495 ■ "Reduce or Repay" in *Canadian Business* (Vol. 80, November 5, 2007, No. 22, pp. 35)
Pub: Rogers Media
Ed: Regan Ray. **Description:** The new greenhouse gas (GHG) policy of Alberta, Canada requires about 100 industrial facilities that emit over 100,000 tons of GHG per year to reduce emissions by 12 percent by the end of 2007. Facilities that fail to comply will pay $15 per ton of GHG emission beyond target. The economic impacts of the regulation are evaluated.

27496 ■ "Reform or Perish" in *Canadian Business* (Vol. 82, April 27, 2009, No. 7, pp. 20)
Pub: Rogers Media
Ed: Al Rosen. **Description:** It is believed that Canada needs to fix its financial regulatory framework in order to provide more oversight on accounting procedures that is often left up to auditors. While the U.S. has constantly rebuilt its regulatory framework, Canada has not instituted reforms on its regulations. Canada entered the recession with a strong system but needs to build more substance into it.

27497 ■ "Regarding Warren" in *Canadian Business* (Vol. 80, November 5, 2007, No. 22, pp. 29)
Pub: Rogers Media
Ed: Jeff Sanford. **Description:** Berkshire Hathaway's Warren Buffet believes that investing in energy shares is profitable, however, he warns investors about volatility in prices. Buffet, the second richest man in the world, forecasts that the value of the Canadian dollar will continue to rise. Buffet's investments are also discussed.

27498 ■ "Region and City Need Influx of Youth" in *Crain's Detroit Business* (Vol. 24, April 14, 2008, No. 15, pp. 8)
Pub: Crain Communications, Inc.
Description: Discusses an upcoming report from Michigan Future Inc. which finds that young professionals, including those with children, are interested in living in an active urban environment. It also states that because many of those young professionals are entrepreneurial in nature, oftentimes businesses follow.

27499 ■ "Rep Contracts: Simple, Clear, Fair" in *Agency Sales Magazine* (Vol. 39, September-October 2009, No. 9, pp. 3)
Pub: MANA
Ed: Bryan C. Shirley. **Description:** Things that a manufacturer and a sales representative needs to strive for when creating an Agreement for Representation includes an agreement that is simple and complete, one that covers all the needs of both parties and is fair, equitable, and balanced. Sales representatives need to make more sales calls and find new opportunities during this recession.

27500 ■ "Reply! Grows at Unprecedented Rate, Rips Beta Off Its Marketplace" in *Marketing Weekly News* (September 19, 2009, pp. 149)
Pub: Investment Weekly News
Description: Profile of Reply.com, a leader in locally-targeted Internet marketing, announced significant growth in terms of revenue, enhanced features and services and new categories since launching its beta Reply! Marketplace platform. Even in the face of an economic downturn, the company has posted over 50 percent revenue growth in the Real Estate and Automotive categories.

27501 ■ "Reps Continue to Move to International Trade" in *Agency Sales Magazine* (Vol. 39, September-October 2009, No. 9, pp. 24)
Pub: MANA
Ed: Jack Foster. **Description:** Sales representatives should get involved and look into international trade if they want to be successful in the future. The weak U.S. dollar, labor costs, and the low cost of transportation are factors that drive the trend towards international trade.

27502 ■ "Research Highlights Disengaged Workforce" in *Workforce Management* (Vol. 88, November 16, 2009, No. 12, pp. 22)
Pub: Crain Communications, Inc.
Ed: Ed Frauenheim. **Description:** Most researchers have documented a drop in employee engagement during the recession due to such factors as layoffs, restructuring and less job security.

27503 ■ "Research and Markets Adds Report: Cyprus: Convergence, Broadband and Internet Market" in *Wireless News* (September 4, 2009)
Pub: Close-Up Media
Description: Overview of a new report by Research and Markets entitled, "Cyprus Convergence, Broadband and Internet Market - Overview, Statistics and Forecasts." Highlights include information regarding broadband accounts which now account for the majority of household Internet connections.

27504 ■ "Research and Markets Adds Report: Ghana: Convergence, Broadband and Internet Market" in *Wireless News* (September 4, 2009)
Pub: Close-Up Media
Description: Overview of a new report by Research and Markets entitled, "Ghana Convergence, Broadband and Internet Market - Overview, Statistics and Forecasts." Ghana was among the first countries in Africa connected to the Internet and to introduce ADSL broadband services; however, only 30 of the 140 licensed ISP's are operational making the sector highly competitive.

27505 ■ "Research Note" in *International Journal of Globalisation and Small Business* (Vol. 4, September 21, 2010, No. 1, pp. 92)
Pub: Publishers Communication Group
Ed: Alexander Bode, Tobias B. Talmon l'Armee, Simon Alig. **Description:** The cluster concept has steadily increased its importance during the past years both from practitioners' and reearchers' points of view. Simultaneously, many corporate networks are established. Researchers from different areas (business management, economic social and geographical science) are trying to explain both phenomena.

27506 ■ "Restaurants Dish Up Meal Deals To Attract Customers" in *Crain's Detroit Business* (Vol. 24, October 6, 2008, No. 40, pp. 1)
Pub: Crain Communications, Inc.
Ed: Nathan Skid. **Description:** Restaurateurs are devising many creative and rewarding incentives to get customers to frequent their establishments during this economic crisis. Innovative ways in which even higher-end establishments are drawing in business are discussed.

27507 ■ "Restaurants Slammed by Economy" in *Business Courier* (Vol. 24, April 4, 2008, No. 52, pp. 1)
Pub: American City Business Journals, Inc.
Ed: Lisa Biank Fasig. **Description:** Restaurants in Cincinnati are closing some of their stores due to growing costs of fuel, eggs and meat. The establishments are also affected by lower consumer spending that was brought on by unemployment, higher grocery prices and foreclosures. The economic problems in Cincinnati are also compared to those in other cities.

27508 ■ "Restaurants Stewing Over Food Prices" in *The Business Journal-Milwaukee* (Vol. 25, August 22, 2008, No. 48, pp. A1)
Pub: American City Business Journals, Inc.
Ed: David Doege. **Description:** Many restaurant operators in the Milwaukee area are changing their menus, increasing prices and decreasing workers' hours amid the soaring prices of commodities. The prices of some staples have risen by over 50 percent since 2006. The impacts of the continued rise in food prices are examined further.

27509 ■ *The Retail Revolution: How Wal-Mart Created a Brave New World of Business*
Pub: Metropolitan Books
Ed: Nelson Lichtenstein. **Released:** July 21, 2009. **Price:** $25.00. **Description:** Comprehensive discussion on how Wal-Mart changed retailing, and its place in the changing global economy.

27510 ■ "Retail Slump Deflates Local Development" in *Business Courier* (Vol. 24, February 29, 2008, No. 47, pp. 1)
Pub: American City Business Journals, Inc.
Ed: Lisa Biank Fasig. **Description:** 2007 sales of the retail industry are the slowest since the year 2003, driving retail stores to reconsider their expansion plans for 2008. A number of retail projects have been delayed, cancelled or altered, including Newport Pavilion, Rivers Crossing, Wal-Mart Supercenters, Legacy Place and Millworks. The impacts of retail slowdown on development projects are analyzed further.

27511 ■ "Retailers Dig In For Holiday Shopping Push" in *Business Review, Albany New York* (Vol. 34, November 30, 2007, No. 35, pp. 1)
Pub: American City Business Journals, Inc.
Ed: Michael DeMasi. **Description:** Tough economic conditions have led to lower consumer spending and retailers in Albany, New York and nationwide experienced mix results during the Black Friday weekend. Local retailers enjoyed higher sales in 2007 compared to 2006 and the National Retail Federation projects that retail sales will climb by four percent. Holiday retail trade forecasts are discussed.

27512 ■ "Retailers Pull Out All Stops to Combat Poor Projections" in *Austin Business JournalInc.* (Vol. 28, November 21, 2008, No. 36, pp. 1)
Pub: American City Business Journals
Ed: Jean Kwon. **Description:** Report from Wachovia Economics Group reports that holiday sales for 2008 are expected to decline by 2 percent and local retailers are planning to boost holiday sales through marketing efforts, which include giving freebies to early shoppers. Details on marketing strategies of several retailers are provided.

27513 ■ *The Return of Depression Economics and the Crisis of 2008*
Pub: W.W. Norton & Company, Inc.
Ed: Paul Krugman. **Price:** $16.95. **Description:** The recipient of the 2008 Nobel Memorial Prize in Economics revises his earlier work from 1999 to reflect the current economic crisis of 2008.

27514 ■ "Return to Wealth; Bank Strategy" in *The Economist* (Vol. 390, January 3, 2009, No. 8612, pp. 56)
Pub: The Economist Newspaper Inc.
Description: UBS' strategy to survive these trying economic times is presented. Statistical data included. UBS has a stronger balance-sheet than most of its investment-banking peers and has reduced its portfolio.

27515 ■ "Revenue Shortfall Leads to Budget Uncertainty" in *Crain's Detroit Business* (Vol. 24, March 10, 2008, No. 10, pp. 26)
Pub: Crain Communications, Inc.
Ed: Amy Lane. **Description:** Michigan's current-year budget may face a $134 million shortfall due to such issues as lower-than-anticipated payment from a 1999 national settlement with the U.S. tobacco industry, overestimated growth in property-tax revenue, the impact of the federal stimulus package and

the potential settlement of a Midland property-tax dispute. The governor's proposed budget for fiscal year for 2009 may face a $249.6 million shortfall.

27516 ■ "The Right Time for REITs" in *Barron's* (Vol. 88, July 14, 2008, No. 28, pp. 32)
Pub: Dow Jones & Co., Inc.
Ed: Mike Hogan. **Description:** Discusses the downturn in U.S. real estate investment trusts so these are worth considering for investment. Several Websites that are useful for learning about real estate investment trusts for investment purposes are presented.

27517 ■ "Rising in the East; Research and Development" in *The Economist* (Vol. 390, January 3, 2009, No. 8612, pp. 47)
Pub: The Economist Newspaper Inc.
Description: Impressive growth of the technological research and development in Asian countries is discussed. Statistical data included.

27518 ■ "Risk and Reward" in *Canadian Business* (Vol. 81, October 13, 2008, No. 17, pp. 21)
Pub: Rogers Media Ltd.
Ed: Calvin Leung. **Description:** Macro-economist and currency analyst Mark Venezia believes that stable financial institutions, free-market reforms, and the role of central banks in keeping inflation and exchange rates stable could make emerging-market bonds strong performers for better future returns. Venezia's other views on emerging-market bonds are discussed.

27519 ■ *The Road from Ruin: How to Revive Capitalism and Put American Back on Top*
Pub: Crown Business
Ed: Matthew Bishop, Michael Green. **Released:** January 26, 2010. **Price:** $27.00. **Description:** Authors show why American companies must respond to the economic crisis with long term vision and a renewed emphasis on values.

27520 ■ "Ronald Taketa" in *Hawaii Business* (Vol. 54, September 2008, No. 3, pp. 28)
Pub: Hawaii Business Publishing
Ed: Shara Enay. **Description:** Interview with Ronald Taketa of the Hawaii Carpenters Union who states that the economic downturn has affected the construction industry as 20 percent of the union's 7,800 members are unemployed. He shares his thoughts about the industry's economic situation, the union's advertisements, and his role as a leader of the union.

27521 ■ "Rough Q1 Begs Question: Is the Crocs Craze Over?" in *Brandweek* (Vol. 49, April 21, 2008, No. 16, pp. 16)
Pub: VNU Business Media, Inc.
Ed: Eric Newman. **Description:** Crocs, a rubber shoemaker, announced last week that it missed its expected first quarter revenues by 15 percent. The popular rubber sandals are suffering in sales due to a number of factors including a tougher economic environment, less expensive, knock-off brands, the cold weather delay of the spring season and fading consumer interest in plastic shoes.

27522 ■ "Rough Trade" in *Canadian Business* (Vol. 79, September 11, 2006, No. 18, pp. 31)
Pub: Rogers Media
Ed: Christina Campbell. **Description:** The divergence between trade policy agreements entered into by Chile and the Canadian government are highlighted. Canada-Chile Free Trade Agreement and the myth around the big benefits to be reaped by bilateral trade policy agreements are discussed.

27523 ■ "Roundtable - The Auto Sector Shifts Gears" in *Mergers & Acquisitions: The Dealmaker's Journal* (March 1, 2008)
Pub: SourceMedia, Inc.
Description: Industry professionals discuss the current state of the automotive sector as well as what they predict for the future of the industry; also provides information for investors about opportunities in the sector.

27524 ■ "Roundy' Pushing Chicago Expansion" in *Milwaukee Business Journal* (Vol. 27, February 12, 2010, No. 20, pp. A1)
Pub: American City Business Journals
Ed: Rich Kirchen. **Description:** Roundy Supermarkets Inc. is expanding in Chicago, Illinois as the Milwaukee-based company is set to open one store in downtown Chicago and another in the Arlington suburb. The store openings have been pushed back to spring and early summer in 2010 due to the economic downturn.

27525 ■ "Running On Empty" in *The Business Journal-Milwaukee* (Vol. 25, July 4, 2008, No. 41, pp. A1)
Pub: American City Business Journals, Inc.
Ed: David Doege. **Description:** Employers are more engaged in offering incentives designed to offset commuting costs. Among the incentives offered are gas cards, parking reimbursement and midyear wage increases. The other efforts to help employees with the costs of going to work are discussed.

27526 ■ "Rust Belt No More: The Demise of Manufacturing" in *Crain's Chicago Business* (Vol. 31, March 31, 2008, No. 13, pp. 52)
Pub: Crain Communications, Inc.
Ed: Sarah A. Klein. **Description:** Discusses the history of manufacturing in the Chicago area as well as the history of manufacturer International Harvester Co.

27527 ■ "A Safety Net in Need of Repair" in *The Economist* (Vol. 390, January 3, 2009, No. 8612, pp. 33)
Pub: The Economist Newspaper Inc.
Description: America's unemployment-insurance scheme is outdated and skimpy compared to other industrialized countries despite the fact that Americans tend to work harder at returning to the job market; the benefits are lower and available for a smaller amount of time and less unemployed workers are even able to collect these benefits. Statistical data included.

27528 ■ "Sales at Furniture Showrooms Sink" in *Puget Sound Business Journal* (Vol. 29, October 10, 2008, No. 25, pp. 1)
Pub: American City Business Journals
Ed: Greg Lamm. **Description:** Furniture showrooms are seeing a drop in sales due to the bad economy. Buyer demand has also fallen because of the slumping real estate market.

27529 ■ "Samll Fortunes" in *Business Courier* (Vol. 27, July 23, 2010, No. 12, pp. 1)
Pub: Business Courier
Ed: Steve Watkins. **Description:** Small banks in Cincinnati, Ohio have been faring well despite the economic crisis, a survey has revealed. Sixty percent of local small banks have capital levels above 15.8 percent median. But regulators are seen to close more banks in 2010 than since the financial crises began.

27530 ■ "Sandi Jackson; Alderman, 7th Ward, City of Chicago" in *Crain's Chicago Business* (Vol. 31, May 5, 2008, No. 18, pp. 31)
Pub: Crain Communications, Inc.
Ed: Sarah A. Klein. **Description:** Profile of Sandi Jackson who is an alderman of the 7th ward of the city of Chicago and is addressing issues such as poverty and crime as well as counting on a plan to develop the former USX Corp. steel mill to revitalize the area's economic climate.

27531 ■ *Saudi Arabia: Moving Towards a Privatized Economy*
Pub: Turnaround Associates
Ed: Andrea H. Pampanini. **Released:** April 2005. **Price:** $30.00. **Description:** An overview of how Saudi Arabia took control of its natural resources and created change in the government, education, and culture of the country. Production of oil and natural gas is control entirely by the Saudi Government, however the book discusses the trend towards privatizing particular sectors of the nation in order to compete globally.

27532 ■ "Saudi Overtures" in *The Business Journal-Portland* (Vol. 25, August 15, 2008, No. 23, pp. 1)
Pub: American City Business Journals, Inc.
Ed: Aliza Earnshaw. **Description:** Saudi Arabia's huge revenue from oil is creating opportunities for Oregon companies as the country develops new cities, industrial zones, and tourism centers. Oregon exported only $46.8 million worth of goods to Saudi Arabia in 2007 but the kingdom is interested in green building materials and methods, renewable energy and water quality control, and nanotechnology all of which Oregon has expertise in.

27533 ■ *Save Your Small Business: 10 Crucial Strategies to Survive Hard Times or Close Down and Move On*
Pub: NOLO
Ed: Ralph Warner, Bethany Laurence. **Released:** August 1, 2009. **Price:** $29.99. **Description:** According to a study among 500 businesses, 44 percent used credit cards in order to meet their firm's needs in the previous six months. Written by a business owner, this book provides twelve strategies to protect personal assets from creditors and survive the current recession.

27534 ■ "SBA-Backed Lending Slides; Economy, Close Scrutiny of Applications Cited" in *Crain's Detroit Business* (March 10, 2008)
Pub: Crain Communications, Inc.
Ed: Nancy Kaffer. **Description:** Due to the state of the economy and a closer scrutiny on applications, Small Business Administration-backed loans are down by a significant margin in one loan program and have decreased slightly across the board. Statistical data included.

27535 ■ "SBA Intervenes to Keep Cash Flowing" in *Business First Columbus* (Vol. 25, November 21, 2008, No. 14, pp. A1)
Pub: American City Business Journals
Ed: Adrian Burns. **Description:** U.S. Small Business Administration's loan volumes fell as it tried to cushion the impact of the economic crisis on small businesses. Large investors have pulled back buying SBA loans due to declining profits, but demand for SBA loans are seen to resurge due to low risk.

27536 ■ "SEC Report On Rating Agencies Falls Short" in *Barron's* (Vol. 88, July 14, 2008, No. 28, pp. 35)
Pub: Dow Jones & Co., Inc.
Ed: Jack Willoughby. **Description:** The Securities and Exchange Commissions report on credit-rating firms should have drawn attention to the slipshod practices in the offerings of collateralized debt obligations. The report fell short of prescribing correctives for the flawed system of these agencies' relationship with their clients.

27537 ■ "Selling Pressures Rise in China" in *Barron's* (Vol. 88, March 10, 2008, No. 10, pp. M9)
Pub: Dow Jones & Company, Inc.
Ed: Mohammed Hadi. **Description:** There are about 1.6 trillion yuan worth of shares up for sale in Chinese stock markets in 2008, adding to the selling pressures in these markets. The Chinese government has imposed restrictions to prevent a rapid rise in selling stocks.

27538 ■ "Sentiment Split on Financials" in *Barron's* (Vol. 88, March 24, 2008, No. 12, pp. M14)
Pub: Dow Jones & Company, Inc.
Ed: Steven M. Sears. **Description:** Experts in the financial sector are split as to whether or not the worst of the financial crisis brought on by the credit crunch is over. Some options traders are trading on are defensive puts, expecting the worst, while investors buying calls are considered as bullish.

27539 ■ "Serious Signal Flashing?" in *Barron's* (Vol. 88, July 7, 2008, No. 27, pp. 11)
Pub: Dow Jones & Co., Inc.
Description: Discusses the Hindenburg Omen, named after the airship disaster of May 1937, which is considered a predictor of market crashes and has

appeared twice in June 2008. There is a 25 percent probability that the US stock market will suffer a crash in the July-October 2008 period.

27540 ■ "A Shallow Pool" in *Canadian Business* (Vol. 81, Summer 2008, No. 9, pp. 44)
Pub: Rogers Media Ltd.
Ed: Joe Castaldo. **Description:** Bank of Canada projected in its 'Monetary Policy Report' a growth rate of 1.4 percent in 2008 and does not expect the economy to fully recover until mid-2010. The Canadian stock market has been recovering although slowly with just a 1.6 percent gain by April 30. Other details on the Canadian equity market are presented.

27541 ■ "Shanghai Butterfly" in *Canadian Business* (Vol. 80, March 12, 2007, No. 6, pp. 69)
Pub: Rogers Media
Ed: Thomas Watson. **Description:** The volatile nature of Shanghai stock markets and its impact on investors and the economy is discussed.

27542 ■ "Shifting Gears" in *Business Journal-Serving Phoenix & the Valley of the Sun* (Vol. 31, November 12, 2010, No. 10, pp. 1)
Pub: Phoenix Business Journal
Ed: Patrick O'Grady. **Description:** Automotive parts recyclers in Arizona are benefiting from the challenging national economic conditions as well as from the green movement. Recyclers revealed that customers prefer recycled parts more because they are cheaper and are more environmentally friendly. Other information about the automotive parts recycling industry is presented.

27543 ■ "Shopped Out; Retailing Gloom" in *The Economist* (Vol. 390, January 3, 2009, No. 8612, pp. 26)
Pub: The Economist Newspaper Inc.
Description: Economic volatility in the retail sector is having an impact on a number of countries around the globe. Europe is experiencing hard economic times as well and unless businesses have a strong business plan banks feel unable to lend the money necessary to tide the retailers over. The falling pound has increased the cost of imported goods and small to midsize retail chains may not be able to weather such an unforgiving economic climate.

27544 ■ "'Short Sales,' A Sign of Housing Troubles, Start Popping Up" in *The Business Review Albany* (Vol. 35, April 11, 2008, No. 1, pp. 1)
Pub: The Business Review
Ed: Michael DeMasi. **Description:** Discusses the number of short sales, where homeowners ask banks to forgive part of their mortgages to sell the properties, which is starting to increase in the Albany, New York area. Real estate agents in the area are taking up crash courses in short selling.

27545 ■ "Should the Fed Regulate Wall Street?" in *Barron's* (Vol. 88, March 24, 2008, No. 12, pp. M15)
Pub: Dow Jones & Company, Inc.
Ed: Randall W. Forsyth. **Description:** Greater regulation of the financial sector by the Federal Reserve is essential for it to survive the crisis it is experiencing. The resulting regulation could be in complete contrast with the deregulation the sector previously experienced.

27546 ■ "Sign Up To Grow Your Business, Generate Jobs" in *Women Entrepreneur* (November 25, 2008)
Pub: Entrepreneur Media Inc.
Ed: Eve Gumpel. **Description:** Nell Merlino has announced the new Make Mine A Million-Dollar Race, which aims to encourage hundreds of thousands of women entrepreneurs to grow their business to revenue goals of $250,00, $500,000 or $1 million and more as well as create 800,000 new jobs in an attempt to stimulate the nation's economy.

27547 ■ "Silicon Valley's Economic Recovery Picking Up Pace" in *Globe & Mail* (January 29, 2007, pp. B13)
Pub: CTVglobemedia Publishing Inc.
Ed: Pui-Wing Tam. **Description:** The addition of 30,000 new jobs, rise in average annual wages and household income, along with other factors that have contributed to Silicon Valley's economic recovery are discussed.

27548 ■ "Single Most Important Problem" in *Small Business Economic Trends* (April 2008, pp. 18)
Pub: National Federation of Independent Business
Ed: William C. Dunkelberg, Holly Wade. **Description:** Two graphs and a table presenting the economic problems encountered by small businesses in the U.S. are provided. The figures presented in the graphs include data from 1986 to 2008.

27549 ■ "Six Leading Economists on What to Expect in the Year Ahead: David Wolf" in *Canadian Business* (Dec. 24, 2007)
Pub: Rogers Media
Ed: David Wolf. **Description:** The Canadian dollar recently hit parity with the U.S. dollar, and the exchange rate is going fast and overvaluation of the Canadian dollar could bring in competition from U.S. products. Details on the impact of the slowdown of the U.S. economy on the exchange rate speed are discussed.

27550 ■ "Six Leading Economists on What to Expect in the Year Ahead: Derek Holt; Housing" in *Canadian Business* (December 24, 2007)
Pub: Rogers Media
Ed: Derek Holt. **Description:** The Canadian subprime mortgage market could take a different turn from that of the U.S. as laws governing Canada's mortgage market indirectly limit the probability of a slowdown. Details on how Canada avoided the slowdown in the housing market and forecasts of new homes for 2008 are discussed.

27551 ■ "Six Leading Economists on What to Expect in the Year Ahead: Glen Hodgson; Canada in Depth" in *Canadian Business* (December 24, 2007)
Pub: Rogers Media
Ed: Glen Hodgson. **Description:** Western Canada is expected to have the best economic performance for 2008 among all of the country's regions with a growth rate of 3.6 percent for Alberta and three percent for British Columbia. Details on the country's growth in real income, trends in the labor market, and the effect of Canadian dollar's parity with the U.S. dollar on exports are discussed.

27552 ■ "Six Leading Economists on What to Expect in the Year Ahead: Peter Buchanan" in *Canadian Business* (December 24, 2007)
Pub: Rogers Media
Ed: Peter Buchanan. **Description:** The world economy is expected to grow by five percent in 2008, which is below the pace of the previous two years. Details on the U.S. credit crunch, the U.S. dollar's depreciation, and the economic expansion of developing economies are discussed.

27553 ■ "Six Things You Can Do To Ride Out a Turbulent Market" in *Hispanic Business* (March 2008, pp. 20-21)
Pub: Hispanic Business
Ed: Hildy Medina, Michael Bowker. **Description:** Experts in the financial industry suggest shifting portfolios; investing in cash; thinking long-term for market investments; investing in foreign bonds, covered calls and preferred stocks; and to rebalance a portfolio in order to survive the downturn in the stock market.

27554 ■ "A Slice of Danish; Fixing Finance" in *The Economist* (Vol. 390, January 3, 2009, No. 8612, pp. 55)
Pub: The Economist Newspaper Inc.
Description: Denmark's mortgage-holders and the county's lending system is presented.

27555 ■ "Sluggish Market Gives Hospitals the Financial Chills" in *The Business Journal-Serving Greater Tampa Bay* (Vol. 28, August 1, 2008)
Pub: American City Business Journals, Inc.
Ed: Margie Manning. **Description:** Operating margins for hospitals in the Tampa Bay, Florida area have been reduced from 2 percent in 2006 to 0.8 percent in 2007 due to a weaker US economy. Total margins, on the other hand, rose from 2.9 percent to 3.3 percent in the same period.

27556 ■ "Small-Business Agenda: Increase Capital, Education, Tax Breaks" in *Crain's Detroit Business* (Vol. 24, March 17, 2008)
Pub: Crain Communications, Inc.
Ed: Nancy Kaffer. **Description:** Discusses the policy suggestions detailed in the Small Business Association of Michigan's entrepreneurial agenda which include five main categories of focus: making entrepreneurial education a higher state priority; increasing capital available to entrepreneurs; using the state's tax structure as an incentive for entrepreneurial growth; getting university research from the lab to the market; and limiting government regulation that's burdensome to small businesses and getting legislative support of entrepreneurial assistance efforts.

27557 ■ *Small Business Clustering Technology: Applications in Marketing, Management, Finance, and IT*
Pub: Idea Group Publishing
Ed: Robert C. MacGregor; Ann Hodgkinson. **Released:** June 2006. **Description:** An overview of the development and role of small business clusters in disciplines that include economics, marketing, management and information systems.

27558 ■ "Small Business Earnings" in *Small Business Economic Trends* (January 2008, pp. 6)
Pub: National Federation of Independent Business
Description: Graph from a survey of small businesses in the U.S. is given, representing actual small business earnings from January 1986 to December 2007. Tables showing actual earnings changes and most important reason for lower earnings are also presented.

27559 ■ "Small Business Inventories" in *Small Business Economic Trends* (April 2008, pp. 14)
Pub: National Federation of Independent Business
Ed: William C. Dunkelberg, Holly Wade. **Description:** Three tables and a graph presenting the inventories of small businesses in the U.S. are provided. The tables include figures on actual inventory changes, inventory satisfaction, and inventory plans.

27560 ■ "Small Business: Just When Hopes Were High" in *Business Week* (January 8, 2007)
Pub: McGraw-Hill Companies
Ed: James Mehring. **Description:** Overview of the reasons for a fall in confidence concerning the economy among small businesses and the affect this could have in the coming year.

27561 ■ "Small Business Outlook" in *Small Business Economic Trends* (March 2008, pp. 4)
Pub: National Federation of Independent Business
Ed: William C. Dunkelberg, Holly Wade. **Description:** Three tables and a graph representing forecasts in business expansions of small businesses in the U.S. are presented. The figures presented in the graph include data from 1986 to 2008.

27562 ■ "Small Business Prices" in *Small Business Economic Trends* (September 2010, pp. 8)
Pub: National Federation of Independent Business
Ed: William C. Dunkelberg, Holly Wade. **Description:** A graph from a survey of small businesses in the U.S. is given, representing business prices from January 1986 to August 2010. Actual prices (last three months) and planned prices (next three months)

were compared in the graph. Tables of actual price changes and price plans from January 2005 to August 2010 are also supplied.

27563 ■ "Small Business Sales" in *Small Business Economic Trends* (July 2010, pp. 7)
Pub: National Federation of Independent Business
Description: A graph from a survey of small businesses in the U.S. is given representing sales from January 1986 to June 2010. Actual sales (prior three months) and expected sales (next three months) were compared in the graph. Tables of actual sales changes and sales expectations from January 2005 to June 2010 are also given.

27564 ■ "Small, But Mighty" in *Employee Benefit News* (Vol. 25, November 1, 2011, No. 14, pp. 32)
Pub: SourceMedia Inc.
Ed: Andrea Davis. **Description:** Three consulting firms are facing the challenge of helping clients understand the new health care reform in a tight economy.

27565 ■ "Smaller Banks Could Face Tough 2008" in *Austin Business JournalInc.* (Vol. 28, January 2, 2009, No. 1, pp. 3)
Pub: American City Business Journals
Ed: Christopher Calnan. **Description:** The turbulence in the banking industry is expected to reach Texas in 2009 and industry insiders believe there will be a shift in deposits from small, regional banks to larger banks due to low consumer confidence. One economist says that a large number of banks are going to go out of business in 2009.

27566 ■ "Smart Year-End Tax Moves" in *Business Owner* (Vol. 35, November-December 2011, No. 6, pp. 8)
Pub: DL Perkins Company
Description: Managing small business and individual taxes is more important in a bad economy. It is imperative to seek all tax incentives that apply to your business.

27567 ■ "Sobering Consequences" in *The Business Journal-Milwaukee* (Vol. 25, July 11, 2008, No. 42, pp. A1)
Pub: American City Business Journals, Inc.
Ed: Rich Rovito. **Description:** Milwaukee Mayor Tom Barrett and Wisconsin Governor Jim Doyle met with MillerCoors management in an effort to convince the company to locate its corporate headquarters in the city. The company is expected to announce its decision by mid-July 2008. It was revealed that the decision-making process is focusing on determining an optimal location for the headquarters.

27568 ■ *Social Enterprise: Developing Sustainable Businesses*
Pub: Palgrave Macmillan
Ed: Frank Martin, Marcus Thompson. **Released:** January 1, 2010. **Price:** $106.00. **Description:** Social enterprises bring people and communities together for economic development and social gain and represent a growing sector of the business community.

27569 ■ *Social Entrepreneurship*
Pub: Palgrave Macmillan
Ed: Johanna Mair; Jeffrey Robinson; Kai Hockerts. **Released:** June 2006. **Price:** $80.00. **Description:** Social entrepreneurship is the process involving innovative approaches to solving social problems while creating economic value.

27570 ■ "Some More Equal Than Others" in *Canadian Business* (Vol. 80, April 23, 2007, No. 9, pp. 23)
Pub: Rogers Media
Ed: Jack Mintz. **Description:** The details of the equalization program to be started by United States to improve economic conditions of Canada are presented.

27571 ■ "Some Relief Possible Following Painful Week" in *Barron's* (Vol. 88, July 14, 2008, No. 28, pp. M3)
Pub: Dow Jones & Co., Inc.
Ed: Kopin Tan. **Description:** Dow Chemical is offering a 74 percent premium to acquire Rohm & Haas' coatings and electronics materials operations. Frontline amassed a 5.6 percent stake in rival Overseas Shipholding Group and a merger between the two would create a giant global fleet with pricing power. Highlights of the U.S. stock market during the week that ended in July 11, 2008 are discussed. Statistical data included.

27572 ■ "Some Women Warming Up to Economy's Prospects" in *Crain's Cleveland Business* (Vol. 30, June 1, 2009, No. 21, pp. 9)
Pub: Crain Communications, Inc.
Ed: Mark Dodosh. **Description:** According to a recent survey conducted by the Center for Women's Business Research and KeyBank focusing on the experience and opinions of women business owners, 48 percent of respondents believe the economy will improve over the next six months. Statistical data included.

27573 ■ "Souled Out" in *Canadian Business* (Vol. 81, March 3, 2008, No. 3, pp. 35)
Pub: Rogers Media
Ed: Calvin Leung. **Description:** According to a survey of over 100 entrepreneurs, 78 percent responded that selling their business was emotionally draining for them. Greig Clark, for example, says that one of the toughest times of his life was selling College Pro Painters, after putting 18 years into that business. The economic impacts of selling out are also examined.

27574 ■ "Sour Grapes" in *Canadian Business* (Vol. 79, November 20, 2006, No. 23, pp. 28)
Pub: Rogers Media
Ed: Michael Mainville. **Description:** The impact of the sanctions imposed by Russia on the Georgian wine exports to Russia is discussed.

27575 ■ "Spectre of Iran War Spooks Oil Markets" in *Globe & Mail* (March 28, 2007, pp. B1)
Pub: CTVglobemedia Publishing Inc.
Ed: Shawn McCarthy. **Description:** The increase in the price of crude oil by $5 a barrel to reach $68 in the United States following speculation over war against Iran, is discussed.

27576 ■ "Spending on Innovation Down Sharply in State" in *Crain's Detroit Business* (Vol. 24, March 10, 2008, No. 10, pp. 7)
Pub: Crain Communications, Inc.
Ed: Chad Halcom. **Description:** Due to such issues as Michigan's uncertain tax structure, a shaky national economy, the credit crunch and mortgage lending crisis, investments in innovation for the state have sharply declined.

27577 ■ "Spillover Effects" in *Crain's Detroit Business* (Vol. 24, October 6, 2008, No. 40, pp. 29)
Pub: Crain Communications, Inc.
Description: Earlier this year, the Detroit Regional Chamber estimated that the Detroit Tiger's baseball team's 81 home games would have a $277 million positive economic impact on the region. Due to the poor performance of the team, fewer fans are spending money on tickets, which translates into fewer dollars coming into the region. Lower viewership on television has also been a result of the Tiger's losing season.

27578 ■ "Stadium Developers Seek a Win With the State" in *The Business Journal-Serving Metropolitan Kansas City* (Vol. 26, August 22, 2008)
Pub: American City Business Journals, Inc.
Ed: Rob Roberts. **Description:** Three Trails Redevelopment LLC is hoping to win $30 million in state tax credits from the Missouri Development Finance Board for the construction of an 18,500-seat Wizards stadium. The project is contingent on state tax incentives and the company remains optimistic about their goal.

27579 ■ "Staffing Firms are Picking Up the Pieces, Seeing Signs of Life" in *Milwaukee Business Journal* (Vol. 27, February 5, 2010, No. 19)
Pub: American City Business Journals
Ed: Rich Rovito. **Description:** Milwaukee, Wisconsin-based staffing firms are seeing signs of economic rebound as many businesses turned to temporary employees to fill the demands for goods and services. Economic observers believe the growth in temporary staffing is one of the early indicators of economic recovery.

27580 ■ "Standard-of-Living Gap With U.S. Closing" in *Globe & Mail* (March 27, 2007, pp. B3)
Pub: CTVglobemedia Publishing Inc.
Ed: Heather Scoffield. **Description:** According to latest report released by Statistics Canada, standard-of-living in Canada has increased considerably in last decade to match-up with American economy. Complete analysis in this context is presented.

27581 ■ "Stars Shine Downtown" in *The Business Journal-Serving Metropolitan Kansas City* (Vol. 26, August 29, 2008, No. 51, pp. 1)
Pub: American City Business Journals, Inc.
Ed: Rob Roberts. **Description:** Movie chain AMC Entertainment Inc. renews its lease for 97,000 square feet of space at Ten Main Center. HNTB Federal Services Corp., meanwhile, is to take up 42,000 square feet at an office building located at 120 W. 12th St. The leases' impacts on downtown office market are examined.

27582 ■ *Start-Up Nation*
Pub: Twelve/Hatchette Book Group
Ed: Dan Senor, Paul Singer. **Released:** 2009. **Price:** $26.99. **Description:** Amid the turmoil in the Middle East, Israel's economy continues to thrive.

27583 ■ "State Budget Woes Hurt Many Vendors, Senior Services" in *Sacramento Business Journal* (Vol. 25, August 15, 2008, No. 24, pp. 1)
Pub: American City Business Journals, Inc.
Ed: Melanie Turner. **Description:** Delays in the passage of the California state budget have adversely affected the health care industry. The Robertson Adult Day Health Care had taken out loans to keep the business afloat. The state Legislature has reduced Medi-Cal reimbursement to health care providers by 10 percent.

27584 ■ "State Expects Increase of $50 Million from Film Bills; Come Back, Al Roker" in *Crain's Detroit Business* (March 24, 2008)
Pub: Crain Communications, Inc.
Ed: Bill Shea. **Description:** Overview of the new film initiative and its incentives designed to entice more film work to Michigan; the measures could bring $50 million to $100 million in movie production work for the rest of this year compared to the $4 million total the state saw last year. Also discusses the show "DEA" which was filmed in Detroit and stars Al Roker.

27585 ■ "State Lawmakers Should Try Raising Jobs, Not Taxes" in *Crain's Chicago Business* (Vol. 31, March 24, 2008, No. 12, pp. 20)
Pub: Crain Communications, Inc.
Ed: Diug Whitley. **Description:** According to U.S. Department of Labor figures through December 2007, Illinois has ranked 45th in the nation in job growth for seven straight months. Many feel that the state would not need to raise taxes if they spent more time working to keep and attract employers that create jobs.

27586 ■ "State Shock Prices Take Large Tumble" in *The Business Journal-Milwaukee* (Vol. 25, September 12, 2008, No. 51, pp. A1)
Pub: American City Business Journals, Inc.
Ed: Rich Rovito. **Description:** Weak economic times have caused the stocks of most publicly traded companies in Wisconsin to dip in 2008. Companies that appeared on the worst performing stocks list also experienced drops in share price to as much as 70 percent. Information about the companies that experienced increases in stock prices is also presented. Statistical data included.

27587 ■ "The State of the Stores" in *Playthings* (Vol. 106, November 1, 2008, No. 10, pp. 8)
Pub: Reed Business Information
Ed: Dana French. **Description:** Investigation into the top twenty-five toy and game retailers shows that

video games and related handheld and console systems as well as computer games were number one with America's children in 2007.

27588 ■ "State Tourism Likely to Decline Two Percent this Year" in *Crain's Detroit Business* (Vol. 24, April 14, 2008, No. 15, pp. 6)
Pub: Crain Communications, Inc.
Ed: Amy Lane. **Description:** Due to such national and state economic conditions such as unemployment, the housing crisis and rising gasoline and food prices, Michigan's tourism industry is likely to decline about 2 percent this year.

27589 ■ "Stay Calm, Bernanke Urges Markets" in *Globe & Mail* (March 1, 2007, pp. B1)
Pub: CTVglobemedia Publishing Inc.
Ed: Brian McKenna. **Description:** The views of Ben Bernanke, the chief of the United States Federal Reserve Board, on the future trends of the United States' economy are presented. The effect of the global stock market trends on the American stock markets is discussed.

27590 ■ "Stay in School: Economy Got You Down?" in *Canadian Business* (Vol. 81, November 10, 2008, No. 19, pp. 98)
Pub: Rogers Media Ltd.
Ed: Graham F. Scott, Jane Bao. **Description:** A guide to Canadian MBA programs is presented. The tuition and length of each program is provided along with each school. Details on whether the universities offer part-time options, diversity, and co-op/internships are also given.

27591 ■ "Steady Spending in Retail" in *Business Week* (September 22, 2008, No. 4100, pp. 13)
Pub: McGraw-Hill Companies, Inc.
Ed: Tara Kalwarski. **Description:** Retail jobs have begun to decline on the national level despite the two percent growth in the industry over the last year; much of the growth has been attributed to the sales of higher-priced oil products.

27592 ■ "Stelco Seeks to Shave Its Fixed Costs" in *Globe & Mail* (March 8, 2007, pp. B1)
Pub: CTVglobemedia Publishing Inc.
Ed: Greg Keenan. **Description:** The plans of Stelco Inc. to control its fixed costs in order to protect itself from economic downturns are discussed.

27593 ■ "Step Up to Help Regionalism Step Forward" in *Crain's Cleveland Business* (Vol. 28, November 12, 2007, No. 45, pp. 10)
Pub: Crain Communications, Inc.
Ed: Rob Briggs; William Currin. **Description:** Discusses the importance of regionalism for Northeast Ohio as being a broad, collaborative approach to spur economic development.

27594 ■ *The Sticking Point Solution: 9 Ways to Move Your Business from Stagnation to Stunning Growth in Tough Economic Times*
Pub: Vanguard Press
Ed: Jay Abraham. **Released:** May 10, 2010. **Price:** $25.95. **Description:** Renowned business consultant, Jay Abraham, reveals the nine ways even successful businesses get stuck, hit plateaus, and fail to achieve their dreams and he explains how to get unstuck and create exponential growth.

27595 ■ "Stitching the City Together" in *Business Courier* (Vol. 24, February 8, 2008, No. 44, pp. 1)
Pub: American City Business Journals, Inc.
Ed: Lucy May. **Description:** Nancy Zimpher, University of Cincinnati president, has been given vital leadership posts in regional development organizations in the area. She sees this as part of her job and of the university's mission of serving the community.

27596 ■ *Street Fighters: The Last 72 Hours of Bears Stearns, the Toughest Firm on Wall Street*
Pub: Portfolio
Ed: Kate Kelly. **Released:** 2009. **Price:** $25.95. **Description:** An account of the investment bank, Bears Stearns fight for survival is documented.

27597 ■ "Stretch Your Advertising Dollars" in *Women Entrepreneur* (January 27, 2009)
Pub: Entrepreneur Media Inc.
Ed: Rosalind Resnick. **Description:** During such poor economic times, most businesses are having to cut their advertising budgets; tips for targeting your advertising dollars toward the customer base most likely to buy your product are given.

27598 ■ "Struggling Community Banks Find Little Help In Wall Street Bailout" in *Crain's Detroit Business* (Vol. 24, September 29, 2008)
Pub: Crain Communications, Inc.
Ed: Tom Henderson. **Description:** Both public and private Michigan bands have been hit hard by poorly performing loan portfolios and although their problems were not caused by high-risk securities but by a longtime statewide recession and a housing slump, these community banks have little hope of seeing any of the bailout money that has been allotted for the larger institutions.

27599 ■ "Struggling States Slashing Health Care For Poor" in *Chicago Tribune* (January 15, 2009)
Pub: McClatchy-Tribune Information Services
Ed: Noam N. Levey. **Description:** Health officials warn that even the huge federal rescue plan may not be enough to restore health services being eliminated due to the economic crisis.

27600 ■ "Stuck With Two Mortgages; The Nightmare When Buyers Upgrade" in *Crain's Chicago Business* (Vol. 31, April 21, 2008, No. 16)
Pub: Crain Communications, Inc.
Ed: Darci Smith. **Description:** Discusses the problem a number of people are facing due to the slump in the housing market: being stuck with two mortgages when they move because their former homes have not sold. Many thought they could afford to move to a larger home, anticipating significant equity appreciation that did not occur; now they are left with lowering their price and competing with the host of new developments.

27601 ■ *Studies of Entrepreneurship, Business and Government in Hong Kong: The Economic Development of a Small Open Economy*
Pub: Edwin Mellen Press
Ed: Fu-Lai Tony Yu. **Released:** November 2006. **Price:** $109.95. **Description:** Institutional and Austrian theories are used to analyze the transformation taking place in Hong Kong's economy.

27602 ■ "Studies Mixed on State's 2008 Retail Outlook" in *Crain's Detroit Business* (Vol. 24, March 24, 2008, No. 12, pp. 28)
Pub: Crain Communications, Inc.
Ed: Nancy Kaffer. **Description:** Marcus and Millichap Real Estate Investment Services and the Michigan Retailers Association have released two separate studies concerning Michigan retailers in 2008. According to its report, MRA is forecasting modest retail growth later this year; however, the study conducted by national commercial real estate brokers Marcus and Millichap predicts increasing vacancy rates, flat employment and decreasing sales for Detroit-area retailers.

27603 ■ "Stung by Recession, Hemmer Regroups with New Strategy" in *Business Courier* (Vol. 27, June 4, 2010, No. 5, pp. 1)
Pub: Business Courier
Ed: Lucy May. **Description:** Paul Hemmer Companies reduced its work force and outsourced operations such as marketing and architecture, in order for the commercial and construction firm to survive the recession. Hammer's total core revenue in 2009 dropped to less than $30 million forcing the closure of its Chicago office.

27604 ■ "Subprime Problems Loom" in *The Business Journal-Portland* (Vol. 25, August 29, 2008, No. 25, pp. 1)
Pub: American City Business Journals, Inc.
Ed: Wendy Culverwell. **Description:** Over half of subprime mortgages in Portland are resetting by the end of 2008, which will cause more problems to the local real estate market. The inventory of unsold homes has also been increasing for over a year. Forecasts for the Portland housing market in relation to mortgage resets are supplied.

27605 ■ *The Subprime Solution: How Today's Global Financial Crisis Happened, and What to Do About It*
Pub: Princeton University Press
Ed: Robert J. Shiller. **Released:** 2009. **Price:** $16. 95. **Description:** Yale economist discusses the worldwide financial crisis and offers plans to reform the system.

27606 ■ "Summary. Economic Trends for Small Business" in *Small Business Economic Trends* (February 2008, pp. 1)
Pub: National Federation of Independent Business
Ed: William C. Dunkelberg, Holly Wade. **Description:** Summary of economic trends for small businesses in the U.S. is provided. Economic indicators such as capital spending, inventories and sales, inflation, and profits are given. Analysis of credit markets is also provided.

27607 ■ *Superfreakonomics*
Pub: Morrow/HarperCollins
Ed: Steven D. Levitt, Stephen J. Dubner. **Released:** October 20, 2009. **Price:** $29.99. **Description:** A scholar and a journalist apply economic thinking to everything.

27608 ■ "The Surplus Shell Game" in *Canadian Business* (Vol. 80, March 12, 2007, No. 6, pp. 72)
Pub: Rogers Media
Description: The effort of successive federal governments in Canada to ensure budget surpluses and its impact on the economy are discussed.

27609 ■ "Survey Distorts Cost of Capitals" in *Canadian Business* (Vol. 83, October 12, 2010, No. 17, pp. 22)
Pub: Rogers Media Ltd.
Ed: Matthew McClearn. **Description:** Swiss bank UBS publishes a study comparing the costs of goods and services in megalopolises every three years. The study ranked Toronto and Montreal outside the Top 30 in 2009, but the two cities jumped to eighth and ninth in a recent update. This change can be contributed to the conversion of prices into Euros before making comparisons.

27610 ■ "Survey: Don't Expect Big Results From Stimulus" in *Crain's Detroit Business* (Vol. 25, June 1, 2009, No. 22)
Pub: Crain Communications Inc. - Detroit
Ed: Nancy Kaffer, Chad Halcom. **Description:** In a recent survey, Michigan business owners, operators or managers showed that 48 percent of respondents oppose the President's stimulus package and believe it will have little or no effect on the economy.

27611 ■ "Survey: More Buyers Expect to Spend Less in Most Media" in *Advertising Age* (Vol. 79, July 7, 2008, No. 26, pp. 3)
Pub: Crain Communications, Inc.
Ed: Megan McIlroy. **Description:** Marketers are decreasing their budgets for advertising in television, radio, newspaper and outdoor due to the economic downturn. Statistical data concerning advertising agencies and marketers included.

27612 ■ "The Survey Says" in *Collections and Credit Risk* (Vol. 14, September 1, 2009, No. 8, pp. 16)
Pub: SourceMedia, Inc.
Ed: Bill Grabarek; Darren Waggoner. **Description:** Revenue for the top accounts receivable management firms rose nearly 20 percent in 2008 despite lower liquidation rates, a poor economy and riskier, albeit cheaper debt portfolios; the trend may continue this year as collection agencies expect revenue, on average, to increase 5.8 percent. Debt buyers, however, found that their revenue fell nearly 7 percent in 2008 and expect it to fall another 12 percent this year.

27613 ■ "Survey Says Commercial Real Estate Headed for Turbulence" in *Commercial Property News* (March 17, 2008)
Pub: Nielsen Company
Description: Commercial real estate sector is declining due to the sluggish U.S. economy. According to a recent survey, national office, retail and hospitality markets are also on the decline.

27614 ■ "A Survival Guide for Crazy Times" in *Canadian Business* (Vol. 81, March 3, 2008, No. 3, pp. 61)
Pub: Rogers Media
Ed: David Wolf. **Description:** Investors should ensure that their portfolios are positioned defensively more than the average as the U.S. and Canadian markets face turbulent times. They should not assume that U.S. residential property is a good place to invest only because prices have dropped and the Canadian dollar is showing strength. Other tips that investors can use during unstable periods are supplied.

27615 ■ "Survival Guide: There Can Be an Upside to Managing a Downturn" in *Canadian Business* (Vol. 81, November 10, 2008, No. 19, pp. 54)
Pub: Rogers Media Ltd.
Ed: Sharda Prashad. **Description:** Canada-based Foxy is already limiting its exposure to retailers who could be a credit problem in case of recession. Retirement Life Communities is entering into fixed-rate and fixed-term loans for them to have sufficient financing to grow. Business owners need to realize that customers want more for less.

27616 ■ "Surviving the Storm" in *Canadian Business* (Vol. 81, July 22, 2008, No. 12-13, pp. 50)
Pub: Rogers Media Ltd.
Ed: Jeff Sanford. **Description:** Investment adviser Harry Dent and finance professor Paul Marsh discuss their views and forecasts on the United States' economic condition. Dent believes advisors should concentrate on wealth preservation rather than on returns. Other views regarding U.S. economic conditions are also presented.

27617 ■ "Suspense Hangs Over Fledging Film Industry" in *Crain's Detroit Business* (Vol. 26, January 18, 2010, No. 3, pp. 3)
Pub: Crain Communications, Inc.
Ed: Bill Shea. **Description:** Overview of the film incentive package which has fostered a growth in the industry with 52 productions completed in 2009, bringing in $223.6 million in gross in-state production expenditures of which the state will refund $87.2 million. Opposition to the incentives has been growing among legislatures who believe that the initiatives cost more than they ultimately bring into the state. Experts believe that the initiatives will remain since they have already fostered economic growth and are good for the state's image.

27618 ■ "Swagelok Boss" in *Crain's Cleveland Business* (Vol. 30, June 29, 2009, No. 25, pp. 4)
Pub: Crain Communications, Inc.
Ed: Dan Shingler. **Description:** Swagelok Company president and CEO has not laid off an employee in its 65 years of existence and said at a recent convention that he plans to keep his 4,000 employees working and inventories at normal levels despite the recession.

27619 ■ "Swirling Debate" in *Business Courier* (Vol. 27, August 20, 2010, No. 16, pp. 1)
Pub: Business Courier
Ed: Lucy May. **Description:** The debate on whether to convert Greater Cincinnati Water Works into a public regional district is seen to impact the city's economic recovery. The utility's service area and customer base has significantly grown.

27620 ■ "Taking Collections" in *Investment Dealers' Digest* (Vol. 75, October 9, 2009, No. 38, pp. 19)
Pub: SourceMedia, Inc.
Ed: Aleksandrs Rozens. **Description:** Although the nation's debt-collection industry has grown with increased reliance by consumers on credit, valuations of these firms have lessened due to the economy which has hurt some of the success of these firms in obtaining the debt back from consumers who are experiencing trying economic times.

27621 ■ "Taking the Over-the-Counter Route to US" in *Barron's* (Vol. 88, July 7, 2008, No. 27, pp. 24)
Pub: Dow Jones & Co., Inc.
Ed: Eric Uhlfelder. **Description:** Many multinational companies have left the New York Stock Exchange and allowed their shares to trade over-the-counter. The companies have taken advantage of a 2007 SEC rule allowing publicly listed foreign companies to change trading venues if less than 5 percent of global trading volume in the past 12 months occurred in the US.

27622 ■ "Tampa Condo Conversion Sells for $14.8 Million Less" in *The Business Journal-Serving Greater Tampa Bay* (Vol. 28, September 5, 2008)
Pub: American City Business Journals, Inc.
Ed: Janet Leiser. **Description:** Former apartment complex Village Oaks at Tampa, which was converted to condominiums, has been sold to Tennessee-based real estate investment trust Mid-America Apartment Communities Inc. for $21.2 million in August 2008. The amount was $14.2 million less than what developer Radco Management LLC paid for in 2005.

27623 ■ "Tao of Downfall" in *International Journal of Entrepreneurship and Small Business* (Vol. 11, August 31, 2010, No. 2, pp. 121)
Pub: Publishers Communication Group
Ed: Wenxian Zhang, Ilan Alon. **Description:** Through historical reviews and case studies, this research seeks to understand why some initially successful entrepreneurs failed in the economic boom of past decades. Among various factors contributing to their downfall are a unique political and business environment, fragile financial systems, traditional cultural influences and personal characteristics.

27624 ■ "Tech Godfather Steve Walker Winding Down Howard Venture Fund" in *Baltimore Business Journal* (Vol. 27, December 11, 2009, No. 31)
Pub: American City Business Journals
Ed: Scott Dance. **Description:** Steve Walker, president of venture capital fund firm Walker Ventures, will be closing the Howard County, Maryland-based firm as the economic situation is finding it difficult to recover investor's money. According to Walker, the economy also constrained investors from financing venture funds. Despite the closure, Walker will continue his work in the local angel investing community.

27625 ■ "TechLift Strives to Fill in Gaps in Entrepreneurial Support Efforts" in *Crain's Cleveland Business* (November 12, 2007)
Pub: Crain Communications, Inc.
Ed: Marsha Powers. **Description:** Profile of the program, TechLift, a new business model launched by NorTech, that is aiming to provide assistance to technology-based companies that may not be a good fit for other entrepreneurial support venues.

27626 ■ "Tempel Steel To Expand Its Chicago Plant" in *Chicago Tribune* (August 22, 2008)
Pub: McClatchy-Tribune Information Services
Ed: James P. Miller. **Description:** Tempel Steel Co. is no longer considering transferring a Libertyville factory's production to Mexico; the company has responded to government incentives and will instead shift that work to its plant on Chicago's North Side.

27627 ■ "That Empty Feeling" in *Crain's Cleveland Business* (Vol. 28, October 15, 2007, No. 41, pp. 1)
Pub: Crain Communications, Inc.
Ed: Stan Bullard. **Description:** Townhouses, cluster homes and condominiums lured both buyers and builders for most of this decade but now that market is suffering to an even greater degree than the single-family home market. Statistical data included.

27628 ■ "That Vision Thing" in *Canadian Business* (Vol. 80, December 25, 2006, No. 1, pp. 78)
Pub: Rogers Media
Description: Suggestions for better Canadian tax policy and making airspace competitive among other things, to improve the economy in 2007, are presented.

27629 ■ "That's About It for Quantitative Easing" in *Barron's* (Vol. 89, July 20, 2009, No. 29, pp. M11)
Pub: Dow Jones & Co., Inc.
Ed: Brian Blackstone. **Description:** US Federal Reserve appears to have decided to halt quantitative easing, causing bond prices to drop and yields to rise. The yield for the 1-year Treasury bond rose more than 0.3 percentage point to about 3.65 percent.

27630 ■ "The Next 20 Years: How Customer and Workforce Attitudes Will Evolve" in *Harvard Business Review* (Vol. 85, July-August 2007, No. 7-8)
Pub: Harvard Business School Publishing
Ed: Neil Howe, William Strauss. **Description:** Identification of social categories inhabited by age groups is used to calculate how consumer and employee opinions and behavior will change, and how this will impact economic development and corporate growth.

27631 ■ "There's More Upside in Germany" in *Barron's* (Vol. 90, September 6, 2010, No. 36, pp. M7)
Pub: Barron's Editorial & Corporate Headquarters
Ed: Jonathan Buck. **Description:** Germany's stocks have gone up since the beginning of 2010, and investors can still benefit. These stocks will benefit from Germany's stellar economic performance and the relative weakness of the Euro. The prospects of the shares of Daimler and Hochtief are discussed.

27632 ■ "Things Fall Apart" in *Canadian Business* (Vol. 80, October 8, 2007, No. 20, pp. 187)
Pub: Rogers Media
Ed: Jeff Sanford. **Description:** Infrastructure crisis in Canada and in other countries in North America is examined. Incidents that demonstrate this crisis, such as the collapse of a bridge in Minneapolis and the collapse of an overpass in Quebec, Canada are presented. It is estimated that the reconstruction in the country will cost between C$44 billion and C$200 billion.

27633 ■ "Things Will Improve, or Not: a Chartered Financial Analyst Explains It All" in *Canadian Business* (Vol. 81, November 10, 2008)
Pub: Rogers Media Ltd.
Description: Myles Zyblock expects the global economic slowdown to deepen over the next six to nine months. Zyblock addressed the Toronto CFA Society at their annual dinner in October 2008. He stressed a tight correlation between the credit ratio and asset prices and predicts the S&P 500 to be up by 11 percent by October 2009.

27634 ■ "Think Disruptive! How to Manage In a New Era of Innovation" in *Strategy & Leadership* (Vol. 38, July-August 2010, No. 4, pp. 5-10)
Pub: Emerald Inc.
Ed: Brian Leavy, John Sterling. **Description:** The views expressed by Scott Anthony, president of an innovation consultancy Innosight, on the need for corporate leaders to apply disruptive innovation in a recessionary environment are presented. His suggestion that disruptive innovation is the only way to survive during the economic crisis is discussed.

27635 ■ "Thomas D'Aquino" in *Canadian Business* (Vol. 80, November 19, 2007, No. 23, pp. 92)
Pub: Rogers Media
Ed: Calvin Leung. **Description:** Thomas D'Aquino is the CEO and president of the Canadian Council of Chief Executives since 1981. D'Aquino thinks he has the best job in Canada because he can change the

way policies are made and the way people think. Details of his career as a lawyer and CEO and his views on Canada's economy are provided.

27636 ■ "The Three Amigos" in *Canadian Business* (Vol. 81, March 17, 2008, No. 4, pp. 19)
Pub: Rogers Media
Ed: Rachel Pulfer. **Description:** Mexican president Felipe Calderon said that Mexico exported 30 percent more to Europe and 25 percent more to other countries in Latin America in 2006 in light of the downturn in the U.S. economy. Calderon made this announcement in a speech at Harvard University while protestors marched outside protesting against NAFTA.

27637 ■ "Three Trails Blazes Tax Credit Deal" in *The Business Journal-Serving Metropolitan Kansas City* (Vol. 27, November 7, 2008, No. 9)
Pub: American City Business Journals, Inc.
Ed: Rob Roberts. **Description:** Three Trails Redevelopment LLC plans to redevelop the Bannister Mall area. The Missouri Development Finance Board is expected to approve $30 million in tax credits for the project. A verbal agreement on the terms and conditions has already been reached according to the agency's executive director.

27638 ■ "Tightening Economy Squeezes Business Travel" in *HRMagazine* (Vol. 53, August 2008, No. 8, pp. 19)
Pub: Society for Human Resource Management
Ed: Kathy Gurchiek. **Description:** New surveys show that some companies are not cutting out business travel, they are using cheaper hotels and cutting back on trade shows and conference travel. Statistical data included.

27639 ■ "Time for a Leap Of Faith?" in *Women Entrepreneur* (November 18, 2008)
Pub: Entrepreneur Media Inc.
Ed: Cynthia McKay. **Description:** Starting a new business, despite the downturn in the economy, can prove to be a successful endeavor if one has the time, energy and most importantly a good idea.

27640 ■ "Time to Leave the Party?" in *Barron's* (Vol. 88, March 24, 2008, No. 12, pp. M16)
Pub: Dow Jones & Company, Inc.
Ed: Andrea Hotter. **Description:** Prices of commodities such as gold, copper, crude oil, sugar, cocoa, and wheat have fallen from their all-time highs set in the middle of March 2008. Analysts, however, caution that this decline in prices may be temporary, and that a banking crisis may trigger new price rises in commodities.

27641 ■ "Time is Right for Fiscal Authority" in *Canadian Business* (Vol. 83, July 20, 2010, No. 11-12, pp. 24)
Pub: Rogers Media Ltd.
Ed: Jacqueline Nelson. **Description:** A survey of Canadian CEOs show that only 5 percent of them believe that the world is in a severe recession. Almost 80 percent of them believe that economic recessions and depressions are caused by failures of the free market and the government.

27642 ■ "A Timely Matter" in *Canadian Business* (Vol. 81, March 31, 2008, No. 5, pp. 12)
Pub: Rogers Media
Description: Discusses the committee responsible for restructuring $33 billion of asset-backed commercial paper which has moved back their implementation plan by a month citing complexities. British Columbia has surpassed the $1 billion mark in fiscal '07-'08 from their oil and gas rights. Biovail Corp. founder Eugene Melnyk said he had lost confidence in the management of the company.

27643 ■ "Tiptoeing Beyond Treasuries" in *Barron's* (Vol. 88, March 31, 2008, No. 13, pp. M6)
Pub: Dow Jones & Company, Inc.
Ed: Michael S. Derby. **Description:** Risk-free assets like treasuries are still a good place for cash even if market conditions have calmed down and Treasury yields are low. Investors looking for yield and safety might want to consider Treasury inflation-indexed securities that are attractive given new inflation pressures.

27644 ■ "To Keep Freight Rolling, Springfield Must Grease the Hub" in *Crain's Chicago Business* (Vol. 31, April 21, 2008, No. 16, pp. 22)
Pub: Crain Communications, Inc.
Ed: Paul O'Connor. **Description:** Discusses the importance of upgrading Chicago's continental-hub freight rail system which is integral to moving international products as well as domestic ones. Global tonnage is expected to double by 2020 and unless more money is designated to upgrade the infrastructure the local and national economy will suffer.

27645 ■ "Today's Business Sale Climate" in *Business Owner* (Vol. 35, September-October 2011, No. 5, pp. 10)
Pub: DL Perkins Company
Description: Despite the weak economy, there is a surplus of individuals wanting to purchase a small business. The Small Business Administration loan guarantees program helps with its loans for purchase/ sale of business assistance.

27646 ■ "Top 50 Exporters" in *Hispanic Business* (Vol. 30, July-August 2008, No. 7-8, pp. 42)
Pub: Hispanic Business, Inc.
Ed: Hildy Medina. **Description:** Increases in exports revenues reported by food exporters and green companies in a time of economic slowdown in the U.S are described. Food exporters have benefited from the growth of high-volume grocery stores in underdeveloped countries and the German governments' promotion of solar energy has benefited the U.S. solar heating equipment and solar panel manufactures.

27647 ■ "Top 50 In Profits" in *Canadian Business* (Vol. 81, Summer 2008, No. 9, pp. 116)
Pub: Rogers Media Ltd.
Description: Royal Bank of Canada topped the Investor 500 by profits list despite the slower economic growth in Canada and the U.S. The bank was in the runner-up position in the 2007. RBC's growth strategy is through hefty acquisitions in the U.S. A table ranking the top 50 companies in Canada in terms of profits is presented.

27648 ■ "Top 100 Consolidate Gains" in *Hispanic Business* (Vol. 30, July-August 2008, No. 7-8, pp. 30)
Pub: Hispanic Business, Inc.
Ed: Richard Kaplan. **Description:** Data developed by HispanTelligence on the increase in revenue posted by the top 100 fastest-growing U.S. Hispanic firms over the last five years is reported. Despite the economic downturn, the service sector, IT and health suppliers showed an increase in revenue whereas construction companies showed a marginal slump in revenue growth.

27649 ■ "Top Private Companies" in *Baltimore Business Journal* (Vol. 28, August 27, 2010, No. 16, pp. 1)
Pub: Baltimore Business Journal
Ed: Gary Haber. **Description:** The combined revenue of the 100 largest private firms in Maryland's Baltimore region dropped from about $22.7 billion in 2008 to $21 billion in 2009, an annual decrease of more than 7 percent. To survive the recession's impact, these firms resorted to strategies such as government contracting and overseas expansion.

27650 ■ "Tory or Liberal, Blue or Red, the Impact of the Election is All in Your Head" in *Globe & Mail* (January 14, 2006, pp. B19)
Pub: CTVglobemedia Publishing Inc.
Ed: Derek DeCloet. **Description:** The effect of the outcome of 2006 Canadian federal elections on stock markets is discussed.

27651 ■ "Tough Climate for Nurseries" in *Crain's Cleveland Business* (Vol. 30, June 29, 2009, No. 25, pp. 1)
Pub: Crain Communications, Inc.
Ed: Stan Bullard. **Description:** After 81 years in the business, Sunnybrook Farms & Nursery is closing its doors. The owner sites the bad economy along with cold weather the reason for lack of sales. Other nursery owners discuss the bad economy and weather conditions and how they are affecting their business.

27652 ■ "Tough Sell: Senior Projects Hustle to Keep Buyers" in *Puget Sound Business Journal* (Vol. 29, November 21, 2008, No. 31, pp.)
Pub: American City Business Journals
Ed: Heidi Dietrich. **Description:** Plans to move to retirement communities are being postponed by seniors in Washington's Puget Sound area due to difficulty selling their current homes in the slow economy. Retirement communities are trying to lure clients by offering new finance programs and sales plans.

27653 ■ "Trade Winds" in *Canadian Sailings* (June 30, 2008)
Pub: Commonwealth Business Media
Ed: Peter Malkovsky. **Description:** Trade between Canada and the United States is discussed as well as legislation concerning foreign trade and the future of this trade relationship.

27654 ■ *Trading Places: SMEs in the Global Economy, A Critical Research Handbook*
Pub: Edward Elgar Publishing, Incorporated
Ed: Lloyd-Reason. **Released:** September 2006. **Price:** $110.00. **Description:** An overview of international research for small and medium-sized companies wishing to expand in the global economy.

27655 ■ "Train Now to Get the Competitive Edge" in *Contractor* (Vol. 56, October 2009, No. 10, pp. 58)
Pub: Penton Media, Inc.
Ed: Merry Beth Hall. **Description:** Due to the harsh economic climate, mechanical contractors would be well-served to train their employees while they have time to take them out of the field. This will help ensure that they are not behind when the economic recovery happens. Suggestions on how to choose the best type of training are presented.

27656 ■ "Travel Leery" in *Crain's Chicago Business* (Vol. 31, March 31, 2008, No. 13, pp. 3)
Pub: Crain Communications, Inc.
Description: Due to the rise in airline prices and a possible recession, many companies are starting to change their travel policies and limit travel spending.

27657 ■ *The Trillion Dollar Meltdown: Easy Money, High Rollers, and the Great Credit Crash*
Pub: Public Affairs
Ed: Charles R. Morris. **Released:** 2009. **Price:** $22. 95. **Description:** Former banker believes that Wall Street and the financial community have too much power in America. He estimates that writedowns and defaults of residential mortgages, commercial mortgages, junk bonds, leveraged loans, credit cards, and complex securitized bonds could reach $1 trillion.

27658 ■ "Trillium Turmoil" in *Canadian Business* (Vol. 81, December 8, 2008, No. 21, pp. 16)
Pub: Rogers Media Ltd.
Ed: Jeff Sanford. **Description:** Ontario's manufacturing success in the past was believed to have been built by the 1965 Canada-U.S. automotive pact and by advantages such as low-cost energy. The loss of these advantages along with the challenging economic times has hurt Ontario's manufacturing industry.

27659 ■ "Trimming Costs, But Not Looking It" in *Crain's Chicago Business* (Vol. 31, November 17, 2008, No. 46, pp. 35)
Pub: Crain Communications, Inc.
Ed: Shia Kapos. **Description:** Advice is given concerning ways in which to keep up appearances of success during these troubled financial times.

27660 ■ "Trust Tax Under Fire as Drain on Revenue" in *Globe & Mail* (April 9, 2007, pp. B1)
Pub: CTVglobemedia Publishing Inc.
Ed: Steven Chase. **Description:** The economic aspects of the implementation of the trust levy by the Canadian government are discussed. The acquisition of Canadian income trusts by Canadian and international financial institutions is described.

27661 ■ "Turbulent Skies" in *The Business Journal-Portland* (Vol. 25, August 29, 2008, No. 25, pp. 1)
Pub: American City Business Journals, Inc.
Ed: Erik Siemers. **Description:** Small airlines are struggling to keep their commercial services amid the troubled commercial airline sector. Small communities, for example, were expected to pony up about $650,000 in revenue guarantees each in order to convince SkyWest Airlines to offer two direct flights to Portland daily beginning October 12, 2008. The trends in the commercial airline industry are analyzed.

27662 ■ "Turbulent Times and Golden Opportunity" in *Business Strategy Review* (Vol. 21, Spring 2010, No. 1, pp. 34)
Pub: Wiley-Blackwell
Ed: Don Sull. **Description:** For those feeling storm-tossed by today's economy, the author believes there's much to learn from Carnival Cruise Lines, a company that discovered that turbulence often has an upside.

27663 ■ "The Turkey Has Landed" in *Canadian Business* (Vol. 79, November 20, 2006, No. 23, pp. 38)
Pub: Rogers Media
Ed: Erik Heinrich. **Description:** The design and construction of Toronto Pearson International Airport to handle domestic, international and transborder flights in one facility is discussed.

27664 ■ "Turmoil Means Changes For Retailers" in *The Business Journal-Serving Metropolitan Kansas City* (Vol. 27, October 10, 2008, No. 4)
Pub: American City Business Journals, Inc.
Ed: Suzanna Stagemeyer. **Description:** Impacts of the financial crisis on Kansas Metropolitan Area retailers are varied. Rob Dalzell, for instance, found it difficult to secure a loan for his new self-serve yogurt store Yummo. The trends in retailing in the area are examined further as well as ways in which local businesses are changing in an attempt to stay solvent during the economic downturn.

27665 ■ "A Turn in the South" in *The Economist* (Vol. 390, January 3, 2009, No. 8612, pp. 34)
Pub: The Economist Newspaper Inc.
Description: Overview of Charleston, South Carolina, a region that lost its navy base in 1996, which had provided work for more than 22,000 people; the city developed a plan called Noisette in order to redevelop the area and today the economy is healthier and more diversified than it was a decade ago. Charleston was described as among the best cities for doing business by Inc. Magazine and seems to be handling the downturn of the economy fairly well. Statistical data regarding growth, business and population is included.

27666 ■ "Twenty Years of Advocacy and Education" in *Women Entrepreneur* (January 18, 2009)
Pub: Entrepreneur Media Inc.
Ed: Eve Gumpel. **Description:** Profile of Sharon Hadary who served as executive director of the Center for Women's Business Research for two decades; Hadary discusses what she has learned about women business owners, their impact on the economy and what successful business owners share in common.

27667 ■ "Uncle Volodya's Flagging Christmas Spirit; Russia" in *The Economist* (Vol. 390, January 3, 2009, No. 8612, pp. 22)
Pub: The Economist Newspaper Inc.
Description: Overview of Russia's struggling economy as well as unpopular government decisions such as raising import duties on used foreign vehicles so as to protect Russian carmakers.

27668 ■ "Understanding the Economy: People Worry That a Recession Is Coming" in *Inc.* (December 2007, pp. 103-104)
Pub: Gruner & Jahr USA Publishing
Ed: Joseph H. Ellis. **Description:** It is suggested that by the time a recession arrives, the worst economic damage has already occurred.

27669 ■ "Unemployment Rates" in *The Economist* (Vol. 390, January 3, 2009, No. 8612, pp. 75)
Pub: The Economist Newspaper Inc.
Description: Countries that are being impacted the worst by rising unemployment rates are those that have also been suffering from the housing market crisis. Spain has been the hardest hit followed by Ireland. America and Britain are also seeing levels of unemployment that indicate too much slack in the economy.

27670 ■ "Union Questions Patrick Cudahy Layoffs" in *Business Journal-Milwaukee* (Vol. 28, December 3, 2010, No. 9, pp. A1)
Pub: Milwaukee Business Journal
Ed: Rich Ravito. **Description:** United Food and Commercial Workers Local 1473 is investigating Patrick Cudahy Inc.'s termination of 340 jobs. The union said the company has violated the law for failing to issue proper notice of a mass layoff.

27671 ■ "The Union of Town and Gown" in *Entrepreneur* (Vol. 37, October 2009, No. 10, pp. 47)
Pub: Entrepreneur Media, Inc.
Ed: Jason Daley. **Description:** Ten of the best entrepreneurial initiatives involving cities and local universities in the US are described. Cities and universities are joining up for these efforts to strengthen local economies and stop brain drain.

27672 ■ "U.S. Economy's Underlying Strengths Limit Recession Threat" in *Hispanic Business* (Vol. 30, April 2008, No. 4, pp. 14)
Pub: Hispanic Business
Ed: Dr. Juan B. Solana. **Description:** Large and small businesses as well as consumers and policy-makers are attempting to identify the areas of risk and loss created by the economic crisis; analysts are now estimating that U.S. mortgage losses could reach the $380 to $400 billion mark. Also discusses the falling of wages and the rising of unemployment. Statistical data included.

27673 ■ "U.S. Recession Officially Over: Is Recovery Ever Going to Arrive?" in *Montana Business Quarterly* (Vol. 49, Spring 2011, No. 1, pp. 6)
Pub: Bureau of Business & Economic Research
Ed: Patrick M. Barkey. **Description:** Ten predictions regarding American's economy for 2012 are listed.

27674 ■ *United States Taxes and Tax Policy*
Pub: Cambridge University Press
Ed: David G. Davies. **Released:** January 22, 2010. **Price:** $34.99. **Description:** This book expands the information on taxes found in public finance texts by using a combination of institutional, factual, theoretical and empirical information. It also stresses the economic effects of taxes and tax policy.

27675 ■ "Univest Charter Switch Signals Banking Trend" in *Philadelphia Business Journal* (Vol. 30, September 2, 2011, No. 29, pp. 1)
Pub: American City Business Journals Inc.
Ed: Jeff Blumenthal. **Description:** Univest Corporation of Pennsylvania changed from a federal to state charter because of cost savings and state agency has greater understanding of the intricacies of the local economy. The Pennsylvania Department of Banking has also received inquiries from seven other banks about doing the same this year.

27676 ■ "Up In the Air" in *The Business Journal-Serving Greater Tampa Bay* (Vol. 28, July 18, 2008, No. 30, pp. 1)
Pub: American City Business Journals, Inc.
Ed: Margie Manning. **Description:** Views and information on Busch Gardens and on its future, are presented. The park's 3,769 employees worry for their future, after tourism industry experts have expressed concerns on possible tax cuts and other cost reductions. The future of the park, which ranks number 19 as the most visited park in the world, is expected to have a major impact on the tourism industry.

27677 ■ "Up On The Farm" in *Canadian Business* (Vol. 81, March 31, 2008, No. 5, pp. 23)
Pub: Rogers Media
Ed: John Gray. **Description:** Agricultural products have outperformed both energy and metal and even the prospect of a global economic slowdown does not seem to hinder its prospects. The Organization for Economic Cooperation and Development sees prices above historic equilibrium levels during the next ten years given that fuel and fertilizers remain high and greater demand from India and China remain steady

27678 ■ "An Updated Ranking of Academic Journals in Economics" in *Canadian Journal of Economics* (Vol. 44, November 2011, No. 4, pp. 1525)
Pub: Blackwell Publishers Ltd.
Ed: Pantelis Kalaitzidakis, Theofanis P. Mamuneas, Thanasis Stengos. **Description:** An updated list showing the ranking of economic journals (2003) is presented; however this present study differs methodologically from an earlier study by using a rolling window of years between 2003 and 2008, for each year counting the number of citations of articles published in the previous ten years.

27679 ■ "The Upside of Fear and Loathing" in *Barron's* (Vol. 88, March 24, 2008, No. 12, pp. 11)
Pub: Dow Jones & Company, Inc.
Ed: Michael Santoli. **Description:** Fear and risk aversion prevalent among investors may actually serve to cushion the decline and spark a rally in US stock prices. Surveys of investors indicate rising levels of anxiety and bearishness, indicating a possible positive turnaround.

27680 ■ "USAmeriBank Deals for Growth" in *The Business Journal-Serving Greater Tampa Bay* (Vol. 28, September 26, 2008, No. 40, pp. 1)
Pub: American City Business Journals, Inc.
Ed: Margie Manning. **Description:** It is believed that the pending $14.9 million purchase of Liberty Bank by USAmeriBank could be at the forefront of a trend. Executives of both companies expect the deal to close by the end of 2008. USAmeriBank will have $430 million in assets and five offices in Pinellas, Florida once the deal is completed.

27681 ■ "Valenti: Roots of Financial Crisis Go Back to 1998" in *Crain's Detroit Business* (Vol. 24, October 6, 2008, No. 40, pp. 25)
Pub: Crain Communications, Inc.
Ed: Tom Henderson; Nathan Skid. **Description:** Interview with Sam Valenti III who is the chairman and CEO of Valenti Capital L.L.C., a wealth-management firm; Valenti discusses in detail the history that led up to the current economic crisis as well as his prediction for the future of the country.

27682 ■ "VC Investing Down 63 Percent" in *Austin Business JournalInc.* (Vol. 29, January 29, 2010, No. 47, pp. 1)
Pub: American City Business Journals
Ed: Christopher Calnan. **Description:** Venture capital investments in the Austin, Texas area have declined by about 63 percent from $590.1 million in 2008 to

$219.2 million in 2009. Deal volume remained steady at 53 local company fundings, but the median deal value declined from $6.5 million in 2008 to $3 million in 2009. Details on several local deals are presented.

27683 ■ "Venture Gap" in *Canadian Business* (Vol. 81, March 17, 2008, No. 4, pp. 82)
Pub: Rogers Media
Ed: Joe Castaldo. **Description:** Money raised by Canadian venture capitalist firms has been declining since 2001. A strong venture capital market is important if Canada is to build innovative companies. Fixing Canada's tax policy on foreign investments is a start in reviving the industry.

27684 ■ "The Visitor Rebound" in *Canadian Business* (Vol. 80, November 5, 2007, No. 22, pp. 23)
Pub: Rogers Media
Ed: Graham Silnicki. **Description:** Overnight visits to Canada are expected to fall by 5.3 percent in 2008, however spending is expected to drop by only 2 percent. Senior economist Alex Fritsche thinks that tourism from the U.S. will improve in 2009; the reasons for the expected growth in 2009 are examined.

27685 ■ "Vital Signs: The Big Picture" in *Canadian Business* (Vol. 81, Summer 2008, No. 9, pp. 153)
Pub: Rogers Media Ltd.
Description: Results of the Investor 500 showing percentage of companies with positive returns, most actively traded companies over the past six months and market capitalization by industry are presented. Stock performance and revenues of publicly held corporations in Canada are also provided.

27686 ■ "Viva Brazil" in *Business Strategy Review* (Vol. 21, Autumn 2010, No. 3, pp. 24)
Pub: Wiley-Blackwell
Ed: Georgina Peters. **Description:** Brazil's current status as a major emerging market with a boundless economic horizon is a radical shift from its place in the world in the late 1960s to the mid 1990s. Lessons Brazil can teach other countries are outlined.

27687 ■ "Viva La Evolucion" in *Canadian Business* (Vol. 80, February 12, 2007, No. 4, pp. 63)
Pub: Rogers Media
Ed: Denis Seguin. **Description:** The rise of Cuba as an importance source of oil and its significance for the Canadian economy is discussed.

27688 ■ "Voices: Breaking the Corruption Habit" in *Business Strategy Review* (Vol. 21, Autumn 2010, No. 3, pp. 67)
Pub: Blackwell Publishers Ltd.
Ed: David De Cremer. **Description:** In times of crisis, it seems natural that people will work together for the common good. The author cautions that, on the contrary, both economic and social research proves otherwise. Steps for organizations to take to prevent corrupt behaviors are investigated.

27689 ■ "Wait a Minute!" in *Entrepreneur* (Vol. 37, September 2009, No. 9, pp. 76)
Pub: Entrepreneur Media, Inc.
Ed: Jennifer Wang. **Description:** Advice on how entrepreneurs in the United States should secure funding in view of the economic crisis is presented. Enough interest should be stimulated so as to secure a follow-up meeting. Investors should be asked questions that would encourage them to tell stories related to the downturn.

27690 ■ "Wake-Up Call" in *Canadian Business* (Vol. 80, October 8, 2007, No. 20, pp. 58)
Pub: Rogers Media
Ed: Andrea Mandel-Campbell. **Description:** The need for Canadian companies to develop global marketing strategies is discussed. Thomas Caldwell, chairman of Caldwell Securities, believes the country's average performance in global markets should be a cause for alarm. The factors affecting the country's current economic state is also presented.

27691 ■ "Walker Seeks More Business Participation" in *Business Journal-Milwaukee* (Vol. 28, December 10, 2010, No. 10, pp. A1)
Pub: Milwaukee Business Journal
Ed: Rich Kirchen. **Description:** Wisconsin governor Scott Walker is seeking the aid of Milwaukee business leaders to participate in resolving the challenges posed by the economic crisis. Walker is aiming to create 250,000 jobs. He is also planning to call a special session of the legislature to enact strategies to jumpstart the economy.

27692 ■ "Wannabe Buyers Take Their Own Sweet Time" in *Crain's Chicago Business* (Vol. 31, April 21, 2008, No. 16, pp. 50)
Pub: Crain Communications, Inc.
Ed: Lisa Bertagnoli. **Description:** Although all factors are in place for a robust real-estate market in the Chicago area: low interest rates, plenty of inventory and the region's relatively strong employment, buyers are taking their time and doing more research in order to see how bad the economy will get.

27693 ■ "Want Some of This?" in *Canadian Business* (Vol. 80, April 9, 2007, No. 8, pp. 71)
Pub: Rogers Media
Ed: Jeff Sanford. **Description:** The economic impact of growing private equity in Canada is discussed.

27694 ■ "The War for Good Jobs; The World Will IBe Led with Economic Force" in *Gallup Management Journal* (September 7, 2011)
Pub: Gallup
Ed: Jim Clifton. **Description:** Gallup's chairman believes the next world war will be for good jobs and the winner will triumph with economic force, driven primarily by job creation and quality GDP growth.

27695 ■ "Water Works Spinoff Could Make Big Splash" in *Business Courier* (Vol. 24, October 19, 2008, No. 27, pp. 1)
Pub: American City Business Journals, Inc.
Ed: Dan Monk. **Description:** Cincinnati, Ohio city manager Milton Dohoney proposed to spin off the city-owned Greater Cincinnati Water Works into a regionally focused water district that could allow the city to receive millions of dollars in annual dividends. A feasibility study is to be conducted by a team of outside consultants and city staffers and is expected to be finished by summer of 2008.

27696 ■ *The Way We'll Be: The Zogby Report on the Transformation of the American Dream*
Pub: Crown Business
Ed: John Zogby. **Released:** 2009. **Price:** $26.00. **Description:** According to a recent poll, the next generation of Americans are not as concerned about making money as they are about making a difference in the world.

27697 ■ "We May Finally Find the Silver Lining" in *Crain's Detroit Business* (Vol. 24, April 7, 2008, No. 14, pp. 8)
Pub: Crain Communications, Inc.
Ed: Description: Discusses a possible economic turnaround for Michigan which could be brought forth with such things as the new film initiative incentives which may make filming in the state more appealing than filming in Canada due to the weakened state of the dollar and more exportation from Michigan companies.

27698 ■ "Weathering the Economic Storm" in *Playthings* (Vol. 107, January 1, 2009, No. 1, pp. 10)
Pub: Reed Business Information
Ed: J. Tol Broome Jr. **Description:** Six steps for toy companies to survive the economic turndown are outlined: Outline your business model; seek professional input; meet with your banker; cut your costs; manage your inventory; and use your trade credit.

27699 ■ "The Weeks Ahead" in *Crain's New York Business* (Vol. 24, January 14, 2008, No. 2, pp. 20)
Pub: Crain Communications, Inc.
Description: Listing of events in the Detroit area include conferences addressing entrepreneurialism, economic development, and women business ownership.

27700 ■ "Weighing the Write-Off" in *Baltimore Business Journal* (Vol. 28, September 10, 2010, No. 18, pp. 1)
Pub: Baltimore Business Journal
Ed: Daniel J. Sernovitz. **Description:** President Barrack Obama has proposed to let business write off their investments in plant and equipment upgrades under a plan aimed at getting the economy going. The plan would allow a company to write off 100 percent of the depreciation for their new investments at one time instead of over several years.

27701 ■ "What Are You Afraid Of?" in *Entrepreneur* (Vol. 37, July 2009, No. 7, pp. 79)
Pub: Entrepreneur Media, Inc.
Ed: Lindsay Holloway. **Description:** According to a survey of entrepreneurs in the US, failure, economic uncertainty, not having enough personal time, being their own boss, and staying afloat are the biggest fears when starting a business. Advice on how to deal with these fears is also given.

27702 ■ "What Are Your Party's Legislative Priorities for 2008?" in *Hawaii Business* (Vol. 53, January 2008, No. 7, pp. 22)
Pub: Hawaii Business Publishing
Description: Discusses the Democratic Party of Hawaii which will prioritize giving more opportunities to earn a living a wage in 2008, according to the party chairwoman Jeani Withington. The Republican Party chairman Willes K. Lee, meanwhile, states that his party will seek to enhance the local business climate. The political parties' plans for Hawaii for the year 2008 are presented in detail.

27703 ■ "What to Do in an Economic Upswing Before It's too Late" in *Agency Sales Magazine* (Vol. 39, November 2009, No. 10, pp. 36)
Pub: MANA
Ed: John Graham. **Description:** Some marketing suggestions for businesses as the economy recovers are presented. These include not waiting for the economy to change and telling your brand's story. Showing people what you can do for them and changing doubters into believers is also advised.

27704 ■ "What Ever Happened to TGIF?" in *Barron's* (Vol. 88, March 10, 2008, No. 10, pp. M3)
Pub: Dow Jones & Company, Inc.
Ed: Kopin Tan. **Description:** US stock markets fell in early March 2008 to their lowest level in 18 months, venturing close to entering a bear market phase. The S&P 500 has dropped an average of 0.78 percent on Fridays for 2008.

27705 ■ "What Has Sergey Wrought?" in *Barron's* (Vol. 89, July 13, 2009, No. 28, pp. 8)
Pub: Dow Jones & Co., Inc.
Ed: Alan Abelson. **Description:** Sergey Aleynikov is a computer expert that once worked for Goldman Sachs but he was arrested after he left the company and charged with theft for bringing with him the code for the company's proprietary software for high-frequency trading. The stock market has been down for four straight weeks as of July 13, 2009 which reflects the reality of how the economy is still struggling.

27706 ■ "What Recovery?" in *Canadian Business* (Vol. 82, April 27, 2009, No. 7, pp. 18)
Pub: Rogers Media
Ed: Rachel Pulfer. **Description:** U.S. markets have rallied on the end of March 2009 but experts and analysts believe that it could be short-lived. Market rallies were found to be common during recessions and are not indicative of economic recovery. Meanwhile, it is believed that employment will be a key factor that will determine the U.S. economic recovery.

27707 ■ "What's Holding Down Small Business?" in *Business Owner* (Vol. 35, November-December 2011, No. 6, pp. 3)
Pub: DL Perkins Company
Description: According to a recent survey conducted by the National Federation of Independent Business, demand is the number one reason for slow growth to any small business in today's economy.

27708 ■ "What's More Important: Stag or Inflation?" in *Barron's* (Vol. 88, July 14, 2008, No. 28, pp. M8)
Pub: Dow Jones & Co., Inc.
Ed: Randall W. Forsyth. **Description:** Economists are divided on which part of stagflation, an economic situation in which inflation and economic stagnation occur simultaneously and remain unchecked for a period of time, is more important. Some economists say that the Federal government is focusing on controlling inflation while others see the central bank as extending its liquidity facilities to the financial sector.

27709 ■ "When Profit Is Not the Incentive" in *Business North Carolina* (Vol. 28, February 2008, No. 2, pp. 42)
Pub: Business North Carolina
Ed: Amanda Parry. **Description:** Novant Health is North Carolina's fifth-largest private-sector employer and one of the largest nonprofit companies. Nonprofits grew 35 percent in North Carolina from 1995 to 2003.

27710 ■ "Where Are the Vultures?" in *Mergers & Acquisitions: The Dealmaker's Journal* (March 1, 2008)
Pub: SourceMedia, Inc.
Ed: Ken MacFadyen. **Description:** Although the real estate market is distressed, not many acquisitions are being made by distress private equity investors; this is due, in part, to the difficulty in assessing real estate industry firms since it is a sector which is so localized.

27711 ■ "Where Canada Meets the World" in *Canadian Business* (Vol. 80, October 8, 2007, No. 20, pp. 86)
Pub: Rogers Media
Ed: Zena Olijnyk. **Description:** An overview of facilities within Canada's borders that contributes to the country's economy is presented. The facilities include fishing vessels and seaports. Agencies that regulate the borders such as the Canada Border Services Agency and the Department of Fisheries and Oceans are also presented.

27712 ■ "Where Next?" in *Business Strategy Review* (Vol. 21, Summer 2010, No. 2, pp. 20)
Pub: Wiley-Blackwell
Description: The emergence of large, vibrant and seemingly unstoppable new markets has been the good news story of the past decade. Brazil, Russia, India and China (BRIC) are among those who have emerged blinking into the new economy.

27713 ■ "Where Oil-Rich Nations Are Placing Their Bets" in *Harvard Business Review* (Vol. 86, September 2008, No. 9, pp. 119)
Pub: Harvard Business School Press
Ed: Rawi Abdelal; Ayesha Khan; Tarun Khanna. **Description:** Investment strategies of the Gulf Cooperation Council nations are examined in addition to how these have impacted the global economy and capitalism.

27714 ■ "Where's the Lava" in *Hawaii Business* (Vol. 53, November 2007, No. 5, pp. 18)
Pub: Hawaii Business Publishing
Ed: Jason Ubay. **Description:** Hawaii Volcanoes National Park used to allow visitors to drive to the end of the paved coastal park road and view flowing lava that came from Kilauea until it reached the sea. On Father's Day morning in June 2007, Kilauea began erupting outside the park and the lava flows inland to Kahaualea and Wao Kele O Puna natural area reserves. In July 2007 321,217 visitors came to the park, a 14 percent increase compared to the same month in 2006.

27715 ■ "Whiplashed? That's a Bullish Sign" in *Barron's* (Vol. 88, March 31, 2008, No. 13, pp. 34)
Pub: Dow Jones & Company, Inc.
Ed: Richard W. Arms. **Description:** Huge volatility often occurs just ahead of a substantial rally, according to an analysis of the volatility in the Dow Jones Index since 2000. The Average Percentage Change based on a 10-day moving average of volatility is a way to measure the level of fear in the market and reveals when buying or selling have been overdone.

27716 ■ *Who's Your City? How the Creative Economy is Making Where to Live the Most Important Decision of Your Life*
Pub: Basic Books
Ed: Richard Florida. **Released:** 2009. **Price:** $26.95. **Description:** Richard Florida disagrees with the notion that under globalization, a leveling has taken away the economic advantages of any place in particular. Florida believes that globalization has also created higher-level economic activities such as innovation, design, finance, and media to cluster in a smaller number of locations.

27717 ■ "Why Change?" in *Canadian Business* (Vol. 80, October 8, 2007, No. 20, pp. 9)
Pub: Rogers Media
Ed: Joe Chidley. **Description:** The need for economic change in Canada is discussed. Despite the country's economic growth and low unemployment rate, economic reform is needed in order to maximize its economic potential in the future. Other reasons for the need to further develop its economy, such as the rise of manufacturing and service industries in Asia and the emergence of regional trade pacts in South America are also tackled.

27718 ■ "Why the Rally Should Keep Rolling...for Now" in *Barron's* (Vol. 89, July 27, 2009, No. 30, pp. M3)
Pub: Dow Jones & Co., Inc.
Ed: Kopin Tan. **Description:** Stocks rallied for the second straight week as of July 24, 2009 and more companies reported better than expected earnings but the caveat is that companies are beating estimates chiefly by slashing expenses and firing workers. The regulatory risks faced by CME Group and the IntercontinentalExchange are discussed as well as the shares of KKR Private Equity Investors LP.

27719 ■ "Wikinomics: The Sequel" in *Business Strategy Review* (Vol. 21, Summer 2010, No. 2, pp. 64)
Pub: Wiley-Blackwell
Description: Ever-optimistic Don Tapscott and Anthony Williams, coauthors of Wikinomics and individually, of a number of other books that study the Internet and its relation to society, are now working on a new book, one for which they're using the Internet to determine its title.

27720 ■ "Wild-Goose Chaser" in *Entrepreneur* (Vol. 37, September 2009, No. 9, pp. 96)
Pub: Entrepreneur Media, Inc.
Ed: Jason Daley. **Description:** Geese Police owner David Marcks says he discovered that trained collies could chase geese off golf courses, which started his business. He gives new franchises two dogs to start their business. The company has fared well even during the economic crisis.

27721 ■ "Will Small Business be Stimulated" in *Entrepreneur* (Vol. 37, July 2009, No. 7, pp. 18)
Pub: Entrepreneur Media, Inc.
Ed: Jennifer Wang. **Description:** Steven Strauss, Alberto G. Alvarado, Jeff Rosenweig, Al Gordon, and Theresa Alfaro Daytner share their views on how the American Recovery and Reinvestment Act of 2009, also known as the economic stimulus, will affect small businesses. Their backgrounds are also provided.

27722 ■ "Wing and a Prayer" in *Canadian Business* (Vol. 81, November 10, 2008, No. 19, pp. 70)
Pub: Rogers Media Ltd.
Ed: Sean Silcoff. **Description:** The 61st Annual National Business Aviation Association convention in Orlando, Florida saw unabashed display of wealth and privilege, but the U.S. market meltdown and possible economic crash has raised questions on the industry's future. Statistical details included.

27723 ■ "Winners and Losers" in *Crain's Detroit Business* (Vol. 25, June 22, 2009, No. 25, pp. 18)
Pub: Crain Communications Inc. - Detroit
Description: Rankings for Detroit's 50 top-compensated CEOs has changed due to the economic recession. The biggest changes are discussed.

27724 ■ *The Wisdom of Crowds: Why the Many Are Smarter Than the Few and How Collective Wisdom Shapes Business, Economies, Societies and Nations*
Pub: Doubleday Canada, Limited
Ed: James Surrowiecki. **Released:** May 2004. **Description:** The premise that the many are smarter than the few and its impact on business, economics, societies and nations is discussed.

27725 ■ "With the Indian Market, You Take the Good With the Bad" in *Globe & Mail* (March 23, 2007, pp. B11)
Pub: CTVglobemedia Publishing Inc.
Ed: David Parkinson. **Description:** The performance of Bombay Stock Exchange in the month of February 2007 is analyzed. The impact of growing economy on the stock market performance is also analyzed.

27726 ■ "With New Listings, Business Brokers See Hope" in *Business Courier* (Vol. 27, September 3, 2010, No. 18, pp. 1)
Pub: Business Courier
Ed: Lucy May. **Description:** Business brokers in Cincinnati, Ohio are expecting better prices in view of the strengthening economy.

27727 ■ "WNY Casing In On Loonie's Climb" in *Business First Buffalo* (November 23, 2007, pp. 1)
Pub: American City Business Journals, Inc.
Ed: Scott Thomas. **Description:** Economy of Western New York has rebounded since the 9/11 recession and the rise of the Canadian dollar, which has contributed to the areas economic growth. Canadian shoppers are frequenting markets in the area due to the parity of the U.S. and Canadian dollar. Details of the cross-border shopping and its impact in WNY are discussed.

27728 ■ "Wobbling Economy" in *The Business Journal-Serving Metropolitan Kansas City* (Vol. 27, September 26, 2008, No. 2, pp. 1)
Pub: American City Business Journals, Inc.
Ed: Rob Roberts. **Description:** Real estate developers in Kansas City Metropolitan Area are worried of the possible impacts of the crisis at Wall Street. They expect tightening of the credit market, which will result in difficulty of financing their projects. The potential effects of the Wall Street crisis are examined further.

27729 ■ "Woes Portend Consumer Shift" in *The Business Journal-Serving Metropolitan Kansas City* (Vol. 27, September 26, 2008, No. 2, pp. 1)
Pub: American City Business Journals, Inc.
Ed: Suzanna Stagemeyer. **Description:** Black Bamboo owner Tim Butt believes that prolonged tightening of the credit market will result in consumer spending becoming more cash-driven that credit card driven. The financial crisis has already constricted spending among consumers. Forecasts for the US economy are provided.

27730 ■ "Work To Do" in *Canadian Business* (Vol. 81, July 22, 2008, No. 12-13, pp. 22)
Pub: Rogers Media Ltd.
Ed: Jane Bao. **Description:** Recruiting firm Manpower revealed that 36 percent of Canadian employers had trouble filling positions in 2007, highlighting the labor shortage and the need to bring in more workers. Underemployment of immigrants costs up to $6 billion to Canada's economy every year. Other views regarding Canada's labor shortage and on its economic impact are presented.

27731 ■ "The World Is Your Hospital" in *Canadian Business* (Vol. 81, July 22, 2008, No. 12-13, pp. 62)
Pub: Rogers Media Ltd.
Ed: Sharda Prashad. **Description:** Medical tourism is seen as a booming industry around the world and is expected to grow to around $40 billion in 2010. Key information regarding medical tourism and services are presented. Views on the possible impact of medical tourism on Canada's health care industry, as well as medical tourism opportunities in Canada, are also given.

27732 ■ "A World of Opportunity: Foreign Markets Offer Diversity to Keen Investors" in *Canadian Business* (Vol. 81, Summer 2008, No. 9)
Pub: Rogers Media Ltd.
Ed: Andrew Wahl. **Description:** International Monetary Fund projected in its 'World Economy Outlook' that there is a 25 percent chance that a global recession will occur in 2008 and 2009. Global growth rate is forecasted at 3.7 percent in 2008. Inflation in Asia emerging markets and forecasts on stock price indexes are presented.

27733 ■ "The World Tomorrow" in *Canadian Business* (Vol. 81, December 24, 2007, No. 1, pp. 35)
Pub: Rogers Media
Ed: Zena Olijnyk. **Description:** Global economy is predicted to be in a difficult period as analysts expect a slowdown in economic growth. Germany's Deutsche Bank wrote in a report about 'growth recession' that the chances of the world growth falling below two percent being one in three. Forecasts on other global economic aspects are explored.

27734 ■ "Worry No. 1 at Auto Show" in *Crain's Detroit Business* (Vol. 24, January 21, 2008, No. 3, pp. 1)
Pub: Crain Communications Inc. - Detroit
Ed: Brent Snavely. **Description:** Recession fears clouded activity at the 2008 Annual North American International Auto Show. Automakers are expecting to see a drop in sales due to slow holiday retail spending as well as fallout from the subprime lending crisis.

27735 ■ *The Worst-Case Scenario Business Survival Guide*
Pub: John Wiley & Sons, Inc.
Released: September 28, 2009. **Price:** $17.95. **Description:** Since 1999, the Worst-Case Scenario survival handbooks have provided readers with real answers for the most extreme situations. Now, in a time of economic crisis, the series returns with a new, real-world guide to avoiding the worst business cataclysms.

27736 ■ "The Worst Lies Ahead for Wall Street; More Losses Certain" in *Crain's New York Business* (Vol. 24, January 21, 2008, No. 3, pp. 1)
Pub: Crain Communications, Inc.
Ed: Aaron Elstein. **Description:** Due to the weakening economy, many financial institutions will face further massive losses forcing them to borrow more at higher interest rates and dragging down their earnings for years to come. The effects on commercial real estate and credit card loans are also discussed as well as the trend to investing in Asia and the Middle East.

27737 ■ "Yamasaki Lays Off Last of U.S. Workers, to Vacate World Headquarters in Troy" in *Crain's Detroit Business* (Jan. 11, 2010)
Pub: Crain Communications, Inc.
Ed: Chad Halcom. **Description:** Overview of the impact on the local economy resulting from the closing of Yamasaki Associates, Inc.'s world headquarters located in Troy. The architectural firm notified the last of its employees that they would, indeed be laid off effective December 31.

27738 ■ "Year-End Tax Tips" in *Hawaii Business* (Vol. 53, December 2007, No. 6, pp. 136)
Pub: Hawaii Business Publishing
Ed: Kathleen Bryan. **Description:** Tax planning tips for the end of 2007, in relation to the tax breaks that are scheduled to expire, are presented. Among the tax breaks that will be expiring at the 2007 year-end are sales tax deduction in the state and local level, premiums on mortgage insurance, and deduction on tuition. The impacts of these changes are discussed.

27739 ■ "You Can Rebuild It" in *Entrepreneur* (Vol. 37, July 2009, No. 7, pp. 28)
Pub: Entrepreneur Media, Inc.
Ed: Robert Kiyosaki. **Description:** Entrepreneurs, during tough times, should melt down old business strategies and start rebuilding the business. The business and its customers should be redefined in order to maximize marketing efforts and stay afloat when business slows down. Personal experiences in melting down a business and starting over are also given.

27740 ■ "Young Adult, Childless May Help Fuel Post-Recession Rebound" in *Pet Product News* (Vol. 64, November 2010, No. 11, pp. 4)
Pub: BowTie Inc.
Description: Pet industry retailers and marketers are encouraged to tap into the young adult and childless couple sectors to boost consumer traffic and sales to pre-recession levels. Among young adult owners, pet ownership increased from 40 percent in 2003 to 49 percent in 2009. Meanwhile, the childless couple sector represented 63 percent of all dog/cat owners in 2009.

27741 ■ "Your Bottom Line: How To Bring In Dollars When Times Are Tough" in *Small Business Opportunities* (November 2007)
Pub: Harris Publications Inc.
Ed: Description: Adding a new product or promoting a product in a new way can help any small business during hard economic times.

27742 ■ "Your Exposure to Bear Stearns" in *Barron's* (Vol. 88, March 17, 2008, No. 11, pp. 45)
Pub: Dow Jones & Company, Inc.
Ed: Tom Sullivan; Jack Willoughby. **Description:** Bear Stearns makes up 5.5 percent of Pioneer Independence's portfolio, 1.4 percent of Vanguard Windsor II's portfolio, 1.2 percent of Legg Mason Value Trust, about 1 percent of Van Kampen Equity & Income, and 0.79 percent of Putnam Fund for Growth & Income. Ginnie Mae securities are now trading at 1.78 percentage points over treasuries due to the mortgage crises.

27743 ■ "Your Guide to Local Style Business" in *Hawaii Business* (Vol. 53, December 2007, No. 6, pp. 36)
Pub: Hawaii Business Publishing
Ed: David K. Choo. **Description:** Discusses the importance of studying the Hawaiian culture when doing business locally. It was observed that geographical aspects increase emphasis on culture and lifestyle more than the need to rectify false imaging do. Details of how locals adhere to their culture are supplied.

TRADE PERIODICALS

27744 ■ *ACCRA Research in Review*
Pub: American Chamber of Commerce Researchers Association
Contact: Sean Mcnamara
Ed: Dr. Kenneth E. Poole, Editor. **Released:** Quarterly. **Price:** Included in membership. **Description:** Carries information on research methodology specific to the study of community economic development.

27745 ■ *American Institute for Economic Research—Research Reports*
Pub: American Institute for Economic Research
Ed: Larry Pratt, Editor. **Released:** Semimonthly. **Price:** $59. **Description:** Presents the results of the institute's research, including analyses of significant economic developments and their implications, especially the statistical indications of business-cycle changes.

27746 ■ *Business Facilities*
Pub: Group C Communications Inc.
Contact: Judy Nowell, Advertising Production Coord.
E-mail: jnowell@groupc.com
Released: Monthly. **Description:** Professional magazine focusing on corporate expansion, commercial/industrial real estate, and economic development.

27747 ■ *Economic Development*
Pub: Wakeman/Walworth Inc.
Ed: Keyes Walworth, Editor. **Released:** Weekly, 48/year. **Price:** $245, U.S. and Canada; $265, elsewhere; $435, two years U.S. and Canada; $480, two years elsewhere. **Description:** Covers state efforts to attract new industry, jobs, commerce, and tourism, including such factors as environmental requirements, mass transportation policies, highway construction plans, utility rates, changes in labor laws, tax policies, and enterprise zones. Provides information on urban development programs as affected by growth control legislation, state construction programs, and building codes.

27748 ■ *Economic Development Research Focus*
Pub: Economic Development Institute
Contact: Robert Lann
E-mail: robert.lann@edi.gatech.edu
Ed: Lincoln S. Bates, Editor, lincoln.bates@edi.gatech.edu. **Released:** 3/year. **Price:** Free. **Description:** Reports on the progress and results of studies and activities undertaken by the Center for Economic Development Services. Covers relevant topics, legislation and resources; and presents success stories. Recurring features include notices of publications available, and departments titled Georgia Text, and What Works.

27749 ■ *Entrepreneurship and Regional Development*
Pub: Taylor & Francis Group Journals
Contact: Gerald Sweeney, Founding Ed.
Released: 8/yr. **Price:** $357; $748 institutions online only; $788 institutions print and online. **Description:** Journal containing information on economic development - entrepreneurial vitality and innovation - as local and regional phenomena.

27750 ■ *Future Economic Trends*
Pub: Conservative Publishing Corp.
Ed: C.J. Jones, Editor. **Released:** Monthly. **Price:** $149 per year; $79 new subscriber. **Description:** Covers economic and political science in an historical perspective. Provides financial survival advice and the destruction of the U.S. economy and the dollar. Recurring features include Feature Article, History Tells Us, Hard Money, and As We Go to Press.

27751 ■ *International Trade Reporter*
Pub: Bureau of National Affairs Inc.
Contact: Linda G. Botsford, Managing Editor
Released: Weekly. **Price:** $1,159. **Description:** Covers current international trade policies of the U.S. and of major U.S. trading partners. Topics include bilateral negotiations, customs, export/import policy, foreign investment, standards, taxation, and other related issues. Recurring features include a calendar of events, reports of meetings, and notices of publications available.

27752 ■ *Journal of Economics and Management Strategy*
Pub: John Wiley & Sons Inc.
Contact: Jamea J. Anton, Co-Ed.
Ed: Daniel F. Spulber, Editor, editjems@kellogg.northwestern.edu. **Released:** Quarterly. **Price:** $58 print & online; $85 print & online; $57 other countries print & online; $55 online; $81 online; $53 other countries online; $395 institutions print & online; $395 institutions print & online; $311 institutions, other countries print & online. **Description:** Journal providing a forum for research and discussion on competitive strategies of managers and the organizational structure of firms.

27753 ■ *Quarterly Journal of Business & Economics*
Pub: University of Nebraska
Contact: Margo Young, Managing Editor
E-mail: myoung1@unl.edu
Ed: Gordon V. Karels, Editor. **Released:** Quarterly. **Price:** $24; $45 institutions; $37 out of country; $55 institutions, other countries. **Description:** Journal reporting on finance and economics.

27754 ■ *Utah Department of Workforce Services Workforce Information*
Pub: Utah Department of Workforce Services
Ed: Kenneth Jensen, Editor. **Released:** Monthly. **Price:** Free. **Description:** Offers economic data and analysis for the state of Utah.

VIDEOCASSETTES/ AUDIOCASSETTES

27755 ■ *Small Business in a Big World*
Instructional Video
2219 C St.
Lincoln, NE 68502
Ph:(402)475-6570
Free: 800-228-0164
Fax:(402)475-6500
Co. E-mail: feedback@insvideo.com
URL: http://www.insvideo.com
Price: $99.00. **Description:** Demonstrates how small business has contributed to the overall economy. Includes profiles of small retail, service, manufacturing, professional, high tech, wholesale, and warehousing operations at work. **Availability:** VHS.

TRADE SHOWS AND CONVENTIONS

27756 ■ National Association Business Economics Annual Meeting
National Association for Business Economics
1233 20th St. NW, No. 505
Washington, DC 20036
Ph:(202)463-6223
Co. E-mail: nabe@nabe.com
URL: http://www.nabe.com/
Released: Annual. **Principal Exhibits:** Business economics products and services.

CONSULTANTS

27757 ■ Consulting, Appraisals & Studies Ltd.
111 W Jackson Blvd.
Chicago, IL 60604
Ph:(312)939-7775
Contact: Alfred K. Eckersberg, President
Scope: Real estate and planning consultants offering economic market analyses, feasibility studies, appraisals, development and investment evaluations, fiscal impact reviews and counseling for private and public sector clients. Projects have involved housing, retail shopping and services, industrial, office, hotels and motels, recreational, institutional and public facilities. Other services include demographic surveys and social and economic impacts, with specialized expertise in rehab and redevelopment, historical preservation and urban planning and zoning. Industries served: Business, financial, real estate, developers and government agencies in the U.S. and Canada.

27758 ■ HyettPalma Inc.
1600 Prince St., Ste. 110
Alexandria, VA 22314
Ph:(703)683-5126
Fax:(703)836-5887
Co. E-mail: info@hyettpalma.com
URL: http://www.hyettpalma.com
Contact: Dolores P. Palma, President
Scope: Specializes in economic development in downtown and commercial districts. The firm services feature comprehensive economic enhancement strategies, market analysis, business retention, creation and attraction strategies, business clustering strategies and business district audits. **Publications:** "Creating the Future Downtown," 2002; "Lure Businesses to Your Downtown—By Making Life Easier for Them," NYCOM, Apr, 2001; "Recruiting Developers: Using Rfps To Package Projects"; "Focus Groups For Downtown"; "Business Clustering: How To Leverage Sales"; "The Arts "Hook" Downtown," 2001; "The Arts Help Revitalize Downtowns," 2001; "Making Downtown Renaissance a Reality," 2000; "Assistance Program Helps Revitalize Conroe, Texas," 2000. **Seminars:** Trends in the Revitalization of Pennsylvania's Downtowns Through the Blueprints for Pennsylvania's Downtowns Program, York, 2005; America Downtown-New Thinking, New Life, Dec, 2005; Americas Downtown Renaissance: Retail Revitalization and More, NYS Tug Hill Commission, 2003; Indiana Downtown; Creating the Future Downtown; How to Revitalize Your Downtown; Trends in the Revitalization of America's Downtowns, Pennsylvania League of Cities and Municipalities, 2003; Indiana Downtown, Indiana Association of Cities and Towns, 2003; Creating the Future Downtown, Indiana Association of Cities and Towns, 2003; How to Revitalize Your Downtown, 2002. **Special Services:** America Downtown[R]; Indiana Downtown[R].

27759 ■ New Commons
545 Pawtucket Ave., Studio 106A
PO Box 116
Pawtucket, RI 02860
Ph:(401)351-7110
Fax:(401)351-7158
Co. E-mail: info@newcommons.com
URL: http://www.newcommons.com
Contact: Robert Leaver, Principal
E-mail: rleaver@atsnewcommons.com
Scope: Builder of agile human networks to champion innovation and mobilize change; to pursue business opportunities; to custom design agile organizations and communities, to foster civic engagement. Clients include organizations on-profits, corporations, government agencies, educational institutions; networks-Trade/professional groups, IT services collaborations, service-sharing collectives; and communities- municipalities, states and statewide agencies, regional collaborations. **Publications:** "Plexus Imperative," Sep, 2005; "Creating 21st Century Capable Innovation Systems," Aug, 2004; "Call to Action: Building Providences Creative and Innovative Economy"; "Getting Results from Meetings"; "The Entrepreneur as Artist," Commonwealth Publications; "Leader and Agent of Change," Commonwealth Publications; "Achieving our Providence: Lessons of City-Building," Commonwealth Publications. **Seminars:** Introduction to Social Computing (Web 2.0), Jan, 2009; Every Company Counts, Jun, 2009; Facilitating for Results; Story-Making and Story-Telling.

COMPUTERIZED DATABASES

27760 ■ *ABI/INFORM*
ProQuest LLC
789 E Eisenhower Pky.
PO Box 1346
Ann Arbor, MI 48106-1346
Ph:(734)761-4700
Free: 800-521-0600
Fax:(734)761-6450
Co. E-mail: info@proquest.com
URL: http://www.proquest.com
Description: Contains approximately 6 million full text or bibliographic citations to articles from more than 800 business and management publications worldwide. **Availability:** Online: Wolters Kluwer Health, ProQuest LLC, ProQuest LLC, Questel SA, STN International, Colorado Alliance of Research Libraries, Financial Times Ltd., LexisNexis Group, ProQuest LLC. **Type:** Full text; Bibliographic; Image.

27761 ■ *Claritas Update Demographics*
The Nielsen Co.
770 Broadway
New York, NY 10003-9595
URL: http://www.claritas.com/sitereports/default.jsp
Description: Contains 2000 data, current-year estimates, and five-year projections of key demographics, including data on households, populations, families, income, age, and race. **Availability:** Online: The Nielsen Co; CD-ROM: The Nielsen Co; Diskette: The Nielsen Co;Magnetic Tape: The Nielsen Co. **Type:** Statistical.

27762 ■ *County and City Data Book*
U.S. Census Bureau
4600 Silver Hill Rd.
Washington, DC 20233-0001
Ph:(301)457-4100
Free: 800-923-8282
Fax:(301)457-4714
Co. E-mail: webmaster@census.gov
URL: http://www.census.gov
Description: Contains demographic, economic, and geographic data on U.S. counties and cities. Includes 220 data items for states and counties, 200 data items for cities, and 33 data items for places of 2500 or more. Covers 3141 counties, 1100 incorporated cities of 5000 or more persons, and 11,000 places of 2500 or more persons. Includes detailed information on cities with 25,000 or more inhabitants. Coverage includes land area, population, households, vital statistics, labor force, education, crime, and, for cities, form of government, Moody's bond rating, climate, and residential energy consumption. Address such topics as age, money and personal income, population, housing ownership and value, births and deaths, business, banking, climate, employment, and more. Data are collected from federal agencies and private organizations. Public domain software enables the user to search by states, counties, cities of more than 25,000, and places of more than 2500. Downloadable as PDF file. Corresponds to *County and City Data Book* print edition. **Availability:** Online: U.S. Census Bureau; CD-ROM: U.S. Census Bureau. **Type:** Statistical.

LIBRARIES

27763 ■ Canada–Newfoundland and Labrador Business Service Centre
West Block, Confederation Bldg.
PO Box 8700
St. John's, NL, Canada A1B 4J6
Ph:(709)729-7000
Fax:(709)729-0654
Co. E-mail: mike.howley@acoa-apeca.gc.ca
URL: http://www.intrd.gov.nl.ca/intrd/department/branches/sibd/cnlbsc.html
Contact: Mike Howley, Mgr.
Scope: Marketing, small business, economic and regional development. **Services:** Copying; SDI; centre open to the public. **Holdings:** 10,000 books; 20 VF drawers of subject files; Standard Industrial Classification (SIC) files. **Subscriptions:** 300 journals and other serials.

27764 ■ LECG, LLC Library
2000 Powell St., Ste. 600
Emeryville, CA 94608
Ph:(510)985-6700
Fax:(510)653-9898
Co. E-mail: nadams@lecg.com
URL: http://www.lecg.com
Contact: Nancy Adams, Libn.
Scope: Economics, business, antitrust. **Services:** Library open to the public by appointment only. **Holdings:** 2500 books. **Subscriptions:** 50 journals and other serials; 4 newspapers.

27765 ■ Ontario Ministry of Economic Development and Trade–InfoSource
900 Bay St.
Hearst Block, 6th Fl.
Toronto, ON, Canada M7A 2E1
Ph:(416)325-6666
Fax:(416)325-6688
Co. E-mail: info@edt.gov.on.ca
URL: http://www.ontariocanada.com/ontcan/1medt/en/home_en.jsp
Contact: Janice Somers, Info.Spec.
Scope: Trade, industry, small business, management, company information, economic development. **Services:** Copying; scanning. **Holdings:** 200 books; microfiche; 20 CD-ROMs.

27766 ■ U.S.D.A.–National Agricultural Library–Rural Information Center (10301)
10301 Baltimore Ave., Rm. 132
Beltsville, MD 20705
Ph:(301)504-5547
Free: 800-633-7701
Fax:(301)504-5181
Co. E-mail: ric@nal.usda.gov
URL: http://ric.nal.usda.gov
Contact: William Thomas, Coord.
Scope: Economic development; small business development; city and county government services; government and private grants and funding sources; rural communities; community leadership; natural resources. **Services:** Center open to the public. **Holdings:** Figures not available.

27767 ■ University of Kentucky–Business & Economics Information Center
B&E Info. Ctr., Rm. 116
335-BA Gatton College of Business & Economics
Lexington, KY 40506-0034
Ph:(859)257-5868
Fax:(859)323-9496
Co. E-mail: mrazeeq@pop.uk.edu
URL: http://www.uky.edu//Provost/academicprograms.html
Contact: Michael A. Razeeq, Bus.Ref.Libn.
Scope: Business, economics, business management, marketing, finance, accounting. **Services:** Library open to the public for reference use only.

27768 ■ West Virginia University–College of Business and Economics–Bureau of Business and Economic Research (P.O.)
P.O. Box 6527
Morgantown, WV 26506-6025
Ph:(304)293-7831
Fax:(304)293-5652
Co. E-mail: bebureau@mail.wvu.edu
URL: http://be.wvu.edu/bber
Contact: Tom S. Witt, Dir.
Scope: Economics, West Virginia economy. **Services:** Library not open to the public. **Holdings:** 300 books; 600 other cataloged items. **Subscriptions:** 12 journals and other serials; 4 newspapers.

RESEARCH CENTERS

27769 ■ Arizona State University–JPMorgan Chase Economic Outlook Center
W.P. Carey School of Business
PO Box 874011
Tempe, AZ 85287-4011
Ph:(480)965-5543
Free: 800—448-0432
Fax:(480)965-5458
Co. E-mail: wpcareyeoc@asu.edu
URL: http://wpcarey.asu.edu/seid/EOC
Contact: Lee McPheters, Dir.
E-mail: wpcareyeoc@asu.edu
Scope: Economic and business climate forecasts for Arizona and the western United States, including California, Utah, Nevada, Oregon, New Mexico, Colorado, Idaho, Washington, and Texas. **Services:** Forecasting newsletters and economic analysis. **Publications:** Mexico Consensus Economic Forecast (quarterly); Western Blue Chip Economic Forecast (10/year).

27770 ■ Atlantic Institute for Market Studies
Cogswell Tower, Ste. 1302
2000 Barrington St.
Halifax, NS, Canada B3J 3K1
Ph:(902)429-1143
Fax:(902)425-1393
Co. E-mail: aims@aims.ca
URL: http://www.aims.ca/
Contact: Charles Cirtwill, Pres./CEO
E-mail: aims@aims.ca
Scope: Current and emerging economic and public policy issues facing Atlantic Canadians and Canadians more generally, including the economic and social characteristics and potentials of Atlantic Canada and its four constituent provinces. **Publications:** AIMS On-Line Newsletter; Books; Papers. **Educational Activities:** Conferences, meetings, seminars; Lectures; Training programs.

27771 ■ Atlantic Provinces Economic Council–Conseil Économique Des Provinces De L'Atlantique
5121 Sackville St., Ste. 500
Halifax, NS, Canada B3J 1K1
Ph:(902)422-6516
Fax:(902)429-6803
Co. E-mail: elizabeth.beale@apec-econ.ca
URL: http://www.apec-econ.ca
Contact: Elizabeth Beale, Pres./CEO
E-mail: elizabeth.beale@apec-econ.ca
Scope: Economic development of the Atlantic Region of Canada by monitoring and analyzing current and emerging economic trends and policies. **Services:** Consulting. **Educational Activities:** Business Outlook Conference (annually), held each fall; Forums and dinners.

27772 ■ Ball State University–Bureau of Business Research
Whitinger Business Bldg., Rm. 149
2000 W University Ave.
Muncie, IN 47306
Ph:(765)285-5926
Fax:(765)285-8024
Co. E-mail: mhicks@bsu.edu
URL: http://cms.bsu.edu/Academics/CentersandInstitutes/BBR.aspx
Contact: Michael J. Hicks PhD, Dir.
E-mail: mhicks@bsu.edu
Scope: Business and economics, including special studies designed to contribute to policy research, economic development and growth of eastern/central Indiana. Compiles and disseminates current economic and business data. **Services:** Publication Services, develop, design, produce hard copy and electronic publications for college and community clients. **Publications:** American Journal of Business (semiannually); Indiana Business Bulletin (weekly). **Educational Activities:** Policy Papers for statewide business and law makers (monthly), published economic impact and analysis of current issues; Research Support, editing, data analysis, computer statistical services to faculty; Staff monograph and paper seminars (monthly), faculty.

27773 ■ Baylor University–Center for Business and Economic Research
Economics Department
Hankamer School of Business
PO Box 98003
Waco, TX 76798
Ph:(254)710-4146
Fax:(254)710-6142
Co. E-mail: tom_kelly@baylor.edu
URL: http://www.baylor.edu/business/economic_research
Contact: Dr. Thomas M. Kelly, Dir.
E-mail: tom_kelly@baylor.edu
Scope: Local business and economic conditions. Conducts community economic base studies and supplies social and economic data to local agencies. Compiles and releases monthly indexes of business activity, indexes of consumer prices, and estimates of retail sales to newspapers. Tabulates and analyzes census and other data as requested by local agencies.

27774 ■ Center for the Study of Economics
413 S 10th St.
Philadelphia, PA 19147
Ph:(215)923-7800
Fax:(215)923-7801
Co. E-mail: barbara@urbantools.org
URL: http://www.urbantoolsconsult.org
Contact: R. Joshua Vincent, CEO
E-mail: barbara@urbantools.org
Scope: Property tax reform, land value taxation, recession, and inflation. **Services:** Consulting. **Publications:** Incentive Taxation.

27775 ■ Centre for the Study of Living Standards–Centre d'étude des niveaux de vie
111 Sparks St., Ste. 500
Ottawa, ON, Canada K1P 5B5
Ph:(613)233-8891
Fax:(613)233-8250
Co. E-mail: info@csls.ca
URL: http://www.csls.ca
Contact: Andrew Sharpe PhD, Exec.Dir.
E-mail: info@csls.ca
Scope: Trends in and determinants of productivity, living standards and economic and social well being. **Services:** Database development (occasionally). **Publications:** CSLS Research Reports (10/year); International Productivity Monitor (semiannually).

27776 ■ Chapman University–A. Gary Anderson Center for Economic Research
1 University Dr.
Orange, CA 92866
Ph:(714)997-6693
Fax:(714)997-6601
Co. E-mail: adibi@chapman.edu
URL: http://www.chapman.edu/argyros/asbecenters/acer/Default.asp
Contact: Esmael Adibi PhD, Dir.
E-mail: adibi@chapman.edu
Scope: Economics and business in the U.S. and California, as well as in Orange County, Los Angeles County, and the Inland Empire in California. **Services:** Consulting. **Publications:** Economic & Business Review (semiannually); Local business surveys; Newsletter; Working papers. **Educational Activities:** Chapman University Economic Forecast Conference (annually), each December; Workshops, conferences.

27777 ■ East Tennessee State University–Bureau of Business and Economic Research
222 Sam Wilson Hall
College of Business & Technology
PO Box 70700
Johnson City, TN 37614-1710
Ph:(423)439-5677
Fax:(423)439-8381
Co. E-mail: smitjl01@etsu.edu
URL: http://www.etsu.edu/cbat/bureau
Contact: Jon L. Smith PhD, Dir.
E-mail: smitjl01@etsu.edu
Scope: Regional business conditions and the economic development of northeast Tennessee and the Tri-Cities Metropolitan Statistical Area (MSA) (Johnson City, Kingsport, and Bristol). Assists faculty and students in research efforts. **Services:** Business Development Program; Economic feasibility (impact) studies; Global research; Implementation of pay systems; Regional development information. **Publications:** East Tennessee Business Indicators; Labor Market Report; Tri-Cities Retail Sales Report (quarterly). **Educational Activities:** Business programs; Economic Development Seminars; Workforce Development Seminars.

27778 ■ Fort Lewis College–Office of Economic Analysis and Business Research
Durango, CO 81301
Ph:(970)247-7624
Fax:(970)247-7623
Co. E-mail: walker_d@fortlewis.edu
URL: http://soba.fortlewis.edu/econoweb/
Contact: Deborah Walker, Dir.
E-mail: walker_d@fortlewis.edu
Scope: Economics and local economic conditions. **Services:** Conducts contract research and serves as a clearinghouse linking college faculty and the business community. **Publications:** Four Corners Economic Quarterly (quarterly).

27779 ■ Georgia Southern University–Bureau of Business Research and Economic Development
PO Box 8153-01
Statesboro, GA 30460-8151
Ph:(912)478-0872

Fax:(912)478-5581
Co. E-mail: ehsibbald@georgiasouthern.edu
URL: http://www.bbred.org
Contact: Dr. Edward Sibbald, Interim Dir.
E-mail: ehsibbald@georgiasouthern.edu
Scope: Local economic development, economic forecasting, regional economics, and public finance. **Services:** Consulting and assistance for local businesses and communities.

27780 ■ Georgia State University–Economic Forecasting Center
PO Box 3988
Atlanta, GA 30302-3988
Ph:(404)413-7260
Fax:(404)413-7264
Co. E-mail: rdhawan@gsu.edu
URL: http://robinson.gsu.edu/efc/index.html
Contact: Prof. Rajeev Dhawan PhD, Dir.
E-mail: rdhawan@gsu.edu
Scope: National, regional, and state economic analysis and forecasting. Studies include econometric descriptions of the United States, the Southeast, Georgia, and the Atlanta metropolitan area, including short-term interest rates, long-term bond issues, foreign competition, and currency stability. The Center's objective is to provide economic commentary and analysis to the public and to the business community in particular. **Services:** Entitles sponsors to all data collected or produced by the Center and to one or two private meetings yearly with the Center director. **Publications:** Forecast of Georgia and Atlanta (quarterly); Forecast of the Nation (quarterly); Southeast States Indicators (quarterly). **Educational Activities:** Economic Forecasting Conference (quarterly); Facilities for research on forecasting and related topics; Instructs students in applied economics; Sponsors' Seminar (quarterly).

27781 ■ Hawaii Business, Economic Development, and Tourism Department–Research and Economic Analysis Division
PO Box 2359
Honolulu, HI 96804
Ph:(808)586-2355
Fax:(808)586-2377
Co. E-mail: library@dbedt.hawaii.gov
URL: http://hawaii.gov/dbedt/info/economic
Contact: Richard C. Lim, Dir.
E-mail: library@dbedt.hawaii.gov
Scope: Business, economic development, tourism. **Services:** Statistical and economic information to the public. **Publications:** Hawaii's Economy (occasionally); Quarterly Statistical and Economic Report; State of Hawaii Data Book (annually). **Educational Activities:** Census data workshops and meetings.

27782 ■ Indiana University Bloomington–Indiana Business Research Center
Kelley School of Business
100 S College Ave., Ste. 240
Bloomington, IN 47404
Ph:(812)855-5507
Fax:(812)855-7763
Co. E-mail: conover@indiana.edu
URL: http://www.ibrc.indiana.edu
Contact: Dr. Jerry N. Conover, Dir.
E-mail: conover@indiana.edu
Scope: Indiana's economic development, population trends, state and local economic indicators, and information technology. **Publications:** InContext (bimonthly); Indiana Business Review (quarterly). **Educational Activities:** Public presentations and training.

27783 ■ Interuniversity Research Centre on Quantitative Economics
C.P. 6128, succursale Centre-ville
Montreal, QC, Canada H3C 3J7
Ph:(514)343-6557
Fax:(514)343-5831
Co. E-mail: emanuela.cardia@umontreal.ca
URL: http://www.cireq.umontreal.ca
Contact: Emanuela Cardia PhD, Dir.
E-mail: emanuela.cardia@umontreal.ca
Scope: Theoretical and applied econometrics, decision theory, macroeconomics policies and financial markets as well as environmental problems. **Publications:** Annual report; Research papers. **Educational Activities:** Conferences; Seminars (periodically); Special lectures.

27784 ■ Jacksonville State University–Center for Economic Development
College of Commerce & Business Administration
Jacksonville, AL 36265-1602
Ph:(256)782-5324
Fax:(256)782-5179
Co. E-mail: pshaddix@jsu.edu
URL: http://www.jsu.edu/depart/ced/
Contact: Pat W. Shaddix, Dir.
E-mail: pshaddix@jsu.edu
Scope: Industrial needs analysis for cities and counties and business research, including retail and service studies. Special projects include economic development strategies for Alabama counties and marketing plan considerations for local governments, including Best Fit Studies. **Services:** Maintains a small business development center; State Data Center affiliate. **Publications:** JSU Economic Update; Monographs. **Educational Activities:** Supervisory training, planning.

27785 ■ North Dakota State University–Institute for Business and Industry Development
2718 Gateway Ave., Ste. 104
Bismarck, ND 58503
Ph:(701)328-9718
Fax:(701)328-9721
Co. E-mail: kathleen.tweeten@ndsu.edu
URL: http://www.ag.ndsu.nodak.edu/ibid
Contact: Kathleen Tweeten, Dir.
E-mail: kathleen.tweeten@ndsu.edu
Scope: Business and community economic development. **Services:** Engineering extension services.

27786 ■ Plattsburgh State University of New York–Technical Assistance Center
194 US Oval
Plattsburgh, NY 12903
Ph:(518)564-2214
Fax:(518)564-3220
Co. E-mail: tac@plattsburgh.edu
URL: http://www.plattsburgh.edu/offices/centers/tac/index.php
Contact: Howard Lowe, Dir.
E-mail: tac@plattsburgh.edu
Scope: Regional economic development, project development and implementation for public and private enterprises. Specialties include data/demographic research, tourism studies and seminars, telecommunications, and Geographic Information System GIS. **Publications:** A Guide to State, Regional, County, and Local Business Financing Programs for Northern New York (annually); NY County demographic profiles (7/year). **Awards:** Needs assessments, economic impact analyses, competitive intelligence; Telecommunications network planning and development; Tourism marketing conversion analyses.

27787 ■ Princeton University–Research Program in Development Studies
367 Wallace Hall
Woodrow Wilson School of Public & International Affairs
Princeton, NJ 08544
Ph:(609)258-2177
Fax:(609)258-5974
Co. E-mail: accase@princeton.edu
URL: http://www.princeton.edu/rpds
Contact: Prof. Anne C. Case, Dir.
E-mail: accase@princeton.edu
Scope: Economic development, particularly in health and microeconomics. **Publications:** Working Paper Series. **Educational Activities:** Research seminars in economic development for staff and graduate students of the School (biweekly).

27788 ■ Simon Fraser University–Centre for Sustainable Community Development
TASC2 8900
Faculty of Environment
8888 University Dr.
Burnaby, BC, Canada V5A 1S6
Ph:(778)782-5849
Fax:(778)782-8788
Co. E-mail: roseland@sfu.ca
URL: http://www.sfu.ca/cscd
Contact: Prof. Mark Roseland PhD, Dir.
E-mail: roseland@sfu.ca
Scope: Community economic development through access to knowledge, programs, markets, and funds. **Services:** ced-net, a worldwide discussion group of CED participants.

27789 ■ State University of New York College at Oneonta–Center for Economic and Community Development
Ravine Pky.
Oneonta, NY 13820
Ph:(607)436-2792
Fax:(607)436-2786
Co. E-mail: hayest@oneonta.edu
URL: http://www.oneonta.edu/advancement/cecd
Contact: Timothy Hayes, Dir.
E-mail: hayest@oneonta.edu
Scope: Community, government, and marketing surveys; downtown development studies and marketing research, including business start-up consultation; economic impact analysis, community priorities planning, evaluation services. **Educational Activities:** Industry and government conferences (occasionally); Leadership Otsego (quadrennially), leadership training for community members.

27790 ■ Texas A&M International University–Texas Center for Border Economic and Enterprise Development
5201 University Blvd.
Laredo, TX 78041-1900
Ph:(956)326-2546
Fax:(956)326-2544
Co. E-mail: baldogarcia@tamiu.edu
URL: http://texascenter.tamiu.edu
Contact: Baldomero Garcia, Prog.Mgr.
E-mail: baldogarcia@tamiu.edu
Scope: International trade and border economic enterprise and development. **Services:** Data accessible by Internet. **Publications:** Border Business Indicators International Trade journal (monthly). **Educational Activities:** Internet home pages; Maquila visits; USIA delegations.

27791 ■ University of Alberta–Institute for Public Economics
8-26 HM Tory
Department of Economics
Edmonton, AB, Canada T6G 2H4
Ph:(780)492-7198
Fax:(780)492-3300
Co. E-mail: rascah@ualberta.ca
URL: http://www.uofaweb.ualberta.ca/ipe
Contact: Bob Ascah PhD, Dir.
E-mail: rascah@ualberta.ca
Scope: Public economics, including the public sector and its influence on the economy and society. **Publications:** Working papers. **Educational Activities:** Lectures, Conferences, Forums.

27792 ■ University of Colorado at Boulder–Carl McGuire Center for International Studies
Department of Economics
256 UCB
Boulder, CO 80309-0256
Ph:(303)492-6394
Fax:(303)492-8960
Co. E-mail: wolfgang.keller@colorado.edu
URL: http://www.colorado.edu/Economics/mcguire
Contact: Wolfgang Keller PhD, Dir.
E-mail: wolfgang.keller@colorado.edu
Scope: Organized within the Economics Department, the Center conducts research and graduate training in a broad range of topics relating to international economics, including international trade and finance, international trade negotiations, monetary theory and policy, economic development, and macroeconomics. Offers students in international economics exposure to interdisciplinary study involving the University's programs in international politics, conflict and peace

studies, and international business. **Educational Activities:** Workshop in international economics for graduate students and faculty of the Economics Department.

27793 ■ University of Connecticut–Connecticut Center for Economic Analysis
341 Mansfield Rd., U-1240
Storrs, CT 06269-1240
Ph:(860)486-0614
Fax:(860)486-4463
Co. E-mail: fred.carstensen@uconn.edu
URL: http://ccea.uconn.edu
Contact: Prof. Fred V. Carstensen, Dir.
E-mail: fred.carstensen@uconn.edu
Scope: Economic analysis, including state and local finance, economic impact, policy analysis, cluster analysis, assessment of fiscal structure, dynamic REMI forecasting, econometrics, bench-marketing, labor, and health economics. **Publications:** The Connecticut Economy (quarterly). **Educational Activities:** CCEA Outlook (quarterly), forecast of state employment and gross output; Economic Outlook Conferences (periodically).

27794 ■ University of Maryland at College Park–Center for International Economics
4118D Tydings Hall
Department of Economics
College Park, MD 20742
Ph:(301)405-3548
Fax:(301)405-7835
Co. E-mail: mendozae@econ.umd.edu
URL: http://www.econ.umd.edu/about/centers/CEI
Contact: Prof. Enrique G. Mendoza
E-mail: mendozae@econ.umd.edu
Scope: International economics. **Educational Activities:** Conferences; Graduate Training Program; Professional Training Program in International Economics.

27795 ■ University of North Texas–Center for Economic Development and Research
1155 Union Cir., No. 310469
Denton, TX 76203
Ph:(940)565-4049
Fax:(940)565-4658
Co. E-mail: tclower@unt.edu
URL: http://www.unt.edu/cedr
Contact: Terry L. Clower PhD, Dir.
E-mail: tclower@unt.edu
Scope: Applied economics, business, and public policy, particularly in the areas of economic development, fiscal analysis, energy policy, economic forecasting, and public policy. **Publications:** Perspectives (semiannually).

27796 ■ University of Texas at Austin–Bureau of Business Research
2815 San Gabriel St.
Austin, TX 78705
Ph:(512)475-7813
Co. E-mail: bkellison@ic2.utexas.edu
URL: http://www.ic2.utexas.edu/bbr
Contact: Dr. J. Bruce Kellison, Assoc.Dir.
E-mail: bkellison@ic2.utexas.edu
Scope: Economics and business in Texas, including economic development and planning, natural resources. **Services:** Free information, on the state economy and demography by phone. **Publications:** Texas Business Review (bimonthly). **Educational Activities:** Conferences and workshops, related to the economy of Texas.

27797 ■ University of Texas—Pan American–Center for Entrepreneurship and Economic Development
1201 W University Dr.
Edinburg, TX 78539-2999
Ph:(956)381-3361
Fax:(956)381-2322
Co. E-mail: arriola@panam.edu
URL: http://www.coserve.org/ceed
Contact: Roland S. Arriola
E-mail: arriola@panam.edu
Scope: South Texas business assistance and economic research, focusing on business plans, economic area profiles, economic impact studies, economic development planning, market feasibility studies, international trade, urban and rural commercial revitalization, industrial park development and feasibility, geographic information systems, and land use surveys. The center also has a bi-national agreement with Mexico to provide Mexican business and demographic information for U.S. businesses. These services are provided to businesses, local government, economic development organizations, and the community in general. The center has an agreement with the rural empowerment zone to provide management and technical assistance to the communities. **Publications:** Border Chronicle; Red Factbook. **Educational Activities:** Seminars and workshops; Training in economic development.

27798 ■ University of Utah–Bureau of Economic and Business Research
1645 E Campus Center Dr., Rm. 401
Salt Lake City, UT 84112-9302
Ph:(801)581-6333
Fax:(801)581-3354
Co. E-mail: bureau@business.utah.edu
URL: http://www.bebr.utah.edu
Contact: James A. Wood, Dir.
E-mail: bureau@business.utah.edu
Scope: Economics and business with emphasis on development of economy and resources of the state. **Services:** Inquiry service for individuals and businesses. **Publications:** Utah Construction Report (quarterly); Utah Economic and Business Review (quarterly).

27799 ■ University of Wisconsin—Superior–Northern Center for Community and Economic Development
Erlanson Hall 305D
PO Box 2000
Superior, WI 54880-2898
Ph:(715)394-8208
Fax:(715)394-8592
Co. E-mail: jhembd@uwsuper.edu
URL: http://www.uwsuper.edu/ncced
Contact: Dr. Jerry Hembd, Dir.
E-mail: jhembd@uwsuper.edu
Scope: Regional and local economic development, including area economic profiles surveys, and statistical analyses. **Services:** Consulting. **Educational Activities:** Training.

27800 ■ Williams College–Center for Development Economics
1065 Main St.
Williamstown, MA 01267
Ph:(413)597-2148
Fax:(413)597-4076
Co. E-mail: rachel.louis@williams.edu
URL: http://cde.williams.edu
Contact: Rachel Louis, Asst.Dir.
E-mail: rachel.louis@williams.edu
Scope: Problems of economic development, emphasizing external trade and finance policies, domestic resource and investment policies, industrialization and technology strategies, and developing countries. **Publications:** Research Memorandum Series. **Educational Activities:** Public seminars (occasionally).

Education and Training

START-UP INFORMATION

27801 ■ "218 More Programs" in *Entrepreneur* (Vol. 35, November 2007, No. 11, pp. 96)
Pub: Entrepreneur Media Inc.
Description: List of 218 colleges and universities in the U.S. offering entrepreneurship programs is presented.

27802 ■ "Can You Say $1 Million? A Language-Learning Start-Up Is Hoping That Investors Can" in *Inc.* (Vol. 33, November 2011, No. 9, pp. 116)
Pub: Inc. Magazine
Ed: April Joyner. **Description:** Startup, Verbling is a video platform that links language learners and native speakers around the world. The firm is working to raise money to hire engineers in order to build the product and redesign their Website.

27803 ■ *Entrepreneurship with Online Learning Center Access Card*
Pub: McGraw-Hill Higher Education
Ed: Robert D. Hirich; Michael P. Peters; Dean A. Shepherd. **Released:** October 2006. **Price:** $103.25. **Description:** Book instructs students on entrepreneurial processes that include starting a new business.

27804 ■ "Franchises with an Eye on Chicago" in *Crain's Chicago Business* (Vol. 34, March 14, 2011, No. 11, pp. 20)
Pub: Crain Communications Inc.
Description: Profiles of franchise companies seeking franchisees for the Chicago area include: Extreme Pita, a sandwich shop; Hand and Stone, offering massage, facial and waxing services; Molly Maid, home-cleaning service; Primrose Schools, private accredited schools for children 6 months to 6 hears and after-school programs; Protect Painters, residential and light-commercial painting contractor; and Wingstop, a restaurant offering chicken wings in nine flavors, fries and side dishes.

27805 ■ "Fun And Easy Gold Mines" in *Small Business Opportunities* (Fall 2008)
Pub: Entrepreneur Media Inc.
Description: Twenty-five businesses that cater to the booming children's market are profiled; day care services, party planning, special events video-making, tutoring, personalized children's toys and products and other services geared toward the kids market are included.

27806 ■ "Online Fortunes" in *Small Business Opportunities* (Fall 2008)
Pub: Entrepreneur Media Inc.
Description: Fifty hot, e-commerce enterprises for the aspiring entrepreneur to consider are featured; virtual assistants, marketing services, party planning, travel services, researching, web design and development, importing as well as creating an online store are among the businesses featured.

27807 ■ "Rehab Will Turn Hospital Into Incubator" in *The Business Journal-Serving Metropolitan Kansas City* (Vol. 26, September 12, 2008)
Pub: American City Business Journals, Inc.
Ed: Rob Roberts. **Description:** Independence Regional Health Center will be purchased by CEAH Realtors and be converted into the Independence Regional Entrepreneurial Center, a business incubator that will house startups and other tenants. Other details about the planned entrepreneurial center are provided.

27808 ■ "SBA Streamlines Loans and Ramps Up Web Presence" in *Hispanic Business* (January-February 2008, pp. 64)
Pub: Hispanic Business
Description: Federal government's Small Business Administration offers informational resources and tools to individuals wishing to start a new company as well as those managing existing firms. The site consists of over 20,000 pages with information, advice and tips on starting, financing and managing any small business. Free online courses are also provided.

27809 ■ *Start Your Own Tutoring and Test Prep Business: Your Step-by-Step Guide to Success*
Pub: Entrepreneur Press
Ed: Rich Mintzer. **Released:** September 9, 2010. **Price:** $17.95. **Description:** Are you an advocate of higher learning? Do you enjoy teaching others? Are you interested in starting a business that makes money and a positive impact? Keys for starting a successful tutoring and test preparation small business are presented.

27810 ■ "Top 25 Graduate Programs" in *Entrepreneur* (Vol. 35, November 2007, No. 11, pp. 92)
Pub: Entrepreneur Media Inc.
Description: List of the top twenty-five graduate entrepreneurship programs of different colleges and universities in the U.S. for 2007, as ranked by Entrepreneur Magazine and the Princeton Review, is presented.

27811 ■ "Top 25 Undergrad Programs" in *Entrepreneur* (Vol. 35, November 2007, No. 11, pp. 88)
Pub: Entrepreneur Media Inc.
Description: List of the top twenty-five undergraduate entrepreneurship programs of different colleges and universities in the U.S. for 2007, as ranked by Entrepreneur Magazine and the Princeton Review, is highlighted.

27812 ■ "Top of the Class" in *Entrepreneur* (Vol. 35, November 2007, No. 11, pp. 82)
Pub: Entrepreneur Media Inc.
Ed: Nichole L. Torres. **Description:** Education in entrepreneurship is being pursued by many students and it is important to understand what entrepreneurship program fits you. Aspiring entrepreneurs should also ask about the program's focus. Considerations searched for by students regarding the particular school they chose to study entrepreneurship are discussed.

27813 ■ "UM-Dearborn to Launch Program for Entrepreneurs" in *Crain's Detroit Business* (Vol. 24, April 14, 2008, No. 15, pp. 7)
Pub: Crain Communications, Inc.
Ed: Chad Halcom. **Description:** Starting this fall the University of Michigan-Dearborn will begin its Product Realization and Technology Commercialization Program for entrepreneurs and innovators with lab-tested, high-technology products. Ultimately, 20 businesses will each work with the university in creating a customer base, commercializing a new high-tech product or process and connecting with venture capitalists who may invest in the new companies.

ASSOCIATIONS AND OTHER ORGANIZATIONS

27814 ■ AACSB International
777 S Harbour Island Blvd., Ste. 750
Tampa, FL 33602-5730
Ph:(813)769-6500
Fax:(813)769-6559
Co. E-mail: mediarelations@aacsb.edu
URL: http://www.aacsb.edu
Contact: Duncan Elliott
Description: Represents educational institutions, businesses, and other entities devoted to the advancement of management education. Works to advance quality management education worldwide through accreditation. **Publications:** *Achieving Quality and Continuous Improvement Through Self-Evaluation and Peer Review* (annual); *eNewsline* (monthly); *Guide to Doctoral Programs in Business and Management* (periodic); *Salary Survey* (annual).

27815 ■ American Association of Teachers of Italian
Indiana University
Dept. of French and Italian
Ballentine Hall 642
Bloomington, IN 47405-6601
Co. E-mail: ancvitti@indiana.edu
URL: http://www.aati-online.org
Contact: Antonio C. Vitti, Pres.
Description: Professional society of college and secondary school teachers and others interested in Italian language and culture. Promotes study of Italian language, literature, and culture in schools. Maintains speakers' bureau; compiles statistics. Works with Italian government and universities to sponsor special seminars and with Italian-American organizations for the promotion of the Italian language in the K-12 schools. **Publications:** *AATI Newsletter* (semiannual).

27816 ■ American Society for Training and Development
1640 King St.
Box 1443
Alexandria, VA 22314-2746

Ph:(703)683-8100
Free: 800-628-2783
Fax:(703)683-1523
Co. E-mail: customercare@astd.org
URL: http://www.astd.org
Contact: Tony Bingham, Pres./CEO
Description: Promotes workplace learning and performance; represents the field to U.S. federal and state policymakers through education, policy development, grassroots support and work in coalitions with other national organizations in business, education and labor. Offers the Human Performance Improvement Certificate Program. **Publications:** *ASTD Buyer's Guide and Consultants Directory*; *Infoline Plus* (monthly); *TD Magazine* .

27817 ■ ASTD
Box 1443
Alexandria, VA 22313-1443
Ph:(703)683-8100
Free: 800-628-2783
Fax:(703)683-8103
Co. E-mail: customercare@astd.org
URL: http://www.astd.org
Contact: Tony Bingham, Pres./CEO
Description: Represents workplace learning and performance professionals. **Publications:** *ASTD Buyer's Guide* (annual); *Info-Line: Tips, Tools, and Intelligence for Trainers* (monthly); *Learning Circuits* (monthly).

27818 ■ Canadian Association of Independent Schools
PO Box 3013
St. Catharines, ON, Canada L2R 7C3
Ph:(905)684-5658
Fax:(905)684-5057
Co. E-mail: execassist@cesi.edu
URL: http://www.cais.ca
Contact: Anne-Marie Kee, Exec. Dir.
Description: Private schools. Promotes excellence in independent education. Represents members' interests. **Telecommunication Services:** electronic mail, execdir@cesi.edu.

27819 ■ Canadian Federation of University Women–Federation Canadienne des Femmes Diplomees des Universites
251 Bank St., Ste. 305
Ottawa, ON, Canada K2P 1X3
Ph:(613)234-8252
Fax:(613)234-8221
Co. E-mail: cfuwgen@rogers.com
URL: http://www.cfuw.org
Contact: Robin Jackson, Exec. Dir.
Description: Women graduates from accredited universities from around the world. Promotes continuing education for women. Fosters communication and fellowship among members. Advocates for status of women and human rights and equality rights. **Publications:** *The Communicator* (periodic).

27820 ■ Canadian Network for Innovation in Education–Reseau canadien pour l'innovation en education
260 Dalhousie St., Ste. 204
Ottawa, ON, Canada K1N 7E4
Ph:(613)241-0018
Fax:(613)241-0019
Co. E-mail: cnie-rcie@cnie-rcie.ca
URL: http://www.cnie-rcie.ca
Contact: Lorraine Carter, Pres.
Description: Educators, students, and other individuals with an interest in distance education. Promotes advancement in the field of distance education. Encourages use of new technologies in distance education. **Publications:** *Asynchronous Learning Networks* (periodic); *Canadian Journal of Learning and Technology* (semiannual).

27821 ■ A Commitment to Training and Employment for Women
215 Spadina Ave., Ste. 350
Toronto, ON, Canada M5T 2C7
Ph:(416)599-3590
Fax:(416)599-2043
Co. E-mail: info@actew.org
URL: http://www.actew.org
Contact: Ursule Critoph, Co-Chair
Description: Serves as umbrella organization of agencies, networks, and groups working on the local level to support existing education and training opportunities for women (particularly lower income, refugee, and older women). Encourages the creation of new programs. Conducts research, lobbying, and advocacy.

27822 ■ Community College Business Officers
PO Box 5565
Charlottesville, VA 22905-5565
Ph:(434)293-2825
Fax:(434)245-8453
Co. E-mail: info@ccbo.org
URL: http://www.ccbo.org
Contact: Dr. Bob Hassmiller CAE, Exec. Dir.
Description: Represents business officers. Works to support business officers. .

27823 ■ National Black MBA Association
180 N Michigan Ave., Ste. 1400
Chicago, IL 60601
Ph:(312)236-2622
Fax:(312)236-0390
Co. E-mail: mail@nbmbaa.org
URL: http://www.nbmbaa.org
Contact: William W. Wells Jr., Chm.
Description: Business professionals, lawyers, accountants, and engineers concerned with the role of blacks who hold advanced management degrees. Works to create economic and intellectual wealth for the black community. Encourages blacks to pursue continuing business education; assists students preparing to enter the business world. Provides programs for minority youths, students, and professionals, and entrepreneurs including workshops, panel discussions, and Destination MBA seminar. Sponsors job fairs. Works with graduate schools. Operates job placement service. **Publications:** *National Black MBA Association—Newsletter* (monthly); *NBMBAA Program Book* (annual).

27824 ■ National Business Education Association
1914 Association Dr.
Reston, VA 20191-1596
Ph:(703)860-8300
Fax:(703)620-4483
Co. E-mail: nbea@nbea.org
URL: http://www.nbea.org
Contact: Janet M. Treichel, Exec. Dir.
Description: Teachers of business subjects in secondary and postsecondary schools and colleges; administrators and research workers in business education; businesspersons interested in business education; teachers in educational institutions training business teachers; high school and college students preparing for careers in business. **Publications:** *Keying In* (quarterly); *NBEA Yearbook* (annual).

EDUCATIONAL PROGRAMS

27825 ■ ACCS - Advanced Cisco Campus Switching (Onsite)
Seminar Information Service, Inc.
20 Executive Park, Ste. 120
Irvine, CA 92614
Ph:(949)261-9104
Free: 877-SEM-INFO
Fax:(949)261-1963
Co. E-mail: info@seminarinformation.com
URL: http://www.seminarinformation.com
Price: $3,295.00. **Description:** Covers Catalyst 6000 Series Architecture; Catalyst 2948G-L3 Configuration; Layer 2 and Layer3 Forwarding; Switching Quality of Service Fundamentals and Configuration; Dynamic and Private VLANs; VLAN Access Control Lists; MLS and CEF Operation; High Availability Options for the 6000 Series; FlexWan Configuration and Operation; and Catalyst 6000 Hybrid to Native IOS Conversion. **Locations:** Ottawa, CN; Atlanta, GA; Toronto, CN; and San Jose, CA.

27826 ■ Adobe Acrobat I
EEI Communications
66 Canal Center Plz., Ste. 200
Alexandria, VA 22314
Ph:(703)683-7453
Free: 888-253-2762
Fax:(703)683-7310
Co. E-mail: train@eeicom.com
URL: http://www.eeicom.com/training
Price: $745.00. **Description:** Covers creating PDF documents, including using hyperlinks, bookmarks, sound clips, and security. **Locations:** Silver Spring, MD; Alexandria, VA; and Hunt Valley, MD.

27827 ■ Adobe After Effects I
EEI Communications
66 Canal Center Plz., Ste. 200
Alexandria, VA 22314
Ph:(703)683-7453
Free: 888-253-2762
Fax:(703)683-7310
Co. E-mail: train@eeicom.com
URL: http://www.eeicom.com/training
Price: $1,065.00. **Description:** Covers using After Effects to create digital composites, smooth 2-D animations, and elaborate special effects. **Locations:** Alexandria, VA.

27828 ■ Adobe Director I
EEI Communications
66 Canal Center Plz., Ste. 200
Alexandria, VA 22314
Ph:(703)683-7453
Free: 888-253-2762
Fax:(703)683-7310
Co. E-mail: train@eeicom.com
URL: http://www.eeicom.com/training
Price: $745.00. **Description:** Covers how to create interactive training applications, electronic marketing pieces, and presentations utilizing Macromedia Director. **Remarks:** Formerly known as Macromedia Authorware. **Locations:** Silver Spring, MD; Alexandria, VA; Hunt Valley, MD; and Columbia, MD.

27829 ■ Adobe Director II
EEI Communications
66 Canal Center Plz., Ste. 200
Alexandria, VA 22314
Ph:(703)683-7453
Free: 888-253-2762
Fax:(703)683-7310
Co. E-mail: train@eeicom.com
URL: http://www.eeicom.com/training
Price: $1,065.00. **Description:** Seminar introduces Lingo, Director's programming language. **Remarks:** Formerly known as Macromedia Authorware. **Locations:** Silver Spring, MD; Alexandria, VA; Hunt Valley, MD; and Columbia, MD.

27830 ■ Adobe Flash I
EEI Communications
66 Canal Center Plz., Ste. 200
Alexandria, VA 22314
Ph:(703)683-7453
Free: 888-253-2762
Fax:(703)683-7310
Co. E-mail: train@eeicom.com
URL: http://www.eeicom.com/training
Price: $745.00. **Description:** Covers the basics of Flash including creating animation on the Web that downloads fast and takes up less file space. **Remarks:** Formerly known as Macromedia Authorware. **Locations:** Silver Spring, MD; and Alexandria, VA.

27831 ■ Adobe Flash II
EEI Communications
66 Canal Center Plz., Ste. 200
Alexandria, VA 22314
Ph:(703)683-7453
Free: 888-253-2762
Fax:(703)683-7310
Co. E-mail: train@eeicom.com
URL: http://www.eeicom.com/training
Price: $1,065.00. **Description:** Covers advanced techniques including planning, organizing, and creating a Flash project. **Remarks:** Formerly known as Macromedia Authorware. **Locations:** Silver Spring, MD; and Alexandria, VA.

27832 ■ Adobe FrameMaker I
EEI Communications
66 Canal Center Plz., Ste. 200
Alexandria, VA 22314
Ph:(703)683-7453
Free: 888-253-2762
Fax:(703)683-7310
Co. E-mail: train@eeicom.com
URL: http://www.eeicom.com/training
Price: $1,065.00. **Description:** Covers paragraph designs, color use, graphics, headers and footers, tables, and advanced editing techniques. **Locations:** Silver Spring, MD; Alexandria, VA; Hunt Valley, MD; and Columbia, MD.

27833 ■ Adobe FrameMaker II
EEI Communications
66 Canal Center Plz., Ste. 200
Alexandria, VA 22314
Ph:(703)683-7453
Free: 888-253-2762
Fax:(703)683-7310
Co. E-mail: train@eeicom.com
URL: http://www.eeicom.com/training
Price: $745.00. **Description:** Covers cross-references, footnotes, creating a book file, hyperlinks, and exporting to HTML and PDF. **Locations:** Alexandria, VA.

27834 ■ Adobe Illustrator I
EEI Communications
66 Canal Center Plz., Ste. 200
Alexandria, VA 22314
Ph:(703)683-7453
Free: 888-253-2762
Fax:(703)683-7310
Co. E-mail: train@eeicom.com
URL: http://www.eeicom.com/training
Price: $745.00. **Description:** Covers basic graphic design features, including creating geometric shapes and free forms, using type, creating graphs, and using the manipulation tools. **Locations:** Silver Spring, MD; and Alexandria, VA.

27835 ■ Adobe Illustrator II
EEI Communications
66 Canal Center Plz., Ste. 200
Alexandria, VA 22314
Ph:(703)683-7453
Free: 888-253-2762
Fax:(703)683-7310
Co. E-mail: train@eeicom.com
URL: http://www.eeicom.com/training
Price: $745.00. **Description:** Covers some advanced features of Illustrator, including custom brush patterns, blending modes, effects and styles, and image maps. **Locations:** Silver Spring, MD; and Alexandria, VA.

27836 ■ Adobe Illustrator III
EEI Communications
66 Canal Center Plz., Ste. 200
Alexandria, VA 22314
Ph:(703)683-7453
Free: 888-253-2762
Fax:(703)683-7310
Co. E-mail: train@eeicom.com
URL: http://www.eeicom.com/training
Price: $745.00. **Description:** Covers one- and two-point perspective, shadows, geometric depth, and masking and pathfinders. **Locations:** Silver Spring, MD; and Alexandria, VA.

27837 ■ Adobe InDesign CS4 Master Class for Designers Training
EEI Communications
66 Canal Center Plz., Ste. 200
Alexandria, VA 22314
Ph:(703)683-7453
Free: 888-253-2762
Fax:(703)683-7310
Co. E-mail: train@eeicom.com
URL: http://www.eeicom.com/training
Price: $895.00. **Description:** Master Adobe InDesign CS4's styles, text processing capabilities, table-creation tools, automation features, and in-document creativity enhancements to free up countless hours from smaller tasks and concentrate on designing. **Locations:** Silver Spring, MD; Hunt Valley, MD; Columbia, MD; and Alexandria, VA.

27838 ■ Adobe InDesign I
EEI Communications
66 Canal Center Plz., Ste. 200
Alexandria, VA 22314
Ph:(703)683-7453
Free: 888-253-2762
Fax:(703)683-7310
Co. E-mail: train@eeicom.com
URL: http://www.eeicom.com/training
Price: $745.00. **Description:** Covers basic techniques for creating graphic-intensive documents including editing master pages, placeholder frames, applying color, and flowing and threading text. **Locations:** Silver Spring, MD; Alexandria, VA; and Hunt Valley, MD.

27839 ■ Adobe InDesign II
EEI Communications
66 Canal Center Plz., Ste. 200
Alexandria, VA 22314
Ph:(703)683-7453
Free: 888-253-2762
Fax:(703)683-7310
Co. E-mail: train@eeicom.com
URL: http://www.eeicom.com/training
Price: $745.00. **Description:** Covers techniques for creating graphic-intensive documents including typography, decorative and special font features, exporting documents, importing and linking graphics, drawing straight and curved segments, and advanced frame techniques. **Locations:** Silver Spring, MD; Alexandria, VA; and Hunt Valley, MD.

27840 ■ Adobe InDesign with InCopy for Workgroups Training
EEI Communications
66 Canal Center Plz., Ste. 200
Alexandria, VA 22314
Ph:(703)683-7453
Free: 888-253-2762
Fax:(703)683-7310
Co. E-mail: train@eeicom.com
URL: http://www.eeicom.com/training
Price: $425.00. **Description:** Learn a professional writing and editing program that tightly integrates with Adobe InDesign for a complete solution, including assigning editors to work on parts of pages, spreads, or entire documents in parallel with designers, significantly decreasing the production time for projects. **Locations:** Alexandria, VA.

27841 ■ Adobe Photoshop I
EEI Communications
66 Canal Center Plz., Ste. 200
Alexandria, VA 22314
Ph:(703)683-7453
Free: 888-253-2762
Fax:(703)683-7310
Co. E-mail: train@eeicom.com
URL: http://www.eeicom.com/training
Price: $745.00. **Description:** Covers the basic photo manipulation features of Photoshop. **Locations:** Silver Spring, MD; Alexandria, VA; and Hunt Valley, MD.

27842 ■ Adobe Photoshop II
EEI Communications
66 Canal Center Plz., Ste. 200
Alexandria, VA 22314
Ph:(703)683-7453
Free: 888-253-2762
Fax:(703)683-7310
Co. E-mail: train@eeicom.com
URL: http://www.eeicom.com/training
Price: $1,065.00. **Description:** Covers intermediate techniques including channel and masking, paths, layering, spot techniques, proper file formatting, and gamuts and color transition issues. **Locations:** Silver Spring, MD; and Alexandria, VA.

27843 ■ Adobe Photoshop III: Tips and Tricks
EEI Communications
66 Canal Center Plz., Ste. 200
Alexandria, VA 22314
Ph:(703)683-7453
Free: 888-253-2762
Fax:(703)683-7310
Co. E-mail: train@eeicom.com
URL: http://www.eeicom.com/training
Price: $425.00. **Description:** Covers advanced Photoshop techniques and effects. **Locations:** Silver Spring, MD; and Alexandria, VA.

27844 ■ Adobe Premiere I
EEI Communications
66 Canal Center Plz., Ste. 200
Alexandria, VA 22314
Ph:(703)683-7453
Free: 888-253-2762
Fax:(703)683-7310
Co. E-mail: train@eeicom.com
URL: http://www.eeicom.com/training
Price: $745.00. **Description:** Covers an introduction to video capture and video editing utilizing Premiere. **Locations:** Silver Spring, MD; and Alexandria, VA.

27845 ■ Advanced Grammar Roundtable
EEI Communications
66 Canal Center Plz., Ste. 200
Alexandria, VA 22314
Ph:(703)683-7453
Free: 888-253-2762
Fax:(703)683-7310
Co. E-mail: train@eeicom.com
URL: http://www.eeicom.com/training
Price: $745.00. **Description:** Discuss various philosophies about grammar, the origins of grammar rules and the case against "rule-based" grammar, diagram sentences, review grammar concepts as needed, examine particles, determiners and interrupters, examine the difference between an absolute phrase and a descriptive one. **Locations:** Silver Spring, MD; and Alexandria, VA.

27846 ■ Advanced PC Configuration, Troubleshooting and Data Recovery: Hands-On (Onsite)
Seminar Information Service, Inc.
20 Executive Park, Ste. 120
Irvine, CA 92614
Ph:(949)261-9104
Free: 877-SEM-INFO
Fax:(949)261-1963
Co. E-mail: info@seminarinformation.com
URL: http://www.seminarinformation.com
Price: $2,890.00. **Description:** Learn how to: Recover lost files and directories; Revive non-bootable floppies and hard disks; Create emergency rescue disks to recover crashed Windows systems; Detect, isolate and contain damage from virus programs; Create full disk images for complete backups; Remove unwanted start-up programs from the Registry; Examine system status with Windows XP Computer Management tools; Install and configure a simple TCP/IP network. **Locations:** Waltham, MA; Rockville, MD; Reston, VA; Philadelphia, PA; Irving, TX; Roseland, NJ; Alexandria, VA; and New York, NY.

27847 ■ Advertising Research (Onsite)
Seminar Information Service, Inc.
20 Executive Park, Ste. 120
Irvine, CA 92614
Ph:(949)261-9104
Free: 877-SEM-INFO
Fax:(949)261-1963
Co. E-mail: info@seminarinformation.com
URL: http://www.seminarinformation.com
Price: $1,895.00. **Description:** Provides a practical and a comprehensive framework for classifying various advertising research methods based on what they measure, how they measure it and how good they are at it. Participants will be able to evaluate and select among the numerous procedures used in practice to facilitate key advertising decisions. **Locations:** San Francisco, CA; and Chicago, IL.

27848 ■ Air Conditioning & Refrigeration
American Trainco
9785 S Maroon Cir., Ste. 300
PO Box 3397
Englewood, CO 80112
Ph:(303)531-4560

Free: 877-978-7246
Fax:(303)531-4565
Co. E-mail: Sales@AmericanTrainco.com
URL: http://www.americantrainco.com
Price: $990.00. **Description:** Course designed for anyone who needs to understand basic operation, maintenance, and troubleshooting of air conditioning and refrigeration systems in order to improve efficiencies and uptime at their industrial plants and large building facilities. **Locations:** Cities throughout the United States.

27849 ■ AMA's PMP Exam Prep Express
American Management Association
600 AMA Way
Saranac Lake, NY 12983-5534
Ph:(212)586-8100
Free: 877-566-9441
Fax:(518)891-0368
Co. E-mail: customerservice@amanet.org
URL: http://www.amaseminars.org
Price: $2,195.00 for non-members; $1,995.00 for AMA members; and $1,708.00 for General Services Administration (GSA) members. **Description:** Three-day seminar to increase the probability of obtaining your PMP. **Locations:** New York, NY; Washington, DC; Arlington, VA; Morristown, NJ; Los Angeles, CA; and Chicago, IL.

27850 ■ Arc Flash Protection & Electrical Safety 70E
American Trainco
9785 S Maroon Cir., Ste. 300
PO Box 3397
Englewood, CO 80112
Ph:(303)531-4560
Free: 877-978-7246
Fax:(303)531-4565
Co. E-mail: Sales@AmericanTrainco.com
URL: http://www.americantrainco.com
Price: $990.00. **Description:** Training course designed to save lives, prevent disabling injuries, and prevent damage to plants, buildings and equipment. Participants learn about personal safety for working on or around electrical systems and equipment, how to use proper materials and procedures for doing electrical work, and the potential consequences for themselves and others if they don't. **Locations:** Cities throughout the United States.

27851 ■ Assertiveness Training
American Management Association
600 AMA Way
Saranac Lake, NY 12983-5534
Ph:(212)586-8100
Free: 877-566-9441
Fax:(518)891-0368
Co. E-mail: customerservice@amanet.org
URL: http://www.amaseminars.org
Price: $2,195.00 for non-members; $1,995.00 for AMA members; and $1,708.00 for General Services Administration (GSA) members. **Description:** Three-day seminar to enhance your assertiveness skills at all levels in the organization. **Locations:** Chicago, IL; New York, NY; San Francisco, CA; Atlanta, GA; Washington, DC; Dallas, TX; and Arlington, VA.

27852 ■ Basic Electricity for the Non Electrician
American Trainco
9785 S Maroon Cir., Ste. 300
PO Box 3397
Englewood, CO 80112
Ph:(303)531-4560
Free: 877-978-7246
Fax:(303)531-4565
Co. E-mail: Sales@AmericanTrainco.com
URL: http://www.americantrainco.com
Price: $990.00. **Description:** Understanding and working with industrial electricity. **Locations:** Cities throughout the United States.

27853 ■ Basic Problem Solving Techniques (Onsite)
Seminar Information Service, Inc.
20 Executive Park, Ste. 120
Irvine, CA 92614
Ph:(949)261-9104
Free: 877-SEM-INFO
Fax:(949)261-1963
Co. E-mail: info@seminarinformation.com
URL: http://www.seminarinformation.com
Price: $370.00. **Description:** With the help of several qualitative, quantitative, and creative problem solving methods participants develop their ability to recognize and solve problems through their own efforts. **Locations:** Waukesha, WI.

27854 ■ Basics of Commercial Contracting
Seminar Information Service, Inc.
20 Executive Park, Ste. 120
Irvine, CA 92614
Ph:(949)261-9104
Free: 877-SEM-INFO
Fax:(949)261-1963
Co. E-mail: info@seminarinformation.com
URL: http://www.seminarinformation.com
Price: $995.00. **Description:** Learn the key practical and legal principles applicable to business dealings, as well as a thorough understanding of the Uniform Commercial Code (UCC) **Locations:** Las Vegas, NV; and Washington, DC.

27855 ■ Best Practices in Java Programming: Hands-On (Onsite)
Seminar Information Service, Inc.
20 Executive Park, Ste. 120
Irvine, CA 92614
Ph:(949)261-9104
Free: 877-SEM-INFO
Fax:(949)261-1963
Co. E-mail: info@seminarinformation.com
URL: http://www.seminarinformation.com
Price: $2,890.00. **Description:** Learn how to: Apply Java best practices to increase productivity and build fast, secure and reliable applications; Optimize the compilation, deployment and testing of software applications; Solve architectural problems with proven design patterns and advanced language features; Code securely in Java and authenticate with industry-standard security frameworks; Maximize software performance; Improve the reliability of threaded applications; Extend application functionality non-intrusively. **Locations:** Schaumburg, IL; Rockville, MD; Ottawa, CN; and New York, NY.

27856 ■ Boiler Operation, Maintenance & Safety
American Trainco
9785 S Maroon Cir., Ste. 300
PO Box 3397
Englewood, CO 80112
Ph:(303)531-4560
Free: 877-978-7246
Fax:(303)531-4565
Co. E-mail: Sales@AmericanTrainco.com
URL: http://www.americantrainco.com
Price: $990.00. **Description:** Seminar designed to teach building and facility maintenance personnel how to service their own boiler safely reducing the need for outside service contractors, while at the same time increases your confidence and comfort level in operating and maintaining your own broilers. **Locations:** Cities throughout the United States.

27857 ■ Building Applications with Microsoft Access 2007: Hands-On (Onsite)
Seminar Information Service, Inc.
20 Executive Park, Ste. 120
Irvine, CA 92614
Ph:(949)261-9104
Free: 877-SEM-INFO
Fax:(949)261-1963
Co. E-mail: info@seminarinformation.com
URL: http://www.seminarinformation.com
Price: $2,890.00. **Description:** Learn how to: Develop distributable applications with Microsoft Access 2007; Incorporate user specifications to enhance application functionality; Customize applications by dynamically setting properties and executing methods; Assemble expressions into VBA statements using variables and intrinsic functions; Control program flow with loops and decision-making logic; Apply Data Access Objects (DAO) to incorporate business rules; Centralize the error handling process. **Locations:** Ottawa and Toronto, CN.

27858 ■ Business Process Reengineering for Competitive Advantage (Onsite)
Seminar Information Service, Inc.
20 Executive Park, Ste. 120
Irvine, CA 92614
Ph:(949)261-9104
Free: 877-SEM-INFO
Fax:(949)261-1963
Co. E-mail: info@seminarinformation.com
URL: http://www.seminarinformation.com
Price: $2,890.00. **Description:** Learn how to: Select, organize and implement a business reengineering project using CLAMBRE/UML; Achieve competitive advantage by capitalizing on technology opportunities and the application of UML tools; Maximize customer satisfaction by matching process design to customer needs; Identify typical symptoms of business process dysfunction; Redesign workflow and structure successfully within the business; Ensure best practice through the application of business patterns. **Locations:** Ottawa, CN; Schaumburg, IL; Toronto, CN; Reston, VA; Irving, TX; and New York, NY.

27859 ■ C Programming for Non-C Programmers
Seminar Information Service, Inc.
20 Executive Park, Ste. 120
Irvine, CA 92614
Ph:(949)261-9104
Free: 877-SEM-INFO
Fax:(949)261-1963
Co. E-mail: info@seminarinformation.com
URL: http://www.seminarinformation.com
Price: $2,495.00. **Description:** Provides an accelerated introduction to the most essential components of the C++ language on the first day, followed by four days focus on object-oriented programming with C++. **Locations:** Cities throughout the United States. .

27860 ■ Certified Ethical Hacker (Onsite)
Seminar Information Service, Inc.
20 Executive Park, Ste. 120
Irvine, CA 92614
Ph:(949)261-9104
Free: 877-SEM-INFO
Fax:(949)261-1963
Co. E-mail: info@seminarinformation.com
URL: http://www.seminarinformation.com
Price: $3,295.00. **Description:** Learn to footprint organizations, perform port scanning, and exploit a variety of systems and architectures, including hands-on labs. You'll also receive the CEH study guide, Certified Ethical Hacker Exam Prep, CDs packed with security tools, templates, and white papers, practice exam questions, and an exam voucher. **Locations:** Atlanta, GA; Dallas, TX; and Morristown, NJ.

27861 ■ Chilled Water Systems
American Trainco
9785 S Maroon Cir., Ste. 300
PO Box 3397
Englewood, CO 80112
Ph:(303)531-4560
Free: 877-978-7246
Fax:(303)531-4565
Co. E-mail: Sales@AmericanTrainco.com
URL: http://www.americantrainco.com
Price: $990.00. **Description:** Learn to control your systems and properly maintain them, getting the most out of them. **Locations:** Cities throughout the United States.

27862 ■ Creative Problem Solving and Strategic Thinking
Fred Pryor Seminars & CareerTrack
5700 Broadmoor St., Ste. 300
Mission, KS 66202
Free: 800-780-8476
Fax:(913)967-8849
Co. E-mail: customerservice@pryor.com
URL: http://www.pryor.com
Price: $199.00; $199.00 for groups of 5 or more. **Description:** Learn an innovative approach to problem solving. **Locations:** Cities throughout the United States.

27863 ■ Critical Thinking Skills-Strategic Planning in Action
Seminar Information Service, Inc.
20 Executive Park, Ste. 120
Irvine, CA 92614
Ph:(949)261-9104
Free: 877-SEM-INFO
Fax:(949)261-1963
Co. E-mail: info@seminarinformation.com
URL: http://www.seminarinformation.com
Price: $460.00. **Description:** Seminar provides participants with tools, techniques and the critical thinking skills to identify their critical measures of success, the requirements of internal and external customers, including the strengths and weaknesses of their staff. **Locations:** Waukesha, WI.

27864 ■ Dealing with Competing Demands (Canada)
Canadian Management Centre
150 York St., 5th Fl.
Toronto, ON, Canada M5H 3S5
Ph:(416)214-5678
Free: 877-262-2519
Fax:(416)214-6047
Co. E-mail: cmcinfo@cmctraining.org
URL: http://www.cmctraining.org
Price: $2,395.00 Canadian for non-members; $2,195,00 Canadian for CMC members. **Description:** Covers the skills necessary to manage your objectives with success, including prioritizing, realistic objectives, effective use of communication to meet your goals, and utilize control stress. **Locations:** Toronto, ON.

27865 ■ Defending Windows Networks
Seminar Information Service, Inc.
20 Executive Park, Ste. 120
Irvine, CA 92614
Ph:(949)261-9104
Free: 877-SEM-INFO
Fax:(949)261-1963
Co. E-mail: info@seminarinformation.com
URL: http://www.seminarinformation.com
Price: $2,995.00. **Description:** Lab-intensive to illustrate defense techniques against real-world threats, instead of simply addressing software security features, including how attacks are performed, how they can compromise a Windows Server Network Infrastructure, and how you can lock down the network. **Locations:** Ottawa, Halifax, Montreal, and Toronto CN.

27866 ■ Deploying Intrusion Detection Systems: Hands-On (Onsite)
Seminar Information Service, Inc.
20 Executive Park, Ste. 120
Irvine, CA 92614
Ph:(949)261-9104
Free: 877-SEM-INFO
Fax:(949)261-1963
Co. E-mail: info@seminarinformation.com
URL: http://www.seminarinformation.com
Price: $2,890.00. **Description:** Learn how to: Detect and respond to network- and host-based intruder attacks; Integrate intrusion detection systems (IDS) into your current network topology; Analyze IDS alerts using the latest tools and techniques; Identify methods hackers use to attack systems; Recognize detection avoidance schemes; Stop attackers with Intrusion Prevention Systems (IPSs). **Locations:** Rockville, MD.

27867 ■ Deploying Virtual Server and Workstation Technology: Hands-On (Onsite)
Seminar Information Service, Inc.
20 Executive Park, Ste. 120
Irvine, CA 92614
Ph:(949)261-9104
Free: 877-SEM-INFO
Fax:(949)261-1963
Co. E-mail: info@seminarinformation.com
URL: http://www.seminarinformation.com
Price: $2,890.00. **Description:** Learn how to: Implement VMware and Microsoft virtual machine (VM) technologies; Combine Windows and Linux workstations and servers on a single platform; Leverage VMs to build testing, support and training environments; Partition physical servers to decrease operating costs; Migrate from physical to virtual machines; Manage VMs throughout the enterprise. **Locations:** Reston, VA; and Rockville, MD.

27868 ■ Designing and Building Great Web Pages: Hands-On (Onsite)
Seminar Information Service, Inc.
20 Executive Park, Ste. 120
Irvine, CA 92614
Ph:(949)261-9104
Free: 877-SEM-INFO
Fax:(949)261-1963
Co. E-mail: info@seminarinformation.com
URL: http://www.seminarinformation.com
Price: $2,890.00. **Description:** Learn to build powerful Web content that effectively conveys your message; Create graphical content using Photoshop CS2, Fireworks 8 and Flash 8; Develop Web page content with FrontPage and Dreamweaver 8; Generate complex Web pages using Cascading Style Sheets, tables and layers; and Enhance Web pages with special effects and DHTML. **Locations:** Rockville, MD; Ottawa, CN; Reston, VA; and New York, NY.

27869 ■ Developing Effective Software Estimation Techniques (Onsite)
Seminar Information Service, Inc.
20 Executive Park, Ste. 120
Irvine, CA 92614
Ph:(949)261-9104
Free: 877-SEM-INFO
Fax:(949)261-1963
Co. E-mail: info@seminarinformation.com
URL: http://www.seminarinformation.com
Price: $2,490.00. **Description:** Learn how to prepare a software project estimate through an iterative process; Develop an initial estimate using the expert judgment method; Apply historical data for greater precision in an estimate; Refine the size or scope estimate using a component-based method; Perform Function Point calculations to determine the magnitude of a project; Translate a size or scope estimate into a time, schedule and cost estimate. **Locations:** Toronto and Ottawa, CN.

27870 ■ Developing Effective Training (Onsite)
Seminar Information Service, Inc.
20 Executive Park, Ste. 120
Irvine, CA 92614
Ph:(949)261-9104
Free: 877-SEM-INFO
Fax:(949)261-1963
Co. E-mail: info@seminarinformation.com
URL: http://www.seminarinformation.com
Price: $1,495.00. **Description:** Provides less experienced trainers with an overview of the training process and shows them how to make each element yield effective learning results. **Locations:** New York, NY.

27871 ■ Developing SQL Queries for SQL Server: Hands-On (Onsite)
Seminar Information Service, Inc.
20 Executive Park, Ste. 120
Irvine, CA 92614
Ph:(949)261-9104
Free: 877-SEM-INFO
Fax:(949)261-1963
Co. E-mail: info@seminarinformation.com
URL: http://www.seminarinformation.com
Price: $2,890.00. **Description:** Learn how to develop complex and robust SQL queries for SQL Server 2005 and SQL Server 2000; Query multiple tables with inner joins, outer joins and self joins; Transform data with built-in functions; Summarize data using aggregation and grouping; Execute analytic functions to calculate ranks; Build simple and correlated subqueries. **Locations:** Cities throughout the United States.

27872 ■ Digital Photography Techniques
EEI Communications
66 Canal Center Plz., Ste. 200
Alexandria, VA 22314
Ph:(703)683-7453
Free: 888-253-2762
Fax:(703)683-7310
Co. E-mail: train@eeicom.com
URL: http://www.eeicom.com/training
Price: $745.00. **Description:** Covers using a digital camera, and manipulating digital pictures with Photoshop. **Locations:** Silver Spring, MD; Alexandria, VA; Hunt Valley, MD; and Columbia, MD.

27873 ■ Diversity Train-the-Trainer
Seminar Information Service, Inc.
20 Executive Park, Ste. 120
Irvine, CA 92614
Ph:(949)261-9104
Free: 877-SEM-INFO
Fax:(949)261-1963
Co. E-mail: info@seminarinformation.com
URL: http://www.seminarinformation.com
Price: $1,695.00. **Description:** Designed to build the confidence, knowledge, and skills of individuals charged with conducting high impact, relevant, and involved diversity education and training in their organization. **Locations:** New York, NY.

27874 ■ Effective Training Techniques for Group Leaders
Seminar Information Service, Inc.
20 Executive Park, Ste. 120
Irvine, CA 92614
Ph:(949)261-9104
Free: 877-SEM-INFO
Fax:(949)261-1963
Co. E-mail: info@seminarinformation.com
URL: http://www.seminarinformation.com
Price: $370.00 for non-members; $265.00 for The Management Association, Inc. members. **Description:** Provides group leaders precise and practical methods to train their employees. Leaders also learn to spot worker training needs and provide effective on-the-job training. **Locations:** Palatine, IL; and Waukesha, WI.

27875 ■ Electrical Ladder Drawings, Schematics & Design
American Trainco
9785 S Maroon Cir., Ste. 300
PO Box 3397
Englewood, CO 80112
Ph:(303)531-4560
Free: 877-978-7246
Fax:(303)531-4565
Co. E-mail: Sales@AmericanTrainco.com
URL: http://www.americantrainco.com
Price: $990.00. **Description:** Training will include exercises where participants create schematic diagrams based on circuit descriptions, as well as interpreting schematic drawings so that they can provide verbal or written circuit descriptions and an understanding of several types of drawings and diagrams including Block, Pictorial, One-line, Wiring, Terminal, and Schematic. **Locations:** Cities throughout the United States.

27876 ■ Electrical Troubleshooting & Preventive Maintenance
American Trainco
9785 S Maroon Cir., Ste. 300
PO Box 3397
Englewood, CO 80112
Ph:(303)531-4560
Free: 877-978-7246
Fax:(303)531-4565
Co. E-mail: Sales@AmericanTrainco.com
URL: http://www.americantrainco.com
Price: $990.00. **Description:** Two-day seminar designed for anyone who needs to sharpen their electrical troubleshooting skills in order to increase efficiencies and uptime at their industrial plant or building facility. **Locations:** Cities throughout the United States.

27877 ■ Electronic Editing
EEI Communications
66 Canal Ctr. Plz., Ste. 200
Alexandria, VA 22314-5507
Ph:(703)683-7453
Free: 888-253-2762

Fax:(703)683-7310
Co. E-mail: train@eeicom.com
URL: http://www.eeicom.com/training
Price: $745.00. **Description:** Seminar that covers marking copy using style sheets, tracking changes and comparing documents, using the "search and replace" function, analyzing global changes, writing macros to make repetitive tasks simpler, checking references against citations, and develop a systematic approach to electronic manuscripts. **Locations:** Alexandria, VA.

27878 ■ Forensic Photoshop
EEI Communications
66 Canal Center Plz., Ste. 200
Alexandria, VA 22314
Ph:(703)683-7453
Free: 888-253-2762
Fax:(703)683-7310
Co. E-mail: train@eeicom.com
URL: http://www.eeicom.com/training
Price: $745.00. **Description:** Designed for law enforcement and Homeland Security personnel that outlines the processes for using Photoshop in a forensic environment. **Locations:** Silver Spring, MD; Hunt Valley, MD; Columbia, MD; and Alexandria, VA.

27879 ■ Functional Gage Design
Seminar Information Service, Inc.
20 Executive Park, Ste. 120
Irvine, CA 92614
Ph:(949)261-9104
Free: 877-SEM-INFO
Fax:(949)261-1963
Co. E-mail: info@seminarinformation.com
URL: http://www.seminarinformation.com
Price: $795.00. **Description:** Learn about Gage design principles/tolerances; Ways to avoid commonly used but improper gaging and inspection techniques; Inspection machines; Substitute systems; Surface plate inspection and more. **Locations:** Rolling Meadows, IL.

27880 ■ Generators & Emergency Power
American Trainco
9785 S Maroon Cir., Ste. 300
PO Box 3397
Englewood, CO 80112
Ph:(303)531-4560
Free: 877-978-7246
Fax:(303)531-4565
Co. E-mail: Sales@AmericanTrainco.com
URL: http://www.americantrainco.com
Price: $990.00. **Description:** Learn what you can do, and should do with generators, to make sure your facility will keep running even when the electricity to your facility doesn't. **Locations:** Cities throughout the United States.

27881 ■ Hands-On UNIX and Linux Tools and Utilities (Onsite)
Seminar Information Service, Inc.
20 Executive Park, Ste. 120
Irvine, CA 92614
Ph:(949)261-9104
Free: 877-SEM-INFO
Fax:(949)261-1963
Co. E-mail: info@seminarinformation.com
URL: http://www.seminarinformation.com
Price: $2,890.00. **Description:** Become an expert builder and user of UNIX/Linux tools and utilities, including how to employ standard, programmable text filters to manipulate text and data, build shell scripts to automate routine tasks, and achieve significant productivity gains by matching the mix of tools to the task at hand. **Locations:** New York, NY.

27882 ■ How to Conduct Your Own Energy Audit
American Trainco
9785 S Maroon Cir., Ste. 300
PO Box 3397
Englewood, CO 80112
Ph:(303)531-4560
Free: 877-978-7246
Fax:(303)531-4565
Co. E-mail: Sales@AmericanTrainco.com
URL: http://www.americantrainco.com
Price: $990.00. **Description:** Two-day hands-on seminar shows you how to find quick and inexpensive ways to immediately cut energy costs at your plant or facility. **Locations:** Orange County, CA; and Orlando, FL.

27883 ■ HVAC Controls & Air Distribution
American Trainco
9785 S Maroon Cir., Ste. 300
PO Box 3397
Englewood, CO 80112
Ph:(303)531-4560
Free: 877-978-7246
Fax:(303)531-4565
Co. E-mail: Sales@AmericanTrainco.com
URL: http://www.americantrainco.com
Price: $990.00. **Description:** Learn how to "control" their controls, and how to use fundamental air distribution principles for achieving consistent HVAC comfort and efficiency in buildings, plants and facilities. **Locations:** Cities throughout the United States.

27884 ■ Improving Editing Skills
EEI Communications
66 Canal Center Plz., Ste. 200
Alexandria, VA 22314
Ph:(703)683-0683
Free: 888-253-2762
Fax:(703)683-4915
Co. E-mail: train@eeicom.com
URL: http://www.eeicom.com/training
Price: $425.00. **Description:** Covers the editorial issues such as active and passive voice, lists, redundancy, and sentence construction. **Locations:** Silver Spring, MD; and Alexandria, VA.

27885 ■ Installing, Configuring, and Troubleshooting Microsoft SQL Server (Onsite)
Seminar Information Service, Inc.
20 Executive Park, Ste. 120
Irvine, CA 92614
Ph:(949)261-9104
Free: 877-SEM-INFO
Fax:(949)261-1963
Co. E-mail: info@seminarinformation.com
URL: http://www.seminarinformation.com
Price: $899.00. **Description:** Learn to manage your database projects efficiently, knowledgeable and effectively. **Locations:** Cities throughout the United States.

27886 ■ Instrumentation, Process Measurement & Control
American Trainco
9785 S Maroon Cir., Ste. 300
PO Box 3397
Englewood, CO 80112
Ph:(303)531-4560
Free: 877-978-7246
Fax:(303)531-4565
Co. E-mail: Sales@AmericanTrainco.com
URL: http://www.americantrainco.com
Price: $990.00. **Description:** Learn why it is necessary to measure what is going on with your systems and equipment, how to measure it, and what those measurements may mean in terms of action that should be taken to eliminate future downtime and unnecessary expense. **Locations:** Ontario, CA; Kansas City, MO; Philadelphia, PA; Salt Lake, UT; and Arlington, VA.

27887 ■ Integrating Forms and Databases on the Web
EEI Communications
66 Canal Center Plz., Ste. 200
Alexandria, VA 22314
Ph:(703)683-7453
Free: 888-253-2762
Fax:(703)683-7310
Co. E-mail: train@eeicom.com
URL: http://www.eeicom.com/training
Price: $1,065.00. **Description:** Covers the basics of integrating a database with the world wide web using a Microsoft Access database, active server pages, or Microsoft's Internet Information Server. **Locations:** Silver Spring, MD; Alexandria, VA; Hunt Valley, MD; and Columbia, MD.

27888 ■ Introduction to OS X
EEI Communications
66 Canal Ctr. Plz., Ste. 200
Alexandria, VA 22314-5507
Ph:(703)683-7453
Free: 888-253-2762
Fax:(703)683-7310
Co. E-mail: train@eeicom.com
URL: http://www.eeicom.com/training
Price: $425.00. **Description:** Seminar designed for beginning MAC users, which serves as the foundation for all MAC courses. **Locations:** Silver Spring, MD; Alexandria, VA; Hunt Valley, MD; and Columbia, MD.

27889 ■ Introduction to System and Network Security (Onsite)
Seminar Information Service, Inc.
20 Executive Park, Ste. 120
Irvine, CA 92614
Ph:(949)261-9104
Free: 877-SEM-INFO
Fax:(949)261-1963
Co. E-mail: info@seminarinformation.com
URL: http://www.seminarinformation.com
Price: $2,890.00. **Description:** Learn to analyze your exposure to information assurance threats and protect your organization's systems and data; Reduce your susceptibility to an attack by deploying firewalls, data encryption and other countermeasures; Manage risks emanating from inside the organization and from the Internet; Protect network users from hostile applications and viruses; Identify the security risks that need to be addressed within your organization. **Locations:** Cities throughout the United States.

27890 ■ Introduction to Windows
EEI Communications
66 Canal Center Plz., Ste. 200
Alexandria, VA 22314
Ph:(703)683-7453
Free: 888-253-2762
Fax:(703)683-7310
Co. E-mail: train@eeicom.com
URL: http://www.eeicom.com/training
Price: $425.00. **Description:** Covers introduction to the PC and the basics of Windows. **Locations:** Silver Spring, MD; Alexandria, VA; Hunt Valley, MD; and Columbia, MD.

27891 ■ Inventory Control for Maintenance
American Trainco
9785 S Maroon Cir., Ste. 300
PO Box 3397
Englewood, CO 80112
Ph:(303)531-4560
Free: 877-978-7246
Fax:(303)531-4565
Co. E-mail: Sales@AmericanTrainco.com
URL: http://www.americantrainco.com
Price: $990.00. **Description:** Focus on building an inventory management system that will lead to better control through optimization of inventory quantities, organization of inventory and access to inventory. **Locations:** Orange County, CA; and Orlando, FL.

27892 ■ Java for Non-Programmers
EEI Communications
66 Canal Center Plz., Ste. 200
Alexandria, VA 22314
Ph:(703)683-7453
Free: 888-253-2762
Fax:(703)683-7310
Co. E-mail: train@eeicom.com
URL: http://www.eeicom.com/training
Price: $1,065.00. **Description:** Covers the basics of Java and how to use it for developing websites. **Locations:** Silver Spring, MD; Alexandria, VA; Hunt Valley, MD; and Columbia, MD.

27893 ■ Macromedia Authorware I
EEI Communications
66 Canal Center Plz., Ste. 200
Alexandria, VA 22314
Ph:(703)683-7453

Free: 888-253-2762
Fax:(703)683-7310
Co. E-mail: train@eeicom.com
URL: http://www.eeicom.com/training
Price: $1,695.00. **Description:** Covers how to utilize Authorware to develop presentations, quizzes, interactive hypertext, Help systems, and glossaries. **Remarks:** Formerly known as Macromedia Authorware. **Locations:** Silver Spring, MD; Alexandria, VA; Hunt Valley, MD; and Columbia, MD.

27894 ■ Maintenance Welding
American Trainco
9785 S Maroon Cir., Ste. 300
PO Box 3397
Englewood, CO 80112
Ph:(303)531-4560
Free: 877-978-7246
Fax:(303)531-4565
Co. E-mail: Sales@AmericanTrainco.com
URL: http://www.americantrainco.com
Price: $990.00. **Description:** Learn welding techniques, welding processes, metal and filler selection, cutting processes, new fabrications, troubleshooting defects, welding repair, personal safety, managing costs, record keeping and more. **Locations:** Cities throughout the United States.

27895 ■ Managing Stress Productively (Onsite)
Seminar Information Service, Inc.
20 Executive Park, Ste. 120
Irvine, CA 92614
Ph:(949)261-9104
Free: 877-SEM-INFO
Fax:(949)261-1963
Co. E-mail: info@seminarinformation.com
URL: http://www.seminarinformation.com
Price: $225.00. **Description:** Learn to deal with the pressures of work and to meet the challenges of stress-related problems. **Locations:** Waukesha, WI; and Appleton, WI.

27896 ■ Mastering Microsoft Project
Seminar Information Service, Inc.
20 Executive Park, Ste. 120
Irvine, CA 92614
Ph:(949)261-9104
Free: 877-SEM-INFO
Fax:(949)261-1963
Co. E-mail: info@seminarinformation.com
URL: http://www.seminarinformation.com
Price: $499.00; $449.00 each for 4 or more. **Description:** Learn how to import tasks into your project from any source; how to pull resources from Microsoft Outlook Active Directory and other sources; merge multiple projects into a single master project; and take advantage of templates and Wizards that can reduce your project planning time. **Locations:** Cities throughout the United States.

27897 ■ Mastering QuickBooks Seminars and QuickBooks Classes
Seminar Information Service, Inc.
20 Executive Park, Ste. 120
Irvine, CA 92614
Ph:(949)261-9104
Free: 877-SEM-INFO
Fax:(949)261-1963
Co. E-mail: info@seminarinformation.com
URL: http://www.seminarinformation.com
Price: $449.00. **Description:** Discover how QuickBooks can make you and your business more successful. **Locations:** Cities throughout the United States.

27898 ■ Microsoft Access 2003/2007 - I
EEI Communications
66 Canal Center Plz., Ste. 200
Alexandria, VA 22314
Ph:(703)683-7453
Free: 888-253-2762
Fax:(703)683-7310
Co. E-mail: train@eeicom.com
URL: http://www.eeicom.com/training
Price: $745.00. **Description:** Covers basic database concepts using Access. **Locations:** Alexandria, VA.

27899 ■ Microsoft Access 2003/2007 - II
EEI Communications
66 Canal Center Plz., Ste. 200
Alexandria, VA 22314
Ph:(703)683-7453
Free: 888-253-2762
Fax:(703)683-7310
Co. E-mail: train@eeicom.com
URL: http://www.eeicom.com/training
Price: $745.00. **Description:** Covers database concepts including table design and relationships, advanced query, functions, and form and report techniques. **Locations:** Alexandria, VA.

27900 ■ Microsoft Access 2003: A Comprehensive Hands-On Introduction - Building a Foundation for Client/Server Database Applications (Onsite)
Seminar Information Service, Inc.
20 Executive Park, Ste. 120
Irvine, CA 92614
Ph:(949)261-9104
Free: 877-SEM-INFO
Fax:(949)261-1963
Co. E-mail: info@seminarinformation.com
URL: http://www.seminarinformation.com
Price: $3,190.00. **Description:** Learn how to: Design robust relational database applications using Microsoft Access 2003; Develop client/server database front-ends; Build database applications quickly using Form, Table, Report and Query wizards; Link to ODBC and OLE-DB data sources to leverage enterprise security; Create and integrate macros into your applications; Implement advanced Access reporting features. **Locations:** New York, NY; Alexandria, VA; Reston, VA; Atlanta, GA; Rockville, MD; Irving, TX; and El Segundo, CA.

27901 ■ Microsoft Access 2007: A Comprehensive Hands-On Introduction (Onsite)
Seminar Information Service, Inc.
20 Executive Park, Ste. 120
Irvine, CA 92614
Ph:(949)261-9104
Free: 877-SEM-INFO
Fax:(949)261-1963
Co. E-mail: info@seminarinformation.com
URL: http://www.seminarinformation.com
Price: $2,890.00. **Description:** Learn how to: Utilize Microsoft Access 2007 to design robust database applications; Apply Form, Table, Report and Query wizards to quickly build database applications; Create and integrate macros into your applications; Quickly modify forms and reports with selective filtering, sorting and grouping; Implement advanced Access reporting features; Link to SharePoint and SQL Server data systems. **Locations:** New York, NY; Ottawa, CN; and Rockville, MD.

27902 ■ Microsoft Excel 2003/2007 - I
EEI Communications
66 Canal Center Plz., Ste. 200
Alexandria, VA 22314
Ph:(703)683-7453
Free: 888-253-2762
Fax:(703)683-7310
Co. E-mail: train@eeicom.com
URL: http://www.eeicom.com/training
Price: $745.00. **Description:** Covers the basics of creating simple and complex spreadsheets, including absolute and relative formulas, formatting cells and cell ranges, control pages, working with multiple sheets, and using templates. **Locations:** Silver Spring, MD; and Alexandria, VA.

27903 ■ Microsoft FrontPage
EEI Communications
66 Canal Center Plz., Ste. 200
Alexandria, VA 22314
Ph:(703)683-7453
Free: 888-253-2762
Fax:(703)683-7310
Co. E-mail: train@eeicom.com
URL: http://www.eeicom.com/training
Price: $745.00. **Description:** Covers using FrontPage to develop websites. **Locations:** Silver Spring, MD; Alexandria, VA; Hunt Valley, MD; and Columbia, MD.

27904 ■ Microsoft Office
Fred Pryor Seminars & CareerTrack
5700 Broadmoor St., Ste. 300
Mission, KS 66202
Free: 800-944-8503
Fax:(913)967-8849
Co. E-mail: customerservice@pryor.com
URL: http://www.careertrack.com
Price: $49.00; $44.00 for groups of 5 or more. Covers using Microsoft Office programs to improve work efficiency, create better looking documents, and eliminate repetitive tasks. **Locations:** Cities throughout the United States.

27905 ■ Microsoft PowerPoint 2003/2007 - I
EEI Communications
66 Canal Center Plz., Ste. 200
Alexandria, VA 22314
Ph:(703)683-7453
Free: 888-253-2762
Fax:(703)683-7310
Co. E-mail: train@eeicom.com
URL: http://www.eeicom.com/training
Price: $745.00. **Description:** Covers creating slides and electronic presentations utilizing PowerPoint. **Locations:** Alexandria, VA.

27906 ■ Microsoft Project 2003/2007 - I
EEI Communications
66 Canal Center Plz., Ste. 200
Alexandria, VA 22314
Ph:(703)683-7453
Free: 888-253-2762
Fax:(703)683-7310
Co. E-mail: train@eeicom.com
URL: http://www.eeicom.com/training
Price: $745.00. **Description:** Covers using Project to successfully manage projects, including using Gantt charts, resource leveling, and establishing task dependencies. **Locations:** Alexandria, VA.

27907 ■ Microsoft Project: Managing Multiple and Complex Projects (Onsite)
Seminar Information Service, Inc.
20 Executive Park, Ste. 120
Irvine, CA 92614
Ph:(949)261-9104
Free: 877-SEM-INFO
Fax:(949)261-1963
Co. E-mail: info@seminarinformation.com
URL: http://www.seminarinformation.com
Price: $1,890.00. **Description:** Learn how to: Leverage Microsoft Project Professional tools and techniques in a multi-project environment; Reorganize large or complex projects into master and subprojects; Optimize resource assignments across projects and resolve over allocations; Track schedule, completeness and budget on complex projects and for distributed teams; Connect project managers, teams and data across the organization; Integrate third-party applications to facilitate data sharing and accessibility. **Locations:** New York, NY; and Ottawa, CN.

27908 ■ Microsoft Word 2003/2007 - I
EEI Communications
66 Canal Center Plz., Ste. 200
Alexandria, VA 22314
Ph:(703)683-7453
Free: 888-253-2762
Fax:(703)683-7310
Co. E-mail: train@eeicom.com
URL: http://www.eeicom.com/training
Price: $425.00. **Description:** Covers how to create basic documents using Word. **Locations:** Alexandria, VA.

27909 ■ Microsoft Word 2003/2007 - II
EEI Communications
66 Canal Center Plz., Ste. 200
Alexandria, VA 22314

Ph:(703)683-7453
Free: 888-253-2762
Fax:(703)683-7310
Co. E-mail: train@eeicom.com
URL: http://www.eeicom.com/training
Price: $425.00. **Description:** Covers techniques including creating styles and sections, newspaper-style layouts, creating charts, and adding clip art. **Locations:** Alexandria, VA.

27910 ■ Microsoft Word 2003/2007 - III
EEI Communications
66 Canal Center Plz., Ste. 200
Alexandria, VA 22314
Ph:(703)683-7453
Free: 888-253-2762
Fax:(703)683-7310
Co. E-mail: train@eeicom.com
URL: http://www.eeicom.com/training
Price: $425.00. **Description:** Covers advanced Word skills including running, recording, and running macros, creating custom toolbars, creating online forms, working with master documents, and creating table of contents and indexes. **Locations:** Alexandria, VA.

27911 ■ Motor Selection, Maintenance, Testing & Replacement
American Trainco
9785 S Maroon Cir., Ste. 300
PO Box 3397
Englewood, CO 80112
Ph:(303)531-4560
Free: 877-978-7246
Fax:(303)531-4565
Co. E-mail: Sales@AmericanTrainco.com
URL: http://www.americantrainco.com
Price: $495.00. **Description:** Seminar designed for anyone whose work is affected by motors at their facility, whether they are mechanics doing the work, a supervisor in charge of fixing problems, or purchasing agents responsible for saving money. **Locations:** Anchorage, AK; and Honolulu, HI.

27912 ■ Moving Ahead: Breaking Behavior Patterns That Hold You Back
American Management Association
600 AMA Way
Saranac Lake, NY 12983-5534
Ph:(212)586-8100
Free: 877-566-9441
Fax:(518)891-0368
Co. E-mail: customerservice@amanet.org
URL: http://www.amaseminars.org
Price: $2,095.00 for non-members; $1,895.00 for AMA members; and $1,623.00 for General Services Administration (GSA) members. **Description:** Covers resolution techniques for bad workplace behaviors. **Locations:** New York, NY; San Francisco, CA; Washington, DC; Atlanta, GA; and Chicago, IL.

27913 ■ Online Marketing and Search Engine Optimization
EEI Communications
66 Canal Ctr. Plz., Ste. 200
Alexandria, VA 22314-5507
Ph:(703)683-7453
Free: 888-253-2762
Fax:(703)683-7310
Co. E-mail: train@eeicom.com
URL: http://www.eeicom.com/training
Price: $745.00. **Description:** Covers how to increase traffic to your online site to market your products and services using the Web, including creating and implementation of your plan, setting a budget, redesigning Web site for search engine optimization, tips and tricks, promotion hints, tips, and advice, and how to measure your Internet marketing results. **Locations:** Alexandria, VA.

27914 ■ Personal Success Strategies (Onsite)
Seminar Information Service, Inc.
20 Executive Park, Ste. 120
Irvine, CA 92614
Ph:(949)261-9104
Free: 877-SEM-INFO
Fax:(949)261-1963
Co. E-mail: info@seminarinformation.com
URL: http://www.seminarinformation.com
Price: $370.00. **Description:** Develop a plan to eliminate weaknesses that inhibit success and replace them with positive actions. **Locations:** Waukesha, WI.

27915 ■ PLC Programming & Applications
American Trainco
9785 S Maroon Cir., Ste. 300
PO Box 3397
Englewood, CO 80112
Ph:(303)531-4560
Free: 877-978-7246
Fax:(303)531-4565
Co. E-mail: Sales@AmericanTrainco.com
URL: http://www.americantrainco.com
Price: $990.00. **Description:** Provides skills needed to organize, plan, write, enter, test, and document SLC500 programs using the basic programming instructions and RSLogix software. **Locations:** Cities throughout the United States.

27916 ■ PLCs for Non-Programmers
American Trainco
9785 S Maroon Cir., Ste. 300
PO Box 3397
Englewood, CO 80112
Ph:(303)531-4560
Free: 877-978-7246
Fax:(303)531-4565
Co. E-mail: Sales@AmericanTrainco.com
URL: http://www.americantrainco.com
Price: $990.00. **Description:** Seminar designed for maintenance technicians, electricians, or other non-programmers who need a general understanding of automation and Programmable Logic Controllers. **Locations:** Cities throughout the United States.

27917 ■ Plumbing & Pipefitting for Plants & Buildings
American Trainco
9785 S Maroon Cir., Ste. 300
PO Box 3397
Englewood, CO 80112
Ph:(303)531-4560
Free: 877-978-7246
Fax:(303)531-4565
Co. E-mail: Sales@AmericanTrainco.com
URL: http://www.americantrainco.com
Price: $990.00. **Description:** Covers the necessary requirements to follow code and safety regulations while providing the student with a practical foundation to quickly identify problems and solve them on their own, whether it's a low-pressure water supply line problem, drippy valve or a clogged drain trap. **Locations:** Phoenix, AZ; Orange County, CA; Sacramento, CA; and Denver, CO.

27918 ■ Power Excel: Making Better Decisions (Onsite)
Seminar Information Service, Inc.
20 Executive Park, Ste. 120
Irvine, CA 92614
Ph:(949)261-9104
Free: 877-SEM-INFO
Fax:(949)261-1963
Co. E-mail: info@seminarinformation.com
URL: http://www.seminarinformation.com
Price: $1,890.00. **Description:** Learn how to: Leverage advanced features of Microsoft Excel to facilitate business decisions; Perform 'what-if' analysis for developing budget and project plans; Predict potential business developments using trend analysis; Consolidate and process multidimensional worksheets; Summarize and analyze large amounts of data using PivotTables and Excel features; Automate Excel processes and enhance worksheet models; Generate interactive Web-based worksheet models. **Locations:** Cities throughout the United States and Toronto, CN.

27919 ■ PowerPoint Unplugged
600 AMA Way
Saranac Lake, NY 12983-5534
Ph:(212)586-8100
Free: 877-566-9441
Fax:(518)891-0368
Co. E-mail: customerservice@amanet.org
URL: http://www.amaseminars.org
Price: $1,445.00 for non-members; $1,295.00 for AMA members; and $1,109.00 for General Services Administration (GSA) members. **Description:** Learn when to use and not to use PowerPoint for presentations, gain practical tips for effective interaction between the presenter and the screen, computer, and projector, and learn graphic design basics to create effective visuals. **Locations:** New York, NY; Arlington, VA; Chicago, IL; Washington, DC; and Atlanta, GA.

27920 ■ Predictive Maintenance and Condition Monitoring
American Trainco
9785 S Maroon Cir., Ste. 300
PO Box 3397
Englewood, CO 80112
Ph:(303)531-4560
Free: 877-978-7246
Fax:(303)531-4565
Co. E-mail: Sales@AmericanTrainco.com
URL: http://www.americantrainco.com
Price: $990.00. **Description:** Provides the fundamentals of PdM and condition monitoring applicable to plants, facilities, and manufacturing lines. **Locations:** Orange County, CA; and Orlando, FL.

27921 ■ Preparing for the Project Management Professional PMP Exam (Onsite)
Seminar Information Service, Inc.
20 Executive Park, Ste. 120
Irvine, CA 92614
Ph:(949)261-9104
Free: 877-SEM-INFO
Fax:(949)261-1963
Co. E-mail: info@seminarinformation.com
URL: http://www.seminarinformation.com
Price: $3,190.00. **Description:** Learn how to: Prepare to pass the PMP(r) exam; Navigate the process groups and knowledge areas of the PMBOK(r) Guide 3rd Edition; Identify and map the inputs and outputs of the PMBOK(r) Guide processes; Align your project management knowledge with PMBOK(r) Guide terminology and definitions; Analyze PMBOK(r) Guide tools and techniques essential for PMP(r) exam success; Improve your exam-taking techniques through PMP(r)-style practice questions; Create a personalized plan for self-study to focus your efforts after the course. **Locations:** Rockville, MD; Philadelphia, PA; Chicago, IL; Reston, VA; Baltimore, MD; New York, NY; and Toronto, CN.

27922 ■ Programming Boot Camp
EEI Communications
66 Canal Center Plz., Ste. 200
Alexandria, VA 22314
Ph:(703)683-7453
Free: 888-253-2762
Fax:(703)683-7310
Co. E-mail: train@eeicom.com
URL: http://www.eeicom.com/training
Price: $745.00. **Description:** Covers basic concepts of scripting languages and tools, including JavaScript and Visual Basic. **Locations:** Silver Spring, MD; Alexandria, VA; Hunt Valley, MD; and Columbia, MD.

27923 ■ C Programming: Hands-On (Onsite)
Seminar Information Service, Inc.
20 Executive Park, Ste. 120
Irvine, CA 92614
Ph:(949)261-9104
Free: 877-SEM-INFO
Fax:(949)261-1963
Co. E-mail: info@seminarinformation.com
URL: http://www.seminarinformation.com
Price: $2,890.00. **Description:** Learn how to: Create, compile and run C programs using Visual Studio 2005; Write and understand C language constructs, syntax and classes; Leverage the architecture and namespaces of the .NET Framework library; Manage the Common Language Infrastructure (CLI) to integrate C with Visual Basic 2005 and C++; Develop .NET components in C for desktop and distributed multi-tier applications. **Locations:** Toronto, CN; Rock-

ville, MD; Irving, TX; New York, NY; El Segundo, CA; Alexandria, VA; Schaumburg, IL; Reston, VA; and Roseland, NJ.

27924 ■ Programming Microsoft Access 2003: Hands-On - Building Database Applications with Access and VBA (Onsite)
Seminar Information Service, Inc.
20 Executive Park, Ste. 120
Irvine, CA 92614
Ph:(949)261-9104
Free: 877-SEM-INFO
Fax:(949)261-1963
Co. E-mail: info@seminarinformation.com
URL: http://www.seminarinformation.com
Price: $2,890.00. **Description:** Learn how to: Develop applications with Microsoft Access 2003 using Visual Basic for Applications (VBA); Identify and populate event properties to satisfy design specifications; Modify object properties and invoke object methods to customize applications; Create VBA statements using variables and built-in functions; Build loops and decision logic; Apply Data Access Objects (DAO) to incorporate business rules; Integrate Access with external applications through automation. **Locations:** Reston, VA; and New York, NY.

27925 ■ The Project Planning Workshop (Canada)
Canadian Management Centre
150 York St., 5th Fl.
Toronto, ON, Canada M5H 3S5
Ph:(416)214-5678
Free: 877-CMC-2500
Fax:(416)214-6047
Co. E-mail: cmcinfo@cmctraining.org
URL: http://www.cmctraining.org
Price: $1,995.00 Canadian for non-members; $1,845.00 Canadian for CMC members. **Description:** Two-day seminar covers the applicable tools, templates and proven practices to plan real life work projects. **Locations:** Toronto, ON.

27926 ■ Pump Repair & Maintenance
American Trainco
9785 S Maroon Cir., Ste. 300
PO Box 3397
Englewood, CO 80112
Ph:(303)531-4560
Free: 877-978-7246
Fax:(303)531-4565
Co. E-mail: Sales@AmericanTrainco.com
URL: http://www.americantrainco.com
Price: $990.00. **Description:** Learn common sense pump maintenance and repair techniques to keep facilities and equipment up and running. **Locations:** Cities throughout the United States.

27927 ■ Pumps & Pump Systems
Seminar Information Service, Inc.
20 Executive Park, Ste. 120
Irvine, CA 92614
Ph:(949)261-9104
Free: 877-SEM-INFO
Fax:(949)261-1963
Co. E-mail: info@seminarinformation.com
URL: http://www.seminarinformation.com
Price: $985.00. **Description:** Learn to identify the real problems causing pump failure, and how to avoid repeating those problems in the future. **Locations:** Cities throughout the United States.

27928 ■ QuarkXPress I
EEI Communications
66 Canal Center Plz., Ste. 200
Alexandria, VA 22314
Ph:(703)683-7453
Free: 888-253-2762
Fax:(703)683-7310
Co. E-mail: train@eeicom.com
URL: http://www.eeicom.com/training
Price: $745.00. **Description:** Covers basic desktop publishing skills including creating and saving documents, formatting text and paragraphs, and manipulating graphics. **Locations:** Alexandria, VA.

27929 ■ QuarkXPress II
EEI Communications
66 Canal Center Plz., Ste. 200
Alexandria, VA 22314
Ph:(703)683-7453
Free: 888-253-2762
Fax:(703)683-7310
Co. E-mail: train@eeicom.com
URL: http://www.eeicom.com/training
Price: $745.00. **Description:** Covers desktop publishing skills including paragraph and character style sheets, libraries, master pages, tracking and kerning, and processing colors. **Locations:** Silver Spring, MD; Alexandria, VA; Hunt Valley, MD; and Columbia, MD.

27930 ■ QuarkXPress III
EEI Communications
66 Canal Center Plz., Ste. 200
Alexandria, VA 22314
Ph:(703)683-7453
Free: 888-253-2762
Fax:(703)683-7310
Co. E-mail: train@eeicom.com
URL: http://www.eeicom.com/training
Price: $425.00. **Description:** Covers advanced desktop publishing skills including building table of contents and indexes, creating PostScript files, working with books, and synchronizing documents. **Locations:** Alexandria, VA.

27931 ■ Resume Writing
EEI Communications
66 Canal Center Plz., Ste. 200
Alexandria, VA 22314
Ph:(703)683-7453
Free: 888-253-2762
Fax:(703)683-7310
Co. E-mail: train@eeicom.com
URL: http://www.eeicom.com/training
Price: $425.00. **Description:** Learn to create an exceptional resume that helps you compete successfully for the job you want, as well as how to customize your resume and cover letter for each targeted employer in just a few strokes. **Locations:** Alexandria, VA.

27932 ■ Search Engine Optimization Training
EEI Communications
66 Canal Center Plz., Ste. 200
Alexandria, VA 22314
Ph:(703)683-7453
Free: 888-253-2762
Fax:(703)683-7310
Co. E-mail: train@eeicom.com
URL: http://www.eeicom.com/training
Price: $745.00. **Description:** Learn how to increase traffic to your Web site and get your products and services visible on the Web. **Locations:** Alexandria, VA.

27933 ■ Speed Reading with Evelyn Wood Reading Dynamics
Fred Pryor Seminars & CareerTrack
5700 Broadmoor St., Ste. 300
Mission, KS 66202
Free: 800-780-8476
Fax:(913)967-8849
Co. E-mail: customerservice@pryor.com
URL: http://www.pryor.com
Price: $149.00; $139.00 for groups of 5 or more. **Description:** Learn Evelyn Wood's basic concepts, how to increase your reading rate, note-taking, studying and listening skills and develop better memory, recall and comprehension. **Locations:** Cities throughout the United States.

27934 ■ Steam Systems Maintenance, Safety & Optimization
American Trainco
9785 S Maroon Cir., Ste. 300
PO Box 3397
Englewood, CO 80112
Ph:(303)531-4560
Free: 877-978-7246
Fax:(303)531-4565
Co. E-mail: Sales@AmericanTrainco.com
URL: http://www.americantrainco.com
Price: $990.00. **Description:** This course will teach you how to keep your steam system working efficiently and how to fix common problems and work safely reducing energy loss. **Locations:** Cities throughout the United States.

27935 ■ Style Summit: Editorial Evolution in the Internet Era
EEI Communications
66 Canal Ctr. Plz., Ste. 200
Alexandria, VA 22314-5507
Ph:(703)683-7453
Free: 888-253-2762
Fax:(703)683-7310
Co. E-mail: train@eeicom.com
URL: http://www.eeicom.com/training
Price: $745.00. **Description:** Covers simplifying the editorial process, including issues such as nouns used as verbs (E-mail me), e-jargon and acronyms, and informal usages that seem to break the rules (like vs. such as; more vs. over). **Locations:** Silver Spring, MD; Alexandria, VA; Hunt Valley, MD; and Columbia, MD.

27936 ■ Technical Writing: A Comprehensive Hands-On Introduction (Onsite)
Seminar Information Service, Inc.
20 Executive Park, Ste. 120
Irvine, CA 92614
Ph:(949)261-9104
Free: 877-SEM-INFO
Fax:(949)261-1963
Co. E-mail: info@seminarinformation.com
URL: http://www.seminarinformation.com
Price: $2,890.00. **Description:** Learn how to: Write clear, effective technical = documents, including user manuals and technical reports; Assess your target audience and develop documents to meet their needs; Choose the appropriate writing style to communicate to specialized audiences; Build effective sentences, paragraphs and sections that explain information clearly; Employ diagrams, tables, charts and other graphical tools effectively; Create informative and interesting content that your readers will comprehend and utilize. **Locations:** Rockville, MD; Ottawa, CN; and Alexandria, VA.

27937 ■ Troubleshooting Mechanical Drive Systems & Rotating Equipment
American Trainco
9785 S Maroon Cir., Ste. 300
PO Box 3397
Englewood, CO 80112
Ph:(303)531-4560
Free: 877-978-7246
Fax:(303)531-4565
Co. E-mail: Sales@AmericanTrainco.com
URL: http://www.americantrainco.com
Price: $990.00. **Description:** Provide a new perspective on troubleshooting mechanical and rotating equipment and learn about basic mechanical applications, failures, life expectancy and maintenance shafts, bearings, couplings, chains, sprockets, bushings, gears, belts, sheaves and other mechanical components. You'll learn what data to measure, track and trend so that when equipment fails you can get quick answers to what is wrong, as well as fix the real problems with your equipment and not just the symptoms. **Locations:** Cities throughout the United States.

27938 ■ Understanding & Troubleshooting Hydraulics
American Trainco
9785 S Maroon Cir., Ste. 300
PO Box 3397
Englewood, CO 80112
Ph:(303)531-4560
Free: 877-978-7246
Fax:(303)531-4565
Co. E-mail: Sales@AmericanTrainco.com
URL: http://www.americantrainco.com
Price: $990.00. **Description:** Provides the basic building blocks and information you need to become proficient in working with industrial hydraulics and

fluid power, whether a small mobile unit or large industrial installation. **Locations:** Cities throughout the United States.

27939 ■ Uninterruptable Power Supply (UPS) Maintenance and Readiness
American Trainco
9785 S Maroon Cir., Ste. 300
PO Box 3397
Englewood, CO 80112
Ph:(303)531-4560
Free: 877-978-7246
Fax:(303)531-4565
Co. E-mail: Sales@AmericanTrainco.com
URL: http://www.americantrainco.com
Price: $495.00. **Description:** Seminar designed for personnel responsible for the UPS systems in industrial plants, public facilities, and commercial buildings. **Locations:** Sacramento, CA; and San Diego, CA.

27940 ■ Variable Frequency Drives
American Trainco
9785 S Maroon Cir., Ste. 300
PO Box 3397
Englewood, CO 80112
Ph:(303)531-4560
Free: 877-978-7246
Fax:(303)531-4565
Co. E-mail: Sales@AmericanTrainco.com
URL: http://www.americantrainco.com
Price: $990.00. **Description:** Learn how to troubleshoot common VFD problems, take care of your own equipment, and avoid costly repairs or service repairs, including how to identify hazards associated with working on VFDs, an understanding of the importance of safe work practices, recognition of the main components of a VFD system, and the different methods of controlling a VFD. **Locations:** Cities throughout the United States.

27941 ■ Visual Design I
EEI Communications
66 Canal Center Plz., Ste. 200
Alexandria, VA 22314
Ph:(703)683-7453
Free: 888-253-2762
Fax:(703)683-7310
Co. E-mail: train@eeicom.com
URL: http://www.eeicom.com/training
Price: $745.00. **Description:** Covers the history of type, typography's role in visual communication, structural line, space and kinetic lines, the elements of line, shape and space, and typography and type anatomy. **Locations:** Alexandria, VA.

27942 ■ Visual Design II
EEI Communications
66 Canal Center Plz., Ste. 200
Alexandria, VA 22314
Ph:(703)683-7453
Free: 888-253-2762
Fax:(703)683-7310
Co. E-mail: train@eeicom.com
URL: http://www.eeicom.com/training
Price: $745.00. **Description:** Covers the principles of texture and the diverse approaches to the element of value. Explore monochromatic, analogous and complementary combinations from Itten's color wheel. **Locations:** Alexandria, VA.

27943 ■ Visual Design III
EEI Communications
66 Canal Center Plz., Ste. 200
Alexandria, VA 22314
Ph:(703)683-7453
Free: 888-253-2762
Fax:(703)683-7310
Co. E-mail: train@eeicom.com
URL: http://www.eeicom.com/training
Price: $745.00. **Description:** Covers the compositional elements of line, plane, and form combined with neutral tones, and the Bauhaus and Constructivist theory as it relates to compositional tension and movement created by design. **Locations:** Alexandria, VA.

27944 ■ Visual Design IV
EEI Communications
66 Canal Center Plz., Ste. 200
Alexandria, VA 22314
Ph:(703)683-7453
Free: 888-253-2762
Fax:(703)683-7310
Co. E-mail: train@eeicom.com
URL: http://www.eeicom.com/training
Price: $745.00. **Description:** With focus on the works of Malevich and Escher as a foundation, learn the attributes of shape in positive and negative space, organic and geometric differences, metamorphosis, and symbolism. **Locations:** Alexandria, VA.

27945 ■ Water Treatment for Boilers, Chillers & Cooling Towers
American Trainco
9785 S Maroon Cir., Ste. 300
PO Box 3397
Englewood, CO 80112
Ph:(303)531-4560
Free: 877-978-7246
Fax:(303)531-4565
Co. E-mail: Sales@AmericanTrainco.com
URL: http://www.americantrainco.com
Price: $495.00. **Description:** One-day seminar to take the mystery out of creating, and stabilizing high water quality for your HVAC systems. **Locations:** Cities throughout the United States.

27946 ■ Windows Vista: A Hands-On Introduction (Onsite)
Seminar Information Service, Inc.
20 Executive Park, Ste. 120
Irvine, CA 92614
Ph:(949)261-9104
Free: 877-SEM-INFO
Fax:(949)261-1963
Co. E-mail: info@seminarinformation.com
URL: http://www.seminarinformation.com
Price: $2,890.00. **Description:** Learn how to: Install and maintain Windows Vista in a professional environment; Navigate and configure Windows Vista; Create and manage users and groups; Protect resources with rights, access control and encryption; Implement and troubleshoot network and Internet connectivity; Improve application compatibility to maximize user productivity. **Locations:** Cities throughout the United States; Ottawa, CN; and Toronto, CN.

27947 ■ The Women's Conference
Fred Pryor Seminars & CareerTrack
5700 Broadmoor St., Ste. 300
Mission, KS 66202
Free: 800-944-8503
Fax:(913)967-8849
Co. E-mail: customerservice@pryor.com
URL: http://www.careertrack.com
Price: $149.00; $139.00 for groups of 5 or more. **Description:** Covers the following topics: enhancing your career and professional development; expert communication skills just for women; and the women's professional toolbox. **Locations:** Cities throughout the United States.

27948 ■ Writing the Perfect Business E-Mail
EEI Communications
66 Canal Ctr. Plz., Ste. 200
Alexandria, VA 22314-5507
Ph:(703)683-7453
Free: 888-253-2762
Fax:(703)683-7310
Co. E-mail: train@eeicom.com
URL: http://www.eeicom.com/training
Price: $425.00. **Description:** Seminar that covers e-mails that get read and are understood, including keeping it short and simple, make it useful, spelling, grammar, and other problems, controlling emotion, writing attachments that get read, progress reports, instructions, and evaluations and recommendations. **Locations:** Silver Spring, MD; Alexandria, VA; Hunt Valley, MD; and Columbia, MD.

DIRECTORIES OF EDUCATIONAL PROGRAMS

27949 ■ *American Society Training and Development Buyer's Guide and Consultant Directory*
Pub: American Society for Training & Development
Released: Annual. **Covers:** Over 580 suppliers and consultants in the training and development of employees.

REFERENCE WORKS

27950 ■ "2007 Best Schools for Hispanics: Head of the Class" in *Hispanic Business* (September 2007, pp. 34, 36, 38)
Pub: Hispanic Business
Ed: Hildy Medina. **Description:** Stanford's business school recruits Hispanic students through the Charles P. Bonini Partnership for Diversity Fellowship program. A listing of the top schools for business, engineering, law, and medicine for Hispanics are included.

27951 ■ "The 2007 Black Book" in *Hawaii Business* (Vol. 53, December 2007, No. 6, pp. 43)
Pub: Hawaii Business Publishing
Description: Brief biographies of 364 top executives in Hawaii are presented. Information on their educational achievement, membership in associations, hobbies, family, present position and the company they work for are supplied.

27952 ■ "2010 Book of Lists" in *Austin Business JournalInc.* (Vol. 29, December 25, 2009, No. 42, pp. 1)
Pub: American City Business Journals
Description: Rankings of companies and organizations within the business services, finance, healthcare, hospitality and travel, insurance, marketing and media, professional services, real estate, education and technology industries in Austin, Texas are presented. Rankings are based on sales, business size, and other statistics.

27953 ■ "2010 Book of Lists" in *Business Courier* (Vol. 26, December 26, 2009, No. 36, pp. 1)
Pub: American City Business Journals, Inc.
Description: Rankings of companies and organizations within the business services, education, finance, health care, hospitality and tourism, real estate, and technology industries in the Cincinnati, Ohio-Northern Kentucky area are presented. Rankings are based on sales, business size, or other statistics.

27954 ■ "2010 Book of Lists" in *Tampa Bay Business Journal* (Vol. 30, December 22, 2009, No. 53, pp. 1)
Pub: American City Business Journals
Description: Rankings of companies and organizations within the human resources, banking and finance, business services, healthcare, real estate, technology, hospitality and travel, and education industries in the Greater Tampa Bay area are presented. Rankings are based on sales, business size, and more.

27955 ■ "A Quick Guide to NATE" in *Indoor Comfort Marketing* (Vol. 70, February 2011, No. 2, pp. 12)
Pub: Industry Publications Inc.
Description: Guide for training and certification in the North American Technician Excellence award.

27956 ■ "ACC Game Development Program Opens" in *Austin Business JournalInc.* (Vol. 28, October 31, 2008, No. 33, pp. 1)
Pub: American City Business Journals
Ed: Sandra Zaragoza. **Description:** Austin, Texas-based Austin Community College has launched its Game Development Institute. The institute was created to meet the gaming industry's demand for skilled workers. One hundred students have enrolled with the institute.

27957 ■ "Active Duty" in *Crain's Cleveland Business* (Vol. 28, November 26, 2007, No. 47, pp. 3)
Pub: Crain Communications, Inc.
Ed: David Bennett. **Description:** Discusses the Veteran Workforce Training Program, sponsored by the Volunteers of America - Greater Ohio; the program is meant to provide employment training for military veterans and to assist them in transitioning back into the work force.

27958 ■ "Advantage Tutoring Center" in *Bellingham Business Journal* (Vol. February 2010, pp. 16)
Pub: Sound Publishing Inc.
Ed: Ashley Mitchell. **Description:** Profile of the newly opened Advantage Tutoring, owned by Mary and Peter Morrison. The center offers programs ranging from basic homework help to subject-specific enrichment.

27959 ■ *Ahead of the Curve: Two Years at Harvard Business School*
Pub: Penguin Group USA Inc.
Ed: Philip Delves Broughton. **Released:** 2009. **Price:** $25.95. **Description:** A behind-the-scenes glimpse at Harvard Business School is given. The author believes Harvard succeeds in transforming students into business leaders but feels they are failing them in every other way.

27960 ■ "All Fired Up!" in *Small Business Opportunities* (November 2008)
Pub: Entrepreneur Media Inc.
Ed: Stan Roberts. **Description:** Profile of Brixx Wood Fired Pizza, which has launched a franchising program due to the amount of interest the company's founders received over the years; franchisees do not need experience in the food industry or pizza restaurant service business in order to open a franchise of their own because all franchisees receive comprehensive training in which they are educated on all of the necessary tools to effectively run the business.

27961 ■ "The Americans Are Coming" in *The Economist* (Vol. 390, January 3, 2009, No. 8612, pp. 44)
Pub: The Economist Newspaper Inc.
Description: Student recruitment consultancies, which help place international students at universities in other countries and offer services such as interpreting or translating guidelines, are discussed; American universities who have shunned these agencies in the past; the result has been that America underperforms in relation to its size with a mere 3.5 percent of students on its campuses that are from abroad.

27962 ■ "Angels for the Jobless; Church Volunteer Groups Give Career Guidance" in *Crain's Detroit Business* (Vol. 24, March 31, 2008, No. 13)
Pub: Crain Communications, Inc.
Ed: Sherri Begin. **Description:** St. Andrew Catholic Church, located in Rochester, offers the St. Andrew Career Mentoring Ministry, a program that brings in professionals who volunteer to aid those seeking jobs or, in numerous cases, new careers.

27963 ■ "Applying to Colleges? Consultants Can Demystify the Process" in *Palm Beach Post* (September 3, 2011)
Pub: Palm Beach Post
Ed: Susan Salisbury. **Description:** More parents are turning to college consultants to help guide them through the process of applying to and choosing the right college or university. These specialized consultants assist with every detail for several years and students can reach them 24/7; costs can vary from several hundred dollars to $10,000 depending on services.

27964 ■ "Apprenticeship: Earn While You Learn" in *Occupational Outlook Quarterly* (Vol. 54, Fall 2010, No. 3, pp. 24)
Pub: U.S. Bureau of Labor Statistics
Description: Paid training, or apprenticeships, are examined. Registered apprenticeship programs conform to certain guidelines and industry-established training standards and may be run by businesses, trade or professional associations, or partnerships with business and unions.

27965 ■ "Aquatic Medications Engender Good Health" in *Pet Product News* (Vol. 64, November 2010, No. 11, pp. 47)
Pub: BowTie Inc.
Ed: Madelaine Heleine. **Description:** Pet supply manufacturers and retailers have been exerting consumer education and preparedness efforts to help aquarium hobbyists in tackling ornamental fish disease problems. Aquarium hobbyists have been also assisted in choosing products that facilitate aquarium maintenance before disease attacks their pet fish.

27966 ■ "Are There Material Benefits To Social Diversity?" in *Hispanic Business* (Vol. 30, September 2008, No. 9, pp. 10)
Pub: Hispanic Business, Inc.
Ed: Brigida Benitez. **Description:** Diversity in American colleges and universities, where students view and appreciate their peers as individuals and do not judge them on the basis of race, gender, or ethnicity is discussed. The benefits of diversity in higher education are also acknowledged by the U.S. Supreme Court and by leading American corporations.

27967 ■ "Artexpo Celebrates 30th Anniversary" in *Art Business News* (Vol. 34, November 2007, No. 11, pp. 18)
Pub: Pfingsten Publishing, LLC
Description: In honor of its 30th anniversary Artexpo New York 2008 will be an unforgettable show offering a collection of fine-art education courses for both trade and consumer attendees and featuring a variety of artists working in all mediums.

27968 ■ "Asterand Eyes Jump to Ann Arbor; TechTown Tenant" in *Crain's Detroit Business* (Vol. 25, June 22, 2009)
Pub: Crain Communications Inc. - Detroit
Ed: Tom Henderson. **Description:** Asterand PLC is considering a move to Ann Arbor from its current location as anchor tenant at TechTown, an incubator and technology park associated with Wayne State University. The university believes the Ann Arbor location's rent is too expensive for the tissue bank company.

27969 ■ "ASU Explores Russian Partnership" in *The Business Journal - Serving Phoenix and the Valley of the Sun* (Vol. 28, September 5, 2008)
Pub: American City Business Journals, Inc.
Ed: Mike Sunnucks. **Description:** Arizona State University is planning to partner with Russia-based St. Petersburg State University (SPSU) regarding research, faculty and student exchange, and other joint efforts. SPSU is one of Russia's leading scientific and research institutions. Arizona State's partnerships with other foreign colleges are also mentioned.

27970 ■ "At This Bakery, Interns' Hope Rises Along With the Bread" in *Chicago Tribune* (October 31, 2008)
Pub: McClatchy-Tribune Information Services
Ed: Mary Schmich. **Description:** Profile of Sweet Miss Givings Bakery and its diverse founder, interns and employees; the bakery was founded by Stan Sloan, an Episcopal priest who started the business to help fund his ministry; Sloan saw a need for jobs for those living with HIV and other disabilities and through the bakery the interns learn the skills needed to eventually find work elsewhere.

27971 ■ "ATI Now Ready to Pounce on Biotech" in *Austin Business JournalInc.* (Vol. 28, August 22, 2008, No. 23, pp. 1)
Pub: American City Business Journals
Ed: Laura Hipp. **Description:** Austin Technology Incubator has entered the biotechnology sector through a program of the University of Texas incubator. The company's bioscience program was set off by a grant from the City of Austin worth $125,000. The growth of Austin's biotechnology sector is examined.

27972 ■ "The Balancing Act: How Busy Executives Make Their Lives Work" in *Black Enterprise* (Vol. 37, February 2007, No. 7, pp. 118)
Pub: Earl G. Graves Publishing Co. Inc.
Ed: Marcia A. Reed-Woodard. **Description:** More than 70 percent of women with children work outside the home, according to a 2005 survey conducted by the U.S. Department of Labor Bureau. One of the biggest struggles these women face is balancing family with career aspirations and climbing the corporate ranks.

27973 ■ "Banks Deposit Reassurance, Calm Customers" in *The Business Journal-Serving Greater Tampa Bay* (Vol. 28, August 22, 2008)
Pub: American City Business Journals, Inc.
Ed: Margie Manning. **Description:** Community banks in the Tampa Bay Area are training tellers and other customer care workers to help reassure customers that their deposits are safe. Other measures to reassure depositors include joining a network that allows banks to share deposits. Additional information on moves community banks are making to reassure consumers is presented.

27974 ■ *Barron's Guide to Graduate Business Schools*
Pub: Barron's Educational Series Inc.
Contact: Eugene Miller, Author
Released: Biennial, latest edition 15th; published August, 2007. **Price:** $18.99, individuals paperback; list price; $17.09, individuals web price. **Covers:** More than 600 colleges offering graduate business degrees, including Master of Business Administration. **Entries Include:** Institution name, address, phone, fax, e-mail, website, enrollment, description of graduate program, admission requirements, availability of financial aid, library and computer facilities, placement programs. Includes information on applications, selection of school, tests, etc. **Arrangement:** Geographical. **Indexes:** Institution name.

27975 ■ "BC Forest Safety Council Unveils Supervisor Course to Respond to Industry Demands" in *Canadian Corporate News* (May 14, 2007)
Pub: Comtex News Network Inc.
Description: BC Forest Safety Council launched the sector's first supervisor training program that will lead to certification of forest supervisors in response to an industry-wide demand for standardized safety training for supervisors

27976 ■ "The Bell Tolls for Thee" in *Canadian Business* (Vol. 81, March 3, 2008, No. 3, pp. 36)
Pub: Rogers Media
Ed: Andrew Wahl. **Description:** Bell Canada has formed the Canadian Coalition for Tomorrow's IT Skills to solve the shortage of technology talent in the country. Canada's total workforce has only around 4%, or 600,000 people employed in information technology-related fields. The aims of the Bell-led coalition, which is supported by different industry associations and 30 corporations, are investigated.

27977 ■ "Best Foot Forward" in *Canadian Business* (Vol. 80, October 22, 2007, No. 21, pp. 115)
Pub: Rogers Media
Ed: Jeremy Shinewald. **Description:** Jeremy Shinewald's mbaMission admissions consulting business helps prospective MBA students with essay writing, mock interview preparation and school selection. The consulting fee for application to one school is $2,250. Details of the business schools' MBA programs and tuition fees are explored.

27978 ■ "Better Card Collecting" in *Canadian Business* (Vol. 80, January 15, 2007, No. 2, pp. 66)
Pub: Rogers Media
Ed: Sarah B. Hood. **Description:** Tips on how to collect business cards and use them for enhancing one's business performance are presented. Targeting specific people, taking notes and giving follow ups are some suggestions.

27979 ■ "The BIG Picture" in *Crain's Cleveland Business* (Vol. 30, June 22, 2009, No. 24, pp. 12)
Pub: Crain Communications, Inc.
Ed: Arielle Kass. **Description:** Entrepreneurs are quick to praise their colleges and universities and attribute both personal and business success to them.

27980 ■ "Biggest UM Landlords" in *Crain's Detroit Business* (Vol. 25, June 15, 2009, No. 24, pp. 1)
Pub: Crain Communications Inc. - Detroit
Description: University of Michigan will purchase the two million-square-foot Pfizer campus in June 2009. The university is the largest occupier of commercial real estate off campus in and around Ann Arbor, Michigan.

27981 ■ "Biz U: Cool for School" in *Entrepreneur* (Vol. 35, October 2007, No. 10, pp. 144)
Pub: Entrepreneur Media Inc.
Ed: Nichole L. Torres. **Description:** Forming a high technology business while still in college has its advantages such as having information resources nearby and having students from various fields to ask for help and advice. School business competitions are also helpful in building networks with investors. Ways that the college environment can be useful to aspiring entrepreneurs, particularly to those who are into high technology business, are discussed.

27982 ■ "Bold Goals Will Require Time" in *Contractor* (Vol. 56, October 2009, No. 10, pp. S2)
Pub: Penton Media, Inc.
Ed: Ted Lower. **Description:** Offering a broad range of courses is the Radiant Panel Association (RPA), an organization that holds education as its top priority. The RPA must lead the industry by raising the educational bar for future installers.

27983 ■ "Bond Hill Cinema Site To See New Life" in *Business Courier* (Vol. 27, October 29, 2010, No. 26, pp. 1)
Pub: Business Courier
Ed: Dan Monk. **Description:** Avondale, Ohio's Corinthian Baptist Church will redevelop the 30-acre former Showcase Cinema property to a mixed-use site that could feature a college, senior home, and retail. Corinthian Baptist, which is one of the largest African-American churches in the region, is also planning to relocate the church.

27984 ■ "Book Smart" in *Hawaii Business* (Vol. 53, December 2007, No. 6, pp. 39)
Pub: Hawaii Business Publishing
Ed: David K. Choo. **Description:** Different parts of a biography entry in the Black Book are examined in relation to their usage in starting a conversation with an executive. The second part, which is the educational background, is considered the most significant of all, due to the amount of information given. The importance of making connections in Hawaii is discussed.

27985 ■ "Boosting Corporate Entrepreneurship Through HRM Practices" in *Human Resource Management* (Vol. 49, July-August 2010, No. 4)
Pub: John Wiley
Ed: Ralf Schmelter, Rene Mauer, Christiane Borsch, Malte Brettel. **Description:** A study was conducted to determine which human resource management (HRM) practices promote corporate entrepreneurship (CE) in small and medium-sized enterprises (SMEs). Findings indicate that staff selection, staff development, training, and staff rewards on CE have a strong impact on SMEs.

27986 ■ "Brad Wall" in *Canadian Business* (Vol. 82, April 27, 2009, No. 7, pp. 9)
Pub: Rogers Media
Ed: Joe Castaldo. **Description:** Saskatchewan Premier Brad Wall believes that the mood in the province is positive, as its economy is one of the few that is expected to post growth in 2009. Wall actively promotes the province in job fairs, offering $20,000 in tuition for recent college and university graduates that relocate in the province for seven years. Wall's views on the province's economy and challenges are presented.

27987 ■ "Bridging the Academic-Practitioner Divide in Marketing Decision Models" in *Journal of Marketing* (Vol. 75, July 2011, No. 4, pp. 196)
Pub: American Marketing Association
Ed: Gary L. Lilien. **Description:** A study to determine the reason for the relatively low level of practical use of the many marketing models is presented. Changing the incentive and reward systems for marketing academics, practitioners, and intermediaries can bring about adoption and implementation improvements. Those changes could be beneficial by bridging the academic-practitioner divide.

27988 ■ "Bridging the Talent Gap Through Partnership and Innovation" in *Canadian Business* (Vol. 81, October 27, 2008, No. 18, pp. 88)
Pub: Rogers Media Ltd.
Description: Research revealed that North America is short by more than 60,000 qualified networking professionals. Businesses, educators and communities are collaborating in order to address the shortfall.

27989 ■ "Budget Woes Endanger E-Prep Progress" in *Crain's Cleveland Business* (Vol. 30, June 22, 2009, No. 24, pp. 6)
Pub: Crain Communications, Inc.
Ed: Brian Tucker. **Description:** The future of the Entrepreneurship Preparatory School located in Cleveland is being threatened by State budget concerns. The charter school requires all students to wear uniforms, respect discipline, and attend for longer hours and more weeks.

27990 ■ *Business Black Belt: Develop the Strength, Flexibility and Agility to Run Your Company*
Pub: Career Press, Inc.
Ed: Burke Franklin. **Released:** November 1, 2010. **Price:** $15.99. **Description:** Manual offering insights that will enable anyone to become successful in small business. Seventy short chapters included topics such as attitude, management, marketing, selling, employees, money, MBAs, lawyers, consultants, and investors.

27991 ■ "Business Plan Refines Focus" in *Business Journal Portland* (Vol. 27, December 10, 2010, No. 41, pp. 1)
Pub: Portland Business Journal
Ed: Wendy Culverwell. **Description:** Organizers of the Oregon Business Plan's Leadership Summit 2010 seek the opinions of nearly 1,000 business, education, political, and civic leaders in an effort to address how to rehabilitate Oregon's economy. The opinion-seeking actions recognize the organizers' belief that the economic fate of the state depends on rural Oregon.

27992 ■ *The Campus CEO: The Student Entrepreneur's Guide to Launching a Multi-Million Dollar Business*
Pub: Kaplan Books
Ed: Randal Pinkett. **Released:** February 2007. **Price:** $21.00 (CND). **Description:** Tips for generating income, while attending college is presented to students.

27993 ■ "Canada Tomorrow" in *Canadian Business* (Vol. 80, October 8, 2007, No. 20, pp. 14)
Pub: Rogers Media
Ed: Donald J. Johnston. **Description:** An assessment of Canada's future in terms of its educational, social, and economic environment is presented. Concerns regarding the country's educational system such as the declining interest in science and technology and the possible lack of teachers in the future are discussed. In terms of its social and economic aspects, the need to support entrepreneurs and other qualified people is explained.

27994 ■ "Canadian Research Generates Innovation and Prosperity" in *Canadian Business* (Vol. 81, October 27, 2008, No. 18, pp. 87)
Pub: Rogers Media Ltd.
Description: Universities play a key role in helping Canadians achieve prosperity, competitiveness, and quality of life by conducting more than a third of Canada's research. Research in universities help train graduates to apply sophisticated knowledge to real problems.

27995 ■ "Cancer-Fighting Entrepreneurs" in *Austin Business Journal* (Vol. 31, August 5, 2011, No. 22, pp. 1)
Pub: American City Business Journals Inc.
Ed: Sandra Zaragoza. **Description:** Cancer Prevention and Research Institute of Texas has invested $10 million in recruiting known faculty to the University of Texas. The move is seen to bolster Austin's position as a major cancer research market. The institute has awarded grants to researchers Jonghwan Kim, Guangbin Dong and Kyle Miller.

27996 ■ "A Capitol Opportunity" in *Hispanic Business* (Vol. 30, September 2008, No. 9, pp. 82)
Pub: Hispanic Business, Inc.
Ed: John Schumacher. **Description:** Launched in 2003, the Polanco fellows program is named after former state Senator Richard Polanco, a founder and chairman of the California Latino Caucus Institute. The program offers young Hispanics a chance to experience public policy and the functioning of the California Capitol through a 12-month, on-the-job Capitol training.

27997 ■ "Casinos See College as Job Jackpot" in *The Business Journal-Serving Metropolitan Kansas City* (Vol. 26, August 1, 2008, No. 47)
Pub: American City Business Journals, Inc.
Ed: Suzanna Stagemeyer. **Description:** Wyandotte County casino managers revealed plans to develop partnerships with Kansas City Kansas Community College. The planned partnership is expected to include curriculum development and degree programs that would help train employees for the planned casinos. Other views and information on the project are presented.

27998 ■ "CBC Chief: Future is Now" in *Business Courier* (Vol. 27, August 13, 2010, No. 15, pp. 1)
Pub: Business Courier
Ed: Lucy May. **Description:** Tom Williams, chairman of the Cincinnati Business Committee (CBC), maintains that politicians and business leaders must cooperate to ensure the competitiveness of the city for the 21st Century. Under Williams' leadership, the CBC has put emphasis on initiatives related to government efficiency, economic development, and public education. Williams' views on a proposed inland port are given.

27999 ■ "CBC and Chrysler Strike Deal" in *Black Enterprise* (Vol. 37, December 2006, No. 5, pp. 36)
Pub: Earl G. Graves Publishing Co. Inc.
Ed: Kiara Ashanti. **Description:** Congressional Black Foundation and Chrysler Financial have partnered to provide financial education to students at historically black colleges and universities. The prime objective of the program is to reduce the number of college students that graduate with poor credit scores and high debt.

28000 ■ "The China Connection" in *Crain's Chicago Business* (Vol. 31, March 24, 2008, No. 12, pp. 26)
Pub: Crain Communications, Inc.
Ed: Samantha Stainburn. **Description:** Interview with Ben Munoz who studied abroad in Beijing, China for three months to study international economics, e-commerce and global leadership.

28001 ■ "A Class Act" in *Hawaii Business* (Vol. 53, March 2008, No. 9, pp. 25)
Pub: Hawaii Business Publishing
Ed: Cathy S. Cruz-George. **Description:** UBoost is a startup company that offers online content for the educational magazine 'Weekly Reader'. The website

features quizzes and allows users to accumulate points and redeem rewards afterward. Other details about the company are discussed.

28002 ■ "Class Management" in *Canadian Business* (Vol. 80, April 23, 2007, No. 9, pp. 64)
Pub: Rogers Media
Ed: Erin Pooley. **Description:** The role of executive MBA programs in improving performance of employees is presented.

28003 ■ "College Opens On St. Luke's Site" in *The Business Journal - Serving Phoenix and the Valley of the Sun* (Vol. 28, September 5, 2008)
Pub: American City Business Journals, Inc.
Ed: Angela Gonzales. **Description:** Fortis College is planning to offer classes in Phoenix, Arizona. It has made its home at the St. Luke's Medical Center. Courses to be offered by the college are also provided.

28004 ■ "The Colt Effect" in *Hawaii Business* (Vol. 53, January 2008, No. 7, pp. 30)
Pub: Hawaii Business Publishing
Ed: David K. Choo. **Description:** Participation at the Bowl Championship Games can help the University of Hawaii financially. Playing at a prominent sports event could provoke donations from alumni and increase enrollment at the university. Examples of universities that earned generous income by becoming a part of prestigious sporting events are presented.

28005 ■ "Companies Urged to Take Steps to Replenish Work Force" in *Crain's Cleveland Business* (Vol. 28, October 29, 2007, No. 43, pp. 9)
Pub: Crain Communications, Inc.
Ed: Mike Verespej. **Description:** If America wants to stay competitive in the global marketplace, experts say that the education system will need serious improvements. According to Thomas J. Donahue, president and CEO of the U.S. Chamber of Commerce, one-third of the K-through-12 students in the United States don't graduate from high school.

28006 ■ "The Competitive Imperative Of Learning" in *Harvard Business Review* (Vol. 86, July-August 2008, No. 8, pp. 60)
Pub: Harvard Business School Press
Ed: Amy C. Edmondson. **Description:** Experimentation and reflection are important components for maintaining success in the business world and are the kind of character traits that can help one keep his or her competitive edge.

28007 ■ "Contractors Debate Maximizing Green Opportunities, Education" in *Contractor* (Vol. 56, November 2009, No. 11, pp. 3)
Pub: Penton Media, Inc.
Ed: Robert P. Mader. **Description:** Attendees at the Mechanical Service Co ntractors Association convention were urged to get involved with their local U.S. Green Building Council chapter by one presenter. Another presenter says that one green opportunity for contractors is the commissioning of new buildings.

28008 ■ "Convention Calendar" in *Black Enterprise* (Vol. 37, November 2006, No. 4, pp. 76)
Pub: Earl G. Graves Publishing Co. Inc.
Description: Listing of conferences targeted at African American executives and business owners.

28009 ■ "Conversation: Historian Geoffrey Jones On Why Knowledge Stays Put" in *Harvard Business Review* (Vol. 86, July-August 2008, No. 8)
Pub: Harvard Business School Press
Ed: Gardiner Morse. **Description:** Geoffrey Jones, Harvard Business School's professor of business history, discusses factors that cause knowledge to concentrate in particular regions, rather than disperse, such as the location of wealth.

28010 ■ "Could UNCC Be Home to Future Med School Here?" in *Charlotte Business Journal* (Vol. 25, July 23, 2010, No. 18, pp. 1)
Pub: Charlotte Business Journal
Ed: Jennifer Thomas. **Description:** University of North Carolina, Charlotte chancellor Phil Dubois is proposing that a medical school be established at the campus. The idea began in 2007 and Dubois' plan is for students to spend all four years in Charlotte and train at the Carolinas Medical Center.

28011 ■ "David Saunders Q&A" in *Canadian Business* (Vol. 80, October 22, 2007, No. 21, pp. 11)
Pub: Rogers Media
Ed: Erin Pooley. **Description:** David Saunders, chairman of the Federation of Business School Deans, talks about the changes in business education in Canada. He stresses that a master's degree in business administration is vital and a good investment that would reap rewards in a business career.

28012 ■ "Day Care for Affluent Drawing a Crowd" in *Business First Columbus* (Vol. 24, August 15, 2008, No. 52, pp. 1)
Pub: American City Business Journals
Ed: Carrie Ghose. **Description:** Day care centers for affluent families have grown in popularity in Columbus, Ohio. Primrose Schools Franchising Company has opened three such schools in the area. Statistical data included.

28013 ■ "Day-Care Center Owner to Argue Against Liquor Store Opening Nearby" in *Chicago Tribune* (March 13, 2008)
Pub: McClatchy-Tribune Information Services
Ed: Matthew Walberg. **Description:** NDLC's owner feels that Greenwood Liquors should not be granted its liquor license due to the claim that the NDLC is not only a day-care center but also a school that employs state-certified teachers.

28014 ■ "Deal Made for Pontiac Home of Film Studio" in *Crain's Detroit Business* (Vol. 25, June 1, 2009, No. 22, pp. 3)
Pub: Crain Communications Inc. - Detroit
Ed: Daniel Duggan. **Description:** Details of the $75 million movie production and training facility in Pontiac, Michigan are revealed.

28015 ■ "Deep Thoughts: Getting Employees to Think Better Requires a Bit of Creative Thinking Itself" in *Canadian Business* (March 17, 2008)
Pub: Rogers Media
Ed: Lauren McKeon. **Description:** Discusses the reason a company needs to make their employees understand that ideas are the stuff of life. For employees to be more creative, they need to cultivate spark moments, play with possibilities, and venture into the unknown.

28016 ■ "Defensive Training" in *Crain's Detroit Business* (Vol. 24, September 22, 2008, No. 38, pp. 11)
Pub: Crain Communications, Inc.
Ed: Robert Ankeny. **Description:** Rising retaliation claims in regards to discrimination complaints are creating an atmosphere in which managers must learn how to avoid or deal with these lawsuits as well as the retaliation that often follows. Examples of cases are given as well as advice for dealing with such problems that may arise in the workplace.

28017 ■ "DePaul To Train Hotel Leaders" in *Chicago Tribune* (September 22, 2008)
Pub: McClatchy-Tribune Information Services
Ed: Kathy Bergen. **Description:** With help from a $7.5 million grant from the Conrad N. Hilton Foundation, DePaul University will dramatically expand its role as a training ground for the tourism-industry with the opening of a School of Hospitality.

28018 ■ "Design program in Athletic Footwear" in *Occupational Outlook Quarterly* (Vol. 55, Fall 2011, No. 3, pp. 21)
Pub: U.S. Bureau of Labor Statistics
Description: The Fashion Institute of Technology offers the only certificate program in performance athletic footwear design in the U.S. The program focuses on conceptualizing and sketching shoe designs and covers ergonomic, anatomical, and material considerations for athletic footwear design.

28019 ■ "Developers Vie for UWM Dorm" in *The Business Journal-Milwaukee* (Vol. 25, July 11, 2008, No. 42, pp. A1)
Pub: American City Business Journals, Inc.
Ed: Rich Kirchen. **Description:** Eight developers are competing to build a 500- to 700-student residence hall for the University of Wisconsin-Milwaukee. The residence hall will probably be developed within two miles of the main campus. It was revealed that the university's real estate foundation will select the successful bidder on July 25, 2008, and construction will begin by January 2009.

28020 ■ "Dick Haskayne" in *Canadian Business* (Vol. 81, March 31, 2008, No. 5, pp. 72)
Pub: Rogers Media
Ed: Andy Holloway. **Description:** Dick Haskayne says that he learned a lot about business from his dad who ran a butcher shop where they had to make a decision on buying cattle and getting credit. Haskayne says that family, friends, finances, career, health, and infrastructure are benchmarks that have to be balanced.

28021 ■ "Dr. Mark Holder" in *Crain's Cleveland Business* (Vol. 30, June 29, 2009, No. 25, pp. 14)
Pub: Crain Communications, Inc.
Ed: Kathy Ames Carr. **Description:** Dr. Mark Holder is the director of the financial engineering program at Kent State University. Dr. Holder discusses his role to help teach his students how to market themselves for finance jobs in a down economy.

28022 ■ "Don't Shoot the Messenger: A Wake-Up Call For Academics" in *Academy of Management Journal* (Vol. 50, No. 5, October 2007, pp. 1020)
Pub: Academy of Management
Ed: David E. Guest. **Description:** Author evaluates two well-known publications: HR Magazine and People Management, to emphasize the role of U.S. academics in communicating management practice.

28023 ■ "Downtowns Must Court Young, CEOs for Cities President Says" in *Crain's Detroit Business* (Vol. 24, October 6, 2008, No. 40, pp. 18)
Pub: Crain Communications, Inc.
Ed: Amy Lane. **Description:** It is important to produce more college graduates, and keep them in Michigan, according to CEOs for Cities President Carol Coletta when she spoke to a session at the West Michigan Regional Policy Conference which was held in September in Grand Rapids. Ways in which city leaders can connect students to communities, resulting in employees who have vested interest in the region, are also discussed.

28024 ■ "Dozens 'Come Alive' in Downtown Chicago" in *Green Industry Pro* (July 2011)
Pub: Cygnus Business Media
Ed: Gregg Wartgow. **Description:** Highlights from the Come Alive Outside training event held in Chicago, Illinois July 14-15, 2011 are shared. Nearly 80 people representing 38 landscape companies attended the event that helps contractors review their services and find ways to sell them in new and various ways.

28025 ■ "The Early Bird Gets the Worm" in *Black Enterprise* (Vol. 37, January 2007, No. 6, pp. 111)
Pub: Earl G. Graves Publishing Co. Inc.
Ed: Tykisha N. Lundy. **Description:** General Motors hosts the Black Enterprise Conference And Expo: Where Deals Are Made at Walt Disney World's Swan and Dolphin Resort, May 9-12. The conference will offer great information to entrepreneurs.

28026 ■ "East Coast Solar" in *Contractor* (Vol. 57, February 2010, No. 2, pp. 17)
Pub: Penton Media, Inc.
Ed: Dave Yates. **Description:** U.S. Department of Energy's Solar Decathlon lets 20 college student-led

teams from around the world compete to design and build a solar-powered home. A mechanical contractor discusses his work as an advisor during the competition.

28027 ■ "An Educated Play on China" in *Barron's* (Vol. 88, June 30, 2008, No. 26, pp. M6)
Pub: Dow Jones & Co., Inc.
Ed: Mohammed Hadi. **Description:** New Oriental Education & Technology Group sells English-language courses to an increasingly competitive Chinese workforce that values education. The shares in this company have been weighed down by worries on the impact of the Beijing Olympics on enrollment and the Sichuan earthquake. These shares could be a great way to get exposure to the long-term growth in China.

28028 ■ "EMU, Spark Plan Business Incubator for Ypsilanti" in *Crain's Detroit Business* (Vol. 23, October 15, 2007, No. 42, pp. 3)
Pub: Crain Communications Inc. - Detroit
Ed: Chad Halcom. **Description:** Eastern Michigan University is seeking federal grants and other funding for a new business incubator program that would be in cooperation with Ann Arbor Spark. The site would become a part of a network of three Spark incubator programs with a focus on innovation in biotechnology and pharmaceuticals.

28029 ■ "Encouraging Study in Critical Languages" in *Occupational Outlook Quarterly* (Vol. 55, Summer 2011, No. 2, pp. 23)
Pub: U.S. Bureau of Labor Statistics
Description: Proficiency in particular foreign languages is vital to the defense, diplomacy, and security of the United States. Several federal programs provide scholarships and other funding to encourage high school and college students to learn languages of the Middle East, China, and Russia.

28030 ■ "Endowments for Colleges Hit Hard in '09" in *Milwaukee Business Journal* (Vol. 27, February 12, 2010, No. 20, pp. A1)
Pub: American City Business Journals
Ed: Corrinne Hess. **Description:** Southeast Wisconsin college endowments declined by as much as 35 percent in 2009 due to the economic downturn. A list of 2009 endowments to colleges in southeast Wisconsin and their percent change from 2008 is presented.

28031 ■ *Enlightened Leadership: Best Practice Guidelines and Time Tools for Easily Implementing Learning Organizations*
Pub: Learning House Publishing, Inc.
Ed: Ralph LoVuolo; Alan G. Thomas. **Released:** May 2006. **Price:** $79.99. **Description:** Innovation and creativity are essential for any successful small business. The book provides owners, managers, and team leaders with the tools necessary to produce "disciplined innovation".

28032 ■ *Enlightened Leadership: Best Practice Guidelines and Timesaving Tools for Easily Implementing Learning Organizations*
Pub: Learning House Publishing, Incorporated
Ed: Alan G. Thomas; Ralph L. LoVuolo; Jeanne C. Hillson. **Released:** September 2006, printable 3 times/year. **Price:** $21.00. **Description:** Book provides the tools required to create a learning organization management model along with a step-by-step guide for team planning and learning. The strategy works as a manager's self-help guide as well as offering continuous learning and improvement for company-wide success.

28033 ■ "Essentially Organic Vending Takes Healthy Snacks to Ohio High School" in *Entertainment Close-Up* (September 13, 2011)
Pub: Close-Up Media
Description: Essentially Organic Vending is offering students a healthy alternative for their snacking. The vending machines will be stocked with nutritious energy options.

28034 ■ "Etextbook Space Heats Up" in *Information Today* (Vol. 28, November 2011, No. 10, pp. 10)
Pub: Information Today, Inc.
Ed: Paula J. Hane. **Description:** The use of etextbooks is expected to grow with the use of mobile devices and tablets. A new group of activists is asking students, faculty members and others to sign a petition urging higher education leaders to prioritize affordable textbooks or free ebooks over the traditional, expensive new books required for classes.

28035 ■ "Etextbooks: Coming of Age" in *Information Today* (Vol. 28, September 2011, No. 8, pp. 1)
Pub: Information Today, Inc.
Ed: Amanda Mulvihill. **Description:** National average for textbooks costs was estimated at $1,137 annually at a 4-year public college for the 2010-2011 school year. Amazon reported selling 105 etextbooks for every 100 print books, while Barnes and Noble announced that their etextbooks were outselling print 3 to 1.

28036 ■ "EVMS Gets Grant to Train Providers for Elder Care" in *Virginian-Pilot* (October 29, 2010)
Pub: Virginian-Pilot
Ed: Elizabeth Simpson. **Description:** Eastern Virginia Medical School received a federal grant to train health providers in elder care. Details of the program are provided.

28037 ■ "Executive Training" in *Black Enterprise* (Vol. 37, December 2006, No. 5, pp. 70)
Pub: Earl G. Graves Publishing Co. Inc.
Ed: Marcia A. Reed-Woodard. **Description:** Roy N. Gundy Jr. was preparing to introduce a new strategic plan within his division and understood that his plan may fail if not executed properly. He discusses his experience in the Wharton School's executive education workshop Implementing Strategy, at the University of Pennsylvania and gives tips on putting strategy into action.

28038 ■ "Experts Strive to Educate on Proper Pet Diets" in *Pet Product News* (Vol. 64, November 2010, No. 11, pp. 40)
Pub: BowTie Inc.
Ed: John Hustace Walker. **Description:** Pet supply manufacturers have been bundling small mammal food and treats with educational sources to help retailers avoid customer misinformation. This action has been motivated by the customer's quest to seek proper nutritional advice for their small mammal pets.

28039 ■ "Export Initiative Launched" in *Philadelphia Business Journal* (Vol. 28, December 11, 2009, No. 43, pp. 1)
Pub: American City Business Journals
Ed: Athena D. Merritt. **Description:** The first initiative that came out of the partnership between the Export-Import Bank of the US, the city of Philadelphia, and the World Trade Center of Greater Philadelphia is presented. A series of export finance workshops have featured Ex-Im Bank resources that can provide Philadelphia businesses with working capital, insurance protection and buyer financing.

28040 ■ "Facilitating and Rewarding Creativity During New Product Development" in *Journal of Marketing* (Vol. 75, July 2011, No. 4, pp. 53)
Pub: American Marketing Association
Ed: James E. Burroughs, Darren W. Dahl, C. Page Moreau, Amitava Chattopadhay, Gerald J. Gorn. **Description:** A study to determine the effects of rewards to creativity in the process of new product development is presented. The findings show that the effect of rewards can be made positive if combined with appropriate creativity training.

28041 ■ "Feds to Pay University $20M" in *Business Courier* (Vol. 27, July 23, 2010, No. 12, pp. 3)
Pub: Business Courier
Ed: James Ritchie. **Description:** The U.S. government is set to pay University Hospital and medical residents who trained there $20 million as part of a tax dispute settlement. Around 1,000 former residents are to receive tax refunds. But the hospital must provide the U.S. Internal Revenue Service with extensive documentation.

28042 ■ "Fighting the Good Fight" in *Inc.* (Vol. 33, October 2011, No. 8, pp. 8)
Pub: Inc. Magazine
Ed: Eric Markowitz. **Description:** Rob Roy, former Navy SEAL, runs SOT-G a firm that offers an 80-hour leadership training course inspired by military combat preparations. Details of the program are outlined.

28043 ■ "Finding Life Behind the Numbers" in *Crain's Chicago Business* (Vol. 31, March 24, 2008, No. 12, pp. 25)
Pub: Crain Communications, Inc.
Ed: Samantha Stainburn. **Description:** Interview with Phillip Capodice who is a graduate student at DePaul University's Kellstadt Graduate School of Business and studied abroad in Lima, Peru where he visited a number of companies including some who are trade partners with the United States.

28044 ■ "Finishing High School Leads to Better Employment Prospects" in *Occupational Outlook Quarterly* (Vol. 55, Summer 2011, No. 2, pp. 36)
Pub: U.S. Bureau of Labor Statistics
Description: Students who drop out of high school are more likely to face unemployment than those who finish. Statistical data included.

28045 ■ "Fitness: Dispelling Rocky Mountain Myths Key to Wellness" in *Employee Benefit News* (Vol. 25, November 1, 2011, No. 14, pp. 12)
Pub: SourceMedia Inc.
Ed: Andrea Davis. **Description:** Andrew Sykes, chairman of Health at Work Wellness Actuaries, states that it is a myth that Colorado is ranked as the healthiest state in America. Sykes helped implement a wellness programs at Brighton School District in the Denver area.

28046 ■ "Five New Scientists Bring Danforth Center $16 Million" in *Saint Louis Business Journal* (Vol. 32, October 7, 2011, No. 6, pp. 1)
Pub: Saint Louis Business Journal
Ed: E.B. Solomont. **Description:** Donald Danforth Plant Science Center's appointment of five new lead scientists has increased its federal funding by $16 million. Cornell University scientist Tom Brutnell is one of the five new appointees.

28047 ■ "Five Steps for Handling Independent Contractors" in *Hawaii Business* (Vol. 53, January 2008, No. 7, pp. 49)
Pub: Hawaii Business Publishing
Ed: Jason Ubay. **Description:** Small companies should be cautious in dealing with independent contractors. They must understand that they cannot dictate specific operational procedures, job duties, standards of conduct and performance standards to the contractors, and they cannot interfere with the evaluation and training of the contractors' employees. Tips on negotiating with independent contractors are given.

28048 ■ "Follow the ABCs of Buying a Business" in *Women Entrepreneur* (September 10, 2008)
Pub: Entrepreneur Media Inc.
Ed: Nina Kaufman. **Description:** Buying a business will likely result in the largest single asset one will ever own. A list of steps one can take in order to educate and protect themselves is provided.

28049 ■ "Forget the Elaborate Business Plans, Kids With Passion Are Our Next Great Entrepreneurs" in *Inc.* (October 2007, pp. 87-88)
Pub: Gruner & Jahr USA Publishing
Description: George Gendron, founder and executive director of the Innovation and Entrepreneurship Program at Clark University, stresses the importance of encouraging business students in his entrepreneur-

ial program to follow their passion. The program is dedicated to real-world entrepreneurship by creating businesses rather than business plans.

28050 ■ "Forward Motion" in *Green Industry Pro* (July 2011)
Pub: Cygnus Business Media
Ed: Gregg Wartgow. **Description:** Several landscape contractors have joined this publication's Working Smarter Training Challenge over the last year. This process is helping them develop ways to improve work processes, boost morale, drive out waste, reduce costs, improve customer service, and be more competitive.

28051 ■ "Funbrain Launches Preschool Content" in *Marketing to Women* (Vol. 21, March 2008, No. 3, pp. 3)
Pub: EPM Communications, Inc.
Description: Funbrain.com launches The Moms and Kids Playground, a section of the website devoted to activities and games for moms and kids aged 2 to 6; content aims at building early computer skills and to teach basic concepts such as counting and colors.

28052 ■ "Future Autoworkers will Need Broader Skills" in *Crain's Detroit Business* (Vol. 25, June 8, 2009, No. 23, pp. 13)
Pub: Crain Communications Inc. - Detroit
Ed: Ryan Beene. **Description:** Auto industry observers report that new workers in the industry will need advanced skills and educational backgrounds in engineering and technical fields because jobs in the factories will become more technology-based and multidisciplinary.

28053 ■ "The Future Is Another Country; Higher Education" in *The Economist* (Vol. 390, January 3, 2009, No. 8612, pp. 43)
Pub: The Economist Newspaper Inc.
Description: Due to the growth of the global corporation, more ambitious students are studying at universities abroad; the impact of this trend is discussed.

28054 ■ "Get With the Program" in *Entrepreneur* (Vol. 36, April 2008, No. 4, pp. 130)
Pub: Entrepreneur Media, Inc.
Ed: Nichole L. Torres. **Description:** Entrepreneurship initiatives help college students get connected with other students, teach them about how to start their own business while still in school, and help with funding. Some of these programs are the Harold Grinspoon Charitable Foundation's Entrepreneurship Initiative and the Syracuse Campus-Community Entrepreneurship Initiative.

28055 ■ "Give 'Em a Break" in *Entrepreneur* (Vol. 35, November 2007, No. 11, pp. 32)
Pub: Entrepreneur Media Inc.
Ed: J.J. Ramberg. **Description:** Andy Walter and Peer Pedersen founded Blue Orchid Capital, a fund of hedge funds, and Steamboat Foundation a foundation that helps college students find high-profile summer internships. Details on the fund and the foundation are presented.

28056 ■ "Giving Biotech Startups a Hand" in *Philadelphia Business Journal* (Vol. 28, January 8, 2010, No. 47, pp. 1)
Pub: American City Business Journals
Ed: John George. **Description:** Elkins Park, Pennsylvania-based BioStrategy Partners is a virtual life sciences incubator that is seeking to improve the dull ranking of Philadelphia in the small business vitality index of life sciences. BioStrategy provides technology and business development services to startup life sciences companies and university-based research projects.

28057 ■ "Glendale Pumping $29 Million Into Redevelopment" in *The Business Journal - Serving Phoenix and the Valley of the Sun* (Vol. 28, August 1, 2008, No. 48, pp. 1)
Pub: American City Business Journals, Inc.
Ed: Mike Sunnucks. **Description:** Glendale City is planning to invest $29 million to improve city infrastructure like roadways and water and sewer lines over the next five years. Glendale's city council is also planning to hold a workshop on the redevelopment projects in September 2008. Other views and information on the redevelopment project, are presented.

28058 ■ "Going for the APEX" in *Women In Business* (Vol. 62, September 2010, No. 3, pp. 28)
Pub: American Business Women's Association
Description: Information about the American Business Women's Association (ABWA) professional development tools, which keep members focused on personal excellence, is presented. The organization recently launched the APEX (Achieving Personal Excellence) Award to honor women who are making a commitment to themselves.

28059 ■ "Goodbye, Locker Room: Hello, Boardroom" in *Inc.* (Vol. 33, October 2011, No. 8, pp. 30)
Pub: Inc. Magazine
Ed: Issie Lapowsky, Kasey Wehrum. **Description:** In 2005, the National Football League started the NFL Business Management and Entrepreneurial Program. Since the onset of the program, 700 players have participated in the program which takes place at the business schools of Harvard, the University of Pennsylvania, Northwestern and Stanford.

28060 ■ "Groomers Eye Profit Growth Through Services" in *Pet Product News* (Vol. 64, December 2010, No. 12, pp. 26)
Pub: BowTie Inc.
Ed: Kathleen M. Mangan. **Description:** Pet groomers can successfully offer add-on services by taking into account insider customer knowledge, store image, and financial analysis in the decision-making process. Many pet groomers have decided to add services such as spa treatments and training due to a slump in the bathing and grooming business. How some pet groomers gained profitability through add-on services is explored.

28061 ■ "Group Learning" in *Academy of Management Review* (October 2007, pp. 1041)
Pub: ScholarOne, Inc.
Ed: Jeanne M. Wilson, Paul S. Goodman, Matthew A. Cronin. **Description:** The processes that constitute group learning in order to undertake necessary modifications are covered.

28062 ■ "Growing Your Business Through BPI Certification" in *Indoor Comfort Marketing* (Vol. 70, May 2011, No. 5, pp. 12)
Pub: Industry Publications Inc.
Ed: Scott Vadino. **Description:** Profile of the Building Performance Institute and the ways BPI certification will help grow a heating, ventilation, cooling firm.

28063 ■ "Guts Not Included" in *Canadian Business* (Vol. 81, March 31, 2008, No. 5, pp. 46)
Pub: Rogers Media
Ed: Andrew Wahl. **Description:** Executives need the vision to create a strategy that prepares for an uncertain future in light of growing global competition. Canadian business leaders have the right skills and education but do not have enough tolerance for risk.

28064 ■ "Head of the Class" in *Entrepreneur* (Vol. 37, October 2009, No. 10, pp. 59)
Pub: Entrepreneur Media, Inc.
Description: Top 25 graduate and undergraduate entrepreneurship programs in the US for 2009 as ranked by The Princeton Review are listed. Babson College in Wellesley, Massachusetts topped both categories.

28065 ■ "Henry Mintzberg: Still the Zealous Skeptic and Scold" in *Strategy and Leadership* (Vol. 39, March-April 2011, No. 2, pp. 4)
Pub: Emerald Group Publishing Inc.
Ed: Robert J. Allio. **Description:** Henry Mintzberg, professor at the McGill University in Montreal, Canada, shares his thoughts on issues such as inappropriate methods in management education and on trends in leadership and management. Mintzberg believes that US businesses are facing serious management and leadership challenges.

28066 ■ "Higher Education" in *Canadian Business* (Vol. 79, October 23, 2006, No. 21, pp. 129)
Pub: Rogers Media
Ed: Erin Pooley; Laura Bogomolny; Joe Castaldo; Michelle Magnan. **Description:** Details of some Canadian business schools, where students can simultaneously pursue a master of business administration degree and also be employed on a part time basis, are presented.

28067 ■ "Hire Education" in *Canadian Business* (Vol. 79, September 11, 2006, No. 18, pp. 114)
Pub: Rogers Media
Ed: Erin Pooley. **Description:** Study results showing the perceptions of students while considering full-time employment and the attributes they look for in their future employers are presented.

28068 ■ "His Brother's Keeper: a Mentor Learns the True Meaning of Leadership" in *Black Enterprise* (Vol. 37, December 2006, No. 5, pp. 69)
Pub: Earl G. Graves Publishing Co. Inc.
Ed: Laura Egodigwe. **Description:** Interview with Keith R. Wyche of Pitney Bowes Management Services which discusses the relationship between a mentor and mentee as well as sponsorship.

28069 ■ "Hit the Books" in *Entrepreneur* (Vol. 36, April 2008, No. 4, pp. 74)
Pub: Entrepreneur Media, Inc.
Ed: Nichole L. Torres. **Description:** Lists of the top business schools in different U.S. universities are presented. These lists are categorized according to best professors, best classroom experience, most competitive students, greatest opportunity for women, and greatest opportunity for minority students. The lists, compiled by the Princeton Review, are based on student opinion.

28070 ■ "Hitting the E-Books" in *Inc.* (Vol. 33, September 2011, No. 7, pp. 36)
Pub: Inc. Magazine
Ed: Shivani Vora. **Description:** Textbooks may be getting cheaper for college students now that they can use electronic textbooks that can be read on a laptop or tablet. The market is growing about 50 percent annually. Statistical data included.

28071 ■ "Holy Wasabi! Sushi Not Just For Parents Anymore" in *Chicago Tribune* (March 13, 2008)
Pub: McClatchy-Tribune Information Services
Ed: Christopher Borrelli. **Description:** Wicker Park cooking school, The Kid's Table, specializes in cooking classes for pre-teens; Elena Marre who owns the school was surprised when she was asked to plan a children's party in which she would teach a course in sushi making. More and more adolescents and small children are eating sushi.

28072 ■ "Home Grown" in *Hawaii Business* (Vol. 53, November 2007, No. 5, pp. 51)
Pub: Hawaii Business Publishing
Ed: Jolyn Okimoto Rosa. **Description:** Discusses a program that focuses on Native Hawaiian entrepreneurs and offers business training at the Kapiolani Community College; upon completion of the program, participants may apply for a loan provided by the Office of Hawaiian Affairs (OHA) to help them start their business. OHA plans to present the restructured loan program in November 2007, with aims of shortening the loan process.

28073 ■ "Hopkins' Security, Reputation Face Challenges in Wake of Slaying" in *Baltimore Business Journal* (Vol. 28, August 6, 2010, No. 13)
Pub: Baltimore Business Journal
Ed: Gary Haber. **Description:** The slaying of Johns Hopkins University researcher Stephen Pitcairn has not tarnished the reputation of the elite school in Baltimore, Maryland among students. Maintaining Hopkins' reputation is important since it is Baltimore's largest employer with nearly 32,000 workers. Insights on the impact of the slaying among the Hopkins' community are also given.

28074 ■ *How to Hire, Train, and Keep the Best Employees for Your Small Business*
Pub: Atlantic Publishing Company
Ed: Dianna Podmoroff. **Released:** June 2004. **Price:** $29.95. **Description:** Costs of hiring, training, and lost productivity costs related to losing employees.

28075 ■ "How to Survive This Mess" in *Crain's Chicago Business* (Vol. 31, April 14, 2008, No. 15, pp. 18)
Pub: Crain Communications, Inc.
Ed: Christina Le Beau. **Description:** Small business owners can make it through a possible recession with preparations such as reviewing their balance sheet and cash flow every week and spotting trends then reacting quickly to them.

28076 ■ "How Will You Ever Replace Yourself?" in *Canadian Business* (Vol. 83, August 17, 2010, No. 13-14, pp. 77)
Pub: Rogers Media Ltd.
Ed: Jacqueline Nelson. **Description:** SoftBank founder and CEO masayoshi Son created his very own school called SoftBank Academia in order to pick a successor that will follow his footprint. Son's strategy is extreme but other corporate leaders should pay attention to succession planning.

28077 ■ "Human Resource Management: Challenges for Graduate Education" in *Business Horizons* (Vol. 51, March-April 2008, No. 2, pp. 151)
Pub: Elsevier Advanced Technology Publications
Ed: James C. Wimbush. **Description:** Human resource management education at the master's and doctoral degree levels is discussed. There is an ever-increasing need to produce human resource managers who understand the value of human resource management as a strategic business contributor. uman

28078 ■ "Innovation Station" in *Canadian Business* (Vol. 80, October 8, 2007, No. 20, pp. 42)
Pub: Rogers Media
Ed: Andrew Wahl. **Description:** Study and teaching of entrepreneurship at the University of Waterloo is discussed. Research projects in the university are expected to be influential in Canada's economic development. In spite of the success of these studies, financing is still a problem for the university, especially in technological innovations.

28079 ■ "The Innovator: Rob McEwen's Unique Vision of Philanthropy and Business" in *Canadian Business* (Vol. 81, November 10, 2008, No. 19)
Pub: Rogers Media Ltd.
Ed: Alex Mlynek. **Description:** Rob McEwen says that his donation to the Schulich School of Business is his first large donation. He went to the University Health Network and was told about their pan for regenerative medicine, helping him make the decision. McEwan wants to be involved in philanthropy in the areas of leadership and education.

28080 ■ "Innovators Critical in Technical Economy" in *Crain's Cleveland Business* (Vol. 28, November 5, 2007, No. 44, pp. 10)
Pub: Crain Communications, Inc.
Ed: Peter Rea. **Description:** Discusses the importance to attract, develop and retain talented innovators on Ohio's economy. Also breaks down the four fronts on which the international battle for talent is being waged.

28081 ■ "Integrating Business Core Knowledge through Upper Division Report Composition" in *Business Communication Quarterly* (December 2007)
Pub: Sage Publications USA
Ed: Joy Roach, Daniel Tracy, Kay Durden. **Description:** An assignment that integrates subjects and encourages the use of business communication report-writing skills is presented. This assignment is designed to complement business school curricula and help develop critical thinking and organizational skills.

28082 ■ *International Entrepreneurship Education Issues and Newness*
Pub: Edward Elgar Publishing, Incorporated
Ed: Fayolle. **Released:** August 2006. **Price:** $120.00. **Description:** Entrepreneurial education, focusing on economic, political and social needs of a changing world; ideas for reassessing, redeveloping, and renewing curricula and methods for teaching entrepreneurship are offered.

28083 ■ "International Growth" in *Black Enterprise* (Vol. 38, July 2008, No. 12, pp. 64)
Pub: Earl G. Graves Publishing Co. Inc.
Ed: Marcia A. Reed-Woodard. **Description:** Becoming an increasingly smaller portion of the global business environment is the U.S. economy. Christopher Catlin, an associate with Booz Allen Hamilton, a technology management and strategy-consulting firm, shares what he has learned about the global market.

28084 ■ *International Handbook of Women and Small Business Entrepreneurship*
Pub: Edward Elgar Publishing, Incorporated
Ed: Sandra L. Fielden, Marilyn Davidson. **Released:** December 2006. **Price:** $50.00. **Description:** The number of women entrepreneurs is growing at a faster rate than male counterparts worldwide. Insight into the phenomenon is targeted to scholars and students of women in management and entrepreneurship as well as policymakers and small business service providers.

28085 ■ *Introduction to Business*
Pub: The McGraw-Hill Companies
Ed: Laura Portolese Dias, Amit J. Shah. **Released:** January 1, 2009. **Price:** $70.94. **Description:** Introduction to business course discusses the changing educational environment for teaching business courses in colleges and universities.

28086 ■ "Is Business Ethics Getting Better? A Historical Perspective" in *Business Ethics Quarterly* (Vol. 21, April 2011, No. 2, pp. 335)
Pub: Society for Business Ethics
Ed: Joanne B. Ciulla. **Description:** The question 'Is Business Ethics Getting Better?' as a heuristic for discussing the importance of history in understanding business and ethics is answered. The article uses a number of examples to illustrate how the same ethical problems in business have been around for a long time. It describes early attempts at the Harvard School of Business to use business history as a means of teaching students about moral and social values. In the end, the author suggests that history may be another way to teach ethics, enrich business ethics courses, and develop the perspective and vision in future business leaders.

28087 ■ "It's Not Rocket Science" in *Hispanic Business* (September 2007, pp. 30, 32)
Pub: Hispanic Business
Ed: Hildy Medina. **Description:** Profile of France Cordova, president of Purdue University. Cordova has established many diversity programs at the school.

28088 ■ "Jean-Rober's 'oui'" in *Business Courier* (Vol. 27, August 6, 2010, No. 14, pp. 1)
Pub: Business Courier
Ed: Dan Monk. **Description:** Jean-Robert de Cavel will open his new restaurant in Cincinnati, Ohio. The culinary arts program at Cincinnati State Technical and Community College offered him $100,000 to be its 'chef in residence'. He was able to energize students, boost enrollment, and increase the stature of the culinary program.

28089 ■ "Kids, Computers and the Social Networking Evolution" in *Canadian Business* (Vol. 81, October 27, 2008, No. 18, pp. 93)
Pub: Rogers Media Ltd.
Ed: Penny Milton. **Description:** Social networking was found to help educate students in countries like the U.S., Canada and Mexico. Schools that embrace social networking teach students how to use computers safely and responsibility in order to counter threats to children on the Internet.

28090 ■ "Knowing Is Growing: Five Strategies To Develop You and Your Business" in *Black Enterprise* (Vol. 38, November 2007, No. 4, pp. 106)
Pub: Earl G. Graves Publishing Co. Inc.
Ed: Erinn R. Johnson. **Description:** Five strategies for growing a small business are listed by Andrew Morrison, founder of the Small Business Camp. The camp provides training, coaching, and marketing services to entrepreneurs.

28091 ■ "Knox County Schools Debate Outsourcing Janitorial Services" in (March 29, 2011)
Pub: Knoxville News Sentinel
Ed: Lola Alapo. **Description:** Custodial services of Knox County Schools in Tennessee may be outsourced in move to save money for the school district. Details of the proposed program are included.

28092 ■ "The Labor Crunch is Coming" in *Canadian Business* (Vol. 80, December 25, 2006, No. 1, pp. 74)
Pub: Rogers Media
Description: The need for skilled and educated workforce to meet labor shortage in future in Canada is discussed.

28093 ■ *The Leadership Challenge*
Pub: Jossey-Bass Publishers
Ed: James M. Kouzes, Barry Z. Posner. **Released:** June 30, 1995. **Price:** $22.00. **Description:** According to research by the authors, people can make extraordinary things happen by liberating the leader within everyone around them. This handbook gives practical tips to aspire leaders in retail, manufacturing, government, community, church and school settings.

28094 ■ "Leadership Training" in *Black Enterprise* (Vol. 37, January 2007, No. 6, pp. 56)
Pub: Earl G. Graves Publishing Co. Inc.
Ed: Sonia Alleyne. **Description:** Profile of Theopolis Holman, Group Vice-President of Duke Energy, who discusses how he prepared for the merger between Duke Energy and Cinergy. Holman oversees a division of 9,000 service contractors and employees.

28095 ■ "Leaks in the Pipeline" in *Hispanic Business* (September 2007, pp. 18, 20, 22, 24)
Pub: Hispanic Business
Ed: Holly Ocasio Rizzo. **Description:** Graduate schools need to focus on domestic diversity in order to attract Hispanic students in a growing global economy.

28096 ■ "Learning by Doing: Engaging Students through Learner-Centered Activities" in *Business Communication Quarterly* (Dec. 2007, pp. 451)
Pub: Sage Publications USA
Ed: Karl L. Smart, Nancy Csapo. **Description:** Active learning techniques, such as the Puzzle Brain Spark activity, allow students to engage in learning activities that allow deeper thinking, critical thinking, and problem solving ability that develop business management skills.

28097 ■ "Lessons Learned from Instructional Design Theory" in *Business Communication Quarterly* (December 2007, pp. 414)
Pub: Sage Publications USA
Ed: Lisa A. Burke. **Description:** Instructors should present course information to business students in a way that enhances understanding and should use presentation techniques that students may eventually use; course materials should be kept relevant and simple.

28098 ■ "The Life Changers" in *Canadian Business* (Vol. 81, October 27, 2008, No. 18, pp. 86)
Pub: Rogers Media Ltd.
Description: The first season of 'The Life Changers' was produced in September 2007 to feature stories about research and development (R&D) efforts by

universities in Atlantic Canada. The program addresses the need to inform the public about university R&D and its outcomes.

28099 ■ "Local Researchers Get Cash Infusion" in *Business Courier* (Vol. 26, October 9, 2009, No. 24, pp. 1)
Pub: American City Business Journals, Inc.
Ed: James Ritchie. **Description:** Cincinnati's Children's Hospital Medical Center and the University of Cincinnati researchers are set to receive at least $56 million from the stimulus bill. The cash infusion has reenergized research scientists and enhances Cincinnati's national clout as a major research center.

28100 ■ "The Long View: Roberta Bondar on Science and the Need for Education" in *Canadian Business* (Vol. 81, October 27, 2008, No. 18)
Pub: Rogers Media Ltd.
Ed: Alex Mlynek. **Description:** Roberta Bondar believes that energy and renewable energy is a critical environmental issue faced by Canada today. Bondar is the first Canadian woman and neurologist in space.

28101 ■ "Macomb County, OU Eye Business Incubator" in *Crain's Detroit Business* (Vol. 24, February 11, 2008, No. 6, pp. 1)
Pub: Crain Communications Inc. - Detroit
Ed: Chad Halcom. **Description:** Officials in Macomb County, Michigan are discussing plans to create a defense-themed business incubator in the county. Macomb County was awarded $282,000 in federal budget appropriation for the project.

28102 ■ "Making the Most of Milk to Revive a Falling Market" in *Farmer's Weekly* (March 28, 2008, No. 320)
Pub: Reed Business Information
Description: DairyCo, eight of whom are working dairy farmers, aim to promote a feeding campaign for better herd health, provide research into efficient labor use, and sponsor discussion groups to enhance business skills.

28103 ■ "Making Waves" in *Business Journal Portland* (Vol. 27, November 26, 2010, No. 39, pp. 1)
Pub: Portland Business Journal
Ed: Erik Siemers. **Description:** Corvallis, Oregon-based Columbia Power Technologies LLC is about to close a $2 million Series A round of investment initiated by $750,000 from Oregon Angel Fund. The wave energy startup company was formed to commercialize the wave buoy technology developed by Oregon State University researchers.

28104 ■ "Managing the Facebookers; Business" in *The Economist* (Vol. 390, January 3, 2009, No. 8612, pp. 10)
Pub: Economist Newspaper Ltd.
Description: According to a report from PricewaterhouseCoopers, a business consultancy, workers from Generation Y, also known as the Net Generation, are more difficult to recruit and integrate into companies that practice traditional business acumen. 61 percent of chief executive managers say that they have trouble with younger employees who tend to be more narcissistic and more interested in personal fulfillment with a need for frequent feedback and an overprecise set of objectives on the path to promotion which can be hard for managers who are used to a different relationship with their subordinates. Older bosses should prepare to make some concessions to their younger talent since some of the issues that make them happy include cheaper online ways to communicate and additional coaching, both of which are good for business.

28105 ■ *Managing for Success: The Latest in Management Thought and Practice from Canada's Premier Business School*
Pub: HarperAudio
Ed: Monica Fleck. **Released:** December 2000. **Description:** Canadian business school offers insight into the latest management skills of the nation's business leaders.

28106 ■ "Mandel Site Favored For UWM Hall" in *The Business Journal-Milwaukee* (Vol. 25, September 19, 2008, No. 52, pp. A1)
Pub: American City Business Journals, Inc.
Description: University of Wisconsin-Milwaukee student residence hall's leading location is a site pushed by Mandel Group Inc. Real estate sources say that the developer's proposal offers the best opportunity for business development and the least conflict with nearby neighborhoods. Plans for the Mandel site are presented.

28107 ■ "Manufacturers Urged to Adapt to Defense" in *Crain's Cleveland Business* (Vol. 30, June 22, 2009, No. 24, pp. 3)
Pub: Crain Communications, Inc.
Ed: Dan Shingler. **Description:** Manufacturers in Northeast Ohio are making products for the military from steel, polymers or composite materials. The U.S. Department of Defense is teaching companies to work with titanium and other advanced metals in order to further manufacture for the military.

28108 ■ "Market Forces" in *Canadian Business* (Vol. 79, October 23, 2006, No. 21, pp. 93)
Pub: Rogers Media
Ed: Erin Pooley. **Description:** The tremendous rise in the number of business schools offering Master of business administration degree in Canada and the depletion in the quality of education provided in these business schools is discussed.

28109 ■ "Marketing Scholarship 2.0" in *Journal of Marketing* (Vol. 75, July 2011, No. 4, pp. 225)
Pub: American Marketing Association
Ed: Richard J. Lutz. **Description:** A study of the implications of changing environment and newer collaborative models for marketing knowledge production and dissemination is presented. Crowdsourcing has become a frequently employed strategy in industry. Academic researchers should collaborate more as well as the academe and industry, to make sure that important problems are being investigated.

28110 ■ "MBA Essentials: Real-Life Instruction" in *Women In Business* (Vol. 61, October-November 2009, No. 5, pp. 28)
Pub: American Business Women's Association
Ed: Leigh Elmore. **Description:** University of Kansas School of Business allied itself with the American Business Women's Association (ABWA) which led to the formation of the ABWA-KU MBA essentials program. With this program, ABWA members are exposed to graduate-level coursework that delves on business topics, such as strategy and operations.

28111 ■ "MBA Guide 2008" in *Canadian Business* (Vol. 81, November 10, 2008, No. 19, pp. 92)
Pub: Rogers Media Ltd.
Ed: Sharda Prashad. **Description:** Escalating tuition costs for an MBA degree means that the return on investment could take longer. One study found that MBA degree holders who graduated during recessionary times earned less than those who graduated during good economic times.

28112 ■ *MBA In a Day*
Pub: John Wiley and Sons, Inc.
Ed: Steven Stralser, PhD. **Released:** 2004. **Price:** $34.95. **Description:** Management professor presents important concepts, business topics and strategies that can be used by anyone to manage a small business or professional practice. Topics covered include: human resources and personal interaction, ethics and leadership skills, fair negotiation tactics, basic business accounting practices, project management, and the fundamentals of economics and marketing.

28113 ■ "MBAs Plus Designers Equals New Life for Business" in *Globe & Mail* (April 24, 2007, pp. B1)
Pub: CTVglobemedia Publishing Inc.
Ed: Gordon Pitts. **Description:** The need for Canadian companies to combine the skills of management graduates and designers to achieve corporate growth is discussed.

28114 ■ "Meet UT's New Business Mind" in *Austin Business Journal* (Vol. 31, May 13, 2011, No. 10, pp. A1)
Pub: American City Business Journals Inc.
Ed: Sandra Zaragoza. **Description:** University of Texas (UT) chief commercialization officer, Dr. Richard Miller, has opened a satellite office in Silicon Valley, California in the hopes of luring Californian investors to the science and technology at UT. The satellite office is just one of Miller's efforts to reshape and widen the commercialization of UT-Austin. Insights into Miller's long-term view approach to commercialization are also covered.

28115 ■ "Mentoring Support" in *Black Enterprise* (Vol. 38, July 2008, No. 12, pp. 64)
Pub: Earl G. Graves Publishing Co. Inc.
Description: With his relocation from his multicultural team in New York to the less diverse Scripps Networks' headquarters in Knoxville, Earl Cokley has made it a top priority to push for more diversity and mentoring opportunities within the management of the media and marketing company.

28116 ■ "Mettle Detector" in *Canadian Business* (Vol. 79, July 17, 2006, No. 14-15, pp. 63)
Pub: Rogers Media
Ed: Calvin Leung. **Description:** The difficulties faced in completing the Certified Financial Analyst course, and the rewards one can expect after its completion, are discussed.

28117 ■ *Microtrends: The Small Forces Behind Tomorrow's Big Changes*
Pub: Business Plus
Ed: Mark J. Penn. **Released:** 2007. **Price:** $25.99. **Description:** Political pollster and lead presidential campaign strategist for Hillary Clinton, identifies seventy-five microtrends he believes are changing the social and cultural landscape in the U.S. and globally. The book covers the areas of health and wellness, technology, education and more.

28118 ■ "MindLeaders' Online Training Courses Come to ePath Learning" in *Information Today* (Vol. 26, February 2009, No. 2, pp. 4)
Pub: Information Today, Inc.
Description: MindLeaders has partnered with ePath Learning to provide clients with over 2,200 new online courses. ePath's integrated Learning Management Service (iLMS) allows organizations to create online training programs for employees.

28119 ■ "Mitch D'Olier" in *Hawaii Business* (Vol. 53, November 2007, No. 5, pp. 27)
Pub: Hawaii Business Publishing
Ed: Cathy S. Cruz-George. **Description:** Mitch D'Olier chief executive officer of Kaneohe Ranch/ Harold K.L. Castle Foundation thinks that achievement gaps are a nationwide problem and that the Knowledge is Power Program is one of the programs that focuses on achievement gaps in some communities across the US. He also provides his insights on education in Hawaii and the current shortage of teachers.

28120 ■ "Moooove Over, Sodas: Okaloosa to Get Dairy Vending Machines for Two Schools" in *Northwest Florida Daily News* (September 27, 2001)
Pub: Freedom Communications
Ed: Katie Tammen. **Description:** Two Okaloosa County high schools will be offering more lunch options by installing refrigerated vending machines featuring dairy-related food.

28121 ■ "More Cuts On the Way At Ag School" in *Business First-Columbus* (December 14, 2007, pp. A1)
Pub: American City Business Journals, Inc.
Ed: Carrie Ghose. **Description:** Program cuts at Ohio State University's Agriculture School are discussed. A voluntary retirement incentive to reduce staff was approved by the University's trustees. Since 2000, the College of Food, Agricultural and Environmental Sciences' staff have decreased by 21 percent,

while the faculty experienced a 25 percent reduction. According to Bobby Moser, the college's dean, the institution is looking for other ways to generate income.

28122 ■ "More Sales Leads, Please: Or, What Happened When Frontline Selling Started Practicing What It Preaches" in *Inc.* (November 2007)
Pub: Gruner & Jahr USA Publishing
Description: Frontline Selling located in Oakland, New Jersey helps train sales teams to generate and convert sales leads. The consulting firm doubled their marketing budget to increase their own sales.

28123 ■ "Natalie Peterson; Corporate Counsel, Steris Corp., 39" in *Crain's Cleveland Business* (Vol. 28, November 19, 2007, No. 46, pp. F-14)
Pub: Crain Communications, Inc.
Ed: Chuck Soder. **Description:** Profile of Natalie Peterson, corporate counsel for Steris Corp., a manufacturer of sterilization products; Peterson's blue-collar background did not detour her from her collegiate goals although she hardly knew how to fill out a college application. After graduating from Stanford Law School in 1997, she opted to return to Cleveland in lieu of more lucrative job offers in San Francisco. She has joined the school board and has participated in the 3Rs program, in which lawyers visit public schools in Cleveland to get students thinking about career choices and talk about constitutional law.

28124 ■ "Native Wisdom" in *Canadian Business* (Vol. 80, October 8, 2007, No. 20, pp. 121)
Pub: Rogers Media
Ed: Bernd Christmas. **Description:** Roles of Canadian indigenous peoples in the country's economic development are discussed. It is believed that empowering Canadian natives to contribute to the country's economy will positively affect the country's future. The need for education in preparing natives for the global economy is also tackled.

28125 ■ "Nat'l Instruments Connects with Lego" in *Austin Business JournalInc.* (Vol. 28, August 22, 2008, No. 23, pp. 1)
Pub: American City Business Journals
Ed: Laura Hipp. **Description:** Austin-based National Instruments Corporation has teamed with Lego Group from Denmark to create a robot that can be built by children and can be used to perform tasks. Lego WeDo, their latest product, uses computer connection to power its movements. The educational benefits of the new product are discussed.

28126 ■ "Negotiating Tips" in *Black Enterprise* (Vol. 37, December 2006, No. 5, pp. 70)
Pub: Earl G. Graves Publishing Co. Inc.
Description: Sekou Kaalund, head of strategy, mergers & acquisitions at Citigroup Securities & Fund Services, states that "Negotiation skills are paramount to success in a business environment because of client, employee, and shareholder relationships". He discusses how the book by George Kohlrieser, Hostage at the Table: How Leaders Can Overcome Conflict, Influence Others, and Raise Performance, has helped him negotiate more powerfully and enhance his skills at conflict-resolution.

28127 ■ "'Netting Degrees: More Professionals Continuing Their Education Online" in *Hispanic Business* (September 2007, pp. 62, 64)
Pub: Hispanic Business
Ed: Hildy Medina. **Description:** Traditional universities and private institutions offer online courses to professionals wishing to further their education.

28128 ■ "New Approach Could Boost Ivory Tower Innovation" in *Business Journal-Portland* (Vol. 24, November 16, 2007, No. 37, pp. 1)
Pub: American City Business Journals, Inc.
Ed: Aliza Earnshaw. **Description:** New approach which aims to help universities move to a corporate structure, secure funds, and find professional managers is being explored. Accelerator Corporation was able to help six companies through its funding. Joe Tanous who is behind Oregon's State University's enhanced commercialization, would like to apply the same approach Accelerator used to help Oregon State University, the University of Oregon, Portland State University and Oregon Health and Science University.

28129 ■ "New Career Center Opens at Right Time: Laid-Off Freightliner Workers Will Need Help" in *Charlotte Observer* (February 1, 2007)
Pub: Knight-Ridder/Tribune Business News
Ed: Gail Smith-Arrants. **Description:** Rowan-Cabarrus Community College announced the opening of its new career development center that will help area workers train for new careers.

28130 ■ "The New Schools" in *Black Enterprise* (February 2008)
Pub: Earl G. Graves Publishing Co. Inc.
Ed: Kinsley Kanu, Jr. **Description:** Ten educational programs to help top executives keep pace with the ever-changing market trends while gaining perspective on innovation and new ideas are examined.

28131 ■ "No Fast Cash Class" in *Black Enterprise* (Vol. 37, December 2006, No. 5, pp. 72)
Pub: Earl G. Graves Publishing Co. Inc.
Ed: Description: There are no shortcuts to a obtaining a career as a financial planner. Certified Financial Planner Board of Standards has specific requirements for certification which include having a bachelor's degree from an accredited U.S. school before candidates are even eligible for taking the certification exam. Other criteria and requirements are discussed.

28132 ■ "No, Management Is Not a Profession" in *Harvard Business Review* (Vol. 88, July-August 2010, No. 7-8, pp. 52)
Pub: Harvard Business School Publishing
Ed: Richard Barker. **Description:** An argument is presented that management is not a profession, as it is less focused on mastering a given body of knowledge than it is on obtaining integration and collaboration skills. Implications for teaching this new approach are also examined.

28133 ■ "Nonprofit Ready to Get More Girls into 'STEM' Jobs" in *Austin Business JournalInc.* (Vol. 29, December 25, 2009, No. 42, pp. 1)
Pub: American City Business Journals
Ed: Sandra Zaragoza. **Description:** Girlstart has completed its $1.5 million capital campaign to buy the building it will care the Girlstart Tech Center. Girlstart is a nonprofit organization that prepares girls for science, technology, engineering and mathematics or STEM careers. Details of the program are highlighted.

28134 ■ "Nurturing Talent for Tomorrow" in *Restaurants and Institutions* (Vol. 118, September 15, 2008, No. 14, pp. 90)
Pub: Reed Business Information
Description: Hormel Foods Corporation and The Culinary Institute of America (CIA) have teamed to develop The Culinary Enrichment and Innovation Program that supports future culinary leaders by providing creative and competitive staff development. Sixteen students attend four three-day sessions at the CIA's campus in Hyde Park, New York; sessions include classroom teaching, one-on-one interaction with leading culinarians, and hands-on kitchen time.

28135 ■ "Oakland County to Survey Employers on Needed Skills" in *Crain's Detroit Business* (Vol. 24, April 14, 2008, No. 15, pp. 30)
Pub: Crain Communications, Inc.
Ed: Chad Halcom. **Description:** In an attempt to aid educators and attract talent, Oakland County plans to collect data from 1,000 local employers on workforce skills they need now or will need soon.

28136 ■ *The Official Guide for GMAT Verbal Review, 2nd Edition*
Pub: John Wiley & Sons, Inc.
Ed: Graduate Management Admissions Council. **Released:** August 17, 2009. **Price:** $17.95. **Description:** The only official verbal review for the GMAT from the creators of the test. The guide provides questions, answers, and explanations and targets study and helps improve verbal skills by focusing on the ability to read and comprehend written material, to reason and evaluate arguments, and to correct written material to conform to Standard English.

28137 ■ "On Beyond Powerpoint: Presentations Get a Wake-Up Call" in *Inc.* (November 2007, pp. 58-59)
Pub: Gruner & Jahr USA Publishing
Ed: Michael Fitzgerald. **Description:** New software that allows business presentations to be shared online are profiled, including ProfCast, audio podcasts for sales, marketing, and training; SmartDraw2008, software that creates professional graphics; Dimdim, an open-Web conferencing tool; Empressr, a hosted Web service for creating, managing, and sharing multimedia presentations; Zentation, a free tool that allows users to watch slides and a videos of presenter; Spresent, a Web-based presentation tool for remote offices or conference calls.

28138 ■ "On the Clock" in *Canadian Business* (Vol. 82, April 27, 2009, No. 7, pp. 28)
Pub: Rogers Media
Ed: Sarka Halas. **Description:** Survey of 100 Canadian executives found that senior managers can be out of a job for about nine months before their careers are adversely affected. The nine month mark can be avoided if job seekers build networks even before they lose their jobs. Job seekers should also take volunteer work and training opportunities to increase their changes of landing a job.

28139 ■ "On Their Own: Bronx High School Students Open a Bank Branch" in *Black Enterprise* (Vol. 38, February 2008, No. 7, pp. 42)
Pub: Earl G. Graves Publishing Co. Inc.
Ed: Jessica Jones. **Description:** Students at Fordham Leadership Academy for Business and Technology in New York City opened a student-run bank branch at their high school. The business paid high school seniors $11 per hour to work as tellers. Students were also taught interviewing basics.

28140 ■ "One Hundred Years of Excellence in Business Education: What Have We Learned?" in *Business Horizons* (January-February 2008)
Pub: Elsevier Advanced Technology Publications
Ed: Frank Acito, Patricia M. McDougall, Daniel C. Smith. **Description:** Business schools have to be more innovative, efficient and nimble, so that the quality of the next generation of business leaders is improved. The Kelley School of Business, Indiana University ahs long been a leader in business education. The trends that influence the future of business education and useful success principles are discussed.

28141 ■ "One Laptop Per Child Weighs Going For-Profit" in *Boston Business Journal* (Vol. 31, May 20, 2011, No. 17, pp. 1)
Pub: Boston Business Journal
Ed: Mary Moore. **Description:** Nonprofit organization One Laptop Per Child is thinking of shifting into a for-profit structure in order to raise as much as $10 million in capital to achieve its goal of distributing more XO laptops to poor children worldwide. The organization has distributed 2 million computers since 2008 with Uruguay, Peru and Rwanda as its biggest markets.

28142 ■ "Online Training Requires Tools, Accessories" in *Contractor* (Vol. 56, September 2009, No. 9, pp. 67)
Pub: Penton Media, Inc.
Ed: Larry Drake. **Description:** Importance of the right equipment and tools to members of the United States plumbing industry undergoing online training is

discussed. Portable devices such as Blackberrys and I-phones could be used for online training. The use of headphones makes listening easier for the trainee.

28143 ■ "The Outcome of an Organization Overhaul" in *Black Enterprise* (Vol. 41, December 2010, No. 5)
Pub: Earl G. Graves Publishing Co. Inc.
Ed: Tamara E. Holmes. **Description:** Savvy business owners understand the need for change in order to stay competitive and be successful. This article examines how to manage change as well as what strategies can help employees to get with the program faster.

28144 ■ "Palace Adds Marketing Arm; College Sponsorships First Step In New Effort" in *Crain's Detroit Business* (October 1, 2007)
Pub: Crain Communications Inc. - Detroit
Ed: Bill Shea. **Description:** Palace Sports and Entertainment is restructuring itself from operating the Detroit Piston's basketball team and concert venues into a marketing company that also runs sports teams and venues. The firm signed a deal to handle sponsorship sales for colleges and universities.

28145 ■ "Past Promises Haunt Project" in *The Business Journal-Portland* (Vol. 25, August 1, 2008, No. 21, pp. 1)
Pub: American City Business Journals, Inc.
Ed: Aliza Earnshaw. **Description:** Oregon University System and Oregon Health and Science University will face the state Legislature to defend their request for a $250 million in state bonds to fund a life-sciences collaborative research building. The project is meant to help grow the Oregon bioscience industry. Comments from industry observers and legislators are also presented.

28146 ■ "The People Puzzle; Re-Training America's Workers" in *The Economist* (Vol. 390, January 3, 2009, No. 8612, pp. 32)
Pub: The Economist Newspaper Inc.
Description: With thousands of workers losing their jobs, America is now facing the task of getting them back to work. With an overall unemployment rate of 6.7 percent, the federal government has three main ways for leading workers back to employment: training them for new jobs, providing unemployment insurance in order to replace lost wages during the period of job-hunting; and matching employers who desire a skill with workers who have that skill. Specialized staffing agencies provide employers and potential employees with the help necessary to find a job in some of the more niche markets.

28147 ■ "Perfecting Customer Services" in *Pet Product News* (Vol. 64, November 2010, No. 11, pp. 18)
Pub: BowTie Inc.
Description: Pet supply retailers are encouraged to emphasize customer experience and sales representatives' knowledge of the store's product offerings to foster repeat business. Employee protocols could be implemented to improve customer interaction. Other guidelines on developing a pet supply retail environment that advances repeat business are presented.

28148 ■ "Physics for Females" in *Occupational Outlook Quarterly* (Vol. 55, Summer 2011, No. 2, pp. 22)
Pub: U.S. Bureau of Labor Statistics
Description: Free resources to help females investigate careers in medical physics and health physics are available from the American Physical Society. The booklet is designed for girls in middle and high school and describes the work of 15 women who use physics to solve medical mysteries, discover planets, research new materials, and more.

28149 ■ *Planning Your Future*
Pub: AMIDEAST Publications
Released: Irregular. **Price:** $29.95, individuals first class mail; $13, other countries international mail. **Covers:** over 1,000 printed and electronic sources of information on education and training for approximately 150 careers, including accredited programs, nontraditional education, internships, and disabled student services. **Entries Include:** Title name, date of publication, order address. **Arrangement:** Alphabetical by Occupation. **Indexes:** Alphabetical by Publisher, subject and title.

28150 ■ "PMA Launches Online Education Program" in *Contractor* (Vol. 56, October 2009, No. 10, pp. 8)
Pub: Penton Media, Inc.
Description: Plumbing & Mechanical Association of Georgia launched an online program that covers technical and business management that will help contractors run their businesses. Future courses will include math for plumbers, graywater systems, and recession-proofing your business.

28151 ■ *The Portable MBA in Entrepreneurship*
Pub: John Wiley & Sons, Inc.
Ed: Andrew Zacharakis, William D. Bygrave. **Released:** December 9, 2010. **Price:** $34.95. **Description:** An updated and revised new edition of the comprehensive guide to modern entrepreneurship that tracks the core curriculum of leading business schools.

28152 ■ "Post-Prison Center Idea Rankles OTR" in *Business Courier* (Vol. 26, November 27, 2009, No. 31, pp. 1)
Pub: American City Business Journals, Inc.
Ed: Lucy May. **Description:** Cincinnati officials and community leaders oppose Firetree Ltd.'s plan to launch a residential program for federal offenders near the School for the Creative and Performing Arts in Over-the-Rhine. Firetree, a Pennsylvania-based reentry center services firm, proposed a five-year contract with the Federal Bureau of Prisons based on a letter to Cincinnati Police Chief Thomas Streicher.

28153 ■ "The Power of ABWA" in *Women In Business* (Vol. 62, September 2010, No. 3, pp. 36)
Pub: American Business Women's Association
Ed: Leigh Elmore. **Description:** Information about the internship received by Erica Rockley at American Business Women's Association (ABWA) headquarters is presented. Rockley received heartfelt professional advice the days she spent at the office. She also learned the importance of networking.

28154 ■ "Pre-K Pressure" in *Hawaii Business* (Vol. 53, October 2007, No. 4, pp. 32)
Pub: Hawaii Business Publishing
Ed: David K. Choo. **Description:** Kindergarten admission in Hawaii is becoming more competitive. Parents, for example, prepare their children for the kindergarten admissions process by bringing them to the schools before the interview or by paying for tutorial services. The impacts of increased competition in school admissions on the life of Hawaiian children are discussed.

28155 ■ "The Preparation Gap" in *Hawaii Business* (Vol. 53, February 2008, No. 8, pp. 37)
Pub: Hawaii Business Publishing
Ed: Ashley Hamershock. **Description:** Discussion of the educational gap in Hawaii's workforce is being addressed by educational workshops that aim to improve students' knowledge in science, technology, math, and engineering, and prepare them for their entry into the workforce. Education beyond high school is required for jobs to be filled in the coming years.

28156 ■ "Prison Farms are Closing, but the Manure Remains" in *Canadian Business* (Vol. 83, August 17, 2010, No. 13-14, pp. 9)
Pub: Rogers Media Ltd.
Ed: Steve Maich. **Description:** The explanation given by Canada's government ministers on planned closure of the prison farms and scrapping of the long form census are designed by mixing of spin, argument and transparent justification. The defense should have been plausible but the ministers could not handle the simple questions about statistics and prison job training with pretense.

28157 ■ "Programs Provide Education and Training" in *Contractor* (Vol. 56, September 2009, No. 9, pp. 56)
Pub: Penton Media, Inc.
Ed: William Feldman; Patti Feldman. **Description:** Opportunity Interactive's Showroom v2 software provides uses computer graphics to provide education and training on HVAC equipment and systems. It can draw heat pump balance points for a specific home. Meanwhile, Simutech's HVAC Training Simulators provide trainees with 'hands-on' HVACR training.

28158 ■ "Promoting Academic Programs Using Online Videos" in *Business Communication Quarterly* (December 2007, pp. 478)
Pub: Sage Publications USA
Ed: Thomas Clark, Julie Stewart. **Description:** Xavier Entrepreneurial Center successfully used online videos to promote the effectiveness of its academic programs. Online videos are a cost-effective way of publicizing academic programs.

28159 ■ "PSU Launches $90 Million Project" in *The Business Journal-Portland* (Vol. 25, July 18, 2008, No. 19, pp. 1)
Pub: American City Business Journals, Inc.
Ed: Aliza Earnshaw. **Description:** Portland State University (PSU) has launched a $90-million project for a new business school building, which is to be located at Southwest Market and Southwest Park. The business school is expected to move in to its new 130,000-suqare-foot building by 2013. PSU business school needs to raise $30 million for the project.

28160 ■ "Reaching Your Potential" in *Harvard Business Review* (Vol. 86, July-August 2008, No. 8, pp. 45)
Pub: Harvard Business School Press
Ed: Robert S. Kaplan. **Description:** Being proactive in developing one's career is an important part of entrepreneurship. Keys to successful development include knowing oneself and one's goals, and taking calculated risks.

28161 ■ "Real Estate Ambitions" in *Black Enterprise* (Vol. 37, January 2007, No. 6, pp. 101)
Pub: Earl G. Graves Publishing Co. Inc.
Ed: Description: National Real Estate Investors Association is a nonprofit trade association for both advanced as well as novice real estate investors that offers information on builders to contractors to banks. When looking to become a real estate investor utilize this organization, talk to various investors like the president of your local chapter, let people know your aspirations, and see if you can find a partner who has experience in the field. Resources included.

28162 ■ "Real-Life Coursework for Real-Life Business People" in *Women In Business* (Vol. 63, Summer 2011, No. 2, pp. 22)
Pub: American Business Women's Association
Ed: Leigh Elmore. **Description:** American Business Women's Association National Women's Leadership Conference provides members with academic business training courses. Members can take a variety of MBA-level courses that are taught by University of Kansas School of Business professors. Courses include marketing, management, leadership and communication and decision making.

28163 ■ "Real-Time Computer-Mediated Communication" in *Business Communication Quarterly* (December 2007, pp. 466)
Pub: Sage Publications USA
Ed: Amy Newman. **Description:** Technology-based simulation for business students to respond to emails and instant messages is presented. The simulation allows students to handle volume business correspondence at work with organizational context and under real-word business situations.

28164 ■ "Rebels' Cause: Adult Stem Cell" in *Austin Business Journal* (Vol. 31, June 3, 2011, No. 13, pp. 1)
Pub: American City Business Journals Inc.
Ed: Sandra Zaragoza. **Description:** MedRebels Foundation was launched in February 2011 with the goal of providing millions of dollars for research fund-

ing, education and advocacy for adult stem cell-focused medicine. The foundation, whose major contributor is SpineSmith LP, is a collaboration of other adult stem cell-related companies and nonprofit partners. It hopes to raise $200,000 by the end of 2011.

28165 ■ "Recovery on Tap for 2010?" in *Orlando Business Journal* (Vol. 26, January 1, 2010, No. 31, pp. 1)
Pub: American City Business Journals
Ed: Melanie Stawicki Azam, Richard Bilbao, Christopher Boyd, Anjali Fluker. **Description:** Economic forecasts for Central Florida's leading business sectors in 2010 are presented. These sectors include housing, film and TV, sports business, law, restaurants, aviation, tourism and hospitality, banking and finance, commercial real estate, retail, health care, insurance, higher education, and manufacturing. According to some local executives, Central Florida's economy will slowly recover in 2010.

28166 ■ "Red One and The Rain Chronicles" in *Michigan Vue* (Vol. 13, July-August 2008, No. 4, pp. 30)
Pub: Entrepreneur Media Inc.
Ed: Evan Cornish. **Description:** Troy-based film school the Motion Picture Institute (MPI) implemented the latest technology by shooting the second of their trilogy, "The Rain Chronicles", on the Red One camera. This is the first feature film in Michigan to utilize this exciting new camera, which includes proprietary software for rendering and color correction. Brian K. Johnson heads up the visual effects team as visual effects supervisor and lead CG artist. His company, Dream Conduit Studios, had to tackle the task of employing the new work flow through a post-production pipeline that would allow him to attack complex visual effects shots, many of which were shot with a moving camera, a technique rarely seen in films at this budgetary level where the camera is traditionally locked off.

28167 ■ "Region to Be Named Innovation Hub" in *Business Courier* (Vol. 27, July 2, 2010, No. 9, pp. 1)
Pub: Business Courier
Ed: Dan Monk. **Description:** The selection of Cincinnati's consumer-marketing cluster as a 'Hub of Innovation' by the Ohio Department of Development could boost Cincinnati's chances of receiving $100 million in grants from Ohio's Third Frontier program and other funding sources. Implications of the University of Cincinnati's designation as a Center of Excellence in Advanced Transportation and Aerospace are also discussed.

28168 ■ "Region Ready to Dig Deeper into Tech Fund" in *Business Courier* (Vol. 26, October 30, 2009, No. 27, pp. 1)
Pub: American City Business Journals, Inc.
Ed: James Ritchie. **Description:** Southwest Ohio region aims for a bigger share in the planned renewal of Ohio's Third Frontier technology funding program. Meanwhile, University of Cincinnati vice president Sarah Degen will be appointed to the program's advisory board if the renewal proceeds.

28169 ■ "Regional Talent Network Unveils Jobs Web Site" in *Crain's Cleveland Business* (Vol. 30, June 1, 2009, No. 21, pp. 11)
Pub: Crain Communications, Inc.
Description: Regional Talent Network launched WhereToFindHelp.org, a Website designed to act as a directory of all Northeast Ohio resources that can help employers recruit and job seekers look for positions. The site also lists organizations offering employment and training services.

28170 ■ "Revisiting Rep Coping Strategies" in *Agency Sales Magazine* (Vol. 39, December 2009, No. 11, pp. 32)
Pub: MANA
Ed: Jack Foster. **Description:** Independent manufacturers representatives should become a well-rounded and complete businessman with continued education. The new type of representative is a problem solver and the resource for answering questions. Employing the concept of synergistic selling is also important to salespeople.

28171 ■ "The Right Stuff" in *Canadian Business* (Vol. 79, October 23, 2006, No. 21, pp. 151)
Pub: Rogers Media
Ed: Laura Bogomolny. **Description:** The profile of Linda Duxbury, the winner of the Sprott MBA Students Society 2003-04 Best teacher award as well as Carleton University Students' Association 2002-03 award, is presented.

28172 ■ "The Right Time for REITs" in *Barron's* (Vol. 88, July 14, 2008, No. 28, pp. 32)
Pub: Dow Jones & Co., Inc.
Ed: Mike Hogan. **Description:** Discusses the downturn in U.S. real estate investment trusts so these are worth considering for investment. Several Websites that are useful for learning about real estate investment trusts for investment purposes are presented.

28173 ■ "The Role for Canada's Research Universities" in *Canadian Business* (Vol. 81, October 27, 2008, No. 18, pp. 84)
Pub: Rogers Media Ltd.
Description: Great students tend to be the foundation of a great research-intensive university, enabling it to attract great teachers and researchers. Success is likely to attract the brightest graduate students to do research, leading to further success.

28174 ■ "Rosewood Site Faces Big Cleanup" in *Baltimore Business Journal* (Vol. 27, February 6, 2010, No. 40, pp. 1)
Pub: American City Business Journals
Ed: Daniel J. Sernovitz. **Description:** Environmental assessment report states that Maryland's Rosewood Center for the Developmentally Disabled has significant amounts of toxic chemicals, which could impact Stevenson University's decision to purchase the property. Senator Robert A. Zirkin believes that the state should pay for the cleanup, which is expected to cost millions.

28175 ■ "SAGE Publications Announced a Partnership with Which Medical Device" in *Information Today* (Vol. 28, November 2011, No. 10, pp. 15)
Pub: Information Today, Inc.
Description: SAGE Publications has partnered with Which Medical Device to offer insights, tutorials, and reviews of medical devices.

28176 ■ "St. Rose Professor Builds Contractors and Micro-Doctors" in *Business Review, Albany New York* (Vol. 34, December 28, 2007, No. 39)
Pub: American City Business Journals, Inc.
Ed: Robin K. Cooper. **Description:** Mike Mathews is an associate professor at the College of Saint Rose School of Business and one of the founders of the Center for Micro Enterprises Development, which provides training programs on business planning and management. Details of the business school's curricula and foundations are discussed.

28177 ■ "Scholarships for Minority Students" in *Occupational Outlook Quarterly* (Vol. 54, Fall 2010, No. 3, pp. 25)
Pub: U.S. Bureau of Labor Statistics
Description: Gates Millennium Scholars scholarship is awarded to minority students with leadership skills, a good GPA, and college aspirations.

28178 ■ "Second Chance Counselor" in *Business Courier* (Vol. 27, July 2, 2010, No. 9, pp. 1)
Pub: Business Courier
Ed: Lucy May. **Description:** Stephen Tucker, director of workforce development for the Urban League of Greater Cincinnati, is an example of how ex-offenders can be given chances for employment after service jail sentences. How the Urban Leagues' Solid Opportunities for Advancement job training program helped Tucker and other ex-offenders is discussed.

28179 ■ "Selling With Strengths; Talent Trumps Training" in *Gallup Management Journal* (March 24, 2011)
Pub: Gallup
Description: What are the strengths of salespeople, and how can organizations develop them? What do great sales managers do differently? The authors of, 'Strengths Based Selling' answer these questions and others, including: why money is overrated as a motivator.

28180 ■ "Senate OKs Funds for Promoting Tourism" in *Crain's Detroit Business* (Vol. 24, March 31, 2008, No. 13, pp. 6)
Pub: Crain Communications, Inc.
Ed: Amy Lane. **Description:** Discusses the Senate proposal which allocates funds for Michigan tourism and business promotion as well as Michigan's No Worker Left Behind initiative, a program that provides free tuition at community colleges and other venues to train displaced workers for high-demand occupations.

28181 ■ "Senators Predict Online School Changes" in *Puget Sound Business Journal* (Vol. 29, September 19, 2008, No. 22, pp. 1)
Pub: American City Business Journals
Ed: Clay Holtzman. **Description:** State senators promise to create new legislation that would tighten the monitoring and oversight of online public schools. The officials are concerned about the lack of oversight of the programs as well as lack of knowledge about content of the lessons.

28182 ■ "The Service Imperative" in *Business Horizons* (Vol. 51, January-February 2008, No. 1, pp. 39)
Pub: Elsevier Advanced Technology Publications
Ed: Mary Jo Bitner, Stephen W. Brown. **Description:** The importance of services is growing in developing countries like India and China, but little attention is given to service research, education and innovation. The 'service imperative' seeks to promote the advancement of services. The scope, objectives and philosophy of the service imperative platform are outlined.

28183 ■ "Sewing Is a Life Skill; Teaching To Sew Is An Art" in *Virginia-Pilot* (August 31, 2010)
Pub: Virginian-Pilot
Ed: Jamesetta Walker. **Description:** In conjunction with National Sewing Month, the American Sewing Guild is sponsoring a two-day workshop featuring Stephanie Kimura.

28184 ■ "Small-Business Agenda: Increase Capital, Education, Tax Breaks" in *Crain's Detroit Business* (Vol. 24, March 17, 2008)
Pub: Crain Communications, Inc.
Ed: Nancy Kaffer. **Description:** Discusses the policy suggestions detailed in the Small Business Association of Michigan's entrepreneurial agenda which include five main categories of focus: making entrepreneurial education a higher state priority; increasing capital available to entrepreneurs; using the state's tax structure as an incentive for entrepreneurial growth; getting university research from the lab to the market; and limiting government regulation that's burdensome to small businesses and getting legislative support of entrepreneurial assistance efforts.

28185 ■ "Some Good Earners: Preparing Prison Inmates to Start Businesses Upon Their Release" in *Inc.* (Vol. 31, January-February 2009, No. 1)
Pub: Mansueto Ventures LLC
Ed: Mike Hoffman. **Description:** Prison Entrepreneurship Program (PEP) is a nonprofit organization that works with the Texas Department of Criminal Justice to teach entrepreneurship to prison inmates. Profiled is Hans Becker, owner of Armadillo Tree and Shrub in Dallas; Becker studied the PEP program while serving five years in prison and started his successful company when released.

28186 ■ "Spotlight; 'Classroom Focus' at Encyclopaedia Britannica" in *Crain's Chicago Business* (Vol. 34, October 24, 2011, No. 42, pp. 6)
Pub: Crain Communications Inc.
Ed: Paul Merrion. **Description:** Profile of Gregory Healy, product officer for Encyclopaedia Britannica is

presented. Healy took the position in May 2010 and is focused on online offerings of their publication and to make them more useful to teachers.

28187 ■ "Staples Advantage Receives NJPA National Contract for Janitorial Supplies" in *Professional Services Close-Up* (April 22, 2011)
Pub: Close-Up Media
Description: Staples Advantage, the business-to-business division of Staples Inc. was awarded a contract for janitorial supplies to members of the National Joint Powers Alliance (NJPA). NJPA is a member-owned buying cooperative serving public and private schools, state and local governments, and nonprofit organizations.

28188 ■ *StartingUp Now Facilitator Guide*
Pub: StartingUp Now
Ed: L. Jenkins. **Released:** September 11, 2011. **Price:** $29.95. **Description:** Guide for those teaching entrepreneurship using StartingUp Now; the guide provides 24 lesson plans for each of the 24 steps/ chapters in the book.

28189 ■ "Stay in School: Economy Got You Down?" in *Canadian Business* (Vol. 81, November 10, 2008, No. 19, pp. 98)
Pub: Rogers Media Ltd.
Ed: Graham F. Scott, Jane Bao. **Description:** A guide to Canadian MBA programs is presented. The tuition and length of each program is provided along with each school. Details on whether the universities offer part-time options, diversity, and co-op/internships are also given.

28190 ■ "Stop the Madness" in *Hawaii Business* (Vol. 53, October 2007, No. 4, pp. 10)
Pub: Hawaii Business Publishing
Ed: Kelli Abe Trifonovitch. **Description:** Discusses the number of parents paying for kindergarten admissions tutorials for their kids which has increased, as parents want to improve their children's chances of being admitted at a prestigious school. Some schools in Hawaii are not in favor of this trend, and they actually rate an applicant negatively if his or her answers seem to be too rehearsed. Some of the lessons in the admissions tutorials are discussed.

28191 ■ "Storytelling Star of Show for Scripps" in *Business Courier* (Vol. 26, November 13, 2009, No. 29, pp. 1)
Pub: American City Business Journals, Inc.
Ed: Dan Monk. **Description:** Rich Boehne, CEO Of the EW Scripps Company in Cincinnati has authorized a new training program in storytelling for employees at Scripps' 10 television stations. He believes that the training will improve the quality of broadcasting content. His plans to improve quality of newspaper content are also discussed.

28192 ■ "Study Puts Hub On Top of the Tech Heap" in *Boston Business Journal* (Vol. 30, November 26, 2010, No. 44, pp. 1)
Pub: Boston Business Journal
Ed: Galen Moore. **Description:** The Ewing Marion Kauffman Foundation ranked Massachusetts at the top in its evaluations of states' innovative industries, government leadership, and education. Meanwhile, research blog formDs.com also ranked Massachusetts number one in terms of venture-capital financings per capita.

28193 ■ "Suddenly, Sewing Is Hip Again for Kids, Moms and Crafters" in *Atlanta Journal-Constitution* (August 29, 2010)
Pub: Atlanta Journal-Constitution
Ed: Rosalind Bentley. **Description:** Across Atlanta, Georgia, along with the entire nation, sewing classes are increasing in popularity.

28194 ■ "Survey: Don't Expect Big Results From Stimulus" in *Crain's Detroit Business* (Vol. 25, June 1, 2009, No. 22)
Pub: Crain Communications Inc. - Detroit
Ed: Nancy Kaffer, Chad Halcom. **Description:** In a recent survey, Michigan business owners, operators or managers showed that 48 percent of respondents oppose the President's stimulus package and believe it will have little or no effect on the economy.

28195 ■ "Teachable Moments: Worth Every Penny" in *Pet Product News* (Vol. 64, December 2010, No. 12, pp. 34)
Pub: BowTie Inc.
Ed: Cheryl Reeves. **Description:** Pet bird retailers can attain both outreach to customers and enhanced profitability by staging educational events such as the annual Parrot Palooza event of Burlington, New Jersey-based Bird Paradise. Aside from attracting a global audience, Parrot Palooza features seminars, workshops, classes, and bird-related contests.

28196 ■ "Ted Stahl: Executive Chairman" in *Inside Business* (Vol. 13, September-October 2011, No. 5, pp. NC6)
Pub: Great Lakes Publishing Company
Ed: Miranda S. Miller. **Description:** Profile of Ted Stahl, who started working in his family's business when he was ten years old is presented. The firm makes dies for numbers and letters used on team uniforms. Another of the family firms manufactures stock and custom heat-printing products, equipment and supplies. It also educates customers on ways to decorate garments with heat printing products and offers graphics and software for customers to create their own artwork.

28197 ■ "Texas State Poised for Boom" in *Austin Business JournalInc.* (Vol. 29, January 29, 2010, No. 47, pp. 1)
Pub: American City Business Journals
Ed: Sandra Zaragoza. **Description:** Texas State University, San Marcos has seen its student population grow to 30,800 and the university is set for $633 million in construction projects to address demand for student housing and building expansions and renovations. Details on the buildings and student housing plans for the projects are provided.

28198 ■ "The Way I Work: Kim Kleeman" in *Inc.* (October 2007, pp. 110-112, 114)
Pub: Gruner & Jahr USA Publishing
Ed: Leigh Buchanan. **Description:** Profile of Kim Kleemna, founder and president of ShakespeareSquared, a firm that develops educational materials, including lesson plans, teacher guides, activity workbooks, and discussion guides for large publishers. Kleeman talks about the challenges she faces running her nearly all-women company while maintaining a balance with her family.

28199 ■ "The Thinker" in *Canadian Business* (Vol. 81, March 31, 2008, No. 5, pp. 52)
Pub: Rogers Media
Ed: Andrew Wahl. **Description:** Mihnea Moldoveanu provides much of the academic rigor that underpins Roger Martin's theories on how to improve the way business leaders think. Moldoveanu is also a classically trained pianist and founder of Redline Communications and has a mechanical engineering degree from MIT on top of his astounding knowledge on many academic fields.

28200 ■ "Thinking Aloud: Julian Franks" in *Business Strategy Review* (Vol. 21, Autumn 2010, No. 3, pp. 35)
Pub: Blackwell Publishers Ltd.
Ed: Stuart Crainer. **Description:** Julian Franks is Academic Director of the Centre for Corporate Governance at London Business School and lead investigator for a 1.4 million (sterling pounds) grand for research into corporate governance.

28201 ■ "Top Marks" in *Canadian Business* (Vol. 79, October 23, 2006, No. 21, pp. 143)
Pub: Rogers Media
Ed: Erin Pooley; Laura Bogomolny. **Description:** Profiles of some top grade master of business administration students like Hogan Mullally and Will mercer, belonging to reputed business schools, are presented.

28202 ■ "Trade Craft: Take Pride in Your Trade, Demand Excellence" in *Contractor* (Vol. 56, October 2009, No. 10, pp. 24)
Pub: Penton Media, Inc.
Ed: Al Schwartz. **Description:** There is a need for teaching, developing, and encouraging trade craft. An apprentice plumber is not only versed in the mechanical aspects of the trade but he also has a working knowledge of algebra, trigonometry, chemistry, and thermal dynamics. Contractors should be demanding on their personnel regarding their trade craft and should only keep and train the very best people they can hire.

28203 ■ "Train Now to Get the Competitive Edge" in *Contractor* (Vol. 56, October 2009, No. 10, pp. 58)
Pub: Penton Media, Inc.
Ed: Merry Beth Hall. **Description:** Due to the harsh economic climate, mechanical contractors would be well-served to train their employees while they have time to take them out of the field. This will help ensure that they are not behind when the economic recovery happens. Suggestions on how to choose the best type of training are presented.

28204 ■ "Training Center Wants to be College" in *Austin Business JournalInc.* (Vol. 29, November 13, 2009, No. 36, pp. A1)
Pub: American City Business Journals
Ed: Sandra Zaragoza. **Description:** Texas-based CyberTex Institute, a job training center, has established technical careers in an effort to obtain federal accreditation as a college. A college status would allow CyperTex to extend financial assistance to students. Aside from potentially having an enlarged student body and expanded campus, CyberTex would be allowed to engage in various training programs.

28205 ■ "Training Essential For Growth; It Doesn't Have To Cost Much" in *Crain's Detroit Business* (Vol. 24, January 21, 2008, No. 3, pp. 14)
Pub: Crain Communications Inc. - Detroit
Ed: Sheena Harrison. **Description:** Employee training is essential for small companies to achieve growth.

28206 ■ *Training Resources*
Pub: American Society for Training & Development
Released: Annual, December. **Entries Include:** Company name, contact information and name, profile, list of products and services. **Database Covers:** Businesses and individual consultants offering products, services, and equipment for sale to persons in corporate training and human resource development. **Arrangement:** Alphabetical. **Indexes:** Subject, geographical, industry focus.

28207 ■ "Training the Troops: Battlefield Simulations Bring Growth to UNITECH" in *Black Enterprise* (Vol. 38, February 2008, No. 7, pp. 30)
Pub: Earl G. Graves Publishing Co. Inc.
Ed: Cliff Hocker. **Description:** Universal Systems and Technology (UNITECH) received a total of over $45 million U.S. Department of Defense orders during September and October 2007. UNITECH designs and manufactures battlefield simulation devices used to train troops in the Army and Marine Corps.

28208 ■ "Trend: Tutors to Help You Pump Up the Staff" in *Business Week* (September 22, 2008, No. 4100, pp. 45)
Pub: McGraw-Hill Companies, Inc.
Ed: Reena Janaj. **Description:** High-level managers are turning to innovation coaches in an attempt to obtain advice on how to better sell new concepts within their companies. Individuals as well as consulting firms are now offering this service.

28209 ■ "Trinity Western University Offers Project Management Course" in *Bellingham Business Journal* (Vol. February 2010, pp. 4)
Pub: Sound Publishing Inc.
Description: Trinity Western University in Bellinham, Washington is offering a new certification program in project management. Students who take and pass the certification examination of the International Project Management Institutes will lead to positions in many industries. Details of the program are provided.

28210 ■ *Trump University Entrepreneurship 101*
Pub: John Wiley & Sons, Incorporated
Ed: Mike Gordon. **Released:** January 2007. **Price:** $21.95. **Description:** Entrepreneurs, past, present or future, will find this book helpful. The book covers

three objectives: to energize readers to be courageous when taking steps toward an entrepreneurial goal, works to demystify the entrepreneurial process, and to help individuals improve success.

28211 ■ "U Overhauling Its Janitorial Program, but Custodians Taking Exception" in *Saint Paul Pioneer Press* (August 20, 2011)
Pub: McClatchy-Tribune Regional News
Ed: Mila Koumpilova. **Description:** University of Minnesota developed a new team cleaning approach for its campus. The new custodian program will save $3.1 million annually while providing a cleaner campus. The union representing the custodians questions both claims.

28212 ■ "UA, BP Test Unmanned Aircraft" in *Alaska Business Monthly* (Vol. 27, October 2011, No. 10, pp. 8)
Pub: Alaska Business Publishing Company
Ed: Nancy Pounds. **Description:** University of Alaska Fairbanks Geophysical Institute and BP Exploration Alaska tested the oil-spill capabilities of an unmanned aircraft. The aircraft will be used to gather 3-D ariel data to aid in oil-spill cleanup.

28213 ■ "UA Turns Ann Arbor Green" in *Contractor* (Vol. 56, September 2009, No. 9, pp. 5)
Pub: Penton Media, Inc.
Ed: Robert P. Mader. **Description:** Instructors at the United Association of Plumbers and Steamfitters have studied the latest in green and sustainable construction and service at the Washtenaw Community College in Michigan. Classes included building information modeling, hydronic heating and cooling and advanced HVACR troubleshooting. The UA is currently focusing on green training.

28214 ■ "UAlbany on the Hunt for New Brand" in *Business Review, Albany New York* (Vol. 34, October 5, 2007, No. 27, pp. 1)
Pub: American City Business Journals, Inc.
Ed: Richard A. D'Errico. **Description:** State University of New York at Albany is working on a new marketing and branding initiative to help communicate its message better. The initiative is for the school to better understand its target audiences and their perception of the university.

28215 ■ "UC May Expand into Old Ford Plant" in *Business Courier* (Vol. 26, December 25, 2009, No. 35, pp. 1)
Pub: American City Business Journals, Inc.
Ed: Dan Monk. **Description:** Developer Stuart Lichter is planning to acquire University of Cincinnati (UC) as a tenant at a two-story office building on a 132-acre site where a vacant Ford transmission plant is located. Details of the transaction are outlined.

28216 ■ "UMKC, Hospital Drill Down on Deal" in *The Business Journal-Serving Metropolitan Kansas City* (Vol. 26, July 18, 2008, No. 45, pp. 1)
Pub: American City Business Journals, Inc.
Ed: Rob Roberts. **Description:** University of Missouri Kansas City and Children's Mercy Hospital are negotiating the hospital's potential acquisition of the university's School of Dentistry building. The deal would transfer the 240,000-square foot dental school building to Children's Mercy. Plans for a new dental school building for the UMKC are also presented.

28217 ■ "University Book Store Inc.: an Act of Independence" in *Retail Merchandiser* (Vol. 51, September-October 2011, No. 5, pp. 68)
Pub: Phoenix Media Corporation
Ed: Lori Sichtermann. **Description:** University Book Store Inc. is a campus bookstore located at the University of Washington, in Seattle. The book store provides more than $1 million in UW customer rebates and discounts annually and donated more than $800,000 in UW student scholarships.

28218 ■ "Up Against the Ropes: A Professional Coach May Help" in *Black Enterprise* (Vol. 37, December 2006, No. 5, pp. 72)
Pub: Earl G. Graves Publishing Co. Inc.
Ed: Description: Executive coaching is now a $1 billion industry. The coaching process itself and traits to look for in a coach are discussed.

28219 ■ "An Updated Ranking of Academic Journals in Economics" in *Canadian Journal of Economics* (Vol. 44, November 2011, No. 4, pp. 1525)
Pub: Blackwell Publishers Ltd.
Ed: Pantelis Kalaitzidakis, Theofanis P. Mamuneas, Thanasis Stengos. **Description:** An updated list showing the ranking of economic journals (2003) is presented; however this present study differs methodologically from an earlier study by using a rolling window of years between 2003 and 2008, for each year counting the number of citations of articles published in the previous ten years.

28220 ■ "Using Teaching Teams to Encourage Active Learning" in *Business Communication Quarterly* (December 2007, pp. 457)
Pub: Sage Publications USA
Ed: Lisa E. Gueldenzoph. **Description:** The practice of dividing classes into teaching teams to encourage active learning is studied. Students in business management courses become more involved in the learning process with this technique and collaborate to enhance better understanding of course content.

28221 ■ "USM Focuses on Turning Science Into New Companies, Cash" in *Boston Business Journal* (Vol. 29, July 1, 2011, No. 8, pp. 1)
Pub: American City Business Journals Inc.
Ed: Alexander Jackson. **Description:** University System of Maryland gears up to push for its plan for commercializing its scientific discoveries which by 2020 could create 325 companies and double the $1.4 billion the system's eleven schools garner in yearly research grants. It is talking with University of Utah and University Maryland, Baltimore to explore ways to make this plan a reality.

28222 ■ "UT Deans Serious about Biz" in *Austin Business Journal* (Vol. 31, May 20, 2011, No. 11, pp. 1)
Pub: American City Business Journals Inc.
Ed: Sandra Zaragoza. **Description:** Dean Thomas Gilligan of the University of Texas, McCombs School of Business and engineering school Dean Gregory Fenves have partnered to develop a joint engineering and business degree. Their partnership has resulted in an undergraduate course on initiating startups.

28223 ■ "The Valuation of Players" in *Canadian Business* (Vol. 80, October 22, 2007, No. 21, pp. 39)
Pub: Rogers Media
Ed: Jeff Sanford. **Description:** Business professionals are supplementing their Masters in Business Administration degrees with CBV or chartered business valuator. CBVs are trained, not only in business tangibles, but also in business intangibles such as market position, reputation, intellectual property, and patent. Details of employment opportunities for chartered business valuators are discussed.

28224 ■ "Verdict: Few Legal Jobs" in *Boston Business Journal* (Vol. 31, June 17, 2011, No. 21, pp. 1)
Pub: Boston Business Journal
Ed: Lisa van der Pool. **Description:** Law school graduates in Massachusetts are finding it harder to find work as the legal job market remains weak. The national employment rate for the 2010 law school class fell to 87.6 percent, while only 68.4 percent held jobs that require passing the bar examination.

28225 ■ "Vision for Camden in Better Focus" in *Philadelphia Business Journal* (Vol. 30, September 30, 2011, No. 33, pp. 1)
Pub: American City Business Journals Inc.
Ed: Natalie Kostelni. **Description:** More than $500 million worth of projects aimed at redeveloping the downtown and waterfront areas of Camden, New Jersey are being planned. These include the construction of residential, commercial, and education buildings.

28226 ■ "What Businesses Can Do: Growing the Supply of Highly Skilled Graduates" in *Canadian Business* (Vol. 81, October 27, 2008, No. 18)
Pub: Rogers Media Ltd.
Description: Employers in Canada have expressed concerns over the findings of various studies that revealed current and projected labor shortages in the country. A low birthrate and an aging population is contributing to the problem. Ways businesses can increase the supply of highly skilled workers in Canada is presented.

28227 ■ "What School Did You Attend?" in *Hawaii Business* (Vol. 53, December 2007, No. 6, pp. 14)
Pub: Hawaii Business Publishing
Ed: Kelli Abe Trifonovitch. **Description:** Discusses the question "what school did you attend?" which is observed to be the most important inquiry in Hawaiian business discourse. The principle behind the question is based on establishing connections. The relation between the aforementioned inquiry and Hawaiian culture is explained.

28228 ■ "What's Working Now: In Providing Jobs for North Carolinians" in *Business North Carolina* (Vol. 28, February 2008, No. 2, pp. 16)
Pub: Business North Carolina
Ed: Edward Martin, Frank Maley. **Description:** Individuals previously employed in the furniture, tobacco, or textile manufacturing sectors have gone back to school to be trained in new sectors in the area such as life sciences, finances and other emerging sectors.

28229 ■ "Wheatfield First Choice for Canadian Manufacturer" in *Business First Buffalo* (November 23, 2007, pp. 1)
Pub: American City Business Journals, Inc.
Ed: James Fink. **Description:** Niagara County Industrial Development Agency is preparing an enticement program that would lure automotive parts manufacturer Pop & Lock Corporation to shift manufacturing operations to Wheatfield, Niagara County, New York. The package includes job-training grants and assistance for acquiring new machinery. Details of the plan are included.

28230 ■ "Where to Buy the Right MBA" in *Canadian Business* (Vol. 79, October 23, 2006, No. 21, pp. 99)
Pub: Rogers Media
Ed: Erin Pooley; Laura Bogomolny; Joe Castaldo; Michelle Magnan; Claire Gagne. **Description:** Details of Canadian graduate business schools offering Master of business administration degree are presented.

28231 ■ "Where New Economy Initiative Grants Have Gone" in *Crain's Detroit Business* (Vol. 25, June 1, 2009, No. 22, pp. M014)
Pub: Crain Communications Inc. - Detroit
Description: Listing of grants totaling $20.5 million focusing on talent development, attraction and retention; innovation and entrepreneurship; and shifting to a culture that values learning, work and innovation, is presented.

28232 ■ "The WIN Library" in *Women In Business* (Vol. 61, August-September 2009, No. 4, pp. 36)
Pub: American Business Women's Association
Ed: Leigh Elmore. **Description:** Women's Instructional Network (WIN) offers members of the American Business Women's Association with information about the organization and 15 Team Tools learning modules to help further the learning of business women. Other training programs and services offered by WIN are presented.

28233 ■ "A Woman's Advantage" in *Black Enterprise* (Vol. 38, December 2007, No. 5, pp. 86)
Pub: Earl G. Graves Publishing Co. Inc.
Ed: Marcia Reed-Woodard. **Description:** Leadership development is essential for any small business. Simmons College's Strategic Leadership for Women

educational course offers a five-day program for professional women teaching powerful strategies to perform, compete, and win in the workplace.

28234 ■ "Women as 21st Century Leaders" in *Women In Business* (Vol. 63, Summer 2011, No. 2, pp. 26)
Pub: American Business Women's Association

Ed: Leigh Elmore. **Description:** American Business Women's Association and Park University have partnered to provide a leadership training program to attendees of the 2011 National Women's Leadership Conference. The courses will incorporate introduction to concepts, development of critical thinking skills and direct application through exercises. Comments from executives are also included.

28235 ■ "Women and Higher Education" in *Montly Labor Review* (Vol. 133, September 2010, No. 9, pp. 70)
Pub: Bureau of Labor Statistics

Description: The increase in people going to college has been mostly among women. Statistical data included.

28236 ■ "Work Force: In the Mix" in *Entrepreneur* (Vol. 35, October 2007, No. 10, pp. 109)
Pub: Entrepreneur Media Inc.

Ed: Mark Henricks. **Description:** A study of 708 companies' diversity programs shows that diversity training alone is not the most effective way of increasing diversity in management. It was found that one effective way of putting minorities and women in management teams is to give a team or a person the task of improving diversity in the company. The reason why accountability succeeds in diversifying the workforce is discussed.

28237 ■ "Work Less, Earn More" in *Canadian Business* (Vol. 80, March 12, 2007, No. 6, pp. 30)
Pub: Rogers Media

Ed: Erin Pooley. **Description:** Expert advice on ways to work efficiently to complete the job instead of extending work hours is presented.

28238 ■ *Working Papers, Chapters 1-14 for Needles/Powers/Crosson's Financial and Managerial Accounting*
Pub: Cengage South-Western

Ed: Belverd E. Needles, Marian Powers, Susan V. Crosson. **Released:** May 10, 2010. **Price:** $62.95. **Description:** Appropriate accounting forms for completing all exercises, problems and cases in the text are provided for financial management of a small company.

28239 ■ "The World Is Your Oyster" in *Canadian Business* (Vol. 80, October 22, 2007, No. 21, pp. 140)
Pub: Rogers Media

Ed: Regan Ray. **Description:** Business graduates are not that keen on working abroad. Fortune 500 companies are requiring executives to have a multi-country focus. The skill required for jobs abroad, as well as employment opportunities are discussed.

28240 ■ "The World is Their Classroom" in *Crain's Chicago Business* (Vol. 31, March 24, 2008, No. 12, pp. 24)
Pub: Crain Communications, Inc.

Ed: Samantha Stainburn. **Description:** Due to globalization more business students are studying abroad; 89 percent of eligible students in its executive MBA program went overseas in 2007 compared to 15 percent ten years ago.

28241 ■ "Young Entrepreneur Gets Some Recognition and Some Help for College" in *Philadelphia Inquirer* (August 30, 2010)
Pub: Philadelphia Inquirer

Ed: Susan Snyder. **Description:** Profile of Zachary Gosling, age 18, who launched an online auction Website from his bedroom, using advertising and sponsorship funds rather than charging fees to users.

TRADE PERIODICALS

28242 ■ *AACE Bonus Briefs*
Pub: American Association for Career Education

Ed: Pat Nellor Wickwire, Editor. **Released:** Quarterly. **Price:** Included in membership. **Description:** Contains brief papers by American Association for Career Education members on current issues in careers, education, and employment.

28243 ■ *AACE Distinguished Member Series*
Pub: American Association for Career Education

Ed: Pat Nellor Wickwire, Editor. **Released:** Periodic. **Price:** Included in membership. **Description:** Publication of the American Association for Career Education. Provides information on careers, education, and employment.

28244 ■ *AACSB Newsline*
Pub: AACSB—American Assembly of Collegiate Schools of Business
Contact: Roxanna Motchan

Ed: Becky Johnson, Editor. **Released:** 4/yr. **Price:** $25 /year; $35 elsewhere. **Description:** Covers issues and events affecting management education, and Association projects and activities. Recurring features include notices of publications available and news of educational opportunities.

28245 ■ *California Special Education Alert*
Pub: LRP Publications
Contact: Steve Bevilacquar, Editorial Dir.

Released: Monthly. **Price:** $260 plus $27 s/h. **Description:** Assists California special education administrators comply with changing special education laws, regulations, and policies on the state and federal level to avoid litigation. Recurring features include letters to the editor, interviews, and reports of meetings.

28246 ■ *The Chemical Educator*
Pub: The Chemical Educator
Contact: Clifford LeMaster, Editor-in-Chief
E-mail: chemeducator@gmail.org

Released: Bimonthly. **Price:** $29.95; $149.95 institutions print archive edition available separately; $10 single issue shipping. **Description:** Online journal for chemical educators with a print archive version.

28247 ■ *Multimedia Internet@Schools*
Pub: Information Today Inc.

Released: Bimonthly. **Price:** $45.95 U.S.; $60 Canada and Mexico; $69 other countries; $86 U.S. 2 years; $132 U.S. 3 years. **Description:** Consumer guide to high-tech school products. Includes purchasing recommendations, cost-saving tips, and technical advice. Written for and by K-12 school professionals.

28248 ■ *School Scene*
Pub: Technology Student Association (TSA)
Contact: Lynda Haitz

Ed: Jane Wright, Editor. **Released:** 3x/yr. **Price:** Included in membership. **Description:** Functions as a member newsletter for the Technology Student Association. Dedicated to preparing membership for the challenges of a dynamic world by promoting personal growth and opportunities. Also provides competitive event news and tips, along with conference news. Recurring features include interviews, a calendar of events, reports of meetings, news of educational opportunities, and notices of publications available.

28249 ■ *Teach Magazine*
Pub: TEACH Magazine
Contact: Vinicio Scarci, Art Ed.

Released: 5/yr. **Price:** $18.95 Canada; $28.95 other countries. **Description:** Educational publication featuring reproducible teaching units.

28250 ■ *Thimband-The Newsletter*
Pub: Continuus
Contact: A. Doyle

Ed: A.C. Doyle, Editor. **Released:** Annual. **Price:** $6. **Description:** Provides useful information for homemakers and consumers.

VIDEOCASSETTES/ AUDIOCASSETTES

28251 ■ *Adult Learning? You've Got to Be Kidding!*
American Society for Training and Development (ASTD)
1640 King St.
Box 1443
Alexandria, VA 22313-2043
Ph:(703)683-8100
Free: 800-628-2783
Fax:(703)683-8103
URL: http://www.astd.org

Released: 1989. **Description:** A look at the seven steps to becoming an all-star trainer in business and industry. Describes how to use the principles of learning theory to improve training sessions. Focuses on the issues of the adult learner, including fear of failure, new technology vs. past experience, and bureaucractic systems. **Availability:** VHS; 3/4U.

28252 ■ *Basic Techniques in Practical Chemistry*
TMW Media Group
2321 Abbot Kinney Blvd., Ste. 101
Venice, CA 90291
Ph:(310)577-8581
Free: 800-262-8862
Fax:(310)574-0886
Co. E-mail: general@tmwmedia.com
URL: http://www.tmwmedia.com

Released: 1997. **Price:** $395.00. **Description:** Ten-volume series provide hands on presentations and precise, analytical content that make difficult chemistry understandable for all levels. **Availability:** VHS.

28253 ■ *Charley Chapters: Contraction Action*
Media, Inc.
PO Box 496
Media, PA 19063
Ph:(610)565-2844
Free: 800-523-0118
Fax:(610)565-3614
URL: http://www.mediaincorporated.com

Released: 1996. **Price:** $225.00. **Description:** Explains the rules for changing two words into one. **Availability:** VHS.

28254 ■ *Charley Chapters: Root Words, Prefixes, and Suffixes*
Media, Inc.
PO Box 496
Media, PA 19063
Ph:(610)565-2844
Free: 800-523-0118
Fax:(610)565-3614
URL: http://www.mediaincorporated.com

Released: 1996. **Price:** $225.00. **Description:** Provides lessons for making spelling easier. **Availability:** VHS.

28255 ■ *Charley Chapters: Suffixes and Their Rule Changes*
Media, Inc.
PO Box 496
Media, PA 19063
Ph:(610)565-2844
Free: 800-523-0118
Fax:(610)565-3614
URL: http://www.mediaincorporated.com

Released: 1996. **Price:** $225.00. **Description:** Explains the rules for the ways words change when suffixes are added. **Availability:** VHS.

28256 ■ *Charley Chapters: Writing with Synonyms, Antonyms, and the Thesaurus*
Media, Inc.
PO Box 496
Media, PA 19063
Ph:(610)565-2844
Free: 800-523-0118

Fax:(610)565-3614
URL: http://www.mediaincorporated.com
Released: 1995. **Price:** $225.00. **Description:** Explains how to expand vocabulary and writing skills. **Availability:** VHS.

28257 ■ *Common Miracles: The New American Revolution in Learning*
MPI Home Video
16101 S. 108th Ave.
Orland Park, IL 60467
Ph:(708)460-0555
Free: 800-323-0442
Fax:(708)873-3177
URL: http://www.mpihomevideo.com
Released: 1997. **Price:** $19.98. **Description:** Peter Jennings examines the future of education. **Availability:** VHS.

28258 ■ *Disney Presents Bill Nye the Science Guy Sampler III*
Buena Vista Home Entertainment
500 S. Buena Vista St.
Burbank, CA 91521-1120
Free: 800-723-4763
URL: http://www.bvhe.com
Price: $199.00. **Description:** Collection of 10 full-length shows featuring lessons in archeology, volcanoes, inventions, animal locomotion, and more. **Availability:** VHS.

28259 ■ *The Eisenhower Era, 1940-1960*
Buena Vista Home Entertainment
500 S. Buena Vista St.
Burbank, CA 91521-1120
Free: 800-723-4763
URL: http://www.bvhe.com
Price: $699.00. **Description:** Twenty-volume series covers four thematic units: World War II, The Cold War, The Eisenhower Presidency (Domestic Policy), and The Eisenhower Presidency (Foreign Policy). Includes teacher's guide, companion software, and activities. **Availability:** VHS.

28260 ■ *Got a Problem? Solve It!*
Sunburst Technology
1550 Executive Dr.
Elgin, IL 60123
Free: 888-492-8817
Fax:888-800-3028
Co. E-mail: service@sunburst.com
URL: http://www.sunburst.com
Released: 1997. **Price:** $59.95. **Description:** Four vignettes present positive strategies for logical thinking and problem solving. On-screen questions promote classroom discussions. **Availability:** VHS.

28261 ■ *Helping Your Child Succeed in School*
Tapeworm Video Distributors
25876 The Old Road 141
Stevenson Ranch, CA 91381
Ph:(661)257-4904
Fax:(661)257-4820
Co. E-mail: sales@tapeworm.com
URL: http://www.tapeworm.com
Price: $18.95. **Description:** Six part video series discussing aspects of all stages of learning and development. **Availability:** VHS.

28262 ■ *Hola Amigos Boxed Set*
Monterey Home Video
566 St. Charles Dr.
Thousand Oaks, CA 91360-3953
Ph:(805)494-7199
Free: 800-424-2593
Fax:(805)496-6061
Co. E-mail: customerservice@montereymedia.com
URL: http://www.montereymedia.com
Released: 1997. **Price:** $54.95. **Description:** Three-volume set uses songs and games to provide a gentle introduction to the Spanish language. **Availability:** VHS.

28263 ■ *How to Be a Better Trainer*
GPN Educational Media
1550 Executive Drive
Elgin, IL 60123
Ph:(402)472-2007
Free: 800-228-4630
Fax:800-306-2330
Co. E-mail: askgpn@smarterville.com
URL: http://www.shopgpn.com
Price: $249.95. **Description:** Three-volume series introduces employers, managers and teachers to the elements and techniques of effective training. **Availability:** VHS.

28264 ■ *Johnny Tremain*
Buena Vista Home Entertainment
500 S. Buena Vista St.
Burbank, CA 91521-1120
Free: 800-723-4763
URL: http://www.bvhe.com
Released: 1997. **Price:** $99.00. **Description:** Presents reenactments of historical figures and events such as the Boston Tea Party, Paul Revere, and Samuel Adams. **Availability:** VHS.

28265 ■ *Just the Facts Learning Series: The Great American State Quiz*
Leslie T. McClure
PO Box 1223
Pebble Beach, CA 93953
Ph:(831)656-0553
Fax:(831)656-0555
Co. E-mail: leslie@411videoinfo.com
URL: http://www.411videoinfo.com
Released: 1997. **Price:** $14.95. **Description:** Presents a fun way to learn about the states and capitals. **Availability:** VHS.

28266 ■ *Science in Action*
TMW Media Group
2321 Abbot Kinney Blvd., Ste. 101
Venice, CA 90291
Ph:(310)577-8581
Free: 800-262-8862
Fax:(310)574-0886
Co. E-mail: general@tmwmedia.com
URL: http://www.tmwmedia.com
Released: 1997. **Price:** $119.00. **Description:** Six-volume series explains basic scientific concepts and principles in an easy-to-understand manner. **Availability:** VHS.

28267 ■ *Something Special*
Educational Activities, Inc.
PO Box 87
Baldwin, NY 11510
Free: 800-797-3223
Fax:(516)623-9282
URL: http://www.edact.com
Released: 1997. **Price:** $19.95. **Description:** Teaches movement vocabulary skills and promotes self-esteem. **Availability:** VHS.

28268 ■ *The Story of Joshua and the Battle of Jericho*
MPI Home Video
16101 S. 108th Ave.
Orland Park, IL 60467
Ph:(708)460-0555
Free: 800-323-0442
Fax:(708)873-3177
URL: http://www.mpihomevideo.com
Released: 1997. **Price:** $12.98. **Description:** Animated bible story. **Availability:** VHS.

28269 ■ *Table Time for Tots*
Tapeworm Video Distributors
25876 The Old Road 141
Stevenson Ranch, CA 91381
Ph:(661)257-4904
Fax:(661)257-4820
Co. E-mail: sales@tapeworm.com
URL: http://www.tapeworm.com
Released: 1997. **Price:** $14.95. **Description:** Introduces children to the basic food groups using poem and song. **Availability:** VHS.

28270 ■ *Training 101: Principles, Processes and People Every Trainer Should Know*
American Society for Training and Development (ASTD)
1640 King St.
Box 1443
Alexandria, VA 22313-2043
Ph:(703)683-8100
Free: 800-628-2783
Fax:(703)683-8103
URL: http://www.astd.org
Released: 1989. **Description:** A video overview of training, designed to give trainers more competence and confidence. Basic processes and concepts are explained and human resource development experts present descriptions of their work. **Availability:** VHS; 3/4U.

28271 ■ *Transformations: Science, Technology, and Society*
Karol Media
Hanover Industrial Estates
375 Stewart Rd.
PO Box 7600
Wilkes Barre, PA 18773-7600
Ph:(570)822-8899
Free: 800-526-4773
Co. E-mail: sales@karolmedia.com
URL: http://www.karolmedia.com
Released: 1997. **Price:** $125.00. **Description:** Eight-volume series designed to motivate learning and enhance science instruction. **Availability:** VHS.

28272 ■ *Volcanoes: Cauldrons of Fury*
MPI Home Video
16101 S. 108th Ave.
Orland Park, IL 60467
Ph:(708)460-0555
Free: 800-323-0442
Fax:(708)873-3177
URL: http://www.mpihomevideo.com
Price: $19.98. **Description:** Examines the causes, history and future of volcanoes. **Availability:** VHS.

TRADE SHOWS AND CONVENTIONS

28273 ■ Michigan Association for Computer Users in Learning Conference
Michigan Association for Computer Users in Learning
3410 Belle Chase Way, Ste. 100
Holt, MI 48842-0518
Ph:(517)694-9756
Fax:(517)694-9773
Co. E-mail: macul@macul.org
URL: http://www.macul.org
Released: Annual. **Audience:** Educational technology professionals. **Principal Exhibits:** Computer and educational equipment, supplies, and services.

CONSULTANTS

28274 ■ AMC International Inc.
864 S Robertson Blvd., Ste. 207
PO Box 11292
Los Angeles, CA 90035
Ph:(310)652-5620
Fax:(310)652-6709
Co. E-mail: inquiry@amcusa.com
Contact: Abe Moradian, President
Scope: Offers day to day business management, business turn around, marketing strategies, development or refinement of corporate mission, and merger and acquisition evaluations. Industries served all.

28275 ■ American English Academy
111 N Atlantic Blvd., Ste. 112
Monterey Park, CA 91754
Ph:(626)457-2800
Fax:(626)457-2808
Co. E-mail: admission@aea-usa.com
URL: http://www.aea-usa.com
Contact: Charles Policky, President
Scope: Specializes in providing on-site English language and communication development for corporations and individuals. Also develops and delivers training in speaking, writing, pronunciation, grammar, and idioms with an emphasis on business communication. Offers individual, small group, intensive, and long-distance learning. Programs tailor-made for each client.

28276 ■ Art Munin Consulting
c/o Assistant Dean of Students Office
Depaul University, Student Ctr.
Chicago, IL 60614-3673
Ph:(773)316-2276
Co. E-mail: art@artmunin.com
URL: http://www.artmunin.com
Contact: Art Munin, Principle
Scope: Consulting firm committed to advancing multicultural education and imparting advocacy. Expands the opportunities to engage people in conversations about diversity and social justice. Other areas of interest include counseling skills, crisis response, improving the campus climate for bi/multiracial students, sexual assault, GLBT advocacy, team building, and other diversity-related training topics. **Publications:** "Would they still have written if they knew I had to go home and tell my wife?," 2009; "The leadership bookshelf," 2009; "Improving the campus environment for bi/multiracial students," Peter Lang Publishing, 2009; "Empathy: Love the sinner, hate the sin. About Campus," 2007; "Factors influencing the ally development of college students". **Seminars:** White Privilege 101; Locating Justice; Targeting the Majority in Diversity Education; Art of War - Targeting the Majority in Multicultural Education; Higher Education: The Gate-Keeper to the Middle Class; Who Are Our Transgendered Students?; The Basics of Diversity Training; Retreats; Ethics and Leadership: Making Choices for Social Justice.

28277 ■ Beeline Learning Solutions
14911 Quorum Dr., Ste. 120
Dallas, TX 75254
Ph:(972)813-0465
Fax:(972)386-8667
Co. E-mail: info@consultingpartners.com
URL: http://www.beeline.com
Contact: Debra Gann, Managering Director
E-mail: gann@atsconsultingpartners.com
Scope: Consulting firm offering technology, content, and services addressing recruitment and sourcing, talent management, and learning and performance optimization. Solutions offered include contingent workforce solutions, vendor management software, talent management solutions, recruitment process outsourcing, performance management, applicant tracking, learning management and eLearning. **Special Services:** Beeline[R].

28278 ■ Blackmon Roberts Group Inc.
4000 Ponce De Leon Blvd., Ste. 470
Coral Gables, FL 33145
Ph:(863)802-1280
Fax:(863)802-1290
Co. E-mail: dbeinformation@blackmonroberts.com
URL: http://www.blackmonroberts.com
Contact: Willie Barnes, Principal
Scope: Technical support consultant in technical writing, planning, research, needs analysis, marketing and training, offers training programs from cultural sensitivity issues to effective listening skills.

28279 ■ Business Education Associates
4 Long Hill Rd.
PO Box 4
Bethel, CT 06801
Ph:(203)798-6035
Contact: Robert J. Popp, President
E-mail: bob@ashfordgrp.com
Scope: Offers tailored management education programs. Has been designed to meet the business education needs of companies implementing new systems and companies to re-educate users of existing systems. **Publications:** "The Ashford Group and TQuist Partner to Provide High Impact Manufacturing Solutions"; "The Future of ERP"; "Winning the Implementation Game". **Special Services:** Building Manufacturing Excellence.

28280 ■ Business Improvement Architects
33 Riderwood Dr.
Toronto, ON, Canada M2L 2X4
Ph:(416)444-8225
Free: (866)346-3242
Fax:(416)444-6743
Co. E-mail: info@bia.ca
URL: http://www.bia.ca
Contact: Susan Lee, Principle
E-mail: slee@atsbia.ca
Scope: Provides the following services: strategic planning, leadership development, innovation and project and quality management. Specialize in strategic planning, change management, leadership assessment, and development of skills. **Publications:** "Avoiding Pit falls to Innovation"; "Create a New Dimension of Performance with Innovation"; "The Power of Appreciation in Leadership"; "Why It Makes Sense To Have a Strategic Enterprise Office"; "Burning Rubber at the Start of Your Project"; "Accounting for Quality"; "How Pareto Charts Can Help You Improve the Quality of Business Processes"; "Managing Resistance to Change". **Seminars:** The Innovation Process. . .From Vision to Reality, San Diego, Oct, 2007; Critical Thinking, Kuala Lump or, Sep, 2007; Critical Thinking, Brunei, Sep, 2007; Delivering Project Assurance, Auckland, Jun, 2007; From Crisis to Control: A New Era in Strategic Project Management, Prague, May, 2007; What Project Leaders Need to Know to Help Them Sleep Better At Night, London, May, 2007; Innovation Process. . .From Vision To Reality, Orlando, Apr, 2007. **Special Services:** Project Planning Tool[TM].

28281 ■ Center for Personal Empowerment
102 N Main St., Ste. 1
Columbia, IL 62236-1702
Ph:(618)281-3565
Free: 888-657-1530
Fax:(618)476-7083
Co. E-mail: personalempowerment@wholenet.net
Contact: Cherri Hendrix, Vice President
Scope: Private consultations and trainings to educate on how to determine which emotions, events, beliefs from the past prevent you from achieving success. Methods used include time line therapy, news linguistic programming and hypnosis. Behavior modification through NLP trainings. **Seminars:** NLP Practitioner Training; Hypnosis Certification Training; Lifemap Seminars.

28282 ■ Competitive Edge Inc.
241 E Crestwood Rd.
PO Box 2418
Peachtree City, GA 30269
Ph:(770)487-6460
Fax:(770)487-2919
Co. E-mail: judy@competitiveedgeinc.com
URL: http://www.competitiveedgeinc.com
Contact: Judy I. Suiter, President
E-mail: judy@competitiveedgeinc.com
Scope: Human resources consulting firm providing customized training and software solutions to assist clients in optimizing their human intellectual capital through effective selection, coaching, and training. Works with a network of consultants that are located throughout the United States, Canada, and Europe. **Publications:** "Beteenden och drivkrafter"; "Energizing People: Unleashing The Power of DISC"; "The Ripple Effect: How the Global Model of Endorsement Opens Doors to Success"; "The Journey - Quotes to keep your boat afloat"; "The Universal Language DISC Reference Manual "; "Exploring Values: Releasing the Power of Attitudes"; "COMPETITIVE PRODUCTS REVIEW BOOK"; "The Mother Of All Minds". **Seminars:** How to Recruit and Retain High Performing Employees; The Importance of Values Matching For Sales Selection; How to Build a High Performance Team; Dynamic Communication Skills; Creating Nurturing Customer Relationships; Your Attitude Is Showing; Sales Strategy Index; Validity Study.

28283 ■ Daniel Bloom and Associates Inc.
11517 128th Ave. N
PO Box 1233
Largo, FL 33779
Ph:(727)581-6216
Fax:(727)216-8532
Co. E-mail: dan@dbaiconsulting.com
URL: http://www.dbaiconsulting.com
Contact: Sharon Megiel, Principle
E-mail: dan@dbaiconsulting.com
Scope: Human resources management consultant with a specialization in corporate relocation. Offers clients a turn key service aimed at meeting the unique relocation needs of their employees. Develops and implements training programs within the relocation industry. **Publications:** "Where Have All the Elders Gone," Aug, 2002; "Recoup Your Hiring Investment," Brainbuzz.com, Aug, 2000; "Managing Your Lump Sum Program," Brainbuzz.com, Jun, 2000; "Buyer Value Options," Brainbuzz.com, Apr, 2000; "Just Get Me There". **Seminars:** Chaos in the Workplace: Multiple Generational Interactions; Training Effectiveness: Is the Cost Justified?; Human Capital Resource Management: A Six-Sigma Based Approach to Paving Your Way to the Table; Welcome to My World.

28284 ■ Donna Cornell Enterprises Inc.
68 N Plank Rd., Ste. 204
Newburgh, NY 12550-2122
Ph:(845)565-0088
Free: 888-769-3792
Fax:(845)565-0084
Co. E-mail: rc@cornellcareercenter.com
Contact: Donna Cornell, President
E-mail: rc@cornellcareercenter.com
Scope: Offers services in career consultant, professional search, job placement and national professional search. **Publications:** "The Power of the Woman Within"; "Juggling it All!"; "Journey: A Woman's Guide to Success"; "Shatter the Traditions".

28285 ■ donphin.com Inc.
1001 B Ave., Ste. 200
Coronado, CA 92118
Ph:(619)550-3533
Free: 800-234-3304
Fax:(619)600-0096
Co. E-mail: inquiry@donphin.com
URL: http://www.donphin.com
Contact: Donald A. Phin, CEO
E-mail: don@donphin.com
Scope: Offers a comprehensive approach to understanding and applying a broad range of business principles: legal compliance issues, management concerns, health and safety, customer service, marketing, information management. Industries served: All developing small businesses. **Publications:** "Doing Business Right!"; "HR That Works!"; "Lawsuit Free! How to Prevent Employee Lawsuits"; "Building Powerful Employment Relationships!"; "Victims, Villains and Heroes: Managing Emotions in The Workplace". **Seminars:** Doing Business Right!; HR That Works!; Building Powerful Employment Relationships; Lawsuit Free!.

28286 ■ Dorn & Associates Inc.
8506 Bass Lake Rd.
Minneapolis, MN 55428-5304
Ph:(763)533-7689
Fax:(763)533-1143
Contact: Chad L. Dorn, Vice President
E-mail: chad@dorn-associates.com
Scope: Services include accounting, marketing, employment partnership, new doctor agreements, personnel issues and human resources assessment, practice management, practice merger acquisition sale and liquidation, practice surveys and valuation, staff development and training.

28287 ■ Full Voice
3217 Broadway Ave., Ste. 300
Kansas City, MO 64111
Ph:(816)941-0011
Free: 800-684-8764
Fax:(816)931-8887
Co. E-mail: info@infullvoice.com
URL: http://www.fullvoice.us
Contact: Michienne Dixon, Principle
E-mail: garrett@infullvoice.com
Scope: Vocal performance training firm offering consulting services and personal training sessions in the implementation of effective vocal communication techniques for the development of business relationships and career enhancement. Formalizes a program of proven techniques into a practical method of helping individuals improve their ability to better present themselves when speaking in a professional situation. Industries served: All. **Publications:** "You Can Sound Like You Know What You're Saying". **Seminars:** You Can Sound Like You Know What You're Saying; The Psychology of Vocal Performance; Security. . .the Ability to Accept Change; Knowing. .

.the Key to Relaxed Public Communication; The Effective Voice for Customer Service Enhancement; You Can Speak With Conviction; How To Make Yours a Championship Team; Functional English For Foreign Trade. **Special Services:** FULL VOICE™.

28288 ■ Harding & Co.
511 Harvard Ave.
Swarthmore, PA 19081
Ph:(973)763-9284
Fax:(973)763-9347
Co. E-mail: fharding@hardingco.com
URL: http://www.hardingco.com
Contact: Gary Pines, Principle
E-mail: gpines@atshardingco.com
Scope: Firm specializes in sales management, client development and employee training. **Publications:** "Cross-Selling Success: A Rainmakers Guide to Professional Account Development," Aug, 2002; "Rain Making: The Professional's Guide to Attracting New Clients"; "Creating Rainmakers: The Managers Guide to Training Professionals to Attract New Clients".

28289 ■ Hills Consulting Group Inc.
6 Partridge Ct.
Novato, CA 94945-1315
Ph:(415)898-3944
Contact: Michael R. Hills, President
Scope: Specializes in strategic planning; marketing surveys; market research; customer service audits; new product development; competitive analysis; and sales forecasting.

28290 ■ Interpersonal Coaching & Consulting
1516 W Lake St., Ste. 2000S
Minneapolis, MN 55408
Ph:(612)381-2494
Fax:(612)381-2494
Co. E-mail: mail@interpersonal-coaching.com
URL: http://www.interpersonal-coaching.com
Contact: Mary Belfry, Partner
E-mail: mail@interpersonal-coaching.com
Scope: Provides coaching and consulting to businesses and organizations. Assesses the interpersonal workplace through interviews, assessment instruments and individual group settings. Experienced as a therapist for over a decade. **Seminars:** Sexual harassment and discrimination issues.

28291 ■ Mandalay Associates L.L.C.
190 El Cerrito Plz.
PO Box 226
El Cerrito, CA 94530-4002
Ph:(510)526-4651
Fax:(510)526-5774
Scope: Business management firm specializes in conflict resolution, employee relations, employment and placement, organizational analysis and development, human resources program development, program and project management, and staff development and training.

28292 ■ Milestone Inc.
PO Box 630
Dedham, MA 02027
Ph:(781)467-1200
Fax:(781)467-0299
Co. E-mail: bob@milestoneideas.com
URL: http://www.milestoneideas.com
Contact: William J. Heater, Mgr
E-mail: bob@milestoneideas.com
Scope: Facilitates 100 business creativity and innovation growth sessions per year. Assists to: Discover new growth strategies and planning options; create new ideas, new promises, value propositions, products and programs; identify and integrate customer passions in new and surprising ways; realize higher returns on involvement, interest and investment; refine processes, accelerate innovative growth and build better teams. **Publications:** "Can your brand tell a bigger story". **Seminars:** Ideas in Action; Double-Gesturing; Growth in a period of no growth; Strike while the iron is cold; Natural Creative Strategies; The Enduring Power of Open Ended Creativity; Ideation Techniques to Drive Brand Value. **Special Services:** Milestone®; IMMERgENT®; SmartAlec.

28293 ■ National Pediculosis Association Inc.
50 Kearney Rd.
PO Box 610189
Newton, MA 02461
Free: 800-446-4672
Fax:800-235-1305
Co. E-mail: npa@headlice.org
URL: http://www.headlice.org
Contact: Linda Menditto, Dir of Operations
E-mail: dza@headlice.org
Scope: Consultants in head lice and scabies management, treatment, prevention, and education. Specializes in monitoring health policy administration in schools and trends in the treatment of head lice. Emphasis is on educational activities. Industries served: schools, health professionals, medical professionals, child care centers, health departments, hospitals, HMO's, clinics, libraries, parents, PTA's, camps, military bases, and churches. **Publications:** "All out Comb out".

28294 ■ ProActive English
4355 SE 29th Ave.
Portland, OR 97202
Ph:(503)231-2906
Co. E-mail: infopae@proactive-english.com
URL: http://www.proactive-english.com
Contact: David Kertzner, Managing Director
E-mail: dkertzner@atsproactive-english.com
Scope: Offers on-site individual and small group language and communication training. Sets up learning plans tailored to the needs and schedules of managers and executives who are non-native English speakers. Serves all industries. **Seminars:** Communicating in Business Situations; Presentations and Pronunciation; Tailored Curriculum; One-on-One Programs.

28295 ■ Professional Psychological Services
4130 Linden Ave., Ste. 309
Dayton, OH 45432-3034
Ph:(937)254-7301
Fax:(937)254-2117
Co. E-mail: ppsdocs@aol.com
Contact: Dr. Keith Vukasinovich, Principle
Scope: Offers clinical services, human relations training, multicultural and pluralistic training, and staff development and training.

28296 ■ Sandy Corp.
1149 W 190th St.
Gardena, CA 90248
Ph:(248)649-0800
Free: 800-733-4739
Fax:(248)729-4700
Co. E-mail: info@sandycorp.com
URL: http://www.sandycorp.com
Contact: Phil Werber, Vice President
Scope: It provides the design, development and production of specific consulting, training, communicating and evaluating programs to help clients improve the capabilities of their people to such a level that consistent performance on the job becomes a visible, valued competitive strength.

28297 ■ Tamayo Consulting Inc.
169 Saxony Rd., Ste. 112
Encinitas, CA 92024-6779
Ph:(760)479-1352
Free: 800-580-9606
Fax:(760)479-1465
Co. E-mail: info@tamayoconsulting.com
URL: http://www.tamayoconsulting.com
Contact: Diane West, Principal
E-mail: jdreyer@atsearthlink.net
Scope: Training and consulting firm specializing in leadership and team development. Industries served: private, non-profit, government, educational. **Seminars:** Presentation AdvantEdge Program; Lead point Development Program; Supervisor Development Programs.

28298 ■ Tel-Advise
5635 Highland Rd., Ste. 100
Cleveland, OH 44143-2007
Ph:(440)646-9861
Fax:(216)274-9200
Contact: Russell Vidrine, Principle
Scope: Computers system designers and consultants. **Publications:** "Spanning the Globe".

28299 ■ Training Systems Plus
742 Brent Dr.
PO Box 185
Mulvane, KS 67110-1245
Ph:(316)777-1337
Fax:(316)777-0802
Co. E-mail: chastrain@cox.net
Contact: Charles M. Cadwell, President
E-mail: chastrain@cox.net
Scope: Provides management and training systems to businesses to improve operational profitability as well as individual management and employee performance. Activities include consultation, job descriptions, evaluation forms, training seminars, training materials, operations manuals and employee handbooks. **Seminars:** Effective Classroom Instruction; Training System Design; Interviewing and Selecting; Performance Management, Leadership Skills.

FRANCHISES AND BUSINESS OPPORTUNITIES

28300 ■ Canadian School of Natural Nutrition
10720 Yonge St., Ste. 220
Richmond Hill, ON, Canada L4C 3C9
Ph:(905)737-8729
Free: 800-569-9938
Fax:(905)737-7830
Co. E-mail: hq@csnn.ca
URL: http://www.csnn.ca
No. of Franchise Units: 4. **No. of Company-Owned Units:** 9. **Founded:** 1994. **Franchised:** 1996. **Description:** private vocational school offering adult education leading to professional designations: RHN-Reg. Holistic Nutritionist, and RECP-Reg, ElderCare Practitioner. Franchisees are licensed to distribute CSNN curriculum material to students through classroom education. CSNN offers two programs: Natural Nutrition and Elder Care. CSNN is privately owned, incorporated as 3393291 Canada Inc. **Equity Capital Needed:** $70,000 Canadian Capital. **Franchise Fee:** $12,000. **Training:** Ongoing.

28301 ■ Club Scientific
636 Steels Bridge Rd.
Canton, GA 30114
Ph:(678)880-6460
No. of Franchise Units: 4. **No. of Company-Owned Units:** 8. **Founded:** 1987. **Franchised:** 2007. **Description:** Science enrichment program. **Equity Capital Needed:** $56,825-$84,720. **Franchise Fee:** $20,000-$24,500. **Royalty Fee:** 6%. **Financial Assistance:** Limited in-house financing available. **Training:** Provides 4 days training at headquarters, 4 days at franchisee's location and ongoing support.

28302 ■ Cybertary
1217 Pleasant Grove Blvd., Ste. 100
Roseville, CA 95678
Ph:(916)781-7799
Free: 888-CYB-TARY
Fax:877-CYB-TARY
Co. E-mail: Franchise@Cybertary.com
URL: http://www.CybertaryFranchise.com
No. of Franchise Units: 23. **Founded:** 2005. **Franchised:** 2006. **Description:** Virtual assistant (VA) industry providing on-demand administrative support to businesses, entrepreneurs, and busy people through a nationwide team network to meet the needs of any business. This home-based B2B service offers low overhead and a flexible schedule. **Equity Capital Needed:** $39,500-$78,500. **Franchise Fee:** $37,500-$56,250. **Royalty Fee:** 5%+. **Financial Assistance:** 50% down, balance financed over 1 year and applies to franchise fee and startup costs. **Training:** Receive 4 days of intensive training before you launch your business & 90 days of weekly one-on-one coaching sessions to build your business once you are up and running.

28303 ■ Drama Kids International, Inc.
525-K E Market St., Ste. 250
Leesburg, VA 20176
Free: (866)809-1055
Co. E-mail: dramakids@starpower.net
URL: http://www.dramakids.com
No. of Franchise Units: 54. **Founded:** 1979. **Franchised:** 1989. **Description:** After-school developmental drama program. Curriculum uses fun & creative drama activities so kids ages 5-17 act confidently and speak clearly. **Equity Capital Needed:** $19,000-$57,950. **Franchise Fee:** $17,000-$48,500. **Royalty Fee:** 8-9%. **Financial Assistance:** Third party financing available. **Training:** Formal initial training followed up with additional 'in-school' handson training, assistance in setting up class locations, pre-opening, postopening assistance, and site visits. Field support provided on an ongoing basis.

28304 ■ E.nopi
50 Passaic St.
Hackensack, NJ 07601
Ph:(201)498-1212
Free: 888-835-1212
Fax:(201)498-1218
No. of Franchise Units: 125. **No. of Company-Owned Units:** 513. **Founded:** 1976. **Franchised:** 1976. **Description:** Supplemental education. **Equity Capital Needed:** $43,100-$89,500. **Franchise Fee:** $12,000. **Royalty Fee:** $15/student. **Financial Assistance:** Limited third party financing available. **Training:** Offers 16 hours+ training at headquarters, at franchisee's location and ongoing.

28305 ■ Estrada Strategies Franchise Inc.
3400 Inland Empire Blvd., Ste. 101
Ontario, CA 91764
Ph:(909)476-3510
Fax:(909)476-3511
No. of Franchise Units: 2. **No. of Company-Owned Units:** 1. **Founded:** 2000. **Franchised:** 2006. **Description:** Executive coaching programs. **Equity Capital Needed:** $43,300-$77,200. **Franchise Fee:** $25,000. **Royalty Fee:** Varies. **Financial Assistance:** No. **Training:** Training at corporate headquarters, onsite and ongoing support provided.

28306 ■ Fastrackids International, Ltd.
6900 E Belleview Ave., 1st Fl.
Greenwood Village, CO 80111
Ph:(303)224-0200
Free: 888-576-6888
Fax:(303)224-0222
Co. E-mail: info@fastrackids.com
URL: http://www.fastrackids.com
No. of Franchise Units: 150. **Founded:** 1998. **Franchised:** 1998. **Description:** An accelerated learning system for children. **Equity Capital Needed:** $33,800-$183,500. **Franchise Fee:** $22,000. **Financial Assistance:** Company will assist in obtaining financing or in some instances provide limited financing. **Managerial Assistance:** Newsletters, a web site, and a procedures manual. **Training:** Provides initial training, periodic regional seminars, an annual international conference, sales/telemarketing assistance, and classroom facilitation tips.

28307 ■ Frozen Ropes Training Centers
12 Elkay Dr.
Chester, NY 10918
Ph:(845)469-7331
Fax:(845)469-6742
No. of Franchise Units: 8. **No. of Company-Owned Units:** 1. **Founded:** 1994. **Franchised:** 2003. **Description:** Baseball & softball instruction. **Equity Capital Needed:** $219,800-$276,200. **Franchise Fee:** $45,000. **Royalty Fee:** 3-6%. **Financial Assistance:** No.

28308 ■ Ho Math & Chess Learning Centre
2265 W 41st St., Ste. 4
Vancouver, BC, Canada V6M 2A3
Ph:(604)266-4321
Fax:(604)266-0974
No. of Franchise Units: 6. **No. of Operating Units:** 21. **Founded:** 1995. **Franchised:** 2004. **Description:** Math & chess learning program. **Equity Capital Needed:** $25,150. **Franchise Fee:** $2,100. **Royalty Fee:** None. **Financial Assistance:** No. **Training:** 1 week training provided at headquarters.

28309 ■ KidzArt
KidzArt Texas LLC
1001 Laurence Ave., Ste. E
Jackson, MI 49201
Ph:888-813-2287
Free: 800-379-8302
Fax:(517)338-5300
Co. E-mail: info@kidzart.com
URL: http://www.kidzart.com
No. of Franchise Units: 65. **Founded:** 1997. **Franchised:** 2002. **Description:** Offers children's products and education services. **Equity Capital Needed:** $15,045-$38,150, includes working capital and franchise fee. **Franchise Fee:** $9,900-$19,900. **Financial Assistance:** Third party SBA registry approved franchisee. **Training:** Offers 1 week business/operations training and cutting edge franchisee support; conferences, monthly training calls, one on one quick start coaching and ongoing support.

28310 ■ KnowledgePoints Inc.
5 Centerpoint Dr., Ste. 250
Lake Oswego, OR 97035
Ph:(503)270-5100
Fax:(503)270-5117
No. of Franchise Units: 46. **No. of Company-Owned Units:** 1 **Founded:** 1999. **Franchised:** 2003. **Description:** Tutoring programs. **Equity Capital Needed:** $89,350-$150,250. **Franchise Fee:** $22,500. **Royalty Fee:** 8%. **Financial Assistance:** Third party financing available. **Training:** Provides 6 days training at headquarters, 3 weeks at franchisee's location, and ongoing support for franchisee & managers.

28311 ■ Kumon North America, Inc.
Glenpointe Centre E
300 Frank W Burr Blvd., Ste. 6
Teaneck, NJ 07666
Free: (866)633-0740
Fax:(201)692-3130
Co. E-mail: franchise@kumon.com
URL: http://www.kumonfranchise.com
No. of Franchise Units: 1,350. **No. of Company-Owned Units:** 24. **Founded:** 1958. **Franchised:** 1980. **Description:** North America provider of supplemental math and learning material. The learning center caters to all ages and abilities from pre-school through high school. **Equity Capital Needed:** $50,000-$70,000 cash; $150,000 net worth, $67,763-$145,320 initial investment. **Franchise Fee:** $1,000. **Training:** Kumon has offices worldwide to provide training, support and onsite consultation to franchisees.

28312 ■ Language Leaders Franchising LLC
Foreign Language Network, L.L.C.
401 W. State St.
Geneva, IL 60134
Ph:(630)377-8794
No. of Company-Owned Units: 1. **Founded:** 1998. **Franchised:** 2004. **Description:** Foreign language education and interpreting. **Equity Capital Needed:** $18,700-$107,000. **Franchise Fee:** $10,000-$90,000. **Royalty Fee:** 15%. **Financial Assistance:** In-house assistance with franchise fee. **Training:** 2 days training at headquarters.

28313 ■ LearningRX Franchise Corp.
LearningRx, Inc.
5085 List Dr., Ste. 201
Colorado Springs, CO 80919
Ph:(719)264-8808
Free: 800-535-5441
No. of Franchise Units: 59. **No. of Company-Owned Units:** 2. **Founded:** 1987. **Franchised:** 2003. **Description:** One on one brain skills and reading training. **Equity Capital Needed:** $26,000-$88,000. **Franchise Fee:** $12,500-$42,500. **Financial Assistance:** No. **Training:** Yes.

28314 ■ The LiceSquad Inc.
Lice Squad Canada Inc.
3A King St.
Cookstown, ON, Canada L0L 1L0
Ph:(705)458-4448
Free: 888-542-3778
Fax:(705)458-8887
Co. E-mail: help@licesquad.com
URL: http://www.licesquad.com
No. of Franchise Units: 8. **No. of Company-Owned Units:** 10. **Founded:** 2001. **Franchised:** 2002. **Description:** Join Canada's leading head lice removal and Education Company. Low start up costs and proven potential. Perfect for those in the nursing, hairdressing and child care fields. Our clients include schools, families, camps and other child care organizations. Our home- based business model allows flexibility. Enjoy both family and career. 15 successful LiceSquad franchises operating in Ontario with master franchises available. **Equity Capital Needed:** $15,000 investment required; start-up capital required $5,000. **Franchise Fee:** $20,000. **Training:** Provides training (excluding travel/hotel costs).

28315 ■ Little City Kids LLC
10127 Northwestern Ave.
Franksville, WI 53126
Ph:(262)884-4226
Fax:(262)884-4230
Co. E-mail: littlecitykids@tds.net
URL: http://www.littlecitykids.com
No. of Company-Owned Units: 1. **Founded:** 1998. **Franchised:** 2004. **Description:** Educational playcare for your child. The environment is set into action in an interactive world filled with imagination stations, innovative online curriculum and team teaching methods. We offer two models, the Little City Kids model is for children ages 2-13 years and the Itty Bitty Kids model adds infant and toddler care. **Equity Capital Needed:** $118,000-$189,000. **Franchise Fee:** $35,000. **Royalty Fee:** 7%. **Financial Assistance:** No. **Training:** Thorough training includes administrative and facility management, operating procedures, development procedures, staff hiring, curriculum and team teaching methods.

28316 ■ The Mad Science Group
8360 Bougainville St., Ste. 201
Montreal, QC, Canada H4P 2G1
Ph:(514)344-4181
Free: 800-586-5231
Fax:(514)344-6695
Co. E-mail: joel@madscience.org
URL: http://www.madscience.org
No. of Franchise Units: 200. **Founded:** 1985. **Franchised:** 1995. **Description:** Mad Science is a service company specializing in fun hands on educational science for children. We send trained instructors with all required materials and supplies to conduct onsite activities to schools and other organizations dealing with kids. Our franchisees are sales marketing oriented individuals who enjoy a hands-on owner operated business that enriches children and contributes to the community. **Equity Capital Needed:** $10,000-$23,500 franchise fee, $25,000 equipment package; $20,000-$30,000 working capital. **Franchise Fee:** $10,000-$23,500. **Financial Assistance:** Yes. **Training:** 6 day training at corporate headquarters followed by 5 day training onsite.

28317 ■ Math Monkey Knowledge Centers
56 Winchester Rd.
Newton, MA 02458
Ph:(954)384-1050
Free: 877-468-6284
No. of Franchise Units: 14. **No. of Company-Owned Units:** 1. **Founded:** 2006. **Franchised:** 2006. **Description:** After school enrichment program. **Equity Capital Needed:** $99,000-$164,000. **Franchise Fee:** $31,500. **Royalty Fee:** 6%. **Financial Assistance:** Limited third party financing available. **Training:** 2 weeks training at headquarters included, 2 weeks at franchisee's location, 1 week at existing franchise location, online seminars and ongoing support.

28318 ■ Mathnasium Learning Centers
5120 W Goldleaf Cir., Ste. 130
Los Angeles, CA 90056
Ph:(323)421-8000
Free: 877-531-MATH
Fax:(310)943-2111
Co. E-mail: franchise@mathnasium.com
URL: http://www.mathnasium.com
No. of Franchise Units: 313. **No. of Company-Owned Units:** 1. **Founded:** 2002. **Franchised:** 2003. **Description:** Mathnasium provides the most effective mathematics in education available to grade school children after school, in an attractive neighborhood learning center environment. The Mathnasium Method, developed over 30 years of hands-on experience, is engaging for students and builds confidence as it builds real understanding. Created to address a real need in the market by a team with unparalleled success in the industry, the business model is strong and the opportunity is now. **Equity Capital Needed:** $78,300-$107,500 initial investment range. **Franchise Fee:** $19,500. **Financial Assistance:** No. **Training:** Complete initial training at corporate headquarters and ongoing support.

28319 ■ Motion Golf LLC
55 Lane Rd.
Fairfield, NJ 07004
Free: (866)-585-6033
No. of Company-Owned Units: 3. **Founded:** 2006. **Franchised:** 2007. **Description:** Golf swing analysis, instruction, and club fitting. **Equity Capital Needed:** $250,000 (Express/kiosk option available). **Franchise Fee:** $79,500. **Royalty Fee:** 6%. **Financial Assistance:** Limited third party financing available. **Training:** 1 week at franchisee's location.

28320 ■ Online Trading Academy
18004 Sky Park Cir. S, Ste. 140
Irvine, CA 92614
Ph:(949)608-6020
Fax:(949)608-6026
No. of Franchise Units: 16. **Founded:** 1998. **Franchised:** 2004. **Description:** Stock-trading instruction. **Equity Capital Needed:** $209,800-$388,000. **Franchise Fee:** $80,000-$200,000. **Royalty Fee:** 10%. **Financial Assistance:** Third party financing available. **Training:** Offers 2 weeks training at headquarters, 1 week at franchisees location and ongoing support.

28321 ■ Oxford Learning Centers
747 Hyde Park Rd., Ste. 230
London, ON, Canada N6H 3S3
Ph:(519)473-1207
Free: 888-559-2212
Fax:(519)473-6086
Co. E-mail: franchise@oxfordlearning.com
URL: http://www.oxfordlearning.com
No. of Franchise Units: 104. **No. of Company-Owned Units:** 5. **Founded:** 1984. **Franchised:** 1991. **Description:** Oxford is an educational franchise in Canada, which provides extensive training in all fields. **Equity Capital Needed:** $140,000-$210,000 + applicable taxes. **Franchise Fee:** $40,000 + applicable taxes. **Training:** Provides 2 weeks training and ongoing support.

28322 ■ Parisi Speed School
291 Franklin Ave.
Wyckoff, NJ 07481
Ph:(201)847-1938
Fax:(201)540-0143
No. of Franchise Units: 44. **No. of Company-Owned Units:** 5. **Founded:** 1992. **Franchised:** 2005. **Description:** Youth performance training. **Equity Capital Needed:** $132,500-$300,100. **Franchise Fee:** $29,900. **Royalty Fee:** $1,000/month. **Financial Assistance:** Limited third party financing available.

28323 ■ Parmasters Golf Training Centers
29 Evergreen Dr.
Whitby, ON, Canada L1N 6S6
Ph:(905)721-7593
Free: (866)966-0676
Fax:(416)352-1537
Co. E-mail: andre_ferris@parmastersgolf.com
URL: http://www.parmastersfranchise.com
No. of Franchise Units: 27. **No. of Company-Owned Units:** 7. **Founded:** 2000. **Franchised:** 2001. **Description:** Year-round indoor golf training center. **Equity Capital Needed:** $300,000-$2,500,000. **Franchise Fee:** $50,000.

28324 ■ Pathways Education & Training Centers, Inc.
333 S Parkside Cir.
St. George, UT 84770
Ph:(435)674-1331
Free: (866)845-6463
Fax:(435)674-1831
No. of Franchise Units: 6. **No. of Company-Owned Units:** 1. **Founded:** 2000. **Franchised:** 2005. **Description:** Brain integration program. **Equity Capital Needed:** $20,000. **Financial Assistance:** No. **Training:** Yes.

28325 ■ Spirit of Math Schools
178 Willowdale Ave.
Toronto, ON, Canada M2N 4Y8
Ph:(416)223-1985
Fax:(416)946-1902
Co. E-mail: franchising@spiritofmath.com
URL: http://www.spiritofmath.com
No. of Franchise Units: 13. **No. of Company-Owned Units:** 10. **Founded:** 1992. **Franchised:** 2004. **Description:** Offers an after-school classroom program for high performing students. It develops as skill-based understanding of math focusing on problem solving, co-operation and numeric skills and produces some of the top math students in the nation. **Equity Capital Needed:** $32,000-$70,000. **Franchise Fee:** $39,000. **Financial Assistance:** Yes. **Training:** A comprehensive training and support program is provided.

28326 ■ Thinkertots
Thinkertots Franchise Inc.
22214 Union Tpke.
Bayside, NY 11364
Ph:(718)740-1616
No. of Franchise Units: 4. **No. of Company-Owned Units:** 1. **Founded:** 1998. **Franchised:** 2005. **Description:** Educational parent/child classes. **Equity Capital Needed:** $42,000-$160,000. **Franchise Fee:** $15,000-$25,000. **Financial Assistance:** No. **Training:** Yes.

28327 ■ The Whole Child Learning Co.
2200 Kraft Drive, Ste. 1350
Blacksburg, VA 24060
Ph:(540)443-9252
Free: 888-317-3535
Fax:(540)242-3214
URL: http://www.wholechild.com
No. of Franchise Units: 36. **No. of Company-Owned Units:** 4. **Founded:** 1996. **Franchised:** 1999. **Description:** Educational services for children. **Equity Capital Needed:** $32,600-$38,800. **Franchise Fee:** $29,500. **Royalty Fee:** 7%. **Financial Assistance:** Yes. **Training:** Yes.

28328 ■ Young Rembrandts - The Power Of Drawing
Young Rembrandts Franchise, Inc.
23 N Union St.
Elgin, IL 60123
Ph:(847)742-6999
Free: (866)300-6010
Fax:(847)742-7197
Co. E-mail: yr@youngrembrandts.com
URL: http://www.youngrembrandts.com
No. of Franchise Units: 80. **Founded:** 1988. **Franchised:** 2001. **Description:** Developed a proven method that ensures artistic and academic success for every child. Our unique method and original curriculum teaches drawing, the fundamental skill of visual arts to children ages 3 1/2 to 12. **Equity Capital Needed:** Liquid $50,000; $100,000 net. **Franchise Fee:** $31,500. **Financial Assistance:** No. **Training:** Provides 1 week initial training program for up to 2 people at corporate office. This covers sales, marketing, the Young & Rembrandts method, classroom training and more. We provide complete operation and training manuals, and continual training and coaching calls and an Annual Conference.

COMPUTERIZED DATABASES

28329 ■ *Health & Wellness InSite*
Thomson Reuters
610 Opperman Dr.
Eagen, MN 55122
Free: 800-477-4300
Co. E-mail: gale.contentlicensing@cengage.com
URL: http://www.insite2.gale.com
Description: Contains complete information about health, medicine, fitness, and nutrition. Provides access to 170 of the world's leading professional and consumer health publications, including *The Lancet* and *Nutrition Today*; 550 health and medical pamphlets; 200,000 health-related articles from more than 3000 other publications; and 1800 overviews of different diseases and medical conditions published by Clinical Reference Systems, Ltd. Includes six medical reference books: *Columbia University College of Physicians & Surgeons Complete Home Medical Guide; Mosby's Medical, Nursing, and Allied Health Dictionary; Consumer Health Information Source Book; The People's Book of Medical Tests; USP DI-Vol. II Advice for the Patient; Drug Information in Lay Language;* and *The Complete Directory for People With Chronic Illness.*. Allows searches by article title, article type, author, company name, person discussed in the article, publication name, publication date range, publication type, target audience, ticker symbol, words in the title, and words that appear anywhere in the article. **Availability:** Online: Thomson Reuters. **Type:** Full text.

LIBRARIES

28330 ■ American Society for Training and Development ASTD Information Center
1640 King St.
PO Box 1443
Alexandria, VA 22313-2043
Ph:(703)683-8100
Free: 800-628-2783
Fax:(703)683-1523
Co. E-mail: customercare@astd.org
URL: http://www.astd.org
Contact: Greg Bindner, Mgr.
Scope: Human resource development - general, management, training, career development, Organization development, consulting skills. **Services:** Library open to national members of the Society. **Holdings:** 3000 bound volumes. **Subscriptions:** 60 journals and other serials.

28331 ■ National Association for Industry-Education Cooperation Library
235 Hendricks Blvd.
Buffalo, NY 14226-3304
Ph:(716)834-7047
Fax:(716)834-7047
Co. E-mail: naiec@pcom.net
URL: http://www2.pcom.net/naiec/
Contact: Dr. Donald M. Clark, Pres./CEO
Scope: Industry involvement in education to further continuous system wide school improvement, work force preparation, economic development. **Services:** Library open to members. **Holdings:** 1340 books; 45 bound periodical volumes; 2 AV programs; 89 manuscripts.

RESEARCH CENTERS

28332 ■ Center for Entrepreneurial Studies and Development
College of Engineering & Mineral Research, Ste. B
West Virginia University
1062 Maple Dr.
Morgantown, WV 26505
Ph:(304)293-5551

Fax:(304)293-6707
Co. E-mail: chadsell@mail.cesd.wvu.edu
URL: http://www.cesd.wvu.edu
Contact: Carl Hadsell, Mng.Dir.
E-mail: chadsell@mail.cesd.wvu.edu

Scope: Business operations improvement, employee training, management, and systems development. Operations improvement studies focus on quality control, materials handling systems, cost reduction, work standards development, facilities utilization and planning, work methods, inventory control systems, and computer applications. Employee training focuses on supervisory development, quality training, and problem solving. Management studies focus on management development programs, organization development, steering committee development, facilitation, incentives, and small business organizations. Systems studies focus on business plan development. **Services:** Competitive and economic development strategies; Market assessment and development; Operational improvements; Performance management; Provides assistance in new product or service development.

28333 ■ Center for Occupational Research and Development
PO Box 21689
Waco, TX 76702-1689
Ph:(254)772-8756
Free: 800—972-2766
Fax:(254)772-8972
Co. E-mail: hinckley@cord.org
URL: http://www.cord.org
Contact: Richard C. Hinckley PhD, Pres./CEO
E-mail: hinckley@cord.org

Scope: Educational research and evaluation; designs and develops instructional materials and curricula for grades 7-14; creates innovative applications of educational technology. **Services:** Consulting and coordination services; Forms networks and partnerships. **Publications:** Newsletter (monthly); White papers. **Educational Activities:** Curricula development; Teacher workshops.

28334 ■ Illinois State Board of Education–Data Analysis and Progress Reporting Division
100 N 1st St.
Springfield, IL 62777
Ph:(217)782-3950
Fax:(217)524-7784
Co. E-mail: gjohnson@isbe.net
URL: http://www.isbe.net/research/Default.htm
Contact: Gayle Johnson, Admin.
E-mail: gjohnson@isbe.net

Scope: Education policy.

28335 ■ Indiana University Bloomington–Center for Evaluation and Education Policy
1900 E 10th St.
Bloomington, IN 47406-7512
Ph:(812)855-4438
Free: 800—511-6575
Fax:(812)856-5890
Co. E-mail: jplucker@indiana.edu
URL: http://ceep.indiana.edu
Contact: Prof. Jonathan Plucker PhD, Dir.
E-mail: jplucker@indiana.edu

Scope: Program evaluation and policy research, primarily on education issues but also in healthcare. **Publications:** Policy Bulletins (monthly); Policy Reports; Special Reports and Technical Studies.

28336 ■ Indiana University Bloomington–Center for Postsecondary Research
Eigenmann Hall, Ste. 419
1900 E 10th St.
Bloomington, IN 47406-7512
Ph:(812)856-5824
Free: (866)-435-6773
Fax:(812)856-5150
Co. E-mail: vatorres@indiana.edu
URL: http://cpr.iub.edu/index.cfm
Contact: Vasti Torres, Dir.
E-mail: vatorres@indiana.edu

Scope: Policy issues and issues related to student learning and personal development, including student engagement, student persistence and attrition, institutional advancement, enrollment management and marketing, program evaluation, institutional culture, student learning and personal development, and equity and access in higher education. **Publications:** National Survey of Student Engagement (annually).

28337 ■ Indiana University Bloomington–Center for the Study of Institutions, Population, and Environmental Change
408 N Indiana Ave.
Bloomington, IN 47408-3799
Ph:(812)855-2230
Fax:(812)855-2634
Co. E-mail: cipec@indiana.edu
URL: http://www.indiana.edu/lAtcipec
Contact: Prof. Tom Evans PhD, Dir.
E-mail: cipec@indiana.edu

Scope: Processes of change in forest environments as mediated by institutional arrangements, demographic factors, and other major human driving forces.

28338 ■ Indiana University-Purdue University at Indianapolis–Center for the Study of Religion and American Culture
425 University Blvd., Rm. 417
Indianapolis, IN 46202-5140
Ph:(317)274-8409
Fax:(317)278-3354
Co. E-mail: pgoff@iupui.edu
URL: http://www.iupui.edu/lAtraac/
Contact: Dr. Philip K. Goff, Dir.
E-mail: pgoff@iupui.edu

Scope: Relationship between religion and aspects of American culture. **Publications:** News from the Center for the Study of Religion and American Culture (semiannually); Religion and American Culture: A Journal of Interpretation (semiannually). **Educational Activities:** Public lectures, conferences, and symposia; Young Scholars in American Religion Program.

28339 ■ Indiana University-Purdue University at Indianapolis–CyberLab
799 W Michigan St., ET 232
Indianapolis, IN 46202
Ph:(317)278-2630
Fax:(317)278-9171
Co. E-mail: cyberlab@iupui.edu
URL: http://www.iupui.edu/lAtsolctr/research/details.php?id=247
Contact: Ali Jafari PhD, Dir.
E-mail: cyberlab@iupui.edu

Scope: Worldwide web applications in teaching and learning, especially course management portals, campus portals, agent-based learning environment, and intelligent user interfaces.

28340 ■ Indiana University-Purdue University at Indianapolis–Nuclear Magnetic Resonance Laboratory
402 N Blackford St., Rm. 154
Indianapolis, IN 46202
Ph:(317)274-6900
Fax:(317)274-2393
Co. E-mail: bray@iupui.edu
URL: http://www.physics.iupui.edu/NMR.html
Contact: Bruce D. Ray
E-mail: bray@iupui.edu

Scope: Structure-function relationships of biological macromolecules, using the techniques of nuclear magnetic resonance (NMR). The research is interdisciplinary, bringing together researchers from the School of Science and the School of Medicine. **Educational Activities:** Training, for scientists interested in learning or using NMR techniques.

28341 ■ Indiana University-Purdue University at Indianapolis–Peirce Edition Project
0010 Education/Social Work
Indianapolis, IN 46202-5157
Ph:(317)274-3374
Fax:(317)274-2170
Co. E-mail: adetienn@iupui.edu
URL: http://www.iupui.edu/lAtpeirce
Contact: Prof. Andre De Tienne, Dir.
E-mail: adetienn@iupui.edu

Scope: American philosophy and culture, focusing on the writings of scientist and philosopher Charles S. Peirce. **Publications:** Peirce Project News (periodically); Writings of Charles S. Peirce: A Chronological Edition (occasionally). **Educational Activities:** Indianapolis Peirce Seminar (periodically), lecture series where the speakers are scholars or researchers that are Peirce Project visitors willing to share the latest stage of their research with the Project's specialists and philosophy students.

28342 ■ Institute for Forensic Imaging
9855 Crosspoint Blvd., Ste. 126
Fishers, IN 46256
Ph:(317)356-0245
Fax:(317)842-6974
Co. E-mail: jward@ifi-indy.org
URL: http://www.ifi-indy.org/
Contact: Joe Ward, Exec.Dir.
E-mail: jward@ifi-indy.org

Scope: Forensic imaging in the investigation of crimes and legal questions. **Services:** Consulting; Research. **Educational Activities:** College courses, through the School of Informatics at IUPUI (Indiana University Purdue University Indianapolis); Student centered training; Training programs, certified by the Indiana Law Enforcement Academy.

28343 ■ Massachusetts Institute of Technology–Center for Technology, Policy and Industrial Development–International Motor Vehicle Program
Bldg. E40-207
1 Amherst St.
Cambridge, MA 02139-4307
Ph:(617)253-8973
Fax:(617)253-7140
Co. E-mail: imvpmail@mit.edu
URL: http://imvp.mit.edu
Contact: John Paul MacDuffie, Co-Dir.
E-mail: imvpmail@mit.edu

Scope: Product development, supply chain management, manufacturing, organization and human resources, distribution and marketing, environmental issues, and mobility in the motor vehicle industry. **Publications:** Working papers. **Educational Activities:** Workshops (periodically).

28344 ■ Massachusetts Institute of Technology–Japan Program
MIT Bldg., Rm. E40-455
77 Massachusetts Ave.
Cambridge, MA 02139-4307
Ph:(617)258-2449
Fax:(617)258-7432
Co. E-mail: samuels@mit.edu
URL: http://web.mit.edu/misti/mit-japan
Contact: Dr. Richard J. Samuels, Dir.
E-mail: samuels@mit.edu

Scope: Japan and Asia, in particular Japanese foreign policy with regard to China, Asian energy and security, the changing role of Japan's technology at home and abroad. **Publications:** MIT Japan Science, Technology & Management Report; Newsletter (monthly); Sponsor Update (quarterly); Working Papers Series. **Educational Activities:** Japan Target Seminars, for technologically sophisticated professionals in business and government.

28345 ■ Massachusetts Institute of Technology–Program on the Pharmaceutical Industry
77 Massachusetts Ave., E19-611
Cambridge, MA 02139-4307
Ph:(617)253-0257

Fax:(617)253-0687
Co. E-mail: ghirsch@mit.edu
URL: http://web.mit.edu/cbi/index.html
Contact: Gigi Hirsch PhD, Exec.Dir.
E-mail: ghirsch@mit.edu
Scope: Competitiveness, performance, and productivity in the pharmaceutical field.

28346 ■ Rice University–Center for Education
6100 Main St., MS-147
PO Box 1892
Houston, TX 77005-1892
Ph:(713)348-5145
Fax:(713)348-4229
Co. E-mail: lmcneil@rice.edu
URL: http://centerforeducation.rice.edu
Contact: Prof. Linda McSpadden McNeil PhD, Dir.
E-mail: lmcneil@rice.edu
Scope: Teacher development, reorganization of schools, student evaluation methods, and educational policy and urban schools. **Publications:** Center-Piece.

28347 ■ Rice University–Center for the Study of Languages
6100 Main St., MS 36
Houston, TX 77005
Ph:(713)348-5844
Fax:(713)348-5846
Co. E-mail: wfreeman@rice.edu
URL: http://langcenter.rice.edu
Contact: Prof. Wendy Freeman PhD, Dir.
E-mail: wfreeman@rice.edu
Scope: Language teaching and learning. **Educational Activities:** Seminar, in language methodology; Seminar, in language methodology; Workshops.

28348 ■ University of Connecticut–Institute for Teaching and Learning
Center for Undergraduate Education
386 Fairfield Rd., Unit 2142
Storrs, CT 06269-2142
Ph:(860)486-2686
Fax:(860)486-5724
Co. E-mail: kb@uconn.edu
URL: http://www.itl.uconn.edu/
Contact: Dr. Keith Barker, Dir.
E-mail: kb@uconn.edu
Scope: Teaching and learning methods, pedagogy, media use and distance learning, and technology use in the classroom and online. **Services:** Consulting; Instructional design. **Publications:** The Journal of Graduate Teaching Assistant Development; TA Handbook. **Educational Activities:** Workshops, conferences.

28349 ■ University of Delaware–Delaware Education Research and Development Center
Pearson Hall
College of Human Services, Education & Public Policy
Newark, DE 19716
Ph:(302)831-4433
Fax:(302)831-4438
Co. E-mail: jbuttram@udel.edu
URL: http://www.rdc.udel.edu
Contact: Joan Buttram PhD, Dir.
E-mail: jbuttram@udel.edu
Scope: Educational practice, policy reform, program evaluation.

28350 ■ University of Toronto–Ontario Institute for Studies in Education–Centre for Teacher Development
252 Bloor St. W
Toronto, ON, Canada M5S 1V6
Ph:(416)978-0227
Fax:(416)926-4754
Co. E-mail: ckosnik@oise.utoronto.ca
URL: http://www.oise.utoronto.ca/cted/index.html
Contact: Dr. Clare Kosnik, Hd.
E-mail: ckosnik@oise.utoronto.ca
Scope: Teacher education and development, including pre-service, induction, and in-service. **Publications:** Newsletter (semiannually). **Educational Activities:** CTD Conference (biennially), in late October/early November, attended by educators, holistic practitioners, education officials; Holistic Educators meetings and seminars (monthly), held on Saturdays, attended by educators who specialize holistic learning and teaching.

28351 ■ University of Toronto–Ontario Institute for Studies in Education–International Centre for Educational Change
252 Bloor St. W
Toronto, ON, Canada M5S 1V6
Ph:(416)978-1161
Fax:(416)926-4741
Co. E-mail: sanderson@oise.utoronto.ca
URL: http://icec.oise.utoronto.ca
Contact: Stephen Anderson, Actg.Dir.
E-mail: sanderson@oise.utoronto.ca
Scope: Processes of educational change, including scheduling, teaching, curriculum, caring, assessment and decision-making; large-scale reform efforts, large-scale assessment, evaluation of programs and policies. **Services:** Practical field development, professional development activities, and consulting. **Educational Activities:** Study groups, presentations, discussions, and debates.

Electronic Commerce/E-Business

START-UP INFORMATION

28352 ■ *101 Internet Businesses You Can Start from Home: How to Choose and Build Your Own Successful E-Business*
Pub: Maximum Press
Ed: Susan Sweeney. **Released:** June 2006. **Price:** $29.95. **Description:** Guide for starting and growing an Internet business; information for developing a business plan, risk levels, and promotional techniques are included.

28353 ■ *202 Things You Can Buy and Sell for Big Profits*
Pub: Entrepreneur Press
Ed: James Stephenson; Jason R. Rich. **Released:** July 2008. **Price:** $19.95. **Description:** Become an entrepreneur at selling new and used products. This handbook will help individuals cash in on the boom in reselling new and used products online. A new section defines ways to set realistic goals while distinguishing between 'get-rich schemes' and long term, viable businesses. A discussion about targeting and reaching the right customer base is included, along with finding and obtaining the service support needed for starting a new business.

28354 ■ *Complete Idiot's Guide to Starting an Ebay Business*
Pub: Penguin Books (USA) Incorporated
Ed: Barbara Weltman, Malcolm Katt. **Released:** February 2008. **Price:** $19.95 (US), $29.00 (Canadian). **Description:** Guide for starting an eBay business includes information on products to sell, how to price merchandise, and details for working with services like PayPal, and how to organize fulfillment services.

28355 ■ *Design and Launch Your eCommerce Business in a Week*
Pub: Entrepreneur Press
Ed: Jason R. Rich. **Released:** July 2008. **Price:** $17.95. **Description:** Guide to help anyone start an online business in one week; included tips for Website design.

28356 ■ *Design and Launch Your Online Boutique in a Week*
Pub: Entrepreneur Press
Ed: Melissa Campanelli. **Released:** June 2008. **Price:** $17.95. **Description:** Guide to start an online boutique includes information on business planning, Website design and funding.

28357 ■ *E-Preneur*
Pub: Career Press, Inc.
Ed: Richard Goossen. **Released:** April 2008. **Price:** $15.99. **Description:** Entrepreneurs in the new virtual marketplace are examined. The book surveys and explains the field of Web 2.0 and entrepreneurs successfully using the virtual marketplace.

28358 ■ *EBay Business Start-up Kit: 100s of Live Links to All the Information and Tools You Need*
Pub: NOLO
Ed: Richard Stim. **Released:** July 2008. **Price:** $24.99. **Description:** Interactive kit that connects user directly to EBay is presented.

28359 ■ *eBay Business the Smart Way*
Pub: AMACOM
Ed: Joseph T. Sinclair. **Released:** June 6, 2007. **Price:** $17.95. **Description:** eBay commands ninety percent of all online auction business. Computer and software expert and online entrepreneur shares information to help online sellers get started and move merchandise on eBay. Tips include the best ways to build credibility, find products to sell, manage inventory, create a storefront Website, and more.

28360 ■ *Entrepreneurship with Online Learning Center Access Card*
Pub: McGraw-Hill Higher Education
Ed: Robert D. Hirich; Michael P. Peters; Dean A. Shepherd. **Released:** October 2006. **Price:** $103.25. **Description:** Book instructs students on entrepreneurial processes that include starting a new business.

28361 ■ *How to Start a Home-Based Mail Order Business*
Pub: Globe Pequot Press
Ed: Georganne Fiumara. **Released:** January 2005. **Price:** $17.95. **Description:** Step-by-step guide for starting and growing a home-based mail order business. Information about equipment, pricing, online marketing, are included along with worksheets and checklists for planning.

28362 ■ *How to Start a Home-Based Online Retail Business*
Pub: Globe Pequot Press
Ed: Jeremy Shepherd. **Released:** February 2007. **Price:** $18.95. **Description:** Information for starting an online retail, home-based business is shared.

28363 ■ *How to Start an Internet Sales Business*
Pub: Lulu.com
Ed: Dan Davis. **Released:** August 2005. **Price:** $19.95. **Description:** Small business guide for launching an Internet sales company. Topics include business structure, licenses, and taxes.

28364 ■ "Online Fortunes" in *Small Business Opportunities* (Fall 2008)
Pub: Entrepreneur Media Inc.
Description: Fifty hot, e-commerce enterprises for the aspiring entrepreneur to consider are featured; virtual assistants, marketing services, party planning, travel services, researching, web design and development, importing as well as creating an online store are among the businesses featured.

28365 ■ "Power Up" in *Entrepreneur* (Vol. 35, November 2007, No. 11, pp. 140)
Pub: Entrepreneur Media Inc.
Ed: Amanda C. Kooser. **Description:** PowerSeller is a status in the Internet company eBay, wherein sellers average at least $1,000 in sales per month for three consecutive months. There are five tiers in the PowerSeller status, which ranges from Bronze to Titanium. Launching startups at eBay can help entrepreneurs pick up a wide customer base, but getting and maintaining PowerSeller status is a challenge.

28366 ■ *Scrapbooking for Profit: Cashing in on Retail, Home-Based and Internet Opportunities*
Pub: Allworth Press
Ed: Rebecca Pittman. **Released:** June 2005. **Price:** $19.95 (US), $22.95 (Canadian). **Description:** Eleven strategies for starting a scrapbooking business, including brick-and-mortar stores, home-based businesses, and online retail and wholesale outlets.

28367 ■ *Start Your Own Blogging Business, Second Edition*
Pub: Entrepreneur Press
Released: July 1, 2010. **Price:** $17.95. **Description:** Interviews with professional bloggers from some of the most popular blogs on the Internet will help anyone interested in starting their own blogging business.

28368 ■ *Start Your Own Business on eBay, 2nd Edition*
Pub: Entrepreneur Press
Ed: Jacquelyn Lynn. **Released:** May 2007. **Price:** $19.95. **Description:** Tips for starring a new online business on eBay are shared.

28369 ■ *Start Your Own Net Services Business*
Pub: Entrepreneur Press
Released: February 1, 2009. **Price:** $17.95. **Description:** Web design, search engine marketing, new-media online, and blogging, are currently the four most popular web services available. This book provides information to start a net service business.

28370 ■ *Starting an Ebay Business for Canadians for Dummies*
Pub: John Wiley & Sons, Incorporated
Ed: Marsha Collier; Bill Summers. **Released:** February 2007. **Price:** $35.99. **Description:** Tips for turning a hobby into a successful online eBay company.

28371 ■ *Starting an iPhone Application Business for Dummies*
Pub: Wiley Publishing
Ed: Aaron Nicholson, Joel Elad, Damien Stolarz. **Released:** October 26, 2009. **Price:** $24.99. **Description:** Ways to create a profitable, sustainable business developing and marketing iPhone applications are profiled.

28372 ■ *Starting a Yahoo! Business for Dummies*
Pub: John Wiley & Sons, Incorporated
Ed: Rob Snell. **Released:** June 2006. **Price:** $24.99. **Description:** Rob Snell offers advice for turning online browsers into buyers, increase online traffic, and build an online store from scratch.

28373 ■ *Starting a Yahoo! Business For Dummies*
Pub: John Wiley & Sons, Incorporated
Ed: Rob Snell. **Released:** May 27, 2006. **Price:** $24.99. **Description:** Advice helps turn Web browsers into buyers, boost online traffic, and information to launch a profitable online business.

28374 ■ "Startup Aims to Cut Out Coupon Clipping" in *The Business Journal-Serving Metropolitan Kansas City* (Vol. 26, August 15, 2008, No. 49)
Pub: American City Business Journals, Inc.
Ed: Suzanna Stagemeyer. **Description:** TDP Inc., who started operations 18 months ago, aims to transform stale coupon promotions using technology by digitizing the entire coupon process. The process is expected to enable consumers to hunt coupons online where they will be automatically linked to loyalty cards. Other views and information on TDP and its services are presented.

28375 ■ "Truthfully Speaking" in *Entrepreneur* (Vol. 35, November 2007, No. 11, pp. 118)
Pub: Entrepreneur Media Inc.
Ed: Amanda C. Kooser. **Description:** Internet startup guru Guy Kawasaki talks about his new Web venture Truemors and shares tips on creating a successful Web-based company.

28376 ■ "Virtual Playground" in *Entrepreneur* (Vol. 36, March 2008, No. 3, pp. 112)
Pub: Entrepreneur Media Inc.
Ed: Amanda C. Kooser. **Description:** The growing number of children visiting virtual worlds provides opportunity for entrepreneurs to start online businesses catering to this market. Entrepreneurs need to be aware of the Children's Online Privacy Protection Act with regard to collecting children's information. Details of other things to know about with reference to these businesses are examined.

ASSOCIATIONS AND OTHER ORGANIZATIONS

28377 ■ Internet Alliance
1615 L St. NW, Ste. 1100
Washington, DC 20036-5624
Ph:(202)861-2407
Co. E-mail: tammy@internetalliance.org
URL: http://www.internetalliance.org
Contact: Tammy Cota, Exec. Dir.
Description: Companies offering Internet services. Seeks to "build the confidence and trust necessary for the Internet to become the global mass market medium of the 21st century". Represents members' commercial and regulatory interests; conducts promotional activities; facilitates communication and cooperation among members. **Publications:** *CyberBrief* (daily).

EDUCATIONAL PROGRAMS

28378 ■ Developing Web E-Commerce Applications
EEI Communications
66 Canal Center Plz., Ste. 200
Alexandria, VA 22314
Ph:(703)683-7453
Free: 888-253-2762
Fax:(703)683-7310
Co. E-mail: train@eeicom.com
URL: http://www.eeicom.com/training
Price: $1,065.00. **Description:** Experienced Web producers will learn how to build a shopping cart/order management system for secure transaction processing using the scripting languages ColdFusion and PHP. **Locations:** Silver Spring, MD; Hunt Valley, MD; Columbia, MD; and Alexandria, VA.

REFERENCE WORKS

28379 ■ "3Par: Storing Up Value" in *Barron's* (Vol. 90, August 30, 2010, No. 35, pp. 30)
Pub: Barron's Editorial & Corporate Headquarters
Ed: Mark Veverka. **Description:** Dell and Hewlett Packard are both bidding for data storage company 3Par. The acquisition would help Dell and Hewlett Packard provide customers with a one-stop shop as customers move to a private cloud in the Internet.

28380 ■ *6 Steps to Free Publicity*
Pub: ReadHowYouWant.com, Ltd.
Ed: Marcia Yudkin. **Released:** July 9, 2010. **Price:** $15.99. **Description:** Six steps to help promote a small business are given. The history of the Internet and its use to help provide free publicity to small firms is outlined.

28381 ■ *10 Steps to Successful Social Networking for Business*
Pub: American Society for Training and Development
Ed: Darin Hartley. **Released:** July 1, 2010. **Price:** $19.95. **Description:** Designed for today's fast-paced, need-it-yesterday business environment and for the thousands of workers who find themselves faced with new assignments, responsibilities, and requirements and too little time to learn what they must know.

28382 ■ "3.4 Million Votes Cast in 2011 eBay Motors People's Pick Poll – Winners Announced at SEMA Show" in *Benzinga.com* (, 2011)
Pub: Benzinga.com
Ed: Benzinga Staff. **Description:** eBay Motors sponsored the 2011 People's Picks survey, an annual poll inviting car enthusiasts to vote on their favorite auto thing, ranging from the best camshaft, favorite ignition, to favorite muscle car. More than 3.4 million votes were counted this year. A complete profile of eBay Motors is also provided.

28383 ■ "55-Alive! Wants To Be MySpace for the Baby Boomer Set. Can It Raise $250,000?" in *Inc.* (October 2007, pp. 50)
Pub: Gruner & Jahr USA Publishing
Description: Profile of 55-Alive! The online community created especially for individuals over the age of 50. The Website offers blogs, a dating section, listings for recreational vehicles for sale, movie reviews, advertising and articles of interest to users.

28384 ■ *202 Things You Can Make and Sell for Big Profits*
Pub: Entrepreneur Press
Ed: James Stephenson. **Released:** September 2005. **Price:** $19.95. **Description:** Instructions for 202 products that can be made and sold over the Internet.

28385 ■ *Advanced Selling for Dummies*
Pub: John Wiley and Sons, Inc.
Ed: Ralph R. Roberts; Joe Kraynak (As told to). **Released:** September 2007. **Price:** $21.99. **Description:** This book explores topics such as: visualizing success (includes exercises), investing and reinvesting in your own success, harnessing media and multimedia outlets, calculating risks that stretch your limits, creating lasting relationships, finding balance to avoid burnout and more. This guide is for salespeople who have already read 'Selling for Dummies' and now want forward-thinking, advanced strategies for recharging and reenergizing their careers and their lives. Blogging, Internet leads and virtual assistants are also discussed.

28386 ■ "AllHipHop.com's Founders Thought a Weeklong Event Would Raise the Company'" in *Inc.* (February 2008, pp. 48-51)
Pub: Gruner & Jahr USA Publishing
Ed: Kermit Pattison. **Description:** Co-founders Greg Watkins and Chuck Creekmur, planned a weeklong festival to promote their company, AllHipHop.com; the event nearly ruined the firm. The online firm provides news about hip hop artists and the industry and is updated daily.

28387 ■ "American Chemistry Council Launches Flagship Blog" in *Ecology,Environment & Conservation Business* (October 29, 2011, pp. 5)
Pub: HighBeam Research
Description: American Chemistry Council (ACC) launched its blog, American Chemistry Matters, where interactive space allows bloggers to respond to news coverage and to discuss policy issues and their impact on innovation, competitiveness, job creation and safety.

28388 ■ "Analyzing the Analytics" in *Entrepreneur* (Vol. 37, October 2009, No. 10, pp. 42)
Pub: Entrepreneur Media, Inc.
Ed: Mikal E. Belicove. **Description:** Startups can maximize Web analytics by using them to monitor traffic sources and identify obstacles to converting them into targeted behaviors . Startups should set trackable Web site goals and continuously track traffic and conversion rates.

28389 ■ "Ann Arbor Google's Growth Dips" in *Crain's Detroit Business* (Vol. 25, June 8, 2009, No. 23, pp. 3)
Pub: Crain Communications Inc. - Detroit
Ed: Bill Shea. **Description:** Global recession has slowed the growth of Google Inc. Three years ago, when Google moved to Ann Arbor, Michigan it estimated it would provide 1,000 new jobs within five years, so far the firm employs 250.

28390 ■ "Another California Firm On Way" in *Austin Business Journal* (Vol. 31, May 6, 2011, No. 9, pp. 1)
Pub: American City Business Journals Inc.
Ed: Christopher Calnan. **Description:** Main Street Hub Inc. is planning to build a facility in Austin, Texas. The company helps businesses manage their online reputations. Main Street has selected Aquila Commercial LLC as its real estate broker.

28391 ■ "Anthem Leading the Way in Social Tech Revolution" in *Inside Business* (Vol. 13, September-October 2011, No. 5, pp. 1B3)
Pub: Great Lakes Publishing Company
Ed: Ryan Clark. **Description:** Anthem Blue Cross and Blue Shield is leading the way in social technology. The firm's social media initiatives to promote itself are outlined.

28392 ■ "Anything Could Happen" in *Inc.* (March 2008, pp. 116-123)
Pub: Gruner & Jahr USA Publishing
Ed: Max Chafkin. **Description:** Profile of Evan Williams, founder of Blogger and Twitter, a new type of technology idea; Williams answers ten questions and share insight into growing both of his companies.

28393 ■ "Aptitudes for Apps" in *Boston Business Journal* (Vol. 31, July 1, 2011, No. 23, pp. 3)
Pub: Boston Business Journal
Ed: Kyle Alspach. **Description:** Startups Apperian Inc. and Kinvey Inc. are aiming to accelerate the development and deployment of mobile applications and have received fund pledges from Boston-area venture capital firms.

28394 ■ "Are Offline Pushes Important to E-Commerce?" in *DM News* (Vol. 31, September 14, 2009, No. 23, pp. 10)
Pub: Haymarket Media, Inc.
Description: With the importance of Internet marketing and the popularity of ecommerce increasing experts debate the relevance of more traditional channels of advertising.

28395 ■ "Are You Ready To Do It Yourself? Discipline and Self-Study Can Help You Profit From Online Trading" in *Black Enterprise* (Feb. 2008)
Pub: Earl G. Graves Publishing Co. Inc.
Ed: Steve Garmhausen. **Description:** Steps to help individuals invest in stocks online is given by an expert broker. Discount brokerage houses can save money for online investors.

28396 ■ "Area VCs Take Praise, Lumps, on Web site" in *Boston Business Journal* (Vol. 27, October 26, 2007, No. 39, pp. 1)
Pub: American City Business Journals Inc.
Ed: Jesse Noyes. **Description:** TheFunded.com is a social networking site that allows entrepreneurs to rate venture capitalists and post their comments. Information about venture capitalist firms such as size and the partners behind it are also provided.

28397 ■ "Art of the Online Deal" in *Farm Industry News* (March 25, 2011)
Pub: Penton Business Media Inc.
Description: Farmers share advice for shopping online for machinery; photos, clean equipment, the price, equipment details, and online sources topped their list.

28398 ■ "As Seen On TV" in *Canadian Business* (Vol. 80, November 5, 2007, No. 22, pp. 93)
Pub: Rogers Media
Ed: Zena Olijnyk. **Description:** StarBrand Media Inc. is one of the companies providing fans with information on how and where to purchase the items that television characters are using. StarBrand created the style section found on different television shows' Websites, such as that of the Gossip Girl and Smallville. The benefits of using sites like StarBrand are evaluated.

28399 ■ "As Technology Changes, So Must African American Business" in *Black Enterprise* (Vol. 41, August 2010, No. 1, pp. 61)
Pub: Earl G. Graves Publishing Co. Inc.
Ed: Sonya A. Donaldson. **Description:** Social media is essential to compete in today's business environment, especially for African American firms.

28400 ■ "Ask Inc." in *Inc.* (October 2007, pp. 73-74)
Pub: Gruner & Jahr USA Publishing
Description: An online marketing research firm investigates the use of online communities such as MySpace and Second life in order to recruit individuals to answer surveys.

28401 ■ "Atlific Adds Management of 4 Hotels to Its Portfolio in Fort McMurray" in *Canadian Corporate News* (May 16, 2007)
Pub: Comtex News Network Inc.
Description: Atlific Hotels & Resorts took over management for Merit Inn & Suites, The Merit Hotel, The Nomad Hotel and The Nomad Suites in Fort McMurray. The company feels that they will be able to increase the hotels' abilities to promote their services through their vast network of sales personnel and marketing and e-commerce team.

28402 ■ "Attention, Please" in *Entrepreneur* (Vol. 36, April 2008, No. 4, pp. 52)
Pub: Entrepreneur Media, Inc.
Ed: Andrea Cooper. **Description:** Gurbaksh Chahal created his own company ClickAgents at the age of 16, and sold it two years later for $40 million to ValueClick. He then founded BlueLithium, an online advertising network on behavioral targeting, which Yahoo! Inc. bought in 2007 for $300 million. Chahal, now 25, talks about his next plans and describes how BlueLithium caught Yahoo's attention.

28403 ■ "Attract More Online Customers: Make Your Website Work Harder for You" in *Black Enterprise* (Vol. 37, November 2006, No. 4, pp. 66)
Pub: Earl G. Graves Publishing Co. Inc.
Ed: Description: Having an impressive presence on the Internet has become crucial. Detailed advice on making your website serve your business in the best way possible is included.

28404 ■ "Auctions and Bidding: a Guide for Computer Scientists" in *ACM Computing Surveys* (Vol. 43, Summer 2011, No. 2, pp. 10)
Pub: Association for Computing Machinery
Ed: Simon Parsons, Juan A. Rodriguez-Aguilar, Mark Klein. **Description:** There are various actions: single dimensional, multi-dimensional, single-sided, double-sided, first-price, second-price, English, Dutch, Japanese, sealed-bid, and these have been extensively discussed and analyzed in economics literature. This literature is surveyed from a computer science perspective, primarily from the viewpoint of computer scientists who are interested in learning about auction theory, and to provide pointers into the economics literature for those who want a deeper technical understanding. In addition, since auctions are an increasingly important topic in computer science, the article also looks at work on auctions from the computer science literature. The aim is to identify what both bodies of work tell us about creating electronic auctions.

28405 ■ "AVG Introduces Security Software Suite for SMBs 551179" in *eWeek* (October 12, 2010)
Pub: Ziff Davis Enterprise
Description: AVG Technologies is offering its AVG Internet Security 2011 Business Edition and AVG Anti-Virus Business Edition designed to give Internet-active SMB owners protection. The system protects online transactions and email communications as well as sensitive customer data and AVG Anti-Virus 2011 Business edition offers real-time protection against the latest online threats.

28406 ■ "Babynut.com to Shut Down" in *Bellingham Business Journal* (Vol. February 2010, pp. 3)
Pub: Sound Publishing Inc.
Description: Saralee Sky and Jerry Kilgore, owners of Babynut.com will close their online store. The site offered a free online and email newsletter to help mothers through pregnancy and the first three years of their child's life. Products being sold at clearance prices include organic and natural maternity and nursing clothing, baby and toddler clothes, books on pregnancy, and more.

28407 ■ "Banking on Twitter" in *Baltimore Business Journal* (Vol. 27, February 6, 2010, No. 40, pp. 1)
Pub: American City Business Journals
Ed: Gary Haber. **Description:** Ways that banks are using Twitter, Facebook and other social networking sites to provide customer services is discussed. First Mariner Bank is one of those banks that are finding the social media platform as a great way to reach customers. Privacy issues regarding this marketing trend are examined.

28408 ■ "The Bankrate Double Pay" in *Barron's* (Vol. 88, March 24, 2008, No. 12, pp. 27)
Pub: Dow Jones & Company, Inc.
Ed: Neil A. Martin. **Description:** Shares of Bankrate may rise as much as 25 percent from their level of $45.08 a share due to a strong cash flow and balance sheet. The company's Internet business remains strong despite weakness in the online advertising industry and is a potential takeover target.

28409 ■ "Banks Fall Short in Online Services for Savvy Traders" in *Barron's* (Vol. 88, March 17, 2008, No. 11, pp. 35)
Pub: Dow Jones & Company, Inc.
Ed: Theresa W. Carey. **Description:** Banc of America Investment Services, WellsTrade, and ShareBuilder are at the bottom of the list of online brokerages because they offer less trading technologies and product range. Financial shoppers miss out on a lot of customized tools and analytics when using these services.

28410 ■ "BayTSP, NTT Data Corp. Enter Into Reseller Pact to Market Online IP Monitoring" in *Professional Services Close-Up* (Sept. 11, 2009)
Pub: Close-Up Media
Description: Due to incredible interest from distributors and content owners across Asia, NTT Data Corp. will resell BayTSP's online intellectual property monitoring, enforcement, business intelligence and monetization services in Japan.

28411 ■ "BBB Hires Marketing Firm to Attract More Businesses" in *Baltimore Business Journal* (Vol. 27, January 1, 2010, No. 35, pp. 1)
Pub: American City Business Journals
Ed: Julekha Dash. **Description:** Better Business Bureau (BBB) of Greater Maryland hired Bystry Carson & Associates Ltd. to assist in its rebranding efforts in order to entice more businesses. Bystry Carson will promote BBB's new mission at lectures, seminars, and networking events, as well as educate businesses about the agency through blogs and Twitter. BBB's services are also outlined.

28412 ■ "BDC Launches New Online Business Advice Centre" in *Internet Wire* (July 13, 2010)
Pub: Comtex
Description: The Business Development Bank of Canada (BDC) offers entrepreneurs the chance to use their new online BDC Advice Centre in order to seek advice regarding the challenges of entrepreneurship. Free online business tools and information to help both startups and established firms are also provided.

28413 ■ "Before You Hit Send: Crafting Workplace E-Mails to Avoid Mishaps" in *Black Enterprise* (Vol. 38, January 2008, No. 6, pp. 85)
Pub: Earl G. Graves Publishing Co. Inc.
Ed: Tennille M. Robinson. **Description:** Tips to use before sending an office email our presented. It is important to keep emails looking professional.

28414 ■ *Behind the Cloud*
Pub: Jossey-Bass
Ed: Marc Benioff, Carlye Adler. **Released:** 2010. **Price:** $27.95. **Description:** Salesforce.com is the world's most successful business-to-business cloud-computing company that sells an online service that helps businesses manage sales, customer service, and marketing functions.

28415 ■ "Being all a-Twitter" in *Canadian Business* (Vol. 81, December 8, 2008, No. 21, pp. 22)
Pub: Rogers Media Ltd.
Ed: Andrew Wahl. **Description:** Marketing experts suggest that advertising strategies have to change along with new online social media. Companies are advised to find ways to incorporate social software because workers and customers are expected to continue its use.

28416 ■ "Best Buy's CEO On Learning to Love Social Media" in *Harvard Business Review* (Vol. 88, December 2010, No. 12, pp. 43)
Pub: Harvard Business School Publishing
Ed: Brian J. Dunn. **Description:** Effective utilization of online social networks to enhance brand identity, connect with consumers, and address bad publicity scenarios is examined.

28417 ■ "Beyond YouTube: New Uses for Video, Online and Off" in *Inc.* (October 2007, pp. 53-54)
Pub: Gruner & Jahr USA Publishing
Ed: Leah Hoffmann. **Description:** Small companies are using video technology for embedding messages into email, broadcasting live interactive sales and training seminars, as well as marketing campaigns. Experts offer insight into producing and broadcasting business videos.

28418 ■ *The Big Switch*
Pub: W. W. Norton & Company, Inc.
Ed: Nicholas Carr. **Released:** January 19, 2009. **Price:** $16.95 paperback. **Description:** Today companies are dismantling private computer systems and tapping into services provided via the Internet. This shift is remaking the computer industry, bringing competitors such as Google to the forefront ant threatening traditional companies like Microsoft and Dell. The book weaves together history, economics, and technology to explain why computing is changing and what it means for the future.

28419 ■ *The Big Switch: Rewiring the World, From Edison to Google*
Pub: W.W. Norton & Company
Ed: Nicholas Carr. **Released:** 2009. **Price:** $25.95. **Description:** Companies such as Google, Microsoft, and Amazon.com are building huge centers in order to create massive data centers. Together these centers form a giant computing grid that will deliver the digital universe to scientific labs, companies and homes in the future. This trend could bring about a

new, darker phase for the Internet, one where these networks could operate as a fearsome entity that will dominate the lives of individuals worldwide.

28420 ■ "Blacks Go Broadband: High Speed Internet Adoption Grows Among African Americans" in *Black Enterprise* (Vol. 38, February 2008)
Pub: Earl G. Graves Publishing Co. Inc.
Ed: Cliff Hocker. **Description:** Number of black households using broadband Internet services tripled since 2005 according to a survey conducted by Pew Internet and American Life Project.

28421 ■ "Bloomberg Law Upgraded Its Online Legal Research Platform" in *Information Today* (Vol. 28, September 2011, No. 8, pp. 28)
Pub: Information Today, Inc.
Description: Bloomberg Law upgraded its online legal research platform for law practices. The new services includes a redesigned interface, improved search capabilities, and expanded collaboration and workflow features, while maintaining it comprehensive law resources such as mergers and acquisitions, antitrust, and securities.

28422 ■ "Boise-based Highway 12 Invests in Crowdsourcing Platform" in *Idaho Business Review* (September 24, 2010)
Pub: Dolan Media Newswires
Ed: Simon Shifrin. **Description:** The only venture capital fund in Idaho, Highway 12 Ventures, is funding Kapost a new company that helps news Websites, blogs and other online venues to pull content from a larger network of writers.

28423 ■ "Boom and Bust in the Book Biz" in *Canadian Business* (Vol. 83, August 17, 2010, No. 13-14, pp. 16)
Pub: Rogers Media Ltd.
Ed: Jordan Timm. **Description:** Electronic book marketplace is booming with Amazon.com's e-book sales for the Kindle e-reader exceeding the hardcover sales. Kobo Inc. has registered early success with its Kobo e-reader and has partnered with Hong Kong telecom giant on an e-book store.

28424 ■ "Boosting Strategy With An Online Community" in *Business Strategy Review* (Vol. 21, Spring 2010, No. 1, pp. 40)
Pub: Wiley-Blackwell
Ed: Lynda Gratton, Joel Casse. **Description:** A program that merged online communities with strategic development and implementation at Nokia has provided valuable lessons about new ways employees are able to engage and interact.

28425 ■ "Boosting Your Merchant Management Services With Wireless Technology" in *Franchising World* (Vol. 42, August 2010, No. 8, pp. 27)
Pub: International Franchise Association
Ed: Michael S. Slominski. **Description:** Franchises should have the capability to accept credit cards away from their businesses. This technology will increase sales.

28426 ■ "Borders Previews New Web Site" in *Crain's Detroit Business* (Vol. 23, October 8, 2007, No. 41, pp. 4)
Pub: Crain Communications Inc. - Detroit
Ed: Sheena Harrison. **Description:** Borders Group Inc. previewed its new Website that allows customers to buy items that include the Magic Shelf, a virtual bookcase that displays available recommended books, movies and music.

28427 ■ "Bottoms Up!" in *Entrepreneur* (Vol. 36, April 2008, No. 4, pp. 128)
Pub: Entrepreneur Media, Inc.
Ed: Amanda C. Kooser. **Description:** Jill Bernheimer launched her online alcohol business Domaine547 in 2007, and encountered challenges as legal issues over the licensing and launching of the business took about seven months to finish. Domain547 features blog and forum areas. Marketing strategy that connects to the social community is one of the ways to reach out to customers.

28428 ■ "Brands' Mass Appeal" in *ADWEEK* (Vol. 51, June 14, 2010, No. 24)
Pub: Nielsen Business Media Inc.
Ed: Lisa Thorell, James Sherret. **Description:** Engineering/science crowdsourced projects tend to result from posting and/or publishing interim results as well as from other talents building upon those results to produce even better results. However, the author does not see the same results in the creative world.

28429 ■ "Brief: US-Business/eBay Earnings Rise 31 Per Cent" in *Denver Post* (July 21, 2011)
Pub: Denver Post
Ed: Andy Goldberg. **Description:** eBay's strong performance in second quarter 2011 is being attributed to Paypal online payments division. eBay's online auction sites reported gross merchandise volume up 34 percent. Statistical data included.

28430 ■ "Brite-Strike Tactical Launches New Internet Marketing Initiatives" in *Internet Wire* (September 15, 2009)
Pub: Comtex News Network, Inc.
Description: Brite-Strike Tactical Illumination Products, Inc. has enlisted the expertise of Internet marketing guru Thomas J. McCarthy to help revamp the company's Internet campaign. An outline of the Internet marketing strategy is provided.

28431 ■ "Broadband Reaches Access Limits in Europe" in *Information Today* (Vol. 26, February 2009, No. 2, pp. 22)
Pub: Information Today, Inc.
Ed: Jim Ashling. **Description:** Eurostat (the Statistical Office of the European communities) reports results from is survey regarding Internet use by businesses throughout its 27-member states. Iceland, Finland and the Netherlands provide the most access at broadband speeds, followed by Belgium, Spain and France.

28432 ■ "Building a Better Twitter Brand: My Foray Into Social Analytics" in *Inc.* (Vol. , pp.)
Pub: Inc. Magazine
Ed: John Brandon. **Description:** A small business using Twitter to research and promote the firm decided to test some Web-based dashboards that allow you to manage and analyze accounts on multiple social media networks including Facebook, Twitter, and LinkedIn.

28433 ■ "Building Your Business: A Strong Web Presence Is a Must" in *Black Enterprise* (Vol. 38, December 2007, No. 5, pp. 74)
Pub: Earl G. Graves Publishing Co. Inc.
Ed: Tennille M. Robinson. **Description:** Building a strong presence on the Internet is crucial to any growing business. Websites can provide information or sell merchandise, but the site must also make sure the customer knows how to use and navigate around within the site. Common mistakes to avoid when designing a small business Website are outlined.

28434 ■ "The Business Case for Mobile Content Acceleration" in *Streaming Media* (November 2011, pp. 78)
Pub: Information Today Inc.
Ed: Dan Rayburn. **Description:** Last holiday season, eBay became a mobile commerce (m-commerce) giant when sales rose by 134 percent, as most online retailers offered customers the ability to purchase items using their mobile devices.

28435 ■ "Business Forecast: Stormy and Successful" in *Women In Business* (Vol. 62, June 2010, No. 2, pp. 12)
Pub: American Business Women's Association
Ed: Kathleen Leighton. **Description:** Stormy Simon, vice president of customer service at Overstock.com is a self-made career woman who started out as a temporary employee in the company in 2001. She was not able to attend college because she had two sons to care for after her divorce. Simon got involved in advertising and media buying and shares her love for business.

28436 ■ "Buy Local to Land Great Deals" in *Inside Business* (Vol. 13, September-October 2011, No. 5, pp. SS8)
Pub: Great Lakes Publishing Company
Description: Buy Lakewood! Loyalty Program offers residents great bargains for shopping at local retailers. Residents sign up online and the city mails them a letter of appreciations along with a key card. Showing the key card at any participating businesses listed on the Website will provide discounts.

28437 ■ "Campaigner Survey: 46 Percent of Small Businesses Use Email Marketing" in *Wireless News* (November 21, 2009)
Pub: Close-Up Media
Description: Almost half (46 percent) of small businesses surveyed by Campaigner's 2009 State of Small Business Online Marketing, say that they rely on email marketing to help them find new customers, keep existing ones and grow their businesses. The survey also found that 36 percent of small businesses plan to begin using email marketing over the next year. The trend to utilize Internet marketing tools is allowing small businesses to grow faster and generate higher revenues than those that are not using these mediums.

28438 ■ "Capturing Generation Y: Ready, Set, Transform" in *Credit Union Times* (Vol. 21, July 14, 2010, No. 27, pp. 20)
Pub: Summit Business Media
Ed: Senthil Kumar. **Description:** The financial services sector recognizes that Generation Y will have a definite impact on the way business is conducted in the future. The mindset of Generation Y is social and companies need to use networking tools such as Facebook in order to reach this demographic.

28439 ■ "The China Connection" in *Crain's Chicago Business* (Vol. 31, March 24, 2008, No. 12, pp. 26)
Pub: Crain Communications, Inc.
Ed: Samantha Stainburn. **Description:** Interview with Ben Munoz who studied abroad in Beijing, China for three months to study international economics, e-commerce and global leadership.

28440 ■ "Chris Curtis Preaches the Gospel of Internet Success" in *Black Enterprise* (Vol. 38, March 2008, No. 8, pp. 56)
Pub: Earl G. Graves Publishing Co. Inc.
Ed: Anthony Calypso. **Description:** Profile of the Web Business Ownership Series, a collection of 20 free seminars that help small businesses learn about the Web development process.

28441 ■ "Click Here to Book" in *Caterer & Hotelkeeper* (October 28, 2011, No. 288)
Pub: Reed Reference Publishing
Ed: Ross Bentley. **Description:** Customers expectations are determined by the quality of a Website when booking hotel rooms.

28442 ■ "A Click In the Right Direction: Website Teaches Youth Financial Literacy" in *Black Enterprise* (Vol. 38, December 2007, No. 5)
Pub: Earl G. Graves Publishing Co. Inc.
Ed: Nicole Norfleet. **Description:** Profile of Donald Lee Robinson who launched SkillsThatClick, a Website that teaches young individuals ages 12 to 15 about money management. Robinson shares how he used his Navy career as a model for designing the site.

28443 ■ "ClickFuel Unveils Internet Marketing Tools for Small Businesses" in *Internet Wire* (October 19, 2009)
Pub: Comtex News Network, Inc.
Description: ClickFuel, a firm that manages, designs and tracks marketing campaigns has unveiled a full software suite of affordable services and technology solutions designed to empower small business owners and help them promote and grow their businesses through targeted Internet marketing campaigns.

28444 ■ *Clicking Through: A Survival Guide for Bringing Your Company Online*
Pub: Bloomberg Press
Ed: Jonathan I. Ezor. **Released:** October 1999. **Description:** Summary of legal compliance issues faced by small companies doing business on the Internet, including copyright and patent laws.

28445 ■ "Clicks For Cash: Earning More From Your Website" in *Inc.* (December 2007, pp. 64-65)
Pub: Gruner & Jahr USA Publishing
Ed: Michael Fitzgerald. **Description:** Ways to use a company's Website to generate revenue are discussed. Free services for placing ads include Google AdSense, AdBrite, AuctionAds, Chitkia eMiniMalls, Vizu Answers, and Value Click; profiles of each service are presented.

28446 ■ "Clicks From Round the World: Simplifying International E-Commerce" in *Inc.* (Volume 32, December 2010, No. 10, pp. 146)
Pub: Inc. Magazine
Ed: Ryan Underwood. **Description:** By 2014, global e-commerce spending is expected to increase more than 90 percent, with much of that growth coming from Latin America.

28447 ■ "Cloudy Future for VMware?" in *Barron's* (Vol. 90, September 13, 2010, No. 37, pp. 21)
Pub: Barron's Editorial & Corporate Headquarters
Ed: Jonathan R. Laing. **Description:** VMWare dominated the virtualization market for years, but it may be ending as it faces more competition from rivals that offer cloud computing services. The company's stocks are also expensive and are vulnerable to the smallest mishap.

28448 ■ "Complete Discovery Source, Inc. (CDS) Receives Minority Owned Business Certification" in *Internet Wire* (December 14, 2010)
Pub: Comtex
Description: Complete Discovery Source Inc. (CDS) was granted Minority-Owned Business Enterprise status by the New York State Department of Economic Development. The certification provides CDS, an end-to-end eDiscovery services provider, with access to contracting opportunities with 130 government agencies throughout New York state.

28449 ■ *The Complete Guide to Google Adwords: Secrets, Techniques, and Strategies You Can Learn to Make Millions*
Pub: Atlantic Publishing Company
Released: December 1, 2010. **Price:** $24.95. **Description:** Google AdWords, when it launched in 2002 signaled a fundamental shift in what the Internet was for so many individuals and companies. Learning and understanding how Google AdWords operates and how it can be optimized for maximum exposure, boosting click through rates, conversions, placement, and selection of the right keywords, can be the key to a successful online business.

28450 ■ "Connections: United We Gab" in *Entrepreneur* (Vol. 35, October 2007, No. 10, pp. 60)
Pub: Entrepreneur Media Inc.
Ed: Mike Hogan. **Description:** T-Mobile and AT&T introduced dual-mode service to consumers, helping them to switch between cellular and Wi-Fi networks easily. These services, such as Hotspot@Home, reduces the cost of long distance calls by routing them over the Internet with the use of WiFi. Benefits of dual mode service, such as lower hardware price and better call coverage are given.

28451 ■ "Consumer Electronics: Brick and Mortar Vs. Online" in *Retail Merchandiser* (Vol. 51, September-October 2011, No. 5, pp. 15)
Pub: Phoenix Media Corporation
Description: Brick and mortar retailers with Websites are discovering that the Internet is used more for research than purchasing when it comes to electronics products. According to a recent study conducted by The NPD Group shows that 56 percent of consumers research televisions online before purchasing, but only 19 percent actually buy them online.

28452 ■ "Consumer Trust in E-Commerce Web Sites: a Meta-Study" in *ACM Computing Surveys* (Vol. 43, Fall 2011, No. 3, pp. 14)
Pub: Association for Computing Machinery
Ed: Patricia Beatty, Ian Reay, Scott Dick, James Miller. **Description:** Trust is at once an elusive, imprecise concept, and a critical attribute that must be engineered into e-commerce systems. Engineering trust is examined.

28453 ■ *Content Rich: Writing Your Way to Wealth on the Web*
Pub: 124 S Mercedes Rd.
Ed: Jon Wuebben. **Released:** April 2008. **Price:** $19.95. **Description:** A definitive search engine optimization (SEO) copywriting guide for search engine rankings and sales conversion. It includes topics not covered in other books on the subject and targets the small to medium sized business looking for ways to maximize online marketing activities as well as designers and Web developers seeking to incorporate more SEO techniques into design and content.

28454 ■ "Contest Produce Ad Designs on a Dime" in *San Diego Business Journal* (Vol. 31, August 23, 2010, No. 31, pp. 1)
Pub: San Diego Business Journal
Ed: Mike Allen. **Description:** San Diego-based Prova.fm runs design contests for clients such as the U.S. Postal Service. The client then chooses the best entry from the contest. Prova.fm relies on the Internet to deliver a range of possible graphic solutions and allowing the customer to make the right selection for its business through a process called crowdsourcing.

28455 ■ "Conversations with Customers" in *Business Journal Serving Greater Tampa Bay* (Vol. 31, December 31, 2010, No. 1, pp. 1)
Pub: Tampa Bay Business Journal
Description: Tampa Bay, Florida-based businesses have been using social media to interact with customers. Forty percent of businesses have been found to have at least one social media platform to reach customers and prospects.

28456 ■ "Coping with the Web" in *Agency Sales Magazine* (Vol. 39, December 2009, No. 11, pp. 52)
Pub: MANA
Ed: Karen Saunders. **Description:** When branding your company on the Internet, strategy should first be discussed with the website designer and the target and niche audience should also be defined. Describing "what" and "how" the product or service is offering is also important. In addition, perception, the logo, and the tag line are some elements that are needed to create a brand.

28457 ■ "Copyright Clearance Center (CCC) Partnered with cSubs" in *Information Today* (Vol. 28, November 2011, No. 10, pp. 14)
Pub: Information Today, Inc.
Description: Copyright Clearance Center (CCC) partnered with cSubs to integrate CCC's point-of-content licensing solution RightsLink Basic directly into cSubs workflow. The partnership will allow cSubs' customers a user-friendly process for obtaining permissions. Csubs is a corporate subscription management service for books, newspapers, and econtent.

28458 ■ "The Copyright Evolution" in *Information Today* (Vol. 28, November 2011, No. 10, pp. 1)
Pub: Information Today, Inc.
Ed: Nancy Davis Kho. **Description:** For information professionals, issues surrounding copyright compliance have traditionally been on the consumption side. However, today, content consumption is only half the program because blogging, tweeting, and commenting is a vital part of more standard duties for workers as corporations aim to create authentic communications with customers.

28459 ■ *Crossing the Chasm: Marketing and Selling Disruptive Products to Mainstream Customers*
Pub: HarperInformation
Ed: Geoffrey A. Moore. **Released:** September 2002. **Price:** $17.95. **Description:** A guide for marketing in high-technology industries, focusing on the Internet.

28460 ■ "Crowdsourcing their Way into One Big Mess" in *Brandweek* (Vol. 51, October 25, 2010, No. 38, pp. 26)
Pub: Nielsen Business Media, Inc.
Ed: Gregg S. Lipman. **Description:** The Gap, was counting on crowdsourcing to provide feedback for its new logo, but it did not prove positive for the retailer. However, a massive outcry of negative opinion, via crowdsourcing, may not always equal valid, constructive criticism.

28461 ■ *Crowdsourcing: Why the Power of the Crowd is Driving the Future of Business*
Pub: Crown Business
Ed: Jeff Howe. **Released:** 2009. **Price:** $26.95. **Description:** Small businesses are shown how to use social networks online to promote goods and services.

28462 ■ *Crush It!*
Pub: HarperStudio/HarperCollins
Ed: Gary Vaynerchuk. **Released:** 2009. **Price:** $19.99. **Description:** Ways the Internet can help entrepreneurs turn their passions into successful companies.

28463 ■ "Cyber Thanksgiving Online Shopping a Growing Tradition" in *Marketing Weekly News* (December 12, 2009, pp. 137)
Pub: Investment Weekly News
Description: According to e-commerce analysts, Thanksgiving day is becoming increasingly important to retailers in terms of online sales. Internet marketers are realizing that consumers are already searching for Black Friday sales and if they find deals on the products they are looking for, they are highly likely to make their purchase on Thanksgiving day instead of waiting.

28464 ■ "Cyberwise" in *Black Enterprise* (Vol. 41, September 2010, No. 2, pp. 49)
Pub: Earl G. Graves Publishing Co. Inc.
Ed: Marcia Wade Talbert. **Description:** Advice is given to assist in selling an online store called theupscalegaragesale.com. A listing of business brokers specializing in the sale of Internet businesses is included.

28465 ■ "Datran Media Executives to Lead Industry Debates Across Q1 Conferences" in *Internet Wire* (January 22, 2010)
Pub: Comtex News Network, Inc.
Description: Datran Media, an industry-leading digital marketing technology company, will be sending members of its management team to several conferences in the early part of the first quarter of 2010; discussions will include Internet marketing innovations, e-commerce and media distribution.

28466 ■ "Dear Customer: Managing E-Mail Campaigns" in *Inc.* (March 2008, pp. 58-59)
Pub: Gruner & Jahr USA Publishing
Ed: Ryan Underwood. **Description:** Internet services that help firms manage their online business including email marketing, to manage subscriber lists, comply with spam regulations, monitor bouncebacks, and track potential customers are profiled. Constant Contact, MobileStorm Stun, Campaign Monitor, Pop Commerce, Emma, and StrongMail E-mail Server are among software and services highlighted.

28467 ■ *Designing Websites for Every Audience*
Pub: F & W Publications, Incorporated
Ed: Ilise Benun. **Released:** January 2003. **Description:** Twenty-five case studies targeting six difference audiences are used to help a business design, or make over, a Website.

28468 ■ "DHS Finalizes Rules Allowing Electronic I-9s" in *HR Specialist* (Vol. 8, September 2010, No. 9, pp. 5)
Pub: Capitol Information Group Inc.
Description: U.S. Department of Homeland Security issued regulations that give employers more flexibility to electronically sing and store I-9 employee verification forms.

28469 ■ *Digital Divide: Civic Engagement, Information Poverty, and the Internet Worldwide*
Pub: Cambridge University Press
Ed: Pippa Norris. **Released:** January 22, 2010. **Price:** $28.99. **Description:** The expansive growth of the Internet is intensifying existing inequalities between the information rich and poor. The book examines the evidence for access and use of the Internet in 179 countries and discusses the global divide that is evident between industrialized and developing societies.

28470 ■ "The Digital Revolution is Over. Long Live the Digital Revolution!" in *Business Strategy Review* (Vol. 21, Spring 2010, No. 1, pp. 74)
Pub: Wiley-Blackwell
Ed: Gianvito Lanzolla, Jamie Anderson. **Description:** Many businesses are now involved in the digital marketplace. The authors argue that the new reality of numerous companies offering overlapping products means that it is critical for managers to understand digital convergence and to observe the imperatives for remaining competitive.

28471 ■ "Do-It-Yourself Portfolio Management" in *Barron's* (Vol. 89, July 13, 2009, No. 28, pp. 25)
Pub: Dow Jones & Co., Inc.
Ed: Mike Hogan. **Description:** Services of several portfolio management web sites are presented. These web sites include MarketRiders E.Adviser, TD Ameritrade and E*Trade.

28472 ■ "Dollar General Selects GSI Commerce to Launch Its eCommerce Business" in *Benzinga.com* (October 29, 2011)
Pub: Benzinga.com
Ed: Benzinga Staff. **Description:** Dollar General Corporation chose GSI Commerce, a leading provider of ecommerce and interactive marketing solutions, to launch its online initiative. GSI Commerce is an eBay Inc. company.

28473 ■ "Dots Sings To New Tune With Its Radio Station" in *Crain's Cleveland Business* (Vol. 30, June 15, 2009, No. 23, pp. 7)
Pub: Crain Communications, Inc.
Description: Dots LLC, a women's clothing retailer, has launched an online radio station on its Website. The station plays the in-store music to customers while they are shopping online.

28474 ■ *Double or Nothing: How Two Friends Risked It All to Buy One of Las Vegas' Legendary Casinos*
Pub: HarperBusiness
Ed: Tom Breitling, with Cal Fussman. **Released:** March 2008. **Price:** $24.95. **Description:** Founders of a successful Internet travel agency share their experience from startup to selling the company.

28475 ■ "Dramatic Results: Making Opera (Yes, Opera) Seem Young and Hip" in *Inc.* (October 2007, pp. 61-62)
Pub: Gruner & Jahr USA Publishing
Description: Profile of Peter Gelb, who turned New York's Metropolitan Opera into one of the most media-savvy organizations in the country, using a multifaceted marketing strategy through the media. Gelb used streaming audio and simulcasts on satellite radio and movie theaters to promote a message that opera is hip.

28476 ■ "Drive Traffic To Your Blog" in *Women Entrepreneur* (January 13, 2009)
Pub: Entrepreneur Media Inc.
Ed: Lesley Spencer Pyle. **Description:** Internet social networking has become a vital component to marketing one's business. Tips are provided on how to establish a blog that will attract attention to one's business and keep one's customers coming back for more.

28477 ■ *e-Business, e-Government and Small and Medium-Size Enterprises: Opportunities and Challenges*
Pub: Idea Group Publishing
Ed: Brian J. Corbitt, Nabeel A.Y. Al-Qirim. **Released:** February 2004. **Price:** $64.95. **Description:** Electronic commerce and information technology research in small and medium-sized enterprises (SMEs). Policymakers, legislators, researchers and professionals address significant issues of importance to the small business sector.

28478 ■ *E-Commerce in Regional Small to Medium Enterprises*
Pub: Idea Group Publishing
Ed: Robert MacGregor. **Released:** July 2007. **Price:** $99.95. **Description:** Strategies small to medium enterprises (SMEs) need to implement in order to compete with larger, global businesses and the role electronic commerce plays in this process are outlined. Studies of e-commerce in multiple regional areas, focusing on the role of business size, business sector, market focus, gender of CEO, and education level of the CEO are discussed.

28479 ■ *e-Riches 2.0: Next-Generation Marketing Strategies for Making Million Online*
Pub: AMACOM
Ed: Scott Fox. **Released:** May 27, 2009. **Price:** $25.00. **Description:** Beginner's guide to using the Internet to help grow business, including the best ways to use email lists and newsletters, RSS feeds, online viral marketing, social networking, microblogging, online video and radio/podcasts, tele-seminars and webinars, search engine keyword advertising and affiliate program advertising.

28480 ■ "eBay Business Looking Up" in *Zacks* (July 26, 2011)
Pub: Comtex News Network Inc.
Ed: Sejuti Banerjea. **Description:** eBay reported solid revenue growth for 2011 second quarter, keeping in line with the Zacks Consensus Estimate, and third quarter earnings are expected to be higher. eBay's new strategy is to direct traffic to bigger sellers with improved customer service, making this good for eBay businesses.

28481 ■ "EBay Finally Gaining Traction in China" in *San Jose Mercury News* (October 26, 2011)
Pub: San Jose Mercury News
Ed: John Boudreau. **Description:** eBay has developed a new strategy in China that allows exporters of every type of merchandise to sell directly to eBays 97 million overseas users.

28482 ■ *EBay Income: How ANYONE of Any Age, Location, and/or Background Can Build a Highly Profitable Online Business with eBay (Revised 2nd Edition)*
Pub: Atlantic Publishing Company
Released: December 1, 2010. **Price:** $24.95. **Description:** A complete overview of eBay is given and guides any small company through the entire process of creating the auction and auction strategies, photography, writing copy, text and formatting, multiple sales, programming tricks, PayPal, accounting, creating marketing, merchandising, managing email lists, advertising plans, taxes and sales tax, best time to list items and for how long, sniping programs, international customers, opening a storefront, electronic commerce, buy-it now pricing, keywords, Google marketing and eBay secrets.

28483 ■ "eBay Inc. Completes Acquisition of Zong" in *Benzinga.com* (October 29, 2011)
Pub: Benzinga.com
Ed: Benzinga Staff. **Description:** eBay Inc. acquired Zong, a provider of payments through mobile carrier billing. Terms of the agreement are outlined.

28484 ■ "eBay Introduces Open Commerce Ecosystem" in *Entertainment Close-Up* (October 24, 2011)
Pub: Close-Up Media
Description: eBay's new X.commerce is an open commerce ecosystem that will arm developers and merchants with the technology tools required to keep pace with the ever-changing industry. X.commerce brings together the technology assets and developer communities of eBay, PayPal, Magento and partners to expand on eBays vision for enabling commerce.

28485 ■ "eBay and Jonathan Adler Team to Launch 'The eBay Inspiration Shop'" in *Entertainment Close-Up* (October 25, 2011)
Pub: Close-Up Media
Description: Designer Jonathan Adler partnered with eBay to create a collection of new must-have merchandise for the fall season. Top trendsetters, including actors, designers, bloggers, stylists, editors, photographers, models and musicians helped curate the items being featured in the windows by sharing their shopping wish lists with users.

28486 ■ *The Ebay Seller's Tax and Legal Answer Book*
Pub: AMACOM
Ed: Cliff Ennico. **Released:** April 30, 2007. **Price:** $19.95. **Description:** Helps sellers using Ebay to file taxes properly, while saving money.

28487 ■ *Ebay the Smart Way: Selling, Burying, and Profiting on the Web's Number One Auction Site*
Pub: AMACOM
Ed: Joseph T. Sinclair. **Released:** May 2007. **Price:** $17.95. **Description:** Resource to help individuals sell, buy and profit using the Internet auction site Ebay.

28488 ■ *Effective Web Presence Solutions for Small Businesses: Strategies for Successful Implementation*
Pub: IGI Global
Ed: Stephen Burgess,, Carmine Sellitto, Stergios Karanasio, Stan Karanasios. **Released:** March 1, 2009. **Price:** $165.00. **Description:** Business strategies to implement a Web presence for any small business, is examined, focusing on website development.

28489 ■ "Elanco Challenges Bayer's Advantage, K9 Advantix Ad Claims" in *Pet Product News* (Vol. 64, November 2010, No. 11, pp. 11)
Pub: BowTie Inc.
Description: Elanco Animal Health has disputed Bayer Animal Health's print and Web advertising claims involving its flea, tick, and mosquito control products Advantage and K9 Advantix. The National Advertising Division of the Council of Better Business Bureaus recommended the discontinuation of ads, while Bayer Animal Health reiterated its commitment to self-regulation.

28490 ■ *Electronic Commerce*
Pub: Course Technology
Ed: Gary Schneider, Bryant Chrzan, Charles McCormick. **Released:** May 1, 2010. **Price:** $117.95. **Description:** E-commerce can open the door to more opportunities than ever before for small business. Packed with real-world examples and cases, the book delivers comprehensive coverage of emerging online technologies and trends and their influence on the electronic marketplace. It details how the landscape of online commerce is evolving, reflecting changes in the economy and how business and society are responding to those changes. Balancing technological issues with the strategic business aspects of successful e-commerce, the new edition includes expanded coverage of international issues, social networking, mobile commerce, Web 2.0 technologies, and updates on spam, phishing, and identity theft.

28491 ■ *Electronic Commerce: Technical, Business, and Legal Issues*
Pub: Prentice Hall PTR
Ed: Oktay Dogramaci; Aryya Gangopadhyay; Yelena Yesha; Nabil R. Adam. **Released:** August 1998. **Description:** Provides insight into the goals of using the

Internet to grow a business in the areas of networking and telecommunication, security, and storage and retrieval; business areas such as marketing, procurement and purchasing, billing and payment, and supply chain management; and legal aspects such as privacy, intellectual property, taxation, contractual and legal settlements.

28492 ■ *Email Marketing by the Numbers: How to Use the World's Greatest Marketing Tool to Take Any Organization to the Next Level*
Pub: John Wiley and Sons Inc.
Ed: Chris Baggott. **Released:** April 2007. **Price:** $29.99 (CND). **Description:** Tips for using email to market small business products and services are provided.

28493 ■ *Emerging Business Online: Global Markets and the Power of B2B Internet Marketing*
Pub: FT Press
Ed: Lara Fawzy, Lucas Dworksi. **Released:** October 1, 2010. **Price:** $49.99. **Description:** An introduction into ebocube (emerging business online), a comprehensive proven business model for Internet B2B marketing in emerging markets.

28494 ■ "Empowered" in *Harvard Business Review* (Vol. 88, July-August 2010, No. 7-8, pp. 94)
Pub: Harvard Business School Publishing
Ed: Josh Bernoff, Ted Schadler. **Description:** HERO concept (highly empowered and resourceful operative) which builds a connection between employees, managers, and IT is outlined. The resultant additional experience and knowledge gained by employees improves customer relationship management.

28495 ■ "Endeca Gears Up for Likely IPO Bid" in *Boston Business Journal* (Vol. 31, July 1, 2011, No. 23, pp. 1)
Pub: Boston Business Journal
Ed: Kyle Alspach. **Description:** Endeca Inc. is readying itself for its plans to register as a public company. The search engine technology leader is enjoying continued growth with revenue up by 30 percent in 2010 while its expansion trend makes it an unlikely candidate for an acquisition.

28496 ■ *The Essential Online Solution: The 5-Step Formula for Small Business Success*
Pub: John Wiley & Sons, Incorporated
Ed: Rick Segel; Barbara Callan-Bogia. **Released:** October 2006. **Price:** $22.95. **Description:** Strategies to help any small business increase its online presence and compete with big retail chains. Tips for success Web design are included.

28497 ■ *Essentials of Entrepreneurship and Small Business Management*
Pub: Prentice Hall PTR
Ed: Thomas W. Zimmerer; Norman M. Scarborough; Doug Wilson. **Released:** February 2007. **Price:** $106. 67. **Description:** New venture creation and the knowledge required to start a new business are shared. The challenges of entrepreneurship, business plans, marketing, e-commerce, and financial considerations are explored.

28498 ■ "Etextbook Space Heats Up" in *Information Today* (Vol. 28, November 2011, No. 10, pp. 10)
Pub: Information Today, Inc.
Ed: Paula J. Hane. **Description:** The use of etextbooks is expected to grow with the use of mobile devices and tablets. A new group of activists is asking students, faculty members and others to sign a petition urging higher education leaders to prioritize affordable textbooks or free ebooks over the traditional, expensive new books required for classes.

28499 ■ "Etextbooks: Coming of Age" in *Information Today* (Vol. 28, September 2011, No. 8, pp. 1)
Pub: Information Today, Inc.
Ed: Amanda Mulvihill. **Description:** National average for textbooks costs was estimated at $1,137 annually at a 4-year public college for the 2010-2011 school year. Amazon reported selling 105 etextbooks for every 100 print books, while Barnes and Noble announced that their etextbooks were outselling print 3 to 1.

28500 ■ "Etiquette, Common Sense Often Lag Behind Smarter Devices" in *Crain's Cleveland Business* (Vol. 28, October 22, 2007, No. 42, pp. 21)
Pub: Crain Communications, Inc.
Ed: Chrissy Kadleck. **Description:** Discusses the importance of good etiquette in regards to electronic communication both within as well as outside the business world.

28501 ■ "F1 Makes Room(s) for Aspiring Entrepreneur" in *Austin Business Journal* (Vol. 31, July 1, 2011, No. 17, pp. 1)
Pub: American City Business Journals Inc.
Ed: Vicky Garza. **Description:** Formula One fan and graphic designer Danielle Crespo cashes in on the June 17, 2012 racing event in Austin, Texas via hosting a Website that allows users to book hotel rooms. She invested less than $100 and long hours on this enterprise which now has 74,000-plus visitors.

28502 ■ *The Facebook Effect: The Inside Story of the Company That Is Connecting the World*
Pub: Simon & Shuster
Ed: David Kirkpatrick. **Released:** June 8, 2010. **Price:** $26.00. **Description:** There's never been a Website like Facebook: more than 350 million people have accounts, and if the growth rate continues, by 2013 every Internet user worldwide will have his or her own page. No one's had more access to the inner workings of the phenomenon than Kirkpatrick, a senior tech writer at Fortune magazine. Written with the full cooperation of founder Mark Zuckerberg, the book follows the company from its genesis in a Harvard dorm room through its successes over Friendster and MySpace, the expansion of the user base, and Zuckerberg's refusal to sell.

28503 ■ *The Facebook Era: Tapping Online Social Networks to Build Better Products, Reach New Audiences, and Sell More Stuff*
Pub: Prentice Hall
Ed: Clara Shih. **Price:** $24.99. **Description:** The '90s were about the World Wide Web of information and the power of linking Web pages. Today it's about the World Wide Web of people and the power of the social graph. Online social networks are fundamentally changing the way we live, work, and interact. They offer businesses immense opportunities to transform customer relationships for profit: opportunities that touch virtually every business function, from sales and marketing to recruiting, collaboration to executive decision-making, product development to innovation.

28504 ■ *Facebook Marketing: Designing Your Next Marketing Campaign*
Pub: Que
Ed: Justin R. Levy. **Released:** May 1, 2010. **Price:** $24.99. **Description:** Detailed steps are given in order to develop, use, and create awareness for any business. The book provides detailed instructions, along with case studies from known brands, for launching marketing campaigns on Facebook.

28505 ■ "Facebook Purchased Push Pop Press" in *Information Today* (Vol. 28, October 2011, No. 9, pp. 12)
Pub: Information Today, Inc.
Description: Facebook purchased Push Pop Press, a digital publishing company that developed a multi-touch interface for ebook publishing on the iPad.

28506 ■ "Fifty Percent of Global Online Retail Visits Were to Amazon, eBay and Alibaba in June 2011" in *Benzinga.com* (October 29, 2011)
Pub: Benzinga.com
Ed: Benzinga Staff. **Description:** Current statistics and future forecasts through the year 2015 for Amazon, eBay and Alibaba are explored.

28507 ■ "Financo Panel Lauds Product, Online Marketing" in *Home Textiles Today* (Vol. 31, January 25, 2010, No. 3, pp. 1)
Pub: Reed Business Information, Inc.
Ed: James Mammarella. **Description:** Overview of the Financo Annual Merchandising Industry Chief Executives Event during which there was much discussion on the merits of e-commerce, online marketing as well as the traditional methods of brand recognition and retailing.

28508 ■ "Five Low-Cost Home Based Startups" in *Women Entrepreneur* (December 16, 2008)
Pub: Entrepreneur Media Inc.
Ed: Lesley Spencer Pyle. **Description:** During tough economic times, small businesses have an advantage over large companies because they can adjust to economic conditions more easily and without having to go through corporate red tape that can slow the implementation process. A budding entrepreneur may find success by taking inventory of his or her skills, experience, expertise and passions and utilizing those qualities to start a business. Five low-cost home-based startups are profiled. These include starting an online store, a virtual assistant service, web designer, sales representative and a home staging counselor.

28509 ■ "Fly Phishing" in *Canadian Business* (Vol. 80, October 22, 2007, No. 21, pp. 42)
Pub: Rogers Media
Ed: Andy Holloway. **Description:** Symantec Corporation's report shows consumers and companies have effectively installed network defenses that prevent unwanted access. Phishing packages are readily available and are widely used. Other details of the Internet Security Threat Report are presented.

28510 ■ "For Apple, It's Showtime Again" in *Barron's* (Vol. 90, August 30, 2010, No. 35, pp. 29)
Pub: Barron's Editorial & Corporate Headquarters
Ed: Eric J. Savitz. **Description:** Speculations on what Apple Inc. will unveil at its product launch event are presented. These products include a possible new iPhone Nano, a new update to its Apple TV, and possibly a deal with the Beatles to distribute their songs over iTunes.

28511 ■ "For MySpace, A Redesign to Entice Generation Y" in *The New York Times* (October 27, 2010, pp. B3)
Pub: The New York Times Company
Ed: Miguel Helft. **Description:** MySpace is redesigning its Website in order to attract individuals from the Generation Y group.

28512 ■ "ForeSee Finds Satisfaction On Web Sites, Bottom Line" in *Crain's Detroit Business* (Vol. 24, February 25, 2008, No. 8, pp. 3)
Pub: Crain Communications Inc. - Detroit
Ed: Tom Henderson. **Description:** Ann Arbor-based ForeSee Results Inc. evaluates user satisfaction on Web sites. The company expects to see an increase of 40 percent in revenue for 2008 with plans to expand to London, Germany, Italy and France by the end of 2009.

28513 ■ "Free Speech Vs. Privacy in Data Mining" in *Information Today* (Vol. 28, September 2011, No. 8, pp. 22)
Pub: Information Today, Inc.
Ed: George H. Pike. **Description:** The U.S. Constitution does not explicitly guarantee the right of privacy. Organizations and businesses that require obtaining and disseminating information can be caught in the middle of privacy rights. The long-term impact on data mining, Internet marketing, and Internet privacy issues are examined.

28514 ■ *Freelancing for Journalists*
Pub: Routledge
Ed: Diana Harris. **Released:** January 1, 2010. **Price:** $110.00. **Description:** Comprehensive guide showing the specific skills required for those wishing to freelance in newspapers, magazines, radio, television, and as online journalists.

28515 ■ "Fresh Direct's Crisis" in *Crain's New York Business* (Vol. 24, January 14, 2008, No. 2, pp. 3)
Pub: Crain Communications, Inc.
Ed: Lisa Fickenscher. **Description:** Freshdirect, an Internet grocery delivery service, finds itself under siege from federal immigration authorities, customers and labor organizations due to its employment practice of hiring illegals. At stake is the grocer's reputation as well as its ambitious growth plans, including an initial public offering of its stock.

28516 ■ "Friendly Ice Cream Corporation" in *Ice Cream Reporter* (Vol. 23, August 20, 2010, No. 9, pp. 8)
Pub: Ice Cream Reporter
Description: Friendly Ice Cream Corporation appointed Andrea M. McKenna as vice president of marketing and chief marketing officer.

28517 ■ *From Entrepreneur to Infopreneur: Make Money with Books, E-Books, and Other Information Products*
Pub: John Wiley & Sons, Incorporated
Ed: Stephanie Chandler. **Released:** November 2006. **Price:** $19.95. **Description:** Infopreneurs sell information online in the forms of books, e-books, special reports, audio and video products, seminars, and more.

28518 ■ "The Future of Work" in *Black Enterprise* (Vol. 41, August 2010, No. 1, pp. 65)
Pub: Earl G. Graves Publishing Co. Inc.
Ed: Annya M. Lott. **Description:** Technology, globalization, and outsourcing will continue to shape the future of work. Social media is a means for small companies to market goods and services.

28519 ■ "gdgt: The New Online Home for Gadget Fans" in *Hispanic Business* (July-August 2009, pp. 15)
Pub: Hispanic Business
Ed: Jeremy Nisen. **Description:** Profile of the new online Website for gadget lovers. The site combines a leek interface, gadget database, and social networking-type features which highlights devices for the consumer.

28520 ■ "Generation Y Chooses the Mobile Web" in *PR Newswire* (November 24, 2010)
Pub: PR Newswire Association LLC
Description: Generation Y individuals between the ages of 18 - 27 use their mobile phones to browse the Internet more often than a desktop or laptop computer, according to a survey conducted by Opera, a Web browser company.

28521 ■ "Get Paid and Get Moving" in *Entrepreneur* (Vol. 37, October 2009, No. 10, pp. 38)
Pub: Entrepreneur Media, Inc.
Description: GoPayments application from Intuit allows mobile telephones to process payments like credit card terminals. The application costs $19.95 a month and can be used on the Internet browsers of mobile telephones.

28522 ■ "Get Sold On eBay" in *Entrepreneur* (Vol. 36, March 2008, No. 3, pp. 94)
Pub: Entrepreneur Media Inc.
Ed: Marcia Layton Turner. **Description:** Entrepreneurs are increasingly using eBay to sell products. Some tips to start selling products through eBay include: starting with used items, developing a niche to sell specific products, and researching product pricing. Other tips with regard to starting an eBay business are covered.

28523 ■ "Get Them Talking" in *Entrepreneur* (Vol. 36, February 2008, No. 2, pp. 50)
Pub: Entrepreneur Media Inc.
Ed: Heather Clancy. **Description:** Yelp.com is an Internet search site that presents businesses across the U.S., sorted according to the number of customer reviews they have received. One to five stars are used by the reviewers, or yelpers, to rate businesses. Details on how the International Orange day spa benefited from Yelp are discussed.

28524 ■ *Getting Clients and Keeping Clients for Your Service Business*
Pub: Atlantic Publishing Company
Ed: Anne M. Miller; Gail Brett Levine. **Released:** August 28, 2008. **Price:** $24.95 paperback. **Description:** Tips are offered to help any small service business identify customers, brand and grow the business, as well as development of logos, brochures and Websites.

28525 ■ "Ghouls, Goblins, and Harry Potter: Cashing In On Halloween" in *Inc.* (Vol. 33, October 2011, No. 8, pp. 24)
Pub: Inc. Magazine
Ed: Darren Dahl. **Description:** Costume Craze, an online costume retailer reports $13.2 million in sales last year. Originally the family business started out as a software company called StaticAdvantage, but switched gears.

28526 ■ *Global E-Commerce: Impacts of National Environment and Policy*
Pub: Cambridge University Press
Ed: Kenneth L. Kraemer; Jason Dedrick; Nigel P. Melville; Kevin Zhu. **Released:** August 2006. **Price:** $75.00. **Description:** Global assessment of the impact of e-business on companies as well as countries.

28527 ■ *Global Electronic Business Research: Opportunities and Directions*
Pub: Idea Group Publishing
Ed: Nabeel A.Y. Al-Qirim. **Released:** December 2005. **Price:** $ 74.95. **Description:** Importance electronic commerce research plays in small to medium-sized enterprises in various countries.

28528 ■ "Global Imagery in Online Advertisements" in *Business Communication Quarterly* (December 2007, pp. 487)
Pub: Sage Publications USA
Ed: Geraldine E. Hynes, Marius Janson. **Description:** Respondents from six countries were interviewed about their reactions to two online ads to determine cultural differences in understanding advertising elements. Universal appeals and cultural values determine the effectiveness of symbols in online advertising.

28529 ■ "Google Places a Call to Bargain Hunters" in *Advertising Age* (Vol. 79, September 29, 2008, No. 36, pp. 13)
Pub: Crain Communications, Inc.
Ed: Abbey Klaassen. **Description:** Google highlighted application developers who have created tools for its Android mobile phone in the device's unveiling; applications such as ShopSavvy and CompareEverywhere help shoppers to find bargains by allowing them to compare prices in their local areas and across the web.

28530 ■ *The Google Story: Inside the Hottest Business, Media, and Technology Success of Our Time*
Pub: Random Housing Publishing Group
Ed: David A. Vise; Mark Malseed. **Price:** $26.00.

28531 ■ "Google's Next Stop: Below 350?" in *Barron's* (Vol. 88, March 10, 2008, No. 10, pp. 17)
Pub: Dow Jones & Company, Inc.
Ed: Jacqueline Doherty. **Description:** Share prices of Google Inc. are expected to drop from their level of $433 each to below $350 per share. The company is expected to miss its earnings forecast for the first quarter of 2008, and its continued aggressive spending on non-core areas will eventually bring down earnings.

28532 ■ "Googly Eyed" in *Entrepreneur* (Vol. 36, February 2008, No. 2, pp. 48)
Pub: Entrepreneur Media Inc.
Ed: Mike Hogan. **Description:** Linux has developed desktops that boot into the Google toolbar and applications. These desktops include: Zonbu, Everex gPCTC2502, and Asus Eee PC 4G mini laptop. Details on the applications of these desktops are discussed.

28533 ■ "Government Says Self-Regulation of Online Privacy is Coming Up Short" in *Advertising Age* (Vol. 81, December 6, 2010, No. 43, pp. 1)
Pub: Crain Communications, Inc.
Ed: Edmund Lee. **Description:** U.S. Federal Trade Commission and the Department of Commerce are concerned about the current state of digital privacy and stated that self-regulation has not been sufficient to date.

28534 ■ "Grand Bohemian Hotel in Orlando, Fla. Takes Lead in Wedding Planning" in *Benzinga.com* (August 4, 2011)
Pub: Benzinga.com
Ed: Benzinga Staff. **Description:** MAD-Marketing launched a newly-designed Website for the Grand Bohemian Hotel in Orlando, Florida. The site features the hotel's wedding vanity site to help target prospective couples planning their weddings.

28535 ■ "Grooming Your Online Persona" in *Women In Business* (Vol. 62, June 2010, No. 2, pp. 36)
Pub: American Business Women's Association
Ed: Diane Stafford. **Description:** Employees' use of online social networks could become a basis on how their employers, clients, or business partners would judge them. Personal details, pictures and other online data should be filtered to avoid inappropriate or uncomfortable situations and distinguish personal from professional or work life.

28536 ■ *Groundswell: Winning in a World Transformed by Social Technologies*
Pub: Harvard Business School Press
Ed: Charlene Li; Josh Bernoff. **Released:** April 21, 2008. **Price:** $29.95. **Description:** Individuals are using online social technologies such as blogs, social networking sites, YouTube, and podcasts to discuss products and companies, write their own news, and find their own deals. When consumers you've never met are rating your company's products in public forums with which you have no experience or influence, your company is vulnerable. This book teaches the tools and data necessary to turn this treat into an opportunity.

28537 ■ "Group-Buying Site Hones In on Hispanics" in *Austin Business Journal* (Vol. 31, July 1, 2011, No. 17, pp. 1)
Pub: American City Business Journals Inc.
Ed: Vicky Garza. **Description:** Descuentl Libre is a new group-buying site from Austin, Texas that targets the Hispanic market, offering discounts of practical items and family-friendly activities. The Hispanic market constitutes 17 percent of the U.S. population and spends $23 billion yearly online.

28538 ■ *Grown Up Digital: How the Net Generation Is Changing Your World*
Pub: The McGraw-Hill Companies
Ed: Don Tapscott. **Released:** 2009. **Price:** $27.95. **Description:** As baby boomers retire, business needs to understand what makes the Internet work for business.

28539 ■ *Guerrilla Marketing for the New Millennium*
Pub: Morgan James Publishing, LLC
Ed: Jay Conrad Levinson. **Released:** September 2005. **Price:** $14.00. **Description:** Steps to successfully market a small business on the Internet.

28540 ■ *Guerrilla Marketing: Put Your Advertising on Steroids*
Pub: Morgan James Publishing, LLC
Ed: Jay Conrad Levinson. **Released:** December 2005. **Price:** $14.00. **Description:** Marketing concepts to successfully advertise any Internet business, featuring the ten most successful advertising campaigns of the 20th Century.

28541 ■ "Haagen-Dazs Recruits Shop Owners through Facebook" in *Ice Cream Reporter* (Vol. 23, November 20, 2010, No. 12, pp. 1)
Pub: Ice Cream Reporter
Description: Haagen-Dazs Shoppe Company is using Facebook, the leading social media, to recruit new franchises.

28542 ■ "Happy Blogging" in *Black Enterprise* (Vol. 38, January 2008, No. 6, pp. 47)
Pub: Earl G. Graves Publishing Co. Inc.
Ed: Sonya A. Donaldson. **Description:** Individual seeks advice for setting up a Website and starting a blog; Squarespace and Weebly both offer Web design.

28543 ■ "Harlequin Leads the Way" in *Marketing to Women* (Vol. 22, July 2009, No. 7, pp. 1)
Pub: EPM Communications, Inc.
Description: Although the publishing industry has been slow to embrace new media options, the Internet is now a primary source for reaching women readers. Harlequin has been eager to court their female consumers over the Internet and often uses women bloggers in their campaigns strategies.

28544 ■ "Harley-Davidson Moves to Unconventional Marketing Plan" in *Business Journal-Milwaukee* (Vol. 28, November 26, 2010, No. 8, pp. A1)
Pub: Milwaukee Business Journal
Ed: Rich Rovito. **Description:** Harley Davidson Inc. hired Boulder, Colorado-based Victors & Spoils, an agency that specializes in crowdsourcing, to implement a new creative marketing model. Under the plan, Harley Davidson will draw on the ideas of its brand enthusiasts to help guide the brand's marketing direction.

28545 ■ "Harness the Internet to Boost Equipment Sales" in *Indoor Comfort Marketing* (Vol. 70, July 2011, No. 7, pp. 24)
Pub: Industry Publications Inc.
Ed: Richard Rutigliano. **Description:** Advice is given to increase HVAC/R equipment sales using the Internet.

28546 ■ "Health-Care Highway" in *Saint Louis Business Journal* (Vol. 32, October 14, 2011, No. 7, pp. 1)
Pub: Saint Louis Business Journal
Ed: Angela Mueller. **Description:** Around $2.6 billion will be invested in health care facilities along the Highway 64/40 corridor in St. Louis, Missouri. Mercy Hospital is planning to invest $19 million in a virtual care center. St. Elizabeth's Hospital on the other hand, will purchase 105 acres in the corridor.

28547 ■ "Helping Customers Fight Pet Waste" in *Pet Product News* (Vol. 64, November 2010, No. 11, pp. 52)
Pub: BowTie Inc.
Ed: Sandy Robins. **Description:** Pet cleaning products manufacturers have been enjoying high sales figures by paying attention to changing pet ownership trends and environmental awareness. Meanwhile, the inclusion of user-friendly features in these products has also been boosted by the social role of pets and the media attention to pet waste. How manufacturers have been responding to this demand is explored.

28548 ■ *Here Come the Regulars: How to Run a Record Label on a Shoestring Budget*
Pub: Faber & Faber, Inc.
Ed: Ian Anderson. **Released:** October 1, 2009. **Price:** $15.00. **Description:** Author, Ian Anderson launched his own successful record label, Afternoon Records when he was 18 years old. Anderson shares insight into starting a record label, focusing on label image, budget, blogging, potential artists, as well as legal aspects.

28549 ■ "HER's: the Future is Free" in *Benzinga.com* (October 29, 2011)
Pub: Benzinga.com
Ed: Benzinga Staff. **Description:** In order to create and maintain electronic health records that connects every physician and hospital it is essential to create a reliable, easy-to-use, certified Web-based ambulatory ERH using an ad-supported model. eBay seems to be the company showing the most potential for improving services to physicians and consumers, but requires sellers to pay fees based upon sales price.

28550 ■ "The Hired Guns" in *Business Courier* (Vol. 26, November 13, 2009, No. 29, pp. 1)
Pub: American City Business Journals, Inc.
Ed: Lisa Biank Fasig. **Description:** YourForce has nearly 6,000 retired scientists and researchers who work together in helping Procter & Gamble (P&G) and other companies in addressing various project needs. Operating as an online innovation community, YourEncore is a result of P&G's Connect + Develop program.

28551 ■ "Hitting the E-Books" in *Inc.* (Vol. 33, September 2011, No. 7, pp. 36)
Pub: Inc. Magazine
Ed: Shivani Vora. **Description:** Textbooks may be getting cheaper for college students now that they can use electronic textbooks that can be read on a laptop or tablet. The market is growing about 50 percent annually. Statistical data included.

28552 ■ "Hoover's Mobile, MobileSP Now Available" in *Information Today* (Vol. 26, February 2009, No. 2, pp. 29)
Pub: Information Today, Inc.
Description: Hoover's Inc. introduced its Hoover's Mobile for iPhone, BlackBerry and Windows Mobile smartphones along with Hoover's MobileSP for BlackBerry and Windows Mobile. Both products allow users to access customer, prospect, and partner information; analyze competitors; prepare for meetings; and find new opportunities. In addition, MobileSP adds one-click calling to executives, GPS-enabled location searches, advanced search and list building, and a custom call queue and a 'save to contacts' capabilities.

28553 ■ *Housecleaning Business: Organize Your Business - Get Clients and Referrals - Set Rates and Services*
Pub: The Globe Pequot Press
Ed: Laura Jorstad, Melinda Morse. **Released:** June 1, 2009. **Price:** $18.95. **Description:** This book shares insight into starting a housecleaning businesses. It shows how to develop a service manual, screen clients, serve customers, select cleaning products, competition, how to up a home office, using the Internet to grow the business and offering green cleaning options to clients.

28554 ■ "How to Boost Your Super Bowl ROI" in *Advertising Age* (Vol. 80, December 7, 2009, No. 41, pp. 3)
Pub: Crain's Communications
Ed: Abbey Klaassen. **Description:** Internet marketing is essential, even for the corporations that can afford to spend $3 million on a 30-second Super Bowl spot; last year, Super Bowl advertising reached an online viewership of 99.5 million while 98.7 million people watched the game on television validating the idea that public relations must go farther than a mere television ad campaign. Social media provides businesses with a longer shelf life for their ad campaigns. Advice is also given regarding ways in which to strategize a smart and well-thought plan for utilizing the online marketing options currently available.

28555 ■ *How to Get Rich on the Internet*
Pub: Morgan James Publishing, LLC
Ed: Ted Ciuba. **Released:** August 2004. **Price:** $19.95. **Description:** Interviews with successful Internet entrepreneurs provide insight into marketing products and services online using minimal investment. The importance of a sound marketing ad campaign using the Internet is discussed; maintaining a database and Website will automatically carry out business transactions daily. Suggestions for various types of businesses to run online are given.

28556 ■ "How Good Advice 'Online' Can Attract Customers" in *Indoor Comfort Marketing* (Vol. 70, August 2011, No. 8, pp. 20)
Pub: Industry Publications Inc.
Ed: Richard Rutigilano. **Description:** Online marketing tips for heating and cooling small businesses are explained.

28557 ■ "How I Did It: Jack Ma" in *Inc.* (January 2008, pp. 94-102)
Pub: Gruner & Jahr USA Publishing
Ed: Rebecca Fannin. **Description:** Profile of Jack Ma, who started as a guide and interpreter for Western tourists in Hangzhou. Ma used the Internet to build Alibaba.com, China's largest business-to-business site and one of the hottest IPOs in years.

28558 ■ *How to Make Money with Social Media: Using New and Emerging Media to Grow Your Business*
Pub: FT Press
Ed: Jamie Turner, Reshma Shah. **Released:** October 1, 2010. **Price:** $24.99. **Description:** Marketers, executives, entrepreneurs are shown more effective ways to utilize Internet social media to make money. This guide brings together both practical strategies and proven execution techniques for driving maximum value from social media marketing.

28559 ■ "How to Make Your Website Really Sell" in *Entrepreneur* (Vol. 37, September 2009, No. 9, pp. 79)
Pub: Entrepreneur Media, Inc.
Ed: David Port. **Description:** Advice on how to succeed in Internet marketing is presented. Offering visitors purchase incentives on the home page is encouraged. Delivery of customized landing pages and content is also recommended.

28560 ■ "How to Manage Successful Crowdsourcing Projects" in *eWeek* (September 29, 2010)
Pub: Ziff Davis Enterprise
Description: The advantages, challenges and pitfalls faced when using crowdsourcing to improve a business are outlined. Crowdsourcing helps to eliminate the need to rely on an internal workforce and the need to forecast task volume.

28561 ■ *How to Market and Sell Your Art, Music, Photographs, and Handmade Crafts Online*
Pub: Atlantic Publishing Group, Inc.
Ed: Lee Rowley. **Released:** May 2008. **Price:** $24.95. **Description:** The book provides all the basics for starting and running an online store selling arts, crafts, photography or music. There are more than 300 Websites listed to help anyone market and promote their arts and/or crafts online.

28562 ■ *How to Open and Operate a Financially Successful Bookstore on Amazon and Other Web Sites: With Companion CD-ROM*
Pub: Atlantic Publishing Company
Released: December 1, 2010. **Price:** $39.95. **Description:** This book was written for every used book aficionado and bookstore owner who currently wants to take advantage of the massive collection of online resources available to start and run your own online bookstore business.

28563 ■ *How to Start and Run a Home-Based Landscaping Business*
Pub: Globe Pequot Press
Ed: Owen E. Dell. **Released:** December 2005. **Price:** $18.95. **Description:** Guide to starting and running a successful home-based landscaping business, including tips for marketing on the Internet.

28564 ■ "How To Get a Loan the Web 2.0 Way" in *Black Enterprise* (Vol. 41, December 2010, No. 5, pp. 23)
Pub: Earl G. Graves Publishing Co. Inc.
Ed: John Simons. **Description:** People are turning to online peer-to-peer network for personal loans as banks are lending less money.

28565 ■ "How-To Workshops Teach Sewing, Styles" in *St. Louis Post-Dispatch* (September 14, 2010)
Pub: St. Louis Post-Dispatch
Ed: Kalen Ponche. **Description:** Profile of DIY Style Workshop in St. Charles, Missouri, where sewing, designing and teaching is offered. The shop is home base for DIY Style, a Website created by mother and daughter to teach younger people how to sew.

28566 ■ *How to Use the Internet to Advertise, Promote, and Market Your Business or Web Site: With Little or No Money*
Pub: Atlantic Publishing Company
Released: December 1, 2010. **Price:** $24.95. **Description:** Information is given to help build, promote, and make money from your Website or brick and mortar store using the Internet, with minimal costs.

28567 ■ "I Hear You're Interested In a..." in *Inc.* (January 2008, pp. 40-43)
Pub: Gruner & Jahr USA Publishing
Ed: Leah Hoffmann. **Description:** Four tips to help any small business generate sales leads online are examined.

28568 ■ *I'm on LinkedIn - Now What? (Second Edition): A Guide to Getting the Most Out of LinkedIn*
Pub: Happy About
Ed: Diane Danielson. **Released:** January 7, 2009. **Price:** $19.95. **Description:** Designed to help get the most out of LinkedIn, the popular business networking site and follows the first edition and includes the latest and great approaches using LinkedIn. With over 32 million members there is a lot of potential to find and develop relationships to help in your business and personal life, but many professionals find themselves wondering what to do once they sign up. This book explains the different benefits of the system and recommends best practices (including LinkedIn Groups) so that you get the most out of LinkedIn.

28569 ■ *Information Technology for the Small Business: How to Make IT Work For Your Company*
Pub: TAB Computer Systems, Incorporated
Ed: T.J. Benoit. **Released:** June 2006. **Price:** $17. 95. **Description:** Basics of information technology to help small companies maximize benefits are covered. Topics include pitfalls to avoid, email and Internet use, data backup, recovery and overall IT organization.

28570 ■ "InnoCentive Announces Next Generation Crowdsourcing Platform" in *Internet Wire* (June 15, 2010)
Pub: Comtex
Description: InnoCentive, Inc., a world leader in open innovation, is launching InnoCentive@Work3, a third generation of its @Work enterprise platform for collaborative-driven innovation for companies. The product will help clients solve critical business and technical issues by tapping information both inside and outside of a company.

28571 ■ *Integration Marketing: How Small Businesses Become Big Businesses and Big Businesses Become Empires*
Pub: John Wiley & Sons, Inc.
Ed: Mark Joyner. **Released:** May 1, 2009. **Price:** $22.95. **Description:** Leading Internet marketing expert offers a marketing methodology to grow any business.

28572 ■ "Internet Marketing and Social Media Knowledge Vital for SMBs" in *Internet Wire* (November 24, 2009)
Pub: Comtex News Network, Inc.
Description: Small and medium-size businesses must learn to market themselves over the Internet in order to succeed and grow in today's marketplace. Web Marketing Today offers the largest source of the most important information concerning doing business on the Internet including e-commerce, email marketing and social networking opportunities.

28573 ■ "Internet and Mobile Media" in *MarketingMagazine* (Vol. 115, September 27, 2010, No. 13, pp. 60)
Pub: Rogers Publishing Ltd.
Description: Market data covering the Internet and mobile media in Canada is given.

28574 ■ "Internet Translation Service Helps Burmese" in *News-Sentinel* (May 10, 2011)
Pub: New-Sentinel
Ed: Ellie Bogue. **Description:** Catherine Kasper Place, Parkview Health Community Outreach, Allen County-Fort Wayne Department of Health and Advantage Health have partnered to help the Burmese Community in the area by providing an online service that links doctors' offices with translators in order to provide better healthcare.

28575 ■ "Israeli Spam Law May Have Global Impact" in *Information Today* (Vol. 26, February 2009, No. 2, pp. 28)
Pub: Information Today, Inc.
Ed: David Mirchin. **Description:** Israels new law, called Amendment 40 of the Communications Law, will regulate commercial solicitations including those sent without permission via email, fax, automatic phone dialing systems, or short messaging technologies.

28576 ■ "iSymmetry's Technological Makeover Or, How a Tech Company Finally Grew Up and Discovered the World Wide Web" in *Inc.* (October 2007)
Pub: Gruner & Jahr USA Publishing
Description: Profile of iSymmetry, an Atlanta, Georgia-based IT recruiting firm, covering the issues the company faces keeping its technology equipment up-to-date. The firm has devised a program that will replace its old server-based software systems with on-demand software delivered via the Internet, known as software-as-a-service. Statistical information included.

28577 ■ "It's Back to Business for the Ravens" in *Boston Business Journal* (Vol. 29, July 29, 2011, No. 12, pp. 1)
Pub: American City Business Journals Inc.
Ed: Scott Dance. **Description:** The Baltimore Ravens football team has been marketing open sponsorship packages following the end of the National Football League lockout. Team officials are working to get corporate logos and slogans on radio and television commercials and online advertisements.

28578 ■ "It's a Hit" in *Entrepreneur* (Vol. 36, March 2008, No. 3, pp. 110)
Pub: Entrepreneur Media Inc.
Ed: John Jantsch. **Description:** Entrepreneurs use the Web to market business and keeping relevant content in the Website is important to address questions from customers. Other considerations in marketing businesses online include: interacting with site visitors, using Web applications for project collaboration and file storage, and encouraging customers to post reviews.

28579 ■ "It's a New Game: Killerspin Pushes Table Tennis to Extreme Heights" in *Black Enterprise* (Vol. 37, October 2006, No. 3, pp. 73)
Pub: Earl G. Graves Publishing Co. Inc.
Ed: Bridget McCrea. **Description:** Profile of Robert Blackwell and his company Killerspin L.L.C., which is popularizing the sport of table tennis. Killerspin has hit $1 million in revenues due to product sales primarily generated through the company's website, magazines, DVDs, and event ticket sales.

28580 ■ "Jo-Ann Fabric and Craft Stores Joins ArtFire.com to Offer Free Online Craft Marketplace" in *Internet Wire* (January 26, 2010)
Pub: Comtex News Network, Inc.
Description: Jo-Ann Fabric and Craft Stores has entered into a partnership with ArtFire.com which will provide sewers and crafters all the tools they need in order to make and sell their products from an online venue.

28581 ■ "Joe Wikert, General Manager, O'Reilly Technology Exchange" in *Information Today* (Vol. 26, February 2009, No. 2, pp. 21)
Pub: Information Today, Inc.
Ed: Jamie Babbitt. **Description:** Joe Wikert, general manager of O'Reilly Technology Exchange discusses his plans to develop a free content model that will evolve with future needs. O'Reilly's major competitor is Google. Wikert plans to expand the firm's publishing program to include print, online, and in-person products and services.

28582 ■ "Johnson Publishing Expands: Moving Into Television and Internet To Extend Brand" in *Black Enterprise* (October 2007)
Pub: Earl G. Graves Publishing Co. Inc.
Ed: Tamara E. Holmes. **Description:** Johnson Publishing Company has followed the lives of black families in both Ebony and Jet magazines. The media firm has expanded its coverage by developing entertainment content for television, the Internet and other digital arenas.

28583 ■ "Keep Them Posted" in *Entrepreneur* (Vol. 35, October 2007, No. 10, pp. 39)
Pub: Entrepreneur Media Inc.
Ed: Gwen Moran. **Description:** Survey by the Pew Internet and American Life Project found that 12 million American adults maintain blogs, which are created for personal and business reasons. Blogs are effective in giving a business a personal touch while informing the public about its operations and products. Tips on how to create an effective business blog are presented.

28584 ■ "Kids, Computers and the Social Networking Evolution" in *Canadian Business* (Vol. 81, October 27, 2008, No. 18, pp. 93)
Pub: Rogers Media Ltd.
Ed: Penny Milton. **Description:** Social networking was found to help educate students in countries like the U.S., Canada and Mexico. Schools that embrace social networking teach students how to use computers safely and responsibility in order to counter threats to children on the Internet.

28585 ■ "Know the Facts About Natural Gas!" in *Indoor Comfort Marketing* (Vol. 70, August 2011, No. 8, pp. 26)
Pub: Industry Publications Inc.
Description: AEC Activity Update is presented on the American Energy Coalition's Website.

28586 ■ "Kodak Offers Cloud-Based Operating Option" in *American Printer* (Vol. 128, June 1, 2011, No. 6)
Pub: Penton Media Inc.
Description: Kodak partnered with VMware to offer its first Virtual Operating Environment option for Kodak Unified Workflow Solutions. The new feature enables cost savings, increased efficiency and failover protection.

28587 ■ "Kuno Creative to Present B2B Social Media Campaign Webinar" in *Entertainment Close-Up* (August 25, 2011)
Pub: Close-Up Media
Description: Kuno Creative, an inbound marketing agency, will host Three Steps of a Successful B2B Social Media Campaign. The firm is a provider of Website development, branding, marketing strategy, public relations, Internet marketing, and inbound marketing.

28588 ■ "Last Founder Standing" in *Conde Nast Portfolio* (Vol. 2, June 2008, No. 6, pp. 124)
Pub: Conde Nast Publications, Inc.
Ed: Kevin Maney. **Description:** Interview with Amazon CEO Jeff Bezos in which he discusses the economy, the company's new distribution center and the hiring of employees for it, e-books, and the overall vision for the future of the firm.

28589 ■ "Lavante, Inc. Joins Intersynthesis, Holistic Internet Marketing Company" in *Internet Wire* (November 5, 2009)
Pub: Comtex News Network, Inc.
Description: Lavante, Inc., the leading provider of on-demand vendor information and profit recovery audit solutions for Fortune 1000 companies has chosen Intersynthesis, a new holistic Internet marketing firm, as a provider of pay for performance services. Lavante believes that Intersynthesis' expertise and knowledge combined with their ability to develop integrated strategies, will help them fuel more growth.

28590 ■ "Legislating the Cloud" in *Information Today* (Vol. 28, October 2011, No. 9, pp. 1)
Pub: Information Today, Inc.
Description: Internet and telecommunications industry leaders are asking for legislation to address the emerging market in cloud computing. Existing communications laws do not adequately govern the modern Internet.

28591 ■ "Lights, Camera, Action: Tools for Creating Video Blogs" in *Inc.* (Volume 32, December 2010, No. 10, pp. 57)
Pub: Inc. Magazine
Ed: John Brandon. **Description:** A video blog is a good way to spread company news, talk about products, and stand out among traditional company blogs. New editing software can create two- to four-minute blogs using a webcam and either Windows Live Essentials, Apple iLife 2011, Powerdirector 9 Ultra, or Adobe Visual Communicator 3.

28592 ■ "Looking Out for the Little Guys" in *Black Enterprise* (Vol. 38, October 2007, No. 3, pp. 58)
Pub: Earl G. Graves Publishing Co. Inc.
Ed: Kaylyn Kendall Dines. **Description:** Biz Tech-Connect is a Web portal that offers free online and social networking, along with four modules that help small businesses with marketing and advertising, communications and mobility, financial management, and customer relationship management.

28593 ■ "Looking To Leap?" in *Black Enterprise* (Vol. 38, January 2008, No. 6, pp. 64)
Pub: Earl G. Graves Publishing Co. Inc.
Ed: Tennille M. Robinson. **Description:** Websites and organizations providing resources for any young entrepreneur wishing to start a new business are outlined.

28594 ■ "A Love of Likes" in *Boston Business Journal* (Vol. 31, July 8, 2011, No. 24, pp. 1)
Pub: Boston Business Journal
Ed: Lisa van der Pool. **Description:** An increasing number of companies in Boston, Massachusetts have been keen on getting Facebook 'likes' from people. Business owners realize that Facebook 'likes' could generate sales and based on some studies, equate to specific dollar values.

28595 ■ *Low-Budget Online Marketing for Small Business*
Pub: Self-Counsel Press Inc.
Ed: Holly Berkley. **Released:** August 2006. **Price:** $14.95, include CD-ROM. **Description:** Low-budget advertising campaigns are presented to help market any small business.

28596 ■ "Luxe Hotels on a Budget" in *Inc.* (Volume 32, December 2010, No. 10, pp. 60)
Pub: Inc. Magazine
Ed: Adam Baer. **Description:** Off & Away Website allows users to vie for discounted hotel rooms at more than 100 luxury properties. To compete, uses buy $1 bids and each time an individual bids the price of the room goes up by 10 cents.

28597 ■ "MaggieMoo's Ice Cream and Treatery" in *Ice Cream Reporter* (Vol. 23, September 20, 2010, No. 10, pp. 7)
Pub: Ice Cream Reporter
Description: MaggieMoo's Ice Cream and Treatery has launched a new Website where visitors can learn about the brands newest ice cream innovations.

28598 ■ *Mail Order in the Internet Age*
Pub: Morgan James Publishing, LLC
Ed: Ted Ciuba. **Released:** May 2004. **Price:** $19.95. **Description:** Direct response market, or mail order, for marketing and selling a product or service is discussed, with emphasis on how direct marketing compares favorably to other methods in terms of speed, ease, profitability, and affordability. Advice is given for writing ads; seminars to attend; and newsletters, mailing lists and magazines in which to subscribe.

28599 ■ "Making It Click" in *Barron's* (Vol. 88, March 17, 2008, No. 11, pp. 31)
Pub: Dow Jones & Company, Inc.
Ed: Theresa W. Carey. **Description:** Listing of 23 online brokers that are evaluated based on their trade experience, usability, range of offerings, research amenities, customer service and access, and costs. TradeStation Securities takes the top spot followed by thinkorswim by just a fraction.

28600 ■ "Mapping the Social Internet" in *Harvard Business Review* (Vol. 88, July-August 2010, No. 7-8, pp. 32)
Pub: Harvard Business School Publishing
Description: Chart compares and contrasts online social networks in selected countries.

28601 ■ *Marketing 2.0: Bridging the Gap between Seller and Buyer through Social Media Marketing*
Pub: Wheatmark
Ed: Bernie Borges. **Released:** July 14, 2009. **Price:** $22.95. **Description:** Winning strategies to attract people to your company and your employees using social media site on the Internet are outlined.

28602 ■ "Marketing in the Digital World: Here's How to Craft a Smart Online Strategy" in *Black Enterprise* (Vol. 40, July 2010, No. 12, pp. 47)
Pub: Earl G. Graves Publishing Co. Inc.
Ed: Sonya A. Donaldson. **Description:** Social media is an integral part of any small business plan in addressing marketing, sales, and branding strategies.

28603 ■ "Marketing Scholarship 2.0" in *Journal of Marketing* (Vol. 75, July 2011, No. 4, pp. 225)
Pub: American Marketing Association
Ed: Richard J. Lutz. **Description:** A study of the implications of changing environment and newer collaborative models for marketing knowledge production and dissemination is presented. Crowdsourcing has become a frequently employed strategy in industry. Academic researchers should collaborate more as well as the academe and industry, to make sure that important problems are being investigated.

28604 ■ *Marketing in a Web 2.0 World - Using Social Media, Webinars, Blogs, and More to Boost Your Small Business on a Budget*
Pub: Atlantic Publishing Company
Ed: Peter VanRysdam. **Released:** June 1, 2010. **Price:** $24.95. **Description:** Web 2.0 technologies have leveled the playing field for small companies trying to boost their presence by giving them an equal voice against larger competitors. Advice is given to help target your audience using social networking hubs.

28605 ■ *Marketing Without Money for Small and Midsize Businesses: 300 FREE and Cheap Ways to Increase Your Sales*
Pub: Halle House Publishing
Ed: Nicholas E. Bade. **Released:** July 2005. **Price:** $16.95. **Description:** Three hundred practical low-cost or no-cost strategies to increase sales, focusing on free advertising, free marketing assistance, and free referrals to the Internet.

28606 ■ *Marketing Your Product*
Pub: Self-Counsel Press, Incorporated
Ed: Donald Cyr, Douglas Gray. **Released:** September 2009. **Price:** $20.95. **Description:** Tips for marketing any product in today's competitive consumer environment. One chapter focuses on using the Internet as a marketing tool.

28607 ■ "Mattel's Got a Monster Holiday Hit, But Will Franchise Have Staying Power?" in *Advertising Age* (Vol. 81, December 6, 2010, No. 43)
Pub: Crain Communications, Inc.
Ed: Beth Snyder Bulik. **Description:** Monster High transmedia play expands beyond dolls to merchandise, apparel and entertainment.

28608 ■ *Maximum Marketing, Minimum Dollars: The Top 50 Ways to Grow Your Small Business*
Pub: Kaplan Books
Ed: Kim Gordon. **Released:** April 2006. **Price:** $24.00. **Description:** Marketing tips to increase sales are presented. Small business owners will learn to maximize marketing with 50 innovative and affordable methods, including online marketing.

28609 ■ "Media Giant Remakes Itself: Job Cuts Signal Journal Sentinel's Focus on New Products" in *Business Journal-Milwaukee* (Oct. 12, 2007)
Pub: American City Business Journals, Inc.
Ed: Rich Kirchen. **Description:** Milwaukee Journal Sentinel is reducing its workforce by offering separation pay, and is willing to consider layoffs if the separation program fails. The downsizing is a result of lowered revenue, which was caused by the decline in printed news demand and increase in online competition. Strategies that the Journal Sentinel are employing, such as developing new products, to increase revenue are presented.

28610 ■ "Media Terminology" in *MarketingMagazine* (Vol. 115, September 27, 2010, No. 13, pp. 80)
Pub: Rogers Publishing Ltd.
Description: Media terminology is provided.

28611 ■ "Media Wars" in *Canadian Business* (Vol. 83, August 17, 2010, No. 13-14, pp. 32)
Pub: Rogers Media Ltd.
Ed: Thomas Watson. **Description:** Canada's newspaper industry has changed considerably with The Glove, under Philip Crawley, positioned as corporate Canada's newspaper of record. However, the National Post under Paul Godfrey is making a comeback by re-launching it as the flagship of a national chain of so-called digital first news organizations.

28612 ■ "Microsoft Releases Office Security Updates" in *Mac World* (Vol. 27, November 2010, No. 11, pp. 66)
Pub: Mac Publishing
Ed: David Dahlquist. **Description:** Office for Mac and Mac Business Unit are Microsoft's pair of security- and stability-enhancing updates for Office 2008 and Office 2004. The software will improve the stability and compatibility and fixes vulnerabilities that would allow attackers to overwrite Mac's memory with malicious code.

28613 ■ *Million Dollar Website: Simple Steps to Help You Compete with the Big Boys-Even on a Small Business Budget*
Pub: Prentice Hall Press
Ed: Lori Culwell. **Released:** May 9, 2010. **Price:** $19.95. **Description:** Resource for any small business owner wishing to build a successful Website in order to compete with big box stores.

28614 ■ "MindLeaders' Online Training Courses Come to ePath Learning" in *Information Today* (Vol. 26, February 2009, No. 2, pp. 4)
Pub: Information Today, Inc.
Description: MindLeaders has partnered with ePath Learning to provide clients with over 2,200 new online courses. ePath's integrated Learning Management Service (iLMS) allows organizations to create online training programs for employees.

28615 ■ "Mobility: So Happy Together" in *Entrepreneur* (Vol. 35, October 2007, No. 10, pp. 64)
Pub: Entrepreneur Media Inc.
Ed: Heather Clancy. **Description:** Joshua Burnett, CEO and founder of 9ci, uses index cards to keep track of what he needs to do despite the fact that he has a notebook computer, cell phone and PDA. Kim Hahn, a media entrepreneur, prefers jotting her ideas down in a spiral notebook, has a team that would organize her records for her, and a personal assistant that would keep track of changes to her schedule. Reasons why these entrepreneurs use old-fashioned methods along with new technology are given.

28616 ■ "More Leading Retailers Using Omniture Conversion Solutions to Boost Sales and Ecommerce Performance" in *Internet Wire* (Sept. 22,2009)

Pub: Comtex News Network, Inc.

Description: Many retailers are utilizing Omniture conversion solutions to improve the performance of their ecommerce businesses; recent enhancements to Omniture Merchandising and Omniture Recommendations help clients drive increased conversion to their Internet ventures.

28617 ■ "Most Viewed Stories, Videos on farmindustrynews.com in 2010" in *Farm Industry News* (January 4, 2011)

Pub: Penton Business Media Inc.

Description: The top ten most popularly viewed stories and videos presented on farmindustrynews.com Website are listed.

28618 ■ "Moving Into the Digital Space: How New Media Create Opportunities for Minorities" in *Black Enterprise* (February 2008)

Pub: Earl G. Graves Publishing Co. Inc.

Ed: Sonia Alleyne. **Description:** The Internet is becoming an alternative to traditional sources of entertainment; nearly 16 percent of American households who use the Internet watch television online. One such Internet show features a variety of African American lifestyles.

28619 ■ "My Favorite Tool for Managing Expenses" in *Inc.* (Volume 32, December 2010, No. 10, pp. 60)

Pub: Inc. Magazine

Ed: J.J. McCorvey. **Description:** Web-based service called Expensify is outlined. The service allows companies to log expenses while away from the office using the service's iPhone application.

28620 ■ "Nationwide Bank Ready for December Conversion" in *Business First-Columbus* (October 12, 2007, pp. A1)

Pub: American City Business Journals, Inc.

Ed: Adrian Burns. **Description:** Nationwide Bank will increase marketing to its customers, including the 45,000 that came from the acquisition of Nationwide Federal Credit Union in December 2006. Upgrading its online banking system and Website will bring the company and its services closer to clients. The influence of the insurance industry on the bank's marketing strategy is also examined.

28621 ■ "Navigate to Better Direct Response Messaging Through Search Marketing" in *DM News* (Vol. 32, January 18, 2010, No. 2, pp. 26)

Pub: Haymarket Media, Inc.

Ed: Mark Simon. **Description:** Important lessons to apply when utilizing Internet marketing schemes include telling your customers you have what they want to buy, provide them with discounts or ways to save additional money and drive them to a customized destination like an Online store.

28622 ■ *Nerds on Wall Street: Math, Machines and Wired Markets*

Pub: John Wiley & Sons, Inc.

Ed: David J. Leinweber. **Released:** May 27, 2009. **Price:** $39.95. **Description:** The history of technology and how it will transform investing and trading on Wall Street is outlined.

28623 ■ "Net Profits: Get a Social Life" in *Entrepreneur* (Vol. 35, October 2007, No. 10, pp. 140)

Pub: Entrepreneur Media Inc.

Ed: Amanda C. Kooser. **Description:** Social networking sites such as Facebook and MySpace have millions of users, a sign that social networking is a growing industry. One way to enter this industry is target marketing, like Med3Q, a site for health-conscious individuals had done. How Med3q is earning through online advertising and sponsors is explained.

28624 ■ "Netflix Gets No Respect" in *Barron's* (Vol. 89, July 27, 2009, No. 30, pp. 26)

Pub: Dow Jones & Co., Inc.

Ed: Tiernan Ray. **Description:** Netflix met expectations when they announced their second quarter sales but their shares still fell by almost 10 percent. Analysts say their entry into the "streaming video" business is a mixed bag since customers are increasingly buying the cheaper monthly plan and this is dragging the economics of the business.

28625 ■ "'Netting Degrees: More Professionals Continuing Their Education Online" in *Hispanic Business* (September 2007, pp. 62, 64)

Pub: Hispanic Business

Ed: Hildy Medina. **Description:** Traditional universities and private institutions offer online courses to professionals wishing to further their education.

28626 ■ "The New Basics of Marketing" in *Inc.* (February 2008, pp. 75-81)

Pub: Gruner & Jahr USA Publishing

Ed: Leigh Buchanan. **Description:** New tools for marketing a business or service include updating or upgrading a Website, using email or texting, or advertising on a social Internet network.

28627 ■ "The New Face of Social Media" in *Hispanic Business* (December 2010)

Pub: Hispanic Business

Ed: Gary D. Fackler. **Description:** Latina bloggers carve out a new niche in social media that helps preserve their unique cultural identities.

28628 ■ "The New Guard" in *Entrepreneur* (Vol. 36, February 2008, No. 2, pp. 46)

Pub: Entrepreneur Media Inc.

Ed: Amanda C. Kooser. **Description:** A natural language search engine is being developed by Powerset for better online searching. Zannel Inc. offers Instant Media Messaging platform, which allows for social networking using phones. Ning is an online platform that allows users to customize and control their social networks.

28629 ■ "New Wave of Business Security Products Ushers in the Kaspersky Anti-Malware Protection System" in *Internet Wire* (October 26, 2010)

Pub: Comtex

Description: Kaspersky Anti-Malware System provides anti-malware protection that requires minimal in-house resources for small businesses. The system offers a full range of tightly integrated end-to-end protection solutions, ensuring unified protection across an entire network, from endpoint and mobile device protection to file server, mail server, network storage and gateway protection. It provides flexible centralized management, immediate threat visibility and a level of responsiveness not seen in other anti-malware approaches.

28630 ■ "A New Way to Tell When to Fold" in *Barron's* (Vol. 88, July 7, 2008, No. 27, pp. 27)

Pub: Dow Jones & Co., Inc.

Ed: Theresa W. Carey. **Description:** Overview of the Online trading company SmartStops, a firm that aims to tell investors when to sell the shares of a particular company. The company's Web site categorizes stocks as moving up, down, or sideways, and calculates exit points for individual stocks based on an overall market trend.

28631 ■ "New Ways to Catch a Thief" in *Barron's* (Vol. 88, March 10, 2008, No. 10, pp. 37)

Pub: Dow Jones & Company, Inc.

Ed: Theresa W. Carey. **Description:** Online brokerage firms employ different methods to protect the accounts of their customers from theft. These methods include secure Internet connections, momentary passwords, and proprietary algorithms.

28632 ■ "The Next Dimension" in *Entrepreneur* (Vol. 35, November 2007, No. 11, pp. 62)

Pub: Entrepreneur Media Inc.

Ed: Heather Clancy. **Description:** Entrepreneurs can make use of virtual worlds like Second Life to promote their products or services. Details and cautions on the use of virtual worlds are discussed.

28633 ■ "Nobody Knows What To Do" in *Barron's* (Vol. 88, March 17, 2008, No. 11, pp. 40)

Pub: Dow Jones & Company, Inc.

Ed: Mark Veverka. **Description:** Attendees of the South by Southwest Interactive conference failed to get an insight on how to make money on the Web from former Walt Disney CEO Michael Eisner when Eisner said there's no proven business model for financing projects. Eisner said he finances his projects with the help of his connections to get product-placement deals.

28634 ■ "Nowspeed and OneSource to Conduct Webinar" in *Internet Wire* (December 14, 2009)

Pub: Comtex News Network, Inc.

Description: OneSource, a leading provider of global business information, and Nowspeed, an Internet marketing agency, will conduct a webinar titled "How to Develop Social Media Content That Gets Results" in order to provide marketers insight into how to develop and optimize effective social media content to get consumer results that translate into purchases and lead generation.

28635 ■ "Obama Plan May Boost Maryland Cyber Security" in *Boston Business Journal* (Vol. 29, May 20, 2011, No. 2, pp. 1)

Pub: American City Business Journals Inc.

Ed: Scott Dance. **Description:** May 12, 2011 outline of the cyber security policies of President Obama may improve the cyber security industry in Maryland as the state is home to large defense and intelligence activities. Details of the proposed policies are discusses as well as their advantages to companies that deal in developing cyber security plans for other companies.

28636 ■ "Old Spice Guy (Feb.-July 2010)" in *Canadian Business* (Vol. 83, August 17, 2010, No. 13-14, pp. 23)

Pub: Rogers Media Ltd.

Ed: Andrew Potter. **Description:** Old Spice Guy was played by ex-football player and actor Isaiah Mustafa who made the debut in the ad for Old Spice Red Zone body wash that was broadcast during Super Bowl XLIV in February 2010. Old Spice Guy has become one of social marketing success but was cancelled in July when online viewership started to wane.

28637 ■ "On Beyond Powerpoint: Presentations Get a Wake-Up Call" in *Inc.* (November 2007, pp. 58-59)

Pub: Gruner & Jahr USA Publishing

Ed: Michael Fitzgerald. **Description:** New software that allows business presentations to be shared online are profiled, including ProfCast, audio podcasts for sales, marketing, and training; SmartDraw2008, software that creates professional graphics; Dimdim, an open-Web conferencing tool; Empressr, a hosted Web service for creating, managing, and sharing multimedia presentations; Zentation, a free tool that allows users to watch slides and a videos of presenter; Spresent, a Web-based presentation tool for remote offices or conference calls.

28638 ■ "The One Thing You Must Get Right When Building a Brand" in *Harvard Business Review* (Vol. 88, December 2010, No. 12, pp. 80)

Pub: Harvard Business School Publishing

Ed: Patrick Barwise, Sean Meehan. **Description:** Four uses for new media include: communicating a clearly defined customer promise, creating trust via delivering on the promise, regularly improving on the promise, and innovating past what is familiar.

28639 ■ "Online All the Time" in *Retail Merchandiser* (Vol. 51, July-August 2011, No. 4, pp. 18)

Pub: Phoenix Media Corporation

Description: Ecommerce sales are rising at a steady pace and for cross-channel retailers it is boosting sales in the weak economy. Online sales are expected to reach $188 billion in 2011, boasting a 13.7 rate of growth.

28640 ■ "Online Book Sales Surpass Bookstores" in *Information Today* (Vol. 28, September 2011, No. 8, pp. 11)
Pub: Information Today, Inc.
Ed: Cindy Martine. **Description:** Online book sales outpaced bookstore purchases in the United States, signaling a shift in the US book industry. Statistical data included.

28641 ■ "Online Forex Broker Tadawul FX Intros Arabic Website" in *Entertainment Close-Up* (June 23, 2011)
Pub: Close-Up Media
Description: Online forex broker, Tadawul FX, launched its Arabic language Website, noting that the Middle East is a key market for the investment firm.

28642 ■ "Online Marketing: Puppy Power: Using a New Tool Called a Widget To Boost Your Brand" in *Inc.* (November 2007, pp. 55-56)
Pub: Gruner & Jahr USA Publishing
Ed: Dan Brody. **Description:** Widgets look like small television screens posted on Websites, blogs or desktops with a company's brand or logo. It can display any type of information or image, including sports scores, news headlines, weather reports, animated graphics, or a slide show. Profiles of CarDomain Network, Babystrology, DailyPuppy.com, AnchorBank and more are included.

28643 ■ "Online Pet Medication Store Supports Free Vaccinations for Cats" in *Internet Wire* (August 31, 2010)
Pub: Comtex
Description: Pethealth Inc., The Petango Store will help to support The Humane Society of Tampa Bay's efforts by offering free feline vaccinations for the cat's entire lifetime that is adopted between September 1, 2010 and February 28, 2010. The cat must be one year or older at time of adoption.

28644 ■ "Online Postings Really Influence Older Women" in *Marketing to Women* (Vol. 22, July 2009, No. 7, pp. 8)
Pub: EPM Communications, Inc.
Description: Women over the age of 55 are more likely to be swayed to purchase a product by referrals from others, including Online postings by strangers. Another key influence is associated with the brand's ability to address their lifestyle needs.

28645 ■ "Online Radio That's Cool, Addictive, Free, and Just Maybe A Lasting Business" in *Inc.* (October 2007, pp. 100-106, 108)
Pub: Gruner & Jahr USA Publishing
Ed: Stephanie Clifford. **Description:** Profile of the Internet radio company, Pandora, whose founder, Tim Westergren discusses his business plans to fruition. The station has over eight million loyal listeners, advertisers and a database of 500,000 songs.

28646 ■ "Online Reverse Auctions: Common Myths Versus Evolving Reality" in *Business Horizons* (September-October 2007, pp. 373)
Pub: Elsevier Technology Publications
Ed: Tobias Schoenherr, Vincent A. Mabert. **Description:** Common misconceptions about online reverse auctions are examined based on the data obtained from 30 case study companies. Strategies for maintaining a good buyer-supplier relationship and implications for firms and supply managers are presented.

28647 ■ "Online Security Crackdown: Scanning Service Oversees Site Security at David's Bridal" in (Vol. 84, July 2008, No. 7, pp. 46)
Pub: Chain Store Age
Ed: Samantha Murphy. **Description:** Online retailers are beefing up security on their Websites. Cyber thieves use retail systems in order to gain entry to consumer data. David's Bridal operates over 275 bridal showrooms in the U.S. and has a one-stop wedding resource for new brides planning weddings.

28648 ■ "Online Translation Service Aids Battlefield Troops" in *Product News Network* (August 30, 2011)
Pub: Thomas Publishing Company
Description: Linquist online service, LinGo Link provides real-time interpreter support to military troops overseas. Interpreters skilled in multiple languages and dialects are used in various areas and in multiple instances without requiring physical presence. The service is available through commercial cellular or WiFi services or tactical communications network. The system accommodates exchange of audio, video, photos, and text during conversations via smartphones and mobile peripheral devices.

28649 ■ "The Open Mobile Summit Opens in San Francisco Today: John Donahoe CEO eBay to Keynote" in *Benzinga.com* (November 2, 2011)
Pub: Benzinga.com
Ed: Benzinga Staff. **Description:** eBay's CEO, John Donahoe was keynote speaker at the 4th Annual Open Mobile Summit held in San Francisco, California. eBay is one of the 130 companies participating as speakers at the event.

28650 ■ *Open Source Solutions for Small Business Problems*
Pub: Charles River Media
Ed: John Locke. **Released:** May 2004. **Price:** $35. 95. **Description:** Open source software provides solutions to many small business problems such as tracking electronic documents, scheduling, accounting functions, managing contact lists, and reducing spam.

28651 ■ "Optimize.ca Supplies Free Online Financial Advice" in *Entertainment Close-Up* (October 9, 2010)
Pub: Close-Up Media Inc.
Description: Optimize.ca provides free online financial advice, focusing on instant savings for their mutual funds and other banking products while improving rates of return and overall financial health.

28652 ■ *Outsourcing: Information Technology, Original Equipment Manufacturer, Leo, Oursourcing, Offshoring Research Network, Crowdsourcing*
Pub: General Books LLC
Released: May 1, 2010. **Price:** $14.14. **Description:** Chapters include information for outsourcing firms and how to maintain an outsourcing business.

28653 ■ "Over and Out" in *Entrepreneur* (Vol. 36, February 2008, No. 2, pp. 25)
Pub: Entrepreneur Media Inc.
Ed: Julie Moline. **Description:** Ben Wolin, owner of Waterfront Media that operates wellness and health Websites, had employed the services of human resource consulting firm to advise him in regard to overtime pay. Guidelines on how to avoid overtime pay violations are presented.

28654 ■ "Pagetender LLC Releases Website Design Package for HubSpot Users" in *Internet Wire* (September 30, 2009)
Pub: Comtex News Network, Inc.
Description: Profile of Pagetender LLC, a Certified HubSpot partner, who announced a Website Design Package marketed specifically for HubSpot Owner and Marketer users. This packaged was developed for small to medium sized businesses that want a website designed or their current site redesigned on HubSpot's Content Management System. Companies that would like a more robust site have the option of adding Flash development, ecommerce and photo galleries.

28655 ■ "P&G to Mine E-Commerce Potential" in *Business Courier* (Vol. 26, September 18, 2009, No. 21, pp. 1)
Pub: American City Business Journals, Inc.
Ed: Lisa Biank Fasig. **Description:** Procter & Gamble (P&G) is looking to turn the hits to the company's Websites into increased sales. The program will include a shop now option to track all emerging sales.

28656 ■ "Paper a la Carte" in *American Printer* (Vol. 128, June 1, 2011, No. 6)
Pub: Penton Media Inc.
Description: Blurb, the online publishing platform, launched ProLine which features Mohawk Superfine and Mohawk proPhoto papers. ProLine papers offer two finishes: Pearl Photo and Uncoated.

28657 ■ "PC Connection Acquires Cloud Software Provider" in *New Hampshire Business Review* (Vol. 33, March 25, 2011, No. 6, pp. 8)
Pub: Business Publications Inc.
Description: Merrimack-based PC Connection Inc. acquired ValCom Technology, a provider of cloud-based IT service management software. Details of the deal are included.

28658 ■ "PD Targeting Audience Growth with Web Initiatives" in *Crain's Cleveland Business* (Vol. 30, June 29, 2009, No. 25, pp. 1)
Pub: Crain Communications, Inc.
Ed: Kathy Ames Carr. **Description:** Plain Dealer's publisher C.Z. Egger has his news organization focusing on online offerings in order to build circulation of its newspaper. The 167-year-old paper boasts 1,305,203 readers in print and online weekly.

28659 ■ "People; E-Commerce, Online Games, Mobile Apps" in *Advertising Age* (Vol. 80, October 19, 2009, No. 35, pp. 14)
Pub: Crain's Communications
Ed: Nat Ives. **Description:** Profile of People Magazine and the ways in which the publisher is moving its magazine forward by exploring new concepts in a time of declining newsstand sales and advertising pages; among the strategies are e-commerce such as the brand People Style Watch in which consumers are able highlight clothing and jewelry and then connect to retailers' sites and a channel on Taxi TV, the network of video-touch screens in New Your City taxis.

28660 ■ "People; E-Commerce, Online Games, Mobile Apps: This Isn't Your Mom's People" in *Advertising Age* (Vol. 80, October 19, 2009, No. 35)
Pub: Crain's Communications
Ed: Nat Ives. **Description:** Profile of People Magazine and the ways in which the publisher is moving its magazine forward by exploring new concepts in a time of declining newsstand sales and advertising pages; among the strategies are e-commerce such as the brand People Style Watch in which consumers are able highlight clothing and jewelry and then connect to retailers' sites and a channel on Taxi TV, the network of video-touch screens in New Your City taxis.

28661 ■ "The Perfect Fit" in *Small Business Opportunities* (Fall 2007)
Pub: Harris Publications Inc.
Description: Launched in 2004, Jigsaw provides an online database of more than 5.5 million business contacts and company information for entrepreneurs.

28662 ■ "Plan Your Future with My Next Move" in *Occupational Outlook Quarterly* (Vol. 55, Summer 2011, No. 2, pp. 22)
Pub: U.S. Bureau of Labor Statistics
Description: My Next Move, an online tool offering a variety of user-friendly ways to browse more than 900 occupations was created by the National Center for O NET Development for the US Department of Labor's Employment and Training Administration. Clicking on an occupation presents a one-page profile summarizing key information for specific careers.

28663 ■ *Planet Google: One Company's Audacious Plan to Organize Everything We Know*
Pub: Free Press
Ed: Randall Stross. **Released:** 2009. **Price:** $26.00. **Description:** The book examines Google, the leader in Internet search engines.

28664 ■ "Play By Play: These Video Products Can Add New Life to a Stagnant Website" in *Black Enterprise* (Vol. 41, December 2010, No. 5)
Pub: Earl G. Graves Publishing Co. Inc.
Ed: Marcia Wade Talbert. **Description:** Web Visible, provider of online marketing products and services, cites video capability as the fastest-growing Website feature for small business advertisers. Profiles of various devices for adding video to a Website are included.

28665 ■ "Points of Light Sells MissionFish to eBay" in *Non-Profit Times* (Vol. 25, May 15, 2011, No. 7, pp. May 15, 2011)
Pub: NPT Publishing Group Inc.
Description: eBay purchased MissionFish, a subsidiary of Points of Light Institute for $4.5 million. MissionFish allows eBay sellers to give proceeds from sales to their favorite nonprofit organization and helps nonprofits raise funds by selling on eBay.

28666 ■ "The Power of Negative Thinking" in *Inc.* (Volume 32, December 2010, No. 10, pp. 43)
Pub: Inc. Magazine
Ed: Jason Fried. **Description:** A Website is software and most businesses have and need a good Website to generate business. Understanding for building a powerful Website is presented.

28667 ■ *The Power of Social Networking: Using the Whuffie Factor to Build Your Business*
Pub: Crown Business Books
Ed: Tara Hunt. **Released:** May 4, 2010. **Price:** $15. 00. **Description:** This book shows how any small business can harness its power by increasing whuffie, the store of social capital that is the currency of the digital world. Blogs and social networks such as Facebook and Twitter are used to help grow any small firm.

28668 ■ "Pro Livestock Launches Most Comprehensive Virtual Sales Barn for Livestock and Breed Stock" in *Benzinga.com* (October 29, 2011)
Pub: Benzinga.com
Ed: Benzinga Staff. **Description:** Pro Livestock Marketing launched the first online sales portal for livestock and breed stock. The firm has designed a virtual sales barn allowing individuals to purchase and sell cattle, swine, sheep, goats, horses, rodeo stock, show animals, specialty animals, semen and embryos globally. It is like an eBay for livestock and will help ranchers and farmers grow.

28669 ■ "Promote Your Business Through New Media" in *Business Week* (November 5, 2009)
Pub: McGraw-Hill Companies
Ed: Karen E. Klein. **Description:** Traditional public relations strategies are becoming more and more outdated due to the rapid shift in Internet marketing opportunities. Ideas for marketing your company online are presented.

28670 ■ "Promoting Academic Programs Using Online Videos" in *Business Communication Quarterly* (December 2007, pp. 478)
Pub: Sage Publications USA
Ed: Thomas Clark, Julie Stewart. **Description:** Xavier Entrepreneurial Center successfully used online videos to promote the effectiveness of its academic programs. Online videos are a cost-effective way of publicizing academic programs.

28671 ■ "Promotions Create a Path to Better Profit" in *Pet Product News* (Vol. 64, December 2010, No. 12, pp. 1)
Pub: BowTie Inc.
Ed: Joan Hustace Walker. **Description:** Pet store retailers can boost small mammal sales by launching creative marketing and promotions such as social networking and adoption days.

28672 ■ "Providers Ride First Wave of eHealth Dollars" in *Boston Business Journal* (Vol. 31, June 10, 2011, No. 20, pp. 1)
Pub: Boston Business Journal
Ed: Julie M. Donnelly. **Description:** Health care providers in Massachusetts implementing electronic medical records technology started receiving federal stimulus funds. Beth Israel Deaconess Medical Center was the first hospital to qualify for the funds.

28673 ■ "Punta Gorda Interested in Wi-Fi Internet" in *Charlotte Observer* (February 1, 2007)
Pub: Knight-Ridder/Tribune Business News
Ed: Steve Reilly. **Description:** Punta Gorda officials are developing plans to provide free wireless Internet services to businesses and residents.

28674 ■ "Putting the App in Apple" in *Inc.* (Vol. 30, November 2008, No. 11, pp.)
Pub: Mansueto Ventures LLC
Ed: Nitasha Tiku. **Description:** Aftermarket companies are scrambling to develop games and widgets for Apple's iPhone. Apple launched a kit for developers interested in creating iPhone-specific software along with the App Store, and an iTunes spinoff. Profiles of various software programs that may be used on the iPhone are given.

28675 ■ "Putting SogoTrade Through Its Paces" in *Barron's* (Vol. 89, July 27, 2009, No. 30, pp. 27)
Pub: Dow Jones & Co., Inc.
Ed: Theresa W. Carey. **Description:** SogoTrade options platform streams options quotes in real time and lets users place a trade in several ways. The site also features notable security tactics and is a reasonable choice for bargain-seekers. OptionsXpress' Xtend platform lets users place trades and get real time quotes.

28676 ■ "Q&A Patrick Pichette" in *Canadian Business* (Vol. 81, October 13, 2008, No. 17, pp. 6)
Pub: Rogers Media Ltd.
Ed: Andrew Wahl. **Description:** Patrick Pichette finds challenge in taking over the finances of an Internet company that has a market cap of about $140 billion. He feels, however, that serving as Google's chief financial officer is nothing compared to running Bell Canada Enterprises (BCE). Pichette's other views on Google and BCE are presented.

28677 ■ "Quickoffice's MobileFiles Pro App Enables Excel Editing On-the-Go" in *Information Today* (Vol. 26, February 2009, No. 2, pp. 31)
Pub: Information Today, Inc.
Description: Quickoffice Inc. introduced MobileFiles Pro, which features editable Microsoft Office functionality for the iPone and iPod touch. The application allows users to edit and save Microsoft Excel files in .xls format, transfer files to and from PC and Mac desktops via Wi-Fi, and access and synchronize with Apple MobileMe accounts.

28678 ■ "Real-Time Computer-Mediated Communication" in *Business Communication Quarterly* (December 2007, pp. 466)
Pub: Sage Publications USA
Ed: Amy Newman. **Description:** Technology-based simulation for business students to respond to emails and instant messages is presented. The simulation allows students to handle volume business correspondence at work with organizational context and under real-word business situations.

28679 ■ "Reaping Social-Media Rewards" in *Canadian Business* (Vol. 83, July 20, 2010, No. 11-12, pp. 19)
Pub: Rogers Media Ltd.
Ed: Lyndsie Bourgon. **Description:** Foursquare is a social network which provides benefits such as discounts to users who show loyalty to a business or a brand. One marketing executive believes Foursquare is a good platform for loyalty programs and is an inexpensive alternative to Aeroplan.

28680 ■ "Recovery2.0: a Work in Progress" in *Tampa Bay Business Journal* (Vol. 30, December 18, 2009, No. 52, pp. 3)
Pub: American City Business Journals
Ed: Margaret Cashill. **Description:** The debut of the Recovery.gov 2.0 version has raised questions regarding the Website's price tag, which will cost nearly $18 million. Tampa, Florida-based GSL Solutions Inc. president Michael Gaines believes the Websites created with existing technologies tend to cost less than custom development. The difference between Recovery.org and Recovery.gov are explained.

28681 ■ "Recruiting 2.0" in *Entrepreneur* (Vol. 35, November 2007, No. 11, pp. 100)
Pub: Entrepreneur Media Inc.
Ed: Andrea Cooper. **Description:** Technology is becoming a tool to help small companies find the best employees. Firms can look into social networking sites to see recommendations from the applicants' colleagues. Tips on how to select the employees online are listed.

28682 ■ "Regional Talent Network Unveils Jobs Web Site" in *Crain's Cleveland Business* (Vol. 30, June 1, 2009, No. 21, pp. 11)
Pub: Crain Communications, Inc.
Description: Regional Talent Network launched WhereToFindHelp.org, a Website designed to act as a directory of all Northeast Ohio resources that can help employers recruit and job seekers look for positions. The site also lists organizations offering employment and training services.

28683 ■ "Reinventing Marketing to Manage the Environmental Imperative" in *Journal of Marketing* (Vol. 75, July 2011, No. 4, pp. 132)
Pub: American Marketing Association
Ed: Philip Kotler. **Description:** Marketers must now examine their theory and practices due to the growing recognition of finite resources and high environmental costs. Companies also need to balance more carefully their growth goals with the need to purse sustainability. Insights on the rise of demarketing and social marketing are also given.

28684 ■ "Remodeled Stores Help Fabric Retailer Stitch Up Profit Growth" in *Investor's Business Daily* (January 7, 2010, pp. A06)
Pub: Investor's Business Daily
Ed: Marilyn Much. **Description:** Overview of the successful plan implemented by Darrell Webb for Jo-Ann Fabric and Craft stores to stimulate growth and generate revenue; changes include better inventory controls and remodeling; statistical data included.

28685 ■ "Remote Control: Working From Wherever" in *Inc.* (February 2008, pp. 46-47)
Pub: Gruner & Jahr USA Publishing
Ed: Ryan Underwood. **Description:** New technology allows workers to perform tasks from anywhere via the Internet. Profiles of products to help connect to your office from afar include, LogMein Pro, a Web-based service that allowsaccess to a computer from anywhere; Xdrive, an online service that allows users to store and swap files; Basecamp, a Web-based tools that works like a secure version of MySpace; MojoPac Freedom, is software that allows users to copy their computer's desktop to a removable hard drive and plug into any PC; WatchGuard Firebox X Core e-Series UTM Bundle, hardware that blocks hackers and viruses while allowing employees to work remotely; TightVNC, a free open-source software that lets you control another computer via the Internet.

28686 ■ "Renren Partners With Recruit to Launch Social Wedding Services" in *Benzinga.com* (June 7, 2011)
Pub: Benzinga.com
Ed: Benzinga Staff. **Description:** Renren Inc. and Recruit Company Ltd. partnered to build a wedding social media catering to engaged couples and newlyweds in China. The platform will integrate online wedding related social content and offline media such as magazine and wedding exhibitions.

28687 ■ "Renren Partnership With Recruit to Launch Social Wedding Services" in *Benzinga.com* (June 7, 2011)
Pub: Benzinga.com
Ed: Benzinga Staff. **Description:** Renren Inc., the leading real name social networking Internet platform in China has partnered with Recruit Company Limited, Japan's largest human resource and classified media group to form a joint venture to build a wedding social media catering to the needs of engaged couples and newlyweds in China.

28688 ■ "Rep. Loretta Sanchez Holds a Hearing on Small Business Cyber Security" in *Political/Congressional Transcript Wire* (July 29, 2010)
Pub: CQ Roll Call
Description: U.S. House Committee on Armed Services, Subcommittee on Terrorism, Unconventional Threats and Capabilities held a hearing on small business cyber security innovation.

28689 ■ "Research and Markets Adds Report: Asian - Internet Market" in *Health and Beauty Close-Up* (January 19, 2010)
Pub: Close-Up Media
Description: Overview of Research and Markets new report regarding Internet marketing and e-commerce in the Asian region; statistical data included.

28690 ■ "Research and Markets Adds Report: USA - Internet Market - Analysis, Statistics and Forecasts" in *Wireless News* (January 15, 2010)
Pub: Close-Up Media
Description: According to Research and Markets new report concerning the United State's Internet market, e-commerce and Online advertising are expected to recover strongly in 2010.

28691 ■ "The Return of the Infomercial" in *Canadian Business* (Vol. 83, September 14, 2010, No. 15, pp. 19)
Pub: Rogers Media Ltd.
Ed: James Cowan. **Description:** Infomercials or direct response ads have helped some products succeed in the marketplace. The success of infomercials is due to the cheap advertising rates, expansion into retail stores and the products' oddball appeal. Insights into the popularity of infomercial products on the Internet and on television are given.

28692 ■ "Ric Elis/Dan Feldstein" in *Charlotte Business Journal* (Vol. 25, December 31, 2010, No. 41, pp. 6)
Pub: Charlotte Business Journal
Ed: Ken Elkins. **Description:** Charlotte, North Carolina-based Internet marketing firm Red Ventures has grown significantly. General Atlantic has purchased stakes in Red Ventures.

28693 ■ "Rise Interactive, Internet Marketing Agency, Now Offers Social Media Training and Advisory Services" in *Internet Wire* (Nov. 4, 2009)
Pub: Comtex News Network, Inc.
Description: Profile of Rise Interactive, a full-service Internet marketing agency which has recently added social media to its list of offerings; the agency touts that its newest service gives their clients the power to have ongoing communication with current and potential customers on the sites they are most actively visiting.

28694 ■ "Ritchie Bros. Breaks Record for Internet Sales at Fort Worth Site During Multi-Million Dollar Unreserved Auction" in *Canadian Corporate News*
Pub: Comtex News Network Inc.
Description: Ritchie Bros. Auctioneers, the world's largest auctioneer of trucks and industrial equipment, conducted a large unreserved auction at its permanent auction facility in Fort Worth, Texas, in which the company broke the record for Internet sales with bidders using the company's online bidding service, rbauctionBid-Live. Internet bidders purchased more than 440 lots in the auction.

28695 ■ "ROIonline Announces Streaming Video Products" in *Marketing Weekly News* (December 5, 2009, pp. 155)
Pub: Investment Weekly News
Description: ROIonline LLC, an Internet marketing firm serving business-to-business and the industrial marketplace, has added streaming video options to the Internet solutions it offers its clients; due to the huge increase of broadband connections, videos are now commonplace on the Internet and can often convey a company's message in a must more efficient, concise and effective way that will engage a website's visitor thus delivering a high return on a company's investment.

28696 ■ "Rumor Has It" in *Entrepreneur* (Vol. 35, October 2007, No. 10, pp. 30)
Pub: Entrepreneur Media Inc.
Ed: Chris Penttila. **Description:** Some entrepreneurs like Ren Moulton and Dan Scudder regard rumor sites and product blogs as great sources of market research. However, there are legal issues that must be studied before using these Internet sites in marketing and product development. The use and limitations of rumor sites and product blogs are provided.

28697 ■ *Salesforce.com Secrets of Success: Best Practices for Growth and Profitability*
Pub: Prentice Hall Business Publishing
Ed: David Taber. **Released:** May 15, 2009. **Price:** $34.99. **Description:** Guide for using Salesforce.com; it provides insight into navigating through user groups, management, sales, marketing and IT departments in order to achieve the best results.

28698 ■ *The Savvy Gal's Guide to Online Networking (Or What Would Jane Austen Do?)*
Pub: Booklocker.com Inc.
Ed: Diane K. Daneilson, Lindsey Pollak. **Released:** August 10, 2007. **Price:** $14.95. **Description:** It is a truth universally acknowledged that a woman in search of a fabulous career must be in want of networking opportunities. Or so Jane Austen would say if she were writing, or more likely, blogging today. So begins the must-read guide to networking in the 21st Century. Authors and networking experts share the nuts, bolts and savvy secrets that businesswomen need in order to use technology to build professional relationships.

28699 ■ *The Savvy Girl's Guide to Online Networking (Or What Would Jane Austen Do?)*
Pub: Booklocker.com Inc.
Ed: Diane K. Danielson; Lindsey Pollak. **Released:** August 10, 2007. **Price:** $14.95. **Description:** The book offers tips, tactics and etiquette for businesswomen wishing to build professional relationships via email, online networks, blogs, and message boards.

28700 ■ *Say Everything: How Blogging Began, What It's Becoming, and Why It Matters*
Pub: Crown Business
Ed: Scott Rosenberg. **Released:** 2009. **Price:** $26.00. **Description:** A history of Internet blogs that explains how they started and why they matter to any small business.

28701 ■ "Scientific American Builds Novel Blog Network" in *Information Today* (Vol. 28, September 2011, No. 8, pp. 12)
Pub: Information Today, Inc.
Ed: Kurt Schiller. **Description:** Scientific American launched a new blog network that joins a diverse lineup of bloggers cover various scientific topics under one banner. The blog network includes 60 bloggers providing insights into the ever-changing world of science and technology.

28702 ■ "Scitable Puts Nature Education on the Map" in *Information Today* (Vol. 26, February 2009, No. 2, pp. 29)
Pub: Information Today, Inc.
Description: Nature Education, a division of the Nature Publishing Group, released its first product, Scitable, a free online resource for undergraduate biology students and educators. The service includes over 180 overviews of key genetics concepts as well as social networking features, including groups and functionality, that lets students work with classmates and others. Teachers can use the service to set up public or private groups for students.

28703 ■ "Search and Discover New Opportunities" in *DM News* (Vol. 31, December 14, 2009, No. 29, pp. 13)
Pub: Haymarket Media, Inc.
Ed: Chantal Tode. **Description:** Although other digital strategies are gaining traction in Internet marketing, search marketing continues to dominate this advertising forum. Companies like American Greetings, which markets e-card brands online, are utilizing social networking sites and affiliates to generate a higher demand for their products.

28704 ■ *The Search: How Google and Its Rival Rewrote the Rules of Business and Transformed Our Culture*
Pub: Penguin Group Incorporated
Ed: John Battelle. **Released:** October 3, 2006. **Price:** $14.95. **Description:** Provides a history of Internet search technology.

28705 ■ *Selling Online: Canada's Bestselling Guide to Becoming a Successful E-Commerce Merchant*
Pub: John Wiley and Sons Canada Ltd.
Ed: Jim Carroll; Rick Broadhead. **Released:** September 6, 2002. **Description:** Helps individuals build online retail enterprises; this updated version includes current tools, information and success strategies, how to launch an online storefront, security, marketing strategies, and mistakes to avoid.

28706 ■ "Senators Predict Online School Changes" in *Puget Sound Business Journal* (Vol. 29, September 19, 2008, No. 22, pp. 1)
Pub: American City Business Journals
Ed: Clay Holtzman. **Description:** State senators promise to create new legislation that would tighten the monitoring and oversight of online public schools. The officials are concerned about the lack of oversight of the programs as well as lack of knowledge about content of the lessons.

28707 ■ *The SEO Manifesto: A Practical and Ethical Guide to Internet Marketing and Search Engine Optimization*
Pub: Cape Project Management Inc.
Ed: Dan Tousignant, Pamela Gobiel. **Released:** December 5, 2011. **Price:** $14.99. **Description:** Comprehensive guide for each phase of launching an online business; chapters include checklists, process descriptions, and examples.

28708 ■ "Serials Solutions Launches 360 Resource Manager Consortium Edition" in *Information Today* (Vol. 26, February 2009, No. 2, pp. 32)
Pub: Information Today, Inc.
Description: Serials Solutions new Serials Solutions 360 Resource Manager Consortium Edition helps consortia, groups and member libraries with their e-resource management services. The products allows users to consolidate e-resource metadata and acquisition information into one place, which enables groups to manage holdings, subscriptions, licensing, contacts, and cost information and to streamline delivery of information to members.

28709 ■ "Sharing the Micro Wealth" in *Entrepreneur* (Vol. 37, July 2009, No. 7, pp. 46)
Pub: Entrepreneur Media, Inc.
Ed: Jennie Dorris. **Description:** Step-by-step guide is presented on how Kiva.org, a website which allows people to make microloans to entrepreneurs across the world, works. The website, founded by Matt Flannery, raises $1 million weekly and it will add U.S. entrepreneurs to its list of loan recipients in June 2010. Other features of Kiva.org are discussed.

28710 ■ "Shoestring-Budget Marketing" in *Women Entrepreneur* (January 5, 2009)
Pub: Entrepreneur Media Inc.
Ed: Maria Falconer. **Description:** Pay-per-click search engine advertising is the traditional type of e-marketing that may not only be too expensive for

certain kinds of businesses but also may not attract the quality customer base a business looking to grow needs to find. Social networking websites have become a mandatory marketing tool for business owners who want to see growth in their sales; tips are provided for utilizing these networking websites in order to gain more visibility on the Internet which can, in turn, lead to the more sales.

28711 ■ "Silverpop Recognized for Email Marketing Innovations by Econsultancy" in *Marketing Weekly News* (January 23, 2010, pp. 124)
Pub: Investment Weekly News
Description: Econsultancy, a respected source of insight and advice on digital marketing and e-commerce, recognized Silverpop, the world's only provider of both marketing automation solutions and email marketing specifically tailored to the unique needs of B2C and B2B marketers at Econsultancy's 2009 Innovation Awards.

28712 ■ "Simplifying Social Media for Optimum Results" in *Franchising World* (Vol. 42, August 2010, No. 8, pp. 12)
Pub: International Franchise Association
Ed: Paul Segreto. **Description:** Keys to effective technology usage requires the development of an integrated plan, choosing the most complementary tools and implementing well-planned strategies.

28713 ■ "Sites Set" in *Entrepreneur* (Vol. 35, November 2007, No. 11, pp. 112)
Pub: Entrepreneur Media Inc.
Ed: Nichole L. Torres. **Description:** Marketing information online can be a good bui9sness if you know who to target. Partnering with other online companies to provide information services that cater to specific groups of people is also helpful.

28714 ■ "Siteworx Earns 4 Interactive Media Awards in Q1 of 2011" in *Entertainment Close-Up* (, 2011)
Pub: Close-Up Media
Description: Details of the four awards Siteworx earned for its achievements in Web development and design are outlined.

28715 ■ "Skype Ltd. Acquired GroupMe" in *Information Today* (Vol. 28, October 2011, No. 9, pp. 12)
Pub: Information Today, Inc.
Description: Skype Ltd. acquired GroupMe, a group messaging company that allows users to form impromptu groups where they can text message, share data, and make conference calls for free and is supported on Android, iPhone, BlackBerry, and Windows phones.

28716 ■ "Small Budget, Big Impact" in *Small Business Opportunities* (Summer 2010)
Pub: Harris Publications Inc.
Ed: Hilary J.M. Topper. **Description:** Ways to use social media to get in from of a target audience for small businesses are examined.

28717 ■ *Small Business Clustering Technology: Applications in Marketing, Management, Finance, and IT*
Pub: Idea Group Publishing
Ed: Robert C. MacGregor; Ann Hodgkinson. **Released:** June 2006. **Description:** An overview of the development and role of small business clusters in disciplines that include economics, marketing, management and information systems.

28718 ■ *Small Business for Dummies*
Pub: John Wiley & Sons, Incorporated
Ed: Eric Tyson, Jim Schell. **Released:** March 2008. **Price:** $21.99. **Description:** Advice for launching and growing a small business; insights into using the Internet as business tool are included.

28719 ■ *Small Business Management*
Pub: John Wiley & Sons, Incorporated
Ed: Margaret Burlingame. **Released:** March 2007. **Price:** $44.95. **Description:** Advice for starting and running a small business as well as information on the value and appeal of small businesses, is given. Topics include budgets, taxes, inventory, ethics, e-commerce, and current laws.

28720 ■ *Small Business Taxes Made Easy: How to Increase Your Deductions, Reduce What You Owe, and Boost Your Profits*
Pub: McGraw-Hill Companies
Ed: Eva Rosenberg. **Released:** December 2004. **Price:** $16.95. **Description:** Tax expert gives advice to small business owners regarding tax issues. TaxMamma.com, run by Eva Rosenberg, is one of the top seven tax advice Websites on the Internet.

28721 ■ *SMEs and New Technologies: Learning E-Business and Development*
Pub: Palgrave Macmillan
Ed: Banji Oyelaran-Oyeyinka; Kaushalesh Lal. **Released:** October 2006. **Price:** $85.00. **Description:** Adoption and learning of new information technologies in developing nations is covered. New technologies are opening opportunities for small companies in these countries.

28722 ■ *The Social Media Bible: Tactics, Tools, and Strategies for Business Success*
Pub: John Wiley & Sons, Inc.
Ed: Lon Safko, David Brake. **Released:** June 17, 2009. **Price:** $29.95. **Description:** Information is given to build or transform a business into social media, where customers, employees, and prospects connect, collaborate, and champion products and services in order to increase sales and to beat the competition.

28723 ■ "Social Media By the Numbers: Social-Media Marketing Is All the Rage" in *Inc.* (Vol. 33, November 2011, No. 9, pp. 70)
Pub: Inc. Magazine
Ed: J.J. McCorvey, Issie Lapowsky. **Description:** Six strategies to help small businesses use social media sites such as Facebook and Twitter to promote their companies are presented.

28724 ■ "Social Media Event Slated for March 25" in *Bellingham Business Journal* (Vol. February 2010, pp. 3)
Pub: Sound Publishing Inc.
Description: Center for Economic Vitality (CEV) and the Technology Alliance Group (TAG) will host the 2010 Social Media Conference at the McIntyre Hall Performing Arts & Conference Center in Mt. Vernon, Washington. The event will provide networking opportunities for attendees.

28725 ■ "Social Networkers for Hire" in *Black Enterprise* (Vol. 40, December 2009, No. 5, pp. 56)
Pub: Earl G. Graves Publishing Co., Inc.
Ed: Brittany Hutson. **Description:** Companies are utilizing social networking sites in order to market their brand and personally connect with consumers and are increasingly looking to social media specialists to help with this task. Aliya S. King is one such web strategist, working for ICED Media by managing their Twitter, Facebook, YouTube and Flickr accounts for one of their publicly traded restaurant clients.

28726 ■ "Social Networks in the Workplace" in *Strategy & Leadership* (Vol. 38, July-August 2010, No. 4, pp. 50-53)
Pub: Emerald Inc.
Ed: Daniel Burrus. **Description:** The opinions of futurist Daniel Burrus on a novel trend called 'Business 2.0', which involves the use of social networking applications as business tools, are presented. His suggestion that personal social networking technology can be used by businesses to improve collaboration, problem solving, and leadership communications to achieve continuous value innovation is discussed.

28727 ■ "Sometimes, Second Impressions Count Most" in *Canadian Business* (Vol. 83, October 12, 2010, No. 17, pp. 11)
Pub: Rogers Media Ltd.
Ed: Richard Branson. **Description:** Developing a favorable impression at the first point of contact is imperative for businesses. Managers who want their organizations to make positive first and second impressions need to learn to balance the Web's labor-saving efficiencies with human assistants. The importance of considering the customer relations value in company Websites is also explained.

28728 ■ "Sounders Kicking Ball to Fans" in *Puget Sound Business Journal* (Vol. 29, November 28, 2008, No. 32, pp. 1)
Pub: American City Business Journals
Ed: Greg Lamm. **Description:** Major League Soccer expansion team, Seattle Sounders FC, hopes to build fan support leading to its inaugural season 2009-2010 by tapping online social networks. The club launched fan clubs with actual powers over its decision making and Websites similar to Facebook.

28729 ■ "Startup on Cusp of Trend" in *Austin Business JournalInc.* (Vol. 29, January 8, 2010, No. 44, pp. 1)
Pub: American City Business Journals
Ed: Christopher Calnan. **Description:** Austin-based Socialware Inc. introduced a new business called social middleware, which is a software that is layered between the company network and social networking Website used by workers. The software was designed to give employers a measure of control over content while allowing workers to continue using online social networks.

28730 ■ "Startup to Serve Bar Scene" in *Austin Business JournalInc.* (Vol. 29, December 18, 2009, No. 41, pp. 1)
Pub: American City Business Journals
Ed: Christopher Calnan. **Description:** Startup ATX Innovation Inc. of Austin, Texas has developed a test version of TabbedOut, a Web-based tool that would facilitate mobile phone-based restaurant and bar bill payment. TabbedOut has been tested by six businesses in Austin and will be available to restaurant and bar owners for free. Income would be generated by ATX through a 99-cent convenience charge per transaction.

28731 ■ *Stealing MySpace: The Battle to Control the Most Popular Website in America*
Pub: Random House
Ed: Julia Angwin. **Released:** 2009. **Price:** $27.00. **Description:** Information regarding Rupert Murdoch's outwitting Viacom's Tom Freston and details of the deal are presented.

28732 ■ *Success Secrets of Social Media Marketing Superstars*
Pub: Entrepreneur Press
Ed: Mitch Meyerson. **Released:** June 1, 2010. **Price:** $21.95. **Description:** Provides access to the playbooks of social media marketers who reveal their most valuable strategies and tactics for standing out in the new online media environment.

28733 ■ "Sunbrella Engages Consumers Via Social Media" in *Home Textiles Today* (Vol. 31, May 24, 2011, No. 13, pp. 4)
Pub: Reed Business Information
Description: Performance fabric brand Sunbrella is marketing to social media, such as Facebook and Twitter, in order to boost consumer interest and retailer support.

28734 ■ "Sylvie Collection Offers a Feminine Perspective and Voice in Male Dominated Bridal Industry" in *Benzinga.com* (October 29, 2011)
Pub: Benzinga.com
Ed: Benzinga Staff. **Description:** Bridal jewelry designer Sylvie Levine has created over 1,000 customizable styles of engagement rings and wedding bands and is reaching out to prospective new brides through a new Website, interactive social media campaign and monthly trunk show appearances.

28735 ■ "Taking the Steps Into the Clouds" in *New Hampshire Business Review* (Vol. 33, March 25, 2011, No. 6, pp. 19)
Pub: Business Publications Inc.
Ed: Tim Wessels. **Description:** Cloud services include Internet and Web security, spam filtering, message archiving, work group collaboration, IT asset management, help desk and disaster recovery backup.

28736 ■ "Tap the iPad and Mobile Internet Device Market" in *Franchising World* (Vol. 42, September 2010, No. 9, pp. 43)
Pub: International Franchise Association
Ed: John Thomson. **Description:** The iPad and other mobile Internet devices will help franchise owners interact with customers. It will be a good marketing tool for these businesses.

28737 ■ "Technology Drivers to Boost Your Bottom Line" in *Franchising World* (Vol. 42, August 2010, No. 8, pp. 15)
Pub: International Franchise Association
Ed: Dan Dugal. **Description:** Technological capabilities are expanding quickly and smart franchises should stay updated on all the new developments, including smart phones, global positioning systems, and social media networks.

28738 ■ "Technology: What Seems To Be the Problem? Self Service Gets a Tune-Up" in *Inc.* (February 2008, pp. 43-44)
Pub: Gruner & Jahr USA Publishing
Ed: Darren Dahl. **Description:** Self-service software can save companies money when responding to customer service phone calls, text or email messages. More companies are relying on alternatives such as automated Web-based self-service systems.

28739 ■ "Tee Off Online" in *Black Enterprise* (Vol. 37, January 2007, No. 6, pp. 52)
Pub: Earl G. Graves Publishing Co. Inc.
Ed: James C. Johnson. **Description:** The E-Com Resource Center is one of many resources that are available for those interested in starting an e-commerce business. One of the first steps is to create a business plan, of which there are free samples available at BPlans.com.

28740 ■ "Tell Us What You Really Think Collecting Customer Feedback" in *Inc.* (Vol. 30, December 2008, No. 12, pp. 52)
Pub: Mansueto Ventures LLC
Ed: Ryan Underwood. **Description:** According to a recent survey, nearly 77 percent of online shoppers review consumer-generated reviews of products before making a purchase.

28741 ■ "The Way I Work" in *Inc.* (March 2008, pp. 102-104, 106)
Pub: Gruner & Jahr USA Publishing
Ed: Hannah Clark Steiman. **Description:** Profile of Howard Lefkowitz, CEO of Vegas.com, a Website that allows visitors to book flights, reserve hotel rooms, buy show tickets, make spa appointments, and coordinate any and all aspects of a trip to Las Vegas. The firm also runs brick-and-mortar box offices and concierge desks at various cities.

28742 ■ "Things Really Clicking for Macy's Online" in *Business Courier* (Vol. 24, November 30, 2008, No. 33, pp. 1)
Pub: American City Business Journals, Inc.
Ed: Lisa Biank Fasig. **Description:** Retailer Macy's online division Macys.com are projecting sales at $1billion in 2007, compared to $620 million in 2006. Macy's new online features and products and the growth of online retail sector are also discussed.

28743 ■ "Thomas Industrial Network Unveils Custom SPEC" in *Entertainment Close-Up* (March 3, 2011)
Pub: Close-Up Media
Description: Thomas Industrial Network assists custom manufacturers and industrial service providers a complete online program called Custom SPEC which includes Website development and Internet exposure.

28744 ■ "Tim Tebow Foundation to Hold Pink 'Cleats for a Cure' Auction" in *Travel & Leisure Close-Up* (October 20, 2011)
Pub: Close-Up Media
Description: Tim Tebow Foundation partnered with XV Enterprises to hold the 'Cleats for a Cure' auction on eBay. Tebow is auctioning off a pair of pink cleans he wore during the Denver Broncos vs. Tennessee Titans game October 3, 2010. All funds will go toward finding a cure for breast cancer.

28745 ■ *Titanium EBay: A Tactical Guide to Becoming a Millionaire PowerSeller*
Pub: Penguin Group Incorporated
Ed: Skip McGrath. **Released:** June 2006. **Price:** $24. 95. **Description:** Advice is given to help anyone selling items on eBay to become a Power Seller, an award presented based on monthly gross merchandise sales.

28746 ■ "Tool-o-Rama" in *Barron's* (Vol. 90, September 6, 2010, No. 36)
Pub: Barron's Editorial & Corporate Headquarters
Description: New trading tool features from several online brokers are discussed. The new features from Fidelity, ChoiceTrade, JunoTrade and TradeKing are examined. Investors can now screen exchanged traded funds in the same way as stocks with Fidelity, while ChoiceTrade can run in any browser without the need to install additional plug-ins.

28747 ■ "Tool Time" in *Entrepreneur* (Vol. 36, March 2008, No. 3, pp. 90)
Pub: Entrepreneur Media Inc.
Ed: Nichole A. Torres. **Description:** DaVinci Institute holds an annual event in Colorado to display new products and inventions. Innovative Design Engineering Animation is a consulting company that helps inventors develop product through various stages. NineSigma Inc. has an online marketplace where inventors can post ideas for clients needing new products.

28748 ■ "Traffic's Up: Website's Down Preventing Costly Crashes" in *Inc.* (March 2008, pp. 55-56)
Pub: Gruner & Jahr USA Publishing
Ed: Darren Dahl. **Description:** Grid Web hosting protects a small company's Website when a sudden burst of Internet traffic hits enabling it to continue rather than be crippled. Options can vary in cost from $4 to $1,000 monthly and include using a shared server, grid server, virtual private server, or a dedicated server. The article explains each option.

28749 ■ "Try a Little Social Media" in *American Printer* (Vol. 128, June 1, 2011, No. 6)
Pub: Penton Media Inc.
Description: Social media helps keep Ussery Printing on customers radar. Jim David, VP of marketing for the firm, states that 350 people following them on Facebook are from the local area.

28750 ■ "TW Trade Shows to Offer Seminars On Niche Selling, Social Media" in *Travel Weekly* (Vol. 69, October 4, 2010, No. 40, pp. 9)
Pub: NorthStar Travel Media LLC
Description: Travel Weekly's Leisure World 2010 and Fall Home Based Travel Agent Show focused on niche selling, with emphasis on all-inclusives, young consumers, groups, incentives, culinary vacations, and honeymoon or romance travel.

28751 ■ "Twitter Hack: Made in Japan? User Says Attack Showed Security Flaw" in *Houston Chronicle* (September 24, 2010, pp. 3)
Pub: Houston Chronicle
Ed: Tomoko A. Hosaka. **Description:** Details of the attack on Twitter caused by a Japanese computer hacker are revealed.

28752 ■ *Twitterville: How Businesses Can Thrive in the New Global Neighborhoods*
Pub: Portfolio Hardcover
Ed: Shel Israel. **Price:** $23.95. **Description:** Twitter is the most rapidly adopted communication tool in history, going from zero to ten million users in just over two years. On Twitter, word can spread faster than wildfire. Companies no longer have the option of ignoring the conversation. Unlike other hot social media spaces, Twitterville is dominated by professionals, not students. And despite its size, it still feels like a small town. Twitter allows people to interact much the way they do face-to-face, honestly and authentically.

28753 ■ "Two Ways to Find New Customers" in *Inc.* (Vol. 31, January-February 2009, No. 1, pp. 41)
Pub: Mansueto Ventures LLC
Description: Latest software programs that help sales staff connect to new leads are profiled. Salesconx provides online leads while Demandbase reports users on a particular Website.

28754 ■ *The Ultimate Guide to Electronic Marketing for Small Business: Low-Cost/High Return Tools and Techniques That Really Work*
Pub: John Wiley & Sons, Incorporated
Ed: Tom Antion. **Released:** June 2005. **Price:** $19.95 (US), $25.99 (Canadian). **Description:** Online marketing techniques for small business to grow and increase sales.

28755 ■ "Understanding Persuasive Online Sales Messages from eBay Auctions" in *Business Communication Quarterly* (December 2007, pp. 482)
Pub: Sage Publications USA
Ed: Barbara Jo White, Daniel Clapper, Rita Noel, Jenny Fortier, Pierre Grabolosa. **Description:** eBay product listings were studied to determine the requirements of persuasive sales writing. Potential sellers should use the proper keywords and make an authentic description with authentic photographs of the item being auctioned.

28756 ■ "U.S. Enters BlackBerry Dispute Compromise Sought Over Security Issues" in *Houston Chronicle* (August 6, 2010)
Pub: Houston Chronicle
Ed: Matthew Lee. **Description:** U.S. State Department is working for a compromise with Research in Motion, manufacturer of the BlackBerry, over security issues. The Canadian company makes the smartphones and foreign governments believe they pose a security risk.

28757 ■ "Universal Music Sues Grooveshark's Parent" in *Wall Street Journal Eastern Edition* (November 22 , 2011, pp. B5)
Pub: Dow Jones & Company Inc.
Ed: Ethan Smith. **Description:** Escape Media Group Inc., the parent company of online-music service Grooveshark, and seven of its executives have been sued by Universal Music Group, which alleges patent infringement involving its sound recordings. The executives are alleged to have uploaded thousands of songs onto Grooveshark.

28758 ■ "Unlimited Priorities Strengthens Executive Team" in *Entertainment Close-Up* (November 1, 2011)
Pub: Close-Up Media
Description: Founder and president of Unlimited Priorities Corporation, Iris L. Hanney, added two executive level professionals to her team. The new employees will help increase the firm's capabilities in social media and information technology.

28759 ■ "Up To Code? Website Eases Compliance Burden for Entrepreneurs" in *Black Enterprise* (Vol. 38, March 2008, No. 8, pp. 48)
Pub: Earl G. Graves Publishing Co. Inc.
Ed: Robin White-Goode. **Description:** Business.gov is a presidential E-government project created to help small businesses easily find, understand, and comply with laws and regulations pertaining to a particular industry.

28760 ■ "Uptick in Clicks: Nordstrom's Online Sales Surging" in *Puget Sound Business Journal* (Vol. 29, August 22, 2008, No. 18, pp. 1)
Pub: American City Business Journals
Ed: Gregg Lamm. **Description:** Nordstrom Inc.'s online division grew its sales by 15 percent in the second quarter of 2008, compared to 2007's 4.3 percent in overall decline. The company expects their online net sales to reach $700 million in 2008 capturing eight percent of overall sales.

28761 ■ "Utah Technology Council: Social Media Is Here to Stay; Embrace It" in *Wireless News* (December 14, 2009)
Pub: Close-Up Media
Description: Social media outlets such as Facebook and Twitter are blurring the lines between advertising, public relations, branding and marketing; businesses must stop thinking in terms of traditional marketing versus Internet marketing if they want to succeed in today's marketing climate.

28762 ■ "A View to a Killer Business Model" in *Black Enterprise* (Vol. 40, December 2009, No. 5, pp. 50)
Pub: Earl G. Graves Publishing Co., Inc.
Ed: Sonya A. Donaldson. **Description:** Profile of Gen2Media Corp., a production, technology and Internet marketing firm based in Florida with offices in New York; Gen2Media is utilizing the advances in technology to now include video in its online marketing offerings.

28763 ■ "Virgin America Flies with V&S on Web" in *ADWEEK* (Vol. 51, July 12 2010, No. 27, pp. 31)
Pub: Nielsen Business Media Inc.
Description: Victors & Spoils, a crowdsourcing agency is examined.

28764 ■ "Vistaprint Survey Indicates that Online Marketing Taking Hold Among Small Businesses" in *Internet Wire* (December 10, 2009)
Pub: Comtex News Network, Inc.
Description: According to a comprehensive survey from Vistaprint N.V., small businesses are very likely to increase their use of Internet marketing strategies such as paid and organic search, email marketing, social media networking and custom websites over the next year. Trends continue to show that more small businesses are indeed adapting to the changing marketplace and are more willing to diversify their marketing strategies than ever before.

28765 ■ "Web-Based Marketing Excites, Challenges Small Business Use" in *Colorado Springs Business Journal* (January 20, 2010)
Pub: Dolan Media Co.
Ed: Becky Hurley. **Description:** Business-to-business and consumer-direct firms alike are using the fast-changing Web technologies to increase sales, leads and track consumer behavior but once a company commits to an Online marketing plan, experts believe, they must be prepared to consistently tweak and overhaul content and distribution vehicles in order to keep up.

28766 ■ "Web-Preneuring" in *Small Business Opportunities* (May 2008)
Pub: Harris Publications Inc.
Description: 1&1 Internet provides known servers with more than 6.84 million customers through contracts with both consumer and business users. It operates five secure data centers housing 40,000 servers that process more than 5 billion monthly emails.

28767 ■ "Web to Print" in *American Printer* (Vol. 128, August 1, 2011, No. 8)
Pub: Penton Media Inc.
Description: Jerry Kennelly, CEO and founder of Tweak.com believes that Web-to-Design is middleware with no content. His firm offers an easy to use interface that flows right into the printer's workflow with no additional costs.

28768 ■ "Web Sight: Do You See What I See?" in *Entrepreneur* (Vol. 35, October 2007, No. 10, pp. 58)
Pub: Entrepreneur Media Inc.
Ed: Heather Clancy. **Description:** Owners of Trunkt, a boutique in New York that showcases independent designs, have created a new style of Website called Trunkt.org. The Website allows buyers to select the products they want to see and designers can choose anytime which of their items will be displayed on the site. An explanation of the strategy that helped bring Trunkt closer to its clients is presented.

28769 ■ "Web Traffic Numbers Facing Scrutiny" in *Boston Business Journal* (Vol. 27, November 2, 2007, No. 40, pp. 1)
Pub: American City Business Journals Inc.
Ed: Jesse Noyes. **Description:** Interactive Advertising Bureau (IAB) held a summit meeting with major industry players in an effort to create more transparent standards for measuring Internet traffic. The terms at issue were registered users, unique visitors, time spent and retention.

28770 ■ "Web Translation Made Simple" in *Inc.* (Vol. 33, October 2011, No. 8, pp. 44)
Pub: Inc. Magazine
Ed: Adam Baer. **Description:** Smartling is a Web-based service that translates sites into more than 50 foreign languages. The software will begin translation right after setting up the account.

28771 ■ "Webadvertising" in *MarketingMagazine* (Vol. 115, September 27, 2010, No. 13, pp. 70)
Pub: Rogers Publishing Ltd.
Description: Website advertising in Canada is examined.

28772 ■ "Web.Preneuring: How Local TV Ads and Online Marketing Can Help You Win Big" in *Small Business Opportunities* (January 2008)
Pub: Harris Publications Inc.
Ed: David Waxman. **Description:** Spot Runner, an Internet-based advertising agency offers low-cost local business television ads. The company secures the ad buy, places and tracks the ads, and analyzes viewership and demographics for clients.

28773 ■ "What the Future Holds for Consumers" in *Black Enterprise* (Vol. 41, August 2010, No. 1, pp. 47)
Pub: Earl G. Graves Publishing Co. Inc.
Ed: Sheiresa Ngo. **Description:** The way people purchase goods and service has changed with technology. With an increased focus on security (as well as privacy and fairness) the U.S. Congress began regulating the credit card industry with the Fair Credit Reporting Act of 1970 and the Credit Card Accountability, Responsibility, and Disclosure (CARD) Act of 2009.

28774 ■ "What's Your Personal Social Media Strategy?" in *Harvard Business Review* (Vol. 88, November 2010, No. 11, pp. 127)
Pub: Harvard Business School Publishing
Ed: Soumitra Dutta. **Description:** Identification of four distinct sectors and how they interrelate to social media is given. The sectors are personal and private; professional and private; personal and public; and professional and public. Appropriate topics and types of social media are discussed for each.

28775 ■ "What's Your Social Media Strategy?" in *Black Enterprise* (Vol. 41, November 2010, No. 4, pp. 75)
Pub: Earl G. Graves Publishing Co. Inc.
Ed: Denise Campbell. **Description:** Advice for using social media sites such as Twitter, Facebook and LinkedIn as a professional networking tool is given.

28776 ■ "White Cat Media Tells You Where to Get a Bargain. Now It's Shopping for $1.5 Million" in *Inc.* (March 2008, pp. 48)
Pub: Gruner & Jahr USA Publishing
Ed: Athena Schindelheim. **Description:** Profile of White Cat Media which runs two shopping Websites: SheFinds.com for fashion and beauty items, and MomFinds.com for mothers. The New York City firm reported revenues for 2007 at $400,000 and is looking for funding capital in the amount of $1.7 million.

28777 ■ "Why LinkedIn is the Social Network that Will Never Die" in *Advertising Age* (Vol. 81, December 6, 2010, No. 43, pp. 2)
Pub: Crain Communications, Inc.
Ed: Irina Slutsky. **Description:** Despite the popularity of Facebook, LinkIn in will always be a source for professionals who wish to network.

28778 ■ "Why Some Get Shaften By Google Pricing" in *Advertising Age* (Vol. 79, July 14, 2008, No. 7, pp. 3)
Pub: Crain Communications, Inc.
Ed: Abbey Klaassen. **Description:** Google's search advertising is discussed as well as the company's pricing structure for these ads.

28779 ■ "Why We'll Never Escape Facebook" in *Canadian Business* (Vol. 83, June 15, 2010, No. 10, pp. 28)
Pub: Rogers Media Ltd.
Ed: James Cowan, Tamara Shopsin, Jason Fulford. **Description:** Facebook users are growing in numbers despite criticism of the site's privacy policies that have put the onus of keeping anonymous to the user. Facebook's business model and its growing influence on the Internet are discussed.

28780 ■ "Why You Need a New-Media 'Ringmaster'" in *Harvard Business Review* (Vol. 88, December 2010, No. 12, pp. 78)
Pub: Harvard Business School Publishing
Ed: Patrick Spenner. **Description:** The concept of ringmaster is applied to brand marketing. This concept includes integrative thinking, lean collaboration skills, and high-speed decision cycles.

28781 ■ "Wi-Fi On Steroids: Will WiMAX Provide the Juice For Souped-Up Connections?" in *Black Enterprise* (November 2007)
Pub: Earl G. Graves Publishing Co. Inc.
Ed: Fiona Haley. **Description:** WiMAX, Worldwide Interoperability for Microwave Access in the U.S. WiMax is technology that moves data and connects faster and at greater distances than before.

28782 ■ *Wikinomics: How Mass Collaboration Changes Everything*
Pub: Penguin Group Incorporated
Ed: Don Tapscott; Anthony D. Williams. **Released:** April 2008. **Price:** $27.95. **Description:** Research and information about the every changing world of the Internet is provided to help small businesses.

28783 ■ "Wikinomics: The Sequel" in *Business Strategy Review* (Vol. 21, Summer 2010, No. 2, pp. 64)
Pub: Wiley-Blackwell
Description: Ever-optimistic Don Tapscott and Anthony Williams, coauthors of Wikinomics and individually, of a number of other books that study the Internet and its relation to society, are now working on a new book, one for which they're using the Internet to determine its title.

28784 ■ "Will mCommerce Make Black Friday Green?" in *Retail Merchandiser* (Vol. 51, September-October 2011, No. 5, pp. 8)
Pub: Phoenix Media Corporation
Ed: Scott Miller. **Description:** Retailers speculate the possibilities of mobile commerce and are implementing strategies at their stores. Consumers using mobile devices accounted for only 0.1 percent of visits to retail Websites on Black Friday 2009 and rose to 5.6 percent in 2010; numbers are expected to rise for 2011.

28785 ■ "Winner: Private Company, Less Than $100M" in *Crain's Detroit Business* (Vol. 25, June 22, 2009, No. 25)
Pub: Crain Communications Inc. - Detroit
Ed: Tom Henderson. **Description:** Profile of ForeSee Results, an Ann Arbor, Michigan-based firm that uses the University of Michigan American Consumer Satisfaction Index to help businesses measure satisfaction with their Websites.

28786 ■ *Winner Take All: How Competitiveness Shapes the Fate of Nations*
Pub: Basic Books
Ed: Richard J. Elkus Jr. **Released:** 2009. **Price:** $27.00. **Description:** American government and misguided business practices has allowed the U.S. to fall behind other countries in various market sectors such as cameras and televisions, as well as information technologies. It will take a national strategy to for America to regain its lead in crucial industries.

28787 ■ "Wireless: Full Service" in *Entrepreneur* (Vol. 35, October 2007, No. 10, pp. 60)
Pub: Entrepreneur Media Inc.

Ed: Amanda C. Kooser. **Description:** Palm Foleo, the $599 smart phone enables users to access and compose email, browse the Internet, view documents and play Powerpoint files. It weighs 2.5 pounds and has a 10-inch screen. Other features, such as built-in WiFi are described.

28788 ■ "Women Clicking to Earn Virtual Dollars" in *Sales and Marketing Management* (November 11, 2009)
Pub: Nielsen Business Media, Inc.

Ed: Stacy Straczynski. **Description:** According to a new report from Internet marketing firm Q Interactive, women are increasingly playing social media games where they are able to click on an ad or sign up for a promotion to earn virtual currency. Research is showing that this kind of marketing may be a potent tool, especially for e-commerce and online stores.

28789 ■ "Women Workers Spend Lunchtime on Fridays Shopping Online" in *Marketing to Women* (Vol. 23, November 2010, No. 11, pp. 8)
Pub: EPM Communications, Inc.

Description: Forty percent of women shop online during work hours, particularly on Fridays. The largest number of women make these purchases during their lunch break. Demographics are included.

28790 ■ "WordStream Announces a Pair of Firsts for SEO and PPC Keyword Research Tools" in *Internet Wire* (November 10, 2009)
Pub: Comtex News Network, Inc.

Description: WordSteam, Inc., a provider of pay-per-click (PPC) and search engine optimization (SEO) solutions for continuously expanding and optimizing search marketing efforts has released two new features in their flagship Keyword Management solution; these tools will allow marketers to analyze data from paid search, organic search and estimated totals from keyword suggestion tools side-by-side.

28791 ■ *Work at Home Now*
Pub: Career Press, Inc.

Ed: Christine Durst, Michael Haaren. **Released:** October 9, 2010. **Price:** $14.99. **Description:** There are legitimate home-based jobs and projects that can be found on the Internet, but trustworthy guidance is scarce. There is a 58 to 1 scam ratio in work at-home advertising filled with fraud.

28792 ■ "Xtium Has Its Head in the Clouds" in *Philadelphia Business Journal* (Vol. 30, September 23, 2011, No. 32, pp. 1)
Pub: American City Business Journals Inc.

Ed: Peter Key. **Description:** Philadelphia-based cloud computing firm Xtium LLC received an $11.5 million first-round investment from Boston-Massachusetts-based OpenView Venture Partners. Catering to midsize businesses and unit of bigger firms, Xtium offers disaster-recovery, hosting, and managed-information-technology-infrastructure services.

28793 ■ "The Yahoo Family Tree" in *Conde Nast Portfolio* (Vol. 2, June 2008, No. 6, pp. 34)
Pub: Conde Nast Publications, Inc.

Ed: Blaise Zerega. **Description:** Yahoo, founded in 1994 by Stanford students Jerry Yang and David Filo, is still an Internet powerhouse. The company's history is also outlined as well as the reasons in which Microsoft desperately wants to acquire the firm.

28794 ■ "Yahoo! - Microsoft Pact: Alive Again?" in *Barron's* (Vol. 89, July 27, 2009, No. 30, pp. 8)
Pub: Dow Jones & Co., Inc.

Ed: Mark Veverka. **Description:** Yahoo! reported higher than expected earnings in the second quarter of 2009 under CEO Carol Bartz who has yet to articulate her long-term vision and strategy for turning around the company. The media reported that Yahoo! and Microsoft are discussing an advertising-search partnership which should benefit both companies.

28795 ■ "Yammer Gets Serious" in *Inc.* (Volume 32, December 2010, No. 10, pp. 58)
Pub: Inc. Magazine

Ed: Eric Markowitz. **Description:** Yammer, an internal social network for companies, allows coworkers to share ideas and documents in real-time. Details of this service are included.

28796 ■ "You Are What They Click" in *Entrepreneur* (Vol. 37, July 2009, No. 7, pp. 43)
Pub: Entrepreneur Media, Inc.

Ed: Mikal Belicove. **Description:** Hiring the right website design firm is the first stage in building an online business, and this involves various factors such as price, technical expertise, and talent. Writing a request for proposal (RFP) detailing the website's details, which include purpose, budget and audience, is the first step the process. Other tips in finding the right web designer are given.

28797 ■ *Your First Year in Real Estate: Making the Transition from Total Novice to Successful Professional*
Pub: Crown Business Books

Ed: Dirk Zeller. **Released:** $August 3, 2010. **Price:** $20.00. **Description:** Zeller helps new realtors to select the right company, develop mentor and client relationships, using the Internet and social networking to stay ahead of competition, to set and reach career goals, to stay current in the market, and more.

28798 ■ "Your Turn in the Spotlight" in *Inc.* (Volume 32, December 2010, No. 10, pp. 57)
Pub: Inc. Magazine

Ed: John Brandon. **Description:** Examples of three video blogs created by entrepreneurs to promote their businesses and products are used to show successful strategies. Wine Library TV promotes a family's wine business; SHAMA.TV offers marketing tips and company news; and Will It Blend? promotes sales of a household blender.

28799 ■ *YouTube and Video Marketing: An Hour a Day*
Pub: Sybex

Ed: Greg Jarboe. **Released:** August 10, 2009. **Price:** $29.99. **Description:** The importance of online video marketing for businesses is stressed. Tips for developing and implementing video marketing are outlined.

28800 ■ "Zeon Solutions Teams with Endeca for SaaS Version of Endeca InFront" in *Entertainment Close-Up* (October 25, 2011)
Pub: Close-Up Media

Description: Zeon Solutions, an enterprise e-commerce and Website development firm announced a special licensing partnership with Endecca Technologies. Endeca is an information management software company that provides small and mid-size retailers with high-performance Customer Experience Management technology.

TRADE PERIODICALS

28801 ■ *Business 2.0*
Pub: eCompany Now

Released: Monthly. **Price:** $6.99; $10 two years; $9.65 Canada; $13.75 two years in Canada. **Description:** Trade magazine covering electronic commerce and business.

CONSULTANTS

28802 ■ BIA/Kelsey
15120 Enterprise Ct.
Chantilly, VA 20151
Ph:(609)921-7200
Fax:(703)803-3299
Co. E-mail: info@bia.com
URL: http://www.kelseygroup.com
Contact: Bobbi Loy-Luster, Vice President
E-mail: pkelsey@atskelseygroup.com
Scope: A provider of research and fact-based analysis focusing on local advertising and electronic commerce. **Publications:** "Penetration of Online Media Surpasses Traditional Media for First Time Among Small-Business Advertisers," Aug, 2009; "Rapid Adoption of Advanced Mobile Devices Driving Increased Mobile Local Search Activity, According to The Kelsey Group," Nov, 2008; "Online Consumer Generated Reviews Have Significant Impact on Offline Purchase Behavior," Nov, 2007. **Seminars:** Drilling Down on Local: Marketplaces, The Westin Seattle, Seattle, Washington, Apr, 2008; The Future of Local Search in Europe, London, Jun, 2007; DDC2006?Directory Driven Commerce Conference, Hyatt Century Plaza, LA, Sep, 2006; Drilling Down on Local: Targeting the On-Demand Marketplace, 2005.

28803 ■ Digital Deli Inc.
3145 Geary Blvd., Ste. 532
San Francisco, CA 94118-3316
Ph:(415)387-7653
Free: 800-557-3354
Fax:(415)387-7656
Co. E-mail: sales@thedeli.com
Contact: Brian Thomas, Vice President
E-mail: blt@atsthedeli.com
Scope: Specializes in interactive marketing development. Provides strategic and tactical planning for interactive media. Specializes in marketing communications.

28804 ■ Digitas Inc.
33 Arch St.
Boston, MA 02110-1424
Ph:(617)867-1000
Fax:(617)867-1111
Co. E-mail: contact@digitasinc.com
URL: http://www.digitas.com
Contact: Brian Roberts, CFO
Scope: Helps clients determine how to use the Internet and emerging technologies to create new business models and enterprise-wide customer value propositions to gain competitive advantages, improved market share, and enhanced profitability. Technology, architecture, and infrastructure service marketing and creative services were focused on enabling brands to connect with the right customer at the right time through the right channels in the most effective way possible. Performance measurement provides the ultimate yardstick and continuous feedback mechanisms.

28805 ■ HyperClick Online Services
PO Box 235555
Honolulu, HI 96823-3509
Ph:(808)539-2545
Co. E-mail: hyperclick@hawaii.rr.com
Contact: Jan Zastrow, Owner
E-mail: zastrow@hawaii.edu
Scope: An information management consulting firm that offers customized digital information products, services, and training. Specializes in building educational and business solutions for real-world end-users. Provides distance learning consultation and course-ware; web publishing, web site analysis and evaluation reports; digitized collections; Internet training; online research and reference; information architecture, content development and interactivity; editing and copy-editing. **Publications:** "Pssst! Anybody Listening? Hand held Audio May Be the Next Big Thing," E Content, Jul, 2001; "It's a Small World After All: Content for Wireless & Mobile Appliances," E Content, May, 2001; "Click to Talk: Web Phones Spell Opportunity for Libraries," Online, Feb, 2001.

28806 ■ Inspired Arts Inc.
4225 Executive Sq., Ste. 1160
PO Box 1009
La Jolla, CA 92037
Ph:(619)623-3525
Free: 800-851-4394

Fax:(619)623-3534
Contact: Brian Kent, Principle
Scope: Provides Internet business solutions and web design services. Specializes in Internet business plans, website development, e-business and online marketing. **Seminars:** E-Commerce: Gone with the Net; The E-Business Buzz; Online Marketing: The Second Ten Commandments.

28807 ■ Organic Inc.
555 Market St., 4th Fl.
San Francisco, CA 94105-2873
Ph:(415)581-5300
Fax:(415)581-5400
Co. E-mail: newbiz@organic.com
URL: http://www.organic.com
Contact: Troy Young, Exec VP
E-mail: marita@organic.com
Scope: Strategic consulting, e-business, marketing solutions, e-commerce website creation, customer service and fulfillment.

28808 ■ Sapient Corp.
131 Dartmouth St., 3rd Fl.
Cambridge, MA 02116
Ph:(617)621-0200
Fax:(617)621-1300
Co. E-mail: info@sapient.com
URL: http://www.sapient.com
Contact: Alan Herrick, Senior Vice President, COO
Scope: The company offers its services in the areas of business and information technology (IT) strategy, business applications, business intelligence, marketing, and outsourcing. Its business and IT strategy services include business-process consulting, business applications and enterprise architecture planning, e-business and Web strategy, IT governance and advisory services, and program management office. **Publications:** "Here Today, Gone Tomorrow: How to Get the Most Out of Your Ads," Mar, 2009; "New Media Age," Dec, 2005.

28809 ■ Spherix Inc.
12051 Indian Creek Ct.
Beltsville, MD 20705
Ph:(301)897-2540
Free: (866)774-3749
Fax:(301)897-2567
Co. E-mail: info@spherix.com
URL: http://www.biospherics.com
Contact: Thomas B. Peter, Director
Scope: Provides health sciences consulting services that provides scientific and strategic support for suppliers, manufacturers, distributors and retailers of: Conventional foods, biotechnology-derived foods, medical foods, infant formulas, food ingredients, dietary supplements, food contact substances, pharmaceuticals, medical devices, consumer products and industrial chemicals and pesticides. Provides teleservices, ebusinesses, and IT solutions for the health and information industries. **Publications:** "Viking found no life on Mars, and, just as important, it found why there can be no life". **Special Services:** Naturlose^{R}.

28810 ■ Sterling Strategies Corp.
1821 Walden Office Sq.
Schaumburg, IL 60173
Ph:(847)925-5440
Co. E-mail: info@sterlingstrategies.com
Contact: Herbert Ritchell, Principle
E-mail: rlall@sterlingstrategies.com
Scope: A management consulting firm providing strategic planning services to the information technology industry.

28811 ■ Stratamar Inc.
5661 Seapine Rd.
Hilliard, OH 43026
Ph:(614)946-4614
Fax:(614)529-2945
Co. E-mail: info@stratamar.com
URL: http://www.stratamar.com
Contact: Nancy Brown, Owner
E-mail: neilbrown@stratamar.com
Scope: A full-spectrum strategic marketing consulting company. Areas of concentration include product development, product management, strategic planning, development and implementation of tactical marketing plans, and Internet marketing. The primary focus is upon maximizing the benefit/cost ratio of promotions through the use of direct marketing, low cost media, and the like. **Publications:** "Business Plans," Feb, 2006.

COMPUTERIZED DATABASES

28812 ■ *BtoB*
Crain Communications Inc.
1155 Gratiot Ave.
Detroit, MI 48207
Ph:(313)446-6000
Free: 800-678-2427
Fax:(313)446-1616
Co. E-mail: info@crain.com
URL: http://www.crain.com
Description: Contains news, articles, and features from the monthly print version of *BtoB*, as well as content exclusive to the online version. Contains daily news reports, analysis, and articles on business-to-business marketing and related issues. Includes coverage of e-commerce and current business events. Includes editorials and feature articles from the monthly magazine. **Availability:** Online: Crain Communications Inc. **Type:** Full text.